The Heath Anthology of American Literature

Volume A

Beginnings to 1800

The Heath Anthology of American Literature

SIXTH EDITION

Volume A

Beginnings to 1800

Paul Lauter
Trinity College
General Editor

Richard Yarborough
University of California, Los Angeles
Associate General Editor

John Alberti
Northern Kentucky University
Editor, Instructor's Guide

Mary Pat Brady
Cornell University

Jackson R. Bryer
University of Maryland

King-Kok Cheung
University of California, Los Angeles

Kirk Curnutt
Troy University

Anne Goodwyn Jones
Allegheny College

James Kyung-Jin Lee
University of California, Santa Barbara

Wendy Martin
Claremont Graduate University

Quentin Miller
Suffolk University

Bethany Schneider
Bryn Mawr College

Ivy T. Schweitzer
Dartmouth College

Sandra A. Zagarell
Oberlin

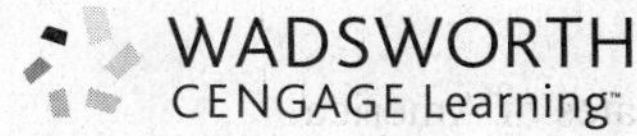

Australia • Brazil • Japan • Korea • Mexico • Singapore • Spain • United Kingdom • United States

The Heath Anthology of American Literature, Sixth Edition
Paul Lauter et al.

Publisher: Patricia Coryell

Sponsoring Editor: Joann Kozyrev

Marketing Manager: Tom Ziolkowski

Senior Development Editor: Kathy Sands-Boehmer

Senior Project Editor: Rosemary Winfield

Art and Design Manager: Jill Haber

Photo Editor: Stacey Dong

Composition Buyer: Chuck Dutton

New Title Project Manager: Patricia O'Neill

Editorial Assistant: Daisuke Yasutake

Marketing Associate: Bettina Chiu

Editorial Assistant: Paola Moll

Cover: © Burstein Collection/Corbis

Credits continue on page A-1, which constitutes an extension of the copyright page.

Library of Congress Catalog Card Number: 2008922122

ISBN-13: 978-0-618-89799-5

ISBN-10: 0-618-89799-2

Wadsworth
20 Channel Center Street
Boston, MA 02210
USA

Cengage Learning is a leading provider of customized learning solutions with office locations around the globe, including Singapore, the United Kingdom, Australia, Mexico, Brazil, and Japan. Locate your local office at **www.cengage.com/global**

Cengage Learning products are represented in Canada by Nelson Education, Ltd.

To learn more about Wadsworth, visit **www.cengage.com/wadsworth**

Purchase any of our products at your local college store or at our preferred online store **www.CengageBrain.com**

Printed in the United States of America
5 6 12 11 10

CONTENTS

An excerpt from "Treatise Concerning Religious Affections" is found in the Cluster: Religion and Spirituality—on Nature and Nature's God on page 662.

PREFACE

In this sixth edition of *The Heath Anthology of American Literature,* we have extended the innovative tradition established by the very first edition of the anthology. That first edition implemented the slogan of the Reconstructing American Literature project that led to the publication of the *Heath Anthology:* "So that the work of Frederick Douglass, Mary Wilkins Freeman, Agnes Smedley, Zora Neale Hurston, and others is read with the work of Nathaniel Hawthorne, Henry James, William Faulkner, Ernest Hemingway, and others." Consequently, that first edition, while providing very rich selections of traditionally canonical authors, also contained the widest selection of writing by women and authors of diverse racial, ethnic, and regional origins ever assembled in an academic textbook. That is still the case in the sixth edition of the *Heath Anthology*—still innovating, still leading.

The *Heath Anthology*'s breadth and depth of coverage is extended in this sixth edition. Volume A includes entries from Northeast woodlands tribes as well as a section on New Netherland literature. Volume B contains significant newly anthologized texts like Phoebe Cary's hilarious poetic parodies, Hawthorne's striking early story "Alice Doane's Appeal," and a substantial selection from Julia Ward Howe's strange and long-unavailable *The Hermaphrodite.* Volume C now offers an independent entry by accomplished nineteenth-century poet Sarah Piatt and one of the English-language fiction and poetry by the versatile Japanese writer Yone Noguchi. Volume D now includes poems and stories by Américo Paredes, relevant commentaries on culture by period thinkers such as Walter Lippmann, Gilbert Seldes, and Margaret Sanger, as well as new selections from Gertrude Stein, Katherine Anne Porter, and John Steinbeck. Two of the most prominent living fiction writers—Philip Roth and Don DeLillo—are represented for the first time in Volume E.

One major objective of the *Heath Anthology* has always been to enable students to understand literary texts in relation to the cultural and historical contexts out of which they developed and to which they initially spoke. One innovation for this edition has been to provide four clusters in each volume on similar cultural and historical issues—Nature and Religion; Aesthetics; America in the World, the World in America; and E Pluribus Unum. These clusters consist of shorter selections that are relevant to each topic. They can be used as the basis for self-contained assignments or studied in relation to the primary texts in each volume. With the *Heath Anthology*'s unusually wide selection, they provide instructors with broadened opportunities to help students perceive continuity and change in the literary and cultural history of what is now the United States.

Another major goal of the *Heath Anthology* has been to broaden our understanding of what constitutes the "literary." On the one hand, we want to provide students with a large selection of well-known texts whose literary power and cultural relevance had been established by generations of critics and teachers—William

Bradford's "Of Plymouth Plantation," Benjamin Franklin's *Autobiography,* "Young Goodman Brown," "Self-Reliance," "Civil Disobedience," "Annabel Lee," "Daisy Miller," "The Open Boat," *The Waste Land,* "Hills Like White Elephants," "Sonny's Blues," "Howl." At the same time, we wish to provide exemplary texts that, because of their forms or subjects, have seldom been taught and often little read. Thus, we include, for example, "sorrow songs" or spirituals, nineteenth-century folk songs and stories, *corridos* and blues lyrics, and poems written on the walls of Angel Island prison by Chinese detainees. Likewise, we include nonfictional forms such as the spiritual autobiographies of Thomas Shepard and Elizabeth Ashbridge, sketches by Fanny Fern, polemical letters by Angelina and Sarah Grimké, columns by Finley Peter Dunne, José Martí's important "Our America," Randolph Bourne's "Trans-National America," Martin Luther King's "I Have a Dream," and chapters from Gloria Anzaldúa's *Borderlands / La Frontera.* The sixth edition extends this goal by including journal entries from several members of the Lewis and Clark expedition, letters protesting Cherokee removal, "proletarian" folk songs, a number of graphic narratives by Art Spiegelman, Lynda Barry, and others. In addition, each volume includes a glossy insert of paintings, photographs, book jackets, and documents that illuminate the culture of each historical period. These reproductions are, we think, not only attractive in themselves but useful as objects of study parallel to the volume's literary texts.

The *Heath Anthology* has also from its beginning balanced longer complete works with shorter texts by the wide variety of authors included in our anthology. Thus, for example, the sixth edition includes the full texts of Royall Tyler's "The Contrast," Mercy Otis Warren's "The Group," Melville's "Benito Cereno" and "Billy Budd," Frederick Douglass's *Narrative,* Abraham Cahan's "The Imported Bridegroom," Kate Chopin's *The Awakening,* Nella Larsen's *Passing,* Arthur Miller's *The Crucible,* among many other longer works. At the same time, student preferences and instructor suggestions have led us to make available, packaged with the anthology, a choice of a number of important longer works in *separate* volumes of the New Riverside series. These include *The Scarlet Letter, Typee, The Portrait of a Lady, Huckleberry Finn, The Red Badge of Courage,* and *The Damnation of Theron Ware.* The availability of these independent volumes not only satisfies student preferences for such separate texts but provides instructors with increased variety in terms of easily accessible novels that they can teach along with the anthology's basic selections.

The particular character of the *Heath Anthology* has always depended on the participation in the project of a wide community of scholars and teachers. Unlike other anthologies, the *Heath* includes introductory notes that have been written by scholars who specialize in a particular author. In their diverse yet consistent approaches, these notes illustrate for students how writing about literature is not limited to any single standard. More important, perhaps, these contributing editors, together with readers, consultants, and users of the anthology, have provided guidance to our unusually large and diverse editorial board as we determine the changes that will make the anthology most useful. The *Heath* community has also remained active in constructing the complementary materials that have made the *Heath Anthology,* despite the unique diversity of its content, particularly user friendly. These include the twice-yearly *Heath Newsletter,* which is designed in particular to support teaching innovation; the *Instructor's Guide* (online and in paper), edited by John Alberti, which offers suggestions for approaching texts and authors, model assignments, and useful exam and discussion questions; and the innovative *Heath Anthology* web site. The *Heath* website, available at college.hmco.com/pic/lautervolA6e, contains the *Instructor's Guide,* a detailed time line, bibliographical materials, and links to a large number of visual and auditory resources that are very useful in the classroom.

Changes in individual volumes reflect the *Heath Anthology*'s continuing commitment to bringing contemporary scholarship into classroom practice:

- In Volume A, we have reorganized the Native American entries to better reflect current scholarship and to include a broader representation of native cultures. In addition to drawing on recent scholarship on New Netherland life, we have extended the literature of exploration forward to the nineteenth century with the expedition of Lewis and Clark to the northwest.

- In Volume B, in addition to the changes mentioned above, the four new clusters will help to focus classroom discussion of critical early nineteenth-century phenomena like the Second Great Awakening, the rise of the abolitionist movement, the conflict over expansionism and Indian "removal," and the debates over reform in the rapidly industrializing and urbanizing United States. These clusters help make clear how deeply involved the writers of the early nineteenth century were with the world that they helped shape and to which they spoke.

- Volume C has added or restored a broad range of works, including Charles Chesnutt's "Po' Sandy," Kate Chopin's "The Storm" and "The Story of an Hour," Henry James's "The Beast in the Jungle," Sarah Orne Jewett's "The Foreigner," Alice Dunbar-Nelson's "Mr. Baptiste" and "The Praline Woman," Sui-Sin Far's "The Wisdom of the New," and an additional story by Jack London, "Koolau the Leper." We have added two new sheafs—"A Latino Chorus for Social Change" and "Filipino and Filipina Writing"—and restored the "Sheaf of Poetry by Late Nineteenth-Century American Women" to its original size. We have grouped the literature by writers from New Orleans in a subsection on "New Orleans and America" that features the life and culture of that city. Finally, our four clusters adapt the themes common to all five volumes to the rich, variegated, and often contentious circumstances of the United States between 1865 and 1910

- Volume D continues to demonstrate the diversity of the literary period known as modernism by introducing readers to the array of modernisms that constitute it—the hermetic experiments of Ezra Pound and T. S. Eliot, the more commercial expression of loss and uncertainty in popular efforts by F. Scott Fitzgerald and Edna St. Vincent Millay, the ethnically complex fusion of African American and dominant-culture aesthetics that typify the Harlem Renaissance, and the political activism of the proletarian movement of the 1930s and its internal debates over the social functions of art. Volume D now includes the full text of Nella

Larsen's *Passing,* as well as revised selections from Katherine Anne Porter, Richard Wright, John Steinbeck, and other writers. These changes have been undertaken in an effort to reconceptualize reputations, confront pedagogical complacencies, and reignite interest in overlooked works. The major change from previous editions of this volume is the inclusion of four clusters that are designed to dramatize the upheavals that characterized the first half of the American twentieth century. Despite the avowals of some of its leading figures, these excerpts demonstrate that the literature of modernism did not exist outside of history—the explosion of consumerism, the rise of popular-culture appropriations of modernist ideals in advertising, and such hot-button topics as immigration, racial discrimination, and the regulation of political freedom. In keeping with the mission of reiterating this fact, another significant change to this edition is the addition of a folk music cluster that demonstrates the narrative continuities between popular music and the written word.

- Volume E has been revised to reflect changes in the notion of what can be called contemporary. The new structure of the volume advances the idea that the years including and surrounding the Vietnam War mark a turning point in literary tastes, styles, and subjects. Two distinct periods of literary history are beginning to emerge—from the end of World War II to the early 1970s and from the mid-1970s to the present. The latter period, more than any other in history, reflects American literature's consciousness of its diversity, a consciousness that *Heath Anthology* editors have labored to uncover in earlier periods.

Acknowledgments

We want to extend our thanks to all of the contributing editors who devoted their time and scholarship to introductory notes, choices of texts, and teaching materials. For the current edition, they include Paula Bernat Bennett (Emerita), Southern Illinois University; Renée Bergland, Simmons College; Mary Pat Brady, Cornell University; Hillary Chute, Harvard University; Denise Cruz, Indiana University; Gene Jarrett, Boston University; Daniel Heath Justice, University of Toronto; Ann Keniston, University of Nevada, Reno; James Kyung-Jin Lee, University of California, Santa Barbara; Katherine E. Ledford, Appalachian State University; Viet Nguyen, University of Southern California; Robert Dale Parker, University of Illinois at Urbana-Champaign; Elizabeth Petrino, Fairfield University; Ramón Saldívar, Stanford University; Lavina Shankar, Bates College; Scott Slovic, University of Nevada, Reno; Mayumi Takada, Bryn Mawr College; Darlene Unrue, University of Nevada, Las Vegas; and Joanne van der Woude, Columbia University.

Thanks to Oberlin College for funding student researchers and to Amanda Shubert and Hillary Smith for the incomparable work they have done in that capacity. We also want to thank student researchers Carson Thomas and Kyle Lewis from Dartmouth College for excellent editorial help.

We especially want to thank those who reviewed this edition: Jennifer Adkison, Idaho State University; John Battenburg, California Polytechnic State University; Michael Berndt, Normandale Community College; Patricia Bostian, Central Piedmont Community College; Steve Brahlek, Palm Beach Community College; Amy Braziller, Red Rocks Community College; Francis Broussard, Southeastern Louisiana University; Mark Cantrell, University of Miami; Adrienne Cassel, Sinclair Community College; Susan Castillo, Kings College, London; Linda Coblentz, University of Houston–Downtown; Linda Daigle, Houston Community College; Cynthia Denham, Snead State Community College; Robert Dunne, Central Connecticut State University; Philip Egan, Western Michigan; Gregory Eislien, Kansas State; Michael Elliott, Emory University; Brad Evans, Rutgers University; Paul Ferlazzo, Northern Arizona University; Tom Fick, Southeastern Louisiana University; Africa R. Fine, Palm Beach Community College; Joe Fulton, Baylor University; Eric Gardner, Saginaw Valley State University; Susan Gilmore, Central Connecticut State University; Yoshinobu Hakutani, Kent State University; Emily Hegarty, Nassau Community College; Kathleen Hicks, Arizona State University; Rebecca Hite, Southeastern Louisiana University; Barbara Hodne, University of Minnesota Minneapolis; Martha Holder, Wytheville Community College; Daniel Heath Justice, University of Toronto; Homer Kemp, Tennessee Technical University; Kristie Knott, Westfield State College; Camille Langston, St. Mary's University; Katherine Ledford, Appalacian State University; Max Loges, Lamar University; Christopher Lukasik, Purdue University; Stephen Mathis, North Haverhill Community College; Brian Norman, Idaho State University; John Parks, Miami University; Cyrus Patell, New York University; Joan Reeves, Northeast Alabama Community College; Carla Rineer, Millersville University; Jane Rosecrans, J. Sargeant Reynolds Community College; Michael Sirmons, Austin Community College; Scott Slawinski, Western Michigan; Emily Todd, Westfield State College; Gregory Tomso, University of West Florida; Bill Toth, Western New Mexico University; Joanne Van der Wonde, Columbia University; Mark Van Wienen, Northern Illinois; Bryan Waterman, New York University; Megan Wesling, University of California, Santa Cruz; and Susan Wolstenholme, Cayuga Community College.

We also want to thank those who contributed to this as well as to earlier editions of this work: Susan Abbotson, Rhode Island College; Thomas P. Adler, Purdue University; Jesse Alemán, University of New Mexico; Elizabeth Ammons, Tufts University; William L. Andrews, University of Kansas; Frances R. Aparicio, University of Michigan; Elaine Sargent Apthorp, San Jose State University; Evelyn Avery, Towson State University; Liahna Babener, Montana State University; Barbara A. Bardes, Loyola University of Chicago; Helen Barolini; Marleen Barr, Virginia Polytechnic Institute and State University; Sam S. Baskett, Michigan State University; Rosalie Murphy Baum, University of South Florida; Herman Beavers, University of Pennsylvania; Eileen T. Bender, Indiana University at Bloomington; Renée L. Bergland, Simmons College; Juda Bennett, The College of New Jersey; Carol Marie Bensick, University of California, Riverside; David Bergman, Towson State University; Susan L. Blake, Lafayette College; Michael Boccia, Tufts University; Robert H. Brinkmeyer, Jr., University of Mississippi; Joanna Brooks, San Diego State University; Carol A. Burns, Southern Illinois University Press; Cynthia Butos, Trinity College; John F. Callahan, Lewis and Clark College; Jane Campbell, Purdue University, Calumet; Christine Cao, University of California, Los Angeles; Jean Ferguson Carr, University of Pittsburgh; Juliana Chang, Santa Clara University; Allan Chavkin,

Southwest Texas State University; Bell Gale Chevigny (Emeritus), Purchase College, State University of New York; Randolph Chilton, University of St. Francis; Beverly Lyon Clark, Wheaton College; C. B. Clark, Oklahoma City University; Amanda J. Cobb, New Mexico State University; Arthur B. Coffin, Montana State University; the late Constance Coiner, Binghamton University, State University of New York; James W. Coleman, University of North Carolina at Chapel Hill; Martha E. Cook, Longwood College; Angelo Costanzo, Shippensburg University; Patti Cowell, Colorado State University; John W. Crowley, Syracuse University; Sister Martha Curry, Wayne State University; Walter C. Daniel, University of Missouri–Columbia Cathy N. Davidson, Duke University; Sharon L. Dean, Rivier College; Jane Krause DeMouy; Dorothy L. Denniston, Brown University; Kathryn Zabelle Derounian-Stodola, University of Arkansas at Little Rock; Joseph Dewey, University of Pittsburgh at Johnstown; the late Margaret Dickie, University of Georgia; Elizabeth Maddock Dillon, Northeastern University; Joanne Dobson, Fordham University; Raymond F. Dolle, Indiana State University; Sheila Hurst Donnelly, Orange County Community College; Carole K. Doreski, Daniel Webster College; Michael J. Drexler, Brown University; Sally Ann Drucker, North Carolina State University; Arlene A. Elder, University of Cincinnati; the late Everett Emerson (Emeritus), University of North Carolina at Chapel Hill; Bernard F. Engel, Michigan State University; Hugh English, City University of New York; Betsy Erkkila, Northwestern University; Lillian Faderman, California State University, Fresno; Charles Fanning, Southern Illinois University; Robert M. Farnsworth, University of Missouri–Kansas City; Dominika Ferens, Wroclaw University; Laraine Fergenson, City University of New York, Bronx Community College; Judith Fetterley, University at Albany, State University of New York; Joseph Fichtelberg, Hofstra University; Cheryl J. Fish, Manhattan Community College, City University of New York; Lucy M. Freibert, University of Louisville; George S. Friedman, Towson State University; Susan Stanford Friedman, University of Wisconsin–Madison; Albert Furtwangler, Mount Allison University; Diana Hume George, Pennsylvania State University at Erie, The Behrend College; Allison Giffen, New Mexico State University; Leah Blatt Glasser, Mount Holyoke College; Wendell P. Glick, University of Minnesota; William Goldhurst, University of Florida; Rita K. Gollin, State University of New York, Geneseo; Suzanne Gossett, Loyola University of Chicago; Philip Gould, Brown University; Maryemma Graham, University of Kansas; Theodora Rapp Graham, Pennsylvania State University, Harrisburg; Robert M. Greenberg, Temple University; Barry Gross, Michigan State University; James Guimond, Rider College; Minrose C. Gwin, University of New Mexico; Alfred Habegger; Joan F. Hallisey, Regis College; Jeffrey A. Hammond, St. Mary's College of Maryland; Earl N. Harbert, Northeastern University; Sharon M. Harris, University of Connecticut; Susan K. Harris, University of Kansas; Trudier Harris, University of North Carolina–Chapel Hill; Ellen Louise Hart, University of California, Santa Cruz; the late William L. Hedges, Goucher College; Joan D. Hedrick, Trinity College; Allison Heisch, San Jose State University; Robert Hemenway, University of Kentucky; Desirée Henderson, University of Texas at Arlington; Kristin Herzog, University of Massachusetts, Lowell; Donald R. Hettinga, Calvin College; Danielle Hinrichs, University of Southern California; Hilary W. Holladay, Independent Scholars Association of the North Carolina Triangle at Chapel Hill; Elvin Holt, Southwest Texas State University; Kenneth Alan Hovey, University of Texas at San Antonio; Akasha (Gloria) Hull, University of California, Santa Cruz; James M. Hutchisson, The Citadel; Susan Clair Imbarrato, Minnesota State University, Moorhead; Gregory S. Jackson, Rutgers University; Ronna C. Johnson, Tufts University; Paul Jones, University of North Carolina–Chapel Hill; Joyce Ann Joyce, Temple University; Nancy Carol Joyner, Western Carolina University; Rose Yalow Kamel, University of Sciences in Philadelphia; Carolyn L. Karcher, Temple University; Janet Kaufman, University of Iowa; Richard S. Kennedy, Temple University; Carol Farley Kessler, Pennsylvania State University; Elizabeth L. Keyser, Hollins University; Karen L. Kilcup, University of North Carolina–Greensboro; Daniel Y. Kim, Brown University; Elaine H. Kim, University of California, Berkeley; Marcy Jane Knopf-Newman, Boise State University; Maureen Konkle, University of Missouri Columbia; Michael Kreyling, Vanderbilt University; Lawrence La Fountain-Stokes, University of Michigan, Ann Arbor; Him Mark Lai; David M. Larson, Cleveland State University; Estella Lauter, University of Wisconsin–Green Bay; Barry Leeds, Central Connecticut State University; George S. Lensing, University of North Carolina–Chapel Hill; James A. Levernier, University of Arkansas at Little Rock; Walter K. Lew, University of California, Los Angeles; Cliff Lewis, University of Massachusetts at Lowell; Patricia Liggins-Hill, University of San Francisco; Genny Lim, New College of California; Shirley Geok-lin Lim, University of California, Santa Barbara; John Lowe, Louisiana State University; Juanita Luna-Lawhn, San Antonio College; Etta Madden, Southwest Missouri State University; Joseph Mancini, Jr., George Washington University; Daniel Marder, University of Tulsa; Robert A. Martin; Derek C. Maus, University of North Carolina–Chapel Hill; Kate McCullough, Cornell University; Deborah E. McDowell, University of Virginia; Joseph R. McElrath, Florida State University; Peggy McIntosh, Wellesley College Center for Research on Women; the late Nellie Y. McKay, University of Wisconsin–Madison; D. H. Melhem, Union for Experimenting Colleges and Universities; Michael J. Mendelsohn, University of Tampa; Gabriel Miller, Rutgers University; James A. Miller, George Washington University; Jeanne-Marie A. Miller, Howard University; Keith D. Miller, Arizona State University; Arthenia J. Bates Millican; Daniel Moos, Rhode Island College; James S. Moy, University of Wisconsin–Madison; Joel Myerson, University of South Carolina; Cary Nelson, University of Illinois at Urbana–Champaign; Margaret F. Nelson, Oklahoma State University; Charles H. Nichols (Emeritus), Brown University; Vera Norwood, University of New Mexico; Michael O'Brien, Miami University; Margaret Anne O'Connor, University of North Carolina–Chapel Hill; Genaro M. Padilla, University of California, Berkeley; Linda Pannill, Transylvania University; James W. Parins, University of Arkansas at Little Rock; Grace H. Park, University of California, Los Angeles; Vivian M. Patraka, Bowling Green State University; John J. Patton, Atlantic Cape Community College; James Robert Payne, New Mexico State University; Richard Pearce, Wheaton College; Michael W. Peplow, Western International University; Ronald Primeau, Central Michigan University; John Purdy, Western Washington University; Jennifer L. Randisi, University of California, Berkeley; Geoffrey Rans, University of Western Ontario; Julius Rowan Raper, University of North Carolina–Chapel Hill; Kelly Reames; John M. Reilly, Howard University; Thelma Shinn Richard, Arizona State University; Phillip M. Richards, Colgate University; Marilyn Richardson; John-Michael Rivera, University of Colorado; Evelyn Hoard Roberts,

Saint Louis Community College at Meramec; James A. Robinson, University of Maryland; William H. Robinson, Rhode Island College; Kenneth M. Roemer, University of Texas at Arlington; Judith Roman-Royer, Indiana University East; Nicholas D. Rombes, Jr., Pennsylvania State University; the late Lora Romero, Stanford University; Robert C. Rosen, William Paterson University; Deborah S. Rosenfelt, University of Maryland; Karen E. Rowe, University of California, Los Angeles; A. LaVonne Brown Ruoff (Emrita), University of Illinois at Chicago; Roshni Rustomji-Kerns, Stanford University; Doreen Alvarez Saar, Drexel University; Enrique Sacerio-Garí, Bryn Mawr College; Douglas C. Sackman, University of Puget Sound; Ramón Saldívar, Stanford University; Sonia Saldívar-Hull, University of California, Los Angeles; Thomas Scanlan, Ohio University; Gary Scharnhorst, University of New Mexico; Judith Scheffler, West Chester University; Bethany Ridgway Schneider, Bryn Mawr College; George J. Searles, Mohawk Valley Community College; Cynthia Secor, Higher Education Resource Services, Mid-America, at the University of Denver; David S. Shields, University of South Carolina; Thelma J. Shinn, Arizona State University; Frank C. Shuffelton, University of Rochester; Peggy Skaggs, Angelo State University; Katharine Capshaw Smith, University of Connecticut; Beth Helen Stickney, City University of New York; Catharine R. Stimpson, New York University; Janis P. Stout, Texas A & M University; Jim Sullivan, Mira Costa College; the late Claudia Tate, Princeton University; Ronnie Theisz, Black Hills State University; John Edgar Tidwell, University of Kansas; Eleanor Q. Tignor, City University of New York, La Guardia Community College; Jane Tompkins, University of Illinois at Chicago; Steven C. Tracy; Eleanor W. Traylor, Howard University; Richard Tuerk, Texas A&M University–Commerce; Bonnie TuSmith, Northeastern University; George Uba, California State University, Northridge; Paula Uruburu, Hofstra University; Donald Vanouse, State University of New York College at Oswego; Daniel Walden, Pennsylvania State University; Arthur E. Waterman, Georgia State University; Sybil Weir, San Jose State University; Judith Wellman, State University of New York College at Oswego; James L. W. West III, Pennsylvania State University; Thomas R. Whitaker, Yale University; Barbara A. White, University of New Hampshire; Margaret B. Wilkerson, University of California, Berkeley; the late Kenny J. Williams, Duke University; Marcellette G. Williams, Michigan State University; James C. Wilson, University of Cincinnati; Norma Clark Wilson, University of South Dakota; Amy E. Winans, Susquehanna University; Kate H. Winter, State University of New York at Albany; Frederick Woodard, University of Iowa; Jean Fagan Yellin (Emeritus), Pace University; Amy Marie Yerkes, Johns Hopkins University; Judith Yung, University of California, Santa Cruz.

The Heath Anthology of American Literature

Volume A

Beginnings to 1800

BEGINNINGS TO 1700

When he was captured in December 1607 by a large band of Algonkians hunting deer, Captain John Smith was taken by the *werowance*—the headman, or tribal chief—of the group to be the white werowance of the Jamestown colony that had arrived in the area the year before. According to native custom, it was inappropriate to put werowances to death, so Smith's fate could be determined only by Powhatan, the hereditary chief of the Algonkians who had expanded his realm north from the present-day Carolinas into the tidewater Virginia area. Smith was taken to Powhatan's residence, where he impressed the native chief with his self-confident bravery and his seemingly supernatural pocket compass. Powhatan evidently invoked an Algonkian custom and in a ceremony of transformation adopted Smith as a subordinate werowance into his group. The ceremony involved his eleven- or twelve-year-old daughter, Pocahontas. But as Smith told the story years later in his *Generall Historie of Virginia, New-England, and the Summer Isles* (1624), it looked very different:

having feasted him after their best barbarous manner they could, a long consultation was held, but the conclusion was, two great stones were brought before Powhatan: then as many as could layd hands on him, dragged him to them, and thereon laid his head, and being ready with their clubs, to beate out his braines, Pocahontas the Kings dearest daughter, when no intreaty could prevaile, got his head in her armes, and laid her owne upon his to save him from death: whereat the Emperour was contented he should live to make him hatchets, and her bells, beads, and copper; for they thought him as well of all occupations as themselves.

Smith's story of Pocahontas emerged among English-speakers as a tale of the charity and bravery of a young Indian maiden who was willing to sacrifice her life in order to save a man of superior merit. In the nineteenth century, it attained the status of a myth justifying colonial conquest, and in the twentieth century, it became emblematic of the European imposition of "otherness" on inhabitants of the New World. And thus the story remained for centuries, until anthropologists and ethnographers began to dismantle the assumptions behind the tale. These assumptions stem from one key belief—that the explorers who had come to the Americas were much superior to the Native Americans already there because of their race, religion, and so-called "civilization." Such ethnocentrism, the attitude that one's own culture is superior to any other, characterized the attitudes held by European settlers—whether Spanish or French or English—who came to the Americas and confronted the various indigenous peoples.

What of those peoples? We know now, for instance, that the Jamestown colonists arrived at a time when the eastern native groups were experiencing cultural change. When Smith met Powhatan, Powhatan was in the midst of consolidating control over about thirty different groups in the Chesapeake region. Tribal populations had suffered devastation from European diseases brought to the Indians, who had no natural immunities to such diseases, before Jamestown was founded. The groups had disintegrated and scattered in the face of European intrusion. Powhatan, who appeared in immense dignity before his amalgamated peoples, took advantage of the opportunity to consolidate power into his own Algonkian band. In fact, some scholars suggest that had the process of Powhatan's empire-building continued without the further interruption of the Europeans, indigenous states not unlike those of the Aztec, Incan, or Mayan groups of Central and South America might have established themselves over the course of the next centuries.

When Powhatan adopted Smith as a werowance, he was, at least in the minds of his own people, subjecting Smith to his own power. When Powhatan then used his quasi-alliance with Smith to trade for European goods that appealed to his native allies, he was further augmenting his own power. Smith himself observed that everything that was stolen from Jamestown found its way into Powhatan's hands, illustrating the redistributive power of the chief. Finally, when Powhatan married Pocahontas to the English settler and tobacco planter John Rolfe in 1614, he was cementing a guarded peace with the white settlers. Powhatan, then, used Smith and the English (not to mention his own daughter) to demonstrate his considerable power to his own people.

Native American Culture and Traditions

Captain John Smith may have been ethnocentric, but he was also one of the first to point out the falseness of the common European view that Native Americans lacked the attributes of what the West considered an organized society: law, inheritance, religion, and systematic agriculture. In fact, the native peoples of the Americas had centuries-old traditions, traditions antedating Christianity and western European social organizations, traditions from which they derived their own cultural stories about the origin of all peoples, the existence of what could be construed as good and evil in the world, the development of different societies, the development of agriculture, and so forth. They did not consider themselves primitive peoples.

The term *Indian* was the misnomer Columbus gave the peoples he met in October 1492 in the Bahamas because he thought he had found the Indies (until he died, he persisted in this belief). The term *Native Americans* derives from the fact that the migrations of these peoples antedated the arrival of the Spanish in the fifteenth century as well as the settlement of Indo-European speakers in western Europe. According to many anthropologists, the forerunners of the Native American population, often called Paleo-Indians, probably arrived in the Americas more than 30,000 years ago, having traveled a now submerged land connection between Asia and North America at the site of the Bering Strait. Nomadic peoples, they hunted game and gathered wild fruits and greens for sustenance, and they eventually spread—over the course of many centuries—through North and South America. Natives living in central Mexico began to cultivate food crops about 5,500 years ago, and the innovation of agricultural production curtailed their nomadic existence; most started to live more stationary lives.

In the areas now known as Mexico and Guatemala (Mesoamerica), the most advanced Native American civilizations—the Aztec and the Maya—evolved from great empires characterized by large cities, ceremonial sites with massive pyramid-like temples, hereditary rule by an elite of warrior-priests, and agricultural production of food. The Aztecs, warlike peoples, had consolidated control over central Mexico by the time the Spanish arrived there. The Mayan civilization, already in decline by the time the Spanish came, had invented systems of writing and mathematics, along with a calendar. Such developments had begun to disappear from historical record by the time the English arrived in the sixteenth century: the Spanish invaders of the fifteenth century had deliberately destroyed native cities and cultures to signify Spanish domination. On the sites that had once held Aztec, Mayan, and Incan temples, the Spanish built cathedrals and monasteries. And, despite the occasional intervention of priests, the Spanish burned or otherwise destroyed the vestiges of any written records they found. The native peoples to the north of these ancient civilizations fared somewhat better because the English, French, and Dutch, not immediately interested in colonizing the lands they found, did not so fully and systematically interfere with the native populations. However, the changes foisted upon these native groups were no less incontrovertible.

Knowledge of Native American culture as it was *then* is not available from written records; instead, what little we know about these peoples has been pieced together from various material artifacts, such as stone implements, pottery pieces, and shards, and from oral stories as they have been passed as traditions down through scores of generations of native peoples. What the traditions reveal is that the peoples encountered by Europeans upon their arrival in North America were well adapted to their environments: those who lived in environments not well suited to agriculture, like the Paiutes and Shoshonis, who inhabited the part of the Great Basin now known as Nevada and Utah, continued in seasonal movements; those who combined agriculture with fishing, gathering, and hunting, like the Chinooks of present-day Washington and Oregon, the Arikaras of the Missouri River Valley, and the Algonkians of what is now eastern Canada and northeastern United States, tended to remain in relatively defined territories in which they made occasional seasonal movements within a circumscribed land area. Their languages, social and political structures, and religions differed widely yet were derived from models that had evolved, sometimes patrilineally (along male birth lines) and sometimes matrilineally (through the female line), over the course of centuries. When the Europeans arrived in the fifteenth century, they confronted a wide variety of cultures—perhaps four to six million people. These peoples spoke well over a thousand different languages. No wonder they did not like being grouped together as if they were one people; no wonder, too, that they did not at first consider uniting to repel the European invaders.

Native American religions reflected cultural practices. For the most part, Native Americans were polytheistic, believing in a multitude of gods. Their religious rituals often related to their chief means of subsistence, which varied. Native Americans who relied upon agriculture, like the Pueblo peoples of the present-day American Southwest, who began raising squash and beans about 3,000 years ago, tended to evoke major deities associated with cultivation, and their chief festivals centered on planting and harvest. By contrast, those Native Americans whose subsistence was based upon hunting and gathering, like the Siouan-speaking tribes of the Great Plains, associated their religious practices with animals, and their major festivals were related to hunting. Unlike the religious practices of the patriarchally determined European societies, which placed men at the fore of their familial, social, and religious systems, some Native American groups gave prominent religious roles to women. In the East, for instance, the Six Nations, or Iroquois peoples, gave women the most prominent religious positions; Iroquois women performed most of their societies' agricultural chores. If Europeans returned to Europe with conflicting reports about the Native Americans they encountered, it was due in part to the diversity of Indian cultures.

Given their manner of living, their social and political organizations, and their religions, Native Americans generally had little use for written records. They relied instead upon group traditions and group memory. Their lives in constant flux from seasonal change or tribal intrusion, Native Americans valued highly the oratorical skills by which their traditions could be transmitted to the group and to later generations. Tellers told stories of the development and peopling of the world, of the group's determination of places to live, of the presence of good and evil in the world. Full of rhythm and repetition, these oral forms—ceremonial or popular songs, prayers, chants or incantations, and historical narratives—resemble dramatic performances. In addition to speaking, a narrator enacts scenes, sometimes adopting different voices and gestures for different characters, sometimes moving around, within a circumscribed area, in order to reflect particular tribally known—and tribally significant—places and times. In Navajo ritual, for instance, a speaker or chanter will work within a sand-painted circle inside a hogan (a consecrated dwelling), selecting symbolic postures and voices so as to invoke, in a ritually correct performance, particular Holy People, the supernatural beings of the Navajos. Thus, an individual speaking voice reinforces communal values, creating or recreating in both spoken word and physical gesture a culturally significant moment in the tribal formation or belief system.

Early Native American oral forms are known today primarily through written transmissions that, precisely because they are written, cannot represent the cultural norms and circumstances under which the literature originally emerged. Readers today must read Native American songs or chants or narratives in the absence of a generally well-known, accompanying cultural "text"—the narrator, the narrative scene, and the cultural assumptions—from which the forms emerged. And even the words that we today reproduce in anthologies are not the words, not the languages, the Native Americans used. Most North American native works from the early period are transcriptions that were made mostly in the late nineteenth and early twentieth centuries, when anthropologists and ethnographers first sought to record native traditions and languages just as the Native Americans who carried on their own traditions and languages were banished to reservations

Even the few older written forms that survive—primarily the works of the Mayas of Central America—have been linguistically transformed by being recorded in the Spanish language soon after the Mayas were conquered by the Spanish. *The Book of Chilam Balam of Chumayel* (as it is called in the twentieth-century English translation) contains the Mayan chant, "The Beginning of Sickness," which speaks of the time before the Spanish arrived, a time when the Mayas felt in harmony with their environment, and so expresses the Mayan perception of the result of the Spanish conquest:

Then they adhered to their reason.
There was no sin;
in the holy faith their lives were passed.
There was then no sickness;
they had then no aching bones;
they had then no high fever;
they had then no smallpox;
they had then no burning chest;
they had then no abdominal pains;
they had then no consumption;
they had then no headache.
At the time the course of humanity was
    orderly.
The foreigners made it otherwise when
    they arrived here.
They brought shameful things when
    they came [. . .]
this was the cause of our sickness also.
There were no more lucky days for us;
we had no sound judgment.
At the end of our loss of vision,
and of our shame,
everything shall be revealed.

The Europeans Arrive

The Book of Chilam Balam of Chumayel also offers the Mayan version of the arrival of the Spanish:

They came from the east when they
arrived.
Then Christianity also began.
The fulfillment of its prophecy is
ascribed to the east [. . .]
Then with the true God, the true *Dios,*
came the beginning of our misery.
It was the beginning of tribute,
the beginning of church dues,
the beginning of strife with purse-
snatching,
the beginning of strife with blow-guns;
the beginning of strife by trampling on
people,
the beginning of robbery with violence,
the beginning of forced debts,
the beginning of debts enforced by false
testimony,
the beginning of individual strife,
a beginning of vexation.

It was an intrusion that forced upon Mayan culture a complete transformation. One of only a few contemporary views available, the poem reveals the motive for the Spanish exploration: colonization and wealth. But it also reveals the extent to which, in the absence of the known language of the speakers, their language must have been transformed to accommodate the language of the conquerer. Before the Spanish arrived, the Mayan language would have had no word for "Christianity," nor for the many other elements associated with a money-based economy (e.g., "purse"). With the onslaught of the Christianizing Spanish, the Mayas adapted to and adopted the language—and thus the culture—of their invaders. With Spanish as the mediating language, the Mayas would never again experience their culture within its own linguistic construct.

This is an important point to remember, for the Spanish likewise faced a linguistic barrier: how were they to name the peoples they encountered and forced to assimilate into their own culture? The Spanish language, too, was shaped by experiences Spaniards had in Europe and in world travel. But how were they to record phenomena they had no language to describe? In some instances, the Spanish adopted native names. More simply, they renamed things, like the land they found, thus inscribing their own colonial expectations. In the language and attitude of the conqueror, Columbus promptly renamed the island he found in the Bahamas *San Salvador,* claiming it for the king and queen of Spain. Absolutely sure that he had reached the Indies, he called the people *los Indios,* Indians.

There is an odd irony in this: the Spanish had come upon a land they didn't want, a land perceived as an obstruction rather than an expectation, a land they were seeking to get around, not inhabit. When Spain sent its fleets westward in the fifteenth century, it was looking for a passage to the east, to Asia, which offered the riches—and the African slaves—that neighboring Portugal had acquired a century earlier. A century after the Spanish, the French likewise sent expeditions through the northeast portion of the present-day United States, searching for a legendary "Northwest Passage" to Asia and the Far East. In the process of exploring and then of naming anew, the Spanish came to realize what they had come upon. Before long, Europeans generally acknowledged that a significant section of the world, a section about which they had known nothing, was available to them.

The Spanish and French were among the first to dispatch exploratory voyages. Among the leaders of early voyages was the Florentine Amerigo Vespucci, who explored the South American coast in 1499. He was the first to publish the idea among Europeans that a new continent had been found; the lands were credited by name to him, as *America.* More than five hundred years earlier, Norse explorers had briefly colonized present-day Newfoundland; before that, according to some accounts, the Chinese had explored the coast of what is now southern California. In addition, recent archaeological work suggests that African ships had visited the Americas by, if not before, the early fourteenth century. Spain controlled the seas in the late medieval and early Renaissance era. Once Spain announced that land across the ocean was available to the west, all Europe became interested in western exploration. The accounts of explorers like John Cabot (1497), Giovanni da Verrazano (1524), Jacques Cartier (1534), and Henry Hudson (1609–1610)—all of whom searched for a Northwest Passage—held Europe's attention. Each new account seemed more promising and fascinating than the last. The public demanded stories about the intriguing "new" land and its inhabitants; monarchs sought information about the possibilities of enlarging their empires and increasing their treasuries; the pope saw possibilities of extending the Catholic Church in missionary efforts.

Except for Portugal, a poorer country that had nonetheless effected, in the fifteenth century, the introduction of African slaves into Europe, only Spain was in a position—due to a reinvigorated monarchy that encouraged dominion over the seas—to move immediately into the areas Europeans had discovered in what is now Central and South America, Florida and the southeastern United States, and the southwestern United States (through the West and Pacific Northwest). By the 1520s, the Spanish dreams of wealth and dominion were realized: Cortés conquered the Aztec Empire when he gained the capital city, Tenochtitlán, an achievement that encouraged the Aztecs to kill their ruler, Moctezuma; the Aztec treasures of gold and silver were claimed for Spain. While the explorations of conquistadores like Juan Rodríguez Cabrillo, who sailed along the California coast, Hernando de Soto, who explored the Mississippi River, and Francisco Vásquez de Coronado, who explored the Southwest, proved less monetarily valuable, those of Francisco Pizarro, who explored western and coastal South America, were fruitful for Spain. Pizarro conquered and enslaved the Incas in 1535, claiming for Spain the richest silver mines in the world. Within half a century after Columbus's voyages, Spain controlled—as its own possessions—the most extensive empire known since ancient Rome.

The quickly acquired wealth exacted its own demands on Spain, however. The economy of Spain could not easily adapt to the new-found gold and silver; rapid inflation caused Spanish products to become overpriced in international trade, eventually bringing about the collapse of Spain's world-renowned textile manufactures, among scores of other businesses. The South American mines showed signs of giving out by the middle of the seventeenth century, and Spain's economy crumbled. In addition, the missionary efforts of the Catholic Church created—from the very start—problems for the wealth-seeking colonizers. A 1493 Papal Bull, expressing the desire to Christianize Native Americans rather than enslave them, prevented open aggression against the native populations. A 1542 Spanish law forbidding the enslavement of the Native Americans temporarily interfered with colonizing efforts. The Spaniards quickly turned instead to the African slave trade for their labor force. The colonists, mostly men, formed relations with native and later black women, which created the racially mixed population of present-day Latin America. Finally, when the English defeated the Spanish Armada in 1588, Spain lost its century-long control of the rich lands and the seas to the west.

England and France watched greedily while Spain extended its empire, and both countries took advantage of Spain's losses as the sixteenth century progressed. France had early established outposts for trade—

largely furs from the Native Americans for European metalworks and cloth—in the eastern portions of what is now North America. While searching for a Northwest Passage, the French established control over fur traffic at Quebec (1608) and Montreal (1642) and along the St. Lawrence River. Although the interests of France were largely for trade with the native peoples rather than enslavement of them, the French presence nonetheless influenced native societies, which shifted to some extent from subsistence hunting or agriculture to trapping and trade. Combined with the trading activities of the Swedish at Fort Christina on the Delaware River, founded in 1638, and the Dutch at New Amsterdam and Fort Orange, founded in 1624, French activities had a significant impact upon the interests and resources of Native Americans.

But it was finally the English who, though they arrived last, had the most extensive influence on North America. Seeking wealth and colonization to match Spain's, England began sending exploratory parties to the eastern seaboard in the 1580s. English efforts proved largely unsuccessful until England eventually changed its endeavor from accelerated colonization to agricultural community-making. Unlike Spain, France, and the Netherlands, England finally succeeded when it sent large numbers of men—and some women—to set up agriculturally based communities. Efforts at Jamestown would largely have failed (and nearly did fail) had not John Smith, despite the reservations and open hostility of the men who landed with him in 1607, insisted upon a daily regimen of work, planting, and hunting, during the first year of settlement. England's control of the tobacco planting and trade shortly followed the Jamestown settlement. When religious and social changes in England caused the English Separatists, better known as the Pilgrims, to leave Holland and settle at Plymouth in 1620 and the Congregationalists, better known as the Puritans, to leave England and settle at Massachusetts Bay in 1630, England's endeavors to dominate the New World were fully confirmed.

None of these early settlements would have succeeded without the aid of friendly native neighbors. As we have seen, cordial relations with the Algonkian confederation held the key to English survival at Jamestown. The colonists learned from the Algonkians how to hunt and fish, and most importantly, how to cultivate corn and tobacco. Furthermore, the colonists learned the importance of trade with the Native Americans. The Separatists who settled in the area they called Plymouth in 1620 had set sail on the *Mayflower* with a group of adventurers bound for the upper reaches of the Virginia area. Having gone off course, they arrived at what is now Cape Cod as winter was setting in. Although they were, as a group, more willing than the Virginia colonists to work, they could not plant crops so late in the season. As it was, by spring only half of the *Mayflower*'s passengers were alive. The Pokanokets (or Wampanoags) on Cape Cod had suffered terrible losses in an epidemic (probably of smallpox) in the years 1616–1618. Massasoit, their leader, quickly signed a protective treaty with the colonists, supplying them with the foodstuffs essential for survival and showing them how to hunt, fish, and plant crops.

Aid from their native neighbors was also essential to the survival of the larger colonial effort at Massachusetts Bay. Unlike the privately funded efforts at Jamestown and Plymouth, the Puritan colony was chartered by King Charles I. But like the earlier efforts, it made the "civilization" and religious conversion of natives a central motivating factor in the justification for colonization. English missionizing in the North and the South, however, would not get underway in earnest for several decades, during which time the English traded with many tribes, made treaties for land and protection, expanded ruthlessly into native territories, and played one tribe against the other. Although English colonizing efforts differed from the efforts of Spain and France and the Netherlands, they also differed from each other. Jamestown was settled predominantly by upper-class men who were less willing to work at subsistence living and had little similarity beyond their elite class assumptions. The New England communities fared better first, because women were brought *from the start,* thus ensuring essential repopulation at the earliest colonial stage; second, because the "middling" and merchant class background of the people generally made them accept field labor; and third, because many of the settlers had a common ideological goal, the development of, as John Winthrop (borrowing from the biblical book of Matthew) phrased it, a "city upon a hill."

New World Cultures

The Puritans were, like the Jamestown settlers, ethnocentric, and they brought with them a consuming hegemonic vision of a community dedicated to the fulfillment of God's vision. That God's vision might differ if one were not a Puritan occurred only to the most radical—and reviled—among them. Theirs was a community based upon the individual's acceptance of his or her status, including its educational and financial prerogatives, which they believed to be God-given in both church and state: men above women, whites above all other races, Protestant English above all other cultures. The Spanish, too, worked largely from the belief that theirs was the one true course for glory, whether that glory was signified by wealth acquired here (as with the conquistadores) or hereafter (as with the missionary priests). The patriarchal assumptions held by Renaissance and late Renaissance European societies, both Catholic and Protestant, subjected women and other cultures to a hierarchy of power invested in the husband, the governor, and God. The Americas merely offered a new arena for Europe to work out its ages-old rivalries, as Spain, France, the Netherlands, and England vied over souls and resources.

But these cultures did not vie for dominion without resistance from Native Americans. Thirty years after Pedro Menéndez de Avilés, along with a group of soldiers, priests, and settlers, established Spain's first permanent settlement in North America (St. Augustine, Florida, 1565), a similar group led by Juan de Oñate colonized New Mexico. Their mutual goals of finding wealth and Christianizing native peoples spurred them to make ruthless encroachments upon Native Americans. Native laborers were forced to destroy their own religious places and set up monasteries and to work the Spaniards' fields and care for their livestock. Spanish settlers and missionaries, based at Santa Fe (beginning in 1610), saw success meet their efforts for a half-century before the Pueblos revolted. In 1680, under the leadership of Popé, a respected medicine man whom the Pueblos called Tío Pepe, the Pueblos drove the Spanish intruders from New Mexico. Their uprising continued until Spanish authority was restored, at least in name, in 1692, when Spain decided upon a policy of cooperation with rather than coercion of the Pueblo peoples.

A less systematic but no less harmful repression of the Native Americans occurred at the hands of the English. In their continued incursions on Native American lands and culture, the English settlers likewise forced the Native Americans to strike back at the intruders. At the outset the Powhatan confederacy established peaceable connections with the English, even to the point where racial intermarriage was encouraged—as it was in New Spain. But when the continually expanding Virginia tobacco culture took away the best Algonkian lands and threatened encroachment upon additional Algonkian territories, stripping them of trees and fertile planting areas, the Powhatan confederacy attacked

Rules and Precepts That Are Observed in the College

1. When any scholar is able to understand Tully, or suchlike classical Latin author extempore, and make and speak true Latin in verse and prose, *suo ut aiunt Marte* [by his own effort, as they say]; and decline perfectly the paradigms of nouns and verbs in the Greek tongue, let him then and not before be capable of admission into the college.

2. Let every student be plainly instructed and earnestly pressed to consider well the main end of his life and studies is *to know God and Jesus Christ which is eternal life* (John 17:3), and therefore to lay Christ in the bottom as the only foundation of all sound knowledge and learning. And seeing the Lord only gives wisdom, let everyone seriously set himself by prayer in secret to seek it of Him (Prov. 2:3).

3. Everyone shall so exercise himself in reading the Scriptures twice a day that he shall be ready to give such an account of his proficiency therein, both in theoretical observations of the language and logic, and in practical and spiritual truths, as his tutor shall require, according to his ability; seeing *the entrance of the word giveth light, it giveth understanding to the simple* (Ps. 119:130).

Anon., "Account of Harvard College," 1643

the Virginia colony in 1622. Not until 1646 did the Powhatans reach an uneasy treaty with the English. By the early 1670s, however, Virginians wanted the rich lands north of the York River, lands that had been ceded to native groups in earlier treaties. A series of raids and counter-raids between planters and the powerful Susquehannock tribe during the winter of 1676 led white planters to rally behind a recently arrived planter, Nathaniel Bacon, who wanted "to ruine and extirpate all Indians in generall." After a "rebellion" that nearly tore the colony apart, the Virginia House of Burgesses negotiated a treaty in 1677 that opened the disputed lands to white settlers.

Similar problems over lands and peoples occurred in the English settlements to the north. The Pequot War (1637) signaled the end of peaceable relations between whites and natives in the Connecticut River Valley area. Provoked by English raids on their villages that continued from 1636 into 1637, the Pequots, having attempted, but failing to gain support from other local bands, attacked the new town of Wethersfield in April 1637; they killed nine and captured two young women who were eventually returned unharmed. A retaliatory party of Massachusetts Bay settlers, aided by some of their Narragansett allies, attacked and burned the key Pequot town on the Mystic River. At least four hundred people—many of them women and children—were killed, and the few survivors were captured and enslaved. War erupted again forty years later over the fertile Connecticut River Valley, led by Metacomet, known to the colonists as King Philip, the son of Massasoit, leader of the Pokanoket or Wampanoag band. Resenting the intrusions of the English on his ancestral lands, Metacomet sought the support of the neighboring Nipmucks and Narragansetts. In the fall of 1675, the three native groups made joint attacks upon settlements in the Connecticut River Valley, and in the winter and spring of 1676, they attacked Plymouth and burned Providence to the ground. Despite scarce food and ammunition stores, the natives were largely successful until the English were aided by "praying" (converted) Indians. They regained control over the valley when Metacomet was killed in ambush in the autumn of 1676; his wife and son were captured and sold to the West Indian slave trade. The New England Indian alliance never gathered force again, and the devastating consequences of the war set New England's development back several decades.

Another important factor in New World cultures was the presence of slavery. Africans had traveled to the Americas with the earliest exploring parties from Spain, including those directed by Coronado and Cabeza de Vaca. Indeed, a black man named Pedro Alonso Niño is said to have participated in the first expedition of Columbus. Records indicate that the transatlantic slave trade began in 1502, when the Spanish brought the first Africans to work plantations in the West Indies. Balboa's 1513 expedition to the Pacific included thirty slaves, and slaves accompanied Hernando de Soto on his Mississippi exploration in 1539. The best-known (because of written records) of these early slave travelers, Estévan (also called Estevanico and Esteban), explored with Cabeza de Vaca and Fray Marcos de Niza the areas that are now Arizona and New Mexico and lived with Cabeza de Vaca among the Indians. Then, in the late 1530s, he served as a guide for Fray Marcos de Niza in his search for the Seven Cities of Cíbola. Blacks also accompanied Alarçon and Coronado and were with Menéndez at the founding of St. Augustine.

Initially, the Spanish attempted to draw their slave labor from the indigenous peoples of the New World. In addition to practical problems encountered in this effort, both the Catholic Church and the Spanish government eventually prohibited their enslavement. In 1517, in protesting the exploitation of natives, the Spanish missionary Bartolomé de Las Casas proposed the use of African slaves instead. Permission to import Africans was soon granted, and by the mid-sixteenth century roughly ten thousand blacks were being brought into the Spanish colonies annually. By the time the English developed their own settlements in the Caribbean and North America, the Spanish had held Africans in slavery for over a century.

Historical evidence seems to suggest that the blacks who arrived during the first two to three decades of English settlement came as indentured servants, which meant that they eventually became free. Such servants arrived at Jamestown on a Dutch vessel in 1619, only twelve years after the founding of the settlement. Precisely because indentured servants could eventually become free and move off the lands they had worked, planters in the South came to rely upon the slave market for laborers. The increasing demand for slaves meant that larger and larger groups of Africans were captured on their homelands and sold into bondage. Some, like those taken to South Carolina, were skilled agricultural laborers, and they taught their owners much about survival and success in an environment like that in the Carolina lowlands. The South was not the only place where English acquired slaves, however. Africans were first imported into Connecticut in 1629 and in 1637 into Massachusetts, which in 1641 became the first colony to legalize slavery in its legal code. Also at about this time New England ships became actively involved in the slave trade. By the end of the seventeenth century, African or West Indian slaves were increasingly more common in the households of the well-to-do from Massachusetts Bay to Florida, Jamestown to Santa Fe and beyond.

As the plantation-based economy of the southern colonies expanded, the importation of slaves accelerated rapidly. Not surprisingly, with the swelling black population came greater numbers of slave escapes and revolts. Indeed, in a number of areas, fugitive slaves called "maroons" (from the Spanish *cimarrones*) had established independent communities and were creating trouble for local white settlements. Elsewhere, some blacks found refuge with Native Americans after their flight from slavery. In retaliation for this and other rebellious black behavior, whites enacted increasingly strict slave codes in order to regulate the behavior of their human property. One of the most important legal actions relating to the treatment of blacks was the law—first passed in Virginia in 1662—which stipulated that the status of a child would follow that of its mother. In combination with the forbidding of interracial marriage, and also of sexual contact between black men and white women, this legislation decriminalized the systematic rape of black women and insured that the numerous illegitimate slave offspring of white males would have no right to freedom and, in fact, would serve to enrich the slaveowner's human stock. The most tragic result of these developments was the rampant sexual abuse of black women.

Gradually, the morality of slavery as an institution began to be called into question by some of the colonists. In 1652, for example, Rhode Island passed the first antislavery law, although the law was not strictly enforced. Then, in 1688, Quakers in the Philadelphia area became one of the first organized groups to denounce the enslavement of blacks publicly. In 1700, the New England jurist Samuel Sewall wrote a pamphlet condemning slavery. John Woolman, the influential Quaker diarist, also wrote and campaigned against the practice. By 1711, the Quaker denomination generally had taken a strong abolitionist position. From this point on, the slavery issue, and the question of racial difference on which it rested, presented America with one of its most vexing dilemmas.

New World cultures were, by definition, hybrid, multi-racial and multicultural. Furthermore, what the historical record indicates is that the United States of America emerged from a multi-national competition for dominance and possession rather than an establishment of utopian communities in isolated colonies that eventually clashed, in the nineteenth century, as culture met culture in the farther reaches of the American continent. Such competition initiated the tradition of bloody, no-quarter struggles among European claimants to American space that inevitably caught up the native populations, who in the end would suffer the greatest casualties. It also initiated another tradition: the literature of the Americas, whose founding texts offer epic tales not in English, but in French and Spanish. It was in these languages that the unique problems of the textualization of America were first confronted.

New World Literatures

The explorers and settlers who came to the New World left cultures that were experiencing enormous transformations. Tales of the New World only fed imaginations already attuned to wonder because of the invention of moveable type for printing presses, the revival of classical Greek and Roman literature and architecture, and the rise of the arts—painting, sculpture, and architecture. The Renaissance occurred largely for the privileged classes; with the possibility of a developing print culture, however, information and knowledge would never again be the sole province of the intellectuals or well-to-do.

The privileged form of writing during the Renaissance was poetry, especially epic poetry. Christian epic poetry, from Tasso to Spenser and later to Milton, informed the imaginations of those who believed that the lands to the west provided them with a special opportunity to work out their own spiritual journeys. Thus, New England poet Anne Bradstreet transformed the popular epic poem of the (now obscure) French Protestant poet Guilliame du Bartas, and Michael Wigglesworth penned the first bestseller in North America, *The Day of Doom,* a dramatization of the Last Judgment in epic proportions, which many people committed to memory. Although comparatively few books of poetry were published in the Americas during the century, everybody, it seemed, was reading and writing poetry.

Because fiction was banned by the Spanish crown as a genre potentially subversive of centralized authority, poetry was the most popular form of literature in Latin America. A contest held in Mexico in 1585, for instance, attracted more than three hundred entries fashioned after Spanish models. In the first decade of the century, Gaspar Perez de Villagrá memorialized the conquest of New Mexico in epic verse modeled on Renaissance masters, and at the end of the century, Sor Juana Inés de la Cruz, a child prodigy and nun, wrote brilliant allegories, lyrics, and philosophical satires responding acerbically to aspersions cast upon her sex.

In the northern colonies, poems often circulated in manuscript among families and communities or were published as broadsides and hawked in the streets. They appeared in the early almanacs, were copied into church and town records, and were preserved in letters, journals, and what people called "commonplace books." Translation was a popular form, and the first book printed on a New England press in 1640 was a group translation of David's Psalms known as *The Bay Psalm Book.* By contrast, in the Virginia colony, George Sandys, an English immigrant, continued his translations of Ovid's *Metamorphoses* (1626). These two early projects reveal the different orientation of colonial regions. Other popular poetic forms were the pas-

II. On the Nativity Conditions of Slavery (December 1662)

Whereas some doubts have arisen whether children got by an Englishman upon a Negro woman should be slave or free, *be it therefore enacted and declared by this present Grand Assembly,* that all children born in this country shall be held bond or free only according to the condition of the mother; and that if any Christian shall commit fornication with a Negro man or woman, he or she so offending shall pay double the fines imposed by the former act.

V. On the Killing of Slaves (October 1669)

Whereas the only law in force for the punishment of refractory servants resisting their master, mistress, or overseer cannot be inflicted upon Negroes, nor the obstinacy of many of them be suppressed by other than violent means, *be it enacted and declared by this Grand Assembly* if any slave resists his master (or other by his master's order correcting him) and by the extremity of the correction should chance to die, that his death shall not be accounted a felony, but the master (or that other person appointed by the master to punish him) be acquitted from molestation, since it cannot be presumed that premeditated malice (which alone makes murder a felony) should induce any man to destroy his own estate.

Virginia Slave Laws

toral and lyric, the religious meditation and elegy, and some verse drama. Later, verse satire emerged as a significant form.

Prose also saw increased development. Essays and pamphlets abounded on cultural matters from poetry to theology, behavioral guides, and character studies. With the European voyages to the westward lands, exploration, promotional, and travel literature emerged in Europe as the most significant prose form, with narratives ranging from the informative, such as Hakluyt's *Principal Navigations and Discoveries of the English Nation,* to the utopian, such as Thomas More's *Utopia.* Sermons formed a large part of colonial prose writing, especially in New England, along with other theological tracts and treatises. History writing and scientific studies, especially of the teeming and seemingly exotic natural world, both gained an enormous impetus from New World exploration and settlement. Travelers and settlers wrote letters and kept often voluminous journal and diaries, and there was the occasional satire. But travel literature dominated the prose forms until it was surpassed in popularity by the most important prose romance of the day, Cervantes's *Don Quixote* (1605–1615).

All of these genres provided a record of experience according to Old World values, modified by New World encounters. Settlers, like Roger Williams and Cotton Mather, attempted to record Native American speech but were frustrated by language systems that were structured entirely differently—oral in origin and glyphic in form. Furthermore, European responses to the newly found lands and people were thoroughly predetermined by linguistic and cultural constructs. The linguistic construct was predominantly Spanish and later English, and the cultural construct was Christian, ethnocentric, and patriarchal.

Although European explorers considered the new lands to be the possessions of their monarchs, they had no familiar language to describe the remarkable world they encountered. In European writing about contact, the new had to be conveyed in terms of the old, and the result was a continual comparison and contrast with European materials and images. Or writers described the New World in terms of the ideals and desires of the Old World. For example, when Arthur Barlowe's expedition reached the shoals off the coast of Virginia in 1584, Barlowe reported that they encountered "so strong a smell as if we had been in the midst of some delicate garden, abounding with all kinds of oderiferous flowers." Almost a half-century later, John Winthrop made the identical comment upon reaching the shores of the Massachusetts Bay. Barlowe described the Indians as "the most gentle, loving, and faithful, void of all guile, and treason, and such as lived after the manner of the golden age." This idyllic picture was less a reflection of what he might have seen and more a reflection of his reading in classical literature, the Bible, and other travel accounts. Like other travel writers of the era, Barlowe presents the new in terms of the familiar but, at the same time, also sees the new as a lost ideal or prelapsarian paradise, "the golden age" of innocence and guilelessness, or the gilded, legendary cities of Cíbola, allegedly sighted by Cabeza de Vaca and Fray Marcos de Niza. More provocatively, like John Donne in his Elegie XIX, "To His Mistris Going to Bed," Barlowe evokes "America" as the desired Other—discovered, deciphered like a cryptic book that gives up its secrets only to the special few, dominated, explored, and possessed.

Because the very experiences of explorers and settlers were predetermined by their ideologies, their writings construct events to conform to those expectations. The Puritans' settlement narratives, from William Bradford's *Of Plymouth Plantation* to Mary Rowlandson's captivity narrative—an important example of this most "American" of genres—were shaped to conform to their ideological needs. The Puritans believed all events occurred according to the providential will of God. All crises were tests or trials offered by Satan to try one's faith. Thus, when Bradford reports that his surveying party found native corn buried in the ground, he understood this as God's provision for and approval of the Separatist journey. Likewise, when Mary Rowlandson speaks of the remarkable providences that enabled her Wampanoag captors, during the fierce fighting of Metacomet's War, to elude the English army, she does not acknowledge native endurance or military savvy but rather interprets English setbacks as an all-powerful God's testing her spiritual mettle. In histories, diaries, poems, and sermons, Puritan writers searched relentlessly for biblical precedent and for the shaping hand of God in all events. It is not surprising that their descriptions of the world they found, that "howling wilderness," were so skewed for so long.

Representations of the New World were also conditioned by writers' awareness that interest in newness alone would not elicit continued funding of expensive exploratory voyages. Thus, images of America from the outset were shaped by financial concerns and the need to bring back items of value that would enrich the imperial powers. Columbus, for example, collected samples of exploitable natural objects, from aloe trees to natives, as visible proof of the potential return on investments. When later voyages failed to deliver on the promised material gains, he switched to verbal justifications, depicting the New World as the long-sought-for source of creation, marshaling both ancient "science" and the Bible to his defense. When Cabeza de Vaca found himself in the opprobrious position of having to explain the utter failure of an expedition to which he had been assigned as the guardian of the emperor's investment, he claimed to have seen signs of precious metals. Having failed to bring back any, he offered an explanation his Catholic patron could appreciate: his material failure was evidence of divine providence's plan for his transformation into a religious healer, a voice crying in the wilderness, a born-again Christian with the message of a New World man. These precarious overlays of European ideals and desires mapped onto the American geography began a tradition that continues to this day.

The dream of America has been a dream primarily of material but also of spiritual domination. The earliest narratives combine stories of strange environments and fantastic beliefs with the potential benefits of immediate exploitation and eventual "civilization" and religious conversion of natives. Europeans aimed at acquiring both territory for their home countries and converts for Christianity. Whether searching for the fabled spice lands of Marco Polo or dreaming of the terrestrial Paradise, envisioning Eldorado or tracing routes taken by earlier explorers, the chroniclers of exploration wrote about their attempts to decipher, encode, and thus control this strange new world, and to accommodate themselves to the challenges of the new environments.

The genres and literature they brought to the New World often served a disciplinary as well as an accommodating function. Thus, Villagrá rendered the Spanish massacre of the Acoma in courtly verses redolent of Virgil, casting ruthless conquest into the noble art of warfare. In Cotton Mather's magisterial history of the Massachusetts Bay colony, John Winthrop was not merely a clever and important governor of the colony; he was "an American Nehemiah," just as the other Puritan fathers found their counterparts in the Bible or in ancient Greece and Rome. Likewise, the natives were initially angelic and later, more often, demonic. Writers compensated for their sense of powerlessness and disorientation by imagining and textually reproducing their cultural superiority over the native populations they encountered, as they all too often tried to prove their cultural superiority through the use of violence, which is thematized as textual violence as well. From the earliest narratives, dreams of wealth and conquest commingle with dreams of saving souls from eternal perdition, reflecting a multi-national competition not only for particular spaces but for entire peoples.

But the explorers and settlers were not left untouched by the processes they initiated. The interplay of cultural forces produced a tension in which the European writer, while preserving a semblance of an Old World identity, becomes a different self. Over and over the European narrator recalls the sense of being lost in the immensity of the unchartered Americas—as when Columbus faced the strange behavior of his navigational tools that left him literally disoriented; Cabeza de Vaca wandered at the whim of Gulf waters or Indian masters; Laudonnière was unable to decipher a native ritual in which he perceived himself to be the guest of honor; Coronado walked through grasslands so vast that an army left no trace of where it had passed; Champlain became lost in the endless forest while following a beautiful, exotic bird he wished to capture. Thus, the roles of conquerer and conquered invert, and the lines of power are blurred. Stranded among native peoples, Cabeza de Vaca learned to adjust and adapt to a culture he had once deplored. His narrative of captivity is one of many such narratives—a truly "American" genre—that details the dynamic process by which the European comes to accept the Other's world. He finally learned that he was fully comfortable among neither native people nor the Spanish, when he was again found. Who were the civilized, who the barbaric? Who exemplified Christian virtues, and who merely gave them lipservice? The uneasy journey into another culture becomes a kind of otherworldly journey into a new self, a journey that perhaps best signifies the process of becoming an American embodied in the emerging literatures of the New World.

Indigenous Literary Traditions

Imagination is, like other cultural expressions, deeply informed by and expressive of the geographic and social contexts from which it finds inspiration. Imagination shapes both our lived experiences and our understandings of those experiences. To understand "American" literature, we must consider the many imaginative influences that comprise—and contest—the expressive relationship between nation and imagination.

Although the narrative traditions of indigenous peoples of the Americas have long been represented as almost exclusively oral, many communities were familiar with textual expression long before the arrival of Europeans. Indigenous peoples in this hemisphere have communicated their ideas through symbols, ideograms, and other representational means on a wide range of materials. These materials include Mayan and Aztecan codices, Dakota winter counts, Lenape and Haudenosaunee wampum belts, Anishinaabe birchbark scrolls, and Haida crest poles, among others.

These texts complement rather than supplant oral performance traditions. As a result, we can see the adoption of alphabetic writing by Native peoples after European invasion as a natural extension of these other communicative media, rather than an inevitable deviation from oral traditions.

In considering indigenous literary traditions, we must be attentive to a wide range of textual expressions and their ongoing relationships to living traditions of oratory. Included in this range are medical formulae books, songs, treaties, letters, autobiographies, and histories, as well as poems, short stories, novels, illustrated fiction and nonfiction, plays, and other texts.

Oral traditions predate the very concept of "America" but have been challenged, at various times, by forces outside their source communities. Of particular significance was the arrival of a strange and often hostile new people on the shores of what is now the Bahamas, an arrival that would transform the entire world and bring heretofore unknown wealth to some inhabitants of Europe and incalculable misery to millions who lived in North and South America.

The world into which Christopher Columbus and his crew sailed in 1492 was unlike anything he had expected in his own imagination, and far different from the representations in most conventional histories. Columbus believed he had found a swift trade route to India. Instead, he discovered what many indigenous peoples in the East call Turtle Island. This name originates from a creation story in which a spirit-woman falls from the sky world to this world, which was all water, and lands on the back of a giant turtle, the only solid thing to stand on. A muskrat descends to the bottom of the world-ocean and returns with soil, which the spirit-woman spreads around creating the landmass we now call North America.

Columbus's context was informed by dramatic religious, cultural, and political conflict. His first journey coincided with the expulsion of Jews from Spain and the looming dispersal of the Muslim Moors within the following decade. An ambitious trader, explorer, and seafarer, he carried with him the brutal ethnocentrism and xenophobia that marked Spanish politics of the time. Among the many "souvenirs" he brought back to present to King Ferdinand and Queen Isabella were gold, parrots, and Taino captives. Although not the first group of

Europeans to reach the Americas—Viking sailors had a short-lived settlement in "Vinland" off the east coast of present-day Canada in the eleventh century—the Columbian voyage marked the first wave of invasion and the expropriation of resources that would fund the transformation of some of Europe's bickering, provincial feudal monarchs into wealthy imperial powers with ambitions of global domination.

Yet far from being the *terra nullis*—"empty land"—of later settler mythology, the hemisphere that would become "the Americas" for Europeans was already widely inhabited. Tens of millions of people from thousands of rich and diverse civilizations were living in varied and complicated relationships with one another, their respective ecosystems, and various cosmologies of spiritual beings who were intimately involved with human and more-than-human affairs. Among these many and assorted peoples there were few connecting threads of shared worldview, economy, language, political organization, or social structure; what they shared, at first, was a hemisphere—and later, the experience of colonization by successive waves of European colonists.

In 1492, the land known to Algonquin speakers as "Turtle Island" was far from an isolated backwater. Though physically separated from the mainland, its culture was complex and its interaction with other nations in the hemisphere was extensive. In the south, in what is now Mexico City, the Aztec Triple Alliance pursued its imperial ambitions from its capital, Tenochtitlán, one of the largest cities in the world, with political and economic influence and architecture that rivaled and often surpassed its most powerful European counterparts. In what is now southern Ontario and northeastern New England, the Haudenosaunee Confederacy, an alliance of once-rival tribal nations, had come together under the Great Law of Peace in the twelfth century to form what would become one of the world's oldest representative governments. The hereditary Coast Salish chiefdoms of the upper Pacific coast in present-day Washington and British Columbia solidified social, spiritual, and political ties through highly ritualized give-away ceremonies known as potlatches. Complex and long-lasting trade networks stretched across the North American continent to bring West Coast dentalia shells to the Great Plains, East Coast wampum to the Great Lakes, southwestern turquoise to Mesoamerica, and spread social and ceremonial traditions between culturally and linguistically diverse regions.

These few examples illustrate the difficulty of a broad term like "Native American" as well as a category such as "Native American literature." Distinguishing between the textual and the oral can be useful and informative when placed in a larger understanding of their mutual interconnectedness, which in turn reflects the many other connections between peoples. If we think of "American literature" as literature that emerges from the people of the land itself, we are challenged to confront the fact that it does not begin with the rise of the United States, or even with the arrival of Columbus. Instead, it begins in the land-rooted memory of the first peoples of this hemisphere.

Though undeniably challenged by the devastations of alien diseases, military and missionary assaults, oppressive economic policies, land dispossessions, and social and political intrusions brought by European nations and their descendants, indigenous nations are still very much alive and very much rooted in the lands now collectively known as the Americas. Indigenous oral and literary traditions continue to express the beliefs, values, perspectives, and imaginative possibilities of the first peoples of this hemisphere, and they draw on a long and rich history of both textual production and oral performance.

Daniel Heath Justice
University of Toronto

Native American Oral Literatures

At the moment when Native Americans first entered the consciousness of the European kingdoms through the Columbian contacts, more than ten million people occupied present-day North America, living in different patterns of settlement, with different economies, different ways of tracing ancestry, and different structures for distributing authority and responsibility. Only the broadest and thinnest generalizations can link these differences under a single title as "Native American." Among them, they spoke more than 350 languages and developed complex genre systems of verbal art within the familiar categories of speech, chant, and song. Today, two million of their descendants live in the United States, and in America, north of Mexico, perhaps as many as 200 languages are still spoken. Far from being the plain and casual utterances the foreign invaders often took them to be, the oral literatures of these Native American communities are distinguishable by form, content, style, and features of performance well-known to the native communities in which they have evolved. These works thus correspond well to the most fundamental notions of literature, however much their themes, forms, and styles may differ from Euro-American traditions.

The principal difference, of course, is the mode of presentation. Oral literatures are performed in the presence of audiences that evaluate the manner of performance as well as the content. Evaluation is not reserved for the conclusion of the performance; it is an ongoing activity reflected in degrees of attention and overt comment. Audiences apprehend the structure of a story through the slightly varied repetitions of incident, respond to characterizations highlighted by changes in the voice volume and pitch, or wait in the full silence of a pause. The canons of aesthetic value for performance differ from community to community and within each community from genre to genre. Oral literature is less a tradition of texts than a tradition of performances. This difference between the joint, contemporary realization of an oral performance and the delayed collaboration between an author and a reader through a text is worth reflecting on. Within the limits imposed by translation and textualizations, contemporary readers can usefully read these texts aloud, weighing line breaks, punctuation and sentence length in an attempt to simulate the experience of an oral literature. Each performance, then, is unique, but its uniqueness is modulated by a framework of expectations. Many works exist in different versions, while others have been rigidly governed by sanctions which restricted variation. This interplay between conservation and innovation is the very life of the oral tradition, and, as the Yuchi story and the Seneca story of "How America Was Discovered" witness, contact with Europeans has been an important element of that dynamic.

In Europe the Age of the Book coincided with the Age of Discovery. For this reason and others, most of the European newcomers were slow to recognize the existence of these Native American literatures. The terrible but transparent irony is that the process of recording them did not begin in earnest until the nineteenth century, when Native American communities themselves were being pressed to the brink of annihilation. While there is little doubt that the long-term effect of the European presence has been to reduce Native American populations and undermine the integrity of their cultures, nevertheless many Indian communities today still sustain viable oral literatures, preserving old forms and evolving new ones, while literacy has enabled the emergence of masterful writing in English by Native American authors.

The transformation of oral literature into literary texts, a process which includes both transcription and translation, is not simply a technical problem of how to write down spoken words. Every act of textualization reflects the nature of the non-Indian audience at which it is aimed and the specific interests motivating it. Differences in audience and interest substantially affect the form of the textualization and the nature of the Euro-American and Indian collaboration required to produce change. Most of the first Europeans understood language as a tool through which one could have access to important cultural information about Native Americans. Acts of textualization always employed the Latin alphabet, which obscured differences in sound and style, and the block or paragraph format (familiar from European conventions for expository writing), which obscured differences in genre forms. Moreover, in the act of textualization, what began as dialogue or first-person direct address was often reduced to depersonalized statements framed in the grammatical third person, thus obscuring the Native American speaker. In this way Indian-authored utterances were re-presented to non-Indian audiences as authoritative Indian texts.

The need for information useful for advancing the aims of religious, economic, or political colonization was not the only reason for textualizing oral literatures. As early as the sixteenth century, some of the Spanish priests and the Nahua converts they had educated began textualizing the oral poetry of the Aztecs. Their interest was in those forms of discourse most closely analogous to categories recognized in the West as literature. Recording of native materials was usually undertaken by individuals interested in representing Native Americans in a light most favorable to Europeans. One result was that such acts of textualization, especially those in English that began in earnest in the nineteenth century, often re-presented native verbal art in forms and styles most closely resembling whatever was the current conventional Western notion of the literary. This was true whether those producing the texts were Indian, as in the case of David Cusick or Arthur Parker, or non-Indian. A comparison of their texts in this volume reveals just how different the models of "literariness" can be; indeed, comparison can open a valuable avenue of inquiry into the social and aesthetic values implicit in textmaking and the agents and audiences involved in that activity.

By and large, the textualizations that have proven most durable are those produced by linguists and anthropologists in this century. Careful transcription and translation has secured texts, such as Ruth Bunzel's Zuni texts in this volume, that closely approximate both the individual voice and cultural aesthetics. In this way, these texts make available a singular instance of a story or song that has been circulating orally for perhaps hundreds of years. Today, newer models of textmaking provide for recording patterns of sound and silence or employ culturally distinctive grammatical markers to structure texts.

These oral works have emerged from a confluence of forces, but we can still usefully ask familiar questions about them. For example, anthropologists interested in recording stories as representative cultural or linguistic documents often ignored the creative role of the individual singer or storyteller and contributed to a misconception about anonymous or communal authorship. Authoring is a cultural role, burdened by many assumptions. In most Indian societies, some stories and songs are considered common property, while others are the property of a particular social or religious group, and still others are said to belong to individuals. These notions of ownership differ from contemporary Western notions that emphasize individual ownership as private property and authorship as Romantic and "inspired." To focus on the role of the individual author, when known, such as in the Aztec or Inuit poetry, is to raise the same kinds of questions we ask of any author's attempt to negotiate a respect for tradition with a desire for innovation within the framework of communal sanctions.

Similarly, we may rightly ask familiar questions about verisimilitude, about the text's representation of the world. Understanding character motivation, image, or theme, however, requires expending some effort to understand cultural values and beliefs about the shape of the world and human nature, often very different from the reader's own, as an appropriate context for interpretation. It is only one's intimate but nevertheless learned familiarity with the cultural values and beliefs of one's own community which makes them seem "natural" or "universal." And the same may be said for aesthetic judgments, which often emerge from a reader's almost instinctive comparison between the work at hand and works judged to be similar in form, theme, or style. But using the appearance of similarity to establish an intertextual context for evaluation often fails to weigh the work justly, because the intertextual tradition against which it is judged is European or American, not Siouan, Zuni, or Seneca. In short, aesthetic values emerge from rather than transcend specific cultural contexts, and we quickly discover the limits of our own assumptions and knowledge in encountering literatures from outside the more familiar Euro-American traditions.

In developing a sample of the oral literatures of Native America for inclusion in this anthology, a number of values had to be weighed and balanced. While it is important to emphasize, for example, that Native American oral literatures not only survive, but in many cases, flourish today alongside contemporary Native American writing, these texts were placed at the beginning of the volume, although most of them were recorded, as the dates appended to them attest, in the nineteenth and twentieth centuries. The placement was meant to highlight the depth of oral traditions, for some of these stories and songs were certainly told for centuries and reflect pre-contact cultural realities. We wish to underscore the fact that humanity's experience on this continent was articulated in complex forms long before the Europeans came. Columbus did not enter a silent world. Also, the wish to offer a number of texts of different genres from within a single culture had to be balanced by an equally important commitment to represent the cultural diversity of Native American peoples. Another difficult challenge was to choose works which were at once complex enough in form, theme, and language to adequately represent the multiplicity of interests, beliefs, and values that shaped them, while not requiring the development of a critical apparatus so extensive and cumbersome that it would overshadow the literature. Individual works were not chosen because they were "masterworks"; indeed, while a Zuni would place a very high value on "Sayatasha's Night Chant" or a Lakota on the story of White Buffalo Calf Pipe Woman, it is doubtful they would single out any one work from their literatures as a "masterwork." Such tendencies toward canonization reflect our interests, not those of native communities. Among the many genres of verbal art actualized by performance at different times and in different settings throughout the year, the stories and songs included in this anthology were valuable for many reasons. And their interest for us as a secondary audience will to some degree be different from their interest for their original audience.

In the end, with each fresh encounter, the reader must struggle, with imagination and understanding, to modulate his or her own individual interests with those of the author, community, and world from which the text emerged.

Andrew O. Wiget
New Mexico State University
Daniel Heath Justice
University of Toronto

Creation/Emergence Accounts

Native American stories, rich in tradition, are inextricably rooted in the things of tribal experiences; and, because they are oral rather than written, the tales rely upon a performance dimension that is lost to a reader. For instance, some Navajo and Iroquois stories are told in complex performances that, for an understanding of their fullest dimensions, require the audience's knowledge of the location of particular places where events occurred and the specific voices in which certain characters are speaking. Ritual dances in both cultures ascribe to certain locations inside the audience circle the geographical places afar off that are mentioned in the stories. Sand paintings, in the Navajo traditions, are ritualistic and sacred, for they symbolize sacred places and sacred acts that inform the Navajo stories being told. The creation story of the Iroquois similarly relies upon the experiences known to the listeners; the long houses of the sky dwellers in the Iroquois creation story resemble the long houses traditional in Iroquois culture. Native American stories, then—whether they are chants, songs, or narratives—rely upon a performance, a dramatic presentation that the written word for the most part cannot convey.

Cycles of stories relate to the Native Americans' subsistence experiences—planting, hunting, and fishing—and to life experiences—birth, puberty, and death. Other stories explain the more distant origin of the world and emergence of the people, the development of the particular Native American population and crucial events in the history of that population, and the uncertain nature of human existence. The latter groups of stories are offered here—stories of origin and emergence, historical narratives, and trickster tales.

Origin and Emergence Stories are complex symbolic tales that typically dramatize the tribal explanation of the origin of the earth and its people; establish the central relationships among people, the cosmos or universe, and the other creatures (flora and fauna) of the earth; distinguish gender roles and social organization for the tribe; account for the distinctive aspects of climate and topography of the tribe's homeland; and tell of the origins of the tribe's most significant social institutions and activities. Given the great numbers of Native American tribes, it can be expected that some of the stories offer interesting similarities while others suggest great differences among tribes.

Several different types of origin tales are prominent in the Native American canon. The two most common are the Emergence story, found throughout the southwestern United States, and the Earth-Diver story, which predominates throughout Canada and the eastern region. The Earth-Diver story tells of a great flood that covered the earth and of beings who are borne upon the water until, after several failed attempts, an animal brings up enough mud from beneath the water to begin the magical creation of the earth. David Cusick, a Tuscarora Indian whose tribe was allied to the Iroquoian Confederacy, began the history of his people with a version of the Earth-Diver story. Because it resembled that of Noah and the flood of the biblical tradition, many Euro-Americans considered the Indians to be descended from the Lost Tribes of Israel, a group of ten tribes that, after the conquest and destruction of ancient Israel, never returned. It is possible that the biblical stories and the Native Americans' stories have an ancient, common antecedent.

Native American tales more frequently differ, however, from the stories of biblical tradition. For most of the pueblo dwellers and many other Native American groups, people did not originate in a protoworld (like Eden) but rather in the womb of the Earth Mother, from which they were called out into the daylight of their Sun Father. Most widely developed among agricultural peoples, the Emergence story narrates the original passage from darkness to light, from chaos to order, and from undetermined to distinctly human form. The dynamic of evolution—that life evolves from one form to another—serves as a fundamental metaphor for transformations of all kinds. If one is ill, or if the community is without rain or food, restoration can be achieved by a ritual return to the place of Emergence and recovery of the original power from that place.

Both the Emergence and Earth-Diver stories are part of much longer narratives, in which they are followed by migration stories, as in the Zuni search for the Center of the World, or **Culture Hero Stories,** like the Navajo story of Changing Woman and the Hero Twins. Culture Hero Stories dramatize a people's belief about how a remarkable individual altered the original world and social order to its culturally accepted norm. The events in these stories account for the origin of distinctive cultural beliefs, values and practices. So, for example, the Lakota tell how a supernatural woman, White Buffalo Calf Pipe Woman, brought to them the sacred pipe and taught them how to pray with it to the Great Spirit. The Seneca tell of a young man named Gaqka or Crow who went to the south and, listening to the earth, learned all the stories, and brought back storytelling to the Seneca.

The biblical stories of Genesis, which most Europeans believed, functioned in a similar manner for the colonists. Yet a comparison of Native American origin tales and biblical stories illuminates profound cultural differences. Generally speaking, Native Americans traditionally did not believe in a single supreme, autonomous, and eternal being who established the conditions under which all beings must exist. Nor did they consider humans as having a radically different nature from the rest of earth's inhabitants, which they conceived of as intelligent, self-willed, and communicative. Given such beliefs, Native Americans found that the proper relation between people and the earth should be one of familial and personal respect, a relation honorable because of a kinship derived from a common beginning.

Perhaps most importantly, no Native American origin myth identifies anything at all analogous to the Christian belief in sin or a fall from the grace of a god. That is, there is no evil pre-condition, no lost harmony and balance, in the Native American interpretation of origin. Thus, there is likewise no story similar to that of the Christian savior. Many Native American tales, by contrast, explain that people and the universe at the same time moved from chaos and disorder to balance and harmony. These stories offer examples of prototypical relationships that show reciprocal and cyclic evolution, an evolution tied to a very particular place. Jews and Christians over the centuries have transported to each new settlement the divine commission given to Adam at the moment of creation. The Zuni, the Navajo, the Iroquois, indeed each Native American people, lived in a particular homeland known to be their own since their beginning, given to them, as the Zuni myth so aptly expresses it, as their Center. For most Native Americans this Center was both a specific life-sustaining environment and a compelling identity-sustaining idea, especially in times of tribal trouble. To move or be moved from their Center was, for these Native Americans, unthinkable.

As the Native Americans' stories of their origin, religious life, and social activity differed markedly from the Europeans', so did their stories explaining life's uncertainties. **Trickster Tales** illustrate a testing of the limits of cultural formation and practice. That is, Native American stories about trickster characters—people in the form of Coyote, Raven, or Rabbit—feature humorous and often scandalous attempts to violate the established customs and values of the tribe. The Trickster figure, stereotyped as alone and wandering on the margins of the social world, frequently engages in socially unacceptable acts to call attention to the arbitrary and tentative nature of established cultural patterns. For instance, when Raven cures a girl in the Tsimshian story by imitating the behavior of the medicine men (in order to gain both material and sexual rewards), Raven's actions cast doubt upon both the motives and methods used by medicine men, thus urging the audience to distinguish between the *role* a person plays in society and the *character* of the person in the role. Both scandalous and instructive, trickster stories ultimately offer cultural lessons. Told with relish, the stories ironically provide useful and necessary correctives to cultural self-satisfaction.

Whether the stories are socially corrective trickster tales or emergence or historical narratives, these and other Native American genres show the people aspiring for harmonious interaction with the earth. Native American communities continually return in prayer and ritual, story and song, to the fundamental relationships established as part of their tribal identity. At the same time, many contemporary Native American writers, who have never participated in the life of a tribal community, have discovered a new strength in old traditions. The ancient stories endure, despite radical changes in the circumstances of the people who produced them and who tell them today, because they provide a structure of meaning and value at once intellectually satisfying and imaginatively compelling.

Andrew O. Wiget
New Mexico State University

PRIMARY WORKS

Washington Matthews, *Navajo Legends,* 1897; John R. Swanton, *Tlingit Myths and Texts,* Bulletin Thirty-Nine of the Bureau of American Ethnology, 1909; Franz Boas, *Tsimshian Mythology,* Thirty-First Annual Report of the Bureau of American Ethnology, 1916; Stith Thompson, *Tales of the North American Indian,* 1929, 1973; Ruth Bunzel, "Zuni Origin Myths," Forty-Seventh Annual Report of the Bureau of American Ethnology, 1930; Edmund Nequatewa, *Truth of a Hopi,* 1936, 1967; John Bierhorst, *The Red Swan: Myths and Tales of the American Indians,* 1976; G. E. Lankford, *Native American Legends,* 1987.

Talk Concerning the First Beginning (Zuni)[1]

Yes, indeed. In this world there was no one at all. Always the sun came up; always he went in. No one in the morning gave him sacred meal; no one gave him prayer sticks; it was very lonely.[2] He said to his two children:[3] "You will go into the fourth womb. Your fathers, your mothers, kä-eto·we, tcu-eto·we, mu-eto·we, le-eto·we, all the society priests, society pekwins, society bow priests, you will bring out yonder into the light of your sun father."[4] Thus he said to them. They said, "But how shall we go in?" "That will be all right." Laying their lightning arrow across their rainbow bow, they drew it. Drawing it and shooting down, they entered.

When they entered the fourth womb it was dark inside. They could not distinguish anything. They said, "Which way will it be best to go?" They went toward the west. They met someone face to face. They said, "Whence come you?" "I come from over this way to the west." "What are you doing going around?" "I am going around to look at my crops. Where do you live?" "No, we do not live any place. There above our father the Sun, priest, made us come in. We have come in," they said. "Indeed," the younger brother said. "Come, let us see," he said. They laid down their bow. Putting underneath some dry brush and some dry grass that was lying about, and putting the bow on top, they kindled fire by hand. When they had kindled the fire, light came out from the coals. As it came out, they blew on it and it caught fire. Aglow! It is growing light. "Ouch! What have you there?" he said. He fell down crouching. He had a slimy horn, slimy tail, he was slimy all over, with webbed hands. The elder brother said, "Poor thing! Put out the light." Saying thus, he put out the light. The youth said, "Oh dear, what have you there?" "Why, we have fire," they said. "Well, what (crops) do you have coming up?" "Yes, here are our things coming up." Thus he said. He was going around looking after wild grasses.

He said to them, "Well, now, let us go." They went toward the west, the two leading. There the people were sitting close together. They questioned one another. Thus they said, "Well, now, you two, speak. I think there is something to say. It will

[1]The Zuni Indians, inheritors of the ancient Anasazi and Mogollon cultures, live in the Southwest, primarily in New Mexico. Their agricultural subsistence enabled them to develop large pueblos along the Zuni River valley. Visited by the Spanish expedition seeking the fabled Seven Cities of Cibola, they drove off the Spanish in 1539–1540. The Spanish eventually established a mission among the Zuni in 1629, and the Zuni joined in the Pueblo Revolt of 1680. Today the population of their New Mexico reservation exceeds 8,000.

[2]There is a reciprocal gift-giving relationship between the Sun Father and all creatures, including people. According to Zuni tradition, the Sun Father gives corn and breath, the gifts of life. In return, the Zuni offer corn meal and downy feathers, symbolizing clouds and breath, which are attached to ritually painted sticks. Both are deposited at shrines near Zuni.

[3]The two children are the Ahaiyute, the War God Hero Twins.

[4]Zuni people are organized into religious societies, each responsible for a different aspect of the community's welfare. The *-eto:we* are fetishes, each representing that spirit, originating deep within the womb of the earth, which is the foundational force of each society. The Pekwin is the sun priest who keeps the ritual calendar; the Bow Priests govern warfare and regulate social behavior. In bringing all these from the earth's fourth womb onto the earth's surface, the War God Twins are assisting at the birth of the Zuni tribe, the "daylight people."

not be too long a talk. If you let us know that we shall always remember it." "That is so, that is so," they said. "Yes, indeed, it is true. There above is our father, Sun. No one ever gives him prayer sticks; no one ever gives him sacred meal; no one ever gives him shells. Because it is thus we have come to you, in order that you may go out standing yonder into the daylight of your sun father. Now you will say which way (you decide)." Thus the two said. "Hayi! Yes, indeed. Because it is thus you have passed us on our roads.[5] Now that you have passed us on our roads here where we stay miserably, far be it from us to speak against it. We can not see one another. Here inside where we just trample on one another, where we just spit on one another, where we just urinate on one another, where we just befoul one another, where we just follow one another about, you have passed us on our roads. None of us can speak against it. But rather, as the priest of the north says, so let it be. Now you two call him." Thus they said to the two, and they came up close toward the north side. . . .

They met the north priest on his road. "You have come," he said. "Yes, we have come. How have you lived these many days?" "Here where I live happily you have passed me on my road. Sit down." When they were seated he questioned them. "Now speak. I think there is something to say. It will not be too long a talk. So now, that you will let me know." "Yes, indeed, it is so. In order that you may go out standing there into the daylight of your sun father we have passed you on your road. However you say, so shall it be." "Yes, indeed, now that you have passed us on our road here where we live thus wretchedly, far be it from me to talk against it. Now that you have come to us here inside where we just trample on one another, where we just spit on one another, where we just urinate on one another, where we just befoul one another, where we just follow one another about, how should I speak against it?" so he said. Then they arose. They came back. Coming to the village where they were sitting in the middle place, there they questioned one another. "Yes, even now we have met on our roads. Indeed there is something to say; it will not be too long a talk. When you let me know that, I shall always remember it," thus they said to one another. When they had spoken thus, "Yes, indeed. In order that you may go out standing into the daylight of your sun father, we have passed you on your road," thus they said. "Hayi! Yes, indeed. Now that you have passed us on our road here where we cannot see one another, where we just trample on one another, where we just urinate on one another, where we just befoul one another, where we just follow one another around, far be it from me to speak against it. But rather let it be as my younger brother, the priest of the west shall say. When he says, 'Let it be thus,' that way it shall be. So now, you two call him." Thus said the priest of the north and they went and stood close against the west side. . . .[6]

"Well, perhaps by means of the thoughts of someone somewhere it may be that we shall go out standing into the daylight of our sun father." Thus he said.

[5]A formulaic phrase, suggesting something like destiny. Everyone's life, and indeed the life of the community, can be imagined as a "road"; to "pass another on the road" is to acknowledge converging destinies.

[6]The Twins visit the Priest of the North first, since he is the senior priest. The Zuni order lists according to the cardinal directions, moving "sunwise" (counterclockwise), beginning at the north. In the section omitted, priests for the other three directions are consulted in similar passages. Four is a sacred number, signifying wholeness or completion.

Then the two thought. "Come on, let us summon our grandson," thus they said. They went. They came to where humming bird[7] was staying. "You have come?" "Yes, how have you lived these days?" "Where I live happily these days you have passed me on my road. Sit down." When they had sat down: "Well, now, speak. I think there is something to say; it will not be too long a talk. So now if you let me know that, I shall always remember it." "Yes, indeed, it is so. When our fathers, kä-eto·we, tcu-eto·we, mu-eto·we, le-eto·we, the society priests, go out standing into the daylight of their sun father, you shall be the one to look for their road; for that we have summoned you." "Is that so?" Saying this, they went. When they got there, he questioned them. "Well, even now you summoned me. Surely there is something to say. It will not be too long a talk. So now when you let me know that I shall always remember it." Thus he said. "Yes, indeed, it is so. When our fathers, käeto·we, tcu-eto·we, mu-eto·we, leeto·we, the society priests, go out into the daylight of their sun father, that you shall be the one to look for their road, for that we have summoned you." Thus the two said. He went out toward the south. He went on. Coming back to his starting place, nothing was visible. Farther out he went. Coming back to the same place, nothing was visible. Then for the third time he went. Coming back to the same place, nothing was visible. For the fourth time he went close along the edge of the sky. Coming back to the same place, nothing was visible. He came. Coming where kä-eto·we were staying, "Nothing is visible." "Hayi!" "Yes. Well, I am going now." "Very well, go." He went.

The two said, "What had we better do now? That many different kinds of feathered creatures, the ones who go about without ever touching the ground, have failed." Thus the two said. "Come, let us talk with our grandson, locust. Perhaps that one will have a strong spirit because he is like water."[8] Thus they said. They went. Their grandson, locust, they met. "You have come." "Yes, we have come." "Sit down. How have you lived these days?" "Happily." "Well, even now you have passed me on my road. Surely there is something to say; it will not be too long a talk. So now when you let me know that, that I shall always remember." Thus he said. "Yes, indeed, it is so. In order that our fathers, käeto·we, tcu-eto·we, mu-eto·we, le-eto·we, the society priests, may go out standing into the daylight of their sun father, we have come to you." "Is that so?" Saying this, they went. When they arrived they sat down. Where they were sitting, he questioned them. "Well, just now you came to me. Surely there is something to say; it will not be too long a talk. So now if you let me know that, that I shall always remember." "Yes, indeed. In order that our fathers, kä-eto·we, tcu-eto·we, mu-eto·we, le-eto·we, the society priests, may go out standing into the daylight of their sun father, we have summoned you." "Indeed?" Saying this, locust rose right up. He goes up. He went through into another world. And again he goes right up. He went through into another world. And again he goes right up. Again he went through into another world. He goes right up. When he had just gone a little way his strength gave out, he came back to where kä-eto·we were staying and said, "Three times I went through and the fourth time my strength gave out." "Hayi! Indeed?" Saying this, he went.

[7]Consistent with the Zuni pattern of fourfold repetition, three other birds had tried to find a way out before the hummingbird succeeded.

[8]That is, like water, he can go through anything solid. [Bunzel's note]

When he had gone the two thought. "Come, let us speak with our grandson, Reed Youth. For perhaps that one with his strong point will be all right." Saying this, they went. They came to where Reed Youth stayed. "You have come?" "Yes; how have you lived these days." "Where I stay happily you have passed me on my road. Sit down." Thus he said. They sat down. Then he questioned them. "Yes. Well, even now you have passed me on my road. I think there is something to say; it will not be too long a talk. When you let me know that, that I shall always remember." Thus he said. "Yes, indeed, in order that our fathers, kä-eto·we, tcu-eto·we, mu-eto·we, le-eto·we, the society priests, may go out standing into the daylight of their sun father, we have come to you." "Hayi! Is that so?" Having spoken thus, they went. When they arrived they sat down. There he questioned them. "Yes, even now that you have summoned me I have passed you on your roads. Surely there is something to say; it will not be too long a talk. When you let me know that, that I shall always remember." "Yes, indeed, it is so. In order that our fathers, käeto·we, tcu-eto·we, mu-eto·we, leeto·we, the society priests, may go forth standing into the daylight of their sun father, we have summoned you." Thus they said. "Hayi! Is that so?" Saying this, he went out. Where Locust had gone out he went out. The first time he passed through, the second time he passed through, the third time he passed through. Having passed through the fourth time and come forth standing into the daylight of his sun father, he went back in. Coming back in he came to where kä-eto·we were staying. "You have come?" Thus they said. "Yes," he said. "Far off to see what road there may be you have gone. How may it be there now?" Thus they said. "Yes, indeed, it is so. There it is as you wanted it. As you wished of me, I went forth standing into the daylight of my sun father now." Thus he said. "Halihi! Thank you!" "Now I am going." "Go." Saying this, he went.

After he had gone they were sitting around. Now as they were sitting around, there the two set up a pine tree for a ladder. They stayed there. For four days they stayed there. Four days, they say, but it was four years. There all the different society priests sang their song sequences for one another. The ones sitting in the first row listened carefully. Those sitting next on the second row heard all but a little. Those sitting on the third row heard here and there. Those sitting last on the fourth row heard just a little bit now and then. It was thus because of the rustling of the dry weeds.

When their days there were at an end, gathering together their sacred things they arose. "Now what shall be the name of this place?" "Well, here it shall be sulphur-smell-inside-world; and furthermore, it shall be raw-dust world." Thus they said. "Very well. Perhaps if we call it thus it will be all right." Saying this, they came forth.

After they had come forth, setting down their sacred things in a row at another place, they stayed there quietly. There the two set up a spruce tree as a ladder. When the ladder was up they stayed there for four days. And there again the society priests sang their song sequences for one another. Those sitting on the first row listened carefully. Those sitting there on the second row heard all but a little. Those sitting there on the third row heard here and there. Those sitting last distinguished a single word now and then. It was thus because of the rustling of some plants. When their days there were at an end, gathering together their sacred things there they arose. "Now what shall it be called here?" "Well, here it shall be called soot-inside-world, because we still can not recognize one another." "Yes, perhaps if it is called thus it will be all right." Saying this to one another, they arose.

Passing through to another place, and putting down their sacred things in a row, they stayed there quietly. There the two set up a piñon tree as a ladder. When the piñon tree was put up, there all the society priests and all the priests went through their song sequences for one another. Those sitting in front listened carefully. Those sitting on the second row heard all but a little. Those sitting behind on the third row heard here and there. Those sitting on the fourth row distinguished only a single word now and then. This was because of the rustling of the weeds.

When their days there were at an end, gathering together their sacred things they arose. Having arisen, "Now what shall it be called here?" "Well, here it shall be fog-inside-world, because here just a little bit is visible." "Very well, perhaps if it is called thus it will be all right." Saying this, rising, they came forth.

Passing through to another place, there the two set down their sacred things in a row, and there they sat down. Having sat down, the two set up a cottonwood tree as a ladder. Then all the society priests and all the priests went through their song sequences for one another. Those sitting first heard everything clearly. Those sitting on the second row heard all but a little. Those sitting on the third row heard here and there. Those sitting last on the fourth row distinguished a single word now and then. It was thus because of the rustling of some plants.

When their days there were at an end, after they had been there, when their four days were passed, gathering together their sacred possessions, they arose. When they arose, "Now what shall it be called here?" "Well, here it shall be wing-inner-world, because we see our sun father's wings."[9] Thus they said. They came forth.

Into the daylight of their sun father they came forth standing. Just at early dawn they came forth. After they had come forth there they set down their sacred possessions in a row. The two said, "Now after a little while when your sun father comes forth standing to his sacred place you will see him face to face. Do not close your eyes." Thus he said to them. After a little while the sun came out. When he came out they looked at him. From their eyes the tears rolled down. After they had looked at him, in a little while their eyes became strong. "Alas!" Thus they said. They were covered all over with slime. With slimy tails and slimy horns, with webbed fingers, they saw one another. "Oh dear! is this what we look like?" Thus they said.

Then they could not tell which was which of their sacred possessions. Meanwhile, nearby an old man of the Dogwood clan[10] lived alone. Spider said to him, "Put on water. When it gets hot, wash your hair." "Why?" "Our father, our mothers, kä-eto·we, tcu-eto·we, mu-eto·we, le-eto·we, all the society priests, into the daylight of their sun father have come forth standing. They can not tell which is which. You will make this plain to them." Thus she said. "Indeed? Impossible. From afar no one can see them. Where they stay quietly no one can recognize them." Thus he said. "Do

[9]The "wings" are the rays of sunlight slanting into this world through the Emergence hole in the sky above, which opens onto the earth's surface, the "daylight world." This is the last of the four lower worlds.

[10]The first Pekwin, or Sun Priest, keeper of the ritual calendar, a hereditary responsibility in the Dogwood clan. His hair-washing is an act of spiritual as well as physical purification.

not say that. Nevertheless it will be all right. You will not be alone. Now we shall go." Thus she said. When the water was warm he washed his hair.

Meanwhile, while he was washing his hair, the two said, "Come let us go to meet our father, the old man of the Dogwood clan. I think he knows in his thoughts; because among our fathers, kä-eto·we, tcu-eto·we, mu-eto·we, le-eto·we, we can not tell which is which." Thus they said. They went. They got there. As they were climbing up, "Now indeed! They are coming." Thus Spider said to him. She climbed up his body from his toe. She clung behind his ear. The two entered. "You have come," thus he said. "Yes. Our father, how have you lived these days?" "As I live happily you pass me on my road. Sit down." They sat down. "Well, now, speak. I think some word that is not too long, your word will be. Now, if you let me know that, remembering it, I shall live." "Indeed it is so. Our fathers, kä-eto·we, tcu-eto·we, mu-eto·we, le-eto·we, all the society priests, into the daylight of their sun father have risen and come out. It is not plain which is which. Therefore we have passed you on your road." "Haiyi, is that so? Impossible! From afar no one can see them. Where they stay quietly no one can recognize them." Thus he said. "Yes, but we have chosen you." Thus the two said. They went. When they came there, "My fathers, my mothers, how have you lived these days?" "Happily, our father, our child. Be seated." Thus they said. He sat down. Then he questioned them. "Yes, now indeed, since you have sent for me, I have passed you on your road. I think some word that is not too long your word will be. Now if you let me know that, remembering it, I shall always live."

Thus he said. "Indeed, it is so. Even though our fathers, our mothers, kä-eto·we, tcu-eto·we, mu-eto·we, le-eto·we, have come out standing into the daylight of their sun father, it is not plain which of these is which. Therefore we have sent for you." Thus they said. "Haiyi, Well, let me try." "Impossible. From afar no one can see them. Where they stay quietly no one can tell which is which." "Well, let me try." Thus he said. Where they lay in a row he stood beside them. Spider said to him, "Here, the one that lies here at the end is kä-eto·we and these next ones touching it are tcu-eto·we, and this next one is le-eto·we, and these next ones touching it are mu-eto·we." Thus she said. He said, "Now this is kä-eto·we, and these all touching it are tcu-eto·we, and this one is le-eto·we, and all these touching it are mu-eto·we." Thus he said. "Halihi! Thank you. How shall be the cycle of the months for them?" Thus he said: "This one Branches-broken-down. This one No-snow-on-the-road. This one Little-sand-storms. This one Great-sand-storms. This the Month-without-a-name. This one Turn-about. This one Branches-broken-down. This one No-snow-on-the-road. This one Little-sand-storms. This one Great-sand-storms. This the Month-without-a-name. This one Turn-about. Thus shall be all the cycle of the months." "Halihi! Thank you. Our father, you shall not be poor. Even though you have no sacred possessions toward which your thoughts bend, whenever Itiwana is revealed to us, because of your thought, the ceremonies of all these shall come around in order. You shall not be a slave." This they said. They gave him the sun. "This shall be your sacred possession." Thus they said. When this had happened thus they lived.

Four days—four days they say, but it was four years—there they stayed. When their days were at an end, the earth rumbled. The two said, "Who was left behind?" "I do not know, but it seems we are all here." Thus they said. Again the earth rumbled. "Well, does it not seem that some one is still left behind?" Thus, the two said.

They went. Coming to the place where they had come out, there they stood. To the mischief-maker and the Mexicans[11] they said, "Haiyi! Are you still left behind?" "Yes." "Now what are you still good for?" Thus they said. "Well, it is this way. Even though kä-eto·we have issued forth into the daylight, the people do not live on the living waters of good corn; on wild grasses only they live. Whenever you come to the middle you will do well to have me. When the people are many and the land is all used up, it will not be well. Because this is so I have come out." Thus he said. "Haiyi! Is that so? So that's what you are. Now what are you good for?" Thus they said. "Indeed, it is so. When you come to the middle, it will be well to have my seeds. Because kä-eto·we do not live on the good seeds of the corn, but on wild grasses only. Mine are the seeds of the corn and all the clans of beans." Thus he said. The two took him with them. They came to where kä-eto·we were staying. They sat down. Then they questioned him. "Now let us see what you are good for." "Well, this is my seed of the yellow corn." Thus he said. He showed an ear of yellow corn. "Now give me one of your people." Thus he said. They gave him a baby. When they gave him the baby it seems he did something to her. She became sick. After a short time she died. When she had died he said, "Now bury her." They dug a hole and buried her. After four days he said to the two, "Come now. Go and see her." The two went to where they had come out. When they got there the little one was playing in the dirt. When they came, she laughed. She was happy. They saw her and went back. They came to where the people were staying. "Listen! Perhaps it will be all right for you to come. She is still alive. She has not really died." "Well, thus it shall always be." Thus he said.[12]

Gathering together all their sacred possessions, they came hither. To the place called since the first beginning, Moss Spring, they came.[13] There they set down their sacred possessions in a row. There they stayed. Four days they say, but it was four years. There the two washed them. They took from all of them their slimy tails, their slimy horns. "Now, behold! Thus you will be sweet." There they stayed.

When their days were at an end they came hither. Gathering together all their sacred possessions, seeking Itiwana, yonder their roads went. To the place called since the first beginning Massed-cloud Spring, they came. There they set down their sacred possessions in a row. There they stayed quietly. Four days they stayed. Four days they say, but it was four years. There they stayed. There they counted up the days. For kä-eto·we, four nights and four days. With fine rain caressing the earth, they passed their days. The days were made for le-eto·we, mu-eto·we. For four days and four nights it snowed. When their days were at an end there they stayed.

When their days were at an end they arose. Gathering together all their sacred possessions, hither their roads went. To the place called since the first beginning Mist Spring their road came. There they sat down quietly. Setting out their sacred posses-

[11]The mischief-maker is Coyote, the Trickster. The Mexicans have been introduced as emerging later because they were not part of the emerging Zuni people. The linking of Coyote and the Mexicans makes a negative comment about historical Zuni relations with the Spanish.

[12]This symbolic story of the first death in exchange for corn suggests the reciprocal relationship between life and death.

[13]One of dozens of springs that mark the route of the migration from the Emergence Place to Zuni, the Center of the World.

sions in a row, they sat down quietly. There they counted up the days for one another. They watched the world for one another's waters. For kä-eto·we, four days and four nights, with heavy rain caressing the earth they passed their days. When their days were at an end the days were made for le-eto·we and mu-eto·we. Four days and four nights with falling snow the world was filled. When their days were at an end, there they stayed.

When all their days were passed, gathering together all their sacred possessions, hither their road went. To Standing-wood Spring they came. There they sat down quietly. Setting out their sacred possessions in a row, they stayed quietly. There they watched one another's days. For kä-eto·we, four days and four nights with fine rain caressing the earth, they passed their days. When all their days were at an end, the days were made for le-eto·we and mu-eto·we. For four days and four nights, with falling snow, the world was filled. When all their days were at an end, there they stayed.

When all their days were passed, gathering together their sacred possessions, and arising, hither they came. To the place called since the first beginning Upuilima they came. When they came there, setting down their sacred possessions in a row, they stayed quietly. There they strove to outdo one another. There they planted all their seeds. There they watched one another's days for rain. For kä-eto·we, four days with heavy rain caressing the earth. There their corn matured. It was not palatable, it was bitter. Then the two said, "Now by whose will will our corn become fit to eat?" Thus they said. They summoned raven. He came and pecked at their corn, and it became good to eat. "It is fortunate that you have come." With this then, they lived.

When their days were at an end they arose. Gathering together their sacred possessions, they came hither. To the place called since the first beginning, Cornstalk-place they came. There they set down their sacred possessions in a row. There they stayed four days. Four days they say, but it was four years. There they planted all their seeds. There they watched one another's days for rain. During kä-eto·we's four days and four nights, heavy rain fell. During le-eto·we's and mu-eto·we's four days and four nights, the world was filled with falling snow. Their days were at an end. Their corn matured. When it was mature it was hard. Then the two said, "By whose will will our corn become soft? Well, owl." Thus they said. They summoned owl. Owl came. When he came he pecked at their corn and it became soft.

Then, when they were about to rise, the two said, "Come, let us go talk to the corn priest." Thus they said. They went. They came to where the corn priest stayed. "How have you lived these days?" "As we are living happily you have passed us on our road. Sit down." They sat down. There they questioned one another. "Well, speak. I think some word that is not too long, your word will be. Now, if you let me know that, remembering it, I shall always live." "Indeed, it is so. To-morrow, when we arise, we shall set out to seek Itiwana. Nowhere have we found the middle. Our children, our women, are tired. They are crying. Therefore we have come to you. To-morrow your two children will look ahead. Perhaps if they find the middle when our fathers, our mothers, kä-eto·we, tcu-eto·we, mu-eto·we, le-eto·we, all the society priests, come to rest, there our children will rest themselves. Because we have failed to find the middle." "Haiyi! Is that so? With plain words you have passed us on our road. Very well, then, thus it shall be." Thus he said. The two went.

Next morning when they were about to set out they put down a split ear of corn and eggs. They made the corn priest stand up. They said, "Now, my children, some of you will go yonder to the south. You will take these." Thus he said (indicating) the tip of the ear and the macaw egg. And then the ones that were to come this way took the base of the ear and the raven egg. Those that were to go to the south took the tip of the ear and the macaw egg. "Now, my children, yonder to the south you will go. If at any time you come to Itiwana, then some time we shall meet one another."[14] Thus they said. They came hither.

They came to the place that was to be Katcina village. The girl got tired. Her brother said, "Wait, sit down for a while. Let me climb up and look about to see what kind of a place we are going to." Thus he said. His sister sat down. Her brother climbed the hill. When he had climbed up, he stood looking this way. "Eha! Maybe the place where we are going lies in this direction. Maybe it is this kind of a place." Thus he said and came down. Meanwhile his sister had scooped out the sand. She rested against the side of the hill. As she lay sleeping the wind came and raised her apron of grass. . . . As he came down he saw her. He desired her. He lay down upon his sister and copulated with her. His sister awoke. "Oh, dear, oh, dear," she was about to say (but she said,) "Watsela, watsela." Her brother said, "Ah!" He sat up. With his foot he drew a line. It became a stream of water. The two went about talking. The brother talked like Koyemci. His sister talked like Komakatsik. The people came.

"Oh alas, alas! Our children have become different beings."[15] Thus they said. The brother speaking: "Now it will be all right for you to cross here." Thus he said. They came and went in. They entered the river. Some of their children turned into water snakes. Some of them turned into turtles. Some of them turned into frogs. Some of them turned into lizards. They bit their mothers. Their mothers cried out and dropped them. They fell into the river. Only the old people reached the other side. They sat down on the bank. They were half of the people. The two said, "Now wait. Rest here." Thus they said. Some of them sat down to rest. The two said (to the others), "Now you go in. Your children will turn into some kind of dangerous animals and will bite you. But even though you cry out, do not let them go. If, when you come out on the other side, your children do not again become the kind of creatures they are now, then you will throw them into the water." Thus they said to them. They entered the water. Their children became different creatures and bit them. Even though they cried out, they crossed over. Then their children once more became the

[14]This passage, which represents the first major social division of the emergent community, is understood to establish Zuni's relationship to Indian tribes to the south.

[15]A very important event in the migration narrative: in breaking the incest taboo, the brother and sister have reversed the process of physical and social evolution, and they suffer the consequences in their own persons; their language is confused, their appearance deformed. Nevertheless, their mistake has useful consequences. The line they draw becomes a river separating the Emergence World into two domains. At this moment on the river, all kinds of transformations are possible. When some of the children return to their pre-emergence water-creature form, they are dropped by the parents and sink to the bottom of the river, where they become the kachinas whose transformative powers provide an eternal source of renewal for the Zuni. They promise to return to Zuni with rain and moisture when they are called.

kind of creatures they had been. "Alas! Perhaps had we done that it would have been all right." Now all had crossed over.

There setting down their sacred possessions in a row, they stayed quietly. They stayed there quietly for four days. Thus they say but they stayed for four years. There each night they lived gaily with loud singing. When all their time was passed, the two said, "Come, let us go and talk to Ne'we·kwe." Thus they said. They went to where the Ne'we·kwe were staying. They came there. "How have you passed these days?" "Happily. You have come? Be seated." They sat down. Then they questioned them. "Now speak. I think some word that is not too long your word will be. If you let me know that, remembering it I shall always live." "Indeed it is so. To-morrow we shall arise. Our fathers, our mothers, kä-eto·we, tcu-eto·we, mu-eto·we, le-eto·we, all the society priests, are going to seek the middle. But nowhere have we come to the middle. Our children and our women are tired. They are crying now. Therefore we have passed you on your road. To-morrow you will look ahead. If perhaps somewhere you come to Itiwana there our children will rest." Thus they said. "Alas! but we are just foolish people. If we make some mistake it will not be right." Thus he said. "Well, that is of no importance. It can't be helped. We have chosen you." Thus they said. "Well indeed?" "Yes. Now we are going." "Go ahead." The two went out.

They came (to where the people were staying). "Come, let us go and speak to our children." Thus they said. They went. They entered the lake. It was full of katcinas. "Now stand still a moment. Our two fathers have come." Thus they said. The katcinas suddenly stopped dancing. When they stopped dancing they said to the two, "Now our two fathers, now indeed you have passed us on our road. I think some word that is not too long your word will be. If you will let us know that we shall always remember it." Thus he said. "Indeed it is so. To-morrow we shall arise. Therefore we have come to speak to you." "Well indeed? May you go happily. You will tell our parents, 'Do not worry.' We have not perished. In order to remain thus forever we stay here. To Itiwana but one day's travel remains. Therefore we stay near by. When our world grows old and the waters are exhausted and the seeds are exhausted, none of you will go back to the place of your first beginning. Whenever the waters are exhausted and the seeds are exhausted you will send us prayer sticks. Yonder at the place of our first beginning with them we shall bend over to speak to them. Thus there will not fail to be waters. Therefore we shall stay quietly near by." Thus they said to them. "Well indeed?" "Yes. You will tell my father, my mother, 'Do not worry.' We have not perished." Thus they said. They sent strong words to their parents. "Now we are going. Our children, may you always live happily." "Even thus may you also go." Thus they said to the two. They went out. They arrived. They told them. "Now our children, here your children have stopped. 'They have perished,' you have said. But no. The male children have become youths, and the females have become maidens. They are happy. They live joyously. They have sent you strong words. 'Do not worry,' they said." "Haiyi! Perhaps it is so."

They stayed overnight. Next morning they arose. Gathering together all their sacred possessions, they came hither. They came to Hanlipinka. Meanwhile the two Ne'we·kwe looked ahead. They came to Rock-in-the-river. There two girls were washing a woolen dress. They killed them. After they had killed them they scalped them. Then someone found them out. When they were found out, because they were raw people, they wrapped themselves in mist. There to where kä-eto·we were staying they came. "Alack, alas! We have done wrong!" Thus they said. Then they set the days for the enemy. There they watched one another's days for rain. Kä-eto·we's four days and four nights passed with the falling of heavy rain. There where a waterfall issued from a cave the foam arose. There the two Ahaiyute appeared. They came to where kä-eto·we were staying. Meanwhile, from the fourth innerworld, Unasinte, Uhepololo, Kailuhtsawaki, Hattunka, Oloma, Catunka, came out to sit down in the daylight. There they gave them the comatowe song cycle.[16] Meanwhile, right there, Coyote was going about hunting. He gave them their pottery drum. They sang comatowe.

After this had happened, the two said, "Now, my younger brother, Itiwana is less than one day distant. We shall gather together our children, all the beast priests, and the winged creatures, this night." They went.[17] They came yonder to Comkäkwe. There they gathered together all the beasts, mountain lion, bear, wolf, wild cat, badger, coyote, fox, squirrel; eagle, buzzard, cokapiso, chicken hawk, bald-headed eagle, raven, owl. All these they gathered together. Now squirrel was among the winged creatures, and owl was among the beasts. "Now my children, you will contest together for your sun father's daylight. Whichever side has the ball, when the sun rises, they shall win their sun father's daylight." Thus the two said. "Indeed?" They went there. They threw up the ball. It fell on the side of the beasts. They hid it. After they had hidden it, the birds came one by one but they could not take it. Each time they paid four straws. They could not take it.

At this time it was early dawn. Meanwhile Squirrel was lying by the fireplace. Thus they came one by one but they could not take it. Eagle said, "Let that one lying there by the fireplace go." They came to him and said, "Are you asleep?" "No. I am not asleep." "Oh dear! Now you go!" Thus they said. "Oh no, I don't want to go," he said. He came back. "The lazy one does not wish to." Thus they said. Someone else went. Again they could not take it. Now it was growing light. "Let that one lying by the fireplace go." Thus they said. Again Buzzard went. "Alas, my boy, you go." "Oh, no, I don't feel like it." Thus he said. Again he went back. "He does not want to," he said. Again some one else went. Again they did not take it. Now it was growing light. Spider said to him, "Next time they come agree to go." Thus she said. Then again they said, "Let that one lying by the fireplace go." Thus they said; and again someone went. When he came there he said, "Alas, my boy, you go." "All right, I shall go." Thus he said and arose. As he arose Spider said to him, "Take that stick." He took up a stick, so short. Taking it, he went. Now the sun was about to rise. They came there. Spider said to him, "Hit those two sitting on the farther side." Thus she said. Bang! He knocked them down. He laid them down. Then, mountain lion, who was standing right there, said, "Hurry up, go after it. See whether you can take it." Thus he said. Spider said to him, "Say to him, 'Oh, no, I don't want to take it.' So she said." "Oh, no, I don't want to take it. Perhaps there is nothing inside. How should

[16]The first culpable death provokes the return of the War God Twins who give the people the *comatowe* ceremonial for relieving the guilt associated with killing in war.

[17]The Contest for Daylight story, which is widespread throughout Native America, is told here to account for the characteristic behaviors of different species. It leads directly to a comment about the deaths of animals. Though it is not mentioned, the killing of animals must also be done in a ritually prescribed way in order not to repudiate the Sun, the Father and gift-giver.

I take it? There is nothing in there." "That is right. There is nothing in there. All my children are gathered together. One of them is holding it. If you touch the right one, you will take it." "All right." Now Spider is speaking: "No one who is sitting here has it. That one who goes about dancing, he is holding it." Thus she said. He went. He hit Owl on the hand. The white ball came out. He went. He took up the hollow sticks and took them away with him. Now the birds hid the ball. Spider came down. Over all the sticks she spun her web. She fastened the ball with her web. Now the animals came one by one. Whenever they touched a stick, she pulled (the ball) away. Each time they paid ten straws. The sun rose. After sunrise, he was sitting high in the sky. Then the two came. They said, "Now, all my children, you have won your sun father's daylight, and you, beasts, have lost your sun father's daylight. All day you will sleep. After sunset, at night, you will go about hunting. But you, owl, you have not stayed among the winged creatures. Therefore you have lost your sun father's daylight. You have made a mistake. If by daylight, you go about hunting, the one who has his home above will find you out. He will come down on you. He will scrape off the dirt from his earth mother and put it upon you. Then thinking, 'Let it be here,' you will come to the end of your life. This kind of creature you shall be." Thus they said. They stayed there overnight. The animals all scattered.

The two went. They came to where kä-eto·we were staying. Then they arose. Gathering together all their sacred possessions, they arose. Le-eto·we said, "Now, my younger brothers, hither to the north I shall take my road. Whenever I think that Itiwana has been revealed to you, then I shall come to you." Thus he said, and went to the north. Now some woman, seeing them, said, "Oh dear! Whither are these going?" Thus she said:

> Naiye heni aiye
> Naiye heni aiye.

In white stripes of hail they went.

Meanwhile kä-eto·we came hither. They came to House Mountain. When they came there they would not let them pass through. They fought together. A giant went back and forth before them. Thus they fought together.[18] Thus evening came. In the evening they came back to Hanlipinka. Next day they went again. In heavy rain they fought together. In the evening they went back again. Next morning they went again for the third time. Again they fought together. The giant went back and forth in front. Even though she had arrows sticking in her body she did not die. At sunset they went back again. Next morning they went. They came there, and they fought together. Still they would not surrender. The giant went back and forth in front. Although she was wounded with arrows, she would not surrender. Ahaiyute said, "Alas, why is it that these people will not let us pass? Wherever may her heart be, that one that goes back and forth? Where her heart should be we have struck her, yet she does not surrender. It seems we can not overcome her. So finally go up to where

[18]The slaying of a giant, who stands in the way of peaceful settlement of the land, is a common theme in southwestern Native literatures. This should be compared with a similar episode in the Navajo story "Changing Woman and the Hero Twins," where the giant is named Yéitso, the "Great Fear." The giant is slain with the help of the Sun.

your father stays. Without doubt he knows." Thus he said. His younger brother climbed up to where the sun was.

It was nearly noon when he arrived. "You have come?" "Yes, I have come." "Very well, speak. I think some word that is not too long your word will be. So if you let me know that, I shall always remember it." Thus he said. "Indeed, it is so. Our fathers, our mothers, kä-eto·we, tcu-eto·we, mu-eto·we, le-eto·we, all the society priests, have issued forth into the daylight. Here they go about seeking Itiwana. These people will not let them pass. Where does she have her heart, that one who goes back and forth before them? In vain have we struck her where her heart should be. Even though the arrows stick in her body, she does not surrender." "Haiyi! For nothing are you men! She does not have her heart in her body. In vain have you struck her there. Her heart is in her rattle." Thus he said. "This is for you and this is for your elder brother." Thus he said, and gave him two turquoise rabbit sticks. "Now, when you let these go with my wisdom I shall take back my weapons." "Haiyi! Is that so? Very well, I am going now." "Go ahead. May you go happily." Thus he said. He came down. His elder brother said to him, "Now, what did he tell you?" "Indeed, it is so. In vain do we shoot at her body. Not there is her heart; but in her rattle is her heart. With these shall we destroy her." Thus he said, and gave his brother one of the rabbit sticks. When he had given his brother the rabbit stick, "Now go ahead, you." Thus he said. The younger brother went about to the right. He threw it and missed. Whiz! The rabbit stick went up to the sun. As the rabbit stick came up the sun took it. "Now go ahead, you try." Thus he said. The elder brother went around to the left. He threw it. As he threw it, zip! His rabbit stick struck his rattle. Tu—-n! They ran away. As they started to run away, their giant died. Then they all ran away. The others ran after them. They came to a village. They went into the houses. "This is my house;" "This is my house;" and "This is mine." Thus they said. They went shooting arrows into the roof. Wherever they first came, they went in. An old woman and a little boy this big and a little girl were inside.

In the center of their room was standing a jar of urine.[19] They stuffed their nostrils with känaite flowers and with cotton wool. Then they thrust their noses into the jar. The people could see them. "Oh, dear! These are ghosts!" Thus they said. Then the two said to them, "Do not harm them, for I think they know something. So even though it is dangerous they are still alive." Thus they said. The two entered. As they came in they questioned them. "And now do you know something? Therefore, even though it is dangerous, you have not perished." "Well, we have a sacred object." "Indeed! Very well, take them. We shall go. Your fathers, your mothers, kä-eto·we, tcu-eto·we, mu-eto·we, le-eto·we, you will pass on their roads. If your days are the same as theirs you will not be slaves. It does not matter that he is only a little boy. Even so, he will be our father. It does not matter that she is a little girl, she will be our mother." Thus he said. Taking their sacred object they went. They came to where kä-eto·we were staying. There they said to them, "Now make your days." "Oh, no! We shall not be first. When all your days are at an end, then we shall add on our days." Thus they said. Then they worked for kä-eto·we. Kä-eto·we's days were made. Four days

[19]The stench of urine is believed to repel ghosts. That the family inside are ghosts suggests that they have a special power. By obtaining the object, the Twins have provided a way for the people to be free from being terrorized by ghosts.

and four nights, with fine rain falling, were the days of kä-eto·we. When their days were at an end, the two children and their grandmother worked. Their days were made. Four days and four nights, with heavy rain falling, were their days. Then they removed the evil smell. They made flowing canyons. Then they said, "Halihi! Thank you! Just the same is your ceremony. What may your clan be?" "Well, we are of the Yellow Corn clan." Thus they said. "Haiyi! Even though your eton·e is of the Yellow Corn clan, because of your bad smell, you have become black. Therefore you shall be the Black Corn clan." Thus they said to them.[20]

Then they arose. Gathering together all their sacred possessions, they came hither, to the place called, since the first beginning, Halona-Itiwana, their road came. There they saw the Navaho helper, little red bug. "Here! Wait! All this time we have been searching in vain for Itiwana. Nowhere have we seen anything like this." Thus they said. They summoned their grandchild, water bug. He came. "How have you lived these many days?" "Where we have been living happily you have passed us on our road. Be seated." Thus they said. He sat down. Then he questioned them. "Now, indeed, even now, you have sent for me. I think some word that is not too long your word will be. So now, if you will let me know that, I shall always remember it." "Indeed, it is so. Our fathers, our mothers, kä-eto·we, tcu-eto·we, mu-eto·we, le-eto·we, all the society priests, having issued forth into the daylight, go about seeking the middle. You will look for the middle for them. This is well. Because of your thoughts, at your heart, our fathers, kä-eto·we, tcu-eto·we, mu-eto·we, le-eto·we, will sit down quietly. Following after those, toward whom our thoughts bend, we shall pass our days." Thus they said. He sat down facing the east. To the left he stretched out his arm. To the right he stretched out his arm, but it was a little bent. He sat down facing the north. He stretched out his arms on both sides. They were just the same. Both arms touched the horizon. "Come, let us cross over to the north. For on this side my right arm is a little bent." Thus he said. They crossed (the river). They rested. He sat down. To all directions he stretched out his arms. Everywhere it was the same. "Right here is the middle."[21] Thus he said. There his fathers, his mothers, kä-eto·we, tcu-eto·we, mu-eto·we, le-eto·we, all the society priests, the society pekwins, the society bow priests, and all their children came to rest.

Thus it happened long ago.

1930

[20]This incident accounts for the origin of Zuni clans.

[21]Having completed their physical, religious, and social evolution, the Zuni end their journey in the Middle, the place of achievement and balance, from which no further movement is necessary. The sacred name of Zuni Pueblo is Halona-Itiwana, "The Middle Ant Hill of the World."

Changing Woman and the Hero Twins after the Emergence of the People (Diné-Navajo)[1]

The Navajos now removed to White Standing Rock, where, a few days after they arrived, they found on the ground a small turquoise image of a woman; this they preserved. Of late the monsters had been actively pursuing and devouring the people, and at the time this image was found there were only four persons remaining alive; these were an old man and woman and their two children, a young man and a young woman. Two days after the finding of the image, early in the morning, before they rose, they heard the voice of the Talking God, crying his call of "Wu'hu'hu'hú" so faint and far that they could scarcely hear it. After a while the call was repeated a second time, nearer and louder than at first. Again, after a brief silence, the call was heard for the third time, still nearer and still louder. The fourth call was loud and clear, as if sounded near at hand; as soon as it ceased, the shuffling tread of moccasined feet was heard, and a moment later Talking God stood before them.

He told the four people to come up to the top of *Tsolíhi* after twelve nights had passed, bringing with them the turquoise image they had found, and at once he departed. They pondered deeply on his words, and every day they talked among themselves, wondering why Talking God had summoned them to the mountain.

On the morning of the appointed day they ascended the mountain by a holy trail, and on a level spot, near the summit, they met a party that awaited them there. They found there Talking God, Calling God, White Body (who came up from the lower world with the Navajos), the eleven brothers (of Maid Who Becomes a Bear), the Mirage Stone People, the Daylight People standing in the east, the Blue Sky People standing in the south, the Yellow Light People standing in the west, and the Darkness People standing in the north. White Body stood in the east among the Daylight People, bearing in his hand a small image of a woman wrought in white shell, about the same size and shape as the blue image which the Navajos bore.

Talking God laid down a sacred buckskin with its head toward the west. The Mirage Stone People laid on the buckskin, heads west, the two little images,—of turquoise and white shell,—a white and a yellow ear of corn, the Pollen Boy, and the Grasshopper Girl. On top of all these Talking God laid another sacred buckskin with its head to the east, and under this they now put Wind.

Then the assembled crowd stood so as to form a circle, leaving in the east an opening through which Talking God and Calling God might pass in and out, and they sang the sacred song of Blessingway. Four times the gods entered and raised the cover. When they raised it for the fourth time, the images and the ears of corn were found changed to living beings in human form: the turquoise image had become the Woman Who Changes (or rejuvenates herself); the white shell image had become the White Shell Woman; the white ear of corn had become the White Corn Boy and

[1]The Navajo Indians of the southwest United States migrated from northwestern Canada by about A.D. 1200. They came to the Southwest as a hunting and gathering people; they learned agriculture from the pueblo peoples and in the sixteenth century acquired livestock from the Spanish. Their religious customs are thus somewhat similar to the Hopi people.

the yellow ear of corn, the Yellow Corn Girl. After the ceremony, White Body took Pollen Boy, Grasshopper Girl, White Corn Boy, and Yellow Corn Girl with him into *Tsolíhi;* the rest of the assembly departed, and the two divine sisters, Changing Woman and White Shell Woman,[2] were left on the mountain alone.

The women remained here four nights; on the fourth morning Changing Woman said: "Younger Sister, why should we remain here? Let us go to yonder high point and look around us." They went to the highest point of the mountain, and when they had been there several days Changing Woman said: "It is lonely here; we have no one to speak to but ourselves; we see nothing but that which rolls over our heads (the sun), and that which drops below us (a small dripping waterfall). I wonder if they can be people. I shall stay here and wait for the one in the morning, while you go down among the rocks and seek the other."

In the morning Changing Woman found a bare, flat rock and lay on it with her feet to the east, and the rising sun shone upon her. White Shell Woman went down where the dripping waters descended and allowed them to fall upon her. At noon the women met again on the mountain top and Changing Woman said to her sister: "It is sad to be so lonesome. How can we make people so that we may have others of our kind to talk to?" White Shell Woman answered: "Think, Elder Sister; perhaps after some days you may plan how this is to be done."

Four days after this conversation White Shell Woman said: "Elder Sister, I feel something strange moving within me; what can it be?" and Changing Woman answered: "It is a child. It was for this that you lay under the waterfall. I feel, too, the motions of a child within me. It was for this that I let the sun shine upon me." Soon after the voice of Talking God was heard four times, as usual, and after the last call he and Water Sprinkler[3] appeared. They came to prepare the women for their approaching delivery.

In four days more they felt the commencing throes of labor, and one said to the other: "I think my child is coming." She had scarcely spoken when the voice of the approaching god was heard, and soon Talking God and Water Sprinkler were seen approaching. The former was the accoucheur of Changing Woman, and the latter of White Shell Woman. To one woman a drag-rope of rainbow was given, to the other a drag-rope of sunbeam, and on these they pulled when in pain, as the Navajo woman now pulls on the rope. Changing Woman's child was born first. Talking God took it aside and washed it. He was glad, and laughed and made ironical motions, as if he were cutting the baby in slices and throwing the slices away. They made for the children two baby-baskets, both alike; the foot-rests and the back battens were made of sun-beam, the hoods of rainbow, the side-strings of sheet lightning, and the lacing strings of zigzag lightning. One child they covered with the black cloud, and the other with the female rain.[4] They called the children grandchildren, and they left, promising to return at the end of four days.

[2]Changing Woman represents Nature as cyclical—the seasons, the parts of a day, the ages of an individual life. White Shell Woman is not a separate individual, but Changing Woman in another form. In this version of the story, each conceives a son; yet, Changing Woman alone has conceived twins.

[3]A holy being responsible for rain.

[4]The fundamental principle of the Navajo world is complementarity. All things can be termed male or female and are associated with colors and the cardinal directions. Male rain is the dark thunderstorm; female rain is the light shower.

When the gods returned at the end of four days, the boys had grown to be the size of ordinary boys of twelve years of age. The gods said to them: "Boys, we have come to have a race with you." So a race was arranged that should go all around a neighboring mountain, and the four started,—two boys and two gods. Before the long race was half done the boys, who ran fast, began to flag, and the gods, who were still fresh, got behind them and scourged the lads with twigs of mountain mahogany. Talking God won the race, and the boys came home rubbing their sore backs. When the gods left they promised to return at the end of another period of four days.

As soon as the gods were gone, the Wind whispered to the boys and told them that the old ones were not such fast runners, after all, and that if the boys would practice during the next four days they might win the coming race. So for four days they ran hard, many times daily around the neighboring mountain, and when the gods came back again the youths had grown to the full stature of manhood. In the second contest the gods began to flag and fall behind when half way round the mountain, where the others had fallen behind in the first race, and here the boys got behind their elders and scourged the latter to increase their speed. The elder of the boys won this race, and when it was over the gods laughed and clapped their hands, for they were pleased with the spirit and prowess they witnessed.

The night after the race the boys lay down as usual to sleep; but hearing the women whispering together, they lay awake and listened. They strained their attention, but could not hear a word of what was uttered. At length they rose, approached the women, and said: "Mothers, of what do you speak?" and the women answered: "We speak of nothing." The boys then said: "Grandmothers, of what do you speak?" but the women again replied: "We speak of nothing." The boys then questioned: "Who are our fathers?" "You have no fathers," responded the women; "you are illegitimate." "Who are our fathers?" again demanded the boys, and the women answered: "The round cactus and the sitting cactus are your fathers."[5]

Next day the women made rude bows of juniper wood, and arrows, such as children play with, and they said to the boys: "Go and play around with these, but do not go out of sight from our hut, and do not go to the east." Notwithstanding these warnings the boys went to the east the first day, and when they had travelled a good distance they saw an animal with brownish hair and a sharp nose. They drew their arrows and pointed them toward the sharp-nosed stranger; but before they could shoot he jumped down into a canyon and disappeared. When they returned home they told the women—addressing them as "Mother" and "Grandmother"—what they had seen. The women said: "That is Coyote which you saw. He is a spy for the monster *Téelgeˇt.*". . .[6] Alas, our children! What shall we do to make you hear us? What shall we do to save you? You would not listen to us. Now the spies of the *alien gods* in all quarters of the world have seen you. They will tell their chiefs, and soon the monsters will come here to devour you, as they have devoured all your kind before you."

[5]The mystery of the boys' paternity is linked to that of the monsters they will slay, for they will discover that the Sun is the father of both the slayers and the slain.

[6]This edition of the story eliminates three repetitions of this episode in which the Twins, who should be hiding from the monsters who are terrorizing the people, play in the open where they are observed by spies for the monsters. *Téelgĕt* is a monstrous, horned quadruped.

The next morning the women made a corncake and laid it on the ashes to bake. Then White Shell Woman went out of the *hogán,* and, as she did so, she saw *Yéitso,*[7] the tallest and fiercest of the alien gods, approaching. She ran quickly back and gave the warning, and the women hid the boys under bundles and sticks. *Yéitso* came and sat down at the door, just as the women were taking the cake out of the ashes. "That cake is for me," said *Yéitso.* "How nice it smells!" "No," said Changing Woman, "it was not meant for your great maw." "I don't care," said *Yéitso.* "I would rather eat boys. Where are your boys? I have been told you have some here, and I have come to get them." "We have none," said Changing Woman. "All the boys have gone into the paunches of your people long ago." "No boys?" said the giant. "What, then, has made all the tracks around here?" "Oh! these tracks I have made for fun," replied the woman. "I am lonely here, and I make tracks so that I may fancy there are many people around me." She showed *Yéitso* how she could make similar tracks with her fist. He compared the two sets of tracks, seemed to be satisfied, and went away.

When he was gone, the White Shell Woman went up to the top of a neighboring hill to look around, and she beheld many of the anáye hastening in the direction of her lodge. She returned speedily, and told her sister what she had seen. Changing Woman took four colored hoops, and threw one toward each of the cardinal points,—a white one to the east, a blue one to the south, a yellow one to the west, and a black one to the north. At once a great gale arose, blowing so fiercely in all directions from the *hogán* that none of the enemies could advance against it.

Next morning the boys got up before daybreak and stole away. Soon the women missed them, but could not trace them in the dark. When it was light enough to examine the ground the women went out to look for fresh tracks. They found four footprints of each of the boys, pointing in the direction of the mountain of *Dsilnáotil,* but more than four tracks they could not find. They came to the conclusion that the boys had taken a holy trail, so they gave up further search and returned to the lodge.

The boys travelled rapidly in the holy trail, and soon after sunrise, near *Dsilnáotil,* they saw smoke arising from the ground. They went to the place where the smoke rose, and they found it came from the smoke-hole of a subterranean chamber. A ladder, black from smoke, projected through the hole. Looking down into the chamber they saw an old woman, the Spider Woman,[8] who glanced up at them and said: "Welcome, children. Enter. Who are you, and whence do you two come together walking?" They made no answer, but descended the ladder. When they reached the floor she again spoke to them, asking: "Whither do you two go walking together?" "Nowhere in particular," they answered; "we came here because we had nowhere else to go." She asked this question four times, and each time she received a similar answer. Then she said: "Perhaps you would seek your father?" "Yes," they answered, "if we only knew the way to his dwelling." "Ah!" said the woman, "it is a long and dangerous way to the house of your father, the Sun. There are many of the

[7]The name means "the Great Fear." The monsters were conceived unnaturally in the underworld by women who had turned away from men. Each monster or obstacle the Twins overcome can be understood to represent certain kinds of fears.

[8]In southwestern Native literatures, Spider Woman is a grandmotherly figure whose great wisdom is often placed at the service of humanity.

monsters dwelling between here and there, and perhaps, when you get there, your father may not be glad to see you, and may punish you for coming. You must pass four places of danger,—the rocks that crush the traveller, the reeds that cut him to pieces, the cane cactuses that tear him to pieces, and the boiling sands that overwhelm him. But I shall give you something to subdue your enemies and preserve your lives." She gave them a charm, the feather of the alien gods, which consisted of a hoop with two life-feathers (feathers plucked from a living eagle) attached, and another life-feather to preserve their existence. She taught them also this magic formula, which, if repeated to their enemies, would subdue their anger: "Put your feet down with pollen. Put your hands down with pollen. Put your head down with pollen. Then your feet are pollen; your hands are pollen; your body is pollen; your mind is pollen; your voice is pollen. The trail is beautiful. Be still."[9]

Soon after leaving the house of Spider Woman, the boys came to the rocks that crush.[10] There was here a narrow chasm between two high cliffs. When a traveller approached, the rocks would open wide apart, apparently to give him easy passage and invite him to enter; but as soon as he was within the cleft they would close like hands clapping and crush him to death. These rocks were really people; they thought like men; they were monsters. When the boys got to the rocks they lifted their feet as if about to enter the chasm, and the rocks opened to let them in. Then the boys put down their feet, but withdrew them quickly. The rocks closed with a snap to crush them; but the boys remained safe on the outside. Thus four times did they deceive the rocks. When they had closed for the fourth time the rocks said: "Who are ye; whence come ye two together, and whither go ye?" "We are children of the Sun," answered the boys. "We come from *Dsilnáotil,* and we go to seek the house of our father." Then they repeated the words the Spider Woman had taught them, and the rocks said: "Pass on to the house of your father." When next they ventured to step into the chasm the rocks did not close, and they passed safely on.

The boys kept on their way and soon came to a great plain covered with reeds that had great leaves on them as sharp as knives. When the boys came to the edge of the field of reeds, the latter opened, showing a clear passage through to the other side. The boys pretended to enter, but retreated, and as they did so the walls of reeds rushed together to kill them. Thus four times did they deceive the reeds. Then the reeds spoke to them, as the rocks had done; they answered and repeated the sacred words. "Pass on to the house of your father," said the reeds, and the boys passed on in safety.

The next danger they encountered was in the country covered with cane cactuses. These cactuses rushed at and tore to pieces whoever attempted to pass through them. When the boys came to the cactuses the latter opened their ranks to let the travellers pass on, as the reeds had done before. But the boys deceived them as they had deceived the reeds, and subdued them as they had subdued the reeds, and passed on in safety.

After they had passed the country of the cactus they came, in time, to the land of the rising sands. Here was a great desert of sands that rose and whirled and boiled

[9]This is a prayer for life and peace, symbolized by pollen, which serves to bless their journey.

[10]These mythical places are also identified with real locales in the Navajo world, so that the story accounts for how the landscape came to assume its present form.

like water in a pot, and overwhelmed the traveller who ventured among them. As the boys approached, the sands became still more agitated and the boys did not dare venture among them. "Who are ye?" said the sands, "and whence come ye?" "We are children of the Sun, we came from *Dsilnáotil,* and we go to seek the house of our father." These words were four times said. Then the elder of the boys repeated his sacred formula; the sands subsided, saying: "Pass on to the house of your father," and the boys continued on their journey over the desert of sands.

Soon after this adventure they approached the house of the Sun. As they came near the door they found the way guarded by two bears that crouched, one to the right and one to the left, their noses pointing toward one another. As the boys drew near, the bears rose, growled angrily, and acted as if about to attack the intruders; but the elder boy repeated the sacred words the Spider Woman had taught him, and when he came to the last words, "Be still," the bears crouched down again and lay still. The boys walked on. After passing the bears they encountered a pair of sentinel serpents, then a pair of sentinel winds, and, lastly, a pair of sentinel lightnings. As the boys advanced, all these guardians acted as if they would destroy them; but all were appeased with the words of prayer.

The house of the Sun God was built of turquoise; it was square like a pueblo house, and stood on the shore of a great water. When the boys entered they saw, sitting in the west, a woman; in the south, two handsome young men; and in the north, two handsome young women. The women gave a glance at the strangers and then looked down. The young men gazed at them more closely, and then, without speaking, they rose, wrapped the strangers in four coverings of the sky, and laid them on a shelf.

The boys had lain there quietly for some time when a rattle that hung over the door shook and one of the young women said: "Our father is coming." The rattle shook four times, and soon after it shook the fourth time, the Sun Bearer entered his house. He took the sun off his back and hung it up on a peg on the west wall of the room, where it shook and clanged for some time, going "tla, tla, tla, tla," till at last it hung still.

Then the Sun Bearer turned to the woman and said, in an angry tone: "Who are those two who entered here to-day?" The woman made no answer and the young people looked at one another, but each feared to speak. Four times he asked this question, and at length the woman said: "It would be well for you not to say too much. Two young men came hither to-day, seeking their father. When you go abroad, you always tell me that you visit nowhere, and that you have met no woman but me. Whose sons, then, are these?" She pointed to the bundle on the shelf, and the children smiled significantly at one another.

He took the bundle from the shelf. He first unrolled the robe of dawn with which they were covered, then the robe of blue sky, next the robe of yellow evening light, and lastly the robe of darkness. When he unrolled this the boys fell out on the floor. He seized them, and threw them first upon great, sharp spikes of white shell that stood in the east; but they bounded back, unhurt, from these spikes, for they held their life-feathers tightly all the while. He then threw them in turn on spikes of turquoise in the south, on spikes of haliotis in the west, and spikes of black rock in the north; but they came uninjured from all these trials and the Sun Bearer said: "I wish it were indeed true that they were my children."

He said then to the elder children—those who lived with him,—"Go out and prepare the sweat-house and heat for it four of the hardest boulders you can find. Heat a white, a blue, a yellow, and a black boulder." When the Winds heard this they said: "He still seeks to kill his children. How shall we avert the danger?" The sweat-house was built against a bank. Wind dug into the bank a hole behind the sudatory, and concealed the opening with a flat stone. Wind then whispered into the ears of the boys the secret of the hole and said: "Do not hide in the hole until you have answered the questions of your father." The boys went into the sweat-house, the great hot boulders were put in, and the opening of the lodge was covered with the four sky-blankets. Then the Sun Bearer called out to the boys: "Are you hot?" and they answered: "Yes, very hot." Then they crept into the hiding-place and lay there. After a while the Sun Bearer came and poured water through the top of the sweat-house on the stones, making them burst with a loud noise, and a great heat and steam was raised. But in time the stones cooled and the boys crept out of their hiding-place into the sweat-house. The Sun Bearer came and asked again: "Are you hot?" hoping to get no reply; but the boys still answered: "Yes, very hot." Then he took the coverings off the sweat-house and let the boys come out. He greeted them in a friendly way and said: "Yes, these are my children," and yet he was thinking of other ways by which he might destroy them if they were not.

The four sky-blankets were spread on the ground one over another, and the four young men were made to sit on them, one behind another, facing the east. "My daughters, make these boys to look like my other sons," said the Sun Bearer. The young women went to the strangers, pulled their hair out long, and moulded their faces and forms so that they looked just like their brethren. Then Sun bade them all rise and enter the house. They rose and all went, in a procession, the two strangers last.

As they were about to enter the door they heard a voice whispering in their ears: "St! Look at the ground." They looked down and beheld a spiny caterpillar, who, as they looked, spat out two blue spits on the ground. "Take each of you one of these," said Wind, "and put it in your mouth, but do not swallow it. There is one more trial for you,—a trial by smoking." When they entered the house the Sun Bearer took down a pipe of turquoise that hung on the eastern wall and filled it with tobacco. "This is the tobacco he kills with," whispered Wind to the boys. The Sun Bearer held the pipe up to the sun that hung on the wall, lit it, and gave it to the boys to smoke. They smoked it, and passed it from one to another till it was finished. They said it tasted sweet, but it did them no harm.

When the pipe was smoked out and the Sun Bearer saw the boys were not killed by it, he was satisfied and said: "Now, my children, what do you want from me? Why do you seek me?" "Oh, father!" they replied, "the land where we dwell is filled with monsters, who devour the people. There are Yéitso and the Horned Monster, the Giant Eagle, Those-Who-Slay-With-Their-Eyes, and many others. They have eaten nearly all of our kind; there are few left; already they have sought our lives, and we have run away to escape them. Give us, we beg, the weapons with which we may slay our enemies. Help us to destroy them."

"Know," said the Sun Bearer, "that Yéitso who dwells at *Tsótsil* is also my son, yet I will help you to kill him. I shall hurl the first bolt at him, and I will give you those things that will help you in war." He took from pegs where they hung around the room and gave to each a hat, a shirt, leggings, moccasins, all made of flint,[11] a chain-lightning arrow, a sheet-lightning arrow, a sunbeam arrow, a rainbow arrow, and a great stone knife or knife club. "These are what we want," said the boys. They put on the clothes of flint, and streaks of lightning shot from every joint.

Next morning the Sun Bearer led the boys out to the edge of the world, where the sky and the earth came close together, and beyond which there was no world. Here sixteen wands or poles leaned from the earth to the sky; four of these were of white shell, four of turquoise, four of haliotis shell, and four of red stone. A deep stream flowed between them and the wands. As they approached the stream, the Wind whispered: "This is another trial;" but he blew a great breath and formed a bridge of rainbow, over which the brothers passed in safety. Wind whispered again: "The red wands are for war, the others are for peace;" so when the Sun Bearer asked his sons: "On which wands will ye ascend?" they answered: "On the wands of red stone," for they sought war with their enemies. They climbed up to the sky on the wands of red stone, and their father went with them.

They journeyed on till they came to the sky-hole which is in the centre of the sky. The hole is edged with four smooth, shining cliffs that slope steeply downwards,—cliffs of the same materials as the wands by which they had climbed from the earth to the sky. They sat down on the smooth declivities,—the Sun Bearer on the west side of the hole, the brothers on the east side. The latter would have slipped down had not the Wind blown up and helped them to hold on. The Sun Bearer pointed down and said: "Where do you belong in the world below? Show me your home." The brothers looked down and scanned the land; but they could distinguish nothing; all the land seemed flat; the wooded mountains looked like dark spots on the surface; the lakes gleamed like stars, and the rivers like streaks of lightning. The elder brother said: "I do not recognize the land, I know not where our home is." Now Wind prompted the younger brother, and showed him which were the sacred mountains and which the great rivers, and the younger exclaimed, pointing downwards: "There is the Male Water (San Juan River), and there is the Female Water (Rio Grande); yonder is the mountain of *Tsisnadzini;* below us is *Tsótsil;* there in the west is *Dokoslid;* that white spot beyond the Male Water is *Depentsa;* and there between these mountains is *Dsilnáotil,* near which our home is."[12] "You are right, my child, it is thus that the land lies," said the Sun Bearer. Then, renewing his promises, he spread a streak of lightning; he made his children stand on it,—one on each end,—and he shot them down to the top of *Tsótsil* (Mt. Taylor).

They descended the mountain on its south side and walked toward the warm spring at *Tósato.* As they were walking along under a high bluff, where there is now a white circle, they heard voices hailing them. "Whither are you going? Come hither a while." They went in the direction in which they heard the voices calling and found

[11]Actually, armor, like arrow points and knife blades, made from flint.

[12]These rivers and the sacred boundary mountains (*Depentsa,* Hesperus Peak, in the north; *Tsisnadzini,* the Sangre de Cristo Mountains in the east; *Tsótsil,* Mt. Taylor, in the south; and *Dokoslid,* the San Francisco Peaks, in the east) mark Navajo land, of which *Dsilnáotil,* or Gobernador Knob, is the Center.

four holy people,—Holy Man, Holy Young Man, Holy Boy, and Holy Girl. The brothers remained all night in a cave with these people, and the latter told them all about Yéitso. They said that he showed himself every day three times on the mountains before he came down, and when he showed himself for the fourth time he descended from *Tsótsil* to *Tósato* to drink; that, when he stooped down to drink, one hand rested on *Tsótsil* and the other on the high hills on the opposite side of the valley, while his feet stretched as far away as a man could walk between sunrise and noon.

They left the cave at daybreak and went on to *Tósato,* where in ancient days there was a much larger lake than there is now. There was a high, rocky wall in the narrow part of the valley, and the lake stretched back to where Blue Water is to-day. When they came to the edge of the lake, one brother said to the other: "Let us try one of our father's weapons and see what it can do." They shot one of the lightning arrows at *Tsótsil;* it made a great cleft in the mountain, which remains to this day, and one said to the other: "We cannot suffer in combat while we have such weapons as these."

Soon they heard the sound of thunderous footsteps, and they beheld the head of Yéitso peering over a high hill in the east; it was withdrawn in a moment. Soon after, the monster raised his head and chest over a hill in the south, and remained a little longer in sight than when he was in the east. Later he displayed his body to the waist over a hill in the west; and lastly he showed himself, down to the knees, over *Tsótsil* in the north. Then he descended the mountain, came to the edge of the lake, and laid down a basket which he was accustomed to carry.

Yéitso stooped four times to the lake to drink, and, each time he drank, the waters perceptibly diminished; when he had done drinking, the lake was nearly drained. The brothers lost their presence of mind at sight of the giant drinking, and did nothing while he was stooping down. As he took his last drink they advanced to the edge of the lake, and Yéitso saw their reflection in the water. He raised his head, and, looking at them, roared: "What a pretty pair have come in sight! Where have I been hunting?" (*i.e.,* that I never saw them before). "Throw (his words) back in his mouth," said the younger to the elder brother. "What a great thing has come in sight! Where have we been hunting?" shouted the elder brother to the giant. Four times these taunts were repeated by each party. The brothers then heard Wind whispering quickly, "Akó'! Akó'! Beware! Beware!" They were standing on a bent rainbow just then; they straightened the rainbow out, descending to the ground, and at the same instant a lightning bolt, hurled by Yéitso, passed thundering over their heads. He hurled four bolts rapidly; as he hurled the second, they bent their rainbow and rose, while the bolt passed under their feet; as he discharged the third they descended, and let the lightning pass over them. When he threw the fourth bolt they bent the rainbow very high, for this time he aimed higher than before; but his weapon still passed under their feet and did them no harm. He drew a fifth bolt to throw at them; but at this moment the lightning descended from the sky on the head of the giant and he reeled beneath it, but did not fall. Then the elder brother sped a chain-lightning arrow; his enemy tottered toward the east, but straightened himself up again. The second arrow caused him to stumble toward the south (he fell lower and lower each time), but again he stood up and prepared himself to renew the conflict. The third lightning arrow made him topple toward the west, and the fourth to the north. Then he fell to his knees, raised himself partly again, fell flat on his face, stretched out his limbs, and moved no more.

When the arrows struck him, his armor was shivered in pieces and the scales flew in every direction. The elder brother said: "They may be useful to the people in the future."[13] The brothers then approached their fallen enemy and the younger scalped him. Heretofore the younger brother bore only the name, Child of the Water; but now his brother gave him also the warrior name of He Who Cuts Around. What the elder brother's name was before this we do not know; but ever after he was called Monster Slayer.

They cut off his head and threw it away to the other side of *Tsótsil,* where it may be seen to-day on the eastern side of the mountain.[14] The blood from the body now flowed in a great stream down the valley, so great that it broke down the rocky wall that bounded the old lake and flowed on. Wind whispered to the brothers: "The blood flows toward the dwelling of Those-Who-Slay-With-Their-Eyes; if it reaches them, Yéitso will come to life again." Then Monster Slayer took his flint club, and drew with it across the valley a line. Here the blood stopped flowing and piled itself up in a high wall. But when it had piled up here very high it began to flow off in another direction, and Wind again whispered: "It now flows toward the dwelling of the Bear that Pursues; if it reaches him, Yéitso will come to life again." Hearing this, Monster Slayer again drew a line with his knife on the ground, and again the blood piled up and stopped flowing. The blood of Yéitso fills all the valley to-day, and the high cliffs in the black rock that we see there now are the places where Monster Slayer stopped the flow with his flint club.

They then put the broken arrows of Yéitso and his scalp into his basket and set out for their home near *Dsilnáotil.* When they got near the house, they took off their own suits of armor and hid these, with the basket and its contents, in the bushes. The mothers were rejoiced to see them, for they feared their sons were lost, and they said: "Where have you been since you left here yesterday, and what have you done?" Monster Slayer replied: "We have been to the house of our father, the Sun. We have been to *Tsótsil* and we have slain Yéitso." "Ah, my child," said Changing Woman, "do not speak thus. It is wrong to make fun of such an awful subject." "Do you not believe us?" said Monster Slayer; "come out, then, and see what we have brought back with us." He led the women out to where he had hidden the basket and showed them the trophies of Yéitso. Then they were convinced and they rejoiced, and had a dance to celebrate the victory. . . .[15]

"Surely all the monsters are now killed," said Changing Woman. "This storm must have destroyed them." But Wind whispered into Monster Slayer's ear, "Old Age still lives." The hero said then to his mother: "Where used Old Age to dwell?" His mother would not answer him, though he repeated his question four

[13]By providing the Navajo with flint for blades and arrow points.

[14]Forty miles northeast of Mt. Taylor is Cabezon ("The Head") Peak. Yéitso's blood coagulated into The Malpais, an extensive lava flow south of Mt. Taylor.

[15]This is the first Scalp Dance, which celebrates victory over the enemy while it cleanses the warrior from the effects of contact with enemy dead. After this initial victory, the Twins slay many other monsters and return home after a storm, presuming to have made the world safe and habitable for humankind. In the remarkable encounters which follow, people learn that, although they might have power over some things, the use of power might not always be wise.

times. At last Wind again whispered in his ear and said: "She lives in the mountains of *Depentsa.*"

Next morning he set out for the north, and when, after a long journey, he reached *Depentsa,* he saw an old woman who came slowly toward him leaning on a staff. Her back was bent, her hair was white, and her face was deeply wrinkled. He knew this must be Old Age. When they met he said: "Grandmother, I have come on a cruel errand. I have come to slay you." "Why would you slay me?" she said in a feeble voice, "I have never harmed any one. I hear that you have done great deeds in order that men might increase on the earth, but if you kill me there will be no increase of men; the boys will not grow up to become fathers; the worthless old men will not die; the people will stand still. It is well that people should grow old and pass away and give their places to the young. Let me live, and I shall help you to increase the people." "Grandmother, if you keep this promise I shall spare your life," said Monster Slayer, and he returned to his mother without a trophy.

When he got home Wind whispered to him: "Cold Woman still lives." Monster Slayer said to Changing Woman: "Mother, grandmother, where does Cold Woman dwell?" His mother would not answer him; but Wind again whispered, saying: "Cold Woman lives high on the summits of *Depentsa,* where the snow never melts."

Next day he went again to the north and climbed high among the peaks of *Depentsa,* where no trees grow and where the snow lies white through all the summer. Here he found a lean old woman, sitting on the bare snow, without clothing, food, fire, or shelter. She shivered from head to foot, her teeth chattered, and her eyes streamed water. Among the drifting snows which whirled around her, a multitude of snow-buntings were playing; these were the couriers she sent out to announce the coming of a storm. "Grandmother," he said, "a cruel man I shall be. I am going to kill you, so that men may no more suffer and die by your hand," and he raised his knife-club to smite her. "You may kill me or let me live, as you will. I care not," she said to the hero; "but if you kill me it will always be hot, the land will dry up, the springs will cease to flow, the people will perish. You will do well to let me live. It will be better for your people." He paused and thought upon her words. He lowered the hand he had raised to strike her, saying: "You speak wisely, grandmother; I shall let you live." He turned around and went home.

When Monster Slayer got home from this journey, bearing no trophy, Wind again whispered in his ear and said: "Poverty still lives." He asked his mother where Poverty used to live, but she would not answer him. It was Wind who again informed him. "There are two, and they dwell at *Dsildasdzini.*"

He went to *Dsildasdzini* the next day and found there an old man and an old woman, who were filthy, clad in tattered garments, and had no goods in their house. "Grandmother, grandfather," he said, "a cruel man I shall be. I have come to kill you." "Do not kill us, my grandchild," said the old man: "it would not be well for the people, in days to come, if we were dead; then they would always wear the same clothes and never get anything new. If we live, the clothing will wear out and the people will make new and beautiful garments; they will gather goods and look handsome. Let us live and we will pull their old clothes to pieces for them." So he spared them and went home without a trophy.

The next journey was to seek Hunger, who lived, as Wind told him, at White Spot of Grass. At this place he found twelve of the Hunger People. Their chief was a big, fat man, although he had no food to eat but the little brown cactus. "I am going to be cruel," said Monster Slayer, "so that men may suffer no more the pangs of hunger and die no more of hunger." "Do not kill us," said the chief, "if you wish your people to increase and be happy in the days to come. We are your friends. If we die, the people will not care for food; they will never know the pleasure of cooking and eating nice things, and they will never care for the pleasures of the chase." So he spared also Hunger, and went home without a trophy.

When Monster Slayer came back from the home of Hunger, Wind spoke to him no more of enemies that lived. The Monster Slayer said to his mother: "I think all the monsters must be dead, for every one I meet now speaks to me as a relation; they say to me, 'my grandson,' 'my son,' 'my brother.'" Then he took off his armor—his knife, moccasins, leggings, shirt, and cap—and laid them in a pile; he put with them the various weapons which the Sun had given him, and he sang this song:—

Now Monster Slayer arrives
Here from the house made of the dark stone knives.
From where the dark stone knives dangle on high,
You have the treasures, holy one, not I.

The Child of the Water now arrives,
Here from the house made of the serrate knives.

From where the serrate knives dangle on high,
You have the treasures, holy one, not I.

He who was reared beneath the Earth arrives,
Here from the house made of all kinds of knives.
From where all kinds of knives dangle on high,
You have the treasures, holy one, not I.

The hero, Changing Grandchild, now arrives,
Here from the house made of the yellow knives.
From where the yellow knives dangle on high,
You have the treasures, holy one, not I.[16]

1897

[16]In this song, the Twins bring the story full circle by acknowledging that Changing Woman is really the most powerful being, the one for whom the Sun's weapons have been used, the one whose treasures benefit everyone.

Origin of the Sun Shower (Huron-Wendat)[1]

A young woman, the most beautiful of all women, was not pleased with her suitors, whom she scorned [one after the other] for a very long time. One day, however, a very handsome young man came around, and she fell in love with him. Now she was indeed willing to converse with him; so they soon agreed to marry. The young man said, "Well then, to-morrow at night, I shall come and take you away." The young woman said to her mother, "I am very much in love with him, for he is far more handsome [than the others]. To-morrow, at night, he is going to come and take me along with him." The mother gave her consent.

The next night, the young man came over. The mother saw him as he came into her house. They spoke to each other; and he said, "I have come for your daughter." The old woman replied, "Be it so!"

He went away with the [the young woman]. When they had travelled but a short distance, he said, "Here! let us take the shorter way across the forest yonder." And they went across [the forest], so that, although they had travelled a long way, it did not seem long to her.

Upon reaching home, as he found his mother and three sisters all sitting there together, he brought the young woman in. And the young man and his bride then were married.

Now her husband went out hunting in order to bring back deer meat. And his bride kept on sitting there waiting for him. She was thinking that this was the abode of human beings. But, after a while, she was very much frightened when [she found out that] her husband was a big snake. She had taken him for a young man, but there, in her lap, he rested his head and said, "Louse me!" So she just looked on one side, and then she glanced at the other side. It was only a big snake whose head was in her lap. She cried out, and started up quickly.

[1]From *Huron-Wyandot Traditional Narratives in Translations and Native Texts,* collected by Marius Barbeau (Ottawa: Government of Canada, Dept. of Northern Affairs and National Resources, 1960). The story was told by Catherine Johnson, a fluent speaker of Wyandot and member of the Deer clan, in Wyandotte, Oklahoma, in 1912. Her son, Allen, acted as translator.

The Wendat (Wyandot or Wyandotte) Confederacy was a loose alliance of linguistically and culturally related agricultural peoples in their homeland of Wendake, located in southern Ontario between Georgian Bay and Lake Ontario. The name *Huron* most likely comes from the French word *hure,* or wild boar, referring to the bristling hair fashion among Wendat men.

Given their influential trade location between the farming Haudenosaunee Confederacy to the south and the hunting Algonquin peoples to the north, the Wendat were in the ideal location for Jesuit missionary activities in the mid-fifteenth century. Earlier conflicts with the Haudenosaunee Confederacy increased dramatically with the increased pressures of European colonization, and the Wendat alliance was shattered by 1650. Some survivors were incorporated into various Haudenosaunee communities, though the majority fled to present-day Quebec, Michigan, and Ohio. Later, as a result of the Indian Removal Act of 1830, they emigrated to Kansas and Oklahoma. There are currently around 8,000 Wendats spread between Quebec, Ontario, Michigan, Kansas, and Oklahoma.

The [husband's] mother [spoke to him] and said, "Why did you ever want to marry this woman if really you could not transform yourself [forever] into a human being?" The young woman, by this time, knew that he was not a human being, and she was most frightened. The [husband's] mother scolded him still more bitterly. He [remained] a snake and [the girl] thought, "He was only man-like, [the one] whom I have married."

The mother [took the young woman aside] and said, "Next time, when he goes out hunting again, you had better run back home. I have scolded him; but I shall not be able to prevent him from killing you, as he is one of us, and we are not human beings, but snakes. This really happened because you did not want to get married for so long.[2] That is why he said, 'As it is, I will be transfigured into a human being to marry her.' This could not be so, and he could not forever retain the shape of a human being."

The young woman then took to flight and made for her home, because [the old woman] had said, "Be off, and go straight to the North, and run all the way as fast as you possibly can. It is a long way, but exert yourself to the utmost and run all the way home." Now she started out, running northward with all her might.

When the [young man] came back [from the hunt], nowhere could he see his bride. Soon, finding out that she had run away, he pursued her.

The girl was quite far already, for she had been running as fast as she could. It so happened that the water rose all around her, and it became so deep that she could no longer run along. Now her husband, swimming with his head out of the water, was about to overtake her.

Several men could be seen standing [at a distance]. Their chief shouted [to the young woman] "This way! Come and stand behind me. I shall defend you against him." But the Snake was getting still closer to her, while swimming with his head out of the water. The chief [spoke to his men] saying, "Shoot right there!" So it was done, and they killed the big Snake, the one who had been the young woman's husband. The air at once became dark with smoke, as her protectors were the Thunder [and his three sons, whose darts were lightning].[3] The old man took the young woman along with him. She knew nothing of the place whither she was being taken. This time, she got married to [one of] the Thunder's sons, and soon she gave birth to a child.

She was constantly longing to go down and visit her mother. As she had no idea of the way to her mother's home, the Thunder, her husband, said "I am willing to take you down to your mother's home. But you will have to take the young one along with you and pledge yourself to take the utmost care of him, as he must always be good-natured. He should never strike anybody, for if he does he will surely kill them outright, as he is of our family. And should this happen, I would at once take him away from you."[4]

The chief [Thunder] had three young men with him, his own sons; and the young woman's mother had five sons.

[2]The young woman's vanity has blinded her to the illusory beauty of the transformed snake.

[3]Thunder is a spirit being of great power and benevolence among many Iroquoian peoples. Sometimes a singular spirit, sometimes one of multiple Thunderers, in various stories he engages in battle with a great, murderous serpent who often embodies the dangerous forces of lightning.

[4]Four is a number noted for its spiritual power.

Now the child grew in size. When he had reached his fourth year, he could go out and play with the other boys, and he was given a bow.[5] As the other children [one day] came around, one of them took hold of his bow. The [Thunder-] child at once took it back and drew it at the other boy; and a thunder peal resounded.

The Thunder [his father] looked for the woman, and the air became filled with smoke. When the smoke cleared off, nowhere was the Thunder-child to be seen. His father had fulfilled his promise, for he had said to his wife, "I will take him away from you if he breaks the custom and kills anybody."

Then the Thunder spoke again to the young woman, and said, "I have now taken him along with me, and whenever it rains while the sun is shining, the people will think and say that Tsijutoon, the Wyandot, is making the rain."

Wohpe and the Gift of the Pipe (Lakota)

Finger[1]

In the long ago the Lakotas were in camp and two young men lay upon a hill watching for signs. They saw a long way in the distance a lone person coming, and they ran further toward it and lay on another hill hidden so that if it were an enemy they would be able to intercept it or signal to the camp. When the person came close, they saw that it was a woman and when she came nearer that she was without clothing of any kind except that her hair was very long and fell over her body like a robe. One young man said to the other that he would go and meet the woman and embrace her and if he found her good, he would hold her in his tipi. His companion cautioned him to be careful for this might be a buffalo woman who could enchant him and take him with her to her people and hold him there forever. But the young man would not

[5]Though the Thunder is kind, he and his descendants are also beings of extraordinary power that can be dangerous if their passions are unrestrained.

[1]James R. Walker was a physician to the Oglala at the Pine Ridge (South Dakota) Reservation from 1896 to 1914. Faced with the tremendous medical problems on the reservation, especially tuberculosis, he sought the assistance of the medicine men to help him understand and serve the Lakotas. They began to teach him the stories and ceremonies of the Lakotas, stating, "We will do this so you may know how to be a medicine man for the people. . . . We will tell you of the ceremonies as if you were an Oglala who wished to take part in them."

Finger, an old and very conservative Oglala holy man who was very helpful in enabling Walker to understand some of the most complex Oglala beliefs, told this story on March 25, 1914, in response to Walker's inquiries about how the pipe came to the Lakotas. *Wohpe* is one of the forms of the *wakan tanka,* which is often described singularly as the Great Spirit, but which, according to Oglala holy man George Sword, has sixteen different aspects. *Wohpe* is feminine and the mediator between earth and sky, so she is recognized in nature as the meteor or falling star. She is familiarly personified, though not named in this narrative, as White Buffalo Calf Woman. She is responsible for bringing to the Lakotas the seven principal rites, of which the pipe is one. This text is taken from James R. Walker, *Lakota Belief and Ritual,* 1980.

be persuaded and met the woman on the hill next to where they had watched her. His companion saw him attempt to embrace her and there was a cloud closed about them so that he could not see what happened. In a short time the cloud disappeared and the woman was alone. She beckoned to the other young man and told him to come there and assured him that he would not be harmed. As she spoke in the Lakota language the young man thought she belonged to his people and went to where she stood.

When he got there, she showed him the bare bones of his companion and told him that the Crazy Buffalo had caused his companion to try to do her harm and that she had destroyed him and picked his bones bare. The young man was very much afraid and drew his bow and arrow to shoot the woman, but she told him that if he would do as she directed, no harm would come to him and he should get any girl he wished for his woman, for she was *wakan*[2] and he could not hurt her with his arrows. But if he refused to do as she should direct, or attempt to shoot her, he would be destroyed as his companion had been. Then the young man promised to do as she should bid him.

She then directed him to return to the camp and call all the council together and tell them that in a short time they would see four puffs of smoke under the sun at midday. When they saw this sign they should prepare a feast, and all sit in the customary circle to have the feast served when she would enter the camp, but the men must all sit with their head bowed and look at the ground until she was in their midst. Then she would serve the feast to them and after they had feasted she would tell them what to do: that they must obey her in everything; that if they obeyed her in everything they would have their prayers to the *Wakan Tanka* answered and be prosperous and happy; but that if they disobeyed her or attempted to do her any harm, they would be neglected by *Wakan Tanka* and be punished as the young man who had attempted to embrace her had been.

Then she disappeared as a mist disappears so that the young man knew that she was *wakan.* He returned to the camp and told these things to the people and the council decided to do as she had instructed the young man. They made preparation for the feast and in a few days they saw four puffs of black smoke under the sun at midday, so they prepared for a feast and all dressed in their best clothing and sat in the circle ready to be served and every man bowed his head and looked toward the ground. Suddenly the women began uttering low exclamations of admiration, but all the men steadily kept their eyes toward the ground except one young man and he looked toward the entrance of the camp. He saw a puff of black smoke which blew into his eyes and a voice said, "You have disobeyed me and there will be smoke in your eyes as long as you live." From that time, that young man had very sore eyes and all the time they were as if biting smoke was in them.

Then the woman entered the circle and took the food and served it, first to the little children and then to the women and then she bade the men to look up. They did so and saw a very beautiful woman dressed in the softest deer skin which was

[2]Wakan is customarily translated as "sacred" or "holy," but it more precisely means anything charged with power which can only be approached through ritual.

ornamented with fringes and colors more beautiful than any woman of the Lakota had ever worked. Then she served the men with food, and when they had feasted she told them that she wished to serve them always; that they had first seen her as smoke and that they should always see her as smoke. Then she took from her pouch a pipe and willow bark and Lakota tobacco and filled the pipe with the bark and tobacco and lighted it with a coal of fire.[3]

She smoked a few whiffs and handed the pipe to the chief and told him to smoke and hand it to another. Thus the pipe was passed until all had smoked. She then instructed the council how to gather the bark and the tobacco and prepare it, and gave the pipe into their keeping, telling them that as long as they preserved this pipe she would serve them. But she would serve them in this way. When the smoke came from the pipe she would be present and hear their prayers and take them to the *Wakan Tanka* and plead for them that their prayers should be answered.

After this she remained in this camp for many days and all the time she was there everyone was happy for she went from tipi to tipi with good words for all. When the time came for her to go, she called all the people together and bade the women to build a great fire of dried cottonwood, which they did. Then she directed all to sit in a circle about the fire and the shaman to have an abundance of sweetgrass. She stood in the midst of the circle and when the fire had burned to coals she directed the shaman to place on it the sweetgrass. This made a cloud of smoke and the woman entered the smoke and disappeared. Then the shamans knew that it was *Wohpe* who had given the pipe and they appointed a custodian for it with instructions that it was to be kept sacred and used only on the most solemn and important occasions. With due ceremony they made wrappers for the pipe so that it is *wakan*. The shamans instructed the people that they could make other pipes and use them and that *Wohpe* would be in the smoke of any such pipe if smoked with proper solemnity and form.

Thus it was that the Beautiful Woman brought the pipe to the Lakotas.

1980

[3]The pipe is used in all rituals and is therefore the central integrating element in Lakota ritual life. In its complex forms of stone, wood, feathers, and animal carvings, it also represents the Lakota cosmos. The smoke offered to the four directions carried prayer to Wakan Tanka. Bonds between groups, vows to *Wakantanka,* and prophecies were validated by means of the pipe, and any transgressions against it would cause the offender or his family to suffer misfortune or even death. Thus the pipe could not be desecrated by word or deed, and it could only be handled by persons properly trained in its protocol.

The Origin of Stories (Seneca)

There was once a boy who had no home. His parents were dead and his uncles would not care for him. In order to live this boy, whose name was Gaqka, or Crow, made a bower of branches for an abiding place and hunted birds and squirrels for food.[1]

He had almost no clothing but was very ragged and dirty. When the people from the village saw him they called him Filth-Covered-One, and laughed as they passed by, holding their noses. No one thought he would ever amount to anything, which made him feel heavy-hearted. He resolved to go away from his tormentors and become a great hunter.

One night Gaqka found a canoe. He had never seen this canoe before, so he took it. Stepping in he grasped the paddle, when the canoe immediately shot into the air, and he paddled above the clouds and under the moon. For a long time he went always southward. Finally the canoe dropped into a river and then Gaqka paddled for shore.

On the other side of the river was a great cliff that had a face that looked like a man. It was at the forks of the river where this cliff stood. The boy resolved to make his home on the top of the cliff and so climbed it and built a bark cabin.

The first night he sat on the edge of the cliff he heard a voice saying, "Give me some tobacco." Looking around the boy, seeing no one, replied, "Why should I give tobacco?"

There was no answer and the boy began to fix his arrows for the next day's hunt. After a while the voice spoke again, "Give me some tobacco."

Gaqka now took out some tobacco and threw it over the cliff. The voice spoke again: "Now I will tell you a story."

Feeling greatly awed the boy listened to a story that seemed to come directly out of the rock upon which he was sitting. Finally the voice paused, for the story had ended. Then it spoke again saying, "It shall be the custom hereafter to present me with a small gift for my stories." So the boy gave the rock a few bone beads. Then the rock said, "Hereafter when I speak, announcing that I shall tell a story you must say, 'Nio,' and as I speak you must say 'Hĕ″,' that I may know that you are listening. You must never fall asleep but continue to listen until I say 'Dā̆neho nigagā̆is.' (So thus finished is the length of my story). Then you shall give me presents and I shall be satisfied."[2]

[1]The theme that stories originated in the earth or elsewhere beyond human understanding and are only communicated to humans either through dreams or magical agents (such as this speaking cliff) confirms a deep belief in the seriousness of stories as chartering original relations among all the elements of the universe. The motif of the despised orphan who alone is capable and worthy of receiving sacred knowledge is widespread. This text is taken from Arthur C. Parker, *Seneca Myths and Folk Tales,* 1923.

[2]In many oral literatures, stories are marked off from other forms of discourse by opening and closing formulas. Audiences are often required to indicate their attentiveness and imaginative participation by responding with formulaic words. The value and importance of storytelling is further signalled by giving gifts to the storyteller and to the earth.

The next day the boy hunted and killed a great many birds. These he made into soup and roasts. He skinned the birds and saved the skins, keeping them in a bag.

That evening the boy sat on the rock again and looked westward at the sinking sun. He wondered if his friend would speak again. While waiting he chipped some new arrow-points, and made them very small so that he could use them in a blow gun. Suddenly, as he worked, he heard the voice again. "Give me some tobacco to smoke," it said. Gaqka threw a pinch of tobacco over the cliff and the voice said, "Hau'nio''," and commenced a story. Long into the night one wonderful tale after another flowed from the rock, until it called out, "So thus finished is the length of my story." Gaqka was sorry to have the stories ended but he gave the rock an awl made from a bird's leg and a pinch of tobacco.

The next day the boy hunted far to the east and there found a village. Nobody knew who he was but he soon found many friends. There were some hunters who offered to teach him how to kill big game, and these went with him to his own camp on the high rock. At night he allowed them to listen to the stories that came forth from the rock, but it would speak only when Gaqka was present. He therefore had many friends with whom to hunt.

Now after a time Gaqka made a new suit of clothing from deer skin and desired to obtain a decorated pouch. He, therefore, went to the village and found one house where there were two daughters living with an old mother. He asked that a pouch be made and the youngest daughter spoke up and said, "It is now finished. I have been waiting for you to come for it." So she gave him a handsome pouch.

Then the old mother spoke, saying, "I now perceive that my future son-in-law has passed through the door and is here." Soon thereafter, the younger woman brought Gaqka a basket of bread and said, "My mother greatly desires that you should marry me." Gaqka looked at the girl and was satisfied, and ate the bread. The older daughter was greatly displeased and frowned in an evil manner.

That night the bride said to her husband, "We must now go away. My older sister will kill you for she is jealous." So Gaqka arose and took his bride to his own lodge. Soon the rock spoke and began to relate wonder stories of things that happened in the old days. The bride was not surprised, but said, "This standing rock, indeed, is my grandfather. I will now present you with a pouch into which you must put a trophy for every tale related."

All winter long the young couple stayed in the lodge on the great rock and heard all the wonder tales of the old days. Gaqka's bag was full of stories and he knew all the lore of former times.

As springtime came the bride said, "We must now go north to your own people and you shall become a great man." But Gaqka was sad and said, "Alas, in my own country I am an outcast and called by an unpleasant name."

The bride only laughed, saying, "Nevertheless we shall go north."

Taking their pelts and birdskins, the young couple descended the cliff and seated themselves in the canoe. "This is my canoe," said the bride. "I sent it through the air to you."

The bride seated herself in the bow of the canoe and Gaqka in the stern. Grasping a paddle he swept it through the water, but soon the canoe arose and went through the air. Meanwhile the bride was singing all kinds of songs, which Gaqka learned as he paddled.

When they reached the north, the bride said, "Now I shall remove your clothing and take all the scars from your face and body." She then caused him to pass through a hollow log, and when Gaqka emerged from the other end he was dressed in the finest clothing and was a handsome man.

Together the two walked to the village where the people came out to see them. After a while Gaqka said, "I am the boy whom you once were accustomed to call 'Cia''dō– dă'.' I have now returned." That night the people of the village gathered around and listened to the tales he told, and he instructed them to give him small presents and tobacco. He would plunge his hand in his pouch and take out a trophy, saying, "Ho ho! So here is another one!" and then looking at his trophy would relate an ancient tale.

Everybody now thought Gaqka a great man and listened to his stories. He was the first man to find out all about the adventures of the old-time people. That is why there are so many legends now.

1923

Iroquois or Confederacy of the Five Nations (Haudenosaunee-Iroquois)[1]

By the tradition of the Five Nations it appears that in their early history, they were frequently engaged in petty wars one with another, as well also with tribes living north of the lakes. The Five Nations, on account of their small numbers, suffered more by these wars than their neighbors, until there sprang up among the Onondagas a man more formidable in war than a whole tribe or nation. He consequently became the terror of all the surrounding nations, especially of the Cayugas and Senecas. This man, so formidable and whose cabin was as impregnable as a tower, is said to have had a head of hair, the ends of each terminating in a living snake; the ends of his fingers, and toes, his ears, nose & lips, eye brows & eye lashes all terminated in living snakes. He required in war, no bow and arrow, no battle axe or war club, for he had but to look upon his enemies, & they fell dead—so great was the power of the snakes that enshrouded him. He was a warrior by birth, and by his great power he had become the military despot of all the surrounding nations. And when he marched against his enemies they fled before his fatal sight.

Among the Onondagas there lived a man renowned for his wisdom, and his great love of peace. For a long time he had watched with great anxiety the increasing power of this military despot who on account of his snakey habilaments, was known

[1]The Iroquois were a confederacy of five nations—the Cayuga, Mohawk, Oneida, Onondaga, and Seneca Indians. These five Indian groups, later joined by the Tuscarora, joined together about 1450 under the legendary leadership of Dekanawida (probably a Huron) and Hiawatha (a Mohawk). Because they lived in what is now the Northeast, largely in present-day New York state, the Iroquois confederacy successfully slowed the westward expansion of the Europeans until nearly the middle of the eighteenth century.

by the applicable name Tadodahoh, or Atotahoh, signifying tangled because the snakes seemed to have tangled themselves into his hair; he saw bands of noble warriors fall before his fatal look. He revolved in his mind by what means he could take from the Tadodahoh his power, and also to divest him of his snakey appendages. He well knew that he could not wrest his power from him, unless he could put into his hands some means by which he could still exercise power and influence. He therefore concluded to call a general council, of the Five Nations, and to invite to this council the Tadodahoh, at which council he proposed to lay before the wise men a plan of Union that would secure not only amity and peace among themselves, and a perpetual existence as a confederacy but they would render themselves formidable & superior in power to any nation on the Continent. He accordingly called a council to be held upon the east bank of the Onondaga Lake, and to this council the Tadodahoh was invited, who it is said lived near the shores of Lake Ontario a short distance from Irondequoit Bay. He accepted the invitation and proceeded to the place. He occupied the council grounds alone, for no one would approach near to him, although great numbers had come to attend. The projector of the alliance alone proceeded to the grounds and into the presence of the Tadodahoh. He proceeded to divulge his plan when he was informed that his daughter had died whom he had left at home sick. He drew his robe about him, covering himself completely, and mourned for her. (His style of mourning was afterwards adopted by the Confederacy as the custom to mourn for sachems just before another was to be installed in his place.) He mourned night and day, and in his mourning which he did in a kind of song, he repeated the whole plan of Union. And when he had finished, no one of the wise men seemed to understand or comprehend his meaning and objects. Daganowedah, the projector of the plan of alliance, being provoked at their dullness of comprehension, which resulted more from their ignorance of civil matters than dullness of comprehension, arose in the night and travelled towards the east. He had not travelled far when he struck a small lake, and anyone could go around it sooner than to cross it in a canoe. Yet he chose to make a canoe of bark and go across it. It seems that he did not wish to deviate from a straight line. While he was crossing the lake, his canoe ran upon what he supposed to be a sand bar; he put his paddle down into the water to ascertain the cause of the stopping of the boat; in taking out his paddle he found a quantity of small shells, he took pains to put a sufficient quantity into his canoe, and after going ashore, he made a pouch of a young deer skin, and put these shells into it, after having first made a number of belts, and put the rest into strings of equal lengths. To this he gave the name of wampum, and the belts and strings he had made of the shells, he converted into the records of his wise sayings & the entire plan of his project of alliance.

He then proceeded on his journey, and he had not travelled far when he came to an Indian castle.[2] Without calling a council he began to rehearse his plan of alliance, by means of his belts and strings of wampum. But the people of this castle were unable to comprehend the benefits of his project, and talked of him as crazy. When he heard what they were saying concerning him, he proceeded on his journey, sorrowing that he could not find a people who would listen to the words of wisdom. He at length came to another settlement, which was one of the Mohawk castles. Here again

[2]A settlement.

he rehearsed his plan of Union. Still his sayings were incomprehensible to that people. They however listened carefully for the purpose of ascertaining what it was that he could talk so long upon. All that they could understand of it, was the manner in which councils were to be called. A council was accordingly called and he invited to attend. They invited him for the purpose of giving him an opportunity to say in council and before a large number what he had been so long saying in the open fields. But after he had taken his seat in council and nothing was said or done, no exchange of wampum belts (for he had lent them a belt with which to call a council), he arose and again went into the fields and there repeated his speeches. He concluded by saying that they too were ignorant, and knew nothing about transacting civil matters. This was reported to the Grand Chief of the Mohawks and again he called another council and invited Daganowedah. When the council was opened and the wise man had taken his seat, the Mohawk Chief presented to him a belt of wampum, with a request that whatever he should have to say, should be said in open council. If he was a messenger from another tribe, they would hear in open council what were their wishes. He merely replied that he was the messenger of no one; that he had conceived a noble plan of alliance, but had not found a nation wise enough to comprehend its benefits, and thus he had travelled and should continue so to travel until he found support. He then rehearsed in open council his plan of Union, which though they could not comprehend it, was pronounced by all to be a noble project. Daganowedah the Onondaga wise man was immediately adopted into the Mohawk Nation, nor could the Onondagas afterwards claim him, since they first rejected his project of Alliance. He was also made a chief of the Mohawk Nation, and was to exercise equal power with the original Mohawk chief. They were to live in the same lodge, and to be, in every respect, equals.

But he had lived with the original chief but a short time, when he was ordered about as though he had been a mere servant. To this a free spirit will ever revolt, he therefore left him, and again went into the fields. He was asked why he left the house of his friend. He replied that he had not been treated as a friend or visitor, but as a slave. The original chief begged his pardon, and solicited him to return. He did, and was thenceforth treated with great regard. Daganowedah at length suggested the propriety of sending runners to the west, from whence he had come, to ascertain what may be doing from whence he had come. He wanted runners to go and seek the smoke of the council fire. The chief of the Mohawks at once called upon some runners to go towards the west in search of the smoke of a council fire. The guardian bird of the runners was the heron; they accordingly took upon themselves the form of herons. They went towards the west, but flying too high they did not see the smoke of the council fire of Onondaga. They proceeded as far west as Sandusky in Ohio, where they were unable to transform or change themselves again into men. Another set of runners were then sent out, who took upon them the form or shape of crows. They found the smoke of the council fire at Onondaga and so reported.

Daganowedah then proposed to send a few runners to the council to inform them that they had found a wise man of the Onondaga nation, who had conceived a plan of Union, and to request that he might be heard before the Great Tadodahoh. This was done; and as soon as the council at Onondaga heard where their wise man had gone, they sent a deputation to recall him. Daganowedah had in the mean time made arrangement with the Mohawk Chief to act as his spokesman when they should be in council. He was also to take the lead in the file, and to perform all the duties necessary to the completion of the Alliance, but he was to act as Daganowedah should direct. His reason for choosing a spokesman, was that he had not been heard when the council first opened, and that probably they might listen to a wise man of the Mohawks. To this arrangement the Mohawk agreed. He agreed also to divest Tadodahoh of his snakes, and to make him as other men, except that he should clothe him in civil power as the Head of the Confederacy that should be formed. They then proceeded with a delegation of the Mohawks to the council grounds at Onondaga. When they had arrived they addressed Todadahoh the great military despot. The Mohawk divested him of his snakes, and for this reason he was styled Hayowenthah, or one who takes away or divests.

The plan of alliance was at first simple. It provided for the establishment of a confederacy, enjoying a democratic form of government. The civil and legislative power was to be vested in a certain number of wise men who should be styled civil sachems, and the military and executive power in another set of men who should be styled military sachems. The Union was to be established as a family organization, the Mohawks, Onondagas and Senecas to compose the Fathers and the Cayugas and Oneidas the children. This plan was adopted.[3]

Iktomi and the Dancing Ducks[1] (Christine Dunham, Oglala Sioux)

This is about a man who is very cunning, crafty and sly. He could fool anybody and get by with just about anything. He also was lazy, stupid and a briber. Because of all this and because he was a coward and couldn't be trusted, he was called Iktomi.

One day Iktomi was walking along by a pond where a flock of ducks were swimming. He stopped to watch them for awhile. Right away his mind started working on how he could get a few of them for his dinner. Finally he had an idea. He filled his sack with grass, which he carried on his back. Walking as if he were in a hurry, he

[3]This text was transcribed about 1850 by Ely S. Parker, a full Seneca born on the Tonawanda Seneca Reservation in New York state. Educated at a mission school and then sent to Canada, Parker eventually returned to New York, learned English, and studied law, only to be denied legal practice because he was Indian. He worked on the Genesee Valley canal as an engineer until he was appointed superintendent of construction of the custom house and marine hospital at Galena, Illinois. Parker entered into Civil War conflict in 1863, serving as secretary to General Grant, whom he had known at Galena. Having remained in the army after the war until 1869, Parker served until 1871 as President Grant's commissioner of Indian affairs. When Parker died in 1895, he was a member of the New York City police department.

Parker wrote about this narrative, "I cannot tell how much reliance can be placed upon this tradition, which is more of an allegory than real. The main facts of its origin may be embodied in the allegory, while it has been painted up by the imagination of the Indians."

[1]Recorded in 1973 on the Rosebud Reservation, by R. D. Theisz. Christine Dunham is a member of the Brulé subdivision of the Lakota. The title is attributed by the editor of the present anthology.

passed close to where the ducks could see him. Sure enough, the ducks saw him with the load on his back and called out to him, "Brother, where are you going? What is that you carry in your sack?" Sly old Iktomi pretended not to hear them. So they swam closer to the edge of the pond and called out again, "What do you carry and why are you in a hurry?" Iktomi hurried along and said, "Do not delay me; I'm in a hurry!" Now the ducks were really curious. They asked again what was in the sack that made it look so heavy. Iktomi stopped and said he had a lot of songs in that sack and he was taking them to some people who wanted them for a dance. The ducks were very delighted to hear this and wanted to have the songs for themselves, so that they might dance, too. That was just what Iktomi wanted. So he let the ducks talk him into staying with them, so they could hear the songs and dance, too. Iktomi made the ducks promise to do exactly what he wanted them to do, otherwise he would take his songs and leave. This worried the ducks, but they agreed to do whatever was asked of them. Now Iktomi had them build a sweat tipi of small poles and branches while he sat in the shade and watched them work. How hungry he was! His mouth was watering and his stomach was growling, for he had nothing to eat all that morning. The ducks finished the tipi and were ready for the dance. Inside the tipi they were to dance around in a circle. Iktomi sat at the opening of the sweat tipi and started his song. "Dance with your eyes closed! Dance with your eyes closed! He who opens them, his eyes will turn red." On and on he sang. Faster and faster danced the ducks with their eyes shut. Iktomi had emptied his sack and started to put the ducks he had killed into it. He had been singing while he was wringing their necks until one little duck—a mud hen—opened her eyes and saw what Iktomi was doing. She screamed, "Fly, fly away or Iktomi will wipe us out!" But it was too late. The little duck was the only one left. She got away, but her eyes turned red and from then on, she has been a loner. Now you see her swimming by herself. Iktomi took his sack of ducks and as lazy as he was started the process of cleaning the ducks over an open fire. While his meal was cooking, Iktomi thought he would take a nap in the shade of some trees. He closed his eyes and was about to sleep when he heard a groaning and squeaky noise. He looked up and saw two tall young trees rubbing together each other whenever the wind blew. The rubbing of the branches was what made the noises. Iktomi said to them, "Don't fight! You are brothers. Be good to each other!" But the wind blew and the groaning and squeaky noise went on. Iktomi couldn't sleep, and he was very angry with them. He climbed up one tree and said, "I told you not to fight!" And put his arm between the branches. At about that time the wind quit blowing and there hung Iktomi, high up between the trees. Iktomi screamed and hollered. He cried, threatened, begged and pleaded to be let free or his dinner would burn. But the wind just kept still, so he continued to hang there. Then to make things worse along came a coyote, trotting along and minding his own business. The least of his concerns was Iktomi. But he never would have noticed the man except that Iktomi had to open his mouth to call to the coyote to stay away from his dinner which was cooking over the fire. Now, the coyote being hungry and curious and in no hurry, turned and sniffed around until he found the ducks ready to eat. He stuffed himself and licking his chops, went about his way again. Poor Iktomi was still begging the trees to let him go. About the time the coyote left, the wind blew and Iktomi fell to the ground. He picked himself up and went to his ducks, but all that was left was the bones. How angry Iktomi was! He muttered to himself, "He who steals my food will pay with his life!" Iktomi set out to find the coyote. Soon he saw the coyote napping in the sun. Iktomi thought to himself, "I told you I would find you." Then he built a big fire and was going to grab the coyote by his hind legs and throw him in the fire, but the coyote outsmarted him and kicked Iktomi in instead. Iktomi never bothered the coyote again.

Man's Dependence on Animals (Anishinaabe Ojibway)[1]

When the world was flooded, all the land animals perished; only the fishes and birds and animals who lived in the water survived.

With their prescience and preknowledge, the animals sensed the supernatural conception of man in the spirit-woman. It was their feeling of compassion for the spirit woman that prompted the animals to invite her down to rest upon the turtle's back.[2] Even the smallest and the least of the animals, the muskrat, served. When all the others failed, the muskrat brought back from the bottom of the sea the small portion of soil requested by the spirit woman. Without the animals the world would not have been; without the animals the world would not be intelligible.[3]

At birth man was helpless. Again it was the animals who assisted the spirit woman in nourishing the newborn infants by bringing fruits, vegetables, berries, and drink, while the birds and butterflies brought joy.

That winter, when food was scarce and the winds cold, the animals sheltered man. The bear, who loved the newborn beings, offered his flesh so that the Anishi-

[1]From Basil Johnston, *Ojibway Heritage* (Toronto: McClelland and Stewart, 1976). The Anishinaabeg (or "Human Beings")—also known as *Ojibways* (from a word meaning the puckered seam of a moccasin or referring to the writing of pictographs on birchbark) or *Chippewas* (a corruption of *Ojibway*)—are collectively the largest indigenous people north of Mexico, with current population estimates of more than 300,000 across reserves in Ontario, Manitoba, and western Quebec in present-day Canada and reservations in Michigan, Wisconsin, North Dakota, and Minnesota in the United States.

The Anishinaabe historically relied more on hunting than agriculture, as demonstrated by their important role as guides, trappers, and pelt preparers in the fur trade, although wild rice harvesting was and continues to be of great cultural importance. In Anishinaabe oral traditions, the teacher-trickster Nanabush (Nanabozho or Waynabozho are two of many variant spellings) is a frequent figure, eliciting both respect and amusement, although animals also play similar roles, as in this narrative.

[2]This spirit-woman fell from the sky world to this world, which was all water. The only thing solid enough for her to stand on was the back of a giant turtle. The muskrat descended to the bottom of the world-ocean and returned with soil, which the spirit-woman spread around to become the landmass we now call North America. Thus, its name among many indigenous peoples of the east is Turtle Island.

[3]A common theme in many indigenous traditions is the dependence of humanity on the rest of the natural world, especially animals, who are often referred to as elder siblings and teachers in a kinship relationship of respect and humility.

nabeg would survive.[4] Following the example of the bear, the deer, moose, porcupine, beaver, ground hog, grouse, and goose, and almost every animal being offered himself in sacrifice.

Even when the first man and woman were fully grown and had many descendants, the animals continued to serve. Man relied on the creatures for all his needs. He did not work because there was no need for labour. Life was easy. More and more the Anishnabeg relied upon the animals. And as life was easy for mankind, it was difficult for the animal beings. The animals' burdens became more onerous.

Men and women understood the utterances of the animals; the animals understood man. It was this mutual understanding that enabled man to impose greater burdens upon his brothers. What was worse, man set animal against animal.

Instead of doing his own fishing, man dispatched a loon or a kingfisher to catch fish for him. If he wanted a rabbit, man would send an eagle or a hawk; if he wanted a partridge, he would send a fox; if he wanted the sap of trees, he ordered the woodpecker to drill holes in the trees for him; if he wanted a new lodge, he commanded the beaver and the porcupine to fell the trees. The animals did all the work; man did none.

For a long time the animals served without complaint. But what was worse than burdens was the apparent indifference of the Anishnabeg to the needs of the animals themselves. Little could be collected and stored to keep them during the long winter, and what was set aside, was often taken by man. Service brought poverty.

At last, weary of service, the animals convened a great meeting to gain their freedom.[5] All came at the invitation of the courier.

The bear was chosen to be the first speaker and to act as chairman of the session. He explained the purpose of the meeting. "We are met to decide our destiny. We have been oppressed far too long by man. He has taken our generosity and repaid us with ingratitude; he has taken our labours and repaid us with servitude; he has taken our friendship and fostered enmity among us.

"Either we continue to serve him or we withhold our labours. Are we to continue to serve? We shall come to an end. If we deny our labours we shall live. Should you choose the former, you must resign yourselves to your fate. Should you prefer the latter, then you must consider the manner by which it is to be accomplished. Consider carefully."

The bear had scarcely finished when the groundhog shouted out, "I am for man's death. We have suffered enough. The Anishnabeg have killed us; they have been unkind; and they have subjected us. Only with the death of man will these injustices cease. Man must die."

"Hey! Hey! Let him die," concurred the animals.

"I am for life. I am for mercy," said the dog on rising. "While, it is true, that man has been unkind, he has not been unkind to all. There are many in this company who have not suffered. The cat, the vulture, the whippoorwill, the frog, the butterfly, the mouse, the humming-bird have, all of them, lived and worked, and rested without harm. To them man has been kind. Perhaps he has been somewhat thoughtless. Is

[4]Anishnabeg is one spelling of the plural form of the singular Anishinaabe.

[5]Just like humans, animals gather in social and political communities to debate matters of great importance.

this a good reason to wish him dead? Man does not deserve death; he deserves to live, even as we live."

"Hey! Hey! Let him live," chorused the dog's supporters.

The wolverine rose to his feet, visage dark and threatening. "Let the Anishnabeg neither live or die, but let him suffer. If you have suffered at man's hand you are partly to blame; for he who allows himself to be servile deserves servitude. He bears as much guilt as he who subjects. Man is not entirely to blame, and ought not pay the entire penalty for your folly."

As he sat down, the wolverine taunted, "And if man is to die, who will kill him?"

The meeting buzzed with the consternation of the animals. Questions were asked, "If man is to die, who will kill him?"

All the animals looked at one another, but not one spoke to answer this final question.

"Bear, will you kill him?" asked the wolverine sardonically.

"Yes! The bear! He is strong and brave," shouted the animals.

The bear cringed, turning somewhat grey. "I am too slow. I am unwilling. There are too few of us," he replied to excuse himself.

"Then the wolves must do it. They are fast and strong," offered the wolverine.

Not expecting to be named, the startled wolves managed to sputter, "We cannot, and we dare not. Man is too clever."

"Cowards!" jeered the wolverine. "The rattlesnake shall do it."

But the rattlesnakes refused saying, "We are too slow. Man is too swift. We are not big enough."

While the debate raged, a dog stole away from the meeting. A vigilant wolf spied him and trailed him.

The debate continued and became a clamour. The bear, realizing that nothing could be resolved with opinion divided and feelings heated, called the meeting to order. "We cannot kill man. He is too strong, too many, and too cunning. Nor should we want to kill him or injure him. He, too, is entitled to life and well being. We can resolve our state without man's death."

It was at this time that the wolf dragged the errant dog into the meeting and near the central fire.

Without waiting to be asked to speak, the wolf angrily shouted above the din. The whimpering of the dog and the ululating snarl of the wolf instilled silence.

"This dog has betrayed us. He must be punished. A little while ago he made off almost unnoticed. But I saw him and followed. He went directly to the village of the Anishnabeg and divulged what we were discussing. This one and all the dogs must be punished."

The assembled animals were outraged. They seized the dogs and began to pummel them. But though the bear was as outraged as his brothers, he maintained his composure. He thundered out, "Brothers, it is too late. To kill the dogs would be without purpose and substance. Rather let him endure his servitude. Let him serve man. Let him hunger. Let him hunt for man. Let him guard man. Let him know man's fickleness."

Turning to the dog, the bear speaking on behalf of his brothers said, "For your betrayal, you shall no longer be regarded as a brother among us. Instead of man, we shall attack you. Worse than this, from now on you shall eat only what man has left, sleep in the cold and rain, and receive kicks as a reward for your fidelity."

The bear turned again to the crowd. "To make it difficult for man to enslave us again, no longer will we speak the same language. Instead we shall speak in different languages. From now on we shall live to ourselves, for ourselves. Let men learn to fend for themselves without our help."[6]

With that the meeting broke up, and the animals went their separate ways.

Origin of Disease and Medicine (Cherokee)[1]

In the old days the beasts, birds, fishes, insects, and plants could all talk, and they and the people lived together in peace and friendship. But as time went on the people increased so rapidly that their settlements spread over the whole earth, and the poor animals found themselves beginning to be cramped for room. This was bad enough, but to make it worse Man invented bows, knives, blowguns, spears, and hooks, and began to slaughter the larger animals, birds, and fishes for their flesh or their skins, while the smaller creatures, such as the frogs and worms, were crushed and trodden upon without thought, out of pure carelessness or contempt. So the animals resolved to consult upon measures for their common safety.

The Bears were the first to meet in council in their townhouse under Kuwâ´hĭ mountain,[2] the "Mulberry place," and the old White Bear chief presided. After each in turn had complained of the way in which Man killed their friends, ate their flesh, and used their skins for his own purposes, it was decided to begin war at once against him. Some one asked what weapons Man used to destroy them. "Bows and arrows,

[6]To protect themselves from further abuse by humans, animals make their languages unintelligible to humanity. Animals still provide knowledge to humans, but that knowledge is now dependent on careful observation, an effort that requires humility, care, and respect.

[1]From James Mooney, *Myths of the Cherokee* (1900) (Mineola, NY: Dover Publications, 1995). Although known as the *Ani-yunwiya,* or "The Real Human Beings" in their own language, the name *Cherokee* comes from a Muskogee word meaning either "people of another speech," referring to their Iroquoian language (unique among Muskogean and Siouan peoples in the southeastern United States), or "people who live in caves," a reference to their territories in the upper reaches of the Appalachian mountain range in the southeastern United States.

One of the most powerful tribal nations during the time of the American Revolution, the Cherokees became a constitutional republic in the early nineteenth century. Under the authority of the 1830 Indian Removal Act, most Cherokees were forced in 1838 and 1839 to move to what is now eastern Oklahoma and western Arkansas; others emigrated to Texas and Mexico. There are currently three Cherokee governments in the United States with a combined citizenry of nearly 300,000—the Cherokee Nation and the United Keetoowah Band of Cherokee Indians in Oklahoma and the Eastern Band of Cherokee Indians in North Carolina.

[2]Now known as Clingman's Dome, the tallest mountain in the Great Smoky Mountains National Park.

of course," cried all the Bears in chorus. "And what are they made of?" was the next question. "The bow of wood, and the string of our entrails," replied one of the Bears. It was then proposed that they make a bow and some arrows and see if they could not use the same weapons against Man himself. So one Bear got a nice piece of locust wood and another sacrificed himself for the good of the rest in order to furnish a piece of his entrails for the string. But when everything was ready and the first Bear stepped up to make the trial, it was found that in letting the arrow fly after drawing back the bow, his long claws caught the string and spoiled the shot. This was annoying, but some one suggested that they might trim his claws, which was accordingly done, and on a second trial it was found that the arrow went straight to the mark. But here the chief, the old White Bear,[3] objected, saying it was necessary that they should have long claws in order to be able to climb trees. "One of us has already died to furnish the bowstring, and if we now cut off our claws we must all starve together. It is better to trust to the teeth and claws that nature gave us, for it is plain that man's weapons were not intended for us."

No one could think of any better plan, so the old chief dismissed the council and the Bears dispersed to the woods and thickets without having concerted any way to prevent the increase of the human race. Had the result of the council been otherwise, we should now be at war with the Bears,[4] but as it is, the hunter does not even ask the Bear's pardon when he kills one.

The Deer next held a council under their chief, the Little Deer, and after some talk decided to send rheumatism to every hunter who should kill one of them unless he took care to ask their pardon for the offense. They sent notice of their decision to the nearest settlement of Indians and told them at the same time what to do when necessity forced them to kill one of the Deer tribe. Now, whenever the hunter shoots a Deer, the Little Deer, who is swift as the wind and can not be wounded, runs quickly up to the spot and, bending over the blood-stains, asks the spirit of the Deer if it has heard the prayer of the hunter for pardon. If the reply be "Yes," all is well, and the Little Deer goes on his way; but if the reply be "No," he follows on the trail of the hunter, guided by the drops of blood on the ground, until he arrives at his cabin in the settlement, when the Little Deer enters invisibly and strikes the hunter with rheumatism, so that he becomes at once a helpless cripple. No hunter who has regard for his health ever fails to ask pardon of the Deer for killing it, although some hunters who have not learned the prayer may try to turn aside the Little Deer from his pursuit by building a fire behind them in the trail.

Next came the Fishes and Reptiles, who had their own complaints against Man. They held their council together and determined to make their victims dream of snakes twining about them in slimy folds and blowing foul breath in their faces, or to make them dream of eating raw or decaying fish, so that they would lose appetite, sicken, and die. This is why people dream about snakes and fish.

[3]In Cherokee color symbolism, white represents wisdom and peace. Cherokee leadership was generally divided between white (peaceful or beloved) leaders and red (war) leaders, with white leaders generally being older men and women.

[4]In another Cherokee story, bears were once human beings who went wild and surrendered their humanity for a more leisurely life of hunting and gathering.

Finally the Birds, Insects, and smaller animals came together for the same purpose, and the Grubworm was chief of the council. It was decided that each in turn should give an opinion, and then they would vote on the question as to whether or not Man was guilty. Seven votes should be enough to condemn him. One after another denounced Man's cruelty and injustice toward the other animals and voted in favor of his death. The Frog spoke first, saying: "We must do something to check the increase of the race, or people will become so numerous that we shall be crowded from off the earth. See how they have kicked me about because I'm ugly, as they say, until my back is covered with sores;" and here he showed the spots on his skin. Next came the Bird—no one remembers now which one it was—who condemned Man "because he burns my feet off," meaning the way in which the hunter barbecues birds by impaling them on a stick set over the fire, so that their feathers and tender feet are singed off. Others followed in the same strain. The Ground-squirrel alone ventured to say a good word for Man, who seldom hurt him because he was so small, but this made the others so angry that they fell upon the Ground-squirrel and tore him with their claws, and the stripes are on his back to this day.

They began then to devise and name so many new diseases, one after another, that had not their invention at last failed them, no one of the human race would have been able to survive. The Grubworm grew constantly more pleased as the name of each disease was called off, until at last they reached the end of the list, when some one proposed to make menstruation sometimes fatal to women.[5] On this he rose up in his place and cried: "*Wadãn´!* [Thanks!] I'm glad some more of them will die, for they are getting so thick that they tread on me." The thought fairly made him shake with joy, so that he fell over backward and could not get on his feet again, but had to wriggle off on his back, as the Grubworm has done ever since.

When the Plants, who were friendly to Man, heard what had been done by the animals, they determined to defeat the latters' evil designs. Each Tree, Shrub, and Herb, down even to the Grasses and Mosses, agreed to furnish a cure for some one of the diseases named, and each said: "I shall appear to help Man when he calls upon me in his need." Thus came medicine; and the plants, every one of which has its use if we only knew it,[6] furnish the remedy to counteract the evil wrought by the revengeful animals. Even weeds were made for some good purpose, which we must find out for ourselves. When the doctor does not know what medicine to use for a sick man the spirit of the plant tells him.

[5]Menstruation in Cherokee tradition is a period associated with spiritual cleansing and women's inherent power, so the animals' decision to make it fatal is a particularly dire threat.

[6]In Cherokee traditions, the connection to plants is even more significant, as First Woman, from whom all Cherokees descend, is Selu, the Corn-Mother, the spiritual and physical personification of maize (*Zea mays*). Wild tobacco (*Nicotiana rustica*) and the eastern red cedar (*Juniperus virginiana*) are respected for their spiritual and purification properties.

Raven and Marriage (Tlingit)[1]

Next Raven married the daughter of a chief named Fog-over-the salmon. It was winter, and they were without food, so Raven wanted salmon very much. His wife made a large basket and next morning washed her hands in it. When she got through there was a salmon there. Both were very glad, and cooked and ate it. Every day afterward she did the same thing until their house was full of drying salmon. After that, however, Raven and his wife quarreled, and he hit her on the shoulder with a piece of dried salmon. Then she ran away from him, but, when he ran after her and seized her, his hands passed right through her body. Then she went into the water and disappeared forever, while all of the salmon she had dried followed her. He could not catch her because she was the fog. After that he kept going to his father-in-law to beg him to have his wife come back, but his father-in-law said, "You promised me that you would have respect for her and take care of her. You did not do it, therefore you can not have her back."

Then Raven had to leave this place, and went on to another town where he found a widower. He said to this man, "I am in the same fix as you. My wife also has died." Raven wanted to marry the daughter of the chief in that town, so he said, "Of course I have to marry a woman of as high caste as my first wife. That is the kind I am looking for." But *TsAgwâ´n,* a bird, who was also looking for a high-caste wife, followed Raven about all the time. He said to the people, "That man is telling stories around here. His first wife left him because he was cruel to her." For this reason they refused to give the girl to him. Then he said to the chief, "If I had married your daughter you would have had a great name in the world. You will presently see your daughter take up with some person who is a nobody, and, when they speak of you in the world, it will always be as Chief-with-no-name. You may listen to this *TsAgwâ´n* if you want to, but you will be sorry for it. He is a man from whom no good comes. Hereafter this *TsAgwâ´n* will live far out at sea. And I will tell you this much, that neither *TsAgwâ´n* nor myself will get this woman." This is why *TsAgwâ´n* is now always alone. Raven also said to the chief, "You will soon hear something of this daughter of yours." All the high-caste men wanted to marry this woman, but she would not have them.

Going on again, Raven came to an old man living alone, named *DAmnā´djî,* and said to him, "Do you know the young daughter of the chief close by here?" "Yes, I know her." "Why don't you try to marry her?" "I can't get her. I know I can't, so I don't want to try." Then Raven said, "I will make a medicine to enable you to get her." "But I have no slave," said the old man; "to get her a man must have slaves." "Oh!" said Raven, "you do not have to have a slave to get her. She will take a liking to you and nobody can help it. She will marry you. Her father will lose half of his

[1]The Tlingit Indians are a northwest coastal group that occupied the southeastern coast of Alaska from Yakutat Bay to Cape Fox. Their abundant food supply from hunting, fishing, and gathering afforded the Tlingits ample time in winter to develop complex social systems and religious ceremonies. They lived in cedar plank dwellings, and they traded freely with the Russians, Americans, and English.

property." Then he made the old man look young, got feathers to put into his hair and a marten-skin robe to put over him so that he appeared very handsome. But Raven said to him, "You are not going to look like this all of the time. It is only for a day or so."

After this the rejuvenated man got into his skin canoe, for this was well to the north, and paddled over to where the girl lived. He did not ask her father's consent but went directly to her, and she immediately fell in love with him. Although so many had been after her she now said, "I will marry you. I will go with you even if my father kills me for it."

When the chief's slaves found them in the bedroom at the rear of the house, they said to the chief, "Your daughter is married." So her mother looked in there and found it was true. Then her father said, "Come out from that room, daughter." He had already told his slaves to lay down valuable furs on the floor for his daughter and her husband to sit on. He thought if she were already married it was of no use for him to be angry with her. So the girl came out with her husband, and, when her father saw him he was very glad, for he liked his looks, and he was dressed like a high-caste person.

Then the chief related to his son-in-law how a fellow came along wanting to marry his daughter, and how *TsAgwâ´n* had come afterward and told him that he had been cruel to his first wife. Said the chief, "This man had a wife. His first wife is living yet. I don't want to hurt his wife's feelings."

After that his son-in-law said, "My father told me to start right out after him today in my canoe." He was in a hurry to depart because he was afraid that all of his good clothing would leave him. He said to his wife, "Take only your blanket to use on the passage, because I have plenty of furs of every description at home." So she took nothing but her marten-skin robe and a fox robe.

As she lay in the canoe, however, with her head resting on his lap she kept feeling drops of water fall upon her face, and she said many times, "What is that dripping on my face?" Then he would say, "It must be the water splashing from my paddle," but it was really the drippings that fall from an old man's eyes when he is very filthy. Her husband had already become an old man again and had lost his fine clothing, but she could not see it because her face was turned the other way. When the woman thought that they were nearly at their destination she raised herself to look out, glanced at her husband's face, and saw that he was an altogether different man. She cried very hard.

After they had arrived at his town the old man went from house to house asking the people to take pity on him and let him bring his wife to one of them, because he knew that his own house was not fit for her. These, however, were some of the people that had wanted to marry this woman, so they said, "Why don't you take her to your own fine house? You wanted her." Meanwhile she sat on the beach by the canoe, weeping. Finally the shabby sister of this old man, who was still older than he, came down to see her and said, "See here, you are a high-caste girl. Everybody says this man is your husband, and you know he is your husband, so you better come up to the house with me." Then she saw the place where he lived, and observed that his bed was worse than that of one of her father's slaves. The other people also paid no attention to her, although they knew who she was, because she had married this man. They would eat after everybody else was through, and, while he was eating, the people of the town would make fun of him by shouting out, "*DAmnā'djî's* father-in-law and his brothers-in-law are coming to his grand house to see him." Then he would run out to see whether it were so and find that they were making fun of him. Every morning, while he was breakfasting with his wife, the people fooled him in this way.

Although he had not said so, the father-in-law and the brothers-in-law of *DAmnā'djî* thought that he was a very high-caste person because he was dressed so finely. So they got together all their expensive furs to visit him, and they had one canoe load of slaves, which they intended to give him, all dressed withn green feathers from the heads of mallard drakes. One morning the people again shouted, "*DAmnā'djî*'s father-in-law and his brothers-in-law are coming to see him." Running out to look this time, he saw canoe after canoe coming, loaded down deep. Then he did not know what to do. He began to sweep out the house and begged some boys to help him clean up, but they said, "You clean up yourself. Those are your people coming." The people of the place also began hiding all of their basket-work pots, and buckets.

As they came in, the people in the canoes sang together and all of them were iridescent with color. They were very proud people. Then the old man begged the boys to carry up the strangers' goods, but they replied as before, "You carry them up yourself. You can do it." So the strangers had to bring up their own things into the house and sit about without anyone telling them where. The old man's sister was crying all the time. Then the strangers understood at once what was the matter and felt very sorry for these old people.

After that the old man kept saying to the boys who came in to look at his visitors, "One of you go after water," but they answered, "Go after water yourself. You can do it." He tried to borrow a basket for his guests to eat off of, but they all said, "Use your basket. What did you go and get that high-caste girl for? You knew that you couldn't afford it. Why didn't you get a poor person like yourself instead of a chief's daughter? Now you may know that it isn't fun to get a high-caste person when one is poor." His brothers-in-law and his father-in-law felt ashamed at what they heard, and they also felt badly for him. Then the old woman gave her brother a basket that was unfit for the chief's slaves to eat out of, and he ran out to get water for his guests.

When he got there, however, and was stooping down to fill his basket, the creek moved back from him and he followed it. It kept doing this and he kept running after it until he came to the mountain, where it finally vanished into a house. Running into this, he saw a very old woman sitting there who said to him, "What are you after? Is there anything I can do for you?" He said, "There is much that you can do for me, if you can really do it. My friends are very mean to me. My father-in-law and the other relations of my wife have all come to my place to visit me. I married a very high-caste woman, and the people of my place seem to be very mean about it. I am very poor and have nothing with which to entertain them." He told all of his troubles to her from the beginning, and, when he was through, she said, "Is that all?" "Yes, that is all." Then the woman brushed back his hair several times with her hand, and lo! he had a head of beautiful hair, while his ragged clothes changed into valuable ones. He was handsomer and better clothed than at the time when he first obtained his wife. The old basket he had also turned into a very large beautiful basket. Then she said to him, "There is a spring back in the corner. Go there and uncover it and dip that basket as far down as you can reach." He did so and, when he drew it out, it was full of dentalia.

Now *DAmnā'djî* returned home very quickly, but nobody recognized him at first except his wife and those who had seen him when he went to get her. After he gave water to his guests, and they could see dentalia shells at the bottom. The house was now filled with spectators, and those who had made fun of him were very much ashamed of themselves. After he had given them water, he gave them handfuls of dentalia, for which his father-in-law and his brothers-in-law gave him slaves, valuable furs, and other property. So he became very rich and was chief of that town. That is why the Indians do the same now. If a brother-in-law gives them the least thing they return much more than its value.

Now he had a big house built, and everything that he said had to be done. The people that formerly made fun of him were like slaves to him. He also gave great feasts, inviting people from many villages. But, after he had become very great among them, he was too hard upon the people of his town. His wife was prouder than when she was with her father and if boys or anyone else displeased her they were put to death.

As they were now very proud and had plenty of people to work for them, the husband and wife spent much time sitting on the roof of their house looking about. One spring the woman saw a flock of swans coming from the southeast, and said, "Oh! there is a high-caste person among those birds that I was going to marry." Another time they went up, and a flock of geese came along. Then she again said to her husband, "Oh! there is the high-caste person I was going to marry." By and by some sandhill cranes flew past, and she repeated the same words. But, when the brants came over, and she spoke these words, they at once flew down to her and carried her off with them. Her husband ran after the brants underneath as fast as he could, and every now and then some of her clothing fell down, but he was unable to overtake her.

When the birds finally let this woman drop, she was naked and all of her hair even was gone. Then she got up and walked along the beach crying, and she made a kind of apron for herself out of leaves. Continuing on along the beach, she came upon a red snapper head, which she picked up. She wandered on aimlessly, not knowing what to do, because she was very sad at the thought of her fine home and her husband. Presently she saw smoke ahead of her and arrived at a house where was an old woman. She opened the door, and the old woman said, "Come in." Then she said to the old woman, "Let us cook this red snapper head." "Yes, let us cook it," said the latter. After they had eaten it, the old woman said to her, "Go along the beach and try to find something else." So she went out and found a sculpin. Then she came back to the house and cooked that, but, while they were eating, she heard many boys shouting, and she thought they were laughing at her because she was naked. She looked around but saw no one. Then the old woman said to her, "Take the food out to that hole." She went outside with the tray and saw an underground sweathouse out of which many hands protruded. This was the place from which the shouting came. She handed the tray down and it was soon handed up again with two fine fox skins in it. Then the old woman said to her, "Make your clothing out of these furs," and so she did.

After she had put the skins on, this old woman said, "Your father and mother live a short distance away along this beach. You better go to them. They are living at a salmon creek." So the girl went on and soon saw her father and mother in a canoe far out where her father was catching salmon. But, when she ran down toward the canoe to meet them, her father said to his wife, "Here comes a fox." As he was looking for something with which to kill it, she ran back into the woods.

Then she felt very badly, and returned to the old woman crying. "Did you see your father?" said the latter. "Yes." "What did he say to you?" "He took me for a fox. He was going to kill me." Then the old woman said, "Yes, what else do you think you are? You have already turned into a fox. Now go back to your father and let him kill you."

The woman went to the same place again and saw her father still closer to the shore; and she heard him say, "Here comes that big fox again." Then she ran right up to him, saying to herself, "Let him kill me," and he did so. Years ago all the high-caste people wore bracelets and necklaces, and each family had its own way of fixing them. Now, as this woman was skinning the fox, she felt something around its foreleg. She looked at it and found something like her daughter's bracelet. Afterward she also cut around the neck and found her daughter's necklace. Then she told her husband to come and look saying, "Here on this fox are our daughter's necklace and bracelet." So they cried over the fox and said, "Something must have made her turn into a fox." They knew how this fox ran toward them instead of going away.

Now they took the body of the fox, placed it upon a very nice mat, and laid another over it. They put eagle's down, which was always kept in bags ready for use, on the body, crying above it all the time. They also began fasting, and all of her brothers and relations in that village fasted with them. All cleaned up their houses and talked to their Creator. One midnight, after they had fasted for many days, they felt the house shaking, and they heard a noise in the place where the body lay. Then the father and mother felt very happy. The mother went there with a light and saw that her daughter was in her own proper shape, acting like a shaman. Then the woman named the spirts in her. The first she mentioned was the swan spirit, the next the goose spirit, the next the sand-hill crane spirit, the next the brant spirit. Another spirit was the red-snapper-head spirit which called itself Spirit-with-a-*labret*-in-its-chin, and another the fox spirit. Now the father and mother of this woman were very happy, but her husband lost all of his wealth and became poor again.[2]

1909

[2]The complex social systems of the Tlingits usually kept young men from marrying women of higher social standing.

Creation of the Whites (Yuchi)[1]

It was out upon the ocean. Some sea-foam formed against a big log floating there. Then a person emerged from the sea-foam and crawled out upon the log. He was seen sitting there. Another person crawled up, on the other side of the log. It was a woman. They were whites. Soon the Indians saw them, and at first thought that they were sea-gulls, and they said among themselves, "Are they not white people?" Then they made a boat and went out to look at the strangers more closely.

Later on the whites were seen in their house-boat. Then they disappeared.

In about a year they returned, and there were a great many of them. The Indians talked to them but they could not understand each other. Then the whites left.

But they came back in another year with a great many ships. They approached the Indians and asked if they could come ashore. They said, "Yes." So the whites landed, but they seemed to be afraid to walk much on the water. They went away again over the sea.

This time they were gone a shorter time; only three months passed and they came again. They had a box with them and asked the Indians for some earth to fill it. It was given to them as they desired. The first time they asked they had a square box, and when that was filled they brought a big shallow box. They filled this one too. Earth was put in them and when they were carried aboard the ship the white men planted seed in them and many things were raised. After they had taken away the shallow box, the whites came back and told the Indians that their land was very strong and fertile. So they asked the Indians to give them a portion of it that they might live on it. The Indians agreed to do it, the whites came to the shore, and they have lived there ever since.

1987

[1]The Yuchis, in the seventeenth and eighteenth centuries, moved from the southern Appalachian Mountains southward and eastward into the lowlands. Though thriving, they were removed in the 1830s to the new territory assigned to the Creeks, west of the Mississippi, and retained representation in the Creek National Assembly.

Among some of the Southeast Indians, the origin of the people is ascribed not to emergence (as in the Zuni narrative, for instance), but rather to the sun, sky, moon, sea, ashes, eggs, and plants. The Yuchis call themselves the "Offspring of the Sun." White people, in Yuchi narrative, have a separate origin and are said to come from sea foam.

An interesting version of the following story appears among the Hitchitis, another group that originally occupied the Southeast. As told in J. R. Swanton's *Early History of the Creek Indians,* according to the Hitchitis, the whites who came to them brought whiskey: After staying a while at the ocean's shore, "people came across the water to visit them. These were the white people, and the Indians treated them hospitably, and at that time they were on very friendly terms with each other. The white people disappeared, however, and when they did so they left a keg of something which we know was whiskey. A cup was left with this, and the Indians began pouring whiskey into this cup and smelling it, all being much pleased with the odor. Some went so far as to drink a little. They became intoxicated and began to reel and stagger and butt each other with their heads. Then the white people came back and the Indians began trading peltries, etc., for things which the white people had."

The Arrival of the Whites (Lenape-Delaware)[1]

Version 1: "Indian Account of the First Arrival of the Dutch at New York Island" As Told to John Heckewelder

The relation I am going to make was taken down many years since from the mouth of an intelligent Delaware Indian, and may be considered as a correct account of the tradition existing among them of this momentous event. I give it as much as possible in their own language.

A great many years ago, when men with a white skin had never yet been seen in this land, some Indians who were out a fishing, at a place where the sea widens, espied at a great distance something remarkably large floating on the water, and such as they had never seen before. These Indians immediately returning to the shore, apprised their countrymen of what they had observed, and pressed them to go out with them and discover what it might be. They hurried out together, and saw with astonishment the phenomenon which now appeared to their sight, but could not agree upon what it was; some believed it to be an uncommonly large fish or animal, while others were of the opinion it must be a very big house floating on the sea. At length the spectators concluded that this wonderful object was moving towards the land, and that it must be an animal or something else that had life in it; it would therefore be proper to inform all the Indians on the inhabited islands of what they had seen, and put them on their guard. Accordingly they sent off a number of runners and watermen to carry the news to their scattered chiefs, that they might send off in every direction for the warriors, with a message that they should come immediately. These arriving in numbers, and having themselves viewed the strange appearance, and observing that it was actually moving towards the entrance of the river or bay; concluded it to be a remarkably large house in which the Mannitto (the Great or Supreme Being) himself was present,[2] and that he probably was coming to visit them. By this time the chiefs were assembled at York island, and deliberating in what manner they should receive their Mannitto on his arrival. Every measure was taken to be well provided

[1]From Brian Swan, ed., *Algonquin Spirit: Contemporary Translations of the Algonquian Literatures of North America* (Lincoln: U of Nebraska P, 2005). Sharing the name *Delaware* with the lands and waterways of their homeland (all named after Baron De La Warr, the governor of the Virginia colony from 1610 to 1611), the Lenni Lenape are referred to by other Algonquin-speaking peoples as elder grandfathers and were accorded great respect as progenitors of other tribes.

A tribal nation with influence extending to the Ohio River valley to the west and the Appalachian mountains to the south, the Lenape were vital trading and political partners with early Dutch colonists and the young United States. After being displaced by white settlers and the policies of the 1830 Indian Removal Act, most Lenape emigrated to what is now Oklahoma. The largest Lenape communities today are located in Oklahoma and in the province of Ontario in Canada.

[2]Among many Algonquin speakers, a *manitou* is a spirit-being of great power. There are multiple *Manitou,* but the greatest of these, *Kitche Manitou,* sometimes referred to as "the Great Spirit," is more accurately understood as "the Great Mystery," whose dreams compelled him to bring creation into existence.

with plenty of meat for a sacrifice. The women were desired to prepare their best victuals. All the idols or images were examined and put in order, and a grand dance was supposed not only to be an agreeable entertainment for the Great Being, but it was believed that it might, with the addition of a sacrifice, contribute to appease him if he was angry with them. The conjurers were also set to work, to determine what this phenomenon portended, and what the possible result of it might be. To these and to the chiefs and wise men of the nations, men, women, and children were looking up for advice and protection. Distracted between hope and fear, they were at a loss what to do; a dance, however, commenced in great confusion. While in this situation, fresh runners arrive declaring it to be a large house of various colours, and crowded with living creatures. It appears now to be certain, that it is the great Mannitto, bringing them some kind of game, such as he had not given them before, but other runners soon after arriving declare that it is positively a house full of human beings, of quite a different colour from that of the Indians, and dressed differently from them; that in particular one of them was dressed entirely in red, who must be the Mannitto himself.

They are hailed from the vessel in a language they do not understand, yet they shout or yell in return by way of answer, according to the custom of their country; many are for running off to the woods, but are pressed by others to stay, in order not to give offence to their visitor, who might find them out and destroy them. The house, some say, large canoe, at last stops, and a canoe of a smaller size comes on shore with the red man, and some others in it; some stay with his canoe to guard it. The chiefs and wise men, assembled in council, form themselves into a large circle, towards which the man in red clothes approaches with two others. He salutes them with a friendly countenance, and they return the salute after their manner. They are lost in admiration; the dress, the manners, the whole appearance of the unknown strangers is to them a subject of wonder; but they are particularly struck with him who wore the red coat all glittering with gold lace, which they could in no manner account for. He, surely, must be the great Mannitto, but why should he have a white skin? Meanwhile, a large Hackhack (*Hackhack is properly a gourd; but since they have seen glass bottles and decanters, they call them by the same name*) is brought by one of his servants, from which an unknown substance is poured out into a small cup or glass, and handed to the supposed Mannitto. He drinks—has the glass filled again, and hands it to the chief standing next to him. The chief receives it, but only smells the contents and passes it on to the next chief, who does the same. The glass or cup thus passes through the circle, without the liquor being tasted by any one, and is upon the point of being returned to the red clothed Mannitto, when one of the Indians, a brave man and a great warrior, suddenly jumps up and harangues the assembly on the impropriety of returning the cup with its contents. It was handed to them, says he, by the Mannitto, that they should drink out of it, as he himself had done. To follow his example would be pleasing to him; but to return what he had given them might provoke his wrath, and bring destruction on them. And since the orator believed it for the good of the nation that the contents offered them should be drunk, and as no one else would do it, he would drink it himself, let the consequence be what it might; it was better for one man to die, than that a whole nation should be destroyed. He then took up the glass, and bidding the assembly a solemn farewell, at once drank up its whole contents. Every eye was fixed on the resolute chief, to see what effect the unknown liquor would produce. He soon began to stagger, and at last fell prostrate on the ground. His companions now bemoan his fate, he falls into a sound sleep, and they think he has expired. He wakes again, jumps up and declares, that he has enjoyed the most delicious sensations, and that he never before felt himself so happy as after he had drunk the cup. He asks for more, his wish is granted; the whole assembly then imitate him, and all become intoxicated.[3]

After this general intoxication had ceased, for they say that while it lasted the whites had confined themselves to their vessel, the man with the red clothes returned again, and distributed presents among them, consisting of beads, axes, hoes, and stockings such as the white people wear. They soon became familiar with each other, and began to converse by signs. The Dutch made them understand that they would not stay here, that they would return home again, but would pay them another visit the next year, when they would bring them more presents, and stay with them awhile; but as they could not live without eating, they should want a little land of them to sow seeds, in order to raise herbs and vegetables to put into their broth.

They went away as they had said, and returned in the following season, when both parties were much rejoiced to see each other; but the whites laughed at the Indians, seeing that they knew not the use of the axes and hoes they had given them the year before; for they had these hanging to their breasts as ornaments, and the stockings were made use of as tobacco pouches. The whites now put handles to the former for them, and cut trees down before their eyes, hoed up the ground, and put the stockings on their legs. Here, they said, a general laughter ensued among the Indians, that they had remained ignorant of the use of such valuable implements, and had borne the weight of such heavy metal hanging to their necks, for such a length of time. They took every white man they saw for an inferior Mannitto attendant upon the supreme Deity who shone superior in the red and laced clothes. As the whites became daily more familiar with the Indians, they at last proposed to stay with them, and asked only for so much ground for a garden spot as, they said, the hide of a bullock would cover or encompass, which hide was spread before them. The Indians readily granted this apparently reasonable request; but the whites then took a knife, and beginning at one end of the hide, cut it up to a long rope, not thicker than a child's finger, so that by the time the whole was cut up, it made a great heap; they then took the rope at one end, and drew it gently along, carefully avoiding its breaking. It was drawn out into a circular form, and being closed at its ends, encompassed a large piece of ground. The Indians were surprised at the superior wit of the whites (these Dutchmen were probably acquainted with what is related of Queen Dido in ancient history,[4] and thus turned their classical knowledge to a good account), but did not wish to content with them about a little land, as they had still enough themselves. The white and red men lived contentedly together for a long time, though the

[3]Although fermented drinks were not unknown among indigenous peoples before the introduction of European alcohol, especially in Mesoamerica, their uses were generally within specific ritual contexts very different from the manipulative trade practices described here.

[4]In classical tradition, Dido (or Elissa) was the Phoenician founder and ruler of the city-state of Carthage, which at its height was the chief rival of Rome. As in this narrative, Dido similarly bargained for land with the inhabitants of her new home, asking for just enough land as could be surrounded by an ox hide. She then cut the hide into strips and circled an entire hill, which then became the foundations of her empire.

former from time to time asked for more land, which was readily obtained, and thus they gradually proceeded higher up the Mahicannittuck [Hudson River], until the Indians began to believe that they would soon want all their country, which in the end proved true. (Heckewelder 1876, 71–76)

Version 2: "First Acquaintance with the Whites" As Told by Captain Pipe to C. C. Trowbridge (1824)

The tradition of their first acquaintance with the whites has been minutely related by Mr. Heckewelder and agrees in substance with the account now given of that important event. Capt. Pipe says that in those days the Indians were accustomed to worship annually as they now do, in a large building prepared and kept for that purpose. At one of these meetings an old man prophesied the coming of some important and extraordinary events and a few days after a ship hove in sight and a boat with some of the officers came on shore. The Indians, supposing the crew to be inferior deities sent by the great Spirit, spread beaver skins upon the ground for them to walk upon. The whites refused to comply and pointed to their hats endeavouring to make them understand the value and proper use of the skins, but they were compelled to accept the politeness of their new acquaintances who surrounded them and drove them on the skins. When they arrived at the great council house or place of worship one of them took a cup and filling it with liquor drank of it and offered it to the astonished spectators. The cup passed around, refused by all. At length three brave men supposing the Deity would be offended by their stubbornness resolved to undertake the dreadful task, and having drunk the contents of the cup they were taken out of the lodge and seated upon a log. The effect of the liquor soon prostrated them to the ground, and their recovery was despaired of. However they were closely watched and at length one of them lifted up his head and demanded more of the poison. In time they all recovered and their account of its pleasing effects induced others to join, and its use soon became universal.

After becoming familiar with them the whites solicited them to give a small piece of land upon which they might build a fire to prepare their food. They demanded only a piece as large as a Bullocks hide and the request was readily granted, when to their great astonishment the bullocks hide was soaked in water and cut into a small cord with which the land was surrounded. However, they determine to overlook the deception and be more wary in future. The whites presented them with Axes, hoes etc. and departed, promising to revisit them the next year.

Upon their return they were not a little amused to see the Indians walking about with these things suspended from their necks as ornaments. They taught them their use, trafficked a little with them,[5] and at length told them that they wanted more lands, because it was impossible from the smallness of the size of the first grant, to

[5]European horticultural methods differed significantly from those of indigenous peoples, which were specifically suited to the plants and soils of this land. Many Europeans judged these differences as deficiency because they assumed that farming could only be done within the standards of their own cultural production. This also served to undermine traditional practices of manufacture and make Native populations dependent on European trade goods.

build a fire upon it without being incommoded with the smoke. It was therefore resolved to add to the first piece a quantity large enough to hold the chair of the whites, without the influence of the smoke. Upon this the bottom of the chair, which was composed of small cords, was taken out and like the hide, stretched around the lands. This second deception determined them never to give more lands without fixing some boundary understood by both parties distinctly. (Weslager 1972, 475–76)

Version 3: "The Coming of the Whites" As Told in Lenape by Willie Longbone in 1939 to Carl Voegelin

A long time ago when the whites came across the water the Lenape did not know that they were coming. One man said in his version song, "Someone wants to come to see us. He will come across the water." A warrior said, "I'll kill him when I see him."

The next year they saw a ship coming in this direction, and the chief [who had the vision] said, "Now that's the one. The one coming is our elder brother," but the warrior said, "Not mine!" When the whites had arrived, the warrior began to say, "I want to overpower him," but the man [chief] said, "This one is our older brother, that's what I said! [Na nën ndëluwèn]" The white man said, "Oh, [repeating the Lenape world *ndëluwèn*], you must be a Delaware!" That is the reason they began to call the Lenape "Delaware." [At this point the sound on the record becomes very distorted, but then it resumes as] "What do you want?" He [the white man] said, "I want a little piece of land, only as much as a cowhide will cover. Will you give it to me?"

[The Lenape answered], "Oh yes, we can give you that much." Ah, but they did not use just the cowhide. They began to cut it into little thin strips so that when stretched out it encircled a large piece of land. [End of recording].

Version 4: "The White People Are Still Fooling Us" As Told in Lenape by Bessie Snake of the Delaware Tribe of Western Oklahoma in 1978 to Jim Rementer and Bruce Pearson

This one when he was first here, he wanted to fool us, our elder brother [white people]. They said, "We will treat you good for as long as the creek flows and our uncle, the sun, moves and as long as the grass grows every spring, for that long I will take care of you people and I will be friends to you people," he said. He just wanted to fool us, and it seems that he is still fooling us.

Then he said, "I will give you this red flag." He said, "As long as you keep this, you give us a little piece of land as much as [will be covered by] a cow we will kill and then skin him." Then they did not take the hide off but cut it into very small pieces. Then they [the Delawares] looked good at it. It was a big piece of land our Lenape ancestors of long ago gave to them. They thought that the land was only to be as big as the hide they put on the ground, but it was a big piece.

Then they said, "You did not say, 'I want to cut it up!'" Then he [white man] said, "Now you have already finished signing this paper!" Now that is where our money now comes from that we receive, and we are still fighting it. It was said at that time, "We will treat you good and you will be given everything." This is true, he does give us everything.

Then [to] those deceased chiefs they [the whites] gave to them an axe and a hoe for them to use. Then they [the chiefs] just put them on their necks. The white man told them, "That is not the way to use it putting it on your neck. I will give you something else to wear around your neck." Then he handed them back to him and he took them. Then he put them on handles so they can take ahold of them.

Then the white man told him, "This is how it is used when you plant something to make rows. Now this axe is used to cut trees or to cut wood or make a log house; that is what you use to make it." Then he [the Lenape] said, "All right!" Then from then on they always used it.

Then I told my daughter and my grandchildren that they are still fooling us.

Version 5: "Prediction of the Arrival of the White People" As Told by Nora Thompson Dean, 2002

Long ago there was a Lenape man who had remarkable powers. He would often go and meditate. He was able to foresee the future. One day he told his people, "Soon we will have visitors. They will be real white, fair-skinned people, and they will come from the east in a huge vessel. They are a people who will change our way of life."

Not many people believed him, but finally one day the Lenape people saw a ship coming in. And when these men got out of their boat, the Lenape people were much amazed as they had light skin, blue eyes, and light hair. They were very stunned and dumbfounded, but most of the Lenape were so glad that these visitors had come that they put down furs for them to walk on.

But some Lenape wanted to kill the white people and said, "We don't want these people here. We'll just kill them." But the powerful man said, "No, they came to me in a vision. We will not kill them. They might be our brothers. They might bring us good things. They are going to bring us good things, eventually. We want to treat them good."

And so they did. They put furs down for the white people to sit and walk on. They gave the white people seeds, food, and other things they needed. That's the way the prediction was told a long time ago about the arrival of the white people.

Ritual Poetry, Song, and Ceremony

In the world's numerous oral literatures, poetry is song, whether the psalms of David, the lyrics of Orpheus, or the meditations of Tecayahuatzin. The movement from recitation to chant and song is often correlated with other factors, such as increasing seriousness, emotional intensity, or complexity of linguistic form. In short, like other poetry song consists of affectively charged, sophisticated language. Ritual poetry, created for communal expression, is widespread in Native America; lyric poetry, which articulates an individual response, is far less common.

Ritual poetry both commemorates and creates. In a wide variety of settings, it transports participants back to the time of origin recalling the prototypical events and persons who gave structure and meaning, life and health, to this world, or it calls them forward to belief in a new world to come. In either case, the symbolic language and narrative form of most ritual poetry aims to re-create the sacred in the present moment. The complex Navajo healing ceremonials transform the patient's home into the world just after the emergence, and heal by identifying the patient with the culture heroes Monster-Slayer and Born-for-Water, who rid the world of monsters. Similarly, whole communities regularly seek to be restored to their original fecundity in cyclic ceremonials, which anthropologists call world-renewal rituals. In some cultures, ritual poetry may be quite brief and imagistic, achieving its impact through repetition which induces in the participants a powerful sense of imaginative transport. In other cultures, it may be quite long and predominantly narrative, drawing heavily upon its mythic subtext. In either case, it is usually marked by conventionalized symbolic expressions called formulae, which may be as short as a phrase or as long as several lines (block formula).

"Sayatasha's Night Chant" is a fine instance of Native American ritual poetry. It is sung as part of the extensive Zuni world-renewal ceremonial commonly called Shalako, after the ten-foot tall masked impersonations of those spirits. The formal name of the ceremony, however, means "The Coming of the Gods," and refers to the fact that the kachinas, who are patron spirits of both the earth's forces and the Zuni ancestral dead, promised at the beginning of time to return every December to the village in the high desert of New Mexico with seeds and moisture to renew life for the coming year. The gods return incarnated in the persons of masked, costumed men, who have spent most of the previous year in arduous preparation for these sacred responsibilities. Thus begins the half-year-long season in which the kachinas are present and visible among men until their going home in late summer. Throughout this season, everyone at Zuni is busy in fulfilling ritual obligations, which are accompanied by complex songs and prayers, rich in agricultural and environmental symbolism, for the aim of Zuni religion is nothing less than to promote the continuance of life.

The poem is chanted in unison by the Shalako priests, a section at a time with breaks in between, over the course of the eighth night of Shalako, the whole performance, with accompanying rituals, taking about six hours. The narrative structure of the poem has two distinct sections. The first is an extended flashback consisting of several elements: the events of the previous New Year when Pautiwa chose and consecrated the present Sayatasha narrator (ll. 1–103); a more limited flashback in which Sayatasha recounts his formal investiture and the immediate preparation for this Shalako which began forty-nine days before (ll. 104–379); and the recounting of his visits during this preparatory period to the sacred shrines where he contacted the rain-making ancestral spirits, while retracing the route of the Zuni aboriginal migration to their present home (ll. 380–520). The second section narrates contemporary occurrences taking place on the eighth night of Shalako, the house consecration and the gift of seed, game and human fertility (ll. 521–758), and the concluding litany of blessings (ll. 759–774).

Looking more closely at the chant, we can describe it as a singular manifestation of a more basic pattern recurrent throughout the world, including Native America: the quest for power. Having assumed the responsibility to be the Sayatasha impersonator, the narrator obliges himself to present the needs of the community to those who can answer them. Especially important here is his visit to Kothluwalawa, the Zuni "Heaven" and Kachina village, to which he comes as a man, but from which he leaves fully invested as Sayatasha the kachina (ll. 178–379). Endowed with the kachina's power to promote life and growth, symbolized by the pouch of all seeds which was given to him, he returns to Zuni to confer these blessings upon his people. His ability as masked impersonator to represent both humans and kachinas enables him to serve as a mediator between the two communities. Not all Native American ritual poetry is as long or as formulaic as "Sayatasha's Night Chant," but however different Native American tribes have been and are from each other, they continue to create the majority of their oral poetry in ritual contexts.

Other forms of ritual poetry, including shorter prayers and dream songs, often compressed speech and imagery in poetic language and form. The two Cherokee formulas included here use a prescribed seven-part form that is rigidly followed and a color symbolism laden with cultural significance as key elements in reconfiguring reality through magical speech. These brief, but socially sanctioned forms contrast with other more private forms. In the Pima deer-hunting song, the hunter enters into the spirit of the hunted, imagining and vocalizing the delirium of the deer in its death throes. In the prayer before going into battle, a Blackfeet man addresses the Sun and asks to be delivered from the fate he dreamed. Other shorter forms are genuine lyrics, individually composed to focus through concentrated language and song an intense emotional response to personal experience. The several songs of love and war included here, though brief, were sung repeatedly to deepen the singer's recovery of the original experience.

Lyric poetry, which articulates a uniquely individualized response, is less common than ritual poetry. This may not have been the reality in the community, however, so much as a bias in the record. Because the anthropologists who recorded texts were often more interested in collecting oral literature that reflected a density of cultural beliefs, especially mythic narratives and ritual material, individualized works were less often recorded. As a result, we have been denied access to those voices who individualized the common experience. Instead of the factions and differences within a community, we are left, as a result of this historical bias, with an artificial sense of a common "cultural" response that contributes to the creation of stereotypes. Yet the insouciance of the Makah woman To'ak's reply to the vain man who was courting her or the plea of Victoria to mothers in his community suggests that every community rings with many voices, not always in harmony, and reminds us again that our concept of other cultures is shaped for us by those who do the recording. Among the early anthropologists, the most diligent recorder of the names and social situations of Indian singers and storytellers was Frances Densmore, who devoted her life to recording the music and sung poetry of Native America.

Nevertheless, among a few Native peoples the creation of lyric poetry was culturally celebrated as an artistic act of the highest order. Among the Aztecs, indeed, it mimed the actions of the Lord of the Close and the Near, the Creator who created himself, for whom invention was the fundamental principle of being and the entire world his mask. The creation of poetry was a task for well-educated Aztec nobles. Individual composers like Tecayhuatzin, Ayocuan, or Nezahualcoyotl earned re-nown for their poetry, which celebrated the transience of life even as the Aztec empire was at its height, a theme which they articulated repeatedly by subtly manipulating a small but rich poetic vocabulary of flowers and jewels. Life, precious as jade or quetzal feather, could be shattered like the former, crushed like the latter. They thought of themselves as cut flowers, captured for a moment in time, decaying in the very instant their beauty is being contemplated. Life, so solid, so apparently real, was thus an illusion. Only by creating art, by imitating the Lord of the Close and the Near, could they aspire to immortality. So well-known were these songs, that more than seventy-five years after the death of Nezahualcoyotl they were still being sung, this time to Spanish-educated, Christianized Aztecs who recorded them and insured their composers' immortality.

Inuit (Eskimo) lyric poetry, with its often violent imagery, its pained, urgent voice, its short stanzas and simple refrains is very different in content, tone, and structure from the cool, contemplative, and complex Aztec lyrics. Inuit poetry was not, after all, the poetry of an educated and secure elite, but a poetry of the masses, of men and women who struggled to create life and beauty in a brutal environment wrapped for months in darkness. In the silence of the snowy night, abroad on the heaving ice, however, they waited for the words that would name their experience. "Songs are thoughts," Orpingalik said, "sung out with the breath when people are moved by great forces and ordinary speech no longer suffices. Man is moved just like the ice flow sailing here and there out in the current. His thoughts are driven by a flowing force when he feels joy, when he feels sorrow. Thoughts can wash over him like a flood, making his blood come in gasps, and his heart throb. Something like an abatement in the weather will keep him thawed up, and then it will happen that we, who always think we are small, will feel still smaller. And we will fear to use words. But it will happen that the words we need will come of themselves. When the words we want to use shoot up by themselves—we get a new song." Orpingalik's words communicate the origins of Inuit poetry, not unlike Wordsworth's "emotion recollected in tranquility," but many of the songs themselves suggest that a good deal of forethought and anxiety went into composing as well. All of this poetry was for public performance, after all, the equivalent of publication; there were evidently no closet poets among the Inuit. Well-wrought poetry was valued. As one Inuit poet commented, "The most festive thing of all is joy in beautiful, smooth words and our ability to express them."

Andrew O. Wiget
New Mexico State University
Daniel Heath Justice
University of Toronto

PRIMARY WORKS

Ruth Bunzel, "Zuni Ritual Poetry," *Forty-Seventh Annual Report of the Bureau of American Ethnology,* 1930; *Eskimo Poems from Canada and Greenland,* trans. Tom Lowenstein, 1973; John Bierhorst, *Four Masterworks of American Indian Literature,* 1974; John Bierhorst, *Cantares Mexicanos,* 1986.

Sayatasha's Night Chant (Zuni)

And now indeed it has come to pass.
When the sun who is our father
Had yet a little ways to go to reach his left-hand altar,[1]

Our daylight father,
Pekwin of the Dogwood clan,
Desired the waters, the seeds
Of his fathers,
Priests of the masked gods.
Then our fathers,
Sharing one another's desire, sat down together
In the rain-filled room
Of those that first came into being.
Yonder following all the springs,
They sought those ordained to bring long life to man,
Those that stand upright,
But (like the waters of the world),
Springing from one root, are joined together fast.
At the feet of some fortunate one
Offering prayer meal,
Turquoise, corn pollen,
Breaking the straight young shoots,
With their warm human hands
They held them fast[2]
Taking the massed cloud robe of their grandfather, turkey man,
Eagle's mist garment,
The thin cloud wings and massed cloud tails
Of all the birds of summer,
With these four times clothing their plume wands,
They made the plume wands into living beings.

[1]"*I.e.,* the south, therefore at the winter solstice," [Bunzel's note]. Most of the poem (ll. 1–520), which is sung on the eighth night of Shalako, is an elaborate flashback recounting the events that have led up to this moment. Thus, the Pekwin or Sun Priest began preparations for this year's Shalako a year ago by gathering the priests, "the fathers," in the kiva, a subterranean room for prayer and planning which is entered through the roof. The kiva is called a "rain-filled room" because its form symbolizes the wet, lower worlds from which the Zuni emerged onto this earth's surface. (See "Talk Concerning the First Beginning.") When they enter the kiva, the priests symbolically enter the lower world of their preemergence, whence all creative transformations originate.

[2]Willow shoots are gathered to be made into prayer sticks. As the block formula which follows (ll. 24–45) indicates, through the prayerful intention of the priests, these prayer sticks are endowed with spirit so that they can communicate man's intentions to the kachinas, the ancestral spirit powers of the world. (cf. ll. 114–20).

With the flesh of their mother,
Cotton woman,
Even a thread badly made,
A soiled cotton thread,
Four times encircling their wand they made their belts;
With rain-bringing prayer feathers
They made them into living beings.
With the flesh of their two mothers,
Black paint woman,
Clay woman,
Clothing their plume wands with flesh,
They made them into living beings.
When they said, "Let it be now,"
The ones who are our fathers
Commissioned with prayers
The prayer wands that they had fashioned.

When the sun who is our father,
Had gone in to sit down at his ancient place,
Then over toward the south,
Whence the earth is clothed anew,
Our father, Kawulia Pautiwa,
Perpetuating what had been since the first beginning
Again assumed human form.[3]
Carrying his fathers' finished plume wands
He made his road come hither.
Wherever he thought, "Let it be here,"
Into his fathers' rain-filled room,
He made his road to enter.
And when our sun father,
Had yet a little ways to go
To go in to sit down at his ancient place,
Yonder from all sides
Rain-bringing birds,
Pekwin, priest
From where he stays quietly,
Made his road come forth.
Making his road come hither,
Into his fathers' rain-filled room,
He made his road to enter.
With his wings,

[3]Pautiwa is pekwin of the Kachinas, who have a social organization in their underwater village, Kothluwala, which parallels that of Zuni. Here he is impersonated by a Zuni, though not wearing Pautiwa's distinctive mask. Of masking, Bunzel notes, "The impersonator dons a mask and becomes the god, and inversely the god assumes human form. As a matter of fact, in the evening the impersonator comes unmasked, the mask having been previously taken to the Kiva."

His fathers' cloud house he fashioned,
Their bed of mist he spread out,
Their life-giving road of meal he sent forth
Their precious spring he prepared.[4]
When all was ready,
Our father, Käwulia Pautiwa
Reaching his house chiefs,
His pekwin
His bow priests,
He made his road to go in.
Following one road,
Sitting down quietly
A blessed night
The divine ones
With us, their children, came to day.

Next day, when our sun father
Had come out standing to his sacred place,
Saying, "Let it be now."
Over there to the south,
Whence the earth is clothed anew,
Our father, Käwulia Pautiwa,
Perpetuating what had been since the first beginning,
Again assumed human form.
Carrying his waters,
Carrying his seeds,
Carrying his fathers' precious plume wands,
He made his road come forth.
He made his road come hither.
The country of the Corn priests,
Four times he made his road encircle.
Yonder wherever all his kiva children's rain-filled roads come out
His precious plume wands
He laid down.
Then turning he went back to his own country.

My father picked up the prayer plume,
And with the precious prayer plume
Me he appointed.
The moon, who is our mother,
Yonder in the west waxed large;
And when standing fully grown against the eastern sky,

[4]As the Zuni pekwin prepares an altar of sand-painted images in the kiva (ll. 69–73), his kachina counterpart, Pautiwa, approaches the pueblo in order to appoint all those who will serve as impersonators of the kachinas for the next year, including the Sayatasha impersonator (ll. 100–107).

She made her days,
For my fathers,
Rain maker priests,
Priests of the masked gods.
I fashioned prayer plumes into living beings.
My own common prayer plume,
I fastened to the precious prayer plume of my fathers.
At the place since the first beginning called "cotton hanging,"
I brought my fathers prayer plumes.
Drawing my prayer plumes toward them,
They spoke to those inside the place of our first beginning.[5]
Yonder following all the springs,
On all the mossy mountains,
In all the wooded places,
At the encircling ocean,
With my prayer plumes,
With my sacred meal,
With my sacred words,
They talked to those within.
Winter,
Summer,
Through the cycle of the months,
Though my prayer plumes were but poor ones,
There toward the south,
Wherever my fathers' roads come out
I continued to give them prayer plumes.

And when the cycle of months was at an end[6]
My fathers made their rain roads come in
To their fathers,
Their mothers,
Those that first came into being.
Sharing one another's desire, they sat down together.
With the flesh of their mother,
Cotton woman,
Even a cord badly made,
A soiled cotton cord,
With this four times

[5]Throughout the year, the Sayatasha impersonator has visited all the sacred springs around Zuni, depositing at these shrines the prayer sticks by means of which the needs of the Zuni people are communicated to the ancestral rain-making spirits in the springs.

[6]*I.e.,* the many months of prayer and ritual obligations which consumed most of the year having been completed, the 49-day preparatory period, starting in mid-October, begins, during which a single knot is untied each day from a knotted day-count cord (l. 147) until the beginning of Shalako in early December.

They made the day counts into living beings.
Saying, "Let it be now,"
They sent for me.
I came to my fathers,
Where they were waiting for me.
With their day count
They took hold of me fast.
Carrying their day count
I came back to my house.
Saying, "Let it be now,"
And carrying the prayer plumes which I had prepared,
Yonder to the south
With prayers, I made my road go forth.
To the place ever since the first beginning called "Ants go in,"
My road reached.[7]
There where my fathers' water-filled roads come out,
I gave them plume wands;
I gave them prayer feathers;
There I asked for light for you.
That you may grow old,
That you may have corn,
That you may have beans,
That you may have squash,
That you may have wheat,
That you may kill game,
That you may be blessed with riches,
For all this I asked.
Then over toward the west
Where the road of my fathers comes in,
I gave them plume wands.

And now, when all of their days were past,[8]
Over toward the west,
Where the gray mountain stands,

[7]The man who has been given the role of the Sayatasha reports that he has indeed fulfilled his obligations by visiting all the springs throughout the year.

[8]The man who is impersonating Sayatasha visits Kothlawalawa, the Kachinas' underwater village, sometimes popularly called "Zuni Heaven," the source of life and renewal. There his "father," the actual kachina Sayatasha (represented by the chief Zuni kachina priest) invests him as Sayatasha. This involves two rites, ritual smoking and baptism with cornmeal, which are part of other Zuni ceremonials, and for which block formulas are used. Smoke is a complex symbol at Zuni, associated with mist and rain, with breath and life, and with thought and intention, all comprehended by the distinctive formulaic phrase: "I added to their hearts (breath)." Smoking is also a sign of peace and marks reciprocal relations as among kin (ll. 230–234). The ritual smoking formula occurs several times (ll. 205–33, 421–47, 597–620). Baptism with prayer meal is an act of physical blessing (ll. 190–200, 401–416, 584–91). The cornmeal, like pollen, fertilizes that upon which it lands.

And the blue mountain,
Where rain always falls,
Where seeds are renewed,
Where life is renewed,
Where no one ever falls down,
At the abiding place
Of those who are our children,
There I met them on their roads.
There where the one who is my father
Had prepared my seat
Four times my father sprinkled prayer meal.
On the crown of my head
Four times he sprinkled prayer meal.
And after he had sprinkled prayer meal on his rain seat,
Following him,
My prayer meal
Four times I sprinkled.
My father's rain seat
I stood beside.
My father took hold of me.
Presenting me to all the directions, he made me sit down.
When I had sat down,
My father
Took his grandson,
Reed youth.
Within his body,
He bored a hole going through him.
Four times drawing toward him his bag of native tobacco,
Into the palm of his hand
He measured out the tobacco.
Within his body
He placed mist.
He took his grandmother by the hand,
And made her sit down in the doorway.
Having made her sit in the doorway,
Four times inhaling, he drew the mist through.
With the mist
He added to the hearts
Of the rain maker priests of all directions.
It is well;
Praying that the rain makers
Might not withhold their misty breath,
With his prayers
He added to their hearts.
He handed it to me.
Four times inhaling,
Into my body

I made the mist pass through.
Then with the mist,
I added to the hearts of my fathers of all the directions.
When this was at an end,
We greeted one another with terms of kinship:
Father,
Son; elder brother, younger brother; uncle, nephew; grandfather, grandson; ancestor, descendant.
With this many words we greeted one another.
When all this was at an end,
My father questioned me:
"Yes, now indeed
You have passed us on our roads.
Surely you will have something to say, some words that are not too long."
Thus he spoke to me.

"Yes, indeed it is so.
Back at the New Year,
All my fathers
Desiring something,
With their precious prayer plume
Appointed me.
Yonder toward the south,
At all the places where the roads of the rain makers come out,
I have continued to offer you prayer plumes.
Now that the cycle of your months is at an end,
Now that the counted number of your days has been told off
Now that this many days
Anxiously we have awaited your day,
Now this day,
We have reached the appointed time.
Now I have passed you on your roads."
Thus I spoke to them.

When I had spoken thus,
Hurriedly, without delay,
My father took hold of me.[9]
From the very soles of my feet
Even to the crown of my head
He clothed me all over with all things needful.
When all this was at an end,

[9]Sayatasha the kachina now invests the man who will impersonate him, not only costuming him for his public ceremonial appearances in the kachina's stead, but more importantly supplying him with all the requisite elements for renewing life at Zuni and empowering him to effectively bless the people with fertility.

Then also with that which is called my belt,
His prayer meal,
He covered my navel.
With his bundle that covered it all over.
He took hold of me,
His bundle reached all around my body.
When all this was at an end,
Then also the different kinds of seeds four times he placed over
my navel.
All different kinds of seeds his bundle contained:
The seeds of the yellow corn,
The seeds of the blue corn,
The seeds of the red corn,
The seeds of the white corn,
The seeds of the speckled corn,
The seeds of the black corn,
And also that by means of which you may have firm flesh,
Namely, the seeds of the sweet corn;
And also those which will be your sweet tasting delicacies,
Namely, all the clans of beans—
The yellow beans,
The blue beans
The red beans,
The white beans,
The spotted beans,
The black beans,
The large beans,
The small beans,
The little gray beans,
The round beans,
The string beans,
Then also those that are called the ancient round things—
The striped squash,
The crooked-neck squash.
The watermelons,
The sweet melons,
And also those which you will use to dip up your clear water,
Namely, the gourds;
And then also the seeds of the piñon tree,
The seeds of the juniper tree,
The seeds of the oak tree,
The seeds of the peach tree,
The seeds of the black wood shrub,
The seeds of the first flowering shrub,
The seeds of the kapuli shrub.
The seeds of the large yucca,

The seeds of the small yucca,
The seeds of the branched cactus,
The seeds of the brown cactus,
The seeds of the small cactus;
And then also the seeds of all the wild grasses—
The evil smelling weeds,
The little grass,
Tecukta,
Kucutsi,
O'co,
Apitalu,
Sutoka,
Mololoka,
Piculiya
Small piculiya,
Hamato
Mitaliko;
And then also the seeds of those that stand in their doorways,
Namely the cat-tails,
The tall flags,
The water weeds,
The water cress,
The round-leafed weed;
Across my navel
His bundle reached.
And then also, the yellow clothing bundle of the priest of the north,
The blue clothing bundle of the priest of the west,
The red clothing bundle of the priest of the south,
The white clothing bundle of the priest of the east,
The many colored bundle of the priest of the above,
The dark colored bundle of the priest of the below;
Across my navel
His bundle reached.

When all this was at an end,
My father spoke to me:[10]
"Thus you will go.
Your daylight fathers,
Your daylight mothers,
Your daylight children
You will pass on their roads.

[10]The spirit of the ancestral dead, who, clothed with clouds, are partly responsible for bringing rain, promise to come to Zuni when the impersonator of Sayatasha, Rain Priest of the North, calls. The description is a block formula, repeated in ll. 480 ff.

And wherever you come to rest,
We shall come to you.
Assuredly none of us shall be left behind—
All the men,
Those with snow upon their heads,
With moss on their faces,
With skinny knees, no longer upright, and leaning on canes,
Even all of these;
And furthermore the women,
Even those who are with child,
Carrying one child on the back,
Holding another on a cradle board,
Leading one by the hand,
With yet another going before,
Even all of us,
Our daylight fathers,
Our daylight mothers,
Our children,
We shall pass on their roads."

Thus my father said.
Having spoken thus,
He took hold of me.
Presenting me to all the directions he made me arise.
With his prayer meal
Four times he sprinkled his water-filled ladder.[11]
After him,
Four times I sprinkled my prayer meal.
Taking four steps,
Four times striding forward,
Standing, I came out.

[Having come out standing,
Yonder to all directions I looked;
I looked toward the north,
I looked toward the west,
I looked toward the south,
I looked toward the east.
Hither, toward the place of dawn,
I saw four roads going side by side.
Along the middle road,
Four times my prayer meal I sprinkled.

[11]Because the kiva is meant to represent a spring, "a rain-filled room," the ladder descending into it from the roof is called "water-filled."

There I made the sound of the water-filled breath of the priest of
the north.
Taking four steps,
Four times striding forward,
To the place known since the first beginning as Great Lake,[12]
My road came.

Where my father's road comes out
I stood in the doorway.
That which formed my belt,
My prayer meal,
Four times sprinkling inside,
I opened their curtain of scum.
After that,
Four times sprinkling prayer meal inside
Standing I came in.
When I came in standing,
My father
Hurrying without delay
Where he had prepared his rain seat,
His prayer meal
Four times he sprinkled.
On the top of my head
His prayer meal
Four times he sprinkled.
After him
Four times sprinkling my prayer meal,
My father's rain seat
I stood beside.
As I stood up beside it
My father took hold of me,
Yonder to all the directions presenting me,
He made me sit down.

Having seated me
The one who is my father
Took the water bringing cigarettes which he had prepared.
Four times drawing it toward him,
He took his grandmother by the hand
And made her sit down in the doorway,

[12]One of the 29 sacred springs visited by the Zuni during their post-emergence migration in search of their present home. At each spring, the Sayatasha impersonator actually enters the spring, moving aside the algae scum, which is imagined as a curtain serving as a door for the "rain-filled room" (l. 400). At each of the 29 springs, the baptism with corn meal and the ritual smoking occur, inviting the ancestral rain-making spirits residing in the spring to return to Zuni.

Four times inhaling, he drew the mist through
With the mist
He added to the hearts of fathers,
Rain maker priests.
Thus it is well;
In order that the rain makers may not withhold their misty breath.
With mist he added to their hearts.
When all this was at an end,
My father handed it to me.
Four times inhaling, I drew the mist through.
Into my body drawing the misty breath,
With the mist
I added to the hearts of my fathers.
This is well;
In order that the rain makers may not withhold their misty breath,
With mist I added to their hearts.
When all this was at an end,
We greeted one another with terms of kinship:
Father,
Son; elder brother, younger brother; uncle, nephew; grandfather, grandson; ancestor, descendant.
With these words we greeted one another.

When all this was at an end
My father questioned me:
"Yes, now at this time
You have passed us on our roads.
Surely you will have something to say, some word that is not too long,
If you let us know that,
I shall know it for all time."
Thus my father spoke.
When he had spoken thus, (I answered)
"Yes, indeed it is so.
Yonder to the south,
Following wherever your roads come out,
I have been bringing you prayer sticks,
I have been bringing you prayer feathers.
Now this day,
Having reached the appointed time,
I have passed you on your roads."
"Is that so. With plain words you have come to us.
We are clothed with your prayer sticks;
We hold your prayer meal;
With your prayer plumes in our hair we are sitting in here waiting.
Here where we are just standing around,
Where we are just sitting on our haunches,

You have come to us.[13]
When the sun who is our father
Has yet a little ways to go,
Before he goes in to sit down at his sacred place,
Nearby your daylight fathers,
Your daylight mothers,
Your children,
You will pass on their roads.
Wherever you come to rest,
All together we shall come to you.
All the men,
Those with snow upon their heads, with moss upon their faces,
With skinny knees,
No longer upright but leaning on canes;
And the women,
Even those who are with child,
Carrying one upon the back,
Holding another on the cradle board,
Leading one by the hand,
With yet another going before.
Yes, with all of these,
Your daylight fathers,
Your daylight mothers,
Your children,
You will pass on their roads,
And wherever you come to rest
We shall come to you."
Thus my father spoke.

When he had spoke thus,
He took hold of me.
Yonder to all the directions
Presenting me
He made me arise.
After he had made me arise
With his prayer meal
His water-filled ladder
He sprinkled.
After him sprinkling my prayer meal
Standing, I came out.][14]

[13]The relationship between men and spirits is not a compulsive but a generous one. The spirits, it seems, need to feel needed and have been waiting for the Zuni to request their assistance.

[14]The bracketed portion of the text, ll. 380–509, is repeated 29 times, the only change being the substitution in l. 393 of the name of a different one of the 29 springs, which the Zuni visited during their post-emergence migration. By visiting each of these springs in order, the Sayatasha impersonator reenacts that mythic migration search for the Center of the world.

Coming out standing
Yonder to all directions I looked.
I looked to the north,
I looked to the west,
I looked to the south,
I looked to the east,
Hither toward Itiwana I saw four roads going side by side.
Along the middle road,
My prayer meal
Four times I sprinkled before me.
Then I made the sound of the rain-filled breath of the rain maker
priest of the below.

Taking four steps,
Four times striding forward,
Where descends the watery road.
Of my daylight fathers,
My daylight mothers,
I stood.
Then I consecrated the place
Where my father's watery road descends.[15]
That none of his children might fall from the ladder,
Having still one rung left to go,
Having still two rungs left to go,
Having still three rungs left to go,
Having still four rungs left to go;
In order that none of his children should fall down
I consecrated the place where his watery road descends.
When all this was at an end
The one who is my father
On the crown of my head
Four times sprinkled prayer meal.
Four times he threw prayer meal upward.
Then after him,
My prayer meal
Sprinkling before me,
Where my father's water-filled road ascends
I made my road ascend.
The one who is my father
Four times sprinkled prayer meal before him.

[15]The flashback portion of the chant ends here, as the narration of the Sayatasha impersonator has caught up with events. On this eighth night of Shalako, he has entered into the Shalako house, a home representing the Zuni community as a family. He consecrates the house by rooting it in the earth, like a living plant (ll. 554–68), so that there may be long life (ll. 529, 534) and fertility (ll. 570–82).

After him
Four times sprinkling prayer meal before me,
Standing, I came in.
As standing I came in
I could scarcely see all my fathers,
So full was his house.

Then my father's rain-filled room
I rooted at the north,
I rooted at the west,
I rooted at the south,
I rooted at the east,
I rooted above,
Then in the middle of my father's roof,
With two plume wands joined together,
I consecrated his roof.
This is well;
In order that my father's offspring may increase,
I consecrated the center of his roof.
And then also, the center of my father's floor,
With seeds of all kinds,
I consecrated the center of his floor.
This is well;
In order that my father's fourth room
May be bursting with corn,
That even in his doorway,
The shelled corn may be scattered before the door,
The beans may be scattered before the door,
That his house may be full of little boys,
And little girls,
And people grown to maturity;
That in his house
Children may jostle one another in the doorway,
In order that it may be thus,
I have consecrated the rain-filled room
Of my daylight father,
My daylight mother.

When all this was at an end,
The one who is my father
Four times sprinkled prayer meal
Where he had prepared my seat.
Following him,
Four times sprinkling prayer meal before me,
Where my father had prepared my seat,
I stood beside it.
My father took hold of me.

Presenting me to all the directions, he made me sit down.
After my father had seated me,
The rain invoking cigarette which he had prepared
My father drew toward him.
He took his grandmother by the hand
And made her sit in the doorway.
Having seated her in the doorway,
Four times inhaling he made the mist pass through;
Into his body
He drew the misty breath.
With the mist he added to the hearts of his fathers.
This is well:
That the rain makers may not withhold their misty breath,
With mist
He added to the hearts of his fathers.
He handed it to me.
Four times inhaling I made the mist pass through;
Into my warm body
I drew the misty breath.
With mist I added to the hearts of my fathers.
This is well:
That the rain makers may not withhold their misty breath,
With mist I added to their hearts.
When all this was at an end,
We greeted one another with terms of kinship:
Father,
Son, elder brother, younger brother; uncle, nephew; grandfather, grandson; ancestor, descendant.
With this many words we greeted one another.

When all this was at an end,
My daylight father questioned me:
"Yes, now indeed
You have passed us on our roads,
The one whom all our fathers,
Desiring something,
Appointed at the New Year.
Yonder to the south
Wherever emerge the precious roads of our fathers,
Rain maker priests,
Rain maker Pekwins,
Rain maker bow priests.
With your prayer plumes—poorly made though they were,
You have asked for light for us.
Now this day, the appointed time has come."

Thus my father said to me.
Now our fathers,[16]
Shola-witsi, pekwin priest,
Sayatasha, bow priest,
Hututu, bow priest,
The two Yamuhakto, bow priests,
Perpetuating their rite,
Have once more assumed human form.
Their seeds,
Their riches,
Their fecundity,
The seeds of the yellow corn,
The seeds of the blue corn,
The seeds of the red corn,
The seeds of the white corn,
The seeds of the speckled corn,
The seeds of the black corn,
The seeds of the sweet corn,
All the clans of beans,
All the ancient round things,
The seeds of all the different trees,
The seeds of all the wild weeds,
I carry over my navel.
Those which we brought,
These seeds we now leave here
In the rain-filled rooms
Of our daylight fathers,
Our daylight mothers.

When in the spring,
Your earth mother is enriched with living waters,
Then in all your water-filled fields,
These, with which you will renew yourselves,
Your mothers,
All the different kinds of corn,
Within your earth mother
You will lay down.
With our earth mother's living waters,
They will once more become living beings.
Into the daylight of our sun father
They will come out standing.
They will stand holding out their hands to all the directions,

[16]Sholawitsi, the little Fire God, represents the Sun and carries a fawn skin full of different seeds. Hututu, the Rain Priest of the South, is the deputy of Sayatasha, Rain Priest of the North. The Yamuhakto are patron spirits of the forests and game animals. All are represented by masked impersonators.

Calling for water.
And from somewhere,
Our fathers with their fresh water
Will come to them.
Their fresh waters
They will drink in.
They will clasp their children in their arms;
Their young will finish their roads.
Into your house,
You will bring them,
To be your beloved ones.
In order that you may live thus,
In the rain-filled rooms
Of our daylight fathers,
Our daylight mothers,
Our daylight children,
The seeds which we brought tied about our waists
We leave here now.
This is well;
That going but a little ways from their house
Our fathers may meet their children;[17]
That going about, as they say,
With your water-filled breath
(You may meet) antelope,
Mountain goats.
Does,
Bucks,
Jack rabbits,
Cottontails,
Wood rats,
Small game—even little bugs;
So that thus going out from your houses,
With the flesh of these
You may satisfy your hunger.

This is well;
In order that my daylight father's rain-filled rooms,
May be filled with all kinds of clothing,
That their house may have a heart,[18]
That even in his doorway

[17]As the parallelism suggests, these are the game animals. The ceremonial of which this chant is a part, while focusing primarily on agricultural imagery, is a world renewal ceremony to promote fertility in all living persons, whether animal, vegetable, or human. Indeed, given the corn-flesh and animal-human transformations that are central to the Zuni creation story, all life is one and all creatures are persons. See "Talk Concerning the First Beginning," [Zuni], above.

[18]"An empty house 'has no heart.' The heart of a house is anything which has been used by human beings." [Bunzel's note]

The shelled corn may be spilled before his door,
That beans may be spilled before his door,
That wheat may be spilled outside the door,
(That the house may be full of) little boys,
And little girls,
And men and women grown to maturity,
That in his house
Children may jostle one another in the doorway,
In order that it may be thus,
With two plume wands joined together,
I have consecrated the center of his roof.
Praying for whatever you wished,
Through the winter,
Through the summer,
Throughout the cycle of the months,
I have prayed for light for you.
Now this day,
I have fulfilled their thoughts.
Perpetuating the rite of our father,
Sayatasha, bow priest,
And giving him human form
I have passed you on your roads.
My divine father's life-giving breath,
His breath of old age,
His breath of waters,
His breath of seeds,
His breath of riches,
His breath of fecundity,
His breath of power,
His breath of strong spirit,
His breath of all good fortune whatsoever,
Asking for his breath,
And into my warm body
Drawing his breath,
I add to your breath now.
Let no one despise the breath of his fathers,
But into your bodies,
Draw their breath.
That yonder to where the road of our sun father comes out,
Your roads may reach;
That clasping hands,
Holding one another fast,
You may finish your roads,[19]

[19]This exhortation captures the purpose of this Zuni ceremonial in which a representative from the human community seeks the life-giving aid ("the breath") of the ancestral spirits ("the fathers") and brings it back to renew the community ("add to our breath"). Only continuity with the past can insure continuance in the future.

To this end, I add to your breath now.
Verily, so long as we enjoy the light of day
May we greet one another with love;[20]
Verily, so long as we enjoy the light of day
May we wish one another well,
Verily may we pray for one another.
To this end, my fathers,
My mothers,
My children:
May you be blessed with light;
May your roads be fulfilled;
May you grow old;
May you be blessed in the chase;
To where the life-giving road of your sun father comes out
May your roads reach;
May your roads all be fulfilled.

1930

The Singer's Art (Aztec)[1]

I polish the jade to brilliance,
I arrange the black-green feathers,
I ponder the roots of the song,
I order in rank the yellow feathers,
  So that a beautiful song I sing.
I strike the jade continuously
To break out light from the flower's blossoming,
  Only to honor the Lord of the Close and the Near.

The yellow plumes of the troupial,
The black-green of the trogon,
The crimson of the rosy spoonbill,
I freshly arrange.
  My noble song, sounding golden tones,
  My song I will sing.

[20]"Literally, 'call one another by terms of relationship,'" [Bunzel note], as in I. 619. A more appropriate translation than "love," which is burdened by Western Romantic notions, may be: "May we greet one another as family."

[1]From Daniel Brinton, *Ancient Nahuatl Poetry* (Philadelphia, 1890). Trans. from the Nahuatl by Andrew Wiget. Composing a poem is compared to fine craftsmanship in other valued materials, precious stones and rare feathers.

A golden finch my song is proclaimed.
I sing it in the place of the raining flowers,[2]
  Before the face of the Lord of the Close and the Near.

A song good in its origins,
From the place whence comes the gold I bring it forth.
To the heavens I uncover the song I sing.
  A golden finch, a glittering jade it is.
I will make blossom a beautiful new song.
I will bring forth the perfume of mixed flowers to sweeten my song,
Before the face of the Lord of the Close and the Near.

The rosy spoonbill answers me,
When my bell-toned song reaches
The place of beautiful new songs.
  A polished jewel, a jade precious and brilliant.
  Of deepest green, it is made,
  A spring flower prepared to perfume the heavens.
  To the place of rosy flowers,
  Toward there I sing my song.

I choose the colors,
I mix the flowers,
In the place of beautiful new songs.
  A polished jewel, a jade precious and brilliant.
  Of deepest green, it is made,
  A spring flower prepared to perfume the heavens.
  To the place of rosy flowers,
  Toward there I sing my song.

I am honored, I am made glad,
Chasing the much-prized flower, the aroma of the rose in the place of song.
So that with sweetness my heart is filled.
Wave after wave I send to buffet my heart.
I inhale the perfume;
My soul becomes drunk.
I so long for the place of beauty.
The place of flowers, the place of my fulfillment,
That with flowers my soul is made drunk.

1890

[2]A metaphor for the Aztec Paradise, the home of the Sun and of song.

Two Songs[1] (Aztec)

I

We came only to sleep,
We came only to dream.
It is not so, it is not so,
That we came to endure on earth.

II

We become as the verdant spring.
Our hearts are rejuvenated,
Burst forth anew.
But our bodies are as the flowers:
Some blossom; they wither away.

Is it yet true there is living on earth?
Not forever on earth; but a moment here.
If it is jade, it shatters.
If it is gold, it crumbles.
If it is feather, it rends.
Not forever on earth; but a moment here.

1973

Like Flowers Continually Perishing[1] (Ayocuan Aztec)

Lo! From within the womb of the heavens they come,
The beautiful flower, the beautiful song.
Our eagerness destroys them,
Our diligence destroys them.
Truly perhaps even those of the Prince of the Chichimecs,[2]
    Tecoyahuatzin.
With his flowers, let all enjoy themselves!

[1]From the *Cantares Mexicanos.* Trans. by Arthur J. O. Anderson, in his *Grammatical Examples, Exercises and Review, for Use with "Rules of the Aztec Language."* (Salt Lake City: U Utah, 1973).

[1]From Birgitta Leander, *Flor y Canto* (Mexico: Instituto Nacional Indigenista, 1972). Trans. from the Nahuatl by Andrew Wiget.

[2]Another name for the Aztecs.

The exotic perfume of flowers filters down,
Friendship, a rain of precious flowers,
Plumes of white heron interlaced
With the precious cut flowers.
In the place of the branches,
They go about sipping at the flowers,
The lords and the nobles.

Yet you, O golden, belling bird!
How beautiful our song,
How beautifully you intone it!
There among the wreathed flowers,
There among the branching flowers, there you sing.

Perhaps you are this precious bird, O Giver of Life?[3]
Perhaps thus you have spoken, you, the god?
From the beginning, when you sit viewing the dawn,
You set about singing.

Eagerly my heart desires it,
The shield flowers,
The flowers of the Giver of Life.
  What shall my heart do?
  In vain we come to this place,
  We come to live on earth.

Yet only like these am I to be,
Like flowers continually perishing.
Will my name endure anywhere?
Will my fame end here on earth?
At least the flower, at least the song remains!
  What shall my heart do?
  In vain we come to this place,
  We come to live on earth.

Let us be content, O my friends!
Here there is embracing.
In a world of flowers we are living.
Of these not one will be destroyed,
The flower, the song.
They live in the house of the Giver of Life.

How brief an instant here on earth!
Will it be like this also in the next place of living?

[3]Another name for the Creator, the Lord of the Close and the Near.

Will there be rejoicing there? Friends?
Is it only here we come to know ourselves,
On earth?

1972

Moved (Uvavnuk, Inglulik Eskimo-Inuit)[1]

The great sea stirs me.
The great sea sets me adrift.
It sways me like a weed
On a river stone.

The sky's height stirs me.
The strong wind blows through my mind.
It carries me away
And moves my inward parts with joy.

1973

Improvised Greeting (Takomaq, Iglulik Eskimo-Inuit)[1]

Ajaja-aja-jaja.
The lands around my dwelling
Are more beautiful
From the day
When it is given me to see
Faces I have never seen before.
All is more beautiful,
All is more beautiful,
And life is thankfulness.

[1]From *Eskimo Poetry from Canada and Greenland.* Trans. Tom Lowenstein. (Pittsburgh: U Pittsburgh P, 1973). Uvavnuk entered the hut singing this song. Afterward she explained that she had been looking up at the night sky when a star rushed down, struck her and gave her this song. References to the sea, wind, and sky all allude to *silap inue,* the "Great Weather," the supernatural being who animates the environment.

[1]From Knud Rasmussen, *Intellectual Culture of the Iglulik Eskimo.* Report of the Fifth Thule Expedition. 7:1 (1929). This woman composed this song spontaneously as she brewed tea to greet Rasmussen.

These guests of mine
Make my house grand.
Ajaja-aja-jaja.

1929

Song[1] (Copper Eskimo-Inuit)

And I thought over again
My small adventures
As with a shore wind I drifted out
In my kayak
and thought I was in danger.

My fears,
Those small ones
That I had thought so big
For all the vital things
I had to get and reach.
And yet there is only
One great thing.
The only thing:
To live to see in huts and on journeys
The great day that dawns
And the light that fills the world.

1942

Widow's Song[1] (Quernertoq, Copper Eskimo-Inuit)

Why will people
have no mercy on me?
Sleep comes hard
since Maula's[2] killer

[1]From Knud Rasmussen, *The Mackenzie Eskimo.* Ed. H. Ostermann. Report of the Fifth Thule Expedition, 1921–24. 10:2 (Copenhagen, 1942).

[1]From *Eskimo Poetry from Canada and Greenland.* Trans. Tom Lowenstein. (Pittsburgh: U Pittsburgh P, 1973).
[2]Maula, her husband.

showed no mercy.
Ijaja-ijaja.

Was the agony I felt so strange
when I saw the man I loved
thrown on the earth
with bowed head?
Murdered by enemies,
worms have forever deprived him
of his homecoming.
Ijaja-ijaja.

He was not alone
in leaving me.
My little son
has vanished
to the shadow-land.
Ijaja-ijaja.

Now I'm like a beast
caught in the snare
of my hut.
Ijaja-ijaja.

Long will be my journey
on the earth.
It seems as if
I'll never get beyond
the foot-prints that I make.
Ijaja-ijaja.

A worthless amulet[3]
is all my property;
while the northern light
dances its sparkling steps
in the sky.
Ijaja-ijaja.

1973

[3]Amulets made of bone, wood, and stone represent the individual's spirit-helper whose protection is essential for survival.

My Breath[1] (Netsilik Eskimo-Inuit)

My breath . . . this is what I call my song, because it is as important for me to sing it as it is to draw breath.

This is my song: a powerful song.
Unaija-unaija.
Since autumn I have lain here,
helpless and ill,
as if I were my own child.

Sorrowfully, I wish my woman
to another hut,
another man for refuge,
firm and safe as the winter-ice.
Unaija-unaija.

And I wish my woman
a more fortunate protector,
now I lack the strength
to raise myself from bed.
Unaija-unaija.

Do you know yourself?
How little of yourself you understand!
Stretched out feebly on my bench,
my only strength is in my memories.
Unaija-unaija.

Game! Big game,
chasing ahead of me!
Allow me to relive that!
Let me forget my frailty,
by calling up the past.
Unaija-unaija.

I bring to mind that great white one,
the polar bear,
approaching with raised hind-quarters,
his nose in the snow—
convinced, as he rushed at me,
that of the two of us,

[1]From *Eskimo Poetry from Canada and Greenland.* Trans. Tom Lowenstein. (Pittsburgh: U Pittsburgh P, 1973).

he was the only male!
Unaija-unaija.

Again and again he threw me down:
but spent at last,
he settled by a hump of ice,
and rested there,
ignorant that I was going to finish him.
He thought he was the only male around!
But I too was a man!
Unaija-unaija.

Nor will I forget that great blubbery one,
the fjord-seal, that I slaughtered
from an ice-floe before dawn,
while friends at home
were laid out like the dead,
feeble with hunger,
famished with bad luck.
Unaija-unaija.

I hurried home,
laden with meat and blubber,
as though I were just running across the ice
to view a breathing-hole.
Yet this had been an old and cunning bull,
who'd scented me at once—
but before he had drawn breath,
my spear was sinking
through his neck.
Unaija-unaija.

This is how it was.
Now I lie on my bench,
too sick even to fetch
a little seal oil for my woman's lamp.
Time, time scarcely seems to pass,
though dawn follows dawn,
and spring approaches the village.
Unaija-unaija.

How much longer must I lie here?
How long? How long must she go begging
oil for the lamp,
reindeer-skins for her clothes,
and meat for her meal?
I, a feeble wretch:

she, a defenceless woman.
Unaija-unaija.

Do you know yourself?
How little of yourself you understand!
Dawn follows dawn,
and spring is approaching the village.
Unaija-unaija.

1973

Deer Hunting Song (Virsak Vai-i, O'odham)[1]

At the time of the White Dawn;
At the time of the White Dawn,
I arose and went away.
    At Blue Nightfall I went away.

I ate the thornapple leaves[2]
    and the leaves made me dizzy.
I drank the thornapple flowers
    and the drink made me stagger.

The hunter, Bow-remaining,
    he overtook and killed me,
cut and threw my horns away.
    The hunter, Reed-remaining,
he overtook me and killed me,
    cut and threw my feet away.

Now the flies become crazy
    and they drop with flapping wings.
The drunken butterflies sit
    with opening and shutting wings.

1985

[1]This song was sung by Virsak Vai-i and recorded by Frank Russell on the Gila River Reservation in Arizona in 1902. Vai-i's people, whom Russell and other Americans knew as the Pima, call themselves O'odham, "the people." Historically organized in patrilineages, they live on the Gila River and Salt River Reservations in Arizona. This text is from Frank Russell, *The Pima Indians,* 1985.

[2]A species of Datura with psychochemical properties. The deer speaks in this poem of being sickened by it. This deer-hunting song, like many other hunting songs, was also used by medicine men for curing. This song was used for curing illnesses that had symptoms of dizziness and vomiting.

Song of Repulse to a Vain Lover (To'ak, Makah)[1]

Keep away
Just a little touch of you
is sufficient.

1939

A Dream Song (Annie Long Tom, Clayoquot)[1]

Do not listen to the other singing.
Do not be afraid to sing your own song.

1939

Song of the Drum (Lewis Mitchell, Passamaquoddy)[1]

Nil nulopin naka ntotolitehmen pokuhulakon.
Nil ntotoli wiqtahan weyossisok . . .

[1]This song was recorded by Frances Densmore from Helen Irving during Densmore's work on the Makah Reservation at Neah Bay, Washington, during the summers of 1923 and 1926. Historically, the Makah were great whalers and lived by hunting sea mammals and fishing. Densmore wrote: "The composer of this song was a blind woman named To'ak. The interpreter remembered her and said that she sat against the wall all day, singing and tapping her knuckles on the wall as an accompaniment. Her name refers to a beach and was thought to mean a pile of valuables on the shore. To'ak belonged to the Ozette band of Makah. There was no one to take care of her and she drifted from one family to another, but people were glad to have her because she was always so happy." This text is from Frances Densmore, *Nootka and Quileute Music,* 1939.

[1]This song was also recorded by Densmore during her Neah Bay fieldwork. Annie Long Tom, a Clayoquot, was the widow of a Makah man who survived by seasonal work and making baskets for sale. She received many of her songs in dreams. According to Densmore, "Annie Long Tom has a drum with which she accompanies her songs as she sits alone in her house. In describing some of her dream songs, she said the melodies came to her at night when she was asleep . . . [she] dreamed this song at the time when the Shaker religion came to Neah Bay. The Shaker religion is now established in the village, having a commodious building and many adherents, but Mrs. Long Tom has never attended the meetings. At first she debated the matter in her own mind, but a crow came to her in a dream and gave her this song, so she held aloof from the new religion." This text is from Frances Densmore, *Nootka and Quileute Music,* 1939.

[1]From Brian Swann, ed., *Algonquin Spirit: Contemporary Translations of the Algonquian Liter-*

pemotonek naka ona peciw wucowsonol n'ciksitmakon
n'pokuhulakon.

Nulopin naka ntotolitehmen pokuhulakon.
Peciw mecikiskak petagik ntasitemgok pokuhulakonok
naka na kci Apolahsomwehsit cenisu 'ciksotomon npokuhulakon.

Nulopin naka n'pokuhulakton.
Nitte Cipelahq naka n'ciksotomakun npokuhulakon.
Eltaqak pecite kci Wocawson 'conekehla unoski
naka 'ciksitomon eltaqak npokuhulakon.

Nulopin naka n'tokotomon npokuhulakon.
Peciw te Lumpeqinuwok moskapasuwok naka 'ciksotomoniyia
npokuhulakon
naka na Atwosskonikess conaqtihike naka 'ciksotomon
n'pokuhulakon.

Nulopin naka ntokotomon npokuhulakon
naka kei Aputamkon
muskessin tehna nekom 'ciksotomon npokuhulakon.

Pesahqetuwok, petakiyik, wucowsonol, mecikiskakiyil,
Atwosskonikess, Apolahsomwehsit, Lumpeqinuwok, Cipelahq,
mpsiu mace petapasuwok naciciksotomoniya eltaqahk npokuhulakon.

Translation:

I sit down and I am beating the drum.
I am drawing[2] them in . . .
and even the winds listen to my drum.

I sit down and I am beating the drum.
Even storm clouds[3] and thunder reply with their drums;
and more, Apolahsomwehsit the great whirlwind stopped and
listened to my drum.

I sit down with my drum.
And Cipelahq (that great monster) listened to my drum.

atures of North America (Lincoln: U of Nebraska P, 2005). The Algonquin-speaking Passamaquoddies and their close relatives the Penobscots are, along with the Abenakis, referred to as "people of the Dawnland," referring to their traditional homelands on the northeastern edge of present-day Maine and southwestern New Brunswick. Early relationships with French traders and missionaries were generally good, whereas there were numerous conflicts with the English. After years of displacement and subsequent negotiation and litigation, the Passamaquoddy land base has risen to 200,000 acres in Maine, and the population currently exceeds 800.

2 *wiqtahan:* Literally, hooking them in.

3 *mecitiskak:* Literally, bad weather.

The great Wind Bird, making noise, suddenly stopped moving its wings
and listened to the sound of my drum.

I sit down and I am striking my drum
Even the water creatures[4] rise out[5] of the water and listen to my drum
and more, Atwosskonikess[6] stops chopping and he listens to my drum.

I sit down and I beat my drum and the great sea serpent Aputamkon[7]
he also comes out, he listens to my drum.

Lightnings, thunders, winds, storm clouds,
Atwosskonikess, whirlwind, water creatures, Cipelahq;
they begin to come to me, following[8] the sound of my drum.

Song of War (Blackfeet)[1]

Old man on high [Sun],
help me,
that I may be saved from my dream!
Give me a good day!
I pray you, pity me!

1911

[4]*lumpeqinuwok:* Literally, creatures that live under water.

[5]*moskapasuwok:* Literally, they start coming out.

[6]Prince says this is "an invisible being who roams the forest armed with a stone hatchet with which he occasionally fells trees with a single blow." John Dyneley Prince, "Notes on Passamaquoddy Literature," *Annals of the New York Academy of Science* 13 (1901): 381–86. David Francis, Passamaquoddy elder and linguist, says the word means "caterpillar" or "inchworm" (in Swann, *Algonquin Spirit,* p. 96 n. 15).

[7]David Francis says the name means "his face is turned inside out"—that is, concave (in Swann, *Algonquin Spirit,* p. 97 n. 17). Prince says this is a "bugaboo" with long red hair that lived under the water, invoked to frighten children. Prince, "Notes on Passamaquoddy Literature," 386 n. 4.

[8]*mace petapasuwok naciciksotomoniya:* Literally, they start walking over here, they change direction to listen to it.

[1]Historically the Blackfeet were primarily buffalo hunters who lived on high plains in Montana and Alberta, where today they have reservations. Like other Plains peoples, the Blackfeet view the Sun as the giver of life and the being to whom prayer is ultimately directed. The sense of dependence and humility expressed in the plea for "pity" was a deeply felt part of the ethos of many Plains tribes. "Warfare" consisted principally of raiding and retaliation. This warrior sings that he may be saved from a dream which has made him anxious about going into battle. This text is from C. C. Uhlenbeck, *Original Blackfoot Texts,* 1911.

Song of War (Odjib'we,[1] Anishinabe-Ojibway[2])

The Sioux women
pass to and fro wailing.
As they gather up their wounded men
the voice of their weeping comes back to me.[3]

1913

War Song (Young Doctor,[1] Makah)[2]

The only reason I do not cut off your head[3]
is that your face would have a crying expression
when I carried it.

1939

[1]Densmore writes, "When Odjib'we was a boy his paternal grandfather, two of the latter's brothers, and two of his own brothers, were killed by the Sioux. Hatred filled his heart and he determined to hunt and kill the Sioux. Thus at an early age he chose the career of a warrior."

[2]The Anishinabe, called Chippewa by Anglo-Americans, historically occupied the wooded lake country of Minnesota and Wisconsin and far western Ontario. Pressures on their land forced them into conflict with the Sioux nations, originally also woodland peoples from the same area, and the two groups became bitter enemies. Frances Densmore recorded this song on the White Earth Reservation in Minnesota in the first decade of this century. She writes, "[Chippewa] War songs are of four kinds: dream songs of individual warriors, songs concerning war charms and medicines, songs of the conduct of war expeditions, and those which commemorate success." Today many war songs are sung as social songs. This text is from Frances Densmore, *Chippewa Music II,* 1913.

[3]This song is one of three Densmore recorded from Odjib'we connected with an expedition against the Sioux, their traditional enemies encamped in a village on the upper waters of the Minnesota River. Densmore notes, "A war party of more than a hundred Chippewa attacked this village and the first man killed was the Sioux Chief. During the fight, the Sioux women rushed out and dragged back the wounded men that they might not be scalped."

[1]Densmore wrote that Young Doctor was "formerly a medicine man. In the early morning he goes fishing, being able to manage a boat although he is so crippled he cannot stand upright. His store and his work in wood and stone carving occupy his time during the day and he is constantly busy."

[2]This song was recorded during Frances Densmore's fieldwork on the Makah Reservation at Neah Bay, Washington during the summers of 1923 and 1926. This text is from Frances Densmore, *Nootka and Quileute Music,* 1939.

[3]The pointedness of the sarcasm in this song derives from the Makah custom of beheading their enemies, which, Densmore says, they attributed "to the mythical personage Kwati, who stole the box containing the daylight. The owner of the box overtook Kwati, regained the box, and killed him. When Kwati was about to be killed, he said they must not bury him but must cut off his head, take it home and let it lie on a smooth sandy beach for four days, then put it on a pole, stick the pole upright in the sand, and let it remain there until it fell."

Song of War (Two Shields, Lakota)[1]

As the young men go by,
I was looking for him.
It surprises me anew
that he is gone.
It is something
to which I can not
be reconciled.

1918

Song of War (Victoria, Tohono O'odham)[1]

Men shouting "Brother," men shouting "Brother,"—
Among the mountains they have taken
little Apache children
where the sun went down in sorrow.
All women, what shall we do
to realize this.[2]

1929

[1]Densmore recorded this song from Two Shields during her fieldwork on the Standing Rock Reservation in South Dakota, which occupied her from 1911 to 1914. She provides no information on Two Shields. The Lakota are one of three dialectically distinct groups known to Anglo-Americans as the Sioux, a French corruption of a Chippewa word. This text is from Frances Densmore, *Teton Sioux Music,* 1918.

[1]Densmore recorded this song during fieldwork in November and December of 1920 near Sells, Arizona, where the Tohono O'odham, known to ethnographers as the Papago, have a reservation. Densmore described Victoria [sic] as "an aged member of his tribe. . . . His voice is weak but he knows many songs." This text is from Frances Densmore, *Papago Music,* 1929.

[2]Densmore writes, "When the warriors approached the village, the women, especially the relatives of the warriors, went to meet them, to receive the trophies they brought. The warriors danced on their way to the village, and on reaching the village they went to every house and danced. When they were finished, they stopped until evening, when the scalp dance began. Captives, as well as scalps, were brought by the returning warriors, and [this song] is concerning children taken captive among the Apaches." Apaches were ancient tribal enemies of the Tohono O'odham. This song points to the tragic irony of the women among the victors identifying with the mothers among their enemies.

Thanksgiving Address[1] (Haudenosaunee-Iroquois)

We gather together and see that the cycle of life continues. As human beings, we have been given the responsibility to live in balance and harmony with each other and with all of creation. So now, we bring our minds together as one as we give greetings and thanks to each other as People.

Now our minds are one.

We are thankful for our mother, the earth, for she gives us all that we need for life. She sustains and supports us as our feet move upon her. We are joyful in knowing that she continues to care for us as she has from the beginning of time. To our Mother, we send greetings and thanks.

Now our minds are one.

We give thanks to the waters for quenching our thirst and providing us with strength. Water is life, and we are thankful for its purity. We know its power in many forms—waterfalls and rain, mists, and streams, rivers and oceans. With one mind, we send greetings and thanks to the spirit of the Water.

Now our minds are one.

We turn our minds to all of the fish of the world. They cleanse and purify the waters of life, and they offer themselves to us as food. So we turn now to the Fish and send our greetings and thanks.

Now our minds are one.[2]

[1]From Alfred Taiaiake, *Wasáse: Indigenous Pathways of Action and Freedom* (Peterborough, ON: Broadview, 2005). The Haudenosaunee (Iroquois) Confederacy is one of the oldest continuing political alliances in the world, dating perhaps to the twelfth century. According to tradition, it was formed by five battling nations who came together under the "Great Law of Peace" proposed by the Wendat-Seneca visionary Dekanawidah, the Peacemaker. The founding nations were the Mohawks on the eastern frontier, Senecas at "the western door," with the Oneidas, Onondagas, and Cayugas between them; the Tuscaroras joined the Confederacy in the eighteenth century.

Having effectively dealt with both English and French colonists, thus establishing itself as a major power in lower Canada and the northern United States, the Confederacy was variously a significant political influence, an eager trading partner, and an unmistakable military threat to the early United States. The combined population of the Confederacy today is well over 100,000, with communities in Quebec and Ontario in Canada and New York, Wisconsin, and Oklahoma in the United States.

[2]The Thanksgiving Address is a ritual invocation of kinship and respect and a reminder of humanity's responsibilities to the rest of creation that is still recited at both important and commonplace gatherings. It affirms a shared purpose and relationship and also expresses appreciation to the various peoples of the more-than-human world for their own contributions to the well being of all. All beings share value by virtue of merely existing, but all also have both rights and responsibilities and active agents in this world.

5 Now we turn our minds to the many kinds of life-sustaining plant life in the fields and forests. The earth is covered with plants growing and working many wonders. With our minds gathered together, we give thanks and look forward to seeing Plant Life continue in all its diversity for many generations to come.

Now our minds are one.

With one mind, we turn to offer special thanks to all of the food plants. Since the beginning of time, the grains, vegetables, beans, and berries have helped people survive. We honour all of the Food Plants together as one and send them greetings and thanks.

Now our minds are one.

Now we turn to the medicines of the natural world. From the beginning, they have taken away our sickness. We are grateful they are always waiting to heal us. And we are happy there are special people among us who hold knowledge of the healing plants. With one mind, we send greetings and thanks to the Medicines and to the Medicine Keepers.

Now our minds are one.

We gather our minds together to send greetings and thanks to all the animal life of the world. We honour their wisdom and their strength. Animals have many lessons to teach us human beings, and they offer themselves to us as sustenance. We coexist with them where we live and in the forests and mountains. We are glad that the Animals are still here, and we hope that it will always be so.

Now our minds are one.

We now turn our thoughts to the trees. The earth has many families of beautiful trees, each with their own instructions and duties. Some trees provide us with shelter and shade, others with fruit and the other useful things we need to survive. Trees are symbols of peace, strength, and a reverence for life for peoples all over the world. With one mind, we greet and give thanks to the Trees.

Now our minds are one.

10 We put our minds together as one and thank all the birds who fly about in the sky. Their beautiful songs each day remind us to enjoy and appreciate life. To all the Birds—from the smallest to the largest—we send our joyful greetings and thanks.

Now our minds are one.

We are thankful for the powers we know as the Four Winds. We hear their voices in the moving air as they refresh us and purify the air we breathe. From the Four Directions they bring the change of seasons and messages. The Four Winds give us strength. With one mind, we send our greetings and thanks to the Four Winds.

Now our minds are one.

Now we turn to the west and our grandfathers, the thunder beings.[3] With their voices lightning and thunder, they bring the water that renews all life. We bring our minds together as one to send greetings and thanks to our grandfathers, the Thunderers.

Now our minds are one.

We now send greetings and thanks to our eldest brother, the sun. Each and every day he travels the sky from the east to the west, bringing with him the light of a new day. He is the source of all fires and of all life. With one mind, we send greetings and thanks to our brother, the Sun.

Now our minds are one.

We now put our minds together and give thanks to our oldest grandmother, the moon, who lights the night sky and governs the movement of the ocean tides. Her strength and wisdom are inside and around all women. By her changing face we mark the changing seasons, and it is the moon who watches over the arrival of children here on earth. With one mind, we send greetings and thanks to our grandmother, the Moon.

Now our minds are one.

We give thanks to the stars who are spread across the sky like bright sparks. We see them in the night, helping the moon to light the darkness and bringing dew to the fields and gardens. When we travel at night, they guide our way. With our minds gathered together as one, we send greetings and thanks to all of the Stars.

Now our minds are one.

We gather our minds to greet and thank all the enlightened teachers who have come to inspire and help the people throughout the ages. When we forget the Original Teachings and how to live in harmony, they remind us of the way we were instructed to live as people. With one mind, we send greetings and thanks to these caring Teachers.

Now our minds are one.

Now we turn our thoughts to the Creator and to the life-force of the universe. We send greetings and thanks for all the gifts of creation. Everything we need to live a good life is here in our natural world. For all of the love that is still around us, we gather our minds together as one and send our choicest words of greetings and thanks for the power of love, life, and of creation.

Now our minds are one.

We have now arrived at the place where we end our words. In thanking and acknowledging all of the things we have named, we did not

[3]As with most indigenous peoples, the Haudenosaunee recognize kinship as extending beyond human-exclusive genealogy. This broader sense of relationship encompasses a range of beings, both physical and spiritual.

intend to leave anything out. If something was forgotten, we leave it to each of you to send such greetings as we have spoken, and to offer gratitude in your own way.

Onen enska neiokwanikonra. Now our minds are one.

Formula to Attract a Woman (Cherokee)[1]

(1)

Now![2] In the Seventh Heaven all of You rest, You Little Men, You
Great Wizards!
All of You fail in nothing.
(I have just informed all of You.)[3]

Now You and I have just come to "remake" the Brown Tobacco.[4]
(This is my name, _______; these are my people, _______.)
Now You and I have just come to draw away the soul of a woman.

Then your thoughts are not to wander away!
Your soul is to be mine!
What the Brown Dog said to you, say to her![5]

Now you will be making a shadow behind me where I am walking.
"I have just come to 'remake' for you the White Tobacco!"
Now you will be standing about behind me where I am walking.

[1]From Jack Frederick Kilpatrick and Anna Gritts Kilpatrick, eds., *Walk in Your Soul: Love Incantations of the Oklahoma Cherokees* (Dallas: Southern Methodist UP, 1965), pp. 29–32. The Cherokees had many magical formulas, called *i:gawe:sdi,* words that focused or directed thought. Many of these were recorded by medicine men in manuscript books in the Cherokee syllabary. This one was recorded in southeast Adair County, Oklahoma.

These magical formulas feature repetition of key words, a structure highlighted by the most sacred number seven, the use of the pronoun *I,* and a long pause during which the speaker thinks intently on the purpose of the ritual. They may be recited, sung, or simply thought and are often used to infuse tobacco with magical power. This is an example of an "attracting" formula that draws the affections of the woman to whom it is directed. There are four sections, representing the holistic and balancing function of four in Cherokee tradition.

[2]"Now!" is a rhetorical formalism that prefaces a new thought and invokes the attention of the addressed spirit-beings. Seven is the Cherokee number signifying wholeness and totality. The "Little Men" and "Great Wizards" are references to relatives of Thunder, a powerful and benevolent figure in Cherokee tradition.

[3]The present tense form of the formula is an invocation of the desired effect. Thus, by stating the requested condition in the present tense, the words themselves help to actualize the results.

[4]To "remake" tobacco is to ritually imbue it with power.

[5]According to Cherokee ethnologists Jack and Anna Gritts Kilpatrick, "'Brown Dog' is the ceremonial designation for a divining pebble. The incantatory says to himself: 'You know what her future is fated to be. Tell the girl what it is.' Successive statements of the *i:gawé:sdi* (all the requisite four of them are written out) gradually change the 'color' of that future until the spell finally comes to rest upon the 'blue' of *uhí:so?dí,* the hue of love-longing."

(2)

Now! In the Seventh Heaven all of You rest, You Little Men, You
Great Wizards!
All of You fail in nothing.
(I have just informed all of You.)

Now You and I have just come to "remake" the Brown Tobacco.
(This is my name, ______; these are my people, ______.)
Now You and I have just come to draw away the soul of a woman.

Then your thoughts are not to wander away!
Your soul is to be mine!
What the White Dog said to you, say to her!

Now you will be making a shadow behind me where I am walking.
"I have just come to 'remake' for you the White Tobacco!"
Now you will be standing about behind me where I am walking.

(3)

Now! In the Seventh Heaven all of You rest, You Little Men, You
Great Wizards!
All of You fail in nothing.
(I have just informed all of You.)
Now You and I have just come to "remake" the Brown Tobacco.
(This is my name, ______; these are my people, ______.)
Now You and I have just come to draw away the soul of a woman.

Then your thoughts are not to wander away!
Your soul is to be mine!
What the Black Dog said to you, say to her!
Now you will be making a shadow behind me where I am walking.
"I have just come to 'remake' for you the White Tobacco!"
Now you will be standing about behind me where I am walking.

(4)

Now! In the Seventh Heaven all of You rest, You Little Men, You
Great Wizards!
All of You fail in nothing.
(I have just informed all of You.)

Now You and I have just come to "remake" the Brown Tobacco.
(This is my name, ______; these are my people, ______.)
Now you and I have just come to draw away the soul of a woman.

Then your thoughts are not to wander away!
Your soul is to be mine!
What the Blue Dog said to you, say to her!

Now you will be making a shadow behind me where I am walking.
"I have just come to 'remake' for you the White Tobacco!"
Now you will be standing behind me where I am walking.

Formula for Going to the Water (Cherokee)[1]

Now, listen! Now the road has just come to lie at your feet. Now the White Cloth has just fallen down.[2] Now the white perfumes have been brought. "Now, scatter them!" he has just come to say. (Seven Times.)

Long Person, you are in repose. Nothing can overpower you.

Now you are going to elevate my soul. You are going to renew it. Ha! Now you have just come to elevate it. Long Person, I have just come bearing my soul.

Long Person, you have just come to pronounce the Edict: "Ha! Take your rest in the First Heaven (July)."[3]

You Maker, it was too confining. He will be able to fulfill the Edict. Ha! Nothing can ever overpower you. He will be able to fulfill the Edict.

To the Second Heaven farther on I have come bearing my soul.

Long Person, you have just come to pronounce the Edict: "Take your rest through August." You maker, it was too confining.

[1]From Alan Kilpatrick, ed., *The Night Has a Naked Soul: Witchcraft and Sorcery among the Western Cherokee* (Syracuse: Syracuse UP, 1997), pp. 112–113. A spiritual state of purification is necessary to ensure success for Cherokee medicine, and the "going to water" ceremony helps to purify both body and spirit. This particularly poetic formula was written by medicine man Dlanus Toyanisi around 1940 and collected by Alan Kilpatrick's parents, the famed Cherokee ethnographers Jack and Anna Gritts Kilpatrick. The "Long Person" referred to here is the river spirit who abides in the water. According to Alan Kilpatrick, the formula "was recited at daybreak while the subject to be cleansed stood at the edge of a flowing stream, facing the rising sun in the east. At the conclusion of the recitation, the patient underwent a symbolic immersion in the water, a laving repeated either four or seven times."

[2]Kilpatrick explains Cherokee color symbolism (what he calls "buttressing devices" for the formulas) as follows: "The color black, *gv:hnáge*, is often associated with the most extreme forms of physical illness or with death itself. . . . Blue is most often associated with that peculiar Cherokeean melancholic state of love sickness, or uneasiness, known as *uhí:so?dí*. . . . Red is a metaphorical color that, in the Cherokee ethos, connotes victory or good fortune. . . . The ethereal color white is usually employed to connote a transcendental state of peaceful calm or bliss."

[3]Kilpatrick explains: "In 'Going to the Water' rites, which have been employed to divine the longevity of a patient, folk healers often refer to a standardized framework of seven successive heavens to which the patient's soul may aspire to elevate itself." Each heaven represents a year of extended life. Thus, the seventh heaven is a prediction of a significantly longer life span.

Long Person, I have come bearing my soul.

Ha! He will be able to fulfill the Edict: "In the Third Heaven farther on, September, take your rest." Ha! Maker, it was too confining.

Long Person, I have come bearing my soul.

Ha! He will be able to fulfill the Edict. Ha! Nothing can ever overpower you.

To the Fourth Heaven farther on I have come bearing my soul.

"Ha! Through October take your rest." You Maker, it was too confining.

Long Person, I have come bearing my soul.

Ha! He will be able to fulfill the Edict.

To the Fifth Heaven farther on I have come bearing my soul.

"Take your rest through November." You Maker, it was too confining.

Long Person, I have come bearing my soul.

Ha! He will be able to fulfill the Edict. Ha! Nothing can ever overpower you. Ha! He will be able to fulfill the Edict.

To the Sixth Heaven farther on I have come bearing my soul.

"Through December (it was too confining)—"take your rest." You Maker, Long Person, you have just come to pronounce the Edict.

To the Seventh Heaven farther on I have come bearing my soul. Now it has become part of a congregation there. Listen, you Maker, now you are going to renew my soul. Now you are going to elevate it.

Out beyond where I stand here you are calling exultantly. You can fail in nothing. Now you are going to renew my soul. You are going to elevate it. You are going to renew it.

He will use the White Walking Stick.[4] You will be holding the White Walking Stick at a slant.

You maker, now my soul here below—

"I have just come to breathe upon it," he said. "I am standing here. I have just come to prolong it."

On high the stars are peeping out. He loves you deeply. Now you have just come to pronounce the Edict.

"My soul—"I have just come to breathe upon it."

Here the forest is swaying. Out beyond here, Panther, you are calling exultantly. He loves you deeply. The Edict—Ha! You will be able to fulfill it. You great Wizard! He sees what you will be doing just beyond. Long Person, you are calling exultantly. You come by calling exultantly. He is young.

"I have just come to breathe upon it."

"Now you are going to elevate my soul to your breast."

"You will stand again."

"My name is ______. My clan is ______.

[4]According to Kilpatrick, this is "an ethereal metaphor for old age."

Cluster: America in the World/ The World in America

When Columbus set out with his small fleet from Spain in 1492, he was not seeking "America" but rather an elusive place described by classical and pre-Renaissance sources as *el Paraiso terrenal,* an earthly Eden imaginatively located as far east as India. Until his death, the intrepid admiral insisted that this is what he "discovered" when he landed on the islands of the Caribbean, exemplifying the tenacity with which Europeans, even those who had traveled to the New World, clung to their preconceptions. Scholars now agree that the Europeans' primary responses to the early reports were wholly self-referential and, largely, self-justifying. Like many other explorers, as well as armchair adventurers, Columbus proved nearly incapable of seeing this new world except through the lenses and the desires of the old. "Both the theologians of the Sacred Scriptures and the learned philosophers had rightly said the Earthly Paradise is in the Far East," he declared, and so he named the inhabitants he met "los indios," and cited the Greek naturalist Pliny to explain the origin of the pearls offered to him by the islanders or a curvature in the earth, shaped "something like a woman's nipple," that he discerned on this third voyage. "There is nothing of the modem empiricist" about Columbus's attitude, according to Tzvetan Todorov; rather, it is a " 'finalist' strategy," like that employed by the church fathers, where the ultimate meaning is already known, and interpretation, even the perception, of material reality merely shows us the path to that meaning.

Thus, the lust for conquest; the intense flurry of consumerism and passion for collecting artifacts, commodities, and peoples; the zeal of religious conversion; and even the determination of settlement all illuminate European concerns and anxieties. Roland Greene has recently argued that early promotional literature enticed financial backers with an approach that he calls Petrarchan, evoking an eroticized yearning for an alluringly ambiguous imagined "other." This mode only thinly veiled the power relations characteristic of the early inventions of America. These constructions took a number of different forms, some filtered through Columbus's "Indian" lens, including images of noble or quasi-Christian savages and ignoble cannibals, Amazons, pygmies and giants, Cyclops and other freakish creatures, lost cities of gold and Ages of Gold, worlds of pastoral innocence, potential utopias, and new Edens. The power of these fictions is exemplified by John Dees, who, almost a century after Columbus, made several presentations to Queen Elizabeth I, in which he argued that the fables of ancient conquest of America by figures like King Arthur, King Malgo, the Welsh Prince Madoc, St. Brendan the Navigator, and the Scottish Prince Icarus, later recounted in Book Two of Spenser's *The Faerie Queen* (1596), constituted legal proof of English sovereignty over this fabulous new land.

The excerpts in this cluster represent some prominent imaginary constructions of America. Thomas More's influential satire, *Utopia,* describes an idealistic communal society, based in part on Plato's *Republic* and Plutarch' s account of Sparta under Lycurgus's rule, which stands in stark contrast to the tumultuous England of the early sixteenth century in which More was trying to make his way. Although *utopia* means "no place," More's fictitious narrator, a Portuguese called Raphael Hythloday (whose surname is a learned joke, Greek for"knowledgeable in nonsense"), claims to have traveled to the New World with Amerigo Vespucci, whose account appeared in 1507. While scholars speculate that More may have based Hythloday's vision on reports of Mayan or Incan societies, the excerpt describes the widely acknowledged principle of *vacuum domicilium,* which legitimates the peaceful possession of apparently vacant land by improving it. Invoked by John Winthrop, governor of the Massachusetts Bay Colony, to justify Puritan land grabbing, this principle ultimately caused the dispossession of indigenous peoples, who were hunters, gatherers, and seasonal migrants and practiced an ecological form of agriculture that required the cyclical fallowing of fields.

Although the Renaissance in Europe was a time of expanding mental and physical horizons, the prevailing attitude, fostered by Catholic and Protestant zealots, was one of insularity, ethnocentrism, and intolerance. Moral thought was shaped by seemingly absolute and irreconcilable oppositions—good or evil, civilization or barbarism—which made the acceptance of different structures of belief and social organization almost impossible. The French essayist Michel de Montaigne was one of the few European intellectuals to resist the reigning absolutism. Profoundly shaken by reports coming out of the New World and a probable encounter with Tupinamba Indians brought from Brazil to Rouen, he composed his essay "Of Cannibals" as a critique of European violence, dogmatism, and unreflecting superiority. Using exotic American culture filtered through classical ideals as the basis for comparison and critique of his own nominally "civilized" world, Montaigne mobilized the trope of the noble savage as the source of "naked truth," a strategy that had a profound and not altogether positive influence on the imaginative constructions of the Americas.

An important facet of this trope of innocence was the convention of gendering the New World as the virginal, unclaimed body of a woman, which was thus vulnerable to ravishment and required masculine protection. By the 1570s, Emopean artists and mapmakers had popularized an allegorical image of America as an indigenous woman. One of the most revealing of these images is Jan van der Straet's drawing of Vespucci's "discovery" of America, which circulated widely in an engraving by Theodor Galle (page 110). Naked, and reclining on a hammock surrounded by indigenous flora and fauna, the female figure reaches languidly toward the cloaked and armored explorer, who wields a cruciform staff and banner, a sword, and an astrolabe. The motto reads, "Americen Americus retexit, & Semel vocavit inde semper excitam" (Americus rediscovers America; he called her once and thenceforth she was always awake). While Vespucci's fully rigged ship waits at anchor in the upper left-hand corner, in the center of the background other naked females roast a human leg in the signal "American" act of cannibalism, linking femininity and savagery. Michel de Certeau calls this "an inaugural scene" in which "the discourse of power . . . will use the New World as if it were a blank, 'savage' page on which Western desire will be written."

A seemingly playful instance of such "writing that conquers" is John Donne's "Elegie XIX," his witty response to Sir Walter Raleigh's proposed "seduction" of America, which employs figures of sexual difference to explore the dynamics of desire underlying this fantasy of conquest. The poem's male speaker imagines himself as an explorer who discovers and possesses a beloved explicitly apostrophized as "America." Her silence characterizes her as Europeans hoped the New World would be—unoccupied, receptive, and innocent, though not, however, a new Eve but a new Eden welcoming the new Adam into a paradise of one. This gendered fantasy, which justified conquest under the guise of heterosexual love, achieves popular form in the myth of Pocahontas's rescue of John Smith, and the Barbadian legend of Inkle and Yarico.

Finally, Francis Bacon offered his vision of the ideal commonwealth in the posthumously published fragment entitled *New Atlantis.* According to Greek legend, the island of Atlantis had a perfected political system and was the center of civilization until an earthquake caused it to sink into the ocean. Often compared to More's *Utopia,* Bacon's vision is based upon empirical science and on Machiavelli's critique of classical utopias. Bacon describes Spanish sailors setting out from Peru, en route to China and Japan, who encounter instead a Pacific island called Bensalem, which may have been modeled on the accounts of highly developed civilizations found in Central and South America. Though their relative peacefulness was a much lauded contrast to the strife, poverty, and violence endemic to European culture, it did not prevent these cultures from being subdued and ultimately destroyed.

Ivy Schweitzer
Dartmouth College

from Utopia

Thomas More 1478–1535

But if so be that the multitude throughout the whole iland pass and exceed the due number, then they chews out of every city certain citizens, and build up a town under their own laws in the next land where the inhabitants have much waste and unoccupied ground, receiving also the inhabitants to them if they will join and dwell together. They, thus joining and dwelling together, do easily agree in one fashion of living, and that to the great wealth of both the peoples. For they so bring the matter about by their laws that the ground which before was neither good nor profitable for the one nor the other is now sufficient and fruitful enough for them both. But if the inhabitants of that land will not dwell with them, to be ordered by their laws, then they drive them out of those bounds which they have limited and appointed out for themselves. And if they resist, then they make war against them. For they count this the most just cause of war, when any people, holdeth a piece of ground void and vacant, to no good or profitable use, keeping others from the use and possession of it, which notwithstanding by the law of nature ought thereof to be nourished and relieved. . . .

1516

from Of Cannibals

Michel de Montaigne 1533–1592

These nations, then, seem to me barbarous in this sense, that they have been fashioned very little by the human mind, and are still very close to their original naturalness. The laws of nature still rule them, very little corrupted by ours. . . . I am sorry that Lycurgus and Plato did not know of them; for it seems to me that what we actually see in these nations surpasses not only all the pictures in which poets have idealized the golden age and all their inventions in imagining a happy state of man, but also the conceptions and the very desire of philosophy. They could not imagine a naturalness so pure and simple as we see by experience; nor could they believe that our society could be maintained with so little artifice and human solder. This is a nation,

I should say to Plato, in which there is no sort of traffic, no knowledge of letters, no science of numbers, no name for a magistrate or for political superiority, no custom of servitude, no riches or poverty, no contracts, no successions, no partitions, no occupations but leisure ones, no care for any but common kinship, no clothes, no agriculture, no metal, no use of wine or wheat. The very words signify lying, treachery, dissimulation, avarice, envy, belittling, pardon—unheard of. How far from this perfection would he find the republic that he imagined: *Men fresh sprung from the gods* [Seneca].

1580

Theodor Galle 1571–1633
after a drawing by Jan van der Straet [Stradanus]

America, c. 1575

John Donne 1573–1631

Elegie XIX

To his Mistris Going to Bed

Come, Madame, come, all rest my powers defie,
Until I labour, I in labour lye.
The foe oft-times, having the foe in sight,
Is tir'd with standing, though they never fight.
Off with that girdle, like heavens zone glistering
But a farre fairer world encompassing.
Unpin that spangled brest-plate, which you weare
That th'eyes of busy fooles may be stopt there:
Unlace your selfe, for that harmonious chime
Tells me from you that now 'tis your bed time.
Off with that happy buske, whom I envye
That still can be, and still can stand so nigh.
Your gownes going off such beauteous state reveales
As when from flowery meades th'hills shadow steales.
Off with your wyrie coronet and showe
The hairy dyadem which on you doth growe.
Off with those shoes: and then safely tread
In this loves hallow'd temple, this soft bed.
In such white robes heaves Angels us'd to bee
Receiv'd by men; Thou Angel bring'st with thee
A heaven like Mahomets Paradise; and though
Ill spirits walk in white, we easily know
By this these Angels from an evill sprite:
They set our haires, but these the flesh upright.
  Licence my roving hands, and let them goe
Behind, before, above, between, below.
Oh my America, my new found lande,
My kingdome, safeliest when with one man man'd,
My myne of precious stones, my Empiree,
How blest am I in this discovering thee.
To enter in these bonds is to be free,
Then where my hand is set my seal shall be.
  Full nakedness, all joyes are due to thee.
As soules unbodied, bodies uncloth'd must bee
To taste whole joyes. Gems which you women use
Are as Atlanta's balls, cast in mens viewes,
That when a fooles eye lighteth on a gem

His earthly soule may covet theirs not them.
Like pictures, or like bookes gay coverings made
For laymen, are all women thus arraid;
Themselves are mystique bookes, which only wee
Whom their imputed grace will dignify
Must see reveal'd. Then since I may knowe,
As liberally as to a midwife showe
Thy selfe; cast all, yea this white linnen hence.
Here is no pennance, much lesse innocence.
  To teach thee, I am naked first: Why than
What need'st thou have more covering than a man.

1580s or 1590s

Francis Bacon 1561–1626

from New Atlantis

[W]ithin less than the space of one hundred years, the great Atlantis was utterly lost and destroyed, not by a great earthquake . . . but by a particular deluge of inundation. . . . But it is true that the same inundation was not deep, not past forty foot in most places from the ground, so that although it destroyed man and beast generally, yet some few wild inhabitants of the wood escaped. . . . So as marvel you not at the thin population of America, nor at the rudeness and ignorance of the people, for you must account your inhabitants of America as a young people, younger a thousand years at the least than the rest of the world, for that there was so much time between the universal flood and their particular inundation. For the poor remnant of human seed which remained in their mountains peopled the country again slowly, by little and little; and being simple and savage people (not like Noah and his sons, which was the chief family of the earth) they were not able to leave letters, arts, and civility to their posterity. . . . In the youth of a State, arms do flourish; in the middle age of a State, learning; and the both of them together for a time; and in the declining age of a State, mechanical arts and merchandise.

1627

New Spain

Columbus's establishment of a base at Hispaniola (present-day Haiti) provided Spain with the opportunity for wide exploration fanning out along the Caribbean basin. Juan Ponce de León reached Florida in 1513, about the time Vasco Nuñez de Balboa crossed the Isthmus of Panama and found the Pacific Ocean. Less than ten years later, Cortés seized the wealth—and history—of the Aztecs. Other conquistadores went northward: Juan Rodriguez Cabrillo sailed along the California coast; Hernando de Soto discovered the Mississippi River; and Francisco Vásquez de Coronado explored the Southwest. The way was open for Spain to conquer a vast dominion in the Americas, a desire due in part to the riches found by Cortés among the Aztecs and by Francisco Pizarro among the Incas, and in part because of the souls of Native Americans to be gained for the Catholic Church. With Portugal and with Pope Alexander VI, Spain had signed the Treaty of Tordesillas in 1494. This treaty gave Spain dominion over all of the Americas except Brazil; Brazil and Africa were given over to Portuguese dominance.

The Spanish system of colonization was under the tight control of the Spanish crown. Wealth in the colonies came from exploitation of the native population and of slaves taken from Africa. Laws adopted in 1542 forbade the taking of native people as slaves but allowed for the system of *encomienda,* in which native people were required to pay tribute to local conquistadores, later simply to the wealthiest leading officials in the territories. Through the mid-sixteenth century, it was the *encomienda* system that enabled native labor to substitute for slave labor. Thereafter, and for the next century and a half, thousands of Africans were captured and transported annually to the Spanish colonies, where they worked under intolerable conditions on large sugar and coffee plantations.

Missionary activity was supposed to facilitate but often competed with the activity of the colonizers. Franciscan, Dominican, Augustinian, and later Jesuit missionaries all sought at first to eradicate native faith practices. When these efforts were unsuccessful, missionaries tended to content themselves with sacramental instruction. The goal of the missionaries was not simply conversion but the complete education and hispanicization of native society. An essential function of this effort was *congregación,* the establishing of nucleated settlements apart from indigenous settlements. In this, Spanish missionary efforts and methods differed markedly from the Récollets and Jesuits of New France, who established their missions amid the sparse settlements and woods of the North.

In the early seventeenth century, two missionary regions had been established in northwestern New Spain, one in the south (Sonora), where missionary work was under Jesuit auspices, and one in the north (New Mexico), where the Franciscans established their missions. According to estimates made by the fathers, who in 1630 claimed as many as 60,000 christianized Indians in ninety Pueblos served by fifty priests, the missionary efforts were flourishing among the Pueblos. What became clear by the end of the century, however, is that Native Americans' nominal acceptance of the mission system, and of Catholicism generally, was not a result of actual conversion to Christianity. In proscribing

Written by jurist Palacios Rubios of the Council of Castile to satisfy the growing need that Spaniards felt for more specific justification of their conquest of the New World, this document exemplifies the injustice and cruelty of European self-rationalization. It was designed to be read to indigenous people and offer them the opportunity to convert and subject themselves peacefully to Spanish rule before conquistadores launched their military attack. Delivered in a language incomprehensible to these auditors, it nevertheless lays the blame for the ensuing violence, death, theft, and enslavement on native recalcitrance.

On the part of the king, Don Ferdinand, and of Doña Juana, his daughter, queen of Castile and León, subduers of the barbarous nations, we their servants notify and make known to you, as best we can, that the Lord our God, living and eternal, created the heaven and the earth, and one man and one woman, of whom you and we, and all the men of the world, were and are descendants, as well as all those who come after us. But on account of the multitude which has sprung from this man and woman in five thousand years since the world was created, it was necessary that some men should go one way and some another, and that they should be divided into many kingdoms and provinces, for in one alone they could not be sustained.

Of all these nations God our lord gave charge to one man called St. Peter, that he should be lord and superior to all the men in the world, that all should obey him, and that he should be the head of the whole human race, wherever men should live, and under whatever law, sect, or belief they should be; and he gave him the world for his kingdom and jurisdiction.

And he commanded him to place his seat in Rome, as the spot most fitting to rule the world from; but also he permitted him to have his seat in any other part of the world, and to judge and govern all Christians, Moors, Jews, Gentiles, and all other sects. This man was called Pope, as if to say Admirable Great Father and Governor of men. The men who lived in that time obeyed that St. Peter and took him for lord, king, and superior of the universe. So also they have regarded the others who after him have been elected to the pontificate, and so has it been continued even till now, and will continue till the end of the world.

One of these pontiffs, who succeeded that St. Peter as lord of the world, in the dignity and seat which I have before mentioned, made donation of these islands and mainland to the aforesaid king and queen and to their successors, our lords, with all that there are in these territories, as is contained in certain writings which passed upon the subject as aforesaid, which you can see if you wish.

So their highnesses are kings and lords of these islands and mainland by virtue of this donation; and some islands, and indeed almost all those to whom this had been notified, have received and served their highnesses, as lords and kings, in the way that subjects ought to do, with good will, without any resistance, immediately, without delay, when they were informed of the aforesaid facts. And also they received and obeyed the priests whom their highnesses sent to preach to them and to teach them our holy faith; and all these, of their own free will, without any reward or condition have become Christians, and are so, and the highnesses have joyfully and graciously received them, and they have also commanded them to be treated as their subjects and vassals; and you too are held and obliged to do the same. Wherefore, as best we can, we ask and require that you consider what we have said to you, and that you take the time that shall be necessary to understand and deliberate upon it, and that you acknowledge the Church as the ruler and superior of the whole world, and the high priest called Pope, and in his name the king and queen Doña Juana our lords, in his place, as superiors and lords and kings of these islands and this mainland by virtue of the said donation, and that you consent and permit that these religious fathers declare and preach to you the aforesaid.

If you do so you will do well, and that which you are obliged to do to their highnesses, and we in their name shall receive you in all love and charity, and shall leave you your wives and your children and your lands free without servitude, that you may do with them and with yourselves freely what you like and think best, and they shall not compel you to turn Christians unless you yourselves, when informed of the truth, should wish to be converted to our holy Catholic faith, as almost all the inhabitants of the rest of the islands have done. And besides this, their highnesses award you many privileges and exemptions and will grant you many benefits.

But if you do not do this or if you maliciously delay in doing it, I certify to you that with the help of God we shall forcefully enter into your country and shall make war against you in all ways and manners that we can, and shall subject you to the yoke and obedience of the Church and of their highnesses; we shall take you and your wives and your children and shall make slaves of them, and as such shall sell and dispose of them as their highnesses may command; and we shall take away your goods and shall do to you all the harm and damage that we can, as to vassals who do not obey and refuse to receive their lord and resist and contradict him; and we protest that the deaths and losses which shall accrue from this are your fault, and not that of their highnesses, or ours, or of these soldiers who come with us. And that we have said this to you and made this Requerimiento we request the notary here present to give us his testimoney in writing, and we ask the rest who are present that they should be witnesses of this Requerimiento.

—Palacios Rubios, "Requerimiento," ca. 1512

native ceremonies and dances, in suppressing and destroying ceremonial objects, especially those associated with kachina practices, in publicly punishing native priests and medicine men, the reverend fathers and their military assistants merely pushed Native Americans underground in their efforts to retain native ways and ultimately initiated the backlash that resulted in the Pueblo Revolt of 1680.

The important image of the Virgin of Guadalupe is a syncretic figure that bridged the cultures instead of exacerbating their opposition. She represents a merging of Old and New World religions, symbolized by the Catholic Virgin Mary and the Nahuatl Tonantzin. The figure suggests the power of the dominant order to impose its religious forms *and* the perseverance of native belief systems, which had to adapt to the culture of the colonizers. This image had the potential to mediate between the races, yet despite its mediatory function, native resistance to Spanish rule continued even after the Reconquest by Diego de Vargas, which lasted from 1692 to 1694. A Hopi oral narrative in these selections provides an important native perspective on the advent of the Spanish in the Southwest and the ensuing Pueblo Revolt. Long-simmering resentment erupted into numerous rebellions over the centuries, revolts often waged under the banner of the Virgin of Guadalupe.

Over the years, and as a result of interactions and intermarriage among the Spanish, Indians, and Africans, the population and culture of New Spain became increasing mixed or "mestizo." The earliest literature from this region, however, was written largely by explorers, conquistadores, and colonial administrators from the educated and aristocratic classes. Much of it was published in Spain and directed at sophisticated Spanish readers at court and church; thus, it drew on Spanish literary styles and fashions of the day. Nevertheless, the first printing press in the Americas was founded in Mexico City in 1539, more than half a century before the English even ventured to establish colonies in the New World.

The travel, exploration, and contact literature represented in these selections embodies European attitudes about cultural superiority and the justification of empire. Columbus cannot understand the new places he has stumbled on, except in comparison (usually negative) with Madrid or Seville. Fray Marcos de Niza, following in the footsteps of Coronado, whets the imagination of his readers with tales of the mythical Seven Cities of Cíbola and their untold wealth. Almost a half-century before the English establish their first permanent colony, Spain and France clashed decisively over disputed claims to Florida and the Carolinas. From 1565 to 1568, Pedro Menéndez de Avilés fought and defeated French explorers seeking new fields of conquest and conversion for their Huguenot (Protestant) faith, which was being repressed harshly in France. The Spanish conquest of Florida led to the establishment of the oldest city of European origin in North America, St. Augustine, Florida, and positioned the Spanish for a push into Virginia. Gaspar Pérez de Villagrá, a former courtier of King Philip II and a scholar with a classical education, versified the subduing of the Acoma and other momentous engagements in the progress of conquest in his epic poem, *The History of New Mexico.*

Cabeza de Vaca's narrative of the ill-fated plan of Pánfilo de Narváez to explore the Gulf coast in 1528 begins as a narrative of conquest but quickly transforms into what some have considered one of the first expressions of the "American" experience. After becoming a captive and a slave, a faith healer and a wanderer, Cabeza de Vaca is rendered unrecognizable to the Spanish who ultimately find him, and to himself. His liminal experiences in the new land, his loss of power and position, and his adaptation to a culture he formerly deplored change him ineluctably into something new that reflects the newness of the

Although somewhat out of fashion in the Middle Ages, the ideas of the classical Greek philosopher, Aristotle (384–322 BCE), were revived and gained popularity during the Renaissance in Europe. In his description of the household from Politics, Aristotle propounded a theory of "natural slavery," which later apologists of conquest marshaled in their justification of the use of force against indigenous people. Aristotle identified a category of men who, like women and children, did not possess rational faculties sufficiently developed to control their passions but had just enough reason to recognize their inferiority and need to be ruled by superiors. While "natural slaves" willingly submit to their subordination, the problem remained how to determine who fit into this category. Aristotle suggested three solutions—physical determinism, genetic transmission (through mothers), and outsider ("barbarian") status—all of which contributed in different ways to the association of "natural slavery" with racial or ethnic identity. In the famous debate in Valladolid in 1550–1551, Juan Ginés de Sepúlveda, a prominent humanist and Greek scholar, invoked Aristotle's theory to justify the legal use of force in the conversion of Amerindians against the accusations of cruelty mounted by Fray Bartolomé de Las Casas. Although this debate established Las Casas as the premier defender of the Indians, the Aristotelian argument mounted by Sepúlveda had far-reaching and devastating effects on European views about the "naturalness" of enslavement for some groups of people.

But is there any one thus intended by nature to be a slave, and for whom such a condition is expedient and right, or rather is not all slavery a violation of nature?

There is no difficulty in answering this question, on grounds both of reason and of fact. For that some should rule and others be ruled is a thing not only necessary, but expedient; from the hour of their birth, some are marked out for subjection, others for rule.

And there are many kinds both of rulers and subjects (and that rule is the better which is exercised over better subjects—for example, to rule over men is better than to rule over wild beasts; for the work is better which is executed by better workmen, and where one man rules and another is ruled, they may be said to have a work); for in all things which form a composite whole and which are made up of parts, whether continuous or discrete, a distinction between the ruling and the subject element comes to light. Such a duality exists in living creatures, but not in them only; it originates in the constitution of the universe; even in things which have no life there is a ruling principle, as in a musical mode. But we are wandering from the subject. We will therefore restrict ourselves to the living creature, which, in the first place, consists of soul and body: and of these two, the one is by nature the ruler, and the other the subject. But then we must look for the intentions of nature in things which retain their nature, and not in things which are corrupted. And therefore we must study the man who is in the most perfect state both of body and soul, for in him we shall see the true relation of the two; although in bad or corrupted natures the body will often appear to rule over the soul, because they are in an evil an unnatural condition. At all events we may firstly observe in living creatures both a despotical and a constitutional rule; for the soul rules the body with a despotical rule, whereas the intellect rules the appetites with a constitutional and royal rule. And it is clear that the rule of the soul over the body, and of the mind and the rational element over the passionate, is natural and expedient; whereas the equality of the two or the rule of the inferior is always hurtful. The same holds good of animals in relation to men; for tame animals have a better nature than wild, and all tame animals are better off when they are ruled by man; for then they are preserved. Again, the male is by nature superior, and the female inferior; and the one rules, and the other is ruled; this principle, of necessity, extends to all mankind. Where then there is such a difference as that between soul and body, or between men and animals (as in the case of those whose business is to use their body, and who can do nothing better), the lower sort are by nature slaves, and it is better for them as for all inferiors that they should be under the rule of a master. For he who can be, and therefore is, another's, and he who participates in rational principle enough to apprehend, but not to have, such a principle, is a slave by nature. Whereas the lower animals cannot even apprehend a principle; they obey their instincts. And indeed the use made of slaves and of tame animals is not very different; for both with their bodies minister to the needs of life. Nature would like to distinguish between the bodies of freemen and slaves, making the one strong for servile labour, the other upright, and although useless for such services, useful for political life in the arts both of war and peace. But the opposite often happens—that some have the souls and others have the bodies of freeman. And doubtless if men differed from one another in the mere forms of their bodies as much as the statues of the Gods do from men, all would acknowledge that the inferior class should be slaves of the superior. And if this is true of the body, how much more just that a similar distinction should exist in the soul? but the beauty of the body is seen, whereas the beauty of the soul is not seen. It is clear, then, that some men are by nature free, and others slaves, and that for these latter slavery is both expedient and right.

—Aristotle, "On Natural Slavery," from *Politics,* 350 BCE

world he has stumbled upon. More than a century and a half later, in a Mexico with an established university and educated creole class, a girl child and intellectual prodigy explores new cultural territory of a different sort. Sor Juana Inés de la Cruz, as she is known, joins a convent in order to preserve herself from marriage, and amasses an impressive collection of books. From her cell issues a steady stream of poetic meditations, witty and acerbic satires, verse dramas, and a defense of women's rights to knowledge and personhood that earned her the title she shares with Anne Bradstreet: "Tenth Muse of the New World."

Christopher Columbus 1451–1506

An accomplished merchant and seaman with more than twenty years of experience in the maritime commerce of Mediterranean and Atlantic trade routes, Christopher Columbus sailed from Spain in 1492 to enrich the treasury and expand the empire of a cash-strapped, militant Catholic monarchy. Explicitly framing his journey as an extension of Fernando and Isabel's defeat of the Moors and expulsion of Jews earlier that same year, Columbus's *Diario,* or journal, of the first voyage (1492–1493) articulates these economic and colonial rationales as it describes the land and peoples of the Bahamas, Cuba, and Hispaniola (Haiti and the Dominican Republic). When hoped-for precious metals and other marketable commodities do not immediately appear on these Caribbean islands, Columbus works to place his "discoveries" within European traditions of travel writing, cartography, geography, and theology. He struggles to reconcile the new, "exotic," and unexpected of the Americas with the traditional, desired, and familiar of Europe's culture and economy.

Most of what we know today as the journals of Columbus are redactions made by Fray Bartolemé de las Casas, perhaps as many as forty years after the death of Columbus. Although Las Casas presents himself as a faithful transcriber, some scholars question his influence on both the style and the substance of the journals. These reservations are most acute when it comes to descriptions of Indians, for whom Las Casas had much greater sympathy than did Columbus. Accurate estimates of Indian populations before Columbus arrived continue to elude historians, but the destruction of as much as four-fifths of the original population of Hispaniola in Columbus's lifetime provides an essential starting point for any reading of his written representations of Indians.

Columbus failed in his quest to discover a western route to the fabled riches of India or Cipangu (Japan), but his first voyage laid the foundation for Spanish control of potentially rich territories. To publicly authenticate their claims to the Caribbean, the Spanish monarchs established an enduring link between the politics of empire and the written accounts of explorers, by publishing excerpts from the journals along with a letter that Columbus had composed during his return trip. Fernando and Isabel quickly equipped Columbus for a second voyage (1493–1496), during which he explored Puerto Rico, the Virgin Islands, Jamaica, Cuba, and the Lesser Antilles and attempted to establish a colony on Hispaniola. No journal of this trip survives, but extant records indicate that Columbus's poor management of the colony and his controversial decision to enslave Taino Indians for sale in Europe undermined his credibility in Spain.

During his third voyage (1498–1500),

Columbus landed on Trinidad, formally took possession of the coast of Venezuela, and then sailed to Hispaniola, where he so alienated the Spanish colonists with his inflexible governance that he was arrested and sent back to Spain as a prisoner. In the journal, Columbus puzzles over unexpected compass readings recorded during his travels. Influenced by the cosmography of Pierre de Martyr's *Imago Mundi* (a copy of which he had heavily annotated), Columbus concluded that the Orinoco River must lead to the "Terrestial Paradise," or Garden of Eden. Although Columbus had explored a similar idea during the return trip from his first voyage, this later articulation underscores the interpretive challenges that he encounters when he situates his new observations of sea, land, and stars within a pre-Columbian, European world view. From giving each landfall and sighting a Catholic name to compiling religious texts in his "Book of Prophecies," Columbus frames his explorations not as the opening of a new world but as a Spanish Catholic fulfillmen of Old Testament traditions.

Restored to good graces (but stripped of governing authority) by Fernando and Isabel, Columbus embarked on a fourth voyage (1502–1504), during which he explored Central America in search of a passage to the Indian Ocean. After being stranded on Jamaica for more than a year, Columbus returned to Spain with his already fragile health ruined. He died two years later (1506), a wealthy but bitter man who felt unappreciated by his monarchs and uncertain of his legacy.

Jim Sullivan
MiraCosta College

PRIMARY WORKS

Journal of the First Voyage to America by Christopher Columbus, 1825 (first voyage); J. M. Cohen, ed. and trans., *The Four Voyages of Columbus,* 1969 (third voyage); Oliver Dunn and James Kelley, ed. and trans., *The Diario of Christopher Columbus's First Voyage to America,* 1989.

from Journal of the First Voyage to America, 1492–1493[1]

Sunday, Oct. 21st [1492].[2] At 10 o'clock, we arrived at a cape of the island, and anchored, the other vessels in company. After having dispatched a meal, I went ashore, and found no habitation save a single house, and that without an occupant; we had no doubt that the people had fled in terror at our approach, as the house was completely furnished. I suffered nothing to be touched, and went with my captains and some of the crew to view the country. This island even exceeds the others in beauty and fertility. Groves of lofty and flourishing trees are abundant, as also large lakes, surrounded and overhung by the foliage, in a most enchanting manner. Everything looked as green as in April in Andalusia. The melody of the birds was so exquisite that one was never willing to part from the spot, and the flocks of parrots obscured the heavens. The diversity in the appearance of the feathered tribe from those of our

[1]This extract begins with what Las Casas identifies as an extended direct quotation of Columbus.

[2]On October 12, Columbus landed on an island referred to by its natives as Guanahani. He renamed it San Salvador. By October 21, Columbus was still exploring various islands of the Bahamas.

country is extremely curious. A thousand different sorts of trees, with their fruit were to be met with, and of a wonderfully delicious odour. It was a great affliction to me to be ignorant of their natures, for I am very certain they are all valuable; specimens of them and of the plants I have preserved. Going round one of these lakes, I saw a snake,[3] which we killed, and I have kept the skin for your Highnesses; upon being discovered he took to the water, whither we followed him, as it was not deep, and dispatched him with our lances; he was seven spans in length; I think there are many more such about here. I discovered also the aloe tree, and am determined to take on board the ship to-morrow, ten quintals of it, as I am told it is valuable. While we were in search of some good water, we came upon a village of the natives about half a league from the place where the ships lay; the inhabitants on discovering us abandoned their houses, and took to flight, carrying off their goods to the mountain. I ordered that nothing which they had left should be taken, not even the value of a pin. Presently we saw several of the natives advancing towards our party, and one of them came up to us, to whom we gave some hawk's bells and glass beads, with which he was delighted. We asked him in return, for water, and after I had gone on board the ship, the natives came down to the shore with their calabashes full, and showed great pleasure in presenting us with it. I ordered more glass beads to be given them, and they promised to return the next day. It is my wish to fill all the water casks of the ships at this place, which being executed, I shall depart immediately, if the weather serve, and sail round the island, till I succeed in meeting with the king, in order to see if I can acquire any of the gold, which I hear he possesses. Afterwards I shall set sail for another very large island which I believe to be *Cipango,*[4] according to the indications I receive from the Indians on board. They call the Island *Colba,*[5] and say there are many large ships, and sailors there. This other island they name *Bosio,*[6] and inform me that it is very large; the others which lie in our course, I shall examine on the passage, and according as I find gold or spices in abundance, I shall determine what to do; at all events I am determined to proceed on to the continent, and visit the city of *Guisay*[7] where I shall deliver the letters of your Highnesses to the *Great Can,*[8] and demand an answer, with which I shall return.

Monday, Oct. 22d. Through the night, and today we remained waiting here to see if the king, or any others would bring us gold or anything valuable. Many of the natives visited us, resembling those of the other islands, naked like them, and painted white, red, black and other colours; they brought javelins and clews of cotton to barter, which they exchanged with the sailors for bits of glass, broken cups, and fragments of earthenware. Some of them wore pieces of gold at their noses; they readily gave them away for hawk's bells and glass beads; the amount collected in this manner, however, was very inconsiderable. Any small matter they received from us, they

[3]Probably an iguana, a valued food among the Indians.

[4]Marco Polo's name for Japan. Polo's *Description of the World* (1299) was the primary source for Columbus's ideas about the geography of Asia.

[5]Cuba.

[6]A variation of Bohío. Columbus translated this name as "abounding in gold." It most likely referred to the island that Columbus renamed La Isla Española (known as Ayti or "mountainous land" to its natives).

[7]Hangzou, China.

[8]A reference to the Mongol dynasty of Kublai Khan, which controlled China from 1279 to 1368. By 1492 the Ming dynasty (1368–1644) ruled China, but Europeans, isolated from China by Turkish control of trade routes, did not know this.

held in high estimation, believing us to have come from heaven. We took in water for the ships from a lake in the neighbourhood of this cape, which I have named *Cabo del Isleo:* in this lake Martin Alonzo Pinzon, captain of the Pinta, killed a snake similar to that of yesterday, seven spans long. I ordered as much of the aloe to be collected as could be found.

Tuesday, Oct. 23d. It is now my determination to depart for the island of *Cuba,* which I believe to be *Cipango,* from the accounts I have received here, of the multitude and riches of the people. I have abandoned the intention of staying here and sailing round the island in search of the king, as it would be a waste of time, and I perceive there are no gold mines to be found. Moreover it would be necessary to steer many courses in making the circuit, and we cannot expect the wind to be always favourable. And as we are going to places where there is great commerce, I judge it expedient not to linger on the way, but to proceed and survey the lands we met with, till we arrive at that most favourable for our enterprise. It is my opinion that we shall find much profit there in spices; but my want of knowledge in these articles occasions me the most excessive regrets, inasmuch as I see a thousand sorts of trees, each with its own species of fruit, and as flourishing at the present time, as the fields in Spain, during the months of May and June; likewise a thousand kinds of herbs and flowers, of all which I remain in ignorance as to their properties, with the exception of the aloe, which I have directed to-day to be taken on board in large quantities for the use of your Highnesses. I did not set sail to-day for want of wind, a dead calm and heavy rain prevailing. Yesterday it rained much without cold; the days here are hot, and the nights mild like May in Andalusia.

Wednesday, Oct. 24th. At midnight weighed anchor and set sail from *Cabo del Isleo* of the island of *Isabela,* being in the North part, where I had remained preparing to depart for the island of *Cuba,* in which place the Indians tell me I shall find a great trade, with abundance of gold and spices, and large ships, and merchants; they directed me to steer toward the W.S.W., which is the course I am pursuing. If the accounts which the natives of the islands and those on board the ships have communicated to me by signs (for their language I do not understand) may be relied on, this must be the island of *Cipango,* of which we have heard so many wonderful things; according to my geographical knowledge it must be somewhere in this neighbourhood. . . .[9]

The Indians on board told them that the island of *Cuba* was distant from thence a voyage of a day and a half in their canoes, which are small things, made of a log, and carrying no sail. Departed for *Cuba,* which from the Indians signifying to them the abundance of gold and pearls there, as well as the magnitude of the island, they doubted not, was Cipango.

Sunday, Oct. 28th. Continued on S.S.W., in quest of the island of *Cuba,* keeping close to the shore. They entered a fine river, free from shallows and all other obstructions, which in fact is the case with all the coast here, the shore being very bold. The mouth of the river had a depth of water of twelve fathoms, and a breadth sufficient for ships to beat in. They anchored within the river, and the Admiral states that the prospect here exceeded in beauty anything he ever saw, the river being surrounded with trees of the most beautiful and luxuriant foliage of a singular appear-

[9]Las Casas ends his direct quotation of Columbus here and resumes his third-person narration.

ance, and covered with flowers and fruits of all sorts. Birds were here in abundance singing most delightfully. Great numbers of palm trees were noticed, different from those of Guinea, and ours, wanting their particular manner of bark; they were of a moderate height, and bore very large leaves, which the natives use for coverings to their houses. The land appeared quite level. The Admiral went ashore in the boat, and found two dwellings, which he supposed to be those of fishermen, and that the owners had fled; he found in one of them a dog unable to bark. Both houses contained nets of palm, lines, horn fish-hooks, harpoons of bone, and other implements for fishing, as also many fire-places, and each seemed to be adapted to the reception of a large number of persons. The Admiral gave orders that nothing should be touched, which directions were adhered to. The grass was as high as it is in Andalusia in April and May, and they found purslain and strawberry-blite in abundance. They returned on board the boat and ascended the river some distance, where the Admiral says it was exceedingly pleasant to behold the delightful verdure and foliage which presented itself, not to mention the birds in the neighbourhood; the whole offered a scene of such enchantment that it was hardly possible to part from it. He declares this to be the most beautiful island ever seen, abounding in good harbours, and deep rivers, with a shore upon which it appears that the sea never breaks high, as the grass grows down to the water's edge, a thing which never happens where the sea is rough. Indeed a high sea they had not as yet experienced among these islands. This isle, he says, is full of pleasant mountains, which are lofty, although not of great extent, the rest of the country is high, after the manner of Sicily, abounding in streams, as they understood from the Indians of *Guanahani,* which were on board the ships, who informed them by signs that it contained ten large rivers, and was of such a size that with their canoes they could not sail round it in twenty days. When the ships were sailing towards the island, some of the natives put off from the shore in two canoes, and perceiving the Spaniards entering into the boat and rowing towards the mouth of the river to sound for an anchorage, they took to flight. The Indians told them there were mines of gold here and pearls, and the Admiral observed mussels and other indications of these articles in the neighbourhood. They further informed him that there came large ships hither from the *Great Can,* and that the main land was distant ten days' voyage. The Admiral named this river and port *San Salvador*. . . . [10]

Thursday, Nov. 1st. At sunrise the Admiral sent the boats to land to visit the houses they saw there; they found the inhabitants all fled, but after some time they espied a man; the Admiral then dispatched one of his Indians on shore, who called out to him from a distance and bade him not be fearful, as the Spaniards were a friendly people, not injuring anyone, nor belonging to the *Great Can,* but on the contrary, had made many presents of their goods among the inhabitants of the islands. The natives having ascertained that no ill was intended them, gathered confidence, and came in above sixteen canoes to the ships, bringing cotton yarn and other things, which the Admiral ordered should not be taken from them, as he wished them to understand that he was in search of nothing but gold, which they call *nucay.* All day the canoes kept passing between the ships and the shore. The Admiral saw no gold among them, but remarks having observed an Indian with a bit of wrought silver at

[10]The Bay of Nipé in the eastern part of Cuba.

his nostrils, which he conceived to be an indication of the existence of that metal in the country. The Indians informed them by signs that within three days there would come many traders from the interior to purchase the goods of the Spaniards, to whom they would communicate news of the king, who as far as could be learned from the signs of the natives, was about four days' journey distant. They informed the Spaniards also that many persons had been dispatched to inform the king respecting the Admiral. These people were found to be of the same race and manners with those already observed, without any religion that could be discovered; they had never remarked the Indians whom they kept on board the ships to be engaged in any sort of devotion of their own, but they would, upon being directed, make the sign of the cross, and repeat the *Salve* and *Ave Maria* with the hands extended towards heaven. The language is the same throughout these islands, and the people friends to one another, which the Admiral says he believes to be the case in all the neighbouring parts, and that they are at war with the *Great Can,* whom they call *Cavila,* and his country *Bafan.* These people go naked like the rest. The river here he describes as deep, and having a bold shore at the mouth, where ships may lay close to the land; the water of the river salt for a league upwards when it becomes very fresh. It is certain, says the Admiral, that this is the continent, and that we are in the neighbourhood of *Zayto* and *Guinsay,* a hundred leagues more or less distant from the one or the other. . . .

Sunday, Nov. 4th. Early in the morning the Admiral went on shore in the boat to shoot birds, and at his return, Martin Alonzo Pinzon came to him with two pieces of cinnamon, saying that a Portuguese on board his vessel had seen an Indian with two large handfuls of it, but was afraid to purchase it on account of the prohibition of the Admiral, and furthermore that the Indian had some reddish things resembling nutmegs. The boatswain of the Pinta declared he had seen cinnamon trees. The Admiral went to the place but found none. He showed some of the natives pepper and cinnamon which he had brought from Castile, they recognized it as he declares, and intimated to him by signs that much of it was to be found not far from thence to the southeast. He likewise showed them gold and pearls, and was informed by some old men that these existed in great abundance in a place which they called *Bohio,* being worn by the people at their necks, ears, arms and legs. They had, according to the same account, large ships, and carried on traffic, and this was all at the southeast. They further informed him that at a distance there were men with one eye only, and others with faces like dogs, who were man-eaters, and accustomed upon taking a prisoner, to cut his throat, drink his blood, and dismember him. The Admiral then determined to return to his ship and wait for the men whom he had sent into the country, when he was resolved to depart in quest of the regions which had been described to him, unless he should receive such accounts from the interior as would induce him to stay. He says "these people are very mild and timorous, naked as I have described the others, without weapons or laws. The soil is very fertile abounding with *mames,*[11] a root like a carrot, with a taste of chestnuts; beans likewise are here, very dissimilar to ours, also cotton, growing spontaneously among the mountains; I am of opinion that this is gathered at all seasons of the year, as I observed upon a sin-

[11]Cassava.

gle tree blossoms, pods unripe, and others burst open. A thousand other productions, which are doubtless of great value, I remarked, but find it impossible to describe them. . . ."

Tuesday, Nov. 6th. Last night, says the Admiral, the two men whom I had sent into the country returned, and related as follows. After having travelled a dozen leagues they came to a town containing about fifty houses, where there were probably a thousand inhabitants, every house containing a great number; they were built in the manner of large tents. The inhabitants received them after their fashion with great ceremony; the men and women flocked to behold them, and they were lodged in their best houses. They signified their admiration and reverence of the strangers by touching them, kissing their hands and feet, and making signs of wonder. They imagined them come from heaven, and signified as much to them. They were feasted with such food as the natives had to offer. Upon their arrival at the town they were led by the arms of the principal men of the place, to the chief dwelling, here they gave them seats, and the Indians sat upon the ground in a circle round them. The Indians who accompanied the Spaniards explained to the natives the manner in which their new guests lived, and gave a favourable account of their character. The men then left the place, and the women entered, and seated themselves around them in the same manner, kissing their hands and feet, and examining whether they were flesh and bone like themselves. They entreated them to remain there as long as five days. The Spaniards showed them the cinnamon, pepper and other spices which they had received from the Admiral, and they informed them by signs that there was much of these in the neighbourhood at the southeast, but they knew not of any in this place. The Spaniards not discovering any great number of towns here, resolved to return to the ships, and had they chosen to admit the natives to accompany them, might have been attended back by more than five hundred men and women, who were eager to bear them company, thinking they were returning to heaven. They took none along with them but one of the principal inhabitants with his son; with these the Admiral held some conversation, and showed them great civilities; the Indian described to him by signs many countries and islands in these parts, and the Admiral thought to carry him home to Spain, but says he was unable to find whether the Indian was willing. At night he seemed to grow fearful, and wished to go on shore; the Admiral says that having the ship aground he thought it not advisable to oppose him, and so let him return, requesting him to come back the next morning, but they saw him no more. The Spaniards upon their journey met with great multitudes of people, men and women with firebrands in their hands and herbs to smoke after their custom.[12] No village was seen upon the road of a larger size than five houses, but all the inhabitants showed them the same respect. Many sorts of trees were observed, and herbs and odoriferous flowers. Great numbers of birds they remarked, all different from those of Spain except the nightingales, who entertained them with their songs, and the partridges and geese, which were found in abundance. Of quadrupeds they described none except dumb dogs. The soil appeared fertile and under good cultivation, producing the *mames* aforementioned and beans very dissimilar to ours, as

[12]The Spanish probably saw tobacco on October 6, but they first saw it smoked during this five-day expedition inland.

well as the grain called panic-grass. They saw vast quantities of cotton, spun and manufactured, a single house contained above five hundred *arrobas,*[13] four thousand quintals might be collected here per annum. The Admiral says it appears to him that they do not sow it, but that it is productive the whole year round; it is very fine with an exceeding long staple. Everything which the Indians possessed they were ready to barter at a very low price; a large basket of cotton they would give for a leather thong, or other trifling thing which was offered them. They are an inoffensive, unwarlike people, naked, except that the women wear a very slight covering at the loins; their manners are very decent, and their complexion not very dark, but lighter than that of the inhabitants of the Canary Islands. "I have no doubt, most serene Princes," says the Admiral, "that were proper devout and religious persons to come among them and learn their language, it would be an easy matter to convert them all to Christianity, and I hope in our Lord that your Highnesses will devote yourselves with much diligence to this object, and bring into the church so many multitudes, inasmuch as you have exterminated those who refused to confess the Father, Son and Holy Ghost, so that having ended your days (as we are all mortal) you may leave your dominions in a tranquil condition, free from heresy and wickedness, and meet with a favourable reception before the eternal Creator, whom may it please to grant you a long life and great increase of kingdoms and dominions, with the will and disposition to promote, as you always have done, the holy Christian religion, Amen.

"This day I launched the ship, and made ready to depart in the name of God, next Thursday, for the S.E. in quest of gold and spices, as well as to discover the country." These are the words of the Admiral, who expected to sail on Thursday, but the wind being contrary, detained him till the twelfth day of November.

Monday, Nov. 12th. They sailed from the port and river *de Mares* at daybreak: they directed their course in search of an island which the Indians on board affirmed repeatedly was called *Babeque,*[14] where as they related by signs, the inhabitants collected gold at night by torchlight upon the shore, and afterwards hammered it into bars. In order to reach this island they directed to steer East by South. Having sailed eight leagues along the coast, they discovered a river, and four leagues further onward, another, very large, exceeding in size all which they had seen. The Admiral was unwilling to remain, and put into either of them, for two reasons, the first and principal one, because the wind and weather were favourable to proceed to the above-mentioned island of *Babeque;* the other was, that were there any large towns near the sea, they might easily be discovered, but in case they were far up the rivers, they could only be reached by ascending the stream in small vessels, which those of his fleet were not. A desire, therefore, not to waste time determined him not to explore these rivers, the last of which was surrounded with a well-peopled country; he named it *Rio del Sol.*[15] He states that the Sunday previous he had thought it would be well to take a few of the natives from the place where the ships lay for the purpose of carrying them to Spain, that they might acquire our language, and inform us what their country contained, besides becoming Christians and serving us at their return as interpreters, "for I have observed," says he, "that these people have no religion,

[13]Five hundred *arrobas* (twenty-five pounds) would be more than six tons.

[14]Native name for an island (probably Great Inagua) southeast of the part of Cuba that Columbus explored.

[15]Puerto del Padre.

neither are they idolaters, but are a very gentle race, without the knowledge of any iniquity; they neither kill, nor steal, nor carry weapons, and are so timid that one of our men might put a hundred of them to flight, although they will readily sport and play tricks with them. They have a knowledge that there is a God above, and are firmly persuaded that we have come from heaven. They very quickly learn such prayers as we repeat to them, and also to make the sign of the cross. Your Highnesses should therefore adopt the resolution of converting them to Christianity, in which enterprise I am of opinion that a very short space of time would suffice to gain to our holy faith multitudes of people, and to Spain great riches and immense dominions, with all their inhabitants; there being, without doubt, in these countries vast quantities of gold, for the Indians would not without cause give us such descriptions of places where the inhabitants dug it from the earth, and wore it in massy bracelets at their necks, ears, legs, and arms. Here are also pearls and precious stones, and an infinite amount of spices. In the river *de Mares,*[16] which I left last evening, there is undoubtedly a great deal of mastick, and the quantity might be increased, for the trees transplanted easily take root; they are of a lofty size, bearing leaves and fruit like the lentisk; the tree, however, is taller and has a larger leaf than the lentisk, as is mentioned by Pliny, and as I have myself observed in the island of Scio in the Archipelago. I ordered many of these trees to be tapped in order to extract the resin, but as the weather was rainy all the time I was in the river, I was unable to procure more than a very small portion, which I have preserved for your Highnesses. It is possible also that this is not the proper season for collecting it, which, it is likely, may be in the spring, when they begin to put forth their blossoms; at present the fruit upon them is nearly ripe. Great quantities of cotton might be raised here, and sold, as I think, profitably, without being carried to Spain, but to the cities of the *Great Can,* which we shall doubtless discover, as well as many others belonging to other sovereigns; these may become a source of profit to your Highnesses by trading thither with the productions of Spain and the other European countries. Here also is to be found abundance of aloe, which, however, is not a thing of very great value, but the mastick assuredly is, being met with nowhere else except in the before-mentioned island of Scio, where, if I remember rightly, it is produced to the amount of fifty thousand ducats' value in a year. The mouth of this river forms the best harbour I have yet seen, being wide, deep and free from shoals, with a fine situation for a town and fortification where ships may lie close along the shore, the land high, with a good air and fine streams of water. Yesterday a canoe came to the ship with six young men; five of them came on board, whom I ordered to be detained, and have them with me; I then sent ashore to one of the houses, and took seven women and three children: this I did that the Indians might tolerate their captivity better with their company, for it has often happened that the Portuguese have carried the natives from Guinea to Portugal for the purpose of learning their language, and when this was done and they returned with them to Guinea, expecting by reason of the good treatment they had showed them, and the presents they had given them, to find great benefit in their use, they have gone among their own people and never appeared more. Others have done

[16]Located in the Bay of Gibara, the northernmost point of Cuba reached during the first voyage.

differently, and by keeping their wives, have assured themselves of their possession. Besides, these women will be a great help to us in acquiring their language, which is the same throughout all these countries, the inhabitants keeping up a communication among the islands by means of their canoes. This is not the case in Guinea, where there are a thousand different dialects, one tribe not understanding another. This evening came on board the husband of one of the women and father of the three children, which were a boy and two girls; he intreated me to let him accompany them, which I very willingly granted; the natives whom I had taken from here were all so delighted at this as to induce me to think them his relations. He is a person of about forty-five years of age." All this is in the exact words of the Admiral; he also says that he found the weather somewhat cold, and being in the winter, thought it not advisable to prosecute his discoveries any farther towards the north. . . .

1825

from Narrative of the Third Voyage, 1498–1500

Each time I sailed from Spain to the Indies I found that when I reached a point a hundred leagues west of the Azores, the heavens, the stars, the temperature of the air and the waters of the sea abruptly changed. I very carefully verified these observations, and found that, on passing this line from north to south, the compass needle, which had previously pointed north-east, turned a whole quarter of the wind to the north-west. It was as if the seas sloped upwards on this line. I also observed that here they were full of a vegetation like pine branches loaded with fruit similar to that of the mastic. This weed is so dense that on my first voyage I thought we had reached shallows, and that the ships might run aground. We had not seen a single strand of weed before we came to that line. I noticed that when we had passed it the sea was calm and smooth, never becoming rough even in a strong wind. I found also that westwards of this line the temperature of the air was very mild and did not change from winter to summer. Here the Pole Star describes a circle of five degrees in diameter, and when it is at its lowest the Guards[1] point towards the right. It then rises continuously until they point to the left. It then stands at five degrees, and from there it sinks until they are again on the right.

On this present voyage I sailed from Spain to Madeira, from Madeira to the Canaries, and then to the Cape Verde Islands. From here, as I have already said, I followed a southward course in order to cross the Equator. On reaching a point exactly on the parallel which passes through Sierra Leone in Guinea, I found such heat and such strength in the sun's rays that I was afraid I might be burnt. Although it rained and the sky was overcast, I remained in a state of exhaustion until the Lord gave me a fair wind and the desire to sail westwards, encouraged by the thought that, on

[1]Stars in the constellation Ursa Minor used to determine the relationship between Polaris and the true North Pole.

reaching the line of which I have spoken, I should find a change in temperature. On coming to this line I immediately found very mild temperatures which became even milder as I sailed on. But I found no corresponding change in the stars. At nightfall the Pole Star stood at five degrees, with the Guards pointing straight overhead, and later, at midnight, it had risen to ten degrees, and at daybreak stood at fifteen degrees, with the Guards pointing downwards.[2] I found the sea as smooth as before, but not the same vegetation. I was greatly surprised by this behaviour of the Pole Star and spent many nights making careful observations with the quadrant, but found that the plumb line always fell to the same point. I regard this as a new discovery, and it may be established that here the heavens undergo a great change in a brief space.

I have always read that the world of land and sea is spherical. All authorities and the recorded experiments of Ptolemy and the rest, based on the eclipses of the moon and other observations made from east to west, and on the height of the Pole Star made from north to south, have constantly drawn and confirmed this picture, which they held to be true. Now, as I said, I have found such great irregularities that I have come to the following conclusions concerning the world: that it is not round as they describe it, but the shape of a pear, which is round everywhere except at the stalk, where it juts out a long way; or that it is like a round ball, on part of which is something like a woman's nipple. This point on which the protuberance stands is the highest and nearest to the sky. It lies below the Equator, and in this ocean, at the farthest point of the east, I mean by the farthest point of the east the place where all land and islands end. . . .

Ptolemy and the other geographers believed that the world was spherical and that the other hemisphere was as round as the one in which they lived, its centre lying on the island of Arin, which is below the Equator between the Arabian and Persian gulfs; and that the boundary passes over Cape St Vincent in Portugal to the west, and eastward to China and the *Seres.*[3] I do not in the least question the roundness of that hemisphere, but I affirm that the other hemisphere resembles the half of a round pear with a raised stalk, as I have said, like a woman's nipple on a round ball. Neither Ptolemy nor any of the other geographers had knowledge of this other hemisphere, which was completely unknown, but based their reasoning on the hemisphere in which they lived, which is a round sphere, as I have said.

Now that your Highnesses have commanded navigation, exploration and discovery, the nature of this other hemisphere is clearly revealed. For on this voyage I was twenty degrees north of the Equator in the latitude of Hargin[4] and the African mainland, where the people are black and the land very parched. I then went to the Cape Verde Islands, whose inhabitants are blacker still, and the farther south I went the greater the extremes. In the latitude in which I was, which is that of Sierra Leone, where the Pole Star stood at five degrees at nightfall, the people are completely black, and when I sailed westwards from there the heats remained excessive. On passing the line of which I have spoken, I found the temperatures growing milder, so

[2]The change from the five-degree circles "described" by the Pole Star earlier in this journal entry to the ten- and fifteen-degree circles noted here contributes to Columbus's conclusion about the earth's shape.

[3]Classical Roman name for the Chinese.

[4]Arguin, an island off the northern coast of Mauritania in western Africa.

that when I came to the island of Trinidad, where the Pole Star also stands at five degrees at nightfall, both there and on the mainland opposite the temperatures were extremely mild. The land and the trees were very green and as lovely as the orchards of Valencia in April, and the inhabitants were lightly built and fairer than most of the other people we had seen in the Indies. Their hair was long and straight and they were quicker, more intelligent and less cowardly. The sun was in Virgo above their heads and ours. All this is attributable to the very mild climate in those regions, and this in its turn to the fact that this land stands highest on the world's surface, being nearest to the sky, as I have said. This confirms my belief that the world has this variation of shape which I have described, and which lies in this hemisphere that contains the Indies and the Ocean Sea, and stretches below the Equator. This argument is greatly supported by the fact that the sun, when Our Lord made it, was at the first point of the east; in other words the first light was here in the east, where the world stands at its highest. Although Aristotle believed that the Antarctic Pole, or the land beneath it, is the highest part of the world and nearest to the sky, other philosophers contest it, saying that the land beneath the Arctic Pole is the highest. This argument shows that they knew one part of the world to be higher and nearer to the sky than the rest. It did not strike them however that, for the reasons of shape that I have set down, this part might lie below the Equator. And no wonder, since they had no certain information about this other hemisphere, only vague knowledge based on deduction. No one had ever entered it or gone in search of it until now when your Highnesses commanded me to explore and discover these seas and lands. . . .

Holy Scripture testifies that Our Lord made the earthly Paradise in which he placed the Tree of Life. From it there flowed four main rivers: the Ganges in India, the Tigris and the Euphrates in Asia, which cut through a mountain range and form Mesopotamia and flow into Persia, and the Nile, which rises in Ethiopia and flows into the sea at Alexandria.

I do not find and have never found any Greek or Latin writings which definitely state the worldly situation of the earthly Paradise, nor have I seen any world map which establishes its position except by deduction. Some place it at the source of the Nile in Ethiopia. But many people have travelled in these lands and found nothing in the climate or altitude to confirm this theory, or to prove that the waters of the Flood which covered, etc., etc. . . . reached there. Some heathens tried to show by argument that it was in the Fortunate Islands (which are the Canaries); and St Isidore, Bede, Strabo, the Master of Scholastic History,[5] St Ambrose and Scotus and all learned theologians agree that the earthly Paradise is in the East, etc.

I have already told what I have learnt about this hemisphere and its shape, and I believe that, if I pass below the Equator, on reaching these higher regions I shall find a much cooler climate and a greater difference in the stars and waters. Not that I believe it possible to sail to the extreme summit or that it is covered by water, or that it is even possible to go there. For I believe that the earthly Paradise lies here, which no one can enter except by God's leave. I believe that this land which your Highnesses have commanded me to discover is very great, and that there are many

[5]Twelfth-century theologian Petrus Comestor, author of *Historia Scolastica.*

other lands in the south of which there have never been reports. I do not hold that the earthly Paradise has the form of a rugged mountain, as it is shown in pictures, but that it lies at the summit of what I have described as the stalk of a pear, and that by gradually approaching it one begins, while still at a great distance, to climb towards it. As I have said, I do not believe that anyone can ascend to the top. I do believe, however, that, distant though it is, these waters may flow from there to this place which I have reached, and form this lake. All this provides great evidence of the earthly Paradise, because the situation agrees with the beliefs of those holy and wise theologians and all the signs strongly accord with this idea. For I have never read or heard of such a quantity of fresh water flowing so close to the salt and flowing into it, and the very temperate climate provides a further confirmation. If this river does not flow out of the earthly Paradise, the marvel is still greater. For I do not believe that there is so great and deep a river anywhere in the world.

1969

Cluster: Aesthetics and Criticism—Paradigms of Cultural Encounters

Changing conceptions of encounters between Europeans and Native Americans, as well as shifting ideas of what constitutes an encounter, engender multiple versions of American literary history. As ideas of frontier and encounter are re-envisioned, so too is the canon of American literature; formerly neglected texts come to be seen as important or essential, while others fall out of favor. The belief in an expanding frontier in which Europeans met and displaced Native Americans in a linear movement from East to West led to an emphasis on New England texts and Puritan experiences as the originary foundations of the American experience and literary legacy. Critics like Philip Gura raised questions about New England's monolithic presence in literary studies: "If the relationship between discourses and power really fascinates so many of us in early American literature, we had better move beyond the shoals of Cape Cod." New ideas about what constitutes American literature encourage us to travel not only beyond New England but also across national and geographic boundaries.

The first acquaintance of cultures includes a meeting of languages and identities, complicating our notions of a national literature. As William Spengemann suggests, American literature cannot be contained within its linguistic roots, because its language is not American but English, linking its history and development to England and other English-speaking countries. Furthermore, he points out that "Americans have written in many languages, all of which (with the exception of the indigenous tongues) transcend the political and physical boundaries of America and form distinct linguistic worlds, each with its own history and geography." The conceptual frameworks of critics like Gura and Spengemann made way for a proliferation of new models of cultural encounter and for increased attention to previously ignored or marginalized narratives. Through various models of cultural contact, critics have encouraged us to rethink our belief in singular origins and our definitions of America and literature, yielding a more expansive and inclusive literary canon.

Frederick Jackson Turner articulated the deeply rooted myth of westward expansion and frontier in his famous essay, "The Significance of the Frontier in American History." The frontier myth equates the movement of European settlers westward with the proliferation of civilization, technology, and destiny for European Americans. Since Turner published his essay in 1893, literary, historical, and cultural critics have discussed the limitations of Turner's thesis, recognizing that this myth speaks from a singularly European point of view, neglects the land's diverse Native American communities, gives credence to the violence of expansion in the name of "civilization" and "progress," and reinforces a linear and uncomplicated notion of encounter. Subsequent critics have sought to reopen the frontier and redefine it, emphasizing the ways in which people of different lives and ideas meet each other and negotiate business, enforce ideologies, adapt beliefs, and respond to oppression.

All intercultural meetings on the American continent cannot be understood through a single paradigm. Andew Wiget calls attention to the uniqueness of each encounter and the enormous differences that characterize meetings between specific tribes and groups of Europeans. His model emphasizes the centrality of stories and traditions and the intertextual as well as multicultural nature of encounter. Each encounter includes a collision of stories that represent sometimes incompatible, deeply held beliefs and world views. During migration, Wiget explains, literature is a "means of both legitimating and accounting for [people's] own sense of their present identity, not only in terms of how they differ from other groups but in terms of how they resemble them." Reading both familiar and unfamiliar stories of migration and origin helps us to envision how various communities "understand the very dynamic of the migration experience in radically opposed ways."

Wiget and Annette Kolodny, like William Spengemann, have focused on language as a tool of mediation and a chronicle of hybridity and change during encounter. Kolodny rejects the traditional notion of the frontier, with its ahistorical connotations of unpopulated land and "uncivilzed" people and favors the concept of *la frontera,* or borderlands, a "liminal landscape of changing meanings on which distinct human cultures first encounter one another's 'otherness' and appropriate, accommodate, or domesticate it through language." Through this model of encounter, we understand the frontier not as a line drawn across the continent, dividing East from West, but as an expanse of land and array of languages producing multiple encounters that take place sporadically rather than progressively, changing lives and cultures through mediation.

Like Kolodny's borderlands, Mary Louise Pratt's "contact zones" express the vastness and multiplicity of early American encounters. She defines such places as "social spaces where disparate cultures meet, clash, and grapple with each other, often in highly asymmetrical relations of domination and subordination—like colonialism, slavery, or their aftermaths as they are lived out across the globe today." Pratt emphasizes the inequality of power relations in colonial conquest and encourages us to consider the intersections of conquest, colonialism, imperialism, and slavery, all brought together in travel narratives. Rather than presenting a unifying theory, though, Pratt offers a way to recognize the disunity and differences in how communities meet each other, react, and change throughout their interactions. The contact zone is an improvisational space of activity and transformation in which each group reconstitutes its own identity through encounter.

Paul Gilroy's discussion of encounter travels the furthest from Turner's frontier in the sense that it departs from the land as a determination of and influence on human encounter, thereby transgressing national and geographic borders. The ship, recalling the Middle Passage as well as later trade and travel, serves as an icon of encounter based on economy, politics, race, and industry. Gilroy writes,

> *A concern with the Atlantic as a cultural and political system has been forced on black historiograhy and intellectual history by the economic and historical matrix in which plantation slavery—capitalism with its clothes off—was one special moment. The fractal patterns of cultural and political exchange and transformation that we try and specify through manifestly inadequate theoretical terms like creolisation and syncretism indicate how both enthnicities and political cultures have been made anew in ways that are significant not simply for the peoples of the Caribbean but for Europe, for Africa, especially Liberia and Sierra Leone, and of course, for black America. (15)*

By focusing on how encounters of ethnicities and races create and define the nation and its literature, Gilroy suggests that we pay too little attention to how these encounters engender new identities and historical trends in multiple communities and political spaces. Gilroy takes a wider view of encounter that enables literary historians to see the oppressive meeting of Africans and Europeans as a network of interactions that changed and continue to influence developing identities in the Americas, Europe and Africa.

The "trans-American imaginary," described by Paula M. L. Moya and Ramón Saldívar, takes our border crossings in the often neglected directions of north and south. They write, "Indeed, the influences on American literature of nations other than England and idioms that do not originate in the English language have been unevenly and inadequately incorporated into the larger narrative of American literary historiography." Emerging from the active and influential field of Latino and Latina studies, these scholars contribute their knowledge of writers whose perspectives come from positions that are both "marginal" and "dual cultural" to create a new notion of American literature that is both intercultural and transnational.

What was once a narrow, ethnocentric, and unidirectional line of inquiry is now a complex network of human relationships, necessary terrain for understanding American language and literature.

WORKS CITED

Paul Gilroy, *The Black Atlantic: Modernity and Double Consciousness* (Cambridge, MA: Harvard University Press, 1993); Philip F. Gura, "Turning Our World Upside Down: Reconceiving Early American Literature," *American Literature* 63.1 (March 1991): 104–112; Annette Kolodny, "Letting Go Our Grand Obsessions: Notes Toward a New Literary History of the American Frontiers," *American Literature* 64.1 (March 1992): 1–18; Paula M. L. Moya and Ramón Saldívar, "Fictions of the Trans-American Imaginary," *Modern Fiction Studies* 49 (Spring 2003): 1–18; Mary Louise Pratt, *Imperial Eyes: Travel Writing and Transculturation* (London: Routledge, 1992); William C. Spengemann, "American Things / Literary Things: The Problem of American Literary History," *American Literature* 57.3 (October 1985): 456–481; Frederick Jackson Turner, "The Significance of the Frontier in American History" (Washington: Government Printing Office, 1894); Andrew Wiget, "Reading Against the Grain: Origin Stories and American Literary History," *American Literary History* 3.2 (Summer 1991): 209–231.

Frederick Jackson Turner 1861–1932

from The Significance of the Frontier in American History

The frontier is the line of most rapid and effective Americanization. The wilderness masters the colonist. It finds him a European in dress, industries, tools, modes of travel, and thought. It takes him from the railroad car and puts him in the birch canoe. It strips him of the garments of civilization, and arrays him in the hunting shirt and moccasin. It puts him in the log cabin of the Cherokee and the Iroquois, and runs an Indian palisade around him. Before long he has gone to planting Indian corn and plowing with a sharp stick; he shouts the war cry and takes the scalp in orthodox Indian fashion. In short, at the frontier the environment is at first too strong for the man. He must accept the conditions which it furnishes, or perish, and so he fits himself into the Indian clearings and follows the Indian trails. Little by little he transforms the wilderness, but the outcome is not the old Europe. . . . The fact is that here is a new product that is American. *As successive terminal moraines result from successive glaciations, so each frontier leaves its traces behind it, and when it becomes a settled area the region still partakes of the frontier characteristics.* Thus the advance of the frontier has meant a steady movement away from the influence of Europe, a steady growth of independence on American lines. And to study this advance, the men who grew up under these conditions, and the political economic, and social results of it, is to study the really American part of our history.

1893

Andrew Wiget

from Reading Against the Grain: Origin Stories and American Literary History

Though cognizant of more proximate historical causes, the New Englanders viewed the Indian wars in biblical terms, either extending the Exodus subtext to identify their opponents as Canaanites to be displaced from the Promised Land or redefining them in New Testament terms as devils come out of the "howling desart" to afflict the backsliders and test the faithful. Despite the efforts of John Eliot, the "praying Indians" were few and, for the most part, unfavored. The reality of frequent bloody, if small-scale, encounters undergirded the ideological predisposition against Indians. The Spanish, on the other hand, encountered widely scattered populations of Indians concentrated into "pueblos" or towns, with complex rituals, visible social structure, and developed agriculture—Indians, in other words, who corresponded much more to the Virgilian picture of fallen greatness. This reality supported the policy of Catholic countries to convert rather than conquer. . . . Catholic policy was based not on Calvin's view of a depraved humanity and on Exodus typology but on the reason and the creation theology of Genesis.

1991

Annette Kolodny

from Letting Go Our Grand Obsessions: Notes Toward a New Literary History of the American Frontiers

Although we have only recently marked the one-hundredth anniversary of the supposed closing of the frontier, I am recommending that we reopen it, thematizing frontier as a multiplicity of ongoing first encounters over time and land, rather than as linear chronology of successive discoveries and discrete settlements. Noting the passionately contested meanings of this year's five-hundredth anniversary of Columbus's first landing, I am asking that we once and for all eschew the myth of origins—with its habits of either fetishizing or marginalizing race, place, and ethnicity—and, by returning to serious study of the frontier, adopt a model of history that privileges no group's priority and no region's primacy. In the frontier literary history I have projected here, there can be no Ur-landscape because there are so many borderlands, and, over time, even the same site may serve for seriatim first encounters. There can be no paradigmatic first contact because there are so many different kinds of first encounters. And there can be no single overarching story.

1992

Mary Louise Pratt

from Imperial Eyes: Travel Writing and Transculturation

In the attempt to suggest a dialectic and historicized approach to travel writing, I have manufactured some terms and concepts along the way. One coinage that recurs throughout the book is the term "contact zone," which I use to refer to the space of colonial encounters, the space in which people geographically and historically separated come into contact with each other and establish ongoing relations, usually involving conditions of coercion, radical inequality, and intractable conflict. I borrow the term "contact" here from its use in linguistics, where the term contact language refers to improvised languages that develop among speakers of different native languages who need to communicate with each other consistently, usually in the context of trade. Such languages begin as pidgins, and are called creoles when they come to have native speakers of their own. Like the societies of the contact zone, such languages are commonly regarded as chaotic, barbarous, lacking in structure. . . . "Contact Zone" in my discussion is often synonymous with "colonial frontier." But while the latter term is grounded within a European expansionist perspective (the frontier is a frontier only with respect to Europe), "contact zone" is an attempt to invoke the spatial and temporal copresence of subjects previously separated by geographic and historical disjunctures, and whose trajectories now intersect. By using the term "contact," I aim to foreground the interactive, improvisational dimensions of colonial encounters so easily ignored or suppressed by diffusionist accounts of conquest and domination. A "contact" perspective emphasizes how subjects are constituted in and by their relations to each other. It treats the relations among colonizers and colonized, or travelers and "travelees," not in terms of separateness or apartheid, but in terms of copresence, interaction, interlocking understandings and practices, often within radically asymmetrical relations of power.

1992

Paul Gilroy

from The Black Atlantic: Modernity and Double Consciousness

If this appears to be little more than a roundabout way of saying that the reflexive cultures and consciousness of the European settlers and those of the Africans they enslaved, the "Indians" they slaughtered, and the Asians they indentured were not, even in situations of the most extreme brutality, sealed off hermetically from each other, then so be it. This seems as though it ought to be an obvious and self-evident observation, but its stark character has been systematically obscured by commentators from all sides of political opinion. Regardless of their affiliation to the right, left, or centre, groups have fallen back on the idea of cultural nationalism, on the overintegrated conceptions of culture which present immutable, ethnic differences as an absolute break in the histories and experiences of "black" and "white" people. Against this choice stands another, more difficult option: the theorisation of creolisation, métissage, mestizaje, and hybridity. From the viewpoint of ethnic absolutism, this would be a litany of pollution and impurity. These terms are rather unsatisfactory ways of naming the processes of cultural mutation and restless (dis)continuity that exceed racial discourse and avoid capture by its agents.

1993

Paula M. L. Moya and Ramón Saldívar

from Fictions of the Trans-American Imaginary

The trans-American imaginary is "imaginary" to the extent that it figures a very real but fundamentally different snytax of codes, images, and icons, as well as the tacit assumptions, convictions, and beliefs that seek to bind together the varieties of American national discourses. The transnational imaginary is thus to be understood as a chronotope, a contact zone, that is both historical and geographical and that is populated by transnational persons whose lives form an experiential region within which singularly delineated notions of political, social, and cultural identity do not suffice. As we understand it, the trans-American imaginary is an alternative and epistemologically valuable way of describing our place in the world and the literature we teach. It is an interpretive framework that yokes together North and South America instead of New England and England. And although we are not at this point suggesting that this alternative framework will always produce more illuminating interpretations of American literature, we do contend that unless we make more visible the unequal relations of domination that exist in this hemisphere, our conception of American literary history will remain both incomplete and inadequate. A literary historiography that ignores those hemispheric relations effectively obscures certain historical events and makes opaque certain political interests. It has the effect, finally, of devaluing certain kinds of literature—literatures not written in English, literatures written in unofficial vernaculars, literatures that look South and West instead of North and East.

2003

Alvar Núñez Cabeza de Vaca 1490?–1556?

Álvar Núñez Cabeza de Vaca's eight-year ordeal as a lost man in North America belongs, on one level, to a distant era: that of Spanish conquistadors, first contact between Europeans and Native Americans, the exploration of and ignorance about the New World. On another level, however, Cabeza de Vaca's experiences reflect universal, timeless anxieties: the fear of death, of separation from the familiar, of the unknown. This combination of historical specificity and emotional accessibility makes *La Relación* (1542), Cabeza de Vaca's account of his role in the disastrous Spanish expedition of 1527 and of the years he spent searching for a way home, one of the most compelling texts about the Old World/New World interface. It also signals the first exploration of a new literary subject—America—and the beginnings of uniquely American forms of literary expression—such as the captivity narrative—derived from European traditions but responding to novel landscapes, peoples, religions, and circumstances.

Cabeza de Vaca was born in Spain to a prominent family and spent his young adulthood in service to the crown, eventually receiving appointment as treasurer on an expedition led by Pánfilo de Narváez, who intended to found a colony on the Gulf Coast of North America. Narváez and his contemporaries were woefully misinformed about the geography of the region they called *Florida,* believing the Florida peninsula to be only a few days' march from Spanish holdings in Mexico. Upon landing on the coast of the peninsula in 1528. Narváez sent almost the entire party of 300 men ashore, intending to reconnnoiter the land as his ships followed the coastline. This decision, apparently opposed by Cabeza de Vaca and other expedition officials, proved disastrous. The party and ships were soon separated, never to be reunited. Beset by Native Americans, stymied by the difficult terrain, unable to find sufficient food, and rapidly reducing in number due to accident, disease, and Native hostilities, the group constructed five rudimentary barges and put to sea. Two barges containing about eighty men eventually washed up on a coastal island near present-day Galveston, Texas, Narváez's craft among the lost after he abandoned his command. Only four of these men—including Cabeza de Vaca and an African-born slave of one of the surviving Spaniards—endured the nine-year odyssey and found their way overland through Texas and the Southwest to Spanish settlements in northwest Mexico.

La Relación, composed by Cabeza de Vaca shortly after the journey ended in 1536 but not published until 1542, reflects the complexities of interactions between Native peoples and Europeans in a terrain that, for the Spaniards, was not only harsh but also bewilderingly foreign. Cabeza de Vaca recounts his initial condescending attitude toward Natives, his own and his compatriots' total reliance on Native generosity; their enslavement by Natives in Texas; and, finally, his respect for the Native peoples he lived among. Stripped of all material possessions that linked him to the Old World and challenged psychologically and religiously by his predicament, Cabeza de Vaca builds a new identity for himself, becoming a trader and healer among the Natives, using Catholic prayer and symbology as commodities in exchange for food, shelter, and protection. When he and his compatriots finally encounter a group of Spaniards on a slave-taking foray, they have acculturated to such an extent that they have a difficult time convincing the soldiers of their identity. Cabeza de Vaca entered Florida as a conquistador and left Mexico, by his own account, a changed man, opposing the enslavement of Natives and arguing for recognition of their humanity.

Historians, anthropologists, biologists, and geologists have mined *La Relación* for a glimpse into precontact life ways and landscapes in Florida, Texas, and the Southwest. Literary critics have hailed the text as the first American manifestation of both the captivity narrative and the immigrant story and recognized it as a progenitor of the mestizo literary tradition in the New World. Cabeza de Vaca's narrative places suffering and loss in the context of God's divine plan, echoing the form of a Christian conversion tale, the first in the United States literary tradition. With this scholarly attention has come controversy. Historians debate the accuracy of reconstructions of Cabeza de Vaca's route and academics question the accuracy of Cabeza de Vaca's representations of Native peoples, of his fellow Spaniards, and, utimately, of himself. In the Prologue, a letter addressed to the Spanish king, Cabeza de Vaca turns apparent failure into success by positioning himself as a loyal subject of the crown and characterizing his experience as the invaluable commodity. He asserts that while he did not return from the New World with gold or other precious metals, he has brought the king something at least as valuable, if not more so—information about the New World, thus setting the stage for more profitable exploitation of the lands and peoples he illuminates. Some critics read the entire text as a justification for the author's actions with an eye toward securing a future governmental placement, which casts doubt on the genuineness of his altered feelings toward Native Americans. Indeed, Cabeza de Vaca was appointed governor of the territory that would become Paraguay but was accused of misrule, convicted in Spain, and banished to North Africa, although he was eventually cleared of the charges and allowed to return to Spain. Some scholars regard this troubled career as evidence that the new attitude toward Native peoples he expresses in *La Relación* had truly taken root in Spain, making his participation in oppression of Natives problematic.

Ultimately, it may be best to regard *La Relación* as the hybrid text it is—part anthropological observation, part historical narrative, part environmental catalogue, all filtered through traditional literary forms and signaling the beginnings of uniquely American versions of textual representation. As with travel narratives in general—of which *La Relación* is a particularly dramatic example—readers must approach such a seemingly straightforward text with an awareness of the factors that influenced its composition and reception, placing Cabeza de Vaca's emotional relation in larger contexts.

Katherine E. Ledford
Appalachian State University

PRIMARY WORK

Relation of Alvar Nuñez Cabeza de Vaca, trans. Buckingham Smith, 1871; rpt. 1966. (First published in Seville in 1542.)

from Relation of Alvar Núñez Cabeza de Vaca

Prologue

Holy, Imperial, Catholic Majesty.[1]

Among as many princes as we know there have been in the world, I think none could be found whom men have tried to serve with truer will or greater diligence and desire than we see men honoring Your Majesty today. It is quite evident that this is not without great cause and reason; nor are men so ignorant that all of them blindly and arbitrarily pursue this course, since we see not only countrymen, whom faith and duty oblige to do this, but even foreigners strive to exceed their efforts. But even when the desire and will of all makes them equal in this matter, beyond the particular advantage that any one can secure for himself, there is a very great disparity not caused by the shortcoming of any one of them, but only by fortune, or more certainly through no fault of one's own, but only by the will and judgment of God, where it happens that one may come away with more notable services than he expected, while to another everything occurs so to the contrary that he cannot demonstrate any greater witness to his intention than his diligence, and even this is sometimes so obscured that it cannot make itself evident. For myself I can say that on the expedition that by command of Your Majesty I made to the mainland, well I thought that my deeds and services would be as illustrious and self-evident as those of my ancestors, and that I would not have any need to speak in order to be counted among those who with complete fidelity and great solicitude administer and carry out the mandates of Your Majesty, and whom you favor. But since neither my counsel nor diligence prevailed in order that the endeavor upon which we were embarked be completed as service to Your Majesty, and since no expedition of as many as have gone to those lands ever saw itself in such grave dangers or had such a wretched and disastrous end as that which God permitted us to suffer on account of our sins, I had no opportunity to perform greater service than this, which is to bring to Your Majesty an account of all that I was able to observe and learn in the nine years that I walked lost and naked through many and very strange lands, as much regarding the locations of the lands and provinces and the distances among them, as with respect to the foodstuffs and animals that are produced in them, and the diverse customs of many and very barbarous peoples with whom I conversed and lived, plus all the other particularities that I could come to know and understand, so that in some manner Your Majesty may be served. Because although the hope that I had of coming out from among them was always very little, my care and effort to remember everything in detail was always very great. This I did so that if at some time our Lord God should wish to bring me to the place where I am now,[2] I would be able to bear witness to my will and serve Your Majesty, inasmuch as the account of it all is, in my opinion, information not trivial for those who in your name might go to conquer those lands and at the same time bring them to knowledge of the true faith and the true Lord and

[1]Charles V, Holy Roman emperor (1519–1558), king of Spain (as Charles I, 1516–1556).
[2]Castile.

service to Your Majesty. I wrote all this with such sure knowledge that although some very novel things may be read in it, very difficult for some to believe, they can absolutely give them credence and be assured that I am in everything brief rather than lengthy, and it will suffice for this purpose to have offered it to Your Majesty as such, for which I ask that it be received in the name of service, because this alone is what a man who came away naked could carry out with him.

from Chapter VII
The Character of the Country[3]

The country where we came on shore to this town and region of Apalachen, is for the most part level, the ground of sand and stiff earth. Throughout are immense trees and open woods, in which are walnut, laurel and another tree called liquidamber, cedars, savins, evergreen oaks, pines, red-oaks and palmitos like those of Spain. There are many lakes, great and small, over every part of it; some troublesome of fording, on account of depth and the great number of trees lying throughout them. Their beds are sand. The lakes in the country of Apalachen are much larger than those we found before coming there.

In this Province are many maize fields; and the houses are scattered as are those of the Gelves. There are deer of three kinds, rabbits, hares, bears, lions and other wild beasts. Among them we saw an animal with a pocket on its belly, in which it carries its young until they know how to seek food; and if it happen that they should be out feeding and any one come near, the mother will not run until she has gathered them in together. The country is very cold. It has fine pastures for herds. Birds are of various kinds. Geese in great numbers. Ducks, mallards, royal-ducks, fly-catchers, night-herons and partridges abound. We saw many falcons, gerfalcons, sparrow-hawks, merlins, and numerous other fowl.

Two hours after our arrival at Apalachen, the Indians who had fled from there came in peace to us, asking for their women and children, whom we released; but the detention of a cacique by the Governor produced great excitement, in consequence of which they returned for battle early the next day [June 26], and attacked us with such promptness and alacrity that they succeeded in setting fire to the houses in which we were. As we sallied they fled to the lakes near by, because of which and the large maize fields, we could do them no injury, save in the single instance of one Indian, whom we killed. The day following, others came against us from a town on the opposite side of the lake, and attacked us as the first had done, escaping in the same way, except one who was also slain.

We were in the town twenty-five days [July 19], in which time we made three incursions, and found the country very thinly peopled and difficult to travel for the bad passages, the woods and lakes. We inquired of the cacique we kept and the natives we brought with us, who were the neighbors and enemies of these Indians, as to the nature of the country, the character and condition of the inhabitants, of the food and all other matters concerning it. Each answered apart from the rest, that the largest

[3]We pick up Cabeza de Vaca's journey in June, 1528, in northern Florida.

town in all that region was Apalachen; the people beyond were less numerous and poorer, the land little occupied, and the inhabitants much scattered; that thenceforward were great lakes, dense forests, immense deserts and solitudes. We then asked touching the region towards the south, as to the towns and subsistence in it. They said that in keeping such a direction, journeying nine days, there was a town called Aute, the inhabitants whereof had much maize, beans and pumpkins, and being near the sea, they had fish, and that those people were their friends.

In view of the poverty of the land, the unfavorable accounts of the population and of everything else we heard, the Indians making continual war upon us, wounding our people and horses at the places where they went to drink, shooting from the lakes with such safety to themselves that we could not retaliate, killing a lord of Tescuco,[4] named Don Pedro,[5] whom the Commissary brought with him, we determined to leave that place and go in quest of the sea, and the town of Aute of which we were told. . . .

The Indians we had so far seen in Florida are all archers. They go naked, are large of body, and appear at a distance like giants. They are of admirable proportions, very spare and of great activity and strength. The bows they use are as thick as the arm, of eleven or twelve palms in length, which they will discharge at two hundred paces with so great precision that they miss nothing.

Having got through this passage, at the end of a league we arrived at another of the same character, but worse, as it was longer, being half a league in extent. This we crossed freely, without interruption from the Indians, who, as they had spent on the former occasion their store of arrows, had nought with which they dared venture to engage us. Going through a similar passage the next day [July 21], I discovered the trail of persons ahead, of which I gave notice to the Governor, who was in the rear guard, so that though the Indians came upon us, as we were prepared they did no harm. After emerging upon the plain they followed us, and we went back on them in two directions. Two we killed, and they wounded me and two or three others. Coming to woods we could do them no more injury, nor make them further trouble. . . .

from Chapter VIII
We Go from Aute

The next morning we left Aute,[6] and traveled all day before coming to the place I had visited. The journey was extremely arduous. There were not horses enough to carry the sick, who went on increasing in numbers day by day, and we knew of no cure. It was piteous and painful to witness our perplexity and distress. We saw on our arrival how small were the means for advancing farther. There was not any where to go; and if there had been, the people were unable to move forward, the greater part being ill, and those were few who could be on duty. I cease here to relate more of this, because any one may suppose what would occur in a country so remote and

[4]Tezcoco, in Mexico City.

[5]Thought to be the brother of an heir to the Aztec throne, Ixtlilxochitl, dispossessed by his own father. The brothers allied themselves with Cortés against the Aztecs, and Don Pedro commanded an army in the final battle for Mexico City.

[6]The party found their way to Aute, yet found no Christians there, as had been hoped, and left the town August 3.

malign, so destitute of all resource, whereby either to live in it or go out of it; but most certain assistance is in God, our Lord, on whom we never failed to place reliance. One thing occurred, more afflicting to us than all the rest, which was, that of the persons mounted, the greater part commenced secretly to plot, hoping to secure a better fate for themselves by abandoning the Governor and the sick, who were in a state of weakness and prostration. But, as among them were many hidalgos and persons of gentle condition, they would not permit this to go on, without informing the Governor and the officers of your Majesty; and as we showed them the deformity of their purpose, and placed before them the moment when they should desert their captain, and those who were ill and feeble, and above all the disobedience to the orders of your Majesty, they determined to remain, and that whatever might happen to one should be the lot of all, without any forsaking the rest.

After the accomplishment of this, the Governor called them all to him, and of each apart he asked advice as to what he should do to get out of a country so miserable, and seek that assistance elsewhere which could not here be found, a third part of the people being very sick, and the number increasing every hour; for we regarded it as certain that we should all become so, and could pass out of it only through death, which from its coming in such a place was to us all the more terrible. These, with many other embarrassments being considered, and entertaining many plans, we coincided in one great project, extremely difficult to put in operation, and that was to build vessels in which we might go away. This appeared impossible to every one: we knew not how to construct, nor were there tools, nor iron, nor forge, nor tow, nor resin, nor rigging; finally, no one thing of so many that are necessary, nor any man who had a knowledge of their manufacture; and, above all, there was nothing to eat, while building, for those who should labor. Reflecting on all this, we agreed to think of the subject with more deliberation, and the conversation dropped from that day, each going his way, commending our course to God, our Lord, that he would direct it as should best serve Him. . . .

During this time some went gathering shell-fish in the coves and creeks of the sea, at which employment the Indians twice attacked them and killed ten men in sight of the camp, without our being able to afford succor.[7] We found their corpses traversed from side to side with arrows; and for all some had on good armor, it did not give adequate protection or security against the nice and powerful archery of which I have spoken. According to the declaration of our pilots under oath, from the entrance to which we had given the name *Bahía de la Cruz* to this place, we had traveled two hundred and eighty leagues or thereabout. Over all that region we had not seen a single mountain, and had no information of any whatsoever.

Before we embarked there died more than forty men of disease and hunger, without enumerating those destroyed by the Indians. By the twenty-second of the month of September, the horses had been consumed, one only remaining; and on that day we embarked in the following order: In the boat of the Governor went forty-nine men; in another, which he gave to the Comptroller and the Commissary, went as many others; the third, he gave to Captain Alonzo del Castillo and Andrés Dorantes, with forty-eight men; and another he gave to two captains, Tellez and

[7]The group was able to make ready five small boats.

Peñalosa, with forty-seven men. The last was given to the Assessor and myself, with forty-nine men. After the provisions and clothes had been taken in, not over a span of the gunwales remained above water; and more than this, the boats were so crowded that we could not move: so much can necessity do, which drove us to hazard our lives in this manner, running into a turbulent sea, not a single one who went, having a knowledge of navigation.

from Chapter X
The Assault from the Indians

[November 2]I found myself in thirty fathoms. . . .[8] [The Governor] asked me what I thought we should do. I told him we ought to join the boat which went in advance, and by no means to leave her; and, the three being together, we must keep on our way to where God should be pleased to lead. He answered saying that could not be done, because the boat was far to sea and he wished to reach the shore. . . . [B]ut the Governor having in his boat the healthiest of all the men, we could not by any means hold with or follow her. Seeing this, I asked him to give me a rope from his boat, that I might be enabled to keep up with him; but he answered me that he would do no little, if they, as they were, should be able to reach the land that night. I said to him, that since he saw the feeble strength we had to follow him, and do what he ordered, he must tell me how he would that I should act. He answered that it was no longer a time in which one should command another; but that each should do what he thought best to save his own life; that he so intended to act; and saying this, he departed with his boat. . . .

Near the dawn of day [November 5] . . . a wave took us, that knocked our boat out of the water the distance of the throw of a crowbar, and from the violence with which she struck, nearly all the people who were in her like dead, were roused to consciousness. Finding themselves near the shore, they began to move on hands and feet, crawling to land into some ravines.

from Chapter XI
Of What Befel Lope de Oviedo with the Indians

As it appeared to us [Oviedo] was gone a long time, we sent two men that they should look to see what might have happened. They met him near by, and saw that three Indians with bows and arrows followed and were calling to him, while he, in the same way, was beckoning them on. Thus he arrived where we were, the natives remaining a little way back, seated on the shore. Half an hour after, they were supported by one hundred other Indian bowmen, who if they were not large, our fears made giants of them. . . . We gave them beads and hawk-bells, and each of them gave me an arrow, which is a pledge of friendship. They told us by signs that they would return in the morning and bring us something to eat, as at the time they had nothing.

[8]The group neared the entrance to the Mississippi River by November 2, 1528.

from Chapter XXI
Our Cure of Some of the Afflicted

[September 1528: Cabeza de Vaca and his mates, separated from Narváez, have been shipwrecked off the Louisiana/Texas coast, captured and forced to serve the Indians.]

That same night of our arrival, some Indians came to Castillo and told him that they had great pain in the head, begging him to cure them. After he made over them the sign of the cross, and commended them to God, they instantly said that all the pain had left, and went to their houses bringing us prickly pears,[9] with a piece of venison, a thing to us little known. As the report of Castillo's performances spread, many came to us that night sick, that we should heal them, each bringing a piece of venison, until the quantity became so great we knew not where to dispose of it. We gave many thanks to God, for every day went on increasing his compassion and his gifts. After the sick were attended to, they began to dance and sing, making themselves festive, until sunrise; and because of our arrival, the rejoicing was continued for three days.

When these were ended, we asked the Indians about the country farther on, the people we should find in it, and of the subsistence there. They answered us, that throughout all the region prickly pear plants abounded; but the fruit was now gathered and all the people had gone back to their houses. They said the country was very cold, and there were few skins. Reflecting on this, and that it was already winter, we resolved to pass the season with these Indians.

Five days after our arrival, all the Indians went off, taking us with them to gather more prickly pears, where there were other peoples speaking different tongues. After walking five days in great hunger, since on the way was no manner of fruit, we came to a river and put up our houses. We then went to seek the product of certain trees, which is like peas. As there are no paths in the country, I was detained some time. The others returned, and coming to look for them in the dark, I got lost. Thank God I found a burning tree, and in the warmth of it passed the cold of that night. In the morning, loading myself with sticks, and taking two brands with me, I returned to seek them. In this manner I wandered five days, ever with my fire and load; for if the wood had failed me where none could be found, as many parts are without any, though I might have sought sticks elsewhere, there would have been no fire to kindle them. This was all the protection I had against cold, while walking naked as I was born. Going to the low woods near the rivers, I prepared myself for the night, stopping in them before sunset. I made a hole in the ground and threw in fuel which the trees abundantly afforded, collected in good quantity from those that were fallen and dry. About the whole I made four fires, in the form of a cross, which I watched and made up from time to time. I also gathered some bundles of the coarse straw that there abounds, with which I covered myself in the hole. In this way I was sheltered at night from cold. On one occasion while I slept, the fire fell upon the straw, when it began to blaze so rapidly that notwithstanding the haste I made to get out of it, I

[9]Fruit of the cactus.

carried some marks on my hair of the danger to which I was exposed. All this while I tasted not a mouthful, nor did I find anything I could eat. My feet were bare and bled a good deal. Through the mercy of God, the wind did not blow from the north in all this time, otherwise I should have died.

At the end of the fifth day I arrived on the margin of a river, where I found the Indians, who with the Christians, had considered me dead, supposing that I had been stung by a viper. All were rejoiced to see me, and most so were my companions. They said that up to that time they had struggled with great hunger, which was the cause of their not having sought me. At night, all gave me of their prickly pears, and the next morning we set out for a place where they were in large quantity, with which we satisfied our great craving, the Christians rendering thanks to our Lord that he had ever given us his aid.

from Chapter XXIV
Customs of the Indians of That Country

From the Island of Malhado to this land, all the Indians whom we saw have the custom from the time in which their wives find themselves pregnant, of not sleeping with them until two years after they have given birth. The children are suckled until the age of twelve years, when they are old enough to get support for themselves. We asked why they reared them in this manner; and they said because of the great poverty of the land, it happened many times, as we witnessed, that they were two or three days without eating, sometimes four, and consequently, in seasons of scarcity, the children were allowed to suckle, that they might not famish; otherwise those who lived would be delicate having little strength.

If any one chance to fall sick in the desert, and cannot keep up with the rest, the Indians leave him to perish, unless it be a son or a brother; him they will assist, even to carrying on their back. It is common among them all to leave their wives when there is no conformity, and directly they connect themselves with whom they please. This is the course of the men who are childless; those who have children, remain with their wives and never abandon them. When they dispute and quarrel in their towns, they strike each other with the fists, fighting until exhausted, and then separate. Sometimes they are parted by the women going between them; the men never interfere. For no disaffection that arises do they resort to bows and arrows. After they have fought, or had out their dispute, they take their dwellings and go into the woods, living apart from each other until their heat has subsided. When no longer offended and their anger is gone, they return. From that time they are friends as if nothing had happened; nor is it necessary that any one should mend their friendships, as they in this way again unite them. If those that quarrel are single, they go to some neighboring people, and although these should be enemies, they receive them well and welcome them warmly, giving them so largely of what they have, that when their animosity cools, and they return to their town, they go rich.

They are all warlike, and have as much strategy for protecting themselves against enemies as they could have were they reared in Italy in continual feuds. When they are in a part of the country where their enemies may attack them, they place their houses on the skirt of a wood, the thickest and most tangled they can find, and near it make a ditch in which they sleep. The warriors are covered by small pieces of stick through which are loop holes; these hide them and present so false an appearance, that if come upon they are not discovered. They open a very narrow way, entering into the midst of the wood, where a spot is prepared on which the women and children sleep. When night comes they kindle fires in their lodges, that should spies be about, they may think to find them there; and before daybreak they again light those fires. If the enemy comes to assault the houses, they who are in the ditch make a sally; and from their trenches do much injury without those who are outside seeing or being able to find them. When there is no wood in which they can take shelter in this way, and make their ambuscades, they settle on open ground at a place they select, which they invest with trenches covered with broken sticks, having apertures whence to discharge arrows. These arrangements are made for night.

While I was among the Aguenes, their enemies coming suddenly at midnight, fell upon them, killed three and wounded many, so that they ran from their houses to the fields before them. As soon as these ascertained that their assailants had withdrawn, they returned to pick up all the arrows the others had shot, and following after them in the most stealthy manner possible, came that night to their dwellings without their presence being suspected. At four o'clock in the morning the Aguenes attacked them, killed five, and wounded numerous others, and made them flee from their houses, leaving their bows with all they possessed. In a little while came the wives of the Quevenes to them and formed a treaty whereby the parties became friends. The women, however, are sometimes the cause of war. All these nations, when they have personal enmities, and are not of one family, assassinate at night, waylay, and inflict gross barbarities on each other.

from **Chapter XXVII**
We Moved Away and Were Well Received

. . . At sunset we reached a hundred Indian habitations. Before we arrived, all the people who were in them came out to receive us, with such yells as were terrific, striking the palms of their hands violently against their thighs. They brought us gourds bored with holes and having pebbles in them, an instrument for the most important occasions, produced only at the dance or to effect cures, and which none dare touch but those who own them. They say there is virtue in them, and because they do not grow in that country, they come from heaven: nor do they know where they are to be found, only that the rivers bring them in their floods. So great were the fear and distraction of these people, some to reach us sooner than others, that they might touch us, they pressed us so closely that they lacked little of killing us; and without letting us put our feet to the ground, carried us to their dwellings. We were so crowded upon by numbers, that we went into the houses they had made for us. On no account would we consent that they should rejoice over us any more that night. The night long they passed in singing and dancing among themselves; and the next day they brought us all the people of the town, that we should touch and bless them in the way we had done to others among whom we had been. After this performance they presented many arrows to some women of the other town who had accompanied theirs.

The next day we left, and all the people of the place went with us: and when we came to the other Indians we were as well received as we had been by the last. They gave us of what they had to eat, and the deer they had killed that day. Among them we witnessed another custom, which is this: they who were with us took from him who came to be cured, his bow and arrows, shoes and beads if he wore any, and then brought him before us that we should heal him. After being attended to, he would go away highly pleased, saying that he was well. So we parted from these Indians, and went to others by whom we were welcomed. They brought us their sick, which, we having blessed, they declared were sound; he who was healed, believed we could cure him; and with what the others to whom we had administered would relate, they made great rejoicing and dancing, so that they left us no sleep. . . .

from Chapter XXXII
The Indians Give Us the Hearts of Deer

. . . We were in this town three days.[10] A day's journey farther was another town, at which the rain fell heavily while we were there, and the river became so swollen we could not cross it, which detained us fifteen days. In this time Castillo saw the buckle of a sword-belt on the neck of an Indian and stitched to it the nail of a horse shoe. He took them, and we asked the native what they were: he answered that they came from heaven. We questioned him further, as to who had brought them thence: they all responded, that certain men who wore beards like us, had come from heaven and arrived at that river; bringing horses, lances, and swords, and that they had lanced two Indians. In a manner of the utmost indifference we could feign, we asked them what had become of those men: they answered us that they had gone to sea, putting their lances beneath the water, and going themselves also under the water; afterwards that they were seen on the surface going towards the sunset. For this we gave many thanks to God our Lord. We had before despaired of ever hearing more of Christians. Even yet we were left in great doubt and anxiety, thinking those people were merely persons who had come by sea on discoveries. However, as we had now such exact information, we made greater speed, and as we advanced on our way, the news of the Christians continually grew. We told the natives that we were going in search of that people, to order them not to kill nor make slaves of them, nor take them from their lands, nor do other injustice. Of this the Indians were very glad.

We passed through many territories and found them all vacant: their inhabitants wandered fleeing among the mountains, without daring to have houses or till the earth for fear of Christians. The sight was one of infinite pain to us, a land very fertile and beautiful, abounding in springs and streams, the hamlets deserted and

[10]At an earlier point in the narrative, the journal reports that "we called the place Pueblo de los Corazones," on the gulf of Cortés.

burned, the people thin and weak, all fleeing or in concealment. As they did not plant, they appeased their keen hunger by eating roots, and the bark of trees. We bore a share in the famine along the whole way; for poorly could these unfortunates provide for us, themselves being so reduced they looked as though they would willingly die. They brought shawls of those they had concealed because of the Christians, presenting them to us; and they related how the Christians, at other times had come through the land destroying and burning the towns, carrying away half the men, and all the women and the boys, while those who had been able to escape were wandering about fugitives. We found them so alarmed they dared not remain anywhere. They would not, nor could they till the earth; but preferred to die rather than live in dread of such cruel usage as they received. Although these showed themselves greatly delighted with us, we feared that on our arrival among those who held the frontier and fought against the Christians, they would treat us badly, and revenge upon us the conduct of their enemies; but when God our Lord was pleased to bring us there, they began to dread and respect us as the others had done, and even somewhat more, at which we no little wondered. Thence it may at once be seen, that to bring all these people to be Christians and to the obedience of the Imperial Majesty, they must be won by kindness, which is a way certain, and no other is. . . . [11]

from Chapter XXXIII
We See Traces of Christians

When we saw sure signs of Christians, and heard how near we were to them, we gave thanks to God our Lord, for having chosen to bring us out of a captivity so melancholy and wretched. The delight we felt let each one conjecture, when he shall remember the length of time we were in that country, the suffering and perils we underwent. That night I entreated my companions that one of them should go back three days' journey after the Christians who were moving about over the country, where we had given assurance of protection. Neither of them received this proposal well, excusing themselves because of weariness and exhaustion; and although either might have done better than I, being more youthful and athletic, yet seeing their unwillingness, the next morning I took the negro[12] with eleven Indians, and following the Christians by their trail, I traveled ten leagues, passing three villages, at which they had slept.

The day after I overtook four of them on horseback, who were astonished at the sight of me, so strangely habited as I was, and in company with Indians. They stood staring at me a length of time, so confounded that they neither hailed me nor drew near to make an inquiry. I bade them take me to their chief: accordingly we went together half a league to the place where was Diego de Alcaraz, their captain.

[11] As the concluding section here suggests, the advice of Cabeza de Vaca went unheeded, even by the Christians he met. By this time the party had entered northern Mexico.

[12] Estévan, a black member of the Spanish expedition.

After we had conversed, he stated to me that he was completely undone; he had not been able in a long time to take any Indians; he knew not which way to turn, and his men had well begun to experience hunger and fatigue. I told him of Castillo and Dorantes, who were behind, ten leagues off, with a multitude that conducted us. He thereupon sent three cavalry to them, with fifty of the Indians who accompanied him. The negro returned to guide them, while I remained. I asked the Christians to give me a certificate of the year, month and day, I arrived there, and of the manner of my coming, which they accordingly did. From this river to the town of the Christians, named San Miguel, within the government of the province called New Galicia, are thirty leagues.

from Chapter XXXIV
Of Sending for the Christians

Five days having elapsed, Andrés Dorantes and Alonzo del Castillo arrived with those who had been sent after them. They brought more than six hundred persons of that community, whom the Christians had driven into the forests, and who had wandered in concealment over the land. Those who accompanied us so far, had drawn them out, and given them to the Christians, who thereupon dismissed all the others they had brought with them. Upon their coming to where I was, Alcaraz begged that we would summon the people of the towns on the margin of the river, who straggled about under cover of the woods, and order them to fetch us something to eat. This last was unnecessary, the Indians being ever diligent to bring us all they could. Directly we sent our messengers to call them, when there came six hundred souls, bringing us all the maize in their possession. They fetched it in certain pots, closed with clay, which they had concealed in the earth. They brought whatever else they had; but we, wishing only to have the provision, gave the rest to the Christians, that they might divide among themselves. After this we had many high words with them; for they wished to make slaves of the Indians we brought.

In consequence of the dispute, we left at our departure many bows of Turkish shape we had along with us and many pouches. The five arrows with the points of emerald were forgotten among others, and we lost them. We gave the Christians a store of robes of cowhide and other things we brought. We found it difficult to induce the Indians to return to their dwellings, to feel no apprehension and plant maize. They were willing to do nothing until they had gone with us and delivered us into the hands of other Indians, as had been the custom; for if they returned without doing so, they were afraid they should die, and going with us, they feared neither Christians nor lances. Our countrymen became jealous at this, and caused their interpreter to tell the Indians that we were of them, and for a long time we had been lost; that they were the lords of the land who must be obeyed and served, while we were persons of mean condition and small force. The Indians cared little or nothing for what was told them; and conversing among themselves said the Christians lied: that we had come whence the sun rises, and they whence it goes down: we healed the sick, they killed the sound; that we had come naked and barefooted, while they had arrived in clothing and on horses with lances; that we were not covetous of anything, but all that was given to us, we directly turned to give, remaining with nothing; that the others had the only purpose to rob whomsoever they found, bestowing nothing on any one.

In this way they spoke of all matters respecting us, which they enhanced by contrast with matters concerning the others, delivering their response through the interpreter of the Spaniards. To other Indians they made this known by means of one among them through whom they understood us. Those who speak that tongue we discriminately call Primahaitu, which is like saying Vasconyados.[11] We found it in use over more than four hundred leagues of our travel, without another over that whole extent. Even to the last, I could not convince the Indians that we were of the Christians; and only with great effort and solicitation we got them to go back to their residences. We ordered them to put away apprehension, establish their towns, plant and cultivate the soil. . . .

1542

Fray Marcos de Niza 1495?–1542

The party headed by Cabeza de Vaca related tales of a populated area far to the north in which the natives spoke of the fabulously rich "Seven Cities of Cíbola." This stirred hopes of another Mexico awaiting conquest. Antonio de Mendoza, the first viceroy of New Spain, sent the Franciscan Fray Marcos to explore the area, guided by Estévan, Cabeza de Vaca's black companion. Estévan took to breaking the trail, advancing well beyond Fray Marcos and the main party. It was thus that he was killed, under circumstances difficult to confirm, although Fray Marcos would narrate the event as if he had thorough knowledge of it. In the same fashion, Fray Marcos claimed he had seen Cíbola, somewhat as Moses had been allowed to glimpse the promised land he could not enter. His narrative bolstered Cabeza de Vaca's claims, and moved Coronado, the Governor of New Galicia, to organize a massive expedition (see Casteñeda). When it was found, however, that the pueblos, though extraordinary in their construction, were not centers of great wealth, Fray Marcos lost both his reputation and his position with Coronado. Yet his text stands as an example of the rhetoric of promise just over the horizon that would become essential to the American experience, drawing waves of immigrants in search of their fortunes.

Juan Bruce-Novoa
University of California at Irvine

from A Relation of the Reverend Father Fray Marcos de Niza, Touching His Discovery of the Kingdom of Ceuola or Cibola . . .

. . . After the three days were past, many people assembled to go with me, of whom I chose thirty chiefs, who were very well supplied with necklaces of turquoises, some of them wearing as many as five or six strings. With these I took the retinue necessary to carry food for them and me and started on my way. I entered the desert on the ninth day of May. On the first day, by a very wide and well travelled road, we arrived for dinner at a place where there was water, which the Indians showed to me, and in the evening we came again to water, and there I found a shelter which the Indians had just constructed for me and another which had been made for *Stephen*[1] to sleep in when he passed. There were some old huts and many signs of fire, made by people passing to *Cibola*[2] over this road. In this fashion I journeyed twelve days, always very well supplied with victuals of venison, hares, and partridges of the same color and flavor as those of Spain, although rather smaller. . . .

Continuing our journey, at a day's march from Cibola, we met two other Indians, of those who had gone with Stephen, who appeared bloody and with many wounds. At this meeting, they and those that were with me set up such a crying, that out of pity and fear they also made me cry. So great was the noise that I could not ask about Stephen nor of what had happened to them, so I begged them to be quiet that we might learn what had passed. They said to me: "How can we be quiet, when we know that our fathers, sons and brothers who were with Stephen, to the number of more than three hundred men, are dead? And we no more dare go to Cibola, as we have been accustomed." Nevertheless, as well as I could, I endeavored to pacify them and to put off their fear, although I myself was not without need of someone to calm me. I asked the wounded Indians concerning Stephen and as to what had happened. They remained a short time without speaking a word, weeping along with those of their towns. At last they told me that when Stephen arrived at a day's journey from Cibola, he sent his messengers with his calabash to the lord of Cibola to announce his arrival and that he was coming peacefully and to cure them. When the messengers gave him the calabash and he saw the rattles, he flung it furiously on the floor and said: "I know these people; these rattles are not of our style of workmanship; tell them to go back immediately or not a man of them will remain alive." Thus he remained very angry. The messengers went back sad, and hardly dared to tell Stephen of the reception they had met. Nevertheless they told him and he said that they should not fear, that he desired to go on, because, although they answered him badly, they would receive him well. So he went and arrived at the city of Cibola just before sunset, with all his company, which would be more than three hundred men, besides

[1]Estévan served as guide and interpreter. As they traveled, Estévan began to be accompanied by an Indian woman. The friars sent him ahead, into Zuni territory. The Zuni, unfamiliar with black races, killed Estévan.

[2]The Spaniard's name for the Zuni pueblos he found.

many women. The inhabitants would not permit them to enter the city, but put them in a large and commodious house outside the city. They at once took away from Stephen all that he carried, telling him that the lord so ordered. "All that night," said the Indians, "they gave us nothing to eat nor drink. The next day, when the sun was a lance-length high, Stephen went out of the house and some of the chiefs with him. Straightway many people came out of the city and, as soon as he saw them, he began to flee and we with him. Then they gave us these arrow-strokes and cuts and we fell and some dead men fell on top of us. Thus we lay till nightfall, without daring to stir. We heard loud voices in the city and we saw many men and women watching on the terraces. We saw no more of Stephen and we concluded that they had shot him with arrows as they had the rest that were with him, of whom there escaped only us."

In view of what the Indians had related and the bad outlook for continuing my journey as I desired, I could not help but feel their loss and mine. God is witness of how much I desired to have someone of whom I could take counsel, for I confess I was at a loss what to do. I told them that Our Lord would chastize Cibola and that when the Emperor knew what had happened he would send many Christians to punish its people. They did not believe me, because they say that no one can withstand the power of Cibola. I begged them to be comforted and not to weep and consoled them with the best words I could muster, which would be too long to set down here. With this I left them and withdrew a stone's throw or two apart, to commend myself to God, and remained thus an hour and a half. When I went back to them, I found one of my Indians, named Mark, who had come from Mexico, and he said to me: "Father, these men have plotted to kill you, because they say that on account of you and Stephen their kinsfolk have been murdered, and that there will not remain a man or woman among them all who will not be killed." I then divided among them all that remained of dry stuffs and other articles, in order to pacify them. I told them to observe that if they killed me they would do me no harm, because I would die a Christian and would go to heaven, and that those who killed me would suffer for it, because the Christians would come in search of me, and against my will would kill them all. With these and many other words I pacified them somewhat, although there was still high feeling on account of the people killed. I asked that some of them should go to Cibola, to see if any other Indian had escaped and to obtain some news of Stephen, but I could not persuade them to do so. Seeing this, I told them that, in any case, I must see the city of Cibola and they said that no one would go with me. Finally, seeing me determined, two chiefs said that they would go with me.

With these and with my own Indians and interpreters, I continued my journey till I came within sight of Cibola. It is situated on a level stretch on the brow of a roundish hill. It appears to be a very beautiful city, the best that I have seen in these parts; the houses are of the type that the Indians described to me, all of stone with their storeys and terraces, as it appeared to me from a hill whence I could see it. The town is bigger than the city of Mexico.[3] At times I was tempted to go to it, because I knew that I risked nothing but my life, which I had offered to God the day I

[3]A clear exaggeration.

commenced the journey; finally I feared to do so, considering my danger and that if I died, I would not be able to give an account of this country, which seems to me to be the greatest and best of the discoveries. When I said to the chiefs who were with me how beautiful Cibola appeared to me, they told me that it was the least of the seven cities, and that Totonteac is much bigger and better than all the seven, and that it has so many houses and people that there is no end to it. Viewing the situation of the city, it occurred to me to call that country the new kingdom of St. Francis, and there, with the aid of the Indians, I made a big heap of stones and on top of it I placed a small, slender cross, not having the materials to construct a bigger one. I declared that I placed that cross and landmark in the name of Don Antonio de Mendoza, viceroy and governor of New Spain for the Emperor, our lord, in sign of possession, in conformity with my instructions. I declared that I took possession there of all the seven cities and of the kingdoms of Tontonteac and Acus and Marata, and that I did not go to them, in order that I might return to give an account of what I had done and seen.

Then I started back, with more more fear than food, and went to meet the people whom I had left behind, with the greatest haste I could make. I overtook them after two day's march and went with them till we had passed the desert and arrived at their home. Here I was not made welcome as previously, because the men as well as the women indulged in much weeping for the persons killed at Cibola. Without tarrying I hastened in fear from that people and that valley. The first day I went ten leagues, then I went eight and again ten leagues, without stopping till I had passed the second desert.

On my return, although I was not without fear, I determined to approach the open tract, situated at the end of the mountain ranges, of which I said above that I had some account. As I came near, I was informed that it is peopled for many days' journey towards the east, but I dared not enter it, because it seemed to me that we must go to colonize and to rule that other country of the seven cities and the kingdoms I have spoken of, and that then one could see it better. So I forebore to risk my person and left it alone to given an account of what I had seen. However, I saw, from the mouth of the tract seven moderate-sized towns at some distance, and further a very fresh valley of very good land, whence rose much smoke. I was informed that there is much gold in it and that the natives of it deal in vessels and jewels for the ears and little plates with which they scrape themselves to relieve themselves of sweat, and that these people will not consent to trade with those of the other part of the valley; but I was not able to learn the cause for this. Here I placed two crosses and took possession of all this plain and valley in the same manner as I had done with the other possessions, according to my instructions. From there I continued my return journey, with all the haste I could, till I arrived at the town of San Miguel, in the province of Culiacan, expecting to find there Francisco Vazquez de Coronado, governor of New Galicia. As I did not find him there, I continued my journey to the city of Compostella, where I found him. From there I immediately wrote word of my coming to the most illustrious lord, the viceroy of New Spain, and to our father provincial, Friar Antonio of Ciudad-Rodrigo, asking him to send me orders what to do.

I omit here many particulars which are not pertinent; I simply tell what I saw and what was told me concerning the countries where I went and those of which I was given information, in order to make a report to our father provincial, that he may show it to the father of our order, who may advise him, or to the council of the order, at whose command I went, that they may give it to the most illustrious lord, the viceroy of New Spain, at whose request they sent me on this journey.—*Fray Marcos de Niza, vice comissarius.*

1539

Pedro de Casteñeda 1510?–1570?

As Fray Marcos de Niza set out to verify Cabeza de Vaca's accounts, Viceroy Mendoza also was preparing for a full-scale exploration to be launched out of the northern province of New Galicia. To secure it as a base, he appointed as governor his protegé Francisco Vásquez de Coronado. When Fray Marcos returned with glowing tales of Cíbola, Coronado was commissioned to lead a land expedition of some two thousand people—including at least three women—and almost as many animals while a fleet under Hernando de Alarcón proceeded up the Gulf of California. The venture set out with great expectations.

Disappointment soon replaced optimism when the capture of Cíbola (Zuni) revealed Fray Marcos's penchant for hyperbole. The friar was sent back, but Coronado continued farther and farther into the heart of the continent following other voices of exaggerated promises. The most infamous was offered by "the Turk," a Plains Indian, who convinced the Spaniards that Quivira was the city of their dreams. Coronado led a splinter group as far as central Kansas, encountering the Wichita, who were numerous but not rich in gold. He also encountered herds of buffalo and described the ocean-like plains that centuries later would swallow wagon trains from the east. Coronado eventually returned south in failure, the purpose of his mission—gold and the location of another Mexico City—having eluded him.

Little is known of Pedro de Casteñeda, who recorded the account of Coronado's journey over twenty years after the event. A native of Najera in northern Spain, he had established himself at the Spanish outpost at Culiacan, in northwestern Mexico, at the time Coronado formed his expedition.

Juan Bruce-Novoa
University of California at Irvine

PRIMARY WORK

Pedro de Casteñeda, *The Journey of Coronado, 1540–1542,* trans. George Parker Winship, 1904.

from The Narrative of the Expedition of Coronado

Chapter XXI
Of how the army returned to Tiguex[1] and the general reached Quivira.

The general started from the ravine with the guides that the Teyas[2] had given him. He appointed the alderman Diego Lopez his army-master, and took with him the men who seemed to him to be most efficient, and the best horses. The army still had some hope that the general would send for them, and sent two horsemen, lightly equipped and riding post, to repeat their petition.

The general arrived—I mean, the guides ran away during the first few days and Diego Lopez had to return to the army for guides, bringing orders for the army to return to Tiguex to find food and wait there for the general. The Teyas, as before, willingly furnished him with new guides. The army waited for its messengers and spent a fortnight here, preparing jerked beef to take with them. It was estimated that during this fortnight they killed 500 bulls.[3] The number of these that were there without any cows was something incredible. Many fellows were lost at this time who went out hunting and did not get back to the army for two or three days, wandering about the country as if they were crazy, in one direction or another, not knowing how to get back where they started from, although this ravine extended in either direction so that they could find it. Every night they took account of who was missing, fired guns and blew trumpets and beat drums and built great fires, but yet some of them went off so far and wandered about so much that all this did not give them any help, although it helped others. The only way was to go back where they had killed an animal and start from there in one direction and another until they struck the ravine or fell in with somebody who could put them on the right road. It is worth noting that the country there is so level that at midday, after one has wandered about in one direction and another in pursuit of game, the only thing to do is to stay near the game quietly until sunset, so as to see where it goes down, and even then they have to be men who are practiced to do it. Those who are not, had to trust themselves to others.

The general followed his guides until he reached Quivira, which took forty-eight days' marching, on account of the great detour they had made toward Florida.[4] He was received peacefully on account of the guides whom he had. They asked the Turk why he had lied and had guided them so far out of their way. He said that his country was in that direction and that, besides this, the people at Cicuye had asked him to lead them off on to the plains and lose them, so that the horses would die when their provisions gave out, and they would be so weak if they ever returned that they

[1]The region of the New Mexican pueblo settlements.

[2]The Spanish name for the Indians they encountered in Texas. It meant "friend" in the native language.

[3]Buffalo.

[4]Texas was considered part of Florida, and it appeared as such on early maps.

would be killed without any trouble, and thus they could take revenge for what had been done to them.[5] This was the reason why he had led them astray, supposing that they did not know how to hunt or to live without corn, while as for the gold, he did not know where there was any of it. He said this like one who had given up hope and who found that he was being persecuted, since they had begun to believe Ysopete[6] who had guided them better than he had, and fearing lest those who were there might give some advice by which some harm would come to him. They garroted him, which pleased Ysopete very much, because he had always said that Ysopete was a rascal and that he did not know what he was talking about and had always hindered his talking with anybody. Neither gold nor silver nor any trace of either was found among these people. Their lord wore a copper plate on his neck and prized it highly.

The messengers whom the army had sent to the general returned, as I said, and then, as they brought no news except what the alderman had delivered, the army left the ravine and returned to the Teyas, where they took guides who led them back by a more direct road. They readily furnished these, because these people are always roaming over this country in pursuit of the animals and so know it thoroughly. They keep their road in this way: In the morning they notice where the sun rises and observe the direction they are going to take, and then shoot an arrow in this direction. Before reaching this they shoot another over it, and in this way they go all day toward the water where they are to end the day. In this way they covered in 25 days what had taken them 37 days going, besides stopping to hunt cows on the way. They found many salt lakes on this road, and there was a great quantity of salt. There were thick pieces of it on top of the water bigger than tables, as thick as four or five fingers. Two or three spans down under water there was salt which tasted better than that in the floating pieces, because this was rather bitter. It was crystalline. All over these plains there were large numbers of animals like squirrels[7] and a great number of their holes.

On its return the army reached the Cicuye river more than 30 leagues below there—I mean below the bridge they had made when they crossed it, and they followed it up to that place. In general, its banks are covered with a sort of rose bushes, the fruit of which tastes like muscatel grapes.[8] They grow on little twigs about as high up as a man. It has the parsley leaf. There were unripe grapes and currants and wild marjoram. The guides said this river joined that of Tiguex more than 20 days from here, and that its course turned toward the east. It is believed that it flows into the mighty river of the Holy Spirit (Espiritu Santo)[9] which the men with Don Hernando de Soto discovered in Florida. A painted Indian woman ran away from Juan de Saldibar and hid in the ravines about this time, because she recognized the country of Tiguex where she had been a slave. She fell into the hands of some Spaniards who had entered the country from Florida to explore it in this direction.

[5]The Spanish used force to subdue the Pueblo Indians.

[6]Another member of the Plains Indian tribe found in captivity with the Pueblos. From the beginning he had tried to alert the Spanish to Turk's lies.

[7]The first report of the extensive prairie dog towns common to the southwestern United States.

[8]Reports of the lush growth of edible plants encouraged later settlers who came to make permanent agricultural settlements.

[9]The Mississippi.

After I got back to New Spain I heard them say that the Indian told them that she had run away from other men like them nine days, and that she gave the names of some captains; from which we ought to believe that we were not far from the region they discovered, although they said they were more than 200 leagues inland. I believe the land at that point is more than *600 leagues*[10] across from sea to sea.

As I said, the army followed the river up as far as Cicuye, which it found ready for war and unwilling to make any advances toward peace or to give any food to the army. From there they went on to Tiguex where several villages had been reinhabited, but the people were afraid and left them again.

1904

Gaspar Pérez de Villagrá 1555–1620

Villagrá was the official chronicler, military outfitter, and missionizer of the Juan de Oñate expedition (1598–1608) that explored and then established permanent Spanish settlements in north central New Mexico. This expedition also generated the first drama and the first epic poem of European origin, *Historia de la Nueva México* (1610), in the present U.S. territory.

While Oñate, interested in mineral wealth, dispatched his troops in wide-ranging forays into the surrounding areas, the settlers in his party wanted him to concentrate on securing the colony for agriculture and livestock raising. Conflicts were inevitable. To add to Oñate's problems, one of the forays provoked violence at the Acoma pueblo. The ensuing battle set an ominous precedent for European–Native American encounters, repeated from New England to Patagonia by colonizers of different national origins.

The Acoma pueblo, which had received the Coronado expedition in friendship sixty years earlier, submitted peacefully to Oñate. However, when a small band of Spaniards abused their welcome, the Acomas killed thirteen soldiers, including the commanding officer Juan de Saldívar. Oñate sent Vicente de Saldívar on a punitive expedition against the fortress-like city high on a mesa. After days of struggle, in which the Spaniards deployed artillery to level the village, the Acomas were decimated, with some 800 killed. Those who surrendered were indentured, many after having one foot severed as punishment.

Villagrá, in the literary fashion of the era, composed his chronicle in epic verse. With one eye on recording events and the other on the demands of his craft and genre, the poet/chronicler filtered facts through a grid of Renaissance literary conventions, juxtaposing brutal genocide and the elegance of classic verse.

Juan Bruce-Novoa
University of California at Irvine

Amy E. Winans
Dickinson College

[10]Approximately 2,400 miles.

PRIMARY WORKS

Historia de la Nueva México, 1616; *Historia de la Nueva México, 1610,* trans. and ed. M. Encinias, A. Rodríguez, and J. P. Sánchez, 1992.

from The History of New Mexico[1]

from Canto I

Which sets forth the outline of the history and the location of New Mexico, and the reports had of it in the traditions of the Indians, and of the true origin and descent of the Mexicans.

I sing of arms and the heroic man,
The being, courage, care, and high emprise
Of him whose unconquered patience,
Though cast upon a sea of cares,
In spite of envy slanderous,
Is raising to new heights the feats,
The deeds, of those brave Spaniards who,
In the far India of the West,
Discovering in the world that which was hid,
'Plus ultra' go bravely saying
By force of valor and strong arms,
In war and suffering as experienced
As celebrated now by pen unskilled.
I beg of thee, most Christian Philip,[2]
Being the Phoenix of New Mexico
Now newly brought forth from the flames
Of fire and new produced from ashes
Of the most ardent faith, in whose hot coals
Sublime your sainted Father and our lord
We saw all burned and quite undone,
Suspend a moment from your back
The great and heavy weight which bears you down
Of this enormous globe which, in all right,
Is by your arm alone upheld,
And, lending, O great King, attentive ear,
Thou here shalt see the load of toil,

[1]This text is taken from M. Encinias, A. Rodríguez, and J. P. Sánchez, trans. and ed., *Historia de la Nueva México, 1610,* 1992.

[2]Philip III, King of Spain, 1598–1621.

Of calumny, affliction, under which
Did plant the evangel holy and the Faith of Christ
That Christian Achilles whom you wished
To be employed in such heroic work.
And if in fortune good I may succeed
In having you, my Monarch, listener,
Who doubts that, with a wondering fear,
The whole round world shall listen too
To that which holds so high a King intent.
For, being favored thus by you,
It being no less to write of deeds worthy
Of being elevated by the pen
Than to undertake those which are no less
Worthy of being written by this same pen,
'Tis only needed that those same brave men
For whom this task I undertook
Should nourish with their great, heroic valor
The daring flight of this my pen,
Because I think that this time we shall see
The words well equaled by the deeds.
Hear me, great King, for I am witness
Of all that here, my Lord, I say to you.
Beneath the Arctic Pole, in height
Some thirty-three degrees, which the same
Are, we know, of sainted Jerusalem,
Not without mystery and marvel great,
Are spread, extended, sown, and overflow
Some nations barbarous, remote
From the bosom of the Church,[3] where
The longest day of all the year contains and has
Some fourteen hours and a half when it arrives,
The furious sun, at the rising of Cancer,
Through whose zenith he doth usually pass
The image of Andromeda and Perseus,
Whose constellation always influences
The quality of Venus and Mercury.
And shows to us its location in longitude,
According as most modern fixed meridian
Doth teach us and we practice,
Two hundred just degrees and seventy
Into the temperate zone and the fourth clime,
Two hundred long leagues from the place

[3]Villagrá placed the expedition among those that sought the continued expansion of the Catholic Church, represented in the Acts of the Apostles as moving westward from Jerusalem, to Asia Minor, to Rome, and then westward.

Where the Sea of the North[4] and Gulf of Mexico
Approach the most and nearest to the coast
On the southeast; and to the side
Toward the rough Californio[5] and Sea of the Pearls[6]
The distance in that direction is about the same
Toward where the southwest wind strikes the coast
And from the frozen zone its distance is
About five hundred full long leagues;
And in a circle round we see it hold,
Beneath the parallel, if we should take
The height of thirty-seven degrees,
Five thousand goodly Spanish leagues,
Whose greatness it is a shame it should be held
By so great sum of people ignorant
About the blood of Christ, whose holiness
It causes pain to think so many souls know not.
From these new regions[7] 'tis notorious,
Of public voice and fame, that there descended
Those oldest folk of Mexico
Who to the famous city, Mexico,
Did give their name, that it might be
Memorial eternal of their name, and lasting,
In imitation of wise Romulus
Who put a measure to the walls of Rome. . . .

Canto XIV

How the River of the North was discovered and the trials that were borne in discovering it, and of things that happened until arriving at the point of taking possession of the land.

The value of a thing undertaken
Is esteemed and praised and raised aloft
In such proportion as that is esteemed
With which it is accomplished, gained, and won.
This I do say, great lord, so that I may
Make clearer the great greatness, excellence,
Of warlike exercise practiced
By all those heroes valorous
Who, in exchange for toil and suffering,
Life and blood, have bought and won
Only the famous name of soldiers,

[4]The Atlantic Ocean.
[5]The Colorado River.
[6]The Gulf of California.
[7]That the ancient races came from northern regions is an allusion to the myth of Aztlán, renewed by Chicano literature of the 1960s.

To whose high excellence 'tis proper
To see and to observe in every way
That 'tis useless to bear the trials
Miseries, afflictions, and fatigues
That bloody war always entails
If in the middle of its course unstoppable
Their spirit breaks and becomes cowardly.
And, not to come to such disgrace,
Our tired forces sinking down,
Seeing no port agreeable, sweet,
When the noble Polca,[1] content,
Her farewell said, had gone to her country,
As goes the huntsman who has lost
A great gyrfalcon, falcon, or saker.
Shouting among the valleys and hills,
Calling it with anxiety,
Showing the lure until he sees him safe
Perched on his hand, where, happily,
Without a memory of his recent fright,
He dandles him and pets him and smooths down
His ruffled plumage, and appeases him,
So went the beautiful barbarian, I think,
She went eagerly after her Milco,
And we, lord, resolute anew,
Did journey more than fifty days,
Suffering heavy mischances.
And as it had unceasing rained on us
For seven long, hard days' journeyings,
Our clothing sticking to our flesh,
No one of us had any thought
Of coming out with life from that affair.
We went through rough and craggy lands.
Of Arabs and of rude barbarians
And other deserts, wild and perilous,
Upon whose wide and spacious soil
No Christian foot had ever trod.
In which long time we did consume
The poor provisions we had brought,
And all with difficulty fed
Their tired bodies, all worn out,
Only with coarse roots indigestible.
Driving against the hardness of our fate
We ever held unto our course,

[1]Polca, and the later-mentioned Milco, are two Indians who served as guides for Oñate's expedition.

Now through thick briars and ravines,
Entangled in whose harsh forests
Even our strong cuisses[2] were torn,
Now over high and rugged peaks,
Over whose summits we did drive
Our tired horses on before,
Panting and tired and quite worn out,
On foot and hindered by all our arms,
Our swollen feet, now quite naked
And shoeless, without shoes we still did set
On cliffs and ragged looming rocks,
Now over lofty dunes of sand,
So ardent, burning, and fervent
That, wounded by their strong reflection,
Our miserable eyes, burnt up
'Neath our hard helmets, failed us quite.
And as the end of what is hoped
Alone is nourished, thewed, sustained,
By valor and the ring of hope,
Hoping, we did those tasks that were
But lighter, more endurable, and easier borne.
And since a ready diligence
Lent to a careful toil
Is mother of all good outcome,
We had that same, discovering the pass
That the astute barbarian told us of,
Marking the lands all round about
The sites and places that he showed
When we with Milco captured him.
And, like Magellan through his strait,
We all pass through it,
Worn down with toil, now quite worn out
By the force of the rigorous fate
Which with a strong and heavy hand
So pressed us down, afflicted us.
Four complete days did pass away
In which we drank no drop of water there,
And now the horses, being blind,
Did give themselves most cruel blows
And bumps against the unseen trees,
And we, as tired as they,
Exhaling living fire and spitting forth
Saliva more viscous than pitch,
Our hope given up, entirely lost,

[2]Chest armor made of thick leather.

Were almost all wishing for death.
But the great Providence, pitying,
Which is always more quick in helping us
As we more firmly trust in it,
The fifth day opened us the door
And we all, happily, did come upon the roaring River
Of the North, for which we all had undergone
Such care and such enormous toil.
Unto whose waters the weak horses
Creeping, staggering much, approached
And, all there plunging in their heads,
Two of them drank to such extent
They there, together, burst and died,
And two more, blind, went in so far
That, by the current snatched away,
They also died, with water satisfied.
And as in public taverns there do use
To lie upon the floor some wretched ones,
Drunk from the wine they have imbibed,
So our companions remained,
Stretched out upon the watery sand,
As swollen, dropsical, gasping,
As they had all been toads,
The whole river seeming to them but small
To extinguish and abate their thirst.
And as if in the fresh Elysian Fields
We had arrived, there to refresh ourselves,
Such, lord, there did appear to us
All those beaches and banks,
Among whose goodly pasture the horses
Were gladly grazing and resting
Their tired and exhausted bones
From the laborious, weary road.
And in the pleasant wood we all
With much pleasure did roam about
'Mid fresh and well-leaved poplar groves
Whose beautiful, agreeable shades
Gave invitation to our weary limbs,
By their own prostrate trunks nearby
To rest together with them there.
Through their green branches, spreading wide,
As exceeding chaste bees do go,
With buzzing dull and comforting,
Traveling from one thyme to the next
Tasting the best of many flowers,
Likewise among those lofty trunks,
With dainty, sweet-intoned song,

There flew a million little birds,
Whose graceful, unembarrassed throats
And lyric tongues did sing the praise
Of that All-powerful Lord who had made them.
And even the waters of the harsh river,
At flood, a furious, roaring stream,
Were all flowing and pouring down
As peaceful, suave, pleasing, and mild
As though they were a quiet pool
Over wide flats and well spread out,
And, too, with many kinds of fish
Most excellently rich and abounding.
We found, beside this, much hunting,
Of many cranes and ducks and geese,
Upon which the astute, prompt hunters there
Made good use of their harquebuses.[3]
And having hunted and fished much,
From out the fire-bearing flints
We struck their hidden fires and made
A great and excellent campfire,
And on huge spits and in the coals
We put a huge supply of meat and fish,
Placing with liberal hands all that
Our eager appetites did ask
To conquer in completest sort
Their great desire for savory food.
And like that memorable dove
Which, after the great storm had passed,
Returned with the green olive branch,[4]
Not otherwise, we all returned,
Filled wholly with content and joy,
Which is the true reward of work.
And when we came to the army
We were received with much festivity,
And, as 'tis always needed and is pleasant, too,
To bring to memory the toils,
The miseries, fatigues, we have endured
When the fierce war was on,
The Sergeant Major, drawn by this pleasure,
Related unto all the camp,
The General being present, those events,
Journeys, occurrences, endured

[3]Guns.
[4]The reference is to Noah's ark, an image that Villagrá repeats. [Translators' note.]

Until at last we came unto the shores,
The banks and groves of that river,
Under whose widely spreading trees
We took our ease after all our fatigues.
And as it always causes great relief
To know one suffers not alone,
When he had done, the skillful General
Took to himself the floor and as a comfort
For our sad trials now gone by,
Told of the trials that his men
Had also borne and undergone,
And how one of them was so hard
That the camp came to the edge of ruin.
And 'twas that, March coming on hot
And settling down with burning suns,
Water began to fail to such extent
That, with their throats all miserably dry,
The tender children, women, and the men,
Afflicted, ruined, quite burnt up,
Did beg for aid from sovereign God,
This being the final remedy
That they could have in such distress.
And the sad, tired animals,
Feeble as those of Nineveh,[5]
Worn down by unchecked fast,
Thus all did show themselves worn out
By the weather that they had borne.[6]
And as He always favors and assists
With His immense sovereign goodness
The ones who truly ask and beg of Him,
The sky, being clear and very calm
In all directions, was disturbed
By huge black clouds, heavy laden,
And without lightening or thunder
They shed and poured down such water
That oxen laden with their yokes
Did satisfy their killing thirst.
And when the afflicted army
Was quite entirely appeased,
The beauty of the sun's bright rays
Was spread so widely over all
That not a single cloud held back

[5]Villagrá recalls the Old Testament, *Nahum* 1–3. [Translators' note.]

[6]This long description of drought echoes that in Statius's *Thebaid* IV. [Translators' note.]

His bright splendor from any place.
And so, for this cause, they did give
The place that holy water fell
The name of "Water of the Miracle" that it
Might have its memory prolonged eternally
And never throughout all time be forgot.
O sovereign God, with what swiftness dost Thou
Assist us in our need if we have but
Such faith as but a grain of mustard-seed
May measure, weigh, and balance with!
Blessed be such a gift and its use
Not only that the lofty clouds
Out of their season might pour water down,
But that the most massive mountains
Might move and change their locations
And the swift-flying sun might halt
His powerful course and hold it back
For no more than the order of a noble Man
At whose feet there do yield and crouch
All things, both great and small,
Finally, as a man upheld
By hands so great and wonderful.
It seems his greatness continued
To carry on this camp as His,
Being sometimes burdened with great woes
And others aided with a thousand joys,
A certain, direct, and true voyage
Of those great laborers who raised
Heroic buildings for his Church.
For, marching thus for many days,
They came unto the waters of this river,
And, like the Trojan memorable
Who was favored and protected
By Neptune's water trident
After the whirlwind and great storm,[7]
The Governor with all his camp
Came to a safe and pleasant port,
And to his sore-tried soldiery
He gave permission free to rest
Upon those cooling banks and shores.
And as good government does no consist
In industry of no more than the present time,

[7]The reference is to Aeneas, the *Aeneid* I, 177. [Translators' note]

But in a timely foresight of
What afterward may trouble us,
The Governor ordered that without delay
The Sergeant should set out at once
With five chosen companions,
All skillful in swimming, to seek
Some safe ford through the swift river
So that by it all this your camp
Might pass safely and without fear.
And carrying that order out
There went Caravajal, Antonio Sánchez,
The great Cristóbal Sánchez and Araujo,
And I, too, with them, that I might
Complete the number of the five.
And, traveling all together, studiously,
Careful in search for some good ford,
We suddenly did come upon
Some thatched huts from whence there came out
Great numbers of barbarian warriors.
And as that place was all marshy
And we could not well use arms,
We went ahead toward the barbarians
Showing ourselves agreeable friends.
And as giving even breaks rocks,
Giving them of the clothes we had
We made them so peaceful, friendly, to us
That four of them did come with us
And showed to us a goodly ford.
For which reason the prudent General
Ordered that all the four be clothed
And treated with much regalement,
Wherefore all four went down the stream
And, as a sign of peace, brought back
A great number of fresh caught fish.
And, ordering us to make proper return,
He then did cause to be made there,
Within a pleasant, leafy wood,
A graceful church, one with a nave
Of such a size that all the camp at once
Might be contained in it without crowding.
Within whose shelter, holy and religious,
They sang a very solemn Mass,
And the learned Commissary, with wisdom,
Did speak a famous sermon, well thought out.
And when the services were done
They did present a great drama

The noble Captain Farfán had composed,[8]
Whose argument was but to show to us
The great reception of the Church
That all New Mexico did give,
Congratulating it upon its arrival,
Begging, with thorough reverence,
And kneeling on the ground, it would wash out
Its faults with that holy water
Of precious Baptism which they brought,
With which most salutary sacrament
We saw many barbarians cleansed
When we were traveling through their lands.
There were solemn and pleasing festivals
Of splendid men on horseback,
And in honor of that illustrious day
A gallant squadron was released
From that illustrious Captain Cárdenas,
A soldier of courage, modesty
And who, O lord, has served you well.
He, thinking that the expedition
Would be unable to set out,
Remained, so that he never afterward
Could overtake this camp of yours,
Wherefore his standard then was given
To Diego Núñez. And with that we then
Did take possession of that land
Making some record of the case,
Which it is well I give to you,
Nor skip a letter, for it imports much
As being the statement of the General himself.

Canto XXX[1]

How the new General, having given orders to his soldiers, went to take leave of Luzcoija, and the battle he had with the Spaniards, and the things that happened.

[8]Farfán's play, now lost, would undoubtedly be the first literary work created in what is today the United States. [Translators' note.]

[1]On July 11, 1958, Oñate established temporary headquarters near San Juan Pueblo, north of present-day Santa Fe, before setting out for the west with the main body of the expedition. Near the end of October 1598, Oñate met with some leaders at Acoma, a pueblo built atop a high, isolated mesa, and elicited from them what be judged to be promises of cooperation and allegiance. Then he moved west to Zuni and Hopi. The smaller force following Oñate, led by Juan de Saldívar, was on December 4. Villagrá's narrative culminates in the for the retaliatory attack on Acoma by Vicente de Saldívar, Juan's brother.

When man enkindles himself against right
And forces his desires to bend themselves
To undertake a thing that has no plan,
With what ease he doth mark and note
What is in favor, what against that thing
That he wills to undertake against justice.
Gicombo, then, fearing and foreseeing,
Being prudent, skillful, and cautious,
That Zutacapán and all the people
Together would fail him at any time,
Did make them bind themselves and take an oath
According to their laws, rites, and customs,
As Hannibal once swore upon the fanes
And altars of his gods that he would be
Ever a mortal foe to the Romans,
So that they would keep inviolate,
Subject to penalties, controls, and force,
The conditions made and agreed.
The ceremony done and done also
The vile and superstitious oath taking,
He, with his own hand, did select
Five hundred brave barbarian warriors
And ordered them to go in a body
Unto a great cavern, by nature made,
Near to the two ditches we have mentioned,
Purposing, when your men should pass that place,
That they should sally forth from their ambush and
Deprive them, then and there, of all their lives.
And when he'd posted them and entrusted
To brave Bempol, Chumpo, Zutancalpo,
To Calpo, Buzcoico, and Ezmicaio,[2]
To each of these a squadron well-chosen,
The better to trap us into their hands
He carefully gave us to understand
That all the town was deserted.
And when the shining sun had gone to rest
And the dark bodies had been plunged
Into deep shadows, and in silence deep
All living things remained at rest,

[2]Like Gicombo, these men—whose historical identity is now lost in the Spanish transliterations—were Acoma leaders who had urged peace. After the first violent encounter following the attack on Juan de Saldívar's party, a council is convened in which Gicombo is named war captain. All agree that, despite the reservations about defeating the Spanish, they will unite with the aggressive-minded faction led by Zutacapán, Villagrá's real villain.

From the sea came forth the night,
Enveloping the earth in a dark veil.
And before all the stars had run
The mighty course which they do take,
He went to take leave of Luzcoija,
Who was awaiting him in that same place
Where he had chosen to leave her, wounded
Deeply by that love which did burn in her.
And when she saw him, overcome,
Like a mild turtledove which, lost
From its sweet company, roosts not
Nor takes repose on flowering branches,
But on the dry and leafless trees,
And like a tender mother who carries
Her tender child about with her, hanging
About her lovely neck, and, filled with love,
Yearns over him and grows tender
In loving fire, and wastes away,
So this poor woman, conquered by her love,
Making two fountains of her tears,
Did there raise her discouraged voice:
"If the dear pure love I have had for you,
A thousand times more loving you than my own soul,
Deserveth that you give me some comfort,
I beg of you, my lord, not to permit
A flower so tender to wither
Which you have made me think was e'er
To you more pleasing, sweet, and beautiful
Than the life which you live and do enjoy.
By which dear gift I beg of you
That if you come, lord, but to go,
You take my life, for I cannot
Live without you a single hour."
And she became expectantly quiet,
Awaiting a reply, and then spoke out
The sad barbarian: "Madam, I swear
Now by the beauty of those eyes
Which are the peace and light of mine,
And by those lips with which you hide
Those lovely oriental pearls,
And by those soft, delicate hands
Which hold me in such sweet prison,
That now I cannot make excuse
From going to battle against Spain.
Wherefore you must rouse your courage
And strengthen mine, so this sad soul
May return but to look on you,

For though 'tis true it fears your loss
It has firm hope to enjoy you.
And though I die a thousand times I swear
I shall return to see and console you,
And that, dear love, you may understand this
I leave you as ransom my heart and soul."
And so he took his leave, for now
The morning light was appearing,
And, entering the cavern with his men,
The light came fast and embroidered
All of the sky with bright red clouds.
At this great time and conjuncture
The Father Fray Alonso, saying mass,
Did celebrate the day of his name saint,
And having given communion to us all,
Turned from the altar and addressed us thus:
"Ye valiant cavaliers of Christ
And of our most holy laws defenders,
I have not to exhort you to the Church
For as her noble sons you have always
Taken great pains to serve and respect her.
By Jesus Christ I ask and beg of you,
And by His holy blood, that you restrain
Your keen swords, in so far as possible,
From shedding the blood of the enemy,
For thus the valor of the Spaniards is,
To conquer without blood and death whom they attack.
And since you carry God within your souls,
May He bless all of you and may His powerful hand
Protect you, and I, in His name,
Do bless you all." And having thus
Received the blessing from this holy Father there,
We then climbed to the lofty passageway,
Whence we all saw from afar off
That all the pueblo was deserted quite
And that no living soul was seen.
For this reason thirteen immediately
Did pass both ditches from the passageway
Without the Sergeant's order or his permission,
And hardly had they, all together, occupied
The further side when all at once
There charged from the horrible cave
The valiant Gicombo, roaring loud.
And, like the young whale which, wounded
By keen harpoon and deadly steel,
Projects on high thick clouds of spume
And lashes the sea with his tail and cleaves

The water here and there, rising
His spacious back, and, in anger
Snorting and restless, doth stir up
A thousand whirlpools in the deep, so he,
Enraged, his mighty weapons lifted high,
Attacked with them and struck at all.
Seeing the enemy so near at hand
Our men did, in a volley, fire
Their ready harquebuses and, though many
Were stricken down, they yet were forced,
Unable to load a second time,
To come to swords, and in the hot melee,
Mixed with each other, we could not
Give any aid to them because they had
Taken that beam by which they crossed
Unto the second ditch and did not note
They left the first without means of crossing.
All thus involved in such confusion,
Plunging their daggers and the sharp edges
Of their swift swords into a great slaughter
Of miserable, shattered bodies,
They made a fearful butchery.
And so, proud, brave, and fiery
There the two valorous brothers,
Cristóbal Sánchez and Francisco Sánchez,
Captain Quesada and Juan Piñero,
Francisco Vázquez and Manuel Francisco,
Cordero, Juan Rodríguez, Pedraza,
Like to the fingers of the human hand,
Which, being unequal, yet combine
Each with the others and do form,
When closed, a fist that doth destroy
Some strong substance and crushes it,
All joined together in one band,
Each with the others, and charged in.
And, opening great wounds, they shed
From the barbarian breasts and sides,
Eyes, heads, and legs, and from their throats,
Swift-flowing streams of their fresh blood,
And through these great and fearful mouths
Their fearful souls did take swift flight,
All going thence so not to fall
Into such powerful hands. And then
Carrasco, Isasti, Casas, Montesinos,
Their swords red up to their elbows,
Were plying well their brawny arms
When Zutancalpo and great Buzcoico,

With reinforcements, came and did drive back
Your Spaniards, and with so great a force
That, all cornered upon a slope
Which was a trifle deep and protected,
By rain of rocks which they discharged
Upon them, though they wounded none,
Yet so swift and so overwhelming
They were burying them beyond all help.
The brave youth then, seeing that little ship
So overwhelmed and now about to sink,
Shouted with a great voice that someone should
Immediately go and bring a beam.
Hearing this, then, I did fall back,
For, lord, I thought he spoke to me,
Some nine paces and, like to Curtius,
I was running, near desperate,
Toward the first ditch and the Sergeant,
Thinking that I would be dashed to pieces,
Did grasp me by the shield, and, had he not
Loosed me no doubt that had been
The last test I had made of fortune in my life.
But, as he loosed me quickly, I gathered
Momentum for that leap to such effect
That finally I jumped the ditch and then,
Not free from fear and trembling, I took
The log as best I might and dragged,
And, passage made between the ditches,
Your men did quickly pass over.
And hardly had the trumpet blared aloud
When, from the slope on which they were,
Our friends so dear who were buried
Did all come forth, as needs must be
Upon the trumpet's sound shall rise,
On that day of the ultimate judgment,
All of the dead from out their sepulchers.
And seeing that all the lost ground
Was now regained by our men,
Bursting with shame and with sense of disgrace,
Like fiery coals that were buried
And came from the ashes ablaze,
Fiercer than courageous lions
They all did charge, being aided by
Captain Romero and Juan Velarde,
Carabajal, Bañuelos, and Archuleta,
De Lorenzo, Salado, and de Zubia
And many other noble Castilians
Who to the right and left dispatched

Idolaters most swiftly from this life.
Because of this the strong Zutancalpo,
With brave Gicombo and Buzcoico,
Just as the sea in tumult and tempest
Doth boil all over, raising up
Huge crests of water, high summits
Wetting the high heaven, and haughtily
Swells and increases, moans and roars,
And breaks and foams its wild fury
On mighty rocks, and does not rest
So long as the winds temper not
The force of their blasts nor do show themselves
All temperate in peaceful calm,
So were these brave, ferocious barbarians,
Who, urging on their men, did order them
To speed from their swift ready bows
A flight of arrows full as numerous
As the thick drops of water and hailstones
That the high heaven rains or hails.
By whose sharp force sorely wounded
They left Quesada and the ensign, too,
Carabajal and good Antonio Hernández,
Francisco García, and Lizama.
At this, Asencio de Archuleta
Did set firmly against his breast
The stock of his harquebus and did align
The rear sight with the front sight in such wise
That, not knowing how 'twas or where he shot,
He shot through, with four heavy balls,
The greatest comrade and the dearest friend
Whom the poor man had ever in his life.
O divine Shepherd, how You stretch
Your most holy crook out and direct it
To that sad, disobedient sheep
Which we have seen of its free will
Departing very far from out the fold.
Their just punishment is well shown
By unhappy Salado, for, seeing
Eight deadly mouths there open wide
In back and breast and in his sides,
Shrugging his shoulders and raising
His eyes unto the lofty Heavens,
The poor wretch thus did raise his voice to God:
"Lord, it is two years since I have confessed
No matter how my friends have begged me to.
I know, my Lord, I have offended Thee
And I beg only that Thou wait for me

'Till I wash off the stains with which I have
Contaminated my sad soul, redeemed
By that most precious blood You shed."
Hearing of this misfortune, then did come
The Sergeant Major in a mighty haste,
And that he might confess he then ordered
That six good soldiers should take him down.
And he, understanding that aid,
Did beg of him with much sincerity
That since he had alone given offense
To God, our Lord, it be allowed to him
To seek his remedy alone.
Seeing how sincerely he begged
He pleased him in this, but, appearing nonchalant,
He ordered that those men should go with him.
Now, as they followed, he came to a cliff
Of a great height, whereon he saw
A fearful demon who did say to him:
"O valorous soldier, if you now desire
To leave this sad life in triumph,
Throw yourself off here, for I, in these hands,
Will hold your body so that it cannot
Receive an injury in any place."
The sad christian one, hearing this,
Though filled with fear and suspicion,
Summoning courage, answered thus:
"Begone from here, accursed! Tempt me not,
For I am God's soldier, and if I have followed
Your vain standards, this is no time
For such calamity." And, turning back
His tired feet, he then followed
The proper road and clambered down
Unto the Father's tent, where, just as soon
As he confessed his faults and was absolved,
He there lay senseless, for his soul had gone.
The Angels praise you, O my God,
That You thus cure our wounds and show to us
That however You afflict and destroy
The miserable body You gave us,
The soul yet lives and is raised up
Unto the highest height and excellence
That doth await and expect us.
And since the storm of battle as it goes
Grows hotter, and since I do feel myself
Without the strength or courage to continue it,
I wish to stop here that I may write it.

1992

The Apparition of the Virgin of Guadalupe in 1531

Tradition has it that a miraculous apparition of the Virgin Mary took place near Mexico City in 1531, as the following text relates. The Virgin of Guadalupe is a syncretic religious figure. She represents a particular form of the Virgin Mary, mother of Jesus Christ, and as such she mediates between humans and God the Father. She is the symbolic mother of all Catholics. At the same time, her brown skin and Indian features make her a Native American Virgin Mother. In addition, she appeared to a poor Indian. Finally, her apparition was on a sacred site traditionally associated with a female Indian god of fertility, Tonantzin. For centuries she has been the image of miscegenation incarnate, the blending of Spanish and Indian worlds.

In the eighteenth century, when American independence movements were stirring throughout the colonies, Mexican nationalists turned the Virgin of Guadalupe into an image of cultural and political nationalism. Her image became the standard of a war of independence, and the miscegenation of Spanish and Indian was deemphasized in favor of an image of New World hybridity, the *mestizo.* While she competes regionally with other forms of the Virgin, like Our Lady of Conquest in New Mexico or La Virgin de San Juan in Texas, Guadalupe has become a central icon of Mexican American culture. Her image appears in statues on home altars, painted in murals on the side of buildings, tattooed on biceps and etched into windows of low-rider, customized automobiles. Her image serves many different functions, from religious to political, turning up in churches, picket lines, and Chicano literature. She is generally associated with the struggle for civil rights, although her symbol cannot be divorced from traditional values of Catholicism, women, and the family.

Andrew Wiget
New Mexico State University

PRIMARY WORK

Donald Demarest and Coley Taylor, eds., *The Dark Virgin: The Book of Our Lady of Guadalupe,* 1956.

History of the Miraculous Apparition of the Virgin of Guadalupe in 1531[1]

Herein is told, in all truth, how by a great miracle the illustrious Virgin, Blessed Mary, Mother of God, Our Lady, appeared anew, in the place known as Tepeyacac.

She appeared first to an Indian named Juan Diego; and later her divine Image appeared in the presence of the first Bishop of Mexico, Don Fray Juan de Zumárraga; also there are told various miracles which have been done. It was ten years after the beginning of bringing water from the mountain of Mexico, when the arrow and the shield had been put away, when in all parts of the country there was tranquillity which was beginning to show its light, and faith and knowledge of Him was being taught through Whose favor we have our being, Who is the only true God.

In the year 1531, early in the month of December, it happened that an humble Indian, called Juan Diego, whose dwelling, it is said, was in Quahutítlan, although for divine worship he pertained to Tlatilolco, one Saturday very early in the morning, while he was on his way to divine worship according to his custom, when he had arrived near the top of the hill called Tepeyacac, as it was near dawn, he heard above the hill a singing like that when many choice birds sing together, their voices resounding as if echoing throughout the hills; he was greatly rejoiced; their song gave him rapture exceeding that of the bell-bird and other rare birds of song.

Juan Diego stopped to wonder and said to himself: *Is it I who have this good fortune to hear what I hear? Or am I perhaps only dreaming? Where am I? Perhaps this is the place the ancients, our forefathers, used to tell about—our grandfathers—the flowery land, the fruitful land? Is it perchance the earthly paradise?*

And while he was looking towards the hilltop, facing the east, from which came the celestial song, suddenly the singing stopped and he heard someone calling as if from the top of the hill, saying: *Juan.* Juan Diego did not dare to go there where he was being called; he did not move, perhaps in some way marvelling; yet he was filled with great joy and delight, and then, presently, he began to climb to the summit where he was called.

And, when he was nearing it, on the top of the peak he saw a lady who was standing there who had called him from a distance, and, having come into her presence, he was struck with wonder at the radiance of her exceeding great beauty, her garments shining like the sun; and the stones of the hill, and the caves, reflecting the brightness of her light were like precious gold; and he saw how the rainbow clothed the land so that the cactus and other things that grew there seemed like celestial plants, their leaves and thorns shining like gold in her presence. He made obeisance and heard her voice, her words, which rejoiced him utterly when she asked, very tenderly, as if she loved him:

[1]The original version of this text was published in Náhuatl, the language of the Aztecs, by Bachiller Luis Lazo de Vega, Chaplain of the Sanctuary of Our Lady of Guadalupe, in 1649, over a century after the event. The text is believed to be the work of Antonio Valeriano, a contemporary of Juan Diego and Bishop Zumárraga. The story of the Virgin's appearance is essentially an oral tradition, however, and to this day it is maintained as such among Mexican-Americans.

Listen, xocoyote[2] mio, Juan, where are you going?

And he replied: *My Holy One, my Lady, my Damsel, I am on my way to your house at Mexico-Tlatilulco; I go in pursuit of the holy things which our priests teach us.*

Whereupon She told him, and made him aware of her divine will, saying: *You must know, and be very certain in your heart, my son, that I am truly the eternal Virgin, holy Mother of the True God, through Whose favor we live, the Creator, Lord of Heaven, and the Lord of the Earth. I very much desire that they build me a church here, so that in it I may show and may make known and give all my love, my mercy and my help and my protection-I am in truth your merciful mother-to you and to all the other people dear to me who call upon me, who search for me, who confide in me; here I will hear their sorrow, their words, so that I may make perfect and cure their illnesses, their labors, and their calamities. And so that my intention may be made known, and my mercy, go now to the episcopal palace of the Bishop of Mexico and tell him that I send you to tell him how much I desire to have a church built here, and tell him very well all that you have seen and all that you have heard; and be sure in your heart that I will pay you with glory and you will deserve much that I will repay you for your weariness, your work, which you will bear diligently doing what I send you to do. Now hear my words, my dear son, and go and do everything carefully and quickly.*

Then he humbled himself before her and said: *My Holy One, my Lady, I will go now and fulfill your commandment.*

And straightway he went down to accomplish that with which he was charged, and took the road that leads straight to Mexico.

And when he had arrived within the city, he went at once to the episcopal palace of the Lord Bishop, who was the first [Bishop] to come, whose name was Don Fray Juan de Zumárraga, a religious of St. Francis. And having arrived there, he made haste to ask to see the Lord Bishop, asking his servants to give notice of him. After a good while they came to call him, and the Bishop advised them that he should come in; and when he had come into his presence, he knelt and made obeisance, and then after this he related the words of the Queen of Heaven, and told besides all that he had seen and all that he had heard. And [the Bishop] having heard all his words and the commandment as if he were not perfectly persuaded, said in response:

My son, come again another time when we can be more leisurely; and I will hear more from you about the origin of this; I will look into this about which you have come, your will, your desire.

And he departed with much sorrow because he had not been able to convince him of the truth of his mission.

Thereupon he returned that same day and went straightway to the hill where he had seen the Queen of Heaven, who was even then standing there where he had first seen Her, waiting for him, and he, having seen Her, made obeisance, kneeling upon the ground, and said:

My Holy One, most noble of persons, My Lady, my Xocoyota, my Damsel, I went there where You sent me; although it was most difficult to enter the house of the Lord

[2]*Xocoyote:* This Náhuatl word is variously translated into Spanish as if it were "my little son" or "my dear son." *Xocoyota* is the form for "daughter."

Bishop, I saw him at last, and in his presence I gave him your message in the way You instructed me; he received me very courteously, and listened with attention; but he answered as if he could not be certain and did not believe; he told me: Come again another time when we can be at leisure, and I will hear you from beginning to end; I will look into that about which you come, what it is you want and ask me for. He seemed to me, when he answered, to be thinking perhaps that the church You desire to have made here was perchance not Your will, but a fancy of mine. I pray You, my Holy One, my Lady, my Daughter, that any one of the noble lords who are well known, reverenced and respected be the one to undertake this so that Your words will be believed. For it is true that I am only a poor man; I am not worthy of being there where You send me; pardon me, my Xocoyota, I do not wish to make your noble heart sad; I do not want to fall into your displeasure.

Then the always noble Virgin answered him, saying: *Hear me, my son, it is true that I do not lack for servants or ambassadors to whom I could entrust my message so that my will could be verified, but it is important that you speak for me in this matter, weary as you are; in your hands you have the means of verifying, of making plain my desire, my will; I pray you, my xocoyote, and advise you with much care, that you go again tomorrow to see the Bishop and represent me; give him an understanding of my desire, my will, that he build the church that I ask; and tell him once again that it is the eternal Virgin, Holy Mary, the Mother of God, who sends you to him.*

And Juan Diego answered her, saying: *Queen of Heaven, my Holy One, my Damsel, do not trouble your heart, for I will go with all my heart and make plain Your voice, Your words. It is not because I did not want to go, or because the road is stony, but only because perhaps I would not be heard, and if I were heard I would not be believed. I will go and do your bidding and tomorrow in the afternoon about sunset I will return to give the answer to your words the Lord Bishop will make; and now I leave You, my Xocoyota, my Damsel, my Lady; meanwhile, rest You.*

With this, he went to his house to rest. The next day being Sunday, he left his house in the morning and went straightway to Tlatilulco, to attend Mass and the sermon. Then, being determined to see the Bishop, when Mass and the sermon were finished, at ten o'clock, with all the other Indians he came out of the church; but Juan Diego left them and went to the palace of the Lord Bishop. And having arrived there, he spared no effort in order to see him and when, after great difficulty, he did see him again, he fell to his knees and implored him to the point of weeping, much moved, in an effort to make plain the words of the Queen of Heaven, and that the message and the will of the most resplendent Virgin would be believed; that the church be built as She asked, where She wished it.

But the Lord Bishop asked Juan Diego many things, to know for certain what had taken place, questioning him: Where did he see Her? What did the Lady look like whom he saw? And he told the Lord Bishop all that he had seen. But although he told him everything exactly, so that it seemed in all likelihood that She was the Immaculate Virgin, Mary most pure, the beloved Mother of Our Lord Jesus Christ, the Bishop said he could not be certain. He said: It is not only with her words that we have to do, but also to obtain that for which she asks. It is very necessary to have some sign by which we may believe that it is really the Queen of Heaven who sends you.

And Juan Diego, having heard him, said to the Lord Bishop: *My Lord, wait for whatever sign it is that you ask for, and I will go at once to ask the Queen of Heaven, who sent me.* And the Lord Bishop, seeing that he had agreed, and so that he should not be confused or worried, in any way, urged him to go; and then, calling some of his servants in whom he had much confidence, he asked them to follow and to watch where he went and see whomsoever it was that he went to see, and with whom he might speak. And this was done accordingly, and when Juan Diego reached the place where a bridge over the river, near the hill, met the royal highway, they lost him, and although they searched for him everywhere they could not find him in any part of that land. And so they returned, and not only were they weary, but extremely annoyed with him, and upon their return they abused him much with the Lord Bishop, over all that had happened, for they did not believe in him; they said that he had been deceiving him, and had imagined all that he had come to relate to him, or perhaps he had dreamed it, and they agreed and said that if he should come again they would seize him and chastise him severely so that he would not lie another time.

The next day, Monday, when Juan Diego was to bring some sign by which he might be believed, he did not return, since, when he arrived at his house, an uncle of his who was staying there, named Juan Bernardino, was very ill of a burning fever; Juan Diego went at once to bring a doctor and then he procured medicine; but there still was no time because the man was very ill. Early in the morning his uncle begged him to go out to bring one of the priests from Tlatilulco so that he might be confessed, for he was very certain that his time had come to die, now that he was too weak to rise, and could not get well.

And on Tuesday, very early in the morning, Juan Diego left his house to go to Tlatilulco to call a priest, and as he was nearing the hill on the road which lies at the foot of the hill towards the west, which was his usual way, he said to himself: *If I go straight on, without doubt I will see Our Lady and She will persuade me to take the sign to the Lord Bishop; let us first do our duty; I will go first to call the priest for my poor uncle; will he not be waiting for him?*

With this he turned to another road at the foot of the slope and was coming down the other side towards the east to take a short cut to Mexico; he thought that by turning that way the Queen of Heaven would not see him, but She was watching for him, and he saw Her on the hilltop where he had always seen Her before, coming down that side of the slope, by the shortest way, and She said to him:

Xocoyote mio, where are you going? What road is this you are taking?

And he was frightened; it is not known whether he was disgusted with himself, or was ashamed, or perhaps he was struck with wonder; he prostrated himself before Her and greeted her, saying: *My Daughter, my Xocoyota, God keep You, Lady. How did You waken? And is your most pure body well, perchance? My Holy One, I will bring pain to your heart-for I must tell You, my Virgin, that an uncle of mine, who is Your servant, is very sick, with an illness so strong that without doubt he will die of it; I am hastening to Your house in Mexico to call one of Our Lord's dear ones, our priests, to come to confess him, and when I have done that, then I will come back to carry out Your commandment. My Virgin, my Lady, forgive me, be patient with me until I do my duty, and then tomorrow I will come back to You.*

And having heard Juan Diego's explanation, the most holy and immaculate Virgin replied to him:

Listen, and be sure, my dear son, that I will protect you; do not be frightened or grieve, or let your heart be dismayed; however great the illness may be that you speak of, am I not here, I who am your mother, and is not my help a refuge? Am I not of your kind?[3] *Do not be concerned about your uncle's illness, for he is not now going to die; be assured that he is now already well. Is there anything else needful?* (And in that same hour his uncle was healed, as later he learned.)

And Juan Diego, having heard the words of the Queen of Heaven, greatly rejoiced and was convinced, and besought Her that She would send him again to see the Lord Bishop, to carry him some sign by which he could believe, as he had asked.

Whereupon the Queen of Heaven commanded him to climb up to the top of the hill where he had always seen her, saying: *Climb up to the top of the hill, my xocoyote, where you have seen me stand, and there you will find many flowers; pluck them and gather them together, and then bring them down here in my presence.*

Then Juan Diego climbed up the hill and when he had reached the top he marvelled to see blooming there many kinds of beautiful flowers of Castile, for it was then very cold, and he marvelled at their fragrance and odor. Then he began to pluck them, and gathered them together carefully, and wrapped them in his mantle, and when he had finished he descended and carried to the Queen of Heaven all the flowers he had plucked. She, when she had seen them, took them into her immaculate hands, gathered them together again, and laid them in his cloak once more and said to him:

My xocoyote, all these flowers are the sign that you must take to the Bishop; in my name tell him that with this he will see and recognize my will and that he must do what I ask; and you who are my ambassador worthy of confidence, I counsel you to take every care that you open your mantle only in the presence of the Bishop, and you must make it known to him what is that you carry, and tell him how I asked you to climb to the top of the hill to gather the flowers. Tell him also all that you have seen, so that you will persuade the Lord Bishop and he will see that the church is built for which I ask.

And the Queen of Heaven having acquainted him with this, he departed, following the royal highway which leads directly to Mexico; he traveled content, because he was persuaded that now he would succeed; he walked carefully, taking great pains not to injure what he was carrying in his mantle; he went glorying in the fragrance of the beautiful flowers. When he arrived at the Bishop's palace, he encountered his majordomo and other servants and asked them to tell the Bishop that he would like to see him; but none of them would, perhaps because it was still very early in the morning or, perhaps recognizing him, they were vexed or, because they knew how others of their household had lost him on the road when they were following him. They kept him waiting there a long time; he waited very humbly to see if they would call him, and when it was getting very late, they came to him to see what it was he was carrying as a proof of what he had related. And Juan Diego, seeing that he

[3]The Virgin identifies herself as an Indian.

could not hide from them what he was carrying, when they had tormented him and jostled him and knocked him about, let them glimpse that he had roses, to deliver himself from them; and they, when they saw that they were roses of Castile, very fragrant and fresh, and not at all in their season, marvelled and wanted to take some of them. Three times they made bold to take them, but they could not because, when they tried to take them, they were not roses that they touched, but were as if painted or embroidered. Upon this, they went to the Lord Bishop to tell him what they had seen, and that the Indian who was there often before had come again and wanted to see him, and that they had kept him waiting there a long time.

The Lord Bishop, having heard this, knew that now this was the sign that should persuade him whether what the Indian had told him was true. He straightway asked that he be brought in to see him.

Having come into his presence, Juan Diego fell to his knees (as he had always done) and again related fully all that he had seen, and full of satisfaction and wonder he said: *My Lord, I have done that which you asked me; I went to tell my Holy One, the Queen of Heaven, the beloved Virgin Mary, Mother of God, how you asked me for some sign that you might believe that it was She who desired you to build Her the church for which She asked. And also I told Her how I had given my word that I would bring you some sign so that you could believe in what She had put in my care, and She heard with pleasure your suggestion and found it good, and just now, early this morning, She told me to come again to see you and I asked Her for the sign that I had asked Her to give me, and then She sent me to the hilltop where I have always seen Her, to pluck the flowers that I should see there. And when I had plucked them, I took them to the foot of the mountain where She had remained, and She gathered them into her immaculate hands and then put them again into my mantle for me to bring them to you. Although I knew very well that the hilltop was not a place for flowers, since it is a place of thorns, cactuses, caves and mezquites, I was not confused and did not doubt Her. When I reached the summit I saw there was a garden there of flowers with quantities of the fragrant flowers which are found in Castile; I took them and carried them to the Queen of Heaven and She told me that I must bring them to you, and now I have done it, so that you may see the sign that you ask for in order to do Her bidding, and so that you will see that my word is true. And here they are.*

Whereupon he opened his white cloak, in which he was carrying the flowers, and as the roses of Castile dropped out to the floor, suddenly there appeared the most pure image of the most noble Virgin Mary, Mother of God, just exactly as it is, even now, in Her holy house, in Her church which is named Guadalupe;[4] and the Lord Bishop, having seen this, and all those who were with him, knelt down and gazed with wonder; and then they grew sad, and were sorrowful, and were aghast,

[4]The original significance of this word is unclear. It is probably a Hispanic form of a compound derived from the Náhuatl (Aztec) word for "snake," *coatl,* and the Spanish word for "crush, trample," *llope.* Thus, *coatl-llope,* "she crushes the serpent." Interestingly, the image described here is clearly modelled on traditional Catholic figures of Immaculate Mary, Queen of Heaven, statues of whom (based on Genesis 3:15) feature the Virgin standing on a half-moon, crushing with her foot the Devil, represented as a snake. In addition, the Aztec culture hero is Quetzalcoatl, the Plumed Serpent, and the Virgin is requesting that her Cathedral be built over the site of an Aztec place of worship, which, in fact, it was.

and the Lord Bishop with tenderness and weeping begged Her forgiveness for not having done Her bidding at once. And when he had finished, he untied from Juan Diego's neck the cloak on which was printed the figure of the Queen of Heaven. And then he carried it into his chapel; and Juan Diego remained all that day in the house of the Bishop, who did not want him to go. And the following day the Bishop said to him: *Come, show us where it is the Queen of Heaven wishes us to build Her church.* And when he had shown them where it was, he told them that he wanted to go to his house to see his uncle Juan Bernardino who had been very ill and he had set out for Tlatilulco to get a priest to confess him, but the Queen of Heaven had told him that he was already cured.

They did not let him go alone, but went with him to his house, and when they arrived there, they saw that his uncle was well and that nothing was now the matter with him; and the uncle wondered much when he saw such a company with his nephew, and all treating him with great courtesy, and he asked him: *How is it they treat you this way? And why do they reverence you so much?*

And Juan Diego told him that when he had gone from the house to call a confessor for him, he saw the Queen of Heaven on the hill called Tepeyacac and She had sent him to Mexico to see the Lord Bishop to have a church built for Her. And that She had also told him not to worry about his uncle, that he was now well.

Whereupon his uncle showed great joy and told him that it was true that at that very hour he had been healed, and that he himself had seen exactly that same Person, and that She had told him how She had sent him to Mexico to see the Bishop, and also that when he saw him again, to tell him all that he had seen also, and how, miraculously, he had been restored to health, and that the most holy Image of the Immaculate Virgin should be called Santa María de Guadalupe.

And after this they brought Juan Bernardino into the Lord Bishop's presence so that he might tell him under oath all that he had just related; and the Bishop kept the two men (that is, Juan Diego and Juan Bernardino) as his guests in his own house several days until the church for the Queen of Heaven was built where Juan Diego had shown them. And the Lord Bishop moved the sacred Image of the Queen of Heaven, which he had in his chapel, to the cathedral so that all the people could see it.

All the city was in a turmoil upon seeing Her most holy portrait; they saw that it had appeared miraculously, that no one in the world had painted it on Juan Diego's mantle; for this, on which the miraculous Image of the Queen of Heaven appeared, was *ayate,* a coarse fabric made of cactus fibre, rather like homespun, and well woven, for at that time all the Indian people covered themselves with *ayate,* except the nobles, the gentlemen and the captains of war, who dressed themselves in cloaks of cotton, or in cloaks made of wool.

The esteemed *ayate* upon which the Immaculate Virgin, Our Sovereign Queen, appeared unexpectedly is made of two pieces sewn together with threads of cotton; the height of Her sacred Image from the sole of Her foot to the top of Her head measures six hands, and one woman's hand. Her sacred face is very beautiful, grave, and somewhat dark; her precious body, according to this, is small; her hands are held at her breast; the girdle at her waist is violet; her right foot only shows, a very little, and her slipper is earthen in color; her robe is rose-colored; in the shadows it appears deeper red, and it is embroidered with various flowers outlined in gold; pendant at her throat is a little gold circlet which is outlined with a black line around it; in the middle it has a cross; and one discovers glimpses of another, inner vestment of white cotton, daintily gathered at her wrists. The outer mantle which covers her from her head almost to her feet is of heavenly blue; half-way down its fullness hangs in folds, and it is bordered with gold, a rather wide band of gold thread, and all over it there are golden stars which are in number forty-six. Her most holy head is turned towards the right and is bending down; and on her head above her mantle she wears a shining gold crown, and at her feet there is the new moon with its horns pointed upward; and exactly in the middle of it the Immaculate Virgin is standing, and, it would seem also, in the middle of the sun, since its rays surround her everywhere. These rays number a hundred; some are large and others are small; those on each side of her sacred face and those above her head number twelve, in all they number fifty on each side. And outside the edges of this and her robes She is encircled with white clouds. This divine Image as it is described stands above an angel, half of whose body only appears, since he is in the midst of clouds. The angel's outstretched arms hold the edges of her outer robes as they hang in folds near her sacred feet. His garment is of rosy color with a gold ornament at his neck; his wings are made or composed of various sizes of feathers, and it seems as if he were very happy to be accompanying the Queen of Heaven.

1649

Sor Juana Inés de la Cruz 1648–1695

Known to her contemporaries as "the Phoenix of Mexico" and "the Tenth Muse," Sor Juana Inés de la Cruz has been characterized as the greatest lyrical poet of colonial Mexico. Born the illegitimate daughter of a Basque landowner and a creole mother, she was by all accounts an intellectual prodigy; at the age of eight, she is said to have written a *loa,* a brief dramatic poem, about the Sacraments. Word of her precocity and erudition won her an invitation to the viceregal court of Mexico, where her intellectual agility, personal charisma, and charm made a considerable impact.

In seventeenth-century Mexico, it was not possible for women to pursue university studies, and the only path open to women who wished to dedicate themselves to learning was the religious life. In the words of Sor Juana Inés herself, "And so I entered the religious life, knowing that life there entailed certain conditions (I refer to superficial, and not fundamental, regards) most repugnant to my nature; but given the total antipathy I felt for marriage, I deemed convent life the least unsuitable and the most honorable I could elect. . . ." Thus, at the age of twenty-one, Juana Inés de la Cruz entered the convent of San Jeronimo, where she assembled a sizable collection of books and manuscripts and dedicated herself to a life of study, writing, and religious devotions. Later, at the convent of Santa Paula, she lived in some comfort, surrounded by her books and her collections of folk art and scientific instruments.

New Spain in the seventeenth century was a rigidly hierarchical culture, and roles for women were limited to the domestic sphere, the court, and the convent; women who ventured beyond these bounds and who challenged existing gender norms were cruelly ostracized. Given the caliber of her literary production and her fearlessness in expounding views that were considered unorthodox at the time, it was perhaps inevitable that Sor Juana Inés would attract censure as well as recognition. In 1691 she entered into a debate with the Portuguese Jesuit Father Antonio Vieira, an able and lucid rhetorician, regarding the biblical episode in which Jesus washes the feet of his disciples. According to Vieira, Christ washed the disciples' feet for the sake of love itself; Sor Juana maintained that this act was proof of his love for humanity. The ecclesiastical authorities saw her dissent from the views of such a prominent male theologian as insolent, and the bishop of Puebla, using the female pseudonym Sor Filotea, wrote her a letter demanding that she restrict herself to her religious duties and give up her intellectual pursuits. Sor Juana Inés's reply is a masterpiece of irony, logic, and rhetorical skill, a Baroque theatrical performance in which she manipulates existing stereotypes of femininity in order to demonstrate the hypocrisy and intellectual poverty of her male counterparts. In one of her sonnets, Sor Juana denounces the persecution to which she was subjected for pursuing her intellectual vocation:

> In my pursuit, World, why such
>   diligence?
> What my offence, when I am thus
>   inclined,
> insuring elegance affect my mind,
> not that my mind affect an
>   elegance?
> I have no love of riches or finance,
> and thus do I most happily, I find,
> expend finances to enrich my
>   mind
> and not mind expend upon finance.
> I worship beauty not, but vilify
> that spoil of time that mocks
>   eternity,
> nor less, deceitful treasures glorify,
> but hold foremost, with greatest
>   constancy,
> consuming all the vanity in life,
> and not consuming life in vanity.

On the pressures she faced as a woman and thinker, she once commented plaintively, "Women feel that men surpass them, and that I seem to place myself on a level with men; some wish that I did not know so much; others say that I ought to know more to merit such applause; elderly women do not wish that other women know more than they; young women, that others present a good appearance; and one and all wish me to conform to the rules of their judgement; so that from all sides comes such a singular martyrdom as I deem none other has ever experienced."

The poetry of Sor Juana Inés de la Cruz shares many features with Spanish Baroque poetry of the period, with its classical allusions and imagery. Although her work has been compared to that of the Spanish poet Gongora in its dazzling and often convoluted language effects, her irony recalls that of the satirist Quevedo, another distinguished Spanish writer, with its elegant Baroque play of light and shadow, reality and illusion. The texts of Sor Juana Inés, however, are radically different from those of her Old World counterparts and are characterized by her recourse not only to European but also to indigenous verse forms and Mexican motifs. Her poetry demonstrates an effortless command of stylistic conventions, while conveying a genuinely radical political message regarding the gender norms of New Spain and the emergence of a genuine creole identity among the Mexicans of her day.

The final years of Sor Juana Inés were difficult ones for Mexico, with epidemics, natural catastrophes, and civil unrest. Some scholars suggest that Sor Juana blamed herself for this state of affairs, and indeed she signed a document in her own blood renouncing the intellectual life and reaffirming her religious faith. Finally, however, she was compelled to sell most of her library, donating the money to the poor and devoting herself to spiritual concerns. She died on April 17, 1695, after nursing her sister nuns during a plague epidemic in Mexico City.

Susan Castillo
King's College, London

PRIMARY WORK

Sor Juana Inés de la Cruz, *Poems, Protest, and a Dream,* trans. Dorothy Sayers Peden, 1997.

48 In Reply to a Gentleman from Peru, Who Sent Her Clay Vessels While Suggesting She Would Better Be a Man

Kind Sir, while wishing to reply,
my Muses[1] all have taken leave,
and none, even for charity,
will aid me now I wish to speak;

and though we know these Sisters nine[2]
good mothers are of wit and jest,
not one, once having heard your verse,
will dare to jest at my behest.

The God Apollo[3] listens, rapt,
and races on, so high aloft
that those who guide his Chariot
must raise their voices to a shout.

To hear your lines, fleet Pegasus[4]
his lusty breathing will retain,
that no one fear his thunderous neigh
as your verses are declaimed.

Checking, against nature's order,
altering crystalline watercourse,

[1]The nine goddesses who presided over poetry, music, dancing, and all the liberal arts: Clio, Euterpe, Thalia, Melpomene, Terpsichore, Erato, Polyhymnia, Calliope, and Urania.
[2]The Muses.
[3]Apollo, Greek god of poetry and the sun, was often depicted flanked by the Muses.
[4]The winged horse of poetry, sprung from the head of Medusa.

Helicon[5] stays its gurgling water,
Agannipe,[6] her murmuring source:

for, having heard your murmuring,
the Nine Daughters all concede,
beside your verses they are wanting,
unfit to study at your feet.

Apollo sets aside the wand
that he employs to mark the beat,
because, on seeing you, he knows
he cannot justly take the lead.

And thus, acknowledge it I must,
I cannot scribe the verses owed
unless, perhaps, compassionate,
keen inspiration you bestow.

Be my Apollo, and behold
(as your light illumines me)
how my lyre will then be heard
the length and breadth of land and sea.

Though humble, oh, how powerful
my invocation's consequence,
I find new valor in my breast,
new spirit given utterance!

Ignited with unfamiliar fervour,
my pen bursting into flame,
while giving due to famed Apollo
I honor Navarrete's[7] name.

Traveling where none has trod,
expression rises to new heights,
and, revering in new invention,
finds in itself supreme delight.

Stammering with such abundance
my clumsy tongue is tied with pain:
much is seen, but little spoken,
some is known, but none explained.

[5]Mountain near the Gulf of Corinth, sacred to Apollo.
[6]The fountain at the foot of Mount Helicon.
[7]Surname of the gentleman from Peru (of the poem's title).

You will think that I make mock;
no, nothing further from the truth,
to prophesy, my guiding spirit
is lacking but a fine hair's breadth.

But if I am so little able
to offer you sufficient praise,
to form the kind of compliment
that only your apt pen may phrase,

what serve me then to undertake it?
to venture it, what good will serve?
if mine be pens that write in water,
recording lessons unobserved.

That they themselves elucidate,
I now leave your eulogies:
as none to their measure correspond,
none can match them in degree,

and I turn to giving thanks
for your fair gifts, most subtly made;
Art lifts a toast to appetite
in lovely Vessels of fragrant clay.

Earthenware, so exquisite
that Chile properly is proud,
though it is not gold or silver
that gives your gift its wide renown

but, rather, from such lowly matter
forms emerge that put to shame
the brimming Goblets made of gold
from which Gods their nectar drained.

Kiss, I beg, the hands that made them,
though judging by the Vessels' charm
—such grace can surely leave no doubt—
yours were the hands that gave them form.

As for the counsel that you offer,
I promise you, I will attend
with all my strength, although I judge no strength
on earth can en-Tarquin:[8]

[8]Tarquinius Superbus, seventh and last king of Rome, was said to have been deposed because his son Sextus raped Lucretia. Dorothy Sayers Peden suggests in a footnote to her translation that the verb invented by Sor Juana Inés broadly means "to turn a woman into a man." Another reading is that she is asserting the inviolate nature of her own ideas.

for here we have no Salmacis,[9]
whose crystal water, so they tell,
to nurture masculinity
possesses powers unexcelled.

I have no knowledge of these things,
except that I came to this place
so that, if true that I am female,
none substantiate that state.

I know, too, that they were wont
to call wife, or woman, in the Latin
uxor, only those who wed,
though wife or woman might be virgin.

So in my case, it is not seemly
that I be viewed as feminine,
as I will never be a woman
who may as woman serve a man.[10]

I know only that my body,
not to either state inclined,
is neuter, abstract, guardian
of only what my Soul consigns.

Let us renounce this argument,
let others, if they will, debate;
some matters better left unknown
no reason can illuminate.

Generous gentleman from Peru,
proclaiming such unhappiness,
did you leave Lima any art,
given the art you brought to us?

You must know that law of Athens
by which Aristides[11] was expelled:
it seems that, even if for good,
it is forbidden to excel.

[9]Here Sor Juana Inés refers ironically to the fountain of Salmacis, which rendered effeminate any man who, like Hermaphroditus, drank of its waters.

[10]Either due to her state as a nun or to her refusal to accept subordinate status.

[11]An Athenian statesman and general (530–468 B.C.), called "the Just" for his impartiality. According to tradition, an illiterate Athenian, tired of Aristedes' fame, asked him to write the name Aristedes on a ballot demanding his ostracism from the state. Without revealing his identity, Aristedes complied and was expelled.

He was expelled for being good,
and other famous men as well;
because to tower over all
is truly unforgivable.

He who always leads his peers
will by necessity invite
malicious envy, as his fame
will rob all others of the light.

To the degree that one is chosen
as the target for acclaim,
to that same measure, envy trails
in close pursuit, with perfect aim.

Now you are banished from Peru
and welcomed in my Native Land,
we see the Heavens grant to us
the blessing that Peru declined.

But it is well that such great talent
live in many different zones,
for those who are with greatness born
should live not for themselves alone.

94 Which Reveals the Honorable Ancestry of a High-Born Drunkard

Alfeo claims he comes from kings,
he boasts of blood of royal hue,
he speaks of queens with *diamond* rings,
whose *hearts* pump only royal blue.

The truth is, his line brandished *clubs,*
his House is the House of Topers,[1]
but have no doubt, when in his cups,
he's king —in *spades*—the King of Jokers.

[1]Drunkards.

317 Villancico VI, from Santa Catarina, 1691[1]

Refrain

Victor! Victor! Catherine,
who with enlightenment divine
persuaded all the learned men,
she who with triumph overcame
—with knowledge truly sovereign—
the pride and arrogance profane
of those who challenged her, in vain
Victor! Victor! Victor!

Verses

There in Egypt, all the sages
by a woman were convinced
that gender is not of the essence
in matters of intelligence.
Victor! Victor!

A victory, a miracle;
though more prodigious than the feat
of conquering, was surely that
the men themselves declared defeat.
Victor! Victor!

How wise they were, these Prudent Men,
acknowledging they were outdone,
for one conquers when one yields
to wisdom greater than one's own.
Victor! Victor!

Illumination shed by truth
will never by mere shouts be drowned;
persistently, its echo rings,

[1]A *villancico* is a religious song, an element in the lyrical play by Sor Juana Inés about St. Catherine of Alexandria, a young noblewoman known for her erudition and religious ardor. The Roman emperor Maximinus, persecutor of Christians in the third century, was said to have assembled the greatest philosophers to confound her. When Catherine refuted their arguments, they were burned alive. Later, an attempt was made to break her on a spiked wheel, but it fell to pieces and she was unhurt. The analogies with the situation of Sor Juana Inés and her theological disputes with Father Antonio Vieira and with Bishop Sahagun are evident.

above all obstacles resounds.
Victor! Victor!

None of these Wise Men was ashamed
when he found himself convinced,
because, in being Wise, he knew
his knowledge was not infinite.
Victor! Victor!

It is of service to the Church
that women argue, tutor, learn,
for He Who granted women reason
would not have them uninformed.
Victor! Victor!

How haughtily they must have come,
the men that Maximin[2] convened,
though at their advent arrogant,
they left with wonder and esteem.
Victor! Victor!

Persuaded, all of them, with her,
gave up their lives unto the knife:
how much good might have been lost,
were Catherine less erudite!
Victor! Victor!

No man, whatever his renown,
accomplished such a victory,
and we know that God, through her,
honored femininity.
Victor! Victor!

Too brief, the flowering of her years,
but ten and eight, the sun's rotations,
but when measuring her knowledge,
who could sum the countless ages?
Victor! Victor!

Now all her learned arguments
are lost to us (how great the grief).
But with her blood, if not with ink,
she wrote the lesson of her life.
Victor! Victor!
Tutelar and holy Patron,

[2]Maximinus. See previous note.

Catherine, the Shrine of Arts;
long may she illumine Wise Men,
she who Wise to Saints converts.
Victor! Victor!

Don Antonio de Otermín fl. 1680

At the end of the seventeenth century, the Kingdom of New Mexico, as it was called, was the jewel of the northern frontier of Spain's American empire. It was also the central cog in the defensive line that held that frontier. To be governor of such a province was both a great honor and a tremendous responsibility. From 1678 to 1683 the honor fell to Don Antonio de Otermín, but his honor turned to shame when he became the first governor forced to surrender his province to native rebels.

In 1680 about 2,800 Spanish settlers lived in New Mexico, with many more Indians interacting with them in the colonial system. The settlements were located in the north-central area of the present state, in the upper valley of the Rio Grande. For a century, since the arrival of Oñate, the colony had been evolving a culture of its own, already distinct from that of New Spain far to the south. Agriculture, sheep herding, buffalo hunting, and some mining were staples of the economy. Franciscan missionaries still staffed the churches, although the long-standing settlement could no longer be considered a recently opened territory.

Yet the native population had not been incorporated well into the church, and the Franciscans continually pressured them to convert. As long as that pressure respected certain limits, the missionaries were tolerated, but toward the second half of the 1600s the missionaries' zeal led them to interfere with the Indians' private practices. They preached against the use of kiva ceremonies, and they attempted to destroy native symbolic objects, such as masks and kachina dolls. At the same time, the demands for forced labor from both the state and the church left almost no time for the natives to cultivate their own lands. The situation was intolerable. As a result, the Indians, under the leadership of Popé, a Tewa religious leader known among his people as Tío Pepe, united in a well-organized, surprise attack that swept the Spaniards out of northern New Mexico. In the process, twenty-one of the thirty-two Franciscans were killed; many churches were destroyed (like the enormous structure at Pecos, the largest church built in the U.S. territory until St. Patrick's Cathedral in New York City, centuries later); and the governor's palace was taken over by the ruler of the coalition.

Otermín's letter, like Cabeza de Vaca's a century and a half before, is an attempt to justify failure. The governor had lost an entire province, miles of territory, a century of accumulated investments in land and livestock and buildings. Even more, he had allowed the "lowly" natives to defeat the representatives of the royal crown. In 1681 his attempt to retake the territory was beaten back, only proving the seriousness of the rebellion and the need for a large and concerted campaign of reconquest. The disgrace echoed throughout the empire, causing deep preoccupation lest the story spread and lead to more uprisings. Otermín's tale of the irresistible forces allied against him, the confusion into which the Spaniards were thrown, and the flight for their lives might easily have been read as a judgment on the state of the empire itself, and the consequences could have been disastrous. Latin America in general was not that much different from New Mexico; the façade of control was precarious. Otermín's defeat was the equivalent of Custer's last stand two centuries later, a revelation of defeat which temporarily shocked the Spanish colonizers and spurred aggressive military action.

Juan Bruce-Novoa
University of California at Irvine

PRIMARY WORK

C. W. Hackett, ed., *Historical Documents Relating to New Mexico, Nueva Vizcaya, and Approaches Thereto, to 1773,* 3 vols., 1937.

Letter on the Pueblo Revolt of 1680

My very reverend father, Sir, and friend, most beloved Fray Francisco de Ayeta: The time has come when, with tears in my eyes and deep sorrow in my heart, I commence to give an account of the lamentable tragedy, such as has never before happened in the world, which has occurred in this miserable kingdom and holy *custodia,*[1] His Divine Majesty having thus permitted it because of my grievous sins. Before beginning my narration I desire, as one obligated and grateful, to give yourreverence the thanks due for the demonstrations of affection and kindness which you have given in your solicitude in ascertaining and inquiring for definite notices about both my life and those of the rest in this miserable kingdom, in the midst of persistent reports which had been circulated of the deaths of myself and the others, and for sparing neither any kind of effort nor large expenditures. For this only Heaven can reward your reverence, though I do not doubt that his Majesty (may God keep him) will do so.

After I sent my last letter to your reverence by the *maese de campo,*[2] Pedro de Leyba, while the necessary things were being made ready alike for the escort and in the way of provisions, for the most expeditious despatch of the returning carts and their guards, as your reverence had enjoined me, I received information that a plot for a general uprising of the Christian Indians was being formed and was spreading rapidly. This was wholly contrary to the existing peace and tranquillity in this miserable kingdom, not only among the Spaniards and natives, but even on the part of the heathen enemy, for it had been a long time since they had done us any considerable damage. It was my misfortune that I learned of it on the eve of the day set for the beginning of the said uprising, and though I immediately, at that instant, notified the lieutenant-general on the lower river and all the other *alcaldes mayores*[3]—so that they could take every care and precaution against whatever might occur, and so that they could make every effort to guard and protect the religious ministers and the

[1]Guardianship.
[2]A military officer.
[3]A category of civil official combining the functions of mayor and judge. The reference here includes Native American officials.

temples—the cunning and cleverness of the rebels were such, and so great, that my efforts were of little avail. To this was added a certain degree of negligence by reason of the [report of the] uprising not having been given entire credence, as is apparent from the ease with which they captured and killed both those who were escorting some of the religious, as well as some citizens in their houses, and, particularly, in the efforts that they made to prevent my orders to the lieutenant-general passing through. This was the place where most of the forces of the kingdom were, and from which I could expect some help, but of three orders which I sent to the said lieutenant-general, not one reached his hands. The first messenger was killed and the others did not pass beyond Santo Domingo, because of their having encountered on the road the certain notice of the deaths of the religious[4] who were in that convent, and of the *alcalde mayor,* some other guards, and six more Spaniards whom they captured on that road. Added to this is the situation of this kingdom which, as your reverence is aware, makes it so easy for the said [Indian] alcaldes to carry out their evil designs, for it is entirely composed of *estancias,*[5] quite distant from one another.

On the eve [of the day] of the glorious San Lorenzo, having received notice of the said rebellion from the governors of Pecos and Tanos, [who said] that two Indians had left the Theguas, and particularly the pueblo of Thesuque,[6] to which they belonged, to notify them to come and join the revolt, and that they [the governors] came to tell me of it and of how they were unwilling to participate in such wickedness and treason, saying that they now regarded the Spaniards as their brothers, I thanked them for their kindness in giving the notice, and told them to go to their pueblos and remain quiet. I busied myself immediately in giving the said orders which I mentioned to your reverence, and on the following morning as I was about to go to mass there arrived Pedro Hidalgo, who had gone to the pueblo of Thesuque, accompanying Father Fray Juan Pio, who went there to say mass. He told me that the Indians of the said pueblo had killed the said Father Fray Pio and that he himself had escaped miraculously. [He told me also] that the said Indians had retreated to the sierra with all the cattle and horses belonging to the convent, and with their own.

The receipt of this news left us all in the state that may be imagined. I immediately and instantly sent the *maese de campo,* Francisco Gómez, with a squadron of soldiers sufficient to investigate this case and also to attempt to extinguish the flame of the ruin already begun. He returned here on the same day, telling me that [the report] of the death of the said Fray Juan Pio was true. He said also that there had been killed that same morning Father Fray Tomás de Torres, *guardián* of Nambé, and his brother, with the latter's wife and a child, and another resident of Thaos, and also Father Fray Luis de Morales, *guardián* of San Ildefonso, and the family of Francisco de Anaya; and in Poxuaque Don Joseph de Goitia, Francisco Ximénez, his wife and family, and Doña Petronila de Salas with ten sons and daughters; and that they had robbed and profaned the convents and [had robbed] all the haciendas of those murdered and also all the horses and cattle of that jurisdiction and La Cañada.

Upon receiving this news I immediately notified the *alcalde mayor* of that district to assemble all the people in his house in a body, and told him to advise at once the

[4]The uprising was aimed specifically at the missionaries who threatened the Native American religious and political hegemony.

[5]Farms.

[6]Native American villages in the upper Rio Grande valley, between present-day Santa Fe and Taos.

alcalde mayor of Los Taos to do the same. On this same day I received notice that two members of a convoy had been killed in the pueblo of Santa Clara, six others having escaped by flight. Also at the same time the *sargento mayor,*[7] Bernabe Márquez, sent to ask me for assistance, saying that he was surrounded and hard pressed by the Indians of the Queres and Tanos nations. Having sent the aid for which he asked me, and an order for those families of Los Cerrillos to come to the villa, I instantly arranged for all the people in it and its environs to retire to the *casas reales.*[8] Believing that the uprising of the Tanos and Pecos might endanger the person of the reverend father custodian, I wrote him to set out at once for the villa, not feeling reassured even with the escort which the lieutenant took, at my orders, but when they arrived with the letter they found that the Indians had already killed the said father custodian; Father Fray Domingo de Vera; Father Fray Manuel Tinoco, the minister *guardián* of San Marcos, who was there; and Father Fray Fernando de Velasco, *guardián* of Los Pecos, near the pueblo of Galisteo, he having escaped that far from the fury of the Pecos. The latter killed in that pueblo Fray Juan de la Pedrosa, two Spanish women, and three children. There died also at the hands of the said enemies in Galisteo Joseph Nieto, two sons of *Maestre de Campo* Leiba, Francisco de Anaya, the younger, who was with the escort, and the wives of *Maestre de Campo* Lieba and Joseph Nieto, with all their daughters and families. I also learned definitely on this day that there had died in the pueblo of Santo Domingo fathers Fray Juan de Talabán, Fray Francisco Antonio Lorenzana, and Fray Joseph de Montesdoca, and the *alcalde mayor,* Andrés de Peralta, together with the rest of the men who went as escort.

Seeing myself with notices of so many and such untimely deaths, and that not having received any word from the lieutenant-general was probably due to the fact that he was in the same exigency and confusion, or that the Indians had killed most of those on the lower river, and considering also that in the pueblo of Los Taos the fathers *guardianes* of that place and of the pueblo of Pecuries might be in danger, as well as the *alcalde mayor* and the residents of that valley, and that at all events it was the only place from which I could obtain any horses and cattle—for all these reasons I endeavored to send a relief of soldiers. Marching out for that purpose, they learned that in La Cañada, as in Los Taos and Pecuries, the Indians had risen in rebellion, joining the Apaches of the Achos nation.[9] In Pecuries they had killed Francisco Blanco de la Vega, a *mulata* belonging to the *maese de campo,* Francisco Xavier, and a son of the said *mulata.*[10] Shortly thereafter I learned that they also killed in the pueblo of Taos the father *guardián,* Fray Francisco de Mora, and Father Fray Mathías Rendón, the *guardián* of Pecuries, and Fray Antonio de Pro, and the *alcalde mayor,* as well as another fourteen or fifteen soldiers, along with all the families of the inhabitants of that valley, all of whom were together in the convent. Thereupon I sent an order to the *alcalde mayor,* Luis de Quintana, to come at once to the villa with all the people whom he had assembled in his house, so that, joined with those of us who were in the *casa reales,* we might endeavor to defend ourselves against the enemy's

[7]Sergeant-major.

[8]Central public buildings; governor's palace.

[9]The Pueblos and Apaches were enemies, so this comment indicates the extreme danger represented by pan-Indianism spurred by the common opposition to European colonialism.

[10]Woman of black and white racial mixture. The fact that she "belonged to" an official alludes to the presence of slavery in the colonies, although she could have been a servant.

invasions. It was necessarily supposed that they would join all their forces to take our lives, as was seen later by experience.

On Tuesday, the thirteenth of the said month, at about nine o'clock in the morning, there came in sight of us in the suburb of Analco, in the cultivated field of the hermitage of San Miguel, and on the other side of the river of the villa, all the Indians of the Tanos and Pecos nations and the Querez of San Marcos, armed and giving war-whoops. As I learned that one of the Indians who was leading them was from the villa and had gone to join them shortly before, I sent some soldiers to summon him and tell him on my behalf that he could come to see me in entire safety, so that I might ascertain from him the purpose for which they were coming. Upon receiving this message he came to where I was, and, since he was known, as I say, I asked him how it was that he had gone crazy too—being an Indian who spoke our language, was so intelligent, and had lived all his life in the villa among the Spaniards, where I had placed such confidence in him—and was now coming as a leader of the Indian rebels. He replied to me that they had elected him as their captain, and that they were carrying two banners, one white and the other red, and that the white one signified peace and the red one war. Thus if we wished to choose the white it must be [upon our agreeing] to leave the country, and if we chose the red, we must perish, because the rebels were numerous and we were very few; there was no alternative, inasmuch as they had killed so many religious and Spaniards.

On hearing his reply, I spoke to him very persuasively, to the effect that he and the rest of his followers were Catholic Christians, [asking] how they expected to live without the religious; and said that even though they had committed so many atrocities, still there was a remedy, for if they would return to the obedience of his Majesty they would be pardoned; and that thus he should go back to his people and tell them in my name all that had been said to him, and persuade them to [agree to] it and to withdraw from where they were; and that he was to advise me of what they might reply. He came back from there after a short time, saying that his people asked that all classes of Indians who were in our power be given up to them, both those in the service of the Spaniards and those of the Mexican nation of that suburb of Analco. He demanded also that his wife and children be given up to him, and likewise that all the Apache men and women whom the Spaniards had captured in war [be turned over to them], inasmuch as some Apaches who were among them were asking for them. If these things were not done they would declare war immediately, and they were unwilling to leave the place where they were because they were awaiting the Taos, Pecuries, and Theguas nations, with whose aid they would destroy us.

Seeing his determination, and what they demanded of us, and especially the fact that it was untrue that there were any Apaches among them, because they were at war with all of them, and that these parleys were intended solely to obtain his wife and children and to gain time for the arrival of the other rebellious nations to join them and besiege us, and that during this time they were robbing and sacking what was in the said hermitage and the houses of the Mexicans, I told him (having given him all the preceding admonitions as a Christian and a Catholic) to return to his people and say to them that unless they immediately desisted from sacking the houses and dispersed, I would send to drive them away from there. Whereupon he went back, and his people received him with peals of bells and trumpets, giving loud shouts in sign of war.

With this, seeing after a short time that they not only did not cease the pillage but were advancing toward the villa with shamelessness and mockery, I ordered all the soldiers to go out and attack them until they succeeded in dislodging them from that place. Advancing for this purpose, they joined battle, killing some at the first encounter. Finding themselves repulsed, they took shelter and fortified themselves in the said hermitage and the houses of the Mexicans, from which they defended themselves a part of the day with the firearms that they had and with arrows. Having set fire to some of the houses in which they were, thus having them surrounded and at the point of perishing, there appeared on the road from Thesuque a band of the people whom they were awaiting, who were all the Teguas. Thus it was necessary to go to prevent these latter from passing on to the villa, because the *casas reales* were poorly defended; whereupon the said Tanos and Pecos fled to the mountains and the two parties joined together, sleeping that night in the sierra of the villa. Many of the rebels remained dead and wounded, and our men retired to the *casas reales* with one soldier killed and the *maese de campo,* Francisco Gómez, and some fourteen or fifteen soldiers wounded, to attend them and entrench and fortify ourselves as best we could.

On the morning of the following day, Wednesday, I saw the enemy come down all together from the sierra where they had slept, toward the villa. Mounting my horse, I went out with the few forces that I had to meet them, above the convent. The enemy saw me and halted, making ready to resist the attack. They took up a better position, gaining the eminence of some ravines and thick timber, and began to give war-whoops, as if daring me to attack them.

I paused thus for a short time, in battle formation, and the enemy turned aside from the eminence and went nearer the sierras, to gain the one which comes down behind the house of the *maese de campo,* Francisco Gómez. There they took up their position, and this day passed without our having any further engagements or skirmishes than had already occurred, we taking care that they should not throw themselves upon us and burn the church and the houses of the villa.

The next day, Thursday, the enemy obliged us to take the same step as on the day before of mounting on horseback in fighting formation. There were only some light skirmishes to prevent their burning and sacking some of the houses which were at a distance from the main part of the villa. I knew well enough that these dilatory tactics were to give time for the people of the other nations who were missing to join them in order to besiege and attempt to destroy us, but the height of the places in which they were, so favorable to them and on the contrary so unfavorable to us, made it impossible for us to go and drive them out before they should all be joined together.

On the next day, Friday, the nations of the Taos, Pecuries, Hemes, and Querez having assembled during the past night, when dawn came more than 2,500 Indians fell upon us in the villa, fortifying and entrenching themselves in all its houses and at the entrances of all the streets, and cutting off our water, which comes through the *arroyo*[11] and the irrigation canal in front of the *casas reales.* They burned the holy temple and many houses in the villa. We had several skirmishes over possession of the water, but seeing that it was impossible to hold even this against them, and almost all the soldiers of the post being already wounded, I endeavored to fortify myself in the *casas reales* and to make a defense without leaving their walls. [The Indians were] so dexterous and so

[11]*Arroyos* are great cuts in the land where rain water collects and forms streams.

bold that they came to set fire to the doors of the fortified tower of Nuestra Señora de las Casas Reales, and, seeing such audacity, and the manifest risk that we ran of having the *casas reales* set on fire, I resolved to make a sally into the plaza of the said *casas reales* with all my available force of soldiers, without any protection, to attempt to prevent the fire which the enemy was trying to set. With this endeavor we fought the whole afternoon, and, since the enemy, as I said above, had fortified themselves and made embrasures in all the houses, and had plenty of arquebuses, powder, and balls. They did us much damage. Night overtook us thus and God was pleased that they should desist somewhat from shooting us with arquebuses and arrows. We passed this night, like the rest, with much care and watchfulness, and suffered greatly from thirst because of the scarcity of water.

On the next day, Saturday, they began at dawn to press us harder and more closely with gunshots, arrows, and stones, saying to us that now we should not escape them, and that besides their own numbers, they were expecting help from the Apaches whom they had already summoned. They fatigued us greatly on this day, because all was fighting, and above all we suffered from thirst, as we were already oppressed by it. At nightfall, because of the evident peril in which we found ourselves by their gaining the two stations where cannon were mounted, which we had at the doors of the *casas reales,* aimed at the entrances of the streets, in order to bring them inside it was necessary to assemble all the forces that I had with me, because we realized that this was their [the Indians'] intention. Instantly all the said Indian rebels began a chant of victory and raised war-whoops, burning all the houses of the villa, and they kept us in this position the entire night, which I assure your reverence was the most horrible that could be thought of or imagined, because the whole villa was a torch and everywhere were war chants and shouts. What grieved us most were the dreadful flames from the church and the scoffing and ridicule which the wretched and miserable Indian rebels made of the sacred things, intoning the *alabado*[12] and the other prayers of the church with jeers.

Finding myself in this state, with the church and the villa burned, and with the few horses, sheep, goats, and cattle which we had without feed or water for so long that many had already died, and the rest were about to do so, and with such a multitude of people, most of them children and women, so that our numbers in all came to about a thousand persons, perishing with thirst—for we had nothing to drink during these two days except what had been kept in some jars and pitchers that were in the *casas reales*—surrounded by such a wailing of women and children, with confusion everywhere, I determined to take the resolution of going out in the morning to fight with the enemy until dying or conquering. Considering that the best strength and armor were prayers to appease the Divine wrath, though on the preceding days the poor women had made them with fervor, that night I charged them to do so increasingly, and told the father *guardián* and the other two religious to say mass for us at dawn, and exhort all alike to repentance for their sins and to conformance with the Divine will, and to absolve us from guilt and punishment. These things being done, all of us who could mounted our horses, and the rest [went] on foot with their arquebuses, and some Indians who were in our service with their bows and arrows,

[12]Hymn in praise of the sacrament of the Holy Eucharist.

and in the best order possible we directed our course toward the house of the *maese de campo,* Francisco Xavier, which was the place where (apparently) there were the most people and where they had been most active and boldest. On coming out of the entrance to the street it was seen that there was a great number of Indians. They were attacked in force, and though they resisted the first charge bravely, finally they were put to flight, many of them being overtaken and killed. Then turning at once upon those who were in the streets leading to the convent, they also were put to flight with little resistance. The houses in the direction of the house of the said *maestre de campo,* Francisco Xavier, being still full of Indians who had taken refuge in them, and seeing that the enemy with the punishment and deaths that we had inflicted upon them in the first and second assaults were withdrawing toward the hills, giving us a little room, we laid siege to those who remained fortified in the said houses. Though they endeavored to defend themselves, and did so, seeing that they were being set afire and that they would be burned to death, those who remained alive surrendered and much was made of them. The deaths of both parties in this and the other encounters exceeded three hundred Indians.

Finding myself a little relieved by this miraculous event, though I had lost much blood from two arrow wounds which I had received in the face and from a remarkable gunshot wound in the chest on the day before, I immediately had water given to the cattle, the horses, and the people. Because we now found ourselves with very few provisions for so many people, and without hope of human aid, considering that our not having heard in so many days from the people on the lower river would be because of their all having been killed, like the others in the kingdom, or at least of their being or having been in dire straits, with the view of aiding them and joining with them into one body, so as to make the decisions most conducive to his Majesty's service, on the morning of the next day, Monday, I set out for La Isleta,[13] where I judged the said comrades on the lower river would be. I trusted in Divine Providence, for I left without a crust of bread or a grain of wheat or maize, and with no other provisions for the convoy of so many people except four hundred animals and two carts belonging to private persons, and, for food, a few sheep, goats, and cows.

In this manner, and with this fine provision, besides a few small ears of maize that we found in the fields, we went as far as the pueblo of La Alameda, where we learned from an old Indian whom we found in a maize-field that the lieutenant-general with all the residents of his jurisdictions had left some fourteen or fifteen days before to return to El Paso to meet the carts. This news made me very uneasy, alike because I could not be persuaded that he would have left without having news of me as well as of all the others in the kingdom, and because I feared that from his absence there would necessarily follow the abandonment of this kingdom. On hearing this news I acted at once, sending four soldiers to overtake the said lieutenant-general and the others who were following him, with orders that they were to halt wherever they should come up with them. Going in pursuit of them, they overtook them at the place of Fray Cristóbal. The lieutenant-general, Alonso Garcia, overtook me at the place of Las Nutrias, and a few days' march thereafter I encountered the maese de campo, Pedro de Leiba, with all the people under his command, who were

[13]The Native Americans from Isleta were taken south by Otermín when he retreated after the failed campaign of 1681, and they resettled in Isleta Sur southeast of El Paso, Texas.

escorting these carts and who came to ascertain whether or not we were dead, as your reverence had charged him to do, and to find me, ahead of the supply train. I was so short of provisions and of everything else that at best I should have had a little maize for six days or so.

Thus, after God, the only succor and relief that we have rests with your reverence and in your diligence. Wherefore, and in order that your reverence may come immediately, because of the great importance to the service of God and the king of your reverence's presence here, I am sending the said *maese de campo,* Pedro de Leyba, with the rest of the men whom he brought so that he may come as escort for your reverence and the carts or mule-train in which we hope you will bring us some assistance of provisions. Because of the haste which the case demands I do not write at more length, and for the same reason I cannot make a report at present concerning the above to the señor viceroy, because the *autos*[14] are not verified and there has been no opportunity to conclude them. I shall leave it until your reverence's arrival here. For the rest I refer to the account which will be given to your reverence by the father secretary, Fray Buene Ventura de Berganza. I am slowly overtaking the other party, which is sixteen leagues from here, with the view of joining them and discussing whether or not this miserable kingdom can be recovered. For this purpose I shall not spare any means in the service of God and of his Majesty, losing a thousand lives if I had them, as I have lost my estate and part of my health, and shedding my blood for God. May He protect me and permit me to see your reverence in this place at the head of the relief. September 8, 1680. Your servant, countryman, and friend kisses your reverence's hand. DON ANTONIO DE OTERMIN.

1937

The Coming of the Spanish and the Pueblo Revolt (Hopi)

Among Native American tales, historical narratives frequently relate the encounter with European colonizers and efforts to resist their domination. In this Hopi narrative of the coming of the Spanish, we find what some native groups call "memory culture" embracing centuries of time as if it existed on one chronological level. The story relates events in the absence of a linear historical sense which would locate events according to their relationship in real time. In other words, the story collapses chronology, telling centuries of happenings within one time-reference.

Many stories of this vast historical literature are of value for Euro-Americans, for they tell of colonization and its rejection from the Native American perspective. The Hopi narrative, with its unflattering picture of Franciscan missionizing—substantiated in large measure by documentary records—stands in stark contrast to Villagrá's Catholic vision of the conquest as a glorious march of the cross. More importantly, the story highlights the profound differences between the two cultures, differences even centuries of contact have not altered. The Spanish understood native religions as paganism and felt duty-bound to eradicate them, for the good of the individual native as well as for the larger community. Indians, on the other

[14]Official reports.

hand, questioned a God who commanded them to abandon their kachina religion, knowing that extinction was the logical consequence of suppressing a traditional religion that had secured rain, food, and life itself, since their emergence into the day-world. While some tribes would forge a close working relationship with the colonizers—Spanish and Anglo-Americans—the Hopis pride themselves on never having given in or up.

Andrew Wiget
New Mexico State University

PRIMARY WORK

Edmund Nequatewa, *Truth of a Hopi,* 1936, 1967.

The Coming of the Spanish and the Pueblo Revolt (Hopi)[1]

It may have taken quite a long time for these villages to be established. Anyway, every place was pretty well settled down when the Spanish came.[2] The Spanish were first heard of at Zuni and then at Awatovi. They came on to Shung-opovi, passing Walpi. At First Mesa, Siky-atki was the largest village then, and they were called Si-kyatki, not Walpi. The Walpi people were living below the present village on the west side. When the Spaniards came, the Hopi thought that they were the ones they were looking for—their white brother, the Bahana, their savior.[3]

The Spaniards visited Shung-opovi several times before the missions were established. The people of Mishongovi welcomed them so the priest who was with the white men built the first Hopi mission at Mishongovi. The people of Shung-opovi were at first afraid of the priests but later they decided he was really the Bahana, the savior, and let him build a mission at Shung-opovi.

Well, about this time the Strap Clan were ruling at Shung-opovi and they were the ones that gave permission to establish the mission. The Spaniards, whom they called Castilla, told the people that they had much more power than all their chiefs and a whole lot more power than the witches. The people were very much afraid of them, particularly if they had much more power than the witches. They were so scared that they could do nothing but allow themselves to be made slaves. Whatever they wanted done must be done. Any man in power that was in this position the Hopi

[1]The Hopi Indians, descendants of the Anasazi who had occupied cliff dwellings, occupy a number of pueblos in northeastern Arizona. Agricultural in their culture and economy, they had their own complex social and religious customs when they were subjected to the missionary efforts of the Spanish in 1629; Coronado had visited them in 1540. They joined the Pueblo Revolt of 1680.

[2]The first Spaniard to visit the Hopi was Coronado in 1540. Other expeditions followed. The Catholic missions, staffed by Franciscan priests, were established there in the beginning of the seventeenth century.

[3]The Hopis, like the Aztecs, believed that a fair-skinned culture hero would return from exile in the East to establish peace and prosperity. This belief in the *Bahana* had been greatly influenced by Christianity by the time the present narrative was published in 1936, but it is clear from available evidence that both Cortez in Mexico and the Spanish priests at Hopi used it as a means of entrance into the community.

called *Tota-achi,* which means a grouchy person that will not do anything himself, like a child. They couldn't refuse, or they would be slashed to death or punished in some way. There were two *Tota-achi.*

The missionary did not like the ceremonies. He did not like the Kachinas and he destroyed the altars and the customs. He called it idol worship and burned up all the ceremonial things in the plaza.

When the Priests started to build the mission, the men were sent away over near the San Francisco peaks to get the pine or spruce beams. These beams were cut and put into shape roughly and were then left till the next year when they had dried out. Beams of that size were hard to carry and the first few times they tried to carry these beams on their backs, twenty to thirty men walking side by side under the beam. But this was rather hard in rough places and one end had to swing around. So finally they figured out a way of carrying the beam in between them. They lined up two by two with the beam between the lines. In doing this, some of the Hopis were given authority by the missionary to look after these men and to see if they all did their duty. If any man gave out on the way he was simply left to die. There was great suffering. Some died for lack of food and water, while others developed scabs and sores on their bodies.

It took a good many years for them to get enough beams to Shung-opovi to build the mission. When this mission was finally built, all the people in the village had to come there to worship, and those that did not come were punished severely. In that way their own religion was altogether wiped out, because they were not allowed to worship in their own way. All this trouble was a heavy burden on them and they thought it was on account of this that they were having a heavy drought at this time. They thought their gods had given them up because they weren't worshiping the way they should.[4]

Now during this time the men would go out pretending they were going on a hunting trip and they would go to some hiding place, to make their prayer offerings. So today, a good many of these places are still to be found where they left their little stone bowls in which they ground their copper ore to paint the prayer sticks. These places are called *Puwa-kiki,* cave places. If these men were caught they were severely punished.

Now this man, Tota-achi (the Priest)[5] was going from bad to worse. He was not doing the people any good and he was always figuring what he could do to harm them. So he thought out how the water from different springs or rivers would taste and he was always sending some man to these springs to get water for him to drink, but it was noticed that he always chose the men who had pretty wives. He tried to send them far away so that they would be gone two or three days, so it was not very long until they began to see what he was doing. The men were even sent to the Little Colorado River to get water for him, or to Moencopi. Finally, when a man was sent out he'd go out into the rocks and hide, and when the night came he would come

[4]The Hopi religion, like that of the Zunis and other pueblos, uses mask dancing to invoke the assistance of the ancestral dead and the kachinas in securing life-giving rain for the crops. Spanish missionary policy was to destroy native religion by disrupting ceremonies and by destroying all ritual objects, especially masks, which they identified with the Devil.

[5]The precise identity of this priest is unclear. Several priests served at Shungopovi prior to the Pueblo Revolt. Fr. José Trujillo, who came to the Hopi from service in the Philippines, was a charismatic, intense, religious zealot. Fr. Salvador de Guerra, who preceded him, was transferred from Shungopovi to Jemez, much farther east, as discipline for having tortured the Indians in his charge. It is likely that this Tota-achi is a corporate figure, whose image conflates the memory of the misdeeds of several individuals.

home. Then, the priest, thinking the man was away, would come to visit his wife, but instead the man would be there when he came. Many men were punished for this.

All this time the priest, who had great power, wanted all the young girls to be brought to him when they were about thirteen or fourteen years old. They had to live with the priest. He told the people they would become better women if they lived with him for about three years. Now one of these girls told what the Tota-achi were doing and a brother of the girl heard of this and he asked his sister about it, and he was very angry. This brother went to the mission and wanted to kill the priest that very day, but the priest scared him and he did nothing. So the Shung-opovi people sent this boy, who was a good runner, to Awatovi to see if they were doing the same thing over there, which they were. So that was how they got all the evidence against the priest.

Then the chief at Awatovi sent word by this boy that all the priests would be killed on the fourth day after the full moon. They had no calendar and that was the best way they had of setting the date. In order to make sure that everyone would rise up and do this thing on the fourth day the boy was given a cotton string with knots in it and each day he was to untie one of these knots until they were all out and that would be the day for the attack.[6]

Things were getting worse and worse so the chief of Shung-opovi went over to Mishongnovi and the two chiefs discussed their troubles. "He is not the savior and it is your duty to kill him," said the chief of Shung-opovi. The chief of Mishongnovi replied, "If I end his life, my own life is ended."

Now the priest would not let the people manufacture prayer offerings, so they had to make them among the rocks in the cliffs out of sight, so again one day the chief of Shung-opovi went to Mishongnovi with tobacco and materials to make prayer offerings. He was joined by the chief of Mishongnovi and the two went a mile north to a cave. For four days they lived there heartbroken in the cave, making *pahos*. Then the chief of Mishongnovi took the prayer offerings and climbed to the top of the Corn Rock and deposited them in the shrine, for according to the ancient agreement with the Mishongnovi people it was their duty to do away with the enemy.

He then, with some of his best men, went to Shung-opovi, but he carried no weapons. He placed his men at every door of the priest's house. Then he knocked on the door and walked in. He asked the priest to come out but the priest was suspicious and would not come out. The chief asked the priest four times and each time the priest refused. Finally, the priest said, "I think you are up to something."

The chief said, "I have come to kill you." "You can't kill me," cried the priest, "you have no power to kill me. If you do, I will come to life and wipe out your whole tribe."

The chief returned, "If you have this power, then blow me out into the air; my gods have more power than you have.[7] My gods have put a heart into me to enter

[6]The Pueblo Revolt of August 13, 1680, was a concerted, successful effort of the Pueblo Indian communities to throw off Spanish military and religious oppression. Many soldiers and perhaps as many as 28 priests were killed in the uprising. The remaining colonists retreated south to El Paso del Norte and did not reestablish control over the northern frontier until Vargas's reconquest in 1692. The present narrative views the events at Hopi as a solution to a particular problem and not as part of a larger action.

[7]The debate between the Mishongnovi and Shungopovi chiefs indicates that the core of the Hopi interest in this narrative is religious, not military, conflict. Christianity fails because a drought follows the suppression of the kiva religion and because the priest fails to live up to his own culture's Christ-like ideal and the Hopi's ideal of the *Bahana*.

your home. I have no weapons. You have your weapons handy, hanging on the wall. My gods have prevented you from getting your weapons."

The old priest made a rush and grabbed his sword from the wall. The chief of Mishongnovi yelled and the doors were broken open. The priest cut down the chief and fought right and left but was soon overpowered, and his sword taken from him.

They tied his hands behind his back. Out of the big beams outside they made a tripod. They hung him on the beams, kindled a fire and burned him.

1936

Don Diego de Vargas ?–1704

Diego de Vargas Zapata y Luján Ponce de León y Contreras was appointed captain-general and governor of New Mexico in 1691, charged with a territorial reconquest that was already in progress, as Vargas's comments on his predecessor's violent battles indicate. Eleven years before, the Indians had organized under the Tewa religious leader Popé to drive out the Spaniards. For a decade, the colonists and some loyal natives waited in northern Mexico for the territory to be reclaimed. The project, however, was slow in advancing, for the Indians held the fortress-like mesa and resisted fiercely. By the time Vargas took command, few Christian colonists remained in El Paso. Fewer still wanted to return; they required forceful convincing by Vargas.

Meanwhile, however, the French had designs on the northern provinces of the Spanish empire. In 1681, Count de Peñalosa, a Peruvian-born ex-governor of New Mexico, had presented to the French government a project for the conquest of territory lying east of New Mexico and another proposal to conquer the Mexican province of New Biscaya with its rich mineral wealth. Peñalosa's plan proposed the taking of the territory from the mouth of the Rio Grande to San Diego on the Pacific coast, and including the Mines in Parral and the city of Durango. At the same time, the French were cultivating alliances with Plains Indians, especially the Pawnees, and moving into the heartland from their bases in the Great Lakes area. All of this made it imperative to Spain that New Mexico be retaken and settled as part of the defense of the empire. The Conde de Galve, viceroy of New Spain, meant to fortify the entire northern frontier. To carry out this plan, New Mexico was essential.

Vargas achieved his assignment with deliberate professionalism. On September 14, 1692, with the theatricality of European ceremony, he officially reclaimed the Plaza of Santa Fe. By 1693 he could compose the report that follows. His discourse is that of the panoptic ruler, viewing his kingdom as a great circle fanning out from the center, which he occupies with the authority of his royal commission. At the same time, his projection of settlements and numbers of colonizers are veiled pleas for support. Yet there is a security, even a calmness in his tone—perhaps the arrogance his countrymen would accuse him of when he stood trial a few years later for allegedly abusing his authority. There are no flights of literary fancy here, just the description of the lay of the land. Vargas, having carried out his charge, surveyed his holdings, apparently secure in the power of his government to reclaim all they saw, although in truth unconquered tribes surrounded him. The reconquest was so important to the empire that the viceroy commissioned one of Mexico's best writers, Carlos Sigüenza y Góngora, to write a tract celebrating the victory. *Mercurio Volante* recounted in stirring literary style Vargas's success. The empire had been restored.

Yet, by 1695, Vargas ordered a careful questioning of a band of Apaches who had arrived to trade of stories about the large number of French who were moving into the plains of Cíbola. The menace was so convincing that Vargas wrote the central government in Mexico to request artillery to prepare his defenses before the French arrived. In 1696, the Pueblos rebelled again, killing priests and settlers, but not all of the tribes joined, and Vargas, with great personal bravery, was able to quell the rebellion. Next he faced accusations of abuse, house arrest, and a bitter power struggle—yet once again he survived to regain authority.

The French never reached New Mexico in Vargas's lifetime, but no governor of New Mexico would ever again be able to write a letter as calm and secure as the letter that appears below. The reconquest was more than the end of an Indian revolt, it was the beginning of the end of New Mexico's isolation at the edge of the Spanish empire. New Mexico would not fall to a foreign power for another century and a half, but its position at the end of the seventeenth century was already shifting to that of an international crossroads. Vargas's letter can be read as a calm before the storm.

Juan Bruce-Novoa
University of California at Irvine

PRIMARY WORK

Coronado Cuarto Centennial Publications, 1540–1940; vol. 4, 1940.

from Letter on the Reconquest of New Mexico, 1692

Excellent Sir:

I scarcely arrived from my happy conquest, on the twentieth of December last, when two hours later the courier arrived with the answer to that which, with testimony of the records, I sent to your Excellency from the villa of Santa Fe, notifying your Highness through them and the letter of transmittal of what had been conquered up to the said day. A happy day, luck, and good fortune were attained, your Excellency, through the impulse which, fervently, spurred by the faith and as a loyal vassal of his Majesty, led me to undertake the said enterprise, considering that it is a region so large as to be a kingdom, all of which was in rebel hands for the past twelve years, and only on the confines of which was it known that they had been visited. For their safety, they were living on the mesas, the approaches to which made it difficult to invade them without their being assured of victory. All these conditions could have justly embarrassed me, but, realizing that the defense of my faith and my king were of greater importance, I scorned them and put into execution the said enterprise. . . .

I acknowledge the command and order of your Excellency, made in agreement with the real junta de hacienda,[1] in which you say, order, and command that I

[1]The royal administration.

should continue in the region. I wrote your Excellency, telling you that upon my return from subduing and conquering the Pecos, the Keres tribes living on various mesas, and the Jémez, I would make entry to the rock of Acoma and the provinces of Zuñi and Moqui, should I consider it possible for the horses to travel two hundred leagues. I answer that despite great obstacles, as attested in the records, I made the said entry which I had previously proposed to your Excellency with doubt; having also succeeded in obtaining some *almagre* earth, or vermilion,[2] which is believed to contain quicksilver ore, and having made known the new route which might be used for transit from the said kingdom, for his Majesty, should it contain quicksilver. With great interest I embarked upon the discovery of the said route and crossing, and, having come out at the pueblo of Socorro on the tenth of December last, there was such continuous snow and ice that on the following day we found the river frozen over. And we found that to return to the said villa and its surrounding pueblos by this route would be a waste of time and unfruitful, for it entailed the danger of the enemy Apaches as well as their partisans in this region of El Paso. I decided to hasten there so that the inhabitants would have the defense and garrison of the arms of their presidio and in order that the horses might gain strength and recuperate in order that I might carry out your Excellency's orders.

With regard to the transportation of the families which may be found at this pueblo of El Paso, I decided to visit them in order to make a census list, which I am sending to your Excellency so that your Highness may have record of the exact number of children and other persons who are under the care of each family. Those who can be taken unburdened will go, trusting that your Excellency will take into consideration my report which I referred to in the letter of remission adjoined to the said census. As for the return of the inhabitants who have withdrawn and who live in the kingdoms of [New] Vizcaya and [New] Galicia, I have decided to go in person in order effectively to persuade them, for I shall endeavor to find those who are living in haciendas and known localities, and in the settlements, announcing your Excellency's order and command to the royal authorities, and with their assistance they also will be made known by the proclamation which I will have published. And I shall make known therein that all those who desire to come and colonize the said kingdom will be promised all that which is contained in your Excellency's order. I will enlist them all with their privileges, paying the expenses of those who are to be transported, not only to this pueblo of El Paso, but as far as the villa of Santa Fe. In order that your Excellency may be entirely without anxiety with regard to the said colonization, I shall at all costs set out from this pueblo of El Paso with both groups of settlers upon my return from the said kingdoms, providing that your Excellency, in view of this, will send me the necessary sum, in response to the same and with the same courier. He will find me at the camp of Sombrerete collecting the twelve thousand pesos which your Excellency has placed to my account, if it is not obtainable at Guadiana. For I shall also visit that place for the purpose of enlisting some people, as those obtained for these parts must be of good quality, campaigners and persons agile in the pursuit of this war. . . .

[2]Vermillion indicates the presence of cinnabar, the prime source of mercury, which is indispensable for refining silver. The mention of vermillion held out the possibility of an important mineral resource which could justify expenditures on the colony of New Mexico.

As for the settlement of the region, the soldiers needed for its presidio, its defense and safety, and that of the lives of the religious, I repeat to your Excellency my opinion that five hundred families are necessary for the settlement of the villa and the following districts, not counting the one hundred soldiers necessary for the presidio at the villa of Santa Fe.

While I was there I examined and appraised the land. And, nine days after its conquest, having taken the road to the pueblo of Galisteo, which is the wagon road, and having entered the pueblo of the Pecos tribe, I returned to the said villa by way of the short road through the mountains, which the said tribes travel on foot and on horseback. I then went to the pueblos of the Tegua and Tano tribes, continued to that of Picuríes, and from there to that of Taos. Having seen the said thirteen pueblos and inspected the character of their lands, pastures, water supply, and wood, I find that the only place adequate for the founding of the said villa is its existing site, setting it up and establishing it on this side [*sic*] of the arroyo where it overlooks and dominates the pueblo and stronghold occupied there by the Tegua and Tano tribes, which comprises what was formerly the major portion of the palace and royal houses of the governor, and those of the inhabitants of the said villa who left as a result of their rebellion. They have extended and raised the walls, and fortified them, so that the said pueblo is walled. Besides, in La Ciénega and its lowland, the waters gather from the surrounding mountains and mesas, and the said stronghold being near by, it is in the shade, and for that reason it is hidden from the sun in the morning, and in the afternoon it also is without the sun's rays. And, due to the climate and temperature of the said kingdom, which is extremely cold, cloudy, and abounding in water, with heavy frosts and ice, and due to its shade and thick fog and mists of known and evident detriment, the said place is unsatisfactory.

The favor granted to the said natives, which I promised them at the time of their conquest, is not prejudicial to the said colonists, rather it is to their interest to settle at the place where I established my encampment on the day of my entry there. It is located a musket shot distance away. Its land dominates and overlooks the said stronghold, the place having sufficient height so that the artillery may control and cause much respect from the enemy. Also the surrounding country is well supplied with wood, farm lands, and pastures. These can be reserved, setting aside and reserving from the entrance at Las Bocas along the road to Santo Domingo, a distance of seven leagues. And as for the pueblo of La Ciénega, which I found abandoned, if some Keres Indians should repopulate it, it will be with the *tasación*[3] of five hundred varas, from the door of the church to the four cardinal points, and no more. Also with regard to the abandoned hacienda of El Alamo, to whomsoever lays claim to it will be given the lands with limits, but without liability claims with regard to the said horses.

With regard to the abandoned hacienda which is located a distance of two leagues from there, beyond the arroyo or river called the Seco, also to its owner [*sic*], in the same manner, if he wishes to settle it, and the aforesaid length and distance, with its entrances and exits, will be reserved as the common land not only for the horses and mules of the inhabitants who settle there, but also for those of

[3]Measurement.

the soldiers of the presidio. And also, the said place should be settled because it has dry land, with very little gravel, and is clear, getting the sun all day, and enjoying the winds from every direction.

With regard to its settlers, as many as one hundred and fifty families may enter and settle the said villa, as well as the one hundred presidial soldiers, who may cover the land with their arms by being established at this central point which controls a distance of ninety leagues in the following manner: thirty-two long leagues to the pueblo of Taos, to the north, thirty leagues to the pueblos of the Jémez and the Keres of Sia, which are between the south and west, and thirty leagues to the pueblo of Isleta, which is to the west. At the said place they will be assured of having provisions, whether or not the weather is good, and should the population be augmented such that they will need additional sources of supply, the one hundred and fifty families may settle part of the land; for, the said kingdom having the protection of the arms of the presidio, many will decide to settle on the haciendas which they formerly had and which they abandoned at the time of the uprising. The number of those which are occupied will be shared with the families hailing from other parts.

It is my wish, with those with whom I enter, including the soldiers, that they should, first and foremost, personally build the church and holy temple, setting up in it before all else the patroness of the said kingdom and villa, who is the one that was saved from the ferocity of the savages, her title being Our Lady of the Conquest. And so, with the aid of the soldiers and settlers, the foundations will be laid and the walls of the holy temple raised, bringing at the same time, by means of the oxen that will be taken, the timber necessary. At the same time the said construction will be hastened, so that by our example the conquered will be moved to build gladly their churches in their pueblos, which I hope will be accomplished. . . .

With regard to the settlement at the pueblo of Taos, which is on the frontier, and the most distant one of the kingdom, where the Apaches continually make their entry, it will be necessary to place one hundred settlers there. This pueblo has a site even more favorable for settlement, because its valleys are very broad, and it has many arroyos, wood, and pastures, and the land is very fertile and will yield good crops and is very suitable for the raising of all types of livestock, large and small. The said number of settlers, backed by the strength of the arms of the presidio of the said villa, will make it impossible for the enemy easily to swoop down on the pueblos of the said tribes; and also those who rebuild and resettle their haciendas may live in safety, for on the way to this pueblo there are many abandoned sites which were pointed out to me and named by their previous owners.

At the pueblo of Pecos, a distance of eight leagues from Santa Fe, fifty families may be settled, for it is also an Apache frontier and is surrounded by very mountainous country, very adaptable to ambush. And so, if it is settled, and with the said arms at the said villa, it will be possible to prevent the thefts and deaths otherwise facilitated by easy entry. It is very fertile land, which responds with great abundance to all the types of seeds that are planted.

Between the pueblos of Santo Domingo and Cochití, the original inhabitants of this kingdom who so desire may settle, should the Indians of the Keres tribe not come down to occupy the said pueblos. Those of Cochití are living on the mesa and mountain of La Cieneguilla, a distance of four leagues away; and those of

Santo Domingo are living on the mesa of the Cerro Colorado with the Keres Indians of Captain Malacate who were absent from their pueblo of Sia at the time General Don Domingo Jironza, my predecessor, burned it and captured those who escaped from fire and arms. And so the people of this Keres tribe are living on the said mesas, which are those of the said two pueblos and the one of Sia. From what they told me on the mesa of the Cerro Colorado, where they again have their pueblo, it is doubtful that they will return to resettle the one of Sia, which was burned by General Don Domingo. They said that they would not return to the pueblo for the additional reason that the land is nitrous, lacks sufficient water, is without wood, and is very sterile, and that if they should descend they would settle in the canyon between the pueblo of Sia and that of abandoned Santa Ana.

In the vicinity of this pueblo of Santa Ana, another fifty settlers may be established, because it has good lands and also because they are necessary to close the way to the enemy Apache; and so that the fathers who minister to the Keres Indians, and those of the Jémez tribe, may have the said settlers near by for their protection, and may, without fear of risking their lives, minister to them, punish them, and reprehend them as the case might be.

In the abandoned pueblo of Jémez, the walls of the church and most of the houses of the dwellings are standing, in which pueblo, should the Indians who are living on the mesa of the canyon remain there, one hundred residents can be settled. It has plenty of lands for planting and pastures, with water and very fertile, and the settlement of the said place would be very important because the Apaches make entry there, by virtue of which some of the Indians are rebellious in spirit and are our enemies.

From the hacienda of "La Angostura," two leagues from the pueblo of "La Angostura," that is, San Felipe, to the abandoned pueblo of Sandía, and one league from the abandoned pueblo of Puaray, at the said first one of Sandía Spaniards also may be settled. The walls of the church and some houses, although badly damaged, may be repaired. The lands are good, with their irrigation ditches. The said pueblos are on the camino real, and it would be very desirable to settle the region with another one hundred colonists, who will be able to live very comfortably and prosperously. It is a distance of twenty leagues from the said villa and will be of great value for the protection of the haciendas which extend from "Las Huertas."

At a distance of ten leagues, on the said camino real, on the other side of the river, there is situated the pueblo of Isleta, which is abandoned. The walls of the church are in good condition, as are most of the houses of the Indians of the Tegua nation who were withdrawn by General Don Antonio de Otermín when he made the entry in the year of 'eighty-one, at the expense of his Majesty, in the time of his Excellency, the viceroy, Conde de Paredes. The natives of the said tribe now live in some miserable huts in the pueblo of Isleta, in this district of El Paso, and so it will be desirable to restore them to their pueblo. They will be assured success in cultivating the fields which they plant at the pueblo, because the lands are extensive, in a good climate, and can be easily irrigated. And they will be protected if the said intervening haciendas called "Las Huertas" are settled, along with those extending from Las Barrancas, and those toward the abandoned pueblos of Alamillo and Sevilleta, whose natives are scattered and restless, and with the settlement of the said haciendas and the pueblo referred to, it will be possible to restore them to their pueblos.

Continuing a distance of ten leagues, Socorro is found, which may be settled with the Indians who at present occupy this one of Socorro in this district of El Paso, and they may be joined by the Piros, who are few, and who live in the pueblo of Senecú in this district, for it is a vast and fertile land; it has its irrigation ditches, and some of the walls of the convent are in good condition. Senecú, which the Piros occupied previously, a distance of ten leagues away, should not be settled because the river has damaged the land, and furthermore it is on a frontier infested with many Apaches. If it is the wish of some to settle the abandoned haciendas, it will be useful for the protection of the said Indians, and it will also prepare the way for the filling in and occupying of the land. The above is only the form in which the settlement should be made, in order that the natives of the said tribes, aware of the neighboring settlers and of the armed strength of the presidio, may be kept in submission, and so that our holy faith may be spread among them, and their children may join it with full obedience, and the missionaries, their teachers of Christian doctrine, may not find themselves alone and afraid to teach them, as I repeat, the doctrines of our holy faith.

As for the natives of the rock of Acoma, since they are a distance of twenty-four leagues from Isleta, and also those of the province of Zuñi, they may be left as they are. But as for those of the province of Moqui, in case the said vermilion earth is found not to contain quicksilver ore, it is my opinion that they should be removed from their pueblos to the abandoned ones of Alamillo and Sevilleta and the region between them, for in this way they will be safe and their missionaries will have control over them, for otherwise they would undergo great risk.

1693

New France

In 1897, historian Francis Parkman asserted in *The Jesuits in North America in the Seventeenth Century* that "Spanish civilization crushed the Indian; English civilization scorned and neglected him; [and] French civilization embraced and cherished him." This assessment shows an anti-Spanish bias typical of Parkman's era, and it romanticizes French treatment of Native Americans. While it is doubtful that a pacific religious takeover of peoples is any less damaging to them than their enslavement or displacement, whether by the *encomienda* system of the Spanish or the township system of the English, the French, if one considers their missionary efforts alone, treated Native Americans in a more respectful manner than their Spanish and English neighbors.

The French Empire in North America began with the potential missionary efforts initiated by Jacques Cartier, who explored for France the North American territories (now Quebec) accessible via the St. Lawrence in the 1530s and 1540s. The French were ostensibly searching for souls to convert to Catholicism, if King François I's 1540 announcement is to believed. Speaking of his intent to sponsor a permanent French colony in the "new" world, the king said he was seeking "to do something pleasing to God our creator and redeemer and which may lead to the augmentation of His Holy sacred name and of our mother Holy Catholic Church of whom we are called and named the first son." Yet Jacques Cartier's 1541 return expedition to North America—though it was intended "to establish the Christian Religion in a country of savages separated from France by all the extent of the earth"—carried only six churchmen in a vessel loaded with men and equipment; indeed, "two goldsmiths and lapidaries (workers in gems)" were much higher up on the list than these churchmen. If Cartier held high hopes for a religious mission, these hopes were nonetheless modified by equal aspirations for material gains.

The French were ultimately searching for a Northwest Passage to Asia, so that they could develop their own trade systems to compete with those already established by Portugal and Spain. In establishing relations with the native peoples of the Northeast, they were hoping to learn of trading and mining opportunities equal to those found by Spain in Mesoamerica. A key factor in French colonizing efforts was learning native languages. Cartier exchanged French boys for native boys, an exchange that Samuel de Champlain half a century later would continue. It seems that the French first sought mastery of native languages for purposes of exploration, then for missionary efforts, and finally for the steady development of a system of fur trade, which ultimately became the economic and intersocietal mainstay of New France.

Unlike their Spanish and English counterparts, the French did not seek the extermination or displacement of native peoples, largely, it seems, because they needed native allies for the fur trade and for raids against their Spanish and English neighbors. French activities in the Northeast nonetheless had a significant impact upon the area's indigenous population. The Abenakis of present-day Maine, for instance, grew to rely upon trade for food with the Massachusetts to the south, because the Abenakis began to devote their energies to trapping fur-bearing animals for trade with the French. Native lives were not in jeopardy, perhaps, but native livelihoods, indeed entire ways of looking at the material world, would irrevocably change as a result of contact with the French and with Europeans generally.

Samuel de Champlain, a geographer, is often credited with the success of the development of New France, for he played a major role in establishing good relations with native peoples of the Northeast. Indeed, the alliance between the French and natives in the area was so strong that well into the eighteenth century, English settlers in New England and the Middle Atlantic area feared French and Indian encroachment. Some of the fears of the Protestant English related to the Catholicism of the French and the Indians among whom Jesuit missionaries were working. Champlain persistently sought Jesuit missionaries for Quebec; when the Jesuits went to Acadia instead, he asked for "some good friars, with zeal and affection for the glory of God, whom I might persuade to send or come themselves with me to this country to try to plant there the faith." Among the Franciscan Récollets of Brouage he found some "good friars." A poor order, vowed to poverty, they had no funds to maintain missionaries, but they had no strong fears of living among natives. The missionary work of the Jesuits and the Récollets was persistent, if ill funded; their efforts did not always coincide with the efforts of fur traders, but their influence was widespread and well known.

In the mid-sixteenth century, Spain had defeated France in disputes over lands in Florida and the Carolinas, and during the seventeenth century, England and France clashed continually over control of the vast new continent. Constant skirmishing and border raiding erupted into full-scale hostilities known as King William's War (1689–97), during which England seized Nova Scotia. By the end of the war and the beginning of the eighteenth century, the French controlled—through missionary efforts or trading posts, or both—large portions of present-day Canada down into what is now the state of Illinois. France also had lucrative colonies in the West Indies, where African slaves labored on large, productive sugar plantations. The French occupied the mouth of the Mississippi and asserted a claim to its vast watershed. This occupation enabled wide-ranging exploratory parties to cross westward in the hope of finding gold mines and an overland route to the Pacific. The English feared that the French would form a vast and strong connection along the Mississippi and up to Canada, thus cutting off the possibility of English expansion westward.

French exploration writers like Laudonnière and Champlain share many of the assumptions of other European explorers, but these particular selections highlight important aspects of the power dynamics of conquest and contact. While Laudonnière's ignorance of native language and custom makes the ritual he is recounting seem obscure, Champlain has become a new center of meaning for the Hurons, who realize that they must safeguard his life so as not to incur the wrath of the imperial power that has redirected their lives and values. Father Isaac Jogues's narrative is just one of many extremely popular *Jesuit Relations* (reports from Jesuit missions in New France) compiled and published in France during the seventeenth century. Like many of his fellow missionaries, Jogues welcomed suffering, hardship, and even death, in the service of his monarch and his God. As "captivity narratives," these reports contrast sharply with the captivity tales emerging from New Spain and New England. Not only do they express different attitudes toward the Native Americans as potential religious converts, but they challenge the prevailing conception of that most "American" of genres.

René Goulaine de Laudonnière c. 1529–1582 (or fl. 1562–1582)

Although divided by France's bloody and destructive religious wars, Catholic and Huguenot (French Protestant) leaders found common purpose in their desire to challenge Spain's claims to southeastern North America and to discover precious metals and other commodities to bolster the French economy. In 1564, René de Laudonnière, an accomplished Huguenot sea captain, led a second French attempt to colonize Florida at Fort Caroline, near the mouth of the St. John's River.

Because the French colonists did not plant their own crops and did not receive promised supplies from France, they soon found themselves completely dependent upon the Timucua Indians for food. This selection from Laudonnière's account of the colony, written to justify his leadership to an unstable monarchy, describes a French officer's duplicitous attempt to maintain neutrality among warring Indian chiefdoms. To avoid alienating a coastal chief, the officer, a Captain Vasseur, contrived an elaborate lie about killing some of the tribal leader's enemies when, in fact, the French had just returned from forming an alliance with those same enemies. This tense political backdrop further complicates the linguistic and cultural obstacles for the colonists as they struggle to interpret the violent and emotionally charged Indian ceremony described in the passage. Commemorating earlier suffering at the hands of Indian enemies, the ritualized torture described here may also suggest the host tribe's skepticism about the French commitment to the coastal Indian's political and military objectives.

Ultimately, tensions with the Indians were not as devastating to the colony as European international conflicts were. In 1565, Spain's Philip II sent a small fleet to destroy Fort Caroline because he considered the Protestant outpost a dangerous threat to Catholic Spain's Caribbean trade routes and claims to sovereignty over Florida. Although Laudonnière and a few others escaped to France, the Spanish expedition destroyed the French colony, executed hundreds of Huguenot prisoners, and founded St. Augustine, the first permanent settlement in what is now the United States.

Jim Sullivan,
MiraCosta College

PRIMARY WORK

A Notable Historie Containing Foure Voyages Made by Certaine French Captaines unto Florida, trans. Richard Hakluyt, 1587; rpt. by H. Stevens, Sons and Stiles, 1964.

from A Notable Historie Containing Foure Voyages Made by Certaine French Captaines unto Florida[1]

The good cheere being done, and the discourses ended, my men embarked themselves againe with intention to bring me those good newes unto the fort *Caroline.* But after they had sayled a very long whyle downe the river, and were come within three

[1]The text is Hakluyt's, slightly modernized.

leagues of us, the tide was so strong against them, that they were constrayned to goe on land, and to retire themselves because of the night unto the dwelling of a certain *Paracoussy*[2] named *Molona,* which shewed himselfe very glad of their arrival: for he desired to know some newes of *Thimogoua,*[3] and thought that the French men went thither for none other occasion but for to invade them. Which captain *Vasseur* perceiving dissembled so wel, that he made him beleeve that he went to *Thimogoua,* with none other intention, but to subdue them, and to destroy them with the edge of the sword without mercy, but that their purpose had not such successe as they desired, because that the people of *Thimogoua* being advertised of this enterprise, retired into the woods, and saved themselves by flight: yet neverthelesse they had taken some as they were flying away which carried to newes thereof unto their fellowes. The *Paracoussy* was so glad of this relation, that he enterrupted him, and asked *Vasseur* of the beginning and maner of his execution, and praied him that he would shew him by signes how all things passed. Immediatly *Frauncis la Caille* the seargeant of my band took his sword in his hand, saying that with the point thereof he had thrust through two Indians which ran into the woods, and that his companions had done no lesse for their parts. And that if fortune had so favoured them, that they had not bin discovered by the men of *Thimogoua,* they had had a victorie most glorious and worthy of eternall memory. Hereupon the *Paracoussy* shewed himselfe so wel satisfied, that he could not devise how to gratifie our men, which he caused to come into his house to feast them more honorably: and having made captaine *Vasseur* to sit next him, and in his own chaire (which the Indians esteeme for the chiefest honour) and then underneath him two of his sonnes, goodly and might fellowes, he commanded al the rest to place themselves as they thought good. This done, the Indians came according to their good custom, to present their drink *Cassine* to the *Paracoussy,* and then to certaine of his chiefest friends, and the Frenchmen. Then he which brought it set the cup aside, and drew out a little dagger which hung stucke up in the roofe of the house, and like a mad man he lift his head aloft, and ran apace, and went and smote an Indian which sate alone in one of the corners of the hall, crying with a loud voyce, *Hyou,* the poore Indian stirring not at al for the blow, which he seemed to endure paciently. He which held the dagger went quickly to put the same in his former place, and began again to give us drink, as he did before: but he had not long continued, and had scarcely given 3. or 4. thereof, but he left his bowle againe, tooke the dagger in his hand, and quickly returned unto him which he had stroken before, to whom he gave a very sore blow on the side, crying *Hyou,* as he had done before: then he went to put the dagger in his place, and set him self down among the rest. A little while after, he that had bin stroken fel down backwards, stretching out his armes and legs as if he had bin ready to yeld up the latter gaspe. And then the younger soone of the *Paracoussy* apparrelled in a long white skin, fel down at the feet of him that was fallen backward, weeping bitterly halfe a quarter of an houre: after two other of his brethren clad in like apparel, came about him that

[2]Tribal chief or leader. The various "paracoussy" described in this passage were brothers of Saturiwa, the regional chieftain of the coastal Timucua who lived near Fort Caroline.

[3]Roughly translated as "ancient and natural enemies," *Thimogoua* specifically refers to the more powerful inland Timucua groups led by Chief Utina, who eventually became an ally of the Spanish.

was so stricken, and began to sigh pitifully. Their mother bearing a little infant in her arms came from another part, and going to the place where her sonnes were, at the first she used infinit numbers of outcries, then one while lifting up her eies to heaven, an other while falling down unto the ground, she cried so dolefully, that her lamentable mournings would have moved the most hard and stonie heart in the world with pity. Yet this sufficed not, for there came in a company of young gyrles which did never lyn weeping for a long while in the place where the Indian was fallen down, whom afterward they took, and with the saddest gestures they could devise, caried him away into another house a little way of from the great hal of the *Paracoussy,* and continued their weepings and mournings by the space of two long houres: in which meane while the Indians ceassed not to drink Cassine, but with such silence that one word was not heard in the parler. *Vasseur* beeing grieved that hee understood not these ceremonies, demaunded of the *Paracoussy* what these thinges meant: which answered him slowly, *Thimogoua, Thimogoua,* with out saying any more. Beeing more displeased then he was before with so slight an answeare, he turned unto another Indian the *Paracoussyes* brother, who was a *Paracoussy* as well as his brother, called *Malica,* which made him a like answere as he did at the first, praying him to aske no more of these matters, and to have patience for that time. The subtile old *Paracoussy* praied him within a while after to shew him his sword, which he would not deny him, thinking that hee would have behelde the fashion of his weapons: but he soone perceived that it was to another end: for the old man holding it in his hand, beheld it a long while on every place to see if he could find any blood upon it which might shew that any of their enemies had bin killed: (for the Indians are woont to bring their weapons wherwith their enemies have bin defeated with some blood upon them, for a token of their victories.) But seeing no signe thereof upon it, he was upon the point to say unto him, that he had killed none of the men of *Thimogoua,* when as *Vasseur* preventing that which he might object, declared and shewed to him by signes the maner of his enterprise, adding that by reason of the 2. Indians which he had slaine, his sword was so bloudy, that he was inforced to wash and make it cleane a long while in the river: which the old man beleeved to be like to be true, and made no maner of reply thereunto. *Vasseur, la Caille,* and their other companions went out of the hall to go into the roome whither they had carried the Indian: there they found the *Paracoussy* sitting upon tapistries made of smal reeds, which was at meat after the Indian fashion, and the Indian that was smitten hard by him, lying upon the selfsame tapistry, about whom stood the wife of the *Paracoussy,* with all the young damsels which before bewailed him in the hall: which did nothing els but warme a great deale of mosse in steede of napkins to rub the Indians side. Hereupon our men asked the *Paracoussy* again, for what occasion the Indian was so persecuted in his presence: he answered, that this was nothing els but a kind of ceremony wherby they would cal to mind the death and persecutions of the *Paracoussies* their ancestors executed by their enemy *Thimogoua:* alledging moreover, that as often as he himself, or any of his friends and alies returned from the countrey, without they brought the heads of their enimies, or without bringing home some prisoner, he used for a perpetual memory of al his predecessors, to beate the best beloved of all his children, with the selfsame weapons, wherewith they had bin killed in times past: to the ende that by renewing of the wounde their death should be lamented afresh.

1587

Samuel de Champlain 1570?–1635

In 1609, when Samuel Champlain ventured out from the newly founded Quebec in search of trade with Indians, future converts to Christianity, and a "great inland sea" that would provide access to Asia, he had already fought in the fifteenth-century wars of religion of his native France, voyaged to the Spanish Caribbean, mapped the coast of northeastern America from Maine to Cape Cod, and spent three years exploring New France (Canada). His journal documents his interest in the North American landscape as a source of commodities and his early alliance with Algonkian, Montagnais, and Huron Indians, who made his access to the interior contingent upon French military support against rival Iroquois nations.

Champlain's account of his first battle with the Iroquois contradicts other known accounts of Iroquois war tactics. The regimented military formations and Champlain's heroic role in the encounter seem to reflect European cultural notions of war and Champlain's personal ambitions more than the likely realities of this attack. These discrepancies aside, Champlain narrates a turning point in North American history. His use of European military technology in support of his Indian allies drove the Iroquois into alliance with first the Dutch and then the British. Eventually, this powerful Anglo-Iroquois partnership cost the French their North American territories and motivated them to support the rebellious colonists in their war for independence.

The second selection from Champlain's journals presented here describes his experience with the Hurons after another battle with the Iroquois. The French explorer's story of finding his way through the woods testifies to his stamina and courage, and the concerns that the Hurons had about losing him confirm Champlain's importance to French and Indian relations. But this incident also demonstrates that Champlain was, in effect, a prisoner of the Hurons, whose guides also functioned as his guards. In 1615, Champlain's Indian allies determined where and when the man whom historians would later dub "the founder of New France" traveled and traded. In this sense, early political, economic, and military power relationships between North American Indians and the French were not as one-sided as Champlain's writings attempt to depict them.

Jim Sullivan
MiraCosta College

PRIMARY WORK

The Voyages of Samuel de Champlain, 1604–1618, ed. W. L. Grant, 1907.

from The Voyages of Samuel de Champlain, 1604–1618

from The Voyages to the Great River St. Lawrence, 1608–1612

[An Encounter with the Iroquois]

We set out on the next day,[1] continuing our course in the river as far as the entrance of the lake. There are many pretty islands here, low, and containing very fine woods and meadows, with abundance of fowl and such animals of the chase as stags, fallow-deer, fawns, roe-bucks, bears, and others, which go from the main land to these islands. We captured a large number of these animals. There are also many beavers, not only in this river, but also in numerous other little ones that flow into it. These regions, although they are pleasant, are not inhabited by any savages, on account of their wars; but they withdraw as far as possible from the rivers into the interior, in order not to be suddenly surprised.

The next day we entered the lake,[2] which is of great extent, say eighty or a hundred leagues long, where I saw four fine islands, ten, twelve, and fifteen leagues long, which were formerly inhabited by the savages, like the River of the Iroquois; but they have been abandoned since the wars of the savages with one another prevail. There are also many rivers falling into the lake, bordered by many fine trees of the same kinds as those we have in France, with many vines finer than any I have seen in any other place; also many chestnut-trees on the border of this lake, which I had not seen before. There is also a great abundance of fish, of many varieties; among others, one called by the savages of the country *Chaousarou,*[3] which varies in length, the largest being, as the people told me, eight or ten feet long. I saw some five feet long, which were as large as my thigh; the head being as big as my two fists, with a snout two feet and a half long, and a double row of very sharp and dangerous teeth. Its body is, in shape, much like that of a pike; but it is armed with scales so strong that a poniard[4] could not pierce them. Its color is silver-gray. The extremity of its snout is like that of swine. This fish makes war upon all others in the lakes and rivers. It also possesses remarkable dexterity, as these people informed me, which is exhibited in the following manner. When it wants to capture birds, it swims in among the rushes, or reeds, which are found on the banks of the lake in several places, where it puts its snout out of water and keeps perfectly still: so that, when the birds come and light on its snout, supposing it to be only the stump of a tree, it adroitly closes it, which it had kept ajar, and pulls the birds by the feet down under water. The savages gave me the head of one of them, of which they make great account, saying that, when they have the headache, they bleed themselves with the teeth of this fish on the spot where they suffer pain, when it suddenly passes away.

Continuing our course over this lake on the western side, I noticed, while ob-

[1]July 13, 1609.
[2]Lake Champlain.
[3]"Garpike."
[4]Dagger.

serving the country, some very high mountains[5] on the eastern side, on the top of which there was snow. I made inquiry of the savages whether these localities were inhabited, when they told me that the Iroquois dwelt there, and that there were beautiful valleys in these places, with plains productive in grain, such as I had eaten in this country, together with many kinds of fruit without limit. They said also that the lake extended near mountains, some twenty-five leagues distant from us, as I judge. I saw, on the south, other mountains,[6] no less high than the first, but without any snow. The savages told me that these mountains were thickly settled, and that it was there we were to find their enemies; but that it was necessary to pass a fall[7] in order to go there (which I afterwards saw), when we should enter another lake,[8] nine or ten leagues long. After reaching the end of the lake, we should have to go, they said, two leagues by land, and pass through a river[9] flowing into the sea on the Norumbegue coast, near that of Florida, whither it took them only two days to go by canoe, as I have since ascertained from some prisoners we captured, who gave me minute information in regard to all they had personal knowledge of, through some Algonquin interpreters, who understood the Iroquois language.

Now, as we began to approach within two or three days' journey of the abode of their enemies, we advanced only at night, resting during the day. But they did not fail to practise constantly their accustomed superstitions, in order to ascertain what was to be the result of their undertaking; and they often asked me if I had had a dream, and seen their enemies, to which I replied in the negative. Yet I did not cease to encourage them, and inspire in them hope. When night came, we set out on the journey until the next day, when we withdrew into the interior of the forest, and spent the rest of the day there. About ten or eleven o'clock, after taking a little walk about our encampment, I retired. While sleeping, I dreamed that I saw our enemies, the Iroquois, drowning in the lake near a mountain, within sight. When I expressed a wish to help them, our allies, the savages, told me we must let them all die, and that they were of no importance. When I awoke, they did not fail to ask me, as usual, if I had had a dream. I told them that I had, in fact, had a dream. This, upon being related, gave them so much confidence that they did not doubt any longer that good was to happen to them.

When it was evening, we embarked in our canoes to continue our course; and, as we advanced very quietly and without making any noise, we met on the 29th of the month the Iroquois, about ten o'clock at evening, at the extremity of a cape[10] which extends into the lake on the western bank. They had come to fight. We both began to utter loud cries, all getting their arms in readiness. We withdrew out on the water, and the Iroquois went on shore, where they drew up all their canoes close to each other and began to fell trees with poor axes, which they acquire in war sometimes, using also others of stone. Thus they barricaded themselves very well.

Our forces also passed the entire night, their canoes being drawn up close to each other, and fastened to poles, so that they might not get separated, and that they might be all in readiness to fight, if occasion required. We were out upon the water, within arrow range of their barricades. When they were armed and in array, they

[5]The Green Mountains of Vermont.
[6]The Adirondacks.
[7]Ticonderoga.
[8]Lake George.
[9]The Hudson.
[10]Crown Point.

despatched two canoes by themselves to the enemy to inquire if they wished to fight, to which the latter replied that they wanted nothing else: but they said that, at present, there was not much light, and that it would be necessary to wait for daylight, so as to be able to recognize each other; and that, as soon as the sun rose, they would offer us battle. This was agreed to by our side. Meanwhile, the entire night was spent in dancing and singing, on both sides, with endless insults and other talk; as, how little courage we had, how feeble a resistance we should make against their arms, and that, when day came, we should realize it to our ruin. Ours also were not slow in retorting, telling them they would see such execution of arms as never before, together with an abundance of such talk as is not unusual in the siege of a town. After this singing, dancing, and bandying words on both sides to the fill, when day came, my companions and myself continued under cover, for fear that the enemy would see us. We arranged our arms in the best manner possible, being, however, separated, each in one of the canoes of the savage Montagnais.[11] After arming ourselves with light armor, we each took an arquebuse,[12] and went on shore. I saw the enemy go out of their barricade, nearly two hundred in number, stout and rugged in appearance. They came at a slow pace towards us, with a dignity and assurance which greatly amused me, having three chiefs at their head. Our men also advanced in the same order, telling me that those who had three large plumes were the chiefs, and that they had only these three, and that they could be distinguished by these plumes, which were much larger than those of their companions, and that I should do what I could to kill them. I promised to do all in my power, and said that I was very sorry they could not understand me, so that I might give order and shape to their mode of attacking their enemies, and then we should, without doubt, defeat them all; but that this could not now be obviated, and that I should be very glad to show them my courage and good-will when we should engage in the fight.

As soon as we had landed, they began to run for some two hundred paces towards their enemies, who stood firmly, not having as yet noticed my companions, who went into the woods with some savages. Our men began to call me with loud cries; and, in order to give me a passage-way, they opened in two parts, and put me at their head, where I marched some twenty paces in advance of the rest, until I was within about thirty paces of the enemy, who at once noticed me, and halting, gazed at me, as I did also at them. When I saw them making a move to fire at us, I rested my musket against my cheek, and aimed directly at one of the three chiefs. With the same shot, two fell to the ground; and one of their men was so wounded that he died some time after. I had loaded my musket with four balls. When our side saw this shot so favorable for them, they began to raise such loud cries that one could not have heard it thunder. Meanwhile, the arrows flew on both sides. The Iroquois were greatly astonished that two men had been so quickly killed, although they were equipped with armor woven from cotton thread, and with wood which was proof against their arrows. This caused great alarm among them. As I was loading again, one of my companions fired a shot from the woods, which astonished them anew to such a degree that, seeing their chiefs dead, they lost courage, and took to flight,

[11] "Mountain People"—the French name for a Canadian, Algonkian-speaking Indian tribe, courted by the French.

[12] A portable matchlock gun dating from the fifteenth century.

abandoning their camp and fort, and fleeing into the woods, whither I pursued them, killing still more of them. Our savages also killed several of them, and took ten or twelve prisoners. The remainder escaped with the wounded. Fifteen or sixteen were wounded on our side with arrow-shots; but they were soon healed.

After gaining the victory, our men amused themselves by taking a great quantity of Indian corn and some meal from their enemies, also their armor, which they had left behind that they might run better. After feasting sumptuously, dancing and singing, we returned three hours after, with the prisoners. The spot where this attack took place is in latitude 43° and some minutes, and the lake was called Lake Champlain.

from The Voyages of 1615

[Champlain, among the Huron, Lost in the Woods]

When they first went out hunting,[1] I lost my way in the woods, having followed a certain bird that seemed to me peculiar. It had a beak like that of a parrot, and was of the size of a hen. It was entirely yellow, except the head which was red, and the wings which were blue, and it flew by intervals like a partridge. The desire to kill it led me to pursue it from tree to tree for a very long time, until it flew away in good earnest. Thus losing all hope, I desired to retrace my steps, but found none of our hunters, who had been constantly getting ahead, and had reached the enclosure. While trying to overtake them, and going, as it seemed to me, straight to where the enclosure was, I found myself lost in the woods, going now on this side now on that, without being able to recognize my position. The night coming on, I was obliged to spend it at the foot of a great tree, and in the morning set out and walked until three o'clock in the afternoon, when I came to a little pond of still water. Here I noticed some game, which I pursued, killing three or four birds, which were very acceptable, since I had had nothing to eat. Unfortunately for me there had been no sunshine for three days, nothing but rain and cloudy weather, which increased my trouble. Tired and exhausted I prepared to rest myself and cook the birds in order to alleviate the hunger which I began painfully to feel, and which by God's favor was appeased.

When I had made my repast I began to consider what I should do, and to pray God to give me the will and courage to sustain patiently my misfortune if I should be obliged to remain abandoned in this forest without counsel or consolation except the Divine goodness and mercy, and at the same time to exert myself to return to our hunters. Thus committing all to His mercy I gathered up renewed courage, going here and there all day, without perceiving any foot-print or path, except those of wild beasts, of which I generally saw a good number. I was obliged to pass here this night also. Unfortunately I had forgotten to bring with me a small compass which would have put me on the right road, or nearly so. At the dawn of day, after a brief repast, I set out in order to find, if possible, some brook and follow it, thinking that it must of necessity flow into the river on the border of which our hunters were encamped.

[1]Champlain was in the company of the Huron Indians in northern Canada in the fall of 1615.

Having resolved upon this plan, I carried it out so well that at noon I found myself on the border of a little lake, about a league and a half in extent, where I killed some game, which was very timely for my wants; I had likewise remaining some eight or ten charges of powder, which was a great satisfaction.

I proceeded along the border of this lake to see where it discharged, and found a large brook, which I followed until five o'clock in the evening, when I heard a great noise, but on carefully listening failed to perceive clearly what it was. On hearing the noise, however, more distinctly, I concluded that it was a fall of water in the river which I was searching for. I proceeded nearer, and saw an opening, approaching which I found myself in a great and far-reaching meadow, where there was a large number of wild beasts, and looking to my right I perceived the river, broad and long. I looked to see if I could not recognize the place, and walking along on the meadow I noticed a little path where the savages carried their canoes. Finally, after careful observation, I recognized it as the same river, and that I had gone that way before.

I passed the night in better spirits than the previous ones, supping on the little I had. In the morning I re-examined the place where I was, and concluded from certain mountains on the border of the river that I had not been deceived, and that our hunters must be lower down by four or five good leagues. This distance I walked at my leisure along the border of the river, until I perceived the smoke of our hunters, where I arrived to the great pleasure not only of myself but of them, who were still searching for me, but had about given up all hopes of seeing me again. They begged me not to stray off from them any more, or never to forget to carry with me my compass, and they added: If you had not come, and we had not succeeded in finding you, we should never have gone again to the French, for fear of their accusing us of having killed you. After this he was very careful of me when I went hunting, always giving me a savage as companion, who knew how to find again the place from which he started so well that it was something very remarkable.

1907

The Jesuit Relations

The *Jesuit Relations,* a series of reports from Jesuit missions in New France, were published annually in Paris between 1632 and 1673. The Society of Jesus, a Roman Catholic male order founded in 1540 by Ignatius Loyola (1491–1556) and whose members were known as Jesuits, viewed the preparation of such reports as part of their worldwide missionary program. But the *Relations* do more than narrate the Jesuits' spiritual progress: they also present detailed views of the state of the French colony, accounts of expeditions to the interior of North America, and descriptions of the diverse Native American cultures of eastern Canada and the Great Lakes. The *Relations* were published by the French royal printer and seem to have reached a large audience. The excerpt below, for instance, includes testimony from Anne of Austria, the French queen, that she finds the story of Isaac Jogues's sufferings more powerful than any romance.

In 1632, the year of the first *Relation,* the French began to rebuild settlements along the St. Lawrence River and to re-establish trade alliances with Montagnais, Huron, and Algonkian peoples, all of which had been disrupted by an English attack in 1629. In order to obtain greater control over the religiously divided colony and to compete with English settlements to the south, Cardinal Richelieu, the powerful chief minister of King Louis XIII, formed the Company of New France to manage the colony's affairs. The company excluded from Canada both the Huguenots, French Protestants who had controlled the New France trade, and the Franciscan Récollets, rivals of the Jesuits. Richelieu granted the Jesuits a monopoly on missionary work and allowed them to operate as negotiators in the fur trade. By 1640, although the French population in Canada remained under four hundred, the Jesuits had amassed large landholdings and had sponsored the construction in Quebec of a college to educate the sons of French settlers, a hospital, and a convent for Ursuline nuns.

During this decade, the focus of the Jesuit missionary effort was Huronia, a region lying to the east of Lake Huron. The Hurons were sedentary agriculturalists who also served as intermediaries in the fur trade, delivering high-quality furs from the north to French ships. The Jesuits had built five chapels in the Huron country by the late 1630s and were anticipating great spiritual success. Explanations for the relatively high number of Huron converts to Catholicism vary. Some scholars argue that the Jesuits' importance in the economy of Huronia compelled the Hurons to follow their spiritual direction; others suggest that Hurons may have turned to the Jesuits' religion when they began to suffer the effects of epidemic diseases.

However, in the early 1640s tensions between the French and their major enemy, the five Iroquois tribes, rose dramatically. The Five Nations were enduring population losses from disease and the economic challenge posed by French, Dutch, and English fur-trading companies, who sought alliances with rival Native American groups. In 1642, the Iroquois began a series of attacks upon the Hurons, themselves an Iroquoian-speaking people but long the enemies of the Five Nations. These attacks, known as "mourning-wars," were intended not simply to spread death or destruction but to capture enemies. Following an often grueling initiation period, these captives were either adopted into the clan or executed. By the 1650s, the Iroquois had forced the Jesuits to abandon their missions in Huronia and sparked a massive migration of Indian refugee populations to the west.

Father Isaac Jogues's narrative, the centerpiece of the *Relation* for the year 1647, provides one view of the devastating French-Iroquois wars. Jogues's first encounter with the Mohawks, one of the five Iroquois tribes, came in 1642, when he was captured along with several Frenchmen and Huron converts while traveling from the Huron country to Quebec. The Mohawks kept Jogues and the other captives, resisting ransom overtures, until Jogues managed to evade his captors and escape to the Dutch. Despite the tortures he endured, Jogues's captivity was not entirely a nightmarish experience. Indeed, his ability to withstand punishment enhanced his reputation among the Mohawks. Jogues was adopted into the Wolf clan and visited Mohawk territory in 1646 to initiate a Jesuit mission in Iroquoia. The mission was short-lived: shortly after he returned to the Mohawks in 1647, Jogues was put to death, perhaps by Bear clan members angry over an outbreak of sickness that they blamed on the Jesuit.

The following account should not be read as eyewitness testimony. Father Jerome Lalemant, the superior of the Jesuit missions in Canada, drew from Jogues's letters and those of other Jesuits when preparing this *Relation;* the text was further edited by Jesuits in Paris before its publication. In its published form, the narrative effectively conveys the devotion of both Jogues and the Huron converts to their faith, while providing only limited insight into Mohawk views of the same events. Jogues's story circulated widely, and readers may wish to consider why it became so popular in seventeenth-century France. This narrative should also be compared with other colonial "captivity narratives" like that of Mary Rowlandson or John Williams. Unlike those two captives, Jogues actually seeks to return to his captors. What tone does Jogues adopt to describe the sufferings he endures? What might captivity itself have meant for a missionary and a group of converts prepared and even eager to die for their faith?

John Pollack
University of Pennsylvania

PRIMARY WORKS

Original French edition: *Relation de ce qui s'est passé de plus remarquable és Missions des Peres de la Compagnie de Jesus, en la Nouvelle France sur le grand fleuve de S. Laurens en l'annee 1647,* 1648. French critical edition: Lucien Campeau, ed., *Monumenta novae franciae,* vol. VII, 1994. This English translation is taken from *The Jesuit Relations and Allied Documents* (general ed. Reuben Gold Thwaites), selected and edited by Edna Kenton, 1925.

from The Relation of 1647, by Father Jerome Lalemant.[1]

How Father Jogues Was Taken by the Iroquois, and What He Suffered on His First Entrance into their Country

Father Isaac Jogues had sprung from a worthy family of the City of Orleans.[2] After having given some evidence of his virtue in our Society, he was sent to New France, in the year 1638. In the same year he went up to the Hurons, where he sojourned until the thirteenth of June in the year 1642, when he was sent to Kebec[3] upon the affairs of that important and arduous Mission.

From that time until his death, there occurred many very remarkable things,—of which one cannot, without guilt, deprive the public. What has been said of his labors in the preceding Relations, come, for the most part, from some Savages,[4] companions in his sufferings. But what I am about to set down has issued from his own pen and his own lips.

The Reverend Father Hiersome L'alemant, at that time Superior of the Mission among the Hurons, sent for him, and proposed to him the journey to Kebec,—a frightful one, on account of the difficulty of the roads, and very dangerous because of the ambuscades of the Hiroquois,[5] who massacred, every year, a considerable

[1]Lalemant (also referred to as Father Hiersome L'alemant) became the superior of the New France missions in 1645. As superior, he was responsible for assembling, editing, and sending to Paris the letters and narrative that made up each *Relation.* Note, though, that Lalemant takes pains to assure readers that this account comes directly from Jogues's "own lips."

[2]On the Loire River, in central France.

[3]Quebec.

[4]The *Relations* and other French colonial documents refer to the native peoples of Canada either by tribal names or, collectively, as *sauvages.* Allies of the French were often called *nos sauvages,* "our savages."

[5]Iroquois.

number of the Savages allied to the French. Let us hear him speak upon his subject and upon the result of his journey:

"Authority having made me a simple proposition, and not a command, to go down to Kebec, I offered myself with all my heart. So there we were, on the way and in the dangers all at once. We were obliged to disembark forty times, and forty times to carry our boats and all our baggage amid the currents and waterfalls that one encounters on this journey of about three hundred leagues. At last, thirty-five days after our departure from the Hurons, we arrived, much fatigued, at Three Rivers;[6] thence we went down to Kebec. Our affairs being finished in fifteen days, we solemnly observed the feast of St. Ignace;[7] and the next day, we left Three Rivers, in order to go up again to the country whence we came. The first day was favorable to us; the second caused us to fall into the hands of the Iroquois.

"We were forty persons, distributed in several canoes; the one which kept the vanguard, having discovered on the banks of the great river some tracks of men, recently imprinted on the sand and clay, gave us warning. A landing was made: some say that these are footprints of the enemy, others are sure that they are those of Algonquins, our allies. In this dispute, Eustache Ahatsistari exclaimed: 'Be they friends or enemies, it matters not; they are not in greater number than we; let us advance and fear nothing.'

"We had not yet made a half-league, when the enemy, concealed among the grass and brushwood, rises with a great outcry, discharging at our canoes a volley of balls. The noise so greatly frightened a part of our Hurons that they abandoned their canoes and weapons in order to escape by flight into the depth of the woods. We were four French,—one of whom, being in the rear, escaped with the Hurons, who abandoned him before approaching the enemy. Eight or ten, both Christians and Catechumens,[8] joined us; they oppose a courageous front to the enemy. But, having perceived that another band—of forty Hiroquois, who were in ambush on the other side of the river—was coming to attack them, they lost courage; insomuch that those who were least entangled fled.

"A Frenchman named René Goupil,[9] whose death is precious before God, was surrounded and captured, along with some of the most courageous Hurons. I was watching this disaster," says the Father, "from a place very favorable for concealing me from the sight of the enemy, but this thought could never enter my mind. 'Could I indeed,' I said to myself, 'abandon our French and leave those good Neophytes[10] and those poor Catechumens, without giving them the help which the Church of my God has entrusted to me?' Flight seemed horrible to me. 'It must be,' I said in my heart, 'that my body suffer the fire of earth, in order to deliver these poor souls from the flames of Hell; it must die a transient death, in order to procure for them an eternal life.' My conclusion being reached without great opposition from my feelings, I call the

[6]The French settlement at Three Rivers lay seventy miles upriver from Quebec on the St. Lawrence.

[7]A Catholic feast day honoring St. Ignatius Loyola, the founder of the Jesuit order, and observed on July 31.

[8]Catechumens were Christian converts who had not yet been baptized.

[9]Goupil, from Anjou, France, was a novice or *donné,* that is, a layman in training for the Jesuit order.

[10]Neophytes were newly baptized Christian converts.

one of the Hiroquois who had remained to guard the prisoners. He advances and, having seized me, puts me in the number of those whom the world calls miserable. Finally they brought that worthy Christian Captain named Eustache, who, having perceived me, exclaimed, 'Ah, my Father, I had sworn to you that I would live or die with you.' The sight of him piercing my heart, I do not remember the words that I said to him.

"Another Frenchman, named Guillaume Couture, seeing that the Hurons were giving way, escaped like them into those great forests; and, as he was agile, he was soon out of the enemy's grasp. But, remorse having seized him because he had forsaken his Father and his comrade, he stops quite short. The dread of being regarded as perfidious makes him face about; he encounters five stout Hiroquois. One of these aims at him, but, his arquebus having missed fire, the Frenchman did not miss him,—he laid him, stone-dead, on the spot; the other four Hiroquois fell upon him with a rage of Lions, or rather of Demons. Having stripped him bare as the hand, they bruised him with heavy blows of clubs. . . . In short, they pierced one of his hands with a javelin, and led him, tied and bound in this sad plight, to the place where we were. Having recognized him, I escape from my guards and fall upon his neck. The Hiroquois at first remained quite bewildered; then, all at once,—imagining perhaps that I was applauding that young man because he had killed one of their captains,—they fell upon me with a mad fury, they belabored me with thrusts and with blows from sticks and war-clubs, flinging me to the ground, half dead. When I began to breathe again, those who had not struck me, approaching, violently tore out my finger nails; and then biting, one after another, the ends of my two fore-fingers, destitute of their nails, caused me the sharpest pain,—grinding and crushing them as if between two stones, even to the extent of causing splinters or little bones to protrude.[11] They treated the good René Goupil in the same way, without doing, at that time, any harm to the Hurons.

"As I saw them engrossed in examining and distributing our spoils, I sought also for my share. I visit all the captives; I baptize those who were not yet baptized; I encourage those poor wretches to suffer with constancy, assuring them that their reward would far exceed the severity of their torments. I ascertained on this round of visits, that we were twenty-two captives, without counting three Hurons killed on the spot.

"So there we were, on the way to be led into a country truly foreign. It is true that, during the thirteen days that we spent on that journey, I suffered in the body torments almost unendurable, and, in the soul, mortal anguish; hunger, the fiercely burning heat, the threats and hatred of those Leopards, the pain of our wounds,—which, for not being dressed, became putrid even to the extent of breeding worms,—caused us, in truth, much distress. But all these things seemed light to me in comparison with an inward sadness which I felt at the sight of our earliest and most ardent Christians of the Hurons. I had thought that they were to be the pillars of the rising church, and I saw them become the victims of death. The ways closed for a long time to the salvation of so many peoples made me die every hour in the depth of my soul.

"Eight days after our departure from the shores of the great river of saint Lawrence, we met two hundred Hiroquois, who were coming in pursuit of the

[11]These tortures focusing upon the captives' hands may have been intended to prevent captives from holding weapons, as well as to make their prisoner status clearly visible.

French and of the Savages, our allies. At this encounter we were obliged to sustain a new shock. It is a belief among these Barbarians that those who go to war are the more fortunate in proportion as they are cruel toward their enemies; I assure you that they made us thoroughly feel the force of that wretched belief.

"Accordingly, having perceived us, they first thanked the Sun for having caused us to fall into the hands of their Fellow-countrymen. That done, they set up a stage on a hill; then they seek sticks or thorns according to their fancy. Being thus armed, they form in line,—a hundred on one side, and a hundred on the other,—and make us pass, all naked, along that way of fury and anguish.[12] I had not accomplished the half of this course when I fell to the earth under the weight of that hail and of those redoubled blows. Seeing that I had not fallen by accident, and that I did not rise again for being too near death, they entered upon a cruel compassion; their rage was not yet glutted, and they wished to conduct me alive into their own country. I would be too tedious if I were to set down in writing all the rigor of my sufferings. . . .

"I had always thought, indeed, that the day on which the whole Church rejoices in the glory of the Blessed Virgin—her glorious and triumphant Assumption—would be for us a day of pain.[13] We arrived on the eve of that sacred day at a little river,[14] distant from the first village of the Hiroquois about a quarter of a league. We found on its banks many men and youths. They led us in triumph into that first village; all the youth were outside the gates, arranged in line,—armed with sticks, and some with iron rods, which they easily secure, on account of their vicinity to the Dutch.[15] Here follows the order which was observed at that funereal and pompous entry. They made one Frenchman march at the end, and another in the middle of the Hurons, and me the very last. We were following one another at an equal distance; and, that our executioners might have more leisure to beat us at their ease, some Hiroquois thrust themselves into our ranks in order to prevent us from running and from avoiding any blows. . . . Such was our entrance into that Babylon. Hardly could we arrive as far as the scaffold which was prepared for us, so exhausted were we; our bodies were all livid, and our faces all stained with blood. But more disfigured than all was René Goupil, so that nothing white appeared in his face except his eyes. . . .

"Evening having come, they made us descend, in order to be taken into the cabins as the sport of the children. They gave us for food a very little Indian corn simply boiled in water; then they made us lie down on pieces of bark, binding us by the hands and feet to four stakes fastened in the ground. Oh, my God, what nights! To remain always in an extremely constrained position; to be unable to stir or to turn, under the attack of countless vermin which assailed us on all sides; to be burdened with wounds, some recent and others all putrid; not to have sustenance for the half of one's life, in truth, these torments are great, but God is infinite. At Sunrise they

[12]Jogues and his companions were met outside the village palissade by a "gantlet," two lines of villagers who beat them with sticks. Once inside the village, they were tied to a "scaffold," where they were subject to further beatings and humiliations.

[13]August 15, the day on which Catholics mark the passage or "assumption" of the Virgin Mary, the mother of Jesus, into Heaven following her death. Jogues uses the occasion to recall the sufferings of Jesus rather than the joy usually associated with the Assumption.

[14]The Mohawk River, in what is now upper New York State.

[15]The Mohawks were in frequent contact with their trading partners the Dutch, who had established a trading post at Fort Orange (present-day Albany) in the late 1620s.

led us back to our scaffold, where we spent three days and three nights in the sufferings I have just described.

"The three days having expired, they parade us into two other villages, where we make our entrance as into the first; these villages are several leagues distant from one another. The sentence decreed in the Council is intimated to me; the following night is to be (as they say) the end of my torments and of my life. My soul is well pleased with these words, but not yet was my God,—he willed to prolong my martyrdom. Those Barbarians reconsidered the matter, exclaiming that life ought to be spared to the Frenchmen, or, rather, their death postponed.[16] They thought to find more moderation at our forts, on account of us. They accordingly sent Guillaume Couture into the largest village, and René Goupil and I were lodged together in another. Life being granted us, they did us no more harm. But, alas, it was then that we felt at leisure the torments which had been inflicted on us. They gave us for beds the bark of trees, and for refreshment a little Indian meal, and sometimes a bit of squash, half raw. Our hands and fingers being all in pieces, they had to feed us like children. Patience was our Physician. Some women, more merciful, regarded us with much charity, and were unable to look at our sores without compassion."

God Preserves Father Isaac Jogues after the Murder of His Companion. He Instructs Him in a Very Remarkable Manner

When these poor captives had recovered a little of their strength, the principal men of the country talked of conducting them back to Three Rivers, in order to restore them to the French. But, as their captors could not agree, the Father and his companions endured, more than ever, the pangs of death. These Barbarians are accustomed to give prisoners, whom they do not choose to put to death, to the families who have lost some of their relatives in war. These prisoners take the place of the deceased, and are incorporated into that family, which alone has the right to kill them or let them live. But when they retain some public prisoner, like the Father, without giving him to any individual, this poor man is every day within two finger-lengths of death.

The young Frenchman who was the Father's companion was accustomed to caress the little children, and to teach them to make the sign of the Cross. An old man, having seen him make this sacred sign on the forehead of his grandson, said to a nephew of his: "Go and kill that dog; that act will cause some harm to my grandson." Father Jogues leads him to a grove near the village, and explains to him the dangers in which they stood.[17] While they were returning, the nephew of that old man, and another Savage, armed with hatchets and watching for an opportunity, go to meet them. One of the men says to the Father, "March forward," and at the same time he breaks the head of poor René Goupil, who, on falling and expiring, pronounced the Holy name of Jesus.[18] "Give me a moment's time," the Father said to them, suppos-

[16] While captives underwent torture, Iroquois village headmen and matrons would debate whether they should be killed or adopted into the village.

[17] Jogues apparently had been forewarned that the Mohawks had decided against releasing the French and would kill them instead.

[18] Goupil was killed on September 29, 1642.

ing that they would accord him the same favor as to his companion. "Get up," they reply; "thou wilt not die this time."

That young man, or that blessed martyr, being thus slain, the Father returns to his cabin; his people apply their hands to his breast, in order to feel whether fear did not agitate his heart. Having found it steady, they said to him: "Do not again leave the village, unless thou art accompanied by some one of us; they intend to beat thee to death; look out for thyself." He knew very well that they were seeking his life; a Huron, who had given him some shoes out of compassion, came to ask them of him again,—"Because," he said to him, "soon thou wilt have no more use for them, and another would use them." The Father gave them back to him, understanding very well what he meant to tell him. In brief, this good Father was every day like a bird on the branch; his life held only by a thread; and it seemed to him that at every moment some one was about to cut it; but he who held the end of it was not willing to let it go so soon.

The Father Is Given as a Servant to Some Hunters. He Suffers, He Is Consoled, He Exercises His Zeal in His Journeys

They gave this poor Father to some families, to serve them as a menial in their hunts; he follows them at the approach of Winter and makes thirty leagues with them, serving them through two months, as a slave. All his clothes sheltered him no more than would a shirt and a sorry pair of drawers; his stockings and his shoes made like tennis slippers, and of a leather just as thin, without any soles,—in a word, he was all in rags. As they did not account him fit for hunting, they gave him a woman's occupation,—that is to cut and bring the wood to keep up the cabin fire.[19] The chase beginning to furnish supplies, he could to some extent repair his strength,—meat not being stinted to him; but when he saw that they were offering to the Demon of the chase all that they took, he told them plainly that he would never eat of flesh sacrificed to the devil. He therefore contented himself with a very little sagamité,[20] and even then he had it but seldom, because, gorged with meat, they despised their dry cornmeal.

He secretly confessed to one of our Fathers that God tried him exceedingly in that journey, and that he saw himself a long time without any other support than Faith alone; his desolation was so great, and the sight of his miseries appeared to him so frightful that he knew not in what direction to turn. He had recourse to prayer; he would go to the woods as soon as it was morning, bringing back even more wood than was needed to keep up the fire which burns day and night in their cabins. His task done, he withdrew alone upon a hill covered with spruce trees, and there he spent eight or ten hours in prayer. He continued these exercises during forty days, without house, without fire, without other shelter than the sky and the woods, and a miserable scrap of I know not what, almost as transparent as the air. Those of his

[9]Although Jogues did not fully realize it, Iroquois women were responsible for a wide variety of tasks: preparing meat from hunts; planting and tending fields of corn, beans, and squash; and gathering wood, berries, and nuts. Women also controlled most aspects of village life, including keeping the "cabin fire" in the longhouse. Iroquois societies were matrilineal—that is, lineages were traced through the maternal line.

[20]A dietary staple for many northern tribes, *sagamité* consists of corn meal boiled and combined with any of the following: animal fats, meat, fish, berries, dried fruits, or nuts.

cabin, having perceived his retreat, and supposing that he was there preparing some spells in order to make men die, they tormented him from time to time, playing upon him a thousand tricks. In fine, they regarded him as an abomination,—even to the degree that whatever he touched was polluted and contaminated among them, so that he might not use any of the articles in the cabin. He had his thighs and legs cracked and split by the rigor of the cold, not having wherewith to cover himself.

From the month of August till the end of March,[21] the Father was every day in the pains and terrors of death. A lesser courage had died a hundred times from apprehension. It is easier to die all at once than to die a hundred times. Toward the end of April, a Savage Captain from the country of the Sokoquiois[22] appeared in the land of the Hiroquois, laden with presents, which he came to offer for the ransome and deliverance of a Frenchman named Ondesson,—thus the Hurons and the Hiroquois named Father Jogues.[23] This embassy gave some credit to the Father, and caused him to be regarded for a short time with more compassionate eyes; but these Barbarians, having accepted the gifts, nevertheless did not set him at liberty,—violating the law of nations, and the law accepted among these tribes.

In the months of May and June, the Father wrote several letters, by warriors who were coming to hunt men upon the great stream of the Saint Lawrence; he told them that they should fasten these letters to some poles on the banks of that river. Be this as it may, one of them was delivered to Monsieur the Governor, on the occasion which we have described in Chapter 12 of the Relation for the year 1642, where a copy of that letter is written at full length.

About that time, some Hiroquois Captains going to visit some small nations tributary to them, in order to get some presents,—that man who had the Father in custody, being of the party, led him in his train; his design was to display the triumphs of the Hiroquois over even the nations which are in Europe. There was never Anchorite[24] more abstemious than this poor captive on that journey; his living was only a little wild purslane[25] which he went to gather in the fields, with which he made a soup without other seasoning than clear water. They gave him, indeed, certain seeds to eat,—but so insipid and so dangerous that they served as a very quick poison to those who knew not how to prepare them; and he would not touch them.

The Father Escapes from the Hiroquois and Proceeds to France, through the Intervention of the Dutch. He returns to Canada. Having Arrived There, He Makes a Journey to the Country of the Iroquois

Upon the return from this journey, they command the Father to accompany some fishermen, who conducted him seven or eight leagues below a Dutch settlement. While he was engaged in that exercise, he learned from some Iroquois who came to

[21] 1642–1643.

[22] The Western Abenaki, from the region of the northern Connecticut River. This group had recently become allies of the French, and hence the Sokoki "Captain" offers to ransom Jogues.

[23] The renaming of captives was common practice among Iroquois peoples.

[24] Anchorites were Christian hermits of the second and third centuries who fled worldly material comforts in order to live in cloistered communities.

[25] A trailing weed with yellow flowers.

that quarter that they were awaiting him in the village to burn him. This news was the occasion of his deliverance. The Dutch having given him the opportunity to enter a ship, the Iroquois complained of it,—he was withdrawn and conducted to the house of the Captain, who gave him in custody to an old man, until they should have appeased these Barbarians. In a word, if they had persevered in their demand, and rejected some presents that were made to them, the Father would have been given up into their hands, to be the object of their fury and food for their fires. Now, while they were awaiting the opportunity to send him back to Europe, he remained six weeks under the guard of that old man, who lodged him in an old garret. The Minister[26] visited him sometimes, and bethinking himself one day to ask how they treated him; he answered that they brought him very few things. "I suspect as much," the Minister answers, "for that old man is a great miser, who no doubt retains most of the provisions that are sent you."

In this garret where the Father was, there was a recess to which his Guard continually led Hiroquois Savages, in order to sell some produce which he locked up there: this recess was made of planks so slightly joined that one might easily have passed his fingers into the openings. "I am astonished," says the Father, "that those Barbarians did not hundreds of times discover me; I saw them without difficulty. I concealed myself behind casks, bending myself into a constrained posture which gave me gehenna and torture two, three, or four hours in succession, and that very often. To go down to the court of the dwelling was casting myself headlong; for every place was filled with those who were seeking to put me to death."

Finally, the Governor of the country,[27] sending a bark of one hundred tons to Holland, sent the Father back at the beginning of the month of November.

They anchored in a port of England, toward the end of December. On Christmas eve he embarked in I know not what boat or little bark laden with mineral coal, which landed him the next day on the coast of lower Brittany. Finally, on the fifth of January, 1644, he was knocking at the door of our College at Rennes.

The porter, seeing him in such plight, clad in garments so incongruous, did not recognize him. The Father besought him to bring the Father Rector, that he might impart to him, he said, some news from Canada. The Father Rector was putting on the Sacerdotal vestments, in order to go and celebrate holy Mass, but the porter having told him that a poor man, come from Canada, was asking for him, that word "poor" touched him. "Perhaps," he said to himself, "he is in haste, and he may be in need." He then lays aside the sacred vestments with which he was partly robed; he goes to find him; the Father, without revealing his identity, offers him letters signed by the Governor of the Dutch; before reading these he puts various questions to the Father, without recognizing him; and then, at last, he asks him if he were indeed acquainted with Father Isaac Jogues. "I know him very well," he answers. "We have had word that he was taken by the Hiroquois; is he dead? is he still captive? Have not those Barbarians slain him?" "He is at liberty, and it is he, my Reverend Father, who speaks to you," and thereupon he falls upon his knees to receive his blessing. The Father Rector, overcome with an unaccustomed joy, embraces him, and has him enter the house; every one hastens thither; the joy and consolation of a deliverance

[26]Johannes Megapolensis, a Protestant minister at Fort Orange.

[27]Willem Kieft, governor of New Netherland.

so little expected interrupt their words. In fine, they regard him as a Lazarus raised from the dead,—who is destined to go and die for the last time in the country where he has already suffered so many deaths.

From Rennes he comes to Paris: the Queen having heard mention of his sufferings, says aloud: "Romances are feigned, but here is a genuine combination of great adventures." She wished to see him; her eyes were touched with compassion at the sight of the cruelty of the Hiroquois. He made no long sojourn in France; the spring of the year 1644, having come, he betook himself to la Rochelle in order to cross back to the country of his martyrdom,—where, having arrived, he was sent to Montreal. Peace being made with the Hiroquois,[28] the Father was taken from Montreal, to go and lay the foundations of a Mission in their country, which was named "The Mission of the martyrs." On the sixteenth of May, 1646, this good Father left Three Rivers in company with Sieur Bourdon, the engineer of Monsieur the Governor. They arrived (back) at Three Rivers,—having accomplished their embassy,—the 29th of the month of June.

Father Isaac Jogues Returns for the Third Time to the Country of the Hiroquois, Where He Is Put to Death

Hardly had the poor Father been refreshed among us two or three months, when he recommenced his expeditions; on the twenty-fourth of September, in the same year, 1646, he embarks with a young Frenchman, in a canoe conducted by some Hurons, in order to return to the land of his crosses. He had strong premonitions of his death. We have learned that was slain directly upon his entrance into that country full of murder and blood: here follows a letter announcing this:

"For the rest, I have not much to tell you, except how the French arrived, on the 17th of this present month of October, 1647, at the fort of the Maquois.[29] The very day of their coming, they began to threaten them, saying: 'You will die tomorrow: be not astonished. But we will not burn you; have courage; we will strike you with the hatchet and will set your heads on the palings,' (that is to say, on the fence about their village), 'so that when we capture your brothers they may still see you.' You must know that it was only the nation of the bear which put them to death; the nations of the wolf and the turtle did all that they could to save their lives, and said to the nation of the bear: 'Kill us first.' But, alas, they are not in life for all that. Know, then, that on the 18th, in the evening, when they came to call Isaac to supper, he got up and went away with that Barbarian to the lodge of the bear. There was a traitor with his hatchet behind the door, who, on entering, split open his head; then, immediately, he cut it off, and set it on the palings. The next day, very early, he did the same to the other man, and their bodies were thrown into the river. Monsieur, I have not been able to know or to learn from any Savage why they have killed them."

Such is what the Dutch have written of the death of Father Isaac Jogues.

[28]A truce that lasted less than a year, in 1646.

[29]The Mohawks.

Chesapeake

"Virginia," when Queen Elizabeth granted Sir Walter Ralegh a patent for its exploration, was a vast track of land stretching from New England to Florida. The Spanish, who already had settlements in Florida and missions in present-day Georgia and South Carolina, had attempted to found a mission among the Virginia Indians as early as the 1570s but were unsuccessful. The colony at Jamestown, made famous by the histories of John Smith, was the first *successful* English attempt to found a permanent settlement in North America. Unlike most of the later English colonies, Virginia was settled largely by non-Puritan Anglicans and people of secular and commercial interests. It became the oldest English colony, known as the "old dominion," and played an important role in the colonial politics of the southeastern region as well as the emerging nation.

Jamestown was not the first attempt by the English to establish a colony in the New World. In the early 1580s, England had tried but failed to establish its first colony at Roanoke Island on what is now the Outer Banks of North Carolina. Thomas Harriot and John White sailed on the second expedition to this area in 1585, during which the settlement was founded. They brought back notable records of their trip: Harriot, in his *Brief and True Report,* excerpted below; and John White, in a series of watercolors detailing the natural and native world, which were later reproduced as engravings by the German editor Theodor DeBry. Harriot's *Report* was largely promotional, intended to dispel negative rumors about the colonial endeavor and attract prospective investors and backers. Although we are most interested in the last section, which provides a detailed description of native life, his contemporaries were more concerned with the first three sections, which describe the potential for extracting profit from the new land and the resources (food, building materials) needed for establishing settlements. Harriot depicted the natives as "very ingenious" and thought they could be easily "brought to civility, and the embracing of true religion." Although it is possible that religious concerns acted as a cover for economic interests, the two were closely linked for English colonizers, as was the use of military force to ensure discipline in the colonies.

Ralph Lane was left in charge of the small colony, and it was his inordinate use of military force that demoralized his own soldiers and intimidated the formerly tractable Indians. Fearing that chief Wingina was about to betray him and exterminate the colony, Lane pursued and beheaded the chief. But when a ship carrying reinforcements and supplies for the further exploration of the Chesapeake was wrecked in a great storm, Lane abandoned the colony. Ralegh made another attempt. He reduced the strong military presence, and, most important, included women and children for the first time. Under the leadership of John White, this group sailed in 1587 and landed at Roanoke, where Manteo, a Croatoan Indian who had gone back to England with the first expedition and returned with White's, was christened and admitted to the Church of England (also known as the Anglican Church). Five days later, White's granddaughter, named Virginia Dare, was delivered, the first English child to be born in the New World. Despite these momentous events, when White returned in 1590, after protracted attempts to resupply a ship and make for the colony during the war with Spain that was fought at sea, he found the settlement razed and the colonists mysteriously disappeared. None of the theories about what happened at Roanoke have been proved, but this failure curtailed English colonizing efforts for almost twenty years, and it predisposed the English to regard the Indians as untrustworthy and an obstacle to further settlement.

In May 1607, a small expedition financed by a group of private investors including John Smith arrived in Chesapeake Bay, explored the James River, and selected a site on a small peninsula for the establishment of what would be the first permanent English settlement in the New World. This success came at a great cost, however. Of the 144 men who originally set sail from England, only 104 survived the voyage. By January 1608, only 38 of the original colonists still survived. The precariousness of the situation necessitated John Smith's famous policy, "he who does not work shall not eat," which forced the aristocrats and gentlemen who looked down upon Smith, a mere captain, to work in order to survive. One of these aristocrats, Edward Maria Wingfield, a gentleman from a distinguished family and a veteran of the wars in Ireland and the Netherlands, became the first "president" of the colony and even accused Smith of fomenting mutiny on the voyage over. But Wingfield was removed from office in disgrace after only a few months, because of squabbling over food supplies and status, and Smith instituted a regimen of work and established trade with the native Powhatans. Both of these strategies saved the colonists from starvation. Wingfield's version of the events, though thoroughly self-interested, provides a useful counterpart to Smith's more widely known narratives in the *True Relation,* and the *General History,* and sheds light on the economic, political, and class conflicts that rent the fledgling settlement.

One of the most important aspects of Smith's account is the insight it provides into relations between the colonists and Native Americans. The English believed that social order and cultural progress depended upon a hierarchical universe in which relations among people of different classes and among the divine, human, and nonhuman worlds were fixed and immutable. Thus, though God ruled the world, man (gender specific) had, according to the Book of Genesis, "dominion over the fish of the sea, and over the fowl of the air, and over the cattle, and over all the earth, and over every thing that creepeth upon the earth" (Genesis 2:26). Furthermore, there was a general consensus among the English that advancing the glory of God included not only spreading the Gospel to the benighted natives but also augmenting the honor and power of the English nation through the accumulation of wealth and profit. A loud, angelic voice in the Book of Revelation declares, "Worthy is the Lamb that was slain to receive power, and riches, and wisdom, and strength, and honor, and glory, and blessing" (5:12). The "Lamb" symbolized the sacrificed Christ, but Anglicans understood themselves to be the rightful inheritors of that sacrifice, so they believed that godliness, wealth, and power were ineluctably linked.

By contrast, the Powhatans, like many native peoples in North America, conceived of the universe as a living entity of which they, as humans, were an integral part, along with animals and spirits who were equally as important. The world, they believed, was not created for human benefit, nor was life created for the pursuit of profit. Chief Powhatan, at the time of his famous encounter with John Smith, was extending his domains and consolidating his empire, but he understood the strategic necessity of acknowledging Smith as a powerful leader as well, and encouraging intermarriage as a way of producing peace.

Nevertheless, the ethnocentrism and materialism of the English eventually led to the decimation of the Indians and their concentration on inland reservations, far from the rich coastal lands of their ancestors. Virginia, like the other southern colonies established in the latter part of the seventeenth century by King Charles II and his son James II, adopted what came to be known as *staple agriculture,* the production of one staple product not native to the region like sugar, cotton, silk, or tobacco. Extremely labor intensive, this form of agriculture required a stable labor force, and by the 1670s, colonies like Virginia were becoming more and more dependent on slave labor imported from Africa and the West Indies. But the shortage of labor affected lower classes of whites as well. Both the letter by Richard Frethorne and the ballad by James Revel reveal the hardships faced by the lower orders of society—indentured servants and conscripted criminals—in a class-ridden colonial society dominated by a planter aristocracy.

They are also an important corrective to the promotional and self-promotional writings of those in power. Class issues and conflicts with native populations over land produced a volatile series of events that came to be called Bacon's Rebellion in 1676. Playing upon the dissatisfaction of the lower and middle classes who wanted Indian lands to be available to them for purchase and who felt the colonial government of Sir William Berkeley to be unresponsive to their plight, Nathaniel Bacon set off a firestorm of anti-Indian sentiment that threatened to tear the colony apart. Only Bacon's sudden death from dysentery in 1676 stopped the rebellion from spiraling out of control, but his seductive rhetoric linked white racial solidarity and a notion of "the people's rights" in a powerful way that would color American ideology for centuries to come.

Thomas Harriot 1560–1621

Thomas Harriot, an Oxford-trained scientist, naturalist, and mathematician, wrote one of the most influential and best known sixteenth-century English colonial texts. First published in 1588, *A Briefe and True Report of the New Found Land of Virginia* was based on Harriot's voyage to the New World in 1585 on the second Roanoke expedition led by Sir Richard Grenville, Sir Walter Ralegh's brother-in-law. Two years later, Theodor DeBry published Harriot's *A Briefe and True Report* again, this time with copperplate engravings based on the watercolor drawings of John White, who had accompanied Harriot on the 1585 expedition. Not only did *A Briefe and True Report* offer readers a wealth of information on the flora and fauna of Virginia, it is widely recognized as one of the most detailed early English ethnographies of the native populations of North America. Indeed, its stature as an ethnography would not be surpassed until well into the seventeenth century with the writings of John Smith, William Wood, Roger Williams, and others.

Reflecting the highly decentralized nature of English colonialism, Harriot's *A Briefe and True Report* served as a model for almost all subsequent English colonial promotional pamphlets. Rather than being funded and controlled centrally by the monarchy, as was usually the case with the colonies of Spain and Portugal, England's colonies were the product of joint-stock companies, whereby a number of individual investors pooled their resources to purchase the supplies and equipment necessary for colonial exploration. The promotional pamphlet, therefore, emerged as one of the most effective vehicles for convincing wary investors of the significant financial potential of England's fledgling colonial enterprises. Although the particular advantages of colonial investment changed over the next century, the central structural fact of English colonialism did not: England's colonies would remain dependent on periodic infusions of capital from England well into the seventeenth century. And as long as that was the case, the promotional pamphlet, of which *A Briefe and True Report* is the prototype, remained a staple of the English publishing and bookselling trades.

While Harriot devotes most of his text to the considerable number of "merchantable commodities" to be found in Virginia—commodities ranging from luxury items, such as furs and pearls, to strategically significant materials, such as timber and iron—he also spends a considerable amount of time describing the ease with which the land in the New World could be farmed. In these parts of his text, Harriot reminds us that the colonial enterprise was not exclusively an investment opportunity for the very rich, who would reap profits from the importation of valuable raw materials. In addition to serving as sources for these materials, the colonies, in Harriot's vision, would also be places where the younger sons of the gentry might live and prosper and where idle English laborers, displaced by enclosures, might make themselves productive members of a new society. For this other group of people, who were interested in investing not their capital but rather their labor in the colonial enterprise, the agricultural potential of the land was of primary interest. Moreover, Harriot's depiction of the colonial geography as conducive to the family-oriented enterprise of farming might have been intended to allay widespread English fears that colonies might become sites of licentious and criminal behavior.

One need not be a cynic to observe that financial gain was probably the single largest incentive for colonial undertaking. In colonial promotional pamphlets like Harriot's, however, readers are almost always reassured that the handsome material gains will not come at the expense of the salvation of the soul. For the English, the easiest way to care for their own souls was to look after the souls of the native inhabitants. It is with this fact in mind that we should read Harriot's account of "the nature and maners of the people." In this part of his text, Harriot shows himself acutely aware of the antipathy of the English toward the whole notion of colonial enterprise—an antipathy born largely out of a fear that English colonizers might commit the same sorts of atrocities as the Spanish. Harriot, accordingly, attempts to reassure potential investors that the English settlers will be able to convince the Virginia natives to submit to their rule. In phrasing that is at once ominous and upbeat, Harriot opines, they shall "have cause both to feare and love us, that shall inhabite with them." The reality, of course, was that the leader of Harriot's expedition, Sir Richard Grenville, and his successor, Ralph Lane, relied much more heavily on fear and coercion than on love and cooperation. It was, in all likelihood, the harsh treatment of the natives by the English that led to the mysterious disappearance of the English settlers on Roanoke Island not long after the initial publication of Harriot's text. Hence, although Harriot's pamphlet may have exerted an enduring influence on colonial writing, its influence was probably undermined by the immediate perception of colonialism as a risky activity.

Thomas Scanlan
Ohio University

PRIMARY WORK

Thomas Harriot, *A Briefe and True Report of the New Found Land of Virginia* (London, 1588).

from A Briefe and True Report of the New Found Land of Virginia

To the Adventurers, Favourers, and Welwillers of the enterprise for the inhabiting and planting in Virginia.

Since the first undertaking by Sir Walter Ralegh to deale in the action of discovering of that countrey which is now called and knowen by the name of Virginia, many voyages having beene thither made at sundry times to his great charge; as first in the yere 1584, and afterwards in the yeres 1585, 1586, and now of late this last yeere 1587:[1] there have bene divers and variable reports, with some slanderous and shamefull speeches bruted abroad by many that returned from thence: especially of that discovery which was made by the Colony transported by Sir Richard Grinvile[2] in the yere 1585, being of all others the most principall, and as yet of most effect, the time of their abode in the countrey being a whole yere, when as in the other voyage before they stayed but sixe weeks, and the others after were onely for supply and transportation, nothing more being discovered then had bene before. Which reports have not done a little wrong to many that otherwise would have also favoured and adventured in the action, to the honour and benefit of our nation, besides the particular profit and credit which would redound to themselves the dealers therein, as I hope by the sequel of events, to the shame of those that have avouched the contrary, shall be manifest, if you the adventurers, favourers and welwillers doe but either increase in number, or in opinion continue, or having beene doubtfull, renew your good liking and furtherance to deale therein according to the woorthinesse thereof already found, and as you shall understand hereafter to be requisit. Touching which woorthinesse through cause of the diversity of relations and reports, many of your opinions could not be firme, nor the minds of some that are well disposed be setled in any certaintie.[3]

I have therefore thought it good, being one that have beene in the discoverie, and in dealing with the naturall inhabitants specially imployed: and having therefore seene and knowen more then the ordinary, to impart so much unto you of the fruits of our labours, as that you may know how injuriously the enterprise is slandered, and that in publique maner at this present, chiefly for two respects.

First, that some of you which are yet ignorant or doubtfull of the state thereof, may see that there is sufficient cause why the chiefe enterpriser with the favour of her Majesty, notwithstanding such reports, hath not onely since continued the action by sending into the countrey againe, and replanting this last yeere a new Colony, but is

[1]Harriot's *Briefe and True Report* was based on his participation in the 1585 expedition. The 1587 expedition was to end disastrously and led to the "lost colony" of Roanoke.

[2]Sir Richard Grenville was Sir Walter Ralegh's brother-in-law and leader of the 1587 expedition to Virginia.

[3]Although scholars have found very few first-hand accounts critical of England's colonial efforts, Harriot's claims here are generally believed to be true, as many other early English colonial promotional texts refer to widespread criticism of the colonizing enterprise.

also ready, according as the times and meanes will affoord, to follow and prosecute the same.

Secondly, that you seeing and knowing the continuance of the action, by the view hereof you may generally know and learne what the countrey is, and thereupon consider how your dealing therein, if it proceed, may returne you profit and gaine, be it either by inhabiting and planting, or otherwise in furthering thereof.

And least that the substance of my relation should be doubtfull unto you, as of others by reason of their diversitie, I will first open the cause in a few words, wherefore they are so different, referring my selfe to your favourable constructions, and to be adjudged of, as by good consideration you shall finde cause.

Of our company that returned, some for their misdemeanour and ill dealing in the countrey have bene there worthily punished, who by reason of their bad natures, have maliciously not onely spoken ill of their Governours, but for their sakes slandered the countrey it selfe. The like also have those done which were of their consort.[4] . . .

The ground they never fatten with mucke, dung, or any other thing, neither plow nor digge it as we in England, but onely prepare it in sort as followeth. A few dayes before they sowe or set, the men with woodden instruments made almost in forme of mattocks or hoes with long handles: the women with short peckers or parers, because they use them sitting, of a foot long, and about five inches in breadth, doe onely breake the upper part of the ground to raise up the weeds, grasse, and olde stubbes of corne stalks with their roots. The which after a day or two dayes drying in the Sunne, being scrapt up into many small heaps, to save them labour for carying them away, they burne into ashes. And whereas some may thinke that they use the ashes for to better the ground, I say that then they would either disperse the ashes abroad, which wee observed they do not, except the heaps be too great, or els would take speciall care to set their corne where the ashes lie, which also wee finde they are carelesse of. And this is all the husbanding of their ground that they use.

Then their setting or sowing is after this maner. First for their corne, beginning in one corner of the plot, with a pecker they make a hole, wherein they put foure graines, with care that they touch not one another (about an inch asunder) & cover them with the molde againe: and so thorowout the whole plot making such holes, and using them after such maner, but with this regard, that they be made in ranks, every ranke differing from other halfe a fadome or a yard, and the holes also in every ranke as much. By this meanes there is a yard spare ground betweene every hole: where according to discretion here and there, they set as many Beanes and Peaze; in divers places also among the seeds of Macocquer, Melden, and Planta solis.[5]

The ground being thus set according to the rate by us experimented, an English acre conteining forty pearches in length, and foure in breadth, doth there yeeld in croppe or ofcome of corne, Beanes and Peaze, at the least two hundred London bushels, besides the Macocquer, Melden, and Planta solis; when as in England forty bushels of our Wheat yeelded out of such an acre is thought to be much.

I thought also good to note this unto you, that you which shall inhabit, and plant there, may know how specially that countrey corne is there to be preferred before

[4]Colonial promoters were eager to demonstrate their willingness to discipline the members of their own expeditions.

[5]Respectively, a melon or gourd, an herb, and an herb with a yellow flower.

ours: besides, the manifold wayes in applying it to victual, the increase is so much, that small labor & paines is needful in respect of that which must be used for ours. For this I can assure you that according to the rate we have made proofe of, one man may prepare and husband so much ground (having once borne corne before) with lesse then foure and twenty houres labour, as shall yeeld him victual in a large proportion for a twelvemoneth, if he have nothing els but that which the same ground will yeeld, and of that kinde onely which I have before spoken of: the sayd ground being also but of five and twenty yards square. And if need require, but that there is ground enough, there might be raised out of one and the selfesame ground two harvests or ofcomes: for they sow or set, and may at any time when they thinke good, from the midst of March untill the end of June: so that they also set when they have eaten of their first croppe. In some places of the countrey notwithstanding they have two harvests, as we have heard, out of one and the same gound. . . .

There is an herbe which is sowed apart by it selfe, and is called by the inhabitants Uppowoc: in the West Indies it hath divers names, according to the severall places and countreys where it groweth and is used: the Spanyards generally call it Tabacco. The leaves thereof being dried and brought into pouder, they use to take the fume or smoake thereof, by sucking it thorow pipes made of clay, into their stomacke and head; from whence it purgeth superfluous fleame and other grosse humours, and openeth all the pores and passages of the body: by which meanes the use thereof not onely preserveth the body from obstructions, but also (if any be, so that they have not bene of too long continuance) in short time breaketh them: whereby their bodies are notably preserved in health, and know not many grievous diseases, wherewithall we in England are often times afflicted.

This Uppowoc is of so precious estimation amongst them, that they thinke their gods are marvellously delighted therewith: whereupon sometime they make hallowed fires, and cast some of the pouder therin for a sacrifice: being in a storme upon the waters, to pacifie their gods, they cast some up into the aire and into the water: so a weare for fish being newly set up, they cast some therein and into the aire: also after an escape of danger, they cast some into the aire likewise: but all done with strange gestures, stamping, sometime dancing, clapping of hands, holding up of hands, and staring up into the heavens, uttering therewithall, and chattering strange words and noises.

We our selves, during the time we were there, used to sucke it after their maner, as also since our returne, and have found many rare and woonderfull experiments of the vertues thereof: of which the relation would require a volume by it selfe: the use of it by so many of late, men and women of great calling, as els, and some learned Physicians also, is sufficient witnesse. . . .

Of the nature and maners of the people.

It resteth I speake a word or two of the naturall inhabitants, their natures and maners, leaving large discourse thereof until time more convenient hereafter: nowe onely so farre foorth, as that you may know, how that they in respect of troubling our inhabiting and planting, are not to be feared, but that they shall have cause both to feare and love us, that shall inhabite with them.

They are a people clothed with loose mantles made of deere skinnes, and aprons of the same round about their middles, all els naked, of such a difference of statures onely as wee in England, having no edge tooles or weapons of yron or steele to offend us withall, neither knowe they how to make any: those weapons that they have, are onely bowes made of Witch-hazle,[6] and arrowes of reedes, flat edged truncheons also of wood about a yard long, neither have they any thing to defend themselves but targets made of barkes, and some armours made of sticks wickered together with thread.

Their townes are but small, and neere the Sea coast but fewe, some contayning but tenne or twelve houses; some 20. the greatest that we have seene hath bene but of 30. houses: if they bee walled, it is onely done with barkes of trees made fast to stakes, or els with poles onely fixed upright, and close one by another.

Their houses are made of small poles, made fast at the tops in round forme after the maner as is used in many arbories in our gardens of England, in most townes covered with barkes, and in some with artificiall mats made of long rushes, from the tops of the houses downe to the ground. The length of them is commonly double to the breadth, in some places they are but 12. and 16. yards long, and in other some we have seene of foure and twentie.

In some places of the Countrey, one onely towne belongeth to the government of a Wiroans or chiefe Lord, in other some two or three, in some sixe, eight, and more: the greatest Wiroans that yet wee had dealing with, had but eighteene townes in his government, and able to make not above seven or eight hundreth fighting men at the most. The language of every government is different from any other, and the farther they are distant, the greater is the difference.

Their maner of warres amongst themselves is either by sudden surprising one an other most commonly about the dawning of the day, or moone-light, or els by ambushes, or some subtile devises. Set battels are very rare, except it fall out where there are many trees, where either part may have some hope of defence, after the delivery of every arrow, in leaping behind some or other.

If there fall out any warres betweene us and them, what their fight is likely to bee, wee having advantages against them so many maner of wayes, as by our discipline, our strange weapons and devises else, especially Ordinance great and small, it may easily bee imagined: by the experience wee have had in some places, the turning up of their heeles, against us in running away was their best defence.

In respect of us they are a people poore, and for want of skill and judgement in the knowledge and use of our things, doe esteeme our trifles[7] before things of greater value: Notwithstanding, in their proper maner (considering the want of such meanes as we have), they seeme very ingenious. For although they have no such tooles, nor any such crafts, Sciences and Artes as wee, yet in those things they doe, they shew excellencie of wit. And by how much they upon due consideration shall finde our maner of knowledges and crafts to exceede theirs in perfection, and speede for doing or execution, by so much the more is it probable that they should desire our friendship and love, and have the greater respect for pleasing and obeying us.

[6]Witch hazel was a small deciduous shrub found in Virginia.

[7]European explorers typically traded "trifles" of little value, such as toys, coins, and cooking implements, for commodities that they valued more highly.

Whereby may bee hoped, if meanes of good government be used, that they may in short time bee brought to civilitie, and the imbracing of true Religion.

Some religion they have already, which although it be farre from the trueth, yet being as it is, there is hope it may be the easier and sooner reformed.

They beleeve that there are many gods, which they call Mantoac,[8] but of different sorts & degrees, one onely chiefe and great God, which hath bene from all eternitie. Who, as they affirme, when hee purposed to make the world, made first other gods of a principall order, to be as meanes and instruments to be used in the creation and government to follow, and after the Sunne, moone, and starres as pettie gods, and the instruments of the other order more principal. First (they say) were made waters, out of which by the gods was made all diversitie of creatures that are visible or invisible.

For mankinde they say a woman was made first, which by the working of one of the gods, conceived and brought foorth children: And in such sort they say they had their beginning. But how many yeeres or ages have passed since, they say they can make no relation, having no letters nor other such meanes as we to keepe Records of the particularities of times past, but onely tradition from father to sonne.

They thinke that all the gods are of humane shape, and therefore they represent them by images in the formes of men, which they call Kewasowok, one alone is called Kewas: them they place in houses appropriate or temples, which they call Machicomuck, where they worship, pray, sing, and make many times offrings unto them. In some Machicomuck we have seene but one Kewas, in some two, and in other some three. The common sort thinke them to be also gods.

They beleeve also the immortalitie of the soule, that after this life as soone as the soule is departed from the body, according to the workes it hath done, it is either caried to heaven the habitacle of gods, there to enjoy perpetuall blisse and happinesse, or els to a great pitte or hole, which they thinke to be in the furthest parts of their part of the world toward the Sunne set, there to burne continually: the place they call Popogusso.

For the confirmation of this opinion, they tolde me two stories of two men that had bene lately dead and revived againe, the one happened but few yeeres before our comming into the Countrey of a wicked man, which having bene dead and buried, the next day the earth of the grave being seene to move, was taken up againe, who made declaration where his soule had bene, that is to say, very neere entring into Popogusso, had not one of the gods saved him, and gave him leave to returne againe, and teach his friends what they should do to avoyd that terrible place of torment. The other happened in the same yeere we were there, but in a towne that was 60. miles from us, and it was told me for strange newes, that one being dead, buried, and taken up againe as the first, shewed that although his body had lien dead in the grave, yet his soule was alive, & had travailed farre in a long broad way, on both sides whereof grew most delicate and pleasant trees, bearing more rare and excellent fruits, then ever hee had seene before, or was able to expresse, and at length came to most brave and faire houses, neere which he met his father that had bene dead before, who gave him great charge to goe backe againe, and shew his friendes what good they were to

[8]The god Harriot here refers to as Mantoac is called Manitoo in other colonial texts.

doe to enjoy the pleasures of that place, which when he had done he should after come againe.

What subtiltie soever be in the Wiroances and priestes, this opinion worketh so much in many of the common and simple sort of people, that it maketh them have great respect to their Governours, and also great care what they doe, to avoyd torment after death, and to enjoy blisse, although notwithstanding there is punishment ordeined for malefactours, as stealers, whoremongers, and other sorts of wicked doers, some punished with death, some with forfeitures, some with beating, according to the greatnesse of the facts.

And this is the summe of their Religion, which I learned by having speciall familiaritie with some of their priests. Wherein they were not so sure grounded, nor gave such credite to their traditions and stories, but through conversing with us they were brought into great doubts of their owne, and no small admiration of ours, with earnest desire in many, to learne more then wee had meanes for want of perfect utterance in their language to expresse.

Most things they sawe with us, as Mathematicall instruments, sea Compasses, the vertue of the load-stone in drawing yron, a perspective glasse whereby was shewed many strange sights, burning glasses, wilde firewoorkes, gunnes, bookes, writing and reading, springclockes that seeme to goe of themselves and many other things that wee had were so strange unto them, and so farre exceeded their capacities to comprehend the reason and meanes how they should be made and done, that they thought they were rather the workes of gods then of men, or at the leastwise they had bene given and taught us of the gods. Which made many of them to have such opinion of us, as that if they knew not the trueth of God and Religion already, it was rather to bee had from us whom God so specially loved, then from a people that were so simple, as they found themselves to be in comparison of us. Whereupon greater credite was given unto that wee spake of, concerning such matters.

Many times and in every towne where I came, according as I was able, I made declaration of the contents of the Bible, that therein was set foorth the true and onely God, and his mightie workes, that therein was conteined the true doctrine of salvation through Christ, with many particularities of Miracles and chiefe points of Religion, as I was able then to utter, and thought fit for the time. And although I told them the booke materially and of it selfe was not of any such vertue, as I thought they did conceive, but onely the doctrine therein conteined: yet would many be glad to touch it, to embrace it, to kisse it, to holde it to their breastes and heads, and stroke over all their body with it, to shew their hungry desire of that knowledge which was spoken of.

The Wiroans with whom we dwelt called Wingina, and many of his people would bee glad many times to be with us at our Prayers, and many times call upon us both in his owne towne, as also in others whither hee sometimes accompanied us, to pray and sing Psalmes, hoping thereby to be partaker of the same effects which we by that meanes also expected.

Twise this Wiroans was so grievously sicke that he was like to die, and as he lay languishing, doubting of any helpe by his owne priestes, and thinking hee was in such danger for offending us and thereby our God, sent for some of us to pray and bee a meanes to our God that it would please him either that he might live, or after death dwell with him in blisse, so likewise were the requests of many others in the like case.

On a time also when their corne began to wither by reason of a drought which happened extraordinarily, fearing that it had come to passe by reason that in some thing they had displeased us, many would come to us and desire us to pray to our God of England, that he would preserve their Corne, promising that when it was ripe we also should be partakers of the fruit.

There could at no time happen any strange sicknesse, losses, hurts, or any other crosse unto them, but that they would impute to us the cause or meanes thereof, for offending or not pleasing us. One other rare and strange accident, leaving others, wil I mention before I end, which moved the whole Countrey that either knew or heard of us, to have us in wonderfull admiration.

There was no towne where wee had any subtile devise practised against us, wee leaving it unpunished or not revenged (because we sought by all meanes possible to win them by gentlenesse) but that within a few dayes after our departure from every such Towne, the people began to die very fast,[9] and many in short space, in some Townes about twentie, in some fourtie, and in one sixe score, which in trueth was very many in respect of their numbers. This happened in no place that we could learne, but where we had bin, where they used some practise against us, & after such time. The disease also was so strange, that they neither knewe what it was, nor how to cure it, the like by report of the oldest men in the Countrey never happened before, time out of minde. A thing specially observed by us, as also by the naturall inhabitants themselves. Insomuch that when some of the inhabitants which were our friends, and especially the Wiroans Wingina, had observed such effects in foure or five Townes to followe their wicked practises, they were perswaded that it was the worke of our God through our meanes, and that we by him might kill and slay whom we would without weapons, and not come neere them. And thereupon when it had happened that they had understanding that any of their enemies had abused us in our journeys, hearing that we had wrought no revenge with our weapons, and fearing upon some cause the matter should so rest: did come and intreate us that we would be a meanes to our God that they as others that had dealt ill with us might in like sort die, alleadging how much it would bee for our credite and profite, as also theirs, and hoping furthermore that we would doe so much at their requests in respect of the friendship we professed them.

Whose entreaties although wee shewed that they were ungodly, affirming that our God would not subject himselfe to any such prayers and requests of men: that indeede all things have bene and were to be done according to his good pleasure as he had ordeined: and that we to shewe our selves his true servants ought rather to make petition for the contrary, that they with them might live together with us, be made partakers of his trueth, and serve him in righteousnesse, but notwithstanding in such sort, that wee referre that, as all other things, to bee done according to his divine will and pleasure, and as by his wisedome he had ordeined to be best.

Yet because the effect fell out so suddenly and shortly after according to their desires, they thought neverthelesse it came to passe by our meanes, & that we in using such speeches unto them, did but dissemble the matter, and therefore came unto

[9]A reminder that far greater numbers of native inhabitants were killed by disease than by warfare.

us to give us thankes in their maner, that although we satisfied them not in promise, yet in deedes and effect we had fulfilled their desires.

This marveilous accident in all the Countrey wrought so strange opinions of us, that some people could not tell whether to thinke us gods or men, and the rather because that all the space of their sicknes, there was no man of ours knowen to die, or that was specially sicke: they noted also that we had no women amongst us, neither that we did care for any of theirs.

Some therefore were of opinion that we were not borne of women, and therefore not mortal, but that we were men of an old generation many yeeres past, then risen againe to immortalitie.

Some would likewise seeme to prophecie that there were more of our generation yet to come to kill theirs and take their places, as some thought the purpose was by that which was already done. Those that were immediatly to come after us they imagined to be in the aire, yet invisible and without bodies, and that they by our intreatie and for the love of us, did make the people to die in that sort as they did, by shooting invisible bullets into them.

To confirme this opinion, their Phisitions (to excuse their ignorance in curing the disease) would not be ashamed to say, but earnestly make the simple people beleeve, that the strings of blood that they sucked out of the sicke bodies, were the strings wherewithall the invisible bullets were tied and cast. Some also thought that wee shot them our selves out of our pieces, from the place where wee dwelt, and killed the people in any such Towne that had offended us, as wee listed, how farre distant from us soever it were. And other some said, that it was the speciall worke of God for our sakes, as we our selves have cause in some sort to thinke no lesse, whatsoever some doe, or may imagine to the contrary, specially some Astrologers, knowing of the Eclipse of the Sunne[10] which we saw the same yeere before in our voyage thitherward, which unto them appeared very terrible. And also of a Comet which began to appeare but a fewe dayes before the beginning of the saide sicknesse. But to exclude them from being the speciall causes of so speciall an accident there are further reasons then I thinke fit at this present to be alleadged. These their opinions I have set downe the more at large, that it may appeare unto you that there is good hope they may be brought through discreete dealing and government to the imbracing of the trueth, and consequently to honour, obey, feare and love us.

And although some of our company towards the end of the yeere, shewed themselves too fierce in slaying some of the people in some Townes, upon causes that on our part might easily enough have bene borne withall: yet notwithstanding, because it was on their part justly deserved, the alteration of their opinions generally and for the most part concerning us is the lesse to be doubted. And whatsoever else they may be, by carefulnesse of our selves neede nothing at all to be feared.[11]

1588

[10]Harriot tells a story that is strikingly similar to the one told by Christopher Columbus, who, because he was able to predict a solar eclipse, convinced the native populations to submit to him.

[11]Harriot is vague about the hostilities between the English and the natives, probably because he doesn't want to worry potential investors.

Edward Maria Wingfield 1560?–1613?

The early years of the Jamestown colony, established in Virginia in 1607, were fraught with difficulty. The initial group consisted of a fractious company of 104 men and boys, among them effete gentry with few practical skills, adventurers beguiled by visions of the riches to be extracted from the New World, and artisans whose abilities were of little use in the primitive conditions at hand. On the whole, they were ill equipped for the hard labor needed to sustain the settlement.

Life at Jamestown proved calamitous from the outset. The colony was erected on swampy ground where dank air and mosquito infestation made conditions unhealthful. Attention was immediately diverted to the futile search for gold and a water route to the West. Assuming that they would be kept in supplies by the Virginia Company, the men made few attempts to raise food; a fire in the first winter destroyed most of the buildings and wiped out the few remaining food stores not contaminated by rats. The absence of wives and families as well as class tensions contributed to social instability, and much energy was dissipated in drink and idleness. Antagonistic relations with local tribes resulted in continuing strife. Weakened by the stresses of settlement, the colonists fell victim to a barrage of lethal diseases, and within months of their arrival, fewer than half of the original group were alive.

The struggle for survival was augmented by ineffectual governance. The first president of Jamestown was Edward Maria Wingfield, a former military commander and adventurer who was elected according to the provisions of the Virginia Company charter of 1606. One of the seven original members of the Royal Council appointed to administer the colony, Wingfield was a well-meaning but indecisive leader who proved unable to reconcile the divided company. Wingfield's aristocratic lineage estranged him from working-class colonists; his unwillingness to endorse favored status for "gentlemen" lost him the support of fellow councillors; and his Roman Catholic background was suspect in the primarily Protestant band.

The atmosphere of distrust among the councillors was heightened by the pressures of sickness, famine, and cold, and within months of his election, Wingfield was under fire from the Council. Charged with pillaging the company stores (a serious accusation in a time of severe deprivation), practicing atheism (it was observed that he neglected to carry a Bible on his person), and assorted other complaints, Wingfield was summarily deposed from the "Presidentship," prompting an administrative crisis that was not quelled until John Smith was elected to that office in 1608.

Following his removal, Wingfield penned *A Discourse of Virginia,* a defense of his own actions and a narrative that provides one of the few eyewitness accounts of the struggle to settle Jamestown. Paired with other early documents such as Bradford's *Of Plymouth Plantation,* Morton's *The New English Canaan,* and especially Winthrop's "Speech to the General Court" recorded in his *Journal,* Wingfield's chronicle illuminates the personal pressures facing colonial leaders and identifies a number of critical political and social issues central to the founding of democratic governments in the New World.

Liahna Babener
Montana State University

PRIMARY WORK

A Discourse of Virginia, 1608.

from A Discourse of Virginia

[Here Followeth What Happened in James Town, in Virginia, after Captain Newport's Departure for England.]

Captain Newport,[1] having always his eyes and ears open to the proceedings of the Colony, three or four days before his departure asked the President[2] how he thought himself settled in the government—whose answer was that no disturbance could endanger him or the Colony but it must be wrought either by Captain Gosnold or Mr. Archer.[3] For the one was strong with friends and followers, and could if he would; and the other was troubled with an ambitious spirit, and would if he could. The Captain gave them both knowledge of this, the President's opinion, and moved them with many entreaties to be mindful of their duties to His Majesty and the Colony.

June, 1607, the 22nd: Captain Newport returned for England, for whose good pasage and safe return we made many prayers to our Almighty God.

June the 25th, an Indian came to us from the great Powhatan[4] with the word of peace—that he desired greatly our friendship, that the werowances[5] Pasyaheigh and Tapahanah should be our friends, that we should sow and reap in peace or else he would make wars upon them with us. This message fell out true; for both those werowances have ever since remained in peace and trade with us. We rewarded the messenger with many trifles which were great wonders to him. This Powhatan dwelleth 10 miles from us, upon the River Pamunkey[6] which lies north from us. . . .

July—the 3rd of July, seven or eight Indians presented the President a deer from Pamaonke, a werowance desiring our friendship. They inquired after our shipping, which the President said was gone to Croutoon.[7] They fear much our ships; and therefore he would not have them think it far from us. Their werowance had a hatchet sent him. They were well contented with trifles. A little after this came a deer to the President from the Great Powhatan. He and his messengers were pleased with the like trifles. The President likewise bought, diverse times, deer of the Indians, beavers and other flesh, which he always caused to be equally divided among the Colony.

About this time diverse of our men fell sick. We missed above forty before September did see us, amongst whom was the worthy and religious gentleman Capt. Bartholomew Gosnold, upon whose life stood a great part of the good success and fortune of our government and Colony. In his sickness time the President did easily foretell his own deposing from his command—so much differed the President and the other councillors in managing the government of the Colony.

July—the 7th of July, Tapahanah, a werowance dweller on Salisbury side,[8] hailed us with the word of peace. The President, with a shallop well manned, went to him.

[1]Commander of the expedition's flagship and one of the original seven Councillors.
[2]Wingfield refers to himself in the third person as "the President" through most of the narrative.
[3]Both members of the original Council.
[4]Chief ruler over the Algonkians in tidewater Virginia.
[5]Local chieftains.
[6]York River.
[7]Indian town thought to be where the survivors of the ill-fated Roanoke settlement might have gone in 1587.
[8]South shore of the James River.

He found him sitting on the ground crosslegged, as is their custom, with one attending on him which did often say, "This is the werowance Tapahanah"; which he did likewise confirm with stroking his breast. He was well enough known, for the President had seen him diverse times before. His countenance was nothing cheerful, for we had not seen him since he was in the field against us; but the President would take no knowledge thereof, and used him kindly, giving him a red waistcoat which he did desire. Tapahanah did inquire after our shipping. He received answer as before. He said his old store was spent, that his new was not at full growth by a foot, [and] that as soon as any was ripe he would bring it; which promise he truly performed.

The —— of ——[9] Mr. Kendall[10] was put off from being of the Council and committed to prison, for that it did manifestly appear he did practice to sow discord between the President and Council. Sickness had not now left us six able men in our town. God's only mercy did now watch and ward for us; but the President hid this our weakness carefully from the savages, never suffering them in all this time to come into our town.

September—the 6th of September, Pasyaheigh sent us a boy that was run from us. This was the first assurance of his peace with us; besides, we found them no cannibals.[11] The boy observed the men and women to spend the most part of the night in singing or howling, and that every morning the women carried all the little children to the river side; but what they did there he did not know. The rest of the werowances do likewise send our men renegades to us home again, using them well during their being with them; so as now, they being well rewarded at home at their return, they take little joy to travel abroad without passports.

The Council demanded some larger allowance for themselves, and from some sick [persons], their favorites—which the President would not yield unto without their warrants. . . . He prayed them further to consider the long time before we expected Capt. Newport's return, the uncertainty of his return (if God did not favor his voyage), the long time before our harvest would be ripe, and the doubtful peace that we had with the Indians (which they would keep no longer than opportunity served to do us mischief).

It was then therefore ordered that every meal of fish or flesh should excuse the allowance for porridge, both against the sick and [against the] whole. The Council, therefore, sitting again upon this proposition, instructed in the former reasons and order, did not think fit to break the former order by enlarging their allowance. . . . Now was the common store of oil, vinegar, sack, and aquavita all spent, saving two gallons of each. The sack [was] reserved for the Communion Table, the rest for such extremities as might fall upon us, which the President had only made known to Capt. Gosnold of which course he liked well. The vessels were, therefore, bunged up.[12] When Mr. Gosnold was dead, the President did acquaint the rest of the Council with the said remnant; but, Lord, how they then longed to sup up that little remnant! For they had now emptied all their own bottles, and all others that they could smell out.

[9]In this and subsequent references, omitted dates are left out of the original manuscript.

[10]One of the original seven Councillors.

[11]Rumors and stories had been widely circulated that some of the indigenous tribes were cannibalistic, a belief shared by John Smith. Such fears were the product of European prejudices and anxieties about native people and had no basis in fact.

[12]Stopped up with a cork.

A little while after this the Council did again fall upon the President for some better allowance for themselves and some few [of] the sick, their privates. The President protested he would not be partial; but, if one had anything of him, every man should have his portion according to their places. Nevertheless [he said] that, upon [being shown] their warrants, he would deliver what [it] pleased them to demand. If the President had at that time enlarged the proportion according to their request, without doubt in very short time he had starved the whole company. He would not join with them, therefore, in such ignorant murder without their own warrant.

The President, well seeing to what end their impatience would grow, desired them earnestly and oftentimes to bestow the Presidentship among themselves, [and said] that he would obey, [as] a private man, as well as they could command. But they refused to discharge him of the place, saying they might not do it; for that he did His Majesty good service in it. In this meantime the Indians did daily relieve us with corn and flesh, that in three weeks the President had reared up 20 men able to work; for, as his store increased, he mended the common pot, he had laid up, besides, provision for three weeks' wheat beforehand.

By this time the Council had fully plotted to depose Wingfield, their then President, and had drawn certain articles in writing amongst themselves, and took their oaths upon the Evangelists to observe them—the effect whereof was, first: to depose the then President; to make Mr. Ratcliffe[13] the next President; not to depose the one the other; not to take the deposed President into Council again; not to take Mr. Archer into the Council, or any other, without the consent of every one of them. To these [articles] they had subscribed, as out of their own mouths at several times it was easily gathered. Thus had they forsaken His Majesty's government, [as] set us down in the instructions, and made it a triumvirate. It seemeth Mr. Archer was nothing acquainted with these articles. Though all the rest crept out of his notes and commentaries that were preferred against the President, yet it pleased God to cast him into the same disgrace and pit that he prepared for another, as will appear hereafter.

September—the 10th of September, Mr. Ratcliffe, Mr. Smith, and Mr. Martin[14] came to the President's tent, with a warrant subscribed under their hands, to depose the President, saying they thought him very unworthy to be either President or of the Council; and therefore discharged him of both. He answered them that they had eased him of a great deal of care and trouble [and] that, long since, he had diverse times proffered them the place at an easier rate. And [he said] further, that the President ought to be removed (as appeareth in His Majesty's instructions for our government) by the greater number of 13 voices, Councillors, [and] that they were but three;[15] and therefore [he] wished them to proceed advisedly. But they told him if they did him wrong they must answer [for] it. Then said the deposed President, "I am at your pleasure. Dispose of me as you will, without further garboils."[16]

I will now write what followeth in my own name, and give the new President his

[13]Another of the original seven Council members who was later elected to succeed Wingfield; he experienced similar problems of leadership and was also deposed within a year. John Smith then became President.

[14]Members of the original Council.

[15]Of the original seven Councillors, Newport had sailed for England; Gosnold had now died; Kendall had been deposed; leaving—aside from Wingfield—Ratcliff, Smith, and Martin.

[16]Confusion.

title. I shall be the briefer, being thus discharged. I was committed to a sergeant, and sent to the pinnace; but I was answered with, "If they did me wrong, they must answer [for] it."

The 11th of September, I was sent for to come before the President and Council upon their court day. They had now made Mr. Archer recorder of Virginia. The President made a speech to the Colony that he thought it fit to acquaint them why I was deposed. (I am now forced to stuff my paper with frivolous trifles, that our grave and worthy Council may the better strike those veins where the corrupt blood lieth, and that they may see in what manner of government the hope of the Colony now travaileth.) First, Master President said that I had denied him a penny-whistle, a chicken, a spoonful of beer, and served him with foul corn; and with that [he] pulled some grain out of a bag, showing it to the company. Then started up Mr. Smith and said that I had told him plainly how he lied; and that I said though we were equal here, yet, if he were in England, [I] would scorn his name. . . . Mr. Martin followed with, "He reporteth that I do slack the service in the Colony, and do nothing but tend my pot, spit, and oven; but he hath starved my son and denied him a spoonful of beer. I have friends in England shall be revenged on him, if ever he come in London."

I asked Mr. President if I should answer these complaints and whether he had aught else to charge me withal. With that he pulled out a paper book, loaded full with articles against me, and gave them [to] Mr. Archer to read. I told Mr. President and the Council that, by the instructions for our government, our proceeding ought to be verbal, and I was there ready to answer; but they said they would proceed in that order. I desired a copy of the articles and time given me to answer them likewise by writing; but that would not be granted. I bade them then please themselves. Mr. Archer then read some of the articles—when, on the sudden, Mr. President said, "Stay, stay! We know not whether he will abide our judgment, or whether he will appeal to the King." [He said] to me, "How say you: will you appeal to the King, or no?" I apprehended presently that God's mercy had opened me a way, through their ignorance, to escape their malice; for I never knew how I might demand an appeal. Besides, I had secret knowledge how they had forejudged me to pay five-fold for anything that came to my hands, whereof I could not discharge myself by writing; and that I should lie in prison until I had paid it.

The Captain Merchant had delivered me our merchandise, without any note of the particulars, under my hand; for himself had received them in gross. I likewise, as occasion moved me, spent them in trade or by gift amongst the Indians. So likewise did Capt. Newport take of them. . . . And disposed of them as was fit for him. Of these, likewise, I could make no account; only I was well assured I had never bestowed the value of three penny-whistles to my own use nor to the private use of any other; for I never carried any favorite over with me, or entertained any there. I was all [to] one and one to all. Upon these considerations I answered Mr. President and the Council that His Majesty's hands were full of mercy and that I did appeal to His Majesty's mercy. Then they committed me prisoner again to the master of the pinnace, with these words, "Look to him well; he is now the King's prisoner."

Then Mr. Archer pulled out of his bosom another paper book full of articles against me, desiring that he might read them in the name of the Colony. I said I stood there, ready to answer any man's complaint whom I had wronged; but no one man spoke one word against me. Then was he willed to read his book, whereof I complained;

but I was still answered, "If they do me wrong, they must answer [for] it." I have forgotten the most of the articles, they were so slight (yet he glorieth much in his penwork). I know well the last—and a speech that he then made savored well of a mutiny—for he desired that by no means I might lie prisoner in the town, lest both he and others of the Colony should not give such obedience to their command as they ought to do; which goodly speech of his they easily swallowed.

But it was usual and natural to this honest gentleman, Mr. Archer, to be always hatching of some mutiny in my time. He might have appeared an author of three several mutinies. And he (as Mr. Pearsy [Percy] sent me word) had bought some witnesses' hands against me to diverse articles, with Indian cakes (which was no great matter to do after my deposal, and considering their hunger), persuasions, and threats. At another time he feared not to say, openly and in the presence of one of the Council, that, if they had not deposed me when they did, he had gotten twenty others to himself which should have deposed me. But this speech of his was likewise easily digested. Mr. Crofts[17] feared not to say that, if others would join with him, he would pull me out of my seat and out of my skin too. Other would say (whose names I spare) that, unless I would amend their allowance, they would be their own carvers. For these mutinous speeches I rebuked them openly, and proceeded no further against them, considering therein of men's lives in the King's service there. One of the Council was very earnest with me to take a guard about me. I answered him I would [have] no guard but God's love and my own innocence. In all these disorders was Mr. Archer a ringleader.

When Mr. President and Mr. Archer had made an end of their articles above mentioned, I was again sent prisoner to the pinnace; and Mr. Kendall, taken from thence, had his liberty, but might not carry arms. All this while the savages brought to the town such corn and flesh as they could spare. Pasyaheigh, by Tapahanah's mediation, was taken into friendship with us. The Councillors, Mr. Smith especially, traded up and down the river with the Indians for corn; which relieved the Colony well.

As I understand by a report, I am much charged with starving the Colony. I did always give every man his allowance faithfully, both of corn, oil, aquavita, etc., as was by the Council proportioned; neither was it bettered after my time, until, towards the end of March, a biscuit was allowed to every working man for his breakfast, by means of the provision brought us by Capt. Newport, as will appear hereafter. It is further said I did much banquet and riot. I never had but one squirrel roasted, whereof I gave part to Mr. Ratcliffe, then sick—yet was that squirrel given me. I did never heat a flesh-pot but when the common pot was so used likewise. Yet how often Mr. President's and the Councillor's spits have night and day been endangered to break their backs—so laden with swans, geese, ducks, etc.! How many times their flesh-pots have swelled, many hungry eyes did behold to their great longing. And what great thieves and thieving there hath been in the common store since my time—I doubt not but it is already made known to his Majesty's Council for Virginia.

The 17th day of September I was sent for to the Court to answer a complaint exhibited against me by Jehu Robinson; for [he charged] when I was President I did say [that] he with others had consented to run away with the shallop to Newfoundland. At

[17]One of the original settlers, classified officially as a "gentleman."

another time I must answer Mr. Smith for [the charge] that I had said he did conceal an intended mutiny. I told Mr. Recorder those words would bear no actions—that one of the causes was done without the limits mentioned in the patent granted to us. And therefore [I] prayed Mr. President that I might not be thus lugged with these disgraces and troubles; but he did wear no other eyes or ears than grew on Mr. Archer's head. The jury gave the one of them 100 pounds and the other 200 pounds damages for slander. Then Mr. Recorder did very learnedly comfort me, [saying] that if I had wrong I might bring my writ of error in London; whereat I smiled.

I, seeing their law so speedy and cheap, desired justice for a copper kettle which Mr. Croft did detain from me. He said I had given it him. I did bid him bring his proof for that. He confessed he had no proof. Then Mr. President did ask me if I would be sworn I did not give it him. I said I knew no cause why to swear for mine own [property]. He asked Mr. Croft if he would make oath I did give it him; which oath he took, and won my kettle from me, that was in that place and time worth half his weight in gold. Yet I did understand afterwards that he would have given John Capper the one half of the kettle to have taken the oath for him; but he would [have] no copper on that price. I told Mr. President I had not known the like law, and prayed they would be more sparing of law until we had more wit or wealth. [I said] that laws were good spies in a populous, peaceable, and plentiful country, where they did make the good men better and stayed the bad from being worse; yet we were so poor as they did but rob us of time that might be better employed in service in the Colony.

The —— day of —— the President did beat James Read, the smith. The smith struck him [back] again. For this he was condemned to be hanged; but before he was turned off the ladder he desired to speak with the President in private—to whom he accussed Mr. Kendall of a mutiny, and so escaped himself. What indictment Mr. Recorder framed against the smith I know not; but I know it is familiar for the President, Councillors, and other officers, to beat men at their pleasure. One lieth sick till death, another walketh lame, the third crieth out of all his bones; which miseries they do take upon their consciences to come to them by this their alms of beating. Were this whipping, lawing, beating, and hanging in Virginia known in England, I fear it would drive many well-affected minds from this honorable action of Virginia.

This smith, coming aboard the pinnace . . . two or three days before his arraignment, brought me commendations from Mr. Pearsy [Percy], Mr. Waller, Mr. Kendall, and some others, saying they would be glad to see me on shore. I answered him they were honest gentlemen and had carried themselves very obediently to their governors. I added further that upon Sunday if the weather were fair I would be at the sermon. Lastly, I said that I was so sickly, starved, [and] lame, and did lie so cold and wet in the pinnace, as I would be dragged thither before I would go thither any more. Sunday proved not fair; I went not to the sermon.

The —— day of —— Mr. Kendall was executed, being shot to death for a mutiny. In the arrest of his judgement he alleged to Mr. President that his name was Sicklemore, not Ratcliffe,[18] and so [he] had no authority to pronounce judgement. Then Mr. Martin pronounced judgment.

[18]There was apparently some confusion over Ratcliffe's correct name. His name appeared in the Virginia Charter as "Captain John Sicklemore, alias Ratcliffe."

Somewhat before this time the President and Council had sent for the keys of my coffers, supposing that I had some writings concerning the Colony. I requested that the Clerk of the Council might see what they took out of my coffers; but they would not suffer him or any other. Under color hereof they took my books of accounts and all my notes that concerned the expenses of the Colony, and instructions under the Captain Merchant's hand of the store of provisions, diverse other books, and trifles of my own proper goods, which I could never recover. Thus was I made good prize on all sides.

The—— day of—— the President commanded me to come on shore, which I refused, as not rightfully deposed. And [I] desired that I might speak to him and the Council in the presence of ten of the best sort of the gentlemen. With much entreaty some of them were sent for. Then I told them I was determined to go into England to acquaint our Council there with our weakness. I said further [that] their laws and government were such as I had no joy to live under them any longer, that I did much mislike their triumvirate, having forsaken His Majesty's instructions for our government; and therefore prayed there might be more made of the Council. I said further I desired not to go into England, if either Mr. President or Mr. Archer would go, but was willing to take my fortune with the Colony; and [I] did also proffer to furnish them with £100 towards the fetching home [of] the Colony, if the action was given over. They did like of none of my proffers, but made diverse shot at me in the pinnace. I, seeing their resolutions, went ashore to them—where, after I had stayed a while in conference, they sent me to the pinnace again.

December—the 10th of December Mr. Smith went up the river of the Chickahominy to trade for corn. He was desirous to see the head of that river; and, when it was not possible with the shallop, he hired a canoe and an Indian to carry him up further. The river . . . grew worse and worse. Then he went on shore with his guide and left Robinson and Emmery, two of our men in the canoe—which were presently slain by the Indians, Pamunkey's [Pamaonke's] men. And he himself [was] taken prisoner, and by the means of his guide his life was saved. And Pamunkey [Pamaonke], having him prisoner, carried him to his neighbors' werowances to see if any of them knew him for one of those which had been, some two or three years before us, in a river amongst them northward and [had] taken away some Indians from them by force. At last he brought him to the great Powhatan (of whom before we had no knowledge), who sent him home[19] to our town the 8th of January.

During Mr. Smith's absence the President did swear Mr. Archer one of the Council, contrary to his oath taken in the articles agreed upon between themselves (before spoken of), and contrary to the King's instructions, and without Mr. Martin's consent; whereas there were no more but the President and Mr. Martin then of the Council.

Mr. Archer, being settled in his authority, sought how to call Mr. Smith's life in question, and had indicted him upon a chapter in Leviticus[20] for the death of his two men. He had had his trial the same day of his return and, I believe, his hanging the same or the next day—so speedy is our law there. But it pleased God to send Captain

[19]Powhatan . . . sent him home: An allusion to the famous episode in which Smith was taken captive by the chief and later released.

[20]Leviticus 24:19–21.

Newport unto us the same evening, to our unspeakable comfort; whose arrival saved Mr. Smith's life and mine, because he took me out of the pinnace and gave me leave to lie in the town. Also by his coming was prevented a parliament, which the new Councillor, Mr. Recorder, intended there to summon. Thus error begot error.

Captain Newport, having landed, lodged, and refreshed his men, employed some of them about a fair storehouse, others about a stove, and his mariners about a church—all which works they finished cheerfully and in short time.

January—the 7th of January our town was almost quite burnt[21] with all our apparel and provision; but Captain Newport healed our wants, to our great comforts, out of the great plenty sent us by the provident and loving care of our worthy and most worthy Council.

This vigilant Captain, slacking no opportunity that might advance the prosperity of the Colony, having settled the company upon the former works, took Mr. Smith and Mr. Scrivener (another Councillor of Virginia, upon whose discretion liveth a great hope of the action) [and] went to discover the River Pamunkey on the further side whereof dwelleth the Great Powhatan, and to trade with him for corn. This river lieth north from us, and runneth east and west. I have nothing but by relation of that matter, and therefore dare not make any discourse thereof, lest I might wrong the great desert which Captain Newport's love to the action hath deserved—especially himself being present, and best able to give satisfaction thereof. I will hasten, therefore, to his return.

March—the 9th of March he returned to Jamestown with his pinnace well laden with corn, wheat, beans, and peas to our great comfort and his worthy commendations.

By this time the Council and Captain, having attentively looked into the carriage both of the Councillors and other officers, removed some officers out of the store, and Captain Archer, a Councillor whose insolency did look upon that little himself with great-sighted spectacles, derogating from others' merits by spewing out his venomous libels and infamous chronicles upon them, as doth appear in his own handwriting; for which, and other worse tricks, he had not escaped the halter, but that Captain Newport interposed his advice to the contrary.

Captain Newport, having new dispatched all his business and set the clock in a true course (if so the Council will keep it), prepared himself for England upon the 10th of April, and arrived at Blackwall on Sunday, the 21st of May, 1608.

1608

John Smith 1580–1631

John Smith has often been described by scholars as a swashbuckling colonial statesman, a self-made man who in his writing proffered the hope that through hard work and enterprise his readers too could realize the American dream. Born in

[21] A reference to the fire that had destroyed most of the colony's provisions and buildings in the early winter of 1607–1608.

Lincolnshire, England, to a yeoman farmer and his wife, Smith completed a grammar school education and was subsequently apprenticed to a merchant in nearby King's Lynn. Soon after his father's death, however, he left his apprenticeship to begin his career as a soldier and joined the British volunteers fighting in the Dutch war of independence from Spain. He later joined the Austrian forces fighting against the Turks and was soon promoted to captain for his work in Hungary. While battling the Turks, he was captured and sold into slavery. In one of his last works, *The True Travels, Adventures, and Observations of Captaine John Smith, in Europe, Asia, Affrica, and America* (1630), Smith would vividly dramatize his daring escape and travels through Russia, Poland, and Transylvania. Upon his return to England in 1605, Smith grew interested in plans to colonize Virginia. When the Virginia Company's first colonists sailed the following year, Smith sailed with them as one of the seven councillors.

Unlike the Puritan settlements that were later established in Massachusetts, the goals of the Jamestown colony were primarily commercial rather than religious from the outset. The organizers of the Virginia Company and many of the first settlers were inspired by Spain's model of colonization; profit for the company's stockholders was to be accumulated through conquest and the discovery of gold, not agriculture. The Jamestown population, particularly during the colony's early years, was almost entirely composed of men, many of whom were of the elite classes and did not expect to have to grow the food the settlement needed for its survival. Unlike the Puritan settlements which would rely upon strong, hierarchical religious and familial structures and on common goals to unite their members, the Jamestown settlement, troubled by quarreling colonists with competing interests, was in a precarious position from its inception.

Even before becoming president in 1608, Smith worked to make survival, not gold, the settlement's priority. He spent much of his time exploring the region and negotiating with Native Americans for food. As president, Smith organized the building of houses, fortifications, and a church, and he instituted a policy of military discipline. His policy that "he who does not work shall not eat" was extremely unpopular, particularly among members of the elite classes. But, as Smith clearly surmised, this was the policy that kept the colonists alive: during Smith's administration the survival rate among colonists rose dramatically to more than ninety percent.

Recognizing that the colony's relations with the surrounding Native American populations were crucial to its survival, Smith sent young men to live among the Native Americans to learn their language, customs, and methods of agriculture. Smith realized that knowledge of the surrounding populations was a prerequisite to establishing strong and vital trade relations. Although Smith's policies helped the colony survive, it remained unable to produce a profit for its investors. In 1609 the Virginia Company decided to reorganize the colony by sending five hundred new settlers and replacing Smith and his government. Before the new president could arrive, however, a serious wound from a gunpowder explosion forced Smith to return to England.

Despite repeated offers of his services to the colony, Smith was never to return to Virginia. He soon shifted his attention to promoting colonization in the region he would name "New England," obtaining valuable information about the region's natural history and geography during his voyage there in 1614. When his further attempts at colonization of "New England" were blocked by weather, pirates, and lack of funding, he turned his efforts to writing about colonization.

Much of Smith's writing, beginning with his first work, *A True Relation . . . of*

Virginia (1608) served the dual purpose of promoting colonization and establishing Smith's own reputation as exemplary colonizer. To this end in his best-known work, *The Generall Historie of Virginia, New-England, and the Summer Isles* (1624), Smith drew on his own earlier writings on Virginia and New England and the writing of others. Although this and other works fall into the genre of travel writing, popularized by Richard Hakluyt's *The Principall Navigations, Voiages and Discoveries of the English Nation* (1589), they differ in that—as Smith was always quick to remind his readers—their writer had firsthand experience with the colonial enterprise. As Smith asserted at the opening of *The Generall Historie,* "I am no Compiler by hearsay, but have beene a real Actor." Indeed, whether he is contending with other writers, the gold-digging settlers, the Virginia Company, or Powhatan, it is the voice of this actor that we hear most consistently throughout his work.

Of the numerous adventures Smith recounts in *The Generall Historie* none is better known than the account of his captivity in the court of Powhatan and Pocahontas's "saving" his life. Because Pocahontas made no appearance in Smith's first account of the story in *A True Relation,* some have doubted its veracity and challenged Smith's reliability as historian. More significant than the issue of the accuracy of this story, however, is the relative positioning of the two cultures within the story itself. Pocahontas's apparent willingness to offer her own life in place of Smith's is a romanticized depiction of a Native American's willingness to yield to the interests of the "superior" civilization. The scene depicts the paradigm that appears throughout many later colonialist writings, in which Native Americans readily submit to the advance of a European civilization they accept as superior to their own.

Smith devoted much of the third book of *The General Historie* to a description of the interaction between the two very different civilizations. Less concerned with the ethics of colonization than the sheer survival of the colony, Smith formulated a controversial policy toward the Native Americans. From their arrival at Jamestown, the colonists had found themselves in a rather embarassing position: not only were they unable to feed themselves, but they were dependent upon "inferior" people for food. Despite the Virginia Company's continual requests for a gentler policy toward the Native Americans, Smith sought to intimidate and control the Powhatans through shows of force. Even as he negotiated with Powhatan for the food upon which the colony depended for its very survival, Smith continued his ongoing argument with Powhatan regarding the necessity of the English wearing their arms while in his presence.

Smith's final work, *Advertisements for the Unexperienced Planters of New England* (1631), is a summation of Smith's ideas about colonization based upon his experiences in Virginia and his knowledge of New England. The Massachusetts Bay Colony came much closer than the Virginia settlement to epitomizing Smith's ideal; with its emphasis on private property, it drew settlers from the "middling group" of English society who were willing to work hard. Reflecting back, once again, on his Virginia experience, Smith described his accomplishments in the face of the many obstacles he had confronted. To the end Smith lamented the fact that despite his lifelong devotion to the cause of colonization, his expertise and accomplishments had never been sufficiently appreciated.

Amy E. Winans
Susquehanna University

PRIMARY WORKS

A True Relation of . . . Virginia, 1608; *A Description of New England,* 1616; *The Generall Historie of Virginia, New-England, and the Summer Isles,* 1624; *The True Travels, Adventures, and Observations of Captaine John Smith,* 1630; *Advertisements for the Unexperienced Planters of New England, or Anywhere,* 1631; *The Complete Works of Captain John Smith (1580–1631),* 3 vols., ed. P. L. Barbour, 1986; Karen Ordahl Kupperman, ed., *Captain John Smith,* 1988.

from The Generall Historie of Virginia, New-England, and the Summer Isles[1]

from Book III, Chapter 2 [Smith as captive at the court of Powhatan in 1608]

At last they brought him[2] to *Meronocomoco* [*5 Jan. 1608*], where was *Powhatan* their Emperor. Here more than two hundred of those grim Courtiers stood wondering at him, as he had beene a monster; till *Powhatan* and his trayne had put themselves in their greatest braveries. Before a fire upon a seat like a bedsted, he sat covered with a great robe, made of *Rarowcun*[3] skinnes, and all the tayles hanging by. On either hand did sit a young wench of 16 or 18 yeares, and along on each side the house, two rowes of men, and behind them as many women, with all their heads and shoulders painted red: many of their heads bedecked with the white downe of Birds; but every one with something: and a great chayne of white beads about their necks. At his entrance before the King, all the people gave a great shout. The Queene of *Appamatuck* was appointed to bring him water to wash his hands, and another brought him a bunch of feathers, in stead of a Towell to dry them: having feasted him after their best barbarous manner they could, a long consultation was held, but the conclusion was, two great stones were brought before *Powhatan:* then as many as could layd hands on him, dragged him to them, and thereon laid his head, and being ready with their clubs, to beate out his braines, *Pocahontas* the Kings dearest daughter, when no intreaty could prevaile, got his head in her armes, and laid her owne upon his to save him from death: whereat the Emperour was contented he should live to make him hatchets, and her bells, beads, and copper; for they thought him aswell of all occupations as themselves. For the King himselfe will make his owne robes, shooes, bowes, arrowes, pots; plant, hunt, or doe any thing so well as the rest.

They say he bore a pleasant shew,
But sure his heart was sad.
For who can pleasant be, and rest,

[1]*The Generall Historie* was first published in London in 1624. This text, slightly modified, is taken from *The Complete Works of Captain John Smith,* 3 vols., 1986.

[2]Smith. Smith wrote this version of his captivity entirely in the third person.

[3]Raccoon.

That lives in feare and dread:
And having life suspected, doth
It still suspected lead.[4]

Two dayes after [*7 Jan. 1608*], *Powhatan* having disguised himselfe in the most fearefullest manner he could, caused Captain *Smith* to be brought forth to a great house in the woods, and there upon a mat by the fire to be left alone. Not long after from behinde a mat that divided the house, was made the most dolefullest noyse he ever heard; then *Powhatan* more like a devill then a man, with some two hundred more as blacke as himselfe, came unto him and told him now they were friends, and presently he should goe to *James* towne, to send him two great gunnes, and a gryndstone, for which he would give him the Country of *Capahowosick,* and for ever esteeme him as his sonne *Nantaquoud.* So to *James* towne with 12 guides *Powhatan* sent him. That night [*7 Jan. 1608*] they quarterd in the woods, he still expecting (as he had done all this long time of his imprisonment) every houre to be put to one death or other: for all their feasting. But almightie God (by his divine providence) had mollified the hearts of those sterne *Barbarians* with compassion. The next morning [*8 Jan.*] betimes they came to the Fort, where *Smith* having used the Salvages with what kindnesse he could, he shewed *Rawhunt, Powhatans* trusty servant, two demi-Culverings[5] and a millstone to carry *Powhatan:* they found them somewhat too heavie; but when they did see him discharge them, being loaded with stones, among the boughs of a great tree loaded with Isickles, the yce and branches came so tumbling downe, that the poore Salvages ran away halfe dead with feare. But at last we regained some conference with them, and gave them such toyes; and sent to *Powhatan,* his women, and children such presents, as gave them in generall full content. . . . Now ever once in foure or five dayes, *Pocahontas* with her attendants, brought him so much provision, that saved many of their lives, that els for all this had starved with hunger.

Thus from numbe death our good God sent reliefe,
The sweete asswager of all other griefe.

His relation of the plenty he had seene, especially at *Werawocomoco,* and of the state and bountie of *Powhatan,* (which till that time was unknowne) so revived their dead spirits (especially the love of *Pocahontas*[6]) as all mens feare was abandoned.

from Book III, Chapter 8 [Smith's journey to Pamaunkee]

The 12 of January we arrived at Werowocomoco, where the river was frozen neare halfe a myle from the shore; but to neglect no time, the President with his Barge so far had approached by breaking the ice, as the ebbe left him amongst those oasie shoules, yet rather then to lye there frozen to death, by his owne example he taught

[4]Taken from Fotherby's translation of Euripides.

[5]Demi-culverins: small cannons.

[6]Pocahontas married John Rolfe, a tobacco planter, in 1613. Smith maintained that the marriage resulted in "friendly trade and commerce" with the Powhatans. In 1616 Pocahontas traveled to England (with her husband and infant son), where she died the following year.

them to march neere middle deepe, a flight shot through this muddy frozen oase. When the Barge floated, he appoynted two or three to returne her aboord the Pinnace. Where for want of water in melting the ice, they made fresh water, for the river there was salt. But in this march Master Russell, (whom none could perswade to stay behinde) being somewhat ill, and exceeding heavie, so overtoyled himselfe as the rest had much adoe (ere he got ashore) to regaine life into his dead benummed spirits. Quartering in the next houses we found, we sent to Powhatan for provision, who sent us plentie of bread, Turkies, and Venison; the next day having feasted us after his ordinary manner, he began to aske us when we would be gone: fayning he sent not for us, neither had he any corne; and his people much lesse: yet for fortie swords he would procure us fortie Baskets. The President shewing him the men there present that brought him the message and conditions, asked Powhatan how it chanced he became so forgetfull; thereat the King concluded the matter with a merry laughter, asking for our Commodities, but none he liked without gunnes and swords, valuing a Basket of Corne more precious then a Basket of Copper; saying he could eate his Corne, but not the Copper.

Captaine Smith seeing the intent of this subtill Salvage began to deale with him after this manner.

> *Powhatan, though I had many courses to have made my provision, yet beleeving your promises to supply my wants, I neglected all to satisfie your desire: and to testifie my love, I send you my men for your building, neglecting mine owne. What your people had you have engrossed, forbidding them our trade: and now you thinke by consuming the time, we shall consume for want, not having to fulfill your strange demands. As for swords and gunnes, I told you long agoe I had none to spare; and you must know those I have can keepe me from want: yet steale or wrong you I will not, nor dissolve that friendship we have mutually promised, except you constraine me by our bad usage.*

The King having attentively listned to this Discourse, promised that both he and his Country would spare him what he could, the which within two dayes they should receive. Yet Captaine Smith, sayth the King,

> *some doubt I have of your comming hither, that makes me not so kindly seeke to relieve you as I would: for many doe informe me, your comming hither is not for trade, but to invade my people, and possesse my Country, who dare not come to bring you corne, seeing you thus armed with your men. To free us of this feare, leave aboord your weapons, for here they are needlesse, we being all friends, and for ever Powhatans.*

With many such discourses they spent the day, quartering that night in the Kings houses. The next day he renewed his building, which hee little intended should proceede. For the Dutch-men finding his plentie, and knowing our want, and perceiving his preparations to surprise us, little thinking we could escape both him and famine; (to obtaine his favour) revealed to him so much as they knew of our estates and projects, and how to prevent them. One of them being of so great a spirit, judgement, and resolution, and a hireling that was certaine of his wages for his labour, and ever well used both he and his Countrymen; that the President knew not whom better to trust; and not knowing any fitter for that imployment, had sent him as a spy to discover Powhatans intent, then little doubting his honestie, nor could ever be certaine of his villany till neare halfe a yeare after.

Whilst we expected the comming in of the Country, we wrangled out of the King ten quarters of Corne for a copper Kettell, the which the President perceiving him much to affect, valued it at a much greater rate; but in regard of his scarcity he would accept it, provided we should have as much more the next yeare, or els the Country of Monacan. Wherewith each seemed well contented, and Powhatan began to expostulate the difference of Peace and Warre after this manner.

> *Captaine Smith, you may understand that I having seene the death of all my people thrice, and not any one living of those three generations but my selfe; I know the difference of Peace and Warre better then any in my Country. But now I am old and ere long must die, my brethren, namely Opitchapam, Opechancanough, and Kekataugh, my two sisters, and their two daughters, are distinctly each others successors. I wish their experience no lesse then mine, and your love to them no lesse then mine to you. But this bruit from Nandsamund, that you are come to destroy my Country, so much affrighteth all my people as they dare not visit you. What will it availe you to take that by force you may quickly have by love, or to destroy them that provide you food. What can you get by warre; when we can hide our provisions and fly to the woods? whereby you must famish by wronging us your friends. And why are you thus jealous of our loves seeing us unarmed, and both doe, and are willing still to feede you, with that you cannot get but by our labours? Thinke you I am so simple, not to know it is better to eate good meate, lye well, and sleepe quietly with my women and children, laugh and be merry with you, have copper, hatchets, or what I want being your friend: then be forced to flie from all, to lie cold in the woods, feede upon Acornes, rootes, and such trash, and be so hunted by you, that I can neither rest, eate, nor sleepe; but my tyred men must watch, and if a twig but breake, every one cryeth there commeth Captaine Smith: then must I fly I know not whether: and thus with miserable feare, end my miserable life, leaving my pleasures to such youths as you, which through your rash unadvisednesse may quickly as miserably end, for want of that, you never know where to finde. Let this therefore assure you of our loves, and every yeare our friendly trade shall furnish you with Corne; and now also, if you would come in friendly manner to see us, and not thus with your guns and swords as to invade your foes.*

To this subtill discourse, the President thus replyed.

> *Seeing you will not rightly conceive of our words, we strive to make you know our thoughts by our deeds; the vow I made you of my love, both my selfe and my men have kept. As for your promise I find it every day violated by some of your subjects: yet we finding your love and kindnesse, our custome is so far from being ungratefull, that for your sake onely, we have curbed our thirsting desire of revenge; els had they knowne as well the crueltie we use to our enemies, as our true love and courtesie to our friends. And I thinke your judgement sufficient to conceive, as well by the adventures we have undertaken, as by the advantage we have (by our Armes) of yours: that had we intended you any hurt, long ere this we could have effected it. Your people comming to James Towne are entertained with their Bowes and Arrowes without any exceptions; we esteeming it with you as it is with us, to weare our armes as our apparell. As for the danger of our enemies, in such warres consist our chiefest pleasure: for your riches we have no use: as for the hiding your provision, or by your flying*

to the woods, we shall not so unadvisedly starve as you conclude, your friendly care in that behalfe is needlesse, for we have a rule to finde beyond your knowledge.

Many other discourses they had, till at last they began to trade. But the King seeing his will would not be admitted as a law, our guard dispersed, nor our men disarmed, he (sighing) breathed his minde once more in this manner.

Captaine Smith, I never use any Werowance so kindely as your selfe, yet from you I receive the least kindnesse of any. Captaine Newport gave me swords, copper, cloathes, a bed, tooles, or what I desired; ever taking what I offered him, and would send away his gunnes when I intreated him: none doth deny to lye at my feet, or refuse to doe what I desire, but onely you; of whom I can have nothing but what you regard not, and yet you will have whatsoever you demand. Captaine Newport you call father, and so you call me; but I see for all us both you will doe what you list, and we must both seeke to content you. But if you intend so friendly as you say, send hence your armes, that I may beleeve you; for you see the love I beare you, doth cause me thus nakedly to forget my selfe.

Smith seeing this Salvage but trifle the time to cut his throat, procured the Salvages to breake the ice, that his Boate might come to fetch his corne and him: and gave order for more men to come on shore, to surprise the King, with whom also he but trifled the time till his men were landed: and to keepe him from suspicion, entertained the time with this reply.

Powhatan you must know, as I have but one God, I honour but one King; and I live not here as your subject, but as your friend to pleasure you with what I can. By the gifts you bestow on me, you gaine more then by trade: yet would you visit mee as I doe you, you should know it is not our custome, to sell our curtesies as a vendible commodity. Bring all your countrey with you for your guard, I will not dislike it as being over jealous. But to content you, tomorrow I will leave my Armes, and trust to your promise. I call you father indeed, and as a father you shall see I will love you: but the small care you have of such a childe caused my men perswade me to looke to my selfe.

By this time Powhatan having knowledge his men were ready whilest the ice was a breaking, with his luggage women and children, fled. Yet to avoyd suspicion, left two or three of the women talking with the Captaine, whilest hee secretly ran away, and his men that secretly beset the house. Which being presently discovered to Captaine Smith, with his pistoll, sword, and target hee made such a passage among these naked Divels; that at his first shoot, they next him tumbled one over another, and the rest quickly fled some one way some another: so that without any hurt, onely accompanied with John Russell, hee obtained the *corps du guard.* When they perceived him so well escaped, and with his eighteene men (for he had no more with him a shore) to the uttermost of their skill they sought excuses to dissemble the matter: and Powhatan to excuse his flight and the sudden comming of this multitude, sent our Captaine a great bracelet and a chaine of pearle, by an ancient Oratour that bespoke us to this purpose, perceiving even then from our Pinnace, a Barge and men departing and comming unto us.

Captaine Smith, our Werowance is fled, fearing your gunnes, and knowing when the ice was broken there would come more men, sent these numbers but to guard his corne from stealing, that might happen without your knowledge: now though some bee hurt by your misprision, yet Powhatan is your friend and so will for ever continue. Now since the ice is open, he would have you send away your corne, and if you would have his company, send away also your gunnes, which so affright his people, that they dare not come to you as hee promised they should.

Then having provided baskets for our men to carry our corne to the boats, they kindly offered their service to guard our Armes, that none should steale them. A great many they were of goodly well proportioned fellowes, as grim as Divels; yet the very sight of cocking our matches, and being to let fly, a few wordes caused them to leave their bowes and arrowes to our guard, and beare downe our corne on their backes; wee needed not importune them to make dispatch. But our Barges being left on the oase by the ebbe, caused us stay till the next high-water, so that wee returned againe to our old quarter. Powhatan and his Dutch-men brusting[7] with desire to have the head of Captaine Smith, for if they could but kill him, they thought all was theirs, neglected not any oportunity to effect his purpose. The Indians with all the merry sports they could devise, spent the time till night: then they all returned to Powhatan, who all this time was making ready his forces to surprise the house and him at supper. Notwithstanding the eternall all-seeing God did prevent him, and by a strange meanes. For Pocahontas his dearest jewell and daughter, in that darke night came through the irksome woods, and told our Captaine great cheare should be sent us by and by: but Powhatan and all the power he could make, would after come kill us all, if they that brought it could not kill us with our owne weapons when we were at supper. Therefore if we would live shee wished us presently to bee gone. Such things as shee delighted in, he would have given her: but with the teares running downe her cheekes, shee said shee durst not be seene to have any: for if Powhatan should know it, she were but dead, and so shee ranne away by her selfe as she came. . . .

1624

from A Description of New England[1]

[Appeal for settlers to plant a colony in New England]

Who can desire more content, that hath small meanes; or but only his merit to advance his fortune, then to tread, and plant that ground hee hath purchased by the hazard of his life? If he have but the taste of virtue and magnanimitie, what to such a minde can bee more pleasant, then planting and building a foundation for his Posteritie, gotte from the rude earth, by Gods blessing and his owne industrie, without prejudice to any? If hee have any graine of faith or zeale in Religion, what can hee

[7]Bursting.

[1]*A Description of New England* was first published in London in 1616. This text, slightly modified, is taken from *The Complete Works of Captain John Smith,* 3 vols., 1986.

doe lesse hurtfull to any: or more agreeable to God, then to seeke to convert those poore Salvages to know Christ, and humanitie, whose labors with discretion will triple requite thy charge and paines? What so truely su[i]tes with honour and honestie, as the discovering things unknowne? erecting Townes, peopling Countries, informing the ignorant, reforming things unjust, teaching virtue; and gaine to our Native mother-countrie a kingdom to attend her: finde imployment for those that are idle, because they know not what to doe: so farre from wronging any, as to cause Posteritie to remember thee; and remembring thee, ever honour that remembrance with praise? . . .

I have not beene so ill bred, but I have tasted of *Plenty* and *Pleasure,* as well as *Want* and *Miserie:* nor doth necessitie yet, or occasion of discontent, force me to these endeavors: nor am I ignorant what small thanke I shall have for my paines; or that many would have the Worlde imagine them to be of great judgement, that can but blemish these my designes, by their witty objections and detractions: yet (I hope) my reasons with my deeds, will so prevaile with some, that I shall not want imployment in these affaires, to make the most blinde see his owne senselessnesse, and incredulity; Hoping that gaine will make them affect that, which Religion, Charity, and the Common good cannot. It were but a poore device in me, To deceive my selfe; much more the King, State, my Friends and Countrey, with these inducements: which, seeing his Majestie hath given permission, I wish all sorts of worthie, honest, industrious spirits, would understand: and if they desire any further satisfaction, I will doe my best to give it: Not to perswade them to goe onley; but goe with them: Not leave them there; but live with them there. I will not say, but by ill providing and undue managing, such courses may be taken, [that] may make us miserable enough: But if I may have the execution of what I have projected; if they want to eate, let them eate or never digest Me. If I performe what I say, I desire but that reward out of the gaines [which] may su[i]te my paines, quality, and condition. And if I abuse you with my tongue, take my head for satisfaction. If any dislike at the yeares end, defraying their charge, by my consent they should freely returne. I feare not want of companie sufficient, were it but knowne what I know of those Countries; and by the proofe of that wealth I hope yearely to returne, if God please to blesse me from such accidents, as are beyond my power in reason to prevent: For, I am not so simple to thinke, that ever any other motive then wealth, will ever erect there a Commonweale; or draw companie from their ease and humours at home, to stay in *New England* to effect my purposes. And lest any should thinke the toile might be insupportable, though these things may be had by labour, and diligence: I assure my selfe there are who delight extreamly in vaine pleasure, that take much more paines in *England,* to enjoy it, then I should doe heere [*New England*] to gaine wealth sufficient: and yet I thinke they should not have halfe such sweet content: for, our pleasure here is still gaines; in *England* charges and losse. Heer nature and liberty affords us that freely, which in *England* we want, or it costeth us dearely. What pleasure can be more, then (being tired with any occasion a-shore, in planting Vines, Fruits, or Hearbs, in contriving their owne Grounds, to the pleasure of their owne mindes, their Fields, Gardens, Orchards, Buildings, Ships, and other works, &c.) to recreate themselves before their owne doores, in their owne boates upon the Sea; where man, woman and childe, with a small hooke and line, by angling, may take diverse sorts of excellent fish, at their pleasures? And is it not pretty sport, to pull up two pence, six pence, and twelve pence, as fast as you can ha[u]le and veare a line? He is a very bad fisher [that] cannot kill in one day with his hooke and line, one, two, or three hundred Cods: which dressed and dried, if they be sould there for ten shillings the hundred, though in England they will give more than twentie, may not both the servant, the master, and marchant, be well content with this gaine? If a man worke but three dayes in seaven, he may get more then hee can spend, unlesse he will be excessive. Now that Carpenter, Mason, Gardiner, Taylor, Smith, Sailer, Forgers, or what other, may they not make this a pretty recreation though they fish but an houre in a day, to take more then they eate in a weeke? or if they will not eate it, because there is so much better choice; yet sell it, or change it, with the fisher men, or marchants, for any thing they want. And what sport doth yeeld a more pleasing content, and lesse hurt or charge then angling with a hooke; and crossing the sweete ayre from Ile to Ile, over the silent streames of a calme Sea? Wherein the most curious may finde pleasure, profit, and content. Thus, though all men be not fishers: yet all men, whatsoever, may in other matters doe as well. For necessity doth in these cases so rule a Commonwealth, and each in their severall functions, as their labours in their qualities may be as profitable, because there is a necessary mutuall use of all.

For Gentlemen, what exercise should more delight them, then ranging dayly those unknowne parts, using fowling and fishing, for hunting and hawking? and yet you shall see the wilde-haukes give you some pleasure, in seeing them stoope (six or seaven after one another) an houre or two together, at the skuls of fish in the faire harbours, as those a-shore at a foule; and never trouble nor torment yourselves, with watching, mewing, feeding, and attending them: nor kill horse and man with running and crying, *See you not a hawk?* For hunting also: the woods, lakes, and rivers affoord not onely chase sufficient, for any that delights in that kinde of toyle, or pleasure; but such beasts to hunt, that besides the delicacy of their bodies for food, their skins are so rich, as may well recompence thy dayly labour, with a Captains pay.

For labourers, if those that sowe hemp, rape, turnups, parsnips, carrats, cabidge, and such like; give 20, 30, 40, 50 shillings yearely for an acre of ground, and meat drinke and wages to use it, and yet grow rich; when better, or at least as good ground, may be had, and cost nothing but labour; it seems strange to me, any such should there grow poore.

My purpose is not to perswade children from their parents; men from their wives; nor servants from their masters: onely, such as with free consent may be spared: But that each parish, or village, in Citie or Countrey, that will but apparell their fatherlesse children, of thirteene or fourteen years of age, or young mar[r]ied people, that have small wealth to live on; heere by their labour may live exceeding well: provided alwaies that first there bee a sufficient power to command them, houses to receive them, meanes to defend them, and meet provisions for them; for, any place may bee overlain: and it is most necessarie to have a fortresse (ere this grow to practice) and sufficient masters (as, Carpenters, Masons, Fishers, Fowlers, Gardiners, Husbandmen, Sawyers, Smiths, Spinsters,[2] Taylors, Weavers, and such like) to take ten, twelve, or twentie, or as ther is occasion, for Apprentises. The Masters by this may

[2]Spinners.

quicklie growe rich; these may learne their trades themselves, to doe the like; to a generall and an incredible benefit, for King, and Countrey, Master, and Servant. . . .

Religion, above all things, should move us (especially the Clergie) if wee were religious, to shewe our faith by our workes; in converting those poore salvages, to the knowledge of God, seeing what paines the *Spanyards* take to bring them to their adulterated faith. Honor might move the Gentrie, the valiant, and industrious; and the hope and assurance of wealth, all; if wee were that we would seeme, and be accounted. Or be we so far inferior to other nations, or our spirits so far dejected, from our auncient predecessors, or our mindes so [set] upon spoile, piracie, and such villany, as to serve the *Portugall, Spanyard, Dutch, French,* or *Turke,* (as to the cost of *Europe,* too many dooe) rather then our God, our King, our Country, and our selves? excusing our idlenesse, and our base complaints, by want of imploiement; when heere is such choise of all sorts, and for all degrees, in the planting and discovering these North parts of *America*. . . .

But, to conclude, *Adam* and *Eve* did first beginne this innocent worke, To plant the earth to remaine to posteritie, but not without labour, trouble, and industrie. *Noe,* and his family, beganne againe the second plantation; and their seede as it still increased, hath still planted new Countries, and one countrie another: and so the world to that estate it is. But not without much hazard, travell,[3] discontents, and many disasters. Had those worthie Fathers, and their memorable off-spring not beene more diligent for us now in these Ages, then wee are to plant that yet unplanted, for the after livers: Had the seede of *Abraham,* our Saviour Christ, and his Apostles, exposed themselves to no more daungers to teach the Gospell, and the will of God then wee; Even wee our selves, had at this present beene as Salvage, and as miserable as the most barbarous Salvage yet uncivilized. . . . Then seeing we are not borne for our selves, but each to helpe other, and our abilities are much alike at the houre of our birth, and the minute of our death: Seeing our good deedes, or our badde, by faith in Christs merits, is all we have to carrie our soules to heaven, or hell: Seeing honour is our lives ambition; and our ambition after death, to have an honourable memorie of our life: and seeing by noe meanes wee would bee abated of the dignities and glories of our Predecessors; let us imitate their vertues to bee worthily their successors.

1616

[3]Travail.

from Advertisements for the Unexperienced Planters of New-England, or Anywhere, Or the Path-way to Experience to Erect a Plantation[1] [Review of the colonies planted in New England and Virginia]

from **Chapter 1**

The Warres in *Europe, Asia,* and *Affrica,* taught me how to subdue the wilde Salvages in *Virginia* and *New-England,* in *America;* which now after many a stormy blast of ignorant contradictors, projectors, and undertakers, both they and I have beene so tossed and tortured into so many extremities, as despaire was the next wee both expected, till it pleased God now at last to stirre up some good mindes, that I hope will produce glory to God, honour to his Majesty, and profit to his Kingdomes: although all our Plantations have beene so foyled and abused, their best good willers have beene for the most part discouraged, and their good intents disgraced, as the generall History of them will at large truly relate [to] you.

Pardon me if I offend in loving that I have cherished truly, by the losse of my prime fortunes, meanes, and youth: If it over-glad me to see Industry her selfe adventure now to make use of my aged ende[a]vours, not by such (I hope) as rumour doth report, a many of discontented Brownists,[2] Anabaptists, Papists, Puritans, Separatists, and such factious Humorists.[3] for no such they will suffer among them, if knowne, as many of the chiefe of them [*John Winthrop &c.*] have assured mee; and the much conferences I have had with many of them, doth confidently perswade me to write thus much in their behalfe.

I meane not the Brownists of *Leyden* and *Amsterdam* at *New-Plimoth,*[4] who although by accident, ignorance, and wilfulnesse, [they] have endured, with a wonderfull patience, many losses and extremities; yet they subsist and prosper so well, not any of them will abandon the Country, but to the utmost of their powers increase their numbers. But of those which are gone within this eighteene moneths [*April 1629–Oct. 1630*] for Cape *Anne,* and the Bay of the *Massachusets.* Those which are their chiefe Undertakers are Gentlemen of good estate, some of 500, some a thousand pound land a yeere, all which they say they will sell for the advancing [of] this harmlesse and pious worke; men of good credit and well-beloved in their Country [*district*], not such as flye for debt, or any scandall at home; and are good Catholike

[1] *Advertisements* was first published in London in 1631. This text, slightly modified, is taken from *The Complete Works of Captain John Smith,* 3 vols., 1986.

[2] Followers of Robert Browne (1550–1633), who formulated the principles of Congregationalism and led a group of Separatists to Holland in 1582.

[3] People driven by a single humor, eccentrics.

[4] The Pilgrims. As Separatists who had fled to Holland, they were commonly referred to as Brownists, the better-known group of Separatists that had done the same thing earlier, though Browne was not their leader.

Protestants according to the reformed Church of *England,* if not, it is well they are gone. The rest of them men of good meanes, or Arts, Occupations, and Qualities, much more fit for such a businesse, and better furnished of all necessaries if they arrive well, than was ever any Plantation went out of *England.* I will not say but some of them may be more precise than needs, nor that they all be so good as they should be; for Christ had but twelve apostles, and one was a traitor: and if there be no dissemblers among them, it is more than a wonder; therefore doe not condemne all for some. But however they have as good authority from his Majesty as they could desire: if they doe ill, the losse is but their owne; if well, a great glory and exceeding good to this Kingdome, to make good at last what all our former conclusions have disgraced. Now they take not that course the *Virginia* company did for the Planters there, their purses and lives were subject to some few here in *London* who were never there, that consumed all in Arguments, Projects, and their owne conceits: every yeare trying new conclusions, altering every thing yearely as they altered opinions, till they had consumed more than two hundred thousand pounds, and neere eight thousand mens lives.

It is true, in the yeere of our Lord 1622. they were, the Company in *England* say 7. or 8. thousand: the Counsell in *Virginia* say but 2200. or thereabouts, English indifferently well furnished with most necessaries, and many of them grew to that height of bravery, living in that plenty and excesse, that went thither not worth any thing, [that] made the Company here thinke all the world was Oatmeale there; and all this proceeded by surviving those that died: nor were they ignorant to use as curious tricks there as here, and out of the juice of Tabacco, which at first they sold at such good rates, they regarded nothing but Tabacco; a commodity then so vendable, it provided them all things. And the loving Salvages their kinde friends, they trained so well up to shoot in a Peece, to hunt and kill them fowle, they became more expert than our owne Country-men; whose labours were more profitable to their Masters in planting Tabacco and other businesse.

This superfluity caused my poore beginnings [to be] scorned, or to be spoken of but with much derision, that never sent Ship from thence fraught, but onely some small quantities of Wainscot, Clap-board, Pitch, Tar, Rosin, Sope-ashes, Glasse, Cedar, Cypresse, Blacke Walnut, Knees for Ships, Ash for Pikes, Iron Ore none better, some Silver Ore but so poore it was not regarded; better there may be, for I was no Mineralist; some Sturgion, but it was too tart of the Vinegar (which was of my owne store, for little came from them which was good); and Wine of the Countries wilde Grapes, but it was too sowre; yet better than they sent us any, [which was] in two or three years but one Hogshead of Claret. . . .

Now because I sent not their ships full fraught home with those commodities; they kindly writ to me, if we failed the next returne, they would leave us there as banished men, as if houses and all those commodities did grow naturally, only for us to take at our pleasure; with such tedious Letters, directions, and instructions, and most contrary to that was fitting, we did admire [*wonder*] how it was possible such wise men could so torment themselves and us with such strange absurdities and impossibilities: making Religion their colour, when all their aime was nothing but present profit, as most plainly appeared, by sending us so many Refiners, Goldsmiths, Jewellers, Lapidaries, Stone-cutters, Tobacco-pipe-makers, Imbroderers, Perfumers, Silkemen, with [not only] all their appurtenances but materialls, and all those had great summes out of the common stocke; and [were] so many spies and super-intendents over us, as if they supposed we would turne Rebels, all striving to suppresse and advance they knew not what. . . . Much they blamed us for not converting the Salvages, when those they sent us were little better, if not worse; nor did they all, convert any of those [*natives*] we sent them to *England* for that purpose. So doating of Mines of gold, and the South Sea; that all the world could not have devised better courses to bring us to ruine than they did themselves, with many more such like strange conceits. . . .

from Chapter 9

Now if you but truly consider how many strange accidents have befallen those plantations and my selfe; how oft up, how oft downe, sometimes neere despaire, and ere long flourishing; how many scandals and Spanolized English[5] have sought to disgrace them, bring them to ruine, or at least hinder them all they could; how many have shaven and couzened both them and me, and their most honourable supporters and well-willers: [you] cannot but conceive Gods infinite mercy both to them and me. Having beene a slave to the Turks, prisoner amongst the most barbarous Salvages, after my deliverance commonly discovering and ranging those large rivers and unknowne Nations with such a handfull of ignorant companions that the wiser sort often gave mee [up] for lost, alwayes in mutinies [*i.e., of others*] wants and miseries, blowne up with gunpowder; A long time [a] prisoner among the French Pyrats, from whom escaping in a little boat by my selfe, and adrift all such a stormy winter night, when their ships were split, more than a hundred thousand pound lost [which] they had taken at sea, and most of them drowned upon the Ile of *Ree,* not farre from whence I was driven on shore in my little boat &c. Any many a score of the worst of winter moneths [have] lived in the fields: yet to have lived neere 37. yeares [1593–1630] in the midst of wars, pestilence and famine, by which many an hundred thousand have died about mee, and scarce five living of them [that] went first with me to *Virginia:* and [yet to] see the fruits of my labours thus well begin to prosper: though I have but my labour for my paines, have I not much reason both privately and publikely to acknowledge it and give God thankes, whose omnipotent power onely delivered me, to doe the utmost of my best to make his name knowne in those remote parts of the world, and his loving mercy to such a miserable sinner.

1631

[5]Englishmen who supported Spain or adopted Spanish ways.

Richard Frethorne fl. 1623

Richard Frethorne was a young Englishman who came over to the New World in 1623 as an indentured servant and settled in Virginia, near the Jamestown colony. Other than the three letters to his parents included here, there is no historical record of his life. The letters, however, provide an illuminating picture of the hardships of colonization in the early seventeenth century, especially for the class of indentured servants.

Combatting homesickness, disease, hunger, discomfort, and isolation, Frethorne and his fellow settlers struggled to make a success of their fledgling community. But life in early Virginia was particularly difficult because of the shortage of supplies, the prevalence of disease, and tense relations with the Native Americans. On March 22, 1622, the Powhatan chief Opechancanough organized an attack on English settlements across the colony that killed between three hundred and four hundred people. This attack, ignited by the recent murder of the great warrior Nemattanew by the English, was intended to curb English expansion into native lands. As a result, the English abandoned many outlying settlements and moved closer to or into Jamestown itself, increasing the incidence of disease and death in the overcrowded village. The English retaliated by destroying Indian crops. Frethorne alludes to this attack, in which eighty people from his outlying settlement died, and which motivated the fear and harsh policies of the settlers toward the Indians. Tensions between the two groups escalated over the next decade and climaxed in another attack by Opechancanough in 1641, in which nearly four hundred English colonists were killed. It is not surprising, as Frethorne recounts, that many longed to be "redeemed out of Egypt" and return to their former lives across the Atlantic.

Liahna Babener
Montana State University

Ivy Schweitzer
Dartmouth College

PRIMARY WORKS

Richard Frethorne, Letter to his father and mother, March 20, April 2–3, 1623, in Susan Kingsbury, ed., *The Records of the Virginia Company of London* (Washington, D.C.: U.S. Government Printing Office, 1935), 4: 58–62.

from Richard Frethorne, to His Parents (Virginia, 1623)

Loving and kind father and mother:

My most humble duty remembered to you, hoping in God of your good health, as I myself am at the making hereof. This is to let you understand that I your child am in a most heavy case by reason of the nature of the country, [which] is such that it causeth much sickness, as the scurvy and the bloody flux and diverse other diseases, which maketh the body very poor and weak. And when we are sick there is nothing to comfort us; for since I came out of the ship I never ate anything but peas, and loblollie (that is, water gruel). As for deer or venison I never saw any since I came into this land. There is indeed some fowl, but we are not allowed to go and get it, but must work hard both early and late for a mess of water gruel and a mouthful of bread and beef. A mouthful of bread for a penny loaf must serve for four men which is most pitiful. . . . People cry out day and night—Oh! that they were in England without their limbs—and would not care to lose any limb to be England again, yea, though they beg from door to door. For we live in fear of the enemy every hour, yet we have had a combat with them on the Sunday before Shrovetide,[1] and we took two alive and made slaves of them. But it was by policy, for we are in great danger; for our plantation is very weak by reason of the death and sickness of our company. For we came but twenty for the merchants, and they are half dead just; and we look every hour when two more should go. Yet there came some four other men yet to live with us, of which there is but one alive; and our Lieutenant is dead, and his father and his brother. And there was some five or six of the last year's twenty, of which there is but three left, so that we are fain to get other men to plant with us; and yet we are but 32 to fight against 3000 if they should come. And the nighest help that we have is ten miles of us, and when the rogues overcame this place last they slew 80 persons. How then shall we do, for we lie even in their teeth? They may easily take us, but that God is merciful and can save with few as well as with many, as he showed to Gilead.[2] . . .

And I have nothing to comfort me, nor there is nothing to be gotten here but sickness and death, except that one had money to lay out in some things for profit. But I have nothing at all—no, not a shirt to my back but two rags (2), nor no clothes but one poor suit, nor but one pair of shoes, but one pair of stockings, but one cap, but two bands. My cloak is stolen by one of my own fellows, and to his dying hour [he] would not tell me what he did with it; but some of my fellows saw him have butter and beef out of a ship, which my cloak, I doubt [not], paid for. So that I have not a penny, nor a penny worth, to help me to either spice or sugar or strong waters, without the which one cannot live here. For as strong beer in England doth fatten and strengthen them, so water here doth wash and weaken these here [and] only keeps life and soul together. But I am not half a quarter so strong as I was in England, and all is for want of victuals; for I do protest unto you that I have eaten more in [one] day at home than I have allowed me here for a week. You have given more than my day's allowance to a beggar at the door; and if Mr. Jackson had not relieved me, I should be in a poor case. But he like a father and she like a loving mother doth still help me. . . .

Goodman Jackson pitied me and made me a cabin to lie in . . . which comforted me more than peas or water gruel. Oh, they be very godly folks, and love me very well, and will do anything for me. And he much marvelled that you would send me a servant to the Company; he saith I had been better knocked on the head. And indeed so I find it now, to my great grief and misery; and saith that if you love me you will redeem me suddenly, for which I do entreat and beg. And if you cannot get the merchants to redeem me for some little money, then for God's sake get a gathering or entreat some good folks to lay out some little sum of money in meal and cheese and butter and beef. Any eating meat will yield great profit. Oil and vinegar

[1]The three days before Ash Wednesday, formerly set aside as a period of confession and a time of festivity preceding Lent in Christian practice.

[2]A region east of the Jordan River settled in biblical times by, among others, Israelites who were successfully defended in battle against vastly superior numbers of invaders by Judas Maccabeus and his warriors.

is very good; but, father, there is great loss in leaking. But for God's sake send beef and cheese and butter, or the more of one sort and none of another. But if you send cheese, it must be very old cheese; and at the cheesemonger's you may buy very good cheese for twopence farthing or halfpenny, that will be liked very well. But if you send cheese, you must have a care how you pack it in barrels; and you must put cooper's chips between every cheese, or else the heat of the hold will rot them. And look whatsoever you send me—be it never so much—look, what[ever] I make of it, I will deal truly with you. I will send it over and beg the profit to redeem me; and if I die before it come, I have entreated Goodman Jackson to send you the worth of it, who hath promised he will. . . . Good father, do not forget me, but have mercy and pity my miserable case. I know if you did but see me, you would weep to see me; for I have but one suit. . . . Wherefore, for God's sake, pity me. I pray you to remember my love to all my friends and kindred. I hope all my brothers and sisters are in good health, and as for my part I have set down my resolution that certainly will be; that is, that the answer of this letter will be life or death to me. Therefore, good father, send as soon as you can; and if you send me any thing let this be the mark.

ROT

Richard Frethorne,
Martin's Hundred

The names of them that be dead of the company [that] came over with us to serve under our Lieutenants:

John Flower
John Thomas
Thos. Howes
John Butcher
John Sanderford
Rich. Smith
John Olive
Thos. Peirsman
William Cerrell
George Goulding

Jos. Johnson
our lieutenant, his
father and brother
Thos. Giblin
George Banum
a little Dutchman
one woman
one maid
one child

All these died out of my master's house, since I came; and we came in but at Christmas, and this is the 20th day of March. And the sailors say that there is two-thirds of the 150 dead already. And thus I end, praying to God to send me good success that I may be redeemed out of Egypt. So *vale in Christo.*

Loving father, I pray you to use this man very exceeding kindly, for he hath done much for me, both on my journey and since. I entreat you not to forget me, but by any means redeem me; for this day we hear that there is 26 of Englishmen slain by the Indians. And they have taken a pinnace[3] of Mr. Pountis, and have gotten pieces, armor, swords, all things fit for war; so that they may now steal upon us and we cannot know them from English till it is too late—that they be upon us—and then there is no mercy. Therefore if you love or respect me as your child, release

[3]A small sailing boat, often used as a scout for a larger vessel.

me from the bondage and save my life. Now you may save me, or let met be slain with infidels. Ask this man—he knoweth that all is true and just that I say here. If you do redeem me, the Company must send for me to my Mr. Harrod; for so is this Master's name. April, the second day,

Your loving son,
Richard Frethorne

Moreover, on the third day of April we heard that after these rogues had gotten the pinnace and had taken all furnitures [such] as pieces, swords, armor, coats of mail, powder, shot and all the things that they had to trade withal, they killed the Captain and cut off his head. And rowing with the tail of the boat foremost, they set up a pole and put the Captain's head upon it, and so rowed home. Then the Devil set them on again, so that they furnished about 200 canoes with above 1000 Indians, and came, and thought to have taken the ship; but she was too quick for them—which thing was very much talked of, for they always feared a ship. But now the rogues grow very bold and can use pieces, some of them, as well or better than an Englishman; for an Indian did shoot with Mr. Charles, my master's kinsman, at a mark of white paper, and he hit it at the first, but Mr. Charles could not hit it. But see the envy of these slaves, for when they could not take the ship, then our men saw them threaten Accomack, that is the next plantation. And now there is no way but starving; . . . For they had no crop last year by reason of these rogues, so that we have no corn but as ships do relieve us, nor we shall hardly have any crop this year; and we are as like to perish first as any plantation. For we have but two hogsheads of meal left to serve us this two months, . . . that is but a halfpennyloaf a day for a man. Is it not strange to me, think you? But what will it be when we shall go a month or two and never see a bit of bread, as my master doth say we must do? And he said he is not able to keep us all. Then we shall be turned up to the land and eat barks of trees or molds of the ground; therefore with weeping tears I beg of you to help me. Oh, that you did see my daily and hourly sighs, groans, and tears, and thumps that I afford mine own breast, and rue and curse the time of my birth, with holy Job. I thought no head had been able to hold so much water as hath and doth daily flow from mine eyes.

But this is certain: I never felt the want of father and mother till now; but now, dear friends, full well I know and rue it, although it were too late before I knew it. . . .

Your loving son,
Richard Frethorne
Virginia, 3rd April, 1623

1881

Nathaniel Bacon 1647–1677

Even four hundred years after his death, Nathaniel Bacon remains a source of controversy. Some writers have called him the leader of the first American movement against unrepresentative governmental authority. Bacon's Rebellion (1675–77), these writers tell us, represents the first stirrings of the American urge for representative democracy that would explode one hundred years later in the American Revolution.

Others have painted Bacon in a less flattering light. These writers have him as the key figure in the development of modern American racial classifications and the racism that accompanies those classifications. Still other writers have argued that the significance of the rebellion has been overblown by later generations who have misread it as a precursor of the future rather than a reflection of the past.

At his birth in 1647, Bacon seemed an unlikely candidate for any of these roles. Born into an English family of high social rank, Bacon was headed for the life of a gentleman squire on a lavish estate, the same as generations of his family before him. He married in 1670, but his father-in-law, Sir Edward Duke, saw something so unacceptable in him that he disinherited his daughter Elizabeth. A few years after his marriage, Bacon's mishandling of financial matters led his own father to send him to Virginia, where he settled upriver from the capital of Jamestown in the hopes of profiting from the lucrative fur trade with local Indians.

However, colonial Virginia was not a place where newcomers, even newcomers of social distinction, found life easy. By 1670, the colonial population had grown to about thirty thousand, but fewer than about 10 percent could be considered successful planters. Most were tenants, foremen, laborers, indentured servants, or slaves. Bacon, too, had a difficult time making his plantations a success, even though he quickly began receiving favorable treatment from the colony's governor, William Berkeley, his cousin by marriage.

Like the vast majority of Virginia colonists at the time, Berkeley was born in England but spent considerable time in the colonies, serving two terms as governor. Berkeley enjoyed great popularity during his first term, from 1641 to 1652. Removed from office in 1652 when he refused to side with the Puritan Commonwealth government in the English Civil War, Berkeley returned to power in 1660 but without the wide support he had earlier received. His refusal to call new elections of the local assembly, which thus sat continuously for fourteen years, his taxation policies, and his clear favoritism toward elite Virginians helped produce a climate of unrest among the majority of colonial Virginians in the years following the restoration of the English monarchy.

The events known as Bacon's Rebellion began soon after Bacon's arrival in 1676, when a dispute between a group of Doeg Indians and English colonists over livestock turned deadly. Tensions among the colonists and between the colonists and the Indians had been simmering for some time. After English settlers were killed, though, a good number of the colonists wanted the Virginia authorities to organize a force to attack the local Indians, regardless of their involvement in the dispute, on the grounds that all Indians were alike in being enemies to the English. Berkeley decided against launching a large-scale attack. Instead, he proposed building a series of forts that would double as trading posts. His attempt to prevent indiscriminate strikes against all Indians while making a tidy profit for himself only served to provoke the colonists. Settlers on the south side of the James River, who were most antagonistic to local Indians as well as most abused by Berkeley's trading policies, staged a rally to protest Berkeley's plan. Bacon had also suffered losses in the aftermath of the dispute between Doegs and colonists, and he agreed to lead the colonists against the local Indians. He no doubt believed his good relations with the governor and his high social standing provided sufficient grounds for assuming leadership of the colonial force, though whether he had overstepped his authority became the subject of considerable dispute in the following months.

The forces led by Bacon initially attacked only the local Indians, but the war soon turned into a civil conflict when Berkeley issued a proclamation labeling as traitors all those aligned with Bacon. Bacon's forces were able to capture and burn the capital, and they had control of most of the colony for at least three months. But Bacon died suddenly of natural causes, and the rebellion ended soon afterward. In all, the hostilities lasted only about one year. When troops from England arrived, Berkeley was removed from office and taken to England to explain his actions. While there, he, too, died of natural causes. The conflict was so serious, according to the king's agents, that the colonists were thought to be willing to transfer their allegiance—and the profits to be had from the tobacco trade—to a foreign monarch.

Whatever the historical legacy of Bacon's Rebellion—whether the birthplace of American freedom, American racism, some combination of both, or an outcome unrelated to the history of a nation not yet even imagined—the events spawned an outpouring of plays, poems, novels, and histories. The English playwright Aphra Behn's *The Widow Ranter* (1689), for instance, used the rebellion to examine the changing notions of nobility in English society, and the satiric poem "The History of Colonial Nathaniel Bacon's Rebellion in Virginia" (1731) by the so-called "poet Laurette" of Maryland, Ebenezer Cooke, cast Bacon and his collaborators as a "Publick Evil" whose actions threatened to undermine royally sanctioned authority. After the Revolutionary War, American novelists across the political spectrum seized on the opportunity to use the rebellion of these very English subjects as a stage for investigating where a distinctively American culture could be said to begin and, in the process, helping to re-imagine what it meant to be American in the first place.

James Egan
Brown University

PRIMARY WORK

"Proclamations of Nathaniel Bacon," 1676.

Nathaniel Bacon Esq'r his Manifesto Concerning the Present Troubles in Virginia[1]

If vertue be a sin, if Piety be guilt, all the Principles of morality goodness and Justice be perverted, Wee must confesse That those who are now called Rebells may be in danger of those high imputations, Those loud and severall Bull would affright Innocents and render the defence of our Brethren and the enquiry into our sad and heavy oppressions, Treason. But if there bee as sure there is, a just God to appeal too, if Religion and Justice be a sanctuary here, If to plead youre cause of the oppressed, If sincerely to aime at his Majesties[2] Honour and the Publick good without any reservation or by Interest, If to stand in the Gap after soe much blood of our dear Brethren bought and sold, If after the losse of a great part of his Majesties Colony deserted and dispeopled,[3] freely with our lives and estates to indeavor to save the

[1]The text is from "Proclamations of Nathaniel Bacon," *Virginia Historical Magazine* 1 (1893): 55–63, with some modifications.

[2]Bacon refers here to King Charles II, who assumed the monarchy in 1660 after the English Commonwealth, the authority that had replaced the monarchy during the English Civil War, abdicated power.

[3]The phrase "deserted and dispeopled" refers to land English colonists had recently left or from which they had been forced off by local Indians, land the colonists argued was legally the property of the English monarch, who had authorized English subjects rather than Indians to occupy it.

remaynders bee Treason God Almighty Judge and lett guilty dye. But since wee cannot in our hearts find one single spott of Rebellion or Treason or that wee have in any manner aimed at the subverting youre setled Government or attempting of the Person of any either magistrate or private man not with standing the severall Reproaches and Threats of some who for sinister ends were disaffected to us and censured our ino[cent] and honest designes, and since al people in all places where wee have yet bin can attest our civill quiet peaseable behaviour farre different from that of Rebellion and tumultuous persons let Trueth be bold and all the world know the real Foundations of pretended guilt. Wee appeale to the Country itselfe what and of what nature their Oppressions have bin or by what Caball[4] and mistery the designes of many of those whom wee call great men have bin transacted and caryed on, but let us trace these men in Authority and Favour to whose hands the dispensation of the Countries wealth has been commited; let us observe the sudden Rise of their Estates composed with the Quality in which they first entered this Country Or the Reputation they have held here amongst wise and discerning men, And lett us see wither their extractions and Education have not bin vile, And by what pretence of learning and vertue they could soe soon into Imployments of so great Trust and consequence, let us consider wither any Publick work for our safety and defence or for the Advancement and propogation of Trade, liberall Arts or sciences is here Extant in any [way] adaquate to our vast chardg, now let us compare these things togit[her] and see what spounges have suckt up the Publique Treasure and wither it hath not bin privately contrived away by unworthy Favourites and juggling Parasites whose tottering tunes have bin repaired and supported at the Publique chardg. Now if it be so Judg what greater guilt can bee then to offer to pry into these and to unriddle the misterious wiles of a powerfull Cabal let all people Judge what can be of more dangerous Import then to suspect the soe long Safe proceedings of Some of our Grandees and wither People may with safety open their Eyes in soe nice a Concerne.

Another main article of our Guilt is our open and manifest aversion of all, not onely the Foreign but the protected and Darling Indians, this wee are informed is Rebellion of a deep dye For that both the Governour and Councell are by Colonell Coales Assertion bound to defend the Queen and the Appamatocks with their blood.[5] Now whereas we doe declare and can prove that they have bin for these Many years enemies to the King and Country, Robbers and Theeves and Invaders of

[4]Intrigue or conspiracy.

[5]Bacon refers here to Governor Berkeley and the members of his appointed council who advised him on colonial matters, one of whom was Colonel William Cole, a particular favorite of Berkeley's. In support of Berkeley's insistence that the colonists treat the various Indian groups as distinctly different communities, Colonel Cole had argued that the Pamunkey and Appomattox Indians were the colonists' allies whom the colonists, he said, "ought to defend . . . with our blood." The "Queen" is the leader of the Pamunkeys, who had recently been asked by local legislature to allow some of her warriors to work as spies and guides for the English in their attacks against hostile Indian groups. Indeed, the practice of using one Indian group to spy on another was common in the English colonies, and the Pamunkeys had already lost a number of their people—including the Queen's husband, Tottopottomoi—while working for the English. The decision by one group of Indians to side with the English was not necessarily a sign of their support for English actions. Such decisions more often had to do with the particular Indian group's attempt to negotiate the increasingly complicated, violent conflicts between Indians and English.

his Majesties Right and our Interest and Estates, but yet have by persons in Authority bin defended and protected even against his Majesties loyall Subjects and that in soe high a Nature that even the Complaints and oaths of his Majesties Most loyall Subjects in a lawfull Manner proffered by them against those barborous Outlawes have bin by youre right honourable Governour rejected and youre Delinquents from his presence dismissed not only with pardon and indemnitye but with all incouragement and favour, Their Fire Arms soe destructfull to us and by our lawes prohibited, Commanded to be restored them, and open Declaration before Witness made That they must have Ammunition although directly contrary to our law. Now what greater guilt can be then to oppose and indeavour the destruction of these Honest quiet neighbours of ours.

Another main article of our Guilt is our Design not only to ruine and extirpate all Indians in Generall but all Manner of Trade and Commerce with them, Judge who can be innocent that strike at this tender Eye of Interest; Since the Right honourable the Governour hath bin pleased by his Commission to warrant this Trade who dare oppose it, or opposing it can be innocent. Although Plantations be deserted, the blood of our dear Brethren Spilt, on all Sides our complaints, continually Murder upon Murder renewed upon us, who may or dare think of the generall Subversion of all Mannor of Trade and Commerce with our enemies who can or dare impeach any of * * * Traders at the Heades of the Rivers if contrary to the wholesome provision made by lawes for the countries safety, they dare continue their illegall practises and dare asperse[6] ye right honourable Governours wisdome and Justice soe highly to pretend to have his warrant to break that law which himself made. Who dare say That these Men at the Heads of the Rivers buy and sell our blood, and doe still notwithstanding the late Act made to the contrary,[7] admit Indians painted and continue to Commerce, although these things can be proved yet who dare bee soe guilty as to doe it.

Another Article of our Guilt is To Assert all those neighbour Indians as well as others to be outlawed, wholly unqualifyed for the benefitt and Protection of the law, For that the law does reciprocally protect and punish, and that all people offending must either in person or Estate make equivalent satisfaction or Restitution according

[6]To spread false and injurious charges against a person.

[7]On May 10, Berkeley called for a new election for the House of Burgesses, the local assembly formed in 1620s that was the first representative legislature in the English American colonies. The newly elected members supported, for the most part, the rebel positions, and when they met in June passed a number of bills that addressed rebel concerns, including acts that extended the vote to colonists who did not own land and acts that sought to prevent colonial authorities from abusing their privileges. Bacon refers in this sentence to two bills passed by this assembly. The first both declared war "against the barbarous Indians" and named Bacon "generall and commander in chiefe of the forces raised," granting him what was referred to as "his commission," a power that was not, in fact, the assembly's to give. The second bill sought to allay critics of the governor's monopoly of the fur trade, which, the rebels claimed, had led him to defend the Indians. This second bill repealed an earlier act favorable to Berkeley and his favorites, which "permitted five persons in each county to trade with the Indians," and it criminalized trade with those Bacon labels "Indians painted"—in other words, those who were considered at war with the English. Of course, the distinction between Indians who were England's allies and those who were its enemies was often not recognized by the colonists who opposed the governor.

to the manner and merit of youre Offences Debts or Trespasses; Now since the Indians cannot according to the tenure and forme of any law to us known be prosecuted, Seised or Complained against, Their Persons being difficulty distinguished or known, Their many nations languages, and their subterfuges such as makes them incapeable to make us Restitution or satisfaction would it not be very guilty to say They have bin unjustly defended and protected these many years.

If it should be said that the very foundation of all these disasters the Grant of the Beaver trade to the Right Honourable Governour was illegall and not granteable by any power here present as being a monopoly, were not this to deserve the name of Rebell and Traytor.

Judge therefore all wise and unprejudiced men who may or can faithfully or truly with an honest heart attempt youre country's good, their vindication and libertie without the aspersion of Traitor and Rebell, since as soe doing they must of necessity gall such tender and dear concernes, But to manifest Sincerity and loyalty to the World, and how much wee abhorre those bitter names, may all the world know that we doe unanimously desire to represent our sad and heavy grievances to his most sacred Majestie as our Refuge and Sanctuary, where wee doe well know that all our Causes will be impartially heard and Equall Justice administered to all men.

The Declaration of the People[8]

For having upon specious pretences of Publick works raised unjust Taxes upon the Commonalty for the advancement of private Favourits and other sinnister ends but noe visible effects in any measure adequate.

For not having dureing the long time of his Government in any measure advanced this hopefull Colony either by Fortification, Townes or Trade.

For having abused and rendered Contemptible the Majesty of Justice, of advancing to places of judicature scandalous and Ignorant favourits.

For having wronged his Majesties Prerogative and Interest by assuming the monopoley of the Beaver Trade.

By having in that unjust gaine Bartered and sould his Majesties Country and the lives of his Loyal Subjects to the Barbarous Heathen.

For having protected favoured and Imboldened the Indians against his Majesties most Loyall subjects never contriveing requireing or appointing any due or proper means of satisfaction for their many Invasions Murthers and Robberies Committed upon us.

For having when the Army of the English was Just upon the Track of the Indians, which now in all places Burne Spoyle and Murder, and when wee might with ease have destroyed them who then were in open Hostility for having expresly Countermanded and sent back our Army by passing his word for the peaceable demean-

[8]The declaration was issued by Bacon on July 30, 1676. It was not produced by the people of Virginia at large, as its title might suggest to a modern reader, or even by any small but representative portion of those people. Instead, the remarks represent Bacon's declaration on behalf of the colonists, and, by implication, they demonstrate his sense that he had the authority and social position that allowed him to speak on behalf of those he considered his social inferiors.

our of the said Indians, who imediately prosecuted their evill Intentions Committing horrid Murders and Robberies in all places being protected by the said Engagement and word pass'd of him the said Sir William Berkley having ruined and made desolate a great part of his Majesties Country, have now drawne themselves into such obscure and remote places and are by their successes soe imboldened and confirmed and by their Confederacy soe strengthened that the cryes of Bloud are in all places and the Terrour and consternation of the People soe great, that they are now become not only a difficult, but a very formidable Enemy who might with ease have been destroyed &c. When upon the Lord Outcries of blood the Assembly had with all care raised and framed an Army for the prevention of future Mischiefs and safeguard of his Majesties Colony.

For having with only the privacy of some few favourits without acquainting the People, only by the Alteration of a Figure forged a Commission by wee know not what hand, not only without but against the Consent of the People, for raising and effecting of Civill Warrs, and distractions, which being happily and without Bloodshedd prevented.[9]

For having the second tyme attempted the same thereby, calling downe our Forces from the defence of the Frontiers, and most weake Exposed Places, for the prevention of civill Mischief and Ruine amongst ourselves, whilst the barbarous Enemy in all places did Invade murder and spoyle us his Majesties most faithful subjects.

Of these the aforesaid Articles wee accuse Sir William Berkely, as guilty of each and every one of the same, and as one who hath Traiterously attempted, violated and Injured his Majesties Interest here, by the losse of a great Part of his Colony, and many of his Faithfull and Loyall subjects by him betrayed, and in such a barbarous and shamefull manner exposed to the Incursions and murthers of the Heathen.

And we further declare these the Ensueing Persons in this List, to have been his wicked, and pernitious Councellors, Aiders and Assisters against the Commonality in these our Cruell Commotions.

Sir Henry Chicherly, Knt.,	Jos. Bridger,
Col. Charles Wormley,	William Clabourne,
Phil. Dalowell,	Thos. Hawkins, Juni'r,
Robert Beverly	William Sherwood,
Robert Lee,	Jos. Page, Clerk,
Thos. Ballard,	Jo. Cliffe, Clerk

[9]Bacon here refers to Berkeley's ill-fated attempt to regain control of the colony in what has become known as the Gloucester Petition. On June 22, Berkeley had granted Bacon the authority—referred to in the documents as "his commission"—to command troops against the Indians. After Bacon's men had subsequently—and, in their eyes, with the authority of the governor—taken supplies gathered by Berkeley's supporters in Gloucester County for their own assault against the Indians, Berkeley's supporters responded with their own petition, in the name of the inhabitants of the county, pleading for the governor's protection against Bacon's men. When Berkeley went to Gloucester, he declared that the commission he had granted Bacon was given under duress and thus was invalid, and he called on the people to join him against Bacon. While many of the events of the rebellion are in dispute, all parties agree that the people of Gloucester did not answer Berkeley's call to arms because they were unwilling to take up arms against Bacon and his men.

William Cole, Hubberd Farrell,
Richard Whitacre, John West,
Nicholas Spencer, Thos. Reade.
Mathew Kemp.

And wee doe further demand, That the said Sir William Berkley, with all the Persons in this List, be forthwith delivered upp, or surrender themselves, within foure dayes, after the notice hereof, or otherwise wee declare, as followeth. That in whatsoever place, or shipp, any of the said Persons shall reside, be hide, or protected, Wee doe declare, that the Owners, masters, or Inhabitants of the said places, to be Confederates, and Traitors to the People, and the Estates of them, as alsoe of all the aforesaid Persons to be Confiscated, This wee the Commons of Virginia doe declare desiring a prime Union among ourselves, that wee may Joyntly, and with one Accord defend ourselves against the Common Enemye. And Let not the Faults of the guilty, be the Reproach of the Innocent, or the Faults or Crimes of ye Oppressors divide and separate us, who have suffered by theire oppressions.

These are therefore in his Majesties name, to Command you forthwith to seize, the Persons above mentioned, as Traytors to ye King and Countrey, and them to bring to Middle Plantation,[10] and there to secure them, till further Order, and in Case of opposition, if you want any other Assistance, you are forthwith to demand it in the Name of the People of all the Counties of Virginia.

1676 1893

James Revel 1640s?–?

Little is known of James Revel other than what he tells us in his poem. If we take the narrator of the poem to be a figure for its author, which the poem leads us to do, it would appear that Revel was a convicted felon for whom transportation to Virginia served as punishment. So little can be confirmed about Revel's life from sources outside the poem, though, that some scholars question his very existence. Since the earliest known version of the poem dates from the eighteenth century, he might have been the creation of an enterprising publisher looking to capitalize on the popularity of Daniel Defoe's tales of transported convicts, such as *Moll Flanders.* Why, then, do scholars believe that, whether or not Revel was a real person or the product of a printer's imagination, at the very least the poem itself was produced in the seventeenth century?

One argument in favor of the poem being a seventeenth-century work concerns the history of transportation tales in English literature. According to John Melville Jennings, who not only recovered Revel's poem from obscurity but also published the most extensive discussion of it,

[10]The site of present-day Williamsburg, Virginia. In August 1676, Bacon met with several of his supporters who were also of the gentleman class at Middle Plantation. At the meeting, Bacon asked them to take an oath pledging their support for him against Berkeley. Some of those who agreed to support Bacon later insisted that they did so only to avoid the prospect of his appointing people of lesser social stature as leaders if he succeeded in replacing Berkeley as the colony's legal authority.

tales of felons transported across the Atlantic existed at least one hundred years before Defoe put them in his fiction. One reason for the frequency of such stories can be seen in the sheer numbers of those who were transported. At least thirty thousand people convicted of crimes in England were transported to the colonies during the seventeenth and eighteenth centuries. Judges were empowered to make a choice: either sentencing individuals to death or sending them to the colonies. Protests by colonial agents led to the suspension of transportation from 1671 to 1717, but the widespread sense that England was threatened by a wave of crime in the early eighteenth century led to the resumption of the practice.

Criminals were not the only "undesirable elements" of society sent to the colonies. Early advocates of English colonization in the sixteenth and seventeenth centuries claimed that England's colonies could be used as a place to send various unwanted subjects. Critics, satirists, and many colonists themselves complained of this use of the colonies in the seventeenth century, citing it as an impediment to economic development and a sign of the colony's degraded culture. However they portrayed such "undesirable elements" in the colonies, the figure of the colonial convict became a staple if not a cliché in seventeenth-century literature about the colonies, a tradition that would continue in work by colonial Americans and about colonial America into the eighteenth century both before and after Defoe's novels.

Second, internal evidence in the poem suggests that only someone with an intimate knowledge of seventeenth-century Virginia could have written the piece. Revel notes that he lived in Rappahannock County for twelve of his fourteen years in Virginia. The name Rappahannock disappeared from Virginia place names and was relegated to memory when, in 1692, the county was split into two new counties, Richmond and Essex. It is very unlikely that an eighteenth-century writer simply trying to capitalize on the popularity of a recent novel would seek to authenticate his narrative by going to the trouble of mentioning the name of a long-dead county whose very existence was known to precious few.

And lest we take the absence of any surviving seventeenth-century edition of Revel's poem as a sure sign of its eighteenth-century origins, we should remember that the work was no doubt issued in an inexpensive edition known as a chapbook. In the decades following the English Civil War, the market for printed material expanded to include more and more members of the middling ranks. Printers issued numerous works that would appeal to the interests and concerns of these new consumers, but to keep prices within the range of the little disposable income such people were able to accumulate, the works were often of such poor quality that chapbooks were literally read to pieces. Few chapbooks or other inexpensive printed materials remain from the seventeenth or eighteenth centuries. Revel's poem, then, serves as a useful reminder of important literary traditions that existed alongside and, at least in some sense, in competition with the works of often more "mainstream" writers, writers whose works were issued in more durable editions. Revel's poem gives us a glimpse of the tastes, interests, and concerns of readers who do not represent the wealthy or elite parts of society.

James Egan
Brown University

PRIMARY WORK

"The Poor Unhappy Transported Felon's Sorrowful Account of his Fourteen Years Transportation, at Virginia, in America."

The Poor, Unhappy Transported Felon[1]

[*Tune of "Death and the Lady"*[2]]

My loving Countrymen pray lend an Ear,
To this Relation which I bring you here,
My sufferings at large I will unfold,
Which tho' 'tis strange, 'tis true as e'er was told,
Of honest parents I did come (tho' poor,)
Who besides me had never Children more;
Near Temple Bar was born their darling son,
And for some years in virtue's path did run.
My parents in me took great delight,
And brought me up at School to read and write,
And cast accompts likewise, as it appears,
Until that I was aged thirteen years.
Then to a Tin-man I was Prentice bound,
My master and mistress good I found,
They lik'd me well, my business I did mind,
From me my parents comfort hop'd to find.
My master near unto Moorfields did dwell,
Where into wicked company I fell;
To wickedness I quickly was inclin'd,
Thus soon is tainted any youthful mind.
I from my master then did run away,
And rov'd about the streets both night and day:
Did with a gang of rogues a thieving go,
Which filled my parents heart with grief and woe.
At length my master got me home again,
And used me well, in hopes I might reclaim,
My father tenderly to me did say,
My dearest child, what made you run away?
If you had any cause at all for grief,
Why came you not to me to seek relief?
I well do know you did for nothing lack,
Food for your belly and cloaths to your back.
My mother cry'd, dear son I do implore,
That you will from your master go no more,
Your business mind, your master ne'er forsake,
Lest you again to wicked courses take.

[1]The text is a slightly modified version of "The Poor Unhappy Transported Felon's Sorrowful Account of his Fourteen Years Transportation at Virginia in America," ed. John Melville Jennings, *Virginia Historical Magazine* (1948): 180–94.

[2]A popular folksong. It was not uncommon for printed ballads to be set to the music of well-known folksongs.

I promis'd fair, but yet could not refrain,
But to my vile companions went again:
For vice when once, alas! it taints the mind,
Is not soon rooted out again we find.
With them again I did a thieving go,
But little did my tender parents know,
I follow'd courses that could be so vile,
My absence griev'd them, being their only child[,]
A wretched life I liv'd, I must confess,
In fear and dread and great uneasiness;
Which does attend such actions that's unjust,
For thieves can never one another trust.
Strong liquor banish'd all the thoughts of fear,
But Justice stops us in our full career:
One night was taken up one of our gang,
Who five impeach'd & three of these were hang'd.
I was one of the five was try'd and cast,
Yet transportation I did get at last;
A just reward for my vile actions past,
Thus justice overtook me at the last.
My Father griev'd, my mother she took on,
And cry'd, Alas! alas! my only Son:
My Father cry'd, It cuts me to the heart,
To think on such a cause as this we part.
To see them grieve thus pierc'd my very soul,
My wretched case I sadly did condole;
With grief and shame my eyes did overflow,
And had much rather chuse to die than go.
In vain I griev'd, in vain my parents weep,
For I was quickly sent on board the Ship:
With melting kisses and a heavy heart,
I from my dearest parents then did part.

Part II

In a few Days we left the river quite,
And in short time of land we lost the sight,
The Captain and the sailors us'd us well,
But kept us under lest we should rebel.
We were in number much about threescore,
A wicked lowsey crew as e'er went o'er;
Oaths and Tobacco with us plenty were,
For most did smoak, and all did curse and swear.
Five of our number in our passage died,
Which were thrown into the Ocean wide:
And after sailing seven Weeks and more,

We at Virginia all were put on shore.
  Where, to refresh us, we were wash'd and cleaned
That to our buyers we might the better seem;
Our things were gave to each they did belong,
And they that had clean linnen put it on.
  Our faces shav'd, comb'd out our wigs and hair,
That we in decent order might appear,
Against the planters did come down to view,
How well they lik'd this fresh transported crew.
  The Women s[e]parated from us stand,
As well as we, by them for to be view'd;
And in short time some men up to us came,
Some ask'd our trades, and others ask'd our names.
  Some view'd our limbs, and other's turn'd us round
Examening like Horses, if we're sound,
What trade are you, my Lad, says one to me,
A Tin-man, Sir, that will not do, says he[.]
  Some felt our hands and view'd our legs and feet,
And made us walk, to see we were compleat;
Some view'd our teeth, to see if they were good,
Or fit to chew our hard and homely Food.
  If any like our look, our limbs, our trade,
The Captain then a good advantage made:
For they a difference made it did appear,
'Twixt those for seven and for fourteen year.
  Another difference there is alow'd,
They who have money have most favour show'd;
For if no cloaths nor money they have got,
Hard is their fate, and hard will be their lot.
  At length a grim old Man unto me came,
He ask'd my trade, and likewise ask'd my Name:
I told him I a Tin-man was by trade,
And not quite eighteen years of age I said.
  Likewise the cause I told that brought me there,
That I for fourteen years transported were,
And when he this from me did understand,
He bought me of the Captain out of hand.

Part III

Down to the harbour I was took again,
  On board of a sloop, and loaded with a chain;
Which I was forc'd to wear both night and day,
For fear I from the Sloop should get away.
  My master was a man but of ill fame,

Who first of all a Transport thither came;
In Reppahannock county we did dwell,
Up Reppahannock river known full well,
And when the Sloop with loading home was sent
An hundred mile we up the river went
The weather cold and very hard my fare,
My lodging on the deck both hard and bare.
At last to my new master's house I came,
At the town of Wicocc[o]moco[3] call'd by name,
Where my Europian clothes were took from me,
Which never after I again could see.
A canvas shirt and trowsers then they gave,
With a hop-sack frock in which I was to slave:
No shoes nor stockings had I for to wear,
Nor hat, nor cap, both head and feet were bare.
Thus dress'd into the Field I nex[t] must go,
Amongst tobacco plants all day to hoe,
At day break in the morn our work begun,
And so held to the setting of the Sun.
My fellow slaves were just five Transports more,
With eighteen Negroes, which is twenty four:
Besides four transport women in the house,
To wait upon his daughter and his Spouse.
We and the Negroes both alike did fare,
Of work and food we had an equal share;
But in a piece of ground we call our own,
The food we eat first by ourselves were sown,
No other time to us they would allow,
But on a Sunday we the same must do:
Six days we slave for our master's good,
The seventh day is to produce our food.
Sometimes when that a hard days work we've done,
Away unto the mill we must be gone;
Till twelve or one o'clock a grinding corn,
And must be up by daylight in the morn.
And if you run in debt with any one,
It must be paid before from thence you come;
For in publick places they'll put up your name,
That every one their just demands may claim.
And if we offer for to run away,
For every hour we must serve a day;
For every day a Week, They're so severe,

[3]Wicomico was a seventeenth-century Virginia location, but it was not in Rappahannock County, as the narrator claims, but in the adjoining county of Northumberland.

For every week a month, for every month a year
But if they murder, rob or steal when there,
Then straightway hang'd, the Laws are so severe;
For by the Rigour of that very law
They're much kept under and to stand in awe.

Part IV

At length, it pleased God I sick did fall
But I no favour could receive at all,
For I was Forced to work while I could stand,
Or hold the hoe within my feeble hands.
   Much hardships then in deed I did endure,
No dog was ever nursed so I'm sure,
More pity the poor Negroe slaves bestowed
Than my inhuman brutal master showed.
   Oft on my knees the Lord I did implore,
To let me see my native land once more;
For through God's grace my life I would amend
And be a comfort to my dearest friends.
   Helpless and sick and being left alone,
I by myself did use to make my moan;
And think upon my former wicked ways,
How they had brought me to this wretched case.
   The Lord above who saw my Grief and smart,
Heard my complaint and knew my contrite heart,
His gracious Mercy did to me afford,
My health again was unto me restor'd.
   It pleas'd the Lord to grant me so much Grace,
That tho' I was in such a barbarous place,
I serv'd the Lord with fervency and zeal,
By which I did much inward comfort feel.
   Thus twelve long tedious years did pass away,
And but two more by law I had to stay:
When Death did for my cruel Master call,
But that was no relief to us at all.
   The Widow would not the Plantation hold,
So we and that were both for to be sold,
A lawyer rich who at James-Town did dwell,
Came down to view it and lik'd it very well.
   He bought the Negroes who for life were slaves,
But no transported Fellons would he have,
So we were put like Sheep into a fold,
There unto the best bidder to be sold.

Part V

A Gentleman who seemed something grave,
Unto me said, how long are you to slave;
Not two years quite, I unto him reply'd,
That is but very short indeed he cry'd.
He ask'd my Name, my trade, and whence I came
And what vile Fate had brought me to that shame?
I told him all at which he shook his head,
I hope you have seen your folly now, he said,
I told him yes and truly did repent,
But that which made me most of all relent
That I should to my parents prove so vile,
I being their darling and their only child.
He said no more but from me short did turn,
While from my Eyes the tears did trinkling run,
To see him to my overseer go,
But what he said to him I do not know.
He straightway came to me again,
And said no longer here you must remain,
For I have bought you of that Man said he,
Therefore prepare yourself to come with me.
I with him went with heart oppressed with woe,
Not knowing him, or where I was to go;
But was surprised very much to find,
He used me so tenderly and kind.
He said he would not use me as a slave,
But as a servant if I well behav'd;
And if I pleased him when my time expir'd,
He'd send me home again if I required.
My kind new master did at James Town dwell;
By trade a Cooper,[4] and liv'd very well:
I was his servant on him to attend,
Thus God, unlook'd for raised me up a friend.

Part VI

Thus did I live in plenty and at ease,
Having none but my master for to please,
And if at any time he did ride out,
I with him rode the country round about.

[4]A craftsman who makes and repairs wooden vessels formed of staves and hoops, such as casks, buckets, and tubs.

And in my heart I often cry'd to see,
So many transport fellons there to be;
Some who in England had lived fine and brave,
Were like old Horses forced to drudge and slave.
At length my fourteen years expired quite,
Which fill'd my very soul with fond delight;
To think I shoud no longer there remain,
But to old England once return again.
My master for me did express much love,
And as good as his promise to me prov'd:
He got me ship'd and I came home again
With joy and comfort tho' I went asham'd,
My Father and my Mother wel[l] I found,
Who to see me, with Joy did much abound:
My Mother over me did weep for Joy,
My Father cry'd once more to see my Boy;
Whom I thought dead, but does alive remain,
And is resumed to me once again;
I hope God has so wrought upon your mind,
No more wickedness you'll be inclined,
I told them all the dangers I went thro'
Likewise my sickness and my hardships too;
Which fill'd their tender hearts with sad surprise,
While tears ran trinkling from their aged eyes.
I begg'd them from all grief to refrain,
Since God had brought me to them home again,
The Lord unto me so much grace will give,
For to work for you both while I live,
My country men take warning e'er too late,
Lest you should share my hard unhappy fate;
Altho' but little crimes you here have done,
Consider seven or fourteen years to come,
Forc'd from your friends and country for to go,
Among the Negroes to work at the hoe;
In distant countries void of all relief,
Sold for a slave because you prov'd a thief.
Now young men with speed your lives amend,
Take my advice as one that is your friend:
For tho' so slight you make of it while here,
Hard is your lot when once the[y] get you there.

c. 1680s after 1750s

New Netherland

The role of the Dutch in shaping American literature and culture through their colony New Netherland (which is now commonly referred to in the singular) has long been overlooked. The interest of the United Provinces, known as the Netherlands, in America began in 1602 when they chartered the United East India Company to find a passage to the Indies and claim any unchartered territory their ships encountered along the way. In 1609, the English explorer Henry Hudson sailed a United East India ship named the *Halve Maen* (Half Moon) up the river now named after him as far as Albany and claimed the land for the Netherlands.

Although passage to India remained elusive, Hudson's voyage opened the area for a lucrative fur trade and, soon after, colonization, which began in 1624. But when settlements in the north proved unsafe due to a war between Mohawk and Mahican tribes, Peter Minuit, the director general of the newly formed Dutch West India Company, came to the newly organized province and negotiated an agreement with the indigenous people to settle the island of Manhattan in exchange for sixty guilders' worth of trinkets—the famous so-called purchase. Minuit began building Fort New Amsterdam, a settlement attractive to farmers and merchants who came, not because of religious persecution or destitution but to make their fortunes. Until Britain passed the Navigation Acts in 1651, Dutch traders traded freely with New England and Virginia and a hearty entrepreneurial spirit reigned.

New Netherland differed from New England in the remarkable diversity of its settlers. At least half of the province, which grew to about 9,000 by 1664, was not Dutch but German, Swedish, and Finnish, as well as English. A number of "half free" African slaves also lived in the area, making yearly payments to the West India Company to maintain their freedom. In 1654, a group of twenty-three Jews arrived in New Amsterdam from the New Holland colony in Brazil. They were segregated and allowed to practice their religion but not build a synagogue.

As the colony prospered, Britain maneuvered to take it over, arguing that it had prior claim to the land through John Cabot's explorations in 1498. All through the early seventeenth century, the Dutch and British regarded each other as competitors in trade and engaged in a series of wars for control of New Netherland. In 1664, Charles II officially made New Netherland a British colony and sent over a fleet to seize control. In September of that year, Director General Pieter Stuyvesant surrendered Fort Amsterdam, which was renamed Fort James, and the city of New Amsterdam and the colony were renamed New York. Although the Dutch briefly regained control of the colony in the second Anglo-Dutch war of 1665 to 1667, the land was returned to the British in 1674 and remained an important British military stronghold up to and during the Revolutionary War, until it was liberated in 1783.

Although the early literary productions of New Netherland include a rich store of poetry and prose, most of it rarely included in anthologies of American literature, we begin our section on the region with the writing of a colorful and significant figure. In his 2005 prize-winning book on the early history of New Netherland, Russell Shorto wrote that Adriaen Van der Donck's *Description of the New Netherland* (*Beschrijvinge van Nieuw-Nederlandt*) "is considered a classic of early American literature, but it has been forgotten by history [because] it was written in the language not of the eventual masters of the American colonies but of their bitter rival"—the Dutch (*The Island at the Center of the World,* 2005). The traditional exclusion of this text has led students and scholars to disregard a valuable source of information on the indigenous population and ignore the presence of one of Europe's major imperial powers in North America.

Van der Donck's *Description* gains real relevance when it is read not as the single representative of a forgotten colony but rather within the larger context of colonial cultural production. Careful comparison to Thomas Harriot and Roger Williams, whose descriptions of encounters with the New World can be found in the section on New England, for example, reveals how ethnographic descriptions and concomitant imperial attitudes develop and change over time. In this way, Van der Donck's text forms an enlightening introduction to the literature and culture of New Netherland, and an essential contribution to the canon of early American literature.

Adriaen Van der Donck (1620?–1655)

Adriaen Van der Donck's *Description* offers an account of what was one of the largest European territories in America—stretching from modern Schenectady down the Hudson River and from Martha's Vineyard along the Atlantic coast to the Delaware. After it was claimed as a province by the Netherlands in 1614, the area initially functioned as a profitable trading post rather than as a settlement colony. As a result, Dutch colonists found themselves easily outnumbered and unable to protect their holdings from frequent incursions by the English, to whom the territory was ceded in 1674. Despite the colony's brief existence, the Dutch model of imperial diplomacy and trade relations—in which the Europeans did not seek to convert the indigenous population to their way of life—influenced both the English and French. Texts from New Netherland render this contribution as well as serving as a vivid reminder of the diverse and mutable reality of colonial America.

Van der Donck's *Description* concisely depicts the specific situation of Dutch America and illustrates the larger promise and problems of New World settlement. Adriaen Van der Donck studied law in Leiden before he was hired to become *schout* (sheriff) of Rensselaerwyck, a large estate near modern Albany. After his arrival in 1641, however, he quickly quarreled with other colonial officials and eagerly assessed tracts of land that he would like to own himself, angering his employer, Van Rensselaer, who did not renew his contract after three years. Van der Donck chose to remain in the area and helped secure a peace treaty with the Mohawks in 1645. As a reward, he was granted a large tract of land of about 24,000 acres near New Amsterdam, the Dutch settlement on Manhattan Island. He became known as "the Jonckheer" (gentleman or squire), in reference to his estate and possibly his personal demeanor. His former possessions are still called by his nickname—Joncker, or Yonkers, New York.

As an independent property owner, Van der Donck joined the chorus of settlers who complained about the policies of the (Dutch) West India Company, which governed New Netherlands. By far the most educated man in Dutch America, Van der Donck perhaps felt called to keep a record of the colonists' grievances: taxes and fees were too high, trade with the Indians should be facilitated, and substantial numbers of new settlers were needed. These complaints culminated in the *Remonstrance* (*Vertoogh*), a petition presented by Van der Donck to the Dutch government to grant more power to landowners. The *Remonstrance* has sometimes—most recently by Russell Shorto in his lively narrative of New Netherland, mentioned above—been misread as a proto-democratic tract. Van der Donck's concerns, however, were more personal and financial in nature: he did not strive to institute representative government or enfranchise the average citizens of Dutch America.

Yet Parliament did not prove receptive to Van der Donck's protests: he was forbidden to leave the country and, wiling away his time in Holland, expanded his initial essay into *A Description of the New Netherland (Beschrijvinge van Nieuw-Nederlandt)*. This little book enjoyed instant popularity and was the primary source of information and inspiration for many New World land owners, most notably William Penn, who formed a Quaker settlement on the holdings named after his father—Pennsylvania. Van der Donck's luck did not improve when he was finally allowed to return to his estate. He died in 1655, probably killed by Indians during a minor military skirmish.

The *Description* is ultimately an odd mix of propaganda and complaint. It seeks to draw new settlers to the colony while inveighing against the initiatives of the West India Company that, according to Van der Donck, make life in New Netherland unbearable. The dual populist and political goals of this text aptly illustrate the complexities of the early colonial situation. Van der Donck's exhaustive catalogue of natural resources, for example, is framed by his concerns about English encroachment. Similarly, the descriptions of the Indians are, he writes, intended as "a memorial of them" for the time when "the Christians have multiplied and the natives have disappeared and melted away." Van der Donck thus describes cultures (Mahican and Mohawk) and a colony (Dutch America) that he knows will not last. His ambiguous celebration of the territory, replete with the nostalgia that is inherent in the idealized pastoral mode and tropes of noble savagery, fittingly captures the short-lived existence of New Netherland.

Joanne van der Woude
Columbia University

PRIMARY WORKS

A Description of the New Netherlands, ed. Thomas F. O'Donnell, 1968; *Remonstrance of New Netherland,* trans. E. B. O'Callaghan, 1856.

SECONDARY WORKS

Russell Shorto, *The Island at the Center of the World: The Epic Story of Dutch Manhattan and the Forgotten Colony That Shaped America,* 2005.

from A Description of the New Netherlands

from **Part I. The Land**

from When, and by Whom, New Netherlands Was First Discovered

This country was first found and discovered in the year of our Lord 1609; when, at the cost of the incorporated East India Company, a ship named the *Half-Moon* was fitted out to discover a westerly passage to the kingdom of China. This ship was commanded by Hendrick Hudson, as captain and supercargo, who was an Englishman by birth, and had resided many years in Holland, during which he had been in the employment of the East India Company. . . .

from Why This Country Is Called New Netherlands . . .

The country having been first found or discovered by the Netherlanders, and keeping in view the discovery of the same, it is named the New Netherlands. That this country was first found or discovered by the Netherlanders, is evident and clear from the fact, that the Indians or natives of the land, many of whom are still living, and with whom I have conversed, declare freely, that before the arrival of the Lowland ship, the *Half-Moon,* in the year 1609, they (the natives) did not know that there were any other people in the world than those who were like themselves, much less any people who differed so much in appearance from them as we did. Their men on the breasts and about the mouth were bare, and their women like ours, hairy; going unclad and almost naked, particularly in summer, while we are always clothed and covered. When some of them first saw our ship approaching at a distance, they did not know what to think about her, but stood in deep and solemn amazement, wondering whether it were a ghost or apparition, coming down from heaven, or from hell. Others of them supposed her to be a strange fish or sea monster. When they discovered men on board, they supposed them to be more like devils than human beings. Thus they differed about the ship and men. A strange report was also spread about the country concerning our ship and visit, which created a great astonishment and surprise amongst the Indians. These things we have frequently heard them declare, which we hold as certain proof that the Netherlanders were the first finders or discoverers and possessors of the New Netherlands. There are Indians in the country, who remember a hundred years, and if there had been any other people here before us, they would have known something of them, and if they had not seen them themselves, they would have heard an account of them from others. There are persons who believe that the Spaniards have been here many years ago, when they found the climate too cold to their liking, and again left the country; and that the maize or Turkish corn, and beans found among the Indians, were left with them by the Spaniards. This opinion or belief is improbable, as we can discover nothing of the kind from the Indians. They say that their corn and beans were received from the southern Indians, who received their seed from a people who resided still farther south, which may well be true, as the Castilians have long since resided in Florida. The maize may have been among the Indians in the warm climate long ago; however, our Indians say that they did eat roots and the bark of trees instead of bread, before the introduction of Indian corn or maize.

from Of the Limits of the New Netherlands, and How Far the Same Extend . . .

On the south side, the country is bounded by Virginia. Those boundaries are not yet well defined, but in the progress of the settlement of the country, the same will be determined without difficulty. On the northeast the New Netherlands abut upon New England, where there are differences on the subject of boundaries, which we wish were well settled. On the north, the river of Canada stretches a considerable distance, but to the northwest it is still undefined and unknown. Many of our Netherlanders have been far into the country, more than seventy or eighty miles from the river and seashore. We also frequently trade with the Indians, who come more than ten and twenty days' journey from the interior, and who have been farther off to catch beavers, and they know of no limits to the country, and when spoken to on the subject, they deem such enquiries to be strange and singular. Therefore we may safely say, that we know not how deep, or how far we extend inland. . . .

from Part II, of the Manners and Peculiar Customs of the Natives of the New Netherlands

from First—Of Their Bodily Form and Appearance, and Why We Named Them *(Wilden)* Wild Men

Having briefly remarked on the situation and advantages of the country, we deem it worth our attention to treat concerning the nature of the original native inhabitants of the land; that after the Christians have multiplied and the natives have disappeared and melted away, a memorial of them may be preserved.

Their appearance and bodily form, as well of the men as of the women, are well proportioned, and equal in height to the Netherlanders, varying little from the common size. Their limbs are properly formed, and they are sprightly and active. They can run very fast for a long time, and they can carry heavy packs. To all bodily exertions they are very competent, as far as their dispositions extend; but to heavy slavish labour the men have a particular aversion, and they manage their affairs accordingly, so that they need not labour much. . . . Their yellowness is no fault of nature; but it is caused by the heat of the scorching sun, which is hotter and more powerful in that country than in Holland, which from generation to generation has been shining on that people, and exhibits its effects stronger. Although this yellowness of the skin appears more or less on all this race, still we find very comely men and women amongst them. It is true that they appear singular and strange to our nation, because their complexion, speech and dress are so different, but this, on acquaintance, is disregarded. Their women are well favoured and fascinating. Several of our Netherlanders were connected with them before our women came over, and remain firm in their attachments. Their faces and countenances are as various as they are in Holland, seldom very handsome, and rarely very ugly, and if they were instructed as our women are, there then would be little or no difference in their qualifications. . . .

from Of the Food and Substance of the Indians

In eating and drinking the Indians are not excessive, even in their feast-days. They are cheerful and well satisfied when they have a sufficiency to support nature, and to satisfy hunger and thirst. It is not with them as it is here in Holland, where the greatest, noblest, and richest live more luxuriously than a *Calis,* or a common man; but with them meat and drink are sufficient and the same for all. Their common drink is water from a living spring or well, when it can be had, wherein they seldom fail, as in days of old. Sometimes in the season of grapes, and when they have fresh meat or fish, and are well pleased, they will press out the juice of the grapes and drink it new. They never make wine or beer. Brandy or strong drink is unknown to them, except to those who frequent our settlements, and have learned that beer and wine taste better than water. . . .

from Of Their Religion, and Whether They Can Be Brought Over to the Christian Faith

The natives are all heathen and without any religious devotions. Idols are neither known nor worshipped among them. When they take an oath they swear by the sun, which, they say, sees all things. They think much of the moon, and believe it has great influence over vegetation. Although they know all the planets from the other stars, by appropriate names, still they pay no idolatrous worship to the same, yet by the planets and other signs they are somewhat weatherwise. The offering up of prayers, or the making of any distinction between days, or any matter of the kind, is unknown among them. They neither know or say any thing of God; but they possess great fear of the devil, who they believe causes diseases, and does them much injury. When they go on a hunting or fishing excursion they usually cast a part of what is first taken into the fire, without using any ceremony on the occasion, then saying, "stay thou devil, eat thou that." They love to hear us speak of God and of our religion, and are very attentive and still during divine service and prayers, and apparently are inclined to devotion; but in truth they know nothing about it, and live without any religion, or without any inward or outward godly fear, nor do they know of any superstition or idolatry; they only follow the instilled laws of nature, therefore some suppose they can easily be brought to the knowledge and fear of God. Among some nations the word Sunday is known by the name *Kintowen.* The oldest among them say that in former times the knowledge and fear of God had been known among them, and they remark, that since they can neither read nor write, in process of time the Sunday will be forgotten, and all knowledge of the same lost. Their old men, when we reason earnestly with them on the matter, seem to feel pensive or sorrowful, but manifest no other emotions or agitations—when we reprove them for bad conduct and reason with them on its impropriety, and say that there is a God in heaven above whom they offend, their common answer is, "We do not know that God, we have never seen him, we know not who he is—if you know him and fear him, as you say you do, how does it happen that so many thieves, drunkards, and evil-doers are found among you. Certainly that God will punish you severely, because he has warned you to beware of those deeds, which he has never done to us. We know nothing about it, and therefore we do not deserve such punishment." Very seldom do they adopt our religion, nor have there been any political measures taken for their conversion. When their children are young some of them are frequently taken into our families for assistants, who are, according to opportunity, instructed in our religion, but as soon as they are grown up, and turn lovers and associate again with the Indians, they forget their religious impressions and adopt the Indian customs. The Jesuits have taken great pains and trouble in Canada to convert the Indians to the Roman Church, and outwardly many profess that religion; but inasmuch as they are not well instructed in its fundamental principles, they fall off lightly and make sport of the subject and its doctrine.

In the year 1639, when a certain merchant, who is still living with us, went into that country to trade with an Indian chief who spoke good French, after he had drank two or three glasses of wine, they began to converse on the subject of religion. The chief said that he had been instructed so far that he often said mass among the Indians, and that on a certain occasion the place where the altar stood caught fire by accident, and our people made preparations to put out the fire, which he forbade them to do, saying that God, who stands there, is almighty, and he will put out the fire himself; and we waited with great attention, but the fire continued till all that was burned up, with your almighty God himself and with all the fine things about him. Since that time I have never held to that religion, but regard the sun and moon much more, as being better than all your Gods are; for they warm the earth and cause the fruits to grow, when your lovely Gods cannot preserve themselves from the fire. In the whole country I know no more than one Indian who is firm in his religious profession, nor can any change be expected among them, as long as matters are permitted to remain as heretofore. . . .

New England

For centuries it has been argued that the motivations that brought the English Puritans to North America were primarily religious. More recently, however, social historians have speculated that the rise of Puritanism in England might have been a consequence of distinct social changes taking place there. Between 1530 and 1680, the population in England doubled; people were living longer; babies were surviving into (at least) young adulthood; childbearing less frequently resulted in the death of the mother. The dramatic demographic shift created tension in an already troubled economy: fewer consumable goods were available for more people, which brought a rise in prices, made worse as the number of workers increased and real wages dropped. Social tensions added to the problem: the well-to-do, alarmed at the rising population of the lower classes, feared what might be the disappearance of their traditional ways of life. The English Reformation was only part of the picture, albeit an important one.

The mid-sixteenth century to the mid-seventeenth century was a turbulent period of religious controversy, persecution, and civil war that climaxed in the regicide of King Charles I in 1649, the protectorate of Oliver Cromwell (leader of the Puritan parliamentary forces), and finally the restoration of the monarchy in 1660. When Henry VIII broke with the Roman Catholic Church for refusing to grant him a divorce, he established the Church of England, or Anglican Church, in 1534. For the most part, this church differed little from the Catholic Church, except that the English monarch, not the pope, was its head. Some reformers thought that Henry and his short-lived successor, Edward VI, did not go far enough. European reformers like Martin Luther (1483–1546), a German monk whose criticism of the Catholic Church in 1517 is said to have begun the Reformation, and John Calvin (1509–1564), a French cleric and lawyer who settled in Geneva and was very influential among English Protestants, argued for less ritual and fewer mediating structures like priests and Latin masses. Luther called for a "priesthood of all believers," and Calvin emphasized the total depravity of humanity and double predestination (to salvation and damnation). English Protestants, many of whom studied with Calvin in Geneva, sought greater change in the Anglican Church.

But when Mary Tudor, Henry VIII's eldest daughter, came to the throne, she returned the Church of England to papal control, and she persecuted dissenters, many of whom fled to the European continent. In 1558, her half-sister Elizabeth succeeded her and firmly re-established the Protestant church. Relative peace reigned for the rest of the century, but political and theological divisions developed when Elizabeth's successor, James I (also James VI of Scotland), the first Stuart king, and his son Charles I, came to the throne. Both kings—but especially Charles, who married the Catholic daughter of the king of Spain—were suspected of sympathizing with Catholics and of turning back the Reformation.

The Church of England was headed by the monarch and a ruling episcopacy similar in organization to the Catholic Church hierarchy. "Independents," however, rejected this top-down structure. These Protestants fell into two main groups:

Presbyterians and Congregationalists. English Presbyterians, like Scottish Presbyterians, still believed in a national church but wanted it governed by a central representative body composed of ordained and lay people. Congregationalists rejected national church governance in favor of small groups of worshipers who came together in self-governing congregations, overseen by ministers, elders, and deacons selected by the community. These "Independent" groups represented a political as well as religious threat to the centralized Church of England.

Charles's adviser William Laud, archbishop of Canterbury, advocated more elaborate church ritual and liturgy and forced nonconforming Protestant ministers to sign the Thirty-nine Articles of the Church of England, which included an acknowledgment of the divine right of the national church. Some English Protestants, like the "separatists" who fled first to Holland and then to Plymouth (William Bradford dubbed them "Pilgrims"), considered the Church of England so corrupt that it was not salvageable. Others, like the Congregationalists who later founded and settled Massachusetts Bay, believed that the Church of England could be purified from within. But because they would not "conform" to Laud's High-Church doctrine, the "Puritans" were silenced, removed from their churches, prevented from other employment, and imprisoned. Many immigrated to Massachusetts Bay Colony in the decades following its founding in 1630, and they attempted to establish a Puritan commonwealth there as a model and beacon for Old England, which was rife with economic problems and religious and civil unrest.

Religion was a daily presence in the lives of the Puritans who came to the New World. Followers of Calvin, they believed that God had predestined their souls for heaven or for hell and that even devout believers in Christ could do nothing to alter their predetermined fate. Because mere belief did not assure salvation, constant vigilance and self-examination, on the individual and communal levels, formed a necessary part of the Puritans' primary duties as Christians. With heaven the destination for only a few—the "elect," the "saints," or (following Old Testament terminology) the "chosen ones"—they believed that only those who could give a convincing narrative of their conversion and spiritual life should enter into church membership. For a time, civic privileges, like the franchise, were only open to male church members. The interior examination of one's soul thus influenced the external arena of social action. Self-questioning was, to some extent, a kind of pre-condition to social place. But even the most pious continually doubted their place with God, and many, like John Winthrop and Samuel Sewall, kept diaries in which they carefully detailed and examined everyday occurrences for signs of God's hand in their endeavors.

The common purpose of the New England Puritans surely contributed to their survival. Their later prosperity—although they considered it a sign of God's hand working favorably among them—brought about their dispersal. The community relied upon the necessary interdependence of its individuals, with the Old Testament model of the patriarch (in New England, the governor) at the head of the state and the church. Modeling their society upon the one they had left, the Puritans established a patriarchal community: just as God the father directed the endeavors of the elect church, so did the husband and father direct the activities of the family, which included not just his wife and children but his servants and slaves as well.

This patriarchal hierarchical structure in church and family, a structure founded on "Christian Charity" (the model of love that John Winthrop spoke of on board the *Arbella*), was modified by their conception of mutual consent. The covenantal nature of their faith—the belief that God had made an agreement with them by choosing them, of all other people, to come to America and they had a responsibility to uphold their end of the contract—coalesced with the covenantal relationships they established on the familial and church level. The Mayflower Compact (1620), like the Fundamental Orders of Connecticut (1639), established social systems that reflected their beliefs in covenanted communities based upon the mutual consent of those so governed. The Puritans signaled their religious and governmental goals by establishing compact towns with churches and common grounds at their centers. Their communal endeavor, their attempt to establish a "city upon a hill," required a uniformity that brought them through the most difficult times of the earliest settlement but also quashed dissent.

Not surprisingly, trouble emerged from the start. Encroachments upon the Connecticut River Valley brought a war with the Pequots, who were native to the area, in 1637. Roger Williams had warned in 1635 that England had no right to be giving away charters to lands held by Native Americans and that the Puritans had no right to impose themselves and their faith on all people. His advocacy of toleration threatened disunity, and he was banished from Massachusetts. He founded the town of Providence, known for its tolerance of all faiths, on Narragansett Bay.

Another dissenter, Anne Marbury Hutchinson, brought even greater challenge to Massachusetts Bay authorities. Arguing that the elect could communicate with God directly and get assurance of salvation, Hutchinson threatened the structure of the institutional church, because her religious assumptions denied the necessity for a minister's mediating efforts. As a midwife, she first gained many followers among the women in Massachusetts Bay. When the husbands of her women followers started to join them for Bible study in Hutchinson's home instead of in church, authorities grew uneasy. Hutchinson was brought before the General Court of Massachusetts in 1637, ostensibly because she threatened religious orthodoxy. But she threatened the patriarchal hierarchy as well. Puritans believed that all people were equal before God but that women were inferior to men because they were tainted by Eve's guilt. The magistrates who tried Anne Hutchinson commented upon her "masculine" behavior as much as they commented upon her religious beliefs. John Winthrop accused her of setting wife against husband. Another judge was more indignant: "You have stept out of your place," he adjudged, continuing, "you have rather bine a Husband than a Wife and a preacher than a Hearer; and a Magistrate than a Subject." Anne Hutchinson was expelled from Massachusetts Bay in 1637.

When it was clear that the Massachusetts Bay settlers were surviving the ordeal of colonization, greater numbers of settlers came over in what historians have called the "Great Migration" (1629–40). Some of the new colonists were Puritans; others were merchants and artisans simply bent upon making their way in the English colonies. The numbers of people emigrating combined with the increasing population (children born in New England survived in greater proportions than their counterparts in England in the seventeenth century) to require larger Puritan landholdings and a dispersal of the once centralized population. There were societal changes for Puritan and non-Puritan alike.

A key change was that fewer and fewer people wished to attend to the rigor of Puritan church discipline. By 1662, the New England clergy had established the Half-Way Covenant, which offered admission to one of two church sacraments (baptism but not the taking of the Lord's Supper) to the children of baptized church members. The Half-Way Covenant enabled those who were *born of members* who had expressed a visible sainthood—but who had not themselves experienced God's grace—to attend church sacraments. The relaxation of church rigor, it was believed, might encourage more people to attend to the state of their souls—and to attend church. For traditionalists, the introduction of the Half-Way Covenant was a doleful sign that God's chosen people were failing.

The necessity of the Half-Way Covenant, the growth of dissenting opinions, the increasingly debilitating Indian wars, and the widespread secularization—all contributed to an era of self-doubt for the Puritan patriarchy. Although it was part of the functioning of the Puritan faith that individuals continually concern themselves with their soul's state, individual self-doubt transformed into a kind of communal self-doubt. Some thought the devil had arisen in the unwary New England community. Some saw it as the chastisement of a vengeful Lord ready at any moment to strike at the failing community of saints. These various social and religious crises culminated in the Salem witch trials of the 1690s.

Some historians argue that this social upheaval resulted from the growing tensions in a land-hungry community with an overabundance of unmarried women. Others argue that the trials represented communal Puritan doubt turned into self-mutilation. By the end of the debacle, twenty-seven people were convicted of witchcraft, fifty more had "confessed," and one hundred others were imprisoned and awaiting trial. Twenty people died as accused witches. An additional two hundred had been accused but never went to trial. Public embarrassment, doubt, and collective sorrow brought a speedy end to this communal trauma, which significantly weakened the hold of traditional Puritanism in New England. By the turn of the century, a more progressive theology was taking hold in New England, and the region had transformed from a struggling colony to a populous, powerful province.

Although other narratives, like Thomas Morton's *New English Canaan* and various letters by Roger Williams, give accounts of the settlement of New England quite unflattering to the Puritans, the Puritan version dominated, as did Puritan discourse. Based upon the relative "plainness" of the Geneva Bible, which Puritans preferred to the more lyrical Anglican King James version, this discourse depended upon the themes and figures of the Old and New Testament. Thus, like the Israelites of old, Bradford's pilgrims searching for their holy city were engaged in an epic battle not just for their own survival but for the hereafter. Winthrop's band of Congregationalists, as Winthrop exhorted them on board the flagship *Arbella* during the initial crossing, "must be knit together in this work as one man," so that they could "find that the God of Israel is among us," making them "a praise and glory, that men shall say of succeeding plantations: the lord make it like that of New England."

The Puritans implemented their social and religious ideology by linking it closely to literacy and the acculturation of children, servants, slaves, and, later, Indians. Protestant theology made individuals responsible for their own spiritual progress, which depended, in some measure, upon reading the word of God. Michael Wigglesworth's bestselling epic poem, *The Day of Doom* (1662), was so popular because it offered a veritable catechism of Puritan belief in easily memorizable verses. *The Bay Psalm Book* (1640) and *The New England Primer* (earliest extant copy from 1683), both of which used the same sing-song ballad measure as Wigglesworth's poem, also promoted acculturation into Puritan values through the acquisition of literacy. A good illustration of this is the very first rhyme a child encountered in the *Primer*'s famous illustrated alphabet for the letter A: "In Adam's Fall, / We Sinned all." The message could not be clearer.

These examples illustrate as well the dominant Puritan aesthetic, which regarded the arts as subservient to the great end of religious edification and stressed content over form, order and logic over beauty and gracefulness. Distrustful of the senses and the imagination when not controlled and directed by the enlightened will, Puritan ministers like Cotton Mather cautioned their readers against the "intoxication of the Circean cup" of poetry and argued that the goal of rhetorical forms was to bring listeners or readers to a clearer understanding of divine law and so open their hearts to the saving effects of grace. The most effective "means" of grace was the voice of an inspired preacher; thus eloquence in public performance was a most valued accomplishment, especially in the form of the sermon, which Puritan ministers produced unstintingly. Sermons were also a vehicle for the airing of controversial issues, such as the sermons by Samuel Sewall and Cotton Mather on the keeping and religious education of slaves.

Music, except for religious hymns, was not encouraged, and stage plays were banned in New England until well into the eighteenth century. But everyone was reading and writing poetry, and distinctive poetic forms flourished in New England, such as the religious meditation, the acrostic and anagram, the elegy, the jeremiad. Anne Bradstreet's early poetry indicates her familiarity with Renaissance forms and literary models, as well as her sense of trespassing on male literary turf; her later poetry evolves a feminine and New World voice. Edward Taylor wrote in various forms—the meditation, the psalm paraphrase, the religious epic, the elegy—and adapted the metaphysical "wit" of English religious poets like George Herbert and John Donne to reflect a frontier landscape and a particularly Puritan aesthetic in which the very operations of language reveal the divine. His aesthetic dilemma as a Puritan poet—how can I, a fallen man, represent God's infinity—was finally inseparable from his spiritual pursuit of salvation.

The requirement for self-examination and the production of a conversion narrative for church membership attuned Puritans to their inner psychological states and encouraged the writing of journals, diaries, and especially spiritual autobiographies. By recording their experiences, Puritans could map their journeys toward salvation and read their lives and the world around them for "signs" of divine favor or disfavor. Thomas Shepard's brief autobiography provides remarkable insight into the lives of the early settlers, and Samuel Sewall's extensive journal depicts changes in New England over half a century. Winthrop's journal focuses on public events and is connected to another important prose genre of this period, history writing, exemplified by Bradford's account of Plymouth Plantation and Cotton Mather's sweeping history of New England.

Finally, the distinctly New World genre of the captivity narrative takes a particularly Puritan form in the examples by Mary Rowlandson and John Williams. Both a minister and a minister's wife fall victim to wars precipitated by European colonialism and are forced to experience life among peoples they were taught to abhor—Indians and French Catholics. Gender, race, and class are salient issues for both these writers, whose accounts struggle to square an ideologically rigid Puritan worldview with the often harsh realities of the New World.

Thomas Morton 1579?–1647?

Little is known about Morton's early life except that he became a lawyer in the "west countries" of England and married in 1621. In 1622 he first sailed to New England and in 1626 established himself as head of a trading post at Passonagessit, which he renamed "Ma-re Mount" (or, as Bradford spelled it, "Merry-mount"). There he offended the neighboring Separatist Puritan settlement by erecting a maypole and cavorting with the Indians, to whom, according to Bradford, he sold guns. He was arrested by Miles Standish, the military leader at Plymouth, and sent back to England in 1628. He returned, however, acquitted of the charges against him in 1629, but in 1630 his property at Ma-re Mount was seized or burned by Puritan authorities. He was once again banished to England where he worked with the anti-Puritan Anglican authorities in an unsuccessful attempt to undermine the Massachusetts Bay Company. He returned to New England in 1643, was imprisoned for slander by the authorities in Boston in the winter of 1644–1645, and died two years later in Maine (then part of the Massachusetts colony), where he had finally settled. His only literary work is *New English Canaan* (1637), best known for its satire of Puritans in general and the Separatists in particular.

Throughout *New English Canaan,* Thomas Morton often resorts to brief essays and loosely related anecdotes rather than constructing a continuous historical narration. The lack of narrative continuity can be attributed in large part to the generically hybrid status of the text. Although it is most often referred to by critics as a promotional tract, Morton's *New English Canaan* also read at times like a natural history, an ethnography, and a political pamphlet. In the first two sections of his three-part text, Morton follows the format adhered to by many other writers of promotional literature: he offers readers information about New England's native inhabitants and its natural resources. Echoing opinions voiced by early English explorers and colonial commentators like Thomas Harriot and Richard Hakluyt, Morton argues that New England is a valuable region inhabited by friendly natives, a region that well deserves English colonization.

In the third part of *New English Canaan,* Morton makes explicit his larger purpose in writing his tract—namely to suggest that England's colonial effort is being hampered by the Separatist colonists of Plymouth and their Puritan allies. In this section of his text, Morton offers readers an alternative version of many of the same events of 1620–30 that William Bradford recounts from an opposing point of view in his history of Plymouth Plantation. In his version, Morton tries to counter Bradford's portrayal of him as a lawless and unscrupulous troublemaker. Instead, he suggests that his various disputes with the Plymouth colonists resulted from their own intolerance and lack of respect for someone who does not adhere to their austere brand of Christianity. In so doing, Morton provides an English context within which to read his version of colonial events. Morton's English readers would have readily recognized him as a "Cavalier," a term used loosely to refer to English people who supported the authority of the king and the Church of England and opposed the political and religious reforms advocated by the Puritans.

In addition to his endorsement of the politics of the Cavaliers, Morton embraces their literary values as well. Rejecting texts written in the so-called "plain style" favored by the Puritans, Cavaliers generally preferred writing that drew attention to itself with its ornate or flowery style. The three opening dedicatory poems, written by supporters of Morton and included in the 1637 edition of the text, suggest that Morton wished to appeal to a readership that valued things explicitly literary. And by self-consciously fashioning his *New English Canaan* as a flamboyantly mock-heroic epic, Morton would have pleased just such an audience. The same can be said for Morton's other literary flourishes, such as attaching titles like those found in Jacobean comedy to his main characters. Referring to himself as "the Great Monster" and to Miles Standish as "Captain Shrimp," Morton turns his caricature of the Puritans into a parody of knightly romance in the manner of *Don Quixote.* To the extent that Morton adheres to the stylistic tastes of the Cavaliers, he reveals the ways in which American colonial writing was often produced against the backdrop of the English literary landscape.

In spite of their disagreements on political, social, and literary questions, Puritans and their opponents all agreed on the importance of the native populations in the English colonial enterprise. Morton's flattering portrayal of the native inhabitants reminds us of this fact and of the crucial role that Native Americans played in England's attempts to construct a national identity through its colonial endeavors. The English were determined to differentiate their methods from those of their Catholic rivals, especially the Spanish, who were portrayed in early exploratory accounts as using violence and coercion. Morton's repeated assertions about the humanity and civility of his Native American neighbors, therefore, had considerable appeal for English readers who hoped that their nation could achieve its colonial ambitions without using undue force. By implying that the Plymouth colonists have squandered the goodwill of the native inhabitants, Morton casts doubt on the likelihood of their achieving one of England's most publicly articulated colonial objectives—the peaceful cohabitation with, and eventual conversion of, native populations.

Even when he is not attacking the Plymouth colonists explicitly, Morton attempts to undermine their credibility by indirect means. For instance, he intends his audience to read his sympathetic portrait of the native people against his equally unflattering portrayal of the Puritans. In contrast to the "precise separatists," as he calls them, Morton shows how the Indians adhere to a natural religion supported by the virtues of hospitality to strangers and respect for authority. Instead of striving for personal wealth, they prefer to enjoy and share nature's bounty. This core of common humanity Morton shares with them and finds supported by his own Anglicanism, with its traditional celebration of saints' days, like that upon which Morton set up the infamous maypole. He asserts that the Puritans, by contrast, condemn natural pleasure, are inhospitable, respect neither king nor church tradition, and live only for what they consider the "spirit" but Morton considers private gain. Morton hopes, thereby, to convince English readers that he is better equipped to serve their national interests than are his rivals. Although he did not succeed, he produced an important and entertaining counternarrative to the prevailing Puritan version.

Kenneth Alan Hovey
University of Texas at San Antonio

Thomas Scanlan
Ohio University

PRIMARY WORK

New English Canaan, 1637.

from New English Canaan

from **Book I, Containing the originall of the Natives, their manners & Customes, with their tractable nature and love towards the English**

from **Chapter IV Of their Houses and Habitations**

. . . They use not to winter and summer in one place, for that would be a reason to make fuell scarse; but, after the manner of the gentry of Civilized natives, remoove for their pleasures; some times to their hunting places, where they remaine keeping good hospitality for that season; and sometimes to their fishing places, where they abide for that season likewise: and at the spring, when fish comes in plentifully, they have meetinges from severall places, where they exercise themselves in gaminge and playing of juglinge trickes and all manner of Revelles, which they are deligted in; [so] that it is admirable to behould what pastime they use of severall kindes, every one striving to surpasse each other. After this manner they spend their time.

from **Chapter VI Of the Indians apparrell**

. . . Mantels made of Beares skinnes is an usuall wearinge, among the Natives that live where the Beares doe haunt: they make shooes of Mose skinnes, which is the principall leather used to that purpose; and for want of such lether (which is the strongest) they make shooes of Deeres skinnes, very handsomly and commodious; and, of such deeres skinnes as they dresse bare, they make stockinges that comes within their shooes, like a stirrop stockinge, and is fastned above at their belt, which is about their middell; Every male, after hee attaines unto the age which they call Pubes, wereth a belt about his middell, and a broad peece of lether that goeth betweene his leggs and is tuckt up both before and behinde under that belt; and this they weare to hide their secreats of nature, which by no meanes they will suffer to be seene, so much modesty they use in that particular. . . .

Their women have shooes and stockinges to weare likewise when they please, such as the men have, but the mantle they use to cover their nakednesse with is much longer then that which the men use; for, as the men have one Deeres skinn, the women have two soed together at the full lenght, and it is so lardge that it trailes after them like a great Ladies trane; and in time I thinke they may have their Pages to beare them up; and where the men use but one Beares skinn for a Mantle, the women have two soed together; and if any of their women would at any time shift one, they take that which they intend to make use of, and cast it over them round, before they shifte away the other, for modesty, being unwilling to be seene to discover their nakednesse; and the one being so cast over, they slip the other from under them in a decent manner, which is to be noted in people uncivilized; therein they seeme to have as much modesty as civilized people, and deserve to be applauded for it.

Chapter VIII
Of their Reverence, and respect to age

It is a thing to be admired, and indeede made a president, that a Nation yet uncivilized should more respect age then some nations civilized, since there are so many precepts both of divine and humane writers extant to instruct more Civill Nations: in that particular, wherein they excell, the younger are allwayes obedient unto the elder people, and at their commaunds in every respect without grummbling; in all councels, (as therein they are circumspect to do their acciones by advise and councell, and not rashly or inconsiderately,) the younger mens opinion shall be heard, but the old mens opinion and councell imbraced and followed: besides, as the elder feede and provide for the younger in infancy, so doe the younger, after being growne to yeares of manhood, provide for those that be aged: and in distribution of Acctes the elder men are first served by their dispensator;[1] and their counsels (especially if they be powahs) are esteemed as oracles amongst the younger Natives.

The consideration of these things, mee thinkes, should reduce some of our irregular young people of civilized Nations, when this story shall come to their knowledge, to better manners, and make them ashamed of their former error in this kinde, and to become hereafter more duetyfull; which I, as a friend, (by observation having found,) have herein recorded for that purpose.

Chapter XVI
Of their acknowledgment of the Creation, and immortality of the Soule

Although these Salvages are found to be without Religion, Law, and King (as Sir William Alexander[2] hath well observed,) yet are they not altogether without the knowledge of God (historically); for they have it amongst them by tradition that God made one man and one woman, and bad them live together and get children, kill deare, beasts, birds, fish and fowle, and what they would at their pleasure; and that their posterity was full of evill, and made God so angry that hee let in the Sea upon them, and drowned the greatest part of them, that were naughty men, (the Lord destroyed so;) and they went to Sanaconquam, who feeds upon them (pointing to the Center of the Earth, where they imagine is the habitation of the Devill:) the other, (which were not destroyed,) increased the world, and when they died (because they were good) went to the howse of Kytan, pointing to the setting of the sonne; where they eate all manner of dainties, and never take paines (as now) to provide it.

Kytan makes provision (they say) and saves them that laboure; and there they shall live with him forever, voyd of care. And they are perswaded that Kytan is hee that makes corne growe, trees growe, and all manner of fruits.

[1]One who dispenses goods, a steward.

[2]Scottish poet and statesman (1567?–1640), who founded and colonized Nova Scotia in the 1620s.

And that wee that use the booke of Common prayer[3] doo it to declare to them, that cannot reade, what Kytan has commaunded us, and that wee doe pray to him with the helpe of that booke; and doe make so much accompt of it, that a Salvage (who had lived in my howse before hee had taken a wife, by whome hee had children) made this request to mee, (knowing that I allwayes used him with much more respect than others,) that I would let his sonne be brought up in my howse, that hee might be taught to reade in that booke: which request of his I granted; and hee was a very joyfull man to thinke that his sonne should thereby (as hee said) become an Englishman; and then hee would be a good man.

I asked him who was a good man; his answere was, hee that would not lye, nor steale.

These, with them, are all the capitall crimes that can be imagined; all other are nothing in respect of those; and hee that is free from these must live with Kytan for ever, in all manner of pleasure.

from Chapter XX
That the Salvages live a contended life

A Gentleman and a traveller, that had bin in the parts of New England for a time, when hee retorned againe, in his discourse of the Country, wondered, (as hee said,) that the natives of the land lived so poorely in so rich a Country, like to our Beggers in England. Surely that Gentleman had not time or leasure whiles hee was there truely to informe himselfe of the state of that Country, and the happy life the Salvages would leade weare they once brought to Christianity.

I must confesse they want the use and benefit of Navigation, (which is the very sinnus[4] of a flourishing Commonwealth,) yet are they supplied with all manner of needefull things for the maintenance of life and lifelyhood. Foode and rayment are the cheife of all that we make true use of; and of these they finde no want, but have, and may have, them in a most plentifull manner. . . .

Now since it is but foode and rayment that men that live needeth, (though not all alike,) why should not the Natives of New England be sayd to live richly, having no want of either? Cloaths are the badge of sinne; and the more variety of fashions is but the greater abuse of the Creature: the beasts of the forrest there doe serve to furnish them at any time when they please: fish and flesh they have in greate abundance, which they both roast and boyle.

They are indeed not served in dishes of plate[5] with variety of Sauces to procure appetite; that needs not there. The rarity of the aire, begot by the medicinable quality of the sweete herbes of the Country, alwayes procures good stomakes to the inhabitants.

I must needs commend them in this particular, that, though they buy many commodities of our Nation, yet they keepe but fewe, and those of speciall use.

They love not to bee cumbered with many utensilles, and although every proprietor knowes his owne, yet all things, (so long as they will last), are used in

[3]The book containing the liturgical services and prayers of the Church of England.

[4]Sinews.

[5]Gold or silver.

common amongst them: A bisket cake given to one, that one breakes it equally into so many parts as there be persons in his company, and distributes it. Platoes Commonwealth[6] is so much practised by these people.

According to humane reason, guided onely by the light of nature, these people leades the more happy and freer life, being voyde of care, which torments the mindes of so many Christians: They are not delighted in baubles, but in usefull things.

from Book III, Containing a description of the People that are planted there, what remarkable Accidents have happened there since they were setled, what Tenents they hould, together with the practise of their Church

from Chapter I
Of a great League made with the Plimmouth Planters after their arrivall, by the Sachem of those Territories

The Sachem of the Territories where the Planters of New England are setled, that are the first of the now Inhabitants of New Canaan, not knowing what they were, or whether they would be freindes or foes, and being desirous to purchase their freindship that hee might have the better Assurance of quiet tradinge with them, (which hee conceived would be very advantagious to him,) was desirous to prepare an ambassador, with commission to treat on his behalfe, to that purpose; and having one that had beene in England (taken by a worthlesse man out of other partes, and after left there by accident,) this Salvage[7] hee instructed how to behave himselfe in the treaty of peace; and the more to give him incouragement to adventure his person amongst these new come inhabitants, which was a thinge hee durst not himselfe attempt without security or hostage, promised that Salvage freedome, who had beene detained there as theire Captive: which offer hee accepted, and accordingly came to the Planters, salutinge them with wellcome in the English phrase, which was of them admired to heare a Salvage there speake in their owne language, and used him great courtesie: to whome hee declared the cause of his comminge, and contrived the businesse so that hee brought the Sachem and the English together, betweene whome was a firme league concluded, which yet continueth.

from Chapter V
Of a Massacre made upon the Salvages at Wessaguscus

[T]he Plimmouth men . . . came in the meane time to Wessaguscus, and there pretended to feast the Salvages of those partes, bringing with them Porke and thinges

[6]The communal society described in Plato's *Republic.*

[7]Morton has apparently conflated Squanto, the Indian who was kidnapped by Captain Thomas Hunt, with Samoset, the Indian who first greeted the Pilgrims.

for the purpose, which they sett before the Salvages. They eate thereof without suspition of any mischeife, who were taken upon a watchword given, and with their owne knives, (hanging about their neckes,) were by the Plimmouth planters stabd and slaine: one of which were hanged up there, after the slaughter. . . .

The Salvages of the Massachusetts, that could not imagine from whence these men should come, or to what end, seeing them performe such unexpected actions; neither could tell by what name properly to distinguish them; did from that time afterwards call the English Planters Wotawquenange, which in their language signifieth stabbers, or Cutthroates: and this name was received by those that came there after for good, being then unacquainted with the signification of it, for many yeares following.

from Chapter VII
Of Thomas Mortons entertainement at Plimmouth, and castinge away upon an Island

This man arrived in those parts, and, hearing newes of a Towne that was much praised, he was desirous to goe thither, and see how thinges stood; where his entertainement was their best, I dare be bould to say: for, although they had but 3. Cowes in all, yet had they fresh butter and a sallet of egges in dainty wise, a dish not common in a wildernes. There hee bestowed some time in the survey of this plantation. His new come servants, in the meane time, were tane to taske, to have their zeale appeare, and questioned what preacher was among their company; and finding none, did seeme to condole their estate as if undone, because no man among them had the guift to be in Jonas steade, nor they the meanes to keepe them in that path so hard to keepe.[8]

Our Master, say they, reades the Bible and the word of God, and useth the booke of common prayer: but this is not the meanes, the answere is: the meanes, they crie, alas, poore Soules where is the meanes? you seeme as if betrayed, to be without the meanes: how can you be stayed from fallinge headlonge to perdition? *Facilis descensus averni:*[9] the booke of common prayer, sayd they, what poore thinge is that, for a man to reade in a booke? No, no, good sirs, I would you were neere us, you might receave comfort by instruction: give me a man hath the guiftes of the spirit, not a booke in hand. I doe professe sayes one, to live without the meanes is dangerous, the Lord doth know.

By these insinuations, like the Serpent, they did creepe and winde into the good opinion of the illiterate multitude, that were desirous to be freed and gone to them, no doubdt, (which some of them after confessed); and little good was to be done one them after this charme was used: now plotts and factions how they might get loose. . . . [B]ut their Master to prevent them caused the sales and oares to be brought a shore, to make a tilt if neede should be, and kindled fire, broched that Hogshed, and caused

[8]According to Morton, the Pilgrims at Plymouth considered themselves to have preachers who had the "gifts of the spirit" and who could dispense "the means of salvation" (the word of God properly preached). Morton's company lacked such a Puritan preacher. Jonah in the Bible was the one worshipper of God in a ship full of pagans.

[9]"The descent to the underworld is easy" (Virgil, *Aeneid* 6.126).

them fill the can with lusty liqour, Claret sparklinge neate; which was not suffered to grow pale and flatt, but tipled of with quick dexterity: the Master makes a shew of keepinge round,[10] but with close lipps did seeme to make longe draughts, knowinge the wine would make them Protestants;[11] and so the plot was then at large disclosed and discovered. . . .

from Chapter XIV
Of the Revells of New Canaan

The Inhabitants of Pasonagessit, (having translated the name of their habitation from that ancient Salvage name to Ma-re Mount, and being resolved to have the new name confirmed for a memorial to after ages,) did devise amongst themselves to have it performed in a solemne manner, with Revels and merriment after the old English custome; [they] prepared to sett up a Maypole upon the festivall day of Philip and Jacob,[12] and therefore brewed a barrell of excellent beare and provided a case of bottles, to be spent, with other good cheare, for all commers of that day. And because they would have it in a compleat forme, they had prepared a song fitting to the time and present occasion. And upon Mayday they brought the Maypole to the place appointed, with drumes, gunnes, pistols and other fitting instruments, for that purpose; and there erected it with the help of Salvages, that came thether of purpose to see the manner of our Revels. A goodly pine tree of 80. foote longe was reared up, with a peare of buckshorns nayled one somewhat neare unto the top of it: where it stood, as a faire sea marke for directions how to finde out the way to mine Hoste of Ma-re Mount.[13] . . .

The setting up of this Maypole was a lamentable spectacle to the precise seperatists, that lived at new Plimmouth. They termed it an Idoll; yea, they called it the Calfe of Horeb, and stood at defiance with the place, naming it Mount Dagon;[14] threatning to make it a woefull mount and not a merry mount. . . .

There was likewise a merry song made, which, (to make their Revells more fashionable,) was sung with a Corus, every man bearing his part; which they performed in a daunce, hand in hand about the Maypole, whiles one of the Company sung and filled out the good liquor, like gammedes and Jupiter.[15]

[10]Drinking as much as his companions.

[11]Instead of "precise Seperatists" like the Pilgrims.

[12]The feast day of St. Philip and St. James, celebrated on May 1 by the Church of England.

[13]Morton's name for himself. "Host," in this case, suggests hosteler or innkeeper.

[14]The calf of Horeb was the golden figure of a calf destroyed as a false idol by Moses in Exodus 32. Dagon was the false idol of the Philistines (I Samuel 5).

[15]Ganymede is the cup-bearer of Jupiter, the king of the gods in Roman mythology.

The Songe

Cor.

Drinke and be merry, merry, merry boyes;
Let all your delight be in the Hymens[16] joyes;
Iô[17] to Hymen, now the day is come,
About the merry Maypole take a Roome.
  Make greene garlons, bring bottles out
  And fill sweet Nectar freely about.
  Uncover thy head and feare no harme,
  For hers good liquor to keepe it warme.
Then drinke and be merry, &c.
Iô to Hymen, &c.
  Nectar is a thing assign'd
  By the Deities owne minde
  To cure the hart opprest with greife,
  And of good liquors is the cheife.
Then drinke, &c.
Iô to Hymen, &c.
  Give to the Mellancolly man
  A cup or two of't now and than;
  This physick will soone revive his bloud,
  And make him be of a merrier moode.
Then drinke, &c.
Iô to Hymen, &c.
  Give to the Nymphe thats free from scorne
  No Irish stuff[18] nor Scotch over worne.
  Lasses in beaver coats come away,
  Yee shall be welcome to us night and day.
To drinke and be merry &c.
Iô to Hymen, &c.

This harmeles mirth made by younge men, (that lived in hope to have wifes brought over to them, that would save them a laboure to make a voyage to fetch any over,) was much distasted of the precise Seperatists, that keepe much a doe about the tyth of Muit and Cummin,[19] troubling their braines more than reason would require about things that are indifferent: and from that time sought occasion against my honest Host of Ma-re Mount, to overthrow his ondertakings and to destroy his plantation quite and cleane. . . .

[16]Hymen is the Roman god of marriage.

[17]A Latin word meaning "hurrah," generally used in celebrations of Hymen.

[18]Cloth.

[19]The Pharisees are accused in Matthew 23:23 of paying "tithe of mint and anise and cummin" while omitting "weightier matters of the law, judgment, mercy, and faith."

Some of them affirmed that the first institution [of the Maypole] was in memory of a whore; not knowing that it was a Trophe erected at first in honor of Maja, the Lady of learning which they despise, vilifying the two universities[20] with uncivile termes, accounting what is there obtained by studdy is but unnecessary learning; not considering that learninge does inable mens mindes to converse with eliments of a higher nature then is to be found within the habitation of the Mole.

Chapter XV
Of a great Monster supposed to be at Ma-re-Mount; and the preparation made to destroy it

The Seperatists, envying the prosperity and hope of the Plantation at Ma-re Mount, (which they perceaved beganne to come forward, and to be in a good way for gaine in the Beaver trade,) conspired together against mine Host especially, (who was the owner of that Plantation,) and made up a party against him; and mustred up what aide they could, accounting of him as a great Monster.

Many threatening speeches were given out both against his person and his Habitation, which they divulged should be consumed with fire: And taking advantage of the time when his company, (which seemed little to regard theire threats,) were gone up into the Inlands to trade with the Salvages for Beaver, they set upon my honest host at a place called Wessaguscus, where, by accident, they found him. The inhabitants there were in good hope of the subvertion of the plantation at Mare Mount, (which they principally aymed at;) and the rather because mine host was a man that indeavoured to advaunce the dignity of the Church of England; which they, (on the contrary part,) would laboure to vilifie with uncivile termes: enveying against the sacred booke of common prayer, and mine host that used it in a laudable manner amongst his family, as a practise of piety.

There hee would be a meanes to bringe sacks to their mill, (such is the thirst after Beaver,) and helped the conspiratores to surprise mine host, (who was there all alone;) and they chardged him, (because they would seeme to have some reasonable cause against him to sett a glosse upon their mallice,) with criminall things; which indeede had beene done by such a person, but was of their conspiracy; mine host demaunded of the conspirators who it was that was author of that information, that seemed to be their ground for what they now intended. And because they answered they would not tell him, hee as peremptorily replyed, that hee would not say whether he had, or he had not done as they had bin informed.

The answere made no matter, (as it seemed,) whether it had bin negatively or affirmatively made; for they had resolved what hee should suffer, because, (as they boasted,) they were now become the greater number: they had shaked of their shackles of servitude, and were become Masters, and masterles people.

It appeares they were like beares whelpes in former time, when mine hosts plantation was of as much strength as theirs, but now, (theirs being stronger,) they, (like overgrowne beares,) seemed monsterous. In breife, mine host must indure to be their prisoner untill they could contrive it so that they might send him for England, (as

[20]Oxford and Cambridge.

they said,) there to suffer according to the merrit of the fact which they intended to father upon him; supposing, (belike,) it would proove a hainous crime.

Much rejoycing was made that they had gotten their capitall enemy, (as they concluded him;) whome they purposed to hamper in such sort that hee should not be able to uphold his plantation at Ma-re Mount.

The Conspirators sported themselves at my honest host, that meant them no hurt, and were so joccund that they feasted their bodies, and fell to tippeling as if they had obtained a great prize; like the Trojans when they had the custody of Hippeus pinetree horse.[21]

Mine host fained greefe, and could not be perswaded either to eate or drinke; because hee knew emptines would be a meanes to make him as watchfull as the Geese kept in the Roman Cappitall:[22] whereon, the contrary part, the conspirators would be so drowsy that hee might have an opportunity to give them a slip, insteade of a tester.[23] Six persons of the conspiracy were set to watch him at Wessaguscus: But hee kept waking; and in the dead of night, (one lying on the bed for further suerty,) up gets mine Host and got to the second dore that he was to passe, which, notwithstanding the lock, hee got open, and shut it after him with such violence that it affrighted some of the conspirators.

The word, which was given with an alarme, was, ô he's gon, he's gon, what shall wee doe, he's gon! The rest, (halfe a sleepe,) start up in a maze, and, like rames, ran theire heads one at another full butt in the darke.

Theire grande leader, Captaine Shrimp,[24] tooke on most furiously and tore his clothes for anger, to see the empty nest, and their bird gone.

The rest were eager to have torne theire haire from theire heads; but it was so short that it would give them no hold.[25] Now Captaine Shrimp thought in the losse of this prize, (which hee accoumpted his Master peece,) all his honor would be lost for ever.

In the meane time mine Host was got home to Ma-re Mount through the woods, eight miles round about the head of the river Monatoquit that parted the two Plantations, finding his way by the helpe of the lightening, (for it thundered as hee went terribly;) and there hee prepared powther, three pounds dried, for his present imployement, and foure good gunnes for him and the two assistants left at his howse, with bullets of severall sizes, three hounderd or there-abouts, to be used if the conspirators should pursue him thether: and these two persons promised theire aides in the quarrell, and confirmed that promise with health in good rosa solis.[26]

Now Captaine Shrimp, the first Captaine in the Land, (as hee supposed,) must doe some new act to repaire this losse, and, to vindicate his reputation, who had

[21]The famous wooden horse made by Epeius (incorrectly called Hippeus, "horseman"). The Trojans welcomed it into their city, unaware that it was filled with Greek soldiers, and they lost the Trojan War as a result.

[22]According to the Roman historian Livy, the squawking of geese in the Capitol warned the citizens of Rome that enemies were approaching while they slept and, thereby saved the city.

[23]"The slip, instead of a tip." A tester is a British coin of the sixteenth century.

[24]Miles Standish.

[25]Some Puritans wore their hair short and went without wigs; they were sometimes called "Round-heads."

[26]Cordial made of spirits (usually brandy) with spice and sugar.

sustained blemish by this oversight, begins now to study, how to repaire or survive his honor: in this manner, callinge of Councell, they conclude.

Hee takes eight persons more to him, and, (like the nine Worthies of New Canaan,) they imbarque with preparation against Ma-re-Mount, where this Monster of a man, as theire phrase was, had his denne; the whole number, had the rest not bin from home, being but seaven, would have given Captaine Shrimpe, (a quondam Drummer,) such a wellcome as would have made him wish for a Drume as bigg as Diogenes tubb,[27] that hee might have crept into it out of sight.

Now the nine Worthies are approached, and mine Host prepared: having intelligence by a Salvage, that hastened in love from Wessaguscus to give him notice of their intent.

One of mine Hosts men prooved a craven: the other had prooved his wits[28] to purchase a little valoure, before mine Host had observed his posture.

The nine worthies comming before the Denne of this supposed Monster, (this seaven headed hydra, as they termed him,) and began, like Don Quixote against the Windmill, to beate a parly, and to offer quarter, if mine Host would yeald; for they resolved to send him for England; and bad him lay by his armes.

But hee, (who was the Sonne of a Souldier,) having taken up armes in his just defence, replyed that hee would not lay by those armes, because they were so needefull at Sea, if hee should be sent over. Yet, to save the effusion of so much worty bloud, as would have issued out of the vaynes of these 9. worthies of New Canaan, if mine Host should have played upon them out at his port holes, (for they came within danger like a flocke of wild geese, as if they had bin tayled one to another, as coults to be sold at a faier,) mine Host was content to yeelde upon quarter; and did capitulate with them in what manner it should be for more certainety, because hee knew what Captaine Shrimpe was.

Hee expressed that no violence should be offered to his person, none to his goods, nor any of his Howsehold: but that hee should have his armes, and what els was requisit for the voyage: which theire Herald retornes, it was agreed upon, and should be performed.

But mine Host no sooner had set open the dore, and issued out, but instantly Captaine Shrimpe and the rest of the worties stepped to him, layd hold of his armes, and had him downe: and so eagerly was every man bent against him, (not regarding any agreement made with such a carnall man,) that they fell upon him as if they would have eaten him: some of them were so violent that they would have a slice with scabbert, and all for haste; untill an old Souldier, (of the Queenes, as the Proverbe is,) that was there by accident, clapt his gunne under the weapons, and sharply rebuked these worthies for their unworthy practises. So the matter was taken into more deliberate consideration.

Captaine Shrimpe, and the rest of the nine worthies, made themselves, (by this outragious riot,) Masters of mine Host of Ma-re Mount, and disposed of what hee had at his plantation.

[27]Diogenes, the ancient Greek philosopher, is supposed to have made his home in a tub.
[28]Gotten drunk.

This they knew, (in the eye of the Salvages,) would add to their glory, and diminish the reputation of mine honest Host; whome they practised to be ridd of upon any termes, as willingly as if hee had bin the very Hidra of the time.

Chapter XVI
How the 9. worthies put mine Host of Ma-re-Mount into the inchaunted Castle at Plimmouth, and terrified him with the Monster Briareus[29]

The nine worthies of New Canaan having now the Law in their owne hands, (there being no generall Governour in the Land; nor none of the Seperation that regarded the duety they owe their Soveraigne, whose naturall borne Subjects they were, though translated out of Holland, from whence they had learned to worke all to their owne ends, and make a great shewe of Religion, but no humanity,) for they were now to sit in Counsell on the cause.

And much it stood mine honest Host upon to be very circumspect, and to take Eacus[30] to taske; for that his voyce was more allowed of then both the other: and had not mine Host confounded all the arguments that Eacus could make in their defence, and confuted him that swaied the rest, they would have made him unable to drinke in such manner of merriment any more. So that following this private counsell, given him by one that knew who ruled the rost, the Hiracano ceased that els would split his pinace.

A conclusion was made and sentence given that mine Host should be sent to England a prisoner. But when hee was brought to the shipps for that purpose, no man durst be so foole hardy as to undertake carry him. So these Worthies set mine Host upon an Island, without gunne, powther, or shot or dogge or so much as a knife to get any thinge to feede upon, or any other cloathes to shelter him with at winter then a thinne suite which hee had one at that time. Home hee could not get to Ma-re-Mount. Upon this Island hee stayed a moneth at least, and was releeved by Salvages that tooke notice that mine Host was a Sachem of Passonagessit, and would bringe bottles of strong liquor to him, and unite themselves into a league of brother hood with mine Host; so full of humanity are these infidels before those Christians.

From this place for England sailed mine Host in a Plimmouth shipp, (that came into the Land to fish upon the Coast,) that landed him safe in England at Plimmouth: and hee stayed in England untill the ordinary time for shipping to set forth for these parts, and then retorned: Noe man being able to taxe him of any thinge.

But the Worthies, (in the meane time,) hoped they had bin ridd of him.

1637

[29]The hundred-armed monster that, according to Roman myth, fought the Titans and guarded hell.

[30]One of the three judges of the underworld in Greek mythology, here used to refer to one of the leaders of Plymouth, probably Thomas Fuller.

John Winthrop 1588–1649

At the time of John Winthrop's birth in Groton, England, the *Mayflower* had not yet departed for the New World, but the economic and religious upheavals of the coming years would spawn a large emigration of people (not all Puritans) to New England. At the age of fourteen, Winthrop entered Trinity College, and within only two years he married the first of four wives. By eighteen, he was a justice of the peace and shortly thereafter a steward for the manor on which he had been raised—a job that provided him with the administrative skills that would serve him well in New England. His "wild and dissolute" boyhood, as he would later describe it, soon gave way to austere self-abasement and "an insatiable thirst" to know God, a thirst that would shape not only his own private life but his conception of civil government. As governor of the Massachusetts Bay Colony for twelve of the nineteen years during which he lived there, Winthrop was integral in influencing—and recording—the social, political, and religious growth of the colony.

Although he was not personally oppressed by the economic hardships that had befallen England by the 1620s (he was one of a few thousand wealthy men in England), he was nonetheless distressed at the economic and religious conditions around him. As early as 1622 Winthrop had referred to England as "this sinfull land," plagued by poverty, unemployment, inequitable taxation, and a bureaucratic legal system. Later he would write that "this Land grows weary of her Inhabitants," and continue with a blistering attack against the religious and educational systems of England. Furthermore, the monarchy in England was becoming increasingly hostile to Puritanism, favoring instead Catholicism, which resulted in the silencing of many ministers who refused to conform.

However, it seems as if Winthrop's decision to depart for the New World was rather sudden. Only in the Cambridge Agreement of 1629, made less than a year before the *Arbella* set sail, did the Congregationalist Puritans officially decide to plant a colony in New England. The charter, which granted the Massachusetts Bay Company the right to settle in New England, is unique in that no provision was made for a designated meeting place for the administration of the company, thus freeing it to establish a government in New England. The company was lucky to have been granted such a liberal charter, since only six days after it was officially granted, King Charles dissolved Parliament. Winthrop was elected governor of the company in 1629, and he left, with nearly four hundred other people, for New England aboard the *Arbella* the following year.

Winthrop envisioned "a city of God" as the Utopian foundation for the new society that he and his fellow Puritans would be building, and he fully expected that the hardships they would face in the wilderness would test their sainthood. This new land would be an opportunity for the Puritans, according to Winthrop, to *practice* what had only been *professed* in England. He longed for the transformation of abstract Christian ideals into concrete gestures that would pervade daily living. Yet this new land, however fertile for spiritual rejuvenation, was also a wellspring of new temptations. Although wealth was certainly one indicator of status in the Puritan community, it was also a source of conflict for the Puritans in New England, who struggled to reconcile God, commerce, and individualism. Although the new society would extol charity and a strong sense of community, Winthrop did not hesitate to note that God designated that "some must be rich some poor, some high and eminent in power and dignitie; others mean and in subjection." This conflict between the physical and incorporeal reflects the paradoxical Puritan conception of freedom and authority. In 1645, responding to charges that he had exceeded the powers of his office, Winthrop delivered in his own defense a speech that epitomizes this struggle in Puritan religious and political thought. In it, he deftly distinguished between natural and civil liberties, designating the former as the ability to do evil as well as good—a trait he felt the colonists had in common with "the beasts"—and the latter as the liberty to do what is "good, just, and honest." He argued that this second form of liberty cannot exist without authority. Having chosen to live under this authority (of either Christ or the magistrates in the colony), the colonists must obey.

Perhaps the most formidable challenge that Winthrop, as well as the entire Puritan oligarchy, would face was the threat posed by Anne Hutchinson, whom Winthrop described in his journal as "a woman of ready wit and bold spirit." In what would later become known as the Antinomian controversy, Hutchinson, who had been influenced by John Cotton, argued that good works were no indication of God's favor. And since the elect were guaranteed salvation, the church's mediating role between God and man was obsolete. In her home she held religious meetings, which were quite popular. Her interpretation of the Covenant of Grace threatened the religious and patriarchal hierarchy since it could have led to the collapse of distinctions of birth, education, and wealth. For a while little was done to stop Hutchinson, and a plurality of openly expressed ideas abounded in Boston. Along with her compatriots, she was soon censured, however, and banished from Boston.

A *Modell of Christian Charity,* a sermon probably delivered at Southampton before the departure of the fleet, is perhaps one of Winthrop's more famous writings—important because it eloquently forwards a spiritual blueprint of sorts for the "city upon a Hill." Written as a series of questions, answers, and objections, a rhetorical maneuver that reflects Winthrop's legal training, the sermon was, in part, a plea for a real *community* in which "the care of the public must oversway all private respects" and in which its inhabitants must "bear one another's burthens." In a more immediate sense, however, it also served to assuage tensions among the tired, waterbound passengers of the *Arbella.*

Although Winthrop's journal, which he began aboard the *Arbella,* is historically significant because it charts the Puritans' progress in the New World, it is perhaps even more significant because it charts Puritan thought. Much of what we know about the colony's social, political, and religious strata comes from Winthrop's journal. And America's first flirtations with democracy, indeed America's eventual conception of liberty itself, are rooted in the conflicts and contradictions of Puritan thinking, reflected in the writings of John Winthrop.

Nicholas D. Rombes, Jr.
University of Detroit Mercy

PRIMARY WORKS

A. Forbes, ed., *The Winthrop Papers,* 1929–45; Richard S. Dunn and Laetitia Yeandle, eds., *The Journal of John Winthrop, 1630–1649,* 1996.

from A Modell of Christian Charity[1]

Christian Charitie

A Modell Hereof

God Almightie in his most holy and wise providence hath soe disposed of the Condicion of mankinde, as in all times some must be rich some poore, some highe and eminent in power and dignitie; others meane and in subjeccion.

The Reason Hereof

1. REAS: *First,* to hold conformity with the rest of his workes, being delighted to shewe forthe the glory of his wisdome in the variety and differance of the Creatures and the glory of his power, in ordering all these differences for the preservacion and good of the whole, and the glory of his greatnes that as it is the glory of princes to have many officers, soe this great King will have many Stewards counting himselfe more honoured in dispenceing his guifts to man by man, then if hee did it by his owne immediate hand.

2. REAS: *Secondly,* That he might have the more occasion to manifest the worke of his Spirit: first, upon the wicked in moderateing and restraineing them: soe that the riche and mighty should not eate upp the poore, nor the poore, and dispised rise upp against theire superiours, and shake off theire yoake; 2ly in the regenerate in exerciseing his graces in them, as in the greate ones, theire love mercy, gentlenes, temperance etc., in the poore and inferiour sorte, theire faithe patience, obedience etc:

3. REAS: Thirdly, That every man might have need of other, and from hence they might be all knitt more nearly together in the Bond of brotherly affeccion: from hence it appeares plainely that noe man is made more honourable then another or more wealthy etc., out of any perticuler and singuler respect to himselfe but for the glory of his Creator and the Common good of the Creature, Man; Therefore God still reserves the propperty of these guifts to himselfe as Ezek: 16. 17. he there calls wealthe his gold and his silver etc.[2] Prov: 3. 9. he claimes theire service as his due honour the Lord with thy riches etc.[3] All men being thus (by divine providence) rancked into two sortes, riche and poore; under the first, are comprehended all such as are able to live comfortably by theire owne meanes duely improved; and all others are poore according to the former distribution. There are two rules whereby wee are to walke one towards another: JUSTICE and MERCY. These are allwayes distinguished

[1]Although it was thought that Winthrop preached his lay sermon aboard the *Arbella,* some time before the colonists set foot on America, recent scholarship argues that he delivered it at Southampton on the eve of the departure. The text is taken from *The Winthrop Papers,* ed. A. Forbes. The manuscript of the sermon seems to have been circulated widely during Winthrop's lifetime.

[2]"Thou hast also taken thy fair jewels of my gold and my silver, which I had given thee, and madest to thyself images of men, and didst commit whoredom with them."

[3]"Honor the Lord with thy substance, and with the first fruits of all thine increase: so shall thy barns be filled with plenty, and thy presses burst out with new wine."

in theire Act and in theire object, yet may they both concurre in the same Subject in eache respect; as sometimes there may be an occasion of shewing mercy to a rich man, in some sudden danger of distresse, and allsoe doeing of meere Justice to a poor man in regard of some perticuler contract etc. There is likewise a double Lawe by which wee are regulated in our conversacion one towardes another: in both the former respects, the lawe of nature and the lawe of grace, or the morrall lawe or the lawe of the gospell, to omitt the rule of Justice as not propperly belonging to this purpose otherwise then it may fall into consideracion in some perticuler Cases: By the first of these lawes man as he was enabled soe withall [is] commaunded to love his neighbour as himselfe;[4] upon this ground stands all the precepts of the morrall lawe, which concernes our dealings with men. To apply this to the works of mercy this lawe requires two things first that every man afford his help to another in every want or distresse. Secondly, That hee performe this out of the same affeccion, which makes him carefull of his owne good according to that of our Saviour Math: [7.12] Whatsoever ye would that men should doe to you.[5] This was practised by Abraham and Lott in entertaineing the Angells and the old man of Gibea.[6]

The Lawe of Grace or the Gospell hath some differance from the former as in these respectes, first the lawe of nature was given to man in the estate of innocency; this of the gospell in the estate of regeneracy:[7] 2ly, the former propounds one man to another, as the same fleshe and Image of god, this as a brother in Christ allsoe, and in the Communion of the same spirit and soe teacheth us to put a difference betweene Christians and others. Doe good to all especially to the household of faith; upon this ground the Israelites were to putt a difference betweene the brethren of such as were strangers though not of the Canaanites.[8] 3ly. The Lawe of nature could give noe rules for dealeing with enemies for all are to be considered as freinds in the estate of innocency, but the Gospell commaunds love to an enemy. proofe. If thine Enemie hunger feede him; Love your Enemies doe good to them that hate you Math: 5.44.

This Lawe of the Gospell propoundes likewise a difference of seasons and occasions: there is a time when a christian must sell all and give to the poore as they did in the Apostles times.[9] There is a tyme allsoe when a christian (though they give not all yet) must give beyond theire abillity, as they of Macedonia. Cor:2.6. likewise community of perills calls for extraordinary liberallity and soe doth Community in some speciall service for the Churche. Lastly, when there is noe other meanes whereby our Christian brother may be releived in this distresse, wee must help him beyond our

[4]Matthew 5:43; 19:19.

[5]"All things therefore whatsoever ye would that men should do unto you even so do ye also unto them: for this is the law of the prophets" (Matthew 7:12).

[6]Genesis 18:1–2 tells of Abraham's entertainment of the angels. Lot, Abraham's nephew, defended two angels against a mob and thus escaped the destruction of the city of Sodom (Genesis 19:1–14). In Judges 19:16–21, an old citizen of Gibeah sheltered a Levite or traveling priest, defending him from enemies.

[7]In the Garden of Eden, mankind was naturally innocent; when Adam and Eve fell from innocence, they entered an unregenerate state. Mankind was redeemed from sin when Christ came, offering salvation to those who would believe. Those who believed in Christ became regenerate and were saved.

[8]Canaan was the Israelites' promised land.

[9]Luke 18:22.

ability, rather then tempt God, in putting him upon help by miraculous or extraordinary meanes.

This duty of mercy is exercised in the kindes, Giveing, lending, and forgiveing. . . .

Haveing allready sett forth the practise of mercy according to the rule of gods lawe, it will be usefull to lay open the groundes of it allsoe being the other parte of the Commaundement and that is the affeccion from which this exercise of mercy must arise, the Apostle tells us that this love is the fullfilling of the lawe,[10] not that it is enough to love our brother and soe noe further; but in regard of the excellency of his partes giveing any motion to the other as the Soule to the body and the power it hath to sett all the faculties on worke in the outward exercise of this duty as when wee bid one make the clocke strike he doth not lay hand on the hammer which is the immediate instrument of the sound but setts on worke the first mover or maine wheele, knoweing that will certainely produce the sound which hee intends; soe the way to drawe men to the workes of mercy is not by force of Argument from the goodnes or necessity of the worke, for though this course may enforce a rationall minde to some present Act of mercy as is frequent in experience, yet it cannot worke such a habit in a Soule as shall make it prompt upon all occasions to produce the same effect but by frameing these affeccions of love in the hearte which will as natively bring forthe the other, as any cause doth produce the effect.

The diffinition which the Scripture gives us of love is this Love is the bond of perfection.[11] First, it is a bond, or ligament. 2ly, it makes the worke perfect. There is noe body but consistes of partes and that which knitts these partes together gives the body its perfeccion, because it makes eache parte soe contiguous to other as thereby they doe mutually participate with eache other, both in strengthe and infirmity in pleasure and paine, to instance in the most perfect of all bodies, Christ and his church make one body: the severall partes of this body considered aparte before they were united were as disproportionate and as much disordering as soe many contrary quallities or elements but when christ comes and by his spirit and love knitts all these partes to himselfe and each to other, it is become the most perfect and best proportioned body in the world, Eph: 4. 16. "Christ, by whome all the body being knitt together by every joynt for the furniture thereof, according to the effectuall power which is in the measure of every perfeccion of partes; a glorious body without spott or wrinckle the ligaments hereof being Christ or his love for Christ is love, I John: 4. 8." Soe this definition is right; Love is the bond of perfeccion.

From hence wee may frame these Conclusions.

1 first all true Christians are of one body in Christ I. Cor. 12. 12. 13. 17. [27.] Ye are the body of Christ and members of [your] parte.

2ly. The ligamentes of this body which knitt together are love.

3ly. Noe body can be perfect which wants its propper ligamentes.

4ly. All the partes of this body being thus united are made soe contiguous in a speciall relacion as they must needes partake of each others strength and infirmity,

[10]Paul, in Romans 13:10; 9:31.

[11]Colossians 3:14. Winthrop probably used the Geneva version of the Bible, which reads "love, which is the bond of perfectnesse." Quotations in these notes are from the King James version of the Bible, which is more commonly available.

joy, and sorrowe, weale and woe. I Cor: 12. 26. If one member suffers, all suffer with it; if one be in honour, all rejoyce with it.

5ly. This sensiblenes and Sympathy of each others Condicions will necessarily infuse into each parte a native desire and endeavour, to strengthen, defend, preserve, and comfort the other.

To insist a little on this Conclusion being the product of all the former the truthe hereof will appeare both by precept and patterne i. John 3. 10. yee ought to lay downe your lives for the brethren Gal: 6. 2. beare ye one anothers burthens and soe fulfill the lawe of Christ.

For patterns wee have that first of our Saviour whoe out of his good will in obedience to his father, becomeing a parte of this body, and being knitt with it in the bond of love, found such a native sensiblenes of our infirmities and sorrowes as hee willingly yeilded himselfe to deathe to ease the infirmities of the rest of his body and soe heale theire sorrowes: from the like Sympathy of partes did the Apostles and many thousands of the Saintes lay downe theire lives for Christ againe, the like wee may see in the members of this body among themselves. 1 Rom. 9. Paule could have beene contented to have beene seperated from Christ that the Jewes might not be cutt off from the body: It is very observable which hee professeth of his affectionate part[ak]eing with every member: whoe is weake (saith hee) and I am not weake? whoe is offended and I burne not;[12] and againe. 2 Cor: 7. 13. therefore wee are comforted because yee were comforted. of Epaphroditus he speaketh Phil: 2. 30.[13] that he regarded not his owne life to [do] him service soe Phebe. and others are called the servantes of the Churche,[14] now it is apparant that they served not for wages or by Constrainte but out of love, the like wee shall finde in the histories of the churche in all ages: the sweete Sympathie of affeccions which was in the members of this body one towardes another, theire chearfullness in serveing and suffering together, how liberall they were without repineing, harbourers without grudgeing, and helpfull without reproacheing, and all from hence they had fervent love amongst them, which onely make[s] the practise of mercy constant and easie.

The next consideracion is how this love comes to be wrought; Adam in his first estate was a perfect modell of mankinde in all theire generacions, and in him this love was perfected in regard of the habit, but Adam Rent in himselfe from his Creator, rent all his posterity allsoe one from another, whence it comes that every man is borne with this principle in him, to love and seeke himselfe onely and thus a man continueth till Christ comes and takes possession of the soule, and infuseth another principle, love to God and our brother. And this latter haveing continuall supply from Christ, as the head and roote by which hee is united get the predominency in the soule, soe by little and little expells the former I John 4. 7. love cometh of god and every one that loveth is borne of god, soe that this love is the fruite of the new birthe, and none can have it but the new Creature, now when this quallity is thus formed in the soules of men it workes like the Spirit upon the drie bones Ezek. 37. [7] bone came to bone, it gathers together the scattered bones of perfect old man

[12] 2 Corinthians 11:29.

[13] In Philippians 2:25–30, Paul tells the Philippians he will send them Epaphroditus, "my brother and companion in labor."

[14] Romans 16:1.

Adam and knitts them into one body againe in Christ whereby a man is become againe a liveing soule.

The third Consideracion is concerning the exercise of this love, which is twofold, inward or outward, the outward hath beene handled in the former preface of this discourse, for unfolding the other wee must take in our way that maxime of philosophy, Simile simili gaudet or like will to like; for as it is things which are carved with disafeccion to eache other, the ground of it is from a dissimilitude or *[blank]* ariseing from the contrary or different nature of the things themselves, soe the ground of love is an apprehension of some resemblance in the things loved to that which affectes it. This is the cause why the Lord loves the Creature, soe farre as it hath any of his Image in it, he loves his elect because they are like himselfe, he beholds them in his beloved sonne: soe a mother loves her childe, because shee throughly conceives a resemblance of herselfe in it. Thus it is betweene the members of Christ, each discernes by the worke of the spirit his owne Image and resemblance in another, and therefore cannot but love him as he loves himselfe: Now when the soule which is of a sociable nature findes any thing like to it selfe, it is like Adam when Eve was brought to him, shee must have it one with herselfe this is fleshe of my fleshe (saith shee) and bone of my bone shee conceives a greate delighte in it, therefore shee desires nearenes and familiarity with it: shee hath a greate propensity to doe it good and receives such content in it, as feareing the miscarriage of her beloved shee bestowes it in the inmost closett of her heart, shee will not endure that it shall want any good which shee can give it, if by occasion shee be withdrawne from the Company of it, shee is still lookeing towardes the place where shee left her beloved, if shee heare it groane shee is with it presently, if shee finde it sadd and disconsolate shee sighes and mournes with it, shee hath noe such joy, as to see her beloved merry and thriveing, if shee see it wronged, shee cannot beare it without passion, she setts noe boundes of her affeccions, nor hath any thought of reward, shee findes recompence enoughe in the exercise of her love towardes it, wee may see this Acted to life in Jonathan and David.[15] Jonathan a valiant man endued with the spirit of Christ, soe soone as hee Discovers the same spirit in David had presently his hearte knitt to him by this linement of love, soe that it is said he loved him as his owne soule, he takes soe great pleasure in him that hee stripps himselfe to adorne his beloved, his fathers kingdome was not soe precious to him as his beloved David, David shall have it with all his hearte, himselfe desires noe more but that hee may be neare to him to rejoyce in his good hee chooseth to converse with him in the wildernesse even to the hazzard of his owne life, rather then with the greate Courtiers in his fathers Pallace; when hee sees danger towards him, hee spares neither care paines, nor perill to divert it, when Injury was offered his beloved David, hee could not beare it, though from his owne father, and when they must parte for a Season onely, they thought theire heartes would have broake for sorrowe, had not theire affeccions found vent by aboundance of Teares: other instances might be brought to shewe the nature of this affeccion as of Ruthe and Naomi[16] and many others, but this truthe is cleared enough. If any shall object that it is not possible that love should be bred or upheld without hope of requitall,

[15]David and Jonathan appear in 1 Samuel 19ff.

[16]Ruth refused to leave her mother-in-law, Naomi, during a time of trouble: "For whither thou goest, I will go; and where thou lodgest, I will lodge" (Ruth 1:16).

it is graunted but that is not our cause, for this love is allwayes under reward it never gives, but it allwayes receives with advantage: first, in regard that among the members of the same body, love and affection are reciprocall in a most equall and sweete kinde of Commerce. 2ly [3ly], in regard of the pleasure and content that the exercise of love carries with it as wee may see in the naturall body the mouth is at all the paines to receive, and mince the foode which serves for the nourishment of all the other partes of the body, yet it hath noe cause to complaine; for first, the other partes send backe by secret passages a due proporcion of the same nourishment in a better forme for the strengthening and comforteing the mouthe. 2ly the labour of the mouthe is accompanied with such pleasure and content as farre exceedes the paines it takes: soe is it in all the labour of love, among christians, the partie loveing, reapes love againe as was shewed before, which the soule covetts more then all the wealthe in the world. 2ly [4ly]. noething yeildes more pleasure and content to the soule then when it findes that which it may love fervently, for to love and live beloved is the soules paradice, both heare and in heaven: In the State of Wedlock there be many comfortes to beare out the troubles of that Condicion; but let such as have tryed the most, say if there be any sweetnes in that Condicion comparable to the exercise of mutuall love.

From the former Consideracions ariseth these Conclusions.

1 First, This love among Christians is a reall thing not Imaginarie.

2ly. This love is as absolutely necessary to the being of the body of Christ, as the sinewes and other ligaments of a naturall body are to the being of that body.

3ly. This love is a divine, spirituall nature, free, active, strong, Couragious, permanent, under valueing all things beneathe its propper object, and of all the graces this makes us nearer to resemble the virtues of our heavenly father.

4ly, It restes in the love and wellfare of its beloved, for the full and certaine knowledge of these truthes concerning the nature use, [and] excellency of this grace, that which the holy ghost hath left recorded 1. Cor. 13. may give full satisfaccion which is needfull for every true member of this lovely body of the Lord Jesus, to worke upon theire heartes, by prayer, meditacion, continuall exercise at least of the speciall [power] of this grace till Christ be formed in them and they in him all in eache other knitt together by this bond of love.

It rests now to make some applicacion of this discourse by the present designe which gave the occasion of writeing of it. Herein are 4 things to be propounded: first the persons, 2ly, the worke, 3ly, the end, 4ly the meanes.

1. For the persons, wee are a Company professing our selves fellow members of Christ, In which respect onely though wee were absent from eache other many miles, and had our imploymentes as farre distant, yet wee ought to account our selves knitt together by this bond of love, and live in the exercise of it, if wee would have comforte of our being in Christ, this was notorious in the practise of the Christians in former times, as is testified of the Waldenses[17] from the mouth of one of the adversaries Aeneas Sylvius,[18] mutuo [solent amare] penè antequam norint, they use to love any of theire owne religion even before they were acquainted with them.

[17]The Waldenses were followers of Pater Valdes, an early French reformer.

[18]Aeneas Sylvius Piccolomini (1405–1464), Pope Pius II, scholar and historian.

2ly. for the worke wee have in hand, it is by a mutuall consent through a speciall overruleing providence, and a more then an ordinary approbation of the Churches of Christ to seeke out a place of Cohabitation and Consorteshipp under a due forme of Government both civill and ecclesiasticall. In such cases as this the care of the publique must oversway all private respects, by which not onely conscience, but meare Civill pollicy doth binde us; for it is a true rule that perticuler estates cannott subsist in the ruine of the publique.

3ly. The end is to improve our lives to doe more service to the Lord the comforte and encrease of the body of christe whereof wee are members that our selves and posterity may be the better preserved from the Common corrupcions of this evill world to serve the Lord and worke out our Salvation under the power and purity of his holy Ordinances.

4ly for the meanes whereby this must bee effected, they are 2fold, a Conformity with the worke and end wee aime at, these wee see are extraordinary, therefore wee must not content our selves with usuall ordinary meanes; whatsoever wee did or ought to have done when wee lived in England, the same must wee doe and more allsoe where wee goe: That which the most in theire Churches maineteine as a truthe in profession onely, wee must bring into familiar and constant practise, as in this duty of love wee must love, brotherly, without dissimulation; wee must love one another with a pure hearte fervently; wee must beare one anothers burthens; wee must not looke onely on our owne things, but allsoe on the things of our brethren; neither must wee think that the lord will beare with such faileings at our hands as hee dothe from those among whome wee have lived, and that for 3 Reasons.

1. In regard of the more neare bond of mariage, betweene him and us, wherein he hath taken us to be his after a most strickt and peculiar manner which will make him the more Jealous of our love and obedience soe he tells the people of Israell, you onely have I knowne of all the families of the Earthe therefore will I punishe you for your Transgressions.

2ly, because the lord will be sanctified in them that come neare him. Wee know that there were many that corrupted the service of the Lord some setting upp Alters before his owne, others offering both strange fire and strange Sacrifices allsoe; yet there came noe fire from heaven, or other sudden Judgement upon them as did upon Nadab and Abihu[19] whoe yet wee may thinke did not sinne presumptuously.

3ly When God gives a speciall Commission he lookes to have it stricktly observed in every Article, when hee gave Saule a Commission to destroy Amaleck hee indented with him upon certaine Articles and because hee failed in one of the least, and that upon a faire pretence, it lost him the kingdome, which should have beene his reward, if hee had observed his Commission:[20] Thus stands the cause betweene God and us, wee are entered into Covenant with him for this worke,[21] wee have

[19]"And Nadab and Abihu, the sons of Aaron, took either of them his censer, and put fire therein, and put incense thereon, and offered strange fire before the Lord, which he commanded them not. And there went out fire from the Lord, and devoured them, and they died before the Lord" (Leviticus 10:1–2). To Winthrop, punishment is greater for the chosen people than for unbelievers.

[20]Saul agreed to destroy the Amalekites and their possessions, yet he spared their sheep and oxen. Because Saul disobeyed, he was rejected as king (1 Samuel 15:1–34).

[21]A covenant is like a legal contract. God promised to protect the Israelites if they were faithful and followed His word.

taken out a Commission, the Lord hath given us leave to drawe our owne Articles wee have professed to enterprise these Accions upon these and these ends, wee have hereupon besought him of favour and blessing: Now if the Lord shall please to heare us, and bring us in peace to the place wee desire, then hath hee ratified this Covenant and sealed our Commission, [and] will expect a strickt performance of the Articles contained in it, but if wee shall neglect the observacion of these Articles which are the ends wee have propounded, and dissembling with our God, shall fall to embrace this present world and prosecute our carnall intencions, seekeing greate things for our selves and our posterity, the Lord will surely breake out in wrathe against us, be revenged of such a perjured people, and make us knowe the price of the breache of such a Covenant.

Now the onely way to avoyde this shipwracke and to provide for our posterity is to followe the Counsell of Micah, to doe Justly, to love mercy, to walke humbly with our God.[22] For this end, wee must be knitt together in this worke as one man, wee must entertaine each other in brotherly Affeccion, wee must be willing to abridge our selves of our superfluities, for the supply of others necessities, wee must uphold a familiar Commerce together in all meekenes, gentlenes, patience and liberallity, wee must delight in eache other, make others Condicions our owne, rejoyce together, mourne together, labour, and suffer together, allwayes having before our eyes our Commission and Community in the worke, our Community as members of the same body, soe shall wee keepe the unitie of the spirit in the bond of peace,[23] the Lord will be our God and delight to dwell among us, as his owne people and will commaund a blessing upon us in all our wayes, soe that wee shall see much more of his wisdome, power, goodnes, and truthe then formerly wee have beene acquainted with, wee shall finde that the God of Israell is among us, when tenn of us shall be able to resist a thousand of our enemies, when hee shall make us a prayse and glory, that men shall say of succeeding plantacions: the lord make it like that of New England: for wee must Consider that wee shall be as a City upon a Hill,[24] the eyes of all people are uppon us; soe that if wee shall deale falsely with our god in this worke wee have undertaken and soe cause him to withdrawe his present help from us, wee shall be made a story and a by-word through the world, wee shall open the mouthes of enemies to speake evill of the ways of god and all professours for Gods sake; wee shall shame the faces of many of gods worthy servants, and cause theire prayers to be turned into Cursses upon us till we be consumed out of the good land whether wee are goeing: And to Shutt upp this discourse with that exhortacion of Moses that faithfull servant of the Lord in his last farewell to Israell Deut. 30.[25] Beloved there is now sett before us life, and good, deathe and evill in that wee are Commaunded

[22]Micah 6:8; 7:9.

[23]Ephesians 4:4.

[24]"Ye are the light of the world. A city that is set on a hill cannot be hid. Neither do men light a candle, and put it under a bushel, but on a candlestick; and it giveth light unto all that are in the house" (Matthew 5:14–15).

[25]"And it shall come to pass, when all these things are come upon thee, the blessing and the curse, which I have set before thee, and thou shalt call them to mind among all the nations, whither the Lord thy God hath driven thee, and shalt return unto the Lord thy God, and shalt obey his voice according to all that I command thee this day, thou and thy children, with all thine heart, and with all thy soul; that then the Lord thy God will turn thy captivity, and have compassion upon thee, and will return and gather thee from all the nations, whither the Lord thy God hath scattered thee" (Deuteronomy 30:1–3).

this day to love the Lord our God, and to love one another to walke in his wayes and to keepe his Commaundements and his Ordinance, and his lawes, and the Articles of our Covenant with him that wee may live and be multiplyed, and that the Lord our God may blesse us in the land whether wee goe to possesse it: But if our heartes shall turne away soe that wee will not obey, but shall be seduced and worshipp other Gods our pleasures, and proffitts, and serve them; it is propounded unto us this day, wee shall surely perishe out of the good Land whether wee passe over this vast Sea to possesse it;

Therefore lett us choose life,
that wee, and our Seede,
may live; by obeyeing his
voyce, and cleaveing to him,
for hee is our life, and
our prosperity.

1838

from The Journal of John Winthrop

[July 5, 1632] At Watertown there was (in the view of divers witnesses) a great combat between a mouse and a snake; and, after a long fight, the mouse prevailed and killed the snake. The pastor of Boston, Mr. Wilson, a very sincere, holy man, hearing of it, gave this interpretation: That the snake was the devil; the mouse was a poor contemptible people, which God had brought hither, which should overcome Satan here, and dispossess him of his kingdom. Upon the same occasion, he told the governor,[1] that, before he was resolved to come into this country, he dreamed he was here, and that he saw a church arise out of the earth, which grew up and became a marvellous goodly church.

[December 27, 1633] The governor and assistants met at Boston, and took into consideration a treatise, which Mr. Williams[2] (then of Salem) had sent to them, and which he had formerly written to the governor and council of Plymouth, wherein, among other things, he disputes their right to the lands they possessed here, and concluded that, claiming by the king's grant, they could have no title, nor otherwise, except they compounded with the natives. For this, taking advice with some of the most judicious ministers, (who much condemned Mr. Williams's error and presumption,) they gave order, that he should be convented[3] at the next court, to be censured, etc. There were three passages chiefly whereat they were much offended: 1, for that he chargeth King James to have told a solemn public lie, because in his patent he blessed God that he was the first Christian prince that had discovered this land; 2, for that he chargeth him and others with blasphemy for calling Europe Christendom, or the Christian world; 3, for that he did personally apply to our present king, Charles, these three places in the Revelations, viz., [*blank*].

[1]Winthrop himself.
[2]Roger Williams (c. 1603–1683) was called to the First Church of Boston but refused the post because the Congregationalist Puritans would not separate from the Anglican Church.
[3]Summoned to appear.

Mr. Endicott being absent, the governor wrote to him to let him know what was done, and withal added divers arguments to confute the said errors, wishing him to deal with Mr. Williams to retract the same, etc. Whereto he returned a very modest and discreet answer. Mr. Williams also wrote to the governor,[4] and also to him and the rest of the council, very submissively, professing his intent to have been only to have written for the private satisfaction of the governor, etc., of Plymouth, without any purpose to have stirred any further in it, if the governor here had not required a copy of him; withal offering his book, or any part of it, to be burnt.

At the next court he appeared penitently, and gave satisfaction of his intention and loyalty. So it was left, and nothing done in it.

[January 20, 1634] Hall and the two others, who went to Connecticut November 3, came now home, having lost themselves and endured much misery. They informed us that the small pox was gone as far as any Indian plantation was known to the west, and much people dead of it, by reason whereof they could have no trade.

At Naragansett, by the Indians' report, there died seven hundred; but, beyond Pascataquack, none to the eastward.

[January 24, 1634] The governor and council met again at Boston, to consider of Mr. Williams's letter, etc., when, with the advice of Mr. Cotton[5] and Mr. Wilson, and weighing his letter, and further considering of the aforesaid offensive passages in his book, (which, being written in very obscure and implicative phrases, might well admit of doubtful interpretation,) they found the matters not to be so evil as at first they seemed. Whereupon they agreed, that, upon his retraction, etc., or taking an oath of allegiance to the king, etc., it should be passed over.

[January 11, 1636] The governor[6] and assistants met at Boston to consider about Mr. Williams, for that they were credibly informed, that, notwithstanding the injunction laid upon him (upon the liberty granted him to stay till the spring) not to go about to draw others to his opinions, he did use to entertain company in his house, and to preach to them, even of such points as he had been censured for; and it was agreed to send him into England by a ship then ready to depart. The reason was, because he had drawn above twenty persons to his opinion, and they were intended to erect a plantation about the Naragansett Bay, from whence the infection would easily spread into these churches, (the people being, many of them, much taken with the apprehension of his godliness). Whereupon a warrant was sent to him to come presently to Boston, to be shipped, etc. He returned answer, (and divers of Salem came with it,) that he could not come without hazard of his life, etc. Whereupon a pinnace[7] was sent with commission to Capt. Underhill, etc., to apprehend him, and carry him aboard the ship, (which then rode at Natascutt;) but, when they came at his house, they found he had been gone three days before; but whither they could not learn.

He had so far prevailed at Salem, as many there (especially of devout women) did embrace his opinions, and separated from the churches, for this cause, that some

[4]Edward Winslow was governor in 1633.

[5]John Cotton (1584–1652), an influential preacher in the colony, was pastor of the First Church of Boston.

[6]John Hays (1594–1654). Winthrop was re-elected governor in 1637.

[7]A small sailing boat, often used as a scout for a larger vessel.

of their members, going into England, did hear the ministers there, and when they came home the churches here held [to be in] communion with them.

[October 21, 1636] One Mrs. Hutchinson,[8] a member of the church of Boston, a woman of a ready wit and bold spirit, brought over with her two dangerous errors: 1. That the person of the Holy Ghost dwells in a justified[9] person. 2. That no sanctification can help to evidence to us our justification—From these two grew many branches; as, 1. Our union with the Holy Ghost, so as a Christian remains dead to every spiritual action, and hath no gifts nor graces, other than such as are in hypocrites, nor any other sanctification but the Holy Ghost himself.

There joined with her in these opinions a brother of hers, one Mr. Wheelwright, a silenced minister sometimes in England.

[October 25, 1636] The other ministers in the bay, hearing of these things, came to Boston at the time of a general court, and entered conference in private with them, to the end they might know the certainty of these things; that if need were, they might write to the church of Boston about them, to prevent (if it were possible) the dangers, which seemed hereby to hang over that and the rest of the churches. At this conference, Mr. Cotton was present, and gave satisfaction to them, so as he agreed with them all in the point of sanctification, and so did Mr. Wheelwright; so as they all did hold, that sanctification did help to evidence justification. The same he had delivered plainly in public, divers times; but, for the indwelling of the person of the Holy Ghost, he held that still, as some other of the ministers did, but not union with the person of the Holy Ghost, (as Mrs. Hutchinson and others did,) so as to amount to a personal union.

[November 1, 1637] There was great hope that the late general assembly would have had some good effect in pacifying the troubles and dissensions about matters of religion; but it fell out otherwise. For though Mr. Wheelwright and those of his party had been clearly confuted and confounded in the assembly, yet they persisted in their opinions, and were as busy in nourishing contentions (the principal of them) as before.

The court also sent for Mrs. Hutchinson, and charged her with divers matters, as her keeping two public lectures every week in her house, whereto sixty or eighty persons did usually resort, and for reproaching most of the ministers (viz., all except Mr. Cotton) for not preaching a covenant of free grace, and that they had not the seal of the spirit, nor were able ministers of the New Testament; which were clearly proved against her, though she sought to shift it off. And, after many speeches to and fro, at last she was so full as she could not contain, but vented her revelations; amongst which this was one, that she had it revealed to her, that she should come into New England, and should here be persecuted, and that God would ruin us and our posterity, and the whole state, for the same. So the court proceeded and banished her; but, because it was winter, they committed her to a private house, where she was well provided, and her own friends and the elders permitted to go to her, but none else.

[8]Anne Hutchinson (1591–1643), like Roger Williams, was cast out of the Massachusetts Bay Colony. With Williams's assistance, she settled on the outskirts of Providence.

[9]One chosen for salvation by God.

The court called also Capt. Underhill, and some five or six more of the principal, whose hands were to the said petition; and because they stood to justify it, they were disfranchised, and such as had public places were put from them.

The court also ordered, that the rest, who had subscribed the petition, (and would not acknowledge their fault, and which near twenty of them did,) and some others, who had been chief stirrers in these contentions, etc., should be disarmed. This troubled some of them very much, especially because they were to bring them in themselves; but at last, when they saw no remedy, they obeyed.

All the proceedings of this court against these persons were set down at large, with the reasons and other observations, and were sent into England to be published there, to the end that all our godly friends might not be discouraged from coming to us, etc.

[March, 1638] While Mrs. Hutchinson continued at Roxbury,[10] divers of the elders and others resorted to her, and finding her to persist in maintaining those gross errors beforementioned, and many others, to the number of thirty or thereabout, some of them wrote to the church at Boston, offering to make proof of the same before the church, etc., 15; whereupon she was called, (the magistrates being desired to give her license to come,) and the lecture was appointed to begin at ten. (The general court being then at Newtown, the governor[11] and the treasurer, being members of Boston, were permitted to come down, but the rest of the court continued at Newtown.) When she appeared, the errors were read to her. The first was, that the souls of men are mortal by generation, but, after, made immortal by Christ's purchase. This she maintained a long time; but at length she was so clearly convinced by reason and scripture, and the whole church agreeing that sufficient had been delivered for her conviction, that she yielded she had been in an error. Then they proceeded to three other errors: 1. That there was no resurrection of these bodies, and that these bodies were not united to Christ, but every person united hath a new body, etc. These were also clearly confuted, but yet she held her own; so as the church (all but two of her sons) agreed she should be admonished, and because her sons would not agree to it, they were admonished also.

Mr. Cotton pronounced the sentence of admonition with great solemnity, and with much zeal and detestation of her errors and pride of spirit. The assembly continued till eight at night, and all did acknowledge the special presence of God's spirit therein; and she was appointed to appear again the next lecture day.

[March 22, 1638] Mrs. Hutchinson appeared again; (she had been licensed by the court, in regard she had given hope of her repentance, to be at Mr. Cotton's house, that both he and Mr. Davenport[12] might have the more opportunity to deal with her;) and the articles being again read to her, and her answer required, she delivered it in writing, wherein she made a retractation of near all, but with such explanations and circumstances as gave no satisfaction to the church; so as she was required to speak further to them. Then she declared, that it was just with God to leave her to herself, as He had done, for her slighting His ordinances, both magistracy and ministry; and confessed that what she had spoken against the magistrates at the court (by way of revelation) was rash and ungrounded; and desired the church to pray for

[10]Near Boston.

[11]Winthrop himself.

[12]John Davenport (1597–1670), a Puritan minister.

her. This gave the church good hope of her repentance; but when she was examined about some particulars, as that she had denied inherent righteousness, etc., she affirmed that it was never her judgment; and though it was proved by many testimonies, that she had been of that judgment, and so had persisted, and maintained it by argument against divers, yet she impudently persisted in her affirmation, to the astonishment of all the assembly. So that, after much time and many arguments had been spent to bring her to see her sin, but all in vain, the church, with one consent, cast her out. Some moved to have her admonished once more; but, it being for manifest evil in matter of conversation, it was agreed otherwise; and for that reason also the sentence was denounced by the pastor, matter of manners belonging properly to his place.

After she was excommunicated, her spirits, which seemed before to be somewhat dejected, revived again, and she gloried in her sufferings, saying, that it was the greatest happiness, next to Christ, that ever befell her. Indeed, it was a happy day to the churches of Christ here, and to many poor souls, who had been seduced by her, who, by what they heard and saw that day, were (through the grace of God) brought off quite from her errors, and settled again in the truth. . . .

After two or three days, the governor sent a warrant to Mrs. Hutchinson to depart this jurisdiction before the last of this month, according to the order of court, and for that end set her at liberty from her former constraint, so as she was not to go forth of her own house till her departure; and upon the 28th she went by water to her farm at the Mount, where she was to take water, with Mr. Wheelwright's wife and family, to go to Pascataquack; but she changed her mind, and went by land to Providence, and so to the island in the Naragansett Bay, which her husband and the rest of that sect had purchased of the Indians.

[September, 1638] . . . Mrs. Hutchinson, being removed to the Isle of Aquiday, in the Naragansett Bay, after her time was fulfilled, that she expected deliverance of a child, was delivered of a monstrous birth, which, being diversely related in the country, (and, in the open assembly at Boston, upon a lecture day, [was] declared by Mr. Cotton to be twenty-seven several lumps of man's seed, without any alteration or mixture of anything from the woman, and thereupon gathered that it might signify her error in denying inherent righteousness, but that all was Christ in us, and nothing of ours in our faith, love, etc.). Hereupon the governor wrote to Mr. Clarke, a physician and a preacher to those of the island, to know the certainty thereof. . . .

[July 3 1645] Then was the deputy governor desired by the court to go up and take his place again upon the bench, which he did accordingly, and the court being about to arise, he desired leave for a little speech, which was to this effect.

> I suppose something may be expected from me, upon this charge that is befallen me, which moves me to speak now to you; yet I intend not to intermeddle in the proceedings of the court, or with any of the persons concerned therein. Only I bless God, that I see an issue of this troublesome business. I also acknowledge the justice of the court, and for mine own part, I am well satisfied, I was publicly charged, and I am publicly and legally acquitted, which is all I did expect or desire. And though this be sufficient for my justification before men, yet not so before the God, who hath seen so much amiss in my dispensations (and even in this affair) as calls me to be humble. For to be publicly and criminally charged in this court, is matter of humiliation, (and I desire to make a right use of it,) notwithstanding I be

thus acquitted. If her father had spit in her face, (saith the Lord concerning Miriam,[13]) should she not have been ashamed seven days? Shame had lien upon her, whatever the occasion had been. I am unwilling to stay you from your urgent affairs, yet give me leave (upon this special occasion) to speak a little more to this assembly. It may be of some good use, to inform and rectify the judgments of some of the people, and may prevent such distempers as have arisen amongst us. The great questions that have troubled the country, are about the authority of the magistrates and the liberty of the people. It is yourselves who have called us to this office, and being called by you, we have our authority from God, in way of an ordinance, such as hath the image of God eminently stamped upon it, the contempt and violation whereof hath been vindicated with examples of divine vengeance. I entreat you to consider, that when you choose magistrates, you take them from among yourselves, men subject to like passions as you are. Therefore when you see infirmities in us, you should reflect upon your own, and that would make you bear the more with us, and not be severe censurers of the failings of your magistrates, when you have continual experience of the like infirmities in yourselves and others. We account him a good servant, who breaks not his covenant. The covenant between you and us is the oath you have taken of us, which is to this purpose, that we shall govern you and judge your causes by the rules of God's laws and our own, according to our best skill. When you agree with a workman to build you a ship or house, etc., he undertakes as well for his skill as for his faithfulness, for it is his profession, and you pay him for both. But when you call one to be a magistrate, he doth not profess nor undertake to have sufficient skill for that office, nor can you furnish him with gifts, etc., therefore you must run the hazard of his skill and ability. But if he fail in faithfulness, which by his oath he is bound unto, that he must answer for. If it fall out that the case be clear to common apprehension, and the rule clear also, if he transgress here, the error is not in the skill, but in the evil of the will: it must be required of him. But if the case be doubtful, or the rule doubtful, to men of such understanding and parts as your magistrates are, if your magistrates should err here, yourselves must bear it.

For the other point concerning liberty, I observe a great mistake in the country about that. There is a twofold liberty, natural (I mean as our nature is now corrupt) and civil or federal. The first is common to man with beasts and other creatures. By this, man, as he stands in relation to man simply, hath liberty to do what he lists; it is a liberty to evil as well as to good. This liberty is incompatible and inconsistent with authority, and cannot endure the least restraint of the most just authority. The exercise and maintaining of this liberty makes men grow more evil, and in time to be worse than brute beasts: *omnes sumus licentia deteriores.*[14] This is that great enemy of truth and peace, that wild beast, which all the ordinances of God are bent against, to restrain and subdue it. The other kind of liberty I call civil or federal, it may also be termed moral, in reference to the covenant between God and man, in the moral law, and the politic covenants and constitutions, amongst men themselves. This liberty is the proper end and object of authority, and cannot subsist without it; and it is a liberty to that only which is good, just, and honest. This

[13]Moses' and Aaron's sister. "And the Lord said to Moses, If her father had but spit in her face, should she not be ashamed seven days? Let her be shut out from the camp seven days, and after that let her be received in again" (Numbers 12:14).

[14]We are all the worse for license.

liberty you are to stand for, with the hazard (not only of your goods, but) of your lives, if need be. Whatsoever crosseth this, is not authority, but a distemper thereof. This liberty is maintained and exercised in a way of subjection to authority; it is of the same kind of liberty wherewith Christ hath made us free. The woman's own choice makes such a man her husband; yet being so chosen, he is her lord, and she is to be subject to him, yet in a way of liberty, not of bondage; and a true wife accounts her subjection her honor and freedom, and would not think her condition safe and free, but in her subjection to her husband's authority. Such is the liberty of the church under the authority of Christ, her king and husband; his yoke is so easy and sweet to her as a bride's ornaments; and if through forwardness or wantonness, etc., she take it off, at any time, she is at no rest in her spirit, until she take it up again; and whether her lord smiles upon her, and embraceth her in his arms, or whether he frowns, or rebukes, or smites her, she apprehends the sweetness of his love in all, and is refreshed, supported, and instructed by every such dispensation of his authority over her. On the other side, ye know who they are that complain of this yoke and say, let us break their bands, etc., we will not have this man to rule over us. Even so, brethren, it will be between you and your magistrates. If you stand for your natural corrupt liberties, and will do what is good in your own eyes, you will not endure the least weight of authority, but will murmur, and oppose, and be always striving to shake off that yoke; but if you will be satisfied to enjoy such civil and lawful liberties, such as Christ allows you, then will you quietly and cheerfully submit unto that authority which is set over you, in all the administrations of it, for your good. Wherein, if we fail at any time, we hope we shall be willing (by God's assistance) to hearken to good advice from any of you, or in any other way of God; so shall your liberties be preserved, in upholding the honor and power of authority amongst you.

The deputy governor having ended his speech, the court arose, and the magistrates and deputies retired to attend their other affairs. . . .

1826

William Bradford 1590–1657

Born into a Yorkshire family of yeoman farmers, William Bradford's early misfortune must have made him more receptive to the religious fervor and sense of community that Puritanism later provided. By the age of seven, Bradford was orphaned of both parents and a grandfather, and soon was sent to live with his uncles, who raised him as a farmer. His fragile health and sense of isolation allowed him plenty of time to read his Bible, and when at the age of twelve he heard the sermons of Richard Clyfton, a nonconformist minister, Bradford felt spiritually moved. Despite the scorn of family and friends, Bradford in 1606 became a member of this group of Separatists who had formed their own congregation in the village of Scrooby under the direction of Clyfton, John Robinson, his later successor to the pulpit, and William Brewster, the group's pre-eminent elder. Because of pressure to conform to the hierarchy of the Anglican Church, the Scrooby group in 1608 fled to Holland and eventually settled in Leyden. After one disastrous business venture, William Bradford became a weaver.

In 1620 part of the Leyden congregation, along with an assortment of less pious emigrants, departed on the *Mayflower* to establish a settlement where they could maintain a church of "ancient purity" freed from European entanglements. In November they arrived off the shores of what is now Cape Cod, Massachusetts (somewhat farther north than they had intended), and in December disembarked at Plymouth. Since John Robinson had stayed behind in Leyden, William Brewster became the settlers' spiritual leader, preaching regularly on Sundays; because of the Separatist emphasis upon spontaneity, other members gave short, impromptu sermons as they wished. When Plymouth's first governor, John Carver, died in 1621, Bradford was elected to take his place. The governor wielded extensive powers by contemporary standards: chief judge and jury, superintendant of agriculture and trade, and secretary of state. During his lifetime Bradford was re-elected to the position thirty times, serving almost continuously, for a total term of thirty-three years until his death in 1657.

In 1630 William Bradford wrote the first book of his history, *Of Plymouth Plantation.* Perhaps the settlement that year of a much larger, and potentially overshadowing, Puritan colony at Massachusetts Bay prompted Bradford to begin his history. He put aside the manuscript until 1644, when he finished the eleventh chapter, and, between 1646 and 1650, he brought the account of the colony's struggles and achievements through the year 1646.

Surprisingly, Bradford's unfinished manuscript was not published until 1856. It had remained in the Bradford family until 1728, when Reverend Thomas Prince placed it in his personal library in Boston's Old South Church. During the American Revolution, the manuscript was lost, presumably stolen by a British soldier during the British occupation of Boston (1775–1776). In 1855, scholars intrigued by references to Bradford in two books on the history of the Episcopal Church in America (both written in England) located the manuscript in the bishop of London's library at Lambeth Palace. In 1897, after a protracted legal battle, *Of Plymouth Plantation* was returned to Massachusetts. The unfinished manuscript of *Of Plymouth Plantation* is not Bradford's only literary effort—he wrote a journal of Plymouth's first year, some poems, and a series of dialogues—but it constitutes his greatest literary achievement. For Bradford the history of the Plymouth settlers closely followed the plot of the Old Testament. The Puritans' journey to the New World indicated a covenanted relationship with God for which God's relationship with the Israelites provided a model and a guide. This interpretive strategy, known as *typology,* influenced a number of later New England historians such as Nathaniel Morton, Cotton Mather, and Thomas Prince.

The way in which Bradford composed *Of Plymouth Plantation* should remind us that his history is not a yearly chronicle of events but a retrospective attempt to interpret God's design for his "saints," that exclusive group of believers predestined for eternal salvation. Like the Puritan journal, the genre of Puritan history served a distinctly *useful* purpose in enhancing spiritual life. Bradford hoped to demonstrate the workings of divine providence for the edification of future generations, and since all temporal events theoretically conveyed divine meaning, the texture of Bradford's writing is as rich in historical detail as it is patterned on the language of the Geneva Bible. The word choice and cadence of Bradford's prose manifested a constant reminder of the biblical precedent for Puritan history. Yet a major tension in his narrative involves the difficulty in interpreting the providential will. As Bradford repeatedly encounters human wickedness and duplicity, *Of Plymouth Plantation* increasingly reveals its author's perplexity over the apparent ambiguity of divine providence. Bradford maintains his piety, but he is forced to acknowledge his perception of an infinite gulf between man and God. Such an acknowledgment amplifies the narrative's tone of humility, established at the outset, in Bradford's declaration that he shall write in the Puritan "plain style" of biblical simplicity and concrete image, and tell the "simple truth" as well as his "slender judgment" would permit.

Many readers have noted the elegiac note of sadness on which *Of Plymouth Plantation* ends. If Bradford's realization that "so uncertain are the mutable things of this unstable world" dictates his humility throughout, his final entries particularly pronounce a sense of loss. In the eulogy to William Brewster (included below) Bradford lamented, most of all, the disappearance of a communitarian vision embodied by the first-generation founders like Brewster and John Robinson. To Bradford, those first emigrants whom he called "Pilgrims" exemplified the value of community and sense of purpose that were presumably waning in the 1640s as second-generation inhabitants and new immigrants looked for better farmland. *Of Plymouth Plantation* thus speaks a message characteristic of much of the literature of immigration: the paradoxical nature of prosperity and success, the sense that, in this case, the founding of the first successful British settlement in New England led only to fragmentation and dispersal.

Philip Gould
Brown University

Michael Drexler
Brown University

PRIMARY WORKS

Mourt's Relation, 1622; *Of Plymouth Plantation,* ed. S. E. Morison, 1952, 1959; "A Dialogue Between Young Men Born in New England and Sundry Ancient Men that Came Out of Holland and Old England," n.d.

from Of Plymouth Plantation

And first of the occasion and inducements thereunto; the which, that I may truly unfold, I must begin at the very root and rise of the same. The which I shall endeavour to manifest in a plain style, with singular regard unto the simple truth in all things; at least as near as my slender judgment can attain the same.

from Book I
from Chapter I
The Separatist Interpretation of the Reformation in England 1550–1607

It is well known unto the godly and judicious, how ever since the first breaking out of the light of the gospel in our honourable nation of England,[1] (which was the first of nations whom the Lord adorned therewith after the gross darkness of popery which had covered and overspread the Christian world), what wars and oppositions ever since, Satan hath raised, maintained and continued against the Saints,[2] from

[1]The Protestant Reformation.
[2]Not the canonical saints of the Roman Catholic church, but faithful Christians in general, a term often applied simply to all Puritans.

time to time, in one sort or other. Sometimes by bloody death and cruel torments; other whiles imprisonments, banishments and other hard usages; as being loath his kingdom should go down, the truth prevail and the churches of God revert to their ancient purity and recover their primitive order, liberty and beauty.

But when he could not prevail by these means against the main truths of the gospel, but that they began to take rooting in many places, being watered with the blood of the martyrs and blessed from Heaven with a gracious increase; he then began to take him to his ancient stratagems, used of old against the first Christians. That when by the bloody and barbarous persecutions of the heathen emperors he could not stop and subvert the course of the gospel, but that it speedily overspread, with a wonderful celerity, the then best known parts of the world; he then began to sow errours, heresies and wonderful dissensions amongst the professors[3] themselves, working upon their pride and ambition, with other corrupt passions incident to all mortal men, yea to the saints themselves in some measure, by which woeful effects followed. As not only bitter contentions and heartburnings, schisms, with other horrible confusions; but Satan took occasion and advantage thereby to foist in a number of vile ceremonies, with many unprofitable canons and decrees, which have since been as snares to many poor and peaceable souls even to this day. . . .

So many, therefore, of these professors as saw the evil of these things in these parts, and whose hearts the Lord had touched with heavenly zeal for His truth, they shook off this yoke of antichristian bondage, and as the Lord's free people joined themselves (by a covenant of the Lord) into a church estate, in the fellowship of the gospel, to walk in all His ways made known, or to be made known unto them, according to their best endeavours, whatsoever it should cost them, the Lord assisting them.[4] And that it cost them something this ensuing history will declare. . . .

from Chapter IX
Of their Voyage, and how they Passed the Sea; and of their Safe Arrival at Cape Cod[5]

September 6. These troubles being blown over, and now all being compact together in one ship, they put to sea again with a prosperous wind, which continued divers

[3] Those who profess true Christianity, a term often applied simply to all Puritans.

[4] A paraphrase of the words of the covenant that people made when they formed a Separatist (later Congregational) church.

[5] In a previous chapter Bradford offers a number of reasons that compelled a minority of the Leyden group to leave for America. A treaty between Holland and Spain was due to expire in 1621, and some of the Separatists were afraid of a Spanish (and Catholic) invasion of the Low Countries. Some of the Leyden group were also concerned about their children's potential assimilation into Dutch society. Moreover, the Dutch were lax in maintaining the purity of the sabbath day. The Leyden group received two successive patents from the Virginia Company (which were eventually useless because of their accidental arrival in New England, north of the Company's domain), and although King James I did not grant them religious toleration, he did promise not to interfere with them, so long as they maintained themselves peacefully. Some of the economic arrangements with the financial backers in London proved to be difficult as well. Finally, because one of their ships, the *Speedwell,* was forced to turn back because of a leak, those members still willing to make the voyage joined the *Mayflower* which then departed for a second time with 101 passengers, about 35 of whom were Separatists.

days together, which was some encouragement unto them; yet, according to the usual manner, many were afflicted with seasickness. And I may not omit here a special work of God's providence. There was a proud and very profane young man, one of the seamen, of a lusty, able body, which made him the more haughty; he would alway be contemning the poor people in their sickness and cursing them daily with grievous execrations; and did not let to tell them that he hoped to help to cast half of them overboard before they came to their journey's end, and to make merry with what they had; and if he were by any gently reproved, he would curse and swear most bitterly. But it pleased God before they came half seas over, to smite this young man with a grievous disease, of which he died in a desperate manner, and so was himself the first that was thrown overboard. Thus his curses light on his own head, and it was an astonishment to all his fellows for they noted it to be the just hand of God upon him. . . .

But to omit other things (that I may be brief) after long beating at sea they fell with that land which is called Cape Cod; the which being made and certainly known to be it, they were not a little joyful. After some deliberation had amongst themselves and with the master of the ship, they tacked about and resolved to stand for the southward (the wind and weather being fair) to find some place about Hudson's River for their habitation. But after they had sailed that course about half the day, they fell amongst dangerous shoals and roaring breakers, and they were so far entangled therewith as they conceived themselves in great danger; and the wind shrinking upon them withal, they resolved to bear up again for the Cape and thought themselves happy to get out of those dangers before night overtook them, as by God's good providence they did. And the next day they got into the Cape Harbor[6] where they rid in safety. . . .

Being thus arrived in a good harbor, and brought safe to land, they fell upon their knees and blessed the God of Heaven who had brought them over the vast and furious ocean, and delivered them from all the perils and miseries thereof, again to set their feet on the firm and stable earth, their proper element. And no marvel if they were thus joyful, seeing wise Seneca[7] was so affected with sailing a few miles on the coast of his own Italy, as he affirmed, that he had rather remain twenty years on his way by land than pass by sea to any place in a short time, so tedious and dreadful was the same unto him.

But here I cannot but stay and make a pause, and stand half amazed at this poor people's present condition; and so I think will the reader, too, when he well considers the same. Being thus passed the vast ocean, and a sea of troubles before in their preparation (as may be remembered by that which went before), they had now no friends to welcome them nor inns to entertain or refresh their weatherbeaten bodies; no houses or much less towns to repair to, to seek for succour. It is recorded in Scripture as a mercy to the Apostle and his shipwrecked company, that the barbarians showed them no small kindness in refreshing them,[8] but these savage barbarians, when they met with them (as after will appear) were readier to fill their sides full of

[6]Now Provincetown harbor. The *Mayflower* was at sea sixty-five days, arriving in November 1620.

[7]Roman statesman, playwright, and Stoic philosopher (3? B.C.–A.D. 65?).

[8]Acts 28:2.

arrows than otherwise. And for the season it was winter, and they that know the winters of that country know them to be sharp and violent, and subject to cruel and fierce storms, dangerous to travel to known places, much more to search an unknown coast. Besides, what could they see but a hideous and desolate wilderness, full of wild beasts and wild men—and what multitudes there might be of them they knew not. Neither could they, as it were, go up to the top of Pisgah to view from this wilderness a more goodly country to feed their hopes,[9] for which way soever they turned their eyes (save upward to the heavens) they could have little solace or content in respect of any outward objects. For summer being done, all things stand upon them with a weather-beaten face, and the whole country, full of woods and thickets, represented a wild and savage hue. If they looked behind them, there was the mighty ocean which they had passed and was now as a main bar and gulf to separate them from all the civil parts of the world. If it be said they had a ship to succour them, it is true; but what heard they daily from the master and company? But that with speed they should look out a place (with their shallop[10]) where they would be, at some near distance; for the season was such as he would not stir from thence till a safe harbor was discovered by them, where they would be, and he might go without danger; and that victuals consumed apace but he must and would keep sufficient for themselves and their return. Yea, it was muttered by some that if they got not a place in time, they would turn them and their goods ashore and leave them. Let it also be considered what weak hopes of supply and succour they left behind them, that might bear up their minds in this sad condition and trials they were under; and they could not but be very small. It is true, indeed, the affections and love of their brethren at Leyden was cordial and entire towards them, but they had little power to help them or themselves; and how the case stood between them and the merchants at their coming away hath already been declared.

What could now sustain them but the Spirit of God and His grace? May not and ought not the children of these fathers rightly say: "Our fathers were Englishmen which came over this great ocean, and were ready to perish in this wilderness; but they cried unto the Lord, and He heard their voice and looked on their adversity,"[11] etc. "Let them therefore praise the Lord, because He is good: and His mercies endure forever." "Yea, let them which have been redeemed of the Lord, shew how He hath delivered them from the hand of the oppressor. When they wandered in the desert wilderness out of the way, and found no city to dwell in, both hungry and thirsty, their soul was overwhelmed in them. Let them confess before the Lord His lovingkindness and His wonderful works before the sons of men."[12]

[9]As Moses viewed the Promised Land in Numbers 23:14; Deuteronomy 3:27.

[10]A small, open boat used in shallow water.

[11]Bradford's adaptation of Deuteronomy 26:5, 7.

[12]Psalm 107:1–5, 8.

from Book II
Chapter XI
The Remainder of Anno 1620

[The Mayflower Compact]

I shall a little return back, and begin with a combination made by them before they came ashore; being the first foundation of their government in this place.[13] Occasioned partly by the discontented and mutinous speeches that some of the strangers amongst them had let fall from them in the ship: That when they came ashore they would use their own liberty, for none had power to command them, the patent they had being for Virginia and not for New England, which belonged to another government, with which the Virginia Company had nothing to do. And partly that such an act by them done, this their condition considered, might be as firm as any patent, and in some respects more sure.

The form was as followeth

IN THE NAME OF GOD, AMEN.

We whose names are underwritten, the loyal subjects of our dread Sovereign Lord King James, by the Grace of God of Great Britain, France, and Ireland King, Defender of the Faith, etc.

Having undertaken, for the Glory of God and advancement of the Christian Faith and Honour of our King and Country, a Voyage to plant the First Colony in the Northern Parts of Virginia, do by these presents solemnly and mutually in the presence of God and one of another, Covenant and Combine ourselves together into a Civil Body Politic, for our better ordering and preservation and furtherance of the ends aforesaid; and by virtue hereof to enact, constitute and frame such just and equal Laws, Ordinances, Acts, Constitutions and Offices, from time to time, as shall be thought most meet and convenient for the general good of the Colony, unto which we promise all due submission and obedience. In witness whereof we have hereunder subscribed our names at Cape Cod, the 11th of November, in the year of the reign of our Sovereign Lord King James, of England, France and Ireland the eighteenth, and of Scotland the fifty-fourth. Anno Domini 1620.[14]

After this they chose, or rather confirmed, Mr. John Carver (a man godly and well approved amongst them) their Governor for that year. And after they had provided a place for their goods, or common store (which were long in unlading for want of boats, foulness of the winter weather and sickness of divers) and begun some small cottages for their habitation; as time would admit, they met and consulted of laws and orders, both for their civil and military government as the necessity of their condition did require, still adding thereunto as urgent occasion in several times, and as cases did require.

In these hard and difficult beginnings they found some discontents and murmurings arise amongst some, and mutinous speeches and carriages in other; but they were soon quelled and overcome by the wisdom, patience, and just and equal car-

[13]This is commonly referred to as the Mayflower Compact.

[14]Forty-one men signed the Mayflower Compact.

riage of things, by the Governor and better part, which clave faithfully together in the main.

[The Starving Time]

But that which was most sad and lamentable was, that in two or three months' time half of their company died, especially in January and February, being the depth of winter, and wanting houses and other comforts; being infected with the scurvy and other diseases which this long voyage and their inaccommodate condition had brought upon them. So as there died some times two or three of a day in the foresaid time, that of 100 and odd persons, scarce fifty remained. And of these, in the time of most distress, there was but six or seven sound persons who to their great commendations, be it spoken, spared no pains night nor day, but with abundance of toil and hazard of their own health, fetched them wood, made them fires, dressed them meat, made their beds, washed their loathsome clothes, clothed and unclothed them. In a word, did all the homely and necessary offices for them which dainty and queasy stomachs cannot endure to hear named; and all this willingly and cheerfully, without any grudging in the least, showing herein their true love unto their friends and brethren; a rare example and worthy to be remembered. Two of these seven were Mr. William Brewster, their reverend Elder, and Myles Standish, their Captain and military commander, unto whom myself and many others were much beholden in our low and sick condition. And yet the Lord so upheld these persons as in this general calamity they were not at all infected either with sickness or lameness. And what I have said of these I may of many others who died in this general visitation, and others yet living; that whilst they had health, yea, or any strength continuing, they were not wanting to any that had need of them. And I doubt not but their recompense is with the Lord.

But I may not here pass by another remarkable passage not to be forgotten. As this calamity fell among the passengers that were to be left here to plant, and were hasted ashore and made to drink water that the seamen might have the more beer, and one[15] in his sickness desiring but a small can of beer, it was answered that if he were their own father he should have none. The disease began to fall amongst them also, so as almost half of their company died before they went away, and many of their officers and lustiest men, as the boatswain, gunner, three quartermasters, the cook and others. At which the Master was something strucken and sent to the sick ashore and told the Governor he should send for beer for them that had need of it, though he drunk water homeward bound.

But now amongst his company there was far another kind of carriage in this misery than amongst the passengers. For they that before had been boon companions in drinking and jollity in the time of their health and welfare, began now to desert one another in this calamity, saying they would not hazard their lives for them, they should be infected by coming to help them in their cabins; and so, after they came to lie by it, would do little or nothing for them but, "if they died, let them die." But such of the passengers as were yet aboard showed them what mercy they could, which

[15]Bradford himself.

made some of their hearts relent, as the boatswain (and some others) who was a proud young man and would often curse and scoff at the passengers. But when he grew weak, they had compassion on him and helped him; then he confessed he did not deserve it at their hands, he had abused them in word and deed. "Oh!" (saith he) "you, I now see, show your love like Christians indeed one to another, but we let one another lie and die like dogs." Another lay cursing his wife, saying if it had not been for her he had never come this unlucky voyage, and anon cursing his fellows, saying he had done this and that for some of them; he had spent so much and so much amongst them, and they were now weary of him and did not help him, having need. Another gave his companion all he had, if he died, to help him in his weakness; he went and got a little spice and made him a mess of meat once or twice. And because he died not so soon as he expected, he went amongst his fellows and swore the rogue would cozen him, he would see him choked before he made him any more meat; and yet the poor fellow died before morning.

[Indian Relations]

All this while the Indians came skulking about them, and would sometimes show themselves aloof off, but when any approached near them, they would run away; and once they stole away their tools where they had been at work and were gone to dinner. But about the 16th of March, a certain Indian came boldly amongst them and spoke to them in broken English, which they could well understand but marveled at it. At length they understood by discourse with him, that he was not of these parts, but belonged to the eastern parts where some English ships came to fish, with whom he was acquainted and could name sundry of them by their names, amongst whom he had got his language. He became profitable to them in acquainting them with many things concerning the state of the country in the east parts where he lived, which was afterwards profitable unto them; as also of the people here, of their names, number and strength, of their situation and distance from this place, and who was chief amongst them. His name was Samoset. He told them also of another Indian whose name was Squanto, a native of this place, who had been in England and could speak better English than himself.

Being, after some time of entertainment and gifts dismissed, a while after he came again, and five more with him, and they brought again all the tools that were stolen away before, and made way for the coming of their great Sachem, called Massasoit. Who, about four or five days after, came with the chief of his friends and other attendance, with the aforesaid Squanto. With whom, after friendly entertainment and some gifts given him, they made a peace with him (which hath now continued this 24 years) in these terms:

1. That neither he nor any of his should injure or do hurt to any of their people.

2. That if any of his did hurt to any of theirs, he should send the offender, that they might punish him.

3. That if anything were taken away from any of theirs, he should cause it to be restored; and they should do the like to his.

4. If any did unjustly war against him, they would aid him; if any did war against them, he should aid them.

5. He should send to his neighbours confederates to certify them of this, that they might not wrong them, but might be likewise comprised in the conditions of peace.

6. That when their men came to them, they should leave their bows and arrows behind them.

After these things he returned to his place called Sowams, some 40 miles from this place, but Squanto continued with them and was their interpreter and was a special instrument sent of God for their good beyond their expectation. He directed them how to set their corn, where to take fish, and to procure other commodities, and was also their pilot to bring them to unknown places for their profit, and never left them till he died. . . .

from Chapter XIV
Anno Domini 1623

[End of the "Common Course and Condition"]

All this while no supply was heard of, neither knew they when they might expect any. So they began to think how they might raise as much corn as they could, and obtain a better crop than they had done, that they might not still thus languish in misery. At length, after much debate of things, the Governor (with the advice of the chiefest amongst them) gave way that they should set corn every man for his own particular, and in that regard trust to themselves; in all other things to go on in the general way as before. And so assigned to every family a parcel of land, according to the proportion of their number, for that end, only for present use (but made no division for inheritance) and ranged all boys and youth under some family. This had very good success, for it made all hands very industrious, so as much more corn was planted than otherwise would have been by any means the Governor or any other could use, and saved him a great deal of trouble, and gave far better content. The women now went willingly into the field, and took their little ones with them to set corn; which before would allege weakness and inability; whom to have compelled would have been thought great tyranny and oppression.

The experience that was had in this common course and condition, tried sundry years and that amongst godly and sober men, may well evince the vanity of that conceit of Plato's[16] and other ancients applauded by some of later times; that the taking away of property and bringing in community into a commonwealth would make them happy and flourishing; as if they were wiser than God. For this community (so far as it was) was found to breed much confusion and discontent and retard much employment that would have been to their benefit and comfort. For the young men, that were most able and fit for labour and service, did repine that they should spend their time and strength to work for other men's wives and children without any recompense. The strong, or man of parts, had no more in division of victuals and clothes

[16]Plato's idea of a communistic society depicted in *The Republic.*

than he that was weak and not able to do a quarter the other could; this was thought injustice. The aged and graver men to be ranked and equalized in labours and victuals, clothes, etc., with the meaner and younger sort, thought it some indignity and disrespect unto them. And for men's wives to be commanded to do service for other men, as dressing their meat, washing their clothes, etc., they deemed it a kind of slavery, neither could many husbands well brook it. Upon the point all being to have alike, and all to do alike, they thought themselves in the like condition, and one as good as another; and so, if it did not cut off those relations that God hath set amongst men, yet it did at least much diminish and take off the mutual respects that should be preserved amongst them. And would have been worse if they had been men of another condition. Let none object this is men's corruption, and nothing to the course itself. I answer, seeing all men have this corruption in them, God in His wisdom saw another course fitter for them. . . .

from **Chapter XIX**
Anno Domini 1628

[Thomas Morton of Merrymount]

About some three or four years before this time, there came over one Captain Wollaston (a man of pretty parts[17]) and with him three or four more of some eminency, who brought with them a great many servants, with provisions and other implements for to begin a plantation. And pitched themselves in a place within the Massachusetts which they called after their Captain's name, Mount Wollaston. Amongst whom was one Mr. Morton, who it should seem had some small adventure of his own or other men's amongst them, but had little respect amongst them, and was slighted by the meanest servants. Having continued there some time, and not finding things to answer their expectations nor profit to arise as they looked for, Captain Wollaston takes a great part of the servants and transports them to Virginia, where he puts them off at good rates, selling their time to other men; and writes back to one Mr. Rasdall (one of his chief partners and accounted their merchant) to bring another part of them to Virginia likewise, intending to put them off there as he had done the rest. And he, with the consent of the said Rasdall, appointed one Fitcher to be his Lieutenant and govern the remains of the Plantation till he or Rasdall returned to take further order thereabout. But this Morton abovesaid, having more craft than honesty (who had been a kind of pettifogger of Furnival's Inn) in the others' absence watches an opportunity (commons being but hard amongst them) and got some strong drink and other junkets and made them a feast; and after they were merry, he began to tell them he would give them good counsel. "You see," saith he, "that many of your fellows are carried to Virginia, and if you stay till this Rasdall return, you will also be carried away and sold for slaves with the rest. Therefore I would advise you to thrust out this Lieutenant Fitcher, and I, having a part in the Plantation, will receive you as my partners and consociates; so may you be free from service, and we will converse,

[17]A clever man, intellectually gifted at least in a superficial way.

plant, trade, and live together as equals and support and protect one another," or to like effect. This counsel was easily received, so they took opportunity and thrust Lieutenant Fitcher out o' doors, and would suffer him to come no more amongst them, but forced him to seek bread to eat and other relief from his neighbours till he could get passage for England.

After this they fell to great licentiousness and led a dissolute life, pouring out themselves into all profaneness. And Morton became Lord of Misrule, and maintained (as it were) a School of Atheism. And after they had got some goods into their hands, and got much by trading with the Indians, they spent it as vainly in quaffing and drinking, both wine and strong waters in great excess (and, as some reported) £10 worth in a morning. They also set up a maypole, drinking and dancing about it many days together, inviting the Indian women for their consorts, dancing and frisking together like so many fairies, or furies, rather; and worse practices. As if they had anew revived and celebrated the feasts of the Roman goddess Flora, or the beastly practices of the mad Bacchanalians. Morton likewise, to show his poetry composed sundry rhymes and verses, some tending to lasciviousness, and others to the detraction and scandal of some persons, which he affixed to this idle or idol maypole. They changed also the name of their place, and instead of calling it Mount Wollaston they call it Merry-mount, as if this jollity would have lasted ever. But this continued not long, for after Morton was sent for England (as follows to be declared) shortly after came over that worthy gentleman Mr. John Endecott, who brought over a patent under the broad seal for the government of the Massachusetts. Who, visiting those parts, caused that maypole to be cut down and rebuked them for their profaneness and admonished them to look there should be better walking. So they or others now changed the name of their place again and called it Mount Dagon.[18]

Now to maintain this riotous prodigality and profuse excess, Morton, thinking himself lawless, and hearing what gain the French and fishermen made by trading of pieces, powder and shot to the Indians, he as the head of this consortship began the practice of the same in these parts. And first he taught them how to use them, to charge and discharge, and what proportion of powder to give the piece, according to the size or bigness of the same; and what shot to use for fowl and what for deer. And having thus instructed them, he employed some of them to hunt and fowl for him, so as they became far more active in that employment than any of the English, by reason of their swiftness of foot and nimbleness of body, being also quicksighted and by continual exercise well knowing the haunts of all sorts of game. So as when they saw the execution that a piece would do, and the benefit that might come by the same, they became mad (as it were) after them and would not stick to give any price they could attain to for them; accounting their bows and arrows but baubles in comparison of them.

And here I may take occasion to bewail the mischief that this wicked man began in these parts, and which since, base covetousness prevailing in men that should know better, has now at length got the upper hand and made this thing common, notwithstanding any laws to the contrary. So as the Indians are full of pieces all over, both fowling pieces, muskets, pistols, etc. They have also their moulds to make shot of all sorts, as musket bullets, pistol bullets, swan and goose shot, and of smaller

[18]The "false idol" of the Philistines (Judges 16:23).

sorts. Yea some have seen them have their screw-plates to make screw-pins themselves when they want them, with sundry other implements, wherewith they are ordinarily better fitted and furnished than the English themselves. Yea, it is well known that they will have powder and shot when the English want it nor cannot get it; and that in a time of war or danger, as experience hath manifested, that when lead hath been scarce and men for their own defense would gladly have given a groat a pound, which is dear enough, yet hath it been bought up and sent to other places and sold to such as trade it with the Indians at 12*d* the pound. And it is like they give 3*s* or 4*s* the pound, for they will have it at any rate. And these things have been done in the same times when some of their neighbours and friends are daily killed by the Indians, or are in danger thereof and live but at the Indians' mercy. Yea some, as they have acquainted them with all other things, have told them how gunpowder is made, and all the materials in it, and that they are to be had in their own land; and I am confident, could they attain to make saltpeter, they would teach them to make powder.

O, the horribleness of this villainy! How many both Dutch and English have been lately slain by those Indians thus furnished, and no remedy provided; nay, the evil more increased, and the blood of their brethren sold for gain (as is to be feared) and in what danger all these colonies are in is too well known. O that princes and parliaments would take some timely order to prevent this mischief and at length to suppress it by some exemplary punishment upon some of these gain-thirsty murderers, for they deserve no better title, before their colonies in these parts be overthrown by these barbarous savages thus armed with their own weapons, by these evil instruments and traitors to their neighbours and country! But I have forgot myself and have been too long in this digression; but now to return.

This Morton having thus taught them the use of pieces, he sold them all he could spare, and he and his consorts determined to send for many out of England and had by some of the ships sent for above a score. The which being known, and his neighbours meeting the Indians in the woods armed with guns in this sort, it was a terror unto them who lived stragglingly and were of no strength in any place. And other places (though more remote) saw this mischief would quickly spread over all, if not prevented. Besides, they saw they should keep no servants, for Morton would entertain any, how vile soever, and all the scum of the country or any discontents would flock to him from all places, if this nest was not broken. And they should stand in more fear of their lives and goods in short time from this wicked and debased crew than from the savages themselves.

So sundry of the chief of the straggling plantations, meeting together, agreed by mutual consent to solicit those of Plymouth (who were then of more strength than them all) to join with them to prevent the further growth of this mischief, and suppress Morton and his consorts before they grew to further head and strength. Those that joined in this action, and after contributed to the charge of sending him for England, were from Piscataqua, Naumkeag, Winnisimmet, Wessagusset, Nantasket and other places where any English were seated. Those of Plymouth being thus sought to by their messengers and letters, and weighing both their reasons and the common danger, were willing to afford them their help though themselves had least cause of fear or hurt. So, to be short, they first resolved jointly to write to him, and in a friendly and neighbourly way to admonish him to forbear those courses, and sent a messenger with their letters to bring his answer.

But he was so high as he scorned all advice, and asked who had to do with him, he had and would trade pieces with the Indians, in despite of all, with many other scurrilous terms full of disdain. They sent to him a second time and bade him be better advised and more temperate in his terms, for the country could not bear the injury he did. It was against their common safety and against the King's proclamation. He answered in high terms as before; and that the King's proclamation was no law, demanding what penalty was upon it. It was answered, more than he could bear—His Majesty's displeasure. But insolently he persisted and said the King was dead and his displeasure with him, and many the like things. And threatened withal that if any came to molest him, let them look to themselves for he would prepare for them.

Upon which they saw there was no way but to take him by force; and having so far proceeded, now to give over would make him far more haughty and insolent. So they mutually resolved to proceed, and obtained of the Governor of Plymouth to send Captain Standish and some other aid with him, to take Morton by force. The which accordingly was done. But they found him to stand stiffly in his defense, having made fast his doors, armed his consorts, set divers dishes of powder and bullets ready on the table; and if they had not been over-armed with drink, more hurt might have been done. They summoned him to yield, but he kept his house and they could get nothing but scoffs and scorns from him. But at length, fearing they would do some violence to the house, he and some of his crew came out, but not to yield but to shoot; but they were so steeled with drink as their pieces were too heavy for them. Himself with a carbine, overcharged and almost half filled with powder and shot, as was after found, had thought to have shot Captain Standish; but he stepped to him and put by his piece and took him. Neither was there any hurt done to any of either side, save that one was so drunk that he ran his own nose upon the point of a sword that one held before him, as he entered the house; but he lost but a little of his hot blood.

Morton they brought away to Plymouth, where he was kept till a ship went from the Isle of Shoals for England, with which he was sent to the Council of New England, and letters written to give them information of his course and carriage. And also one was sent at their common charge to inform their Honours more particularly and to prosecute against him. But he fooled of the messenger, after he was gone from hence, and though he went for England yet nothing was done to him, not so much as rebuked, for aught was heard, but returned the next year. Some of the worst of the company were dispersed and some of the more modest kept the house till he should be heard from. But I have been too long about so unworthy a person, and bad a cause. . . .

from **Chapter XXIII**
Anno Domini 1632

[Prosperity Brings Dispersal of Population]

Also the people of the Plantation began to grow in their outward estates, by reason of the flowing of many people into the country, especially into the Bay of the Massachusetts. By which means corn and cattle rose to a great price, by which many were much enriched and commodities grew plentiful. And yet in other regards this benefit turned to their hurt, and this accession of strength to their weakness. For now as their stocks increased and the increase vendible, there was no longer any holding them together, but now they must of necessity go to their great lots. They could not otherwise keep their cattle, and having oxen grown they must have land for plowing and tillage. And no man now thought he could live except he had cattle and a great deal of ground to keep them, all striving to increase their stocks. By which means they were scattered all over the Bay quickly and the town in which they lived compactly till now was left very thin and in a short time almost desolate.

And if this had been all, it had been less, though too much; but the church must also be divided, and those that had lived so long together in Christian and comfortable fellowship must now part and suffer many divisions. First, those that lived on their lots on the other side of the Bay, called Duxbury, they could not long bring their wives and children to the public worship and church meetings here, but with such burthen as, growing to some competent number, they sued to be dismissed and become a body of themselves. And so they were dismissed about this time, though very unwillingly. But to touch this sad matter, and handle things together that fell out afterward; to prevent any further scattering from this place and weakening of the same, it was thought best to give out some good farms to special persons that would promise to live at Plymouth, and likely to be helpful to the church or commonwealth, and so tie the lands to Plymouth as farms for the same; and there they might keep their cattle and tillage by some servants and retain their dwellings here. And so some special lands were granted at a place general called Green's Harbor, where no allotments had been in the former division, a place very well meadowed and fit to keep and rear cattle good store. But alas, this remedy proved worse than the disease; for within a few years those that had thus got footing there rent themselves away, partly by force and partly wearing the rest with importunity and pleas of necessity, so as they must either suffer them to go or live in continual opposition and contention. And other still, as they conceived themselves straitened or to want accommodation, broke away under one pretence or other, thinking their own conceived necessity and the example of others a warrant sufficient for them. And this I fear will be the ruin of New England, at least of the churches of God there, and will provoke the Lord's displeasure against them.

from Chapter XXVIII
Anno Domini 1637

[The Pequot War]

In the fore part of this year, the Pequots fell openly upon the English at Connecticut, in the lower parts of the river, and slew sundry of them as they were at work in the fields, both men and women, to the great terrour of the rest, and went away in great pride and triumph, with many high threats. They also assaulted a fort at the river's mouth, though strong and well defended; and though they did not there prevail, yet it struck them with much fear and astonishment to see their bold attempts in the face of danger.[19] Which made them in all places to stand upon their guard and to prepare for resistance, and earnestly to solicit their friends and confederates in the Bay of Massachusetts to send them speedy aid, for they looked for more forcible assaults. Mr. Vane, being then Governor, writ from their General Court to them here to join with them in this war . . .

In the meantime, the Pequots, especially in the winter before, sought to make peace with the Narragansetts, and used very pernicious arguments to move them thereunto: as that the English were strangers and began to overspread their country, and would deprive them thereof in time, if they were suffered to grow and increase. And if the Narragansetts did assist the English to subdue them, they did but make way for their own overthrow, for if they were rooted out, the English would soon take occasion to subjugate them. And if they would hearken to them they should not need to fear the strength of the English, for they would not come to open battle with them but fire their houses, kill their cattle, and lie in ambush for them as they went abroad upon their occasions; and all this they might easily do without any or little danger to themselves. The which course being held, they well saw the English could not long subsist but they would either be starved with hunger or be forced to forsake the country. With many the like things; insomuch that the Narragansetts were once wavering and were half minded to have made peace with them, and joined against the English. But again, when they considered how much wrong they had received from the Pequots, and what an opportunity they now had by the help of the English to right themselves; revenge was so sweet unto them as it prevailed above all the rest, so as they resolved to join with the English against them, and did.

The Court here agreed forthwith to send fifty men at their own charge; and with as much speed as possibly they could, got them armed and had made them ready under sufficient leaders, and provided a bark to carry them provisions and tend upon them for all occasions. But when they were ready to march, with a supply from the Bay, they had word to stay; for the enemy was as good as vanquished and there would be no need.

I shall not take upon me exactly to describe their proceedings in these things, because I expect it will be fully done by themselves who best know the carriage and circumstances of things. I shall therefore but touch them in general. From Connecticut, who were most sensible of the hurt sustained and the present danger, they set out a party of men, and another party met them from the Bay, at Narragansetts', who were to join with them. The Narragansetts were earnest to be gone before the English were well rested and refreshed, especially some of them which came last. It should seem their desire was to come upon the enemy suddenly and undiscovered. There was a bark of this place, newly put in there, which was come from Connecticut, who did encourage them to lay hold of the Indians' forwardness, and to show as great forwardness as they, for it would encourage them, and expedition might prove to their great

[19]The English had accused the Pequot of three recent murders and in retaliation had sent a raiding expedition into Connecticut to demand that the murderers be handed over to them. Rebuffed, the English burned and looted Pequot lands, and the violence that Bradford describes here was in response to both that expedition and the construction of the English fort at Old Saybrook at the mouth of the Connecticut River.

advantage. So they went on, and so ordered their march as the Indians brought them to a fort of the enemy's (in which most of their chief men were) before day. They approached the same with great silence and surrounded it both with English and Indians, that they might not break out; and so assaulted them with great courage, shooting amongst them, and entered the fort with all speed. And those that first entered found sharp resistance from the enemy who both shot at and grappled with them; others ran into their houses and brought out fire and set them on fire, which soon took in their mat; and standing close together, with the wind all was quickly on a flame, and thereby more were burnt to death than was otherwise slain; It burnt their bowstrings and made them unserviceable; those that scaped the fire were slain with the sword, some hewed to pieces, others run through with their rapiers, so as they were quickly dispatched and very few escaped. It was conceived they thus destroyed about 400 at this time. It was a fearful sight to see them thus frying in the fire and the streams of blood quenching the same, and horrible was the stink and scent thereof; but the victory seemed a sweet sacrifice,[20] and they gave the praise thereof to God, who had wrought so wonderfully for them, thus to enclose their enemies in their hands and give them so speedy a victory over so proud and insulting an enemy. . . .

from **Chapter XXIX**
Anno Domini 1638

[Great and Fearful Earthquake]

This year, about the first or second of June, was a great and fearful earthquake. It was in this place heard before it was felt. It came with a rumbling noise or low murmur, like unto remote thunder. It came from the northward and passed southward; as the noise approached nearer, the earth began to shake and came at length with that violence as caused platters, dishes and such-like things as stood upon shelves, to clatter and fall down. Yea, persons were afraid of the houses themselves. It so fell out that at the same time divers of the chief of this town were met together at one house, conferring with some of their friends that were upon their removal from the place, as if the Lord would hereby show the signs of His displeasure, in their shaking a-pieces and removals one from another. However, it was very terrible for the time, and as the men were set talking in the house, some women and others were without the doors, and the earth shook with that violence as they could not stand without catching hold of the posts and pales that stood next them. But the violence lasted not long. And about half an hour, or less came another noise and shaking, but neither so loud nor strong as the former, but quickly passed over and so it ceased. It was not only on the seacoast, but the Indians felt it within land, and some ships that were upon the coast were shaken by it. So powerful is the mighty hand of the Lord, as to make both the earth and sea to shake, and the mountains to tremble before Him, when He pleases. And who can stay His hand?[21]

[20]Leviticus 2:1–2. Bradford thus places the Pequot War in a line of great battles waged by God's chosen people.

[21]Daniel 4:35 and Haggai 2:6.

It was observed that the summers for divers years together after this earthquake were not so hot and seasonable for the ripening of corn and other fruits as formerly, but more cold and moist, and subject to early and untimely frosts by which, many times, much Indian corn came not to maturity. But whether this was any cause I leave it to naturalists to judge.

from Chapter XXXII Anno Domini 1642

[Wickedness Breaks Forth]

Marvelous it may be to see and consider how some kind of wickedness did grow and break forth here, in a land where the same was so much witnessed against and so narrowly looked unto, and severely punished when it was known, as in no place more, or so much, that I have known or heard of; insomuch that they have been somewhat censured even by moderate and good men for their severity in punishments. And yet all this could not suppress the breaking out of sundry notorious sins (as this year, besides other, gives us too many sad precedents and instances), especially drunkenness and uncleanness. Not only incontinency between persons unmarried, for which many both men and women have been punished sharply enough, but some married persons also. But that which is worse, even sodomy and buggery (things fearful to name) have broke forth in this land oftener than once.

I say it may justly be marveled at and cause us to fear and tremble at the consideration of our corrupt natures, which are so hardly bridled, subdued and mortified; nay, cannot by any other means but the powerful work and grace of God's Spirit. But (besides this) one reason may be that the Devil may carry a greater spite against the churches of Christ and the gospel here, by how much the more they endeavour to preserve holiness and purity amongst them and strictly punisheth the contrary when it ariseth either in church or commonwealth; that he might cast a blemish and stain upon them in the eyes of [the] world, who use to be rash in judgment. I would rather think thus, than that Satan hath more power in these heathen lands, as some have thought, than in more Christian nations, especially over God's servants in them.

2. Another reason may be, that it may be in this case as it is with waters when their streams are stopped or dammed up. When they get passage they flow with more violence and make more noise and disturbance than when they are suffered to run quietly in their own channels; so wickedness being here more stopped by strict laws, and the same more nearly looked unto so as it cannot run in a common road of liberty as it would and is inclined, it searches everywhere and at last breaks out where it gets vent.

3. A third reason may be, here (as I am verily persuaded) is not more evils in this kind, nor nothing near so many by proportion as in other places; but they are here more discovered and seen and made public by due search, inquisition and due punishment; for the churches look narrowly to their members, and the magistrates over all, more strictly than in other places. Besides, here the people are but few in comparison of other places which are full and populous and lie hid, as it were, in a wood or thicket and many horrible evils by that means are never seen nor known; whereas

here they are, as it were, brought into the light and set in the plain field, or rather on a hill, made conspicuous to the view of all. . . .

But it may be demanded how came it to pass that so many wicked persons and profane people should so quickly come over into this land and mix themselves amongst them? Seeing it was religious men that began the work and they came for religion's sake? I confess this may be marveled at, at least in time to come, when the reasons thereof should not be known; and the more because here was so many hardships and wants met withal. I shall therefore endeavour to give some answer hereunto.

1. And first, according to that in the gospel, it is ever to be remembered that where the Lord begins to sow good seed, there the envious man will endeavour to sow tares.[22]

2. Men being to come over into a wilderness, in which much labour and service was to be done about building and planting, etc., such as wanted help in that respect, when they could not have such as they would, were glad to take such as they could; and so, many untoward servants, sundry of them proved, that were thus brought over, both men and womenkind who, when their times were expired, became families of themselves, which gave increase hereunto.

3. Another and a main reason hereof was that men, finding so many godly disposed persons willing to come into these parts, some began to make a trade of it, to transport passengers and their goods, and hired ships for that end. And then, to make up their freight and advance their profit, cared not who the persons were, so they had money to pay them. And by this means the country became pestered with many unworthy persons who, being come over, crept into one place or other.

4. Again, the Lord's blessing usually following His people as well in outward as spiritual things (though afflictions be mixed withal) do make many to adhere to the People of God, as many followed Christ for the loaves' sake (John vi.26) and a "mixed multitude" came into the wilderness with the People of God out of Egypt of old (Exodus xii.38). So also there were sent by their friends, some under hope that they would be made better; others that they might be eased of such burthens, and they kept from shame at home, that would necessarily follow their dissolute courses. And thus, by one means or other, in 20 years' time it is a question whether the greater part be not grown the worser? . . .

[A Horrible Case of Bestiality]

And after the time of the writing of these things befell a very sad accident of the like foul nature in this government, this very year, which I shall now relate. There was a youth whose name was Thomas Granger. He was servant to an honest man of Duxbury, being about 16 or 17 years of age. (His father and mother lived at the same time at Scituate.) He was this year detected of buggery, and indicted for the same, with a mare, a cow, two goats, five sheep, two calves and a turkey. Horrible it is to mention, but the truth of the history requires it. He was first discovered by one that accidentally saw his lewd practice towards the mare. (I forbear particulars.) Being upon it examined and committed, in the end he not only confessed the fact with that beast at that time, but sundry times before and at several times with all the rest of the forenamed in his indictment. And this his free confession was not only in private to

[22]Matthew 13:24–30.

the magistrates (though at first he strived to deny it) but to sundry, both ministers and others; and afterwards, upon his indictment, to the whole Court and jury; and confirmed it at his execution. And whereas some of the sheep could not so well be known by his description of them, others with them were brought before him and he declared which were they and which were not. And accordingly he was cast by the jury and condemned, and after executed about the 8th of September, 1642. A very sad spectacle it was. For first the mare and then the cow and the rest of the lesser cattle were killed before his face, according to the law, Leviticus xx.15; and then he himself was executed. The cattle were all cast into a great and large pit that was digged of purpose for them, and no use made of any part of them.

Upon the examination of this person and also of a former that had made some sodomitical attempts upon another, it being demanded of them how they came first to the knowledge and practice of such wickedness, the one confessed he had long used it in old England; and this youth last spoken of said he was taught it by another that had heard of such things from some in England when he was there, and they kept cattle together. By which it appears how one wicked person may infect many, and what care all ought to have what servants they bring into their families.

from Chapter XXXIII
Anno Domini 1643

[The Life and Death of Elder Brewster]

I am to begin this year with that which was a matter of great sadness and mourning unto them all. About the 18th of April died their Reverend Elder and my dear and loving friend Mr. William Brewster, a man that had done and suffered much for the Lord Jesus and the gospel's sake, and had borne his part in weal and woe with this poor persecuted church above 36 years in England, Holland and in this wilderness, and done the Lord and them faithful service in his place and calling. And notwithstanding the many troubles and sorrows he passed through, the Lord upheld him to a great age. He was near fourscore years of age (if not all out) when he died. He had this blessing added by the Lord to all the rest; to die in his bed, in peace, amongst the midst of his friends, who mourned and wept over him and ministered what help and comfort they could unto him, and he again recomforted them whilst he could. His sickness was not long, and till the last day thereof he did not wholly keep his bed. His speech continued till somewhat more than half a day, and then failed him, and about nine or ten a clock that evening he died without any pangs at all. A few hours before, he drew his breath short, and some few minutes before his last, he drew his breath long as a man fallen into a sound sleep without any pangs or gaspings, and so sweetly departed this life unto a better. . . .

I cannot but here take occasion not only to mention but greatly to admire the marvelous providence of God! That notwithstanding the many changes and hardships that these people went through, and the many enemies they had and difficulties they met withal, that so many of them should live to very old age! It was not only this reverend man's condition (for one swallow makes no summer as they say) but many more of them did the like, some dying about and before this time and many still living, who attained to sixty years of age, and to sixty-five, divers to seventy and above, and some near eighty as he did. It must needs be more than ordinary and above natural reason, that so it should be. For it is found in experience that change of air, famine or unwholesome food, much drinking of water, sorrows and troubles, etc., all of them are enemies to health, causes of many diseases, consumers of natural vigour and the bodies of men, and shorteners of life. And yet all of these things they had a large part and suffered deeply in the same. They went from England to Holland, where they found both worse air and diet than that they came from; from thence, enduring a long imprisonment as it were in the ships at sea, into New England; and how it hath been with them here hath already been shown, and what crosses, troubles, fears, wants and sorrows they had been liable unto is easy to conjecture. So as in some sort they may say with the Apostle, 2 Corinthians xi.26, 27, they were "in journeyings often, in perils of waters, in perils of robbers, in perils of their own nation, in perils among the heathen, in perils in the wilderness, in perils in the sea, in perils among false brethren; in weariness and painfulness, in watching often, in hunger and thirst, in fasting often, in cold and nakedness."

What was it then that upheld them? It was God's visitation that preserved their spirits. Job x.12: "Thou hast given me life and grace, and thy visitation hath preserved my spirit." He that upheld the Apostle upheld them. "They were persecuted, but not forsaken, cast down, but perished not."[23] "As unknown, and yet known; as dying, and behold we live; as chastened, and yet not killed"; 2 Corinthians vi.9.

God, it seems, would have all men to behold and observe such mercies and works of His providence as these are towards His people, that they in like cases might be encouraged to depend upon God in their trials, and also to bless His name when they see His goodness towards others. Man lives not by bread only, Deuteronomy viii.3. It is not by good and dainty fare, by peace and rest and heart's ease in enjoying the contentments and good things of this world only that preserves health and prolongs life; God in such examples would have the world see and behold that He can do it without them; and if the world will shut their eyes and take no notice thereof, yet He would have His people to see and consider it. Daniel could be better liking with pulse than others were with the king's dainties.[24] Jacob, though he went from one nation to another people and passed through famine, fears and many afflictions, yet he lived till old age and died sweetly and rested in the Lord,[25] as infinite others of God's servants have done and still shall do, through God's goodness, notwithstanding all the malice of their enemies, "when the branch of the wicked shall be cut off before his day" (Job xv.32) "and the bloody and deceitful men shall not live [out] half their days"; Psalm lv.23.

[The New England Confederation and the Narragansetts]

By reason of the plottings of the Narragansetts ever since the Pequots' War the Indians were drawn into a general conspiracy against the English in all parts, as was in part discovered the year before; and now made more plain and evident by many discoveries and free confessions of sundry Indians upon several occasions from divers places, concurring in one. With such other concurring circumstances as gave them sufficiently to understand the truth thereof. And to think of means how to prevent

[23]II Corinthians 4:9.
[24]Daniel 1:8–16.
[25]Genesis 47:28; 49:33.

the same and secure themselves. Which made them enter into this more near union and confederation following.

These were the articles of agreement in the union and confederation which they now first entered into. And in this their first meeting held at Boston the day and year abovesaid, amongst other things they had this matter of great consequence to consider on:

The Narragansetts, after the subduing of the Pequots, thought to have ruled over all the Indians about them. But the English, especially those of Connecticut, holding correspondency and friendship with Uncas, sachem of the Mohegan Indians which lived near them (as the Massachusetts had done with the Narragansetts) and he had been faithful to them in the Pequot War, they were engaged to support him in his just liberties and were contented that such of the surviving Pequots as had submitted to him should remain with him and quietly under his protection. This did much increase his power and augment his greatness, which the Narragansetts could not endure to see. But Miantonomo,[26] their chief sachem, an ambitious and politic man, sought privately and by treachery, according to the Indian manner, to make him away by hiring some to kill him. Sometime they assayed to poison him; that not taking, then in the night time to knock him on the head in his house or secretly to shoot him, and suchlike attempts. But none of these taking effect, he made open war upon him (though it was against the covenants both between the English and them, as also between themselves and a plain breach of the same). He came suddenly upon him with 900 or 1000 men, never denouncing any war before. The other's power at that present was not above half so many, but it pleased God to give Uncas the victory and he slew many of his men and wounded many more; but the chief of all was, he took Miantonomo prisoner.

And seeing he was a great man, and the Narragansetts a potent people and would seek revenge, he would do nothing in the case without the advice of the English, so he, by the help and direction of those of Connecticut, kept him prisoner till this meeting of the Commissioners. The Commissioners weighed the cause and passages as they were clearly represented and sufficiently evidenced betwixt Uncas and Miantonomo; and the things being duly considered, the Commissioners apparently saw that Uncas could not be safe whilst Miantonomo lived; but either by secret treachery or open force, his life would be still in danger. Wherefore they thought he might justly put such a false and blood-thirsty enemy to death; but in his own jurisdiction, not in the English plantations. And they advised in the manner of his death all mercy and moderation should be showed, contrary to the practice of the Indians, who exercise tortures and cruelty. And Uncas having hitherto showed himself a friend to the English, and in this craving their advice, if the Narragansett Indians or others shall unjustly assault Uncas for this execution, upon notice and request the English promise to assist and protect him as far as they may against such violence.

This was the issue of this business. The reasons and passages hereof are more at large to be seen in the acts and records of this meeting of the Commissioners. . . . And Uncas followed this advice and accordingly executed him in a very fair manner according as they advised, with due respect to his honour and greatness.[27]

[26] Miantonomo was attempting to forge a pan-Indian alliance in New England, in an effort to ward the English off Native American lands. To succeed, Miantonomo had to attack Uncas, a faithful ally of the English.

[27] The supposedly "very fair manner" in which Uncas executed Miantonomo was this: Miantonomo was bound and slain by a hatchet wielded by Uncas's brother.

from Chapter XXXIV Anno Domini 1644

[*Proposal to Remove to Nauset*]

Mr. Edward Winslow was chosen Governor this year.

Many having left this place (as is before noted) by reason of the straitness and barrenness of the same and their finding of better accommodations elsewhere more suitable to their ends and minds; and sundry others still upon every occasion desiring their dismissions, the church began seriously to think whether it were not better jointly to remove to some other place than to be thus weakened and as it were insensibly dissolved.[28] Many meetings and much consultation was held hereabout, and divers were men's minds and opinions. Some were still for staying together in this place, alleging men might here live if they would be content with their condition, and that it was not for want or necessity so much that they removed as for the enriching of themselves. Others were resolute upon removal and so signified that here they could not stay; but if the church did not remove, they must. Insomuch as many were swayed rather than there should be a dissolution, to condescend to a removal if a fit place could be found that might more conveniently and comfortably receive the whole, with such accession of others as might come to them for their better strength and subsistence; and some such-like cautions and limitations.

So as, with the aforesaid provisos, the greater part consented to a removal to a place called Nauset, which had been superficially viewed and the good will of the purchasers to whom it belonged obtained, with some addition thereto from the Court. But now they began to see their errour, that they had given away already the best and most commodious places to others, and now wanted themselves. For this place was about 50 miles from hence, and at an outside of the country remote from all society; also that it would prove so strait as it would not be competent to receive the whole body, much less be capable of any addition or increase; so as, at least in a short time, they should be worse there than they are now here. The which with sundry other like considerations and inconveniences made them change their resolutions. But such as were before resolved upon removal took advantage of this agreement and went on, notwithstanding; neither could the rest hinder them, they having made some beginning.[29]

And thus was this poor church left, like an ancient mother grown old and forsaken of her children, though not in their affections yet in regard of their bodily presence and personal helpfulness; her ancient members being most of them worn away by death, and these of later time being like children translated into other families, and she like a widow left only to trust in God.[30] Thus, she that had made many rich became herself poor.[31] . . .

[28]Bradford and likeminded Pilgrims welcomed the establishment of new towns and churches in the Colony by newcomers, as at Scituate and Taunton, but they wanted the original Plymouth church, including members of the second generation, to stick together.

[29]After looking it over twice, a committee of the Plymouth church reported that there was not enough room for all.

[30]I Timothy 5:5.

[31]II Corinthians 6:10.

Roger Williams 1603?–1683

Banished in his time, beloved in ours, Roger Williams represents a paradoxical early expression of the American ideals of democracy and religious freedom. William Bradford described him as "godly and zealous . . . but very unsettled in judgment" with "strange opinions." John Winthrop said Williams held "diverse new and dangerous opinions." Cotton Mather vilified him as a kind of Don Quixote, the "first rebel against the divine-church order in the wilderness" with a "windmill" whirling so furiously in his head that "a whole country in America [is] like to be set on fire." Providence, Rhode Island, which prospered under his tolerance, became a haven for heretics, runaways, and malcontents, a "Rogue's Island."

Since the nineteenth century, Americans have enshrined Roger Williams as a symbol of liberty of individual conscience and toleration of racial and religious differences, an apostle of civil and spiritual freedom. But Williams's liberal inclusiveness was paradoxical, since it was based on his own rigid adherence to the doctrine of separatism. He was a friend of the Narragansett Indians and defender of religious dissenters because he was a devout Separatist Puritan, whose political ideas were founded on his belief that Christianity must be free from the "foul embrace" of civil authority. Rather than liberalism, it was his literalism—his literal-minded reading of Christian scripture—that led him toward policies of religious tolerance.

Williams grew up in the Smithfield district of London, a center of Separatist activity. In 1617 his skill at shorthand earned him the patronage of Sir Edward Coke, who enrolled him at Cambridge in 1623, where Williams completed a B.A. in 1627 and began an M.A. Having "forsaken the university" for Puritanism, he became a chaplain in 1629. His religious beliefs grew increasingly radical. He met John Winthrop and John Cotton, who would become his chief adversary. On December 10, 1630, Williams sailed with the Great Migration.

His unorthodoxy started trouble almost as soon as the Puritans arrived in February 1631. Called to be minister of Boston's First Church, he told the community he "durst not officiate to an unseparated people." He insisted that they separate and repent worshiping with the Church of England. Also, he denounced magistrates for punishing violations of the Sabbath, arguing that they had no authority to enforce the first four Commandments, thus beginning a battle with the Puritan leaders over separation of church and state. Moving first to Plymouth and then to Salem, he continued to preach three extreme positions: (1) the Puritans should become Separatists (a position that endangered the Massachusetts Bay Company charter and the relative freedom it granted); (2) the charter was invalid because Christian kings had no right to heathen lands (a position based on separation of spiritual and material prerogatives); and (3) the civil magistrates had no jurisdiction over matters of conscience and soul, only material and social matters (a position that undermined the Puritan oligarchy). The governor and magistrates saw the dangerous implications of Williams's positions, and on July 8, 1635, he was indicted for heresy and divisiveness, then sentenced to banishment on October 9. To avoid deportation, Williams fled south to an Indian settlement in January 1636.

He purchased land from the Narragansetts and founded Providence, where he devoted himself to creating a heavenly city on earth. Exiles followed him, including Anne Hutchinson, and dissenters of all kinds from Quakers to Jews. In 1643, Williams sailed for England to incorporate Providence, Newport, and Portsmouth under a charter that recognized separation of church and state. After the Puritan execution of King Charles I invalidated the charter, he again voyaged to England in 1651 and returned with a second patent in 1654 that assured political stability. As president of the General Assembly, he guided the policies of the colony, such as welcoming Quakers. For most of his life he held offices, continuing to fight for Indian rights and his religious principles. His last major public role was as negotiator for the Narragansetts during King Philip's War. Tragically, he failed to keep them out of the conflict; consequently, Providence was burned and the tribe was wiped out.

His first and most artistic work is *A Key into the Language of America,* which was published in London in 1643, when Williams was getting the charter from Charles I. Each chapter begins with an *"Implicite Dialogue,"* Narragansett on the left, English on the right. This section is followed by a focused "Observation" on the topic, followed by a "*generall* Observation" that draws cultural and spiritual conclusions and offers moral instruction through meditation and analogy. The chapters end with emblematic poems that satirize English civilized degeneracy and sympathize with Indian barbaric virtue. These poems express Williams's view of the tragic effects of the colonizing process. The book is a massive sociolinguistic project that shows sensitivity to Native American's language and admiration for their culture, while at the same time offering a lament that these pagans are damned. The text presents a paradox: the Indians had to be civilized before they could be Christianized, but civilizing them often destroyed their natural virtue. Throughout the book, this paradox suggests ironic comparisons of civilization with barbarism.

In his other important works, polemical tracts, Williams used his Cambridge training in medieval disputation to compose prolix, rhetorical, erudite arguments, loaded with biblical and classical allusions and quotations. For example, *Mr. Cotton's Letter* presents Williams's version of his banishment, defending his Separatist position, citing intolerance in Massachusetts, and characterizing Cotton as a self-righteous bigot. Williams's most famous work, *The Bloody Tenent of Persecution,* is a refutation of Cotton's tenet justifying persecution for personal beliefs. In a dialogue between Truth and Peace, the first half of *The Bloody Tenent* is a point-by-point rebuttal and a plea for liberty of conscience as a human right. The second half argues that a government is granted power by the people, most of whom are unregenerate. As delegates of the people, therefore, magistrates could not interfere with religion, for the unregenerate have no power in Christ's church. His most famous letter is "To the Town of Providence" (January 1655), written to settle a controversy that divided the town over religious autonomy and civil restraint. While defending a government's right to require civil obedience, he also shows that liberty of conscience does not lead to anarchy. As a septuagenarian he engaged in a vehement debate with the Quakers and wrote a seemingly uncharacteristic denunciation of "the cursed sect" and their leader, George Fox. Although opposed to their fanatic assurance of their infallibility and "inner light," which he felt repudiated the Bible and Christ, he never wanted them subjected to legal persecution. He met their threat to social peace in his heavenly city by arguing against their errors, remaining true to his principles of religious toleration.

Raymond F. Dolle
Indiana State University

Renée Bergland
Simmons College

PRIMARY WORKS

A Key into the Language of America, 1643; *The Bloody Tenent of Persecution for Cause of Conscience, Discussed in a Conference betweene Truth and Peace,* 1644; *Mr. Cotton's Letter Lately Printed, Examined, and Answered,* 1644; *Queries of the Highest Consideration,* 1644; *Christenings Make Not Christians,* 1645; *The Bloody Tenent Yet More Bloudy by Mr. Cotton's Endeavor to Wash it White in the Blood of the Lambe,* 1652; *Experiments of Spiritual Life and Health,* 1652; *The Fourth Paper Presented by Major Butler,* 1652; *The Hireling Ministry None of Christs,* 1652; *George Fox Digg'd Out of His Burrowes,* 1676; *The Complete Writings of Roger Williams,* 6 vols., ed. J. Hammond Trumball, 1866–1874; rpt. with an additional volume by Perry Miller, 1963; *The Correspondence of Roger Williams,* 2 vols., ed. Glenn LaFantasie, 1988.

from A Key into the Language of America[1]

[Preface]
To my Deare and Welbeloved Friends and Countreymen, in old and new England

I present you with a *Key;* I have not heard of the like, yet framed, since it pleased God to bring that mighty *Continent of America* to light: Others of my Countrey-men have often, and excellently, and lately written of the *Countrey* (and none that I know beyond the goodnesse and worth of it.) This *Key,* respects the *Native Language* of it, and happily may unlocke some *Rarities* concerning the *Natives* themselves, not yet discovered.

I drew the *Materialls* in a rude lumpe at Sea,[2] as a private *helpe* to my owne memory, that I might not by my present absence *lightly lose* what I had so *dearely bought* in some few years *hardship,* and *charges* among the *Barbarians;* yet being reminded by some, what pitie it were to bury those *Materialls* in my *Grave* at land or Sea; and withall, remembring how oft I have been importun'd by *worthy friends,* of all sorts, to afford them some helps this way.

I resolved (by the assistance of the *most High*) to cast those *Materialls* into this *Key, pleasant* and *profitable* for *All,* but speally for my *friends* residing in those parts:

A little *Key* may open a *Box,* where lies a *bunch* of *Keyes.*

With this I have entred into the secrets of those *Countries,* where ever *English* dwel about two hundred miles, betweene the *French* and *Dutch* Plantations; for want of this, I know what grosse *mistakes* my selfe and others have run into.

There is a mixture of this *Language North* and *South,* from the place of my abode, about six hundred miles; yet within the two hundred miles (aforementioned)

[1]Subtitled *An help to the Language of the Natives in that part of America, called New-England,* the *Key* was first published in London in 1643. This text, slightly modernized, is taken from *The Complete Writings of Roger Williams,* 7 vols., 1963.

[2]Williams composed *A Key* during his two-month transatlantic crossing in 1643.

their *Dialects* doe exceedingly differ;[3] yet not so, but (within that compasse) a man may, by this *helpe,* converse with *thousands* of *Natives* all over the *Countrey:* and by such converse it may please the *Father of Mercies* to spread *civilitie,* (and in his owne most holy season) *Christianitie;* for *one Candle* will light *ten thousand,* and it may please *God* to blesse a *little Leaven* to season the *mightie Lump* of those *Peoples* and *Territories. . . .*

And because to this Question, some put an edge from the boast of the Jesuits in *Canada* and *Maryland,* and especially from the wonderfull conversions made by the Spaniards and Portugalls in the *West-Indies,* besides what I have here written, as also, beside what I have observed in the Chapter of their Religion! I shall further present you with a briefe Additionall discourse concerning this Great Point, being comfortably perswaded that that Father of Spirits, who was graciously pleased to perswade *Japhet*[4] (the Gentiles) to dwell in the Tents of *Shem*[5] (the Jewes) will in his holy season (I hope approaching) perswade, these Gentiles of *America* to partake of the mercies of *Europe,* and then shall bee fulfilled what is written, by the Prophet *Malachi,*[6] from the rising of the Sunne in *(Europe)* to the going down of the same (in *America*) my Name shall be great among the Gentiles.) So I desire to hope and pray,

Your unworthy Country-man
Roger Williams

Directions for the use of the Language

1. A Dictionary *or* Grammer *way* I *had consideration of, but purposely avoided, as not so accommodate to the Benefit of all, as I hope this Forme is.*

2. A Dialogue *also I had thoughts of, but avoided for brevities sake, and yet (with no small paines) I have so framed every Chapter and the matter of it, as I may call it an Implicite Dialogue.*

3. *It is framed chiefly after the* Narrogánset *Dialect, because most spoken in the Countrey, and yet (with attending to the variation of peoples and Dialects) it will be of great use in all parts of the Countrey.*

4. *Whatever your occasion bee either of Travell, Discourse, Trading & c. turne to the Table which will direct you to the Proper Chapter.*

5. *Because the Life of all Language is in the Pronuntiation, I have been at the paines and charges to Cause the Accents, Tones, or sounds to be affixed, (which some understand, according to the* Greeke *Language, Acutes, Graves, Circumflexes) for example, in the second leafe*[7] *in the word* Ewò *He: the sound or Tone must not be put on* E, *but* wò *where the grave Accent is.*

In the same leafe, in the word Ascowequássin, *the sound must not be on any of the Syllables, but on* quáss, *where the Acute or sharp sound is.*

In the same leafe in the word Anspaumpmaûntam, *the sound must not be on any other syllable but* Maûn, *where* the Circumflex *or long sounding Accent is.*

[3]The Indians in the region spoke dialects of the Algonkian language family, which included Narragansett.

[4]The third son of Noah, traditionally progenitor of the Medes and Greeks.

[5]The eldest son of Noah, ancestor of the Semitic peoples.

[6]See Malachi 1.11.

[7]On page two.

6. *The* English *for every* Indian *word or phrase stands in a straight line directly against the* Indian: *yet sometimes there are two words for the same thing (for their Language is exceeding copious, and they have five or six words sometimes for one thing) and then the* English *stands against them both: for example in the second leafe,*

Cowáunckamish & Cuckquénamish.	*I pray your Favour.*

Chapter XI
Of Travell

Máyi.	*A way.*
Mayúo?	*Is there a way?*
Mat mayanúnno.	*There is no way.*
Peemáyagat.	*A little way.*
Mishimmáyagat.	*A great path.*
Machípscat.	*A stone path.*

Obs. It is admirable to see, what paths their naked hardned feet have made in the wildernesse in most stony and rockie places.

Nnatotemúckaun.	*I will aske the way.*
Kunnatótemous.	*I will inquire of you.*
Kunnatotemì?	*Doe you aske me?*
Tou nishin méyi?	*Where lies the way?*
Kokotemíinnea méyi.	*Shew me the way.*
Yo áinshick méyi.	*There the way lies.*
Kukkakótemous.	*I will shew you.*
Yo cummittamáyon.	*There is the way you must goe.*
Yo chippachâusin.	*There the way divides.*
Maúchatea.	*A guide.*
Máuchase.	*Be my guide.*

Obs. The wildernesse being so vast, it is a mercy, that for a hire a man shall never want guides, who will carry provisions, and such as hire them over the Rivers and Brookes, and find out often times hunting-houses, or other lodgings at night.

Anóce wénawash.	*Hire him.*
Kuttánnoonsh.	*I will hire you.*
Kuttaúnckquittaunch.	*I will pay you.*
Kummuchickónckquatous.	*I will pay you well.*
Tocketaonckquittíinnea?	*What wil you give me?*
Cummáuchanish.	*I will conduct you.*
Yó aûnta.	*Let us goe that way.*
Yò cuttâunan.	*Goe that way.*
Yo mtúnnock.	*The right hand.*
Yo nmúnnatch.	*The left hand.*

Cowéchaush.	*I will goe with you.*
Wétash.	*Goe along.*
Cowéchaw ewò.	*He will goe with you.*
Cowechauatímmin.	*I will goe with you.*
Wechauatíttea.	*Let us accompany.*
Taûbot wétáyean.	*I thanke you for your company.*

Obs. I have heard of many *English* lost, and have oft been lost my selfe, and my selfe and others have often been found, and succoured by the *Indians.*

Pitchcowáwwon.	*You will lose your way.*
Meshnowáwwon.	*I lost my way.*
Nummauchèmin, Ntanniteímmin.	*I will be going.*
Mammauchêtuck.	*Let us be going.*
Ânakiteunck.	*He is gone.*
Memauchêwi ánittui, Memauchegushánnick, Anakugushánnick.	*They are gone.*
Tunnockuttòme, Tunnockkuttoyeâim?	*Whither goe you?*
Tunnockkuttínshem, Nnegónshem.	*I will goe before.*
Cuppompáish.	*I will stay for you.*
Negónshesh.	*Goe before.*
Mittummayaûcup.	*The way you went before.*
Cummáttanish.	*I will follow you.*
Cuppahímmin.	*Stay for me.*
Tawhich quaunqua quêan?	*Why doe you run so?*
Nowecóntum púmmishem.	*I have a mind to travell.*
Konkenuphshâuta.	*Let us goe apace.*
Konkenúppe.	*Goe apace.*
Michéme nquanunquaquêmin.	*I have run alwayes.*
Yo ntoyamâushem.	*I goe this pace.*

Obs. They are generally quick on foot, brought up from the breasts to running: their legs being also from the wombe stretcht and bound up in a strange way on their Cradle backward, as also annointed; yet have they some that excell: so that I have knowne many of them run betweene fourescoure or an hundred miles in a Summers day, and back within two dayes: they doe also practice running of *Races;* and commonly in the Summer, they delight to goe without shoes, although they have them hanging at their backs: they are so exquisitely skilled in all the body and bowels of the Countrey (by reason of their huntings) that I have often been guided twentie, thirtie, sometimes fortie miles through the woods, a streight course, out of any path.

Yò wuchê.	*From hence.*
Tounúckquaque yo wuchê?	*How far from hence?*

Yò anúckquaque.	*So farre.*
Yo anuckquaquêse.	*So little a way.*
Waunaquêse.	*A little way.*
Aukeewushaûog.	*They goe by land.*
Mìshoon hómwock.	*They goe* or *come by water.*
Naynayoûmewot.	*A Horse.*
Wunnìa, naynayoûmewot.	*He rides on Horse-back.*

Obs. Having no Horses, they covet them above other Cattell,[8] rather preferring ease in riding, then their profit and belly, by milk and butter from Cowes and Goats, and they are loth to come to the *English* price for any.

Aspumméwi.	*He is not gone by.*
Aspumméwock.	*They are not gone by.*
Awánick payánchick?	*Who come there?*
Awanick negonsháchick?	*Who are these before us?*
Yo cuppummesicómmin.	*Crosse over into the way there.*
Cuppì-machàug.	*Thick wood: a Swamp.*

Obs. These thick Woods and Swamps (like the Boggs to the *Irish*) are the Refuges for Women and children in Warre, whil'st the men fight. As the Country is wondrous full of Brookes and Rivers, so doth it also abound with fresh ponds, some of many miles compasse.

Níps -nipsash.	*Pond: Ponds.*
Wèta: wétedg.	*The Woods on fire.*
Wussaumpatámmin.	*To View* or *looke about.*
Wussaum patámoonck.	*A Prospect.*
Wuttocékémin.	*To wade.*
Tocekétuck.	*Let us wade.*
Tou wuttáuqussin?	*How deepe?*
Yò ntaúqussin.	*Thus deep.*
Kunníish.	*I will carry you.*
Kuckqússuckqun.	*You are heavy.*
Kunnâukon.	*You are light.*
Pasúckquish.	*Rise.*
Anakish: maúchish.	*Goe.*
Quaquìsh.	*Runne.*
Nokus káuatees.	*Meet him.*
Nockuskauatítea.	*Let us meet.*
Neenmeshnóckuskaw.	*I did meet.*

Obs. They are joyfull in meeting of any in travell, and will strike fire either with stones or sticks, to take Tobacco, and discourse a little together.

[8]Farm animals.

Mesh Kunnockqus kauatímmin?	*Did you meet? &c.*
Yò Kuttauntapímmin.	*Let us rest here.*
Kussackquêtuck.	*Let us sit downe.*
Yo appíttuck.	*Let us sit here.*
Nissówanis, Nissowànishkaûmen.	*I am weary.*
Nickqússaqus.	*I am lame.*
Ntouagonnausinnúmmin.	*We are distrest undone,* or *in misery.*

Obs. They use this word properly in wandring toward Winter night, in which case I have been many a night with them, and many times also alone, yet alwayes mercifully preserved.

Teâno wonck nippéeam.	*I will be here by and by againe.*
Mat Kunníckansh.	*I will not leave you.*
Aquie Kunnickatshash	*Doe not leave me.*
Tawhítch nickatshiêan?	*Why doe you forsake me?*
Wuttánho.	*A staffe.*
Yò íish Wuttánho.	*Use this staffe.*

Obs. Sometimes a man shall meet a lame man or an old man with a Staffe: but generally a Staffe is a rare sight in the hand of the eldest, their Constitution is so strong. I have upon occasion travelled many a score, yea many a hundreth mile amongst them, without need of stick or staffe, for any appearance of danger amongst them: yet it is a rule amongst them, that it is not good for a man to travell without a Weapon nor alone.

Taquáttin.	*Frost.*
Auke taquátsha.	*The ground is frozen.*
Séip taquáttin.	*The River is frozen.*
Now ánnesin.	*I have forgotten.*
Nippittakûnnamun.	*I must goe back.*

Obs. I once travelled with neere 200 who had word of neere 700 Enemies in the way, yet generally they all resolved that it was a shame to feare and goe back.

Nippanishkokómmin, Npussagokommìn.	*I have let fall something.*
Mattaâsu.	*A little way.*
Naûwot.	*A great way.*
Náwwatick.	*Farre off at Sea.*
Ntaquatchuwaûmen.	*I goe up hill.*
Taguatchòwash.	*Goe up hill.*
Wáumsu.	*Downe hill.*
Mauúnshesh.	*Goe slowly* or *gently.*
Mauanisháuta.	*Let us goe gently.*

Tawhìtch cheche qunnuwáyean?	*Why doe you rob me?*
Aquie chechequnnuwásh.	*Doe not rob me.*
Chechequnnuwáchick.	*Robbers.*
Chechequnníttin.	*There is a Robbery committed.*
Kemineantúock.	*They murder each other.*

Obs. If any Robbery fall out in Travell, between Persons of diverse States, the offended State sends for Justice; If no Justice bee granted and recompence made, they grant out a kind of Letter of Mart to take satisfaction themselves, yet they are carefull not to exceed in taking from others, beyond the Proportion of their owne losse.

Wúskont àwaùn nkemineíucqun.	*I feare some will murther mee.*

Obs. I could never heare that Murthers or Robberies are comparably so frequent, as in parts of *Europe* amongst the English, French, &c.

Cutchachewussímmin.	*You are almost there.*
Kiskecuppeeyáumen.	*You are a little short.*
Cuppeeyáumen.	*Now you are there.*
Muckquétu.	*Swift.*
Cummúmmuckquete.	*You are swift.*
Cussásaqus.	*You are slow.*
Sassaqushâuog.	*They are slow.*
Cuttinneapúmmishem?	*Will you passe by?*
Wuttineapummushâuta, Keeatshaûta.	*Let us passe by.*
Ntinneapeeyaûmen.	*I come for no busines.*
Acoûwe.	*In vaine* or *to no purpose.*
Ntackówwepeyaùn.	*I have lost my labour.*
Cummautússakou.	*You have mist him.*
Kihtummâyi-wussáuhumwi.	*He went just now forth.*
Pittúckish.	*Goe back.*
Pittuckétuck.	*Let us goe back.*
Pónewhush.	*Lay downe your burthen.*

Generall Observations of their Travell

As the same Sun shines on the Wildernesse that doth on a Garden! so the same faithfull and all sufficient God, can comfort, feede and safely guide even through a desolate howling Wildernesse.

More particular:

God makes a Path, provides a Guide,
And feeds in Wildernesse!

His glorious Name while breath remaines,
O that I may confesse.

Lost many a time, I have had no Guide,
No House, but hollow Tree!
In stormy Winter night no Fire,
No Food, no Company:

In him I have found a House, a Bed,
A Table, Company:
No Cup so bitter, but's made sweet,
When God shall Sweet'ning be.

from Chapter XXI
Of Religion, the soule, &c.

Manìt-manittó-wock.	*God, Gods.*

Obs. He that questions whether God made the World, the *Indians* will teach him. I must acknowledge I have received in my converse with them many Confirmations of those two great points, *Heb.* 11. 6. *viz:*

1. That God is.
2. That hee is a rewarder of all them that diligently seek him.

They will generally confesse that God made all: but then in speciall, although they deny not that *English-mans* God made *English* Men, and the Heavens and Earth there! yet their Gods made them and the Heaven, and Earth where they dwell.

Nummusquaunamúckqun manìt.	*God is angry with me*

Obs. I have heard a poore *Indian* lamenting the losse of a child at break of day, call up his Wife and children, and all about him to Lamentation, and with abundance of teares cry out! O God thou hast taken away my child! thou art angry with me: O turne thine anger from me, and spare the rest of my children.

If they receive any good in hunting, fishing, Harvest &c. they acknowledge God in it.

Yea, if it be but an ordinary accident, a fall, &c. they will say God was angry and did it, *musquántum manit* God is angry. But herein is their Misery.

First they branch their God-head into many Gods.

Secondly, attribute it to Creatures.

First, many Gods: they have given me the Names of thirty seven, which I have, all which in their solemne Worships they invocate: as *Kautántowwit* the great *South-West* God, to whose House all soules goe, and from whom came their Corne, Beanes, as they say.

Wompanànd.	*The Easterne God.*
Chekesuwànd.	*The Westerne God.*
Wunnanaméanit.	*The Northerne God.*

Sowwanànd.	*The Southerne God.*
Wetuómanit.	*The house God.*

Even as the Papists have their He and Shee Saint Protectors as St. *George,* St. *Patrick,* St. *Denis,* Virgin *Mary,* &c.

Squáuanit.	*The Womans God.*
Muckquachuckquànd.	*The Childrens God.*

Obs. I was once with a *Native* dying of a wound, given him by some murtherous *English* (who rob'd him and run him through with a Rapier, from whom in the heat of his wound, he at present escaped from them, but dying of his wound, they suffered Death at new *Plymouth,* in *New-England,*[9] this *Native* dying call'd much upon *Muckquachuckquànd,* which of other *Natives* I understood (as they believed) had appeared to the dying young man, many yeares before, and bid him when ever he was in distresse call upon him.

Secondly, as they have many of these fained Deities: so worship they the Creatures in whom they conceive doth rest some Deitie:

Keesuckquànd.	*The Sun God.*
Nanepaûshat.	*The Moone God.*
Paumpágussit.	*The Sea.*
Yotáanit.	*The Fire God.*

Supposing that Deities be in these, &c.

When I have argued with them about their Fire-God: can it say they be, but this fire must be a God, or Divine power, that out of a stone will arise in a Sparke, and when a poore naked *Indian* is ready to starve with cold in the House, and especially in the Woods, often saves his life, doth dresse all our Food for us, and if it be angry will burne the House about us, yea if a spark fall into the drie wood, burnes up the Country, (though this burning of the Wood to them they count a Benefit both for destroying of vermin, and keeping downe the Weeds and thickets?)

Praesentem narrat quaelibet herba Deum,

Every little Grasse doth tell,
The sons of Men, there God doth dwell.

Besides there is a generall Custome amongst them, at the apprehension of any Excellency in Men, Women, Birds, Beasts, Fish, &c. to cry out *Manittóo,* that is, it is a God, as thus if they see one man excell others in Wisdome, Valour, strength, Activity &c. they cry out *Manittóo* A God: and therefore when they talke amongst themselves of the *English* ships, and great buildings, of the plowing of their Fields, and especially

[9]Four runaway servants from Plymouth murdered a Narragansett in the summer of 1638. Williams demanded justice for the murder in a letter to Winthrop. Bradford described the crime, trial, and execution of the murderers in his *History of Plymouth Plantation.*

of Bookes and Letters, they will end thus: *Manittôwock* They are Gods: *Cummanittôo,* you are a God, &c. A strong Conviction naturall in the soule of man, that God is; filling all things, and places, and that all Excellencies dwell in God, and proceed from him, and that they only are blessed who have that Jehovah their portion.

Nickómmo. *A Feast or Dance.*

Of this Feast they have publike, and private and that of two sorts.

First in sicknesse, or Drouth, or Warre, or Famine.

Secondly, after Harvest, after hunting, when they enjoy a caulme of Peace, Health, Plenty, Prosperity, then *Nickómmo* a Feast, especially in Winter, for then (as the Turke saith of the Christian, rather the Antichristian,) they run mad once a yeare) in their kind of Christmas feasting.

Powwáw. *A Priest.*
Powwaûog. *Priests.*

Obs. These doe begin and order their service, and Invocation of their Gods, and all the people follow, and joyne interchangeably in a laborious bodily service, unto sweating, especially of the Priest, who spends himselfe in strange Antick Gestures, and Actions even unto fainting.

In sicknesse the Priest comes close to the sick person, and performes many strange Actions about him, and threaten and conjures out the sicknesse. They conceive that there are many Gods or divine Powers within the body of a man: In his pulse, his heart, his Lungs, &c.

I confesse to have most of these their customes by their owne Relation, for after once being in their Houses and beholding what their Worship was, I durst never bee an eye witnesse, Spectatour, or looker on, least I should have been partaker of Sathans Inventions and Worships, contrary to *Ephes.* 5. 14.[10]

Nanouwétea. *An over-Seer and Orderer of their Worship.*
Neen nanowwúnnemun. *I will order or oversee.*

They have an exact forme of King, Priest, and Prophet, as was in Israel typicall of old in that holy Land of *Canaan,* and as the Lord Jesus ordained in his spirituall Land of *Canaan* his Church throughout the whole World: their Kings or Governours called *Sachimaüog,* Kings, and *Atauskowaũg* Rulers doe govern: Their Priests, performe and manage their Worship: Their wise men and old men of which number the Priests are also,) whom they call *Taupowaüog* they make solemne speeches and Orations, or Lectures to them, concerning Religion, Peace, or Warre and all things.

Nowemaúsitteem. *I give away at the Worship.*

He or she that makes this *Nickòmmo* Feast or Dance, besides the Feasting of sometimes twenty, fifty, an hundreth, yea I have seene neere a thousand persons at

[10]Ephesians 5:11: "Take no part in the unfruitful works of darkness, but instead expose them."

one of these Feasts) they give I say a great quantity of money, and all sort of their goods (according to and sometimes beyond their Estate) in severall small parcells of goods, or money, to the value of eighteen pence, two Shillings, or thereabouts to one person: and that person that receives this Gift, upon the receiving of it goes out, and hollowes thrice for the health and prosperity of the Party that gave it, the Mr. or Mistris of the Feast.

Nowemacaũnash.	*Ile give these things.*
Nitteaũguash.	*My money.*
Nummaumachíuwash.	*My goods.*

Obs. By this Feasting and Gifts, the Divell drives on their worships pleasantly (as he doth all false worships, by such plausible Earthly Arguments of uniformities, universalities, Antiquities, Immunities, Dignities, Rewards, unto submitters, and the contrary to Refusers) so that they run farre and neere and aske

Awaun. Nákommit?	*Who makes a Feast?*
Nkekinneawaûmen.	*I goe to the Feast.*
Kekineawaũi.	*He is gone to the Feast.*

They have a modest Religious perswasion not to disturb any man, either themselves *English, Dutch,* or any in their Conscience, and worship, and therefore say:

Aquiewopwaũwash. Aquiewopwaũwock.	*Peace, hold your peace.*
Peeyaúntam.	*He is at Prayer.*
Peeyaúntamwock.	*They are praying.*
Cowwéwonck.	*The Soule,*

Derived from *Cowwene* to sleep, because say they, it workes and operates when the body sleepes. *Míchachunck* the soule, in a higher notion, which is of affinity, with a word signifying a looking glasse, or cleere resemblance, so that it hath its name from a cleere sight or discerning, which indeed seemes very well to suit with the nature of it.

Wuhóck.	*The Body.*
Nohòck: cohòck.	*My body, your body.*
Awaunkeesitteoúwincohòck:	*Who made you?*
Tunna-awwa commítchichunck-kitonckquèan?	*Whither goes your soule when you die?*
An. Sowánakitaũwaw.	*It goes to the South-West.*

Obs. They beleive that the soules of Men and Women goe to the Sou-west, their great and good men and Women to *Cautàntouwit* his House, where they have hopes (as the Turkes have of carnall Joyes): Murtherers thieves and Lyers, their Soules (say they) wander restlesse abroad.

Now because this Book (by Gods good providence) may come into the hand of many fearing God, who may also have many an opportunity of occasionall discourse with some of these their wild brethren and Sisters, and may speake a word for their and our glorious Maker, which may also prove some preparatory Mercy to their

Soules: I shall propose some proper expressions concerning the Creation of the World, and mans Estate, and in particular theirs also, which from my selfe many hundreths of times, great numbers of them have heard with great delight, and great convictions: which who knowes (in Gods holy season) may rise to the exalting of the Lord Jesus Christ in their conversion, and salvation?

Nétop Kunnatótemous.	*Friend, I will aske you a Question.*
Natótema:	*Speake on.*
Tocketunnántum?	*What thinke you?*
Awaun Keesiteoûwin Kéesuck?	*Who made the Heavens?*
Aûke Wechêkom?	*The Earth, the Sea?*
Mittauke.	*The World.*

Some will answer *Tattá* I cannot tell, some will answer *Manittôwock* the Gods.

Tasuóg, Maníttowock.	*How many Gods bee there?*
Maunaũog Mishaúnawock.	*Many, great many.*
Nétop machàge.	*Friend, not so.*
Pausuck naúnt manìt.	*There is onely one God.*
Cuppíssittone.	*You are mistaken.*
Cowauwaúnemun.	*You are out of the way.*

A phrase which much pleaseth them, being proper for their wandring in the woods, and similitudes greatly please them.

Kukkakótemous, wâchit-quáshouwe.	*I will tell you, presently.*
Kuttaunchemókous.	*I will tell you newes.*
Paûsuck naúnt manít kéesittin keesuck, &c	*One onely God made the Heavens, &c.*
Napannetashèmittan naugecautúmmonab nshque.	*Five thousand yeers agoe and upwards.*
Naũgom naũnt wukkesittínnes wâme teâgun.	*He alone made all things.*
Wuche mateâg	*Out of nothing.*
Quttatashuchuckqúnnacaus-keesitínnes wâme.	*In six dayes he made all things.*
Nquittaqúnne. Wuckéesitin wequâi.	*The first day Hee made the Light.*
Néesqunne. Wuckéesitin Keésuck.	*The Second day Hee made the Firmament.*
Shúckqunne wuckéesitin Aũke kà wechêkom.	*The third day hee made the Earth and Sea.*
Yóqunne wuckkéesitin Nip-paũus kà Nanepaũshat.	*The fourth day he made the Sun and the Moon.*
Neenash-mamockíuwash wêquanantíganash.	*Two great Lights.*

Kà wáme anócksuck.	*And all the Starres.*
Napannetashúckqunne Wuck-éesittin pussuckfeésuck wâme.	*The fifth day hee made all the Fowle.*
Keesuckquíuke.	*In the Ayre, or Heavens.*
Ka wáme namaũsuck. Wechekommíuke.	*And all the Fish in the Sea.*
Quttatashúkqunne wuckkeésit-tin penashímwockwamè	*The sixth day hee made all the Beasts of the Field.*
Wuttàke wuchè wuckeesittin. pausuck Enìn, *or,* Enefkée-tomp.	*Last of all he made one Man*
Wuche mishquòck.	*Of red Earth,*
Ka wesuonckgonnakaûnes Adam, túppautea mish-quòck.	*And call'd him Adam, or red Earth.*
Wuttàke wuchè, Câwit mish-quock.	*Then afterward, while Adam, or red Earth slept.*
Wuckaudnúmmenes manit peetaũgon wuche Adam.	*God tooke a rib from Adam, or red Earth.*
Kà wuchè peteaũgon.	*And of that rib he made One*
Wukkeefitinnes paũsuck squàw.	*woman,*
Kà pawtouwúnnes Adâmuck.	*And brought her to Adam.*
Nawônt Adam wuttúnnawaun nuppeteâgon ewò.	*When Adam saw her, he said, his is my bone.*
Enadatashúckqunne, aquêi.	*The seventh day hee rested,*
Nagaû wuchè quttatashúck-qune anacaũsuock English-mánuck.	*And therefore Englishmen worke six dayes.*
Enadatashuckqunnóckat taubataũmwock.	*On the seventh day they praise God.*

Obs. At this Relation they are much satisfied, with a reason why (as they observe) the *English* and *Dutch,* &c. labour six dayes, and rest and worship the seventh.

Besides, they will say, Wee never heard of this before: and then will relate how they have it from their Fathers, that *Kautántowwit* made one man and woman of a stone, which disliking, he broke them in pieces, and made another man and woman of a Tree, which were the Fountaines of all mankind.

They apprehending a vast difference of Knowledge betweene the *English* and themselves, are very observant of the *English* lives: I have heard them say to an Englishman (who being hindred, broke a promise to them) You know God, Will you lie Englishman? . . .

The generall Observation *of* Religion, &c.

The wandring Generations of *Adams* lost posteritie,[11] having lost the true and living God their Maker, have created out of the nothing of their owne inventions many false and fained Gods and Creators.

More particular:

Two sorts of men shall naked stand.
Before the burning ire
Of him that shortly shall appeare,
In dreadfull flaming fire.

First, millions know not God, nor for
His *knowledge, care to seeke:*
Millions have knowledge store, but in
Obedience are not meeke.

If woe to Indians, *Where shall* Turk,
Where shall appeare the Jew?
O, where shall stand the Christian false?
O blessed then the True.

Chapter XXII
Of their Government and Justice

Sâchim- maûog.	*King, Kings.*
Sachimaûonck.	*A Kingdome* or *Monarchie.*

Obs. Their Government is Monarchicall, yet at present the chiefest government in the Countrey is divided betweene a younger *Sachim,* Miantunnômu, and an elder *Sachim,* Caunoúnicus, of about fourescore yeeres old, this young mans Uncle: and their agreement in the Government is remarkable:

The old *Sachim* will not be offended at what the young *Sachim* doth: and the young *Sachim* will not doe what hee conceives will displease his Uncle.

Saunks.	*The Queen, or Sachims Wife.*
Saunckssquûaog.	*Queenes.*
Otân-nash.	*The towne, townes.*
Otânick.	*To the towne.*
Sachimmaacómmock.	*A Princes house,* which according to their condition, is farre different from the

[11]A popular theory about the origins of the Indians was that they were descended from the Ten Lost Tribes of Israel, which were carried into captivity by the King of Assyria.

	other house, both in capacity or receit;[12] and also the finenesse and quality of their Mats.
Ataúskawaw -wáuog.	*Lord, Lords.*
Wauôntam.	*A Wise man* or *Counsellour.*
Wauóntakick.	*Wise men.*
Enátch *or* eàtch Keèn anawáyean.	*Your will shall be law.*
Enàtch neèn ánowa.	*Let my word stand.*
Ntínnume.	*He is my man.*
Ntacquêtunck ewò.	*He is my subject.*
Kuttackquêtous	*I will* [*be*] *subject to you.*

Obs. Beside their generall subjection to the highest *Sachims,* to whom they carry presents: They have also particular Protectors, under *Sachims,* to whom they also carry presents, and upon any injury received, and complaint made, these Protectors will revenge it.

Ntannôtam.	*I will revenge it.*
Kuttannótous.	*I will revenge you.*
Miâwene.	*A Court* or *meeting.*
Wèpe cummiâwene.	*Come to the meeting.*
Miawêtuck.	*Let us meet.*
Wauwháutowash.	*Call a meeting.*
Miawêmucks.	*At a meeting.*
Miawéhettit.	*When they meet.*

Obs. The *Sachims,* although they have an absolute Monarchie over the people; yet they will not conclude of ought that concernes all, either Lawes, or Subsidies, or warres, unto which the people are averse, and by gentle perswasion cannot be brought.

Peyaùtch naûgum.	*Let himselfe come here.*
Pétiteatch.	*Let him come.*
Mishaúntowash.	*Speake out.*
Nanántowash.	*Speake plaine.*
Kunnadsíttamen wèpe.	*You must inquire after this.*
Wunnadsittamútta.	*Let us search into it.*
Neen pitch-nnadsíttamen.	*I will inquire into it.*
Machíssu ewò.	*He is naught.*
Cuttiantacompàwwem.	*You are a lying fellow.*
Cuttiantakiskquáwquaw.	*You are a lying woman.*
Wèpe cukkúmmoot.	*You have stole.*
Mat méshnawmônash.	*I did not see those things.*
Mat mèsh nummám menash.	*I did not take them.*

[12]Receptiveness, hospitality.

Wèpe kunnishquêko cummiskissâwwaw.	*You are fierce and quarrelsome.*

Obs. I could never discerne that excesse of scandalous sins amongst them, which *Europe* aboundeth with. Drunkennesse and gluttony, generally they know not what sinnes they be; and although they have not so much to restraine them (both in respect of knowledge of God and Lawes of men) as the *English* have, yet a man shall never heare of such crimes amongst them of robberies, murthers, adulteries, &c. as amongst the *English:* I conceive that the glorious Sunne of so much truth as shines in *England,* hardens our *English* hearts; for what the Sunne softeneth not, it hardens.

Tawhìtch yò enêan?	*Why doe you so?*
Tawhìtch cummootóan?	*Why doe you steale?*
Tawhìtch nanompanieân?	*Why are you thus idle* or *base?*
Wewhepapúnnoke.	*Bind him.*
Wèpe kunnishaûmis.	*You kild him.*
Wèpe kukkemineantín.	*You are the murtherer.*
Sasaumitaúwhitch.	*Let him be whipt.*
Upponckquittaúwhitch	*Let him be imprisoned.*
Nìppitch ewò.	*Let him die.*
Níphéttitch.	*Let them die.*
Nìss-Nìssoke.	*Kill him.*
Púm-púmmoke.	*Shoot him.*

Obs. The most usuall Custome amongst them in executing punishments, is for the *Sachim* either to beat, or whip, or put to death with his owne hand, to which the common sort most quietly submit: though sometimes the *Sachim* sends a secret Executioner, one of his chiefest Warriours to fetch of a head, by some sudden unexpected blow of a Hatchet, when they have feared Mutiny by publike execution.

Kukkeechequaûbenitch.	*You shall be hanged.*
Níppansínnea.	*I am innocent.*
Uppansìnea-ewo.	*He is innocent.*
Matmeshnowaûwon.	*I knew nothing of it.*
Nnowaûtum.	*I am sorry.*
Nummachiemè.	*I have done ill.*
Aumaúnemoke.	*Let it passe,* or *take away this accusation.*
Konkeeteatch Ewo.	*Let him live.*
Konkeeteáhetti.	*Let them live.*

Observation Generall, of their Government.

The wildest of the sonnes of Men have ever found a necessity, (for preservation of themselves, their Families and Properties) to cast themselves into some Mould or forme of Government.

More particular:

Adulteries, Murthers, Robberies, Thefts,
Wild Indians *punish these!*
And hold the Scales of Justice so,
That no man farthing leese.
When Indians *heare the horrid filths,*
Of Irish, English *Men,*
The horrid Oaths and Murthers late,
Thus say these Indians *then:*

We weare no Cloaths, have many Gods,
And yet our sinnes are lesse:
You are Barbarians, Pagans wild,
Your Land's the Wildernesse.

1643

To the Town of Providence[1]

[Providence?]

Loving Friends and Neighbours

It pleaseth GOD, yet to continue this great Liberty of our Town-Meetings, for which, we ought to be humbly thankful, and to improve these Liberties to the Praise of the Giver, and to the Peace and Welfare of the Town and Colony, without our own private Ends.[2]—I thought it my Duty, to present you with this my impartial Testimony, and Answer to a Paper sent you the other Day from my Brother,—*That it is Blood-Guiltiness, and against the Rule of the Gospel, to execute Judgment upon Transgressors, against the private or public Weal.*[3]—That ever I should speak or write a Tittle[4] that tends to such an infinite Liberty of Conscience, is a Mistake; and which I have ever disclaimed and abhorred. To prevent such Mistakes, I at present shall only propose this Case.—There goes many a Ship to Sea, with many a Hundred Souls in one Ship, whose Weal and Woe is common; and is a true Picture of a Common-Wealth, or an human Combination, or Society.[5] It hath fallen out sometimes, that both *Papists* and *Protestants, Jews,* and *Turks,* may be embarqued into one Ship. Upon which Supposal, I do affirm, that all the Liberty of Conscience that ever I pleaded for, turns upon these two Hinges, that none of the *Papists, Protestants, Jews,* or *Turks,* be forced to come to the Ships Prayers or Worship; nor, secondly, compelled

[1]Written ca. January 1654–1655. Undated, but believed to have been written after Williams's return to Providence from England in 1654. This text is taken from *The Correspondence of Roger Williams,* ed. Glenn LaFantasie, 1988.

[2]The controversy that divided the community may have been the issue of compulsory military service and its implications for religious autonomy and civil obedience.

[3]This work is lost and the author unknown.

[4]Dot, least bit.

[5]This analogy is Williams's reply to the argument that a citizen could not be prosecuted for resisting civil law if he claimed that it violated his private conscience. This fallacious idea was based on a misreading of *The Bloody Tenent.*

from their own particular Prayers or Worship, if they practice any. I further add, that I never denied, that notwithstanding this Liberty, the Commander of this Ship ought to command the Ship's Course; yea, and also to command that Justice, Peace, and Sobriety, be kept and practised, both among the Seamen and all the Passengers. If any Seamen refuse to perform their Service, or Passengers to pay their Freight;—if any refuse to help in Person or Purse, towards the Common Charges, or Defence;—if any refuse to obey the common Laws and Orders of the Ship, concerning their common Peace and Preservation;—if any shall mutiny and rise up against their Commanders, and Officers;—if any shall preach or write, that there ought to be no Commanders, nor Officers, because all are equal in CHRIST, therefore no Masters, nor Officers, no Laws, nor Orders, no Corrections nor Punishments—I say, I never denied, but in such Cases, whatever is pretended, the Commander or Commanders may judge, resist, compel, and punish such Transgressors, according to their Deserts and Merits. This, if seriously and honestly minded, may, if it so please the Father of Lights, let in some Light, to such as willingly shut not their Eyes.—I—remain, studious of our common Peace and Liberty,—

Roger Williams

c. 1654 1874

Testimony of Roger Williams relative to his first coming into the Narragansett country

Narragansett, June 18, 1682.

I testify, as in the presence of the all-making and all-seeing God, that about fifty years since,[1] I coming into this Narragansett country, I found a great contest between three Sachems, two, (to wit, Canonicus and Miantonomo) were against Ousamaquin, on Plymouth side, I was forced to travel between them three, to pacify, to satisfy all their and their dependents' spirits of my honest intentions to live peaceably by them. I testify, that it was the general and constant declaration, that Canonicus his father had three sons, whereof Canonicus was the heir, and his youngest brother's son, Miantonomo, (because of youth,) was his marshal and executioner, and did nothing without his uncle Canonicus' content; and therefore I declare to posterity, that were it not for the favor God gave me with Canonicus, none of these parts, no, not Rhode Island, had been purchased or obtained, for I never got any thing out of Canonicus but by gift.[2] I also profess, that very inquisitive of what the title or denomination Narragansett should come, I heard that Narragansett was so named from a little is-

[1]Williams fled from Salem to Seekonk, Narragansett Bay, in January 1636. This text, slightly modernized, is taken from *The Complete Writings of Roger Williams,* 7 vols., 1963.

[2]On March 24, 1638, Williams obtained a "Town Evidence" deed from the Narragansett sachems.

land between Puttiquomscut and Musquomacuk on the sea and fresh water side. I went on purpose to see it; and about the place called Sugar Loaf Hill, I saw it, and was within a pole of it, but could not learn why it was called Narragansett. I had learned, that the Massachusetts was called so, from the Blue Hills, a little island thereabout; and Canonicus' father and ancestors, living in these southern parts, transferred and brought their authority and name into those northern parts, all along by the sea-side, as appears by the great destruction of wood all along near the sea-side and I desire posterity to see the gracious hand of the Most High, (in whose hands are all hearts) that when the hearts of my countrymen and friends and brethren failed me, his infinite wisdom and merits stirred up the barbarous heart of Canonicus to love me as his son to his last gasp, by which means I had not only Miantonomo and all the lowest Sachems my friends, but Ousamaquin also, who because of my great friendship with him at Plymouth, and the authority of Canonicus, consented freely, being also well gratified by me, to the Governor Winthrop and my enjoyment of Prudence, yea of Providence itself, and all the other lands I procured of Canonicus which were upon the point, and in effect whatsoever I desired of him; and I never denied him or Miantonomo whatever they desired of me as to goods or gifts or use of my boats or pinnace, and the travels of my own person, day and night, which, though men know not, nor care to know, yet the all-seeing Eye hath seen it, and his all-powerful hand hath helped me. Blessed be his holy name to eternity.

Roger Williams

c. 1682 — 1963

Thomas Shepard 1605–1649

Born in the same year as the symbolic defeat of Catholicism in England in the discovery of Guy Fawkes's infamous Gunpowder Plot—the 1605 Catholic conspiracy to blow up the king and House of Lords—Thomas Shepard began life in a society rent by religious schisms. The first half of the seventeenth century was a turbulent time in the developing English Reformation, marked by extraordinary levels of intolerance and violence that would culminate in the regicide of Charles I in 1649. Religious persecution in the sixteenth century had resulted mostly from the competition between Catholic and Protestant world-views, as the throne passed from the Protestant convert Henry VIII and his short-lived son, Edward VI, to the Roman Catholic Queen Mary, and back to the Protestant Elizabeth I. But by the early seventeenth century, the Protestant church was firmly established in England, and in the absence of a unifying papal threat, political and theological divisions within the Protestant church began to widen.

Protestantism in England broke down into two primary factions: one was the Church of England, consisting of High-Church and Low-Church parties, with the monarch at its head and a ruling episcopacy similar in organization to the Catholic Church hierarchy; the other was the Puritan faction, divided into two principal camps, Presbyterians and Congregationalists. The

New England Puritans were Congregationalists. Unlike the Scottish Presbyterians, with their churches regulated by a central governing body known as the presbytery, the Congregationalist Puritans viewed each church—the congregation, deacons, ruling elders, and minister—as an autonomous body responsible for regulating the conduct of the members of its own community.

Because autonomous congregations were perceived as a threat to the political chain of command, critics of the New England Puritans labeled them Separatists, subject-citizens who denied the authority of church and state. The New England Puritans were not Separatists to the degree that their counterparts who removed to Holland in the early part of James's reign were. Rather, they were noncomformists, who, while accepting allegiance to the king, denied fealty to the Church of England. This was not an easy distinction to maintain, for the king was head of the church, and to dissent from the episcopacy could be construed as treason against king and state. The Puritans further objected that the Anglican Church had not gone far enough in its reform. They came to see Archbishop William Laud's High-Church party as promoting Roman Catholic liturgy and elaborate religious iconography pleasing to the Stuart kings, suspected Catholic sympathizers. The Puritans earned their name as noncomformists because they refused to sign Laud's Thirty-nine Articles of the Church of England, which mandated uniformity among the clergy by a signed avowal of High-Church liturgy and the "divine right of the episcopacy," a doctrine that held that the members of the bishopric had their commission directly from the Holy Spirit. Those like Shepard who refused to sign the oath were turned out of the pulpits and officially "silenced."

Shepard's autobiography and journal are among the most trenchant accounts of the persecution of the Puritans under Laud. Such persecution initiated the Great Migration (1629–1640) of nearly 20,000 Anglican dissenters to New England, and it inspired these Puritans to forge a covenant alliance with God in the New World and to build a holy city—a New Jerusalem—whose light would shine not only over the New World but also across the Atlantic to the shores of their native land. The first half of Shepard's autobiography chronicles his role in the Protestant skirmishes and the early part of the Puritan Revolt, even as it models for his New England posterity the good fight each Christian must undertake to defend the true church.

This tradition of life-writing (autobiography, journals, and conversion narratives) was a vital part of Puritan spiritual life. Puritans like Shepard discovered their predestined membership in the Invisible Church—those Christians preordained for salvation—by a constant scrutiny both of their own inner impulses and of the natural occurrences in the world around them. They believed that the human soul and the larger natural world operated as an elaborate sign system, which when read in the appropriate way conveyed God's will. Because, as *The New England Primer* phrased it, "In Adam's Fall/We Sinned all," the Puritans believed that humans had lost the ability to communicate directly with God and so instead had to rely upon his message indirectly conveyed through a sophisticated interpretive system—the reading of dreams, historical events, and natural occurrences, such as shipwrecks, deaths, earthquakes, and Indian attacks. Nowhere is this more poignant than in Shepard's interpretation of the death of his wife and child as a sign of his having placed too great a "store" in earthly things. They were taken prematurely, he writes, because he loved them too much. Recording such reflections allowed each individual to analyze and arrange the data and to construct a narrative that explained the world and one's place in it.

Such master narratives of God's plan for a community, however, were never wholly free from personal and imperial interests and were thus friendly to ideologies of racial and gender superiority and colonial expansionism. Shepard's autobiography indeed offers a celebratory account of most of the prominent Puritan players in the early drama of New England, even as it seeks to justify the brutal Pequot War (1636–1637) and the horrible, sweeping violence of Puritan retaliation against Native Americans for what were isolated Indian attacks. And we cannot lightly dismiss Shepard's signature role as one of Anne Hutchinson's principal inquisitors in the Antinomian purge. Far from being disgraceful only to modern sensibilities, both of these events achieved infamy in their own day.

Puritan life-writing powerfully shaped the individual's identity in the act of narrating experience. One interpreted the discrete events of life, and then used those interpretations to weave a larger fabric of meaning, to shape a spiritual destiny. Like Mary Rowlandson's captivity narrative, Shepard's autobiography validated his membership among God's chosen. Why, after all, would God allow him to encounter so many evils—religious persecution, near imprisonment, a perilous wreck at sea, the deaths of his wife and children, and Indian attacks—and to prevail over them if not to bring him to an awareness of God's saving grace? Just as Rowlandson's narrative attempts to bring meaning to the randomness of the violent world she encounters, Shepard's autobiography attempts to translate a historical record—a catalog of personal and national events—into a logical demonstration of God's preordained design. By making a temporal connection between his birth and Fawkes's terrorist attack on Parliament, Shepard suggests a powerful affinity between autobiography and allegory. Generations of Christians would, after all, view Shepard's narrative as a guide to understanding their own role in sacred history. Shepard points out precisely this narrative purpose when, by prefacing his autobiography with a letter to his son, he dedicates his life's story to family posterity—a posterity that five generations later would include Abigail Adams, wife of the second U.S. president and mother of the fifth. Such a correlation between New England's secular history and sacred design helps explain the national tendency to interchange American history and providential destiny.

Gregory S. Jackson
Rutgers University

PRIMARY WORK

John Albro, ed., *The Works of Thomas Shepard,* 3 vol. (1853; rpt., 1967).

Autobiography

[*My Birth and Life.*][1]

In the year of Christ 1604,[2] upon the 5th day of November, called the Powder Treason day, and that very hour of the day wherein the Parliament should have been blown up by Popish priests, I was then born, which occasioned my father to give me this name, Thomas,[3] because, he said, I would hardly *believe* that ever any such wickedness should be attempted by men against so religious and good [a] Parliament.

My father's name was William Shepard, born in a little poor town in Northamptonshire called Fossecut, near Towcester, and being a prentice to one Mr. Bland, a grocer, he married one of his daughters of whom he begat many children—three sons: John, William, and Thomas; and six daughters: Ann, Margaret, Mary, Elizabeth, Hester, Sarah—of all which only John, Thomas, Anna, and Margaret are still living in the town where I was born, viz., Towcester, in Northamptonshire, six miles distant from the town of Northampton in Old England.

I do well remember my father and have some little remembrance of my mother. My father was a wise, prudent man, the peacemaker of the place, and toward his latter end much blessed of God in his estate and in his soul. For there being no good ministry in the town, he was resolved to go and live at Banbury in Oxfordshire under a stirring ministry, having bought a house there for that end. My mother was a woman much afflicted in conscience, sometimes even unto distraction of mind, yet was sweetly recovered again before she died. I being the youngest, she did bear exceeding great love to me and made many prayers for me. But she died when I was about four years old, and my father lived and married a second wife, not dwelling in the same town, of whom he begat two children, Samuel and Elizabeth, and died when I was about ten years of age.

But while my father and mother lived, when I was about three years old, there was a great plague in the town of Towcester which swept away many in my father's family, both sisters and servants. I being the youngest, and best beloved of my mother, was sent away the day the plague brake out to live with my aged grandfather and grandmother in Fossecut, a most blind town and corner, and those I lived with also being very well to live, yet very ignorant. And there was I put to keep geese and other such country work, all that time much neglected of them, and afterward sent

[1]Shepard prefaces the original manuscript of his autobiography, completed around 1646, with a letter to his eldest son, Thomas Shepard Jr. (1635–1677), which begins with the following dedication: "To My Dear son Thomas Shepard with whom I leave these records of God's great kindness to him, not knowing that I shall live to tell them myself with my own mouth, that so he may learn to know and love the great and most high God, the God of his father."

[2]A slip of the pen in the original manuscript; Shepard was born in 1605, the year of the Gunpowder Plot.

[3]"Doubting Thomas": Christ's Apostle who, upon seeing his newly resurrected Lord, asked to touch the nail prints left in the flesh by crucifixion as proof that the person before him was indeed Jesus risen from the dead (John 20:25).

from them unto Adthrop, a little blind town adjoining, to my uncle, where I had more content, but did learn to sing and sport as children do in those parts and dance at their Whitsun Ales,[4] until the plague was removed and my dear mother dead, who died not of the plague, but of some other disease after it. And being come home, my sister Ann married to one Mr. Farmer, and my sister Margaret loved me much, who afterward married to my father's prentice, viz., Mr. Mapler.[5] And my father married again to another woman, who did let me see the difference between my own mother and a stepmother. She did seem not to love me, but incensed my father often against me; it may be that it was justly also for my childishness. And having lived thus for a time, my father sent me to school to a Welshman, one Mr. Rice, who kept the free school in the town of Towcester. But he was exceeding curst and cruel, and would deal roughly with me, and so discouraged me wholly from desire of learning that I remember I wished oftentimes myself in any condition, to keep hogs or beasts, rather than to go to school and learn.

But my father at last was visited with sickness, having taken some cold upon some pills he took, and so had the hickets[6] with his sickness a week together, in which time I do remember I did pray very strongly and heartily for the life of my father, and made some covenant, if God would do it, to serve Him the better, as knowing I should be left alone if he was gone. Yet the Lord took him away by death, and so I was left fatherless and motherless when I was about ten years old, and was committed to my stepmother to be educated, who therefore had my portion, which was a £100, which my father left me. But she neglecting my education very much, my brother John, who was my only brother alive, desired to have me out of her hands and to have me with him, and he would bring me up for the use of my portion; and so at last it was granted. And so I lived with this my eldest brother, who showed much love unto me, and unto whom I owe much, for him God made to be both father and mother unto me. And it happened that the cruel schoolmaster died and another[7] came into his room to be a preacher also in the town, who was an eminent preacher in those days and accounted holy, but afterward turned a great apostate and enemy to all righteousness, and I fear did commit the unpardonable sin. Yet it so fell out, by God's good providence, that this man stirred up in my heart a love and desire of the honor of learning, and therefore I told my friends I would be a scholar; and so the Lord blessed me in my studies, and gave me some knowledge of the Latin and Greek tongues, but much ungrounded in both. But I was studious, because I was ambitious of learning and being a scholar; and hence when I could not take notes of the sermon, I remember I was troubled at it, and prayed the Lord earnestly that he would help me to note sermons. And I see cause of wondering at the Lord's providence therein, for as soon as ever I had prayed (after my best fashion) Him for it, I presently, the next Sabbath, was able to take notes, who the precedent Sabbath could do nothing at all that way.

So I continued till I was about fifteen years of age, and then was conceived to be ripe for the University; and it pleased the Lord to put it into my brother's heart to

[4]Whitsun Ales: "a parish festival formerly held at Whitsuntide [Day of Pentecost], marked by feasting, sports, and merry-making" (OED). The Puritans disapproved of such festivities.

[5]Variously printed in extant texts as "Mapler" or "Waples."

[6]Hiccups.

[7]William Cluer, a graduate of Emmanuel College, Cambridge, became a Master of the school on September 23, 1617.

provide and to seek to prepare a place for me there, which was done in this manner. One Mr. Cockerill,[8] Fellow of Emmanuel College in Cambridge, being a Northamptonshire man, came down into the country to Northampton, and so sent for me, who, upon examination of me, gave my brother encouragement to send me up to Cambridge. And so I came up, and though I was very raw and young, yet it pleased God to open the hearts of others to admit me into the College a pensioner, and so Mr. Cockerill became my tutor.[9] But I do here wonder, and I hope shall bless the Lord forever in heaven, that the Lord did so graciously provide for me; for I have oft thought what a woful estate I had been left in if the Lord had left me in that profane, ignorant town of Towcester where I was born, that the Lord should pluck me out of that sink and Sodom, who was the least in my father's house, forsaken of father and mother, yet that the Lord should fetch me out from thence by such a secret hand.

The first two years I spent in Cambridge was in studying and in much neglect of God and private prayer, which I had sometime used; and I did not regard the Lord at all, unless it were at some fits. The third year, wherein I was Sophister, I began to be foolish and proud, and to show myself in the Public Schools, and there to be a disputer about things which now I see I did not know then at all, but only prated about them. And toward the end of this year when I was most vile (after I had been next unto the gates of death by the small pox the year before), the Lord began to call me home to the fellowship of his grace; which was in this manner:

(1) I do remember that I had many good affections (but blind and unconstant) oft cast into me since my father's sickness by the spirit of God wrestling with me; and hence I would pray in secret. And hence, when I was at Cambridge, I heard old Doctor Chadderton,[10] the master of the College when I came. And the first year I was there, to hear him, upon a sacrament day, my heart was much affected, but I did break loose from the Lord again. And half a year after I heard Mr. Dickinson common-place in the Chapel upon those words, "I will not destroy it for ten's sake,"[11] and then again was much affected; but I shook this off also and fell from God to loose and lewd company, to lust and pride and gaming, and bowling and drinking. And yet the Lord left me not; but a godly scholar, walking with me, fell to discourse about the misery of every man out of Christ, viz., that whatever they did was sin, and this did much affect me. And at another time when I did light in godly company, I heard them discourse about the wrath of God, and the terror of it, and how intolerable it was, which they did present by fire: how intolerable the torment of that was for a time—what then would eternity be? And this did much awaken me, and I began to pray again. But then by loose company I came to dispute in the schools, and there to join to loose scholars of other colleges and was fearfully left of God and fell to drink with them. And I drank so much one day that I was dead

[8]Daniel Cockerell (master's degree, 1612; Fellow, 1612–1621).

[9]Shepard was admitted as pensioner (a scholarship student) on February 10, 1620.

[10]Laurence Chaderton (1536–1640) graduated Christ's College, Cambridge, in 1567 and became Master of Emmanuel College, Cambridge, (1584–1622). Both of these colleges (particularly Emmanuel, which was founded by a Puritan), and Cambridge University in general, would for the next century be the nursery of Puritanism, training the vast majority of divines who emigrated to New England. In his life of more than a century, Chaderton was to become a leading force in England's Reformation and the ascendancy of Puritanism.

[11]Genesis 18:32.

drunk, and that upon a Saturday night, and so was carried from the place I had drinked at and did feast at unto a scholar's chamber, one Bassett, of Christ's College, and knew not where I was until I awakened late on that Sabbath and sick with my beastly carriage. And when I awakened, I went from him in shame and confusion, and went out into the fields, and there spent that Sabbath lying hid in the cornfields where the Lord, who might justly have cut me off in the midst of my sin, did meet me with much sadness of heart and troubled my soul for this and other my sins which then I had cause and leisure to think of. And now, when I was worst, He began to be best unto me, and made me resolve to set upon a course of daily meditation about the evil of sin and my own ways. Yet although I was troubled for this sin, I did not know my sinful nature all this while.

(2) The Lord therefore sent Dr. Preston[12] to be Master of the College; and Mr. Stone[13] and others commending his preaching to be most spiritual and excellent, I began to listen unto what he said. The first sermon he preached was Romans xii. "Be renewed in the spirit of your mind." In opening which point, viz., the change of heart in a Christian, the Lord so bored my ears, as that I understood what he spake, and the secrets of my soul were laid open before me—the hypocrisy of all my good things I thought I had in me—as if one had told him of all that ever I did, of all the turnings and deceits of my heart, insomuch as that I thought he was the most searching preacher in the world, and I began to love him much, and to bless God I did see my frame and my hypocrisy, and self and secret sins, although I found a hard heart and could not be affected with them.

(3) I did therefore set more constantly upon the work of daily meditation, sometimes every morning, but constantly every evening before supper; and my chief meditation was about the evil of sin, the terror of God's wrath, day of death, beauty of Christ, the deceitfulness of the heart, &c. But principally I found this my misery: sin was not my greatest evil, did lie light upon me as yet, yet I was much afraid of death and the flames of God's wrath. And this I remember, I never went out to meditate in the fields but I did find the Lord teaching me somewhat of myself, or Himself, or the vanity of the world I never saw before. And hence I took out a little book I have every day into the fields, and writ down what God taught me lest I should forget them; and so the Lord encouraged me and I grew much. But in my observation of myself, I did see my atheism. I questioned whether there were a God, and my unbelief whether Christ was the Messiah, whether the Scriptures were God's word or no. I felt all manner of temptations to all kind of religions, not knowing which I should choose, whether education might not make me believe what I had believed, and whether, if I had been educated up among the Papists, I should not have been as verily persuaded that Popery is the truth, or Turkism is the truth. And at last I heard of

[12]John Preston (1587–1628) was a convert of John Cotton and one of the most distinguished Puritan writers of his generation, successfully disputing Bishop Thomas Morton's attack on Cambridge; he replaced Chaderton as Master of Emmanuel College (1622–1628).

[13]Samuel Stone (1602–1663) graduated Emmanuel College, Cambridge, in Shepard's class (1623, M.A. in 1627). Suspended for nonconformity in 1630, he departed three years later for New England, where with Thomas Hooker he served the churches at Newton, Massachusetts (renamed Cambridge in 1637), and Hartford, Connecticut, named for Stone's birthplace.

Grindleton,[14] and I did question whether that glorious estate of perfection might not be the truth, and whether old Mr. Rogers's *Seven Treatises* and the *Practice of Christianity,*[15] the book which did first work upon my heart, whether these men were not all legal men and their books so. But the Lord delivered me at last from them, and in the conclusion after many prayers, meditations, duties, the Lord let me see three main wounds in my soul: (1) I could not feel sin as my greatest evil; (2) I could do nothing but I did seek myself in it, and was imprisoned there, and though I desired to be a preacher, yet it was honor I did look to like a vile wretch in the use of God's gifts I desired to have; (3) I felt a depth of atheism and unbelief in the main matters of salvation and whether the Scriptures were God's word. These things did much trouble me, and in the conclusion did so far trouble me that I could not read the Scriptures or hear them read without secret and hellish blasphemy, calling all into question and all Christ's miracles. And hereupon I fell to doubt whether I had not committed the unpardonable sin; and because I did question whether Christ did not cast out devils from Beelzebub, &c., I did think and fear I had. And now the terrors of God began to break in like floods of fire into my soul.

For three quarters of a year this temptation did last, and I had some strong temptations to run my head against walls and brain and kill myself. And so I did see, as I thought, God's eternal reprobation of me, a fruit of which was this dereliction to these doubts and darkness, and I did see God like a consuming fire and an everlasting burning, and myself like a poor prisoner leading to that fire; and the thoughts of eternal reprobation and torment did amaze my spirits, especially at one time upon a Sabbath day at evening. And when I knew not what to do (for I went to no Christian and was ashamed to speak of these things), it came to my mind that I should do as Christ, when he was in an agony. He prayed earnestly; and so I fell down to prayer. And being in prayer, I saw myself so unholy and God so holy that my spirits began to sink. Yet the Lord recovered me and poured out a spirit of prayer upon me for free mercy and pity; and in the conclusion of the prayer, I found the Lord helping me to see my unworthiness of any mercy, and that I was worthy to be cast out of his sight and to leave myself with him to do with me what he would; and then, and never until then, I found rest. And so my heart was humbled and cast down, and I went with a stayed heart unto supper late that night and so rested here, and the terrors of the Lord began to assuage sweetly. Yet when these were gone, I felt my senselessness of sin and bondage to self and unconstancy and losing what the Lord had wrought and my heartlessness to any good and loathing of God's ways. Whereupon walking in the fields the Lord dropped this meditation into me, "Be not discouraged therefore be-

[14]The "Grindletonians," named for the town of Grindleton in Yorkshire where their leader Roger Brereley was curate, were Donatists or perfectionists, who believed that the spirit of the Lord could so fill the soul that there would be no room left for sin. Their infamy, increasing over time, was largely a fiction of their first detractor, Stephen Denison, who wrote *The White Wolf* (1627), a sermon misrepresenting the Grindleton church. Tried for heresy, Brereley was exonerated by Archbishop Tobias Matthew.

[15]Richard Rogers (1550?–1618) graduated Christ's College, Cambridge, in 1565. His *Seven Treatises* (1603), abridged as *The Practise of Christianity* in 1618, is one of the seminal theological treatises on Puritanism, widely influential in establishing the systematic appearance of "orthodoxy" in New England. His son Ezekiel emigrated to Massachusetts as the first minister at Rowley.

cause thou art so vile, but make this double use of it: first, loathe thyself the more; secondly, feel a greater need and put a greater price upon Jesus Christ who only can redeem thee from all sin." And this I found of wonderful use to me in all my course whereby I was kept from sinkings of heart and did beat Satan, as it were, with his own weapons. And I saw Christ teaching me this before any man preached any such thing unto me. And so the Lord did help me to loathe myself in some measure, and to say oft, Why shall I seek the glory and good of myself, who am the greatest enemy, worse then the Devil can be, against myself, which self ruins me and blinds me, &c.? And thus God kept my heart exercised, and here I began to forsake my loose company wholly and to do what I could to work upon the hearts of other scholars and to humble them and to come into a way of holy walking in our speeches and otherwise. But yet I had no assurance Christ was mine.

(4) The Lord therefore brought Dr. Preston to preach upon that text, 1 Corinthians 1:30: "Christ is made unto us wisdom, righteousness, sanctification, and redemption." And when he had opened how all the good I had, all the redemption I had, it was from Jesus Christ, I did then begin to prize him, and he became very sweet unto me, although I had heard many a time Christ freely offered by his ministry, if I would come in and receive him as Lord and Saviour and husband. But I found my heart ever unwilling to accept of Christ upon these terms. I found them impossible for me to keep [on] that condition; and Christ was not so sweet as my lust. But now the Lord made himself sweet to me, and to embrace him and to give up myself unto him. But yet after this I had many fears and doubts.

(5) I found, therefore, the Lord revealing free mercy, and that all my help was in that to give me Christ, and to enable me to believe in Christ and accept of him; and here I did rest.

(6) The Lord also letting me see my own constant vileness in everything, put me to this question, Why did the Lord Jesus keep the law, had no guile in his heart, had no unbrokenness, but holiness there? Was it not for them that did want it? And here I saw Christ Jesus's righteousness for a poor sinner's ungodliness, but yet questioned whether ever the Lord would apply this and give this unto me.

(7) The Lord made me see that so many as receive him, he gives power to be the sons of God (John 1:12). And I saw the Lord gave me a heart to receive Christ with a naked hand, even naked Christ; and so the Lord gave me peace.

And thus I continued till I was six years' standing, and then went, half a year before I was Master of Arts, to Mr. Weld's[16] house at Tarling in Essex, where I enjoyed the blessing of his and Mr. Hooker's[17] ministry at Chelmesford. But before I came

[16]Thomas Weld (1595–1661) graduated Trinity College, Cambridge, in 1614 (master's degree in 1618). At this time he was vicar at Terling, Essex; in 1632, he immigrated to Boston, as minister of the Roxbury Church. In 1641, along with Peter Hugh and William Hibbins, Weld acted as agent of the Massachusetts General Court to England, where in 1646 he repatriated and served as rector of St. Mary's Church in Newcastle until his death.

[17]Thomas Hooker (1586?–1647) graduated Emmanuel College, Cambridge, in 1608 (master's degree in 1611). Dismissed from the pulpit for nonconformity, he left for Delft and then Rotterdam, Holland, where he served the church with the renowned William Ames. He joined John Cotton and Samuel Stone in London in 1633, and all three emigrated to New England that summer. Hooker settled at Newtown with a large following, but later in 1633 he relocated with his church to New Haven, leaving the settlement intact for Shepard and his followers.

there, I was very solicitous what would become of me when I was Master of Arts, for then my time and portion would be spent. But when I came thither, and had been there some little season, until I was ready to be Master of Arts, one Dr. Wilson[18] had purposed to set up a Lecture, and given £30 per annum to the maintenance of it. And when I was among those worthies in Essex, where we had monthly fasts, they did propound it unto me to take the Lecture[19] and to set it up at a great town in Essex, called Cogshall; and so Mr. Weld especially pressed me unto it, and wished me to seek God about it. And after fasting and prayer, the ministers in those parts of Essex had a day of humiliation, and they did seek the Lord for direction where to place the Lecture; and toward the evening of that day they began to consider whether I should go to Cogshall, or no. Most of the ministers were for it, because it was a great town, and they did not know any place [that] did desire it but they. Mr. Hooker only did object against my going thither, for being but young and unexperienced, and there being an old, yet sly and malicious minister in the town who did seem to give way to it to have it there, did therefore say it was dangerous and uncomfortable for little birds to build under the nests of old ravens and kites.

But while they were thus debating it, the town of Earles-Colne, being three miles off from Essex,[20] hearing that there was such a Lecture to be given freely, and considering that the Lecture might enrich that poor town, they did therefore just at this time of the day come to the place where the ministers met, viz., at Terling, in Essex, and desired that it might be settled there for three years (for no longer was it to continue in any place, because it was conceived if any good was done, it would be within such a time; and then, if it went away from them, the people in a populous town would be glad to maintain the man themselves; or if no good was done, it was pity they should have it any longer.) And when they thus came for it, the ministers with one joint consent advised me to accept of the people's call and to stay among them if I found, upon my preaching a little season with them, that they still continued in their desires for my continuance there.

And thus I, who was so young, so weak, and unexperienced, and unfit for so great a work, was called out by twelve or sixteen ministers of Christ to the work, which did much encourage my heart; and for the Lord's goodness herein I shall, I hope, never forget his love. For I might have been cast away upon a blind place, without the help of any ministry about me. I might have been sent to some gentleman's house to have been corrupted with the sins in it. But this I have found; the Lord was not content to take me from one town to another, but from the worst town I think in the world to the best place for knowledge and learning, viz., to Cambridge. And there the Lord was not content to give me good means, but the best means and ministry and help of private Christians, for Dr. Preston and Mr. Goodwin[21] were the

[18]Edmund Wilson, doctor and brother of Reverend John Wilson of First Church, Boston

[19]Funded by wealthy Puritans, such lectureships were often established in parts of the country with a shortage of churches and ministers.

[20]Actually, Coggeshall, a market town in Essex.

[21]Thomas Goodwin (1600–1680) graduated Christ's College, Cambridge, in 1616. In 1634, he was expelled from his lectureship at Trinity Church, Cambridge, for nonconformity. Oliver Cromwell appointed him president of Magdalen College, Oxford, in 1650, a position he lost in 1660 when the monarchy was restored.

most able men for preaching Christ in this latter age. And when I came from thence, the Lord sent me to the best country in England, viz., to Essex, and set me in the midst of the best ministry in the country by whose monthly fasts and conferences I found much of God. And thus the Lord Jesus provided for me of all things of the best.

So being resolved to go unto Earles-Colne in Essex after my commencing Master of Arts and my sinful taking of orders about a fortnight after of the Bishop of Peterborough, viz., [Bishop] Dove,[22] I came to the town and boarded in Mr. Cosins his house, an aged, but godly and cheerful Christian, and schoolmaster in the town, and by whose society I was much refreshed, there being not one man else in all the town that had any godliness but him that I could understand. So having preached upon the Sabbath day out of 2 Corinthians 5:19, all the town gave me a call and set to their hands in writing; and so I saw God would have me to be there, but how to be there and continue there, I could not tell. Yet I sinfully got a license to officiate the cure of the Bishop of London's register before my name was known, and by virtue of that I had much help.

But when I had been here a while, and the Lord had blessed my labors to divers in and out of the town, especially to the chief house in the town, the Priory, to Mr. Harlakenden's[23] children, where the Lord wrought mightily upon his eldest son, Mr. Richard (now dwelling there), and afterward on Mr. Roger,[24] who came over with me to New England and died here, Satan then began to rage, and the commissaries, registers, and others began to pursue me, and to threaten me, as thinking I was a nonconformable man, when for the most of that time I was not resolved either way, but was dark in those things. Yet the Lord, having work to do in the place, kept me, a poor, ignorant thing, against them all until such time as my work was done. By strange and wonderful means, notwithstanding all the malice of the ministers round about me, the Lord had one way or other to deliver me.

The course I took in my preaching was, first, to show the people their misery; secondly, the remedy, Christ Jesus; thirdly, how they should walk answerable to his mercy, being redeemed by Christ. And so I found the Lord putting forth his strength in my extreme weakness and not forsaking of me when I was so foolish, as I have wondered since why the Lord hath done any good to me and by me.

So the time of three years being expired, the people would not let me go, but gathered about £40 yearly for me. And so I was intended to stay there, if the Lord would, and prevailed to set up the Lecture in the town of Towcester where I was born, as knowing no greater love I could express to my poor friends than thus. And so Mr. Stone (Dr. Wilson giving way thereto) had the Lecture and went to Towcester with it, where the Lord was with him. And thus I saw the Lord's mercy following me to make me a poor instrument of sending the Gospel to the place of my nativity.

[22]Thomas Dove (1555–1630) graduated Pembroke Hall, Cambridge, around 1574. His eloquence in the pulpit earned him the office of chaplain to Queen Elizabeth I. In 1600, he was named bishop of Peterborough (1601–1630). Judging from Laud's repeated criticism, Dove seems to have had Low-Church sympathies.

[23]Richard Harlakenden (1600–1677) married Alice Mildmay, cousin to John Winthrop. His wealth enabled him to support Puritan ministers who were turned out of the pulpit. He emigrated with Shepard aboard the *Defence* in 1635 and settled in Newtown, remaining one of Shepard's closest friends.

[24]Roger Harlakenden (1611–1638), younger brother of Richard, embarked for New England with Shepard. He settled in Newtown among Shepard's congregation and died three years later of smallpox.

So when I had preached a while at Earles-Colne, about half a year, the Lord saw me unfit and unworthy to continue me there any longer; and so the Bishop of London, Mountain,[25] being removed to York, and Bishop Laud[26] (now Archbishop) coming in his place, a fierce enemy to all righteousness, and a man fitted of God to be a scourge to his people, he presently (having been not long in the place) sent for me up to London, and there, never asking me whether I would subscribe (as I remember) but what I had to do to preach in his diocese, chiding also Dr. Wilson for setting up this Lecture in his diocese, after many railing speeches against me, forbade me to preach; and not only so, but if I went to preach any where else, his hand would reach me. And so God put me to silence there, which did somewhat humble me, for I did think it was for my sins the Lord set him thus against me. . . .

Yet when I was thus silenced, the Lord stirred me up friends. The house of the Harlakendens were so many fathers and mothers to me; and they and the people would have me live there though I did nothing but stay in the place. But remaining about half a year after this silencing among them, the Lord let me see into the evil of the English ceremonies, cross, surplice, and kneeling. And the Bishop of London, viz., Laud, coming down to visit, he cited me to appear before him at the Court at Reldon,[27] where I appearing, he asked me what I did in the place, and I told him I studied. He asked me, what? I told him the Fathers. He replied, I might thank him for that, yet charged me to depart the place. I asked him whither should I go? To the University, said he. I told him I had no means to subsist there. Yet he charged me to depart the place.

Now, about this time, I had great desire to change my estate by marriage, and I had been praying three years before that the Lord would carry me to such a place where I might have a meet yoke-fellow. And I had a call at this time to go to Yorkshire, to preach there in a gentleman's house. But I did not desire to stir till the Bishop tired me out of this place. For the Bishop having thus charged me to depart, and being two days after to visit at Dunmow, in Essex, Mr. Weld, Mr. Daniel Rogers,[28] Mr. Ward,[29] Mr. Marshall,[30] Mr. Wharton,[31] consulted together whether it

[25]George Montaigne (or Mountain) (1569–1628), favorite of King James, was successively bishop of Lincoln, London, and Durham (1617–1628). A staunch advocate of Laud's High-Church party, he was named archbishop of York in 1628.

[26]William Laud (1573–1645) graduated St. Johns College, Oxford, in 1590. He enjoyed the special favor of Kings James I and Charles I, served in prominent positions at Oxford University, and was named archbishop of Canterbury in 1633. He was rigorous in his prosecution of nonconforming Puritans, and his policies were largely responsible for the large numbers of emigrants to New England. He was executed in 1645 during the Puritan Revolt.

[27]Possibly Peldon, near Colchester, Essex.

[28]Daniel Rogers (1573–1652) graduated Christ's College, Cambridge, in 1595; he was the son of Richard Rogers and archenemy of Laud. He protected Cambridge University against Anglican Church incursion and was suspended from the pulpit in 1629 for nonconformity.

[29]This is likely Nathaniel Ward (1578?–1652), who graduated Emmanuel College, Cambridge, in 1599 (master's degree in 1603). Expelled from the pulpit in 1633 for nonconformity, he emigrated to Agawam (later Ipswich), Massachusetts, where he played a significant role in drafting the "Body of Liberties," the new colony's bill of rights. He repatriated to England in 1646, publishing his *The Simple Cobler of Aggawam in America,* widely held as one of the most "literary" of all seventeenth-century Puritan writings.

[30]Stephen Marshall (1594?–1655) graduated Emmanuel College, Cambridge, in 1618. Although he signed the Thirty-nine Articles, he was suspected by the episcopacy of nonconformity. At this time he was serving as vicar of Finchingfield, Essex.

[31]Samuel Wharton, vicar of Felsted, Essex.

was best to let such a swine to root up God's plants in Essex, and not to give him some check. Whereupon it was agreed upon privately at Braintry that some should speak to him and give him a check.

So Mr. Weld and I travelling together had some thoughts of going to New England. But we did think it best to go first unto Ireland and preach there and to go by Scotland thither. But when we came to the church, Mr. Weld stood and heard without (being excommunicated by him). I, being more free, went within. And after sermon, Mr. Weld went up to hear the Bishop's speech, and being seen to follow the Bishop, the first thing he did was to examine Mr. Weld what he did to follow him and to stand upon holy ground. Thereupon he was committed to the pursuivant, and bound over to answer it at the High Commission. But when Mr. Weld was pleading for himself, and that it was ignorance that made him come in, the Bishop asked him whither he intended to go, whether to New England, and if so, whether I would go with him. While he was thus speaking, I came into the crowd and heard the words. Others bid me go away. But neglecting to do it, a godly man pulled me away with violence out of the crowd; and as soon as ever I was gone, the apparitor calls for Mr. Shepard, and the pursuivant was sent presently after to find me out. But he that pulled me away (Mr. Holbeech[32] by name, a schoolmaster at Felsted, in Essex) hastened our horses, and away we rid as fast as we could. And so the Lord delivered me out of the hand of that lion a third time.

And now I perceived I could not stay in Colne without danger; and hereupon receiving a letter from Mr. Ezekiel Rogers,[33] then living at [Rowley] in Yorkshire, to encourage me to come to the knight's house, called Sir Richard Darley, dwelling at a town called Buttercrambe, and the knight's two sons, viz., Mr. Henry and Mr. Richard Darley, promising me £20 a year for their part, and the knight promising me my table, and the letters sent to me crying with that voice of the man of Macedonia, "Come and help us." Hereupon I resolved to follow the Lord to so remote and strange a place, the rather because I might be far from the hearing of the malicious Bishop Laud, who had threatened me if I preached any where. So when I was determined to go, the gentleman sent a man to me to be my guide in my journey, who coming for me, with much grief of heart I forsook Essex and Earles-Colne, and they me, going, as it were, now I knew not whither.

So as we travelled (which was five or six days together near unto winter) the Lord sent much rain and ill weather, insomuch as the floods were up when we came near Yorkshire and hardly passable. At last we came to a town called Ferrybridge, where the waters were up and ran over the bridge for half a mile together and more. So we hired a guide to lead us. But when he had gone a little way, the violence of the water was such that he first fell in, and after him another man, who was near drowning before my eyes. Whereupon my heart was so smitten with fear of the danger and

[32]Martin Holbeach, headmaster of Felsted School, where several prominent Puritans were educated prior to attending university.

[33]Ezekiel Rogers (1590–1661), son of Richard Rogers, graduated Bennet College, Cambridge (master's degree from Christ's College, Cambridge). Suspended from his post as a private chaplain for refusing to read *The Book of Sports,* he emigrated to New England in 1638 with a following from Yorkshire. He founded Rowley, becoming minister of the first church, and established the first cotton and woolen mills in New England.

my head so dizzied with the running of the water that had not the Lord immediately upheld me and my horse also, and so guided it, I had certainly perished that bout. But the Lord was strong in my weakness. And we went on by some little direction upon the bridge and at last I fell in, yet in a place where the waters were not so violent, but I sat upon my horse, which, being a very good horse, clambered up upon the bridge again. But Mr. Darley's man, for fear of me, fell in also but came out safe again. And so we came to the dry land where we had a house, and shifted ourselves, and went to prayer, and blessed God for this wonderful preservation of us. And the Lord made me then to profess that I looked now upon my life as a new life given unto me, which I saw good reason to give up unto him and his service. And truly, about this time, the Lord, that had dealt only gently with me before, began to afflict me and to let me taste how good it was to be under his tutoring. So I came to York late upon Saturday night, and having refreshed ourselves there, I came to Buttercrambe to Sir Richard's house that night, very wet and late, which is about seven miles off from York.

Now as soon as I came into the house, I found divers of them at dice and tables. And Mr. Richard Darley, one of the brothers, being to return to London the Monday after, and being desirous to hear me preach, sent me speedily to my lodging (the best in the house), and so I preached the day after once; and then he departed the day after, having carefully desired my comfortable abode there. But I do remember I never was so low sunk in my spirit as about this time. For, first, I was now far from all friends. Secondly, I was I saw in a profane house, not any sincerely good. Thirdly, I was in a vile, wicked town and country. Fourthly, I was unknown and exposed to all wrongs. Fifthly, I was unsufficient to do any work and my sins were upon me, &c.; and hereupon I was very low and sunk deep. Yet the Lord did not leave me comfortless, for though the lady was churlish, yet Sir Richard was ingenious, and I found in the house three servants, viz., Thomas Fugill,[34] Mrs. Margaret Touteville, the knight's kinswoman, that was afterward my wife, and Ruth Bushell (now married to Edward Michelson)[35] very careful of me; which somewhat refreshed me.

But it happened that when I had been there a little while there was a marriage of one Mr. Allured, a most profane young gentleman, to Sir Richard's daughter, and I was desired to preach at their marriage, at which sermon the Lord first touched the heart of Mistress Margaret with very great terrors for sin and her Christless estate. Whereupon others began to look about them, especially the gentlewoman lately married, Mistress Allured, and the Lord brake both their hearts very kindly. Then others in the family, viz., Mr. Allured, he fell to fasting and prayer and great reformation. Others also were reformed and their hearts changed—the whole family brought to external duties—but I remember none in the town or about it brought home. And thus the Lord was with me and gave me favor and friends and respect of all in the family; and the Lord taught me much of his goodness and sweetness. And when he had fitted a wife for me, he then gave me her who was a most sweet, humble woman,

[34]Thomas Fugill, one of the principal settlers of New Haven in 1638, was excommunicated from the church on the charge of embezzlement due probably to an innocent accounting error.

[35]Edward and Ruth Michelson settled in Cambridge, Massachusetts, among Shepard's congregation.

full of Christ, and a very discerning Christian, a wife who was most incomparably loving to me, and every way amiable and holy, and endued with a very sweet spirit of prayer. And thus the Lord answered my desires. When my adversaries intended most hurt to me, the Lord was then best unto me and used me the more kindly in every place. For the Lord turned all the sons and Sir Richard and Mr. Allured so unto me that they not only gave her freely to be my wife, but enlarged her portion also. And thus I did marry the best and fittest woman in the world unto me after I had preached in this place about a twelvemonth, for which mercy to me in my exiled condition in a strange place, I did promise the Lord that this mercy should knit my heart the nearer to Him, and that his love should constrain me. But I have ill requited the Lord since that time and forgot myself and my promise also.

But now when we were married, in the year 1632,[36] she was unwilling to stay at Buttercrambe, and I saw no means of likelihood of abode there. For Bishop Neale[37] coming up to York, no friends could procure my liberty of him, without subscription. And hereupon the Lord gave me a call to Northumberland, to a town called Heddon, five miles beyond Newcastle, which, when I had considered of and saw no place but that to go unto and saw the people very desirous of it and that I might preach there in peace, being far from any Bishops, I did resolve to depart thither. And so being accompanied with Mr. Allured to the place, I came not without many fears of enemies. And my poor wife full of fears, it was not a place of subsistence with any comfort to me there. But the good Lord, who all my life followed me, made this place the fittest for me; and I found many sweet friends and Christian acquaintance, Mistress Sherbourne maintaining me, and Mistress Fenwick lending us the use of her house; and so God comforted us in our solitary and yet married condition many ways.

Now when I was here, the Lord blessed my poor labors both to the saints and to sundry others about and in Newcastle, and I came here to read and know more of the ceremonies, church government and estate, and the unlawful standing of Bishops than in any other place. I lived at Mistress Fenwick's house for a time, about a twelvemonth or half a year, and then we went and dwelt alone in a town near Heddon, called [Haherze], in a house which we found haunted with the Devil, as we conceived. For when we came into it, a known witch went out of it. And being troubled with noises four or five nights together, we sought God by prayer to remove so sore a trial, and the Lord heard and blessed us there and removed the trouble. But after we were settled, the Bishop put in a priest who would not suffer me to preach publicly any more. Hereupon the means was used to the Bishop of Durham, Bishop Morton,[38] and he professed he durst not give me liberty, because Laud had taken notice

[36]July 23, 1632.

[37]Richard Neile (1562–1640) graduated St. John's College, Cambridge, in 1580. He declared himself "adversary of the Puritan faction." He was successively bishop of Rochester, Linchfield, Lincoln, Durham, and Winchester (1608–1631) and in this capacity helped to elevate Laud's career. In 1631 he was elected archbishop of York, a position he held until his death.

[38]Thomas Morton (1564–1659) graduated St. John's College, Cambridge, in 1584. He was successively bishop of Chester, Linchfield, and Durham, the last from 1632 to 1659. A man of Low-Church sympathies, Morton took no active part in Laud's coercive campaign for uniformity, rather attempting to win noncomformists and recusants through disputation. He was most famously the mentor of poet-priest John Donne and the bishop who pardoned Richard Mather.

of me. So I preached up and down in the country and at last privately in Mr. Fenwick's house. And there I stayed till Mr. Cotton,[39] Mr. Hooker, Stone, Weld, went to New England, and hereupon most of the godly in England were awakened and intended much to go to New England. And I having a call by divers friends in New England to come over, and many in Old England desiring me to go over and promising to go with me, I did hereupon resolve to go thither, especially considering the season. And thus the Lord blessed me in this dark country, and gave me a son, called Thomas, anno 1633, my poor wife being in sore extremities four days, by reason she had an unskilful midwife. But as the affliction was very bitter, so the Lord did teach me much by it, and I had need of it, for I began to grow secretly proud and full of sensuality, delighting my soul in my dear wife more than in my God, whom I had promised better unto; and my spirit grew fierce in some things and secretly mindless of the souls of the people. But the Lord, by this affliction of my wife, learnt me to desire to fear him more and to keep his dread in my heart. And so, seeing I had been tossed from the south to the north of England and now could go no farther, I then began to listen to a call to New England.

The reasons which swayed me to come to New England were many. (1) I saw no call to any other place in Old England nor way of subsistence in peace and comfort to me and my family. (2) Divers people in Old England of my dear friends desired me to go to New England, there to live together; and some went before, and writ to me of providing a place for a company of us, one of which was John Bridge;[40] and I saw divers families of my Christian friends who were resolved thither to go with me. (3) I saw the Lord departing from England when Mr. Hooker and Mr. Cotton were gone, and I saw the hearts of most of the godly set and bent that way; and I did think I should feel many miseries if I stayed behind. (4) My judgment was then convinced not only of the evil of ceremonies, but of mixed communion, and joining with such in sacraments, though I ever judged it lawful to join with them in preaching. (5) I saw it my duty to desire the fruition of all God's ordinances, which I could not enjoy in Old England. (6) My dear wife did much long to see me settled there in peace and so put me on to it. (7) Although it was true I should stay and suffer for Christ, yet I saw no rule for it now the Lord had opened a door of escape. Otherwise, I did incline much to stay and suffer, especially after our sea storms. (8) Though my ends were mixed and I looked much to my own quiet, yet the Lord let me see the glory of those liberties in New England and made me purpose, if ever I should come over, to live among God's people as one come out from the dead to his praise—though since

[39]John Cotton (1584–1652) graduated Trinity College, Cambridge, in 1603 (master's degree in 1606). He was vicar of St. Botolph's in Lincolnshire (1612–1632) when he was summoned to appear before the Court of High Commission for nonconformity. He embarked for New England in 1633 aboard the *Griffin* with Hooker, Stone, Edmund Quincy, and John Haynes. His authority in Boston was challenged by the orthodoxy, including Shepard and Winthrop, during the Antinomian controversy, until he recanted his position, abandoning Anne Hutchinson and many former followers to their fate of excommunication and exile in Rhode Island. He wrote the defining treatise on the theory and methods of Congregationalism, *The Way of the Churches of Christ in New England* (1645).

[40]John Bridge, Thomas Hooker's and Shepard's predecessor at Newtown (Cambridge after 1637), Massachusetts, arriving in 1632.

I have seen, as the Lord's goodness, so my own exceeding weakness to be as good as I thought to have been.

And although they did desire me to stay in the north and preach privately, yet (1) I saw that this time could not be long without trouble from King Charles. (2) I saw no reason to spend my time privately when I might possibly exercise my talent publicly in New England. (3) I did hope my going over might make them to follow me. (4) I considered how sad a thing it would be for me to leave my wife and child (if I should die) in that rude place of the north, where was nothing but barbarous wickedness generally, and how sweet it would be to leave them among God's people, though poor. (5) My liberty in private was daily threatened, and I thought it wisdom to depart before the pursuivants came out, for so I might depart with more peace and lesser trouble and danger to me and my friends. And I knew not whether God would have me to hazard my person and comfort of me and all mine for a disorderly manner of preaching privately (as it was reputed) in those parts.

So after I had preached my farewell sermon at Newcastle, I departed from the north in a ship laden with coals for Ipswich, about the beginning of June, after I had been about a year in the north, the Lord having blessed some few sermons and notes to divers in Newcastle, from whom I parted filled with their love. And so the Lord gave us a speedy voyage from thence to Ipswich in Old England, whither I came in a disguised manner with my wife and child and maid, and stayed a while at Mr. Russell's house, another while at Mr. Collins his house, and then went down to Essex to the town where I had preached, viz., Earles-Colne, to Mr. Richard Harlakenden's house where I lived privately, but with much love from them all, as also from Mr. Joseph Cooke,[41] and also with friends at London and Northamptonshire. And truly I found this time of my life—wherein I was so tossed up and down and had no place of settling, but kept secret in regard of the Bishops—the most uncomfortable and fruitless time, to my own soul especially, that ever I had in my life. And therefore I did long to be in New England as soon as might be, and the rather because my wife, having weaned her first son Thomas, had conceived again and was breeding, and I knew no place in England where she could lie in without discovery of myself, danger to myself and all my friends that should receive me, and where we could not but give offence to many if I should have my child not baptized. And, therefore, there being divers godly Christians resolved to go toward the latter end of the year if I would go, I did therefore resolve to go that year, the end of that summer I came from the north. And the time appointed for the ship to go out was about a month or fortnight before Michaelmas (as they there call it). The ship was called the Hope, of Ipswich. The master of it, a very able seaman, was Mr. Gurling, who professed much love to me, who had got this ship of 400 tons from the Danes, and, as some report, it was by some fraud. But he denied it, and being a man very loving and full of fair promises of going at the time appointed, and an able seaman, hence we resolved to adventure that time, though dangerous in regard of the approaching winter.

[41]John Russell and Joseph Cooke immigrated to New England in 1635 with Thomas Shepard and Roger Harlakenden; Shepard, his brother George, and Samuel Shepard are registered in the ship's manifest as Harlakenden's servants. They settled with Thomas Shepard's company at Newtown. Edward Collins arrived the following year and served as deacon under Shepard's leadership.

Now here the Lord's wonderful terror and mercy to us did appear. For being come to Ipswich with my family at the time appointed, the ship was not ready, and we stayed six or eight weeks longer than the time promised for her going. And so it was very late in the year and very dangerous to go to sea. And, indeed, if we had gone, doubtless we had all perished upon the seas, it being so extreme cold and tempestuous winter. But yet we could not go back, when we had gone so far. And the Lord saw it good to chastise us for rushing onward too soon and hazarding ourselves in that manner; and I had many fears, and much darkness (I remember) overspread my soul, doubting of our way. Yet I say we could not now go back. Only I learnt from that time never to go about a sad business in the dark, unless God's call within as well as that without be very strong, and clear, and comfortable.

So that in the year 1634, about the beginning of the winter, we set sail from Harwich. And having gone some few leagues on to the sea, the wind stopped us that night, and so we cast anchor in a dangerous place. And on the morning the wind grew fierce, and rough against us full, and drave us toward the sands. But the vessel being laden too heavy at the head, would not stir for all that which the seamen could do, but drave us full upon the sands near Harwich harbour; and the ship did grate upon the sands, and was in great danger. But the Lord directed one man to cut some cable or rope in the ship, and so she was turned about and was beaten quite backward toward Yarmouth, quite out of our way.

But while the ship was in this great danger, a wonderful miraculous providence did appear to us. For one of the seamen, that he might save the vessel, fell in when it was in that danger, and so was carried out a mile or more from the ship and given for dead and gone. The ship was then in such danger that none could attend to follow him; and when it was out of the danger it was a very great hazard to the lives of any that should take the skiff to seek to find him. Yet it pleased the Lord that, being discerned afar off floating upon the waters, three of the seamen adventured out upon the rough waters, and at last, about an hour after he fell into the sea, (as we conjectured), they came and found him floating upon the waters, never able to swim but supported by a divine hand all this while. When the men came to him they were glad to find him, but concluded he was dead, and so got him into the skiff, and when he was there tumbled him down as one dead. Yet one of them said to the rest, "Let us use what means we can, if there be life, to preserve it," and thereupon turned his head downward for the water to run out. And having done so, the fellow began to gasp and breathe. Then they applied other means they had; and so he began at last to move and then to speak, and by that time he came to the ship, he was pretty well and able to walk. And so the Lord showed us his great power, whereupon a godly man in the ship then said, "This man's danger and deliverance is a type of ours, for he did fear dangers were near unto us, and that yet the Lord's power should be shown in saving of us."

For so indeed it was. For the wind did drive us quite backward out of our way and gave us no place to anchor at until we came unto Yarmouth Roads—an open place at sea, yet fit for anchorage, but otherwise a very dangerous place. And so we came thither through many uncomfortable hazards within thirty hours and cast anchor in Yarmouth Roads, which when we had done upon a Saturday morning, the Lord sent a most dreadful and terrible storm of wind from the west, so dreadful that to this day the seamen call it *Windy Saturday,* that it also scattered many ships on divers coasts at that time, and divers ships were cast away. One among the rest, which was the seaman's ship who came with us from Newcastle, was cast away, and he and all his men perished. But when the wind thus arose, the master cast all his anchors, but the storm was so terrible that the anchors broke and the ship drave toward the sands, where we could not but be cast away. Whereupon the master cries out that we were dead men, and thereupon the whole company [got] to prayer. But the vessel still drave so near to the sands that the master shot off two pieces of ordnance to the town for help to save the passengers. The town perceived it and thousands came upon the walls of Yarmouth and looked upon us, hearing we were New England men, and pitied much and gave us for gone because they saw other ships perishing near unto us at that time, but could not send any help unto us though much money was offered by some to hazard themselves for us.

So the master not knowing what to do, it pleased the Lord that there was one Mr. Cock, a drunken fellow but no seaman, yet one that had been at sea often, and would come in a humor unto New England with us, whether it was to see the country, or no, I cannot tell. But sure I am, God intended it for good unto us to make him an instrument to save all our lives, for he persuaded the master to cut down his mainmast. The master was unwilling to it, and besotted, not sensible of ours and his own loss. At last this Cock calls for hatchets, tells the master, "If you be a man, save the lives of your passengers, cut down your mainmast." Hereupon he encouraged all the company who were forlorn and hopeless of life; and the seamen presently cut down the mast aboard, just at that very time wherein we all gave ourselves for gone to see neither Old nor New England nor faces of friends any more, there being near upon two hundred passengers in the ship. And so when the mast was down, the master had one little anchor left and cast it out. But the ship was driven away toward the sands still; and the seamen came to us and bid us look (pointing to the place) where our graves should shortly be, conceiving also that the wind had broke off this anchor also. So the master professed he had done what he could and therefore now desired us to go to prayer. So Mr. Norton[42] in one place and myself in another part of the ship, he with the passengers, and myself with the mariners above decks, went to prayer and committed our souls and bodies unto the Lord that gave them.

Immediately after prayer, the wind began to abate, and the ship stayed, for the last anchor was not broke (as we conceived) but only rent up with the wind, and so drave and was drawn along, ploughing the sands with the violence of the wind, which abating after prayer, though still very terrible, the ship was stopped just when it was ready to be swallowed up of the sands, a very little way off from it. And so we rid it out, yet not without fear of our lives though the anchor stopped the ship, because the cable was let out so far that a little rope held the cable, and the cable the little anchor, and the little anchor the great ship in this great storm. But when one of the company perceived that we were so strangely preserved, had these words, "That

[42]John Norton (1606–1663) graduated Peter House, Cambridge, in 1623 (master's degree in 1627). He became curate at Bishop's Stortford, Hertfordshire. He emigrated in 1635, one year after his escape aboard this vessel, and served as minister at Ipswich in Massachusetts (1636–1652); he then succeeded John Cotton as minister at First Church in Boston (1652) and acted with Simon Bradstreet as agent for the colony in London in 1662.

thread we hang by will save us," for so we accounted of the rope fastened to the anchor in comparison of the fierce storm. And so indeed it did, the Lord showing his dreadful power towards us and yet his unspeakable rich mercy to us, who, in depths of mercy, heard, nay helped us, when we could not cry through the disconsolate fears we had out of these depths of seas and miseries.

This deliverance was so great that I then did think if ever the Lord did bring me to shore again I should live like one come and risen from the dead. This is one of those living mercies the Lord hath shown me, a mercy to myself, to my wife and child then living, and to my second son, Thomas, who was in this storm but in the womb of his dear mother, who might then have perished and been cut off from all hope of means and mercy, and unto my dear friends then with me, viz., brother Champney, Frost, Goff,[43] and divers others, most dear saints, and also to all with me. And how would the name of the Lord suffered if we had so perished. That the Lord Jesus should have respect to me, so vile and one at that time full of many temptations and weaknesses, amazed [me] much, and deeply afraid of God's terror, yet supported. I desire this mercy may be remembered of my children and their children's children when I am dead and cannot praise the Lord in the land of the living any more.

And so we continued that night, many sick, many weak and discouraged, many sad hearts. Yet upon the Sabbath morning we departed and went out of the ship—I fear a little too soon, for we should have spent that day in praising of Him. Yet we were afraid of neglecting a season of providence in going out while we had a calm; and many sick folk were unfit for that work and had need of refreshing at shore. So, upon the Sabbath-day morning, boats came to our vessel from the town, and so my dear wife and child went in the first boat. But here the Lord saw that these waters were not sufficient to wash away my filth and sinfulness, and therefore he cast me into the fire as soon as ever I was upon the sea in the boat, for there my first-born child, very precious to my soul and dearly beloved of me, was smitten with sickness. The Lord sent a vomiting upon it, whereby it grew faint, and nothing that we could use could stop its vomiting, although we had many helps at Yarmouth. And this was a very bitter affliction to me. And the Lord now showed me my weak faith, want of fear, pride, carnal content, immoderate love of creatures, and of my child especially, and begat in me some desires and purposes to fear his name. But yet the Lord would not be entreated for the life of it, and after a fortnight's sickness, at last it gave up the ghost when its mother had given it up to the Lord, and was buried at Yarmouth, where I durst not be present lest the pursuivants should apprehend me and I should be discovered, which was a great affliction, and very bitter to me and my dear wife. And hereby I saw the Lord did come near to me, and I did verily fear the Lord would take away my wife also, if not myself, not long after.

And these afflictions, together with the Lord's crossing us and being so directly against our voyage, made me secretly willing to stay and suffer in England, and my heart was not so much toward New England. Yet this satisfied me, that seeing there

[43]Richard Champney (?–1669), arrived in Cambridge, Massachusetts, with his wife Jane some time in 1635 and served in the church there with Shepard; Edmund Frost and his wife Thomasine served with Shepard at Cambridge; Edward Goffe served as representative to the General Court of Massachusetts in 1646 and 1650.

was a door opened of escape, why should I suffer? And I considered how unfit I was to go to such a good land with such an unmortified, hard, dark, formal, hypocritical heart; and therefore no wonder if the Lord did thus cross me. And the Lord made me fear my affliction came in part for running too far in a way of separation from the mixed assemblies in England, though I bless God I have ever believed that there are true churches in many parishes in England, where the Lord sets up able men and ministers of his Gospel, and I have abhorred to refuse to hear any able minister in England.

So that now I having buried my first-born, and being in great sadness, and not knowing where to go nor what to do, the Lord sent Mr. Roger Harlakenden and my brother, Samuel Shepard,[44] to visit me after they had heard of our escape at sea, who much refreshed us and clave to me in my sorrows. And being casting about where to go and live, Mr. Bridge,[45] then minister in Norwich, sent for me to come and live with him; and being come, one Mistress Corbet, who lived five miles off Norwich, an aged, eminent, godly gentlewoman, hearing of my coming, and that by being with Mr. Bridge might hazard his liberty by countenancing of me, she did therefore freely offer to me a great house of hers, standing empty at a town called Bastwick. And there the Lord stirred up her heart to show all love to me, which did much lighten and sweeten my sorrows. And I saw the Lord Jesus's care herein to me, and saw cause of trusting him in times of straits, who set me in such a place, where I lived for half a year, all the winter long, among and with my friends (Mr. Harlakenden dwelling with me and bearing all the charge of housekeeping) and far from the notice of my enemies, where we enjoyed sweet fellowship one with another and also with God, in a house which was fit to entertain any prince for fairness, greatness and pleasantness.

Here the Lord hid us all the winter long, and when it was fit to travel in the spring, we went up to London, Mr. Harlakenden not forsaking me all this while, for he was a father and mother to me. And when we came to London to Mistress Sherborne, not knowing what to do nor where to live privately, the Lord provided a very private place for us where my wife was brought to bed and delivered of my second son, Thomas, and none but our friends did know of it. And so by this means, my son was not baptized until we came to New England the winter following, being born in London, April 5, 1635. One remarkable deliverance my wife had when we were coming up to London. Mr. Burrows, the minister, kindly entertained us about a fortnight in the way. And when my wife was there, being great with child, she fell down from the top of a pair of stairs to the bottom. Yet the Lord kept her and the child also safe from that deadly danger.

When we had been also at London for a time and began to be known in the place, my wife was brought to bed. The Lord put it into our hearts to remove to another place in Mr. Eldred's house in London, which stood empty. And the very night we were all come away, then came the pursuivants and others to search after us, but the Lord delivered us out of their hands. And so, when the Lord had recovered my

[44]Samuel Shepard arrived with his elder brother Thomas, settled in Cambridge, and helped build Harvard College. He returned to England in 1645, relocated to Ireland, and served in a number of prominent civil positions throughout his life.

[45]William Bridge, a graduate of Cambridge University.

wife, we began to prepare for a removal once again to New England. And the Lord seemed to make our way plain: (1) because I had no other call to any place in England; (2) many more of God's people resolved to go with me, as Mr. Roger Harlakenden and Mr. Champney, &c.; (3) the Lord saw our unfitness and the unfitness of our going the year before. And therefore giving us good friends to accompany us and good company in the ship, we set forward about the tenth of August, 1635, with myself, wife, and my little son Thomas, and other precious friends, having tasted much of God's mercy in England and lamenting the loss of our native country when we took our last view of it.

In our voyage upon the sea, the Lord was very tender of me, and kept me from the violence of sea-sickness. In our coming we were refreshed with the society of Mr. Wilson,[46] [and] Mr. Jones,[47] by their faith and prayers and preaching. The ship we came in was very rotten and unfit for such a voyage, and therefore the first storm we had, we had a very great leak, which did much appall and affect us. Yet the Lord discovered it unto us when we were thinking of returning back again and much comforted our hearts. We had many storms, in one of which my dear wife took such a cold and got such weakness, as that she fell into a consumption of which she afterward died. And also the Lord preserved her with the child in her arms from imminent and apparent death. For by the shaking of the ship in a violent storm, her head was pitched against an iron bolt, and the Lord miraculously preserved the child and recovered my wife. This was a great affliction to me and was a cause of many sad thoughts in the ship how to behave myself when I came to New England. My resolutions I have written down in my little book.

And so the Lord after many sad storms and wearisome days, and many longings to see the shore, the Lord brought us to the sight of it upon October 2, anno 1635; and upon October the 3d, we arrived, with my wife, child, brother Samuel, Mr. Harlakenden, Mr. Cookes, &c., at Boston with rejoicing in our God after a longsome voyage,[48] my dear wife's great desire being now fulfilled, which was to leave me in safety from the hand of my enemies and among God's people, and also the child under God's precious ordinances.

Now when we came upon shore, we were kindly saluted and entertained by many friends, and were the first three days in the house of Mr. Cottington,[49] being Treasurer at that time, and that with much love.

[46]John Wilson (1591?–1667) graduated King's College, Cambridge, in 1610. He was removed from his pulpit by the bishop of Norwich. He crossed to New England with Winthrop's party in 1630, without his wife Elizabeth, a daughter of Sir John and Lady Mansfield. He returned for her in 1635, later served as first minister of First Church in Charlestown (1630–1633), and then shared a pulpit with John Cotton (1633–1667) when the church moved to Boston.

[47]John Jones (?–1665?) served with Peter Bulkley at Concord (1635–1644), then served at Fairfield, Connecticut (1644–1665).

[48]The passage took fifty-four days from August 10, 1635.

[49]William Coddington (1601–1678), known as the "Father of Rhode Island," was a principal founder of Boston and served as treasurer of the Bay Colony. He fell from grace among the Boston magistrates for having taken Anne Hutchinson's side against Shepard, Winthrop, and Dudley in the Antinomian controversy. He removed to Aquidneck, Rhode Island, founded Newport, and served as governor of Aquidneck and later of the united plantations of Rhode Island and Providence. Near the end of his life he converted to Quakerism.

When we had been here two days, upon the Monday, October 5, we came (being sent for by friends at Newtown) to them, to my brother Mr. Stone's house. And that congregation being upon their removal to Hartford at Connecticut, myself and those that came with me found many houses empty and many persons willing to sell; and hence our company bought off their houses to dwell in until we should see another place fit to remove unto. But having been here some time, divers of our brethren did desire to sit still and not to remove further, partly because of the fellowship of the churches, partly because they thought their lives were short, and removals to new plantations full of troubles, partly because they found sufficient for themselves and their company. Hereupon there was a purpose to enter into church fellowship, which we did the year after about the end of the winter, a fortnight after which my dear wife Margaret died, being first received into church fellowship, which as she much longed for, so the Lord did so sweeten it unto her that she was hereby exceedingly cheered and comforted with the sense of God's love, which continued until her last gasp.

No sooner were we thus set down and entered into church fellowship but the Lord exercised us and the whole country with the opinions of Familists, begun by Mistress Hutchinson,[50] raised up to a great height by Mr. Vane,[51] too suddenly chosen Governor, and maintained too obscurely by Mr. Cotton, and propagated too boldly by the members of Boston and some in other churches. By means of which division by these opinions, the ancient and received truth came to be darkened, God's name to be blasphemed, the churches' glory diminished, many godly grieved, many wretches hardened, deceiving and being deceived, growing worse and worse. The principal opinion and seed of all the rest was this, viz., that a Christian should not take any evidence of God's special grace and love toward him by the sight of any graces or conditional evangelical promises to faith or sanctification, in way of ratiocination (for this was evidence, and so a way of works), but it must be without the sight of any grace, faith, holiness, or special change in himself, by immediate revelation in an absolute promise. And because that the whole Scriptures do give such clear, plain, and notable evidences of favor to persons called and sanctified, hence they said that a second evidence might be taken from thence, but no first evidence. But from hence it arose, that as all error is fruitful, so this opinion did gender above

[50]Anne Hutchinson (1591–1643) became the focus of the Antinomian heresy in Boston in 1635. Her insistence on an inner illumination of the spirit divided the local clergy into those, like Shepard, Winthrop, and Wilson, who she alleged preached a "covenant of works" and those, like herself, John Cotton, and former Bay colonist Roger Williams, who taught a "covenant of grace." Her opponents accused her of teaching a religion that absolved those adhering to it from obedience to civil law, thus the name "Antinomian," or "against the law." She died in an Indian massacre.

[51]Sir Henry Vane (1613–1662) studied first at Magdalen Hall, Oxford, and then at Leyden. He sailed for Massachusetts in 1635 aboard the *Abigail*. He was defeated by John Winthrop in 1637 after one year as governor of the Bay Colony. The harsh criticism he received for his support of Anne Hutchinson hastened his departure the same year for England. There he assisted Roger Williams in securing the Rhode Island charter in 1644. For assisting in the overthrow of Archbishop Laud and supporting Oliver Cromwell and the Protectorate, he was imprisoned by Charles II in 1660, tried for treason, and executed.

a hundred monstrous opinions in the country, which the elders perceiving, having used all private brotherly means with Mr. Cotton first, and yet no healing, hereupon they publicly preached both against opinions publicly and privately maintained. And I account it no small mercy to myself that the Lord kept me from that contagion and gave me any heart or light to see through those devices of men's heads, although I found it a most uncomfortable time to live in contention. And the Lord was graciously pleased by giving witness against them, to keep this poor church spotless and clear from them.

This division in the Church began to trouble the Commonwealth. Mr. Wheelwright,[52] a man of a bold and stiff conceit of his own worth and light, preached (as the Court judged) a seditious sermon, stirring up all sorts against those that preached a covenant of works, meaning all the elders in the country that preached justification by faith and assurance of it by sight of faith and sanctification, being enabled thereto by the spirit. The troubles thus increasing, and all means used for crushing and curing these sores, a Synod[53] was thought of and called from the example Acts 15, wherein, by the help of all the elders joined together, those errors, through the grace and power of Christ were discovered, the defenders of them convinced and ashamed, the truth established, and the consciences of the saints settled, there being a most wonderful presence of Christ's spirit in that Assembly, held at Cambridge anno 1637, about August, and continued a month together in public agitations. For the issue of this Synod was this:

(1) The Pequot Indians were fully discomfited, for as the opinions arose, wars did arise, and when these began to be crushed by the ministry of the elders, and by opposing Mr. Vane and casting him and others from being magistrates, the enemies began to be crushed and were perfectly subdued by the end of the Synod.

(2) The magistrates took courage and exiled Mr. Wheelwright, Mistress Hutchinson, and divers Islanders,[54] whom the Lord did strangely discover, giving most of them over to all manner of filthy opinions, until many that held with them before were ashamed of them. And so the Lord, within one year, wrought a great change among us.

At this time I cannot omit the goodness of God as to myself, so to all the country, in delivering us from the Pequot furies. These Indians were the stoutest, proudest, and most successful in their wars of all the Indians. Their chief sachem was Sasakus, a proud, cruel, unhappy, and headstrong prince, who, not willing to be guided by the persuasions of his fellow, an aged sachem, Monanattuck, nor fearing the revenge of the English, having first sucked the blood of Captain Stone and Mr.

[52]John Wheelwright (1594–1679) was brother-in-law of Anne Hutchinson and chief supporter with Vane of Anne Hutchinson. A decade later he would turn from the excesses of the Hutchinsonians.

[53]When doctrinal differences among the churches threatened unity in the colony, as during the Antinomian controversy (1635–1637), the Massachusetts General Court called a synod, a general conference in which the ministers and elders of the churches throughout the colony came together to broker theological compromises and impose doctrinal uniformity, often by exiling recalcitrant factions.

[54]Islanders of Aquidneck in present-day Rhode Island were the separate followers of both Roger Williams and Anne Hutchinson.

Oldham,[55] found it so sweet, and his proceedings for one whole winter so successful that, having besieged and killed about four men that kept Saybrook fort, he adventured to fall upon the English up the river at Wethersfield, where he slew nine or ten men, women, and children at unawares and took two maids prisoners, carrying them away captive to the Pequot country. Hereupon, those upon the river first gathered about seventy men and sent them into Pequot country to make that the seat of war and to revenge the death of those innocents whom they barbarously and most unnaturally slew. These men marched two days and nights from the way of the Naraganset unto Pequot, being guided by those Indians, then the ancient enemies of the Pequots. They intended to assault Sasakus's fort, but falling short of it the second night, the providence of God guided them to another nearer, full of stout men, and their best soldiers, being, as it were, cooped up there to the number of three or four hundred in all for the divine slaughter by the hand of the English. These, therefore, being all night making merry and singing the death of the English the next day, toward break of the day, being very heavy with sleep, the English drew near within the sight of the fort, very weary with travel and want of sleep, at which time five hundred Naragansets fled for fear and only two of the company stood to it to conduct them to the fort and the door and entrance thereof. The English being come to it, awakened the fort with a peal of muskets directed into the midst of their wigwams, and after this, some undertaking to compass the fort without, some adventured into the fort upon the very faces of the enemy, standing ready with their arrows ready bent to shoot whoever should adventure. But the English, casting by their pieces, took their swords in their hands (the Lord doubling their strength and courage) and fell upon the Indians, where a hot fight continued about the space of an hour. At last, by the direction of one Captain Mason,[56] their wigwams were set on fire, which being dry, and contiguous one to another, was most dreadful to the Indians, some burning, some bleeding to death by the sword, some resisting till they were cut off, some flying were beat down by the men without, until the Lord had utterly consumed the whole company, except four or five girls they took prisoners and dealt with them at Saybrook as they dealt with ours at Wethersfield. And 'tis verily thought, scarce one man escaped unless one or two to carry forth tidings of the lamentable end of their fellows. And of the English not one man was killed, but one by the musket of an Englishman (as was conceived). Some were wounded much; but all recovered, and restored again.

Thus the Lord having delivered the country from war with Indians and Familists (who arose and fell together), he was pleased to direct the hearts of the magistrates (then keeping Court ordinarily in our town, because of these stirs at Boston) to think of erecting a school or college, and that speedily, to be a nursery of knowledge in these deserts and supply for posterity. And because this town (then called Newtown)

[55]According to early Puritan historians, the murders of Captain John Stone in 1633 and the trader John Oldham in 1636 precipitated the 1637 Pequot War. Later historians have redistributed a large portion of the blame for the war to Governor John Vane's July 26, 1636, authorization of John Endecott's punitive expedition against the Pequots for allegedly threatening an uprising.

[56]John Mason (1600?–1672), soldier and colonial magistrate, saw service in England before coming to New England in 1633. He served as commander of the Connecticut forces in the Pequot War. He later founded the towns of Windsor and Norwich and held prominent offices in the government of Connecticut, including deputy governor (1660–1669).

was through God's great care and goodness kept spotless from the contagion of the opinions, therefore at the desire of some of our town, the Deputies of the Court, having got Mr. Eaton to attend the school, the Court for that and sundry other reasons determined to erect the college here, which was no sooner done, but the chief of the magistrates and elders sent to England to desire help to forward this work. But they all neglecting us (in a manner), the Lord put it into the heart of one Mr. Harvard,[57] who died worth £1600, to give half his estate to the erecting of the school. The man was a scholar and pious in his life and enlarged towards the country and the good of it in life and death.

But no sooner was this given but Mr. Eaton[58] (professing eminently, yet falsely and most deceitfully, the fear of God) did lavish out a great part of it, and being for his cruelty to his scholars, especially to one Briscoe, as also for some other wantonness in life, not so notoriously known, driven [from] the country, the Lord about a year after graciously made up the breach by one Mr. Dunster,[59] a man pious, painful, and fit to teach, and very fit to lay the foundations of the domestical affairs of the college, whom God hath much honored and blessed.

The sin of Mr. Eaton was at first not so clearly discerned by me. Yet after more full information, I saw his sin great, and my ignorance and want of wisdom and watchfulness over him, very great, for which I desire to mourn all my life, and for the breach of his family.

But thus the Lord hath been very good unto me in planting the place I live in with such a mercy to myself, such a blessing to my children and the country, such an opportunity of doing good to many by doing good to students, as the school is.

After this I fell sick after Mr. Harlakenden's death, my most dear friend and most precious servant of Jesus Christ. And when I was very low and my blood much corrupted, the Lord revived me, and after that took pleasure in me to bless my labors that I was not altogether useless nor fruitless. And not only to speak by me to his people, but likewise to print my *Notes upon the Nine Principles,* I intended to proceed on with in Yorkshire, but never intended them or imagined they should be for

[57]John Harvard (1607–1638) graduated Emmanuel College, Cambridge, in 1631. He emigrated to New England with wife Anna around 1637. The Harvards were lifelong members of the church at Charlestown, where Shepard frequently served as a guest preacher. In a bequest likely secured with the assistance of Shepard, Harvard gave half of his estate—approximately £850 and his personal library of 260 volumes—to the founding of the first college, named after him by the grateful General Court in 1639.

[58]Nathaniel Eaton (1609?–1674) graduated Trinity College, Cambridge, in 1629. He studied in Leyden under the renowned William Ames until 1637, when he emigrated to Massachusetts with his two brothers, the eldest of whom was destined to be governor of the New Haven Colony for nineteen years. Prized for his learning, Eaton was made head of Harvard in 1639 with a gift from the General Court of 500 acres. He was charged shortly after for "avarice," for withholding food from his students, and for cruelty in the severe use of corporal punishment. Later charged with embezzlement, he escaped first to Virginia and eventually back to England. Shepard held himself responsible for not having detected Eaton's defects of character.

[59]Henry Dunster (1609–1659) graduated Magdalene College, Cambridge, in 1631 (master's degree in 1634). He arrived in New England in 1640. He was named Harvard's first president for his learning; he was proficient in Hebrew, Greek and Latin. Forced to resign the presidency over rumor of his Anabaptist heresy in 1654, he retired to Scituate, where he was a minister until his death.

the press. Yet six of them being finished in Old England and printed,[60] and the other three desired, I finished (the Lord helping) those at Cambridge, and so sent them to England, where they also are printed,[61] which I do not glory in (for I know my weakness), that my name is up by this means, but that the Lord may be pleased to do some good by them there in my absence. For I have seen the Lord making improvement of my weak abilities as far as they could reach and of myself to the utmost, which I desire to bless his name forever for.

The year after those wars in the country, God having taken away my first wife, the Lord gave me a second, the eldest daughter of Mr. Hooker,[62] a blessed stock. And the Lord hath made her a great blessing to me to carry on matters in the family with much care and wisdom, and to seek the Lord God of her father.

The first child I had by her, being a son, died (through the weakness of the midwife) before it saw the sun, even in the very birth. The second, whom the Lord I bless hath hitherto spared (viz., my little Samuel)[63] is yet living. The third son (viz., my son John) after sixteen weeks departed on the Sabbath day morning, a day of rest, to the bosom of rest to Him who gave it, which was no small affliction and heart-breaking to me that I should provoke the Lord to strike at my innocent children for my sake.

The Lord thus afflicting yet continued peace to the country, that amazing mercy when all England and Europe are in a flame. The Lord hath set me and my children aside from the flames of the fires in Yorkshire and Northumberland whence if we had not been delivered, I had been in great afflictions and temptations, very weak and unfit to be tossed up and down and to bear violent persecution. The Lord therefore hath showed his tenderness to me and mine in carrying me to a land of peace, though a place of trial, where the Lord hath made the savage Indians (who conspired the death of all the English by Miantinomo upon a sudden, if Uncas could have been cut off first, who stood in their way, and determined an open war upon us by the privy suggestions of some neutral English on the Island) to seek for peace from us upon our own terms, without bloodshed, August 26, 1645.

But the Lord hath not been wont to let me live long without some affliction or other, and yet ever mixed with some mercy. And therefore, April the 2d, 1646, as he gave me another son, John, so he took away my most dear, precious, meek, and loving wife in child-bed after three weeks' lying in, having left behind her two hopeful branches, my dear children, Samuel and John. This affliction was very heavy to me, for in it the Lord seemed to withdraw his tender care for me and mine, which he graciously manifested by my dear wife; also refused to hear prayer, when I did think he would have hearkened and let me see his beauty in the land of the living in restoring of her to health again; also, in taking her away in the prime time of her life, when she might have lived to have glorified the Lord long; also, in threatening me to proceed in rooting out my family, and that he would not stop, having begun here, as in Eli, for not being zealous enough against the sins of his sons. And I saw that if I had profited by former afflictions of this nature, I should not have had this scourge. But I am the Lord's, and He may do with me what he will. He did teach me to prize a little grace gained by a cross as a sufficient recompense for all outward losses.

[60]*The Sincere Convert* (London, 1640).

[61]*The Sound Believer* (London, 1645).

[62]Joanna Hooker.

[63]Samuel Shepard the younger (1641–1668) was ordained minister at Rowley, where he served until his early death.

But this loss was very great. She was a woman of incomparable meekness of spirit, toward myself especially, and very loving, of great prudence to take care for and order my family affairs, being neither too lavish nor sordid in anything, so that I knew not what was under her hands. She had an excellency to reprove for sin and discern the evils of men. She loved God's people dearly, and [was] studious to profit by their fellowship, and therefore loved their company. She loved God's word exceedingly, and hence was glad she could read my notes, which she had to muse on every week. She had a spirit of prayer, beyond ordinary of her time and experience. She was fit to die long before she did die, even after the death of her first-born, which was a great affliction to her. But her work not being done then, she lived almost nine years with me and was the comfort of my life to me; and the last sacrament before her lying-in, seemed to be full of Christ and thereby fitted for heaven. She did oft say she should not outlive this child; and when her fever first began (by taking some cold), she told me so, that we should love exceedingly together, because we should not live long together. Her fever took away her sleep; want of sleep wrought much distemper in her head and filled it with fantasies and distractions, but without raging. The night before she died, she had about six hours' unquiet sleep. But that so cooled and settled her head that when she knew none else, so as to speak to them, yet she knew Jesus Christ, and could speak to him; and therefore, as soon as she awakened out of sleep, she brake out into a most heavenly, heart-breaking prayer, after Christ, her dear Redeemer, for the spirit of life, and so continued praying until the last hour of her death, "Lord, though I [am] unworthy, Lord, one word, one word," &c.; and so gave up the ghost.

Thus God hath visited and scourged me for my sins and sought to wean me from this world. But I have ever found it a difficult thing to profit even but a little by the sorest and sharpest afflictions.

c. 1646 1853, 1972

Anne Bradstreet 1612?–1672

Anne Dudley Bradstreet is among the best known of early North American poets, the first in the British colonies to have a book of poetry published. She was born in England to Dorothy Yorke, whom Cotton Mather described as "a gentlewoman whose extract and estate were considerable," and Thomas Dudley, steward to the Earl of Lincoln at Sempringham. As a child she had access to private tutors and the Earl's library, a circumstance that allowed her educational opportunities unusual for women of her time. Her family was part of the nonconformist group of Puritans actively planning for the settlement of Massachusetts Bay Colony. In 1628, Anne Dudley married Simon Bradstreet (also nonconformist), and in 1630 (with Winthrop's group) she arrived with her husband and parents in Massachusetts. Many years later she wrote to her children of her first impressions of North America, where she "found a new world and new manners, at which [her] heart rose. But after [she] was convinced it was the way of God, [she] submitted to it and joined to the church at Boston."

The Bradstreets soon left Boston for Newtown (now Cambridge), then Ipswich, and after 1644 they moved to North An-dover, where Bradstreet remained until her death in 1672. While her husband and her father began long careers in public service to the new colony, she raised eight children and wrote poetry. *The Tenth Muse Lately Sprung Up in America* was published in London in 1650 at the insistence of John Woodbridge, Bradstreet's brother-in-law. The poems had evidently circulated among various members of Bradstreet's family. Taking a manuscript copy to London, Woodbridge inserted a preface to assure readers of the book's authenticity:

. . . the worst effect of his [the reader's] reading will be unbelief, which will make him question whether it be a woman's work, and ask, is it possible? If any do, take this as an answer from him that dares avow it; it is the work of a woman, honored, and esteemed where she lives, for her gracious demeanor, her eminent parts, her pious conversation, her courteous disposition, her exact diligence in her place, and discreet managing of her family occasions, and more than so, these poems are the fruit but of some few hours, curtailed from her sleep and other refreshments.

Woodbridge's care to point out that Bradstreet's poems were not written in neglect of family duties says much about Renaissance suspicions regarding literary women.

The 1650 edition of Bradstreet's poems contains her early conventional verse: quaternions, elegies, and dialogues that reveal more about the literary influences upon her writing (Quarles, DuBartas, Sylvester, Sidney, Spenser, Thomas Dudley) than about her responses to a new environment. Despite opposition from "carping tongues" who said her "hand a needle better fits" than a pen, Bradstreet continued to write. A Boston edition of her poems appeared posthumously in 1678, with a substantial quantity of new material, much of it her finest work.

This later work, from which most of the selections included here are taken, develops from the conventional public verse of the first edition to more private themes of family, love, nature, sorrow, faith, and resignation. However varied the subject matter, Bradstreet's poetry consistently reflects the Puritan spiritual and communal vision that informed her life. Furhter, the assertiveness about women's abilities in public pieces such as "The Prologue" grows into an uninhibited use of images drawn from women's experiences, particularly her own. In her mature poems, as in the prose meditations she left to her children, Bradstreet "avoided encroaching upon other's conceptions, because [she] would leave [them] nothing but [her] own." The poet's voice becomes distinct and individual, revealing tensions between conventional literary subject matter and her own experience, between rebellion against and acquiescence to her frontier circumstances, between her love of this world and her concern for the afterlife of Puritan doctrine. While Bradstreet's didactic motives frequently remain, they become less overt. She intends no moralizing in verse, but simply to react to her own experiences. With those personal reactions, she occasionally makes the Puritan aesthetic within which she worked satisfy a larger aesthetic, one more accessible to modern readers. As the first widely recognized woman poet in a North American literature not known for its attention to women writers, Anne Bradstreet is a model for future generations.

Pattie Cowell
Colorado State University

PRIMARY WORKS

The Tenth Muse Lately Sprung Up in America, 1650; *Several Poems Compiled with Great Variety of Wit and Learning,* 1678, rpt. 1758; *The Works of Anne Bradstreet in Prose and Verse,* ed. John Harvard Ellis, 1867; *The Works of Anne Bradstreet,* ed. Jeannine Hensley, 1967; *The Complete Works of Anne Bradstreet,* ed. Joseph R. McElrath Jr. and Allan P. Robb, 1981.

The Prologue [To Her Book][1]

1

To sing of wars, of captains, and of kings,
Of cities founded, commonwealths begun,
For my mean[2] pen are too superior things:
Or how they all or each their dates have run,
Let poets and historians set these forth,
My obscure lines shall not so dim their worth.

2

But when my wond'ring eyes and envious heart
Great Bartas'[3] sugar'd lines do but read o'er
Fool I do grudge the Muses[4] did not part
'Twixt him and me that overfluent store;
A Bartas can do what a Bartas will,
But simple I according to my skill.

3

From schoolboy's tongue no rhet'ric we expect,
Nor yet a sweet consort from broken strings,
Nor perfect beauty where's a main defect:
My foolish, broken, blemish'd Muse so sings,
And this to mend, alas, no art is able,
'Cause nature made it so irreparable.

4

Nor can I, like that fluent sweet tongu'd Greek,
Who lisp'd at first,[5] in future times speak plain;
By art he gladly found what he did seek,
A full requital of his striving pain.

[1]It is surmised that this prologue was originally written for "Quaternions," Bradstreet's epic on the history of mankind and the "four monarchies." In *The Tenth Muse* (1650), the poem stood as an introductory address.

[2]Low or humble.

[3]Guillaume de Salluste du Bartas (1544–1590), French writer of religious epics, was admired by the Puritans.

[4]The Greek Muses were nine female deities of the arts and sciences. Calliope, mentioned in stanza 6, was the muse of epic poetry.

[5]The Greek orator Demosthenes (c. 383–322 B.C.) was born with a lisp.

Art can do much, but this maxim's most sure:
A weak or wounded brain admits no cure.

5

I am obnoxious to each carping tongue
Who says my hand a needle better fits,
A poet's pen all scorn I should thus wrong,
For such despite they cast on female wits:
If what I do prove well, it won't advance,
They'll say it's stol'n, or else it was by chance.

6

But sure the antique Greeks were far more mild,
Else of our sex, why feigned they those Nine,
And poesy made Calliope's own child;
So 'mongst the rest they placed the arts divine,
But this weak knot, they will full soon untie,
The Greeks did nought, but play the fools and lie.

7

Let Greeks be Greeks, and women what they are,
Men have precedency and still excel,
It is but vain unjustly to wage war;
Men can do best, and women know it well.
Preeminence in all and each is yours;
Yet grant some small acknowledgment of ours.

8

And oh ye high flown quills[6] that soar the skies,
And ever with your prey still catch your praise,
If e'er you deign these lowly lines your eyes,
Give thyme or parsley wreath, I ask no bays;[7]
This mean and unrefined ore of mine
Will make your glist'ring gold but more to shine.

1650

[6]Quills were used as pens.
[7]Laurels, foliage from a tree in southern Europe used by the ancient Greeks as a crown of honor.

In Honour of . . . Queen Elizabeth

The Proem

Although, great Queen, thou now in silence lie
Yet thy loud herald Frame doth to the sky
Thy wondrous worth proclaim in every clime,
And so hath vow'd while there is world or time.
So great's thy glory and thine excellence,
The sound thereof rapts every human sense,
That men account it no impiety,
To say thou wert a fleshly Diety:
Thousands bring offerings (though out of date)
Thy world of honours to accumulate,
'Mongst hundred hecatombs[1] of roaring verse,
Mine bleating stands before they royal hearse.
Thou never didst nor canst thou now disdain
T' accept the tribute of a loyal brain.
Thy clemency did erst[2] esteem as much
The acclamations of the poor as rich,
Which makes me deem my rudeness is no wrong,
Though I resound thy praises 'mongst the throng.

The Poem

No Phoenix pen,[3] nor Spenser's[4] poetry,
No Speed's[5] nor Camden's[6] learned history,
Eliza's works, wars, praise, can e're compact;
The world's the theatre where she did act.
No memories nor volumes can contain
The 'leven Olympiads[7] of her happy reign.
Who was so good, so just, so learn'd, so wise,
From all the kings on earth she won the prize.
Nor say I more than duly is her due,

[1]A large number or quantity.
[2]In the past, formerly.
[3]A reference to the work of Sir Philip Sidney (1554–1586), the English poet in whose memory an anthology of poems called *The Phoenix Nest* (1593) was collected.
[4]Edmund Spenser (1552?–1599), English poet and author of *The Faerie Queene,* a celebration of Queen Elizabeth.
[5]John Speed (1522?–1629), who published a *Historie of Great Britaine.*
[6]William Camden (1551–1623), English historian whose Latin *Annales* of Queen Elizabeth's reign became available in English in 1625.
[7]In ancient Greece, time was reckoned by the four-year intervals between Olympic Games. This phrase suggests the long duration of Queen Elizabeth's reign, from 1558 to 1603, roughly the length of eleven Olympiads.

Millions will testify that this is true.
She hath wip'd off th' aspersion of her sex,
That women wisdom lack to play the rex:[8]
Spain's monarch says not so, nor yet his host:
She taught them better manners, to their cost.[9]
The Salic law,[10] in force now had not been,
If France had ever hop'd for such a queen.
But can you, doctors, now this point dispute,
She's argument enough to make you mute.
Since first the sun did run his ne'er run race,
And earth had once a year, a new old face,
Since time was time, and man unmanly man,
Come show me such a Phoenix[11] if you can.
Was ever people better rul'd than hers?
Was ever land more happy freed from stirs?
Did ever wealth in England more abound?
Her victories in foreign coasts resound;
Ships more invincible than Spain's, her foe,
She wracked, she sacked, she sunk his Armado;
Her stately troops advanc'd to Lisbon's wall,[12]
Don Anthony in's right there to install.
She frankly helped Frank's brave distressed king,
The states united now her fame do sing.
She their protectrix was; they well do know
Unto our dread virago,[13] what they owe.
Her nobles sacrific'd their noble blood,
Nor men nor coin she spar'd to do them good.
The rude untamed Irish, she did quell,
Before her picture the proud Tyrone fell.[14]
Had ever prince such counsellors as she?
Herself Minerva[15] caus'd them so to be.
Such captains and such soldiers never seen,
As were the subjects of our Pallas[16] Queen.
Her seamen through all straits the world did round;

[8]Latin word for "king."

[9]Philip II of Spain assembled a large fleet to invade England in 1588. The English defeated this "Invincible Armada" in one of the most famous naval battles in history.

[10]The legal code of the Salic Franks, one provision of which excluded women from the line of succession to a throne.

[11]The legendary, long-lived bird that burned itself to ashes and then rose from the ashes to live again.

[12]Elizabeth sent Sir Francis Drake with a large fleet to attack Portugal in 1589. Her aim was to establish Don Antonio of Crato (1531–1595) as king. Drake failed to take Lisbon, and Elizabeth's purpose was defeated.

[13]A woman who possesses great stature, strength, and courage.

[14]Hugh O'Neill, second earl of Tyrone (c. 1540–1616), an Irish leader opposed to English rule, was forced to submit to the Crown in 1603.

[15]Roman goddess of wisdom.

[16]Athena, Greek goddess of wisdom.

Terra incognita[17] might know the sound.
Her Drake[18] came laden home with Spanish gold;
Her Essex[19] took Cadiz, their Herculean hold.
But time would fail me, so my tongue would too,
To tell of half she did, or she could do.
Semiramis[20] to her is but obscure,
More infamy than fame she did procure.
She built her glory but on Babel's walls,[21]
World's wonder for a while, but yet it falls.
Fierce Tomris,[22] (Cyrus' heads-man), Scythians' queen,
Had put her harness off, had she but seen
Our Amazon in th' Camp of Tilbury,[23]
Judging all valour and all majesty
Within that princess to have residence,
And prostrate yielded to her excellence.
Dido,[24] first foundress of proud Carthage walls,
(Who living consummates her funerals)
A great Eliza, but compar'd with ours,
How vanisheth her glory, wealth, and powers.
Profuse, proud Cleopatra,[25] whose wrong name,
Instead of glory, prov'd her country's shame:
Of her what worth in stories to be seen,
But that she was a rich Egyptian queen.
Zenobya,[26] potent empress of the East,
And of all these, without compare the best,
Whom none but great Aurelius[27] could quel;

[17]Latin for "unknown territory," "unexplored land."

[18]Sir Francis Drake (1540?–1596), circumnavigator of the world, was knighted by Queen Elizabeth in 1581. He commanded one of the divisions of the English fleet against the Spanish Armada in 1588. In 1585 and again in 1589 he raided Spanish cities and destroyed much Spanish shipping.

[19]Robert Devereux, second earl of Essex (1566–1601), captured Cádiz in 1596.

[20]In Greek legend, queen of Assyria, famous in war.

[21]Described in Genesis 11, the walls of the tower of Bable were designed to reach to the heavens. God confused the language of the tower's builders, scattering them throughout the earth and forcing them to leave their project unfinished.

[22]The Messagetae queen Tomyris or Tomiris, whose army defeated and killed Cyrus the Great (c. 600–530 B.C.). Herodotus described her vengeance on Cyrus for the death of her son: Cyrus's severed head was placed in a skin full of blood to carry out Tomyris's pre-battle promise to give him his fill of blood if he attacked.

[23]Shortly before their engagement with the Spanish Armada in 1588, Elizabeth reviewed and gave a rousing speech to a detachment of her troops camped at Tilbury on the north bank of the Thames. Some accounts claim she wore armor, hence the reference to "Our Amazon."

[24]Legendary queen of Carthage in Virgil's *Aeneid.* Carthage was an ancient North African city and state located on the Mediterranean coast northeast of modern Tunis.

[25]Queen of Egypt, who lived from 69 to 30 B.C., mistress of Julius Caesar and Mark Antony.

[26]Zenobia, from A.D. 267 to 272 queen of Palmyra, an ancient city on the northern edge of the Syrian Desert.

[27]Aurelian (c. A.D. 215–275), Roman emperor who defeated Zenobia at Palmyra in 272.

Yet for our Queen is no fit parallel.
She was a Phoenix queen, so shall she be,
Her ashes not reviv'd, more Phoenix she.
Her personal perfections, who would tell,
Must dip his pen in th' Heleconian well,[28]
Which I may not, my pride doth but aspire
To read what others write, and so admire.
Now say, have women worth? or have they none?
Or had they some, but with our Queen is't gone?
Nay masculines, you have thus taxed us long,
But she, though dead, will vindicate our wrong.
Let such as say our sex is void of reason,
Know 'tis a slander now, but once was treason.
But happy England which had such a queen;
Yea happy, happy, had those days still been:
But happiness lies in a higher sphere,
Then wonder not Eliza moves not here.
Full fraught with honour, riches and with days
She set, she set, like Titan[29] in his rays.
No more shall rise or set so glorious sun
Until the heaven's great revolution;
If then new things their old forms shall retain,
Eliza shall rule Albion[30] once again.

Her Epitaph

Here sleeps the queen, this is the royal bed
Of th' damask rose, sprung from the white and red,
Whose sweet perfume fills the all-filling air:
This rose is wither'd, once so lovely fair.
On neither tree did grow such rose before,
The greater was our gain, our loss the more.

Another

Here lies the pride of queens, pattern of kings,
So blaze it, Fame, here's feathers for thy wings.
Here lies the envied, yet unparalled prince,
Whose living virtues speak (though dead long since).
If many worlds, as that fantastic fram'd,
In every one be her great glory fam'd.

1643

[28]A well those waters flowed from Mount Helicon in Greece, site of a temple dedicated to the Muses.

[29]The sun.

[30]Latin name for England.

The Author to Her Book[1]

Thou ill-form'd offspring of my feeble brain,
Who after birth did'st by my side remain,
Till snatcht from thence by friends, less wise than true,
Who thee abroad expos'd to public view,
Made thee in rags halting to th' press to trudge,
Where errors were not lessened (all may judge).
At thy return my blushing was not small,
My rambling brat (in print) should mother call;
I cast thee by as one unfit for light,
Thy visage was so irksome in my sight;
Yet being mine own, at length affection would
Thy blemishes amend, if so I could:
I wash'd thy face, but more defects I saw,
And rubbing off a spot, still made a flaw.
I stretcht thy joints to make thee even feet,
Yet still thou run'st more hobbling than is meet;
In better dress to trim thee was my mind,
But nought save homespun cloth i' th' house I find;
In this array, 'mongst vulgars may'st thou roam,
In critic's hands, beware thou dost not come;
And take thy way where yet thou art not known,
If for thy father asked, say thou had'st none:
And for thy mother, she alas is poor,
Which caus'd her thus to send thee out of door.

1678

To Her Father with Some Verses

Most truly honored, and as truly dear,
If worth in me, or ought[1] I do appear,
Who can of right better demand the fame,
Then may your worthy self from whom it came?
The principle might yield a greater sum,[2]
Yet handled ill, amounts but to this crumb;
My stock's so small, I know not how to pay,

[1]Bradstreet's book, *The Tenth Muse,* was published in London in 1650. It is thought that she wrote this poem in 1666, when a second edition seemed to have been considered.

[1]Anything.
[2]Principal, or primary capital, yields interest.

My bond[3] remains in force unto this day;
Yet for part payment take this simple mite,
Where nothing's to be had kings loose their right;
Such is my debt, I may not say forgive,
But as I can, I'll pay it while I live:
Such is my bond, none can discharge but I,
Yet paying is not paid until I die.

1678

The Flesh and the Spirit

In secret place where once I stood
Close by the banks of Lacrim[1] flood,
I heard two sisters reason on
Things that are past and things to come;
One flesh was called, who had her eye
On wordly wealth and vanity;
The other Spirit, who did rear
Her thoughts unto a higher sphere:
Sister, quoth Flesh, what liv'st thou on,
Nothing but meditation?
Doth contemplation feed thee so
Regardlessly to let earth go?
Can speculation satisfy
Notion[2] without reality?
Dost dream of things beyond the moon,
And dost thou hope to dwell there soon?
Hast treasures there laid up in store
That all in th' world thou count'st but poor?
Art fancy sick, or turned a sot
To catch at shadows which are not?
Come, come, I'll show unto thy sense,
Industry hath its recompense.
What canst desire, but thou may'st see
True substance in variety?
Dost honor like? Acquire the same,
As some to their immortal fame,
And trophies to thy name erect

[3]Contract.
[1]*Lacrima,* in Latin, means "tear."
[2]Knowledge, from the Latin, *notio.*

Which wearing time shall ne'er deject.
For riches doth thou long full sore?
Behold enough of precious store.
Earth hath more silver, pearls, and gold,
Than eyes can see or hands can hold.
Affect's thou pleasure? Take thy fill,
Earth hath enough of what you will.
Then let not go, what thou may'st find
For things unknown, only in mind.

Spirit: Be still thou unregenerate[3] part,
Disturb no more my settled heart,
For I have vowed (and so will do)
Thee as a foe still to pursue.
And combat with thee will and must,
Until I see thee laid in th' dust.
Sisters we are, yea, twins we be,
Yet deadly feud 'twixt thee and me;
For from one father are we not,
Thou by old Adam wast begot.
But my arise is from above,
Whence my dear Father I do love.
Thou speak'st me fair, but hat'st me sore,
Thy flatt'ring shows I'll trust no more,
How oft thy slave, hast thou me made,
When I believed what thou hast said,
And never had more cause of woe
Than when I did what thou bad'st do.
I'll stop mine ears at these thy charms,
And count them for my deadly harms.
Thy sinful pleasures I do hate,
Thy riches are to me no bait,
Thine honors do, nor will I love;
For my ambition lies above.
My greatest honor it shall be
When I am victor over thee,
And triumph shall with laurel head,
When thou my captive shalt be led,
How I do live, thou need'st not scoff,
For I have meat thou know'st not of;[4]
The hidden manna[5] I do eat,
The word of life it is my meat.
My thoughts do yield me more content

[3]Not "saved," unrepentant.
[4]See John 4:32.
[5]The Israelites miraculously received manna, or food from heaven, when they were in the wilderness (Exodus 16:15). Mystical "hidden manna" is promised in Revelation 2:17.

Than can thy hours in pleasure spent.
Nor are they shadows which I catch,
Nor fancies vain at which I snatch,
But reach at things that are so high,
Beyond thy dull capacity;
Eternal substance I do see,
With which enriched I would be.
Mine eye doth pierce the heavens and see
What is invisible to thee.
My garments are not silk nor gold,
Nor such like trash which earth doth hold,
But royal robes I shall have on,
More glorious than the glist'ring sun;
My crown not diamonds, pearls, and gold,
But such as angels' heads enfold.
The city where I hope to dwell,[6]
There's none on earth can parallel;
The stately walls both high and strong,
Are made of precious jasper stone;
The gates of pearl, both rich and clear,
And angels are for porters there;
The streets thereof transparent gold,
Such as no eye did e'er behold;
A crystal river there doth run,
Which doth proceed from the Lamb's throne.
Of life, there are the waters sure,
Which shall remain forever pure,
Nor sun, nor moon, they have no need,
For glory doth from God proceed.
No candle there, nor yet torchlight,
For there shall be no darksome night.
From sickness and infirmity
For evermore they shall be free;
Nor withering age shall e'er come there,
But beauty shall be bright and clear;
This city pure is not for thee,
For things unclean there shall not be.
If I of heaven may have my fill,
Take thou the world and all that will.

1678

[6]The heavenly city of the New Jerusalem is described in lines 85 to 106; they are based on Revelations 21:10–27 and 22:1–5.

Before the Birth of One of Her Children

All things within this fading world hath end,
Adversity doth still our joys attend;
No ties so strong, no friends so dear and sweet,
But with death's parting blow is sure to meet.
The sentence past is most irrevocable,
A common thing, yet oh inevitable;
How soon, my dear, death may my steps attend,
How soon't may be thy lot to lose thy friend,
We both are ignorant, yet love bids me
These farewell lines to recommend to thee,
That when that knot's untied that made us one,
I may seem thine, who in effect am none.
And if I see not half my days that's due,
What nature would, God grant to yours and you;
The many faults that well you know I have,
Let be interr'd in my oblivion's grave;
If any worth or virtue were in me,
Let that live freshly in thy memory,
And when thou feel'st no grief, as I no harms,
Yet love thy dead, who long lay in thine arms:
And when thy loss shall be repaid with gains,
Look to my little babes, my dear remains.
And if thou love thy self, or loved'st me,
These O protect from step-dame's injury.[1]
And if chance to thine eyes shall bring this verse,
With some sad sighs honor my absent hearse;
And kiss the paper for thy love's dear sake,
Who with salt tears this last farewell did take.

1678

To My Dear and Loving Husband

If ever two were one, then surely we.
If ever man were loved by wife, then thee;
If ever wife was happy in a man,
Compare with me, ye women, if you can.
I prize thy love more than whole mines of gold
Or all the riches that the East doth hold.

[1]Bradstreet alludes to tales of evil stepmothers.

My love is such that rivers cannot quench,
Nor ought but love from thee, give recompense.
Thy love is such I can no way repay,
The heavens reward thee manifold, I pray.
Then while we live, in love let's so persevere
That when we live no more, we may live ever.

1678

A Letter to Her Husband, Absent upon Public Employment

My head, my heart, mine eyes, my life, nay more,
My joy, my magazine[1] of earthly store,
If two be one, as surely thou and I,
How stayest thou there, whilst I at Ipswich[2] lie?
So many steps, head from the heart to sever,
If but a neck, soon should we be together:
I, like the earth this season, mourn in black,
My sun is gone so far in's zodiac,
Whom whilst I 'joy'd, nor storms, nor frosts I felt,
His warmth such frigid colds did cause to melt.
My chilled limbs now numbed lie forlorn;
Return, return sweet Sol from Capricorn;[3]
In this dead time, alas, what can I more
Then view those fruits which through thy heat I bore?
Which sweet contentment yield me for a space,
True living pictures of their father's face.
O strange effect! now thou art southward gone,
I weary grow, the tedious day so long;
But when thou northward to me shalt return,
I wish my sun may never set, but burn
Within the Cancer[4] of my glowing breast,
The welcome house of him my dearest guest.
Where ever, ever stay, and go not thence,
Till nature's sad decree shall call thee hence;
Flesh of thy flesh, bone of thy bone,
I here, thou there, yet both but one.

1678

[1]Warehouse.
[2]Town north of Boston, Massachusetts.
[3]When Sol (the Sun) is in Capricorn (the tenth zodiacal sign), it is winter.
[4]When the sun is in Cancer (the fourth sign of the zodiac), it is summer.

In Memory of My Dear Grandchild Elizabeth Bradstreet, Who Deceased August, 1665, Being a Year and Half Old

Farewell dear babe, my heart's too much content,
Farewell sweet babe, the pleasure of mine eye,
Farewell fair flower that for a space was lent,
Then ta'en away unto eternity.
Blest babe, why should I once bewail thy fate,
Or sigh thy days so soon were terminate,
Sith thou art settled in an everlasting state.

2

By nature trees do rot when they are grown,
And plums and apples thoroughly ripe do fall,
And corn and grass are in their season mown,
And time brings down what is both strong and tall.
But plants new set to be eradicate,
And buds new blown to have so short a date,
Is by His hand alone that guides nature and fate.

1678

On My Dear Grandchild Simon Bradstreet, Who Died on 16 November, 1669, being but a Month, and One Day Old

No sooner came, but gone, and fall'n asleep,
Acquaintance short, yet parting caused us weep;
Three flowers, two scarcely blown, the last i' th' bud,
Cropt by th' Almighty's hand; yet is He good.
With dreadful awe before Him let's be mute,
Such was His will, but why, let's not dispute,
With humble hearts and mouths put in the dust,
Let's say He's merciful as well as just.
He will return and make up all our losses,
And smile again after our bitter crosses
Go pretty babe, go rest with sisters twain;
Among the blest in endless joys remain.

1678

Upon the Burning of Our House July 10th, 1666

In silent night when rest I took
For sorrow near I did not look
I wakened was with thund'ring noise
And piteous shrieks of dreadful voice.
That fearful sound of "Fire!" and "Fire!"
Let no man know is my desire.
I, starting up, the light did spy,
And to my God my heart did cry
To strengthen me in my distress
And not to leave me succorless.
Then, coming out, beheld a space
The flame consume my dwelling place.
And when I could no longer look,
I blest His name that gave and took,
That laid my goods now in the dust.
Yea, so it was, and so 'twas just.
It was His own, it was not mine,
Far be it that I should repine;
He might of all justly bereft
But yet sufficient for us left.
When by the ruins oft I past
My sorrowing eyes aside did cast,
And here and there the places spy
Where oft I sat and long did lie:
Here stood that trunk, and there that chest,
There lay that store I counted best.
My pleasant things in ashes lie,
And them behold no more shall I.
Under thy roof no guest shall sit,
Nor at thy table eat a bit.
No pleasant tale shall e'er be told,
Nor things recounted done of old.
No candle e'er shall shine in thee,
Nor bridegroom's voice e'er heard shall be.
In silence ever shall thou lie,
Adieu, Adieu, all's vanity.
Then straight I 'gin my heart to chide,
And did thy wealth on earth abide?
Didst fix thy hope on mold'ring dust?
The arm of flesh didst make thy trust?
Raise up thy thoughts above the sky
That dunghill mists away may fly.

Thou hast an house on high erect,
Framed by that mighty Architect,
With glory richly furnished,
Stands permanent though this be fled.
It's purchased and paid for too
By Him who hath enough to do.
A price so vast as is unknown
Yet by His gift is made thine own;
There's wealth enough, I need no more,
Farewell, my pelf, farewell my store.
The world no longer let me love,
My hope and treasure lies above.

1666

To My Dear Children

This book by any yet unread,
I leave for you when I am dead,
That being gone, here you may find
What was your living mother's mind.
Make use of what I leave in love,
And God shall bless you from above.

My dear children,

I, knowing by experience that the exhortations of parents take most effect when the speakers leave to speak, and those especially sink deepest which are spoke latest, and being ignorant whether on my death bed I shall have opportunity to speak to any of you, much less to all, thought it the best, whilst I was able, to compose some short matters (for what else to call them I know not) and bequeath to you, that when I am no more with you, yet I may be daily in your remembrance (although that is the least in my aim in what I now do), but that you may gain some spiritual advantage by my experience. I have not studied in this you read to show my skill, but to declare the truth, not to set forth myself, but the glory of God. If I had minded the former, it had been perhaps better pleasing to you, but seeing the last is the best, let it be best pleasing to you.

The method I will observe shall be this: I will begin with God's dealing with me from my childhood to this day.

In my young years, about 6 or 7 as I take it, I began to make conscience of my ways, and what I knew was sinful, as lying, disobedience to parents, etc., I avoided it. If at any time I was overtaken with the like evils, it was as a great trouble, and I could not be at rest 'till by prayer I had confessed it unto God. I was also troubled at the neglect of private duties though too often tardy that way. I also found much comfort in reading the Scriptures, especially those places I thought most concerned my condition, and as I grew to have more understanding, so the more solace I took in them.

In a long fit of sickness which I had on my bed I often communed with my heart and made my supplication to the most High who set me free from that affliction.

But as I grew up to be about 14 or 15, I found my heart more carnal, and sitting loose from God, vanity and the follies of youth take hold of me.

About 16, the Lord laid His hand sore upon me and smote me with the smallpox. When I was in my affliction, I besought the Lord and confessed my pride and vanity, and He was entreated of me and again restored me. But I rendered not to Him according to the benefit received.

After a short time I changed my condition and was married, and came into this country, where I found a new world and new manners, at which my heart rose. But after I was convinced it was the way of God, I submitted to it and joined to the church at Boston.

After some time I fell into a lingering sickness like a consumption together with a lameness, which correction I saw the Lord sent to humble and try me and do me good, and it was not altogether ineffectual.

It pleased God to keep me a long time without a child, which was a great grief to me and cost me many prayers and tears before I obtained one, and after him gave me many more of whom I now take the care, that as I have brought you into the world, and with great pains, weakness, cares, and fears brought you to this, I now travail in birth again of you till Christ be formed in you.

Among all my experiences of God's gracious dealings with me, I have constantly observed this, that He hath never suffered me long to sit loose from Him, but by one affliction or other hath made me look home, and search what was amiss; so usually thus it hath been with me that I have no sooner felt my heart out of order, but I have expected correction for it, which most commonly hath been upon my own person in sickness, weakness, pains, sometimes on my soul, in doubts and fears of God's displeasure and my sincerity towards Him; sometimes He hath smote a child with a sickness, sometimes chastened by losses in estate, and these times (through His great mercy) have been the times of my greatest getting and advantage; yea, I have found them the times when the Lord hath manifested the most love to me. Then have I gone to searching and have said with David, "Lord, search me and try me, see what ways of wickedness are in me, and lead me in the way everlasting," and seldom or never but I have found either some sin I lay under which God would have reformed, or some duty neglected which He would have performed, and by His help I have laid vows and bonds upon my soul to perform his righteous commands.

If at any time you are chastened of God, take it as thankfully and joyfully as in greatest mercies, for if ye be His, ye shall reap the greatest benefit by it. It hath been no small support to me in times of darkness when the Almighty hath hid His face from me that yet I have had abundance of sweetness and refreshment after affliction and more circumspection in my walking after I have been afflicted. I have been with God like an untoward child, that no longer than the rod has been on my back (or at least in sight) but I have been apt to forget Him and myself, too. Before I was afflicted, I went astray, but now I keep Thy statutes.

I have had great experience of God's hearing my prayers and returning comfortable answers to me, either in granting the thing I prayed for, or else in satisfying my mind without it, and I have been confident it hath been from Him, because I have found my heart through His goodness enlarged in thankfulness to Him.

I have often been perplexed that I have not found that constant joy in my pilgrimage and refreshing which I supposed most of the servants of God have, although He hath not left me altogether without the witness of His holy spirit, who hath oft given me His word and set to His seal that it shall be well with me. I have sometimes tasted of that hidden manna that the world knows not, and have set up my Ebenezer, and have resolved with myself that against such a promise, such tastes of sweetness, the gates of hell shall never prevail; yet have I many times sinkings and droopings, and not enjoyed that felicity that sometimes I have done. But when I have been in darkness and seen no light, yet have I desired to stay myself upon the Lord, and when I have been in sickness and pain, I have thought if the Lord would but lift up the light of His countenance upon me, although He ground me to powder, it would be but light to me; yea, oft have I thought were I in hell itself and could there find the love of God toward me, it would be a heaven. And could I have been in heaven without the love of God, it would have been a hell to me, for in truth it is the absence and presence of God that makes heaven or hell.

Many times hath Satan troubled me concerning the verity of the Scriptures, many times by atheism how I could know whether there was a God; I never saw any miracles to confirm me, and those which I read of, how did I know but they were feigned? That there is a God my reason would soon tell me by the wondrous works that I see, the vast frame of the heaven and the earth, the order of all things, night and day, summer and winter, spring and autumn, the daily providing for this great household upon the earth, the preserving and directing of all to its proper end. The consideration of these things would with amazement certainly resolve me that there is an Eternal Being. But how should I know He is such a God as I worship in Trinity, and such a Saviour as I rely upon? Though this hath thousands of times been suggested to me, yet God hath helped me over. I have argued thus with myself. That there is a God, I see. If ever this God hath revealed himself, it must be in His word, and this must be it or none. Have I not found that operation by it that no human invention can work upon the soul, hath not judgments befallen divers who have scorned and contemned it, hath it not been preserved through all ages maugre all the heathen tyrants and all of the enemies who have opposed it? Is there any story but that which shows the beginnings of times, and how the world came to be as we see? Do we not know the prophecies in it fulfilled which could not have been so long foretold by any but God Himself?

When I have got over this block, then have I another put in my way, that admit this be the true God whom we worship, and that be his word, yet why may not the Popish religion be the right? They have the same God, the same Christ, the same word. They only enterpret it one way, we another.

This hath sometimes stuck with me, and more it would, but the vain fooleries that are in their religion together with their lying miracles and cruel persecutions of the saints, which admit were they as they term them, yet not so to be dealt withal.

The consideration of these things and many the like would soon turn me to my own religion again.

But some new troubles I have had since the world has been filled with blasphemy and sectaries, and some who have been accounted sincere Christians have been carried away with them, that sometimes I have said, "Is there faith upon the earth?" and I have not known what to think; but then I have remembered the works of Christ that so it must be, and if it were possible, the very elect should be deceived. "Behold," saith our Saviour, "I have told you before." That hath stayed my heart, and I can now say, "Return, O my Soul, to thy rest, upon this rock Christ Jesus will I build my faith, and if I perish, I perish"; but I know all the Powers of Hell shall never prevail against it. I know whom I have trusted, and whom I have believed, and that He is able to keep that I have committed to His charge.

Now to the King, immortal, eternal and invisible, the only wise God, be honour, and glory for ever and ever, Amen.

This was written in much sickness and weakness, and is very weakly and imperfectly done, but if you can pick any benefit out of it, it is the mark which I aimed at.

1867

Mercury Shew'd Apollo, Bartas *Book*

Mercury shew'd *Apollo, Bartas* Book,
Minerva this, and wisht him well to look,
And tell uprightly, which did which excell,
He view'd and view'd, and vow'd he could not tel.
They did him Hemisphear his mouldy nose,
With's crackt leering-glasses, for it would pose
The best brains he had in's old pudding-pan,
Sex weigh'd, which best, the Woman, or the Man?
He peer'd, and por'd, and glar'd, and said for wore
I'me even as wise now, as I was before:
They both 'gan laugh, and said, it was no mar[ve]l
The Auth'ress was as right *Du Bartas* Girle.
Good sooth quoth the old Don, tel ye me so,
I muse whither at length these Girls will go;
It half revives my chil frost-bitten blood,
To see a woman once do, ought, that's good;
And shod by *Chaucers* Boots, and *Homers* Furrs,
Let Men look to't, least Women wear the Spurrs.

Nathaniel Ward, 1678

Nathaniel Ward's "Mercury shew'd Apollo, Bartas Book" was written for Anne Bradstreet and prefaced Bradstreet's Several Poems, *the 1678 enlarged and corrected edition of* The Tenth Muse.

Michael Wigglesworth 1631–1705

Upon Michael Wigglesworth's death in 1705, his gravestone was inscribed, "Here lies Intered in Silent Grave Below/ Mauldens Physician For Soul and Body too." Wigglesworth served as minister and physician in the Massachusetts town of Malden for over fifty years, but poems rather than sermons would sustain his reputation throughout the colonies during the seventeenth century. *The Day of Doom* and *Meat Out of the Eater,* both bestselling expressions of conservative Puritan theology, urged Puritans to repent their sins and to seek redemption. Presenting the basic tenets of Puritan belief in a jogging verse form called "fourteeners," *The Day of Doom* was purchased, memorized, and recited by Puritans throughout the colonies and England. Today, Wigglesworth's candid diary and persuasive poetry serve as fascinating glosses on Puritan experience.

Born in Yorkshire, England in 1631, Wigglesworth was raised by devout parents who left England in 1638 to join the growing community of Puritans in Massachusetts Bay. He excelled in his studies from a young age, and his parents eventually sent him to the newly established Harvard College in 1648. Arriving at Harvard with thoughts of studying medicine, he soon began to struggle with, define, and express the religious and philosophical ideas that would form the substance of his writings and make him an influential minister and poet. Reflecting on God's grace and examining his own soul—an experience of salvation central to Puritan theology—Wigglesworth postponed his medical studies to prepare for the ministry. He rejected several ministerial positions, however, in order to remain at Harvard for his master's degree and as a tutor. Intensely devoted to his students, Wigglesworth struggled endlessly to place God foremost in his mind at all times.

Wigglesworth's *Diary* records his thoughts and conversations with God during his tutoring years at Harvard, his marriage to a cousin, Mary Reyner, and his agonizing decision to accept a pastorship in Malden. The diary reveals the Puritan's constant self-scrutiny and unceasing search for signs of God's favor or displeasure. He returns again and again to his most unrelenting sins: pride, lack of affection for his parents, especially his father, and attachment to things of the world rather than the divine. With remarkable emotional intensity, he describes his worries about his sexuality and his frequent bouts of illness. Exhaustion, weak lungs, and a chronic sore throat kept Wigglesworth from performing his full duties as pastor of Malden. He compensated for this shortcoming by becoming active in his community as a physician and as a poet. After the death of his wife, he began writing verse, preaching to the world through a medium kinder to his malady. He responded to his frustrated parishioners in the preface to *The Day of Doom:*

> Some think my voice is strong,
> Most times when I do Preach:
> But ten days after what I feel
> And suffer, few can reach.

In *The Day of Doom,* Wigglesworth sought to make more present that day that should never leave the Puritan mind: the Day of Judgment. The Last Judgment comes without warning in the poem, instructing readers that they must constantly ready themselves for God by considering each action in life in the light of God's judgment in death. The fervency of Wigglesworth's literary plea for rectitude was, in part, a response to the growth of materialism and the decline of spiritualism in the colonies. Through a poetic parable of goats (the damned) and sheep (the saved), Wigglesworth delineated punishments for the wicked and rewards for the virtuous, balancing God's mercy and justice. Easily accessible and directed at a broad audience,

The Day of Doom provided comfort to many generations of believers. The first edition, published in 1662, sold out within a year, and the volume was reprinted many times in both America and England. Unable to lecture consistently in his own parish, Wigglesworth preached compellingly to an enormous audience throughout the colonies. His next publication, *Meat Out of the Eater,* fell just short of the popularity of his first book. The title derives from the Biblical story of Samson and suggests that blessing arises from suffering, a theme perpetually present in Wigglesworth's own life as he attempted to turn physical ailment into spiritual health. Wigglesworth's jeremiad about the colonies' spiritual apathy, "God's Controversy with New-England," was written in 1662 but remained unpublished for two centuries.

Wigglesworth became embroiled in his own New England controversy when he married his unbaptized servant, Martha Mudge, in 1679. His influence in the colony, however, continued unabated. In the latter part of his life, Wigglesworth's health improved, and he became a more vigorous spiritual leader. After Martha Mudge's death, he married for a third time, became a Fellow at Harvard, and began preaching more often and energetically. As the colony as a whole grew less orthodox and wavered in its respect for members of the clergy, Wigglesworth still claimed considerable admiration. He continued to heal both body and soul through his medicine, his ministry, and his poetry until his death in 1705.

Danielle Hinrichs
University of Southern California

PRIMARY WORKS

The Day of Doom, 1662; *Meat Out of the Eater,* 1670, 1717; *Riddles Unriddled, or, Christian Paradoxes,* 1689; "God's Controversy with New-England," 1662, 1873; Edmund S. Morgan, ed., *The Diary of Michael Wigglesworth, 1653–1657,* 1970; Ronald A. Bosco, ed., *The Poems of Michael Wigglesworth,* 1989.

from The Diary of Michael Wigglesworth

[*February 15, 1653.*] Pride I feel still again and again abounding, self-admiration, though destroying my self daly. god gracious and bountifull in bestowing in directing me and mine, but I unthankfully wickedly making gods gifts subservient to my vain glory. ah Lord I am vile, I desire to abhor my self (o that I could!) before thee for these things. *I find such unresistable torments of carnal lusts or provocation unto the ejection of seed that I find my self unable to read any thing to inform me about my distemper because of the prevailing or rising of my lusts. This I have procured to my self. God hath brought this to my eye this day Thou hast destroyed thy self but in me is thy help Lord let me find help in thee though I have destroyed my self by my iniquity*[1]

[*February 25–27, 1653.*] . . . After noon god pleased to giue some affection and to warm my heart a little with the loue and grace of christ coming and dwelling amongst us. yet in the fore part of the sermon I found my spirit so distracted *with*

[1]Italics indicate portions of the diary written in a shorthand code.

vain thoughts and so disquieted within me, because one of my pupils was ill and absent from the ordinances, that I could not attend to the word, I could not cry for help scarcely to heaven nor see the evill of those impatient disquietments yet I desir'd a heart to cry for help, and the lord set me free at length from them. yet sundry times this day pride prevald over me. And some fears because I feel not loue to god as I should, but more loue to man, least I should loue man more than god. I am laden with a body of death, and could almost be willing to be dissolved and be with christ free'd from this sinful flesh, saue that I fear my state and haue some misgiuings; yet I desire to be made sincere, what is amis lord amend! . . .

[*March 2, 1653.*] This day was brought news of that dreadful disaster at Boston by fire; which came to pass the very night before Mr. Mitchels[2] lecture concerning god['s] judgements, and how abused they aggravate sin. thus god seals his word with his dreadful works. my heart was much affected and dejected within me upon deep thoughts of these things and what I had heard god speak to me in his word, (for he met with sundry of my sins and gaue dreadful examples of gods judgments that should haue warned me from them) yet afterward, o amazing prodigious, overpowering prevalency of wickedness,! pride again, and again most fearfully after all those shakings, awaknings, and almost sinkings of spirit, discovered its power over me. ah Lord! my king, my god, thee thee I provoke, and wert thou got a god indeed, infinite in thy grace fire and brimstone, or a flood of wrath had seized on me long ere now. why hast thou not pluck't away from me by some sad stroke my dearest ones? am I better, nay how far am I viler than they to whom thou hast done this. . . .

[*April 5, 1653.*] On thursday morning the Lord was pleas'd to give me somewhat a heart-breaking meditation of him. so that I thought and will the Lord now again return and embrace me in the arms of his dearest love? wil he fall upon my neck and kiss me? for he was pleased to giue in some secret and silent evidence of his love.

[*June 12, 1653.*] And why do vain thoughts still lodge within me upon thy day, amidst thy worship? ah my God, why is there yet such a prophane spirit let loose to trample my soul under foot, as that I cannot see the evils, be sensible of the plagues of my owne heart when I am waiting to hear thee speak in thy ordinances? when I should receiv good from thee I grow unsensible of my need of grace for my self: hence I mind with greater affection what concerneth others good than my owne. My heart is no sooner beginning to be awakened, affected, broken for my sins, (as it began yesterday) but my goodness (if any there be) is like the morning dew that is dried up. . . .

[*July 4–5, 1653.*] *In the 2 next days I found so much of a spirit of pride and secret joying in some conceived excellence in my self which is too hard for me and I cant prevail over and also so much secret vice and vain thoughts in holy duties and thereby weariness of them and such filthy lust also flowing from my fond affection to my pupils while in their presence on the third day after noon that I confess myself an object of God's loathing as my sins is of my own and pray God make it so more to me*

[*October 24, 1653.*] . . . On the 2d day at night in my sleep I dream'd of the approach of the great and dreadful day of judgment; and was thereby exceedingly

[2]Jonathan Mitchel (d. 1668), pastor and Harvard alumnus.

awakned in spirit (as I thought) to follow god with teares and crys until he gaue me some hopes of his gracious good wil toward me.

[*March 12, 1654.*] . . . The sabbath evening and the next day I was much distressed in conscience, seing a stable dore of Mr Mitchels beat to and fro with the wind, whither, I should out of duty shut it or not; no temptations perplex me so sorely as such like, when I am not clear concerning my duty

my fear is lest my wil should blind reason. this made me seriously and solemly cry to heaven for light to my mind, and grace to obey with chearfulness all gods wil. And still I cry, Lord leav me not to er from thy ways

subdue the enmity of my heart in tender mercy for thy name sake: pitty my poor fainting decaying body. . . .

[*April 25, 1654.* Wigglesworth returns from a voyage to New Haven.] Coming through the wilderness we were overtaken with a great and dreadful tempest of rain and wind. where I beheld the mighty power of god as wel by land as by sea. For all the trees of the Forrest bowed and bended like a bow over our heads as we rid along and divers we heard fall; and about 40 I suppose we see in our way that were newly blown down. I thought how good it was to haue this great god for a mans friend, For loe! how easily he could arm all his creatures against his enemies? And at this time the Lord let in sweet peace and confidence into my heart in the hopes of his favour. For which tast of his sweetness I wil bless his name as Long as I live.

[*August 5, 1654.*] But ah how apt am I to kick with the heel Jesurun[3] like and lightly to esteem the rock of my salvation? how soon haue I forgotten his wonderful works? A mind distracted with a thousand vanitys sabbath dayes and week days when I should be musing of the things of god. But where is my sorrow and bitter mourning for these prophanations of gods ordinances? a thing so grievous to my God. It hath bin some grief to me that I am so unprofitable a servant, that I cannot serv god in my calling aiming at his glory, and doing it as his work. I haue begged this mercy but alas! I cannot attain it, but I lose myself and my love to god amidst my multitude of occasions. My heart is hurried now this way, now that way by divers lusts; one while anxiously sollicitous, another while pleasing my self with this or that creature, this or that project, but ah! where is my walking with god, and rejoycing in the light of his countenance? . . .

[*February 15, 1655.*) . . . To continue in a single estate, Is both uncomfortable many wayes, and dangerous (as I conceiv) to my life, and exposeth to sin, and contrary to engagement of affections, and Friends expectations, and lyable to the harsh sensure of the world that expecteth the quite contrary: To change my condition endangers to bring me into a pining and loathsom diseas,[4] to a wretched life and miserable death, the beginnings whereof I do already feel at sometimes, and dread more than death; and consequently I fear it would be injurious to another besides my self, whom I least desire to injure.

[3]Variant spelling of Jeshurun, the biblical name for Israel. See Deuteronomy 32:15, "But Jeshurun waxed fat, and kicked: thou art waxen fat, thou art grown thick, thou art covered with fatness; then he forsook God which made him, and lightly esteemed the Rock of his salvation."

[4]Wigglesworth believed that he had gonorrhea, though doctors informed him that he did not. Whether he did indeed have this disease is not known, but most scholars assert that it is unlikely.

[*May 18, 1655.*] At the time appointed with fear and trembling I came to Rowley to be marryed.[5] The great arguments unto me were, 1: Physicians counsel:[6] 2ly the institution of marryage by god himself for the preservation of purity and chastity, which with most humble and hearty prayers I have begged and stil wil beg of the Lord. so that I went about the business which god call'd me to attend And consummated it now is by the will of god May 18. 1655./ oh Lord! let my cry come up unto thee for all the blessings of a marryed estate, A heart sutable thereto, chastity especially thereby, and life and health if it be thy will. oh crown thy own ordinance with thy blessing, that it may appear it is not in vain to wait upon thee in the wayes of thy own appointment *I feel the stirrings of my former distemper even after the use of marriage the next day which makes me exceeding afraid. I know not how to keep company with my dearest friend but it is with me as formerly in some days already.* oh pitty the poorest and vilest of thy creatures for the Lords sake, And let not thy servants be a curs each to other but a blessing in this new relation

[*September 15, 1655.*] God will guide and provide.

He hath done so in troubles as great as these and therefore he can do it and will do it

In Memoriall of his former mercys received in answer to prayer and off all his goodnes hitherto I wil erect

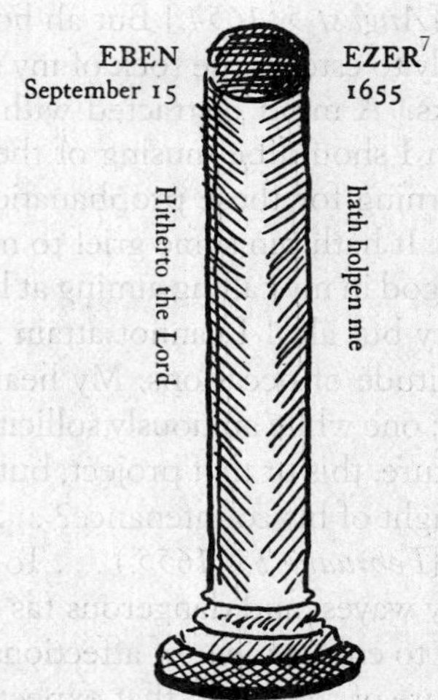

A pillar to the prayse of his grace
O Dulcis memoria
difficultatis praeteritae!

Olim haec (quae nunc incumbunt
mala, haec inquam)
Meminisse juvabit.

Quae mala nunc affligunt, postea in
Laudem dei, nostramque voluptatem cedent

Quis triumphum caneret, quis spoliis onustus
rederet victor, si numquam dimicaret?[8]

[5]Wigglesworth's first marriage, to his cousin Mary Reyner.

[6]Wigglesworth wrote to three prominent men in the colony, two of whom were physicians, for advice on his illness and a potential marriage. After some discussion, all advised him to marry.

[7]1 Samuel 7:12. "Then Samuel took a stone, and set it between Mizpeh and Shen, and called the name of it Eben-ezer, saying, Hitherto hath the Lord helped us."

[8]Oh Sweet memory
of past troubles!

One day we will remember with pleasure
these trials (these trials, I say,
which now tend to an evil outcome)

The ills which now afflict us will later
yield to the praise of God and to our pleasure

Who would sing the triumph, who would
return a victor
charged with spoils, if he never fought?

(Translated from the Latin by Eva Cherniavsky.)

some *night pollution escaped me notwithstanding my earnest prayer to the contrary which brought to mind my old sins now too much forgotten (as near as I remember the thoughts that then I had) together with my later sins unto seeming one that had received so many mercies from the Lord O unthankfulness unthankfulness when shall I get rid of thee.*

[*February 1656.*] February 20 toward night being wednesday my wife began to travail, and had sore paines. The nearnes of my bed to hers made me hear all the nois. her pangs pained my heart, broke my sleep the most off that night, I lay sighing, sweating, praying, almost fainting through wearines before morning. The next day. the spleen much enfeebled me, and setting in with grief took away my strength, my heart was smitten within me, and as sleep departed from myne eyes so my stomack abhorred meat. I was brought very low and knew not how to pass away another night; For so long as my love lay crying I lay sweating, and groaning. I was now apt to be hasty and impatient, but the Lord made me desirous to stoop to his wil (if he should take away her whom he had given, much more) if he should onely prolong her pains (himself supporting) and in time restore her. Being brought to this the Lord gaue some support to my heart. After about midnight he sent me the glad tidings of a daughter[9] that and the mother both living; after she had been in paines about 30 houres or more. oh Let the Lord be magnifyd who heareth the poor chatterings of his prisoners; who wil lay no more than he enableth to bear. . . .

[*January 11, 1657.*] Sabbath. Lord I am not worthy to be owned or pittied by thee, a sink of sin! so frowardly passionate, so earthly and carnal as I have bin this week past. for the Lords sake hide not away thy face this day. oh! when wilt thou come to me? when wilt thou mortify these lusts, when wilt thou giue me a heart to savour the things of god above all other things? oh that it might be this day! I wil beg, I wil wait for the Lord's salvation. . . .

A Song of Emptiness,[1]
To fill up the Empty Pages following.

Vanity of Vanities[2]

Vain, frail, short liv'd, and miserable Man,
Learn what thou art when thine estate is best:
A restless Wave o'th' troubled Ocean,
A Dream, a lifeless Picture finely drest:

[9]Wigglesworth's first child, Mercy, was born on February 22, 1656.

[1]First published in the final pages of *The Day of Doom* in 1662.

[2]A popular poetic theme echoing Ecclesiastes 1:2.

A Wind, a Flower, a Vapour, and a Bubble,
A Wheel that stands not still, a trembling Reed,
A rolling Stone, dry Dust, light Chaff, and Stubble,
A Shadow of Something, but nought indeed.

Learn what deceitful toyes, and empty things,
This World, and all its best Enjoyments bee:
Out of the Earth no true Contentment springs,
But all things here are vexing Vanitee.

For what is *Beauty,* but a fading Flower?
Or what is *Pleasure,* but the Devils bait,
Whereby he catcheth whom he would devour,
And multitudes of Souls doth ruinate?

And what are *Friends* but mortal men, as we?
Whom Death from us may quickly separate;
Or else their hearts may quite estranged be,
And all their love be turned into hate.

And what are *Riches* to be doted on?
Uncertain, fickle, and ensnaring things;
They draw Mens Souls into Perdition,
And when most needed, take them to their wings.

Ah foolish Man! that sets his heart upon
Such empty Shadows, such wild Fowl as these,
That being gotten will be quickly gone,
And whilst they stay increase but his disease

As in a Dropsie, drinking draughts begets,[3]
The more he drinks, the more he still requires:
So on this World whoso affection sets,
His Wealths encrease encreaseth his desires.

O happy Man, whose portion is above,
Where Floods, where Flames, where Foes cannot bereave him;
Most wretched man, that fixed hath his love
Upon this World, that surely will deceive him!

For, what is *Honour?* What is *Sov'raignty,*
Whereto mens hearts so restlesly aspire?
Whom have they Crowned with Felicity?
When did they ever satisfie desire?

[3]The painful accumulation of fluid in the body.
Draughts or drafts: great gulps of liquid.

The Ear of Man with hearing is not fill'd:
To see new sights still coveteth the Eye:
The craving Stomack though it may be still'd,
Yet craves again without a new supply.

All Earthly things, a man's Cravings answer not,
Whose little heart would all the World contain,
(If all the World should fall to one man's Lot)
And notwithstanding empty still remain.

The *Eastern Conquerour*[4] was said to weep,
When he the *Indian* Ocean did view,
To see his Conquest bounded by the Deep,
And no more Worlds remaining to subdue.

Who would that man in his Enjoyments bless,
Or envy him, or covet his estate,
Whose gettings do augment his greediness,
And make his wishes more intemperate?

Such is the wonted and the common guise
Of those on Earth that bear the greatest Sway:
If with a few the case be otherwise
They seek a Kingdom that abides for ay.

Moreover they, of all the Sons of men,
that Rule, and are in highest places set,
Are most inclin'd to scorn their Bretheren
And God himself (without great grace) forget.

For as the Sun doth blind the gazer's eyes,
That for a time they nought discern aright:
So Honour doth befool and blind the Wise,
And their own Lustre 'reaves[5] them of their sight.

Great are their Dangers, manifold their Cares,
Thro which, whilst others Sleep, they scarcely Nap;
And yet are oft surprized unawares,
And fall unweeting[6] into Envies Trap.

The mean Mechanick[7] finds his kindly rest,
All void of fear Sleepeth the County-Clown,

[4]Alexander the Great (356–323 B.C.), king of Macedonia.
[5]Bereaves, dispossesses.
[6]Unknowing.
[7]Poor laborer.

When greatest Princes often are distrest,
And cannot Sleep upon their Beds of Down.

Could *Strength* or *Valour* men Immortalize,
Could *Wealth* or *Honour* keep them from decay,
There were some cause the same to Idolize,
And give the lye to that which I do say.

But neither can such things themselves endure
Without the hazard of a Change one hour,
Nor such as trust in them can they secure
From dismal dayes, or Deaths prevailing pow'r.

If *Beauty* could the beautiful defend
From Death's dominion, than fair *Absalom*[8]
Had not been brought to such a shameful end:
But fair and foul into the Grave must come.

If *Wealth* or *Scepters* could Immortal make,
then wealthy *Croesus,*[9] wherefore are thou dead?
If *Warlike force,* which makes the World to quake,
Then why is *Julius Caesar*[10] perished?

Where are the *Scipio's*[11] Thunder-bolts of War?
Renowned *Pompey,*[12] *Caesars* Enemie?
Stout *Hannibal,*[13] *Romes* Terror known so far?
Great *Alexander,*[14] what's become of thee?

If *Gifts* and *Bribes* Death's favour might but win,
If *Power,* if force, or *Threatnings* might it fray,

[8]2 Samuel 18. After attempting to usurp power from his father, King David, Absalom is slain and thrown into the forest.

[9]Croesus (560–c. 547 B.C.), king of Lydia, attained legendary wealth. He was captured by Cyrus, king of Persia, but was miraculously saved from death on a burning funeral pyre.

[10]Julius Caesar (100–44 B.C.), Roman general, achieved great military success and became dictator of Rome. Conspirators who had been his friends murdered him.

[11]Several members of the Scipio family occupied important military positions in ancient Rome. Cnaeus Cornelius Scipio Calvas (d. 211 B.C.) and Publius Cornelius Scipio (d. c. 211 B.C.) attempted to thwart Hannibal's invasion of Italy. Publius Cornelius Scipio Nasica Serapio (d. c. 132 B.C.) led conspirators who murdered Tiberius Gracchus. Quintas Caecilius Metellus Pius Scipio (d. 46 B.C.), governor of Syria, resisted Julius Caesar's rule and stabbed himself to avoid capture.

[12]Cnaeus Pompeius Magnus (106–48 B.C.), Roman general, fought Julius Caesar in civil war. Pompey was defeated at Pharsalus and assassinated in Egypt.

[13]Hannibal (247–c. 183 B.C.), Carthaginian general and renowned tactician, successfully invaded Italy, almost reached Rome, but was forced to withdraw. He poisoned himself when threatened with Roman capture.

[14]Alexander the Great sought to conquer the entire Persian Empire and beyond. He died of fever, his empire struggling and unfinished.

All these, and more, had still surviving been:
But all are gone, for Death will have no Nay.

Such is this World with all her Pomp and Glory,
Such are the men whom worldly eyes admire:
Cut down by Time, and now become a Story,
That we might after better things aspire.

Go boast thy self of what thy heart enjoyes,
Vain Man! triumph in all thy worldly Bliss:
Thy best enjoyments are but Trash and Toyes:
Delight thy self in that which worthless is.

Omnia praetereunt praeter amare Deum.[15]

The Bay Psalm Book (1640) *The New England Primer (1683?)*

The Bay Psalm Book and *The New England Primer* were, next to the Bible, the most commonly owned books in seventeenth-century New England. Together, they served to disseminate Puritan values for over a hundred years. Designed to be inexpensive and easily portable, they addressed the Puritan concern for having personal faith reconfirmed in daily activity. They established the basic texts of Puritan culture, setting them to familiar hymn tunes and pictured alphabets, thus enabling singing, recitation, and memorization. These books made possible individual participation in the culture, but they also represent the authoritative disciplining of that individuality through culturally sanctioned texts and behavior.

In 1647, the Massachusetts courts warned against that "old deluder, Satan," who strove "to keep men from the knowledge of the Scriptures, . . . by keeping them in an unknown tongue." *The Bay Psalm Book* addressed this warning by translating the Hebrew psalms of David into idiomatic, metrical English to be sung by the entire congregation both in church and at home. *The New England Primer* offered every child ("and apprentice") the chance to learn to read the catechism and a set of moral precepts. Both books insisted on the cultural and religious importance of reading in the vernacular instead of in a language available only to university-trained clergy. The 1647 court hoped that "learning may not be buried in the grave of the fathers in the church and commonwealth."

The Bay Psalm Book was the collaborative project of over twelve leading Puritan divines and the first publishing venture of the Massachusetts colony. The 1700 copies of the first edition provided Puritans with "a plain and familiar translation" designed to represent more "faithfully" the Hebrew psalms than did the version used by the Pilgrims of neighboring Plymouth. As John Cotton wrote in 1643, the translation was "as near the original as we could

[15] Latin: "All things pass by except the love of God."

express it in our English tongue." In his preface, Cotton defended the Puritans' version as attending to "Conscience rather than Elegance, fidelity rather than poetry": "If therefore the verses are not always so smooth and elegant as some may desire or expect; let them consider that God's Altar needs not our polishings." Often printed in England and Scotland as well as in the colonies, the psalter went through over fifty editions in the next century. Revised by Richard Lyon and Henry Dunster (the first president of Harvard) in 1651, and three more times in the 1700s (once by Cotton Mather), *The Bay Psalm Book* was widely used until it was supplanted in the eighteenth century by psalters written by Nahum Tate and Nicholas Brady (1696), by Isaac Watts (1719), and by John and Charles Wesley (1737). Psalm singing continued to be considered an important means by which the general population could learn the cultural text through the eighteenth century and into the nineteenth century. Emerson, describing the singing of the psalms during the 1835 bicentennial celebration of Concord, spoke with a kind of reverence about the psalm singing: "It was a noble ancient strain, & had the more effect from being 'deaconed' out, a line at a time, after the fashion of our grandfathers, & sung by the whole congregation."

The New England Primer, which is estimated to have sold five million copies of its various versions from 1683 to 1830, offered the Puritan child literacy and religious training combined. By means of an illustrated alphabet, moral sentences, poems, and a formal catechism (either the Westminster Assembly's "Shorter Catechism" or John Cotton's "Spiritual Milk for Babes"), the child was to be "both instructed in his Duty, and encouraged in his Learning." The book was the practical outgrowth of the colony's insistence on the importance of widespread literacy as a means for salvation and civic order. A 1642 law required town leaders to inquire into the training of children, "especially their ability to read and understand the principles of Religion and the Capital laws of the country." The *Primer*'s exemplary poem by the martyred John Rogers exhorts children to treasure the "little Book" of their father's words, to "Lay up [God's] Laws within your heart, and print them in your thought." The young readers of the *Primer,* like Rogers's children, were not just the "Heirs of earthly Things"; they were expected to inherit and preserve the cultural and religious values of the community, to be responsible for "that part,/ which never shall decay" as long as each generation learned the words and creeds, the promises and definitions upon which Puritan culture was based.

Both the *Psalm Book* and the *Primer* are evolving texts, whose frequent revisions show their valued yet contested status as cultural transmissions. They are the product neither of a single author nor of one historical period, but embody the changing values of a changing society and show the influence of new events and situations, of variation in language and literary taste. Although both books clearly advance a dominant ideology, insisting on specific religious beliefs and moral precepts, they also show concern for making creeds responsive to the particular historical circumstances of the colonists. The preface to the *Psalm Book* warns against mere imitation of ancient poetry, advocating instead that "every nation without scruple might follow . . . their own country poetry." The *Psalm Book* was revised to satisfy the desire for "a little more Art," in reaction to changing practices of church singing and under the influence of neoclassical and Latin poetry. The introduction to the 1752 revision justified changes because "the Flux of Languages has rendered several Phrases in it obsolete, and the Mode of Expression in various Places less acceptable." The 1758 revision sought to elevate "diminutive Terms" into "more grand and noble Words" (changing, for example, "Hills" to "Mountains," "Floods" to "Seas") and to match diction more closely with mood ("for *grand Ideas,* I seek the *most majestick Words;* for *tender Sentiments,* the *softest Words*").

The *Primer* proved even more chameleon, as it was adapted to different geographical areas (e.g., *The Albany Primer, The Pennsylvania Primer*) and to different ethnic groups (an *Indian Primer* of 1781 was a dual-language text, designed for Mohawk children "to acquire the spelling and reading of their own: As well as to get acquainted with the English Tongue, which for that purpose is put on the opposite page"). Although certain sections of the *Primer* were regularly retained (especially the catechism, the pictured alphabet, and John Rogers's poem), revisions over time show the influence of events (the American Revolution, the evangelical movement of the 1800s) and changes in attitudes (the softening of attitudes toward punishment and sin, the move toward more secularized moral education), as well as changes in children's literature. In later, more secularized versions, naughty children are threatened not with tempests and the consuming fire, but with losing "Oranges, Apples, Cakes, or Nuts," and the grim poem of the martyr is printed in uneasy conjunction with Isaac Watts's soothing "Cradle Song." The value of literacy as a route to eternal salvation becomes, in a 1790 English revision, the promise of economic advancement. An 1800 version even replaces the trademark illustrated alphabet with a milder verse, "A was an apple-pie." Thus the *Psalm Book* and the *Primer,* in their multiple versions, both chronicle and foster historical change. They are central texts of Puritan culture, and they mark the subsequent transformations and uses of that culture.

Jean Ferguson Carr
University of Pittsburgh

PRIMARY WORKS

John Cotton, John Wilson, Peter Bulkely, and others, *The Whole Booke of Psalms Faithfully Translated into English Metre,* known as *The Bay Psalm Book,* 1640; revised 1651, 1718, 1752, 1758; reprint 1862; facsimile reprint 1903, 1956. *The New England Primer* or *Milk for Babes,* 1683?; *The New England Primer Enlarged,* 1687; facsimile reprint of the earliest extant edition (1727) 1897, 1962; Denise D. Knight, ed. *Cotton Mather's Verse in English,* 1989.

from The Bay Psalm Book

from the Preface by John Cotton

The singing of Psalms, though it breathe forth nothing but holy harmony, and melody: yet such is the subtlety of the enemy, and the enmity of our nature against the Lord, and his wayes, that our hearts can find matter of discord in this harmony, and crotchets of division in this holy melody. . . . There have been three questions especially stirring concerning singing. First, what psalms are to be sung in churches? whether David's and other scripture psalms, or the psalms invented by the gifts of godly men in every age of the church. Secondly, if scripture psalms, whether in their own words, or in such meter as English poetry is wont to run in? Thirdly, by whom are they to be sung? whether by the whole churches together with their voices? or by one man singing alone and the rest joining in silence and in the close saying amen.

Touching the first, certainly the singing of David's psalms was an acceptable worship of God, not only in his own, but in succeeding times. . . . So that if the singing David's psalms be a moral duty and therefore perpetual; then we under the New Testament are bound to sing them as well as they under the Old; . . . [y]et we read that they are commanded to sing in the words of David and Asaph,[1] which were ordinarily to be used in the public worship of God: and we doubt not but those that are wise will easily see; that those set forms of psalms of God's own appointment not of man's conceived gift or humane imposition were sung in the Spirit by those holy Levites, as well as their prayers were in the spirit which themselves conceived, the Lord not then binding them therin to any set forms; and shall set forms of psalms appointed of God not be sung in the spirit now, which others did then?. . . .

As for the scruple that some take at the translation of the book of psalms into meter, because David's psalms were sung in his own words without meter, we answer—First, there are many verses together in several psalms of David which run in rhythms . . . which shews at least the lawfulness of singing psalms in English rhythms.

Secondly, the psalms are penned in such verses as are suitable to the poetry of the Hebrew language, and not in the common style of such other books of the Old Testament as are not poetical; now no Protestant doubteth but that all the books of the scripture should by Gods ordinance be extant in the mother tongue of each nation, that they may be understood of all, hence the psalms are to be translated into our English tongue; and if in our English tongue we are to sing them, then as all our English songs (according to the course of our English poetry) do run in metre, so ought David's psalms to be translated into meter, that so we may sing the Lord's songs, as in our English tongue so in such verses as are familiar to an English ear. . . . [B]ut the truth is, as the Lord hath hid from us the Hebrew tunes, lest we should think our selves bound to imitate them, so also the course and frame (for the most part) of their Hebrew poetry, that we might not think our selves bound to imitate that, but that every nation without scruple might follow as the graver sort of tunes of their own country songs, so the graver sort of verses of their own country poetry.

Neither let any think, that for the metre sake we have taken liberty or poetical license to depart from the true and proper sense of David's words in the Hebrew verses, no; but it hath been one part of our religious care and faithful endeavour, to keep close to the original text.

As for other objections taken from the difficulty of *Ainsworth's* tunes,[2] and the corruptions in our common psalm books,[3] we hope they are answered in this new edition of psalms which we here present to God and his Churches. For although we have cause to bless God in many respects for the religious endeavours of the trans-

[1]Asaph, who composed several of the psalms, was the chief of the Levites, whom David appointed "to minister before the ark of the Lord, and to record, and to thank and praise the Lord God of Israel" (I Chronicles 16:4).

[2]Henry Ainsworth, minister of the English Church in Amsterdam, translated the psalms in 1612 and included "singing notes" in his book. His version of the psalms was used by the Plymouth Pilgrims.

[3]The Puritans objected to the influential Sternhold-Hopkins translation of 1562, which was attached to the Book of Common Prayer.

lators of the psalms into metre usually annexed to our Bibles, yet it is not unknown to the godly learned that they have rather presented a paraphrase than the words of David translated according to the rule 2 *Chron.* 29, 30,[4] and that their addition to the words, detractions from the words are not seldom and rare, but very frequent and many times needless (which we suppose would not be approved of if the psalms were so translated into prose) and that their variations of the sense, and alterations of the sacred text too frequently, may justly minister matter of offence to them that are able to compare the translation with the text; of which failings, some judicious have oft complained, others have been grieved, whereupon it hath been generally desired, that as we do enjoy other, so (if it were the Lords will) we might enjoy this ordinance also in its native purity: we have therefore done our endeavour to make a plain and familiar translation of the psalms and words of David into English metre, and have not so much as presumed to paraphrase to give the sense of his meaning in other words; we have therefore attended herein as our chief guide the original, shunning all additions, except such as even the best translators of them in prose supply, avoiding all material detractions from words or sense. . . .

As for our translations, we have with our English Bibles[5] (to which next to the Original we have had respect) used the Idioms of our own tongue in stead of Hebraisms, lest they might seem English barbarisms. . . .

If therefore the verses are not always so smoothe and elegant as some may desire or expect, let them consider that God's Altar needs not our polishings: Ex. 20.[6] for we have respected rather a plain translation, than to smooth our verses with the sweetnes of any paraphrase, and so have attended Conscience rather than Elegance, fidelity rather than poetry, in translating the Hebrew words into English language, and David's poetry into English metre; that so we may sing in Sion the Lord's songs of praise according to his own will; until he take us from hence, and wipe away all our tears, and bid us enter into our master's joy to sing eternal Hallelujahs.

1640

Psalm 1

O Blessed man, that in th'advice
 Of wicked doeth not walk:
Nor stand in sinners way, nor sit
 In chair of scornful folk.

[4]"Moreover Hezekiah the king and the princes commanded the Levites to sing praise unto the Lord with the words of David, and of Asaph the seer" (II Chronicles 29:30).

[5]The Puritans used primarily the Geneva Bible (1560), although they made occasional reference to the King James version (1611).

[6]"An altar of earth thou shalt make unto me. . . . And if thou wilt make me an altar of stone, thou shalt not build it of hewn stone: for if thou lift up thy tool upon it, thou hast polluted it" (Exodus 20:24–25).

But in the law of Jehovah
  Is his longing delight:
And in his law doth meditate,
  By day and eke by night.

And he shall be like to a tree
  Planted by water-rivers:
That in his season yields his fruit,
  And his leaf never withers.

And all he doth, shall prosper well,
  The wicked are not so:
But they are like unto the chaff,
  Which wind drives to and fro.

Therefore shall not ungodly men,
  Rise to stand in the doom,
Nor shall the sinners with the just,
  In their assembly come.

For of the righteous men, the Lord
  Acknowledgeth the way:
But the way of ungodly men,
  Shall utterly decay.

1640

Psalm 6

To the chief musician on Neginoth upon Sheminith, a Psalm of David

Lord in thy wrath rebuke me not,
  nor in thy hot wrath chasten me.
Pity me Lord, for I am weak,
  Lord heal me, for my bones vexed be.
Also my soul is troubled sore:
  how long Lord wilt thou me forsake?
Return O Lord, my soul release:
  O save me for thy mercy's sake.
In death no mem'ry is of thee,
  and who shall praise thee in the grave?
I faint with groans; all night my bed
  swims; I with tears my couch washed have.
Mine eye with grief is dim and old:
  because of all mine enemies.

But now depart away from me,
all ye that work iniquities:
For Jehovah ev'n now hath heard
the voice of these my weeping tears.
Jehovah hear my humble suit,
Jehovah doth receive my prayers,
Let all mine enemies be asham'd
and greatly troubled let them be;
Yea let them be returned back,
and be ashamed suddenly.

1640

Psalm 8

To the chief Musician upon Gittith, a Psalm of David

O Lord our God in all the earth
How's thy name wondrous great—
Who hast thy glorious majesty
Above the heavens set.

Out of the mouth of sucking babes,
Thy strength thou didst ordain,
That thou mightst still the enemy,
And them that thee disdain.

When I thy fingers' work, thy Heav'ns,
The moon and stars consider
Which thou hast set: What's wretched man
That thou dost him remember?

Or what's the Son of man, that thus
Him visited thou hast?
For next to Angels, thou hast him
A little lower plac't,

And hast with glory crowned him,
And comely majesty:
And on thy works hast given him
Lordly authority.

All hast thou put under his feet,
All sheep and oxen, yea

And beasts of field. Fowls of the air,
  And fishes of the sea,

And all that pass through paths of seas.
  O Jehovah our Lord,
How wondrously magnificent
  Is thy name through the world?

1640

Psalm 19

To the chief musician, a Psalm of David

The heavens do declare
  The majesty of God:
Also the firmament shows forth
  His handiwork abroad.

Day speaks to day, knowledge
  Night hath to night declar'd.
There neither speech nor language is,
  Where their voice is not heard.

Through all the earth their line
  Is gone forth, and unto
The utmost end of all the world,
  Their speeches reach also:

A Tabernacle he
  In them pitched for the Sun,
Who Bridegroom-like from 's chamber goes,
  Glad Giant's-race to run.

The Lord's law perfect is,
  The soul converting back:
God's testimony faithful is,
  Makes wise who wisdom lack.

The statutes of the Lord
  Are right, and glad the heart:
The Lord's commandment is pure,
  Light doth to eyes impart.

Jehovah's fear is clean,
  And doth endure forever:

The judgments of the Lord are true,
And righteous altogether.

Than gold, than much fine gold.
More to be prized are,
Than honey, and the honeycomb,
Sweeter they are by far.

Also thy servant is
Admonished from hence:
And in the keeping of the same
Is a full recompense.

Who can his errors know?
From secret faults cleanse me.
And from presumptuous sins, let thou
kept back thy servant be:

Let them not bear the rule
In me, and then shall I
Be perfect, and shall cleansed be
From much iniquity.

Let the words of my mouth,
And the thoughts of my heart,
Be pleasing with thee, Lord, my Rock,
Who my redeemer art.

1640

Psalm 23

A Psalm of David

The Lord to me a shepherd is,
Want therefore shall not I.
He in the folds of tender grass
Doth cause me down to lie:

To waters calm me gently leads,
Restore my soul doth he,
He doth in paths of righteousness
For his name's sake lead me.

Yea though in valley of death's shade
I walk, none ill I'll fear:

Because thou art with me, thy rod
  And staff my comfort are.

For me a table thou hast spread,
  In presence of my foes:
Thou dost anoint my head with oil,
  My cup it overflows.

Goodness and mercy surely shall
  All my days follow me:
And in the Lord's house I shall dwell
  So long as days shall be.

1640

PSALM 23

A Psalm of David.

The LORD is my shepherd: I shall not want.
2 He maketh me to lie down in green pastures: he leadeth me beside the
still waters.
3 He restoreth my soul: he leadeth me in the paths of righteousness for
his name's sake.
4 Yea, though I walk through the valley of the shadow of death, I will
fear no evil: for thou art with me; thy rod and thy staff they comfort me.
5 Thou preparest a table before me in the presence of mine enemies:
thou anointest my head with oil: my cup runneth over.
6 Surely goodness and mercy shall follow me all the days of my life: and
I will dwell in the house of the LORD for ever.

The Bible, Authorized King James Version

1611

Psalm 137

The rivers on of Babylon
there when we did sit down:
Yea even then we mourned, when
we remembered Sion.
Our harps we did hang it amid,
upon the willow tree.
Because there they that us away
led in captivity,
Requir'd of us a song, and thus
asked mirth, us waste who laid,
Sing us among a Sion's song,
unto us then they said.
The Lord's song sing can we? being
in stranger's land. Then let
Loose her skill my right hand, if I
Jerusalem forget.
Let cleave my tongue my palate on,
if mind thee do not I:
If chief joys o'er I prize not more
Jerusalem my joy.
Remember Lord, Edom's sons' word,
unto the ground said they,
It raze, it raze, when as it was
Jerusalem her day.
Blesst shall he be, that payeth thee,
daughter of Babylon,
Who must be waste: that which thou hast
rewarded us upon.
O happy he shall surely be
that taketh up, that eke
Thy little ones against the stones
doth into pieces break.

1640

from The New England Primer[1]

Alphabet

A In *Adam's* Fall
We Sinned all.

B Thy Life to Mend
This *Book* Attend.

C The *Cat* doth play
And after slay.

D A *Dog* will bite
A Thief at night.

E An *Eagle's* flight
Is out of sight.

F The Idle *Fool*
Is whipt at School.

G As runs the *Glass*
Man's life doth pass.

H My *Book* and *Heart*
Shall never part.

J *Job* feels the Rod
Yet blesses GOD.

K Our KING the
good
No man of blood.

L The *Lion* bold
The *Lamb* doth hold.

M The *Moon* gives light
In time of night.

N *Nightengales* sing
In Time of Spring.

O The Royal Oak
it was the Tree
That sav'd His
Royal Majestie.

P *Peter* denies
His Lord and cries

Q *Queen Esther* comes
in Royal State
To Save the JEWS
from dismal Fate

R *Rachel* doth mourn
For her first born.

S *Samuel* anoints
Whom God appoints.

T *Time* cuts down all
Both great and small.

U Uriah's beauteous Wife
Made David seek his
Life.

W *Whales* in the Sea
God's Voice obey.

X *Xerxes* the great did
die,
And so must you & I.

Y *Youth* forward slips
Death soonest nips.

Z *Zacheus* he
Did climb the Tree
His Lord to see,

[1]The pictured alphabet and "The Death of John Rogers" probably appeared in the earliest versions of the *Primer.* Later versions revised these items and added new material. Items are dated by their first inclusion in the *Primer.*

Now the Child being entred in his Letters and Spelling, let him learn these and such like Sentences by Heart, whereby he will be both instructed in his Duty, and encouraged in his Learning.

1683?

The Dutiful Child's Promises

I Will fear GOD, and honour the KING.
I will honour my Father & Mother.
I will Obey my Superiours.
I will Submit to my Elders,
I will Love my Friends.
I will hate no Man.
I will forgive my Enemies, and pray to God for them.
I will as much as in me lies keep all God's Holy Commandments.
I will learn my Catechism.
I will keep the Lord's Day Holy.
I will Reverence God's Sanctuary,
For our GOD is a consuming Fire.

1727

Verses

I in the Burying Place may see
Graves shorter there than I;
From Death's Arrest no Age is free,
Young Children too may die;
My God, may such an awful Sight,
Awakening be to me!
Oh! that by early Grace I might
For Death prepared be.

[1727][2]

* * *

[2]This poem, originally titled "The Child Seeing the Funeral of Another Child," was Part VI of Cotton Mather's "Instructions for Children," first printed in his *The A.B.C. of Religion* (Boston, 1713). In Mather's version, the Graves are "not so long as I." The poem appeared in the 1727 edition on pages that no longer exist. The text used here appeared in later editions of the *Primer.*

Good Children must,

Fear God all Day,	Love Christ alway,
Parents obey,	In Secret Pray,
No false thing say,	Mind little Play,
By no Sin stray,	Make no delay,

In doing Good.

1727

* * *

Awake, arise, behold thou hast
Thy Life a Leaf, thy Breath a Blast;
At Night lye down prepar'd to have
Thy sleep, thy death, thy bed, thy grave.

1727

The Death of John Rogers[3]

Mr. *John Rogers,* Minister of the Gospel in *London,* was the first Martyr in Q *Mary's* Reign, and was burnt at *Smithfield, February* the fourteenth, 1554 His Wife, with nine small Children, and one at her Breast, following him to the Stake, with which sorrowful sight he was not in the least daunted, but with wonderful Patience died couragiously for the Gospel of Jesus Christ.

Some few Days before his Death, he writ the following Exhortation to his Children.

Give ear my Children to my words,
  whom God hath dearly bought,
Lay up his Laws within your heart,
  and print them in your thought,
I leave you here a little Book,
  for you to look upon;
That you may see your Fathers face,
  when he is dead and gone.
Who for the hope of heavenly things,

[3]This popular English poem was first printed in 1559. It appears in the various versions of the *Primer* with illustrations of Rogers's family watching the scene of his martyrdom.

while he did here remain,
Gave over all his golden Years
to Prison and to Pain.
Where I among my Iron Bands,
inclosed in the dark,
Not many days before my Death
I did compose this Work.
And for Example to your Youth,
to whom I wish all good;
I send you here God's perfect Truth,
and seel it with my Blood
To you my Heirs of earthly Things,
which I do leave behind,
That you may read and understand,
and keep it in your mind.
That as you have been Heirs of thet
which once shall wear away,
you also may possess that part,
which never shall decay.

. . .

1683?

Mary White Rowlandson [Talcott] 1637?–1711

Mary White Rowlandson's narrative of her three-month captivity by Algonkian Indians during King Philip's War (1675–1678) was one of the first bestsellers in American literature. Four editions of the *The Soveraignty and Goodness of GOD, Together With the Faithfulness of His Promises Displayed; Being a Narrative of the Captivity and Restauration of Mrs. Mary Rowlandson* appeared in 1682, and it remained a popular success into the early nineteenth century. In moments of national crisis such as the American Revolution, new editions of Rowlandson's text figured prominently in the discourse of national rights and of God's challenges to the nation. More than thirty editions have been published to date, and the *Narrative* is acknowledged as a major contribution to an early American genre, the captivity narrative, which extends back to the period of European exploration. (See, for instance, the Hopi account, "The Coming of the Spanish.") The genre was explored by many other early writers, including John Gyles and Elizabeth Meader Hanson, who experienced real-life captivities. Early novels (most notably, Catharine Maria Sedgwick's *Hope Leslie* and James Fenimore Cooper's *The Last of the Mohicans*) again expanded the genre when their authors crafted fictionalized versions of captivity narratives.

Thus, one woman's trauma-ridden experience of captivity became an icon of a national ideology.

Mary White was born in Somerset, England, probably in 1637. With her parents, Joan and John White, she and her nine siblings emigrated to New England, settling first in Salem, Massachusetts, and finally in the frontier town of Lancaster, Massachusetts. Around 1656 she married the Reverend Joseph Rowlandson of Lancaster. Their first child, Mary, died just after her third birthday; three other children were born to the Rowlandsons.

When the events that led to King Philip's War began to emerge in New England, a forty-year period of relative tranquillity between the colonists and the indigenous people of the region was destroyed, and Rowlandson's comfortable life in Lancaster was shattered. Inter-colonial and inter-tribal differences—between the governments of Plymouth, Massachusetts Bay, and Rhode Island on the one hand, and between Algonkian tribes such as the Wampanoags, Narragansetts, and the Mohegans on the other—created an atmosphere of strained relations that abetted the outbreak of war. The major impetus for King Philip's War, however, was the continuing encroachment by Euro-American settlers onto lands occupied by the Algonkians.

In 1664, the leaders of Plymouth Colony seized Wamsutta, a Wampanoag chief, hoping to convince Wamsutta to relinquish an early pact with England that granted his people full rights to their land, so Plymouth Colony could purchase the land. While in captivity, Wamsutta died, and Metacom became chief and agreed to the colonists' demands. Yet the colonists continued their unprecedented encroachment. Ironically, in 1671 the leadership of Plymouth Colony demanded that Metacom (or "Philip," as the white settlers referred to him) appear before them to answer charges of aggression. Then, in 1674 events escalated into a series of retributive acts, the facts of which are blurred by charges and counter-charges. A "praying Indian," John Sassamon, was murdered; the colonists assumed Metacom's people were responsible, and they executed three Wampanoags in retaliation. On June 20, 1675, Metacom counter-retaliated by leading an attack on the village of Swansea, Massachusetts. At this point, the colonies of Massachusetts Bay and Rhode Island joined with Plymouth and sent combined troops in pursuit of Metacom. War was officially declared on September 9, 1675. King Philip's War lasted for almost three years; it devastated the New England region and decimated the Algonkians.

The war completely altered Mary Rowlandson's life as well. On February 10, 1676, a group of Narragansett Indians attacked the village of Lancaster. Joseph Rowlandson was in Boston attempting to raise aid for the defense of Lancaster. Mary Rowlandson and their three children—Joseph (age 14), Mary (age 10), and Sarah (age 6)—were taken captive, and many of her relatives and neighbors were killed or also taken captive. The events of Rowlandson's captivity are related in her autobiographical narrative, as she closely details the twenty "removes" that she and her captors underwent. Sarah died within a week of the attack. Rowlandson was ransomed on May 2, 1676, but it was several weeks later before she and her husband were able to effect the release of their two remaining children.

For a year after their reunion, the Rowlandsons remained in Boston; in 1677 they sought to re-establish their lives when Joseph Rowlandson accepted a position in Wethersfield, Connecticut, and the family resettled in that community. He died less than two years later, however. Following seventeenth-century expectations, Mary remarried on August 6, 1679. Her second husband was Captain Samuel Talcott, a Harvard-educated farmer and community leader. As a member of the War Council during the years of King Philip's War, Talcott undoubtedly empathized with the trauma Rowlandson had endured. Mary Rowlandson Talcott lived for a decade after her second husband's death in 1691, but she did not marry again. At the age of seventy-three, she died in Wethersfield on January 5, 1711.

Although thirty years eclipsed the 1682 publication of Rowlandson's narrative and her death, the *Narrative* remains her only known comment on her months of captivity. The narrative was written in the years between her ransom and Joseph's death; she asserted that her purpose in writing about her experiences was simply for the edification of her children and friends.

In the Puritan culture, which repressed women's public speaking and writing, the decision to publish her account was almost as exceptional as the experience itself. Several reasons may be considered for the encouragement of the publication of this text. Attesting to her experiences as God's means of testing her faith, Rowlandson's text appeared at a time when Congregationalist church membership had declined in New England. The decision to publish her narrative, therefore, had the support of the leading Congregationalist clergymen, including Increase Mather, who is assumed to be the author of a preface that accompanied the first editions. In a broader sense, the text also supported the colonists' negative representations of Native Americans as "savages" who inhabited Satan's domain. Through such depictions, the dominant culture could thus argue that the removal of the Algonkians and other native peoples was in the "national" interest.

The *Narrative* is also a powerful account of one woman's endurance in captivity and of the psychological means and behavioral adaptations she used to survive. Although her account reflected her religious beliefs and prejudices, she also honestly expressed her opinions about the personal, psychological consequences of her experiences.

Sharon M. Harris
Texas Christian University

PRIMARY WORK

"The Soveraignty and the Goodness of GOD, Together With the Faithfulness of His Promises Displayed; Being a Narrative of the Captivity and Restauration of Mrs. Mary Rowlandson . . . ," 1682.

from A Narrative of the Captivity and Restauration of Mrs. Mary Rowlandson

Preface to the Reader

It was on Tuesday, Feb. 1, 1675, in the afternoon, when the *Narrhagansets'*[1] Quarters (in or toward the *Nipmug* Country, whither they were now retired for fear of the *English* Army, lying in their own Country) were the second time beaten up by the Forces of the United Colonies,[2] who thereupon soon betook themselves to flight, and were all the next day pursued by the *English,* some overtaken and destroyed. But on Thursday, Feb. 3, the *English,* having now been six days' on their March from their Headquarters in Wickford, in the Narrhaganset Country, toward and after the enemy, and Provision grown exceeding short; insomuch that they were fain to kill some Horses for the supply, especially of their *Indian* Friends, they were necessitated to consider what was best to be done; and about noon (having hitherto followed the Chase as hard as they might) a Council was called, and though some few were of another mind, yet it was concluded, by far the greater part of the Council of War, that the Army should desist the pursuit, and retire; the forces of Plimouth and the Bay to the next town of the Bay, and Connecticut forces to their own next towns, which determination was immediately put in execution: The consequent whereof, as it was not difficult to be foreseen by those that knew the causeless enmity of these *Barbarians* against the *English,* and the malicious and revengeful spirit of these Heathen; so it soon proved dismal.

The *Narrhagansets* were now driven quite from their own Country, and all their Provisions there hoarded up, to which they durst not at present return, and being so numerous as they were, soon devoured those to whom they went, whereby both the one and the other were now reduced to extreme straits, and so necessitated to take the first and best opportunity for supply, and very glad no doubt of such an opportunity as this, to provide for themselves, and make spoile of the *English* at once; and seeing themselves thus discharged of their pursuers, and a little refreshed after their flight, the very next week, on Thursday, Feb. 10, they fell with a mighty force and fury upon Lancaster.[3] which small Town, remote from aid of others, and not being Garrison'd as it might, the Army being now come in, and as the time indeed required (the design of the *Indians* against that place being known to the English some time before) was not able to make effectual resistance; but notwithstanding the utmost endeavour of the Inhabitants, most of the buildings were turned into ashes, many People (Men, Women, and Children) slain, and others captivated. The most solemn and remarkable part of this Tragedy may that justly be reputed which fell upon the Family of that Reverend Servant of God, Mr Joseph Rowlandson, the faithful Pastor of the Church of Christ in that place, who, being gone down to the Council of the Massachusets, to seek aid for the defence of the place, at his return found the Town in

[1]Native American tribe traditionally located in Rhode Island.

[2]Massachusetts, Connecticut, and Plymouth colonies.

[3]Lancaster, Massachusetts. A frontier village thirty miles west of Boston, one of many attacked during King Philip's War.

flames or smoke, his own house being set on fire by the Enemy, through the disadvantage of a defective Fortification, and all in it consumed; his precious yoke-fellow, and dear Children, wounded and captivated (as the issue evidenced, and the following Narrative declares) by these cruel and barbarous Salvages. A sad Catastrophe! Thus all things come alike to all: None knows either love or hatred by all that is before him. 'Tis no new thing for God's precious ones to drink as deep as others, of the Cup of common Calamity: take just *Lot* (yet captivated) for instance, beside others. But it is not my business to dilate on these things, but only in few words introductively to preface to the following script, which is a Narrative of the wonderfully awful, wise, holy, powerful, and gracious providence of God, toward that worthy and precious Gentlewoman, the dear Consort of the said Reverend Mr Rowlandson, and her Children with her, as in casting of her into such a waterless pit, so in preserving, supporting, and carrying through so many such extream hazards, unspeakable difficulties and disconsolateness, and at last delivering her out of them all, and her surviving Children also. It was a strange and amazing dispensation that the Lord should so afflict his precious Servant, and Hand-maid: It was as strange, if not more, that he should so bear up the spirits of his Servant under such bereavements, and of his Hand-maid under such Captivity, travels, and hardships (much too hard for flesh and blood) as he did, and at length deliver and restore. But he was their Saviour, who hath said, *When thou passes through the Waters, I will be with thee, and through the Rivers, they shall not overflow thee: when thou walkest through the Fire, thou shalt not be burnt, nor shall the flame kindle upon thee,* Isai. xliii ver. 3; and again, *He woundeth, and his hands make whole; he shall deliver thee in six troubles, yea, in seven there shall no evil touch thee: In Famine he shall redeem thee from death; and in War from the power of the sword,* Job v. 18, 19, 20. Methinks this dispensation doth bear some resemblance to those of *Joseph, David,* and *Daniel,*[4] yea, and of the three children[5] too, the stories whereof do represent us with the excellent textures of divine providence, curious pieces of divine work: And truly so doth this, and therefore not to be forgotten, but worthy to be exhibited to, and viewed and pondered by all, that disdain not to consider the operation of his hands.

The works of the Lord (not only of Creation, but of Providence also, especially those that do more peculiarly concern his dear ones, that are as the apple of his eye, as the signet upon his hand, the delight of his eyes, and the object of his tenderest care) are great, sought out of all those that have pleasure therein; and of these, verily, this is none of the least.

This Narrative was Penned by this Gentlewoman her self, to be to her a *Memorandum* of God's dealing with her, that she might never forget, but remember the same, and the several circumstances thereof, all the daies of her life. A pious scope, which deserves both commendation and imitation. Some Friends having obtained a sight of it, could not be so much affected with the many passages of working providence discovered therein, as to judge it worthy of publick view, and altogether unmeet that such works of God should be hid from present and future Generations; and therefore though this Gentlewoman's modesty would not thrust it into the Press,

[4]God saves Joseph from prison (Genesis 39), David from Goliath (1 Samuel 17), and Daniel from the den of lions (Daniel 6).

[5]Shadrach, Meshach, and Abed-nego are cast into fire, but God protects them from harm (Daniel 3).

yet her gratitude unto God, made her not hardly perswadable to let it pass, that God might have his due glory, and others benefit by it as well as her selfe.

I hope by this time none will cast any reflection upon this Gentlewoman, on the score of this publication of her Affliction and Deliverance. If any should, doubtless they may be reckoned with the nine Lepers, of whom it is said, *Were there not ten cleansed? where are the nine?*[6] but one returning to give God thanks. Let such further know, that this was a dispensation of publick note and of Universal concernment; and so much the more, by how much the nearer this Gentlewoman stood related to that faithful Servant of God, whose capacity and employment was publick, in the House of God, and his Name on that account of a very sweet savour in the Churches of Christ. Who is there of a true Christian spirit, that did not look upon himself much concerned in this bereavement, this Captivity in the time thereof, and in this deliverance when it came, yea, more than in many others? And how many are there to whom, so concerned, it will doubtless be a very acceptable thing, to see the way of God with this Gentlewoman in the aforesaid dispensation, thus laid out and pourtrayed before their eyes.

To conclude, Whatever any coy phantasies may deem, yet it highly concerns those that have so deeply tasted how good the Lord is, to enquire with *David, What shall I render to the Lord for all his benefits to me?* Psal. cxvi. 12. He thinks nothing too great: yea, being sensible of his own disproportion to the due praises of God, he calls in help: *O magnifie the Lord with me, let us exalt his Name together, Psal.* xxxiv. 3. And it is but reason that our praises should hold proportion with our prayers; and that as many have helped together by prayer for the obtaining of this mercy, so praises should be returned by many on this behalf; and forasmuch as not the general but particular knowledge of things makes deepest impression upon the affections, this Narrative particularizing the several passages of this providence, will not a little conduce thereunto: and therefore holy David, in order to the attainment of that end, accounts himself concerned to declare what God had done for his Soul, *Psal.* lxvi. 16. *Come and hear, all ye that fear God, and I will declare what God hath done for my Soul,* i.e. *for his Life.* See ver. 9, 10. *He holdeth our soul in life, and suffers not our feet to be moved; for thou our God hast proved us: thou hast tried us, as silver is tried.* Life-mercies are heart-affecting mercies; of great impression and force, to enlarge pious hearts in the praises of God, so that such know not how but to talk of God's acts, and to speak of and publish his wonderful works. Deep troubles, when the waters come in unto the Soul, are wont to produce vows: Vows must be paid: *It is better not vow, than to vow and not pay.*[7] I may say, that as none knows what it is to fight and pursue such an enemy as this, but they that have fought and pursued them: so none can imagine, what it is to be captivated, and enslaved to such Atheistical, proud, wild, cruel, barbarous, brutish, (in one word,) diabolical Creatures as these, the worst of the heathen; nor what difficulties, hardships, hazards, sorrows, anxieties, and perplexities, do unavoidably wait upon such a condition, but those that have tried it. No serious spirit then (especially knowing any thing of this Gentlewoman's Piety) can imagine but that the vows of God are upon her. Excuse her then if she come thus into the publick, to pay those Vows. Come and hear what she hath to say.

[6]Luke 17:17.
[7]Ecclesiastes 5:5.

I am confident that no Friend of divine Providence, will ever repent his time and pains spent in reading over these sheets, but will judge them worth perusing again and again.

Here *Reader,* you may see an instance of the Sovereignty of God, who doth what he will with his own as well as others; and who may say to him, *what dost thou?*[8] here you may see an instance of the Faith and Patience of the Saints, under the most heart-sinking Tryals; here you may see, the Promises are breasts full of Consolation, when all the World besides is empty, and gives nothing but sorrow. That God is indeed the supream Lord of the World: ruling the most unruly, weakening the most cruel and salvage: granting his People mercy in the sight of the most unmerciful: curbing the lusts of the most filthy, holding the hands of the violent, delivering the prey from the mighty, and gathering together the out-casts of Israel. Once and again, you have heard, but here you may see, that power belongeth unto God: that our God is the God of Salvation: and to him belong the issues from Death. That our God is in the Heavens, and doth whatever pleases him. Here you have *Samson's* riddle exemplified, and that great promise, *Rom.* viii. 28, verified: *Out of the Eater comes forth meat, and sweetness out of the strong;*[9] The worst of evils working together for the best good. How evident is it that the Lord hath made this Gentlewoman a gainer by all this Affliction, that she can say, 'tis good for her, yea better that she hath been, than she should not have been, thus afflicted.

Oh how doth God shine forth in such things as these!

Reader, if thou gettest no good by such a Declaration as this, the fault must needs be thine own. Read, therefore, peruse, ponder, and from hence lay up something from the experience of another, against thine own turn comes: that so thou also through patience and consolation of the Scripture mayest have hope.

PER AMICUM[10]

On the tenth of February 1675, Came the Indians with great numbers upon Lancaster; Their first coming was about Sun-rising; hearing the noise of some Guns, we looked out; several Houses were burning, and the Smoke ascending to Heaven. There were five persons taken in one house, the Father, and the Mother and a sucking Child, they knockt on the head; the other two they took and carried away alive. There were two others, who being out of their Garison[1] upon some occasion were set upon; one was knockt on the head, the other escaped: Another their was who running along was shot and wounded, and fell down; he begged of them his life, promising them Money (as they told me) but they would not hearken to him but knockt him in head, and stript him naked, and split open his Bowels. Another seeing many of the Indians about his Barn, ventured and went out, but was quickly shot down. There were three others belonging to the same Garison who were killed; the Indians getting

[8]Job 9:12.

[9]Judges 14:14.

[10]Latin: "By a Friend." This anonymous preface is often attributed to Increase Mather, Puritan minister, political leader, and president of Harvard College.

[1]One of six fortified houses in Lancaster. Only the Rowlandson house fell to the Indians upon attack.

up upon the roof of the Barn, had advantage to shoot down upon them over their Fortification. Thus these murtherous wretches went on, burning, and destroying before them.

At length they came and beset our own house, and quickly it was the dolefullest day that ever mine eyes saw. The House stood upon the edg of a hill; some of the Indians got behind the hill, others into the Barn, and others behind any thing that could shelter them; from all which places they shot against the House, so that the Bullets seemed to fly like hail; and quickly they wounded one man among us, then another, and then a third, About two hours (according to my observation, in that amazing time) they had been about the house before they prevailed to fire it (which they did with Flax and Hemp, which they brought out of the Barn, and there being no defence about the House, only two Flankers[2] at two opposite corners and one of them not finished) they fired it once and one ventured out and quenched it, but they quickly fired it again, and that took. Now is the dreadfull hour come, that I have often heard of (in time of War, as it was the case of others) but now mine eyes see it. Some in our house were fighting for their lives, others wallowing in their blood, the House on fire over our heads, and the bloody Heathen ready to knock us on the head, if we stirred out. Now might we hear Mothers and Children crying out for themselves, and one another, Lord, What shall we do? Then I took my Children[3] (and one of my sisters, hers) to go forth and leave the house: but as soon as we came to the dore and appeared, the Indians shot so thick that the bullets rattled against the House, as if one had taken an handfull of stones and threw them, so that we were fain to give back. We had six stout Dogs belonging to our Garrison, but none of them would stir, though another time, if any Indian had come to the door, they were ready to fly upon him and tear him down. The Lord hereby would make us the more acknowledge his hand, and to see that our help is always in him. But out we must go, the fire increasing, and coming along behind us, roaring, and the Indians gaping before us with their Guns, Spears and Hatchets to devour us. No sooner were we out of the House, but my Brother in Law[4] (being before wounded, in defending the house, in or near the throat) fell down dead, wherat the Indians scornfully shouted, and hallowed, and were presently upon him, stripping off his cloaths, the bulletts flying thick, one went through my side, and the same (as would seem) through the bowels and hand of dear Child in my arms.[5] One of my elder Sisters Children, named William, had then his Leg broken, which the Indians perceiving, they knockt him on head. Thus were we butchered by those merciless Heathen, standing amazed, with the blood running down to our heels. My eldest Sister being yet in the House, and seeing those wofull sights, the Infidels haling Mothers one way, and Children another, and some wallowing in their blood: and her elder Son telling her that her Son William was dead, and my self was wounded, she said, And, Lord, let me dy with them; which was no sooner said, but she was struck with a Bullet, and fell down dead over the threshold. I hope she is reaping the fruit of her good labours, being faithfull to the service of God in her place. In her younger years she lay under much trouble

[2]Projections or bastions of fortified houses from which defenders could position themselves against their attackers.

[3]Joseph, Mary, and Sarah Rowlandson.

[4]John Divoll, husband of Rowlandson's younger sister, Hannah.

[5]Rowlandson's younger daughter, Sarah.

upon spiritual accounts, till it pleased God to make that precious Scripture take hold of her heart, 2 Cor. 12. 9. *And he said unto me, my Grace is sufficient for thee.* More then twenty years after I have heard her tell how sweet and comfortable that place was to her. But to return: The Indians laid hold of us, pulling me one way, and the Children another, and said, Come go along with us; I told them they would kill me: they answered, If I were willing to go along with them, they would not hurt me.

Oh the dolefull sight that now was to behold at this House! *Come, behold the works of the Lord, what dissolations he had made in the Earth.* Of thirty seven persons who were in this one House, none escaped either present death, or a bitter captivity, save only one,[6] who might say as he, Job 1. 15, *And I only am escaped alone to tell the News.* There were twelve killed, some shot, some stab'd with their Spears, some knock'd down with their Hatchets. When we are in prosperity, Oh the little that we think of such dreadfull sights, and to see our dear Friends, and Relations ly bleeding out their heart-blood upon the ground. There was one who was chopt into the head with a Hatchet, and stript naked, and yet was crawling up and down. It is a solemn sight to see so many Christians lying in their blood, some here, and some there, like a company of Sheep torn by Wolves, All of them stript naked by a company of hell-hounds, roaring, singing, ranting and insulting, as if they would have torn our very hearts out; yet the Lord by his Almighty power preserved a number of us from death, for there were twenty-four of us taken alive and carried Captive.

I had often before this said, that if the Indians should come, I should chuse rather to be killed by them then taken alive but when it came to the tryal my mind changed; their glittering weapons so daunted my spirit, that I chose rather to go along with those (as I may say) ravenous Beasts, then that moment to end my dayes; and that I may the better declare what happened to me during that grievous Captivity, I shall particularly speak of the severall Removes we had up and down the Wilderness.

The First Remove[7]

Now away we must go with those Barbarous Creatures, with our bodies wounded and bleeding, and our hearts no less than our bodies. About a mile we went that night, up upon a hill within sight of the Town, where they intended to lodge. There was hard by a vacant house (deserted by the English before, for fear of the Indians). I asked them whither I might not lodge in the house that night to which they answered, what will you love English men still? this was the dolefullest night that ever my eyes saw. Oh the roaring, and singing and danceing, and yelling of those black creatures in the night, which made the place a lively resemblance of hell. And as miserable was the wast that was there made, of Horses, Cattle, Sheep, Swine, Calves, Lambs, Roasting Pigs, and Fowl (which they had plundered in the Town) some roasting, some lying and burning, and some boyling to feed our merciless Enemies; who were joyful enough though we were disconsolate. To add to the dolefulness of the former day, and the dismalness of the present night: my thoughts ran upon my losses

[6]Ephraim Roper. Rowlandson was unaware that three children had also escaped.

[7]After each move, the group remained encamped for several days.

and sad bereaved condition. All was gone, my Husband gone (at least separated from me, he being in the Bay,[8] and to add to my grief, the Indians told me they would kill him as he came homeward) my Children gone, my Relations and Friends gone, our House and home and all our comforts within door, and without, all was gone, (except my life) and I knew not but the next moment that might go too. There remained nothing to me but one poor wounded Babe, and it seemed at present worse than death that it was in such a pitiful condition, bespeaking Compassion, and I had no refreshing for it, nor suitable things to revive it. Little do many think what is the savageness and bruitishness of this barbarous Enemy, I[9] even those that seem to profess more than others among them, when the English have fallen into their hands.

Those seven that were killed at Lancaster the summer before upon a Sabbath day, and the one that was afterward killed upon a week day, were slain and mangled in a barbarous manner, by one-ey'd John[10] and Marlborough's Praying Indians,[11] which Capt. Mosely brought to Boston, as the Indians told me.

The Second Remove

But now, the next morning, I must turn my back upon the Town, and travel with them into the vast and desolate Wilderness, I knew not whither. It is not my tongue, or pen can express the sorrows of my heart, and bitterness of my spirit, that I had at this departure: but God was with me, in a wonderfull manner, carrying me along, and bearing up my spirit, that it did not quite fail. One of the Indians carried my poor wounded Babe upon a horse, I went moaning all along, I shall dy, I shall dy. I went on foot after it, with sorrow that cannot be exprest. At length I took it off the horse, and carried it in my armes till my strength failed, and I fell down with it: Then they set me upon a horse with my wounded Child in my lap, and there being no furniture upon the horse back, as we were going down a steep hill, we both fell over the horses head, at which they like inhumane creatures laught, and rejoyced to see it, though I thought we should there have ended our dayes, as overcome with so many difficulties. But the Lord renewed my strength still, and carried me along, that I might see more of his Power; yea, so much that I could never have thought of, had I not experienced it.

After this it quickly began to snow, and when night came on, they stopt: and now down I must sit in the snow, by a little fire, and a few boughs behind me, with my sick Child in my lap; and calling much for water, being now (through the wound) fallen into a violent Fever. My own wound also growing so stiff, that I could scarce sit down or rise up; yet so it must be, that I must sit all this cold winter night upon the cold snowy ground, with my sick Child in my armes, looking that every hour would be the last of its life; and having no Christian friend near me, either to comfort or help me. Oh, I may see the wonderfull power of God, that my Spirit did not utterly sink under my affliction: still the Lord upheld me with his gracious and mercifull Spirit, and we were both alive to see the light of the next morning.

[8] *I.e.,* in or near Boston.

[9] Ay.

[10] One-eyed John, also known as Monoco and Apequinsah.

[11] "Praying Indians" refers to a settlement of Christianized Indians at Marlborough, Massachusetts.

The Third Remove[12]

The morning being come, they prepared to go on their way. One of the Indians got up upon a horse, and they set me up behind him, with my poor sick Babe in my lap. A very wearisome and tedious day I had of it; what with my own wound, and my Childs being so exceeding sick, and in a lamentable condition with her wound. It may be easily judged what a poor feeble condition we were in, there being not the least crumb of refreshing that came within either of our mouths, from Wednesday night to Saturday night, except only a little cold water. This day in the afternoon, about an hour by Sun, we came to the place where they intended, *viz*[13] an Indian Town, called Wenimesset, Norward of Quabaug[14] When we were come, Oh the number of Pagans (now merciless enemies) that there came about me, that I may say as David, Psal. 27. 13, *I had fainted, unless I had believed,* etc. The next day was the Sabbath: I then remembered how careless I had been of Gods holy time, how many Sabbaths I had lost and mispent, and how evily I had walked in Gods sight; which lay so close unto my spirit, that it was easie for me to see how righteous it was with God to cut off the thread of my life, and cast me out of his presence for ever. Yet the Lord still shewed mercy to me, and upheld me; and as he wounded me with one hand, so he healed me with the other. This day there came to me one Robbert Pepper (a man belonging to Roxbury) who was taken in Captain Beers his Fight, and had been now a considerable time with the Indians; and up with them almost as far as Albany, to see king Philip,[15] as he told me, and was now very lately come into these parts. Hearing, I say, that I was in this Indian Town, he obtained leave to come and see me. He told me, he himself was wounded in the leg at Captain Beers his Fight; and was not able some time to go, but as they carried him, and as he took Oaken leaves and laid to his wound, and through the blessing of God he was able to travel again. Then I took Oaken leaves and laid to my side, and with the blessing of God it cured me also; yet before the cure was wrought, I may say, as it is in Psal. 38. 5, 6. *My wounds stink and are corrupt, I am troubled, I am bowed down greatly, I go mourning all the day long.* I sat much alone with a poor wounded Child in my lap, which moaned night and day, having nothing to revive the body, or cheer the spirits of her, but in stead of that, sometimes one Indian would come and tell me one hour, that your Master will knock your Child in the head, and then a second, and then a third, your Master[16] will quickly knock your Child in the head.

This was the comfort I had from them, miserable comforters are ye all, as he said.[17] Thus nine dayes I sat upon my knees, with my Babe in my lap, till my flesh was raw again; my Child being even ready to depart this sorrowfull world, they bade me carry it out to another Wigwam (I suppose because they would not be troubled with such spectacles) Whither I went with a very heavy heart, and down I sat with the picture of death in my lap. About two houres in the night, my sweet Babe like a Lambe departed this life, on Feb. 18, 1675. It being about six yeares, and five months old. It was nine dayes from the first wounding, in this miserable condition, without

[12]The third remove ended at an Indian village, Menameset, on the Ware River; this is now New Braintree, Massachusetts.

[13]Latin: namely.

[14]Now Brookfield, Massachusetts.

[15]The Wampanoag leader, Metacom, also known as Metacomet.

[16]Rowlandson's Indian captor and owner.

[17]Job 16:1–2.

any refreshing of one nature or other, except a little cold water. I cannot, but take notice, how at another time I could not bear to be in the room where any dead person was, but now the case is changed; I must and could ly down by my dead Babe, side by side all the night after. I have thought since of the wonderfull goodness of God to me, in preserving me in the use of my reason and senses, in that distressed time, that I did not use wicked and violent means to end my own miserable life. In the morning, when they understood that my child was dead they sent for me home to my Masters Wigwam: (by my Master in this writing, must be understood Quanopin, who was a Saggamore, and married King Phillips wives Sister; not that he first took me, but I was sold to him by another Narrhaganset Indian, who took me when first I came out of the Garison). I went to take up my dead child in my arms to carry it with me, but they bid me let it alone: there was no resisting, but goe I must and leave it. When I had been at my masters wigwam, I took the first opportunity I could get, to go look after my dead child: when I came I askt them what they had done with it? then they told me it was upon the hill: then they went and shewed me where it was, where I saw the ground was newly digged, and there they told me they had buried it: There I left that Child in the Wilderness, and must commit it, and my self also in this Wilderness-condition, to him who is above all. God having taken away this dear Child, I went to see my daughter Mary, who was at this same Indian town, at a Wigwam not very far off, though we had little liberty or opportunity to see one another. She was about ten years old, and taken from the door at first by a Praying Ind and afterward sold for a gun. When I came in sight, she would fall a weeping; at which they were provoked, and would not let me come near her, but bade me be gone; which was a heart-cutting word to me. I had one Child dead, another in the Wilderness, I knew nor where, the third they would not let me come near to: *Me* (as he said) *have ye bereaved of my Children, Joseph is not, and Simeon is not, and ye will take Benjamin also, all these things are against me.* I could not sit still in this condition, but kept walking from one place to another. And as I was going along, my heart was even overwhelm'd with the thoughts of my condition, and that I should have Children, and a Nation which I knew not ruled over them. Whereupon I earnestly entreated the Lord, that he would consider my low estate, and shew me a token for good, and if it were his blessed will, some sign and hope of some relief. And indeed quickly the Lord answered, in some measure, my poor prayers: for as I was going up and down mourning and lamenting my condition, my Son came to me, and asked me how I did; I had not seen him before, since the destruction of the Town, and I knew not where he was, till I was informed by himself, that he was amongst a smaller percel of Indians, whose place was about six miles off; with tears in his eyes, he asked me whether his Sister Sarah was dead; and told me he had seen his Sister Mary; and prayed me, that I would not be troubled in reference to himself. The occasion of his coming to see me at this time, was this: There was, as I said, about six miles from us, a smal Plantation of Indians, where it seems he had been during his Captivity: and at this time, there were some Forces of the Ind. gathered out of our company, and some also from them (among whom was my Sons master) to go to assault and burn Medfield: In this time of the absence of his master, his dame brought him to see me. I took this to be some gracious answer to my earnest and unfeigned desire. The next day, *viz.* to this, the Indians returned from Medfield, all the company, for those that belonged to the other smal company, came thorough the Town that now we were at. But before they came to us, Oh! the outragious roaring and hooping that there was: They began their din about a mile before they came to us. By their noise and hooping they signified how many they had destroyed (which was at that time twenty three.)[18] Those that were with us at home, were gathered together as soon as they heard the hooping, and every time that the other went over their number, these at home gave a shout, that the very Earth rung again: And thus they continued till those that had been upon the expedition were come up to the Sagamores Wigwam; and then, Oh, the hideous insulting and triumphing that there was over some Englishmens scalps that they had taken (as their manner is) and brought with them, I cannot but take notice of the wonderfull mercy of God to me in those afflictions, in sending me a Bible. One of the Indians that came from Medfield fight, had brought some plunder, came to me, and asked me, if I would have a Bible, he had got one in his Basket. I was glad of it, and asked him, whether he thought the Indians would let me read? he answered, yes: So I took the Bible, and in that melancholy time, it came into my mind to read first the 28. Chap. of Deut.,[19] which I did, and when I had read it, my dark heart wrought on this manner, That there was no mercy for me, that the blessing were gone, and the curses come in their room, and that I had lost my opportunity. But the Lord helped me still to go on reading till I came to Chap. 30 the seven first verses, where I found, there was mercy promised again, if we would return to him by repentance; and though we were scatered from one end of the Earth to the other, yet the Lord would gather us together, and turn all those curses upon our Enemies. I do not desire to live to forget this Scripture, and what comfort it was to me. . . .

The Fourth Remove

. . . Heart-aking thoughts here I had about my poor Children, who were scattered up and down among the wild beasts of the forrest: My head was light and dissey (either through hunger or hard lodging, or trouble or altogether) my knees feeble, my body raw by sitting double night and day, that I cannot express to man the affliction that lay upon my Spirit, but the Lord helped me at that time to express it to himself. I opened my Bible to read, and the Lord brought that precious Scripture to me, Jer. 31. 16. *Thus saith the Lord, refrain thy voice from weeping, and thine eyes from tears, for thy work shall be rewarded, and they shall come again from the land of the Enemy.* This was a sweet Cordial to me, when I was ready to faint, many and many a time have I sat down, and weept sweetly over this Scripture. At this place we continued about four dayes.

The Fifth Remove[20]

The occasion (as I thought) of their moving at this time, was, the English Army,[21] it being near and following them: For they went, as if they had gone for their lives, for

[18]The Indian custom of whooping signaled the number of enemy killed and captured in the battle.

[19]Recital of blessings for obedience to God and curses for disobedience.

[20]This remove included crossing the Baquag River in Orange.

[21]The colonial militia, consisting of Massachusetts and Connecticut forces under Captain Thomas Savage.

some considerable way, and then they made a stop, and chose some of their stoutest men, and sent them back to hold the English Army in play whilst the rest escaped: And then, like Jehu,[22] they marched on furiously, with their old, and with their young: some carried their old decrepit mothers, some carried one, and some another. Four of them carried a great Indian upon a Bier; but going through a thick Wood with him, they were hindered, and could make no hast; whereupon they took him upon their backs, and carried him, one at a time, till they came to Bacquaug River. Upon a Friday, a little after noon we came to this River. When all the company was come up, and were gathered together, I thought to count the number of them, but they were so many, and being somewhat in motion, it was beyond my skil. In this travel, because of my wound, I was somewhat favoured in my load; I carried only my knitting work and two quarts of parched meal:[23] Being very faint I asked my mistriss to give me one spoonfull of the meal, but she would not give me a taste. They quickly fell to cutting dry trees, to make Rafts to carry them over the river: and soon my turn came to go over: By the advantage of some brush which they had laid upon the Raft to sit upon, I did not wet my foot (which many of themselves at the other end were mid-leg deep) which cannot but be acknowledged as a favour of God to my weakned body, it being a very cold time. I was not before acquainted with such kind of doings or dangers. *When thou passeth through the waters I will be with thee, and through the Rivers they shall not overflow thee,* Isai. 43.2. A certain number of us got over the River that night, but it was the night after the Sabbath before all the company was got over. On the Saturday they boyled an old Horses leg which they had got, and so we drank of the broth, as soon as they thought it was ready, and when it was almost all gone, they filled it up again.

The first week of my being among them, I hardly ate any thing; the second week, I found my stomach grow very faint for want of something; and yet it was very hard to get down their filthy trash: but the third week, though I could think how formerly my stomach would turn against this or that, and I could starve and dy before I could eat such things, yet they were sweet and savoury to my taste. I was at this time knitting a pair of white cotton stockins for my mistriss; and had not yet wrought upon a Sabbath day; when the Sabbath came they bade me go to work; I told them it was the Sabbath day, and desired them to let me rest, and told them I would do as much more to morrow; to which they answered me, they would break my face. And here I cannot but take notice of the strange providence of God in preserving the heathen: They were many hundreds, old and young, some sick, and some lame, many had Papooses at their backs, the greatest number at this time with us, were Squaws, and they travelled with all they had, bag and baggage, and yet they got over this River aforesaid; and on Munday they set their Wigwams on fire, and away they went: On that very day came the English Army after them to this River, and saw the smoak of their Wigwams, and yet this River put a stop to them. God did not give them courage or activity to go over after us; we were not ready for so great a mercy as victory and deliverance; if we had been, God would have found out a way for the English to have passed this River, as well as for the Indians with their Squaws and Children, and all their Luggage. *Oh that my People had hearkened to me, and Israel had walked in my*

[22]King of Israel (c. 843–816 B.C.).
[23]A favorite traveling food.

ways, I should soon have subdued their Enemies, and turned my hand against their Adversaries, Psal. 81: 13.14.

The Eighth Remove[24]

On the morrow morning we must go over the River, *i.e.* Connecticot, to meet with King Philip; two Cannoos ful, they had carried over, the next Turn I my self was to go; but as my foot was upon the Cannoo to step in, there was a sudden out-cry among them, and I must step back; and instead of going over the River, I must go four or five miles up the River farther Northward. Some of the Indians ran one way, and some another. The cause of this rout was, as I thought, their espying some English Scouts, who were thereabout. In this travel up the River, about noon the Company made a stop, and sate down; some to eat, and others to rest them. As I sate amongst them, musing of things past, my Son Joseph unexpectedly came to me: we asked of each others welfare, bemoaning our dolefull condition, and the change that had come upon uss. We had Husband and Father, and Children, and Sisters, and Friends, and Relations, and House, and Home, and many Comforts of this Life: but now we may say, as Job, *Naked came I out of my Mothers Womb, and naked shall I return: The Lord gave, and the Lord hath taken away, Blessed be the Name of the Lord.*[25] I asked him whither he would read; he told me, he earnestly desired it, I gave him my Bible, and he lighted upon that comfortable Scripture, Psal. 118. 17, 18. *I shall not dy but live, and declare the works of the Lord: the Lord hath chastened me sore, yet he hath not given me over to death.* Look here, Mother (sayes he) did you read this? And here I may take occasion to mention one principall ground of my setting forth these Lines: even as the Psalmist sayes, To declare the Works of the Lord, and his wonderfull Power in carrying us along, preserving us in the Wilderness, while under the Enemies hand, and returning of us in safety again, And His goodness in bringing to my hand so many comfortable and suitable Scriptures in my distress.[26] But to Return, We travelled on till night; and in the morning, we must go over the River to Philip's Crew. When I was in the Cannoo, I could not but be amazed at the numerous crew of Pagans that were on the Bank on the other side. When I came ashore, they gathered all about me, I sitting alone in the midst: I observed they asked one another questions, and laughed, and rejoyced over their Gains and Victories. Then my heart began to fail: and I fell a weeping which was the first time to my remembrance, that I wept before them. Although I had met with so much Affliction, and my heart was many times ready to break, yet could I not shed one tear in their sight: but rather had been all this while in a maze, and like one astonished: but now I may say as, Psal. 137. 1. *By the Rivers of Babylon, there we sate down: yea, we wept when we remembered Zion.* There one of them asked me, why I wept, I could hardly tell what to say: yet I answered, they would kill me: No, said he, none will hurt you. Then came one of them and gave me two spoon-fulls of Meal to comfort me, and another gave me half a pint of Pease; which was more worth than many Bushels at

[24]To Coasset in South Vernon, Vermont.

[25]Job 1:21.

[26]Rowlandson probably had Psalm 145:4 in mind: "One generation shall praise thy works to another and shall declare thy mighty acts."

another time. Then I went to see King Philip, he bade me come in and sit down, and asked me whether I woold smoke it (a usual Complement nowadayes amongst Saints and Sinners)[27] but this no way suited me. For though I had formerly used Tobacco, yet I had left it ever since I was first taken. It seems to be a Bait, the Devil layes to make men loose their precious time: I remember with shame, how formerly, when I had taken two or three pipes, I was presently ready for another, such a bewitching thing it is: But I thank God, he has now given me power over it; surely there are many who may be better imployed than to ly sucking a stinking Tobacco-pipe.

Now the Indians gather their Forces to go against North-Hampton: over-night one went about yelling and hooting to give notice of the design. Whereupon they fell to boyling of Ground-nuts, and parching of Corn (as many as had it) for their Provision: and in the morning away they went. During my abode in this place, Philip spake to me to make a shirt for his boy, which I did, for which he gave me a shilling: I offered the mony to my master, but he bade me keep it: and with it I bought a piece of Horse flesh. Afterwards he asked me to make a Cap for his boy, for which he invited me to Dinner. I went, and he gave me a Pancake, about as big as two fingers; it was made of parched wheat, beaten, and fryed in Bears grease, but I thought I never tasted pleasanter meat in my life. . . .

The Twelfth Remove

It was upon a Sabbath-day-morning, that they prepared for their Travel. This morning I asked my master whither he would sell me to my Husband; he answered me *Nux,*[28] which did much rejoyce my spirit. My mistriss, before we went, was gone to the burial of a Papoos, and returning, she found me sitting and reading in my Bible; she snatched it hastily out of my hand, and threw it out of doors; I ran out and catcht it up, and put it into my pocket, and never let her see it afterward. Then they packed up their things to be gone, and gave me my load: I complained it was too heavy, whereupon she gave me a slap in the face, and bade me go; I lifted up my heart to God, hoping the Redemption was not far off: and the rather because their insolency grew worse and worse.

But the thoughts of my going homeward (for so we bent our course) much cheared my Spirit, and made my burden seem light, and almost nothing at all. But (to my amazement and great perplexity) the scale was soon turned: for when we had gone a little way, on a sudden my mistriss gives out, she would go no further, but turn back again, and said, I must go back again with her, and she called her *Sannup,* and would have had him gone back also, but he would not, but said, He would go on, and come to us again in three dayes. My Spirit was upon this, I confess, very impatient, and almost outragious. I thought I could as well have dyed as went back: I cannot declare the trouble that I was in about it; but yet back again I must go. As soon as I had an opportunity, I took my Bible to read, and that quieting Scripture came to my hand, Psal. 46. 10. *Be still, and know that I am God.* Which stilled my spirit for the present: But a sore time of tryal, I concluded, I had to go through, My master

[27] Among believers (saints) as well as the unregenerate.

[28] Yes.

being gone, who seemed to me the best friend that I had of an Indian, both in cold and hunger, and quickly so it proved. Down I sat, with my heart as full as it could hold, and yet so hungry that I could not sit neither: but going out to see what I could find, and walking among the Trees, I found six Acorns, and two Ches-nuts, which were some refreshment to me. Towards Night I gathered me some sticks for my own comfort, that I might not ly a-cold: but when we came to ly down they bade me go out, and ly some-where-else, for they had company (they said) come in more than their own: I told them, I could not tell where to go, they bade me go look; I told them, if I went to another Wigwam they would be angry, and send me home again. Then one of the Company drew his sword, and told me he would run me thorough if I did not go presently. Then was I fain to stoop to this rude fellow, and to go out in the night, I knew not whither. Mine eyes have seen that fellow afterwards walking up and down Boston, under the appearance of a Friend-Indian, and severall others of the like Cut. I went to one Wigwam, and they told me they had no room. Then I went to another, and they said the same; at last an old Indian bade me come to him, and his Squaw gave me some Ground-nuts; she gave me also something to lay under my head, and a good fire we had: and through the good providence of God, I had a comfortable lodging that night. In the morning, another Indian bade me come at night, and he would give me six Ground-nuts, which I did. We were at this place and time about two miles from Connecticut River. We went in the morning to gather Ground-nuts, to the River, and went back again that night. I went with a good load at my back (for they when they went, though but a little way, would carry all their trumpery with them) I told them the skin was off my back, but I had no other comforting answer from them than this, That it would be no matter if my head were off too.

The Thirteenth Remove[29]

Instead of going toward the Bay, which was that I desired, I must go with them five or six miles down the River into a mighty Thicket of Brush: where we abode almost a fortnight. Here one asked me to make a shirt for her Papoos, for which she gave me a mess of Broth, which was thickened with meal made of the Bark of a Tree, and to make it the better, she had put into it about a handful of Pease, and a few roasted Ground-nuts. I had not seen my son a pritty while, and here was an Indian of whom I made inquiry after him, and asked him when he saw him: he answered me, that such a time his master roasted him, and that himself did eat of piece of him, as big as his two fingers, and that he was very good meat: But the Lord upheld my Spirit, under this discouragement; and I considered their horrible addictedness to lying, and that there is not one of them that makes the least conscience of speaking of truth. In this place, on a cold night, as I lay by the fire, I removed a stick that kept the heat from me, a Squaw moved it down again, at which I lookt up, and she threw a handfull of ashes in mine eyes; I thought I should have been quite blinded, and have never seen more: but lying down, the water run out of my eyes, and carried the dirt with it, that by the morning, I recovered my sight again. Yet upon this, and the like occasions, I hope it is not too much to say with Job, *Have pitty upon me, have pitty upon me, O*

[29]The encampment shifted to Hindsdale, New Hampshire, near the Connecticut River.

ye my Friends, for the Hand of the Lord has touched me.[30] And here I cannot but remember how many times sitting in their Wigwams, and musing on things past, I should suddenly leap up and run out, as if I had been at home, forgetting where I was, and what my condition was: But when I was without, and saw nothing but Wilderness, and Woods, and a company of barbarous heathens, my mind quickly returned to me, which made me think of that, spoken concerning Sampson, who said, *I will go out and shake my self as at other times, but he wist not that the Lord was departed from him.*[31] About this time I began to think that all my hopes of Restoration would come to nothing. I thought of the English Army, and hoped for their coming, and being taken by them, but that failed. I hoped to be carried to Albany, as the Indians had discoursed before, but that failed also. I thought of being sold to my Husband, as my master spake, but in stead of that, my master himself was gone, and left behind, so that my Spirit was now quite ready to sink. I asked them to let me go out and pick up some sticks, that I might get alone, And poure out my heart unto the Lord. Then also I took my Bible to read, but I found no comfort here neither, which many times I was wont to find: So easie a thing it is with God to dry up the Streames of Scripture-comfort from us. Yet I can say, that in all my sorrows and afflictions, God did not leave me to have my impatience work towards himself, as if his wayes were unrighteous. But I knew that he laid upon me less then I deserved. Afterward, before this dolefull time ended with me, I was turning the leaves of my Bible, and the Lord brought to me some Scriptures, which did a little revive me, as that Isai. 55. 8, *For my thoughts are not your thoughts, neither are your wayes my ways, saith the Lord.* And also that, Psal. 37. 5, *Commit thy way unto the Lord, trust also in him, and he shal bring it to pass.* About this time they came yelping from Hadly, where they had killed three English men, and brought one Captive with them, *viz.* Thomas Read. They all gathered about the poor Man, asking him many Questions. I desired also to go and see him; and when I came, he was crying bitterly, supposing they would quickly kill him. Whereupon I asked one of them, whether they intended to kill him; he answered me, they would not: He being a little cheared with that, I asked him about the wel-fare of my Husband, he told me he saw him such a time in the Bay, and he was well, but very melancholly. By which I certainly understood (though I suspected it before) that whatsoever the Indians told me respecting him was vanity and lies. Some of them told me, he was dead, and they had killed him: some said he was Married again, and that the Governour wished him to Marry; and told him he should have his choice, and that all perswaded I was dead. So like were these barbarous creatures to him who was a lyer from the beginning.[32]

As I was sitting once in the Wigwam here, Phillips Maid came in with the Child in her arms, and asked me to give her a piece of my Apron, to make a flap for it, I told her I would not: then my Mistriss bad me give it, but still I said no: the maid told me if I would not give her a piece, she would tear a piece off it: I told her I would tear her Coat then, with that my Mistriss rises up, and takes up a stick big enough to have killed me, and struck at me with it, but I stept out, and she struck the stick into the Mat of the Wigwam. But while she was pulling of it out, I ran to the Maid and gave her all my Apron, and so that storm went over.

[30]Job 19:21.
[31]Judges 16:20.
[32]Satan.

Hearing that my Son was come to this place, I went to see him, and told him his Father was well, but melancholly: he told me he was as much grieved for his Father as for himself; I wondered at his speech, for I thought I had enough upon my spirit in reference to my self, to make me mindless of my Husband and every one else: they being safe among their Friends. He told me also, that a while before, his Master (together with other Indians) where[33] going to the French for Powder; but by the way the Mohawks met with them, and killed four of their Company which made the rest turn back again, for it might have been worse with him, had he been sold to the French, than it proved to be in his remaining with the Indians.

I went to see an English Youth in this place, one John Gillberd of Springfield. I found him lying without dores, upon the ground; I asked him how he did? he told me he was very sick of a flux,[34] with eating so much blood: They had turned him out of the Wigwam, and with him an Indian Papoos, almost dead, (whose Parents had been killed) in a bitter cold day, without fire or clothes: the young man himself had nothing on, but his shirt and wastcoat. This sight was enough to melt a heart of flint. There they lay quivering in the Cold, the youth round like a dog; the Papoos stretcht out, with his eyes and nose and mouth full of dirt, and yet alive, and groaning. I advised John to go and get to some fire: he told me he could not stand, but I perswaded him still, lest he should ly there and die: and with much adoe I got him to a fire, and went my self home. As soon as I was got home, his Masters Daughter came after me, to know what I had done with the English man, I told her I had got him to a fire in such a place. Now had I need to pray Pauls Prayer, 2 Thess. 3. 2. *That we may be delivered from unreasonable and wicked men.* For her satisfaction I went along with her, and brought her to him; but before I got home again, it was noised about, that I was running away and getting the English youth, along with me; that as soon as I came in, they began to rant and domineer: asking me Where I had been, and what I had been doing? and saying they would knock him on the head: I told them, I had been seeing the English Youth, and that I would not run away, they told me I lyed, and taking up a Hatchet, they came to me, and said they would knock me down if I stirred out again; and so confined me to the Wigwam. Now may I say with David, 2 Sam. 24. 14. *I am in a great strait.* If I keep in, I must dy with hunger, and if I go out, I must be knockt in head. This distressed condition held that day, and half the next; And then the Lord remembred me, whose mercyes are great. Then came an Indian to me with a pair of stockings that were too big for him, and he would have me ravel them out, and knit them fit for him. I shewed my self willing, and bid him ask my mistriss if I might go along with him a little way; she said yes, I might, but I was not a little refresht with that news, that I had my liberty again. Then I went along with him, and he gave me some roasted Ground-nuts, which did again revive my feeble stomach.

Being got out of her sight, I had time and liberty again to look into my Bible: Which was my Guid by day, and my Pillow by night. Now that comfortable Scripture presented it self to me, Isa. 54. 7. *For a smal moment have I forsaken thee, but with great mercies will I gather thee.* Thus the Lord carried me along from one time to another, and made good to me this precious promise, and many others. Then my

[33]Were.
[34]Dysentery.

Son came to see me, and I asked his master to let him stay a while with me, that I might comb his head, and look over him, for he was almost overcome with lice. He told me, when I had done, that he was very hungry, but I had nothing to relieve him; but bid him go into the Wigwams as he went along, and see if he could get any thing among them. Which he did, and it seems tarried a little too long; for his Master was angry with him, and beat him, and then sold him. Then he came running to tell me he had a new Master, and that he had given him some Groundnuts already. Then I went along with him to his new Master who told me he loved him: and he should not want. So his Master carried him away, and I never saw him afterward, till I saw him at Pascataqua in Portsmouth.

That night they bade me go out of the Wigwam again: my Mistrisses Papoos was sick, and it died that night, and there was one benefit in it, that there was more room. I went to a Wigwam, and they bade me come in, and gave me a skin to ly upon, and a mess of Venson and Ground-nuts, which was a choice Dish among them. On the morrow they buried the Papoos, and afterward, both morning and evening, there came a company to mourn and howle with her: though I confess, I could not much condole with them. Many sorrowfull dayes I had in this place: often getting alone; *like a Crane, or a Swallow, so did I chatter: I did mourn as a Dove, mine eyes ail with looking upward. Oh, Lord, I am oppressed; undertake for me,* Isa. 38. 14. I could tell the Lord as Hezeckiah, ver. 3. *Remember now O Lord, I beseech thee, how I have walked before thee in truth.*[35] Now had I time to examine all my wayes: my Conscience did not accuse me of un-righteousness toward one or other: yet I saw how in my walk with God, I had been a careless creature. As David said, *Against thee, thee only have I sinned:*[36] and I might say with the poor Publican, *God be merciful unto me a sinner.*[37] On the Sabbath-dayes, I could look upon the Sun and think how People were going to the house of God, to have their Souls refresht; and then home, and their bodies also: but I was destitute of both; and might say as the poor Prodigal, *he would fain have filled his belly with the husks that the Swine did eat, and no man gave unto him.* Luke 15. 16. For I must say with him, *Father I have sinned against Heaven, and in thy sight,*[38] ver. 21. I remembred how on the night before and after the Sabbath, when my Family was about me, and Relations and Neighbours with us, we would pray and sing, and then have a comfortable Bed to ly down on: but in stead of all this, I had only a little Swill for the body, and then like a Swine, must ly down on the ground. I cannot express to man the sorrow that lay upon my Spirit, the Lord knows it. Yet that comfortable Scripture would often come to my mind, *For a small moment have I forsaken thee, but with great mercies will I gather thee.*[39]

The Fifteenth Remove

We went on our travel, I having got one handful of Ground nuts for my support that day: they gave me my load, and I went on cheerfully, (with the thoughts of going homeward) having my burden more on my back than my spirit; we came to Baquaug

[35]Isaiah 38:3.
[36]Psalm 51:4.
[37]Luke 6:36.
[38]Luke 15:21.
[39]Isaiah 54:7.

River again that day, near which we abode a few days. Sometimes one of them would give me a Pipe, another a little Tobacco, another a little Salt; which I would change for a little Victuals. I cannot but think what a Wolvish appetite persons have in a starving condition; for many times, when they gave me that which was hot, I was so greedy, that I should burn my mouth, that it would trouble me hours after; and yet I should quickly do the same again. And after I was thoroughly hungry, I was never again satisfied; for though sometimes it fell out that I got enough, and did eat till I could eat no more, yet I was as unsatisfied as I was when I began. And now could I see that Scripture verified, (there being many Scriptures which we do not take notice of, or understand, till we are afflicted,) *Mic.* vi. 14, *Thou shalt eat and not be satisfied.* Now might I see more than ever before, the miseries that sin hath brought upon us. Many times I should be ready to run out against the Heathen, but that Scripture would quiet me again, *Amos* iii. 6, *Shall there be evil in the City and the Lord hath not done it?* The Lord help me to make a right improvement of his word, and that I might learn that great lesson, *Mic.* vi. 8, 9, *He hath shewed thee, O Man, what is good; and what doth the Lord require of thee but to do justly, and love mercy, and walk humbly with thy God? Hear ye the rod, and who hath appointed it.* . . .

The Eighteenth Remove

We took up our packs, and along we went; but a wearsome day I had of it. As we went along I saw an *English-man* stript naked, and lying dead upon the ground, but knew not who it was. Then we came to another Indian Town, where we stayed all night: In this Town there were four *English Children,* Captives: and one of them my own Sister's: I went to see how she did, and she was well, considering her Captive condition. I would have tarried that night with her, but they that owned her would not suffer it. Then I went to another Wigwam, where they were boiling Corn and Beans, which was a lovely sight to see; but I could not get a taste thereof. Then I went into another Wigwam, where there were two of the *English Children:* The Squaw was boiling horses feet; then she cut me off a little piece, and gave one of the *English Children* a piece also: Being very hungry, I had quickly eat up mine; but the Child could not bite it, it was so tough and sinewy, but lay sucking, gnawing, chewing, and slobbering it in the mouth and hand; then I took it of the Child, and eat it myself; and savoury it was to my taste.

That I may say as *Job,* chap. vi. 7, *The things that my Soul refused to touch are as my sorrowful meat.* Thus the Lord made that pleasant and refreshing which another time would have been an Abomination. Then I went home to my Mistress's Wigwam; and they told me I disgraced my Master with begging; and if I did so any more they would knock me on the head: I told them, they had as good knock me on the head as starve me to death.

The Nineteenth Remove

They said, when we went out, that we must travel to Wachuset this day. But a bitter weary day I had of it, travelling now three dayes together, without resting any day between. At last, after many weary steps, I saw Wachuset hills, but many miles off. Then we came to a great Swamp, through which we travelled, up to the knees in mud and water, which was heavy going to one tyred before. Being almost spent, I thought I should have sunk down at last, and never gat out; but I may say, as in Psal. 94. 18, *When my foot slipped, thy mercy, O Lord, held me up.* Going along, having indeed my life, but little spirit, Philip, who was in the Company, came up and took me by the hand, and said, Two weeks more and you shal be Mistress again. I asked him, if he spake true? he answered, Yes, and quickly you shal come to your master again; who had been gone from us three weeks. After many weary steps we came to Wachuset, where he was: and glad I was to see him. He asked me, When I washt me? I told him not this month, then he fetcht me some water himself, and bid me wash, and gave me the Glass to see how I lookt; and bid his Squaw give me something to eat: so she gave me a mess of Beans and meat, and a little Ground-nut Cake. I was wonderfully revived with this favour shewed me, Psal. 106. 46, *He made them also to be pittied, of all those that carried them Captives.*

My master had three Squaws, living sometimes with one, and sometimes with another one, this old Squaw, at whose Wigwam I was, and with whom my Master had been those three weeks. Another was Wattimore, with whom I had lived and served all this while: A severe and proud Dame she was, bestowing every day in dressing her self neat as much time as any of the Gentry of the land: powdering her hair, and painting her face, going with Neck-laces, with Jewels in her ears, and Bracelets upon her hands: When she had dressed her self, her work was to make Girdles of Wampom and Beads. The third Squaw was a younger one, by whom he had two Papooses. By that time I was refresht by the old Squaw, with whom my master was, Wettimores Maid came to call me home, at which I fell a weeping. Then the old Squaw told me, to encourage me, that if I wanted victuals, I should come to her, and that I should ly there in her Wigwam. Then I went with the maid, and quickly came again and lodged there. The Squaw laid a Mat under me, and a good Rugg over me; the first time I had any such kindness shewed me. I understood that Wettimore thought, that if she should let me go and serve with the old Squaw, she would be in danger to loose, not only my service, but the redemption-pay also. And I was not a little glad to hear this; being by it raised in my hopes, that in Gods due time there would be an end of this sorrowfull hour. Then came an Indian, and asked me to knit him three pair of Stockins, for which I had a Hat, and a silk Handkerchief. Then another asked me to make her a shift, for which she gave me an Apron.

Then came Tom and Peter,[40] with the second Letter from the Council, about the Captives. Though they were Indians, I gat them by the hand, and burst out into tears; my heart was so full that I could not speak to them; but recovering my self, I asked them how my husband did, and all my friends and acquaintance? they said, They are all very well but melancholy. They brought me two Biskets, and a pound of Tobacco. The Tobacco I quickly gave away; when it was all gone, one asked me to give him a pipe of Tobacco, I told him it was all gone; then began he to rant and threaten. I told him when my Husband came I would give him some: Hang him Rogue (sayes he) I will knock out his brains, if he comes here. And then again, in the same breath they would say, That if there should come an hundred without Guns, they would do them no hurt. So unstable and like mad men they were. So that fearing the worst, I durst

[40]Christian Indians Tom Dublet and Peter Conway, who were negotiating for ransom.

not send to my Husband, though there were some thoughts of his coming to Redeem and fetch me, not knowing what might follow. For there was little more trust to them then to the master they served. When the Letter was come, the Saggamores met to consult about the Captives, and called me to them to enquire how much my husband would give to redeem me, when I came I sate down among them, as I was wont to do, as their manner is: Then they bade me stand up, and said, they were the General Court.[41] They bid me speak what I thought he would give. Now knowing that all we had was destroyed by the Indians, I was in a great strait: I thought if I should speak of but a little, it would be slighted, and hinder the matter; if of a great sum, I knew not where it would be procured: yet at a venture, I said Twenty pounds, yet desired them to take less; but they would not hear of that, but sent that message to Boston, that for Twenty pounds I should be redeemed. It was a Praying-Indian that wrote their Letter for them. There was another Praying Indian, who told me, that he had a brother, that would not eat Horse; his conscience was so tender and scrupulous (though as large as hell, for the destruction of poor Christians). Then he said, he read that Scripture to him, 2 Kings, 6. 25. *There was a famine in Samaria, and behold they beseiged it, untill an Asses head was sold for fourscore pieces of silver, and the fourth part of a Kab of Doves dung, for five pieces of silver.* He expounded this place to his brother, and shewed him that it was lawfull to eat that in a Famine which is not at another time. And now, sayes he, he will eat Horse with any Indian of them all. There was another Praying-Indian, who when he had done all the mischief that he could, betrayed his own Father into the English hands, thereby to purchase his own life. Another Praying-Indian was at Sudbury-fight,[42] though, as he deserved, he was afterward hanged for it. There was another Praying Indian, so wicked and cruel, as to wear a string about his neck, strung with *Christian* Fingers. Another Praying *Indian,* when they went to *Sudbury* Fight, went with them, and his Squaw also with him, with her Papoos at her back: before they went to that Fight, they got a company together to *Powaw:* the manner was as followeth. There was one that kneeled upon a *Deerskin,* with the Company round him in a Ring, who kneeled, striking upon the Ground with their hands, and with sticks, and muttering or humming with their Mouths. Besides him who kneeled in the ring, there also stood one with a Gun in his hand: Then he on the Deer-skin made a speech and all manifested assent to it; and so they did many times together. Then they bade him with the Gun go out of the ring, which he did; but when he was out they called him in again; but he seemed to make a stand; then they called the more earnestly, till he returned again. Then they all sang. Then they gave him two Guns, in either hand one. And so he on the Deer-skin began again; and at the end of every Sentence in his speaking, they all assented, humming or muttering with their Mouthes, and striking upon the Ground with the Hands. Then they bade him with the two Guns go out of the Ring again: which he did a little way. Then they called him in again, but he made a stand, so they called him with greater earnestness: but he stood reeling and wavering, as if he knew not whether he should stand or fall, or which way to go. Then they called him with exceeding great vehemency, all of them, one and another: after a little while, he turned in, staggering as he went, with his Arms stretched out; in either hand a Gun. As soon

[41]In imitation of the Colonial Assembly of Massachusetts.

[42]An April 18 attack on Sudbury, Massachusetts.

as he came in, they all sang and rejoyced exceedingly a while. And then he upon the Deer-skin, made another speech, unto which they all assented in a rejoycing manner: and so they ended their business, and forthwith went to *Sudbury* Fight. To my thinking they went without any scruple but that they should prosper and gain the Victory. And they went out not so rejoycing, but that they came home with as great a Victory. For they said they had killed two Captains, and almost an hundred men. One *Englishman* they brought alive with them; and he said, it was too true, for they had made sad work at Sudbury, as indeed it proved. Yet they came home without that rejoycing and triumphing over their victory, which they were wont to shew at other times, but rather like Dogs (as they say) which have lost their ears. Yet I could not perceive that it was for their own loss of men: They said, they had not lost above five or six: and I missed none, except in one Wigwam. When they went, they acted as if the Devil had told them that they should gain the victory: and now they acted, as if the Devil had told them they should have a fall. Whither it were so or no, I cannot tell, but so it proved, for quickly they began to fall, and so held on that Summer, till they came to utter ruine. . . .

The Twentieth Remove[43]

It was their usual manner to remove, when they had done any mischief, lest they should be found out: and so they did at this time. We went about three or four miles, and there they built a great Wigwam, big enough to hold an hundred Indians, which they did in preparation to a great day of Dancing. They would say now amongest themselves, that the Governour would be so angry for his loss at Sudbury, that he would send no more about the Captives, which made me grieve and tremble. My Sister being not far from the place where we now were, and hearing that I was here, desired her master to let her come and see me, and he was willing to it, and would go with her: but she being ready before him, told him she would go before, and was come within a Mile or two of the place; Then he overtook her, and began to rant as if he had been mad; and made her go back again in the Rain; so that I never saw her till I saw her in Charlestown. But the Lord requited many of their ill doings, for this Indian her Master, was hanged afterward at Boston. The Indians now began to come from all quarters, against their merry dancing day. Among some of them came one Goodwife Kettle. I told her my heart was so heavy that it was ready to break: so is mine too said she, but yet said, I hope we shall hear some good news shortly. I could hear how earnestly my Sister desired to see me, and I as earnestly desired to see her: and yet neither of us could get an opportunity. My Daughter was also now about a mile off, and I had not seen her in nine or ten weeks, as I had not seen my Sister since our first taking. I earnestly desired them to let me go and see them: yea, I intreated, begged, and perswaded them, but to let me see my Daughter; and yet so hard hearted were they, that they would not suffer it. They made use of their tyrannical power whilst they had it: but through the Lords wonderfull mercy, their time was now but short.

[43]This remove, from April 28–May 2, was to an encampment near the southern end of Wachusett Lake, Princeton, Massachusetts.

On a Sabbath day, the Sun being about an hour high in the afternoon, came Mr. John Hoar[44] (the Council permitting him, and his own foreward spirit inclining him) together with the two fore-mentioned Indians, Tom and Peter, with their third Letter from the Council. When they came near, I was abroad: though I saw them not, they presently called me in, and bade me sit down and not stir. Then they catched up their Guns, and away they ran, as if an Enemy had been at hand; and the Guns went off apace. I manifested some great trouble, and they asked me what was the matter? I told them, I thought they had killed the English-man (for they had in the mean time informed me that an English-man was come) they said, No; They shot over his Horse and under, and before his Horse; and they pusht him this way and that way, at their pleasure: shewing what they could do: Then they let them come to their Wigwams. I begged of them to let me see the English-man, but they would not. But there was I fain to sit their pleasure. When they had talked their fill with him, they suffered me to go to him. We asked each other of our welfare, and how my Husband did, and all my Friends? He told me they were all well, and would be glad to see me. Amongst other things which my Husband sent me, there came a pound of Tobacco: which I sold for nine shillings in Money: for many of the Indians for want of Tobacco, smoaked Hemlock, and Ground-Ivy. It was a great mistake in any, who thought I sent for Tobacco: for through the favour of God, that desire was overcome. I now asked them, whither I should go home with Mr. Hoar? They answered No, one and another of them: and it being night, we lay down with that answer; in the morning, Mr. Hoar invited the Saggamores to Dinner; but when we went to get it ready, we found that they had stollen the greatest part of the Provision Mr. Hoar had brought, out of his Bags, in the night. And we may see the wonderfull power of God, in that one passage, in that when there was such a great number of the Indians together, and so greedy of a little good food; and no English there, but Mr. Hoar and my self: that there they did not knock us in the head, and take what we had: there being not only some Provision, but also Trading cloth,[45] a part of the twenty pounds agreed upon: But instead of doing us any mischief, they seemed to be ashamed of the fact, and said, it were some Matchit Indian[46] that did it. Oh, that we could believe that there is no thing too hard for God! God shewed his Power over the Heathen in this, as he did over the hungry Lyons when Daniel was cast into the Den.[47] Mr. Hoar called them betime to Dinner, but they ate very little, they being so busie in dressing themselves, and getting ready for their Dance: which was carried on by eight of them, four Men and four Squaws: My master and mistress being two. He was dressed in his Holland shirt,[48] with great Laces sewed at the tail of it, he had his silver Buttons, his white Stockins, his Garters were hung round with Shillings, and he had Girdles of Wampom[49] upon his head and shoulders. She had a Kersey Coat,[50] and covered with Girdles of Wampom from the Loins upward: her armes from her elbows to her

[44]Delegated by Rowlandson's husband to represent him at the Council for the Sagamore Indians and to bargain for Mrs. Rowlandson's redemption.

[45]Cloth used for barter.

[46]A bad Indian.

[47]See Daniel 6:1–29.

[48]Linen.

[49]Polished shell beads used by the Indians as currency.

[50]Coarse cloth, ribbed and woven from long wool.

hands were covered with Bracelets; there were handfulls of Necklaces about her neck, and severall sorts of Jewels in her ears. She had fine red Stokins and white Shoos, her hair powdered and face painted Red, that was alwayes before Black. And all the Dancers were after the same manner. There were two other singing and knocking on a Kettle for their musick. They keep hopping up and down one after another, with a Kettle of water in the midst, standing warm upon some Embers, to drink of when they were dry. They held on till it was almost night, throwing out Wampom to the standers by. At night I asked them again, if I should go home? They all as one said No, except[51] my Husband would come for me. When we were lain down, my Master went out of the Wigwam, and by and by sent in an Indian called James the Printer[52] who told Mr. Hoar, that my Master would let me go home to-morrow, if he would let him have one pint of Liquors. Then Mr. Hoar called his own Indians, Tom and Peter, and bid them go and see whither he would promise it before them three: and if he would, he should have it; which he did, and he had it. Then Philip[53] smelling the business cal'd me to him, and asked me what I would give him, to tell me some good news, and speak a good word for me. I told him, I could not tell what to give him, I would any thing I had, and asked him what he would have? He said, two Coats and twenty shillings in Mony, and half a bushel of seed Corn, and some Tobacco. I thanked him for his love: but I knew the good news as well as the crafty Fox. My Master after he had had his drink, quickly came ranting into the Wigwam again, and called for Mr. Hoar, drinking to him, and saying, He was a good man: and then again he would say, Hang him Rogue: Being almost drunk, he would drink to him, and yet presently say he should be hanged. Then he called for me. I trembled to hear him, yet I was fain to go to him, and he drank to me, shewing no incivility. He was the first Indian I saw drunk all the while that I was amongst them. At last his Squaw ran out, and he after her, round the Wigwam, with his mony jingling at his knees: But she escaped him: But having an old Squaw he ran to her: and so through the Lords mercy, we were no more troubled that night. Yet I had not a comfortable nights rest: for I think I can say, I did not sleep for three nights together. The night before the Letter came from the Council, I could not rest, I was so full of feares and troubles, God many times leaving us most in the dark, when deliverance is nearest: yea, at this time I could not rest night nor day. The next night I was overjoyed, Mr. Hoar being come, and that with such good tidings. The third night I was even swallowed up with the thoughts of things, *viz.* that ever I should go home again; and that I must go, leaving my Children behind me in the Wilderness; so that sleep was now almost departed from mine eyes.

On Tuesday morning they called their General Court (as they call it) to consult and determine, whether I should go home or no: And they all as one man did seemingly consent to it, that I should go home; except Philip, who would not come among them.

But before I go any further, I would take leave to mention a few remarkable passages of providence, which I took special notice of in my afflicted time.

[51]Unless.

[52]Indian who assisted Reverend John Eliot in his printing of the Bible.

[53]An Indian who aided Rowlandson earlier in the journey.

1. Of the fair opportunity lost in the long March, a little after the Fort-fight, when our English Army was so numerous, and in pursuit of the Enemy, and so near as to take several and destroy them: and the Enemy in such distress for food, that our men might track them by their rooting in the earth for Ground-nuts, whilest they were flying for their lives. I say, that then our Army should want Provision, and be forced to leave their pursuit and return homeward: and the very next week the Enemy came upon our Town, like Bears bereft of their whelps, or so many ravenous Wolves, rending us and our Lambs to death. But what shall I say? God seemed to leave his People to themselves, and order all things for his own holy ends. *Shal there be evil in the City and the Lord hath not done it?*[54] *They are not grieved for the affliction of Joseph, therefore shal they go Captive, with the first that go Captive.*[55] It is the Lords doing, and it should be marvelous in our eyes.

2. I cannot but remember how the Indians derided the slowness, and dulness of the English Army, in its setting out. For after the desolations at Lancaster and Medfield, as I went along with them, they asked me when I thought the English Army would come after them? I told them I could not tell: It may be they will come in May, said they. Thus did they scoffe at us, as if the English would be a quarter of a year getting ready.

3. Which also I have hinted before, when the English Army with new supplies were sent forth to pursue after the enemy, and they understanding it, fled before them till they came to Baquaug River, where they forthwith went over safely; that that River should be impassable to the English. I can but admire to see the wonderfull providence of God in preserving the heathen for farther affliction to our poor Countrey. They could go in great numbers over, but the English must stop: God had an over-ruling hand in all those things.

4. It was thought, if their Corn were cut down, they would starve and dy with hunger: and all their Corn that could be found, was destroyed, and they driven from that little they had in store, into the Woods in the midst of Winter; and yet how to admiration did the Lord preserve them for his holy ends, and the destruction of many still amongst the English! strangely did the Lord provide for them; that I did not see (all the time I was among them) one Man, Woman, or Child, die with hunger.

Though many times they would eat that, that a Hog or a Dog would hardly touch; yet by that God strengthned them to be a scourge to his People.

The chief and commonest food was Ground-nuts: They eat also Nuts and Acorns, Harty-choaks,[56] Lilly roots, Ground-beans, and several other weeds and roots, that I know not.

They would pick up old bones, and cut them to pieces at the joynts, and if they were full of wormes and magots, they would scald them over the fire to make the vermine come out, and then boile them, and drink up the Liquor, and then beat the great ends of them in a Morter, and so eat them. They would eat Horses guts, and ears, and all sorts of wild Birds which they could catch: also Bear, Vennison, Beaver, Tortois, Frogs, Squirrels, Dogs, Skunks, Rattle-snakes; yea, the very Bark of Trees; besides all sorts of creatures, and provision which they plundered from the English. I can but stand in admiration to see the wonderful power of God, in providing for such a vast number of our Enemies in the Wilderness, where there was nothing to be

[54]Amos 3:6.
[55]Amos 6:6–7.
[56]The Jerusalem artichoke, which grows wild in North America.

seen, but from hand to mouth. Many times in a morning, the generality of them would eat up all they had, and yet have some forther supply against they wanted. It is said, Psal. 81. 13, 14. *Oh, that my People had hearkned to me, and Israel had walked in my wayes, I should soon have subdued their Enemies, and turned my hand against their Adversaries.* But now our perverse and evil carriages in the sight of the Lord, have so offended him, that instead of turning his hand against them, the Lord feeds and nourishes them up to be a scourge to the whole Land.

5. Another thing that I would observe is, the strange providence of God, in turning things about when the Indians was at the highest, and the English at the lowest. I was with the Enemy eleven weeks and five dayes, and not one Week passed without the fury of the Enemy, and some desolation by fire and sword upon one place or other. They mourned (with their black faces) for their own lossess, yet triumphed and rejoyced in their inhumane, and many times devilish cruelty to the English. They would boast much of their Victories; saying, that in two hours time they had destroyed such a Captain, and his Company at such a place; and such a Captain and his Company in such a place; and such a Captain and his Company in such a place: and boast how many Towns they had destroyed, and then scoffe, and say, They had done them a good turn, to send them to Heaven so soon. Again, they would say, This Summer that they would knock all the Rogues in the head, or drive them into the Sea, or make them flie the Countrey: thinking surely, Agag-like,[57] *The bitterness of Death is past.*[58] Now the Heathen begins to think all is their own, and the poor Christians hopes to fail (as to man) and now their eyes are more to God, and their hearts sigh heaven-ward: and to say in good earnest, *Help Lord, or we perish:* When the Lord had brought his people to this, that they saw no help in any thing but himself: then he takes the quarrel into his own hand: and though they had made a pit, in their own imaginations, as deep as hell for the Christians that Summer, yet the Lord hurll'd them selves into it. And the Lord had not so many wayes before to preserve them, but now he hath as many to destroy them.

But to return again to my going home, where we may see a remarkable change of Providence: At first they were all against it, except my Husband would come for me; but afterwards they assented to it, and seemed much to rejoyce in it; some askt me to send them some Bread, others some Tobacco, others shaking me by the hand, offering me a Hood and Scarfe to ride in; not one moving hand or tongue against it. Thus hath the Lord answered my poor desire, and the many earnest requests of others put up unto God for me. In my travels an Indian came to me, and told me, if I were willing, he and his Squaw would run away, and go home along with me: I told him No: I was not willing to run away, but desired to wait Gods time, that I might go home quietly, and without fear. And now God hath granted me my desire. O the wonderfull power of God that I have seen, and the experience that I have had: I have been in the midst of those roaring Lyons, and Salvage Bears, that feared neither God, nor Man, nor the Devil, by night and day, alone and in company: sleeping all sorts together, and yet not one of them ever offered me the least abuse of unchastity to me, in word or action. Though some are ready to say, I speak it for my own credit; But I speak it in the presence of God, and to his Glory. Gods Power is as great now, and

[57]King of Amalek; defeated by Saul and thought himself spared but was slain instead by Samuel.

[58]I Samuel 15:32.

as sufficient to save, as when he preserved Daniel in the Lions Den: or the three Children in the fiery Furnace. I may well say as his Psal. 107. 12, *Oh give thanks unto the Lord for he is good, for his mercy endureth for ever.*[59] Let the Redeemed of the Lord say so, whom he hath redeemed from the hand of the Enemy, especially that I should come away in the midst of so many hundreds of Enemies quietly and peacably, and not a Dog moving his tongue. So I took my leave of them, and in coming along my heart melted into tears, more then all the while I was with them, and I was almost swallowed up with the thoughts that ever I should go home again. About the Sun going down, Mr. Hoar, and my self, and the two Indians came to Lancaster, and a solemn sight it was to me. There had I lived many comfortable years amongst my Relations and Neighbours, and now not one Christian to be seen, nor one house left standing. We went on to a Farm house that was yet standing, where we lay all night: and a comfortable lodging we had, though nothing but straw to ly on. The Lord preserved us in safety that night, and raised us up again in the morning, and carried us along, that before noon, we came to Concord. Now was I full of joy, and yet not without sorrow: joy to see such a lovely sight, so many Christians together, and some of them my Neighbours: There I met with my Brother, and my Brother in Law, who asked me, if I knew where his Wife was? Poor heart! he had helped to bury her, and knew it not; she being shot down by the house was partly burnt: so that those who were at Boston at the desolation of the Town, and came back afterward, and buried the dead, did not know her. Yet I was not without sorrow, to think how many were looking and longing, and my own Children amongst the rest, to enjoy that deliverance that I had now received, and I did not know whither ever I should see them again. Being recruited with food and raiment we went to Boston that day, where I met with my dear Husband, but the thoughts of our dear Children, one being dead, and the other we could not tell where, abated our comfort each to other. I was not before so much hem'd in with the merciless and cruel Heathen, but now as much with pittiful, tender-hearted and compassionate Christians. In that poor, and destressed, and beggerly condition I was received in, I was kindly entertained in severall Houses: so much love I received from several (some of whom I knew, and others I knew not) that I am not capable to declare it. But the Lord knows them all by name: The Lord reward them seven fold into their bosoms of his spirituals, for their temporals. The twenty pounds the price of my redemption was raised by some Boston Gentlemen, and Mrs. Usher, whose bounty and religious charity, I would not forget to make mention of. Then Mr. Thomas Shepard of Charlstown received us into his House, where we continued eleven weeks; and a Father and Mother they were to us. And many more tender-hearted Friends we met with in that place. We were now in the midst of love, yet not without much and frequent heaviness of heart for our poor Children, and other Relations, who were still in affliction. The week following, after my coming in, the Governour and Council sent forth to the Indians again; and that not without success; for they brought in my Sister, and Good-wife Kettle: Their not knowing where our Children were, was a sore tryal to us still, and yet we were not without secret hopes that we should see them again. That which was dead lay heavier upon my spirit, than those which were alive and amongst the Heathen; thinking how it suffered with its wounds, and I was no way able to relieve it; and how it was buried by the Heathen in the Wilderness from among all Christians. We were

[59]Daniel 3:13–30.

hurried up and down in our thoughts, sometime we should hear a report that they were gone this way, and sometimes that; and that they were come in, in this place or that: We kept enquiring and listning to hear concerning them, but no certain news as yet. About this time the Council had ordered a day a publick Thanks-giving:[60] though I thought I had still cause of mourning, and being unsettled in our minds, we thought we would ride toward the Eastward, to see if we could hear any thing concerning our Children. And as we were riding along (God is the wise disposer of all things) between Ipswich and Rowly we met with Mr. William Hubbard, who told us that our Son Joseph was come in to Major Waldrens, and another with him, which was my Sisters Son. I asked him how he knew it? He said, the Major himself told him so. So along we went till we came to Newbury; and their Minister being absent, they desired my Husband to Preach the Thanks giving for them; but he was not willing to stay there that night, but would go over to Salisbury, to hear further, and come again in the morning; which he did, and Preached there that day. At night, when he had done, one came and told him that his Daughter was come in at Providence: Here was mercy on both hands: Now hath God fulfiled that precious Scripture which was such a comfort to me in my distressed condition. When my heart was ready to sink into the Earth (my Children being gone I could not tell whither) and my knees trembled under me, And I was walking through the valley of the shadow of Death: Then the Lord brought, and now has fulfilled that reviving word unto me: *Thus saith the Lord, Refrain thy voice from weeping, and thine eyes from tears, for thy Work shall be rewarded, saith the Lord, and they sall come again from the Land of the Enemy.*[61] Now we were between them, the one on the East, and the other on the West: Our Son being nearest, we went to him first, to Portsmouth, where we met with him, and with the Major also: who told us he had done what he could, but could not redeem him under seven pounds; which the good People thereabouts were pleased to pay. The Lord reward the Major, and all the rest, though unknown to me, for their labour of Love. My Sisters Son was redeemed for four pounds, which the Council gave order for the payment of. Having now received one of our Children, we hastened toward the other; going back through Newbury, my Husband preached there on the Sabbath-day: for which they rewarded him many fold.

On Munday we came to Charlstown, where we heard that the Governour of Road-Island had sent over for our Daughter, to take care of her, being now within his Jurisdiction: which should not pass without our acknowledgments. But she being nearer Rehoboth than Road-Island, Mr. Newman went over, and took care of her, and brought her to his own House. And the goodness of God was admirable to us in our low estate, in that he raised up passionate[62] Friends on every side to us, when we had nothing to recompance any for their love. The Indians were now gone that way, that it was apprehended dangerous to go to her: But the Carts which carried Provision to the English Army, being guarded, brought her with them to Dorchester, where we received her safe: blessed be the Lord for it, For great is his Power, and he can do whatsoever seemeth him good. Her coming in was after this manner: She was travelling one day with the Indians, with her basket at her back; the company of Indians were got before her, and gone out of sight, all except one Squaw; she followed

[60]June 29, 1676.
[61]Jeremiah 31:16.
[62]Compassionate.

the Squaw till night, and then both of them lay down, having nothing over them but the heavens, and under them but the earth. Thus she travelled three dayes together, not knowing whither she was going: having nothing to eat or drink but water, and green Hirtle-berries.[63] At last they came into Providence, where she was kindly entertained by several of that Town. The Indians often said, that I should never have her under twenty pounds: But now the Lord hath brought her in upon free-cost, and given her to me the second time. The Lord make us a blessing indeed, each to others. Now have I seen that Scripture also fulfilled, Deut. 30:4, 7. *If any of thine be driven out to the outmost parts of heaven, from thence will the Lord thy God gather thee, and from thence will he fetch thee. And the Lord thy God will put all these curses upon thine enemies, and on them which hate thee, which persecuted thee.* Thus hath the Lord brought me and mine out of that horrible pit, and hath set us in the midst of tender-hearted and compassionate Christians. It is the desire of my soul, that we may walk worthy of the mercies received, and which we are receiving.

Our Family being now gathered together (those of us that were living) the South Church in Boston hired an House for us: Then we removed from Mr. Shepards, those cordial Friends, and went to Boston, where we continued about three quarters of a year: Still the Lord went along with us, and provided graciously for us. I thought it somewhat strange to set up House-keeping with bare walls; but as Solomon sayes, *Mony answers all things,*[64] and that we had through the benevolence of Christian-friends, some in this Town, and some in that, and others: And some from England, that in a little time we might look, and see the House furnished with love. The Lord hath been exceeding good to us in our low estate, in that when we had neither house nor home, nor other necessaries; the Lord so moved the hearts of these and those towards us, that we wanted neither food, nor raiment for our selves or ours, Prov. 18. 24. *There is a Friend which sticketh closer than a Brother.* And how many such Friends have we found, and now living amongst? And truly such a Friend have we found him to be unto us, in whose house we lived, *viz.* Mr. James Whitcomb, a Friend unto us near hand, and afar off.

I can remember the time, when I used to sleep quietly without workings in my thoughts, whole nights together, but now it is other wayes with me. When all are fast about me, and no eye open, but his who ever waketh, my thoughts are upon things past, upon the awfull dispensation of the Lord towards us; upon his wonderfull power and might, in carrying of us through so many difficulties, in returning us in safety, and suffering none to hurt us. I remember in the night season, how the other day I was in the midst of thousands of enemies, and nothing but death before me: It is then hard work to perswade my self, that ever I should be satisfied with bread again. But now we are fed with the finest of the Wheat, and, as I may say, With honey out of the rock:[65] In stead of the Husk, we have the fatted Calf.[66] The thoughts of these things in the particulars of them, and of the love and goodness of God towards us, make it true of me, what David said of himself, Psal. 6. 5.[67] *I watered my Couch with my tears.* Oh! the wonderfull power of God that mine eyes have seen, affording matter enough for my thoughts to run in, that when others are sleeping mine eyes are weeping.

[63]Huckleberries.
[64]Ecclesiastes 10:19.
[65]Psalm 81:16.
[66]Luke 15:23.
[67]Psalm 6:6.

I have seen the extrem vanity of this World: One hour I have been in health, and wealth, wanting nothing: But the next hour in sickness and wounds, and death, having nothing but sorrow and affliction.

Before I knew what affliction meant, I was ready sometimes to wish for it. When I lived in prosperity, having the comforts of the World about me, my relations by me, my Heart chearfull, and taking little care for any thing; and yet seeing many, whom I preferred before my self, under many tryals and afflictions, in sickness, weakness, poverty, losses, crosses, and cares of the World, I should be sometimes jealous least I should have my portion in this life, and that Scripture would come to my mind. Heb. 12. 6 *For whom the Lord loveth he chasteneth, and scourgeth every Son whom he receiveth.* But now I see the Lord had his time to scourge and chasten me. The portion of some is to have their afflictions by drops, now one drop and then another; but the dregs of the Cup, the Wine of astonishment, like a sweeping rain that leaveth no food, did the Lord prepare to be my portion. Affliction I wanted, and affliction I had, full measure (I thought) pressed down and running over; yet I see, when God calls a Person to any thing, and through never so many difficulties, yet he is fully able to carry them through and make them see, and say they have been gainers thereby. And I hope I can say in some measure, As David did, *It is good for me that I have been afflicted.* The Lord hath shewed me the vanity of these outward things. That they are the Vanity of vanities, and vexation of spirit; that they are but a shadow, a blast, a bubble, and things of no continuance. That we must rely on God himself, and our whole dependance must be upon him. If trouble from smaller matters begin to arise in me, I have something at hand to check my self with, and say, why am I troubled? It was but the other day that if I had had the world, I would have given it for my freedom, or to have been a Servant to a Christian. I have learned to look beyond present and smaller troubles, and to be quieted under them, as Moses said, Exod. 14. 13. *Stand still and see the salvation of the Lord.*

1682

Edward Taylor 1642?–1729

Celebrated today as colonial America's most prolific and inventive poet, Edward Taylor was virtually unpublished in his lifetime. Not until the twentieth century did Thomas Johnson unearth Taylor's long-buried manuscripts at the Yale University Library and in 1937 publish the first selections from Taylor's *Preparatory Meditations* (1682–1725) and *Gods Determinations touching his Elect* (c. 1680). These collections revealed Taylor to be a frontier parson with a secret passion for the confessional lyrics and versified theological allegories popular among seventeenth-century English poets and clerics. Despite Taylor's prominence as minister of the Congregational Church in Westfield for fifty-eight years until his death on June 24, 1729, details of his life remain rudimentary.

Most likely born in 1642 in Sketchley, Leicestershire, England, the son of a yeoman farmer, Taylor often adopts quaint colloquialisms and the imagery of provincial farming and weaving in his later poems. According to great-grandson Henry Wyllys Taylor's family memoir (1848), Taylor studied at Cambridge University, although certain proof is lacking. As a

Protestant dissenter, he was buoyed by Oliver Cromwell's Puritan Commonwealth (1649–1660), but after the Restoration under Charles II, his refusal to sign the 1662 Act of Uniformity probably prevented Taylor from teaching school, worshiping, or pursuing a licensed clerical career. His earliest verse and later sermons virulently satirize "Popish" and Anglican worship as well as other heresies (such as Quakerism) that threatened an orthodox Calvinist theology and congregational polity.

Brimming with nautical observations, Taylor's *Diary* (1668–1671) catalogs his Atlantic crossing, from the April 26, 1668, departure to his safe deliverance on July 5 in the Massachusetts Bay Colony. After conferring with President Charles Chauncy, he entered Harvard University on July 23 as an upperclassman, where he served two years as college butler and was chamberfellow with diarist Samuel Sewall, a lifelong friend and correspondent. When he departed on November 27, 1671, for Westfield, Taylor journeyed, "not without much apprehension," through the Connecticut Valley's rugged forests. Despite his fears, Taylor settled energetically into his multiple roles as farmer, rural physician, and minister to a frequently endangered band of the pioneering Puritan elect, who were called to Sabbath worship by "beat of drum." After delays occasioned by Indian warfare and other early hardships, the first church at Westfield was formally organized on August 27, 1679. The gathering of local elders and neighboring clergy included Northampton's Solomon Stoddard, with whom Taylor would later split bitterly over differences in administering the Lord's Supper. Delivered on this occasion, Taylor's spiritual "Relation" and his "Foundation Day Sermon," now in the Westfield *Church Records,* are among his earliest extant prose writings. As penitent sinner, Taylor recounts his personal conversion and acceptance of God's grace, and as community preacher, he leads his congregation to the founding of a "Particular Church" over which he would preside for another fifty years as spiritual guide, disciplinary statesman, and piously learned theologian.

Although Taylor wrote several *pro forma* funeral elegies for public figures and a verse declamation defending the English language, these early literary efforts (1668–1671) were somberly pedantic exercises. But in his next attempts at occasional verse (1674–1683), he sought for more varied lyrical forms: acrostics and love poems to his wife-to-be, miniature allegories on insects or domestic objects, as in "Huswifery," and spiritualized contemplations of natural "occurants," such as "The Ebb & Flow." Among the most moving poems is the anguished pathos of "Upon Wedlock, & Death of Children" (1682?). On November 5, 1674, Taylor married Elizabeth Fitch, who bore him eight children, five of whom died in infancy; his second wife (1692), Ruth Wyllys, produced six children. With its heart-wrenching revelation of how premature death tests one's submission to God's will, "Upon Wedlock, & Death of Children" resembles the elegies of Anne Bradstreet, whose 1678 second edition of poems Taylor owned. His 1689 funeral elegy for Elizabeth Fitch, "My Onely Dove," echoes, though not without "Gust of Sorrows groan," the customary eulogistic praise for a Puritan woman as "Mistriss, Mother, Wife." During this early period, Taylor also inaugurated his first version (1674–1675) of metrical paraphrases of the Psalms (1–9, 18). He transcribed a second version, of virtually all different Psalms (11–39, 48–49), during the early 1680s. The paraphrases are a self-conscious tutorial in versification, imitative of the English Sternhold-Hopkins psalter and the Massachusetts *Bay Psalm Book.* In the occasional poems as well as Psalm paraphrases, Taylor's distinctive meditative voice begins to emerge, perhaps as a result of his identification with David's gift of hymn-like poesy or the inspiration of "occurant" contemplations.

During the late 1670s and early 1680s, Taylor also brought together his vision of Christian salvation history with varied verse experiments to create his first major poem, *Gods Determinations touching his Elect: and The Elects Combat in their Conversion, and Coming up to God in Christ together with the Comfortable Effects thereof.* Having imaginatively re-enacted God's "Glorious Handywork" of cosmic creation and the debate between Justice and Mercy over humankind's destiny, the collection of thirty-five poems traces Christ's combat with Satan for three ranks of elect human souls, then culminates with the redeemed "Saints'" final joyful acceptance of "Church Fellowship Rightly Attended." Taylor's own ministerial "warfare" to rescue his Westfield flock from Indian attacks and second-generation backsliding would have been a likely stimulus, as well as a need to maintain doctrinal purity by admitting only regenerate converts to the church and Lord's Supper. Critics today often praise Taylor's occasional lyrics because they appeal to post-romantic sensibilities, but the formally didactic history of spiritual combat was commonplace in an age that valued plain-style rationality and in which Taylor might turn for models to John Milton's *Paradise Lost,* John Bunyan's *The Holy War,* Michael Wigglesworth's *The Day of Doom,* and countless sermons and tracts.

Whether inspired by his occasional verse or the patterned deliberateness of the Psalm paraphrases and *Gods Determinations,* Taylor inaugurated in 1682 the *Preparatory Meditations before my Approach to the Lords Supper,* two extended series of 217 poems—and his greatest artistic achievement. Generally composed after he had drafted a sermon or preaching notes, the poems are private meditations, "Chiefly upon the Doctrin preached upon the Day of administration," in which Taylor applies to his own soul lessons gleaned from the sacrament day's Biblical text, which doubles as the poem's title. Like *The Temple* (1633) by Anglican George Herbert, with whom Taylor is most often compared, the *Preparatory Meditations* belongs to a tradition of meditative writing in verse and prose. Taylor's purpose is self-examination, to root out sins that infect his soul and to cultivate instead a heart receptive to God's sweet grace and readied to hymn "New Psalms on Davids Harpe to thee."

As a preacher and Puritan, debased by his human condition, Taylor felt spiritually unworthy of God's grace. His poetic petitions to God and Christ serve as ritualized cathartic cleansings and as twofold preparations of the soul: first, for the imminent preaching of God's Word to his Westfield congregation and administering of the Lord's Supper; second, as a saint's lifelong preparation for the heavenly union with Christ. As the *Treatise Concerning the Lord's Supper* (1693–1694) indicates, Taylor reacted vehemently against Solomon Stoddard's liberalizing doctrine that permitted all church members to partake of the Lord's Supper as a "converting ordinance." By contrast, Taylor demanded an "Evangelicall Preparation"; those desiring to partake of the Lord's Supper were expected to make a prior spiritual relation of conversion and, by practicing "prayer, meditation, and self-examination," to cultivate a proper "festival frame of spirit." Meditation, therefore, provided a means for examining the heart and for contemplating the feast's benefits, mainly its nature as a covenant seal and commemoration of Christ's sacrifice.

But these poems also became Taylor's private spiritual diary, a preparation not merely for his own earthly Supper, but for the eternal feast at which Taylor, like the heavenly angels, would be wed as a "Loving Spouse" to the Bridegroom Christ forever. Not surprisingly, the second series of meditations evolves thematically from Old Testament types (1–30) that foreshadow Christ, then focuses on New Testament Christology (2.42–56) and the Supper (2.102–111), and culminates with a twelve-year study of Canticles (2.115–165). The

Song of Solomon was regarded as one of the Bible's most poetic books and a clearly predictive allegory of Christ's promised marriage with the redeemed church and saints. With its lavishly sensuous metaphors of feasts, gardens, lovers' wooing, anatomized beauties, and marital union, it might also have been Taylor's own visionary preparation for death. After suffering a severe illness in 1720, he composed three versions of "A Valediction to all the World preparatory for Death 3^d^ of the 11^m^ 1720" (January 1721) and two variants of "A Fig for thee Oh! Death," which in their renouncing of earth's splendors and defying of death's terrors complement the heavenly visions of the final Canticles poems.

Although Taylor's reputation will undoubtedly rest upon the *Preparatory Meditations,* these poems account for a mere twenty-five percent of the output from an immensely imaginative mind that also produced twenty thousand lines of *A Metrical History of Christianity.* But the plethora of Psalm and Job paraphrases, elegies, acrostics, love poems, allegorical histories, meditations, and occasional lyrics, written during a lifetime spent in New England, give ample proof that the wilderness frontier did not deaden but instead nourished Taylor's latent poetic talent. Taylor's themes are sin inherited from Adam's fall and salvation in which Christ's curative mercy tempers God's justice; God's providential design that makes history a script for redemption; the Old Testament's predictive typology fulfilled in the New Testament; the Lord's Supper as a spiritual commemoration of Christ's body and blood; and the Supper as a mere shadow of the eternal marriage feast to come.

Taylor inherited an exegetical and poetic tradition that was rooted in the Calvinist belief in the literal text and sole authority of Scripture as God's Word, from which spiritual meanings might be drawn only within strict frameworks of prudent interpretation. He struggles rebelliously against the limits of a fallen language and "Goose quill-slabbred draughts," so inadequate to the divine subject that demands a "Transcendent style." But, through the repeated task of poetic composition and soul-searching examination, he underscores his desire to perfect both faith and art. Even though they were not published, the care with which Taylor transcribed the minor poems, *Gods Determinations,* and the *Preparatory Meditations* into four hundred manuscript pages of the leather-bound "Poetical Works" suggests his intent to preserve these poetic offerings. For the modern reader, they are a truly rare find, from a man described by his grandson Ezra Stiles as "of quick passions, yet serious and grave. Exemplary in piety, and for a very sacred observance of the Lord's day," but only long after his death known as New England's premier poet.

Karen E. Rowe
University of California at Los Angeles

PRIMARY WORKS

The Poetical Works of Edward Taylor, ed. Thomas H. Johnson, 1939; *The Poems of Edward Taylor,* ed. Donald E. Stanford, 1960, abridged edition 1963, rpt. 1989; *Edward Taylor's Christographia,* ed. Norman S. Grabo, 1962; *A Transcript of Edward Taylor's Metrical History of Christianity,* ed. Donald E. Stanford, 1962, rpt. 1977; *The Diary of Edward Taylor,* ed. Francis Murphy, 1964; *Edward Taylor's Treatise Concerning the Lord's Supper,* ed. Norman S. Grabo, 1965; *The Unpublished Writings of Edward Taylor;* vol. 1, *Edward Taylor's "Church Records" and Related Sermons;* vol. 2, *Edward Taylor vs. Solomon Stoddard: The Nature of the Lord's Supper;* vol. 3, *Edward Taylor's Minor Poetry,* ed. Thomas M. and Virginia L. Davis, 1981; *Harmony of the Gospels,* 4 vols., ed. Thomas M. and Virginia L. Davis, 1983; *Upon the Types of the Old Testament,* 2 vols., ed. Charles W. Mignon, 1989.

from Gods Determinations[1]

The Preface

Infinity, when all things it beheld
In Nothing, and of Nothing all did build,
Upon what Base was fixt the Lath, wherein
He turn'd this Globe, and riggalld[2] it so trim?
Who blew the Bellows of his Furnace Vast?
Or held the Mould wherein the world was Cast?
Who laid its Corner Stone?[3] Or whose Command?
Where stand the Pillars upon which it stands?
Who Lac'de and Fillitted[4] the earth so fine,
With Rivers like green Ribbons Smaragdine?[5]
Who made the Sea's its Selvedge,[6] and it locks
Like a Quilt Ball[7] within a Silver Box?
Who Spread its Canopy? Or Curtains Spun?
Who in this Bowling Alley bowld the Sun?
Who made it always when it rises set
To go at once both down, and up to get?
Who th'Curtain rods made for this Tapistry?
Who hung the twinckling Lanthorns in the Sky?
Who? who did this? or who is he? Why, know
Its Onely Might Almighty this did doe.
His hand hath made this noble worke which Stands
His Glorious Handywork not made by hands.
Who spake all things from nothing; and with ease
Can speake all things to nothing, if he please.
Whose Little finger at his pleasure Can
Out mete[8] ten thousand worlds with halfe a Span:

[1]Taylor's "debate" sequence of thirty-five poems explores the human soul's progress from the world's creation and fall of man to the redemption of Christian souls through Christ's crucifixion. Christ's mercy triumphs over justice—the punishment that man deserves for his disobedience—and the soul is finally carried to heaven to share in the joys of the Resurrection. The complete title of the sequence is *Gods Determinations touching his Elect: and The Elects Combat in their Conversion, and Coming up to God in Christ together with the Comfortable Effects thereof* (probably completed about 1680; transcribed in final form in 1681–1682). Text is from Stanford, ed., *Poems.*

[2]Verb from the noun *riggal,* a ring-like mark, or a groove in wood or stone.

[3]See Job 38:4–11.

[4]Filleted, bound, or girded as with an ornamental band or material strip.

[5]Consisting of a smaragd (precious bright green stone); of an emerald green.

[6]Border of woven material to prevent unraveling.

[7]Treasured pincushions, exquisitely decorated with needlework, even laced with silver thread and green silk, were kept in boxes; stuffed ball cushions covered with salvaged embroidered fabric could be suspended from the girdle.

[8]To measure out; apportion; the noun means a boundary mark or line, a limit.

Whose Might Almighty can by half a looks
Root up the rocks and rock the hills by th'roots.
Can take this mighty World up in his hande,
And shake it like a Squitchen[9] or a Wand.[10]
Whose single Frown will make the Heavens shake
Like as an aspen leafe the Winde makes quake.
Oh! what a might is this Whose single frown
Doth shake the world as it would shake it down?[11]
Which All from Nothing fet,[12] from Nothing, All:
Hath All on Nothing set, lets Nothing fall.
Gave All to nothing Man indeed, whereby
Through nothing man all might him Glorify.
In Nothing then imbosst the brightest Gem
More pretious than all pretiousness in them.
But Nothing man did throw down all by Sin:
And darkened that lightsom Gem in him.
 That now his Brightest Diamond is grown
 Darker by far than any Coalpit Stone.

c. 1680 1939

The Souls Groan to Christ for Succour

Good Lord, behold this Dreadfull Enemy
 Who makes me tremble with his fierce assaults,
I dare not trust, yet feare to give the ly,
 For in my soul, my soul finds many faults.
 And though I justify myselfe to's face:
 I do Condemn myselfe before thy Grace.

He strives to mount my sins, and them advance
 Above thy Merits, Pardons, or Good Will
Thy Grace to lessen, and thy Wrath t'inhance
 As if thou couldst not pay the sinners bill.
 He Chiefly injures thy rich Grace, I finde
 Though I confess my heart to sin inclin'de.

Those Graces which thy Grace enwrought in mee,
 He makes as nothing but a pack of Sins.

[9]Altered form of quitch, a species of couch-grass or weed, or a variant of escutcheon, a shield depicting a coat of arms.

[10]A walking cane, young sapling, switch, sceptre, or ceremonial staff.

[11]Earthquakes rocked England in 1661, April 3, 1668 (twenty-three days before Taylor's departure), 1678, and 1680, and were often read as providential signs of God's power and judgment.

[12]Fetch, to bring from a distance, in a sweeping movement; to summon by force.

He maketh Grace no grace, but Crueltie,
Is Graces Honey Comb, a Comb of Stings?
This makes me ready leave thy Grace and run.
Which if I do, I finde I am undone.

I know he is thy Cur,[1] therefore I bee
Perplexed lest I from thy Pasture stray.
He bayghs, and barks so veh'mently at mee.
Come rate[2] this Cur, Lord, breake his teeth I pray.
Remember me I humbly pray thee first.
Then halter up this Cur that is so Curst.

c. 1680 1939

Christs Reply

Peace, Peace, my Hony, do not Cry,
My Little Darling, wipe thine eye,
Oh Cheer, Cheer up, come see.
Is anything too deare, my Dove,[1]
Is anything too good, my Love
To get or give for thee?

If in the severall[2] thou art
This Yelper fierce will at thee bark:
That thou art mine this shows.
As Spot barks back the sheep again
Before they to the Pound[3] are ta'ne,
So he and hence 'way goes.

But yet this Cur that bayghs so sore
Is broken tootht, and muzzled sure,
Fear not, my Pritty Heart.
His barking is to make thee Cling
Close underneath thy Saviours Wing.
Why did my sweeten start?

[1]A worthless, low-bred, or snappish dog.
[2]To scold or rebuke angrily or violently.
[1]See Song of Solomon 2:10–14, 5:2, 6:9, where Solomon's love for the Shulamite maiden, his bride and Dove, serves as a figure for God's love of Israel and an allegory of Christ's love for His heavenly Bride, the individual soul, and the Church.
[2]Privately owned land, especially enclosed pastures not held in common; divided, existing apart, hence the soul is torn between Christ and the Devil.
[3]Enclosure to shelter sheep or cattle.

And if he run an inch too far,
I'le Check his Chain, and rate the Cur.
My Chick, keep clost to mee.
The Poles shall sooner kiss, and greet[4]
And Paralells shall sooner meet
Than thou shalt harmed bee.

He seeks to aggrivate thy sin
And screw[5] them to the highest pin,[6]
To make thy faith to quaile.
Yet mountain Sins like mites should show
And then these mites for naught should goe
Could he but once prevaile.

I smote thy sins upon the Head.[7]
They Dead'ned are, though not quite dead:
And shall not rise again.
I'l put away the Guilt thereof,
And purge its Filthiness cleare off:
My Blood doth out the stain.

And though thy judgment was remiss
Thy Headstrong Will too Wilfull is.
I will Renew the same.
And though thou do too frequently
Offend as heretofore hereby
I'l not severly blaim.

And though thy senses do inveagle
Thy Noble Soul to tend the Beagle,
That t'hunt her games forth go.
I'le Lure her back to me, and Change
Those fond[8] Affections that do range
As yelping beagles doe.

Although thy sins increase their race,
And though when thou hast sought for Grace,
Thou fallst more than before
If thou by true Repentence Rise,

[4]See George Herbert's "The Search," lines 41–44.

[5]To torture by means of a thumbscrew; figuratively, to extort by moral or physical pressure.

[6]A tuning peg for regulating the tension of a stringed musical instrument; a figure applied also to the torture rack.

[7]See Genesis 3:15. After Adam and Eve commit the original sin, God curses their tempter, the serpent (Satan or the Devil), and prophesies that the seed of woman, Christ, through his death and resurrection, will bruise the serpent's head, thereby vanquishing sin, death, and Satan forever (Revelation 12:9).

[8]Foolish.

And Faith makes me thy Sacrifice,
  I'l pardon all, though more.

Though Satan strive to block thy way
By all his Stratagems he may:
  Come, come though through the fire.
For Hell that Gulph of fire for sins,
Is not so hot as t'burn thy Shins.
  Then Credit not the Lyar.

Those Cursed Vermin Sins that Crawle
All ore thy Soul, both Greate, and small
  Are onely Satans own:
Which he in his Malignity
Unto thy Souls true Sanctity
  In at the doors hath thrown.

And though they be Rebellion high,
Ath'ism[9] or Apostacy:[10]
  Though blasphemy it bee:
Unto what Quality, or Sise
Excepting one, so e're it rise.
  Repent, I'le pardon thee.

Although thy Soule was once a Stall
Rich hung with Satans nicknacks all;
  If thou Repent thy Sin,
A Tabernacle in't I'le place
Fild with Gods Spirit, and his Grace.
  Oh Comfortable thing!

I dare the World therefore to show
A God like me, to anger slow:
  Whose wrath is full of Grace.
Doth hate all Sins both Greate, and small:
Yet when Repented, pardons all.
  Frowns with a Smiling Face.

As for thy outward Postures each,
Thy Gestures, Actions, and thy Speech,
  I Eye and Eying spare,

[9]Disbelief in the existence of deity and rejection of all religious faith and practice.

[10]Apostasy, or renouncing of a religious faith. Though the term essentially implies total abandonment of what one has religiously professed (*i.e.,* faith in Christ) as opposed to mere heresy or schism, for the Puritan it meant mankind's rebellion against God's decrees and, consequently, his fall and ruin.

If thou repent. My Grace is more
Ten thousand times still tribled ore
Than thou canst want, or ware.

As for the Wicked Charge he makes,
That he of Every Dish first takes
Of all thy holy things.
Its false, deny the same, and say,
That which he had he stool away
Out of thy Offerings.[11]

Though to thy Griefe, poor Heart, thou finde
In Pray're too oft a wandring minde,
In Sermons Spirits dull.
Though faith in firy furnace[12] flags,
And Zeale in Chilly Seasons lags.
Temptations powerfull.

These faults are his, and none of thine
So far as thou dost them decline.
Come then receive my Grace.
And when he buffits thee therefore
If thou my aid, and Grace implore
I'le shew a pleasant face.

But still look for Temptations Deep,
Whilst that thy Noble Sparke doth keep
Within a Mudwald Cote.
These White Frosts and the Showers that fall
Are but to whiten thee withall.
Not rot the Web they smote.

If in the fire where Gold is tride
Thy Soule is put, and purifide
Wilt thou lament thy loss?
If silver-like this fire refine
Thy Soul and make it brighter shine:
Wilt thou bewaile the Dross?

[11]The Israelites made sacrificial offerings to God of the first fruits of their labor (grain or animals) as a holy gift of worship and an expiation for sins, expressing the desire for God's purification and forgiveness. Christ here accuses Satan of having taken from Adam and Eve, hence all mankind, the bounty of Eden out of which our first parents might provide offerings of praise and thanksgiving to God.

[12]See Daniel 3 for the account of Shadrach, Meshach, and Abednego in the fiery furnace.

Oh! fight my Field: no Colours fear:
I'l be thy Front, I'l be thy reare.
Fail not: my Battells fight.
Defy the Tempter, and his Mock.
Anchor thy heart on mee thy Rock.[13]
I do in thee Delight.

c. 1680 1939

The Joy of Church Fellowship rightly attended[1]

In Heaven soaring up, I dropt an Eare
On Earth: and oh! sweet Melody:
And listening, found it was the Saints[2] who were
Encoacht for Heaven that sang for Joy.
For in Christs Coach they sweetly sing;
As they to Glory ride therein.

Oh! joyous hearts! Enfir'de with holy Flame!
Is speech thus tassled[3] with praise?
Will not your inward fire of Joy contain;
That it in open flames doth blaze?
For in Christ's Coach Saints sweetly sing,
As they to Glory ride therein.

And if a string do slip, by Chance, they soon
Do screw it up[4] again: whereby
They set it in a more melodious Tune
And a Diviner Harmony.
For in Christs Coach they sweetly sing
As they to Glory ride therein.

In all their Acts, publick, and private, nay
And secret too, they praise impart.
But in their Acts Divine and Worship, they
With Hymns do offer up their Heart.

[13]See Exodus 17:6. The Rock of Horeb becomes a type of Christ the Rock (I Corinthians 10:4), smitten so that the spirit of life flows from Him to all who drink. In Matthew 16:18 and I Peter 2:4–8, Christ and his disciples, especially Peter, are referred to as the rock (*petra,* or massive rock) or cornerstone upon which the Church is built.

[1]This is the final poem in *Gods Determinations,* in which Taylor visualizes the redeemed saints entering into Church fellowship, meaning the Church on earth (the coach) which also foreshadows the saints' journey after death and the eternal fellowship after Christ's Second Coming and the Final Judgment.

[2]The "visible Saints," who were church members when alive.

[3]Tasselled, or adorned with a tassel.

[4]To tighten or adjust tuning pegs regulating the tension or pitch of a string on a musical instrument.

Thus in Christs Coach they sweetly sing
As they to Glory ride therein.

Some few not in; and some whose Time, and Place
Block up this Coaches way do goe
As Travellers afoot, and so do trace
The Road that gives them right thereto
While in this Coach these sweetly sing
As they to Glory ride therein.

c. 1680 1937

from Occasional Poems[1]

4. *Huswifery*[1]

Make mee, O Lord, thy Spining Wheele compleat.
Thy Holy Words my Distaff make for mee.
Make mine Affections thy Swift Flyers neate
And make my Soule thy holy Spoole to bee.
My Conversation make to be thy Reele
And reele the yarn there on Spun of thy Wheele.[2]

Make me thy Loome then, knit therein this Twine:
And make thy Holy Spirit, Lord, winde quills:[3]
Then weave the Web thyselfe. The yarn is fine.
Thine Ordinances make my Fulling Mills.[4]
Then dy the same in Heavenly Colours Choice,
All pinkt[5] with Varnisht Flowers of Paradise.

[1]What remains in the "Poetical Works" manuscript is a torn fragment of the heading "*** occurrants occasioning what follow" that introduces a section of eight numbered poems, probably copied in the early 1680s. Allegorizations of natural events, or what Taylor calls "occurants," was common among Puritan theologians and writers. Texts are from Davis and Davis, eds., *Minor Poetry.*

[1]The function or province of a woman (usually married) who manages household affairs, often with skill and thrift. Taylor's "huswifery," or housekeeping, here means weaving more particularly and alludes to a linen cloth between fine and coarse for family uses.

[2]In this stanza Taylor refers to the parts of a spinning wheel: the distaff holds the flax or raw wool; flyers control the spinning; the spool or spindle twists the yarn; and the reel takes up the finished thread.

[3]To wind thread or yarn on a quill, *i.e.,* a bobbin, spool, or spindle.

[4]A mill in which cloth is beaten with wooden mallets and cleansed with fuller's earth or soap. To "full" also means to shrink and thicken woolen cloth by moistening, heating, and pressing.

[5]Ornamented by cutting or punching eyelet-holes, figures, or letters; said of flounces, frills, ribbons, which have raw edges cut into scallops, jags, or narrow points.

Then cloath therewith mine Understanding, Will,
Affections, Judgment, Conscience, Memory
My Words, & Actions, that their Shine may fill
My wayes with glory and thee glorify.
Then mine apparell shall display before yee
That I am Cloathd in Holy robes for glory.

c. 1682–83 1937

6. *Upon Wedlock, & Death of Children*[1]

A Curious Knot[2] God made in Paradise,
And drew it out inamled neatly Fresh.
It was the True-Love Knot, more Sweet than spice
And Set with all the flowres of Graces dress.
Its Weddens Knot, that ne're can be unti'de.
No Alexanders Sword[3] can it divide.

The Slips[4] here planted, gay & glorious grow:
Unless an Hellish breath do sindge their Plumes.
Here Primrose, Cowslips, Roses, Lilies blow,[5]
With Violets & Pinkes that voide perfumes.
Whose beautious leaves ore lai'd with Hony Dew.
And Chanting birds Cherp out sweet Musick true.

When in this Knot I planted was, my Stock
Soon knotted, & a manly flower out brake.[6]
And after it my branch again did knot
Brought out another Flowre its Sweet breathd mate.[7]
One knot gave one tother the tothers place.
Whence Checkling[8] Smiles fought in each others face.

[1]Stanzas 5 and 7 were originally printed in Cotton Mather's *Right Thoughts in Sad Hours* (London, 1689) and are among Taylor's only poetry known to have been published in his lifetime. Taylor married Elizabeth Fitch of Norwich in November 1674. Stanford dates this poem to 1682, based upon references to the first four of Taylor's fourteen children.

[2]A flower or garden bed. Figuratively, it refers to the "True-Love Knot" or intimate bond of union (as between Adam and Eve) in marriage, to the original Covenant of Works uniting God and man, which was broken and superseded by the Covenant of Grace, and to the wedding knot, that spiritually joins the saint or "Bride" to the beloved "Bridegroom," Christ.

[3]Alexander the Great (356–323 B.C.), King of Macedonia, famous for his military conquests, cut the Gordian knot, devised by the King of Phrygia, when he learned that anyone who could undo it would rule Asia.

[4]Cuttings (stems, roots, twigs) of a plant used for replanting or grafting.

[5]Bloom.

[6]Samuel Taylor, born August 27, 1675, survived to maturity.

[7]Elizabeth Taylor, born December 27, 1676, died on December 25, 1677 (see line 20).

[8]From an obsolete verb, to checkle, meaning to laugh violently or giddily; closely related to chuckling. Taylor commonly creates puns, perhaps here from "cheek."

But oh! a glorious hand from glory came
Guarded with Angells, soon did Crop this flowre
Which almost tore the root up of the same
At that unlookt for, Dolesom, darksome houre.
In Pray're to Christ perfum'de[9] it did ascend,
And Angells bright did it to heaven tend.

But pausing on't, this Sweet perfum'd my thought,
Christ would in Glory have a Flowre, Choice, Prime,
And having Choice, chose this my branch forth brought;
Lord take't. I thanke thee, thou takst ought of mine,
It is my pledg in glory, part of mee
Is now in it, Lord, glorifi'de with thee.

But praying ore my branch, my branch did Sprout
And bore another manly flower, & gay[10]
And after that another, Sweet brake out,[11]
The which the former hand soon got away.
But oh! the tortures, Vomit, Screechings, groans,
And Six weeks Fever would pierce hearts like Stones.

Griefe o're doth flow: & nature fault would finde
Were not thy Will, my Spell Charm, Joy, & Gem:
That as I said, I say, take, Lord, they're thine.
I piecemeale pass to Glory bright in them.
I joy, may I sweet Flowers for Glory breed,
Whether thou getst them green, or lets them Seed.

c. 1682 1937

[9]In the Old Testament, incense offerings (types of prayer and praise) were regularly given up to God by the High Priests, and perfumed oils were used for cleansing and anointing (see Exodus 30). But Taylor may also have in mind the continuing analogy with flowers and possibly the preparation of the body for burial.

[10]James Taylor, born on October 12, 1678, lived to maturity.

[11]Abigail, born August 6, 1681, died August 22, 1682.

from Preparatory Meditations[1]

First Series

Prologue

Lord, Can a Crumb of Dust the Earth outweigh,
Outmatch all mountains, nay the Chrystall Sky?
Imbosom in't designs that shall Display
And trace into the Boundless Deity?
Yea hand a Pen whose moysture doth guild ore
Eternall Glory with a glorious glore.

If it its Pen had of an Angels Quill,[2]
And Sharpend on a Pretious Stone ground tite,
And dipt in Liquid Gold, and mov'de by Skill
In Christall leaves should golden Letters write
It would but blot and blur yea jag, and jar
Unless thou mak'st the Pen, and Scribener.

I am this Crumb of Dust which is design'd
To make my Pen unto thy Praise alone,
And my dull Phancy[3] *I would gladly grinde*
Unto an Edge on Zions Pretious Stone.[4]
And Write in Liquid Gold upon thy Name
My Letters till thy glory forth doth flame.

[1]Composed as self-examinations preparatory to the Lord's Supper, 217 meditations, dated from 1682 to 1725, survive in the manuscript "Poetical Works." The dates suggest that Taylor administered the Supper at irregular intervals, but the frequent clusters on a single text and lengthy series on biblical themes indicate that he composed sermon series and the accompanying poems over extended periods of time. His topics included Old Testament types (2.1–18, 20–30, 58–61, 70–71), Christ's nature and qualifications (2.42–56), the Lord's Supper (2.102–111), and the Song of Solomon (2.115–153, 156–157B, 160–165). Extant sermons have been published in *Upon the Types of the Old Testament* and *Edward Taylor's Christographia.* Taylor dates his sermons and poems according to an ecclesiastical calendar with the first month being March and the twelfth being February. Both Taylor's and, as needed, the commonly accepted Gregorian year [in brackets] are given below. The complete title of the text is *Preparatory Meditations before my Approach to the Lords Supper. Chiefly upon the Doctrin preached upon the Day of administration* from Stanford, ed., *Poems.*

[2]The tube or barrel of a feather from a large bird (often a goose) formed into a pen by pointing and slitting the lower end; loosely used for a feather, poetically for a wing.

[3]Fancy, a mental image or representation; imagination, especially of a delusive sort, but used during the Renaissance to refer to the power of conception and representation in art and poetry.

[4]See Revelation 21:11, 19–21, describing the heavenly city, the New Jerusalem, garnished with precious stones, streets of gold, and transparent glass. Throughout Revelation (14:3, 19:9, 21:5) a heavenly voice instructs John to "write."

Let not th'attempts breake down my Dust I pray
Nor laugh thou them to scorn but pardon give.
Inspire this Crumb of Dust till it display
Thy Glory through't: and then thy dust shall live.
Its failings then thou'lt overlook I trust,
They being Slips slipt from thy Crumb of Dust.

Thy Crumb of Dust breaths two words from its breast,
That thou wilt guide its pen to write aright
To Prove thou art, and that thou art the best
And shew thy Properties to shine most bright.
And then thy Works will shine as flowers on Stems
Or as in Jewellary Shops, do jems.

Undated [1682?] 1937

[6.] *Another Meditation at the same time.*[1]

Am I thy Gold? Or Purse, Lord, for thy Wealth;
Whether in mine, or mint refinde for thee?
Ime counted so, but count me o're thyselfe,
Lest gold washt face, and brass in Heart I bee.
I Feare my Touchstone[2] touches when I try
Mee, and my Counted Gold too overly.

Am I new minted by thy Stamp indeed?
Mine Eyes are dim; I cannot clearly see.
Be thou my Spectacles that I may read
Thine Image, and Inscription stampt on mee.
If thy bright Image do upon me stand
I am a Golden Angell[3] in thy hand.

Lord, make my Soule thy Plate: thine Image bright
Within the Circle of the same enfoile.
And on its brims in golden Letters write
Thy Superscription in an Holy style.

[1]Unlike most of the meditations, this one lacks a date and a biblical verse, but the manuscript positions it between Meditation 1.5 (September 1683) and Meditation 1.7 (February 1684).

[2]A smooth, fine-grained, black or dark-colored variety of quartz or jasper, used for testing the quality of gold and silver alloys; that which serves to test the genuineness or value of anything.

[3]An English coin (1470–1634) showing the archangel Michael slaying the dragon. See also Revelation 8–11 for the seven archangels heralding Christ's Second Coming and the New Jerusalem.

Then I shall be thy Money, thou my Hord:
Let me thy Angell bee, bee thou my Lord.

Undated [1683?] 1939

8. *Meditation. Joh. 6.51. I am the Living Bread.*[1]

I kening[2] through Astronomy Divine
The Worlds bright Battlement,[3] wherein I spy
A Golden Path my Pensill cannot line,
From that bright Throne unto my Threshold ly.
And while my puzzled thoughts about it pore
I finde the Bread of Life in't at my doore.

When that this Bird of Paradise[4] put in
This Wicker Cage (my Corps) to tweedle praise
Had peckt the Fruite forbad: and so did fling
Away its Food; and lost its golden dayes;
It fell into Celestiall Famine sore:
And never could attain a morsell more.

Alas! alas! Poore Bird, what wilt thou doe?
The Creatures field no food for Souls e're gave.
And if thou knock at Angells dores they show
An Empty Barrell: they no soul bread have.
Alas! Poore Bird, the Worlds White[5] Loafe is done.
And cannot yield thee here the smallest Crumb.

In this sad state, Gods Tender Bowells[6] run
Out streams of Grace: And he to end all strife
The Purest Wheate in Heaven, his deare-dear Son

[1]See John 6:22–59. As elsewhere in the *Preparatory Meditations,* Taylor here composes a short series of Meditations (1:8–10) on linked biblical texts and themes focusing upon Christ's flesh and blood as elements of the Lord's Supper. Fulfilling the Old Testament type of the manna which God provided daily for the Israelites (Exodus 16), Christ offers his body, the "living bread that came down from heaven," as a token or sign, which is "given for the life of the world."

[2]To discover by sight or signs and derive knowledge through instruction, here of divine astronomy. A kenning also denotes the distance bounding the range of ordinary vision, especially a marine measure of twenty miles; a dry measure of a half bushel, or a vessel containing that quantity of meal or grain. A kenning-glass is a spy-glass or small telescope.

[3]"Like a jasper stone, clear as crystal," bright light radiates from the New Jerusalem, whose parapets (battlements) mark the outer reaches of the new heavenly city of "pure gold, like clear glass," prophesied in Revelation 21–22. Enclosed within are God Almighty's white throne and the eternal paradise promised to redeemed saints after the Final Judgment.

[4]The soul is analogous to a "Bird of Paradise" housed within the body's cage.

[5]Israel's manna is "like coriander seed, white; and the taste of it was like wafers made with honey" (Exodus 16:31).

[6]Intestines or interior of the body; seat of tenderness, pity, and grace; the heart.

Grinds, and kneads up into this Bread of Life.
Which Bread of Life from Heaven down came and stands
Disht on thy Table up by Angells Hands.[7]

Did God mould up this Bread in Heaven, and bake,
Which from his Table came, and to thine goeth?
Doth he bespeake thee thus, This Soule Bread take.
Come Eate thy fill of this thy Gods White Loafe?[8]
Its Food too fine for Angells, yet come, take
And Eate thy fill. Its Heavens Sugar Cake.

What Grace is this knead in this Loafe? This thing
Souls are but petty things it to admire.
Yee Angells, help: This fill would to the brim
Heav'ns whelm'd-down[9] Chrystall meele Bowle, yea and higher.
This Bread of Life dropt in thy mouth, doth Cry.
Eate, Eate me, Soul, and thou shalt never dy.

June 8, 1684 1937

from Preparatory Meditations *Second Series*

1. *Meditation. Col. 2.17. Which are Shaddows of things to come and the body is Christs*

Oh Leaden heeld. Lord, give, forgive I pray.
Infire my Heart: it bedded is in Snow.
I Chide myselfe seing myselfe decay.
In heate and Zeale to thee, I frozen grow.
File my dull Spirits: make them sharp and bright:
Them firbush[1] for thyselfe, and thy delight.

[7]See also John 6:1–14 for Christ's miracle of feeding the five thousand with barley loaves and fishes, which is linked with the Passover (a type also of the Lord's Supper) and which precedes His declaration as the living bread.

[8]In the sacrament of the Lord's Supper, instituted by Christ (Luke 22:19), the bread spiritually signifies Christ's body "broken" during the crucifixion, His incarnate sacrifice to expiate mankind's sins, and God's grace and promise of eternal life to faithful communicants who are invited to come and eat.

[9]Turned upside down, as a dish or vessel to cover something. The *Oxford English Dictionary* quotes an illuminating passage from Dryden: "That the earth is like a trencher [wooden platter] and the Heavens a dish whelmed over it." In Revelation 15:7 seven angels carry "seven golden bowls [vials]" of God's wrath, but Taylor here envisions the new heavens as an inverted crystal bowl beaming forth eternally radiant light.

[1]Set on fire, using a fuel (firebrush, or firbrush, the needle foliage of fir trees) to ignite flames; sharpen, as a needle from the fir bush; a play on words with "firebrand," meaning one who inflames the passions.

My Stains are such, and sinke so deep, that all
The Excellency in Created Shells
Too low, and little is to make it fall
Out of my leather Coate wherein it dwells.
This Excellence is but a Shade to that
Which is enough to make my Stains go back.

The glory of the world slickt up in types
In all Choise things chosen to typify,
His glory upon whom the worke doth light,
To thine's a Shaddow, or a butterfly.
How glorious then, my Lord, art thou to mee
Seing to cleanse me, 's worke alone for thee.

The glory of all Types[2] doth meet in thee.
Thy glory doth their glory quite excell:
More than the Sun excells in its bright glee
A nat, an Earewig, Weevill, Snaile, or Shell.
Wonders in Crowds start up; your eyes may strut
Viewing his Excellence, and's bleeding cut.

Oh! that I had but halfe an eye to view
This excellence of thine, undazled: so
Therewith to give my heart a touch anew
Untill I quickned am, and made to glow.
All is too little for thee: but alass
Most of my little all hath other pass.

Then Pardon, Lord, my fault: and let thy beams
Of Holiness pierce through this Heart of mine.
Ope to thy Blood a passage through my veans.
Let thy pure blood my impure blood refine.
Then with new blood and spirits I will dub
My tunes upon thy Excellency good.

1693 1960

[2]In *Upon the Types of the Old Testament,* Taylor defines a type as "a Certain thing Standing with a Sacred impression set upon it by God to Signify Some good to come as Christ, or the Gospell Concerns in this Life." He composes 36 Sermons and corresponding Meditations 2.1–18, 20–30, 58–61, and 70–71, between 1693 and 1706, to illustrate how Old Testament persons, ceremonies, providences, and seals, foreshadow New Testament fulfillments through Christ and His Church.

26. *Meditation. Heb. 9.13.14. How much more shall the blood of Christ, etc.*

Unclean, Unclean:[1] My Lord, Undone, all vile
Yea all Defild: What shall thy Servant doe?
Unfit for thee: not fit for holy Soile,
Nor for Communion of Saints below.
A bag of botches, Lump of Loathsomeness:
Defild by Touch, by Issue: Leproust flesh.[2]

Thou wilt have all that enter do thy fold
Pure, Cleane, and bright, Whiter than whitest Snow
Better refin'd than most refined Gold:
I am not so: but fowle: What shall I doe?
Shall thy Church Doors be shut, and shut out mee?
Shall not Church fellowship my portion bee?[3]

How can it be? Thy Churches do require
Pure Holiness: I am all filth, alas!
Shall I defile them, tumbled thus in mire?
Or they mee cleanse before I current pass?
If thus they do, Where is the Niter bright
And Sope they offer mee to wash me White?

The Brisk Red heifer's Ashes,[4] when calcin'd,
Mixt all in running Water, is too Weake
To wash away my Filth: The Dooves assign'd
Burnt, and Sin Offerings[5] neer do the feate
But as they Emblemize the Fountain Spring
Thy Blood, my Lord, set ope to wash off Sin.

Oh! richest Grace! Are thy Rich Veans then tapt
To ope this Holy Fountain (boundless Sea)

[1]See Leviticus 13:44–46, instructing lepers to cry "Unclean, unclean," and to be put outside Israel's camp. Leviticus 13 and 14:1–32 record the priest's duty of identifying and ceremonially cleansing leprous persons, using sacrificial rites that Taylor traces more minutely in Meditation 2.27.

[2]In *Upon the Types of the Old Testament* and corresponding Meditations, Taylor categorizes Old Testament types of ceremonial uncleanness by touching (2.26), issues and leprosy (2.27), and moral impurity (2.28).

[3]In Sermons and Meditations 2.26–28, Taylor typologically interprets Old Testament priestly purifications, since "the Discipline enacted by God to fit Such as were Ceremonially unclean, for Church Fellowship under the Legall Dispensation, was typicall of Christ's Evangelicall preparing Such as are Spiritually unclean, for Church Fellowship in the Gospell day."

[4]See Numbers 19 for the purification of those unclean by touching (of a corpse) by the sacrifice of a red heifer.

[5]See Leviticus 15; unclean issues require the sacrifice of two turtledoves as sin and burnt offerings, by which the priest makes atonement.

For Sinners here to lavor off (all sapt
    With Sin) their Sins and Sinfulness away?
    In this bright Chrystall Crimson Fountain flows
    What washeth whiter, than the Swan or Rose.

Oh! wash mee, Lord, in this Choice Fountain, White
    That I may enter, and not sully here
Thy Church, whose floore is pav'de with Graces bright
    And hold Church fellowship with Saints most cleare.
    My Voice all sweet, with their melodious layes
    Shall make sweet Musick blossom'd with thy praise.

June 26, 1698

1957

50. Meditation. Joh. 1.14. Full of Truth[1]

The Artists Hand more gloriously bright,
    Than is the Sun itselfe, in'ts shining glory
Wrought with a stone axe made of Pearle, as light
    As light itselfe, out of a Rock all flory[2]
    Of Precious Pearle,[3] a Box most lively made
    More rich than gold Brimfull of Truth enlaid.

Which Box should forth a race of boxes send
    Teemd from its Womb such as itselfe, to run
Down from the Worlds beginning to its end.
    But, o! this box of Pearle Fell, Broke, undone.
    Truth from it flew: It lost Smaragdine[4] Glory:
    Was filld with Falshood: Boxes teemd of Sory.

The Artist puts his glorious hand again
    Out to the Worke: His Skill out flames more bright
Now than before. The worke he goes to gain,
    He did portray in flaming Rayes of light.
    A Box of Pearle shall from this Sory, pass
    More rich than that Smaragdine Truth-Box was.

[1]Meditations 2.42–56, composed between August 1701 and October 1703, are linked with fourteen corresponding sermons which focus on Christ's nature and qualifications. See the *Christographia.*

[2]Flowery, showy.

[3]Taylor apparently draws upon Revelation 21:18–21, which describes the New Jerusalem's pearly gates, and upon Matthew 13:45–46, which identifies the pearl of great price with the true Church and as a metaphor for Christ.

[4]Of a smaragd (precious bright green stone); emerald green.

Which Box, four thousand yeares, o'r ere 'twas made,
In golden Scutchons[5] lay'd[6] in inke Divine
Of Promises, of a Prophetick Shade,
And in embellishments of Types that shine.
Whose Beames in this Choice pearle-made-Box all meet
And bedded in't their glorious Truth to keep.

But now, my Lord, thy Humane Nature, I
Doe by the Rayes this Scutcheon sends out, finde
Is this Smaragdine Box where Truth doth ly
Of Types, and Promises, that thee out lin'de.
Their Truth they finde in thee: this makes them shine.
Their Shine on thee makes thee appeare Divine.

Thou givst thy Truth to them, thus true they bee.
They bring their Witness out for thee. Hereby
Their Truth appeares emboxt indeed in thee:
And thou the true Messiah shin'st thereby.
Hence Thou, and They make One another true
And They, and Thou each others Glory shew.

Hence thou art full of Truth, and full dost stand,
Of Promises, of Prophesies, and Types.
But that's not all: All truth is in thy hand,
Thy lips drop onely Truth, give Falshood gripes.
Leade through the World to glory, that ne'er ends
By Truth's bright Hand all such as Grace befriends.

O! Box of Truth! tenent[7] my Credence in
The mortase[8] of thy Truth: and Thou in Mee.
These Mortases, and Tenents make so trim,
That They and Thou, and I ne'er severd bee.
Embox my Faith, Lord, in thy Truth a part
And I'st by Faith embox thee in my heart.

December 27, 1702 1960

[5]Escutcheon, as in heraldry, a shield depicting a coat of arms.

[6]From inlayed, to embed a substance of a different kind in a surface.

[7]In carpentry, to join together by fitting a tenon, or projection on a piece of wood, into a mortice, so as to form a secure joint; possibly in the double sense of tenet, to hold firmly a doctrine, dogma, or opinion in religion or philosophy.

[8]Mortise, or mortice, the cavity or hole cut in a piece of timber to receive the shaped end (tenon); mortise and tenon are the component parts of a joint, but it also refers collectively to the method of joining.

115. *Meditation. Cant. 5:10. My Beloved*[1]

What art thou mine? Am I espousd to thee?
What honour's this? It is more bright Renown.
I ought to glory more in this sweet glee
Than if I'd wore greate Alexanders[2] Crown.
Oh! make my Heart loaded with Love ascend
Up to thyselfe, its bridegroom, bright, and Friend.

Her whole delight, and her Belov'de thou art.
Oh! Lovely thou: Oh! grudg my Soule, I say,
Thou straitend standst, lockt up to Earths fine parts
Course matter truly, yellow earth, Hard Clay.
Why should these Clayey faces be the keyes
T'lock, and unlock thy love up as they please?

Lord, make thy Holy Word, the golden Key
My Soule to lock and make its bolt to trig[3]
Before the same, and Oyle the same to play
As thou dost move them off and On to jig[4]
The ripest Fruits that my affections beare
I offer, thee. Oh! my Beloved faire.

Thou standst the brightest object in bright glory
More shining than the shining sun to 'lure.
Unto thyselfe the purest Love. The Stories
Within my Soul can hold refinde most pure
In flaming bundles polishd all with Grace
Most sparklingly about thyselfe t'imbrace.
The most refined Love in Graces mint
In rapid flames is best bestowd on thee

[1]Between September 4, 1713, and October 1725, Taylor culminated his *Preparatory Meditations* with an extended series on the Canticles, or Song of Solomon. Forty-nine of his final fifty-three Meditations poetically explicate consecutive verses from Canticles 5:10–16; 6:1–13; 7:1–6; 5:1; and 2:1, 3–5. Written during a period of severe illness and declining health (1722–1725), the final seven poems (161A–165) are part of Taylor's poignant epithalamium and *ars moriendi,* expressing his desire (as the Bride) for a heavenly, eternal union with Christ the Bridegroom. Regarded as a premier poetic book of the Bible with the most clearly erotic imagery, Solomon's lyrical celebration of his love for the Shulamite maiden was interpreted by Puritan expositors as a figurative revelation of God's love for His covenant people (Israel) and as a spiritual allegory of Christ's love for His heavenly Bride, the Church, and the individual Elect soul. Canticles signifies a lyric, little song, or hymn.

[2]Alexander the Great (356–323 B.C.), King of Macedonia, was famous for his military conquests of Greece, the Persian Empire, and northwestern India.

[3]Hold firm or fast; make faithful, trim, or tidy.

[4]To move up and down, to and fro with a rapid, jerky motion, as in jiggle.

The brightest: metall with Divinest print
Thy tribute is, and ever more shall bee.
The Loving Spouse and thou her Loved Sweet
Make Lovely Joy when she and thee do meet:

Thou art so lovely, pitty 'tis indeed
That any drop of love the Heart can hold
Should be held back from thee, or should proceed
To drop on other Objects, young, or old.
Best things go best together: best agree:
But best are badly usd, by bad that bee.

Thou all o're Lovely art, Most lovely Thou:
Thy Spouse, the best of Loving Ones: Her Love,
The Best of Love: and this she doth avow
Thyselfe. And thus she doth thyself approve.
That object robs thee of thy due that wares
Thy Spouses Love. With thee none in it shares.

Lord fill my heart with Grace refining Love.
Be thou my onely Well-Belov'd I pray.
And make my Heart with all its Love right move
Unto thyselfe, and all her Love display.
My Love is then right well bestow'd, alone
When it obtains thyselfe her Lovely One.

My Best love then shall on Shoshannim[5] play,
Like David[6] her Sweet Musick, and thy praise
Inspire her Songs, that Glory ever may
In Sweetest tunes thy Excellency Glaze.
And thou shalt be that burden of her Song
Loaded with Praise that to thyselfe belong.

September 4, 1713 1960

[5]The Hebrew titles of Psalms 45, 60, 69, and 80 suggest that shoshannim refers to lilies, thought to indicate (a) the popular melody to which these psalms were sung; (b) a lily-shaped long silver trumpet used by priests to announce festivals or assemble the congregation; or (c) an old rite in which revelations, testimony, or omens were taken from lilies, which were also (in Canticles) an emblem of love.

[6]David (Hebrew, beloved; also meaning chieftain) was a shepherd, son of Jesse, who became Israel's second King, of such heroic aspect that he was regarded not only as a lineal ancestor but also as a type of the Messiah. Considered the sweet singer of Israel, he was designated author in the Hebrew titles of seventy-three Psalms, of a song of deliverance, and of a lamentation for Saul and Jonathan, the latter of which Taylor also paraphrased in the "Poetical Works." See I Samuel 16:12 through I Kings 2:11, I Chronicles 11–29, and the Psalms.

from A Valediction to all the World preparatory for Death 3^d of the 11^m 1720[1] (from Version 1)[2]

Cant. 3. Valediction, to the Terraqueous[3] Globe

Thou Realm of Senses, Sensuality
Enchanting e'ry Sense to take its fill,
Cooking up to the Tast Cocksbowl[4] full high.
Unto the Eare's enchanting Melodies Skill,
Unto the Eyes enticing Beauteous Sights
And to the Touch silk downy soft delights;
While in this Earthly Paradise that brings
Things to entice to Sensualities.
Most Sparkling Sights of various sorts of things
Delicious dishes Spic'de Varieties,
Melodies Sounds, & Aromatick Smells
And downy Soft delight enchanting Spells.
While in the Senses markets, Souls, beware
That in their truck[5] thou do not erre nor miss,
Oh never make thy Choicest food & fare
A mess of butterd Cocks crumbs in a Dish.[6]
If I should you hold & ne'er so hard & fast,
You sure would leave me in the lurch at last.
Will I or will I. Hence you Cheats adjue[7]
You will but Gull mee, if I leave not you.

[1]Nearly eighty and after a severe illness in December 1720, Taylor composed this poem as a farewell to earthly things in anticipation of death, which did not come until June 24, 1729. When dating his poems, Taylor used March as the first month of the year; hence, the "Valediction" was written in January 1721. Text is from Davis and Davis, eds., *Minor Poetry.*

[2]The Canticles excerpted here are two of eight in Version 1 from the "Poetical Works" manuscript. The "Valediction" exists in three versions and provides an opportunity to observe Taylor's practice of composing in several stages.

[3]Terraqueous, consisting of land and water.

[4]Cock may refer to (a) the male domestic fowl; (b) a spout to channel liquids and, therefore, a "cocksbowl" or vessel to hold liquids; or (c) a short form of "cockle," a shellfish, oyster, or plant grown in cornfields.

[5]Bartering or exchanging commodities, especially in an underhanded way; short for "truckle," to act subserviently, bend obsequiously.

[6]A delicacy or "pretty dish" of stewed (or preserved) cocks-combs, i.e. rooster's crests (or shellfish?), sometimes stuffed with crumbled meats and spices; possibly the reddish-purple or yellow-orange flowering plant called cockscomb.

[7]Variant of (a) *adieu,* French meaning "I commend you to God," and commonly to bid farewell, with regret at a loss, or a formal leavetaking; or (b) adjure, to charge or entreat solemnly or earnestly, as if under oath or the penalty of a curse; to exorcise an evil spirit by adjuration in God's name.

My Cloaths farewell: no more by mee to be worn
You'l no more warm me, no nor me adorn.
My Bed farewell, my Coverlids & Rug[8]
A Coffin, Grave, or Green turffe I now hug;
My Meat, my Drink & Physick all adjue,
I'me got within Gods Paradise its trew.
Where's my best life & no Physickal here
Is ever needed: Here's the Best best Cheere.
The Tree of Life[9] doth bear mee. Oh food Choice
That is within the pale of Paradise.
And of the pure pure water of the River
Of Gods Stilld Aqua Vitae,[10] I'st drink ever.

. . . .

My House & lands, my Stock & State I finde
Can't ease my tooth's nor Head ach nor my minde;
My Friends & mine acquaintances very deare,
My Deare-Deare Wife & little twigs that peare
Out of my Stock, Bits of myself, I finde
Exceeding dear whom now I leave behinde.
Tho' attending me with pickled Eyes,
Dropping their brine upon my Cask that lies
Gasping for Breath & panting. Oh! I could
My Pickle mix with yours, which if I could
All would not keep me Sweet. My Vessell soon
Would tainte, tho' all your Love & Skill should bloom.
I now do wish you well & say adjue
You'l leave me helpless, if I leave not you.

I leave you all biding you all adjue
You'l soon leave me if I do not leave you.
My study, Books, Pen, Inke, & Paper all
My Office implements off from me fall.
My People, aye & Pulpet leave be hinde
Unto a Voice thence uttering Gods minde
For some more richly laid in, for Christs work
Bringing a richer blessing, & no Shirk
To fill Christs warehous full of Spirituall Trades
And not an empty Sound of Some Vain blades.

[8]A coarse woolen material or coverlet; a heavy bed covering handmade of sturdy linen or wool backing densely set with raised loops of yarn.

[9]See Genesis 2:9, 3:22; Revelation 2:7, 22:2, 14, for the Tree of Life.

[10]Literally, "water of life;" any brandy or spirituous liquor; originally applied by alchemists to ardent spirits. Taylor draws upon references to the waters of Paradise from Revelation 7:17; 21:6; 22:1, 17. Thirty-four lines of the poem, which would normally follow this line, have been omitted in this edition.

But yet my Lord I give thee hearty thanks
Thou'st let me these to tend me to the banks
Of thy high & Eternall glorious Throne
And now do leave them here tho' calld mine Own.
Untill the last day dawns & up then springs
At whose good morrow when the last Trump[11] rings
I do expect these Organs, once again
To Sing thy praises then in Sweeter Strain.
And drest up all in glorious robes Rich Grace
Deckt if it be appeare before the judgments place.
When Angells bright shall bid me then good morrow
Wholy acquitted of all Sin & Sorrow.
And in these Organs with Angellick Phrase
Sing out Gods glory in Ceremoniall Praise,
Which now I laying down tho' ne'er so bright
Till then & therefore bid them all good night.

January 3, 1720 [1721] 1972

A Fig for thee Oh! Death (Version 2)[1]

Thou King of Terrours with thy Gastly Eyes
With Butter teeth, bare bones Grim looks likewise.
And Grizzly Hide, & clawing Tallons, fell,[2]
Opning to Sinners Vile, Trap Door of Hell,
That on in Sin impenitently trip
The Down fall art of the infernall Pit,
Thou struckst thy teeth deep in my Lord's blest Side:
Who dasht it out, & all its venom 'Stroyde.
That now thy Poundrill[3] shall onely dash
My Flesh & bones to bits, & Cask shall clash.[4]
Thou'rt not so frightful now to me, thy knocks

[11]I Corinthians 15:52, signifying the trumpet that heralds the resurrection of the redeemed dead at Christ's Second Coming and the ascension into the New Jerusalem after the millennium and Last Judgment. This passage is just before the well-known I Corinthians 15:55, "O death, where is thy sting? O grave, where is thy victory?" See also Revelation 8, 9, 11.

[1]Version 1 appears in the "Manuscript Book," probably copied in 1723–1724, while the second—and final—version appears in the "Poetical Works," in which Taylor usually transcribed his finished poems. Text is from Davis and Davis, eds., *Minor Poetry.*

[2]Deadly.

[3]A pounder or instrument for crushing by heavy blows into small fragments or powder, such as a pestle or heavy wooden hammer.

[4]His body will feel the resounding blow.

Do crack my shell, its Heavenly kernells box
Abides most safe. Thy blows do breake its Shell,
Thy Teeth its Nut. Cracks are that on it fell
Thence out its kirnell fair & not by worms.
Once Viciated out, new formd forth turns
And on the wings of some bright Angell flies,
Out to bright glory of Gods blissful joyes.
Hence thou to mee with all thy Gastly face
Art not so dreadfull unto mee thro' Grace.
I am resolvde to fight thee, & ne'er yield
Blood up to th' Ears; & in the battle field.
Chassing thee hence: But not for this my flesh,
My Body, my vile harlot, its thy Mess.[5]
Labouring to drown me into Sin's disguise
By Eating & by drinking such evill joyes
Tho' Grace preserv'd mee that I nere have
Surprised been nor tumbled in Such grave.[6]
Hence for my Strumpet I'le ne'er draw my Sword
Nor thee restrain at all by Iron Curb
Nor for her Safty will I 'gainst thee Strive
But let thy frozen grips take her Captive
And her imprison in thy dungeon Cave
And grinde to powder in thy Mill the grave,
[W]hich powder in thy Van[7] thou'st safely keep
[T]ill She hath slept out quite her fatall Sleep.
[W]hen the last Cock shall Crow the last day in
And the Arch Angells Trumpets sound shall ring[8]
Then th' Eye Omniscient seek shall all there round
Each dust death's mill had very findly ground,
Which in death's Smoky furnace well refinde
And each to'ts fellow hath exactly joyn'd,
[I]s raised up anew & made all bright
And Christalized; & top full of delight.
And entertains its Soule again in bliss
And Holy Angells waiting all on this.
The Soule & Body now, as two true Lovers

[5]Dinner.

[6]In the first version Taylor's sense in lines 24–28 becomes clearer: "My harlot body, make thou it, thy Mess,/ That oft ensnared mee with its Strumpets guise/ Of Meats and drinks dainty Sensualities./ Yet Grace ne'er suffer me to turn aside/ As Sinners oft fall in & do abide."

[7]Winnowing basket.

[8]Revelation 8, 9, 11 presents the seven archangels and trumpets that announce Christ's new reign on earth, when the redeemed will be resurrected from the dead. After the millennium and Final Judgment (of the damned), a second resurrection will take place, into the New Jerusalem where the saints will dwell throughout eternity. See also I Corinthians 15.

[E]ry night how do they hug & kiss each other.
[A]nd going hand in hand thus thro' the Skies
[U]p to Eternall glory glorious rise.
[I]s this the Worse thy terrours then can? why
Then Should this grimace at me terrify?
Why comst thou then so slowly? mend thy pace
Thy Slowness me detains from Christ's bright face.
Altho' thy terrours rise to th' highst degree,
[I] still am where I was, a Fig[9] for thee.

Copied 1723–25? 1960

Samuel Sewall 1652–1730

For fifty-six years (1674–1729) Samuel Sewall diligently kept a diary that scholars and historians value for its details about colonial culture, including entries about the weather, births, marriages, arrivals, departures, legal proceedings, and deaths in Sewall's Boston community. As a chronicler of his times, Sewall also provided insight into the psychology of Puritan thought, reading the physical world for its spiritual messages. For example: "Nov. 11 [1675]. Morning proper fair, the weather exceedingly benign, but (to me) metaphoric, dismal, dark and portentous, some prodigies appearing in every corner of the skies; Satterday, June 27th [1685]. It pleaseth God to send Rain on the weary dusty Earth; Wednesday, P. M., July 15 [1685]. Very dark, and great Thunder and Lightening; July, 1 [1707]. A Rainbow is seen just before night, which comforts us against our Distresses." For Puritans like Sewall, natural events conveyed divine meaning. Thunder and lightning portended the awful power of Providence; rainbows brought reassurance. This duality was both Platonic and biblical, suggesting an ideal world mirrored below and open to a method called *typology,* where events from the Old Testament foreshadowed those in the present. As a Puritan, Sewall held to the Doctrine of Preparation and believed he might be called to God at any moment. In order to "prepare," he needed to be in a constant state of self-examination, an onerous and stressful task. David D. Hall points out that although Sewall's notations "represent a mental world very different from our own," the diary also reopens "a world of wonders," as Sewall scanned the skies for divine messages and sincerely tried to reconcile discrepancies.

Samuel Sewall was born on March 28, 1652, at Bishop Stoke, in Hampshire, England. His father was Henry Sewall, a wealthy merchant, and his mother was Jane Drummer Sewall, whose highly regarded merchant family had migrated to the colonies in 1634. In 1661, Sewall's family migrated to New England when Samuel

[9]Fig may refer to (a) a poisoned fig used secretly to destroy an obnoxious person; or (b) the *Fica,* a contemptuous gesture created by thrusting the thumb between two closed fingers into the mouth, thereby offering an obscene insult or crude dismissal. See Micah 4:4; Isaiah 34:4; Revelation 6:12–14.

was nine years old. In Newbury, Sewall resumed his grammar school education under the tutelage of a prominent Oxford and Leyden-trained scholar, Dr. Thomas Parker. Entering Harvard in 1667, he trained for the ministry and for two years roomed with Edward Taylor, who would become a lifelong friend. Sewall received his B.A. in 1673 and his M.A. in 1674. During this time, he met Hannah Hull, whose father, John Hull, was the colonial treasurer, master of the mint, and the wealthiest man in Boston. Hannah and Samuel married on February 28, 1675, a bond lasting forty-two years that produced fourteen children, six of whom survived. When Sewall graduated from Harvard, rather than enter the ministry, he joined his father-in-law as a merchant. He exported turpentine, fish, and furs to the Caribbean and Europe, bringing back luxury items. Unusual for their time, neither Hull nor Sewall engaged in the slave trade. Sewall also held positions as a banker, bookseller, and printer. He was appointed deputy of the General Court (the colonial legislature) in 1683 and managed the colony's printing press. He was a member of the town Council (1684–1725), and he served as chief justice of the Superior Court (1718–1728).

Sewall was married three times: to Hannah Hull until her death in 1717; to Abigail Tilley in 1719 until her death a year later; and to Mary Gibbs in 1722. In one of the more endearing sections of his diary, Sewall narrates his courtship of Madame Katherine Winthrop, who eventually rejected him but not until after receiving several visits and gifts from Sewall of luxuries like sugared almonds, whose amounts he meticulously recorded in his diary as well as the heartaches of a failed romance.

On a very different note are Sewall's political activities. In 1692, he was appointed by Massachusetts governor William Phips to serve as one of nine judges of the Salem witchcraft trials, and he was the only judge to publicly apologize for his participation in the gruesome events. In 1697, after his minister, Samuel Willard, preached on the misguided actions of those dark days, Sewall wrote a formal statement that he presented to Willard and that was publicly displayed. He also entered the statement in his diary. In 1700, Sewall wrote an anti-slavery tract, *The Selling of Joseph,* that condemned the slave trade on two main points: that blacks and whites are all descended from Adam and Eve and therefore slavery is anti-doctrinal, and that indentured servitude with the promise of release was a preferable system. Although there is much to praise about Sewall's pamphlet, Emory Elliott is right to point out that Sewall's anti-slavery stand was not necessarily a call for racial equality. Still, the document predated the abolitionist movement by a hundred years and reminds us that the debate began long before the Civil War. In 1721, Sewall wrote *A Memorial Relating to the Kennebeck Indians,* arguing for humane treatment of Indians. He remained actively involved in his community and entered detailed accounts in his diary to the end. On January 1, 1730, Samuel Sewall died in Boston at the age of seventy-seven.

Susan Clair Imbarrato
Minnesota State University–Moorhead

PRIMARY WORKS

Sidney Kaplan, ed., *The Selling of Joseph: A Memorial,* 1969; M. Halsey Thomas, ed., *The Diary of Samuel Sewall: 1674–1729,* 2 vols., 1973.

from The Diary of Samuel Sewall[1]

Augt. 25. [1692] Fast at the old [First] Church, respecting the Witchcraft, Drought, &c.[2]

Monday, Sept. 19, 1692. About noon, at Salem, Giles Corey[3] was press'd to death for standing Mute; much pains was used with him two days, one after another, by the Court and Capt. Gardner of Nantucket who had been of his acquaintance: but all in vain.

Sept. 20. [1692] Now I hear from Salem that about 18 years agoe, he was suspected to have stamped and press'd a man to death, but was cleared. Twas not remembered till Anne Putnam was told of it by said Corey's Spectre the Sabbath-day night before Execution.[4]

Sept. 20, 1692. The Swan brings in a rich French Prize of about 300 Tuns, laden with Claret, White Wine, Brandy, Salt, Linnen Paper, &c.

Sept. 21. [1692] A petition is sent to Town in behalf of Dorcas Hoar, who now confesses: Accordingly an order is sent to the Sheriff to forbear her Execution, notwithstanding her being in the Warrant to die to morrow. This is the first condemned person who has confess'd.[5]

Nov. 6. [1692] Joseph threw a knop of Brass and hit his Sister Betty on the forhead so as to make it bleed and swell; upon which, and for his playing at Prayertime, and eating when Return Thanks, I whipd him pretty smartly. When I first went in (call'd by his Grandmother) he sought to shadow and hide himself from me behind the head of the Cradle: which gave me the sorrowfull remembrance of Adam's carriage.

Monday, April 29, 1695. The morning is very warm and Sunshiny; in the Afternoon there is Thunder and Lightening, and about 2 P.M. a very extraordinary Storm of Hail, so that the ground was made white with it, as with the blossoms when fallen; 'twas as bigg as pistoll and Musquet Bullets; It broke of the Glass of the new House about 480 Quarrels [squares] of the Front; of Mr. Sergeant's about as much; Col. Shrimpton, Major General, Govr Bradstreet, New Meetinghouse, Mr. Willard, &c. Mr. Cotton Mather dined with us, and was with me in the new Kitchen when this was; He had just been mentioning that more Minister Houses than others proportionably had been smitten with Lightening; enquiring what the meaning of God should be in it. Many Hail-Stones broke throw the Glass and flew to the middle of

[1]Sewall's diary begins on December 3, 1673/4, and ends on October 13, 1728/9. In Sewall's day, England followed the Julian calendar, in which the year began on Lady Day, March 25. This text has been slightly modernized and is from *The Diary of Samuel Sewall,* ed. M. Halsey Thomas, 1973.

[2]Governor William Phips appointed Sewall one of nine judges for the witchcraft trials. Sewall made relatively few entries on this subject during the trials. Fast days were regularly held as communal days of atonement.

[3]Giles Corey was eighty years old. Heavy stones were placed on his chest until he died, a punishment in English law for "standing mute and refusing to plead to an indictment."

[4]While working in the Parris kitchen, twelve-year-old Anne Putnam allegedly studied under Tituba, the Caribbean slave at the center of the accusations. Anne and her mother were main accusers during the trials.

[5]Under English law, even though Dorcas Hoar had already been tried and sentenced, confession saved her from the gallows.

the Room, or farther: People afterward Gazed upon the House to see its Ruins. I got Mr. Mather to pray with us after this awfull Providence; He told God He had broken the brittle part of our house, and prayd that we might be ready for the time when our Clay-Tabernacles should be broken. Twas a sorrowfull thing to me to see the house so far undon again before twas finish'd. It seems at Milton [near Boston] on the one hand, and at Lewis's [the tavern at Lynn] on the other, there was no Hail.[6]

Jany 15. [1697] . . . Copy of the Bill[7] I put up on the Fast day [January 14]; giving it to Mr. Willard as he pass'd by, and standing up at the reading of it, and bowing when finished; in the Afternoon.

Samuel Sewall, sensible of the reiterated strokes of God upon himself and family, and being sensible, that as to the Guilt contracted, upon the opening of the late Commission of Oyer and Terminer[8] at Salem (to which the order for this Day relates) he is, upon many accounts, more concerned than any that he knows of, Desires to take the Blame and Shame of it, Asking pardon of Men, And especially desiring prayers that God, who has an Unlimited Authority, would pardon that Sin and all other his Sins; personal and Relative: And according to his infinite Benignity, and Soveraignty, Not Visit the Sin of him, or of any other, upon himself or any of his, nor upon the Land: But that He would powerfully defend him against all Temptations to Sin, for the future; and vouchsafe him the Efficacious, Saving Conduct of his Word and Spirit.

July, 15. 1698. Mr. Edward Taylor[9] comes to our house from Westfield. *Monday July 18. [1698]* I walk'd with Mr. Edward Taylor upon Cotton Hill, thence to Becon Hill, the Pasture, along the Stone-wall: As came back, we sat down on the great Rock, and Mr. Taylor told me his courting his first wife,[10] and Mr. Fitch his story of Mr. Dod's prayer to God to bring his Affection to close with a person pious, but hard-favoured. Has God answered me in finding out one Godly and fit for me, and shall I part for fancy? When came home, my wife gave me Mr. Tappan's Letter concerning Eliza,[11] which caus'd me to reflect on Mr. Taylor's Discourse. And his Prayer was for pardon of error in our ways—which made me think whether it were not best to overlook all, and go on. This day John Ive, fishing in great Spiepond, is arrested with mortal sickness which renders him in a manner speechless and senseless; dies next day; buried at Charlestown on the Wednesday. Was a very debauched, atheistical man. I was not at his Funeral. Had Gloves sent me, but the knowledge of his notoriously wicked life made me sick of going; and Mr. Mather, the president, came in just as I was ready to step out, and so I staid at home, and by that means lost a Ring: but hope had no loss.[12] Follow thou Me, was I suppose more complied with, than if had left Mr. Mather's company to go to such a Funeral.

[6]The hailstorm was one misfortune in a succession of events that year. On May 22, 1696, Sewall buried a premature son who was stillborn. On December 23, his daughter Sarah (1694–1696) died. Scholars have speculated that these events led Sewall to his decision to ask for forgiveness for his role as a Salem judge. Milton is a town south of Boston.

[7]Sewall's recantation of his participation in the witchcraft trials. He was the only judge to do so publicly.

[8]The phrase "Oyer and Terminer" means "To hear and to determine"; therefore, the court was permitted to hear and determine criminal cases.

[9]A rare visit from his Harvard roommate, Edward Taylor (1642?–1729), the poet and minister at Westfield.

[10]Elizabeth Finch, who had died on July 7, 1689.

[11]Elizabeth Toppan was Sewall's niece, his sister Hannah Sewall Toppan's daughter.

[12]Gloves were sent as invitations to funerals; a ring was given as a token of remembrance.

Fourth-day, June 19, 1700 . . . Having been long and much dissatisfied with the Trade of fetching Negros from Guinea; at last I had a strong Inclination to Write something about it; but it wore off. At last reading Bayne, Ephes. about servants, who mentions Blackamoors; I began to be uneasy that I had so long neglected doing any thing.[13] When I was thus thinking, in come Bror Belknap to shew me a Petition he intended to present to the Genl Court for the freeing a Negro and his wife, who were unjustly held in Bondage. And there is a Motion by a Boston Comittee to get a Law that all Importers of Negros shall pay 40s *per* head, to discourage the bringing of them. And Mr. C. Mather resolves to publish a sheet to exhort Masters to labour their Conversion. Which makes me hope that I was call'd of God to Write this Apology for them; Let his Blessing accompany the same.

Lord's Day, June, 10. 1705. The Learned and pious Mr. Michael Wigglesworth dies at Malden about 9. m. Had been sick about 10. days of a Fever; 73 years and 8 moneths old. He was the Author of the Poem entituled The Day of Doom, which has been so often printed: and was very useful as a Physician.

Febr. 6. [1718] This morning wandering in my mind whether to live a Single or a Married Life;[14] I had a sweet and very affectionat Meditation Concerning the Lord Jesus; Nothing was to be objected against his Person, Parentage, Relations, Estate, House, Home! Why did I not resolutely, presently close with Him! And I cry'd mightily to God that He would help me so to doe! . . .

March, 14. [1718] Deacon Marion comes to me, sits with me a great while in the evening; after a great deal of Discourse about his Courtship—He told [me] the Olivers said they wish'd I would Court their Aunt.[15] I said little, but said twas not five Moneths since I buried my dear Wife. Had said before 'twas hard to know whether best to marry again or no; whom to marry. Gave him a book of the Berlin Jewish Converts.

Sept 5. [1720] Mary Hirst goes to Board with Madam Oliver and her Mother Loyd, Going to Son Sewall's I there meet with Madam Winthrop, told her I was glad to meet her there, had not seen her a great while; gave her Mr. Homes's Sermon.

Sept. 30. [1720] Mr. Colman's Lecture: Daughter Sewall acquaints Madam Winthrop that if she pleas'd to be within at 3. P.M. I would wait on her. She answer'd she would be at home.

October 1. [1720] Satterday, I dine at Mr. Stoddard's: from thence I went to Madam Winthrop's just at 3. Spake to her, saying, my loving wife died so soon and suddenly, 'twas hardly convenient for me to think of Marrying again; however I came to this Resolution, that I would not make my Court to any person without first Consulting with her. Had a pleasant discourse about 7 Single persons sitting in the Foreseat[16] [September] 29th, viz. Madm Rebekah Dudley, Catharine Winthrop, Bridget

[13]Paul Baynes, *A Commentary upon the First Chapter of the Epistle of St. Paul. Written to the Ephesians* (London, 1618). This text inspired Sewall's anti-slavery tract, *The Selling of Joseph,* which was printed five days later on June 24, 1700.

[14]Hannah Hull Sewell died on October 19, 1717. Sewall married Abigail Tilley on October 29, 1719. She died suddenly six months later on May 26, 1720. He married Mary Gibbs on March 29, 1722. She survived him sixteen years and died on July 17, 1746.

[15]Katherine Brattle Winthrop (1664–1725), widow of John Eyre Sr. and of Chief Justice Wait Still Winthrop, was fifty-six at this meeting and had been widowed one year. Chief Justice Winthrop was a friend of Sewall's.

[16]The front pews were usually reserved for widows in the congregation.

Usher, Deliverance Legg, Rebekah Loyd, Lydia Colman, Elizabeth Bellingham. She propounded one and another for me; but none would do, said Mrs. Loyd was about her Age. 11??

Octobr 3. 2. [1720] Waited on Madam Winthrop again; 'twas a little while before she came in. Her daughter Noyes[17] being there alone with me, I said, I hoped my Waiting on her Mother would not be disagreeable to her. She answer'd she should not be against that that might be for her Comfort. I Saluted[18] her, and told her I perceiv'd I must shortly wish her a good Time; (her mother had told me, she was with Child, and within a Moneth or two of her Time). By and by in came Mr. Airs, Chaplain of the Castle,[19] and hang'd up his Hat, which I was a little startled at, it seeming as if he was to lodge there. At last Madam Winthrop came in. After a considerable time, I went up to her and said, if it might not be inconvenient I desired to speak with her. She assented, and spake of going into another Room; but Mr. Airs and Mrs. Noyes presently rose up, and went out, leaving us there alone. Then I usher'd in Discourse from the names in the Fore-seat; at last I pray'd that Katharine [Mrs. Winthrop] might be the person assign'd for me. She instantly took it up in way of Denyal, as if she had catch'd at an Opportunity to do it, saying she could not do it before she was asked. Said that was her mind unless she should Change it, which she believed she should not; could not leave her Children. I express'd my Sorrow that she should do it so Speedily; pray'd her Consideration, and ask'd her when I should wait on her agen. She setting no time, I mention'd that day Sennight.[20] Gave her Mr. Willard's Fountain open'd with the little print and verses; saying I hop'd if we did well read that book,[21] we should meet together hereafter if we did not now. She took the Book, and put it in her Pocket. Took Leave.[22]

1878–82

The Selling of Joseph, A Memorial[1]

Forasmuch as Liberty *is in real value next unto* Life:[2] *None ought to part with it themselves, or deprive others of it, but upon most mature Consideration.*

The Numerousness of Slaves at this day in the Province, and the Uneasiness of them under their Slavery, hath put many upon thinking whether the Foundation of

[17]Katherine Winthrop Jeffries Noyes (1694–?), daughter of Katherine Winthrop and John Eyre, wife of Dr. Oliver Noyes.

[18]*Saluted* means "kissed."

[19]Obadiah Ayers, chaplin of Castle William in Boston Harbor.

[20]A week later, as in "seven-night."

[21]Samuel Willard's *The Fountain Opened: Or, the Great Gospel Privilege of Having Christ Exhibited to Sinful Men* (Boston, 1700).

[22]Sewall continued to court Madam Winthrop until November 7, 1720. Several attempts to negotiate a favorable match for each party made it clear that his suit was without hope.

[1]This first anti-slavery tract by a Puritan was published in Boston by Green and Allen, June 24, 1700. The text has been slightly modernized.

[2]Sewall's translation of a passage from *De conscientia, et eius iure, vel casibus* (1623) by Dr. William Ames (1576–1633), noted English Puritan who had fled to Holland in 1610. Known as "the chief architect of Puritan ecclesiastical theory," Ames died before he could migrate to New England.

it be firmly and well laid; so as to sustain the Vast Weight that is built upon it. It is most certain that all Men, as they are the Sons of *Adam,* are Coheirs; and have equal Right unto Liberty, and all other outward Comforts of Life. *God hath given the Earth* [with all its Commodities] *unto the Sons of Adam, Psal* 115. 16. *And hath made of One Blood, all Nations of Men, for to dwell on all the face of the Earth, and hath determined the Times before appointed, and the bounds of their habitation: That they should seek the Lord. Forasmuch then as we are the Offspring of GOD* &c. *Act* 17. 26, 27, 29. Now although the Title given by the last ADAM, doth infinitely better Mens Estates, respecting GOD and themselves; and grants them a most beneficial and inviolable Lease under the Broad Seal of Heaven, who were before only Tenants at Will: Yet through the Indulgence of GOD to our First Parents after the Fall, the outward Estate of all and every of their Children, remains the same, as to one another. So that Originally, and Naturally, there is no such thing as Slavery. *Joseph* was rightfully no more a Slave to his Brethren, than they were to him: and they had no more Authority to *Sell* him, than they had to *Slay* him. And if *they* had nothing to do to Sell him; the *Ishmaelites* bargaining with them, and paying down Twenty pieces of Silver could not make a Title. Neither could *Potiphar* have any better Interest in him than the *Ishmaelites* had. *Gen.* 37. 20, 27, 28.[3] For he that shall in this case plead *Alteration of Property,* seems to have forfeited a great part of his own claim to Humanity. There is no proportion between Twenty Pieces of Silver, and LIBERTY. The Commodity it self is the Claimer. If *Arabian* Gold be imported in any quantities, most are afraid to meddle with it, though they might have it at easy rates; lest if it should have been wrongfully taken from the Owners, it should kindle a fire to the Consumption of their whole Estate. 'Tis pity there should be more Caution used in buying a Horse, or a little lifeless dust; than there is in purchasing Men and Women: Whenas they are the Offspring of GOD, and their Liberty is,

. . . . *Auro pretiosior Omni.*[4]

And seeing GOD hath said, *He that Stealeth a Man and Selleth him, or if he be found in his hand, he shall surely be put to Death.* Exod. 21. 16. This Law being of Everlasting Equity, wherein Man Stealing is ranked amongst the most atrocious of Capital Crimes: What louder Cry can there be made of that Celebrated Warning,

Caveat Emptor![5]

And all things considered, it would conduce more to the Welfare of the Province, to have White Servants for a Term of Years, than to have Slaves for Life. Few can endure to hear of a Negro's being made free; and indeed they can seldom use their freedom well; yet their continual aspiring after their forbidden Liberty,

[3]Genesis 37:20, "Come now therefore, and let us slay him, and cast him into some pit, and we will say, Some evil beast hath devoured him: and we shall see what will become of his dreams"; 37:27–28, "Come, let us sell him to the Ishmeelites, and let not our hand be upon him; for he is our brother and our flesh. And his brethren were content. Then there passed by Midianites merchantmen; and they drew and lifted up Joseph out of the pit, and sold Joseph to the Ishmeelites for twenty pieces of silver: and they brought Joseph into Egypt."

[4]"More precious than all gold." Isaiah 13:12 reads: "I will make a man more precious then fine gold, even a man above the wedge of gold of Ophir."

[5]"Let the buyer beware!"

renders them Unwilling Servants. And there is such a disparity in their Conditions, Colour & Hair, that they can never embody with us, and grow up into orderly Families, to the Peopling of the Land: but still remain in our Body Politick as a kind of extravasat Blood.[6] As many Negro men as there are among us, so many empty places there are in our Train Bands, and the places taken up of Men that might make Husbands for our Daughters. And the Sons and Daughters of *New England* would become more like *Jacob,* and *Rachel,* if this Slavery were thrust quite out of doors. Moreover it is too well known what Temptations Masters are under, to connive at the Fornication of their Slaves; lest they should be obliged to find them Wives, or pay their Fines. It seems to be practically pleaded that they might be Lawless; 'tis thought much of, that the Law should have Satisfaction for their Thefts, and other Immoralities; by which means, *Holiness to the Lord,* is more rarely engraven upon this sort of Servitude. It is likewise most lamentable to think, how in taking Negros out of *Africa,* and Selling of them here, That which GOD ha's joyned together men do boldly rend asunder; Men from their Country, Husbands from their Wives, Parents from their Children. How horrible is the Uncleanness, Mortality, if not Murder, that the Ships are guilty of that bring great Crouds of these miserable Men, and Women. Methinks, when we are bemoaning the barbarous Usage of our Friends and Kinsfolk in *Africa:* it might not be unseasonable to enquire whether we are not culpable in forcing the *Africans* to become Slaves amongst our selves. And it may be a question whether all the Benefit received by *Negro* Slaves, will balance the Accompt of Cash laid out upon them; and for the Redemption of our own enslaved Friends out of *Africa.* Besides all the Persons and Estates that have perished there.

Obj. 1. *These Blackamores are of the Posterity of* Cham, *and therefore are under the Curse of Slavery.* Gen. 9. 25, 26, 27.[7]

Answ. Of all Offices, one would not begg this; *viz.* Uncall'd for, to be an Executioner of the Vindictive Wrath of God; the extent and duration of which is to us uncertain. If this ever was a Commission; How do we know but that it is long since out of Date? Many have found it to their Cost, that a Prophetical Denunciation of Judgment against a Person or People, would not warrant them to inflict that evil. If it would, *Hazael* might justify himself in all he did against his Master, and the *Israelites,* from 2 *Kings* 8. 10, 12.[8]

But it is possbile that by cursory reading, this Text may have been mistaken. For *Canaan* is the Person Cursed three times over, without the mentioning of *Cham.* Good Expositors suppose the Curse entaild on him, and that this Prophesie was accomplished in the Extirpation of the *Canaanites,* and in the Servitude of the *Gibeonites. Vide Pareum.*[9] Whereas the Blackmores are not descended of *Canaan,*

[6]Blood forced out of the proper vessels; thus Sewall expresses a concern for miscegenation.

[7]Genesis 9:25–27, "And he said, Cursed be Canaan; a servant of servants shall he be unto his brethren. And he said, Blessed be the Lord God of Shem; and Canaan shall be his servant. God shall enlarge Japheth, and he shall dwell in the tents of Shem; and Canaan shall be his servant."

[8]II Kings 8:10, "And Elisha said unto him, Go, say unto him, Thou mayest certainly recover: howbeit the Lord hath shewed me that he shall surely die"; 12, "And Hazael said, Why weepeth my lord? And he answered, Because I know the evil that thou wilt do unto the children of Israel: their strong holds wilt thou set on fire, and their young men wilt thou slay with the sword, and wilt dash their children, and rip up their women with child."

[9]Latin for "See Pareus": David Pareus (1548–1635), a Protestant theologian from Heidelberg.

but of *Cush.* Psal. 68. 31. *Princes shall come out of Egypt* [Mizraim], *Ethiopia* [Cush] *shall soon stretch out her hands unto God.* Under which Names, all *Africa* may be comprehended; and their Promised Conversion ought to be prayed for. *Jer.* 13. 23. *Can the Ethiopian change his skin?* This shows that Black Men are the Posterity of *Cush:* Who time out of mind have been distinguished by their Colour. And for want of the true, *Ovid* assigns a fabulous cause of it.

Sanguine tum credunt in corpora summa vocato
Æthiopum populus nigrum traxisse colorem.

Metamorph. lib. 2.[10]

Obj. 2. *The* Nigers *are brought out of a Pagan Country, into places where the Gospel is Preached.*

Answ. Evil must not be done, that good may come of it. The extraordinary and comprehensive Benefit accruing to the Church of God, and to *Joseph* personally, did not rectify his brethrens Sale of him.

Obj. 3. *The* Africans *have Wars one with another: Our Ships bring lawful Captives taken in those Wars.*

Answ. For ought is known, their Wars are much such as were between *Jacob's* Sons and their Brother *Joseph.* If they be between Town and Town; Provincial, or National: Every War is upon one side Unjust. An Unlawful War can't make lawful Captives. And by Receiving, we are in danger to promote, and partake in their Barbarous Cruelties. I am sure, if some Gentlemen should go down to the *Brewsters* to take the Air, and Fish: And a stronger party from *Hull* should Surprise them, and Sell them for Slaves to a Ship outward bound: they would think themselves unjustly dealt with; both by Sellers and Buyers. And yet 'tis to be feared, we have no other kind of Title to our *Nigers. Therefore all things whatsoever ye would that men should do to you, do ye even so to them: for this is the Law and the Prophets.* Matt. 7. 12.

Obj. 4. Abraham *had Servants bought with his Money, and born in his House.*

Answ. Until the Circumstances of *Abraham's* purchase be recorded, no Argument can be drawn from it. In the mean time, Charity obliges us to conclude, that He knew it was lawful and good.

It is Observable that the *Israelites* were strictly forbidden the buying, or selling one another for Slaves. *Levit.* 25. 39. 46.[11] *Jer.* 34 8. . . . . . . 22.[12] And GOD gaged

[10] In a passage from the myth of Phaeton, Ovid's *Metamorphoses,* Book 2, reads, "It was then, as men think, that the peoples of Ethiopia became black-skinned, since the blood was drawn to the surface of their bodies by the heat."

[11] Leviticus 25:39, "And if thy brother that dwelleth by thee be waxen poor, and be sold unto thee; thou shalt not compel him to serve as a bondservant"; 46, "And ye shall take them as an inheritance for your children after you, to inherit them for a possession; they shall be your bondmen for ever: but over your brethren the children of Israel, ye shall not rule one over another with rigour."

[12] Jeremiah 34:8–22: "This is the word that came unto Jeremiah from the Lord, after that the king Zedekiah had made a covenant with all the people which were at Jerusalem, to proclaim liberty unto them; That every man should let his manservant, and every man his maidservant, being an Hebrew or an Hebrewess, go free; that none should serve himself of them, to wit, of a Jew his brother. Now when all princes, and all the people, which had entered into the covenant, heard that every one should let his manservant, and every one his maidservant, go free, that none should serve themselves of them any more, then they obeyed, and let them go. But after-

His Blessing in lieu of any loss they might conceipt they suffered thereby. *Deut.* 15. 18.[13] And since the partition Wall is broken down, inordinate Self love should likewise be demolished. GOD expects that Christians should be of a more Ingenuous and benign frame of spirit. Christians should carry it to all the World, as the *Israelites* were to carry it one towards another. And for men obstinately to persist in holding their Neighbours and Brethren under the Rigor of perpetual Bondage, seems to be no proper way of gaining Assurance that God ha's given them Spiritual Freedom. Our Blessed Saviour ha's altered the Measures of the ancient Love-Song, and set it to a most Excellent New Tune, which all ought to be ambitious of Learning. *Matt.* 5. 43, 44.[14] *John* 13. 34.[15] These *Ethiopians,* as black as they are; seeing they are the Sons and Daughters of the First *Adam,* the Brethren and Sisters of the Last ADAM, and the Offspring of GOD; They ought to be treated with a Respect agreeable.

Servitus perfecta voluntaria, inter Christianum & Christianum, ex parte servi patientis sæpe est licita, quia est necessaria: sed ex parte domini agentis, & procurando &

ward they turned, and caused the servants and the handmaids, whom they had let go free, to return, and brought them into subjection for servants and for handmaids. Therefore the word of the Lord came to Jeremiah from the Lord, saying, Thus saith the Lord, the God of Israel: I made a covenant with your fathers in the day that I brought them forth out of the land of Egypt, out of the house of bondmen, saying, At the end of seven years let ye go every man his brother an Hebrew, which hath been sold unto thee; and when he hath served thee six years, thou shalt let him go free from thee: but your fathers hearkened not unto me, neither inclined their ear. And ye were now turned, and had done right in my sight, in proclaiming liberty every man to his neighbour; and ye had made a covenant before me in the house which is called by my name: But ye turned and polluted my name, and caused every man his servant, and every man his handmaid, whom he had set at liberty at their pleasure, to return, and brought them into subjection, to be unto you for servants and for handmaids. Therefore saith the Lord: Ye have not hearkened unto me, in proclaiming liberty, every one to his brother, and every man to his neighbour: behold, I proclaim a liberty for you, saith the Lord, to the sword, to the pestilence, and to the famine: and I will make you to be removed into all the kingdoms of the earth. And I will give the men that have transgressed my covenant, which have not performed the words of the covenant which they had made before me, when they cut the calf in twain, and passed between the parts thereof, The princes of Judah, and the princes of Jerusalem, the eunuchs, and the priests, and all the people of the land, which passed between the parts of the calf; I will even give them into the hand of their enemies, and into the hand of them that seek their life: and their dead bodies shall be for meat unto the fowls of the heaven, and to the beasts of the earth. And Zedekiah king of Judah and his princes will I give into the hand of their enemies, and into the hand of them that seek their life, and into the hand of the king of Babylon's army, which are gone up from you. Behold I will command, saith the Lord, and cause them to return to this city; and they shall fight against it, and take it, and burn it with fire: and I will make the cities of Judah a desolation without an inhabitant."

[13]Deuteronomy 15:18, "It shall not seem hard unto thee, when thou sendest him away free from thee; for he hath been worth a double hired servant to thee, in serving thee six years: and the Lord thy God shall bless thee in all that thou doest."

[14]Matthew 5:43–44, "Ye have heard that it hath been said, Thou shalt love thy neighbour, and hate thine enemy. But I say unto you, Love your enemies, bless them that curse you, do good to them that hate you, and pray for them which despitefully use you, and persecute you."

[15]John 13:34, "A new commandment I give unto you, That ye love one another; as I have loved you, that ye also love one another."

exercendo, vix potest esse licita: quia non convenit regulæ illi generali: Quæcunque volueritis ut faciant vobis homines, ita & vos facite eis. Matt. 7. 12.

Perfecta servitus pœnæ, non potest jure locum habere, nisi ex delicto gravi quod ultimum supplicium aliquo modo meretur: quia Libertas ex naturali æstimatione proxime accedit ad vitam ipsam, & eidem a multis præferri solet.

Ames. Cas. Consc. Lib. 5. Cap. 23. Thes. 2, 3.[16]

1700

My Verses upon the New Century [Jan. 1, 1701][1]

Once more! Our GOD, vouchsafe to Shine:
Tame Thou the Rigour of our Clime.
Make haste with thy Impartial Light,
And terminate this long dark Night.

Let the transplanted *English* Vine
Spread further still: still Call it Thine.
Prune it wtih Skill: for yield it can
More Fruit to Thee the Husbandman.

Give the poor *Indians* Eyes to see
The Light of Life: and set them free;
That they Religion may profess,
Denying all Ungodliness.

From hard'ned *Jews* the Vail remove,
Let them their Martyr'd JESUS love;
And Homage unto Him afford,
Because He is their Rightfull LORD.

[16]This passage, taken from William Ames's *De conscientia, et eius iure, vel casibus,* Book 5, Chapter 23, Theses 2, 3, reads, in a translation called *Conscience with the Power and Cases thereof* (London, 1643), "2.2 Perfect servitude, so it be voluntary, is on the patients part often lawfull betweene Christian and Christian, because indeed it is necessary: but on the Masters part who is the agent, in procuring and exercising the authority, it is scarce lawfull; in respect, it thwarts that generall Canon, *What you would have men doe unto you, even so doe unto them; Matth.* 17.12. 3.3, Perfect servitude, by way of punishment, can have no place by right, unlesse for some hainous offence, which might deserve the severest punishment, to wit, death: because our liberty in the naturall account, is the very next thing to life it selfe, yea by many is preferred before it." The passage is taken from "The Fift Booke of the Duties of Man Towards his Neighbour."

[1]This text is taken from a broadside entitled "Wednesday, January 1, 1701. A little before Break-a-Day, at Boston of the Massachusetts." The text has been slightly modernized. On January 1, Sewall remarked in his diary that a group of trumpeters on Boston Common "sounded there till about sunrise."

So false Religions shall decay,
And Darkness fly before bright Day:
So Men shall GOD in CHRIST adore;
And worship Idols vain, no more.

As *Asia*, and *Africa*,
Europa, with *America*;
All Four, in Consort join'd, shall Sing
New Songs of Praise to CHRIST our KING.

1701

Cotton Mather 1663–1728

Cotton Mather was the grandson of two of the most influential first-generation Puritans in Massachusetts: John Cotton, after whom he was named, and Richard Mather. His father, Increase Mather, rose during the first half of Cotton's life to become pastor of Old North Church and president of Harvard College; he also secured a new charter for Massachusetts from King Charles II and selected the first governor and council to serve under it. As the eldest son, Cotton intended to follow in Increase's footsteps. A child prodigy, he graduated from Harvard at age sixteen.

In 1685, Mather matched his father's first accomplishment by becoming the ordained pastor of Old North Church, a position he held until his death. He never became president of Harvard, although he was offered (and refused) the presidency of Yale. He wished to match his father's achievements, yet his political influence never approached that of Increase Mather. In fact, Cotton Mather's influence, like his father's, declined from 1694 on, largely as a result of political changes brought on by the new Massachusetts charter. A more serious embarrassment, however, was the Salem witch trials of 1692, which Increase opposed but Cotton supported.

Cotton's reaction to Salem's alleged witches, while pronounced, was not unusual in an age still absorbed by providences. Seventeenth-century Puritans had inherited a Platonic world-view, believing that the spiritual and the earthly realms overlapped, so that the events of this world were but temporal shadows of an eternal reality. If, as the Puritans believed, God revealed his will in the events of the material world—in the veiled form of storms, martial wins and losses, miraculous cures, and so on—they also believed that the devil influenced the outcome of earthly events, often through his demonic minions: fallen angels, witches, heretics, and "heathens."

Broadly speaking, Mather's narratives of both the Salem witch trials and the Indian wars provide a psychological barometer of the Puritans' anxiety over their perceived status as God's chosen and the status of their colony as a holy community. From the 1660s, a decade in which the Bay Colony buried the majority of its founding generations, Puritan ministers in the second and third generations began to see omens of spiritual decline, clear signs of a gradual abatement of religious fervor and a withdrawing of God's favor. Britain's Puritan Commonwealth had fallen shortly after Oliver Cromwell's death in 1658; and the following three decades brought two Catholic kings to the restored throne. Once again headed by the monarchy, the Anglican

Church renewed its claims of religious hegemony. And as the imperial interests of Great Britain began to outstrip the provincial and religious interests of its colony, the monarchy began a systematic program to strip the Boston leadership of its chartered powers.

Still more devastating, third-generation Puritans, though devout in their spirituality and vigilant in their religious observations, increasingly lacked a genuine conversion experience and were thus unable to provide a testimony of their knowledge of personal salvation. Without this requisite ritual of regeneration—which triggered the individual's transformation from a member of the congregation to a covenant-member of the visible "Church"—an individual could not enter the covenant of "visible saints." By the 1690s, the decade in which Mather would write most of the works anthologized here, the Puritan clergy saw in their community's afflictions the signs of God's displeasure. The French Canadians and their Indian allies began to retaliate after decades of Protestant oppression. And a "knot of witches" in Salem threatened the moral welfare of the colony.

Mather used both the witch trials and the Indian wars to generate a narrative that would encourage a spiritual awakening in the face of widespread religious complacency. Like his grandfather John Cotton, Mather believed that New England was the fulfillment of a bibical "type." Thus the witch trials and Hannah Dustan's Indian captivity were rendered as biblical tropes. While the devil's assault upon Salem was cast as the Philistine attack on Israel—with the role of the prophet-warrior Samuel going to the witch-trial judges—Dustan's captivity, her miraculous escape, and her brutal retaliation upon her sleeping captors were rendered as the Old Testament story of Jael, the Hebrew woman who violently killed a Canaanite king for holding her people captive.

Although his treatment of these "demonic" forces has given him more lasting (if dubious) fame than his scientific writings, Mather was as intrigued by the visible world as he was by the invisible. He was elected to the preeminent scientific body, the Royal Society, in 1713; he was an early proponent of vaccination; and he published such influential scientific works as *The Christian Philosopher* (1720). Careful scientific observation is to be found in his sermons, papers, and personal letters.

Neither the natural nor the supernatural world, however, interested Mather as much as the lives of men, especially his forebears who had founded New England as a celestial empire. Mather's longest and most admired work is the *Magnalia Christi Americana.* At once an encyclopedic account of New England's history and a gallery of its eminent lives, the *Magnalia* attempts to preserve a sense of the colony's sacred mission. To that end, most of Mather's biographies are quite similar, for each New England hero is made to fit a common, saintly pattern from early conversion experience to oracular deathbed scene, and each is highly eulogized. But in each life distinctive features are emphasized, and many of these clearly reflect the author's own reforming interests. For example, Mather emphasized John Eliot's role as "apostle to the Indians" and to African slaves; Mather himself would advocate similar apostolic missions in *The Negro Christianized* (1706) and *India Christiana* (1721). He praised past models to stimulate present action, whether by individuals or by "reforming societies" like those described in *Bonifacius or Essay to Do Good* (1710). Inspired by *Bonifacius,* men like Benjamin Franklin went on to "do good" singly or to form groups devoted to improvement in secular and religious life.

Despite Cotton's failure to match Increase's political career, the son far surpassed the father as a writer. Well over four hundred separate publications marked his literary career, and when he died he left a substantial body of still unpublished manuscripts, including one he considered his masterwork, the *Biblia Americana*. One feature that sets Mather's works apart from those of his contemporaries is their mode of expression. Full of ingenious turns of phrase and richly adorned with allusions, often in Latin, Greek, or Hebrew, this style was aptly described by Mather himself as a golden cloth "stuck with as many jewels as the gown of a Russian ambassador." Such sheer delight in verbal play seems a strange accompaniment to serious Puritan content, but both the style and the religion are deeply rooted in sixteenth-century models. Mather, however, clearly outdid his models—and at a time when Baroque ornamentation and orthodox theology were being simplified; thus, his florid style was often attacked by rationalist critics in his own day. Nevertheless, the rich poetics of his work often has a deeper sense, linking the nation's past with the patterns of sacred history.

Kenneth Alan Hovey
University of Texas at San Antonio

Gregory S. Jackson
Rutgers University

PRIMARY WORKS

Wonders of the Invisible World, 1692; *Decennium Luctuosom: a History of the Long War,* 1699; *Magnalia Christi Americana,* 1702; *The Negro Christianized,* 1706; *Bonifacius,* 1710; *The Christian Philosopher,* 1720; *Manductio ad Ministerium,* 1726.

from The Wonders of the Invisible World[1]

[The Devil Attacks the People of God]

The New Englanders are a people of God settled in those, which were once the devil's territories; and it may easily be supposed that the devil was exceedingly disturbed, when he perceived such a people here accomplishing the promise of old made unto our blessed Jesus, that He should have the utmost parts of the earth for His possession.[2] There was not a greater uproar among the Ephesians, when the

[1]In May 1692, Governor William Phips of Massachusetts appointed a court to "hear and determine" the evidence against Salem residents accused of witchcraft in April and May 1692. The accusations and arrests continued throughout the summer. Phips named William Stoughton, his lieutenant-governor, as chief justice and appointed several lesser magistrates to serve under Stoughton, including John Hathorne (Nathaniel Hawthorne's ancestor), Samuel Sewall, John Richards, Wait Winthrop (grandson of John), and Nathaniel Saltonstall, who resigned from the tribunal in protest after the first trial. Already beginning to feel the resentment of public opinion after the final execution of condemned witches on September 22, 1692, Stoughton and the other judges prevailed upon Cotton Mather to defend the court's decisions, particularly the execution of so many Salem residents. Mather had attended the proceedings in August at the special invitation of John Richards. First published in 1693, this slightly modernized text is taken from the reprint by John Russell Smith (London, 1862).

[2]In Psalm 2:8, God promises his son, "Ask of me, and I shall give thee the heathen for thine inheritance, and the uttermost parts of the earth for thy possession." Mather also likely has in mind the moment when, after his baptism, Jesus is tempted by the devil, who offers him an earthly kingdom.

Gospel was first brought among them,[3] than there was among the powers of the air (after whom those Ephesians walked) when first the silver trumpets of the Gospel here made the joyful sound. The devil thus irritated, immediately tried all sorts of methods to overturn this poor plantation: and so much of the church, as was fled into this wilderness, immediately found the serpent cast out of his mouth a flood for the carrying of it away.[4] I believe that never were more satanical devices used for the unsettling of any people under the sun, than what have been employed for the extirpation of the vine which God has here planted, casting out the heathen, and preparing a room before it, and causing it to take deep root, and fill the land, so that it sent its boughs unto the Atlantic Sea eastward, and its branches unto the Connecticut River westward, and the hills were covered with a shadow thereof.[5] But all those attempts of hell have hitherto been abortive, many an Ebenezer[6] has been erected unto the praise of God, by his poor people here; and having obtained help from God, we continue to this day.[7] Wherefore the devil is now making one attempt more upon us; an attempt more difficult, more surprising, more snarled with unintelligible circumstances than any that we have hitherto encountered; an attempt so critical, that if we get well through, we shall soon enjoy halcyon days with all the vultures of hell trodden under our feet.[8] He has wanted his incarnate legions to persecute us, as the people of God have in the other hemisphere been persecuted: he has therefore drawn forth his more spiritual ones to make an attack upon us. We have been advised by some credible Christians yet alive, that a malefactor, accused of witchcraft as well as murder, and executed in this place more than forty years ago, did then give notice of an horrible plot against the country by witchcraft, and a foundation of witchcraft then laid, which if it were not seasonably discovered, would probably blow up, and pull down all the churches in the country. And we have now with horror seen the discovery of such a witchcraft! An army of devils is horribly broke in upon the place which is the center, and after a sort, the firstborn of our English settlements: and the houses of the good people there are filled with doleful shrieks of their children and servants, tormented by invisible hands, with tortures altogether preternatural. After the mischiefs there endeavored, and since in part conquered, the terrible plague of evil angels hath made its progress into some other places, where other persons have been in like manner diabolically handled. These our poor afflicted neighbors, quickly after they become infected and infested with these demons, arrive to a capacity of discerning those which they conceive the shapes of their troublers; and notwithstanding the great and just suspicion that the demons might impose the

[3]Located on the southwest coast of modern-day Turkey, Ephesus was the ancient Greek port city renowned for its Temple of Diana and for the religious fanaticism of her followers. When Paul arrived to proselytize the Christian gospel, he and his disciples were confronted by a crowd of devotees of Diana (see Acts 19:22–41).

[4]Revelation 12:6, 15.

[5]Mather's description draws parallels between New England as God's Promised Land and the biblical Land of Canaan (Psalm 80:8–12).

[6]Stone of help (1 Samuel 7:12): The Old Testament prophet Samuel commemorated God's aid in defeating the Philistines by marking the enemy's line of retreat with a stone he named Ebenezer.

[7]Mather echoes Paul's unwavering faith in God from the first moment of his conversion (Acts 26:22).

[8]Mather invokes scripture to make a comparison between the Salem witches and the wicked destroyed by God in the great flood (Isaiah 28:3).

shapes of innocent persons in their spectral exhibitions upon the sufferers (which may perhaps prove no small part of the witch-plot in the issue), yet many of the persons thus represented, being examined, several of them have been convicted of a very damnable witchcraft: yea, more than one twenty have confessed, that they have signed unto a book, which the devil showed them, and engaged in his hellish design of bewitching and ruining our land. We know not, at least I know not, how far the delusions of Satan may be interwoven into some circumstances of the confessions; but one would think all the rules of understanding human affairs are at an end, if after so many most voluntary harmonious confessions, made by intelligent persons of all ages, in sundry towns, at several times, we must not believe the main strokes wherein those confessions all agree: especially when we have a thousand preternatural things every day before our eyes, wherein the confessors do acknowledge their concernment, and give demonstration of their being so concerned. If the devils now can strike the minds of men with any poisons of so fine a composition and operation, that scores of innocent people shall unite, in confessions of a crime, which we see actually committed, it is a thing prodigious, beyond the wonders of the former ages, and it threatens no less than a sort of a dissolution upon the world. Now, by these confessions 'tis agreed that the Devil has made a dreadful knot of witches in the country, and by the help of witches has dreadfully increased that knot: that these witches have driven a trade of commissioning their confederate spirits to do all sorts of mischiefs to the neighbors, whereupon there have ensued such mischievous consequences upon the bodies and estates of the neighborhood, as could not otherwise be accounted for: yea, that at prodigious witch-meetings, the wretches have proceeded so far as to concert and consult the methods of rooting out the Christian religion from this country, and setting up instead of it perhaps a more gross diabolism than ever the world saw before. And yet it will be a thing little short of miracle, if in so spread a business as this, the Devil should not get in some of his juggles,[9] to confound the discovery of all the rest.

* * *

But I shall no longer detain my reader from his expected entertainment, in a brief account of the trials which have passed upon some of the malefactors lately executed at Salem, for the witchcrafts whereof they stood convicted. For my own part, I was not present at any of them; nor ever had I any personal prejudice at the persons thus brought upon the stage; much less at the surviving relations of those persons, with and for whom I would be as hearty a mourner as any man living in the world: The Lord comfort them! But having received a command[10] so to do, I can do no other than shortly relate the chief matters of fact, which occurred in the trials of some that were executed, in an abridgment collected out of the court papers on this occasion put into my hands. You are to take the truth, just as it was; and the truth will hurt no good man. There might have been more of these, if my book would not thereby have swollen too big; and if some other worthy hands did not perhaps intend something further in these collections; for which cause I have only singled out four

[9]Tricks or snares.
[10]Mather refers to Stoughton's request that he explain and justify the actions of the Court of Oyer and Terminer.

or five, which may serve to illustrate the way of dealing, wherein witchcrafts use to be concerned; and I report matters not as an advocate, but as an historian.

* * *

V. The Trial of Martha Carrier[11] at the Court of Oyer and Terminer,[12] Held by Adjournment at Salem, August 2, 1692

I. Martha Carrier was indicted for the bewitching certain persons, according to the form usual in such cases, pleading not guilty to her indictment; there were first brought in a considerable number of the bewitched persons who not only made the court sensible of an horrid witchcraft committed upon them, but also deposed that it was Martha Carrier, or her shape, that grievously tormented them, by biting, pricking, pinching and choking of them. It was further deposed that while this Carrier was on her examination before the magistrates, the poor people were so tortured that every one expected their death upon the very spot, but that upon the binding of Carrier they were eased. Moreover the look of Carrier then laid the afflicted people for dead; and her touch, if her eye at the same time were off them, raised them again: which things were also now seen upon her trial. And it was testified that upon the mention of some having their necks twisted almost round, by the shape of this Carrier, she replied, "It's no matter though their necks had been twisted quite off."

II. Before the trial of this prisoner, several of her own children had frankly and fully confessed not only that they were witches themselves, but that this their mother had made them so. This confession they made with great shows of repentance, and with much demonstration of truth. They related place, time, occasion; they gave an account of journeys, meetings and mischiefs by them performed, and were very credible in what they said. Nevertheless, this evidence was not produced against the prisoner at the bar,[13] inasmuch as there was other evidence enough to proceed upon.

III. Benjamin Abbot gave his testimony that last March was a twelvemonth, this Carrier was very angry with him, upon laying out some land near her husband's: her expressions in this anger were that she would stick as close to Abbot as the bark stuck to the tree; and that he should repent of it afore seven years came to an end, so as Doctor Prescot should never cure him. These words were heard by others besides Abbot himself; who also heard her say, she would hold his nose as close to the grindstone as ever it was held since his name was Abbot. Presently after this, he was taken with a swelling in his foot, and then with a pain in his side, and exceedingly tormented. It bred into a sore, which was lanced by Doctor Prescot, and several gallons of corruption[14] ran out of it. For six weeks it continued very bad, and then another

[11]Martha Carrier was one of the most outspoken of the accused. She not only boldly renounced witnesses for lying, but she also questioned the judgment and impartiality of the authorities, shaming John Hathorne for believing "folks that are out of their wits."

[12]"To hear and determine."

[13]Before the court.

[14]An incision was made into the flesh and the infected matter drained.

sore bred in the groin, which was also lanced by Doctor Prescot. Another sore then bred in his groin, which was likewise cut, and put him to very great misery: he was brought unto death's door, and so remained until Carrier was taken, and carried away by the constable, from which very day he began to mend, and so grew better every day, and is well ever since.

Sarah Abbot also, his wife, testified that her husband was not only all this while afflicted in his body, but also that strange, extraordinary and unaccountable calamities befell his cattle; their death being such as they could guess at no natural reason for.

IV. Allin Toothaker testified that Richard, the son of Martha Carrier, having some difference with him, pulled him down by the hair of the head. When he rose again he was going to strike at Richard Carrier but fell down flat on his back to the ground, and had not power to stir hand or foot, until he told Carrier he yielded; and then he saw the shape of Martha Carrier go off his breast.

This Toothaker had received a wound in the wars; and he now testified that Martha Carrier told him he should never be cured. Just afore the apprehending of Carrier, he could thrust a knitting needle into his wound four inches deep; but presently after her being seized, he was thoroughly healed.

He further testified that when Carrier and he some times were at variance, she would clap her hands at him, and say he should get nothing by it; whereupon he several times lost his cattle, by strange deaths, whereof no natural causes could be given.

V. John Rogger also testified that upon the threatening words of this malicious Carrier, his cattle would be strangely bewitched; as was more particularly then described.

VI. Samuel Preston testified that about two years ago, having some difference with Martha Carrier, he lost a cow in a strange, preternatural, unusual manner; and about a month after this, the said Carrier, having again some difference with him, she told him he had lately lost a cow, and it should not be long before he lost another; which accordingly came to pass; for he had a thriving and well-kept cow, which without any known cause quickly fell down and died.

VII. Phebe Chandler testified that about a fortnight before the apprehension of Martha Carrier, on a Lordsday, while the Psalm was singing in the Church, this Carrier then took her by the shoulder and shaking her, asked her, where she lived: she made her no answer, although as Carrier, who lived next door to her father's house, could not in reason but know who she was. Quickly after this, as she was at several times crossing the fields, she heard a voice, that she took to be Martha Carrier's, and it seemed as if it was over her head. The voice told her she should within two or three days be poisoned. Accordingly, within such a little time, one half of her right hand became greatly swollen and very painful; as also part of her face: whereof she can give no account how it came. It continued very bad for some days; and several times since she has had a great pain in her breast; and been so seized on her legs that she has hardly been able to go. She added that lately, going well to the house of God, Richard, the son of Martha Carrier, looked very earnestly upon her, and immediately her hand, which had formerly been poisoned, as is abovesaid, began to pain her greatly, and she had a strange burning at her stomach; but was then struck deaf, so that she could not hear any of the prayer, or singing, till the two or three last words of the Psalm.

VIII. One Foster, who confessed her own share in the witchcraft for which the prisoner stood indicted, affirmed that she had seen the prisoner at some of their witch-meetings, and that it was this Carrier, who persuaded her to be a witch. She confessed that the Devil carried them on a pole to a witch-meeting; but the pole broke, and she hanging about Carrier's neck, they both fell down, and she then received an hurt by the fall, whereof she was not at this very time recovered.

IX. One Lacy, who likewise confessed her share in this witchcraft, now testified, that she and the prisoner were once bodily present at a witch-meeting in Salem Village; and that she knew the prisoner to be a witch, and to have been at a diabolical sacrament, and that the prisoner was the undoing of her and her children by enticing them into the snare of the devil.

X. Another Lacy, who also confessed her share in this witchcraft, now testified, that the prisoner was at the witch-meeting, in Salem Village, where they had bread and wine administered unto them.

XI. In the time of this prisoner's trial, one Susanna Sheldon in open court had her hands unaccountably tied together with a wheel-band[15] so fast that without cutting it, it could not be loosed: it was done by a specter; and the sufferer affirmed it was the prisoner's.

Memorandum. This rampant hag, Martha Carrier, was a person of whom the confessions of the witches, and of her own children among the rest, agreed that the devil had promised her she should be Queen of Hebrews.

from Magnalia Christi Americana; or, The Ecclesiastical History of New-England[1]

from A General Introduction

Dicam hoc propter utilitatem eorum qui Lecturi sunt hoc opus.
Theodoret[2]

I. I WRITE the *Wonders* of the CHRISTIAN RELIGION, flying from the Depravations of *Europe,* to the *American Strand.*[3] And, assisted by the Holy Author of that *Religion,* I do, with all Conscience of *Truth,* required therein by Him, who is the *Truth* itself, Report the *Wonderful Displays* of His Infinite Power, Wisdom, Good-

[15]A metal or leather band or strap that goes around a wooden wheel.

[1]"A History of Christ's Wonderful Works in America." The full subtitle is *The Ecclesiastical History of New-England from its First Planting, in the Year 1620, unto the Year of Our Lord, 1698.* First published in London in 1702; this slightly modernized text is taken from the edition by Thomas Robbins (Hartford, Conn., 1855).

[2]"This I say for the benefit of those who may happen to read the book." This quotation, printed in the original text in Greek as well as Latin, is by Theodoret (393?–457), a Greek bishop and church historian.

[3]See George Herbert, "The Church Militant," 235–36.

ness, and Faithfulness, wherewith His Divine Providence hath *Irradiated* an *Indian Wilderness.*

I Relate the *Considerable Matters,* that produced and attended the First Settlement of COLONIES, which have been Renowned for the Degree of REFORMATION, Professed and Attained by *Evangelical Churches,* erected in those *Ends of the Earth:*[4] And a *field* being thus prepared, I proceed unto a Relation of the *Considerable Matters* which have been acted thereupon.

I first introduce the *Actors,* that have, in a more exemplary manner served those *Colonies;* and give *Remarkable Occurrences,* in the exemplary LIVES of many *Magistrates,* and of more *Ministers,* who so *Lived,* as to leave unto Posterity, *Examples* worthy of *Everlasting Remembrance.*[5]

I add hereunto, the *Notables* of the only *Protestant Univeristy,*[6] that ever *shone* in that Hemisphere of the *New World;* with particular Instances of *Criolians,*[7] in our *Biography,* provoking the *whole World,* with vertuous Objects of Emulation.

I introduce then, the *Actions* of a more Eminent Importance, that have signalized those *Colonies;* Whether the *Establishments,* directed by their *Synods;* with a Rich Variety of *Synodical* and *Ecclesiastical* Determinations;[8] or, the *Disturbances,* with which they have been from all sorts of *Temptations* and *Enemies* Tempestuated; and the *Methods* by which they have still weathered out each *Horrible Tempest.*[9]

And into the midst of these *Actions,* I interpose an entire *Book,* wherein there is, with all possible Veracity, a *Collection* made, of *Memorable Occurrences,* and amazing *Judgments* and *Mercies,* befalling many *particular Persons* among the People of *New-England.*[10]

Let my Readers expect all that I have promised them, in this *Bill of Fare;* and it may be they will find themselves entertained with yet many other Passages, above and beyond their Expectation, deserving likewise a room in *History:* In all which, there will be nothing, but the *Author's* too mean way of preparing so great Entertainments, to Reproach the Invitation . . .

3. It is the History of these PROTESTANTS, that is here attempted: PROTESTANTS that highly honoured and affected *The Church of* ENGLAND, and humbly Petition to be a *Part* of it: But by the Mistake of a few powerful *Brethren,* driven to seek a place for the Exercise of the *Protestant Religion,* according to the Light of their Consciences, in the Desarts of *America.* And in this Attempt I have proposed, not only to preserve and secure the Interest of *Religion,* in the Churches of that little Country *NEW-ENGLAND,* so far as the Lord Jesus Christ may please to Bless it for that End, but also to offer unto the Churches of the *Reformation,* abroad in the World, some small *Memorials,* that may be serviceable unto the Designs of *Reformation,* whereto, I believe, they are quickly to be awakened . . . Tho' the *Reformed Churches* in the *American Regions,* have, by very Injurious Representations of their Brethren (all which they desire to Forget and Forgive!) been many times thrown into

[4]The topic of the first book of the *Magnalia.*

[5]The second book of the *Magnalia* consists of biographies of magistrates, the third of biographies of ministers.

[6]The fourth book describes Harvard and its best students.

[7]Creoles, people of European or African descent naturalized in America.

[8]The topic of the fifth book.

[9]The topic of the seventh and last book.

[10]The topic of the sixth book.

a *Dung-Cart;* yet, as they have been a *precious Odour to God in Christ,* so, I hope, they will be a *precious Odour* unto *His People;* and not only *Precious,* but *Useful* also, when the *History* of them shall come to be considered. A *Reformation of the Church* is coming on, and I cannot but thereupon say, with the dying *Cyrus* to his Children in *Xenophon*[11] . . . *Learn from the things that have been done already, for this is the best way of Learning.* The Reader hath here an Account of *The Things that have been done already. Bernard*[12] upon that Clause in the *Canticles,* [*O thou fairest among Women*] has this ingenious Gloss, *Pulchram, non omnimodo quidem, sed pulchram inter mulieres cam dicit, videlicet cum Distinctione, quatenus et ex hoc amplius reprimatur, & sciat quid desit sibi.*[13] Thus I do not say, That the Churches of *New-England* are the most *Regular* that can be; yet I do say, and am sure, That they are very like unto those that were in the *First Ages* of Christianity. And if I assert, That in the *Reformation* of the Church, the State of it in those *First Ages,* is to be not a little considered, the Great *Peter Ramus,*[14] among others, has emboldened me. . . . In short, The *First Age* was the *Golden Age:* To return unto *That,* will make a Man a *Protestant,* and I may add, a *Puritan.* 'Tis possible, That our Lord Jesus Christ carried some Thousands of *Reformers* into the Retirements of an *American Desart,* on purpose, that, with an opportunity granted unto many of his Faithful Servants, to enjoy the precious *Liberty* of their *Ministry,* tho' in the midst of many *Temptations* all their days, He might there, *To* them first, and then *By* them, give a *Specimen* of many Good Things, which He would have His Churches elsewhere aspire and arise unto: And *This* being done, He knows whether there be not *All done,* that *New-England* was planted for; and whether the Plantation may not, soon after this, *Come to Nothing.* Upon that Expression in the Sacred Scripture, *Cast the unprofitable Servant into Outer Darkness,*[15] it hath been imagined by some, That the *Regiones Exteræ*[16] of *America,* are the *Tenebræ Exteriores,*[17] which the *Unprofitable* are there condemned unto. No doubt, the Authors of those Ecclesiastical Impositions and Severities, which drove the English Christians into the *Dark Regions* of *America,* esteemed those *Christians* to be a very *unprofitable* sort of Creatures. But behold, ye *European* Churches, There are *Golden Candlesticks* [more than *twice Seven times Seven!*][18] in the midst of this *Outer Darkness:* Unto the *upright* Children of *Abraham,* here hath arisen *Light in Darkness.* And let us humbly speak it, it shall be *Profitable* for you to consider the *Light,* which from the midst of this *Outer Darkness,* is now to be Darted over unto the other side of the *Atlantick Ocean.* But we must therewithal ask your Prayers, that these *Golden Candlesticks* may not *quickly* be *Removed out of their place!*

4. But whether *New England* may *Live* any where else or no, it must *Live* in our *History!* . . .

1702

[11]Ancient Greek author (430?–355? B.C.), whose *Anabasis* recounts the accomplishments of the Persian prince, Cyrus the Younger.

[12]St. Bernard of Clairvaux (1090–1153) commenting on Song of Solomon 1:8 ("Canticles" is an alternative name for Song of Solomon).

[13]"He says that she is fair, not in a universal sense, but fair among women, plainly with a distinction, to which extent his praise is qualified and she may know what she lacks."

[14]Pierre de la Ramée (1515–1572), French philosopher and educational reformer who converted to Protestantism.

[15]Matthew 25:30.

[16]Outer regions.

[17]Outer shadows (or darkness).

[18]Revelations 1:12–13, 20; 2:5.

Galeacius Secundus:[1] *The Life of William Bradford, Esq., Governor of Plymouth Colony*

Omnium Somnos illius vigilantia defendit; omnium otium, illius Labor; omnium Delitias, illius Industria; omnium vacationem, illius occupatio.[2]

I. It has been a matter of some observation, that although Yorkshire be one of the largest shires in England; yet, for all the *fires* of martyrdom which were kindled in the days of Queen Mary,[3] it afforded no more *fuel* than one poor *Leaf;* namely, John Leaf, an apprentice, who suffered for the doctrine of the Reformation at the same time and stake with the famous John Bradford.[4] But when the reign of Queen Elizabeth[5] would not admit the Reformation of worship to proceed unto those degrees, which were proposed and pursued by no small number of the faithful in those days, Yorkshire was not the least of the shires in England that afforded suffering *witnesses* thereunto. The Churches there gathered were quickly molested with such a raging persecution, that if the spirit of separation in them did carry them unto a further *extream* than it should have done, one blameable cause thereof will be found in the *extremity* of that persecution.[6] Their troubles made that *cold* country too *hot* for them, so that they were under a necessity to *seek* a retreat in the Low Countries;[7] and yet the watchful malice and fury of their adversaries rendred it almost impossible for them to *find* what they sought. For them to leave their native soil, their lands and their friends, and go into a strange place, where they must hear foreign language, and live meanly[8] and hardly, and in other imployments than that of husbandry, wherein they had been educated, *these* must needs have been such discouragements as could have been conquered by none, save those who "sought first the kingdom of God, and the righteousness thereof."[9] But that which would have made these discouragements the more unconquerable unto an ordinary faith, was the terrible zeal of their enemies to guard all ports, and search all ships, that none of them should be carried off. I will not relate the sad things of this kind then *seen* and *felt* by this people of God; but only exemplifie those trials with one short story. Divers of this people having hired a

[1]"The second Galeazzo"; Mather compares Bradford to Galeazzo Caraccoli (1517–1586), a Neapolitan patrician who forsook his native land to follow the example of Calvin in Geneva. Bradford was elected governor of Plymouth Colony when the first governor, John Carver, died.

[2]"His vigilance defends others' sleep; his labor, their rest; his diligence, their pleasures; his constancy, their leisure."

[3]During her reign (1553–1558), Catholic Queen Mary Tudor ("Bloody Mary") attempted to overturn the state Protestantism established by her father Henry VIII; many Protestants were executed or imprisoned during England's Counter Reformation.

[4]English theologian John Bradford (1510?–1555) was burned at the stake with Leaf on July 1, 1555. Their martyrdom was celebrated in John Foxe's *Book of Martyrs.*

[5]Protestant Queen Elizabeth succeeded to the throne upon Mary's death, and her reign (1558–1603) established the modern Anglican Church.

[6]For more detail on the Protestant conflict between the Anglicans and the Puritans in seventeenth-century England, see the headnote for Thomas Shepard.

[7]The Dutch provinces of Holland and Zeeland.

[8]In poverty.

[9]Matthew 6:33.

Dutchman, then lying at Hull, to carry them over to Holland, he promised faithfully to take them in between Grimsly and Hill;[10] but they coming to the place a day or two too soon, the appearance of such a multitude alarmed the officers of the town adjoining, who came with a great body of soldiers to seize upon them. Now it happened that one boat full of men had been carried aboard, while the women were yet in a bark that lay aground in a creek at low water. The Dutchman perceiving the storm that was thus beginning ashore, swore by the sacrament that he would stay no longer for any of them; and so taking the advantage of a fair wind then blowing, he put out to sea for Zealand. The women thus left near Grimsly-common, bereaved of their husbands, who had been hurried from them, and forsaken of their neighbours, of whom none durst in this fright stay with them, were a very rueful spectacle; some crying for *fear,* some shaking for *cold,* all dragged by troops of armed and angry men from one Justice to another, till not knowing what to do with them, they even dismissed them to shift as well as they could for themselves. But by their singular *afflictions,* and by their Christian *behaviours,* the *cause* for which they exposed themselves did gain considerably. In the mean time, the men at sea found reason to be glad that their families were not with them, for they were surprized with an horrible tempest, which held them for fourteen days together, in seven whereof they saw not sun, moon or star, but were driven upon the coast of Norway. The mariners often despaired of life, and once with doleful shrieks gave over all, as thinking the vessel was foundred: but the vessel rose again, and when the mariners with sunk hearts often cried out, "We sink! we sink!" the passengers, without such distraction of mind, even while the water was running into their mouths and ears, would cheerfully shout, "Yet, Lord, thou canst save! Yet, Lord, thou canst save!" And the Lord accordingly brought them at last safe unto their desired haven: and not long after helped their distressed relations thither after them, where indeed they found upon almost all accounts a *new world,* but a world in which they found that they must live like strangers and pilgrims.

2. Among those devout people was our William Bradford, who was born *Anno 1588,* in an obscure village called Ansterfield, where the people were as unacquainted with the Bible, as the Jews do seem to have been with *part* of it in the days of Josiah;[11] a most ignorant and licentious *people,* and *like unto their priest.* Here, and in some other places, he had a comfortable inheritance left him of his honest parents, who died while he was yet a child, and cast him on the education, first of his grand parents, and then of his uncles, who devoted him, like his ancestors, unto the affairs of husbandry. Soon a long sickness kept him, as he would afterwards thankfully say, from the *vanities of youth,* and made him the fitter for what he was afterwards to undergo. When he was about a dozen years old, the reading of the Scriptures began to cause great impressions upon him; and those impressions were much assisted and improved, when he came to enjoy Mr. Richard Clifton's[12] illuminating ministry, not far from his abode; he was then also further befriended, by being

[10] In Bradford's *History of Plymouth Plantation,* Grimsby and Hull, on the Lincolnshire coast, is near the Humber River. Mather here follows Bradford's account.

[11] Josiah, king of Judah (638–608? B.C.), rediscovered the Book of the Law (Bible) forsaken by his predecessors. See II Kings 22:10ff.

[12] A Puritan minister in the town of Scrooby, Clifton settled with the Scrooby Separatists in Amsterdam.

brought into the company and fellowship of such as were then called professors; though the young man that brought him into it did after become a prophane and wicked *apostate.* Nor could the wrath of his uncles, nor the scoff of his neighbours, now turned upon him, as one of the *Puritans,* divert him from his pious inclinations.

3. At last, beholding how fearfully the evangelical and apostolical *church-form* whereinto the churches of the primitive times were cast by the good spirit of God, had been *deformed* by the apostacy of the succeeding times; and what little progress the Reformation had yet made in many parts of Christendom towards its recovery, he set himself by reading, by discourse, by prayer, to learn whether it was not his duty to withdraw from the communion of the parish-assemblies, and engage with some society of the faithful, that should keep close unto the *written word* of God, as the *rule* of their worship. And after many distresses of mind concerning it, he took up a very deliberate and understanding resolution, of doing so; which resolution he chearfully prosecuted, although the provoked rage of his friends tried all the ways imaginable to reclaim him from it, unto all whom his answer was:

"Were I like to endanger my life, or consume my estate by any ungodly courses, your counsels to me were very seasonable; but you know that I have been diligent and provident in my calling, and not only desirous to augment what I have, but also to enjoy it in your company; to part from which will be as great a cross as can befal me. Nevertheless, to keep a good conscience, and walk in such a way as God has prescribed in his Word, is a thing which I must prefer before you all, and above life it self. Wherefore, since 'tis for a good cause that I am like to suffer the disasters which you lay before me, you have no cause to be either angry with me, or sorry for me; yea, I am not only willing to part with every thing that is dear to me in this world for this cause, but I am also thankful that God has given me an heart to do, and will accept me so to suffer for him."

Some lamented him, some derided him, *all* dissuaded him: nevertheless, the more they did it, the more fixed he was in his purpose to seek the ordinances of the gospel, where they should be dispensed with most of the *commanded purity;* and the sudden deaths of the chief relations which thus lay at him, quickly after convinced him what a folly it had been to have quitted his profession, in expectation of any satisfaction from them. So to Holland he attempted a removal.

4. Having with a great company of Christians hired a ship to transport them for Holland, the master perfidiously betrayed them into the hands of those persecutors, who rifled and ransacked their goods, and clapped their persons into prison at Boston,[13] where they lay for a month together. But Mr. Bradford being a young man of about eighteen, was dismissed sooner than the rest, so that within a while he had opportunity with some others to get over to Zealand, through *perils,* both by *land* and *sea* not inconsiderable; where he was not long ashore ere a viper seized on his hand—that is, an officer—who carried him unto the magistrates, unto whom an envious passenger had accused him as having *fled* out of England. When the magistrates understood the true cause of his coming thither, they were well satisfied with

[13]Boston, England.

him; and so he repaired joyfully unto his brethren at Amsterdam, where the difficulties to which he afterwards stooped in learning and serving of a Frenchman at the working of silks, were abundantly compensated by the delight wherewith he sat under the shadow of our Lord, in his purely dispensed ordinances. At the end of two years, he did, being of age to do it, convert his estate in England into money; but setting up for himself, he found some of his designs by the *providence* of God frowned upon, which he judged a *correction* bestowed by God upon him for certain decays of *internal piety,* whereinto he had fallen; the consumption of his *estate* he thought came to prevent a consumption in his *virtue.* But after he had resided in Holland about half a score years, he was one of those who bore a part in that hazardous and generous enterprise of removing into New-England, with part of the English church at Leyden, where, at their first landing, his dearest consort[14] accidentally falling overboard, was drowned in the harbour; and the rest of his days were spent in the services, and the temptations, of that American wilderness.

5. Here was Mr. Bradford, in the year 1621, unanimously chosen the governour of the plantation: the difficulties whereof were such, that if he had not been a person of more than ordinary piety, wisdom and courage, he must have sunk under them. He had, with a laudable industry, been laying up a treasure of experiences, and he had now occasion to use it: indeed, nothing but an *experienced* man could have been suitable to the necessities of the people. The potent nations of the Indians, into whose country they were come, would have cut them off, if the blessing of God upon *his* conduct had not quelled them; and if his prudence, justice and moderation had not over-ruled them, they had been ruined by their own distempers. One specimen of his demeanour is to this day particularly spoken of.[15] A company of young fellows that were newly arrived, were very unwilling to comply with the governour's order for working abroad on the publick account; and therefore on Christmas-day, when he had called upon them, they excused themselves, with a pretence that it was against their conscience to *work* such a day. The governour gave them no answer, only that he would spare them till they were better informed; but by and by he found them all at *play* in the street, sporting themselves with various diversions; whereupon commanding the instruments of their games to be taken from them, he effectually gave them to understand. "*That it was against his conscience that they should play whilst others were at work:* and that if they had any devotion to the day, they should show it at home in the exercises of religion, and not in the streets with pastime and frolicks," and this gentle reproof put a final stop to all such disorders for the future.

6. For two years together after the beginning of the colony, whereof he was now governour, the poor people had a great experiment of "man's not living by bread alone;"[16] for when they were left all together without one morsel of bread for many months one after another, still the good providence of God relieved them, and supplied them, and this for the most part out of the *sea.* In this low condition of affairs,

[14]His wife.

[15]Following Bradford's account of the incident in his *History* for 1621. Puritans did not consider Christmas Day a holiday.

[16]Luke 4:4.

there was no little exercise for the prudence and patience of the governour, who chearfully bore his part in all: and, that industry might not flag, he quickly set himself to settle *propriety* among the new-planters;[17] foreseeing that while the whole country laboured upon a common stock, the husbandry and business of the plantation could not flourish, as Plato and others long since dreamed that it would, if a *community* were established. Certainly, if the spirit which dwelt in the old puritans, had not inspired these new-planters, they had sunk under the burden of these difficulties; but our Bradford had a double portion of that spirit.

7. The plantation was quickly thrown into a storm that almost overwhelmed it, by the unhappy actions of a minister sent over from England by the adventurers[18] concerned for the plantation; but by the blessing of Heaven on the conduct of the governour, they weathered out that storm. Only the adventurers hereupon breaking to pieces, threw up all their concealments with the infant-colony; whereof they gave this as one reason, "That the planters dissembled with his Majesty and their friends in their petition, wherein they declared for a church-discipline, agreeing with the French and others of the reforming churches in Europe."[19] Whereas 'twas now urged, that they had admitted into their communion a person who at his admission utterly renounced the Churches of England, (which person, by the way, was *that* very man who had made the complaints against them,) and therefore, though they denied the *name* of Brownists,[20] yet they were the thing. In answer hereunto, the very words written by the governour were these:

"Whereas you tax us with dissembling about the *French discipline,* you do us wrong, for we both hold and practice the *discipline* of the French and other Reformed Churches (as they have published the same in the Harmony of Confessions) according to our means, in effect and substance. But whereas you would tie us up to the French *discipline* in every circumstance, you derogate from the *liberty* we have in Christ Jesus. The Apostle Paul would have none to *follow him* in any thing, but wherein he *follows* Christ; much less ought any Christian or church in the world to do it. The French may err, we may err, and other churches may err, and doubtless do in many *circumstances.* That honour therefore belongs only to the *infallible Word of God,* and *pure Testament of Christ,* to be propounded and followed as the only rule and pattern for direction herein to all churches and Christians. And it is too great arrogancy for any man or church to think that he or they have so sounded the Word of God unto the bottom, as precisely to set down the church's discipline without error

[17]Common property.

[18]In 1624, John Lyford and John Oldham arrived at Plymouth and soon attracted a "faction" opposing the colonists' separatism, which charged them with a variety of offenses committed in England. Although both men were convicted and expelled from the colony, Lyford's continued agitation ended in the breakup of the English investors ("adventurers"), who stopped sending provisions to the colony.

[19]The Edict of Nantes (1598) enabled freedom of worship ("liberty of conscience") while preserving the authority of the French crown.

[20]Robert Browne (c. 1550–1633) advocated separation from the Church of England on the grounds that it did not exclude the corrupt. He called instead for independent congregations, an organization of the (Calvinist) church known as Congregationalism.

in substance or circumstances, that no other without blame may digress or differ in any thing from the same. And it is not difficult to shew that the Reformed Churches differ in many *circumstances* among themselves."

By which words it appears how far he was free from that rigid spirit of separation, which broke to pieces the Separatists themselves in the Low Countries, unto the great scandal of the reforming churches.[21] He was indeed a person of a well-tempered spirit, or else it had been scarce possible for him to have kept the affairs of Plymouth in so good a temper for thirty-seven years together; in every one of which he was chosen their governour, except the three years wherein Mr. Winslow, and the two years wherein Mr. Prince, at the choice of the people, took a turn with him.[22]

8. The leader of a people in a wilderness had need be a Moses; and if a Moses had not led the people of Plymouth Colony, when this worthy person was their governour, the people had never with so much unanimity and importunity still called him to lead them.[23] Among many instances thereof, let this one piece of self-denial be told for a memorial of him, wheresoever this History shall be considered: The Patent of the Colony was taken in his name, running in these terms: "To William Bradford his heirs, associates, and assigns." But when the number of the freemen[24] was much increased, and many new townships erected, the General Court[25] there desired of Mr. Bradford, that he would make a surrender of the same into their hands, which he willingly and presently assented unto, and confirmed it according to their desire by his hand and seal, reserving no more for himself than was his proportion, with others, by agreement. But as he found the providence of Heaven many ways recompensing his many acts of self-denial, so he gave this testimony to the faithfulness of the divine promises: "That he had forsaken friends, houses and lands for the sake of the gospel, and the Lord gave them him again." Here he prospered in his estate; and besides a worthy son which he had by a former wife, he had also two sons and a daughter by another, whom he married in this land.

9. He was a person for study as well as action; and hence, notwithstanding the difficulties through which he passed in his youth, he attained unto a notable skill in languages: the Dutch tongue was become almost as vernacular to him as the English; the French tongue he could also manage; the Latin and the Greek he had mastered; but the Hebrew he most of all studied, "Because," he said, "he would see with his own eyes the ancient oracles of God in their native beauty." He was also well skilled

[21]The Separatist movement broke down in England and Holland, primarily because each congregation held itself to be the "purer" church.

[22]Edward Winslow (1595–1655) and Thomas Prince (1600–1673).

[23]Moses was the lawgiver who led the Israelites out of bondage in Egypt (meant to represent England) to the Promised Land of Canaan (meant to represent Massachusetts).

[24]Those who worked on their own, for themselves, rather than as indentured servants.

[25]The supreme legislative body of the Massachusetts Bay Colony; the Bay Colony established in 1630 by the "Puritans"—almost identical in religious belief to Bradford's "Pilgrims"—absorbed the Plymouth Colony under its leadership.

in History, in Antiquity, and in Philosophy; and for Theology he became so versed in it, that he was an irrefragable disputant against the *errors,* especially those of Anabaptism,[26] which with trouble he saw rising in his colony; wherefore he wrote some significant things for the confutation of those errors. But the *crown* of all was his holy, prayerful, watchful, and fruitful walk with God, wherein he was very exemplary.

10. At length he fell into an indisposition of body, which rendred him unhealthy for a whole winter; and as the spring advanced, his health yet more declined; yet he felt himself not what he counted sick, till one day; in the night after which, the God of heaven so filled his mind with ineffable consolations, that he seemed little short of Paul, rapt up unto the unutterable entertainments of Paradise.[27] The next morning he told his friends, "That the good Spirit of God had given him a pledge of his happiness in another world, and the first-fruits of his eternal glory;" and on the day following he died, May 9, 1657, in the 69th year of his age—lamented by all the colonies of New-England, as a common blessing and father to them all.

O mihi si Similis Contingat Clausula Vitæ![28]

Plato's brief description of a governour, is all that I will now leave as his character, in an

EPITAPH.[29]

MEN are but FLOCKS: BRADFORD beheld their need,
And long did them at once both rule and feed.

1702

[26]Anabaptists did not believe in the baptism of infants, and they sought to separate church affairs from the affairs of the state.

[27]In 2 Corinthians 12:1–4, Paul describes the divine revelations that helped him through his suffering.

[28]"Oh, that I might reach a similar end of life!"

[29]The Greek philosopher Plato (427?–347 B.C.) wrote about republican states. In the original publication, Mather provided the Greek for the following: "The shepherd, the provider of the human flock." His verse epitaph carries the same effect.

from Decennium Luctuosum:[1] An History of Remarkable Occurrences in the Long [Indian] War[2]

[Hannah Dustan's Captivity]

Article XXV
A Notable Exploit: *dux femina facti.*[3]

On March 15, 1697, the salvages made a descent upon the skirts of Haverhill, murdering and captivating about thirty-nine persons, and burning about half a dozen houses. In this broil, one Hannah Dustan,[4] having lain in about a week, attended with her nurse, Mary Neff,[5] a body of terrible Indians drew near unto the house where she lay, with designs to carry on their bloody devastations. Her husband hastened from his employments abroad unto the relief of his distressed family; and first bidding *seven* of his *eight* children (which were from *two* to *seventeen* years of age) to get away as fast as they could unto some garrison in the town, he went in to inform his wife of the horrible distress come upon them. Ere she could get up, the fierce Indians were got so near, that, utterly desparing to do her any service, he ran out after his children; resolving that on the horse which he had with him, he would ride away with *that* which he should in this extremity find his affections to pitch most upon, and leave the rest unto the care of the Divine Providence. He overtook his children, about forty rod from his door; but then such was the *agony* of his parental affections, that he found it impossible for him to distinguish any one of them from the rest; wherefore he took up a courageous resolution to live and die with them all. A party of Indians came up with him; and now, though they fired at him, and he fired at them, yet he manfully kept at the reer of his *little army* of unarmed children, while

[1] "A melancholy decade."

[2] The complete title is *Decennium Luctuosum: An History of Remarkable Occurrences in the Long War, which New-England hath had with the Indian Salvages, from the year 1688, to the year 1698.* The work was originally published anonymously in Boston in 1699; Mather later reprinted it in Book VII, Appendix of *Magnalia Christi Americana.* Also referred to as "King William's War" by the colonists, the Long War was a ten-year war between the Massachusetts colonists and an Indian alliance composed of several New England and Canadian tribes. The war was precipitated by the continued encroachment of white settlements, broken treaties, and the trespassing of colonists on the Indian fishing grounds along the Saco River, and it was likely further inflamed by the French Canadians, who also resented English imperialism. In the attack upon Haverhill, the Indians were reported to have killed or taken captive forty colonists.

[3] "A woman guides the venture" (Latin).

[4] Hannah Dustan (1657–1736) married Thomas Dustan (variously recorded as Duston, Dustin and Durston) on December 3, 1677, and bore thirteen children, eight of whom were living at the time of her captivity. Shortly after their escape, Dustan and her companions traveled to Boston to relate their experience to the Massachusetts General Court. Among those present to hear the story firsthand were Cotton Mather and Samuel Sewall, both of whom recorded a version of the story in their diaries. The General Court gave the former captives a monetary reward for their "heroic deeds" and a bounty for the Indian scalps.

[5] Mary Neff was a widow who apparently had only recently come to stay with the Dustan family as a nurse to Hannah and her newborn child.

they marched off with the pace of a child of five years old; until, by the singular providence of God, he arrived safe with them all unto a place of safety about a mile or two from his house.[6] But his house must in the mean time have more dismal *tragedies* acted at it. The nurse, trying to escape with the new-born infant, fell into the hands of the formidable salvages; and those furious tawnies coming into the house, bid poor Dustan to rise immediately. Full of astonishment, she did so; and sitting down in the chimney with an heart full of most fearful *expectation,* she saw the raging dragons rifle all that they could carry away, and set the house on fire. About nineteen or twenty Indians now led these away, with about half a score other English captives; but ere they had gone many steps, they dash'd out the brains of the infant against a tree; and several of the other captives, as they began to tire in the sad journey, were soon sent unto their long home; the salvages would presently bury their hatchets in their brains, and leave their carcases on the ground for birds and beasts to feed upon. However, Dustan (with her nurse) notwithstanding her present condition, travelled that night about a dozen miles, and then kept up with their new masters in a long travel of an hundred and fifty miles, more or less, within a few days ensuing, without any sensible damage in their health, from the hardships of their *travel,* their *lodging,* their *diet,* and their many other difficulties.

These two poor women were now in the hands of those whose "tender mercies and cruelties;" but the good God, who hath all "hearts in his own hands," heard the sighs of these prisoners, and gave them to find unexpected favour from the master who hath laid claim unto them. That Indian family consisted of twelve persons; two stout men, three women, and seven children; and for the shame of many an English family, that has the character of *prayerless* upon it, I must now publish what these poor women assure me. 'Tis this: in obedience to the instructions which the French have given them, they would have *prayers* in their family no less than thrice every day; in the morning, at noon, and in the evening; nor would they ordinarily let their children *eat* or *sleep,* without first saying their prayers.[7] Indeed, these *idolaters* were, like the rest of their whiter brethen, *persecutors,* and would not endure that these poor women should retire to their English prayers, if they could hinder them. Nevertheless, the poor women had nothing but fervent prayers to make their lives comfortable or tolerable; and by being daily sent out upon business, they had opportunities, together and asunder, to do like another Hannah, in "pouring out their souls before the Lord."[8] Nor did their praying friends among our selves forbear to "pour out" supplications for them. Now, they could not observe it without some wonder, that their Indian master sometimes when he saw them dejected, would say unto them, "What need you trouble your self? If your God will have you delivered, you shall be so!" And it seems our God would have it so to be. This Indian family was now travelling with these two captive women, (and an English youth taken from Worcester, a

[6]The Dustan farm lay about two miles outside the village of Haverhill, Massachusetts.

[7]Mather does not miss the opportunity to point out to his Protestant readers that the Indians were converts to Roman Catholicism and thus allied to the French in Canada. By depicting the Indians as "idolaters" and "persecutors," Mather links them to the Puritan representation of papacy as a threat to Protestantism.

[8]Mather alludes to the biblical Hannah, the mother of Samuel, who wept and prayed for a child (1 Samuel 1:1–18).

year and a half before),[9] unto a rendezvouz of salvages, which they call a *town,* some where beyond Penacook; and they still told these poor women that when they came to this town, they must be stript, and scourg'd, and run the *gantlet*[10] through the whole army of Indians. They said this was the *fashion* when the captives first came to a town; and they derided some of the faint-hearted English, which, they said, fainted and swoon'd away under the *torments* of this discipline. But on April 30,while they were yet, it may be, about an hundred and fifty miles from the Indian town, a little before break of day, when the whole crew was in a *dead sleep,* (reader, see if it prove not so!) one of these women took up a resolution to imitate the action of Jael upon Siseria;[11] and being where she had not her own *life* secured by any *law* unto her, she thought she was not forbidden by any *law* to take away the *life* of the *murderers* by whom her child had been butchered. She heartened the nurse and the youth to assist her in this enterprize; and all furnishing themselves with hatchets for the purpose, they struck such home blows upon the heads of their sleeping oppressors, that ere they could any of them struggle into any effectual resistance, "at the feet of these poor prisoners, they bow'd, they fell, they lay down; at their feet they bow'd, they fell; where they bow'd, there they fell down dead."[12] Only one squaw escaped, sorely wounded, from them in the dark; and one boy, whom they reserved asleep, intending to bring him away with them, suddenly waked, and scuttled away from this desolation. But cutting off the scalps of the ten wretches, they came off, and received *fifty pounds*[13] from the General Assembly of the province, as a recompence of their action; besides which, they received many "presents of congratulation" from their more private friends; but none gave 'em a greater taste of bounty than Colonel Nicholson, the Governour of Maryland, who, hearing of their action, sent 'em a very generous token of his favour.

[9]Samuel Lennardson had been taken prisoner in an attack on Worcester, Massachusetts, about eight months before the attack on Haverhill. By "English youth," Mather simply means a British subject, like himself.

[10]A gauntlet consists of two parallel rows of people, between which a person—often stripped of clothing—is forced to run. As the person proceeds, he or she is physically assaulted from both sides. The gauntlet was an initiation ceremony, although among the colonists it became an example of propaganda supporting the myth of Indian "savagery."

[11]Jael, the wife of Heber the Kenite, killed Sisera, the Canaanite king who held Israel captive, by driving a spike through his skull as he slept in her tent (see Judges 4:17–22; 5:6–7).

[12]See Judges 5:27.

[13]Hannah received twenty-five pounds and Neff and Lennardson ten each for their "bravery."

from The Negro Christianized[1]

It is a *Golden Sentence,* that has been sometimes quoted from *Chrysostom;* That *for a man to know the Art of Alms, is more than for a man to be Crowned with the Diadem of Kings: But to Convert one Soul unto God, is more than to pour out Ten Thousand Talents into the Baskets of the Poor.*[2] Truly, to Raise a *Soul,* from a dark State of Ignorance and Wickedness, to the Knowledge of GOD, and the Belief of CHRIST, and the practice of our Holy and Lovely RELIGION; 'Tis the noblest Work, that ever was undertaken among the Children of men. An Opportunity to Endeavour the CONVERSION of a Soul, from a Life of *Sin,* which is indeed a woeful *Death,* to Fear God, and Love CHRIST, and by a Religious Life to Escape the *Paths of the Destroyer;* it cannot but be Acceptable to all that have themselves had in themselves Experience of such a *Conversion.* And such an Opportunity there is in your Hands, O all you that have any Negroes in your Houses; an Opportunity to try, Whether you may not be the Happy *Instruments,* of Converting, the *Blackest* Instances of *Blindness* and *Baseness,* into admirable *Candidates* of Eternal Blessedness. Let not this Opportunity be Lost; if you have any concern for *Souls,* your Own or Others; but, make a Trial, Whether by your Means, the most *Bruitish* of Creatures upon Earth may not come to be disposed, in some Degree, like the *Angels* of Heaven; and the *Vassals* of Satan, become the *Children* of God. Suppose these Wretched *Negroes,* to be the Offspring of *Cham*[3] (which yet is not so very certain,) yet let us make a Trial, Whether the CHRIST who *dwelt in the Tents of Shem,*[4] have not some of His Chosen among them; Let us make a Trial, Whether they that have been Scorched and Blacken'd by the Sun of *Africa,* may not come to have their Minds Healed by the more Benign *Beams* of the *Sun of Righteousness.*

It is come to pass by the *Providence* of God, without which there comes nothing to pass, that Poor Negroes are cast under your Government and Protection. You take them into your *Families;* you look on them as part of your *Possessions;* and you Expect from their Service, a Support, and perhaps an Increase, of your other *Possessions.* How agreeable would it be, if a Religious Master or Mistress thus attended, would now think with themselves! *Who can tell but that this Poor Creature may belong to the Election of God! Who can tell, but that God may have sent this Poor Creature into my Hands, that so One of the Elect may by my means be Called; & by my Instruction be made Wise unto Salvation! The glorious God will put an unspeakable Glory upon me, if it may be so!* The Considerations that would move you, To Teach

[1]The complete title is *The Negro Christianized. An Essay to Excite and Assist that Good Work, The Instruction of Negro-Servants in Christianity.* The work was first published in 1706.

[2]In his *Homilies on First Corinthians,* Homily III, John Chrysostom (c. 347–407) argues that "although thou give countless treasure unto the poor, thou wilt do no such work as he who converteth one soul."

[3]In Genesis 9:22–27, Ham (or Cham), Noah's second son, has the temerity to gaze upon his father as he lies drunk and naked. For that offense, Noah curses Ham, the progenitor of Canaan, condemning him to be a "servant of servants" (v. 25). This biblical passage was used by eighteenth- and nineteenth-century apologists for U.S. slavery, who saw Africans as Ham's descendants.

[4]In Genesis 9:27, Noah declares that God shall "dwell in the tents of Shem," his oldest son. Since "Canaan shall be his servant," Mather argues that cursed servants may nevertheless be redeemed in godly households.

your *Negroes* the *Truths* of the Glorious Gospel, as far as you can, and bring them, if it may be, to Live according to those *Truths,* a *Sober,* and a *Righteous,* and a *Godly* Life; They are *Innumerable;* And, if you would after a *Reasonable* manner consider, the Pleas which we have to make on the behalf of *God,* and of the *Souls* which He has made, one would wonder that they should not be *Irresistible. Show your selves Men,* and let *Rational Arguments* have their Force upon you, to make you treat, not as *Bruits* but as *Men,* those *Rational Creatures* whom God has made your *Servants.*

For,

First; The Great GOD *Commands* it, and *Requires* it of you; to do what you can that *Your Servants,* may also be *His.* It was an Admonition once given; Eph. 5.9.[5] *Masters, Know that your Master is in Heaven.* You will confess, That the God of Heaven is your *Master.* If your *Negroes* do not comply with your *Commands,* into what Anger, what Language, Perhaps into a misbecoming *Fury,* are you transported? But you are now to attend unto the *Commands* of your more Absolute *Master;* and they are His *Commands* concerning your *Negroes* too. What can be more Expressive; than those words of the Christian Law? Col. 4.1. *Masters, give unto your Servants, that which is Just & Equal, knowing that ye also have a Master in Heaven.* Of what *Servants* is this Injunction to be understood? Verily, of *Slaves.* For *Servants* were generally such, at the time of Writing the New Testament. Wherefore, *Masters,* As it is *Just & Equal,* that your *Servants* be not *Over-wrought,*[6] and that while they *Work* for you, you should *Feed* them, and *Cloath* them, and afford convenient *Rest* unto them, and make their Lives comfortable; So it is *Just* and *Equal,* that you should Acquaint them, as far as you can, with the way to Salvation by JESUS CHRIST. You deny your *Master in Heaven,* if you do nothing to bring your *Servants* unto the Knowledge and Service of that glorious *Master.* One Table of the *Ten Commandments,* has this for the Sum of it; *Thou shalt Love thy Neighbour as thy self.* Man, Thy *Negro* is thy *Neighbour.* T'were an Ignorance, unworthy of a *Man,* to imagine otherwise. Yea, if thou dost grant, *That God hath made of one Blood, all Nations of men,* he is thy *Brother* too. Now canst thou *Love* thy *Negro,* and be willing to see him ly under the Rage of Sin, and the Wrath of God? Canst thou *Love* him, and yet refuse to do any thing, that his miserable Soul may be rescued from Eternal miseries? Oh! Let thy *Love* to that Poor *Soul,* appear in thy concern, to make it, if thou canst, as happy as thy own! We are Commanded, Gal. 6.10. *As we have opportunity let us Do Good unto all men, especially unto them, who are of the Houshold of Faith.* Certainly, we have *Opportunity,* to *Do Good* unto our *Servants,* who are of our *own Houshold;* certainly, we may do something to *make them Good,* and bring them to be of the *Houshold of Faith.* In a word, All the Commandments in the Bible, which bespeak our *Charity* to the *Souls* of others, and our *Endeavour* that the *Souls* of others may be delivered from the Snares of Death; every one of these do oblige us, to do what we can, for the *Souls* of our *Negroes.* They are more nearly *Related* unto us, than many others are; we are more fully *capable* to do for them, than for many others. . . .

Yea, the pious *Masters,* that have instituted their *Servants* in Christian Piety, will even in this Life have a sensible *Recompence.* The more *Serviceable,* and Obedient

[5]Mather's or a printer's error for Ephesians 6:9. [6]Overworked.

and obliging Behaviour of their *Servants* unto them, will be a sensible & a notable *Recompence.* Be assured, Syrs; Your *Servants* will be the *Better Servants,* for being made *Christian Servants.* To *Christianize* them aright, will be to *fill them with all Goodness. Christianity* is nothing but a very Mass of Universal *Goodness.* Were your *Servants* well tinged with the Spirit of *Christianity,* it would render them exceeding *Dutiful* unto their *Masters,* exceeding *Patient* under their *Masters,* exceeding faithful in their Business, and afraid of speaking or doing any thing that may justly displease you. It has been observed, that those *Masters* who have used their *Negroes* with most of *Humanity,* in allowing them all the Comforts of Life, that are necessary and *Convenient* for them, (Who have remembered, that by the Law of God, even an *Ass* was to be relieved, When *Sinking under his Burden,*[7] and an *Ox* might not be *Muzzled* when *Treading out the Corn;*[8] and that if a *Just man will regard the Life of his Beast,* he will much more allow the comforts of life to and not hide himself *from his own Flesh:*) have been better *Serv'd,* had more work done for them, and better done, than those *Inhumane Masters,* who have used their *Negroes* worse than their *Horses.* And those *Masters* doubtless, who use their *Negroes* with most of *Christianity,* and use most pains to inform them in, and conform them to, *Christianity,* will find themselves no losers by it. *Onesimus*[9] was doubtless a *Slave:* but this poor *Slave,* on whose behalf a great Apostle of God was more than a little concerned; yea, one Book in our Bible was Written on his behalf! When he was *Christianized,* it was presently said unto his *Master,* Philem. 11. *In time past he was unprofitable to thee, but now he will be profitable.* But many *Masters* whose *Negroes* have greatly vexed them, with miscarriages, may do well to examine, Whether Heaven be not chastising of them, for their failing in their Duty about their *Negroes.* Had they done more, to make their *Negroes* the knowing and willing *Servants* of God, it may be, God would have made their *Negroes* better *Servants* to them. Syrs, you may Read your *Sin* in the *Punishment.*

And now, what *Objection* can any Man Living have, to refund the force of these *Considerations*? Produce the *cause,* O Impiety, *Bring forth thy strong reasons,* and let all men see what Idle and silly cavils, are thy best *Reasons* against this Work of God.

It has been cavilled, by some, that it is questionable Whether the *Negroes* have *Rational Souls,* or no. But let that *Bruitish* insinuation be never Whispered any more. Certainly, their *Discourse,* will abundantly prove, that they have *Reason. Reason* showes it self in the *Design* which they daily act upon. The vast improvement that *Education* has made upon *some* of them, argues that there is a *Reasonable Soul* in *all* of them. An old Roman, and Pagan, would call upon the Owner of such Servants, *Homines tamen esse memento.*[10] They are *Men,* and not *Beasts* that you have bought,

[7]A reference to Exodus 23:5.

[8]See Deuteronomy 25:4. In 1 Corinthians 9:9, Paul, referring to this Mosaic law protecting draught animals, asks rhetorically, "Doth God take care for oxen?" Also see 1 Timothy 5:17–18, where the protection of oxen prompts Paul to claim that one who labors "in the word and doctrine . . . is worthy of his reward."

[9]In his Epistle to Philemon, Paul asks pardon for the slave boy Onesimus, who has been his companion in prison and whom he has converted. *Onesimus* means "useful" or "profitable."

[10]"But remember that they are men."

and they must be used accordingly. 'Tis true; They are *Barbarous.* But so were our own *Ancestors.* The *Britons* were in many things as *Barbarous,* but a little before our Saviours Nativity, as the *Negroes* are at this day if there be any Credit in *Caesars Commentaries. Christianity* will be the best cure for this *Barbarity.* Their *Complexion* sometimes is made an Argument, why nothing should be done for them. A *Gay* sort of argument! As if the great God went by the *Complexion* of Men, in His Favours to them! As if none but *Whites* might hope to be Favoured and Accepted with God! Whereas it is well known, That the *Whites,* are the least part of Mankind. The biggest part of Mankind, perhaps, are *Copper-Coloured;* a sort of *Tawnies.* And our *English* that inhabit some Climates, do seem growing apace to be not much unlike unto them. As if, because a people, from the long force of the African *Sun & Soil* upon them, (improved perhaps, to further Degrees by maternal imaginations, and other accidents,) are come at length to have the small *Fibres* of their *Veins,* and the Blood in them, a little more Interspersed thro their Skin than other People, this must render them less valuable to Heaven then the rest of Mankind? Away with such Trifles. The God who *looks on the Heart,* is not moved by the colour of the *Skin;* is not more propitious to one *Colour* than another. Say rather, with the Apostle; Acts 10.34, 35. *Of a truth I perceive, that God is no respector of persons; but in every Nation, he that feareth Him and worketh Righteousness, is accepted with Him.* Indeed their *Stupidity* is a *Discouragement.* It may seem, unto as little purpose, to *Teach,* as to *wash an Ethopian.* But the greater their *Stupidity,* the greater must be our *Application.* If we can't learn them so much as we *Would,* let us learn them as much as we *Can.* A little divine *Light* and *Grace* infused into them, will be of great account. And the more *Difficult* it is, to fetch such *forlorn things* up out of the perdition whereinto they are fallen, the more *Laudable* is the undertaking: There will be the more of a *Triumph,* if we prosper in the undertaking. Let us encourage our selves from that word; Mat. 3.9 *God is able of these Stones, to raise up Children unto Abraham.*

Well; But if the *Negroes* are *Christianized,* they will be *Baptized;* and their *Baptism* will presently entitle them to their *Freedom;* so our *Money* is thrown away.

Man, If this were true; that a *Slave* bought with thy *Money,* were by thy means brought unto the *Things that accompany Salvation,* and thou shouldest from this time have no more Service from him, yet thy *Money* were not thrown away. That Man's *Money will perish with him,* yet he had rather the *Souls* in his Family should *Perish,* than that he should lose a little *Money.* And suppose it were so, that *Baptism* gave a legal Title to *Freedom.*[11] Is there no guarding against this Inconvenience? You may by sufficient *Indentures,* keep off the things, which you reckon so Inconvenient. But it is all a Mistake. There is no such thing. What *Law* is it, that Sets the *Baptized Slave* at *Liberty?* Not the *Law of Christianity:* that allows of *Slavery;* Only it wonderfully Dulcifies, and Mollifies, and Moderates the Circumstances of it. *Christianity* directs a *Slave,* upon his embracing the *Law of the Redeemer,* to satisfy himself, *That he is the Lords Free-man,* tho' he continues a *Slave.* It supposes, (Col. 3.11.) That there are *Bond* as well as *Free,* among those that have been *Renewed in the Knowledge and Image of Jesus Christ.* Will the *Canon-law* do it? No; The *Canons* of Numberless *Councils,*

[11]Popular belief, stimulated by such English works as Morgan Godwin's *The Negro's & Indians Advocate* (1680), held that baptism conferred manumission. The 1729 Yorke-Talbot decision confirmed Mather's claim that baptism was irrelevant to this context.

mention, the *Slaves* of *Christians,* without any contradiction. Will the *Civil Law* do it? No: Tell, if you can, any part of *Christendom,* wherein *Slaves* are not frequently to be met withal. But is not *Freedom* to be claim'd for a *Baptised Slave,* by the *English* Constitution? The English *Laws,* about *Villains,*[12] or, *Slaves,* will not say so; for by those *Laws,* they may be granted *for Life,* like a *Lease,* and passed over with a *Mannor,* like other *Goods or Chattels.* And by those *Laws,* the Lords may sieze the Bodies of their *Slaves* even while a Writt, *De libertate probanda,*[13] is depending. These English *Laws* were made when the *Lords* & the *Slaves,* were both of them *Christians;* and they stand still unrepealed. If there are not now such *Slaves* in *England* as formerly, it is from the *Lords,* more than from the *Laws.* The *Baptised* then are not thereby entitled unto their *Liberty.* Howbeit, if they have arrived unto such a measure of *Christianity,* that *some are forbid Water for the Baptising of them,* it is fit, that they should enjoy those *comfortable circumstances* with us, which are due to them, not only as the *Children* of *Adam,* but also as our *Brethren,* on the same level with us in the expectations of a blessed Immortality, thro' the *Second Adam.* Whatever Slaughter the Assertion may make among the pretensions which are made unto *Christianity,* yet while the *sixteenth* Chapter of *Matthew* is in the Bible,[14] it must be asserted; the *Christian,* who cannot so far *Deny himself,* can be no *Disciple* of the Lord JESUS CHRIST. But, O Christian, thy *Slave* will not Serve thee one jot the worse for that *Self denial.*

The way is now cleared, for the work that is proposed: that excellent WORK, The Instruction of the Negroes in the Christian Religion.

A CATECHISM shall be got ready for them; first a *Shorter,* then a *Larger;* Suited unto their poor Capacities.

They who cannot themselves *Personally* so well attend the *Instruction* of the *Negroes,* may employ and reward those that shall do it for them. In many *Families,* the *Children* may help the *Negroes,* to Learn the *Catechism,* or their well-instructed and well-disposed *English Servants* may do it: And they should be *Rewarded* by the *Masters,* when they do it.

In a Plantation of many *Negroes,* why should not a *Teacher* be hired on purpose, to instil into them the principles of the *Catechism*?

Or, if the *Overseers* are once *Catechised* themselves, they may soon do the Office of *Catechisers* unto those that are under them.

However, Tis fit for the *Master* also *Personally* to enquire into the progress which his *Negroes* make in *Christianity,* and not leave it *Entierly* to the management of others.

There must be *Time* allow'd for the *Work.* And why not The Lords-Day? The precept of God concerning the *Sabbath,* is very positive; *Remember the SABBATH-DAY, to keep it Holy. Thou shalt not then do any work, thou nor thy Son, nor thy Daughter, thy Man-Servant, nor thy Maid-Servant.*[15] By virtue of this precept, we do

[12]The term for a feudal serf. In *Chamberline v. Marley* (1696–1697), villeinage was used to claim that English law supported absolute ownership of persons and property.

[13]"Proving freedom."

[14]In Matthew 16:24, Jesus exhorts his followers, "If any man will come after me, let him deny himself, and take up his cross, and follow me."

[15]Exodus 20:8, 10.

even demand, The Lords-Day, for the *Negroes:* that they may be permitted the Freedom of The Lords-Day, and not be then unnecessarily diverted from attending on such *means of Instruction,* as may be afforded unto them. . . .[16]

1706

from Bonifacius. . . . with Humble Proposals . . . *to Do Good in the World*[1]

[Proposal concerning reforming societies]

REFORMING SOCIETIES, or *Societies for the Supression of Disorders,* have begun to grow somewhat into fashion; and it is one of the best *omens* that the world has upon it. *Behold, how great a matter a little* of this heavenly *fire* may kindle! Five or six gentlemen in *London,* began with an heroic resolution, and association, to encounter the torrent of wickedness, which was carrying all before it in the nation. More were soon added unto them; and though they met with great opposition, from *wicked spirits,* and these *incarnate* as well as *invisible,* and some in *high places*[2] too, yet they proceeded with a most honorable and invincible courage. Their *success,* if not proportionable to their *courage,* yet was far from *contemptible.* In the *punishments* inflicted on them who transgressed the laws of *good morality,* there were soon offered many thousands of *sacrifices,* unto the holiness of GOD. Hundreds of *houses* which were the *chambers* of Hell, and the *scandals* of earth, were soon extinguished. There was a remarkable check soon given to raging *profanity;* and the Lord's Day was not openly and horribly profaned as formerly. And among other *essays to do good,* they scattered thousands of *good books,* that had a tendency to reform the evil manners of the people. It was not long before this excellent example was followed in other parts of the *British* Empire. Virtuous men of diverse qualities and persuasions, became the members of the *societies:* persons high and low, Con[forming] and Noncon[forming],[3] united; the union became formidable to the Kingdom of Darkness. The report of the *societies* flew over the seas; the pattern was followed in other countries; men of wisdom

[16]In the brief conclusion to *The Negro Christianized,* not printed here, Mather proposes a particular catechism and prayer for the spiritual edification of African slaves, and he exhorts them to bear their earthly burdens in this life so that they may receive their reward in the next.

[1]The complete title is *Bonifacius. An Essay upon the Good, that is to be Devised to Answer the Great End of Life, and to Do Good while They Live.* This text was first published in 1710.

[2]Mather alludes to Ephesians 6:12, "For we wrestle not against flesh and blood, but against principalities, against powers, against the rulers of the darkness of this world, against spiritual wickedness in high places." Although "high places" refers to the preternatural power of Satan, Mather puns on the phrase to implicate the Anglican bishopric of his grandfather's generation.

[3]"Conforming" refers to Anglican clergy; "Nonconforming" to the Puritans, who refused to sign Archbishop William Laud's Act of Conformity and were thus denied communion and expelled from the ministry.

in remote parts of *Europe* have made their joyful remark upon them, *that they cause unspeakable good, and annunciate a more illustrious state of the Church of God, which is to be expected,*

The repetition of these passages, is enough to make way for the Proposal:

That a fit number in a neighborhood, whose hearts God has touched with a *zeal to do good,* would combine into a *society,* to meet, when and where they shall agree, and consider that case, "What are the DISORDERS that we may see rising among us? And what may be done, either by ourselves immediately, or by others through our advice, to suppress those disorders?" That they would obtain if they can, the presence of a *minister* with them, and every time they meet, have a *prayer* wherein the glorious Lord shall be called upon, to bless the design, direct and prosper it. That they would also have a *justice of peace,* if it may be, to be a member of the Society. That they once in half a year choose two *stewards,* to dispatch the *business* and *messages* of the *Society,* and manage the *votes* in it; who shall nominate unto the *Society,* their successors, when their term is expired. That they would have a faithful *treasurer,* in whose hands their *stock of charity* may be deposited: and a *clerk,* to keep a convenient *record* of *transactions* and *purposes.* And, finally, that they do with as *modest* and *silent* a conduct as may be, carry on all their undertakings.

I will finish the PROPOSAL, by reciting the POINTS OF CONSIDERATION which the SOCIETIES may have read unto them from time to time at their meetings, with a due *pause* upon each of them, for anyone to offer what he please upon it.

I. Is there any REMARKABLE DISORDER in the place that requires our endeavor for the suppression of it? And in what good, fair, likely way may we endeavor it?

II. "Is there any PARTICULAR PERSON, whose *disorderly behaviors* may be so scandalous and so notorious, that we may do well to send unto the said person our charitable *admonitions?* Or, are there any *contending persons,* whom we should admonish, to quench their *contentions?*

John Williams 1664–1729

The Reverend John Williams was the minister of Deerfield, Massachusetts, in February 1704 when he was taken captive by Abenaki Indians following a bloody predawn raid on the frontier village by French and Indian forces. Although citizens of Deerfield were on the lookout for an attack and had built a stockade around the town, deep snowdrifts allowed a force of some three hundred French Canadians, Abenakis, and Caughnawaga Mohawks to scramble over the stockade and destroy the town, burning many of the houses, killing residents, and taking more than one hundred inhabitants as captives, many of whom would not survive the march north to Canada. *The Redeemed Captive Returning to Zion* is William's account of his forced march to Canada following his capture and of the two and a half years he subsequently spent in captivity—eight weeks with the Abenakis, the remainder in French Catholic communities near Montreal.

Deerfield was a precarious outpost of

English colonialism at the turn of the eighteenth century. Originally settled in 1672, the village was abandoned in 1676 after Indian attacks during King Philip's War. The town was resettled in 1682, and Williams arrived to serve as the town's spiritual leader in 1686. As the French and English engaged in battles in Europe—in this case, the War of Spanish Succession—border skirmishes between French and English colonists in North America became more active, and both sides employed Indians to asssist in their war efforts. The 1704 attack on Deerfield was thus an incident in what the colonists called Queen Anne's War (the second of the four French and Indian Wars), a war that was based on hostilities a continent away but nonetheless offered the occasion for territorial warfare in New England and Canada.

John Williams was the grandson of Robert Williams, who emigrated from Norwich to Roxbury in 1637, and the son of Samuel Williams, a shoemaker and large landholder, who became deacon and later Ruling Elder in the Roxbury church of John Eliot. He attended Roxbury Latin School; graduated from Harvard in 1683; became Congregational minister of Deerfield in 1686; and married Eunice Mather, niece of Increase Mather and stepdaughter of Solomon Stoddard, in 1687. Williams and his wife had eight children: John Williams Jr., age 6; and Jerusha Williams, 6 weeks, were killed in the raid on Deerfield. Of the remaining six, five (Samuel, 15; Esther, 13; Stephen, 10; Eunice, 7; and Warham, 4) were taken captive and marched to Canada. Williams's oldest son, Eleazar, also 15, was away from Deerfield at the time of the attack. Williams's wife was killed during the march to Canada. Williams was a prominent and well-connected member of the New England clergy, and his captivity was a matter of great concern throughout the colony. Governor Joseph Dudley negotiated the final terms of his release in 1706—terms that involved the exchange of the notorious French pirate Baptiste for Williams and other New Englanders. After his release, Williams returned to Deerfield and later married his wife's cousin, Abigail Allen Bissell. He wrote the tale of his captivity in 1707, shortly after his "redemption." The narrative was extremely popular and eventually went through six editions over the course of the century.

Williams's narrative describes the battle in Deerfield and the long march through the snow; the death of his wife, who, having given birth only a few weeks earlier, could not keep up with the prisoners and was killed by the Indians; the cruelties and kindnesses of the Indians; Williams's attempts to obtain news about his children, who had been separated from him; his efforts to serve members of his congregation who were scattered among Indian and French settlements; his purchase by the French and Jesuit efforts to convert him; his correspondence with his son Samuel, who briefly converted to Catholicism; and Williams's return home after more than two years of bondage, with all of his remaining children except Eunice, then ten, who chose, to her father's enduring consternation, to remain with the Indians.

The narrative is unusual among captivity narratives because Williams spends the greater part of his captivity among the French, not among Indians. Yet for the Puritan Williams, the dangerously foreign religion of Catholicism poses a threat equal to that of the "savagery" of Indian culture. Throughout the narrative, Williams details his continued resistance to the pressures of the Jesuits to convert and his attempts to save his children and other New Englanders from the double threat of absorption into French Catholic or Indian culture. His son Samuel does briefly convert to Catholicism, and his daughter Eunice does become a fully adopted member of the Caughnawaga Mohawks, a tribe of Catholic Indians living outside Montreal. The narrative tells of Williams's sorrow upon learning that Eunice can no longer speak English. Seven years after his release, Williams returned to her village and met with her, but, as he wrote to a friend, "she is obstinately resolved to live and dye here, and will not so much as give me one pleasant look."

The narrative also functions as a jeremiad. It warns New Englanders that they have fallen away from their unique covenant with God, and it demonstrates "the anger of God" toward his "professing people" and the patience of Christians who are suffering "the will of God in very trying public calamities!" Williams seeks to offer an account of his captivity—to render his painful plight meaningful—and thus ascribes both personal and collective meaning to his experiences in the violent cultural, religious, economic, and political power struggles among the French, British, and Indians that roiled New England during the eighteenth century.

Rosalie Murphy Baum
University of South Florida

Elizabeth Maddock Dillon
Northeastern University

PRIMARY WORKS

The Redeemed Captive Returning to Zion, 1707, facsimile, 1966; critical, modernized text, ed., Edward W. Clark, 1976.

from The Redeemed Captive Returning to Zion[1]

[The Dedication: To His Excellency, Joseph Dudley, Esq.][2]

It would be unaccountable stupidity in me not to maintain the most lively and awful sense of divine rebukes which the most holy God has seen meet in spotless sovereignty to dispense to me, my family, and people in delivering us into the hands of those that hated us, who led us into a strange land: my soul has these still in remembrance and is humbled in me; however, God has given us plentiful occasion to sing of mercy as well as judgment. The wonders of divine mercy, which we have seen in the land of our captivity and deliverance therefrom, cannot be forgotten without incurring the guilt of the blackest ingratitude.

To preserve the memory of these, it has been thought advisable to publish a short account of some of those signal appearances of divine power and goodness for hoping it may serve to excite the praise, faith, and hope of all that love God, and may peculiarly serve to cherish a grateful spirit, and to render the impressions of God's mighty works indelible on my heart, and on those that with me have seen the wonders of the Lord and tasted of His salvation: that we may not fall under that heavy charge made against Israel of old, Psalms 78:11, 42: "They forgot His works and the

[1]The complete title of Williams's narrative is *The Redeemed Captive Returning to Zion. A Faithful History of Remarkable Occurrences in the Captivity and the Deliverance of Mr. John Williams, Minister of the Gospel.* Zion is a city of God, the ideal nation envisaged by the Israelites.

[2]Joseph Dudley was governor of the Massachusetts Bay Colony at the time of Williams's release from captivity. His son, William, assisted in making the arrangements for Williams's release. [Clark's note.]

wonders He showed them. They remembered not His hand, nor the day that He delivered them from the enemy."

[The Attack]

On the twenty-ninth of February 1704, not long before break of day, the enemy came in like a flood upon us, our watch being unfaithful: an evil, whose awful effects in a surprisal of our fort, should bespeak all watchmen to avoid, as they would not bring the charge of blood upon themselves. They came to my house in the beginning of the onset and, by their violent endeavors to break open doors and windows with axes and hatchets, awakened me out of sleep; on which I leaped out of bed, and running toward the door, perceived the enemy making their entrance into the house. I called to awaken two soldiers in the chamber and returned towards my bedside for my arms. The enemy immediately broke into the room, I judge to the number of twenty, with painted faces and hideous acclamations. I reached up my hands to the bedtester for my pistol, uttering a short petition to God for everlasting mercies for me and mine on the account of the merits of our glorified redeemer, expecting a present passage through the Valley of the Shadow of Death, saying in myself as Isaiah 38:10–11: "I said in the cutting off my days, 'I shall go to the gates of the grave. I am deprived of the residue of my years.' I said, 'I shall not see the Lord, even the Lord, in the land of the living. I shall behold man no more with the inhabitants of the world.'" Taking down my pistol, I cocked it and put it to the breast of the first Indian who came up, but my pistol missing fire, I was seized by three Indians who disarmed me and bound me naked, as I was in my shirt, and so I stood for near the space of an hour. Binding me, they told me they would carry me to Quebec. My pistol missing fire was an occasion of my life's being preserved, since which I have also found it profitable to be crossed in my own will. The judgment of God did not long slumber against one of the three which took me, who was a captain, for by sunrising he received a mortal shot from my neighbor's house, who opposed so great a number of French and Indians as three hundred and yet were no more than seven men in an ungarrisoned house.

I cannot relate the distressing care I had for my dear wife, who had lain-in but a few weeks before, and for my poor children, family, and Christian neighbors. The enemy fell to rifling the house and entered in great numbers into the house. I begged of God to remember mercy in the midst of judgment, that He would so far restrain their wrath as to prevent their murdering of us, that we might have grace to glorify His name, whether in life or death, and, as I was able, committed our state to God. The enemies who entered the house were all of them Indians and Mohawks, insulted over me awhile, holding hatchets over my head threatening to burn all I had. But yet God beyond expectation made us in a great measure to be pitied, for though some were so cruel and barbarous as to take and carry to the door two of my children and murder them, as also a Negro woman, yet they gave me liberty to put on my clothes, keeping me bound with a cord on one arm, till I put on my clothes to the other, and then changing my cord, they let me dress myself and then pinioned me again. [They] gave liberty to my dear wife to dress herself and our children.

About sun an hour high we were all carried out of the house for a march and saw many of the houses of my neighbors in flames, perceiving the whole fort, one excepted, to be taken. Who can tell what sorrows pierced our souls when we saw ourselves carried away from God's sanctuary to go into a strange land exposed to so many trials, the journey being at least three hundred miles we were to travel, the snow up to the knees, and we never inured to such hardships and fatigues, the place we were to be carried to a popish country? . . .

[The Journey Northward]

After this we went up the mountain and saw the smoke of the fires in the town and beheld the awful desolations of our town, and, before we marched any farther, they killed a sucking child of the English. There were slain by the enemy of the inhabitants of our town to the number of thirty-eight besides nine of the neighboring towns. We traveled not far the first day; God made the heathen so to pity our children that, though they had several wounded persons of their own to carry upon their shoulders for thirty miles before they came to the river, yet they carried our children, incapable of traveling, upon their shoulders and in their arms.

When we came to our lodging-place the first night,[3] they dug away the snow and made some wigwams, cut down some of the small branches of spruce trees to lie down on, and gave the prisoners somewhat to eat, but we had but little appetite. I was pinioned and bound down that night, and so I was every night while I was with the army. Some of the enemy who brought drink with them from the town fell to drinking, and in their drunken fit they killed my Negro man, the only dead person I either saw at the town or on the way. In the night an Englishman made his escape; in the morning I was called for and ordered by the general[4] to tell the English that, if any more made their escape, they would burn the rest of the prisoners.

He that took me was unwilling to let me speak with any of the prisoners as we marched; but on the morning of the second day, he being appointed to guard the rear, I was put into the hands of my other master who permitted me to speak to my wife when I overtook her and to walk with her to help her in her journey. On the way we discoursed of the happiness of them who had a right to a house not made with hands, eternal in the heavens and God for a father and a friend; as also that it was our reasonable duty quietly to submit to the will of God and to say the will of the Lord be done. My wife told me her strength of body began to fail and that I must expect to part with her, saying she hoped God would preserve my life and the lives of some, if not all of our children with us, and commended to me, under God, the care of them. She never spoke any discontented word as to what had befallen us, but with suitable expressions justified God in what had befallen us.

We soon made a halt in which time my chief surviving master came up, upon which I was put upon marching with the foremost, and so made to take my last farewell of my dear wife, the desire of my eyes, and companion in many mercies and afflictions. Upon our separation from each other we asked, for each other, grace sufficient for what God should call us to. After our being parted from one another, she spent the few remaining minutes of her stay in reading the holy Scriptures, which she was wont personally every day to delight her soul in reading, praying, meditating of

[3]Greenfield Meadows, five miles north of Deerfield.

[4]François Hertel de Rouville.

and over, by herself in her closet, over and above what she heard out of them in our family worship.

I was made to wade over a small river and so were all the English, the water above knee-deep, the stream very swift; and after that to travel up a small mountain; my strength was almost spent before I came to the top of it. No sooner had I overcome the difficulty of that ascent, but I was permitted to sit down and be unburdened of my pack; I sat pitying those who were behind and entreated my master to let me go down and help up my wife, but he refused and would not let me stir from him. I asked each of the prisoners as they passed by me after her, and heard that in passing through the abovesaid river, she fell down and was plunged over head and ears in the water; after which she traveled not far, for at the foot of this mountain the cruel and bloodthirsty savage who took her, slew her with his hatchet at one stroke, the tidings of which were very awful; and yet such was the hard-heartedness of the adversary that my tears were reckoned to me as a reproach.[5]

My loss and the loss of my children was great; our hearts were so filled with sorrow that nothing but the comfortable hopes of her being taken away in mercy, to herself, from the evils we were to see, feel, and suffer under (and joined to the assembly of the spirits of just men made perfect, to rest in peace and joy unspeakable, and full of glory, and the good pleasure of God thus to exercise us) could have kept us from sinking under at that time. That Scripture, Job 1:21, "Naked came I out of my Mother's womb, and naked shall I return thither. The Lord gave and the Lord hath taken away, blessed be the name of the Lord," was brought to my mind and from it that an afflicting God was to be glorified, with some other places of Scripture to persuade to a patient bearing my afflictions.

[Over the Green Mountains and into Canada]

My march on the French River[6] was very sore, for, fearing a thaw, we traveled a very great pace; my feet were so bruised and my joints so distorted by my traveling in snowshoes that I thought it impossible to hold out. One morning a little before break of day my master came and awakened me out of my sleep, saying, "Arise, pray to God, and eat your breakfast, for we must go a great way today." After prayer I arose from my knees, but my feet were so tender, swollen, bruised, and full of pain that I could scarce stand upon them without holding onto the wigwam. And then the Indians said, "You must run today."

I answered, "I could not run."

My master, pointing to his hatchet, said to me, "Then I must dash out your brains and take off your scalp."

I said, "I suppose then you will do so, for I am not able to travel with speed." He sent me away alone on the ice.

About sun half an hour high he overtook me for I had gone very slowly, not thinking it possible to travel five miles. When he came up, he called [to] me to run;

[5]Williams's wife, Eunice, was killed at the Green River, at the foot of the Leyden Hills. A monument was erected at the spot of her death.

[6]The Onion or Winooski River, which flows into Lake Champlain at present-day Burlington, Vermont.

I told him [that] I could go no faster; he passed by without saying one word more so that sometimes I scarce saw anything of him for an hour together. I traveled from about break of day till dark, never so much as set down at noon to eat warm victuals, eating frozen meat which I had in my coat pocket as I traveled. We went that day two of their day's journey as they came down. I judge we went forty or forty-five miles that day. God wonderfully supported me and so far renewed my strength that in the afternoon I was stronger to travel than in the forenoon. My strength was restored and renewed to admiration. We should never distrust the care and compassion of God who can give strength to them who have no might and power to them who are ready to faint.

When we entered on the lake,[7] the ice was very rough and uneven, which was very grievous to my feet that could scarce endure to be set down on the smooth ice on the river: I lifted up my cry to God in ejaculatory requests that He would take notice of my state and some way or other relieve me. I had not marched above half a mile before there fell a moist snow about an inch and a half deep that made it very soft for my feet to pass over the lake to the place where my master's family was—wonderful favors in the midst of trying afflictions!

We went a day's journey from the lake to a small company of Indians who were hunting; they were after their manner kind to me and gave me the best they had, which was mooseflesh, groundnuts, and cranberries but not bread; for three weeks together I ate no bread. After our stay there and undergoing difficulties in cutting of wood, [I] suffered from lousiness having lousy old clothes of soldiers put upon me when they stripped me of mine to sell to the French soldiers of the army. We again began a march for Chambly; we stayed at a branch of the lake and feasted two or three days on geese we killed there.

[The Jesuits at St. Francis Fort]

That night we arrived at the fort called St. Francis, where we found several poor children who had been taken from the Eastward the summer before, a sight very affecting, they being in habit very much like Indians and in manner very much symbolizing with them.[8] At this fort lived two Jesuits, one of which was made Superior of the Jesuits at Quebec. One of these Jesuits met me at the fort gate and asked me to go into the church and give God thanks for preserving my life; I told him I would do that in some other place. When the bell rang for evening prayers, he that took me bid me go, but I refused. . . .

My master took hold of my hand to force me to cross myself, but I struggled with him and would not suffer him to guide my hand; upon this he pulled off a crucifix from his own neck and bade me kiss it, but I refused once again. He told me he would dash out my brains with his hatchet if I refused. I told him I should sooner choose death than to sin against God; then he ran and caught up his hatchet and acted as though he would have dashed out my brains. Seeing I was not moved, he

[7]Lake Champlain.

[8]Taking on the symbols or trappings of Indian life, for example, dress, language, customs. For Williams, most disturbing would be the adopting of the symbols of Catholicism, such as wearing a cross, carrying a rosary; or praying before statues.

threw down his hatchet, saying he would first bite off all my nails if I still refused; I gave him my hand and told him I was ready to suffer. He set his teeth in my thumbnails and gave a grip with his teeth, and then said, "No good minister, no love God, as bad as the devil," and so left off.

I have reason to bless God who strengthened me to withstand; by this he was so discouraged as nevermore to meddle with me about my religion. I asked leave of the Jesuits to pray with those English of our town that were with me, but they absolutely refused to give us any permission to pray one with another and did what they could to prevent our having any discourse together. . . .

[At Montreal]

When I came to Montreal, which was eight weeks after my captivity, the Governor de Vaudreuil redeemed me out of the hands of the Indians, gave me good clothing, took me to his table, gave me the use of a very good chamber, and was in all respects relating to my outward man courteous and charitable to admiration. At my first entering into his house, he sent for my two children who were in the city that I might see them and promised to do what he could to get all my children and neighbors out of the hands of the savages. My change of diet after the difficulties of my journeys caused an alteration of my body; I was physicked, blooded, and very tenderly taken care of in my sickness.

The governor redeemed my eldest daughter[9] out of the hands of the Indians, and she was carefully tended in the hospital until she was well of her lameness and by the governor provided for with respect during her stay in the country. My youngest child was redeemed by a gentlewoman in the city as the Indians passed by.[10] After the Indians had been at their fort[11] and discoursed with the priests, they came back and offered to the gentlewoman a man for the child, alleging that the child could not be profitable to her, but the man would, for he was a weaver and his service would much advance the design she had of making cloth. But God overruled so far that this temptation to the woman prevailed not for an exchange, for had the child gone to the Indian fort in an ordinary way, it had abode there still, as the rest of the children carried there do.

The governor gave orders to certain officers to get the rest of my children out of the hands of the Indians and as many of my neighbors as they could. After six weeks a merchant of the city obtained my eldest son,[12] who was taken to live with him; he took a great deal of pains to persuade the savages to part with him. An Indian came to the city (Sagamore George of Penacook) from Cowass and brought word of my son Stephen's being near Cowass, and some money was put into his hand for his redemption and a promise of full satisfaction if he brought him; but the Indian proved unfaithful, and I never saw my child till a year after.

The governor ordered a priest to go along with me to see my youngest daughter among the Mohawks and endeavor her ransom.[13] I went with him; he was very courteous to me, and, from his parish which was near the Mohawk fort,[14] he wrote a letter

[9]Esther.
[10]Warham.
[11]The St. Louis Mission at Caughnawaga.
[12]Samuel, the eldest son held captive.
[13]Eunice.
[14]The St. Louis Mission at Caughnawaga.

to the Jesuit to desire him to send my child to see me and to speak with them that took her to come along with [her].

But the Jesuit wrote back a letter that I should not be permitted to speak with or see my child; if I came, that my labor would be lost, and that the Mohawks would as soon part with their hearts as my child. At my return to the city I with a heavy heart carried the Jesuit's letter to the governor who, when he read it, was very angry and endeavored to comfort me, assuring me I should see her and speak with her, and he would to his utmost endeavor her ransom. Accordingly he sent to the Jesuits who were in the city and bade them improve their interest for the obtaining the child.

After some days he went with me in his own person to the fort. When we came there, he discoursed with the Jesuits after which my child was brought into the chamber where I was. I was told I might speak with her but should be permitted to speak to no other English person there. My child was about seven years old; I discoursed with her near an hour; she could read very well and had not forgotten her catechism. And [she] was very desirous to be redeemed out of the hands of the Mohawks and bemoaned her state among them, telling me how they profaned God's Sabbaths and said she thought that a few days before they had been mocking the devil, and that one of the Jesuits stood and looked on them.

I told her she must pray to God for His grace every day. She said she did as she was able and God helped her. But, says she, "They force me to say some prayers in Latin, but I don't understand one word of them; I hope it won't do me any harm." I told her she must be careful she did not forget her catechism and the Scriptures she had learned by heart. She told the captives after I was gone, as some of them have informed me, almost everything I spoke to her and said she was much afraid she should forget her catechism, having no one to instruct her. I saw her once a few days after in the city but had not many minutes of time with her, but what time I had I improved to give her the best advice I could.

The governor labored much for her redemption, at last he had a promise of it in case he would procure for them an Indian girl in her place. Accordingly he sent up the river[15] some hundreds of leagues for one, but it was refused when offered by the governor: he offered them a hundred pieces of eight for her redemption, but it was refused. His lady went over to have begged her from them, but all in vain; [she is] there still and has forgotten to speak English. Oh! That all who peruse this history would join in their fervent requests to God, with whom all things are possible, that this poor child, and so many others of our children who have been cast upon God from the womb and are now outcast ready to perish, might be gathered from their dispersions and receive sanctifying grace from God! . . .

One day one of the Jesuits came to the governor and told the company there that he never saw such persons as were taken from Deerfield. Said he, "The Mohawks will not suffer any of their prisoners to abide in their wigwams while they themselves are at Mass but carry them with them to the church, and they can't be prevailed with to fall down on their knees to pray there, but no sooner are they returned to their wigwams, but they fall down on their knees to prayer." He said [that] they could do nothing with the grown persons there, and they hindered the children's complying.

[15]The St. Lawrence River.

Whereupon the Jesuits counseled the Mohawks to sell all the grown persons from the fort—a stratagem to seduce poor children! Oh Lord! Turn the counsels of these Ahithophels[16] into foolishness, and make the counsels of the heathen of none effect!

Here I observed they were wonderfully lifted up with pride after the return of Captain Montigny from Northampton[17] with news of success; they boasted of their success against New England. And they sent out an army as they said of seven hundred men, if I mistake not, two hundred of which were French, in company of which army went several Jesuits, and [they] said [that] they would lay desolate all the places on Connecticut River. The superior of the priests told me their general was a very prudent and brave commander of undaunted courage, and he doubted not but they should have great success. This army went away in such a boasting, triumphant manner that I had great hopes God would discover and disappoint their designs; our prayers were not wanting for the blasting such a bloody design.[18]

The superior of the priests said to me, "Don't flatter yourselves in hopes of a short captivity, for," said he, "there are two young princes contending for the kingdom of Spain, and a third, [and] that care is to be taken for his establishment on the English throne."[19] And [he] boasted what they would do to Europe, and that we must expect not only [in] Europe but in New England the establishment of popery.

I said, "Glory not, God can make great changes in a little time and revive His own interest and yet save His poor afflicted people."

Said he, "The time for miracles is past, and in the time of the last war the king of France was, as it were, against all the world and yet did very great things, but now the kingdom of Spain is for him, and the Duke of Bavaria, and the Duke of Savoy, etc." And spoke in a lofty manner of great things to be done by them and having the world, as I may say, in subjection to them.

[At Quebec]

All means were used to seduce poor souls. I was invited one day to dine with one of chief note. As I was going, [I] met with the superior of the Jesuits coming out of the house, and he came in after dinner; and presently it was propounded to me, if I would stay among them and be of their religion, I should have a great and honorable

[16]Ahithopel was a false counselor to King David; he joined in Absalom's plot to overthrow his father according to the second book of Samuel.

[17]Northampton, Massachusetts, is located seventeen miles south of Deerfield on the Connecticut River.

[18]The Marquis de De Vaudreuil, governor of Canada, sent a force of about 700 Indians and 125 French soldiers to attack English towns along the Connecticut River in the summer of 1704, but according to a report by de Vaudreuil, a French soldier deserted upon reaching New England and caused a panic among the Indian troops, who retreated before engaging in any attack.

[19]The princes contending for the Spanish throne were Philip, grandson of Louis XIV of France, and the Austrian archduke Charles. In addition to supporting Philip's claim to the Spanish throne, Louis XIV contended that James II, the Stuart king deposed in England's Puritan revolution, was the rightful heir to the British throne. In response to Louis XIV, William of England entered an alliance with Holland and Austria against France, and his successor, Queen Anne, joined Holland and Austria in declaring war on France in 1702, thus beginning the War of Spanish Succession, known in the colonies as Queen Anne's War.

pension from the king every year. The superior of the Jesuits turned to me and said, "Sir, you have manifested much grief and sorrow for your neighbors and children; if you will comply with this offer and proposal, you may have all your children with you, and here will be enough for an honorable maintenance for you and them."

I answered, "Sir, if I thought your religion to be true, I would embrace it freely without any such offer, but so long as I believe it to be what it is, the offer of the whole world is of no more value to me than a blackberry." And [I] manifested such an abhorrence of this proposal that I speedily went to take my leave and be gone.

"Oh! Sir," said he, "set down, why [are you] in such a hurry, you are alone in your chamber, divert yourself a little longer," and fell to other discourse. And within half an hour says again, "Sir, I have one thing earnestly to request of you, I pray pleasure me!"

I said, "Let your Lordship speak."

Said he, "I pray come down to the place tomorrow morning and honor me with your company in my coach to the great church, it being a saint's day."

I answered, "Ask me anything wherein I can serve you with a good conscience, and I am ready to gratify you, but I must ask your excuse here," and immediately went away from him. Returning unto my chamber, I gave God thanks for His upholding of me and also made an inquiry with myself whether I had by any action given encouragement for such a temptation.

[Redemption]

We have reason to bless God who has wrought deliverance for so many, and yet to pray to God for a door of escape to be opened for the great number yet behind, not much short of a hundred,[20] many of which are children, and of these not a few among the savages and having lost the English tongue, will be lost and turn savages in a little time unless something extraordinary prevent.

The vessel that came for us in its voyage to Canada struck a bar of sand, and there lay in very great hazard for four tides, and yet they saw reason to bless God for striking there, for had they got over the bar, they should at midnight in a storm of snow have run upon a terrible ledge of rocks.

We came away from Quebec October twenty-five [1706] and by contrary winds and a great storm we were retarded, and then driven back nigh the city, and had a great deliverance from shipwreck, the vessel striking twice on a rock in that storm. But through God's goodness we all arrived in safety at Boston November twenty-one, the number of captives fifty-seven, two of which were my children. I have yet a daughter of ten years of age and many neighbors whose case bespeaks your compassion and prayers to God to gather them, being outcasts ready to perish.

1707

[20]The remaining captives were not all from Deerfield but included English captured from other towns as well.

A Sheaf of Seventeenth-Century Anglo-American Poetry

Despite the distance from London literary circles and the rigorous demands of colonial life, colonists read and wrote a great deal of poetry in seventeenth-century America. Heirs of the Renaissance, educated colonists, like their English contemporaries, read classical poets as well as the chief "moderns": Sidney, Jonson, Donne, Herbert, Quarles, and later, Milton and Dryden. Many colonists considered themselves heirs of the Reformation as well, and they cherished the poetry of the Bible, especially David's Psalms and Solomon's Song. Finally, British Americans were avid readers of each other's verse. Poems were circulated in manuscript, exchanged in letters, read aloud in families, copied into diaries and commonplace books, committed to memory, and sometimes published.

Considered the most stately and moving form of language, poetry offered a popular vehicle for commemorating important events in personal and public life. Such New World occasions as the death of a local political or religious leader, conflicts with Native Americans, a bountiful harvest, or a crippling drought were addressed in adaptations of Old World poetic forms: the elegy, the epic, the ballad, the verse satire. Private lyrics commemorated personal and domestic events: spiritual episodes, courtship, family love, deliverance from illness, the death of a loved one. Whether public or private, poetry helped reveal the preordained order presumed to govern human lives—a goal especially important to settlers facing the illegibility of a strange new world. Poetic wit, defined far more broadly than today, offered a means of connecting the particular with the general, of discovering one's place on the cosmic and cultural map.

For many New Englanders, that map was biblical and religious; in the more secular middle and southern colonies, it was often English, patriotic, and mercantile. Puns, conceits, emblems, anagrams, and acrostics served as verbal tools for confirming harmony beneath a chaotic surface. This baroque or metaphysical tendency, as much a habit of mind as a literary style, often joined seemingly disparate and even contradictory elements: classical mythology with Biblical literalism, a sensitivity to nature with a celebration of commerce, a lament for societal corruption with extreme pride of place, verbal play with earnest piety, sensory imagery with otherworldly devotion. Such juxtapositions reflected post-Elizabethan verbal exuberance and an unremitting drive to make sense of things—especially to reconcile Old World culture with New World realities. Seeking to celebrate and internalize pre-existent truths rather than to create new truths, most poets wrote for specific purposes: to teach, to preach, to warn, to inspire, to console, and to entertain. To read their work is to rediscover an important early role of poetry in confirming cultural values and identity.

The era's major poets—Anne Bradstreet, Michael Wigglesworth, Edward Taylor, and Ebenezer Cook—appear elsewhere in the anthology, as do selections from the Bay Psalm Book, which had considerable influence on Puritan poetry. Poems in English can also be found in the selections from John Smith, Thomas Morton, Roger Williams, Cotton Mather, Samuel Sewall, and Sarah Kemble Knight. Poetry was also the most popular form of literature in Spanish-speaking America, since the promulgation of fiction in the colonies was banned by the Spanish crown.

A contest held in Mexico in 1585, for instance, attracted more than three hundred entries fashioned after Spanish models, a good half-century before the first book of poetry came out of the British colonies. It is instructive to read Gaspar Perez de Villagrá's epic on the conquest of Mexico, or Sor Juana Inés de la Cruz's lyrics and satires, both in the anthology, alongside works by their English-speaking contemporaries. The poets gathered in this section, arranged by date of birth, further underscore the range and diversity of early Anglo-American poetry.

Jeffrey A. Hammond
St. Mary's College of Maryland

Ivy Schweitzer
Dartmouth College

PRIMARY WORKS

Harrison T. Meserole, ed., *American Poetry of the Seventeenth Century,* 1968, 1985; Kenneth Silverman, ed., *Colonial American Poetry,* 1968; Pattie Cowell, ed., *Women Poets in Pre-Revolutionary America 1650–1775,* 1981.

Thomas Tillam (?–c. 1676)

Seeking refuge in New England on the eve of the English Civil War, Tillam wrote this short lyric on his first sight of America. His verse expresses the heady idealism of many Puritan immigrants, but it is also tinged with a note of warning. For unknown reasons, Tillam did not remain in New England. During the Commonwealth period he returned to England, where he wrote several works with millenarian themes, until he was imprisoned after the Restoration of the monarchy. In 1661, and now a Baptist, he left England for good and settled in Heidelberg, Germany, the leader of a small, communal religious group.

Uppon the first sight of New-England June 29, 1638[1]

Hayle holy-land, wherin our holy lord
Hath planted his most true and holy word
Hayle happye people who have dispossest
Your selves of friends, and meanes, to find some rest
For your poore wearied soules, opprest of late

[1]The text is from *Seventeenth-Century American Poetry,* ed. H. Meserole, 1968.

For Jesus-sake, with Envye, spight, and hate
To you that blessed promise truly's given[2]
Of sure reward, which you'l receve in heaven
Methinks I heare the Lambe of God thus speake
Come my deare little flocke, who for my sake
Have lefte your Country, dearest friends, and goods
And hazarded your lives o'th raginge floods
Posses this Country; free from all anoye
Heare I'le bee with you, heare you shall Injoye
My sabbaths, sacraments, my minestrye
And ordinances in their puritye
But yet beware of Sathans wylye baites
Hee lurkes among you, Cunningly hee waites
To Catch you from mee; live not then secure
But fight 'gainst sinne, and let your lives be pure
Prepared to heare your sentence thus expressed
Come yee my servants of my father Blessed[3]

1633 1944

John Wilson c. 1588–1667

According to Cotton Mather, John Wilson, the learned and pious teacher and minister of the first church established in Charlestown, later the First Church of Boston, was beloved by many. In addition, he "had so nimble a Faculty of putting his Devout Thoughts into *Verse,* that he Signalized himself by the Greatest *Frequency,* perhaps, that ever Man used, of sending *Poems* to all Persons, in all Places, on all Occasions" and thus "was a *David* unto the *Flocks* of our Lord in the *Wilderness.*" Educated at King's College, Cambridge, where he came into contact with Puritan ideas, Wilson sailed with the first group to come to Massachusetts Bay led by John Winthrop. In London in 1626 he published a lengthy poem for children entitled *A Song or, Story, For the Lasting Remembrance of diuerse famous works, which God hath done in our time,* better known as *A Song of Deliverance,* the title of the second edition published in Boston in 1680. In New England, he was prolific but published little, circulating most of his poems in manuscript. He especially excelled at composing funeral elegies based on anagrams of the name of the departed, sometimes squeezing up to six anagrams and elegies, in English and Latin, from the names of particularly eminent divines, such as his series on Thomas Shepard and John Norton. His anagrammatic elegy on Abigail Tompson, mother of the poet Benjamin Tompson, while conventionally pious, is notable for its use of the woman's voice with its gentle critique of her minister husband's inability to communicate the joys of heaven.

[2]Matthew 19:29.

[3]Matthew 25:34.

Anagram made by mr John Willson of Boston upon the Death of Mrs. Abigaill Tompson, And sent to her husband in virginia, while he was sent to preach the gospell yr.[1]

i am gon to all bliss[2]
The blessed news i send to thee is this:
That i am goon from thee unto all bliss,
Such as the saints & angells do enjoy,
Whom neither Deuill, world, nor flesh anoiy.
To bliss of blisses i am gon: to him
Who as a bride did for him selfe me trimm.
Thy bride i was, a most unworthy one,
But to a better bridegroom i am gon,
Who doth a Count me worthy of him selfe,
Tho i was neuer such a worthles elfe.
He hath me Cladd with his own Righteousness,
And for the sake of it he doth me bless.
Thou didst thy part to wash me, but his grace
Hath left no spott nor wrincle on my face.
Thou little thinkst, or Canst at all Conceiue,
What is the bliss that i do now receiue.
When oft i herd thee preach & pray & sing
I thought that heauen was a glorious thing,
And i belieud, if any knew, twas thou
That knewest what a thing it was; but now
I see thou sawest but a glimpse, and hast
No more of heauen but a little taste,
Compared with that which hear we see & have,
Nor Canst haue more till thou art past the graue.
Thou neuer touldst me of the Tyth,[3] nor yet
The hundred thousand thousand part of it.
Alas, Dear Soule, how short is all the fame
Of the third heauens, where i translated amm!
O, if thou euer louest me at all,
Whom thou didst by such loueing titles Call,
Yea, if thou louest Christ, (as who doth more?)

[1]The text, with slight modifications, is from *Handkerchiefs from Paul, being Pious and Consolatory Verses of Puritan Massachusetts,* ed. Kenneth Murdock, 1927. In 1642, Tompson and two other missionaries went down to Virginia at the request of several struggling nonconformist churches there, but the colonial authorities were so hostile to nonconformists that the men returned in 1643.

[2]The letters in this line can be rearranged to spell "Abigaill Tomsson" (with an extra *l* and an *s* in place of the *p* in "Tompson."

[3]From the word *tithe,* meaning "one-tenth."

Then do not thou my Death too much deplore.
Wring not thy hand, nor sigh nore mourn, nor weep,
All tho thine Abigaill be faln a sleep.
This but her body—that shall ryse again;
In Christs sweet bosom doth her soule remain.
Mourn not as if thou hadst no hope of me;
Tis i, tis i hau Caus to pitty thee.
O turne thy sighings into songs of prais
Unto the name of god; lett all thy Days
Be spent in blessing of his name for thiss:
That he hath brought me to this place of bliss.
It was a blessed, a thrice blessed, snow
Which to the meeting i then waded through,
When pierced i was upon my naked skinn
Up to the middle, the deep snow within.
There neuer was more happie way i trodd,
That brought me home so soone unto my god
Instead of Braintry Church; Conducting mee
Into a better Church, where now i see,
Not sinfull men, But Christ & those that are
Fully exempt from euery spot & skarr
Of sinfull guilt, where I no longer need
Or word or seale my feeble soul to feede,
But face to face i do behould the lamb,
Who down from heauen for my saluation Came,
And thither is asended up again,
Me to prepare a place whear in to Raign,
Where we do allways hallaluiahs sing,
Where i do hope for thee to Come err long
To sing thy part in this most glorious song.

1643 1927

John Josselyn c. 1610–post-1692

Born in Essex, England, Josselyn journeyed in 1637–38 to New England to visit his brother and other Puritan leaders and ramble through the unfamiliar countryside. He claimed to have delivered to John Cotton, minister of the First Church, the translation of the Psalms into English by poet Francis Quarles. From his observations of the natural phenomena of the New World, he wrote *New-England's Rarities Discovered*, published in London in 1672. These "rarities" apparently included the indigenous women of New England, whom he compares to other women in his unabashedly objectifying "Verses" inspired by a picture of a European "savage," a gypsy woman. The stormy crossing to America inspired his lines on an Atlantic tempest.

Verses made sometime since upon the Picture of a young and handsome Gypsie, not improperly transferred upon the Indian Squa[1]

The Poem

Whether White or Black be best
Call your Senses to the quest;
And your touch shall quickly tell
The Black in softness doth excel
And in smoothness; but the Ear,
What, can that a Colour hear?
No, but 'tis your Black ones Wit
That doth catch, and captive it.
And if Slut and Fair be one,
Sweet and Fair, there can be none:
Nor can ought so please the test
As what's brown and lovely drest:
And who'll say, that that is best
To please one sense, displease the rest?
Maugre[2] then all that can be sed
In flattery of White and Red:
Those flatterers themselves must say
That darkness was before the Day;
And such perfection here appears
It neither Wind nor Sun-shine fears.

1672

[1]The texts of both poems by Josselyn are from *Seventeenth-Century American Poetry*, ed. H. Meserole, 1968.

[2]In spite of, notwithstanding.

[And the bitter storm augments; the wild winds wage]

And the bitter storm augments; the wild winds wage
War from all parts, and joyn with the Seas rage.
The sad clouds sink in showers; you would have thought,
That highswoln-seas even unto Heaven had wrought;
And Heaven to Seas descended: no star shown;
Blind night in darkness, tempests, and her own
Dread terrours lost; yet this dire lightning turns
To more fear'd light; the Sea with lightning Burns.
The Pilot knew not what to chuse or Hy,[1]
Art stood amaz'd in Ambiguity.

1674

John Saffin 1626–1710

Before his family made his personal *Notebook* public at the beginning of the twentieth century, Saffin was known as a lawyer, judge, and very successful merchant in Boston whom diarist Samuel Sewall mocked as "wigg'd and powder'd with pretense." Their disagreements went much deeper as the short verse "The Negroes Character" makes clear, but Saffin's wig also points to his position and sophistication. Born in Somerset, England, of a well-to-do family, he emigrated as a youngster and grew up in the cultured town of Scituate, Massachusetts. Although he never attended a university, this environment encouraged his social ambitions and belletristic leanings. Saffin was a shrewd and inventive merchant, whose trade included slaves as well as plunder from foreign ships. His volatile personality made him many enemies, and when he fell out of favor politically, he retired in 1687 to Bristol, Rhode Island. His last years were also marked by his bitter feud with Sewall over the freeing of Saffin's slave—and by extension, the justice of slave-owning in general. The complex and vexing legal case in which both were involved dragged on in the courts for a long time. Saffin's *Notebook* contains about fifty poems, making him a prolific poet by colonial standards. The poems are unusually varied for the time—love poems, elegies, acrostics, satires, and occasional verse—and are remarkable for their intimate subjects and personal voice.

[1]Hie, to advance quickly to some destination or mark.

[Sweetly (my Dearest) I left thee asleep][1]

Sweetly (my Dearest) I left thee asleep
Which Silent parting made my heart to weep,
Faine would I wake her, but Love did Reply
O wake her not, So sweetly let her Lye.
But must I goe, O must I Leave her So,
So ill at Ease: involv'd in Slumbering wo
Must I goe hence: and thus my Love desert
Unknown to Her, O must I now Depart;
Thus was I hurried with such thoughts as these,
Yet loath to Rob thee of thy present Ease,
Or rather senceless payn: farewell thought I,
My Joy my Deare in whom I live or Dye
Farewell Content, farewell fare Beauty's light
And the most pleasing Object of my Sight;
I must begone, Adieu my Dear, Adieu
Heavens grant good Tideings I next heare from you
Thus in sad Silence I alone and mute,
My lips bad thee farewell, with a Salute.
And so went from thee; turning back againe
I thought one kiss to little then Stole twaine
And then another: but no more of this,
Count with your Self how many of them you miss.
now my love soon let me from thee heare
Of thy good health, that may my Spirits Cheare
Acquaint me with such passages as may
Present themselves since I am come away
And above all things let me thee Request
To bee both Chearfull quiet and at Rest
In thine own Spirit, and let nothing move
Thee unto Discontent my Joy my Love.
Hopeing that all things shall at last Conduce
Unto our Comfort and a Blessed use
Considering that those things are hardly gain'd
Are most Delightfull when they are Attain'd.
Gold Crowns are heavy: Idalian[2] Burns
And Lovers Days are good, and bad by turns
But yet the Consummation will Repay
The Debt thats due many a happy Day
Which that it may so be, Ile Heaven Implore

[1]The texts of both poems by Saffin are from *Seventeenth-Century American Poetry,* ed. H. T. Meserole, 1968.

[2]Idalium, an ancient city in southern Cyprus, became the center of the cult of Aphrodite, goddess of love.

To grant the fame henceforth forever more
And so farewell, farewell fair Beautys light
Ten thousand times Adieu my Dear Delight.
Your Ever loveing friend whilest Hee
Desolved is: or Cease to bee.

1928

The Negroes Character[1]

Cowardly and cruel are those *Blacks* Innate
Prone to Revenge, Imp of inveterate hate.
He that exasperates them soon espies
Mischief and Murder in their very eyes.
Libidinous, Deceitful, False and Rude,
The spume Issue of Ingratitude.
The Premises consider'd, all may tell,
How near good *Joseph* they are parallel.

1701

[1]This poem concludes Saffin's "A Briefe and Candid Answer to a late Printed Sheet, Entitled, The Selling of Joseph. 1701." In 1700, Samuel Sewall, a judge and leading citizen of Boston, published the first anti-slavery text in the colonies, "The Selling of Joseph," after hearing the appeal of the slave Adam against his master, who had reneged on a promise of freedom after a specified time of work. John Saffin, Adam's master, was a judge in the same court as Sewall. Saffin published his response to Sewall, and the terms of their debate persisted into the nineteenth century. Using the example of Joseph's brothers selling him into slavery in Egypt (see Genesis 37:27), Sewall argued that no one had the authority to steal a person's liberty; furthermore, Sewall argued that slavery corrupted the slave owner and the community. Saffin agreed that Negroes were "Creatures of God," but he believed them so inferior as to invalidate the comparison with Joseph. He reasoned that "God . . . hath Ordained different degrees and orders of men," and he claimed that there was biblical support for slavery, not the least of which was the example of Abraham. Furthermore, to free slaves would be to impose an unfair financial loss on owners; and, he warned, when free, Negroes would have to be transported abroad or "they will be a plague to this Country."

George Alsop 1636?–1673?

Alsop was baptized at St. Martin in the Fields in June 1636. Despite his wide reading, evident in his book, *A Character of the Province of Mary-Land* (1666), Alsop was probably born into humble circumstances. A loyal follower of King Charles I, Alsop seems to have feared unhappy political recriminations when Oliver Cromwell rose to power, so he signed an indenture that brought him to Maryland in 1658. He spent four years of his indenture near Baltimore before returning to England, where he wrote *A Character,* a lively promotional tract that blended pastoral and commercial themes.

Trafique is Earth's Great Atlas[1]

Trafique[2] is Earth's great *Atlas,* that supports
The pay of Armies, and the height of Courts,
And makes Mechanicks[3] live, that else would die
Meer starving Martyrs to their penury:[4]
None but the Merchant of this thing can boast,
He, like the Bee, comes loaden from each Coast,
And to all Kingdoms, as within a Hive,
Stows up those Riches that doth make them thrive:
Be thrifty, *Mary-Land,* keep what thou hast in store,
And each years Trafique to thy self get more.

1666

Sarah Whipple Goodhue 1641–1681

Of the poets collected in this group, Sarah Whipple Goodhue was the first native-born writer. She was born into a middle-class family of merchants; she married Joseph Goodhue (1639–1697), who was to become a leader of Ipswich, her native town. Her volume, *The Copy of a Valedictory* (1681), a religious and monitory book written in anticipation of her death, was published after she died giving birth to twins.

[1]Text is from H. T. Meserole, ed., *American Poetry of the Seventeenth Century*, 1985.
[2]Commerce, trade
[3]Tradesmen, laborers.
[4]Poverty.

Lines to Her Family[1]

My first, as thy name is Joseph, labor so in knowledge to increase,
As to be freed from the guilt of thy sins, and enjoy eternal peace.

Mary, labor so to be arrayed with the hidden man of the heart,
That with Mary thou mayst find thou hast chosen the better part.[2]

William, thou hast that name for thy grandfather's sake,
Labor so to tread in his steps, as over sin conquest thou mayst make.

Sarah, Sarah's daughter thou shalt be, if thou continuest in doing well,
Labor so in holiness among the daughters to walk, as that thou may
excel.
So my children all, if I must be gone, I with tears bid you all farewell.
The Lord bless you all.

Now, dear husband, I can do no less than turn unto thee,
And if I could, I would naturally mourn with thee:

. . . .

O dear heart, if I must leave thee and thine here behind,
Of my natural affection here is my heart and hand.

1681

Benjamin Tompson 1642–1714

Among the first native-born Anglo-American poets, Tompson was born into a family of zealous Puritans. He became a schoolmaster for several towns around Boston, his most famous pupil being Cotton Mather. Tompson's fame as a poet arose from his volume *New Englands Crisis* (1676) and its revision *New Englands Tears* (London, 1676), a verse epic treating the war with the Algonkian Confederation during the 1670s as a test of the faith of the elect in New England.

[1]The texts of both poems by Goodhue are from *Women Poets in Pre-Revolutionary America*, ed. P. Cowell, 1981.

[2]See Romans 7:22: "For I delight in the law of God after the inward man." Martha and Mary represented the active and the contemplative life (Luke 10:41–42)

Chelmsfords Fate[1]

Ere famous *Winthrops* bones are laid to rest
The pagans *Chelmsford* with sad flames arrest,
Making an artificial day of night
By that plantations formidable light.
Here's midnight shrieks and Soul-amazing moanes,
Enough to melt the very marble stones:
Fire-brands and bullets, darts and deaths and wounds
Confusive outcryes every where resounds:
The natives shooting with the mixed cryes,
With all the crueltyes the foes devise
Might fill a volume, but I leave a space
For mercyes still successive in there place
Not doubting but the foes have done their worst,
And shall by heaven suddenly be curst.
Let this dear Lord the sad Conclusion be
Of poor New-Englands *dismal tragedy.*
Let not the glory of thy former work
Blasphemed be by pagan Jew or Turk:
But in its funeral ashes write thy Name
So fair all Nations may expound the same:
Out of her ashes let a Phoenix rise
That may outshine the first and be more wise.

1676

A Supplement

What meanes this silence of *Harvardine* quils
While *Mars*[1] triumphant thunders on our hills.
Have pagan priests their Eloquence confin'd
To no mans use but the mysterious mind?
Have Pawawas[2] charm'd that art which was so rife
To crouch to every Don[3] that lost his life?
But now whole towns and Churches fire and dy

[1]Text is adapted from H. T. Meserole, ed., *American Poetry of the Seventeenth Century*.

[1]Roman god of war.

[2]Powwows: Native American religious figures who cured the sick and wounded and presided over dances preparatory for war.

[3]University professor. In the first decades of the Puritan commonwealth, many elegies were composed on the deaths of eminent members of the community

Without the pitty of an *Elegy.*
Nay rather should my quils were they all swords
Wear to the hilts in some lamenting words.
I dare not stile them poetry but truth,
The dwingling products of my crazy youth.
If these essayes shall raise some quainter pens
Twil to the Writer make a rich amends.

1676

Richard Steere 1643?–1721

Steere was born to a clothworker at Chertsey, Surrey (about twenty miles north of London), and educated at a local singing school and then at a Latin grammar school. Apprenticed to the cordwainer's trade in London, Steere became a staunch Whig and avoided Charles II's suppression of Whigs by taking ship to New England in 1683. He settled in New London, Connecticut, where he became a merchant, but soon moved to Southold, Long Island, to protest local persecution of Quakers. His major work, *The Daniel Catcher* (1713), was an anti-Catholic answer to John Dryden's *Absalom and Achitophel.* Steere's verse has an unusual range and quality among early Anglo-American poets.

On a Sea-Storm nigh the Coast[1]

All round the Horizon black Clouds appear;
A Storm is near:
Darkness Eclipseth the Sereener Sky,
The Winds are high,
Making the Surface of the Ocean Show
Like mountains Lofty, and like Vallies Low.

The weighty Seas are rowled from the Deeps
In mighty heaps,
And from the Rocks Foundations do arise
To Kiss the Skies
Wave after Wave in Hills each other Crowds,
As if the Deeps resolv'd to Storm the Clouds.

How did the Surging Billows Fome and Rore
Against the Shore

[1]Text is from H. T. Meserole, ed., *American Poetry of the Seventeenth Century.*

Threatning to bring the Land under their power
And it Devour:
Those Liquid Mountains on the Clifts were hurld
As to a Chaos they would shake the World.

The Earth did Interpose the Prince of Light,
'Twas Sable night:
All Darkness was but when the Lightnings fly
And Light the Sky,
Night, Thunder, Lightning, Rain, and *raging* Wind,
To make a Storm had all their forces joyn'd.

c. 1700

Anna Tompson Hayden 1648–1720

Anna Tompson Hayden was half-sister to Benjamin Tompson and Joseph Tompson, in whose journal all of her known poems have been preserved. She married Ebenezer Hayden of Boston and had one child, born in 1679. Hayden's two extant poems are elegiac; they reveal an acceptance of death in humble accord with God's plan.

Upon the Death of Elizabeth Tompson[1]

A lovely flow'r cropt in its prime
By Death's cold fatal hand;
A warning here is left for all
Ready prepar'd to stand.
For none can tell who shall be next,
Yet all may it expect;
Then surely it concerneth all,
Their time not to neglect.
How many awful warnings that
Before us oft are set,
That as a flaming sword to mind
Our youth hath often met,
To stop them in their course
And mind them of their end,

[1]Text is from P. Cowell, ed., *Women Poets in Pre-Revolutionary America.* The complete title of the poem in manuscript in Joseph Tompson's copybook is: "Upon the Death of that Desirable Young Virgin, Elizabeth Tompson, Daughter of Joseph and Mary Tompson of Bilerika, Who Deceased in Boston Out of the House of Mr. Legg, 24 August, 1712, Aged 22 Years."

To make them to consider
Whither their ways to tend.
We see one suddenly taken hence
That might have lived as long
For the few years she'd lived here
As any she lived among.
Her harmless blameless life
Will stand for her defence,
And be an honor to her name
Now she is gone from hence.

A Supplement

Charity bids us hope that she'll among those virgins be,
When Christ shall come to reign,[2]
Whom he will own among the wise,
And for his entertain.

1712

Elizabeth Sowle Bradford 1663?–1731

Elizabeth Bradford was born to a Quaker printer in London, and she married her father's apprentice, William Bradford, in 1685, the same year the couple set off for Philadelphia. She eventually settled with William in New York, where they established a thriving printing business. When they printed an edition of *War with the Devil* (1707) by Baptist minister Benjamin Keach, both Bradfords contributed poems to the volume. Elizabeth Bradford's poem follows.

To the Reader, in Vindication of this Book[1]

One or two lines to thee I'll here commend,
This honest poem to defend
From calumny, because at this day,
All poetry there's many do gain-say,
And very much condemn, as if the same
Did worthily deserve reproach and blame.
If any book in verse, they chance to spy,

[2]A reference to the parable of the wise virgins, whose lamps were trimmed and filled with oil in preparation for the bridegroom (Matt. 25:1–13).

[1]Text is from P. Cowell, ed., *Women Poets in Pre-Revolutionary America.*

Away profane, they presently do cry:
But though this kind of writing some dispraise,
Sith men so captious are in these our days,
Yet I dare say, how e'er the scruple rose,
Verse hath express'd as secret things as prose.
Though some there be that poetry abuse,
Must we therefore, not the same method use?
Yea, sure, for of my conscience 'tis the best,
And doth deserve more honor than the rest.
For 'tis no humane knowledge gain'd by art,
But rather 'tis inspir'd into the heart
By divine means; for true divinity
Hath with this science great affinity:
Though some through ignorance, do it oppose,
Many do it esteem, far more than prose:
And find also that unto them it brings
Content, and hath been the delight of kings.
David, although a king, yet was a poet,
And Solomon, also, the Scriptures show it.
Then what if for all this some should abuse it?
I'm apt to think that angels do embrace it,
And though God giv't here but in part to some,
Saints shall hav't perfect in the world to come.[2]

1707

Roger Wolcott 1679–1767

Wolcott rose to become governor of Connecticut in 1750 but began life in humble circumstances. His mother taught him to read and write, and he was apprenticed to a clothier, setting up in his own successful business at twenty. After marrying, he moved to South Windsor, Connecticut, to take up farming, and he embarked on a long career in public service as selectman, town magistrate, lawyer, military leader, and eventually governor. His poetry reflects Puritan themes and Baroque styles. A contemporary of the poet Edward Taylor and an orthodox Calvinist, he wrote the first book of poetry to be published in Connecticut, *Poetical Meditations, Being the Improvement of Some Vacant Hours* (1725). His remarkable historical poem in epic style on the founding and rechartering of the colony, excerpted here, imbues the events with near mythic status.

[2]The Book of Revelation foretold that saints in heaven would sing "a new song before the throne" (Rev. 14:3).

from A Brief Account of the Agency of the Honorable John Winthrop, Esq; In the Court of King Charles the Second, *Anno Dom.* 1662 When he Obtained for the Colony of Connecticut His Majesty's Gracious Charter[1]

. . . "Chear'd with the sight [of land] they set all Sails a-trip,[2]
"And rais'd the *English Ensign* on their Ship.
"Brave Youths with eager Strokes bend knotty Oars,
"Glad shouts bring chearful Eccho's from the Shores.
"As when the Wounded Amorous doth spy,
"His Smiling Fortune in his Ladys Eye,
"O how his Veins and Breast swell with a Flood,
"Of pleasing Raptures that revive his Blood?
"And grown impatient now of all Delays,
"No longer he Deliberating stays;
"But thro' the Force of her resistless Charms,
"He throws him Soul & Body in her Arms.
"So we amazed at these seen Delights,
"Which to fruition every sense Invites
"Our eager Mind already Captive made,
"Grow most Impatient now to be delay'd.
"This most Delightful Country to Possess,
"And forward with Industrious speed we press
"Upon the Virgin Stream who had as yet,
"Never been Violated with a Ship;
"Upon the Banks King *Aramamet* Stood,
"And round about his Wondering Multitude . . .
"Whence come you? Seek you with us *Peace* or *War*?
"*Brittons* you see, say they, and we are come,
From *England* happiest Seat in *Christendom,*
"Where Mighty Charles Obligeth *Sea* & *Land*
"To yield Obedience to his Scept'red Hand,
"Nor came we here to Live with you in Wars,
"As He knows best that made Sun Moon & Stars.
"But rather here to Live with you in Peace,
"Till Day and Nights Successive Changes cease.

[1]The text, from the first edition of Wolcott's *Poetical Meditations,* is from a transcript by David Shields. Upon the restoration of Charles II to the English throne, John Winthrop, Jr., son of Governor Winthrop of Massachusetts Bay Colony, went to England to express the colony's loyalty and have its charter confirmed. In the almost fifteen-hundred-line poem, Winthrop narrates to Charles the story of the founding of the colony.

[2]Hoisted up and ready for trimming.

"This we propose and this if you approve
"And do Respect our Neighbourhood and Love,
"Then Sell us Land, whereon we *Towns* may Plant,
"And join with us in Friendly covenant.
"What you propse, (quoth he,) is Just & Good,
"And I shall e're Respect your Neighbourhood;
"Land you may have, we Value not the Soil,
"Accounting Tillage too severe a Toil." . . .

. . . "Now Fortunes shews to the beholders sight,
A very Dreadful, yet a Doubtful Fight.[3]
"Whilst Mighty Men born in far Distant Land,
"Stood Foot to Foot engaging Hand to Hand. . . .
"Never did *Pequots* fight with greater Pride:,
"Never was *English* Valour Better try'd.
"Never was Ground soak't with more Gallant blood,
"Than the *Aceldama*[4] whereupon we stood.
"Sometimes one Party Victory soon Expect,
"As soon their eager Hopes are Counterchect.
"And those that seem'd as Conquered before,
"Repel with greater force the Conqueror.
"Three times the Pequots seemed to be beat:
"As many times they made their Foes retreat.
"And now our hope and help for Victory,
"Chiefly Depended from the Arm on High . . .
"But O what Language or what Tongue can tell,
"This dreadful Emblem of the flames of Hell?
"No Fantasie sufficient is to Dream,
"A Faint Idea of their Woes Extream.
"Some like unlucky Comets do appear,
"Rushing along the Streets with flagrant hair:
"Some seeking safety Clamber up the wall,
"Then down again with Blazing fingers Fall.
"In this last Hour of Extremity,
"Friends and Relations met in Company:
"But all in vain their tender Sympathy,
"Cannot allay but makes their Misery.
"The Paramour here met his amorous Dame,
Whose eyes had often set his heart in flame:
"Urg'd with the Motives of her Love and Fear,

[3]A description of the battle of Mystic, during the Pequot War (1636–1637), in which British forces set fire to the Pequot stronghold and massacred the inhabitants.

[4]Greek representation of the Aramaic phrase meaning "field of blood." This was the name given to any field in the vicinity of Jerusalem purchased with the blood money paid to and then confiscated from Judas Iscariot, betrayer of Jesus. It has come to mean any scene of slaughter or butchery.

"She runs and Clasps her arms about her Dear:
"Where weeping on his bosom as she Lies,
"And Languisheth on him she sets her Eyes;
"Till those bright Lamps do with her life Expire,
"And Leave him Weltering in a double fire."
"The Fair & Beauteous Bride with all her Charms,
"This night lay Melting in her Bridegrooms arms.
"This Morning in his bosom yields her Life,
"While he dyes Sympathizing with his Wife.
"In Love relation and in Life the same,
"The same in Death, both dy in the same Flame.
"Their Souls united both at once repair,
"Unto their place appointed thro' the air.
"The Gracious Father here stood looking on,
"His little Brood with deep affection,
"They round about him at each quarter stands,
"With piteous looks, Each lifts his little Hands
"To him for shelter, and then nearer throng,
"Whilst piercing Cries for help flow from each Tongue,
"Fain would he give their miseries relief;
"Tho' with the forfeiture of his own life;
"But finds his power too short to shield off harms,
"The torturing flame Arrests them in his arms.
"The tender Mother with like Woes opprest,
"Beholds her Infant frying at her breast;
"Crying and looking on her, as it fryes;
"Till death shuts up its heart affecting Eyes.
"The Conquering flame long Sorrows doth prevent,
"And Vanquisht Life soon breaks Imprisonment,
"Souls leave their Tenements gone to decay,
"And fly untouched through the flames away.
"Now all with speed to final ruin hast,
"And soon this Tragick scene is overpast.
"The Towns its Wealth high Battlements & Spires,
"Now Sinketh Weltring in conjoining Fires."

1725

Mary French 1687?–?

Mary French has survived in literary history because her 104-line poem to her sister, upon a captivity among Indians, was printed by Cotton Mather in his volume, *Good Fetch'd Out of Evil* (Boston, 1706). French had been captured at age sixteen during a 1703 Indian raid on Deerfield, Massachusetts. Forbidden to meet together for worship in their own Puritan faith, the captives were evidently pushed by their captors to accept Catholicism.

from A Poem Written by a Captive Damsel[1]

Dear sister, Jesus does you call
To walk on in his ways.
I pray make no delay at all,
Now in your youthful days.
O turn to him, who has you made,
While in your tender years,
For as the withering grass we fade,
Which never more appears.
But if that God should you afford
A longer life to live,
Remember that unto the Lord
The praises you do give.

. . . .

That earthly things are fading flow'rs
We by experience see;
And of our years and days and hours
We as observers be.
Of all degrees, and every age,
Among the dead we find;
Many there fell by bloody rage,
When we were left behind.
Let us be silent then this day
Under our smarting rod.
Let us with patience meekly say,
It is the will of God.
Of friends and parents we're bereaved,
Distresst and left alone;
Lord, we thy spirit oft have grieved:
And now as doves we moan.

. . . .

Dear sister, bear me in your mind;
Learn these few lines by heart;
Alas, an aching heart I find,
Since we're so long to part.
But to the care of God on high
Our cause we will commend.
For your soul sake these lines now I
Your loving sister send.

1706

[1]Text is from P. Cowell, *Women Poets in Pre-Revolutionary America.* The complete title of the poem was "A Poem Written By a Captive Damsel, About Sixteen or Seventeen Years of Age, Who Being [Told?] That Her Younger Sister at a Distance From Her [Would?] Be Led Away by the Popish [Demons?], Address'd Her in these Lines."

EIGHTEENTH CENTURY

Eighteenth-century Americans witnessed significant changes in their lives—changes demographic, economic, and, of course, political. In many ways, the alterations in the colonial demography and economy that took place in the first half of the century contributed to the key political event—the Revolutionary War—that took place in the latter part of the century.

One of the most striking shifts was demographic. Compared to life in Europe, where population was dense and more urban, life in the colonies was healthier, especially in the colonies north of Virginia. The population grew naturally as more children survived to adulthood and as women married at younger ages. Many Europeans, whether as independent farmers or as indentured workers, ventured across the Atlantic. Unlike the earlier migrations, however, those of the eighteenth century were marked by increasing numbers of non-English settlers. By 1775, half the population south of New England was of non-English origin. The institution of slavery and the vast Spanish territory in Florida both account in part for this figure. About 275,000 black slaves were brought to the colonies during the century. Spanish missionaries continued their movement into both Florida and the Southwest, where Franciscans set up chains of missions. By the late eighteenth century, Spain had dominion over a vast territory extending from California, initially colonized in 1769, through Texas, settled largely after 1700, to the Gulf coast. Yet the largest immigration movement in the English colonies occurred along the eastern seaboard, where non-English settlers—Scotch-Irish, German, Scottish, and, to a lesser extent, Dutch, French Huguenots, and Jews (usually coming from the Netherlands)—began to arrive in increasing numbers as the century progressed.

Ethnic diversity, combined with the healthful circumstances of life in eighteenth-century America, strengthened the population and helped bring about a rising standard of living. In his 1751 pamphlet *Observations Concerning the Increase of Mankind,* Benjamin Franklin predicted that in another century "the greatest Number of Englishmen will be on this [the American] side the water." In light of population statistics, Franklin was correct in his assessment. In 1650, the overall Euro-American population had been 52,000, the size of a small city today. By 1700, the European American and African American population had grown to 250,000, and by 1730, that figure had more than doubled. By 1775, this population had expanded to 2.5 million; by the 1790s, it was 3.5 million. According to some historians, such a rate of population growth—doubling nearly every twenty years—is unparalleled in recorded history.

Franklin's speculations about the resulting economic and trade gains were also borne out. Generally speaking, the standard of living was on the rise for all property-owning Americans. Household inventories show the acquisition of amenities, such as earthenware and a variety of metal utensils to replace the wooden items previously used. Indeed, after 1750, the presence of luxury items like silver and silver plate in homes of the wealthy and English ceramics and teapots in homes of the "middling" sort suggests that the standard of living for colonial Americans was quickly rising. Yet this rise was not evenly distributed. By midcentury, signs of an increasingly poorer urban population indicate that those already owning property were gaining, those who had no property were not. There was very little available land in areas already settled by white colonists, making land more expensive for everyone. In addition, the greater number of children surviving in each family put pressure on cities, for the children of country people sought increasingly scarce work in the cities nearby.

Furthermore, the colonies were subject to European powers and the fluctuations caused by the impact of European wars and by variations in overseas demands for American products. But wars and trade variations affected the colonies differently. The New England area, marked by rocky terrain and great pine forests, could be farmed for subsistence but not for crops for exportation; thus, merchant sea trade and shipbuilding predominated. New England traders benefited financially from the slave trade, as the South made increasing demands for slave importation. Because New Englanders were dependent upon the seas for their livelihoods, the imperial wars between England and other European nations seriously disrupted trade patterns and work opportunities.

The most significant European war to affect the colonies was King George's War, known in Europe as the War of the Austrian Succession (1739–1748). England in 1739 had declared war on Spain. New England initially gained from increased shipbuilding and the need for sailors, but the region suffered heavy losses after 1744, when France joined Spain against England and England started losing to the combined power of its two neighboring antagonists. The war took a great toll on New England men and supplies both at sea and on land. New Englanders were taxed heavily to pay for their own militia's capture of the French fortress of Louisbourg at the mouth of the St. Lawrence River in 1745, and they resented the 1748 Treaty of Aix-la-Chapelle, which gave Louisbourg back to the French.

By contrast, the Middle Colonies—New York, Pennsylvania, and New Jersey—prospered during this period. The greater fertility of the soil provided larger and richer farms for the white population that could afford land. The farms required tenant farmers and provided work for people in the area. The Middle Colonies gained from the greater wartime demand for foodstuffs. By midcentury, the economy in Philadelphia and New York surpassed that of Boston, which had deteriorated under the wartime situation.

The Chesapeake area and the Lower South also benefited from the European wartime demand for food and supplies. After 1745, some Chesapeake planters began to convert tobacco fields to wheat and corn to meet the demand; but most kept their fields in tobacco, thus taking advantage of a world trade market that brought for tobacco nearly double the price of grain produce. To handle the labor-intensive work of tobacco planting and curing, Chesapeake planters escalated their acquisition of a slave force, whose size was surpassed only by that in areas to the south.

The Lower South—the Carolinas and Georgia—depended entirely upon staple crops and slave labor. In midcentury, tobacco and rice crops climbed in value, despite some minor setbacks in trade caused by King George's War, so that the South as a region generally became richer than the North. South Carolina, for instance, had the highest average wealth per freeholder in Anglo-America by the time of the Revolutionary War. Its large slave force, which grew larger by natural increase, brought the dominant whites in the area a vast affluence, unparalleled in the colonies.

But the land seemed too small to fulfill

the dreams and expectations of all immigrants, and many coveted the territory westward, where Native Americans in increasing numbers were forced to resettle. Westward movement, with its consequent displacement of native populations, seemed the only recourse to the dominant culture. As they had from the earliest days of exploration, the Europeans viewed the Native Americans as formidable but ultimately subduable foes. English domination resulted in part from superior military weaponry and in part from the native peoples' unwillingness to form alliances with traditional foes against their newest, common enemy, the English. Yet the indigenous peoples determined that they could use antagonisms among European powers to forestall European encroachment: they could remain neutral as the Spanish, English, and French attacked one another, or they could threaten alliance with one European power against another.

The natives' policies of neutrality, with the added threat of potentially antagonistic alliance, worked well in the East until the time of the Great War for Empire—the French and Indian War—in the middle of the eighteenth century. The Iroquois Confederacy dominated the Northeast territory from the earliest days of European exploration until the first half of the eighteenth century. First composed of five Indian nations, the Mohawks, Oneidas, Onondagas, Cayugas, Senecas—and, in 1722, joined by the Tuscaroras—the Confederacy until the early 1750s managed to remain relatively free of territorial agitation. In 1701, the Confederacy officially adopted a policy of neutrality toward the Europeans but engaged in trade with the French, thus enabling the latter to locate strategically placed trading posts along the Ohio River. Trouble for the Iroquois began when English fur traders pushed into the Ohio country in 1752, causing French traders there to fortify existing outposts along the rivers and to build new ones southward from Lake Erie.

Fearing French intrusion in lands potentially English, a delegation from seven northern and middle colonies met at Albany, New York, in June 1754. At this meeting, later called the Albany Congress, the colonial delegates adopted a plan of union for mutual legislation and support, and they agreed to seek an English-Iroquois alliance and thus create a coordinated defense of the English colonies. The plan came too late, however. Governor Robert Dinwiddie of Virginia had already pushed Virginia militia into present-day western Pennsylvania, where the French had established a stronghold at the juncture of the Allegheny and Monangahela Rivers (now Pittsburgh). Dinwiddie's inexperienced troops suffered a serious defeat against the French. Taking the English failure as a sign of ineptitude and future losses, the Iroquois Confederacy joined forces with the French.

For a time, the Indians' decision seemed appropriate, as suggested by the July 1755 defeat—memorably recorded in Franklin's *Autobiography*—of General Braddock near Fort Duquesne. English and colonial losses continued until July 1758, when the fort at Louisbourg was recaptured. A year later, French defenses were broken at Quebec. The English eventually won the war, and England gained—at the Treaty of Paris, signed in 1763—the major North American holdings of the French. In addition, England obtained Spanish Florida; Spain, having joined France against England toward the end of the war, ceded Florida to the English in return for its gain of French holdings in Louisiana.

Now all along the eastern seaboard natives found themselves forced ever farther westward into central North America, away from their homelands. Similar developments occurred in the South, where English inroads against the Creeks and Cherokees provoked a Cherokee attack in 1760. In the Northwest Territory, extending from present-day western Pennsylvania to western Michigan, English encroachments reached crisis proportions in 1763. In an unprecedented move, Pontiac, an Ottawa war chief, brought about an alliance among the Ottawas, Chippewas, Hurons, Potawatomis, Delawares, Shawnees, and even a portion of the Mingoes (Pennsylvania Iroquois). During the spring of 1763, the Indians besieged a number of forts in the territory and raided the Pennsylvania and Virginia frontiers unimpeded, until Pontiac, in late October, suspended the attacks for the winter.

English response to the frontier situation was ineffectual for the most part. In a Proclamation of 1763, for example, the English government declared that the source waters of rivers flowing eastward to the Atlantic from the Appalachian Mountains should be the colonists' western boundary. But English settlers had already passed the boundary by the time the Proclamation of 1763 was enacted.

A complicated hierarchy of authority was evolving at the time. Native Americans were increasingly dominated by white frontier settlers who themselves were under the dominion of governments located largely in the East, from Savannah and Charleston to Philadelphia, New York, and Boston. Yet those centers of power were themselves theoretically directed by an overseas authority, the English king and Parliament. But the overseas government consistently revealed itself to know less and less about the colonies. Furthermore, ethnic diversity and economic ability led American colonists into a broader questioning of the values of the mother country. American intellectuals were in a prime position to test the political, scientific, and philosophical "truths" about which their European counterparts could only theorize.

The Enlightenment and the Great Awakening

Like their European counterparts, educated colonists were well aware of the scientific findings of Sir Isaac Newton (1642–1727) and the political, scientific, and philosophical theorizing of Thomas Hobbes (1588–1679) and John Locke (1632–1704). Most intellectuals would readily have concurred with Alexander Pope's pronouncement in the *Essay on Man* (1733–1734):

> Know then Thyself, presume not God to scan;
> The proper Study of Mankind is *Man*.

And they would have agreed with Pope's assertion that Newton showed the superiority of humankind in his ability to "unfold all Nature's Laws." Interest in science, given credence by the 1660 founding of the Royal Society, was promulgated in the eighteenth century in both poetry and prose. Some writers, like Cotton Mather, followed Newton's thinking and considered that the study of humans and nature would add to the progress of human knowledge and thus to the greater glory of God. Others worked from Newton's scientific discoveries—the laws of gravitation and the refraction of light—and dispensed with his insistence that these discoveries revealed God's hand in a harmonious universe and well-ordered natural world.

As Isaac Newton was influential in the areas of science and theology, so his contemporaries, Thomas Hobbes and John Locke, were influential in psychological, political, and philosophical inquiry. Both Hobbes and Locke sought ways to argue against medieval scholasticism and the Renaissance neo-Platonists' intuitional philosophy, which was based upon the assumption that humankind was given, *a priori,* innate knowledge by God. Hobbes, insisting upon the absolute power of the state, studied human psychology and asserted that people in the state of nature formed social groups out of fear and the need for mutual protection. Locke, born two generations later, argued that each person was born with a *tabula rasa,* a blank slate, upon which experience inscribed knowledge. Human knowledge was thus, for Locke and his followers, accrued according to experience, not divinely given at birth and sanctioned by intuition. Locke's view of human nature was more favorable than Hobbes's, and his conception of government—for mutual benefit—more readily adaptable to life in the colonies during the eighteenth century.

Many colonists, especially of the "middling" group but also the politically influential elite, by midcentury had absorbed popularized versions of enlightenment philosophy promoted by what has come to be called the Scottish Common Sense "school," an outgrowth of the Scottish Enlightenment. These writers and philosophers were responding to the theories of Newton, Hobbes, and Locke, as well as to the intellectual, economic, social, and political turmoil in Europe. Colonists were attracted to Adam Ferguson (1723–1816), whose social theories called into question the prevailing assumptions about the state of nature. They admired Henry Home, Lord Kames (1696–1782), for his theories of jurisprudence, which advanced views of historical relativism. For history, they read David Hume (1711–1776) and William Robertson (1721–1793). For moral philosophy, Francis Hutcheson (1694–1746) and Adam Smith (1723–1790) provided bases for progressive views of human nature. Even in medicine, intellectuals in the colonies tended to look to Edinburgh until well after the Revolution.

For colonists in the eighteenth century, the central philosopher of common sense was Thomas Reid (1710–1796), whose appeal was democratic and utilitarian. Reid answered the philosophical skepticism of David Hume, which undermined the philosophical basis of Newton's science by throwing doubt on the necessary link between cause and effect. Rather than arguing the particulars of what can or cannot be proved by reasoning, Reid insisted that philosophers should, on the grounds of experience, consensus, and necessity, assume that the human mind can know actual objects and that "a wise and good Author of nature" will "continue the same laws of nature, and the same connections of things, for a long time." A reasonable and predictable God is close to the deity of Jefferson and Paine. And the practical philosophy of reliance upon moral and sensory impressions appealed to people who were about to create what they argued could be a rational and predictable future.

> Among the natural rights of the colonists are these: first, a right to life; second, to liberty; third, to property; together with the right to support and defend them in the best manner they can. These are evident branches of, rather than deductions from, the duty of self-preservation, commonly called the first law of nature.
>
> All men have a right to remain in a state of nature as long as they please; and in case of intolerable oppression, civil or religious, to leave the society they belong to, and enter into another.
>
> When men enter into society, it is by voluntary consent; and they have a right to demand and insist upon the performance of such conditions and previous limitations as form an equitable original compact.
>
> Every natural right not expressly given up, or, from the nature of a social compact, necessarily ceded, remains.
>
> Samuel Adams, "The Rights of the Colonists," 1772

The rise of empirical science—the inquiry into natural phenomena—in the late seventeenth and early eighteenth centuries made the colonies a good testing-place for scientific, political, and philosophical beliefs. There, as never before, European assumptions about nature and human nature could be tested. Some intellectuals, like Jonathan Edwards, found in the American testing-place ample demonstration of the theological certainties of Newton, that evidence of God's hand was everywhere apparent in the natural world. Others, like Franklin and Jefferson, found political and social evidence for the position of Locke and the Common Sense philosophers on government, and they developed arguments insisting upon the necessary and infallible progress of human affairs.

Given the immense changes in the eighteenth century, it is no wonder that some people wanted reassurance of God's steadying presence. One of the strongest American supporters of Newtonian and Lockean philosophy was Jonathan Edwards (1703–1758), a quiet and introspective minister whose preaching and writing ignited one of America's largest evangelical movements. At a time when strict Puritan practice was giving way to a more ecumenical Protestant approach to salvation, Edwards used the most recent scientific and philosophical treatises to insist upon his own devout belief in the necessity for each person to have a felt experience of God's grace in order to be assured of salvation. He rejected the liberalism of his maternal grandfather, Solomon Stoddard, who had helped introduce the Half-Way Covenant in New England. Edwards held that such a liberalizing transformation of strict Puritan doctrine was "repugnant to the design and tenor of the gospel." His reading in the works of Newton, Locke, and their followers suggested to him, first, that God's hand was evident in all the natural creation, and second, that careful inquiry into one's relationship with God could create the psychological state necessary to achieve a felt presence of the godhead. For Edwards, it was not sufficient to comprehend God mentally; one had to experience the truth of the Gospel. His reading in Locke convinced him that sense impressions could convey signs of God's presence.

For a time, he was successful. In 1735, his congregation seemed to be "seized," he later said, "with a deep concern about their eternal salvation." A revival began to spread to other congregations in the neighboring communities. News of the awakening in western Massachusetts spread to Boston, where it was publicized and debated. With only minor setbacks, the awakening continued to flourish in New England settlements, only to become more widespread by the late 1730s. The years 1738 and 1739 brought reports of a wide evangelical movement in England, then in the southern and middle colonies, under the work of English evangelist George Whitefield (1714–1770). Whitefield reached New England in 1740, where congregation after congregation was moved to evangelical fervor and spiritual outpouring and renewal. The Great Awakening, as it was called, was at its height. With its emphasis on individual experience above time-honored authority, the Great Awakening was, in effect, a large and democratic movement in the colonies. Anyone, it seemed—rich or poor, black or Native American or white—could awaken and so join, on an equal footing, in a national movement toward salvation. A key factor of the Great Awakening was the extent to which it drew people from non-elite and rural culture into a communal identity.

Other Americans took the same intellectual tradition Edwards followed and began to suggest, like the Europeans they read, that salvation for humankind was not in the hands of God but in the hands of humans. These intellectuals thought that Newton's scientific discoveries would light the way to a more perfect human community. Known as Deists, they argued that the structure of the universe, not the Bible, attested to God. Whereas Christian theologians believed that God intervened directly and immediately in human life, Enlightenment philosophers like Benjamin Franklin considered God a kind of supreme architect or watchmaker who designed the world, set it in motion, and then left it to operate on its own. It was up to people, not God, to see that the world functioned for the good of all, not just those who happened to belong to one religious sect or another. Religious fanaticism was an object worthy only of satire—as Franklin's "A Witch Trial at Mount Holly" (1730) suggests. Rather than religious belief, people should inquire into doing good in the world.

The Society of Friends, or Quakers as they were commonly called, flourished in the eighteenth century and implemented their theories of equality and toleration in their social practice. Welsh, Irish, Dutch, and German Quakers had in the late seventeenth century established themselves in Pennsylvania, where Quaker William Penn had formed a colony. Pacifist and egalitarian in principles, the Quakers became known for their tolerance of all peoples, which brought to Pennsylvania a number of Native American groups from western Maryland, Virginia, and North Carolina along with many European immigrants. Quakers believed that all the creation was God's and that the individual's experience of God's love could manifest itself as an inner light of harmony expressed outwardly as love for all in God's world. Their egalitarian practice was evident in their meetinghouse, where both men and women could pray or speak if they felt moved to do so, and in countinghouse. The Quakers were the first group to work in behalf of freedom of worship for black slaves and the first to seek, in a Yearly Meeting notice from the 1680s, the abolition of slavery. They resisted paying taxes for war and doing military service. Their simplified way of living ran counter to the materialism of the eighteenth-century colonies.

Daily Life and the Woman's Sphere

Quakers were the first group of Euro-Americans to allow women full voice in religious meeting and in the home. For the most part, the Euro-American community continued in the well-established patriarchal social tradition that allocated to men certain social privileges outside the home, privileges associated with church and state affairs, that were not available to women. For the most part, it was the men of the elite class who established themselves as public voices.

White men and women who could afford the leisure time required for writing lived primarily in the plantation South and in northern cities. Such leisure time was a luxury in the colonies, where an overwhelming majority—more than ninety percent of the population—lived in rural areas. Given the abundance of literature that has survived, we tend to forget that nearly all adult white men and women lived and worked on farms. Whether a man was a miller or blacksmith and whether his wife ran a small business selling the family's surplus produce, both engaged in those activities in addition to their central tasks of farming.

Rural women typically worked on household affairs—food preparation (milking cows and making butter, planting and harvesting of gardens, in addition to cooking and canning), clothing manufacture (from spinning the thread for the cloth to cutting and sewing garments), and cleaning (making the soap, then washing clothes in a nearby water source or carrying the water home). Life was not easy for such women, and their chores were performed in addition to training the five to eight children they bore. It is no wonder, then, that the diaries of women frequently contain entries made up entirely of descriptions of chores they accomplished or complaints about personal weakness and sickness. Men in eighteenth-century households also experienced heavy workloads. Their wives' gardens were for the family; their own pastures were usually cultivated for market. They planted and cultivated large fields, ran herds of cattle into pastures, and slaughtered animals for home and city markets. In households governed largely by the seasons and by available light, the accomplishment of such arduous chores necessitated the help of children or, in wealthier households, servants or slaves.

For the small percentage of the population that lived in cities, life took on a different character. Mercantile in nature and usually coastal or riverside in location, city life was dominated by the market, which brought in foodstuffs and wares from rural areas and goods imported from abroad. The cities offered more opportunity for socializing, and wealthier urbanites had leisure time for reading, walking or riding, card-playing, dancing, and attending plays or concerts. News from London and the rest of Europe, as well as news from other colonies, appeared in local newspapers. Printers and presses increased in number as the century progressed: by the middle of the eighteenth century, every major city had at least one newspaper, and some cities had two or three. Twenty-six newspapers were published weekly by 1765. Competing for a relatively small readership, newspapers regularly announced the "latest news" and "newest imported goods."

City life and work opportunities tended to attract rural workers, single women, and widows. Women, whether unmarried or widowed with children, could rarely run farmsteads without the aid of adult men, so they tended to seek work in the cities for their own livelihoods, as nurses or midwives, seamstresses, servants, or prostitutes. Only unmarried women or widows could legally run independent businesses, and very few had the capital necessary to open up their own businesses (shops, inns, or boardinghouses). The common-law system of *coverture,* in which a married woman became one person with her husband, who was given all legal rights to her personal property, prevented married women from seeking work or social activity outside the domestic sphere.

More than ninety-five percent of black families were held as slaves. The majority of South Carolina's population was black; in Georgia, about half the population and, in the Chesapeake, forty percent was black. In these areas, the average household held about ten workers as slaves. And, given the size of such plantation households, workers' labors were specialized. Men typically worked as blacksmiths, woodworkers, and field workers, while women worked the dairies or made clothing or food. But only about twenty percent of the slaves engaged in specialized labor. By far the majority—especially on the larger plantations—were assigned to the fields. James Grainger's long poem, *The Sugar Cane* (1764), describes the situation of black slaves in the West Indies, a more intense version of conditions in the South. Anxiety about controlling the slave population revealed a fascination with "the other" born of fear and desire for "mastery" over the black slave body.

Because most slaves were prevented from learning to read and write, stories by blacks tended to be passed down orally. Autobiographical accounts like *The Interesting Narrative of the Life of Olaudah Equiano, or Gustavus Vassa, the African* (1789) provide rare glimpses into the lives of slaves. The importance of oral expression in African culture encouraged slaves to maintain a vitality of expression in their new American surroundings, a vitality lost on white masters who did not understand the symbolic resilience of their slaves' oral transmissions.

Literacy and Education

Colonial life, especially in the first half of the eighteenth century, was hierarchically structured, men over women, whites over blacks and Native Americans. Power was concentrated in the hands of the dominant class. The abundance of writing from this era might suggest that most British Americans could both read and write. Yet most—almost all blacks, half the white women, and one-fifth the white men—could do neither. Colonial culture was—at least in the first half of the eighteenth century, before the market economy started to develop and printing presses became fully established—an oral culture, one that depended upon the person-to-person transmission of information.

By midcentury, this situation began to shift. The newer elite culture, made up of merchants and tradesmen in cities and northern farmers and southern rural plantation-holders, was aligned with the printed medium, individual rather than communal accomplishment, and the city. Literacy, less essential in a rurally based and orally oriented society like that of early-eighteenth-century America, became a sign of status and thus an accomplishment. Parents who held property sent their male children to study, usually with the local minister, in preparation for collegiate training in one of the newly founded universities—schools now known as the College of William and Mary (chartered, 1693; established, 1726); Princeton (1747); Columbia (1754); Brown (1765); Rutgers (1766)—or to Harvard (1636) or Yale (1701). Except for the first Native American students at Princeton and Dartmouth (originally Moor's Indian School), education was for the propertied elite. Indeed, the wealthiest families sent their children to Europe—usually London or Edinburgh—for college.

Very few families sent women to study at the minister's home, much less to college. Yet public (or dame) schools were established on an increasingly frequent basis in the eastern seaboard cities and even in urban areas in the countryside. Consequently, by midcentury, more and more children—male and female—were being trained in reading and writing. Along with a rudimentary intellectual education, usually in reading but not in writing, girls from elite families might also receive instruction in music, dancing, and fancy needlework, these three abilities signifying genteel status.

In contrast, the vast majority of slaves received only such formal education as their white masters deemed necessary for them to perform their duties. Because slaveholders—especially in the South—believed that literacy made it harder for slaves to accept their place, many governments passed laws making it illegal to teach slaves to read and write. The relatively small number of free blacks in the English colonies had only slightly better educational opportunities, for most schools did not enroll black students. By comparison, Native Americans seemed to fare somewhat better. Between the 1730s and 1760s, a flurry of Indian education experiments took place in the Middle Colonies especially. As a result, a number of Native Americans received formal educations. Yet only a small proportion of the total population of Native Americans was selected for training, which itself was determined by the Christianizing attitudes of the whites who ran the schools.

Revolution and Confederation

Demographic differences in the colonies generally affected Americans' attitudes toward revolution against England. For example, in the South, where the population was most racially mixed, white colonists' zeal for revolution was countered by their interest in keeping their slave territory free of intrusion and slave revolts. The American Revolution confronted nonwhites with the complex dilemma of determining allegiance. For the majority of African Americans, the choices were especially stark: possible emancipation versus continued enslavement. At the outset of the war, the willingness of free northern blacks to support the rebellion was dramatized most memorably by the case of Crispus Attucks, an ex-slave who was one of the first people killed in the revolutionary cause when he was shot by British troops in the Boston Massacre in 1770. Then, in

1775, African Americans played active roles in the engagements at Lexington, Concord, and Bunker Hill, and in the efforts of the Green Mountain Boys in Vermont.

However, in late 1775, blacks were officially barred from the American military, partially because of fear among slaveholders that arming them would prove disruptive. Moving to take advantage of the colonists' paranoia, in November 1775 the British attempted to destabilize the colonial workforce in the South by offering freedom to male slaves and indentured servants who joined their side. This action forced George Washington and the Continental Congress to reverse their decision on the enlistment of blacks. In addition, it served to consolidate support for the Revolution—especially in the South, where many whites had initially remained loyal to England. The British attempt to undermine the slave system enabled "patriot" American propagandists to argue successfully that any serious division among whites could render the southern colonies, where blacks often made up half or more of the population, vulnerable to slave insurrections.

Likewise, fear of attack by Native Americans brought white settlers on the western frontier into the Revolution in support of the rebel Americans. The Indians, frustrated and displaced by whites' pressures on their homelands, might have been willing to use a British alliance to retaliate against the colonists, who seemed increasingly uninterested in the rights of Native Americans. Although the Proclamation of 1763 did not protect Native Americans from incursions, it did suggest to them that British officials in London respected their claims to lands more fully than did the colonists who had overrun their territories. When Lord Dunmore's War erupted in western Virginia in 1774, the way seemed clear for an Indian alliance with the British. Out of self-defense and their awareness that colonial relations with the Indians were very poor, revolutionaries sought Native Americans' neutrality in the conflict. The Cherokees were the only large group to attack Americans—on the western borders of settlements in the Carolinas and Virginia, in the summer of 1776—during the Revolutionary War. Other groups heeded the message of the Second Continental Congress that the war was "a family quarrel between us and Old England," that "you Indians are not concerned in it."

Problems in the "family," between the colonies and England, had emerged at least as early as the 1750s. As a result of the French and Indian War, often called the Great War for Empire or the Seven Years War, which concluded with the 1763 Treaty of Paris, the British treasury was depleted. Convinced that the colonists should contribute to the cost of their own defense, members of Parliament passed a series of taxes designed to enhance the English treasury at the Americans' expense. The first of these, the Sugar Act of 1764, led to a colonial boycott of English goods. The Stamp Act of 1765 brought a similar response, along with more direct action: the Stamp Act Congress drafted a "Declaration of Rights and Grievances" for presentation to king and Parliament. As tempers flared on both sides of the Atlantic, conciliatory voices grew silent. Evidently seeking to affirm its authority, Parliament passed a series of measures—the Declaratory Act, the Townshend Acts, the Tea Act, the Coercive Acts—that proved inimical to the colonists. Although some of these measures were repealed, the colonists were ready for open revolt by 1776.

Even before the Declaration of Independence, however, the Boston Massacre (1770) and the Boston Tea Party (1773) had mobilized anti-British resistance, which erupted into armed skirmishes at Lexington and Concord in 1775. Significant open warfare, after the Declaration was made, occurred in New York City, where George Washington's patriot forces lost to the British regulars and Hessian mercenaries in June, 1776. The British expected a brief campaign of decisive victories. They planned for the war to be over in 1776. George Washington, commander-in-chief of the American army, considered winning battles less important than preventing major losses. He lacked regular troops—the Continental Army never numbered more than 18,500 men—but he nonetheless found the necessary militia at crucial times. Washington lost his first battle over New York City in 1776; his retreat across New Jersey allowed the British to occupy New York and New Jersey. Wintering at Valley Forge, Washington's troops faced what Thomas Paine in *The American Crisis* called "the times that try men's souls." The colonial militia rallied and struck back—during Christmas-time, 1776, and the early part of 1777—at the battles of Trenton and Princeton. In the meantime, the British general William Howe, having plotted with Joseph Galloway and other Tories (pro-British sympathizers) in Philadelphia, left New York City and took over Philadelphia in 1777. But the Americans had a victory in upper New York, where the militia under the command of General Horatio Gates surrounded British general Burgoyne late in the year. As a result, officials in London decided that a shift in command and in strategy was necessary. They sent Sir Henry Clinton to replace Howe in Philadelphia. In 1778, the French joined the American colonists against the English.

The British set about attacking the South in 1779 and 1780. Charleston, the most important city in the American South, fell to British forces in May 1780; South Carolina was under attack throughout the year. American retaliation in South Carolina began in October 1780, in the west Appalachians, where a group of "over-mountain men" defeated a large party of loyalists and redcoats. In 1781, American generals Nathanael Greene and Daniel Morgan confronted British regiments under Tarleton and Cornwallis in the Carolinas. When Cornwallis withdrew his troops to the tip of the Virginia peninsula between the York and James Rivers, Washington quickly advanced over seven thousand troops southward and, with the aid of the Comte de Grasse, who brought a French fleet from the West Indies, forced a British surrender there in October 1781. By November 1782, a preliminary peace agreement was reached at Paris; it was formally signed in September 1783.

The years immediately following the end of the Revolution were extremely difficult for the new nation. A post-war economic depression created restlessness among farmers, and the U.S. government under the Articles of Confederation (1781) failed to establish control over the states. Cries for a more effective national government increased. As a result, the men who gathered in Philadelphia in 1787 to work out a revision of the Articles dismantled the old system in favor of a new form of government. They wrote a Constitution that based its authority on neither God nor a king but on the people, from whom all power would emanate. Reprinted in all newspapers in the states, the constitutional articles produced a controversy over ratification that led to a bitter debate between federalists, those interested in strong central government, and anti-federalists, who preferred regional interests to rule over national ones. Sectional differences emerged as southerners feared the loss of power due to their agriculturally based economy in the face of northern merchant and industrial enterprise. In spite of the strong opposition to centralization, the Constitution was ratified in 1788, and George Washington was inaugurated as first president of the United States in 1789.

The ratification of the Constitution signaled a shift in political ideology, a shift best reflected in the phrase "We, the People," which began the document and created a basis for common identity while being sufficiently vague to permit a range of complex interpretations. The

Constitution set up a system designed to prevent any one faction from gaining absolute control by providing for checks and balances among the executive, the legislative, and the judicial branches of the government. Committed to the efficacy of compromise, the men who devised the Constitution hoped to unify conflicting sections of American society.

A Nation of Disparate Peoples

Underlying the constitutional debate about power was an ideological debate about the basis of human nature: Were humans innately depraved, and did they thus need strong, centralized governmental control to prevent them from pursuing unrestrained self-interest? Or was human nature basically good—or, if not basically good, improvable—and thus deserving of the freedom necessary for progressive achievement? It was a vexing issue, one that in many ways resembled the religious controversies of earlier centuries, in which Puritans argued that humankind deserved the constraints and chastisement of an angry God, while Catholics and Anglicans argued that humankind could, through good works, achieve salvation. Yet the constitutional debate of the eighteenth century took its premises not so much from religious beliefs as from seventeenth- and eighteenth-century philosophical positions. Some American political theorists—John Adams most prominently—looked with skepticism upon liberal conceptions of progress, and they argued that governmental restraints were necessary because people could not be trusted to behave well. Other political theorists—Jefferson, most notably—favored the notion that scientific rationalism could free people for personal and civic betterment. The debate about the nature of the American government was officially over once the Constitution was ratified, yet the debate about human nature has not ceased, as Americans still attempt to establish just who "We, the People" are and how extensive our rights might be.

With the ratification of the Constitution, a new era was at hand. In 1775, about half the population, white and black, was under sixteen years of age. This is a significant figure. Americans tend to consider the men who devised the Constitution, honorifically called the Founding Fathers, as sage elder statesmen. Except for Franklin, however, most of them were just reaching the height of their legal careers. The Constitution was for their children and the future great nation they envisioned. Once the Constitution was devised and ratified, the real challenge emerged: leaders would have to make such a youthful and diverse population accept the radically new form of government.

The youthful age of colonists at the time of the Revolution perhaps contributed to the greater impetus, after the Revolution, to establish an educational system for most Americans. During most of the century, education had been available for the well-to-do, a personal benefit obtainable through private means. After the Revolution, however, education was needed to serve a public purpose. Two very important changes in educational practice occurred in America during the late 1780s and the 1790s: states became willing to fund public elementary schools from tax monies, and schooling was improved for girls. At this time, demographics worked in favor of women's education: the new generation of mothers would have to be instructed in order to raise and educate civic-minded sons and daughters. Some, like Judith Sargent Murray, argued in behalf of women's education on the grounds that women were as intellectually capable as men.

The logic of equality and natural rights, on which the Revolution had been fought, fueled progressive arguments about gender and racial equality. One female "Matrimonial Republican" argued, contrary to the patriarchal social assumptions of her day, that "marriage ought never to be considered as a contract between a superior and an inferior, but a reciprocal union of interest." In New Jersey, unmarried women, widows, and free blacks even seized voting rights in 1776. Yet most eighteenth-century Americans, regardless of gender, considered women's place to be in the home, as wives and mothers subject to the authority of husbands and fathers. Free blacks and women were disenfranchised by the New Jersey state legislature in 1807. Revolutionary fervor notwithstanding, deeply held attitudes could not be overturned so quickly.

But social changes were imminent. A great deal of internal migration occurred in post-revolutionary America: between five and ten percent of the population moved each year, usually westward. When poor white southern farmers moved westward into Kentucky and Tennessee, then to the rich lands in western Georgia or to the Gulf coast, they displaced their entire households, including their slaves. Amid the social upheaval, evangelical religion offered many the only sense of social cohesion they had. A Second Great Awakening began about 1800 in the western areas, this time among Baptist, Presbyterian, and Methodist groups. Both women and blacks formed significant portions of those spiritually awakened, and they preached as well, exhorting both white and black listeners to universal salvation. This awakening, coincident with the constitutional disestablishment of a state religion and increased racial ferment in the Upper South, produced the first signs of the collective empowering of blacks and women at the level of non-elite culture. In this regard, the work of ministers like Lemuel Haynes stands as a significant achievement.

Members of minority groups felt empowered locally, perhaps, but they had little voice in the larger, public debate about their status in the new world they had a major part in creating. Slaves, free blacks, Mexicans, and Native Americans had almost no part in the process of establishing norms and scant opportunity to voice their objections to the established practices of the dominant white culture. Discrimination against these groups was already entrenched—in both law and custom—and white Americans were well on the way to developing a coherent racist theory that would justify the oppression of non-whites. Some groups—for example, white slaveholders—even began to call into question the very humanity of non-white peoples—specifically, blacks—as a way to maintain their power in a nation that had just proclaimed that "*all* men [sic] are created equal."

Blacks did not let such racism go unanswered. Benjamin Banneker set about directly challenging Jefferson's assumption—expressed in his influential *Notes on the State of Virginia* (1787)—of blacks' intellectual inferiority. Banneker—a free black surveyor, astronomer, mathematician, and almanac-maker—sent Thomas Jefferson a copy of his latest almanac in 1791. Jefferson complimented Banneker on his ability but suggested to him that he was an exception among blacks.

Other blacks attacked whites for their hypocritical support of slavery in a supposedly free society. In 1789, Olaudah Equiano attacked the institution of slavery, denouncing it as an arbitrary value system that, where the rights of African Americans were concerned, promoted Christianity in principle but not in practice. Because white churches often refused to minister to black parishioners, two black ministers, Absalom Jones and Richard Allen, founded the Free African Society in 1787, an organization that eventually developed into the African Methodist Episcopal Church. In response to the wide evangelical success of several black ministers during the Second Great Awakening, other writers, supported by members of the clergy, spoke of slavery as a social imbalance "unbecoming the excellence of true religion."

You say that you are sent to instruct us how to worship the Great Spirit agreeably to His mind, and, if we do not take hold of the religion which you white people teach, we shall be unhappy hereafter. You say that you are right and we are lost. How do we know this to be true? We understand that your religion is written in a book. If it was intended for us as well as you, why has not the Great Spirit given to us, and not only to us, but why did He not give to our forefathers the knowledge of that book, with the means of understanding it rightly? We only know what you tell us about it. How shall we know when to believe, being so often deceived by the white people?

Brother, you say there is but one way to worship and serve the Great Spirit. If there is but one religion, why do you white people differ so much about it? Why not all agreed, as you can all read the book?

Brother, we do not understand these things. We are told that your religion was given to your forefathers and has been handed down from father to son. We also have a religion which was given to our forefathers and has been handed down to us, their children. We worship in that way. It teaches us to be thankful for all the favors we receive, to love each other, and to be united. We never quarrel about religion.

Brother, the Great Spirit has made us all, but He has made a great difference between His white and red children. He has given us different complexions and different customs. To you He has given the arts. To these He has not opened our eyes. We know these things to be true. Since He has made so great a difference between us in other things, why may we not conclude that He has given us a different religion according to our understanding? The Great Spirit does right. He knows what is best for His children; we are satisfied.

Sagoyewatha (Red Lion), 1805

Blacks struggled with the question of how they could participate in American society. Some, like Prince Hall, who brought together the first black Masonic order in 1775, advocated the development of separate social institutions for blacks. In 1777, Hall, with the assistance of a contingent of free blacks in Boston, petitioned the Massachusetts House of Representatives to abolish slavery, arguing that freedom was "the natural right of all men—and their children who were born in this land of liberty." To disregard the cause of freedom was to be in violation of the "law of nature and of a nation." In behalf of free blacks, Hall petitioned for public education for children of tax-paying blacks. The petition was denied.

Whites faced similar questions about integration. Some, like Ezra Stiles, president of Yale, advocated the colonization of free blacks in West Africa. In January 1787, Prince Hall, with seventy-three other blacks, petitioned the Massachusetts General Court (the state legislature) for financial or other assistance for blacks to emigrate to Africa. Emigration westward seemed another answer to disempowered blacks. Around the year 1779, the black Jean Baptiste Point du Sable established a trading post on the southern shore of Lake Michigan, an area that eventually became the city of Chicago. In 1781, a small group of *pobladores,* or settlers, established the *Pueblo de Nuestra Senora la Reina de los Angeles de Porciuncula* in California. Of the forty-four *pobladores,* twenty-six were either of black or a mixture of black and Hispanic ancestry. These Afro-Mexicans created the founding location of present-day Los Angeles.

But the emigration of free blacks was hardly a workable solution to an overwhelming cultural problem, the institution of slavery. In the decades following the Revolution, the northern states chose to address the issue by abolishing slavery—either immediately or over a predetermined number of years. In 1777 Vermont became the first state to ban slavery within its borders; by 1783, Massachusetts had done likewise. In 1780, Pennsylvania set up a plan for gradual emancipation, as did Connecticut and Rhode Island in 1784. Other northern states devised similar legislation. The possibility of this trend spreading to the South grew dimmer with each passing year, however, for the southern economic system was far more directly dependent upon slave labor than was that of the North. Furthermore, with Eli Whitney's invention of the cotton gin in 1793, the South became even more economically dependent upon cotton and, in turn, upon slave labor.

The sectional differences between North and South over the slave question were publicly evident at least as far back as 1776, when Thomas Jefferson removed a statement attacking Great Britain for its support of the slave trade from the Declaration of Independence he had drafted. Considering that twenty-five of the fifty-five delegates to the Constitutional Convention in 1787 were slaveholders, it is hardly surprising that the Constitution itself bespoke an uneasy compromise on an issue over which, Americans painfully learned, there could be no compromise. The strategy adopted at the time was to appease the southern interests by allowing three-fifths of the total number of slaves to be included in the population totals for each state in determining taxation and the apportionment of votes in the House of Representatives. In return, the South permitted the inclusion of a clause stipulating that the importation of slaves would be illegal after twenty years. Thus, not only did the Constitution have no effect whatsoever upon the internal slave trade, but it forbade states to harbor fugitive slaves, and it left unaddressed the rights of free blacks.

These concessions also led to further concessions to proslavery interests. For example, in 1803, Congress allowed slavery in the newly purchased Louisiana territory. At the close of 1819 twenty-two states had been admitted to statehood, eleven slave (Virginia, Maryland, Delaware, Kentucky, Tennessee, North Carolina, South Carolina, Georgia, Alabama, Mississippi, and Louisiana) and eleven free (Massachusetts, Connecticut, Rhode Island, Vermont, New Hampshire, New York, New Jersey, Pennsylvania, Ohio, Indiana, and Illinois). The political balance had been maintained by an alternating pattern of admission of slave and free states. When Missouri and Maine petitioned Congress for statehood at the close of 1819, northern fears arose that, through the vehicle of Missouri statehood, slavery would ultimately extend northward to the Canadian border. In 1820, Congress passed the Missouri Compromise, which decreed that free and slave states would be admitted into the Union in equal numbers and drew a line limiting the expansion of slavery.

Yet these steps did little to address the fundamental issue of whether the United States, having just successfully waged a war of liberation, was ready to confront the extent to which large groups of Americans were not free. In retrospect, we now see that the Revolution and the first decades of the new republic marked but one stage in this nation's ongoing struggle to reconcile its extraordinary idealism with a social reality that so clearly ran counter to the principles upon which it was founded.

From the Plow, to the Sword, to the Book

During the eighteenth century, the colonies progressed from largely independent, rural regions to unified political bodies strong enough to win the Revolutionary War, and then to states that, with written legislation, became inextricably interdependent political entities. Still, given the regional differences and the diverse population, the forging of a single national identity would be difficult. The situation provided an unusual opportunity for writers. A great number of increasingly educated readers required reading material, and the presses that became fully established in revolutionary and post-revolutionary Anglo-America had to suit the demands of a wide readership.

Yet writers were in a quandary. Many continued to write patriotic works and political treatises. The writing of other types of works, especially fiction, was more difficult. There was one key problem: writers and their readers were used to looking to Europe, especially to England, for cultural and artistic models. Yet part of the message of the revolutionary era had been that Americans were more virtuous than their luxury-loving European counterparts. Writers wishing to produce anything not specifically patriotic would face the dilemma of convincing their audience that their works offered instruction in virtue.

The most popular writers, whether they wrote plays, poems, or novels, managed to persuade their audience that their texts would inculcate virtue and dispel vice. Thus, Royall Tyler's *The Contrast* (1787) offers a "manly" view of sobriety, honesty, and industry in contrast with the foppishness of Billy Dimple's Europeanized actions. Other authors, like novelist William Hill Brown (*The Power of Sympathy,* 1789), chose to detail the actions of seductive Europeans in order to warn young women away from them. This was a popular ploy: novelists provided sensational and lurid details of just the behavior they wished readers to find reprehensible. Susanna Rowson and Hannah Webster Foster, for example, delineated Europeanized social practices while ostensibly extolling virtue. Like the legal and social institutions that were fostered during the era, literature was considered a means by which specifically American cultural norms could be reinforced.

When the French Revolution of 1789 turned into the French bloodbath of 1793, Americans took an increasingly negative look at their European neighbors, fearing that mob action might spread to America. In the face of farmers' uprisings and skirmishes with native peoples in frontier areas, politicians argued that strong central government was needed to forestall excessive and irrational behavior. Writers vehemently attacked the excess emotionalism that might lead to anarchy. The rise in Europe of gothicism—with its emphasis upon darkness and secrecy, psychological confusion, and amorality—was taken by Americans to be evidence of yet another sign of European degeneracy. Notably, Charles Brockden Brown, who experimented with gothicism, found that in America novels about ventriloquism and sleepwalking, fratricide and revenge, would not sell to the troubled populace of the 1790s. The revolutionary generation was seeking conformity; cultural norms were being established to keep the body politic under control.

The cultural norms were politically conservative, patriarchal, and white-dominant. Yet if minority cultures would be held in subjection, they would nonetheless show signs of having learned an important lesson from the dominant culture: the power of the word to move masses of people.

During the 1780s and 1790s, white women, African Americans, and Native Americans were finding voice for their positions as never before. The elite might control the government and, by extension, most social practices—including that of "literature"—but it could not very easily control the voices of those who for the first time in America were—at least in theory—offered rights to free speech.

To Native Americans, the right to free speech was a small freedom in the face of the near-total loss of homelands. In addition to Revolutionary War veterans who had been granted lands in the Ohio territory in lieu of payment for their wartime services, thousands of new settlers were migrating westward, onto lands held by the natives, many of whom preferred hunting to agriculture. Native Americans, some of them age-old enemies, were forced to share lands over which they had for centuries had full and independent control. Eastern native groups, the relative newcomers to the western territories, were displaced from the land itself and forced to abandon traditional modes of subsistence. Where formerly they had pursued agriculture, they found themselves amid unfriendly hunting groups. Rights to lands westward were granted to white settlers, at the expense of the varied populations and cultures of Native Americans.

They found their own leader in Tecumseh, a Shawnee whose Algonkian family had settled in the Ohio area a century before his birth in 1768. The Constitution spoke of "We, the People," but Tecumseh quickly realized that "We" did not freely include Native Americans. Watching both English and French maneuvers as the War of 1812 was developing, Tecumseh decided that the time was opportune for Native Americans to unite against the Americans for one last struggle. Adopting some of the phraseology of the white leaders whose activities he deplored, Tecumseh delivered a series of speeches that made him famous as an Indian orator. In an oration reported to have been given before the Choctaws, Tecumseh—whose name in Shawnee, prophetically, means Falling Star or Meteor—argued:

. . . But what need is there to speak of the past? It speaks for itself and asks, Where today are the Pequot? Where are the Narraganset, the Mohican, the Pocanoket and many other once powerful tribes of our people? They have vanished before the avarice and oppression of the white man, as snow before a summer sun. In the vain hope of defending alone their ancient possessions, they have fallen in wars. . . . Look abroad over their once beautiful country, and what see you now? Nought but the ravages of the paleface destroyers. So it will be with you Choctaw and Chickasaw! . . .

Before the palefaces came among us, we enjoyed the happiness of unbounded freedom and were acquainted with neither wants nor oppression. How is it now? Need and oppression are our lot—for are we not controlled in everything, and dare we move without asking by your leave? Are we not being stripped day by day of the little that remains of our ancient liberty? . . . Then let us by unity of action destroy them all, which we now can do, or drive them back whence they came. To fight or to be exterminated is now our only choice . . .

Tecumseh joined the British during the War of 1812 and died on Canadian soil in the Battle of the Thames, Ontario. Tecumseh's oration to the Choctaws, the conclusion of which resembles Washington's presidential Farewell Address, provides a telling reminder that "We, the People" would continue through succeeding centuries to speak and to fight for the right of self-determination.

Settlement and Religion

The early part of the eighteenth century remained focused on continuing exploration and settlement, as isolated colonial outposts, especially along the eastern seaboard, expanded, defended themselves against the skirmishes and open hostilities between imperial powers and their native allies, and united through the growing unrest that would culminate in the Anglo-American colonists' War for Independence from England. The writings in this section suggest the range of social and religious transformations that resulted from increasing population and new economic and political patterns. The autobiographical writings, especially, reveal the extent to which writers found their places in the new American world by writing out their experiences of it.

From the time of colonial contact, travel journals were a significant literary genre in America. To a greater extent than earlier travel accounts, the journals by eighteenth-century writers offer more social critique of manners and colonial institutions. Writers often traversed territory already explored by others, so they wrote less about the natural world they experienced and more about the people they encountered along the way. The journal of Sarah Kemble Knight, who journeyed from Boston to New York to settle a private estate, is a classic in this regard. Witty, sophisticated, and downright humorous by turns, Knight's account contributes to the comic and secular traditions in New England writing, even as it indicates the depth of knowledge and range of independence widows could attain in a region still dominated by Puritan patriarchal values. The travel account of the Baron de Lahontan records his exploration of the territory along the Wisconsin and Mississippi Rivers in 1688–1689. Fresh from an unsuccessful campaign against the Iroquois on Lake Ontario in 1684 and a stint as commander of Fort Saint Joseph (now Niles, Michigan) in 1687, Lahontan was impressed with the power of the native inhabitants of the New World, and his presentation influenced the growth of primitivism in France and England. His account, considered one of the best works on New France, was a source for Anglo-American naturalists and historians like Robert Beverley and William Byrd. Byrd's *History of the Dividing Line* was, like Knight's journal, circulated privately and thus "published" in the way that many manuscripts were published in the early part of the century. After his return from a public mission to determine the boundary between Virginia and North Carolina, Byrd composed a private, coterie version of the events of his trip in the picaresque style, with himself as the comic hero. His official, or public, *History* evokes the secular literature of the day—travel journals, scientific and philosophical treatises, and natural histories—and offers insight into Anglo-colonial conflicts.

The selections from Jonathan Edwards, Elizabeth Ashbridge, John Woolman, and Francisco Palou suggest the various countervailing spiritual tendencies of the age. All wrote during a time when, in general, spiritual questions seemed to many people less important than secular ones, but the spiritual renewals that swept the colonies throughout the century suggest an underlying hunger for spiritual grounding. Their evangelical calling to write of their own, or others', religious experience suggests their desire to offer models of spiritual reformation to a backsliding people and a materialist culture. Edwards was probably the greatest thinker of the century, a truly international figure who used Enlightenment assertions about the sensory nature of human knowledge to bring people to a felt conviction of orthodox Puritan doctrine. Concerned with the psychology of religious experience, he observed himself and others closely, producing compelling accounts of spiritual conversions during the first Great Awakening as well as his own experiences. His "Personal Narrative" falls into the venerable tradition of the spiritual autobiography, popularized in the seventeenth century by John Bunyan's *Pilgrim's Progress* (1678) and a favorite genre of New England Puritan writers. Edwards's particular emphasis on the sensible beauty of God's creation embraces earlier Puritan typology and anticipates Emersonian Romanticism. His famous sermon, "Sinners in the Hands of an Angry God," was only one of the hundreds he wrote and delivered, but it played a crucial role in fanning the flames of religious renewal in New England.

The journals of Elizabeth Ashbridge and John Woolman represent the best writings in this era from the Quaker tradition. Edwards's emphasis on the felt experience of God's grace may have resembled the central Quaker conception of the "Inner Light," but in most other ways Quakerism diverged sharply from Puritan doctrine. Rejecting Calvinist ideas of innate depravity and original sin, Quakers believed in a God of love who extended salvation to all. While Puritan spiritual autobiography centered upon the conversion experience, Quaker journals emphasized the importance of the converted believer's witnessing in his or her life and actions. Ashbridge's remarkable narrative details the multiple burdens of a woman throwing off the traditional authority of church and husband, confronting domestic violence and social ostracism, in order to find her personal beliefs and public voice. Worldly concerns kept Woolman, who probably had read Ashbridge's earlier work, fettered and made God's love inaccessible. Just as a simplified material life allowed him to experience the "Inner Light" and witness to others, Woolman applied Quaker principles to current, pressing social issues of poverty, slavery, inequality, and war.

Changes in the Spanish mission to convert the Indians during the eighteenth century are reflected in Francisco Palou's life of Junípero Serra. Spain faced increasing problems with its colonies in the Americas during this century. Revenues and exports were suffering, and territorial battles added to the expense of colonization, despite reforms instituted by King Charles III at midcentury. Tensions increased in New Mexico, where local civil agents vied with missionaries for diminishing power over native populations. But as Franciscan efforts in New Mexico flagged, they found new impetus in California. The Catholic Church entered California in 1769 from Baja in the south and founded its first mission that year at San Diego and its last in Sonoma in 1823. Although the missionary efforts in this area supervised by Junípero Serra were, for the most part, pacific, the overall missionary program of the Spanish imposed resettlement on native peoples and banned their indigenous religious practices, causing incalculable damage including a considerable reduction of the native population all along the California coast. Francisco Palou, also a dedicated missionary, wrote his account of Serra to promulgate a model of the virtuous Christian life they both strove to live as an embodiment of their conception of the mission in New Spain. We must read such interested narratives of the spiritual life as we read other accounts of religious colonialism in the New World, against the economic realities of imperial agendas and the material effects upon native cultures.

Sarah Kemble Knight 1666–1727

Since its publication in 1825, Sarah Kemble Knight's journal, composed as an account of her roundtrip journey from Boston to New York in 1704–1705, has remained an early American literary landmark, partly because of the larger-than-life character it reveals and partly because it records an arduous journey not usually undertaken by a woman. In addition to providing a funny, often racy, account of the people and places she encounters along the way, Knight paints a vivid verbal picture of New England backwoods settlements and of middle-class social aspirations. Typical of the picaro, she views the wilderness as romantic and literary, colonized and domesticated, dangerous yet comic and amoral. Unlike many other latter-day Puritans who considered the frontier dangerous, Knight considered it challenging.

The first daughter of Thomas Kemble and Elizabeth Trerice Kemble, Sarah was born in Boston. Sometime between 1688 and 1689, she married Richard Knight, who was apparently much older than she. Tradition holds that Richard Knight was a shipmaster and agent in London for an American company and that Sarah Kemble was his second wife, but neither claim can be confirmed. Their one child, Elizabeth, was born in Boston on May 8, 1689. Even before Richard Knight died (probably in 1706), his wife seems to have taken over many of his business responsibilities. She evidently attained some degree of business and legal acumen, skills she used in settling estates. In fact, she made the trip her journal documents to settle the estate of her cousin Caleb Trowbridge, who left a young widow. Sarah Kemble Knight kept a shop and house on Moon Street in Boston. That she also ran a writing school attended by Benjamin Franklin is more likely rumor than fact. When her daughter married John Livingston of New London, Connecticut, Knight, now widowed, moved to be near her. Knight seems to have continued some business activities in Connecticut; when she died, her estate was valued at £1800.

Knight's work might be expected to fall into the tradition of Puritan journal-keeping, yet its content, style, and tone seem un-Puritan indeed. First, Knight's journal is primarily a series of stories, not a history, whose heroine is more like Chaucer's Wife of Bath (who is also a social climber) than the self-effacing stereotype of Puritan womanhood. Second, Knight's style is worldly and literary. And third, her tone encompasses several different types of humor. As Julia Stern so astutely points out, the journal's focus on things oral—eating and speaking—constitutes its main narrative thrust.

Kathryn Zabelle Derounian-Stodola
University of Arkansas at Little Rock

PRIMARY WORK

The Journals of Madam Knight, and Rev. Mr. Buckingham, from the Original Manuscripts, written in 1704 and 1710, 1825, in *Journeys in New Worlds: Early American Women's Narratives,* ed. William L. Andrews (1990).

The Journal of Madam Knight[1]

Monday, Octb'r. ye second, 1704.—About three o'clock afternoon, I begun my Journey from Boston to New-Haven; being about two Hundred Mile. My Kinsman, Capt. Robert Luist, waited on me as farr as Dedham, where I was to meet ye Western post.[2]

I vissitted the Reverd. Mr. Belcher,[3] ye Minister of ye town, and tarried there till evening, in hopes ye post would come along. But he not coming, I resolved to go to Billingses where he used to lodg, being 12 miles further. But being ignorant of the way, Madm Billings,[4] seing no persuasions of her good spouses or hers could prevail with me to Lodg there that night, Very kindly went wyth me to ye Tavern, where I hoped to get my guide, And desired the Hostess to inquire of her guests whether any of them would go with mee. But they being tyed by the Lipps to a pewter engine, scarcely allowed themselves time to say what clownish * * *.

***Peices of eight, I told her no, I would not be accessary to such extortion.

Then John shan't go, sais shee. No, indeed, shan't hee; And held forth at that rate a long time, that I began to fear I was got among the Quaking tribe, beleeving not a Limbertong'd sister among them could out do Madm. Hostes.

Upon this, to my no small surprise, son John arrose, and gravely demanded what I would give him to go with me? Give you, sais I, are you John? Yes, says he, for want of a Better; And behold! this John look't as old as my Host, and perhaps had bin a man in the last Century. Well, Mr. John, sais I, make your demands. Why, half a pss. of eight and a dram, sais John. I agreed, and gave him a Dram (now) in hand to bind the bargain.

My hostess catechis'd John for going so cheep, saying his poor wife would break her heart***His shade on his Hors resembled a Globe on a Gate post. His habitt, Hors and furniture, its looks and goings Incomparably answered the rest.

Thus Jogging on with an easy pace, my Guide telling mee it was dangero's to Ride hard in the Night, (whch his horse had the sence to avoid,) Hee entertained me with the Adventurs he had passed by late Rideing, and eminent Dangers he had escaped, so that, Remembring the Hero's in Parismus and the Knight of the Oracle,[5] I didn't know but I had mett wth a Prince disguis'd.

When we had Ridd about an how'r, wee come into a thick swamp, wch. by Reason of a great fogg, very much startled mee, it being now very Dark. But nothing

[1]Knight's *Journal* was first published, along with that of Reverend Thomas Buckingham of Hartford, in New York, 1825, by Theodore Dwight. Since then, the journal has gone through a number of editions, among them one by Perry Miller and Thomas Johnson (1938), the source of the present text. This edition places superscript letters on the line; for the most part, Miller's and Johnson's notes are printed below.

The original manuscript, now lost, was evidently torn in two places, and a few manuscript sheets were lost. In the present text, these places where manuscript has been lost are marked by asterisks. We print the journal in its entirety.

[2]Dispatch messenger who carried mail from stage to stage.

[3]The Reverend Joseph Belcher (1669–1723).

[4]Mrs. Belcher, wife of the pastor.

[5]References to the romances *The History of Parismus* (1598), by Emmanuel Ford, and *The Famous History of Montelion, Knight of the Oracle* (earliest surviving edition 1633).

dismay'd John: Hee had encountered a thousand and a thousand such Swamps, having a Universall Knowledge in the woods; and readily Answered all my inquiries wch. were not a few.

In about an how'r, or something more, after we left the Swamp, we come to Billinges, where I was to Lodg. My Guide dismounted and very Complasantly help't me down and shewd the door, signing to me wth his hand to Go in; wch I Gladly did—But had not gone many steps into the Room, ere I was Interogated by a young Lady I understood afterwards was the Eldest daughter of the family, with these, or words to this purpose, (viz.) Law for mee—what in the world brings You here at this time a night?—I never see a woman on the Rode so Dreadfull late, in all the days of my versall life. Who are You? Where are You going? I'me scar'd out of my witts—with much now of the same Kind. I stood aghast, Prepareing to reply, when in comes my Guide—to him Madam turn'd, Roreing out: Lawfull heart, John, is it You?—how de do! Where in the world are you going with this woman? Who is she? John made no Ansr. but sat down in the corner, fumbled out his black Junk,[6] and saluted that instead of Debb; she then turned agen to mee and fell anew into her silly questions, without asking me to sitt down.

I told her shee treated me very Rudely, and I did not think it my duty to answer her unmannerly Questions. But to get ridd of them, I told her I come there to have the post's company with me to-morrow on my Journey, &c. Miss star'd awhile, drew a chair, bid me sitt, And then run up stairs and putts on two or three Rings, (or else I had not seen them before,) and returning, sett herself just before me, showing the way to Reding, that I might see her Ornaments, perhaps to gain the more respect. But her Granam's new Rung[7] sow, had it appeared, would affected me as much. I paid honest John wth money and dram according to contract, and Dismist him, and pray'd Miss to shew me where I must Lodg. Shee conducted me to a parlour in a little back Lento,[8] wch was almost fill'd wth the bedsted, wch was so high that I was forced to climb on a chair to gitt up to ye wretched bed that lay on it; on wch having Stretcht my tired Limbs, and lay'd my head on a Sad-colourd pillow, I began to think on the transactions of ye past day.

Tuesday, October ye third, about 8 in the morning, I with the Post proceeded forward without observing any thing remarkable; And about two, afternoon, Arrived at the Post's second stage, where the western Post mett him and exchanged Letters. Here, having called for something to eat, ye woman bro't in a Twisted thing like a cable, but something whiter; and laying it on the bord, tugg'd for life to bring it into a capacity to spread; wch having wth great pains accomplished, shee serv'd in a dish of Pork and Cabage, I suppose the remains of Dinner. The sause was of a deep Purple, wch I tho't was boil'd in her dye Kettle; the bread was Indian, and every thing on the Table service Agreeable to these. I, being hungry, gott a little down; but my stomach was soon cloy'd, and what cabbage I swallowed serv'd me for a Cudd the whole day after.

Having here discharged the Ordnary[9] for self and Guide, (as I understood was the custom,) About Three afternoon went on with my Third Guide, who Rode very

[6]A pipe for smoking.
[7]*I.e.,* having a ring through the snout.
[8]A lean-to room.
[9]An ordinary was an eating house or tavern providing meals at a fixed price.

hard; and having crossed Providence Ferry, we come to a River wch they Generally Ride thro'. But I dare not venture; so the Post got a Ladd and Cannoo to carry me to tother side, and hee rid thro' and Led my hors. The Cannoo was very small and shallow, so that when we were in she seem'd redy to take in water, which greatly terrified mee, and caused me to be very circumspect, sitting with my hands fast on each side, my eyes stedy, not daring so much as to lodg my tongue a hair's breadth more on one side of my mouth then tother, nor so much as think on Lott's wife, for a wry thought would have oversett our wherey:[10] But was soon put out of this pain, by feeling the Cannoo on shore, wch I as soon almost saluted with my feet; and Rewarding my sculler, again mounted and made the best of our way forwards. The Rode here was very even and ye day pleasant, it being now near Sunsett. But the Post told mee we had neer 14 miles to Ride to the next Stage, (where we were to Lodg.) I askt him of the rest of the Rode, foreseeing wee must travail in the night. Hee told mee there was a bad River we were to Ride thro', wch was so very firce a hors could sometimes hardly stem it: But it was but narrow, and wee should soon be over. I cannot express The concern of mind this relation sett me in: no thoughts but those of the dang'ros River could entertain my Imagination, and they were as formidable as varios, still Tormenting me with blackest Ideas of my Approaching fate—Sometimes seing my self drowning, otherwhiles drowned, and at the best like a holy Sister Just come out of a Spiritual Bath in dripping Garments.

Now was the Glorious Luminary,[11] wth his swift Coursers arrived at his Stage, leaving poor me wth the rest of this part of the lower world in darkness, with which *wee* were soon Surrounded. The only Glimering we now had was from the spangled Skies, Whose Imperfect Reflections rendered every Object formidable. Each lifeless Trunk, with its shatter'd Limbs, appear'd an Armed Enymie; and every little stump like a Ravenous devourer. Nor could I so much as discern my Guide, when at any distance, which added to the terror.

Thus, absolutely lost in Thought, and dying with the very thoughts of drowning, I come up wth the post, who I did not see till even with his Hors: he told mee he stopt for mee; and wee Rode on Very deliberatly a few paces, when we entred a Thickett of Trees and Shrubbs, and I perceived by the Hors's going, we were on the descent of a Hill, wch, as wee come neerer the bottom, 'twas totaly dark wth the Trees that surrounded it. But I knew by the Going of the Hors wee had entred the water, wch my Guide told mee was the hazzardos River he had told me off; and hee, Riding up close to my Side, Bid me not fear—we should be over Imediatly. I now ralyed all the Courage I was mistriss of, Knowing that I must either Venture my fate of drowning, or be left like ye Children in the wood. So, as the Post bid me, I gave Reins to my Nagg; and sitting as Stedy as Just before in the Cannoo, in a few minutes got safe to the other side, which hee told mee was the Narragansett country.

Here We found great difficulty in Travailing, the way being very narrow, and on each side the Trees and bushes gave us very unpleasent welcomes wth their Branches and bow's, wch wee could not avoid, it being so exceeding dark. My Guide, as before so now, putt on harder than I, wth my weary bones, could follow; so left mee and the way beehind him. Now Returned my distressed aprehensions of the place

[10] A wherry was a light rowing boat for transporting river passengers.

[11] The moon.

where I was: the dolesome woods, my Company next to none, Going I knew not whither, and encompased wth Terrifying darkness; The least of which was enough to startle a more Masculine courage. Added to which the Reflections, as in the afternoon of ye day that my Call was very Questionable, wch till then I had not so Prudently as I ought considered. Now, coming to ye foot of a hill, I found great difficulty in ascending; But being got to the Top, was there amply recompenced with the friendly Appearance of the Kind Conductress of the night, Just then Advancing above the Horisontall Line. The Raptures wch the Sight of that fair Planett produced in mee, caus'd mee, for the Moment, to forgett my present wearyness and past toils; and Inspir'd me for most of the remaining way with very divirting tho'ts, some of which, with the other Occurances of the day, I reserved to note down when I should come to my Stage. My tho'ts on the sight of the moon were to this purpose:

Fair Cynthia,[12] all the Homage that I may
Unto a Creature, unto thee I pay;
In Lonesome woods to meet so kind a guide,
To Mee's more worth than all the world beside.
Some Joy I felt just now, when safe got or'e
Yon Surly River to this Rugged shore,
Deeming Rough welcomes from these clownish Trees,
Better than Lodgings wth Nereidees.[13]
Yet swelling fears surprise; all dark appears—
Nothing but Light can disipate those fears.
My fainting vitals can't lend strength to say,
But softly whisper, O I wish 'twere day.
The murmur hardly warm'd the Ambient air,
E're thy Bright Aspect rescues from dispair:
Makes the old Hagg her sable mantle loose,
And a Bright Joy do's through my Soul diffuse.
The Boistero's Trees now Lend a Passage Free,
And pleasent prospects thou giv'st light to see.

From hence wee kept on, with more ease than before: the way being smooth and even, the night warm and serene, and the Tall and thick Trees at a distance, especially when the moon glar'd light through the branches, fill'd my Imagination wth the pleasent delusion of a Sumpteous citty, fill'd wth famous Buildings and churches, wth their spiring steeples, Balconies, Galleries and I know not what: Granduers wch I had heard of, and wch the stories of foreign countries had given me the Idea of.

Here stood a Lofty church—there is a steeple,
And there the Grand Parade—O see the people!
That Famous Castle there, were I but nigh,
To see the mote and Bridg and walls so high—
They'r very fine! sais my deluded eye.

Being thus agreably entertain'd without a thou't of any thing but thoughts themselves, I on a suden was Rous'd from these pleasing Imaginations, by the Post's

[12]Poetic name for the moon personified as a goddess.

[13]The Nereides were sea nymphs.

sounding his horn, which assured mee hee was arrived at the Stage, where we were to Lodg: and that musick was then most musickall and agreeable to mee.

Being come to mr. Havens', I was very civilly Received, and courteously entertained, in a clean comfortable House; and the Good woman was very active in helping off my Riding clothes, and then ask't what I would eat. I told her I had some Chocolett, if shee would prepare it; which with the help of some Milk, and a little clean brass Kettle, she soon effected to my satisfaction. I then betook me to my Apartment, wch was a little Room parted from the Kitchen by a single bord partition; where, after I had noted the Occurrances of the past day, I went to bed, which, tho' pretty hard, Yet neet and handsome. But I could get no sleep, because of the Clamor of some of the Town tope-ers in next Room, Who were entred into a strong debate concerning ye Signifycation of the name of their Country, (viz.) *Narraganset.* One said it was named so by ye Indians, because there grew a Brier there, of a prodigious Highth and bigness, the like hardly ever known, called by the Indians Narragansett; And quotes an Indian of so Barberous a name for his Author; that I could not write it. His Antagonist Replyed no—It was from a Spring it had its name, wch hee well knew where it was, which was extreem cold in summer, and as Hott as could be imagined in the winter, which was much resorted too by the natives, and by them called Narragansett, (Hott and Cold,) and that was the originall of their places name—with a thousand Impertinances not worth notice, wch He utter'd with such a Roreing voice and Thundering blows with the fist of wickedness on the Table, that it peirced my very head. I heartily fretted, and wish't 'um tongue tyed; but wth as little succes as a freind of mine once, who was (as shee said) kept a whole night awake, on a Jorny, by a country Left.[14] and a Sergent, Insigne and a Deacon, contriving how to bring a triangle into a Square. They kept calling for tother Gill,[15] wch while they were swallowing, was some Intermission; But presently, like Oyle to fire, encreased the flame. I set my Candle on a Chest by the bed side, and setting up, fell to my old way of composing my Resentments, in the following manner:

I ask thy Aid, O Potent Rum!
To Charm these wrangling Topers Dum.
Thou hast their Giddy Brains possest—
The man confounded wth the Beast—
And I, poor I, can get no rest.
Intoxicate them with thy fumes:
O still their Tongues till morning comes!

And I know not but my wishes took effect, for the dispute soon ended wth 'tother Dram; and so Good night!

Wednesday, Octobr 4th. About four in the morning, we set out for Kingston (for so was the Town called) with a french Docter in our company. Hee and ye Post put on very furiously, so that I could not keep up with them, only as now and then they'd stop till they see mee. This Rode was poorly furnished wth accommodations for Travellers, so that we were forced to ride 22 miles by the post's account, but neerer thirty by mine, before wee could bait so much as our Horses, wch I exceedingly complained

[14]Lieutenant. Sometimes still pronounced, and formerly spelled, *leftenant.*

[15]Measure used for wine.

of. But the post encourag'd mee, by saying wee should be well accommodated anon at mr. Devills, a few miles further. But I questioned whether we ought to go to the Devil to be helpt out of affliction. However, like the rest of Deluded souls that post to ye Infernal denn, Wee made all possible speed to this Devil's Habitation; where allitting, in full assurance of good accommodation, wee were going in. But meeting his two daughters, as I suposed twins, they so neerly resembled each other, both in features and habit, and look't as old as the Divel himselfe, and quite as Ugly, We desired entertainm't, but could hardly get a word out of 'um, till with our Importunity, telling them our necesity, &c. they call'd the old Sophister, who was as sparing of his words as his daughters had bin, and no, or none, was the reply's hee made us to our demands. Hee differed only in this from the old fellow in to'ther Country: hee let us depart. However, I thought it proper to warn poor Travailers to endeavour to Avoid falling into circumstances like ours, wch at our next Stage I sat down and did as followeth:

May all that dread the cruel feind of night
Keep on, and not at this curs't Mansion light.
'Tis Hell; 'tis Hell! and Devills here do dwell:
Here dwells the Devill—surely this's Hell.
Nothing but Wants: a drop to cool yo'r Tongue
Cant be procur'd these cruel Feinds among.
Plenty of horrid Grins and looks sevear,
Hunger and thirst, But pitty's bannish'd here—
The Right hand keep, if Hell on Earth you fear!

Thus leaving this habitation of cruelty, we went forward; and arriving at an Ordinary about two mile further, found tollerable accommodation. But our Hostes, being a pretty full mouth'd old creature, entertain'd our fellow travailer, ye french Docter, wth Inumirable complaints of her bodily infirmities; and whispered to him so lou'd, that all ye House had as full a hearing as hee: which was very divirting to ye company, (of which there was a great many,) as one might see by their sneering. But poor weary I slipt out to enter my mind in my Jornal, and left my Great Landly with her Talkative Guests to themselves.

From hence we proceeded (about ten forenoon) through the Narragansett country, pretty Leisurely; and about one afternoon come to Paukataug River, wch was about two hundred paces over, and now very high, and no way over to to'ther side but this. I darid not venture to Ride thro, my courage at best in such cases but small, And now at the Lowest Ebb, by reason of my weary, very weary, hungry and uneasy Circumstances. So takeing leave of my company, tho' wth no little Reluctance, that I could not proceed wth them on my Jorny, Stop at a little cottage Just by the River, to wait the Waters falling, wch the old man that lived there said would be in a little time, and he would conduct me safe over. This little Hutt was one of the wretchedest I ever saw a habitation for human creatures. It was suported with shores enclosed with Clapbords, laid on Lengthways, and so much asunder, that the Light come throu' every where; the doore tyed on wth a cord in ye place of hinges; The floor the bear earth; no windows but such as the thin covering afforded, nor any furniture but a Bedd wth a glass Bottle hanging at ye head on't; an earthan cupp, a small pewter Bason, A Bord wth sticks to stand on, instead of a table, and a block or two in ye corner instead of chairs. The family were the old man, his wife and two Children; all and every part being the picture of poverty. Notwithstanding both the Hutt and its Inhabitance were very clean and tydee: to the crossing the Old Proverb, that bare walls make giddy hows-wifes.

I Blest myselfe that I was not one of this misserable crew; and the Impressions their wretchedness formed in me caused mee on ye very Spott to say:

Tho' Ill at ease, A stranger and alone,
All my fatigu's shall not extort a grone.
These Indigents have hunger with their ease;
Their best is wors behalfe then my disease.
Their Misirable hutt wch Heat and Cold
Alternately without Repulse do hold;
Their Lodgings thyn and hard, their Indian fare,
The mean Apparel which the wretches wear,
And their ten thousand ills wch can't be told,
Makes nature er'e 'tis midle age'd look old.
When I reflect, my late fatigues do seem
Only a notion or forgotten Dreem.

I had scarce done thinking, when an Indian-like Animal come to the door, on a creature very much like himselfe, in mien and feature, as well as Ragged cloathing; and having 'litt, makes an Awkerd Scratch wth his Indian shoo, and a Nodd, sitts on ye block, fumbles out his black Junk, dipps it in ye Ashes, and presents it piping hott to his muscheeto's, and fell to sucking like a calf, without speaking, for near a quarter of an hower. At length the old man said how do's Sarah do? who I understood was the wretches wife, and Daughter to ye old man: he Replyed—as well as can be expected, &c. So I remembred the old say, and suposed I knew Sarah's case. Butt hee being, as I understood, going over the River, as ugly as hee was, I was glad to ask him to show me ye way to Saxtons, at Stoningtown; wch he promising, I ventur'd over wth the old mans assistance; who having rewarded to content, with my Tattertailed guide, I Ridd on very slowly thro' Stoningtown, where the Rode was very Stony and uneven. I asked the fellow, as we went, divers questions of the place and way, &c. I being arrived at my country Saxtons, at Stonington, was very well accommodated both as to victuals and Lodging, the only Good of both I had found since my setting out. Here I heard there was an old man and his Daughter to come that way, bound to N. London; and being now destitute of a Guide, gladly waited for them, being in so good a harbour, and accordingly, Thirsday, Octobr ye 5th, about 3 in the afternoon, I sat forward with neighbour Polly and Jemima, a Girl about 18 Years old, who hee said he had been to fetch out of the Narragansetts, and said they had Rode thirty miles that day, on a sory lean Jade, wth only a Bagg under her for a pillion, which the poor Girl often complain'd was very uneasy.

Wee made Good speed along, wch made poor Jemima make many a sow'r face, the mare being a very hard trotter; and after many a hearty and bitter Oh, she at length Low'd out: Lawful Heart father! this bare mare hurts mee Dingeely,[16] I'me

[16]Apparently Knight's own coined intensifier meaning "extremely."

direfull sore I vow; with many words to that purpose: poor Child sais Gaffer—she us't to serve your mother so. I don't care how mother us't to do, quoth Jemima, in a pasionate tone. At which the old man Laught, and kik't his Jade[17] o' the side, which made her Jolt ten times harder.

About seven that Evening, we come to New London Ferry: here, by reason of a very high wind, we mett with great difficulty in getting over—the Boat tos't exceedingly, and our Horses capper'd at a very surprizing Rate, and set us all in a fright; especially poor Jemima, who desired her father to say so jack to the Jade, to make her stand. But the careless parent, taking no notice of her repeated desires, She Rored out in a Passionate manner: Pray suth father, Are you deaf? Say so Jack to the Jade, I tell you. The Dutiful Parent obey's; saying so Jack, so Jack, as gravely as if hee'd bin to saying Catechise after Young Miss, who with her fright look't of all coullers in ye Rain Bow.

Being safely arrived at the house of Mrs. Prentices in N. London, I treated neighbour Polly and daughter for their diverting company, and bid them farewell; and between nine and ten at night waited on the Revd Mr. Gurdon Saltonstall,[18] minister of the town, who kindly Invited me to Stay that night at his house, where I was very handsomely and plentifully treated and Lodg'd; and made good the Great Character I had before heard concerning him: viz. that hee was the most affable, courteous, Genero's and best of men.

Friday, Octor 6th. I got up very early, in Order to hire somebody to go with mee to New Haven, being in Great parplexity at the thoughts of proceeding alone; which my most hospitable entertainer observing, himselfe went, and soon return'd wth a young Gentleman of the town, who he could confide in to Go with mee; and about eight this morning, wth Mr. Joshua Wheeler my new Guide, takeing leave of this worthy Gentleman, Wee advanced on towards Seabrook. The Rodes all along this way are very bad, Incumbred wth Rocks and mountainos passages, wch were very disagreeable to my tired carcass; but we went on with a moderate pace wch made ye Journy more pleasent. But after about eight miles Rideing, in going over a Bridge under wch the River Run very swift, my hors stumbled, and very narrowly 'scaped falling over into the water; wch extreemly frightened mee. But through God's Goodness I met with no harm, and mounting agen, in about half a miles Rideing, come to an ordinary, were well entertained by a woman of about seventy and vantage, but of as Sound Intellectuals as one of seventeen. Shee entertain'd Mr. Wheeler wth some passages of a Wedding awhile ago at a place hard by, the Brides-Groom being about her Age or something above, Saying his Children was dredfully against their fathers marrying, wch shee condemned them extreemly for.

From hence wee went pretty briskly forward, and arriv'd at Saybrook ferry about two of the Clock afternoon; and crossing it, wee call'd at an Inn to Bait, (foreseeing we should not have such another Opportunity till we come to Killingsworth.) Landlady come in, with her hair about her ears, and hands at full pay scratching. Shee told us shee had some mutton wch shee would broil, wch I was glad to hear;

[17]Contemptuous name for an inferior, vicious, or worn-out horse.

[18]Gurdon Saltonstall (1666–1724), minister at New London, was a celebrated preacher. He sat at one time as Chief Justice of the Supreme Court of the Connecticut Colony.

But I supose forgot to wash her scratchers; in a little time shee brot it in; but it being pickled, and my Guide said it smelt strong of head sause, we left it, and pd sixpence a piece for our Dinners, wch was only smell.

So wee putt forward with all speed, and about seven at night come to Killingsworth, and were tollerably well with Travillers fare, and Lodgd there that night.

Saturday, Oct. 7th, we sett out early in the Morning, and being something unaquainted wth the way, having ask't it of some wee mett, they told us wee must Ride a mile or two and turne down a Lane on the Right hand; and by their Direction wee Rode on but not Yet comeing to ye turning, we mett a Young fellow and ask't him how farr it was to the Lane which turn'd down towards Guilford. Hee said wee must Ride a little further, and turn down by the Corner of uncle Sams Lott. My Guide vented his Spleen at the Lubber; and we soon after came into the Rhode, and keeping still on, without any thing further Remarkabell, about two a clock afternoon we arrived at New Haven, where I was received with all Posible Respects and civility. Here I discharged Mr. Wheeler with a reward to his satisfaction, and took some time to rest after so long and toilsome a Journey; And I Inform'd myselfe of the manners and customs of the place, and at the same time employed myselfe in the afair I went there upon.

They are Govern'd by the same Laws as wee in Boston, (or little differing,) thr'out this whole Colony of Connecticot, And much the same way of Church Government, and many of them good, Sociable people, and I hope Religious too: but a little too much Independant in their principalls, and, as I have been told, were formerly in their Zeal very Riggid in their Administrations towards such as their Lawes made Offenders, even to a harmless Kiss or Innocent merriment among Young people. Whipping being a frequent and counted an easy Punishment, about wch as other Crimes, the Judges were absolute in their Sentances. They told mee a pleasant story about a pair of Justices in those parts, wch I may not omit the relation of.

A negro Slave belonging to a man in ye Town, stole a hogs head from his master, and gave or sold it to an Indian, native of the place. The Indian sold it in the neighbourhood, and so the theft was found out. Thereupon the Heathen was Seized, and carried to the Justices House to be Examined. But his worship (it seems) was gone into the feild, with a Brother in office, to gather in his Pompions.[19] Whither the malefactor is hurried, And Complaint made, and satisfaction in the name of Justice demanded. Their Worships cann't proceed in form without a Bench: whereupon they Order one to be Imediately erected, which, for want of fitter materials, they made with pompions—which being finished, down setts their Worships, and the Malefactor call'd, and by the Senior Justice Interrogated after the following manner. You Indian why did You steal from this man? You sho'dn't do so—it's a Grandy wicked thing to steal. Hol't Hol't, cryes Justice Junr, Brother, You speak negro to him. I'le ask him. You sirrah, why did You steal this man's Hoggshead? Hoggshead? (replys the Indian,) me no stomany. No? says his Worship; and pulling off his hatt, Patted his own head with his hand, sais, Tatapa—You, Tatapa—you; all one this. Hoggs-head all one this. Hah! says Netop, now me stomany that. Whereupon the Company fell into a great fitt of Laughter, even to Roreing. Silence is comanded, but to no

[19]Pumpkins.

effect: for they continued perfectly Shouting. Nay, sais his worship, in an angry tone, if it be so, *take mee off the Bench*.

Their Diversions in this part of the Country are on Lecture days and Training days mostly:[20] on the former there is Riding from town to town.

And on training dayes The Youth divert themselves by Shooting at the Target, as they call it, (but it very much resembles a pillory,) where hee that hitts neerest the white has some yards of Red Ribbin presented him, wch being tied to his hattband, the two ends streeming down his back, he is Led away in Triumph, wth great applause, as the winners of the Olympiack Games. They generally marry very young: the males oftener as I am told under twentie than above; they generally make public wedings, and have a way something singular (as they say) in some of them, viz. Just before Joyning hands the Bridegroom quitts the place, who is soon followed by the Bridesmen, and as it were, dragg'd back to duty—being the reverse to ye former practice among us, to steal ms Pride.

There are great plenty of Oysters all along by the sea side, as farr as I Rode in the Collony, and those very good. And they Generally lived very well and comfortably in their famelies. But too Indulgent (especially ye farmers) to their slaves: sufering too great familiarity from them, permitting them to sit at Table and eat with them, (as they say to save time,) and into the dish goes the black hoof as freely as the white hand. They told me that there was a farmer lived nere the Town where I lodgd who had some difference wth his slave, concerning something the master had promised him and did not punctualy perform; wch caused some hard words between them; But at length they put the matter to Arbitration and Bound themselves to stand to the award of such as they named—wch done, the Arbitrators Having heard the Allegations of both parties, Order the master to pay 40s to black face, and acknowledge his fault. And so the matter ended: the poor master very honestly standing to the award.

There are every where in the Towns as I passed, a Number of Indians the Natives of the Country, and are the most salvage of all the salvages of that kind that I had ever Seen: little or no care taken (as I heard upon enquiry) to make them otherwise. They have in some places Landes of their owne, and Govern'd by Law's of their own making;—they marry many wives and at pleasure put them away, and on the ye least dislike or fickle humour, on either side, saying *stand away* to one another is a sufficient Divorce. And indeed those uncomely *Stand aways* are too much in Vougue among the English in this (Indulgent Colony) as their Records plentifully prove, and that on very trivial matters, of which some have been told me, but are not proper to be Related by a Female pen, tho some of that foolish sex have had too large a share in the story.

If the natives committ any crime on their own precincts among themselves, ye English takes no Cognezens of. But if on the English ground, they are punishable by our Laws. They mourn for their Dead by blacking their faces, and cutting their hair, after an Awkerd and frightfull manner; But can't bear You should mention the names of their dead Relations to them: they trade most for Rum, for wch theyd hazzard their

[20]Lecture days, when the weekly religious lecture took place, were on Thursdays. Training days were specifically appointed for militia drill.

very lives; and the English fit them Generally as well, by seasoning it plentifully with water.

They give the title of merchant to every trader; who Rate their Goods according to the time and spetia they pay in: viz. Pay, mony, Pay as mony, and trusting. *Pay* is Grain, Pork, Beef, &c. at the prices sett by the General Court that Year; *mony* is pieces of Eight, Ryalls, or Boston or Bay shillings (as they call them,) or Good hard money, as sometimes silver coin is termed by them; also Wampom, vizt. Indian beads wch serves for change. *Pay as mony* is provisions, as aforesd one Third cheaper then as the Assembly or Genel Court sets it; and *Trust* as they and the mercht agree for time.

Now, when the buyer comes to ask for a comodity, sometimes before the merchant answers that he has it, he sais, *is Your pay redy?* Perhaps the Chap Reply's Yes: what do You pay in? say's the merchant. The buyer having answered, then the price is set; as suppose he wants a sixpenny knife, in pay it is 12d—in pay as money eight pence, and hard money its own price, viz. 6d. It seems a very Intricate way of trade and what Lex Mercatoria[21] had not thought of.

Being at a merchants house, in comes a tall country fellow, wth his alfogeos[22] full of Tobacco; for they seldom Loose their Cudd, but keep Chewing and Spitting as long as they'r eyes are open,—he advanc't to the midle of the Room, makes an Awkward Nodd, and spitting a Large deal of Aromatick Tincture, he gave a scrape with his shovel like shoo, leaving a small shovel full of dirt on the floor, made a full stop, Hugging his own pretty Body with his hands under his arms, Stood staring rown'd him, like a Catt let out of a Baskett. At last, like the creature Balaam Rode on, he opened his mouth and said: have You any Ribinen for Hatbands to sell I pray? The Questions and Answers about the pay being past, the Ribin is bro't and opened. Bumpkin Simpers, cryes its confounded Gay I vow; and beckning to the door, in comes Jone Tawdry, dropping about 50 curtsees, and stands by him: hee shows her the Ribin. *Law, You,* sais shee, *its right Gent,*[23] do You, take it, *tis dreadfull pretty.* Then she enquires, *have You any hood silk I pray?* wch being brought and bought, Have You any *thred silk to sew it wth* says shee, wch being accomodated wth they Departed. They Generaly stand after they come in a great while speachless, and sometimes dont say a word till they are askt what they want, which I Impute to the Awe they stand in of the merchants, who they are constantly almost Indebted too; and must take what they bring without Liberty to choose for themselves; but they serve them as well, making the merchants stay long enough for their pay.

We may Observe here the great necessity and bennifitt both of Education and Conversation; for these people have as Large a portion of mother witt, and sometimes a Larger, than those who have bin brought up in Citties; But for want of emprovements, Render themselves almost Ridiculos, as above. I should be glad if they would leave such follies, and am sure all that Love Clean Houses (at least) would be glad on't too.

[21]Latin for "the law of merchants," that is, the legally recognized commercial system.

[22]Alfogeos, or Spanish saddlebags, also referred to a baboon's cheeks. Thus Knight uses this word in a humorously derogatory way.

[23]Genteel.

They are generaly very plain in their dress, throuout all ye Colony, as I saw, and follow one another in their modes; that You may know where they belong, especially the women, meet them where you will.

Their Cheif Red Letter day is St. Election,[24] wch is annualy Observed according to Charter, to choose their Govenr: a blessing they can never be thankfull enough for, as they will find, if ever it be their hard fortune to loose it. The present Govenor in Conecticott is the Honlbe John Winthrop Esq.[25] A Gentleman of an Ancient and Honourable Family, whose Father was Govenor here sometime before, and his Grand father has bin Govr of the Massachusetts. This gentleman is a very curteous and afable person, much Given to Hospitality, and has by his Good services Gain'd the affections of the people as much as any who had bin before him in that post.

Decr 6th. Being by this time well Recruited and rested after my Journy, my business lying unfinished by some concerns at New York depending thereupon, my Kinsman, Mr. Thomas Trowbridge of New Haven, must needs take a Journy there before it could be accomplished, I resolved to go there in company wth him, and a man of the town wch I engaged to wait on me there. Accordingly, Dec. 6th we set out from New Haven, and about 11 same morning came to Stratford ferry; wch crossing, about two miles on the other side Baited our horses and would have eat a morsell ourselves, But the Pumpkin and Indian mixt Bred had such an Aspect, and the Barelegg'd Punch so awkerd or rather Awfull a sound, that we left both, and proceeded forward, and about seven at night come to Fairfield, where we met with good entertainment and Lodg'd; and early next morning set forward to Norowalk, from its halfe Indian name *North-walk,* when about 12 at noon we arrived, and Had a Dinner of Fryed Venison, very savoury. Landlady wanting some pepper in the seasoning, bid the Girl hand her the spice in the little *Gay* cupp on ye shelfe. From hence we Hasted towards Rye, walking and Leading our Horses neer a mile together, up a prodigios high Hill; and so Riding till about nine at night, and there arrived and took up our Lodgings at an ordinary, wch a French family kept. Here being very hungry, I desired a fricasee, wch the Frenchman undertakeing, mannaged so contrary to my notion of Cookery, that I hastned to Bed superless; And being shewd the way up a pair of stairs wch had such a narrow passage that I had almost stopt by the Bulk of my Body; But arriving at my apartment found it to be a little Lento Chamber furnisht amongst other Rubbish with a High Bedd and a Low one, a Long Table, a Bench and a Bottomless chair,—Little Miss went to scratch up my Kennell wch Russelled as if shee'd bin in the Barn amongst the Husks, and supose such was the contents of the tickin—nevertheless being exceeding weary, down I laid my poor Carkes (never more tired) and found my Covering as scanty as my Bed was hard. Annon I heard another Russelling noise in Ye Room—called to know the matter—Little miss said shee was making a bed for the men; who, when they were in Bed, complained their leggs lay out of it by reason of its shortness—my poor bones complained bitterly not being used to such Lodgings, and so did the man who was with us; and poor I made but one Grone, which was from the time I went to bed to the time I Riss, which was about three in the morning, Setting up by the Fire till Light, and having discharged

[24]Knight's colloquial manner of indicating that Election Days were officially observed.

[25]Fitz-John Winthrop (1638–1707), eldest son of Governor John Winthrop, was Governor of Connecticut from 1698 to 1707.

our ordinary wch was as dear as if we had had far Better fare—wee took our leave of Monsier and about seven in the morn come to New Rochell a french town, where we had a good Breakfast. And in the strength of that about an how'r before sunsett got to York. Here I applyd myself to Mr. Burroughs, a merchant to whom I was recommended by my Kinsman Capt. Prout, and received great Civilities from him and his spouse, who were now both Deaf but very agreeable in their Conversation, Diverting me with pleasant stories of their knowledge in Brittan from whence they both come, one of which was above the rest very pleasant to me viz. my Lord Darcy had a very extravagant Brother who had mortgaged what Estate hee could not sell, and in good time dyed leaving only one son. Him his Lordship (having none of his own) took and made him Heir of his whole Estate, which he was to receive at the death of his Aunt. He and his Aunt in her widowhood held a right understanding and lived as become such Relations, shee being a discreat Gentlewoman and he an Ingenios Young man. One day Hee fell into some Company though far his inferiors, very freely told him of the Ill circumstances his fathers Estate lay under, and the many Debts he left unpaid to the wrong of poor people with whom he had dealt. The Young gentleman was put out of countenance—no way hee could think of to Redress himself—his whole dependance being on the Lady his Aunt, and how to speak to her he knew not—Hee went home, sat down to dinner and as usual sometimes with her when the Chaplain was absent, she desired him to say Grace, wch he did after this manner:

Pray God in Mercy take my Lady Darcy
Unto his Heavenly Throne,
That little John may live like a man,
And pay every man his own.

The prudent Lady took no present notice, But finishd dinner, after wch having sat and talk't awhile (as Customary) He Riss, took his Hatt and Going out she desired him to give her leave to speak to him in her Clossett, Where being come she desired to know why hee prayed for her Death in the manner aforesaid, and what part of her deportment towards him merritted such desires. Hee Reply'd, none at all, But he was under such disadvantages that nothing but that could do him service, and told her how he had been affronted as above, and what Impressions it had made upon him. The Lady made him a gentle reprimand that he had not informed her after another manner, Bid him see what his father owed and he should have money to pay it to a penny, And always to lett her know his wants and he should have a redy supply. The Young Gentleman charm'd with his Aunts Discrete management, Beggd her pardon and accepted her kind offer and retrieved his fathers Estate, &c. and said Hee hoped his Aunt would never dye, for shee had done better by him than hee could have done for himself.—Mr. Burroughs went with me to Vendue[26] where I bought about 100 Rheem of paper wch was retaken in a flyboat from Holland and sold very Reasonably here—some ten, some Eight shillings per Rheem by the Lott wch was ten Rheem in a Lott. And at the Vendue I made a great many acquaintances amongst the good women of the town, who curteosly invited me to their houses and generously entertained me.

[26]Place of public sale or auction.

The Cittie of New York is a pleasant, well compacted place, situated on a Commodius River wch is a fine harbour for shipping. The Buildings Brick Generaly, very stately and high, though not altogether like ours in Boston. The Bricks in some of the Houses are of divers Coullers and laid in Checkers, being glazed look very agreeable. The inside of them are neat to admiration, the wooden work, for only the walls are plasterd, and the Sumers and Gist[27] are plained and kept very white scowr'd as so is all the partitions if made of Bords. The fire places have no Jambs (as ours have) But the Backs run flush with the walls, and the Hearth is of Tyles and is as farr out into the Room at the Ends as before the fire, wch is Generally Five foot in the Low'r rooms, and the peice over where the mantle tree should be is made as ours with Joyners work, and as I supose is fasten'd to iron rodds inside. The House where the Vendue was, had Chimney Corners like ours, and they and the hearths were laid wth the finest tile that I ever see, and the stair cases laid all with white tile which is ever clean, and so are the walls of the Kitchen wch had a Brick floor. They were making Great preparations to Receive their Govenor, Lord Cornbury[28] from the Jerseys, and for that End raised the militia to Gard him on shore to the fort.

They are Generaly of the Church of England and have a New England Gentleman for their minister, and a very fine church set out with all Customary requisites. There are also a Dutch and Divers Conventicles as they call them, viz. Baptist, Quakers, &c. They are not strict in keeping the Sabbath as in Boston and other places where I had bin, But seem to deal with great exactness as farr as I see or Deall with. They are sociable to one another and Curteos and Civill to strangers and fare well in their houses. The English go very fasheonable in their dress. But the Dutch, especially the middling sort, differ from our women, in their habitt go loose, were French muches wch are like a Capp and a head band in one, leaving their ears bare, which are sett out wth Jewells of a large size and many in number. And their fingers hoop't with Rings, some with large stones in them of many Coullers as were their pendants in their ears, which You should see very old women wear as well as Young.

They have Vendues very frequently and make their Earnings very well by them, for they treat with good Liquor Liberally, and the Customers Drink as Liberally and Generally pay for't as well, by paying for that which they Bidd up Briskly for, after the sack has gone plentifully about, tho' sometimes good penny worths are got there. Their Diversions in the Winter is Riding Sleys about three or four Miles out of Town, where they have Houses of entertainment at a place called the Bowery, and some go to friends Houses who handsomely treat them. Mr. Burroughs cary'd his spouse and Daughter and myself out to one Madame Dowes, a Gentlewoman that lived at a farm House, who gave us a handsome Entertainment of five or six Dishes and choice Beer and metheglin,[29] Cyder, &c. all which she said was the produce of her farm. I believe we mett 50 or 60 slays that day—they fly with great swiftness and some are so furious that they'le turn out of the path for none except a Loaden Cart. Nor do they spare for any diversion the place affords, and sociable to a degree, they'r Tables being as free to their Naybours as to themselves.

[27]Beams and joints.

[28]Edward Hyde, Lord Cornbury, governor of New York, 1702–1708.

[29]Alcoholic drink made with fermented honey; spiced mead.

Having here transacted the affair I went upon and some other that fell in the way, after about a fortnight's stay there I left New-York with no Little regrett, and Thursday, Dec. 21, set out for New Haven wth my Kinsman Trowbridge, and the man that waited on me about one afternoon, and about three come to half-way house about ten miles out of town, where we Baited and went forward, and about 5 come to Spiting Devil, Else Kings bridge,[30] where they pay three pence for passing over with a horse, which the man that keeps the Gate set up at the end of the Bridge receives.

We hoped to reach the french town and Lodg there that night, but unhapily lost our way about four miles short, and being overtaken by a great storm of wind and snow which set full in our faces about dark, we were very uneasy. But meeting one Gardner who lived in a Cottage thereabout, offered us his fire to set by, having but one poor Bedd, and his wife not well, &c. or he would go to a House with us, where he thought we might be better accommodated—thither we went, But a surly old shee Creature, not worthy the name of woman, who would hardly let us go into her Door, though the weather was so stormy none but shee would have turnd out a Dogg. But her son whose name was gallop, who lived Just by Invited us to his house and shewed me two pair of stairs, viz. one up the loft and tother up the Bedd, wch was as hard as it was high, and warmed it with a hott stone at the feet. I lay very uncomfortably, insomuch that I was so very cold and sick I was forced to call them up to give me something to warm me. They had nothing but milk in the house, wch they Boild, and to make it better sweetened wth molasses, which I not knowing or thinking oft till it was down and coming up agen wch it did in so plentifull a manner that my host was soon paid double for his portion, and that in specia. But I believe it did me service in Cleering my stomach. So after this sick and weary night at East Chester, (a very miserable poor place,) the weather being now fair, Friday the 22d Dec. we set out for New Rochell, where being come we had good Entertainment and Recruited ourselves very well. This is a very pretty place well compact, and good handsome houses, Clean, good and passable Rodes, and situated on a Navigable River, abundance of land well fined and Cleerd all along as wee passed, which caused in me a Love to the place, wch I could have been content to live in it. Here wee Ridd over a Bridge made of one entire stone of such a Breadth that a cart might pass with safety, and to spare—it lay over a passage cutt through a Rock to convey water to a mill not farr off. Here are three fine Taverns within call of each other, very good provision for Travailers.

Thence we travailed through Merrinak, a neet, though little place, wth a navigable River before it, one of the pleasantest I ever see—Here were good Buildings, Especialy one, a very fine seat, wch they told me was Col. Hethcoats, who I had heard was a very fine Gentleman. From hence we come to Hors Neck, where wee Baited,[31] and they told me that one Church of England parson officiated in all these three towns once every Sunday in turns throughout the Year; and that they all could but poorly maintaine him, which they grudg'd to do, being a poor and quarelsome crew as I understand by our Host; their Quarelling about their choice of Minister, they chose to have none—But caused the Government to send this Gentleman to them.

[30]Spuyten Duyvil Creek, at Kingsbridge. The creek divides Manhattan Island from the mainland.

[31]Stopped at an inn to feed the horses and refresh the passengers.

Here wee took leave of York Government, and Descending the Mountainos passage that almost broke my heart in ascending before, we come to Stamford, a well compact Town, but miserable meeting house, wch we passed, and thro' many and great difficulties, as Bridges which were exceeding high and very tottering and of vast Length, steep and Rocky Hills and precipices, (Buggbears to a fearful female travailer.) About nine at night we come to Norrwalk, having crept over a timber of a Broken Bridge about thirty foot long, and perhaps fifty to ye water. I was exceeding tired and cold when we come to our Inn, and could get nothing there but poor entertainment, and the impertinant Bable of one of the worst of men, among many others of which our Host made one, who, had he bin one degree Impudenter, would have outdone his Grandfather. And this I think is the most perplexed night I have yet had. From hence, Saturday, Dec. 23, a very cold and windy day, after an Intolerable night's Lodging, wee hasted forward only observing in our way the Town to be situated on a Navigable river wth indiferent Buildings and people more refind than in some of the Country towns wee had passed, tho' vicious enough, the Church and Tavern being next neighbours. Having Ridd thro a difficult River wee come to Fairfield where wee Baited and were much refreshed as well with the Good things wch gratified our appetites as the time took to rest our wearied Limbs, wch Latter I employed in enquiring concerning the Town and manners of the people, &c. This is a considerable town, and filled as they say with wealthy people—have a spacious meeting house and good Buildings. But the Inhabitants are Litigious, nor do they well agree with their minister, who (they say) is a very worthy Gentleman.[32]

They have aboundance of sheep, whose very Dung brings them great gain, with part of which they pay their Parsons sallery, And they Grudg that, prefering their Dung before their minister. They Lett out their sheep at so much as they agree upon for a night; the highest Bidder always caries them, And they will sufficiently Dung a Large quantity of Land before morning. But were once Bitt by a sharper who had them a night and sheared them all before morning—From hence we went to Stratford, the next Town, in which I observed but few houses, and those not very good ones. But the people that I conversed with were civill and good natured. Here we staid till late at night, being to cross a Dangerous River ferry, the River at that time full of Ice; but after about four hours waiting with great difficulty wee got over. My fears and fatigues prevented my here taking any particular observation. Being got to Milford, it being late in the night, I could go no further; my fellow travailer going forward, I was invited to Lodg at Mrs.——, a very kind and civill Gentlewoman, by whom I was handsomely and kindly entertained till the next night. The people here go very plain in their apparel (more plain than I had observed in the towns I had passed) and seem to be very grave and serious. They told me there was a singing Quaker living there, or at least had a strong inclination to be so, His Spouse not at all affected that way. Some of the singing Crew come there one day to visit him, who being then abroad, they sat down (to the woman's no small vexation) Humming and singing and groneing after their conjuring way—Says the woman are you singing quakers? Yea says They—Then take my squalling Brat of a child here and sing to it

[32]Joseph Webb (1666–1732), minister in Fairfield, Connecticut, from 1694 to 1732.

says she for I have almost split my throat wth singing to him and cant get the Rogue to sleep. They took this as a great Indignity, and mediately departed. Shaking the dust from their Heels left the good woman and her Child among the number of the wicked.

This is a Seaport place and accomodated with a Good Harbour, But I had not opportunity to make particular observations because it was Sabbath day—This Evening.

December 24. I set out with the Gentlewomans son who she very civilly offered to go with me when she see no parswasions would cause me to stay which she pressingly desired, and crossing a ferry having but nine miles to New Haven, in a short time arrived there and was Kindly received and well accommodated amongst my Friends and Relations.

The Government of Connecticut Collony begins westward towards York at Stanford (as I am told) and so runs Eastward towards Boston (I mean in my range, because I dont intend to extend my description beyond my own travails) and ends that way at Stonington—And has a great many Large towns lying more northerly. It is a plentiful Country for provisions of all sorts and its Generally Healthy. No one that can and will be dilligent in this place need fear poverty nor the want of food and Rayment.

January 6th. Being now well Recruited and fitt for business I discoursed the persons I was concerned with, that we might finnish in order to my return to Boston. They delayd as they had hitherto done hoping to tire my Patience. But I was resolute to stay and see an End of the matter let it be never so much to my disadvantage—So January 9th they come again and promise the Wednesday following to go through with the distribution of the Estate which they delayed till Thursday and then come with new amusements. But at length by the mediation of that holy good Gentleman, the Rev. Mr. James Pierpont, the minister of New Haven, and with the advice and assistance of other our Good friends we come to an accommodation and distribution, which having finished though not till February, the man that waited on me to York taking the charge of me I sit out for Boston. We went from New Haven upon the ice (the ferry being not passable thereby) and the Rev. Mr. Pierpont wth Madam Prout Cuzin Trowbridge and divers others were taking leave wee went onward without any thing Remarkabl till wee come to New London and Lodged again at Mr. Saltonstalls—and here I dismist my Guide, and my Generos entertainer provided me Mr. Samuel Rogers of that place to go home with me—I stayed a day here Longer than I intended by the Commands of the Honble Govenor Winthrop to stay and take a supper with him whose wonderful civility I may not omitt. The next morning I Crossed ye Ferry to Groton, having had the Honor of the Company, of Madam Livingston (who is the Govenors Daughter) and Mary Christophers and divers others to the boat—And that night Lodgd at Stonington and had Rost Beef and pumpkin sause for supper. The next night at Haven's and had Rost fowle, and the next day wee come to a river which by Reason of Ye Freshetts coming down was swell'd so high wee feard it impassable and the rapid stream was very terryfying—However we must over and that in a small Cannoo. Mr. Rogers assuring me of his good Conduct, I after a stay of near an how'r on the shore for consultation went into the Cannoo, and Mr. Rogers paddled about 100 yards up the Creek by the shore side, turned into the swift stream and dexterously steering her in a moment wee come to the other side as swiftly passing as an arrow shott out of the Bow by a strong arm. I staid on ye shore till Hee returned to fetch our horses, which he caused to swim over himself bringing the furniture in the Cannoo. But it is past my skill to express the Exceeding fright all their transactions formed in me. Wee were now in the colony of the Massachusetts and taking Lodgings at the first Inn we come too had a pretty difficult passage the next day which was the second of March by reason of the sloughy ways then thawed by the Sunn. Here I mett Capt. John Richards of Boston who was going home, So being very glad of his Company we Rode something harder than hitherto, and missing my way in going up a very steep Hill, my horse dropt down under me as Dead; this new surprize no little hurt me meeting it Just at the Entrance into Dedham from whence we intended to reach home that night. But was now obliged to gett another Hors there and leave my own, resolving for Boston that night if possible. But in going over the Causeway at Dedham the Bridge being overflowed by the high waters comming down I very narrowly escaped falling over into the river Hors and all wch twas almost a miracle I did not—now it grew late in the afternoon and the people having very much discouraged us about the sloughy way wch they said wee should find very difficult and hazardous it so wrought on mee being tired and dispirited and disapointed of my desires of going home that I agreed to Lodg there that night wch wee did at the house of one Draper, and the next day being March 3d wee got safe home to Boston, where I found my aged and tender mother and my Dear and only Child in good health with open arms redy to receive me, and my Kind relations and friends flocking in to welcome mee and hear the story of my transactions and travails I having this day bin five months from home and now I cannot fully express my Joy and Satisfaction. But desire sincearly to adore my Great Benefactor for thus graciously carying forth and returning in safety his unworthy handmaid.

1825

Louis Armand de Lom d'Arce, Baron de Lahontan 1666–1715

Louis Armand de Lom d'Arce, Baron of Lahontan, was born into an aristocratic family in 1666 in Mont-de-Marsan, France. His father, Isaac de Lom, Sieur d'Arce, was a distinguished civil engineer who was seventy-two-years old at the time of his son's birth. Not surprisingly, Lahontan was orphaned at an early age, but his inheritance turned out to be little more than an encumbered estate. His family helped him obtain a cadetship in a Bourbon regiment; later he entered the marine corps, the body in charge of France's colonies, in a position considered a fast track to advancement for young noblemen. Charles Bragelonne, a relative of Lahontan's, was one of the Company of the Hundred Associates, created by Cardinal Richelieu in 1627 to spur colonization in the New World and granted a complete monopoly of the lucrative fur trade in New France. In 1683, the governor of New France petitioned the French court to send eight hundred regular troops as reinforcements against the Iroquois. Among this detachment was the young baron, then only seventeen years old.

Lahontan remained in Quebec for the next ten years and spent time not only in garrison in Montreal but also exploring the surrounding countryside and acquainting himself with the languages and cultures of the native inhabitants of Canada. He describes a hunting trip spent "In a Canow upon several Rivers, Marshes and Pools, that disembogue in the Champlain Lake, being accompany'd with thirty or forty of the Savages that are very expert in Shooting and Hunting, and perfectly well acquainted with the proper places for finding Water-foul, Deer, and other fallow Beasts." His enjoyment of the wilderness did not prevent him from reading the classical authors, and he remarks urbanely: "Besides the pleasure of so many different sorts of Diversion, I was likewise entertained in the Woods with the company of the honest old Gentlemen that lived in former Ages. Honest Homer, the amiable Anacreon, and my dear Lucian, were my inseparable companions. Aristotle too desired passionately to go along with us, but my Canow was too little to hold his bulky Equipage of Perpatetick Silogisms: so that he was e'en fain to trudge back to the Jesuits, who vouchasafed him a very honorable Reception."

Lahontan's account of his travels, *New Voyages to North-America,* was first published in 1703 as the desperate act of a bankrupt fugitive. Written mostly in the form of letters to someone described as an "old relation" to whom Lahontan had promised letters in exchange for financial assistance, it was translated into English, under the patronage of the Duke of Devonshire, as well as into German, Dutch, and Italian. With its accounts of adventures at sea, its portraits of the colonial society of New France and of the culture of native Canadian groups, its recounting of native traditional stories, and its risqué and irreverent descriptions of marriage and courtship not only among French settlers but also among Canadian Indians, its success is easy to understand. One of the most fascinating parts is a dialogue between a fictional version of Lahontan and a Huron called Adario, in which the latter is presented as a rational human being uncorrupted by society and its deceits. The figure of Adario, the prototype of the Noble Savage, would have an incalculable effect on French Enlightenment thinkers such as Voltaire and Rousseau.

Susan Castillo
King's College London

PRIMARY WORK

New Voyages to North-America, containing an Account of the Several Nations of that vast Continent; their Customs, Commerce, and Way of Navigation upon the Lakes and Rivers; the Several Attempts of the English and French to dispossess one another; with the Reasons of the Miscarriage of the former; and the various Adventures between the French, and the Iroquois Confederates of England, from 1683 to 1694, in Two Volumes, translator anonymous (London: Printed for H. Bonwick, 1703).

from New Voyages to North-America . . . from 1683 to 1694, in Two Volumes

from Volume I
A Discourse of the Interest of the French, and of the English, in North-America

Since New France and New England subsist only upon cod-fishery and the fur trade, it is the interest of these two colonies to enlarge the number of the ships employed in the fishery, and to encourage the savages to hunt and shoot beavers, by furnishing them with what arms and ammunition they have occasion for. It is well known that there is a great consumption of codfish in the Southern countries of Europe, and that few commodities meet with a better and readier market, especially if they are good and well-cured.

Those who allege that the destruction of the Iroquois would promote the interest of the colonies of New France are strangers to the true interest of that country; for if that were once accomplished, the savages who are now the French allies would turn their greatest enemies, as being then rid of their earlier fears. They would not fail to call in the English, by reason that their commodities are at once cheaper and more esteemed than ours; and by that means the whole commerce of that wide country would be wrested out of our hands.

I conclude therefore that it is the interest of the French to weaken the Iroquois but not to see them entirely defeated. I own that at this day they are too strong, insomuch that they cut the throats of the savages [who are] our allies every day. They have nothing less in view than to cut off all the Nations they know, let their situation be never so remote from their country.[1] It is our business to reduce them to one half of the power they are now possessed of, if it were possible; but we do not go the right way to work.[2] Above these thirty years, their ancient counselors have still remonstrated to the warriors of the Five Nations[3] that it was expedient to cut off all the savage nations of Canada in order to ruin the commerce of the French, and then to dislodge them from the Continent. With this view they have carried the war about four or five hundred leagues off their country, after the destroying of several different nations in several places. . . .

To allege that these barbarians have a dependence upon the English is a foolish plea: for they are so far from owning any dependence, that when they go to New York to truck[4] their skins, they have the confidence to put rates upon the goods they have occasion for when the merchants offer to raise their price. I have intimated already several times that their respect for the English is tacked to the occasion they have to make use of them; that this is the only motive which induces them to treat the English as their brethren and their friends; and that if the French would sell them

[1]That is, no matter how far these other native nations were from Iroquois lands.

[2]That is, we are not going about this in the right way.

[3]The Iroquois Confederacy among the Mohawk, Oneida, Onondaga, Cayuga, and Seneca nations.

[4]Trade.

the necessaries of life, as well as arms and ammunition, at easier rates, they would not make many journeys to the English colonies. This is a consideration that ought to be chiefly in our view; for if we minded it to the purpose, they would be cautious of insulting our savage confederates as well as ourselves. The Governors General of Canada would do well to employ the sensible men of the country that are acquainted with our confederates, in pressing them to live in a good correspondence with one another, without waging war among themselves. . . .

To conclude: I must say the English in these colonies are too careless and lazy; the French *coureurs de bois*[5] are much readier for enterprises, and the Canadians are certainly more vigilant and more active. It behooves the inhabitants of New York to enlarge their fur trade by well-concerted enterprises; and those of New England, to render the cod-fishing more beneficial to the colony by taking such measures as other people would, if they were as advantageously seated.

from Volume II
New Voyages to America, Giving an Account of the Customs, Commerce, Religion and Strange Opinions of the Savages of that Country

A Discourse of the Habit, Houses, Complexion and Temperament of the Savages of North America

I have read some histories of Canada, which were written at several times by the monks,[6] and must own that they have given some plain and exact descriptions of such countries as they knew; but at the same time they are widely mistaken in their accounts of the manners and customs of the savages. The Récollets[7] brand the savages for stupid, gross and rustic persons, incapable of thought or reflection. But the Jesuits give them other sort of language,[8] for they entitle them to good sense, to a tenacious memory, and to a quick apprehension seasoned with a solid judgement. The former allege that it is to no purpose to preach the Gospel to a sort of people that have less knowledge than the brutes. On the other hand the latter (I mean the Jesuits) give it out, that these savages take pleasure in hearing the word of God, and readily apprehend the meaning of the Scriptures. In the meantime, it is no difficult matter to point to the reasons that influence the one and the other to such allegations; the mystery is easily unraveled by those who know that these two orders cannot set their horses together in Canada.[9]

[5]Fur trappers and traders.

[6]Probably the *Jesuit Relations,* forty volumes of which were published in Paris from 1632 to 1673.

[7]A French Catholic religious order that did much missionary work in New France.

[8]That is, describe them in different terms.

[9]Lahontan is implying that the differences in the attitude of the two rival orders toward the native peoples of Canada resulted from the varying success of their respective missions.

I have seen so many impertinent accounts of this country, and those written by authors that passed for saints, that I now begin to believe that all History is one continued series of Pyrrhonism.[10] Had I been unacquainted with the language of the savages, I might have credited all that was said of them; but the opportunity I had of conversing with that people served to undeceive me, and gave me to understand, that the Récollets and the Jesuits content themselves with glancing at things without taking notice of the (almost) invincible aversion of the savages to the truths of Christianity. Both the one and the other had good reason to be cautious of touching upon that string. In the meantime suffer me to acquaint you, that upon this head I only speak of the savages of Canada, excluding those that live beyond the River of Mississippi, of whose manners and customs I could not acquire a perfect scheme, by reason that I was unacquainted with their languages, not to mention that I had not time to make any long stay in their country. In the Journal of my voyage upon the long River, I acquainted you that they are a very polite people, which you will likewise infer from the circumstances in that discourse.

Those who represented the savages to be as rough as bears, never had the opportunity of seeing them; for they have neither beard nor hair in any part of their body, not so much as under their arm-pits. This is true of both sexes, if I may credit those who ought to know better than I. Generally they are proper well-made persons, and fitter companions to American than to European women. The Iroquois are of a larger stature, and withal more valiant and cunning than the other nations; but at the same time they are neither so nimble nor so dexterous at the exercises of war of hunting, which they never go about but in great numbers. The Illinois, the Oumamis,[11] and the Outagamins,[12] with some other adjacent nations, are of an indifferent size, and run like greyhounds, if the comparison be allowable. The Ottawa, and most of the other savages to the northward (excepting the Sauteurs[13] and the Clistinos[14]) are cowardly, ugly, and ungainly fellows; but the Hurons are a brave, active and daring people, resembling the Iroquois in their stature and countenance.

All the savages are of a sanguine constitution, inclining to an olive color, and generally speaking they have good faces and proper persons. It is a great rarity to find any among them that are lame, hunchbacked, one-eyed, blind, or dumb. Their eyes are large and black as well as their hair; their teeth are white like ivory, and the breath that springs from their mouth in expiration is as pure as the air that they suck in in inspiration, notwithstanding they eat no bread; which shows that we are mistaken in Europe, in fancying that the eating of meat without bread makes one's breath stink. They are neither so strong nor so vigorous as most of the French are in raising of weights with their arms, or carrying of burdens on their backs; but to make amends for that, they are indefatigable and inured to hardships, insomuch that the inconveniences of cold or heat have no impression upon them; their whole time being spent in the way of exercise, whether in running up and down at hunting and fishing, or in dancing and playing at foot-ball, or such games as require the motion of the legs.

[10]A system of philosophy based on the teachings of Pyrrho, a Greek sceptic of the third century B.C., who taught the impossibility of attaining certainty of knowledge.

[11]Miami.

[12]Fox.

[13]Ojibwa or Anishinabe.

[14]Cree.

The savages are very healthy, and unacquainted with an infinity of diseases that plague the Europeans, such as palsy,[15] dropsy,[16] gout, phtisick,[17] asthma, gravel,[18] and the stone.[19] But at the same time they are liable to the smallpox, and to pleurisies.[20] If a man dies at the age of sixty years, they think he dies young, for they commonly live to eighty or a hundred; nay, I met with two that were turned of a hundred several years.[21] But there are some of them that do not live so long, because they voluntarily shorten their lives by poisoning themselves, as I shall show you elsewhere. In this point they seem to join issue with Zeno[22] and the Stoics, who vindicate self-murder; and from thence I conclude, that the Americans[23] are as great fools as these great philosophers.

from A Short View of the Humors and Customs of the Savages

The savages are utter strangers to distinctions of property, for what belongs to one is equally another's. If any one of them be in danger at the Beaver Hunting, the rest fly to his assistance without being so much as asked. If his fusee[24] bursts, they are ready to offer him their own. If any of his children be killed or taken by the enemy, he is preferently furnished with as many slaves as he has occasion for. Money is in use with none of them but those that are Christians, who live in the suburbs of the towns. The others will not touch or so much as look upon silver, but give it the odious name of the French Serpent. They will tell you that among us the people murder, plunder, defame, and betray one another for money, that the husbands make merchandise of their wives, and the mothers of their daughters, for the lucre of that metal. They think it unaccountable that one man should have more than another, and that the rich should have more respect than the poor. In short, they say, the name of savages which we bestow upon them would fit ourselves better, since there is nothing in our actions that bears an appearance of wisdom. Such as have been in France were continually teasing us with the faults and disorders they observed in our towns, as being occasioned by money. It is in vain to remonstrate to them how useful the distinction of property is for the support of a society: they make a jest of what is to be said on that head. In fine, they neither quarrel nor fight nor slander one another. They scoff at arts and sciences, and laugh at the difference of degrees which is observed with us. They brand us for slaves, and call us miserable souls whose life is not worth having, alleging that we degrade ourselves in subjecting ourselves to one man who possesses the whole power, and is bound by no law but his own will; that we have continual jars[25] among ourselves; that our children rebel against their parents; that we imprison one another, and publicly promote our own destruction. Besides, they value themselves above anything that you can imagine, and this is the reason they always

[15]Paralysis of the limbs.
[16]Abnormal retention of fluids.
[17]Tuberculosis.
[18]Gallstones.
[19]Kidney stones.
[20]Diseases of the lungs.
[21]They were several years older than 100.
[22]A Greek philosopher (342?–270? B.C.) of the Stoic school known for his logical powers; Aristotle called him the founder of dialectic.
[23]Native Americans.
[24]Probably a mistranslation of *fusil* or musket.
[25]Conflicts.

give for it: That one is as much Master as another, and since men are all made of the same clay there should be no distinction or superiority among them. They pretend that their contented way of living far surpasses our riches; that all our sciences are not so valuable as the art of leading a peaceful calm life; that a man is not a man with us any farther than riches will make him; but among them the true qualifications of a man are to run well, to hunt, to bend the bow and manage the fuzee,[26] to work a canoe, to understand war, to know forests, to subsist upon a little, to build cottages, to fell trees, and to be able to travel a hundred leagues in a wood without any guide or other provision than his bow and arrows. They say we are great cheats in selling them bad wares four times dearer than they are worth, by way of exchange for their beaver skins; that our fuzees are continually bursting and laming them, after they have paid sufficient prices for them. I wish I had time to recount the innumerable absurdities they are guilty of relating to our customs, but to be particular upon that head would be a work of ten or twelve days. . . .

They pay an infinite deference to old age. The son that laughs at his father's advice shall tremble before his grandfather. In a word, they take the ancient men for oracles, and follow their counsel accordingly. If a man tells his son it is time he should marry, or go to the war, or the hunting, or shooting, he shall answer carelessly, "That's valient, I thought so." But if his grandfather tell him so, the answer is, "That's good. It shall be done." If by chance they kill a partridge, a goose, or a duck, or catch any delicate fish, they never fail to present it to their oldest relations.

The savages are wholly free from care. They do nothing but eat, drink, sleep, and ramble about in the night when they are at their villages. Having no set hours for meals, they eat when they are hungry, and commonly do it in a large company, feasting here and there by turns. The women and girls do the same among themselves, and do not admit any men into their company at that time. . . . It is not to be denied but the savages are a very sensible people, and are perfectly well acquainted with the interest of their nations. They are great moralists, especially when they criticize on the manners of the Europeans, and are mightily upon their guard in our company, unless it be with such as they are intimately acquainted with. In other matters they are incredulous and obstinate to the last degree, and are not able to distinguish between a chimerical supposition and an undoubted truth, or between a fair and a false consequence. . . .

from An Account of the Amours and Marriages of the Savages

I could recount a thousand curious things relating to the courtship and the way of marrying among the savages; but the relation of so many particulars would be too tedious, for which reason I shall only confine myself to what is most essential on that subject.

It may be justly said that the men are as cold and indifferent as the girls are passionate and warm. The former love nothing but war and hunting, and their utmost ambition reaches no farther. When they are at home and have nothing to do, they run with the match, that is, they are nightwalkers. The young men do not marry until they are thirty years of age, for they pretend that the enjoyment of women does so

[26]Musket.

enervate[27] them that they have not the same measure of strength to undergo great fatigues, and that their hams[28] are too weak for long marches or quick pursuits. In pursuance of this thought, it is alleged that those who have married, or strolled in the nights too often, are taken by the Iroquois, by reason of the weakness of their limbs, and the decay of their vigor. But after all, we must not imagine that they live chaste until that age; for they pretend that excessive continence occasions vapors, disorders of the kidneys, and a suppression of urine, so that it is necessary for their health to have a run once a week.

If the savages were capable of being subjected to the Empire of Love, they must needs have an extraordinary command of themselves to disguise the just jealousy they might have of their mistresses, and at the same time to carry it fair with their rivals. I know the humor of the savages better than a great many French people that have lived among them all their lifetime, for I studied their customs so narrowly and exactly that all their conduct of life is as perfectly well known to me, as if I had been among them all my lifetime. And it is this exact knowledge that prompts me to say that they are altogether strangers to that blind fury which we call love. They content themselves with a tender friendship that is not liable to all the extravagancies that the passion of love raises in such breasts as harbor it. In a word, they live with such tranquility that one may call their love simple goodwill, and their discretion upon that head is unimaginable. Their friendship is firm, but free of transport, for they are very careful in preserving the liberty and freedom of their heart, which they look upon as the most valuable treasure upon earth. From whence I conclude that they are not altogether so savage as we are.

. . . Some young women will not hear of a husband through a principle of debauchery. That sort of women are called *Ickoue ne Kioussa,* i.e., Hunting Women, for they commonly accompany the huntsmen in their diversions. To justify their conduct, they allege that they find themselves to be of too indifferent a temper to brook the conjugal yoke, to be too careless for the bringing up of children, and too impatient to bear the passing of the whole winter in the village. Thus it is that they cover and disguise their lewdness. Their parents or relations dare not censure their vicious conduct; on the contrary, they seem to approve of it, in declaring, as I said before, that their daughters have the command of their own bodies and may dispose of their persons as they think fit, they being at liberty to do what they please. In short, the children of these common women are accounted a lawful issue, and entitled to all the privileges of other children, abating for[29] one thing, namely, that the noted warriors or counselors will not accept them for their sons in law, and that they cannot enter into alliance with certain ancient families, though at the same time these families are not possessed of any peculiar right or pre-eminence. The Jesuits do their utmost to prevent the lewd practices of these whores by preaching to their parents that their indulgence is very disagreeable to the Great Spirit, that they must answer before God for not confining their children to the measures of continence and chastity, and that a fire is kindled in the other world to torment them for ever unless they take more care to correct vice.

[27]Weaken.
[28]Buttocks.

[29]Except for.

To such remonstrances the men reply, "That's admirable," and the women usually tell the good fathers[30] in a deriding way that if their threats be well grounded, the mountains of the other world must consist of the ashes of souls.

1703

William Byrd II 1674–1744

William Byrd II is a key literary figure from the first half of the eighteenth century in British America. Engaging in the many genres then available to the educated cosmopolitan elite, Byrd wrote treatises dealing with medicine, science, and agriculture, as well as political briefs, diaries, character sketches, letters, and travel narratives. Especially in his *History of the Dividing Line,* Byrd developed a distinctive style that posed satire against disinterested observation. Such a style aptly recorded the contradictory life of a genteel colonial who understood that, for English readers, the New World made him both a suspect stranger *and* a valuable witness.

Byrd's father, William Byrd I (1652–1704), emigrated from England in the late 1660s to inherit from his uncle a growing fur trade and some 3,000 acres of land on the Virginia frontier; he became very knowledgeable about the geography of the interior and a valuable negotiator with local Indian tribes. He married Mary Horsmanden Filmer, a member of the Cavalier elite who had fled Cromwell's England. The elder Byrd participated with Nathaniel Bacon in a rebellion against the royally appointed Governor William Berkeley, but ultimately Byrd ended up on Berkeley's side. He was elected to the House of Burgesses the next year and was appointed a member of the governor's Council in 1682.

When William Byrd II was seven, he was sent across the ocean to the Felsted school in Essex to receive a genteel education. Never close with his wards there, he only received brief letters from his father with words such as "improve your time, and bee carefull to serve God as you ought, without which you cannot expect to doe well here or hereafter." At Felsted, Byrd assiduously collected the various attributes of an English gentleman; he read manuals such as Henry Peacham's *Compleat Gentleman* and learned Greek, Latin, Hebrew, French, and Italian. From the time he traveled to England, Byrd saw his father only twice more before his father's death. Evidently he felt haunted enough by this distant but formidable paternal presence that years later, in the winter of 1710, Byrd recorded in his diary, "I had my father's grave opened to see him but he was so wasted there was not anything to be distinguished."

In 1690, Byrd was sent to Rotterdam to study commerce, but upon his return to England he decided instead to pursue law at the Middle Temple. In these years, frequenting court circles, spas, and coffeehouses, Byrd came to know well-placed noblemen and noblewomen, literati, and men of science. He befriended figures on both sides of the great intellectual contest between the "Moderns," who believed that, especially in matters of science, modern learning superseded ancient knowledge, and the "Ancients," who believed in the abiding superiority of the classical world. Byrd was elected to the central institution of the "New Science," the Royal Society of London, brought to Society meetings live American specimens such as the rattlesnake and the female opossum, and published in its *Transactions* "An Account of

[30]The Jesuits.

a Negro-Boy that is dappel'd in several Places of his Body with White Spots."

Byrd returned to Virginia to inherit his father's estate and his lucrative post as receiver general in 1705. He married Lucy Parke, the daughter of a colonial governor who was soon after assassinated in Antigua. It was at this time that Byrd began keeping a diary that he would write in, confess to, and regulate himself by almost every day for the next thirty-five years. In this secret diary, in shorthand cipher, he would record his daily regimen of rising early, reading Greek or Hebrew, dancing (moving through a series of morally inflected postures), praying, eating, speaking with "his people" (servants and slaves), and walking in his garden with his wife; in the same terse form, he recorded his nightmares, sexual transgressions, acts of corporal punishment, and the death of his infant son.

On a trip to England with Byrd in 1716, Lucy died of smallpox, leaving him two little girls in Virginia. Byrd spent most of the following decade in London arguing Virginia's political and economic causes before the British government (and rebelling against his colony's lieutenant governor much as his father had done decades before), amassing the largest book collection in the colonies, and courting English heiresses, who rejected him largely because of his colonial status. He finally married Maria Taylor, a woman he was "completely crazy about" because she "spoke Greek, the tongue of the Muses." During this time, he wrote flattering verse sketches that were printed in *Tunbrigalia* in 1719, displayed his bookish knowledge of the healing arts in *A Discourse concerning the Plague* (1721), and mocked women's superstitions in *The Female Creed* (1725). These years represented an important stage in his maturation: after repeated political and romantic failures, Byrd came to accept his colonial situation, seeing life on a Virginia plantation surrounded by "his people" less as a curse and more as a dignified responsibility in the mode of the Old Testament patriarchs. After 1726, as he acquired thousands of acres of land to the west and tried to encourage a colony of Swiss immigrants to settle there, rebuilt his father's estate, entertained and wrote to important naturalists, and founded the future cities of Richmond and Petersburg, Byrd came to understand the unique opportunities of his American environment.

In the spring of 1728, Byrd was appointed to lead the Virginia members of a commission to survey and settle the boundary line between Virginia and North Carolina. To encourage individuals to buy property inland and thus expand both colonies westward, the two governments needed to clarify which should govern and tax the disputed land along the border. As Virginia was the first English colony in North America and a royal colony, whereas the later-established North Carolina was owned by a group of Lords Proprietors, Virginians felt great interest in demarcating their territory—not only geographically but socially—from a colony they believed to be inferior. Byrd kept a longhand journal throughout the trip for official purposes. Over the next few years he transformed it first into the *Secret History of the Line* and finally into *The History of the Dividing Line.* The *Secret History,* dealing with unseemly acts of sexual aggression and male squabbling, was intended for a small audience of Byrd's intimates. The *History,* "improved" by learned citations to classical sources, to other travel narratives, and to natural histories, was intended for a larger public. The unresolved play in these texts between two versions of American reality offers us, on the one hand, a panegyric devoted to civilization's westward progress and, on the other, a satire of its wilderness degeneration. Such a bifurcated narrative line is a dizzying and fascinating one to tread.

Susan Scott Parrish
University of Michigan

PRIMARY WORKS

The Prose Works of William Byrd, ed. Louis B. Wright, 1966; *The Secret Diary of William Byrd of Westover, 1709–1712,* ed. Louis B. Wright and Marion Tinling, 1941; *William Byrd of Virginia: The London Diary (1717–1721) and Other Writings,* ed. Louis B. Wright and Marion Tinling, 1958; *Another Secret Diary of William Byrd of Westover, 1739–1741,* ed. Maude Woodfin, trans. Marion Tinling, 1942; *The Correspondence of the Three William Byrds,* ed. Marion Tinling, 1977.

from The History of the Dividing Line betwixt Virginia and North Carolina *and* The Secret History of the Line[1]

Before I enter upon the Journal of the Line between Virginia and North Carolina, it will be necessary to clear the way to it, by shewing how the other British Colonies on the Main have, one after the other, been carved out of Virginia, by Grants from his Majesty's Royal Predecessors. All that part of the Northern American Continent now under the Dominion of the King of Great Britain, and Stretching quite as far as the Cape of Florida, went *at first under the General Name of Virginia.*

The only Distinction, in those early Days, was, that all the Coast to the Southward of Chesapeake Bay was called South Virginia, and all to the Northward of it, North Virginia.

The first Settlement of this fine Country was owing to that great Ornament of the British Nation, Sir Walter Raleigh, who obtained a Grant thereof from Queen Elizabeth of ever-glorious Memory, by Letters Patent, dated March the 25th, 1584. . . .

As it happen'd some Ages before to be the fashion to Santer to the Holy Land,[2] and go upon other Quixot Adventures, so it was now grown the Humour to take a Trip to America. The Spaniards had lately discovered Rich Mines in their Part of the West Indies, which made their Maritime Neighbours eager to do so too. This Modish Frenzy being still more Inflam'd by the Charming Account given of Virginia, by the first Adventurers, made many fond of removeing to such a Paradise.

Happy was he, and still happier She, that cou'd get themselves transported, fondly expecting their Coarsest Utensils, in that happy place, would be of Massy Silver.

This made it easy for the Company to procure as many Volunteers as they wanted for their new Colony. . . .

These Wretches were set Ashoar not far from Roanoak Inlet, but by some fatal disagreement, or Laziness, were either Starved or cut to Pieces by the Indians.

Several repeated Misadventures of this kind did, for some time, allay the Itch of Sailing to this New World; but the Distemper broke out again about the Year 1606.

[1]The texts of *The History of the Dividing Line betwixt Virginia and North Carolina* and *The Secret History* are taken from *The Prose Works of William Byrd,* ed. Louis B. Wright (Cambridge, 1966). For the convenience of the reader, we are providing, in sequence, the texts of both the official history and the secret history. The secret history appears in italics.

[2]The Crusades of the Middle Ages.

Then it happened that the Earl of Southampton and several other Persons, eminent for their Quality and Estates, were invited into the Company, who apply'd themselves once more to People the then almost abandon'd Colony. For this purpose they embarkt about an Hundred men, most of them Reprobates of good Familys, and related to some of the company, who were men of Quality and Fortune.

The Ships that carried them made a Shift to find a more direct way to Virginia, and ventured thro the Capes into the Bay of Chesapeak. The same Night they came to an Anchor at the Mouth of Powatan, the same as James River, where they built a Small Fort at a Place call'd Point Comfort.

This Settlement stood its ground from that time forward in spite of all the Blunders and Disagreement of the first Adventurers, and the many Calamitys that befel the Colony afterwards.

The six gentlemen who were first named of the company by the Crown, and who were empowered to choose an annual President from among themselves, were always engaged in Factions and Quarrels, while the rest detested Work more than Famine. At this rate the Colony must have come to nothing, had it not been for the vigilance and Bravery of Capt. Smith, who struck a Terrour into all the Indians round about. This Gentleman took some pains to perswade the men to plant Indian corn, but they look upon all Labor as a Curse. They chose rather to depend upon the Musty Provisions that were sent from England: and when they fail'd they were forct to take more pains to Seek for Wild Fruits in the Woods, than they would have taken in tilling the Ground. Besides, this Exposed them to be knockt on the head by the Indians, and gave them Fluxes into the Bargain, which thind the Plantation very much. To Supply this mortality, they were reinforct the year following with a greater number of People, amongst which were fewer Gentlemen and more Labourers, who, however, took care not to kill themselves with Work.

These found the First Adventurers in a very starving condition, but relieved their wants with the fresh Supply they brought with them. From Kiquotan they extended themselves as far as James-Town, where like true Englishmen, they built a Church that cost no more than Fifty Pounds, and a Tavern that cost Five hundred.

They had now made peace with the Indians, but there was one thing wanting to make that peace lasting. The Natives could, by no means, perswade themselves that the English were heartily their Friends, so long as they disdained to intermarry with them. And, in earnest, had the English consulted their own Security and the good of the Colony—Had they intended either to Civilize or Convert these Gentiles, they would have brought their Stomachs to embrace this prudent Alliance.

The Indians are generally tall and well-proportion'd, which may make full Amends for the Darkness of their Complexions. Add to this, that they are healthy & Strong, with Constitutions untainted by Lewdness, and not enfeebled by Luxury. Besides, Morals and all considered, I cant think the Indians were much greater Heathens than the first Adventurers, who, had they been good Christians, would have had the Charity to take this only method of converting the Natives to Christianity. For, after all that can be said, a sprightly Lover is the most prevailing Missionary that can be sent amongst these, or any other Infidels.

Besides, the poor Indians would have had less reason to Complain that the English took away their Land, if they had received it by way of Portion with their Daughters. Had such Affinities been contracted in the Beginning, how much Bloodshed had been prevented, and how populous would the Country have been, and, consequently, how considerable? Nor wou'd the Shade of the Skin have been any reproach at this day; for if a Moor may be washt white in 3 Generations, Surely an Indian might have been blancht in two. . . .

About the same time New England was pared off from Virginia by Letters Patent, bearing date April the 10th, 1608. Several Gentlemen of the Town and Neighbourhood of Plymouth obtain'd this Grant, with the Ld Chief Justice Popham at their Head.

Their Bounds were Specified to Extend from 38 to 45 Degrees of Northern Latitude, with a Breadth of one Hundred Miles from the Sea Shore. The first 14 Years, this Company encounter'd many Difficulties, and lost many men, tho' far from being discouraged, they sent over Numerous Recruits of Presbyterians, every year, who for all that, had much ado to stand their Ground, with all their Fighting and Praying.

But about the year 1620, a Large Swarm of Dissenters fled thither from the Severities of their Stepmother, the Church. These Saints conceiving the same Aversion to the Copper Complexion of the Natives, with that of the first Adventurers to Virginia, would, on no Terms, contract Alliances with them, afraid perhaps, like the Jews of Old, lest they might be drawn into Idolatry by those Strange Women.

Whatever disgusted them I cant say, but this false delicacy creating in the Indians a Jealousy that the English were ill affected towards them, was the Cause that many of them were cut off, and the rest Exposed to various Distresses.

This Reinforcement was landed not far from Cape Codd, where, for their greater Security they built a Fort, and near it a Small Town, which in Honour of the Proprietors, was call'd New Plymouth. But they Still had many discouragements to Struggle with, tho' by being well Supported from Home, they by Degrees Triumph't over them all.

Their Bretheren, after this, flockt over so fast, that in a few Years they extended the Settlement one hundred Miles along the Coast, including Rhode Island and Martha's Vineyard.

Thus the Colony throve apace, and was throng'd with large Detachments of Independents and Presbyterians, who thought themselves persecuted at home.

Tho' these People may be ridiculd for some Pharisaical Particularitys in their Worship and Behaviour, yet they were very useful Subjects, as being Frugal and Industrious, giving no Scandal or bad Example, at least by any Open and Public Vices. By which excellent Qualities they had much the Advantage of the Southern Colony, who thought their being Members of the Establish't Church sufficient to Sanctifie very loose and Profligate Morals. For this Reason New England improved much faster than Virginia, and in Seven or Eight Years New Plimouth, like Switzerland, seemed too Narrow a Territory for its Inhabitants. . . .

Both the French and the Spaniards had, in the Name of their Respective Monarchs, long ago taken Possession of that Part of the Northern Continent that now goes by the Name of Carolina; but finding it Produced neither Gold nor Silver, as they greedily expected, and meeting such returns from the Indians as their own Cruelty and Treachery deserved, they totally abandond it. In this deserted Condition that country lay for the Space of 90 Years, till King Charles the 2d, finding it a DERELICT, granted it away to the Earl of Clarendon and others, by His Royal Charter, dated March the 24th, 1663. The Boundary of that Grant towards Virginia was a due West Line from Luck-Island, (the same as Colleton Island), lying in 36 degrees N. Latitude, quite to the South Sea.

But afterwards Sir William Berkeley, who was one of the Grantees and at that time Governour of Virginia, finding a Territory of 31 Miles in Breadth between the Inhabited Part of Virginia and the above-mentioned Boundary of Carolina, advisd the Lord Clarendon of it. And His Lordp had Interest enough with the King to obtain a Second Patent to include it, dated June the 30th, 1665.

In the mean time, the People on the Frontiers Entered for Land, & took out Patents by Guess, either from the King or the Lords Proprietors. But the Crown was like to be the loser by this Incertainty, because the Terms both of taking up and seating Land were easier much in Carolina. The Yearly Taxes to the Public were likewise there less burdensom, which laid Virginia under a Plain disadvantage.

This Consideration put that Government upon entering into Measures with North Carolina, to terminate the Dispute, and settle a Certain Boundary between the two colonies.

The Governor and Council of Virginia in the year 1727 received an express order from His Majesty to appoint commissioners who, in conjunction with others to be named by the government of North Carolina, should run the line betwixt the two colonies. The rule these gentlemen were directed to go by was a paper of proposals formerly agreed on between the two governors, at that time Spotswood and Eden.[3] *It would be a hard thing to say of so wise a man as Mr. Spotswood thought himself that he was overreached, but it has appeared upon trial that Mr. Eden was much better informed how the land lay than he. However, since the King was pleased to agree to these unequal proposals, the government of Virginia was too dutiful to dispute them. They therefore appointed Steddy*[4] *and Merryman commissioners on the part of Virginia to execute that order and Astrolabe*[5] *and Capricorn to be the surveyors. But Merryman dying, Firebrand and Meanwell*[6] *made interest to fill his place. Most of the Council inclined to favor the last, because he had offered his services before he knew that any pay would belong to the place. But Burly, one of the honorable board, perceiving his friend Firebrand would lose it if it came to the vote, proposed the expedient of sending three commissioners upon so difficult and hazardous an expedition. To this a majority agreed, being unwilling to be thought too frugal of the public money. Accordingly, they were both joined with Steddy in this commission. When this was over, Steddy proposed that a chaplain might be allowed to attend the commissioners, by reason they should have a number of men with them sufficient for a small congregation and were to pass through an ungodly country where they should find neither church nor minister; that, besides, it would be an act of great charity to give the gentiles of that part of the world an opportunity to christen both them and their children. This being unanimously consented to, Dr. Humdrum*[7] *was named upon Steddy's recommendation.*

Of all these proceedings notice was dispatched to Sir Richard Everard, Governor of North Carolina, desiring him to name commissioners on the part of that province to meet those of Virginia the spring following. In consequence whereof that government named

[3]Colonel Alexander Spotswood, Lieutenant-Governor of Virginia, and Sir Charles Eden, Governor of North Carolina.

[4]Byrd's name for himself.

[5]William Mayo.

[6]Richard Fitz-William, Surveyor-General of Customs for the Southern Colonies, and William Dandridge.

[7]The Reverend Peter Fountain.

Jumble,[8] *Shoebrush,*[9] *Plausible,*[10] *and Puzzlecause, being the flower and cream of the Council of that province. The next step necessary to be taken was for the commissioners on both sides to agree upon a day of meeting at Currituck Inlet in order to proceed on this business, and the fifth of March was thought a proper time, because then Mercury and the moon were to be in conjunction. . . .*

[March 6] . . . After both Commissions were considered, the first Question was, where the Dividing Line was to begin. This begat a Warm debate; the Virginia Commissioners contending, with a great deal of Reason, to begin at the End of the Spitt of Sand, which was undoubtedly the North Shore of Currituck Inlet. But those of Carolina insisted Strenuously, that the Point of High Land ought rather to be the Place of Beginning, because that was fixt and certain, whereas the Spitt of Sand was ever Shifting, and did actually run out farther now than formerly. The Contest lasted some Hours, with great Vehemence, neither Party receding from their Opinion that Night. But next Morning, Mr. M[oseley] to convince us he was not that Obstinate Person he had been represented, yielded to our Reasons, and found Means to bring over his Collegues.

Here we began already to reap the Benefit of those Peremptory Words in our Commission, which in truth added some Weight to our Reasons. Nevertheless, because positive proof was made by the Oaths of two Credible Witnesses, that the Spitt of Sand had advanced 200 Yards towards the Inlet since the Controversy first began, we were willing for Peace-sake to make them that allowance. Accordingly we fixed our Beginning about that Distance North of the Inlet, and there Ordered a Cedar-Post to be driven deep into the Sand for our beginning. While we continued here, we were told that on the South Shore, not far from the Inlet, dwelt a Marooner, that Modestly call'd himself a Hermit, tho' he forfeited that Name by Suffering a wanton Female to cohabit with Him.

His Habitation was a Bower, cover'd with Bark after the Indian Fashion, which in that mild Situation protected him pretty well from the Weather. Like the Ravens, he neither plow'd nor sow'd, but Subsisted chiefly upon Oysters, which his Handmaid made a Shift to gather from the Adjacent Rocks. Sometimes, too, for Change of Dyet, be sent her to drive up the Neighbour's Cows, to moisten their Mouths with a little Milk. But as for raiment, he depended mostly upon his Length of Beard, and She upon her Length of Hair, part of which she brought decently forward, and the rest dangled behind quite down to her Rump, like one of Herodotus's East Indian Pigmies.[11]

Thus did these Wretches live in a dirty State of Nature, and were mere Adamites, Innocence only excepted.

[March] 8 . . . [W]e rowed up an arm of the sound called the Back Bay till we came to the head of it. There we were stopped by a miry pocosin[12] full half a mile in breadth, through which we were obliged to daggle on foot, plunging now and then,

[8]Chief Justice Christophe Gale.

[9]John Lovick.

[10]William Little.

[11]Herodotus, a Greek living under Persian rule in the fifth century B.C., wrote a history of the Greco-Persian war, the first great narrative history of the ancient world. Byrd, writing a history of the New World, must have been drawing a parallel.

[12]A low, flat, swampy region.

though we picked our way, up to the knees in mud. At the end of this charming walk we gained the terra firma of Princess Anne County. In that dirty condition we were afterwards obliged to foot it two miles as far as John Heath's plantation, where we expected to meet the surveyors and the men who waited upon them. . . .

All the people in the neighborhood flocked to John Heath's to behold such rarities as they fancied us to be. The men left their beloved chimney corners, the good women their spinning wheels, and some, of more curiosity than ordinary, rose out of their sick beds to come and stare at us. They looked upon us as a troop of knights-errant who were running this great risk of our lives, as they imagined, for the public weal: and some of the gravest of them questioned much whether we were not all criminals condemned to this dirty work for offenses against the state.

8. . . . Amongst other spectators came two girls to see us, one of which was very handsome and the other very willing. However, we only saluted them, and if we committed any sin at all, it was only in our hearts.

9. In the morning we walked with the surveyors to the line, which cut through Eyland's plantation, and came to the banks of North River. Hither the girls abovementioned attended us, but an old woman came along with them for the security of their virtue. . . .

10. The Sabbath happened very opportunely, to give some ease to our jaded people, who rested religiously from every work but that of cooking the kettle. We observed very few cornfields in our walks and those very small, which seemed the stranger to us because we could see no other tokens of husbandry or improvement. But upon further inquiry we were given to understand people only made corn for themselves and not for their stocks, which know very well how to get their own living. Both cattle and hogs ramble into the neighboring marshes and swamps, where they maintain themselves the whole winter long and are not fetched home till the spring. Thus these indolent wretches during one half of the year lose the advantage of the milk of their cattle, as well as their dung, and many of the poor creatures perish in the mire, into the bargain, by this ill management. Some who pique themselves more upon industry than their neighbors will now and then, in compliment to their cattle, cut down a tree whose limbs are loaded with the moss aforementioned. The trouble would be too great to climb the tree in order to gather this provender, but the shortest way (which in this country is always counted the best) is to fell it, just like the lazy Indians, who do the same by such trees as bear fruit and so make one harvest for all. By this bad husbandry milk is so scarce in the winter season that were a big-bellied woman to long for it she would tax her longing. And, in truth, I believe this is often the case, and at the same time a very good reason why so many people in this province are marked with a custard complexion.

The only business here is raising of hogs, which is managed with the least trouble and affords the diet they are most fond of. The truth of it is, the inhabitants of North Carolina devour so much swine's flesh that it fills them full of gross humors.[13] For want, too, of a constant supply of salt, they are commonly obliged to eat it fresh, and that begets the highest taint of scurvy. Thus, whenever a severe cold happens to

[13] According to the medical theory of the time, these were the bodily fluids whose composition controlled health and character.

constitutions thus vitiated, 'tis apt to improve into the yaws, called there very justly the country distemper. This has all the symptoms of the pox, with this aggravation, that no preparation of mercury will touch it. First it seizes the throat, next the palate, and lastly shows its spite to the poor nose, of which 'tis apt in a small time treacherously to undermine the foundation. This calamity is so common and familiar here that it ceases to be a scandal, and in the disputes that happen about beauty the noses have in some companies much ado to carry it. Nay, tis said that once, after three good pork years, a motion had like to have been made in the House of Burgesses, that a man with a nose should be incapable of holding any place of profit in the province; which extraordinary motion could never have been intended without some hopes of a majority.

Thus, considering the foul and pernicious effects of eating swine's flesh in a hot country, it was wisely forbid and made an abomination to the Jews, who lived much in the same latitude with Carolina.

11. . . . We had encamped so early that we found time in the evening to walk near half a mile into the woods. There we came upon a family of mulattoes that called themselves free, though by the shyness of the master of the house, who took care to keep least in sight, their freedom seemed a little doubtful. It is certain many slaves shelter themselves in this obscure part of the world, nor will any of their righteous neighbors discover them. On the contrary, they find their account in settling such fugitives on some out-of-the way corner of their land to raise stocks for a mean and inconsiderable share, well knowing their condition makes it necessary for them to submit to any terms. Nor were these worthy borderers content to shelter runaway slaves, but debtors and criminals have often met with the like indulgence. But if the government of North Carolina have encouraged this unneighborly policy in order to increase their people, it is no more than what ancient Rome did before them, which was made a city of refuge for all debtors and fugitives and from that wretched beginning grew up in time to be mistress of great part of the world. And, considering how Fortune delights in bringing great things out of small, who knows but Carolina may, one time or other, come to be the seat of some other great empire?

11. . . . In the meanwhile, Shoebrush and I took a walk into the woods and called at a cottage where a dark angel surprised us with her charms. Her complexion was a deep copper, so that her fine shape and regular features made her appear like a statue en bronze *done by a masterly hand. Shoebrush was smitten at the first glance and examined all her neat proportions with a critical exactness. She struggled just enough to make her admirer more eager, so that if I had not been there, he would have been in danger of carrying his joke a little too far.*

12. . . . I retired early to our camp at some distance from the house, while my colleagues tarried withindoors and refreshed themselves with a cheerful bowl. In the gaiety of their hearts, they invited a tallow-faced wench that had sprained her wrist to drink with them, and when they had raised her in good humor they examined all her hidden charms and played a great many gay pranks. While Firebrand, who had the most curiosity, was ranging over her sweet person, he picked off several scaps as big as nipples, the consequence of eating too much pork. The poor damsel was disabled from making any resistance by the lameness of her hand; all she could do was to sit still and make the fashionable exclamation of the country, "Flesh alive and tear it!" and, by what I can understand, she never spake so properly in her life.

One of the representatives of North Carolina made a midnight visit to our camp, and his curiosity was so very clamorous that it waked me, for which I wished his nose as flat as any of his porcivorous countrymen.

14. *This Morning early the Men began to make up the Packs they were to carry on their Shoulders into the Dismal. They were victual'd for 8 Days, which was judg'd sufficient for the Service. Those Provisions with the Blankets & other Necessaries loaded the Men with a Burthen of 50 or 60^{lb} for Each. Orion*[14] *helpt most of all to make these Loads so heavy, by taking his Bed, and several changes of Raiment, not forgeting a Suit for Sundays along with him. This was a little unmercifull, which with his peevish Temper made him no Favorite. We fixt them out about ten in the Morning, & then Meanwell, Puzzlecause, & I went along with them, resolving to enter them fairly into this dreadful Swamp, which no body before ever had either the Courage or Curiosity to pass.*[15] *But Firebrand & Shoebrush chose rather to toast their Noses over a good Fire, & Spare their dear Persons. After a March of 2 Miles thro' very bad way, the Men sweating under their Burthens, we arriv'd at the Edge of the Dismal, where the Surveyors had left off the Night before. Here Steddy thought proper to encourage the Men by a short harangue to this effect. "Gentlemen, we are at last arriv'd at this dreadfull place, which til now has been thought unpassable. Tho' I make no doubt but you will convince every Body, that there is no difficulty which may not be conquer'd by Spirit & constancy. You have hitherto behaved with so much Vigour, that the most I can desire of you, is to persevere unto the End; I protest to You the only reason we don't Share in Your Fatigue, is, the fear of adding to Your Burthens, (which are but too heavy already,) while we are Sure we can add nothing to your Resolution. I shall say no more, but only pray the Almighty to prosper your Undertaking, & grant we may meet on the other Side in perfect Health & Safety." The Men took this Speech very kindly, and answer'd it in the most cheerful manner, with 3 Huzzas. Immediately we enter'd the Dismal, 2 Men clearing the way before the Surveyors, to enable them to take their Sight. The Reeds which grew about 12 feet high, were so thick, & so interlaced with Bamboe-Briars, that our Pioneers were forc't to open a Passage. The Ground, if I may properly call it so, was so Spungy, that the Prints of our Feet were instantly fill'd with Water. Amongst the Reeds here & there stood a white Cedar, commonly mistaken for Juniper. Of this Sort was the Soil for about half a Mile together, after which we came to a piece of high land about 100 Yards in Breadth. We were above 2 Hours scuffling thro' the Reeds to this Place, where we refresh't the poor Men. Then we took leave, recommending both them & the Surveyors to Providence. We furnish'd Astrolabe with Bark & other Medicines, for any of the People, that might happen to be Sick, not forgetting 3 Kinds of Rattle-Snake Root made into Doses in case of Need. . . .*

15. . . . At the end of eighteen miles we reached Timothy Ivy's plantation, where we pitched our tent for the first time and were furnished with everything the place afforded. We perceived the happy effects of industry in this family, in which every one looked tidy and clean and carried in their countenances the cheerful marks of plenty. We saw no drones there, which are but too common, alas, in that part of the world. Though, in truth, the distemper of laziness seizes the men oftener much

[14]Alexander Irvine, professor of mathematics at William and Mary College.

[15]The Great Dismal Swamp, at the time forty miles long and covering an area of about 2,000 square miles, was named by Byrd.

than the women. These last spin, weave, and knit, all with their own hands, while their husbands, depending on the bounty of the climate, are slothful in everything but getting of children, and in that only instance make themselves useful members of an infant colony.

15. . . . Timothy Ives . . . supplied us with everything that was necessary. He had a tall, straight daughter of a yielding, sandy complexion, who having the curiosity to see the tent, Puzzlecause gallanted her thither, and might have made her free of it had not we come seasonably to save the damsel's chastity. Here both our cookery and bedding were more cleanly than ordinary. The parson lay with Puzzlecause in the tent to keep him honest or, peradventure, to partake of his diversion if he should be otherwise.

16. . . . We passed by no less than two Quaker meetinghouses, one of which had an awkward ornament on the west end of it that seemed to ape a steeple. I must own I expected no such piece of foppery from a sect of so much outside simplicity. That persuasion prevails much in the lower end of Nansemond County, for want of ministers to pilot the people a decenter way to Heaven. The ill reputation of tobacco planted in those lower parishes makes the clergy unwilling to accept of them, unless it be such whose abilities are as mean as their pay.[16] Thus, whether the churches be quite void or but indifferently filled, the Quakers will have an opportunity of gaining proselytes. 'Tis a wonder no popish[17] missionaries are sent from Maryland to labor in this neglected vineyard, who we know have zeal enough to traverse sea and land on the meritorious errand of making converts. Nor is it less strange that some wolf in sheep's clothing arrives not from New England to lead astray a flock that has no shepherd. People uninstructed in any religion are ready to embrace the first that offers. 'Tis natural for helpless man to adore his Maker in some form or other, and were there any exception to this rule, I should suspect it to be among the Hottentots of the Cape of Good Hope and of North Carolina.

17. . . . One thing may be said for the inhabitants of that province, that they are not troubled with any religious fumes and have the least superstition of any people living. They do not know Sunday from any other day, any more than Robinson Crusoe did, which would give them a great advantage were they given to be industrious. But they keep so many Sabbaths every week that their disregard of the seventh day has no manner of cruelty in it, either to servants or cattle.

18. . . . We made the best of our way to Mr. Thomas Speight's, who appeared to be a grandee of North Carolina. There we arrived about four, though the distance could not be less than twenty-five miles. Upon our arrival our poor landlord made a shift to crawl out upon his crutches, having the gout in both his knees. He bid us welcome, and a great bustle was made in the family about our entertainment. We saw two truss[18] *damsels stump about very industriously, that were handsome enough upon a march.*

19. . . . My landlord's daughter, Rachel, offered her service to wash my linen and regaled me with a mess of hominy, tossed up with rank butter and glyster sugar. This I was forced to eat to show that nothing from so fair a hand could be disagreeable. She was a smart lass, and, when I desired the parson to make a memorandum of his christenings that we might keep an account of the good we did, she asked me very pertly who

[16]Clergy were often paid in tobacco.
[17]Catholic.
[18]Compact, shapely.

was to keep an account of the evil? I told her she should be my secretary for that if she would go along with me.

25. . . . Our landlord had not the good fortune to please Firebrand with our dinner, but, surely, when people do their best, a reasonable man would be satisfied. But he endeavored to mend his entertainment by making hot love to honest Ruth, who would by no means be charmed either with his persuasion or his person. While the master was employed in making love to one sister, the man made his passion known to the other; only he was more boisterous and employed force when he could not succeed by fair means. Though one of the men rescued the poor girl from this violent lover but was so much his friend as to keep the shameful secret from those whose duty it would have been to punish such violations of hospitality. . . .

[25] . . . Surely there is no place in the world where the inhabitants live with less labor than in North Carolina. It approaches nearer to the description of Lubberland[19] than any other, by the great felicity of the climate, the easiness of raising provisions, and the slothfulness of the people. Indian corn is of so great increase that a little pains will subsist a very large family with bread, and then they may have meat without any pains at all, by the help of the low grounds and the great variety of mast that grows on the high land. The men, for their parts, just like the Indians, impose all the work upon the poor women. They make their wives rise out of their beds early in the morning, at the same time that they lie and snore till the sun has risen one-third of his course and dispersed all the unwholesome damps. Then, after stretching and yawning for half an hour, they light their pipes, and, under the protection of a cloud of smoke, venture out into the open air; though if it happen to be never so little cold they quickly return shivering into the chimney corner. When the weather is mild, they stand leaning with both their arms upon the cornfield fence and gravely consider whether they had best go and take a small heat at the hoe but generally find reasons to put it off till another time. Thus they loiter away their lives, like Solomon's sluggard,[20] with their arms across, and at the winding up of the year scarcely have bread to eat. To speak the truth, 'tis a thorough aversion to labor that makes people file off to North Carolina, where plenty and a warm sun confirm them in their disposition to laziness for their whole lives. . . .

27. . . . Within three or four miles of Edenton[21] the soil appears to be a little more fertile, though it is much cut with slashes, which seem all to have a tendency toward the Dismal.[22] This town is situate on the north side of Albemarle Sound, which is there about five miles over. A dirty slash runs all along the back of it, which in the summer is a foul annoyance and furnishes abundance of that Carolina plague, mosquitoes. There may be forty or fifty houses, most of them small and built without expense. A citizen here is counted extravagant if he has ambition enough to aspire to a brick chimney. Justice herself is but indifferently lodged, the courthouse having much of the air of a common tobacco house. I believe this is the only metropolis in the Christian or Mahometan world where there is neither church, chapel, mosque, synagogue, or any other place of public worship of any sect or religion

[19]Imaginary land of plenty without labor.

[20]Proverbs 6:6–11.

[21]Then the unofficial capital of North Carolina, an important commercial center named after Governor Eden.

[22]Small swampy areas; The Great Dismal Swamp.

whatsoever. What little devotion there may happen to be is much more private than their vices. The people seem easy without a minister as long as they are exempted from paying him. Sometimes the Society for Propagating the Gospel has had the charity to send over missionaries to this country; but, unfortunately, the priest has been too lewd for the people, or, which oftener happens, they too lewd for the priest. For these reasons these reverend gentlemen have always left their flocks as arrant heathen as they found them. Thus much, however, may be said for the inhabitants of Edenton, that not a soul has the least taint of hypocrisy or superstition, acting very frankly and aboveboard in all their exercises.

Provisions here are extremely cheap and extremely good, so that people may live plentifully at a trifling expense. Nothing is dear but law, physic, and strong drink, which are all bad in their kind, and the last they get with so much difficulty that they are never guilty of the sin of suffering it to sour upon their hands. Their vanity generally lies not so much in having a handsome dining room as a handsome house of office:[23] in this kind of structure they are really extravagant. They are rarely guilty of flattering or making any court to their governors but treat them with all the excesses of freedom and familiarity. They are of opinion their rulers would be apt to grow insolent if they grew rich, and for that reason take care to keep them poorer and more dependent, if possible, than the saints in New England used to do their governors. They have very little coin, so they are forced to carry on their home traffic with paper money. This is the only cash that will tarry in the country, and for that reason the discount goes on increasing between that and real money and will do so to the end of the chapter. . . .

April 1. . . . Wherever we passed we constantly found the borderers laid it to heart if their land was taken into Virginia; they chose much rather to belong to Carolina, where they pay no tribute, either to God or to Caesar. Another reason was that the government there is so loose and the laws are so feebly executed that, like those in the neighborhood of Sidon formerly, everyone does just what seems good in his own eyes.[24] If the Governor's hands have been weak in that province, under the authority of the Lords Proprietors, much weaker, then, were the hands of the magistrate, who, though he might have had virtue enough to endeavor to punish offenders, which very rarely happened, yet that virtue had been quite impotent for want of ability to put it in execution. Besides, there might have been some danger, perhaps, in venturing to be so rigorous, for fear of undergoing the fate of an honest justice in Currituck precinct. This bold magistrate, it seems, taking upon him to order a fellow to the stocks for being disorderly in his drink, was for his intemperate zeal carried thither himself and narrowly escaped being whipped by the rabble into the bargain.

5. Our surveyors made an elegant plat of our line from Currituck Inlet to the place where they left off, containing the distance of seventy-three miles and thirteen poles.[25] *Of this exact copies were made and, being carefully examined, were both signed by the commissioners of each colony. . . . The poor chaplain was the common butt at which all our company aimed their profane wit and gave him the title of "Dean Pip," because instead of a pricked line he had been so maidenly as to call it a pipped line. I left the com-*

[23]Outbuilding.
[24]Judges 21:25; Matthew 11:21–22.
[25]A pole is a unit of measure equal to a rod, 16½ feet.

pany in good time, taking as little pleasure in their low wit as in their low liquor, which was rum punch. . . .

7. . . . In the morning we dispatched a runner to the Nottoway town to let the Indians know we intended them a visit that evening, and our honest landlord was so kind as to be our pilot thither, being about four miles from his house. Accordingly, in the afternoon we marched in good order to the town, where the female scouts, stationed on an eminence for that purpose, had no sooner spied us but they gave notice of our approach to their fellow citizens by continual whoops and cries, which could not possibly have been more dismal at the sight of their most implacable enemies. This signal assembled all their great men, who received us in a body and conducted us into the fort.

This fort was a square piece of ground, enclosed with substantial puncheons or strong palisades about ten feet high and leaning a little outwards to make a scalade more difficult. Each side of the square might be about a hundred yards long, with loopholes at proper distances through which they may fire upon the enemy. Within this enclosure we found bark cabins sufficient to lodge all their people in case they should be obliged to retire thither. These cabins are no other but close arbors made of saplings, arched at the top and covered so well with bark as to be proof against all weather. The fire is made in the middle, according to the Hibernian[26] fashion, the smoke whereof finds no other vent but at the door and so keeps the whole family warm, at the expense both of their eyes and complexion. The Indians have no standing furniture in their cabins but hurdles[27] to repose their persons upon which they cover with mats or deerskins. We were conducted to the best apartments in the fort, which just before had been made ready for our reception and adorned with new mats that were very sweet and clean.

The young men had painted themselves in a hideous manner, not so much for ornament as terror. In that frightful equipage they entertained us with sundry war dances, wherein they endeavored to look as formidable as possible. The instrument they danced to was an Indian drum, that is, a large gourd with a skin braced taut over the mouth of it. The dancers all sang to this music, keeping exact time with their feet while their head and arms were screwed into a thousand menacing postures.

Upon this occasion the ladies had arrayed themselves in all their finery. They were wrapped in their red and blue matchcoats, thrown so negligently about them that their mahogany skins appeared in several parts, like the Lacedaemonian damsels of old. Their hair was braided with white and blue peak and hung gracefully in a large roll upon their shoulders.

This peak consists of small cylinders cut out of a conch shell, drilled through and strung like beads. It serves them both for money and jewels, the blue being of much greater value than the white for the same reason that Ethiopian mistresses in France are dearer than French, because they are more scarce. The women wear necklaces and bracelets of these precious materials when they have a mind to appear lovely. Though their complexions be a little sad-colored, yet their shapes are very straight and well proportioned. Their faces are seldom handsome, yet they have an air of innocence and bashfulness that with a little less dirt would not fail to make them desirable. Such charms might have had their full effect upon men who had been so long

[26]Irish.

[27]Wattles, frames interwoven with branches.

deprived of female conversation but that the whole winter's soil was so crusted on the skins of those dark angels that it required a very strong appetite to approach them. The bear's oil with which they anoint their persons all over makes their skins soft and at the same time protects them from every species of vermin that use to be troublesome to other uncleanly people.

We were unluckily so many that they could not well make us the compliment of bedfellows according to the Indian rules of hospitality, though a grave matron whispered one of the commissioners very civilly in the ear that if her daughter had been but one year older she should have been at his devotion. It is by no means a loss of reputation among the Indians for damsels that are single to have intrigues with the men; on the contrary, they account it an argument of superior merit to be liked by a great number of gallants. However, like the ladies that game, they are a little mercenary in their amours and seldom bestow their favors out of stark love and kindness. But after these women have once appropriated their charms by marriage, they are from thenceforth faithful to their vows and will hardly ever be tempted by an agreeable gallant or be provoked by a brutal or even by a fumbling husband to go astray.

The little work that is done among the Indians is done by the poor women, while the men are quite idle or at most employed only in the gentlemanly diversions of hunting and fishing. In this, as well as in their wars, they now use nothing but firearms, which they purchase of the English for skins. Bows and arrows are grown into disuse, except only amongst their boys. Nor is it ill policy, but on the contrary very prudent, thus to furnish the Indians with firearms, because it makes them depend entirely upon the English, not only for their trade but even for their subsistence. Besides, they were really able to do more mischief while they made use of arrows, of which they would let silently fly several in a minute with wonderful dexterity, whereas now they hardly ever discharge their firelocks more than once, which they insidiously do from behind a tree and then retire as nimbly as the Dutch horse used to do now and then formerly in Flanders.

We put the Indians to no expense but only of a little corn for our horses, for which in gratitude we cheered their hearts with what rum we had left, which they love better than they do their wives and children. Though these Indians dwell among the English and see in what plenty a little industry enables them to live, yet they choose to continue in their stupid idleness and to suffer all the inconveniences of dirt, cold, and want rather than disturb their heads with care or defile their hands with labor.

The whole number of people belonging to the Nottoway town, if you include women and children, amount to about two hundred. These are the only Indians of any consequence now remaining within the limits of Virginia. The rest are either removed or dwindled to a very inconsiderable number, either by destroying one another or else by the smallpox and other diseases. Though nothing has been so fatal to them as their ungovernable passion for rum, with which, I am sorry to say it, they have been but too liberally supplied by the English that live near them.

And here I must lament the bad success Mr. Boyle's charity has hitherto had toward converting any of these poor heathens to Christianity.[28] Many children of our

[28]Robert Boyle (1627–1691), the famous English scientist, bequeathed £4000 from his estate to go to "pious and charitable uses." £45 per annum went to William and Mary College for the education of Indians.

neighboring Indians have been brought up in the College of William and Mary. They have been taught to read and write and been carefully instructed in the principles of the Christian religion till they came to be men. Yet after they returned home, instead of civilizing and converting the rest, they have immediately relapsed into infidelity and barbarism themselves. . . .

I am sorry I can't give a better account of the state of the poor Indians with respect to Christianity, although a great deal of pains has been and still continues to be taken with them. For my part, I must be of opinion, as I hinted before, that there is but one way of converting these poor infidels and reclaiming them from barbarity, and that is charitably to intermarry with them, according to the modern policy of the Most Christian King in Canada and Louisiana. Had the English done this at the first settlement of the colony, the infidelity of the Indians had been worn out at this day with their dark complexions, and the country had swarmed with people more than it does with insects. It was certainly an unreasonable nicety that prevented their entering into so good-natured an alliance. All nations of men have the same natural dignity, and we all know that very bright talents may be lodged under a very dark skin. The principal difference between one people and another proceeds only from the different opportunities of improvement. The Indians by no means want understanding and are in their figure tall and well proportioned. Even their copper-colored complexion would admit of blanching, if not in the first, at the farthest in the second, generation. I may safely venture to say, the Indian women would have made altogether as honest wives for the first planters as the damsels they used to purchase from aboard the ships. 'Tis strange, therefore, that any good Christian should have refused a wholesome, straight bedfellow, when he might have had so fair a portion with her as the merit of saving her soul.

8. *When we were dressed, Meanwell and I visited most of the princesses at their own apartments, but the smoke was so great there, the fire being made in the middle of the cabins, that we were not able to see their charms. Prince James's princess sent my wife a fine basket of her own making, with the expectation of receiving from her some present of ten times its value. An Indian present, like those made to princes, is only a liberality put out to interest and a bribe placed to the greatest advantage.*

I could discern by some of our gentlemen's linen, discolored by the soil of the Indian ladies, that they had been convincing themselves in the point of their having no fur.[29] . . .

[October] 10. We began this day very luckily by killing a Brace of Turkeys & One Deer, so that the Plenty of our Breakfast this Morning, made amends for the Shortness of our Supper last Night. This restor'd good Humour to the Men, who had a mortal Aversion to fasting. As I lay in my Tent, I overheard one of them, call'd James Whitlock, wish that he were at home. From this I reprov'd him publickly, asking him whether it was the Danger, or the Fatigue of the Journey that disheartén'd him, wondring how he cou'd be tired so soon of the Company of so many Brave Fellows. So reasonable a Reprimand put an effectual Stop to all Complaints, and no Body after that day was ever heard so much as to wish himself in Heaven. A small distance from our Camp we crost a Creek which we call'd Cocquade Creek, because we there began to wear the Beards of Wild Turkey-Cocks in our Hats by way of Cocquade. . . .

[29]Because of the summer heat and the seasonal crops, from April to September the survey was discontinued, as Byrd explains in his letter of May 20, 1729.

October 13. . . . In the evening we examined our friend Bearskin[30] concerning the religion of his country, and he explained it to us without any of that reserve to which his nation is subject. He told us he believed there was one supreme god, who had several subaltern deities under him. And that this master god made the world a long time ago. That he told the sun, the moon, and stars their business in the beginning, which they, with good looking-after, have faithfully performed ever since. That the same power that made all things at first has taken care to keep them in the same method and motion ever since. He believed that God had formed many worlds before he formed this, but that those worlds either grew old and ruinous or were destroyed for the dishonesty of the inhabitants. That God is very just and very good, ever well pleased with those men who possess those godlike qualities. That he takes good people into his safe protection, makes them very rich, fills their bellies plentifully, preserves them from sickness and from being surprised or overcome by their enemies. But all such as tell lies and cheat those they have dealings with he never fails to punish with sickness, poverty, and hunger and, after all that, suffers them to be knocked on the head and scalped by those that fight against them.

He believed that after death both good and bad people are conducted by a strong guard into a great road, in which departed souls travel together for some time till at a certain distance this road forks into two paths, the one extremely level and the other stony and mountainous. Here the good are parted from the bad by a flash of lightning, the first being hurried away to the right, the other to the left. The right-hand road leads to a charming, warm country, where the spring is everlasting and every month is May; and as the year is always in its youth, so are the people, and particularly the women are bright as stars and never scold. That in this happy climate there are deer, turkeys, elks, and buffaloes innumerable, perpetually fat and gentle, while the trees are loaded with delicious fruit quite throughout the four seasons. That the soil brings forth corn spontaneously, without the curse of labor, and so very wholesome that none who have the happiness to eat of it are ever sick, grow old, or die. Near the entrance into this blessed land sits a venerable old man on a mat richly woven, who examines strictly all that are brought before him, and if they have behaved well, the guards are ordered to open the crystal gate and let them enter into the land of delight. The left-hand path is very rugged and uneven, leading to a dark and barren country where it is always winter. The ground is the whole year round covered with snow, and nothing is to be seen upon the trees but icicles. All the people are hungry yet have not a morsel of anything to eat except a bitter kind of potato, that gives them the dry gripes and fills their whole body with loathsome ulcers that stink and are insupportably painful. Here all the women are old and ugly, having claws like a panther with which they fly upon the men that slight their passion. For it seems these haggard old furies are intolerably fond and expect a vast deal of cherishing. They talk much and exceedingly shrill, giving exquisite pain to the drum of the ear, which in that place of the torment is so tender that every sharp note wounds it to the quick. At the end of this path sits a dreadful old woman on a monstrous toadstool, whose head is covered with rattlesnakes instead of tresses, with glaring white eyes that strike a terror unspeakable into all that behold her. This hag pro-

[30]An Indian who had joined them to help hunt game.

nounces sentence of woe upon all the miserable wretches that hold up their hands at her tribunal. After this they are delivered over to huge turkey buzzards, like harpies, that fly away with them to the place above-mentioned. Here, after they have been tormented a certain number of years according to their several degrees of guilt, they are again driven back into this world to try if they will mend their manners and merit a place the next time in the regions of bliss.

This was the substance of Bearskin's religion and was as much to the purpose as could be expected from a mere state of nature, without one glimpse of revelation or philosophy. It contained, however, the three great articles of natural religion: the belief of a god, the moral distinction betwixt good and evil, and the expectation of rewards and punishments in another world. Indeed, the Indian notion of a future happiness is a little gross and sensual, like Mahomet's Paradise. But how can it be otherwise in a people that are contented with Nature as they find her and have no other lights but what they receive from pur-blind tradition?

14. . . . This was the first time we had ever been detained a whole day in our camp by the rain and therefore had reason to bear it with the more patience.

As I sat in the tent, I overheard a learned conversation between one of our men and the Indian. He ask[ed] the Englishman what it was that made that rumbling noise when it thundered. The man told him merrily that the god of the English was firing his great guns upon the god of the Indians, which made all that roaring in the clouds, and that the lightning was only the flash of those guns. The Indian, carrying on the humor, replied very gravely he believed that might be the case indeed, and that the rain which followed upon the thunder must be occasioned by the Indian god's being so scared he could not hold his water. . . .

20. . . . And now I mention the northern Indians, it may not be improper to take notice of their implacable hatred to those of the south. Their wars are everlasting, without any peace, enmity being the only inheritance among them that descends from father to son, and either party will march a thousand miles to take their revenge upon such hereditary enemies . . . 'Tis amazing to see their sagacity in discerning the track of a human foot, even amongst dry leaves, which to our shorter sight is quite undiscoverable. If by one or more of those signs they be able to find out the camp of any southern Indians, they squat down in some thicket and keep themselves hush and snug till it is dark: then, creeping up softly, they approach near enough to observe all the motions of the enemy. And about two o'clock in the morning, when they conceive them to be in a profound sleep, for they never keep watch and ward, pour in a volley upon them, each singling out his man. The moment they have discharged their pieces they rush in with their tomahawks and make sure work of all that are disabled. Sometime, when they find the enemy asleep round their little fire, they first pelt them with little stones to wake them, and when they get up, fire in upon them, being in that posture a better mark than when prostrate on the ground.

They that are killed of the enemy or disabled, they scalp: that is, they cut the skin all round the head just below the hair, and then, clapping their feet to the poor mortal's shoulders, pull the scalp off clean and carry it home in triumph, being as proud of those trophies as the Jews used to be of the foreskins of the Philistines.[31] This way of scalping was practiced by the ancient Scythians, who used these hairy scalps as

[31]I Samuel 18:25–27.

towels at home and trappings for their horses when they went abroad. They also made cups of their enemies' skulls, in which they drank prosperity to their country and confusion to all their foes.

The prisoners they happen to take alive in these expeditions generally pass their time very scurvily. They put them to all the tortures that ingenious malice and cruelty can invent. And (what shows the baseness of the Indian temper in perfection) they never fail to treat those with greatest inhumanity that have distinguished themselves most by their bravery, and if he be a war captain, they do him the honor to roast him alive and distribute a collop to all that had a share in stealing the victory. Though who can reproach the poor Indians for this, when Homer makes his celebrated hero, Achilles, drag the body of Hector at the tail of his chariot for having fought gallantly in defense of his country? Nor was Alexander the Great, with all his famed generosity, less inhuman to the brave Tyrians, two thousand of which he ordered to be crucified in cold blood for no other fault but for having defended their city most courageously against him during a siege of seven months. And what was still more brutal, he dragged —— alive at the tail of his chariot through all the streets, for defending the town with so much vigor.

They are very cunning in finding out new ways to torment their unhappy captives, though, like those of hell, their usual method is by fire. Sometimes they barbecue them over live coals, taking them off every now and then to prolong their misery; at other times they will stick sharp pieces of lightwood all over their bodies and, setting them on fire, let them burn down into the flesh to the very bone. And when they take a stout fellow that they believe able to endure a great deal, they will tear all the flesh off his bones with red-hot pincers. While these and suchlike barbarities are practicing, the victors are so far from being touched with tenderness and compassion that they dance and sing round these wretched mortals, showing all the marks of pleasure and jollity. And if such cruelties happen to be executed in their towns, they employ their children in tormenting the prisoners, in order to extinguish in them betimes all sentiments of humanity. In the meantime, while these poor wretches are under the anguish of all this inhuman treatment, they disdain so much as to groan, sigh, or show the least sign of dismay or concern so much as in their looks: on the contrary, they make it a point of honor all the time to soften their features and look as pleased as if they were in the actual enjoyment of some delight; and if they never sang before in their lives, they will be sure to be melodious on this sad and dismal occasion. So prodigious a degree of passive valor in the Indians is the more to be wondered at, because in all articles of danger they are apt to behave like cowards. And what is still more surprising, the very women discover on such occasions as great fortitude and contempt, both of pain and death, as the gallantest of their men can do.

30. . . . I gave order that four men should set off early and clear the way, that the baggage horses might travel with less difficulty and more expedition. We followed them about eleven, and, the air being clear, we had a fair prospect of the mountains both to the north and south. That very high one to the south with the precipice at the west end we called the Lover's Cure, because one leap from thence would put a sudden period both to his passion and his pain. On the highest ledge, that stretched away to the northeast, rose a mount in the shape of a maiden's breast, which for that reason we called by that innocent name. . . .

This being His Majesty's birthday, we drank his health in a dram of excellent cherry brandy but could not afford one drop for the Queen and the royal issue. We therefore remembered them in water as clear as our wishes. And because all loyal rejoicings should be a little noisy, we fired canes instead of guns, which made a report as loud as a pistol, the heat expanding the air shut up within the joints of this vegetable and making an explosion. . . .

30. . . . In the evening we pitched our tent near Miry Creek, though an uncomfortable place to lodge in, purely for the advantage of the canes. Our hunters killed a large doe and two bears, which made all other misfortunes easy. Certainly no Tartar[32] ever loved horseflesh or Hottentot[33] guts and garbage better than woodsmen do bear. The truth of it is, it may be proper food perhaps for such as work or ride it off, but, with our chaplain's leave, who loved it much, I think it not a very proper diet for saints, because 'tis apt to make them a little too rampant. And, now, for the good of mankind and for the better peopling an infant colony, which has no want but that of inhabitants, I will venture to publish a secret of importance which our Indian disclosed to me. I asked him the reason why few or none of his countrywomen were barren. To which curious question he answered, with a broad grin upon his face, they had an infallible secret for that. Upon my being importunate to know what the secret might be, he informed me that if any Indian woman did not prove with child at a decent time after marriage, the husband, to save his reputation with the women, forthwith entered into a bear diet for six weeks, which in that time makes him so vigorous that he grows exceedingly impertinent to his poor wife, and 'tis great odds but he makes her a mother in nine months. And thus much I am able to say besides for the reputation of the bear diet, that all the married men of our company were joyful fathers within forty weeks after they got home, and most of the single men had children sworn to them within the same time, our chaplain always excepted, who, with much ado, made a shift to cast out that importunate kind of devil by dint of fasting and prayer.

31. . . . We took up our camp at Miry Creek and regaled ourselves with one buck and two bears, which our men killed in their march. Here we promoted our chaplain from the deanery of Pip to the bishopric of Beardom. For as those countries where Christians inhabit are called Christendom, so those where bears take up their residence may not improperly go by the name of Beardom. And I wish other bishops loved their flock as entirely as our Doctor loves his.

November 4. . . . John Ellis, who was one of the men we had sent to bring up the tired horses, told us a romantic adventure which he had with a bear on Saturday last. He had straggled from his company and treed a young cub. While he was new priming his gun to shoot at it, the old gentlewoman appeared, who, seeing her heir apparent in distress, came up to his relief. The bear advanced very near to her enemy, reared up on her posteriors, and put herself in guard. The man presented his piece at her, but, unfortunately, it only snapped, the powder being moist. Missing his fire in this manner, he offered to punch her with the muzzle of his gun, which Mother Bruin, being aware of, seized the weapon with her paws and by main strength wrenched it out of his hand. Being thus fairly disarmed and not knowing in the fright but the bear might turn his own cannon upon him, he thought it prudent to retire as fast as his legs could carry him. The brute, being grown more bold by the flight of her adversary, immediately pursued, and for some time it was doubtful whether fear made one run faster or fury the other. But after a fair course of forty yards, the poor man had the mishap to stumble over a stump

[32]Mongol peoples who conquered Asia and eastern Europe in the thirteenth century.

[33]People of southern Africa.

and fell down at his full length. He now would have sold his life a pennyworth, but the bear, apprehending there might be some trick in this fall, instantly halted and looked very earnestly to observe what the man could mean. In the meantime, he had with much presence of mind resolved to make the bear believe he was dead by lying breathless on the ground, upon the hopes that the bear would be too generous to kill him over again. He acted a corpse in this manner for some time, till he was raised from the dead by the barking of a dog belonging to one of his companions. Cur came up seasonably to his rescue and drove the bear from her pursuit of the man to go and take care of her innocent cub, which she now apprehended might fall into a second distress.

15. . . . I drew out the men after dinner and harangued them on the subject of our safe return in the following terms:

"Friends and fellow travelers, it is with abundance of pleasure that I now have it in my power to congratulate your happy arrival among the inhabitants. You will give me leave to put you in mind how manifestly Heaven has engaged in our preservation. No distress, no disaster, no sickness of any consequence has befallen any one of us in so long and so dangerous a journey. We have subsisted plentifully on the bounty of Providence and been day by day supplied in the barren wilderness with food convenient for us. This is surely an instance of divine goodness never to be forgotten, and, that it may still be more complete, I heartily wish that the same protection may have been extended to our families during our absence." . . .

22. . . . We arrived at Coggins Point about four, where my servants attended with boats in order to transport us to Westover. I had the happiness to find all the family well. This crowned all my other blessings and made the journey truly prosperous, of which I hope I shall ever retain a grateful remembrance. Nor was it all that my people were in good health, but my business was likewise in good order. Everyone seemed to have done their duty, by the joy they expressed at my return. My neighbors had been kind to my wife, when she was threatened with the loss of her son and heir. Their assistance was kind as well as seasonable, when her child was threatened with fatal symptoms and her husband upon a long journey exposed to great variety of perils. Thus, surrounded with the most fearful apprehensions, Heaven was pleased to support her spirits and bring back her child from the grave and her husband from the mountains, for which blessings may we be all sincerely thankful.

1841, 1929

Letter to Mrs. Jane Pratt Taylor[1]

Virginia, the 10th of October, 1735

If my dear cousen Taylor be not a little indulgent, she will be apt to think me a troublesome correspondent this year. It's now the fourth time I have broke in upon

[1]Widow of Thomas Taylor, the brother of Byrd's second wife.

her meditations, which is pretty fair for one who lives quite out of the latitude of news, and adventures, nor can pick up one dash of scandal to season a letter withall. 'Tis a mighty misfortune for an epistolizer not to live near some great city like London or Paris, where people play the fool in a well-bred way, & furnish their neighbours with discourse. In such places stories rowle about like snow balls, & gather variety of pretty circumstances in their way, til at last they tell very well, & serve as a good entertainment for a country cousen.

But alas what can we poor hermits do, who know of no intrigues, but such as are carry'd on by the amorous turtles, or some such innocent lovers? Our vices & disorders want all that wit & refinement, which make them palatable to the fine world. We are unskild in the arts of makeing our follys agreable, nor can we dress up the D——so much to advantage, as to make him pass for an angel of light. Therefore without a little invention, it would not be possible for one of us anchorites to carry on a tolerable correspondence, but like French historians, where we don't meet with pretty incidents, we must e'en make them, & lard a little truth with a great deal of fiction.

Perhaps you'll think the story I am going to tell you of this poetical sort. We have here an Italian bona roba,[2] whose whole study is to make her person charming, which to be sure will sound very strangely in the ears of an English lady. Those who understand physognomy suspect this dear creature has been a Venetian cortezan, because her whole mien & every motion proves she has been traind up in the art of pleaseing. She does not only practice graces at her glass, but by her skill in opticks, has instructed her eyes to reflect their rays in a very mischeivous manner. In a word she knows how to make the most of every part that composes her lovely frame, as you will see by the harmless adventure that follows.

You must know the two little hillucks in her bosome have lost a pretty deal of their natural firmness & elasticity. This is reacond a disadvantage to a fine neck not easy to be repaird, but she has an invention to brace them up again to a maiden protuberancy. She has a silver pipe made so exceedingly small at one end, that 'twill enter the narrow orifice of the nipple. At the other end of the tube her fille de chambre[3] blows with all her might, til the breast swells & struts like any blown bladder. This is no sooner performd, but a composition of wax, rosin & Spanish brown is nimbly applyd to hinder the imprisond wind from escapeing. Thus she preserves all the charms of the horizontal chest, without the German artifice of bolstering it up with a douzen of napkins. And 'tis moreover so hard and thrummy, that if any of the monsters with eight legs and no eyelids shoud presume to stray that way, she may fairly crack them upon it.

But as no human skil is ever so perfect, as to be secure from misadventures, so you will be sorry for what befell this gentlewoman one day at a ball. It happend she had deckt herself with all her artificial ornaments, but the warmth of the weather, joind with the agility of her motion, occasiond so copious a perspiration, that it softend & dissolvd the cement smeard upon her mammels. By this accident the doors being set open, the wind unluckily rusht forth, as fast as it well coud do, thro' so narrow a channel, & produced a sound that was a little unseemly. And that too not

[2]Wench.
[3]Maid.

in seperate notes, but with a long winded blast, which a genius to musick might have modulated into a tune. It is not easy to tell you, whether the company was more diverted, or the seignora more confounded at this accident: but so much is certain, that we were all surprizd at the unusual length of the noise, & the quarter from whence it sallyd out. We vertuosos[4] took, her immediately for one of those bellyspeaker's[5] whose gift it is to make a voice seem to issue out of any part of their body. The religious part of the company which consisted chiefly of old women, concluded her to be a demonaique, in the power of some evil spirit who chose to play his gambols in so fair an habitation. While we were taken up in debating upon this uncommon event, the unfortunate person slunk away thro' the crowd, & has never appeard out of her doors since.

Heaven be praisd I am able to tell my dear cousen Taylor that we are all in chearfull good health. We often discourse you in effigie, and call the painter a bungler for falling so short of the original. I hope you are not grown so thin as he has made you, because a lady can't loose her enbonpoint, without haveing some of her health go along with it. May you keep that jewel intire, 'til Time himself grow sick with age & all his iron teeth drop out of his head. I am without one word of a lye my dear cousen Taylors most &c.

1901

[4]Amateur scientists or collectors of curiosities. [5]Ventriloquists.

Cluster: Religion and Spirituality— On Nature and Nature's God

Some contemporary readers might wince when William Bradford, writing of the voyage from England to America, describes as an act of God the washing overboard of a cursing sailor. Bradford had no such qualms. His God worked in precisely this way, as the Bible asserts, "ordering all things together for the good of those who love the Lord." Bradford and his co-religionists imbued the operations of nature, individual actions, and the maneuverings of nations with this providential notion of history. All might seem to be independent and locally initiated natural or human events, but the believer could see in each the hand of God and knew otherwise.

These conceptions of God, humanity, and nature collapsed under the weight of the new science, which demanded that any ideas not derived, as John Locke put it, from sensation or reflection were not true knowledge. They could not be tested or verified by experience or reason. Such a reorientation toward the empirical clearly challenged religious beliefs, as later generations of Puritan divines understood, when they worried about the reliability of the spectral "evidence," as it was called, that was introduced at the Salem witch trials. Nevertheless, religion soon adopted the language of sensation and the test of experience. Jonathan Edwards, the great Puritan theologian, argued that "spiritual understanding consists primarily of a sense of the heart and derives from a real, "sensible knowledge" of God "in which more than the mere intellect is concerned." The emotional experiences engendered by Edwards's preaching on the "sense of the heart" are the core of the evangelical movement that swept the colonies in the 1730s under the banner of the Great Awakening. Benjamin Franklin, Edwards's contemporary, was less sanguine and united pragmatism and empiricism in his recollection that "revelation had indeed no weight with me, as such; but I entertain'd opinion that, though certain actions might not be bad because they were forbidden by it, or good because it commanded them, yet probably these actions might be forbidden because they were bad for us, or commanded because they were beneficial to us, in their own natures, all the circumstances of things considered." From here it was only a short step to dispense with revelation entirely, and claim, as did the Revolutionary polemicist Tom Paine, "my mind is my own church," in the first chapter of a work aptly titled *The Age of Reason*.

"Nature's God," as Jefferson would name him, revealed his design through the orderliness of creation, an idea as old as medieval Catholicism and once held in faith but now confirmed in science. Certainly this was the case with physics and cosmology. Isaac Newton did nothing less than describe the operations of the universe mathematically, with no reference to God required. Developments moved more slowly in the biological sciences. Still, it was clear to intellectuals like the British poet Alexander Pope that the orderly universe was composed of systems within systems, characterized by "strong connexions, nice dependencies, / Gradations just." American poets, like Ann Eliza Bleecker, writing during the Revolution, and Philip Freneau, writing in its aftermath, appealed to nature for moral guidance. Enlightened minds struggled to understand this new conception of the universe in relation to the prevailing paradigm of the Great Chain of Being, a sense of systematic hierarchy reaching from God through angels and humans down through creatures and plants to stones and nothingness. Slavery and other social ills raised questions about whose interests were served by promoting a concept of hierarchy such as this, which seemed to teach, in Pope's words, that "whatever is, is right." In the century before the debate about evolution, it was one thing for enlightened minds like the Comte du Buffon to believe that all species ever created must still exist somewhere and that no new species have ever been created, and yet another thing to ask ourselves the meaning of physcial differences in determining species, whether in something as newly remarkable as the first dinosaur bones or as anciently familiar as race and gender. Those passages in Jefferson's *Notes on the State of Virginia* about relative passions and intelligence of Indians and slaves, about interracial and interspecies sexual relations, and the nature and effect of skin pigmentation, however embarrassing to today's readers, are reported as reasonable inferences within the existing scientific paradigms. In the eighteenth century, as in the present one, science was charged with social and political implications.

The political consequences of viewing God in these terms were not lost on the American Revolutionaries. James Otis unabashedly drew upon nature's God for metaphors of order and design to represent the American political will to self-government, not as a revolutionary disruption of the natural order but as a necessary and natural evolution. Jefferson, in the Declaration of Independence, would pick up this theme, arguing that revolution is a necessary corrective, "in the course of human events," to the arbitrariness of idiosyncratic, monarchical rule. If the Christian monarch justified his arbitrariness by an appeal to the example of an arbitrary, demanding Old Testament deity, citizens claimed their liberty from nature's God, who endowed people with natural, inalienable rights. Happiness, then, did not, as formerly, consist of submitting one's own will to the arbitrary will of God and king. Rather, happiness returned to its fundamental etymological sense of moment, opportunity, or occasion, as in "happen" or "mishap," and the pursuit of happiness, as in the Declaration, was understood to be a natural right, given by nature's God, to shape one's own vision of the future through empowering choices.

A century had elapsed between the Salem witch trials and Tom Paine's *Age of Reason.* Two revolutions had irrevocably altered the political landscape, redefining humans from subjects to citizens. It all began with the new scientific temperament that, in insisting on empirical evidence, turned our attention away from the world beyond to the world of nature and supplanted the biblical God with nature's God.

Andrew Wiget
New Mexico State University

John Locke 1632–1704

from Essay Concerning Human Understanding

Chapter I. Of Ideas in general, and their Original

1. *Idea is the object of thinking.* Every man being conscious to himself that he thinks; and that which his mind is applied about whilst thinking being the ideas that are there, it is past doubt that men have in their minds several ideas,—such as are those expressed by the words whiteness, hardness, sweetness, thinking, motion, man, elephant, army, drunkenness, and others: it is in the first place then to be inquired, How he comes by them?

I know it is a received doctrine, that men have native ideas, and original characters, stamped upon their minds in their very first being. This opinion I have at large examined already; and, I suppose what I have said in the foregoing Book will be much more easily admitted, when I have shown whence the understanding may get all the ideas it has; and by what ways and degrees they may come into the mind;—for which I shall appeal to every one's own observation and experience.

2. *All ideas come from sensation or reflection.* Let us then suppose the mind to be, as we say, white paper, void of all characters, without any ideas:—How comes it to be furnished? Whence comes it by the vast store which the busy and boundless fancy of man has painted on it with an almost endless variety? Whence has it all the materials of reason and knowledge? To this I answer, in one word, from EXPERIENCE. In that all our knowledge is founded; and from that it ultimately derives itself. Our observation employed either, about external sensible objects, or about the internal operations of our minds perceived and reflected on by ourselves, is that which supplies our understandings with all the materials of thinking. These two are the fountains of knowledge, from whence all the ideas we have, or can naturally have, do spring.

3. *The objects of sensation one source of ideas.* First, our Senses, conversant about particular sensible objects, do convey into the mind several distinct perceptions of things, according to those various ways wherein those objects do affect them. And thus we come by those ideas we have of yellow, white, heat, cold, soft, hard, bitter, sweet, and all those which we call sensible qualities; which when I say the senses convey into the mind, I mean, they from external objects convey into the mind what produces there those perceptions. This great source of most of the ideas we have, depending wholly upon our senses, and derived by them to the understanding, I call SENSATION.

4. *The operations of our minds, the other source of them.* Secondly, the other fountain from which experience furnisheth the understanding with ideas is,—the perception of the operations of our own mind within us, as it is employed about the ideas it has got;—which operations, when the soul comes to reflect on and consider, do furnish the understanding with another set of ideas, which could not be had from things without. And such are perception, thinking, doubting, believing, reasoning, knowing, willing, and

all the different actings of our own minds;—which we being conscious of, and observing in ourselves, do from these receive into our understandings as distinct ideas as we do from bodies affecting our senses. This source of ideas every man has wholly in himself; and though it be not sense, as having nothing to do with external objects, yet it is very like it, and might properly enough be called internal sense. But as I call the other SENSATION, so I call this REFLECTION, the ideas it affords being such only as the mind gets by reflecting on its own operations within itself. By reflection then, in the following part of this discourse, I would be understood to mean, that notice which the mind takes of its own operations, and the manner of them, by reason whereof there come to be ideas of these operations in the understanding. These two, I say, viz. external material things, as the objects of SENSATION, and the operations of our own minds within, as the objects of REFLECTION, are to me the only originals from whence all our ideas take their beginnings. The term operations here I use in a large sense, as comprehending not barely the actions of the mind about its ideas, but some sort of passions arising sometimes from them, such as is the satisfaction or uneasiness arising from any thought.

5. *All our ideas are of the one or the other of these.* The understanding seems to me not to have the least glimmering of any ideas which it doth not receive from one of these two. External objects furnish the mind with the ideas of sensible qualities, which are all those different perceptions they produce in us; the mind furnishes the understanding with ideas of its own operations.

These, when we have taken a full survey of them, and their several modes, combinations, and relations, we shall find to contain all our whole stock of ideas; and that we have nothing in our minds which did not come in one of these two ways. Let any one examine his own thoughts, and thoroughly search into his understanding; and then let him tell me, whether all the original ideas he has there, are any other than the objects of his senses, or of the operations of his mind, considered as objects of his reflection. And how great a mass of knowledge soever he imagines to be lodged there, he will, upon taking a strict view, see that he has not any idea in his mind but what one of these two have imprinted;—though perhaps, with infinite variety compounded and enlarged by the understanding, as we shall see hereafter.

1690

Alexander Pope 1632–1704

from Essay on Man, Epistle I

I

Say first, of God above or Man below
What can we reason but from what we know?

Of man what see we but his station here,
From which to reason, or to which refer?
Thro' worlds unnumber'd tho' the God be known,
'Tis ours to trace him only in our own.
He who thro' vast immensity can pierce,
See worlds on worlds compose one universe,
Observe how system into system runs,
What other planets circle other suns,
What varied being peoples every star,
May tell why Heav'n has made us as we are:
But of this frame, the bearings and the ties,
The strong connexions, nice dependencies,
Gradations just, has thy pervading soul
Look'd thro'; or can a part contains the whole?
Is the great chain that draws all to agree,
And drawn supports, upheld by God or thee?

VII

Far as creation's ample range extends,
The scale of sensual, mental powers ascends.
Mark how it mounts to man's imperial race
From the green myriads in the peopled grass:
What modes of sight betwixt each wide extreme,
The mole's dim curtain and the lynx's beam:
Of smell, the headlong lioness between
And hound sagacious on the tainted green:
Of hearing, from the life that fills the flood
To that which warbles thro' the vernal wood.
The spider's touch, how exquisitely fine,
Feels at each thread, and lives along the line:
In the nice bee what sense so subtly true,
From pois'nous herbs extracts the healing dew!
How instinct varies in the grovelling swine,
Compared, half-reas'ning elephant, with thine!
For ever seperate, yet for ever near!
Remembrance and reflection how allied!
What thin partitions Sense from Thought divide!
And middle natures how they long to join,
Yet never pass th'insuperable line!
Without this just gradation could they be
Subjected these to those, or all to thee!
The powers of all subdued by thee alone,
Is not thy Reason all these powers in one?

X

Cease, then, nor Order imperfection name;
Our proper bliss depends on what we blame.
Know thy own point: this kind, this due degree
Of blindness, weakness, Heav'n bestows on thee.
Submit: in this or any other sphere,
Secure to be as bless'd as thou canst bear;
Safe in the hand of one disposing Power,
Or in the natal or the mortal hour.
All Nature is but Art unknown to thee;
All chance direction, which thou canst not see;
All discord, harmony not understood;
All partial evil, universal good:
And spite of Pride, in erring Reason's spite,
One truth is clear, *Whatever is, is right.*

1733

Jonathan Edwards 1703–1758

from Treatise Concerning Religious Affections

1. Love to Christ: "Whom having not yet seen, ye love." The world was ready to wonder, what strange principle it was, that influenced them to expose themselves to so great sufferings, to forsake the things that were seen, and renounce all that was dear and pleasant, which was the object of sense. They seemed to the men of the world about them, as though they were beside themselves, and to act as though they hated themselves; there was nothing in their view, that could induce them thus to suffer, and support them under, and carry them through such trials. But although there was nothing that was seen, nothing that the world saw, or that the Christians themselves ever saw with their bodily eyes, that thus influenced and supported them, yet they had a supernatural principle of love to something unseen; they love Jesus Christ, for they saw him spiritually whom the world saw not, and whom they themselves had never seen with bodily eyes. . . .

God has endued the soul with two faculties: one is that by which it is capable of perception and speculation, or by which it discerns, and views, and judges of things; which is called the understanding. The other faculty is that by which the soul does not merely perceive and view things, but is some way inclined with respect to the things it views or considers; either is inclined to them, or is disinclined and averse from them; or is the faculty by which the soul does not behold things, as an indifferent unaffected spectator, but either as liking or disliking, pleased or displeased, approving or rejecting. This faculty is called by various names; it is sometimes called the inclination: and, as it has respect to the actions that are determined and governed by it, is called the will: and the mind, with regard to the exercises of this faculty, is often called the heart.

The exercises of this faculty are of two sorts; either those by which the soul is carried out towards the things that are in view, in approving of them, being pleased with them, and inclined to them; or those in which the soul opposes the things that are in view, in disapproving of them, and in being displeased with them, averse from them, and rejecting them.

And as the exercises of the inclination and will of the soul are various in their kinds, so they are much more various in their degrees. There are some exercises of pleasedness or displeasedness, inclination or disinclination, wherein the soul is carried but a little beyond the state of indifference.—And there are other degrees above this, wherein the approbation or dislike, pleasedness or aversion, are stronger, wherein we may rise higher and higher, till the soul comes to act vigorously and sensibly, and the actings of the soul are with that strength, that (through the laws of the union which the Creator has fixed between the soul and the body) the motion of the blood and animal spirits begins to be sensibly altered; whence oftentimes arises some bodily sensation, especially about the heart and vitals, that are the fountain of the fluids of the body: from whence it comes to pass, that the mind, with regard to the exercises of this faculty, perhaps in all nations and ages, is called the heart. And it is to be noted, that they are these more vigorous and sensible exercises of this faculty that are called the affections.

The will, and the affections of the soul, are not two faculties; the affections are not essentially distinct from the will, nor do they differ from the mere actings of the will, and inclination of the soul, but only in the liveliness and sensibleness of exercise. . . .

Such seems to be our nature, and such the laws of the union of soul and body, that there never is in any case whatsoever, any lively and vigorous exercise of the will or inclination of the soul, without some effect upon the body, in some alteration of the motion of its fluids, and especially of the animal spirits. And, on the other hand, from the same laws of the union of the soul and body, the constitution of the body, and the motion of its fluids, may promote the exercise of the affections. But yet it is not the body, but the mind only, that is the proper seat of the affections. The body of man is no more capable of being really the subject of love or hatred, joy or sorrow, fear or hope, than the body of a tree, or than the same body of man is capable of thinking and understanding. As it is the soul only that has ideas, so it is the soul only that is pleased or displeased with its ideas. As it is the soul only that thinks, so it is the soul only that loves or hates, rejoices or is grieved at what it thinks of. Nor are these motions of the animal spirits, and fluids of the body, anything properly belonging to the nature of the affections, though they always accompany them, in the present state; but are only effects or concomitants of the affections that are entirely distinct from the affections themselves, and no way essential to them; so that an unbodied spirit may be as capable of love and hatred, joy or sorrow, hope or fear, or other affections, as one that is united to a body. . .

Spiritual understanding consists primarily in a sense of heart of that spiritual beauty. I say, a sense of heart; for it is not speculation merely that is concerned in this kind of understanding; nor can there be a clear distinction made between the two faculties of understanding and will, as acting distinctly and separately, in this matter. When the mind is sensible of the sweet beauty and amiableness of a thing, that implies a sensibleness of sweetness and delight in the presence of the idea of it: and this sensibleness of the amiableness or delightfulness of beauty, carries in the very nature of it the sense of the heart; or an effect and impression the soul is the subject of, as a substance possessed of taste, inclination and will.

There is a distinction to be made between a mere notional understanding wherein the mind only beholds things in the exercise of a speculative faculty; and the sense of the heart, wherein the mind does not only speculate and behold, but relishes and feels. That sort of knowledge, by which a man has a sensible perception of amiableness and loathsomeness, or of sweetness and nauseousness, is not just the same sort of knowledge with that by which he knows what a triangle is, and what a square is. The one is mere speculative knowledge, the other sensible knowledge, in which more than the mere intellect is concerned; the heart is the proper subject of it, or the soul, as a being that not only beholds, but has inclination, and is pleased or displeased. And yet there is the nature of instruction in it; as he has perceived the sweet taste of honey, knows much more about it, than he who has only looked upon, and felt of it.

1746

James Otis 1725–1783

from The Discourse of Nature and Government

Is not government founded on *grace*? No. Nor on *force*? No. Nor on *compact*? Nor *property*? Not altogether on either. Has it *any* solid foundation, any chief cornerstone but what accident, chance, or confusion may lay one moment and destroy the next? I think it has an everlasting foundation in the *unchangeable will of* GOD, the author of nature, whose laws never vary. The same omniscient, omnipotent, infinitely good and gracious Creator of the universe who has made it necessary that what we call matter should *gravitate* for the celestial bodies to roll round their axes, dance their orbits, and perform various revolutions in that beautiful order and concert which we all admire has made it *equally* necessary that from *Adam and Eve* to these degenerate days the different sexes should sweetly *attract* each other, form societies of *single* families, of which *larger* bodies and communities are naturally, mechanically, and necessarily combined as the dew of heaven and the soft distilling rain is collected by the all enlivening heat of the sun. *Government* is therefore most evidently founded *on the necessities of our nature.* It is by no means an *arbitrary* thing depending merely on human *compact* or *human will* for its existence.

1764

Anna Eliza Bleecker 1752–1783

On the Immensity of Creation

Oh! could I borrow some celestial plume,
This narrow globe should not confine me long
In its contracted sphere—the vast expanse,
Beyond where thought can reach, or eye can glance,
My curious spirit, charm'd should taverse o'er,
New worlds to find, new systems to explore:
When these appear'd, again I'd urge my flight
Till all creation open'd to my sight.
Ah! unavailing wish, absurd and vain,
Fancy return and drop thy wing again;
Could'st thou more swift than light move steady on,
Thy sight as broad, and piercing as the sun,
And Gabriel's years too added to thy own;
Nor Gabriel's sight, nor thought, nor rapid wing,
Can pass the immense domains of th' eternal King;
The greatest seraph in his bright abode
Can't comprehend the labors of a God.
Proud reason fails, and is confounded here;
—Man how contemptible thou dost appear!
What art thou in this scene?—Alas! no more
Than a small atom to the sandy shore,
A drop of water to a boundless sea,
A single moment to eternity.

1773

Philip Freneau 1752–1832

On the Universality and Other Attributes of the God of Nature

All that we see, about, abroad,
What is it all, but nature's God?
In meaner works discover'd here
No less than in the starry sphere.

In seas, on earth, this God is seen;
All that exist, upon him lean;
He lives in all, and never stray'd
A moment from the works he made.

His system fix'd on general laws
Bespeaks a wise creating cause;
Impartially he rules mankind
And all that on this globe we find.

Unchanged in all that seems to change,
Unbounded space is his great range;
To one vast purpose always true,
No time, with him, is old or new.

In all the attributes divine
Unlimited perfectings shine;
In these enwrapt, in these complete,
All virtues in that centre meet.

This power who doth all powers transcend,
To all intelligence a friend,
Exists, *the greatest and the best*[1]
Throughout all worlds, to make them blest.

All that he did he first approved
He all things into *being* loved;

[1] "Jupiter optimus, maximus,—Cicero," [Freneau's note.]

O'er all he made he still presides,
For them in life, or death provides.

1815

Thomas Paine 1737–1809

from The Age of Reason[1]

Chapter I
The Author's Profession of Faith

It has been my intention, for several years past, to publish my thoughts upon religion; I am well aware of the difficulties that attend the subject, and from that consideration, had reserved it to a more advanced period of life. I intended it to be the last offering I should make to my fellow-citizens of all nations, and that at a time when the purity of the motive that induced me to it could not admit of a question, even by those who might disapprove the work.

The circumstance that has now taken place in France, of the total abolition of the whole national order of priesthood, and of everything appertaining to compulsive systems of religion, and compulsive articles of faith, has not only precipitated my intention, but rendered a work of this kind exceedingly necessary, lest, in the general wreck of superstition, of false systems of government, and false theology, we lose sight of morality, of humanity, and of the theology that is true.

As several of my colleagues, and others of my fellow-citizens of France, have given me the example of making their voluntary and individual profession of faith, I also will make mine; and I do this with all that sincerity and frankness with which the mind of man communicates with itself.

I believe in one God, and no more; and I hope for happiness beyond this life.

I believe in the equality of man, and I believe that religious duties consist in doing justice, loving mercy, and endeavouring to make our fellow-creatures happy.

But, lest it should be supposed that I believe many other things in addition to these, I shall, in the progress of this work, declare the things I do not believe, and my reasons for not believing them.

I do not believe in the creed professed by the Jewish church, by the Roman church, by the Greek church, by the Turkish church, by the Protestant church, nor by any church that I know of. My own mind is my own church.

[1]The first part of the *Age of Reason* was published in 1794; the second part, in 1795 in France and in 1796 in England.

All national institutions of churches, whether Jewish, Christian, or Turkish, appear to me no other than human inventions set up to terrify and enslave mankind, and monopolize power and profit.

I do not mean by this declaration to condemn those who believe otherwise; they have the same right to their belief as I have to mine. But it is necessary to the happiness of man, that he be mentally faithful to himself. Infidelity does not consist in believing, or in disbelieving; it consists of professing to believe what he does not believe.

It is impossible to calculate the moral mischief, if I may so express it, that mental lying has produced in society. When a man has so far corrupted and prostituted the chastity of his mind, as to subscribe his professional belief to things he does not believe, he has prepared himself for the commission of every other crime. He takes up the trade of a priest for the sake of gain, and, in order to qualify himself for that trade, he begins with a perjury. Can we conceive anything more destructive to morality than this?

Soon after I had published the pamphlet COMMON SENSE, in America, I saw the exceeding probability that a revolution in the system of government would be followed by a revolution in the system of religion. The adulterous connection of church and state, wherever it had taken place, whether Jewish, Christian, or Turkish, had so effectually prohibited, by pains and penalties, every discussion upon established creeds, and upon first principles of religion, that until the system of government should be changed, those subjects could not be brought fairly and openly before the world; but that whenever this should be done, a revolution in the system of religion would follow. Human inventions and priest-craft would be detected; and man would return to the pure, unmixed, and unadulterated belief of one God, and no more.

Jonathan Edwards 1703–1758

Nearly a century after the landing of the *Mayflower* at Plymouth, the writer who, according to novelist William Dean Howells, "first gave our poor American provinciality world standing" was born in East Windsor, a new settlement in the Connecticut River valley. Edwards's father Timothy was a well-read Harvard graduate who held the sole pastorship of the small town's Congregational church. Edwards's maternal grandfather, Solomon Stoddard, pastor of a much larger and more influential congregation upriver in Northampton, Massachusetts, was, like Edwards, a significant theologian. Opposing his more conservative peers, Stoddard devised a policy of relaxing the requirements for full membership in the established church.

Edwards was prepared for college by his father and matriculated in 1716 to the recently opened Collegiate School (later Yale University), which Cotton Mather had helped to found in hopes of counteracting the "liberal" drift of the younger generation of faculty at Harvard. During Edwards's junior year, the College received a major gift of recent books in science and philosophy, a gift that introduced Edwards and his classmates to such famous authors as Sir Isaac Newton and John Locke. Valedictorian of his class, Edwards received his B.A. in 1720. He remained in New Haven for postgraduate study until 1722, when he accepted a job as pastor of a Presbyterian church (identical in theology but more formal and hierarchical in governance than the Congregational churches of his father and grandfather) in New York City.

After nine months, Edwards left the New York pastorate to complete a master's thesis in theology in New Haven. From the year 1720, he had made sporadic entries in a conventional personal diary, but returning home after taking his graduate degree, he began making voluminous notes on his original inquiries in physical science, theology, and philosophy. At the urging of his father, Edwards prepared a scientific paper on the so-called flying spider, and his father sent it to a member of the British Royal Society. In 1724, Edwards accepted an appointment as a tutor at Yale.

Edwards left the College in 1726 to return to the ministry, settling down as assistant to his grandfather Stoddard at Northampton and then, after Stoddard's death in 1729, as sole pastor of the Northampton congregation. He married Sarah Pierrepont, the daughter of a New Haven minister whom he had known since college. In response to influential colleagues who proclaimed the soul's power to affect its own conversion, Edwards preached in 1734 a series of corrective sermons emphasizing the Calvinist (but in fact traditionally Augustinian and Pauline) tenet of the passivity of the convert before God's all-powerful offer of grace.

In 1735, Edwards's more "evangelical" emphasis brought about a number of conversions in the Northampton congregation. Hearing of the revival in Northampton, the Reverend Benjamin Colman, pastor of Boston's "liberal" Brattle Street Church (founded in Edwards's childhood to open a pulpit to theological opponents of the Mathers), asked Edwards to prepare an authoritative account of the awakening. Published by Colman in pamphlet form, Edwards's letter had a wide circulation, spreading his fame among Protestants on both sides of the Atlantic. While the pamphlet remained in circulation, Edwards expanded and re-wrote it for book publication as *A Faithful Narrative of the Surprising Work of God* (published in America in 1737 and in England later the same year).

Northampton's small revival seemed temperate compared to the sensation attending the 1739–1740 colonial tour of a young English preacher, George Whitefield, who had an established reputation in Britain in the "methodist" or evangelical Anglican movement. Whitefield traveled throughout the provinces of British North America from Georgia to Massachusetts. Barred from speaking by local ministers and universities, he evoked thousands of conversions among audiences. Meanwhile, within the native anti-Anglican establishment, Presbyterian and Congregational alike, homebred American awakeners like Gilbert Tennent and Joseph Davenport achieved effects similar to Whitefield's.

Particularly in scholarly New England, the Great Awakening drove American ministers to their pens. Some defended, some denounced as heresy, the conversions and the itinerant evangelical preaching that had produced them. Edwards, who was at one with his contemporary Benjamin Franklin in finding Whitefield personally likeable, nevertheless perceived the statements of both parties as confused. With the premise that ministers could not meaningfully celebrate or condemn the particular emotional experiences of converts without having a clear theory of the place of emotion in religion, and trusting that clarification of the terms and points at issue would be welcome in the debate, Edwards devoted himself to producing a systematic study. Edwards's *Treatise Concerning Religious Affections* attempted to transcend the politicized issues by lifting the discussion to a philosophical plane. While too subtle to have a direct practical effect on the passions of the time, the book became indispensable to such major modern philosophers and psychologists of religion as William James.

For Edwards as author, the results of the Awakening were happy; for Edwards as pastor, they ultimately were not. Emboldened by the increase in parishioners testifying to grace-begetting experiences, in 1748 Edwards attempted to abolish Stoddard's practice of admitting to the Lord's Supper anyone who had been baptized, returning instead to the original "New England Way" of first requiring formal profession of a saving experience. Although a considerable number of the seriously devout in Northampton were prepared to accept Edwards's reform, many—reflecting the decreased respect for local ministerial authority that was becoming the legacy of the Awakening's itinerant revivalists—were not. In 1750, in a climate of accumulated family rivalries, Edwards's attempted return to pre-Stoddard membership requirements became the formal issue over which his congregation ultimately voted in sufficient numbers to dismiss him.

With his family of eleven surviving children, Edwards remained in Northampton, working on various writing projects. In spite of financial hardship, Edwards refused to return to ministry, rejecting pastorships in the American South and as far away as Scotland, opting instead for an administrative position at a Congregational mission for the Housatonic Indians at Stockbridge, on the western border of Massachusetts. Compared to his pastoral responsibilities, administrative duties posed no intellectual competition for Edwards's primary work as an author.

The fourth year after he moved to Stockbridge, Edwards produced a book that was instantly accepted as a major contribution to an international debate on human self-determination. Edwards's *Careful and Strict Enquiry into the modern prevailing Notions of that Freedom of Will Which is supposed to be essential to . . . Praise and Blame* (familiarly called *The Freedom of the Will*) would be used as a standard textbook at Yale and other colleges for decades. Here, Edwards averred that people enter the world in a state of total depravity and carry no disposition to good or bad action. The sole liberty people possess, in Edwards's view, is the liberty that "I *can* do, if I *will*." Yet the will, Edwards concluded in this treatise, is not free; it is determined by motives toward "apparent *good*" or "that which is agreeable." So long as people can do what they will to do, Edwards argued, they are free. *Freedom of the Will* was a complicated treatise for complicated philosophical times.

In 1757, Edwards was called to another post, again in administration, this time as president of the College of New Jersey at Nassau Hall (now Princeton). He was at first disposed to resist the offer but finally agreed to take the post. Ahead of his family, Edwards traveled alone to Princeton. He had barely arrived when, in the aftermath of a failed inoculation for smallpox, he died at age fifty-five. Before his death, publishers in Northampton, Boston, New York, and London had published twenty-four original titles by Edwards, making him indisputably one of the few major figures in colonial American literary history.

Edwards seems to have early dedicated himself to speculative thought, laid speculation aside for the practical purposes of marriage and child rearing, then turned again to speculative writing shortly before he died. He clearly pursued his writing with the expectation of eventual publication, yet, as he got further and further behind on his projects, he evidently accepted that the audience he was addressing was one of the future.

Carol M. Bensick
University of California at Riverside

Wendy Martin
Claremont Graduate University

PRIMARY WORKS

A Faithful Narrative of the Surprising Work of God in the Conversions of Many Hundred Souls . . . , 1737; *A Treatise Concerning Religious Affections,* 1746; *A Careful and Strict Enquiry into the modern prevailing Notions of that Freedom of Will, Which is supposed to be essential to . . . Praise and Blame,* 1754; *The Great Christian Doctrine of Original Sin defended; Evidences of it's Truth produced and Arguments to the Contrary answered,* 1758; Samuel Hopkins, ed., *The Life and Character of the Late Rev. Mr. Jonathan Edwards,* 1765; John E. Smith et al., eds., *A Jonathan Edwards Reader,* 1995; Henry Stout, ed., *The Works of Jonathan Edwards,* 17 vols., 1957–1998.

from Images of Divine Things[1]

7. That the things of the world are ordered [and] designed to shadow forth spiritual things, appears by the Apostle's arguing spiritual things from them. I Cor. 15:36, "Thou fool, that which thou sowest is not quickened, except it die." If the sowing of seed and its springing were not designedly ordered to have an agreeableness to the resurrection, there could be no sort of argument in that which the Apostle alleges; either to argue the resurrection itself or the manner of it, either its certainty, or probability, or possibility. See how the Apostle's argument is thus founded (Heb. 9:16–17) about the validity of a testament.

8. Again, it is apparent and allowed that there is a great and remarkable analogy in God's works. There is a wonderful resemblance in the effects which God produces, and consentaneity in his manner of working in one thing and another, throughout all nature. It is very observable in the visible world. Therefore 'tis allowed that God does purposely make and order one thing to be in an agreeableness and harmony with another. And if so, why should not we suppose that he makes the inferior in imitation of the superior, the material of the spiritual, on purpose to have a resemblance and shadow of them? We see that even in the material world God makes one part of it strangely to agree with another; and why is it not reasonable to suppose he makes the whole as a shadow of the spiritual world?

63. In the manner in which birds and squirrels that are charmed by serpents go into their mouths and are destroyed by them, is a lively representation of the manner in which sinners under the gospel are very often charmed and destroyed by the devil. The animal that is charmed by the serpent seems to be in great exercise and fear, screams and makes ado, but yet don't flee away. It comes nearer to the serpent, and then seems to have its distress increased and goes a little back again, but then comes still nearer than ever, and then appears as if greatly affrighted and runs or flies back again a little way, but yet don't flee quite away, and soon comes a little nearer and a little nearer with seeming fear and distress that drives 'em a little back between whiles, until at length they come so [near] that the serpent can lay hold of them: and so they become their prey.

Just thus, oftentimes sinners under the gospel are bewitched by their lusts. They have considerable fears of destruction and remorse of conscience that makes 'em hang back, and they have a great deal of exercise between while, and some partial reformations, but yet they don't flee away. They won't wholly forsake their beloved lusts, but return to 'em again; and so whatever warnings they have, and whatever checks of conscience that may exercise 'em and make [them] go back a little and stand off for a while, yet they will keep their beloved sin in sight, and won't utterly break off from it and forsake [it], but will return to it again and again, and go a little

[1]Edwards wrote *Images of Divine Things* over many years, compiling his thoughts and reflections concerning the expression of the divine in the material world. His manuscripts indicate that sometime between 1737 and 1741 he changed the title of his work from *Shadows of Divine Things* to *Images of Divine Things.* The work has also been published with the title *Images or Shadows of Divine Things.*

further and a little further, until Satan remedilessly makes a prey of them. But if anyone comes and kills the serpent, the animal immediately escapes. So the way in which poor souls are delivered from the snare of the devil is by Christ's coming and bruising the serpent's head.

70. If we look on these shadows of divine things as the voice of God, purposely, by them, teaching us these and those spiritual and divine things, to show of what excellent advantage it will be, how agreeably and clearly it will tend to convey instruction to our minds, and to impress things on the mind, and to affect the mind. By that we may as it were hear God speaking to us. Wherever we are and whatever we are about, we may see divine things excellently represented and held forth, and it will abundantly tend to confirm the Scriptures, for there is an excellent agreement between these things and the Holy Scriptures.

158. The way in which most of the things we use are serviceable to us and answer their end is in their being strained, or hard-pressed, or violently agitated. Thus the way in which the bow answers its end is in hard straining of it to shoot the arrow and do the execution; the bow that won't bear straining is good for nothing. So it is with a staff that a man walks with: it answers its end in being hard-pressed. So it is with many of the members of our bodies, our teeth, our feet, etc.; and so with most of the utensils of life, an ax, a saw, a flail, a rope, a chain, etc. They are useful and answer their end by some violent straining, pressure, agitation, collision or impulsion, and they that are so weak not to bear the trial of such usage are good for nothing.

Here is a lively representation of the way in which true and sincere saints (which are often in Scripture represented as God's instruments or utensils) answer God's end, and serve and glorify him in it: by enduring temptation, going through hard labor, suffering, or self-denial or such service or strains hard upon nature and self. Hypocrites are like a broken tooth, a foot out of joint, a broken staff, a deceitful bow, which fail when pressed or strained.

212. The immense magnificence of the visible world, its inconceivable vastness, the incomprehensible height of the heavens, etc. is but a type of the infinite magnificence, height and glory of God's work in the spiritual world: the most incomprehensible expression of his power, wisdom, holiness and love, in what is wrought and brought to pass in that world; and in the exceeding greatness of the moral and natural good, the light, knowledge, holiness and happiness which shall be communicated to it. And therefore to that magnificence of the world, height of heaven, those things are often compared in such expressions, "Thy mercy is great above the heavens, thy truth reacheth [unto the clouds]"; "Thou hast set thy glory above the heavens," etc.[2] See no 21.

1728 1948

[2]Psalm 108:4; Psalm 8:1.

On Sarah Pierrepont[1]

They say there is a young lady in [New Haven] who is beloved of that almighty Being, who made and rules the world, and that there are certain seasons in which this great Being, in some way or other invisible, comes to her and fills her mind with exceeding sweet delight, and that she hardly cares for anything, except to meditate on him—that she expects after awhile to be received up where he is, to be raised out of the world and caught up into heaven; being assured that he loves her too well to let her remain at a distance from him always. There she is to dwell with him, and to be ravished with his love, favor and delight, forever. Therefore, if you present all the world before her, with the richest of its treasures, she disregards it and cares not for it, and is unmindful of any pain or affliction. She has a strange sweetness in her mind, and sweetness of temper, uncommon purity in her affections; is most just and praiseworthy in all her actions; and you could not persuade her to do anything thought wrong or sinful, if you would give her all the world, lest she should offend this great Being. She is of a wonderful sweetness, calmness and universal benevolence of mind; especially after those times in which this great God has manifested himself to her mind. She will sometimes go about, singing sweetly, from place to [place]; and seems to be always full of joy and pleasure; and no one knows for what. She loves to be alone, and to wander in the fields and on the mountains, and seems to have someone invisible always conversing with her.

c. 1723 | 1829–30

Sarah Pierrepont Edwards's (1710–1758) written testimony of her religious conversion in 1742. Her husband, Jonathan Edwards, drew heavily upon her testimony for his influential work Some Thoughts Concerning the Present Revival of Religion in New England *(1743).*

I continued in a sweet and lively sense of Divine things, until I retired to rest. That night, which was Thursday night, Jan. 28, was the sweetest night I ever had in my life. I never before, for so long a time together, enjoyed so much of the light, and rest and sweetness of heaven in my soul, but without the least agitation of body during the whole time. The great part of the night I lay awake, sometimes asleep, and sometimes between sleeping and waking. But all night I continued in a constant, clear and lively sense of the heavenly sweetness of Christ's excellent and transcendent love, of his nearness to me, and of my dearness to him; with an inexpressibly sweet calmness of soul in an entire rest in him. I seemed to myself to perceive a glow of divine love come down from the heart of Christ in heaven, into my heart, in a constant stream, like a stream or pencil of sweet light. At the same time, my heart and soul all flowed out in love to Christ; so that there

[1]This passage was originally untitled and written in a book ostensibly given to Sarah Pierrepont by Jonathan Edwards in 1723. The subject is believed to be Sarah Pierrepont, whom Edwards married in 1727.

seemed to be a constant flowing and reflowing of heavenly and divine love, from Christ's heart to mine; and I appeared to myself to float or swim, in these bright, sweet beams of the love of Christ, like the motes swimming in the beams of the sun, or the streams of his light which came in at the window. My soul remained in a kind of heavenly elysium. So far as I am capable of making a comparison, I think that what I felt each minute, during the continuance of the whole time, was worth more than all the outward comfort and pleasure, which I had enjoyed in my whole life put together. It was a pure delight, which fed and satisfied the soul. It was pleasure, without the least sting, or any interruption. It was a sweetness, which my soul was lost in. It seemed to be all that my feeble frame could sustain, of that fulness of joy, which is felt by those, who behold the face of Christ, and share his love in the heavenly world. There was but little difference, whether I was asleep or awake, so deep was the impression made on my soul; but if there was any difference, the sweetness was greatest and most uninterrupted, while I was asleep.

As I awoke early the next morning, which was Friday, I was led to think of Mr. Williams of Hadley preaching that day in the town, as had been appointed; and to examine my heart, whether I was willing that he, who was a neighbouring minister, should be extraordinarily blessed, and made a greater instrument of good in the town, than Mr. Edwards; and was enabled to say, with respect to that matter, "Amen, Lord Jesus!" and to be entirely willing, if God pleased, that he should be the instrument of converting every soul in the town. My soul acquiesced fully in the will of God, as to the instrument, if his work of renewing grace did but go on.

from A Faithful Narrative of the Surprising Work of God[1]

. . . There is a vast difference, as has been observed, in the degree, and also in the particular manner of persons' experiences, both at and after conversion; some have grace working more sensibly in one way, others in another. Some speak more fully of

[1]When Reverend Benjamin Colman (1673–1747) of Boston's Brattle Street Church learned of Edwards's remarkable conversions of parishioners in western Massachusetts, he wrote to Edwards requesting an account of the "great awakening." Edwards replied in a letter dated May 30, 1735, telling of a number of conversions at Northampton and in neighboring communities. Impressed, Colman published Edwards's letter in 1736. The published letter was then sent to some clergymen in London. Its popularity there induced Edwards to expand his account of the Great Awakening. The revised account was published in London late in 1737 as *A Faithful Narrative of the Surprising Work of God in the Conversion of Many Hundred Souls in Northampton and the Neighboring Towns . . . in the Province of Massachusetts Bay in New England. A Faithful Narrative* was so popular that it went through three editions and twenty printings between 1737 and 1739.

This selection has been taken from Edwards's *Works,* ed. S. Austin (1808).

a conviction of the justice of God in their condemnation; others more of their consenting to the way of salvation by Christ; some more of the actings of love to God and Christ: some more of acts of affiance, in a sweet and assured conviction of the truth and faithfulness of God in his promises; others more of their choosing and resting in God as their whole and everlasting portion, and of their ardent and longing desires after God, to have communion with him; others more of their abhorrence of themselves for their past sins, and earnest longings to live to God's glory for their time to come: some have their minds fixed more on God; others on Christ, as I have observed before, but it seems evidently to be the same work, the same thing done, the same habitual change wrought in the heart; it all tends the same way, and to the same end; and 'tis plainly the same spirit that breathes and acts in various persons. There is an endless variety in the particular manner and circumstances in which persons are wrought on, and an opportunity of seeing so much of such a work of God will shew that God is further from confining himself to certain steps, and a particular method, in his work on souls, than it may be some do imagine. I believe it has occasioned some good people amongst us, that were before too ready to make their own experiences a rule to others, to be less censorious and more extended in their charity. The work of God has been glorious in its variety, it has the more displayed the manifoldness and unsearchableness of the wisdom of God, and wrought more charity among its people.

There is a great difference among those that are converted as to the degree of hope and satisfaction that they have concerning their own state. Some have a high degree of satisfaction in this matter almost constantly: and yet it is rare that any do enjoy so full an assurance of their interest in Christ, that self-examination should seem needless to them; unless it be at particular seasons, while in the actual enjoyment of some great discovery, that God gives of his glory and rich grace in Christ, to the drawing forth of extraordinary acts of grace. But the greater part, as they sometimes fall into dead frames of spirit, are frequently exercised with scruples and fears concerning their condition.

They generally have an awful apprehension of the dreadfulness and undoing nature of a false hope; and there has been observable in most a great caution, lest in giving an account of their experiences, they should say too much, and use too strong terms. And many after they have related their experiences, have been greatly afflicted with fears, lest they have played the hypocrite, and used stronger terms than their case would fairly allow of; and yet could not find how they could correct themselves.

I think that the main ground of the doubts and fears that persons, after their conversion, have been exercised with about their own state, has been that they have found so much corruption remaining in their hearts. At first their souls seem to be all alive, their hearts are fixed, and their affections flowing; they seem to live quite above the world, and meet with but little difficulty in religious exercises; and they are ready to think it will always be so. Though they are truly abased under a sense of their vileness by reason of former acts of sin, yet they are not then sufficiently sensible what corruption still remains in their hearts; and therefore are surprised when they find that they begin to be in dull and dead frames, to be troubled with wandering thoughts in the time of public and private worship, and to be utterly unable to keep themselves from 'em; also when they find themselves unaffected at seasons in which, they think, there is the greatest occasion to be affected; and when they feel worldly dispositions working in them, and it may be pride and envy, and stirrings of revenge, or some ill spirit towards some person that has injured them, as well as other workings of indwelling sin: their hearts are almost sunk with the disappointment; and they are ready presently to think that all this they have met with is nothing, and that they are mere hypocrites.

They are ready to argue, that if God had indeed done such great things for them, as they hoped, such ingratitude would be inconsistent with it. They cry out of the hardness and wickedness of their hearts; and say there is so much corruption, that it seems to them impossible that there should be any goodness there: and many of them seem to be much more sensible how corrupt their hearts are, than ever they were before they were converted; and some have been too ready to be impressed with fear, that instead of becoming better, they are grown much worse, and make it an argument against the goodness of their state. But in truth, the case seems plainly to be, that now they feel the pain of their own wounds; they have a watchful eye upon their hearts, that they don't use to have: they take more notice what sin is there, and sin is now more burdensome to 'em, they strive more against it, and feel more of the strength of it.

They are somewhat surprised that they should in this respect find themselves so different from the idea that they generally had entertained of godly persons; for though grace be indeed of a far more excellent nature than they imagined; yet those that are godly have much less of it, and much more remaining corruption, than they thought. They never realized it, that persons were wont to meet with such difficulties, after they were once converted. When they are thus exercised with doubts about their state, through the deadness of their frames of spirit, as long as these frames last, they are commonly unable to satisfy themselves of the truth of their grace, by all their self-examination. When they hear of the signs of grace laid down for 'em to try themselves by, they are often so clouded that they don't know how to apply them: they hardly know whether they have such and such things in them or no, and whether they have experienced them or not: that which was sweetest, and best and most distinguishing in their experiences, they can't recover a sense or idea of. But on a return of the influences of the Spirit of God, to revive the lively actings of grace, the light breaks through the cloud, and doubting and darkness soon vanish away.

Persons are often revived out of their dead and dark frames by religious conversation: while they are talking of divine things, or ever they are aware, their souls are carried away into holy exercises with abundant pleasure. And oftentimes, while they are relating their past experiences to their Christian brethren, they have a fresh sense of them revived, and the same experiences in a degree again renewed. Sometimes while persons are exercised in mind with several objections against the goodness of their state, they have Scriptures, one after another, coming to their minds, to answer their scruples and unravel their difficulties, exceeding apposite and proper to their circumstances; by which means their darkness is scattered; and often before the bestowment of any new remarkable comforts, especially after long continued deadness and ill frames, there are renewed humblings, in a great sense of their own exceeding vileness and unworthiness, as before their first comforts were bestowed.

Many in the country have entertained a mean thought of this great work that there has been amongst us, from what they have heard of impressions that have been made on persons' imaginations. But there have been exceeding great misrepresentations and innumerable false reports concerning that matter. 'Tis not, that I know of, the profession or opinion of any one person in the town, that any weight is to be laid on anything seen with the bodily eyes: I know the contrary to be a received and established principle amongst us. I cannot say that there have been no instances of persons that have been ready to give too much heed to vain and useless imaginations; but they have been easily corrected, and I conclude it will not be wondered at, that a congregation should need a guide in such cases, to assist them in distinguishing wheat from chaff. But such impressions on the imagination as have been more usual, seem to me to be plainly no other than what is to be expected in human nature in such circumstances, and what is the natural result of the strong exercise of the mind, and impressions on the heart.

I do not suppose that they themselves imagined that they saw anything with their bodily eyes; but only have had within them ideas strongly impressed, and as it were, lively pictures in their minds: as for instance, some when in great terrors, through fear of hell, have had lively ideas of a dreadful furnace. Some, when their hearts have been strongly impressed, and their affections greatly moved with a sense of the beauty and excellency of Christ, it has wrought on their imaginations so, that together with a sense of his glorious spiritual perfections, there has arisen in the mind an idea of one of glorious majesty, and of a sweet and a gracious aspect. So some, when they have been greatly affected with Christ's death, have at the same time a lively idea of Christ hanging upon the cross, and of his blood running from his wounds; which things won't be wondered at by them that have observed how strong affections about temporal matters will excite lively ideas and pictures of different things in the mind.

. . . There have indeed been some few instances of impressions on persons' imaginations, that have been something mysterious to me, and I have been at a loss about them; for though it has been exceeding evident to me by many things that appeared in them, both then (when they related them) and afterwards, that they indeed had a great sense of the spiritual excellency of divine things accompanying them; yet I have not been able well to satisfy myself, whether their imaginary ideas have been more than could naturally arise from their spiritual sense of things. However, I have used the utmost caution in such cases; great care has been taken both in public and in private to teach persons the difference between what is spiritual and what is merely imaginary. I have often warned persons not to lay the stress of their hope on any ideas of any outward glory, or any external thing whatsoever, and have met with no opposition in such instructions. But 'tis not strange if some weaker persons, in giving an account of their experiences, have not so prudently distinguished between the spiritual and imaginary part; which some that have not been well affected to religion, might take advantage of.

There has been much talk in many parts of the country, as though the people have symbolized with the Quakers,[2] and the Quakers themselves have been moved with such reports; and came here, once and again, hoping to find good waters to fish in; but without the least success, and seemed to be discouraged and have left off coming. There have also been reports spread about the country, as though the first occasion of so remarkable a concern on people's minds here, was an apprehension

[2]Those who heard about the Great Awakening sometimes compared the Puritans' conversion experiences to those of the Quakers. Yet Quaker experience of the inward light differed, like their theology, from Puritan conversion.

that the world was near to an end, which was altogether a false report. Indeed, after this stirring and concern became so general and extraordinary, as has been related, the minds of some were filled with speculation, what so great a dispensation of divine providence might forebode: and some reports were heard from abroad, as though certain divines and others thought the conflagration was nigh; but such reports were never generally looked upon [as] worthy of notice.

The work that has now been wrought on souls is evidently the same that was wrought in my venerable predecessor's days;[3] as I have had abundant opportunity to know, having been in the ministry here two years with him, and so conversed with a considerable number that my grandfather thought to be savingly converted in that time; and having been particularly acquainted with the experiences of many that were converted under his ministry before. And I know no one of them, that in the least doubts of its being the same spirit and the same work. Persons have now no otherwise been subject to impressions on their imaginations than formerly: the work is of the same nature, and has not been attended with any extraordinary circumstances, excepting such as are analogous to the extraordinary degree of it before described. And God's people that were formerly converted, have now partook of the same shower of divine blessing in the renewing, strengthening, edifying influences of the Spirit of God, that others have, in his converting influences; and the work here has also been plainly the same with that which has been wrought in those of other places that have been mentioned, as partaking of the same blessing. I have particularly conversed with persons about their experiences that belong to all parts of the county, and in various parts of Connecticut, where a religious concern has lately appeared; and have been informed of the experiences of many others by their own pastors.

'Tis easily perceived by the foregoing account that 'tis very much the practice of the people here to converse freely one with another of their spiritual experiences; which is a thing that many have been disgusted at. But however our people may have, in some respects, gone to extremes in it, yet 'tis doubtless a practice that the circumstances of this town, and [of] neighboring towns, has naturally led them into. Whatsoever people are in such circumstances, where all have their minds engaged to such a degree in the same affair, that 'tis ever uppermost in their thoughts; they will naturally make it the subject of conversation one with another when they get together, in which they will grow more and more free: restraints will soon vanish; and they will not conceal from one another what they meet with. And it has been a practice which, in the general, has been attended with many good effects, and what God has greatly blessed amongst us. But it must be confessed, there may have been some ill consequences of it; which yet are rather to be laid to the indiscreet management of it than to the practice itself: and none can wonder, if among such a multitude some fail of exercising so much prudence in choosing the time, manner, and occasion of such discourse, as is desirable.

1736

[3]Edwards became a colleague of his grandfather, Reverend Solomon Stoddard, in Northampton in 1726.

Personal Narrative[1]

I had a variety of concerns and exercises about my soul from my childhood; but had two more remarkable seasons of awakening, before I met with that change, by which I was brought to those new dispositions, and that new sense of things, that I have since had. The first time was when I was a boy, some years before I went to college, at a time of remarkable awakening in my father's congregation. I was then very much affected for many months, and concerned about the things of religion, and my soul's salvation; and was abundant in duties. I used to pray five times a day in secret, and to spend much time in religious talk with other boys; and used to meet with them to pray together. I experienced I know not what kind of delight in religion. My mind was much engaged in it, and had much self-righteous pleasure; and it was my delight to abound in religious duties. I, with some of my school-mates joined together, and built a booth in a swamp, in a very secret and retired place, for a place of prayer. And besides, I had particular secret places of my own in the woods, where I used to retire by myself; and used to be from time to time much affected. My affections seemed to be lively and easily moved, and I seemed to be in my element, when engaged in religious duties. And I am ready to think, many are deceived with such affections, and such a kind of delight, as I then had in religion, and mistake it for grace.

But in process of time, my convictions and affections wore off; and I entirely lost all those affections and delights, and left off secret prayer, at least as to any constant performance of it; and returned like a dog to his vomit, and went on in ways of sin.[2]

Indeed, I was at some times very uneasy, especially towards the latter part of the time of my being at college. 'Till it pleas'd God, in my last year at college, at a time when I was in the midst of many uneasy thoughts about the state of my soul, to seize me with a pleurisy;[3] in which he brought me nigh to the grave, and shook me over the pit of hell.

But yet, it was not long after my recovery, before I fell again into my old ways of sin. But God would not suffer me to go on with any quietness; but I had great and violent inward struggles: 'till after many conflicts with wicked inclinations, and repeated resolutions, and bonds that I laid myself under by a kind of vows to God, I was brought wholly to break off all former wicked ways, and all ways of known outward sin; and to apply myself to seek my salvation, and practice the duties of religion: But without that kind of affection and delight, that I had formerly experienced. My concern now wrought more by inward struggles and conflicts, and self-reflections. I made seeking my salvation the main business of my life. But yet it seems to me, I sought after a miserable manner: Which has made me some times since to question, whether ever it issued in that which was saving; being ready to doubt, whether such miserable seeking was ever succeeded. But yet I was brought to seek salvation, in a

[1]Written during or after January 1739, Edwards's account of his spiritual life was not published until after his death, when his friend Samuel Hopkins published it as "An Account of His Conversion, Experiences, and Religious Exercises," in *The Life and Character of the Late Rev. Mr. Jonathan Edwards* (1765).

[2]"As a dog returneth to his vomit, so a fool returneth to his folly" (Proverbs 26:11).

[3]An illness in the respiratory system.

manner that I never was before. I felt a spirit to part with all things in the world, for an interest in Christ. My concern continued and prevailed, with many exercising thoughts and inward struggles; but yet it never seemed to be proper to express my concern that I had, by the name of terror.

From my childhood up, my mind has been wont to be full of objections against the doctrine of God's sovereignty, in choosing whom he would to eternal life, and rejecting whom he pleased; leaving them eternally to perish, and be everlastingly tormented in hell. It used to appear like a horrible doctrine to me. But I remember the time very well, when I seemed to be convinced, and fully satisfied, as to this sovereignty of God, and his justice in thus eternally disposing of men, according to his sovereign pleasure. But never could give an account, how, or by what means, I was thus convinced; not in the least imagining, in the time of it, nor a long time after, that there was any extraordinary influence of God's spirit in it; but only that now I saw further, and my reason apprehended the justice and reasonableness of it. However, my mind rested in it; and it put an end to all those cavils and objections, that had 'till then abode with me, all the preceding part of my life. And there has been a wonderful alteration in my mind, with respect to the doctrine of God's sovereignty, from that day to this; so that I scarce ever have found so much as the rising of an objection against God's sovereignty, in the most absolute sense, in showing mercy to whom he will show mercy, and hardening and eternally damning whom he will.[4] God's absolute sovereignty, and justice, with respect to salvation and damnation, is what my mind seems to rest assured of, as much as of any thing that I see with my eyes; at least it is so at times. But I have often times since that first conviction, had quite another kind of sense of God's sovereignty, than I had then. I have often since, not only had a conviction, but a *delightful* conviction. The doctrine of God's sovereignty has very often appeared, an exceeding pleasant, bright and sweet doctrine to me: and absolute sovereignty is what I love to ascribe to God. But my first conviction was not with this.

The first that I remember that ever I found any thing of that sort of inward, sweet delight in God and divine things, that I have lived much in since, was on reading those words, I Tim. i. 17. "Now unto the king eternal, immortal, invisible, the only wise God, be honor and glory for ever and ever, Amen." As I read the words, there came into my soul, and was as it were diffused thro' it, a sense of the glory of the Divine Being; a new sense, quite different from any thing I ever experienced before. Never any words of scripture seemed to me as these words did. I thought with myself, how excellent a being that was; and how happy I should be, if I might enjoy that God, and be wrapt up to God in Heaven, and be as it were swallowed up in Him. I kept saying, and as it were singing over these words of scripture to myself; and went to prayer, to pray to God that I might enjoy him; and prayed in a manner quite different from what I used to do; with a new sort of affection. But it never came into my thought, that there was any thing spiritual, or of a saving nature in this.

From about that time, I began to have a new kind of apprehensions and ideas of Christ, and the work of redemption, and the glorious way of salvation by Him. I had an inward, sweet sense of these things, that at times came into my heart; and my soul

[4]"Therefore hath he mercy on whom he will have mercy, and whom he will he hardeneth" (Romans 9:18).

was led away in pleasant views and contemplations of them. And my mind was greatly engaged, to spend my time in reading and meditating on Christ; and the beauty and excellency of His person, and the lovely way of salvation, by free grace in Him. I found no books so delightful to me, as those that treated of these subjects. Those words Cant. ii. I. used to be abundantly with me: *I am the Rose of Sharon, the lily of the valleys.* The words seemed to me, sweetly to represent, the loveliness and beauty of Jesus Christ. And the whole Book of Canticles[5] used to be pleasant to me; and I used to be much in reading it, about that time. And found, from time to time, an inward sweetness, that used, as it were, to carry me away in my contemplations; in what I know not how to express otherwise, than by a calm, sweet abstraction of soul from all the concerns of this world; and a kind of vision, or fix'd ideas and imaginations, of being alone in the mountains, or some solitary wilderness, far from all mankind, sweetly conversing with Christ, and wrapt and swallowed up in God. The sense I had of divine things, would often of a sudden as it were, kindle up a sweet burning in my heart; an ardor of my soul, that I know not how to express.

Not long after I first began to experience these things, I gave an account to my father, of some things that had pass'd in my mind. I was pretty much affected by the discourse we had together. And when the discourse was ended, I walked abroad alone, in a solitary place in my father's pasture, for contemplation. And as I was walking there, and looked up on the sky and clouds; there came into my mind, a sweet sense of the glorious majesty and grace of God, that I know not how to express. I seemed to see them both in a sweet conjunction: majesty and meekness join'd together: it was a sweet and gentle, and holy majesty; and also a majestic meekness; an awful sweetness; a high, and great, and holy gentleness.

After this my sense of divine things gradually increased, and became more and more lively, and had more of that inward sweetness. The appearance of every thing was altered: there seem'd to be, as it were, a calm, sweet cast, or appearance of divine glory, in almost every thing. God's excellency, his wisdom, his purity and love, seemed to appear in every thing; in the sun, moon and stars; in the clouds, and blue sky; in the grass, flowers, trees; in the water, and all nature; which used greatly to fix my mind. I often used to sit and view the moon, for a long time; and so in the day time, spent much time in viewing the clouds and sky, to behold the sweet glory of God in these things: in the mean time, singing forth with a low voice, my contemplations of the Creator and Redeemer. And scarce any thing, among all the works of nature, was so sweet to me as thunder and lightning. Formerly, nothing had been so terrible to me. I used to be a person uncommonly terrified with thunder: and it used to strike me with terror, when I saw a thunder-storm rising. But now, on the contrary, it rejoiced me. I felt God at the first appearance of a thunder-storm. And used to take the opportunity at such times to fix myself to view the clouds, and see the lightnings play, and hear the majestic and awful voice of God's thunder: which often times was exceeding entertaining, leading me to sweet contemplations of my great and glorious God. And while I viewed, used to spend my time, as it always seem'd natural to me, to sing or chant forth my meditations; to speak my thoughts in soliloquies, and speak with a singing voice.

[5]Canticles is another name for the Song of Solomon.

I felt then a great satisfaction as to my good estate. But that did not content me.[6] I had vehement longings of soul after God and Christ, and after more holiness; wherewith my heart seemed to be full, and ready to break: which often brought to my mind, the words of the psalmist, Psal. cxix. 28. *My soul breaketh for the longing it hath.* I often felt a mourning and lamenting in my heart, that I had not turned to God sooner, that I might have had more time to grow in grace. My mind was greatly fix'd on divine things; I was almost perpetually in the contemplation of them. Spent most of my time in thinking of divine things, year after year. And used to spend abundance of my time, in walking alone in the woods, and solitary places, for meditation, soliloquy and prayer, and converse with God. And it was always my manner, at such times, to sing forth my contemplations. And was almost constantly in ejaculatory prayer, wherever I was. Prayer seem'd to be natural to me; as the breath, by which the inward burnings of my heart had vent.

The delights which I now felt in things of religion, were of an exceeding different kind, from those forementioned, that I had when I was a boy. They were totally of another kind; and what I then had no more notion or idea of, than one born blind has of pleasant and beautiful colors. They were of a more inward, pure, soul-animating and refreshing nature. Those former delights, never reached the heart; and did not arise from any sight of the divine excellency of the things of God; or any taste of the soul-satisfying, and life-giving good, there is in them.

My sense of divine things seemed gradually to increase, 'till I went to preach at New York;[7] which was about a year and a half after they began. While I was there, I felt them, very sensibly, in a much higher degree, than I had done before. My longings after God and holiness, were much increased. Pure and humble, holy and heavenly Christianity, appeared exceeding amiable to me. I felt in me a burning desire to be in every thing a complete Christian; and conformed to the blessed image of Christ: and that I might live in all things, according to the pure, sweet and blessed rules of the gospel. I had an eager thirsting after progress in these things. My longings after it, put me upon pursuing and pressing after them. It was my continual strife day and night, and constant inquiry, How I should be more holy, and live more holily, and more becoming a child of God, and disciple of Christ. I sought an increase of grace and holiness, and that I might live an holy life, with vastly more earnestness, than ever I sought grace, before I had it. I used to be continually examining myself, and studying and contriving for likely ways and means, how I should live holily, with far greater diligence and earnestness, than ever I pursued any thing in my life: But with too great a dependence on my own strength; which afterwards proved a great damage to me. My experience had not then taught me, as it has done since, my extreme feebleness and impotence, every manner of way; and the innumerable and bottomless depths of secret corruption and deceit, that there was in my heart. However, I went on with my eager pursuit after more holiness; and sweet conformity to Christ.

The Heaven I desired was a heaven of holiness; to be with God, and to spend my eternity in divine love, and holy communion with Christ. My mind was very much taken up with contemplations on heaven, and the enjoyments of those there; and

[6]Edwards here speaks of his spiritual state.

[7]Edwards assisted as a pastor in New York at a Presbyterian Church from 1722 until April 1723. He speaks in this passage of the felt presence he had of Christ.

living there in perfect holiness, humility and love. And it used at that time to appear a great part of the happiness of heaven, that there the saints could express their love to Christ. It appear'd to me a great clog and hindrance and burden to me, that what I felt within, I could not express to God, and give vent to, as I desired. The inward ardor of my soul, seem'd to be hindered and pent up, and could not freely flame out as it would. I used often to think, how in heaven, this sweet principle should freely and fully vent and express itself. Heaven appeared to me exceeding delightful as a world of love. It appeared to me, that all happiness consisted in living in pure, humble, heavenly, divine love.

I remember the thoughts I used then to have of holiness. I remember I then said sometimes to myself, I do certainly know that I love holiness, such as the gospel prescribes. It appeared to me, there was nothing in it but what was ravishingly lovely. It appeared to me, to be the highest beauty and amiableness, above all other beauties: that it was a *divine* beauty; far purer than any thing here upon earth; and that every thing else, was like mire, filth and defilement, in comparison of it.

Holiness, as I then wrote down some of my contemplations on it, appeared to me to be of a sweet, pleasant, charming, serene, calm nature. It seemed to me, it brought an inexpressible purity, brightness, peacefulness and ravishment to the soul: and that it made the soul like a field or garden of God, with all manner of pleasant flowers; that is all pleasant, delightful and undisturbed; enjoying a sweet calm, and the gently vivifying beams of the sun. The soul of a true Christian, as I then wrote my meditations, appear'd like such a little white flower, as we see in the spring of the year; low and humble on the ground, opening its bosom, to receive the pleasant beams of the sun's glory; rejoicing as it were, in a calm rapture; diffusing around a sweet fragrancy; standing peacefully and lovingly, in the midst of other flowers round about; all in like manner opening their bosoms, to drink in the light of the sun.

There was no part of creature-holiness, that I then, and at other times, had so great a sense of the loveliness of, as humility, brokenness of heart and poverty of spirit: and there was nothing that I had such a spirit to long for. My heart as it were panted after this, to lie low before God, and in the dust; that I might be nothing, and that God might be all; that I might become as a little child.[8]

While I was there at New York, I sometimes was much affected with reflections on my past life, considering how late it was, before I began to be truly religious; and how wickedly I had lived 'till then: and once so as to weep abundantly, and for a considerable time together.

On January 12, 1722-3. I made a solemn dedication of myself to God, and wrote it down; giving up myself, and all that I had to God; to be for the future in no respect my own; to act as one that had no right to himself, in any respect. And solemnly vowed to take God for my whole portion and felicity; looking on nothing else as any part of my happiness, nor acting as if it were: and his law for the constant rule of my obedience: engaging to fight with all my might, against the world, the flesh and the devil, to the end of my life. But have reason to be infinitely humbled, when I consider, how much I have fail'd of answering my obligation.

[8]"Verily, I say unto you, Whosoever shall not receive the kingdom of God as a little child, he shall not enter therein" (Mark 10:15).

I had then abundance of sweet religious conversation in the family where I lived, with Mr. John Smith, and his pious mother. My heart was knit in affection to those, in whom were appearances of true piety; and I could bear the thoughts of no other companions, but such as were holy, and the disciples of the blessed Jesus.

I had great longings for the advancement of Christ's kingdom in the world. My secret prayer used to be in great part taken up in praying for it. If I heard the least hint of any thing that happened in any part of the world, that appear'd to me, in some respect or other, to have a favorable aspect on the interest of Christ's kingdom, my soul eagerly catch'd at it; and it would much animate and refresh me. I used to be earnest to read public news-letters, mainly for that end; to see if I could not find some news favorable to the interest of religion in the world.

I very frequently used to retire into a solitary place, on the banks of Hudson's river, at some distance from the city, for contemplation on divine things, and secret converse with God; and had many sweet hours there. Sometimes Mr. Smith and I walked there together, to converse of the things of God; and our conversation used much to turn on the advancement of Christ's kingdom in the world, and the glorious things that God would accomplish for his church in the latter days.

I had then, and at other times, the greatest delight in the holy Scriptures, of any book whatsoever. Often-times in reading it, every word seemed to touch my heart. I felt an harmony between something in my heart, and those sweet and powerful words. I seem'd often to see so much light, exhibited by every sentence, and such a refreshing ravishing food communicated, that I could not get along in reading. Used often-times to dwell long on one sentence, to see the wonders contained in it; and yet almost every sentence seemed to be full of wonders.

I came away from New York in the month of April, 1723, and had a most bitter parting with Madam Smith and her son. My heart seemed to sink within me, at leaving the family and city, where I had enjoyed so many sweet and pleasant days. I went from New York to Weathersfield[9] by water. As I sail'd away, I kept sight of the city as long as I could; and when I was out of sight of it, it would affect me much to look that way, with a kind of melancholy mixed with sweetness. However, that night after this sorrowful parting, I was greatly comforted in God at Westchester, where we went ashore to lodge: and had a pleasant time of it all the voyage to Saybrook.[10] It was sweet to me to think of meeting dear Christians in heaven, where we should never part more. At Saybrook we went ashore to lodge on Saturday, and there kept sabbath; where I had a sweet and refreshing season, walking alone in the fields.

After I came home to Windsor, remained much in a like frame of my mind, as I had been in at New York, but only sometimes felt my heart ready to sink, with the thoughts of my friends at New York. And my refuge and support was in contemplations on the heavenly state; as I find in my diary of May 1, 1723. It was my comfort to think of that state, where there is fulness of joy; where reigns heavenly, sweet, calm and delightful love, without alloy; where there are continually the dearest expressions of this love; where is the enjoyment of the persons loved, without ever parting; where these persons that appear so lovely in this world, will really be inexpressibly

[9]Wethersfield, Connecticut.

[10]Westchester, New York, and Saybrook, Connecticut.

more lovely, and full of love to us. And how sweetly will the mutual lovers join together to sing the praises of God and the Lamb![11] How full will it fill us with joy, to think, that this enjoyment, these sweet exercises will never cease or come to an end; but will last to all eternity!

Continued much in the same frame in the general, that I had been in at New York, till I went to New Haven, to live there as tutor of the college; having some special seasons of uncommon sweetness: particularly once at Boston, in a journey from Boston, walking out alone in the fields. After I went to New Haven, I sunk in religion; my mind being diverted from my eager and violent pursuits after holiness, by some affairs that greatly perplexed and distracted my mind.

In September, 1725, was taken ill at New Haven; and endeavoring to go home to Windsor, was so ill at the North Village, that I could go no further: where I lay sick for about a quarter of a year. And in this sickness, God was pleased to visit me again with the sweet influences of His spirit. My mind was greatly engaged there on divine, pleasant contemplations, and longings of soul. I observed that those who watched with me, would often be looking out for the morning, and seemed to wish for it. Which brought to my mind those words of the psalmist, which my soul with sweetness made its own language. *My soul waitest for the Lord, more than they that watch for the morning, I say, more than they that watch for the morning.*[12] And when the light of the morning came, and the beams of the sun came in at the windows, it refreshed my soul from one morning to another. It seemed to me to be some image of the sweet light of God's glory.

I remember, about that time, I used greatly to long for the conversion of some that I was concerned with. It seem'd to me, I could gladly honor them, and with delight be a servant to them, and lie at their feet, if they were but truly holy.

But some time after this, I was again greatly diverted in my mind, with some temporal concerns, that exceedingly took up my thoughts, greatly to the wounding of my soul: and went on through various exercises, that it would be tedious to relate, that gave me much more experience of my own heart, than ever I had before.

Since I came to this town,[13] I have often had sweet complacency in God, in views of his glorious perfections, and the excellency of Jesus Christ. God has appeared to me, a glorious and lovely being, chiefly on the account of His holiness. The holiness of God has always appeared to me the most lovely of all His attributes. The doctrines of God's absolute sovereignty, and free grace, in showing mercy to whom He would show mercy; and man's absolute dependence on the operations of God's Holy Spirit, have very often appeared to me as sweet and glorious doctrines. These doctrines have been much my delight. God's sovereignty has ever appeared to me, as great part of His glory. It has often been sweet to me to go to God, and adore Him as a sovereign God, and ask sovereign mercy of Him.

I have loved the doctrines of the gospel: They have been to my soul like green pastures. The gospel has seem'd to me to be the richest treasure; the treasure that I have most desired, and longed that it might dwell richly in me. The way of salvation by Christ, has appeared in a general way, glorious and excellent, and most pleasant

[11]In Revelation, the Lamb is the symbol of Christ.

[12]Psalm 130:6.

[13]In 1726, Edwards went to Northampton, Massachusetts, to assist his grandfather in parish duties.

and beautiful. It has often seem'd to me, that it would in a great measure spoil heaven, to receive it in any other way. That Text has often been affecting and delightful to me, Isai. xxxii. 2. *A man shall be an hiding place from the wind, and a covert from the tempest etc.*

It has often appear'd sweet to me, to be united to Christ; to have Him for my head, and to be a member of His body: and also to have Christ for my teacher and prophet. I very often think with sweetness and longings and pantings of soul, of being a little child, taking hold of Christ, to be led by Him through the wilderness of this world. That text, Matth. xviii. at the beginning, has often been sweet to me, *Except ye be converted, and become as little children etc.* I love to think of coming to Christ, to receive salvation of Him, poor in spirit, and quite empty of self; humbly exalting Him alone; cut entirely off from my own root, and to grow into, and out of Christ: to have God in Christ to be all in all; and to live by faith on the Son of God, a life of humble, unfeigned confidence in Him. That Scripture has often been sweet to me, Psal. cxv. I. *Not unto us, O Lord, not unto us, but unto Thy name give glory, for Thy mercy, and for Thy truth's sake.* And those words of Christ, *Luk. x. 21. In that hour Jesus rejoiced in spirit, and said, I thank thee, O Father, Lord of heaven and earth, that Thou hast hid these things from the wise and prudent, and hast revealed them unto babes: Even so Father, for so it seemed good in Thy sight.* That sovereignty of God that Christ rejoiced in, seemed to me to be worthy to be rejoiced in; and that rejoicing of Christ, seemed to me to show the excellency of Christ, and the spirit that He was of.

Sometimes only mentioning a single word, causes my heart to burn within me: or only seeing the Name of Christ, or the name of some attribute of God. And God has appeared glorious to me, on account of the Trinity. It has made me have exalting thoughts of God, that he subsists in three persons; Father, Son, and Holy Ghost.

The sweetest joys and delights I have experienced, have not been those that have arisen from a hope of my own good estate; but in a direct view of the glorious things of the gospel. When I enjoy this sweetness, it seems to carry me above the thoughts of my own safe estate. It seems at such times a loss that I cannot bear, to take off my eye from the glorious, pleasant object I behold without me, to turn my eye in upon myself, and my own good estate.

My heart has been much on the advancement of Christ's kingdom in the world. The histories of the past advancement of Christ's kingdom, have been sweet to me. When I have read histories of past ages, the pleasantest thing in all my reading has been, to read of the kingdom of Christ being promoted. And when I have expected in my reading, to come to any such thing, I have lotted upon it all the way as I read. And my mind has been much entertained and delighted, with the Scripture promises and prophecies, of the future glorious advancement of Christ's kingdom on earth.

I have sometimes had a sense of the excellent fulness of Christ, and His meetness and suitableness as a Saviour; whereby He has appeared to me, far above all, the chief of ten thousands.[14] And His blood and atonement has appeared sweet, and His righteousness sweet; which is always accompanied with an ardency of spirit, and inward strugglings and breathings and groanings, that cannot be uttered, to be emptied of myself, and swallowed up in Christ.

[14]"My beloved is white and ruddy, the chiefest among ten thousand" (Song of Solomon 5:10).

Once, as I rid out into the woods for my health, *Anno*[15] 1737; and having lit from my horse in a retired place, as my manner commonly has been, to walk for divine contemplation and prayer; I had a view, that for me was extraordinary, of the glory of the Son of God; as mediator between God and man; and his wonderful, great, full, pure and sweet grace and love, and meek and gentle condescension. This grace, that appear'd to me so calm and sweet, appear'd great above the heavens. The person of Christ appear'd ineffably excellent, with an excellency great enough to swallow up all thought and conception, which continued, as near as I can judge, about an hour; which kept me, the bigger part of the time, in a flood of tears, and weeping aloud. I felt withal, an ardency of soul to be, what I know not otherwise how to express, than to be emptied and annihilated; to lie in the dust, and to be full of Christ alone; to love Him with a holy and pure love; to trust in Him; to live upon Him; to serve and follow Him, and to be totally wrapt up in the fullness of Christ; and to be perfectly sanctified and made pure, with a divine and heavenly purity. I have several other times, had views very much of the same nature, and that have had the same effects.

I have many times had a sense of the glory of the third person in the Trinity, in His office of sanctifier; in His holy operations communicating divine light and life to the soul. God in the communications of His Holy Spirit, has appear'd as an infinite fountain of divine glory and sweetness; being full and sufficient to fill and satisfy the soul: pouring forth itself in sweet communications, like the sun in its glory, sweetly and pleasantly diffusing light and life.

I have sometimes had an affecting sense of the excellency of the word of God, as a word of life; as the light of life; a sweet, excellent, life-giving word: accompanied with a thirsting after that word, that it might dwell richly in my heart.

I have often since I lived in this town, had very affecting views of my own sinfulness and vileness; very frequently so as to hold me in a kind of loud weeping, sometimes for a considerable time together: so that I have often been forced to shut myself up.[16] I have had a vastly greater sense of my own wickedness, and the badness of my heart, since my conversion, than ever I had before. It has often appeared to me, that if God should mark iniquity against me, I should appear the very worst of all mankind; of all that have been since the beginning of the world to this time: and that I should have by far the lowest place in hell. When others that have come to talk with me about their soul concerns, have expressed the sense they have had of their own wickedness, by saying that it seem'd to them, that they were as bad as the devil himself; I thought their expressions seemed exceeding faint and feeble, to represent my wickedness. I thought I should wonder, that they should content themselves with such expressions as these, if I had any reason to imagine, that their sin bore any proportion to mine. It seemed to me, I should wonder at myself, if I should express *my* wickedness in such feeble terms as they did.

My wickedness, as I am in myself, has long appear'd to me perfectly ineffable, and infinitely swallowing up all thought and imagination; like an infinite deluge, or infinite mountains over my head. I know not how to express better, what my sins appear to me to be, than by heaping infinite upon infinite, and multiplying infinite by

[15]The year.

[16]Take to meditation alone in my room.

infinite. I go about very often, for this many years, with these expressions in my mind, and in my mouth, "Infinite upon infinite. Infinite upon infinite!" When I look into my heart, and take a view of my wickedness, it looks like an abyss infinitely deeper than hell. And it appears to me, that were it not for free grace, exalted and raised up to the infinite height of all the fulness and glory of the great Jehovah,[17] and the arm of His power and grace stretched forth, in all the majesty of His power, and in all the glory of His sovereignty; I should appear sunk down in my sins infinitely below hell itself, far beyond sight of every thing, but the piercing eye of God's grace, that can pierce even down to such a depth, and to the bottom of such an abyss.

And yet, I ben't in the least inclined to think, that I have a greater conviction of sin than ordinary. It seems to me, my conviction of sin is exceeding small, and faint. It appears to me enough to amaze me, that I have no more sense of my sin. I know certainly, that I have very little sense of my sinfulness. That my sins appear to me so great, don't seem to me to be, because I have so much more conviction of sin than other Christians, but because I am so much worse, and have so much more wickedness to be convinced of. When I have had these turns of weeping and crying for my sins, I thought I knew in the time of it, that my repentance was nothing to my sin.

I have greatly longed of late, for a broken heart, and to lie low before God. And when I ask for humility of God, I can't bear the thoughts of being no more humble, than other Christians. It seems to me, that tho' their degrees of humility may be suitable for them; yet it would be a vile self-exaltation in me, not to be the lowest in humility of all mankind. Others speak of their longing to be humbled to the dust. Tho' that may be a proper expression for them, I always think for myself, that I ought to be humbled down below hell. 'Tis an expression that it has long been natural for me to use in prayer to God. I ought to lie infinitely low before God.

It is affecting to me to think, how ignorant I was, when I was a young Christian, of the bottomless, infinite depths of wickedness, pride, hypocrisy and deceit left in my heart.

I have vastly a greater sense, of my universal, exceeding dependence on God's grace and strength, and mere good pleasure, of late, than I used formerly to have; and have experienced more of an abhorrence of my own righteousness. The thought of any comfort or joy, arising in me, on any consideration, or reflection on my own amiableness, or any of my performances or experiences, or any goodness of heart or life, is nauseous and detestable to me. And yet I am greatly afflicted with a proud and self-righteous spirit; much more sensibly, than I used to be formerly. I see that serpent rising and putting forth it's head, continually, everywhere, all around me.

Tho' it seems to me, that in some respects I was a far better Christian, for two or three years after my first conversion, than I am now; and lived in a more constant delight and pleasure: yet of late years, I have had a more full and constant sense of the absolute sovereignty of God, and a delight in that sovereignty; and have had more of a sense of the glory of Christ, as a mediator, as revealed in the gospel. On one Saturday night in particular, had a particular discovery of the excellency of the gospel of Christ, above all other doctrines; so that I could not but say to myself; "This is my chosen light, my chosen doctrine": and of Christ, "This is my chosen prophet." It

[17]God, in the Old Testament.

appear'd to me to be sweet beyond all expression, to follow Christ, and to be taught and enlighten'd and instructed by Him; to learn of Him, and live to Him.

Another Saturday night, January, 1738-9, had such a sense, how sweet and blessed a thing it was, to walk in the way of duty, to do that which was right and meet to be done, and agreeable to the holy mind of God; that it caused me to break forth into a kind of a loud weeping, which held me some time; so that I was forced to shut myself up, and fasten the doors. I could not but as it were cry out, "How happy are they which do that which is right in the sight of God! They are blessed indeed, they are the happy ones!" I had at the same time, a very affecting sense, how meet and suitable it was that God should govern the world, and order all things according to his own pleasure; and I rejoiced in it, that God reigned, and that his will was done.

1765

Sinners in the Hands of an Angry God[1]

Deuteronomy 32.35

Their foot shall slide in due time.[2]

In this verse is threatened the vengeance of God on the wicked unbelieving Israelites, who were God's visible people, and who lived under the means of grace,[3] but who, notwithstanding all God's wonderful works towards them, remained (as in verse 28.) void of counsel, having no understanding in them.[4] Under all the cultivations of heaven, they brought forth bitter and poisonous fruit, as in the two verses next preceding the text.[5] The expression I have chosen for my text, "Their foot shall slide in

[1]Edwards delivered this sermon before the congregation at Enfield on Sunday, July 8, 1741. Said to have been one of the quietest, least spectacular of preachers in his own day, Edwards used this sermon during the Great Awakening, when his audiences often broke out in hysteria. According to Reverend Eleazer Wheelock, future president of Dartmouth College, "There was such a breathing of distress, and weeping, that the preacher was obliged to speak to the people and desire silence, that he might be heard" (reported by Benjamin Trumbull in *A Complete History of Connecticut,* 1797).

The text of the sermon is from Sereno Dwight, ed., *The Works of Jonathan Edwards,* vol. 7 (1829–30).

[2]"To me belongeth vengeance, and recompense; their foot shall slide in due time: for the day of their calamity is at hand, and the things that shall come upon them make haste."

[3]The Israelites were given the Ten Commandments. For most Puritans, "means of grace" were the preaching of the word of God and the administration of the two sacraments, baptism and the Lord's Supper.

[4]"They are a nation void of counsel, neither is there any understanding in them" (Deuteronomy 32:28).

[5]"For their vine is of the vine of Sodom, and the fields of Gomorrah: their grapes are grapes of gall, their clusters are bitter: their wine is the poison of dragons, and the cruel venom of asps" (Deuteronomy 32:32–33). Sodom and Gomorrah, cities of wickedness, were destroyed by a rain of fire and sulphur (Genesis 19:28).

due time," seems to imply the following things, relating to the punishment and destruction to which these wicked Israelites were exposed.

1. That they were always exposed to destruction; as one that stands or walks in slippery places is always exposed to fall. This is implied in the manner of their destruction coming upon them, being represented by their foot sliding. The same is expressed, Psalm 73.18: "Surely thou didst set them in slippery places; thou castedst them down into destruction."

2. It implies that they were always exposed to sudden unexpected destruction. As he that walks in slippery places is every moment liable to fall, he cannot foresee one moment whether he shall stand or fall the next; and when he does fall, he falls at once without warning. Which is also expressed in Psalm 73. 18-19: "Surely thou didst set them in slippery places; thou castedst them down into destruction: How are they brought into desolation as in a moment!"

3. Another thing implied is, that they are liable to fall of themselves, without being thrown down by the hand of another; as he that stands or walks on slippery ground needs nothing but his own weight to throw him down.

4. That the reason why they are not fallen already, and do not fall now, is only that God's appointed time is not come. For it is said, that when that due time or appointed times comes, their foot shall slide. Then they shall be left to fall, as they are inclined by their own weight. God will not hold them up in these slippery places any longer, but will let them go; and then, at that very instant, they shall fall into destruction; as he that stands on such slippery declining ground, on the edge of a pit, he cannot stand alone, when he is let go he immediately falls and is lost.

The observation from the words that I would now insist upon is this. "There is nothing that keeps wicked men at any one moment out of hell, but the mere pleasure of God." By the mere pleasure of God, I mean His sovereign pleasure, His arbitrary will, restrained by no obligation, hindered by no manner of difficulty, any more than if nothing else but God's mere will had in the least degree, or in any respect whatsoever, any hand in the preservation of wicked men one moment. The truth of this observation may appear by the following considerations.

1. There is no want of power in God to cast wicked men into hell at any moment. Men's hands cannot be strong when God rises up. The strongest have no power to resist Him, nor can any deliver out of His hands. He is not only able to cast wicked men into hell, but He can most easily do it. Sometimes an earthly prince meets with a great deal of difficulty to subdue a rebel, who has found means to fortify himself, and has made himself strong by the numbers of his followers. But it is not so with God. There is no fortress that is any defense from the power of God. Though hand join in hand, and vast multitudes of God's enemies combine and associate themselves, they are easily broken in pieces. They are as great heaps of light chaff before the whirlwind; or large quantities of dry stubble before devouring flames. We find it easy to tread on and crush a worm that we see crawling on the earth; so it is easy for us to cut or singe a slender thread that any thing hangs by: thus easy is it for God, when he pleases, to cast His enemies down to hell. What are we, that we should think to stand before him, at whose rebuke the earth trembles, and before whom the rocks are thrown down?

2. They deserve to be cast into hell; so that divine justice never stands in the way, it makes no objection against God's using His power at any moment to destroy them.

Yea, on the contrary, justice calls aloud for an infinite punishment of their sins. Divine justice says of the tree that brings forth such grapes of Sodom, "Cut it down, why cumbereth it the ground?" Luke 13.7. The sword of divine justice is every moment brandished over their heads, and it is nothing but the hand of arbitrary mercy, and God's will, that holds it back.

3. They are already under a sentence of condemnation to hell. They do not only justly deserve to be cast down thither, but the sentence of the law of God, that eternal and immutable rule of righteousness that God has fixed between Him and mankind, is gone out against them, and stands against them; so that they are bound over already to hell. John 3.18: "He that believeth not is condemned already." So that every unconverted man properly belongs to hell; that is his place; from thence he is, John 8.23: "Ye are from beneath." And thither he is bound; it is the place that justice, and God's word, and the sentence of his unchangeable law assign to him.

4. They are now the objects of that very same anger and wrath of God that is expressed in the torments of hell. And the reason why they do not go down to hell at each moment is not because God, in whose power they are, is not then very angry with them as He is with many miserable creatures now tormented in hell, who there feel and bear the fierceness of His wrath. Yea, God is a great deal more angry with great numbers that are now on earth: yea, doubtless, with many that are now in this congregation, who it may be are at ease, than He is with many of those who are now in the flames of hell.

So that it is not because God is unmindful of their wickedness, and does not resent it, that He does not let loose His hand and cut them off. God is not altogether such an one as themselves, though they may imagine Him to be so. The wrath of God burns against them, their damnation does not slumber; the pit is prepared, the fire is made ready, the furnace is now hot, ready to receive them; the flames do now rage and glow. The glittering sword is whet, and held over them, and the pit hath opened its mouth under them.

5. The devil stands ready to fall upon them, and seize them as his own, at what moment God shall permit him. They belong to him; he has their souls in his possession, and under his dominion. The scripture represents them as his goods, Luke 11.12. The devils watch them; they are ever by them at their right hand; they stand waiting for them, like greedy hungry lions that see their prey, and expect to have it, but are for the present kept back. If God should withdraw His hand, by which they are restrained, they would in one moment fly upon their poor souls. The old serpent is gaping for them; hell opens it mouth wide to receive them; and if God should permit it, they would be hastily swallowed up and lost.

6. There are in the souls of wicked men those hellish principles reigning that would presently kindle and flame out into hell fire, if it were not for God's restraints. There is laid in the very nature of carnal men a foundation for the torments of hell. There are those corrupt principles, in reigning power in them, and in full possession of them, that are seeds of hell fire. These principles are active and powerful, exceeding violent in their nature, and if it were not for the restraining hand of God upon them, they would soon break out, they would flame out after the same manner as the same corruptions, the same enmity does in the hearts of damned souls, and would beget the same torments as they do in them. The souls of the wicked are in scripture compared to the troubled sea, Isaiah 57.20. For the present, God restrains their wickedness by His mighty power, as He does the raging waves of the troubled sea, saying, "Hitherto

shalt thou come, but no further;"[6] but if God should withdraw that restraining power, it would soon carry all before it. Sin is the ruin and misery of the soul; it is destructive in its nature; and if God should leave it without restraint, there would need nothing else to make the soul perfectly miserable. The corruption of the heart of man is immoderate and boundless in its fury; and while wicked men live here, it is like fire pent up by God's restraints, whereas if it were let loose, it would set on fire the course of nature; and as the heart is now a sink of sin, so if sin was not restrained, it would immediately turn the soul into a fiery oven, or a furnace of fire and brimstone.

7. It is no security to wicked men for one moment that there are no visible means of death at hand. It is no security to a natural man that he is now in health and that he does not see which way he should now immediately go out of the world by any accident, and that there is no visible danger in any respect in his circumstances. The manifold and continual experience of the world in all ages, shows this is no evidence that a man is not on the very brink of eternity, and that the next step will not be into another world. The unseen, unthought-of ways and means of persons going suddenly out of the world are innumerable and inconceivable. Unconverted men walk over the pit of hell on a rotten covering, and there are innumerable places in this covering so weak that they will not bear their weight, and these places are not seen. The arrows of death fly unseen at noonday;[7] the sharpest sight cannot discern them. God has so many different unsearchable ways of taking wicked men out of the world and sending them to hell, that there is nothing to make it appear that God had need to be at the expense of a miracle, or go out of the ordinary course of His providence, to destroy any wicked man at any moment. All the means that there are of sinners going out of the world are so in God's hands, and so universally and absolutely subject to His power and determination, that it does not depend at all the less on the mere will of God whether sinners shall at any moment go to hell than if means were never made use of or at all concerned in the case.

8. Natural men's prudence and care to preserve their own lives, or the care of others to preserve them, do not secure them a moment. To this, divine providence and universal experience do also bear testimony. There is this clear evidence that men's own wisdom is no security to them from death; that if it were otherwise we should see some difference between the wise and politic men of the world, and others, with regard to their liableness to early and unexpected death: but how is it in fact? Ecclesiastes 2.16: "How dieth the wise man? even as the fool."

9. All wicked men's pains and contrivance which they use to escape hell, while they continue to reject Christ, and so remain wicked men, do not secure them from hell one moment. Almost every natural man[8] that hears of hell, flatters himself that he shall escape it; he depends upon himself for his own security; he flatters himself in what he has done, in what he is now doing, or what he intends to do. Every one lays out matters in his own mind how he shall avoid damnation, and flatters himself that he contrives well for himself, and that his schemes will not fail. They hear indeed that there are but few saved, and that the greater part of men that have died heretofore are gone to hell; but each one imagines that he lays out matters better for his own

[6]Job 38:11.

[7]"Thou shalt not be afraid for the terror by night; nor for the arrow that flieth by day" (Psalm 91:5).

[8]One unsaved, not having experienced God's grace.

escape than others have done. He does not intend to come to that place of torment; he says within himself that he intends to take effectual care, and to order matters so for himself as not to fail.

But the foolish children of men miserably delude themselves in their own schemes, and in confidence in their own strength and wisdom; they trust to nothing but a shadow. The greater part of those who heretofore have lived under the same means of grace, and are now dead, are undoubtedly gone to hell; and it was not because they were not as wise as those who are now alive: it was not because they did not lay out matters as well for themselves to secure their own escape. If we could speak with them, and inquire of them, one by one, whether they expected, when alive, and when they used to hear about hell, ever to be the subjects of that misery, we doubtless, should hear one and another reply, "No, I never intended to come here: I had laid out matters otherwise in my mind; I thought I should contrive well for myself: I thought my scheme good. I intended to take effectual care; but it came upon me unexpected; I did not look for it at that time, and in that manner; it came as a thief: Death outwitted me: God's wrath was too quick for me. Oh, my cursed foolishness! I was flattering myself, and pleasing myself with vain dreams of what I would do hereafter; and when I was saying, peace and safety, then suddenly destruction came upon me."

10. God has laid Himself under no obligation by any promise to keep any natural man out of hell one moment. God certainly has made no promises either of eternal life or of any deliverance or preservation from eternal death but what are contained in the covenant of grace,[9] the promises that are given in Christ, in whom all the promises are yea and amen. But surely they have no interest in the promises of the covenant of grace who are not the children of the covenant, who do not believe in any of the promises, and have no interest in the Mediator of the covenant.

So that, whatever some have imagined and pretended about promises made to natural men's earnest seeking and knocking, it is plain and manifest that whatever pains a natural man takes in religion, whatever prayers he makes, till he believes in Christ, God is under no manner of obligation to keep him a moment from eternal destruction.

So that, thus it is that natural men are held in the hand of God, over the pit of hell; they have deserved the fiery pit, and are already sentenced to it; and God is dreadfully provoked, His anger is as great towards them as to those that are actually suffering the executions of the fierceness of His wrath in hell, and they have done nothing in the least to appease or abate that anger, neither is God in the least bound by any promise to hold them up one moment; the devil is waiting for them, hell is gaping for them, the flames gather and flash about them, and would fain lay hold on them, and swallow them up; the fire pent up in their own hearts is struggling to break out: and they have no interest in any Mediator, there are no means within reach that can be any security to them. In short, they have no refuge, nothing to take hold of; all that preserves them every moment is the mere arbitrary will, and uncovenanted, unobliged forbearance of an incensed God.

[9]The Covenant of Works was the original covenant God made with Adam; the Covenant of Grace is a second covenant, made through the intercession of Christ, that if mankind would believe in Christ, mankind would be saved.

Application

The use of this awful subject may be for awakening unconverted persons in this congregation. This that you have heard is the case of every one of you that are out of Christ. That world of misery, that lake of burning brimstone is extended abroad under you. There is the dreadful pit of the glowing flames of the wrath of God; there is hell's wide-gaping mouth open; and you have nothing to stand upon, nor any thing to take hold of; there is nothing between you and hell but the air; it is only the power and mere pleasure of God that holds you up.

You probably are not sensible of this; you find you are kept out of hell, but do not see the hand of God in it; but look at other things, as the good state of your bodily constitution, your care of your own life, and the means you use for your own preservation. But indeed these things are nothing; if God should withdraw His hand, they would avail no more to keep you from falling, than the thin air to hold up a person that is suspended in it.

Your wickedness makes you as it were heavy as lead, and to tend downwards with great weight and pressure towards hell; and if God should let you go, you would immediately sink and swiftly descend and plunge into the bottomless gulf, and your healthy constitution, and your own care and prudence, and best contrivance, and all your righteousness, would have no more influence to uphold you and keep you out of hell, than a spider's web would have to stop a fallen rock. Were it not for the sovereign pleasure of God, the earth would not bear you one moment; for you are a burden to it; the creation groans with you; the creature is made subject to the bondage of your corruption, not willingly; the sun does not willingly shine upon you to give you light to serve sin and Satan; the earth does not willingly yield her increase to satisfy your lusts; nor is it willingly a stage for your wickedness to be acted upon; the air does not willingly serve you for breath to maintain the flame of life in your vitals, while you spend your life in the service of God's enemies. God's creatures are good, and were made for men to serve God with, and do not willingly subserve to any other purpose, and groan when they are abused to purposes so directly contrary to their nature and end. And the world would spew you out, were it not for the sovereign hand of Him who hath subjected it in hope. There are black clouds of God's wrath now hanging directly over your heads, full of the dreadful storm, and big with thunder; and were it not for the restraining hand of God, it would immediately burst forth upon you. The sovereign pleasure of God, for the present, stays His rough wind; otherwise it would come with fury, and your destruction would come like a whirlwind, and you would be like the chaff of the summer threshing floor.

The wrath of God is like great waters that are dammed for the present; they increase more and more, and rise higher and higher, till an outlet is given; and the longer the stream is stopped, the more rapid and mighty is its course when once it is let loose. It is true that judgment against your evil works has not been executed hitherto; the floods of God's vengeance have been withheld; but your guilt in the meantime is constantly increasing, and you are every day treasuring up more wrath; the waters are constantly rising, and waxing more and more mighty; and there is nothing but the mere pleasure of God that holds the waters back, that are unwilling to be stopped, and press hard to go forward. If God should only withdraw His hand from the floodgate, it would immediately fly open, and the fiery floods of the fierceness and wrath of God, would rush forth with inconceivable fury, and would come upon you with omnipotent power; and if your strength were ten thousand times greater than it is, yea, ten thousand times greater than the strength of the stoutest, sturdiest devil in hell, it would be nothing to withstand or endure it.

The bow of God's wrath is bent, and the arrow made ready on the string, and justice bends the arrow at your heart, and strains the bow, and it is nothing but the mere pleasure of God, and that of an angry God, without any promise or obligation at all, that keeps the arrow one moment from being made drunk with your blood. Thus all you that never passed under a great change of heart, by the mighty power of the Spirit of God upon your souls, all you that were never born again, and made new creatures, and raised from being dead in sin, to a state of new, and before altogether unexperienced light and life, are in the hands of an angry God. However you may have reformed your life in many things, and may have had religious affections, and may keep up a form of religion in your families and closets,[10] and in the house of God, it is nothing but His mere pleasure that keeps you from being this moment swallowed up in everlasting destruction. However unconvinced you may now be of the truth of what you hear, by and by you will be fully convinced of it. Those that are gone from being in the like circumstances with you see that it was so with them; for destruction came suddenly upon most of them; when they expected nothing of it and while they were saying, peace and safety: now they see that those things on which they depended for peace and safety, were nothing but thin air and empty shadows.

The God that holds you over the pit of hell, much as one holds a spider or some loathsome insect over the fire, abhors you, and is dreadfully provoked: His wrath towards you burns like fire; He looks upon you as worthy of nothing else but to be cast into the fire; He is of purer eyes than to bear to have you in His sight; you are ten thousand times more abominable in His eyes than the most hateful venomous serpent is in ours. You have offended Him infinitely more than ever a stubborn rebel did his prince; and yet it is nothing but His hand that holds you from falling into the fire every moment. It is to be ascribed to nothing else, that you did not go to hell the last night; that you was suffered to awake again in this world, after you closed your eyes to sleep. And there is no other reason to be given, why you have not dropped into hell since you arose in the morning, but that God's hand has held you up. There is no other reason to be given why you have not gone to hell, since you have sat here in the house of God, provoking His pure eyes by your sinful wicked manner of attending His solemn worship. Yea, there is nothing else that is to be given as a reason why you do not this very moment drop down into hell.

O sinner! Consider the fearful danger you are in: it is a great furnace of wrath, a wide and bottomless pit, full of the fire of wrath, that you are held over in the hand of that God, whose wrath is provoked and incensed as much against you, as against many of the damned in hell. You hang by a slender thread, with the flames of divine wrath flashing about it, and ready every moment to singe it, and burn it asunder; and you have no interest in any Mediator, and nothing to lay hold of to save yourself, nothing to keep off the flames of wrath, nothing of your own, nothing that you ever have done, nothing that you can do, to induce God to spare you one moment. And consider here more particularly,

[10]Places of meditation.

1. Whose wrath it is? It is the wrath of the infinite God. If it were only the wrath of man, though it were of the most potent prince, it would be comparatively little to be regarded. The wrath of kings is very much dreaded, especially of absolute monarchs, who have the possessions and lives of their subjects wholly in their power, to be disposed of at their mere will. Proverbs 20.2: "The fear of a king is as the roaring of a lion: Whoso provoketh him to anger, sinneth against his own soul." The subject that very much enrages an arbitrary prince, is liable to suffer the most extreme torments that human art can invent, or human power can inflict. But the greatest earthly potentates in their greatest majesty and strength, and when clothed in their greatest terrors, are but feeble, despicable worms of the dust, in comparison of the great and almighty Creator and King of heaven and earth. It is but little that they can do, when most enraged, and when they have exerted the utmost of their fury. All the kings of the earth, before God, are as grasshoppers; they are nothing, and less than nothing: both their love and their hatred is to be despised. The wrath of the great King of kings, is as much more terrible than theirs, as His majesty is greater. Luke 12.4–5: "And I say unto you, my friends, Be not afraid of them that kill the body, and after that, have no more that they can do. But I will forewarn you whom you shall fear: fear him, which after he hath killed, hath power to cast into hell: yea, I say unto you, Fear him."

2. It is the fierceness of His wrath that you are exposed to. We often read of the fury of God; as in Isaiah 59.18: "According to their deeds, accordingly he will repay fury to his adversaries." So Isaiah 66.15: "For behold, the Lord will come with fire, and with his chariots like a whirlwind, to render his anger with fury, and his rebuke with flames of fire." And in many other places. So, Revelation 19.15: we read of "the wine press of the fierceness and wrath of Almighty God." The words are exceeding terrible. If it had only been said, "the wrath of God," the words would have implied that which is infinitely dreadful: but it is "the fierceness and wrath of God." The fury of God! the fierceness of Jehovah![11] Oh, how dreadful must that be! Who can utter or conceive what such expressions carry in them! But it is also "the fierceness and wrath of Almighty God." As though there would be a very great manifestation of His almighty power in what the fierceness of His wrath should inflict, as though omnipotence should be as it were enraged, and exerted, as men are wont to exert their strength in the fierceness of their wrath. Oh! then, what will be the consequence! What will become of the poor worms that shall suffer it! Whose hands can be strong? And whose heart can endure? To what a dreadful, inexpressible, inconceivable depth of misery must the poor creature be sunk who shall be the subject of this!

Consider this, you that are here present that yet remain in an unregenerate state. That God will execute the fierceness of His anger implies that He will inflict wrath without any pity. When God beholds the ineffable extremity of your case, and sees your torment to be so vastly disproportioned to your strength, and sees how your poor soul is crushed, and sinks down, as it were, into an infinite gloom; He will have no compassion upon you, He will not forbear the executions of His wrath, or in the least lighten His hand; there shall be no moderation or mercy, nor will God then at all stay His rough wind; He will have no regard to your welfare, nor be at all careful lest you should suffer too much in any other sense, than only that you shall not suf-

[11]The God of the Old Testament.

fer beyond what strict justice requires. Nothing shall be withheld because it is so hard for you to bear. Ezekiel 8.18: "Therefore will I also deal in fury: mine eye shall not spare, neither will I have pity; and though they cry in mine ears with a loud voice, yet I will not hear them." Now God stands ready to pity you; this is a day of mercy; you may cry now with some encouragement of obtaining mercy. But when once the day of mercy is past, your most lamentable and dolorous cries and shrieks will be in vain; you will be wholly lost and thrown away of God as to any regard to your welfare. God will have no other use to put you to, but to suffer misery; you shall be continued in being to no other end; for you will be a vessel of wrath fitted to destruction; and there will be no other use of this vessel, but to be filled full of wrath. God will be so far from pitying you when you cry to Him, that it is said He will only "laugh and mock." Proverbs 1.25–26, etc.[12]

How awful are those words, Isaiah 63.3, which are the words of the great God: "I will tread them in mine anger, and will trample them in my fury, and their blood shall be sprinkled upon my garments, and I will stain all my raiment." It is perhaps impossible to conceive of words that carry in them greater manifestations of these three things, viz., contempt, and hatred, and fierceness of indignation. If you cry to God to pity you, He will be so far from pitying you in your doleful case, or showing you the least regard or favor, that instead of that, He will only tread you under foot. And though He will know that you cannot bear the weight of omnipotence treading upon you, yet He will not regard that, but He will crush you under His feet without mercy; He will crush out your blood, and make it fly and it shall be sprinkled on His garments, so as to stain all His raiment. He will not only hate you, but He will have you in the utmost contempt: no place shall be thought fit for you, but under His feet to be trodden down as the mire of the streets.

3. The misery you are exposed to is that which God will inflict to that end, that He might show what that wrath of Jehovah is. God hath had it on His heart to show to angels and men both how excellent His love is, and also how terrible His wrath is. Sometimes earthly kings have a mind to show how terrible their wrath is, by the extreme punishments they would execute on those that would provoke them. Nebuchadnezzar, that mighty and haughty monarch of the Chaldean empire, was willing to show his wrath when enraged with Shadrach, Meshech, and Abednego; and accordingly gave orders that the burning fiery furnace should be heated seven times hotter than it was before; doubtless, it was raised to the utmost degree of fierceness that human art could raise it.[13] But the great God is also willing to show His wrath, and magnify His awful majesty and mighty power in the extreme sufferings of His enemies. Romans 9.22: "What if God, willing to show his wrath, and to make his power known, endure with much long-suffering the vessels of wrath fitted to destruction?" And seeing this in His design, and what He has determined, even to show how terrible the restrained wrath, the fury and fierceness of Jehovah is, He will do it to effect. There will be something accomplished and brought to pass that will be dreadful with a witness. When the great and angry God hath risen up and

[12] "But ye have set at nought all my counsel, and would none of my reproof: I also will laugh at your calamity; I will mock you when your fear cometh."

[13] Daniel 3:1–30.

executed His awful vengeance on the poor sinner, and the wretch is actually suffering the infinite weight and power of His indignation, then will God call upon the whole universe to behold that awful majesty and mighty power that is to be seen in it. Isaiah 33.12–14: "And the people shall be as the burnings of lime, as thorns cut up shall they be burnt in the fire. Hear ye that are far off, what I have done; yet that are near, acknowledge my might. The sinners in Zion are afraid; fearfulness hath surprised the hypocrites," etc.

Thus it will be with you that are in an unconverted state, if you continue in it; the infinite might, and majesty, and terribleness of the omnipotent God shall be magnified upon you, in the ineffable strength of your torments. You shall be tormented in the presence of the holy angels, and in the presence of the Lamb; and when you shall be in this state of suffering, the glorious inhabitants of heaven shall go forth and look on the awful spectacle, that they may see what the wrath and fierceness of the Almighty is; and when they have seen it, they will fall down and adore that great power and majesty. Isaiah 66.23–24: "And it shall come to pass, that from one new moon to another, and from one sabbath to another, shall flesh come to worship before me, saith the Lord. And they shall go forth and look upon the carcasses of the men that have transgressed against me; for their worm shall not die, neither shall their fire be quenched, and they shall be an abhorring unto all flesh."

4. It is everlasting wrath. It would be dreadful to suffer this fierceness and wrath of Almighty God one moment; but you must suffer it to all eternity. There will be no end to this exquisite horrible misery. When you look forward, you shall see a long forever, a boundless duration before you, which will swallow up your thoughts, and amaze your soul; and you will absolutely despair of ever having any deliverance, and end, any mitigation, any rest at all. You will know certainly that you must wear out long ages, millions of millions of ages, in wrestling and conflicting with this almighty merciless vengeance; and then when you have so done, when so many ages have actually been spent by you in this manner, you will know that all is but a point to what remains. So that your punishment will indeed be infinite. Oh, who can express what the state of a soul in such circumstances is! All that we can possibly say about it gives but a very feeble, faint representation of it; it is inexpressible and inconceivable: For "who knows the power of God's anger?"[14]

How dreadful is the state of those that are daily and hourly in the danger of this great wrath and infinite misery! But this is the dismal case of every soul in this congregation that has not been born again, however moral and strict, sober and religious, they may otherwise be. Oh that you would consider it, whether you be young or old! There is reason to think that there are many in this congregation now hearing this discourse that will actually be the subjects of this very misery to all eternity. We know not who they are, or in what seats they sit, or what thoughts they now have. It may be they are now at ease, and hear all these things without much disturbance, and are now flattering themselves that they are not the persons, promising themselves that they shall escape. If they knew that there was one person, and but one, in the whole congregation, that was to be the subject of this misery, what an awful thing would it be to think of! If we knew who it was, what an awful sight would it be to see such a person! How might all the rest of the congregation lift up a lamentable and

[14]Psalm 90:11.

bitter cry over him! But, alas! instead of one, how many is it likely will remember this discourse in hell? And it would be a wonder, if some that are now present should not be in hell in a very short time, even before this year is out. And it would be no wonder, if some persons, that now sit here, in some seats of this meetinghouse, in health, quiet and secure, should be there before tomorrow morning. Those of you that finally continue in a natural condition, that shall keep out of hell longest will be there in a little time! your damnation does not slumber; it will come swiftly, and, in all probability, very suddenly upon many of you. You have reason to wonder that you are not already in hell. It is doubtless the case of some whom you have seen and known, that never deserved hell more than you, and that heretofore appeared likely to have been now alive as you. Their case is past all hope; they are crying in extreme misery and perfect despair; but here you are in the land of the living and in the house of God, and have an opportunity to obtain salvation. What would not those poor damned hopeless souls give for one day's opportunity such as you now enjoy!

And now you have an extraordinary opportunity, a day wherein Christ has thrown the door of mercy wide open, and stands in calling and crying with a loud voice to poor sinners; a day wherein many are flocking to Him, and pressing into the kingdom of God. Many are daily coming from the east, west, north and south; many that were very lately in the same miserable condition that you are in are now in a happy state, with their hearts filled with love to Him who has loved them, and washed them from their sins in His own blood, and rejoicing in hope of the glory of God. How awful is it to be left behind at such a day! To see so many others feasting, while you are pining and perishing! To see so many rejoicing and singing for joy of heart, while you have cause to mourn for sorrow of heart, and howl for vexation of spirit! How can you rest one moment in such a condition? Are not your souls as precious as the souls of the people at Suffield,[15] where they are flocking from day to day to Christ?

Are there not many here who have lived long in the world, and are not to this day born again? and so are aliens from the commonwealth of Israel, and have done nothing ever since they have lived, but treasure up wrath against the day of wrath? Oh, sirs, your case, in an especial manner, is extremely dangerous. Your guilt and hardness of heart is extremely great. Do you not see how generally persons of your years are passed over and left, in the present remarkable and wonderful dispensation of God's mercy? You had need to consider yourselves, and awake thoroughly out of sleep. You cannot bear the fierceness and wrath of the infinite God. And you, young men, and young women, will you neglect this precious season which you now enjoy, when so many others of your age are renouncing all youthful vanities, and flocking to Christ? You especially have now an extraordinary opportunity; but if you neglect it, it will soon be with you as with those persons who spent all the precious days in youth in sin, and are now come to such a dreadful pass in blindness and hardness. And you, children, who are unconverted, do not you know that you are going down to hell, to bear the dreadful wrath of that God, who is now angry with you every day and every night? Will you be content to be the children of the devil, when so many other children in the land are converted, and are become the holy and happy children of the King of kings?

[15]"A town in the neighborhood" [Edwards's note].

And let every one that is yet of Christ, and hanging over the pit of hell, whether they be old men and women, or middle-aged, or young people, or little children, now hearken to the loud calls of God's word and providence. This acceptable year of the Lord, a day of such great favors to some, will doubtless be a day of as remarkable vengeance to others. Men's hearts harden, and their guilt increases apace at such a day as this, if they neglect their souls; and never was there so great danger of such person being given up to hardness of heart and blindness of mind. God seems now to be hastily gathering in His elect in all parts of the land; and probably the greater part of adult persons that ever shall be saved, will be brought in now in a little time, and that it will be as it was on the great outpouring of the Spirit upon the Jews in the apostles' days;[16] the election will obtain, and the rest will be blinded. If this should be the case with you, you will eternally curse this day, and will curse the day that ever you was born, to see such a season of the pouring out of God's Spirit, and will wish that you had died and gone to hell before you had seen it. Now undoubtedly it is, as it was in the days of John the Baptist, the axe is in an extraordinary manner laid at the root of the trees,[17] that every tree which brings not forth good fruit, may be hewn down and cast into the fire.

Therefore, let everyone that is out of Christ, now awake and fly from the wrath to come. The wrath of Almighty God is now undoubtedly hanging over a great part of this congregation: Let everyone fly out of Sodom: "Haste and escape for your lives, look not behind you, escape to the mountain, lest you be consumed."[18]

1829–30

Elizabeth Ashbridge 1713–1755

Although little is known about Elizabeth Ashbridge beyond what is recorded in her brief autobiography, *Some Account of the Fore Part of the Life of Elizabeth Ashbridge . . . Written by her own Hand many years ago* (1755), the narrative itself provides a portrait of a remarkable woman whose spiritual questing and marital trials reveal much about religious imperatives and gender roles in eighteenth-century American culture. Born to Anglican parents in England, Ashbridge lived a rather adventurous adolescence. Eloping at fourteen, an act prompting permanent estrangement from her authoritarian father, she became a widow within months of her marriage. Banished from her parents' home, she spent several years in Ireland, where she began to seek religious enlightenment. At nineteen she emigrated to the colonies as an indentured servant, hoping to begin a new life. The first part of the *Account* records these experiences and presents a protagonist who even as a young

[16]Peter urged people to conversion, saying, "Save yourselves from this untoward generation. Then they that gladly received his word were baptized: and the same day there were added unto them about three thousand souls" (Acts 2:40–41).

[17]"And now also the axe is laid unto the root of the trees: therefore every tree which brings not forth good fruit is hewn down, and cast into the fire" (Matthew 3:10).

[18]Genesis 19:17.

girl showed signs of the fervent independence and spiritual predilection that would mark her adult life as a convinced (that is, converted) Quaker.

Lamenting that the Anglican ministry was closed to women, she turned to other denominations but found little consolation among the Baptists, Presbyterians, and Catholics with whom she worshiped in search of spiritual truth. Her appeals to the priestly patriarchy of various churches were met with imperious indifference. Ashbridge's indenture to a cruel master whom she had taken for "a very religious man" augmented her sense of the hypocrisy of much that passed for piety; it also impelled her to buy her freedom and marry a worldly suitor named Sullivan who "fell in love with me for my dancing." Not long after, visiting Quaker relations in Pennsylvania, she embraced their religion, a commitment that profoundly changed her.

Despite her initial distaste for the practices of the Society of Friends, which sanctioned—against her early ecclesiastical and social tradition—the preaching of women, Ashbridge was drawn to the beauty and eloquence of the faith, and her conversion is told with simple power. Her newfound spiritual mission made her a more somber and self-directed woman, alienating the husband who had loved her for her mirthful nature. The remainder of the narrative is a poignant account of Ashbridge's struggle to observe her new faith against the growing anger and abuse of her husband. Not until Sullivan's death, told in the *Account,* and her eventual union with Aaron Ashbridge, himself a Quaker, did she find the marital and spiritual harmony she had for so long sought.

Elizabeth Ashbridge's *Account* underscores the importance of life-writing as a tool of female vindication in a patriarchal culture. For its candor and emotional power, for the integrity of the religious sensibility it conveys, and for its illuminating portrayal of domestic relations in colonial America, the narrative merits a significant place in our literary history.

Liahna Babener
Central Washington University

Wendy Martin
Claremont Graduate University

PRIMARY WORKS

Some Account of the Fore-Part of the Life of Elizabeth Ashridge, . . . Wrote by Herself, 1774; *Some Account of the Fore Part of the Life of Elizabeth Ashbridge, . . . Written by her own Hand many years ago,* ed. by Daniel B. Shea, 1990.

from Some Account of the Fore Part of the Life of Elizabeth Ashbridge, . . . Written by her own Hand many years ago[1]

I now began to think of my Relations in Pennsylvania whom I had not yet seen; and having a great Desire that way, Got Leave of my Husband to go & also a Certificate from the Priest on Long Island in order that if I made any stay, I might be receiv'd as a Member wherever I came; Then Setting out, my husband bore me Company to the

[1]This text of the *Account* has been edited by Daniel B. Shea, in *Journeys in New Worlds: Early American Women's Narratives,* ed. W.L. Andrews, 1990.

Blazing Star Ferry, saw me Safe over & then returned. On the way near a place called Maidenhead [New Jersey] I fell from my horse & I was Disabled from Traveling for some time: In the interval I abode at the house of an Honest Like Dutchman, who with his wife were very kind to me, & tho' they had much trouble going to the Doctor and waiting upon me, (for I was Several Days unable to help my self) yet would have nothing for it (which I thought Exceeding kind) but Charged me if ever I came that way again to call and Lodge there.—I mention this because by and by I shall have occasion to remark this Place again.

Hence I came to Trenton [New Jersey] Ferry, where I met with no small Mortification upon hearing that my Relations were Quakers, & what was the worst of all my Aunt a Preacher. I was Sorry to hear it, for I was Exceedingly prejudiced against these People & have often wondered with what face they Could Call them Selves Christians. I Repented my Coming and had a mind to have turned back. At Last I Concluded to go & see them since I was so far on my journey, but Expected little Comfort from my Visit. But see how God brings unforeseen things to Pass, for by my going there I was brought to my Knowledge of his Truth.—I went from Trenton to Philadelphia by Water, thence to my Uncle's on Horseback, where I met with very kind reception; for tho' my Uncle was dead and my Aunt married again, yet both her husband and She received me in a very kind manner.

I had not been there three Hours before I met with a Shock, & my opinion began to alter with respect to these People.—For seeing a Book lying on the Table (& being much for reading) I took it up: My Aunt Observing said, "Cousin that is a Quakers' Book," for Perceiving I was not a Quaker, I suppose she thought I would not like it: I made her no answer but revolving in my mind, "what can these People write about, for I have heard that they Deny the Scriptures & have no other bible but George Fox's Journal,[2] & Deny all the holy Ordinances?" So resolved to read, but had not read two Pages before my very heart burned within me and Tears Issued from my Eyes, which I was Afraid would be seen; . . . I walked into the garden, sat Down, and the piece being Small, read it through before I went in; but Some Times was forced to Stop to Vent my Tears, my heart as it were uttering these involuntary Expressions; "my God must I (if ever I come to the true knowledge of thy Truth) be of this man's Opinion, who has sought thee as I have done & join with these People that a few hours ago I preferred the Papists before? O thou, the God of my Salvation & of my Life, who hast in an abundant manner manifested thy Long Suffering & tender Mercy, Redeeming me as from the Lowest Hell, a Monument of thy grace: Lord, my soul beseecheth thee to Direct me in the right way & keep me from Error, & then According to thy Covenant, I'll think nothing too near to Part with for thy name's Sake. If these things be so, Oh! happy People thus beloved of God."

After I came a little to my Self again I washed my face least any in the House should perceive I had been weeping. But this night got but Little Sleep, for the old Enemy began to Suggest that I was one of those that wavered & was not Steadfast in the faith, advancing several Texts of Scripture against me & them, as, in the Latter Days

[2]Englishman George Fox (1624–1691) was the founder of the Society of Friends and the initiator of the Quaker belief in "inner light" theology. Fox's *Journal,* originally published in 1694, recounted the many persecutions and incarcerations he endured as a result of his belief. It served as a sort of manifesto for Quakers and other religious dissenters who sought freedom of conscience.

there should be those that would deceive the very Elect: & these were they, & that I was in danger of being deluded. Here the Subtile Serpent transformed himself so hiddenly that I verily believed this to be a timely Caution from a good Angel—so resolved to beware of the Deceiver, & for Some weeks Did not touch any of their Books.

The next Day being the first of the week I wanted to have gone to Church, which was Distant about four Miles, but being a Stranger and having nobody to go along with me, was forced to Give it out, & as most of the Family was going to Meeting, I went with them, but with a resolution not to like them, & so it was fully Suffered: for as they sat in silence I looked over the Meeting, thinking with my self, "how like fools these People sit, how much better would it be to stay at home & read the Bible or some good Book, than to come here and go to Sleep." For my Part I was very Sleepy & thought they were no better than my Self. Indeed at Length I fell a sleep, and had like to fallen Down, but this was the last time I ever fell asleep in a Meeting, Tho' often Assaulted with it.

Now I began to be lifted up with Spiritual Pride & thought my Self better than they, but thro' Mercy this did not Last Long, for in a Little time I was brought Low & saw that these were the People to whom I must join.—It may seem strange that I who had Lived so long with one of this Society in Dublin, should yet be so great a Stranger to them. In answer let it be Considered that During the time I was there I never read one of their Books nor went to one Meeting, & besides I had heard such ridiculous stories of them as made me Esteem them the worst of any Society of People; but God that knew the Sincerity of my heart looked with Pity on my Weakness & soon Let me see my Error.

In a few weeks there was an afternoon's Meeting held at my Uncle's to which came that Servant of the Lord Wm. Hammans who was made then Instrumental to the Convincing me of the truth more Perfectly, & helping me over Some great Doubts: tho' I believe no one did ever sit in Greater opposition than I did when he first stood up; but I was soon brought Down for he preached the Gospel with such Power I was forced to give up & Confess it was the truth. As soon as meeting Ended I Endeavoured to get alone, for I was not fit to be seen, I being So broken; yet afterward the Restless adversary assaulted me again, on this wise. In the morning before this meeting, I had been Disputing with my Uncle about Baptism, which was the subject this good Man[3] Dwelt upon, which was handled so Clearly as to answer all my Scruples beyond all objection: yet the Crooked Serpent alleged that the Sermon that I had heard did not proceed from divine Revelation but that my Uncle and Aunt had acquainted the Friend of me; which being Strongly Suggested, I fell to Accusing them with it, of which they both cleared themselves, saying they had not seen him Since my Coming into these Parts until he came into the meeting. I then Concluded he was a messenger sent of God to me, & with fervent Cryes Desired I might be Directed a right and now Laid aside all Prejudice & set my heart open to receive the truth in the Love of it. And the Lord in his own good time revealed to my Soul not only the Beauty there is in truth, & how those should shine that continue faithful to it, but also the Emptiness of all shadows, which in the day were Gloryous, but now he the Son of Glory was come to put an end to them all, & to Establish Everlasting Righteousness in the room thereof, which is a work in the Soul. He likewise let me see that all I had

[3]The minister William Hammans.

gone through was to prepare me for this Day & that the time was near that he would require me to go forth & declare to others what he the God of Mercy had done for my Soul; at which I was Surprized & begged to be Excused for fear I should bring dishonour to the truth, and cause his Holy name to be Evil spoken of.

All the while, I never Let any know the Condition I was in, nor did I appear like a Friend, & fear'd a Discovery. I now began to think of returning to my husband but found a restraint to stay where I was. I then Hired to keep School & hearing of a place for him, wrote desiring him to come to me, but Let him know nothing how it was with me. I loved to go to meetings, but did not like to be seen to go on week days, & therefore to Shun it used to go from my school through the Woods, but notwithstanding all my care the Neighbours that were not friends began to revile me, calling me Quaker, saying they supposed I intended to be a fool and turn Preacher; I then receiv'd the same censure that I (a little above a year before) had Passed on one of the handmaids of the Lord at Boston, & so weak was I, alas! I could not bear the reproach, & in order to Change their Opinions got into greater Excess in Apparel than I had freedom to Wear for some time before I came Acquainted with Friends.

In this Condition I continued till my Husband came, & then began the Tryal of my Faith. Before he reached me he heard I was turned Quaker, at which he stampt, saying, "I'd rather heard She had been dead as well as I Love her, for if so, all my comfort is gone." He then came to me & had not seen me before for four Months. I got up & met him saying, "My Dear, I am glad to see thee," at which he flew in a Passion of anger & said, "the Divel thee thee, don't thee me."[4] I used all the mild means I could to pacify him, & at Length got him fit to go & Speak to my Relations, but he was Alarmed, and as soon as we got alone said, "so I see your Quaker relations have made you one." I told him they had not, which was true, nor had I ever told him how it was with me: But he would have it that I was one, & therefore would not let me stay among them; & having found a place to his mind, hired and came Directly back to fetch me hence, & in one afternoon walked near thirty Miles to keep me from Meeting, the next Day being first Day;[5] & on the Morrow took me to the Afforesaid Place & hired Lodgings at a churchman's house; who was one of the Wardens, & a bitter Enemy to Friends & used to Do all he could to irritate my Husband against them, & would tell me abundance of Ridiculous Stuff; but my Judgement was too Clearly convinced to believe it.

I still did not appear like a Friend, but they all believed I was one. When my Husband and he Used to be making their Diversion & reviling, I used to sit in Silence, but now and then an involuntary Sigh would break from me: at which he would tell my husband: "there, did not I tell you that your wife was a Quaker; & She will be a preacher." Upon which My Husband once in a Great rage came up to me, & Shaking his hand over me, said, "you had better be hanged in that Day." I then, Peter like, in a panick denied my being a Quaker, at which great horror seized upon

[4]In Ashbridge's day, Quakers employed the familiar "thee" and "thou," rather than "you," in everyday speech. Her use of the pronoun in interchanges with her husband confirmed for him her following of Quaker belief and practice. Non-believers often disparaged Quakers for this linguistic practice.

[5]Quakers traditionally refer to the days of the week and the months of the year by numbers rather than the conventional names, associated with pagan deities.

me, which Continued near three Months: so that I again feared that by Denying the Lord that Bought me, the heavens were Shut against me; for great Darkness Surrounded, & I was again plunged into Despair. I used to Walk much alone in the Wood, where no Eye saw nor Ear heard, & there Lament my miserable Condition, & have often gone from Morning till Night and have not broke my Fast.

Thus I was brought so Low that my Life was a burden to me; the Devil seem'd to Vaunt that tho' the Sins of my youth were forgiven, yet now he was sure of Me, for that I had Committed the unpardonable Sin & Hell inevitable would be my portion, & my Torment would be greater than if I had hanged my Self at first. In this Doleful State I had none to bewail my Doleful Condition; & Even in the Night when I Could not Sleep under the painful Distress of mind, if my husband perceived me weeping he would revile me for it. At Length when he and his Friends thought themselves too weak to over Set me (tho' I feared it was all ready done) he went to the Priest at Chester [Pennsylvania] to Advise what to Do with me. This man knew I was a member of the Church,[6] for I had Shewn him my Certificate: his advice was to take me out of Pennsylvania, and find some place where there was no Quakers; and then it would wear off. To this my Husband Agreed saying he did not Care where he went, if he Could but restore me to that Livelyness of Temper I was naturally of, & to that Church of which I was a member. I on my Part had no Spirit to oppose the Proposal, neither much cared where I was, For I seemed to have nothing to hope for, but Dayly Expected to be made a Spectacle of Divine Wrath, & was Possessed with a Thought that it would be by Thunder ere long.

The time of Removal came, & I must go. I was not Suffered to go to bid my Relations farewell; my husband was Poor & kept no horse, so I must travel on foot; we came to Wilmington [Delaware] (fifteen Miles) thence to Philadelphia by Water; here he took me to a Tavern where I soon became the Spectacle & discourse of the Company. My Husband told them, "my wife is a Quaker," & that he Designed if Possible to find out some Place where there was none. "O," thought I, "I was once in a Condition deserving that name, but now it is over with me. O! that I might from a true hope once more have an Opportunity to Confess to the truth;" tho' I was Sure of Suffering all manner of Crueltys, I would not Regard it.

These were my Concerns while he was Entertaining the Company with my Story, in which he told them that I had been a good Dancer, but now he Could get me neither to Dance nor Sing, upon which one of the Company stands up saying, "I'll go fetch my Fiddle, & we'll have a Dance," at which my husband was much pleased. The fiddle came, the sight of which put me in a sad Condition for fear if I Refused my husband would be in a great Passion: however I took up this resolution, not to Comply whatever be the Consequence. He comes to me, takes me by the hand saying, "come my Dear, shake off that Gloom, & let's have a civil Dance; you would now and then when you was a good Churchwoman, & that's better than a Stiff Quaker." I trembling desired to be Excused; but he Insisted on it, and knowing his Temper to be exceeding Cholerick, durst not say much, yet did not Consent. He then pluck'd me round the Room till Tears affected my Eyes, at Sight whereof the Musician Stopt and said, "I'll play no more, Let your wife alone," of which I was Glad.

There was also a man in Company who came from Freehold in East Jersey: he

[6]The Anglican Church.

said, "I see your Wife is a Quaker, but if you will take my advice you need not go so far (for my husband's design was for Staten Island); come & live amongst us, we'll soon cure her of her Quakerism, for we want a School Master & Mistress Too" (I followed the Same Business); to which he agreed, & a happy turn it was for me, as will be seen by and by: and the Wonderfull turn of Providence, who had not yet Abandoned me, but raised a glimmering hope, affording the Answer of peace in refusing to Dance, for which I was more rejoyced than to be made Mistress of much Riches; & in floods of Tears said, "Lord, I dread to ask and yet without thy gracious Pardon I'm Miserable; I therefore fall Down before thy Throne, imploring Mercy at thine hand. O Lord once more I beseech thee, try my Obedience, & then what soever thou Commands, I will Obey, & not fear to Confess thee before men."

Thus was my Soul Engaged before God in Sincerity & he in tender Mercy heard my cries, & in me has Shewn that he Delights not in the Death of a Sinner, for he again set my mind at Liberty to praise him & I longed for an Opportunity to Confess to his Truth, which he shewed me should come, but in what manner I did not see, but believed the word that I had heard, which in a little time was fulfilled to me.— My Husband as afforesaid agreed to go to Freehold, & in our way thither we came to Maidenhead, where I went to see the kind Dutchman before mentioned, who made us welcome & Invited us to stay a day or Two.

While we were here, there was held a great Meeting of the Presbyterians, not only for Worship but Business also: for one of their preachers being Charged with Drunkenness, was this day to have his Trial before a great number of their Priests, &c. We went to it, of which I was afterwards glad. Here I perceived great Divisions among the People about who Should be their Shepherd: I greatly Pitied their Condition, for I now saw beyond the Men made Ministers, & What they Preached for: and which those at this Meeting might have done had not the prejudice of Education, which is very prevalent, blinded their Eyes. Some Insisted to have the old Offender restored, some to have a young man they had upon trial some weeks, a third Party was for sending for one from New England. At length stood up one & Directing himself to the Chief Speaker said "Sir, when we have been at the Expence (which will be no Small Matter) of fetching this Gentleman from New England, may be he'll not stay with us." *Answer,* "don't you know how to make him stay?" *Reply,* "no Sir." "I'll tell you then," said he (to which I gave good attention), "give him a good Salary & I'll Engage he'll Stay." "O" thought I, "these Mercenary creatures: they are all Actuated by one & the same thing, even the Love of Money, & not the regard of Souls." This (Called Reverend) Gentleman, whom these People almost adored, to my knowledge had left his flock on Long Island & moved to Philadelphia where he could get more money. I my self have heard some of them on the Island say that they almost Impoverished themselves to keep him, but not being able to Equal Philadelphia's Invitation he left them without a Shepherd. This man therefore, knowing their Ministry all proceeded from one Cause, might be purchased with the Same thing; surely these and Such like are the Shepherd that regards the fleece more than the flock, in whose mouths are Lies; saying the Lord had sent them, & that they were Christ's Ambassadors, whose Command to those he sent was, "Freely ye have receiv'd, freely give; & Blessed be his holy Name;" so they do to this day.

I durst not say any Thing to my Husband of the Remarks I had made, but laid them up in my heart, & they Served to Strengthen me in my Resolution. Hence we set forward to Freehold, & Coming through Stony Brook [New Jersey] my Husband turned towards me tauntingly & Said, "Here's one of Satan's Synagogues, don't you want to be in it? O I hope to See you Cured of this New Religion." I made no answer but went on, and in a little time, we came to a large run of Water over which was no Bridge, & being Strangers knew no way to escape it, but thro' we must go: he Carried over our Clothes, which we had in Bundles. I took off my Shoes and waded over in my Stockings, which Served some what to prevent the Chill of the Water, being Very Cold & a fall of Snow in the 12 Mo. My heart was Concerned in Prayer that the Lord would Sanctify all my Afflictions to me & give me Patience to bear whatsoever should be suffered to come upon me. We Walked the most part of a mile before we came to the first house, which was a sort of a Tavern. My husband Called for Some Spiritous Liquors, but I got some weakened Cider Mull'd, which when I had Drank of (the Cold being struck to my heart) made me Extremely sick, in so much that when we were a Little past the house I expected I should have Fainted, & not being able to stand, fell Down under a Fence. My husband Observing, tauntingly said, "What's the Matter now; what, are you Drunk; where is your Religion now?" He knew better & at that time I believe he Pitied me, yet was Suffered grievously to Afflict me. In a Little time I grew Better, & going on We came to another Tavern, where we Lodged: the next Day I was Indifferent well, so proceeded, and as we Journeyed a young man Driving an Empty Cart overtook us. I desired my husband to ask the young man to Let us Ride; he did, twas readily granted.

I now thought my Self well off, & took it as a great favour, for my Proud heart was humbled, & I did not regard the Looks of it, tho' the time had been that I would not have been seen in one; this Cart belonged to a man at Shrewsbury [New Jersey] & was to go thro' the place we Designed for, so we rode on (but soon had the Care of the team to our Selves from a failure in the Driver) to the place where I was Intended to be made a prey of; but see how unforeseen things are brought to Pass, by a Providential hand. Tis said and answered, "shall we do Evil that good may Come?" God forbid, yet hence good came to me. Here my husband would have had me Stay while we went to see the Team Safe at home: I Told him, no, since he had led me thro' the Country like a Vagabond, I would not stay behind him, so went on, & Lodged that Night at the man's house who owned the Team. Next morning in our Return to Freehold, we met a man riding on full Speed, who Stopping said to my Husband, "Sir, are you a School Master?" *Answer,* "Yes." "I came to tell you," replied the Stranger, "of Two new School Houses, & want a Master in Each, & are two miles apart." How this Stranger came to hear of us, who Came but the night before, I never knew, but I was glad he was not one Called a Quaker, Least my husband might have thought it had been a Plot; and then turning to my husband I said, "my Dear, look on me with Pity; if thou has any Affections left for me, which I hope thou hast, for I am not Conscious of having Done anything to Alienate them; here is (continued I) an Opportunity to Settle us both, for I am willing to do all in my Power towards getting an Honest Livelihood."

My Expressions took place, & after a Little Pause he consented, took the young man's Directions, & made towards the place, & in our way came to the house of a Worthy Friend, Whose wife was a Preacher, tho' we did not know it. I was Surprized to see the People so kind to us that were Strangers; we had not been long in the house till we were Invited to Lodge there that night, being the Last in the Week.—I said nothing but waited to hear my Master Speak; he soon Consented saying, "My wife has had a Tedious Travel & I pity her"; at which kind Expression I was Affected, for they Were now very Seldom Used to me. The friends' kindness could not proceed from my appearing in the Garb of a Quaker, for I had not yet altered my dress: The Woman of the house, after we had Concluded to Stay, fixed her Eyes upon me & Said, "I believe thou hast met with a deal of Trouble," to which I made but Little Answer. My husband, Observing they were of that sort of people he had so much Endeavoured to shun, would give us no Opportunity for any discourse that night, but the next morning I let the friend know a Little how it was with me. Meeting time came, to which I longed to go, but durst not ask my husband leave for fear of Disturbing him, till we were Settled, & then thought I, "if ever I am favoured to be in this Place, come Life or Death, I'll fight through, for my Salvation is at Stake." The Friend getting ready for Meeting, asked my husband if he would go, saying they knew who were to be his Employers, & if they were at Meeting would Speak to them. He then consented to go; then said the Woman Friend, "& wilt thou Let thy Wife go?," which he denied, making Several Objections, all which She answered so prudently that he Could not be angry, & at Last Consented; & with Joy I went, for I had not been at one for near four Months, & an Heavenly Meeting This was: I now renewed my Covenant & Saw the Word of the Lord made Good, that I should have another Opportunity to Confess his Name, for which my Spirit did rejoice in the God of my Salvation, who had brought Strange things to Pass: May I ever be preserved in Humility, never forgetting his tender Mercies to me.

Here According to my Desire we Settled; my husband got one School & I the Other, & took a Room at a Friend's house a Mile from Each School and Eight Miles from the Meeting House:—before next first day we were got to our new Settlement: & now Concluded to Let my husband to see I was determined to joyn with friends. When first day Came I directed my Self to him in this manner, "My Dear, art thou willing to let me go to a Meeting?," at which he flew into a rage, saying, "No you shan't." I then Drew up my resolution & told him as a Dutyfull Wife ought, So I was ready to obey all his Lawfull Commands, but where they Imposed upon my Conscience, I no longer Durst: For I had already done it too Long, & wronged my Self by it, & tho' he was near & I loved him as a Wife ought, yet God was nearer than all the World to me, & had made me sensible this was the way I ought to go, the which I Assured him was no Small Cross to my own will, yet had Given up My heart, & hoped that he that Called for it would Enable me the residue of my Life to keep it steadyly devoted to him, whatever I Suffered for it, adding I hoped not to make him any the worse Wife for it. But all I could Say was in vain; he was Inflexible & Would not Consent.

I had now put my hand to the Plough, & resolved not to Look back, so went without Leave; but Expected to be immediately followed & forced back, but he did not: I went to one of the neighbours & got a Girl to Show me the way, then went on rejoicing & Praising God in my heart, who had thus far given me Power & another Opportunity to Confess to his Truth. Thus for some time I had to go Eight Miles on foot to Meetings, which I never thought hard; My Husband soon bought a Horse, but would not Let me ride him, neither when my Shoes were worn out would he Let me have a new Pair, thinking by that means to keep me from going to meetings, but this did not hinder me, for I have taken Strings & tyed round to keep them on.

He finding no hard Usage could alter my resolution, neither threatening to beat me, nor doing it, for he several times Struck me with sore Blows, which I Endeavoured to bear with Patience, believing the time would Come when he would see I was in the right (which he Accordingly Did), he once came up to me & took out his pen knife saying, "if you offer to go to Meeting tomorrow, with this knife I'll cripple you, for you shall not be a Quaker." I made him no Answer, but when Morning came, set out as Usual & he was not Suffered to hurt me. In Despair of recovering me himself, he now flew to the Priest for help and told him I had been a very Religious Woman in the way of the Church of England, was a member of it, & had a good Certificate from Long Island, but now was bewitched and turn'd Quaker, which almost broke his heart. He therefore Desired as he was one who had the Care of souls, he would Come and pay me a Visit and use his Endeavours to reclaim me & hoped by the Blessing of God it would be done. The Priest Consented to Come, the time was Set, which was to be that Day two Weeks, for he said he could not come Sooner. My Husband Came home extremely Pleased, & told me of it, at which I smiled Saying, "I hope to be Enabled to give him a reason for the hope that is in me," at the same time believing the Priest would never Trouble me (nor ever did).

Before his Appointed time came it was required of me in a more Publick manner to Confess to the world what I was and to give up in Prayer in a Meeting, the sight of which & the power that attended it made me Tremble, & I could not hold my Self still. I now again desired Death & would have freely given up my Natural Life a Ransom; & what made it harder to me I was not yet taken under the care of Friends, & what kept me from requesting it was for fear I might be overcome & bring a Scandal on the Society. I begged to be Excused till I was joyned to Friends & then I would give up freely, to which I receiv'd this Answer, as tho' I had heard a Distinct Voice: "I am a Covenant keeping God, and the word that I spoke to thee when I found thee In Distress, even that I would never leave thee nor forsake thee If thou would be obedient to what I should make known to thee, I will Assuredly make good: but if thou refuse, my Spirit shall not always strive; fear not, I will make way for thee through all thy difficulties, which shall be many for my name's Sake, but be thou faithfull & I will give thee a Crown of Life." I being then Sure it was God that Spoke said, "thy will O God, be done, I am in thy hand; do with me according to thy Word," & gave up. But after it was over the Enemy came in like a flood, telling me I had done what I ought not, & Should now bring Dishonour to this People. This gave me a Little Shock, but it did not at this time Last Long.

This Day as Usual I had gone on foot. My Husband (as he afterwards told me) lying on the Bed at home, these Words ran thro' him, "Lord where shall I fly to shun thee &c." upon which he arose and seeing it Rain got his horse and Came to fetch me; and Coming just as the Meeting broke up, I got on horseback as quick as possible, least he Should hear what had happened. Nevertheless he heard of it, and as soon as we were got into the woods he began, saying, "What do you mean thus to make my Life unhappy? What, could you not be a Quaker without turning fool after this manner?" I Answered in Tears saying, "my Dear, look on me with Pity, if thou hast any. Canst thou think, that I in the Bloom of my Days, would bear all that thou knowest of & a great deal more than thou knowest not of if I did not believe it to be my Duty?" This took hold of him, & taking my hand he said, "Well, I'll E'en give you up, for I see it don't avail to Strive. If it be of God I can't over throw it, & if it be of your self it will soon fall." I saw tears stand in his Eyes, at which my heart was overcome with Joy, and I would not have Changed Conditions with a Queen.

I already began to reap the fruits of my Obedience, but my Tryal Ended not here, the time being up that the Priest was to come; but no Priest Appeared. My Husband went to fetch him, but he would not come, saying he was busy; which so Displeased my husband, that he'd never go to hear him more, & for Some time went to no place of Worship.—Now the Unwearied adversary found out another Scheme, and with it wrought so Strong that I thought all I had gone through but a little to this: It came upon me in such an unexpected manner, in hearing a Woman relate a book she had read in which it was Asserted that Christ was not the son of God. As soon as She had Spoke these words, if a man had spoke I could not have more distinctly heard these words, "no more he is, it's all a fancy & the Contrivance of men," & an horrour of Great Darkness fell upon me, which Continued for three weeks.

The Exercise I was under I am not Able to Express, neither durst I let any know how it was with me. I again sought Desolate Places where I might make my moan, & have Lain whole nights, & don't know that my Eyes were Shut to Sleep. I again thought my self alone, but would not let go my Faith in him, often saying in my heart, "I'll believe till I Die," & kept a hope that he that had Delivered me out of the Paw of the Bear & out of the jaws of the Devouring Lion, would in his own time Deliver me out of his temptation also; which he in Mercy Did, and let me see that this was for my good, in order to Prepare me for future Service which he had for me to Do & that it was Necessary his Ministers should be dipt into all States, that thereby they might be able to Speak to all Conditions, for which my Soul was thankfull to him, the God of Mercies, who had at Several times redeemed me from great distress, & I found the truth of his Words, that all things should work together for good to those that Loved & feared him, which I did with my whole heart & hope ever shall while I have a being. This happened just after my first appearance, & Friends had not been to talk with me, nor did they know well what to do till I had appeared again, which was not for some time, when the Monthly Meeting appointed four Friends to give me a Visit, which I was Glad of; and gave them Such Satisfaction, that they left me well Satisfy'd. I then joyned with Friends.

My Husband still went to no place of Worship. One day he said, "I'd go to Meeting, only I am afraid I shall hear you Clack, which I cannot bear." I used no persuasions, yet when Meeting time Came, he got the horse, took me behind him & went to Meeting: but for several months if he saw me offer to rise, he would go out, till once I got up before he was aware and then (as he afterwards said) he was ashamed to go, & from that time never did, nor hindered me from going to Meetings. And tho' he (poor man) did not take up the Cross, yet his judgement was Convinced: & sometimes in a flood of tears would say, "My Dear, I have seen the Beauty there is in the Truth, & that thou art in the Right, and I Pray God Preserve thee in it. But as for me the Cross is too heavy, I cannot Bear it." I told him, I hoped he that had given me strength Would also favour him: "O!" said he, "I can't bear the Reproach thou Doest, to be Called turncoat & to become a Laughing Stock to the World; but I'll no Longer hinder thee," which I looked on as a great favour, that my way was thus far made easy, and a little hope remained that my Prayers would be heard on his account.

In this Place he had got linked in with some, that he was afraid would make game of him, which Indeed they already Did, asking him when he Designed to

Commence Preacher, for that they saw he Intended to turn Quaker, & seemed to Love his Wife better since she did than before (we were now got to a little house by our Selves which tho' Mean, & little to put in it, our Bed no better than Chaff, yet I was truly Content & did not Envy the Rich their Riches; the only Desire I had now was my own preservation, & to be Bless'd with the Reformation of my husband). These men used to Come to our house & there Provoke my husband to Sit up and Drink, some times till near day, while I have been sorrowing in a Stable. As I once sat in this Condition I heard my husband say to his Company, "I can't bear any Longer to Afflict my Poor Wife in this manner, for whatever you may think of her, I do believe she is a good Woman," upon which he came to me and said, "Come in, my Dear; God has Given thee a Deal of Patience. I'll put an End to this Practice;" and so he did, for this was the Last time they sat up at Night.

My Husband now thought that if he was in any Place where it was not known that he'd been so bitter against Friends, he Could do better than here. But I was much against his Moving; fearing it would tend to his hurt, having been for some months much Altered for the Better, & would often in a broken and Affectionate Manner condemn his bad Usage to me: I told him I hoped it had been for my Good, even to the Better Establishing me in the Truth, & therefore would not have him to be Afflicted about it, & According to the Measure of Grace received did what I could both by Example and advice for his good: & my Advice was for him to fight thro' here, fearing he would Grow Weaker and the Enemy Gain advantage over him, if he thus fled: but All I could say did not prevail against his Moving; & hearing of a place at Bordentown [New Jersey] went there, but that did not suit; he then Moved to Mount Holly [New Jersey] & there we Settled. He got a good School & So Did I.

Here we might have Done very well; we soon got our house Prettily furnished for Poor folks; I now began to think I wanted but one thing to complete my Happiness, Viz. the Reformation of my husband, which Alas! I had too much reason to Doubt; for it fell out according to my Fears, & he grew worse here, & took much to Drinking, so that it Seem'd as if my Life was to be a Continual scene of Sorrows & most Earnestly I Pray'd to Almighty God to Endure me with Patience to bear my Afflictions & submit to his Providence, which I can say in Truth I did without murmuring or ever uttering an unsavoury expression to the Best of my Knowledge; except once, my husband Coming home a little in drink (in which frame he was very fractious) & finding me at Work by a Candle, came to me, put it out & fetching me a box on the Ear said, "you don't Earn your light;" on which unkind Usage (for he had not struck me for Two Years so it went hard with me) I utter'd these Rash Expressions, "thou art a Vile Man," & was a little angry, but soon recovered & was Sorry for it; he struck me again, which I received without so much as a word in return, & that likewise Displeased him: so he went on in a Distracted like manner uttering Several Expressions that bespoke Despair, as that he now believed that he was predestinated to damnation, & he did not care how soon God would Strike him Dead, & the like. I durst say but Little; at Length in the Bitterness of my Soul, I Broke out in these Words, "Lord look Down on mine Afflictions and deliver me by some means or Other." I was answered, I Should Soon be, & so I was, but in such a manner, as I Verily thought It would have killed me.—In a little time he went to Burlington where he got in Drink, & Enlisted him Self to go a Common soldier to Cuba anno 1740.

I had drank many bitter Cups—but this Seemed to Exceed them all for indeed my very Senses Seemed Shaken; I now a Thousand times blamed my Self for making Such an unadvised request, fearing I had Displeased God in it, & tho' he had Granted it, it was in Displeasure, & Suffered to be in this manner to Punish me; Tho' I can truly say I never Desired his Death, no more than my own, nay not so much. I have since had cause to believe his mind was benefitted by the Undertaking, (which hope makes up for all I have Suffered from him) being Informed he did in the army what he Could not Do at home (Viz) Suffered for the Testimony of Truth. When they Came to prepare for an Engagement, he refused to fight; for which he was whipt and brought before the General, who asked him why he Enlisted if he would not fight; "I did it," said he, "in a drunken frolick, when the Divel had the Better of me, but my judgment is convinced that I ought not, neither will I whatever I Suffer; I have but one Life, & you may take that if you Please, but I'll never take up Arms."—They used him with much Cruelty to make him yield but Could not, by means whereof he was So Disabled that the General sent him to the Hospital at Chelsea,[7] where in Nine Months time he Died & I hope made a Good End, for which I prayed both night & Day, till I heard of his Death.

Thus I thought it my duty to say what I could in his Favour, as I have been obliged to say so much of his hard usage to me, all which I hope Did me good, & altho' he was so bad, yet had Several Good Properties, & I never thought him the Worst of Men. He was one I Lov'd & had he let Religion have its Perfect work, I should have thought my Self Happy in the Lowest State of Life; & I've Cause to bless God, who Enabled me in the Station of a Wife to Do my Duty & now a Widow to Submit to his Will, always believing everything he doeth to be right. May he in all Stations of Life so Preserve me by the arm of Divine Power, that I may never forget his tender mercies to me, the Rememberance whereof doth often Bow my Soul, in Humility before his Throne, saying, "Lord, what was I; that thou should have reveal'd to me the Knowledge of thy Truth, & do so much for me, who Deserved thy Displeasure rather, But in me hast thou shewn thy Long Suffering & tender Mercy; may thou O God be Glorifyed and I abased for it is thy own Works that praise thee, and of a Truth to the humble Soul thou Makest every bitter thing Sweet.—The End.—

1755

John Woolman 1720–1772

John Woolman, sometimes referred to as the "Quaker Saint," was born near the Rancocas River in Burlington County, New Jersey (then West Jersey). His family on both sides had strong roots in the Quaker colony they had helped to settle and then to shape. One of thirteen children, Woolman grew up surrounded by a large and supportive family, and he early displayed a sensitivity for spiritual matters and a love for nature and Quaker traditions. Like many eighteenth-century

[7]In what is now London, England.

Quakers, Woolman had a limited formal education, but he nonetheless valued learning, and evidence suggests that his reading extended far beyond the list of books normally prescribed to members of the Society of Friends, as Quakers are officially called.

In 1749, Woolman married Sarah Ellis, from neighboring Chesterfield. Little is known about Ellis other than Woolman's famous description of her in his *Journal* as "a well inclined damsel." Nevertheless, there is no information to suggest that their marriage was anything but an extremely felicitous one. The couple had two children, but only one, a daughter, survived into adulthood. Prior to his marriage, Woolman assisted a local tailor, and his success led him to establish a business of his own in Mount Holly, New Jersey, where he also managed a large farm, occasionally wrote legal documents, and taught. Because of his well-deserved reputation for honesty and industry, Woolman's business expanded and became more prosperous. Fearing that inordinate wealth and excessive involvement in business endangered his soul by drawing his attention toward worldly matters, Woolman decided early in his marriage to curtail his business activities, limiting them to what was essential for supporting his family. Eventually Woolman gave up mercantile trade altogether and devoted his energies almost exclusively to his family, his farm, and his work as a Quaker spokesperson.

Woolman's deliberate withdrawal from the world of commerce is consistent with Quaker beliefs that life should be conducted in a simple and direct manner and that the internal spiritual world should always take precedence over the external material world. Above all, Quakers believe that all individuals harbor within themselves an innate sense of right and wrong, which they term the "Inner Light." It is the responsibility of the individual, Quakers believe, to cultivate the workings of the "Inner Light" by removing oneself from all unnecessary distractions and encumbrances. In line with this reasoning, Quakers of Woolman's day, like Quakers of today, attempted to practice a simple lifestyle based on hard work, frugality, and contemplation. When politics or business entanglements encroach on their quest for inner harmony, Quakers are simply encouraged to withdraw from the source of conflict. Even Quaker worship is designed to minimize external distractions. Unlike their Puritan, Presbyterian, and Anglican neighbors to the north and south, the Quakers of the Middle Colonies shunned traditional rituals. The typical Quaker meeting consisted simply of a quiet gathering, with men and boys seated on one side of the room and women and girls on the other. If during the meeting a member of the group felt an inner urging or "prompting" to address the assembly, that person would stand and speak. Sometimes, however, Quaker meetings passed in total silence. According to Quaker practice, an individual, whether male or female, who has spoken frequently and wisely on behalf of the spirit is accorded local recognition as a minister but is not required to undergo ordination or any formalized process of theological instruction.

While in his early twenties, Woolman showed signs of a special ministerial calling and was acknowledged a minister by his community. In the years to follow, he pursued his calling wherever his "Inner Light" led him, traveling thousands of miles, often on foot, throughout the colonies and eventually to England. The main focus of his ministry was the abolition of slavery, which he denounced as a "dark gloominess hanging over the land" and an unspeakable injustice.

Woolman's abhorrence of slavery began early in life when the man to whom he was apprenticed asked him to write a bill of sale for a slave belonging to a senior member of the Quakers. His dislike of slavery continued to grow, especially after he had labored in the South and seen firsthand the degradation that slavery brought to both slave and slaveholder. Always quiet and persistent in his determination to convince the world that slavery and Christianity were totally incompatible, Woolman illustrated through his own conduct the principles of compassion and goodwill that formed the central message of his itinerant ministry. He refused, for example, to use sugar products or dyes because these items were obtained largely through reliance on slave labor, and during his travels he insisted on paying a remuneration to any slaves who worked in homes where he lodged. Such behavior was his way of drawing attention to his convictions, and it was apparently not without effect, for he records in the *Journal* instances when he successfully altered the hearts of slaveholders.

In addition to his work on behalf of abolition, Woolman championed the rights of Indians and the poor. On the eve of Pontiac's war with the colonies, Woolman journeyed on a mission of peace to the Wyalusing Indians of western Pennsylvania. He was never in good health, and throughout this trip he was frequently endangered by both the hostilities surrounding him and the primitive living conditions he of necessity endured. Nonetheless, he persisted in his mission and was well received by the Indians. After observing the situation of the Indians and listening to their grievances, Woolman returned home with a severe indictment of frontier traders, on whose greed in selling rum to the Indians he blamed the war then taking place. Eventually Woolman's compassion for the downtrodden led him to England, where he died of smallpox on October 7, 1772, a few months after his arrival.

As a writer, Woolman is best remembered today for the *Journal* that he kept intermittently between 1756 and his death. Published posthumously by the Society of Friends in 1774, Woolman's *Journal* is but one of many first-person accounts of the lives of pious eighteenth-century American Quakers; indeed, it participates in a tradition of journal-writing begun by George Fox himself that continues to the present. It is generally acknowledged, however, that Woolman's *Journal* stands out among others in the genre for its remarkable sense of clarity and conviction; for this reason alone, popular interest in the *Journal* has never slackened.

James A. Levernier
University of Arkansas at Little Rock

Wendy Martin
Claremont Graduate University

PRIMARY WORKS

Considerations on the Keeping of Negroes, 1754; *Journal,* 1774; *A Plea for the Poor,* 1793; *The Journal and Major Essays of John Woolman,* ed. Phillips Moulton, 1971.

from The Journal of John Woolman[1]

[Early Life and Vocation]

I have often felt a motion of love to leave some hints in writing of my experience of the goodness of God, and now, in the thirty-sixth year of my age, I begin this work. I was born in Northampton, in Burlington County in West Jersey, A.D. 1720, and before I was seven years old I began to be acquainted with the operations of divine love. Through the care of my parents, I was taught to read near as soon as I was capable of it, and as I went from school one Seventh Day,[2] I remember, while my companions went to play by the way, I went forward out of sight; and sitting down, I read the twenty-second chapter of the Revelations: "He showed me a river of water, clear as crystal, proceeding out of the throne of God and the Lamb, etc." And in reading it my mind was drawn to seek after that pure habitation which I then believed God had prepared for His servants. The place where I sat and the sweetness that attended my mind remains fresh in my memory.

This and the like gracious visitations[3] had that effect upon me, that when boys used ill language it troubled me, and through the continued mercies of God I was preserved from it. The pious instructions of my parents were often fresh in my mind when I happened amongst wicked children, and was of use to me. My parents, having a large family of children, used frequently on First Days after meeting[4] to put to read in the Holy Scriptures or some religious books, one after another, the rest sitting by without much conversation, which I have since often thought was a good practice. From what I had read and heard, I believed there had been in past ages people who walked in uprightness before God in a degree exceeding any that I knew, or heard of, now living; and the apprehension of there being less steadiness and firmness amongst people in this age than in past ages often troubled me while I was a child.

I had a dream about the ninth year of my age as follows: I saw the moon rise near the west and run a regular course eastward, so swift that in about a quarter of an hour she reached our meridian, when there descended from her a small cloud on a direct line to the earth, which lighted on a pleasant green about twenty yards from the door of my father's house (in which I thought I stood) and was immediately turned into a beautiful green tree. The moon appeared to run on with equal swiftness and soon set in the east, at which time the sun arose at the place where it commonly does in the summer, and shining with full radiance in a serene air, it appeared as pleasant a morning as ever I saw.

[1]Woolman's journal was first published in 1774. The source of this text is Phillips Moulton's edition, *The Journal and Major Essays of John Woolman,* 1971.

[2]Saturday. During Woolman's day, Quakers, or members of the Society of Friends, did not use the seven weekday names, which derive from the names of pagan gods.

[3]Moments when he experienced the felt presence of God.

[4]Quakers worship at "meeting," when they gather together for common prayer. Typically, those gathered together remain silent until a motion to speak emerges in a worshiper.

All this time I stood still in the door in an awful frame of mind, and I observed that as heat increased by the rising sun, it wrought so powerfully on the little green tree that the leaves gradually withered; and before noon it appeared dry and dead. There then appeared a being, small of size, full of strength and resolution, moving swift from the north, southward, called a sun worm.[5]

Another thing remarkable in my childhood was that once, going to a neighbor's house, I saw on the way a robin sitting on her nest; and as I came near she went off, but having young ones, flew about and with many cries expressed her concern for them. I stood and threw stones at her, till one striking her, she fell down dead. At first I was pleased with the exploit, but after a few minutes was seized with horror, as having in a sportive way killed an innocent creature while she was careful for her young. I beheld her lying dead and thought those young ones for which she was so careful must now perish for want of their dam to nourish them; and after some painful considerations on the subject, I climbed up the tree, took all the young birds and killed them, supposing that better than to leave them to pine away and die miserably, and believed in this case that Scripture proverb was fulfilled, "The tender mercies of the wicked are cruel."[6] I then went on my errand, but for some hours could think of little else but the cruelties I had committed, and was much troubled.

Thus He whose tender mercies are over all His works hath placed a principle in the human mind which incites to exercise goodness toward every living creature; and this being singly attended to, people become tender-hearted and sympathizing, but being frequently and totally rejected, the mind shuts itself up in a contrary disposition.

About the twelfth year of my age, my father being abroad, my mother reproved me for some misconduct, to which I made an undutiful reply; and the next First Day as I was with my father returning from meeting, he told me he understood I had behaved amiss to my mother and advised me to be more careful in future. I knew myself blameable, and in shame and confusion remained silent. Being thus awakened to a sense of my wickedness, I felt remorse in my mind, and getting home I retired and prayed to the Lord to forgive me, and do not remember that I ever after that spoke unhandsomely to either of my parents, however foolish in other things.

Having attained the age of sixteen years, I began to love wanton company, and though I was preserved from profane language or scandalous conduct, still I perceived a plant in me which produced much wild grapes. Yet my merciful Father forsook me not utterly, but at times through His grace I was brought seriously to consider my ways, and the sight of my backsliding affected me with sorrow. But for want of rightly attending to the reproofs of instruction, vanity was added to vanity, and repentance to repentance; upon the whole my mind was more and more alienated from the Truth, and I hastened toward destruction. While I meditate on the gulf toward which I travelled and reflect on my youthful disobedience, for these things I weep; mine eye runneth down with water.

Advancing in age the number of my acquaintance increased, and thereby my way grew more difficult. Though I had heretofore found comfort in reading the Holy Scriptures and thinking on heavenly things, I was now estranged therefrom. I knew I was going from the flock of Christ and had no resolution to return; hence serious

[5]This is an imagined event.

[6]Proverbs 12:10.

reflections were uneasy to me and youthful vanities and diversions my greatest pleasure. Running in this road I found many like myself, and we associated in that which is reverse to true friendship.

But in this swift race it pleased God to visit me with sickness, so that I doubted of recovering. And then did darkness, horror, and amazement with full force seize me, even when my pain and distress of body was very great. I thought it would have been better for me never to have had a being than to see the day which I now saw. I was filled with confusion, and in great affliction both of mind and body I lay and bewailed myself. I had not confidence to lift up my cries to God, whom I had thus offended, but in a deep sense of my great folly I was humbled before Him, and at length that Word which is as a fire and a hammer broke and dissolved my rebellious heart. And then my cries were put up in contrition, and in the multitude of His mercies I found inward relief, and felt a close engagement that if He was pleased to restore my health, I might walk humbly before Him.

After my recovery this exercise[7] remained with me a considerable time; but by degrees giving way to youthful vanities, they gained strength, and getting with wanton[8] young people I lost ground. The Lord had been very gracious and spoke peace to me in the time of my distress, and I now most ungratefully turned again to folly, on which account at times I felt sharp reproof but did not get low enough to cry for help. I was not so hardy as to commit things scandalous, but to exceed in vanity and promote mirth was my chief study. Still I retained a love and esteem for pious people, and their company brought an awe upon me.

My dear parents several times admonished me in the fear of the Lord, and their admonition entered into my heart and had a good effect for a season, but not getting deep enough to pray rightly, the tempter when he came found entrance. I remember once, having spent a part of the day in wantonness, as I went to bed at night there lay in a window near my bed a Bible, which I opened, and first cast my eye on the text, "We lie down in our shame, and our confusion covers us."[9] This I knew to be my case, and meeting with so unexpected a reproof, I was somewhat affected with it and went to bed under remorse of conscience, which I soon cast off again.

Thus time passed on; my heart was replenished with mirth and wantonness, while pleasing scenes of vanity were presented to my imagination till I attained the age of eighteen years, near which time I felt the judgments of God in my soul like a consuming fire, and looking over my past life the prospect was moving. I was often sad and longed to be delivered from those vanities; then again my heart was strongly inclined to them, and there was in me a sore conflict. At times I turned to folly, and then again sorrow and confusion took hold of me. In a while I resolved totally to leave off some of my vanities, but there was a secret reserve in my heart of the more refined part of them, and I was not low enough to find true peace. Thus for some months I had great trouble, there remaining in me an unsubjected will which rendered my labours fruitless, till at length through the merciful continuance of heavenly visitations I was made to bow down in spirit before the Lord.

I remember one evening I had spent some time in reading a pious author, and walking out alone I humbly prayed to the Lord for His help, that I might be

[7]Religious outpouring.
[8]Shallow, frivolous.
[9]Jeremiah 3:25.

delivered from all those vanities which so ensnared me. Thus being brought low, He helped me; and as I learned to bear the cross I felt refreshment to come from His presence; but not keeping in that strength which gave victory, I lost ground again, the sense of which greatly affected me; and I sought deserts and lonely places and there with tears did confess my sins to God and humbly craved help of Him. And I may say with reverence He was near to me in my troubles, and in those times of humiliation opened my ear to discipline.

I was now led to look seriously at the means by which I was drawn from the pure Truth, and learned this: that if I would live in the life which the faithful servants of God lived in, I must not go into company as heretofore in my own will, but all the cravings of sense must be governed by a divine principle. In times of sorrow and abasement these instructions were sealed upon me, and I felt the power of Christ prevail over selfish desires, so that I was preserved in a good degree of steadiness. And being young and believing at that time that a single life was best for me, I was strengthened to keep from such company as had often been a snare to me.

I kept steady to meetings, spent First Days after noon chiefly in reading the Scriptures and other good books, and was early convinced in my mind that true religion consisted in an inward life, wherein the heart doth love and reverence God the Creator and learn to exercise true justice and goodness, not only toward all men but also toward the brute creatures; that as the mind was moved on an inward principle to love God as an invisible, incomprehensible being, on the same principle it was moved to love Him in all His manifestations in the visible world; that as by His breath the flame of life was kindled in all animal and sensitive creatures, to say we love God as unseen and at the same time exercise cruelty toward the least creature moving by His life, or by life derived from Him, was a contradiction in itself.

I found no narrowness respecting sects and opinions, but believed that sincere, upright-hearted people in every Society who truly loved God were accepted of Him.

As I lived under the cross and simply followed the openings of Truth,[10] my mind from day to day was more enlightened; my former acquaintance was left to judge of me as they would, for I found it safest for me to live in private and keep these things sealed up in my own breast.

While I silently ponder on that change wrought in me, I find no language equal to it nor any means to convey to another a clear idea of it. I looked upon the works of God in this visible creation and an awfulness covered me; my heart was tender and often contrite, and a universal love to my fellow creatures increased in me. This will be understood by such who have trodden in the same path. Some glances of real beauty may be seen in their faces who swell in true meekness. There is a harmony in the sound of that voice to which divine love gives utterance, and some appearance of right order in their temper and conduct whose passions are fully regulated. Yet all these do not fully show forth that inward life to such who have not felt it, but this white stone and new name is known rightly to such only who have it.[11]

[10]That is, as he remained mindful of Christ's humble sacrifice and awaited the felt experience of God. Quakers called their perceived messages from God "openings."

[11]"To him that overcometh will I give to eat of the hidden manna, and will I give him a white stone, and in the stone a new name written, which no man knoweth saving he that receiveth it": Revelation 2:17.

Now though I had been thus strengthened to bear the cross, I still found myself in great danger, having many weaknesses attending me and strong temptations to wrestle with, in the feelings whereof I frequently withdrew into private places and often with tears besought the Lord to help me, whose gracious ear was open to my cry.

All this time I lived with my parents and wrought on the plantation, and having had schooling pretty well for a planter, I used to improve in winter evenings and other leisure times. And being now in the twenty-first year of my age, a man in much business shopkeeping and baking asked me if I would hire with him to tend shop and keep books. I acquainted my father with the proposal, and after some deliberation it was agreed for me to go.

At home I had lived retired, and now having a prospect of being much in the way of company, I felt frequent and fervent cries in my heart to God, the Father of Mercies, that He would preserve me from all taint and corruption, that in this more public employ I might serve Him, my gracious Redeemer, in that humility and self-denial with which I had been in a small degree exercised in a very private life.

The man who employed me furnished a shop in Mount Holly, about five miles from my father's house and six from his own, and there I lived alone and tended his shop. Shortly after my settlement here I was visited by several young people, my former acquaintance, who knew not but vanities would be as agreeable to me now as ever; and at these times I cried to the Lord in secret for wisdom and strength, for I felt myself encompassed with difficulties and had fresh occasion to bewail the follies of time past in contracting a familiarity with a libertine people. And as I had now left my father's house outwardly, I found my Heavenly Father to be merciful to me beyond what I can express.

By day I was much amongst people and had many trials to go through, but in evenings I was mostly alone and may with thankfulness acknowledge that in those times the spirit of supplication was often poured upon me, under which I was frequently exercised and felt my strength renewed.

In a few months after I came here, my master bought several Scotch menservants from on board a vessel and brought them to Mount Holly to sell,[12] one of which was taken sick and died. The latter part of his sickness he, being delirious, used to curse and swear most sorrowfully, and after he was buried I was left to sleep alone the next night in the same chamber where he died. I perceived in me a timorousness. I knew, however, I had not injured the man but assisted in taking care of him according to my capacity, and was not free to ask anyone on that occasion to sleep with me. Nature was feeble, but every trial was a fresh incitement to give myself up wholly to the service of God, for I found no helper like Him in times of trouble.

After a while my former acquaintance gave over expecting me as one of their company, and I began to be known to some whose conversation was helpful to me. And now, I had experienced the love of God through Jesus Christ to redeem me from many pollutions and to be a succour to me through a sea of conflicts, with

[12]That is, the man for whom Woolman worked bought the indentures of some Scottish men. Laborers commonly contracted to work for a negotiated amount of years, in order to "pay" for their passage to America. The contracts, often taken by shipmasters, would be renegotiated upon arrival in America.

which no person was fully acquainted, and as my heart was often enlarged in this heavenly principle, I felt a tender compassion for the youth who remained entangled in snares like those which had entangled me. From one month to another this love and tenderness increased, and my mind was more strongly engaged for the good of my fellow creatures.

I went to meetings in an awful frame of mind and endeavoured to be inwardly acquainted with the language of the True Shepherd. And one day being under a strong exercise of spirit, I stood up and said some words in a meeting, but not keeping close to the divine opening, I said more than was required of me; and being soon sensible of my error, I was afflicted in mind some weeks without any light or comfort, even to that degree that I could take satisfaction in nothing. I remembered God and was troubled, and in the depth of my distress He had pity upon me and sent the Comforter. I then felt forgiveness for my offense, and my mind became calm and quiet, being truly thankful to my gracious Redeemer for His mercies.[13] And after this, feeling the spring of divine love opened and a concern to speak, I said a few words in a meeting, in which I found peace. This I believe was about six weeks from the first time, and as I was thus humbled and disciplined under the cross, my understanding became more strengthened to distinguish the language of the pure Spirit which inwardly moves upon the heart and taught [me] to wait in silence sometimes many weeks together, until I felt that rise which prepares the creature to stand like a trumpet through which the Lord speaks to His flock.

From an inward purifying, and steadfast abiding under it, springs a lively operative desire for the good of others. All faithful people are not called to the public ministry, but whoever are, are called to minister of that which they have tasted and handled spiritually. The outward modes of worship are various, but wherever men are true ministers of Jesus Christ it is from the operation of His spirit upon their hearts, first purifying them and thus giving them a feeling sense of the conditions of others. This truth was early fixed in my mind, and I was taught to watch the pure opening and to take heed lest while I was standing to speak, my own will should get uppermost and cause me to utter words from worldly wisdom and depart from the channel of the true gospel ministry.

In the management of my outward affairs I may say with thankfulness I found Truth to be my support, and I was respected in my master's family, who came to live in Mount Holly within two year after my going there.

About the twenty-third year of my age, I had many fresh and heavenly openings in respect to the care and providence of the Almighty over his creatures in general, and over man as the most noble amongst those which are visible. And being clearly convinced in my judgment that to place my whole trust in God was best for me, I felt renewed engagements that in all things I might act on an inward principle of virtue and pursue worldly business no further than as Truth opened my way therein.

About the time called Christmas I observed many people from the country and dwellers in town who, resorting to the public houses, spent their time in drinking and

[13]That is, Woolman believed he had not remained close to the original "concern" or divinely inspired motion to speak. He felt as if he had spoken from a selfish or worldly desire, rather than from an understanding disciplined by God's love.

vain sports, tending to corrupt one another, on which account I was much troubled. At one house in particular there was much disorder, and I believed it was a duty laid on me to go and speak to the master of that house. I considered I was young and that several elderly Friends in town had opportunity to see these things, and though I would gladly have been excused, yet I could not feel my mind clear.

The exercise was heavy, and as I was reading what the Almighty said to Ezekiel[14] respecting his duty as a watchman, the matter was set home more clearly; and then with prayer and tears I besought the Lord for His assistance, who in lovingkindness gave me a resigned heart. Then at a suitable opportunity I went to the public house, and seeing the man amongst a company, I went to him and told him I wanted to speak with him; so we went aside, and there in the fear and the dread of the Almighty I expressed to him what rested on my mind, which he took kindly, and afterward showed more regard to me than before. In a few years after, he died middle-aged, and I often thought that had I neglected my duty in that case it would have given me great trouble, and I was humbly thankful to my gracious Father, who had supported me herein.

My employer, having a Negro woman, sold her and directed me to write a bill of sale, the man being waiting who bought her. The thing was sudden, and though the thoughts of writing an instrument of slavery for one of my fellow creatures felt uneasy, yet I remembered I was hired by the year, that it was my master who directed me to do it, and that it was an elderly man, a member of our Society, who bought her; so through weakness I gave way and wrote it, but at the executing it, I was so afflicted in my mind that I said before my master and the Friend that I believed slavekeeping to be a practice inconsistent with the Christian religion. This in some degree abated my uneasiness, yet as often as I reflected seriously upon it I thought I should have been clearer if I had desired to be excused from it as a thing against my conscience, for such it was. And some time after this a young man of our Society spake to me to write an instrument of slavery, he having lately taken a Negro into his house. I told him I was not easy to write it, for though many kept slaves in our Society, as in others, I still believed the practice was not right, and desired to be excused from writing [it]. I spoke to him in good will, and he told me that keeping slaves was not altogether agreeable to his mind, but that the slave being a gift made to his wife, he had accepted of her.

* * *

[Travels through North Carolina]

About this time believing it good for me to settle, and thinking seriously about a companion, my heart was turned to the Lord with desires that He would give me wisdom to proceed therein agreeable to His will; and He was pleased to give me a well-inclined damsel, Sarah Ellis, to whom I was married the 18th day, 8th month, 1749.[15]

[14]The prophet Ezekiel was a watchman for the Israelites, sent to deliver warnings from God; Ezekiel 3:17.

[15]Sarah Ellis (1721–1787), raised near Mount Holly, was a childhood friend of Woolman.

In the fall of the year 1750 died my father Samuel Woolman with a fever, aged about sixty years.[16] In his lifetime he manifested much care for us his children, that in our youth we might learn to fear the Lord, often endeavouring to imprint in our minds the true principles of virtue, and particularly to cherish in us a spirit of tenderness, not only toward poor people, but also towards all creatures of which we had the command.

After my return from Carolina I made some observations on keeping slaves, which I had some time before showed him, and he perused the manuscript, proposed a few alterations, and appeared well satisfied that I found a concern on that account. And in his last sickness as I was watching with him one night, he being so far spent that there was no expectation of his recovery, but had the perfect use of his understanding, he asked me concerning the manuscript, whether I expected soon to offer it to the Overseers of the Press, and after some conversation thereon said, "I have all along been deeply affected with the oppression of the poor Negroes, and now at last my concern for them is as great as ever."[17]

By his direction I had wrote his will in a time of health, and that night he desired me to read it to him, which I did, and he said it was agreeable to his mind. He then made mention of his end, which he believed was now near, and signified that though he was sensible of many imperfections in the course of his life, yet his experience of the power of Truth and of the love and goodness of God from time to time, even till now, was such that he had no doubt but that in leaving this life he should enter into one more happy.

The next day his sister Elizabeth came to see him and told him of the decease of their sister Anne, who died a few days before. He then said, "I reckon sister Anne was free to leave this world." Elizabeth said she was. He then said, "I also am free to leave it," and being in great weakness of body said, "I hope I shall shortly go to rest." He continued in a weighty frame of mind and was sensible till near the last.

2nd day, 9th month, 1751. Feeling drawings in my mind to visit Friends at the Great Meadows, in the upper part of West Jersey, with the unity of our Monthly Meeting I went there and had some searching laborious exercise amongst Friends in those parts, and found inward peace therein.

In the 9th month, 1753, in company with my well-esteemed friend John Sykes,[18] and with unity of Friends, we traveled about two weeks visiting Friends in Bucks County.[19] We laboured in the love of the gospel according to the measure received, and through the mercies of Him who is strength to the poor who trust in Him, we found satisfaction in our visit. And in the next winter, way opening to visit Friends' families within the compass of our Monthly Meeting, partly by the labors of two friends from Pennsylvania, I joined some in it, having had a desire some time that it might go forward amongst us.

[16] Samuel Woolman (1690–1750) had spent his lifetime on the farm on Rancocas River, Burlington County, New Jersey.

[17] Woolman's *Some Considerations on the Keeping of Negroes* was published in 1754.

[18] John Sykes (1682–1771), a Quaker missionary, often accompanied Woolman on his journeys through the middle colonies.

[19] Pennsylvania.

About this time a person at some distance lying sick, his brother came to me to write his will. I knew he had slaves, and asking his brother, was told he intended to leave them slaves to his children. As writing is a profitable employ, as offending sober people is disagreeable to my inclination, I was straitened in my mind; but as I looked to the Lord, He inclined my heart to His testimony, and I told the man that I believed the practice of continuing slavery to this people was not right and had a scruple in mind against doing writings of that kind: that though many in our Society kept them as slaves, still I was not easy to be concerned in it and desired to be excused from going to write the will. I spake to him in the fear of the Lord, and he made no reply to what I said, but went away; he also had some concerns in the practice, and I thought he was displeased with me.

In this case I had a fresh confirmation that acting contrary to present outward interest from a motive of divine love and in regard to truth and righteousness, and thereby incurring the resentments of people, opens the way to a treasure better than silver and to a friendship exceeding the friendship of men.

On the 7th day, 2nd month, 1754, at night, I dreamed that I was walking in an orchard, it appeared to be about the middle of the afternoon; when on a sudden I saw two lights in the east resembling two suns, but of a dull and gloomy aspect. The one appeared about the height of the sun at three hours high, and the other more northward and one-third lower. In a few minutes the air in the east appeared to be mingled with fire, and like a terrible storm coming westward the streams of fire reached the orchard where I stood, but I felt no harm. I then found one of my acquaintance standing near me, who was greatly distressed in mind at this unusual appearance. My mind felt calm, and I said to my friend, "We must all once die, and if it please the Lord that our death be in this way, it is good for us to be resigned." Then I walked to a house hard by, and going upstairs, saw people with sad and troubled aspects, amongst whom I passed into another room where the floor was only some loose boards. There I sat down alone by a window, and looking out I saw in the south three great red streams standing at equal distance from each other, the bottom of which appeared to stand on the earth and the top to reach above the region of the clouds. Across those three streams went less ones, and from each end of such small stream others extended in regular lines to the earth, all red and appeared to extend through the whole southern firmament. There then appeared on a green plain a great multitude of men in a military posture, some of whom I knew. They came near the house, and passing on westward some of them, looking up at me, expressed themselves in a scoffing, taunting way, to which I made no reply; soon after, an old captain of the militia came to me, and I was told these men were assembled to improve in the discipline of war. . . .

Until the year 1756 I continued to retail goods, besides following my trade as a tailor, about which time I grew uneasy on account of my business growing too cumbersome. I began with selling trimmings for garments and from thence proceeded to sell clothes and linens, and at length having got a considerable shop of goods, my trade increased every year and the road to large business appeared open; but I felt a stop in my mind.

Through the mercies of the Almighty I had in a good degree learned to be content with a plain way of living. I had but a small family, that on serious consideration I believed Truth did not require me to engage in much cumbrous affairs. It had been my general practice to buy and sell things really useful. Things that served chiefly to please the vain mind in people I was not easy to trade in, seldom did it, and whenever I did I found it weaken me as a Christian.

The increase of business became my burden, for though my natural inclination was toward merchandise, yet I believed Truth required me to live more free from outward cumbers and there was now a strife in my mind between the two; and in this exercise my prayers were put up to the Lord, who graciously heard me and gave me a heart resigned to His holy will. Then I lessened my outward business, and as I had opportunity told my customers of my intentions that they might consider what shop to turn to, and so in a while wholly laid down merchandise, following my trade as a tailor, myself only, having no apprentice. I also had a nursery of apple trees, in which I employed some of my time—hoeing, grafting, trimming, and inoculating.

In merchandise it is the custom where I lived to sell chiefly on credit, and poor people often get in debt, and when payment is expected, not having wherewith to pay, their creditors often sue for it at law. Having often observed occurrences of this kind, I found it good for me to advise poor people to take such goods as were most useful and not costly.

In the time of trading, I had an opportunity of seeing that too liberal a use of spirituous liquors and the custom of wearing too costly apparel lead some people into great inconveniences, and these two things appear to be often connected one with the other. For by not attending to that use of things which is consistent with universal righteousness, there is an increase of labor which extends beyond what our Heavenly Father intends for us. And by great labor, and often by much sweating in the heat, there is even amongst such who are not drunkards a craving of some liquors to revive the spirits: that partly by the wanton, luxurious drinking of some, and partly by the drinkings of others led to it through immoderate labor, very great quantities of rum are every year expended in our colonies, the greater part of which we should have no need did we steadily attend to pure wisdom.

Where men take pleasure in feeling their minds elevated with strong drink and so indulge their appetite as to disorder their understandings, neglect their duty as members in a family or civil society, and cast off all pretense to religion, their case is much to be pitied. And where such whose lives are for the most part regular, and whose examples have a strong influence on the minds of others, adhere to some customs which strongly draw toward the use of more strong liquor than pure wisdom directs to the use of, this also, as it hinders the spreading of the spirit of meekness and strengthens the hands of the more excessive drinkers, is a case to be lamented.

As the least degree of luxury hath some connection with evil, for those who profess to be disciples of Christ and are looked upon as leaders of the people, to have that mind in them which was also in Him, and so stand separate from every wrong way, is a means of help to the weaker. As I have sometimes been much spent in the heat and taken spirits to revive me, I have found by experience that in such circumstance the mind is not so calm nor so fitly disposed for divine meditation as when all such extremes are avoided, and have felt an increasing care to attend to that Holy Spirit which sets right bounds to our desires and leads those who faithfully follow it to apply all the gifts of divine providence to the purposes for which they were intended. Did such who have the care of great estates attend with singleness of heart to this Heavenly Instructor, which so opens and enlarges the mind that men love their neighbors as themselves, they would have wisdom given them to manage without finding occasion to employ some people in the luxuries of life or to make it necessary for others to labor too hard. But for want of steadily regarding this principle of divine love, a selfish spirit takes place in the minds of people, which is attended with darkness and manifold confusions in the world. . . .

When I was at Newbegun Creek,[20] a Friend was there who labored for his living, having no Negroes, and had been a minister many years. He came to me the next day, and as we rode together he signified that he wanted to talk with me concerning a difficulty he had been under, and related it near as follows, to wit: That as monies had of late years been raised by a tax to carry on the wars, he had a scruple in his mind in regard to paying it and chose rather to suffer distraint of goods than pay it. And as he was the only person who refused it in them parts and knew not that anyone else was in the like circumstance, he signified that it had been a heavy trial upon him, and the more so for that some of his brethren had been uneasy with his conduct in that case, and added that from a sympathy he felt with me yesterday in meeting, he found a freedom thus to open the matter in the way of querying concerning Friends in our parts; whereupon I told him the state of Friends amongst us as well as I was able, and also that I had for some time been under the like scruple. I believed him to be one who was concerned to walk uprightly before the Lord and esteemed it my duty to preserve this memorandum.

From hence I went back into Virginia and had a meeting near James Copeland's; it was a time of inward suffering, but through the goodness of the Lord I was made content. Then to another meeting where through the renewings of pure love we had a very comfortable meeting.

Traveling up and down of late, I have renewed evidences that to be faithful to the Lord and content with his will concerning me is a most necessary and useful lesson for me to be learning, looking less at the effects of my labor than at the pure motion and reality of the concern as it arises from heavenly love. In the Lord Jehovah is everlasting strength, and as the mind by a humble resignation is united to Him and we utter words from an inward knowledge that they arise from the heavenly spring, though our way may be difficult and require close attention to keep in it, and though the manner in which we may be led may tend to our own abasement, yet if we continue in patience and meekness, heavenly peace is the reward of our labors.

From hence I went to Curles Meeting, which, though small, was reviving to the honest-hearted. Thence to Black Creek and Caroline Meetings, from whence, accompanied by William Stanley[21] before-mentioned, we rode to Goose Creek, being much through the woods and about one hundred miles. We lodged the first night at a public house, the second in the woods, and the next day we reached a Friend's house at Goose Creek. In the woods we lay under some disadvantage, having no fireworks, nor bells for our horses, but we stopped some before night and let them feed on wild grass, which was plenty, we the meantime cutting with our knives a store against night, and then tied them; and gathering some bushes under an oak we lay down, but the mosquitoes being plenty and the ground damp, I slept but little.

[20]North Carolina.

[21]William Stanley (1729–1807), of Cedar Creek, Virginia.

Thus lying in the wilderness and looking at the stars, I was led to contemplate the condition of our first parents when they were sent forth from the garden, and considered that they had no house, no tools for business, no garments but what their Creator gave them, no vessels for use, nor any fire to cook roots or herbs. But the Almighty, though they had been disobedient, was a father to them; way opened in process of time for all the conveniences of life. And He who by the gracious influence of His spirit illuminated their understand and showed them what was acceptable to Him and tended to their felicity as intelligent creatures, did also provide means for their happy living in this world as they attended to the manifestations of His wisdom. . . .

1774

from Some Considerations on the Keeping of Negroes[1]

Recommended to the Professors of Christianity of Every Denomination

Introduction

Customs generally approved and opinions received by youth from their superiors become like the natural produce of a soil, especially when they are suited to favourite inclinations. But as the judgments of God are without partiality, by which the state of the soul must be tried, it would be the highest wisdom to forego customs and popular opinions, and try the treasures of the soul by the infallible standard: Truth.

Natural affection needs a careful examination. Operating upon us in a soft manner, it kindles desires of love and tenderness, and there is danger of taking it for something higher. To me it appears an instinct like that which inferior creatures have; each of them, we see, by the ties of nature love self best. That which is a part of self they love by the same tie or instinct. In them it in some measure does the offices of reason, by which, among other things, they watchfully keep and orderly feed their helpless offspring. Thus natural affection appears to be a branch of self-love, good in the animal race, in us likewise with proper limitations, but otherwise is productive of evil by exciting desires to promote some by means prejudicial to others.

Our blessed Saviour seems to give a check to this irregular fondness in nature and, at the same time, a precedent for us: "Who is my mother, and who are my brethren?"—thereby intimating that the earthly ties of relationship are, comparatively, inconsiderable to such who, through a steady course of obedience, have come

[1]First published in 1754, Woolman's *Considerations* argues in behalf of the abolition of slavery. The source of the present text is Phillips Moulton's edition, *The Journal and Major Essays of John Woolman,* 1971.

to the happy experience of the Spirit of God bearing witness with their spirits that they are his children: "And he stretched forth his hands towards his disciples and said, 'Behold my mother and my brethren; for whosoever shall do the will of my Father which is in heaven (arrives at the more noble part of true relationship) the same is my brother, and sister, and mother.'" Mt. 12:48 [–50].

This doctrine agrees well with a state truly complete, where love necessarily operates according to the agreeableness of things or principles unalterable and in themselves perfect. If endeavouring to have my children eminent amongst men after my death be that which no reasons grounded on those principles can be brought to support, then to be temperate in my pursuit after gain and to keep always within the bounds of those principles is an indispensable duty, and to depart from it a dark unfruitful toil.

In our present condition, to love our children is needful; but except this love proceeds from the true heavenly principle which sees beyond earthly treasures, it will rather be injurious than of any real advantage to them. Where the fountain is corrupt, the streams must necessarily be impure.

That important injunction of our Saviour (Mt. 6:33), with the promise annexed, contains a short but comprehensive view of our duty and happiness. If then the business of mankind in this life is to first seek another, if this cannot be done but by attending to the means, if a summary of the means is not to do that to another which (in like circumstances) we would not have done unto us, then these are points of moment and worthy of our most serious consideration.

What I write on this subject is with reluctance, and the hints given are in as general terms as my concern would allow. I know it is a point about which in all its branches men that appear to aim well are not generally agreed, and for that reason I chose to avoid being very particular. If I may happily have let drop anything that may excite such as are concerned in the practice to a close thinking on the subject treated of, the candid amongst them may easily do the subject such further justice as, on an impartial enquiry, it may appear to deserve; and such an enquiry I would earnestly recommend.

Some Consideration on the Keeping of Negroes

"Forasmuch as ye did it to the least of these my brethren, ye did it unto me." Mt. 25:40.

As many times there are different motives to the same actions, and one does that from a generous heart which another does for selfish ends, the like may be said in this case.

There are various circumstances amongst them that keep Negroes, and different ways by which they fall under their care; and, I doubt not, there are many well-disposed persons amongst them who desire rather to manage wisely and justly in this difficult matter than to make gain of it. But the general disadvantage which these poor Africans lie under in an enlightened Christian country having often filled me with real sadness, and been like undigested matter on my mind, I now think it my duty, through divine aid, to offer some thoughts thereon to the consideration of others.

When we remember that all nations are of one blood (Gen. 3:20); that in this world we are but sojourners; that we are subject to the like afflictions and infirmities of body, the like disorders and frailties in mind, the like temptations, the same death and the same judgment; and that the All-wise Being is judge and Lord over us all, it seems to raise an idea of a general brotherhood and a disposition easy to be touched with a feeling of each other's afflictions. But when we forget those things and look chiefly at our outward circumstances, in this and some ages past, constantly retaining in our minds the distinction betwixt us and them with respect to our knowledge and improvement in things divine, natural, and artificial, our breasts being apt to be filled with fond notions of superiority, there is danger of erring in our conduct toward them.

We allow them to be of the same species with ourselves; the odds is we are in a higher station and enjoy greater favours than they. And when it is thus that our Heavenly Father endoweth some of his children with distinguished gifts, they are intended for good ends. But if those thus gifted are thereby lifted up above their brethren, not considering themselves as debtors to the weak nor behaving themselves as faithful stewards, none who judge impartially can suppose them free from ingratitude. When a people dwell under the liberal distribution of favours from heaven, it behooves them carefully to inspect their ways and consider the purposes for which those favours were bestowed, lest through forgetfulness of God and misusing his gifts they incur his heavy displeasure, whose judgments are just and equal, who exalteth and humbleth to the dust as he seeth meet.

It appears by Holy Record that men under high favours have been apt to err in their opinions concerning others. Thus Israel, according to the description of the prophet (Is. 65:5), when exceedingly corrupted and degenerated, yet remembered they were the chosen people of God and could say, "Stand by thyself, come not near me, for I am holier than thou." That this was no chance language, but their common opinion of other people, more fully appears by considering the circumstances which attended when God was beginning to fulfil his precious promises concerning the gathering of the Gentiles.

The Most High, in a vision, undeceived Peter, first prepared his heart to believe, and at the house of Cornelius showed him of a certainty that God was no respecter of persons. The effusion of the Holy Ghost upon a people with whom they, the Jewish Christians, would not so much as eat was strange to them. All they of the circumcision were astonished to see it, and the apostles and brethren of Judea contended with Peter about it, till he having rehearsed the whole matter and fully shown that the Father's love was unlimited, they are thereat struck with admiration and cry out, "Then hath God also to the Gentiles granted repentance unto life!" [Acts 11:18].

The opinion of peculiar favours being confined to them was deeply rooted, or else the above instance had been less strange to them, for these reasons: First, they were generally acquainted with the writings of the prophets, by whom this time was repeatedly spoken of and pointed at. Secondly, our blessed Lord shortly before expressly said, "I have other sheep, not of this fold; them also must I bring," etc. [Jn. 10:16]. Lastly, his words to them after his resurrection, at the very time of his ascension, "Ye shall be witnesses to me not only in Jerusalem, Judea, and Samaria, but to the uttermost parts of the earth" [Acts 1:8].

Those concurring circumstances, one would think, might have raised a strong expectation of seeing such a time. Yet when it came, it proved matter of offense and astonishment.

To consider mankind otherwise than brethren, to think favours are peculiar to one nation and exclude others, plainly supposes a darkness in the understanding. For as God's love is universal, so where the mind is sufficiently influenced by it, it begets a likeness of itself and the heart is enlarged towards all men. Again, to conclude a people froward, perverse, and worse by nature than others (who ungratefully receive favours and apply them to bad ends), this will excite a behavior toward them unbecoming the excellence of true religion.

To prevent such error let us calmly consider their circumstances, and, the better to do it, make their case ours. Suppose, then, that our ancestors and we have been exposed to constant servitude in the more servile and inferior employments of life; that we had been destitute of the help of reading and good company; that amongst ourselves we had had few wise and pious instructors; that the religious amongst our superiors seldom took notice of us; that while others in ease have plentifully heaped up the fruit of our labour, we had received barely enough to relieve nature, and being wholly at the command of others had generally been treated as a contemptible, ignorant part of mankind. Should we, in that case, be less abject than they now are? Again, if oppression be so hard to bear that a wise man is made mad by it (Eccles. 7:7), then a series of those things altering the behaviour and manners of a people is what may reasonably be expected.

When our property is taken contrary to our mind by means appearing to us unjust, it is only through divine influence and the enlargement of heart from thence proceeding that we can love our reputed oppressors. If the Negroes fall short in this, an uneasy, if not a disconsolate, disposition will be awakened and remain like seeds in their minds, producing sloth and many other habits appearing odious to us, with which being free men they perhaps had not been chargeable. These and other circumstances, rightly considered, will lessen that too great disparity which some make between us and them.

Integrity of heart hath appeared in some of them, so that if we continue in the world of Christ (previous to discipleship, Jn. 8:31) and our conduct towards them be seasoned with his love, we may hope to see the good effect of it, the which, in a good degree, is the case with some into whose hands they have fallen. But that too many treat them otherwise, not seeming conscious of any neglect, is, alas! too evident.

When self-love presides in our minds our opinions are biased in our own favour. In this condition, being concerned with a people so situated that they have no voice to plead their own cause, there's danger of using ourselves to an undisturbed partiality till, by long custom, the mind becomes reconciled with it and the judgment itself infected.

To humbly apply to God for wisdom, that we may thereby be enabled to see things as they are and ought to be, is very needful; hereby the hidden things of darkness may be brought to light and the judgment made clear. We shall then consider mankind as brethren. Though different degrees and a variety of qualifications and abilities, one dependent on another, be admitted, yet high thoughts will be laid aside, and all men treated as becometh the sons of one Father, agreeable to the doctrine of Christ Jesus.

He hath laid down the best criterion by which mankind ought to judge of their own conduct, and others judge for them of theirs, one towards another—viz., "Whatsoever ye would that men should do unto you, do ye even so to them." I take it that all men by nature are equally entitled to the equality of this rule and under the indispensable obligations of it. One man ought not to look upon another man or society of men as so far beneath him but that he should put himself in their place in all his actions towards them, and bring all to this test—viz., How should I approve of this conduct were I in their circumstances and they in mine?—Arscott's Considerations, *Part III, Fol. 107.*[2]

This doctrine, being of a moral unchangeable nature, hath been likewise inculcated in the former dispensation: "If a stranger sojourn with thee in your land, ye shall not vex him; but the stranger that dwelleth with you shall be as one born amongst you, and thou shalt love him as thyself." Lev. 19:33, 34. Had these people come voluntarily and dwelt amongst us, to have called them strangers would be proper. And their being brought by force, with regret and a languishing mind, may well raise compassion in a heart rightly disposed. But there is nothing in such treatment which upon a wise and judicious consideration will any ways lessen their right of being treated as strangers. If the treatment which many of them meet with be rightly examined and compared with those precepts, "Thou shalt not vex him nor oppress him; he shall be as one born amongst you, and thou shalt love him as thyself" (Lev. 19:33; Deut. 27:19), there will appear an important difference betwixt them.

It may be objected there is cost of purchase and risk of their lives to them who possess 'em, and therefore needful that they make the best use of their time. In a practice just and reasonable such objections may have weight; but if the work be wrong from the beginning, there's little or no force in them. If I purchase a man who hath never forfeited his liberty, the natural right of freedom is in him. And shall I keep him and his posterity in servitude and ignorance? How should I approve of this conduct were I in his circumstances and he in mine? It may be thought that to treat them as we would willingly be treated, our gain by them would be inconsiderable; and it were, in diverse respects, better that there were none in our country.

We may further consider that they are now amongst us, and those of our nation the cause of their being here, that whatsoever difficulty accrues thereon we are justly chargeable with, and to bear all inconveniences attending it with a serious and weighty concern of mind to do our duty by them is the best we can do. To seek a remedy by continuing the oppression because we have power to do it and see others do it, will, I apprehend, not be doing as we would be done by.

How deeply soever men are involved in the most exquisite difficulties, sincerity of heart and upright walking before God, freely submitting to his providence, is the most sure remedy. He only is able to relieve not only persons but nations in their

[2]This quotation, slightly altered, is found in Alexander Arscott, *Some Considerations Relating to the Present State of the Christian Religion, wherein the Nature, End, and Design of Christianity, as well as the Principle Evidence of the Truth of it, are Explained and Recommended out of the Holy Scriptures; with a General Appeal to the Experience of all Men for Confirmation thereof,* Part III (London, 1734), 78. Arscott (1676–1737), an Oxford graduate, was a schoolmaster. About 1700, to the great dismay of his parents, he became a Quaker. He served many years as clerk of the London Yearly Meeting. He intended this volume as an apologetic for Christianity based on both Scripture and reason, apart from the special point of view of the Friends. All three parts were reprinted in Philadelphia, the first two by Benjamin Franklin in 1732, the third by A. Bradford in 1738 [Moulton's note].

greatest calamities. David, in a great strait when the sense of his past error and the full expectation of an impending calamity as the reward of it were united to the aggravating his distress, after some deliberation saith, "Let me fall now into the hands of the Lord, for very great are his mercies; let me not fall into the hand of man." I Chron. 21:13.

To act continually with integrity of heart above all narrow or selfish motives is a sure token of our being partakers of that salvation which God hath appointed for walls and bulwarks (Is. 5:26; Rom. 15:8), and is, beyond all contradiction, a more happy situation than can ever be promised by the utmost reach of art and power united, not proceeding from heavenly wisdom.

A supply to nature's lawful wants, joined with a peaceful, humble mind, is the truest happiness in this life. And if here we arrive to this and remain to walk in the path of the just, our case will be truly happy. And though herein we may part with or miss of some glaring shows of riches and leave our children little else but wise instructions, a good example, and the knowledge of some honest employment, these, with the blessing of providence, are sufficient for their happiness, and are more likely to prove so than laying up treasures for them which are often rather a snare than any real benefit, especially to them who, instead of being exampled to temperance, are in all things taught to prefer the getting of riches and to eye the temporal distinctions they give as the principal business of this life. These readily overlook the true happiness of man as it results from the enjoyment of all things in the fear of God, and miserably substituting an inferior good, dangerous in the acquiring and uncertain in the fruition, they are subject to many disappointments; and every sweet carries its sting.

It is the conclusion of our blessed Lord and his apostles, as appears by their lives and doctrines, that the highest delights of sense or most pleasing objects visible ought ever to be accounted infinitely inferior to that real intellectual happiness suited to man in his primitive innocence and now to be found in true renovation of mind, and that the comforts of our present life, the things most grateful to us, ought always to be received with temperance and never made the chief objects of our desire, hope, or love, but that our whole heart and affections be principally looking to that city "which hath foundations, whose maker and builder is God" [Heb. 11:10].

Did we so improve the gifts bestowed on us that our children might have an education suited to these doctrines, and our example to confirm it, we might rejoice in hopes of their being heirs of an inheritance incorruptible. This inheritance, as Christians, we esteem the most valuable; and how then can we fail to desire it for our children? Oh, that we were consistent with ourselves in pursuing means necessary to obtain it!

It appears by experience that where children are educated in fullness, ease, and idleness, evil habits are more prevalent than is common amongst such who are prudently employed in the necessary affairs of life. And if children are not only educated in the way of so great temptation, but have also the opportunity of lording it over their fellow creatures and being masters of men in their childhood, how can we hope otherwise than that their tender minds will be possessed with thoughts too high for them?—which by continuance, gaining strength, will prove like a slow current, gradually separating them from (or keeping from acquaintance with) that humility and meekness in which alone lasting happiness can be enjoyed. . . .

1754

Apian, *Charta Cosmographia* (1544). This map, with its representations of mythical beasts and godlike figures, displays European views of the New World. Fantastical images inhabit the cosmos in which the map is depicted. Although North America is only a thin land mass, the areas of Central and South America are beginning to take shape as more and more explorers sailed the coastlines. The mythical images coexist with the emerging empirical knowledge of the Americas.

Hopi pueblo. When the Europeans arrived in North America in the fifteenth century, they were met by perhaps four to six million Native Americans with a wide variety of cultures. This variety can be seen in the structures and communities created by different tribes. The Cherokee in the woodlands of southeastern North American, for example, built wooden-framed houses with the outside covered with wood, bark, or clay. The Hopi adapted to their southwestern landscape by building pueblos, communal homes constructed from stone and adobe. Spanish priests moved into many of the pueblo communities, imposing their religion and ideas of "civilization" on the Native Americans they encountered.

Thomas Smith, *Self-Portrait* (c. 1680). Portraiture was one of the few approved forms of Puritan art. This portrait displays the wealth of the subject in the lace collar at the center of the painting and the opulent background. At the same time, the skull and the poem, signed T.S., emphasize the fleeting existence of the world and its "Joies" and "Toies." The window in the background shows a naval battle in which the subject possibly took part. Portraiture is about how we want to represent ourselves to the world. This self-portrait, with its multiple texts, is a carefully constructed set with the subject stage center.

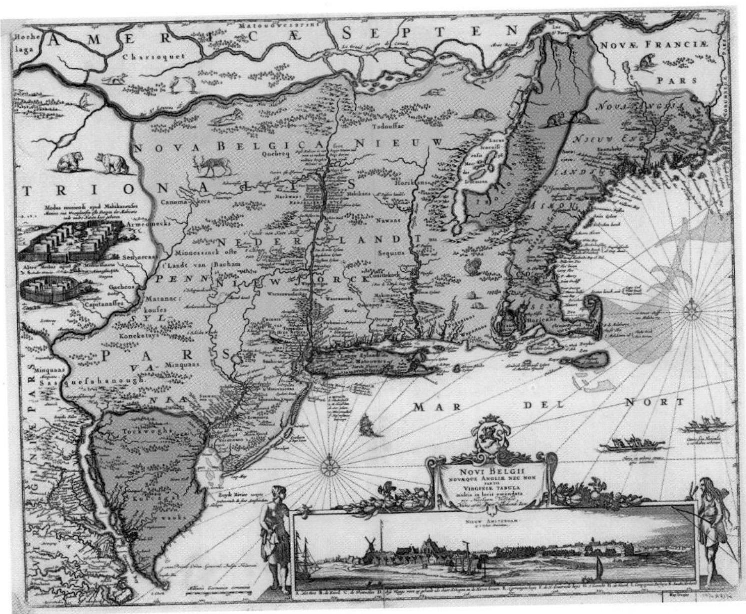

Nicolaes Visscher, Early map of the Dutch colony of New Netherland (c. 1685). After Henry Hudson completed his explorations in the *Half Moon* for the Dutch East India Company in 1609, the Dutch established the colony called New Netherland. Nicolaes Visscher's map, from the mid-seventeenth century, is one of the best-known maps of the region. The map also has an early vignette of New Amsterdam, later renamed New York City in 1664.

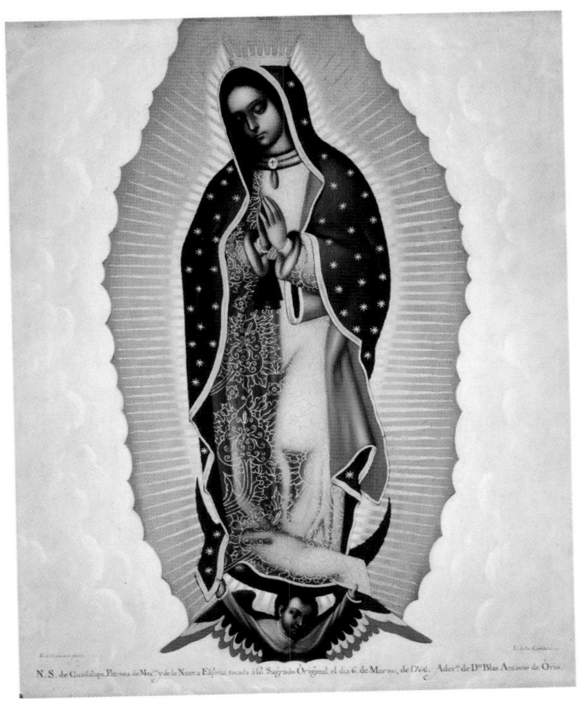

Miguel Cabrera, *La Virgen de Guadalupe* (1766). With her image on everything from tattoos to calendars to jewelry, the Virgin of Guadalupe is one of the best-recognized religious icons in the world. She is a syncretic figure, blending Spanish and Indian worlds and systems of belief. With her darker skin, she is the Native American Virgin Mother.

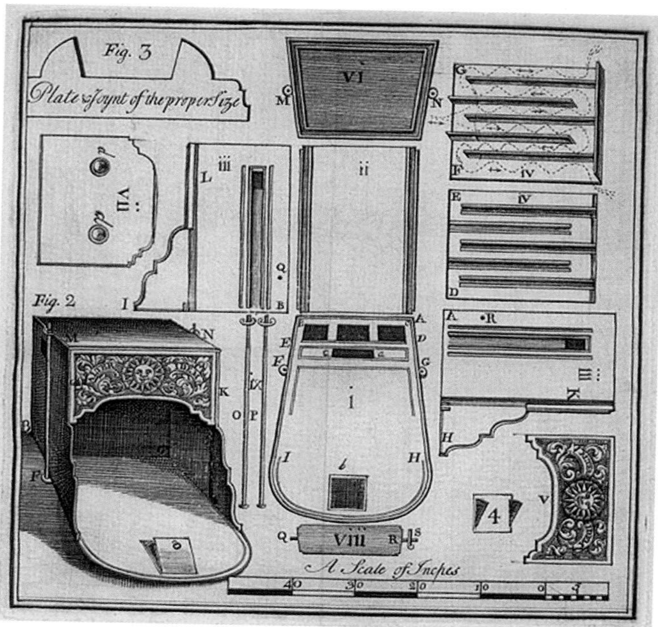

Diagram of a Franklin stove (1744). This diagram accompanies an essay that Benjamin Franklin wrote to promote sales of his stove. By controlling the airflow with a series of partitioned iron plates, the stove loses less heat and thus uses less wood. The stove became so popular that the essay was translated into several languages.

EXPLANATION of the PLATE,
Referring to the Pages where the ſeveral Parts are deſcrib'd, or their Uſes ſhewn.

	Page
i *The Bottom Plate*	
ii *The Back Plate*	14
iii iii *The two Side Plates*	14
iv iv *The two Plates that make up the Air-Box*	14
v *The Front Plate*	15
vi *The Top Plate*	15
vii *The Shutter or Slider*	15
viii *The Regiſter*	15, 20, 21, 22
Fig 2. *The Fire-Place put together*	16, 21, 22
3. *The Section of a Fragment of a Plate, ſhewing the quarter-round Regulets that make the Joints*	16, 35
4. *The Blower, (Bottom upwards)*	14
O P *The two Screw Rods*	21
‡ ‡. *With the prick'd Lines, ſhew the Courſe of the Air thro' the Windings of the Air-Box.*	14

The Capital Letters ſhow the correſponding Parts of the ſeveral Plates.

On the DEVICE of the NEW FIRE-PLACE,
A SUN; *with this Motto*, ALTER IDEM.
i.e. *A ſecond Self*; or, *Another, the ſame.*
By a Friend.

ANOTHER Sun! — 'tis true; — but not THE SAME.
Alike, I own, in Warmth and genial Flame:
But, more obliging than his elder Brother,
This will not ſcorch in Summer, like *the other*;
Nor, when ſharp *Boreas* chills our ſhiv'ring Limbs,
Will *this Sun* leave us for more Southern Climes;
Or, in long Winter Nights, forſake us here,
To chear new Friends in t'other Hemiſphere:
But, faithful ſtill to us, this *new Sun's* Fire,
Warms when we pleaſe, and juſt as we deſire.

Explanation of the diagram of a Franklin stove (1744). Franklin's description of the parts of his stove.

TO BE SOLD, on board the Ship *Bance-Yland*, on tueſday the 6th of *May* next, at *Aſhley-Ferry*; a choice cargo of about 250 fine healthy

NEGROES,

juſt arrived from the Windward & Rice Coaſt. —The utmoſt care has already been taken, and ſhall be continued, to keep them free from the leaſt danger of being infected with the SMALL-POX, no boat having been on board, and all other communication with people from *Charles-Town* prevented.

Auſtin, Laurens, & Appleby.

N. B. Full one Half of the above Negroes have had the SMALL-POX in their own Country.

Advertisement for the sale of Africans (1760).
The merchant firm of Austin, Laurens, and Appleby was a leading importer of slaves during this period.

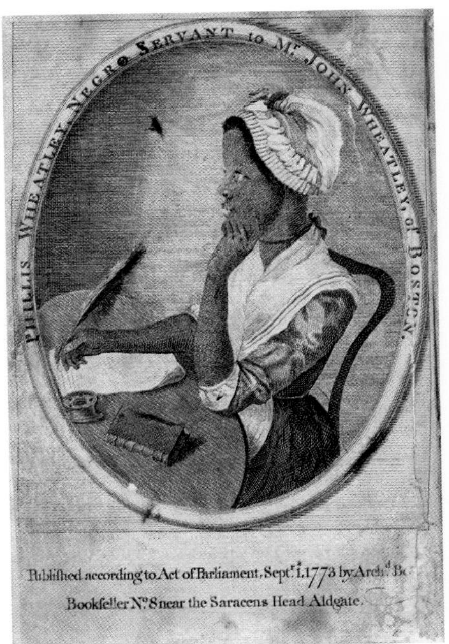

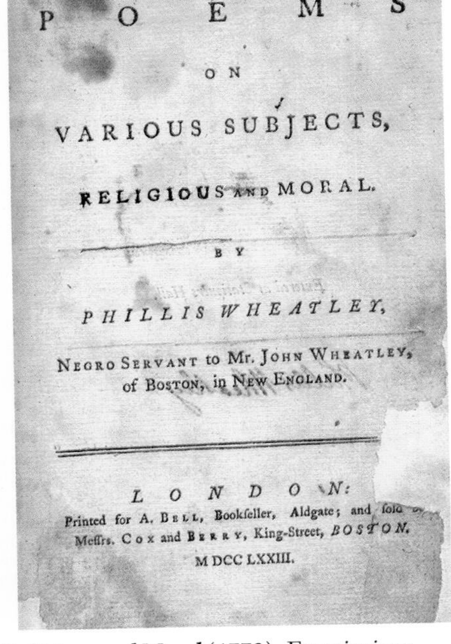
POEMS

ON

VARIOUS SUBJECTS,

RELIGIOUS AND MORAL.

BY

PHILLIS WHEATLEY,

NEGRO SERVANT to Mr. JOHN WHEATLEY, of BOSTON, in NEW ENGLAND.

LONDON:
Printed for A. BELL, Bookſeller, Aldgate; and ſold by Meſſrs. COX and BERRY, King-Street, *BOSTON.*

M DCC LXXIII.

Phillis Wheatley, *Poems on Various Subjects, Religious and Moral* (1773). Frontispiece and title page from the first edition of her book entitled *Poems on Various Subjects, Religious and Moral* printed in London. The illustration and caption stating "Phillis Wheatley, Negro Servant to Mr. John Wheatley, of Boston," emphasizes her unique role as the first published African American poet.

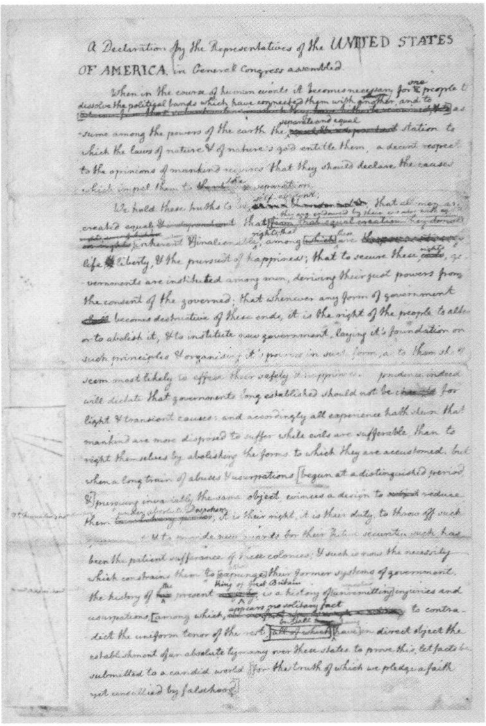

Thomas Jefferson, Draft of the Declaration of Independence (1776). The "original Rough draught" demonstrates how the text changed from Thomas Jefferson's "fair copy" to the final document adopted by Congress on the morning of July 4, 1776. This version shows minor emendations by John Adams and Benjamin Franklin. In his *Autobiography,* Jefferson includes his version and the final version of the Declaration, stating, "As the sentiments of men are known not only by what they receive, but what they reject also, I will state the form of the declaration as originally reported." The very existence of this earlier draft of the document confirms that the signers were aware of its vast historical importance.

Jane Pitford Braddick Peticolas, *Monticello* (c. 1827). This rather idealized image of Monticello displays its beauty set in a kind of Garden of Eden. Monticello stands as the symbol of Jefferson's view of agrarianism as the ideal for America. This watercolor is notable for what it does not include—the slave quarters necessary to maintain the agrarian ideal.

Abigail Adams Hobart, Sampler (1802). Samplers were an important art form in colonial America. They showcased young girls' sewing abilities, a useful skill during this time, and served as a piece of art to be admired and displayed. Since most samplers contain the alphabet, they also exhibit the importance of literacy for girls as well as boys. Abigail Adams Hobart, a member of the prominent New England Adams family, shows buildings at Providence College in her highly decorated sampler.

NEW ENGLAND PRIMER. 11

In Adam's fall
We sinned all.

Thy life to mend,
God's Book attend.

The Cat doth play,
And after slay.

A Dog will bite
A thief at night.

The Eagle's flight
Is out of sight.

The idle Fool
Is whipped at school.

A B C D E F

***The New England Primer* (after 1836).** The Puritans were a well-educated group of colonists who saw books as a way to educate and inculcate their values, especially in the next generation. All children were expected to learn to read and write, which were necessary skills for their religious education. Books such as *The New England Primer* and *The Bay Psalm Book* were in every home along with the Bible. Later revisions display more secularized moral education and adaptation to different regions and ethnic groups.

Francisco Palou 1723–1789

Had he been granted an honorary degree as colleges today grant such degrees, Palou, according to his editor Herbert E. Bolton, would have received this tribute: "Fray Francisco Palou, diligent student, devout Christian, loyal disciple, tireless traveler, zealous missionary, firm defender of the faith, resourceful pioneer, successful mission builder, able administrator, and fair-minded historian of California." Such a tribute seems apt for the man who so successfully memorialized his only rival in the California missionary effort, Fray Junípero Serra.

Born, like Serra (ten years earlier), at Majorca, Spain, Palou entered the Franciscan Order in 1739 and was ordained in 1743. He eagerly joined Serra in the missionary program planned for the Americas; they and other future missionaries reached Vera Cruz, Mexico, in 1749. After several years in missions in Mexico, these Franciscans sought to extend their efforts northward, to replace the Jesuit missionaries who had been expelled from Spanish dominion in 1767 by King Charles III of Spain. Palou and Serra went first to the Baja California missions (1767). They reached Loreto, in Lower (Baja) California, in the spring of 1768. Serra was assigned the next year to Upper (Alta) California missions, which left those in Lower California to Palou's control until 1773.

Palou, wishing to serve with Serra again, chose to serve in the chain of missions in Upper California. He went first to San Diego, then on to Monterey-Carmel, Serra's headquarters. He assisted in the placement of friars, and he collected historical data that survives as some of the only record of these early California years. He was assigned in 1776 to the mission at San Francisco, where he stayed until 1784. Serra's death in Carmel that year left open the presidency of the Upper California missions, a post Palou ably filled until, with failing health, he left in 1785. He died in Mexico, where he completed his life of Serra, most of which he had written in California.

Palou's two works, the *Noticias de la Nueva California* (published in the middle of the nineteenth century) and the biography of Serra, *Relacion historica* (1787), provide key information about early California and the missionary efforts there. He had nearly completed his life of Serra before returning to Mexico. He there added, after much research in the library at San Fernando, the long chapter on Serra's virtues. The book, published in Mexico City, was sent to the royal palace in Madrid, Spain, as well as to Majorca and to the missions in Sonora and California. It received high praise. Fray Junípero Serra's life can serve as a model of discipline and hard work in spite of a revision of history's sense of how the missions he founded affected the native population. More significant is Palou's project of transforming Serra's life into biography, a lengthy, detailed piece of writing, blending epistolary documentation, recreated dialogue, narrative, impassioned exposition, and moralizing. Palou's text stands well as a west-coast balance to Cotton Mather's earlier hagiographies of the Puritan founders in *Magnalia Christi Americana.* Both texts are records of religious heroism in eras that seemed to be fast diminishing before the writers' eyes.

Carla Mulford
Pennsylvania State University

Juan Bruce-Novoa
University of California at Irvine

PRIMARY WORKS

Herbert E. Bolton, tr. and ed., *Historical Memoirs of New California,* 4 vols., 1926; Maynard J. Geiger, tr. and ed., *Palou's Life of Junípero Serra,* 1955.

from Life of Junípero Serra

from **Chapter XXII**
The Expeditions Arrive at the Port of Monterey—The Mission and Presidio of San Carlos Are Founded

What this chapter proposes will be taken care of by the following letter which the Venerable Father wrote to me, in which he announces his arrival at Monterey and what occurred at that port.

Live Jesus, Mary and Joseph!

Reverend Father Lector and President Fray Francisco Palóu

Most dear friend and esteemed Sir:

On May 31, by God's help, after a somewhat distressful sea voyage of a month and a half, this packet-boat, the *San Antonio,* with Don Juan Pérez as captain, arrived and anchored in this beautiful Port of Monterey. It is exactly the same in substance and features as the expedition of Don Sebastián Vizcaíno left it in the year 1603.[1] I was exceedingly comforted when that very night we learned that the over-land expedition had arrived fully eight days before. Father Fray Juan traveled with it. All are enjoying good health. I was further comforted when on the holyday of Pentecost, June 3, in the presence of all the officers of land and sea, together with all their subordinates, near the very same ravine and oak where the [Carmelite] Fathers of the said expedition had celebrated Mass, the altar was prepared, the bells were hung up and rung, the hymn *Veni, Creator* was sung, water was blessed, the large cross and the royal standards were set up and blessed, and I sang the first Mass known to have been celebrated here since that time. Afterwards we sang the *Salve Regina* to Our Lady before a statue given by His Excellency, which stood on the altar. During the Mass I preached to the men. We concluded the ceremonies by singing the *Te Deum.* Thereupon the civil officials performed the formal act of taking possession of the land in the name of the King, our Sovereign (may God save him!). After this we all ate together in the shade by the beach. The entire celebration was accompanied by frequent salvos from the guns aboard ship and ashore. . . .

I beg Your Reverence and earnestly request that two of the group be assigned to these missions, so as to make six with the four who are here, and to establish the Mission of San Buenaventura along the Santa Barbara Channel. It is a section of greater value than that of San Diego or Monterey or of the entire territory thus far discovered. Provisions for that mission have already been sent on two occasions. Up till now, no one has been able to blame the friars for not

[1]Although Spaniards had sailed along the Pacific coast as far as Oregon as early as the 1540s, Monterey Bay was not discovered until the Vizcaíno expedition in 1602. Plans were made to settle the area, but nothing was done until Father Serra established his mission.

having established it; nor would I wish such blame to be attached once the guard is at hand for founding it. The truth is that as long as Father Fray Juan and I are on our feet, it shall not be delayed, because we shall then separate, each one going to his mission. For me it will be the greatest trial to remain alone, with the nearest priest at a distance of eighty leagues. Wherefore I beg Your Reverence to see to it that this utter loneliness of mine does not last too long a time. Father Lasuén ardently desires to come to these missions, and hence Your Reverence may keep him in mind when you have the opportunity to decide on the matter of assigning missionaries.

We are very short of wax for Mass-candles, both here and at San Diego. Nevertheless, tomorrow we are going to celebrate the feast and hold the procession of Corpus Christi, even though it be done in a poor fashion, in order to drive away whatever little devils there may be in this land. If it is possible to send some wax, it will be very helpful to us. Also the incense which I asked for on another occasion. Let Your Reverence not fail to write to His Illustrious Lordship, congratulating him on the discovery of this port and writing whatever may seem proper to you. Cease not to commend us to God. May He preserve Your Reverence for many years in His holy love and grace.

Mission San Carlos de Monterey
June [13], the feast of St. Anthony of Padua, 1770

Your most affectionate friend, companion and servant kisses the hand of Your Reverence.

Fray Junípero Serra

On the very day they took possession of the port, they began the Royal Presidio of San Carlos and founded the mission of the same name. Adjoining the presidio they built a chapel of palings to serve as a temporary church; likewise living quarters with their respective rooms or compartments for the use of the fathers, and the necessary workshops. Both establishments were surrounded by a stockade for their protection. The natives did not show themselves during those days, since the many volleys of artillery and muskets fired by the soldiers had frightened them. But they began to approach after a little while, and the Venerable Father began to offer them gifts to bring about their entrance into the fold of Holy Church and gain their souls, which was the principle purpose of his presence. . . .

The lieutenant of the Catalonian volunteers, Don Pedro Fages, remained in charge of the New Presidio of San Carlos in Monterey. In consideration of the few soldiers he had at his disposal, in accord with the Venerable President he determined to suspend the founding of Mission San Buenaventura until a captain and nineteen soldiers should arrive. These had gone to Old California in February to return with some cattle. However, the captain with the soldiers and cattle returned only as far as San Diego, without sending to Monterey any notice of the fact. The news came only the following year by a ship, as will be seen a little further on. Since for this reason the third mission could not be established, our Venerable Father with his former pupil Fray Juan Crespí applied himself to the conversion of the Indians of Monterey, trying to attract with small gifts those who came to visit him. But since there was no one who knew their language, the missionaries experienced great difficulties in the beginning and up until the time when God desired to open the door to them by means of an Indian boy, a neophyte who had been brought along from Old California. Because of the association which the Venerable Father Junípero ordered him to maintain with the pagans for this precise purpose, he began to understand them and to pronounce some words in their tongue. So by means of this interpreter, Father Junípero was able to explain to the Indians the reason for his coming into their country, which was to guide their souls on the way to heaven.

On December 26 of that year he performed his first baptism in that pagan nation. For the fervent and ardent soul of our Venerable Father, this was the source of inexpressible joy. In time he succeeded in gaining others, and the number of Christians increased, so that three years afterwards, when I arrived at that mission, he had already baptized 165. By the time the Venerable Founder Fray Junípero closed his glorious career, he had baptized 1,014, of whom many had already died, to enjoy God in eternal life through the incessant efforts of that apostolic man.

What greatly aided these conversions, or better, what constituted the principal basis of this important conquest, were the singular marvels and prodigies which God our Lord wrought on behalf of the pagans to make them fear and love the Catholics: fear, so as to restrain them in order that so great a multitude might not treat with impudence so small a number of Christians; and love, that they might listen willingly to the evangelical doctrines which the missionaries had come to teach them, that they might embrace the sweet yoke of our holy law.

In his diary of the second over-land expedition to the Port of Monterey, Father Crespí states on May 24 (as the reader may see for himself) the following:

> *After marching about three leagues, at one o'clock in the afternoon we arrived at the lagoons of salt water by the Point of Pines, toward the northeast, where on the first expedition a second cross had been erected. Before we dismounted, the governor, a soldier and I went to inspect the cross, in order to determine whether we could find any sign of the arrival of the ship there; but we found none. We beheld the cross entirely surrounded by arrows and sticks with many feathers which had been stuck in the ground by the pagans. Also there was a string of sardines, still quite fresh, hanging from a pole at one side of the cross, and another stick with a piece of meat at the foot of the cross; also a little mound of mussels.*

That was a source of great wonder to all, but since they did not know the explanation, they suspended judgment.

Once the newly baptized began to converse in Spanish and the Lower California neophyte understood the Indians' language, the natives on several occasions declared the following: the very first time they saw our people the Indians noticed that all the Spaniards bore on their breasts a very resplendent cross; and when the Spaniards went away from there, leaving that large cross by the beach, the Indians were filled with such fear that they did not dare to approach so sacred an emblem. For they saw the cross shining with bright rays at a time when the rays of the sun which illumined the day were gone and were replaced by the shadows of night. They noticed, however, that the light of the cross grew so bright that it seemed to them to reach the very heavens. On beholding it during the day without these phenomena, and in its natural size, they approached it and tried to win its favor lest they suffer any harm, and in deference to it they made their offerings of meat, fish and mussels. When to their surprise it did not consume what they offered, they placed before it feathers and arrows, showing thereby they desired peace with the Holy Cross and with the people who had erected it there.

Various Indians made this statement at different times (as I have said), and again in the year 1774 when the Venerable Father President returned from Mexico City, before whom they repeated, without the slightest variation, what they had told me the preceding year. This the servant of God, for purposes of edification, wrote to His Excellency the Viceroy, in order to increase his fervor and to encourage him at the same time in the happy realization of this spiritual enterprise. Because of this prodigy and many others which the Lord showed, the conversion of these pagans has continued with all peacefulness and without the conflict of arms. Blessed be God, to Whom be all glory and praise.

from Chapter LVIII The Exemplary Death of the Venerable Father Junípero

. . . I arrived on August 18 at his Mission San Carlos. There I found His Paternity in a very weakened condition, although he was up and around, and with great congestion of the chest. This condition, however, did not prevent him from going to church in the afternoon to recite the catechism and prayers with the neophytes. He concluded the devotions with the tender and pious hymns and versicles composed by the Venerable Father Margil in honor of the Assumption of the Blessed Virgin, whose octave we were celebrating. When I heard him sing with his voice as strong as usual, I remarked to a soldier who was talking to me: "It does not seem that the Father President is very sick." The soldier, who had known him since 1769, answered me: "Father, there is no basis for hope: he is ill. This saintly priest is always well when it comes to praying and singing, but he is nearly finished." . . .

We spoke leisurely on the matters for which he had called me, until the ship arrived. However, I was always in fear he would shortly die, for whenever I would enter into his little room or cell of adobes, I always found him quite interiorly recollected, although his companion told me he had acted this way ever since his faculty to confirm had expired. This, as I have stated before, was on the very day the ship anchored at these missions [of San Francisco]. Five days after I arrived at Monterey, the packet-boat anchored at that port. Immediately the royal surgeon went over to the mission to visit the Reverend Father President. Finding his chest in so bad a condition, he suggested hot poultices to expel the phlegm that had accumulated in the chest. The Father President told him to apply whatever remedy he chose. He did, but with no effect other than to cause further pain to that already worn-out body. But he did not show the least sign of pain, either at this strong application or at the agonies he was suffering. He acted as if he were not sick at all, always up and about as if he were well. When some of the cloth from the supplies of the ship was brought over, with his own hands he began to cut it up and distribute it to the neophytes to cover their nakedness.

On August 25 he told me he was disappointed that the fathers from Missions

San Antonio and San Luis Obispo had not arrived, and that possibly the letters he had written them were delayed. I immediately sent word to the presidio, and the letters were brought over with the information that they had been overlooked. As soon as I saw their contents, an invitation to the fathers for a final farewell, I sent a courier with these letters, adding a message that the fathers should come posthaste, for I feared that our beloved superior would not be long with us because of his very weakened condition. And although the priests set out as soon as they received those letters, they did not arrive in time. The one from Mission San Antonio, which was twenty-five leagues away, arrived after his death and could assist only at his burial. The one from San Luis Obispo, fifty leagues away, arrived three days later and was able to be present at the commemorative services only on the seventh day after his death, as I shall point out later.

On August 26 he arose, weaker still. He told me he had passed a bad night. As a result, he desired to prepare himself for whatever God might decree with regard to him. He remained secluded the entire day, admitting not a single distraction. That night he made his general confession to me amid many tears, and with a clear mind just as if he were well. When this was over, after a brief period of reflection he took a cup of broth and then went to rest, his wish being that no one remain with him in his little room.

As soon as morning dawned on the 27th, I went to visit him and found him saying his breviary, since it was his custom always to commence Matins before daybreak. On the road he always began it as soon as morning dawned. When I asked him how he had spent the night, he answered: "As usual." Nevertheless, he asked me to consecrate a Host and reserve It, and he would let me know when he wanted to receive. I did, and after finishing Mass I returned to tell him, and then he said he would like to receive the Most Holy Viaticum, and that for this he would go to the church. When I told him that was not necessary, that his cell could be fixed up in the best way possible and that the divine Majesty would come to visit him, he said, "No," that he wanted to receive Him in church, since if he could walk there, there was no need for the Lord to come to him. I had to give in and grant his holy desires. He went by himself to the church (more than a hundred yards distant), accompanied by the commandant of the presidio, who came to the ceremony with part of the soldiers (who were joined by the soldiers of the mission); and all the Indians of the town or mission accompanied the sick and devout priest to the church, all of them with great tenderness and piety.

When His Paternity reached the step of the sanctuary, he knelt down before a little table prepared for the ceremony. I came out of the sacristy vested, and on arriving at the altar, as soon as I prepared the incense to begin the devotional ceremony, the fervent servant of God intoned in his natural voice, as sonorous as when he was well, the verse *Tantum ergo Sacramentum,* singing it with tears in his eyes. I gave him the Holy Viaticum, according to the ceremonies of the ritual. When this very devotional function was over, which I had never seen in such circumstances, His Paternity remained in the same posture, kneeling, giving thanks to the Lord. When he was finished, he returned to his little cell accompanied by all the people. Some shed tears from devotion and tenderness, others out of sadness and sorrow because they feared they would be left without their beloved father. He remained alone in his cell in meditation, seated on the chair at the table. When I beheld him thus absorbed, I saw no reason to enter to talk to him. . . .

During the night he felt worse, and he asked to be anointed. This holy sacrament he received seated on an *equipal,* a little stool made of rushes. He recited with us the Litany of All Saints and the Penitential Psalms. He spent the entire night without sleep, the greater part of it on his knees, while he pressed his chest against the boards of his bed. When I suggested that he lie down awhile, he answered that in that position he felt more relieved. Other short periods of the night he spent seated on the floor, leaning against the lap of some of the neophytes. All night long his little cell was filled with these neophytes, drawn there by the great love they had for him as for the father who had begotten them anew in the Lord. When I saw him in this state of exhaustion and leaning against the arms of the Indians, I asked the surgeon how he thought he was. He answered (since the father appeared to be in a very critical state): "It seems to me that this blessed father wants to die on the floor."

I went in soon after and asked him if he wished absolution and the application of the plenary indulgence. He answered "Yes," and prepared himself. On his knees he received the plenary absolution, and I gave him also the plenary indulgence of the Order, with which he was most happy. He passed the entire night in the manner described. The feast of the Doctor of the Church St. Augustine dawned, August 28, and he appeared relieved. He did not experience so much congestion in his chest. During the whole night he had not slept or taken anything. He spent the morning seated on the rush stool, leaning against the bed. This bed consisted of some roughhewn boards, covered by a blanket serving more as a covering than as an aid to rest, for he never used even a sheepskin covering, such as was customary at our college. Along the road he used to do the same thing. He would stretch the blanket and a pillow on the ground, and he would lie down on these to get his necessary rest. He always slept with a crucifix upon his breast, in the embrace of his hands. It was about a foot in length. He had carried it with him from the time he was in the novitiate at the college, nor did he ever fail to have it with him. On all his journeys he carried it with him, together with the blanket and pillow. At his mission and whenever he stopped, as soon as he got up from bed he placed the crucifix upon the pillow. Thus he had it on this occasion when he did not wish to go to bed during the entire night or next morning, on the day when he was to deliver his soul to his Creator.

About ten o'clock in the morning on that feast of St. Augustine, the officers of the frigate came to visit him. . . .

After listening to them, he said: "Well, gentlemen, I thank you that after such a long time, during which we have not seen each other, and after making such a long voyage, you have come from so far off to this port to throw a little earth upon me." On hearing this, the gentlemen and all the rest of us present were surprised, seeing him seated on the little rush stool and hearing him answer everything with full mental faculties. But, scarcely concealing their tears which they could not restrain, they said: "No, Father, we trust that God will still make you well and enable you to continue this conquest." The servant of God (who, if he did not have a foreknowledge of the hour of his death, could not but know that it was near at hand) answered them: "Yes, yes, do me this favor and work of mercy; throw a little bit of earth upon my body, and I shall be greatly indebted to you." And casting his eyes upon me, he said:

"I desire you to bury me in the church, quite close to Father Fray Juan Crespí for the present; and when the stone church is built, they may put me wherever they want."

When my tears allowed me to speak, I said to him: "Father President, if God is pleased to call you to Himself, it will be done as Your Paternity wishes. In that case, I ask Your Paternity out of love and the great affection you have always had for me, that when you arrive in the presence of the Most Blessed Trinity, you adore the Same in my name, and that you be not unmindful of me; and do not forget to pray for all the dwellers in these missions, particularly for those here present." He answered: "I promise, if the Lord in His infinite mercy grants me that eternal happiness, which I do not deserve because of my faults, that I shall pray for all and for the conversion of so many pagans whom I leave unconverted."

Within a short time he asked me to sprinkle his little room with holy water, and I did. When I asked him if he felt some pain, he said "No"; but he asked me to do it so he would have none. He remained in profound silence. All of a sudden, very frightened, he said to me: "Great fear has come upon me; I have a great fear. Read me the Commendation for a Departing Soul, and say it aloud so I can hear it." I did as he asked, while all the gentlemen from the ship assisted. Also present were his priest companion, Fray Matías Noriega, and the surgeon, and many others both from the ship and from the mission. I read for him the Commendation for a Departing Soul, to which the Venerable Father, though dying, responded as if he were well, just sitting there on his little rush stool, moving the hearts of us all to tenderness.

As soon as I finished, he broke out in words full of joy, saying: "Thanks be to God, thanks be to God, all fear has now left me. Thanks be to God, I have no more fear, and so let us go outside." All of us retired to a little outside room with His Paternity. When we noticed this change, we were at one and the same time surprised and happy. . . .

He sat on the chair by the table, picked up his diurnal and began to pray. As soon as he was finished, I told him it was already after one o'clock in the afternoon, and asked him if he would like a cup of broth. He said "Yes." He took it and, after giving thanks, said: "Now, let us go to rest." He walked to his little room where he had his bed. He took off only his mantle and lay down over the boards covered with a blanket, with his holy crucifix mentioned above, in order to rest. We all thought he was going to sleep, as during the whole night he had not slept any. The gentlemen went out to eat. Since I was a little uneasy, after a short time I returned and approached his bed to see if he was sleeping. I found him just as we had left him a little before, but now asleep in the Lord, without having given any sign or trace of agony, his body showing no other sign of death than the cessation of breathing; on the contrary, he seemed to be sleeping. We piously believe that he went to sleep in the Lord a little before two in the afternoon, on the feast of St. Augustine in the year 1784, and that he went to receive in heaven the reward of his apostolic labors.

He ended his laborious life when he was seventy years, nine months and four days old. He lived in the world sixteen years, nine months and twenty-one days; as a religious fifty-three years, eleven months and thirteen days, of which he spent thirty-five years, four months and thirteen days as apostolic missionary. During this time he performed the glorious deeds of which we have read, in which his merits were more numerous than his steps. He lived in continuous activity, occupied in virtuous and holy exercises and in outstanding deeds, all directed to the greater glory of God and the salvation of souls. And would not one who labored so much for them, not labor much more for his own? Much there is that I could say, but this demands more time and more leisure. If God grants me this, and it is His most holy will, I shall not refuse the task of writing something about his heroic virtues for the sake of edification and good example.

As soon as I satisfied myself that we were now orphans, bereft of the amiable company of our venerable superior, that he was not sleeping but actually dead, I ordered the neophytes who were standing there to ring the bells in order to make the news known. As soon as the double peal rang out the sad news, the whole town assembled, weeping over the death of their beloved father who had begotten them anew in the Lord and who was more esteemed by them than if he had been their natural father. All wanted to see him in order to give vent to the sorrow that filled their hearts, and to express it in tears. So great was the crowd of people, including Indians and soldiers and sailors, that it was necessary to close the door in order to place him in the coffin that His Paternity had ordered to be made the day before. And in order to prepare his shroud, we had to do nothing else than to take off his sandals (which the captain of the packet-boat and the Father Chaplain, who were present, received as keepsakes). He remained in the shroud in which he died, that is, the habit, the cowl and the cord, but no inner tunic, for the two which he had for use on his journeys he had sent out to be washed six days before, together with a change of underclothing, which he did not care to use, for he wanted to die wearing only the habit, cowl and cord.

When the venerable corpse was placed in the coffin, and six burning candles were placed about it, the door of his cell was opened, which his saddened sons, the neophytes, immediately entered with their wreaths of wild flowers of varied hues, in order to grace the remains of the deceased Venerable Father. The remains were kept in the cell until nightfall, a continuous concourse of people entering and coming out. They were praying to him and touching rosaries and medals to his venerable hands and face, openly calling him "Holy Father," "Blessed Father," and other names dictated by the love they bore him, and by the heroic virtues which they had witnessed in him during life.

At nightfall we carried the remains to the church in procession. This was composed of the town of neophytes and the soldiers and sailors who remained. The remains were placed on a table surrounded by six lighted candles, and the ceremony was concluded with a response. They asked me to leave the church open in order to keep guard over the remains, and alternately to recite the Rosary for the soul of the deceased. They renewed the watch at set intervals, thus passing the whole night in continual prayer. I consented to this and left two soldiers as a guard to prevent any kind of indiscreet piety or theft, for all desired to obtain some little thing which the deceased had used. Chiefly the seamen and the soldiers, who had known him better and who had a great opinion of the virtue and sanctity of the deceased Venerable Father and who had dealt with him at sea and on land, asked me for some little article from among the things he had used. Although I promised all I would satisfy them after his burial, this was not enough to prevent them from cutting away small pieces of his habit from below, so it would not be noticed, and part of the hair of his tonsure, the guard being unable to restrain them, if it was not that he abetted them and participated in the pious theft. All wanted to obtain some memorial of the deceased, although such was the opinion they had of him that they called such items relics. I tried to correct them and explain it to them.

1787

A Sheaf of Eighteenth-Century Anglo-American Poetry

Before the American Revolution, the English comfortably considered that the course of empire would lead to the progressive betterment of the new colonies. George Berkeley envisioned the westward translation of English empire and the arts when he attempted in 1725 to found a college in Bermuda. Published in 1752, Berkeley's poem, "On the Prospect of Planting Arts and Learning in America," speaks of the "Seat of Innocence" in "Happy Climes," "Where Nature guides and Virtue rules":

> There shall be sung another golden Age,
> The rise of Empire and of Arts,
> The Good and Great inspiring epic Rage,
> The wisest Heads and noblest Hearts.
>
> Not such as *Europe* breeds in her decay;
> Such as she bred when fresh and young,
> When heav'nly Flame did animate her Clay,
> By future Poets shall be sung.
>
> Westward the Course of Empire takes its Way;
> The first four Acts already past,
> A fifth shall close the Drama with the Day;
> Time's noblest Offspring is the last.

For Berkeley and his early-eighteenth-century contemporaries, poetry was still, as it had been in the Renaissance, the privileged literary genre and epic the privileged form. Yet the epic era of European colonization was fast waning, and the demographic changes ocurring in the colonies brought a wider readership that would find prose works, from almanacs to travel journals and fictional vignettes to novels, more appealing and accessible. Poetry—especially epic poetry, based upon the precondition of a classical education—became the province of intellectuals and, to some extent, of pietists.

Even as the colonies engaged in the Revolution that would break down hierarchic social and political structures, the epic impulse remained. Philip Freneau and Hugh Henry Brackenridge, in their 1771 Princeton commencement poem "On the Rising Glory of America," and Joel Barlow in his 1787 *Vision of Columbus,* an attempt to write an American epic, along with many lesser-known poets, would speak of the country's promise and of necessary American progress. That both promise and progress would require less privilege and a more democratic ideology seems to have escaped most of these writers who sought for Americans a place in epic literature like the places held by ancient Greeks and Romans.

Poetry was a signal literary genre of the dominant class, and the dominant poetic voice was public and male. This is not to suggest that men wrote poems only on public issues and that women wrote only on private ones. Nor is it to imply that men did not write on friendship or concerns typically considered "domestic." Yet it is true that men controlled the printing presses and that men's writings more frequently reached print than women's writings. Thus poems on topics of political, social, or literary importance were usually written and published by men through the first half of the century.

Writers generally used the same neoclassical poetic models and methods as their English contemporaries. English neoclassicism had reached its height with the works of Dryden, Pope, and Swift. These poets' interest in the classics was a response to the social chaos caused by the civil wars in seventeenth-century England. They replaced the disruptions in language and meter and the multitudinous poetic conceits of seventeenth-century writers by what they considered precision and control, "correctness" and regularity, in their forms and themes. The marked regularities of eighteenth-century poetic lines were thought to model for readers the regular and harmonious attitudes that writers sought to inculcate in society. Literature, they argued, should be didactic; it should teach those less informed about manners and morals in a refined society. What emerged in the neoclassic era was a highly public and social poetry, where satire flourished and the lyric nearly disappeared.

Like the Anglo-American poetry of the seventeenth century, then, eighteenth-century poetry is marked by its use and transformation of poetic styles common in eighteenth-century England. Anglo-American poets, writing for an audience in England as well as in the colonies, versified colonial experiences in forms common to English readers—pastorals, odes, elegies, and satires. The writers thus proved to their European counterparts their familiarity with the accepted modes of the elite groups that held, as they did during the Renaissance, that poetry was the highest form of written art. By displaying a knowledge of "high" forms—and thus their intellectual and educational equivalence with their English contemporaries—Anglo-American writers could claim for themselves a position in the New World that counterbalanced the tendency of those in English elite society to view all Americans as hard-scrabble hicks trapped in a wilderness.

Two of the most common forms of early-eighteenth-century English poetry are satire and pastoral, both of which had roots in classical Greek and Roman writing. In fact, the classicism of early-eighteenth-century England is often called Augustan, so named after Augustus Caesar, the first Roman emperor. English writers, seeking ways to address contemporary cultural transformations, took refuge in classical forms. Life's complications and uncertainties were more palatable if mocked in satire or transformed into pastoral allegory. American writers, conscious of a world of change not only in England but in the colonies, found these English models useful.

Although the dominant form was public in the earlier part of the eighteenth century, there remained a distinct tradition of pietistic writing, both public and private. Christian epic poetry had reached its height during the Renaissance, and ministers had long been accustomed to writing devotional poems, as the work of Edward Taylor amply demonstrates. Indeed, writers produced a large devotional poetic literature during the middle of the eighteenth century, at the time of the Great Awakening, combining evangelistic fervor with nationalistic calls to a manifest "American" destiny.

At this time of social and political shifts, more and more young men and women required guidance. Education was on the rise, and many more women than ever before were able to read. Some women were trained in writing as well. Often, their writing, like their reading, addressed public concerns. Yet most women who published their writings confined themselves to those matters that society considered within their province, issues domestic and devotional. It is not clear whether women freely chose to publish on these subjects or merely acquiesced in public expectation. However, as the century wore on, the increased public interest in women's education combined with a widespread evangelical movement (beginning with the first Great Awakening and enhanced by the Second Great

Awakening) that enabled women in greater numbers to find voice for their concerns—on both private and public issues—as they had never done before.

Hundreds of poems by colonial women have been preserved over the centuries in print and manuscript, yet few have been readily available. Most remain in manuscript or have been out of print for many decades. Written largely by white women from well-to-do families—Lucy Terry, North America's first black poet, is a significant exception—the poems provide an important addition to our understanding of colonial life. Colonial women poets shared the concerns of their male contemporaries: religion, politics, social events, important public figures, death, love, marriage, war, family. And they wrote in the many poetic forms available to the literate populace of their day: verse letters and plays, elegies and odes to friends or prominent figures, religious meditations, love poems, historical narratives, hymns, social and political satires, translations and paraphrases of the classics and the Bible, poetic dialogues. But these women frequently brought a new perspective to familiar themes and forms. They wrote of conflicts between internalized gender roles and competing aspirations. They wrote of child bearing and rearing, the deaths of children, loving (and not-so-loving) husbands, parents, domestic duties, and home life. In the process, they adapted a range of image and metaphor less available to their male contemporaries.

Hampered by rigid role definitions and social expectations, most colonial women were neither expected nor encouraged to develop artistic or literary talents. The toll of gender-defined work roles and of continuous childbearing was incalculable. If lack of leisure did not prevent women writers from developing their skills, the social stigma attached to stepping outside of conventional gender roles may have. In 1650, Thomas Parker, minister of Newbury, Massachusetts, forcefully clarified colonial attitudes in an open letter to his sister, Elizabeth Avery, in England: "your printing of a book, beyond the custom of your sex, doth rankly smell." Nearly a century later, an anonymous writer in the *Boston Weekly Magazine* for March 2, 1743, explained "to a poetical lady" the social consequences of a woman's insistence upon writing poetry:

What's beauty, wealth and wit beside?
  Nor God, nor man will love her.

The attitudes of the colonial patriarchy provided more subtle obstacles than damaged reputations in the form of publicly voiced condescension that inevitably influenced women's perceptions of themselves and their abilities.

Though colonial society seldom supported their work, colonial women poets encouraged one another. They read the published works of a few well-known women, British and American—Anne Bradstreet, Elizabeth Carter, Lady Mary Wortley Montagu, Elizabeth Singer Rowe, Katherine Philips, Anne Finch, Margaret of Newcastle, Mary Astell, Anne Killigrew, Catherine Macauley, and Elizabeth Montagu among them. In addition, many colonial women poets knew one another personally, corresponded and exchanged their poems. For instance, one of Elizabeth Graeme Fergusson's extant commonplace books was evidently prepared for the New Jersey poet Annis Stockton. Anna Young Smith, Fergusson's niece and ward, occasionally wrote verse. Ann Bleecker's verse was published posthumously by her daughter, Margaretta Faugères, herself a poet. Abigail Dennie almost certainly read the verse of her sister Jane Turell, and her only extant piece is a verse letter to Turell. Other occasions for intellectual and literary contact were fostered when Fergusson followed the tradition of the European salon by initiating regular gatherings of talented women and men at Graeme Park, north of Philadelphia. Annis Stockton held similar salons at Morven, the Stockton estate.

Further evidence of this direct contact among women poets lies in their frequent verses to one another. Susanna Wright wrote poetry to and corresponded with a circle of female friends. Judith Sargent Murray and Sarah Morton exchanged poems in the *Massachusetts Magazine.* Even those women who did not seek publication of their verse circulated their manuscripts among friends. Such networks allowed women to encourage one another in an activity generally unsupported by society at large. Men's networks were more typically those made available through their college or work experiences and the flourishing coffeehouses, which provided a public arena for poetry.

In the selections that follow, we offer a sampling (arranged chronologically according to date of the poets' births) of the variety and versatility of poetic writings by men and women of the northern, middle, and southern colonies in British North America. An examination of the poems by Nathaniel Evans and Thomas Godfrey will show that men, just as much as women, versified their thoughts on friendly associations. Likewise, readers can see the extent to which women wrote on "public" and "political" issues. All of the poets reveal an Anglo-American consciousness of poetic norms established in Europe, and many poets—Cook, Lewis, Dawson, and Godfrey, especially—suggest the extent to which Anglo-American writers sought to test the formal conventions typical of European writings. Readers interested in the poetry of the eighteenth century should consult additional readings—by Jupiter Hammon, Phillis Wheatley, Mercy Otis Warren, Ann Eliza Bleecker, Judith Sargent Murray, Philip Freneau, Timothy Dwight, Joel Barlow—in this anthology.

Pattie Cowell
Colorado State University

Ivy Schweitzer
Dartmouth College

PRIMARY WORKS

Emily Stipes Watts, *The Poetry of American Women from 1632 to 1945,* 1977; Kenneth N. Requa, ed., *Poems of Jane Turell and Martha Brewster,* 1979; Pattie Cowell, ed., *Women Poets in Pre-Revolutionary America, 1650–1775,* 1981; Carla Mulford, ed., *Only for the Eye of a Friend: The Poetry of Annis Boudinot Stockton,* 1995.

Ebenezer Cook 1667–1733

Ebenezer Cook was a tobacco factor (merchant) and plantation owner in Maryland. A prolific writer, he spent much time in London as well as in Maryland. Cook's *The Sot-weed Factor,* first published in London in 1708, is a satire of elitist English expectations about America. The satire is written in the form of Hudibrastic verse, named for Samuel Butler's hilarious satire of Puritans, *Hudibras* (1653–1680). Hudibrastic verse has a Juvenalian (*i.e.,* biting, after the classical writer, Juvenal) satirical stance offered in a form that is jarring to read because of the galloping and potentially monotonous tetrameter lines that end in odd-sounding rhymes. In fact, the incongruity created by "sing-song" lines that might be monotonous except for the unexpected rhymes and odd syntax fosters much of the humor of Hudibrastic verse.

Cook's use of the verse form is doubly satirical. The speaker of *The Sot-weed Factor* speaks as though he were a member of the English elite; he denigrates and mocks Americans as hard-drinking, impious, backwater rogues. Thus, the poem's satire seems on one level to be directed against Americans. Yet the poem really satirizes precisely the English elitist notions about Americans that the speaker holds. The first evidence lies in the fact that the sot-weed factor (tobacco merchant) stands "Erect, with Legs stretch'd wide" (line 67) in a canoe. An American would know that people would not stand in canoes. Other examples repeatedly show the ignorance of the speaker of the poem, who thinks himself superior to the Americans he finds. The last laugh, then, is on the speaker, who thinks himself superior when it is the Americans who really are so.

The text is taken from the original 1708 publication of the poem. Unless otherwise noted, annotations are Cook's, from the original London publication.

The Sot-weed Factor; or, a Voyage to Maryland, &c.[1]

Condemn'd by Fate to way-ward Curse,
Of Friends unkind, and empty Purse;
Plagues worse than fill'd *Pandora*'s Box,
I took my leave of *Albion*'s Rocks:
With heavy Heart, concern'd that I
Was forc'd my Native Soil to fly,
And the *Old World* must bid good-buy.
But Heav'n ordain'd it should be so,
And to repine is vain we know:
Freighted with Fools, from *Plymouth* sound,
To *Mary-Land* our Ship was bound;

[1]Weed that makes one drunk, *i.e.,* tobacco [Ed.].

Where we arriv'd in dreadful Pain,
Shock'd by the Terrours of the Main;
For full three Months, our wavering Boat,
Did thro' the surley Ocean float,
And furious Storms and threat'ning Blasts,
Both tore our Sails and sprung our Masts:
Wearied, yet pleas'd, we did escape
Such Ills, we anchor'd at the *Cape,*[2]
But weighing soon, we plough'd the *Bay,*
To Cove[3] it in *Piscato-way,*[4]
Intending there to open Store,
I put myself and Goods a-shore:
Where soon repair'd a numerous Crew,
In Shirts and Drawers of *Scotch-cloth* Blue.[5]
With neither Stockings, Hat, nor Shooe.
These *Sot-weed* Planters Crowd the Shoar,
In Hue as tawny as a Moor:
Figure so strange, no God design'd,
To be a part of Humane Kind:
But wanton Nature, void of Rest,
Moulded the brittle Clay in Jest,
At last a Fancy very odd
Took me, this was the Land of *Nod;*
Planted at first, when Vagrant *Cain,*
His Brother had unjustly slain:
Then conscious of the Crime he'd done,
From Vengeance dire, he hither run;
And in a Hut supinely dwelt,
The first in *Furs* and *Sot-weed* dealt.
And ever since his Time, the Place,
Has harbour'd a detested Race;
Who when they cou'd not live at Home,
For Refuge to these Worlds did roam;
In hopes by Flight they might prevent,
The Devil and his fell intent;
Obtain from Tripple Tree[6] reprieve,
And Heav'n and Hell alike deceive:
But e're their Manners I display,

[2]By the *Cape,* is meant the *Capes of Virginia,* the first Land on the Coast of *Virginia* and *Mary-Land.* [Cape Henry, Virginia.]

[3]To *Cove* is to lie at Anchor safe in Harbour.

[4]The Bay of *Piscato-way,* the usual place where our Ships come to an Anchor in *Mary-Land* [Evidently, up the Chesapeake Bay and Potomac River to Piscataway Creek; Ed.].

[5]The Planters generally wear Blue *Linnen.*

[6]The gallows [Ed.].

I think it fit I open lay
My Entertainment by the way;
That Strangers well may be aware on,
What homely Diet they must fare on.
To touch that Shoar, where no good Sense is found,
But Conversation's lost, and Maners drown'd.
I crost unto the other side,
A River whose impetuous Tide,
The Savage Borders does divide;
In such a shining odd invention,
I scarce can give its due Dimention.
The *Indians* call this watry Waggon
Canoo, a Vessel none can brag on;[7]
Cut from a *Popular-Tree,* or *Pine,*
And fashion'd like a Trough for Swine:
In this most noble Fishing-Boat,
I boldly put myself a-float;
Standing Erect, with Legs stretch'd wide,
We paddled to the other side:
Where being Landed safe by hap,
As *Sol* fell into *Thetis* Lap.
A ravenous Gang bent on the stroul,
Of Wolves for Prey, began to howl;[8]
This put me in a pannick Fright,
Least I should be devoured quite:
But as I there a musing stood,
And quite benighted in a Wood,
A Female Voice pierc'd thro' my Ears,
Crying, *You Rogue drive home the Steers.*
I listen'd to th' attractive sound,
And straight a Herd of Cattel found
Drove by a Youth, and homewards bound:
Cheer'd with the sight, I straight thought fit,
To ask where I a Bed might get.
The surley Peasant bid me stay,
And ask'd from whom I'de run away.[9]
Surprized at such a saucy Word,
I instantly lugg'd out my Sword;
Swearing I was no Fugitive,
But from *Great-Britain* did arrive,

[7]A *Canoo* is an *Indian* Boat, cut out of the body of a Popler-Tree.

[8]Wolves are very numerous in *Mary-Land.*

[9]'Tis supposed by the Planters, that all unknown Persons are run away from some Master.

In hopes I better there might Thrive.
To which he mildly made reply,
I beg your Pardon, Sir, that I
Should talk to you Unmannerly;
But if you please to go with me,
To yonder House, you'll welcome be.
Encountering soon the smoaky Seat,
The Planter old did thus me greet:
"Whether you come from Gaol or Colledge,
"You're welcome to my certain Knowledge;
"And if you please all Night to stay,
"My Son shall put you in the way.
Which offer I most kindly took,
And for a Seat did round me look;
When presently amongst the rest,
He plac'd his unknown *English* Guest,
Who found them drinking for a whet,
A Cask of Syder on the Fret,[10]
Till Supper came upon the Table,
On which I fed whilst I was able.
So after hearty Entertainment,
Of Drink and Victuals without Payment;
For Planters Tables, you must know,
Are free for all that come and go.
While Pon and Milk,[11] with Mush[12] well stoar'd,
In wooden Dishes grac'd the Board;
With Homine and Syder-pap,[13]
(Which scarce a hungry Dog wou'd lap)
Well stuff'd with Fat, from Bacon fry'd,
Or with *Molossus* dulcify'd.
Then out our Landlord pulls a Pouch
As greasy as the Leather Couch
On which he sat, and straight begun,
To load with Weed his *Indian* Gun;[14]
In length, scarce longer than ones Finger,
Or that for which the Ladies linger.
His Pipe smoak'd out with aweful Grace,
With aspect grave and solemn pace;

[10]Syder-pap is a sort of Food made of Syder and small Homine, like our Oatmeal [*on the Fret:* fermenting; Ed.].

[11]Pon is Bread made of *Indian Corn.*

[12]Mush is a sort of Hasty-Pudding made with Water and *Indian* Flower.

[13]Homine is a Dish that is made of boiled *Indian* Wheat, eaten with Molossus, or Bacon-Fat.

[14]Tobacco Pipe [Ed.].

The reverend Sire walks to a Chest,
Of all his Furniture the best,
Closely confin'd within a Room,
Which seldom felt the weight of Broom;
From thence he lugs a Cag of Rum,
And nodding to me, thus begun:
I find, says he, you don't much care,
For this our *Indian* Country Fare;
But let me tell you, Friend of mine,
You may be glad of it in time,
Tho' now your Stomach is so fine;
And if within this Land you stay,
You'll find it true what I do say.
This said, the Rundlet up he threw,
And bending backwards strongly drew:
I pluck'd as stoutly for my part,
Altho' it made me sick at Heart,
And got so soon into my Head
I scarce cou'd find my way to Bed;
Where I was instantly convey'd
By one who pass'd for Chamber-Maid;
Tho' by her loose and sluttish Dress,
She rather seem'd a *Bedlam-Bess:*[15]
Curious to know from whence she came,
I prest her to declare her Name.
She Blushing, seem'd to hide her Eyes,
And thus in Civil Terms replies;
In better Times, e'er to this Land,
I was unhappily Trapann'd;
Perchance as well I did appear,
As any Lord or Lady here,
Not then a Slave for twice two Year.[16]
My Cloaths were fashionably new,
Nor were my Shifts of Linnen Blue;
But things are changed now at the Hoe,
I daily work, and Bare-foot go,
In weeding Corn or feeding Swine,
I spend my melancholy Time.
Kidnap'd and Fool'd, I hither fled,
To shun a hated Nuptial Bed,[17]

[15]Bedlam was an insane asylum in England [Ed.].

[16]'Tis the Custom for Servants to be obliged for four Years to very servile Work; after which time they have their Freedom.

[17]These are the general Excuses made by *English* Women, which are sold, or sell themselves to *Mary-Land.*

And to my cost already find,
Worse Plagues than those I left behind.
Whate'er the Wanderer did profess,
Good-faith I cou'd not choose but guess
The Cause which brought her to this place,
Was supping e'er the Priest said Grace.
Quick as my Thoughts, the Slave was fled,
(Her Candle left to shew my Bed)
Which made of Feathers soft and good,
Close in the Chimney-corner stood;[18]
I threw me down expecting Rest,
To be in golden Slumbers blest:
But soon a noise disturb'd my quiet,
And plagu'd me with nocturnal Riot;
A Puss which in the ashes lay,
With grunting Pig began a Fray;
And prudent Dog, that Feuds might cease,
Most strongly bark'd to keep the Peace.
This Quarrel scarcely was decided,
By stick that ready lay provided;
But *Reynard* arch and cunning Loon,
Broke into my Appartment soon;
In hot pursuit of Ducks and Geese,
With fell intent the same to seize:
Their Cackling Plaints with strange surprize,
Chac'd Sleeps thick Vapours from my Eyes:
Raging I jump'd upon the Floar,
And like a Drunken Saylor Swore;
With Sword I fiercly laid about,
And soon dispers'd the Feather'd Rout:
The Poultry out of Window flew,
And *Reynard* cautiously withdrew:
The Dogs who this Encounter heard,
Fiercely themselves to aid me rear'd,
And to the Place of Combat run,
Exactly as the Field was won.
Fretting and hot as roasting Capon,
And greasy as a Flitch of Bacon;
I to the Orchard did repair,
To Breathe the cool and open Air;
Expecting there the rising Day,
Extended on a Bank I lay;

[18]Beds stand in the Chimney-corner in this Country.

But Fortune here, that saucy Whore,
Disturb'd me worse and plagu'd me more,
Than she had done the night before.
Hoarse croaking Frogs did 'bout me ring,[19]
Such Peals the Dead to Life wou'd bring,
A Noise might move their Wooden King.[20]
I stuff'd my Ears with Cotten white
For fear of being deaf out-right,
And curst the melancholy Night:
But soon my Vows I did recant,
And Hearing as a Blessing grant;
When a confounded Rattle-Snake,
With hissing made my Heart to ake:
Not knowing how to fly the Foe,
Or whether in the Dark to go;
By strange good Luck, I took a Tree,
Prepar'd by Fate to set me free;
Where riding on a Limb astride,
Night and the Branches did me hide,
And I the Devil and Snake defy'd.
Not yet from Plagues exempted quite,
The curst Muskitoes did me bite;
Till rising Morn' and blushing Day,
Drove both my Fears and Ills away;
And from Night's Errors set me free.
Discharg'd from hospitable Tree;
I did to Planters Booth repair,
And there at Breakfast nobly Fare,
On rashier broil'd of infant Bear:
I thought the Cub delicious Meat,
Which ne'er did ought but Chesnuts eat;
Nor was young Orsin's flesh the worse,
Because he suck'd a Pagan Nurse.[21]
Our Breakfast done, my Landlord stout,
Handed a Glass of Rum about;
Pleas'd with the Treatment I did find,
I took my leave of Oast so kind;
Who to oblige me, did provide,
His eldest Son to be my Guide,
And lent me Horses of his own,

[19]Frogs are called *Virginea* Bells, and make, (both in that Country and *Mary-Land*) during the Night, a very hoarse ungrateful Noise.

[20]A reference to a fable by Aesop in which frogs, dissatisfied with the log they have been given for their king, ask for another king. They are given a crane, which devours them [Ed.].

[21]A reference to the tale *Valentine and Orson,* in which two abandoned infants are saved; one (Valentine) is taken to the court, and the other (Orson) is nursed by a bear [Ed.].

A skittish Colt, and aged Rhoan,
The four-leg'd prop of his Wife *Joan.*
Steering our Barks in Trot or Pace,
We sail'd directly for a place
In *Mary-Land* of high renown,
Known by the Name of *Battle-Town.*
To view the Crowds did there resort,
Which Justice made, and Law their sport,
In that sagacious County Court:
Scarce had we enter'd on the way,
Which thro' thick Woods and Marshes lay;
But *Indians* strange did soon appear,
In hot persuit of wounded Deer;
No mortal Creature can express,
His wild fantastick Air and Dress;
His painted Skin in colours dy'd,
His sable Hair in Satchel ty'd,
Shew'd Savages not free from Pride:
His tawny Thighs, and Bosom bare,
Disdain'd a useless Coat to wear,
Scorn'd Summer's Heat, and Winters Air;
His manly Shoulders such as please,
Widows and Wives, were bath'd in Grease
Of Cub and Bear, whose supple Oil,
Prepar'd his Limbs 'gainst Heat or Toil.
Thus naked Pict in Battel faught,
Or undisguis'd his Mistress sought;
And knowing well his Ware was good,
Refus'd to screen it with a Hood;
His Visage dun, and chin that ne'er
Did Raizor feel or Scissers bear,
Or knew the Ornament of Hair,
Look'd sternly Grim, surpriz'd with Fear,
I spur'd my Horse, as he drew near:
But Rhoan who better knew than I,
The little Cause I had to fly;
Seem'd by his solemn steps and pace,
Resolv'd I shou'd the Specter face,
Nor faster mov'd, tho' spur'd and lick'd,
Than *Balaam's* Ass by Prophet kick'd.[22]
Kekicknitop[23] the Heathen cry'd;

[22]Numbers 22 [Ed.].
[23]*Kekicknitop* is an *Indian* Expression, and signifies no more than this, *How do you do?*

How is it *Tom.* my Friend reply'd:
Judging from thence the Brute was civel,
I boldly fac'd the Courteous Devil;
And lugging out a Dram of Rum,
I gave his Tawny worship some:
Who in his language as I guess,
(My Guide informing me no less,)
Implored the Devil, me to bless.[24]
I thank'd him for his good Intent,
And forwards on my Journey went,
Discoursing as along I rode,
Whether this Race was framed by God
Or whether some Malignant pow'r,
Contriv'd them in an evil hour
And from his own Infernal Look,
Their Dusky form and Image took:
From hence we fell to Argument
Whence Peopled was this Continent.
My Friend suppos'd *Tartarians* wild,
Or *Chinese* from their Home exiled;
Wandering thro' Mountains hid with Snow,
And Rills did in the Vallies flow,
Far to the South of *Mexico:*
Broke thro' the Barrs which Nature cast,
And wide unbeaten Regions past,
Till near those Streams the humane deludge roll'd,
Which sparkling shin'd with glittering Sands of Gold,
And fetch *Pizarro*[25] from the *Iberian* Shoar,[26]
To Rob the Natives of their fatal Stoar.
I Smil'd to hear my young Logician,
Thus Reason like a Politician;
Who ne're by Fathers Pains and Earning
Had got at Mother *Cambridge* Learning;

[24]These *Indians* worship the Devil, and pray to him as we do to God Almighty. 'Tis suppos'd, That *America* was peopl'd from *Scythia* or *Tartaria,* which Borders on *China,* by reason the Tartarians and *Americans* very much agree in their Manners, Arms, and Government. Other Persons are of Opinion, that the *Chinese* first peopled the *West Indies;* Imagining *China* and the Southern part of *America* to be contiguous. Others believe that the *Phoenicians* who were very skilful Mariners, first planted a Colony in the Isles of *America,* and supply'd the Persons left to inhabit there with Women and all other Necessaries; till either the Death or Shipwreck of the first Discoverers, or some other Misfortune occasioned the loss of the Discovery, which had been purchased by the Peril of the first Adventurers.

[25]*Pizarro* was the Person that conquer'd *Peru;* a Man of a most bloody Disposition, base, treacherous, covetous, and revengeful.

[26]*Spanish* Shoar.

Where Lubber youth just free from birch
Most stoutly drink to prop the Church;
Nor with *Grey Groat* had taken Pains
To purge his Head and Cleanse his Reines:[27]
And in obedience to the Colledge,
Had pleas'd himself with carnal Knowlege:
And tho' I lik'd the youngester's Wit,
I judg'd the Truth he had not hit;
And could not choose but smile to think
What they could do for Meat and Drink,
Who o'er so many Desarts ran,
With Brats and Wives in *Caravan;*
Unless perchance they'd got the Trick
To eat no more than Porker sick;
Or could with well contented Maws,
Quarter like Bears upon their Paws.[28]
Thinking his Reasons to confute,
I gravely thus commenc'd Dispute,
And urg'd that tho' a *Chinese* Host,
Might penetrate this *Indian* Coast;
Yet this was certainly most true,
They never cou'd the Isles subdue;
For knowing not to steer a Boat,
They could not on the Ocean float,
Or plant their Sunburnt Colonies,
In Regions parted by the Seas:
I thence inferr'd *Phoenicians* bol,[29]
Discover'd first with Vessels bold
These Western Shoars, and planted here,
Returning once or twice a Year,
With *Naval Stoars* and Lasses kind,
To comfort those were left behind;
Till by the Winds and Tempest toar,
From their intended Golden Shoar;
They suffer'd Ship-wreck, or were drown'd,
And lost the World so newly found.

[27]There is a very bad Custom in some Colledges, of giving the Students *A Groat ad purgandus Rhenes,* which is usually employ'd to the use of the *Donor.*

[28]Bears are said to live by sucking of their *Paws,* according to the Notion of some Learned Authors.

[29]The *Phoenicians* were the best and boldest Saylors of Antiquity, and indeed the only *Persons,* in former Ages, who durst venture themselves on the Main Sea.

But after long and learn'd Contention,
We could not finish our dissention;
And when that both had talk'd their fill,
We had the self same Notion still.
Thus Parson grave well read and Sage,
Does in dispute with Priest engage;
The one protests they are not Wise,
Who judge by Sense and trust their Eyes;[30]
And vows he'd burn for it at Stake,
That Man may God his Maker make;
The other smiles at his Religion,
And vows he's but a learned Widgeon:
And when they have empty'd all their stoar
From Books and Fathers, are not more
Convinc'd or wiser than before.
  Scarce had we finish'd serious Story,
But I espy'd the Town before me,
And roaring Planters on the ground,
Drinking of Healths in Circle round:
Dismounting Steed with friendly Guide,
Our Horses to a Tree we ty'd,
And forwards pass'd amongst the Rout,
To chuse convenient *Quarters* out:
But being none were to be found,
We sat like others on the ground
Carousing Punch in open Air
Till Cryer did the Court declare;
The planting Rabble being met,
Their Drunken Worships likewise set:
Cryer proclaims that Noise shou'd cease,
And streight the Lawyers broke the Peace:
Wrangling for Plaintiff and Defendant,
I thought they ne'er would make an end on't:
With nonsense, stuff and false quotations,
With brazen Lyes and Allegations;
And in the splitting of the Cause,
They us'd such Motions with their Paws,
As shew'd their Zeal was strongly bent,
In Blows to end the Argument.
A reverend Judge, who to the shame
Of all the Bench, cou'd write his Name;[31]
At Petty-fogger took offence,

[30]The *Priests* argue, That our Senses in the point of *Transubstantiation* ought not to be believed, for tho' the Consecrated Bread has all the accidents of Bread, yet they affirm, 'tis the Body of Christ, and not Bread but Flesh and Bones.

[31]In the County-Court of *Maryland,* very few of the Justices of the *Peace* can write or read.

And wonder'd at his Impudence.
My Neighbour *Dash* with scorn replies,
And in the Face of Justice flies:
The Bench in fury streight divide,
And Scribbles take, or Judges side;
The Jury, Lawyers, and their Clyents,
Contending, fight like earth-born Gyants:
But Sheriff wily lay perdue,
Hoping Indictments wou'd ensue,
And when ______________________
A Hat or Wig fell in the way,
He seiz'd them for the *Queen* as stray:
The Court adjourn'd in usual manner,
In Battle Blood, and fractious Clamour:
I thought it proper to provide,
A Lodging for myself and Guide,
So to our Inn we march'd away,
Which at a little distance lay;
Where all things were in such Confusion,
I thought the World at its conclusion:
A Herd of Planters on the ground,
O'er-whelm'd with Punch, dead drunk we found:
Others were fighting and contending,
Some burnt their Cloaths to save the mending.
A few whose Heads by frequent use,
Could better bare the potent Juice,
Gravely debated State Affairs.
Whilst I most nimbly trip'd up Stairs;
Leaving my Friend discoursing oddly,
And mixing things Prophane and Godly:
Just then beginning to be Drunk,
As from the Company I slunk,
To every Room and Nook I crept,
In hopes I might have somewhere slept;
But all the bedding was possest
By one or other drunken Guest:
But after looking long about,
I found an antient Corn-loft out,
Glad that I might in quiet sleep,
And there my bones unfractur'd keep.
I lay'd me down secure from Fray,
And soundly snoar'd till break of Day;
When waking fresh I sat upright,
And found my Shoes were vanish'd quite,
Hat, Wig, and Stockings, all were fled
From this extended *Indian* Bed:
Vext at the Loss of Goods and Chattel,
I swore I'd give the Rascal battel,

Who had abus'd me in this sort,
And Merchant Stranger made his Sport.
I furiously descended Ladder;
No Hare in *March* was ever madder;
In vain I search'd for my Apparel,
And did with Oast and Servants Quarrel;
For one whose Mind did much aspire
To Mischief, threw them in the Fire;[32]
Equipt with neither Hat nor Shooe,
I did my coming hither rue,
And doubtful thought what I should do:
Then looking round, I saw my Friend
Lie naked on a Tables end;
A Sight so dismal to behold,
One wou'd have judg'ed him dead and cold;
When wringing of his bloody Nose,
By fighting got we may suppose;
I found him not so fast asleep,
Might give his Friends a cause to weep:
Rise *Oronooko,* rise, said I,[33]
And from this *Hell* and *Bedlam* fly.
My Guide starts up, and in amaze,
With blood-shot Eyes did round him gaze;
At length with many a sigh and groan,
He went in search of aged Rhoan;
But Rhoan, tho' seldom us'd to faulter,
Had fairly this time slipt his Halter;
And not content all Night to stay
Ty'd up from Fodder, ran away:
After my Guide to ketch him ran,
And so I lost both Horse and Man;
Which Disappointment, tho' so great,
Did only Mirth and Jests create:
Till one more Civil than the rest,
In Conversation for the best,
Observing that for want of Rhoan,
I should be left to walk alone;
Most readily did me intreat,
To take a Bottle at his Seat;
A Favour at that time so great,
I blest my kind propitious Fate;
And finding soon a fresh supply,
Of Cloaths from Stoar-house kept hard by,

[32]'Tis the Custom of the Planters, to throw their own, or any other Persons Hat, Wig, Shooes, or Stockings in the Fire.

[33]Planters are usually call'd by the Name *Oronooko,* from their Planting *Oronooko-Tobacco.*

I mounted streight on such a Steed,
Did rather curb, than whipping need;
And straining at the usual rate,
With spur of Punch which lay in Pate,[34]
E'er long we lighted at the Gate:
Where in an antient *Cedar* House,
Dwelt my new Friend, a Cokerouse;[35]
Whose Fabrick, tho' 'twas built of Wood,
Had many Springs and Winters stood;
When sturdy Oaks, and lofty Pines
Were level'd with Musmelion Vines,[36]
And Plants eradicated were,
By Hurricanes into the air;
There with good Punch and apple Juice,
We spent our Hours without abuse:
Till Midnight in her sable Vest,
Persuaded Gods and Men to rest;
And with a pleasing kind surprize,
Indulg'd soft Slumbers to my Eyes.
Fierce *Ælthon* courser of the Sun.[37]
Had half his Race exactly run;
And breath'd on me a fiery Ray,
Darting hot Beams the following Day,
When snug in Blanket white I lay:
But Heat and *Chinces*[38] rais'd the Sinner,
Most opportunely to his Dinner;
Wild Fowl and Fish delicious Meats,
As good as *Neptune's* Doxy[39] eats,
Began our Hospitable Treat;
Fat Venson follow'd in the Rear,
And Turkies[40] wild Luxurious Chear:
But what the Feast did most commend,
Was hearty welcom from my Friend.
Thus having made a noble Feast,
And eat as well as pamper'd Priest,
Madera strong in flowing Bowls,
Fill'd with extream, delight our Souls;
Till wearied with a purple Flood,
Of generous Wine (the Giant's blood,
As Poets feign) away I made,
For some refreshing verdant Shade;
Where musing on my Rambles strange,

[34]That is, drunk [Ed.].
[35]Cockerouse, is a Man of Quality.
[36]Musmilleon Vines are what we call Musk-milleon Plants.
[37]*Ælthon* is one of the Poetical Horses of the Sun.
[38]*Chinces* are a sort of Vermin like our *Bugs* in *England*.
[39]Sweetheart [Ed.].
[40]Wild Turkies are very good Meat, and prodigiously large in *Maryland*.

And Fortune which so oft did change;
In midst of various Contemplations
Of Fancies odd, and Meditations,
I slumber'd long ________________
Till hazy Night with noxious Dews,
Did Sleep's unwholsom Fetters lose:
With Vapours chil'd, and misty air,
To fire-side I did repair:
Near which a jolly Female Crew,
Were deep engag'ed at *Lanctre-Looe;*[41]
In Nightrails[42] white, with dirty Mein,
Such Sights are scarce in *England* seen:
I thought them first some Witches bent,
On Black Designs in dire Convent.
Till one who with affected air,
Had nicely learn'd to Curse and Swear:
Cry'd Dealing's lost is but a Flam,
And vow'd by G—d she'd keep her *Pam.*[43]
When dealing through the board had run,
They ask'd me kindly to make one;
Not staying often to be bid,
I sat me down as others did:
We scarce had play'd a Round about,
But that these *Indian* Froes[44] fell out.
D—m you, says one, tho' now so brave,
I knew you late a Four-Years Slave;
What if for Planters Wife you go,
Nature design'd you for the Hoe.
Rot you replies the other streight,
The Captain kiss'd you for his Freight;
And if the Truth was known aright,
And how you walk'd the Streets by night,
You'd blush (if one cou'd blush) for shame,
Who from *Bridewell* or *Newgate* came.
From Words they fairly fell to Blows,
And being loath to interpose,
Or meddle in the Wars of Punk,[45]
Away to Bed in hast I slunk.
Waking next day, with aking Head,
And Thirst, that made me quit my Bed;
I rigg'd myself, and soon got up.
To cool my Liver with a Cup
Of *Succahana* fresh and clear,[46]

[41]A card game [Ed.].
[42]Nightgowns [Ed.].
[43]The highest card [Ed.].
[44]Mean-spirited women [Ed.].
[45]Prostitution [Ed.].
[46]*Succahana* is Water.

Not half so good as *English* Beer;
Which ready stood in Kitchin Pail,
And was in fact but *Adam's* Ale;
For Planters Cellars you must know,
Seldom with good *October* flow,[47]
But Perry Quince and Apple Juice,
Spout from the Tap like any Sluce;
Untill the Cask's grown low and stale,
They're forc'd again to Goad and Pail:[48]
The soathing drought scarce down my Throat,
Enough to put a Ship a float,
With Cockerouse as I was sitting,
I felt a Feaver Intermitting;
A fiery Pulse beat in my Veins,
From Cold I felt resembling Pains:
This cursed seasoning I remember,
Lasted from *March* to cold *December;*
Nor would it then its *Quarters* shift
Until by *Cardus*[49] turn'd a drift,
And had my Doctress wanted skill,
Or Kitchin Physick at her will,
My Father's Son had lost his Lands,
And never seen the *Goodwin-Sands:*
But thanks to Fortune and a Nurse
Whose Care depended on my Purse,
I saw myself in good Condition,
Without the help of a Physitian:
At length the shivering ill relieved,
Which long my Head and Heart have grieved;
I then began to think with Care,
How I might sell my *British* Ware,
That with my Freight I might comply,
Did on my Charter party lie:
To this intent, with Guide before,
I tript it to the Eastern Shoar;
While riding near a Sandy Bay,
I met a *Quaker, Yea* and *Nay;*
A Pious Conscientious Rogue,
As e'er woar Bonnet or a Brogue,
Who neither Swore nor kept his Word,
But cheated in the Fear of God;
And when his Debts he would not pay,

[47]That is, the best (October-brewed) ale [Ed.].
[48]A *Goad* grows upon as *Indian* Vine, resembling a Bottle, when ripe it is hollow; this the Planters make use of to drink water out of.
[49]A medicine [Ed.].

By Light within he ran away.
With this sly Zealot soon I struck
A Bargain for my *English* Truck,
Agreeing for ten thousand weight,
Of *Sot-weed* good and fit for freight,
Broad *Oronooko* bright and sound,
The growth and product of his ground;
In Cask that should contain compleat,
Five hundred of Tobacco neat.
The Contract thus betwixt us made,
Not well acquainted with the Trade,
My Goods I trusted to the Cheat,
Whose crop was then aboard the Fleet;
And going to receive my own,
I found the Bird was newly flown:
Cursing this execrable Slave,
This damn'd pretended Godly Knave;
On due Revenge and Justice bent,
I instantly to Counsel went,
Unto an ambodexter *Quack,*[50]
Who learnedly had got the knack,
Of giving Glisters, making Pills,
Of filling Bonds, and forging Wills;
And with a stock of Impudence,
Supply'd his want of Wit and Sense;
With Looks demure, amazing People,
No wiser than a Daw in Steeple;
My Anger flushing in my Face,
I stated the preceeding Case:
And of my Money was so lavish,
That he'd have poyson'd half the Parish,
And hang'd his Father on a Tree,
For such another tempting Fee;
Smiling, said he, the Cause is clear,
I'll manage him you need not fear;
The Case is judg'd, good Sir, but look
In *Galen,* No—in my Lord *Cook,*[51]
I vow to God I was mistook:
I'll take out a Provincial Writ,
And Trounce him for his Knavish Wit;
Upon my life we'll win the Cause,
With all the ease I cure the *Yaws:*[52]

[50]This Fellow was an Apothecary, and turn'd an Attorney at Law.

[51]Galen, the most famous physician of ancient Greece, prepared a handbook on medicine; Sir Edward Coke wrote the *Institutes,* a commentary on the laws [Ed.].

[52]The *Yaws* is the *Pox.*

Resolv'd to plague the holy Brother,
I set one Rogue to catch another;
To try the Cause then fully bent,
Up to *Annapolis*[53] I went,
A City Situate on a Plain,
Where scarce a House will keep out Rain;
The Buildings fram'd with Cyprus rare,
Resembles much our *Southwark* Fair:[54]
But Stranger here will scarcely meet
With Market-place, Exchange, or Street;
And if the Truth I may report,
'Tis not so large as *Tottenham Court.*[55]
St. Mary's[56] once was in repute,
Now here the Judges try the Suit,
And lawyers twice a Year dispute.
As oft the Bench most gravely meet,
Some to get Drunk, and some to eat
A swinging share of Country Treat.
But as for Justice right or wrong,
Not one amongst the numerous throng,
Knows what they mean, or has the Heart,
To give his Verdict on a Stranger's part:
Now Court being call'd by beat of Drum,
The Judges left their Punch and Rum,
When Pettifogger Doctor draws,
His Paper forth, and opens Cause:
And least I shou'd the better get,
Brib'd *Quack* suppress his Knavish Wit.
So Maid upon the downy Field,
Pretends a Force, and Fights to yield:
The Byast Court without delay,
Adjudg'd my Debt in Country Pay;
In Pipe staves, Corn, or Flesh of Boar,[57]
Rare Cargo for the *English* Shoar:
Raging with Grief, full speed I ran,
To joyn the Fleet at *Kicketan;*[58]
Embarqu'd and waiting for a Wind,
I left this dreadful Curse behind.
May Canniballs transported o'er the Sea
Prey on these Slaves, as they have done on me;

[53]The chief [city] of *Mary-land* containing about twenty four *Houses*.

[54]A London fair [Ed.].

[55]A London district [Ed.].

[56]Annapolis became the Maryland capital in 1694 [Ed.].

[57]There is a Law in this Country, the Plaintiff may pay his Debt in Country pay, which consists in the produce of his Plantation.

[58]The homeward bound Fleet meets here. [*Kicketan* is Hampton, Virginia; Ed.].

May never Merchant's, trading Sails explore
This Cruel, this Inhospitable Shoar;
But left abandon'd by the World to starve,
May they sustain the Fate they well deserve:
May they turn Savage, or as *Indians* Wild,
From Trade, Converse, and Happiness exil'd;
Recreant to Heaven, may they adore the Sun,
And into Pagan Superstitions run
For Vengence ripe ________
May Wrath Divine then lay those Regions wast
Where no Man's[59] Faithful, nor a Woman Chast.

1708

Susanna Wright 1697–1784

Susanna Wright was born in Lancashire, England, to Quaker parents who immigrated to Pennsylvania in 1714. By 1728 Wright had settled with her family at Wright's Ferry (later Columbia) in the Susquehanna River valley, where she lived for the rest of her life. She did not marry, but she managed her father's extended household after her mother's death in 1722 and later cared for her brother James's family as well. Her surviving letters to a host of well-known contemporaries reveal that she was not only well connected but also well educated and curious, having the diverse interests that mark Enlightenment minds. She lived at a crossroads between settled society and the Pennsylvania frontier, providing a stopping place for such travelers as Benjamin Franklin, physician Benjamin Rush, and historian Robert Proud. She engaged in scientific study and civic activity, raised prize-winning silkworms, explored the medicinal uses of herbs, and drafted official documents for her less literate neighbors. At least one twentieth-century historian identifies her as a contributor to Franklin's pamphlet denouncing the massacre of the Conestoga Indians. Such efforts made her a prominent citizen. Benjamin Rush recorded in his journal the occasion of his meeting "the famous Suzey Wright a lady who has been celebrated Above half a Century for her wit—good sense & valuable improvements of mind."

Wright was an active participant in a network of Pennsylvania poets, exchanging verse with Hannah Griffitts, Deborah Logan, and Milcah Martha Moore. More than thirty of her poems have been located, most of them in Moore's commonplace book. Wright wrote on many subjects and in a variety of poetic genres. Conventional neoclassical meditations on time, friendship, and labor are complemented by a range of occasional verse, imitations and paraphrases of other poets and of the Bible, devotional pieces, and dialogues. Her longer extant pieces—"To Eliz[a] Norris at Fairhill" and "Anna Boylens Letter to King Henry the 8th," for example—reveal her considerable skill as a poet as well as her daring in moving beyond conventional materials. The verse epistle to her friend Elizabeth Norris urged women to use Enlightenment reverence for reason to undermine the male privilege protected by law:

[59]The Author does not intend by this, any of the *English* Gentlemen resident there.

But womankind call reason to their aid,
And question when or where that law
    was made,
That law divine (a plausible pretence)
Oft urg'd with none, & oft with little
    sense.

Adding to this rational appeal for justice, Wright developed powerful emotional arguments in "Anna Boylens Letter." She was apparently a prolific poet, and it is likely that more of her poems remain to be found. What we have at present suggests they will be worth the effort of the search.

Pattie Cowell
Colorado State University

To Eliz[a] Norris—at Fairhill[1]

Since Adam, by our first fair Mother won
To share her fate, to taste, & be undone,
And that great law, whence no appeal must lie,
Pronounc'd a doom, that he should rule & die,
The partial race, rejoicing to fulfill
This pleasing dictate of almighty will
(With no superior virtue in their mind),
Assert their right to govern womankind.
But womankind call reason to their aid,
And question when or where that law was made,
That law divine (a plausible pretence)
Oft urg'd with none, & oft with little sense,
From wisdom's source no origin could draw,
That form'd the man to keep the sex in awe;
Say Reason governs all the mighty frame,
And Reason rules in every one the same,
No right has man his equal to control,
Since, all agree, there is no sex in soul;
Weak woman, thus in agreement grown strong,
Shakes off the yoke her parents wore too long;
But he, who arguments in vain had tried,
Hopes still for conquest from the yielding side,
Soft soothing flattery & persuasion tries,
And by a feign'd submission seeks to rise,
Steals, unperceiv'd, to the unguarded heart,
        And there reigns tyrant—

But you, whom no seducing tales can gain
To yield obedience, or to wear the chain,

[1]This undated poem is located in the Griffitts manuscripts belonging to the Library Company of Philadelphia. Elizabeth Norris (1704–1779) was a friend of Wright's and sister to Quaker politician and book collector Isaac Norris, Jr. (1701–1766). Fairhill was a Norris family home in Philadelphia, purchased by Isaac Norris, Sr. in 1717.

But set a queen, & in your freedom reign
O'er your own thoughts, of your own heart secure,
You see what joys each erring sex allure,
Look round the most intelligent—how few
But passions sway, or childish joys pursue;
Then bless that choice which led your bloom of youth
From forms & shadows to enlight'ning truth,
Best found when leisure & retirement reign,
Far from the proud, the busy & the vain,
Where rural views soft gentle joys impart,
Enlarge the thought, & elevate the heart,
Each changing scene adorns gay Nature's face,
Ev'n winter wants not its peculiar grace,
Hoar frosts & dews, & pale & summer suns.
Paint each revolving season as it runs,
The showery bow delights your wond'ring eyes,
Its spacious arch, & variegated dyes,
[You] watch the transient colours as they fade,
Till, by degrees, they settle into shade,
Then calm reflect, so regular & fine,
Now seen no more, a fate will soon be mine,
When life's warm stream, chill'd by death's [fey?] hand,
Within these veins a frozen current stands;
Tho' conscious of desert superior far,
Till then, my friend, the righteous claim forbear—
Indulge man in his darling vice of sway,
He only rules those who of choice obey;
When strip'd of power, & plac'd in equal light,
Angels shall judge who had the better right,
All you can do is but to let him see
That woman still shall sure his equal be,
By your example shake his ancient law,
And shine yourself, the finish'd piece you draw.

Anna Boylens Letter to King Henry the 8th[1]

From anxious Thoughts of every future Ill
From these lone Walls which Death & Terror fill,

[1]This poem and the following two are located in the Milcah Martha Moore Commonplace Book in the Quaker Collection at Haverford College. *Milcah Martha Moore's Book,* ed. Catherine La Courreye Blecki and Karin A. Wulf, was published by Pennsylvania State University Press in 1997. King Henry VIII (1491–1547) accused Anne Boleyn (1507?–1536), his second wife, of adultery and ordered her beheaded when she did not produce a male heir.

To you great Sir! a loyal Wife from hence,
Writes to assert her injur'd Innocence.
To you, who on a Throne supremely great
Look down & guide the partial Hand of Fate,
Who rais'd your Subject to a royal Bride,
To the imperial Purples gaudy Pride
And glowing Gems around these Temples ty'd,
You glowing Gems your dazling Rays rebate
And fade thou purple, at thy wearers Fate,
To grandeur rais'd, to Misery cast down
And mourn my sad acquaintance with a Crown,
My Life & Fame must join the Sacrifice
The last alone all peaceful Thought denies,
Renews My Anguish & oe'rflows my Eyes.
For Life & Crown with Patience I forego,
There's no such Charm in filling Thrones below
My Name alone, 'tis Anna Boylens Name
With whose low Station & unspotted Fame
All innocent & happy Days I'd seen,
This harmless Name exalted to a Queen
Is handed infamous to future Times
Loaded with Falshoods blacken'd o'er with Crimes
Y[ou]r. infant Daughter[2] her sad Part must bear,
And with her Mother's Heart her Suff'ring share,
Poor lovely Offspring of a wretched Bed
What are thy hapless Mother's Crimes that shed
This baleful Influence on thy harmless Head?
Thy Father sternly casts thee from his knee,
Whilst each licentious Tongue that rails at me
Points o'er thy opening Years with Infamy,
All Hopes on Earth with Patience I forego
But thee—poor Child left in a World of Woe
May thy dear Life in smoother Channels run
Secure from Ills thy Mother could not shun
All this is Pain, but nothing of Surprise
This Fall I look'd for from my fatal Rise,
From that unhappy Day, my Person pleas'd yr. Eyes.
Such slight Foundations never lasting prove
Where Fancy only lights the Torch of Love,
I see another Fair assume My Place
Who's in your Eyes what Anna Boylen was,
Beware triumphant Beauty how you shine
Those Charms, those Vows & ardours all were mine.
Look on me & beware for as you see,
What I am now, that you shall surely be,

[2]Queen Elizabeth I (1533–1603).

But since my Death & nothing less will do
To bring you to the Bliss you have in View,
May bounteous Heaven the mighty Sin forgive
And not repay, the Injuries I receive,
Yet think, o! think what Crimes will wound yr. Soul,
When your dim Eyes in search of Slumber rowl,
When Lamps burn blue & guilty Tapers fade,
As by your bridal Bed I glide a ghastly Shade,
While sanguine Streams from purple Fountains drain
And all around the gay Apartment stain,
From conscious Guilt will these Illusions rise,
And haunt your Steps & fill your watching Eyes,
For ever raising Tumults in your Breast,
But fear me not for I shall be at Rest.
But at that Day when the last Trumpets Sound,
Shall reach the dead, & break their Sleep profound,
Bones long sepulchred burst their narrow Rooms
And hostile Kings rise trembling from their Tombs,
When nor your Heart, nor mine can lie conceal'd
But ev'ry secret Sin shall stand reveal'd,
Stand full reveal'd that God & Man may see,
How Fate has err'd, & you have injur'd me,
When, but alas all Arguments are vain
To bring your royal wand'ring Heart again
What Innocence unaided & oppress'd
Could do, I've done but who can Pow'r resist.
    I've but one Wish but one Request to make
Let not my Friends be Sufferers for my sake,
All Innocent, humane, & kindly good
May their dear Lives be ransom'd by my Blood,
For ev'ry one the Price I'd freely pay
So many Times could Life be drain'd away,
By what I once have been by what you are,
Happy & great,—by all yr. Joy & Care;
By all things sacred, all your Love forgive,
My Friends their harmless Crimes & let them live,
    Lo! on her bended Knees thus asks yr. Wife,
On terms, you see, she would not ask her Life,
With this I cease, to trouble your Repose,
A few short anxious Hours the stormy Scene will close.

1720 1997

On the Benefit of Labour

Adam from Paradise expell'd,
Was drove into a Locust Field,
Whose rich luxuriant Soils produce,
Nor Fruit, nor Plant, for human Use,
'Till clear'd by Toil, & till'd by Art
With Plenty chear'd his drooping Heart.—
—'Twas thus Relief our Father found
When sent to cultivate the Ground.
For God who knew what Man could bear,
Form'd not his Sentence too severe,
A Life of indolent Repose
Had been the Plan of greater Woes;
While tir'd with Ease too dearly bought,
He past the tedious Hours in Thought,
For Labour only causes Rest,
And calms the Tumults in the Breast.—
    More Leisure to revolve his Fate
Had added Sorrow to the Weight,
Of his unhappy fall'n State.—
While Memory drest the gaudy Scenes
Of Edens never fading Greens,
Of Trees that bloom without Decay,
Where Storms were silent—Zephyrs[1] play,
And Flowers their rifling sweets bestow,
On all the gentle Winds that blow,
With ev'ry Charm that crown'd the Place
Design'd for Adam & his Race:
Our Sire too weak for such a Stroke,
Had sunk beneath the heavy Yoke,
Had on his Breast the Sentence try'd,
Let out his tortur'd Soul & dy'd.—
But kindly to suspend his Doom
For sake of Ages yet to come,
A Life of Action was decreed,
And Labour must produce him Bread;
His Hands the artful Web prepare
To screen him from inclement Air,
And equal Pains a Tent provide
To turn the beating Storm aside.—
—These necessary Toils & Cares

[1]In Greek mythology, Zephyrus personifies the west wind.

For present Wants & future Tears,
Joyn'd to the Curse, a Blessing grow,
And lessen or divert our Woe.

1728 1997

My own Birth Day.—August 4th 1761

Few & evil have the Days of the Years of my Life been.
—[GEN. 47:9].

Were few & Evil stil'd the Patriarchs[1] Days,
Extended to a Length of Years unknown
In this luxurious Age whose swift Decays,
Allow to few so many as my own.
And what are they?—a Vision all the past,
A Bubble on the Waters shining Face,
What yet remain 'till the first transient Blast
Shall leave no more Remembrance of their Place.
Still few & evil, as the Days of old,
Are those allotted to the Race of Man,
And three score Years in sounding Numbers told,
Where's the Amount?—a Shadow & a Span.—
Look back through this long Tide of rolling Years
Since early Reason gave Reflection Birth,
Recall each sad Occasion of thy Tears,
Then say can Happiness be found on Earth?
Pass former Strokes—the recent only name!
A Brother whom no healing Art could save,
In Life's full Prime unnerv'd his manly Frame
From wasting Pains took Refuge in the Grave.—
A Sister who long causeless Anguish knew,
A tender Parent & a patient Wife,
Calmly she bore the bitter Lot she drew,
And clos'd her Sorrows with her Close of Life.
A darling Child, all lovely, all admir'd,
Snatch'd from our Arms in Youths engaging Bloom
A Lazur[2] turn'd e'er his short Date expir'd,
And laid a piteous Object in the Tomb.
Your Memory from my Breast shall never stray

[1]The patriarchs of Israel were Abraham, Isaac, Jacob, and Joseph. See Genesis 12–50.
[2]A poor and diseased person, especially a leper, from the biblical Lazarus, whom Jesus raised from the dead. See John 11ff.

Should years to Patriarchal Age extend,
Thro' Glooms of Night, thro' social Hours of Day
The starting Tear stands ready to descend.—
But tho' I mourn, not without Hope I mourn,
Dear kindred Shades! tho' all unknown yr. Place
Tho' to these Eyes you never must return,
You're safe in the Infinitude of Space.—
One all disposing God who gave you Birth,
That Life sustain'd which his good Pleasure gave,
Then cut you off from ev'ry Claim on Earth,
Is the same guardian God beyond the Grave.
Tho' by impenetrable Darkness veil'd,
Y[ou]r. separate State lies hid from mortal Sight,
The Saviour, Friend of Man, Messiah hail'd,
Brought Life & Immortality to Light.
Rest then my Soul—in these Appointments rest,
And down the Steep of Age pursue thy Way,
With humble Hope, & Faith unfailing blest,
The mortal shall surpass the natal Day.

[Marginal note:]

Soft moving Language, deep Reflection strong
Compose thy pow'rful Harmony of Song. Fidelia

Richard Lewis 1700?–1734

Richard Lewis, a prolific writer, probably came to America from Wales in 1718. He became a schoolmaster and member of the Assembly in Maryland. According to his biographer, J.A. Leo Lemay, no other American poet of the early eighteenth century was so widely reprinted.

Like Ebenezer Cook, Richard Lewis creates a peculiarly American poem using an English poetic model. English pastorals, based upon classical models replete with nymphs and shepherds, idealized rural life and rural scenery in a verse form that emulated the order and harmony of nature. At the hands of English writers like Pope and Philips, the pastoral increasingly began to show the influence of the eighteenth-century realities of English rural life. With its emphasis upon the rural life and its allegorical impulse, the pastoral would have been a welcome form to adapt in America, the place fast turning from a wilderness into a garden. At the hands of Richard Lewis, the pastoral form was transformed into a mode offering a central critique of English poetry because of its pro-American stance. In applying the pastoral tradition to American poetry, Lewis implicitly claimed that American nature was superior to English or European nature as subject, indeed that English and classical poets might have written better had they had America as their topic.

This text is taken from the London *Weekly Register* of January 1, 1732. Unless otherwise noted, annotations are from that publication.

A Journey from Patapsko to Annapolis, April 4, 1730[1]

Me vero primum dulces ante omnia Musae,
Quarum sacra fero ingenti perculsus amore,
Accipiant; Coelique vias & Sydera *monstrent;*——
Sin has ne possim Naturae accedere partes
Frigidus obstiterit circum praecordia Sanguis,
Rura *mihi, &* rigui *placeant in Vallibus* Amnes,
Flumina *amem,* Sylvasque *inglorius.*
—VIRG. *GEOR.* 2[2]

At length the *wintry* Horrors disappear,
And *April* views with Smiles the infant Year;
The grateful Earth from frosty Chains unbound,
Pours out its *vernal* Treasures all around,
Her Face bedeckt with Grass, with Buds the Trees are crown'd.
In this soft Season, 'ere the Dawn of Day,
I mount my Horse, and lonely take my Way,
From woody Hills that shade *Patapsko's* Head,
(In whose deep Vales he makes his stony Bed,
From whence he rushes with resistless Force,
Tho' huge rough Rocks retard his rapid Course,)
Down to *Annapolis,* on that smooth Stream[3]
Which took from fair *Anne-Arundel* its Name.[4]
And now the *Star* that ushers in the Day,[5]
Begins to pale her ineffectual Ray.
The *Moon,* with blunted Horns, now shines less bright,
Her fading Face eclips'd with growing Light;
The fleecy Clouds with streaky Lustre glow,
And Day quits Heav'n to view the Earth below.
Oe'r yon tall *Pines* the *Sun* shews half his Face,
And fires their floating Foliage with his Rays;
Now sheds aslant on Earth his lightsome Beams,
That trembling shine in many-colour'd Streams:
Slow-rising from the Marsh, the Mist recedes,

[1]The Patapsco River meets the Chesapeake Bay at Baltimore, which, in its earliest years, took its name from the river [Ed.].

[2]Ye sacred Muses! with whose beauty fired,
My soul is ravished, and my brain inspired—
Whose priest I am, whose holy fillets wear—
. . . Give me the ways of wandering stars to know,
The depths of heaven above, and earth below:
. . . But, if my heavy blood restrain the flight
Of my free soul, aspiring to the height
Of nature, and unclouded fields of light—
My next desire is, void of care and strife,
To lead a soft, secure, inglorious life— (Virgil, *Georgics,* 2:475–477, 483–487, trans. John Dryden, 1697; the translation Lewis refers to later in the poem) [Ed.]

[3]The Severn River meets the Chesapeake Bay at Annapolis [Ed.].

[4]Anne Arundell was the wife of Cecilius Calvert, eldest son of the first Baron of Baltimore, who founded the colony of Maryland as a refuge for English Roman Catholics [Ed.].

[5]Venus.

The Trees, emerging, rear their dewy Heads;
Their dewy Heads the *Sun* with Pleasure views,
And brightens into Pearls the pendent Dews.
The *Beasts* uprising, quit their leafy Beds,
And to the cheerful *Sun* erect their Heads;
All joyful rise, except the filthy *Swine,*
On obscene Litter stretch'd they snore supine:
In vain the Day awakes, Sleep seals their Eyes,
Till Hunger breaks the Bond and bids them rise.
Mean while the *Sun* with more exalted Ray,
From cloudless Skies distributes riper Day;
Thro' sylvan Scenes my Journey I pursue,
Ten thousand Beauties rising to my View;
Which kindle in my Breast poetic Flame,
And bid me my CREATOR's praise proclaim;
Tho' my low Verse ill-suits the noble Theme.
Here various Flourets grace the teeming Plains,[6]
Adorn'd by Nature's Hand with beauteous Stains;
First-born of *Spring,* here the *Pacone* appears,
Whose golden Root a silver Blossom rears.
In spreading Tufts, see there the *Crowfoot* blue,
On whose green Leaves still shines a globous Dew;
Behold the *Cinque-foil,* with its dazling Dye
Of flaming Yellow, wounds the tender Eye:
But there, enclos'd the grassy *Wheat* is seen,
To heal the aching Sight with cheerful Green.
Safe in yon Cottage dwells the *Monarch-Swain,*
His *Subject-Flocks,* close-grazing, hide the Plain;
For him they live;—and die t'uphold his Reign.
Viands unbought his well-till'd Lands afford,
And smiling *Plenty* waits upon his Board;
Health shines with sprightly Beams around his Head,
And *Sleep,* with downy Wings, o'er-shades his Bed;
His *Sons* robust his daily Labours share,
Patient of Toil, Companions of his Care:
And all their Toils with sweet Success are crown'd.
In graceful Ranks there *Trees* adorn the Ground,
The *Peach,* the *Plum,* the *Apple,* here are found;
Delicious Fruits!——Which from their Kernels rise,
So fruitful is the Soil—so mild the Skies.
The lowly *Quince* yon sloping Hill o'er-shades.
Here lofty *Cherry-Trees* erect their Heads;
High in the Air each spiry Summer waves,

[6]Pacone, or Tumeric root, produces a greenish-white flower in April. Crowfoot is a plant that thrives in water; it has a white flower. Cinque-foil, or Potentilla, blooms with a yellow flower.

Whose Blooms thick-springing yield no Space for Leaves;
Evolving Odours fill the ambient Air,
The *Birds* delighted to the Grove repair:
On ev'ry Tree behold a tuneful Throng,
The vocal Vallies echo to their Song.
    But what is *He,*[7] who perch'd above the rest,
Pours out such various Musick from his Breast!
His Breast, whose Plumes a cheerful White display,
His quiv'ring Wings are dress'd in sober Grey.
Sure, all the *Muses,* this their Bird inspire!
And *He,* alone, is equal to the Choir
Of warbling Songsters who around him play,
While, Echo like, *He* answers ev'ry Lay.
The chirping *Lark* now sings with sprightly Note,
Responsive to her Strain *He* shapes his Throat:
Now the poor widow'd *Turtle* wails her Mate,
While in soft Sounds *He* cooes to mourn his Fate.
Oh, sweet Musician, thou dost far excel
The soothing Song of pleasing *Philomel!*[8]
Sweet is her Song, but in few Notes confin'd;
But thine, thou *Mimic* of the feath'ry Kind,
Runs thro' all Notes!——*Thou* only know'st them *All,*
At once the *Copy,——and th'Original.*
    My *Ear* thus charm'd, mine *Eye* with Pleasure sees,
Hov'ring about the Flow'rs, th'industrious *Bees.*
Like them in Size, the *Humming-Bird* I view,
Like them, *He* sucks his Food, the Honey-Dew,
With nimble Tongue, and Beak of jetty Hue.
He takes with rapid Whirl his noisy Flight,
His gemmy Plumage strikes the Gazer's Sight;
And as he moves his ever-flutt'ring Wings,
Ten thousand Colours he around him flings.
Now I behold the Em'rald's vivid Green,
Now scarlet, now a purple Die is seen;
In brightest Blue, his Breast *He* now arrays,
Then strait his Plumes emit a golden Blaze.
Thus whirring round he flies, and varying still,
He mocks the *Poet's* and the *Painter's* Skill;
Who may forever strive with fruitless Pains,
To catch and fix those beauteous changeful Stains;
While Scarlet now, and now the Purple shines,
And Gold, to Blue its transient Gloss resigns.
Each quits, and quickly each resumes its Place,
And ever-varying Dies each other chase.
Smallest of Birds, what Beauties shine in thee!

[7]The Mock Bird.

[8]The nightingale [Ed.].

A living *Rainbow* on thy Breast I see.
Oh had that *Bard*[9] in whose heart-pleasing Lines,
The *Phoenix* in a Blaze of Glory shines,
Beheld those Wonders which are shewn in Thee,
That *Bird* had lost his Immortality!
Thou in His Verse hadst stretch'd thy flutt'ring Wing
Above all other Birds,—their beauteous King.
But now th'enclos'd Plantation I forsake
And onwards thro' the Woods my Journey take;
The level Road, the longsome Way beguiles,
A blooming Wilderness around me smiles;
Here hardy *Oak,* there fragment *Hick'ry* grows,
Their bursting Buds the tender Leaves disclose;
The tender Leaves in downy Robes appear,
Trembling, they seem to move with cautious Fear,
Yet new to Life, and Strangers to the Air.
Here stately *Pines* unite their whisp'ring Heads,
And with a solemn Gloom embrown the Glades.
See there a green *Savane* opens wide,
Thro' which smooth Streams in wanton Mazes glide;
Thick-branching Shrubs o'er-hang the silver Streams,
Which scarcely deign t'admit the solar Beams.
While with Delight on this soft Scene I gaze,
The *Cattle* upward look, and cease to graze,
But into covert run thro' various Ways.
And now the Clouds in black Assemblage rise,
And dreary Darkness overspreads the Skies,
Thro' which the Sun strives to transmit his Beams,
"But sheds his sickly light in straggling Streams."[10]
Hush'd is the Musick of the wood-land Choir,
Fore-knowing of the Storm, the Birds retire
For Shelter, and forsake the shrubby Plains,
And dumb Horror thro' the Forest reigns;
In that lone House which opens wide its Door,
Safe may I tarry till the Storm is o'er.
Hark how the *Thunder* rolls with solemn Sound!
And see the forceful *Lightning* dart a Wound,
On yon toll Oak!——Behold its Top laid bare!
Its Body rent, and scatter'd thro' the Air
The Splinters fly!——Now—now the *Winds* arise,
From different Quarters of the lowring Skies;
Forth-issuing fierce, the *West* and *South* engage,
The waving Forest bends beneath their Rage:

[9] *Claudian* [(c. 370–c. 404 B.C.) the last important poet of the classical tradition in Latin who wrote mythological epics popular in the Middle Ages (Ed.)].

[10] An allusion to a Dryden translation of Virgil's *Georgics*, I: 550–551: "Or if thro' mists he shoots his sullen beams, / Frugal of light, in loose and straggling streams" [Ed.].

But where the winding Valley checks their Course,
They roar and ravage with redoubled Force;
With circling Sweep in dreadful Whirlwinds move
And from its Roots tear up the gloomy Grove,
Down-rushing fall the Trees, and beat the Ground,
In Fragments flie the shatter'd Limbs around;
Tremble the Under-woods, the Vales resound.
    Follows, with patt'ring Noise, the icy *Hail,*
And *Rain,* fast falling, floods the lowly Vale.
Again the *Thunders* roll, the *Lightnings* fly,
And as they first disturb'd, now clear the Sky;
For lo, the *Gust* decreases by Degrees,
The dying *Winds* but sob amidst the Trees;
With pleasing Softness falls the silver Rain,
Thro' which at first faint-gleaming o'er the Plain,
The Orb of Light scarce darts a watry Ray
To gild the Drops that fall from ev'ry Spray;
But soon the dusky Vapours are dispell'd,
And thro' the Mist that late his Face conceal'd,
Bursts the broad *Sun,* triumphant in a Blaze
Too keen for Sight—Yon Cloud refracts his Rays,
The mingling Beams compose th'*ethereal Bow,*
How sweet, how soft, its melting Colours glow!
Gaily they shine, by heav'nly Pencils laid,
Yet vanish swift,——How soon does *Beauty* fade!
    The *Storm* is past, my Journey I renew,
And a new Scene of Pleasure greets my View:
Wash'd by the copious Rain the gummy *Pine,*
Does cheerful, with unsully'd Verdure shine;
The *Dogwood* Flow'rs assume a snowy white,
The *Maple* blushing gratifies the Sight:
No verdant leaves the lovely *Red-Bud* grace,
Cornation blossoms now supply their Place.
The *Sassafras* unfolds its fragrant Bloom,
The *Vine* affords an exquisite Perfume;
These grateful Scents wide-wafting thro' the Air
The smelling Sense with balmy Odours cheer.
And now the *Birds,* sweet singing, stretch their Throats,
And in one Choir unite their various Notes,
Nor yet unpleasing is the *Turtle's* Voice,
Tho' he complains while other Birds rejoice.
    These vernal Joys, all restless Thoughts controul,
And gently-soothing calm the troubled Soul.
    While such Delights my Senses entertain,
I scarce perceive that I have left the *Plain;*
'Till now the Summit of a *Mount* I gain:
Low at whose sandy Base the *River* glides,
Slow-rolling near their Height his languid Tides;

Shade above Shade, the Trees in rising Ranks,
Cloath with eternal Green his steepy Banks:
The Flood, well pleas'd, reflects their verdant Gleam
From the smooth Mirror of his limpid Stream.
    But see the *Hawk,* who with acute Survey,
Towring in Air predestinates his Prey
Amid the Floods!——Down dropping from on high,
He strikes the *Fish,* and bears him thro' the Sky.
The Stream disturb'd, no longer shews the Scene
That lately stain'd its silver Waves with green;
In spreading Circles roll the troubled Floods,
And to the Shores bear off the pictur'd Woods.
    Now looking round I view the out-stretch'd *Land,*
O'er which the Sight exerts a wide Command;
The fertile Vallies, and the naked Hills,
The Cattle feeding near the chrystal Rills;
The Lawns wide-op'ning to the sunny Ray,
And mazy Thickets that exclude the Day.
A-while the Eye is pleas'd these Scenes to trace,
Then hurrying o'er the intermediate Space,
Far distant Mountains drest in Blue appear,
And all their Woods are lost in empty Air.
    The *Sun* near setting now arrays his Head
In milder Beams and lengthens ev'ry Shade.
The rising Clouds usurping on the Day
A bright Variety of Dies display;
About the wide Horizon swift they fly,
"And chase a Change of Colours round the Sky:[11]
And now I view but half the *flaming Sphere,*
Now one faint Glimmer shoots along the Air,
And all his golden Glories disappear.
    Onwards the *Ev'ning* moves in Habit grey,
And for her Sister *Night* prepares the Way.
The plumy People seek their secret Nests,
To Rest repair the ruminating Beasts.
Now deep'ning Shades confess th' Approach of Night,
Imperfect Images elude the Sight:
From earthly Objects I remove mine Eye,
And view with Look erect the vaulted Sky;
Where dimly-shining now the Stars appear,
At first thin-scatt'ring thro' the misty Air;
Till Night confirm'd, her jetty Throne ascends,
On her the *Moon* in clouded State attends,

[11]An allusion to James Thomson on Summer, in the *Seasons* (1726–1730): "See, how at once the bright effulgent sun, / Rising direct, swift chases from the sky / The short-lived Twilight . . ." (ll. 635–637) [Ed.].

But soon unveil'd her lovely Face is seen,
And *Stars* unnumber'd wait around their Queen;
Rang'd by their MAKER's Hand in just Array,
They march majestic thro' th'ethereal Way.
Are these bright Luminaries hung on high
Only to please with twinkling Rays our Eye?
Or may we rather count each *Star* a *Sun,*
Round which *full peopled Worlds* their Courses run?
Orb above Orb harmoniously they steer
Their various voyages thro' Seas of Air.
Snatch me some *Angel* to those high Abodes,
The Seats perhaps of *Saints* and *Demigods!*
Where such as bravely scorn'd the galling Yoke
Of *vulgar Error,* and her Fetters broke;
Where *Patriots* who fix the publick Good,
In Fields of Battle sacrific'd their Blood;
Where *pious Priests* who Charity proclaim'd,
And *Poets* whom a *virtuous Muse* enflam'd;
Philosophers who strove to mend our Hearts,
And such as polish'd Life with *useful Arts,*
Obtain a Place; when by the Hand of Death
Touch'd, they retire from this poor Speck of Earth;
Their *Spirits* freed from bodily Alloy
Perceive a Fore-taste of that endless Joy,
Which from Eternity hath been prepar'd,
To crown their labours with a vast Reward.
While to these Orbs my wand'ring Thoughts aspire,
A falling *Meteor* shoots his lambent Fire;
Thrown from the heav'nly Space he seeks the Earth,
From whence he first deriv'd his humble Birth.
The *Mind* advis'd by this instructive Sight,
Descending sudden from th'aerial Height,
Obliges me to view a different Scene,
Of more importance to myself, tho' mean.
These distant Objects I no more pursue,
But turning inward my reflective View,
My working Fancy helps me to survey,
In the just Picture of this *April Day,*
My life o'er past,——a Course of thirty *Years*
Blest with few Joys, perplex'd with num'rous Cares.
In the dim Twilight of our *Infancy,*
Scarce can the Eye surrounding Objects see;
Then thoughtless *Childhood* leads us pleas'd and gay,
In Life's fair Morning thro' a flow'ry Way:
The *Youth* in Schools inquisitive of Good,
Science pursues thro' *Learning's* mazy Wood;
Whose lofty Trees, he, to his Grief perceives,
Are often bare of *Fruit,* and only fill'd with *Leaves:*

Thro' lonely Wilds his tedious Journey lies,
At last a brighter Prospect cheers his Eyes;
Now the gay Fields of *Poetry* he views,
And joyous listens to the *tuneful Muse;*
Now *History* affords him vast Delight,
And opens lovely Landscapes to his Sight:
But ah too soon this Scene of Pleasure flies!
And o'er his Head tempestous Troubles rise.
He hears the Thunders roll, he feels the Rains,
Before a friendly Shelter he obtains;
And thence beholds with Grief the furious Storm
The *noon-tide* Beauties of his *Life* deform:
He views the *painted Bow* in distant Skies;
Hence, in his Heart some Gleams of Comfort rise;
He hopes the *Gust* has almost spent its Force,
And that he safely may pursue his Course.
    Thus far *my Life* does with the *Day* agree,
Oh may its coming Stage from Storms be free!
While passing thro' the World's most private Way,
With Pleasure I my MAKER'S Works survey;
Within my Heart let *Peace* a Dwelling find,
Let my *Goodwill* extend to *all Mankind:*
Freed from *Necessity,* and blest with *Health;*
Give me *Content,* let others toil for *Wealth:*
In *busy* Scenes of Life let me exert
A *careful Hand,* and wear an *honest Heart;*
And suffer me my *leisure* Hours to spend,
With chosen *Books,* or a well-natur'd *Friend.*
Thus journeying on, as I advance in Age
May I look back with Pleasure on my Stage;
And as the setting *Sun* withdrew his Light
To rise on other Worlds serene and bright,
Cheerful may I resign my vital Breath,
Nor anxious tremble at th' Approach of *Death;*
Which shall (I hope) but strip me of *my Clay,*
And to a better World my Soul convey.
    Thus musing, I my silent Moments spend,
Till to the *River's* margin I descend,
From whence I may discern my *Journey's* End:
Annapolis adorns its further Shore,
To which the *Boat* attends to bear me o'er.
    And now the moving *Boat* the Flood divides,
While the *Stars* "tremble on the floating Tides;"[12]

[12]Pope's *Rape of the Lock,* Canto II, line 48, reads: "The sunbeams trembling on the floating tide" [Ed.].

Pleas'd with the Sight, again I raise mine Eye
To the Bright Glories of the azure Sky;
And while these Works of God's creative Hand,
The *Moon* and *Stars,* that move at his Command,
Obedient thro' their circling Course on high,
Employ my Sight,——struck with amaze I cry,
ALMIGHTY LORD! whom Heav'n and Earth proclaim,
The *Author* of their universal Frame,
Wilt thou vouchsafe to view the *Son of Man,*
Thy Creature, who but *Yesterday* began,
Thro' animated Clay to draw his Breath,
To-morrow doom'd a Prey to ruthless Death!
TREMENDOUS GOD! May I not justly fear,
That I, unworthy Object of thy Care,
Into this World from thy bright Presence tost,
Am in th'Immensity of *Nature* lost!
And that my Notions of the *World above,*
Are but Creations of my own *Self-Love;*
To feed my coward Heart, afraid to die,
With *fancied* Feasts of *Immortality!*
These Thoughts, which thy amazing Works suggest,
Oh glorious FATHER, rack my troubled Breast.
Yet, GRACIOUS GOD, reflecting that my Frame
From *Thee* deriv'd in animating Flame,
And that what e'er I am, however mean,
By thy Command I enter'd on this Scene
Of Life,——thy wretched *Creature of a Day,*
Condemn'd to travel thro' a tiresome Way;
Upon whose Banks (perhaps to cheer my Toil)
I see thin Verdures rise, and *Daisies* smile:
Poor Comforts these, my Pains t'alleviate!
While on my Head tempestuous Troubles beat.
And must I, when I quit this earthly Scene,
Sink total into *Death,* and never rise again?
No sure,——These *Thoughts* which in my Bosom roll
Must issue from a *never-dying Soul;*
These active *Thoughts* that penetrate the Sky,
Excursive into dark Futurity;
Which hope eternal Happiness to gain,
Could never be bestow'd on *Man* in vain.
To *Thee,* OH FATHER, fill'd with fervent Zeal,
And sunk in humble Silence I appeal;
Take me, my great CREATOR to *Thy Care,*
And gracious listen to my ardent Prayer!
SUPREME OF BEINGS, omnipresent Power!
My great Preserver from my natal Hour,
Fountain of Wisdom, boundless Deity,

OMNISCIENT GOD, my Wants are known to THEE,
With Mercy look on mine Infirmity!
Whatever State thou shalt for me ordain,
Whether my Lot in Life be *Joy* or *Pain;*
Patient let me sustain thy wise Decree,
And learn to *know myself,* and *honour Thee.*

1732

William Dawson 1704–1752

Born in England and educated at Oxford, Dawson moved to Virginia, becoming a tutor in moral philosophy at the College of William and Mary in Williamsburg. He held several important offices in Virginia's colonial government and in 1743 became president of the college. He brought out his collection of verse, *Poems on Several Occasions* (1736), anonymously and published in magazines witty and polished work like the poem below.

The Wager. A Tale[1]

Dare jura Maritis
—HOR.[2]

Two Sparks were earnest in Debate
Touching Man's Life in marry'd State;
The one for Matrimony stood,
And preach'd in grave and solemn Mood,
By Head and Shoulders forcing, oddly,
To tagg each Sentence something Godly,
With many a learned Application
From *Genesis* to *Revelation*—
In Politick's he wisely shew'd,
What Honours *Sparta*'s Laws[3] bestow'd
On those who marry'd in the Prime,
And never lost in a teeming time.
And how the ancient *Roman* Nation
Had the same Rules in Imitation;

[1]*From* the *New York Gazette and Weekly Post-Boy,* 27 Mar. 1749: 323.

[2]"To administer justice to husbands" (Latin), from Horace's *Ars Poetica,* line 398. The passage reads: "This was the wisdom of that time, to separate the public from the private, the sacred from the profane, to prohibit promiscuous lying together, to administer justice to husbands, struggling hard to engrave the laws in wood."

[3]Ancient city-state whose spirit, enforced by stringent laws, was aristocratic, conservative, and militaristic.

And how their Senate oft decreed,
That Men should wed to mend the Breed:
How all those Heroes, whose Renown
Fame's Trump has handed to us down,
For Cities storm'd, and Kingdoms won,
Were each an honest Mother's Son.
How modern *Romans* do, indeed,
Neglect to mind a lawful Breed:
But diverse Practices pursue
Which their Fore-fathers never knew,
And set their whole Affections on
The Scarlet Whore of *Babylon:*[4]
Which we, good *Protestants* o'th'Nation,
Are bound to think abomination;
For which such mortal hate they bear Us,
And curse us bitterly like *Meroz.*[5]
 Dick listen'd to his wise Quotations,
And heard him out with all his Patience,
At length he cry'd, *'Sblood* John (*bar swearing*)
This idle Talk is past all bearing.
You mention old *Lycurgus'*[6] Laws,
And *Spartan* Rules and ancient Saws,
When all this foolish Prittle-prattle,
Is just like *rattle, Bladder, rattle.*
I say, that *Rome*'s a prudent City,
If you don't think so too, 'tis pity.
'Pray, if your Memory don't 'scape ye,
Know you a marry'd Man that's happy?
People may talk and make a Pother,
They're but Decoys for one another.
The *Fox* had ne'er Aversion shewn
To tails—if he had had his own.
So they, that fall into the Gin,
Draw, like *Free-Masons,*[7] others in.
Women, I own, were made for Men,
For their Diversion now and then:
But then, to cap your wisest Sentence,
Pleasure's attended by Repentance.
What we may once repent; a Wife
Makes us repent of *during Life.*

[4]Puritan epithet for the Roman Catholic Church.

[5]See Judges 5:23: "Curse ye Meroz, said the angel of the Lord, curse ye bitterly the inhabitants thereof; because they came not to the help of the Lord, to the help of the Lord against the mighty."

[6]Legendary legislator of Sparta, active around 600 B.C. who turned the luxury- and art-loving Spartans into stern and disciplined, state-directed citizens.

[7]Fraternal organization characterized by secret rituals and passwords.

For whatsoever some pretend,
Wives are but Wives, to their Lives End.
And he that marries, to his Cost,
Will find his Labour not well lost.
As *France*'s King, of high Renown,
Went up the Hill—and so came down.
  John bless'd himself, and scratcht his head,
And looking very wisely, said,
Methinks I smell, in this Discourse,
Free-thinking rank—or something worse.
Don't you think Marriage is a serious
Type of a Tye abstruse, mysterious?
Surely the Text you understand ill,
Else Women you would better handle.
To be our Help-meets in our Need,
When real Friends are Friends indeed,
To share a Part of our Distress,
And, by that Share, to make it less.
To clean our Houses, milk our Kine.
And mind when Boars gallant our Swine;
To drudge about domestick Bus'ness,
And scold at Servants for Remissness:
Are not these Things of mighty Weight,
To ease us, in the marry'd State?
Besides an hundred Things of Course,
That might my Argument enforce,
To strive an hundred Ways t'oblige us,
Which I'll abridge, as being tedious,
Since all the Joys that Life affords,
Are comprehended in few Words;
For don't the Rituals plainly say,
To love, to honour and obey?
  You have it there, indeed says *Dick,*
Obedience is the usual Trick.
They promise it before the Priest,
But saying that, they mean it least:
Or else they take so little Notice,
That what they promise soon forgot is;
For other Thoughts so crowd the Head,
They neither mind what's done or said,
Obedience soon has lost its Force,
And only seems a Word of Course,
And notwithstanding Vows or Oaths
They doff it with their Wedding-Cloaths.
  But since the Rituals, you maintain,
Appear to be positive and plain,
I'll venture with you, if you dare,
A Wager you shall own is fair,

That low Obedience is more common
And oft'ner found, in Man than Woman.
And thus the Matter we'll decide,
A Cart and Horses we'll provide,
Hampers of Eggs shall be the Load,
Thus furnish'd out, we'll take the Road,
At each Plantation make a Stand,
To know who bears the upper Hand.
Where e'er the Wife the Throne,
An Egg we'll leave them and be gone:
But if the woman does obey,
Submitting to her Husband's Sway,
If all his Orders have full Force,
We'll give the Miracle an Horse.
Yet all I'm worth I will engage here,
To half its Value, on this Wager,
That all our Eggs are gone in course,
Before one Husband gets a Horse.
  So said so done—the Wager's laid,
Preliminary Earnest paid,
They Both consult the Men of Law
Authentic Covenants to draw,
And then the hopeful Tour begins,
Both pleas'd—for both were sure to win.
  From that fair Town where rising Day
Does first the House of Law survey,
Where Learning's Seat beholds th'Extreams
Of *Western* Lights departing Beams,[8]
As if contriv'd to let us see
Both one and t'other's Destiny,
Our Travellers jog'd easy on.
Nor left a House uncall'd-upon,
Both where *James*-River's *Northern Shore*
Shrinks from its foamy Currents Roar,
And where *York* River's angry Tide
Impetuous beats its *Southern* Side:
But still where e'er they did advance
Dick seem'd to stand the fairest Chance:
The gentle Husband, at each House,
Gave Way to his superior Spouse,
The Wife took all the Rule upon her,
Just to preserve her Sex's Honour.
The Widow's Houses pass'd no Trial,
Their's was the Sway without Denial,

[8]Williamsburg in Virginia: the Court-House stands at the East End of the City, and the College at the West End. The Towns of Hampton, York, Williamsburgh and James-Town all lie between James-River and York-River. [Dawson's note.]

Whose Cases could admit no Proof,
Elsewhere th'Event was still the same,
The Man obey'd the ruling Dame.
And still those Tyrants were the proudest,
Who oft'nest bred, or scolded loudest. . . .
The Story says, that thus they travel'd
Till luckless *John* was sorely gravel'd
Of Hope and Patience quite bereft,
And only one poor Egg was left:
When Fortune weary of her Spleen
Contriv'd to shew a diff'rent Scene,
And prove that *Dick,* how e'er elate,
Was not above the reach of Fate:
For near that Spring which hands us down
King *Totapotomay*'s Renown,[9]
Arriving at a Planter's Door,
They ask'd, as they'd done oft before
Whose House was that? With surly Phiz,
The Planter answer'd, It was his:
But, Sir, says *Dick, Sans Complement,*[10]
Our Question otherwise was meant,
We want to know who rules the House,
Whether yourself, or else your Spouse?
Walk in, the Planter cry'd we'll try
Who's Master here, my Wife or I.
This Planter had a Hick'ry Stick,
Well-season'd, drubbing proof, and thick,
Oft and on many Causes try'd
To dress and tan his Dearest's Hide,
Whether she lay too long in Bed,
Or left uncomb'd her Daughter's Head;
Or if she fail'd to sweep the House,
Or night and morn to milk the Cows;
Sometimes, for thirst, his Limbs would fail,
And lo! no Gourd was in the Pail!
Sometimes his Beef was over broiled,
At other Times his Coleworts[11]spoil'd;
Or if she fail'd in her Allegiance,
The Hick'ry taught her due Obedience:
As you may see on Muster Days,
When *Nicholas*[12] does his Cudgel raise,

[9]Totapotomay was a chief of the Pamunkey tribe in the 1640's & 50's, who petitioned and received 5,000 acres from the Virginia government where some of his people lived for a time. Bodies of water important in Powhatan cosmology were often named for important people or events. [Ed Ragan]

[10]Without flattery (French).

[11]Any kind of green from the cabbage family.

[12]Late Adjutant-General. [Dawson's note.]

And when his looks the Soldier quails
Who awkward in his Duty fails:
Thus were this Pair in diff'rent Taking,
Imperious he, for Fear she quaking:
He order'd her to wipe his Shoes,
She lowly stoop'd, not durst refuse;
He sent her to the Spring, she went
Nor shew'd the smallest Discontent;
He gave her many Orders more
Which I for Brevity pass o'er,
Until he shew'd to *Dick*'s Disaster,
That he was Sov'reign, Lord, and Master.
Dick gave the Wager now for lost,
And *John* had kindly thank'd his Host
Bidding him choose among the Team
Which Horse the best for him should seem;
The Planter look'd on all around
And chose the Horse he likeliest found;
When as his Wife with angry Voice
Cry'd out, You've made a silly Choice:
Where are your Eyes: What, Can't you see?
You'd better far be rul'd by me.
And make your Choice of that Grey mare,
I'm sure you'll find no better there
The Planter straight the Grey Mare views,
And handles her as Jockeys use;
Adzooks cries he, you're in the Right,
This Grey is better than the White,
So I'll e'en take the Mare away—
Dick interrupting, bid him stay;
My case was desperate I own,
But now the Table's turned, I've won;
You see here, *John,* how Woman rules,
We Men have ever been their Tools:
The surly, and the complaisant,
The sly, the witty, and the gallant,
Spight of their Haughtiness or Funning,
Must yield, or to their Pow'r or Cunning.
Then to the Planter turning round,
I'm glad the Mare's the better found;
But 'tis not worth your While to fret, or
Fume, th' Grey Mare proves the better:
'Tis ev'ry honest Husband's Case,
And will be so, and always was:
My luck has prov'd me not mistaken,
And with this Egg—I've sav'd my Bacon.

1749

Jane Colman Turell 1708–1735

The daughter of Jane Clark and Benjamin Colman, the liberal minister of Boston's Brattle Street Church and president of Harvard College, Jane was a precocious child, lovingly instructed by her father. Ill health and her father's large library allowed her to read widely in divinity, history, and literature. To improve her writing skills, she began a regular correspondence and exchange of verses with her father and composed her first hymn before she was ten. In 1726, she married one of her father's theology students, Ebenezer Turell. She had four children, only one of whom survived her early death at age twenty-seven.

Although Jane Colman Turell was a prolific poet, correspondent, and diarist, the only works that survive are those her husband included in *Some Memoirs of the Life and Death of Mrs. Jane Turell.* He admitted, "I might add to these some Pieces of Wit and Humor, which if published would give a brighter Idea of her to some sort of Readers; but as her Heart was set on graver and better Subjects, and her Pen much oftener employ'd about them, so I chuse to omit them, tho' innocent enough." Turell's father noted that "she was sometimes fir'd with a laudable Ambition of raising the honour of her Sex, who are therefore under Obligations to her. . . ." Her best poetry was written before her marriage—that is, before she was eighteen. Despite masculine censorship, Turell represents a new generation of women who had a consciousness of gender and looked to women as poetic models and whose interests went beyond religious and natural subjects dictated by Puritan culture.

Psalm CXXXVII. Paraphras'd, August 5th, 1725. AETAT. 17.[1]

As on the margin of Euphrates'[2] flood
We wail'd our sins, and mourn'd an angry God:
For God provok'd, to strangers gave our land,
And by a righteous judge condemn'd we stand;
Deep were our groans, our griefs without compare,
With ardent cries, we rent the yielding air.
Born down with woes, no friend at hand was found,
No helper in the waste and barren ground;
Only a mournful willow wither'd there,
Its aged arms by winter storms made bare,
On this our lyres,[3] now useless grown, we hung,
Our lyres by us forsaken and unstrung!

[1]*Aetat:* literally "state" (Latin) but meaning here "age." All of the texts, with slight modification, are from *Women Poets in Pre-Revolutionary America 1650–1775: An Anthology,* ed. Pattie Cowell (Troy: Whitston Publishing Company, 1981).

[2]The river that runs through Babylon, site of the Jewish exile.

[3]Stringed instruments associated with the Greek poets.

We sigh'd in chains, and sunk beneath our woe,
Whilst more insulting our proud tyrants grow.
From hearts opprest with grief they did require
A sacred anthem on the sounding lyre:
Come, now, they cry, regale us with a song,
Music and mirth the fleeting hours prolong.
Shall Babel's daughter hear that blessed sound?
Shall songs divine be sung in heathen ground?
No. Heaven forbid that we should tune our voice,
Or touch the lyre! whilst slaves we can't rejoice.
O Palestina! our once dear abode,
Thou once wert blest with peace, and lov'd by God,
But now art desolate, a barren waste,
Thy fruitful fields by thorns and weeds defac'd.
If I forget Judea's mournful land,
May nothing prosper that I take in hand!
Or if I string the lyre, or tune my voice,
Till thy deliverance cause me to rejoice,
O may my tongue forget her art to move,
And may I never more my speech improve!
Return O Lord! avenge us of our foes,
Destroy the men that up against us rose
Let Eden's sons thy just displeasure know,
And like us serve some foreign conquering foe,
In distant realms, far from their native home,
To which dear seat O let them never come!
Thou Babel's daughter! Author of our woe,
Shalt feel the stroke of some revenging blow;
Thy walls and towers be level'd with the ground,
Sorrow and grief shall in each soul be found
Thrice blest the man, who that auspicious night
Shall seize thy trembling infants in thy sight;
Regardless of thy flowing tears and moans,
And dash the tender babes against the stones.

1725 1735

[Lines on Childbirth]

Phoebus[1] has thrice his yearly circuit run,
The winter's over, and the summer's done;

[1]Phoebus Apollo, god of sunlight in Greek mythology.

Since that bright day on which our hands were join'd,
And to Philander[2] I my all resign'd.

Thrice in my womb I've found the pleasing strife,
In the first struggles of my infant's life:
But O how soon by Heaven I'm call'd to mourn,
While from my womb a lifeless babe is torn?
Born to the grave ere it had seen the light,
Or with one smile had cheer'd my longing sight.

Again in travail pains my nerves are wreck'd,
My eye balls start, my heart strings almost crack'd;
Now I forget my pains, and now I press
Philander's image to my panting breast.
Ten days I hold him in my joyful arms,
And feast my eyes upon his infant charms.
But then the King of Terrors does advance
To pierce its bosom with his iron lance.
Its soul releas'd, upward it takes its flight,
Oh never more below to bless my sight!
Farewell sweet babes I hope to meet above,
And there with you sing the Redeemer's love.

And now O gracious Savior lend thine ear,
To this my earnest cry and humble prayer,
That when the hour arrives with painful throes,
Which shall my burden to the world disclose;
I may deliverance have, and joy to see
A living child, to dedicate to Thee.

1741

On Reading the Warning by Mrs. Singer[1]

Surpris'd I view, wrote by a female pen,
Such a grave warning to the sons of men.
Bold was the attempt and worthy of your lays,
To strike at vice, and sinking virtue raise.

[2]Pseudonym for Turell's husband, Ebenezer.

[1]Elizabeth Singer Rowe (1674–1737) was a popular English writer of hymns, pastorals, and scriptural paraphrases. She wrote several poems reproving sin, including "An Ode on Virtue," which uses historical examples and ends with two extremely virtuous women, Eulalia and Nicetas, who confront sinful men.

Each noble line a pleasing terror gives,
A secret force in every sentence lives.
Inspir'd by virtue you could safety stand
The fair reprover of a guilty land.
You vie with the fam'd prophetess[2] of old.
Burn with her fire, in the same cause grow bold.
Dauntless you undertake th' unequal strife,
And raise dead virtue by your verse to life.
A woman's pen strikes the curs'd serpent's head,
And lays the monster gasping, if not dead.

1725 1735

To My Muse, December 29, 1725

Come gentle muse, and once more lend thine aid,
O bring thy succor to a humble maid!
How often dost thou liberally dispense
To our dull breast thy quick'ning influence!
By thee inspir'd, I'll cheerful tune my voice,
And love and sacred friendship make my choice.
In my pleas'd bosom you can freely pour
A greater treasure than Jove's golden shower.[1]
Come now, fair muse, and fill my empty mind
With rich ideas, great and unconfin'd.
Instruct me in those secret arts that lie
Unseen to all but to a poet's eye.
O let me burn with Sappho's[2] noble fire,
But not like her for faithless man expire.
And let me rival great Orinda's[3] fame,

[2]"Huldah"; a powerful prophetess in Jerusalem who lived "in the college" in Jerusalem and foretold the punishment of the Jews for falling away from their faith. See 2 Kings 22:14ff. [Turell's note.]

[1]Jove or Jupiter, king of the Roman gods (Zeus in Greek mythology) came to Danaë in the form of a golden shower because she had been shut up in a brass tower by her father after the Delphic oracle predicted that he would die by Danaë's son.

[2]Sappho (b. 612 B.C.), native of the isle of Lesbos and a famous Greek lyric poet who headed a group of young girls dedicated to music and poetry. Married with a daughter, Sappho addressed much of her poetry to girls, but the legend that she flung herself into the sea after being rejected by the beautiful youth Phaon has been the subject of many works.

[3]Katherine Philips (1631–1664), English poet and leader of a literary salon in Cardigan, Wales, known as "The Matchless Orinda." Her collection, *Poems,* appeared in 1667.

Or like sweet Philomela's be my name.[4]
Go lead the way, my muse, nor must you stop,
'Till we have gain'd Parnassus' shady top.[5]
'Till I have view'd those fragrant soft retreats,
Those fields of bliss, the muses' sacred seats.
I'll then devote thee to fair virtue's fame,
And so be worthy of a poet's name.

1725 1741

Lucy Terry 1730–1821

Lucy Terry, taken from Africa as a slave, eventually settled in Vermont with her husband, Abijah Prince, a free black from Vermont who bought her freedom. Her only known extant poem, "Bars Fight," was handed down orally for nearly 100 years before being printed in Josiah Holland's *History of Western Massachusetts* in 1855.

Bars Fight[1]

August, 'twas the twenty-fifth,
Seventeen hundred forty-six;
The Indians did in ambush lay,
Some very valiant men to slay,
The names of whom I'll not leave out.
Samuel Allen like a hero fout,[2]
And though he was so brave and bold,
His face no more shall we behold.
Eleazer Hawks was killed outright,
Before he had time to fight,—
Before he did the Indians see,
Was shot and killed immediately.
Oliver Amsden he was slain,
Which caused his friends much grief and pain.
Simeon Amsden they found dead,
Not many rods distant from his head.

[4]Philomela, in Greek mythology, was raped by her brother-in-law, Tereus, who cut out her tongue to silence her. She put her story into a weaving and sent it to her sister, Procne, who took revenge on Tereus by feeding him their son. All three were turned into birds. *Philomela* ("lover of song" in Latin) became the nightingale, the archetypal female poet, and here stands for Elizabeth Singer Rowe.

[5]Mountain in Greece sacred to Apollo and the Muses and thus regarded as the seat of music and poetry.

[1]*Bars* is a colonial term for "meadow."

[2]Probably "fought."

Adonijah Gillett, we do hear,
Did lose his life which was so dear.
John Sadler fled across the water,
And thus escaped the dreadful slaughter.
Eunice Allen see the Indians coming,
And hopes to save herself by running,
And had not her petticoats stopped her,
The awful creatures had not catched her,
Nor tommy hawked her on her head,
And left her on the ground for dead.
Young Samuel Allen, Oh lackaday!
Was taken and carried to Canada.

1885

Thomas Godfrey 1736–1763

Son of Thomas Godfrey (1704–1749), a Philadelphia glazier and member of Benjamin Franklin's Junto Club, Godfrey produced some significant work in his short life. Well known in literary circles in Philadelphia, he was a close friend of the poet Nathaniel Evans and the college provost William Smith. In 1758, he left Philadelphia for Wilmington, North Carolina, to enter business. In 1762, he published the long poem *The Court of Fancy* and also published occasional pieces in local magazines. His most memorable work is a blank-verse play, *The Prince of Parthia, A Tragedy,* which appeared in a posthumous volume, *Juvenile Poems on Various Subjects,* that Evans published in 1765. The play, which echoes Shakespeare's political tragedies, was first staged in 1767. Critic Moses Coit Tyler remarked that "Thomas Godfrey is a true poet, and 'The Prince of Parthia' is a noble beginning of dramatic literature in America."

from The Prince of Parthia, A Tragedy[1]

from Act 1, scene 1

PHRAATES. What a bright hope is ours, when those dread pow'rs
Who rule yon heav'n, and guide the mov'ments here,
Shall call your royal Father to their joys:
In blest *Arsaces* ev'ry virtue meets;

[1]The selections are from *The Prince of Parthia, A Tragedy,* ed. Archibald Henderson (Boston: Little, Brown, 1917). The sons of King Artabanus of Parthia, in order of age, are Arsaces, Verdanes, and Gotarzes. The play details Verdanes's attempts to seize the throne from his brother. Phraates is an officer at the royal court.

He's gen'rous, brave, and wise, and good,
Has skill to act, and noble fortitude
To face bold danger, in the battle firm,
And dauntless as a Lion fronts his foe.
Yet is he sway'd by ev'ry tender passion,
Forgiving mercy, gentleness and love;
Which speak the Hero friend of humankind.

GOTARZES. And let me speak, for 'tis to him I owe
That here I stand, and breathe the common air,
And 'tis my pride to tell it to the world.
One luckless day as in the eager chace
My Courser[2] wildly bore me from the rest,
A monst'rous leopard from a bosky fen
Rush'd forth, and foaming lash'd the ground,
And fiercely ey'd me as his destin'd quarry.
My jav'lin swift I threw, but o'er his head
It erring pass'd, and harmless in the air
Spent all its force; my falchin[3] then I seiz'd,
Advancing to attack my ireful foe,
When furiously the savage sprung upon me,
And tore me to the ground; my treach'rous blade
Above my hand snap'd short, and left me quite
Defenceless to his rage; *Arsaces* then,
Hearing the din, flew like some pitying pow'r,
And quickly freed me from the Monster's paws,
Drenching his bright lance in his spotted breast.

PHRAATES. How different he from arrogant *Vardanes?*
That haughty Prince eyes with a stern contempt
All other Mortals, and with lofty mien
He treads the earth as tho' he were a God.
Nay, I believe that his ambitious soul,
Had it but pow'r to its licentious wishes,
Would dare dispute with Jove the rule of heav'n;
Like a Titanian son with giant insolence,
Match with the Gods, and wage immortal war,
'Til their red wrath should hurl him headlong down,
E'en to destruction's lowest pit of horror.

. . . .

GOTARZES. And yet *Vardanes* owes that hated Brother
As much as I; 'twas summer last, as we
Were bathing in *Euphrates'* flood, *Vardanes*
Proud of strength would seek the further shore;
But 'ere he the mid-stream gain'd, a poignant pain

[2]Horse.

[3]Short sword.

Shot thro' his well-strung nerves, contracting all,
And the stiff joints refus'd their wonted aid.
Loudly he cry'd for help, *Arsaces* heard,
And thro' the swelling waves he rushed to save
His drowning Brother, and gave him life,
And for the boon the Ingrate pays him hate.
. . . . Ingratitude,
Thou hell-born fiend, how horrid is thy form!
The Gods sure let thee loose to scourge mankind,
And save them from an endless waste of thunder.

1765

Annis Boudinot Stockton 1736–1801

Annis Boudinot Stockton, prolific and well-known New Jersey poet, circulated her verse mainly among friends and other women poets. She was well known to the cultural elite of her day, and she wrote several poems to her friend George Washington, among other statesmen. From childhood, Stockton was a close friend of Elizabeth Graeme Fergusson, and, like Fergusson, she held literary salons for an elite Princeton circle. Publications of her pastoral and sentimental verse appeared under her pseudonym, "Amelia" (or Emelia), while other publications, twenty-one in number, appeared under her initials, "A. S.," or anonymously.

To Laura[1]

Permit a sister muse to soar
To heights she never tried before,
And then look up to thee;

For sure each female virtue join'd,
Conspire to make thy lovely mind
The seat of harmony.

Thy fame has reach'd the calm retreat,
Where I secluded from the great,
Have leisure for my lays;

It rais'd ambition in my breast,
Not such as envious souls possess,
Who hate another's praise.

[1]*Laura* is the pen-name of Elizabeth Graeme Fergusson (1737–1801), the friend to whom Stockton sent this verse epistle.

But that which makes me strive to gain,
And ever grateful to retain,
Thy friendship as a prize;

For friendship soars above low rules,
The formal fetters of the schools
She wisely can despise;

So may fair Laura kindly condescend,
And to her bosom take another friend.

1757

Epistle, To Lucius[1]

When lions in the deserts quit their prey
And tuneful birds forsake the leafy spray
When fish for land shall leave the watery main
And rivers to their fountains flow again
When spring shall cease the flow'ry bud to shoot
And autumn mild refuse the blushing fruit
Then and then only could my heart refrain
To vent to thee its pleasure and its pain
But even then thou dearest of thy kind
Thy lov'd Idea would engross my mind
Oh Could my anxious heart but once believe
What my vain thought would tempt me to receive
When thy sweet voice with fascinating grace
Almost persuades me I have power to please
But ah so conscious of my own demerit
In contemplating thee I lose my spirit
When I the treasures of thy mind survey
Like Sheba's queen[2] I shrink and dye away.
But if the powers of genius ever heard
A votaries prayer and e'er that prayer prefer'd
On me may wit and elegance bestow
Some emanation bright some softer glow

[1]Lucius is Stockton's pseudonym for her husband Richard.

[2]According to the biblical story, when she heard reports of the immensity of Solomon's wisdom, the Queen of Sheba traveled to see him and test him. She tested his wits with energy, said his wisdom exceeded the reports she had heard, and bestowed him with gifts before sailing away.

Some sweet atractive that thy heart may twine
(Stronger than beauty) with each nerve of mine
For oh I find on earth no charms for me
But whats Connected with the thought of thee.

1766

A Poetical Epistle, Addressed by a Lady of New Jersey, to Her Niece, upon Her Marriage[1]

Well! my lov'd Niece, I hear the bustle's o'er,
The wedding cake and visits are no more;
The gay ones buzzing round some other bride,
'While you with grave ones grace the fire's side.
Now with your usual sweetness deign to hear,
What from a heart most friendly flows sincere:
Nor do I fear a supercilious Smile—
To pay with gay contempt the muse's toil.
For be assur'd, I never will presume,
Superior sense or judgment to assume;
But barely that which long experience brings,
To men and women, those capricious things,
Nor do I once forget how very sage
Th'advice of Aunts has been in ev'ry age:
On matrimonial themes they all debate—
Wiseacres too who never try'd the state.
And 'twould, I own, appear as truly vain
For me, but to suppose I could attain
New light, upon a subject worn out quite;
And which both Aunts and Authors deem so trite.
But all the nuptial virtues in the class
Of spirit meek, and prudence, I shall pass;
Good nature—sense—of these you've ample store,
And Oeconomicks you have learnt before.
But there are lurking evils that do prove
Under the name of trifles—death to love.—
And from these trifles, all the jarring springs,
And trust me, child, they're formidable things.
First then—with rev'rence treat in ev'ry place,

[1]This poem, written in 1784, probably for Susan Boudinot Bradford, was published in *The Columbian Magazine,* November 1786.

The chosen patron of your future days;
For when you shew him but the least neglect,
Yourself you rifle of your due respect.—
But never let your fondness for him rise,
In words or actions to the prying eyes
Of witnesses—who claim a right to sneer
At all the honey'd words, "My life,—my love,—my dear."
    Nor from your husband should you e'er require
Those epithets, which little minds admire—
Such short restraints will constantly maintain
That pow'r which fondness strives to reach in vain.
And give new joy to the returning hour,
When sweet retirement bars the op'ning door.
Nor do nor say, before the man you love,—
What in its nature must offensive prove;
However closely drawn the mystic ties,
Yet men have always microscopic eyes;
And easily advert to former time,
When nice reserve made females all divine.
"Would she to Damon or Alexis say,
"A thing so rude? and am I less than they?"
    Whene'er your husband means to stay at home,
Whate'er th'occasion—dont consent to roam;
For home's a solitary place to one
Who loves his wife, and finds her always gone.
At least consult the temper of his mind,
If vex'd abroad, he finds himself inclin'd
From public business to relax awhile;
How pleasing then the solace of a smile—
A soft companion to relieve his care,
His joy to heighten—or his grief to share?
    Unbend his thoughts and from the world retire,
Within his sacred home and round his chearful fire;
Nor let him know you've made a sacrifice,
He'll find it out himself: And then he'll prize
Your kind endeavours to promote his ease,
And make the study of your life to please.
    Another rule you'll find of equal weight,
When jars subside, never recriminate;
And when the cloud is breaking from his brow,
Repeat not *what* he said—nor *when* nor *how*.
If he's tenacious, gently give him way—
And tho' 'tis night, if he should say, 'tis day—
Dispute it not—but pass it with a smile;
He'll recollect himself—and pay your toil—
And shew he views it in a proper light;
And no Confusion seek—to do you right:
Just in his humour meet him—no debate,

And let it be your pleasure to forget.
His friends with kindness always entertain,
And tho' by chance he brings them, ne'er complain;
Whate'er's provided for himself and you,
With neatness serv'd, will surely please them too.
Nor e'er restrict him, when he would invite
His friends in form, to spend a day or night:
Some ladies think the trouble is so great,
That all such motions cause a high debate;
And madam pouts and says, I would not mind
How much to company you were inclin'd,
If I had things to entertain genteel;
And could but make my table look as well
As Mrs. A. and Mrs. B. can do;
I'd be as fond of company as you.—
And oft a richer service bribes the feast,
Than suits his purse, and makes himself a jest:
And tho' the good man gains his point at last,
It damps convivial mirth, and poisons the repast.
But you, my dear—if you would wish to shine,
Must always say, *your* friends are also *mine:*
The house is your's, and I will do the best,
To give a chearful welcome to each guest.
Nor are those maxims difficult to cope
When stimulated by so fair a hope,
To reach the summit of domestic bliss;
And crown each day with ever smiling peace.
Now if these lines one caution should contain,
To gain that end, my labour's not in vain;
And be assur'd, my dear, while life endures
With every tender sentiment, I'm your's.

1786

The Vision, an Ode to Washington[1]

'TWAS in a beauteous verdant shade,
Deck'd by the genius of the glade,
With Nature's fragrant stores;
Where Fairy Elves light trip'd the green—

[1]When this poem was published in the *Gazette of the United States,* May 16, 1789, it appeared under this heading: "The following ode was written and inscribed to General Washington, a short time after the surrender of York-Town."

Where Silvan Nymphs were often seen
To strew the sweetest flowers.

Lethean air from tempes vale,
Wafted an aromatic gale,
And lull'd my soul to rest:
I saw, or musing seem'd to see,
The future years of Destiny
That brighten'd all the West.

The Muse array'd in heavenly grace,
Call'd up each actor in his place
Before my wondering eyes,
The magic of the Aonian Maid
The world of Vision wide display'd,
And bid the scenes arise.

I saw great FABIUS[2] come in state,
I saw the British Lion's fate,
The Unicorns dispair;
Conven'd in Secrecy's Divan,
The Chiefs contriv'd the fav'rite plan,
And *York-Town* clos'd the war.

Nor could the dazzling triumph charm
The friends of faction, or its rage disarm—
Fierce to divide, to weaken and subvert:
I saw the Imps of Discord rise—
Intrigue, with little arts, surprise,
*Delude—alarm—*and then the State desert.

My soul grew sick of human things—
I took my Harp, and touch'd the strings,
Full often set to woe;
Conjur'd the gentle Muse to take
The power of future knowledge back—
No more I wish'd to know.

Rash Mortal stop! She cried with zeal,
One secret more I must reveal,
That will renew your prime:
These storms will work the wish'd for cure,
And put the *State* in health so pure,
As to resist old *Time.*

[2]Fabius is Stockton's pseudonym for General Washington.

The free born mind will feel the force,
That Justice is the only source
Of Laws concise and clear;
Their native rights, they will resign
To *Men,* who can those rights define,
And every burthen bear.

The SACRED COMPACT, in a band
Of brothers, shall unite the land,
And Envy's self be dead;
The Body one, and one the soul,
Virtue shall animate the whole,
And FABIUS be the head.

Rous'd from the enthusiastic dream,
By the soft murmur of a stream,
That glided thro' the meads,
I tun'd my lyre to themes refin'd,
While Nature's gentle voices join'd,
To sing the glorious deeds.

When lo! HIMSELF, the CHIEF rever'd,
In native elegance appear'd,
And all things smil'd around
Adorn'd with every pleasing art,
Enthron'd the Sov'reign of each heart,
I saw the HERO crown'd.

1789

Elizabeth Graeme Fergusson 1737–1801

Philadelphian Elizabeth Graeme Fergusson was among the best-known of the middle-colony poets of the eighteenth century, despite the fact that a collected edition of her poems has yet to be published. Her celebrity came from the variety and interest of her poetry and from her prolific and lively correspondence with such notable contemporaries as Benjamin Rush, William Smith, Annis Stockton, and Elias Boudinot. It comes as well from her reputation as a leading salon hostess during the years prior to the Revolution.

Originally engaged to Benjamin Franklin's son, William, Fergusson eventually married Henry Hugh Fergusson in 1772. When her husband remained loyal to the British during the Revolution, Fergusson nearly lost her family estate, Graeme Park, to confiscation. Richard Stockton, Benjamin Rush, Francis Hopkinson, and other prominent leaders intervened on her behalf to secure the property, but Fergusson lived the remainder of her life separated from her husband and in financial difficulty.

Upon the Discovery of the Planet By Mr. Herschel of Bath and By Him Nam'd the Georgium Sidus in Honor of his Britannic Majesty[1]

Whether the optics piercng eyes
Have introduc'd to view,
A distant planet of the skies,
Bright, wonderful, and new?

Or whether we are nearer thrown[2]
To the grand fount of light,
And from that source each mist is flown
That wrapt the star in night?

Too deep this point, a female pen
Dare not such heights explore;
The subject's left to learned men,
Of philosophic lore!

A star is found, that's clear, and hail'd
With Britain's monarch's name:
If terrestrial glory's fail'd,
The Heavens enroll his fame.

c. 1781

On a Beautiful Damask Rose, Emblematical of Love and Wedlock[1]

Queen of the garden! O how oft
Thy praises have been sung!
In numbers eloquent and soft,
To please the fair and young.

O! sure thou wast the first form'd flow'r
Which hail'd young Eden's grove,

[1]Sir William Herschel (1738–1822), noted astronomer who discovered the planet Uranus in 1781 and named it in honor of George III.

[2]This line has an immediate allusion to the shocks that this globe has sustain'd by the late dreadful earthquakes in many parts of the world as it is reported the very poles of the earth are mov'd. [Fergusson's note.]

[1]This poem was published in the *Columbian Magazine,* 3 (May 1789), 312.

The darling of the nuptial bow'r,
And emblem fit for love.

A transient, rich, and balmy sweet
Is in thy fragrance found;
But soon the flow'r and scent retreat—
Thorns left alone to wound.

1789

On the Mind's Being Engrossed by One Subject[1]

When one fond object occupies the mind,
In nature's scenes we still that object find;
And trees, and meads, and sweetly purling rill,
By us made mirrors with ingenious skill,
Reflect the constant subject of our thought;
We view that image in their substance wrought.
The common peasant treads the fresh turn'd soil,
And hopes of future crops his steps beguiles.
The nat'ralist observes each simple's use,
Where lodg'd the healthy, where the baneful juice.
The lover sees his mistress all around
And her sweet voice in vocal birds is found;
He views the brilliant glories of the skies,
But to remind him of her sparkling eyes.
Th' alchemist still anxious seeks the gold,
For this he pierces every cavern's fold:
Trembling to try the magic hazel's pow'r,
Which points attractive to the darling show'r.
While pious Hervey[2] in each plant and tree
Can nought but God and his redeemer see.
When zephyrs[3] play, or when fierce Boreas roars,[4]
The merchant only for his bark[5] implores.
The beau and belle attentive dread the sky,
Lest angry clouds the sprightly scene deny.
But if a coach's procur'd, torrents may pour,
And winds, and tempests, shattered fleets devour.

[1]This poem was published in the *Columbian Magazine,* 3 (July 1789), 437–38.

[2]James Hervey (1714–1758), a devotional writer whose collected works appeared in six volumes in 1769.

[3]Gentle west winds.

[4]Boreas was the Greek god of north wind.

[5]Small boat.

Thus over all, self-love presides supreme,
It cheers the morn, and gives the ev'ning dream.
Though oft we change through life's swift gliding stage,
And seek fresh objects at each varying age,
Here we are constant, faithful to one cause,
Our own indulgence as a center draws.
That faithful inmate makes our breast its home,
From the soft cradle, to the silent tomb.

1789

Nathaniel Evans 1742–1767

Evans was born in Philadelphia to a merchant who wished his son to follow in his footsteps. Yet Evans followed the encouragement of Provost William Smith at the College of Philadelphia instead. After completing an M.A. at the College, Evans traveled to London and was ordained a minister in the Church of England. He took a post as a missionary for the Church, with the Society for the Propagation of the Bible in Foreign Parts, situated in Haddonfield, New Jersey, across the Delaware River from Philadelphia. Although he himself lamented the early death of his friend, Thomas Godfrey, Evans died of tuberculosis at age twenty-five; William Smith gathered his poems and published them, titled *Poems on Several Occasions* (1772).

Hymn to May

Now had the beam of Titan gay[1]
Usher'd in the blissful May,
Scattering from his pearly bed,
Fresh dew on every mountain's head;
Nature mild and debonair,
To thee, fair maid, yields up her care.
May, with gentle plastic hand,
Clothes in flowery robe the land;
O'er the vales the cowslips spreads,
And eglantine beneath the shades;
Violets blue befringe each fountain,
Woodbines lace each steepy mountain;
Hyacinths their sweets diffuse,
And the rose its blush renews;

[1]Apollo, god of the sun, later in the poem called "Sol."

With the rest of Flora's train,
Decking lowly dale or plain.

Through creation's range, sweet May!
Nature's children own thy sway—
Whether in the crystal flood,
Amorous, sport the finny brood;
Or the feather'd tribes declare,
That they breathe thy genial air,
While they warble in each grove
Sweetest notes of artless love;
Or their wound the beasts proclaim,
Smitten with a fiercer flame;
Or the passions higher rise,
Sparing none beneath the skies,
But swaying soft the human mind
With feelings of ecstatic kind—
Through wide creation's range, sweet May!
All Nature's children own thy sway.

Oft will I, (e'er Phosphor's light
Quits the glimmering skirts of night)
Meet thee in the clover field,
Where thy beauties thou shalt yield
To my fancy, quick and warm,
Listening to the dawn's alarm,
Sounded loud by Chanticleer,
In peals that sharply pierce the ear.
And, as Sol his flaming car
Urges up the vaulted air,
Shunning quick the scorching ray,
I will to some covert stray,
Coolly bowers or latent dells,
Where light-footed silence dwells,
And whispers to my heaven-born dream,
Fair Schuylkill, by thy winding stream![2]
There I'll devote full many an hour,
To the still-finger'd Morphean power,
And entertain my thirsty soul
With draughts from Fancy's fairy bowl;
Or mount her orb of varied hue,
And scenes of heaven and earth review.
Nor in milder Eve's decline,
As the sun forgets to shine,

[2]The Schuylkill River winds through the city of Philadelphia.

And sloping down the ethereal plain,
Plunges in the western main,
Will I forbear due strain to pay
To the song-inspiring May;
But as Hesper[3] 'gins to move
Round the radiant court of Jove,
(Leading through the azure sky
All the starry progeny,
Emitting prone their silver light,
To re-illume the shades of night)
Then, the dewy lawn along,
I'll carol forth my grateful song,
Viewing with transported eye
The blazing orbs that roll on high,
Beaming luster, bright and clear,
O'er the glowing hemisphere.
Thus from the early blushing morn,
Till the dappled eve's return,
Will I, in free unlabor'd lay,
Sweetly sing the charming May!

1772

Ode to the Memory of Mr. Thomas Godfrey

O Death! thou victor of the human frame!
The soul's poor fabric trembles at thy name!
How long shall man be urged to dread thy sway,
For those whom thou untimely tak'st away?
Life's blooming spring just opens to our eyes,
And strikes the senses with a sweet surprise,
When thy fierce arm uplifts the fatal blow
That hurls us breathless to the earth below.

* * *

Sudden, as darts the lightning through the sky,
Around the globe thy various weapons fly.
Here war's red engines heap the field with slain,
And pallid sickness there extends thy reign;
Here the soft virgin weeps her lover dead,
There maiden beauty sinks the graceful head;

[3]Hesperus, the planet Venus, as the evening star.

Here infants grieve their parents are no more,
There reverend sires their children's deaths deplore;
Here the sad friend—O! save the sacred name,
Yields half his soul to thy relentless claim;
O pardon, pardon the descending tear!
Friendship commands, and not the muses, here.
O say, thou much loved dear departed shade,
To what celestial region hast thou stray'd?
Where is that vein of thought, that noble fire
Which fed thy soul, and bade the world admire?
That manly strife with fortune to be just,
That love of praise? an honorable thirst!
The Soul, alas! has fled to endless day,
And left its house a mouldering mass of clay.

There, where no fears invade, nor ills molest,
Thy soul shall dwell immortal with the blest;
In that bright realm, where dearest friends no more
Shall from each other's throbbing breasts be tore,
Where all those glorious spirits sit enshrined,
The just, the good, the virtuous of mankind.
There shall fair angels in a radiant ring,
And the great Son of heaven's eternal King,
Proclaim thee welcome to the blissful skies,
And wipe the tears forever from thine eyes.

How did we hope—alas! the hope how vain!
To hear thy future more enripen'd strain;
When fancy's fire with judgment had combined
To guide each effort of the enraptured mind.
Yet are those youthful glowing lays of thine
The emanations of a soul divine;
Who heard thee sing, but felt sweet music's dart
In thrilling transports pierce his captiv'd heart?
Whether soft melting airs attuned thy song,
Or pleased to pour the thundering verse along,
Still nobly great, true offspring of the Nine,
Alas! how blasted in thy glorious prime!
So when first ope the eyelids of the morn,
A radiant purple does the heavens adorn,
Fresh smiling glory streaks the skies around,
And gaily silvers each enamel'd mound,
Till some black storm o'erclouds the ether fair,
And all its beauties vanish into air.

Stranger, whoe'er thou art, by fortune's hand
Toss'd on the baleful Carolinian strand,

Oh! if thou seest perchance the Poet's grave,
The sacred spot with tears of sorrow lave;
Oh! shade it, shade it with ne'er fading bays.
Hallow'd's the place where gentle Godfrey lays.
(So may no sudden dart from death's dread bow,
Far from the friends thou lov'st, e'er lay thee low,)
There may the weeping morn its tribute bring,
And angels shield it with their golden wing,
Till the last trump shall burst the womb of night,
And the purged atoms to their soul unite!

1765

To Benjamin Franklin, Occasioned by Hearing Him Play on the Harmonica[1]

In grateful wonder lost, long had we view'd
Each gen'rous act thy patriot-soul pursu'd;
Our Little State resounds thy just applause,
And, pleas'd, from thee new fame and honour draws:
In thee those various virtues are combin'd,
That form the true pre-eminence of mind.

What wonder struck us when we did survey
The lambent lightnings innocently play,
And down thy rods[2] beheld the dreaded fire
In a swift flame descend—and then expire;
While the red thunders, roaring loud around,
Burst the black clouds, and harmless smite the ground.

Blest use of art! apply'd to serve mankind,
The noble province of the sapient mind!
For this the soul's best faculties were giv'n,
To trace great nature's laws from earth to heav'n!

* * *

Yet not these themes alone thy thoughts command,
Each softer *Science* owns thy fostering hand;
Aided by thee, Urania's[3] heav'nly art,

[1] Instrument invented by Franklin consisting of round glasses of graduated sizes played by the finger.

[2] Alluding to his noble discovery of the use of Pointed Rods of metal for saving houses from damage by lightning [Evans's note].

[3] Urania was the muse of astronomy.

With finer raptures charms the feeling heart;
Th' *Harmonica* shall join the sacred choir,
Fresh transports kindle, and new joys inspire—

Hark! the soft warblings, sounding smooth and clear,
Strike with celestial ravishment the ear,
Conveying inward, as they sweetly roll,
A tide of melting music to the soul;
And sure if aught of mortal-moving strain,
Can touch with joy the high angelic train,
'Tis this enchanting instrument of thine,
Which speaks in accents more than half divine!

1772

Anna Young Smith 1756–1780

Anna Young Smith, a Philadelphia poet, was encouraged in her poetic endeavors by her aunt, poet Elizabeth Fergusson. Smith wrote frequently on politics and feminism as well as on the more conventional subjects of courtship, sensibility, and grief. Several poems were published posthumously under her pseudonym, "Sylvia."

On Reading Swift's Works[1]

Ungenerous bard, whom not e'en Stella's charms
Thy vengeful satire of its sting disarms!
Say when thou dipp'st thy keenest pen in gall,
Why must it still on helpless woman fall?
Why must our "dirt and dullness" fill each line,
Our love of "follies, our desire to shine?"
Why are we drawn as a whole race of fools,
Unsway'd alike by sense or virtue's rules?
Oh! had thy heart with generous candor glowed,
Hadst thou alone on vice thy lash bestow'd,
Had there fair Purity her form imprest,
And had the milder virtues fill'd thy breast;
Thy sprightly page had been by all approv'd,
And what we now admire, we then had loved.
But thy harsh satire, rude, severe, unjust,
Awakes too oft our anger or disgust.
Such are the scenes which still thy pen engage,

[1]First published in the *Universal Asylum and Columbian Magazine,* 5 Sept. 1790: 185. Jonathan Swift (1667–1745) was an Anglo-Irish satirist, author of *Journal to Stella, Gulliver's Travels,* and the biting satire *A Modest Proposal.*

That modesty disdains the shameless page.
'Tis true, we own thy wit almost divine,
And view the diamond 'midst the dunghill shine
Oh, had it sparkled on the breast of youth,
To charm the sage, and to instruct with truth,
To chase the gloom of ignorance away,
And teach mankind with wisdom to be gay;
Thy perfect style, thy wit serenely bright,
Would shed through distant climes their pleasing light;
Mankind would grateful to thy muse attend,
And after ages hail thee as their friend!
But now, so oft filth chokes thy sprightly fire,
We loathe one instant, and the next admire—
Even while we laugh, we mourn thy wit's abuse,
And while we praise thy talents, scorn their use.

Sylvia

1774

An Elegy to the Memory of the American Volunteers, who Fell in the Engagement Between the Massachusetts-Bay Militia, and the British Troops. April 19, 1775.

Let joy be dumb, let mirth's gay carol cease,
See plaintive sorrow comes bedew'd with tears;
With mournful steps retires the cherub peace,
And horrid war with all his train appears.

He comes, and crimson slaughter marks his way,
Stern famine follows in his vengeful tread;
Before him pleasure, hope, and love decay,
And meek-eye'd mercy hangs the drooping head.

Fled like a dream are those delightful hours,
When here with innocence and peace we rov'd
Secure and happy in our native bowers,
Blest in the presence of the youths we lov'd.

The blow is struck, which through each future age
Shall call from pity's eye the frequent tear;
Which gives the brother to the brother's rage,
And dyes with British blood, the British spear.

Where e'er the barb'rous story shall be told,
The British cheek shall glow with conscious shame;
This deed in bloody characters enroll'd,
Shall stain the luster of their former name.

But you, ye brave defenders of our cause,
The first in this dire contest call'd to bleed,
Your names hereafter crown'd with just applause,
Each manly breast with joy-mixt woe shall read;

Your memories, dear to every free-born mind,
Shall need no monument your fame to raise,
Forever in our grateful hearts enshrin'd,
And blest by your united country's praise.

But O permit the muse with grief sincere,
The widow's heart-felt anguish to bemoan,
To join the sisters, and the orphans tear,
Whom this sad day from all they lov'd has torn:

Blest be this humble strain if it imparts
The dawn of peace to but one pensive breast,
If it can hush one sigh that rends your hearts,
Or lull your sorrows to a short liv'd rest.

But vain the hope, too well this bosom knows
How faint is glory's voice to nature's calls:
How weak the balm the laurel wreath bestows,
To heal our breasts, when love or friendship falls.

Yet think, they in their country's cause expir'd,
While guardian angels watch'd their parting sighs,
Their dying breasts with constancy inspir'd,
And bade them welcome to their native skies.

Our future fate is wrapt in darkest gloom
And threat'ning clouds, from which their souls are freed;
Ere the big tempest burst they press the tomb,
Not doom'd to see their much-lov'd country bleed.

O let such thoughts as these assuage your grief,
And stop the tear of sorrow as it flows,
Till Time's all powerful hand shall yield relief,
And shed a kind oblivion o'er your woes.

But oh thou Being infinitely just,
Whose boundless eye with mercy looks on all,

On thee alone thy humbled people trust,
On thee alone for their deliverance call.

Long did thy hand unnumber'd blessings shower,
And crown our land with liberty and peace;
Extend, O lord, again thy saving power,
And bid the horrors of invasion cease.

But if thy awful wisdom has decreed
That we severer evils yet shall know,
By thy Almighty justice doom'd to bleed,
And deeper drink the bitter draughts of woe,

O grant us, Heaven, that constancy of mind
Which over adverse fortune rises still,
Unshaken faith, calm fortitude resign'd,
And full submission to thy holy will.

To Thee, Eternal Parent, we resign
Our bleeding cause and on thy wisdom rest;
With grateful hearts we bless thy power divine,
And own resign'd "Whatever is, is best."

May 2, 1775 1981

Sarah Wentworth Apthorp Morton 1759–1846

Born into Boston "aristocracy," the daughter of two affluent merchant families, Sarah Apthorp had an unusually extensive education and began writing poetry at an early age. In 1781, she married Perez Morton, a young Boston lawyer and noted patriot, and moved into the Apthorp mansion on State Street, where the couple lived until moving to Dorchester in 1791. The Mortons' home became a gathering place for Boston literati, who encouraged Sarah Morton's literary efforts. Until 1788, she circulated her work among friends, thereafter publishing in magazines under the pen name Philenia Constantia. In 1790, she brought out a book-length poem, *Ouâbi: or the Virtues of Nature. An Indian Tale in Four Cantos,* a tale of interracial romance on the Illinois frontier that used native materials in an epic form.

As Morton's literary career flourished, her personal life deteriorated. In 1788, an affair between her husband and her sister Frances, who had borne him a child, became public, and family censure drove Frances to commit suicide. Novelist William Hill Brown used the scandal as the basis for his novel *The Power of Sympathy* (1789). Reconciled with her husband, Morton soon lost a son who lived only a few hours; two of her other five children died prematurely. The only other book Morton published was a collection of poems and "fragments" entitled *My Mind and Its Thoughts* (1823). Dominated by themes of sorrow, betrayal, and resignation, this volume also contains an essay denouncing Mary Wollstonecraft's "pernicious precepts, and still more pernicious practice," although Morton also recognized the necessity that women submit to what she called "the dictatorship of men." She took a firm stand against slavery; her poem "The African Chief" was widely reprinted in the nineteenth century.

PRIMARY WORKS

Ouâbi: on the Virtues of Nature, An Indian Tale, 1790; *My Mind and Its Thoughts,* 1823.

from Ouâbi: or the Virtues of Nature, An Indian Tale. In Four Cantos. By PHILENIA, a Lady of Boston.[1]

Canto I

'Tis not the court, in dazzling splendor gay,
Where soft luxuriance spreads her silken arms,
Where garish fancy leads the soul astray,
And languid nature mourns her slighted charms;

'Tis not the golden hill, nor flowr'y dale,
Which lends my simple muse her artless theme;
But the black forest and uncultur'd vale,
The savage warrior, and the lonely stream.

Where MISSISSIPPI[2] rolls his *parent flood,*
With slope impetuous to the surgy main,
The desert's painted chiefs explore the wood,
Or with the thund'ring war-whoop[3] shake the plain.

There the fierce sachems raise the battle's din,
Or in the stream their active bodies lave,
Or midst the flames their fearless songs begin[4]—
PAIN HAS NO TERRORS TO THE TRULY BRAVE.

[1]Morton cited several sources, such as William Penn and Thomas Jefferson; the story is based on "*Azâkia:* A Canadian Story," from *American Museum* 6 (1789). The notes are Morton's unless otherwise indicated.

[2]*Mississippi,* an Indian name, signifying the great father of rivers. It is subject to no tides, but from its source in the north of the American Continent flows with rapid force, till it empties itself into the Gulph of Mexico.

[3]*War-whoop,* the cry of battle, with which they always make their onset.

[4]The American Indians, after exhausting every species of cruelty and torture upon their most distinguished pensioners, burn them by a distant fire; who expire singing songs of glory and defiance.

There young CELARIO, Europe's fairest boast,
In hopeless exile mourn'd the tedious day;
Now wand'ring slowly o'er the oozy coast,
Now thro the wild woods urg'd his anxious way.

Where the low stooping branch excludes the light,
A piercing shriek assail'd his wounded ear;
Swift as the winged arrow speeds its flight,
He seeks the piteous harbinger of fear.

There a tall Huron rais'd his threat'ning arm,
While round his knees a beauteous captive clung,
Striving to move him with her matchless form,
Or charm him by the magic of her tongue.

Soon as Celario viewed the murd'rous scene,
Quick from his vest the deathful tube he drew;
Its leaden vengeance thunder'd o'er the green,
While from the savage hand the ling'ring hatchet flew.

Low at his feat the breathless warrior lies;
Still the soft captive sickens with alarms,
Calls on OUABI's name with streaming eyes,
While the young victor lives upon her charms.

Her limbs were straighter than the mountain pine,
Her hair far blacker than the raven's wing;
Beauty had lent her form the waving[5] line,
Her breath gave fragrance to the balmy spring.

Each bright perfection open'd on her face,
Her flowing garment wanton'd in the breeze,
Her slender feet the glitt'ring sandals[6] grace,
Her look was dignity, her movement ease.

With spendid beads her braided tresses shone,
Her bending waist a modest girdle bound,
Her pearly teeth outvi'd the cygnet's down—
She spoke—and music follow'd in the sound.

[5]See Hogarth's Line of Beauty. [William Hogarth (1697–1764), English painter, engraver, and satirist. Ed.]

[6]The sandals are ornamented either with little glistening bells, or with a great variety of shining beads and feathers.

SHE.

Great ruler of the winged hour,[7]
AXÂKIA trembles at thy pow'r;
While from thy hand the thunders roll,
Thy charms with lightnings pierce the soul;
Ah! how unlike our sable race,
The snowy lustre of thy face!
That hair of beaming Cynthia's[8] hue,
Those shining eyes of heav'nly blue!
Ah! didst thou leave thy blissful land,
To save me from the murd'rer's hand?

And is Ouâbi still thy care,
The dauntless chief, unknown to fear?

HE.

Cease to call Ouâbi's name,
Give Celario all his claim.
No divinity is here: Spare thy praises, quit thy fear:
Bend no more that beauteous knee,
For I am a slave to thee:
Let my griefs thy pity move,
Heal them with the balm of love.
Far beyond the orient main,
By my rage a youth was slain;
He this daring arm defied,
By this arm the ruffian died:
Exil'd from my native home,
Thro the desert wild I roam;
But if only blest by thee,
All the desert smiles on me.

SHE.

See a graceful form arise![9]
Now it fills my ravish'd eyes,
Brighter than the morning star,
'Tis Ouâbi, fam'd in war:
Close before my bosom spread,
O'er thy preference casts a shade,
Full on him these eyes recline,

[7]It is presumed that Azâkia had never before seen a European, or heard the report of a pistol, as she considers one a deity, and the other his thunder.

[8]Roman goddess of the moon. [Ed.]

[9]The Indian women of America are very chaste after marriage, and if any person makes love to them, they answer, *The Friend that is before my eyes, prevents my seeing you.*

And his person shuts out thine.
Let us to his home retire,
Where he lights the social fire;
Do not thro the desert roam,
Find with me his gentrous home;
There the Illinois obey Great Ouâbi's chosen sway.

1790

Stanzas to a Husband Recently United

In vain upon that hand reclined,
I call each plighted worth my own,
Or rising to thy sovereign mind
Say that it reigns for me alone.

Since, subject to its ardent sway,
How many hearts were left to weep,
To find the granted wish decay,
And the triumphant passion sleep!

Such were of love the transient flame,
Which by the kindling senses led,
To every new attraction came,
And from the known allurement fled.

Unlike the generous care that flows,
With all the rich affections give,
Unlike the mutual hope that knows
But for a dearer self to live.

Was theirs the tender glance to speak
Timid, through many a sparkling tear,
The ever changing hue of cheek,
Its flush of joy, its chill of fear?

Or theirs the full expanded thought,
By taste and moral sense refined,
Each moment with instruction fraught,
The tutor'd elegance of mind?

Be mine the sacred truth that dwells
On One by kindred virtues known,
And mine the chastened glance which tells
That sacred truth to Him alone.

No sordid hope's insidious guise,
No venal pleasure's serpent twine
Invites those soul-illumined eyes,
And blends this feeling heart with thine.

1981

The African Chief

See how the black ship cleaves the main,
High bounding o'er the dark blue wave,
Remurmuring with the groans of pain,
Deep freighted with the princely slave!

Did all the Gods of Afric sleep,
Forgetful of their guardian love,
When the white tyrants of the deep
Betrayed him in the palmy grove?

A chief of Gambia's[1] golden shore,
Whose arm the band of warriors led,
Or more—the lord of generous power,
By whom the foodless poor were fed.

Does not the voice of reason cry,
Claim the first right that nature gave,
From the red scourge of bondage fly,
Nor deign to live a burdened slave?

Has not his suffering offspring clung,
Desponding round his fettered knee;
On his worn shoulder, weeping hung,
And urged one effort to be free?

His wife by nameless wrongs subdued,
His bosom's friend to death resigned;
The flinty path-way drenched in blood,
He saw with cold and frenzied mind.

Strong in despair, then sought the plain,
To heaven was raised his steadfast eye,
Resolved to burst the crushing chain,
Or mid the battle's blast to die.

[1]West African country.

First of his race, he led the band,
Guardless of danger, hurling round,
Till by his red avenging hand,
Full many a despot stained the ground.

When erst Messenia's[2] sons oppressed
Flew desperate to the sanguine field,
With iron clothed each injured breast,
And saw the cruel Spartan yield,

Did not the soul to heaven allied,
With the proud heart as greatly swell,
As when the Roman Decius[3] died,
Or when the Grecian victim fell?[4]

Do later deeds quick rapture raise,
The boon Batavia's[5] William won,
Paoli's[6] time-enduring praise,
Or the yet greater Washington?

If these exalt thy sacred zeal,
To hate oppression's mad control,
For bleeding Afric learn to feel,
Whose Chieftain claimed a kindred soul.

Ah, mourn the last disastrous hour,
Lift the full eye of bootless grief,
While victory treads the sultry shore,
And tears from hope the captive chief.

While the hard race of pallid hue,
Unpracticed in the power to feel,
Resign him to the murderous crew,
The horrors of the quivering wheel,

Let sorrow bathe each blushing cheek,
Bend piteous o'er the tortured slave,
Whose wrongs compassion cannot speak,
Whose only refuge was the grave.

1823

[2]Region in the southwestern Peloponnesus ruled by Polycaon and Messene after Polycaon's exile from Sparta.

[3]Gaius Messius Quintus Traianus Decius (c. 201–251), Roman emperor (249–251). He was the first Roman emperor to institute an organized, empire-wide persecution of the Christians.

[4]"Leonidas." [Morton's note]

[5]City in western New York settled by the Dutch late in the eighteenth century. Batavia became well-known in 1826 when William Morgan, who had written an exposé of the secrets of the Order of the Masons, mysteriously disappeared there.

[6]Pasquale di Paoli (1725–1807), Corsican patriot.

Margaretta Bleecker Faugères 1771–1801

Daughter of Ann Eliza Bleecker (see headnote, p. 1202), Margaretta Bleecker grew up in the shadow of her mother's depression and early death. Her father gave her a superior education, but she rejected his aristocratic pretensions, marrying a French physician, Peter Faugères, on Bastille Day, 1791. Faugères published occasional verse in magazines under the pen name Ella, and many of her poems uncannily prefigure the tone and themes of early Freneau and Edgar Allan Poe. She also collected her mother's extant poetry and prose and published them, along with her own poetry and essays on democratic themes, in 1793. Abusive and profligate, her husband squandered most of Faugères's inheritance and left her and their daughter destitute when he died in 1798. To support herself, Faugères taught school but quickly declined and died early, like her mother, at age thirty.

The following Lines were occasioned by Mr. Robertson's refusing to paint for one Lady, and immediately after taking another lady's likeness 1793[1]

When Laura appear'd, poor APPELLES[2] complain'd,
That his sight was bedim'd, and his optics much pain'd
So his pallet and pencil the artist resign'd,
Lest the blaze of her *beauty* should make him quite blind.
But when fair ANNA enter'd the prospect was chang'd,
The paints and the brushes in order were rang'd;
The artist resum'd his employment again,
Forgetful of labour, and blindness and pain;
And the strokes were so lively that all were assur'd
What the *brunette* had injur'd the *fair one* had cur'd.

1793

[1]The texts, with slight modification, are from *The Posthumous Works of Ann Eliza Bleecker . . . To Which is Added, a Collection of Essays, Prose and Poetical by Margaretta V. Faugères,* ed. Margaretta Faugères (New York: T. and J. Swords, 1793).

[2]Poetical name for the artist, Robertson, after the early Hellenistic court painter, Apelles, considered the greatest artist of antiquity.

To Aribert. October, 1790

Oft' pleas'd my soul looks forward to that day
When struggling to ascend the hills of light,
My spirit bursting from these walls of clay,
Through heav'n's broad arch shall bend its steady flight:

While a few friends attend the lifeless form,
And place it in the bosom of the earth;
Cov'ring it close, to shield it from the storm
And the cold blusters of the whistling north.

Near the sea shore the corpse shall be convey'd;
A small white urn the polish'd stone shall grace,
And a few lines, to tell who there is laid,
Shall *Friendship*'s hand engrave upon the face.

The dark green willow, waving o'er my head,
Shall cast a sadder shade upon the waves;
And many a widow'd swain, and slighted maid,
Shall wear a garland of its weeping leaves:

Far spreads its shadow o'er the pathless vale—
Through its lank boughs the zephyrs sighing pass,
And the low branches, shaken by the gale,
Bend slowly down and kiss the fading grass.

To this lone place the bird of night shall come;
To me shall hie the widow'd turtle too,
And as she perches on the chilly tomb,
Warbles her woes in many a plaintive coo.

There too the trav'ller who hath lost his way,
By the dim glimmer of the moon's pale beam,
Shall spy the marble which conceals my clay,
And rest his weary feet to read the name.

When o'er our world Night's auburn veil is cast,
Oh! should'st thou ever wander near these shores,
Pond'ring the cheerful hours which fled so fast,
With those who were—but are, alas! No more:

To this lone valley let thy footsteps turn—
Here, for a moment rest thy pausing eye;
Just brush the wither'd leaves from off my urn,
And yield the tribute of a friendly sigh.

With thee perhaps *Matilda*[3] too may stray,
To see where lies the friend once held so dear,
And (as she wipes the gath'ring dust away)
May to my mem'ry drop perhaps a tear:

And should some artless, undesigning friend
Enquire "whose head rests here?" him you may tell,
As slowly o'er the sod your steps you bend,
"'Tis Ella rests within this humble cell."

1790 1793

Poems Published Anonymously

Colonial newspapers and magazines were full of poetry. Given the absence of copyright laws, editors were free to pirate materials from whatever publications came to hand or to print verses sent to them by readers. Many poems were published anonymously or pseudonymously. As a consequence, there is no guarantee that the following pieces are by the people described or implied as having written them. What we do know is that they were widely read in the British North American colonies and articulated a gendered topic of lively public interest.

The Lady's Complaint[1]

Custom, alas! doth partial prove,
Nor gives us equal measure;
A pain for us it is to love,
But is to men a pleasure.
They plainly can their thoughts disclose,
Whilst ours must burn within:
We have got tongues, and eyes, in vain,
And truth from us is sin.

Men to new joys and conquests fly,
And yet no hazard run:
Poor we are left, if we deny,
And if we yield, undone.

[3]Pen name of one of Faugères's friends.
[1]First published in the *Virginia Gazette* (ed. Parks), October 22, 1736, p. 3, and reprinted several times.

Then equal laws let custom find,
And neither sex oppress;
More freedom give to womankind,
Or give to mankind less.

1736

Verses Written by a Young Lady, on Women Born to Be Controll'd![1]

How wretched is a woman's fate,
No happy change her fortune knows,
Subject to man in every state.
How can she then be free from woes?

In youth a father's stern command,
And jealous eyes control her will;
A lordly brother watchful stands,
To keep her closer captive still.

The tyrant husband next appears,
With awful and contracted brow;
No more a lover's form he wears,
Her slave's become her sov'reign now.

If from this fatal bondage free,
And not by marriage chains confin'd;
But blest with single life can see,
A parent fond, a brother kind;

Yet love usurps her tender breast,
And paints a Phoenix to her eyes,
Some darling youth disturbs her rest,
And painful sighs in secret rise.

Oh, cruel pow'rs! since you've design'd,
That man, vain man! should bear the sway;
To a slave's fetters add a slavish mind,
That I may cheerfully your will obey.

1743

[1]First published in the *South-Carolina Gazette,* November 21, 1743, p. 3, and reprinted several times.

The Maid's Soliloquy[1]

It must be so—Milton, thou reas'nest well,
Else why this pleasing hope, this fond desire,
This longing after something unpossess'd?
Or whence this secret dread and inward horror
Of dying unespous'd? Why shrinks the soul
Back on itself, and startles at the thought?
'Tis instinct! faithful instinct stirs within us,
'Tis nature's self that points out an alliance,
And intimates an husband to the sex.
Marriage! thou pleasing and yet anxious thought!
Through what variety of hopes and fears,
Through what new scenes, and changes, must we pass:
Th' important state in prospect lies before me,
But shadows, clouds and darkness, rest upon it.
Here will I hold—if Nature prompts the wish,
(And that she does is plain, from all her works)
Our duty and our interest, bid indulge it:
For the great end of nature's law, is bliss.
But yet—in wedlock—women must obey:
I'm weary of these doubts—the priest must end them.
Thus, rashly do I venture loss and gain,
Bondage and pleasure, meet my thoughts at once;
I wed—my liberty is gone for ever:
If happy—then I'm still secure in life.
Love, will then recompense my loss of freedom;
And when my charms shall fade away, my eyes
Themselves grow dim, my stature bend with years,
Then virtuous friendship, shall succeed to love.
Then pleas'd, I'll scorn infirmities, and death,
Renew'd immortal, in a filial race.

1751

[1] Although it was published anonymously, this poem has recently been attributed to Lewis Morris. J. A. Leo Lemay has reported to the editors that the poem appears among the papers of Robert Morris at Rutgers University Library. In manuscript, the poem is titled "Act V. Scene I of Cato Imitated." John T. Shawcross has identified what is so far the earliest known printing in the *Gentleman's Magazine* 17 (January 1747), p. 42, and the poem was frequently reprinted in English periodicals. The earliest North American printing was in the *New York Evening Post,* December 21, 1747, p. 1. At least two other American printings followed, in the *South Carolina Gazette,* March 4, 1751, and the *Newport Mercury,* May 2, 1763.

Native American Political Texts and Oratory

Politics have been significant for indigenous oratory since long before the arrival of Europeans to the Americas. Among many Native peoples, traditional positions of leadership were not predicated on an individual's coercive or punitive power *over* the community. Rather, the community granted authority *to* people based on their ability to convince others to follow their leadership. As such, leadership was explicitly linked to one's rhetorical skills.

Historically, European leaders most often gained their authority through inherited office or rigidly hierarchical structures such as military rank or political patronage; they enforced obedience through violence that was legitimized by colonial institutions. Authority in indigenous communities was generally far less stable, as it depended very much on the community's consent based on the quality of the individual's oratory. There were well-established oratorical protocols both within communities and between peoples, and these were often followed during highly ritualized diplomatic interactions. As so much of daily life revolved around maintaining good relationships between one another and the rest of the world—both physical and spiritual—we should not underestimate the interconnection of the rhetorical and the political.

The complexities of indigenous oratory and its importance to diplomacy did not go unnoticed by Europeans, who soon found it necessary to learn these protocols to form trading or political alliances with indigenous peoples. Even when other cultural aspects of Native nations were interpreted as inferior to those of Europeans, indigenous political oratory was an area of frequent praise, inviting comparisons to the great political orators of classical Greece and Rome. The historical record is rife with translated and transcribed political speeches of Native leaders who spoke eloquently against the ever-increasing geographic and social intrusions of non-Natives. Whether speaking to their own community, other Native peoples, traders, colonial agents, or the powerful leaders of European nations, these orators drew on existing rhetorical conventions and their own creative abilities to engage the imaginations, emotions, and intellects of those who listened.

As Native peoples became familiar with and literate in the languages of the colonial powers, they found new ways of communicating their political and sometimes spiritual concerns to an ever-broadening audience. Some, like Samson Occom (Mohegan), had multiple audiences in mind—those who came to hear him speak in person and those who would likely never meet him but who would read the published versions of his sermons. Similarly, Mahican political leader Hendrick Aupaumut's autobiography is not simply a document that speaks of its author in isolation. It is also a political treatise intended both to explain his people's complicated history and to correct assumptions about his controversial and much-criticized position of loyalty to the United States, in spite of the young nation's overt territorial ambitions.

The history of Native writing in English is very much connected to the varied but enduring political protocols and conventions of indigenous oratory, if not necessarily identical with it. As such, the political dimensions of the writing are significant to the content of these texts and are also fully relevant to their form and function. The political, then, is also the aesthetic: each informs rather than displaces the other.

Daniel Heath Justice
University of Toronto

Handsome Lake (Seneca) 1735–1815

Handsome Lake, who related the original version of this narrative, was a chief in the League of the Iroquois and a half-brother of Cornplanter. He had a vision in the spring of 1799 in which three messengers of the Creator appeared to him in traditional Iroquoian dress and told him that he and the people must abandon alcohol, that witches were corrupting them, and that the people must repent their corruption and ensure that the traditional Strawberry Festival, which celebrated their relationship to the Earth, would be held every year. The other visions that followed apocalyptically predicted the destruction of the world by fire if the return to the old ways was not thorough and immediate. The prophet also rejected any further ceding of Indian lands to whites. Thus began one of the best-documented responses, which anthropologists call revitalization or nativist movements, to European impacts. Handsome Lake's Longhouse Religion prospered to good effect among Iroquois people; seventy-five years later, another revitalization movement, the Ghost Dance of the Great Basin and Plains Indians, would lead to the tragedy at Wounded Knee.

In its re-evaluation of Christian elements and its negative evaluation of the motives and influence of Europeans, this narrative represents an Iroquoian vision of what are today called Columbian consequences. It might be read in conjunction with the earlier Samuel de Champlain selection, and it complements well the works by Samson Occom and Hendrick Aupaumut later in this section.

The narrative was recorded by Arthur C. Parker, himself a Seneca from a distinguished family, who was among the many Native Americans at the turn of the twentieth century who worked singly or with Anglo-American ethnographers to preserve traditions they felt were disappearing under the reservation and allotment systems.

Andrew O. Wiget
New Mexico State University

PRIMARY WORK

A. C. Parker, *Seneca Myths and Folktales,* ed. W. H. Fenton, 1923, 1989.

How America Was Discovered

According to Chief Cornplanter, Handsome Lake taught that America was discovered in the manner here related.

A great queen had among her servants a young minister. Upon a certain occasion she requested him to dust some books that she had hidden in an old chest. Now when the young man reached the bottom of the chest he found a wonderful book which he opened and read. It told that the white men had killed the son of the Creator and it said, moreover, that he had promised to return in three days and then again forty but that he never did. All his followers then began to despair but some said, "He surely will come again some time." When the young preacher read this book he was worried because he had discovered that he had been deceived and that his Lord was not on earth and had not returned when he promised. So he went to some of the chief preachers and asked them about the matter and they answered that he had better seek the Lord himself and find if he were not on the earth now. So he prepared to find the Lord and the next day when he looked out into the river he saw a beautiful island and marveled that he had never noticed it before. As he continued to look he saw a castle built of gold in the midst of the island and he marveled that he had not seen the castle before. Then he thought that so beautiful a palace on so beautiful an isle must surely be the abode of the son of the Creator. Immediately he went to the wise men and told them what he had seen and they wondered greatly and answered that it must indeed be the house of the Lord. So together they went to the river and when they came to it they found that it was spanned by a bridge of gold. Then one of the preachers fell down and prayed a long time and arising to cross the bridge turned back because he was afraid to meet his Lord. Then the other crossed the bridge and knelt down upon the grass and prayed but he became afraid to go near the house. So the young man went boldly over to attend to the business at hand and walking up to the door knocked. A handsome man welcomed him into a room and bade him be of ease. "I wanted you," he said. "You are bright young man; those old fools will not suit me for they would be afraid to listen to me. Listen to me, young man, and you will be rich. Across the ocean there is a great country of which you have never heard. The people there are virtuous, they have no evil habits or appetites but are honest and single-minded. A great reward is yours if you enter into my plans and carry them out. Here are five things. Carry them over to the people across the ocean and never shall you want for wealth, position or power. Take these cards, this money, this fiddle, this whiskey and this blood corruption and give them all to the people across the water. The cards will make them gamble away their goods and idle away their time, the money will make them dishonest and covetous, the fiddle will make them dance with women and their lower natures will command them, the whiskey will excite their minds to evil doing and turn their minds, and the blood corruption will eat their strength and rot their bones."

The young man thought this a good bargain and promised to do as the man had commanded him. He left the palace and when he had stepped over the bridge it was gone, likewise the golden palace and also the island. Now he wondered if he had seen the Lord but he did not tell the great ministers of his bargain because they might try to forstall him. So he looked about and at length found Columbus to whom he told the whole story. So Columbus fitted out some boats and sailed out into the ocean to find the land on the other side. When he had sailed for many days on the water the sailors said that unless Columbus turned about and went home they would behead him but he asked for another day and on that day land was seen and that land was America. Then they turned around and going back reported what they had discovered. Soon a great flock of ships came over the ocean and white men came swarming into the country bringing with them cards, money, fiddles, whiskey and blood corruption.

Now the man who had appeared in the gold palace was the devil and when afterward he saw what his words had done he said that he had made a great mistake and even he lamented that his evil had been so enormous.

1923

Katteuha (Cherokee)

Cherokee politics in the eighteenth century were shaped by two complementary spheres—peace (symbolized by the color white and its Cherokee associations of balance, spiritual wholeness, and purity) and war (symbolized by the conflict, courage, and victory represented by the color red). Among the peace leadership were those known as "Beloved," generally elders who had proven themselves courageous in battle in their younger years and whose later efforts were dedicated toward peace and community harmony.

As in other indigenous communities throughout the southeast, both men and women participated in the political arena. Indeed, Cherokee women had significant influence over foreign and domestic politics of the nation during this period, particularly those women accorded the status of Beloved. Though some had been noted warriors in their younger years, Beloved Women were generally older representatives of peace and calm judgment and had institutionalized authority, which included a voice in council and the right to pardon or condemn prisoners.

This letter is one of a series sent to Benjamin Franklin from Katteuha on matters of political significance to the Cherokee people. The identity of Katteuha has been a matter of some debate. Nanye'hi/ Nancy Ward is the *Ghighau,* or Beloved Woman, most often associated with the peace-town of Chota during this period, so the "Katteuha" of this letter may refer to her, but it more likely refers to a lesser-known but equally politically engaged Beloved Woman of the peace city. There were many women with political influence in the community, not just those whose names appear on surviving documents. Another alternative—given that *Kituwah* is the name of one of the first great Cherokee towns from which the Cherokees are said to be descended and that *Ani-Kituwagi* is one name of the Cherokee people in their own language—is that "Katteuha" refers to a collective authorship of multiple Beloved Women of the politically and historically significant city of Chota.

Daniel Heath Justice
University of Toronto

PRIMARY SOURCES

Virginia Moore Carney, *Eastern Band Cherokee Women: Cultural Persistence in Their Letters and Speeches,* 2005; Theda Perdue, *Cherokee Women: Gender and Culture Change, 1700–1835,* 1998; Karen L. Kilcup, ed., *Native American Women's Writing 1800–1924: An Anthology,* 2000.

Letter from Cherokee Indian Women, to Benjamin Franklin, Governor of the State of Pennsylvania[1]

from Cherokee Indian Women (unpublished)[1]

Brother[2]

8th Sept., 1787.

I am in hopes my Brothers and the Beloved men near the water side will heare from me.[3] This day I filled the pipes that they smoaked in piece, and I am in hopes the smoake has Reached up to the skies above. I here send you a piece of the same Tobacco, and am in hopes you and your Beloved men will smoake it in Friendship—and I am glad in my heart that I am the mother of men that will smoak it in piece.

I am in hopes if you Rightly consider it that woman is the mother of All—and that woman Does not pull Children out of Trees or Stumps nor out of old Logs, but out of their Bodies, so that they ought to mind what a woman says, and look upon her as a mother—and I have Taken the privelage to Speak to you as my own Children, and the same as if you had sucked my Breast—and I am in hopes you have a beloved woman amongst you who will help to put her Children Right if they do wrong, as I shall do the same—the great men have all promised to Keep the path clear and straight, as my Children shall Keep the path clear and white[4] so that the Messengers shall go and come in safety Between us—the old people is never done Talking to their Children—which makes me say so much as I do. The Talk you sent to me was to talk to my Children, which I have done this day, and they all liked my Talk well, which I am in hopes you will heare from me Every now and then that I keep my Children in piece—tho' I am a woman giving you this Talk, I am in hopes that you and all the Beloved men in Congress will pay particular Attention to it, as I am Delivering it to you from the Bottom of my heart, that they will Lay this on the white stool in Congress, wishing them all well and success in all their undertakings—I hold fast the good Talk I Received from you my Brother, and thanks you kindly for your good Talks, and your presents, and the kind usage you have to my son. From

Katteuha,

The Beloved woman of Chota.[5]

Moses Price & Tom Ben, Linchesters.

Endorsed: From Kaattahee, Scolecutta and Kaattahee, Indian Women. His Excellency, Benjamin Franklin, Governor of the State of Pennsylvania.

[1]Cherokee women had significant influence over foreign and domestic politics of the nation in the eighteenth century, particularly those women accorded the status of Beloved. This authority included a voice in council and the right to pardon or condemn prisoners.

[2]In Cherokee social custom, the relationship between a brother and a sister is one of the most important and deserving of respect.

[3]Beloved status belonged to both women and men. It was generally given to elders who had proven themselves courageous in battle in their younger years and whose later efforts were dedicated toward peace and community harmony.

[4]White is the Cherokee color of peace and spiritual wholeness.
[5]Nanye'hi/Nancy Ward was the Beloved Woman most often associated with the peacetown of Chota, so the "Katteuha" of this letter may refer to her, but it also may refer to a lesser-known Beloved Woman or even to a collective authorship of multiple Beloved Women.

Hendrick Aupaumut (Mahican)[1] *1757–1830*

A native diplomat and grand sachem of the Mahicans, Hendrick Aupaumut was an important leader of the Stockbridge Indians during the last forty years of his life. He was described by Timothy Pickering, a special peace agent to the western tribes, as an intelligent man, fluent in English (which he wrote legibly). His elevation to leadership came at a critical time in Stockbridge history.

That history had been remarkable as an example of racial and cultural survival. The Stockbridges, of which the Mahicans formed the largest part, included remnants of tribal groups that had once inhabited the entire Hudson River Valley. At first contact, the Mahicans had controlled the territory on both sides of the river from the Catskills north to Lake Champlain. To the south were other Munsee groups with whom the Mahicans had close relations and with whom they controlled the valley down to Manhattan. By 1700, however, they had been reduced from an estimated 4,000 to about 500 as a result of epidemic diseases, warfare, displacement, and amalgamation with other groups. Their decline continued in the eighteenth century. In 1735, missionaries were sent to the Mahicans and others on the Housatonic River in western Massachusetts, where they established a mission town at Stockbridge, to which were gathered the remnant tribes of the region. In 1740, Moravians established a mission for the Mahicans in New York; when New York officials ordered the Moravians to cease their efforts a few years later, the Mahicans dispersed to Pennsylvania, Canada, and elsewhere, including Stockbridge.

Aupaumut, born at Stockbridge, had been educated by the Moravians. At the outbreak of the Revolutionary War, he and many other Stockbridges enlisted in the Continental Army.

Following the battle of White Plains in 1778, he was commissioned captain and saw extensive service during the remainder of the war. After the war, the Stockbridges decided to move because of terrible losses during the war, the takeover of Stockbridge by whites, and the Stockbridges' susceptibility to the vices of their white neighbors. At the invitation of the Oneidas, they moved to Oneida Creek, New York, in the mid-1780s and established New Stockbridge.

Aupaumut became influential after the removal. By virtue of his loyalty to the United States, he served as an important go-between for the government and the Indians during the early 1790s. When the native groups of the Northwest Territory, encouraged by British intrigue, made war against the frontier settlements, Aupaumut was sent by General Arthur St. Clair in 1791 with a proclamation and offer of peace. At the request of Secretary of War Henry Knox in 1792, he traveled for eleven months among the Delawares, Miamis, Shawnees, and others. After this journey Aupaumut wrote "A Short Narration of My Last Journey to the Western Country," a detailed account of his journey and negotiations with the various peoples. In 1794, he was at the Battle of Fallen Timbers with

[1]A variant of "Mohican" or "Mohegan."

General Wayne and attended a session of the treaty negotiation with the Six Nations and others at Canadaigua; he signed the treaty that was drafted and continued to work as a negotiator for a number of years. In 1808 or 1809 he was seen in Washington with Nicholas Cusick, a Tuscarora, on their way to North Carolina to try to obtain reparations from the North Carolinians for lands that the Tuscaroras had been forced to abandon in the eighteenth century.

By the time of his travels to the Western country, Aupaumut was convinced that the Stockbridges must move farther west. He was afraid of the influence of not only the local whites but the Oneidas, who discouraged farming by the Stockbridge men. When the Oneidas attempted to introduce the religion of Handsome Lake to the Stockbridges, Aupaumut stopped them. In his search for a new home, Aupaumut sought out the Munsees and Delawares who had settled on the White River in Indiana, to whom he was appointed agent in 1808. Attempts of the Stockbridges to find a new home in the West were disrupted by the War of 1812, during which he adamantly opposed the efforts of Tecumseh to organize tribes on the frontier. In 1818 a group migrated to the White River to join the Munsees and Delawares, only to find that the lands had been sold. In 1821, Aupaumut's son Soloman took a small group to Wisconsin, where they settled on Menominee lands and were joined by others from Indiana and New York. In 1828, land was purchased for them on the Fox River, and in 1829, the year before Aupaumut's death, the last Stockbridges, including Aupaumut himself, removed to the West.

Aupaumut's "Narration," sprinkled with flaws in English idioms, attests to the struggle of a Native American, working in a second language, to record an Indian history full of speeches and dramatic episodes. The "Narration" provides the reader with rare insights into Indian manners, diplomacy, and protocol. Aupaumut himself takes on complex dimensions through his narrative. Despite what the colonists had done to his own people, Aupaumut was fiercely loyal to the United States. He had faith that the new nation would treat the Indians fairly. Always the diplomat, he carefully avoided discussing topics that might alienate the Indians, and he presented his audiences with logical arguments, stressing a preference of negotiation over warfare. Written about 1794, the manuscript went unpublished until 1827, after it was found among the papers of Isaac Zane of Philadelphia. Besides this piece, Aupaumut also recorded Mahican tribal traditions in 1791 and was author of a number of speeches and letters published during his lifetime.

Daniel F. Littlefield, Jr.
University of Arkansas at Little Rock

PRIMARY WORK

"History of the Muhheakunnuk Indians," in Jedediah Morse, ed., *First Annual Report of the American Society for Promoting the Civilization and General Improvement of the Indian Tribes of the United States,* 1824; *A Short Narration of My Last Journey to the Western Country,* 1827.

from A Short Narration of My Last Journey to the Western Country[1]

As I have propose to mention—The complaints or arguments of these Indians, and my arguments to convince them in several times, I will now put down.

First principal thing they argue is this—that the white people are deceitful in their dealings with us the Indians; (says they) The white people have taken all our lands from us, from time to time, until this time, and that they will continue the same way, &c. Then I reply and say it has been too much so, because these white people was governed by one Law, the Law of the great King of England; and by that Law they could hold our lands, in spite of our disatisfaction; and we were too fond of their liquors.[2] But now they have new Laws their own, and by these Laws Indians cannot be deceived as usual, &c. And they say, but these Big knifes have take away our lands since they have their own way.[3] And then I tell them, for this very reason the United Sachems[4] invite you to treat with them that you may settle these dificulties—for how can these dificulties settled without you treat with them?

Another thing they mention—says they, the Big knifes have used learning to Civilize Indians: and after they Christianize number of them so as to gain their attention, then they would killed them, and have killed of such 96 in one day at Cosuhkeck,[5] few years ago.

Another instance they mention—that one of the Chiefs of Shawany[6] was friendly to the Big knifes, and Big knifes gave him a flag, that where ever the chief should come a cross the Big knifes, he is to hoist up this flag, then they will meet together in peace. But soon after this agreement was made, the Big knifes came in the town of this Chief; some of the Indians could not trust the Big knifes and run off; but the Chief have such confidence in the words of the Big knifes he hoisted up his flag; but the Big knifes did not regarded, but killed the Chief and number of his friends.

Another instance they mention—that some of the Delawares was with the Big knifes on the service of Americans; but afterward the Big knifes have fall upon them and have killed number of them &c. And since that, every time the Big knifes get ready to come against us, they would sent message to us for peace—then they come to fight us—and they know how to speak good, but would not do good towards Indians &c.

[1]Written about 1794, the *Narration* was not published until 1827 when it appeared in the second volume of the *Memoirs of the Pennsylvania Historical Society.* Accompanied by his brother and other Indians, Aupaumut met in council with a number of tribes including the Delaware, Shawnee, Miami, Wyandot, Ottawa, Chippewa, Potawatomi, and Kickapoo. His narrative is a record not only of speeches and negotiations but also of the complex tribal relations and the intrigues of some well-known historical figures such as Joseph Brant and Simon Girty. What follows is the conclusion of Aupaumut's narrative.

[2]A common complaint throughout Indian history has been that whites subverted Indian society through use of liquors.

[3]These Indians did not use the term "Big knifes" to apply to Americans in general but apparently restricted its use to frontiersmen.

[4]*I.e.,* the leaders of the United States.

[5]An apparent reference to Coshocton, the main town of the Turtle tribe of Delawares destroyed by whites in 1781 at the present site of Coshocton, Ohio.

[6]*I.e.,* Shawnee.

Then I tell them I very sorry to hear these things. If the great men of the United States have the like principal or disposition as the Big knifes had, My nation and other Indians in the East would been along ago anihilated. But they are not so, Especially since they have their Liberty—they begin with new things, and now they endeavour to lift us up the Indians from the ground, that we may stand up and walk ourselves; because we the Indians, hitherto have lay flat as it were on the ground, by which we could not see great way; but if we could stand then we could see some distance. The United States in seeing our situation they put their hands on us, and lead us in the means of Life until we could stand and walk as they are. But on the other hand, the British seeing the Indians in their situation, they would just cover them with blanket and shirt every fall, and the Indians feel themselves warm, and esteem that usage very high—therefore they remain as it were on the ground and could not see great way these many years, &c.

And further I told them, the United Sachems will not speak wrong. Whatever they promise to Indians they will perform. Because out of 30,000 men, they chuse one men to attend in their great Council Fire—and such men must be very honest and wise, and they will do Justice to all people &c. In this way of converseing with them repeatly, make them willing to hear further.

Another thing they urge that the United States could not govern the hostile Big knifes—and that they the Big knifes, will always have war with the Indians. If the United States could govern them, then the peace could stand sure. But the Big knifes are independent, and if we have peace with them, they would make slaves of us.

Then I told them, the reason the Big knifes are so bad, is this because they have run away from their own country of different States, because they were very mischivous, such as theives and robbers and murderes—and their laws are so strict these people could not live there without being often punished; therefore they run off in this contry and become lawless. They have lived such a distance from the United States, that in these several years the Law could not reached them because they would run in the woods, and no body could find them. But at length the people of the United States settle among them, and the Law now binds them; and if they would endeavour to run in the woods as usual, you would then have chance to knock their heads and they know this, therefore they oblige to set still, &c.

And further (says I,) we the Indians have such people also; for instance, here is Kuttoohwoh, or Cherekes;[7] they could not live among their own people in their own Contry, because they have strict Laws, so that if any steals, he must be whipt immediately; and if any commit adultery his ears will be cut off; and if any murders he will be instandly killed, &c. In all my arguments with these Indians, I have as if were oblige to say nothing with regard of the conduct of Yorkers, how they cheat my fathers, how they taken our lands Unjustly, and how my fathers were groaning as it were to their graves, in loseing their lands for nothing, although they were faithful friends to the Whites; and how the white people artfully got their Deeds confirm in

[7]The Cherokees, an Iroquoian-speaking tribe, believed that they migrated from the north, from which they were expelled, and settled in the southeastern part of the continent where the Europeans found them. The Delawares and related tribes called them Kittuwa, after Kituhwa, one of their ancient towns.

their Laws, &c. I say had I mention these things to the Indians, it would agravate their prejudices against all white people, &c.

And here I will also mention the substance of my speech to these Nations, deliverd immediately after Brant's Prohibitory and Cautionary Message delivered.[8] And after the Indians been informed by some Emmissaries, that I and my Companions were sent by the Big knifes to number the Indians, and was to return again with the information, that the White people may judge how many men will be sufficient to fall upon the Indians, &c.

I begin with these words:—

Grandfathers—and Brothers—and friends—attend—[9]

As we have acquaint to each other many things, and as we have agreed that we would set together in council to manifest our sentiments to each other, I will now speak. We have heard various reports of many kinds, for which occasion I will now speak. The Prohibitory Voice of the Mohawks has reachd your ears, that you should not believe the Message I deliver to you, nor to what I say, that I was to deceive you, &c.

My Grandfathers Brothers and friends—

Let us consider the meaning of this Brant's Message—by the sound of it, he point at me as a deceiver or roag, that every nation must be warned. But let us now look back in the path of our forefathers, and see whether you can find one single instance wherein, or how my ancestors or myself have deceived you, or led you one step astray. I say Let us look narrowly, to see whether you can find one bone of yours lay on the ground, by means of my deceitfulness, and I now declare that you cannot found such instance. And further, you may reflect, and see wherein I have speak deceitfully since I come here, that Mohawks should have occasion to stop your ears. But you look back and see heaps of your bones, wherein the Mauquas[10] have deceived you repeatly. I think I could have good reason to tell you not to believe the Message or words of the Mohawks, for they will deceive you greatly as Usual—but I forbear.

Another information reached your ears, that I and my men were sent on purpose to number your nations &c. This also is a Dark Lye, for if you only consider whether I ever ask any of you how many warriors have you, you could easyly know whether I was sent on this Business.

My friends—

I now tell you that the white people well knew your numbers not only your warriors, but your women and children too. (How come they know you would say) because in every fall you gave your numbers to the whites therefore they knew it. Now

[8]Joseph Brant (1747–1807) was a noted Mohawk chief, whose loyalties during and after the American Revolution rested with the British; hence he desired that the western tribes not make peace with the Americans. He did not attend Aupaumut's councils but on September 17, his nephew delivered a message in his behalf, urging the Indians not to be deceived by Aupaumut and declaring that George Washington had laid claim to all their lands.

[9]Common forms of address, indicating respect as well as the political and social relationship among tribal groups.

[10]*I.e.,* Mohawks.

consider, and think whether there is any need on the part of the Whites to sent me to number your nations, &c.

Six strings of wampom delivered.[11]

After this—then they talk among themselves, and then rehearse my speech and heartily thank me for the same.

And the Sachem of Delaware speak and said—

Grandchild—

It is true all what have said, we could not found any instance wherein your ancestors have deceived our fathers, and we cannot find any fault with your words since you meet us in this country &c. But on the other hand, our Uncles have injured us much these many years; and now after they divided, now they wanted to divide us also. And further, it is true we have gave our numbers to the English every year &c.

I have not mention several speeches with wampom delivered by these Indians to me while I was with them, and my last speech to Shawany &c. and many other affairs.

I now have occasion to say that I have been endeavouring to do my best in the business of peace and according to my best knowledge with regard of the desires of the United States, I have press in the minds of friends in the westward repeatly.

But since I arrived at home I understand that my Character is darkened by envious Indians who stayed but few days in Miamie.[12] But for my conduct I will appeal to the nations whom I had Business with last summer, that is if any of my Brothers should doubt of my faithfulness. But this one thing, every wise men well knew, that to employ an enemy or half friend, will never speak well, &c.

With regard to myself, I think it is easy matter to find out whether I was not faithful with the United States in the late war, and whether I have not been faithfull in the work of peace according to abilities in these near two years. I have as it were sacrifice all my own affairs, and my family, for the sake of peace and this last time have gone from home better than Eleven months, and have gone thro a hazardous journeys, and have sufferd with sickness and hunger, and have left my Counsellors with the nations who are for peace, to promote peace and forward every means of peace while I am absent—not only so but I have been pleading and Justifying the Conduct of these people, for which they were well received at their arrival at Miamie. Notwithstand of all this, they brought my Name at Nought. The occasion of my speaking this sort, because of many evil and false reports sounded in the ears of my friends—and I am ready to answer any thing that may be asked respecting to the different Tribes of Indians, &c.—

Hendrick Aupaumut

1827

[11]Wampum belts were commonly used during this time to confirm the authority of the message being delivered.

[12]That is, among the Miami, a tribe in central Ohio.

Voices of Revolution and Nationalism

Modern readers tend too readily to assume that the American Revolution was the result of a consensus of colonial opinion about open revolt against English rule. Yet, as the selections below suggest, several attitudes from the Enlightenment about rebellious agitation emerged during the decades prior to the Revolutionary War. In philosophical terms, the contradictory ideas expressed during the revolutionary era arose from conflicting opinions about human nature and the extent to which humankind could progress. Conservatives held a fairly negative view of human nature. They feared social change, some arguing (along the lines of Thomas Hobbes and later philosophers who followed him) that beastly mobs would result, others (those who followed Calvinist belief) insisting that social disruption would enable Satan to enter the body politic. Those who held more progressive views of human nature and action tended to follow John Locke, Jean-Jacques Rousseau, the Scottish "Common Sense" school, and other philosophers who suggested that social betterment would result from individual freedom, in both inquiry and action. The natural world, they insisted, was harmonious; if people could freely enquire into natural science, they could design systems of government based upon natural principles of harmony. Combined with the social and economic issues that divided the colonies, these philosophical concerns led to a wide ideological debate about armed revolt and confederation.

The ideological debate is represented in the well-known correspondence, late in their lives, between John Adams and Thomas Jefferson. In June 1813, Jefferson assessed his past differences with the conservative Adams in this way:

> *Altho'. . . you expressly disclaim the wish to influence the freedom of enquiry, you predict that that will produce nothing more worthy of transmission to posterity, than the principles, institutions, and systems of education received from their ancestors. I do not consider this as your deliberate opinion. You possess, yourself, too much science, not to see how much is still ahead of you, unexplained and unexplored.*

Given his unfailing interest in natural science and the improvement of government for the betterment of society, Jefferson was a member of what Ralph Waldo Emerson later called "a party of hope." He wanted Adams to leave behind what Emerson labeled "a party of memory." Yet Adams held to his earlier conservative stance. Adams's response to Jefferson was a series of rhetorical questions:

> *Let me now ask you, very seriously my Friend, Where are now in 1813, the Perfection and perfectability of human Nature? Where is now, the progress of the human Mind? Where is the Amelioration of Society? Where the Augmentations of human Comforts? Where the diminutions of human Pains and miseries? . . .*
>
> *When? Where? and how? is the present Chaos to be arranged into Order?*

Order could not result if all people—whites *and* non-whites, men *and* women, elite *and* non-elite—were given a voice in governance.

Chaos of a different but no less destructive sort reigned in the world of Handsome

Lake, a Seneca and chief in the League of the Iroquois. The visions he had in the spring of 1799 called the Iroquois to renew their ancient religion and culture and to resist white appropriation of native lands. Benjamin Franklin accurately assessed the plight of Native Americans as well as the hypocrisy of slaveholding. By contrast, Jefferson, a so-called progressive and idealist, argued, in *Notes on the State of Virginia* (1787), for abolition on the basis of the harm it caused to slave owners and white society in general, and maintained a racialist stance on the intellectual capacity of Africans and African Americans. Furthermore, in his role as president, Jefferson conspired to subdue native independence and appropriate native territory by persuading Native Americans to become agriculturalists and give up their traditional hunting. At the end of the eighteenth century, a former slave named Toussaint L'Overture embodied the fears implicit in the southern colonies' harsh regulation of slaves. Toussaint led a successful insurrection against his French colonial masters on the island of Saint Domingue (present-day Haiti). Not only did he prove the universal appeal and subversive application of revolutionary principles championed by thinkers like Jefferson, but he rejected the image of blacks as passive and became a hero to many people of African descent struggling for rights and equality.

To a greater extent than many Americans have been taught to expect, the literature of the era of revolution and confederation suggests ambiguous stances toward political change and culture. Crèvecoeur's Quaker farmer James is perhaps the best-known fictional example of such cultural ambivalence. James celebrates the economic stability and possibility that "America" represents for white immigrants and Americans, yet he deplores the civil degradation of slavery in the South. He suggests that life among native people would be a natural and beneficial corrective to the present social sterility of "civilized" nations, yet he clearly abhors the idea of life alongside natives as one of the "distresses of the frontiersman," hardly a suitable alternative for white colonists who do not wish to participate in the Revolutionary War. Progressive ideals were at odds, many writers suggested, with colonial experience. Mere sobriety, industry, and frugality—values honored by Crèvecoeur and many writers from his era—could not make a commonwealth.

Despite the evident differences among those in the revolutionary generation, the literature that has informed the American literary tradition has, by and large, been "patriot" literature promoting Enlightenment ideals and American independence. Thus, Benjamin Franklin has come down through the centuries—despite persistent critical caveats against a self-satisfied egotism and a doctrine of conformity—as the pre-eminent American patriot statesman, a Renaissance man whose scientific, philosophical, and political inquiry, along with his diplomacy in all three areas, made life better for all Americans. Like John Smith and Cotton Mather before him, Franklin embraced the ideals of industry and frugality, offering in his autobiography the life of a model American who through his own hard work freed himself of financial worry and, spirit renewed, re-created in himself a new man. This pro-American view of Franklin has dominated the tradition to such an extent that few recognize Franklin's hard-headed realism. Skepticism, he believed, left one "half-melancholy" and without will. Individual improvement could lead to changes in manners, morals, and laws that might better society as a whole.

Anglo-American literature of this era played upon a long tradition of writings about human nature, liberty, and the law, as attested to in the Federalist and Anti-Federalist writing. The educated elite, in both progressive and conservative camps, sought precedents for their actions in the literature of the past. Looking to John Locke, whose *Second Treatise on Civil Government* (1690) proved highly influential, and Enlightenment rationalist thinkers, a multitude of British Commonwealth writers on ancient British liberties, "Common

Sense" philosophers, and ancient and continental sources on human nature, American writers constructed an intriguing argument in behalf of freedom from English domination. They considered that in ancient Brittany the people freely chose to constitute themselves together into one body for their own better protection and governance. The officials of the commonwealth—kings, lords, and commons, all acting together—represented the body of the people and determined laws and enacted statutes for the whole. Yet more recent kings, they insisted, took away the colonists' rights as citizens, forcing them into subjection without offering a suitable position of representation in the English common body, breaking down the British "family."

The "family" argument worked especially well for those writers who sought to negate the assumptions about social hierarchy and political power they found in British politics and propaganda. In the arguments of pro-independence writers, all Britons were alike given ancient liberties. The colonists who came here, whether they were farmers or aristocrats, were of the same family. Family members, they avowed, incurred mutual obligations and so deserved the same rights. Mercy Otis Warren, sister and wife of patriot leaders, composed sharply satirical plays in which greedy and wicked Tories, colonists loyal to the British crown and more often than not neighbors and friends of her family, acted despicably to betray the moral cause of the Revolution. In his influential *Common Sense* (1776), Thomas Paine, a recent English immigrant, argued that England could not properly be called the "mother country," for she had forfeited that right by acting like a "monster" who devoured her young rather than like a nurturing, protective mother. Only a few months after *Common Sense* appeared, Jefferson used the appeal of family and kinship in his draft of the Declaration of Independence to attack King George III as a bad father figure to a nation desperate for paternal protection. The Declaration itself suggested that the King, and not the colonies, was responsible for the breakup of the family: "We have reminded them [Americans' "British Brethren"] of the Circumstances of our Emigration and Settlement here. We have appealed to their native Justice and Magnanimity, and we have conjured them by the Ties of our common Kindred to disavow these Usurpations." Rhetorical appeals like these provided rallying cries for the patriot agitators and helped to effect colonial unity among the disparate colonies.

Benjamin Franklin 1706–1790

Translated into fourteen languages and frequently reprinted in English, Benjamin Franklin's renowned autobiography marks the author's status as noteworthy statesman, man of science, and literary figure in eighteenth-century America. The autobiography often provides the lens through which Franklin's early life as well as his achievements in politics, philosophy, and print culture are viewed, because it both presents interesting details of the life of a founder of the new nation and reminds readers of the ways in which a public persona may be crafted through the written word. That is, Franklin's memoirs present one picture of the author; other writings by and about Franklin provide another. Collectively, these works provide a vivid picture of eighteenth-century political life and literary culture.

Born in Boston to Josiah Franklin and his second wife, Abiah Folger, Benjamin admired his father for his convictions as a religious dissenter who, in coming to

America, sought freedom from persecution; Benjamin Franklin praised his mother for her hearty constitution in bearing and nurturing ten children. He exemplified his parents' worthy characteristics of independence and fortitude and rebelled against his father's wishes that he pursue a career either in service to the church or in the family's business of candle and soap making. Instead, Benjamin was apprenticed at age twelve to his older brother James and began to learn the printing business and to develop his literary skills. Asserting again his need for independence, Benjamin Franklin left Boston for Philadelphia at age seventeen and in the following year (1724) departed Philadelphia for London. Almost two years later, more experienced in the social and economic realities of life, Franklin returned to Philadelphia, where he devoted many years (1726–1757) to establishing himself as a printer and philosopher and to gaining celebrity for his wit, his business acumen, and his political insights.

Franklin's inclination from an early age to initiate his ideas independently and then to elicit followers led to his success as a writer, printer, man of science, and philanthropist. From his inventive mind and willingness to experiment came not only his work with lightning and the well-known "Franklin stove" but also the creation of such public institutions as the free library and the postal system.

His openness to new ideas and his inquisitive nature, as well as his strong work ethic and love of conversation, enabled Franklin to succeed in myriad situations, including those he encountered as he traveled. Both in his early years in Philadelphia and London and in his later life, as an agent of the Pennsylvania legislature in England (c. 1757–1775), emissary to Montreal (1776), and minister to France (1776–1785), Franklin seems to have been able to adapt to his circumstances and to charm those around him.

Franklin's early literary work exhibits the humor and wit that almost all his works exude. The pseudonymously written "Silence Dogood" papers (1722), which appeared in James's newspaper, *The New-England Courant,* mark the beginning of Benjamin's literary career. As he notes in his autobiography, he imitated the essay and verse style characteristic of English periodicals such as *The Spectator,* and popular ballads. Franklin undoubtedly was influenced in his creation and development of literary characters, their speech, and their experiences by Plutarch's *Lives,* John Bunyan's *Pilgrim's Progress,* and Daniel Defoe's numerous narratives, all of which Franklin mentions having read in his youth.

The fictional and witty character Richard Saunders was at the center of Franklin's popular *Poor Richard's Almanac* (1733–1738), for which he became well known in his middle years. The preface to the *Almanac*'s twenty-fifth anniversary edition, known as *The Way to Wealth,* compiles excerpts from prior editions, emphasizing collectively the economic imperative upon which Franklin elaborates in the autobiography. He asserts that, in turn, hard work, frugality, avoidance of vice, restraint from debt, and honesty are intertwining elements of financial success.

Many of Franklin's humorous pieces, which are not without their serious aspects, suggest the need for social change even as they entertain. The "Witch Trial at Mount Holly" (1730), for example, mocks the supposed rationalism of Calvinist religion, as those involved in the trial exhibit prejudices and superstitions arising from ignorance. Written from the perspective of a supposedly unbiased reporter, the piece exaggerates tests of faith and testimonies such as those presented in Cotton Mather's *Wonders of the Invisible World,* even as it implies Franklin's rational and empirical understanding of swimming, drawn from Jean de Thevenot's text on the subject.

In "The Speech of Polly Baker" (1747), as in the *Almanac,* Franklin exhibits his ability to create an entertaining fictional character. The outspoken woman points a finger at men who were unwilling to accept responsibility for their sexual actions, and she forcefully explains that her numerous children are the result of unfulfilled promises made by supposedly honorable gentlemen, such as those before whom she pleads her case. Polly's concluding plea, that a statue be erected in her memory, mocks Mather's memorializing of saints in his *Magnalia Christi Americana* as well as Puritan execution sermons that made object lessons of wayward females. While Baker's rational arguments from Scripture echo the persuasive testimony of the colonial antinomian Anne Hutchinson, they also remind us of the diverse responses of readers, as some might find Baker's speech excessive and passionate rather than rational. Thus "Polly Baker" is no simplistic caricature but embodies the complexities and social concerns that appear within Franklin's other writings and the sensibilities apparent in other eighteenth-century characters.

A staple of the American literary canon at least since D. H. Lawrence included it in *Studies in Classic American Literature* (1923), Franklin's autobiography is most often read as an idealized picture of American manhood. It merits consideration, however, from multiple perspectives: the author's sense of audience, his composing process, his use of thematic and structural commonplaces—of both life writing and eighteenth-century novels—as well as specific incidents that identify the story as unique to Franklin.

The narrative usually appears in a three-part format, designated as much by Franklin's periods of composing as by theme or chronology. Franklin set out to write his memoirs on several different occasions (1771, 1784, 1788, and 1788–1789) and in diverse locales. Part I, written in England and, as Franklin explains, directed at his son in order to provide a model for success, focuses on Franklin's youth and the beginnings of his career as a writer and publisher. Interrupted by the Revolution, Franklin picked up his pen again in France at the encouragement of friends. This second part focuses on Franklin's system of moral development, a method that many may want to attribute to Enlightenment science. Nonetheless, the system of daily reckoning that Franklin advocates is not without its similarities to Puritan patterns of preparation for election. Works like Cotton Mather's *Bonifacius: or Essays to do Good,* a work for which Franklin notes his admiration, also present such a system. Part III, less frequently anthologized and taught than the first two sections, describes Franklin's scientific experiments and involvement with such political activities (through 1757) as the French and Indian War, the free library, and the post office system.

Perhaps unable to visualize his life as complete, Franklin left the autobiography unfinished and unpublished upon his death. Yet his reference to his life as a text whose "errata" might be corrected, were he able to prepare a second edition, reflects not only his immersion in print culture but also suggests his view of himself as the ultimate compositor, framing and presenting the narrative portrait as he wished. In addition, the metaphor reflects Franklin's position as a deist, distancing himself from his Calvinist predecessors and their belief in a sovereign God who elected whom he would. This emphasis on self-reliance throughout the narrative contributes to an objectification, if not diminution, of those around Franklin—never equal, other people, men as well as women, provide the steppingstones to Franklin's position of prominence. Thus the autobiography valuably contributes to our understanding of successful American manhood and the darker side of success in the colonial era and in the early Republic.

The shorter works from Franklin's later life, more poignant and direct than the earlier satirical pieces, reflect his immersion in the political concerns of the young Republic. "Remarks Concerning the Savages" (1784) attempts to dispel myths and present truths about natives, while "On the Slave-Trade" (1790), which appeared pseudonymously in the *Federal Gazette,* presents Franklin's understanding of the economic underpinnings of slavery and the religious arguments used to justify it. Although pessimistic in its conclusions, the piece implies Franklin's involvement with the Pennsylvania Society for the Abolition of Slavery, which elected him its president in 1785.

Franklin's posthumously published "Speech in the Convention" (delivered 1787; published 1837) acknowledges the universality of self-centeredness that approaches tyranny, while it encourages delegates to the Constitutional Convention to support the development of a new system of government. As in the autobiography, this honest recognition of the tension between vanity and humility, between a self-serving work ethic and self-disciplining for civic purposes, marks Franklin's contribution to the ideals of American citizenship.

Franklin's works are fraught with frankness about such incongruities and inconsistencies and entertain with their clever word play and apt presentation of life's complexities. Emphasizing economic enterprise, self-sufficiency, and involvement with the communal good, Franklin and his writing have earned a well-deserved place in studies of American literature. They revise Puritan ideology, reflect transatlantic economic and political life of the eighteenth century, and foreshadow Ralph Waldo Emerson's image of self-reliance and self-improvement as a means of social reform. As such, Franklin's works embody not only key concerns of the Enlightenment but also of American literature.

Etta Madden
Southwest Missouri State University

PRIMARY WORKS

The Writings of Benjamin Franklin, ed. Albert Henry Smyth, 10 vols., 1905–1907; *The Papers of Benjamin Franklin,* ed. Leonard Labaree, et al., 1959; *The Autobiography of Benjamin Franklin: A Genetic Text,* eds. J. A. Leo Lemay and P. M. Zall, 1981; *Benjamin Franklin's Autobiography,* eds. J. A. Leo Lemay and P. M. Zall, 1986; *Benjamin Franklin,* ed. J. A. Leo Lemay, 1987.

The Way to Wealth[1]

Preface to Poor Richard Improved

Courteous Reader,

I have heard that nothing gives an Author so great Pleasure, as to find his Works respectfully quoted by other learned Authors. This Pleasure I have seldom enjoyed;

[1]Franklin prepared this essay, in Father Abraham's voice, for the twenty-fifth anniversary issue of the *Almanac.*

for tho' I have been, if I may say it without Vanity, an *eminent Author* of Almanacks annually now a full Quarter of a Century, my Brother Authors in the same Way, for what Reason I know not, have ever been very sparing in their Applauses; and no other Author has taken the least Notice of me, so that did not my Writings produce me some solid *Pudding,* the great Deficiency of *Praise* would have quite discouraged me.

I concluded at length, that the People were the best Judges of my Merit; for they buy my Works; and besides, in my Rambles, where I am not personally known, I have frequently heard one or other of my Adages repeated, with, *as Poor Richard says,* at the End on't; this gave me some Satisfaction, as it showed not only that my Instructions were regarded, but discovered likewise some Respect for my Authority; and I own, that to encourage the Practice of remembering and repeating those wise Sentences, I have sometimes *quoted myself* with great Gravity.

Judge then how much I must have been gratified by an Incident I am going to relate to you. I stopt my Horse lately where a great Number of People were collected at a Vendue of Merchant Goods. The Hour of Sale not being come, they were conversing on the Badness of the Times, and one of the Company call'd to a plain clean old Man, with white Locks, *Pray, Father* Abraham, *what think you of the Times? Won't these heavy Taxes quite ruin the Country? How shall we be ever able to pay them? What would you advise us to?*—Father *Abraham* stood up, and reply'd, If you'd have my Advice, I'll give it you in short, for a *Word to the Wise is enough,* and *many Words won't fill a Bushel,* as *Poor Richard says.* They join'd in desiring him to speak his Mind, and gathering round him, he proceeded as follows;

"Friends, says he, and Neighbours, the Taxes are indeed very heavy, and if those laid on by the Government were the only Ones we had to pay, we might more easily discharge them; but we have many others, and much more grievous to some of us. We are taxed twice as much by our *Idleness,* three times as much by our *Pride,* and four times as much by our *Folly,* and from these Taxes the Commissioners cannot ease or deliver us by allowing an Abatement. However let us hearken to good Advice, and something may be done for us; *God helps them that help themselves,* as *Poor Richard* says, in his Almanack of 1733.

It would be thought a hard Government that should tax its People one tenth Part of their *Time,* to be employed in its Service. But *Idleness* taxes many of us much more, if we reckon all that is spent in absolute *Sloth,* or doing of nothing, with that which is spent in idle Employments or Amusements, that amount to nothing. *Sloth,* by bringing on Diseases, absolutely shortens Life. *Sloth, like Rust, consumes faster than Labour wears, while the used Key is always bright,* as *Poor Richard* says. But *dost thou love Life, then do not squander Time, for that's the Stuff Life is made of,* as *Poor Richard* says.—How much more than is necessary do we spend in Sleep! forgetting that *The sleeping Fox catches no Poultry,* and that *there will be sleeping enough in the Grave,* as *Poor Richard* says. If Time be of all Things the most precious, *wasting Time* must be, as *Poor Richard* says, *the greatest Prodigality,* since, as he elsewhere tells us, *Lost Time is never found again;* and what we call *Time-enough, always proves little enough.* Let us then up and be doing, and doing to the Purpose; so by Diligence shall we do more with less Perplexity. *Sloth makes all Things difficult, but Industry all easy,* as *Poor Richard* says; and *He that riseth late, must trot all Day, and shall scarce overtake his Business at Night.* While *Laziness travels so slowly, that Poverty soon over-*

takes him, as we read in *Poor Richard,* who adds, *Drive thy Business, let not that drive thee;* and *Early to Bed, and early to rise, makes a Man healthy, wealthy, and wise.*

So what signifies *wishing* and *hoping* for better Times. We may make these Times better if we bestir ourselves. *Industry need not wish,* as *Poor Richard* says, and *He that lives upon Hope will die fasting. There are no Gains, without Pains;* then *Help Hands, for I have no Lands,* or if I have, they are smartly taxed. And, as *Poor Richard* likewise observes, *He that hath a Trade hath an Estate,* and *He that hath a Calling hath an Office of Profit and Honour;* but then the *Trade* must be worked at, and the *Calling* well followed, or neither the *Estate,* nor the *Office,* will enable us to pay our Taxes.—If we are industrious we shall never starve; for, as *Poor Richard* says, *At the working Man's House* Hunger *looks in, but dares not enter.* Nor will the Bailiff or the Constable enter, for *Industry pays Debts, while Despair encreaseth them,* says *Poor Richard.*—What though you have found no Treasure, nor has any rich Relation left you a Legacy, *Diligence is the Mother of Good-luck,* as *Poor Richard* says, *and God gives all Things to Industry.* Then *plough deep, while Sluggards sleep, and you shall have Corn to sell and to keep,* says *Poor Dick.* Work while it is called To-day, for you know not how much you may be hindered To-morrow, which makes *Poor Richard* say, *One To-day is worth two To-morrows;* and farther, *Have you somewhat to do To-morrow, do it To-day.* If you were a Servant, would you not be ashamed that a good Master should catch you idle? Are you then your own Master, *be ashamed to catch yourself idle,* as *Poor Dick* says. When there is so much to be done for yourself, your Family, your Country, and your gracious King, be up by Peep of Day; *Let not the Sun look down and say, Inglorious here he lies.* Handle your Tools without Mittens; remember that *the Cat in Gloves catches no Mice,* as *Poor Richard* says. 'Tis true there is much to be done, and perhaps you are weak handed, but stick to it steadily, and you will see great Effects, for *constant Dropping wears away Stones,* and by *Diligence and Patience the Mouse ate in two the Cable;* and *little Strokes fell great Oaks,* as *Poor Richard* says in his Almanack, the Year I cannot just now remember.

Methinks I hear some of you say, *Must a Man afford himself no Leisure?*—I will tell thee, my Friend, what *Poor Richard* says, *Employ thy Time well if thou meanest to gain Leisure;* and, *since thou art not sure of a Minute, throw not away an Hour.* Leisure, is Time for doing something useful; this Leisure the diligent Man will obtain, but the lazy Man never; so that, as *Poor Richard* says, a *Life of Leisure and a Life of Laziness are two Things.* Do you imagine that Sloth will afford you more Comfort than Labour? No, for as *Poor Richard* says, *Trouble springs from Idleness, and grievous Toil from needless Ease. Many without Labour, would live by their* WITS *only, but they break for want of Stock.* Whereas Industry gives Comfort, and Plenty, and Respect: *Fly Pleasures, and they'll follow you. The diligent Spinner has a large Shift,* and *now I have a Sheep and a Cow, every Body bids me Good morrow;* all which is well said by *Poor Richard.*

But with our Industry, we must likewise be *steady, settled* and *careful,* and oversee our own Affairs *with our own Eyes,* and not trust too much to others; for, as *Poor Richard* says,

I never saw an oft removed Tree,
Nor yet an oft removed Family,
That throve so well as those that settled be.

And again, *Three Removes is as bad as a Fire;* and again, *Keep thy Shop, and thy Shop will keep thee;* and again, *If you would have your Business done, go; If not, send.* And again,

He that by the Plough would thrive,
Himself must either hold or drive.

And again, *The Eye of a Master will do more Work than both his Hands;* and again, *Want of Care does us more Damage than Want of Knowledge;* and again, *Not to oversee Workmen, is to leave them your Purse open.* Trusting too much to others Care is the Ruin of many; for, as the *Almanack* says, *In the Affairs of this World, Men are saved, not by Faith, but by the Want of it;* but a Man's own Care is profitable; for, saith *Poor Dick, Learning is to the Studious,* and *Riches to the Careful,* as well as *Power to the Bold,* and *Heaven to the Virtuous.* And farther, *If you would have a faithful Servant, and one that you like, serve yourself.* And again, he adviseth to Circumspection and Care, even in the smallest Matters, because sometimes *a little Neglect may breed great Mischief;* adding, *For want of a Nail the Shoe was lost; for want of a Shoe the Horse was lost; and for want of a Horse the Rider was lost,* being overtaken and slain by the Enemy, all for want of Care about a Horseshoe Nail.

So much for Industry, my Friends, and Attention to one's own Business; but to these we must add *Frugality,* if we would make our *Industry* more certainly successful. A Man may, if he knows not how to save as he gets, *keep his Nose all his Life to the Grindstone,* and die not worth a *Groat* at last. *A fat Kitchen makes a lean Will,* as *Poor Richard* says; and,

Many Estates are spent in the Getting,
Since Women for Tea forsook Spinning and Knitting,
And Men for Punch forsook Hewing and Splitting.

If you would be wealthy, says he, in another Almanack, *think of Saving as well as of Getting: The* Indies *have not made* Spain *rich, because her* Outgoes *are greater than her* Incomes. Away then with your expensive Follies, and you will not have so much Cause to complain of hard Times, heavy Taxes, and chargeable Families; for, as *Poor Dick* says,

Women and Wine, Game and Deceit,
Make the Wealth small, and the Wants great.

And farther, *What maintains one Vice, would bring up two Children.* You may think perhaps, That a *little* Tea, or a *little* Punch now and then, Diet a *little* more costly, Clothes a *little* finer, and a *little* Entertainment now and then, can be no *great* Matter; but remember what *Poor Richard* says, *Many a* Little *makes a Mickle;* and farther, *Beware of* little *Expences; a small Leak will sink a great Ship;* and again, *Who Dainties love, shall Beggars prove;* and moreover, *Fools make Feasts, and wise Men eat them.*

Here you are all got together at this Vendue of *Fineries* and *Knicknacks.* You call them *Goods,* but if you do not take Care, they will prove *Evils* to some of you. You expect they will be sold *cheap,* and perhaps they may for less than they cost; but if you have no Occasion for them, they must be *dear* to you. Remember what *Poor Richard* says, *Buy what thou hast no Need of, and ere long thou shalt sell thy*

Necessaries. And again, *At a great Pennyworth pause a while:* He means, that perhaps the Cheapness is *apparent* only, and not *real;* or the Bargain, by straitning thee in thy Business, may do thee more Harm than Good. For in another Place he says, *Many have been ruined by buying good Pennyworths.* Again, *Poor Richard* says, *'Tis foolish to lay out Money in a Purchase of Repentance;* and yet this Folly is practised every Day at Vendues, for want of minding the Almanack. *Wise Men,* as *Poor Dick* says, *learn by others Harms, Fools scarcely by their own;* but, *Felix quem faciunt aliena Pericula cautum.* Many a one, for the Sake of Finery on the Back, have gone with a hungry Belly, and half starved their Families; *Silks and Sattins, Scarlet and Velvets,* as *Poor Richard* says, *put out the Kitchen Fire.* These are not the *Necessaries* of Life; they can scarcely be called the *Conveniencies,* and yet only because they look pretty, how many *want* to *have* them. The *artificial* Wants of Mankind thus become more numerous than the *natural;* and, as *Poor Dick* says, *For one poor Person, therè are an hundred* indigent. By these, and other Extravagancies, the Genteel are reduced to Poverty, and forced to borrow of those whom they formerly despised, but who through *Industry* and *Frugality* have maintained their Standing; in which Case it appears plainly, that a *Ploughman on his Legs is higher than a Gentleman on his Knees,* as *Poor Richard* says. Perhaps they have had a small Estate left them, which they knew not the Getting of; they think *'tis Day, and will never be Night;* that a little to be spent out of *so much,* is not worth minding; (*a Child and a Fool,* as *Poor Richard* says, *imagine* Twenty Shillings *and Twenty Years can never be spent*) but, *always taking out of the Meal-tub, and never putting in, soon comes to the Bottom;* then, as *Poor Dick* says, *When the Well's dry, they know the Worth of Water.* But this they might have known before, if they had taken his Advice; *If you would know the Value of Money, go and try to borrow some;* for, *he that goes a borrowing goes a sorrowing;* and indeed so does he that lends to such People, when he goes *to get it in again.—Poor Dick* farther advises, and says,

Fond Pride of Dress, *is sure a very Curse;*
E'er Fancy *you consult, consult your Purse.*

And again, *Pride is as loud a Beggar as Want, and a great deal more saucy.* When you have bought one fine Thing you must buy ten more, that your Appearance may be all of a Piece; but *Poor Dick* says, *'Tis easier to* suppress *the first Desire, than to* satisfy *all that follow it.* And 'tis as truly Folly for the Poor to ape the Rich, as for the Frog to swell, in order to equal the Ox.

Great Estates may venture more,
But little Boats should keep near Shore.

'Tis however a Folly soon punished; for *Pride that dines on Vanity sups on Contempt,* as *Poor Richard* says. And in another Place, *Pride breakfasted with Plenty, dined with Poverty, and supped with Infamy.* And after all, of what Use is this *Pride of Appearance,* for which so much is risked, so much is suffered? It cannot promote Health, or ease Pain; it makes no Increase of Merit in the Person, it creates Envy, it hastens Misfortune.

What is a Butterfly? At best
He's but a Caterpillar drest.
The gaudy Fop's his Picture just,

as *Poor Richard* says.

But what Madness must it be to *run in Debt* for these Superfluities! We are offered, by the Terms of this Vendue, *Six Months Credit;* and that perhaps has induced some of us to attend it, because we cannot spare the ready Money, and hope now to be fine without it. But, ah, think what you do when you run in Debt; *You give to another Power over your Liberty.* If you cannot pay at the Time, you will be ashamed to see your Creditor; you will be in Fear when you speak to him; you will make poor pitiful sneaking Excuses, and by Degrees come to lose your Veracity, and sink into base downright lying; for, as *Poor Richard* says, *The second Vice is Lying, the first is running in Debt.* And again, to the same Purpose, *Lying rides upon Debt's Back.* Whereas a freeborn *Englishman* ought not to be ashamed or afraid to see or speak to any Man living. But Poverty often deprives a Man of all Spirit and Virtue: *'Tis hard for an empty Bag to stand upright,* as *Poor Richard* truly says. What would you think of that Prince, or that Government, who should issue an Edict forbidding you to dress like a Gentleman or a Gentlewoman, on Pain of Imprisonment or Servitude? Would you not say, that you are free, have a Right to dress as you please, and that such an Edict would be a Breach of your Privileges, and such a Government tyrannical? And yet you are about to put yourself under that Tyranny when you run in Debt for such Dress! Your Creditor has Authority at his Pleasure to deprive you of your Liberty, by confining you in Gaol for Life, or to sell you for a Servant, if you should not be able to pay him! When you have got your Bargain, you may, perhaps, think little of Payment; but *Creditors, Poor Richard* tells us, *have better Memories than Debtors;* and in another Place says, *Creditors are a superstitious Sect, great Observers of set Days and Times.* The Day comes round before you are aware, and the Demand is made before you are prepared to satisfy it. Or if you bear your Debt in Mind, the Term which at first seemed so long, will, as it lessens, appear extreamly short. *Time* will seem to have added Wings to his Heels as well as Shoulders. *Those have a short Lent,* saith *Poor Richard, who owe Money to be paid at Easter.* Then since, as he says, *The Borrower is a Slave to the Lender, and the Debtor to the Creditor,* disdain the Chain, preserve your Freedom; and maintain your Independency: Be *industrious* and *free;* be *frugal* and *free.* At present, perhaps, you may think yourself in thriving Circumstances, and that you can bear a little Extravagance without Injury; but,

For Age and Want, save while you may;
No Morning Sun lasts a whole Day,

As *Poor Richard* says.—Gain may be temporary and uncertain, but ever while you live, Expence is constant and certain; and *'tis easier to build two Chimnies than to keep one in Fuel,* as *Poor Richard* says. So *rather go to Bed supperless than rise in Debt.*

Get what you can, and what you get hold;
'Tis the Stone that will turn all your Lead into Gold,

as *Poor Richard* says. And when you have got the Philosopher's Stone, sure you will no longer complain of bad Times, or the Difficulty of paying Taxes.

This Doctrine, my Friends, is *Reason* and *Wisdom;* but after all, do not depend too much upon your own *Industry,* and *Frugality,* and *Prudence,* though excellent Things, for they may all be blasted without the Blessing of Heaven; and therefore ask that Blessing humbly, and be not uncharitable to those that at present seem to want it, but comfort and help them. Remember *Job* suffered, and was afterwards prosperous.

And now to conclude, *Experience keeps a dear School, but Fools will learn in no other, and scarce in that;* for it is true, *we may give Advice, but we cannot give Conduct,* as *Poor Richard* says: However, remember this, *They that won't be counselled, can't be helped,* as *Poor Richard* says: And farther, That *if you will not hear Reason, she'll surely rap your Knuckles.*

Thus the old Gentleman ended his Harangue. The People heard it, and approved the Doctrine, and immediately practised the contrary, just as if it had been a common Sermon; for the Vendue opened, and they began to buy extravagantly, notwithstanding all his Cautions, and their own Fear of Taxes.—I found the good Man had thoroughly studied my Almanacks, and digested all I had dropt on those Topicks during the Course of Five-and-twenty Years. The frequent Mention he made of me must have tired any one else, but my Vanity was wonderfully delighted with it, though I was conscious that not a tenth Part of this Wisdom was my own which he ascribed to me, but rather the *Gleanings* I had made of the Sense of all Ages and Nations. However, I resolved to be the better for the Echo of it; and though I had at first determined to buy Stuff for a new Coat, I went away resolved to wear my old One a little longer. *Reader,* if thou wilt do the same, thy Profit will be as great as mine.

I am, as ever,

Thine to serve thee,

RICHARD SAUNDERS.

July 7, 1757

1758

A Witch Trial at Mount Holly[1]

Burlington, Oct. 12. Saturday last at Mount-Holly, about 8 Miles from this Place, near 300 People were gathered together to see an Experiment or two tried on some Persons accused of Witchcraft. It seems the Accused had been charged with making their Neighbours Sheep dance in an uncommon Manner, and with causing Hogs to speak, and sing Psalms, &c. to the great Terror and Amazement of the King's good and peaceable Subjects in this Province; and the Accusers being very positive that if the Accused were weighed in Scales against a Bible, the Bible would prove too heavy for them; or that, if they were bound and put into the River, they would swim; the said Accused desirous to make their Innocence appear, voluntarily offered to un-

[1]First printed in *The Pennsylvania Gazette,* October 22, 1730.

dergo the said Trials, if 2 of the most violent of their Accusers would be tried with them. Accordingly the Time and Place was agreed on, and advertised about the Country; The Accusers were 1 Man and 1 Woman; and the Accused the same. The Parties being met, and the People got together, a grand Consultation was held, before they proceeded to Trial; in which it was agreed to use the Scales first; and a Committee of Men were appointed to search the Men, and a Committee of Women to search the Women, to see if they had any Thing of Weight about them, particularly Pins. After the Scrutiny was over, a huge great Bible belonging to the Justice of the Place was provided, and a Lane through the Populace was made from the Justices House to the Scales, which were fixed on a Gallows erected for that Purpose opposite to the House, that the Justice's Wife and the rest of the Ladies might see the Trial, without coming amongst the Mob; and after the Manner of Moorfields, a large Ring was also made. Then came out of the House a grave tall Man carrying the Holy Writ before the supposed Wizard, &c. (as solemnly as the Sword-bearer of London before the Lord Mayor) the Wizard was first put in the Scale, and over him was read a Chapter out of the Books of Moses, and then the Bible was put in the other Scale, (which being kept down before) was immediately let go; but to the great Surprize of the Spectators, Flesh and Bones came down plump, and outweighed that great good Book by abundance. After the same Manner, the others were served, and their Lumps of Mortality severally were too heavy for Moses and all the Prophets and Apostles. This being over, the Accusers and the rest of the Mob, not satisfied with this Experiment, would have the Trial by Water; accordingly a most solemn Procession was made to the Mill-pond; where both Accused and Accusers being stripp'd (saving only to the Women their Shifts) were bound Hand and Foot, and severally placed in the Water, lengthways, from the Side of a Barge or Flat, having for Security only a Rope about the Middle of each, which was held by some in the Flat. The Accuser Man being thin and spare, with some Difficulty began to sink at last; but the rest every one of them swam very light upon the Water. A Sailor in the Flat jump'd out upon the Back of the Man accused, thinking to drive him down to the Bottom, but the Person bound, without any Help, came up some time before the other. The Woman Accuser, being told that she did not sink, would be duck'd a second Time; when she swam again as light as before. Upon which she declared, That she believed the Accused had bewitched her to make her so light, and that she would be duck'd again a Hundred Times, but she would duck the Devil out of her. The accused Man, being surpriz'd at his own Swimming, was not so confident of his Innocence as before, but said, *If I am a Witch, it is more than I know.* The more thinking Part of the Spectators were of Opinion, that any Person so bound and plac'd in the Water (unless they were mere Skin and Bones) would swim till their Breath was gone, and their Lungs fill'd with Water. But it being the general Belief of the Populace, that the Womens Shifts, and the Garters with which they were bound help'd to support them; it is said they are to be tried again the next warm Weather, naked.

1730

The Speech of Polly Baker[1]

[The Speech of Miss Polly Baker, before a Court of Judicature, at Connecticut near Boston in New-England; where she was prosecuted the Fifth Time, for having a Bastard Child: Which influenced the Court to dispense with her Punishment, and induced one of her Judges to marry her the next Day.]

May it please the Honourable Bench to indulge me in a few Words: I am a poor unhappy Woman, who have no Money to fee Lawyers to plead for me, being hard put to it to get a tolerable Living. I shall not trouble your Honours with long Speeches; for I have not the Presumption to expect, that you may, by any Means, be prevailed on to deviate in your Sentence from the Law, in my Favour. All I humbly hope is, That your Honours would charitably move the Governor's Goodness on my Behalf, that my Fine may be remitted. This is the Fifth Time, Gentlemen, that I have been dragg'd before your Court on the same Account; twice I have paid heavy Fines, and twice have been brought to Publick Punishment, for want of Money to pay those Fines. This may have been agreeable to the Laws, and I don't dispute it; but since Laws are sometimes unreasonable in themselves, and therefore repealed, and others bear too hard on the Subject in particular Circumstances; and therefore there is left a Power somewhat to dispense with the Execution of them; I take the Liberty to say, That I think this Law, by which I am punished, is both unreasonable in itself, and particularly severe with regard to me, who have always lived an inoffensive Life in the Neighbourhood where I was born, and defy my Enemies (if I have any) to say I ever wrong'd Man, Woman, or Child. Abstracted from the Law, I cannot conceive (may it please your Honours) what the Nature of my Offence is. I have brought Five fine Children into the World, at the Risque of my Life; I have maintain'd them well by my own Industry, without burthening the Township, and would have done it better, if it had not been for the heavy Charges and Fines I have paid. Can it be a Crime (in the Nature of Things I mean) to add to the Number of the King's Subjects, in a new Country that really wants People? I own it, I should think it a Praise-worthy, rather than a punishable Action. I have debauched no other Woman's Husband, nor enticed any Youth; these Things I never was charg'd with, nor has any one the least Cause of Complaint against me, unless, perhaps, the Minister, or Justice, because I have had Children without being married, by which they have missed a Wedding Fee. But, can ever this be a Fault of mine? I appeal to your Honours. You are pleased to allow I don't want Sense; but I must be stupified to the last Degree, not to prefer the Honourable State of Wedlock, to the Condition I have lived in. I always was, and still am willing to enter into it; and doubt not my behaving well in it, having all the Industry, Frugality, Fertility, and Skill in Oeconomy, appertaining to a good Wife's Character. I defy any Person to say, I ever refused an Offer of that Sort: On the contrary, I readily consented to the only Proposal of Marriage that ever was made me, which was when I was a Virgin; but too easily confiding in the Person's Sincerity that

[1]First printed in *The Gentleman's Magazine,* April 1747.

made it, I unhappily lost my own Honour, by trusting to his; for he got me with Child, and then forsook me: That very Person you all know; he is now become a Magistrate of this Country; and I had Hopes he would have appeared this Day on the Bench, and have endeavoured to moderate the Court in my Favour; then I should have scorn'd to have mention'd it; but I must now complain of it, as unjust and unequal, That my Betrayer and Undoer, the first Cause of all my Faults and Miscarriages (if they must be deemed such) should be advanc'd to Honour and Power in the Government, that punishes my Misfortunes with Stripes and Infamy. I should be told, 'tis like, That were there no Act of Assembly in the Case, the Precepts of Religion are violated by my Transgressions. If mine, then, is a religious Offence, leave it to religious Punishments. You have already excluded me from the Comforts of your Church-Communion. Is not that sufficient? You believe I have offended Heaven, and must suffer eternal Fire: Will not that be sufficient? What Need is there, then, of your additional Fines and Whipping? I own, I do not think as you do; for, if I thought what you call a Sin, was really such, I could not presumptuously commit it. But, how can it be believed, that Heaven is angry at my having Children, when to the little done by me towards it, God has been pleased to add his Divine Skill and admirable Workmanship in the Formation of their Bodies, and crown'd it, by furnishing them with rational and immortal Souls. Forgive me, Gentlemen, if I talk a little extravagantly on these Matters; I am no Divine, but if you, Gentlemen, must be making Laws, do not turn natural and useful Actions into Crimes, by your Prohibitions. But take into your wise Consideration, the great and growing Number of Batchelors in the Country, many of whom from the mean Fear of the Expences of a Family, have never sincerely and honourably courted a Woman in their Lives; and by their Manner of Living, leave unproduced (which is little better than Murder) Hundreds of their Posterity to the Thousandth Generation. Is not this a greater Offence against the Publick Good, than mine? Compel them, then, by Law, either to Marriage, or to pay double the Fine of Fornication every Year. What must poor young Women do, whom Custom have forbid to solicit the Men, and who cannot force themselves upon Husbands, when the Laws take no Care to provide them any; and yet severely punish them if they do their Duty without them; the Duty of the first and great Command of Nature, and of Nature's God, *Encrease and Multiply.* A Duty, from the steady Performance of which, nothing has been able to deter me; but for its Sake, I have hazarded the Loss of the Publick Esteem, and have frequently endured Publick Disgrace and Punishment; and therefore ought, in my humble Opinion, instead of a Whipping, to have a Statue erected to my Memory.

1747

An Edict by the King of Prussia[1]

Dantzick, September 5.

We have long wondered here at the Supineness of the English Nation, under the Prussian Impositions upon its Trade entering our Port. We did not till lately know the *Claims,* antient and modern, that hang over that Nation, and therefore could not suspect that it might submit to those Impositions from a Sense of *Duty,* or from Principles of *Equity.* The following *Edict,* just made public, may, if serious, throw some Light upon this Matter.

"FREDERICK, by the Grace of God, King of Prussia, &c. &c. &c. to all present and to come, HEALTH. The Peace now enjoyed throughout our Dominions, having afforded us Leisure to apply ourselves to the Regulation of Commerce, the Improvement of our Finances, and at the same Time the easing our *Domestic Subjects* in their Taxes: For these Causes, and other good Considerations us thereunto moving, We hereby make known, that after having deliberated these Affairs in our Council, present our dear Brothers, and other great Officers of the State, Members of the same, WE, of our certain Knowledge, full Power and Authority Royal, have made and issued this present Edict, viz.

"WHEREAS it is well known to all the World, that the first German Settlements made in the Island of Britain, were by Colonies of People, Subjects to our renowned Ducal Ancestors, and drawn from *their* Dominions, under the Conduct of Hengist, Horsa, Hella, Uffa, Cerdicus, Ida, and others; and that the said Colonies have flourished under the Protection of our august House, for Ages past, have never been *emancipated* therefrom, and yet have hitherto yielded little Profit to the same. And whereas We Ourself have in the last War fought for and defended the said Colonies against the Power of France, and thereby enabled them to make Conquests from the said Power in America, for which we have not yet received adequate Compensation. And whereas it is just and expedient that a Revenue should be raised from the said Colonies in Britain towards our Indemnification; and that those who are Descendants of our antient Subjects, and thence still owe us due Obedience, should contribute to the replenishing of our Royal Coffers, as they must have done had their Ancestors remained in the Territories now to us appertaining: WE do therefore hereby ordain and command, That from and after the Date of these Presents, there shall be levied and paid to our Officers of the Customs, on all Goods, Wares and Merchandizes, and on all Grain and other Produce of the Earth exported from the said Island of Britain, and on all Goods of whatever Kind imported into the same, a *Duty* of *Four and an Half* per Cent. *ad Valorem,* for the Use of us and our Successors. And that the said Duty may more effectually be collected, We do hereby ordain, that all Ships or Vessels bound from Great Britain to any other Part of the World, or from any other Part of the World to Great Britain, shall in their respective Voyages touch at our Port of KONINGSBERG, there to be unladen, searched, and charged with the said Duties.

[1]First printed in *The Public Advertiser,* September 2, 1773.

"AND WHEREAS there have been from Time to Time discovered in the said Island of Great Britain by our Colonists there, many Mines or Beds of Iron Stone; and sundry Subjects of our antient Dominion, skilful in converting the said Stone into Metal, have in Times past transported themselves thither, carrying with them and communicating that Art; and the Inhabitants of the said Island, *presuming* that they had a natural Right to make the best Use they could of the natural Productions of their Country for their own Benefit, have not only built Furnaces for smelting the said Stone into Iron, but have erected Plating Forges, Slitting Mills, and Steel Furnaces, for the more convenient manufacturing of the same, thereby endangering a Diminution of the said Manufacture in our antient Dominion. WE *do therefore* hereby farther ordain, that from and after the Date hereof, no Mill or other Engine for Slitting or Rolling of Iron, or any Plating Forge to work with a Tilt-Hammer, or any Furnace for making Steel, shall be erected or continued in the said Island of Great Britain: And the Lord Lieutenant of every County in the said Island is hereby commanded, on Information of any such Erection within his County, to order and by Force to cause the same to be abated and destroyed, as he shall answer the Neglect thereof to Us at his Peril. But We are nevertheless graciously pleased to permit the Inhabitants of the said Island to transport their Iron into Prussia, there to be manufactured, and to them returned, they paying our Prussian Subjects for the Workmanship, with all the Costs of Commission, Freight and Risque coming and returning, any Thing herein contained to the contrary notwithstanding.

"WE do not however think fit to extend this our Indulgence to the Article of *Wool,* but meaning to encourage not only the manufacturing of woollen Cloth, but also the raising of Wool in our antient Dominions, and to prevent *both,* as much as may be, in our said Island, We do hereby absolutely forbid the Transportation of Wool from thence even to the Mother Country Prussia; and that those Islanders may be farther and more effectually restrained in making any Advantage of their own Wool in the Way of Manufacture, We command that none shall be carried *out of one County into another,* nor shall any Worsted-Bay, or Woollen-Yarn, Cloth, Says, Bays, Kerseys, Serges, Frizes, Druggets, Cloth-Serges, Shalloons, or any other Drapery Stuffs, or Woollen Manufactures whatsoever, made up or mixt with Wool in any of the said Counties, be carried into any other County, or be Waterborne even across the smallest River or Creek, on Penalty of Forfeiture of the same, together with the Boats, Carriages, Horses, &c. that shall be employed in removing them. *Nevertheless* Our loving Subjects there are hereby permitted, (if they think proper) to use all their Wool as *Manure for the Improvement of their Lands.*

"AND WHEREAS the Art and Mystery of making *Hats* hath arrived at great Perfection in Prussia, and the Making of Hats by our remote Subjects ought to be as much as possible restrained. And forasmuch as the Islanders before-mentioned, being in Possession of Wool, Beaver, and other Furs, have *presumptuously* conceived they had a Right to make some Advantage thereof, by manufacturing the same into Hats, to the Prejudice of our domestic Manufacture, WE do therefore hereby strictly command and ordain, that no Hats or Felts whatsoever, dyed or undyed, finished or unfinished, shall be loaden or put into or upon any Vessel, Cart, Carriage or Horse, to be transported or conveyed *out of one County* in the said Island *into another County,* or to *any other Place whatsoever,* by any Person or Persons whatsoever, on Pain of forfeiting the same, with a Penalty of *Five Hundred Pounds* Sterling for every

Offence. Nor shall any Hat-maker in any of the said Counties employ more than two Apprentices, on Penalty of *Five Pounds* Sterling per Month: We intending hereby that such Hat-makers, being so restrained both in the Production and Sale of their Commodity, may find no Advantage in continuing their Business. But lest the said Islanders should suffer Inconveniency by the Want of Hats, We are farther graciously pleased to permit them to send their Beaver Furs to Prussia; and We also permit Hats made thereof to be exported from Prussia to Britain, the People thus favoured to pay all Costs and Charges of Manufacturing, Interest, Commission to Our Merchants, Insurance and Freight going and returning, as in the Case of Iron.

"And lastly, Being willing farther to favour Our said Colonies in Britain, We do hereby also ordain and command, that all the Thieves, Highway and Street-Robbers, House-breakers, Forgerers, Murderers, So[domi]tes, and Villains of every Denomination, who have forfeited their Lives to the Law in Prussia, but whom We, in Our great Clemency, do not think fit here to hang, shall be emptied out of our Gaols into the said Island of Great Britain *for the* BETTER PEOPLING *of that Country.*

"We flatter Ourselves that these Our Royal Regulations and Commands will be thought *just* and *reasonable* by Our much-favoured Colonists in England, the said Regulations being copied from their own Statutes of 10 and 11 Will. III. C. 10, 5 Geo. II. C. 22, 23 Geo. II. C. 29, 4 Geo. I. C. 11, and from other equitable Laws made by their Parliaments, or from Instructions given by their Princes, or from Resolutions of both Houses entered into for the GOOD *Government* of their own Colonies in Ireland and America.

"And all Persons in the said Island are hereby cautioned not to oppose in any wise the Execution of this Our Edict, or any Part thereof, such Opposition being HIGH TREASON, of which all who are *suspected* shall be transported in Fetters from Britain to Prussia, there to be tried and executed according to the *Prussian Law.*

"Such is our Pleasure.

Given at Potsdam this twenty-fifth Day of the Month of August, One Thousand Seven Hundred and Seventy-three, and in the Thirty-third Year of our Reign.

By the KING in his Council

RECHTMAESSIG, *Secr.*"

Some take this Edict to be merely one of the King's *Jeux d'Esprit:* Others suppose it serious, and that he means a Quarrel with England: But all here think the Assertion it concludes with, "that these Regulations are copied from Acts of the English Parliament respecting their Colonies," a very *injurious* one: it being impossible to believe, that a People distinguish'd for their *Love of Liberty,* a Nation so *wise,* so *liberal in its Sentiments,* so *just and equitable* towards its *Neighbours,* should, from mean and *injudicious* Views of *petty immediate Profit,* treat *its own Children* in a Manner so *arbitrary* and TYRANNICAL!

1773

The Ephemera, an Emblem of Human Life

You may remember, my dear friend, that when we lately spent that happy day in the delightful garden and sweet society of the Moulin Joly, I stopt a little in one of our walks, and staid some time behind the company. We had been shown numberless skeletons of a kind of little fly, called an ephemera, whose successive generations, we were told, were bred and expired within the day. I happened to see a living company of them on a leaf, who appeared to be engaged in conversation. You know I understand all the inferior animal tongues: my too great application to the study of them is the best excuse I can give for the little progress I have made in your charming language. I listened through curiosity to the discourse of these little creatures; but as they, in their national vivacity, spoke three or four together, I could make but little of their conversation. I found, however, by some broken expressions that I heard now and then, they were disputing warmly on the merit of two foreign musicians, one a *cousin,* the other a *moscheto;* in which dispute they spent their time, seemingly as regardless of the shortness of life as if they had been sure of living a month. Happy people! thought I, you live certainly under a wise, just, and mild government, since you have no public grievances to complain of, nor any subject of contention but the perfections and imperfections of foreign music. I turned my head from them to an old grey-headed one, who was single on another leaf, and talking to himself. Being amused with his soliloquy, I put it down in writing, in hopes it will likewise amuse her to whom I am so much indebted for the most pleasing of all amusements, her delicious company and heavenly harmony.

"It was," said he, "the opinion of learned philosophers of our race, who lived and flourished long before my time, that this vast world, the Moulin Joly, could not itself subsist more than eighteen hours; and I think there was some foundation for that opinion, since, by the apparent motion of the great luminary that gives life to all nature, and which in my time has evidently declined considerably towards the ocean at the end of our earth, it must then finish its course, be extinguished in the waters that surround us, and leave the world in cold and darkness, necessarily producing universal death and destruction. I have lived seven of those hours, a great age, being no less than four hundred and twenty minutes of time. How very few of us continue so long! I have seen generations born, flourish, and expire. My present friends are the children and grandchildren of the friends of my youth, who are now, alas, no more! And I must soon follow them; for, by the course of nature, though still in health, I cannot expect to live above seven or eight minutes longer. What now avails all my toil and labor, in amassing honey-dew on this leaf, which I cannot live to enjoy! What the political struggles I have been engaged in, for the good of my compatriot inhabitants of this bush, or my philosophical studies for the benefit of our race in general! for, in politics, what can laws do without morals? Our present race of ephemeræ will in a course of minutes become corrupt, like those of other and older bushes, and consequently as wretched. And in philosophy how small our progress! Alas! art is long, and life is short! My friends would comfort me with the idea of a name, they say, I shall leave behind me; and they tell me I have lived long enough to nature and to glory. But what will fame be to an ephemera who no longer exists? And what will become of all history in the eighteenth hour, when the world itself, even the whole Moulin Joly, shall come to its end, and be buried in universal ruin?"

To me, after all my eager pursuits, no solid pleasures now remain, but the reflection of a long life spent in meaning well, the sensible conversation of a few good lady ephemeræ, and now and then a kind smile and a tune from the ever amiable *Brillante*.

1778

Remarks Concerning the Savages of North America

Savages we call them, because their Manners differ from ours, which we think the Perfection of Civility; they think the same of theirs.

Perhaps, if we could examine the Manners of different Nations with Impartiality, we should find no People so rude, as to be without any Rules of Politeness; nor any so polite, as not to have some Remains of Rudeness.

The Indian Men, when young, are Hunters and Warriors; when old, Counsellors; for all their Government is by Counsel of the Sages; there is no Force, there are no Prisons, no Officers to compel Obedience, or inflict Punishment. Hence they generally study Oratory, the best Speaker having the most Influence. The Indian Women till the Ground, dress the Food, nurse and bring up the Children, and preserve and hand down to Posterity the Memory of public Transactions. These Employments of Men and Women are accounted natural and honourable. Having few artifical Wants, they have abundance of Leisure for Improvement by Conversation. Our laborious Manner of Life, compared with theirs, they esteem slavish and base; and the Learning, on which we value ourselves, they regard as frivolous and useless. An Instance of this occurred at the Treaty of Lancaster, in Pennsylvania, *anno* 1744, between the Government of Virginia and the Six Nations. After the principal Business was settled, the Commissioners from Virginia acquainted the Indians by a Speech, that there was at Williamsburg a College, with a Fund for Educating Indian youth; and that, if the Six Nations would send down half a dozen of their young Lads to that College, the Government would take care that they should be well provided for, and instructed in all the Learning of the White People. It is one of the Indian Rules of Politeness not to answer a public Proposition the same day that it is made; they think it would be treating it as a light matter, and that they show it Respect by taking time to consider it, as of a Matter important. They therefore deferr'd their Answer till the Day following; when their Speaker began, by expressing their deep Sense of the kindness of the Virginia Government, in making them that Offer; "for we know," says he, "that you highly esteem the kind of Learning taught in those Colleges, and that the Maintenance of our young Men, while with you, would be very expensive to you. We are convinc'd, therefore, that you mean to do us Good by your Proposal; and we thank you heartily. But you, who are wise, must know that different Nations have different Conceptions of things; and you will therefore not take it amiss, if our Ideas of this kind of Education happen not to be the same with yours.

We have had some Experience of it; Several of our young People were formerly brought up at the Colleges of the Northern Provinces; they were instructed in all your Sciences; but, when they came back to us, they were bad Runners, ignorant of every means of living in the Woods, unable to bear either Cold or Hunger, knew neither how to build a Cabin, take a Deer, or kill an Enemy, spoke our Language imperfectly, were therefore neither fit for Hunters, Warriors, nor Counsellors; they were totally good for nothing. We are however not the less oblig'd by your kind Offer, tho' we decline accepting it; and, to show our grateful Sense of it, if the Gentlemen of Virginia will send us a Dozen of their Sons, we will take great Care of their Education, instruct them in all we know, and make *Men* of them."

Having frequent Occasions to hold public Councils, they have acquired great Order and Decency in conducting them. The old Men sit in the foremost Ranks, the Warriors in the next, and the Women and Children in the hindmost. The Business of the Women is to take exact Notice of what passes, imprint it in their Memories (for they have no Writing), and communicate it to their Children. They are the Records of the Council, and they preserve Traditions of the Stipulations in Treaties 100 Years back; which, when we compare with our Writings, we always find exact. He that would speak, rises. The rest observe a profound Silence. When he has finish'd and sits down, they leave him 5 to 6 Minutes to recollect, that, if he has omitted anything he intended to say, or has any thing to add, he may rise again and deliver it. To interrupt another, even in common Conversation, is reckon'd highly indecent. How different this is from the conduct of a polite British House of Commons, where scarce a day passes without some Confusion, that makes the Speaker hoarse in calling *to Order;* and how different from the Mode of Conversation in many polite Companies of Europe, where, if you do not deliver your Sentence with great Rapidity, you are cut off in the middle of it by the Impatient Loquacity of those you converse with, and never suffer'd to finish it!

The Politeness of these Savages in Conversation is indeed carried to Excess, since it does not permit them to contradict or deny the Truth of what is asserted in their Presence. By this means they indeed avoid Disputes; but then it becomes difficult to know their Minds, or what Impression you make upon them. The Missionaries who have attempted to convert them to Christianity, all complain of this as one of the great Difficulties of their Mission. The Indians hear with Patience the Truths of the Gospel explain'd to them, and give their usual Tokens of Assent and Approbation; you would think they were convinc'd. No such matter. It is mere Civility.

A Swedish Minister, having assembled the chiefs of the Susquehanah Indians, made a Sermon to them, acquainting them with the principal historical Facts on which our Religion is founded; such as the Fall of our first Parents by eating an Apple, the coming of Christ to repair the Mischief, his Miracles and Suffering, &c. When he had finished, an Indian Orator stood up to thank him. "What you have told us," says he, "is all very good. It is indeed bad to eat Apples. It is better to make them all into Cyder. We are much oblig'd by your kindness in coming so far, to tell us these Things which you have heard from your Mothers. In return, I will tell you some of those we had heard from ours. In the Beginning, our Fathers had only the Flesh of Animals to subsist on; and if their Hunting was unsuccessful, they were starving. Two of our young Hunters, having kill'd a Deer, made a Fire in the Woods to broil some Part of it. When they were about to satisfy their Hunger, they beheld a beautiful young Woman descend from the Clouds, and seat herself on that Hill, which you see yonder among the blue Mountains. They said to each other, it is a Spirit that has smelt our broiling Venison, and wishes to eat of it; let us offer some to her. They presented her with the Tongue; she was pleas'd with the Taste of it, and said, 'Your kindness shall be rewarded; come to this Place after thirteen Moons, and you shall find something that will be of great Benefit in nourishing you and your Children to the latest Generations.' They did so, and, to their Surprise, found Plants they had never seen before; but which, from that ancient time, have been constantly cultivated among us, to our great Advantage. Where her right Hand had touched the Ground, they found Maize; where her left hand had touch'd it, they found Kidney-Beans; and where her Backside had sat on it, they found Tobacco." The good Missionary, disgusted with this idle Tale, said, "What I delivered to you were sacred Truths; but what you tell me is mere Fable, Fiction, and Falshood." The Indian, offended, reply'd, "My brother, it seems your Friends have not done you Justice in your Education; they have not well instructed you in the Rules of common Civility. You saw that we, who understand and practise those Rules, believ'd all your stories; why do you refuse to believe ours?"

When any of them come into our Towns, our People are apt to crowd round them, gaze upon them, and incommode them, where they desire to be private; this they esteem great Rudeness, and the Effect of the Want of Instruction in the Rules of Civility and good Manners. "We have," say they, "as much Curiosity as you, and when you come into our Towns, we wish for Opportunities of looking at you; but for this purpose we hide ourselves behind Bushes, where you are to pass, and never intrude ourselves into your Company."

Their Manner of entring one another's village has likewise its Rules. It is reckon'd uncivil in travelling Strangers to enter a Village abruptly, without giving Notice of their Approach. Therefore, as soon as they arrive within hearing, they stop and hollow, remaining there till invited to enter. Two old Men usually come out to them, and lead them in. There is in every Village a vacant Dwelling, called *the Strangers' House.* Here they are plac'd, while the old Men go round from Hut to Hut, acquainting the Inhabitants, that Strangers are arriv'd, who are probably hungry and weary; and every one sends them what he can spare of Victuals, and Skins to repose on. When the Strangers are refresh'd, Pipes and Tobacco are brought; and then, but not before, Conversation begins, with Enquiries who they are, whither bound, what News, &c.; and it usually ends with offers of Service, if the Strangers have occasion of Guides, or any Necessaries for continuing their Journey; and nothing is exacted for the Entertainment.

The same Hospitality, esteem'd among them as a principal Virtue, is practis'd by private Persons; of which Conrad Weiser, our Interpreter, gave me the following Instance. He had been naturaliz'd among the Six Nations, and spoke well the Mohock Language. In going thro' the Indian Country, to carry a Message from our Governor to the Council at Onondaga, he call'd at the Habitation of Canassatego, an old Acquaintance, who embrac'd him, spread Furs for him to sit on, plac'd before him some boil'd Beans and Venison, and mix'd some Rum and Water for his Drink. When he was well refresh'd, and had lit his Pipe, Canassatego began to converse with him; ask'd how he had far'd the many Years since they had seen each other; whence he then came; what occasion'd the Journey, &c. Conrad answered all his Questions;

and when the Discourse began to flag, the Indian, to continue it, said, "Conrad, you have lived long among the white People, and know something of their Customs; I have been sometimes at Albany, and have observed, that once in Seven Days they shut up their Shops, and assemble all in the great House; tell me what it is for? What do they do there?" "They meet there," says Conrad, "to hear and learn *good Things.*" "I do not doubt," says the Indian, "that they tell you so; they have told me the same; but I doubt the Truth of what they say, and I will tell you my Reasons. I went lately to Albany to sell my Skins and buy Blankets, Knives, Powder, Rum, &c. You know I us'd generally to deal with Hans Hanson; but I was a little inclin'd this time to try some other Merchant. However, I call'd first upon Hans, and asked him what he would give for Beaver. He said he could not give any more than four Shillings a Pound; 'but,' says he, 'I cannot talk on Business now; this is the Day when we meet together to learn *Good Things,* and I am going to the Meeting.' So I thought to myself, 'Since we cannot do any Business to-day, I may as well go to the meeting too,' and I went with him. There stood up a Man in Black, and began to talk to the People very angrily. I did not understand what he said; but, perceiving that he look'd much at me and at Hanson, I imagin'd he was angry at seeing me there; so I went out, sat down near the House, struck Fire, and lit my Pipe, waiting till the Meeting should break up. I thought too, that the Man had mention'd something of Beaver, and I suspected it might be the Subject of their Meeting. So, when they came out, I accosted my Merchant. 'Well, Hans,' says I, 'I hope you have agreed to give more than four Shillings a Pound.' 'No,' says he, 'I cannot give so much; I cannot give more than three shillings and sixpence.' I then spoke to several other Dealers, but they all sung the same song,—Three and sixpence,—Three and sixpence. This made it clear to me, that my Suspicion was right; and, that whatever they pretended of meeting to learn *good Things,* the real purpose was to consult how to cheat Indians in the Price of Beaver. Consider but a little, Conrad, and you must be of my Opinion. If they met so often to learn *good Things,* they would certainly have learnt some before this time. But they are still ignorant. You know our Practice. If a white Man, in travelling thro' our Country, enters one of our Cabins, we all treat him as I treat you; we dry him if he is wet, we warm him if he is cold, we give him Meat and Drink, that he may allay his Thirst and Hunger; and we spread soft Furs for him to rest and sleep on; we demand nothing in return. But, if I go into a white Man's House at Albany, and ask for Victuals and Drink, they say, 'Where is your Money?' and if I have none, they say, 'Get out, you Indian Dog.' You see they have not yet learned those little *Good Things,* that we need no Meetings to be instructed in, because our Mothers taught them to us when we were Children; and therefore it is impossible their Meetings should be, as they say, for any such purpose, or have any such Effect; they are only to contrive *the Cheating of Indians in the Price of Beaver.*"[1]

1784

[1]It is remarkable that in all Ages and Countries Hospitality has been allow'd as the Virtue of those whom the civiliz'd were pleas'd to call Barbarians. The Greeks celebrated the Scythians for it. The Saracens possess'd it eminently, and it is to this day the reigning Virtue of the wild Arabs. St. Paul, too, in the Relation of his Voyage and Shipwreck on the Island of Melita says the Barbarous People shewed us no little kindness; for they kindled a fire, and received us every one, because of the present Rain, and because of the Cold.—[Franklin's note].

On the Slave-Trade

To the Editor of the Federal Gazette

March 23d, 1790.

Sir,

Reading last night in your excellent Paper the speech of Mr. Jackson in Congress against their meddling with the Affair of Slavery, or attempting to mend the Condition of the Slaves, it put me in mind of a similar One made about 100 Years since by Sidi Mehemet Ibrahim, a member of the Divan of Algiers, which may be seen in Martin's Account of his Consulship, anno 1687. It was against granting the Petition of the Sect called *Erika,* or Purists, who pray'd for the Abolition of Piracy and Slavery as being unjust. Mr. Jackson does not quote it; perhaps he has not seen it. If, therefore, some of its Reasonings are to be found in his eloquent Speech, it may only show that men's Interests and Intellects operate and are operated on with surprising similarity in all Countries and Climates, when under similar Circumstances. The African's Speech, as translated, is as follows.

"Allah Bismillah, &c. God is great, and Mahomet is his Prophet.

"Have these *Erika* considered the Consequences of granting their Petition? If we cease our Cruises against the Christians, how shall we be furnished with the Commodities their Countries produce, and which are so necessary for us? If we forbear to make Slaves of their People, who in this hot Climate are to cultivate our Lands? Who are to perform the common Labours of our City, and in our Families? Must we not then be our own Slaves? And is there not more Compassion and more Favour due to us as Mussulmen, than to these Christian Dogs? We have now above 50,000 Slaves in and near Algiers. This Number, if not kept up by fresh Supplies, will soon diminish, and be gradually annihilated. If we then cease taking and plundering the Infidel Ships, and making Slaves of the Seamen and Passengers, our Lands will become of no Value for want of Cultivation; the Rents of Houses in the City will sink one half; and the Revenues of Government arising from its Share of Prizes be totally destroy'd! And for what? To gratify the whims of a whimsical Sect, who would have us, not only forbear making more Slaves, but even to manumit those we have.

"But who is to indemnify their Masters for the Loss? Will the State do it? Is our Treasury sufficient? Will the *Erika* do it? Can they do it? Or would they, to do what they think Justice to the Slaves, do a greater Injustice to the Owners? And if we set our Slaves free, what is to be done with them? Few of them will return to their Countries; they know too well the greater Hardships they must there be subject to; they will not embrace our holy Religion; they will not adopt our Manners; our People will not pollute themselves by intermarrying with them. Must we maintain them as Beggars in our Streets, or suffer our Properties to be the Prey of their Pillage? For Men long accustom'd to Slavery will not work for a Livelihood when not compell'd. And what is there so pitiable in their present Condition? Were they not Slaves in their own Countries?

"Are not Spain, Portugal, France, and the Italian states govern'd by Despots, who hold all their Subjects in Slavery, without Exception? Even England treats its Sailors as Slaves; for they are, whenever the Government pleases, seiz'd, and confin'd in Ships of War, condemn'd not only to work, but to fight, for small Wages, or a mere Subsistence, not better than our Slaves are allow'd by us. Is their Condition then made worse by their falling into our Hands? No; they have only exchanged one Slavery for another, and I may say a better; for here they are brought into a Land where the Sun of Islamism gives forth its Light, and shines in full Splendor, and they have an Opportunity of making themselves acquainted with the true Doctrine, and thereby saving their immortal Souls. Those who remain at home have not that Happiness. Sending the Slaves home then would be sending them out of Light into Darkness.

"I repeat the Question, What is to be done with them? I have heard it suggested, that they may be planted in the Wilderness, where there is plenty of Land for them to subsist on, and where they may flourish as a free State; but they are, I doubt, too little dispos'd to labour without Compulsion, as well as too ignorant to establish a good government, and the wild Arabs would soon molest and destroy or again enslave them. While serving us, we take care to provide them with every thing, and they are treated with Humanity. The Labourers in their own Country are, as I am well informed, worse fed, lodged, and cloathed. The Condition of most of them is therefore already mended, and requires no further Improvement. Here their Livers are in Safety. They are not liable to be impress'd for Soldiers, and forc'd to cut one another's Christian Throats, as in the Wars of their own Countries. If some of the religious mad Bigots, who now teaze us with their silly Petitions, have in a Fit of blind Zeal freed their Slaves, it was not Generosity, it was not Humanity, that mov'd them to the Action; it was from the conscious Burthen of a Load of Sins, and Hope, from the supposed Merits of so good a Work, to be excus'd Damnation.

"How grossly are they mistaken in imagining Slavery to be disallow'd by the Alcoran! Are not the two Precepts, to quote no more, '*Masters, treat your Slaves with kindness; Slaves, serve your Masters with Cheerfulness and Fidelity,*' clear Proofs to the contrary? Nor can the Plundering of Infidels be in that sacred Book forbidden, since it is well known from it, that God has given the World, and all that it contains, to his faithful Mussulmen, who are to enjoy it of Right as fast as they conquer it. Let us then hear no more of this detestable Proposition, the Manumission of Christian Slaves, the Adoption of which would, be depreciating our Lands and Houses, and thereby depriving so many good Citizens of their Properties, create universal Discontent, and provoke Insurrections, to the endangering of Government and producing general Confusion. I have therefore no doubt, but this wise Council will prefer the Comfort and Happiness of a whole Nation of true Believers to the Whim of a few *Erika,* and dismiss their Petition."

The Result was, as Martin tells us, that the Divan came to this Resolution; "The Doctrine, that Plundering and Enslaving the Christians is unjust, is at best *problematical;* but that it is the Interest of this State to continue the Practice, is clear; therefore let the Petition be rejected."

And it was rejected accordingly.

And since like Motives are apt to produce in the Minds of Men like Opinions and Resolutions, may we not, Mr. Brown, venture to predict, from this Account, that the Petitions to the Parliament of England for abolishing the Slave-Trade, to say nothing of other Legislatures, and the Debates upon them, will have a similar Conclusion? I am, Sir, your constant Reader and humble Servant,

HISTORICUS.

1790

Speech in the Convention

At the Conclusion of Its Deliberations[1]

Mr. President,

I confess, that I do not entirely approve of this Constitution at present; but, Sir, I am not sure I shall never approve it; for, having lived long, I have experienced many instances of being obliged, by better information or fuller consideration, to change my opinions even on important subjects, which I once thought right, but found to be otherwise. It is therefore that, the older I grow, the more apt I am to doubt my own judgment of others. Most men, indeed, as well as most sects in religion, think themselves in possession of all truth, and that wherever others differ from them, it is so far error. Steele, a Protestant, in a dedication, tells the Pope, that the only difference between our two churches in their opinions of the certainty of their doctrine, is, the Romish Church is *infallible,* and the Church of England is *never in the wrong.* But, though many private Persons think almost as highly of their own infallibility as of that of their Sect, few express it so naturally as a certain French Lady, who, in a little dispute with her sister, said, "But I meet with nobody but myself that is *always* in the right." *"Je ne trouve que moi qui aie toujours raison."*

In these sentiments, Sir, I agree to this Constitution, with all its faults,—if they are such; because I think a general Government necessary for us, and there is no *form* of government but what may be a blessing to the people, if well administered; and I believe, farther, that this is likely to be well administered for a course of years, and can only end in despotism, as other forms have done before it, when the people shall become so corrupted as to need despotic government, being incapable of any other. I doubt, too, whether any other Convention we can obtain, may be able to make a better constitution; for, when you assemble a number of men, to have the advantage of their joint wisdom, you inevitably assemble with those men all their prejudices, their passions, their errors of opinion, their local interests, and their selfish views. From such an assembly can a *perfect* production be expected? It therefore astonishes me, Sir, to find this system approaching so near to perfection as it does; and I think

[1]The date of the speech is September 17, 1787, the final day of the Constitutional Convention.

it will astonish our enemies, who are waiting with confidence to hear, that our councils are confounded like those of the builders of Babel, and that our States are on the point of separation, only to meet hereafter for the purpose of cutting one another's throats. Thus I consent, Sir, to this Constitution, because I expect no better, and because I am not sure that it is not the best. The opinions I have had of its *errors* I sacrifice to the public good. I have never whispered a syllable of them abroad. Within these walls they were born, and here they shall die. If every one of us, in returning to our Constituents, were to report the objections he has had to it, and endeavour to gain Partisans in support of them, we might prevent its being generally received, and thereby lose all the salutary effects and great advantages resulting naturally in our favour among foreign nations, as well as among ourselves, from our real or apparent unanimity. Much of the strength and efficiency of any government, in procuring and securing happiness to the people, depends on *opinion,* on the general opinion of the goodness of that government, as well as of the wisdom and integrity of its governors. I hope, therefore, for our own sakes, as a part of the people, and for the sake of our posterity, that we shall act heartily and unanimously in recommending this Constitution, wherever our Influence may extend, and turn our future thoughts and endeavours to the means of having it *well administered.*

On the whole, Sir, I cannot help expressing a wish, that every member of the Convention who may still have objections to it, would with me on this occasion doubt a little of his own infallibility, and, to make *manifest* our *unanimity,* put his name to this Instrument.

1837

from The Autobiography

Part One

Twyford, at the Bishop of St. Asaph's, 1771.

Dear Son,

I have ever had a Pleasure in obtaining any little Anecdotes of my Ancestors. You may remember the Enquiries I made among the Remains of my Relations when you were with me in England; and the Journey I took for that purpose. Now imagining it may be equally agreeable to you to know the Circumstances of *my* Life, many of which you are yet unacquainted with; and expecting a Week's uninterrupted Leisure in my present Country Retirement, I sit down to write them for you. To which I have besides some other Inducements. Having emerg'd from the Poverty and Obscurity in which I was born and bred, to a State of Affluence and some Degree of Reputation in the World, and having gone so far thro' Life with a considerable Share of Felicity, the conducing Means I made use of, which, with the Blessing of God, so well succeeded, my Posterity may like to know, as they may find some of them suitable to their own Situations, and therefore fit to be imitated. That Felicity, when I reflected on it, has induc'd me sometimes to say, that were it offer'd to my Choice, I should have no Objection to a Repetition of the same Life from its Beginning, only asking the Advantage Authors have in a second Edition to correct some Faults of the first. So would I if I might, besides corr[ectin]g the Faults, change some sinister Accidents and Events of it for others more favourable, but tho' this were deny'd, I should still accept the Offer. However, since such a Repetition is not to be expected, the next Thing most like living one's Life over again, seems to be a *Recollection* of that Life; and to make that Recollection as durable as possible, the putting it down in Writing. Hereby, too, I shall indulge the Inclination so natural in old Men, to be talking of themselves and their own past Actions, and I shall indulge it, without being troublesome to others who thro' respect to Age might think themselves oblig'd to give me a Hearing, since this may be read or not as any one pleases. And lastly, (I may as well confess it, since my Denial of it will be believ'd by no body) perhaps I shall a good deal gratify my own *Vanity.* Indeed I scarce ever heard or saw the introductory Words, *Without Vanity I may say,* &c. but some vain thing immediately follow'd. Most People dislike Vanity in others whatever share they have of it themselves, but I give it fair Quarter wherever I meet with it, being pursuaded that it is often productive of Good to the Possessor and to others that are within his Sphere of Action: And therefore in many Cases it would not be quite absurd if a Man were to thank God for his Vanity among the other Comforts of Life.

And now I speak of thanking God, I desire with all Humility to acknowledge, that I owe the mention'd Happiness of my past Life to his kind Providence, which led me to the Means I us'd and gave them Success. My Belief of this, induces me to *hope,* tho' I must not *presume,* that the same Goodness will still be exercis'd towards me in continuing that Happiness, or in enabling me to bear a fatal Reverse, which I may experience as others have done, the Complexion of my future Fortune being known to him only: and in whose Power it is to bless to us even our Afflictions.

The Notes one of my Uncles (who had the same kind of Curiosity in collecting Family Anecdotes) once put into my Hands, furnish'd me with several Particulars relating to our Ancestors. From these Notes I learnt that the Family had liv'd in the same Village, Ecton in Northamptonshire, for 300 Years, and how much longer he knew not (perhaps from the Time when the Name *Franklin* that before was the Name of an Order of People,[1] was assum'd by them for a Surname, when others took Surnames all over the Kingdom). (Here a Note)[2] on a Freehold of about 30 Acres, aided by the Smith's Business which had continued in the Family till his Time, the eldest Son being always bred to that Business. A Custom which he and my Father both followed as to their eldest Sons. When I search'd the Register at Ecton, I found an Account of their Births, Marriages and Burials, from the Year 1555 only, there being no Register kept in that Parish at any time preceding. By that Register I perceiv'd that I was the youngest Son of the youngest Son for 5 Generations back.

My Grandfather Thomas, who was born in 1598, lived at Ecton till he grew too old to follow Business longer, when he went to live with his Son John, a Dyer at Banbury in Oxfordshire, with whom my Father serv'd an Apprenticeship. There my

[1]In medieval England a *franklin* was a middle-class landowner.

[2]Franklin omitted the note he intended to insert here.

Grandfather died and lies buried. We saw his Gravestone in 1758. His eldest Son Thomas liv'd in the House of Ecton, and left it with the Land to his only Child, a Daughter, who with her Husband, one Fisher of Wellingborough sold it to Mr. Isted, now Lord of the Manor there. My Grandfather had 4 Sons that grew up, viz. Thomas, John, Benjamin and Josiah. I will give you what Account I can of them at this distance from my Papers, and if they are not lost in my Absence, you will among them find many more Particulars. Thomas was bred a Smith under his Father, but being ingenious, and encourag'd in Learning (as all his Brothers like wise were) by an Esquire Palmer then the principal Gentlemen in that Parish, he qualify'd for the Business of Scrivener, became a considerable Man in the County Affairs, was a chief Mover of all publick Spirited Undertakings, for the County, or Town of Northampton and his own Village, of which many Instances were told us at Ecton and he was much taken Notice of and patroniz'd by the then Lord Halifax. He died in 1702, Jan. 6, old Stile, just 4 Years a Day before I was born.[3] The Account we receiv'd of his Life and Character from some old People at Ecton, I remember struck you as something extraordinary from its Similarity to what you knew of mine. Had he died on the same Day, you said one might have suppos'd a Transmigration.

John was bred a Dyer, I believe of Woollens. Benjamin, was bred a Silk Dyer, serving an Apprenticeship at London. He was an ingenious Man, I remember him well, for when I was a Boy he came over to my Father in Boston, and lived in the House with us some Years. He lived to a great Age. His Grandson Samuel Franklin now lives in Boston. He left behind him two Quarto Volumes, M.S. of his own Poetry, consisting of little occasional Pieces address'd to his Friends and Relations, of which the following sent to me, is a Specimen. (Here insert it.)[4] He had form'd a Shorthand of his own, which he taught me, but never practising it I have now forgot it. I was nam'd after this Uncle, there being a particular Affection between him and my Father. He was very pious, a great Attender of Sermons of the best Preachers, which he took down in his Shorthand and had with him many Volumes of them. He was also much of a Politician, too much perhaps for his Station. There fell lately into my Hands in London a Collection he had made of all the principal Pamphlets relating to Publick affairs from 1641 to 1717. Many of the Volumes are wanting, as appears by the Numbering, but there still remains 8 Vols. Folio, and 24 in 4to and 8vo.[5] A Dealer in old Books met with them, and knowing me by my sometimes buying of him, he brought them to me. It seems my Uncle must have left them here when he went to America, which was above 50 Years since. There are many of his Notes in the Margins.

This obscure Family of ours was early in the Reformation, and continu'd Protestants thro' the Reign of Queen Mary, when they were sometimes in Danger of Trouble on Account of their Zeal against Popery.[6] They had got an English Bible, and to conceal and secure it, it was fastned open with Tapes under and within the Frame of

[3]In 1752 the Julian (or "Old Style") calendar replaced the Gregorian (or "New Style") calendar. Franklin's birthday (January 6, Old Style) thus advanced eleven days to January 17 (New Style).

[4]No sample was included.

[5]"Folio," "quarto," and "octavo" refer to book sizes made from sheets with two, four, or eight pages printed on each side.

[6]Queen Mary, who reigned from 1553–1558, attempted to restore Roman Catholicism in Protestant England.

a Joint Stool. When my Great Great Grandfather read in it to his Family, he turn'd up the Joint Stool upon his Knees, turning over the Leaves then under the Tapes. One of the Children stood at the Door to give Notice if he saw the Apparitor coming, who was an Officer of the Spiritual Court.[7] In that Case the Stool was turn'd down again upon its feet, when the Bible remain'd conceal'd under it as before. This Anecdote I had from my Uncle Benjamin. The Family continu'd all of the Church of England till about the End of Charles the 2ds Reign,[8] when some of the Ministers that had been outed for Nonconformity, holding Conventicles[9] in Northamptonshire, Benjamin and Josiah adher'd to them, and so continu'd all their Lives. The rest of the Family remain'd with the Episcopal Church.

Josiah, my Father, married young, and carried his Wife with three Children unto New England, about 1682. The Conventicles having been forbidden by Law, and frequently disturbed, induced some considerable Men of his Acquaintance to remove to that Country, and he was prevail'd with to accompany them thither, where they expected to enjoy their Mode of Religion with Freedom. By the same Wife he had 4 Children more born there, and by a second Wife ten more, in all 17, of which I remember 13 sitting at one time at his Table, who all grew up to be Men and Women, and married. I was the youngest Son and the youngest Child but two, and was born in Boston, N. England.

My Mother the 2d Wife was Abiah Folger, a Daughter of Peter Folger, one of the first Settlers of New England, of whom honourable mention is made by Cotton Mather, in his Church History of that Country, (entitled Magnalia Christi Americana) as a *godly learned Englishman,* if I remember the words rightly. I have heard that he wrote sundry small occasional Pieces, but only one of them was printed which I saw now many Years since. It was written in 1675, in the homespun Verse of that Time and People, and address'd to those then concern'd in the Government there. It was in favour of Liberty of Conscience, and in behalf of the Baptists, Quakers, and other Sectaries, that had been under Persecution; ascribing the Indian Wars and other Distresses, that had befallen the Country to that Persecution, as so many Judgments of God, to punish so heinous an Offence; and exhorting a Repeal of those uncharitable Laws. The whole appear'd to me as written with a good deal of Decent Plainness and manly Freedom. The six last concluding Lines I remember, tho' I have forgotten the two first of the Stanza, but the Purport of them was that his Censures proceeded from *Goodwill,* and there he would be known as the Author,

> because to be a Libeller, (says he)
> I hate it with my Heart.
> From Sherburne Town[10] where now I dwell,
> My Name I do put here,
> Without Offence, your real Friend,
> It is Peter Folgier.

[7]An ecclesiastical court established to eliminate heresy.

[8]Charles II reigned from 1660–1685.

[9]The secret and illegal meetings of religious nonconformists.

[10]"In the Island of Nantucket."—[Franklin's note].

My elder Brothers were all put Apprentices to different Trades. I was put to the Grammar School at Eight Years of Age, my Father intending to devote me as the Tithe[11] of his Sons to the Service of the Church. My early Readiness in learning to read (which must have been very early, as I do not remember when I could not read) and the Opinion of all his Friends that I should certainly make a good Scholar, encourag'd him in this Purpose of his. My Uncle Benjamin too approv'd of it, and propos'd to give me all his Shorthand Volumes of Sermons I suppose as a Stock to set up with, if I would learn his Character.[12] I continu'd however at the Grammar School not quite one Year, tho' in that time I had risen gradually from the Middle of the Class of that Year to be the Head of it, and farther was remov'd into the next Class above it, in order to go with that into the third at the End of the Year. But my Father in the mean time, from a View of the Expence of a College Education which, having so large a Family, he could not well afford, and the mean Living many so educated were afterwards able to obtain, Reasons that he gave to his Friends in my Hearing, altered his first Intention, took me from the Grammar School, and set me to a School for Writing and Arithmetic kept by a then famous Man, Mr. Geo. Brownell, very successful in his Profession generally, and that by mild encouraging Methods. Under him I acquired fair Writing pretty soon, but I fail'd in the Arithmetic, and made no Progress in it.

At Ten Years old, I was taken home to assist my Father in his Business, which was that of a Tallow Chandler and Sope-Boiler.[13] A Business he was not bred to, but had assumed on his Arrival in New England and on finding his Dying Trade would not maintain his Family, being in little Request. Accordingly I was employed in cutting Wick for the Candles, filling the Dipping Mold, and the Molds for cast Candles, attending the Shop, going of Errands, &c. I dislik'd the Trade and had a strong Inclination for the Sea; but my Father declar'd against it; however, living near the Water, I was much in and about it, learnt early to swim well, and to manage Boats, and when in a Boat or Canoe with other Boys I was commonly allow'd to govern, especially in any case of Difficulty; and upon other Occasions I was generally a Leader among the Boys, and sometimes led them into Scrapes, of which I will mention one Instance, as it shows an early projecting public Spirit, tho' not then justly conducted. There was a Salt Marsh that bounded part of the Mill Pond, on the Edge of which at Highwater, we us'd to stand to fish for Minews. By much Trampling, we had made it a mere Quagmire. My Proposal was to build a Wharf there fit for us to stand upon, and I show'd my Comrades a large Heap of Stones which were intended for a new House near the Marsh, and which would very well suit our Purpose. Accordingly in the Evening when the Workmen were gone, I assembled a Number of my Playfellows, and working with them diligently like so many Emmets,[14] sometimes two or three to a Stone, we brought them all away and built our little Wharff. The next Morning the Workmen were surpriz'd at Missing the Stones; which were found in our Wharff; Enquiry was made after the Removers; we were discovered and complain'd of; several of us were corrected by our Fathers; and tho' I pleaded the Usefulness of the Work, mine convinc'd me that nothing was useful which was not honest.

[11]Tenth.
[12]Shorthand system.
[13]A maker of candles and soap.
[14]Ants.

I think you may like to know Something of his Person and Character. He had an excellent Constitution of Body, was of middle Stature, but well set and very strong. He was ingenious, could draw prettily, was skill'd a little in Music and had a clear pleasing Voice, so that when he play'd Psalm Tunes on his Violin and sung withal as he sometimes did in an Evening after the Business of the Day was over, it was extreamly agreable to hear. He had a mechanical Genius too, and on occasion was very handy in the Use of other Tradesmen's Tools. But his great Excellence lay in a sound Understanding, and solid Judgment in prudential Matters, both in private and publick Affairs. In the latter indeed he was never employed, the numerous Family he had to educate and the straitness of his Circumstances, keeping him close to his Trade, but I remember well his being frequently visited by leading People, who consulted him for his Opinion in Affairs of the Town or of the Church he belong'd to and show'd a good deal of Respect for his Judgment and Advice. He was also much consulted by private Persons about their Affairs when any Difficulty occur'd, and frequently chosen an Arbitrator between contending Parties. At his Table he lik'd to have as often as he could, some sensible Friend or Neighbour, to converse with, and always took care to start some ingenious or useful Topic for Discourse, which might tend to improve the Minds of his Children. By this means he turn'd our Attention to what was good, just, and prudent in the Conduct of Life; and little or no Notice was ever taken of what related to the Victuals on the Table, whether it was well or ill drest, in or out of season, of good or bad flavour, preferable or inferior to this or that other thing of the kind; so that I was bro't up in such a perfect Inattention to those Matters as to be quite Indifferent what kind of Food was set before me; and so unobservant of it, that to this Day, if I am ask'd I can scarce tell, a few Hours after Dinner, what I din'd upon. This has been a Convenience to me in travelling, where my Companions have been sometimes very unhappy for want of a suitable Gratification of their more delicate because better instructed Tastes and Appetites.

My Mother had likewise an excellent Constitution. She suckled all her 10 Children. I never knew either my Father or Mother to have any Sickness but that of which they dy'd, he at 89 and she at 85 Years of age. They lie buried together at Boston, where I some Years since plac'd a Marble stone over their Grave with this Inscription

Josiah Franklin
And Abiah his Wife
Lie here interred.
They lived lovingly together in Wedlock
Fifty-five Years.
Without an Estate or any gainful Employment,
By constant labour and Industry,
With God's Blessing,
They maintained a large Family
Comfortably;
And brought up thirteen Children,
And seven Grand Children
Reputably.
From this Instance, Reader,
Be encouraged to Diligence in thy Calling,

And distrust not Providence.
He was a pious & prudent Man,
She a discreet and virtuous Woman.
Their youngest Son,
In filial Regard to their Memory,
Places this Stone.
J.F. born 1655—Died 1744. Ætat[15] 89
A.F. born 1667—died 1752—85

By my rambling Digressions I perceive my self to be grown old. I us'd to write more methodically. But one does not dress for private Company as for a publick Ball. 'Tis perhaps only Negligence.

To return, I continu'd thus employ'd in my Father's Business for two Years, that is till I was 12 Years old; and my Brother John, who was bred to that Business having left my Father, married and set up for himself at Rhodeisland, there was all Appearance that I was destin'd to supply his Place and be a Tallow Chandler. But my Dislike to the Trade continuing, my Father was under Apprehensions that if he did not find one for me more agreable, I should break away and get to Sea, as his Son Josiah had done to his great Vexation. He therefore sometimes took me to walk with him, and see Joiners, Bricklayers, Turners, Braziers,[16] &c. at their Work, that he might observe my Inclination, and endeavour to fix it on some Trade or other on Land. It has ever since been a Pleasure to me to see good Workmen handle their Tools; and it has been useful to me, having learnt so much by it, as to be able to do little Jobs my self in my House, when a Workman could not readily be got; and to construct little Machines for my Experiments while the Intention of making the Experiment was fresh and warm in my Mind. My Father at last fix'd upon the Cutler's Trade, and my Uncle Benjamin's Son Samuel who was bred to that Business in London being about that time establish'd in Boston, I was sent to be with him some time on liking. But his Expectations of a Fee with me displeasing my Father, I was taken home again.

From a Child I was fond of Reading, and all the little Money that came into my Hands was ever laid out in Books. Pleas'd with the Pilgrim's Progress, my first Collection was of John Bunyan's Works, in separate little Volumes.[17] I afterwards sold them to enable me to buy R. Burton's Historical Collections; they were small Chapmen's books and cheap 40 or 50 in all. My Father's little Library consisted chiefly of Books in polemic Divinity, most of which I read, and have since often regretted, that at a time when I had such a Thirst for Knowledge, more proper Books had not fallen in my Way, since it was now resolv'd I should not be a Clergyman. Plutarch's Lives[18] there was, in which I read abundantly, and I still think that time spent to great Advantage. There was also a Book of Defoe's, called an Essay on Projects, and another

[15]Latin: aged.
[16]Woodworkers, bricklayers, latheworkers, brassworkers.
[17]John Bunyan (1628–1688) wrote *The Pilgrim's Progress* (1678).
[18]Plutarch (A.D. 46?–120?) was a Greek biographer; *Parallel Lives* presents the biographies of forty-six noted Greek and Roman figures.

of Dr. Mather's, call'd Essays to do Good which perhaps gave me a Turn of Thinking that had an Influence on some of the principal future Events of my Life.[19]

This Bookish Inclination at length determin'd my Father to make me a Printer, tho' he had already one Son, (James) of that Profession. In 1717 my Brother James return'd from England with a Press and Letters[20] to set up his Business in Boston. I lik'd it much better than that of my Father, but still had a Hankering for the Sea. To prevent the apprehended Effect of such an Inclination, my Father was impatient to have me bound to my Brother. I stood out some time, but at last was persuaded and signed the Indentures, when I was yet but 12 Years old. I was to serve as an Apprentice till I was 21 Years of Age, only I was to be allow'd Journeyman's Wages[21] during the last Year. In a little time I made great Proficiency in the Business, and became a useful Hand to my Brother. I now had Access to better Books. An Acquaintance with the Apprentices of Booksellers, enabled me sometimes to borrow a small one, which I was careful to return soon and clean. Often I sat up in my Room reading the greatest Part of the Night, when the Book was borrow'd in the Evening and to be return'd early in the Morning lest it should be miss'd or wanted. And after some time an ingenious Tradesman Mr. Matthew Adams who had a pretty Collection of Books, and who frequented our Printing House, took Notice of me, invited me to his Library, and very kindly lent me such Books as I chose to read. I now took a Fancy to Poetry, and made some little Pieces. My Brother, thinking it might turn to account encourag'd me, and put me on composing two occasional Ballads. One was called the *Light House Tragedy,* and contain'd an Account of the drowning of Capt. Worthilake with his Two Daughters; the other was a Sailor Song on the Taking of *Teach* or Blackbeard the Pirate. They were wretched Stuff, in the Grubstreet Ballad Stile,[22] and when they were printed he sent me about the Town to sell them. The first sold wonderfully, the Event being recent, having made a great Noise. This flatter'd my Vanity. But my Father discourag'd me, by ridiculing my Performances, and telling me Versemakers were generally Beggars; so I escap'd being a Poet, most probably a very bad one. But as Prose Writing has been of great Use to me in the Course of my Life, and was a principal Means of my Advancement, I shall tell you how in such a Situation I acquir'd what little Ability I have in that Way.

There was another Bookish Lad in Town, John Collins by Name, with whom I was intimately acquainted. We sometimes disputed, and very fond we were of Argument, and very desirous of confuting one another. Which disputacious Turn, by the way, is apt to become a very bad Habit, making People often extreamly disagreable in Company, by the Contradiction that is necessary to bring it into Practice, and thence, besides souring and spoiling the Conversation, is productive of Disgusts and perhaps Enmities where you may have occasion for Friendship. I had caught it by reading my Father's Books of Dispute about Religion. Persons of good Sense, I have since observ'd, seldom fall into it, except Lawyers, University Men, and Men of all Sorts that have been bred at Edinborough. A Question was once some how or other started between Collins and me, of the Propriety of educating the Female Sex in

[19]Daniel Defoe's *Essay Upon Projects* (1697) proposed remedies for economic improvement; Cotton Mather's *Bonafacius* was published in 1710.

[20]Type.

[21]Daily wages.

[22]London's Grub Street was populated with literary hacks.

Learning, and their Abilities for Study. He was of Opinion that it was improper; and that they were naturally unequal to it. I took the contrary Side, perhaps a little for Dispute sake. He was naturally more eloquent, had a ready Plenty of Words, and sometimes as I thought bore me down more by his Fluency than by the Strength of his Reasons. As we parted without settling the Point, and were not to see one another again for some time, I sat down to put my Arguments in Writing, which I copied fair and sent to him. He answer'd and I reply'd. Three or four Letters of a Side had pass'd, when my Father happen'd to find my Papers, and read them. Without entering into the Discussion, he took occasion to talk to me about the Manner of my Writing, observ'd that tho' I had the Advantage of my Antagonist in correct Spelling and pointing[23] (which I ow'd to the Printing House) I fell far short in elegance of Expression, in Method and in Perspicuity, of which he convinc'd me by several Instances. I saw the Justice of his Remarks, and thence grew more attentive to the *Manner* in Writing, and determin'd to endeavour at Improvement.

About this time I met with an odd Volume of the Spectator.[24] It was the third. I had never before seen any of them. I bought it, read it over and over, and was much delighted with it. I thought the Writing excellent, and wish'd if possible to imitate it. With that View, I took some of the Papers, and making short Hints of the Sentiment in each Sentence, laid them by a few Days, and then without looking at the Book, try'd to compleat the Papers again, by expressing each hinted Sentiment at length and as fully as it had been express'd before, in any suitable Words, that should come to hand.

Then I compar'd my Spectator with the Original, discover'd some of my Faults and corrected them. But I found I wanted a Stock of Words or a Readiness in recollecting and using them, which I thought I should have acquir'd before that time, if I had gone on making Verses, since the continual Occasion for Words of the same Import but of different Length, to suit the Measure,[25] or of different Sound for the Rhyme, would have laid me under a constant Necessity of searching for Variety, and also have tended to fix that Variety in my Mind, and make me Master of it. Therefore I took some of the Tales and turn'd them into Verse: And after a time, when I had pretty well forgotten the Prose, turn'd them back again. I also sometimes jumbled my Collections of Hints into Confusion, and after some Weeks, endeavour'd to reduce them into the best Order, before I began to form the full Sentences, and compleat the Paper. This was to teach me Method in the Arrangement of Thoughts. By comparing my work afterwards with the original, I discover'd many faults and amended them; but I sometimes had the Pleasure of Fancying that in certain Particulars of small Import, I had been lucky enough to improve the Method or the Language and this encourag'd me to think I might possibly in time come to be a tolerable English Writer, of which I was extreamly ambitious.

My Time for these Exercises and for Reading, was at Night, after Work or before Work began in the Morning; or on Sundays, when I contrived to be in the Printing house alone, evading as much as I could the common Attendance on publick Worship, which my Father used to exact of me when I was under his Care: And

[23]Punctuation.

[24]A daily periodical published between 1711–1712 containing essays on literature and morality.

[25]Meter.

which indeed I still thought a Duty; tho' I could not, as it seemed to me, afford the Time to practise it.

When about 16 Years of Age, I happen'd to meet with a Book, written by one Tryon,[26] recommending a Vegetable Diet. I determined to go into it. My Brother being yet unmarried, did not keep House, but boarded himself and his Apprentices in another Family. My refusing to eat Flesh occasioned an Inconveniency, and I was frequently chid for my singularity. I made my self acquainted with Tryon's Manner of preparing some of his Dishes, such as Boiling Potatoes or Rice, making Hasty Pudding, and a few others, and then propos'd to my Brother, that if he would give me Weekly half the Money he paid for my Board I would board my self. He instantly agreed to it, and I presently found that I could save half what he paid me. This was an additional Fund for buying Books: But I had another Advantage in it. My Brother and the rest going from the Printing House to their Meals, I remain'd there alone, and dispatching presently my light Repast, (which often was no more than a Bisket or a Slice of Bread, a Handful of Raisins or a Tart from the Pastry Cook's, and a Glass of Water) had the rest of the Time till their Return, for Study, in which I made the greater Progress from that greater Clearness of Head and quicker Apprehension which usually attend Temperance in Eating and Drinking. And now it was that being on some Occasion made asham'd of my Ignorance in Figures, which I had twice failed in learning when at School, I took Cocker's Book of Arithmetick,[27] and went thro' the whole by my self with great Ease. I also read Seller's and Sturmy's Books of Navigation,[28] and became acquainted with the little Geometry they contain, but never proceeded far in that Science. And I read about this Time Locke on Human Understanding, and the Art of Thinking by Messrs. du Port Royal.[29]

While I was intent on improving my Language, I met with an English Grammar (I think it was Greenwood's)[30] at the End of which there were two little Sketches of the Arts of Rhetoric and Logic, the latter finishing with a Specimen of a Dispute in the Socratic Method. And soon after I procur'd Xenophon's Memorable Things of Socrates,[31] wherein there are many Instances of the same Method. I was charm'd with it, adopted it, dropt my abrupt Contradiction, and positive Argumentation, and put on the humble Enquirer and Doubter. And being then, from reading Shaftsbury and Collins,[32] become a real Doubter in many Points of our Religious Doctrine, I found this Method safest for my self and very embarassing to those against whom I used it, therefore I took a Delight in it, practis'd it continually and grew very artful and expert in drawing People even of superior Knowledge into concessions the Consequences of which they did not foresee, entangling them in Difficulties out of which

[26]Thomas Tryon, *The Way to Health, Long Life and Happiness, or a Discourse of Temperance* (1683).

[27]Edward Cocker, *Arithmetic* (1677).

[28]John Seller, *An Epitome of the Art of Navigation* (1681), and Samuel Sturmy, *The Mariner's Magazine; or Sturmy's Mathematical and Practical Arts* (1669).

[29]John Locke, *Essays Concerning Human Understanding* (1690); Antoine Arnauld and Pierre Nicole of Port-Royal translated *Logic: or the Art of Thinking* (1662) from Latin into English (1685).

[30]James Greenwood, *An Essay towards a Practical English Grammar* (1711).

[31]Xenophon, *The Memorable Things of Socrates,* translated by Edward Bysshe (1712).

[32]Anthony Ashley Cooper, third Earl of Shaftesbury (1671–1713), was a religious skeptic, and Anthony Collins (1676–1729), a deist.

they could not extricate themselves, and so obtaining Victories that neither my self nor my Cause always deserved.

I continu'd this Method some few Years, but gradually left it, retaining only the Habit of expressing my self in Terms of modest Diffidence, never using when I advance any thing that may possibly be disputed, the Words, *Certainly, undoubtedly,* or any others that give the Air of Positiveness to an Opinion; but rather say, I conceive, or I apprehend a Thing to be so or so, It appears to me, or I should think it so or so for such and such Reasons, or I imagine it to be so, or it is so if I am not mistaken. This Habit I believe has been of great Advantage to me, when I have had occasion to inculcate my Opinions and persuade Men into Measures that I have been from time to time engag'd in promoting. And as the chief Ends of Conversation are to *inform,* or to be *informed,* to *please* or to *persuade,* I wish wellmeaning sensible Men would not lessen their Power of doing Good by a Positive assuming Manner that seldom fails to disgust, tends to create Opposition, and to defeat every one of those Purposes for which Speech was given us, to wit, giving or receiving Information, or Pleasure: For if you would *inform,* a positive dogmatical Manner in advancing your Sentiments, may provoke Contradiction and prevent a candid Attention. If you wish Information and Improvement from the Knowledge of others and yet at the same time express your self as firmly fix'd in your present Opinions, modest sensible Men, who do not love Disputation, will probably leave you undisturb'd in the Possession of your Error; and by such a Manner you can seldom hope to recommend your self in *pleasing* your Hearers, or to persuade those whose Concurrence you desire. Pope says, judiciously,

> Men should be taught as if you taught them not,
> And things unknown propos'd as things forgot,

farther recommending it to us,

> *To speak tho' sure, with seeming Diffidence.*[33]

And he might have coupled with this Line that which he has coupled with another, I think less properly,

> *For Want of Modesty is Want of Sense.*

If you ask why, *less properly,* I must repeat the Lines;

> Immodest Words admit of *no* Defence;
> *For* Want of Modesty is Want of Sense.[34]

Now is not *Want of Sense* (where a Man is so unfortunate as to want it) some Apology for his *Want of Modesty?* and would not the Lines stand more justly thus?

[33]Alexander Pope, *An Essay on Criticism* (1711), lines 574–575, 567. Franklin is quoting from memory. The first line should read, "Men must be taught as if you taught them not," and the third "And speak, tho' sure, with seeming diffidence."

[34]Often attributed to Pope, the couplet is actually from Wentworth Dillon's *Essay on Translated Verse* (1684), lines 113–114. The second line should read, "For want of decency is want of sense."

Immodest Words admit *but this* Defence,
That Want of Modesty is Want of Sense.

This however I should submit to better Judgments.

My Brother had in 1720 or 21, begun to print a Newspaper. It was the second that appear'd in America,[35] and was called *The New England Courant.* The only one before it, was *the Boston News Letter.* I remember his being dissuaded by some of his Friends from the Undertaking, as not likely to succeed, one newspaper being in their Judgment enough for America. At this time 1771 there are not less than five and twenty. He went on however with the Undertaking, and after having work'd in composing the Types and printing off the Sheets I was employ'd to carry the Papers thro' the Street to the Customers. He had some ingenious Men among his Friends who amus'd themselves by writing little Pieces for this Paper, which gain'd it Credit, and made it more in Demand; and these Gentlemen often visited us. Hearing their Conversations, and their Accounts of the Approbation their Papers were receiv'd with, I was excited to try my Hand among them. But being still a Boy, and suspecting that my Brother would object to printing any Thing of mine in his Paper if he knew it to be mine, I contriv'd to disguise my Hand, and writing an anonymous Paper[36] I put it in at Night under the Door of the Printing House. It was found in the Morning and communicated to his Writing Friends when they call'd in as usual. They read it, commented on it in my Hearing, and I had the exquisite Pleasure, of finding it met with their Approbation, and that in their different Guesses at the Author none were named but Men of some Character among us for Learning and Ingenuity.

I suppose now that I was rather lucky in my Judges: And that perhaps they were not really so very good ones as I then esteem'd them. Encourag'd however by this, I wrote and convey'd in the same Way to the Press several more Papers, which were equally approv'd, and I kept my Secret till my small Fund of Sense for such Performances was pretty well exhausted, and then I discovered[37] it; when I began to be considered a little more by my Brother's Acquaintance, and in a manner that did not quite please him, as he thought, probably with reason, that it tended to make me too vain. And perhaps this might be one Occasion of the Differences that we frequently had about this Time. Tho' a Brother, he considered himself as my Master, and me as his Apprentice; and accordingly expected the same Services from me as he would from another; while I thought he demean'd me too much in some he requir'd of me, who from a Brother expected more Indulgence. Our Disputes were often brought before our Father, and I fancy I was either generally in the right, or else a better Pleader, because the Judgment was generally in my favour: But my Brother was passionate and had often beaten me, which I took extreamly amiss; and thinking my Apprenticeship very tedious, I was continually wishing for some Opportunity of shortening it, which at length offered in a manner unexpected.[38]

[35]Actually the fifth.

[36]The first of the "Silence Dogwood" letters, published in the *Courant* from April 12–October 8, 1722.

[37]Revealed.

[38]"I fancy his harsh and tyrannical Treatment of me, might be a means of impressing me with that Aversion to arbitrary Power that has stuck to me thro' my whole Life." [Franklin's note].

One of the Pieces in our News-Paper, on some political Point which I have now forgotten, gave Offence to the Assembly.[39] He was taken up, censur'd and impris-on'd for a Month by the Speaker's Warrant, I suppose because he would not discover his Author. I too was taken up and examin'd before the Council; but tho' I did not give them any Satisfaction, they contented themselves with admonishing me, and dis-miss'd me; considering me perhaps as an Apprentice who was bound to keep his Master's Secrets. During my Brother's Confinement, which I resented a good deal, notwithstanding our private Differences, I had the Management of the Paper, and I made bold to give our Rulers some Rubs in it, which my Brother took very kindly, while others began to consider me in an unfavourable Light, as a young Genius that had a Turn for Libelling and Satyr. My Brother's Discharge was accompany'd with an Order of the House, (a very odd one) *that James Franklin should no longer print the Paper called the New England Courant.* There was a Consultation held in our Printing House among his Friends what he should do in this Case. Some propos'd to evade the Order by changing the Name of the paper; but my Brother seeing In-conveniences in that, it was finally concluded on as a better Way, to let it be printed for the future under the Name of *Benjamin Franklin.* And to avoid the Censure of the Assembly that might fall on him, as still printing it by his Apprentice, the Con-trivance was, that my old Indenture should be return'd to me with a full Discharge on the Back of it, to be shown on Occasion; but to secure to him the Benefit of my Service I was to sign new Indentures for the Remainder of the Term, which were to be kept private. A very flimsy Scheme it was, but however it was immediately exe-cuted, and the Paper went on accordingly under my Name for several Months. At length a fresh Difference arising between my Brother and me, I took upon me to as-sert my Freedom, presuming that he would not venture to produce the new Inden-tures. It was not fair in me to take this Advantage, and this I therefore reckon one of the first Errata of my Life: But the Unfairness of it weigh'd little with me, when un-der the Impression of Resentment, for the Blows his Passion too often urg'd him to bestow upon me. Tho' he was otherwise not an ill-natur'd Man: Perhaps I was too saucy and provoking.

When he found I would leave him, he took care to prevent my getting Employ-ment in any other Printing-House of the Town, by going round and speaking to every Master, who accordingly refus'd to give me Work. I then thought of going to New York as the nearest Place where there was a Printer: and I was the rather inclin'd to leave Boston, when I reflected that I had already made myself a little obnoxious to the governing Party; and from the arbitrary Proceedings of the Assembly in my Brother's Case it was likely I might if I stay'd soon bring myself into Scrapes; and far-ther that my indiscrete Disputations about Religion began to make me pointed at with Horror by good People, as an Infidel or Atheist. I determin'd on the Point: but my Father now siding with my Brother, I was sensible that If I attempted to go openly, Means would be used to prevent me. My Friend Collins therefore undertook to manage a little for me. He agreed with the Captain of a New York Sloop for my Passage, under the Notion of my being a young Acquaintance of his that had got a naughty Girl with Child, whose Friends would compel me to marry her, and

[39]One of the two Houses of the Massachusetts legislature.

therefore I could not appear or come away publickly. So I sold some of my Books to raise a little Money, Was taken on board privately, and as we had a fair Wind in three Days I found my self in New York near 300 Miles from home, a Boy of but 17, without the least Recommendation to or Knowledge of any Person in the Place, and with very little Money in my Pocket.

My Inclinations for the Sea, were by this time worne out, or I might now have gratify'd them. But having a Trade, and supposing my self a pretty good Workman, I offer'd my Service to the Printer of the Place, old Mr. Wm. Bradford,[40] (who had been the first Printer in Pensilvania, but remov'd from thence upon the Quarrel of Geo. Keith). He could give me no Employment, having little to do, and Help enough already. But, says he, my Son at Philadelphia has lately lost his principal Hand, Aquila Rose, by Death. If you got thither I believe he may employ you. Philadelphia was 100 Miles farther. I set out, however, in a Boat for Amboy,[41] leaving my Chest and Things to follow me round by Sea. In crossing the Bay we met with a Squall that tore our rotten Sails to pieces, prevented our getting into the Kill,[42] and drove us upon Long Island. In our Way a drunken Dutchman, who was a Passenger too, fell over board; when he was sinking I reach'd thro' the Water to his shock Pate[43] and drew him up so that we got him in again. His Ducking sober'd him a little, and he went to sleep, taking first out of his Pocket a Book which he desir'd I would dry for him. It prov'd to be my old favourite Author Bunyan's Pilgrim's Progress in Dutch, finely printed on good Paper with copper Cuts,[44] a Dress better than I had ever seen it wear in its own Language. I have since found that it has been translated into most of the Languages of Europe, and suppose it has been more generally read than any other Book except perhaps the Bible. Honest John was the first that I know of who mix'd Narration and Dialogue, a Method of Writing very engaging to the Reader, who in the most interesting Parts finds himself as it were brought into the Company; and present at the Discourse. Defoe in his Cruso, his Moll Flanders, Religious Courtship, Family Instructor, and other Pieces, has imitated it with Success. And Richardson has done the same in his Pamela, &c.[45]

When we drew near the Island we found it was at a Place where there could be no Landing, there being a great Surf on the stony Beach. So we dropt Anchor and swung round towards the Shore. Some People came down to the Water Edge and hallow'd to us, as we did to them. But the Wind was so high and the Surf so loud, that we could not hear so as to understand each other. There were Canoes on the Shore, and we made Signs and hallow'd that they should fetch us, but they either did not understand us, or thought it impracticable. So they went away, and Night coming on, we had no Remedy but to wait till the Wind should abate, and in the mean time the Boatman and I concluded to sleep if we could, and so crouded into the Scuttle with the Dutchman who was still wet, and the Spray beating over the Head of our

[40]William Bradford (1663–1752), an American printer and father of Franklin's competitor, Andrew Bradford (1686–1742).

[41]Perth Amboy, New Jersey.

[42]Narrow channel separating Staten Island, New York, from New Jersey.

[43]Bushy hair.

[44]Engravings.

[45]Daniel Defoe wrote *Robinson Crusoe* (1719), *Moll Flanders* (1722), *Religious Courtship* (1722), *The Family Instructor* (1715–18). Samuel Richardson wrote *Pamela, or Virtue Rewarded* (1740). Franklin reprinted *Pamela* in 1744, thereby publishing the first novel in the colonies.

Boat, leak'd thro' to us, so that we were soon almost as wet as he. In this Manner we lay all Night with very little Rest. But the Wind abating the next Day, we made a Shift to reach Amboy before Night, having been 30 Hours on the Water without Victuals, or any Drink but a Bottle of filthy Rum: The Water we sail'd on being salt.

In the evening I found my self very feverish, and went in to Bed. But having read somewhere that cold Water drank plentifully was good for a Fever, I follow'd the prescription, sweat plentifully most of the Night, my Fever left me, and in the Morning crossing the Ferry, I proceeded on my Journey, on foot, having 50 Miles to Burlington,[46] where I was told I should find Boats that would carry me the rest of the Way to Philadelphia.

It rain'd very hard all the Day, I was thoroughly soak'd and by Noon a good deal tir'd, so I stopt at a poor Inn, where I staid all Night, beginning now to wish I had never left home. I cut so miserable a Figure too, that I found by the Questions ask'd me I was suspected to be some runaway Servant, and in danger of being taken up on that Suspicion. However I proceeded the next Day, and got in the Evening to an Inn within 8 or 10 Miles of Burlington, kept by one Dr. Brown.[47]

He entered into Conversation with me while I took some Refreshment, and finding I had read a little, became very sociable and friendly. Our Acquaintance continu'd as long as he liv'd. He had been, I imagine, an itinerant Doctor, for there was no Town in England, or Country in Europe, of which he could not give a very particular Account. He had some Letters,[48] and was ingenious, but much of an Unbeliever, and wickedly undertook some Years after to travesty the Bible in doggrel Verse as Cotton had done Virgil.[49] By this means he set many of the Facts in a very ridiculous Light, and might have hurt weak minds if his Work had been publish'd: but it never was. At his House I lay that Night, and the next Morning reach'd Burlington. But had the Mortification to find that the regular Boats were gone, a little before my coming, and no other expected to go till Tuesday, this being Saturday. Wherefore I return'd to an old Woman in the Town of whom I had bought Gingerbread to eat on the Water, and ask'd her Advice; she invited me to lodge at her House till a Passage by Water should offer: and being tired with my foot Travelling, I accepted the Invitation. She understanding I was a Printer, would have had me stay at that Town and follow my Business, being ignorant of the Stock necessary to begin with. She was very hospitable, gave me a Dinner of Ox Cheek with great Goodwill, accepting only of a Pot of Ale in return. And I tho't my self fix'd till Tuesday should come. However walking in the Evening by the Side of the River a Boat came by, which I found was going towards Philadelphia, with several People in her. They took me in, and as there was no Wind, we row'd all the Way; and about Midnight not having yet seen the City, some of the Company were confident we must have pass'd it, and would row no farther, the others knew not where we were, so we put towards the Shore, got into a Creek, landed near an old Fence with the Rails of which we made a Fire, the Night being cold, in October, and there we remain'd till Daylight.

[46]In western New Jersey, about eighteen miles from Philadelphia.

[47]John Browne (c. 1667–1737), a religious skeptic, physician, and innkeeper in Burlington.

[48]Education.

[49]Charles Cotton (1630–1687) wrote the parody, *Scarronides, or the First Book of Virgil Travestied* (1664).

Then one of the Company knew the Place to be Cooper's Creek a little above Philadelphia, which we saw as soon as we got out of the Creek, and arriv'd there about 8 or 9 a Clock, on the Sunday morning, and landed at the Market street Wharff.

I have been the more particular in this Description of my Journey, and shall be so of my first Entry into that City, that you may in your Mind compare such unlikely Beginnings with the Figure I have since made there. I was in my Working Dress, my best Cloaths being to come round by Sea. I was dirty from my Journey; my Pockets were stuff'd out with Shirts and Stockings; I knew no Soul, nor where to look for Lodging. I was fatigu'd with Traveling, Rowing and Want of Rest. I was very hungry, and my whole Stock of Cash consisted of a Dutch Dollar and about a Shilling in Copper. The latter I gave the People of the Boat for my Passage, who at first refus'd it on Account of my Rowing; but I insisted on their taking it, a Man being sometimes more generous when he has but a little Money than when he has plenty, perhaps thro' Fear of being thought to have but little.

Then I walk'd up the Street, gazing about, till near the Market House I met a Boy with Bread. I had made many a Meal on Bread, and inquiring where he got it, I went immediately to the Baker's he directed me to in second Street; and ask'd for Bisket, intending such as we had in Boston, but they it seems were not made in Philadelphia, then I ask'd for a threepenny Loaf, and was told they had none such: so not considering or knowing the Difference of Money and the greater Cheapness nor the Names of his Bread, I bad him give me three penny worth of any sort. He gave me accordingly three great Puffy Rolls. I was surpriz'd at the Quantity, but took it, and having no room in my Pockets, walk'd off, with a Roll under each Arm, and eating the other. Thus I went up Market Street as far as fourth Street, passing by the Door of Mr. Read, my future Wife's Father, when she standing at the Door saw me, and thought I made as I certainly did a most awkward ridiculous Appearance. Then I turn'd and went down Chestnut Street and part of Walnut Street, eating my Roll all the Way, and coming round found my self again at Market Street Wharff, near the Boat I came in, to which I went for a Draught of the River Water, and being fill'd with one of my Rolls, gave the other two to a Woman and her Child that came down the River in the Boat with us and were waiting to go farther. Thus refresh'd I walk'd again up the Street, which by this time had many clean dress'd People in it who were all walking the same Way; I join'd them, and thereby was led into the great Meeting house of the Quakers near the Market. I sat down among them, and after looking round a while and hearing nothing said, being very drowsy thro' Labour and want of Rest the preceding Night, I fell fast asleep, and continu'd so till the Meeting broke up, when one was kind enough to rouse me. This was therefore the first House I was in or slept in, in Philadelphia.

Walking again down towards the River, and looking in the Faces of People, I met a young Quaker Man whose Countenance I lik'd, and accosting him requested he would tell me where a Stranger could get Lodging. We were then near the Sign of the Three Mariners. Here, says he, is one Place that entertains Strangers, but it is not a reputable House; if thee wilt walk with me, I'll show thee a better. He brought me to the Crooked Billet in Water-Street. Here I got a Dinner. And while I was eating it, several sly Questions were ask'd me, as it seem'd to be suspected from my youth and Appearance, that I might be some Runaway. After Dinner my Sleepiness return'd:

and being shown to a Bed, I lay down without undressing, and slept till Six in the Evening; was call'd to Supper; went to Bed again very early and slept soundly till the next Morning. Then I made my self as tidy as I could, and went to Andrew Bradford the Printer's. I found in the Shop the old Man his Father, whom I had seen at New York, and who travelling on horse back had got to Philadelphia before me. He introduc'd me to his Son, who receiv'd me civilly, gave me a Breakfast, but told me he did not at present want a Hand, being lately supply'd with one. But there was another Printer in town lately set up, one Keimer,[50] who perhaps might employ me; if not, I should be welcome to lodge at his House, and he would give me a little Work to do now and then till fuller Business should offer.

The old Gentleman said, he would go with me to the new Printer: And when we found him, Neighbour, says Bradford, I have brought to see you a young Man of your Business, perhaps you may want such a One. He ask'd me a few Questions, put a Composing Stick in my Hand to see how I work'd, and then said he would employ me soon, tho' he had just then nothing for me to do. And taking old Bradford whom he had never seen before, to be one of the Towns People that had a Good Will for him, enter'd into a Conversation on his present Undertaking and Prospects; while Bradford not discovering that he was the other Printer's Father, on Keimer's saying he expected soon to get the greatest Part of the Business into his own Hands, drew him on by artful Questions and starting little Doubts, to explain all his Views, what Interest he rely'd on, and in what manner he intended to proceed. I who stood by and heard all, saw immediately that one of them was a crafty old Sophister, and the other a mere Novice. Bradford left me with Keimer, who was greatly surpriz'd when I told him who the old Man was.

Keimer's Printing House I found, consisted of an old shatter'd Press, and one small worn-out Fount of English,[51] which he was then using himself, composing in it an Elegy on Aquila Rose before-mentioned, an ingenious young Man of excellent Character much respected in the Town, Clerk of the Assembly, and a pretty Poet. Keimer made Verses, too, but very indifferently. He could not be said to write them, for his Manner was to compose them in the Types directly out of his Head; so there being no Copy, but one Pair of Cases,[52] and the Elegy likely to require all the Letter, no one could help him. I endeavour'd to put his Press (which he had not yet us'd, and of which he understood nothing) into Order fit to be work'd with; and promising to come and print off his Elegy as soon as he should have got it ready, I return'd to Bradford's who gave me a little Job to do for the present, and there I lodged and dieted. A few Days after Keimer sent for me to print off the Elegy. And now he had got another Pair of Cases, and a Pamphlet to reprint, on which he set me to work.

These two Printers I found poorly qualified for their Business. Bradford had not been bred to it, and was very illiterate; and Keimer tho' something of a Scholar, was a mere Compositor, knowing nothing of Presswork. He had been one of the French Prophets[53] and could act their enthusiastic Agitations. At this time he did not profess any particular Religion, but something of all on occasion; was very ignorant of

[50]Samuel Keimer (c. 1688–1742). Unsuccessful as a printer, he left Philadelphia in 1730.

[51]Oversized type.

[52]Trays of type containing uppercase and lowercase letters.

[53]Religious sect given to trances.

the World, and had, as I afterwards found, a good deal of the Knave in his Composition. He did not like my Lodging at Bradford's while I work'd with him. He had a House indeed, but without Furniture, so he could not lodge me: But he got me a Lodging at Mr. Read's before-mentioned, who was the Owner of his House. And my Chest and Clothes being come by this time, I made rather a more respectable Appearance in the Eyes of Miss Read, than I had done when she first happen'd to see me eating my Roll in the Street.

I began now to have some Acquaintance among the young People of the Town, that were Lovers of Reading with whom I spent my Evenings very pleasantly and gaining Money by my Industry and Frugality, I lived very agreably, forgetting Boston as much as I could, and not desiring that any there should know where I resided, except my Friend Collins who was in my Secret, and kept it when I wrote to him. At length an Incident happended that sent me back again much sooner than I had intended.

I had a Brother-in-law, Robert Holmes,[54] Master of a Sloop, that traded between Boston and Delaware. He being at New Castle 40 Miles below Philadelphia, heard there of me, and wrote me a Letter, mentioning the Concern of my Friends in Boston at my abrupt Departure, assuring me of their Goodwill to me, and that every thing would be accommodated to my Mind if I would return, to which he exhorted me very earnestly. I wrote an Answer to his Letter, thank'd him for his Advice, but stated my Reasons for quitting Boston fully, and in such a Light as to convince him I was not so wrong as he had apprehended.

Sir William Keith[55] Governor of the Province, was then at New Castle, and Capt. Holmes happening to be in Company with him when my Letter came to hand, spoke to him of me, and show'd him the Letter. The Governor read it, and seem'd surpriz'd when he was told my Age. He said I appear'd a young Man of promising Parts, and therefore should be encouraged: The Printers of Philadelphia were wretched ones, and if I would set up there, he made no doubt I should succeed; for his Part, he would procure me the publick Business, and do me every other Service in his Power. This my Brother-in-Law afterwards told me in Boston. But I knew as yet nothing of it; when one Day Keimer and I being at Work together near the Window, we saw the Governor and another Gentleman (which prov'd to be Col. French, of New Castle) finely dress'd, come directly across the Street to our House, and heard them at the Door. Keimer ran down immediately, thinking it a Visit to him. But the Governor enquir'd for me, came up, and with a Condescension and Politeness I had been quite unus'd to, made me many Compliments, desired to be acquainted with me, blam'd me kindly for not having made my self known to him when I first came to the Place, and would have me away with him to the Tavern where he was going with Col. French to taste as he said some excellent Madeira. I was not a little surpriz'd, and Keimer star'd like a Pig poison'd. I went however with the Governor and Col. French, to a Tavern the Corner of Third Street, and over the Madeira he propos'd my Setting up my Business, laid before me the Probabilities of Success, and both he and Col. French assur'd me I should have their Interest and Influence in procuring the Publick Business of both Governments. On my doubting whether my

[54]Robert Holmes (d. before 1743), husband of Franklin's sister Mary, and a ship's captain.

[55]Sir William Keith (1680–1749), governor of Pennsylvania 1717–1726.

Father would assist me in it, Sir William said he would give me a Letter to him, in which he would state the Advantages, and he did not doubt of prevailing with him. So it was concluded I should return to Boston in the first Vessel with the Governor's Letter recommending me to my Father. In the mean time the Intention was to be kept secret, and I went on working with Keimer as usual, the Governor sending for me now and then to dine with him, a very great Honour I thought it, and conversing with me in the most affable, familiar, and friendly manner imaginable.

About the End of April 1724, a little Vessel offer'd for Boston. I took Leave of Keimer as going to see my Friends. The Governor gave me an ample Letter, saying many flattering things of me to my Father, and strongly recommending the Project of my setting up at Philadelphia, as a Thing that must make my Fortune. We struck on a Shoal in going down the Bay and sprung a Leak, we had a blustering time at Sea, and were oblig'd to pump almost continually, at which I took my Turn. We arriv'd safe however at Boston in about a Fortnight. I had been absent Seven Months and my Friends had heard nothing of me; for my Br. Holmes was not yet return'd; and had not written about me. My unexpected Appearance surpriz'd the Family; all were however very glad to see me and made me Welcome, except my Brother. I went to see him at his Printing-House: I was better dress'd than ever while in his Service, having a genteel new Suit from Head to foot, a Watch, and my Pockets lin'd with near Five Pounds Sterling in Silver. He receiv'd me not very frankly, look'd me all over, and turn'd to his Work again. The Journey-Men were inquisitive where I had been, what sort of a Country it was, and how I lik'd it? I prais'd it much, and the happy Life I led in it; expressing strongly my Intention of returning to it; and one of them asking what kind of Money we had there, I produc'd a handful of Silver and spread it before them, which was a kind of Raree-Show[56] they had not been us'd to, Paper being the Money of Boston. Then I took an Opportunity of letting them see my Watch: and lastly, (my Brother still grum and sullen) I gave them a Piece of Eight to drink[57] and took my Leave. This visit of mine offended him extreamly. For when my Mother some time after spoke to him of a Reconciliation, and of her Wishes to see us on good Terms together, and that we might live for the future as Brothers, he said, I had insulted him in such a Manner before his People that he could never forget or forgive it. In this however he was mistaken.

My Father receiv'd the Governor's Letter with some apparent Surprize; but said little of it to me for some Days; when Capt. Holmes returning, he show'd it to him, ask'd if he knew Keith, and What kind of a Man he was: Adding his Opinion that he must be of small Direction, to think of setting a Boy up in Business who wanted yet 3 Years of Being at Man's Estate. Holmes said what he could in favour of the Project; but my Father was clear in the Impropriety of it; and at last gave a flat Denial to it. Then he wrote a civil Letter to Sir William thanking him for the Patronage he had so kindly offered me, but declining to assist me as yet in Setting up, I being in his Opinion too young to be trusted with the Management of a Business so important, and for which the Preparation must be so expensive.

My Friend and Companion Collins, who was a Clerk at the Post-Office, pleas'd with the Account I gave him of my new Country, determin'd to go thither also: And

[56]A sidewalk peepshow.

[57]He gave them a Spanish dollar for drinks.

while I waited for my Fathers Determination, he set out before me by Land to Rhodeisland, leaving his Books which were a pretty Collection of Mathematicks and Natural Philosophy,[58] to come with mine and me to New York where he propos'd to wait for me. My Father, tho' he did not approve Sir William's Proposition was yet pleas'd that I had been able to obtain so advantageous a Character from a Person of such Note where I had resided, and that I had been so industrious and careful as to equip my self so handsomely in so short a time: therefore seeing no Prospect of an Accommodation between my Brother and me, he gave his Consent to my Returning again to Philadelphia, advis'd me to behave respectfully to the People there, endeavour to obtain the general Esteem, and avoid lampooning and libelling to which he thought I had too much Inclination; telling me, that by steady Industry and a prudent Parsimony, I might save enough by the time I was One and Twenty to set me up, and that if I came near the Matter he would help me out with the rest. This was all I could obtain, except some small Gifts as Tokens of his and my Mother's Love, when I embark'd again for New York, now with their Approbation and their Blessing.

The Sloop putting in at Newport, Rhodeisland, I visited my Brother John, who had been married and settled there some Years. He received me very affectionately, for he always lov'd me. A Friend of his, one Vernon, having some Money due to him in Pensilvania, about 35 Pounds Currency, desired I would receive it for him, and keep it till I had his Directions what to remit it in. Accordingly he gave me an Order. This afterwards occasion'd me a good deal of Uneasiness. At Newport we took in a Number of Passengers for New York: Among which were two young Women, Companions, and a grave, sensible Matron-like Quaker-Woman with her Attendants. I had shown an obliging readiness to do her some little Services which impress'd her I suppose with a degree of Good-will towards me. Therefore when she saw a daily growing Familiarity between me and the two Young Women, which they appear'd to encourage, she took me aside and said, Young Man, I am concern'd for thee, as thou has no Friend with thee, and seems not to know much of the World, or of the Snares Youth is expos'd to; depend upon it those are very bad Women, I can see it in all their Actions, and if thee art not upon thy Guard, they will draw thee into some Danger: they are Strangers to thee, and I advise thee in a friendly Concern for thy Welfare, to have no Acquaintance with them. As I seem'd at first not to think so ill of them as she did, she mention'd some Things she had observ'd and heard that had escap'd my Notice; but not convinc'd me she was right. I thank'd her for her kind Advice, and promis'd to follow it. When we arriv'd at New York, they told me where they liv'd, and invited me to come and see them: but I avoided it. And it was well I did: For the next Day, the Captain miss'd a Silver Spoon and some other Things that had been taken out of his Cabbin, and knowing that these were a Couple of Strumpets, he got a Warrant to search their Lodgings, found the stolen Goods, and had the Thieves punish'd. So tho' we had escap'd a sunken Rock which we scrap'd upon in the Passage, I thought this Escape of rather more Importance to me.

At New York I found my Friend Collins, who had arriv'd there some Time before me. We had been intimate from Children, and had read the same Books together. But he had the Advantage of more time for reading, and Studying and a

[58]Natural science.

wonderful Genius for Mathematical Learning in which he far outstript me. While I liv'd in Boston most of my Hours of Leisure for Conversation were spent with him, and he continu'd a sober as well as an industrious Lad; was much respected for his Learning by several of the Clergy and other Gentlemen, and seem'd to promise making a good Figure in Life: but during my Absence he had acquir'd a Habit of Sotting[59] with Brandy; and I found by his own Account and what I heard from others, that he had been drunk every day since his Arrival at New York, and behav'd very oddly. He had gam'd too and lost his Money, so that I was oblig'd to discharge[60] his Lodgings, and defray his Expenses to and at Philadelphia: Which prov'd extreamly inconvenient to me. The then Governor of N[ew] York, Burnet,[61] Son of Bishop Burnet hearing from the Captain that a young Man, one of his Passengers, had a great many Books, desired he would bring me to see him. I waited upon him accordingly, and should have taken Collins with me but that he was not sober. The Governor treated me with great Civility, show'd me his Library, which was a very large one, and we had a good deal of Conversation about Books and Authors. This was the second Governor who had done me the Honor to take Notice of me, which to a poor Boy like me was very pleasing.

We proceeded to Philadelphia. I received on the Way Vernon's Money, without which we could hardly have finish'd our Journey. Collins wish'd to be employ'd in some Counting House; but whether they discover'd his Dramming by his Breath, or by his Behaviour, tho' he had some Recommendations, he met with no Success in any Application, and continu'd Lodging and Boarding at the same House with me and at my Expense. Knowing I had the Money of Vernon's he was continually borrowing of me, still promising Repayment as soon as he should be in Business. At length he had got so much of it, that I was distress'd to think what I should do, in case of being call'd on to remit it. His Drinking continu'd about which we sometimes quarrel'd, for when a little intoxicated he was very fractious. Once in a Boat on the Delaware with some other young Men, he refused to row in his Turn: I will be row'd home, says he. We will not row you, says I. You must or stay all Night on the Water, says he, just as you please. The others said, Let us row; what signifies it? But my Mind being soured with his other Conduct, I continu'd to refuse. So he swore he would make me row, or throw me overboard; and coming along stepping on the Thwarts towards me, when he came up and struck at me and I clapt my Hand under his Crutch, and rising pitch'd him head-foremost into the River. I knew he was a good Swimmer, and so was under little Concern about him; but before he could get round to lay hold of the Boat, we had with a few Strokes pull'd her out of his Reach. And ever when he drew near the Boat, we ask'd if he would row, striking a few Strokes to slide her away from him. He was ready to die with Vexation, and obstinately would not promise to row; however seeing him at last beginning to tire, we lifted him in; and brought him home dripping wet in the Evening. We hardly exchang'd a civil Word afterwards; and a West India Captain who had a Commission to procure a Tutor for the Sons of a Gentleman at Barbadoes, happening to meet with him, agreed to carry him thither. He left me then, promising to remit me the first Money he should receive in order to discharge the Debt. But I never heard of him after.

[59]Getting drunk.
[60]Pay for.
[61]William Burnet (1688–1729), governor of New York and New Jersey (1720–1728).

The Breaking into this Money of Vernon's was one of the first great Errata of my Life. And this Affair show'd that my Father was not much out in his Judgment when he suppos'd me too young to manage Business of Importance. But Sir William, on reading his Letter, said he was too prudent. There was great Difference in Persons, and Discretion did not always accompany Years, nor was Youth always without it. And since he will not set you up, says he, I will do it myself. Give me an Inventory of the Things necessary to be had from England, and I will send for them. You shall repay me when you are able; I am resolv'd to have a good Printer here, and I am sure you must succeed. This was spoken with such an Appearance of Cordiality, that I had not the least doubt of his meaning what he said. I had hitherto kept the Proposition of my Setting up a Secret in Philadelphia, and I still kept it. Had it been known that I depended on the Governor, probably some Friend that knew him better would have advis'd me not to rely on him, as I afterwards heard it as his known Character to be liberal of Promises which he never meant to keep. Yet unsolicited as he was by me, how could I think his generous Offers insincere? I believ'd him one of the best Men in the World.

I presented him an Inventory of a little Printing House, amounting by my Computation to about £100 Sterling. He lik'd it, but ask'd me if my being on the Spot in England to chuse the Types and see that every thing was good of the kind, might not be of some Advantage. Then, says he, when there, you may make Acquaintances and establish Correspondencies in the Bookselling and Stationary Way. I agreed that this might be advantageous. Then says he, get yourself ready to go with Annis;[62] which was the annual Ship, and the only one at that Time usually passing between London and Philadelphia. But it would be some Months before Annis sail'd, so I continu'd working with Keimer, fretting about the Money Collins had got from me, and in daily Apprehensions of being call'd upon by Vernon, which however did not happen for some Years after.

I believe I have omitted mentioning that in my first Voyage from Boston, being becalm'd off Block Island,[63] our People set about catching Cod and hawl'd up a great many. Hitherto I had stuck to my Resolution of not eating animal Food; and on this Occasion, I consider'd with my Master Tryon, the taking every Fish as a kind of unprovok'd Murder, since none of them had or ever could do us any Injury that might justify the Slaughter. All this seem'd very reasonable. But I had formerly been a great Lover of Fish, and when this came hot out of the Frying Pan, it smelt admirably well. I balanc'd some time between Principle and Inclination: till I recollected, that when the Fish were opened, I saw smaller Fish taken out of their Stomachs: Then thought I, if you eat one another, I don't see why we mayn't eat you. So I din'd upon Cod very heartily and continu'd to eat with other People, returning only now and then occasionally to a vegetable Diet. So convenient a thing it is to be a *reasonable Creature,* since it enables one to find or make a Reason for every thing one has a mind to do.

Keimer and I liv'd on a pretty good familiar Footing and agreed tolerably well: for he suspected nothing of my Setting up. He retain'd a great deal of his old

[62]Thomas Annis, captain of the ship that sailed between England and Philadelphia.

[63]Off the coast of Rhode Island.

Enthusiasms, and lov'd Argumentation. We therefore had many Disputations. I us'd to work him so with my Socratic Method, and had trapann'd him so often by Questions apparently so distant from any Point we had in hand, and yet by degrees led to the Point, and brought him into Difficulties and Contradictions that at last he grew ridiculously cautious, and would hardly answer me the most common Question, without asking first, *What do you intend to infer from that?* However it gave him so high an Opinion of my Abilities in the Confuting Way, that he seriously propos'd my being his Colleague in a Project he had of setting up a new Sect. He was to preach the Doctrines, and I was to confound all Opponents. When he came to explain with me upon the Doctrines, I found several Conundrums[64] which I objected to unless I might have my Way a little too, and introduce some of mine. Keimer wore his Beard at full Length, because somewhere in the Mosaic Law it is said, *thou shalt not mar the Corners of thy Beard.*[65] He likewise kept the seventh day Sabbath; and these two Points were Essentials with him. I dislik'd both, but agreed to admit them upon Condition of his adopting the Doctrine of using no animal Food. I doubt, says he, my Constitution will not bear that. I assur'd him it would, and that he would be the better for it. He was usually a great Glutton, and I promised my self some Diversion in half-starving him. He agreed to try the Practice if I would keep him Company. I did so and we held it for three Months. We had our Victuals dress'd and brought to us regularly by a Woman in the Neighbourhood, who had from me a List of 40 Dishes to be prepar'd for us at different times, in all which there was neither Fish Flesh nor Fowl, and the whim suited me the better at this time from the Cheapness of it, not costing us about 18*d.* Sterling each, per Week. I have since kept several Lents most strictly, Leaving the common Diet for that, and that for the common, abruptly, without the least Inconvenience: So that I think there is little in the Advice of making those Changes by easy Gradations, I went on pleasantly, but poor Keimer suffer'd grievously, tir'd of the Project, long'd for the Flesh Pots of Egypt,[66] and order'd a roast Pig. He invited me and two Women Friends to dine with him, but it being brought too soon upon table, he could not resist the Temptation, and ate it all up before we came.

I had made some Courtship during this time to Miss Read. I had a great Respect and Affection for her, and had some Reason to believe she had the same for me: but as I was about to take a long Voyage, and we were both very young, only a little above 18. it was thought most prudent by her Mother to prevent our going too far at present, as a Marriage if it was to take place would be more convenient after my Return, when I should be as I expected set up in my Business. Perhaps too she thought my Expectations not so wellfounded as I imagined them to be.

My chief Acquaintances at this time were, Charles Osborne, Joseph Watson, and James Ralph; All Lovers of Reading. The two first were Clerks to an eminent

[64]Puzzling questions.

[65]"Ye shall not round the corners of your heads, neither shall thou mar the corners of thy beard" (Leviticus 19:27).

[66]"And the whole congregation of the children of Israel murmured against Moses and Aaron in the wilderness: and the children of Israel said unto them, Would to God that we had died by the hands of the Lord in the land of Egypt, when we sat by the flesh pots, and when we did eat bread to the full" (Exodus 16:2,3).

Scrivener or Conveyancer[67] in the Town, Charles Brogden;[68] the other was Clerk to a Merchant. Watson was a pious sensible young Man, of great Integrity. The others rather more lax in their Principles of Religion, particularly Ralph, who as well as Collins had been unsettled by me, for which they both made me suffer. Osborne was sensible, candid, frank, sincere, and affectionate to his Friends; but in litterary Matters too fond of Criticising. Ralph, was ingenious, genteel in his Manners, and extremely eloquent; I think I never knew a prettier Talker. Both of them great Admirers of Poetry, and began to try their Hands in little Pieces. Many pleasant Walks we four had together on Sundays into the Woods near Skuylkill,[69] where we read to one another and conferr'd on what we read.

Ralph was inclin'd to pursue the Study of Poetry, not doubting but he might become eminent in it and make his Fortune by it, alledging that the best Poets must when they first begin to write, make as many Faults as he did. Osborne dissuaded him, assur'd him he had no Genius for Poetry, and advis'd him to think of nothing beyond the Business he was bred to; that in the mercantile way tho' he had no Stock, he might by his Diligence and Punctuality recommend himself to Employment as a Factor,[70] and in time acquire wherewith to trade on his own Account. I approv'd the amusing one's self with Poetry now and then, so far as to improve one's Language, but no farther. On this it was propos'd that we should each of us at our next Meeting produce a Piece of our own Composing, in order to improve by our mutual Observations, Criticisms and Corrections. As Language and Expression was what we had in View, we excluded all Considerations of Invention, by agreeing that the Task should be a version of the 18th Psalm, which describes the Descent of a Deity. When the Time of our Meeting drew nigh, Ralph call'd on me first, and let me know his Piece was ready. I told him I had been busy, and having little Inclination had done nothing. He then show'd me his Piece for my Opinion; and I much approv'd it, as it appear'd to me to have great Merit. Now, says he, Osborne never will allow the least Merit in any thing of mine, but makes 1000 Criticisms out of mere Envy. He is not so jealous of you. I wish therefore you would take this Piece, and produce it as yours. I will pretend not to have had time, and so produce nothing: We shall then see what he will say to it. It was agreed, and I immediately transcib'd it that it might appear in my own hand. We met. Watson's Performance was read: there were some Beauties in it: but many Defects. Osborne's was read: It was much better. Ralph did it Justice, remark'd some Faults, but applauded the Beauties. He himself had nothing to produce. I was backward, seem'd desirous of being excus'd, had not had sufficient Time to correct; &c. but no Excuse could be admitted, produce I must. It was read and repeated; Watson and Osborne gave up the Contest; and join'd in applauding it immoderately. Ralph only made some Criticisms and propos'd some Amendments, but I defended my Text. Osborne was against Ralph, and told him he was no better a Critic than Poet; so he dropt the Argument. As they two went home together, Osborne express'd himself still more strongly in favour of what he thought my Production, having restrain'd himself before as he said, lest I should think it Flattery. But who would have imagin'd, says he, that Franklin had been capable of such a

67One who draws up leases and deeds to property.
68Charles Brockden (1683–1769).
69Schuylkill River in Philadelphia.
70Business agent.

Performance; such Painting, such Force! such Fire! he has even improv'd the Original! In his common Conversation, he seems to have no Choice of Words; he hesitates and blunders; and yet, good God, how he writes! When we next met, Ralph discover'd the Trick, we had plaid him, and Osborne was a little laught at. This Transaction fix'd Ralph in his Resolution of becoming a Poet. I did all I could to dissuade him from it, but He continued scribbling Verses, till Pope cur'd him.[71] He became however a pretty good Prose Writer. More of him hereafter.

But as I may not have occasion again to mention the other two, I shall just remark here, that Watson died in my Arms a few Years after, much lamented, being the best of our Set. Osborne went to the West Indies, where he became an eminent Lawyer and made Money, but died young. He and I had made a serious Agreement, that the one who happen'd first to die, should if possible make a friendly Visit to the other, and acquaint him how he found things in that Separate State. But he never fulfill'd his Promise.

The Governor, seeming to like my Company, had me frequently to his House; and his Setting me up was always mention'd as a fix'd thing. I was to take with me Letters recommendatory to a Number of his Friends, besides the Letter of Credit to furnish me with the necessary Money for purchasing the Press and Types, Paper, &c. For these Letters I was appointed to call at different times, when they were to be ready, but a future time was still named. Thus we went on till the Ship whose Departure too had been several times postponed was on the Point of sailing. Then when I call'd to take my Leave and Receive the Letters, his Secretary, Dr. Bard,[72] came out to me and said the Governor was extreamly busy, in writing, but would be down at Newcastle[73] before the Ship, and there the Letters would be delivered to me.

Ralph, tho' married and having one Child, had determined to accompany me in this Voyage. It was thought he intended to establish a Correspondence, and obtain Goods to sell on Commission. But I found afterwards, that thro' some Discontent with his Wifes Relations, he purposed to leave her on their Hands, and never return again. Having taken leave of my Friends, and interchang'd some Promises with Miss Read, I left Philadelphia in the Ship, which anchor'd at Newcastle. The Governor was there. But when I went to his Lodging, the Secretary came to me from him with the civillest Message in the World, that he could not then see me being engag'd in Business of the utmost Importance; but should send the Letters to me on board, wish'd me heartily a good Voyage and a speedy Return, &c. I return'd on board, a little puzzled, but still not doubting.

Mr. Andrew Hamilton,[74] a famous Lawyer of Philadelphia, had taken Passage in the same Ship for himself and Son: and with Mr. Denham a Quaker Merchant, and Messrs. Onion and Russel Masters of an Iron Work in Maryland, had engag'd the Great Cabin; so that Ralph and I were forc'd to take up with a Birth in the Steerage: And none on board knowing us, were considered as ordinary Persons. But Mr. Hamilton and his Son (it was James, since Governor[75]) return'd from New Castle to

[71]Ralph defended some writers attacked by Alexander Pope in the first edition of the *Dunciad* (1728). Pope responded in *Sawney* with the couplet: "Silence, ye Wolves! while Ralph to Cynthia howls,/And makes Night hideous—Answer him ye Owls." III, 159–60.

[72]Patrick Baird, a surgeon.

[73]Delaware.

[74]Andrew Hamilton (c. 1678–1741).

[75]James Hamilton (c. 1710–1783), governor of Pennsylvania four times between 1748 and 1773.

Philadelphia, the Father being recall'd by a great Fee to plead for a seized Ship. And just before we sail'd Col. French coming on board, and showing me great Respect, I was more taken Notice of, and with my Friend Ralph invited by the other Gentlemen to come into the Cabin, there being now Room. Accordingly we remov'd thither.

Understanding that Col. French had brought on board the Governor's Dispatches, I ask'd the Captain for those Letters that were to be under my Care. He said all were put into the Bag together; and he could not then come at them; but before we landed in England, I should have an Opportunity of picking them out. So I was satisfy'd for the present, and we proceeded on our Voyage. We had a sociable Company in the Cabin, and lived uncommonly well, having the Addition of all Mr. Hamilton's Stores, who had laid in plentifully. In this Passage Mr. Denham[76] contracted a Friendship for me that continued during his life. The Voyage was otherwise not a pleasant one, as we had a great deal of bad Weather.

When we came into the Channel, the Captain kept his Word with me, and gave me an Opportunity of examining the Bag for the Governor's Letters. I found none upon which my Name was put, as under my Care; I pick'd out 6 or 7 that by the Hand writing I thought might be the promis'd Letters, especially as one of them was directed to Basket the King's Printer,[77] and another to some Stationer. We arriv'd in London the 24th of December, 1724. I waited upon the stationer who came first in my Way, delivering the Letter as from Gov. Keith. I don't know such a Person, says he: but opening the Letter, O, this is from Riddlesden;[78] I have lately found him to be a compleat Rascal, and I will have nothing to do with him, nor receive any Letters from him. So putting the Letter into my Hand, he turn'd on his Heel and left me to serve some Customer. I was surprized to find these were not the Governor's Letters. And after recollecting and comparing Circumstances, I began to doubt his Sincerity. I found my Friend Denham, and opened the whole Affair to him. He let me into Keith's Character, told me there was not the least Probability that he had written any Letters for me, that no one who knew him had the smallest Dependance on him, and he laught at the Notion of the Governor's giving me a Letter of Credit, having as he said no Credit to give. On my expressing some Concern about what I should do: He advis'd me to endeavour getting some Employment in the Way of my Business. Among the Printers here, says he, you will improve yourself; and when you return to America, you will set up to greater Advantage.

We both of us happen'd to know, as well as the Stationer, that Riddlesden the Attorney, was a very Knave. He had half ruin'd Miss Read's Father by drawing him in to be bound for him. By his Letter it appear'd, there was a secret Scheme on the foot to the Prejudice of Hamilton, (Suppos'd to be then coming over with us,) and that Keith was concern'd in it with Riddlesden. Denham, who was a Friend of Hamilton's, thought he ought to be acquainted with it. So when he arriv'd in England, which was soon after, partly from Resentment and Ill-Will to Keith and Riddlesden, and partly from Good Will to him: I waited on him, and gave him the Letter. He thank'd me

[76]Thomas Denham (d. 1728), Philadelphia merchant and Franklin's benefactor.
[77]John Baskett (d. 1742).
[78]William Riddlesden (d. before 1733), a swindler known in Maryland as "a Person of matchless Character in Infamy."

cordially, the Information being of Importance to him. And from that time he became my Friend, greatly to my Advantage afterwards on many Occasions.

But what shall we think of a Governor's playing such pitiful Tricks, and imposing so grossly on a poor ignorant Boy! It was a Habit he had acquired. He wish'd to please every body; and having little to give, he gave Expectations. He was otherwise an ingenious sensible Man, a pretty good Writer, and a good Governor for the People, tho' not for his Constituents the Proprietaries,[79] whose Instructions he sometimes disregarded. Several of our best Laws were of his Planning, and pass'd during his Administration.

Ralph and I were inseparable Companions. We took Lodgings together in Little Britain[80] at 3*s.* 6*d.* per Week, as much as we could then afford. He found some Relations, but they were poor and unable to assist him. He now let me know his Intentions of remaining in London, and that he never meant to return to Philadelphia. He had brought no Money with him, the whole he could muster having been expended in paying his Passage. I had 15 Pistoles:[81] So he borrowed occasionally of me, to subsist while he was looking out for Business. He first endeavoured to get into the Playhouse, believing himself qualify'd for an Actor; but Wilkes,[82] to whom he apply'd, advis'd him candidly not to think of that Employment, as it was impossible he should succeed in it. Then he propos'd to Roberts, a Publisher in Pasternoster Row,[83] to write for him a Weekly Paper like the Spectator, on certain Conditions, which Roberts did not approve. Then he endeavour'd to get Employment as a Hackney Writer[84] to copy for the Stationers and Lawyers about the Temple:[85] but could find no Vacancy.

I immediately got into Work at Palmer's then a famous Printing House in Bartholomew Close;[86] and here I continu'd near a Year. I was pretty diligent; but spent with Ralph a good deal of my Earnings in going to Plays and other Places of Amusement. We had together consum'd all my Pistoles, and now just rubb'd on from hand to mouth. He seem'd quite to forget his Wife and Child, and I by degrees my Engagements with Miss Read, to whom I never wrote more than one Letter, and that was to let her know I was not likely soon to return. This was another of the great Errata of my Life, which I should wish to correct if I were to live it over again. In fact, by our Expences, I was constantly kept unable to pay my Passage.

At Palmer's I was employ'd in composing for the second Edition of Woollaston's Religion of Nature.[87] Some of his Reasonings not appearing to me well-founded, I wrote a little metaphysical Piece, in which I made Remarks on them, It was entitled, *A Dissertation on Liberty and Necessity, Pleasure and Pain.* I inscrib'd it to my Friend Ralph. I printed a small Number. It occasion'd my being more consider'd by Mr. Palmer, as a young Man of some Ingenuity, tho' he seriously expostulated with me

[79]The Penn family, proprietors of Pennsylvania.
[80]A London street near St. Paul's Cathedral.
[81]Spanish gold coins, each worth eighteen English shillings.
[82]Robert Wilks (1665?–1732), London actor.
[83]Center of the printing business.
[84]A copyist.
[85]The Inner and the Middle Temples were two of the four sets of buildings that were London's center for the legal profession.
[86]A small square in London, a center for printers.
[87]Actually the third edition (1725) of *The Religion of Nature Delineated* (1722) by William Wollaston.

upon the Principles of my Pamphlet which to him appear'd abominable. My printing this Pamphlet was another Erratum.[88]

While I lodg'd in Little Britain I made an Acquaintance with one Wilcox a Bookseller, whose Shop was at the next Door. He had an immense Collection of second-hand Books. Circulating Libraries were not then in Use; but we agreed that on certain reasonable Terms which I have now forgotten, I might take, read and return any of his Books. This I esteem'd a great Advantage, and I made as much use of it as I could.

My Pamphlet by some means falling into the Hands of one Lyons, a Surgeon, Author of a Book intituled *The Infallibility of Human Judgment,* it occasioned an Acquaintance between us; he took great Notice of me, call'd on me often, to converse on those Subjects, carried me to the Horns a pale Ale-House in [blank] Lane, Cheapside, and introduc'd me to Dr. Mandevile, Author of the Fable of the Bees[89] who had a Club there, of which he was the Soul, being a most facetious entertaining Companion. Lyons too introduc'd me, to Dr. Pemberton, at Batson's Coffee House, who promis'd to give me an Opportunity some time or other of seeing Sir Isaac Newton, of which I was extremely desirous; but this never happened.

I had brought over a few Curiosities among which the principal was a Purse made of the Asbestos, which purifies by Fire. Sir Hans Sloane[90] heard of it, came to see me, and invited me to his House in Bloomsbury Square, where he show'd me all his Curiosities, and persuaded me to let him add to the Number, for which he paid me handsomely.

In our House there lodg'd a young Woman; a Millener, who I think had a Shop in the Cloisters.[91] She had been genteelly bred, was sensible and lively, and of most pleasing Conversation. Ralph read Plays to her in the Evenings, they grew intimate, she took another Lodging, and he follow'd her. They liv'd together some time, but he being still out of Business, and her Income not sufficient to maintain them with her Child, he took a Resolution of going from London, to try for a Country School, which he thought himself well qualify'd to undertake, as he wrote an excellent Hand, and was a Master of Arithmetic and Accounts. This however he deem'd a Business below him, and confident of future better Fortune when he should be unwilling to have it known that he once was so meanly employ'd, he chang'd his Name, and did me the Honour to assume mine. For I soon after had a Letter from him, acquainting me, that he was settled in a small Village in Berkshire, I think it was, where he taught reading and writing to 10 or a dozen Boys at 6 pence each per Week, recommending Mrs. T. to my Care, and desiring me to write to him directing for Mr. Franklin Schoolmaster at such a Place. He continu'd to write frequently, sending me large Specimens of an Epic Poem, which he was then composing, and desiring my Remarks and Corrections. These I gave him from time to time, but endeavour'd rather to discourage his Proceeding. One of Young's Satires was then just publish'd. I

[88]The pamphlet (1725) denied the existence of vice and virtue, laying Franklin open to charges of atheism.

[89]Bernard Mandeville's *The Fable of the Bees, or Private Vices Public Benefits* was published in 1714.

[90]Hans Sloane (1660–1753) succeeded Newton as president of the Royal Society.

[91]Near St. Bartholomew's Church.

copy'd and sent him a great Part of it, which set in a strong Light the Folly of pursuing the Muses with any Hope of Advancement by them. All was in vain. Sheets of the Poem continu'd to come by every Post. In the mean time Mrs. T. having on his Account lost her Friends and Business, was often in Distress, and us'd to send for me, and borrow what I could spare to help her out of them. I grew fond of her Company, and being at this time under no Religious Restraints, and presuming on my Importance to her, I attempted Familiarities (another Erratum) which she repuls'd with a proper Resentment, and acquainted him with my Behaviour. This made a Breach between us, and when he return'd again to London, he let me know he thought I had cancel'd all the Obligations he had been under to me. So I found I was never to expect his Repaying me what I lent to him or advance'd for him. This was however not then of much Consequence, as he was totally unable. And in the Loss of his Friendship I found my self reliev'd from a Burthen. I now began to think of getting a little Money beforehand; and expecting better Work, I left Palmer's to work at Watt's[92] near Lincoln's Inn Fields, a still greater Printing House. Here I continu'd all the rest of my Stay in London.

At my first Admission into this Printing House, I took to working at Press, imagining I felt a Want of the Bodily Exercise I had been us'd to in America, where Presswork is mix'd with Composing. I drank only Water; the other Workmen, nearly 50 in Number, were great Guzzlers of Beer. On occasion I carried up and down Stairs a large Form of Types in each hand, when others carried but one in both Hands. They wonder'd to see from this and several Instances that the Water-American as they call'd me was *stronger* than themselves who drank *strong* Beer. We had an Alehouse Boy who attended always in the House to supply the Workmen. My Companion at the Press, drank every day a Pint before Breakfast, a Pint at Breakfast with his Bread and Cheese; a Pint between Breakfast and Dinner; a Pint at Dinner; a Pint in the Afternoon about Six o'Clock, and another when he had done his Day's-Work. I thought it a detestable Custom. But it was necessary, he suppos'd, to drink *strong* Beer that he might be *strong* to labour. I endeavour'd to convince him that the Bodily Strength afforded by Beer could only be in proportion to the Grain or Flour of the Barley dissolved in the Water of which it was made; that there was more Flour in a Penny-worth of Bread, and therefore if he would eat that with a Pint of Water, it would give him more Strength than a Quart of Beer. He drank on however, and had 4 or 5 Shillings to pay out of his Wages every Saturday Night for that muddling Liquor; an Expence I was free from. And thus these poor Devils keep themselves always under.

Watts after some Weeks desiring to have me in the Composing Room, I left the Pressmen. A new *Bienvenu*[93] or sum for drink being 5*s.*, was demanded of me by the Compositors. I thought it an Imposition, as I had paid below. The Master thought so too, and forbad my Paying it. I stood out two or three Weeks, was accordingly considered as an Excommunicate, and had so many little Pieces of private Mischief done me, by mixing my Sorts,[94] transposing my Pages, breaking my Matter,[95] &c. &c. if I were ever so little out of the Room, and all ascrib'd to the Chapel Ghost, which they

[92]John Watts (c. 1678–1763).
[93]French: Welcome.
[94]Type characters or letters.
[95]Type set up for printing.

said ever hunted those not regularly admitted, that notwithstanding the Master's Protection, I found myself oblig'd to comply and pay the Money; convinc'd of the Folly of being on ill Terms with those one is to live with continually. I was now on a fair Footing with them, and soon acquir'd considerable influence. I propos'd some reasonable Alterations in their Chapel[96] Laws, and carried them against all Opposition. From my Example a great Part of them, left their muddling Breakfast of Beer and Bread and Cheese, finding they could with me be supply'd from a neighbouring House with a large Porringer of hot Water-gruel, sprinkled with Pepper, crumb'd with Bread, and a Bit of Butter in it, for the Price of a Pint of Beer, viz, three halfpence. This was a more confortable as well as cheaper Breakfast, and kept their Heads clearer. Those who continu'd sotting with Beer all day, were often, by not paying, out of Credit at the Alehouse, and us'd to make Interest with me to get Beer, *their Light,* as they phras'd it, *being out.* I watch'd the Pay table on Saturday Night, and collected what I stood engag'd for them, having to pay some times near Thirty Shillings a Week on their Accounts. This, and my being esteem'd a pretty good Riggite, that is a jocular verbal Satyrist, supported my Consequence in the Society. My constant Attendance, (I never making a St. Monday),[97] recommended me to the Master; and my uncommon Quickness at Composing, occasion'd my being put upon all Work of Dispatch which was generally better paid. So I went on now very agreably.

My Lodging in Little Britain being too remote, I found another in Dukestreet opposite to the Romish Chapel. It was two pair of Stairs backwards at an Italian Warehouse. A Widow Lady kept the House; she had a Daughter and a Maid Servant, and a Journeyman who attended the Warehouse, but lodg'd abroad. After sending to enquire my Character at the House where I last lodg'd, she agreed to take me in at the same Rate, 3*s.* 6*d.* per Week, cheaper as she said from the Protection she expected in having a Man lodge in the House. She was a Widow, an elderly Woman, had been bred a Protestant, being a Clergyman's Daughter, but was converted to the Catholic Religion by her Husband, whose Memory she much revered, had lived much among People of Distinction, and knew a 1000 Anecdotes of them as far back as the Times of Charles the Second. She was lame in her Knees with the Gout, and therefore seldom stirr'd out of her Room, so sometimes wanted Company; and hers was so highly amusing to me; that I was sure to spend an Evening with her whenever she desired it. Our Supper was only half an Anchovy each, on a very little Strip of Bread and Butter, and half a Pint of Ale between us. But the Entertainment was in her Conversation. My always keeping good Hours, and giving little Trouble in the Family, made her unwilling to part with me; so that when I talk'd of a lodging I had heard of, nearer my Business, for 2*s.* a Week, which intent as I now was on saving Money, made some Difference; she bid me not think of it, for she would abate me two Shillings a Week for the future, so I remain'd with her at 1*s.* 6*d.* as long as I staid in London.

In a Garret of her House there lived a Maiden Lady of 70 in the most retired Manner, of whom my Landlady gave me this Account, that she was a Roman

[96] "A Printing House is always called a Chappel by the Workmen." [Franklin's note].

[97] *I.e.,* never taking off Monday as a day of religious observance.

Catholic, had been sent abroad when young and lodg'd in a Nunnery with an Intent of becoming a Nun: but the Country not agreeing with her, she return'd to England, where there being no Nunnery, she had vow'd to lead the Life of a Nun as near as might be done in those Circumstances: Accordingly she had given all her Estate to charitable uses, reserving only Twelve Pounds a Year to live on, and out of this Sum she still gave a great deal in Charity, living her self on Water-gruel only, and using no Fire but to boil it. She had lived many Years in that Garret, being permitted to remain there gratis by successive Catholic Tenants of the House below, as they deem'd it a Blessing to have her there. A Priest visited her, to confess her every Day. I have ask'd her, says my Landlady, how she, as she liv'd, could possibly find so much Employment for a Confessor? O, says she, it is impossible to avoid *vain Thoughts.* I was permitted once to visit her: She was chearful and polite, and convers'd pleasantly. The Room was clean, but had no other Furniture than a Matras, a Table with a Crucifix and Book, a Stool which she gave me to sit on, and a Picture over the Chimney of St. Veronica, displaying her Handkerchief with the miraculous Figure of Christ's bleeding Face on it, which she explain'd to me with great Seriousness. She look'd pale, but was never sick, and I give it as another Instance on how small an Income Life and Health may be supported.

At Watts's Printinghouse I contracted an Acquaintance with an ingenious young Man, one Wygate, who having wealthy Relations, had been better educated than most Printers, was a tolerable Latinist, spoke French, and lov'd Reading. I taught him, and a Friend of his, to swim, at twice going into the River, and they soon became good Swimmers. They introduc'd me to some Gentlemen from the Country who went to Chelsea by Water to see the College[98] and Don Saltero's Curiosities.[99] In our Return, at the Request of the Company, whose Curiosity Wygate had excited, I stript and leapt into the River, and swam from near Chelsea to Blackfryars,[100] performing on the Way many Feats of Activity both upon and under Water, that surpriz'd and pleas'd those to whom they were Novelties. I had from a Child been ever delighted with this Exercise, had studied and practis'd all Thevenot's Motions and Positions,[101] added some of my own, aiming at the graceful and easy, as well as the Useful. All these I took this Occasion of exhibiting to the Company, and was much flatter'd by their Admiration. And Wygate, who was desirous of becoming a Master, grew more and more attach'd to me, on that account, as well as from the Similarity of our Studies. He at length propos'd to me travelling all over Europe together, supporting ourselves everywhere by working at our Business. I was once inclin'd to it. But mentioning it to my good Friend Mr. Denham, with whom I often spent an Hour, when I had Leisure. He dissuaded me from it, advising me to think only of returning to Pensilvania, which he was now about to do.

I must record one Trait of this good Man's Character. He had formerly been in Business at Bristol, but fail'd in Debt to a Number of People, compounded[102] and went to America. There, by a close Application to Business as a Merchant, he

[98]Chelsea Hospital, erected on the site of the former Chelsea College.

[99]James Salter exhibited various curiosities of doubtful authenticity, including the sword of William the Conqueror and the tears of Job.

[100]Three and one half miles.

[101]Melchisédec de Thévenot, *The Art of Swimming* (1699).

[102]Partially settled his debts.

acquir'd a plentiful Fortune in a few Years. Returning to England in the Ship with me, He invited his old Creditors to an Entertainment, at which he thank'd them for the easy Composition they had favor'd him with, and when they expected nothing but the Treat, every Man at the first Remove,[103] found under his Plate an Order on a Banker for the full Amount of the unpaid Remainder with Interest.

He now told me he was about to return to Philadelphia, and should carry over a great Quantity of Goods in order to open a Store there: He propos'd to take me over as his Clerk, to keep his Books (in which he would instruct me) copy his Letters, and attend the Store. He added, that as soon as I should be acquainted with mercantile Business he would promote me by sending me with a Cargo of Flour and Bread &c. to the West Indies, and procure me Commissions from others; which would be profitable, and if I manag'd well, would establish me handsomely. The Thing pleas'd me, for I was grown tired of London, remember'd with Pleasure the happy Months I had spent in Pennsylvania, and wish'd again to see it. Therefore I immediately agreed, on the Terms of Fifty Pounds a Year, Pennsylvania Money; less indeed than my present Gettings as a Compostor, but affording a better Prospect.

I now took Leave of Printing, as I thought for ever, and was daily employ'd in my new Business; going about with Mr. Denham among the Tradesmen, to purchase various Articles, and seeing them pack'd up, doing Errands, calling upon Workmen to dispatch, &c. and when all was on board, I had a few Days Leisure. On one of these Days I was to my Surprize sent for by a great Man I knew only by Name, a Sir William Wyndham[104] and I waited upon him. He had heard by some means or other of my Swimming from Chelsey to Blackfryars, and of my teaching Wygate and another young Man to swim in a few Hours. He had two Sons about to set out on their Travels; he wish'd to have them first taught Swimming; and propos'd to gratify me handsomely if I would teach them. They were not yet come to Town and my Stay was uncertain, so I could not undertake it. But from this Incident I thought it likely, that if I were to remain in England and open a Swimming School, I might get a good deal of Money. And it struck me so strongly, that had the Overture been sooner made me, probably I should not so soon have returned to America. After many Years, you and I had something of more Importance to do with one of these Sons of Sir William Wyndham, become Earl of Egremont, which I shall mention in its Place.

Thus I spent about 18 months in London. Most Part of the Time, I work'd hard at my Business, and spent but little upon my self except in seeing Plays and in Books. My friend Ralph had kept me poor. He owed me about 27 Pounds; which I was now never likely to receive; a great Sum out of my small Earnings. I lov'd him notwithstanding, for he had many amiable Qualities. Tho' I had by no means improv'd my Fortune. But I had pick'd up some very ingenious Acquaintance whose Conversation was of great Advantage to me, and I had read considerably.

We sail'd from Gravesend on the 23rd of July 1726. For the Incidents of the Voyage, I refer you to my Journal, where you will find them all minutely related. Perhaps the most important Part of that Journal is the *Plan*[105] to be found in it which I

[103]First clearing of the plates.

[104]Sir William Wyndham (1687–1740), English politician.

[105]The full text of the "Plan" is lost.

formed at Sea, for regulating my future Conduct in Life. It is the more remarkable, as being form'd when I was so young, and yet being pretty faithfully adhered to quite thro' to old Age. We landed in Philadelphia the 11th of October, where I found sundry Alterations. Keith was no longer Governor, being superceded by Major Gordon:[106] I met him walking the Streets as a common Citizen. He seem'd a little asham'd at seeing me, but pass'd without saying any thing. I should have been as much asham'd at seeing Miss Read, had not her Friends, despairing with Reason of my Return, after the Receipt of my Letter, persuaded her to marry another, one Rogers, a Potter, which was done in my Absence. With him however she was never happy, and soon parted from him, refusing to cohabit with him, or bear his Name It being now said that he had another Wife. He was a worthless Fellow tho' an excellent Workman which was the Temptation to her Friends. He got into Debt, and ran away in 1727 or 28. Went to the West Indies, and died there. Keimer had got a better House, a Shop well supply'd with Stationary, plenty of new Types, a number of Hands tho' none good, and seem'd to have a great deal of Business.

Mr. Denham took a Store in Water Street, where we open'd our Goods. I attended the Business diligently, studied Accounts, and grew in a little Time expert at selling. We lodg'd and boarded together, he counsell'd me as a Father, having a sincere Regard for me: I respected and lov'd him: and we might have gone on together very happily: But in the Beginning of Feby. 1726/7 when I had just pass'd my 21st Year, we both were taken ill. My Distemper was a Pleurisy, which very nearly carried me off: I suffered a good deal, gave up the Point[107] in my own mind, and was rather disappointed when I found my Self recovering; regretting in some degree that I must now some time or other have all that disagreable Work to do over again. I forget what his Distemper was. It held him a long time, and at length carried him off. He left me a small Legacy in a nuncupative Will,[108] as a Token of his Kindness for me, and he left me once more to the wide World. For the Store was taken into the Care of his Executors, and my Employment under him ended: My Brother-in-law Holmes, being now at Philadelphia, advis'd my Return to my Business. And Keimer tempted me with an Offer of large Wages by the Year to come and take the Management of his Printing–House, that he might better attend his Stationer's Shop. I had heard a bad Character of him in London, from his Wife and her Friends, and was not fond of having any more to do with him. I try'd for farther Employment as a Merchant's Clerk; but not readily meeting with any, I clos'd again with Keimer.

I found in *his* House these Hands; Hugh Meredith[109] a Welsh-Pensilvanian, 30 Years of Age, bred to Country Work: honest, sensible, had a great deal of solid Observation, was something of a Reader, but given to drink: Stephen Potts,[110] a young Country Man of full Age, bred to the Same: of uncommon natural Parts, and great Wit and Humour, but a little idle. These he had agreed with at extream low Wages, per Week, to be rais'd a Shilling every 3 Months, as they would deserve by improving in their Business, and the Expectation of these high Wages to come on hereafter

[106]Patrick Gordon (1644–1736), Governor of Pennsylvania, 1726–1736.

[107]Will to live.

[108]An oral will.

[109]Hugh Meredith (c. 1696–c. 1749), later Franklin's business partner.

[110]Stephen Potts (d. 1758), bookseller and tavern keeper.

was what he had drawn them in with. Meredith was to work at Press, Potts at Bookbinding, which he by Agreement, was to teach them, tho' he knew neither one nor t'other. John—a wild Irishman brought up to no Business, whose Service for 4 Years Keimer had purchas'd from the Captain of a Ship. He too was to be made a Pressman. George Webb,[111] an Oxford Scholar, whose Time for 4 Years he had likewise bought intending him for a Compositor: of whom more presently. And David Harry,[112] a Country Boy, whom he had taken Apprentice. I soon perceiv'd that the Intention of engaging me at Wages so much higher than he had been us'd to give, was to have these raw cheap Hands form'd thro' me, and as soon as I had instructed them, then, they being all articled to him, he should be able to do without me. I went on however, very chearfully; put his Printing House in Order, which had been in great Confusion, and brought his Hands by degrees to mind their Business and to do it better.

It was an odd Thing to find an Oxford Scholar in the Situation of a bought Servant. He was not more than 18 Years of Age, and gave me this Account of himself; that he was born in Gloucester, educated at a Grammar School there, had been distinguish'd among the Scholars for some apparent Superiority in performing his Part when they exhibited Plays; belong'd to the Witty Club there, and had written some Pieces in Prose and Verse which were printed in the Gloucester Newspapers. Thence he was sent to Oxford; there he continu'd about a Year, but not well-satisfy'd, wishing of all things to see London and become a Player. At length receiving his Quarterly allowance of 15 Guineas, instead of discharging his Debts, he walk'd out of Town, hid his Gown in a Furz Bush,[113] and footed it to London, where having no Friend to advise him, he fell into bad Company, soon spent his Guineas, found no means of being introduc'd among the Players, grew necessitous, pawn'd his Cloaths and wanted Bread. Walking the Street very hungry, and not knowing what to do with himself, a Crimp's Bill[114] was put into his Hand, offering immediate Entertainment and Encouragement to such as would bind themselves to serve in America. He went directly, sign'd the Indentures, was put into the Ship and came over; never writing a Line to acquaint his Friends what was become of him. He was lively, witty, goodnatur'd, and a pleasant Companion, but idle, thoughtless and imprudent to the last Degree.

John the Irishman soon ran away. With the rest I began to live very agreably; for they all respected me, the more as they found Keimer incapable of instructing them, and that from me they learnt something daily. We never work'd on a Saturday, that being Keimer's Sabbath. So I had two Days for Reading. My Acquaintance with Ingenious People in the Town, increased. Keimer himself treated me with great Civility, and apparent Regard; and nothing now made me uneasy but my Debt to Vernon, which I was yet unable to pay being hitherto but a poor Oeconomist. He however kindly made no Demand of it.

[111]George Webb (b. c. 1709), a printer.
[112]David Harry (1708–1760), later first printer in Barbados.
[113]He hid his academic robe in an evergreen bush.
[114]An advertisement for free passage to the colonies in exchange for labor.

Our Printing-House often wanted Sorts, and there was no Letter Founder in America. I had seen Types cast at James's in London,[115] but without much Attention to the Manner: However I now contriv'd a Mould, made use of the Letters we had, as Puncheons,[116] struck the Matrices[117] in Lead, and thus supply'd in a pretty tolerable way all Deficiencies. I also engrav'd several Things on occasion. I made the Ink, I was Warehouse-man and every thing, in short quite a Factotum.[118]

But however serviceable I might be, I found that my Services became every Day of less Importance, as the other Hands improv'd in the Business. And when Keimer paid my second Quarter's Wages, he let me know that he felt them too heavy, and thought I should make an Abatement. He grew by degrees less civil, put on more of the Master, frequently found Fault, was captious and seem'd ready for an Outbreaking. I went on nevertheless with a good deal of Patience, thinking that his incumber'd Circumstances were partly the Cause. At length a Trifle snapt our Connexion. For a great Noise happening near the Courthouse, I put my Head out of the Window to see what was the Matter. Keimer being in the Street look'd up and saw me, call'd out to me in a loud Voice and angry Tone to mind my Business, adding some reproachful Words, that nettled me the more for their Publicity, all the Neighbours who were looking out on the same Occasion being Witnesses how I was treated. He came up immediately into the Printing-House, continu'd the Quarrel, high Words pass'd on both Sides, he gave me the Quarter's Warning we had stipulated, expressing a Wish that he had not been oblig'd to so long a Warning: I told him his Wish was unnecessary for I would leave him that Instant; and so taking my Hat walk'd out of Doors; desiring Meredith[119] whom I saw below to take care of some Things I left, and bring them to my Lodging.

Meredith came accordingly in the Evening, when we talk'd my Affair over. He had conceiv'd a great Regard for me, and was very unwilling that I should leave the House while he remain'd in it. He dissuaded me from returning to my native Country which I began to think of. He reminded me that Keimer was in debt for all he possess'd, that his Creditors began to be uneasy, that he kept his Shop miserably, sold often without Profit for ready Money, and often trusted without keeping Accounts. That he must therefore fail; which would make a Vacancy I might profit of. I objected my Want of Money. He then let me know, that his Father had a high Opinion of me, and from some Discourse that had pass'd between them, he was sure would advance Money to set us up, if I would enter into Partnership with him. My Time, says he, will be out with Keimer in the Spring. By that time we may have our Press and Types in from London: I am sensible I am no Workman. If you like it, Your Skill in the Business shall be set against the Stock I furnish; and we will share the Profits equally. The Proposal was agreeable, and I consented. His Father was in Town, and approv'd of it, the more as he saw I had great Influence with his Son, had prevail'd on him to abstain long from Dramdrinking,[120] and he hop'd might break him of that wretched Habit entirely, when we came to be so closely connected. I gave an Inventory to the

[115]Thomas James's foundry, the largest in London.

[116]Stamping tools.

[117]Molds for casting type.

[118]Jack-of-all-trades.

[119]Simon Meredith (d. 1745?).

[120]Drinking small measures of alcoholic beverages.

Father, who carry'd it to a Merchant; the Things were sent for; the Secret was to be kept till they should arrive, and in the mean time I was to get work if I could at the other Printing House. But I found no Vacancy there, and so remain'd idle a few Days, when Keimer, on a Prospect of being employ'd to print some Paper-money, in New Jersey, which would require Cuts and various Types that I only could supply, and apprehending Bradford might engage me and get the Jobb from him, sent me a very civil Message, that old Friends should not part for a few Words, the Effect of sudden Passion, and wishing me to return. Meredith persuaded me to comply, as it would give more Opportunity for his Improvement under my daily Instructions. So I return'd, and we went on more smoothly than from some time before. The New Jersey Jobb was obtain'd. I contriv'd a Copper-Plate Press for it, the first that had been seen in the Country. I cut several Ornaments and Checks for the Bills. We went together to Burlington, where I executed the Whole to Satisfaction, and he received so large a Sum for the Work, as to be enabled thereby to keep his Head much longer above Water.

At Burlington I made an Acquaintance with many principal People of the Province. Several of them had been appointed by the Assembly a Committee to attend the Press, and take Care that no more Bills were printed than the Law directed. They were therefore by Turns constantly with us, and generally he who attended brought with him a Friend or two for company. My Mind having been much more improv'd by Reading than Keimer's, I suppose it was for that Reason my Conversation seem'd to be more valu'd. They had me to their Houses, introduc'd me to their Friends and show'd me much Civility, while he, tho' the Master, was a little neglected. In truth he was an odd Fish, ignorant of common Life, fond of rudely opposing receiv'd Opinions, slovenly to extream dirtiness, enthusiastic in some Points of Religion, and a little Knavish withal. We continu'd there near 3 Months, and by that time I could reckon among my acquired Friends, Judge Allen, Samuel Bustill, the Secretary of the Province, Isaac Pearson, Joseph Cooper and several of the Smiths, Members of Assembly, and Isaac Decow the Surveyor General. The latter was a shrewd sagacious old Man, who told me that he began for himself when young by wheeling Clay for the Brickmakers, learnt to write after he was of Age, carry'd the Chain for Surveyors, who taught him Surveying, and he had now by his Industry acquir'd a good Estate; and says he, I foresee, that you will soon work this Man out of his Business and make a Fortune in it at Philadelphia. He had not then the least Intimation of my Intention to set up there or any where. These Friends were afterwards of great Use to me, as I occasionally was to some of them. They all continued their Regard for me as long as they lived.

Before I enter upon my public Appearance in Business it may be well to let you know the then State of my Mind, with regard to my Principles and Morals, that you may see how far those influenc'd the future Events of my Life. My Parents had early given me religious Impressions, and brought me through my Childhood piously in the Dissenting Way.[121] But I was scarce 15 when, after doubting by turns of several Points as I found them disputed in the different Books I read, I began to doubt of Revelation it self. Some Books against Deism fell into my Hands; they were said to

[121]As a Congregationalist, who dissents from the doctrines of the Church of England.

be the Substance of Sermons preached at Boyle's Lectures.[122] It happened that they wrought an Effect on me quite contrary to what was intended by them: For the Arguments of the Deists which were quoted to be refuted, appeared to me much stronger than the Refutations. In short I soon became a thorough Deist. My Arguments perverted some others, particularly Collins and Ralph: but each of them having afterwards wrong'd me greatly without the least Compunction and recollecting Keith's Conduct towards me, (who was another Freethinker) and my own towards Vernon and Miss Read which at Times gave me great Trouble, I began to suspect that this Doctrine tho' it might be true, was not very useful. My London Pamphlet, which had for its Motto those Lines of Dryden

> —Whatever is, is right.—
> Tho' purblind Man.
> Sees but a Part of the Chain, the nearest Link,
> His Eyes not carrying to the equal Beam,
> That poizes all, above.[123]

And from the Attributes of God, his infinite Wisdom, Goodness and Power concluded that nothing could possibly be wrong in the World, and that Vice and Virtue were empty Distinctions, no such Things existing: appear'd now not so clever a Performance as I once thought it; and I doubted whether some Error had not insinuated itself unperceiv'd into my Argument, so as to infect all that follow'd, as is common in metaphysical Reasonings. I grew convinc'd that *Truth, Sincerity and Integrity* in Dealings between Man and Man, were of the utmost Importance to the Felicity of Life, and I form'd written Resolutions, (which still remain in my Journal Book) to practice them ever while I lived. Revelation had indeed no weight with me as such; but I entertain'd an Opinion, that tho' certain Actions might not be bad *because* they were forbidden by it, or good *because* it commanded them; yet probably those Actions might be forbidden *because* they were bad for us, or commanded *because* they were beneficial to us, in their own Natures, all the Circumstances of things considered. And this Persuasion, with the kind hand of Providence, or some guardian Angel, or accidental favourable Circumstances and Situations, or all together, preserved me (thro' this dangerous Time of Youth and the hazardous Situations I was sometimes in among Strangers, remote from the Eye and Advice of my Father) without any *wilful* gross Immorality or Injustice that might have been expected from my Want of Religion. I say *wilful,* because the Instances I have mentioned, had something of *Necessity* in them, from my Youth, Inexperience, and the Knavery of others. I had therefore a tolerable Character to begin the World with, I valued it properly, and determin'd to preserve it.

We had not been long return'd to Philadelphia, before the New Types arriv'd from London. We settled with Keimer, and left him by his Consent before he heard of it. We found a House to hire near the Market, and took it. To lessen the Rent, (which was then but £24 a Year tho' I have since known it let for 70) We took in Tho'

[122] Robert Boyle (1627–1691) established a series of lectures to defend Christianity against skeptics.

[123] The first line is not from John Dryden but from Pope's *Essay on Man* (1733), Epistle I, line 294. The rest is from Dryden's *Oedipus,* Act III, Scene i, lines 244–248.

Godfrey a Glazier[124] and his Family, who were to pay a considerable Part of it to us, and we to board with them. We had scarce opened our Letters and put our Press in Order, before George House, an Acquaintance of Mine, brought a Country-man to us; whom he had met in the Street enquiring for a Printer. All our Cash was now expended in the Variety of Particulars we had been obliged to procure and this Countryman's Five Shillings being our first Fruits, and coming so seasonably, gave me more Pleasure than any Crown I have since earn'd; and from the Gratitude I felt towards House, has made me often more ready than perhaps I should otherwise have been to assist young Beginners.

There are Croakers in every Country always boding its Ruin. Such a one then lived in Philadelphia, a Person of Note, an elderly Man, with a wise Look, and very grave Manner of speaking. His Name was Samuel Mickle. This Gentleman, a Stranger to me, stopt one Day at my Door, and asked me if I was the young Man who had lately opened a new Printing House: Being answer'd in the Affirmative; he said he was sorry for me, because it was an expensive Undertaking and the Expence would be lost; for Philadelphia was a sinking Place, the People already half Bankrupts or near being so; all Appearances of the contrary, such as new Buildings and the Rise of Rents being to his certain Knowledge fallacious, for they were in fact among the Things that would soon ruin us. And he gave me such a Detail of Misfortunes, now existing or that were soon to exist, that he left me half-melancholy. Had I known him before I engag'd in this Business, probably I never should have done it. This Man continu'd to live in this decaying Place; and to declaim in the same Strain, refusing for many Years to buy a House there, because all was going to Destruction, and at last I had the Pleasure of seeing him give five times as much for one as he might have bought it for when he first began his Croaking.

I should have mention'd before, that in the Autumn of the preceding Year I had form'd most of my ingenious Acquaintance into a Club for mutual Improvement, which we call'd the Junto.[125] We met on Friday Evenings. The Rules I drew up requir'd that every Member in his Turn should produce one or more Queries on any Point of Morals, Politics or Natural Philosophy, to be discuss'd by the Company, and once in three Months produce and read an Essay of his own Writing on any Subject he pleased. Our Debates were to be under the Direction of a President, and to be conducted in the sincere Spirit of Enquiry after Truth, without Fondness for Dispute, or Desire of Victory; and to prevent Warmth all Expressions of Positiveness in Opinion, or of direct Contradiction, were after some time made contraband and prohibited under small pecuniary Penalties. The first Members were Joseph Brientnal, A Copyer of Deeds for the Scriveners; a good-natur'd friendly middle-ag'd Man, a great Lover of Poetry, reading all he could meet with, and writing some that was tolerable; very ingenious in many little Nicknackeries, and of sensible Conversation. Thomas Godfrey, a self-taught Mathematician, great in his Way, and afterwards Inventor of what is now call'd Hadley's Quadrant. But he knew little out of his way, and was not a pleasing Companion, as like most Great Mathematicians I have met with, he expected unusual Precision in every thing said, or was forever denying or

[124]One who sets glass for windowpanes.
[125]A small, private, or secret group, from the Spanish word for "joined."

distinguishing upon Trifles, to the Disturbance of all Conversation. He soon left us. Nicholas Scull, a Surveyor, afterwards Surveyor-General, Who lov'd Books, and sometimes made a few Verses. William Parsons, bred a Shoemaker, but loving Reading, had acquir'd a considerable Share of Mathematics, which he first studied with a View to Astrology that he afterwards laught at. He also became Surveyor General. William Maugridge, a Joiner, a most exquisite Mechanic and a solid sensible Man. Hugh Meredith, Stephen Potts, and George Webb, I have Characteris'd before. Robert Grace, a young Gentleman of some Fortune, generous, lively and witty, a Lover of Punning and of his Friends. And William Coleman, then a Merchant's Clerk, about my Age, who had the coolest clearest Head, the best Heart, and the exactest Morals, of almost any Man I ever met with. He became afterwards a Merchant of Great Note, and one of our Provincial Judges: Our Friendship continued without Interruption to his Death upwards of 40 Years.

And the club continu'd almost as long and was the best School of Philosophy, Morals and Politics that then existed in the Province; for our Queries which were read the Week preceding their Discussion, put us on Reading with Attention upon the several Subjects, that we might speak more to the purpose: and here too we acquired better Habits of Conversation, every thing being studied in our Rules which might prevent our disgusting each other. From hence the long Continuance of the Club, which I shall have frequent Occasion to speak farther of hereafter; But my giving this Account of it here, is to show something of the Interest I had, every one of these exerting themselves in recommending Business to us. Brientnal particularly procur'd us from the Quakers, the Printing 40 Sheets of their History, the rest being to be done by Keimer: and upon this we work'd exceeding hard, for the Price was low. It was a Folio, Pro Patria Size, in Pica[126] with Long Primer[127] Notes. I compos'd of it a Sheet a Day, and Meredith work'd it off at Press. It was often 11 at Night and sometimes later, before I had finish'd my Distribution for the next days Work: For the little Jobbs sent in by our other Friends now and then put us back. But so determin'd I was to continue doing a Sheet a Day of the Folio, that one Night when having impos'd my Forms, I thought my Days Work over, one of them by accident was broken and two Pages reduc'd to Pie,[128] I immediately distributed and compos'd it over again before I went to bed. And this Industry visible to our Neighbours began to give us Character and Credit; particularly I was told, that mention being made of the new Printing Office at the Merchants every-night-Club, the general Opinion was that it must fail, there being already two Printers in the Place, Keimer and Bradford; but Doctor Baird (whom you and I saw many Years after at his native Place, St. Andrews in Scotland) gave a contrary Opinion; for the Industry of that Franklin, says he, is superior to any thing I ever saw of the kind: I see him still at work when I go home from Club; and he is at Work again before his Neighbours are out of bed. This struck the rest, and we soon after had Offers from one of them to Supply us with Stationary. But as yet we did not chuse to engage in Shop Business.

I mention this Industry the more particularly and the more freely, tho' it seems to be talking in my own Praise, that those of my Posterity who shall read it, may know

[126]A large volume, set in 12-point type.
[127]10-point type.
[128]A messy pile.

the Use of that Virtue, when they see its Effects in my Favour throughout this Relation.

George Webb, who had found a Female Friend that lent him wherewith to purchase his Time of Keimer, now came to offer himself as a Journeyman to us. We could not then imploy him, but I foolishly let him know, as a Secret, that I soon intended to begin a Newspaper, and might then have Work for him. My Hopes of Success as I told him were founded on this, that the then only Newspaper,[129] printed by Bradford was a paltry thing, wretchedly manag'd, and no way entertaining; and yet was profitable to him. I therefore thought a good Paper could scarcely fail of good Encouragement. I requested Webb not to mention it, but he told it to Keimer, who immediately, to be beforehand with me, published Proposals for Printing one himself, on which Webb was to be employ'd. I resented this, and to counteract them, as I could not yet begin our Paper, I wrote several Pieces of Entertainment for Bradford's Paper, under the Title of the Busy Body which Brientnal continu'd some Months. By this means the Attention of the Publick was fix'd on that Paper, and Keimers Proposals which we burlesqu'd and ridicul'd, were disregarded. He began his Paper however, and after carrying it on three Quarters of a Year, with at most only 90 Subscribers, he offer'd it to me for a Trifle, and I having been ready some time to go on with it, took it in hand directly, and it prov'd in a few Years extreamly profitable to me.[130]

I perceive that I am apt to speak in the singular Number, though our Partnership still continu'd. The Reason may be, that in fact the whole Management of the Business lay upon me. Meredith was no Compositor, a poor Pressman, and seldom sober. My friends lamented my Connection with him, but I was to make the best of it.

Our first Papers made a quite different Appearance from any before in the Province, a better Type and better printed: but some spirited Remarks of my Writing on the Dispute then going on between Govr. Burnet[131] and the Massachusetts Assembly, struck the principal People, occasion'd by the Paper and the Manager of it to be much talk'd of, and in a few Weeks brought them all to be our Subscribers. Their Example was follow'd by many, and our Number went on growing continually. This was one of the first good Effects of my having learnt a little to scribble. Another was, that the leading Men, seeing a News Paper now in the hands of one who could also handle a Pen, thought it convenient to oblige and encourage me. Bradford still printed the Votes and Laws and other Publick Business. He had printed an Address of the House to the Governor in a coarse blundering manner; We reprinted it elegantly and correctly, and sent one to every Member. They were sensible of the Difference, it strengthen'd the Hands of our Friends in the House, and they voted us their Printers for the Year ensuing.

Among my Friends in the House I must not forget Mr. Hamilton before mentioned, who was now returned from England and had a Seat in it. He interested

[129] *The American Weekly Mercury,* established December 22, 1719.

[130] Franklin took over *The Universal Instructor in All Arts and Sciences: and Pennsylvania Gazette* in October 1729, shortened the title to *The Pennsylvania Gazette,* and made it one of the best papers in the Colonies.

[131] William Burnet (1688–1729), Governor of Massachusetts.

himself[132] for me strongly in that Instance, as he did in many others afterwards, continuing his Patronage till his Death. Mr. Vernon about this time put me in mind of the Debt I ow'd him: but did not press me. I wrote him an ingenuous Letter of Acknowledgments, crav'd his Forbearance a little longer which he allow'd me, and as soon as I was able I paid the Principal with Interest and many Thanks. So that *Erratum* was in some degree corrected.

But now another Difficulty came upon me, which I had never the least Reason to expect. Mr. Meredith's Father, who was to have paid for our Printing House according to the Expectations given me, was able to advance only one Hundred Pounds, Currency, which had been paid, and a Hundred more was due to the Merchant; who grew impatient and su'd us all. We gave Bail, but saw that if the Money could not be rais'd in time, the Suit must come to a Judgment and Execution, and our hopeful Prospects must with us be ruined, as the Press and Letters must be sold for Payment, perhaps at half Price. In this Distress two true Friends whose Kindness I have never forgotten nor ever shall forget while I can remember any thing, came to me separately unknown to each other, and without any Application from me, offering each of them to advance me all the Money that should be necessary to enable me to take the whole Business upon my self if that should be practicable, but they did not like my continuing the Partnership with Meredith, who as they said was often seen drunk in the Streets, and playing at low Games in Alehouses, much to our Discredit. These two Friends were William Coleman and Robert Grace.[133] I told them I could not propose a Separation while any Prospect remain'd of the Merediths fulfilling their Part of our Agreement. Because I thought myself under great Obligations to them for what they had done and would do if they could. But if they finally fail'd in their Performance, and our Partnership must be dissolv'd, I should then think myself at Liberty to accept the Assistance of my Friends.

Thus the matter rested for some time. When I said to my Partner, perhaps your Father is dissatisfied at the Part you have undertaken in this Affair of ours, and is unwilling to advance for you and me what he would for you alone: If that is the Case, tell me, and I will resign the whole to you and go about my Business. No says he, my Father has really been disappointed and is really unable; and I am unwilling to distress him farther. I see this is a Business I am not fit for. I was bred a Farmer, and it was a Folly in me to come to Town and put my Self at 30 Years of Age an Apprentice to learn a new Trade. Many of our Welsh People are going to settle in North Carolina where Land is cheap: I am inclin'd to go with them, and follow my old Employment. You may find Friends to assist you. If you will take the Debts of the Company upon you, return to my Father the hundred Pound he has advanc'd, pay my little personal Debts, and give me Thirty Pounds and a new Saddle, I will relinquish the Partnership and leave the whole in your Hands. I agreed to this Proposal. It was drawn up in Writing, sign'd and seal'd immediately. I gave him what he demanded and he went soon after to Carolina; from whence he sent me next Year two long Letters, containing the best Account that had been given of that Country, the Climate, Soil, Husbandry, &c. for in those Matters he was very judicious. I printed them in the Papers, and they gave grate Satisfaction to the Publick.

[132] "I got his Son once £500."—[Franklin's note].

[133] William Coleman (1704–1769), Robert Grace (1709–1766), original members of Franklin's Junto.

As soon as he was gone, I recurr'd to my two Friends; and because I would not give an unkind Preference to either, I took half what each had offered and I wanted, of one, and half of the other; paid off the Company Debts, and went on with the Business in my own Name, advertising that the Partnership was dissolved. I think this was in or about the Year 1729.[134]

About this Time there was a Cry among the People for more Paper-Money, only £15,000, being extant in the Province and that soon to be sunk. The wealthy Inhabitants oppos'd any Addition, being against all Paper Currency, from an Apprehension that it would depreciate as it had done in New England to the Prejudice of all Creditors. We had discuss'd this Point in our Junto, where I was on the Side of Addition, being persuaded that the first small Sum struck in 1723 had done much good, by increasing the Trade Employment, and Number of Inhabitants in the Province, since I now saw all the old Houses inhabited, and many new ones building, where as I remember'd well, that when I first walk'd about the Streets of Philadelphia, eating my Roll, I saw most of the House in Walnut street between Second and Front streets with Bills on their Doors, to be let; and many likewise in Chestnut Street, and other Streets; which made me then think the Inhabitants of the City were one after another deserting it. Our Debates possess'd me so fully of the Subject, that I wrote and printed an anonymous Pamphlet on it, entituled, *The Nature and Necessity of a Paper Currency.* It was well receiv'd by the common People in general; but the Rich Men dislik'd it; for it increas'd and strengthen'd the Clamour for more Money; and they happening to have no Writers among them that were able to answer it, their Opposition slacken'd, and the Point was carried by a Majority in the House. My Friends there, who conceiv'd I had been of some Service, thought fit to reward me, by employing me in printing the Money, a very profitable Jobb, and a great Help to me. This was another Advantage gain'd by my being able to write. The Utility of this Currency became by Time and Experience so evident, as never afterwards to be much disputed, so that it grew soon to £55,000, and in 1739 to £80,000 since which it arose during War to upwards of £350,000. Trade, Building and Inhabitants all the while increasing. Tho' I now think there are Limits beyond which the Quantity may be hurtful.

I soon after obtain'd, thro' my Friend Hamilton, the Printing of the New Castle Paper Money,[135] another profitable Jobb, as I then thought it; small Things appearing great to those in small Circumstances. And these to me were really great Advantages, as they were great Encouragements. He procured me also the Printing of the Laws and Votes of the Government which continu'd in my Hands as long as I follow'd the Business.

I now open'd a little Stationer's Shop. I had in it Blanks of all Sorts the correctest that ever appear'd among us, being assisted in that by my Friend Brientnal; I had also Paper, Parchment, Chapmen's Books, &c. One Whitemash a Compositor I had known in London, an excellent Workman now came to me and work'd with me constantly and diligently, and I took an Apprentice the Son of Aquila Rose. I began now gradually to pay off the Debt I was under for the Printing House. In order to secure

[134]Actually July 14, 1730.
[135]The counties of New-Castle, Kent, and Sussex had the same governor as Pennsylvania but a separate legislature.

my Credit and Character as a Tradesman, I took care not only to be in *Reality* Industrious and frugal, but to avoid all *Appearances* of the Contrary. I drest plainly; I was seen a no Places of idle Diversion; I never went out a-fishing or shooting; a Book, indeed, sometimes debauch'd me from my Work; but that was seldom, snug, and gave no Scandal: and to show that I was not above my Business, I sometimes brought home the Paper I purchas'd at the Stores, thro' the Streets on a Wheelbarrow. Thus being esteem'd an industrious thriving young Man, and paying duly for what I bought, the Merchants who imported Stationary solicited my Custom, others propos'd supplying me with Books, and I went on swimmingly. In the mean time Keimer's Credit and Business declining daily, he was at last forc'd to sell his Printinghouse to satisfy his Creditors. He went to Barbadoes, and there lived some Years, in very poor Circumstances.

His Apprentice David Harry, whom I had instructed while I work'd with him, set up in his Place at Philadelphia, having bought his Materials. I was at first apprehensive of a powerful Rival in Harry, as his Friends were very able, and had a good deal of Interest. I therefore propos'd a Partnership to him; which he, fortunately for me, rejected with Scorn. He was very proud, dress'd like a Gentleman, liv'd expensively, took much Diversion and Pleasure abroad, ran in debt, and neglected his Business, upon which all Business left him; and finding nothing to do, he follow'd Keimer to Barbadoes; taking the Printinghouse with him. There this Apprentice employ'd his former Master as a Journeyman. They quarrel'd often. Harry went continually behindhand, and at length was forc'd to sell his Types, and return to his Country Work in Pensilvania. The Person that bought them, employ'd Keimer to use them, but in a few years he died. Their remain'd now no Competitor with me at Philadelphia, but the old one, Bradford, who was rich and easy, did a little Printing now and then by straggling Hands, but was not very anxious about the Business. However, as he kept the Post Office, it was imagined he had better Opportunities of obtaining News, his Paper was thought a better Distributer of Advertisements than mine, and therefore had many more, which was a profitable thing to him and a Disadvantage to me. For tho' I did indeed receive and send Papers by Post, yet the publick Opinion was otherwise; for what I did send was by Bribing the Riders who took them privately: Bradford being unkind enough to forbid it: which ocasion'd some Resentment on my Part; and I thought so meanly of him for it, that when I afterwards came into his Situation,[136] I took care never to imitate it.

I had hitherto continu'd to board with Godfrey who lived in Part of my House with his Wife and Children, and had one Side of the Shop for his Glazier's Business, tho' he work'd little, being always absorb'd in his Mathematics. Mrs. Godfrey projected a Match for me with a Relation's Daughter, took Opportunities of bringing us often together, till a serious Courtship on my Part ensu'd, the Girl being in herself very deserving. The old Folks encourag'd me by continual Invitations to Supper, and by leaving us together, till at length it was time to explain. Mrs. Godfrey manag'd our little Treaty. I let her know that I expected as much Money with their Daughter as would pay off my Remaining Debt for the Printing-house, which I believe was not

[136]Franklin became the Deputy Postmaster-General for the Colonies in 1753.

then above a Hundred Pounds. She brought me Word they had no such Sum to spare. I said they might mortgage their House in the Loan Office. The Answer to this after some Days was that they did not approve the Match; that on Enquiry of Bradford they had been inform'd the Printing Business was not a profitable one, the Types would soon be worn out and more wanted, that S. Keimer and D. Harry had fail'd one after the other, and I should probably soon follow them; and therefore I was forbidden the House, and the Daughter shut up. Whether this was a real Change of Sentiment, or only Artifice, on a Supposition of our being too far engag'd in Affection to retract, and therefore that we should steal a Marriage, which would leave them at Liberty to give or withold what they pleas'd, I know not: But I suspected the latter, resented it, and went no more. Mrs. Godfrey brought me afterwards some more favourable Accounts of their Disposition, and would have drawn me on again: but I declared absolutely my Resolution to have nothing more to do with that Family. This was resented by the Godfreys, we differ'd, and they removed, leaving me the whole House, and I resolved to take no more Inmates.

But this Affair having turn'd my Thoughts to Marriage, I look'd round me, and made Overtures of Acquaintance in other Places; but soon found that the Business of a Printer being generally thought a poor one, I was not to expect Money with a Wife unless with such a one, as I should not otherwise think agreable. In the mean time, that hard-to-be-govern'd Passion of Youth, had hurried me frequently into Intrigues with low Women that fell in my Way, which were attended with some Expence and great Inconvenience, besides a continual Risque to my Health by a Distemper which of all Things I dreaded, tho' by Great good Luck I escaped it.

A friendly Correspondence as Neighbours and old Acquaintances, had continued between me and Mrs. Read's Family, who all had a Regard for me from the time of my first Lodging in their House. I was often invited there and consulted in their Affairs, wherein I sometimes was of service. I pity'd poor Miss Read's unfortunate Situation, who was generally dejected, seldom chearful, and avoided Company. I consider'd my Giddiness and Inconstancy when in London as in a great degree the Cause of her Unhappiness; tho' the Mother was good enough to think the Fault more her own than mine, as she had prevented our Marrying before I went thither, and persuaded the other Match in my Absence. Our mutual Affection was revived, but there were now great Objections to our Union. That Match was indeed look'd upon as invalid, a preceding Wife being said to be living in England; but this could not easily be prov'd, because of the Distance. And tho' there was a Report of his Death, it was not certain. Then tho' it should be true, he had left many Debts which his Successor might be call'd on to pay. We ventured however, over all these Difficulties, and I [took] her to Wife Sept. 1, 1730.[137] None of the Inconveniencies happened that we had apprehended, she prov'd a good and faithful Helpmate, assisted me much by attending the Shop, we throve together, and have ever mutually endeavour'd to make each other happy. Thus I corrected that great *Erratum* as well as I could.

About this Time our Club meeting, not at a Tavern, but in a little Room of Mr. Grace's set apart for that Purpose; a Proposition was made by me that since our Books

[137]Without proof that Deborah's first husband, John Rogers, was dead, Deborah could not officially remarry. Franklin and Deborah entered into "common law" marriage without a civil or church ceremony.

were often referr'd to in our Disquisitions upon the Queries, it might be convenient to us to have them all together where we met, that upon Occasion they might be consulted; and by thus clubbing our Books to a common Library, we should, while we lik'd to keep them together, have each of us the Advantage of using the Books of all the other Members, which would be nearly as beneficial as if each owned the whole. It was lik'd and agreed to, and we fill'd one End of the Room with such Books as we could best spare. The Number was not so great as we expected; and tho' they had been of great Use, yet some Inconveniencies occurring for want of due Care of them, the Collection after about a Year was separated, and each took his Books home again.

And now I set on foot my first Project of a public Nature, that for a Subscription Library. I drew up the Proposals, got them put into Form by our great Scrivener Brockden, and by the help of my Friends in the Junto, procur'd Fifty Subscribers of 40*s.* each to begin with and 10*s.* a Year for 50 Years, the Term our Company was to continue. We afterwards obtain'd a Charter, the Company being increas'd to 100. This was the Mother of all the N American Subscription Libraries now so numerous. It is become a great thing itself, and continually increasing. These Libraries have improv'd the general Conversation of the Americans, made the common Tradesmen and Farmers as intelligent as most Gentlemen from other Countries, and perhaps have contributed in some degree to the Stand so generally made throughout the Colonies in Defence of their Privileges.

Memo.

Thus far was written with the Intention express'd in the Beginning and therefore contains several little family Anecdotes of no Importance to others. What follows was written many Years after in compliance with the Advice contain'd in these Letters, and accordingly intended for the Publick. The Affairs of the Revolution occasion'd the Interruption.

Letter from Mr. Abel James[138] with Notes of my Life, to be here inserted. Also Letter from Mr. Vaughan[139] to the same purpose

My Dear and honored Friend.

I have often been desirous of writing to thee, but could not be reconciled to the Thoughts that the Letter might fall into the Hands of the British,[140] lest some Printer or busy Body should publish some Part of the Contents and give our Friends Pain and myself Censure.

Some Time since there fell into my Hands to my great Joy about 23 Sheets in thy own hand-writing containing an Account of the Parentage and Life of thyself, directed to thy Son ending in the Year 1730 with which there were Notes[141] likewise in thy writing, a Copy of which I inclose in Hopes it may be a means if thou

[138]Abel James (c. 1726–1790), Philadelphia Quaker merchant.

[139]Benjamin Vaughan (1751–1835), English diplomat. He edited the first general collection of Franklin's works, 1779.

[140]The letter was written to Franklin in Paris in 1782 while Britain was still at war with the Colonies.

[141]Franklin drew up an outline for his autobiography soon after he began to write in 1771.

continuedst it up to a later period, that the first and latter part may be put together, and if it is not yet continued, I hope thou wilt not delay it, Life is uncertain as the Preacher tells us, and what will the World say if kind, humane and benevolent Ben Franklin should leave his Friends and the World deprived of so pleasing and profitable a Work, a Work which would be useful and entertaining not only to a few, but to millions.

The Influence Writings under that Class have on the Minds of Youth is very great, and has no where appeared so plain as in our public Friend's Journal. It almost insensibly leads the Youth into the Resolution of endeavouring to become as good and as eminent as the Journalist. Should thine for Instance when published, and I think it could not fail of it, lead the Youth to equal the Industry and Temperance of thy early Youth, what a Blessing with that Class would such a Work be. I know of no Character living nor many of them put together, who has so much in his Power as Thyself to promote a greater Spirit of Industry and early Attention to Business, Frugality and Temperance with the American Youth. Not that I think the Work would have no other Merit and Use in the World, far from it, but the first is of such vast Importance, that I know nothing that can equal it. . . .

ABEL JAMES

The foregoing letter and the minutes accompanying it being shewn to a friend, I received from him the following:

Paris, January 31, 1783.

My dearest sir,

When I had read over your sheets of minutes of the principal incidents of your life, recovered for you by your Quaker acquaintance; I told you I would send you a letter expressing my reasons why I thought it would be useful to complete and publish it as he desired. Various concerns have for some time past prevented this letter being written, and I do not know whether it was worth any expectation: happening to be at leisure however at present, I shall be writing at least interest and instruct myself; but as the terms I am inclined to use may tend to offend a person of your manners, I shall only tell you how I would address any other person, who was as good and as great as yourself, but less diffident. I would say to him, Sir, I *solicit* the history of your life from the following motives.

Your history is so remarkable, that if you do not give it, somebody else will certainly give it; and perhaps so as nearly to do as much harm, as your own management of the thing might do good.

It will moreover present a table of the internal circumstances of your country, which will very much tend to invite to it settlers of virtuous and manly minds. And considering the eagerness with which such information is sought by them, and the extent of your reputation, I do not know of a more efficacious advertisement than your Biography would give.

All that has happened to you is also connected with the detail of the manners and situation of a *rising* people; and in this respect I do not think that the writings of Caesar and Tacitus can be more interesting to a true judge of human nature and society.

But these, Sir, are small reasons in my opinion, compared with the chance which your life will give for the forming of future great men; and in conjunction with your Art of Virtue, (which you design to publish) of improving the features of private character, and consequently of aiding all happiness both public and domestic.

The two works I allude to, Sir, will in particular give a noble rule and example of *self-education*. School and other education constantly proceed upon false principles, and shew a clumsy apparatus pointed at a false mark; but your apparatus is simple, and the mark a true one; and while parents and young persons are left destitute of other just means of estimating and becoming prepared for a reasonable course in life, your discovery that the thing is in many a man's private power, will be invaluable!

Influence upon the private character late in life, is not only an influence late in life, but a weak influence. It is in youth that we plant our chief habits and prejudices; it is in youth that we take our party as to profession, pursuits, and matrimony. In youth therefore the turn is given; in youth the education even of the next generation is given; in youth the private and public character is determined; and the term of life extending but from youth to age, life ought to begin well from youth; and more especially before we take our party as to our principal objects.

But your Biography will not merely teach self-education, but the education of a wise man; and the wisest man will receive lights and improve his progress, by seeing detailed the conduct of another wise man. And why are weaker men to be deprived of such helps, when we see our race has been blundering on in the dark, almost without a guide in this particular, from the farthest trace of time? Shew then, Sir, how much is to be done, *both to sons and fathers;* and invite all wise men to become like yourself; and other men to become wise.

When we see how cruel statesmen and warriors can be to the humble race, and how absurd distinguished men can be to their acquaintance, it will be instructive to observe the instances multiply of pacific acquiescing manners; and to find how compatible it is to be great and *domestic,* enviable and yet *good-humored.*

The little private incidents which you will also have to relate, will have considerable use, as we want above all things, *rules of prudence in ordinary affairs;* and it will be curious to see how you have acted in these. It will be so far a sort of key to life, and explain many things that all men ought to have once explained to them, to give them a chance of becoming wise by foresight.

The nearest thing to having experience of one's own, is to have other people's affairs brought before us in a shape that is interesting; this is sure to happen from your pen. Your affairs and management will have an air of simplicity or importance that will not fail to strike; and I am convinced you have conducted them with as much originality as if you had been conducting discussions in politics or philosophy; and what more worthy of experiments and system, (its importance and its error considered) than human life!

Some men have been virtuous blindly, others have speculated fantastically, and others have been shrewd to bad purposes; but you, Sir, I am sure, will give under your hand, nothing but what is at the same moment, wise, practical, and good.

Your account of yourself (for I suppose the parallel I am drawing for Dr.

Franklin, will hold not only in point of character but of private history), will shew that you are ashamed of no origin; a thing the more important, as you prove how little necessary all origin is to happiness, virtue, or greatness.

As no end likewise happens without a means, so we shall find, Sir, that even you yourself framed a plan by which you became considerable; but at the same time we may see that though the event is flattering, the means are as simple as wisdom could make them; that is, depending upon nature, virtue, thought, and habit.

Another thing demonstrated will be the propriety of every man's waiting for his time for appearing upon the stage of the world. Our sensations being very much fixed to the moment, we are apt to forget that more moments are to follow the first, and consequently that man should arrange his conduct so as to suit the *whole* of a life. Your attribution appears to have been applied to your *life,* and the passing moments of it have been enlivened with content and enjoyment, instead of being tormented with foolish impatience or regrets. Such a conduct is easy for those who make virtue and themselves their standard, and who try to keep themselves in countenance by examples of other truly great men, of whom patience is so often the characteristic.

Your Quaker correspondent, Sir, (for here again I will suppose the subject of my letter resembling Dr. Franklin,) praised your frugality, diligence, and temperance, which he considered as a pattern for all youth; but it is singular that he should have forgotten your modesty, and your disinterestedness, without which you never could have waited for your advancement, or found your situation in the mean time comfortable; which is a strong lesson to shew the poverty of glory, and the importance of regulating our minds.

If this correspondent had known the nature of your reputation as well as I do, he would have said; your former writings and measures would secure attention to your Biography and Art of Virtue; and your Biography and Art of Virtue, in return, would secure attention to them. This is an advantage attendant upon a various character, and which brings all that belongs to it into greater play; and it is the more useful, as perhaps more persons are at a loss for the *means* of improving their minds and characters, than they are for the time or the inclination to do it.

But there is one concluding reflection, Sir, that will shew the use of your life as a mere piece of biography. This style of writing seems a little gone out of vogue, and yet it is a very useful one; and your specimen of it may be particularly serviceable, as it will make a subject of comparison with the lives of various public cutthroats and intriguers, and with absurd monastic self-tormentors, or vain literary triflers. If it encourages more writings of the same kind with your own, and induces more men to spend lives fit to be written; it will be worth all Plutarch's Lives put together.

But being tired of figuring to myself a character of which every feature suits only one man in the world, without giving him the praise of it; I shall end my letter, my dear Dr. Franklin, with a personal application to your proper self.

I am earnestly desirous then, my dear Sir, that you should let the world into the traits of your genuine character, as civil broils may otherwise tend to disguise or traduce it. Considering your great age, the caution of your character, and your peculiar style of thinking, it is not likely that any one besides yourself can be sufficiently master of the facts of your life, or the intentions of your mind.

Besides all this, the immense revolution of the present period, will necessarily turn our attention towards the author of it; and when virtuous principles have been pretended in it, it will be highly important to shew that such have really influenced; and, as your own character will be the principal one to receive a scrutiny, it is proper (even for its effects upon your vast and rising country, as well as upon England and upon Europe), that it should stand respectable and eternal. For the furtherance of human happiness, I have always maintained that it is necessary to prove that man is not even at present a vicious and detestable animal; and still more to prove that good management may greatly amend him; and it is for much the same reason, that I am anxious to see the opinion established, that there are fair characters existing among the individuals of the race; for the moment that all men, without exception, shall be conceived abandoned, good people will cease efforts deemed to be hopeless, and perhaps think of taking their share in the scramble of life, or at least of making it comfortable principally for themselves.

Take then, my dear Sir, this work most speedily into hand: shew yourself good as you are good, temperate as you are temperate; and above all things, prove yourself as one who from your infancy have loved justice, liberty, and concord, in a way that has made it natural and consistent for you to have acted, as we have seen you act in the last seventeen years of your life. Let Englishmen be made not only to respect, but even to love you. When they think well of individuals in your native country, they will go nearer to thinking well of your country; and when your countrymen see themselves well thought of by Englishmen, they will go nearer to thinking well of England. Extend your views even further; do not stop at those who speak the English tongue, but after having settled so many points in nature and politics, think of bettering the whole race of men.

As I have not read any part of the life in question, but know only the character that lived it, I write somewhat at hazard. I am sure however, that the life, and the treatise I allude to (on the Art of Virtue), will necessarily fulfil the chief of my expectations; and still more so if you take up the measure of suiting these performances to the several views above stated. Should they even prove unsuccessful in all that a sanguine admirer of yours hopes from them, you will at least have framed pieces to interest the human mind; and whoever gives a feeling of pleasure that is innocent to man, has added so much to the fair side of a life otherwise too much darkened by anxiety, and too much injured by pain.

In the hope therefore that you will listen to the prayer addressed to you in this letter, I beg to subscribe myself, my dearest Sir, &c. &c.

BENJ. VAUGHAN.

Part Two Continuation of the Account of My Life Begun at Passy[142] 1784

It is some time since I receiv'd the above Letters, but I have been too busy till now to think of complying with the Request they contain. It might too be much better

[142] A suburb of Paris, France, where Franklin lived while negotiating the Treaty of Paris (1783).

done if I were at home among my Papers, which would aid my Memory and help to ascertain Dates. But my Return being uncertain, and having just now a little Leisure, I will endeavour to recollect and write what I can; if I live to get home, it may there be corrected and improv'd.

Not having any Copy here of what is already written, I know not whether an Account is given of the means I used to establish the Philadelphia publick Library, which from a small Beginning is now become so considerable, though I remember to have come down to near the Time of that Transaction, 1730. I will therefore begin here, with an Account of it, which may be struck out if found to have been already given.

At the time I establish'd my self in Pensylvania, there was not a good Bookseller's Shop in any of the Colonies to the Southward of Boston. In New-York and Philadelphia the Printers were indeed Stationers, they sold only Paper, &c., Almanacks, Ballads, and a few common School Books. Those who lov'd Reading were oblig'd to send for their Books from England. The Members of the Junto had each a few. We had left the Alehouse where we first met, and hired a Room to hold our Club in. I propos'd that we should all of us bring our Books to that Room, where they would not only be ready to consult in our Conferences, but become a common Benefit, each of us being at Liberty to borrow such as he wish'd to read at home. This was accordingly done, and for some time contented us. Finding the Advantage of this little Collection, I propos'd to render the Benefit from Books more common by commencing a Public Subscription Library. I drew a Sketch of the Plan and Rules that would be necessary, and got a skillful Conveyancer, Mr. Charles Brockden to put the whole in Form of Articles of Agreement to be subscribed; by which each Subscriber engag'd to pay a certain Sum down for the first Purchase of Books and an annual Contribution for encreasing them. So few were the Readers at that time in Philadelphia, and the Majority of us so poor, that I was not able with great Industry to find more than Fifty Persons, mostly young Tradesmen, willing to pay down for this purpose Forty shillings each, and Ten Shillings per Annum. On this little Fund we began. The Books were imported. The Library was open one Day in the Week for lending them to the Subscribers, on their Promisory Notes to pay Double the Value if not duly returned. The Institution soon manifested its Utility, was imitated by other Towns and in other Provinces, the Librarys were augmented by Donations, Reading became fashionable, and our People having no publick Amusements to divert their Attention from Study became better acquainted with Books, and in a few Years were observ'd by Strangers to be better instructed and more intelligent than People of the same Rank generally are in other Countries.

When we were about to sign the above-mentioned Articles, which were to be binding on us, our Heirs, &c. for fifty Years, Mr. Brockden, the Scrivener, said to us, "You are young Men, but it is scare probable that any of you will live to see the Expiration of the Term fix'd in this Instrument." A Number of us, however, are yet living: But the Instrument was after a few Years rendered null by a Charter that incorporated and gave Perpetuity to the Company.

The Objections, and Reluctances I met with in Soliciting the Subscriptions, made me soon feel the Impropriety of presenting one's self as the Proposer of any useful Project that might be suppos'd to raise one's Reputation in the smallest degree above that of one's Neighbours, when one has need of their Assistance to accomplish that Project. I therefore put my self as much as I could out of sight, and stated it as a Scheme of a *Number of Friends,* who had requested me to go about and propose it to such as they thought Lovers of Reading. In this way my Affair went on more smoothly, and I ever after practis'd it on such Occasions; and from my frequent Successes, can heartily recommend it. The present little Sacrifice of your Vanity will afterwards be amply repaid. If it remains a while uncertain to whom the Merit belongs, some one more vain than yourself will be encourag'd to claim it, and then even Envy will be dispos'd to do you Justice, by plucking those assum'd Feathers, and restoring them to their right Owner.

This Library afforded me the means of Improvement by constant Study, for which I set apart an Hour or two each Day; and thus repair'd in some Degree the Loss of the Learned Education my Father once intended for me. Reading was the only Amusement I allow'd my self. I spent no time in Taverns, Games, or Frolicks of any kind. And my Industry in my Business continu'd as indefatigable as it was necessary. I was in debt for my Printing-house, I had a young Family coming on to be educated,[143] and I had to contend with for Business two Printers who were establish'd in the Place before me. My Circumstances however grew daily easier: my original Habits of Frugality continuing. And my Father having among his Instructions to me when a Boy, frequently repeated a Proverb of Solomon, *"Seest thou a Man diligent in his Calling, he shall stand before Kings, he shall not stand before mean Men."*[144] I from thence consider'd Industry as a Means of obtaining Wealth and Distinction, which encourag'd me, tho' I did not think that I should ever literally stand before Kings, which however has since happened.—for I have stood before five,[145] and even had the honor of sitting down with one, the King of Denmark, to Dinner.

We have an English Proverb that says,

He that would thrive
Must ask his Wife;

it was lucky for me that I had one as much dispos'd to Industry and Frugality as my self. She assisted me chearfully in my Business, folding and stitching Pamphlets, tending Shop, purchasing old Linen Rags for the Paper-makers, &c. &c. We kept no idle Servants, our Table was plain and simple, our furniture of the cheapest. For instance my Breakfast was a long time Bread and Milk, (no Tea) and I ate it out of a twopenny earthen Porringer with a Pewter Spoon. But mark how Luxury will enter Families, and make a Progress, in Spite of Principle. Being call'd one Morning to Breakfast, I found it in a China Bowl with a Spoon of Silver. They had been bought for me without my Knowledge my Wife, and had cost her the enormous Sum of three and twenty Shillings, for which she had no other Excuse of Apology to make, but that she thought *her* Husband deserv'd a Silver Spoon and China Bowl as well as any of his Neighbours. This was the first Appearance of Plate and China in our House, which afterwards in a Course of Years as our Wealth encreas'd augmented gradually to several Hundred Pounds in Value.

I had been religiously educated as a Presbyterian; and tho' some of the Dogmas of that Persuasion, such as the Eternal Decrees of God, Election, Reprobation, &c.

[143] William, born about 1731; Francis, born 1732; and Sarah, born 1743.

[144] Proverbs 22:29.

[145] Louis XV and Louis XVI of France, George II and George III of England, and Christian VI of Denmark.

appear'd to me unintelligible, others doubtful, I early absented myself from the Public Assemblies of the Sect, Sunday being my Studying-Day, I never was without some religious Principles; I never doubted, for instance, the Existance of the Deity, that he made the World, and govern'd it by his Providence; that the most acceptable Service of God was the doing Good to man; that our Souls are immortal; and that all Crime will be punished and Virtue rewarded either here or hereafter; these I esteem'd the Essentials of every Religion, and being to be found in all the Religions we had in our Country I respected them all, tho' with different degrees of Respect as I found them more or less mix'd with other Articles which without any Tendency to inspire, promote or confirm Morality, serv'd principally to divide us and make us unfriendly to one another. This Respect to all, with an Opinion that the worst had some good Effects, induc'd me to avoid all Discourse that might tend to lessen the good Opinion another might have of his own Religion; and as our Province increas'd in People and new Places of worship were continually wanted, and generally erected by voluntary Contribution, my Mite for such purpose, whatever might be the Sect, was never refused.

Tho' I seldom attended any Public Worship, I had still an Opinion of its Propriety, and of its Utility when rightly conducted, and I regularly paid my annual Subscription for the Support of the only Presbyterian Minister or Meeting we had in Philadelphia. He us'd to visit me sometimes as a Friend, and admonish me to attend his Administrations, and I was now and then prevail'd on to do so, once for five Sundays successively. Had he been, *in my Opinion,* a good Preacher perhaps I might have continued, notwithstanding the occasion I had for the Sunday's Leisure in my Course of Study: But his Discourses were chiefly either polemic Arguments, or Explications of the peculiar Doctrines of our Sect, and were all to me very dry, uninteresting and unedifying, since not a single moral Principle was inculcated or enforc'd their Aim seeming to be rather to make us Presbyterians than good Citizens. At length he took for his Text that Verse on the 4th Chapter of Philippians, *Finally, Brethren, Whatsoever Things are true, honest, just, pure, lovely, or of good report, if there be any virtue, or any praise, think on these Things;*[146] and I imagin'd in a Sermon on such a Text, we could not miss of having some Morality: But he confin'd himself to five Points only as meant by the Apostle, viz. 1. Keeping holy the Sabbath Day. 2. Being diligent in Reading the Holy Scriptures. 3. Attending duly the Publick Worship. 4. Partaking of the Sacrament. 5. Paying a due Respect to God's Ministers. These might be all good Things, but as they were not the kind of good Things that I expected from that Text, I despaired of ever meeting with them from any other, was disgusted, and attended his Preaching no more. I had some Years before compos'd a little Liturgy or Form of Prayer for my own private Use, viz, in 1728. entitled, *Articles of Belief and Acts of Religion.* I return'd to the Use of this, and went no more to the public Assemblies. My Conduct might be blameable, but I leave it without attempting farther to excuse it, my present purpose being to relate Facts, and not to make Apologies for them.

It was about this time that I conceiv'd the bold and arduous Project of arriving at moral Perfection. I wish'd to live without committing any Fault at any time; I would conquer all that either Natural Inclination, Custom, or Company might lead

[146]Philippians 4:8.

me into. As I knew, or thought I knew, what was right and wrong, I did not see why I might not *always* do the one and avoid the other. But I soon found I had undertaken a Task of more Difficulty than I had imagined. While my *Attention was taken up* in guarding against one Fault, I was often surpriz'd by another. Habit took the Advantage of Inattention. Inclination was sometimes too strong for Reason. I concluded at length, that the mere speculative Conviction that it was our Interest to be compleatly virtuous, was not sufficient to prevent our Slipping, and that the contrary Habits must be broken and good ones acquired and established, before we can have any Dependance on a steady uniform Rectitude of Conduct. For this purpose I therefore contriv'd the following Method.

In the various Enumerations of the moral Virtues I had met with in my Reading, I found the Catalogue more or less numerous, as different Writers included more or fewer Ideas under the same Name. Temperance, for Example, was by some confin'd to Eating and Drinking, while by others it was extended to mean the moderating every other Pleasure, Appetite, Inclination or Passion, bodily or mental, even to our Avarice and Ambition. I propos'd to myself, for the sake of Clearness, to use rather more Names with fewer Ideas annex'd to each, than a few Names with more Ideas; and I included under Thirteen Names of Virtues all that at that time occurr'd to me as necessary or desirable, and annex'd to each a short Precept, which fully express'd the Extent I gave to its Meaning.

These Names of Virtues with their Precepts were

1. TEMPERANCE.

Eat not to Dulness.
Drink not to Elevation.

2. SILENCE.

Speak not but what may benefit others or yourself. Avoid trifling Conversation.

3. ORDER.

Let all your Things have their Places. Let each Part of your Business have its Time.

4. RESOLUTION.

Resolve to perform what you ought. Perform without fail what you resolve.

5. FRUGALITY.

Make no Expence but to do good to others or yourself: i.e., Waste nothing.

6. INDUSTRY.

Lose no Time. Be always employ'd in something useful. Cut off all unnecessary Actions.

7. SINCERITY.

Use no hurtful Deceit.
Think innocently and justly; and, if you speak, speak accordingly.

8. JUSTICE.

Wrong none, by doing Injuries or omitting the Benefits that are your Duty.

9. MODERATION.

Avoid Extreams. Forbear resenting Injuries so much as you think they deserve.

10. CLEANLINESS.

Tolerate no Uncleanness in Body, Cloaths or Habitation.

11. TRANQUILITY.

Be not disturbed at Trifles, or at Accidents common or unavoidable.

12. CHASTITY.

Rarely use Venery but for Health or Offspring: Never to Dulness, Weakness, or the Injury of your own or another's Peace or Reputation.

13. HUMILITY.

Imitate Jesus and Socrates.

My Intention being to acquire the *Habitude* of all these Virtues, I judg'd it would be well not to distract my Attention by attempting the whole at once, but to fix it on one of them at a time, and when I should be Master of that, then to proceed to another, and so on till I should have gone thro' the thirteen. And as the previous Acquisition of some might facilitate the Acquisition of certain others, I arrang'd them with that View as they stand above. *Temperance* first, as it tends to produce that Coolness and Clearness of Head, which is so necessary where constant Vigilance was to be kept up, and Guard maintained, against the unremitting Attraction of ancient Habits, and the Force of perpetual Temptations. This being acquir'd and establish'd, *Silence* would be more easy, and my Desire being to gain Knowledge at the same time that I improv'd in Virtue, and considering that in Conversation it was obtain'd rather by use of the Ears than of the Tongue, and therefore wishing to break a Habit I was getting into of Prattling, Punning and Joking, which only made me acceptable to trifling Company, I gave *Silence* the second Place. This, and the next, *Order,* I expected would allow me more Time for attending to my Project and my Studies; RESOLUTION, once become habitual, would keep me firm in my Endeavours to obtain all the subsequent Virtues; *Frugality* and *Industry,* by freeing me from my remaining Debt, and producing Affluence and Independance, would make more easy the Practice of *Sincerity* and *Justice,* &c. &c. Conceiving then that agreable to the Advice of Pythagoras[147] in his Golden Verses daily Examination would be necessary, I contriv'd the following Method for conducting that Examination.

I made a little Book in which I allotted a Page for each of the Virtues. I rul'd each Page with red Ink, so as to have seven Columns, one for each Day of the Week, marking each Column with a Letter for the Day. I cross'd these Columns with thirteen red Lines, marking the Beginning of each Line with the first Letter of one of the Virtues, on which Line and in its proper Column I might mark by a little black Spot every Fault I found upon Examination to have been committed respecting that Virtue upon that Day.

I determined to give a Week's strict Attention to each of the Virtues successively. Thus in the first Week my great Guard was to avoid every the least Offence against Temperance, leaving the other Virtues to their ordinary Chance, only marking every Evening the Faults of the Day. Thus if in the first Week I could keep my first Line

[147]Pythagoras (b. 580 B.C.?), Greek philosopher and mathematician. A note in Franklin's manuscript indicated that he intended to include translated verses: "Let sleep not close your eyes till you have thrice examined the transactions of the day: where have I strayed, what have I done, what good have I omitted?"

marked T clear of Spots, I suppos'd the Habit of that Virtue so much strengthen'd and its opposite weaken'd, that I might venture extending my Attention to include the next, and for the following Week keep both Lines clear of Spots. Proceeding thus to the last, I could go thro' a Course compleat in Thirteen Weeks, and four Courses in a year. And like him who having a Garden to weed, does not attempt to eradicate all the bad Herbs at once, which would exceed his Reach and his Strength, but works on one of the Beds at a time, and having accomplish'd the first proceeds to a Second; so I should have, (I hoped) the encouraging Pleasure of seeing on my Pages the Progress I made in Virtue, by clearing successively my Lines of their Spots, till in the End by a Number of Courses, I should be happy in viewing a clean Book after a thirteen Weeks daily Examination.

Form of the Pages

Temperance.							
Eat not to Dulness. Drink not to Elevation.							
	S	M	T	W	T	F	S
T							
S	●●	●		●		●	
O	●	●	●		●	●	●
R			●			●	
F		●			●		
I			●	●			
S							
I							
M							
Cl.							
T							
Ch.							
H							

This my little Book had for its Motto these Lines from Addison's *Cato;*

Here will I hold: If there is a Pow'r above us,
(And that there is, all Nature cries aloud
Thro' all her Works) he must delight in Virtue,
And that which he delights in must be happy.[148]

Another from Cicero.

O Vitœ Philosophia dux! O Virtulum indagatrix, expultrixque vitiorum! Unus dies bene, et ex preceptis tuis actus, peccanti immortalitati est anteponendus.[149]

Another from the Proverbs of Solomon speaking of Wisdom or Virtue;

Length of Days is in her right hand, and in her Left Hand Riches and Honours; Her Ways are Ways of Pleasantness, and all her Paths are Peace. III, 16, 17.

[148]Joseph Addison, *Cato, A Tragedy* (1713), Act V, Scene i, lines 15–18.

[149]Marcus Tullius Cicero (106–43 B.C.), Roman philosopher and orator. The quotation is from *Tusculan Disputations,* Act V, Scene ii, line 5. Several lines are omitted after *vitiorum.* "Oh philosophy, guide of life! Oh searcher out of virtues and expeller of vices! . . . One day lived well and according to thy precepts is to be preferred to an eternity of sin."

And conceiving God to be the Fountain of Wisdom, I thought it right and necessary to solicit his Assistance for obtaining it; to this End I form'd the following little Prayer, which was prefix'd to my Tables of Examination; for daily Use.

O Powerful Goodness! bountiful Father! merciful Guide! Increase in me that Wisdom which discovers my truest Interests; Strengthen my Resolutions to perform what that Wisdom dictates. Accept my kind Offices to thy other Children, as the only Return in my Prayer for thy continual Favours to me.

I us'd also sometimes a little Prayer which I took from Thomson's Poems. viz

Father of Light and Life, thou Good supreme,
O teach me what is good, teach me thy self!
Save me from Folly, Vanity and Vice,
From every low Pursuit, and fill my Soul
With Knowledge, conscious Peace, and Virtue pure,
Sacred, substantial, neverfading Bliss![150]

The Precept of *Order* requiring that every *Part of my Business should have its allotted Time,* one Page in my little Book contain'd the following Scheme on Employment for the Twenty-four Hours of a natural Day.

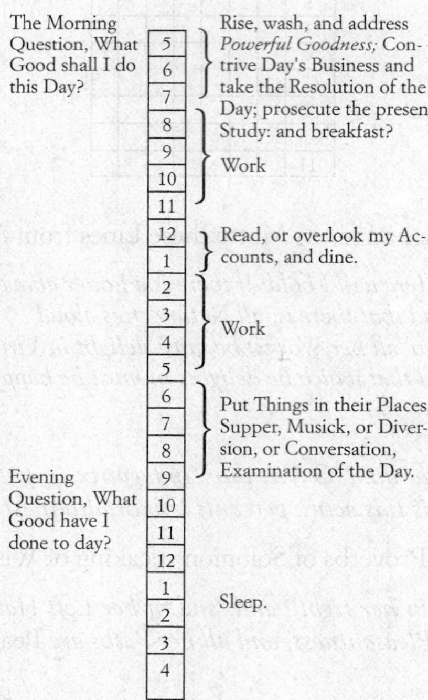

The Morning Question, What Good shall I do this Day?
5
6
7
Rise, wash, and address *Powerful Goodness;* Contrive Day's Business and take the Resolution of the Day; prosecute the present Study: and breakfast?
8
9
10
11
Work
12
1
Read, or overlook my Accounts, and dine.
2
3
4
5
Work
6
7
8
9
Put Things in their Places, Supper, Musick, or Diversion, or Conversation, Examination of the Day.
Evening Question, What Good have I done to day?
10
11
12
1
2
3
4
Sleep.

[150]From James Thomson (1700–1748), *The Seasons,* "Winter" (1726), lines 218–23.

I enter'd upon the Execution of this Plan for Self-Examination, and continu'd it with occasional Intermissions for some time. I was surpriz'd to find myself so much fuller of Faults than I had imagined, but I had the Satisfaction of seeing them diminish. To avoid the Trouble of renewing now and then my little Book, which by scraping out the Marks on the Paper of old Faults to make room for new Ones in a new Course, became full of Holes: I transferr'd my Tables and Precepts to the Ivory Leaves of a Memorandum Book, on which the Lines were drawn with red Ink that made a durable Stain, and on those Lines I mark'd my Faults with a black Lead Pencil, which Marks I could easily wipe out with a wet Sponge. After a while I went thro' one Course only in a Year, and afterwards only one in several years, till at length I omitted them entirely, being employ'd in Voyages and Business abroad with a Multiplicity of Affairs, that interfered, but I always carried my little Book with me.

My scheme of ORDER, gave me the most Trouble, and I found, that tho' it might be practicable where a Man's Business was such as to leave him the Disposition of his Time, that of a Journey-man Printer for instance, it was not possible to be exactly observ'd by a Master, who must mix with the World, and often receive People of Business at their own Hours. *Order* too, with regard to Places for Things, Papers, &c. I found extreamly difficult to acquire. I had not been early accustomed to *Method,* and having an exceeding good Memory, I was not so sensible of the Inconvenience attending Want of Method. This Article therefore cost me so much painful Attention and my Faults in it vex'd me so much, and I made so little Progress in Amendment, and had such frequent Relapses, that I was almost ready to give up the Attempt, and content my self with a faulty Character in that respect. Like the Man who in buying an Ax of a Smith my neighbour, desired to have the whole of its Surface as bright as the Edge; The Smith consented to grind it bright for him if he would turn the Wheel. He turn'd while the Smith press'd the broad Face of the Ax hard and heavily on the Stone, which made the Turning of it very fatiguing. The Man came every now and then from the Wheel to see how the Work went on; and at length would take his Ax as it was without farther Grinding. No, says the Smith, Turn on, turn on; we shall have it bright by and by; as yet 'tis only speckled. Yes, says the Man; but—*I think I like a speckled Ax best.* And I believe this may have been the Case with many who having for want of some such Means as I employ'd found the Difficulty of obtaining good, and breaking bad Habits, in other Points of Vice and Virtue, have given up the Struggle, and concluded that *a speckled Ax was best.* For something that pretended to be Reason was every now and then suggesting to me, that such extream nicety as I exacted of my self might be a kind of Foppery in Morals, which if it were known would make me ridiculous; that a perfect Character might be attended with the Inconvenience of being envied and hated; and that a benevolent Man should allow a few Faults in himself, to keep his Friends in Countenance.

In Truth I found myself incorrigible with respect to *Order;* and now I am grown old, and my Memory bad, I feel very sensibly the want of it. But on the whole, tho' I never arrived at the Perfection I had been so ambitious of obtaining, but fell far short of it, yet I was by the Endeavour a better and a happier Man than I otherwise should have been, if I had not attempted it; As those who aim at perfect Writing by imitating the engraved Copies, tho' they never reach the wish'd for Excellence of those Copies, their Hand is mended by the Endeavour, and is tolerable while it continues fair and legible.

And it may be well my Posterity should be informed, that to this little Artifice, with the Blessing of God, their Ancestor ow'd the constant Felicity of his Life down to his 79th Year in which this is written. What Reserves may attend the Remainder is in the Hand of Providence: But if they arrive the Reflection on past Happiness enjoy'd ought to help his Bearing them with more Resignation. To *Temperance* he ascribes his long-continu'd Health, and what is still left to him of a good Constitution. To *Industry* and *Frugality* the early Easiness of his Circumstances, and Acquisition of his Fortune, with all that Knowledge which enabled him to be an useful Citizen, and obtain'd for him some Degree of Reputation among the Learned. To *Sincerity* and *Justice* the Confidence of his Country, and the honourable Employs it conferr'd upon him. And to the joint Influence of the whole Mass of the Virtues, even in the imperfect State he was able to acquire them, all that Evenness of Temper, and that Chearfulness in Conversation which makes his Company still sought for, and agreable even to his younger Acquaintance. I hope therefore that some of my Descendants may follow the Example and reap the Benefit.

It will be remark'd that, tho' my Scheme was not wholly without Religion there was in it no Mark of any of the distinguishing Tenets of any particular Sect. I had purposely avoided them; for being fully persuaded of the Utility and Excellency of my Method, and that it might be serviceable to People in all Religions, and intending some time or other to publish it, I would not have any thing in it that should prejudice any one of any Sect against it. I purposed writing a little Comment on each Virtue, in which I would have shown the Advantages of possessing it, and the Mischiefs attending its opposite Vice; and I should have called my Book the ART of *Virtue,* because it would have shown the *Means and Manner* of obtaining Virtue, which would have distinguish'd it from the mere Exhortation to be good, that does not instruct and indicate the Means; but is like the Apostle's Man of verbal Charity, who only, without showing to the Naked and the Hungry *how* or where they might get Cloaths or Victuals, exhorted them to be fed and clothed. *James* II, 15, 16.[151]

But it so happened that my Intention of writing and publishing this Comment was never fulfilled. I did indeed, from time to time put down short Hints of the Sentiments, Reasonings, &c. to be made use of in it; some of which I have still by me: But the necessary close Attention to private Business in the earlier part of Life, and public Business since, have occasioned my postponing it. For it being connected in my Mind with a *great and extensive Project* that required the whole Man to execute, and which an unforeseen Succession of Employs prevented my attending to, it has hitherto remain'd unfinish'd.

In this Piece it was my Design to explain and enforce this Doctrine, that vicious Actions are not hurtful because they are forbidden, but forbidden because they are hurtful, the Nature of Man alone consider'd: That it was therefore every one's Interest to be virtuous, who wish'd to be happy even in this World. And I should from this Circumstance, there being always in the World a Number of rich Merchants, Nobility, States and Princes, who have need of honest Instruments for the Management of their Affairs, and such being so rare have endeavoured to convince young

[151] "If a brother or sister be naked, and destitute of daily food. And one of you say unto them, Depart in peace, be ye warmed and filled: notwithstanding ye give them not those things which are needful to the body; what doth it profit?"

Persons, that no Qualities were so likely to make a poor Man's Fortune as those of Probity and Integrity.

My List of Virtues contain'd at first but twelve: But a Quaker Friend having kindly inform'd me that I was generally thought proud; that my Pride show'd itself frequently in Conversation; that I was not content with being in the right when discussing any Point, but was overbearing and rather insolent; of which he convinc'd me by mentioning several Instances; I determined endeavouring to cure myself if I could of this Vice or Folly among the rest, and I added *Humility* to my List, giving an extensive Meaning to the Word. I cannot boast of much Success in acquiring the *Reality* of this Virtue; but I had a good deal with regard to the *Appearance* of it. I made it a Rule to forbear all direct Contradiction to the Sentiments of others, and all positive Assertion of my own. I even forbid myself agreable to the old Laws of our Junto, the Use of every Word or Expression in the Language that imported a fix'd Opinion; such as *certainly, undoubtedly,* &c. and I adopted instead of them, *I conceive, I apprehend,* or *I imagine* a thing to be so or so, or it so appears to me at present. When another asserted something, that I thought an Error, I deny'd my self the Pleasure of contradicting him abruptly, and of showing immediately some Absurdity in his Proposition; and in answering I began by observing that in certain Cases or Circumstances his Opinion would be right, but that in the present case there *appear'd* or *seem'd* to me some Difference, &c. I soon found the Advantage of this Change in my Manners. The Conversations I engag'd in went on more pleasantly. The modest way in which I propos'd my Opinions, procur'd them a readier Reception and less Contradiction; I had less Mortification when I was found to be in the wrong, and I more easily prevail'd with others to give up their Mistakes and join with me when I happen'd to be in the right. And this Mode, which I at first put on, with some violence to natural Inclination, became at length so easy and so habitual to me, that perhaps for these Fifty Years past no one has ever heard a dogmatical Expression escape me. And to this Habit (after my Character of Integrity) I think it principally owing, that I had early so much Weight with my Fellow Citizens, when I proposed new Institutions, or Alterations in the old; and so much Influence in public Councils when I became a Member. For I was but a sad Speaker, never eloquent, subject to much Hesitation in my choice of Words, hardly correct in Language, and yet I generally carried my Points.

In reality there is perhaps no one of our natural Passions so hard to subdue as *Pride.* Disguise it, struggle with it, beat it down, stifle it, mortify it as much as one pleases, it is still alive, and will every now and then peep out and show itself. You will see it perhaps often in this History. For even if I could conceive that I had compleatly overcome it, I should probably by [be] proud of my Humility.

Thus far written at Passy 1784

Part Three [Philadelphia, 1788]

I am now about to write at home (Philadelphia), August 1788, but cannot have the help expected from my papers, many of them being lost in the war. I have, however, found the following. . . .

My being many years in the Assembly, the majority of which were constantly Quakers, gave me frequent opportunities of seeing the embarrassment given them by their principle against war whenever application was made to them by order of the Crown to grant aids for military purposes. They were unwilling to offend government, on the one hand, by a direct refusal and their Friends, the body of Quakers, on the other, by a compliance contrary to their principles—hence a variety of evasions to avoid complying and modes of disguising the compliance when it became unavoidable. The common mode at last was to grant money under the phrase of its being "for the King's use," and never to enquire how it was applied. But if the demand was not directly from the Crown, that phrase was found not so proper, and some other was to be invented. . . .

These embarrassments that the Quakers suffered from having established and published it as one of their principles that no kind of war was lawful, and which being once published, they could not afterwards, however they might change their minds, easily get rid of, reminds me of what I think a more prudent conduct in another sect among us, that of the Dunkers.[152] I was acquainted with one of its founders, Michael Welfare, soon after it appeared. He complained to me that they were grievously calumniated by the zealots of other persuasions, and charged with abominable principles and practices to which they were utter strangers. I told him this had always been the case with new sects and that to put a stop to such abuse, I imagined it might be well to publish the articles of their belief and the rules of their discipline. He said that it had been proposed among them, but not agreed to for this reason: "When we were first drawn together as a society," says he, "it had pleased God to enlighten our minds so far as to see that some doctrines which we once esteemed truths were errors, and that others which we had esteemed errors were real truths. From time to time he has been pleased to afford us further light, and our principles have been improving and our errors diminishing. Now we are not sure that we are arrived at the end of this progression, and at the perfection of spiritual or theological knowledge; and we fear that if we should once print our confession of faith, we should feel ourselves as if bound and confined by it, and perhaps be unwilling to receive further improvement, and our successors still more so, as conceiving what their elders and founders had done to be something sacred, never to be departed from." This modesty in a sect is perhaps a singular instance in the history of mankind, every other sect supposing itself in possession of all truth, and that those who differ are so far in the wrong—like a man travelling in foggy weather: Those at some distance before him on the road he sees wrapped up in the fog, as well as those behind him, and also the people in the fields on each side; but near him all appears clear, tho' in truth he is as much in the fog as any of them. To avoid this kind of embarrassment, the Quakers have of late years been gradually declining the public service in the Assembly and in the magistracy, choosing rather to quit their power than their principle.

In order of time, I should have mentioned before that, having in 1742 invented an open stove for the better warming of rooms and at the same time saving fuel, as the fresh air admitted was warmed in entering, I made a present of the model to Mr. Robert Grace, one of my early friends, who having an iron furnace, found the casting of the plates for these stoves a profitable thing, as they were growing in demand.

[152]Members of a German Baptist sect, also known as Dunkards, many of whom emigrated to Pennsylvania in the early eighteenth century.

To promote that demand, I wrote and published a pamphlet entitled, *An Account of the New-Invented Pennsylvania Fireplaces: Wherein Their Construction and Manner of Operation is Particularly Explained, Their Advantages above Every Other Method of Warming Rooms Demonstrated; and All Objections That Have Been Raised against the Use of Them Answered and Obviated, etc.* This pamphlet had a good effect. Governor Thomas was so pleased with the construction of this stove as described in it that he offered to give me a patent for the sole vending of them for a term of years; but I declined it from a principle which has ever weighed with me on such occasions; viz., *that as we enjoy great advantages from the inventions of others, we should be glad of an opportunity to serve others by any invention of ours, and this we should do freely and generously.* An ironmonger in London, however, after assuming[153] a good deal of my pamphlet, and working up into his own, and making some small changes in the machine, which rather hurt its operation, got a patent for it there, and made, as I was told, a little fortune by it. And this is not the only instance of patents taken out for my inventions by others, tho' not always with the same success, which I never contested, as having no desire of profiting by patents myself and hating disputes. The use of these fireplaces in very many houses both of this and the neighbouring colonies, has been and is a great saving of wood to the inhabitants. . . .

Our city, tho' laid out with a beautiful regularity, the streets large, straight, and crossing each other at right angles, had the disgrace of suffering those streets to remain long unpaved; and in wet weather the wheels of heavy carriages ploughed them into a quagmire so that it was difficult to cross them. And in dry weather the dust was offensive. I had lived near what was called the Jersey Market and saw with pain the inhabitants wading in mud while purchasing their provisions. A strip of ground down the middle of that market was at length paved with brick so that being once in the market they had firm footing, but were often over shoes in dirt to get there. By talking and writing on the subject, I was at length instrumental in getting the street paved with stone between the market and the bricked foot pavement that was on each side next the houses. This for some time gave an easy access to the market, dry-shod. But the rest of the street not being paved, whenever a carriage came out of the mud upon this pavement; it shook off and left its dirt upon it, and it was soon covered with mire, which was not removed, the city as yet having no scavengers.[154] After some enquiry I found a poor, industrious man who was willing to undertake keeping the pavement clean by sweeping it twice a week and carrying off the dirt from before all the neighbours' doors, for the sum of sixpence per month, to be paid by each house. I then wrote and printed a paper, setting forth the advantages to the neighborhood that might be obtained by this small expence: the greater ease in keeping our houses clean, so much dirt not being brought in by people's feet; the benefit to the shops by more custom, as buyers could more easily get at them; and by not having in windy weather the dust blown in upon their goods, etc., etc. I sent one of these papers to each house and in a day or two went round to see who would subscribe an agreement to pay these sixpences. It was unanimously signed and for a time well executed. All the inhabitants of the city were delighted with the cleanliness of the pavement that surrounded the market, it being a convenience to all; and this raised a general desire to have all the streets paved, and made the people more willing

[153]Appropriating

[154]Street cleaners

to submit to a tax for that purpose. After some time I drew a bill for paving the city and brought it into the Assembly. It was just before I went to England in 1757 and did not pass till I was gone, and then with an alteration in the mode of assessment, which I thought not for the better, but with an additional provision for lighting as well as paving the streets, which was a great improvement. It was by a private person, the late Mr. John Clifton, giving a sample of the utility of lamps by placing one at his door that the people were first impressed with the idea of lighting all the city. The honour of this public benefit has also been ascribed to me, but it belongs truly to that gentleman. I did but follow his example and have only some merit to claim respecting the form of our lamps as differing from the globe lamps we at first were supplied with from London. Those we found inconvenient in these respects: They admitted no air below; the smoke therefore did not readily go out above, but circulated in the globe, lodged on its inside, and soon obstructed the light they were intended to afford, giving, besides, the daily trouble of wiping them clean; and an accidental stroke on one of them would demolish it and render it totally useless. I therefore suggested the composing them of four flat panes, with a long funnel above, to draw up the smoke, and crevices admitting air below, to facilitate the ascent of the smoke. By this means they were kept clean, and did not grow dark in a few hours as the London lamps do, but continued bright till morning; and an accidental stroke would generally break but a single pane, easily repaired. I have sometimes wondered that the Londoners did not, from the effect holes in the bottom of the globe lamps used at Vauxhall[155] have in keeping them clean, learn to have such holes in their street lamps. But those holes being made for another purpose, viz., to communicate flame more suddenly to the wick by a little flax hanging down thro' them, the other use of letting in airs seems not to have been thought of. And therefore, after the lamps have been lit a few hours, the streets of London are very poorly illuminated.

The mention of these improvements puts me in mind of one I proposed when in London to Dr. Fothergill,[156] who was among the best men I have known and a great promoter of useful projects. I had observed that the streets when dry were never swept and the light dust carried away, but it was suffered to accumulate till wet weather reduced it to mud; and then after lying some days so deep on the pavement that there was no crossing but in paths kept clean by poor people with brooms, it was with great labour raked together and thrown up into carts open above, the sides of which suffered some of the slush at every jolt on the pavement to shake out and fall, sometimes to the annoyance of foot passengers. The reason given for not sweeping the dusty streets was that the dust would fly into the windows of shops and houses. An accidental occurrence had instructed me how much sweeping might be done in a little time. I found at my door in Craven Street one morning a poor woman sweeping my pavement with a birch broom. She appeared very pale and feeble as just come out of a fit of sickness. I asked who employed her to sweep there. She said, "Nobody. But I am very poor and in distress, and I sweeps before gentlefolkses doors and hopes they will give me something." I bid her sweep the whole street clean and I would give her a shilling. This was at nine o'clock. At twelve she came for the shilling. From the slowness I saw at first in her working, I could scarce believe that the work was done so soon and sent my servant to examine it, who reported that the whole

[155]Vauxhall Gardens, an amusement park on the outskirts of London.

[156]Dr. John Fothergill (1712–1780), noted British physician.

street was swept perfectly clean and all the dust placed in the gutter which was in the middle; and the next rain washed it quite away so that the pavement and even the kennel[157] were perfectly clean. I then judged that if that feeble woman could sweep such a street in three hours, a strong, active man might have done it in half the time. And here let me remark the convenience of having but one gutter in such a narrow street running down its middle instead of two, one on each side near the footway. For where all the rain that falls on a street runs from the sides and meets in the middle, it forms there a current strong enough to wash away all the mud it meets with. But when divided into two channels, it is often too weak to cleanse either and only makes the mud it finds more fluid so that the wheels of carriages and feet of horses throw and dash it up on the foot pavement, which is thereby rendered foul and slippery, and sometimes splash it upon those who are walking. . . .

Some may think these trifling matters not worth minding or relating. But when they consider that tho' dust blown into the eyes of a single person or into a single shop on a windy day is but of small importance, yet the great number of the instances in a populous city and its frequent repetitions give it weight and consequence; perhaps they will not censure very severely those who bestow some attention to affairs of this seemingly low nature. Human felicity is produced not so much by great pieces of good fortune that seldom happen as by little advantages that occur every day. Thus, if you teach a poor young man to shave himself and keep his razor in order, you may contribute more to the happiness of his life than in giving him a thousand guineas. The money may be soon spent, the regret only remaining of having foolishly consumed it. But in the other case he escapes the frequent vexation of waiting for barbers and of their sometimes dirty fingers, offensive breaths, and dull razors. He shaves when most convenient to him and enjoys daily the pleasure of its being done with a good instrument. With these sentiments I have hazarded the few preceding pages, hoping they may afford hints which sometime or other may be useful to a city I love, having lived many years in it very happily—and perhaps to some of our towns in America. . . .

1791

Mercy Otis Warren 1728–1814

Mercy Otis Warren was a poet, dramatist, satirist, patriot propagandist, and historian at a time when women, if they wrote, were confined to *belle-lettres* or religious subject matter. The American Revolution and her particular place in Massachusetts society and politics, however, practically forced Warren into the limelight. She was the third child of James Otis and Mary Allyne, of Barnstable, a farming town south of Plymouth, on Cape Cod. Both families were descended from the earliest Pilgrim settlers. James Otis was a farmer, merchant, and attorney, and his successful practice won him election to the Massachusetts House of Representatives in 1745. Not an educated man himself, Otis wanted his two sons to have an education and hired the Reverend Jonathan Russell to prepare them for college. When Joseph, the oldest

[157]Gutter

son, decided not to attend college, Mercy, the youngest child, was allowed to take his place. She studied the same curriculum as her brother James, except for Latin and Greek, which she read in translation.

Both James and Mercy were exceptional students. Mercy loved history—especially political history—invective, and wit; Sir Walter Ralegh's *History of the World* (1614) became a lifelong model for her. Both of the Otis children studied literature, including Shakespeare, Milton, Dryden, and Pope, and became able writers and rhetoricians. It was the younger James who first uttered the phrase "Taxation without representation is tyranny," which became the battle cry for the American Revolution. In 1754, Mercy married James Warren, a farmer from Plymouth and a Harvard classmate of her brother. They had a long, happy marriage and raised five sons. Like the Otis men, James Warren was elected to the Massachusetts House of Representatives. He served continuously from 1766 to 1778, eventually becoming speaker of the House and president of the Massachusetts Provincial Congress, which had moved to Watertown during the British occupation of Boston. A radical and outspoken activist, he became an active leader in local revolutionary politics.

Because of her family connections, no other woman, with the exception of Abigail Adams, was as intimately involved as Mercy Otis Warren with the political issues of the day. Thus, when Tory supporters brutally beat her brother James in a Boston tavern in 1769, friends in her circle urged her to step in and take his place as a revolutionary polemicist. Warren complied, although a comment by her friend and fellow patriot John Adams suggests the social conventions massed against her. "Tell your wife," Adams wrote to James Warren, that "God Almighty (I use a bold style) has entrusted her with Powers for the good of the World, which, in the Cause of His Providence, he bestows on few of the human race. That instead of being a fault to use them, it would be criminal to neglect them."

Warren used her "Powers" for the revolutionary cause. She wrote numerous letters and poems, which she published anonymously in newspapers. Her most effective efforts at propaganda were a series of satirical plays—the first plays written by an American woman. They appeared in newspapers and as pamphlets, instead of being performed, because Puritan Boston had laws against staging plays and did not have a theater until 1794. Three political plays have been identified as hers: *The Adulateur* (1772), *The Defeat* (1773), and *The Group* (1775), although the only play she acknowledged authorship of was *The Group.* All three focus on the moral evil of the Tory administration in Massachusetts, its hypocrisy, crass ambition, warmongering, and the invidious policies of its arch villain, Governor Thomas Hutchinson. In her biting satires, Warren calls Hutchinson "Rapatio," to contrast him with the self-sacrifice, heroism, and virtue of the patriots. The best of the three is *The Group,* printed below in full, a brilliant defense of the patriot cause. Instead of staging debates in this play, Warren offers a series of dialogues among Tory sympathizers and turncoats, many of whom were connected to her family, in which they drop their public masks to reveal their ignoble choices and reprehensible designs. Although her use of blank verse and allusions to Greek and Roman politics lend the plays a "tragic" tone that later critics found "grandiose," their savage satire was an effective propaganda tool.

At the end of the Revolution, both Warrens fell out with their old friends: James for supporting Daniel Shays and his rebellion; Mercy for her comments on the overly passionate nature of John Adams. In 1781, they purchased the estate of their former antagonist, Governor Hutchinson, but lived there only eight years before moving back to Plymouth, where Warren attended to her writing. In 1790, she brought out the collection *Poems, Dramatic and Miscellaneous* in her own name. It contained two more plays, *The Sack of Rome* and *The Ladies of Castille.* Both works dramatize historical analogues to the American Revolution and explore another important theme in Warren's satires and poetry: the issue of women as writers and revolutionary activists. These historical plays prominently feature women—and mothers—as public orators and rebel leaders. Warren gives them the most stirring speeches; an example from *The Ladies of Castille* is excerpted below.

Warren's most audacious trespass on masculine turf, however, was her *History of the Rise, Progress, and Termination of the American Revolution* in three volumes, which appeared in 1805. It was written over twenty-five years and represents a brilliant and important female intervention in a conventionally masculine field of literature. As Warren states in her preface, she was uniquely positioned to experience events leading up to the Revolution, and she knew well many of the leaders who took part in the various military campaigns. More important, she argues that "every domestic enjoyment depends on the unimpaired possession of civil and religious liberty," so that everyone, including women, had a crucial stake in the winning and maintenance of that liberty.

Ivy Schweitzer
Dartmouth College

PRIMARY WORKS

The Adulateur, 1773; *The Defeat,* 1773; *The Group,* 1775; *Poems, Dramatic and Miscellaneous,* 1790; *History of the Rise, Progress, and Termination of the American Revolution,* 1805; *The Plays and Poems of Mercy Otis Warren,* fac., ed. Benjamin V. Franklin, 1980.

To Fidelio, Long absent on the great public Cause, which agitated all America, in 1776[1]

The hilltops smile o'er all the blooming mead,
As I alone, on Clifford's[2] summit tread;
Traverse the rural walks, the gurgling rills,
Survey the beauties of th' adjacent hills;
Taste the delights of competence and health[3]
Each sober pleasure reason lends to wealth:
Yet o'er the lawn a whispering echo sighs,
Thy friend is absent—my fond heart replies—
Say—do not friendship's joys outweigh the whole?

[1]Fidelio is James Warren, Mercy's husband, who spent many of the war years away from home, as paymaster of the colonial army and director of naval operations. This text is from *Poems, Dramatic and Miscellaneous* (1790). Thanks to Jeffrey Richards for help with these selections.

[2]The Warrens's country home in Plymouth, Massachusetts.

[3]Mercy's brother James Otis, Jr., a patriot, was severely beaten in a tavern by Tory supporters and never regained his mental health. In 1770, Warren wrote the poem "On the Inestimable Blessing of Reason, Occasioned By Its Privation To a Friend Of Very Superior Talents and Virtues."

'Tis social converse, animates the soul.
Thought interchanged, the heavenly spark improves,
And reason brightens by the heart it loves;
While solitude sits brooding o'er her cares,
She oft accelerates the ills she fears;
And though fond hope with silken hand displays,
The distant images of halcyon days,
Her sable brow contracts a solemn air,
That treads too near the threshold of despair;
'Till heaven benign the choicest blessings lend,
The balm of life, a kind and faithful friend:
This highest gift, by heaven indulged, I claim;
Ask, what is happiness?—My friend, I name:
Yet while the state, by fierce internal war,
Shook to the centre, asks his zealous care,
I must submit, and smile in solitude,
My fond affection, my self love subdued:
The times demand exertions of the kind,
A patriot zeal must warm the female mind.
Yet, gentle hope!—come, spread thy silken wing,
And waft me forward to revolving spring;
Or ere the vernal equinox returns,
At worst, before the summer solstice burns,
May peace again erect her cheerful stand,
Disperse the ills which hover o'er the land;
May every virtuous noble minded pair,
Be far removed from the dread din of war;
Then each warm breast where generous friendships glow,
Where all the virtues of the patriot flow,
Shall taste each joy domestic life can yield,
Nor enter more the martial bloody field.

But, hark!—alas! the brave Montgomery dies,[4]
Oh, heaven forbid that such a sacrifice,
My country or my sex should yield again,
Or such rich blood pour o'er the purpled plain:
May guilty traitors satiate the grave,
But let the sword forever—spare the brave;
I weep his fall—I weep the hero slain,
And mingle sighs with his Janetta's pain:
Yet while I weep, and lend the pitying sigh,
I bow the knee, and lift my soul on high,
That virtue, struggling with assiduous pains,
May free this country from despotic chains.
Long life I ask, and blessings to descend,

[4]Richard Montgomery (1738–1775), commander of the American attack on Montreal, was killed during the assault on Quebec. Janet, his wife, was a friend of Warren's.

And crown the efforts of my constant friend;
My early wish, and evening prayer the same,
That virtue, health, and peace, and honest fame,
May hover o'er thee, till time's latest hour,
Commissionate[5] the dread resistless power;
Then gently lay thee by thy Marcia's[6] clay,
'Til both shall rise, and on a tide of day,
Be wafted on, and skim the ambient plains
Through lucid air, and see the God who reigns.

Where cherubims in borrowed lustre shine,
We'll hand in hand our grateful homage join;
Beneath his throne, where listening angels stand,
With raptured seraphs wait his least command.

Clifford Farm, 1776 — 1790

The Group

As Lately Acted, and to be Re-acted to the Wonder of all Superior Intelligences, Nigh Headquarters at Amboyne.[1]

The author has thought proper to borrow the following spirited lines from a late celebrated poet, and offer to the public by way of PROLOGUE, which cannot fail of pleasing at this crisis.

[5]Commissioned.

[6]Warren's pen name.

[1]This satire was inspired by the Boston Tea Party, an act of resistance to the British Parliament's tax on tea. When three ships arrived at Boston harbor carrying tea, angry Bostonians refused to let the cargo come ashore, and Massachusetts governor Thomas Hutchinson refused to let the ships leave until the tea was unloaded. The stalemate ended on December 16, 1773, when a group of patriots dressed as Indians, including Samuel Adams and Paul Revere, boarded the ships and threw the tea overboard. To punish Massachusetts, Parliament passed a series of laws that the colonists called the "Intolerable Acts." One of the laws closed the port of Boston until the owners of the tea had been compensated. Other laws changed the way the colony was governed and restricted the colonists' political freedoms. Through a writ of *mandamus* (Latin for "we command") the royal governor was empowered to appoint councilors to govern in the place of locally elected officials. Hutchinson returned to England, and General Thomas Gage, commander of British troops in North America, became governor of the colony. Protest was so widespread that only about ten of the thirty-six appointed mandamus councilors actually took the oath of office. Many of the councilors had long-standing connections to the Otis-Warren family or to John Adams. Warren's play focuses on tensions among these Tory sympathizers. "Amboyne" is a fictional place. It is doubtful whether the play was ever performed. It first appeared in partial form in the *Boston Gazette,* 23 Jan. 1775, and in the *Massachusetts Spy,* 26 Jan. 1775. The text, with slight modifications, is from the expanded third edition, published in 1775 by Edes and Gill of Boston.

What! arm'd for virtue, and not point the pen,
Brand the bold front of shameless guilty men,
Dash the proud Gamester from his gilded car,
Bare the mean heart which lurks beneath a star,

. . . .

Shall I not strip the gilding off a knave,
Unplac'd, unpension'd, no man's heir or slave?
I will or perish in the gen'rous cause;
Hear this and tremble, ye who 'scape the laws;
Yes, while I live, no rich or noble knave,
Shall walk the world in credit to his grave:
To virtue only, and her friends, a friend,
The world beside may murmur, or commend.[2]

DRAMATIS PERSONAE[3]

Lord Chief Justice HAZLEROD
Judge MEAGRE
Brigadier HATEALL
MONSIEUR de Francois
CRUSTY CROWBAR, Esq.
DUPE,—SECRETARY of State

[2]With minor discrepancies, from Alexander Pope (1688–1744), "First Satire on the Second Book of Horace Imitated" (1733), lines 105–109, 115–122.

[3]All the characters are based on Tory sympathizers. Jeffrey Richards has identified them as follows: Hazelrod is Peter Oliver (1713–1791), Thomas Hutchinson's brother-in-law, chief justice of the Massachusetts Superior Court, and one of the most influential loyalists in Boston; he appeared in the earlier play, *The Adulateur.* Meagre is Foster Hutchinson (1724–1799), Thomas Hutchinson's younger brother, Harvard classmate of James Otis, Jr., and justice of the Superior Court; he also appeared in *The Adulateur.* Hateall is Timothy Ruggles (1711–1798), a profane and contentious lawyer from Plymouth County who was a judicial rival of James Otis, Sr. and had some public disputes with James Otis, Jr., Hum-Humbug is John Erving, Jr. (1727–1816), Harvard class of 1747, a mandamus councilor who took the oath. Sir Sparrow is William Pepperell Sparhawk, the younger (1746–1816), who inherited his grandfather's wealth and in 1774 became the only American baronet with lands in Maine. Hector Mushroom is Colonel John Murray (d. 1794), a merchant notorious for his short temper who served in the Massachusetts General Court (colonial legislature) and was a latecomer to the Hutchinson faction; a mob formed to prevent him from accepting the mandamus post. Beau-Trumps is Daniel Leonard (1740–1829), a lawyer, king's attorney for Bristol County, member of the Massachusetts House of Representatives, and close friend of John Adams; he favored independence until the Boston Tea Party. Dick is Richard Lechmere (1727–1814), who followed his father Thomas in the customs service. Simple Sapling is Nathaniel Ray Thomas (1731–1787), of Marshfield in Plymouth County, Harvard class of 1751, loyalist and wealthy farmer. De Francois is James Boutineau (b. 1710), father-in-law of and attorney for John Robinson, the customs commissioner charged with the beating of James Otis, Jr. in 1769. Crusty Crowbar is Josiah Edson, a Plymouth County resident, Harvard class of 1730, and a friend of Timothy Ruggles. Dupe is Thomas Flucker (1719–1783), a staunch Hutchinson supporter who became provincial secretary and appears in *The Adulateur.* Scriblerius is Harrison Gray (1711–1794), treasurer of Massachusetts from 1753 to 1774 and father-in-law of Warren's brother Samuel Allyne Otis; Batteau is Joshua Loring (1716–1781), commodore of naval forces of Lakes Champlain and Ontario during the French and Indian War and commissioner of revenue. Collateralis is William Browne (1737–1802), classmate of John Adams at Harvard in 1755 and Massachusetts Superior Court judge from Salem. Sylla is General Thomas Gage (1721–1787), British general who commanded all British forces in North America from 1763 to 1774; he replaced Hutchinson as governor of Massachusetts (1774–1775).

HUM-HUMBUG, Esq.	SCRIBLERIUS Fribble
SIR SPARROW Spendall	Commodore BATTEAU
HECTOR MUSHROOM,—Col.	COLLATERALIS,—a new-made Judge
BEAU-TRUMPS	SYLLA[4]
Dick, the PUBLICAN[5]	A LADY
SIMPLE SAPLING, Esq.	

Attended by a swarm of court sycophants, hungry harpies, and unprincipled danglers, collected from the neighboring villages, hovering over the stage in the shape of locusts, led by Massachusettensis in the form of a basilisk; the rear brought up by Proteus,6 bearing a torch in one hand, and a powder flask in the other: The whole supported by a mighty army and navy, from Blunderland, for the laudable purpose of enslaving its best friends.

ACT I

SCENE. *a little dark parlor, guards standing at the door.* HAZLEROD, CRUSTY CROWBAR, SIMPLE SAPLING, HATEALL, and HECTOR MUSHROOM.

SIMPLE. I know not what to think of these sad times,
The people armed—and all resolved to die
Ere they'll submit.—
CRUSTY CROWBAR. I too am almost sick of the parade
Of honors purchased at the price of peace.
SIMPLE. Fond as I am of greatness and her charms
Elate with prospects of my rising name,
Pushed into place,—a place I ne'er expected,
My bounding heart leapt in my feeble breast
And ecstasies entranced my slender brain.—
But yet, ere this I hoped more solid gains,
As my low purse demands a quick supply.—
Poor Sylvia weeps—and urges my return
To rural peace and humble happiness,
As my ambition beggars all her babes.

[4]"Sylla" and "A Lady," are not listed in the original edition's list of characters, although they both appear in the play.

[5]Tax or revenue collector.

[6]In Warren's earlier play *The Defeat* (1773), Proteus, a Greek sea-god who could change shape at will, stands for William Brattle (1706–1776), a wealthy man and militia general who, along with James Otis, Sr. and James, Jr., opposed the Stamp Act. When Brattle switched loyalties, John Adams publicly and privately declared his change of heart a betrayal. The basilisk is a legendary serpent with a lethal breath and glance. Massachusettensis was the pen name of Daniel Leonard (who appears in the play as "Beau-Trumps"; see above), a Tory propagandist who published essays against independence and was opposed by John Adams, writing under the pen name Novanglus. Harpies are mythological monsters with the heads and bodies of women and the wings and claws of birds.

CRUSTY. When first I 'listed in the desperate cause,
And blindly swore obedience to his will,
So wise, so just, so good I thought Rapatio,[7]
That if salvation rested on his word
I'd pin my faith and risk my hopes thereon.
HAZLEROD. And why not now?—What staggers thy belief?
CRUSTY. Himself—his perfidy appears—
It is too plain he has betrayed his country.
And we're the wretched tools by him marked out
To seal its ruins—tear up the ancient forms,
And every vestige treacherously destroy,
Nor leave a trait of freedom in the land.
Nor did I think hard fate would call me up
From drudging o'er my acres,
Treading the glade, and sweating at the plough,
To dangle at the tables of the great;
At bowls and cards, to spend my frozen years,
To sell my friends, my country, and my conscience;
Profane the sacred sabbaths of my God,
Scorned by the very men who want my aid
To spread distress o'er this devoted people.
HAZLEROD. Pho! What misgivings—why these idle qualms,
This shrinking backwards at the bugbear conscience?
In early life I heard the phantom named,
And the grave sages prate of moral sense
Presiding in the bosom of the just;
Or panting thongs about the guilty heart.
Bound by these shackles, long my lab'ring mind
Obscurely trod the lower walks of life,
In hopes by honesty my bread to gain;
But neither commerce, or my conjuring rods,
Nor yet mechanics, or new fangled drills,
Or all the ironmonger's curious arts
Gave me a competence of shining ore,
Or gratified my itching palm for more;
Till I dismissed the bold intruding guest,
And banished conscience from my wounded breast.
CRUSTY. Happy expedient!—Could I gain the art,
Then balmy sleep might sooth my waking lids,
And rest once more refresh my weary soul.
HAZLEROD. Resolved more rapidly to gain my point,
mounted high in justice's sacred seat,
With flowing robes, and head equipped without[8]

[7]Thomas Hutchinson (1711–1780), the hated British administrator and governor of Massachusetts (1771– 1774). "Rapatio," mock-Latin for a rapacious or greedy person, was his name in earlier plays by Warren.

[8]Wearing the wig of a judge.

A heart unfeeling and a stubborn soul,
As qualified as e'er a *Jefferies*[9] was,
Save in the knotty rudiments of law,
The smallest requisite for modern times,
When wisdom, law, and justice, are supplied
By swords, dragoons,[10] and ministerial nods,
Sanctions most sacred in the pander's[11] creed.
I sold my country for a splendid bribe.
Now let her sink—and all the dire alarms
Of war, confusion, pestilence and blood,
And tenfold misery be her future doom—
Let civil discord lift her sword on high,
Nay sheathe its hilt e'en in my brother's blood;
It ne'er shall move the purpose of my soul.
Though once I trembled at a thought so bold,
By Philalethes's[12] arguments convinced
We may live demons, as we die like brutes.
I give my tears, and conscience to the winds.

HATEALL. Curse on their coward fears, and dastard soul
Their soft compunctions and relenting qualms,
Compassion ne'er shall seize my steadfast breast
Though blood and carnage spread through all the land,
Till streaming purple tinge the verdant turf,
Till every street shall float with human gore,
I Nero-like,[13] the capital in flames,
Could laugh to see her glutted sons expire,
Though much too rough my soul to touch the lyre.

SIMPLE. I fear the brave, the injured multitude,
Repeated wrongs, arouse them to resent,
And every patriot like old Brutus[14] stands,
The shining steel half drawn—its glitt'ring point
Scarce hid beneath the scabbard's friendly cell—
Resolved to die, or see their country free.

HATEALL. Then let them die!—*The dogs we will keep down*—
While N——'s my friend, and G—— approves the deed,[15]
Though hell and all its hell-hounds should unite,

[9]George Jeffries (1648–1689), England's Lord Chief Justice, famous for his cruelty.

[10]A kind of carbine or musket, so called from its "breathing fire" like a dragon.

[11]Pimp's.

[12]Pen name of Jonathan Sewall (1728–1796), a lawyer and Tory sympathizer.

[13]The Roman emperor Nero (A.D. 37–68), who watched—some say fiddled—as the city of Rome burned.

[14]Marcus Junius Brutus (c. 85–42 B.C.), a Roman senator and military leader who, after Julius Caesar had assumed dictatorial powers, participated in his assassination.

[15]"G—" is General Thomas Gage, military governor of Massachusetts (1774–1775). "N—" is Frederick Lord North (1732–1792), King George III's prime minister.

I'll not recede to save from swift perdition
My wife, my country, family or friends.
G——'s mandamus I more highly prize
Than all the mandates of the ethereal King.[16]

HECTOR MUSHROOM. Will our abettors in the distant towns
Support us long against the common cause,
When they shall see from 'Hampshire's[17] northern bound
Through the wide western plains to southern shores
The whole united continent in arms?—

HATEALL. They shall—as sure as oaths or bonds can bind.
I've boldly sent my newborn brat abroad,
Th'association of my morbid brain,
To which each minion must affix his name.
As all our hope depends on brutal force
On quick destruction, misery and death,
Soon may we see dark ruin stalk around,
With murder, rapine, and inflicted pains,
Estates confiscate, slav'ry and despair,
Wrecks, halters, axes, gibbeting[18] and chains,
All the dread ills that wait on civil war.
How I could glut my vengeful eyes to see
The weeping maid thrown helpless on the world,
Her sire cut off.—Her orphan brothers stand
While the big tear rolls down the manly cheek.
Robbed of maternal care by grief's keen shaft,
The sorrowing mother mourns her starving babes.
Her murdered lord torn guiltless from her side,
And flees for shelter to the pitying grave
To screen at once from slavery and pain.

HAZLEROD. But more complete I view this scene of woe
By the incursions of a savage foe,[19]
Of which I warned them, if they dare refuse
The badge of slaves, and bold resistance use.
Now let them suffer—I'll no pity feel.

HATEALL. Nor I!—But had I power, as I have the Will
I'd send them murm'ring to the shades of hell.

[16]The writ of mandamus was Parliament's tool for creating a royally appointed council to govern Massachusetts, in the place of the locally elected officials, after the Boston Tea Party.

[17]New Hampshire, one of the thirteen original colonies.

[18]Hangings.

[19]British alliances with native tribes posed a constant threat to the revolutionaries.

ACT II

The scene changes to a large dining room. The table furnished with bowls, bottles, glasses and cards—The group appear sitting round in a restless attitude. In one corner of the room is discovered a small cabinet of books, for the use of the studious and contemplative, containing Hobbes's Leviathan, *Sipthrop's* Sermons, *Hutchinson's* History, Fable of the Bees, Philalethes on Philanthrop, with an appendix by Massachusettensis, Hoyle on Whist, Lives of the Stuarts, Statutes of Henry the Eighth, and William the Conqueror, *Wedderburn's* Speeches and Acts of Parliament for 1774.[20]

Scene I

HATEALL, HAZLEROD, MONSIEUR, BEAU-TRUMPS, SIMPLE, HUMBUG, SIR SPARROW, &c. &c.

SCRIBLERIUS. Thy toast Monsieur,—
Pray, why that solemn phiz?[21]—
Art thou, too, balancing 'twixt right and wrong?
Hast thou a thought so mean as to give up
Thy present good for promise in reversion?[22]
'Tis true hereafter has some feeble terrors,
But ere our grizzly heads are wrapped in clay
We may compound,[23] and make our peace with Heav'n.

MONSIEUR. Could I give up the dread of retribution
The awful reck'ning of some future day,
Like surly Hateall I might curse mankind
And dare the threatened vengeance of the skies.

[20]Thomas Hobbes (1588–1679) was an English philosopher; in *Leviathan* (1651) he argues that humans are innately brutish and selfish and that fear of violent death motivates them to create a state and willingly submit to the authority of a sovereign. "Sipthrop" is a satiric reference to Robert Sibthorpe, a seventeenth-century divine who believed that people should accept their lot in life passively. Governor Thomas Hutchinson published the first volume of his three-volume *History of the Colony and Province of Massachusetts* in 1764. *Fable of the Bees* (1723), by Bernard Mandeville (c. 1670–1733), a Dutch physician and writer living in London, contained a paradoxical defense of the usefulness of vices and provoked a long controversy. Tory propagandist Jonathan Sewall used the pen names Philalethes and Philanthrop. Massachusettenis was the pen name of Daniel Leonard, satirized in the play as Beau-Trumps. Edmond Hoyle (1672–1769) codified the card game whist in *A Short Treatise on the Game of Whist* (1742). The Stuarts ruled Scotland from 1371 to 1707, England from 1603 to 1707, and Great Britain from 1707 to 1714; Henry VIII was king of England from 1509 to 1547; William the Conqueror (1027–1087) led the Norman conquest of England in 1066. The Stuarts, Henry VIII, and William all represent English tyranny. Alexander Wedderburn (1733–1805), England's Lord Chancellor, denounced Benjamin Franklin for publishing private letters written by Governor Hutchinson in 1773 that revealed the governor's hostility to the patriots.

[21]Slang for *physiognomy,* facial expression.

[22]Future possessions.

[23]Settle with a creditor.

Or, like yon apostate,—[*Pointing to* HAZLEROD, *retired to a corner to read Massachusettensis*]—feel but slight remorse
To sell my country for a grasp of gold.
But the impressions of my early youth,
Infixed by precepts of my pious sire,
Are stings and scorpions in my goaded breast.
Oft have I hung upon my parent's knee
And heard him tell of his escape from France.
He left the land of slaves and wooden shoes.
From place to place he sought a safe retreat,
Till fair Bostonia stretched her friendly arm
And gave the refugee both bread and peace.
(Shall I, ungrateful, raze the sacred bonds,
And help to clank the tyrant's iron chains
O'er these blest shores—once the sure asylum
From all the ills of arbitrary sway?)
With his expiring breath he bade his sons
If e'er oppression reached the western world
Resist its force, and break the servile yoke.

SCRIBLERIUS. Well, quit thy post;—Go make thy flatt'ring court
To Freedom's Sons and tell thy baby fears.
Show the soft traces in thy puny heart,
Made by the trembling tongue and quiv'ring lip
Of an old grandsire's superstitious whims.

MONSIEUR. No,—I never can—
So great the itch I feel for titled place,
Some honorary post, some small distinction,
To save my name from dark oblivion's jaws.
I'll hazard all, but ne'er give up my place.
For that I'll see Rome's ancient rites restored,
And flame and faggot blaze in ev'ry street.[24]

BEAU-TRUMPS. That's right, Monsieur,
There's nought on earth that has such tempting charms
As rank and show, and pomp, and glitt'ring dress,
Save the dear counters at belov'd quadrille.[25]
Viner unsoil'd, and Littleton may sleep,
And Coke[26] lie mould'ring on the dusty shelf,
If I, by shuffling, draw some lucky card
That wins the livres[27] or lucrative place.

[24]Roman citizens were accompanied through dangerous streets at night by torchbearers. A faggot is a bundle of burning sticks or twigs.

[25]Quadrille was a popular card game played by four people using a deck of forty cards. Counters are pieces of wood or ivory used to keep score.

[26]Sir Edward Coke (1552–1634), Sir Thomas Littleton (1442–1481), and Charles Viner (1678–1756) were Englishmen who wrote treatises on the law.

[27]Money. *Livre* (French) means "pound," the word for English currency.

HUM-HUMBUG. When sly Rapatio show'd his friends the scroll,
I wondered much to see thy patriot name
Among the list of rebels to the state.
I thought thee one of Rusticus's[28] sworn friends.
BEAU-TRUMPS. When first I entered on the public stage
My country groaned beneath base Brundo's[29] hand.
Virtue looked fair and beckoned to her lure.
Through truth's bright mirror I beheld her charms,
And wished to tread the patriotic path,
And wear the laurels that adorn his fame.
I walked awhile and tasted solid peace
With Cassius, Rusticus and good Hortensius.[30]
And many more, whose names will be revered
When you and I and all the venal herd
Weighed in Nemesis's[31] just, impartial scale,
Are marked with infamy, till time blot out
And in oblivion sink our hated names.
But 'twas a poor unprofitable path,
Nought to be gained, save solid peace of mind.
No pensions, place or title there I found;
I saw Rapatio's arts had struck so deep
And giv'n his country such a fatal wound
None but its foes promotion could expect.
I trimmed, and pimped, and veered, and wav'ring stood,
But half resolved to show myself a knave,
Till the Arch Traitor[32] prowling round for aid,
Saw my suspense and bid me doubt no more;—
He gently bowed, and, smiling, took my hand,
And whispering softly in my listening ear,
Showed me my name among his chosen band,
And laughed at virtue dignified by fools;
Cleared all my doubts, and bid me persevere
In spite of the restraints, or hourly checks
Of wounded friendship, and a goaded mind,
Or all the sacred ties of truth and honor.
COLLATERALIS. Come, 'mongst ourselves we'll e'en speak out the truth.
Can you suppose there yet is such a dupe
As still believes that wretch an honest man?
The latter strokes of his serpentine brain

[28]Probably James Warren, Mercy's husband. *Rusticus,* from Latin, means "related to the country or rustic matters."

[29]Probably Sir Francis Bernard (1712–1779), colonial governor of Massachusetts from 1760 to 1770.

[30]"Hortensius" is probably John Adams, the farmer and lawyer from Quincy, Massachusetts, who was a patriot leader and friend of the Warrens. "Cassius" is Samuel Adams (1722–1803), revolutionary leader and propagandist.

[31]In Greek mythology, the goddess of vengeance.

[32]Satan, who rebelled against God.

Outvie the arts of Machiavel[33] himself;
His Borgian[34] model here is realized,
And the stale tricks of politicians played
Beneath a vizard[35] fair—
—Drawn from the Heav'nly form
Of blest religion weeping o'er the land
For virtue fall'n, and for freedom lost.
BEAU-TRUMPS. I think with you—
—unparalleled his effron'try,
When by chicanery and specious art,
'Midst the distress in which he'd brought the city,
He found a few (by artifice and cunning,
By much industry of his wily friend
The false Philanthrop[36]—sly undermining tool,
Who with the Siren's voice[37]
Deals daily 'round the poison of his tongue),
To speak him fair—and overlook his guilt.
They, by reiterated promise, made
To stand their friend at Britain's mighty court,
And vindicate his native, injured land,
Lent him their names to sanctify his deeds.
But mark the traitor—his high crime glossed o'er
Conceals the tender feelings of the man,
The social ties that bind the human heart.
He strikes a bargain with his country's foes,
And joins to wrap America in flames,
Yet with feigned pity, and Satanic grin,
As if more deep to fix the keen insult,
Or make his life a farce still more complete,
He sends a groan across the broad Atlantic,
And with a phiz of crocodilian stamp
Can weep, and wreathe, still hoping to deceive.[38]
He cries the gath'ring clouds hang thick about her,
But laughs within—then sobs—
—"Alas! my country!"[39]
HUM-HUMBUG. Why so severe, or why exclaim at all,
Against the man who made thee what thou art?

[33]Niccolò Machievelli (1469–1527), Italian political theorist who recommends deceit as a political tactic in his famous treatise on ruling, *The Prince* (1513).

[34]The Borgias were a powerful Italian family, famous for treachery from the fourteenth to sixteenth century.

[35]Mask.

[36]Jonathan Sewall, lawyer and Tory.

[37]In Greek mythology, the Sirens were sea nymphs whose irresistible voices lured sailors to their death.

[38]Crocodile tears are false tears with which crocodiles supposedly lure their victims before devouring them.

[39]When Benjamin Franklin published Governor Thomas Hutchinson's private letters, the governor's contempt for the revolutionaries in Boston became clear. See note 20.

BEAU-TRUMPS. I know his guilt,—I ever knew the man.
Thy father knew him ere we trod the stage.[40]
I only speak to such as know him well.
Abroad, I tell the world he is a saint.
But as for interest, I betrayed my own
With the same views. I ranked among his friends,
But my ambition sighs for something more.
What merits has Sir Sparrow of his own?
And yet a feather graces the fool's cap
Which did he wear for what himself achieved.
'Twould stamp some honor on his latest heir—
But I'll suspend my murm'ring rays awhile
Come t'other glass—and try our luck at loo[41]
And if before the dawn your gold I win,
Or e'er bright Phoebus[42] does his course begin,
The eastern breeze from Britain's hostile shore
Should waft her lofty, floating towers o'er,
Whose waving pendants sweep the wat'ry main
Dip their proud beaks and dance towards the plain,
The destined plains of slaughter and distress,
Laden with troops from Hanover and Hess,[43]
I would invigorate my sinking soul,
For then the continent we might control.
Not all the millions that she vainly boasts
Can cope with veteran barbarian hosts;
But the brave sons of Albion's[44] warlike race,
Their arms, and honors, never can disgrace,
Or draw their swords in such a hated cause
In blood to seal a N—'s[45] oppressive laws.
They'll spurn the service. Britons must recoil,
And show themselves the natives of an isle
Who fought for freedom in the worst of times,
Produced her Hampdens, Fairfaxes and Pyms.[46]
But if by carnage we should win the game,
Perhaps by my abilities and fame,
I might attain a splendid glitt'ring car,
And mount aloft, and sail in liquid air,

[40]Before we were born.
[41]A popular card game.
[42]In Greek mythology, the god of the sun who brings the sunrise.
[43]German provinces from which Britain enlisted mercenaries to fight in the British army in North America.
[44]Ancient name for England.
[45]Lord North's.
[46]John Pym (1583?–1643) and John Hampden (1594–1643) were Puritans who opposed royal autonomy and forced King Charles I to convene the Long Parliament in 1640. Thomas Fairfax (1612–1671) was the commander of the pro-Parliament British army that defeated Charles I at Nasby in 1645.

Like Phaeton[47] I'd then outstrip the wind,
And leave my low competitors behind.

ACT II

Scene II

COLLATERALIS—Dick the PUBLICAN.

PUBLICAN. This dull inaction will no longer do;
Month after month the idle troops have lain,
Nor struck one stroke that leads us to our wish.
The trifling bickerings at the city gates,
Or bold outrages of their midnight routs,
Bring us no nearer to the point in view.
Though much the daily suff'rings of the people,
Commerce destroyed, and government unhinged,
No talk of tame submission yet I hear.

COLLATERALIS. No—not the least—
—they're more resolved than ever.
They're firm, united, bold, undaunted, brave,
And every villa boasts their marshalled ranks,
The warlike clarion sounds through ev'ry street.
Both vig'rous youth, and the gray-headed sire
Bear the fusee[48] in regimental garbs,
Repairing to defend invaded right,
And, if pushed hard, by manly force repel.
And though Britannia sends her legions o'er,
To plant her daggers in her children's breast,
It will rebound—New whetted, the keen point
Will find a sheath in ev'ry tyrant's heart.

PUBLICAN. —What then is to be done?
My finances too low to stand it long.
You well remember—
When stationed there to gripe[49] the honest trader,
How much I plundered from your native town.
Under the sanctions of the laws of trade,
I, the hard earnings of industry,
Filch'd from their hands, and built my nest on high.
And on the spoils I rioted a while,
But soon the unrighteous pelf [50] slipped through my hand.
Nor longer idly could I waste my time,

[47]In Greek mythology, the son of Helios, the earliest god of the sun; he was permitted to drive his father's chariot of the sun but lost control and would have set the world on fire if Zeus had not struck him down with a thunderbolt.

[48]Torch.

[49]Oppress.

[50]Booty.

A num'rous flock was rising round my board,[51]
Who urged to something that might give them bread.
My only game was hither to repair,
And court the proud oppressors of my country,
By the parade of pompous luxury
To win their favor, and obtain a place.
That, with my limbeck,[52] might have kept me on,
But for the cursed, persevering spirit
Of Freedom's Sons—who triumph o'er distress,
Nor will comply with requisitions made
By haughty mandates from corrupted courts
To pay the workmen for the chains they'd forged.

COLLATERALIS. No—though proud Britain wafts her wooden walls[53]
O'er the broad waves and plants them round these coasts,
Shuts up their ports, and robs them of their bread,
They're not dismayed—nor servilely comply
To pay the hunters of the nabob shores
Their high demand for India's pois'nous weed,[54]
Long since a sacrifice to Thetis[55] made,
A rich regale. Now all the wat'ry dames
May snuff Souchong, and sip in flowing bowls
The higher flavored choice Hysonian stream,[56]
And leave their nectar to old Homer's gods.

PUBLICAN. The Group this morn were summoned to the camp;
The council early meets at Sylla's[57] tent,
But for what purpose yet I cannot learn.

COLLATERALIS. Then let us haste; 'tis novel to be called
By Sylla's order, summoned to attend,
So close he keeps his counsels in his breast,
Nor trusts us with manoeuvers of state.
I fear he half despises us himself.
And if he does, we cannot wonder much.
We're made the jest of every idle boy,
Most of us hunted from our rural seats,
Drove from our homes, a prey to guilty fears
When—When dare we return!
And now shut up in this devoted city,
Amidst the pestilence on either hand,
Pursued by every dreadful execration
That the bold tongue of innocence oppressed,
Pours forth in anguish for a ruined state.

[51]Dining table.
[52]An apparatus for distilling; thus, what he could siphon off.
[53]Ships.
[54]Tea. "Nabob": a governor of India during the Mogul Empire.
[55]In Greek mythology, a sea-goddess beloved by Zeus and Poseidon, mother of Achilles.
[56]A green tea. "Souchong": a black tea from China.
[57]General Thomas Gage.

ACT II

Scene III

The fragments of the broken Council appear with trembling servile gestures, showing several applications to the General from the under-tools in distant counties, begging each a guard of myrmidons to protect them from the armed multitudes (which the guilty horrors of their wounded consciences hourly presented to their frighted imaginations) approaching to take speedy vengeance on the court parasites, who had fled for refuge to the camp, by immediate destruction to their pimps, panders, and sycophants left behind.

—SYLLA *walking in great perplexity.*

SYLLA. Pray, how will it comport with my pretense[58]
For building walls, and shutting up the town,
Erecting fortresses, and strong redoubts,[59]
To keep my troops from any bold inroads
A brave, insulted people might attempt,
If I send out my little scattered parties,
And the long-suff'ring, gen'rous patriot's care
Prevents[60] a skirmish?
Though they're the sport of wanton cruel power,
And Hydra-headed[61] ill starts up around,
Till the last hope of a redress cut off,
Their humane feelings urge them to forbear,
And wait some milder means to bring relief.
HATEALL. 'Tis now the time to try their daring tempers.
Send out a few, and if they are cut off,
What are a thousand souls, sent swiftly down
To Pluto's[62] gloomy shades, to tell in anguish?
Half their compeers shall sit pandemonic[63]
Ere we will suffer Liberty to reign,
Or see her Sons triumphant win the day.
I feign would push them to the last extreme,
To draw their swords against their legal king.
Then short's the process to complete destruction.
SECRETARY DUPE. Be not so sanguine—the day is not our own,
And much I fear it never will be won.
Their discipline is equal to our own,
Their valor has been tried,—and in a field
They're not less brave than are a Fred'rick's troops.[64]

[58]Affectation.
[59]Fortifications.
[60]Anticipates.
[61]In Greek mythology, the Hydra was a monster with many heads. When one head was cut off, two would grow back in its place.
[62]In Roman mythology, Pluto was the ruler of the underworld.
[63]In hell.
[64]Frederick II (1712–1786), "the Great," was king of Prussia in 1775.

Those members formidable pour along,
While virtue's banners shroud each warrior's head.
Stern Justice binds the helmet on his brow,
And Liberty sits perched on every shield.
But who's applied and asked the General's aid,
Or wished his peaceful villa such a curse
As posting troops beside the peasant's cot?

JUDGE MEAGRE. None but the very dregs of all mankind,
The stains of nature—the blots of human race.
Yet that's no matter. Still, they are our friends.
'Twill help our projects if we give them aid.

SIMPLE SAPLING. Though my paternal acres are eat up,
My patrimony spent, I've yet an house
My lenient creditors let me improve.
Send up the troops, 'twill serve them well for barracks.
I somehow think 'twould bear a noble sound,
To have my mansion guarded by the king.

SYLLA. Hast thou no sons or blooming daughters there,
To call up all the feelings of a father,
Lest their young minds contaminate by vice
Caught from such inmates, dangerous and vile,
Devoid of virtue, rectitude, or honor,
Save what accords with military fame?
Hast thou no wife who asks thy tender care
To guard her from Bellona's[65] hardy sons,
Who, when not toiling in the hostile field,
Are faithful vot'ries to the Cyprian queen?[66]
Or is her soul of such materials made,
Indelicate, and thoughtless of her fame,
So void of either sentiment or sense,
As makes her a companion fit for thee!

SIMPLE SAPLING. Sylvia's good natured, and no doubt will yield,
And take the brawny vet'rans to her board,
When she's assured 'twill help her husband's fame.
If she complains or murmurs at the plan,
Let her solicit charity abroad.
Let her go out and seek some pitying friend
To give her shelter from the wint'ry blast,
Disperse her children round the neighb'ring cots,
And then—

PUBLICAN. —Then weep thy folly, and her own hard fate!
I pity Sylvia, I knew the beauteous maid

[65]The Roman goddess of war.

[66]Aphrodite, Greek goddess of love, whose cult was located on the isle of Cyprus; *cyprian* is also slang for "prostitute."

Ere she descended to become thy wife.
She silent mourns the weakness of her lord;
For she's too virtuous to approve thy deeds.
HATEALL. Pho!—what's a woman's tears,
Or all the whinings of that trifling sex?
I never felt one tender thought towards them.
When young, indeed, I wedded nut-brown Kate
(Blyth buxom dowager, the jockey's prey),[67]
But all I wished was to secure her dower.
I broke her spirits when I'd won her purse;
For which I'll give a recipe most sure
To ev'ry hen-peck'd husband round the board.
If crabbed words or surly looks won't tame
The haughty shrew, nor bend the stubborn mind,
Then the green hick'ry, or the willow twig,
Will prove a curse for each rebellious dame
Who dare oppose her lord's superior will.[68]
SYLLA. Enough of this. Ten thousand harrowing cares
Tear up my peace, and swell my anxious breast.
I see some mighty victim must appease
An injured nation, tott'ring on the verge
Of wide destruction, made the wanton sport
Of hungry harpies gaping for their prey
Which, if by misadventures they should miss,
The disappointed vulture's angry fang
Will seize the lesser gudgeons[69] of the state
And sacrifice to mad Alecto's[70] rage,
Lest the tide turning, with a rapid course
The booming torrent rushes o'er their heads
And sweeps the "cawing cormorants from earth."
HATEALL. Then strike some sudden blow, and if hereafter
Dangers should rise—then set up for thyself,
And make thy name as famous in Columbia
As ever Caesar's was in ancient Gaul.[71]
Who would such distant provinces subdue,
And then resign them to a foreign lord!
With such an armament at thy command
Why all this cautious prudence?
SYLLA. I only wish to serve my Sovereign well,
And bring new glory to my master's crown,

[67]The victim of anyone who would seduce her—or ride her as a jockey rides a horse.

[68]Warren makes an equation between domestic abuse and political tyranny.

[69]Literally, small fish; metaphorically, people easily fooled.

[70]In Greek mythology, one of the Furies, the goddesses of retribution for blood-guilt.

[71]Gaul was the Roman name for France. "Columbia": the personification of America, named for its "discoverer," Christopher Columbus.

Which can't be done by spreading ruin round
This loyal country—
—Wrought up to madness by oppression's hand.
How much deceived my royal master is
By those he trusts!—but more of this anon.
Were it consistent with my former plan
I'd gladly send my sickly troops abroad
Out from the stench of this infected town,
To breathe some air more free from putrefaction,
To brace their nerves against approaching spring,
If my ill stars should destine a campaign
And call me forth to fight in such a cause,
To quench the gen'rous spark, the innate love
Of glorious freedom, planted in the breast
Of every man who boasts a Briton's name,
Until some base-born lust of foreign growth
Contaminate his soul, till false ambition
Or the sordid hope of swelling coffers,
Poison the mind, and brutalize the man.

COLLATERALIS. I almost wish I never had engaged
To rob my country of her native rights
Nor strove to mount on justice's solemn bench,
By mean submission cringing for a place.
How great the pain, and yet how small the *purchase*!
Had I been dumb, or my right hand cut off,
Ere I so servilely had held it up,
Or given my voice abjectly to rescind
The wisest step that mortal man could take
To curb the talons of tyrannic power,
Outstretched rapacious ready to devour
The fair possessions, by our Maker giv'n
Confirmed by compacts—ratified by Heav'n.

SYLLA. Look o'er the annals of our virtuous sires,
And search the story of Britannia's deeds
From Caesar's ravages to Hampden's fall,[72]
From the good Hampden down to glorious Wolfe
Whose soul took wing on Abraham's fatal plain,
Where the young hero fought Britannia's foes
And vanquished Bourbon's dark, ferocious hosts,
Till the slaves trembled at a George's name.[73]

[72]Julius Caesar invaded Britain in 55 B.C. John Hampden died leading parliamentary forces against Charles I in 1643 during the Puritan Revolution.

[73]James Wolfe (1727–1759), English commander, representing King George, led the attack against the French under the command of General Louis Montcalm (1712–1759), representative of King Louis XV of the house of Bourbon (1710–1774), on the Plains of Abraham in Quebec, winning New France (Canada) for the English. Both commanders died soon after the battle. The "dark, ferocious hosts" are the Indian allies of the French.

'Twas love of freedom drew a Marlborough's[74] sword.
This glorious passion moved a Sidney's pen;[75]
And crowned with bays a Harrington and Locke.[76]
'Tis freedom wreathes the garlands o'er their tombs.
For her how oft have bleeding heroes fall'n!
With the warm fluid gushing from their wounds,
Conveyed the purchase to their distant heirs!
And shall I rashly draw my guilty sword
And dip its hungry hilt in the rich blood
Of the best subjects that a Brunswick boasts,[77]
And for no cause, but that they nobly scorn
To wear the fetters of his venal slaves!
But swift time rolls, and on his rapid wheel
Bears the winged hours, and the circling years.
The cloud-capped morn, the dark, short wintry day,
And the keen blasts of roughened Boreas's[78] breath
Will soon evanish, and approaching spring
Opes with the fate of empires on her wing.

Exit SYLLA.

HAZLEROD *rises in great agitation.*

HAZLEROD This balancing of passions ne'er will do,
And by the scale which virtue holds to reason,
Weighing the business ere he executes,
Doubting, deliberating, half resolved
To be the savior of a virtuous state,
Instead of guarding refugees and knaves,
The buzzing reptiles that crawl 'round his court,
And lick his hand for some delicious crumb,
Or painted plume to grace the guilty brow,
Stained with ten thousand falsities, trumped up
To injure every good and virtuous name
Who won't strike hands and be his country's foe.

[74]John Churchill (1650–1722), first duke of Marlborough, supported William of Orange in the Glorious Revolution of 1688, which defeated Catholic King James II of England.

[75]Algernon Sidney (1622–1683), in his *Discourses Concerning Government* (1698), opposed the dictatorial powers of Oliver Cromwell, made Lord Protector after the execution of Charles I.

[76]John Locke (1632–1704), the English philosopher, argued against the divine right of kings. James Harrington (1611–1677) argued for individual rights in his *Commonwealth of Oceana* (1656) and for election by ballot. "Crowned with bays": in the ancient world, heroes and victors were crowned with wreaths of laurel or bay leaf.

[77]*I.e.,* George III boasts. George was descended from the German house of Brunswick/Lüneberg, through his grandfather, King George I.

[78]In Greek mythology, the god of the north wind.

I'll hasten after, and stir up his soul
To dire revenge and bloody resolutions,
Or the whole fabric falls on which we hang,
And down the pit of infamy we plunge,
Without the spoils we long have hoped to reap.

He crosses the stage hastily and goes out after SYLLA. MEAGRE *and* SECRETARY DUPE *at the further part of the stage.*

MEAGRE. As Sylla passed I marked his anxious brow;
I fear his soul is with compassion moved
For suff'ring virtue, wounded and betrayed;
For Freedom hunted down in this fair field,
The only soil, in these degenerate days,
In which the heavenly goddess can exist.
SECRETARY. Humanity recoils—his heart relucts[79]
To execute the black, the accurst design.
Such I must call it, though thy guilty friends,
Thy subtle brother, laid the artful plan,
"And like the toad squat at the ear of Eve"[80]
Infusing poisons by his snaky tongue,
Push'd Brundo on to tread the thorny path
And plunge his country in ten thousand woes;
Then slyly jostling him behind the scenes,
Stepped in his place for which he long had sighed.[81]
MEAGRE. Yes, all allow he played a master game,
And dealt his cards with such peculiar skill
That every dangler about the court,
As you and I and all might well suppose,
Thought the chains fixed which Brundo only clanked.
But yet unless some speedy method's found
To break the union, and dissolve the bonds
That bind this mighty continent so firm,
Their Congresses, their Covenants, and leagues,
With their Committees,[82] working in each town
With unremitting vigilance and care
To baffle every evil machination
Of all state rooks,[83] who peck about the land,
If not broke up, will ruin all at last.

[79]Is opposed.

[80]From John Milton (1609–1674), *Paradise Lost* (1667), Book 4, Line 800, "Squat like a Toad close at the ear of Eve."

[81]Brundo, or Sir Francis Bernard, who as colonial governor of Massachusetts enforced the Stamp Act. He was recalled to England in 1769, and Thomas Hutchinson, lieutenant governor and brother of Foster (Meagre), took his place.

[82]Committees of Safety, formed by patriots to prepare for war with the British troops.

[83]Rooks are scavenger birds resembling crows; here, metaphorically, swindlers.

Amidst the many scribblers of the age,
Can none be found to set their schemes afloat,
To sow dissension and distrust abroad,
Sap that cement that bears down all before it,
And makes America a match for all
The hostile powers that proud Europe boasts?
SECRETARY. Not all the swarms of prostituted pens,
Nor hireling smatterers scribbling for gain,
From the first pensioned on the northern list[84]
To bigot priests who write from southern shores,[85]
With all their phantoms, bugbears, threats or smiles,
Will e'er persuade them to renounce their claim
To freedom, purchased with their fathers' blood.
How various are the arts already tried,
What pains unwearied to write men to sleep
Or rock them in the cradle of despair,
To doze supinely till they should believe
They'd neither eyes, nor tongues, or strength to move
But at that nod of some despotic lord!
What shifts, evasions, what delusive tales,
What poor prevarication for rash oaths,
What nightly watchings, and what daily cares
To dress up falsehood in some fair disguise,
Or wrap the bantling[86] of their midnight dreams
In the soft vest of friendship to betray,
Then send it forth in every fairly form
To stalk at noontide, giddy with fond hope
That some new gambols[87] might deceive again
Men broad awake, who see through all the cheat.
MEAGRE. There is still hope—why need we yet despair?
The doughty champion of our sinking cause,
The deep "arcana"[88] of whose winding brain
Is fraught with dark expedients to betray,
By the long labors of his vet'ran quill,
By scattering scraps from ev'ry musty code
Of canon, civil, or draconian laws,
Quoting old statutes or defining new,
Treasons, misprisions, riots, routs, cabals,
And insurrections of these stubborn times,
He'll sure prevail and terrify at last,

[84]Loyalists who fled Boston for Nova Scotia, where they received civil posts and pensions from Britain.

[85]The American Episcopal Church, most sympathetic to Britain, was strongest in the southern colonies.

[86]Infant.

[87]Lively games.

[88]Secret knowledge (Latin). "Doughty": brave. The reference is to the Tory propagandist Daniel Leonard, who used the pen name Massachusettensis.

By bringing precedents from those blest days
When royal Stuarts Britain's scepter swayed,
And taught her sons the right divine of kings,
When pains and forfeitures an hundred fold
Were dealt to traitors, puny when compared
To the bold rebels of this continent,
From Merrimack[89] to Mississippi's banks,
Who dare resist a ministerial frown.
In spite of all the truths *Novanglus*[90] tells,
And his cool reasoning argumentive style,
Or master strokes of his unrivaled pen,
They will divide, and wavering, will submit
And take the word of Massachusettensis
That men were born all ready bitted,[91] curbed,
And on their backs the saddles prominent,
For every upstart sycophant to mount.

SECRETARY. Not *Massachusettensis's* oily tongue,
Or retailed nonsense of a Philarene,
Not *Senex's* rant, nor yet dull *Grotius's* pen,[92]
Or the whole group of selfish venal men,
If gathered from cold Zembla's[93] frozen shore
To the warm zone where rapid rivers roar,
Can either coax them, or the least control
The val'rous purpose of their Roman souls.

MEAGRE. Let not thy soft timidity of heart
Urge thee to terms, till the last stake is thrown.
'Tis not my temper ever to forgive,
When once resentment's kindled in my breast.
I hated Brutus[94] for his noble stand
Against the oppressors of his injured country.
I hate the leaders of these restless factions,
For all their generous efforts to be free.
I curse the senate which defeats our bribes,
Who Hazlerod impeached for the same crime.[95]

[89]The Merrimack River begins in southern New Hampshire and flows into Massachusetts.

[90]The pen name of John Adams, patriot writer.

[91]Checked, like horses that have steel bits in their mouths.

[92]Senex ("old man" in Latin) and Grotius are pen names for unidentified Tory sympathizers. Philarene was the pen name of the English satirist Soame Jenys (1704–1787), author of *Objections to the Taxation of Our American Colonies by the Legislature of Great Britain Briefly Considered* (1765).

[93]Nova Zemlya, two large islands in the Arctic Ocean.

[94]Name for James Otis, Jr. (1725–1783), Mercy's older brother, renowned as an orator in the cause of independence; he was brutally beaten in a tavern by Tory sympathizers in 1769 and never fully recovered.

[95]In 1774, the Massachusetts legislature ("senate") impeached Chief Justice Peter Oliver ("Hazelrod"). His opponents successfully argued that taking money from King George III compromised his judicial impartiality.

I hate the people who, no longer gulled,
See through the schemes of our aspiring clan,
And from the rancor of my venomed mind
I look askance on all the human race.
And if they're not to be appalled by fear,
I wish the earth might drink that vital stream
That warms the heart and feeds the manly glow,
The love inherent, planted in the breast,
To equal liberty, conferred on man
By Him who formed the peasant and the king!
Could we erase these notions from their minds,
Then (paramount to these ideal whims,
Utopian dreams of patriotic virtue,
Which long have danced in their distemper'd brains)
We'd smoothly glide on midst a race of slaves,
Nor heave one sigh though all the human race
Were plunged in darkness, slavery and vice.
If we could keep our foothold in the stirrup,
And, like the noble Clodia of old,[96]
Ride o'er the people if they don't give way,
Or wish their fates were all involved in one;
For I've a *brother,* as the Roman dame,
Who would strike off the rebel neck at once.[97]

SECRETARY. No, all is o'er unless the sword decides
Which cuts down kings, and kingdoms oft divides.
By that appeal I think we can't prevail.
Their valor's great, and justice holds the scale.
They fight for Freedom, while we stab the breast
Of every man who is her friend professed.
They fight in Virtue's ever-sacred cause,
While we tread on divine and human laws.
Glory and victory, and lasting fame
Will crown their arms and bless each hero's name!

MEAGRE. Away with all thy foolish, trifling cares;
And to the winds give all thy empty fears.
Let us repair and urge brave Sylla on,
I long to see the sweet revenge begun.
As fortune is a fickle, sportive dame,
She may for us the victory proclaim,
And with success our busy ploddings crown,
Though injured justice stern and solemn frown.

[96]Clodia Pulcher was a Roman noblewoman who was said to have poisoned her first husband, Metellus Celer, in 59 B.C. She was attacked by the orator Cicero for license and self-indulgence.

[97]The Roman emperor Caligula (A.D. 12–41) remarked that he wished the people had a single neck so that he could kill them all with a single stroke. His sister, Agrippina the Younger (A.D. 15?–59), was also known for her cruelty.

Then they shall smart for every bold offence,
Estates confiscated will pay th'expense.
On their lost fortunes we awhile will plume,[98]
And strive to think there is no after-doom.

Ex. Om—[99]

As they pass off the stage the curtain draws up, and discovers to the audience a LADY *nearly connected with one of the principal actors in the group, reclined in an adjoining alcove, who in mournful accents accosts them—thus—*

LADY. What painful scenes are hovering o'er the morn,
When spring again invigorates the lawn!
Instead of the gay landscape's beauteous dyes,
Must the stained field salute our weeping eyes;
Must the green turf, and all the mournful glades,
Drenched in the stream, absorb their dewy heads,
Whilst the tall oak, and quiv'ring willow bends
To make a covert for their country's friends
Denied a grave!—amid the hurrying scene
Of routed armies scouring o'er the plain,
Till British troops shall to Columbia yield,
And Freedom's Sons are masters of the field?
Then o'er the purpled plain the victors tread,
Among the stain to seek each patriot dead
(While Freedom weeps that merit could not save
But conquering heroes must enrich the grave.)
An adamantine[100] monument they rear
With this inscription— *Virtue's Sons lie here!*

FINIS

1775

[98]Pride ourselves, as "a feather in our caps."
[99]*Exeunt omnes:* all exit (Latin).
[100]Very hard and thus imperishable.

from The Ladies of Castille[1]

ACT V

Scene I

MARIA, *with her young Son clad in mourning—a Standard borne before him, on which is represented his Father's Death—accompanied by* ZAMORA *and a Procession of Friends—she addresses the Citizens, Soldiers etc. etc. etc.*

Behold, ye virtuous citizens of Spain,
The remnant of Don Juan's noble house;
See here the son of your late murder'd lord;
Behold his infant innocence that weeps
A father's fall, ere yet he's learn'd to lisp
That sacred name, which cruelty dissolv'd.
If heaven and earth decree the world to Charles—
If Spain's prepar'd to wear the badge of slaves,
And degradation makes the bleeding realm—
Then, in the front of this respected band,
Grant me one boon—that yet some gen'rous arm,
Unstain'd by vice, or dip'd in guiltless blood,
Would smite the breast of this infant son,
And lay him gently in his father's tomb,
As the last heir of Spain's expiring worth
That freedom's genius offers to the gods:—
She stoop'd, and dip'd her target in the gore
That copious rush'd from noble Juan's wounds
'Tis the cement, she cry'd, in stronger league
To bind the liberal and unite the brave
'Tis in this option, wisely did ye judge,
To flourish long beneath her lenient reign;
But if, ungratefully, ye spurn the gift,
And fly the field, and yield the proffer'd prize—
Bend thy weak necks, and servilely submit,
Affronted virtue leaves such dastard slaves

[1]This historical drama was written around 1784 and appeared in *Poems, Dramatic and Miscellaneous* (1790), from which this selection is taken. The play is set in north-central Spain in 1521–1522 and draws a parallel between a rebellion during the reign of Charles I of Spain, who also was emperor of the Holy Roman Empire, and the recently concluded American Revolution. Discontent among Spanish peasants leads members of the Cortes, the Castilian assembly, to demand greater freedom. Royalist forces defeat a rebel army led by Juan de Padilla. Padilla is captured and executed, but Maria, his wife, rallies the citizenry to continue the fight. When she is forced to flee to Portugal, the dreams of democratic reform end.

To faint and tremble at a despot's nod.
I, for myself, a bolder part design;
And here, before the soldiers and the Cortes,[2]
In presence of the eternal King, I swear,
Most solemnly I bind my free born soul,
Ere I will live a slave, and kiss the hand
That o'er my country clanks a servile chain,
I'll light the towers, and perish in the flames,
And smile and triumph in the general wreck.
Come, shew one sample of heroic worth,
Ere ancient Spain, the glory of the west,
Bends abject down—by all the nations scorned:—
Secure the city—barricade the gates,
And meet me arm'd with all the faithful bands:
I'll head the troops, and mount the prancing steed;
The courser guide, and vengeance pour along
Amidst the ranks, and teach the slaves of Charles
Not Semiramis' or Zenobia's[3] fame
Outstrips the glory of Maria's name.

[Exit.

[The people shout, and fly to arms.

1784 1790

from An Address to the Inhabitants of the United States of America[1]

At a period when every manly arm was occupied, and every trait of talent or activity engaged either in the cabinet or the field, apprehensive that amid the sudden convulsions, crowded scenes, and rapid changes that flowed in quick succession, many circumstances might escape the more busy and active members of society, I have been induced to improve the leisure Providence had lent, to record as they passed,

[2]Castilian assembly.

[3]Semiramis, or Sammuramat, was a powerful Assyrian queen who effectively resisted invasion by the Medes and Chaldeans. The legendary queen, mentioned by Greek writers and believed to be the daughter of the Syrian goddess Atargatis, is the heroine of Voltaire's tragedy *Sémiramis,* which Warren might have read. Zenobia (d. after 274) became queen of the Roman colony of Palmyra, in present-day Syria, after the death of her husband, Odaenathus. Zenobia seized Egypt, conquered much of Asia Minor, declared independence from Rome, but eventually was subjugated by the Roman emperor Aurelian.

[1]This is the preface to *The History of the Rise, Progress and Termination of the American Revolution* (3 vols., 1805) and is taken from the first edition.

in the following pages, the new and unexperienced events exhibited in a land previously blessed with peace, liberty, simplicity, and virtue. . . .

Connected by nature, friendship, and every social tie with many of the first patriots, and most influential characters on the continent; in the habits of confidential and epistolary intercourse with several gentlemen employed abroad in the most distinguished stations, and with others since elevated to the highest grades of rank and distinction,[2] I had the best means of information, through a long period that the colonies were in suspense, waiting the operation of foreign courts, and the success of their own enterprising spirit.

The solemnity that covered every countenance, when contemplating the sword uplifted and the horrors of civil war rushing to habitations not inured to scenes of rapine and misery, even to the quiet cottage, where only concord and affection had reigned, stimulated to observation a mind that had not yielded to the assertion that all political attentions lay out of the road of female life.

It is true there are certain appropriate duties assigned to each sex; and doubtless it is the more peculiar province of masculine strength, not only to repel the bold invader of the rights of his country and of mankind, but in the nervous[3] style of manly eloquence, to describe the blood-stained field and relate the story of slaughtered armies.

Sensible of this, the trembling heart has recoiled at the magnitude of the undertaking, and the hand often shrunk back from the task; yet, recollecting that every domestic enjoyment depends on the unimpaired possession of civil and religious liberty, that a concern for the welfare of society ought equally to glow in every human breast, the work was not relinquished. The most interesting circumstances were collected, active characters portrayed, the principles of the times developed, and the changes marked; nor need it cause a blush to acknowledge, a detail was preserved with a view of transmitting it to the rising youth of my country, some of them in infancy, others in the European world, while the most interesting events lowered over their native land. . . .[4]

Not indifferent to the opinion of the world, nor servilely courting its smiles, no further apology is offered for the attempt, though many may be necessary, for the incomplete execution of a design, that had rectitude for its basis, and a beneficent regard for the civil and religious rights of mankind for its motive.

The liberal-minded will peruse with candor, rather than criticise with severity; nor will they think it necessary that any apology should be offered for sometimes introducing characters nearly connected with the author of the following annals; as they were early and zealously attached to the public cause, uniform in their principles, and constantly active in the great scenes that produced the revolution and obtained independence for their country, truth precludes that reserve which might have been proper on less important occasions, and forbids to pass over in silence the

[2]Warren's brother James Otis, Jr., was an important leader in the resistance to England in the 1760s; her husband was paymaster of the army and a leading patriot. She corresponded with John Adams, George Washington, and Thomas Jefferson, among many others.

[3]Sinewy, vigorous.

[4]In particular, her own sons, one of whom, Charles, was in Spain.

names of such as expired before the conflict was finished, or have since retired from public scenes. The historian has never laid aside the tenderness of the sex or the friend; at the same time, she has endeavored, on all occasions, that the strictest veracity should govern her heart, and the most exact impartiality be the guide of her pen.

If the work should be so far useful or entertaining, as to obtain the sanction of the generous and virtuous part of the community, I cannot but be highly gratified and amply rewarded for the effort, soothed at the same time with the idea that the motives were justifiable in the eye of Omniscience. Then, if it should not escape the remarks of the critic, or the censure of party, I shall feel no wound to my sensibility, but repose on my pillow as quietly as ever,—

> While all the distant din the world can keep,
> Rolls o'er my grotto, and but soothes my sleep.

Before this address to my countrymen is closed, I beg leave to observe, that as a new century has dawned upon us, the mind is naturally led to contemplate the great events that have run parallel with, and have just closed the last. From the revolutionary spirit of the times, the vast improvements in science, arts, and agriculture, the boldness of genius that marks the age, the investigation of new theories, and the changes in the political, civil, and religious characters of men, succeeding generations have reason to expect still more astonishing exhibitions in the next. In the meantime, Providence has clearly pointed out the duties of the present generation, particularly the paths which Americans ought to tread. The United States form a young republic, a confederacy which ought ever to be cemented by a union of interests and affection, under the influence of those principles which obtained their independence. These have indeed, at certain periods, appeared to be in the wane; but let them never be eradicated, by the jarring interests of parties, jealousies of the sister states, or the ambition of individuals! It has been observed, by a writer of celebrity, that "that people, government, and constitution is the freest, which makes the best provision for the enacting of expedient and salutary laws."[5] May this truth be evinced to all ages, by the wise and salutary laws that shall be enacted in the federal legislature of America!

May the hands of the executive of their own choice be strengthened more by the unanimity and affection of the people, than by the dread of penal inflictions or any restraints that might repress free inquiry, relative to the principles of their own government and the conduct of its administrators! The world is now viewing America, as experimenting a new system of government, a FEDERAL REPUBLIC, including a territory to which the Kingdoms of Great Britain and Ireland bear little proportion. The practicability of supporting such a system has been doubted by some; if she succeeds, it will refute the assertion that none but small states are adapted to republican government; if she does not, and the union should be dissolved, some ambitious son of Columbia or some foreign adventurer, allured by the prize, may wade to empire

[5]William Paley, *Moral and Political Philosophy,* 1785. [Warren's note.]

through seas of blood, or the friends of monarchy may see a number of petty despots stretching their sceptres over the disjointed parts of the continent. Thus by the mandate of a single sovereign, the degraded subjects of one state, under the bannerets of royalty, may be dragged to sheathe their swords in the bosoms of the inhabitants of another.

The state of the public mind appears at present to be prepared to weigh these reflections with solemnity, and to receive with pleasure an effort to trace the origin of the American revolution, to review the characters that effected it, and to justify the principles of the defection and final separation from the parent state. With an expanded heart, beating with high hopes of the continued freedom and prosperity of America, the writer indulges a modest expectation that the following pages will be perused with kindness and candor: this she claims, both in consideration of her sex, the uprightness of her intentions, and the fervency of her wishes for the happiness of all the human race.

1805

J. Hector St. John de Crèvecoeur 1735–1813

Written from the point of view of an ordinary man, Crèvecoeur's *Letters from an American Farmer* is the first text to ask and answer the question "What is an American?" Although Crèvecoeur was describing life in the British colonies in America, he used his character, James, to portray the new consciousness of emerging American society.

Born in Caen, Normandy, Michel-Guilluame-Jean de Crèvecoeur was the child of Norman landowners. He was educated at the Jesuit Collège Royal de Bourbon. After he left school in 1750, he was sent to England, where he became engaged. The untimely death of his fiancée is believed to be the reason that Crèvecoeur left England to begin a new life in French-held Canada in 1755. He worked as a surveyor and cartographer during the French and Indian War. On December 16, 1759, Crèvecoeur disembarked in New York harbor from a British vessel carrying the defeated French troops back to France and began afresh in the British colonies.

For the next ten years, Crèvecoeur worked as a surveyor, trader, and traveled extensively. In 1765, he became a naturalized citizen of New York. Four years later, he married and began to farm. The outbreak of the American Revolution and the desire to see his children's inheritance secured were the likely reasons that Crèvecoeur decided, in 1778, to return to France. The long and dangerous trip was complicated by the war. After being imprisoned as a spy by the British, he was allowed to leave the colonies in 1780. He sold the manuscript of *Letters from an American Farmer* in 1781 to a London publisher and proceeded to France. When *Letters* was published in 1782, its success catapulted Crèvecoeur into French literary and intellectual circles, where he became associated with the *philosophes,* a group of progressive French intellectuals. In 1784, he wrote a French version of *Letters.* Crèvecoeur returned to America in 1783 as French consul to New York, New Jersey, and Connecticut. He found his wife dead, his farm burned, and his children resettled in Boston. In America, Crèvecoeur continued his scientific studies and worked closely with Thomas Jefferson to unite French and American interests. In 1790, Crèvecoeur left America for the last time.

During the last years of his life, the uncertain political situation in France led him to seek obscurity. In 1801, he published *Voyage dans la Haute Pennsylvanie et dans l'état de New York,* which had little commercial success. He died on November 12, 1813.

The twelve letters of *Letters from an American Farmer* are held together by the movement of the fictional narrator of the text, James, the American farmer, from happiness to despair as he records his life as a farmer and his travels to Martha's Vineyard, Nantucket, and Charlestown. In the opening letters, James celebrates America as a place where the oppressed masses of Europe are able to pursue their own self-interest as independent landowners. In the later letters, he deals with problems already causing divisions within the new society—slavery, and the Revolution. *Letters* is a form of epistolary, philosophical travel narrative that integrates important Enlightenment ideas into descriptions of ordinary American life. It was widely read in the late eighteenth century and frequently translated and reprinted, strongly influencing European perceptions of America. It had some influence on the ideas of the English Romantics, particularly Southey and Coleridge.

Doreen Alvarez Saar
Drexel University

PRIMARY WORKS

Letters from an American Farmer, 1782, 1793; *Lettres d'un Cultivateur Américain,* 1784; *Voyage dans la Haute Pennsylvanie et dans l'état de New York,* 1801; *Sketches of Eighteenth Century America,* ed. Henri L. Bourdin, Ralph H. Gabriel, and Stanley T. Williams, 1925.

from Letters from an American Farmer

from Letter I
Introduction

Who would have thought that because I received you with hospitality and kindness, you should imagine me capable of writing with propriety and perspicuity?[1] Your gratitude misleads your judgement. The knowledge which I acquired from your conversation has amply repaid me for your five weeks' entertainment. I gave you nothing more than what common hospitality dictated; but could any other guest have instructed me as you did? You conducted me, on the map, from one European country to another; told me many extraordinary things of our famed mother country, of which I knew very little, of its internal navigation, agriculture, arts, manufactures, and trade; you guided me through an extensive maze, and I abundantly profited by the journey; the contrast therefore proves the debt of gratitude to be on my side. The treatment you received at my house proceeded from the warmth of my heart and from the corresponding sensibility of my wife; what you now desire must flow from a very limited power of mind; the task requires recollection and a variety of talents which I do not possess. . . .

[1]James addresses Mr. F. B., the fictional recipient of the letters.

My father left me a few musty books, which *his* father brought from England with him; but what help can I draw from a library consisting mostly of Scotch divinity, the *Navigation of Sir Francis Drake,* the *History of Queen Elizabeth,* and a few miscellaneous volumes? Our minister often comes to see me, though he lives upwards of twenty miles distant. I have shown him your letter, asked his advice, and solicited his assistance; he tells me that he hath no time to spare, for that like the rest of us, he must till his farm and is moreover to study what he is to say on the Sabbath. My wife (and I never do anything without consulting her) laughs and tells me that you cannot be in earnest. . . .

Our minister took the letter from my wife and read it to himself; he made us observe the two last phrases, and we weighed the contents to the best of our abilities. The conclusion we all drew made me resolve at last to write. You say you want nothing of me but what lies within the reach of my experience and knowledge; this I understand very well; the difficulty is, how to collect, digest, and arrange what I know? Next, you assert that writing letters is nothing more than talking on paper, which, I must confess, appeared to me quite a new thought. "Well, then," observed our minister, "neighbour James, as you can talk well, I am sure you must write tolerably well also; imagine, then, that Mr. F. B. is still here and simply write down what you would say to him. Suppose the questions he will put to you in his future letters to be asked by his viva-voce, as we used to call it at the college; then let your answers be conceived and expressed exactly in the same language as if he was present. This is all that he requires from you, and I am sure the task is not difficult. He is your friend; who would be ashamed to write to such a person? Although he is a man of learning and taste, yet I am sure he will read your letters with pleasure; if they be not elegant, they will smell of the woods and be a little wild; I know your turn, they will contain some matters which he never knew before. Some people are so fond of novelty that they will overlook many errors of language for the sake of information. We are all apt to love and admire exotics, though they may be often inferior to what we possess; and that is the reason I imagine why so many persons are continually going to visit Italy. That country is the daily resort of modern travellers."

JAMES: I should like to know what is there to be seen so goodly and profitable that so many should wish to visit no other country?

MINISTER: I do not very well know. I fancy their object is to trace the vestiges of a once-flourishing people now extinct. There they amuse themselves in viewing the ruins of temples and other buildings which have very little affinity with those of the present age and must therefore impart a knowledge which appears useless and trifling. I have often wondered that no skilful botanists or learned men should come over here; methinks there would be much more real satisfaction in observing among us the humble rudiments and embryos of societies spreading everywhere, the recent foundation of our towns, and the settlements of so many rural districts. I am sure that the rapidity of their growth would be more pleasing to behold than the ruins of old towers, useless aqueducts, or impending battlements.

JAMES: What you say, minister, seems very true; do go on; I always love to hear you talk.

MINISTER: Do not you think, neighbour James, that the mind of a good and enlightened Englishman would be more improved in remarking throughout these provinces the causes which render so many people happy? In delineating the unnoticed means by which we daily increase the extent of our settlements? How we convert huge forests into pleasing fields and exhibit through these thirteen provinces so singular a display of easy subsistence and political felicity?

In Italy, all the objects of contemplation, all the reveries of the traveller, must have a reference to ancient generations and to very distant periods, clouded with the mist of ages. Here, on the contrary, everything is modern, peaceful, and benign. Here we have had no war to desolate our fields; our religion does not oppress the cultivators; we are strangers to those fuedal institutions which have enslaved so many. Here Nature opens her broad lap to receive the perpetual accession of newcomers and to supply them with food. I am sure I cannot be called a partial American when I say that the spectacle afforded by these pleasing scenes must be more entertaining and more philosophical than that which arises from beholding the musty ruins of Rome. Here everything would inspire the reflecting traveller with the most philanthropic ideas; his imagination, instead of submitting to the painful and useless retrospect of revolutions, desolations, and plagues, would, on the contrary, wisely spring forward to the anticipated fields of future cultivation and improvement to the future extent of those generations which are to replenish and embellish this boundless continent. . . .

JAMES: Oh! Could I express myself as you do, my friend, I should not balance a single instant; I should rather be anxious to commence a correspondence which would do me credit.

MINISTER: You can write full as well as you need, and would improve very fast. Trust to my prophecy, your letters at least will have the merits of coming from the edge of the great wilderness, three hundred miles from the sea and three thousand miles over that sea; this will be no detriment to them, take my word for it. You intend one of your children for the gown; who knows but Mr. F. B. may give you some assistance when the lad comes to have concerns with the bishop. It is good for American farmers to have friends even in England. What he requires of you is but simple—what we speak out among ourselves we call conversation, and a letter is only conversation put down in black and white.

JAMES: You quite persuade me—if he laughs at my awkwardness, surely he will be pleased with my ready compliance. On my part, it will be well meant, be the execution what it may. I will write enough, and so let him have the trouble of sifting the good from the bad, the useful from the trifling; let him select what he may want and reject what may not answer his purpose. After all, it is but treating Mr. F. B. now that he is in London, as I treated him when he was in America under this roof; that is with the best things I had, given with a good intention and the best manner I was able. . . .

Thus, sir, have I given you an unaffected and candid detail of the conversation which determined me to accept of your invitation. I thought it necessary thus to begin and to let you into these primary secrets, to the end that you may not hereafter reproach me with any degree of presumption. You'll plainly see the motives which have induced me to begin, the fears which I have entertained, and the principles on which my diffidence hath been founded. I have now nothing to do but to prosecute my task. Remember, you are to give me my subjects, and on no other shall I write, lest you should blame me for an injudicious choice. However incorrect my style, however inexpert my methods, however trifling my observations may hereafter appear to you, assure yourself they will all be the genuine dictates of my mind, and I hope will prove acceptable on that account. Remember that you have laid the foundation of this correspondence; you well know that I am neither a philosopher, politician, divine, or naturalist, but a simple farmer. I flatter myself, therefore, that you'll receive my letters as conceived, not according to scientific rules to which I am a perfect stranger, but agreeable to the spontaneous impressions which each subject may inspire. This is the only line I am able to follow, the line which Nature has herself traced for me; this was the covenant which I made with you and with which you seemed to be well pleased. Had you wanted the style of the learned, the reflections of the patriot, the discussions of the politician, the curious observations of the naturalist, the pleasing garb of the man of taste, surely you would have applied to some of those men of letters with which our cities abound. But since, on the contrary, and for what reason I know not, you wish to correspond with a cultivator of the earth, with a simple citizen, you must receive my letters for better or worse.

from Letter II On the Situation, Feelings, and Pleasures of an American Farmer

As you are the first enlightened European I had ever the pleasure of being acquainted with, you will not be surprised that I should, according to your earnest desire and my promise, appear anxious of preserving your friendship and correspondence. By your accounts, I observe a material difference subsists between your husbandry, modes, and customs and ours; everything is local; could we enjoy the advantages of the English farmer, we should be much happier, indeed, but this wish, like many others, implies a contradiction; and could the English farmer have some of those privileges we possess, they would be the first of their class in the world. Good and evil, I see, are to be found in all societies, and it is in vain to seek for any spot where those ingredients are not mixed. I therefore rest satisfied and thank God that my lot is to be an American farmer instead of a Russian boor or an Hungarian peasant. I thank you kindly for the idea, however dreadful, which you have given me of their lot and condition; your observations have confirmed me in the justness of my ideas, and I am happier now than I thought myself before. It is strange that misery, when viewed in others, should become to us a sort of real good, though I am far from rejoicing to hear that there are in the world men so thoroughly wretched; they are no doubt as harmless, industrious, and willing to work as we are. Hard is their fate to be thus condemned to a slavery worse than that of our Negroes. Yet when young, I entertained some thoughts of selling my farm. I thought it afforded but a dull repetition of the same labours and pleasures. I thought the former tedious and heavy, the latter few and insipid; but when I came to consider myself as divested of my farm, I then found the world so wide, and every place so full, that I began to fear lest there would be no room for me. My farm, my house, my barn, presented to my imagination objects from which I adduced quite new ideas; they were more forcible than before. Why should not I find myself happy, said I, where my father was before? He left me no good books, it is true; he gave me no other education than the art of reading and writing; but he left me a good farm and his experience; he left me free from debts, and no kind of difficulties to struggle with. I married, and this perfectly reconciled me to my situation; my wife rendered my house all at once cheerful and pleasing; it no longer appeared gloomy and solitary as before; when I went to work in my fields, I worked with more alacrity and sprightliness; I felt that I did not work for myself alone, and this encouraged me much. My wife would often come with her knitting in her hand and sit under the shady tree, praising the straightness of my furrows and the docility of my horses; this swelled my heart and made everything light and pleasant, and I regretted that I had not married before.

I felt myself happy in my new situation, and where is that station which can confer a more substantial system of felicity than that of an American farmer possessing freedom of action, freedom of thoughts, ruled by a mode of government which requires but little from us? I owe nothing but a peppercorn to my country,[2] a small tribute to my king, with loyalty and due respect; I know no other landlord than the lord of all land, to whom I owe the most sincere gratitude. My father left me three hundred and seventy-one acres of land, forty-seven of which are good timothy meadow; an excellent orchard; a good house; and a substantial barn. It is my duty to think how happy I am that he lived to build and to pay for all these improvements; what are the labours which I have to undergo, what are my fatigues, when compared to his, who had everything to do, from the first tree he felled to the finishing of his house? Every year I kill from 1,500 to 2,000 weight of pork, 1,200 of beef, half a dozen of good wethers in harvest; of fowls my wife has always a great stock; what can I wish more? My Negroes are tolerably faithful and healthy; by a long series of industry and honest dealings, my father left behind him the name of a good man; I have but to tread his paths to be happy and a good man like him. I know enough of the law to regulate my little concerns with propriety, nor do I dread its power; these are the grand outlines of my situation, but as I can feel much more than I am able to express, I hardly know how to proceed.

When my first son was born, the whole train of my ideas was suddenly altered; never was there a charm that acted so quickly and powerfully; I ceased to ramble in imagination through the wide world; my excursions since have not exceeded the bounds of my farm, and all my principal pleasures are now centred within its scanty limits; but at the same time, there is not an operation belonging to it in which I do not find some food for useful reflections. This is the reason, I suppose, that when you were here, you used, in your refined style, to denominate me the farmer of feelings; how rude must those feelings be in him who daily holds the axe or the plough, how much more refined on the contrary those of the European, whose mind is improved by education, example, books, and by every acquired advantage! Those feelings, however, I will delineate as well as I can, agreeably to your earnest request.

When I contemplate my wife, by my fireside, while she either spins, knits, darns, or suckles our child, I cannot describe the various emotions of love, of gratitude, of conscious pride, which thrill in my heart and often overflow in involuntary tears. I feel the necessity, the sweet pleasure, of acting my part, the part of an husband and father, with an attention and propriety which may entitle me to my good fortune. It is true these pleasing images vanish with the smoke of my pipe, but though they disappear from my mind, the impression they have made on my heart is indelible. When I play with the infant, my warm imagination runs forward and eagerly anticipates his

[2]Traditional offering.

future temper and constitution. I would willingly open the book of fate and know in which page his destiny is delineated. Alas! Where is the father who in those moments of paternal ecstasy can delineate one half of the thoughts which dilate his heart? I am sure I cannot; then again, I fear for the health of those who are become so dear to me, and in their sicknesses I severely pay for the joys I experienced while they were well. Whenever I go abroad, it is always involuntary. I never return home without feeling some pleasing emotion, which I often suppress as useless and foolish. The instant I enter on my own land, the bright idea of property, of exclusive right, of independence, exalt my mind. Precious soil, I say to myself, by what singular custom of law is it that thou wast made to constitute the riches of the freeholder? What should we American farmers be without the distinct possession of that soil? It feeds, it clothes us; from it we draw even a great exuberancy, our best meat, our richest drink; the very honey of our bees comes from this privileged spot. No wonder we should thus cherish its possession; no wonder that so many Europeans who have never been able to say that such portion of land was theirs cross the Atlantic to realize that happiness. This formerly rude soil has been converted by my father into a pleasant farm, and in return, it has established all our rights; on it is founded our rank, our freedom, our power as citizens, our importance as inhabitants of such a district. These images, I must confess, I always behold with pleasure and extend them as far as my imagination can reach; for this is what may be called the true and the only philosophy of an American farmer.

Pray do not laugh in thus seeing an artless countryman tracing himself through the simple modifications of his life; remember that you have required it; therefore, with candour, though with diffidence, I endeavour to follow the thread of my feelings, but I cannot tell you all. Often when I plough my low ground, I place my little boy on a chair which screws to the beam of the plough—its motion and that of the horses please him; he is perfectly happy and begins to chat. As I lean over the handle, various are the thoughts which crowd into my mind. I am now doing for him, I say, what my father formerly did for me; may God enable him to live that he may perform the same operations for the same purposes when I am worn out and old! I relieve his mother of some trouble while I have him with me; the odoriferous furrow exhilarates his spirits and seems to do the child a great deal of good, for he looks more blooming since I have adopted that practice; can more pleasure, more dignity, be added to that primary occupation? The father thus ploughing with his child, and to feed his family, is inferior only to the emperor of China ploughing as an example to his kingdom. In the evening, when I return home through my low grounds, I am astonished at the myriads of insects which I perceive dancing in the beams of the setting sun. I was before scarcely acquainted with their existence; they are so small that it is difficult to distinguish them; they are carefully improving this short evening space, not daring to expose themselves to the blaze of our meridian sun. I never see an egg brought on my table but I feel penetrated with the wonderful change it would have undergone but for my gluttony; it might have been a gentle, useful hen leading her chicken with a care and vigilance which speaks shame to many women. A cock perhaps, arrayed with the most majestic plumes, tender to its mate, bold, courageous, endowed with an astonishing instinct, with thoughts, with memory, and every distinguishing characteristic of the reason of man. I never see my trees drop their leaves and their fruit in the autumn, and bud again in the spring, without wonder;

the sagacity of those animals which have long been the tenants of my farm astonish me; some of them seem to surpass even men in memory and sagacity. I could tell you singular instances of that kind. What, then, is this instinct which we so debase, and of which we are taught to entertain so diminutive an idea? My bees, above any other tenants of my farm, attract my attention and respect; I am astonished to see that nothing exists but what has its enemy; one species pursues and lives upon the other: unfortunately, our king-birds are the destroyers of those industrious insects, but on the other hand, these birds preserve our fields from the depredation of crows, which they pursue on the wing with great vigilance and astonishing dexterity. . . .

from Letter III
What Is an American?

I wish I could be acquainted with the feelings and thoughts which must agitate the heart and present themselves to the mind of an enlightened Englishman when he first lands on this continent. He must greatly rejoice that he lived at a time to see this fair country discovered and settled; he must necessarily feel a share of national pride when he views the chain of settlements which embellish these extended shores. When he says to himself, "This is the work of my countrymen, who, when convulsed by factions, afflicted by a variety of miseries and wants, restless and impatient, took refuge here. They brought along with them their national genius,[3] to which they principally owe what liberty they enjoy and what substance they possess." Here he sees the industry of his native country displayed in a new manner and traces in their works the embryos of all the arts, sciences, and ingenuity which flourish in Europe. Here he beholds fair cities, substantial villages, extensive fields, an immense country filled with decent houses, good roads, orchards, meadows, and bridges where an hundred years ago all was wild, woody, and uncultivated! What a train of pleasing ideas this fair spectacle must suggest; it is a prospect which must inspire a good citizen with the most heart-felt pleasure. The difficulty consists in the manner of viewing so extensive a scene. He is arrived on a new continent; a modern society offers itself to his contemplation, different from what he had hitherto seen. It is not composed, as in Europe, of great lords who possess everything and of a herd of people who have nothing. Here are no aristocratical families, no courts, no kings, no bishops, no ecclesiastical dominion, no invisible power giving to a few a very visible one, no great manufactures employing thousands, no great refinements of luxury. The rich and the poor are not so far removed from each other as they are in Europe. Some few towns excepted, we are all tillers of the earth, from Nova Scotia to West Florida. We are a people of cultivators scattered over an immense territory, communicating with each other by means of good roads and navigable rivers, united by the silken bands of mild government, all respecting the laws without dreading their power, because they are equitable. We are all animated with the spirit of an industry which is unfettered and unrestrained, because each person works for himself. If he travels through our rural districts, he views not the hostile castle and the haughty

[3]Characteristic national spirit.

mansion, contrasted with the clay-built hut and miserable cabin, where cattle and men help to keep each other warm and dwell in meanness, smoke, and indigence. A pleasing uniformity of decent competence appears throughout our habitations. The meanest of our log-houses is a dry and comfortable habitation. Lawyer or merchant are the fairest titles our towns afford; that of a farmer is the only appellation of the rural inhabitants of our country. It must take some time ere he can reconcile himself to our dictionary, which is but short in words of dignity and names of honour. There, on a Sunday, he sees a congregation of respectable farmers and their wives, all clad in neat homespun, well mounted, or riding in their own humble waggons. There is not among them an esquire, saving the unlettered magistrate. There he sees a parson as simple as his flock, a farmer who does not riot[4] on the labour of others. We have no princes for whom we toil, starve, and bleed; we are the most perfect society now existing in the world. Here man is free as he ought to be, nor is this pleasing equality so transitory as many others are. Many ages will not see the shores of our great lakes replenished with inland nations, nor the unknown bounds of North America entirely peopled. Who can tell how far it extends? Who can tell the millions of men whom it will feed and contain? For no European foot has as yet travelled half the extent of this mighty continent!

The next wish of this traveller will be to know whence came all these people. They are a mixture of English, Scotch, Irish, French, Dutch, Germans, and Swedes. From this promiscuous breed, that race now called Americans have arisen. The eastern provinces must indeed be excepted as being the unmixed descendants of Englishmen. I have heard many wish that they had been more intermixed also; for my part, I am no wisher and think it much better as it has happened. They exhibit a most conspicuous figure in this great and variegated picture; they too enter for a great share in the pleasing perspective displayed in these thirteen provinces. I know it is fashionable to reflect on them, but I respect them for what they have done; for the accuracy and wisdom with which they have settled their territory; for the decency of their manners; for their early love of letters; their ancient college, the first in this hemisphere; for their industry, which to me who am but a farmer is the criterion of everything. There never was a people, situated as they are, who with so ungrateful a soil have done more in so short a time. Do you think that the monarchical ingredients which are more prevalent in other governments have purged them from all foul stains? Their histories assert the contrary.

In this great American asylum, the poor of Europe have by some means met together, and in consequence of various causes; to what purpose should they ask one another what countrymen they are? Alas, two thirds of them had no country. Can a wretch who wanders about, who works and starves, whose life is a continual scene of sore affliction or pinching penury—can that man call England or any other kingdom his country? A country that had no bread for him, whose fields procured him no harvest, who met with nothing but the frowns of the rich, the severity of the laws, with jails and punishments, who owned not a single foot of the extensive surface of this planet? No! Urged by a variety of motives, here they came. Everything has tended to regenerate them: new laws, a new mode of living, a new social system; here they are become men: in Europe they were as so many useless plants, wanting vege-

[4]To waste or spend recklessly.

tative mould[5] and refreshing showers; they withered, and were mowed down by want, hunger, and war; but now, by the power of transplantation, like all other plants they have taken root and flourished! Formerly they were not numbered in any civil lists of their country, except in those of the poor; here they rank as citizens. By what invisible power hath this surprising metamorphosis been performed? By that of the laws and that of their industry. The laws, the indulgent laws, protect them as they arrive, stamping on them the symbol of adoption; they receive ample rewards for their labours; these accumulated rewards procure them lands; those lands confer on them the title of freemen, and to that title every benefit is affixed which men can possibly require. This is the great operation daily performed by our laws. Whence proceed these laws? From our government. Whence that government? It is derived from the original genius and strong desire of the people ratified and confirmed by the crown. This is the great chain which links us all, this is the picture which every province exhibits, Nova Scotia excepted.[6] There the crown has done all; either there were no people who had genius or it was not much attended to; the consequence is that the province is very thinly inhabited indeed; the power of the crown in conjunction with the musketos[7] has prevented men from settling there. Yet some parts of it flourished once, and it contained a mild, harmless set of people. But for the fault of a few leaders, the whole was banished. The greatest political error the crown ever committed in America was to cut off men from a country which wanted nothing but men!

What attachment can a poor European emigrant have for a country where he had nothing? The knowledge of the language, the love of a few kindred as poor as himself, were the only cords that tied him; his country is now that which gives him his land, bread, protection, and consequence; *Ubi panis ibi patria*[8] is the motto of all emigrants. What, then, is the American, this new man? He is either an European or the descendant of an European; hence that strange mixture of blood, which you will find in no other country. I could point out to you a family whose grandfather was an Englishman, whose wife was Dutch, whose son married a French woman, and whose present four sons have now four wives of different nations. *He* is an American, who, leaving behind him all his ancient prejudices and manners, receives new ones from the new mode of life he has embraced, the new government he obeys, and the new rank he holds. He becomes an American by being received in the broad lap of our great Alma Mater.[9] Here individuals of all nations are melted into a new race of men, whose labours and posterity will one day cause great changes in the world. Americans are the western pilgrims who are carrying along with them that great mass of arts, sciences, vigour, and industry which began long since in the East; they will finish the great circle. The Americans were once scattered all over Europe; here they are incorporated into one of the finest systems of population which has ever appeared, and which will hereafter become distinct by the power of the different climates they

[5]Nutrient-rich earth that promotes growth.

[6]Crèvecoeur refers to the British removal of French settlers in 1755. In *Journey into Northern Pennsylvania,* Crèvecoeur says, "About the year 1745, Great Britain, to whom France had just ceded Acadia (today New Scotland-Nova Scotia), instead of keeping it for its former inhabitants, in accordance with the capitulation, snatched from its native land, under some frivolous religious pretext and without compensation . . . this gentle and hard-working people."

[7]Mosquitoes.

[8]Where there is bread, there is one's fatherland.

[9]Fostering mother.

inhabit. The American ought therefore to love this country much better than that wherein either he or his forefathers were born. Here the rewards of his industry follow with equal steps the progress of his labour; his labour is founded on the basis of nature, self-interest; can it want a stronger allurement? Wives and children, who before in vain demanded of him a morsel of bread, now, fat and frolicsome, gladly help their father to clear those fields whence exuberant crops are to arise to feed and to clothe them all, without any part being claimed, either by a despotic prince, a rich abbot, or a mighty lord. Here religion demands but little of him: a small voluntary salary to the minister and gratitude to God; can he refuse these? The American is a new man, who acts upon new principles; he must therefore entertain new ideas and form new opinions. From involuntary idleness, servile dependence, penury, and useless labour, he has passed to toils of a very different nature, rewarded by ample subsistence. This is an American. . . .

Andrew[10] arrived at my house a week before I did, and I found my wife, agreeably to my instructions, had placed the axe in his hands as his first task. For some time, he was very awkward, but he was so docile, so willing, and grateful, as well as his wife, that I foresaw he would succeed. Agreeably to my promise, I put them all with different families, where they were well liked, and all parties were pleased. Andrew worked hard, lived well, grew fat, and every Sunday came to pay me a visit on a good horse, which Mr. P.R. lent him. Poor man, it took him a long time ere he could sit on the saddle and hold the bridle properly. I believe he had never before mounted such a beast, though I did not choose to ask him that question, for fear it might suggest some mortifying ideas. After having been twelve months at Mr. P.R.'s and having received his own and his family's wages, which amounted to eighty-four dollars, he came to see me on a weekday and told me that he was a man of middle age and would willingly have land of his own in order to procure him a home as a shelter against old age, that whenever this period should come, his son, to whom he would give his land, would then maintain him, and thus live altogether; he therefore required my advice and assistance. I thought his desire very natural and praiseworthy, and told him that I should think of it, but that he must remain one month longer with Mr. P.R., who had 3,000 rails to split. He immediately consented. The spring was not far advanced enough yet for Andrew to begin clearing any land, even supposing that he had made a purchase, as it is always necessary that the leaves should be out in order that this additional combustible may serve to burn the heaps of brush more readily.

A few days after, it happened that the whole family of Mr. P.R. went to meeting, and left Andrew to take care of the house. While he was at the door, attentively reading the Bible, nine Indians just come from the mountains suddenly made their appearance and unloaded their packs of furs on the floor of the piazza. Conceive, if you can, what was Andrew's consternation at this extraordinary sight! From the singular appearance of these people, the honest Hebridean[11] took them for a lawless band come to rob his master's house. He therefore, like a faithful guardian, precipitately withdrew and shut the doors; but as most of our houses are without locks, he was reduced to the necessity of fixing his knife over the latch, and then flew upstairs in

[10]A recent arrival from Scotland whose situation illustrates the success of the new emigrants.

[11]From the Hebrides Islands of West Scotland.

quest of a broadsword he had brought from Scotland. The Indians, who were Mr. P.R.'s particular friends, guessed at his suspicions and fears; they forcibly lifted the door and suddenly took possession of the house, got all the bread and meat they wanted, and sat themselves down by the fire. At this instant, Andrew, with his broadsword in his hand, entered the room, the Indians earnestly looking at him and attentively watching his motions. After a very few reflections, Andrew found that his weapon was useless when opposed to nine tomahawks, but this did not diminish his anger; on the contrary, it grew greater on observing the calm impudence with which they were devouring the family provisions. Unable to resist, he called them names in broad Scotch and ordered them to desist and be gone, to which the Indians (as they told me afterwards) replied in their equally broad idiom. It must have been a most unintelligible altercation between this honest Barra[12] man and nine Indians who did not much care for anything he could say. At last he ventured to lay his hands on one of them in order to turn him out of the house. Here Andrew's fidelity got the better of his prudence, for the Indian, by his motions, threatened to scalp him, while the rest gave the war whoop. This horrid noise so effectually frightened poor Andrew that, unmindful of his courage, of his broadsword, and his intentions, he rushed out, left them masters of the house, and disappeared. I have heard one of the Indians say since that he never laughed so heartily in his life. Andrew, at a distance, soon recovered from the fears which had been inspired by this infernal yell and thought of no other remedy than to go to the meeting-house, which was about two miles distant. In the eagerness of his honest intentions, with looks of affright still marked on his countenance, he called Mr. P.R. out and told him with great vehemence of style that nine monsters were come to his house—some blue, some red, and some black; that they had little axes in their hands out of which they smoked; and that like highlanders, they had no breeches; that they were devouring all his victuals; and that God only knew what they would do more. "Pacify yourself," said Mr. P.R.; "my house is as safe with these people as if I was there myself; as for the victuals, they are heartily welcome, honest Andrew; they are not people of much ceremony; they help themselves thus whenever they are among their friends; I do so too in their wigwams, whenever I go to their village; you had better therefore step in and hear the remainder of the sermon, and when the meeting is over, we will all go back in the waggon together."

At their return, Mr. P.R., who speaks the Indian language very well, explained the whole matter; the Indians renewed their laugh and shook hands with honest Andrew, whom they made to smoke out of their pipes; and thus peace was made and ratified according to the Indian custom, by the calumet.[13] . . .

from Letter V
Customary Education and Employment of the Inhabitants of Nantucket

The easiest way of becoming acquainted with the modes of thinking, the rules of conduct, and the prevailing manners of any people is to examine what sort of education they give their children, how they treat them at home, and what they are taught in their places of public worship. At home their tender minds must be early struck with

[12]An island of the Hebrides.

[13]Ceremonial Indian pipe.

the gravity, the serious though cheerful deportment of their parents; they are inured to a principle of subordination, arising neither from sudden passions nor inconsiderate pleasure; they are gently holden by an uniform silk cord, which unites softness and strength. A perfect equanimity prevails in most of their families, and bad example hardly ever sows in their hearts the seeds of future and similar faults. They are corrected with tenderness, nursed with the most affectionate care, clad with that decent plainness from which they observe their parents never to depart: in short, by the force of example, which is superior even to the strongest instinct of nature, more than by precepts, they learn to follow the steps of their parents, to despise ostentatiousness as being sinful. They acquire a taste for that neatness for which their fathers are so conspicuous; they learn to be prudent and saving; the very tone of voice with which they are always addressed establishes in them that softness of diction which ever after becomes habitual. Frugal, sober, orderly parents, attached to their business, constantly following some useful occupation, never guilty of riot, dissipation, or other irregularities, cannot fail of training up children to the same uniformity of life and manners. If they are left with fortunes, they are taught how to save them and how to enjoy them with moderation and decency; if they have none, they know how to venture, how to work and toil as their fathers have done before them. If they fail of success, there are always in this island (and wherever this society prevails) established resources, founded on the most benevolent principles. At their meetings they are taught the few, the simple tenets of their sect, tenets as fit to render men sober, industrious, just, and merciful as those delivered in the most magnificent churches and cathedrals. . . .

The first proprietors of this island, or rather the first founders of this town, began their career of industry with a single whale-boat, with which they went to fish for cod; the small distance from their shores at which they caught it enabled them soon to increase their business, and those early successes first led them to conceive that they might likewise catch the whales, which hitherto sported undisturbed on their banks. After many trials and several miscarriages, they succeeded; thus they proceeded, step by step; the profits of one successful enterprise helped them to purchase and prepare better materials for a more extensive one; as these were attended with little costs, their profits grew greater. The south sides of the island, from east to west, were divided into four equal parts, and each part was assigned to a company of six, which, though thus separated, still carried on their business in common. In the middle of this distance, they erected a mast provided with a sufficient number of rounds, and near it they built a temporary hut, where five of the associates lived, whilst the sixth from his high station carefully looked toward the sea in order to observe the spouting of the whales. As soon as any were discovered, the sentinel descended, the whale-boat was launched, and the company went forth in quest of their game. It may appear strange to you, that so slender a vessel as an American whale-boat, containing six diminutive beings, should dare to pursue and to attack, in its native element, the largest and strongest fish that Nature has created. Yet by the exertions of an admirable dexterity, improved by a long practice, in which these people are become superior to any other whalemen, by knowing the temper of the whale after her first movement, and by many other useful observations, they seldom failed to harpoon it and to bring the huge leviathan on the shores. Thus they went on until the profits they made enabled them to purchase larger vessels, and to pursue them farther when the whales quitted their coasts; those who failed in their enterprises returned to the cod-fisheries. . . . Such were their feeble beginnings, such the infancy and the progress of their maritime schemes; such is now the degree of boldness and activity to which they are arrived in their manhood. . . .

from Letter IX Description of Charles Town; Thoughts on Slavery; on Physical Evil; a Melancholy Scene

Charles Town is, in the north, what Lima is in the south; both are capitals of the richest provinces of their respective hemispheres; you may therefore conjecture that both cities must exhibit the appearances necessarily resulting from riches. Peru abounding in gold, Lima is filled with inhabitants who enjoy all those gradations of pleasure, refinement, and luxury which proceed from wealth. Carolina produces commodities more valuable perhaps than gold because they are gained by greater industry; it exhibits also on our northern stage a display of riches and luxury, inferior indeed to the former, but far superior to what are to be seen in our northern towns. Its situation is admirable, being built at the confluence of two large rivers, which receive in their course a great number of inferior streams, all navigable in the spring for flat boats. Here the produce of this extensive territory concentres; here therefore is the seat of the most valuable exportation; their wharfs, their docks, their magazines,[14] are extremely convenient to facilitate this great commercial business. The inhabitants are the gayest in America; it is called the centre of our beau monde[15] and is always filled with the richest planters in the province, who resort hither in quest of health and pleasure. . . .

The three principal classes of inhabitants are lawyers, planters, and merchants; this is the province which has afforded to the first the richest spoils, for nothing can exceed their wealth, their power, and their influence. They have reached the *ne plus ultra*[16] of worldly felicity; no plantation is secured, no title is good, no will is valid, but what they dictate, regulate, and approve. The whole mass of provincial property is become tributary to this society, which, far above priests and bishops, disdain to be satisfied with the poor Mosaical portion of the tenth.[17] I appeal to the many inhabitants who, while contending perhaps for their right to a few hundred acres, have lost by the mazes of the law their whole patrimony. These men are more properly lawgivers than interpreters of the law and have united here, as well as in most other provinces, the skill and dexterity of the scribe with the power and ambition of the prince; who can tell where this may lead in a future day? The nature of our laws and the spirit of freedom, which often tends to make us litigious, must necessarily throw the greatest part of the property of the colonies into the hands of these gentlemen. In another century, the law will possess in the north what now the church possesses in Peru and Mexico.

[14]Warehouses.
[15]The world of fashion.
[16]The utmost point one can achieve or reach.
[17]Tithe; the Old Testament law that each person should give one-tenth of his possessions to God.

While all is joy, festivity, and happiness in Charles Town, would you imagine that scenes of misery overspread in the country? Their ears by habit are become deaf, their hearts are hardened; they neither see, hear, nor feel for the woes of their poor slaves, from whose painful labours all their wealth proceeds. Here the horrors of slavery, the hardship of incessant toils, are unseen; and no one thinks with compassion of those showers of sweat and tears which from the bodies of Africans daily drop and moisten the ground they till. The cracks of the whip urging these miserable beings to excessive labour are far too distant from the gay capital to be heard. The chosen race eat, drink, and live happy, while the unfortunate one grubs up the ground, raises indigo, or husks the rice, exposed to a sun full as scorching as their native one, without the support of good food, without the cordials of any cheering liquor. This great contrast has often afforded me subjects of the most afflicting meditations. On the one side, behold a people enjoying all that life affords most bewitching and pleasurable, without labour, without fatigue, hardly subjected to the trouble of wishing. With gold, dug from Peruvian mountains, they order vessels to the coasts of Guinea; by virtue of that gold, wars, murders, and devastations are committed in some harmless, peaceable African neighbourhood where dwelt innocent people who even knew not but that all men were black. The daughter torn from her weeping mother, the child from the wretched parents, the wife from the loving husband; whole families swept away and brought through storms and tempests to this rich metropolis! There, arranged like horses at a fair, they are branded like cattle and then driven to toil, to starve, and to languish for a few years on the different plantations of these citizens. And for whom must they work? For persons they know not, and who have no other power over them than that of violence, no other right than what this accursed metal has given them! Strange order of things! Oh, Nature, where art thou? Are not these blacks thy children as well as we? On the other side, nothing is to be seen but the most diffusive misery and wretchedness, unrelieved even in thought or wish! Day after day they drudge on without any prospect of ever reaping for themselves; they are obliged to devote their lives, their limbs, their will, and every vital exertion to swell the wealth of masters who look not upon them with half the kindness and affection with which they consider their dogs and horses. Kindness and affection are not the portion of those who till the earth, who carry burthens, who convert the logs into useful boards. This reward, simple and natural as one would conceive it, would border on humanity; and planters must have none of it!

If Negroes are permitted to become fathers, this fatal indulgence only tends to increase their misery; the poor companions of their scanty pleasures are likewise the companions of their labours; and when at some critical seasons they could wish to see them relieved, with tears in their eyes they behold them perhaps doubly oppressed, obliged to bear the burden of Nature—a fatal present—as well as that of unabated tasks. How many have I seen cursing the irresistible propensity and regretting that by having tasted of those harmless joys they had become the authors of double misery to their wives. Like their masters, they are not permitted to partake of those ineffable sensations with which Nature inspires the hearts of fathers and mothers; they must repel them all and become callous and passive. This unnatural state often occasions the most acute, the most pungent of their afflictions; they have no time, like us, tenderly to rear their helpless offspring, to nurse them on their knees, to enjoy the delight of being parents. Their paternal fondness is embittered by considering that if their children live, they must live to be slaves like themselves; no time is allowed them to exercise their pious office; the mothers must fasten them on their backs and, with this double load, follow their husbands in the fields, where they too often hear no other sound than that of the voice or whip of the taskmaster and the cries of their infants, broiling in the sun. These unfortunate creatures cry and weep like their parents, without a possibility of relief; the very instinct of the brute, so laudable, so irresistible, runs counter here to their master's interest; and to that god, all the laws of Nature must give way. Thus planters get rich; so raw, so inexperienced am I in this mode of life that were I to be possessed of a plantation, and my slaves treated as in general they are here, never could I rest in peace; my sleep would be perpetually disturbed by a retrospect of the frauds committed in Africa in order to entrap them, frauds surpassing in enormity everything which a common mind can possibly conceive. I should be thinking of the barbarous treatment they meet with on shipboard, of their anguish, of the despair necessarily inspired by their situation, when torn from their friends and relations, when delivered into the hands of a people differently coloured, whom they cannot understand, carried in a strange machine over an ever agitated element, which they had never seen before, and finally delivered over to the severities of the whippers and the excessive labours of the field. Can it be possible that the force of custom should ever make me deaf to all these reflections and as insensible to the injustice of that trade and to their miseries as the rich inhabitants of this town seem to be? What, then, is man, this being who boasts so much of the excellence and dignity of his nature among that variety of unscrutable mysteries, of unsolvable problems, with which he is surrounded? The reason why man has been thus created is not the least astonishing! It is said, I know, that they are much happier here than in the West Indies because, land being cheaper upon this continent than in those islands, the fields allowed them to raise their subsistence from are in general more extensive. The only possible chance of any alleviation depends on the humour of the planters, who, bred in the midst of slaves, learn from the example of their parents to despise them and seldom conceive either from religion or philosophy any ideas that tend to make their fate less calamitous, except some strong native tenderness of heart, some rays of philanthropy, overcome the obduracy contracted by habit.

I have not resided here long enough to become insensible of pain for the objects which I every day behold. In the choice of my friends and acquaintance, I always endeavour to find out those whose dispositions are somewhat congenial with my own. We have slaves likewise in our northern provinces; I hope the time draws near when they will be all emancipated, but how different their lot, how different their situation, in every possible respect! They enjoy as much liberty as their masters; they are as well clad and as well fed; in health and sickness, they are tenderly taken care of; they live under the same roof and are, truly speaking, a part of our families. Many of them are taught to read and write, and are well instructed in the principles of religion; they are the companions of our labours, and treated as such; they enjoy many perquisites, many established holidays, and are not obliged to work more than white people. They marry where inclination leads them, visit their wives every week, are as decently clad as the common people; they are indulged in educating, cherishing, and chastising their children, who are taught subordination to them as to their lawful parents: in short, they participate in many of the benefits of our society without being obliged to bear any of its burthens. They are fat, healthy, and hearty; and far from repining at their fate, they think themselves happier than many of the lower class of whites;

they share with their masters the wheat and meat provision they help to raise; many of those whom the good Quakers have emancipated have received that great benefit with tears of regret and have never quitted, though free, their former masters and benefactors.

But is it really true, as I have heard it asserted here, that those blacks are incapable of feeling the spurs of emulation and the cheerful sound of encouragement? By no means; there are a thousand proofs existing of their gratitude and fidelity: those hearts in which such noble dispositions can grow are then like ours; they are susceptible of every generous sentiment, of every useful motive of action; they are capable of receiving lights, of imbibing ideas that would greatly alleviate the weight of their miseries. But what methods have in general been made use of to obtain so desirable an end? None; the day in which they arrive and are sold is the first of their labours, labours which from that hour admit of no respite; for though indulged by law with relaxation on Sundays, they are obliged to employ that time which is intended for rest to till their little plantations. What can be expected from wretches in such circumstances? Forced from their native country, cruelly treated when on board, and not less so on the plantations to which they are driven, is there anything in this treatment but what must kindle all the passions, sow the seeds of inveterate resentment, and nourish a wish of perpetual revenge? They are left to the irresistible effects of those strong and natural propensities; the blows they receive, are they conducive to extinguish them or to win their affections? They are neither soothed by the hopes that their slavery will ever terminate but with their lives or yet encouraged by the goodness of their food or the mildness of their treatment. The very hopes held out to mankind by religion, that consolatory system, so useful to the miserable, are never presented to them; neither moral nor physical means are made use of to soften their chains; they are left in their original and untutored state, that very state wherein the natural propensities of revenge and warm passions are so soon kindled. Cheered by no one single motive that can impel the will or excite their efforts, nothing but terrors and punishments are presented to them; death is denounced if they run away; horrid delaceration if they speak with their native freedom; perpetually awed by the terrible cracks of whips or by the fear of capital punishments, while even those punishments often fail of their purpose.

A clergyman settled a few years ago at George Town, and feeling as I do now, warmly recommended to the planters, from the pulpit, a relaxation of severity; he introduced the benignity of Christianity and pathetically made use of the admirable precepts of that system to melt the hearts of his congregation into a greater degree of compassion toward their slaves than had been hitherto customary. "Sir," said one of his hearers, "we pay you a genteel salary to read to us the prayers of the liturgy and to explain to us such parts of the Gospel as the rule of the church directs, but we do not want you to teach us what we are to do with our blacks." The clergyman found it prudent to withhold any farther admonition. Whence this astonishing right, or rather this barbarous custom, for most certainly we have no kind of right beyond that of force? We are told, it is true, that slavery cannot be so repugnant to human nature as we at first imagine because it has been practised in all ages and in all nations; the Lacedaemonians[18] themselves, those great asserters of liberty, conquered the

[18]Another name for the inhabitants of the Greek city-state of Sparta.

Helotes[19] with the design of making them their slaves; the Romans, whom we consider as our masters in civil and military policy, lived in the exercise of the most horrid oppression; they conquered to plunder and to enslave.[20] What a hideous aspect the face of the earth must then have exhibited! Provinces, towns, districts, often depopulated! Their inhabitants driven to Rome, the greatest market in the world, and there sold by thousands! The Roman dominions were tilled by the hands of unfortunate people who had once been, like their victors, free, rich, and possessed of every benefit society can confer, until they became subject to the cruel right of war and to lawless force. Is there, then, no superintending power who conducts the moral operations of the world, as well as the physical? The same sublime hand which guides the planets round the sun with so much exactness, which preserves the arrangement of the whole with such exalted wisdom and paternal care, and prevents the vast system from falling into confusion—doth it abandon mankind to all the errors, the follies, and the miseries, which their most frantic rage and their most dangerous vices and passions can produce?

The history of the earth! Doth it present anything but crimes of the most heinous nature, committed from one end of the world to the other? We observe avarice, rapine, and murder, equally prevailing in all parts. History perpetually tells us of millions of people abandoned to the caprice of the maddest princes, and of whole nations devoted to the blind fury of tyrants. Countries destroyed, nations alternately buried in ruins by other nations, some parts of the world beautifully cultivated, returned again into their pristine state, the fruits of ages of industry, the toil of thousands in a short time destroyed by few! If one corner breathes in peace for a few years, it is, in turn subjected, torn, and levelled; one would almost believe the principles of action in man, considered as the first agent of this planet, to be poisoned in their most essential parts. We certainly are not that class of beings which we vainly think ourselves to be; man, an animal of prey, seems to have rapine and the love of bloodshed implanted in his heart, nay, to hold it the most honourable occupation in society; we never speak of a hero of mathematics, a hero of knowledge or humanity, no, this illustrious appellation is reserved for the most successful butchers of the world. If Nature has given us a fruitful soil to inhabit, she has refused us such inclinations and propensities as would afford us the full enjoyment of it. Extensive as the surface of this planet is, not one half of it is yet cultivated, not half replenished; she created man and placed him either in the woods or plains and provided him with passions which must forever oppose his happiness; everything is submitted to the power of the strongest; men, like the elements, are always at war; the weakest yield to the most potent; force, subtlety, and malice always triumph over unguarded honesty and simplicity. Benignity, moderation, and justice are virtues adapted only to the humble paths of life; we love to talk of virtue and to admire its beauty while in the shade of solitude and retirement, but when we step forth into active life, if it happen to be in competition with any passion or desire, do we observe it to prevail? Hence so many religious impostors have triumphed over the credulity of mankind and have rendered their frauds the creeds of succeeding generations during the course of many ages until, worn away by time, they have been replaced by new ones. Hence

[19]Inhabitants of Helos in Laconia, an ancient country in southern Greece. Their name became synonymous with slave.

[20]Reference to eighteenth-century political theories which treat Rome as a paradigm of the republican state.

the most unjust war, if supported by the greatest force, always succeeds; hence the most just ones, when supported only by their justice, as often fail. Such is the ascendancy of power, the supreme arbiter of all the revolutions which we observe in this planet; so irresistible is power that it often thwarts the tendency of the most forcible causes and prevents their subsequent salutary effects, though ordained for the good of man by the Governor of the universe. Such is the perverseness of human nature; who can describe it in all its latitude? . . .

. . . Even under those mild climates which seem to breathe peace and happiness, the poison of slavery, the fury of despotism, and the rage of superstition are all combined against man! There only the few live and rule whilst the many starve and utter ineffectual complaints; there human nature appears more debased, perhaps, than in the less favoured climates. The fertile plains of Asia, the rich lowlands of Egypt and of Diarbeck, the fruitful fields bordering on the Tigris and the Euphrates, the extensive country of the East Indies in all its separate districts—all these must to the geographical eye seem as if intended for terrestrial paradises; but though surrounded with the spontaneous riches of nature, though her kindest favours seem to be shed on those beautiful regions with the most profuse hand, yet there in general we find the most wretched people in the world. Almost everywhere, liberty so natural to mankind is refused, or rather enjoyed but by their tyrants; the word slave is the appellation of every rank who adore as a divinity a being worse than themselves, subject to every caprice and to every lawless rage which unrestrained power can give. Tears are shed, perpetual groans are heard, where only the accents of peace, alacrity, and gratitude should resound. There the very delirium of tyranny tramples on the best gifts of nature and sports with the fate, the happiness, the lives of millions; there the extreme fertility of the ground always indicates the extreme misery of the inhabitants!

Everywhere one part of the human species is taught the art of shedding the blood of the other, of setting fire to their dwellings, of levelling the works of their industry: half of the existence of nations regularly employed in destroying other nations. What little political felicity is to be met with here and there has cost oceans of blood to purchase, as if good was never to be the portion of unhappy man. Republics, kingdoms, monarchies, founded either on fraud or successful violence, increase by pursuing the steps of the same policy until they are destroyed in their turn, either by the influence of their own crimes or by more successful but equally criminal enemies.

If from this general review of human nature we descend to the examination of what is called civilized society, there the combination of every natural and artificial want makes us pay very dear for what little share of political felicity we enjoy. It is a strange heterogeneous assemblage of vices and virtues and of a variety of other principles, forever at war, forever jarring, forever producing some dangerous, some distressing extreme. Where do you conceive, then, that nature intended we should be happy? Would you prefer the state of men in the woods to that of men in a more improved situation? Evil preponderates in both; in the first they often eat each other for want of food, and in the other they often starve each other for want of room. For my part, I think the vices and miseries to be found in the latter exceed those of the former, in which real evil is more scarce, more supportable, and less enormous. Yet we wish to see the earth peopled, to accomplish the happiness of kingdoms, which is said to consist in numbers. Gracious God! To what end is the introduction of so many beings into a mode of existence in which they must grope amidst as many errors, commit as many crimes, and meet with as many diseases, wants, and sufferings!

The following scene will, I hope, account for these melancholy reflections and apologize for the gloomy thoughts with which I have filled this letter: my mind is, and always has been, oppressed since I became a witness to it. I was not long since invited to dine with a planter who lived three miles from ——, where he then resided. In order to avoid the heat of the sun, I resolved to go on foot, sheltered in a small path leading through a pleasant wood. I was leisurely travelling along, attentively examining some peculiar plants which I had collected, when all at once I felt the air strongly agitated, though the day was perfectly calm and sultry. I immediately cast my eyes toward the cleared ground, from which I was but a small distance, in order to see whether it was not occasioned by a sudden shower, when at that instant a sound resembling a deep rough voice, uttered, as I thought, a few inarticulate monosyllables. Alarmed and surprised, I precipitately looked all round, when I perceived at about six rods distance something resembling a cage, suspended to the limbs of a tree, all the branches of which appeared covered with large birds of prey, fluttering about and anxiously endeavouring to perch on the cage. Actuated by an involuntary motion of my hands more than by any design of my mind, I fired at them; they all flew to a short distance, with a most hideous noise, when, horrid to think and painful to repeat, I perceived a Negro, suspended in the cage and left there to expire! I shudder when I recollect that the birds had already picked out his eyes; his cheek-bones were bare; his arms had been attacked in several places; and his body seemed covered with a multitude of wounds. From the edges of the hollow sockets and from the lacerations with which he was disfigured, the blood slowly dropped and tinged the ground beneath. No sooner were the birds flown than swarms of insects covered the whole body of this unfortunate wretch, eager to feed on his mangled flesh and to drink his blood. I found myself suddenly arrested by the power of affright and terror; my nerves were convulsed; I trembled; I stood motionless, involuntarily contemplating the fate of this Negro in all its dismal latitude. The living spectre, though deprived of his eyes, could still distinctly hear, and in his uncouth dialect begged me to give him some water to allay his thirst. Humanity herself would have recoiled back with horror; she would have balanced whether to lessen such reliefless distress or mercifully with one blow to end this dreadful scene of agonizing torture! Had I had a ball in my gun, I certainly should have dispatched him, but finding myself unable to perform so kind an office, I sought, though trembling, to relieve him as well as I could. A shell ready fixed to a pole, which had been used by some Negroes, presented itself to me; filled it with water, and with trembling hands I guided it to the quivering lips of the wretched sufferer. Urged by the irresistible power of thirst, he endeavoured to meet it, as he instinctively guessed its approach by the noise it made in passing through the bars of the cage. "Tanky you, white man; tanky you; puta some poison and give me." "How long have you been hanging there?" I asked him. "Two days, and me no die; the birds, the birds; aaah me!" Oppressed with the reflections which this shocking spectacle afforded me, I mustered strength enough to walk away and soon reached the house at which I intended to dine. There I heard that the reason for this slave's being thus punished was on account of his having killed the overseer of the plantation. They told me that the laws of self-preservation rendered such executions necessary, and supported the doctrine of slavery with the arguments generally made use of to justify the practice, with the repetition of which I shall not trouble you at present. Adieu.

from Letter XII
Distresses of a Frontier Man

I wish for a change of place; the hour is come at last that I must fly from my house and abandon my farm! But what course shall I steer, inclosed as I am? The climate best adapted to my present situation and humour would be the polar regions, where six months' day and six months' night divide the dull year; nay, a simple aurora borealis would suffice me and greatly refresh my eyes, fatigued now by so many disagreeable objects. The severity of those climates, that great gloom where melancholy dwells, would be perfectly analogous to the turn of my mind. Oh, could I remove my plantation to the shores of the Obi,[21] willingly would I dwell in the hut of a Samoyed;[22] with cheerfulness would I go and bury myself in the cavern of a Laplander. Could I but carry my family along with me, I would winter at Pello, or Tobolsk,[23] in order to enjoy the peace and innocence of that country. But let me arrive under the pole, or reach the antipodes, I never can leave behind me the remembrance of the dreadful scenes to which I have been witness; therefore, never can I be happy! Happy—why would I mention that sweet, that enchanting word? Once happiness was our portion; now it is gone from us, and I am afraid not to be enjoyed again by the present generation! Whichever way I look, nothing but the most frightful precipices present themselves to my view, in which hundreds of my friends and acquaintances have already perished; of all animals that live on the surface of this planet, what is man when no longer connected with society, or when he finds himself surrounded by a convulsed and a half-dissolved one? He cannot live in solitude; he must belong to some community bound by some ties, however imperfect. Men mutually support and add to the boldness and confidence of each other; the weakness of each is strengthened by the force of the whole. I had never before these calamitous times formed any such ideas; I lived on, laboured and prospered, without having ever studied on what the security of my life and the foundation of my prosperity were established; I perceived them just as they left me. Never was a situation so singularly terrible as mine, in every possible respect, as a member of an extensive society, as a citizen of an inferior division of the same society, as a husband, as a father, as a man who exquisitely feels for the miseries of others as well as for his own! But alas! So much is everything now subverted among us that the very word *misery,* with which we were hardly acquainted before, no longer conveys the same ideas, or, rather, tired with feeling for the miseries of others, every one feels now for himself alone. When I consider myself as connected in all these characters, as bound by so many cords, all uniting in my heart, I am seized with a fever of the mind, I am transported beyond that degree of calmness which is necessary to delineate our thoughts.

[21]River in Siberia.
[22]A member of a Siberian nomadic tribe.
[23]Places in Siberia.

I feel as if my reason wanted to leave me, as if it would burst its poor weak tenement; again, I try to compose myself, I grow cool, and preconceiving the dreadful loss, I endeavour to retain the useful guest.

You know the position of our settlement; I need not therefore describe it. To the west it is inclosed by a chain of mountains, reaching to ——; to the east, the country is as yet but thinly inhabited; we are almost insulated, and the houses are at a considerable distance from each other. From the mountains we have but too much reason to expect our dreadful enemy; the wilderness is a harbour where it is impossible to find them. It is a door through which they can enter our country whenever they please; and, as they seem determined to destroy the whole chain of frontiers, our fate cannot be far distant: from Lake Champlain, almost all has been conflagrated one after another. What renders these incursions still more terrible is that they most commonly take place in the dead of the night; we never go to our fields but we are seized with an involuntary fear, which lessens our strength and weakens our labour. No other subject of conversation intervenes between the different accounts, which spread through the country, of successive acts of devastation, and these, told in chimney-corners, swell themselves in our affrighted imaginations into the most terrific ideas! We never sit down either to dinner or supper but the least noise immediately spreads a general alarm and prevents us from enjoying the comfort of our meals. The very appetite proceeding from labour and peace of mind is gone; we eat just enough to keep us alive; our sleep is disturbed by the most frightful dreams; sometimes I start awake, as if the great hour of danger was come; at other times the howling of our dogs seems to announce the arrival of our enemy; we leap out of bed and run to arms; my poor wife, with panting bosom and silent tears, takes leave of me, as if we were to see each other no more; she snatches the youngest children from their beds, who, suddenly awakened, increase by their innocent questions the horror of the dreadful moment. She tries to hide them in the cellar, as if our cellar was inaccessible to the fire. I place all my servants at the windows and myself at the door, where I am determined to perish. Fear industriously increases every sound; we all listen; each communicates to the other his ideas and conjectures. We remain thus sometimes for whole hours, our hearts and our minds racked by the most anxious suspense: what a dreadful situation, a thousand times worse than that of a soldier engaged in the midst of the most severe conflict! Sometimes feeling the spontaneous courage of a man, I seem to wish for the decisive minute; the next instant a message from my wife, sent by one of the children, puzzling me beside with their little questions, unmans me; away goes my courage, and I descend again into the deepest despondency. At last, finding that it was a false alarm, we return once more to our beds; but what good can the kind of sleep of Nature do to us when interrupted by such scenes! Securely placed as you are, you can have no idea of our agitations, but by hearsay; no relation can be equal to what we suffer and to what we feel. Every morning my youngest children are sure to have frightful dreams to relate; in vain I exert my authority to keep them silent; it is not in my power; and these images of their disturbed imagination, instead of being frivolously looked upon as in the days of our happiness, are on the contrary considered as warnings and sure prognostics of our future fate. I am not a superstitious man, but since our misfortunes, I am grown more timid and less disposed to treat the doctrine of omens with contempt.

Though these evils have been gradual, yet they do not become habitual like other incidental evils. The nearer I view the end of this catastrophe, the more I shudder. But why should I trouble you with such unconnected accounts; men secure and out of danger are soon fatigued with mournful details: can you enter with me into fellowship with all these afflictive sensations; have you a tear ready to shed over the approaching ruin of a once opulent and substantial family? Read this, I pray, with the eyes of sympathy, with a tender sorrow; pity the lot of those whom you once called your friends, who were once surrounded with plenty, ease, and perfect security, but who now expect every night to be their last, and who are as wretched as criminals under an impending sentence of the law.

As a member of a large society which extends to many parts of the world, my connexion with it is too distant to be as strong as that which binds me to the inferior division in the midst of which I live. I am told that the great nation of which we are a part is just, wise, and free beyond any other on earth, within its own insular boundaries, but not always so to its distant conquests; I shall not repeat all I have heard because I cannot believe half of it. As a citizen of a smaller society, I find that any kind of opposition to its now prevailing sentiments immediately begets hatred; how easily do men pass from loving to hating and cursing one another! I am a lover of peace; what must I do? I am divided between the respect I feel for the ancient connexion and the fear of innovations, with the consequence of which I am not well acquainted, as they are embraced by my own countrymen. I am conscious that I was happy before this unfortunate revolution. I feel that I am no longer so; therefore I regret the change. This is the only mode of reasoning adapted to persons in my situation. If I attach myself to the mother country, which is 3,000 miles from me, I become what is called an enemy to my own region; if I follow the rest of my countrymen, I become opposed to our ancient masters: both extremes appear equally dangerous to a person of so little weight and consequence as I am, whose energy and example are of no avail. As to the argument on which the dispute is founded, I know little about it. Much has been said and written on both sides, but who has a judgement capacious and clear enough to decide? The great moving principles which actuate both parties are much hid from vulgar eyes, like mine; nothing but the plausible and the probable are offered to our contemplation. The innocent class are always the victims of the few; they are in all countries and at all times the inferior agents on which the popular phantom is erected; they clamour and must toil and bleed, and are always sure of meeting with oppression and rebuke. It is for the sake of the great leaders on both sides that so much blood must be spilt; that of the people is counted as nothing. Great events are not achieved for us, though it is *by* us that they are principally accomplished, by the arms, the sweat, the lives of the people. Books tell me so much that they inform me of nothing. Sophistry, the bane of freemen, launches forth in all her deceiving attire! After all, most men reason from passions; and shall such an ignorant individual as I am decide and say this side is right, that side is wrong? Sentiment and feeling are the only guides I know. Alas, how should I unravel an argument in which Reason herself has given way to brutality and bloodshed! What then must I do? I ask the wisest lawyers, the ablest casuists, the warmest patriots; for I mean honestly. Great Source of wisdom! Inspire me with light sufficient to guide my benighted steps out of this intricate maze! Shall I discard all my ancient principles, shall I renounce that name, that nation which I held once so respectable? I feel the powerful attraction; the sentiments they inspired grew with my earliest knowledge and were grafted upon the first rudiments of my education. On the other hand, shall I arm myself against that country where I first drew breath, against the playmates of my youth, my bosom friends, my acquaintance? The idea makes me shudder! Must I be called a parricide, a traitor, a villain, lose the esteem of all those whom I love to preserve my own, be shunned like a rattlesnake, or be pointed at like a bear? I have neither heroism not magnanimity enough to make so great a sacrifice. Here I am tied, I am fastened by numerous strings, nor do I repine at the pressure they cause; ignorant as I am, I can pervade the utmost extent of the calamities which have already overtaken our poor afflicted country. I can see the great and accumulated ruin yet extending itself as far as the theatre of war has reached; I hear the groans of thousands of families now ruined and desolated by our aggressors. I cannot count the multitude of orphans this war has made nor ascertain the immensity of blood we have lost. Some have asked whether it was a crime to resist, to repel some parts of this evil. Others have asserted that a resistance so general makes pardon unattainable and repentance useless, and dividing the crime among so many renders it imperceptible. What one party calls meritorious, the other denominates flagitious. These opinions vary, contract, or expand, like the events of the war on which they are founded. What can an insignificant man do in the midst of these jarring contradictory parties, equally hostile to persons situated as I am? And after all, who will be the really guilty? Those most certainly who fail of success. Our fate, the fate of thousands, is, then, necessarily involved in the dark wheel of fortune. Why, then, so many useless reasonings; we are the sport of fate. Farewell education, principles, love of our country, farewell; all are become useless to the generality of us: he who governs himself according to what he calls his principles may be punished either by one party or the other for those very principles. He who proceeds without principle, as chance, timidity, or self-preservation directs, will not perhaps fare better, but he will be less blamed. What are *we* in the great scale of events, we poor defenceless frontier inhabitants? What is it to the gazing world whether we breathe or whether we die? Whatever virtue, whatever merit and disinterestedness we may exhibit in our secluded retreats, of what avail? We are like the pismires destroyed by the plough, whose destruction prevents not the future crop. Self-preservation, therefore, the rule of Nature, seems to be the best rule of conduct; what good can we do by vain resistance, by useless efforts? The cool, the distant spectator, placed in safety, may arraign me for ingratitude, may bring forth the principles of Solon or Montesquieu;[24] he may look on me as wilfully guilty; he may call me by the most opprobrious names. Secure from personal danger, his warm imagination, undisturbed by the least agitation of the heart, will expatiate freely on this grand question and will consider this extended field but as exhibiting the double scene of attack and defence. To him the object becomes abstracted; the intermediate glares; the perspective distance and a variety of opinions, unimpaired by affections, present to his mind but one set of ideas. Here he proclaims the high guilt of the one, and there the right of the other. But let him come and reside with

[24]Solon (638?–559? B.C.), a statesman and poet of ancient Athens; Montesquieu (1689–1755), an eighteenth-century French lawyer and philosopher, author of *The Spirit of the Laws.*

us one single month; let him pass with us through all the successive hours of necessary toil, terror, and affright; let him watch with us, his musket in his hand, through tedious, sleepless nights, his imagination furrowed by the keen chisel of every passion; let his wife and his children become exposed to the most dreadful hazards of death; let the existence of his property depend on a single spark, blown by the breath of an enemy; let him tremble with us in our fields, shudder at the rustling of every leaf; let his heart, the seat of the most affecting passions, be powerfully wrung by hearing the melancholy end of his relations and friends; let him trace on the map the progress of these desolations; let his alarmed imagination predict to him the night, the dreadful night when it may be his turn to perish, as so many have perished before. Observe, then, whether the man will not get the better of the citizen, whether his political maxims will not vanish! Yes, he will cease to glow so warmly with the glory of the metropolis; all his wishes will be turned toward the preservation of his family! Oh, were he situated where I am, were his house perpetually filled, as mine is, with miserable victims just escaped from the flames and the scalping knife, telling of barbarities and murders that make human nature tremble, his situation would suspend every political reflection and expel every abstract idea. My heart is full and involuntarily takes hold of any notion from whence it can receive ideal ease or relief. I am informed that the king has the most numerous, as well as the fairest, progeny of children of any potentate now in the world; he may be a great king, but he must feel as we common mortals do in the good wishes he forms for their lives and prosperity. His mind no doubt often springs forward on the wings of anticipation and contemplates us as happily settled in the world. If a poor frontier inhabitant may be allowed to suppose this great personage the first in our system to be exposed but for one hour to the exquisite pangs we so often feel, would not the preservation of so numerous a family engross all his thoughts; would not the ideas of dominion and other felicities attendant on royalty all vanish in the hour of danger? The regal character, however sacred, would be superseded by the stronger, because more natural one of man and father. Oh! Did he but know the circumstances of this horrid war, I am sure he would put a stop to that long destruction of parents and children. I am sure that while he turned his ears to state policy, he would attentively listen also to the dictates of Nature, that great parent; for, as a good king, he no doubt wishes to create, to spare, and to protect, as she does. Must I then, in order to be called a faithful subject, coolly and philosophically say it is necessary for the good of Britain that my children's brains should be dashed against the walls of the house in which they were reared; that my wife should be stabbed and scalped before my face; that I should be either murthered or captivated; or that for greater expedition we should all be locked up and burnt to ashes as the family of the B——n was? Must I with meekness wait for that last pitch of desolation and receive with perfect resignation so hard a fate from ruffians acting at such a distance from the eyes of any superior, monsters left to the wild impulses of the wildest nature? Could the lions of Africa be transported here and let loose, they would no doubt kill us in order to prey upon our carcasses! But their appetites would not require so many victims. Shall I wait to be punished with death, or else to be stripped of all food and raiment, reduced to despair without redress and without hope? Shall those who may escape see everything they hold dear destroyed and gone? Shall those few survivors, lurking in some obscure corner, deplore in vain the fate of their families, mourn over parents either captivated, butchered, or burnt; roam among our wilds and wait for death at the foot of some tree, without a murmur or without a sigh, for the good of the cause? No, it is impossible! So astonishing a sacrifice is not be to expected from human nature; it must belong to beings of an inferior or superior order, actuated by less or by more refined principles. Even those great personages who are so far elevated above the common ranks of men, those, I mean, who wield and direct so many thunders, those who have let loose against us these demons of war, could they be transported here and metamorphosed into simple planters as we are—they would, from being the arbiters of human destiny, sink into miserable victims; they would feel and exclaim as we do, and be as much at a loss what line of conduct to prosecute. Do you well comprehend the difficulties of our situation? If we stay we are sure to perish at one time or another; no vigilance on our part can save us; if we retire, we know not where to go; every house is filled with refugees as wretched as ourselves; and if we remove, we become beggars. The property of farmers is not like that of merchants, and absolute poverty is worse than death. If we take up arms to defend ourselves, we are denominated rebels; should we not be rebels against Nature, could we be shamefully passive? Shall we, then, like martyrs, glory in an allegiance now become useless, and voluntarily expose ourselves to a species of desolation which, though it ruin us entirely, yet enriches not our ancient masters. By this inflexible and sullen attachment, we shall be despised by our countrymen and destroyed by our ancient friends; whatever we may say, whatever merit we may claim, will not shelter us from those indiscriminate blows, given by hired banditti, animated by all those passions which urge men to shed the blood of others; how bitter the thought! On the contrary, blows received by the hands of those from whom we expected protection extinguish ancient respect and urge us to self defence—perhaps to revenge; this is the path which Nature herself points out, as well to the civilized as to the uncivilized. The Creator of hearts has himself stamped on them those propensities at their first formation; and must we then daily receive this treatment from a power once so loved? The fox flies or deceives the hounds that pursue him; the bear, when overtaken, boldly resists and attacks them; the hen, the very timid hen, fights for the preservation of her chicken, nor does she decline to attack and to meet on the wing even the swift kite. Shall man, then, provided both with instinct and reason, unmoved, unconcerned, and passive see his subsistence consumed and his progeny either ravished from him or murdered? Shall fictitious reason extinguish the unerring impulse of instinct? No; my former respect, my former attachment, vanishes with my safety; that respect and attachment were purchased by protection, and it has ceased. Could not the great nation we belong to have accomplished her designs by means of her numerous armies, by means of those fleets which cover the ocean? Must those who are masters of two thirds of the trade of the world, who have in their hands the power which almighty gold can give, who possess a species of wealth that increases with their desires—must they establish their conquest with our insignificant, innocent blood!

Must I, then, bid farewell to Britain, to that renowned country? Must I renounce a name so ancient and so venerable? Alas, she herself, that once indulgent parent, forces me to take up arms against her. She herself first inspired the most unhappy citizens of our remote districts with the thoughts of shedding the blood of those whom they used to call by the name of friends and brethren. That great nation which now convulses the world, which hardly knows the extent of her Indian kingdoms, which looks toward the universal monarchy of trade, of industry, of riches, of power: why must she strew our poor frontiers with the carcasses of her friends, with the wrecks of our insignificant villages, in which there is no gold? When, oppressed by painful recollection, I revolve all these scattered ideas in my mind, when I contemplate my situation and the thousand streams of evil with which I am surrounded, when I descend into the particular tendency even of the remedy I have proposed, I am convulsed—convulsed sometimes to that degree as to be tempted to exclaim, "Why has the Master of the world permitted so much indiscriminate evil throughout every part of this poor planet, at all times, and among all kinds of people?" It ought surely to be the punishment of the wicked only. I bring that cup to my lips, of which I must soon taste, and shudder at its bitterness. What, then, is life, I ask myself; is it a gracious gift? No, it is too bitter; a gift means something valuable conferred, but life appears to be a mere accident, and of the worst kind: we are born to be victims of diseases and passions, of mischances and death; better not to be than to be miserable. Thus, impiously I roam, I fly from one erratic thought to another, and my mind, irritated by these acrimonious reflections, is ready sometimes to lead me to dangerous extremes of violence. When I recollect that I am a father and a husband, the return of these endearing ideas strikes deep into my heart. Alas! They once made it glow with pleasure and with every ravishing exultation; but now they fill it with sorrow. At other times, my wife industriously rouses me out of these dreadful meditations and soothes me by all the reasoning she is mistress of; but her endeavours only serve to make me more miserable by reflecting that she must share with me all these calamities the bare apprehensions of which I am afraid will subvert her reason. Nor can I with patience think that a beloved wife, my faithful helpmate, throughout all my rural schemes the principal hand which has assisted me in rearing the prosperous fabric of ease and independence I lately possessed, as well as my children, those tenants of my heart, should daily and nightly be exposed to such a cruel fate. Self-preservation is above all political precepts and rules, and even superior to the dearest opinions of our minds; a reasonable accommodation of ourselves to the various exigencies of the times in which we live is the most irresistible precept. To this great evil I must seek some sort of remedy adapted to remove or to palliate it; situated as I am, what steps should I take that will neither injure nor insult any of the parties, and at the same time save my family from that certain destruction which awaits it if I remain here much longer. Could I ensure them bread, safety, and subsistence, not the bread of idleness, but that earned by proper labour as heretofore; could this be accomplished by the sacrifice of my life, I would willingly give it up. I attest before heaven that it is only for these I would wish to live and toil, for these whom I have brought into this miserable existence. I resemble, methinks, one of the stones of a ruined arch, still retaining that pristine form which anciently fitted the place I occupied, but the centre is tumbled down; I can be nothing until I am replaced, either in the former circle or in some stronger one. I see one on a smaller scale, and at a considerable distance, but it is within my power to reach it; and since I have ceased to consider myself as a member of the ancient state now convulsed, I willingly descend into an inferior one. I will revert into a state approaching nearer to that of nature, unencumbered either with voluminous laws or contradictory codes, often galling the very necks of those whom they protect, and at the same time sufficiently remote from the brutality of unconnected savage nature. Do you, my friend, perceive the path I have found out? It is that which leads to the tenants of the great —— village of ——, where, far removed from the accursed neighbourhood of Europeans, its inhabitants live with more ease, decency, and peace than you imagine; who, though governed by no laws, yet find in uncontaminated simple manners all that laws can afford. Their system is sufficiently complete to answer all the primary wants of man and to constitute him a social being such as he ought to be in the great forest of Nature. There it is that I have resolved at any rate to transport myself and family: an eccentric thought, you may say, thus to cut asunder all former connexions and to form new ones with a people whom Nature has stamped with such different characteristics! But as the happiness of my family is the only object of my wishes, I care very little where we are or where we go, provided that we are safe and all united together. . . .

Yes, I will cheerfully embrace that resource; it is a holy inspiration; by night and by day, it presents itself to my mind; I have carefully revolved the scheme; I have considered in all its future effects and tendencies the new mode of living we must pursue, without salt, without spices, without linen, and with little other clothing; the art of hunting we must acquire, the new manners we must adopt, the new language we must speak; the dangers attending the education of my children we must endure. These changes may appear more terrific at a distance perhaps than when grown familiar by practice; what is it to us whether we eat well-made pastry or pounded álagrichés,[25] well-roasted beef or smoked venison, cabbages or squashes? Whether we wear neat homespun or good beaver, whether we sleep on feather-beds or on bearskins? The difference is not worth attending to. The difficulty of the language, the fear of some great intoxication among the Indians, finally the apprehension lest my younger children should be caught by that singular charm, so dangerous at their tender years, are the only considerations that startle me. By what power does it come to pass that children who have been adopted when young among these people can never be prevailed on to readopt European manners? Many an anxious parent have I seen last war who at the return of the peace went to the Indian villages where they knew their children had been carried in captivity, when to their inexpressible sorrow they found them so perfectly Indianized that many knew them no longer, and those whose more advanced ages permitted them to recollect their fathers and mothers absolutely refused to follow them and ran to their adoptive parents for protection against the effusions of love their unhappy real parents lavished on them! Incredible as this may appear, I have heard it asserted in a thousand instances, among persons of credit. In the village of ——, where I purpose to go, there lived, about fifteen years ago, an Englishman and a Swede, whose history would appear moving had I time to relate it. They were grown to the age of men when they were taken; they happily escaped the great punishment of war captives and were obliged to marry the squaws who had saved their lives by adoption. By the force of habit, they became at last thoroughly naturalized to this wild course of life. While I was there, their friends sent them a considerable sum of money to ransom themselves with. The Indians, their old masters, gave them their choice, and without requiring any consideration, told them that they had been long as free as themselves. They chose to remain, and the reasons

[25] Corn kernels used in making a kind of mush.

they gave me would greatly surprise you: the most perfect freedom, the ease of living, the absence of those cares and corroding solicitudes which so often prevail with us, the peculiar goodness of the soil they cultivated, for they did not trust altogether to hunting—all these and many more motives which I have forgot made them prefer that life of which we entertain such dreadful opinions. It cannot be, therefore, so bad as we generally conceive it to be; there must be in their social bond something singularly captivating and far superior to anything to be boasted of among us; for thousands of Europeans are Indians, and we have no examples of even one of those aborigines having from choice become Europeans! There must be something more congenial to our native dispositions than the fictitious society in which we live; or else why should children, and even grown persons, become in a short time so invincibly attached to it? There must be something very bewitching in their manners, something very indelible and marked by the very hands of Nature. For, take a young Indian lad, give him the best education you possibly can, load him with your bounty, with presents, nay with riches, yet he would secretly long for his native woods, which you would imagine he must have long since forgot; and on the first opportunity he can possibly find, you will see him voluntarily leave behind all you have given him and return with inexpressible joy to lie on the mats of his fathers. Mr. —— some years ago received from a good old Indian, who died in his house, a young lad of nine years of age, his grandson. He kindly educated him with his children and bestowed on him the same care and attention in respect to the memory of his venerable grandfather, who was a worthy man. He intended to give him a genteel trade, but in the spring season when all the family went to the woods to make their maple sugar, he suddenly disappeared, and it was not until seventeen months after that his benefactor heard he had reached the village of Bald Eagle, where he still dwelt. Let us say what we will of them, of their inferior organs, of their want of bread, etc., they are as stout and well made as the Europeans. Without temples, without priests, without kings, and without laws, they are in many instances superior to us; and the proofs of what I advance are that they live without care, sleep without inquietude, take life as it comes, bearing all its asperities with unparalleled patience, and die without any kind of apprehension for what they have done or for what they expect to meet with hereafter. What system of philosophy can give us so many necessary qualifications for happiness? They most certainly are much more closely connected with Nature than we are; they are her immediate children: the inhabitants of the woods are her undefiled offspring; those of the plains are her degenerated breed, far, very far removed from her primitive laws, from her original design. It is therefore resolved on. I will either die in the attempt or succeed; better perish all together in one fatal hour than to suffer what we daily endure. I do not expect to enjoy in the village of —— an uninterrupted happiness; it cannot be our lot, let us live where we will; I am not founding my future prosperity on golden dreams. Place mankind where you will, they must always have adverse circumstances to struggle with; from nature, accidents, constitution; from seasons, from that great combination of mischances which perpetually leads us to diseases, to poverty, etc. Who knows but I may meet in this new situation some accident whence may spring up new sources of unexpected prosperity? Who can be presumptuous enough to predict all the good? Who can foresee all the evils which strew the paths of our lives? But after all, I cannot but recollect what sacrifice I am going to make, what amputation I am going to suffer, what transition I am going to experience. Pardon my repetitions, my wild, my trifling reflections; they proceed from the agitations of my mind and the fulness of my heart; the action of thus retracing them seems to lighten the burthen and to exhilarate my spirits; this is, besides, the last letter you will receive from me; I would fain tell you all, though I hardly know how. Oh! In the hours, in the moments of my greatest anguish, could I intuitively represent to you that variety of thought which crowds on my mind, you would have reason to be surprised and to doubt of their possibility. Shall we ever meet again? If we should, where will it be? On the wild shores of ——. If it be my doom to end my days there, I will greatly improve them and perhaps make room for a few more families who will choose to retire from the fury of a storm, the agitated billows of which will yet roar for many years on our extended shores. Perhaps I may repossess my house, if it be not burnt down; but how will my improvements look? Why, half defaced, bearing the strong marks of abandonment and of the ravages of war. However, at present I give everything over for lost; I will bid a long farewell to what I leave behind. If ever I repossess it, I shall receive it as a gift, as a reward for my conduct and fortitude. Do not imagine, however, that I am a stoic—by no means I must, on the contrary, confess to you that I feel the keenest regret at abandoning a house which I have in some measure reared with my own hands. Yes, perhaps I may never revisit those fields which I have cleared, those trees which I have planted, those meadows which, in my youth were a hideous wilderness, now converted by my industry into rich pastures and pleasant lawns. If in Europe it is praiseworthy to be attached to paternal inheritances, how much more natural, how much more powerful must the tie be with us, who, if I may be permitted the expression, are the founders, the creators, of our own farms! When I see my table surrounded with my blooming offspring, all united in the bonds of the strongest affection, it kindles in my paternal heart a variety of tumultuous sentiments which none but a father and a husband in my situation can feel or describe. Perhaps I may see my wife, my children, often distressed, involuntarily recalling to their minds the ease and abundance which they enjoyed under the paternal roof. Perhaps I may see them want that bread which I now leave behind, overtaken by diseases and penury, rendered more bitter by the recollection of former days of opulence and plenty. Perhaps I may be assailed on every side by unforeseen accidents which I shall not be able to prevent or to alleviate. Can I contemplate such images without the most unutterable emotions? My fate is determined; but I have not determined it, you may assure yourself, without having undergone the most painful conflicts of a variety of passions—interest, love of ease, disappointed views, and pleasing expectations frustrated—I shuddered at the review. Would to God I was master of the stoical tranquillity of that magnanimous sect; oh, that I were possessed of those sublime lessons which Appollonius of Chalcis gave to the Emperor Antoninus! I could then with much more propriety guide the helm of my little bark, which is soon to be freighted with all that I possess most dear on earth, through this stormy passage to a safe harbour, and when there, become to my fellow-passengers a surer guide, a brighter example, a pattern more worthy of imitation, throughout all the new scenes they must pass and the new career they must traverse. I have observed, notwithstanding, the means hitherto made use of to arm the principal nations against our frontiers. Yet they have not, they will not take up the hatchet against a people who have done them no harm. The passions necessary to urge these people to war cannot be roused; they cannot feel the stings of vengeance, the thirst of which alone can impel them to shed blood: far superior in their motives of action to the Europeans who, for sixpence per day, may be engaged to shed that of any people on earth. They know nothing of the nature of our disputes; they have no ideas of such revolutions as this; a civil division of a village or tribe are events which have never been recorded in their traditions; many of them know very well that they have too long been the dupes and the victims of both parties, foolishly arming for our sakes, sometimes against each other, sometimes against our white enemies. They consider us as born on the same land, and, though they have no reasons to love us, yet they seem carefully to avoid entering into this quarrel, from whatever motives. I am speaking of those nations with which I am best acquainted; a few hundreds of the worst kind mixed with whites worse than themselves are now hired by Great Britain to perpetuate those dreadful incursions. In my youth I traded with the ——, under the conduct of my uncle, and always traded justly and equitably; some of them remember it to this day. Happily their village is far removed from the dangerous neighbourhood of the whites; I sent a man last spring to it who understands the woods extremely well and who speaks their language; he is just returned, after several weeks' absence, and has brought me, as I had flattered myself, a string of thirty purple wampum[26] as a token that their honest chief will spare us half of his wigwam until we have time to erect one. He has sent me word that they have land in plenty, of which they are not so covetous as the whites; that we may plant for ourselves, and that in the meantime he will procure us some corn and meat; that fish is plenty in the waters of ——, and that the village to which he had laid open my proposals have no objection to our becoming dwellers with them. I have not yet communicated these glad tidings to my wife, nor do I know how to do it; I tremble lest she should refuse to follow me, lest the sudden idea of this removal rushing on her mind might be too powerful. I flatter myself I shall be able to accomplish it and to prevail on her; I fear nothing but the effects of her strong attachment to her relations. I would willingly let you know how I purpose to remove my family to so great a distance, but it would become unintelligible to you because you are not acquainted with the geographical situation of this part of the country. Suffice it for you to know that with about twenty-three miles land carriage, I am enabled to perform the rest by water; and when once afloat, I care not whether it be two or three hundred miles. I propose to send all our provisions, furniture, and clothes to my wife's father, who approves of the scheme, and to reserve nothing but a few necessary articles of covering, trusting to the furs of the chase for our future apparel. Were we imprudently to encumber ourselves too much with baggage, we should never reach to the waters of ——, which is the most dangerous as well as the most difficult part of our journey, and yet but a trifle in point of distance. I intend to say to my Negroes, "In the name of God, be free, my honest lads; I thank you for your past services; go, from henceforth, and work for yourselves; look on me as your old friend and fellow-labourer; be sober, frugal, and industrious, and you need not fear earning a comfortable subsistence." Lest my countrymen should think that I am gone to join the incendiaries of our frontiers, I intend to write a letter to Mr. —— to inform him of our retreat and of the reasons that have urged me to it. The man whom I sent to —— village is to accompany us also, and a very useful companion he will be on every account.

[26]Shells used as money and ornament.

You may therefore, by means of anticipation, behold me under the wigwam; I am so well acquainted with the principal manners of these people that I entertain not the least apprehension from them. I rely more securely on their strong hospitality than on the witnessed compacts of many Europeans. As soon as possible after my arrival, I design to build myself a wigwam, after the same manner and size with the rest in order to avoid being thought singular or giving occasion for any railleries, though these people are seldom guilty of such European follies. I shall erect it hard by the lands which they propose to allot me, and will endeavour that my wife, my children, and myself may be adopted soon after our arrival. Thus becoming truly inhabitants of their village, we shall immediately occupy that rank within the pale of their society, which will afford us all the amends we can possibly expect for the loss we have met with by the convulsions of our own. According to their customs, we shall likewise receive names from them, by which we shall always be known. My youngest children shall learn to swim and to shoot with the bow, that they may acquire such talents as will necessarily raise them into some degree of esteem among the Indian lads of their own age; the rest of us must hunt with the hunter. I have been for several years an expert marksman; but I dread lest the imperceptible charm of Indian education may seize my younger children and give them such a propensity to that mode of life as may preclude their returning to the manners and customs of their parents. I have but one remedy to prevent this great evil, and that is to employ them in the labour of the fields as much as I can; I have even resolved to make their daily subsistence depend altogether on it. As long as we keep ourselves busy in tilling the earth, there is no fear of any of us becoming wild; it is the chase and the food it procures that have this strange effect. Excuse a simile—those hogs which range in the woods, and to whom grain is given once a week, preserve their former degree of tameness, but if, on the contrary, they are reduced to live on ground nuts and on what they can get, they soon become wild and fierce. For my part, I can plough, sow, and hunt as occasion may require; but my wife, deprived of wool and flax, will have no room for industry; what is she then to do? Like the other squaws, she must cook for us the nasaump, the ninchickè,[27] and such other preparations of corn as are customary among these people. She must learn to bake squashes and pompions under the ashes, to slice and smoke the meat of our own killing in order to preserve it; she must cheerfully adopt the manners and customs of her neighbours, in their dress, deportment, conduct, and internal economy, in all respects. Surely if we can have fortitude enough to quit all we have, to remove so far, and to associate with people so different from us, these necessary compliances are but subordinate parts of the scheme. The change of garments, when those they carry with them are worn out, will not be the least of my wife's and daughter's concerns, though I am in hopes that self-love will invent some sort of reparation. Perhaps you would not believe that there are in the woods looking-glasses and paint of every colour; and that the inhabitants take as much pains to adorn their faces and their bodies, to fix their bracelets of silver, and plait their hair as our forefathers the Picts[28] used to do in the time of the Romans. Not that I would wish to see either my wife or daughter adopt those savage

[27]Types of corn porridge.
[28]Non-Celtic peoples who inhabited ancient Great Britain.

customs; we can live in great peace and harmony with them without descending to every article; the interruption of trade hath, I hope, suspended this mode of dress. My wife understands inoculation perfectly well; she inoculated all our children one after another and has successfully performed the operation on several scores of people, who, scattered here and there through our woods, were too far removed from all medical assistance. If we can persuade but one family to submit to it, and it succeeds, we shall then be as happy as our situation will admit of; it will raise her into some degree of consideration, for whoever is useful in any society will always be respected. If we are so fortunate as to carry one family through a disorder, which is the plague among these people, I trust to the force of example we shall then become truly necessary, valued, and beloved; we indeed owe every kind office to a society of men who so readily offer to admit us into their social partnership and to extend to my family the shelter of their village, the strength of their adoption, and even the dignity of their names. God grant us a prosperous beginning; we may then hope to be of more service to them than even missionaries who have been sent to preach to them a Gospel they cannot understand.

As to religion, our mode of worship will not suffer much by this removal from a cultivated country into the bosom of the woods; for it cannot be much simpler than that which we have followed here these many years, and I will with as much care as I can redouble my attention and twice a week retrace to them the great outlines of their duty to God and to man. I will read and expound to them some part of the decalogue, which is the method I have pursued ever since I married.

Half a dozen of acres on the shores of ——, the soil of which I know well, will yield us a great abundance of all we want; I will make it a point to give the overplus to such Indians as shall be most unfortunate in their huntings; I will persuade them, if I can, to till a little more land than they do and not to trust so much to the produce of the chase. To encourage them still farther, I will give a quirn[29] to every six families; I have built many for our poor back-settlers, it being often the want of mills which prevents them from raising grain. As I am a carpenter, I can build my own plough and can be of great service to many of them; my example alone may rouse the industry of some and serve to direct others in their labours. The difficulties of the language will soon be removed; in my evening conversations, I will endeavour to make them regulate the trade of their village in such a manner as that those pests of the continent, those Indian-traders, may not come within a certain distance; and there they shall be obliged to transact their business before the old people. I am in hopes that the constant respect which is paid to the elders, and shame, may prevent the young hunters from infringing this regulation. The son of —— will soon be made acquainted with our schemes, and I trust that the power of love and the strong attachment he professes for my daughter may bring him along with us; he will make an excellent hunter; young and vigorous, he will equal in dexterity the stoutest man in the village. Had it not been for this fortunate circumstance, there would have been the greatest danger; for however I respect the simple, the inoffensive society of these people in their villages, the strongest prejudices would make me abhor any alliance with them in blood, disagreeable no doubt to Nature's intentions, which have

[29]Corn mill.

strongly divided us by so many indelible characters. In the days of our sickness, we shall have recourse to their medical knowledge, which is well calculated for the simple diseases to which they are subject. Thus shall we metamorphose ourselves from neat, decent, opulent planters, surrounded with every conveniency which our external labour and internal industry could give, into a still simpler people divested of everything beside hope, food, and the raiment of the woods: abandoning the large framed house to dwell under the wigwam, and the featherbed to lie on the mat or bear's skin. There shall we sleep undisturbed by frightful dreams and apprehensions; rest and peace of mind will make us the most ample amends for what we shall leave behind. These blessings cannot be purchased too dear; too long have we been deprived of them. I would cheerfully go even to the Mississippi to find that repose to which we have been so long strangers. My heart sometimes seems tired with beating; it wants rest like my eyelids, which fell oppressed with so many watchings.

These are the component parts of my scheme, the success of each of which appears feasible, whence I flatter myself with the probable success of the whole. Still, the danger of Indian education returns to my mind and alarms me much; then again, I contrast it with the education of the times; both appear to be equally pregnant with evils. . . . Whatever success they may meet with in hunting or fishing shall be only considered as recreation and pastime; I shall thereby prevent them from estimating their skill in the chase as an important and necessary accomplishment. I mean to say to them: "You shall hunt and fish merely to show your new companions that you are not inferior to them in point of sagacity and dexterity." Were I to send them to such schools as the interior parts of our settlements afford at present, what can they learn there? How could I support them there? What must become of me; am I to proceed on my voyage and leave them? That I never could submit to. Instead of the perpetual discordant noise of disputes so common among us, instead of those scolding scenes, frequent in every house, they will observe nothing but silence at home and abroad: a singular appearance of peace and concord are the first characteristics which strike you in the villages of these people. Nothing can be more pleasing, nothing surprises an European so much, as the silence and harmony which prevail among them, and in each family, except when disturbed by that accursed spirit given them by the wood rangers in exchange for their furs. If my children learn nothing of geometrical rules, the use of the compass, or of the Latin tongue, they will learn and practise sobriety, for rum can no longer be sent to these people; they will learn that modesty and diffidence for which the young Indians are so remarkable; they will consider labour as the most essential qualification, hunting as the second. They will prepare themselves in the prosecution of our small rural schemes, carried on for the benefit of our little community, to extend them farther when each shall receive his inheritance. Their tender minds will cease to be agitated by perpetual alarms, to be made cowards by continual terrors; if they acquire in the village of —— such an awkwardness of deportment and appearance as would render them ridiculous in our gay capitals, they will imbibe, I hope, a confirmed taste for that simplicity which so well becomes the cultivators of the land. If I cannot teach them any of those professions which sometimes embellish and support our society, I will show them how to hew wood, how to construct their own ploughs, and with a few tools how to supply themselves with every necessary implement, both in the house and in the field. If they are hereafter obliged to confess that they belong to no one particular church, I shall have the consolation of teaching them that great, that primary worship which is the foundation of all others. If they do not fear God according to the tenets of any one seminary, they shall learn to worship Him upon the broad scale of nature. The Supreme Being does not reside in peculiar churches or communities, He is equally the great Manitou[30] of the woods and of the plains; and even in the gloom, the obscurity of those very woods, His justice may be as well understood and felt as in the most sumptuous temples. Each worship with us hath, you know, its peculiar political tendency; there it has none but to inspire gratitude and truth: their tender minds shall receive no other idea of the Supreme Being than that of the Father of all men, who requires nothing more of us than what tends to make each other happy. We shall say with them: "Soungwanèha, èsa caurounkyawga, nughwonshauza neattèwek, nèsalanga." Our Father, be thy will done in earth as it is in great heaven.

Perhaps my imagination gilds too strongly this distant prospect; yet it appears founded on so few and simple principles that there is not the same probability of adverse incidents as in more complex schemes. These vague rambling contemplations which I here faithfully retrace carry me sometimes to a great distance; I am lost in the anticipation of the various circumstances attending this proposed metamorphosis! Many unforeseen accidents may doubtless arise. Alas! It is easier for me in all the glow of paternal anxiety, reclined on my bed, to form the theory of my future conduct than to reduce my schemes into practice. But when once secluded from the great society to which we now belong, we shall unite closer together, and there will be less room for jealousies or contentions. As I intend my children neither for the law nor the church, but for the cultivation of the land, I wish them no literary accomplishments; I pray heaven that they may be one day nothing more than expert scholars in husbandry: this is the science which made our continent to flourish more rapidly than any other. Were they to grow up where I am now situated, even admitting that we were in safety; two of them are verging toward that period of their lives when they must necessarily take up the musket and learn, in that new school, all the vices which are so common in armies. Great God! Close my eyes forever rather than I should live to see this calamity! May they rather become inhabitants of the woods.

Thus then in the village of ——, in the bosom of that peace it has enjoyed ever since I have known it, connected with mild, hospitable people, strangers to *our* political disputes and having none among themselves; on the shores of a fine river, surrounded with woods, abounding with game, our little society, united in perfect harmony with the new adoptive one, in which we shall be incorporated, shall rest, I hope, from all fatigues, from all apprehensions, from our present terrors, and from our long watchings. Not a word of politics shall cloud our simple conversation; tired either with the chase or the labours of the field, we shall sleep on our mats without any distressing want, having learnt to retrench every superfluous one; we shall have but two prayers to make to the Supreme Being, that He may shed His fertilizing dew on our little crops and that He will be pleased to restore peace to our unhappy country. These shall be the only subject of our nightly prayers and of our daily ejaculations; and if the labour, the industry, the frugality, the union of men, can be an agreeable offering to Him, we shall not fail to receive His paternal blessings. . . .

[30]Algonkian "Great Spirit."

O Supreme Being! If among the immense variety of planets, inhabited by thy creative power, thy paternal and omnipotent care deigns to extend to all the individuals they contain, if it be not beneath thy infinite dignity to cast thy eye on us wretched mortals, if my future felicity is not contrary to the necessary effects of those secret causes which thou hast appointed, receive the supplications of a man to whom in thy kindness thou hast given a wife and an offspring; view us all with benignity, sanctify this strong conflict of regrets, wishes, and other natural passions; guide our steps through these unknown paths and bless our future mode of life. If it is good and well meant, it must proceed from thee; thou knowest, O Lord, our enterprise contains neither fraud nor malice nor revenge. Bestow on me that energy of conduct now become so necessary that it may be in my power to carry the young family thou hast given me through this great trial with safety and in thy peace. Inspire me with such intentions and such rules of conduct as may be most acceptable to thee. Preserve, O God, preserve the companion of my bosom, the best gift thou hast given me; endue her with courage and strength sufficient to accomplish this perilous journey. Bless the children of our love, those portions of our hearts; I implore thy divine assistance, speak to their tender minds and inspire them with the love of that virtue which alone can serve as the basis of their conduct in this world and of their happiness with thee. Restore peace and concord to our poor afflicted country; assuage the fierce storm which has so long ravaged it. Permit, I beseech thee, O Father of nature, that our ancient virtues and our industry may not be totally lost and that as a reward for the great toils we have made on this new land, we may be restored to our ancient tranquillity and enabled to fill it with successive generations that will constantly thank thee for the ample subsistence thou hast given them.

The unreserved manner in which I have written must give you a convincing proof of that friendship and esteem of which I am sure you never yet doubted. As members of the same society, as mutually bound by the ties of affection and old acquaintance, you certainly cannot avoid feeling for my distresses; you cannot avoid mourning with me over that load of physical and moral evil with which we are all oppressed. My own share of it I often overlook when I minutely contemplate all that hath befallen our native country.

1782

Thomas Paine 1737–1809

Thomas Paine was a renowned pro-American writer and author of some of the most persuasive texts of the American Revolution. In these texts, he used "plain" language in an attempt to engage people of all classes in the struggle for American independence and the rejection of government based on hereditary monarchy.

Born in 1737 in the English village of Thetford, Paine attended grammar school and apprenticed to his father's trade, becoming a master staymaker. He was unsatisfied with the life of a tradesman, however, and briefly went to sea but soon returned to England. In 1759, he opened his own staymaking business and married Mary

Lambert, a household servant. Mary died less than a year later. In 1762, Paine became a collector of excise taxes, was fired in 1765 for falsifying a report, but was eventually reinstated as a tax collector. In Lewes, Sussex, Paine lodged with the prominent Samuel Ollive family. When Ollive died in 1771, Paine married his daughter and took over Ollive's tobacco shop; but soon thereafter he again lost his position as collector, the tobacco shop failed, and in 1774 he separated from his wife. Paine resolved to start again, but this time in the colonies. During the years that Paine had resided in London and Lewes, he had attended several meetings of radical underground political movements. He had also attended scientific lectures in London, where he had become acquainted with the mathematician George Lewis Scott, who introduced him to Benjamin Franklin.

When Paine arrived in Philadelphia in 1774, he came with letters of introduction from Franklin. He resided in America for only thirteen years, returning to England in 1787, but his impact on the developing nation's political philosophy was immeasurable. As the son of a Quaker, Paine rejected hierarchies in church and state; and as a student of Newtonian science, he viewed the universe as governed by harmony, order, and natural laws. Paine brought these social and political philosophies to bear upon his experiences in America, where old local aristocracies (like those in Philadelphia) were being challenged by the rising artisan class. Paine used his extraordinary rhetorical powers to argue for American independence and to suggest the creation of a harmonious social order, with reason as its guiding influence.

At Franklin's recommendation, Paine became editor of the *Pennsylvania Magazine.* He would become best-known, however, for his major works on the rights of independence and studies of the era in which he lived; these included *Common Sense* (1776), the *Crisis* papers (beginning in December 1776 and ending in April 1783), *The Rights of Man* (1791–1792), and *The Age of Reason* (1794–1796). The increasing tensions between England and America—rooted in England's proclaiming the American colonies to be in a state of rebellion, and emerging in the battles at Lexington and Bunker Hill—led in May 1775 to the convening of the Second Continental Congress in Philadelphia.

On January 9, 1776, Paine published *Common Sense,* which argued for American independence from Great Britain and for a republican form of government as superior to hereditary monarchy. Its impact was extraordinary; an unprecedented twenty-five editions appeared in 1776 alone, and the text was circulated hand-to-hand and read to many others who could not read. Later in his life, Paine claimed that it had sold at least 150,000 copies. The text also represents an important rhetorical shift in political commentaries from an ideology rooted in religion to one centered in secular arguments. *Common Sense* was instrumental in spreading a national spirit that led, six months later, to the creation of the Declaration of Independence. Perhaps the greatest impact of *Common Sense* was its call for a halt to attempts at reconciliation and for an immediate separation from England, but Paine himself always asserted that his main purpose was to "bring forward and establish the representative system of government."

Paine enlisted and served as an aide-de-camp during several battles. It seems that his writings far exceeded any military contribution he might have made. In December 1776, after Washington had been defeated in New York and was retreating from New Jersey into Pennsylvania, Paine began publishing the *Crisis* papers. Fifteen more installments would appear over a seven-year period, but the rousing spirit of the opening lines of the first paper—"These are the times that try men's souls"—would remain a hallmark of revolutionary writings. Paine's literary accomplishments earned him a controversial salaried position from Congress that enabled him to continue writing propaganda to serve the colonial forces.

The last *Crisis* paper appeared in 1783, at the conclusion of the Revolution, and it marked a major transition in Paine's personal life. He was a man of sweeping ideas of political reform and of rhetorical powers, but he seems not to have been patient enough for the establishment of a new government of disparate peoples. In 1787 he returned to England with the intention of raising money to build an iron bridge. When this plan failed, he wrote his second extraordinarily successful work, *The Rights of Man* (1791–1792), intended as a response to Edmund Burke's *Reflections on the Revolution in France* (1790). Paine's argument in *The Rights of Man* against a hereditary monarchy resulted in a charge of sedition, forcing him to flee to France to avoid trial. In France, his second adopted country, his arguments garnered him not only citizenship and a seat in the National Assembly but renown as an advocate of revolution. His status was not long-lived, however. A protest against the execution of Louis XVI, which Paine deemed an act of barbarism rather than of the enlightenment that should result from revolution, led to his imprisonment for ten months as a sympathizer with royalty. The American ambassador James Madison eventually arranged for Paine's release on the grounds of his earlier citizenship in America.

Under Madison's aegis, Paine returned to New York City. He did not, however, regain the status he had acquired during the American Revolution, in large part because of his last major work, *The Age of Reason.* Part I of *The Age of Reason* was published in France; the manuscript was surreptitiously brought to the United States by Joel Barlow. *The Age of Reason* was intended as an exploration of the irrationality of religion and as an advocacy of deism. But in the years since Paine's departure from the colonies, the citizens of the new republic had become far more conservative. *The Age of Reason* was viewed by many Americans as an attack on Christianity and an assertion of atheism. In America and in England, from the pulpit and in newspapers, Thomas Paine was ridiculed and depicted as a threat to Christianity and to democracy.

Paine lived his last years in obscurity in New Rochelle, New York; he died in 1809. His contributions to American literature endure, however. Noted most for his "plain style," Paine insisted on the need to reach all classes of citizens, even those "who can scarcely read." As one of America's foremost pamphleteers, his writings were passionate in their demands for political reform based on republican values.

Sharon M. Harris
Texas Christian University

PRIMARY WORKS

The Writings of Thomas Paine, Moncure D. Conway, ed., 4 vols., 1894–1896.

from Common Sense

Thoughts on the Present State of American Affairs[1]

In the following pages I offer nothing more than simple facts, plain arguments, and common sense: and have no other preliminaries to settle with the reader, than that he will divest himself of prejudice and prepossession, and suffer his reason and his feelings to determine for themselves: that he will put on, or rather that he will not put off, the true character of a man, and generously enlarge his views beyond the present day.

Volumes have been written on the subject of the struggle between England and America. Men of all ranks have embarked in the controversy, from different motives, and with various designs; but all have been ineffectual, and the period of debate is closed. Arms as the last resource decide the contest; the appeal was the choice of the King, and the Continent has accepted the challenge.

It hath been reported of the late Mr. Pelham (who tho' an able minister was not without his faults)[2] that on his being attacked in the House of Commons on the score that his measures were only of a temporary kind, replied, *"they will last my time."* Should a thought so fatal and unmanly possess the Colonies in the present contest, the name of ancestors will be remembered by future generations with detestation.

The Sun never shined on a cause of greater worth. 'Tis not the affair of a City, a County, a Province, or a Kingdom; but of a Continent—of at least one eighth part of the habitable Globe. 'Tis not the concern of a day, a year, or an age: posterity are virtually involved in the contest, and will be more or less affected even to the end of time, by the proceedings now. Now is the seed-time of Continental union, faith and honour. The least fracture now will be like a name engraved with the point of a pin on the tender rind of a young oak; the wound would enlarge with the tree, and posterity read it in full grown characters.

By referring the matter from argument to arms, a new æra for politics is struck—a new method of thinking hath arisen. All plans, proposals, &c. prior to the nineteenth of April, *i.e.* to the commencement of hostilities,[3] are like the almanacks of the last year; which tho' proper then, are superceded and useless now. Whatever was advanced by the advocates on either side of the question then, terminated in one and the same point, viz. a union with Great Britain; the only difference between the parties was the method of effecting it; the one proposing force, the other friendship; but it hath so far happened that the first hath failed, and the second hath withdrawn her influence.

As much hath been said of the advantages of reconciliation, which, like an agreeable dream, hath passed away and left us as we were, it is but right that we should

[1]First published in 1776, the pamphlet carried this title: *Common Sense: Addressed to the Inhabitants of America, on the following Interesting Subjects: I. Of the Origin and Design of Government in General, with Concise Remarks on the English Constitution. II. Of Monarchy and Hereditary Succession. III. Thoughts on the Present State of American Affairs. IV. Of the Present Ability of America, with Some Miscellaneous Reflections.*

[2]Thomas Pelham (1693–1768), prime minister of England, 1743 to 1754.

[3]The Battle of Lexington, in Massachusetts, April 19, 1775.

examine the contrary side of the argument, and enquire into some of the many material injuries which these Colonies sustain, and always will sustain, by being connected with and dependant on Great-Britain. To examine that connection and dependance, on the principles of nature and common sense, to see what we have to trust to, if separated, and what we are to expect, if dependant.

I have heard it asserted by some, that as America has flourished under her former connection with Great-Britain, the same connection is necessary towards her future happiness, and will always have the same effect. Nothing can be more fallacious than this kind of argument. We may as well assert that because a child has thrived upon milk, that it is never to have meat, or that the first twenty years of our lives is to become a precedent for the next twenty. But even this is admitting more than is true; for I answer roundly, that America would have flourished as much, and probably much more, had no European power taken any notice of her. The commerce by which she hath enriched herself are the necessaries of life, and will always have a market while eating is the custom of Europe.

But she has protected us, say some. That she hath engrossed us is true, and defended the Continent at our expense as well as her own, is admitted; and she would have defended Turkey from the same motive, *viz.* for the sake of trade and dominion.

Alas! we have been long led away by ancient prejudices and made large sacrifices to superstition. We have boasted the protection of Great Britain, without considering, that her motive was *interest* not *attachment;* and that she did not protect us from *our enemies* on *our account;* but from *her enemies* on *her own account,* from those who had no quarrel with us on any *other account,* and who will always be our enemies on the *same account.* Let Britain waive her pretensions to the Continent, or the Continent throw off the dependance, and we should be at peace with France and Spain, were they at war with Britain. The miseries of Hanover last war ought to warn us against connections.[4]

It hath lately been asserted in parliament, that the Colonies have no relation to each other but through the Parent Country, *i.e.* that Pennsylvania and the Jerseys, and so on for the rest, are sister Colonies by the way of England; this is certainly a very roundabout way of proving relationship, but it is the nearest and only true way of proving enmity (or enemyship, if I may so call it.) France and Spain never were, nor perhaps ever will be, our enemies as *Americans,* but as our being the *subjects of Great Britain.*

But Britain is the parent country, say some. Then the more shame upon her conduct. Even brutes do not devour their young, nor savages make war upon their families; Wherefore, the assertion, if true, turns to her reproach; but it happens not to be true, or only partly so, and the phrase *parent* or *mother country* hath been jesuitically adopted by the King and his parasites, with a low papistical design of gaining an unfair bias on the credulous weakness of our minds. Europe, and not England, is the parent country of America. This new World hath been the asylum for the persecuted lovers of civil and religious liberty from *every part* of Europe. Hither have they fled, not from the tender embraces of the mother, but from the cruelty of the monster; and

[4]A kingdom that would become a province of Germany; the scene of heavy fighting during the Seven Years' War, particularly the campaigns of 1757. Also the royal house that occupied the British throne from 1714 to 1901.

it is so far true of England, that the same tyranny which drove the first emigrants from home, pursues their descendants still.

In this extensive quarter of the globe, we forget the narrow limits of three hundred and sixty miles (the extent of England) and carry our friendship on a larger scale; we claim brotherhood with every European Christian, and triumph in the generosity of the sentiment.

It is pleasant to observe by what regular gradations we surmount the force of local prejudices, as we enlarge our acquaintance with the World. A man born in any town in England divided into parishes, will naturally associate most with his fellow parishioners (because their interests in many cases will be common) and distinguish him by the name of *neighbour;* if he meet him but a few miles from home, he drops the narrow idea of a street, and salutes him by the nature of *townsman;* if he travel out of the county and meet him in any other, he forgets the minor divisions of street and town, and calls him *countryman, i. e. countyman:* but if in their foreign excursions they should associate in France, or any other part of *Europe,* their local remembrance would be enlarged into that of *Englishmen.* And by a just parity of reasoning, all Europeans meeting in America, or any other quarter of the globe, are *countrymen;* for England, Holland, Germany, or Sweden, when compared with the whole, stand in the same places on the larger scale, which the divisions of street, town, and county do on the smaller ones; Distinctions too limited for Continental minds. Not one third of the inhabitants, even of this province, [Pennsylvania], are of English descent. Wherefore, I reprobate the phrase of Parent or Mother Country applied to England only, as being false, selfish, narrow and ungenerous.

But, admitting that we were all of English descent, what does it amount to? Nothing. Britain, being now an open enemy, extinguishes every other name and title: and to say that reconciliation is our duty, is truly farcical. The first king of England, of the present line (William the Conqueror) was a Frenchman, and half the peers of England are descendants from the same country; wherefore, by the same method of reasoning, England ought to be governed by France.

Much hath been said of the united strength of Britain and the Colonies, that in conjunction they might bid defiance to the world: But this is mere presumption; the fate of war is uncertain, neither do the expressions mean any thing; for this continent would never suffer itself to be drained of inhabitants, to support the British arms in either Asia, Africa, or Europe.

Besides, what have we to do with setting the world at defiance? Our plan is commerce, and that, well attended to, will secure us the peace and friendship of all Europe; because it is the interest of all Europe to have America a free port. Her trade will always be a protection, and her barrenness of gold and silver secure her from invaders.

I challenge the warmest advocate for reconciliation to show a single advantage that this continent can reap by being connected with Great Britain. I repeat the challenge; not a single advantage is derived. Our corn will fetch its price in any market in Europe, and our imported goods must be paid for buy them where we will.

But the injuries and disadvantages which we sustain by that connection, are without number; and our duty to mankind at large, as well as to ourselves, instruct us to renounce the alliance: because, any submission to, or dependance on, Great Britain, tends directly to involve this Continent in European wars and quarrels, and set us at variance with nations who would otherwise seek our friendship, and against whom we have neither anger nor complaint. As Europe is our market for trade, we ought to form no partial connection with any part of it. It is the true interest of America to steer clear of European contentions, which she never can do, while, by her dependance on Britain, she is made the make-weight in the scale of British politics.

Europe is too thickly planted with Kingdoms to be long at peace, and whenever a war breaks out between England and any foreign power, the trade of America goes to ruin, *because of her connection with Britain.* The next war may not turn out like the last, and should it not, the advocates for reconciliation now will be wishing for separation then, because neutrality in that case would be a safer convoy than a man of war. Everything that is right or reasonable pleads for separation. The blood of the slain, the weeping voice of nature cries, 'TIS TIME TO PART. Even the distance at which the Almighty hath placed England and America is a strong and natural proof that the authority of the one over the other, was never the design of Heaven. The time likewise at which the Continent was discovered, adds weight to the argument, and the manner in which it was peopled, encreases the force of it. The Reformation was preceded by the discovery of America: As if the Almighty graciously meant to open a sanctuary to the persecuted in future years, when home should afford neither friendship nor safety.

The authority of Great Britain over this continent, is a form of government, which sooner or later must have an end: And a serious mind can draw no true pleasure by looking forward, under the painful and positive conviction that what he calls "the present constitution" is merely temporary. As parents, we can have no joy, knowing that this government is not sufficiently lasting to ensure any thing which we may bequeath to posterity: And by a plain method of argument, as we are running the next generation into debt, we ought to do the work of it, otherwise we use them meanly and pitifully. In order to discover the line of our duty rightly, we should take our children in our hand, and fix our station a few years farther into life; that eminence will present a prospect which a few present fears and prejudices conceal from our sight.

Though I would carefully avoid giving unnecessary offence, yet I am inclined to believe, that all those who espouse the doctrine of reconciliation, may be included within the following descriptions.

Interested men, who are not to be trusted, weak men who *cannot* see, prejudiced men who will not see, and a certain set of moderate men who think better of the European world than it deserves; and this last class, by an ill-judged deliberation, will be the cause of more calamities to this Continent than all the other three.

It is the good fortune of many to live distant from the scene of present sorrow; the evil is not sufficiently brought to their doors to make them feel the precariousness with which all American property is possessed. But let our imaginations transport us a few moments to Boston;[5] that seat of wretchedness will teach us wisdom, and instruct us for ever to renounce a power in whom we can have no trust. The inhabitants of that unfortunate city who but a few months ago were in ease and

[5]Under siege by the Americans from July 1775 to March 1776.

affluence, have now no other alternative than to stay and starve, or turn out to beg. Endangered by the fire of their friends if they continue within the city, and plundered by the soldiery if they leave it, in their present situation they are prisoners without the hope of redemption, and in a general attack for their relief they would be exposed to the fury of both armies.

Men of passive tempers look somewhat lightly over the offences of Great Britain, and, still hoping for the best, are apt to call out, *Come, come, we shall be friends again for all this.* But examine the passions and feelings of mankind: bring the doctrine of reconciliation to the touchstone of nature, and then tell me whether you can hereafter love, honour, and faithfully serve the power that hath carried fire and sword into your land? If you cannot do all these, then are you only deceiving yourselves, and by your delay bringing ruin upon posterity. Your future connection with Britain, whom you can neither love nor honour, will be forced and unnatural, and being formed only on the plan of present convenience, will in a little time fall into a relapse more wretched than the first. But if you say, you can still pass the violations over, then I ask, hath your house been burnt? Hath your property been destroyed before your face? Are your wife and children destitute of a bed to lie on, or bread to live on? Have you lost a parent or a child by their hands, and yourself the ruined and wretched survivor? If you have not, then are you not a judge of those who have. But if you have, and can still shake hands with the murderers, then are you unworthy the name of husband, father, friend, or lover, and whatever may be your rank or title in life, you have the heart of a coward, and the spirit of a sycophant.

This is not inflaming or exaggerating matters, but trying them by those feelings and affections which nature justifies, and without which we should be incapable of discharging the social duties of life, or enjoying the felicities of it. I mean not to exhibit horror for the purpose of provoking revenge, but to awaken us from fatal and unmanly slumbers, that we may pursue determinately some fixed object. 'Tis not in the power of Britain or of Europe to conquer America, if she doth not conquer herself by delay and timidity. The present winter is worth an age if rightly employed, but if lost or neglected the whole Continent will partake of the misfortune; and there is no punishment which that man doth not deserve, be he who, or what, or where he will, that may be the means of sacrificing a season so precious and useful.

'Tis repugnant to reason, to the universal order of things, to all examples from former ages, to suppose that this Continent can long remain subject to any external power. The most sanguine in Britain doth not think so. The utmost stretch of human wisdom cannot, at this time, compass a plan, short of separation, which can promise the continent even a year's security. Reconciliation is *now* a fallacious dream. Nature hath deserted the connection, and art cannot supply her place. For, as Milton wisely expresses, "never can true reconcilement grow where wounds of deadly hate have pierced so deep." . . .[6]

A government of our own is our natural right: and when a man seriously reflects on the precariousness of human affairs, he will become convinced, that it is infinitely wiser and safer, to form a constitution of our own in a cool deliberate manner, while we have it in our power, than to trust such an interesting event to time and chance.

[6]From *Paradise Lost,* IV, ll. 98–99.

If we omit it now, some Massanello[7] may hereafter arise, who, laying hold of popular disquietudes, may collect together the desperate and the discontented, and by assuming to themselves the powers of government, finally sweep away the liberties of the Continent like a deluge. Should the government of America return again into the hands of Britain, the tottering situation of things will be a temptation for some desperate adventurer to try his fortune; and in such a case, what relief can Britain give? Ere she could hear the news, the fatal business might be done; and ourselves suffering like the wretched Britons under the oppression of the Conqueror. Ye that oppose independance now, ye know not what ye do: ye are opening a door to eternal tyranny, by keeping vacant the seat of government. There are thousands and tens of thousands, who would think it glorious to expel from the Continent, that barbarous and hellish power, which hath stirred up the Indians and the Negroes to destroy us; the cruelty hath a double guilt, it is dealing brutally by us, and treacherously by them.

To talk of friendship with those in whom our reason forbids us to have faith, and our affections wounded thro' a thousand pores instruct us to detest, is madness and folly. Every day wears out the little remains of kindred between us and them; and can there be any reason to hope, that as the relationship expires, the affection will encrease, or that we shall agree better when we have ten times more and greater concerns to quarrel over than ever?

Ye that tell us of harmony and reconciliation, can ye restore to us the time that is past? Can ye give to prostitution its former innocence? neither can ye reconcile Britain and America. The last cord now is broken, the people of England are presenting addresses against us. There are injuries which nature cannot forgive; she would cease to be nature if she did. As well can the lover forgive the ravisher of his mistress, as the Continent forgive the murders of Britain. The Almighty hath implanted in us these unextinguishable feelings for good and wise purposes. They are the Guardians of his Image in our hearts. They distinguish us from the herd of common animals. The social compact would dissolve, and justice be extirpated from the earth, or have only a casual existence were we callous to the touches of affection. The robber and the murderer would often escape unpunished, did not the injuries which our tempers sustain, provoke us into justice.

O! ye that love mankind! Ye that dare oppose not only the tyranny but the tyrant, stand forth! Every spot of the old world is overrun with oppression. Freedom hath been hunted round the Globe. Asia and Africa have long expelled her. Europe regards her like a stranger, and England hath given her warning to depart. O! receive the fugitive, and prepare in time an asylum for mankind.

1776

[7]Thomas Anello, also called Massanello, a fisherman of Naples who aroused his countrymen against Spanish oppression, stirred them to revolt, and became king—all in one day.

from The American Crisis[1]

Number 1

These are the times that try men's souls. The summer soldier and the sunshine patriot will, in this crisis, shrink from the service of their country; but he that stands it *now,* deserves the love and thanks of man and woman. Tyranny, like hell, is not easily conquered; yet we have this consolation with us, that the harder the conflict, the more glorious the triumph. What we obtain too cheap, we esteem too lightly: it is dearness only that gives every thing its value. Heaven knows how to put a proper price upon its goods; and it would be strange indeed if so celestial an article as FREEDOM should not be highly rated. Britain, with an army to enforce her tyranny, has declared that she has a right (*not only to TAX*) but "to BIND *us in* ALL CASES WHATSOEVER,"[2] and if being *bound in that manner,* is not slavery, then is there not such a thing as slavery upon earth. Even the expression is impious; for so unlimited a power can belong only to God.

Whether the independence of the continent was declared too soon, or delayed too long, I will not now enter into as an argument; my own simple opinion is, that had it been eight months earlier, it would have been much better. We did not make a proper use of last winter, neither could we, while we were in a dependent state. However, the fault, if it were one, was all our own, we have none to blame but ourselves. But no great deal is lost yet. All that Howe[3] has been doing for this month past, is rather a ravage than a conquest, which the spirit of the Jerseys,[4] a year ago, would have quickly repulsed, and which time and a little resolution will soon recover.

I have as little superstition in me as any man living, but my secret opinion has ever been, and still is, that God Almighty will not give up a people to military destruction, or leave them unsupportedly to perish, who have so earnestly and so repeatedly sought to avoid the calamities of war, by every decent method which wisdom could invent. Neither have I so much of the infidel in me, as to suppose that He has relinquished the government of the world, and given us up to the care of devils; and as I do not, I cannot see on what grounds the king of Britain can look up to heaven for help against us: a common murderer, a highwayman, or a housebreaker, has as good a pretense as he.

'Tis surprising to see how rapidly a panic will sometimes run through a country. All nations and ages have been subject to them: Britain has trembled like an ague at the report of a French fleet of flat bottomed boats; and in the fourteenth century[5] the whole English army, after ravaging the kingdom of France, was driven back like men petrified with fear; and this brave exploit was performed by a few broken forces collected and headed by a woman, Joan of Arc. Would that heaven might inspire some

[1] *The American Crisis* was originally published in the *Pennsylvania Journal,* December 19, 1776.

[2] Paine quotes the Declaratory Act of Parliament (February 1766).

[3] Lord William Howe (1729–1814), commander of British forces in America from 1775–1778.

[4] Colonial New Jersey was divided into East Jersey and West Jersey until 1702.

[5] Joan of Arc (1412–1431) in fact lived during the fifteenth century.

Jersey maid to spirit up her countrymen, and save her fair fellow sufferers from ravage and ravishment! Yet panics, in some cases, have their uses; they produce as much good as hurt. Their duration is always short; the mind soon grows through them; and acquires a firmer habit than before. But their peculiar advantage is, that they are the touchstones of sincerity and hypocrisy, and bring things and men to light, which might otherwise have lain forever undiscovered. In fact, they have the same effect on secret traitors, which an imaginary apparition would have upon a private murderer. They sift out the hidden thoughts of man, and hold them up in public to the world. Many a disguised Tory[6] has lately shown his head, that shall penitentially solemnize with curses the day on which Howe arrived upon the Delaware.

As I was with the troops at Fort Lee, and marched with them to the edge of Pennsylvania, I am well acquainted with many circumstances, which those who live at a distance know but little or nothing of. Our situation there was exceedingly cramped, the place being a narrow neck of land between the North River and the Hackensack. Our force was inconsiderable, being not one fourth so great as Howe could bring against us. We had no army at hand to have relieved the garrison, had we shut ourselves up and stood on our defence. Our ammunition, light artillery, and the best part of our stores, had been removed, on the apprehension that Howe would endeavor to penetrate the Jerseys, in which case Fort Lee could be of no use to us; for it must occur to every thinking man, whether in the army or not, that these kinds of field forts are only for temporary purposes, and last in use no longer than the enemy directs his force against the particular object, which such forts are raised to defend. Such was our situation and condition at Fort Lee on the morning of the 20th of November, when an officer arrived with information that the enemy with 200 boats had landed about seven miles above: Major General Green,[7] who commanded the garrison, immediately ordered them under arms, and sent express to General Washington at the town of Hackensack, distant by the way of the ferry, six miles. Our first object was to secure the bridge over the Hackensack, which laid up the river between the enemy and us, about six miles from us, and three from them. General Washington arrived in about three quarters of an hour, and marched at the head of the troops towards the bridge, which place I expected we should have a brush for; however, they did not choose to dispute it with us, and the greatest part of our troops went over the bridge, the rest over the ferry, except some which passed at a mill on a small creek, between the bridge and the ferry, and made their way through some marshy grounds up to the town of Hackensack, and there passed the river. We brought off as much baggage as the wagons could contain, the rest was lost. The simple object was to bring off the garrison, and march them on till they could be strengthened by the Jersey or Pennsylvania militia, so as to be enabled to make a stand. We stayed four days at Newark, collected our out-posts with some of the Jersey militia, and marched out twice to meet the enemy, on being informed that they were advancing, though our numbers were greatly inferior to theirs. Howe, in my little opinion, committed a great error in generalship in not throwing a body of forces off from Staten Island through Amboy, by which means he might have seized all our

[6]American who supported continued allegiance to Great Britain during the American Revolution.

[7]Nathaniel Green (1742–1786).

stores at Brunswick, and intercepted our march into Pennsylvania; but if we believe the power of hell to be limited, we must likewise believe that their agents are under some providential control.

I shall not now attempt to give all the particulars of our retreat to the Delaware; suffice it for the present to say, that both officers and men, though greatly harassed and fatigued, frequently without rest, covering, or provision, the inevitable consequences of a long retreat, bore it with a manly and martial spirit. All their wishes centered in one, which was, that the country would turn out and help them to drive the enemy back. Voltaire has remarked that king William[8] never appeared to full advantage but in difficulties and in action; the same remark may be made on General Washington, for the character fits him. There is a natural firmness in some minds which cannot be unlocked by trifles, but which, when unlocked, discovers a cabinet of fortitude; and I reckon it among those kinds of public blessings, which we do not immediately see, that God hath blessed him with uninterrupted health, and given him a mind that can even flourish upon care.

I shall conclude this paper with some miscellaneous remarks on the state of our affairs; and shall begin with asking the following question, Why is it that the enemy have left the New-England provinces, and made these middle ones the seat of war? The answer is easy: New-England is not infested with Tories, and we are. I have been tender in raising the cry against these men, and used numberless arguments to show them their danger, but it will not do to sacrifice a world either to their folly or their baseness. The period is now arrived, in which either they or we must change our sentiments, or one or both must fall. And what is a Tory? Good God! what is he? I should not be afraid to go with a hundred Whigs[9] against a thousand Tories, were they to attempt to get into arms. Every Tory is a coward; for servile, slavish, self-interested fear is the foundation of Toryism; and a man under such influence, though he may be cruel, never can be brave.

But, before the line of irrecoverable separation be drawn between us, let us reason the matter together: Your conduct is an invitation to the enemy, yet not one in a thousand of you has heart enough to join him. Howe is as much deceived by you as the American cause is injured by you. He expects you will all take up arms, and flock to his standard, with muskets on your shoulders. Your opinions are of no use to him, unless you support him personally, for 'tis soldiers, and not Tories, that he wants.

I once felt all that kind of anger, which a man ought to feel, against the mean principles that are held by the Tories: a noted one, who kept a tavern at Amboy, was standing at his door, with as pretty a child in his hand, about eight or nine years old, as I ever saw, and after speaking his mind as freely as he thought was prudent, finished with this unfatherly expression, *"Well! give me peace in my day."*[10] Not a man lives on the continent but fully believes that a separation must some time or other finally take place, and a generous parent should have said, *"If there must be trouble, let*

[8]Voltaire (1694–1778), French philosopher and writer; William III (1650–1702), King of England, 1689–1702.

[9]Americans who opposed continued allegiance to Great Britain and supported the Revolution.

[10]"There shall be peace and truth in my days." Isaiah 39:8.

it be in my day, that my child may have peace"; and this single reflection, well applied, is sufficient to awaken every man to duty. Not a place upon earth might be so happy as America. Her situation is remote from all the wrangling world, and she has nothing to do but to trade with them. A man can distinguish himself between temper and principle, and I am as confident, as I am that God governs the world, that America will never be happy till she gets clear of foreign dominion. Wars, without ceasing, will break out till that period arrives, and the continent must in the end be conqueror; for though the flame of liberty may sometimes cease to shine, the coal can never expire.

America did not, nor does not want force; but she wanted a proper application of that force. Wisdom is not the purchase of a day, and it is no wonder that we should err at the first setting off. From an excess of tenderness, we were unwilling to raise an army, and trusted our cause to the temporary defence of a well-meaning militia. A summer's experience has now taught us better; yet with those troops, while they were collected, we were able to set bounds to the progress of the enemy, and, thank God! they are again assembling. I always considered militia as the best troops in the world for a sudden exertion, but they will not do for a long campaign. Howe, it is probable, will make an attempt on this city, should he fail on this side the Delaware, he is ruined: if he succeeds, our cause is not ruined. He stakes all on his side against a part on ours; admitting he succeeds, the consequence will be, that armies from both ends of the continent will march to assist their suffering friends in the middle states; for he cannot go everywhere, it is impossible. I consider Howe as the greatest enemy the Tories have; he is bringing a war into their country, which, had it not been for him and partly for themselves, they had been clear of. Should he now be expelled, I wish with all the devotion of a Christian, that the names of Whig and Tory may never more be mentioned; but should the Tories give him encouragement to come, or assistance if he come, I as sincerely wish that our next year's arms may expel them from the continent, and the congress appropriate their possessions to the relief of those who have suffered in well-doing. A single successful battle next year will settle the whole. America could carry on a two years war by the confiscation of the property of disaffected persons, and be made happy by their expulsion. Say not that this is revenge, call it rather the soft resentment of a suffering people, who, having no object in view but the *good* of *all,* have staked their *own all* upon a seemingly doubtful event. Yet it is folly to argue against determined hardness; eloquence may strike the ear, and the language of sorrow draw forth the tear of compassion, but nothing can reach the heart that is steeled with prejudice.

Quitting this class of men, I turn with the warm ardor of a friend to those who have nobly stood, and are yet determined to stand the matter out: I call not upon a few, but upon all: not on *this* state, but on *every* state: up and help us; lay your shoulders to the wheel; better have too much force than too little, when so great an object is at stake. Let it be told to the future world, that in the depth of winter, when nothing but hope and virtue could survive, that the city and the country, alarmed at one common danger, came forth to meet and to repulse it. Say not that thousands are gone, turn out your tens of thousands;[11] throw not the burden of the day upon

[11] "Saul hath slain his thousands, and David his ten thousands." I Samuel 18:7.

Providence, but *"show your faith by your works,"*[12] that God may bless you. It matters not where you live, or what rank of life you hold, the evil or the blessing will reach you all. The far and the near, the home counties and the back, the rich and the poor, will suffer or rejoice alike. The heart that feels not now, is dead: the blood of his children will curse his cowardice, who shrinks back at a time when a little might have saved the whole, and made *them* happy. I love the man that can smile in trouble, that can gather strength from distress, and grow brave by reflection. 'Tis the business of little minds to shrink; but he whose heart is firm, and whose conscience approves his conduct, will pursue his principles unto death. My own line of reasoning is to myself as straight and clear as a ray of light. Not all the treasures of the world, so far as I believe, could have induced me to support an offensive war, for I think it murder; but if a thief breaks into my house, burns and destroys my property, and kills or threatens to kill me, or those that are in it, and to *"bind me in all cases whatsoever"*[13] to his absolute will, am I to suffer it? What signifies it to me, whether he who does it is a king or a common man; my countryman or not my countryman; whether it be done by an individual villain, or an army of them? If we reason to the root of things we shall find no difference; neither can any just cause be assigned why we should punish in the one case and pardon in the other. Let them call me rebel, and welcome, I feel no concern from it; but I should suffer the misery of devils, were I to make a whore of my soul by swearing allegiance to one whose character is that of a sottish, stupid, stubborn, worthless brutish man. I conceive likewise a horrid idea in receiving mercy from a being, who at the last day shall be shrieking to the rocks and mountains to cover him, and fleeing with terror from the orphan, the widow, and the slain of America.

There are cases which cannot be overdone by language, and this is one. There are persons, too, who see not the full extent of the evil which threatens them; they solace themselves with hopes that the enemy, if he succeed, will be merciful. It is the madness of folly, to expect mercy from those who have refused to do justice; and even mercy, where conquest is the object, is only a trick of war; the cunning of the fox is as murderous as the violence of the wolf, and we ought to guard equally against both. Howe's first object is, partly by threats and partly by promises, to terrify or seduce the people to deliver up their arms and receive mercy. The ministry[14] recommended the same plan to Gage,[15] and this is what the Tories will call making their peace, *"a peace which passeth all understanding" indeed!*[16] A peace which would be the immediate forerunner of a worse ruin than any we have yet thought of. Ye men of Pennsylvania, do reason upon these things! Were the back counties to give up their arms, they would fall an easy prey to the Indians, who are all armed: this perhaps is what some Tories would not be sorry for. Were the home counties to deliver up their arms, they would be exposed to the resentment of the back counties, who would then have it in their power to chastise their defection at pleasure. And were any one state to give up its arms, *that* state must be garrisoned by all Howe's army of

[12]James 2:18.

[13]Paine quotes the British Declaratory Act of 1766.

[14]The British government.

[15]General Thomas Gage, commander of British forces in America, 1763–1775.

[16]"And the peace of God, which passeth all understanding, shall keep your hearts and minds through Christ Jesus." Philippians 4:7.

Britons and Hessians[17] to preserve it from the anger of the rest. Mutual fear is the principal link in the chain of mutual love, and woe be to that state that breaks the compact. Howe is mercifully inviting you to barbarous destruction, and men must be either rogues or fools that will not see it. I dwell not upon the vapors of imagination; I bring reason to your ears, and, in language as plain as A, B, C, hold up truth to your eyes.

I thank God, that I fear not. I see no real cause for fear. I know our situation well, and can see the way out of it. While our army was collected, Howe dared not risk a battle; and it is no credit to him that he decamped from the White Plains, and waited a mean opportunity to ravage the defenceless Jerseys; but it is great credit to us, that, with a handful of men, we sustained an orderly retreat for near an hundred miles, brought off our ammunition, all our field pieces, the greatest part of our stores, and had four rivers to pass. None can say that our retreat was precipitate, for we were near three weeks in performing it, that the country might have time to come in. Twice we marched back to meet the enemy, and remained out till dark. The sign of fear was not seen in our camp, and had not some of the cowardly and disaffected inhabitants spread false alarms through the country, the Jerseys had never been ravaged. Once more we are again collected and collecting; our new army at both ends of the continent is recruiting fast, and we shall be able to open the next campaign with sixty thousand men, well armed and clothed. This is our situation, and who will may know it. By perseverance and fortitude we have the prospect of a glorious issue; by cowardice and submission, the sad choice of a variety of evils—a ravaged country—a depopulated city—habitations without safety, and slavery without hope—our homes turned into barracks and bawdyhouses for Hessians, and a future race to provide for, whose fathers we shall doubt of. Look on this picture and weep over it! and if there yet remains one thoughtless wretch who believes it not, let him suffer it unlamented.

1776

from The Age of Reason[1]

from Chapter II
Of Missions and Revelations

Every national church or religion has established itself by pretending some special mission from God, communicated to certain individuals. The Jews have their Moses; the Christians their Jesus Christ, their apostles and saints; and the Turks their Mahomet; as if the way to God was not open to every man alike.

Each of those churches shows certain books, which they call *revelation,* or the Word of God. The Jews say that their Word of God was given by God to Moses face to face; the Christians say, that their Word of God came by divine inspiration; and the Turks say, that their Word of God (the Koran) was brought by an angel from

[17]Inhabitants of Hesse, mercenaries who fought for the British in the Revolutionary War.

[1]The first part of the *Age of Reason* was published in 1794; the second part, in 1795 in France and in 1796 in England.

heaven. Each of those churches accuses the other of unbelief; and, for my own part, I disbelieve them all.

As it is necessary to affix right ideas to words, I will, before I proceed further into the subject, offer some observations on the word *revelation.* Revelation when applied to religion, means something communicated *immediately* from God to man.

No one will deny or dispute the power of the Almighty to make such a communication if he pleases. But admitting, for the sake of a case, that something has been revealed to a certain person, and not revealed to any other person, it is revelation to that person only. When he tells it to a second person, a second to a third, a third to a fourth, and so on, it ceases to be a revelation to all those persons. It is revelation to the first person only, and *hearsay* to every other, and, consequently, they are not obliged to believe it.

It is a contradiction in terms and ideas to call anything a revelation that comes to us at second hand, either verbally or in writing. Revelation is necessarily limited to the first communication. After this, it is only an account of some thing which that person says was a revelation made to him and though he may find himself obliged to believe it, it cannot be incumbent on me to believe it in the same manner, for it was not a revelation made to *me,* and I have only his word for it that it was made to *him.*

When Moses told the children of Israel that he received the two tables of the commandments from the hand of God they were not obliged to believe him, because they had no other authority for it than his telling them so; and I have no other authority for it than some historian telling me so, the commandments carrying no internal evidence of divinity with them. They contain some good moral precepts such as any man qualified to be a lawgiver or a legislator could produce himself, without having recourse to supernatural intervention. . . .

When also I am told that a woman, called the Virgin Mary, said, or gave out, that she was with child without any cohabitation with a man, and that her betrothed husband Joseph, said that an angel told him so, I have a right to believe them or not: such a circumstance required a much stronger evidence than their bare word for it: but we have not even this; for neither Joseph nor Mary wrote any such matter themselves. It is only reported by others that *they said so.* It is hearsay upon hearsay, and I do not chuse to rest my belief upon such evidence.

It is, however, not difficult to account for the credit that was given to the story of Jesus Christ being the Son of God. He was born when the heathen mythology had still some fashion and repute in the world, and that mythology had prepared the people for the belief of such a story. Almost all the extraordinary men that lived under the heathen mythology were reputed to be the sons of some of their gods. It was not a new thing at that time to believe a man to have been celestially begotten; the intercourse of gods with women was then a matter of familiar opinion. Their Jupiter, according to their accounts, had cohabited with hundreds; the story therefore had nothing in it either new, wonderful, or obscene; it was conformable to the opinions that then prevailed among the people called Gentiles, or mythologists, and it was those people only that believed it. The Jews, who had kept strictly to the belief of one God, and no more, and who had always rejected the heathen mythology, never credited the story.

It is curious to observe how the theory of what is called the Christian Church, sprung out of the tail of the heathen mythology. A direct incorporation took place in the first instance, by making the reputed founder to be celestially begotten. The trinity of gods that then followed was no other than a reduction of the former plurality, which was about twenty or thirty thousand. The statue of Mary succeeded the statue of Diana of Ephesus.[2] The deification of heroes changed into the canonization of saints. The Mythologists had gods for everything; the Christian Mythologists had saints for everything. The church became as crouded with the one, as the pantheon had been with the other; and Rome was the place of both. The Christian theory is little else than the idolatry of the ancient mythologists, accommodated to the purposes of power and revenue; and it yet remains to reason and philosophy to abolish the amphibious fraud.

from Chapter III
Concerning the Character of Jesus Christ, and His History

Nothing that is here said can apply, even with the most distant disrespect, to the *real* character of Jesus Christ. He was a virtuous and an amiable man. The morality that he preached and practised was of the most benevolent kind; and though similar systems of morality had been preached by Confucius,[3] and by some of the Greek philosophers, many years before, by the Quakers since, and by many good men in all ages, it had not been exceeded by any.

Jesus Christ wrote no account of himself, of his birth, parentage, or anything else. Not a line of what is called the New Testament is of his writing. The history of him is altogether the work of other people; and as to the account given of his resurrection and ascension, it was the necessary counterpart to the story of his birth. His historians, having brought him into the world in a supernatural manner, were obliged to take him out again in the same manner, or the first part of the story must have fallen to the ground.

The wretched contrivance with which this latter part is told, exceeds everything that went before it. . . .

But the resurrection of a dead person from the grave, and his ascension through the air, is a thing very different, as to the evidence it admits of, to the invisible conception of a child in the womb. The resurrection and ascension, supposing them to have taken place, admitted of public and ocular demonstration, like that of the ascension of a balloon, or the sun at noon day, to all Jerusalem at least. A thing which everybody is required to believe, requires that the proof and evidence of it should be equal to all, and universal; and as the public visibility of this last related act was the only evidence that could give sanction to the former part, the whole of it falls to the ground, because that evidence never was given. . . .

The Christian mythologists, after having confined Satan in a pit, were obliged to let him out again to bring on the sequel of the fable. He is then introduced into the

[2]A Roman goddess whose main temple was at Ephesus in Asia Minor—one of the Seven Wonders of the Ancient World. Ephesus later became a center of Christianity.

[3]Chinese philosopher, 551?–478 B.C.

garden of Eden in the shape of a snake, or a serpent, and in that shape he enters into familiar conversation with Eve, who is no ways surprised to hear a snake talk; and the issue of this tête-à-tête is, that he persuades her to eat an apple, and the eating of that apple damns all mankind.

After giving Satan this triumph over the whole creation, one would have supposed that the church mythologists would have been kind enough to send him back again to the pit, or, if they had not done this, that they would have put a mountain upon him, (for they say that their faith can remove a mountain) or have put him under a mountain, as the former mythologists had done, to prevent his getting again among the women, and doing more mischief. But instead of this, they leave him at large, without even obliging him to give his parole. The secret of which is, that they could not do without him; and after being at the trouble of making him, they bribed him to stay. They promised him ALL the Jews, ALL the Turks by anticipation, nine-tenths of the world beside, and Mahomet into the bargain. After this, who can doubt the bountifulness of the Christian Mythology? . . .

That many good men have believed this strange fable, and lived very good lives under that belief (for credulity is not a crime) is what I have no doubt of. In the first place, they were educated to believe it, and they would have believed anything else in the same manner. There are also many who have been so enthusiastically enraptured by what they conceived to be the infinite love of God to man; in making a sacrifice of himself, that the vehemence of the idea has forbidden and deterred them from examining into the absurdity and profaneness of the story. The more unnatural anything is, the more is it capable of becoming the object of dismal admiration.

from Chapter VI
Of the True Theology

But if objects for gratitude and admiration are our desire, do they not present themselves every hour to our eyes? Do we not see a fair creation prepared to receive us the instant we are born—a world furnished to our hands, that cost us nothing? Is it we that light up the sun; that pour down the rain; and fill the earth with abundance? Whether we sleep or wake, the vast machinery of the universe still goes on. Are these things, and the blessings they indicate in future, nothing to us? Can our gross feelings be excited by no other subjects than tragedy and suicide? Or is the gloomy pride of man become so intolerable, that nothing can flatter it but a sacrifice of the Creator?

I know that this bold investigation will alarm many, but it would be paying too great a compliment to their credulity to forbear it on that account. The times and the subject demand it to be done. The suspicion that the theory of what is called the Christian church is fabulous, is becoming very extensive in all countries; and it will be a consolation to men staggering under that suspicion, and doubting what to believe and what to disbelieve, to see the subject freely investigated.

* * * * * * * * *

It is only in the CREATION that all our ideas and conceptions of a *word of God* can unite. The Creation speaketh an universal language, independently of human speech or human language, multiplied and various as they be. It is an ever existing original, which every man can read. It cannot be forged; it cannot be counterfeited; it cannot be lost; it cannot be altered; it cannot be suppressed. It does not depend upon the will of man whether it shall be published or not; it publishes itself from one end of the earth to the other. It preaches to all nations and to all worlds; and this *word of God* reveals to man all that is necessary for man to know of God.

Do we want to contemplate his power? We see it in the immensity of the creation. Do we want to contemplate his wisdom? We see it in the unchangeable order by which the incomprehensible Whole is governed. Do we want to contemplate his munificence? We see it in the abundance with which he fills the earth. Do we want to contemplate his mercy? We see it in his not withholding that abundance even from the unthankful. In fine, do we want to know what God is? Search not the book called the scripture, which any human hand might make, but the scripture called the Creation. . . .

Any person, who has made observations on the state and progress of the human mind, by observing his own, cannot but have observed, that there are two distinct classes of what are called Thoughts; those that we produce in ourselves by reflection and the act of thinking, and those that bolt into the mind of their own accord. I have always made it a rule to treat those voluntary visitors with civility, taking care to examine, as well as I was able, if they were worth entertaining; and it is from them I have acquired almost all the knowledge that I have. As to the learning that any person gains from school education, it serves only, like a small capital, to put him in the way of beginning learning for himself afterwards. Every person of learning is finally his own teacher; the reason of which is, that principles, being of a distinct quality to circumstances, cannot be impressed upon the memory; their place of mental residence is the understanding, and they are never so lasting as when they begin by conception. Thus much for the introductory part.

From the time I was capable of conceiving an idea, and acting upon it by reflection, I either doubted the truth of the christian system, or thought it to be a strange affair; I scarcely knew which it was; but I well remember, when about seven or eight years of age, hearing a sermon read by a relation of mine, who was a great devotee of the church, upon the subject of what is called *Redemption by the death of the Son of God.* After the sermon was ended, I went into the garden, and as I was going down the garden steps (for I perfectly recollect the spot) I revolted at the recollection of what I had heard, and thought to myself that it was making God Almighty act like a passionate man, that killed his son, when he could not revenge himself any other way; and as I was sure a man would be hanged that did such a thing, I could not see for what purpose they preached such sermons. This was not one of those kind of thoughts that had any thing in it of childish levity; it was to me a serious reflection, arising from the idea I had that God was too good to do such an action, and also too almighty to be under any necessity of doing it. I believe in the same manner to this moment; and I moreover believe, that any system of religion that has any thing in it that shocks the mind of a child, cannot be a true system. . . .

Of all the systems of religion that ever were invented, there is none more derogatory to the Almighty, more unedifying to man, more repugnant to reason, and more contradictory in itself, than this thing called Christianity. Too absurd for belief, too impossible to convince, and too inconsistent for practice, it renders the heart torpid, or produces only atheists and fanatics. As an engine of power, it serves the purpose of despotism; and as a means of wealth, the avarice of priests; but so far as respects the good of man in general, it leads to nothing here or hereafter. . . .

It has been the scheme of the Christian church, and of all the other invented systems of religion, to hold man in ignorance of the Creator, as it is of government to hold him in ignorance of his rights. The systems of the one are as false as those of the other, and are calculated for mutual support. The study of theology as it stands in Christian churches, is the study of nothing; it is founded on nothing; it rests on no principles; it proceeds by no authorities; it has no data; it can demonstrate nothing; and admits of no conclusion. Not any thing can be studied as a science without our being in possession of the principles upon which it is founded; and as this is not the case with Christian theology, it is therefore the study of nothing. . . .

It has been by wandering from the immutable laws of science, and the light of reason, and setting up an invented thing called "revealed religion," that so many wild and blasphemous conceits have been formed of the Almighty. The Jews have made him the assassin of the human species, to make room for the religion of the Jews. The Christians have made him the murderer of himself, and the founder of a new religion to supersede and expel the Jewish religion. And to find pretence and admission for these things, they must have supposed his power or his wisdom imperfect, or his will changeable; and the changeableness of the will is the imperfection of the judgement. The philosopher knows that the laws of the Creator have never changed, with respect either to the principles of science, or the properties of matter. Why then is it to be supposed they have changed with respect to man?

I here close the subject. I have shewn in all the foregoing parts of this work that the Bible and Testament are impositions and forgeries; and I leave the evidence I have produced in proof of it to be refuted, if any one can do it; and I leave the ideas that are suggested in the conclusion of the work to rest on the mind of the reader; certain as I am that when opinions are free, either in matters of government or religion, truth will finally and powerfully prevail.

1794

John Adams 1735–1826
Abigail Adams 1744–1818

John Adams was the first vice president of the United States and the second president (1797–1801). He was also a lively intellectual leader in revolutionary Boston and in Congress, an able negotiator abroad, the author of many tracts and essays about government, and a reflective correspondent and philosopher in the decades between his retirement from office and his death at the age of ninety.

Born in 1735 to a well-established family in Braintree, Massachusetts, John Adams married Abigail Smith, the daughter of a Weymouth clergyman, in 1764. Abigail Adams was educated by her grandmother, accompanied her husband on diplomatic missions, spoke compellingly about her Federalist views, and greatly influenced her husband's political career. Together they founded a family that would remain distinguished in the United States well into the twentieth century. Their son,

John Quincy Adams, was president; their grandson, Charles Francis Adams, was minister to Britain during the Civil War; their great-grandson, Henry Adams, was a historian, novelist, and autobiographer.

John Adams graduated from Harvard, taught school in Worcester, and prepared there to become an able lawyer. Throughout his life he was a wide-ranging, perceptive, and retentive reader—peppering his letters and papers with fresh and apt allusions to scores of challenging books. He was also a constant writer—of diary entries, legal notes and records, marginal jottings, ample letters, forceful replies to adversaries, letters to the press, and formal reports and state papers. His major writings contribute to the ideological formation of the new American republic and are products of legal scholarship and argument invaluable for students of political theory and history today. His *Dissertation on the Canon and the Feudal Law* (1765) and the *Novanglus* papers (1774–1775) warned against British attempts to impose English law on the colonies as part of an effort to subvert American liberties. *A Defence of the Constitutions of Government of the United States of America* (1787–1788) argued the cause of republican and federal government at a time crucial for both European and American history. Adams's diaries and letters show him to be a shrewd and witty judge of character; they provide bright sketches of people in exciting moments of American politics and provocative insights into American society.

The marriage of John and Abigail Adams was an alliance of two strong minds. Abigail's letters reflect an alert American woman pressing for a real change of consciousness during the Revolution. These partners combined intellectual and moral questioning through long years of revolution, separation, and public life. They also shared a long decline of fame. John Adams lost the presidential election of 1800, and the couple left Washington early on the morning of Jefferson's inauguration. They remained at home in Massachusetts for the rest of their lives. Disgruntled by his rough treatment by the press and by what he perceived as a general public failure to credit his personal contributions to American political life, Adams began a rambling and defensive autobiography in his retirement, but some of his best writing of this period appears in the letters he exchanged after 1812 with Thomas Jefferson.

Repairing the breach in their friendship that stemmed from the election of 1800, Adams and Jefferson carried on a lively discussion about literature, history, and social ideals until both died on the same day, July 4, 1826. The correspondence between the two was first published as a single text in the twentieth century, renewing interest in the political philosophies of both men. Their discussion about an aristocracy of talent and virtue, for example, raised important questions about individuals in a democratic society and was noticed by Ezra Pound as he was writing his *Cantos*.

Albert Furtwangler
Mount Allison University

Frank Shuffelton
University of Rochester

Wendy Martin
Claremont Graduate University

PRIMARY WORKS

The Adams-Jefferson Letters, ed. Lester J. Cappon, 2 vols., 1959; *Diary and Autobiography of John Adams,* ed. L.H. Butterfield, 4 vols., 1961; *Adams Family Correspondence,* 1963; *The Book of Abigail and John: Selected Letters of the Adams Family 1762–1784,* ed. L.H. Butterfield, Marc Friedlaender and Mary-Jo Kline, 1975.

from Autobiography of John Adams

[John Adams shares a bed with Benjamin Franklin, 1776]

The Taverns were so full We could with difficulty obtain Entertainment. At Brunswick, but one bed could be procured for Dr. Franklin and me, in a Chamber little larger than the bed, without a Chimney and with only one small Window. The Window was open, and I, who was an invalid and afraid of the Air in the night, shut it close. Oh! says Franklin dont shut the Window. We shall be suffocated. I answered I was afraid of the Evening Air, Dr. Franklin replied, the Air within this Chamber will soon be, and indeed is now worse than that without Doors: come! open the Window and come to bed, and I will convince you: I believe you are not acquainted with my Theory of Colds. Opening the Window and leaping into Bed, I said I had read his Letters to Dr. Cooper in which he had advanced, that Nobody ever got cold by going into a cold Church, or any other cold Air: but the Theory was so little consistent with my experience, that I thought it a Paradox: However I had so much curiosity to hear his reasons, that I would run the risque of a cold. The Doctor then began an harrangue, upon Air and cold and Respiration and Perspiration, with which I was so much amused that I soon fell asleep, and left him and his Philosophy together: but I believe they were equally sound and insensible, within a few minutes after me, for the last Words I heard were pronounced as if he was more than half asleep.

[John Adams arrives in Bordeaux in 1778]

The Company their dresses, Equipages, and the furniture were splendid and the Supper very sumptuous. The Conversation at and after Supper was very gay, animated, chearfull and good humoured as it appeared to my Eyes and Ears and feelings but my Understanding had no Share in it. The Language was altogether incomprehensible. The Company were more attentive to me, then I desired; for they often addressed Observations and questions to me, which I could only understand by the Interpretation of Mr. Bond [Bondfield], and the returns of civility on my part could only be communicated [to] me through the same Channel, a kind of conviviality so tædious and irksome, that I had much rather have remained in silent Observation and Reflection. One Anecdote I will relate, because among many others I heard in Bourdeaux it was Characteristic of the manners at that time. One of the most elegant Ladies at Table, young and handsome, tho married to a Gentleman in the Company, was pleased to Address her discourse to me. Mr. Bondfield must interpret the Speech which he did in these Words "Mr. Adams, by your Name I conclude you are descended from the first Man and Woman, and probably in your family may be preserved the tradition which may resolve a difficulty which I could never explain. I never could understand how the first Couple found out the Art of lying together?" Whether her phrase was L'Art de se coucher ensemble, or any other more energetic, I know not, but Mr. Bondfield rendered it by that I have mentioned. To me, whose Acquaintance with Women had been confined to America, where the manners of the Ladies were universally characterised at that time by Modesty, Delicacy and Dignity, this question was surprizing and shocking: but although I believe at first I blushed, I was determined not to be disconcerted. I thought it would be as well for once to set a brazen face against a brazen face and answer a fool according to her folly, and accordingly composing my countenance into an Ironical Gravity I answered her "Madame My Family resembles the first Couple both in the name and in their frailties so much that I have no doubt We are descended from that in Paradise. But the Subject was perfectly understood by Us, whether by tradition I could not tell: I rather thought it was by Instinct, for there was a Physical quality in Us resembling the Power of Electricity or of the Magnet, by which when a Pair approached within a striking distance they flew together like the Needle to the Pole or like two Objects in electric Experiments." When this Answer was explained to her, she replied "Well I know not how it was, but this I know it is a very happy Shock." I should have added "in a lawfull Way" after "a striking distance," but if I had her Ladyship and all the Company would only have thought it Pedantry and Bigottry. This is a decent Story in comparison with many which I heard in Bourdeaux, in the short time I remained there, concerning married Ladies of Fashion and reputation. The decided Advances made by married Women, which I heard related, gave rise to many reflections in my mind which may perhaps be detailed hereafter on some similar Occasions. The first was if such a[re] the manners of Women of Rank, Fashion and Reputation [in] France, they can never support a Republican Government nor be reconciled with it. We must therefore take great care not to import them into America.

1961

Letter from Abigail Adams to John Adams, March 31, 1776

I long to hear that you have declared an independancy—and by the way in the new Code of Laws which I suppose it will be necessary for you to make I desire you would Remember the Ladies, and be more generous and favourable to them than your ancestors. Do not put such unlimited power into the hands of the Husbands. Remember all Men would be tyrants if they could. If perticuliar care and attention is not paid to the Laidies we are determined to foment a Rebelion, and will not hold ourselves bound by any Laws in which we have no voice, or Representation.

That your Sex are Naturally Tyrannical is a Truth so thoroughly established as to admit of no dispute, but such of you as wish to be happy willingly give up the harsh title of Master for the more tender and endearing one of Friend. Why then, not put it out of the power of the vicious and the Lawless to use us with cruelty and indignity with impunity. Men of Sense in all Ages abhor those customs which treat us only as the vassals of your Sex. Regard us then as Beings placed by providence under your protection and in immitation of the Supreem Being make use of that power only for our happiness.

1975

Letter from John Adams to Abigail Adams, April 14, 1776

As to Declarations of Independency, be patient. Read our Privateering Laws, and our Commercial Laws. What signifies a Word.

As to your extraordinary Code of Laws, I cannot but laugh. We have been told that our Struggle has loosened the bands of Government every where. That Children and Apprentices were disobedient—that schools and Colledges were grown turbulent—that Indians slighted their Guardians and Negroes grew insolent to their Masters. But your Letter was the first Intimation that another Tribe more numerous and powerfull than all the rest were grown discontented.—This is rather too coarse a Compliment but you are so saucy, I wont blot it out.

Depend upon it, We know better than to repeal our Masculine systems. Altho they are in full Force, you know they are little more than Theory. We dare not exert our Power in its full Latitude. We are obliged to go fair, and softly, and in Practice you know We are the subjects. We have only the Name of Masters, and rather than give up this, which would compleatly subject Us to the Despotism of the Peticoat, I hope General Washington, and all our brave Heroes would fight. I am sure every good Politician would plot, as long as he would against Despotism, Empire, Monarchy, Aristocracy, Oligarchy, or Ochlocracy.—A fine Story indeed. I begin to think the Ministry as deep as they are wicked. After stirring up Tories, Landjobbers, Trimmers, Bigots, Canadians, Indians, Negroes, Hanoverians, Hessians, Russians, Irish Roman Catholicks, Scotch Renegadoes, at last they have stimulated the [ ] to demand new Priviledges and threaten to rebell.

1975

from Letter from John Adams to Mercy Otis Warren, April 16, 1776

. . . The Ladies I think are the greatest Politicians that I have the Honour to be acquainted with, not only because they act upon the Sublimest of all the Principles of Policy, viz., that Honesty is the best Policy, but because they consider Questions more coolly than those who are heated with Party Zeal and inflamed with the bitter Contentions of active public Life. . . .

The Form of Government, which you admire, when its Principles are pure is admirable, indeed, it is productive of every Thing, which is great and excellent among Men. But its Principles are as easily destroyed, as human Nature is corrupted. Such a Government is only to be supported by pure Religion or Austere Morals. Public Virtue cannot exist in a Nation without private, and public Virtue is the only Foundation of Republics. There must be a positive Passion for the public good, the public Interest, Honour, Power and Glory, established in the Minds of the People, or there can be no Republican Government, nor any real Liberty: and this public Passion must be Superiour to all private Passions. Men must be ready, they must pride themselves, and be happy to sacrifice their private Pleasures, Passions and Interests, nay, their private Friendships and dearest Connections, when they stand in Competition with the Rights of Society.

Is there in the World a Nation, which deserves this Character? There have been several, but they are no more. Our dear Americans perhaps have as much of it as any Nation now existing, and New England perhaps has more than the rest of America. But I have seen all along my Life Such Selfishness and Littleness even in New England, that I sometimes tremble to think that, altho We are engaged in the best Cause that ever employed the Human Heart yet the Prospect of success is doubtful not for Want of Power or of Wisdom but of Virtue.

The Spirit of Commerce, Madam, which even insinuates itself into Families, and influences holy Matrimony, and thereby corrupts the morals of families as well as destroys their Happiness, it is much to be feared is incompatible with that purity of Heart and Greatness of soul which is necessary for an happy Republic.

This Same Spirit of Commerce is as rampant in New England as in any Part of the World. Trade is as well understood and as passionately loved there as any where.

Even the Farmers and Tradesmen are addicted to Commerce; and it is too true that Property is generally the standard of Respect there as much as anywhere. While this is the Case there is great Danger that a Republican Government would be very factious and turbulent there. Divisions in Elections are much to be dreaded. Every man must seriously set himself to root out his Passions, Prejudices and Attachments, and to get the better of his private Interest. The only reputable Principle and Doctrine must be that all Things must give Way to the public.

This is very grave and solemn Discourse to a Lady. True, and I thank God, that his Providence has made me Acquainted with two Ladies at least who can bear it. I think Madam, that the Union of the Colonies, will continue and be more firmly cemented. But We must move slowly. Patience, Patience, Patience! I am obliged to invoke this every Morning of my Life, every Noon and every Evening.

1917

from Letters from John Adams to Abigail Adams, July 3, 1776[1]

[1] . . . Yesterday the greatest Question was decided, which ever was debated in America, and a greater perhaps, never was or will be decided among Men. A Resolution was passed without one dissenting Colony "that these united Colonies, are, and of right ought to be free and independent States, and as such, they have, and

[1]John Adams wrote two letters to Abigail Adams on July 3; the passages here come from the first and second, respectively, with the first letter identified as [1] and the second letter identified as [2].

of Right ought to have full Power to make War, conclude Peace, establish Commerce, and to do all the other Acts and Things, which other States may rightfully do." You will see in a few days a Declaration setting forth the Causes, which have impell'd Us to this mighty Revolution, and the Reasons which will justify it, in the Sight of God and Man. A Plan of Confederation will be taken up in a few days.

When I look back to the Year 1761, and recollect the Argument concerning Writs of Assistance, in the Superiour Court, which I have hitherto considered as the Commencement of the Controversy, between Great Britain and America, and run through the whole Period from that Time to this, and recollect the series of political Events, the Chain of Causes and Effects, I am surprized at the Suddenness, as well as Greatness of this Revolution. Britain has been fill'd with Folly, and America with Wisdom, at least this is my Judgment.—Time must determine. It is the Will of Heaven, that the two Countries should be sundered forever. It may be the Will of Heaven that America shall suffer Calamities still more wasting and Distresses yet more dreadfull. If this is to be the Case, it will have this good Effect, at least: it will inspire Us with many Virtues, which We have not, and correct many Errors, Follies, and Vices, which threaten to disturb, dishonour, and destroy Us.—The Furnace of Affliction produces Refinement, in States as well as Individuals. And the new Governments we are assuming, in every Part, will require a Purification from our Vices, and an Augmentation of our Virtues or they will be no Blessings. The People will have unbounded Power. And the People are extreamly addicted to Corruption and Venality, as well as the Great.—I am not without Apprehensions from this Quarter. But I must submit all my Hopes and Fears, to an overruling Providence, in which, unfashionable as the Faith may be, I firmly believe.

[2] Had a Declaration of Independency been made seven Months ago, it would have been attended with many great and glorious Effects. . . . We might before this Hour, have formed Alliances with foreign States.—We should have mastered Quebec and been in Possession of Canada. . . .

But on the other Hand, the Delay of this Declaration to this Time, has many great Advantages attending it.—The Hopes of Reconciliation, which were fondly entertained by Multitudes of honest and well meaning tho weak and mistaken People, have been gradually and at last totally extinguished.—Time has been given for the whole People, maturely to consider the great Question of Independence and to ripen their Judgments, dissipate their Fears, and allure their Hopes, by discussing it in News Papers and Pamphletts, by debating it, in Assemblies, Conventions, Committees of Safety and Inspection, in Town and County Meetings, as well as in private Conversations, so that the whole People in every Colony of the 13, have now adopted it, as their own Act.—This will cement the Union, and avoid those Heats and perhaps Convulsions which might have been occasioned, by such a Declaration Six Months ago.

But the Day is past. The Second Day of July 1776, will be the most memorable Epocha, in the History of America.—I am apt to believe that it will be celebrated, by succeeding Generations, as the great anniversary Festival. It ought to be commemorated, as the Day of Deliverance by solemn Acts of Devotion to God Almighty. It ought to be solemnized with Pomp and Parade, with Shews, Games,

Sports, Guns, Bells, Bonfires and Illuminations from one End of this Continent to the other from this Time forward forever more.

You will think me transported with Enthusiasm but I am not.—I am well aware of the Toil and Blood and Treasure, that it will cost Us to maintain this Declaration, and support and defend these States.—Yet through all the Gloom I can see the Rays of ravishing Light and Glory. I can see that the End is more than worth all the Means. And that Posterity will tryumph in that Days Transaction, even altho We should rue it, which I trust in God We shall not.

1963

Letter from Abigail Adams to John Adams, June 30, 1778

Now I know you are Safe [in France] I wish myself with you. Whenever you entertain such a wish recollect that I would have willingly hazarded all dangers to have been your companion, but as that was not permitted you must console me in your absence by a Recital of all your adventures, tho methinks I would not have them in all respects too similar to those related of your venerable Colleigue [i.e., Franklin], Whose Mentor like appearence, age and philosiphy must certainly lead the polite scientifick Ladies of France to suppose they are embraceing the God of Wisdom, in a Humane Form, but I who own that I never yet wish'd an Angle whom I loved a Man,[1] shall be full as content if those divine Honours are omitted. The whole Heart of my Friend is in the Bosom of his partner, more than half a score of years has so riveted [it] there that the fabrick which contains it must crumble into Dust e'er the particles can be seperated. I can hear of the Brilliant accomplishment[s] of any of my Sex with pleasure and rejoice in that Liberality of Sentiment which acknowledges them. At the same time I regret the trifling narrow contracted Education of the Females of my own country. I have entertaind a superiour opinion of the accomplishments of the French Ladies ever since I read the Letters of Dr. Sherbear,[2] who professes that he had rather take the opinion of an accomplished Lady in matters of polite writing than the first wits of Itally and should think himself safer with her approbation than of a long List of Literati, and he give[s] this reason for it that Women have in general more delicate Sensations than Men, what touches them is for the most part true in Nature, whereas men warpt by Education, judge amiss from previous prejudice and refering all things to the model of the ancients, condemn that by comparison where no true Similitud ought to be expected.

[1] "Back thro' the paths of pleasing sense I ran, / Nor wish'd an Angel whom I lov'd a Man." Alexander Pope, *Eloisa to Abelard,* lines 69–70.

[2] John Shebbeare, notorious English satirist. Both John and Abigail had read his novel, *Letters on the English Nation* (1755).

But in this country you need not be told how much female Education is neglected, nor how fashonable it has been to ridicule Female learning, tho I acknowled[ge] it my happiness to be connected with a person of a more generous mind and liberal Sentiments.

1975

Abigail Adams's Diary of Her Return Voyage to America, March 30–May 1, 1788

Sunday London March 30. We took our departure from the Bath Hotell where I had been a Fortnight, and sat out for Portsmouth, which we reachd on Monday Evening. We put up at the Fountain Inn. Here we continued a week waiting for the Ship which was detaind by contrary winds in the River. The wind changing we past over to the Isle of Wight and landed at a place call'd Ryed, where we took post Chaises and proceeded to Newport to dine. From thence to Cows where our Ship was to call for us. Here Mr. Adams, myself and two Servants took up our abode at the Fountain Inn kept by a widow woman whose Name is Symes. Our Lodging room very small, and the drawing room Confind and unpleasent. I found myself on the first Night much disposed to be uneasy and discontented. On the next day I requested the Land Lady to let me have a very large Room from whence we had a fine view of the Harbour, vessels, east Cowes and surrounding Hills. I found my Spirits much relieved. Never before experienced how much pleasure was to be derived from a prospect, but I had been long used to a large House, a large Family and many and various cares. I had now got into an unpleasent place without any occupation for mind or Body. Haveing staid at Portsmouth untill I had read all our Books and done all the Work I had left out, I never before experienced to such a degree what the French term enui.[1] Monday took a walk to the Castle and upon a Hill behind it which commanded a pleasent view of the Harbour and Town which is a small villiage subsisting chiefly by fishing and piloting Vessels. Cowes is a safe and commodious Harbour. Here many Boats ply to take up the oyster which is always found in an Infant State. Small Vessels calld Smacks receive them and carry them to Colchester where they throw them again into water where the Sea only flows up by tides, and there they fatten and are again taken up and carried [to] the London market. The Isle of Wight is taken all together a very fertile agreable place 24 miles Long and 12 Broad. Produces great plenty of Grain, Sheep and Cattle, is a hilly country and a very Healthy Situation. On tuesday we went to Newport in order to visit Carisbrook Castle. This is a very ancient Ruins. The first account of it in English History is in the year 1513. This is the castle where Charles the first was kept a prisoner and they shew you the window from whence he attempted to escape. In this castle is a well of such a depth that the water is drawn from it by an ass walking in a wheel like a turn spit dog. The woman

[1]Boredom.

who shew it to us told us it was 300 feet deep. It is Beautifully stoned and in as good order as if finishd but yesterday. She lighted paper and threw [it] down to shew us its depth and dropping in a pin, it resounded as tho a large stone had been thrown in. We went to the Top of the citidal which commands a most extensive prospect. We returnd to Newport to dine. After dinner a Gentleman introduced himself to us by the Name of Sharp. Professed himself a warm and zealous Friend to America. After some little conversation in which it was easy to discover that he was a curious Character he requested that we would do him the Honour to go to his House and drink Tea. We endeavourd [to] excuse ourselves, but he would insist upon it, and we accordingly accepted. He carried us home and introduced to us an aged Father of 90 Years, a very surprizing old Gentleman who tho deaf appeard to retain his understanding perfectly. Mrs. Sharp his Lady appeard to be an amiable woman tho not greatly accustomed to company. The two young Ladies soon made their appearence, the Youngest about 17 very Beautifull. The eldest might have been thought Handsome, if she had not quite spoild herself by affectation. By aiming at politeness she overshot her mark, and faild in that Symplicity of manners which is the principal ornament of a Female Character.

This Family were very civil, polite and Friendly to us during our stay at Cowes. We drank Tea with them on the Sunday following and by their most pressing invitation we dined with them the tuesday following. Mr. Sharp is a poet, a man of reading and appears to possess a good mind and Heart and [is] enthusiastick in favor of America. He collected a number of his Friends to dine with us all of whom were equally well disposed to our Country and had always Reprobated the war against us. During our stay at Cowes we made one excursion to Yarmouth about 15 miles distant from Cowes, but the road being Bad it scarcly repaid us for the trouble as we did not meet with any thing curious. After spending a whole fortnight at Cowes the Ship came round and on Sunday the 20 of April we embarked on Board the ship Lucretia Captain Callihan with three Gentlemen passengers viz. Mr. Murry a Clergyman, Mr. Stewart a grandson of old Captain Erwin of Boston who is going out to Bermudas collector of the Customs in that Island, His parents being British subjects, Mr. Boyd of Portsmouth a young Gentleman who received His Education in this Country.

The wind with which we saild scarcly lasted us 5 hours, but we continued our course untill Monday Evening when it blew such a gale that we were driven back and very glad to get into Portland Harbour. Here we have lain ever since, now 8 days, a Situation not to be desired, yet better far than we should have been either at Sea or in the downs. Whenever I am disposed to be uneasy I reflect a moment upon my preferable Situation to the poor Girl my maid, who is very near her Time,[2] in poor Health and distressingly Sea sick, and I am then silent. I Hush every murmer, and tho much of my anxiety is on her account, I think that God will suit the wind to the shorn Lamb, that we may be carried through our difficulties better than my apprehensions. Trust in the Lord, and do good. I will endeavour to practise this precept. My own Health is better than it has been. We fortunately have a Doctor on Board, and I have taken an old woman out of kindness and given her a passage who seems kind, active and cleaver, is not Sea sick and I hope will be usefull to me. I am much better accommodated than when I came and have not sufferd so much by Sea Sickness. Want

[2] *I.e.,* for giving birth.

of Sleep is the greatest inconvenience I have yet sufferd but I shall not escape so. This day 3 weeks Mr. and Mrs. Smith saild and my dear Grandson just one Year old for New York in the Thyne packet. I fear they will have a bad time as the Westerly Winds have been so strong. God protect them and give us all a happy meeting in our Native Land. We Lie Here near the Town of Weymouth, and our Gentlemen go on shore almost every day which is an amusement to them and really some to me, as they collect something or other to bring Back with them either Mental or Bodily food. This is Sunday 27 April. Mr. Murry preachd us a Sermon. The Sailors made themselves clean and were admitted into the Cabbin, attended with great decency to His discourse from these words, "Thou shalt not take the Name of the Lord thy God in vain, for the Lord will not hold him Guiltless that taketh His Name in vain." He preachd without Notes and in the same Stile which all the Clergymen I ever heard make use of who practise this method, a sort of familiar talking without any kind of dignity yet perhaps better calculated to do good to such an audience, than a more polishd or elegant Stile, but in general I cannot approve of this method. I like to hear a discourse that would read well. If I live to return to America, how much shall I regreet the loss of good Dr. Prices Sermons. They were always a delightfull entertainment to me. I revered the Character and Loved the Man. Tho far from being an orator, his words came from the Heart and reached the Heart. So Humble, so diffident, so liberal and Benevolent a Character does honour to that Religion which he both professes and practises.

On Sunday Eve the wind changed in our favour, so much as to induce the Captain to come to sail. This is Thursday the first of May, but we have made very small progress, the winds have been so light; yesterday we past Sylla and are now out of sight of Land. The weather is very fine and we only want fresher winds. The confinement of a Ship is tedious and I am fully of the mind I was when I came over that I will never again try the Sea. I provided then for my return in the Resolution I took, but now it is absolute. Indeed I have seen enough of the world, small as [it?] has been, and shall be content to learn what is further to be known from the page of History. I do not think the four years I have past abroad the pleasentest part of my Life. Tis Domestick happiness and Rural felicity in the Bosom of my Native Land, that has charms for me. Yet I do not regreet that I made this excursion since it has only more attached me to America.

1961

from Letter from John Adams to Thomas Jefferson, September 2, 1813

. . . Now, my Friend, who are the αριστοι ["aristocrats"]? Philosophy may Answer "The Wise and Good." But the World, Mankind, have by their practice always answered, "the rich the beautiful and well born." And Philosophers themselves in marrying their Children prefer the rich the handsome and the well descended to the wise and good.

What chance have Talents and Virtues in competition, with Wealth and Birth? and Beauty?

Haud facile emergunt, quorum Virtutibus obstant [i.e., obstat]
Res Angusta Domi.

One truth is clear,; by all the World confess'd
Slow rises worth, by Poverty oppress'd.

The five Pillars of Aristocracy, are Beauty Wealth, Birth, Genius and Virtues. Any one of the three first, can at any time over bear any one or both of the two last.

Let me ask again, what a Wave of publick Opinion, in favour of Birth has been spread over the Globe, by Abraham, by Hercules, by Mahomet, by Guelphs, Ghibellines, Bourbons, and a miserable Scottish Chief Steuart? By Zingis by, by, by, a million others? And what a Wave will be spread by Napoleon and by Washington? Their remotest Cousins will be sought and will be proud, and will avail themselves of their descent. Call this Principle, Prejudice, Folly Ignorance, Baseness, Slavery, Stupidity, Adulation, Superstition or what you will. I will not contradict you. But the Fact, in natural, moral, political and domestic History I cannot deny or dispute or question.

And is this great Fact in the natural History of Man? This unalterable Principle of Morals, Philosophy, Policy domestic felicity, and dayly Experience from the Creation; to be overlooked, forgotten neglected, or hypocritically waived out of Sight; by a Legislator? By a professed Writer upon civil Government, and upon Constitutions of civil Government?

Thus far I had written, when your favour of Aug. 22 was laid on my table, from the Post Office. I can only say at present that I can pursue this idle Speculation no farther, at least till I have replied to this fresh proof of your friendship and Confidence. Mrs. A. joins in cordial Thanks, with

John Adams

You may laugh at the introduction of Beauty, among the Pillars of Aristocracy. But Madame Barry says Le veritable Royauté est la B[e]autee ["true royalty is beauty"], and there is not a more certain Truth. Beauty, Grace, Figure, Attitude, Movement, have in innumerable Instances prevailed over Wealth, Birth, Talents Virtues and every thing else, in Men of the highest rank, greatest Power, and sometimes, the most exalted Genius, greatest Fame, and highest Merit.

1963

from Letter from Thomas Jefferson to John Adams, October 28, 1813

. . . I agree with you that there is a natural aristocracy among men. The grounds of this are virtue and talents. Formerly bodily powers gave place among the aristoi. But since the invention of gunpowder has armed the weak as well as the strong with missile death, bodily strength, like beauty, good humor, politeness and other accomplishments, has become but an auxiliary ground of distinction. There is also an artificial aristocracy founded on wealth and birth, without either virtue or talents; for with these it would belong to the first class. The natural aristocracy I consider as the most precious gift of nature for the instruction, the trusts, and government of society. And indeed it would have been inconsistent in creation to have formed man for the social state, and not to have provided virtue and wisdom enough to manage the concerns of the society. May we not even say that that form of government is the best which provides the most effectually for a pure selection of these natural aristoi into the offices of government? The artificial aristocracy is a mischievous ingredient in government, and provision should be made to prevent it's ascendancy. On the question, What is the best provision, you and I differ; but we differ as rational friends, using the free exercise of our own reason, and mutually indulging it's errors. *You* think it best to put the Pseudo-aristoi into a separate chamber of legislation where they may be hindered from doing mischief by their coordinate branches, and where also they may be a protection to wealth against the Agrarian and plundering enterprises of the Majority of the people. I think that to give them power in order to prevent them from doing mischief, is arming them for it, and increasing instead of remedying the evil. For if the coordinate branches can arrest their action, so may they that of the coordinates. Mischief may be done negatively as well as positively. Of this a cabal in the Senate of the U. S. has furnished many proofs. Nor do I believe them necessary to protect the wealthy; because enough of these will find their way into every branch of the legislation to protect themselves. From 15. to 20. legislatures of our own, in action for 30. years past, have proved that no fears of an equalisation of property are to be apprehended from them.

I think the best remedy is exactly that provided by all our constitutions, to leave to the citizens the free election and separation of the aristoi from the pseudo-aristoi, of the wheat from the chaff. In general they will elect the real good and wise. In some instances, wealth may corrupt, and birth blind them; but not in sufficient degree to endanger the society.

1963

from Letter from John Adams to Thomas Jefferson, November 15, 1813

. . . We are now explicitly agreed, in one important point, vizt. That "there is a natural Aristocracy among men; the grounds of which are Virtue and Talents."

You very justly indulge a little merriment upon this solemn subject of Aristocracy. I often laugh at it too, for there is nothing in this laughable world more ridiculous than the management of it by almost all the nations of the Earth. But while We smile, Mankind have reason to say to Us, as the froggs said to the Boys, What is Sport to you is Wounds and death to Us. When I consider the weakness, the folly, the Pride, the Vanity, the Selfishness, the Artifice, the low craft and meaning cunning, the want of Principle, the Avarice the unbounded Ambition, the unfeeling Cruelty of a majority of those (in all Nations) who are allowed an aristocratical influence; and on the other hand, the Stupidity with which the more numerous multitude, not only become their Dupes, but even love to be Taken in by their Tricks: I feel a stronger disposition to weep at their destiny, than to laugh at their Folly.

But tho' We have agreed in one point, in Words, it is not yet certain that We are perfectly agreed in Sense. Fashion has introduced an indeterminate Use of the Word "Talents." Education, Wealth, Strength, Beauty, Stature, Birth, Marriage, graceful Attitudes and Motions, Gait, Air, Complexion, Physiognomy, are Talents, as well as Genius and Science and learning. Any one of these Talents, that in fact commands or influences true Votes in Society, gives to the Man who possesses it, the Character of an Aristocrat, in my Sense of the Word.

Pick up, the first 100 men you meet, and make a Republick. Every Man will have an equal Vote. But when deliberations and discussions are opened it will be found that 25, by their Talents, Virtues being equal, will be able to carry 50 Votes. Every one of these 25, is an Aristocrat, in my Sense of the Word; whether he obtains his one Vote in Addition to his own, by his Birth Fortune, Figure, Eloquence, Science, learning, Craft Cunning, or even his Character for good fellowship and a bon vivant. . . .

A daughter of a green Grocer, walks the Streets in London dayly with a baskett of Cabbage, Sprouts, Dandlions and Spinage on her head. She is observed by the Painters to have a beautiful Face, an elegant figure, a graceful Step and a debonair. They hire her to Sitt. She complies, and is painted by forty Artists in a Circle around her. The scientific Sir William Hamilton outbids the Painters, sends her to Schools for a genteel Education and Marries her. This Lady not only causes the Tryumphs of the Nile of Copinhagen and Trafalgar, but seperates Naples from France and finally banishes the King and Queen from Sicilly. Such is the Aristocracy of the natural Talent of Beauty. Millions of Examples might be quoted from History sacred and profane, from Eve, Hannah, Deborah Susanna Abigail, Judith, Ruth, down to Hellen Madame de Maintenon and Mrs. Fitzherbert. For mercy's sake do not compell me to look to our chaste States and Territories, to find Women, one of whom lett go, would, in the Words of Holopherne's Guards "deceive the whole Earth."[1] . . .

Your distinction between natural and artificial Aristocracy does not appear to me well founded. Birth and Wealth are conferred on some Men, as imperiously by Nature, as Genius, Strength or Beauty. The Heir is honours and Riches, and power has often no more merit in procuring these Advantages, than he has in obtaining an handsome face or an elegant figure. When Aristocracies, are established by human Laws and honour Wealth and Power are made hereditary by municipal Laws and political Institutions, then I acknowledge artificial Aristocracy to commence: but this never commences, till Corruption in Elections becomes dominant and uncontroulable. But this artificial Aristocracy can never last. The everlasting Envys, jealousies, Rivalries and quarrells among them, their cruel rapacities upon the poor ignorant People their followers, compell these to sett up Caesar, a Demagogue to be a Monarch and Master, pour mettre chacun a sa place ["to put each one in his

[1]The reference here is to Emma, Lady Hamilton, whose lover was Admiral, Lord Nelson.

place"]. Here you have the origin of all artificial Aristocracy, which is the origin of all Monarchy. And both artificial Aristocracy, and Monarchy, and civil, military, political and hierarchical Despotism, have all grown out of the natural Aristocracy of "Virtues and Talents." We, to be sure, are far remote from this. Many hundred years must roll away before We shall be corrupted. Our pure, virtuous, public spirited federative Republick will last for ever, govern the Globe and introduce the perfection of Man, his perfectability being already proved by Price Priestly, Condorcet Rousseau Diderot and Godwin.[2] . . .

Your distinction between the aristoi and pseudo aristoi, will not help the matter. I would trust one as soon as the other with unlimited Power. The Law wisely refuses an Oath as a witness in his own cause to the Saint as well as to the Sinner.

1963

Thomas Jefferson 1743–1826

The words written by Thomas Jefferson for the opening of the Declaration of Independence are among the most well known, powerful, and charged in the common historical and literary vocabulary of the United States: "We hold these truths to be self-evident"; "life, liberty and the pursuit of happiness"; and, perhaps most compellingly, "all men are created equal." Jefferson's phrases, and the remainder of the Declaration that he drafted, resonate with the political and social complexities of his own time yet go beyond such specificities to speak to the ideals of United States nationhood. The Declaration and Jefferson's other writings represented here—excerpts from *Notes on the State of Virginia* (1787) and selections from his prodigious letters—reveal an individual, and a young nation, struggling with issues of slavery, racial and cultural distinctiveness, political and national identity, the role of religion in civic life, the shape of government, modes of economic development, and the processes for creating a responsible, educated citizenry.

Jefferson was born at Shadwell, Virginia, in the foothills of the Appalachian Mountains, which marked the frontier in the mid-eighteenth century. His father, Peter Jefferson, was a successful landowner, planter, magistrate, surveyor, and mapmaker. His mother, Jane Randolph, a member of an influential Virginia family. Jefferson graduated from the College of William and Mary in 1762, then studied and practiced law. In 1770, Jefferson began building Monticello, a home and estate that he fashioned throughout his life. In 1772, he married Martha Wayles Skelton, with whom he had six children, only two surviving to adulthood. Martha Jefferson died after ten years of marriage, and Jefferson spent the remainder of his life as a widower.

Jefferson's political life began in colonial government in 1769 with his service as a representative to the Virginia House of Burgesses. A leader of the patriot faction aligning itself against Great Britain's assertions of control over the North American colonies, Jefferson wrote *A Summary View of the Rights of*

[2]Adams's appeal here to American incorruptibility is ironic and satiric.

British America (1774), a pamphlet in which he outlined a theory of natural rights based on the conviction that allegiance to a monarch and a country was voluntary. This startling pamphlet solidified Jefferson's reputation as an important political thinker and eloquent writer and brought him to the attention of people beyond Virginia. After his election to the Second Continental Congress, Jefferson was appointed, in June 1776, to serve as leader of a small committee preparing the Declaration. As primary author, Jefferson drafted the document, which was eventually revised and amended by Congress. Congress's decision to remove Jefferson's condemnation of Great Britain's role in the North American slave trade, with its implicit criticisms of the institution itself, points to the turbulent political atmosphere that Jefferson negotiated. Out of such a complex environment, Jefferson crafted a text that stands with the Constitution and the Bill of Rights as foundational documents of United States nationhood, an articulation, as well, of international concepts of personal and civil liberty.

During the Revolutionary years, Jefferson served Virginia as a member of its new General Assembly (1776–1779) and as governor (1779–1781). Toward the end of his governorship, he was given a semi-official questionnaire circulated by François Marbois, a representative of the French government, asking for information about the American states. Drawing upon his observations and the voluminous notes that he assembled as a lawyer, politician, philosopher, and amateur scientist, Jefferson revised Marbois's original questions into twenty-three "queries" whose answers constitute *Notes on the State of Virginia*, Jefferson's only full-length book. Far exceeding Marbois's questions, Jefferson uses facts about Virginia's rivers, towns, mountains, rocks, and climates as springboards for challenging some of the most prominent scientific theories of his day, including the notion, advanced by the Count de Buffon—the most influential naturalist of Jefferson's time—that both animals and people in the New World were smaller and weaker and therefore degenerate in comparison with their Old World counterparts. Buffon's widely accepted theory had implications for the development of American governmental and social institutions, and Jefferson attacks it with vigor, championing the Native American physique and elements of Native cultures as counterexample.

In *Notes,* Jefferson outlines the processes for establishing a republican government in Virginia and the United States, arguing that such a government, bound by the will of the people and subject to their adjustment, is exemplary. He supports systems of public education, with the goal of making the general public more capable of judicious decisions in civil and moral matters. Because he saw public education as a system where "the principal foundations of future order will be laid," Jefferson considered it society's responsibility to identify intellectually gifted individuals and cultivate their talents, "which nature has sown as liberally among the poor as the rich." As his letter to Nathaniel Burwell shows, however, Jefferson did not consider equal intellectual cultivation of the genders a civic necessity, noting that "a plan of female education has never been a subject of systematic contemplation with me." Jefferson's focus on the responsibility of the individual removed the institution of religion from the power of the state. He supported the concept of "reason and free inquiry" exercised by the individual, rather than the imposition of a state religion.

Jefferson was a strong supporter of

an agrarian-based economy in the United States that was built upon a class of small farmers infused with the individual ideals of civic responsibility, education, and religious freedom. This vision, among other ideas, placed Jefferson in the thick of significant national debates, including the Federalist and Anti-Federalist contention regarding governmental centralization versus state authority. It put him in conflict with Alexander Hamilton, who advocated a strong centralized government, a federal bank, and urban development. *Notes* reveals a constant in Jefferson's thought—local facts signifying transcendent ideals.

Notes also provides a window into Jefferson's attitudes toward slavery and African Americans. A slaveowner himself, Jefferson condemned the institution for its disastrous effects on both black and white people, charging, in the chapter titled "Manners," that white children who grew up witnessing the brutalities inherent in the system, and relying on the labor of others, could not help becoming despots. As a lawmaker, Jefferson proposed measures to end slavery in the United States, but his schemes were never enacted. In the chapter called "Laws," he advocates an emancipation of slaves and transportation of them to distant colonies where they would be "removed beyond the reach of mixture" with whites, a concept of racial separation that he supported throughout his life. He considered it impossible to incorporate former slaves into the white body politic, citing insurmountable prejudices and memories of injustice. He also relied on, and advanced, the then-common belief that black people were of an inferior race to whites. Jefferson's pronouncements on the physical, moral, social, and religious condition of "the" black person and "the" Native American are bankrupt by today's standards but are valuable for illuminating the philosophical and scientific attitudes of his own time. Jefferson initially planned to keep *Notes* out of the public realm, circulating copies among trusted friends and acquaintances. His reputation as an important thinker—and international interest in the fledgling nation—resulted in a clamor for *Notes,* to which he finally assented with publication first in Paris, then in London. *Notes* proved to be an important statement of Enlightenment thought and the first major contribution by an American to the scientific and philosophical sea change.

While Jefferson intellectualized about the evils of slavery, and undoubtedly agonized about its effects—writing, "I tremble for my country when I reflect that God is just"—his private conduct regarding the institution was more circumspect. In an 1814 letter to his former neighbor Edward Coles, Jefferson counseled that abolition, "this doctrine truly christian," should be introduced "softly but steadily," characterizing the national eradication of slavery as an "enterprise for the young." Jefferson freed only seven of his slaves, all members of the slave Sally Hemmings's family, a circumstance that fueled speculation, common in his own time and extending to ours with the support of DNA evidence, that Jefferson fathered at least one, if not all, of Hemmings's children. The nature of the relationship between Jefferson and Hemmings—who was a companion and maid to Jefferson's daughters, a domestic servant at Monticello, and perhaps a half-sister to Jefferson's wife, Martha—remains elusive, but their association attests to the dissonances between public and private engagement with the institution of slavery.

Jefferson served the nation as a member of the Continental Congress (1783–1784), minister to France (1784–1789), and secretary of state (1789–1793). After a brief retirement from public service, he became president for two terms (1801–1809). During his presidency, Jefferson recognized the inevitable conflicts arising from further western expansion of white settlement onto Indian lands and argued, to no avail, for the systemic incorporation of Native Americans into the economic and civic life of the United States. A deeply paternalistic enterprise, his plan for assimilating the Indian, expressed in his letters to Benjamin Hawkins and the Seneca chief Handsome Lake, was rooted in Jefferson's belief in agrarianism, calling for a reorientation of Native cultures away from seminomadic traditions based on hunting and gathering and toward life in settled agricultural communities. This shift, Jefferson believed, would benefit the young nation by reducing the amount of land that Indians needed for subsistence, freeing those lands for white settlement.

Jefferson's attitudes toward the citizenship of Native Americans and African Americans were paradoxical: he believed whites and Indians should "intermix, and become one people," but he opposed the same process with blacks. As this and his attitudes toward educating young men and young women suggest, Jefferson's revolutionary statement that "all men are created equal" came with significant caveats during his day but laid the philosophical foundation for a modern acknowledgment of universal rights, a concept that continues to serve, and challenge, the United States today. The activities of Jefferson's later years, the founding of the University of Virginia (1819) and his donation of his personal library as a seed for the Library of Congress, attest to his fundamental belief that education, and the intellectual freedom that it engenders, is the cornerstone to personhood and nationhood.

Jefferson died on July 4, 1826, the fiftieth anniversary of the signing of the Declaration and within hours of the death of John Adams, a poignant reminder of the role that Jefferson and his compatriots played in the establishment of the United States and a symbolic passing of national political responsibility to younger generations.

Katherine E. Ledford
Appalachian State University

PRIMARY WORKS

The Writings of Thomas Jefferson, ed. Andrew A. Lipscomb and Albert E. Bergh, 1903–1904; *The Papers of Thomas Jefferson,* 1950–; *Notes on the State of Virginia,* ed. William Peden, 1954; *Thomas Jefferson: Writings,* Library of America, ed. Merrill Peterson, 1984.

from Notes on the State of Virginia

from Query VI Productions, Mineral, Vegetable, and Animal, Buffon and the Theory of Degeneracy

It is the opinion of Mons. de Buffon[1] that [humankind in America] furnishes no exception to [the theory of the degeneracy of species in the New World]: "Although the savage of the new world is about the same height as man in our world, this does not suffice for him to constitute an exception to the general fact that all living nature has become smaller on that continent. The savage is feeble, and has small organs of generation; he has neither hair nor beard, and no ardor whatever for his female; although swifter than the European because he is better accustomed to running, he is, on the other hand, less strong in body; he is also less sensitive, and yet more timid and cowardly; he has no vivacity, no activity of mind; the activity of his body is less an exercise, a voluntary motion, than a necessary action caused by want; relieve him of hunger and thirst, and you deprive him of the active principle of all his movements; he will rest stupidly upon his legs or lying down entire days. There is no need for seeking further the cause of the isolated mode of life of these savages and their repugnance for society: the most precious spark of the fire of nature has been refused to them; they lack ardor for their females, and consequently have no love for their fellow men: not knowing this strongest and most tender of all affections, their other feelings are also cold and languid; they love their parents and children but little; the most intimate of all ties, the family connection, binds them therefore but loosely together; between family and family there is no tie at all; hence they have no communion, no commonwealth, no state of society. Physical love constitutes their only morality; their heart is icy, their society cold, and their rule harsh. They look upon their wives only as servants for all work, or as beasts of burden, which they load without consideration with the burden of their hunting, and which they compel without mercy, without gratitude, to perform tasks which are often beyond their strength. They have only few children, and they take little care of them. Everywhere the original defect appears: they are indifferent because they have little sexual capacity, and this indifference to the other sex is the fundamental defect which weakens their nature, prevents its development, and—destroying the very germs of life—uproots society at the same time. Man is here no exception to the general rule. Nature, by refusing him the power of love, has treated him worse and lowered him deeper than any animal."[2] An afflicting picture indeed, which, for the honor of human nature, I am glad to believe has no original. Of the Indian of South America I know nothing; for I would not honor with the appellation of knowledge, what I derive from the fables published of them. These I believe to be just as true as the fables of Æsop. This

[1]Georges Louis Leclerc, Count de Buffon (1707–1788), most eminent natural historian of the age who had argued for the inferior stature and strength of New World life forms.

[2]The quotation from Buffon was originally published in French.

belief is founded on what I have seen of man, white, red, and black, and what has been written of him by authors, enlightened themselves, and writing amidst an enlightened people. The Indian of North America being more within our reach, I can speak of him somewhat from my own knowledge, but more from the information of others better acquainted with him, and on whose truth and judgment I can rely. From these sources I am able to say, in contradiction to this representation, that he is neither more defective in ardor, nor more impotent with his female, than the white reduced to the same diet and exercise: that he is brave, when an enterprize depends on bravery; education with him making the point of honor consist in the destruction of an enemy by stratagem, and in the preservation of his own person free from injury; or perhaps this is nature; while it is education which teaches us to honor force more than finesse: that he will defend himself against an host of enemies, always chusing to be killed, rather than to surrender, though it be to the whites, who he knows will treat him well: that in other situations also he meets death with more deliberation, and endures tortures with a firmness unknown almost to religious enthusiasm with us: that he is affectionate to his children, careful of them, and indulgent in the extreme: that his affections comprehend his other connections, weakening, as with us, from circle to circle, as they recede from the center: that his friendships are strong and faithful to the uttermost extremity: that his sensibility is keen, even the warriors weeping most bitterly on the loss of their children, though in general they endeavour to appear superior to human events: that his vivacity and activity of mind is equal to ours in the same situation; hence his eagerness for hunting, and for games of chance. The women are submitted to unjust drudgery. This I believe is the case with every barbarous people. With such, force is law. The stronger sex therefore imposes on the weaker. It is civilization alone which replaces women in the enjoyment of their natural equality. That first teaches us to subdue the selfish passions, and to respect those rights in others which we value in ourselves. Were we in equal barbarism, our females would be equal drudges. The man with them is less strong than with us, but their woman stronger than ours; and both for the same obvious reason; because our man and their woman is habituated to labour, and formed by it. With both races the sex which is indulged with ease is least athletic. An Indian man is small in the hand and wrist for the same reason for which a sailor is large and strong in the arms and shoulders, and a porter in the legs and thighs.—They raise fewer children than we do. The causes of this are to be found, not in a difference of nature, but of circumstance. The women very frequently attending the men in their parties of war and of hunting, child-bearing becomes extremely inconvenient to them. It is said, therefore, that they have learnt the practice of procuring abortion by the use of some vegetable; and that it even extends to prevent conception for a considerable time after. During these parties they are exposed to numerous hazards, to excessive exertions, to the greatest extremities of hunger. Even at their homes the nation depends for food, through a certain part of every year, on the gleanings of the forest: that is, they experience a famine once in every year. With all animals, if the female be badly fed, or not fed at all, her young perish: and if both male and female be reduced to like want, generation becomes less active, less productive. To the obstacles then of want and hazard, which nature has opposed to the multiplication of wild animals, for the purpose of restraining their numbers within certain bounds, those of labour and of voluntary abortion are added with the Indian. No wonder then if they multiply less than we do.

Where food is regularly supplied, a single farm will shew more of cattle, than a whole country of forests can of buffaloes. The same Indian women, when married to white traders, who feed them and their children plentifully and regularly, who exempt them from excessive drudgery, who keep them stationary and unexposed to accident, produce and raise as many children as the white women. Instances are known, under these circumstances, of their rearing a dozen children. An inhuman practice once prevailed in this country of making slaves of the Indians. It is a fact well known with us, that the Indian women so enslaved produced and raised as numerous families as either the whites or blacks among whom they lived.—It has been said, that Indians have less hair than the whites, except on the head. But this is a fact of which fair proof can scarcely be had. With them it is disgraceful to be hairy on the body. They say it likens them to hogs. They therefore pluck the hair as fast as it appears. But the traders who marry their women, and prevail on them to discontinue this practice, say, that nature is the same with them as with the whites. Nor, if the fact be true, is the consequence necessary which has been drawn from it. Negroes have notoriously less hair than the whites; yet they are more ardent. But if cold and moisture be the agents of nature for diminishing the races of animals, how comes she all at once to suspend their operation as to the physical man of the new world, whom the Count acknowledges to be 'à peu près de mème stature que l'homme de notre monde,'[3] and to let loose their influence on his moral faculties? How has this 'combination of the elements and other physical causes, so contrary to the enlargement of animal nature in this new world, these obstacles to the development and formation of great germs,' been arrested and suspended, so as to permit the human body to acquire its just dimensions, and by what inconceivable process has their action been directed on his mind alone? To judge of the truth of this, to form a just estimate of their genius and mental powers, more facts are wanting, and great allowance to be made for those circumstances of their situation which call for a display of particular talents only. This done, we shall probably find that they are formed in mind as well as in body, on the same module with the 'Homo sapiens Europæus'."[4] The principles of their society forbidding all compulsion, they are to be led to duty and to enterprize by personal influence and persuasion. Hence eloquence in council, bravery and address in war, become the foundations of all consequence with them. To these acquirements all their faculties are directed. Of their bravery and address in war we have multiplied proofs, because we have been the subjects on which they were exercised. Of their eminence in oratory we have fewer examples, because it is displayed chiefly in their own councils. Some, however, we have of very superior lustre. I may challenge the whole orations of Demosthenes and Cicero, and of any more eminent orator, if Europe has furnished more eminent, to produce a single passage, superior to the speech of Logan, a Mingo chief, to Lord Dunmore, when governor of this state. And, as a testimony of their talents in this line, I beg leave to introduce it, first stating the incidents necessary for understanding it. In the spring of the year 1774, a robbery and murder were committed on an inhabitant of the frontiers of Virginia, by two Indians of the Shawanee tribe. The neighbouring whites, according to their

[3]". . . nearly the same size as men of our world."

[4]European man.

custom, undertook to punish this outrage in a summary way. Col. Cresap,[5] a man infamous for the many murders he had committed on those much-injured people, collected a party, and proceeded down the Kanhaway in quest of vengeance. Unfortunately a canoe of women and children, with one man only, was seen coming from the opposite shore, unarmed, and unsuspecting an hostile attack from the whites. Cresap and his party concealed themselves on the bank of the river, and the moment the canoe reached the shore, singled out their objects, and, at one fire, killed every person in it. This happened to be the family of Logan, who had long been distinguished as a friend of the whites. This unworthy return provoked his vengeance. He accordingly signalized himself in the war which ensued. In the autumn of the same year, a decisive battle was fought at the mouth of the Great Kanhaway, between the collected forces of the Shawanees, Mingoes, and Delawares, and a detachment of the Virginia militia. The Indians were defeated, and sued for peace. Logan however disdained to be seen among the suppliants. But, lest the sincerity of a treaty should be distrusted, from which so distinguished a chief absented himself, he sent by a messenger the following speech to be delivered to Lord Dunmore.

'I appeal to any white man to say, if ever he entered Logan's cabin hungry, and he gave him not meat; if ever he came cold and naked, and he clothed him not. During the course of the last long and bloody war, Logan remained idle in his cabin, an advocate for peace. Such was my love for the whites, that my countrymen pointed as they passed, and said, 'Logan is the friend of white men.' I had even thought to have lived with you, but for the injuries of one man. Col. Cresap, the last spring, in cold blood, and unprovoked, murdered all the relations of Logan, not sparing even my women and children. There runs not a drop of my blood in the veins of any living creature. This called on me for revenge. I have sought it: I have killed many: I have fully glutted my vengeance. For my country, I rejoice at the beams of peace. But do not harbour a thought that mine is the joy of fear. Logan never felt fear. He will not turn on his heel to save his life. Who is there to mourn for Logan?—Not one.'

Before we condemn the Indians of this continent as wanting genius, we must consider that letters have not yet been introduced among them. Were we to compare them in their present state with the Europeans North of the Alps, when the Roman arms and arts first crossed those mountains, the comparison would be unequal, because, at that time, those parts of Europe were swarming with numbers; because numbers produce emulation, and multiply the chances of improvement, and one improvement begets another. Yet I may safely ask, How many good poets, how many

[5]Michael Cresap (1742–1775), Maryland frontiersman and soldier. When the accuracy of this account was questioned, particularly Cresap's role, Jefferson made further inquiries and in an appendix to the 1800 Philadelphia edition of *Notes* requested that in later editions the section between the words "In the spring of the year 1774 . . ." and ". . . distinguished as a friend of the whites," be changed to read "In the spring of the year 1774, a robbery was committed by some Indians on certain land-adventurers on the river Ohio. The whites in that quarter, according to their custom, undertook to punish this outrage in a summary way. Captain Michael Cresap, and a certain Daniel Great-house, leading on these parties, surprized, at different times, travelling and hunting parties of the Indians, having their women and children with them, and murdered many. Among these were unfortunately the family of Logan, a chief celebrated in peace and war, and long distinguished as the friend of the whites."

able mathematicians, how many great inventors in arts or sciences, had Europe North of the Alps then produced? And it was sixteen centuries after this before a Newton could be formed. I do not mean to deny, that there are varieties in the race of man, distinguished by their powers both of body and mind. I believe there are, as I see to be the case in the races of other animals. I only mean to suggest a doubt, whether the bulk and faculties of animals depend on the side of the Atlantic on which their food happens to grow, or which furnishes the elements of which they are compounded? Whether nature has enlisted herself as a Cis or Trans-Atlantic partisan? I am induced to suspect, there has been more eloquence than sound reasoning displayed in support of this theory; that it is one of those cases where the judgment has been seduced by a glowing pen: and whilst I render every tribute of honor and esteem to the celebrated Zoologist, who has added, and is still adding, so many precious things to the treasures of science, I must doubt whether in this instance he has not cherished error also, by lending her for a moment his vivid imagination and bewitching language.

So far the Count de Buffon has carried this new theory of the tendency of nature to belittle her productions on this side the Atlantic. Its application to the race of whites, transplanted from Europe, remained for the Abbé Raynal.[6] 'On doit etre etonné (he says) que l'Amerique n'ait pas encore produit un bon poëte, un habile mathematicien, un homme de genie dans un seul art, ou une seule science.[7] 'America has not yet produced one good poet.' When we shall have existed as a people as long as the Greeks did before they produced a Homer, the Romans a Virgil, the French a Racine and Voltaire, the English a Shakespeare and Milton, should this reproach be still true, we will enquire from what unfriendly causes it has proceeded, that the other countries of Europe and quarters of the earth shall not have inscribed any name in the roll of poets.[8] But neither has America produced 'one able mathematician, one man of genius in a single art or a single science.' In war we have produced a Washington, whose memory will be adored while liberty shall have votaries, whose name will triumph over time, and will in future ages assume its just station among the most celebrated worthies of the world, when that wretched philosophy shall be forgotten which would have arranged him among the degeneracies of nature. In physics we have produced a Franklin, than whom no one of the present age has made more important discoveries, nor has enriched philosophy with more, or more ingenious solutions of the phænomena of nature. We have supposed Mr. Rittenhouse[9] second to no astronomer living: that in genius he must be the first, because he is self-taught. As an artist he has exhibited as great a proof of mechanical genius

[6]Guillaume Thomas François Raynal (1713–1796), French historian and *philosophe*.

[7]"One must be astonished that America has yet to produce one good poet, an able mathematician, or a man of genius in a single art or a single science."

[8]Has the world as yet produced more than two poets, acknowledged to be such by all nations? An Englishman, only, reads Milton with delight, an Italian Tasso, a Frenchman the Henriade, a Portuguese Camouens: but Homer and Virgil have been the rapture of every age and nation: they are read with enthusiasm in their originals by those who can read the originals, and in translations by those who cannot. [Jefferson's note]

[9]David Rittenhouse (1732–1796), Philadelphia mathematician and astronomer.

as the world has ever produced. He has not indeed made a world; but he has by imitation approached nearer its Maker than any man who has lived from the creation to this day.[10] As in philosophy and war, so in government, in oratory, in painting, in the plastic art, we might shew that America, though but a child of yesterday, has already given hopeful proofs of genius, as well of the nobler kinds, which arouse the best feelings of man, which call him into action, which substantiate his freedom, and conduct him to happiness, as of the subordinate, which serve to amuse him only. We therefore suppose, that this reproach is as unjust as it is unkind; and that, of the geniuses which adorn the present age, America contributes its full share. For comparing it with those countries, where genius is most cultivated, where are the most excellent models for art, and scaffoldings for the attainment of science, as France and England for instance, we calculate thus. The United States contain three millions of inhabitants; France twenty millions; and the British islands ten. We produce a Washington, a Franklin, a Rittenhouse. France then should have half a dozen in each of these lines, and Great-Britain half that number, equally eminent. It may be true, that France has: we are but just becoming acquainted with her, and our acquaintance so far gives us high ideas of the genius of her inhabitants. It would be injuring too many of them to name particularly a Voltaire, a Buffon, the constellation of Encyclopedists, the Abbé Raynal himself, &c. &c. We therefore have reason to believe she can produce her full quota of genius. The present war having so long cut off all communication with Great-Britain, we are not able to make a fair estimate of the state of science in that country. The spirit in which she wages war is the only sample before our eyes, and that does not seem the legitimate offspring either of science or of civilization. The sun of her glory is fast descending to the horizon. Her philosophy has crossed the Channel, her freedom the Atlantic, and herself seems passing to that awful dissolution, whose issue is not given human foresight to scan.

from Query XI
Aborigines, Original Condition and Origin

When the first effectual settlement of our colony was made, which was in 1607, the country from the sea-coast to the mountains, and from Patowmac to the most southern waters of James river, was occupied by upwards of forty different tribes of Indians. Of these the *Powhatans,* the *Mannahoacs,* and *Monacans,* were the most powerful. Those between the sea-coast and falls of the rivers, were in amity with one another, and attached to the *Powhatans* as their link of union. Those between the falls of the rivers and the mountains, were divided into two confederacies; the tribes inhabiting the head waters of Patowmac and Rappahanoc being attached to the *Mannahoacs;* and those on the upper parts of James river to the *Monacans.* But the *Monacans* and their friends were in amity with the *Mannahoacs* and their friends, and waged joint and

[10]There are various ways of keeping truth out of sight. Mr. Rittenhouse's model of the planetary system has the plagiary appellation of an Orrery; and the quadrant invented by Godfrey, an American also, and with the aid of which the European nations traverse the globe, is called Hadley's quadrant. [Jefferson's note. Thomas Godfrey (1704–1749), a Philadelphia glazier, was a member of Franklin's Junto. See the selection of poetry.]

perpetual war against the *Powhatans.* We are told that the *Powhatans, Mannahoacs,* and *Monacans,* spoke languages so radically different, that interpreters were necessary when they transacted business. Hence we may conjecture, that this was not the case between all the tribes, and probably that each spoke the language of the nation to which it was attached; which we know to have been the case in many particular instances. Very possibly there may have been antiently three different stocks, each of which multiplying in a long course of time, had separated into so many little societies. This practice results from the circumstance of their having never submitted themselves to any laws, any coercive power, any shadow of government. Their only controuls are their manners, and that moral sense of right and wrong, which, like the sense of tasting and feeling, in every man makes a part of his nature. An offence against these is punished by contempt, by exclusion from society, or, where the case is serious, as that of murder, by the individuals whom it concerns. Imperfect as this species of coercion may seem, crimes are very rare among them: insomuch that were it made a question, whether no law, as among the savage Americans, or too much law, as among the civilized Europeans, submits man to the greatest evil, one who has seen both conditions of existence would pronounce it to be the last: and that the sheep are happier of themselves, than under care of the wolves. It will be said, that great societies cannot exist without government. The Savages therefore break them into small ones. . . .

I know of no such thing existing as an Indian monument: for I would not honour with that name arrow points, stone hatchets, stone pipes, and half-shapen images. Of labour on the large scale, I think there is no remain as respectable as would be a common ditch for the draining of lands: unless indeed it be the Barrows, of which many are to be found all over this country. These are of different sizes, some of them constructed of earth, and some of loose stones. That they were repositories of the dead, has been obvious to all: but on what particular occasion constructed, was matter of doubt. Some have thought they covered the bones of those who have fallen in battles fought on the spot of interment. Some ascribed them to the custom, said to prevail among the Indians, of collecting, at certain periods, the bones of all their dead, wheresoever deposited at the time of death. Others again supposed them the general sepulchres for towns, conjectured to have been on or near these grounds; and this opinion was supported by the quality of the lands in which they are found, (those constructed of earth being generally in the softest and most fertile meadow-grounds on river sides) and by a tradition, said to be handed down from the Aboriginal Indians, that, when they settled in a town, the first person who died was placed erect, and earth put about him, so as to cover and support him; that, when another died, a narrow passage was dug to the first, the second reclined against him, and the cover of earth replaced, and so on. There being one of these in my neighbourhood, I wished to satisfy myself whether any, and which of these opinions were just. For this purpose I determined to open and examine it thoroughly. It was situated on the low grounds of the Rivanna, about two miles above its principle fork, and opposite to some hills, on which had been an Indian town. It was of a spheroidical form, of about 40 feet diameter at the base, and had been of about twelve feet altitude, though now reduced by the plough to seven and a half, having been under cultivation about a dozen years. Before this it was covered with trees of twelve inches diameter, and round the base was an excavation of five feet depth and width, from whence the earth had been taken of which the hillock was formed. I first dug superficially in several parts of it, and came to collections of human bones, at different depths, from six inches to three feet below the surface. These were lying in the utmost confusion, some vertical, some oblique, some horizontal, and directed to every point of the compass, entangled, and held together in clusters by the earth. Bones of the most distant parts were found together, as, for instance, the small bones of the foot in the hollow of a scull, many sculls would sometimes be in contact, lying on the face, on the side, on the back, top or bottom, so as, on the whole to give the idea of bones emptied promiscuously from a bag or basket, and covered over with earth, without any attention to their order. The bones of which the greatest numbers remained, were sculls, jaw-bones, teeth, the bones of the arms, thighs, legs, feet, and hands. A few ribs remained, some vertebræ of the neck and spine, without their processes, and one instance only of the bone[1] which serves as a base to the vertebral column. The sculls were so tender, that they generally fell to pieces on being touched. The other bones were stronger. There were some teeth which were judged to be smaller than those of an adult; a scull, which, on a slight view, appeared to be that of an infant, but it fell to pieces on being taken out, so as to prevent satisfactory examination; a rib, and a fragment of the under-jaw of a person about half grown; another rib of an infant; and part of the jaw of a child, which had not yet cut its teeth. This last furnishing the most decisive proof of the burial of children here, I was particular in my attention to it. It was part of the right-half of the under-jaw. The processes, by which it was articulated to the temporal bones, were entire; and the bone itself firm to where it had been broken off, which, as nearly as I could judge, was about the place of the eye-tooth. Its upper edge, wherein would have been the sockets of the teeth, was perfectly smooth. Measuring it with that of an adult, by placing their hinder processes together, its broken end extended to the penultimate grinder of the adult. This bone was white, all the others of a sand colour. The bones of infants being soft, they probably decay sooner, which might be the cause so few were found here. I proceeded then to make a perpendicular cut through the body of the barrow, that I might examine its internal structure. This passed about three feet from its center, was opened to the former surface of the earth, and was wide enough for a man to walk through and examine its sides. At the bottom, that is, on the level of the circumjacent plain, I found bones; above these a few stones, brought from a cliff a quarter of a mile off, and from the river one-eighth of a mile off; then a large interval of earth, then a stratum of bones, and so on. At one end of the section were four strata of bones plainly distinguishable; at the other, three; the strata in one part not ranging with those in another. The bones nearest the surface were least decayed. No holes were discovered in any of them, as if made with bullets, arrows, or other weapons. I conjectured that in this barrow might have been a thousand skeletons. Every one will readily seize the circumstances above related, which militate against the opinion, that it covered the bones only of persons fallen in battle; and against the tradition also, which would make it the common sepulchre of a town, in which the bodies were placed upright, and touching each other. Appearances certainly indicate that it has derived both origin and growth from the accustomary collection of bones, and deposition of them together; that the first collection had been deposited on the common surface of the earth, a few stones put over it, and then a covering of earth, that the second had been

[1]The os sacrum.

laid on this, had covered more or less of it in proportion to the number of bones, and was then also covered with earth; and so on. The following are the particular circumstances which give it this aspect. 1. The number of bones. 2. Their confused position. 3. Their being in different strata. 4. The strata in one part having no correspondence with those in another. 5. The different states of decay in these strata, which seem to indicate a difference in the time of inhumation. 6. The existence of infant bones among them.

But on whatever occasion they may have been made, they are of considerable notoriety among the Indians: for a party passing, about thirty years ago, through the part of the country where this barrow is, went through the woods directly to it, without any instructions or enquiry, and having staid about it some time, with expressions which were construed to be those of sorrow, they returned to the high road, which they had left about half a dozen miles to pay this visit, and pursued their journey. There is another barrow, much resembling this in the low grounds of the South branch of Shenandoah, where it is crossed by the road leading from the Rock-fish gap to Staunton. Both of these have, within these dozen years, been cleared of their trees and put under cultivation, are much reduced in their height, and spread in width, by the plough, and will probably disappear in time. There is another on a hill in the Blue ridge of mountains, a few miles North of Wood's gap, which is made up of small stones thrown together. This has been opened and found to contain human bones, as the others do. There are also many others in other parts of the country.

Great question has arisen from whence came those aboriginal inhabitants of America? Discoveries, long ago made, were sufficient to shew that a passage from Europe to America was always practicable, even to the imperfect navigation of ancient times. In going from Norway to Iceland, from Iceland to Groenland, from Groenland to Labrador, the first traject is the widest: and this having been practised from the earliest times of which we have any account of that part of the earth, it is not difficult to suppose that the subsequent trajects may have been sometimes passed. Again, the late discoveries of Captain Cook, coasting from Kamschatka to California, have proved that, if the two continents of Asia and America be separated at all, it is only by a narrow streight. So that from this side also, inhabitants may have passed into America: and the resemblance between the Indians of America and the Eastern inhabitants of Asia, would induce us to conjecture, that the former are the descendants of the latter, or the latter of the former: excepting indeed the Eskimaux, who, from the same circumstance of resemblance, and from identity of language, must be derived from the Groenlanders, and these probably from some of the northern parts of the old continent. A knowledge of their several languages would be the most certain evidence of their derivation which could be produced. In fact, it is the best proof of the affinity of nations which ever can be referred to. How many ages have elapsed since the English, the Dutch, the Germans, the Swiss, the Norwegians, Danes and Swedes have separated from their common stock? Yet how many more must elapse before the proofs of their common origin, which exist in their several languages, will disappear? It is to be lamented then, very much to be lamented, that we have suffered so many of the Indian tribes already to extinguish, without our having previously collected and deposited in the records of literature, the general rudiments at least of the languages they spoke. Were vocabularies formed of all the languages spoken in North and South America, preserving their appellations of the most common objects in nature, of those which must be present to every nation barbarous or civilised, with the inflections of their nouns and verbs, their principles of regimen and concord, and these deposited in all the public libraries, it would furnish opportunities to those skilled in the languages of the old world to compare them with these, now, or at any future time, and hence to construct the best evidence of the derivation of this part of the human race. . . .

from Query XIV
Laws

. . . Many of the laws which were in force during the monarchy being relative merely to that form of government, or inculcating principles inconsistent with republicanism, the first assembly which met after the establishment of the commonwealth appointed a committee to revise the whole code, to reduce it into proper form and volume, and report it to the assembly.[1] . . . The following are the most remarkable alterations proposed:

To change the rules of descent, so as that the lands of any person dying intestate shall be divisible equally among all his children, or other representatives, in equal degree.

To make slaves distributable among the next of kin, as other moveables.

To have all public expences, whether of the general treasury, or of a parish or county, (as for the maintenance of the poor, building bridges, court-houses, &c.) supplied by assessments on the citizens, in proportion to their property.

To hire undertakers for keeping the public roads in repair, and indemnify individuals through whose lands new roads shall be opened.

To define with precision the rules whereby aliens should become citizens, and citizens make themselves aliens.

To establish religious freedom on the broadest bottom.

To emancipate all slaves born after passing the act. The bill reported by the revisors does not itself contain this proposition; but an amendment containing it was prepared, to be offered to the legislature whenever the bill should be taken up, and further directing, that they should continue with their parents to a certain age, then be brought up, at the public expence, to tillage, arts or sciences, according to their geniusses, till the females should be eighteen, and the males twenty-one years of age, when they should be colonized to such place as the circumstances of the time should render most proper, sending them out with arms, implements of houshold and of the handicraft arts, feeds, pairs of the useful domestic animals, &c. to declare them a free and independant people, and extend to them our alliance and protection, till they shall have acquired strength; and to send vessels at the same time to other parts of the world for an equal number of white inhabitants; to induce whom to migrate hither, proper encouragements were to be proposed. It will probably be asked, Why not retain and incorporate the blacks into the state, and thus save the expence of supplying, by importation of white settlers, the vacancies they will leave? Deep rooted prejudices entertained by the whites; ten thousand recollections, by the blacks, of the

[1]Jefferson was one of three members of the Committee of Revisors [Ed.].

injuries they have sustained; new provocations; the real distinctions which nature has made; and many other circumstances, will divide us into parties, and produce convulsions which will probably never end but in the extermination of the one or the other race.—To these objections, which are political, may be added others, which are physical and moral. The first difference which strikes us is that of colour. Whether the black of the negro resides in the reticular membrane between the skin and scarf-skin, or in the scarf-skin itself; whether it proceeds from the colour of the blood, the colour of the bile, or from that of some other secretion, the difference is fixed in nature, and is as real as if its seat and cause were better known to us. And is this difference of no importance? Is it not the foundation of a greater or less share of beauty in the two races? Are not the fine mixtures of red and white, the expressions of every passion by greater or less suffusions of colour in the one, preferable to that eternal monotony, which reigns in the countenances, that immoveable veil of black which covers all the emotions of the other race? Add to these, flowing hair, a more elegant symmetry of form, their own judgment in favour of the whites, declared by their preference of them, as uniformly as is the preference of the Oranootan for the black women over those of his own species. The circumstance of superior beauty, is thought worthy attention in the propagation of our horses, dogs, and other domestic animals; why not in that of man? Besides those of colour, figure, and hair, there are other physical distinctions proving a difference of race. They have less hair on the face and body. They secrete less by the kidnies, and more by the glands of the skin, which gives them a very strong and disagreeable odour. This greater degree of transpiration renders them more tolerant of heat, and less so of cold, than the whites. Perhaps too a difference of structure in the pulmonary apparatus, which a late ingenious experimentalist has discovered to be the principal regulator of animal heat, may have disabled them from extricating, in the act of inspiration, so much of that fluid from the outer air, or obliged them in expiration, to part with more of it. They seem to require less sleep. A black, after hard labour through the day, will be induced by the slightest amusements to sit up till midnight, or later, though knowing he must be out with the first dawn of the morning. They are at least as brave, and more adventuresome. But this may perhaps proceed from a want of forethought, which prevents their seeing a danger till it be present. When present, they do not go through it with more coolness or steadiness than the whites. They are more ardent after their female: but love seems with them to be more an eager desire, than a tender delicate mixture of sentiment and sensation. Their griefs are transient. Those numberless afflictions, which render it doubtful whether heaven has given life to us in mercy or in wrath, are less felt, and sooner forgotten with them. In general, their existence appears to participate more of sensation than reflection. To this must be ascribed their disposition to sleep when abstracted from their diversions, and unemployed in labour. An animal whose body is at rest, and who does not reflect, must be disposed to sleep of course. Comparing them by their faculties of memory, reason, and imagination, it appears to me, that in memory they are equal to the whites; in reason much inferior, as I think one could scarcely be found capable of tracing and comprehending the investigations of Euclid; and that in imagination they are dull, tasteless, and anomalous. It would be unfair to follow them to Africa for this investigation. We will consider them here, on the same stage with the whites, and where the facts are not apocryphal on which a judgment is to be formed. It will be right to make great allowances for the difference of condition, of education, of conversation, of the sphere in which they move. Many millions of them have been brought to, and born in America. Most of them indeed have been confined to tillage, to their own homes, and their own society: yet many have been so situated, that they might have availed themselves of the conversation of their masters; many have been brought up to the handicraft arts, and from that circumstance have always been associated with the whites. Some have been liberally educated, and all have lived in countries where the arts and sciences are cultivated to a considerable degree, and have had before their eyes samples of the best works from abroad. The Indians, with no advantages of this kind, will often carve figures on their pipes not destitute of design and merit. They will crayon out an animal, a plant, or a country, so as to prove the existence of a germ in their minds which only wants cultivation. They astonish you with strokes of the most sublime oratory; such as prove their reason and sentiment strong, their imagination glowing and elevated. But never yet could I find that a black had uttered a thought above the level of plain narration; never see even an elementary trait of painting or sculpture. In music they are more generally gifted than the whites with accurate ears for tune and time, and they have been found capable of imagining a small catch.[2] Whether they will be equal to the composition of a more extensive run of melody, or of complicated harmony, is yet to be proved. Misery is often the parent of the most affecting touches in poetry.—Among the blacks is misery enough, God knows, but no poetry. Love is the peculiar œstrum of the poet. Their love is ardent, but it kindles the senses only, not the imagination. Religion indeed has produced a Phyllis Whately; but it could not produce a poet.[3] The compositions published under her name are below the dignity of criticism. The heroes of the Dunciad are to her, as Hercules to the author of that poem. Ignatius Sancho has approached nearer to merit in composition; yet his letters do more honour to the heart than the head. They breathe the purest effusions of friendship and general philanthropy, and shew how great a degree of the latter may be compounded with strong religious zeal. He is often happy in the turn of his compliments, and his stile is easy and familiar, except when he affects a Shandean fabrication of words. But his imagination is wild and extravagant, escapes incessantly from every restraint of reason and taste, and, in the course of its vagaries, leaves a tract of thought as incoherent and eccentric, as is the course of a meteor through the sky. His subjects should often have led him to a process of sober reasoning: yet we find him always substituting sentiment for demonstration. Upon the whole, though we admit him to the first place among those of his own colour who have presented themselves to the public judgment, yet when we compare him with the writers of the race among whom he lived, and particularly with the epistolary class, in which he has taken his own stand, we are compelled to enroll him at the bottom of the column. This criticism supposes the letters published under his name to be genuine, and to have received amendment from no other hand; points which

[2]The instrument proper to them is the Banjar, which they brought hither from Africa, and which is the original of the guitar, its chords being precisely the four lower chords of the guitar.

[3]Jefferson is speaking of Phillis Wheatley (1753–1784), a distinguished poet whose writings appear elsewhere in this anthology [Ed.].

would not be of easy investigation. The improvement of the blacks in body and mind, in the first instance of their mixture with the whites, has been observed by every one, and proves that their inferiority is not the effect merely of their condition of life. We know that among the Romans, about the Augustan age especially, the condition of their slaves was much more deplorable than that of the blacks on the continent of America. The two sexes were confined in separate apartments, because to raise a child cost the master more than to buy one. Cato, for a very restricted indulgence to his slaves in this particular, took from them a certain price. But in this country the slaves multiply as fast as the free inhabitants. Their situation and manners place the commerce between the two sexes almost without restraint.—The same Cato, on a principle of œconomy, always sold his sick and superannuated slaves. He gives it as a standing precept to a master visiting his farm, to sell his old oxen, old waggons, old tools, old and diseased servants, and every thing else become useless. 'Vendat boves vetulos, plaustrum vetus, ferramenta vetera, servum senem, servum morbosum, & si quid aliud supersit vendat.' Cato de re rusticâ. c. 2. The American slaves cannot enumerate this among the injuries and insults they receive. It was the common practice to expose in the island of Æsculapius, in the Tyber, diseased slaves, whose cure was like to become tedious. The Emperor Claudius, by an edict, gave freedom to such of them as should recover, and first declared, that if any person chose to kill rather than to expose them, it should be deemed homicide. The exposing them is a crime of which no instance has existed with us; and were it to be followed by death, it would be punished capitally. We are told of a certain Vedius Pollio, who, in the presence of Augustus, would have given a slave as food to his fish, for having broken a glass. With the Romans, the regular method of taking the evidence of their slaves was under torture. Here it has been thought better never to resort to their evidence. When a master was murdered, all his slaves, in the same house, or within hearing, were condemned to death. Here punishment falls on the guilty only, and as precise proof is required against him as against a freeman. Yet notwithstanding these and other discouraging circumstances among the Romans, their slaves were often their rarest artists. They excelled too in science, insomuch as to be usually employed as tutors to their master's children. Epictetus, Terence, and Phædrus, were slaves. But they were of the race of whites. It is not their condition then, but nature, which has produced the distinction.—Whether further observation will or will not verify the conjecture, that nature has been less bountiful to them in the endowments of the head, I believe that in those of the heart she will be found to have done them justice. That disposition to theft with which they have been branded, must be ascribed to their situation, and not to any depravity of the moral sense. The man, in whose favour no laws of property exist, probably feels himself less bound to respect those made in favour of others. When arguing for ourselves, we lay it down as a fundamental, that laws, to be just, must give a reciprocation of right: that, without this, they are mere arbitrary rules of conduct, founded in force, and not in conscience: and it is a problem which I give to the master to solve, whether the religious precepts against the violation of property were not framed for him as well as his slave? And whether the slave may not as justifiably take a little from one, who has taken all from him, as he may slay one who would slay him? That a change in the relations in which a man is placed should change his ideas of moral right and wrong, is neither new, nor peculiar to the colour of the blacks. Homer tells us it was so 2600 years ago.

Ἡμισυ, γαζ τ' ἀρετῆς ἀποαίνυ|αι εὐρύθπα Ζεὺς
'Ανερος, ευτ' ἄν μιν κατὰ δόλιον ἡμαζ ἕλησιν.
Od. 17.323.

Jove fix'd it certain, that whatever day
Makes man a slave, takes half his worth away.

But the slaves of which Homer speaks were whites. Notwithstanding these considerations which must weaken their respect for the laws of property, we find among them numerous instances of the most rigid integrity, and as many as among their better instructed masters, of benevolence, gratitude, and unshaken fidelity.—The opinion, that they are inferior in the faculties of reason and imagination, must be hazarded with great diffidence. To justify a general conclusion, requires many observations, even where the subject may be submitted to the Anatomical knife, to Optical glasses, to analysis by fire, or by solvents. How much more then where it is a faculty, not a substance, we are examining; where it eludes the research of all the senses; where the conditions of its existence are various and variously combined; where the effects of those which are present or absent bid defiance to calculation; let me add too, as a circumstance of great tenderness, where our conclusion would degrade a whole race of men from the rank in the scale of beings which their Creator may perhaps have given them. To our reproach it must be said, that though for a century and a half we have had under our eyes the races of black and of red men, they have never yet been viewed by us as subjects of natural history. I advance it therefore as a suspicion only, that the blacks, whether originally a distinct race, or made distinct by time and circumstances, are inferior to the whites in the endowments both of body and mind. It is not against experience to suppose, that different species of the same genus, or varieties of the same species, may possess different qualifications. Will not a lover of natural history then, one who views the gradations in all the races of animals with the eye of philosophy, excuse an effort to keep those in the department of man as distinct as nature has formed them? This unfortunate difference of colour, and perhaps of faculty, is a powerful obstacle to the emancipation of these people. Many of their advocates, while they wish to vindicate the liberty of human nature, are anxious also to preserve its dignity and beauty. Some of these, embarrassed by the question 'What further is to be done with them?' join themselves in opposition with those who are actuated by sordid avarice only. Among the Romans emancipation required but one effort. The slave, when made free, might mix with, without staining the blood of his master. But with us a second is necessary, unknown to history. When freed, he is to be removed beyond the reach of mixture.

from Query XVII
Religion

. . . The error seems not sufficiently eradicated, that the operations of the mind, as well as the acts of the body, are subject to the coercion of the laws. But our rulers can have authority over such natural rights only as we have submitted to them. The rights of conscience we never submitted, we could not submit. We are answerable for them to our God. The legitimate powers of government extend to such acts only as are injurious to others. But it does me no injury for my neighbour to say there are twenty gods, or no god. It neither picks my pocket nor breaks my leg. If it be said, his testimony in a court of justice cannot be relied on, reject it then, and be the stigma on him. Constraint may make him worse by making him a hypocrite, but it will never make him a truer man. It may fix him obstinately in his errors, but will not cure them. Reason and free enquiry are the only effectual agents against error. Give a loose to them, they will support the true religion, by bringing every false one to their tribunal, to the test of their investigation. They are the natural enemies of error, and of error only. Had not the Roman government permitted free enquiry, Christianity could never have been introduced. Had not free enquiry been indulged, at the æra of the reformation, the corruptions of Christianity could not have been purged away. If it be restrained now, the present corruptions will be protected, and new ones encouraged. Was the government to prescribe to us our medicine and diet, our bodies would be in such keeping as our souls are now. Thus in France the emetic was once forbidden as a medicine, and the potatoe as an article of food. Government is just as infallible too when it fixes systems in physics. Galileo was sent to the inquisition for affirming that the earth was a sphere: the government had declared it to be as flat as a trencher, and Galileo was obliged to abjure his error. This error however at length prevailed, the earth became a globe, and Descartes declared it was whirled round its axis by a vortex. The government in which he lived was wise enough to see that this was no question of civil jurisdiction, or we should all have been involved by authority in vortices. In fact, the vortices have been exploded, and the Newtonian principle of gravitation is now more firmly established, on the basis of reason, than it would be were the government to step in, and to make it an article of necessary faith. Reason and experiment have been indulged, and error has fled before them. It is error alone which needs the support of government. Truth can stand by itself. Subject opinion to coercion: whom will you make your inquisitors? Fallible men; men governed by bad passions, by private as well as public reasons. And why subject it to coercion? To produce uniformity. But is uniformity of opinion desireable? No more than of face and stature. Introduce the bed of Procrustes then, and as there is danger that the large men may beat the small, make us all of a size, by lopping the former and stretching the latter. Difference of opinion is advantageous in religion. The several sects perform the office of a Censor morum over each other. Is uniformity attainable? Millions of innocent men, women, and children, since the introduction of Christianity, have been burnt, tortured, fined, imprisoned; yet we have not advanced one inch towards uniformity. What has been the effect of coercion? To make one half the world fools, and the other half hypocrites. To support roguery and error all over the earth. Let us reflect that it is inhabited by a thousand millions of people. That these profess probably a thousand different systems of religion. That ours is but one of that thousand. That if there be but one right, and ours that one, we should wish to see the 999 wandering sects gathered into the fold of truth. But against such a majority we cannot effect this by force. Reason and persuasion are the only practicable instruments. To make way for these, free enquiry must be indulged; and how can we wish others to indulge it while we refuse it ourselves. But every state, says an inquisitor, has established some religion. No two, say I, have established the same. Is this a proof of the infallibility of establishments? Our sister states of Pennsylvania and New York, however, have long subsisted without any establishment at all. The experiment was new and doubtful when they made it. It has answered beyond conception. They flourish infinitely. Religion is well supported; of various kinds, indeed, but all good enough; all sufficient to preserve peace and order: or if a sect arises, whose tenets would subvert morals, good sense has fair play, and reasons and laughs it out of doors, without suffering the state to be troubled with it. They do not hang more malefactors than we do. They are not more disturbed with religious dissensions. On the contrary, their harmony is unparalleled, and can be ascribed to nothing but their unbounded tolerance, because there is no other circumstance in which they differ from every nation on earth. They have made the happy discovery, that the way to silence religious disputes, is to take no notice of them. Let us too give this experiment fair play, and get rid, while we may, of those tyrannical laws. It is true, we are as yet secured against them by the spirit of the times. I doubt whether the people of this country would suffer an execution for heresy, or a three years imprisonment for not comprehending the mysteries of the Trinity. But is the spirit of the people an infallible, a permanent reliance? Is it government? Is this the kind of protection we receive in return for the rights we give up? Besides, the spirit of the times may alter, will alter. Our rulers will become corrupt, our people careless. A single zealot may commence persecutor, and better men be his victims. It can never be too often repeated, that the time for fixing every essential right on a legal basis is while our rulers are honest, and ourselves united. From the conclusion of this war we shall be going down hill. It will not then be necessary to resort every moment to the people for support. They will be forgotten, therefore, and their rights disregarded. They will forget themselves, but in the sole faculty of making money, and will never think of uniting to effect a due respect for their rights. The shackles, therefore, which shall not be knocked off at the conclusion of this war, will remain on us long, will be made heavier and heavier, till our rights shall revive or expire in a convulsion.

from Query XVIII
Manners . . . Effect of Slavery

It is difficult to determine on the standard by which the manners of a nation may be tried, whether *catholic,*[1] or *particular.* It is more difficult for a native to bring to that standard the manners of his own nation, familiarized to him by habit. There must doubtless be an unhappy influence on the manners of our people produced by the existence of slavery among us. The whole commerce between master and slave is a perpetual exercise of the most boisterous passions, the most unremitting despotism on the one part, and degrading submissions on the other. Our children see this, and learn to imitate it; for man is an imitative animal. This quality is the germ of all education in him. From his cradle to his grave he is learning to do what he sees others do. If a parent could find no motive either in his philanthropy or his self-love, for restraining the intemperance of passion towards his slave, it should always be a sufficient one that his child is present. But generally it is not sufficient. The parent storms,

[1]Universal.

the child looks on, catches the lineaments of wrath, puts on the same airs in the circle of smaller slaves, gives a loose to his worst of passions, and thus nursed, educated, and daily exercised in tyranny, cannot but be stamped by it with odious peculiarities. The man must be a prodigy who can retain his manners and morals undepraved by such circumstances. And with what execration should the statesman be loaded, who permitting one half the citizens thus to trample on the rights of the other, transforms those into despots, and these into enemies, destroys the morals of the one part, and the amor patriæ of the other. For if a slave can have a country in this world, it must be any other in preference to that in which he is born to live and labour for another: in which he must lock up the faculties of his nature, contribute as far as depends on his individual endeavours to the evanishment of the human race, or entail his own miserable condition on the endless generations proceeding from him. With the morals of the people, their industry also is destroyed. For in a warm climate, no man will labour for himself who can make another labour for him. This is so true, that of the proprietors of slaves a very small proportion indeed are ever seen to labour. And can the liberties of a nation be thought secure when we have removed their only firm basis, a conviction in the minds of the people that these liberties are of the gift of God? That they are not to be violated but with his wrath? Indeed I tremble for my country when I reflect that God is just: that his justice cannot sleep for ever: that considering numbers, nature and natural means only, a revolution of the wheel of fortune, an exchange of situation, is among possible events: that it may become probable by supernatural interference! The Almighty has no attribute which can take side with us in such a contest.—But it is impossible to be temperate and to pursue this subject through the various considerations of policy, of morals, of history natural and civil. We must be contended to hope they will force their way into every one's mind. I think a change already perceptible, since the origin of the present revolution. The spirit of the master is abating, that of the slave rising from the dust, his condition mollifying, the way I hope preparing, under the auspices of heaven, for a total emancipation, and that this is disposed, in the order of events, to be with the consent of the masters, rather than by their extirpation.

1785

from Letter to James Madison

Oct. 28, 1785

Dear Sir,—Seven o'clock, and retired to my fireside, I have determined to enter into conversation with you. This is a village of about 15,000 inhabitants when the court is not here, and 20,000 when they are, occupying a valley through which runs a brook and on each side of it a ridge of small mountains, most of which are naked rock. The King comes here, in the fall always, to hunt. His court attend him, as do also the foreign diplomatic corps; but as this is not indispensably required and my finances do not admit the expense of a continued residence here, I propose to come occasionally to attend the King's levees, returning again to Paris, distant forty miles. This being the first trip, I set out yesterday morning to take a view of the place. For this purpose I shaped my course towards the highest of the mountains in sight, to the top of which was about a league.

As soon as I had got clear of the town I fell in with a poor woman walking at the same rate with myself and going the same course. Wishing to know the condition of the laboring poor I entered into conversation with her, which I began by enquiries for the path which would lead me into the mountain: and thence proceeded to enquiries into her vocation, condition and circumstances. She told me she was a day laborer at 8 sous or 4d. sterling the day: that she had two children to maintain, and to pay a rent of 30 livres for her house (which would consume the hire of 75 days), that often she could get no employment and of course was without bread. As we had walked together near a mile and she had so far served me as a guide, I gave her, on parting, 24 sous. She burst into tears of a gratitude which I could perceive was unfeigned because she was unable to utter a word. She had probably never before received so great an aid. This little *attendrissement,*[1] with the solitude of my walk, led me into a train of reflections on that unequal division of property which occasions the numberless instances of wretchedness which I had observed in this country and is to be observed all over Europe.

The property of this country is absolutely concentred in a very few hands, having revenues of from half a million of guineas a year downwards. These employ the flower of the country as servants, some of them having as many as 200 domestics, not laboring. They employ also a great number of manufacturers and tradesmen, and lastly the class of laboring husbandmen. But after all there comes the most numerous of all classes, that is, the poor who cannot find work. I asked myself what could be the reason so many should be permitted to beg who are willing to work, in a country where there is a very considerable proportion of uncultivated lands? These lands are undisturbed only for the sake of game. It should seem then that it must be because of the enormous wealth of the proprietors which places them above attention to the increase of their revenues by permitting these lands to be labored. I am conscious that an equal division of property is impracticable, but the consequences of this enormous inequality producing so much misery to the bulk of mankind, legislators cannot invent too many devices for subdividing property, only taking care to let their subdivisions go hand in hand with the natural affections of the human mind. The descent of property of every kind therefore to all the children, or to all the brothers and sisters, or other relations in equal degree, is a politic measure and a practicable one. Another means of silently lessening the inequality of property is to exempt all from taxation below a certain point, and to tax the higher portions or property in geometrical progression as they rise. Whenever there are in any country uncultivated lands and unemployed poor, it is clear that the laws of property have been so far extended as to violate natural right. The earth is given as a common stock for man to labor and live on. If for the encouragement of industry we allow it to be appropriated, we must take care that other employment be provided to those excluded from the appropriation. If we do not, the

[1]Softening of the heart.

fundamental right to labor the earth returns to the unemployed. It is too soon yet in our country to say that every man who cannot find employment, but who can find uncultivated land, shall be at liberty to cultivate it, paying a moderate rent. But it is not too soon to provide by every possible means that as few as possible shall be without a little portion of land. The small landholders are the most precious part of a state. . . .

from Letter to James Madison

Dec. 20, 1787

. . . I like much the general idea of framing a government, which should go on of itself, peaceably, without needing continual recurrence to the State legislatures. I like the organization of the government into legislative judiciary and executive. I like the power given the legislature to levy taxes, and for that reason solely, I approve of the greater House being chosen by the people directly. For though I think a House so chosen, will be very far inferior to the present Congress, will be very illy qualified to legislate for the Union, for foreign nations, etc., yet this evil does not weigh against the good, of preserving inviolate the fundamental principle, that the people are not to be taxed but by representatives chosen immediately by themselves. I am captivated by the compromise of the opposite claims of the great and little States, of the latter to equal, and the former to proportional influence. I am much pleased, too, with the substitution of the method of voting by person, instead of that of voting by States; and I like the negative given to the Executive, conjointly with a third of either House; though I should have liked it better, had the judiciary been associated for that purpose, or invested separately with a similar power. There are other good things of less moment. I will now tell you what I do not like. First, the omission of a bill of rights, providing clearly, and without the aid of sophism, for freedom of religion, freedom of the press, protection against standing armies, restriction of monopolies, the eternal and unremitting force of the habeas corpus laws, and trials by jury in all matters of fact triable by the laws of the land, and not by the laws of nations. To say, as Mr. Wilson does, that a bill of rights was not necessary, because all is reserved in the case of the general government which is not given, while in the particular ones, all is given which is not reserved, might do for the audience to which it was addressed; but it is surely a *gratis dictum,* the reverse of which might just as well be said; and it is opposed by strong inferences from the body of the instrument, as well as from the omission of the cause of our present Confederation, which had made the reservation in express terms. It was hard to conclude, because there has been a want of uniformity among the States as to the cases triable by jury, because some have been so incautious as to dispense with this mode of trial in certain cases, therefore, the more prudent States shall be reduced to the same level of calamity. It would have been much more just and wise to have concluded the other way, that as most of the States had preserved with jealousy this sacred palladium of liberty, those who had wandered, should be brought back to it;

and to have established general right rather than general wrong. For I consider all the ill as established, which may be established. I have a right to nothing, which another has a right to take away; and Congress will have a right to take away trials by jury in all civil cases. Let me add, that a bill of rights is what the people are entitled to against every government on earth, general or particular; and what no just government should refuse, or rest on inference.

The second feature I dislike, and strongly dislike, is the abandonment, in every instance, of the principle of rotation in office, and most particularly in the case of the President. Reason and experience tell us, that the first magistrate will always be re-elected if he may be re-elected. He is then an officer for life. This once observed, it becomes of so much consequence to certain nations to have a friend or a foe at the head of our affairs, that they will interfere with money and with arms. A Galloman, or an Angloman, will be supported by the nation he befriends. If once elected, and at a second or third election out-voted by one or two votes, he will pretend false votes, foul play, hold possession of the reins of government, be supported by the States voting for him, especially if they be the central ones, lying in a compact body themselves, and separating their opponents; and they will be aided by one nation in Europe, while the majority are aided by another. The election of a President of America, some years hence, will be much more interesting to certain nations of Europe, than ever the election of a King of Poland was. Reflect on all the instances in history, ancient and modern, of elective monarchies, and say if they do not give foundation for my fears; the Roman Emperors, the Popes while they were of any importance, the German Emperors till they became hereditary in practice, the Kings of Poland, the Deys of the Ottoman dependencies. It may be said, that if elections are to be attended with these disorders, the less frequently they are repeated the better. But experience says, that to free them from disorder, they must be rendered less interesting by a necessity of change. No foreign power, nor domestic party, will waste their blood and money to elect a person, who must go out at the end of a short period. The power of removing every fourth year by the vote of the people, is a power which they will not exercise, and if they were disposed to exercise it, they would not be permitted. The King of Poland is removable every day by the diet. But they never remove him. Nor would Russia, the Emperor, etc., permit them to do it. Smaller objections are, the appeals on matters of fact as well as laws; and the binding all persons, legislative, executive, and judiciary by oath, to maintain that constitution. I do not pretend to decide, what would be the best method of procuring the establishment of the manifold good things in this constitution, and of getting rid of the bad. Whether by adopting it, in hopes of future amendment; or after it shall have been duly weighed and canvassed by the people, after seeing the parts they generally dislike, and those they generally approve, to say to them, "We see now what you wish. You are willing to give to your federal government such and such powers; but you wish, at the same time, to have such and such fundamental rights secured to you, and certain sources of convulsion taken away. Be it so. Send together deputies again. Let them establish your fundamental rights by a sacrosanct declaration, and let them pass the parts of the Constitution you have approved. These will give powers to your federal government sufficient for your happiness."

This is what might be said, and would probably produce a speedy, more perfect and more permanent form of government. At all events, I hope you will not be discouraged from making other trials, if the present one should fail. We are never permitted to despair of the commonwealth. I have thus told you freely what I like, and what I dislike, merely as a matter of curiosity; for I know it is not in my power to offer matter of information to your judgment, which has been formed after hearing and weighing everything which the wisdom of man could offer on these subjects. I own, I am not a friend to a very energetic government. It is always oppressive. It places the governors indeed more at their ease, at the expense of the people. The late rebellion in Massachusetts[1] has given more alarm, than I think it should have done. Calculate that one rebellion in thirteen States in the course of eleven years, is but one for each State in a century and a half. No country should be so long without one. Nor will any degree of power in the hands of government, prevent insurrections. In England, where the hand of power is heavier than with us, there are seldom half a dozen years without an insurrection. In France, where it is still heavier, but less despotic, as Montesquieu supposes, than in some other countries, and where there are always two or three hundred thousand men ready to crush insurrections, there have been three in the course of the three years I have been here, in every one of which greater numbers were engaged than in Massachusetts, and a great deal more blood was spilt. In Turkey, where the sole nod of the despot is death, insurrections are the events of every day. Compare again the ferocious depredations of their insurgents, with the order, the moderation and the almost self-extinguishment of ours. And say, finally, whether peace is best preserved by giving energy to the government, or information to the people. This last is the most certain, and the most legitimate engine of government. Educate and inform the whole mass of the people. Enable them to see that it is their interest to preserve peace and order, and they will preserve them. And it requires no very high degree of education to convince them of this. They are the only sure reliance for the preservation of our liberty. After all, it is my principle that the will of the majority should prevail. If they approve the proposed constitution in all its parts, I shall concur in it cheerfully, in hopes they will amend it, whenever they shall find it works wrong. This reliance cannot deceive us, as long as we remain virtuous; and I think we shall be so, as long as agriculture is our principal object, which will be the case, while there remains vacant lands in any part of America. When we get piled upon one another in large cities, as in Europe, we shall become corrupt as in Europe, and go to eating one another as they do there. I have tired you by this time with disquisitions which you have already heard repeated by others a thousand and a thousand times; and therefore, shall only add assurances of the esteem and attachment with which I have the honor to be, dear Sir, your affectionate friend and servant.

P.S. The instability of our laws is really an immense evil. I think it would be well to provide in our constitutions, that there shall always be a twelvemonth between the engrossing a bill and passing it; that it should then be offered to its passage without changing a word; and that if circumstances should be thought to require a speedier passage, it should take two-thirds of both Houses, instead of a bare majority.

1829

[1]Shays's Rebellion.

Letter to Benjamin Banneker[1]

Aug. 30, 1791

SIR

I thank you sincerely for your letter of the 19th instant and for the Almanac it contained. No body wishes more than I do to see such proofs as you exhibit, that nature has given to our black brethren, talents equal to those of the other colors of men, and that the appearance of a want of them is owing merely to the degraded condition of their existence, both in Africa & America. I can add with truth, that no body wishes more ardently to see a good system commenced for raising the condition both of their body & mind to what it ought to be, as fast as the imbecility of their present existence, and other circumstances which cannot be neglected, will admit. I have taken the liberty of sending your Almanac to Monsieur de Condorcet, Secretary of the Academy of Sciences at Paris, and member of the Philanthropic society, because I considered it as a document to which your whole colour had a right for their justification against the doubts which have been entertained of them. I am with great esteem, Sir Your most obed[t] humble servt.

1829

Letter to the Marquis de Condorcet[1]

Aug. 30, 1791

Dear Sir

I am to acknolege the receipt of your favor on the subject of the element of measure adopted by France. Candor obliges me to confess that it is not what I would have approved. It is liable to the inexactitude of mensuration as to that part of the quadrant of the earth which is to be measured, that is to say as to one tenth of the quadrant, and as to the remaining nine tenths they are to be calculated on conjectural data, presuming the figure of the earth which has not yet been proved. It is liable too to the objection that no nation but your own can come at it; because yours is the only nation within which a meridian can be found of such extent crossing the 45th. degree and terminating at both ends in a level. We may certainly say then that this measure is uncatholic, and I would rather have seen you depart from Catholicism in your religion than in your Philosophy.

[1]Banneker was a free-born black, a mathematician, astronomer, and almanac maker. Jefferson was responsible for his appointment to survey the District of Columbia.

[1]The Marquis de Condorcet (1743–1794) was a mathematician and *philosophe,* an acquaintance of Jefferson in Paris, and the author of *Progress of the Human Spirit* (1794).

I am happy to be able to inform you that we have now in the United States a negro, the son of a black man born in Africa, and of a black woman born in the United States, who is a very respectable Mathematician. I procured him to be employed under one of our chief directors in laying out the new federal city on the Patowmac, and in the intervals of his leisure, while on that work, he made an Almanac for the next year, which he sent me in his own handwriting, and which I inclose to you. I have seen very elegant solutions of Geometrical problems by him. Add to this that he is a very worthy and respectable member of society. He is a free man. I shall be delighted to see these instances of moral eminence so multiplied as to prove that the want of talents observed in them is merely the effect of their degraded condition, and not proceeding from any difference in the structure of the parts on which intellect depends.

I am looking ardently to the completion of the glorious work in which your country is engaged. I view the general condition of Europe as hanging on the success or failure of France. Having set such an example of philosophical arrangement within, I hope it will be extended without your limits also, to your dependants and to your friends in every part of the earth.—Present my affectionate respects to Madame de Condorcet, and accept yourself assurance of the sentiments of esteem & attachment with which I have the honour to be Dear Sir Your most obedt & most humble servt,

TH: JEFFERSON

1986

Letter to Edward Coles[1]

Aug. 25, 1814

Dear Sir,—Your favour of July 31, was duly received, and was read with peculiar pleasure. The sentiments breathed through the whole do honor to both the head and heart of the writer. Mine on the subject of slavery of negroes have long since been in possession of the public, and time has only served to give them stronger root. The love of justice and the love of country plead equally the cause of these people, and it is a moral reproach to us that they should have pleaded it so long in vain, and should have produced not a single effort, nay I fear not much serious willingness to relieve them & ourselves from our present condition of moral & political reprobation. From those of the former generation who were in the fulness of age when I came into public life, which was while our controversy with England was on paper only, I soon saw that nothing was to be hoped. Nursed and educated in the daily habit of seeing the degraded condition, both bodily and mental, of those unfortunate beings, not reflecting that that degradation was very much the

[1]Coles, a former neighbor of Jefferson, opposed slavery, so he removed to Illinois with his slaves, where he freed them.

work of themselves & their fathers, few minds have yet doubted but that they were as legitimate subjects of property as their horses and cattle. The quiet and monotonous course of colonial life has been disturbed by no alarm, and little reflection on the value of liberty. And when alarm was taken at an enterprize on their own, it was not easy to carry them to the whole length of the principles which they invoked for themselves. In the first or second session of the Legislature after I became a member, I drew to this subject the attention of Col. Bland, one of the oldest, ablest, & most respected members, and he undertook to move for certain moderate extensions of the protection of the laws to these people. I seconded his motion, and, as a younger member, was more spared in the debate; but he was denounced as an enemy of his country, & was treated with the grossest indecorum. From an early stage of our revolution other & more distant duties were assigned to me, so that from that time till my return from Europe in 1789, and I may say till I returned to reside at home in 1809, I had little opportunity of knowing the progress of public sentiment here on this subject. I had always hoped that the younger generation receiving their early impressions after the flame of liberty had been kindled in every breast, & had become as it were the vital spirit of every American, that the generous temperament of youth, analogous to the motion of their blood, and above the suggestions of avarice, would have sympathized with oppression wherever found, and proved their love of liberty beyond their own share of it. But my intercourse with them, since my return has not been sufficient to ascertain that they had made towards this point the progress I had hoped. Your solitary but welcome voice is the first which has brought this sound to my ear; and I have considered the general silence which prevails on this subject as indicating an apathy unfavorable to every hope. Yet the hour of emancipation is advancing, in the march of time. It will come; and whether brought on by the generous energy of our own minds; or by the bloody process of St Domingo, excited and conducted by the power of our present enemy, if once stationed permanently within our Country, and offering asylum & arms to the oppressed, is a leaf of our history not yet turned over. As to the method by which this difficult work is to be effected, if permitted to be done by ourselves, I have seen no proposition so expedient on the whole, as that as emancipation of those born after a given day, and of their education and expatriation after a given age. This would give time for a gradual extinction of that species of labour & substitution of another, and lessen the severity of the shock which an operation so fundamental cannot fail to produce. For men probably of any color, but of this color we know, brought from their infancy without necessity for thought or forecast, are by their habits rendered as incapable as children of taking care of themselves, and are extinguished promptly wherever industry is necessary for raising young. In the mean time they are pests in society by their idleness, and the depredations to which this leads them. Their amalgamation with the other color produces a degradation to which no lover of his country, no lover of excellence in the human character can innocently consent. I am sensible of the partialities with which you have looked towards me as the person who should undertake this salutary but arduous work. But this, my dear sir, is like bidding old Priam to buckle the armour of Hector "trementibus æquo humeris et inutile ferruncingi." No, I have overlived the generation with which mutual labors & perils begat mutual confidence and influence. This enterprise is for the young; for those who can follow it up, and bear it through to its consummation. It shall have all my prayers, & these are the only weapons of an old man. But in the mean time are you right in abandoning this property, and your country with it? I think not. My opinion has ever been that, until more can be done for them, we should endeavor, with those whom fortune has thrown on our hands, to feed and clothe them well, protect them from all ill usage, require such reasonable labor only as is performed voluntarily by freemen, & be led by no repugnancies to abdicate them, and our duties to them. The laws do not permit us to turn them loose, if that were for their good: and to commute them for other property is to commit them to those whose usage of them we cannot control. I hope then, my dear sir, you will reconcile yourself to your country and its unfortunate condition; that you will not lessen its stock of sound disposition by withdrawing your portion from the mass. That, on the contrary you will come forward in the public councils, become the missionary of this doctrine truly christian; insinuate & inculcate it softly but steadily, through the medium of writing and conversation; associate others in your labors, and when the phalanx is formed, bring on and press the proposition perseveringly until its accomplishment. It is an encouraging observation that no good measure was ever proposed, which, if duly pursued, failed to prevail in the end. We have proof of this in the history of the endeavors in the English parliament to suppress that very trade which brought this evil on us. And you will be supported by the religious precept, "be not weary in well-doing." That your success may be as speedy & complete, as it will be of honorable & immortal consolation to yourself, I shall as fervently and sincerely pray as I assure you of my great friendship and respect.

1899

Letter to Peter Carr[1] [Young Man's Education]

Paris, Aug. 10, 1787

DEAR PETER,—I have received your two letters of Decemb. 30 and April 18, and am very happy to find by them, as well as by letters from Mr. Wythe,[2] that you have been so fortunate as to attract his notice & good will; I am sure you will find this to have been one of the most fortunate events of your life, as I have ever been sensible it was of mine. I inclose you a sketch of the sciences to which I would wish you to apply in such order as Mr. Wythe shall advise; I mention also the books in them worth your reading, which submit to his correction. Many of these are among your father's books, which you should have brought to you. As I do not recollect those of them not in his library, you must write to me for them, making out a catalogue of such as you think you shall have occasion for in 18 months from the date of your

[1]Nephew of Jefferson, son of Martha, his fourth sister, and Dabney Carr.

[2]George Wythe (1726–1809), close friend of Jefferson and self-educated man who became a distinguished Virginia lawyer and politician.

letter, & consulting Mr. Wythe on the subject. To this sketch I will add a few particular observations.

1. Italian. I fear the learning of this language will confound your French and Spanish. Being all of them degenerated dialects of the Latin, they are apt to mix in conversation. I have never seen a person speaking the three languages who did not mix them. It is a delightful language, but late events having rendered the Spanish more useful, lay it aside to prosecute that.

2. Spanish. Bestow great attention on this, & endeavor to acquire an accurate knowledge of it. Our future connections with Spain & Spanish America will render that language a valuable acquisition. The antient history of a great part of America, too, is written in that language. I send you a dictionary.

3. Moral philosophy. I think it lost time to attend lectures in this branch. He who made us would have been a pitiful bungler if he had made the rules of our moral conduct a matter of science. For one man of science, there are thousands who are not. What would have become of them? Man was destined for society. His morality therefore was to be formed to this object. He was endowed with a sense of right & wrong merely relative to this. This sense is as much a part of his nature as the sense of hearing, seeing, feeling; it is the true foundation of morality, & not the το καλον,[3] truth &c. as fanciful writers have imagined. The moral sense, or conscience, is as much a part of man as his leg or arm. It is given to all human beings in a stronger or weaker degree, as force of members is given them in a greater or less degree. It may be strengthened by exercise, as may any particular limb of the body. This sense is submitted indeed in some degree to the guidance of reason; but it is a small stock which is required for this: even a less one than what we call common sense. State a moral case to a ploughman & a professor. The former will encourage as well as direct your feelings. The writings of Sterne[4] particularly form the best course of morality that ever was written. Besides these read the books mentioned in the enclosed paper; and above all things lose no occasion of exercising your dispositions to be grateful, to be generous, to be charitable, to be humane, to be true, just, firm, orderly, courageous &c. Consider every act of this kind as an exercise which will strengthen your moral faculties, & increase your worth.

4. Religion. Your reason is now mature enough to examine this object. In the first place divest yourself of all bias in favour of novelty & singularity of opinion. Indulge them in any other subject rather than that of religion. It is too important, & the consequences of error may be too serious. On the other hand shake off all the fears & servile prejudices under which weak minds are serviley crouched. Fix reason firmly in her seat, and call to her tribunal every fact, every opinion. Question with boldness even the existence of a god; because, if there be one, he must more approve of the homage of reason, than that of blindfold fear. You will naturally examine first the religion of your own country. Read the bible then, as you would read Livy or Tacitus.[5] The facts which are within the ordinary course of

[3]The beautiful (Greek).

[4]Laurence Sterne (1713–1768), English author of *Tristram Shandy* (1760) and *A Sentimental Journey through France and Italy* (1768).

[5]Livy (59 B.C.–A.D. 17) and Tacitus (c. 55–118), Roman historians.

nature you will believe on the authority of the writer, as you do those of the same kind in Livy & Tacitus. The testimony of the writer weighs in their favor in one scale, and their not being against the laws of nature does not weigh against them. But those facts in the bible which contradict the laws of nature, must be examined with more care, and under a variety of faces. Here you must recur to the pretensions of the writer to inspiration from god. Examine upon what evidence his pretensions are founded, and whether that evidence is so strong as that its falsehood would be more improbable than a change in the laws of nature in the case he relates. For example in the book of Joshua we are told the sun stood still several hours.[6] Were we to read that fact in Livy or Tacitus we should class it with their showers of blood, speaking of statues, beasts, &c. But it is said that the writer of that book was inspired. Examine therefore candidly what evidence there is of his having been inspired. The pretension is entitled to your inquiry, because millions believe it. On the other hand you are astronomer enough to know how contrary it is to the law of nature that a body revolving on its axis as the earth does, should have stopped, should not by that sudden stoppage have prostrated animals, trees, buildings, and should after a certain time have resumed its revolution, & that without a second general prostration. Is this arrest of the earth's motion, or the evidence which affirms it, most within the law of probabilities? You will next read the new testament. It is the history of a personage called Jesus. Keep in your eye the opposite pretensions 1. of those who say he was begotten by god, born of a virgin, suspended & reversed the laws of nature at will, & ascended bodily into heaven: and 2. of those who say he was a man of illegitimate birth, of a benevolent heart, enthusiastic mind, who set out without pretensions to divinity, ended in believing them, & was punished capitally for sedition by being gibbeted according to the Roman law which punished the first commission of that offence by whipping, & the second by exile or death *in furcâ*.[7] See this law in the Digest Lib. 48. tit. 19. § 28.3. & Lipsius Lib 2. de cruce. cap 2.[8] These questions are examined in the books I have mentioned under the head of religion, & several others. They will assist you in your inquiries, but keep your reason firmly on the watch in reading them all. Do not be frightened from this inquiry by any fear of its consequences. If it ends in a belief that there is no god, you will find incitements to virtue in the comfort & pleasantness you feel in it's exercise, and the love of others it will procure you. If you find reason to believe there is a god, a consciousness that you are acting under his eye, & that he approves you, will be a vast additional incitement; if that there be a future state, the hope of a happy existence in that increases the appetite to deserve it; if that Jesus was also a god, you will be comforted by a belief of his aid and love. In fine, I repeat that you must lay aside all prejudice on both sides, &

[6]"So the sun stood still in the midst of heaven and hasted not to go down about a whole day" (Joshua 10:13).

[7]On a pillory, or fork-shaped prop, used to punish slaves (Latin).

[8]The *Digest* was a codification of laws compiled for Justinian I, Byzantine emperor (r. 527–565). Jefferson cites Book 48, chapter 19, paragraph 28, sentence 3. Justus Lipsius (1547–1606) was a Flemish humanist, classical scholar, and moral and political philosopher. Jefferson cites his second book, *de cruce* (concerning the cross [Latin]), chapter 2.

neither believe nor reject anything because any other persons, or description of persons have rejected or believed it. Your own reason is the only oracle given you by heaven, and you are answerable not for the rightness but uprightness of the decision. I forgot to observe when speaking of the new testament that you should read the histories of Christ, as well of those whom a council of ecclesiastics have decided for us to be Pseudo-evangelists,[9] those they named Evangelists. Because these Pseudo-evangelists pretended to inspiration as much as the others, and you are to judge their pretensions by your own reason, & not by reason of those ecclesiastics. Most of these are lost. There are some however still extant, collected by Fabricius[10] which I will endeavor to get & send you.

5. Travelling. This makes men wiser, but less happy. When men of sober age travel, they gather knowledge which they may apply usefully for their country, but they are subject ever after to recollections mixed with regret, their affections are weakened by being extended over more objects, & they learn habits which cannot be gratified when they return home. Young men who travel are exposed to all these inconveniences in a higher degree, to others still more serious, and do not acquire that wisdom for which a precious foundation is requisite by repeated & just observations at home. The glare of pomp & pleasure is analogous to the motion of their blood, it absorbs all their affection & attention, they are torn from it as from the only good in this world, and return to their home as to a place of exile & condemnation. Their eyes are for ever turned back to the object they have lost, & it's recollection poisons the residue of their lives. Their first & most delicate passions are hackneyed on unworthy objects here, & they carry home only the dregs, insufficient to make themselves or anybody else happy. Add to this that a habit of idleness, an inability to apply themselves to business is acquired & renders them useless to themselves & their country. These observations are founded in experience. There is no place where your pursuit of knowledge will be so little obstructed by foreign objects as in your own country, nor any wherein the virtues of the heart will be less exposed to be weakened. Be good, be learned, & be industrious, & you will not want the aid of travelling to render you precious to your country, dear to your friends, happy within yourself. I repeat my advice to take a great deal of exercise, & on foot. Health is the first requisite after morality. Write to me often & be assured of the interest I take in your success, as well as of the warmth of those sentiments of attachment with which I am, dear Peter, your affectionate friend.

1787 1899

[9]Non-apostolic writers often inspired by or imitating the apostles and active in the second century A.D. Most of them were disqualified by the Roman Catholic church for inclusion in the New Testament.

[10]Johann Albert Fabricius (1668–1736), German classical scholar and accomplished bibliographer. The fourth book of his *Bibliotheca Latina* (1697) deals with early Christian writers.

from Letter to Benjamin Hawkins [Civilization of the Indians]

Washington, Feb. 18, 1803

. . . Altho' you will receive, thro' the official channel of the War Office, every communication necessary to develop to you our views respecting the Indians, and to direct your conduct, yet, supposing it will be satisfactory to you, and to those with whom you are placed, to understand my personal dispositions and opinions in this particular, I shall avail myself of this private letter to state them generally. I consider the business of hunting as already become insufficient to furnish clothing and subsistence to the Indians. The promotion of agriculture, therefore, and household manufacture, are essential in their preservation, and I am disposed to aid and encourage it liberally. This will enable them to live on much smaller portions of land, and indeed will render their vast forests useless but for the range of cattle; for which purpose, also, as they become better farmers, they will be found useless, and even disadvantageous. While they are learning to do better on less land, our increasing numbers will be calling for more land, and thus a coincidence of interests will be produced between those who have lands to spare, and want other necessaries, and those who have such necessaries to spare, and want lands. This commerce, then, will be for the good of both, and those who are friends to both ought to encourage it. You are in the station peculiarly charged with this interchange and who have it peculiarly in your power to promote among the Indians a sense of the superior value of a little land, well cultivated, over a great deal, unimproved and to encourage them to make this estimate truly. The wisdom of the animal which amputates & abandons to the hunter the parts for which he is pursued should be theirs, with this difference, that the former sacrifices what is useful, the latter what is not. In truth, the ultimate point of rest & happiness for them is to let our settlements and theirs meet and blend together, to intermix, and become one people. Incorporating themselves with us as citizens of the U.S., this is what the natural progress of things will of course bring on, and it will be better to promote than to retard it. Surely it will be better for them to be identified with us, and preserved in the occupation of their lands, than be exposed to the many casualties which may endanger them while a separate people. I have little doubt but that your reflections must have led you to the various ways in which their history may terminate, and to see that this is the one most for their happiness. And we have already had an application from a settlement of Indians to become citizens of the U.S. It is possible, perhaps probable, that this idea may be so novel as that it might shock the Indians, were it even hinted to them. Of course, you will keep it for your own reflection; but, convinced of its soundness, I feel it consistent with pure morality to lead them towards it, to familiarize them to the idea that it is for their interest to cede lands at times to the U.S., and for us thus to procure gratifications to our citizens, from time to time, by new acquisitions of land. From no quarter is there at present so strong a pressure on this subject as from Georgia for the residue of the fork of Oconee & Ockmulgee;[1] and indeed I believe it will be difficult to resist it. As it has been mentioned that the Creeks had at one time made up their minds to sell this, and were only checked in it by some indiscretions of an individual, I am in hopes you will be able to bring them to it again. I beseech you to use your most earnest endeavors; for it will relieve us here from a great pressure, and yourself from the unreasonable suspicions of the Georgians which you notice, that you are more attached to the interests of the Indians than of the U.S., and throw cold water on their willingness to part with lands. It is so easy to excite suspicion, that none are to be wondered at; but I am in hopes it will be in your power to quash them by effecting the object. . . .

1803 1899

Letter to Nathaniel Burwell[1] [A Young Woman's Education]

Monticello, March 14, 1818

DEAR SIR,—Your letter of February 17th found me suffering under an attack of rheumatism, which has but now left me at sufficient ease to attend to the letters I have received. A plan of female education has never been a subject of systematic contemplation with me. It has occupied my attention so far only as the education of my own daughters occasionally required. Considering that they would be placed in a country situation, where little aid could be obtained from abroad, I thought it essential to give them a solid education, which might enable them, when become mothers, to educate their own daughters, and even to direct the course for sons, should their fathers be lost, or incapable, or inattentive. My surviving daughter accordingly, the mother of many daughters as well as sons, has made their education the object of her life, and being a better judge of the practical part than myself, it is with her aid and that of one of her élèves[2] [that I] subjoin a catalogue of the books for such a course of reading as we have practiced.

A great obstacle to good education is the inordinate passion prevalent for novels, and the time lost in that reading which should be instructively employed.

[1]Rivers in Georgia in Creek tribal lands. Over the next several decades, Georgia continued to press the claims of its citizens squatting illegally on Indian lands, carrying them all the way to the U.S. Supreme Court, which in 1831–1832 ruled that Indian tribes were "domestic dependent nations" that the individual states could not subject to their laws. President Andrew Jackson, who supported passage of the 1830 Indian Removal Act, which set up an Indian Territory in what is today Oklahoma for Indians who gave up their eastern homelands, refused to defend the rights of the Cherokee Nation against the depredations of Georgia. The ensuing conflict led one faction of the tribe to sign a treaty that led to the entire group being forcibly marched across more than a thousand miles in midwinter to Indian Territory on what has become known as the "Trail of Tears."

[1]A distinguished Virginian.

[2]Pupils (French).

When this poison infects the mind, it destroys its tone and revolts it against wholesome reading. Reason and fact, plain and unadorned, are rejected. Nothing can engage attention unless dressed in all the figments of fancy, and nothing so bedecked comes amiss. The result is a bloated imagination, sickly judgment, and disgust towards all the real businesses of life. This mass of trash, however, is not without some distinction; some few modelling their narratives, although fictitious, on the incidents of real life, have been able to make them interesting and useful vehicles of sound morality. Such, I think, are Marmontel's new moral tales,[3] but not his old ones, which are really immoral. Such are the writings of Miss Edgeworth,[4] and some of those of Madame Genlis.[5] For a like reason, too, much poetry should not be indulged. Some is useful for forming style and taste. Pope, Dryden, Thompson, Shakspeare, and of the French, Moliere, Racine, the Corneilles,[6] may be read with pleasure and improvement.

The French language, become that of the general intercourse of nations, and from their extraordinary advances, now the depository of all science, is an indispensable part of education for both sexes. In the subjoined catalogue, therefore, I have placed the books of both languages indifferently, according as the one or the other offers what is best.

The ornaments too, and the amusements of life, are entitled to their portion of attention. These, for a female, are dancing, drawing, and music. The first is a healthy exercise, elegant and very attractive for young people. Every affectionate parent would be pleased to see his daughter qualified to participate with her companions, and without awkwardness at least, in the circles of festivity, of which she occasionally becomes a part. It is a necessary accomplishment, therefore, although of short use, for the French rule is wise, that no lady dances after marriage. This is founded in solid physical reasons, gestation and nursing leaving little time to a married lady when this exercise can be either safe or innocent. Drawing is thought less of in this country than in Europe. It is an innocent and engaging amusement, often useful, and a qualification not to be neglected in one who is to become a mother and an instructor. Music is invaluable where a person has an ear. Where they have not, it should not be attempted. It furnishes a delightful recreation for the hours of respite from the cares of the day, and lasts us through life. The taste of this country, too, calls for this accomplishment more strongly than for either of the others.

I need say nothing of household economy, in which the mothers of our country

[3]Jean François Marmontel (1723–1799), French novelist and dramatist who published *Contes moraux* (*Moral Stories,* 1761) and *Mémoires d'un père* (*Memoirs of a Father,* 1804), an autobiographical work.

[4]Maria Edgeworth (1767–1849), Anglo-Irish novelist known for her children's stories and novels of Irish life.

[5]Stéphanie Félicité du Crest de Saint-Aubin, Comtesse de Genlis (1746–1830), French novelist and author of treatises on education that sternly rejected "make-believe" for children.

[6]Alexander Pope (1688–1744), poet and satirist, the epitome of English neoclassicism. John Dryden (1631–1700), English poet, dramatist, and critic, a dominant figure during the Restoration. James Thomson (1700–1748), Scottish-born English poet and forerunner of Romanticism. William Shakespeare (1564–1616), best-known English poet and dramatist of the Elizabethan period. Molière, pen name of Jean Baptiste Poquelin (1622–1673), noted French comic dramatist. Jean Racine (1639–1699), French dramatist who humanized classical French drama. Pierre (1606–1684) and Thomas (1625–1709) Corneille, brothers and dramatists; Pierre is considered the shaper of French classical theater.

are generally skilled, and generally careful to instruct their daughters. We all know its value, and that diligence and dexterity in all its processes are inestimable treasures. The order and economy of a house are as honorable to the mistress as those of the farm to the master, and if either be neglected, ruin follows, and children destitute of the means of living.

This, Sir, is offered as a summary sketch on a subject on which I have not thought much. It probably contains nothing but what has already occurred to yourself and claims your acceptance on no other ground than as a testimony of my respect for your wishes, and of my great esteem and respect.

1818 1899

from Indian Addresses: To Brother Handsome Lake

Washington, November 3, 1802

To BROTHER HANDSOME LAKE:—[1]

I have received the message in writing which you sent me through Captain Irvine, our confidential agent, placed near you for the purpose of communicating and transacting between us, whatever may be useful for both nations. I am happy to learn you have been so far favored by the Divine spirit as to be made sensible of those things which are for your good and that of your people, and of those which are hurtful to you; and particularly see the ruinous effects which the abuse of spirituous liquors have produced upon them. It has weakened their bodies, enervated their minds, exposed them to hunger, cold, nakedness, and poverty, kept them in perpetual broils, and reduced their population. I do not wonder then, brother, at your censures, not only on your own people, who have voluntarily gone into these fatal habits, but on all the nations of white people who have supplied their calls for this article. But these nations have done to you only what they do among themselves. They have sold what individuals wish to buy, leaving to every one to be the guardian of his own health and happiness. Spirituous liquors are not in themselves bad, they are often found to be an excellent medicine for the sick; it is the improper and intemperate use of them, by those in health, which makes them injurious. But as you find that our people cannot refrain from an ill use of them, I greatly applaud your resolution not to use them at all. We have too affectionate a concern for your happiness to place the paltry gain on the sale of these articles in competition

[1]Ganioda'yo (1735–1815), Seneca Indian chief who, upon recovery from a grave illness during which he had visions, began in 1800 to preach a new religion of restraint that combined old beliefs with Christian ethics and provided the Iroquois with a faith that revitalized their civilization. He visited Jefferson to explain his beliefs. See Handsome Lake's "How America Was Discovered," elsewhere in this volume.

with the injury they do you. And as it is the desire of your nation, that no spirits should be sent among them, I am authorized by the great council of the United States to prohibit them. I will sincerely cooperate with our wise men in any proper measures for this purpose, which shall be agreeable to them.

You remind me, brother, of what I said to you, when you visited me the last winter, that the lands you then held would remain yours, and shall never go from you but when you would be disposed to sell. This I now repeat, and will ever abide by. We, indeed, are always ready to buy land; but we will never ask but when you wish to sell; and our laws, in order to protect you against imposition, have forbidden individuals to purchase lands from you; and have rendered it necessary, when you desire to sell, even to a State, that an agent from the United States should attend the sale, see that your consent is freely given, a satisfactory price paid, and report to us what has been done, for our approbation. This was done in the late case of which you complain. The deputies of your nation came forward, in all the forms which we have been used to consider as evidence of the will of your nation. They proposed to sell to the State of New York certain parcels of land, of small extent, and detached from the body of your other lands; the State of New York was desirous to buy. I sent an agent, in whom we could trust, to see that your consent was free, and the sale fair. All was reported to be free and fair. The lands were your property. The right to sell is one of the rights of property. To forbid you the exercise of that right would be a wrong to your nation. Nor do I think, brother, that the sale of lands is, under all circumstances, injurious to your people. While they depended on hunting, the more extensive the forest around them, the more game they would yield. But going from a state of agriculture, it may be as advantageous to a society, as it is to an individual, who has more land than he can improve, to sell a part, and lay out the money in stocks and implements of agriculture, for the better improvement of the residue. A little land well stocked and improved, will yield more than a great deal without stock or improvement. I hope, therefore, that on further reflection you will see this transaction in a more favorable light, both as it concerns the interest of your nation, and the exercise of that superintending care which I am sincerely anxious to employ for their subsistence and happiness. Go on then, brother, in the great reformation you have undertaken. Persuade our red brethren, then to be sober, and to cultivate their lands; and their women to spin and weave for their families. You will soon see your women and children well fed and clothed, your men living happily in peace and plenty, and your numbers increasing from year to year. It will be a great glory to you to have been the instrument of so happy a change, and your children's children, from generation to generation, will repeat your name with love and gratitude forever. In all your enterprises for the good of your people, you may count with confidence on the aid and protection of the United States, and on the sincerity and zeal with which I am myself animated in the furthering of this humane work. You are our brethren of the same land; we wish your prosperity as brethren should do. Farewell.

1802

Federalist and Anti-Federalist Contentions

According to the Articles of Confederation, after the Revolutionary War, the states had entered "into a firm league of friendship with each other." The league was anything but "firm," however. Drafted in 1776 and finally ratified a full five years later, the Articles reflect the fear with which the thirteen states approached the idea of a strong, centralized government necessary to maintain a truly "United" States. With the memory of a powerful monarchy still lingering, the states entered into a confederation that left the national governing body—Congress—pitifully weak. Congressional sessions were often so poorly attended that there were not enough delegates to conduct legal business. And although Congress could declare war and peace and enter into alliances, it was not empowered to raise taxes, make laws, or create a national trade policy. On a theoretical level, the states justified this weak central government by arguing from the assumption that a truly republican government—a representative government without a hereditary executive—was only possible among people inhabiting a small land area populated by people with like interests. Therefore, the argument went, the individual states, rather than a centralized government combining all states, would best serve the interests of the people. The argument shows that a centralized power structure had proven, for the Revolutionary generation, untrustworthy.

The harsh economic and social realities of post-war life in the states seriously undermined visions of peaceful and prosperous confederation. The massive economic disruption in the wake of the war had left many in debt. Unable to repay their creditors, many debtors faced imprisonment, so they often turned to extreme measures to protect themselves. In Rhode Island, for instance, debtors gained control of the legislature and began printing large quantities of paper money, stipulating that creditors must accept the virtually worthless currency for the payment of debts. And in Massachusetts, in what has become known as Shays's Rebellion, armed farmers began surrounding courthouses, denying entrance to judges who would be ruling on their foreclosure and bankruptcy cases. In a standoff between roughly 1,500 farmers and 1,000 militiamen at a federal arsenal in Springfield, four farmers were killed. The rebellion, which occurred only a few months before the Federal Convention, played nicely into the hands of those calling for a more aggressive centralized government. John Adams (1735–1826), for instance, wrote about the "lawless tyrannical rabble" of Massachusetts in his *Defence of the Constitutions of Government of the United States of America* (1787, 1788).

When the Federal Convention finally convened in Philadelphia on May 25, 1787, only seven states—barely a majority—were represented. George Washington chaired the debates, which were conducted secretly so that the delegates could speak their minds freely. The secret deliberations were recorded by James Madison, whose Virginia Plan was influential in determining the ultimate ideology of the Constitution. The plan called for a bicameral (two-house) legislature with broad powers of legislative authority, a federal judiciary, and an executive. A system of checks and balances, by which none of the branches of government could gain supremacy over the others, allayed the fears of many who had worried that either the legislative or the executive branch would become tyrannical. On September 17, the Constitution was finally approved, and the state-by-state battle for ratification began.

Such a brief outline of the Convention debates perhaps incorrectly implies that the acceptance of the Constitution was a foregone conclusion, the inevitable end result of the Revolutionary War. However, the vigorous ratification debates suggest that the Constitution was considered a radical document, even though African Americans, Native Americans, and women—the majority of the nation's inhabitants in 1787—were given no political voice in the Constitution. In the debates for ratification, supporters of the Constitution were called Federalists, while opposers came to be known as Anti-Federalists (a name given them by Federalists who realized the value of stigmatizing their opponents with the negative prefix). The Federalists found it difficult to allay common Anti-Federalist concerns—that individual states would lose their political autonomy under the new Constitution, that a national standing army was a threat to liberty, that officials in the new government would constitute an aristocracy, and that there was no bill of rights guaranteeing individual liberties.

The most famous defenses of the Constitution occur in a series of essays—now called the *Federalist Papers*—by Alexander Hamilton (1757–1804), James Madison (1731–1836), and John Jay (1745–1829). Written under the pseudonym *Publius* (for the Roman, Publius Valerianus, who was called *Publicola,* "people-lover"), the essays appeared first in New York newspapers between October 1787 and May 1788. New York was a crucial state in the ratification contest, for New York's influential governor, George Clinton, opposed the Constitution. If only because its citizens feared being the inhabitants of a lone, independent "nation," New York was eventually won over to the side of the Federalists, with the narrow vote of thirty in favor of the Constitution, twenty-seven opposed. The other states were slowly ratifying the Constitutional articles, perhaps under the influence of the *Publius* essays, which were being reprinted throughout the states. With full ratification (in 1790) by all thirteen states, the *Federalist Papers* entered literary history as important writings indeed.

In Federalist No. 6, Hamilton, echoing the beliefs of English philosopher Thomas Hobbes (1588–1679), argued that human beings are basically "ambitious, vindictive and rapacious." Hamilton used this theory of human nature to argue for a strong national government to check the "factions and convulsions" which would otherwise tear the states apart. And in Federalist No. 10, Madison argued that the only method to control faction without destroying individual liberty was to elect leaders whose "wisdom may best discern the true interest of their country." Although Madison acknowledged that the "unequal distribution of property" was the most prevalent source of faction, he nonetheless mocked "theoretic politicians" who had sought to end faction by "reducing mankind to a perfect equality in their political rights."

The Anti-Federalist argument is represented here in an essay by *Agrippa,* most likely written by one-time librarian of Harvard, James Winthrop. The objections to the Constitution raised by *Agrippa* were shared by many Anti-Federalists. Specifically, *Agrippa* argued that a bill of rights was absolutely necessary, because "we shall [not] always have good men to govern us." Thus, while Federalists like Hamilton used the theory of the innate corruptibility of humankind to argue for a strong central government, Anti-Federalists like *Agrippa* used this same theory to argue for a government whose powers would be restricted by a bill of rights.

On July 4, 1788, once it was learned that the crucial state of Virginia had ratified the Constitution, a large parade took place in Philadelphia. Virtually all classes and vocations were represented in the procession. Judges, lawyers, clergy, veterans, merchants, carpenters, sailors, apprentices, farmers, bricklayers (carrying a banner that read "Both Buildings and Rulers are the Works of our Hands"), coach painters, cabinet makers, food suppliers, bookbinders, printers, blacksmiths and others—all marched in the parade. Prominent Philadelphia doctor Benjamin Rush wrote of the procession that "rank for a while forgot all its claims." For that one moment, at least, it seemed as if the "We" of the Constitution truly represented the people themselves.

Nicholas D. Rombes, Jr.
University of Detroit Mercy

PRIMARY WORKS

The Federalist, ed. Jacob E. Cooke, 1961; *The Complete Anti-Federalist,* 7 vols., ed. Herbert J. Storing, 1981.

The Federalist No. 6 (Alexander Hamilton)

November 14, 1787

To the People of the State of New York.

The three last numbers of this Paper have been dedicated to an enumeration of the dangers to which we should be exposed, in a state of disunion, from the arms and arts of foreign nations. I shall now proceed to delineate dangers of a different, and, perhaps, still more alarming kind, those which will in all probability flow from dissentions between the States themselves, and from domestic factions and convulsions. These have been already in some instances slightly anticipated, but they deserve a more particular and more full investigation.

A man must be far gone in Utopian speculations who can seriously doubt, that if these States should either be wholly disunited, or only united in partial confederacies, the subdivisions into which they might be thrown would have frequent and violent contests with each other. To presume a want of motives for such contests, as an argument against their existence, would be to forget that men are ambitious, vindictive and rapacious. To look for a continuation of harmony between a number of independent unconnected sovereignties, situated in the same neighbourhood, would be to disregard the uniform course of human events, and to set at defiance the accumulated experience of ages.

The causes of hostility among nations are innumerable. There are some which have a general and almost constant operation upon the collective bodies of society: Of this description are the love of power or the desire of preeminence and dominion—the jealousy of power, or the desire of equality and safety. There are others which have a more circumscribed, though an equally operative influence, within their spheres: Such are the rivalships and competitions of commerce between commercial nations. And there are others, not less numerous than either of the former, which take their origin intirely in private passions; in the attachments, enmities, interests, hopes and fears of leading individuals in the communities of which they are members. Men of this class, whether the favourites of a king or of a people, have in too many instances abused the confidence they possessed; and assuming the pretext of some public motive, have not scrupled to sacrifice the national tranquility to personal advantage, or personal gratification.

The celebrated Pericles, in compliance with the resentments of a prostitute,[1] at the expense of much of the blood and treasure of his countrymen, attacked, vanquished and destroyed, the city of the *Samnians.* The same man, stimulated by private pique against the *Megarensians,*[2] another nation of Greece, or to avoid a prosecution with which he was threatened as an accomplice in a supposed theft of the statuary *Phidias,*[3] or to get rid of the accusations prepared to be brought against him for dissipating the funds of the State in the purchase of popularity,[4] or from a combination of all these causes, was the primitive author of that famous and fatal war, distinguished in the Grecian annals by the name of the *Pelopponesian* war; which, after various vicissitudes, intermissions and renewals, terminated in the ruin of the Athenian commonwealth.

The ambitious Cardinal,[5] who was Prime Minister to Henry VIIIth permitting his vanity to aspire to the Tripple-Crown[6] entertained hopes of succeeding in the acquisition of that splendid prize by the influence of the Emperor Charles Vth. To secure the favour and interest of this enterprising and powerful Monarch, he precipitated England into a war with France, contrary to the plainest dictates of Policy, and at the hazard of the safety and independence, as well of the Kingdom over which he presided by his councils, as of Europe in general. For if there ever was a Sovereign who bid fair to realise the project of universal monarchy it was the Emperor Charles Vth, of whose intrigues Wolsey was at once the instrument and the dupe.

The influence which the bigottry of one female,[7] the petulancies of another,[8] and the cabals of a third,[9] had in the co[n]temporary policy, ferments and pacifications of a considerable part of Europe are topics that have been too often descanted upon not to be generally known.

To multiply examples of the agency of personal considerations in the production of great national events, either foreign or domestic, according to their direction would be an unnecessary waste of time. Those who have but a superficial acquaintance with the sources from which they are to be drawn will themselves recollect a variety of instances; and those who have a tolerable knowledge of human nature will not stand in need of such lights, to form their opinion either of the reality or extent of that agency. Perhaps however a reference, tending to illustrate the general principle, may with propriety be made to a case which has lately

[1] Aspasia, vide Plutarch's life of Pericles. (Publius)

[2] Idem. (Publius)

[3] Idem. Phidias was supposed to have stolen some public gold with the connivance of Pericles for the embellishment of the statue of Minerva. (Publius)

[4] Idem. (Publius)

[5] Thomas Wolsey (c. 1475–1530). (Cooke)

[6] Worn by the Popes. (Cooke)

[7] Madame De Maintenon. (Publius) She was secretly married to Louis XIV of France in 1684. The "bigotry" to which Hamilton referred was probably her successful attempt to persuade Louis to persecute the Huguenots. (Cooke)

[8] Dutchess of Marlborough. (Publius) As confidante and adviser to Queen Anne from 1702 to 1710, she was extremely influential in both court and state affairs until her political intrigues and personal arrogance led to a break with the Queen. (Cooke)

[9] Madame De Pompadoure. (Publius) As mistress to Louis XV in the years 1745–1765, she played a prominent part in the court intrigues by which France's ministers were chosen and the nation's policies determined. (Cooke)

happened among ourselves. If SHAYS had not been a *desperate debtor* it is much to be doubted whether Massachusetts would have been plunged into a civil war.[10]

But notwithstanding the concurring testimony of experience, in this particular, there are still to be found visionary, or designing men, who stand ready to advocate the paradox of perpetual peace between the States, though dismembered and alienated from each other. The genius of republics (say they) is pacific; the spirit of commerce has a tendency to soften the manners of men and to extinguish those inflammable humours which have so often kindled into wars. Commercial republics, like ours, will never be disposed to waste themselves in ruinous contentions with each other. They will be governed by mutual interest, and will cultivate a spirit of mutual amity and concord.

Is it not (we may ask these projectors in politics) the true interests of all nations to cultivate the same benevolent and philosophic spirit? If this be their true interest, have they in fact pursued it? Has it not, on the contrary, invariably been found, that momentary passions and immediate interests have a more active and imperious controul over human conduct than general or remote considerations of policy, utility or justice? Have republics in practice been less addicted to war than monarchies? Are not the former administered by men as well as the latter? Are there not aversions, predilections, rivalships and desires of unjust acquisition that affect nations as well as kings? Are not popular assemblies frequently subject to the impulses of rage, resentment, jealousy, avarice, and of other irregular and violent propensities? Is it not well known that their determinations are often governed by a few individuals, in whom they place confidence, and are of course liable to be tinctured by the passions and views of those individuals? Has commerce hitherto done anything more than change the objects of war? Is not the love of wealth as domineering and enterprising a passion as that of power or glory? Have there not been as many wars founded upon commercial motives, since that has become the prevailing system of nations, as were before occasioned b[y] the cupidity of territory or dominion? Has not the spirit of commerce in many instances administered new incentives to the appetite both for the one and for the other? Let experience, the least fallible guide of human opinions, be appealed to for an answer to these inquiries.

Sparta, Athens, Rome and Carthage were all Republics; two of them, Athens and Carthage, of the commercial kind. Yet were they as often engaged in wars, offensive and defensive, as the neighbouring Monarchies of the same times. Sparta was little better than a well regulated camp; and Rome was never sated of carnage and conquest.

Carthage, though a commercial Republic, was the aggressor in the very war that ended in her destruction. Hannibal had carried her arms into the heart of Italy

[10]Shays's Rebellion of 1786 and early 1787 in central and western Massachusetts expressed the discontent which was widespread throughout New England during the economic depression following the Revolution. Led by Daniel Shays, a Revolutionary War veteran and officeholder of Pelham, Massachusetts, the insurgents resorted to armed efforts to intimidate and close the courts to prevent action against debtors. By February of 1787 state troops, under the leadership of Major General Benjamin Lincoln, had suppressed the rebellion. (Cooke)

and to the gates of Rome, before Scipio, in turn, gave him an overthrow in the territories of Carthage and made a conquest of the Commonwealth.

Venice in latter times figured more than once in wars of ambition; 'till becoming an object of terror to the other Italian States, Pope Julius the Second found means to accomplish that formidable league,[11] which gave a deadly blow to the power and pride of this haughty Republic.

The Provinces of Holland, 'till they were overwhelmed in debts and taxes, took a leading and conspicuous part in the wars of Europe. They had furious contests with England for the dominion of the sea; and were among the most persevering and most implacable of the opponents of Louis XIV.

In the government of Britain the representatives of the people compose one branch of the national legislature. Commerce has been for ages the predominant pursuit of that country. Few nations, nevertheless, have been more frequently engaged in war; and the wars, in which that kingdom has been engaged, have in numerous instances proceeded from the people.

There have been, if I may so express it, almost as many popular as royal wars. The cries of the nation and the importunities of their representatives have, upon various occasions, dragged their monarchs into war, or continued them in it contrary to their inclinations, and, sometimes, contrary to the real interests of the State. In that memorable struggle for superiority, between the rival Houses of Austria and Bourbon which so long kept Europe in a flame, it is well known that the antipathies of the English against the avarice of a favourite leader,[12] protracted the war beyond the limits marked out by sound policy and for a considerable time in opposition to the views of the Court.[13]

The wars of these two last mentioned nations have in a great measure grown out of commercial considerations—The desire of supplanting and the fear of being supplanted either in particular branches of traffic or in the general advantages of trade and navigation; and sometimes even the more culpable desire of sharing in the commerce of other nations, without their consent.

The last war but two between Britain and Spain sprang from the attempts of the English merchants, to prosecute an illicit trade with the Spanish main.[14] These unjustifiable practices on their part produced severities on the part of the Spaniards, towards the subjects of Great Britain, which were not more justifiable; because they exceeded the bounds of a just retaliation, and were chargeable with inhumanity and cruelty. Many of the English who were taken on the Spanish coasts were sent to dig in the mines of Potosi; and by the usual progress of a spirit of

[11]The League of Cambray, comprehending the Emperor, the King of France, the King of Arragon, and most of the Italian Princes and States. (Publius)

[12]The Duke of Marlborough. (Publius)

[13]The War of the Spanish Succession, 1701–1714. In 1709 Marlborough, commander-in-chief of the united British and Dutch armies, refused to consider a French plea for peace, although the Tory party in England was opposed to continuing the war. (Cooke)

[14]The War of Jenkins's Ear, which began in 1739 and soon was absorbed into the War of the Austrian Succession (1740–1748). It arose from Spanish reprisals against repeated attempts by Englishmen to circumvent or defy the strict regulations under which Spain allowed a limited amount of trade with her American colonies. (Cooke)

resentment, the innocent were after a while confounded with the guilty in indiscriminate punishment. The complaints of the merchants kindled a violent flame throughout the nation, which soon after broke out in the house of commons, and was communicated from that body to the ministry. Letters of reprisal were granted and a war ensued, which in its consequences overthrew all the alliances[15] that but twenty years before had been formed, with sanguine expectations of the most beneficial fruits.

From this summary of what has taken place in other countries, whose situations have borne the nearest resemblance to our own, what reason can we have to confide in those reveries, which would seduce us into an expectation of peace and cordiality between the members of the present confederacy, in a state of separation? Have we not already seen enough of the fallacy and extravagance of those idle theories which have amused us with promises of an exemption from the imperfections, weaknesses and evils incident to society in every shape? Is it not time to awake from the deceitful dream of a golden age, and to adopt as a practical maxim for the direction of our political conduct, that we, as well as the other inhabitants of the globe, are yet remote from the happy empire of perfect wisdom and perfect virtue?

Let the point of extreme depression to which our national dignity and credit have sunk—let the inconveniences felt everywhere from a lax and ill administration of government—let the revolt of a part of the State of North Carolina[16]—the late menacing disturbances in Pennsylvania[17] and the actual insurrections and rebellions in Massachusetts declare![18]

So far is the general sense of mankind from corresponding with the tenets of those, who endeavor to lull asleep our apprehensions of discord and hostility between the States, in the event of disunion, that it has from long observation of the progress of society become a sort of axiom in politics, that vicinity, or nearness of situation, constitutes nations natural enemies. An intelligent writer expresses himself on this subject to this effect—"NEIGHBOURING NATIONS (says he) are naturally ENEMIES of each other, unless their common weakness forces them to league in a CONFEDERATE REPUBLIC, and their constitution prevents the differences that neighbourhood occasions, extinguishing that secret jealousy, which disposes all States to aggrandise themselves at the expence of their neighbours."[19] This passage, at the same time points out the EVIL and suggests the REMEDY.

PUBLIUS.

1787

[15] *I.e.,* the Continental balance-of-power system established by the Treaty of Utrecht in 1713. (Cooke)

[16] This refers to the establishment in 1784 of a separate state, Franklin, by the inhabitants of four western counties of North Carolina. The opposition of North Carolina and internal dissensions in the infant state led, at the end of 1787, to the submission of the inhabitants of Franklin to the authority of North Carolina. (Cooke)

[17] In 1787 many inhabitants of the Wyoming Valley sought to secede from Pennsylvania and establish a new state. The governor of Pennsylvania responded by ordering "a body of militia to hold themselves in readiness to march thither," an action approved by the state assembly less than a month before this essay was written. (Cooke)

[18] Shays's Rebellion, mentioned earlier in this paper. (Cooke)

[19] Vede Principes des Negotiations par L'Abbe de Mably. (Publius)

The Federalist No. 10 (James Madison)

November 22, 1787

To the People of the State of New York.

Among the numerous advantages promised by a well constructed Union, none deserves to be more accurately developed than its tendency to break and control the violence of faction. The friend of popular governments, never finds himself so much alarmed for their character and fate, as when he contemplates their propensity to this dangerous vice. He will not fail therefore to set a due value on any plan which, without violating the principles to which he is attached, provides a proper cure for it. The instability, injustice and confusion introduced in the public councils, have in truth been the mortal diseases under which popular governments have every where perished; as they continue to be the favorite and fruitful topics from which the adversaries to liberty derive their most specious declamations. The valuable improvements made by the American Constitutions on the popular models, both ancient and modern, cannot certainly be too much admired; but it would be an unwarrantable partiality, to contend that they have as effectually obviated the danger on this side as was wished and expected. Complaints are every where heard from our most considerate and virtuous citizens, equally the friends of public and private faith, and of public and personal liberty; that our governments are too unstable; that the public good is disregarded in the conflicts of rival parties; and that measures are too often decided, not according to the rules of justice, and the rights of the minor party; but by the superior force of an interested and over-bearing majority. However anxiously we may wish that these complaints had no foundation, the evidence of known facts will not permit us to deny that they are in some degree true. It will be found indeed, on a candid review of our situation, that some of the distresses under which we labor, have been erroneously charged on the operation of our governments; but it will be found, at the same time, that other causes will not alone account for many of our heaviest misfortunes; and particularly, for that prevailing and increasing distrust of public engagements, and alarm for private rights, which are echoed from one end of the continent to the other. These must be chiefly, if not wholly, effects of the unsteadiness and injustice, with which a factious spirit has tainted our public administrations.

By a faction I understand a number of citizens, whether amounting to a majority or minority of the whole, who are united and actuated by some common impulse of passion, or of interest, adverse to the rights of other citizens, or to the permanent and aggregate interests of the community.

There are two methods of curing the mischiefs of faction: the one, by removing its causes; the other, by controling its effects.

There are again two methods of removing the causes of faction: the one by destroying the liberty which is essential to its existence; the other, by giving to every citizen the same opinions, the same passions, and the same interests.

It could never be more truly said than of the first remedy, that it is worse than the disease. Liberty is to faction, what air is to fire, an aliment without which it instantly expires. But it could not be a less folly to abolish liberty, which is essential to political life, because it nourishes faction, than it would be to wish the annihilation of air, which is essential to animal life, because it imparts to fire its destructive agency.

The second expedient is as impracticable, as the first would be unwise. As long as the reason of man continues fallible, and he is at liberty to exercise it, different opinions will be formed. As long as the connection subsists between his reason and his self-love, his opinions and his passions will have a reciprocal influence on each other; and the former will be objects to which the latter will attach themselves. The diversity in the faculties of men from which the rights of property originate, is not less an insuperable obstacle to a uniformity of interests. The protection of these faculties is the first object of Government. From the protection of different and unequal faculties of acquiring property, the possession of degrees and kinds of property immediately results; and from the influence of these on the sentiments and views of the respective proprietors, ensues a division of the society into different interests and parties.

The latent causes of faction are thus sown in the nature of man; and we see them every where brought into different degrees of activity, according to the different circumstances of civil society. A zeal for different opinions concerning religion, concerning Government and many other points, as well of speculation as of practice; an attachment to different leaders ambitiously contending for pre-eminence and power; or to persons of other descriptions whose fortunes have been interesting to the human passions, have in turn divided mankind into parties, inflamed them with mutual animosity, and rendered them much more disposed to vex and oppress each other, than to cooperate for their common good. So strong is this propensity of mankind to fall into mutual animosities, that where no substantial occasion presents itself, the most frivolous and fanciful distinctions have been sufficient to kindle their unfriendly passions, and excite their most violent conflicts. But the most common and durable source of factions, has been the various and unequal distribution of property. Those who hold, and those who are without property, have ever formed distinct interests in society. Those who are creditors, and those who are debtors, fall under a like discrimination. A landed interest, a manufacturing interest, a mercantile interest, a monied interest, with many lesser interests, grow up of necessity in civilized nation, and divide them into different classes, actuated by different sentiments and views. The regulation of these various and interfering interests forms the principal task of modern Legislation, and involved the spirit of party and faction in the necessary and ordinary operations of Government.

No man is allowed to be a judge in his own cause; because his interest would certainly bias his judgment, and, not improbably, corrupt his integrity. With equal, nay with greater reason, a body of men, are unfit to be both judges and parties, at the same time; yet, what are many of the most important acts of legislation, but so many judicial determinations, not indeed concerning the rights of single persons, but concerning the rights of large bodies of citizens; and what are the different classes of legislators, but advocates and parties to the causes which they determine? Is a law proposed concerning private debts? It is a question to which the creditors are parties on one side, and the debtors on the other. Justice ought to hold the balance between them. Yet the parties are and must be themselves the judges; and the most numerous party, or in other words, the most powerful faction must be expected to prevail. Shall domestic manufactures be encouraged, and in what degree, by restrictions on foreign manufactures? are questions which would be differently decided by the landed and the manufacturing classes; and probably by neither, with a sole regard to justice and the public good. The apportionment of taxes on the various descriptions of poverty, is an act which seems to require the most exact impartiality; yet, there is perhaps no legislative act in which greater opportunity and temptation are given to a predominant party, to trample on the rules of justice. Every shilling with which they over-burden the inferior number, is a shilling saved to their own pockets.

It is in vain to say, that enlightened statesmen will be able to adjust these clashing interests, and render them all subservient to the public good. Enlightened statesmen will not always be at the helm: Nor, in many cases, can such an adjustment be made at all, without taking into view indirect and remote considerations, which will rarely prevail over the immediate interest which one party may find in disregarding the rights of another, or the good of the whole.

The inference to which we are brought, is, that the causes of faction cannot be removed; and that relief is only to be sought in the means of controling its effects.

If a faction consists of less than a majority, relief is supplied by the republican principle, which enables the majority to defeat its sinister views by regular vote: it may clog the administration, it may convulse the society; but it will be unable to execute and mask its violence under the forms of the Constitution. When a majority is included in a faction, the form of popular government on the other hand enables it to sacrifice to its ruling passion or interest, both the public good and the rights of other citizens. To secure the public good, and private rights, against the danger of such a faction, and at the same time to preserve the spirit and the form of popular government, is then the great object to which our enquiries are directed: Let me add that it is the great desideratum, by which alone this form of government can be rescued from the opprobrium under which it has so long labored, and be recommended to the esteem and adoption of mankind.

By what means is this object attainable? Evidently by one of two only. Either the existence of the same passion or interest in a majority at the same time, must be prevented; or the majority, having such co-existent passion or interest, must be rendered, by their number and local situation, unable to concert and carry into effect schemes of oppression. If the impulse and the opportunity be suffered to coincide, we well know that neither moral nor religious motives can be relied on as an adequate control. They are not found to be such on the injustice and violence of individuals, and lose their efficacy in proportion to the numbers combined together; that is, in proportion as their efficacy becomes needful.

From this view of the subject, it may be concluded, that a pure Democracy, by which I mean, a Society, consisting of a small number of citizens, who assemble and administer the Government in person, can admit of no cure for the mischiefs of faction. A common passion or interest will, in almost every case, be felt by a majority of the whole; a communication and concern results from the form of Government itself; and there is nothing to check the inducements to sacrifice the weaker party, or an obnoxious individual. Hence it is, that such Democracies have ever been spectacles of turbulence and contention; have ever been found incompatible with personal security, or the rights of property; and have in general been as short in their lives, as they have been violent in their deaths. Theoretic politicians, who have patronized this species of Government, have erroneously supposed, that by reducing mankind to a perfect equality in their political rights, they would at the same time, be perfectly equalized and assimilated in their possessions, their opinions, and their passions.

A Republic, by which I mean a Government in which the scheme of representation takes place, opens a different prospect, and promises the cure for which we are seeking. Let us examine the points in which it varies from pure Democracy, and we shall comprehend both the nature of the cure, and the efficacy which it must derive from the Union.

The two great points of difference between a Democracy and a Republic are, first, the delegation of the Government, in the latter, to a small number of citizens elected by the rest: secondly, the greater number of citizens, and greater sphere of country, over which the latter may be extended.

The effect of the first difference is, on the one hand to refine and enlarge the public views, by passing them through the medium of a chosen body of citizens, whose wisdom may best discern the true interest of their country, and whose patriotism and love of justice, will be least likely to sacrifice it to temporary or partial considerations. Under such a regulation, it may well happen that the public voice pronounced by the representatives of the people, will be more consonant to the public good, than if pronounced by the people themselves convened for the purpose. On the other hand, the effect may be inverted. Men of factious tempers, of local prejudices, or of sinister designs, may be intrigue, be corruption or by other means, first obtain the suffrages, and then betray the interests of the people. The question resulting is, whether small or extensive Republics are most favorable to the election of proper guardians of the public wealth and it is clearly decided in favor of the latter by two obvious considerations.

In the first place it is to be remarked that however small the Republic may be, the Representatives must be raised to a certain number, in order to guard against the cabals of a few; and that however large it may be, they must be limited to a certain number, in order to guard against the confusion of a multitude. Hence the number of Representatives in the two cases, not being in proportion to that of the Constituents, and being proportionally greatest in the small Republic, it follows, that if the proportion of fit characters, be not less, in the large than in the small Republic, the former will present a greater option, and consequently a greater probability of a fit choice.

In the next place, as each Representative will be chosen by a greater number of citizens in the large than in the small Republic, it will be more difficult for unworthy candidates to practise with success the vicious arts, by which elections are too often carried; and the suffrages of the people being more free, will be more likely to centre on men who possess the most attractive merit, and the most diffusive and established characters.

It must be confessed, that in this, as in most other cases, there is a mean, on both sides of which inconveniencies will be found to lie. By enlarging too much the number of electors, you render the representative too little acquainted with all their local circumstances and lesser interests; as by reducing it too much, you render him unduly attached to these, and too little fit to comprehend and pursue great and national objects. The Federal Constitution forms a happy combination in this respect; the great and aggregate interests being referred to the national, the local and particular, to the state legislatures.

The other point of difference is, the greater number of citizens and extent of territory which may be brought within the compass of Republican, than of Democratic Government; and it is this circumstance principally which renders factious combinations less to be dreaded in the former, than in the latter. The smaller the society, the fewer probably will be the distinct parties and interests composing it; the fewer the distinct parties and interests, the more frequently will a majority be found of the same party; and the smaller the numbers of individuals composing a majority, and the smaller the compass within which they are placed, the more easily will they concert and execute their plans of oppression. Extend the sphere, and you take in a greater variety of parties and interests; you make it less probable that a majority of the whole will have a common motive to invade the rights of other citizens; or if such a common motive exists, it will be more difficult for all who feel it to discover their own strength, and to act in unison with each other. Besides other impediments, it may be remarked, that where there is a consciousness of unjust or dishonorable purposes, communication is always checked by distrust, in proportion to the number whose concurrence is necessary.

Hence it clearly appears, that the same advantage, which a Republic has over a Democracy, in controling the effects of faction, is enjoyed by a large over a small Republic—is enjoyed by the Union over the States composing it. Does this advantage consist in the substitution of Representatives, whose enlightened views and virtuous sentiments render them superior to local prejudices, and to schemes of injustice? It will not be denied, that the Representation of the Union will be most likely to possess these requisite endowments. Does it consist in the greater security afforded by a greater variety of parties, against the event of any one party being able to outnumber and oppress the rest? In an equal degree does the encreased variety of parties, comprised within the Union, encrease this security? Does it, in fine, consist in the greater obstacles opposed to the concert and accomplishment of the secret wishes of an unjust and interested majority? Here, again, the extent of the Union gives it the most palpable advantage.

The influence of factious leaders may kindle a flame within their particular States but will be unable to spread a general conflagration through the other States: a religious sect, may degenerate into a political faction in a part of the confederacy; but the variety of sects dispersed over the entire face of it, must secure the national Councils against any danger from that source: a rage for paper money, for an abolition of debts, for an equal division of property, or for any other improper or wicked project, will be less apt to pervade the whole body of the Union, than a particular member of it; in the same proportion as such a malady is more likely to taint a particular county or district, than an entire State.

In the extent and proper structure of the Union, therefore, we behold a Republican remedy for the diseases most incident to Republican Government. And according to the degree of pleasure and pride, we feel in being Republicans, ought to be our zeal in cherishing the spirit, and supporting the character of Federalists.

PUBLIUS.

1787

An Anti-Federalist Paper

To the Massachusetts Convention.[1]

Gentlemen,

As it is essentially necessary to the happiness of a free people, that the constitution of government should be established in principles of truth, I have endeavoured, in a series of papers, to discuss the proposed form, with that degree of freedom which becomes a faithful citizen of the commonwealth. It must be obvious to the most careless observer, that the friends of the new plan appear to have nothing more in view than to establish it by a popular current, without any regard to the truth of its principles. Propositions, novel, erroneous and dangerous, are boldly advanced to support a system, which does not appear to be founded in, but in every instance to contradict, the experience of mankind. We are told, that a constitution is in itself a bill of rights; that all power not expressly given is reserved; that no powers are given to the new government which are not already vested in the state governments; and that it is for the security of liberty that the persons elected should have the absolute controul over the time, manner and place of election. These, and an hundred other things of the like kind, though they have gained the hasty assent of men, respectable for learning and ability, are false in themselves, and invented merely to serve a present purpose. This will, I trust, clearly appear from the following considerations.

It is common to consider man at first as in a state of nature, separate from all society. The only historical evidence, that the human species ever actually existed in this state, is derived from the book of Gen.[2] There, it is said, that Adam remained a while alone. While the whole species was comprehended in his person was the only instance in which this supposed state of nature really existed. Ever since the completion of the first pair, mankind appear as natural to associate with their own species, as animals of any other kind herd together. Wherever we meet with their settlements, they are found in clans. We are therefore justified in saying, that a state of society is the natural state of man. Wherever we find a settlement of men, we find also some appearance of government. The state of government is therefore as natural to mankind as a state of society. Government and society appear to be coeval. The most rude and artless form of government is probably the most ancient. This we find to be practised among the Indian tribes in America. With them the whole authority of government is vested in the whole tribe.[3] Individuals depend upon their reputation of valour and wisdom to give them influence. Their government is genuinely democratical. This was probably the first kind of government

[1]First published in the *Massachusetts Gazette,* January 29, 1788.

[2]According to Genesis, Adam dwelled in Eden for a time before Eve was created. "And the Lord God said, It is not good that the man should be alone; I will make him a help meet for him" (Genesis 2:18).

[3]*Agrippa* is referring to the Iroquois nation, a confederacy made up of five tribes, each represented on the governing council. At the time of confederation and indeed even today, readers have commented on the similarity between the representative system of the Iroquois and that evident in the Constitution.

among mankind, as we meet with no mention of any other kind, till royalty was introduced in the person of Nimrod.[4] Immediately after that time, the Asiatick nations seem to have departed from the simple democracy, which is still retained by their American brethren, and universally adopted the kingly form. We do indeed meet with some vague rumors of an aristocracy in India so late as the time of Alexander the great.[5] But such stories are altogether uncertain and improbable. For in the time of Abraham,[6] who lived about sixteen hundred years before Alexander, all the little nations mentioned in the Mosaick history appear to be governed by kings. It does not appear from any accounts of the Asiatick kingdoms that they have practised at all upon the idea of a limitted monarchy. The whole power of society has been delegated to the kings; and though they may be said to have constitutions of government, because the succession to the crown is limitted by certain rules, yet the people are not benefitted by their constitutions, and enjoy no share of civil liberty. The first attempt to reduce republicanism to a system, appears to be made by Moses when he led the Israelites out of Egypt.[7] This government stood a considerable time, about five centuries, till in a frenzy the people demanded a king, that they might resemble the nations about them. They were dissatisfied with their judges, and instead of changing the administration, they madly changed their constitution. However they might flatter themselves with the idea, that an high spirited people could get the power back again when they pleased; they never did get it back, and they fared like the nations about them. Their kings tyrannized over them for some centuries, till they fell under a foreign yoke. This is the history of that nation. With a change of names, it describes the progress of political changes in other countries. The people are dazzled with the splendour of distant monarchies, and a desire to share their glory induces them to sacrifice their domestick happiness.

From this general view of the state of mankind it appears, that all the power of government originally reside in the body of the people; and that when they appoint certain persons to administer the government, they delegate all the powers of government not expressly reserved. Hence it appears, that a constitution does not in itself imply any more than a declaration of the relation which the different parts of the government bear to each other, but does not in any degree imply security to the rights of individuals. This has been the uniform practice. In all doubtful cases the decision is in favour of the government. It is therefore impertinent to ask by what right government exercises powers not expressly delegated. Mr. Wilson,[8] the great oracle of federalism, acknowledges, in his speech to the Philadelphians, the truth of these remarks, as they respect the state governments, but attempts to set up a

[4]Nimrod, famed as a great hunter, was a Babylonian leader who ruled several kingdoms. See Genesis 10:8–12.

[5]Alexander the Great (B.C. 356–323) was King of Macedonia, an ancient kingdom north of Greece, now part of Greece, Bulgaria, and Yugoslavia.

[6]According to the Bible, a covenant was established between Abraham's descendants and God, who told Abraham, "As for me, behold, my covenant is with thee, and thou shalt be a father of many nations" (Genesis 17:4).

[7]See Exodus, chapters 13 and 14, for an account of how Moses led the Israelites out of Egypt. See Judges for a description of the Hebrews' disaffection with their government.

[8]James Wilson (1742–1798) was a supporter of the Constitution. *Agrippa* refers to Wilson's "Address to the Citizens of Philadelphia," given on October 6, 1787.

distinction between them and the continental government. To any body who will be at the trouble to read the new system, it is evidently in the same situation as the state constitutions now possess. It is a compact among the *people* for the purposes of government, and not a compact between states. It begins in the name of the people and not of the states.

It has been shown in the course of this paper, that when people institute government, they of course delegate all rights not expressly reserved. In our state constitution the bill of rights consists of thirty articles. It is evident therefore that the new constitution proposes to delegate greater powers than are granted to our own government, sanguine as the person was who denied it. The complaints against the separate governments, even by the friends of the new plan, are not that they have not power enough, but that they are disposed to make a bad use of what power they have. Surely then they reason badly, when they purpose to set up a government possess'd of much more extensive powers than the present, and subject to much smaller checks.

Bills of rights, reserved by authority of the people, are, I believe, peculiar to America. A careful observance of the abuse practised in other countries has had its just effect by inducing our people to guard against them. We find the happiest consequences to flow from it. The separate governments know their powers, their objects, and operations. We are therefore not perpetually tormented with new experiments. For a single instance of abuse among us there are thousands in other countries. On the other hand, the people know their rights, and feel happy in the possession of their freedom, both civil and political. Active industry is the consequence of their security; and within one year the circumstances of the state and of individuals have improved to a degree never before known in this commonwealth. Though our bill of rights does not, perhaps, contain all the cases in which power might be safely reserved, yet it affords a protection to the persons and possessions of individuals not known in any foreign country. In some respects the power of government is a little too confined. In many other countries we find the people resisting their governours for exercising their power in an unaccustomed mode. But for want of a bill of rights the resistance is always by the principles of their government, a rebellion which nothing but success can justify. In our constitution we have aimed at delegating the necessary powers of government and confining their operation to beneficial purposes. At present we appear to have come very near the truth. Let us therefore have wisdom and virtue enough to preserve it inviolate. It is a stale contrivance to get the people into a passion, in order to make them sacrifice their liberty. Repentance always comes, but it comes too late. Let us not flatter ourselves that we shall always have good men to govern us. If we endeavour to be like other nations we shall have more bad men than good ones to exercise extensive powers. That circumstance alone will corrupt them. While they fancy themselves the vicegerents of God, they will resemble him only in power, but will always depart from his wisdom and goodness.

Agrippa.

1788

Toussaint L'Ouverture 1744?–1803

Toussaint Breda was born into slavery on the Breda plantation in Saint Domingue (present-day Haiti, the western part of the island of Hispaniola). At the time of the French Revolution (1789–1799), Saint Domingue was one of the richest colonies in the world, but it was economically tied to France, forced to ship all of its produce to France and import all goods from the mother country. The colony's economy depended on slave labor to perform the exhausting and relentless work of large sugar and coffee plantations. In a slave culture of inconceivable brutality and atrocity, in which one of every ten slaves died within his or her first four years on the island, Toussaint's godfather, a priest, taught him to read, and his relatively tolerant master afforded him access to a library and the freedom to move throughout the plantation. Toussaint studied and worked as a herdsman, a coachman, and a steward; he also married, which was unusual for slaves, and had children. All around him, slaves resisted the harsh conditions of plantation slavery. Many fled to communities of escaped slaves, called maroon societies, in the unsettled mountains. The maroons' activities reached enormous proportions on August 22, 1791, often called the "Night of Fire." With his own plantation threatened by the fighting, Toussaint accompanied his master to safety before joining the rebels. He became the first former slave to lead his nation.

The name "Toussaint" indicates his birth on the Feast of All Saints day; Breda, the last name, was the name of his master, as was customary. As he fought to rid the colony of slavery, Toussaint shed his own ties to the slave system. A famous remark, attributed to several different military officials, lamented, "That blasted Toussaint always manages to find an opening." Toussaint took the French word for opening, *l'ouverture,* as his name, a marker of his identity. He quickly gained authority through his ability to manage and discipline soldiers and through his skill as a field doctor.

Saint Domingue, a French colony, was greatly influenced by the French Revolution. Toussaint sided first with French royalists, believing that the king of France alone could bring change to Saint Domingue, but he shifted alliances in order to maintain power and continue the fight against slavery. For a time he fought for the Spanish, who controlled the eastern part of the island, but he shifted allegiance again when he learned that the French Republic had abolished slavery. The former slaves took up the ideology of the French Revolution and were heard to sing its songs during battles and to profess its ideas of equality. Ironically, the rebels continued to sing songs of the French Revolution years later when they battled France for control of the island. In his letters and proclamations, Toussaint uses the language of the French Revolution to argue for the end of slavery and for political equality.

The revolution in Saint Domingue was enormously significant throughout the Americas. The United States, Jamaica, and other regions depended on slavery for economic strength. Thomas Jefferson remarked on the implications of the revolution in Saint Domingue for slavery throughout the Americas: if slaves could successfully revolt and become political leaders in Saint Domingue, they might do the same elsewhere. And indeed, in his 1797 "Charge" to the African Masonic Lodge, included in this anthology, Prince Hall, an African American organizer, used the slave revolts in Saint Domingue to illustrate the "freedom and equality" for which his audience should be striving. Toussaint L'Ouverture and the Saint Domingue revolution undermined assumptions of racial inferiority and passivity and served as a striking example of the efficacy of resistance and revolt.

The French portion of the island emancipated its slaves in 1794. The eastern region, controlled by Spain, continued to engage in slavery and foster the slave trade until January 24, 1801, when Toussaint L'Ouverture took over the Spanish colony and freed fifteen thousand slaves. Although this action was, in fact, a French victory, Napoleon supported neither the invasion nor Toussaint's display of independence. In another demonstration of his autonomy, Toussaint in July 1801 issued a constitution that permanently banned slavery on the island and granted himself executive power as governor-general of the island. Although he declared an end to slavery, Toussaint responded to Haiti's economic difficulties by reinstating forced labor on plantations. Former slaves were legally bound to their plantations but earned a portion of the profits derived from their labor. This measure created divergent movements and opinions in a cultural climate already defined by conflicting factions based on class, race, and political position.

Responding to Toussaint's growing power and capitalizing on divisions within Saint Domingue, Napoleon sought to regain control. In 1802, he planned an invasion to be led by his brother-in-law, General Leclerc, that would attempt to reassert French authority and reinstate slavery on the island. Hearing news of an imminent French attack in LeCap, Toussaint ordered the town evacuated and burned. Sixteen thousand French soldiers marched through a city of ashes. Nevertheless, after the desertion of several of his generals, Toussaint surrendered to Leclerc in April and retired to his estate. A month later, he agreed to a meeting with the French general. When Toussaint arrived, he was arrested, deported to France, and imprisoned in Fort de Joux. He died from malnutrition and mistreatment on April 7, 1803. Despite the initial success of the French invasion, the leaders of Saint Domingue won the battle a year later and achieved full political control of the island.

Toussaint's proclamations and letters demonstrate a convergence of the political and the literary. Like Nathaniel Bacon's "Proclamation of 1676," Toussaint's pronouncements often claim to speak for the people and employ biblical citations to provide divine sanction for his actions and ideas. Like other writers of African descent decrying slavery, Toussaint uses Enlightenment ideas against imperialist authority. His political legacy is complicated by the intricate dynamics of Saint Domingue society and by the brutality of its revolutionary history. Several groups fought for political power during the revolution, including *grand blancs* (white plantation owners and French officials), *petit blancs* (white overseers, artisans, shopkeepers, and soldiers), black slaves, and free blacks (often mulattos, who were allowed privileges not given to other blacks). Toussaint's rise to power, therefore, meant not only rejecting white slaveholders but also negotiating with and wresting power from other segments of the population. Toussaint has been remembered as a great hero and as a flawed leader, brutal toward mulattos and too conciliatory toward whites. He remains, nevertheless, a powerful example of the horrors of slavery and the possibilities of resistance in colonial America.

Danielle Hinrichs
University of Southern California

PRIMARY WORKS

Register Containing the Proclamations, Ordinances, and Addresses of General Toussaint L'Ouverture, trans. Eleanor Johnson, Schomburg Collection, undated; J. R. Beard, *Toussaint L'Ouverture: A Biography and Autobiography,* 1971; George F. Tyson, ed., *Toussaint L'Ouverture,* 1973.

Proclamations and Letters

Proclamation of 29 August 1793

Brothers and Friends:

I am Toussaint L'Ouverture. My name is perhaps known to you. I have undertaken to avenge you. I want liberty and equality to reign throughout St. Domingue. I am working towards that end. Come and join me, brothers, and combat by our side for the same cause.

Proclamation on the Villate Affair, March 1796[1]

My heart and my feelings are rent upon learning every day of the new plots of the evil-doers, of these corrupt men, of these guilty men and greatly culpable toward the mother country. It is for you to prepare against their false declamations about which I am going to talk to you as a brother, friend and father; too happy I would be if I could get them to come back to themselves, oblige them to recognize and to renounce their errors, inspire them with wholesome remorse and finally put them back on the right path.

Ah my friends, my brothers, my children!—these men[2] are guilty who try by a few quotations from my letters, to persuade you that I have sworn the Destruction of all men of color,[3] they judge my heart by their own hateful and vindictive heart. It is not color that I am fighting; it is crime that I am pursuing and shall always pursue in whatever place it is hidden; this is the reason that:

Considering that it is my duty to enlighten you, I am going to do it, as briefly and as clearly as I possibly can; I am going to speak to you in the Language of reason, truth and religion.

I have written to certain chiefs to be on guard against men of color, because I knew, before the criminal arrest of the General in Chief, that some men of color were at the head of this infernal conspiracy; because I knew that in several quarters of the Colony, the emissaries of these bold chiefs were preaching disobedience, revolt against the lawfully constituted authorities; you have the proof of it today. Who arrested General Laveux?[4] Who dared bring a heinous and sacrilegious hand upon the

[1]In March 1796, Toussaint and mulatto leader Villate were both lieutenant generals under the French general Laveaux. Seeking to wrest power from Laveaux and Toussaint, Villate claimed to discover a plan to reinstate slavery. He captured Laveaux, imprisoned him, and intended to deport him to France. Toussaint was not involved in the plot and deployed troops to restore order. When Villate's coup failed, Laveaux declared Toussaint a loyal hero. The affair elevated Toussaint's standing in the eyes of the French but aggravated relations between Toussaint and the mulattos opposing his power.

[2]Toussaint is likely referring to Villate and his soldiers, whose failed coup left Toussaint with greater power in the colony.

[3]Toussaint refers to the mulattos as "men of color." Historically, mulattos were allowed privileges not given to blacks, and they formed a political faction that often clashed with black political groups.

[4]Governor-General Etienne Laveaux, the target of Villate's attempted coup.

representatives of the Nation? Men of color; it was quite necessary then that I warn my subordinates to suspect these men. God forbid, however, that I confuse the Innocent ones with the guilty! No, my brothers, I am not prejudiced against any particular class; I know that there are men of color who are estimable and virtuous, irreproachable and I have the great satisfaction of having some of them near me, to whom I accord my Esteem, my Friendship and my Confidence; I love them, because, faithful to their duties, they have not participated in perfidious manoeuvres; I have several of them among my Officers, who have never strayed from the right path; and those as well as all faithful soldiers, can count on me; I cherish all virtuous men; I owe them protection, and they shall always obtain it, when they make themselves worthy of it.

When murders were being committed in the Mountain Port of Paix, in the name Etienne, did I not say that Black men were committing these crimes? Let us be just, when we want to accuse; but does calumny know any Limits?

Religion, I remind you, my brothers, is my Guide, it is the rule of my conduct, whatever others might say; Religion tells us, commands us to give back to Caesar that which belongs to Caesar, and to God that which belongs to God,[5] it commands us to give the most complete subordination to our chiefs, to our superiors. A Colonel wishes his body officers to obey him, a Captain wishes his Lieutenants and second-lieutenants to obey him, the Lieutenant wishes his non-commissioned officers to obey him, and the Officers exact the same obedience from their Companies. Why? because they know that subordination is essential to armed Force; there can be no army without subordination.

Supposing that in the presence of a Captain, a Lieutenant, a second-lieutenant, some rebels were to insult, maltreat and arrest the Colonel; what shall they do? Shall they remain peaceful spectators of that criminal conspiracy? They would become guilty themselves, if they did not put forth their efforts to defend him, to snatch him from the hands of those wicked chiefs and they take it ill that I have hurried to the assistance of my chief, of my superior, of the representative of the Republic: they take it ill that I have arrested those who have participated in this Heinous plot. The French nation is going to judge us. I place into its hands those whom I believe guilty.

Officers, the least insubordination arouses you, you mete out severe punishment, sometimes you even stray from the Law in the severity of your punishments; remember that to command well, you must know how to obey.

And you Colonists, you the beloved Children of the Republic; you, whom this tender mother carries in her bosom, you whom she had overwhelmed with kindness, would allow yourselves to be drawn into the artificial suggestions of the wicked! Ah! my brothers, France has decreed, has sanctioned general Liberty; twenty-five million men have ratified this glorious and consoling Decree for humanity, and you fear that she may return you to your former state of Bondage, while she has so long been fighting for her own Liberty and for the Liberty of all Nations.[6] How mistaken you are!

No, my Friends, you are being deceived, they are jealous of your happiness, they want to rob you of it, and you know the ones who are deceiving you; they are those who slander the intentions, the operations of the Governor general and myself, for

[5]Matthew 22:21.

[6]The Republic of France declared slavery illegal on February 4, 1794. Villate justified his attack by claiming that he found chains on Laveaux's ships, evidence that Laveaux was going to restore slavery.

we act together. Believe me then, my brothers, you know me, you know my Religion, you have regarded me up to this day as your Father, I believe I merit this title, I hope to always merit it, it is so near to my heart. I implore you for your happiness, shun the rebels, the wicked; busy yourselves with work, France, your good Mother, will reward you.

The mask is going to fall, the evil-doers feel that the Day of vengeance is approaching; they would like to have a great many accomplices so as to be assured of Impunity; but let them fall alone into the abyss they have dug under their Feet; the hand of God, the Avenger, is going to weigh down upon them, for one does not always defy the Supreme Being with impunity; they have scorned Religion; they have defied the terrible thunder bolts of a God in His Anger; they feel the earth falling in beneath their feet, and they would like to drag you along with them in the depths of their anguish.

Denounce then the wrong doers, those who slander my intentions and actions. I take God as my witness, who must judge us all, that they are pure; I long only for your happiness; one moment more and you will be convinced of it. Close your ears to the voice of the wicked and the Agitator; God lets him act a short while, but often in the midst of his course, He stops him. Look at the proud Haman, the favorite of Ahasuerus, he would like to have had the humble Mordecai perish unjustly.[7] The Gallows, which he had had prepared for this faithful Israelite, served for himself.

Everywhere the Holy Bible (I am pleased to mention it because it consoles me) everywhere the Holy Bible, tells us of the proud being humbled and of the humble being elevated; everywhere it shows us terrible Examples of Divine Justice against great Criminals; now it is an Antiochus,[8] who satiated with crimes, at the approach of death asks for mercy and does not obtain it: now it is a heinous son, an Absalom,[9] urged to insurrection against the most tender of all Fathers and who died miserably; finally, everywhere it proves to us that great scoundrels are punished sooner or later.

Alas! we ask, in the Example of our Divine Master, only the conversion of the Sinner, that he may come back to himself, that he may recognize his mistakes, his errors, his crimes, that he may renounce them, that he may come back to us, and we are ready to give him the "kiss of peace and of reconciliation."

The present letter will be printed, read, published and posted everywhere where there will be need, in order that the wicked persuaded by my peaceable sentiments, may profit by the pardon that I offer them, and that the Good may be cautioned against the snares of Error and seduction.

[7]In the Old Testament Book of Esther, Ahasuerus, an ancient King of Persia, marries Esther, a Jew. Haman is a prominent member of the king's court who secretly plots against the Jews; and Mordecai, Esther's uncle, is a court servant who resists Haman's power. When Mordecai discovers Haman's plan to kill the Jews, he warns Esther, who tells the king, and Ahasuerus sentences Haman to death on the gallows (Esther 9:25).

[8]Antiochus (c. 324–c. 261 B.C.), king of Syria from 280 to c. 261 B.C. The First and Second Books of Maccabees, in the Apocrypha, describe his atrocities and his dying plea to God, who "now no more would have mercy upon him" (2 Maccabees 9:13).

[9]Absalom, son of King David, stages a coup against his father and declares himself king. Eventually, King David's troops defeat Absalom's armies on the battlefield. Contrary to King David's wishes, Absalom is killed, and his body is thrown into a pit in the forest (2 Samuel 18:9–17).

Letter to the Directory, 5 November 1797[1]

The impolitic and incendiary discourse of Vaublanc[2] has not affected the blacks nearly so much as their certainty of the projects which the proprietors of San Domingo are planning: insidious declarations should not have any effect in the eyes of wise legislators who have decreed liberty for the nations. But the attempts on that liberty which the colonists propose are all the more to be feared because it is with the veil of patriotism that they cover their detestable plans. We know that they seek to impose some of them on you by illusory and specious promises, in order to see renewed in this colony its former scenes of horror. Already perfidious emissaries have stepped in among us to ferment the destructive leaven prepared by the hands of liberticides. But they will not succeed. I swear it by all that liberty holds most sacred. My attachment to France, my knowledge of the blacks, make it my duty not to leave you ignorant either of the crimes which they meditate or the oath that we renew, to bury ourselves under the ruins of a country revived by liberty rather than suffer the return of slavery.

It is for you, Citizens Directors, to turn from over our heads the storm which the eternal enemies of our liberty are preparing in the shades of silence. It is for you to enlighten the legislature, it is for you to prevent the enemies of the present system from spreading themselves on our unfortunate shores to sully it with new crimes. Do not allow our brothers, our friends, to be sacrificed to men who wish to reign over the ruins of the human species. But no, your wisdom will enable you to avoid the dangerous snares which our common enemies hold out for you. . . .

I send you with this letter a declaration which will acquaint you with the unity that exists between the proprietors of San Domingo who are in France, those in the United States, and those who serve under the English banner. You will see there a resolution, unequivocal and carefully constructed, for the restoration of slavery; you will see there that their determination to succeed has led them to envelop themselves in the mantle of liberty in order to strike it more deadly blows. You will see that they are counting heavily on my complacency in lending myself to their perfidious views by my fear for my children.[3] It is not astonishing that these men who sacrifice their country to their interests are unable to conceive how many sacrifices a true love of country can support in a better father than they, since I unhesitatingly base the happiness of my children on that of my country, which they and they alone wish to destroy.

I shall never hesitate between the safety of San Domingo and my personal happiness; but I have nothing to fear. It is to the solicitude of the French Government that I have confided my children. . . . I would tremble with horror if it was into the hands of the colonists that I had sent them as hostages; but even if it were so, let them

[1]The Directory, a rotating committee of five men, held executive power in France between 1795 and 1799.

[2]Vienot Vaublanc led a post-revolutionary movement to reassert France's authority over its colonies. He argued that Saint Domingue was out of control and that power should be recovered from black leaders. Vaublanc was deported in September 1797 for his involvement in a royalist conspiracy. Toussaint, unaware of the deportation, wrote this letter in defense of freedom and equality for the blacks of Saint Domingue.

[3]As a show of faith, Toussaint sent his two sons, Isaac and Placide, to study in France. Later, during his invasion of Saint Domingue, Napoleon sent Toussaint's sons to convince their father to submit to French rule. The sons eventually supported Toussaint and independence.

know that in punishing them for the fidelity of their father, they would only add one degree more to their barbarism, without any hope of ever making me fail in my duty. . . . Blind as they are! They cannot see how this odious conduct on their part can become the signal of new disasters and irreparable misfortunes, and that far from making them regain what in their eyes liberty for all has made them lose, they expose themselves to a total ruin and the colony to its inevitable destruction. Do they think that men who have been able to enjoy the blessing of liberty will calmly see it snatched away? They supported their chains only so long as they did not know any condition of life more happy than that of slavery. But to-day when they have left it, if they had a thousand lives they would sacrifice them all rather than be forced into slavery again. But no, the same hand which has broken our chains will not enslave us anew. France will not revoke her principles, she will not withdraw from us the greatest of her benefits. She will protect us against all our enemies; she will not permit her sublime morality to be perverted, those principles which do her most honour to be destroyed, her most beautiful achievement to be degraded, and her Decree of 16 Pluviôse[4] which so honors humanity to be revoked. *But if, to re-establish slavery in San Domingo, this was done, then I declare to you it would be to attempt the impossible: we have known how to face dangers to obtain our liberty, we shall know how to brave death to maintain it.*

This, Citizens Directors, is the morale of the people of San Domingo, those are the principles that they transmit to you by me.

My own you know. It is sufficient to renew, my hand in yours, the oath that I have made, to cease to live before gratitude dies in my heart, before I cease to be faithful to France and to my duty, before the god of liberty is profaned and sullied by the liberticides, before they can snatch from my hands that sword, those arms, which France confided to me for the defence of its rights and those of humanity, for the triumph of liberty and equality.

[4]The decree abolishing slavery in the French colonies.

Cluster: E Pluribus Unum—On the Discourse of Liberty

Perhaps the only words of Thomas Jefferson that every American knows are "all men are created equal." In fact, neither the sentiment nor the language originates with him. The discourse of liberty, which underlay America's independence in the eighteenth century, has a deep taproot. A hundred years earlier, this discourse had rationalized the execution of one English king and the popular acclamation of another. In the late sixteenth century and early seventeenth century, agitation by men like William Bradford and John Winthrop, to separate from the Church of England in order to voluntarily join in their own covenanted communities, had its philosophical justification in Richard Hooker's *Laws of Ecclesiastical Polity.* But before Hooker, the medieval Catholic philosopher Thomas Aquinas argued that "all men are eligible to rule" because of their fundamental equality in nature. And if, as some suggest, natural rights philosophy ultimately has its origin in classical Stoicism, Aquinas, like many, but not all, American Christians certainly found support for his beliefs in biblical discourse: "There is neither Jew nor Greek, there is neither bond nor free, there is neither male nor female: for ye are all one in Christ Jesus" (Galatians 3:28).

This equality, which remained unclear about the inclusion of women, was based on a certain understanding of human nature, most cogently expressed by John Locke, whose *Second Treatise on Civil Government* (1690), wove these various traditions together into a coherent, liberal theory of natural rights and government by social contract. Relying on Hooker and those who preceded him, Locke argued that man in his natural state is free. Many Europeans, commenting on instances of government by consensus and usufruct approach to the commons, used the Indian peoples of the Americas as the principal exemplar of humankind in its ideal, natural state. As Michel de Montaigne wrote in his essay "Of Cannibals," an Indian tribe "is a nation, would I answer Plato, that hath no kind of traffick, no knowledge of magistrates, no knowledge of Letters, no intelligence of numbers, no name of magistrate, nor of politike superiorite; no use of service, of riches, or of poverty, no contracts, no successions." These absences Montaigne noted not as defects but as unnecessary to the condition of the Indians, required only by civilized people, that is, people in a civil or governed state.

Human beings, Locke argued, may need to surrender some of their freedom in order to join together to protect their life, liberty, and property. These latter, Locke adds, are natural rights, given to all, and are so fundamental to the exercise of our individual liberty as people that they cannot be legitimately taken away or surrendered. They are, in Jefferson's language, "inalienable." Government, then, is constituted by the initiative of individuals freely joining themselves together. Legitimate authority consists of nothing more than the use of power, derived from the citizens' voluntary surrender of some freedom of action, in order to protect other, more fundamental liberties. Though presented as a libel case, the 1735 trial of newspaperman John Peter Zenger actually tested this first principle of democracy. In Zenger's time, one could not criticize the authority of governors and royal appointees, even if the charges were based in fact, without risking a charge for criminal libel and imprisonment. Despite leading comments from the judge, the jury accepted the powerful arguments of Zenger's attorney, Andrew Hamilton, about the necessity of speaking truth to power and found Zenger not guilty, establishing the real freedom of the press in pursuit of truth. It was a lesson deeply ingrained in American colonials, as Jefferson would later write in *Notes on the State of Virginia:* "Error alone needs the protection of government. Truth can stand by itself."

By the 1760s, America was stirred by a heady mix of contractualism, the belief that "government derives its just powers from the consent of the governed," and a radical egalitarianism, especially in the North. In *The Rights of the British Colonies Asserted and Proved,* published in 1764 and widely distributed, James Otis reasserted all the basic elements of natural rights philosophy and then opened the question of race: "The colonists are by the law of nature free-born, as indeed all men are, white or black. . . . Does it follow that 'tis right to enslave a man because he is black? Will short curled hair like wool instead of Christian hair, as 'tis called by those whose hearts are as hard as the nether millstone, help the argument? Can any logical inference in favor of slavery be drawn from a flat nose, a long or short face?" Four years later, after the passage of the repressive and infamous Stamp Act (1765) and Townshend Acts (1765), Hannah Griffits would test that spirit of egalitarianism with her 1768 poem "The Female Patriots," in which she calls for women revolutionaries to arise. And the enslaved poet Phillis Wheatley would commend the Mohegan minister Samson Occom on his "vindication" of the "natural rights" of "negroes." Part of this radical egalitarian spirit came from the natural law tradition, but there were other impulses. Edinburgh scholars of the Common Sense school of philosophy had a great influence throughout the colonies, arguing that, while individuals may differ in a number of ways, they are all equal in having a shared or common moral sense. This moral sense is an essential natural feature of all people, regardless of their physical characteristics, equipping them, as Jefferson writes to his nephew Peter Carr, for the decision making required of individuals joined in a social condition.

Regardless of where one might locate the source of our natural equality, the violence of the American Revolution pulled attention away from our commonality and toward a newly defined common enemy. Three years after hostilities broke out and one year after Jefferson drafted the Declaration of Independence, Prince Hall, in a petition to the government of Massachusetts to abolish slavery, still needed to make the point that equality is not dependent on physical characteristics. In 1795, nearly twenty years after a hopeful Abigail Adams reminded her husband, John, sitting in the Continental Congress in Philadelphia, to "remember the ladies," an anonymous writer felt compelled to publish a poem titled "The Rights of Women." Perhaps more united by what they were against than what they were for, Americans caught up in the war had left fundamental questions of liberty and equality unaddressed. Future generations would struggle to remedy those injustices, pitting mobocracy and demagoguery against the ideals of liberty expressed in earlier discourses of natural rights. Stirred by the horrific violence that "liberté, eqalité, fraternité" had unloosed in the French Revolution, some, like Fisher Ames, candidly doubted the value and longevity of a government founded on the claim that all men are created equal.

Andrew Wiget
New Mexico State University

John Locke 1632–1704

from Concerning Civil Government, Second Essay

Chapter II . . .

4. To understand political power aright, and derive it from its original, we must consider what estate all men are naturally in, and that is, a state of perfect freedom to order their actions, and dispose of their possessions and persons as they think fit, within the bounds of the law of Nature, without asking leave or depending upon the will of any other man.

A state also of equality, wherein all the power and jurisdiction is reciprocal, no one having more than another, there being nothing more evident than that creatures of the same species and rank, promiscuously born to all the same advantages of Nature, and the use of the same faculties, should also be equal one amongst another, without subordination or subjection, unless the lord and master of them all should, by any manifest declaration of his will, set one above another, and confer on him, by an evident and clear appointment, an undoubted right to dominion and sovereignty.

But though this be a state of liberty, yet it is not a state of licence; though man in that state have an uncontrollable liberty to dispose of his person or possessions, yet he has not liberty to destroy himself, or so much as any creature in his possession, but where some nobler use than its bare preservation calls for it. The state of Nature has a law of Nature to govern it, which obliges every one, and reason, which is that law teaches all mankind who will but consult it, that being all equal and independent, no one ought to harm another in his life, health, liberty or possessions; for men being all the workmanship of one omnipotent and infinitely wise Maker; all the servants of one sovereign Master, sent into the world by His order and about His business; they are His property, whose workmanship they are made to last during His, not one another's pleasure.

Chapter VII . . .

87. Man being born, as has been proved, with a title to perfect freedom and an uncontrolled enjoyment of all the rights and privileges of the law of Nature, equally with any other man, or number of men in the world, hath by nature a power not only to preserve his property—that is, his life, liberty, and estate, against the injuries and attempts of other men, but to judge of and punish the breaches of that law in others, as he is persuaded the offence deserves, even with death itself, in crimes where the heinousness of the fact, in his opinion, requires it. But because no political society

can be, nor subsist, without having in itself the power to preserve the property, and in order thereunto punish the offences of all those of that society, there, and there only, is political society where every one of the members hath quitted this natural power, resigned it up into the hands of the community in all cases that exclude him not from appealing for protection to the law established by it. . . .

89. Wherever, therefore, any number of men so unite into one society as to quit every one his executive power of the law of Nature, and to resign it to the public, there and there only is a political or civil society. And this is done wherever any number of men, in the state of Nature, enter into society to make one people one body politic under one supreme government: or else when any one joins himself to, and incorporates with any government already made. For hereby he authorises the society, or which is all one, the legislative thereof, to make laws for him as the public good of the society shall require, to the execution whereof his own assistance (as to his own decrees) is due. And this puts men out of a state of Nature into that of a commonwealth, by setting up a judge on earth with authority to determine all the controversies and redress the injuries that may happen to any member of the commonwealth, which judge is the legislative or magistrates appointed by it. And wherever there are any number of men, however associated, that have no such decisive power to appeal to, there they are still in the state of Nature.

90. And hence it is evident that absolute monarchy, which by some men is counted for the only government in the world, is indeed inconsistent with civil society, and so can be not form of civil government at all.

1795

Andrew Hamilton 1676–1741

Closing Argument in the Libel Trial of John Peter Zenger

It is natural, it is a privilege, I will go farther, it is a right, which all free men claim, that they are entitled to complain when they are hurt. They have a right publicly to remonstrate against the abuses of power in the strongest terms, to put their neighbors upon their guard against the craft or open violence of men in authority, and to assert with courage the sense they have of the blessings of liberty, the value they put upon it, and their resolution at all hazards to preserve it as one of the greatest blessings heaven can bestow.

It is agreed upon by all men that this is a reign of liberty. While men keep within the bounds of truth I hope they may with safety both speak and write their sentiments of the conduct of men in power, I mean of that part of their conduct only which affects the liberty or property of the people under their administration. Were this to be denied, then the next step may make them slaves; for what notions can be entertained of slavery beyond that of suffering the greatest injuries and oppressions without the liberty of complaining, or if they do, to be destroyed, body and estate, for so doing?

It is said and insisted on by Mr. Attorney that government is a sacred thing; that it is to be supported and reverenced; that it is government that protects our persons and estates, prevents treasons, murders, robberies, riots, and all the train of evils that overturns kingdoms and states and ruins particular persons. And if those in the administration, especially the supreme magistrate, must have all their conduct censured by private men, government cannot subsist. This is called a licentiousness not to be tolerated. It is said that it brings the rulers of people into contempt, and their authority not to be regarded, and so in the end the laws cannot be put into execution.

These, I say, and such as these, are the general topics insisted upon by men in power and their advocates. But I wish it might be considered at the same time how often it has happened that the abuse of power has been the primary cause of these evils, and that it was the injustice and oppression of these great men that has commonly brought them into contempt with the people. The craft and art of such men is great, and who that is the least acquainted with history or law can be ignorant of these specious pretenses that have often been made use of by men in power to introduce arbitrary rule, and to destroy the liberties of a free people?". . .

The loss of liberty, to a generous mind, is worse than death. And yet we know that there have been those in all ages who for the sake of preferment, or some imaginary honor, have freely lent a helping hand to oppress, nay to destroy, their country.

This brings to my mind that saying of the immortal [Marcus] Brutus when he looked upon the creatures of Caesar, who were very great men but by no means good men. "You Romans," said Brutus, "if yet I may call you so, consider what you are doing. Remember that you are assisting Caesar to forge those very chains that one day he will make you yourselves wear." This is what every man who values freedom ought to consider. He should act by judgment and not be affection or self-interest; for where those prevail, no ties of either country or kindred are regarded; as upon the other hand, the man who loves his country prefers its liberty to all other considerations, well knowing that without liberty life is a misery. . . .

Thus highly was liberty esteemed in those days, that a father could sacrifice his sons to save his country. But why do I go to heathen Rome to bring instances of the love of liberty? The best blood in Britain has been shed in the cause of liberty; and the freedom we enjoy at this day may be said to be in a great measure owing to the glorious stand the famous Hampden, and others of our countrymen, made against the arbitrary demands and illegal impositions of the times in which they lived; who, rather than give up the rights of Englishmen and submit to pay an illegal tax of no more, I think, than three shillings, resolved to undergo, and for the liberty of their country did undergo, the greatest extremities in that arbitrary and terrible Court of the Star Chamber, to whose arbitrary proceedings—it being composed of the principal men of the realm, and calculated to support arbitrary government—no bounds or limits could be set, nor could any other hand remove the evil but Parliament.

Power may justly be compared to a great river. While kept within its due bounds it is both beautiful and useful. But when it overflows its banks, it is then too impetuous to be stemmed; it bears down all before it, and brings destruction and desolation wherever it comes. If, then, this is the nature of power, let us at least do our duty, and like wise men who value freedom use our utmost care to support liberty, the only bulwark against lawless power, which in all ages has sacrificed to its wild lust and boundless ambition the blood of the best men that ever lived.

I hope to be pardoned, Sir, for my zeal upon this occasion. It is an old and wise caution that when our neighbor's house is on fire we ought to take care of our own. For though—blessed be God I live in a government where liberty is well understood and freely enjoyed, yet experience has shown us all—I am sure it has to me that a bad precedent in one government is soon set up for an authority in another. And therefore I cannot but think it my, and every honest man's, that while we pay all due obedience to men in authority we ought at the same time to be upon our guard against power wherever we apprehend that it may affect ourselves or our fellow subjects.

I am truly very unequal to such an undertaking on many accounts. You see that I labor under the weight of many years, and am bowed down with great infirmities of body. Yet, old and weak as I am, I should think it my duty, if required, to go to the utmost part of the land where my services could be of any use in assisting to quench the flame of prosecutions upon informations, set on foot by the government to deprive a people of the right of remonstrating and complaining, too, of the arbitrary attempts of men in power.

Men who injure and oppress the people under their administration provoke them to cry out and complain, and then make that very complaint the foundation for new oppressions and prosecutions. I wish I could say that there were no instances of this kind.

But to conclude the question before the Court and you, Gentlemen of the jury, is not of small or private concern. It is not the cause of one poor printer, nor of New York alone, which you are now trying. No! It may in its consequence affect every free man that lives under a British government on the main of America. It is the best cause. It is the cause of liberty. And I make no doubt but your upright conduct this day will not only entitle you to the love and esteem of your fellow citizens, but every man who prefers freedom to a life of slavery will bless and honor you as men who have baffled the attempt of tyranny, and by an impartial and uncorrupt verdict have laid a noble foundation for securing to ourselves, our posterity, and our neighbors, that to which nature and laws of our country have given us a right to liberty of both exposing and opposing arbitrary power (in these parts of the world at least) by speaking and writing truth.

1736

Hannah Griffitts 1727–1817

A Quaker who remained single, Hannah Griffitts dedicated herself to the care of other female relations. She wrote many poems during the Revolutionary period, and though critical of the extremism that she saw in Tom Paine's position, in this poem she celebrates and encourages female protest of the harsh measures meted out by the British government, such as the Sugar Act (1764) and the Townshend Duties (1767). Another Philadelphia Quaker and poet, Milcah Martha Moore, preserved this poem in her commonplace book.

The Female Patriots. Address'd to the Daughters of Liberty in America, 1768[1]

Since the men, from a party or fear of a frown,
Are kept by a sugar-plum quietly down,
Supinely asleep—and depriv'd of their sight,
Are stripp'd of their freedom, and robb'd of their right;
If the sons, so degenerate! the blessings despise,
Let the Daughters of Liberty nobly arise;
And though we've no voice but a negative here,
The use of the taxables, let us forbear:—
(Then merchants import till your stores are all full,
May the buyers be few, and your traffic be dull!)
Stand firmly resolv'd, and bid Grenville[2] to see,
That rather than freedom we part with our tea,
And well as we love the dear draught when a-dry,
As American Patriots our taste we deny—
Pennsylvania's gay meadows can richly afford
To pamper our fancy or furnish our board;
And paper sufficient at home still we have,
To assure the wiseacre, we will not sign slave;
When this homespun shall fail, to remonstrate our grief,
We can speak viva voce, or scratch on a leaf;
Refuse all their colors, though richest of dye,
When the juice of a berry our paint can supply,
To humor our fancy—and as for our houses,
They'll do without painting as well as our spouses;
While to keep out the cold of a keen winter morn,
We can screen the north-west with a well polished horn;
And trust me a woman, by honest invention,
Might give this state-doctor a dose of prevention.
    Join mutual in this—and but small as it seems,
We may jostle a Grenville, and puzzle his schemes;
But a motive more worthy our patriot pen,
Thus acting—we point out their duty to men;
And should the bound-pensioners tell us to hush,
We can throw back the satire, by biding them blush.

1787

[1]A brief letter to the editors of the *Pennsylvania Chronicle* introduces "The Female Patriots": "Gentlemen, I send you the inclosed female performance for a place in your paper, if you think it may contribute any thing to the entertainment or reformation of your male readers, and am, Yours, &c. Q.R."

[2]George Grenville (1712–1770), English statesman whose tax policies in the American colonies (e.g., the Revenue Act of 1764 and the Stamp Act of 1765) became one of the causes of the American Revolution.

Phillis Wheatley 1753–1784

Letter to Samson Occom

Feb. 11, 1774[1]

Reverend and honoured Sir,

"I have this day received your obliging kind epistle, and am greatly satisfied with your reasons respecting the negroes, and think highly reasonable what you offer in vindication of their natural rights: Those that invade them cannot be insensible that the divine light is chasing away the thick darkness which broods over the land of Africa; and the chaos which has reigned so long, is converting into beautiful order, and reveals more and more clearly the glorious dispensation of civil and religious liberty, which are so inseparably united, that there is little or no enjoyment of one without the other: Otherwise, perhaps, the Israelites had been less solicitous for their freedom from Egyptian slavery; I do not say they would have been contented without it, by no means; for in every human breast God has implanted a principle, which we call love of freedom; it is impatient of oppression, and pants for deliverance; and by the leave of our modern Egyptians I will assert, that the same principle lives in us. God grant deliverance in his own way and time, and get him honour upon all those whose avarice impels them to countenance and help forward the calamities of their fellow creatures. This I desire not for their hurt, but to convince them of the strange absurdity of their conduct, whose words and actions are so diametrically opposite. How well the cry for liberty, and the reverse disposition for the exercise of oppressive power over others agree—I humbly think it does not require the penetration of a philosopher to determine."—

1774

[1]First printed in the *Connecticut Gazette* for March 11, 1774, probably at the behest of the converted Mohegan Indian minister, the Reverend Samson Occom (1723–1792), the poet's longtime friend, who lived near New London where the *Gazette* was printed. This Wheatley letter was widely reprinted in almost a dozen other New England newspapers, of both Whig and Tory persuasions. The text above is from the printing in the *Newport (R.I.) Mercury* for April 11. This is Phillis Wheatley's strongest anti-slavery statement in print.

When it appeared on April 11, 1774, the letter had the following heading: "The following is an extract of a letter from Phillis, a Negro girl of Mr. Wheatley's, of this town; to the Rev. Samson Occom, dated the 11th of February, 1774."

Thomas Jefferson 1743–1826

from Autobiography of Thomas Jefferson

Congress proceeded the same day to consider the declaration of Independance which had been reported & lain on the table the Friday preceding, and on Monday referred to a commee of the whole. The pusillanimous idea that we had friends in England worth keeping terms with, still haunted the minds of many. For this reason those passages which conveyed censures on the people of England were struck out, lest they should give them offence. The clause too, reprobating the enslaving the inhabitants of Africa, was struck out in complaisance to South Carolina and Georgia, who had never attempted to restrain the importation of slaves, and who on the contrary still wished to continue it. Our northern brethren also I believe felt a little tender under those censures; for tho' their people have very few slaves themselves yet they had been pretty considerable carriers of them to others. The debates having taken up the greater parts of the 2d 3d & 4th days of July were, in the evening of the last, closed the declaration was reported by the commee, agreed to by the house and signed by every member present except Mr. Dickinson. As the sentiments of men are known not only by what they receive, but what they reject also, I will state the form of the declaration as originally reported. The parts struck out by Congress shall be distinguished by a black line drawn under them; & those inserted by them shall be placed in the margin or in a concurrent column.[1]

The Declaration of Independence

When, in the course of human events, it becomes necessary for one people to dissolve the political bands which have connected them with another, and to assume among the powers of the earth the separate and equal station to which the laws of nature and of nature's God entitle them, a decent respect to the opinions of mankind requires that they should declare the causes which impel them to the separation.

We hold these truths to be self evident: that all men are created equal; that they are endowed by their Creator with CERTAIN [*inherent and*] inalienable rights; that among these are life, liberty, and the pursuit of happiness; that to secure these rights, governments are instituted among men, deriving their just powers from the consent of the governed; that whenever any form of government becomes destructive of these ends, it is the right of the people to alter or to abolish it, and to institute new government, laying its foundation on such principles, and organizing its powers in such

[1]Here the parts struck out by Congress are italicized and in brackets; the words added by Congress are in large capitals.

form, as to them shall seem most likely to effect their safety and happiness. Prudence, indeed, will dictate that governments long established should not be changed for light and transient causes; and accordingly all experience hath shown that mankind are more disposed to suffer while evils are sufferable, than to right themselves by abolishing the forms to which they are accustomed. But when a long train of abuses and usurpations, [*begun at a distinguished period and*] pursuing invariably the same object, evinces a design to reduce them under absolute despotism, it is their right, it is their duty to throw off such government, and to provide new guards for their future security. Such has been the patient sufferance of these colonies; and such is now the necessity which constrains them to ALTER [*expunge*] their former systems of government. The history of the present king of Great Britain is a history of REPEATED [*unremitting*] injuries and usurpations, ALL HAVING [*among which appears no solitary fact to contradict the uniform tenor of the rest, but all have*] in direct object the establishment of an absolute tyranny over these states. To prove this, let facts be submitted to a candid world [*for the truth of which we pledge a faith yet unsullied by falsehood*].

He has refused his assent to laws the most wholesome and necessary for the public good.

He has forbidden his governors to pass laws of immediate and pressing importance, unless suspended in their operation till his assent should be obtained; and, when so suspended, he has utterly neglected to attend to them.

He has refused to pass other laws for the accommodation of large districts of people, unless those people would relinquish the right of representation in the legislature, a right inestimable to them, and formidable to tyrants only.

He has called together legislative bodies at places unusual, uncomfortable, and distant from the depository of their public records, for the sole purpose of fatiguing them into compliance with his measures.

He has dissolved representative houses repeatedly [*and continually*] for opposing with manly firmness his invasions on the rights of the people.

He has refused for a long time after such dissolutions to cause others to be elected, whereby the legislative powers, incapable of annihilation, have returned to the people at large for their exercise, the state remaining, in the meantime, exposed to all the dangers of invasion from without and convulsions within.

He has endeavored to prevent the population of these states; for that purpose obstructing the laws for naturalization of foreigners, refusing to pass others to encourage their migrations hither, and raising the conditions of new appropriations of lands.

He has OBSTRUCTED [*suffered*] the administration of justice BY [*totally to cease in some of these states*] refusing his assent to laws for establishing judiciary powers.

He has made [*our*] judges dependent on his will alone for the tenure of their offices, and the amount and payment of their salaries.

He has erected a multitude of new offices, [*by a self-assumed power*] and sent hither swarms of new officers to harass our people and eat out their substance.

He has kept among us in times of peace standing armies [*and ships of war*] without the consent of our legislatures.

He has affected to render the military independent of, and superior to, the civil power.

He has combined with others to subject us to a jurisdiction foreign to our constitutions and unacknowledged by our laws, giving his assent to their acts of pretended legislation for quartering large bodies of armed troops among us; for protecting them by a mock trial from punishment for any murders which they should commit on the inhabitants of these states; for cutting off our trade with all parts of the world; for imposing taxes on us without our consent; for depriving us IN MANY CASES of the benefits of trial by jury; for transporting us beyond seas to be tried for pretended offences; for abolishing the free system of English laws in a neighboring province, establishing therein an arbitrary government, and enlarging its boundaries, so as to render it at once an example and fit instrument for introducing the same absolute rule into these COLONIES [*states*]; for taking away our charters, abolishing our most valuable laws, and altering fundamentally the forms of our governments; for suspending our own legislatures, and declaring themselves invested with power to legislate for us in all cases whatsoever.

He has abdicated government here BY DECLARING US OUT OF HIS PROTECTION, AND WAGING WAR AGAINST US [*withdrawing his governors, and declaring us out of his allegiance and protection*].

He has plundered our seas, ravaged our coasts, burnt our towns, and destroyed the lives of our people.

He is at this time transporting large armies of foreign mercenaries to complete the works of death, desolation and tyranny already begun with circumstances of cruelty and perfidy SCARCELY PARALLELED IN THE MOST BARBAROUS AGES, AND TOTALLY unworthy the head of a civilized nation.

He has constrained our fellow citizens taken captive on the high seas, to bear arms against their country, to become the executioners of their friends and brethren, or to fall themselves by their hands.

He has EXCITED DOMESTIC INSURRECTION AMONG US, AND HAS endeavored to bring on the inhabitants of our frontiers, the merciless Indian savages, whose known rule of warfare is an undistinguished destruction of all ages, sexes and conditions [*of existence*].

[*He has incited treasonable insurrections of our fellow citizens, with the allurements of forfeiture and confiscation of our property.*

He has waged cruel war against human nature itself, violating its most sacred rights of life and liberty in the persons of a distant people who never offended him, captivating and carrying them into slavery in another hemisphere, or to incur miserable death in their transportation hither. This piratical warfare, the opprobrium of INFIDEL powers, is the warfare of the CHRISTIAN king of Great Britain. Determined to keep open a market where MEN should be bought and sold, he has prostituted his negative for suppressing every legislative attempt to prohibit or to restrain this execrable commerce. And that this assemblage of horrors might want no fact of distinguished die, he is now exciting those very people to rise in arms among us, and to purchase that liberty of which he has deprived them, by murdering the people on whom he also obtruded them: thus paying off former crimes committed against the LIBERTIES of one people, with crimes which he urges them to commit against the LIVES of another.]

In every stage of these oppressions we have petitioned for redress in the most humble terms: our repeated petitions have been answered only by repeated injuries.

A prince whose character is thus marked by every act which may define a tyrant is unfit to be the ruler of a FREE people [*who mean to be free. Future ages will scarcely believe that the hardiness of one man adventured, within the short compass of twelve years only, to lay a foundation so broad and so undisguised for tyranny over a people fostered and fixed in principles of freedom.*]

Nor have we been wanting in attentions to our British brethren. We have warned them from time to time of attempts by their legislature to extend AN UNWARRANTABLE [*a*] jurisdiction over US [*these our states*]. We have reminded them of the circumstances of our emigration and settlement here, [*no one of which could warrant so strange a pretension: that these were effected at the expense of our own blood and treasure, unassisted by the wealth or the strength of Great Britain: that in constituting indeed our several forms of government, we had adopted one common king, thereby laying a foundation for perpetual league and amity with them: but that submission to their parliament was no part of our constitution, nor ever in idea, if history may be credited: and,*] we HAVE appealed to their native justice and magnanimity AND WE HAVE CONJURED THEM BY [*as well as to*] the ties of our common kindred to disavow these usurpations which WOULD INEVITABLY [*were likely to*] interrupt our connection and correspondence. They too have been deaf to the voice of justice and of consanguinity. WE MUST THEREFORE [*and when occasions have been given them, by the regular course of their laws, of removing from their councils the disturbers of our harmony, they have, by their free election, re-established them in power. At this very time too, they are permitting their chief magistrate to send over not only soldiers of our common blood, but Scotch and foreign mercenaries to invade and destroy us. These facts have given the last stab to agonizing affection, and manly spirit bids us to renounce forever these unfeeling brethren. We must endeavor to forget our former love for them, and hold them as we hold the rest of mankind, enemies in war, in peace friends. We might have a free and a great people together; but a communication of grandeur and of freedom, it seems, is below their dignity. Be it so, since they will have it. The road to happiness and to glory is open to us, too. We will tread it apart from them, and*] acquiesce in the necessity which denounces our [*eternal*] separation AND HOLD THEM AS WE HOLD THE REST OF MANKIND, ENEMIES IN WAR, IN PEACE FRIENDS!

[2]We therefore the representatives of the United States of America in General Congress assembled, do in the name, and by the authority of the good people of these [*states reject and renounce all allegiance and subjection to the kings of Great Britain and all others who may hereafter claim by, through or under them; we utterly dissolve all political connection which may*

We, therefore, the representatives of the United States of America in General Congress assembled, appealing to the supreme judge of the world for the rectitude of our intentions, do in the name, and by the authority of the good people of these colonies, solemnly publish and declare, that these united colonies are, and of right ought to be free and inde-

[2]In this closing section, where additions and deletions have been lengthy, the editors follow Jefferson's device of printing his version in the left column, and the final adopted text in the right column.

heretofore have subsisted between us and the people or parliament of Great Britain: and finally we do assert and declare these colonies to be free and independent states,] and that as free and independent states, they have full power to levy war, conclude peace, contract alliances, establish commerce, and to do all other acts and things which independent states may of right do.

And for the support of this declaration, we mutually pledge to each other our lives, our fortunes, and our sacred honor.

pendent states; that they are absolved from all allegiance to the British crown, and that all political connection between them and the state of Great Britain is, and ought to be, totally dissolved; and that as free and independent states, they have full power to levy war, conclude peace, contract alliances, establish commerce, and to do all other acts and things which independent states may of right do.

And for the support of this declaration, with a firm reliance on the protection of divine providence, we mutually pledge to each other our lives, our fortunes, and our sacred honor.

The Declaration thus signed on the 4th, on paper, was engrossed on parchment, and signed again on the 2d of August.

Prince Hall 1735?–1807

To the Honorable Council & House of Representatives for the State of Massachusetts-Bay in General Court assembled January 13th 1777.[1]

The Petition of a great number of Negroes who are detained in a state of Slavery in the Bowels of a free & Christian Country Humbly Shewing

That your Petitioners apprehend that they have, in common with all other Men, a natural & unalienable right to that freedom, which the great Parent of the Universe hath bestowed equally on all Mankind, & which they have never forfeited by any compact or agreement whatever—But they were unjustly dragged, by the cruel hand of Power, from their dearest friends, & some of them even torn from the embraces

[1]This is from a typescript of an "improved" version, on file at the Massachusetts Archives, volume 212, p. 132; an original, semi-complete version was published by Jeremy Belknap in the *Massachusetts Historical Collections. Fifth Series,* No. 3 (Boston, 1788).

of their tender Parents. From a populous, pleasant and plentiful Country—& in Violation of the Laws of Nature & of Nation & in defiance of all the tender feelings of humanity, brought hither to be sold like Beasts of Burden, & like them condemned to slavery for Life—Among a People professing the mild Religion of Jesus—A People not insensible of the sweets of rational freedom—Nor without spirit to resent the unjust endeavours of others to reduce them to a State of Bondage & Subjection—Your Honors need not to be informed that a Life of Slavery, like that of your petitioners, deprived of every social privilege, of every thing requisite to render Life even tolerable, is far worse than Non-Existence—In imitation of the laudable example of the good People of these States, your Petitioners have long & patiently waited the event of Petition after Petition by them presented to the legislative Body of this State, & can not but with grief reflect that their success has been but too similar—They can not but express their astonishment, that it has never been considered, that every principle from which America has acted in the course of her unhappy difficulties with Great-Britain, pleads stronger than a thousand arguments in favor of your Petitioners. They therefore humbly beseech your Honors, to give this Petition its due weight & consideration, & cause an Act of the Legislature to be passed, whereby they may be restored to the enjoyment of that freedom which is the natural right of all Men—& their Children (who were born in this Land of Liberty) may not be held as Slaves after they arrive at the age of twenty one years—So may the Inhabitants of this State (no longer chargeable with the inconsistency of acting, themselves, the part which they condemn & oppose in others) be prospered in their present glorious struggles for Liberty; & have those blessings secured to them by Heaven, of which benevolent minds can not wish to deprive their fellow Men.

And your Petitioners, as in Duty Bound shall ever pray.

Lancaster Hill
Peter Bess
Brister Slenten
Prince Hall
Jack Purpont *his mark*
Nero Suneto *his mark*
Newport Symner *his mark*
Job Lock

Negroes Petition to the Honble
Genl Assembly—Mass.
March 18
Judge Sargeant
M. Balton
M. Appleton
Coll. Brooks
M. Stony
W. Lowell
Matter Atlege
W. Davis

1788

Anonymous fl. 1795

RIGHTS OF WOMAN[1]

[by a young lady of this city.]
tune—"God Save America"

God save each Female's right,
Show to her ravish'd sight
Woman is Free
Let Freedom's voice prevail,
And draw aside the vail,
Supreme Effulgence hail,
Sweet Liberty
Man boasts the [noble] cause,
Nor yields supine to laws.
Tyrants ordain:
Let Woman have a share,
Nor yield to slavish fear.
Her equal rights declare,
And well maintain.
Come forth with sense array'd,
Nor ever be dismay'd
To meet the foe,—
Who with assuming hands
Inflict the iron bands,
To obey his rash commands,
And vainly bow.
O let the sacred fire
Of Freedom's voice inspire
A Female too:—
Man makes the cause his own,
And Fame his acts renown,—
Woman thy fears disown,
Assert thy due.
Think of the cruel chain,

[1]From *The Weekly Museum,* New York, 25 Apr. 1795.

Endure no more the pain
Of slavery:—
Why should a tyrant bind
A cultivated mind.
By Reason well rein'd,
Ordained Free.
Why should a Woman lie
In base obscurity,
Her talents hid;
Has Providence assign'd
Her soul to be confin'd.
Is not her gentle mind
By virtue led.
With this engaging charm
Where is so much the harm
For her to stand.
To join the grand applause
Of truth and equal laws,
Or lead the noble cause,
Her feeble hand.
Let snarling cynics frown,
Their maxims I disown.
Their ways detest:—
By Man, your tyrant lord,
Females no more be aw'd,
Let Freedom's sacred word,
Inspire your breast.
Woman aloud rejoice,
Exalt thy feeble voice
In chearful strain;
See Wolstonecraft,[2] a friend,
Your injured rights defend,
Wisdom her steps attend,
The cause maintain.
A voice re-echoing round,
With joyful accents sound,
Woman be Free;
Assert the noble claim,
All selfish arts disdain,
Hark how the note proclaim,
Woman is Free!

1795

[2]Mary Wollstonecraft (1759–1797), English author of *A Vindication of the Rights of Woman* (1792), a controversial feminist tract. Wollstonecraft had a child outside of marriage and an unusual domestic arrangement with her partner, later husband, William Godwin, both of which made her the object of severe derision among critics in America.

Fisher Ames 1758–1808

On the Dangers of Democracy

The theory of a democracy supposes, that the will of the people ought to prevail, and that, as the majority possess not only the better right, but the superiour force, of course, it will prevail. A greater force, they argue, will inevitably overcome a less. When a constitution provides, with an imposing solemnity of details, for the collection of the opinions of a majority of the citizens, every sanguine reader not only becomes assured, that the will of the people must prevail, but he goes further, and refuses to examine the reasons, and to excuse the incivism and presumption of those who can doubt of this inevitable result. Yet common sense and our own recent experiences have shewn, that a combination of a very small minority can effectually defeat the authority of the national will. The votes of a majority may sometimes, though not invariably, shew what ought to be done; but to awe or subdue the force of a thousand men, the government must call out the superiour force of two thousand men. It is, therefore, established the very instant it is brought to the test, that the mere will of a majority is inefficient and without authority. and as to employing a superiour force to procure obedience, which a democratick government has an undoubted right to do, and so, indeed, has every other, it is obvious, that the admitted necessity of this resort completely overthrows all the boasted advantages of the democratick system. For, if obedience cannot be procured by reason, it must be obtained by compulsion; and this is exactly what every other government will do in a like case. . . .

As the boastful pretensions of the democratick system cannot be too minutely exposed, another consideration must be given to the subject.

That government certainly deserves no honest man's love or support, which, from the very laws of its being, carries terrour and danger to the virtuous, and arms the vicious with authority and power. The essence and, in the opinion of many thousands not yet cured of their delusions, the excellence of democracy is, that it invests every citizen with an equal proportion of power. A state consisting of a million of citizens has a million sovereigns, each of whom detests all the other sovereignty but its own. This very boast implies as much of the spirit of turbulence and insubordination, as the utmost energy of any known regular government, even the most rigid, could keep in restraint. It also implies a state of agitation, that is justly terrible to all who love their ease, and of instability, that quenches the last hope of those who would transmit their liberty to posterity. Waving any further pursuit of these reflections, let it be resumed, that, if every man of the million has his ratable share of power in the community, then, instead of restraining the vicious, they also are armed with power, for they take their part: as they are citizens, this cannot be refused them. Now, as they have an interest in preventing the execution of the laws, which, in fact, is the apparent common interest of their whole class, their union will happen of course. The very first moment that they do unite, which it is ten thousand to one will happen before the form of the democracy is agreed upon, and while its plausible constitution is framing, that moment they form a faction, and the pretended efficacy of the democratick system, which is to operate by the power of opinion and persuasion, comes to an end. For an imperium in imperio exists; there is a state within a state, a combination interested and active in hindering the will of the majority from being obeyed.

1795

Patriot and Loyalist Songs and Ballads

The stirrings of men's hearts, the expression of their hopes, desires, and motives, inspired many songs and ballads during one of the most emotional periods in American history, the years of the Revolutionary War. The quality of such works is clearly uneven, sometimes because the verses were produced in haste, sometimes because they were conceived by men and women who never before had channeled their feelings into poetic form. A number of songs and ballads, however, were written by well-known literary or political figures, including Benjamin Franklin, John Dickinson, Francis Hopkinson, Thomas Paine, Jonathan Odell, Joseph Stansbury, David Humphreys, Philip Freneau, and Joel Barlow.

Such expressions, especially the most popular ones, remain invaluable for us today because their repetition and survival suggest that they successfully captured—and thus reflect for us—the hearts and the minds of the people. As the poet Joel Barlow commented, upon entering the Army, "I do not know, whether I shall do more for the cause in the capacity of chaplain, than I could in that of poet; I have great faith in the influence of songs; and shall continue, while fulfilling the duties of my appointment, to write one now and then, and to encourage the taste for them which I find in the camp. One good song is worth a dozen addresses or proclamations."

Although contemporary estimates suggest that political allegiances of the American public during the Revolutionary War were fairly evenly divided—one-third in favor of rebellion, one-third opposed, and one-third indifferent—there appear to be considerably more extant patriot (pro-American) songs and ballads than loyalist (pro-English). Several factors could account for this difference: the efforts of loyalist writers began later than that of the patriots; the loyalist response was less appealing and exciting, because it was largely defensive and based in traditional values and structures; and the defeat of the loyalists and the extensive destruction of loyalist property may have affected the amount of loyalist material preserved.

Generally, both the patriot and loyalist poets and versifiers seized upon opportunities to persuade the American public that their side was winning while their opponents' victories were spurious, that their military leaders were brilliant while their opponents' military leaders were fools, that they were fighting fairly and courageously while their opponents were savage and cruel. The loyalists also emphasized the illegality of the Revolution; the loss of English honor, truth, and loyalty; the strength of the British forces; the advantages of union with England; the dangers of an alliance with France; and the generally disreputable nature of Congress and of the Continental army and its leaders. The patriots emphasized specific recent grievances against England (e.g., the Stamp Act and the Townshend Acts, seen as unfair tax measures); the tyranny and corruption of the English Parliament and King; the need to preserve the accomplishments of America's forefathers; the obligation to protect wives and children; pride in the accomplishments of Congress and in the alliance with France; the willingness to die bravely for a good cause; and the urgency of obtaining liberty and independence. Songs and ballads were also written in honor of heroes and traitors, such as George Washington, Nathan Hale, John André, John Champe, and Benedict Arnold.

These songs and ballads became known through broadsides, pamphlets, newspapers, or word-of-mouth among citizens and soldiers and were usually written to familiar tunes. They compose a rich and lasting contribution to the diverse poetic heritage of the revolutionary period.

Rosalie Murphy Baum
University of South Florida

Wendy Martin
Claremont Graduate University

PRIMARY WORKS

Frank Moore, ed., *Songs and Ballads of the American Revolution,* 1855, rpt. 1964; Frederick C. Prescott and John H. Nelson, eds., *Prose and Poetry of the Revolution,* 1925, 1969; James H. Pickering, ed., *The World Turned Upside Down: Prose and Poetry of the American Revolution,* 1975.

"Patriot" Voices

The Liberty Song[1]

Come join hand in hand, brave Americans all,
And rouse your bold hearts at fair Liberty's call;
No tyrannous acts, shall suppress your just claim,
Or stain with dishonor America's name.
In freedom we're born, and in freedom we'll live;
Our purses are ready,
Steady, Friends, steady,
Not as *slaves,* but as *freemen* our money we'll give.

Our worthy forefathers—let's give them a cheer—
To climates unknown did courageously steer;
Thro' oceans to deserts, for freedom they came,
And, dying, bequeath'd us their freedom and fame.

Their generous bosoms all dangers despis'd,
So highly, so wisely, their birthrights they priz'd;
We'll keep what they gave, we will piously keep,
Nor frustrate their toils on the land or the deep.

The Tree, their own hands had to Liberty rear'd,
They lived to behold growing strong and rever'd;
With transport then cried,—"Now our wishes we gain,
For our children shall gather the fruits of our pain."

How sweet are the labors that freemen endure,
That they shall enjoy all the profit, secure,—

[1]Very popular song with patriots, sung to tune of "Hearts of Oak" (composed by William Boyce). Unknown if this is the original or corrected (less "bold") version by John Dickinson (1732–1808), Philadelphia lawyer, member of both Continental Congresses, author of *Letters from a Farmer in Pennsylvania* (1768). Eight lines contributed to original version by Arthur Lee (1740–92), diplomat, member of Continental Congress, 1781–85. Parody by Henry Hulton was, in turn, parodied by Benjamin Church.

No more such sweet labors Americans know,
If Britons shall reap what Americans sow.

Swarms of placemen and pensioners soon will appear,
Like locusts deforming the charms of the year:
Suns vainly will rise, showers vainly descend,
If we are to drudge for what others shall spend.

Then join hand in hand brave Americans all,
By uniting we stand, by dividing we fall;
In so righteous a cause let us hope to succeed,
For Heaven approves of each generous deed.

All ages shall speak with amaze and applause,
Of the courage we'll show in support of our laws;
To die we can bear,—but to serve we disdain,
For shame is to freemen more dreadful than pain.

This bumper I crown for our sovereign's health,
And this for Britannia's glory and wealth:
That wealth, and that glory immortal may be,
If she is but just, and we are but free.
In freedom we're born, &c.

1768

Alphabet[1]

A, stands for Americans, who scorn to be slaves;
B, for Boston, where fortitude their freedom saves;
C, stands for Congress, which, though loyal, will be free;
D, stands for defence, 'gainst force and tyranny.
Stand firmly, A and Z,
We swear for ever to be free!

E, stands for evils, which a civil war must bring;
F, stands for fate, dreadful to both people and king;
G, stands for George,[2] may God give him wisdom and grace;
H, stands for hypocrite, who wears a double face.

[1]Ballad for children.
[2]George III, King of Great Britain and Ireland during the Revolutionary War.

J, stands for justice, which traitors in power defy,
K, stands for king, who should to such the axe apply;
L, stands for London, to its country ever true,
M, stands for Mansfield,[3] who hath another view.

N, stands for North,[4] who to the House the mandate brings,
O, stands for oaths, binding on subjects not on kings:
P, stands for people, who their freedom should defend,
Q, stands for *quere,*[5] when will England's troubles end?

R, stands for rebels, not at Boston but at home,
S, stands for Stuart,[6] sent by Whigs abroad to roam,
T, stands for Tories, who may try to bring them back,
V, stands for villains, who have well deserved the rack.

W, stands for Wilkes,[7] who us from warrants saved,
Y, for York, the New, half corrupted, half enslaved,
Z, stands for Zero, but means the Tory minions,
Who threatens us with fire and sword, to bias our opinions.
Stand firmly A and Z,
We swear for ever to be free!

1775

The King's own REGULARS; And their Triumphs over the *Irregulars.* A New SONG, To the Tune of, *An old Courtier of the Queen's, and the Queen's old Courtier.*[1]

Since you all will have singing, and won't be said, nay,
I cannot refuse where you so beg and pray;

[3]William Murray, Earl of Mansfield; favored coercion of the Colonies.

[4]Frederick North, Earl of Guilford (known as Lord North); Prime Minister under George III.

[5]Question.

[6]Charles Edward Stuart, English prince known as the Young Pretender; son of James Francis Edward Stuart, the Old Pretender.

[7]John Wilkes, English political reformer; champion of patriots in American Revolution.

[1]Song by Benjamin Franklin (1706–1790); text from William B. Willcox, ed., *The Papers of Benjamin Franklin,* vol. 22, 1982.

So I'll sing you a song—as a body may say.
'Tis of the King's Regulars, who ne'er run way.
O the old Soldiers of the King, and the King's own Regulars.

At Preston Pans[2] we met with some Rebels one day,
We marshall'd ourselves all in comely array:
Our hearts were all stout, and bid our legs stray,
But our feet were wrong headed and took us away.
O the old soldiers, &c.

At Falkirk we resolv'd to be braver,
And recover some credit by better behaviour;
We would not acknowledge feet had done us a favour;
So feet swore they would stand, but—legs ran however.
O the old soldiers, &c.

No troops perform better than we at reviews;
We march and we wheel, and whatever you chuse.
George would see how we fight, and we never refuse;
There we all fight with courage—you may see it in the news.
O the old soldiers, &c.

To Monongehela with fifes and with drums
We march'd in fine order, with cannon and bombs:
That great expedition cost infinite sums;
But a few irregulars cut us all into crumbs.
O the old soldiers, &c.

It was not fair to shoot at us from behind trees:
If they had stood open as they ought before our great Guns we should have beat them with ease.
They may fight with one another that way if they please;
But it is not regular to stand and fight with such rascals as these.
O the old soldiers, &c.

At Fort George and Oswego, to our great reputation,
We shew'd our vast skill in fortification;
The French fired three guns, of the fourth they had no occasion;
For we gave up those forts, not thro' fear—but mere persuasion.
O the old soldiers, &c.

[2]The poem lists battle after battle in which the British regulars were defeated: at Prestonpans and Falkirk, near Edinburgh, Scotland, where they were defeated by Highlanders in 1746; at the Monongahela River near Fort Duquesne, where the French and Indians defeated General Edward Braddock in 1755; at Fort William Henry on Lake George ("Fort George") and at Fort Oswego on Lake Ontario, where they were defeated by General Louis Joseph de Montcalm in 1757; and at Ticonderoga, where General Montcalm defeated General James Abercrombie in 1758.

To Ticonderoga we went in a passion,
Swearing to be revenged on the whole French nation.
But we soon turned tail, without hesitation
Because they fought behind trees, which is not the fashion.
O the old soldiers, &c.

Lord Loudon[3] he was a fine regular General, they say;
With a great regular army he went his way
Against Louisbourg, to make it his prey;
But return'd without seeing it, for he did not feel bold that day.
O the old soldiers, &c.

Grown proud at reviews, great George had no rest,
Each grandsire, he had heard a rebellion suppress.
He wish'd a rebellion, look'd round and saw none,
So resolv'd a rebellion to make of his own—
With the old soldiers, &c.

The Yankees he bravely pitch'd on, because he thought they would
not fight,
And so he sent us over to take away their right,
But least they should spoil our review clothes, he cried braver and
louder,
"For God's sake, brother kings, don't sell the cowards any powder."
O the old soldiers, &c.

Our General with his council of war did advise,
How at Lexington we might the Yankees surprise.
We march'd—and we march'd—all surpriz'd at being beat;
And so our wise General's plan of surprise was complete.
O the old soldiers, &c.

For fifteen miles they follow'd and pelted us, we scarce had time to
pull a trigger;
But did you ever know a retreat perform'd with more vigour?
For we did it in two hours, which sav'd us from perdition,
'Twas not in *going out* but in *returning* consisted our *expedition.*
O the old soldiers, &c.

Says our General, we were forced to take to our arms in our own
defence:
(For *arms* read *legs,* and it will be both truth and sense.)

[3]John Campbell, 4th Earl of Loudoun, failed to attack Louisbourg in 1757.

Lord Percy[4] (says He) I must say something of him in civility,
And that is, I can never enough praise him for his great—agility.
O the old soldiers, &c.

Of their firing from behind fences, he makes a great pother,
Ev'ry fence has two sides; they made use of one, and we only forgot to use the other.
That we turn'd our backs and ran away so fast, don't let that disgrace us;
'Twas only to make good what Sandwich[5] said, "that the Yankees would not face us."
O the old soldiers, &c.

As they could not get before us, how could they look us in the face?
We took care they should not, by scampering away apace;
That they had not much to brag of, is a very plain case.
For if they beat us in the fight, we beat them in the race.
O the old soldiers of the King, and the King's own Regulars.

1775

The Irishman's Epistle to the Officers and Troops at Boston[1]

By my faith, but I think ye're all makers of bulls,
With your brains in your breeches, your——in your skulls,
Get home with your muskets, and put up your swords,
And look in your books for the meaning of words.
You see now, my honies, how much your mistaken.
For Concord by discord[2] can never be beaten.

How brave ye went out with your muskets all bright,
And thought to be-frighten the folks with the sight;
But when you got there how they powder'd your pums,
And all the way home how they pepper'd your——,
And it is not, honeys, a comical crack,

[4]General Thomas Gage sent Sir Hugh Percy to the relief of the wounded Lieutenant-Colonel Francis Smith and his men in the British retreat from Lexington. J. A. Leo Lemay reports that the English troops under Lord Percy played "Yankee Doodle"—to ridicule the Americans—as they marched out of Boston April 19, 1775, on their way to Lexington.

[5]John Montagu, 3rd Earl of Sandwich, was first Lord of Admiralty, 1771–82.

[1]Song especially popular with patriots.

[2]Pun upon the word "Concord."

To be proud in the face, and be shot in the back.

How come ye to think, now, they did not know how.
To be after their firelocks as smartly as you?
Why, you see now, my honies, 'tis nothing at all,
But to pull at the trigger, and pop goes the ball.

And what have you got now with all your designing,
But a town[3] without victuals to sit down and dine in;
And to look on the ground like a parcel of noodles,
And sing, how the Yankees have beaten the Doodles.
I'm sure if you're wise you'll make peace for a dinner,
For fighting and fasting will soon make ye thinner.

Paddy.[4]

1775

The Yankee's Return from Camp[1]

Father and I went down to camp,
  Along with Captain Gooding,
And there we see the men and boys,
  As thick as hasty pudding.
    Chorus—Yankee Doodle, keep it up,
      Yankee Doodle, dandy,
    Mind the music and the step,
      And with the girls be handy.

And there we see a thousand men,
  As rich as 'Squire David;
And what they wasted every day,
  I wish it could be saved.

The 'lasses they eat every day,
  Would keep an house a winter;
They have as much that, I'll be bound,
  They eat it when they're a mind to.

[3]Boston.

[4]Slang for an Irishman.

[1]J. A. Leo Lemay identifies "Yankee Doodle" as "an American folk song," probably dating from the late 1740s. Used occasionally in the pre-Revolutionary period by the English to ridicule the Americans, many variants are extant, some of which were very popular with the patriots.

For the origins and significance of the song, see especially Oscar George Theodore Sonneck, compiler, Library of Congress *Report on "The Star-Spangled Banner," "Hail Columbia," "America," "Yankee Doodle"* (Washington, 1909) and J. A. Leo Lemay, "The American Origins of 'Yankee Doodle'" (*William and Mary Quarterly,* July 1976).

And there we see a swamping gun,
Large as a log of maple,
Upon a deuced little cart,
A load for father's cattle.

And every time they shoot it off,
It takes a horn of powder,
And makes a noise like father's gun,
Only a nation louder.

I went as nigh to one myself,
As Siah's underpinning;
And father when as nigh again,
I thought the deuce was in him.

Cousin Simon grew so bold,
I thought he would have cock'd it;
It scar'd me so, I shrink'd it off,
And hung by father's pocket.

And Captain Davis had a gun,
He kind of clapt his hand on't,
And stuck a crooked stabbing iron
Upon the little end on't.

And there I see a pumpkin shell
As big as mother's bason;
And every time they touch'd it off,
They scamper'd like the nation.

I see a little barrel too,
The heads were made of leather,
They knock'd upon't with little clubs,
And call'd the folks together.

And there was Captain Washington,
And gentlefolks about him,
They say he's grown so tarnal proud,
He will not ride without 'em.

He got him on his meeting clothes,
Upon a slapping stallion,
He set the world along in rows,
In hundreds and in millions.

The flaming ribbons in his hat,
They look'd so taring fine ah,

I wanted pockily to get,
  To give to my Jemimah.

I see another snarl of men
  A digging graves, they told me,
So tarnal long, so tarnal deep,
  They 'tended they should hold me.

It scar'd me so, I hook'd it off,
  Nor stop'd, as I remember,
Nor turn'd about, 'till I got home,
  Lock'd up in mother's chamber.

1775

Nathan Hale[1]

The breezes went steadily thro' the tall pines,
  A saying "oh! hu-ush!" a saying "oh! hu-ush!"
As stilly stole by a bold legion of horse,
  For Hale in the bush, for Hale in the bush.

"Keep still!" said the thrush as she nestled her young,
  In a nest by the road; in a nest by the road.
"For the tyrants are near, and with them appear,
  What bodes us no good, what bodes us no good."

The brave captain heard it, and thought of his home,
  In a cot by the brook; in a cot by the brook.
With mother and sister and memories dear,
  He so gaily forsook; he so gaily forsook.

Cooling shades of the night were coming apace,
  The tattoo had beat; the tattoo had beat.
The noble one sprang from his dark lurking place,
  To make his retreat; to make his retreat.

[1]Nathan Hale, captain in the Continental Army, was captured while on a spying mission by British troops under Sir William Howe. Just before his death, he is purported to have said, "I only regret that I have but one life to lose for my country."

He warily trod on the dry rustling leaves,
  As he pass'd thro' the wood; as he pass'd thro' the wood;
And silently gain'd his rude launch on the shore,
  As she play'd with the flood; as she play'd with the flood.

The guards of the camp, on that dark, dreary night,
  Had a murderous will; had a murderous will.
They took him and bore him afar from the shore,
  To a hut on the hill; to a hut on the hill.

No mother was there, nor a friend who could cheer,
  In that little stone cell; in that little stone cell.
But he trusted in love, from his father above.
  In his heart, all was well; in his heart, all was well.

An ominous owl with his solemn base voice,
  Sat moaning hard by; sat moaning hard by.
"The tyrant's proud minions most gladly rejoice,
  "For he must soon die; for he must soon die."

The brave fellow told them, no thing he restrain'd,
  The cruel gen'ral; the cruel gen'ral.
His errand from camp, of the ends to be gain'd,
  And said that was all; and said that was all.

They took him and bound him and bore him away,
  Down the hill's grassy side; down the hill's grassy side.
'Twas there the base hirelings, in royal array,
  His cause did deride; his cause did deride.

Five minutes were given, short moments, no more,
  For him to repent; for him to repent;
He pray'd for his mother, he ask'd not another,
  To Heaven he went; to Heaven he went.

The faith of a martyr, the tragedy shew'd,
  As he trod the last stage; as he trod the last stage.
And Britons will shudder at gallant Hale's blood,
  As his words do presage, as his words do presage.

"Thou pale king of terrors, thou life's gloomy foe,
  Go frighten the slave, go frighten the slave;
Tell tyrants, to you, their allegiance they owe.
  No fears for the brave; no fears for the brave."

1776

Sir Harry's Invitation[1]

Come, gentlemen Tories, firm, loyal, and true,
Here are axes and shovels, and something to do!
For the sake of our king,
Come, labour and sing;
You left all you had for his honour and glory,
And he will remember the suffering Tory:
We have, it is true,
Some small work to do;
But here's for your pay
Twelve coppers a day,
And never regard what the rebels may say,
But throw off your jerkins and labour away.

To raise up the rampart, and pile up the wall,
To pull down old houses and dig the canal,
To build and destroy—
Be this your employ,
In the day time to work at our fortifications,
And steal in the night from the rebels your rations:
The king wants your aid,
Not empty parade;
Advance to your places
Ye men of long faces,
Nor ponder too much on your former disgraces,
This year, I presume, will quite alter your cases.

Attend at the call of the fifer and drummer,
The French and the Rebels are coming next summer,
And forts we must build
Though Tories are kill'd—
Then courage, my jockies, and work for your king,
For if you are taken no doubt you will swing—
If York we can hold
I'll have you enroll'd;
And after you're dead
Your names shall be read
As who for their monarch both labour'd and bled,
And ventur'd their necks for their beef and their bread.

[1]Ballad by Philip Freneau (1752–1832), often called the "Poet of the Revolution."

The American-born Sir Henry Clinton was left in command of the garrison in New York in 1779 when Sir William Howe embarked on his expedition to conquer Pennsylvania. He was criticized for his treatment of Tory refugees.

'Tis an honour to serve the bravest of nations,
And be left to be hang'd in their capitulations—
Then scour up your mortars
And stand to your quarters,
'Tis nonsense for Tories in battle to run,
They never need fear sword, halberd, or gun;
Their hearts should not fail 'em,
No balls will assail 'em,
Forget your disgraces
And shorten your faces,
For 'tis true as the gospel, believe it or not,
Who are born to be hang'd, will never be shot.

1779

Volunteer Boys[1]

Hence with the lover who sighs o'er his wine,
Cloes and Phillises[2] toasting,
Hence with the slave who will whimper and whine,
Of ardor and constancy boasting.
Hence with love's joys,
Follies and noise,
The toast that I give is the Volunteer Boys.

Nobles and beauties and such common toasts,
Those who admire may drink, sir;
Fill up the glass to the volunteer hosts,
Who never from danger will shrink, sir.
Let mirth appear,
Every heart cheer,
The toast that I give is the brave volunteer.

Here's to the squire who goes to parade
Here's to the citizen soldier;

[1]Frank Moore calls this verse "the best convivial" song of the Revolutionary War and attributes its authorship to Henry Archer, a Scotsman who emigrated to America in 1778 and supported the patriot cause.

[2]Names traditionally used for shepherdesses or rustic maids in pastoral poetry.

Here's to the merchant who fights for his trade,
Whom danger increasing makes bolder,
Let mirth appear,
Union is here,
The toast that I give is the brave volunteer.

Here's to the lawyer, who, leaving the bar,
Hastens where honor doth lead, sir,
Changing the gown for the ensigns of war,
The cause of his country to plead, sir.
Freedom appears,
Every heart cheers,
And calls for the health of the law volunteers.

Here's to the soldier, though batter'd in wars,
And safe to his farm-house retir'd;
When called by his country, ne'er thinks of his scars,
With ardor to join us inspir'd.
Bright fame appears,
Trophies uprear,
To veteran chiefs who became volunteers.

Here's to the farmer who dares to advance
To harvests of honor with pleasure;
Who with a slave the most skilful in France,
A sword for his country would measure.
Hence with cold fear,
Heroes rise here;
The ploughman is chang'd to the stout volunteer.

Here's to the peer, first in senate and field,
Whose actions to titles add grace, sir;
Whose spirit undaunted would never yet yield
To a foe, to a pension or place, sir.
Gratitude here,
Toasts to the peer,
Who adds to his titles, "the brave volunteer."

Thus the bold bands for old Jersey's defence,
The muse hath with rapture review'd, sir;
With our volunteer boys, as our verses commence,
With our volunteer boys they conclude, sir.
Discord or noise,
Ne'er damp our joys,
But health and success to the volunteer boys.

1780

"Loyalist" Voices

When Good Queen Elizabeth Governed the Realm[1]

When good Queen Elizabeth govern'd the realm,
And Burleigh's[2] sage counsels directed the helm,
In vain Spain and France our conquests oppos'd;
For Valor conducted what Wisdom propos'd.
Beef and beer was their food;
Love and Truth arm'd their band;
Their courage was ready—
Steady, boys, steady—
To fight and to conquer by sea and by land.

But since tea and coffee, so much to our grief,
Have taken the place of strong beer and roast beef,
Our laurels have wither'd, our trophies been torn;
And the lions of England French triumphs adorn.
Tea and slops are their food;
They unnerve every hand—
Their courage unsteady
And not always ready—
They often are conquer'd by sea and by land.

St. George views with transport our generous flame:
"My sons, rise to glory, and rival my fame.
Ancient manners again in my sons I behold
And this age must eclipse all the ages of gold."
Beef and beer are our food;
Love and Truth arm our band;
Our courage is steady
And always is ready
To fight and to conquer by sea and by land.

While thus we regale as our fathers of old,
Our manners as simple, our courage as bold,
May Vigor and Prudence our freedom secure

[1]Song by Joseph Stansbury (1742–1809), with Dr. Jonathan Odell (1737–1818), one of the two best-known loyalist poets. Probably composed for a meeting of the Sons of St. George in New York in 1774 or 1775, to the tune of "Hearts of Oak."

[2]William Cecil, 1st Baron Burleigh (1520–98), advisor to Queen Elizabeth.

Long as rivers, or ocean, or stars shall endure.
Beef and beer are our food;
Love and Truth arm our band;
Our courage is steady,
And always is ready
To fight and to conquer by sea and by land.

1774 or 1775

Song for a Fishing Party near Burlington, on the Delaware, in 1776[1]

How sweet is the season, the sky how serene;
On Delaware's banks how delightful the scene;
The Prince of the Rivers, his waves all asleep,
In silence majestic glides on to the deep.

Away from the noise of the fife and the drum,
And all the rude din of Bellona we come;
And a plentiful store of good humor we bring
To season our feast in the shade of Cold Spring.

A truce then to all whig and tory debate;
True lovers of freedom, contention we hate:
For the demon of discord in vain tries his art
To possess or inflame a true *Protestant*[2] heart.

True Protestant friends to fair Liberty's cause,
To decorum, good order, religion and laws,
From avarice, jealousy, perfidy, free;
We wish all the world were as happy as we.

We have wants, we confess, but are free from the care
Of those that abound, yet have nothing to spare:
Serene as the sky, as the river serene,
We are happy to want envy, malice, and spleen.

[1]Song by Dr. Jonathan Odell, described by Moses Coit Tyler as "the most powerful and unrelenting of the Tory satirists."

[2]Dr. Odell appended a note to the third verse: "*Protestant* was a term adopted by a circle of Loyalists."

While thousands around us, misled by a few,
The phantoms of pride and ambition pursue,
With pity their fatal delusion we see;
And wish all the world were as happy as we!

1776

Burrowing Yankees[1]

Ye Yankees who, mole-like, still throw up the earth,
And like them, to your follies are blind from your birth;
Attempt not to hold British troops at defiance,
True Britons, with whom you pretend an alliance.

Mistake not; such blood ne'er run in your veins,
'Tis no more than the dregs, the lees, or the drains:
Ye affect to talk big of your hourly attacks;
Come on! and I'll warrant, we'll soon see your backs.

Such threats of bravadoes serve only to warm
The true British hearts, you ne'er can alarm;
The Lion once rous'd, will strike such a terror,
Shall show you, poor fools, your presumption and error.

And the time will soon come when your whole rebel race
Will be drove from the lands, nor dare show your face:
Here's a health to great *George,* may he fully determine,
To root from the earth all such insolent vermin.

1776

A Birthday Song for the King's Birthday, June 4, 1777[1]

Time was when America hallow'd the morn
On which the lov'd monarch of Britain was born,
Hallow'd the day, and joyfully chanted
    God save the King!

[1]Song especially popular with loyalists.

[1]Song by Dr. Jonathan Odell. Dr. Odell also wrote a birthday ode for the King's birthday in 1776.

Then flourish'd the blessings of freedom and peace,
And plenty flow'd in with a yearly increase.
Proud of our lot we chanted merrily
Glory and joy crown the King!

With envy beheld by the nations around,
We rapidly grew, nor was anything found
Able to check our growth while we chanted
God save the King!
O bless'd beyond measure, had honor and truth
Still nurs'd in our hearts what they planted in youth!
Loyalty still had chanted merrily
Glory and joy crown the King!

But see! how rebellion has lifted her head!
How honor and truth are with loyalty fled!
Few are there now who join us in chanting
God save the King!
And see! how deluded the multitude fly
To arm in a cause that is built on a lie!
Yet are we proud to chant thus merrily
Glory and joy crown the King!

Though faction by falsehood awhile may prevail,
And loyalty suffers a captive in jail,
Britain is rous'd, rebellion is falling:
God save the King!
The captive shall soon be releas'd from his chain;
And conquest restore us to Britain again,
Ever to join in chanting merrily
Glory and joy crown the King!

1777

A Song[1]

Here's a bumper, brave boys, to the health of our king,
Long may he live, and long may we sing,
In praise of a monarch who boldly defends
The laws of the realm, and the cause of his friends.

[1]Song sung to the tune of "Hearts of Oak."

Then cheer up, my lads, we have nothing to fear,
While we remain steady,
And always keep ready,
To add to the trophies of this happy year.

The Congress did boast of their mighty ally,
But George does both France and the Congress defy;
And when Britons unite, there's no force can withstand
Their fleets and their armies, by sea and on land.

Thus supported, our cause we will ever maintain,
And all treaties with rebels will ever disdain;
Till reduc'd by our arms, they are forc'd to confess,
While ruled by Great Britain they ne'er knew distress.

Then let us, my boys, Britain's right e'er defend,
Who regards not her rights, we esteem not our friend;
Then, brave boys, we both France and the Congress defy,
And we'll fight for Great Britain and George till we die.
Then cheer up, my lads, we have nothing to fear,
While we remain steady,
And always keep ready,
To add to the trophies of this happy year.

1779

An Appeal[1]

The old English cause knocks at every man's door,
And bids him stand up for religion and right;
It addresses the rich as well as the poor;
And fair liberty, bids them, like Englishmen fight.
And suffer no wrong,
From a rebel throng,
Who, if they're not quelled, will enslave us ere long;
Most bravely then let us our liberty prize,
Nor suffer the Congress to blind all our eyes;
Or each rebel cut-purse, will soon give us law,
For they are as bad as a Tyler or Straw.[2]

[1]Song sung to the tune of "The Cat Purse"; very popular with Loyalists.

[2]Walter Tyler, English leader of Peasants' Revolt (1381); Jack Straw, one of the leaders of Tyler's rebellion.

From France, D'Estaing[3] to America has come.
The French banditti will rob our estates;
These robbers are all protected by Rome,[4]
Consult but their annals, record but their dates,
It's their politics
To burn heretics,
Or poison by water that's fetch'd from the Styx.[5]
Let Frenchified rebels, in vain then attempt
To bring our own church, or our king to contempt;
For no rebel cut-purse shall e'er give us law,
Should they prove as daring as Tyler or Straw.

The farces of Rome, with carrying her hosts,
Are laugh'd at and jeer'd by the learned and wise,
And all her thin tinsels apparently lost,
Her stories of relics, and sanctified lies.
Each ignorant joke
Believe, or you smoke,
And if we are conquer'd we receive the Pope's yoke;
But despising the counsels of Adams and Lee,[6]
As loyal Americans, we'll die or be free.
For no rebel cut-throat shall e'er give us law.
Should they prove as daring as Tyler or Straw.

Let curses most vile, and anathemas roar,
Let half-ruin'd France, to the Pope tribute pay;
Britain's thundering cannon, shall guard safe our shore;
Great George shall defend us, none else we'll obey.
Then France, join'd by Spain,
May labor in vain,
For soon the Havana[7] shall be ours again.
The French then will scamper and quit every state,
And find themselves bubbled, when *morbleu*[8] it's too late.
For no Frenchman, or rebel imp of the law,
In our old constitution can point out a flaw.

1780

[3]Comte Jean Baptiste Charles Henri Hector d'Estaing, naval commander of French squadron aiding the Patriots.

[4]The loyalists used the colonists' fear of the Roman Catholic Church to suggest the dangers of the patriots' accepting military assistance from the French.

[5]River in Hades.

[6]Richard Henry Lee of Virginia, Samuel Adams of Massachusetts Bay, both prominent defenders of colonial rights.

[7]Country.

[8]The devil!

Journals of the Lewis and Clark Expedition

On August 15, 1806, Private John Colter begged a favor of Captains Meriwether Lewis and William Clark—permission to leave the homeward-bound Corps of Discovery and return to the Yellowstone River as a trapper. Clark thought "the offer a very advantagious one, to him" and Colter's compatriots wished him "every Success." Outfitted with "Some Small articles which [the members of the expedition] did not want and Some powder & lead," Colter turned his face westward again as the group with whom he had adventured for the past two years eagerly looked eastward, anticipating an early fall arrival in St. Louis. Colter's dramatic choice, in which he rejects the expedition's narrative of painful removal from and joyful return to civilization, highlights the complexities of the first overland reconnoiter of the Pacific coast conducted by the relentlessly expanding United States.

The expedition contained three people who did not have the luxury of Colter's ability to petition for a free choice about whether to go east or west, north or south, or even go at all. Clark's "servant" York, an enslaved descendant of Africans, moved at his owner's pleasure and direction. Sacagawea,[1] a young Shoshone woman and one of Toussaint Charbonneau's purchased wives, had to follow her husband wherever he went. And their son, Jean Baptiste, born as the party set out from Fort Mandan in North Dakota for the upper Missouri River, certainly did not have a say in the matter. Reflecting the cultural plurality of the young nation, the Corps of Discovery was heterogeneous but hierarchical. Likewise, the texts that the expedition produced were heterogeneous, reflecting the political, scientific, anthropological, linguistic, and geographical desires of the early nation. Perhaps most striking, though, are the different voices that articulate this corps of discovery—and the voices that do not.

Exploration of the trans-Mississippi West had interested Thomas Jefferson from at least 1783, when he had first proposed the idea of sending an expedition to cross the continent. Motivated by a desire to stymie the British in their project to secure trading dominance in the northwest, Jefferson attained the political and financial power to accomplish his exploration scheme with his election to the presidency in 1801. Jefferson tapped his private secretary, Meriwether Lewis (born in 1774), to lead the endeavor. He then arranged for Lewis, a young man with both military and wilderness travel experience, to be trained in Philadelphia by members of the American Philosophical Society, the premier scientific organization of the time. Lewis studied astronomy, natural history, medicine, and ethnology, reflecting Jefferson's intellectual interest in the Enlightenment.

While geographical discovery was arguably the primary goal of the expedition, linked as that enterprise was to political and economic stability for the young nation, the acquisition of knowledge—of peoples, animals, plants, and minerals as well as places—was the overarching purpose of, as Jefferson dubbed it, the Corps

[1]Clark, who transcribed elements of several Native languages on the journey, consistently sought to accurately represent the sound of Native speech. In all seventeen instances of the young Shoshone woman's name in the journals, the third syllable begins with a hard G. Nicholas Biddle (1786–1844), an early editor of the expedition journals, represented the woman's name as *Sacajawea.* Only recently has the more accurate Sah-cah' gah-we-ah gained prominence. The Hidatsa name, given to the Shoshone woman during her captivity, means "bird woman."

of Discovery. High-minded intellectual inquiry was tempered, however, by practical considerations. The Louisiana Purchase in April 1803 made successful contact with the expanded nation's new Indian "citizens" imperative. "Successful contact" translated into assurances of a peaceful part in, and eventual control over, the lucrative fur trade and the squelching of intertribal rivalries that often resulted in economically disruptive violence.

Both Jefferson and Lewis knew the success of the enterprise depended on the presence of an effective co-commander, someone who could shoulder the burden alone if Lewis were killed or met with an accident. William Clark, an old Army friend of Lewis's, accepted Lewis's proposal to join the expedition. Four years Lewis's senior, Clark possessed qualities of temperament, experience, and fortitude that complemented Lewis's. In one of history's great partnerships, Lewis and Clark worked together to satisfy Jefferson's lifelong curiosity about the West and to launch their young nation's first steps toward hegemony over that territory.

Departing from a camp near St. Louis in the spring of 1804, the Corps of Discovery traveled by water and land in search of a viable northwest route to the Pacific. They returned in September of 1806 with bad news: "in passing from the falls of Missouri across the Rocky Mountains to the navagable waters of the Columbia you have 200 miles of Good road, 140 miles of high Steep rugged Mountain 60 miles of which is Covered from 2 to 8 feet deep with Snow in the last of June." This depressing news could have marked Jefferson's high profile exploration project a failure. Their scientific, ethnographic, and geographic discoveries, however, coupled with the amazing fact that they returned at all, secured for them a warm place in the hearts of many of their fellow citizens and a noteworthy place in history.

The Corps of Discovery's great adventure, a boon to white citizens of the United States in position to take advantage of the land, animal, water, and trade resources identified by the expedition, was far less beneficial to other inhabitants of the continent. Shut out from independent participation in new markets, legions of slaves in the United States gained nothing material from Lewis and Clark's new knowledge.

Most disturbingly, Lewis and Clark's contacts with Native peoples prefigured wholesale destruction of ancient, vibrant Native American cultures in the nineteenth century, casting the heroic character of the expedition into a new light. Members of the Corps of Discovery may have been among the first white men to encounter some Native communities, but their European-American culture's influence preceded them. Lewis and Clark saw remnants of Indian villages abandoned many years before due to the ravages of smallpox; they saw trade goods from white cultures among first-contact tribes; and they witnessed displacements, resource hostilities, and violence between indigenous nations stemming from new trading patterns involving encroaching whites. The trans-Mississippi West was a place undergoing transformation even before the Corps of Discovery set foot in it.

The excerpts from the journals of the expedition presented here represent both the grand scope of the journey itself and a limited number of the voices of the people who participated in that journey.[2] We hear nothing firsthand from Sacagawea, Charbonneau, York, or the many privates in the corps. Frustratingly, only a handful of voices have come down to us from this

[2]All selections come from the Journals of the Lewis and Clark Expedition Online, the definitive University of Nebraska Press edition edited by Gary E. Moulton, at http://lewisandclarkjouirnals.unl.edu/index.html. Each journal entry is preceded by the name of the journalist and the date of composition, if known.

great adventure—those of Lewis, Clark, and four of the sergeants ordered to keep written records of the journey, Patrick Gass, Charles Floyd, Joseph Whitehouse, and John Ordway. Three other members of the party—Robert Frazer, Nathaniel Pryor, and Alexander Willard—may have kept written records, but their journals, if they ever existed, are lost.

The extant journals are treasure troves of information, providing not only ethnographic glimpses into religious practices of Native Americans and the first scientific descriptions of the prairie dog but also linguistic information about both Native American communication and the English spoken by men from a variety of backgrounds at the turn of the nineteenth century. To suggest the sound of their voices, we have preserved their idiosyncratic spelling and punctuation—both of which were still unfixed at the beginning of the nineteenth century. Where clarity of meaning for a modern audience is an issue, we have silently corrected the spelling. The journals offer an opportunity to witness the fluidity of written English before widespread standardization in spelling and punctuation became more common. For example, one researcher has noted that Clark spells the word "Sioux" twenty-seven different ways in the journals! The journalists' varied literary styles contribute to a deeper understanding of the individuality of the men, and one courageous Native woman, who made up the Corps of Discovery.

Katherine E. Ledford
Appalachian State University

[Patrick Gass][3]

On Monday the 14th of May 1804, we left our establishment [. . .] and having crossed the Mississippi proceeded up the Missouri on our intended voyage of discovery, under the command of Captain Clarke. [. . .] The corps consisted of forty-three men (including Captain Lewis and Captain Clarke, who were to command the expedition) part of the regular troops of the United States, and part engaged for this particular enterprize. The expedition was embarked on board a batteau and two periogues.[4] The day was showery and in the evening we encamped on the north bank six miles up the river. Here we had leisure to reflect on our situation, and the nature of our engagements: and, as we had all entered this service as volunteers, to consider how far we stood pledged for the success of an expedition, which the government had projected; and which had been undertaken for the benefit and at the expence of the Union: of course of much interest and high expectation.

The best authenticated accounts informed us, that we were to pass through a country possessed by numerous, powerful and warlike nations of savages, of gigantic stature, fierce, treacherous and cruel; and particularly hostile to white men. And fame had united with tradition in opposing mountains to our course, which human enterprize and exertion would attempt in vain to pass. The determined and resolute character, however, of the corps, and the confidence which pervaded all

[3]Sergeant Patrick Gass (1771–1870) was born in Pennsylvania and joined the army in 1799. Gass published his journal in 1807, the first in print, after substantial editing. He died in Wellsburg, West Virginia, the last known survivor of the Corps of Discovery.

[4]Types of watercraft.

ranks dispelled every emotion of fear, and anxiety for the present; while a sense of duty, and of the honour, which would attend the completion of the object of the expedition; a wish to gratify the expectations of the government, and of our fellow citizens, with the feelings which novelty and discovery invariably inspire, seemed to insure to us ample support in our future toils, suffering and dangers.

[William Clark][5]

July 4th *Wednesday* 1804, [. . .] one of the most butifull Plains, I ever Saw, open & butifully diversified with hills & vallies all presenting themselves to the river covered with grass and a few scattering trees a handsom Creek meandering thro at this place the Kansaw Inds. formerly lived and had a very large Town passed a Creek I observed Spring braking out of the bank, a good Situation for a fort on a hill at the upper part

The Plains of this countrey are covered with a Leek Green Grass, well calculated for the sweetest and most norushing hay—interspersed with Cops [copses] of trees, Spreding their lofty branchs over Pools Springs or Brooks of fine water. Groops of Shrubs covered with the most delicious froot is to be seen in every direction, and nature appears to have exerted herself to butify the Senery by the variety of flowers <raiseing> Delicately and highly flavered raised above the Grass, which Strikes & profumes the Sensation, and amuses the mind throws it into Conjecterng the cause of So magnificent a Senerey [*several words illegible, crossed out*] in a Country thus Situated far removed from the Sivilised world to be enjoyed by nothing but the Buffalo Elk Deer & Bear in which it abounds & [*page torn*] Savage Indians

[Joseph Whitehouse][6]

Wednesday July 4th [1804] This morning we started Early from green point or Ordways Island having a fair wind, and the water being good, we rowed on successfully. this day proved very warm. we left off rowing and went to Towing the

[5]Second Lieutenant William Clark (1770–1838) was born in Virginia but moved to Kentucky when he was fourteen. He joined the army in 1792 and rose to the rank of captain before leaving the military to take care of a family business. Invited back into service by Lewis, whom he had met in the army, Clark received only a second lieutenant's rank for his co-command of the Corps of Discovery. To ensure discipline on the journey, Lewis and Clark concealed Clark's lower rank from the members of the expedition and Clark was addressed by his former rank of Captain. Clark's postexpedition appointments included the governorship of the Missouri Territory and the supervision of United States' relations with Native Americans west of the Mississippi River.

[6]Private Joseph Whitehouse (ca. 1775–?) was probably born in Virginia and moved to Kentucky in about 1784. Involved in some type of disciplinary trouble early in the journey, he had other negative encounters with authority after the expedition, being arrested for debt. He deserted the army in 1817.

boat, but the sand was so hot, that it scalded our feet, some of the Men left the tow rope, and had to put on their Mockasins to keep their feet from being burnt, we passed a River which we called Independance, where we found a Gray horse on the So. West side of said River. we came as far as a Priari, call'd Old town de Caugh, where we encamped, the distance being 16 Miles—

[Meriwether Lewis[7] and Clark]

Camp New Island July 12th 1804

A Court martial consisting of the two commanding officers will convene this day at 1 OCk. P.M. for the trial of such prisoners as may be brought before them; one of the course will act as Judge Advocate.—

The Commanding officers. Capt. M. Lewis & W. Clark constituted themselves a Court martial for the trial of Such prisoners as are *Guilty* of *Capatol Crimes,* and under the rules and articles of *War* punishable by *Death.*

Alexander Willard was brought forward Charged with "*Lying down and Sleeping on his post whilst a Sentinal, on the night* of the 11th. Instant" (by John Ordway Sergeant of the Guard)—

To this Charge the prisoner pleads. *Guilty* of *Lying Down,* and *not Guilty, of Going to Sleep.* The Course after Duly Considering the evidence aduced, are of oppinion that the *Prisoner* Alexdn. Willard is guilty of every part of the Charge exhibited against him. it being a breach of the *rules* and articles of *War* (as well as tending to the probable distruction of the party) do *Sentence* him to receive *One hundred lashes on his bear back, at four different times in equal proportion.*— and order that the punishment Commence this evening at Sunset, and Continue to be inflicted, (by the Guard) every evening untill Completed

[John Ordway][8]

Sunday July 15th 1804. a foggy morning which Detained us untill 7 oClock, Drewyer & Sgt. Floyd went on Shore. we proceded on till Breakfast af[ter] I went on Shore with Capt. Clark on the South Side we Saw fresh Sign on bank of Elk. crossed a creek named faun Creek which came in on the South Side of Missouris. we walked on over a Ridge came to high large praries & hills. we

[7]Captain Meriwether Lewis (1774–1809) was born in Virginia. He joined the army in 1794. After leading the Corps of Discovery, he governed the Louisiana Territory, a political post that exacerbated depressive tendencies in Lewis. He committed suicide in 1809.

[8]Sergeant John Ordway (ca. 1775–ca. 1817) was born in New Hampshire. He joined the army as a young man, from which he was appointed to the Corps of Discovery. His reliability and sense of military duty made him the most faithful and complete journalist of the expedition. He became a wealthy private citizen in Missouri.

walked on   found Some cherries near a handsome Spring River named cherry Run, at which we drank at   the forks then followed it or one branch to the head which came out of a ridge which joined the praries, and went up on a high R. Ridge of prarie where we could See all around for a long distance in the open praries or as far as our eyes could behold, and on the opposite Side of the Missouris we Saw a large & extensive prarie which looked verry handsome

[Clark]

July 22nd, Sunday 1804

[. . .] we concluded to delay at this place a few days and Send for Some of the Chiefs of that nation [Otteaus] to let them Know of the Change of Government, The wishes of our Government to Cultivate friendship with them, the Objects of our journy and to present them with a flag and Some Small presents.

[Clark]

24th August Friday 1804

[. . .] In a northerley direction from the mouth of this Creek in an imence Plain a high Hill is Situated, and appears of a Conic form and by the different nations of Indians in this quarter is Suppose to be the residence of Deavels.   that they are in human form with remarkable large heads and about 18 Inches high, that they are Very watchfull, and are arm'd with Sharp arrows with which they Can Kill at a great distance; they are Said to Kill all persons who are So hardy as to attempt to approach the hill; they State that tradition informs them that many Indians have Suffered by those little people and among others three *Mahar* men fell a Sacrefise to their murceyless fury not many years Since—   So much do the Maha, Souis, Ottoes and other neighbouring nations believe this fable that no Consideration is Suffecient to induce them to apporach the hill

[Ordway]

Thursday 30th [1804]   [. . .] at the hour of 9 oClock the commanding officers had all things in readiness to hold a counsel with the chiefs and warriors of the Souix nation, they Sent a pearogue across for them, they all [c]ame into our Camp in the most friendly manner &C   their was four of them which were always a Singing & playing on their curious Instruments which were as follows, viz.   they had each of them a Thrapple[9] made of a fresh buffelow hide dressed white with Some Small Shot in it and a little bunch of hair tied on it, the head man of the[m] was painted white, the rest of them were painted different colours. when they arived at our Camp & took the Commanding officers by the hand 2 Guns was fired from our bow peace. the colours displaying &-C— [. . .] the talk was finished by our Commanding officers about 4 oClock, [Lewis and Clark] made five Chiefs & Gave Each a Medal & Gave the whole Some preasants, they Gave the Grand Chief [. . .] a red laced coat & a fine cocked hat & red feather & an american flag & a white Shirt &.C. all of which he was much pleased with, they [received] all their presents verry thankfully, & divided them among one another &c— [. . .] after dark we Made a large fire for the Indians to have a war dance, all the young men prepared themselves for the dance. Some of them painted themselves in curious manner Some of the Boys had their faces & foreheads all painted white &C a drum was prepared, the Band began to play on their little Instruments, & the drum beat & they Sang. the young men commenced dancing around the fire. it always began with a whoop & hollow & ended with the Same, and in the intervales, one of the warriors at a time would rise with his weapen & Speak of what he had done in his day, & what warlike actions he had done &.c. this they call merrit &.C they would confess how many they had killed & of what nation they were of & how many horses they had Stole &-C—they Camped along Side of us & behaved honestly & cleaver &C. &C—

[Clark]

10th of October 1804

[. . .] we hear that Some jealousy exists as to the Chiefs to be made— at 1 oclock the Cheifs all assembled under an awning near the Boat, and under the American Flag. we Delivered a Similar Speech to those delivered the Ottoes & Sioux, made three Chiefs, one for each Village and gave them Clothes & flags— 1s Chief is name *Ka-ha-wiss assa* lighting ravin 2d Chief *Po-casse* (Hay) & the 3rd *Piaheto* or Eagles Feather— after the Council was over we Shot the Air gun, which astonished them, & they all left us, I observed 2 Sioux in the Council one of them I had Seen below, they Came to interceed with the Ricaras to Stop us as we were told— the Inds. much astonished at my black Servent, who made him Self more turrible in thier view than I wished him to Do as I am told telling them that before I cought him he was wild & lived upon people, young children was verry good eating Showed them his Strength &c. &c.— Those Indians are not fond of Licquer of any Kind—

[9]Usually means *windpipe* but Ordway uses the word to signify a rattle.

[Ordway]

Monday 15th Oct. [1804] [. . .] at Sunset we Camped [. . .] at a hunting Camp of the R. Ree [Arikara] nation. there was about 30 men & a nomber of women & children at this Camp. [. . .] the Greatest Curiousity to them was York[10] Capt. Clarks Black Man. all the nation made a Great deal of him. the children would follow after him, & if he turned towards them they would run from him & hollow as if they were terreyfied, & afraid of him.

[The party traveled up the Missouri River during the summer and early fall of 1804, constructing a winter camp near present-day Washburn, North Dakota, in late October. The captains named the camp Fort Mandan to reflect their proximity to Mandan-Hidatsa villages. The corps spent the winter hunting and trading their blacksmithing services to the Native Americans for food. Much socializing also took place between the two groups. Lewis and Clark occupied themselves with work on their journals.]

[Clark]

22nd of November Thursday 1804

[. . .] I was alarmed about 10 oClock by the Sentinal, who informed that an Indian was about to Kill his wife in the interpeters fire [quarters] about 60 yards below the works, I went down and Spoke to the fellow about the rash act which he was like to commit and forbid any act of the kind near the fort— Some missunderstanding took place between this man & his wife about 8 days ago, and She came to this place, & Continued with the Squars [Squaws] of the interpeters, 2 days ago She returned to the Village. in the evening of the Same day She came to the interpeters fire appearently much beat, & Stabed in 3 places— We Derected that no man of this party have any intercourse with this woman under the penelty of Punishment— he the Husband observed that one of our Serjeants Slept with his wife & if he wanted her he would give her to him, We derected the Serjeant Odway to give the man Some articles, at which time I told the Indian that I believed not one man of the party had touched his wife except the one he had given the use of her for a night, in his own bed, no man of the party Should touch his Squar [Squaw], or the wife of any Indian, nor did I believe they touch a woman if they

[10]York (ca. 1770–?). An enslaved man of African descent, York had been willed to Clark by Clark's father and was probably a servant and companion to Clark from childhood. More than a personal servant to Clark on the journey, York likely carried a gun and performed his share of duties with the other men. Popular culture tales of York's sexual prowess with indigenous women and of his clownish behavior on the expedition are not supported by the journals and are indicative of racial stereotyping. York struggled for his freedom after the expedition, finally receiving it sometime after 1811.

knew her to be the wife of another man, and advised him to take his Squar [Squaw] home and live hapily together in future,—

[Clark]

Fort Mandan on the N E bank of the Missouries
1600 miles up *Tuesday January the 1st 1805*

The Day was ushered in by the Discharge of two Cannon, we Suffered 16 men with their musick to visit the 1st Village for the purpose of Danceing, by as they Said the perticular request of the Chiefs of that village, about 11 oClock I with an interpeter & two men walked up to the Village (my views were to alay Some little miss understanding which had taken place thro jealousy and mortification as to our treatment towards them[])

I found them much pleased at the Danceing of our men, I ordered my black Servent [York] to Dance which amused the Croud verry much, and Some what astonished them, that So large a man Should be active &c. &.

[Clark]

5th of *January Saturday 1805*

a cold day   Some Snow, Several Indians visit us with their axes to get them mended, I imploy my Self drawing a Connection of the Countrey from what information I have received—   a Buffalow Dance (or Medison) for 3 nights passed in the 1st Village, a curious Custom the old men arrange themselves in a circle & after Smoke a pipe, which is handed them by a young man, Dress up for the purpose, the young men who have their wives back of the circle go to one of the old men with a whining tone and [ask] the old man to take his wife (who presents naked except a robe) and—(or Sleep with him)   the Girl then takes the Old man (who verry often can Scercely walk) and leades him to a Convenient place for the business, after which they return to the lodge, if the Old man (or a white man) returns to the lodge without gratifying the man & his wife, he offers her again and again; (we Sent a man to this [dance] last night, they gave him 4 Girls all this to cause the buffalow to Come near So that They may kill them.

[At Fort Mandan, Lewis and Clark hired the interpreting services of Toussaint Charbonneau, a Canadian trader who lived among the Hidatsas and spoke both French and Hidatsa. Charbonneau's two Native American wives were Shoshone, captives of the Hidatsas, who had learned the Hidatsa language during their captivity. Because Lewis and Clark needed to purchase horses from the Shoshone for an overland trek from the headwaters of the Missouri River to the Columbia River, they needed a way to communicate

with the Shoshone. Charbonneau was an especially attractive employee, since his wives offered that linguistic pathway. Only one of these women, Sacagawea, made the journey with Charbonneau.]

[Lewis]

11th February Monday 1805

[. . .] about five oclock this evening one of the wives of Charbono was delivered of a fine boy. it is worthy of remark that this was the first child which this woman had boarn and as is common in such cases her labour was tedious and the pain violent; Mr. Jessome [another interpreter] informed me that he had freequently adminstered a small portion of the rattle of the rattle-snake, which he assured me had never failed to produce the desired effect, that of hastening the birth of the child; having the rattle of a snake by me I gave it to him and he administered two rings of it to the woman broken in small pieces with the fingers and added to a small quantity of water. Whether this medicine was truly the cause or not I shall not undertake to determine, but I was informed that she had not taken it more than ten minutes before she brought forth perhaps this remedy may be worthy of future experiments, but I must confess that I want faith as to it's efficacy.—

[After sending some members of the party back downriver to St. Louis with reports and scientific samples for President Jefferson, the Corps of Discovery continued its travel up the Missouri River in the spring. They now entered territory they knew little about.]

[Lewis]

Fort Mandan April 7th 1805

[. . .] Our vessels consisted of six small canoes, and two large perogues. This little fleet altho' not quite so rispectable as those of Columbus or Capt. Cook were still viewed by us with as much pleasure as those deservedly famed adventurers ever beheld theirs; and I dare say with quite as much anxiety for their safety and preservation. we were now about to penetrate a country at least two thousand miles in width, on which the foot of civillized man had never trodden; the good or evil it had in store for us was for experiment yet to determine, and these little vessells contained every article by which we were to expect to subsist or defend ourselves. however as this the state of mind in which we are, generally gives the colouring to events, when the immagination is suffered to wander into futurity, the picture which now presented itself to me was a most pleasing one. entertaining as I do, the most confident hope of succeading in a voyage which had formed a da[r]ling project of mine for the last ten years, I could but esteem this moment of [our] departure as among the most happy of my life. The party are in excellent health and sperits, zealously attatched to the enterprise, and anxious to proceed; not a whisper of murmur or discontent to be heard among them, but all act in unison, and with the most perfect harmony

[Lewis]

Tuesday May 14th 1805.

[. . .] In the evening the men in two of the rear canoes discovered a large brown bear [. . .] and six of them went out to attack him, all good hunters; [four of them] [. . .] fired nearly at the same time and put each his bullet through him, [. . .] in an instant this monster ran at them with open mouth, the two who had reserved their fires discharged their pieces at him as he came towards them, both of them struck him, [. . .] this however only retarded his motion for a moment only, the men unable to reload their guns took to flight, the bear pursued and had very nearly overtaken them before they reached the river; two of the party betook themselves to a canoe and the others seperated and concealed themselves among the willows, [. . .] they struck him several times again but the guns served only to direct the bear to them, in this manner he pursued two of them seperately so close that they were obliged to throw aside their guns and pouches and throw themselves into the river [. . .] so enraged was this anamal that he plunged into the river only a few feet behind the second man [. . .] when one of those who still remained on shore shot him through the head and finally killed him; [. . .] [another] occurrence [. . .] I cannot recollect but with the utmost trepidation and horror; this is the upseting and narrow escape of the white perogue   It happened unfortunately for us this evening that Charbono was at the helm of this Perogue [. . .] Charbono cannot swim and is perhaps the most timid waterman in the world; [. . .] Capt. C. and myself were both on shore at that moment, a circumstance which rarely happened; [. . .] we were [. . .] too far distant to be heard or to do more than remain spectators of her fate; in this perogue were embarked, our papers, Instruments, books medicine, a great part of our merchandize and in short almost every article indispensibly necessary to further the views, or insure the success of the enterprise [. . .].   surfice it to say, that the Perogue was under sail when a sudden squawl of wind struck her obliquely [. . .] and instantly upset the perogue and would have turned her completely topsaturva, had it not have been from the resistance made by the oarning against the water; [. . .] the perogue then wrighted but had filled within an inch of the gunwals; Charbono still crying to his god for mercy, had not yet recollected the rudder, nor could the repeated orders of the Bowsman, Cruzat, bring him to his recollection untill he threatend to shoot him instantly if he did not take hold of the rudder and do his duty [. . .] while the perogue lay on her side [. . .] I [. . .] involluntarily droped my gun, threw aside my shot pouch and was in the act of unbuttoning my coat, before I recollected the folly of the attempt I was about to make, which was to throw myself into the river and indevour to swim to the perogue; the perogue was three hundred yard distant the waves so high that a perogue could scarcely live in any situation, the water excessively cold, and the stream rappid; had I undertaken this project therefore, there was a hundred to one but what I should have paid the forfit of my life for the madness of my project, but this had the perogue been lost, I should have valued but little.— After having all matters arranged for the evening as well as the nature of circumstances would permit, we thought it a proper occasion to console ourselves and cheer the sperits of our men and accordingly took a drink of grog and gave each man a gill of sperits.

[Lewis]

Sunday May 26th 1805.

[. . .] In the after part of the day I also walked out and ascended the river hills which I found sufficiently fortiegueing. on arriving to the summit one of the highest points in the neighbourhood I thought myself well repaid for any labour; as from this point I beheld the Rocky Mountains for the first time, [. . .] these points of the Rocky Mountains were covered with snow and the sun shone on it in such manner as to give me the most plain and satisfactory view. while I viewed these mountains I felt a secret pleasure in finding myself so near the head of the heretofore conceived boundless Missouri; but when I reflected on the difficulties which this snowy barrier would most probably throw in my way to the Pacific, and the sufferings and hardships of myself and party in them, it in some measure counterballanced the joy I had felt in the first moments in which I gazed on them; but as I have always held it a crime to anticipate evils I will believe it a good comfortable road untill I am compelled to beleive differently.

[Lewis]

Friday May 31st 1805.

[. . .] The obstructions of rocky points and riffles still continue as yesterday; at those places the men are compelled to be in the water even to their armpits, and the water is yet very cold, and so frequent are those point that they are one fourth of their time in the water, added to this the banks and bluffs along which they are obliged to pass are so slippery and the mud so tenacious that they are unable to wear their mockersons, and in that situation draging the heavy burden of a canoe and walking occasionally for several hundred yards over the sharp fragments of rocks which tumble from the clifts and garish the borders of the river; in short their labour is incredibly painfull and great, yet those faithfull fellows bear it without a murmur. The toe rope of the white perogue, the only one indeed of hemp, and that on which we most depended, gave way today at a bad point, the perogue swung and but slightly touched a rock, yet was very near overseting; I fear her evil gennii will play so many pranks with her that she will go to the bottom some of those days.— Capt. C. walked on shore this morning but found it so excessively bad that he shortly returned. at 12 OCk. we came too for refreshment and gave the men a dram which they received with much cheerfullness, and well deserved.—

The hills and river Clifts which we passed today exhibit a most romantic appearance. [. . .] The water in the course of time in decending from those hills and plains on either side of the river has trickled down the soft sand clifts and worn it into a thousand grotesque figures, which with the help of a little immagination and an oblique view at a distance, are made to represent eligant ranges of lofty freestone buildings, having their parapets well stocked with statuary; collumns of various sculpture both grooved and plain, are also seen supporting long galleries in front of those buildings; in other places on a much nearer approach and with the help of less immagination we see the remains or ruins of eligant buildings; some collumns standing and almost entire with their pedestals and capitals; others retaining their pedestals but deprived by time or accident of their capitals, some lying prostrate an[d] broken [. . .] a number of the small martin which build their nests with clay in a globular form attatched to the wall within those nitches, and which were seen hovering about the tops of the collumns did not the less remind us of some of those large stone buildings in the U' States. As we passed on it seemed as if those scenes of visionary inchantment would never have an end; for here it is too that nature presents to the view of the traveler vast ranges of walls of tolerable workmanship, so perfect indeed are those walls that I should have thought that nature had attempted here to rival the human art of masonry had I not recollected that she had first began her work. [. . .] on these clifts I met with a species of pine which I had never seen, it differs from the pitchpine in the particular of it's leaf and cone, the first being vastly shorter, and the latter considerably longer and more pointed. I saw near those bluffs the most beautifull fox that I ever beheld, the colours appeared to me to be a fine orrange yellow, white and black, I endevoured to kill this anamal but it discovered me at a considerable distance, and finding that I could get no nearer, I fired on him as he ran, and missed him; he concealed himself under the rocks of the clift; it appeared to me to be about the size of the common red fox of the Atlantic states, or rather smaller than the large fox common to this country; convinced I am that it is a distinct species. The appearance of coal continu[e]s but in small quanities, but litt[l]e appearance of birnt hills or pumice stones the mineral salts have in some measure abated and no quarts. we saw a great number of the Bighorn some mule deer and a few buffaloe and Elk, no antelopes or common deer. Drewyer who was with me and myself killed two bighorned anamals; the sides of the Clifts where these anamals resort much to lodg, have the peculiar smell of the sheepfolds. the party killed in addition to our hunt 2 buffaloe and an Elk. the river today has been from 150 to 250 yds. wide but little timber today on the river.

[Lewis]

Thursday June 13th 1805

[. . .] about ninty or a hundred yards [. . .] next the [larboard] bluff is a smooth even sheet of water falling over a precipice of at least eighty feet, the remaining part of about 200 yards on my right formes the grandest sight I ever beheld,[11] [. . .] the irregular and somewhat projecting rocks below receives the water in it's passage down and brakes it into a perfect white foam which assumes a thousand forms in a moment sometimes flying up in jets of sparkling foam to the hight of fifteen or twenty feet and are scarcely formed before large roling bodies of the same beaten and foaming water is thrown over and conceals them. in short the rocks seem to be most happily fixed to present a sheet of the whitest beaten froth for 200 yards in length and about 80 feet perpendicular. the water [. . .] seems to reverberate and being met by the more impetuous courant they role and swell into half formed billows of great hight which rise and again disappear in an instant. [. . .] from the reflection of the sun on the spray or mist which arrises from these falls there is a beatifull rainbow produced which adds not a little to the beauty of this majestically grand senery. after wrighting this imperfect discription I again viewed the falls and was so much disgusted with the imperfect idea which it conveyed of the scene that I determined to draw my pen across it and begin agin, but then reflected that I could not perhaps succeed better than pening the first impressions of the mind; I wished for the pencil of Salvator Rosa[12] or the pen of Thompson,[13] that I might be enabled to give to the enlightened world some just idea of this truly magnifficent and sublimely grand object, which has from the commencement of time been concealed from the view of civilized man; but this was fruitless and vain. I most sincerely regreted that I had not brought a crimee obscura[14] with me by the assistance of which even I could have hoped to have done better but alas this was also out of my reach; I therefore with the assistance of my pen only indeavoured to trace some of the stronger features of this seen by the assistance of which and my recollection aided by some able pencil I hope still to give to the world some faint idea of an object which at this moment fills me with such pleasure and astonishment [. . .]

[After not encountering any Native Americans for quite some time, Lewis and Clark begin to search earnestly for the Shoshone Indians, a mountain tribe from whom they hope to purchase horses and hire a guide to direct them west through the mountains to the Columbia River, which they know drains into the Pacific. They need to traverse the mountains before early fall snows make overland travel impossible and stall them east of the Rockies for another winter. Such an occurrence could have been disastrous considering their dwindling supplies, forcing them to abandon their journey to the Pacific.]

[11]The Great Falls of the Missouri River near present-day Great Falls, Montana. The expedition was forced to portage eighteen miles around this series of falls and rapids, an ordeal that took them about a month.

[12]Salvator Rosa (1615–1673), Italian Baroque painter known for his romantic landscapes and battle scenes.

[13]James Thomson (1700–1748), eighteenth-century Scottish poet who dramatized nature.

[14]Camera obscura, an early photographic device that allowed an artist to trace a scene.

[Lewis]

Saturday July 27th 1805.

[. . .] we begin to feel considerable anxiety with respect to the Snake [Shoshone] Indians. if we do not find them or some other nation who have horses I fear the successfull issue of our voyage will be very doubtfull or at all events much more difficult in it's accomplishment. we are now several hundred miles within the bosom of this wild and mountainous country, where game may rationally be expected shortly to become scarce and subsistence precarious without any information with respect to the country not knowing how far these mountains continue, or where to direct our course to pass them to advantage or intercept a navigable branch of the Columbia, or even were we on such a one the probability is that we should not find any timber within these mountains large enough for canoes if we judge from the portion of them through which we have passed. however I still hope for the best, and intend taking a tramp myself in a few days to find these yellow gentlemen if possible. my two principal consolations are that from our present position it is impossible that the S. W. fork can head with the waters of any other river but the Columbia, and that if any Indians can subsist in the form of a nation in these mountains with the means they have of acquiring food we can also subsist.

[Lewis]

Sunday July 28th 1805.

Our present camp is precisely on the spot that the Snake [Shoshone] Indians were encamped at the time the Minnetares [Hidatsas] of the Knife R. first came in sight of them five years since. from hence they retreated about three miles up Jeffersons river and concealed themselves in the woods, the Minnetares [Hidatsas] pursued, attacked them, killed 4 men 4 women a number of boys, and made prisoners of all the females and four boys, *Sah-cah-gar-we-ah*[15] our Indian woman was one of the female prisoners taken at that time; tho' I cannot discover that she shews any immotion of sorrow in recollecting this events, or of joy in being again restored to her native country; if she has enough to eat and a few trinkets to wear I believe she would be perfectly content anywhere.—[16]

[15]The *r* in the third syllable of the Shoshone woman's name reflects Lewis's Virginia speech patterns and is not predominant in representations of her name throughout the journals.

[16]Contrast this characterization of Sacagawea with Lewis's representation of her meeting with her kinspeople on August 17, 1805.

[Lewis]

Sunday August 11th 1805.

I discovered an Indian on horse back about two miles distance coming down the plain toward us. with my glass I discovered from his dress that he was of a different nation from any that we had yet seen, and was satisfyed of his being a Sosone [Shoshone]; [. . .] I was overjoyed at the sight of this stranger and had no doubt of obtaining a friendly introduction to his nation provided I could get near enough to him to convince him of our being whitemen. I therefore proceeded towards him at my usual pace. when I had arrived within about a mile he made a halt which I did also and unloosing my blanket from my pack, I made him the signal of friendship known to the Indians of the Rocky mountains and those of the Missouri, which is by holding the mantle or robe in your hands at two corners and then throwing up in the air higher than the head bringing it to the earth as if in the act of spreading it, thus repeating three times. [. . .] this signal had not the desired effect, he still kept his position and seemed to view Drewyer and Shields [members of the corps] who were now coming in sight on either hand with an air of suspicions, I would willingly have made them halt but they were too far distant to hear me and I feared to make any signal to them least it should increase the suspicion in the mind of the Indian of our having some unfriendly design upon him. I therefore haistened to take out of my sack some beads a looking glass and a few trinketes which I had brought with me for this purpose and leaving my gun and pouch with McNeal [another member of the corps] advanced unarmed towards him. he remained in the same stedfast poisture untill I arrived in about 200 paces of him when he turn his horse about and began to move off slowly from me; I now called to him in as loud a voice as I could command repeating the word *tab-ba-bone,* which in their language signifyes *white man.* [. . .] when I arrived within about 150 paces I again repeated the word tab-ba-bone and held up the trinkits in my hands and striped up my shirt sleeve to give him an opportunity of seeing the colour of my skin and advanced leasure towards him but he did not remain untill I got nearer than about 100 paces when he suddonly turned his horse about, gave him the whip leaped the creek and disapeared in the willow brush in an instant and with him vanished all my hopes of obtaining horses for the present.

[Lewis]

Monday August 12th 1805

[. . .] the road took us to the most distant fountain of the waters of the mighty Missouri in search of which we have spent so many toilsome days and restless nights. thus far I had accomplished one of those great objects on which my mind has been unalterably fixed for many years, judge then of the pleasure I felt in allying my thirst with this pure and ice cold water [. . .] here I halted a few minutes and rested myself. two miles below McNeal [a member of the party] had exultingly stood with a foot on each side of this little rivulet and thanked his god that he had lived to bestride the mighty & heretofore deemed endless Missouri. after refreshing ourselves we proceeded on to the top of the dividing ridge from which I discovered immense ranges of high mountains still to the West of us with their tops partially covered with snow. I now descended the mountain about ¾ of a mile which I found much steeper than on the opposite side, to a handsome bold running Creek of cold Clear water. here I first tasted the water of the great Columbia river.

[Lewis and a few men, who had gone ahead of Clark and the main party, eventually make contact with the Shoshones and begin negotiations for horses, guides, and information, which they find difficult.]

[Lewis]

Friday August 16th 1805

[. . .] I slept but little as might be well expected, my mind dwelling on the state of the expedition which I have ever held in equal estimation with my own existence, and the fate of which appeared at this moment to depend in a great measure upon the caprice of a few savages who are ever as fickle as the wind. I had mentioned to the chief several times that we had with us a woman of his nation who had been taken prisoner by the Minnetares, and that by means of her I hoped to explain myself more fully than I could do by signs. some of the party had also told the Indians that we had a man with us who was black and had short curling hair, this had excited their curiossity very much. and they seemed quite as anxious to see this monster as they were the merchandize which we had to barter for their horses.

[Lewis]

Saturday August 17th 1805.

[. . .] Capt. Clark arrived with the Interpreter Charbono, and the Indian woman [Sacagawea], who proved to be a sister of the [Shoshone] Chief Cameahwait. the meeting of those people was really affecting, particularly between Sah cah-gar-we-ah and an Indian woman, who had been taken prisoner at the same time with her, and who had afterwards escaped from the Minnetares [Hidatsas] and rejoined her nation.

[After acquiring poor horses and valuable information from the Shoshones, who were suffering from want themselves, the corps enters the mountains and encounters members of the Flathead Nation, who have much better horses.]

[Ordway]

Thursday 5th Sept. 1805. a clear cool morning. the Standing water froze a little. the Indian dogs are so ravinous that they eat Several pair of the mens Moccasons. [. . .] our officers took down Some of their language found it verry troublesome Speaking to them as all they Say to them has to go through Six languages,[17] and hard to make them understand. these natives have the Strangest language of any we have ever yet Seen. they appear to us as though they had an Impedement in their Speech or brogue on their tongue. we think perhaps that they are the welch Indians,[18] &C. they are the likelyest and honestest we have seen and are very friendly to us. they Swaped to us Some of their good horses and took our worn out horses, and appeared to wish to help us as much as lay in their power. accommodated us with pack Saddles and chords by our giving them any Small article in return [towa]rds evening our hunters came in had kild 1 deer.

[In the rugged, wintry Rocky Mountains, members of the corps have a hard time finding enough to eat and are eventually reduced to eating their own horses.]

[Clark]

Wednesday [Sunday] *Septr. 15th 1805*

[. . .] From this mountain I could observe high rugged mountains in every direction as far as I could See. with the greatest exertion we Could only make 12 miles up the mountain and encamped on the top of the mountain near a Bank of old Snow about 3 feet deep lying on the Northern Side of the mountain and in Small banks on the top & leavel parts of the mountain, we melted the Snow to drink, and Cook our horse flesh to eat.

[Gass]

Thursday [September] *19th* [1805]. Having heard nothing from our hunters, we again supped upon some of our portable soup.[19] The men are becoming lean and debilitated, on account of the scarcity and poor quality of the provisions on which we subsist: our horses' feet are also becoming very sore. We have, however, some

[17] Actually five languages: Salishan (the language of the Flatheads), Shoshone, Hidatsa, French, and English.

[18] Referring to a legend that a party of Welshmen led by Prince Madoc had discovered America and settled west of the Mississippi centuries before Columbus entered the hemisphere.

[19] A powder or paste soup mix Lewis had purchased in Philadelphia, planning for such circumstances.

hopes of getting soon out of this horrible mountainous desert, as we have discovered the appearance of a valley or level part of the country about 40 miles ahead. When this discovery was made there was as much joy and rejoicing among the corps, as happens among passengers at sea, who have experienced a dangerous and protracted voyage, when they first discover land on the long looked for coast.

[Lewis]

Sunday September 22nd 1805

[. . .] the pleasure I now felt in having tryumphed over the rocky Mountains and decending once more to a level and fertile country where there was every rational hope of finding a comfortable subsistence for myself and party can be more readily conceived than expressed, nor was the flattering prospect of the final success of the expedition less pleasing.

[The party sells their horses, constructs boats, and purchases other watercraft from the Indians on the west side of the Rocky Mountains. They spend October descending the Columbia, portaging around difficult rapids and falls, and encountering many Native peoples on the river who tell them of the Pacific Ocean below.]

[Clark]

November 7th Thursday 1805

Great joy in camp we are in *View* of the *Ocian,*[20] this great Pacific Octean which we been So long anxious to See. and the roaring or noise made by the waves brakeing on the rockey Shores (as I Suppose) may be heard distinctly

[Gass]

Sunday [November] 16th. [1805] [. . .] We are now at the end of our voyage, which has been completely accomplished according to the intention of the expedition, the object of which was to discover a passage by the way of the Missouri and Columbia rivers to the Pacific ocean; notwithstanding the difficulties, privations and dangers, which we had to encounter, endure and surmount.

[By Christmas, the men had constructed their second, and final, winter camp near present-day Astoria, Oregon, away from the Pacific shore but near the Columbia estuary. Lewis

[20]The Columbia estuary, actually.

and Clark called the camp "Fort Clatsop," in reference to the Native Americans living nearby who had advised them in finding this location. Some debate had occurred among the members of the corps concerning the best place to build the camp. The captains consulted each person in the party, including York and Sacagawea, about where to build. They settled in for a miserable winter of rains. They hunted, traded with the Natives, made salt from ocean water, tanned and sewed leather for clothing, and readied their equipment for the journey home. The journalists recorded cultural information about coastal people.]

[Lewis]

Monday January 6th 1806.

Capt Clark set out after an early breakfast with the party in two canoes;[21] Charbono and his Indian woman [Sacagawea] were also of the party; the Indian woman was very importunate to be permited to go, and was therefore indulged; she observed that she had traveled a long way with us to see the great waters, and that now that monstrous fish was also to be seen, she thought it very hard she could not be permitted to see either (she had never yet been to the Ocean).

[Gass]

Friday [March] *21st.* [1806] [. . .] about 10 o'clock we were visited by some of the Clat- sop Indians. These, and the Chin-ook, Cath-la-mas, Cal-a-mex, and Chiltz nations, who inhabit the seacoast, all dress in the same manner. The men are wholly naked, except a small robe; the women have only the addition of the short petticoat. Their language also is nearly the same; and they all observe the same ceremony of depositing with the remains of the dead all their property, or placing it at their graves. I believe I saw as many as an hundred canoes at one burying-place of the Chin-ooks, on the north side of the Columbia, at its entrance into Hailey's Bay [. . .] These Indians on the coast have no horses, and very little property of any kind, except their canoes. The women are much inclined to venery, and like those on the Missouri are sold to prostitution at an easy rate. An old Chin-ook squaw frequently visited our quarters, with nine girls which she kept as prostitutes. To the honour of the Flatheads, who live on the west side of the Rocky Mountains, and extend some distance down the Columbia, we must mention them as an exception; as they do not exhibit those loose feelings of carnal desire, nor appear addicted to the common customs of prostitution: and they are the only nation on the whole route where any thing like chastity is regarded.

[21] To see a whale that had washed up several miles down the shore.

[Lewis]

Monday March 17th 1806.

[. . .] this morning we gave Delashelwilt[22] a certificate of his good deportment &c. and also a list of our names, after which we dispatched him to his village with his female band. These lists of our names we have given to several of the natives and also pasted up a copy in our room [at Fort Clatsop]. the object of these lists we stated in the preamble of the same as follows "The object of this list is, that through the medium of some civilized person who may see the same, it may be made known to the informed world, that the party consisting of the persons whoes names are hereunto annexed, and who were sent out by the government of the U' States in May 1804 to explore the interior of the Continent of North America, did penetrate the same by way of the Missouri and Columbia Rivers, to the discharge of the latter into the Pacific Ocean, where they arrive on the 14th November 1805, and from whence they departed the [*blank*] day of March 1806 on their return to the United States by the same rout they had come out."— on the back of some of these lists we added a sketch of the connection of the upper branches of the Missouri with those of the Columbia, particularly of it's main S. E. branch, on which we also delineated the track we had come and that we meant to pursue on our return where the same happened to very.

[Anxious to leave behind the monotony and dreariness of their time on the Pacific Coast, the Corps of Discovery begins its homeward journey on March 23, 1806.]

[Lewis]

Sunday April 6th 1806.

[. . .] Capt C. entered one of the appartments of the house and offered several articles to the natives in exchange for wappetoe[23] they appeared to be in an ill humour and positively refused to let him have any. Capt. C. sat himself down near the fire and having a part of a portfire match[24] in his pocket cut off a small peice of it and threw it in the fire; at the same time he took out his pocket compass and by means of a magnet which he had in the top of his inkstand he turned the needle of the compass about very briskly; the match took fire and burned vehemently; the indians astonished and allarmed at these exhibitions, ran and brought several parcels of wappetoe and laid at his feet and begged that he would put out the bad fire; to this he consented; [. . .] they were now much more complaisant [. . .]. during the whole of this farcical scene an old man who was setting by continued to speak

[22]A local Native American leader.

[23]A starchy tuber used as food by Native peoples.

[24]A slow-burning fuse.

with great vehemence apparently imploring his god for protection. Capt. C. gave them an adequate compensation for their roots and having lighted his pipe smoaked with the men.

[During their journey back up the Columbia River, members of the corps consistently encounter Native groups with whom they have contentious relations regarding personal property. Lewis and Clark begin trading for horses, preparing for their second traverse of the Rocky Mountains. Horse thievery becomes a particularly troubling issue.]

[Lewis]

Monday April 21st 1806.

[. . .] I sent several men in search of the horse with orders to return at 10 A. M. with or without the horse being determined to remain no longer with these villains. they stole another tomahawk from us this morning I searched many of them but could not find it. I ordered all the spare poles, paddles and the ballance of our canoe put on the fire as the morning was cold and also that not a particle should be left for the benefit of the indians. I detected a fellow in stealing an iron socket of a canoe pole and gave him several severe blows and made the men kick him out of camp. I now informed the indians that I would shoot the first of them that attempted to steal an article from us. that we were not affraid to fight them, that I had it in my power at that moment to kill them all and set fire to their houses, but it was not my wish to treat them with severity provided they would let my property alone. that I would take their horses if I could [not] find out the persons who had stolen the tommahawks, but that I had rather loose the property altogether than take the horse of an innocent person. the chiefs were present hung their heads and said nothing.

[Lewis]

Monday May 5th 1806.

[. . .] while at dinner an indian fellow verry impertinently threw a poor half starved puppy nearly into my plait by way of derision for our eating dogs[25] and laughed very heartily at his own impertinence; I was so provoked at his insolence that I caught the puppy and threw it with great violence at him and struck him in the breast and face, siezed my tomahawk and shewed him by signs if he repeated his

[25]The corps did not enjoy dried salmon, the staple foodstuff of the Native peoples they traveled among, attributing intestinal distress to its consumption. As they traveled up the Columbia, they subsisted on dog meat. Lewis learned to appreciate it, while Clark did not.

insolence I would tommahawk him, their fellow withdrew apparently much mortifyed and I continued my repast *on dog* without further molestation.

[Lewis]

Saturday May 17th 1806.

I am pleased at finding the river rise so rapidly, it no doubt is attributeable to the melting snows of the mountains; that icy barier which seperates me from my friends and Country, from all which makes life esteemable.— patience, patience—

[Finally, the Corps of Discovery begins to wend its way eastward through the Rocky Mountains.]

[Lewis]

Friday June 27th 1806.

[. . .] we had an extensive view of these stupendous mountains principally covered with snow like that on which we stood; we were entirely surrounded by those mountains from which to one unacquainted with them it would have seemed impossible ever to have escaped; in short without the assistance of our [Native] guides I doubt much whether we who had once passed them could find our way to Travellers rest[26] in their present situation for the marked trees on which we had placed considerable reliance are much fewer and more difficult to find than we had apprehended. these fellows [Native guides] are most admireable pilots; we find the road wherever the snow has disappeared though it be only for a few hundred paces. after smoking the pipe and contemplating this scene sufficient to have damp the sperits of any except such hardy travellers as we have become, we continued our march

[Near present-day Missoula, Montana, Lewis and Clark separate, Lewis taking a small number of men with him through the mountains to explore the Marias River drainage while Clark proceeds with the rest of the party to the Three Forks of the Missouri. Clark's group then splits, some men constructing canoes and descending the Missouri to the Great Falls where they meet up with Lewis while Clark and the remainder of the party explore the Yellowstone River. Hoping to meet new Native American nations, Clark prepared the following speech.]

[26]A campsite near present-day Missoula, Montana, that the Corps of Discovery had used on their trip west. They had cached supplies there.

[Clark]

Children. The Great Spirit has given a fair and bright day for us to meet together in his View that he may inspect us in this all we say and do.

Children I take you all by the hand as the children of your Great father the President of the U. States of America who is the great chief of all the white people towards the riseing sun.

Children This Great Chief who is Benevolent, just, wise & bountifull has sent me and one other of his chiefs (who is at this time in the country of the Blackfoot Indians) to all his red children on the Missourei and its waters quite to the great lake of the West where the land ends and the sun sets on the face of the great water, to know their wants and inform him of them on our return.

Children We have been to the great lake of the west and are now on our return to my country. I have seen all my red children quite to that great lake and talked with them, and taken them by the hand in the name of their great father the great Chief of all the white people.

Children We did not see the [*blank*] or the nations to the North. I have [come] across over high mountains and bad road to this river to see the [*blank*]

[Nation] I have come down the river from the foot of the great snowey mountain to see you, and have looked in every derection for you, without seeing you untill now

Children I heard from some of your people [*blank*] nights past by my horses who complained to me of your people haveing taken 4 [24] of their cummerads.

Children The object of my comeing to see you is not to do you injurey but to do you good the Great Chief of all the white people who has more goods at his command than could be piled up in the circle of your camp, wishing that all his red children should be happy has sent me here to know your wants that he may supply them.

Children Your great father the Chief of the white people intends to build a house and fill it with such things as you may want and exchange with you for your skins & furs at a very low price. & has derected me [to] enquire of you, at what place would be most convenient for to build this house. and what articles you are in want of that he might send them imediately on my return

Children The people in my country is like the grass in your plains noumerous they are also rich and bountifull. and love their red brethren who inhabit the waters of the Missoure

Children I have been out from my country two winters, I am pore naked and [have] nothing to keep off the rain. when I set out from my country I had a plenty but have given it all to my red children whome I have seen on my way to the Great Lake of the West. and have now nothing.

Children Your Great father will be very sorry to here of the [*blank*] stealing the horses of his Chiefs wariors whome he sent out to do good to his red children on the waters of Missoure.

[*two lines illegible*] their ears to his good counsels he will shut them and not let any goods & guns be brought to the red people. but to those who open their Ears to his counsels he will send every thing they want into their country. and build a house where they may come to and be supplyed whenever they wish.

Children Your Great father the Chief of all the white people has derected me to inform his red children to be at peace with each other, and the white people who may come into your country under the protection of the Flag of your great father which you. those people who may visit you under the protection of that flag are good people and will do you no harm

Children Your great father has derected me to tell you not to suffer your young and thoughtless men to take the horses or property of your neighbours or the white people, but to trade with them fairly and honestly, as those of his red children below.

Children The red children of your great father who live near him and have opened their ears to his counsels are rich and hapy have plenty of horses cows & Hogs fowls bread &c. &c. live in good houses, and sleep sound. and all those of his red children who inhabit the waters of the Missouri who open their ears to what I say and follow the counsels of their great father the President of the United States, will in a few years be as hapy as those mentioned &c.

Children It is the wish of your Great father the Chief of all the white people that some 2 of the principal Chiefs of this [*blank*] Nation should Visit him at his great city and receive from his own mouth. his good counsels, and from his own hands his abundant gifts, Those of his red children who visit him do not return with empty hands, he send them to their nation loaded with presents

Children If any one two or 3 of your great chiefs wishes to visit your great father and will go with me, he will send you back next Summer loaded with presents and some goods for the nation. You will then see with your own eyes and here with your own years what the white people can do for you. they do not speak with two tongues nor promis what they can't perform

Children Consult together and give me an answer as soon as possible your great father is anxious to hear from (& see his red children who wish to visit him) I cannot stay but must proceed on & inform him &c.

[Lewis]

July 27th 1806 Sunday.

[. . .] This morning at day light the indians got up and crowded around the fire, J. Fields [sic] who was on post had carelessly laid his gun down behind him near where his brother [Reubin Field] was sleeping, one of the indians the fellow to whom I had given the medal[27] last evening slipped behind him and took his gun

[27] A symbolic gift from the United States given to many Native groups on the expedition.

and that of his brothers unperceived by him, at the same instant two others advanced and seized the guns of Drewyer and myself, J. Fields seeing this turned about to look for his gun and saw the fellow just running off with her and his brothers he called to his brother who instantly jumped up and pursued the indian with him whom they overtook at the distance of 50 or 60 paces from the camp seized their guns and wrested them from him and R Fields as he seized his gun stabbed the indian to the heart with his knife the fellow ran about 15 steps and fell dead; [. . .] having recovered their guns they ran back instantly to the camp; Drewyer who was awake saw the indian take hold of his gun and instantly jumped up and seized her and wrested her from him but the indian still retained his pouch, his jumping up and crying damn you let go my gun awakened me I jumped up and asked what was the matter which I quickly learned when I saw drewyer in a scuffle with the indian for his gun. I reached to seize my gun but found her gone, I then drew a pistol from my holster and turning myself about saw the indian making off with my gun I ran at him with my pistol and bid him lay down my gun which he was in the act of doing when the Fieldses returned and drew up their guns to shoot him which I forbid as he did not appear to be about to make any resistance or commit any offensive act, he dropped the gun and walked slowly off, I picked her up instantly, Drewyer having about this time recovered his gun and pouch asked me if he might not kill the fellow which I also forbid as the indian did not appear to wish to kill us, as soon as they found us all in possession of our arms they ran and indeavored to drive off all the horses I now hollowed to the men and told them to fire on them if they attempted to drive off our horses, they accordingly pursued the main party who were driving the horses up the river and I pursued the man who had taken my gun who with another was driving off a part of the horses which were to the left of the camp, I pursued them so closely that they could not take twelve of their own horses but continued to drive one of mine with some others; at the distance of three hundred paces they entered one of those steep nitches in the bluff with the horses before them being nearly out of breath I could pursue no further, I called to them as I had done several times before that I would shoot them if they did not give me my horse and raised my gun, one of them jumped behind a rock and spoke to the other who turned around and stopped at the distance of 30 steps from me and I shot him through the belly, he fell to his knees and on his right elbow from which position he partly raised himself up and fired at me, and turning himself about crawled in behind a rock which was a few feet from him. he overshot me, being bareheaded I felt the wind of his bullet very distinctly. not having my shotpouch I could not reload my peice and as there were two of them behind good shelters from me I did not think it prudent to rush on them with my pistol which had I discharged I had not the means of reloading untill I reached camp; I therefore returned leasurely towards camp, [. . .]. we reached the camp and began to catch the horses and saddle them and put on the packs. [. . .] we had caught and saddled the horses and began to arrange the packs when the Fieldses returned with four of our horses; we left one of our horses and took four of the best of those of the indian's; while the men were preparing the horses I put four sheilds and two bows and quivers of arrows which had been left on the fire, with sundry other articles; they left all their baggage at our mercy.[28] they had but 2 guns and one of them they left the others were armed with bows and arrows and eyedaggs [daggers]. the gun we took with us. I also retook the flag[29] but left the medal about the neck of the dead man that they might be informed who we were.[30]

[Concerned that the powerful Blackfeet Indians would exact revenge for the murder Joseph Field committed, Lewis and his men rushed to join Clark and the other members of the corps near the mouth of the Yellowstone River. Moving quickly down the Missouri River, the corps returned to their 1804–1805 winter camp at Fort Mandan, made contact with some traders, and set their sights firmly on St. Louis.]

[Clark]

Wednesday 17th September 1806

[. . .] at 11 A. M. we met a Captain McClellin late a Capt. of Artillery of the U States Army ascending [the Missouri River] in a large boat. this gentleman an acquaintance of my friend Capt. Lewis was Somewhat astonished to See us return and appeared rejoiced to meet us. we found him a man of information and from whom we received a partial account of the political State of our Country, we were makeing enquires and exchangeing answers &c. untill near mid night. this Gentleman informed us that we had been long Since given out by the people of the U S Generaly and almost forgotton, the President of the U. States had yet hopes of us; we received some civilities of Capt. McClellin, he gave us Some Biscuits, Chocolate Sugar & whiskey, for which our party were in want and for which we made a return of a barrel of corn & much obliges to him.

[28]George Bird Grinnell (1849–1938), an anthropologist who worked with the Blackfeet, interviewed Wolf Calf (ca. 1793–1895), one of the young men involved in this violent encounter with Lewis and his men. Grinnell concludes that the Blackfeet were frightened by their skirmish with the party and exited the scene as quickly as Lewis and his men did. The impetus for weapon thievery may have had more to do with Native cultural statements of power than with covetousness.

[29]The United States flag, which Lewis had earlier given to this group of Blackfeet.

[30]The preceding acts of violence are the only known moments of bloodshed during the expedition, despite tensions with several other Native groups, particularly the Sioux. Only one other known death occurred in connection with the expedition, that of Sergeant Charles Floyd, a member of the corps, probably of peritonitis caused by a ruptured appendix in the early months of the expedition. Lewis suffered a gunshot wound after this encounter with the Blackfeet, but it was at the hand of one of the party who mistook him for an elk.

[Clark]

Friday 19th of September 1806

Set out this morning a little after day & proceeded on very well the men ply their oars & we descended with great velocity, only Came to once for the purpose of gathering papaws [a fruit], our anxiety as also the wish of the party to proceed on as expeditiously as possible to [get to] the Illinois induce us to continue on without halting to hunt. we Calculate on arriving at the first Settlements on to-morrow evening which is 140 miles, an object of our party is to divide the distance into two days, this day to the Osarge River, and tomorrow to the Charriton a Small french Village—

the party being extreemly anxious to get down ply their oars very well, we Saw Some cows on the bank which was a joyfull Sight to the party and Caused a Shout to be raised for joy we Came in Sight of the little french Village called Charriton. the men raised a Shout and Sprung upon their oars and we soon landed opposit to the Village. our party requested to be permited to fire off their Guns which was alowed & they discharged 3 rounds with a hearty Cheer, which was returned from five tradeing boats which lay opposit the village. [. . .] we purchased of a Citizen two gallons of Whiskey for our party for which we were obliged to give Eight dollars in Cash, an imposition on the part of the Citizen. every person, both French and americans Seem to express great pleasure at our return, and acknowledged them selves much astonished in Seeing us return. they informed us that we were Supposed to have been lost long Since, and were entirely given out by every person &c.

[Ordway]

Tuesday 23rd Sept. 1806. a wet disagreeable morning. we Set out after breakfast and proceeded. on Soon arrived at the Mouth of the Missouri entered the Mississippi River and landed at River deboise where we wintered in 1804. [. . .] 12 oClock we arrived in Site of St. Louis fired three Rounds as we approached the Town and landed opposite the center of the Town, the people gathred on the Shore and Huzzared three cheers. we unloaded the canoes and carried the baggage all up to a Store house in Town. drew out the canoes then the party all considerable much rejoiced that we have the Expedition Completed and now we look for boarding in Town and wait for our Settlement and then we intend to return to our native homes to See our parents once more as we have been So long from them.— finis.

Contested Visions, American Voices

Half-humorously but with the seriousness of one socially and legally disempowered, Abigail Adams added a "by the way" in her letter of March 31, 1776, to her husband John Adams, who was in Philadelphia attending emergency sessions of the Continental Congress. "[B]y the way," she wrote, "in the new Code of Laws which I suppose it will be necessary for you to make I desire you would Remember the Ladies, and be more generous and favourable to them than your ancestors." Her plea for equal rights and equal justice under the law went unheeded. John Adams remarked—in a tone that he probably considered jocular—in his return letter of April 14, 1776, "As to your extraordinary Code of Laws, I cannot but laugh. We have been told that our Struggle has loosened the bands of Government every where. That Children and Apprentices were disobedient—that schools and Colledges were grown turbulent—that Indians slighted their Guardians and Negroes grew insolent to their Masters. But your Letter was the first Intimation that another Tribe more numerous and powerfull than all the rest were grown discontented."

This remarkable and well-known exchange between two remarkable people is by no means the only spoken or written evidence about the extent to which people in disempowered social and legal circumstances—particularly women, African Americans, and Native Americans in Anglo-America—spoke about and openly confronted the boundaries set for them by the elite group of men whose visions of the "just" and "good" shaped post-revolutionary society. Ironically, Enlightenment thinking was no guarantee of enlightened thought or action. The epic poem *The Sugar-Cane* (1764), by the English doctor, naturalist, and poet James Grainger, who spent time on sugar plantations in the West Indies, suggests the remarkably complicated stance that an "enlightened" man might take toward the people who made his living and leisure possible. Grainger simultaneously idealized slavery and mythicized the "negroe" body by representing them in heroic couplets and Virgilian pastoral; the objects of his poetic and scientific scrutiny rarely speak. Other poets in this period, like Philip Freneau, Timothy Dwight, and Joel Barlow, cast the American situation and the American future in epic, heroic terms. Men in the Continental Congress and the Constitutional Convention debated, orated, and published their concerns about equality, laws, rights, and obligations. By contrast, members of disempowered groups struggled to be heard on the present identity and future progress of the nation. Abigail Adams, it should be noted, wrote a private letter to her husband and made her suggestion archly, almost as an aside. What emerges from this varied collection of writings is the sense that for both dominant and subordinate groups, issues of "race," identity, and "nation" were hotly contested.

When Prince Hall, speaking of the "chequered world we live in," called upon his fellow Masons of his African Lodge on June 24, 1797, for forbearance and patience under their trials, he insisted nonetheless that they should "Worship God." The Mohegan Samson Occom wrote in his autobiography that he "found Serenity and Pleasure of Soul, in Serving God," yet he concluded his comments in anguish—"I speak like a fool, but I am Constrained"—referring to the difference whites made "between me and other missionaries" when paying them and giving credit for missionary work. African American Lemuel Haynes, having learned from an early age the Calvinist teachings of the whites in his locale, followed their evangelical faith. But he also contested the congressional assertion "We hold these truths to be self-evident, that all men are created Equal," by pointing to what he considered the illegality of the slave trade and the hypocrisy of the white men who quarreled with Britain's oppression while retaining blacks in bondage. Not many voices spoke out against the dominant group, but those who did represent lines of argument made by feminists, evangelicals, African Americans, and Native Americans that have, over the years, continued a critique of the established culture. These speakers and writers, self-conscious about their own "low" status, found useful ways—through the vehicles of logical argumentation, legal contest, and an evangelical religion that provided many women and blacks especially a strong sense of identity and community—to call into question the constructions of "race" and "nation" that were being established as a founding ideology while the colonies were becoming the so-called united states.

Given the population they represented, the number of women, African Americans, and Native Americans who participated in print culture was, though growing, still very small at the end of the eighteenth and beginning of the nineteenth centuries. Few texts from the era reveal what life was like for these groups from what can be called the "inside" viewpoint. Early slave narratives like the ones by Briton Hammon and Olaudah Equiano, the brief autobiography by Samson Occom and the travel narrative by Hendrick Aupaumut, even the poetry and fictionalized captivity narrative by Ann Eliza Bleecker, provide this insight. They also reveal how difficult it was for an unconstrained minority voice to emerge. Very few blacks and Native Americans could read and write English, and those who could appeared at the discretion of white patrons who "owned" them or trained them. Women, as Judith Sargent Murray discloses in her eloquent appeals for equal educational opportunity, were considered intellectually inferior to men and fit only for domestic tasks. Even women of the upper classes, like Bleecker, were prevented by conservative husbands and the general culture from writing seriously. Most of Bleecker's works were presented as spontaneous effusion or letters to intimates and friends. Murray, an extraordinarily prolific writer and progressive thinker, was the exception, an extremely popular writer who managed to live by her pen.

Members of disempowered groups who did write adopted, consciously or unconsciously, a variety of techniques that enabled their works to be published. For example, Jupiter Hammon, Phillis Wheatley, and Samson Occom—all of whom appear to have been truly pious—found religious narratives, poems, and sermons to be acceptable to white readers. Yet even these writers were forced into accepting the "lower" status of their race. Wheatley's constant reference to herself as an "Ethiop" and Occom's allusions to the Indian Moses Paul as a "despised Creature" served to reinforce the views of dominant whites. On the other hand, Wheatley managed to use her position as a Christianized "Ethiop" to speak to the Cambridge students about a Christianity that offered equality to all who embraced belief. These writers' forthright declarations of religious faith that appeared to entail an admission of the superiority of white Christian culture ironically provided them with the confidence to call white society to task for not living up to its own ideals. The problem such writers faced was finding the means to assert the worthiness of people of color without flatly contradicting the notions, almost universally held among whites, that such people were inferior and thus their writings were not worth reading.

This is not to suggest that print culture of the era was solely concerned with issues of race and identity. The American Revolution produced significant changes in print culture in the colonies, not only in the increase in printing presses the colonists supported, but in the readership and types of works printed. Featuring fiction, advice columns, literary criticism, and poems, literary magazines by the dozens saw print for the first time during the last decade and a half of the eighteenth century. Some folded quickly; others began to flourish as printers and authors searched for the formula that would attract an ever-growing readership. To a surprising extent these magazines were supported by non-elite groups—artisans, servants, and other laborers—as much as by members of the elite classes. Late-eighteenth-century Americans, representatives of a new and nominally democratic republic, were in the midst of a change in literary culture, from one of literary patronage to one of the literary marketplace.

For those who sought a livelihood by the pen, the change was both positive and negative. A writer might no longer have to seek a literary patron for financial support, both for personal costs and for the costs of printing the works dedicated to the patron. The means of literary production—the author's livelihood and press costs—were no longer solely in the hands of the elite class. Thus, an author could more freely express his or her views to the reading public. Yet the author was, in the absence of the system of patronage, forced continually to meet the pleasure of a diverse reading public. No longer did authors seek the goodwill of one or two people. Instead, they sought the goodwill of all "good, courteous readers" (as the dedication formula often went) who would determine the success or failure of their literary ventures. To enter the republic of letters, authors had to accept the right of choice expected by an increasing, financially mobile readership. The marketplace would determine the literary text. And the marketplace itself was subject to change as the political and economic climate shifted.

Most writers, men and women, seem to have promoted the values held by government leaders. Their writings, they often openly insisted, reflected the conception that an educated citizenry, free of the European vices of luxury and corruption, would seek to read fine literature, thus improving its general level of taste, manners, and mores. The last quality was key: most writers of imaginative literature attempted to convince readers that their works would assist in moral improvement. They used several means to accomplish this end, one of the most popular being the insistence upon showing Europeanized depravity in order to warn others—especially young women—away from European vice.

This formula, employed successfully by Royall Tyler, Hannah Foster, and Susanna Rowson, was an American adaptation of that used in English fiction. The insistence that reading fiction could inculcate virtuous action and a "high" moral sense complemented the neoclassical aesthetic, a pragmatic theory of art established by poets earlier in the century. Where previous generations of Puritans descried reading fiction and forbade the performance of plays, poets and writers of this era asserted that their works could help to reform the manners and morals of post-Revolution readers, just as the heightened rhetoric of Revolution-era writers helped to bring about that enormous social and political upheaval. Readers and audiences, they insisted, could learn about virtues and "American" values by watching characters struggle to attain—or retain—their own. Even the failures, like Rowson's Charlotte Temple and Foster's Eliza Wharton, taught the nation an important lesson about the vulnerability of the young and unguided to Europeanized influences and the seductions of unrestrained freedom. Furthermore, the successes, like Tyler's representative American male, Colonel Manly, and his female counterpart, Maria van Rough, who triumph over foppish, Europeanized villains like Billy Dimple, lent a nationalist flavor to these didactic tales.

Although some complained about the utilitarian standards for post-Revolution literature, wondering how poetry or the life of the imagination could flourish in such "chilly climes," writers in America such as Charles Brockden Brown, who did not adopt this formula, did not succeed. Brown became interested in the European theoretical inquiry about human psychology and the unconscious that emerged as followers of John Locke began to develop their own theories about human nature. These theorists argued that artists should seek to instruct the moral sense or faculty that existed in each person. By the end of the eighteenth century, this theory was transformed into an argument in behalf of exploring the interior rather than "correcting" the exterior of the human being. English and European writers were taking up the cause of sentiment, creating works that would excite the passions and emotions of their readers. For some writers, the exploration of human sensibility led to gothicism, an aesthetic movement that favored the natural and primitive, the wild and uncontrolled. It was this newer tradition that intrigued Charles Brockden Brown, who never, while he lived, found a readership in the United States. Like many later authors, Brown would not submit to the notion that art should always attempt to instruct the populace. He would not acquiesce to a fiction conditioned by the marketplace. For Brown, identity was not a national issue but a personal one.

Jupiter Hammon 1711–1806?

With the important exception of Lucy Terry, whose "Bars Fight" (included in this anthology) seems to have been well known, Jupiter Hammon was probably the first known, published black American versifier. His *Evening Thought: Salvation by Christ, With Penetential Cries,* a series of twenty-two quatrains, appeared as a broadside in 1760.

Hammon was born a slave on the Manor House estate of Henry Lloyd at Lloyd's Neck (or Queen's Village) on Long Island, New York, where he and other slave children were offered a rudimentary education at a school built on the premises. Biographical facts about him are scarce, but it seems clear that at an early age Hammon became religiously oriented and may have done some Christian exhorting to whatever black and white audiences he could gather. When he was twenty-two years old, he purchased a Bible from his master for seven shillings and sixpence. All of his known writings in prose and verse are exclusively pietist.

When Henry Lloyd died in 1763, Hammon became the property of Joseph Lloyd, a patriot who was obliged to flee encircling British troops and race with his family and slaves to Stamford and later Hartford, Connecticut. There Hammon published three more verses, two of them appended to prose sermonizings. At Hartford, too, he published "An Essay on Ten Virgins," advertised in *The Connecticut Courant* for December 14, 1779; as no text has yet been found, it is not known if this piece is prose or verse. Composed originally at "Queen's Village, 24th. Sept. 1786," while he was a slave to John Lloyd, Junior, Hammon's prose *Address to the Negroe: In the State of New-York* was printed in 1787 in New York and reprinted the same year in Philadelphia and again in 1806 in New York. He is also thought to have written a set of verses that celebrated the 1782 visit of Prince William Henry (King William IV of England, 1830–1837) to the Lloyd Manor on Long Island. These verses are not known to exist today in manuscript.

Hammon's sermons, written in the revolutionary and post-revolutionary eras, retain an acute consciousness of the gathering political significance of blacks in the period. He mentions the deaths of blacks in the War for Independence, draws upon the jeremiad in order to call for a virtuous black nation within the American nation, and speaks of petitions for freedom on the part of black slaves. Despite the seemingly acquiescent tone of much of his writing, his sermons mount a firm appeal for black moral and social autonomy.

On every single one of Hammon's nine published pieces of prose and verse, acknowledgment—hardly incidental—is made of his being a servant to three generations of the Lloyd family. Indeed, on several of his pieces it is noted that his verse or his prose was printed "with the assistance of his friends," presumably white friends. Thus receiving the approbation of whites and repeatedly urging a resigned black reconciliation of slavery with unthreatening Christianity, it is not at all surprising that Hammon was permitted to publish as much as he did.

Our sense that Hammon's sermons, directed primarily toward blacks, are overheard and even managed by white patrons indicates an important problem in early African American writing. Most writing by blacks in the revolutionary period was published under headnotes that indicated white sanction. Within this context, the reader must decide carefully how to weigh the frequent appeals for liberty and freedom that appear even in such a writer as Hammon. The complex weighing of meanings that such terms assume in the revolutionary rhetoric of white political writers becomes even more complicated in the discourse of blacks.

William H. Robinson
Rhode Island College

Philip M. Richards
Colgate University

PRIMARY WORKS

"An Evening Thought" (1760); "An Address to Miss Phillis Wheatley" (1778); Stanley Ransom, Jr., ed., *America's First Negro Poet: The Complete Works of Jupiter Hammon,* 1970.

An Evening Thought: Salvation by Christ, with Penitential Cries

[Composed by Jupiter Hammon, a Negro belonging to Mr. Lloyd of Queen's Village, on Long Island, the 25th of December, 1760.[1]]

Salvation comes by Jesus Christ alone,
The only Son of God;
Redemption now to every one,
That love his holy Word.
Dear Jesus we would fly to Thee,
And leave off every Sin,
Thy tender Mercy well agree;
Salvation from our King.
Salvation comes now from the Lord,
Our victorious King;
His holy Name be well ador'd,
Salvation surely bring.
Dear Jesus give thy Spirit now,
Thy Grace to every Nation,
That han't the Lord to whom we bow,
The Author of Salvation.
Dear Jesus unto Thee we cry,
Give us thy Preparation;
Turn not away thy tender Eye;
We seek thy true Salvation.
Salvation comes from God we know,
The true and only One;
It's well agreed and certain true,
He gave his only Son.
Lord hear our penetential Cry:
Salvation from above;
It is the Lord that doth supply,
With his Redeeming Love,
Dear Jesus by thy precious Blood,
The World Redemption have:
Salvation comes now from the Lord,
He being thy captive Slave.
Dear Jesus let the Nations cry,
And all the People say,
Salvation comes from Christ on high,

[1]This broadside is in the New York Historical Society. There are extant several mistakenly variant printings of this broadside, which appears, in facsimile, in Sidney Kaplan's *The Black Presence in the Era of the American Revolution 1770–1800,* 1973: p. 172.

Haste on Tribunal Day.
We cry as Sinners to the Lord,
Salvation to obtain;
It is firmly fixt his holy Word,
Ye shall not cry in vain.
Dear Jesus unto Thee we cry,
And make our Lamentation:
O let our Prayers ascend on high;
We felt thy Salvation.
Lord turn our dark benighted Souls;
Give us a true Motion,
And let the Hearts of all the World,
Make Christ their Salvation.
Ten Thousand Angels cry to Thee,
Yea louder than the Ocean.
Thou are the Lord, we plainly see;
Thou art the true Salvation.
Now is the Day, excepted Time;
The Day of Salvation;
Increase your Faith, do not repine:
Awake ye every Nation.
Lord unto whom now shall we go,
Or seek a safe Abode;
Thou hast the Word Salvation too
The only Son of God.
Ho! every one that hunger hath,
Or pineth after me,
Salvation be thy leading Staff,
To set the Sinner free.
Dear Jesus unto Thee we fly;
Depart, depart from Sin,
Salvation doth at length supply,
The Glory of our King.
Come ye Blessed of the Lord,
Salvation gently given;
O turn your Hearts, accept the Word,
Your Souls are fit for Heaven.
Dear Jesus we now turn to Thee,
Salvation to obtain;
Our Hearts and Souls do meet again,
To magnify thy Name.
Come holy Spirit, Heavenly Dove,
The Object of our Care;
Salvation doth increase our Love;
Our Hearts hath felt thy fear.
Now Glory be to God on High,
Salvation high and low;

And thus the Soul on Christ rely,
  To Heaven surely go.
Come Blessed Jesus, Heavenly Dove,
  Accept Repentance here;
Salvation give, with tender Love;
  Let us with Angels share.

1760

An Address to Miss Phillis Wheatly *[sic]*, Ethiopian Poetess, in Boston, who came from Africa at eight years of age, and soon became acquainted with the gospel of Jesus Christ.

Miss Wheatly; pray give me leave to express as follows:

1

O Come you pious youth: adore Eccles. xil. 1.
  The wisdom of thy God,
In bringing thee from distant shore,
  To learn his holy word.

2

Thou mightst been left behind, Psal. cxxxvi. 1,2,3.
  Amidst a dark abode;
God's tender mercy still combin'd,
  Thou hast the holy word.

3

Fair wisdom's ways are paths of peace, Psal. i 1,2,3.
  And they that walk therein, Prov. iii. 7.
Shall reap the joys that never cease,
  And Christ shall be their king.

4

God's tender mercy brought thee here, Psal. ciii. 1,2,3,4.
  Tost o'er the raging main;
In Christian faith thou hast a share,
  Worth all the gold of Spain.

5

While thousands tossed by the sea, Death.
  And others settled down,

God's tender mercy set thee free,
 From dangers still unknown.

6

That thou a pattern still might be, 2 Cor. v. 10.
 To youth of Boston town,
The blessed Jesus set thee free,
 From every sinful wound.

7

The blessed Jesus, who came down, Rom. v. 21.
 Unvail'd his sacred face,
To cleanse the soul of every wound,
 And give repenting grace.

8

That we poor sinners may obtain Psal. xxxiv. 6,7,8.
 The pardon of our sin;
Dear blessed Jesus now constrain,
 And bring us flocking in.

9

Come you, Phillis, now aspire, Mat. vii. 7,8.
 And seek the living God,
So step by step thou mayst go higher,
 Till perfect in the word.

10

While thousands mov'd to distant shore, Psal. 1xxxiv. 1.
 And others left behind,
The blessed Jesus still adore,
 Implant this in thy mind.

11

Thou hast left the heathen shore, Psal. xxxiv. 1,2,3.
 Thro' mercy of the Lord,
Among the heathen live no more,
 Come magnify thy God.

12

I pray the living God may be, Psal. 1xxx. 1,2,3.
 The shepherd of thy soul;
His tender mercies still are free,
 His mysteries to unfold.

13

Thou, Phillis, when thou hunger hast, Psal. x1ii. 1,2,3.
 Or pantest for thy God;

Jesus Christ is thy relief,
Thou hast the holy word.

14

The bounteous mercies of the Lord, Psal. xvi. 10,11.
Are hid beyond the sky,
And holy souls that love his word,
Shall taste them when they die.

15

These bounteous mercies are from God, Psal. xxxiv. 15.
The merits of his Son;
The humble soul that loves his word,
He chooses for his own.

16

Come, dear Phillis, be advis'd, John iv. 13,14.
To drink Samaria's flood:
There nothing is that shall suffice,
But Christ's redeeming blood.

17

While thousands muse with earthly toys, Matth. vi. 33.
And range about the street,
Dear Phillis, seek for heaven's joys,
Where we do hope to meet.

18

When God shall send his summons down, Psal. cxvi. 15.
And number saints together,
Blest angel chant, (triumphant sound)
Come live with me forever.

19

The humble soul shall fly to God, Mat. v. 3,8.
And leave the things of time,
Start forth as 'twere at the first word,
To taste things more divine.

20

Behold! the soul shall waft away, Cor. xv. 51,52,53.
Whene'er we come to die,
And leave its cottage made of clay,
In twinkling of an eye.

21

Now glory be to the Most High, Psal. cl. 6.
United praises given,

By all on earth, incessantly,
And all the host of heav'n.

Composed by JUPITER HAMMON, a
Negro Man belonging to Mr. Joseph
Lloyd, of Queen's Village, / on Long
Island, now in Hartford.

***The above lines are published by the Author, and a number of his friends, who desire to join with him in their best / regards to Miss Wheatly.

Hartford, August 4, 1778

James Grainger 1721?–1766

James Grainger's *The Sugar-Cane* combines elements of writing that were very popular during the eighteenth century: New World exploration narratives, imperial topographical poetry (as in such poems as Denham's "Cooper's Hill" and Pope's "Windsor Forest"), and the encyclopedia writing inspired by Diderot's *Encyclopédie.* Yet the poem also drew upon a "georgic" tradition stretching back to Virgil. Poetically, then, Grainger's *Sugar-Cane* had antecedents in classical writings; topically, the poem created innovations on its classical model. Moving beyond the georgic tradition of providing instruction to an idealized farmer, Grainger also aimed to give the reader practical information. Indeed, Grainger's poem remains one of the best descriptions of work life on an eighteenth-century sugar plantation. In extensive footnotes, *The Sugar-Cane* provides minute details on the history and topography of the various islands of the Antilles, the plant and animal life, and the various diseases and their cures.

The fourth and final book of *The Sugar-Cane,* included here, details the management of the labor force—enslaved Africans—that makes the sugar plantation possible. Grainger's own difficulty in justifying the slave system is evident throughout: he shifts awkwardly between advice of a practical nature offered to the slave buyer and invocations and prayers for amelioration of slave conditions, marked by a sense of hope for the eventual abolition of slavery. Grainger puts a difficult and sometimes anguished description of the management of slaves in place of the georgic's usual culminating celebration of the perfect farm. Along the way, Grainger also provides a poetical version of the standard British defense of slavery (the Spanish started it; Scottish miners are worse off than African slaves) and intriguing insights into the various cultures and manners of the Africans who peopled the West Indian islands.

James Grainger was born about 1721 in Berwickshire in southeast Scotland, the son of a tax collector. He studied medicine at the University of Edinburgh, spent three years as an army surgeon in Scotland and Holland, and made a grand tour of Europe before receiving his M.D. degree in 1753. Moving on to London, Grainger joined the Royal College of Physicians, but he met with difficulty in making a living as a physician. He supplemented his income by writing for various magazines on medical and literary topics and by publishing poetry of his own. A self-taught Latinist, Grainger published translations of classical Latin poems, the most notable being the *Elegies of Tibullus,* which was scathingly reviewed by his one-time friend Tobias Smollett, prompting a bitter exchange of insults in print between the two. His later works include what became the standard reference work on West Indian diseases and a ballad included in Percy's *Reliques of Ancient English Poetry* (1765). His literary interests led to friendships with the key figures in London's cultural world at midcentury: Robert Dodsley, Oliver Goldsmith, Samuel Johnson, Thomas Percy, Sir Joshua Reynolds, William Shenstone. In his *Life of Johnson* (1791), James Boswell recorded Bishop Percy's opinion of Grainger: "He was not only a man of genius and learning, but had many excellent virtues; being one of the most generous, friendly, and benevolent men I ever knew."

In hopes of improving his fortune, Grainger set out in 1759 to the West Indies as a paid companion to John Bourryau, a wealthy friend who owned plantations on the island of St. Christopher (commonly called St. Kitts). Shortly after arriving, Grainger met and married a local heiress, whose family made him manager of their estates. Grainger continued his medical practice on the side, hoping one day to be able to buy his own sugar plantation. His authorship of *The Sugar-Cane* represents his education in the cultivation and manufacture of sugar, combined with his growing interest in the history, geography, and natural history of the islands. Interestingly, the poem also suggests Grainger's continuing interest in medicine. After four years in the Caribbean, Grainger traveled back to London, where he presented his long georgic poem to his circle of literary friends for their opinion. According to Boswell, the manuscript of the poem was read at Sir Joshua Reynolds's house, where the company was amused by Grainger's account of the ravages caused in the sugar cane fields by rats. The amusement caused among this literary group by the explicit descriptions of the conditions of sugar cane plantations demonstrates how unusual was Grainger's innovation of including specific technical and medical terminology in the neoclassical form of the georgic poem. One of the ways Grainger managed to maintain the high tone of the blank verse while also providing accurate and useful information was to use extensive footnotes detailing the various names and uses of local flora and fauna. The effect of reading the complete poem with all its footnotes is to take a sort of grand tour of the West Indies while the islands were at the height of a sugar-and-slavery system that produced more wealth for Great Britain than all the North American colonies combined.

Thomas W. Krise
U.S. Air Force Academy

PRIMARY WORK

The Sugar-Cane: A Poem. In Four Books. With Notes. 1764.

from The Sugar-Cane. A Poem. In Four Books.

from *Book IV: The Genius of Africa*[1]

ARGUMENT

Invocation to the Genius of Africa.[2] *Address. Negroes when bought should be young, and strong. The Congo-negroes*[3] *are fitter for the house and trades, than for the field. The Gold-Coast,*[4] *but especially the Papaw-negroes, make the best field-negroes: but even these, if advanced in years, should not be purchased. The marks of a sound negroe at a negroe sale. Where the men do nothing but hunt, fish or fight, and all field drudgery is left to the women; these are to be preferred to their husbands. The Minnahs*[5] *make good tradesmen, but addicted to suicide. The Mundingos,*[6] *in particular, subject to worms; and the Congas, to dropsical disorders. How salt-water, or new negroes should be seasoned. Some negroes eat dirt. Negroes should be habituated by gentle degrees to field labour. This labour, when compared to that in lead-mines, or of those who work in the gold and silver mines of South America, is not only less toilsome, but far more healthy. Negroes should always be treated with humanity. Praise of freedom. Of the dracunculus, or dragon-worm. Of chigres. Of the yaws. Might not this disease be imparted by inoculation? Of worms, and their multiform appearance. Praise of commerce. Of the imaginary disorders of negroes, especially those caused by their conjurers or Obia-men.*[7] *The composition and supposed virtues of a magic-phiol. Field-negroes should not begin to work before six in the morning, and should leave off between eleven and twelve; and beginning again at two, should finish before sun-set. Of the weekly allowance of negroes. The young, the old, the sickly, and even the lazy, must have their victuals prepared for them. Of negroe-ground, and its various productions. To be fenced in, and watched. Of an American garden. Of the situation of the negroe-huts. How best defended from fire. The great negroe-dance described. Drumming, and intoxicating spirits not to be allowed. Negroes should be made to marry in their masters plantation. Inconveniences arising from the contrary practice. Negroes to be cloathed once a year, and before Christmas. Praise of Lewis XIV,*[8] *for the Code Noir. A body of laws of this kind recommended to the English sugar colonies. Praise of the river Thames. A moon-light landscape and vision.*

[1] Printed here is a slightly modernized version of *The Sugar-Cane,* Book IV, originally published in 1764. The notes are the editor's unless otherwise indicated.

[2] The spirit or personification of Africa.

[3] People from the region around the Congo River in modern Zaire.

[4] The coast of the Gulf of Guinea, in modern Ghana, West Africa.

[5] People from the region around Minna, a city in central Nigeria, north of the Niger river in West Africa.

[6] The Mandingo, or Mande, people of West Africa, a predominantly Muslim tribe, known for their widespread trading activities.

[7] Obia, or Obeah, is the traditional magic of West African polytheistic religion; related to vodun (voodoo) in Haiti.

[8] King Louis XIV of France (1638–1715; reigned 1643–1715), called the Sun King, promulgated the *Code Noir* in 1685, which placed some restrictions upon the power of slave-owners over their slaves.

Genius of Africk! whether thou bestrid'st
The castled elephants or at the source,
(While howls the desart fearfully around,)
Of thine own Niger,[9] sadly thou reclin'st
Thy temples shaded by the tremulous palm,
Or quick papaw,[10] whose top is necklac'd round
With numerous rows of party-colour'd fruit:
Or hear'st thou rather from the rocky banks
Of Rio Grandê,[11] or black Sanaga?[12]
Where dauntless thou the headlong torrent brav'st
In search of gold, to brede thy wooly locks,
On with bright ringlets ornament thine ears,
Thine arms, and ankles: O attend my song.
A muse that pities thy distressful state;
Who sees, with grief, thy sons in fetters bound;
Who wished freedom to the race of man;
Thy nod assenting craves: dread Genius, come!

Yet vain thy presence, vain thy favouring nod;
Unless once more the muses; that erewhile
Upheld me fainting in my past career,
Through Caribbe's cane-isles; kind condescend
To guide my footsteps, through parch'd Libya's wilds;
And bind my sun-burnt brow with other bays,
Than ever deck'd the Sylvan bard before.

Say, will my Melvil,[13] from the public care,
Withdraw one moment, to the muses shrine?
Who smit with thy fair fame, industrious cull
An Indian wreath to mingle with thy bays,
And deck the hero, and the scholar's brow!
Wilt thou, whose mildness smooths the face of war,
Who round the victor-blade the myrtle twin'st,
And mak'st subjection loyal and sincere;
O wilt thou gracious hear the unartful strain,
Whose mild instructions teach, no trivial theme,
What care the jetty African requires?
Yes, thou wilt deign to hear; a man thou art
Who deem'st nought foreign that belongs to man.

* * *

[9]Major river in West Africa.
[10]The fast-growing papaya tree.
[11]Now called the Corubal River, in Guinea and Guinea-Bissau in West Africa.
[12]River in Cameroon, West Africa.
[13]Count de Melvil, a virtuous character in Tobias Smollett's novel *The Adventures of Ferdinand Count Fathom* (1753); he is the benefactor of the dissolute title character, who is, like Grainger, a physician.

In mind, and aptitute for useful toil,
The negroes differ: muse that difference sing.

Whether to wield the hoe, or guide the plane;[14]
Or for domestic uses thou intend'st
The sunny Libyan: from what clime they spring,
It not imports; if strength and youth be theirs.

Yet those from Congo's wide-extended plains,
Through which the long Zaire winds with chrystal stream,
Where lavish Nature sends indulgent forth
Fruits of high favour, and spontaneous seeds
Of bland nutritious quality, ill bear
The toilsome field; but boast a docile mind,
And happiness of features. These, with care,
Be taught each nice mechanic art: or train'd
To houshold offices: their ductile souls
Will all thy care, and all thy gold repay.

But, of the labours of the field demand
Thy chief attention; and the ambrosial cane
Thou long'st to see, with spiry frequence, shade
Many an acre: planter, chuse the slave,
Who sails from barren climes; where art alone,
Offspring of rude necessity, compells
The sturdy native, or to plant the soil,
Or stem vast rivers, for his daily food.

Such are the children of the Golden Coast;
Such the Papaws, of negroes far the best:
And such the numerous tribes, that skirt the shore,
From rapid Volta to the distant Rey.[15]

But, planter, from what coast soe'er they sail,
Buy not the old: they ever sullen prove;
With heart-felt anguish, they lament their home;
They will not, cannot work; they never learn
Thy native language; they are prone to ails;
And oft by suicide their being end.—

Must thou from Africk reinforce thy gang?—
Let health and youth their every sinew firm;
Clear roll their ample eye; their tongue be red;
Broad swell their chest; their shoulders wide expand;
Not prominent their belly; clean and strong

[14]Or plough.

[15]Rivers in modern Ghana, West Africa.

Their thighs and legs, in just proportion rise.
Such soon will brave the fervours of the clime;
And free from ails, that kill thy negroe-train.
A useful servitude will long support.

Yet, if thine own, thy childrens life, be dear;
Buy not a Cormantee,[16] tho' healthy, young.
Of breed too generous for the servile field;
They, born to freedom in their native land,
Chuse death before dishonourable bonds:
Or, fir'd with vengeance, at the midnight hour,
Sudden they seize thine unsuspecting watch,
And thine own poinard[17] bury in thy breast.

At home, the men, in many a sylvan realm,
Their rank tobacco, charm of sauntering minds,
From clayey tubes inhale; or, vacant, beat
For prey the forest; or, in war's dread ranks,
Their country's foes affront: while, in the field,
Their wives plant rice, or yams, or lofty maize,
Fell hunger to repel. Be these thy choice:
They, hardy, with the labours of the Cane
Soon grow familiar; while unusual toil,
And new severities their husbands kill.

The slaves from Minnah[18] are of stubborn breed:
But, when the bill, or hammer, they affect;
They soon perfection reach. But fly, with care,
The Moco-nation;[19] they themselves destroy.

Worms lurk in all: yet, pronest they to worms,
Who from Mundingo[20] sail. When therefore such
Thou buy'st, for sturdy and laborious they,
Straight let some learned leach[21] strong medicines give,
Till food and climate both familiar grow.
Thus, tho' from rise to set, in Phoebus' eye,[22]
They toil, unceasing; yet, at night, they'll sleep,
Lap'd in Elysium;[23] and, each day, at dawn,
Spring from their couch, as blythsome as the sun.

* * *

[16]An African from the region around Cormantyne (or Kormantine), site of a Dutch slaving station in modern Ghana.
[17]A poniard, or dagger.
[18]See footnote 5.
[19]Apparently peoples originating in East Africa, who were associated with, or transported from, the Arab port of Mocha on the Red Sea.
[20]See footnote 6.
[21]A physician, so called because of the physician's former use of leeches to let blood as a cure.
[22]The sun; Phoebus being the title of Apollo as god of the sun.
[23]In classical mythology, the place in the Underworld where virtuous souls rest.

One precept more, it much imports to know.—
The Blacks, who drink the Quanza's[24] lucid stream,
Fed by ten thousand springs, are prone to bloat,
Whether at home or in these ocean-isles;
And tho' nice art the water may subdue,
Yet many die; and few, for many a year,
Just strength attain to labour for their lord.

Would'st thou secure thine Ethiop[25] from those ails,
Which change of climate, change of waters breed,
And food unusual? let Machaon[26] draw
From each some blood, as age and sex require;
And well with vervain,[27] well with sempre-vive,[28]
Unload their bowels.—These, in every hedge,
Spontaneous grow.—Nor will it not conduce
To give what chemists, in mysterious phrase,
Term the white eagle; deadly foe to worms.
But chief do thou, my friend, with hearty food,
Yet easy of digestion, likest that
Which they at home regal'd on; renovate
Their sea-worn appetites. Let gentle work,
Or rather playful exercise, amuse
The novel gang: and far be angry words;
Far ponderous chains; and far disheartening blows.—
From fruits restrain their eagerness; yet if
The acajou, haply, in thy garden bloom,
With cherries,[29] or of white or purple hue,
Thrice wholesome fruit in this relaxing clime!
Safely thou may'st their appetite indulge.
Their arid skins will plump, their features shine:
No rheums, no dysenteric ails torment:
The thirsty hydrops[30] flies.—'Tis even averr'd,
(Ah, did experience sanctify the fact;
How many Lybians[31] now would dig the soil,
Who pine in hourly agonies away!)
This pleasing fruit, if turtle join its aid,
Removes that worst of ails, disgrace of art,
The loathsome leprosy's infectious bane.

* * *

[24]The River Cuanza or Kwanza, in Angola in southwestern Africa.

[25]An inhabitant of Ethiopia, in East Africa, here representing Africans generally.

[26]Physician to the Greeks in the Trojan War, and son of the god of medicine, Aescalapius.

[27]An herbaceous plant, native to Europe.

[28]The houseleek, a succulent European plant with reddish flowers.

[29]The tree which produces this wholesome fruit is tall, shady, and of quick growth. Its Indian name is *Acajou;* hence corruptly called *Cashew* by the English. . . . [Grainger's note.]

[30]Former name for edema, the build-up of fluid in the cavities of the body, often due to kidney failure.

[31]Inhabitants of Libya, in North Africa, here signifying Africans generally.

There are, the muse hath oft abhorrent seen,
Who swallow dirt; (so the chlorotic fair
Oft chalk prefer to the most poignant cates.[32])
Such, dropsy bloats, and to sure death consigns;
Unless restrain'd from this unwholesome food,
By soothing words, by menaces, by blows:
Nor yet will threats, or blows, or soothing words,
Perfect their cure; unless thou, Paean,[33] design'st
By medicine's power their cravings to subdue.

To easy labour first inure thy slaves;
Extremes are dangerous. With industrious search,
Let them fit grassy provender[34] collect
For thy keen stomach'd herds.—But when the earth
Hath made her annual progress round the sun,
What time the conch[35] or bell resounds, they may
All to the Cane-ground, with thy gang, repair.

Nor, Negroe, at thy destiny repine,
Tho' doom'd to toil from dawn to setting sun.
How far more pleasant is thy rural task,
Than theirs who sweat, sequester'd from the day,
In dark tartarean caves, sunk far beneath
The earth's dark surface, where sulphureous flames,
Oft from their vapoury prisons bursting wild,
To dire explosion give the cavern'd deep,
And in dread ruin all its inmates whelm?—
Nor fateful only is the bursting flame;
The exhalations of the deep-dug mine,
Tho' slow, shake from their wings as sure a death.
With what intense severity of pain
Hath the afflicted muse, in Scotia, seen
The miners rack'd, who toil for fatal lead?
What cramps, what palsies shake their feeble limbs,
Who, on the margin of the rocky Drave,[36]
Trace silver's fluent ore? Yet white men these!

How far more happy ye, than those poor slaves,
Who, whilom,[37] under native, gracious chiefs,

[32]Dainty foods.
[33]A surname or title for Apollo, the Greek god of medicine, music, archery, prophecy, and light.
[34]Food for livestock.
[35]Plantations that have no bells assemble their Negroes by sounding a conch-shell. [Grainger's note.]
[36]A river in Hungary, on whose banks are found mines of quicksilver [Grainger's note. Quicksilver is mercury. Ed.].
[37]Formerly.

Incas and emperors, long time enjoy'd
Mild government, with every sweet of life,
In blissful climates? See them dragg'd in chains,
By proud insulting tyrants, to the mines
Which once they call'd their own, and then despis'd!
See, in the mineral bosom of their land,
How hard they toil! how soon their youthful limbs
Feel the decrepitude of age! how soon
Their teeth desert their sockets! and how soon
Shaking paralysis unstrings their frame!
Yet scarce, even then, are they allow'd to view
The glorious God of day, of whom they beg,
With earnest hourly supplications, death;
Yet death slow comes, to torture them the more!

With these compar'd, ye sons of Afric, say,
How far more happy is your lot? Bland health,
Of ardent eye, and limb robust, attends
Your custom'd labour: and, should sickness seize,
With what solicitude are ye not nurs'd!—
Ye Negroes, then, your pleasing task pursue;
And, by your toil, deserve your master's care.

When first your Blacks are novel to the hoe;
Study their humours: Some, soft-soothing words;
Some, presents; and some, menaces subdue;
And some I've known, so stubborn is their kind,
Whom blows, alas! could win alone to toil.

Yet, planter, let humanity prevail.—
Perhaps thy Negroe, in his native land,
Possest large fertile plains, and slaves, and herds:
Perhaps, whene'er he deign'd to walk abroad,
The richest silks, from where the Indus rolls,
His limbs invested in their gorgeous pleats:
Perhaps he wails his wife, his children, left
To struggle with adversity: Perhaps
Fortune, in battle for his country fought,
Gave him a captive to his deadliest foe:
Perhaps, incautious, in his native fields,
(On pleasurable scenes his mind intent)
All as he wandered; from the neighbouring grove,
Fell ambush dragg'd him to the hated main.—
Were they even sold for crimes; ye polish'd, say!
Ye, to whom Learning opes her amplest page!
Ye, whom the knowledge of a living God
Should lead to virtue! Are ye free from crimes?
Ah pity, then, these uninstructed swains;

And still let mercy soften the decrees
Of rigid justice, with her lenient hand.
Oh, did the tender muse possess the power;
Which monarchs have, and monarchs oft abuse:
'Twould be the fond ambition of her soul,
To quell tyrannic sway; knock off the chains
Of heart-debasing slavery; give to man,
Of every colour and of every clime,
Freedom, which stamps him image of his God.
Then laws, Oppression's scourge, fair Virtue's prop,
Offspring of Wisdom! should impartial reign,
To knit the whole in well-accorded strife:
Servants, not slaves; of choice, and not compell'd;
The Blacks should cultivate the Cane-land isles.

Say, shall the muse the various ills recount,
Which Negroe-nations feel? Shall she describe
The worm that subtly winds into their flesh,
All as they bathe them in their native streams?
There, with fell increment, it soon attains
A direful length of harm. Yet, if due skill,
And proper circumspection are employed,
It may be won its volumes to wind round
A leaden cylinder: But, O, beware,
No rashness practise; else 'twill surely snap,
And suddenly, retreating, dire produce
An annual lameness to the tortured Moor.

Nor only is the dragon worm to dread:
Fell, winged insects,[38] which the visual ray
Scarcely discerns, their sable feet and hands
Oft penetrate: and, in the fleshy nest,
Myriads of young produce; which soon destroy
The parts they breed in; if assiduous care,
With art, extract not the prolific foe.

Or, shall she sing, and not debase her lay,
The pest peculiar to the Aethiop-kind.
The yaw's[39] infectious bane?—The infected far
In huts, to leeward, lodge; or near the main.
With heartening food, with turtle, and with conchs;
The flowers of sulphur, and hard niccars[40] burnt,

[38]These, by the English, are called *Chigoes* or *Chigres* [Grainger's note. The modern spelling is "chiggers." Ed.]

[39]Yaws, or frambesia, is an infectious tropical disease of the skin.

[40]The botanical name of this medicinal shrub is Guilandina. . . . [Grainger's note.]

The lurking evil from the blood expel,
And throw it on the surface: There in spots
Which cause no pain, and scanty ichor[41] yield,
It chiefly breaks about the arms and hips,
A virulent contagion!—When no more
Round knobby spots deform, but the disease
Seems at a pause: then let the learned leach
Give, in due dose, live-silver[42] from the mine;
Till copious spitting the whole taint exhaust—
Nor thou repine, tho' half-way round the sun,
This globe, her annual progress shall absolve;
Ere, clera'd, thy slave from all infection shine.
Nor then be confident; successive crops
Of defoedations[43] oft will spot the skin:
These thou, with turpentine and guaiac pods,
Reduc'd by coction to a wholesome draught,
Total remove, and give the blood its balm.

Say, as this malady but once infests
The sons of Guinea, might not skill ingraft
(Thus, the small-pox are happily convey'd;)
This ailment early to thy Negroe-train?

Yet, of the ills which torture Libya's sons,
Worms tyrannize the worst. They, Proteus-like,[44]
Each symptom of each malady assume;
And, under every mask, the assassins kill.
Now, in the guise of horrid spasms, they writhe
The tortured body, and all sense o'er-power.
Sometimes, like Mania,[45] with her head downcast,
They cause the wretch in solitude to pine;
Or frantic, bursting from the strongest chains,
To frown with look terrific, not his own.
Sometimes like Ague,[46] with a shivering mien,
The teeth gnash fearful, and the blood runs chill:
Anon the ferment maddens in the veins,
And a false vigour animates the frame.
Again, the dropsy's bloated mask they steal;
Or, "melt with minings of the hectic fire."[47]

[41]Watery discharge from a wound or sore.
[42]Quicksilver, or mercury.
[43]Pollutions, defilements.
[44]Classical sea deity, able to prophesy, known for assuming various shapes to avoid answering humans' questions about the future.
[45]Personification of mania, or madness.
[46]Personification of ague, or acute fever.
[47]From John Armstrong, *The Art of Preserving Health, A Poem* (1744), III. 202.

. . . .

Nor pine the Blacks, alone, with real ills,
That baffle oft the wisest rules of art:
They likewise feel imaginary woes;
Woes no less deadly. Luckless he who owns
The slave, who thinks himself bewitch'd; and whom,
In wrath, a conjuror's snake-mark'd[48] staff hath struck!
They mope, love silence, every friend avoid;
They inly pine; all aliment reject;
Or insufficient for nutrition take:
Their features droop: a sickly yellowish hue
Their skin deforms; their strength and beauty fly.
Then comes the feverish fiend, with firy eyes,
Whom drowth, convulsions, and whom death surround,
Fatal attendants! if some subtle slave
(Such, Obia-men are stil'd) do not engage,
To save the wretch by antidote or spell.

In magic spells, in Obia, all the sons
Of sable Africk trust:—Ye, sacred nine!
(For ye each hidden preparation know)
Transpierce the gloom, which ignorance and fraud
Have render'd awful; tell the laughing world
Of what these wonder-working charms are made.

Fern root cut small, and tied with many a knot;
Old teeth extracted from a white man's skull;
A lizard's skeleton; a serpent's head:
These mix'd with salt, and water from the spring,
Are in a phial pour'd; o'er these the leach
Mutters strange jargon, and wild circles forms.

Of this possest, each negroe deems himself
Secure from poison; for to poison they
Are infamously prone: and arm'd with this,
Their sable country daemons they defy,

[48]The negroe-conjurors, or Obia-men, as they are called, carry about them a staff, which is marked with frogs, snakes, &c. The blacks imagine that its blow, if not mortal, will at least occasion long and troublesome disorders. A belief in magic is inseparable from human nature, but those nations are most addicted thereto, among whom learning, and of course, philosophy have least obtained. As in all other countries, so in Guinea, the conjurors, as they have more understanding, so are they almost always more wicked than the common herd of their deluded countrymen; and as the negroe-magicians can do mischief, so they can also do good on a plantation, provided they are kept by the white people in proper subordination. [Grainger's note. Obia, or Obeah, related to Voodoo, or Vodun, is the traditional belief system of many West African peoples. Ed.]

Who fearful haunt them at the midnight hour,
To work them mischief. This, diseases fly;
Diseases follow: such its wonderous power!
This o'er the threshold of their cottage hung,
No thieves break in; or, if they dare to steal,
Their feet in blotches, which admit no cure,
Burst loathsome out: but should its owner filch,
As slaves were ever of the pilfering kind,
This from detection screens;—so conjurors swear.

'Till morning dawn, and Lucifer withdraw
His beamy chariot; let not the loud bell
Call forth thy negroes from their rushy couch:
And ere the sun with mid-day fervour glow,
When every broom-bush[49] opes her yellow flower;
Let thy black labourers from their toil desist:
Nor till the broom her every petal lock,
Let the loud bell recall them to the hoe.
But when the jalap her bright tint displays,
When the solanum[50] fills her cup with dew,
And crickets, snakes, and lizards 'gin their coil;
Let them find shelter in their cane-thatch'd huts;
Or, if constrain'd unusual hours to toil,
(For even the best must sometimes urge their gang)
With double nutriment reward their pains.

Howe'er insensate some may deem their slaves,
Nor 'bove the bestial rank; far other thoughts
The muse, soft daughter of humanity!
Will ever entertain.—The Ethiop knows,
The Ethiop feels, when treated like a man;
Nor grudges, should necessity compell,
By day, by night, to labour for his lord.

Not less inhuman, than unthrifty those;
Who, half the year's rotation round the sun,
Deny subsistence to their labouring slaves.
But would'st thou see thy negroe-train encrease,
Free from disorders; and thine acres clad
With groves of sugar: every week dispense
Or English beans, or Carolinian rice;

[49]This small plant, which grows in every pasture, may, with propriety, be termed an American clock; for it begins every forenoon at eleven to open its yellow flowers, which about one are fully expanded, and at two closed. . . . [Grainger's note.]

[50]So some authors name the fire-weed. . . . [Grainger's note.]

Iërne's[51] beef, or Pensilvanian flour;
Newfoundland cod, or herrings from the main
That howls tempestuous round the Scotian isles!

Yet some there are so lazily inclin'd,
And so neglectful of their food, that thou,
Would'st thou preserve them from the jaws of death;
Daily, their wholesome viands must prepare:
With these let all the young, and childless old,
And all the morbid share;—so heaven will bless,
With manifold encrease, thy costly care.

Suffice not this; to every slave assign
Some mountain-ground: or, if waste broken land
To thee belong, that broken land divide.
This let them cultivate, one day, each week;
And there raise yams, and there cassada's root:[52]
From a good daemon's staff cassada sprang,
Tradition says, and Caribbees[53] believe;
Which into three the white-rob'd genius broke,
And bade them plant, their hunger to repel.
There let angola's bloomy bush supply,[54]
For many a year, with wholesome pulse their board.
There let the bonavist,[55] his fringed pods
Throw liberal o'er the prop; while ochra[56] bears
Aloft his slimy pulp, and help disdains.
There let potatos[57] mantle o'er the ground;
Sweet as the cane-juice is the root they bear.
There too let eddas[58] spring in order meet,
With Indian cale,[59] and foodful calaloo:[60]

[51]Ireland's.

[52]To an ancient Caribbean, bemoaning the savage uncomfortable life of his countrymen, a deity clad in white apparel appeared, and told him, he would have come sooner to have taught him the ways of civil life, had he been addressed before. He then showed him sharp-cutting stones to fell trees and build houses; and bade him cover them with the palm leaves. Then he broke his staff in three; which, being planted, soon after produced cassada. . . . [Grainger's note.]

[53]Carib Indians, native inhabitants of the Lesser Antilles of the Caribbean.

[54]This is called *Pidgeon-pea*. . . . [Grainger's note.]

[55]This is the Spanish name of a plant, which produces an excellent bean. . . . [Grainger's note.]

[56]Or *Ockro*. . . . [Grainger's note.]

[57]I cannot positively say, whether these vines are of Indian original or not; but as in their fructification, they differ from potatos at home, they probably are not European. They are sweet. There are four kinds, the red, the white, the long, and round. The juice of each may be made into a pleasant cool drink; and, being distilled, yield an excellent spirit. [Grainger's note.]

[58]. . . This wholesome root, in some of the islands, is called *Edda:* . . . [Grainger's note.]

[59]This green, which is a native of the New World, equals any of the greens in the Old. [Grainger's note.]

[60]Another species of Indian pot herb, no less wholesome than the preceding. These, with mezamby, and the Jamaica pickle-weed, yield to no esculent plants in Europe. This is an Indian name. [Grainger's note.]

While mint, thyme, balm, and Europe's coyer herbs,
Shoot gladsome forth, not reprobate the clime.

This tract secure, with hedges or of limes,
Or bushy citrons, or the shapely tree[61]
That glows at once with aromatic blooms,
And golden fruit mature. To these be join'd,
In comely neighbourhood, the cotton shrub;
In this delicious clime the cotton bursts
On rocky soils.—The coffee also plant;
White as the skin of Albion's lovely fair,
Are the thick snowy fragrant blooms it boasts:
Nor wilt thou, cocô, thy rich pods refuse;
Tho' years, and heat, and moisture they require,
Ere the stone grind them to the food of health.
Of thee, perhaps, and of thy various sorts,
And that kind sheltering tree, thy mother nam'd,[62]
With crimson flowerets prodigally grac'd;
In future times, the enraptur'd muse may sing:
If public favour crown her present lay.

But let some antient, faithful slave erect
His sheltered mansion near; and with his dog,
His loaded gun, and cutlass, guard the whole:
Else negroe-fugitives, who skulk 'mid rocks
And shrubby wilds, in bands will soon destroy
Thy labourer's honest wealth; their loss and yours.

. . . .

It much imports to build thy Negroe-huts,
Or on the sounding margin of the main,
Or on some dry hill's gently-sloping sides,
In streets, at distance due.—When near the beach,
Let frequent coco cast its wavy shade;
'Tis Neptune's tree; and, nourish'd by the spray,
Soon round the bending stem's aerial height,
Clusters of mighty nuts, with milk and fruit
Delicious fraught, hang clattering in the sky.
There let the bay-grape,[63] too, its crooked limbs
Project enormous; of impurpled hue

[61]The orange tree. [Grainger's note.]

[62]. . . It is also called *Cocao* and *Cocô*. . . . those who plant cacao-walks, sometimes screen them by a hardier tree, which the Spaniards aptly term *Madre de Cacao*. . . . [Grainger's note.]

[63]Or sea side grape, as it is more commonly called. . . . [Grainger's note.]

Its frequent clusters grow. And there, if thou
Woud'st make the sand yield salutary food,
Let Indian millet[64] rear its corny reed,
Like arm'd battalions in array of war.
But, round the upland huts, bananas plant;
A wholesome nutriment bananas yield,
And sun-burnt labour loves its breezy shade.
Their graceful screen let kindred plantanes join,
And with their broad vans shiver in the breeze;
So flames design'd, or by imprudence caught,
Shall spread no ruin to the neighbouring roof.

Yet nor the sounding margin of the main,
Nor gently sloping side of breezy hill,
Nor streets, at distance due, imbower'd in trees;
Will half the health, or half the pleasure yield,
Unless some pitying naiad deign to lave,
With an unceasing stream, thy thirsty bounds.

On festal days; or when their work is done;
Permit thy slaves to lead the choral dance,
To the wild banshaw's[65] melancholy sound.
Responsive to the sound, head feet and frame
Move aukwardly harmonious; hand in hand
Now lock'd, the gay troop circularly wheels,
And frisks and capers with intemperate joy.
Halts the vast circle, all clap hands and sing;
While those distinguish'd for their heels and air,
Bound in the center, and fantastic twine.
Meanwhile some stripling, from the choral ring,
Trips forth; and, not ungallantly, bestows
On her who nimblest hath the greensward beat,
And whose flush'd beauties have inthrall'd his soul,
A silver token of his fond applause.
Anon they form in ranks; nor inexpert
A thousand tuneful intricacies weave,
Shaking their sable limbs; and oft a kiss
Steal from their partners; who, with neck reclin'd,
And semblant scorn, resent the ravish'd bliss.
But let not thou the drum their mirth inspire;

[64]Or maise. This is commonly called Guinea-corn, to distinguish it from the great or Indian-corn, that grows in the southern parts of North-America. . . . The Indians, Negroes, and poor white people, make many (not unsavoury) dishes with them. It is also called *Turkey wheat.* The turpentine tree will also grow in the sand, and is most useful upon a plantation. [Grainger's note.]

[65]This is a sort of rude guitar, invented by the Negroes. It produces a wild pleasing melancholy sound. [Grainger's note. The banshaw is a banjo. Ed.]

Nor vinous spirits: else, to madness fir'd,
(What will not bacchanalian frenzy dare?)
Fell acts of blood, and vengeance they pursue.

Compel by threats, or win by soothing arts,
Thy slaves to wed their fellow slaves at home;
So shall they not their vigorous prime destroy,
By distant journeys, at untimely hours,
When muffled midnight decks her raven-hair
With the white plumage of the prickly vine.[66]

Would'st thou from countless ails preserve thy gang;
To every Negroe, as the candle-weed[67]
Expands his blossoms to the cloudy sky,
And moist Aquarius melts in daily showers;
A woolly vestment give, (this Wiltshire weaves)
Warm to repel chill Night's unwholesome dews:
While strong coarse linen, from the Scotian loom,
Wards off the fervours of the burning day.

The truly great, tho' from a hostile clime,
The sacred Nine embalm; then, Muses, chant,
In grateful numbers, Gallic Lewis'[68] praise:
For private murder quell'd; for laurel'd arts,
Invented, cherish'd in his native realm;
For rapine punish'd; for grim famine fed:
For sly chicane expell'd the wrangling bar;
And rightful Themis[69] seated on her throne:
But, chief, for those mild laws his wisdom fram'd,
To guard the Aethiop from tyrannic sway!

Did such, in these green isles which Albion claims,
Did such obtain; the muse, at midnight-hour,
This last brain-racking study had not ply'd:
But, sunk in slumbers of immortal bliss,
To bards had listned on a fancied Thames!

All hail, old father Thames! tho' not from far
Thy springing waters roll; nor countless streams,
Of name conspicuous, swell thy watery store;

[66]This beautiful white rosaceous flower is as large as the crown of one's hat, and only blows at midnight. . . . [Grainger's note.]

[67]This shrub, which produces a yellow flower somewhat resembling a narcissus, makes a beautiful hedge, and blows about November. . . . [Grainger's note.]

[68]King Louis XIV of France; see note 8.

[69]Greek goddess, mother of the Seasons, the Fates, and Prometheus; personification of Justice.

Tho' thou, no Plata,[70] to the sea devolve
Vast humid offerings; thou art king of streams:
Delighted Commerce broods upon thy wave;
And every quarter of this sea-girt globe
To thee due tribute pays; but chief the world
By great Columbus found, where now the muse
Beholds, transported, slow vast fleecy clouds,
Alps pil'd on Alps romantically high,
Which charm the sight with many a pleasing form.
The moon, in virgin-glory, gilds the pole,
And tips yon tamarinds, tips yon Cane-crown'd vale,
With fluent silver; while unnumbered stars
Gild the vast concave with their lively beams.
The main, a moving burnish'd mirror, shines;
No noise is heard, save when the distant surge
With drouzy murmurings breaks upon the shore!—

Ah me, what thunders roll! the sky's on fire!
Now sudden darkness muffles up the pole!
Heavens! what wild scenes, before the affrighted sense,
Imperfect swim!—See! in that flaming scroll,
Which Time unfolds, the future germs bud forth,
Of mighty empires! independent realms!—
And must Britannia, Neptune's favorite queen,
Protect'ress of true science, freedom, arts;
Must she, ah! must she, to her offspring crouch?
Ah, must my Thames, old Ocean's favourite son,
Resign his trident to barbaric streams;
His banks neglected, and his waves unsought,
No bards to sing them, and no fleets to grace?—
Again the fleecy clouds amuse the eye,
And sparkling stars the vast horizon gild—
She shall not crouch; if Wisdom guide the helm,
Wisdom that bade loud Fame, with justest praise,
Record her triumphs! bade the lacquaying winds
Transport, to every quarter of the globe,
Her winged navies! bade the scepter'd sons
Of earth acknowledge her pre-eminence!—
She shall not crouch; if these Cane ocean-isles,
Isles which on Britain for their all depend,
And must for ever; still indulgent share
Her fostering smile: and other isles be given,
From vanquish'd foes.—And, see, another race!
A golden aera dazzles my fond sight!

[70]One of the largest rivers of South America. [Grainger's note.]

That other race, that long'd-for aera, hail!
The British George[71] now reigns, the Patriot King!
Britain shall ever triumph o'er the main.

1764

Samson Occom (Mohegan) 1723–1792

Born in a wigwam in 1723, Samson Occom was the son of Joshua Tomacham and Sarah, reputed to be a descendant of the famous Mohegan chief, Uncas. In an autobiographical sketch, dated September 17, 1768, Occom described the nomadic life led by his parents and their fellow Mohegans during his youth.

At sixteen, Samson was aroused to religious fervor by missionaries, and he began to study English in order to read the scriptures. His conversion to Christianity a year later increased his desire to read. In 1743, twenty-year-old Occom went to study for four years with the Reverend Eleazar Wheelock in Lebanon, Connecticut. Ill health and eyestrain prevented him from studying longer. He accepted in 1749 the invitation of the Montauk Indians of Long Island to become their schoolmaster. In 1751, he married Mary Fowler (a Montauk), who subsequently bore him ten children. To support his rapidly growing family, Occom supplemented his stipend by working as a farmer, fisherman, cooper, and bookbinder. Desperate financial circumstances throughout his life haunted him.

After his ordination in 1759, Occom spent the next year as an itinerant minister in southern New England. In 1761, he became a missionary to the Oneida Indians. Determined to work among his own people, Occom moved his family in 1764 to Mohegan and assisted the Reverend George Whitefield in raising money for Wheelock's Indian Charity School, which became present-day Dartmouth College. Because of his success as a preacher and fund-raiser, Whitefield sent him to Great Britain to raise money for the school. During his two years there, Occom preached over three hundred sermons and raised over £12,000.

After his return, Occom devoted his energies to preaching and working on behalf of Native Americans. Prior to his tour of Great Britain, he had helped the Mohegans try to settle their land claims. Now he became an enthusiastic supporter of a plan formulated by his son-in-law, Joseph Johnson (a Mohegan), to remove the Christian Indians of New England to lands offered by the Oneida in western New York. The Revolutionary War halted this move. In an address, Occom described the dangers of this war to his people. Although he pointed out that the English sought to enslave the colonists, Occom urged Indians not to become embroiled in the quarrels of white people because he felt the war was the work of the devil.

Occom traveled throughout New England in 1784 to preach and raise funds for resettlement of the Christian Indians onto Oneida lands, a cause that absorbed him for the next six years. In 1789, he moved his own family. He spent his last years in continued service to his people, now beset by controversies over land claims. Through his efforts, the Christian Indians withstood Oneida efforts to reclaim their

[71]King George III (1738–1820; reigned 1760–1820).

land and white plots to lease the Christian Indians' land for far less than its worth. When he died in 1792 at age sixty-nine, more than three hundred Indians attended his funeral. His dream of a secure settlement for New England Indians was destined to fail, as were all subsequent resettlements of Indians. After the War of 1812, white encroachment caused the Brothertown and Stockbridge Indians to purchase land from the Hochunk (Winnebago) and Menominee Indians in the Green Bay area of what is now Wisconsin.

Occom published only two works: *A Sermon Preached by Samson Occom, . . . at the Execution of Moses Paul* (1772), the first Indian bestseller, and *Collection of Hymns and Spiritual Songs* (1774). Undoubtedly, the success of the sermon inspired Occom, a fine singer, to publish the collection.

For the first time after his English tour, Occom stepped into the public limelight in 1771 when he preached the execution sermon for Moses Paul, a fellow Christian Mohegan. Ejected from a Bethany tavern for drunkenness, Paul killed the next person to leave—Moses Cook, a prominent citizen of Waterbury, Connecticut. Granted a three-month reprieve by the General Assembly of Connecticut, Paul wrote Occom on July 16, 1771, to ask that he preach at the execution. Held on September 2, 1771, the execution drew a large crowd. It was New Haven's first hanging in twenty years, and it offered a unique opportunity to hear a famous Indian minister preach at the execution of a fellow tribesman. Whites and Native Americans flocked to the event. Occom's forceful and emotional sermon so moved his audience that he was immediately urged to publish it. One of the few temperance sermons published during that period, it achieved particular popularity because of its application to Indians whose drunkenness whites feared.

A. LaVonne Brown Ruoff
University of Illinois at Chicago

PRIMARY WORKS

A Sermon Preached by Samson Occom, Minister of the Gospel, and Missionary of the Indians; at the Execution of Moses Paul an Indian, 1772; *Collection of Hymns and Spiritual Songs,* 1774; Samson Occom, *The Collected Writings of Samson Occom, Mohegan: Leadership and Literature in Eighteenth-Century Native America,* edited by Joanna Brooks, Oxford: Oxford University Press, 2006.

A Short Narrative of My Life[1]

From my Birth till I received the Christian Religion

I was Born a Heathen and Brought up In Heathenism, till I was between 16 & 17 years of age, at a Place Calld Mohegan, in New London, Connecticut, in New England. My Parents Livd a wandering life, for did all the Indians at Mohegan, they

[1]The text is transcribed from Occom's manuscript in the Dartmouth College Library. Conjectural readings appear in brackets. Occom's spelling, capitalization, and punctuation have generally been followed.

Chiefly Depended upon Hunting, Fishing, & Fowling for their Living and had no Connection with the English, excepting to Traffic with them in their small Trifles; and they Strictly maintained and followed their Heathenish Ways, Customs & Religion, though there was Some Preaching among them. Once a Fortnight, in ye Summer Season, a Minister from New London used to come up, and the Indians to attend; not that they regarded the Christian Religion, but they had Blankets given to them every Fall of the Year and for these things they would attend and there was a Sort of School kept, when I was quite young, but I believe there never was one that ever Learnt to read any thing,—and when I was about 10 Years of age there was a man who went about among the Indian Wigwams, and wherever he Could find the Indian Children, would make them read; but the Children Used to take Care to keep out of his way;—and he used to Catch me Some times and make me Say over my Letters; and I believe I learnt Some of them. But this was Soon over too; and all this Time there was not one amongst us, that made a Profession of Christianity——Neither did we Cultivate our Land, nor kept any Sort of Creatures except Dogs, which we used in Hunting; and we Dwelt in Wigwams. These are a Sort of Tents, Covered with Matts, made of Flags. And to this Time we were unaquainted with the English Tongue in general though there were a few, who understood a little of it.

From the Time of our Reformation till I left Mr. Wheelocks

When I was 16 years of age, we heard a Strange Rumor among the English, that there were Extraordinary Ministers Preaching from Place to Place and a Strange Concern among the White People. This was in the Spring of the Year. But we Saw nothing of these things, till Some Time in the Summer, when Some Ministers began to visit us and Preach the Word of God; and the Common People all Came frequently and exhorted us to the things of God, which it pleased the Lord, as I humbly hope, to Bless and accompany with Divine Influences to the Conviction and Saving Conversion of a Number of us; amongst whom I was one that was Imprest with the things we had heard. These Preachers did not only come to us, but we frequently went to their meetings and Churches. After I was awakened & converted, I went to all the meetings, I could come at; & Continued under Trouble of Mind about 6 months; at which time I began to Learn the English Letters; got me a Primer, and used to go to my English Neighbours frequently for Assistance in Reading, but went to no School. And when I was 17 years of age, I had, as I trust, a Discovery of the way of Salvation through Jesus Christ, and was enabl'd to put my trust in him alone for Life & Salvation. From this Time the Distress and Burden of my mind was removed, and I found Serenity and Pleasure of Soul, in Serving God. By this time I just began to Read in the New Testament without Spelling,—and I had a Stronger Desire Still to Learn to read the Word of God, and at the Same Time had an uncommon Pity and Compassion to my Poor Brethren According to the Flesh. I used to wish I was capable of Instructing my poor Kindred. I used to think, if I Could once Learn to Read I would Instruct the poor Children in Reading,—and used frequently to talk with our Indians Concerning Religion. This continued till I was in my 19th year: by this Time I Could Read a bit in the Bible. At this Time my Poor Mother was going to Lebanon, and having had Some Knowledge of Mr. Wheelock and hearing he had a Number of English youth under his Tuition, I had a great Inclination to go to him and be with him a week or a Fortnight, and Desired my Mother to Ask Mr. Wheelock, Whether he would take me a little while to Instruct me in Reading. Mother did so; and when She Came Back, She Said Mr. Wheelock wanted to See me as Soon as possible. So I went up, thinking I Should be back again in a few Days; when I got up there, he received me With kindness and Compassion and in Stead of Staying a Forthnight or 3 Weeks, I Spent 4 Years with him.—After I had been with him Some Time, he began to acquaint his Friends of my being with him, and of his Intentions of Educating me, and my Circumstances. And the good People began to give Some Assistance to Mr. Wheelock, and gave me Some old and Some New Clothes. Then he represented the Case to the Honorable Commissioners at Boston, who were Commission'd by the Honourable Society in London for Propagating the gospel among the Indians in New England and parts adjacent, and they allowed him 60 £ in old Tenor, which was about 6 £ Sterling, and they Continu'd it 2 or 3 years, I can't tell exactly.—While I was at Mr. Wheelock's, I was very weakly and my Health much impaired, and at the End of 4 Years, I over Strained my Eyes to such a Degree, I Could not persue my Studies any Longer; and out of these 4 years I Lost Just about one year;—And was obliged to quit my Studies.

From the Time I left Mr. Wheelock till I went to Europe

As soon as I left Mr. Wheelock, I endeavored to find Some Employ among the Indians; went to Nahantuck, thinking they may want a School Master, but they had one; then went to Narraganset, and they were Indifferent about a School, and went back to Mohegan, and heard a number of our Indians were going to *Montauk,* on Long Island,—and I went with them, and the Indians there were very desirous to have me keep a School amongst them, and I Consented, and went back a while to Mohegan and Some time in November I went on the Island, I think it is 17 years ago last November. I agreed to keep School with them Half a Year, and left it with them to give me what they Pleased; and they took turns to Provide Food for me. I had near 30 Scholars this winter; I had an evening School too for those that could not attend the Day School—and began to Carry on their meetings, they had a Minister, one Mr. *Horton,* the Scotch Society's Missionary; but he Spent, I think two thirds of his Time at Sheenecock, 30 Miles from Montauk.[2] We met together 3 times for Divine Worship every Sabbath and once on every Wednesday evening. I [used] to read the Scriptures to them and used to expound upon Some particular Passages in my own Tongue. Visited the Sick and attended their Burials.—When the half year expired, they Desired me to Continue with them, which I complied with, for another half year, when I had fulfilled that, they were urgent to have me Stay Longer, So I continued amongst them till I was Married, which was about 2 years after I went there.

[2]Both the Shinnecock and Montauk Indians were located on present-day Long Island. Many from both tribes left after 1775 to join Occom at the new Christian Indian town of Brotherton.

And Continued to Instruct them in the Same manner as I did before After I was married a while, I found there was need of a Support more than I needed while I was Single,—and I made my Case Known to Mr. *Buell* and to Mr. *Wheelock,* and also the Needy Circumstances and the Desires of these Indians of my Continuence amongst them and Mr. *Wheelock* and other gentlemen Represented my Circumstances and the Desires of these Indians of my Continuence amongst them, and the Commissioners were so good as to grant £ 15 a year Sterling——And I kept on in my Service as usual, yea I had additional Service; I kept School as I did before and Carried on the Religious Meetings as often as ever, and attended the Sick and their Funerals, and did what Writings they wanted, and often Sat as a Judge to reconcile and Decide their Matters Between them, and had visitors of Indians from all Quarters; and, as our Custom is, we freely Entertain all Visitors. And was fetched often from my Tribe and from others to see into their Affairs Both Religious, Temporal,—Besides my Domestick Concerns. And it Pleased the Lord to Increase my Family fast—and Soon after I was Married, Mr. *Horton* left these Indians and the Shenecock & after this I was [licensed to preach?] and then I had the whole care of these Indians at Montauk, and visited the Shenecock Indians often. Used to Set out Saturdays towards Night and come back again Mondays. I have been obliged to Set out from Home after Sun Set, and Ride 30 Miles in the Night, to Preach to these Indians.—And Some Indians at Shenecock Sent their Children to my School at Montauk; I kept one of them Some Time, and had a Young Man a half year from Mohegan, a Lad from Nahantuck, who was with me almost a year; and had little or nothing for keeping them.

My Method in the School was, as Soon as the Children got together, and took their proper Seats, I Prayed with them, then began to hear them. I generally began (after some of them Could Spell and Read,) With those that were yet in their Alphabets, So around, as they were properly Seated till I got through and I obliged them to Study their Books, and to help one another. When they could not make out a hard word they Brought it to me—and I usually heard them, in the Summer Season 8 Times a Day 4 in the morning, and in ye after Noon.—In the Winter Season 6 Times a Day, As Soon as they could Spell, they were obliged to Spell when ever they wanted to go out. I concluded with Prayer; I generally heard my Evening Scholars 3 Times Round, And as they go out the School, every one, that Can Spell, is obliged to Spell a Word, and to go out Leisurely one after another. I Catechised 3 or 4 Times a Week according to the Assembly's Shorter Catechism, and many Times Proposed Questions of my own, and in my own Tongue. I found Difficulty with Some Children, who were Some what Dull, most of these can soon learn to Say over their Letters, they Distinguish the Sounds by the Ear, but their Eyes can't Distinguish the Letters, and the way I took to cure them was by making an Alphabet on Small bits of paper, and glued them on Small Chips of Cedar after this manner A B & C. I put these on Letters in order on a Bench then point to one Letter and bid a Child to take notice of it, and then I order the Child to fetch me the Letter from the Bench; if he Brings the Letter, it is well, if not he must go again and again till he brings ye right Letter. When they can bring any Letters this way, then I just Jumble them together, and bid them to set them in Alphabetical order, and it is a Pleasure to them; and they soon Learn their Letters this way.—I frequently Discussed or Exhorted my Scholars, in Religious matters.—My Method in our Religious Meetings was this; Sabbath

Morning we Assemble together about 10 o'C and begin with Singing; we generally Sung Dr. Watt's Psalms or Hymns. I distinctly read the Psalm or Hymn first, and then gave the meaning of it to them, after that Sing, then Pray, and Sing again after Prayer. Then proceed to Read from Suitable portion of Scripture, and so Just give the plain Sense of it in Familiar Discourse and apply it to them. So continued with Prayer and Singing. In the after Noon and Evening we Proceed in the Same Manner, and so in Wednesday Evening. Some Time after Mr. Horton left these Indians, there was a remarkable revival of religion among these Indians and many were hopefully converted to the Saving knowledge of God in Jesus. It is to be observed before Mr. Horton left these Indians they had Some Prejudices infused in their minds, by Some Enthusiastical Exhorters from New England, against Mr. Horton, and many of them had left him; by this means he was Discouraged; and Sued a Dismission and was disposed from these Indians. And being acquainted with the Enthusiasts in New England: & the make and the Disposition of the Indians I took a mild way to reclaim them. I opposed them not openly but let them go on in their way, and whenever I had an opportunity, I would read Such pages of the Scriptures, and I thought would confound their Notions, and I would come to them with all Authority, Saying, "thus Saith the Lord"; and by this means, the Lord was pleased to Bless my poor Endeavours, and they were reclaimed, and Brought to hear almost any of the ministers.——I am now to give an Account of my Circumstances and manner of Living. I Dwelt in a Wigwam, a Small Hut with Small Poles and Covered with Matts made of Flags, and I was obligd to remove twice a Year, about 2 miles Distance, by reason of the Scarcity of wood, for in one Neck of Land they Planted their Corn, and in another, they had their wood, and I was obligd to have my Corn carted and my Hay also,—and I got my Ground Plow'd every year, which Cost me about 12 shillings an acre; and I kept a Cow and a Horse, for which I paid 21 shillings every year York currency, and went 18 miles to Mill for every Dust of meal we used in my family. I Hired or Joined with my Neighbours to go to Mill, with a Horse or ox Cart, or on Horse Back, and Some time went myself. My Family Increasing fast, and my Visitors also. I was obligd to contrive every way to Support my Family; I took all opportunities, to get Some thing to feed my Family Daily. I Planted my own Corn, Potatoes, and Beans; I used to be out hoeing my Corn Some times before Sun Rise and after my School is Dismist, and by this means I was able to raise my own Pork, for I was allowed to keep 5 Swine. Some mornings & Evenings I would be out with my Hook and Line to Catch fish, and in the Fall of Year and in the Spring, I used my gun, and fed my Family with Fowls. I Could more than pay for my Powder & Shot with Feathers.[3] At other Times I Bound old Books for Easthampton People, made wooden Spoons and Ladles, Stocked Guns, & worked on Cedar to make Pails, Piggins[4] and Churns & C. Besides all these Difficulties I met with adverse Providence. I bought a Mare, had it but a little while, and she fell into the Quick Sand and Died. After a while Bought another, I kept her about half year, and she was gone, and I never have heard of nor Seen her

[3]Feathers were prized as decorations by white Americans and Europeans and were thus an important exchange item.

[4]A small, wooden pail with a stave for a handle.

from that Day to this; it was Supposed Some Rogue Stole her. I got another and Died with a Distemper, and last of all I Bought a Young Mare, and kept her till She had one Colt, and She broke her Leg and Died, and Presently after the Colt Died also. In the whole I Lost 5 Horse Kind; all these Losses helped to pull me down; and by this Time I got greatly in Debt, and acquainted my Circumstances to Some of my Friends, and they Represented my Case to the Commissioners of Boston, and Interceded with them for me, and they were pleased to vote 15 £ for my Help, and Soon after Sent a Letter to my good Friend at New London, acquainting him that they had Superseded their Vote; and my Friends were so good as to represent my Needy Circumstances Still to them, and they were so good at Last, as to Vote £ 15 and Sent it, for which I am very thankful; and the Revd Mr. Buell was so kind as to write in my behalf to the gentlemen of Boston; and he told me they were much Displeased with him, and heard also once again that they blamed me for being Extravagant; I Can't Conceive how these gentlemen would have me Live. I am ready to impute it to their Ignorance, and I would wish they had Changed Circumstances with me but one month, that they may know, by experience what my Case really was; but I am now fully convinced, that it was not Ignorance, For I believe it can be proved to the world that these Same Gentlemen gave a young Missionary a Single man, *one Hundred Pounds* for one year, and fifty Pounds for an Interpreter, and thirty Pounds for an Introducer; so it Cost them one Hundred & Eighty Pounds in one Single Year, and they Sent too where there was no Need of a Missionary.

Now you See what difference they made between me and other missionaries; they gave me 180 Pounds for 12 years Service, which they gave for one years Services in another Mission.—In my Service (I speak like a fool, but I am Constrained) I was my own Interpreter. I was both a School master and Minister to the Indians, yea I was their Ear, Eye & Hand, as Well as Mouth. I leave it with the World, as wicked as it is, to Judge, whether I ought not to have had half as much, they gave a young man Just mentioned which would have been but £ 50 a year; and if they ought to have given me that, I am not under obligations to them, I owe them nothing at all; what can be the Reason that they used me after this manner? I can't think of any thing, but this as a Poor Indian Boy Said, Who was Bound out to an English Family, and he used to Drive Plow for a young man, and he whipt and Beat him allmost every Day, and the young man found fault with him, and Complained of him to his master and the poor Boy was Called to answer for himself before his master, and he was asked, what it was he did, that he was So Complained of and beat almost every Day. He Said, he did not know, but he Supposed it was because he could not drive any better; but says he, I Drive as well as I know how; and at other Times he Beats me, because he is of a mind to beat me; but says he believes he Beats me for the most of the Time "because I am an Indian".

So I am *ready* to Say, they have used me thus, because I Can't Influence the Indians so well as other missionaries; but I can *assure them* I have endeavoured to teach them as well as I know how;—but I *must Say,* "I believe it is because I am a poor Indian". I Can't help that God has made me So; I did not make my self so.—

1768

A Sermon Preached by Samson Occom[1]

The sacred words that I have chosen to speak from, upon this undesirable occasion are found written in the Epistle of St. Paul to the ROMANS, VI. 23. For the Wages of Sin is Death, but the Gift of God is Eternal Life through Jesus Christ our Lord.

Death is called the king of terrors, and it ought to be the subject of every man and woman's thoughts daily; because it is that unto which they are liable every moment of their lives: And therefore it cannot be unreasonable to think, speak and hear of it at any time, and especially on this mournful occasion; for we must all come to it, how soon we cannot tell; whether we are prepared or not prepared, ready or not ready, whether death is welcome or not welcome, we must feel the force of it: Whether we concern ourselves with death or not, it will concern itself with us. Seeing that this is the case with every one of us, what manner of persons ought we to be in all holy conversation and godliness; how ought men to exert themselves in preparation for death, continually; for they know not what a day or an hour may bring forth, with respect to them. But alas! according to the appearance of mankind in general; death is the least thought of. They go on from day to day as if they were to live here forever, as if this was the only life. They contrive, rack their inventions, disturb their rest, and even hazard their lives in all manner of dangers, both by sea and land; yea, they leave no stone unturned that they may live in the world, and at the same time have little or no contrivance to die well. God and their souls are neglected, and heaven and eternal happiness are disregarded; Christ and his religion are despised—yet most of these very men intend to be happy when they come to die, not considering that there must be great preparation in order to die well. Yea there is none so fit to live as those that are fit to die; those that are not fit to die are not fit to live. Life and death are nearly connected; we generally own that it is a great and solemn thing to die. If this be true, then it is a great and solemn thing to live, for as we live so we shall die. But I say again, how do mankind realize these things? They are busy about the things of this world as if there was no death before them. Dr. *Watts* pictures them out to the life in his psalms.[2]

> See the vain race of mortals move,
> Like shadows o'er the plain,
> They rage and strive, desire and love,
> But all the noise is vain.

[1]First published at New Haven in 1772, the sermon appeared in at least nineteen editions, including a translation into Welsh in 1827. The version reprinted here is the tenth edition, published at Bennington, Vermont.

[2]Isaac Watts (1674–1748), English hymn writer, published *The Psalms of David Imitated in the Language of the New Testament* in 1719. Occom quotes number 613.

Some walk in honour's gaudy show,
Some dig for golden ore,
They toil for heirs they know not who,
And strait are seen no more.

But on the other hand, life is the most precious thing, and ought to be the most desired by all rational creatures. It ought to be prized above all things; yet there is nothing so abused and despised as life, and nothing so neglected: I mean eternal life is shamefully disregarded by men in general, and eternal death is chosen rather than life. This is the general complaint of the Bible from the beginning to the end. As long as Christ is neglected, life is refused, as long as sin is cherished, death is chosen. And this seems to be the woful case of mankind of all nations, according to their appearance in these days: For it is too plain to be denied, that vice and immorality, and floods of iniquity are abounding every where amongst all nations, and all orders and ranks of men, and in every sect of people. Yea there is a great agreement and harmony among all nations, and from the highest to the lowest to practice sin and iniquity; and the pure religion of Jesus Christ is turned out of doors, and is dying without; or, in other words, the Lord Jesus Christ is turned out of doors by men in general, and even by his professed people. "He Came to his own, and his own received him not."[3] But the devil is admitted, he has free access to the houses and hearts of the children of men: Thus life is refused and death is chosen.

But in further speaking upon our text by divine assistance, I shall consider these two general propositions.

I. That sin is the cause of all the miseries that befall the children of men, both as to their bodies and souls, for time and eternity.

II. That eternal life and happiness is the gift of God through Jesus Christ our Lord.

In speaking to the first proposition, I shall first consider the nature of sin; and secondly I shall consider the consequences of sin or the wages of sin, which is death. First then, we are to describe the nature of sin.

Sin is the transgression of the law:—This is the scripture definition of sin.—Now the law of God being holy, just and good; sin must be altogether unholy, unjust and evil. If I was to define sin, I should call it a contrariety to God; and as such it must be the vilest thing in the world; it is full of all evil; it is the evil of evils; the only evil in which dwells no good thing; and it is most destructive to God's creation, wherever it takes effect. It was sin that transformed the very angels in heaven, into devils; and it was sin that caused hell to be made. If it had not been for sin, there never would have been such a thing as hell or devil, death or misery.

And if sin is such a thing as we have just described, it must be worse than the devils in hell itself.—Sin is full of deadly poison; it is full of malignity and hatred against God; against all his divine perfections and attributes, against his wisdom, against his power, against his holiness and goodness, against his mercy and justice, against his law and gospel; yea against his very being and existence. Were it in the power of sin, it would even dethrone God, and set itself on the throne.

[3]John 1:11.

When Christ the Son of the Most High came down from the glorious world above, into this wretched world of sin and sorrow, to seek and to save that which was lost, sin or sinners rose up against him, as soon as he entered our world, and pursued him with hellish malice, night and day, for above thirty years together, till they killed him.

Further, sin is against the Holy Ghost; it opposes all its good and holy operations upon the children of men. When, and wherever there is the out pouring of the Spirit of God, upon the children of men, in a way of conviction and conversion; sin will immediately prompt the devil and his children to rise up against it, and they will oppose the work with all their power, and in every shape. And if open opposition will not do, the devil will mimic the work and thus prevent the good effect.

Thus we find by the scripture accounts, that whenever God raises up men, and uses them as instruments of conviction and conversion, the devil and his instruments will rise up to destroy both the reformers and the reformed. Thus it has been from the early days of christianity to this day. We have found it so in our day. In the time of the outpouring of the Spirit of God in these colonies, to the conviction and reformation of many; immediately sin and the devil influenced numbers to rise up against the good work of God, calling it a delusion, and work of the devil. And thus sin also opposes every motion of the Spirit of God, in the heart of every christian; this makes a warfare in the soul.

2. I shall endeavor to show the sad consequences or effects of sin upon the children of men.

Sin has poisoned them, and made them distracted or fools. The psalmist says, The fool hath said in his heart, there is no God.[4] And Solomon, through his proverbs, calls ungodly sinners fools; and their sin he calls their folly and foolishness.[5] The apostle James says, But the tongue can no man tame, it is an unruly evil, full of deadly poison.[6] It is the heart that is in the first place full of deadly poison. The tongue is only an interpreter of the heart. Sin has vitiated the whole man, both soul and body; all the powers are corrupted; it has turned the minds of men against all good, towards all evil. So poisoned are they according to the prophet, Isa. v. 20. "Wo unto them that call evil good and good evil; that put darkness for light, and light for darkness; that put bitter for sweet, and sweet for bitter." And Christ Jesus saith in John iii. 19, 20. "And this is the condemnation, that light has come into the world, and men have loved darkness rather than light, because their deeds were evil. For every one that doeth evil, hateth the light, neither cometh to the light lest his deeds should be reproved." Sin hath stupified mankind, they are now ignorant of God their Maker; neither do they enquire after him. And they are ignorant of themselves, they know not what is good for them, neither do they understand their danger; and they have no fear of God before their eyes.

Further, sin hath blinded their eyes, so that they cannot discern spiritual things: neither do they see the way that they should go, and they are as deaf as adders, so that they cannot hear the joyful sound of the gospel that brings glad tidings of peace and pardon to sinners of mankind. Neither do they regard the charmer charming

[4]Psalms 14.1.
[5]See Proverbs 12:23, 14:8, 14:24, 15:2.
[6]James 3:8.

never so wisely.—Not only so, but sin has made man proud, though he has nothing to be proud of; for he has lost his excellency, his beauty and happiness; he is a bankrupt and is excommunicated from God; he was turned out of paradise by God himself, and became a vagabond in God's world, and as such he has no right or title to the least crumb of mercy, in the world: Yet he is proud, he is haughty, and exalts himself above God, though he is wretched and miserable, and poor and blind and naked. He glories in his shame. Sin has made him beastly and devilish; yea, he is sunk beneath the beasts, and is worse than the ravenous beasts of the wilderness. He is become ill-natured, cruel and murderous; he is contentious and quarrelsome. I said he is worse than the ravenous beasts, for wolves and bears don't devour their own kind, but man does; yea, we have numberless instances of women killing their own children; such women I think are worse than she-tygers.

Sin has made man dishonest, and deceitful, so that he goes about cheating and defrauding and deceiving his fellow-men in the world: Yea, he has become a cheat himself, he goes about in vain shew; we do not know where to find man.—Sometimes we find as an angel of God; and at other times we find as a devil, even one and the same man. Sin has made a man a liar even from the womb; so there is no believing nor trusting him. The royal psalmist says, "The wicked are estranged from the womb, they go astray as soon as they are born, speaking lies."[7] His language is also corrupted. Whereas he had a pure and holy language, in his innocency, to adore and praise God his Maker, he now curses and swears, and profanes, the holy name of God, and curses and damns his fellow creatures. In a word, man is a most unruly and ungovernable creature, and is become as the wild ass's colt, and is harder to tame than any of God's creatures in this world.—In short, man is worse than all the creatures in this lower world, his propensity is to evil and that continually; he is more like the devil than any creature we can think of: And I think it is not going beyond the word of God, to say man is the most devilish creature in the world. Christ said to his disciples, One of you is a devil; to the Jews he said, Ye are of your father the devil, and the lusts of your father ye will do.[8] Thus every unconverted soul is a child of the devil, sin has made them so.

We have given some few hints of the nature of sin, and the effects of sin on mankind.

We shall in the next place consider the wages or the reward of sin, which is death.

Sin is the cause of all the miseries that attend poor sinful man, which will finally bring him to death, death temporal and eternal. I shall first consider his temporal death.

His temporal death then begins as soon as he is born. Though it seems to us that he is just beginning to live, yet in fact he is just entered into a state of death: St. Paul says, "W[h]erefore, as by one man sin entered into the world, and death by sin; and so death passed upon all men, for that all have sinned."[9] Man is surrounded with ten thousand instruments of death, and is liable to death every moment of his life; a thousand diseases await him on every side continually; the sentence of death has pass'd upon them as soon as they are born; yea they are struck with death as soon as they

[7]Psalms 58:3.
[8]Psalms 58:3.
[9]Romans 5:12.

breathe. And it seems all the enjoyments of men in this world are also poisoned with sin; for God said to Adam after he had sinned, "Cursed is the ground for thy sake, in sorrow shalt thou eat of it all the days of thy life."[10] By this we plainly see that every thing that grows out of the ground is cursed, and all creatures that God hath made for man are cursed also; and whatever God curses is a cursed thing indeed. Thus death and destruction is in all the enjoyments of men in this life, every enjoyment in this world is liable to misfortune in a thousand ways, both by sea and land.

How many ships, that have been loaded with the choicest treasures of the earth have been swallowed up in the ocean, many times just before they enter their desired haven. And vast treasures have been consumed by fire on the land, &c.—And the fruits of the earth are liable to many judgments. And the dearest and nearest enjoyments of men are generally balanced with equal sorrow and grief.—A man and his wife who have lived together in happiness for many years; that have comforted each other in various changes of life, must at last be separated; one or the other must be taken away first by death, and then the poor survivor is drowned in tears, in sorrow, mourning and grief. And when a child or children are taken away by death, the bereaved parents are bowed down with sorrow and deep mourning. When Joseph was sold by his brethren unto the Ishmaelites, they took his coat and rolled it in blood, and carried it to their father, and the good old patriarch knew it to be Joseph's coat, and he concluded that his dear Joseph was devoured by evil beasts; and he was plunged all over in sorrow and bitter mourning, and he refused to be comforted. And so when tender parents are taken away by death, the children are left comfortless. All this is the sad effects of sin—These are the wages of sin.

And secondly we are to consider man's spiritual death, while he is here in this world. We find it thus written in the word of God, "And the Lord God commanded the man, saying of every tree of the garden thou mayst freely eat: but of the tree of knowledge of good and evil, thou shalt not eat of it, for in the day thou eatest thereof thou shalt surely die."[11] And yet he did eat of it, and so he and all his posterity are but dead men. And St. Paul to the Ephesians saith, "You hath he quickened who were dead in trespasses and sins."[12] The great Mr. Henry says, in this place, that unregenerate souls are dead in trespasses and sins.[13] All those who are in their sins, are dead in sins; yea, in trespasses and sins; and which may signify all sorts of sins, habitual and actual; sins of heart and life. Sin is the death of the soul. Wherever that prevails, there is a privation of all spiritual life. Sinners are dead in state, being destitute of the principles and powers of spiritual life; and cut off from God, the fountain of life: and they are dead in law, as a condemned malefactor is said to be a dead man. Now a dead man, in a natural sense, is unactive, and is of no service to the living; there is no correspondence between the dead and the living: There is no agreement or union between them, no fellowship at all between the dead and the living. A dead man is altogether ignorant of the intercourse among the living:—Just so it is with men that are spiritually dead; they have no agreeable activity. Their activity in sin, is their deadness and inactivity towards God. They are of no service to God; and

[10]Genesis 3:17.

[11]Genesis 2:16–17.

[12]Ephesians 2:1.

[13]Mathew Henry (1662–1714), a British nonconformist divine and commentator, is best known for his *Exposition of the Old and New Testament* (1710). Occom cites his commentary on Ephesians 2:1.

they have no correspondence with heaven; and there is no agreement or fellowship between them and the living God; and they are totally ignorant of the agreeable and sweet intercourse there is between God and his children here below: and they are ignorant, and know nothing of that blessed fellowship and union there is among the saints here below. They are ready to say indeed, behold how they love one another! But they know nothing of that love, that the children of God enjoy. As sin is in opposition to God; so sinners are at enmity against God; there is no manner of agreement between them.

Let us consider further. God is a living God, he is all life, the fountain of life; and a sinner is a dead soul; there is nothing but death in him. And now judge ye, what agreement can there be between them! God is a holy and pure God, and a sinner is an unholy and filthy creature;—God is a righteous Being, and a sinner is an unrighteous creature; God is light, and a sinner is darkness itself, &c. Further, what agreement can there be between God and a liar, a thief, a drunkard, a swearer, a profane creature, a whoremonger, an adulterer, an idolater, &c. No one that has any sense, dare say that there is any agreement. Further, as sinners are dead to God, as such, they have no delight in God, and godliness; they have no taste for the religion of Jesus Christ: they have no pleasure in the holy exercise of religion. Prayer is no pleasant work with them; or if they have any pleasure in it, it is not out of love to God, but out of self-love, like the Pharisees of old; they loved to pray in open view of men, that they might have praise from them. And perhaps, they were not careful to pray in secret. These were dead souls, they were unholy, rotten hypocrites, and so all their prayers and religious exercises were cold, dead, and abominable services to God. Indeed they are dead to all the duties that God requires of them: they are dead to the holy bible; to all the laws, commands, and precepts thereof; and to the ordinances of the gospel of the Lord Jesus Christ. When they read the book of God, it is like an old almanack to them, a dead book. But it is because they are dead, and as such, all their services are against God, even their best services are an abomination unto God; yea, sinners are so dead in sin, that the threatenings of God don't move them. All the thunderings and lightnings of Mount-Sinai don't stir them. All the curses of the law are out against them; yea, every time they read these curses in the bible, they are cursing them to their faces, and to their very eyes; yet they are unconcern'd, and go on in sin without fear. And lastly here, sin has so stupified the sinner, that he will not believe his own senses, he won't believe his own eyes, nor his own ears, he reads the book of God, but he does not believe what he reads. And he hears of God, and heaven, and eternal happiness, and of hell and eternal misery; but he believes none of these things; he goes on, as if there were no God, nor heaven and happiness; neither has he any fear of hell and eternal torments; and he sees his fellow-men dropping away daily on every side, yet he goes on carelessly in sin, as if he never was to die. And if he at any time thinks of dying, he hardly believes his own thoughts.——Death is at a great distance, so far off, that he dont concern himself about it, so as to prepare for it. God mournfully complains of his people, that they dont consider;—O that they were wise, that they understood this, that they would consider their latter end.

The next thing I shall consider, is the actual death of the body, or separation between soul and body. At the cessation of natural life, there is no more joy or sorrow; no more hope nor fear, as to the body; no more contrivance and carrying on of business; no more merchandizing and trading; no more farming; no more buying and selling; no more building of any kind, no more contrivance at all to live in the world; no more honor nor reproach; no more praise; no more good report, nor evil report; no more learning of any trades, arts or sciences in the world; no more sinful pleasures, they are all at an end; recreations, visiting, tavern-hunting, musick and dancing, chambering and carousing, playing at dice and cards, or any game whatsoever; cursing and swearing, and profaning the holy name of God, drunkeness, fighting, debauchery, lying and cheating, in this world must cease forever. Not only so, but they must bid an eternal farewell to all the world; bid farewell to all their beloved sins and pleasures; and the places and possessions that knew them once, shall know them no more forever. And further, they must bid adieu to all sacred and divine things. They are obliged to leave the bible, and all the ordinances thereof; and to bid farewell to preachers, and all sermons, and all christian people, and christian conversation; they must bid a long farewell to sabbaths and seasons, and opportunities of worship; yea an eternal farewell to all mercy and all hope; an eternal farewell to God the Father, Son and Holy Ghost, and adieu to heaven and all happiness, to saints and all the inhabitants of the upper world. At your leisure please to read the destruction of Babylon; you will find it written in the 18th of the Revelations.

On the other hand, the poor departed soul must take up its lodging in sorrow, wo and misery, in the lake that burns with fire and brimstone, were the worm dieth not and the fire is not quenched; where a multitude of frightful deformed devils dwell, and the damned ghosts of Adam's race; where darkness, horror and despair reigns, or where hope never comes, and where poor guilty naked souls will be tormented with exquisite torments, even the wrath of the Almighty poured out upon the damned souls; the smoke of their torments ascending up forever and ever; their mouths and nostrils streaming forth with living fire; and hellish groans, cries and shrieks all around them, and merciless devils upbraiding them for their folly and madness, and tormenting them incessantly. And there they must endure the most unsatiable, fruitless desire, and the most overwhelming shame and confusion and the most horrible fear, and the most doleful sorrow, and the most racking despair. When they cast their flaming eyes to heaven, with Dives in torments, they behold an angry GOD, whose eyes are as a flaming fire, and they are struck with ten thousand darts of pain; and the sight of the happiness of the saints above, adds to their pains and aggravates their misery. And when they reflect upon their past folly and madness in neglecting the great salvation in their day, it will pierce them with ten thousand inconceivable torments; it will as it were enkindle their hell afresh; and it will cause them to curse themselves bitterly, and curse the day in which they were born, and curse their parents that were the instruments of their being in the world; yea, they will curse, bitterly curse, and wish that very GOD that gave them their being to be in the same condition with them in hell torments. This is what is called the second death and it is the last death, and an eternal death to a guilty soul.

And O eternity, eternity, eternity! Who can measure it? Who can count the years thereof? Arithmetic must fail, the thoughts of men and angels are drowned in it; how shall we describe eternity? To what shall we compare it? Were it possible to employ a fly to carry off this globe by the small particles thereof, and to carry them to such a distance that it would return once in *ten thousand* years for another particle, and so continue till it has carried off all this globe, and framed them together in some unknown space, till it has made just such a world as this is: After all, eternity would remain the same unexhausted duration. This must be the unavoidable portion of all impenitent sinners, let them be who they will, great or small, honorable or ignoble, rich or poor, bond or free. Negroes, Indians, English, or of what nation soever; all that die in their sins must go to hell together; for the wages of sin is death.

The next thing that I was to consider is this:

That eternal life and happiness is the free gift of God through Jesus Christ our Lord.

Under this proposition I shall now endeavour to show that this life and happiness is.

The life that is mentioned in our text is a spiritual life, it is the life of the soul; from sin to holiness, from darkness to light, a translation from the kingdom and dominion of satan, to the kingdom of God's grace. In other words, it is being restored to the image of God and delivered from the image of satan. And this life consists in union of the soul to God, and communion with God; a real participation of the divine nature, or in the Apostle's words, is a Christ formed within us; I live says he, yet not I but Christ liveth in me.[14] And the Apostle John saith God is love and he that dwelleth in love, dwelleth in God, and God in him.[15] This is the life of the soul. It is called emphatically life, because it is a life that shall never have a period, a stable, a permanent, and unchangeable life, called in the scriptures everlasting life, or life eternal. And the happiness of this life consists in communion with God, or in the spiritual enjoyment of God. As much as a soul enjoys of God in this life, just so much of life and happiness he enjoys or possesses; yea, just so much of heaven he enjoys. A true christian, desires no other heaven but the enjoyment of God; a full and perfect enjoyment of God, is a full and perfect heaven and happiness to a gracious soul.—Further, this life is called eternal life because God has planted a living principle in the soul; and whereas he was dead before, now he is made alive unto God; there is an active principle within him towards God, he now moves towards God in his religious devotions and exercises; is daily comfortably and sweetly walking with God, in all his ordinances and commands; his delight is in the ways of God; he breathes towards God, a living breath, in praises, prayers, adorations and thanksgivings; his prayers are now heard in the heavens, and his praises delight the ears of the Almighty, and his thanksgiving are accepted, so alive is he now to God, that it is his meat and drink, yea more than his meat and drink, to do the will of his heavenly Father. It is his delight, his happiness and pleasure to serve God. He does not drag himself to his duties now, but he does them out of choice, and with alacrity of soul. Yea, so alive is he to God, that he gives up himself and all that he has entirely to God, to be for him and no other; his whole aim is to glorify God, in all things, whether by life or death, all the same to him.

We have a bright example of this in St. Paul. After he was converted, he was all alive to God; he regarded not his life but was willing to spend and be spent in the service of his God; he was hated, revil'd, despised, laughed at, and called all manner of evil names; was scourged, stoned and imprisoned; and all could not stop his activity towards God. He would boldly and courageously go on in preaching the gospel of the Lord Jesus Christ, to poor lost and undone sinners; he would do the work God

[14]Galatians 2:20.
[15]Occom paraphrases I John 4:8, 12–13.

set him about, in spite of all opposition he met with either from men or devils, earth or hell; come death or come life, none of these things moved him, because he was alive unto God. Though he suffered hunger and thirst, cold and heat, poverty and nakedness by day and by night, by sea, and by land, and was in danger always; yet he would serve God amidst all these dangers. Read his amazing account in 2 Cor. 11. 23, and on.

Another instance of marvellous love towards God, we have in Daniel. When there was a proclamation of prohibition, sent by the king to all his subjects forbidding them to call upon their gods for 30 days; which was done by envious men, that they might find occasion against Daniel the servant of the most high God; yet he having the life of God in his soul regarded not the king's decree, but made his petition to his God, as often as he used to do though death was threatened to the disobedient. But he feared not the hell they had prepared; for it seems, the den resembled hell, and the lions represented the devils. And when he was actually cast into the lions den, the ravenous beasts became meek and innocent as lambs, before the prophet, because he was alive unto God; the spirit of the Most High was in him, and the lions were afraid before him. Thus it was with Daniel and Paul; they went through fire and water, as the common saying is, because they had eternal life in their souls in an eminent manner; and they regarded not this life for the cause and glory of God. And thus it has been in all ages with true Christians. Many of the fore-fathers of the English, in this country, had this life and are gone the same way, that the holy Prophets and Apostles went. Many of them went through all manner of sufferings for God; and a great number of them are gone home to heaven, in chariots of fire. I have seen the place in London, called Smithfield, where numbers were burnt to death for the religion of Jesus Christ.[16] And there is the same life in true christians now in these days; and if there should persecutions arise in our day, I verily believe, true christians would suffer with the same spirit and temper of mind, as those did, who suffered in days past.—This is the life which our text speaks of.

We proceed in the next place to show, that this life, which we have described, is the free gift of God, through Jesus Christ our Lord.

Sinners have forfeited all mercy into the hands of divine justice and have merited hell and damnation to themselves; for the wages of sin is everlasting death, but heaven and happiness is a free gift; it comes by favor; and all merit is excluded; and especially if we consider that we are fallen sinful creatures, and there is nothing in us that can recommend us to the favour of God; and we can do nothing that is agreeable and acceptable to God; and the mercies we enjoy in this life are altogether from the pure mercy of God; we are unequal to them. Good old Jacob cried out, under the sense of his unworthiness, "I am less than the least of all thy mercies,"[17] and we have nothing to give unto God if we essay to give all the service that we are capable of, we should give him nothing but what was his own, and when we give up ourselves unto God, both soul and body, we give him nothing; for we were his before; he had a right to do with us as he pleased, either to throw us into hell, or to save us.—There is nothing that we can call our own, but our sins; and who is he that dares to say, I

[16]Smithfield, a market until 1855, was a popular spot for burnings. The last for heresy occurred in 1612 during the reign of James I.

[17]Genesis 32:10.

expect to have heaven for my sins? for our text says, that the wages of sin is death. If we are thus unequal and unworthy of the least mercy in this life, how much more are we unworthy of eternal life? Yet God can find it in his heart to give it. And it is altogether unmerited; it is a free gift to undeserving and hell deserving sinners of mankind: it is altogether of God's sovereign good pleasure to give it. It is of free grace and sovereign mercy, and from the unbounded goodness of God; he was self-moved to it. And it is said that this life is given in and through our Lord Jesus Christ. It could not be given in any other way, but in and through the death and suffering of the Lord Jesus Christ; Christ himself is the gift, and he is the christian's life. "For God so loved the world that he gave his only begotten Son, that whosoever believed in him should not perish but have everlasting life."[18] The word says further, "For by grace ye are saved, through faith, and that not of yourselves it is the gift of God."[19] This is given through Jesus Christ our Lord; it is Christ that purchased it with his own blood; he prepared it with his divine and almighty power; and by the same power, and by the influence of his spirit, he prepares us for it; and by his divine grace preserves us to it. In a word, he is all in all in our eternal salvation; all this is the free gift of God.

I have now gone through what I proposed from my text. And I shall now make some application of the whole.

First to the criminal in particular; and then to the auditory in general.

My poor unhappy Brother MOSES,

As it was your own desire that I should preach to you this last discourse, so I shall speak plainly to you.—You are the bone of my bone, and flesh of my flesh. You are an Indian, a despised creature, but you have despised yourself; yea you have despised God more; you have trodden under foot his authority; you have despised his commands and precepts; And now as God says, be sure your sins will find you out. And now, poor Moses, your sins have found you out, and they have overtaken you this day; the day of your death is now come; the king of terrors is at hand; you have but a very few moments to breathe in this world.—The just law of man, and the holy laws of Jehovah, call aloud for the destruction of your mortal life; God says, "Whoso sheddeth man's blood by man shall his blood be shed."[20] This is the ancient decree of heaven, and it is to be executed by man; nor have you the least gleam of hope of escape, for the unalterable sentence is past: The terrible day of execution is come; the unwelcome guard is about you; and the fatal instruments of death are now made ready; your coffin and your grave, your last lodging are open ready to receive you.

Alas! poor Moses, now you know by sad, by woful experience, the living truth of our text, that the wages of sin is death. You have been already dead; yea, twice dead: By nature spiritually dead. And since the awful sentence of death has been passed upon you, you have been dead to all the pleasures of this life; or all the pleasures, lawful or unlawful, have been dead to you: And death, which is the wages of sin, is standing even on this side of your grave ready to put a final period to your mortal life; and just beyond the grave, eternal death awaits your poor soul, and devils are ready to drag your miserable soul down to their bottomless den, where everlasting wo and horror reigns; the place is filled with doleful shrieks, howls and groans of the

[18]John 3:16.
[19]Ephesians 2:8.
[20]Genesis 9:6.

damned. Oh! to what a miserable, folorn, and wretched condition has your extravagance folly and wickedness brought you! i.e. if you die in your sins. And O! what manner of repentance ought you to manifest! How ought your heart to bleed for what you have done! How ought you to prostrate your soul before a bleeding God! And under self-condemnation, cry out ah Lord, ah Lord, what have I done?—Whatever partiality, injustice and error there may be among the judges of the earth, remember that you have deserved a thousand deaths, and a thousand hells, by reason of your sins, at the hands of a holy God. Should God come out against you in strict justice, alas! what could you say for yourself; for you have been brought up under the bright sunshine, and plain, and loud sound of the gospel; and you have had a good education; you can read and write well; and God has given you a good natural understanding: And therefore your sins are so much more aggravated. You have not sinned in such an ignorant manner as others have done; but you have sinned with both your eyes open as it were, under the light even the glorious light of the gospel of the Lord Jesus Christ.—You have sinned against the light of your own conscience, against your knowledge and understanding; you have sinned against the pure and holy laws of God, the just laws of men; you have sinned against heaven and earth; you have sinned against all the mercies and goodness of God; you have sinned against the whole bible, against the Old and New-Testament; you have sinned against the blood of Christ, which is the blood of the everlasting covenant. O poor Moses, see what you have done! And now repent, repent, I say again repent; see how the blood you shed cries against you, and the avenger of blood is at your heels. O fly, fly, to the blood of the Lamb of God for the pardon of all your aggravated sins.

But let us now turn to a more pleasant theme.—Though you have been a great sinner, a heaven-daring sinner; yet hark and hear the joyful sound from heaven, even from the King of kings, and Lord of lords; that the gift of God is eternal life, through Jesus Christ our Lord. It is the free gift offered to the greatest sinners, and upon their true repentance towards God and faith in the Lord Jesus Christ they shall be welcome to the life they have spoken of: it is offered upon free terms. He that hath no money may come; he that hath no righteousness, no goodness may come, the call is to poor undone sinners; the call is not to the righteous, but sinners calling them to repentance. Hear the voice of the Son of the Most High God, Come unto me all ye that labor and are heavy laden, and I will give you rest.[21] This is a call, a gracious call to you poor Moses, under your present burden and distresses. And Christ alone has a right to call sinners to himself. It would be presumption for a mighty angel to call a poor sinner in this manner; and were it possible for you to apply to all God's creatures, they would with one voice tell you, that it was not in them to help you. Go to all the means of grace, they would prove miserable helps without Christ himself. Yea, apply to all the ministers of the gospel in the world, they would all say, that it was not in them, but would only prove as indexes, to point out to you, the Lord Jesus Christ, the only Saviour of sinners of mankind. Yea, go to all the angels in heaven they would do the same. Yea, go to God the Father himself without Christ, he could not help you, to speak after the manner of men, he would also point to the Lord Jesus Christ, and say this is my beloved Son, in whom I am well pleased hear ye him. Thus you see, poor Moses, that there is none in heaven, or earth, that can help you, but Christ; he

[21]Matthew 11:28.

alone has power to save, and to give life.—God the eternal Father appointed him, chose him, authorized and fully commissioned him to save sinners. He came down from heaven into this lower world, and became as one of us, and stood in our room. He was the second Adam. And as God demanded correct obedience of the first Adam; the second fulfil'd it; and as the first sinned and incurred the wrath and anger of God, the second endured it; he suffered in our room. As he became sin for us, he was a man of sorrows, and acquainted with grief; all our stripes were laid upon him; yea, he was finally condemned, because we were under condemnation; and at last was executed and put to death, for our sins; was lifted up between the heavens and the earth, and was crucified on the accursed tree; his blessed hands and feet were fastened there; there he died a shameful and ignominious death; There he finished the great work of our redemption: There his hearts blood was shed for our cleansing: There he fully satisfied the divine justice of God, for penitent, believing sinners, though they have been the chief of sinners.—O Moses! this is good news to you in this last day of your life; here is a crucified Saviour at hand for your sins; his blessed hands are outstretched, all in a gore of blood for you. This is the only Saviour, an Almighty Saviour, just such as you stand in infinite and perishing need of. O, poor Moses! hear the dying prayer of a gracious Saviour on the accursed tree. Father forgive them for they know not what they do. This was a prayer for his enemies and murderers; and it is for you, if you will now only repent and believe in him. O, why will you die eternally, poor Moses, since Christ has died for sinners? Why will you go to hell from beneath a bleeding Saviour as it were? This is the day of your execution, yet it is the accepted time, it is the day of salvation if you will now believe in the Lord Jesus Christ. Must Christ follow you into the prison by his servants and there intreat you to accept of eternal life, and will you refuse it? Must he follow you even to the gallows, and there beseech of you to accept of him, and will you refuse him? Shall he be crucified hard by your gallows, as it were, and will you regard him not. O poor Moses, now believe on the Lord Jesus Christ with all your heart, and thou shalt be saved eternally. Come just as you are, with all your sins and abominations, with all your filthiness, with all your blood-guiltiness, with all your condemnation, and lay hold of the hope set before you this day. This is the last day of salvation with your soul; you will be beyond the bounds of mercy in a few minutes more. O what a joyful day would it be if you would now openly believe in and receive the Lord Jesus Christ; it would be the beginning of heavenly days with your poor soul; instead of a melancholy day, it would be a wedding day to your soul: It would cause the very angels in heaven to rejoice, and the saints on earth to be glad; it would cause the angels to come down from the realms above, and wait hovering about your gallows, ready to convey your soul to the heavenly mansions. There to taste the possession of eternal glory and happiness, and join the heavenly choirs in singing the songs of Moses and the Lamb: There to set down forever with Abraham, Isaac and Jacob in the kingdom of God's glory; and your shame and guilt shall be forever banished from the place, and all sorrow and fear forever fly away, and tears be wiped from your face; and there shall you forever admire the astonishing and amazing and infinite mercy of God in Christ Jesus, in pardoning such a monstrous sinner as you have been; there you will claim the highest note of praise, for the riches of free grace in Christ Jesus. But if you will not except of a Saviour so freely offered to you in this last day of your life, you must this very day bid a farewell to God the Father Son and holy Ghost, to heaven and all the saints and angels that are there; and you must bid all the saints in this lower world an eternal farewell, and even the whole world. And so I must leave you in the hands of God; and I must turn to the whole auditory.

Sirs.—We may plainly see, from what we have heard, and from the miserable object before us, into what a doleful condition sin has brought mankind, even into a state of death and misery. We are by nature as certainly under the sentence of death from God, as this miserable man is by the just determination of man; for we are all dying creatures, and we are, or ought to be sensible of it; and this is the dreadful fruit of sin. O let us then fly from all appearance of sin; let us fight againgst it with all our might; let us repent and turn to God, and believe on the Lord Jesus Christ, that we may live for ever: Let us all prepare for death, for we know not how soon, nor how suddenly we may be called out of the world.

Permit me in particular, reverend gentlemen and fathers in Israel, to speak a few words to you, though I am very sensible that I need to be taught the first principles of the oracles of God, by the least of you. But since the Providence of God has so ordered it, that I must speak here on this occasion, I beg that you would not be offended nor be angry with me.

God has raised you up from among your brethren, and has qualified and authorized you to do his great work; and you are the servants of the Most High God, and ministers of the Lord Jesus Christ; you are Christ's ambassadors; you are called shepherds, watchmen overseers, or bishops, and you are rulers of the temples of God, or of the assemblies of God's people; you are God's angels, and as such you have nothing to do but to wait on God, and to do the work the Lord Jesus Christ your blessed Lord and Master has set you about, not fearing the face of any man, nor seeking to please men, but your Master. You are to declare the whole counsel of God, and to give a portion to every soul in due season; as a physician gives a portion to his patients, according to their diseases, so you are to give a portion to every soul in due season according to their spiritual maladies: Whether it be agreeable or not agreeable to them, you must give it to them; whether they will love you or hate you for it, you must do your work. Your work is to encounter sin and satan; this was the very end of the coming of Christ into the world, and the end of his death and sufferings; it was to make an end of sin and to destroy the works of the devil. And this is your work still, you are to fight the battles of the Lord. Therefore combine together, and be as terrible as an army with banners; attack this monster sin in all its shapes and windings, and lift up your voices as trumpets and not spare, call aloud, call your people to arms against this common enemy of mankind, that sin may not be their ruin. Call upon all orders ranks and degrees of people, to rise up against sin and satan. Arm your selves with fervent prayer continually, this is a terrible weapon against the kingdom of satan. And preach the death and sufferings, and the resurrection of Jesus Christ; for nothing is so destructive to the kingdom of the devil as this is. But what need I speak any more! Let us all attend, and hear the great Apostle of the Gentiles speak unto us in Eph. 6 ch. from the tenth verse and onward. Finally my bretheren, be strong in the Lord, and in the power of his might; put on the whole armour of God, that ye may be able to stand against the wiles of the devil. For we wrestle not against flesh and blood, but against principalities, against powers, against the rulers of darkness of this world, against spiritual wickedness in high places. Wherefore take unto you the whole armour of God, that ye may be able to stand in the evil day, and having done all, to stand. Stand therefore, having your loins girt about with truth, and having on the breast-plate of righteousness; And your feet shod with the preparation of the gospel of peace: Above all, taking the shield of faith, wherewith ye shall be able to quench all the fiery darts of the wicked: And take the helmet of salvation, and the sword of the spirit, which is the word of God: Praying always with all prayer and supplication in the spirit, and watching therunto with all perseverance, and supplication for all saints.

I shall now address myself to the Indians, my bretheren and kindred according to the flesh.

My poor Kindred,

You see the woful consequences of sin, by seeing this our poor miserable countryman now before us, who is to die this day for his sins and great wickedness. And it was the sin of drunkenness that has brought this destruction and untimely death upon him. There is a dreadful wo denounced from the Almighty against drunkards; and it is this sin, this abominable, this beastly and accursed sin of drunkenness, that has stript us of every desirable comfort in this life; by this we are poor miserable and wretched; by this sin we have no name nor credit in the world among polite nations; for this sin we are despised in the world, and it is all right and just, for we despise ourselves more; and if we don't regard ourselves, who will regard us? And it is for our sins and especially for that accursed, that most devilish sin of drunkenness that we suffer every day. For the love of strong drink we spend all that we have, and every thing we can get. By this sin we can't have comfortable houses, nor any thing comfortable in our houses; neither food nor raiment, nor decent utensils. We are obliged to put up with any sort of shelter just to screen us from the severity of the weather, and we go about with very mean, ragged and dirty clothes, almost naked. And we are half-starved, for the most of the time obliged to pick up any thing to eat. And our poor children are suffering every day for want of the necessaries of life; they are very often crying for want of food, and we have nothing to give them; and in the cold weather they are shivering and crying, being pinched with cold. All this for the love of strong drink. And this is not all the misery and evil we bring on ourselves in this world; but when we are intoxicated with strong drink we drown our rational powers, by which we are distinguished from the brutal creation we unman ourselves, and bring ourselves not only level with the beasts of the field, but seven degrees beneath them; yea we bring ourselves level with the devils; I don't know but we make ourselves worse than devils, for I never heard of drunken devils.

My poor kindred, do consider what a dreadful abominable sin drunkenness is. God made us men, and we chuse to be beasts and devils, God made us rational creatures, and we chuse to be fools. Do consider further, and behold a drunkard and see how he looks when he has drowned his reason; how deformed and shameful does he appear? He disfigures every part of him, both soul and body, which was made after the Image of God. He appears with awful deformity, and his whole visage is disfigured; if he attempts to speak he cannot bring out his words distinct, so as to be understood; if he walks he reels and staggers to and fro, and tumbles down. And see how he behaves, he is now laughing, and then he is crying, he is singing, and the next minute he is mourning, and is all love with every one, and anon he is raging and for fighting, and killing all before him, even the nearest and dearest relations and friends: Yea, nothing it too bad for a drunken man to do. He will do that which he would not do for the world, in his right mind; he may lie with his own sister or daughter as Lot did.

Further, when a person is drunk, he is just good for nothing in the world; he is of no service to himself, to his family, to his neighbours, or his country; and how much more unfit is he to serve God: Yet we are just fit for the service of the devil.

Again, a man in drunkenness is in all manner of dangers, he may be killed by his fellow-men, by wild beasts, and tame beasts; he may fall into the fire, into the water, or into a ditch; or he may fall down as he walks along, and break his bones or his neck; and he may cut him-self with edge-tools. Further if he has any money or any thing valuable, he may lose it all, or may be robbed, or he may make a foolish bargain and be cheated out of all he has.

I believe you know the truth of what I have just now said, many of you by sad experience; yet you will go on still in your drunkenness. Though you have been cheated over and over again, and you have lost your substance by drunkenness, yet you will venture to go on in this most destructive sin. O fools, when will ye be wise?—We all know the truth of what I have been saying, by what we have seen and heard of drunken deaths. How many have been drowned in our rivers, and how many frozen to death in the winter season! yet drunkards go on without fear and consideration: Alas, alas! What will become of all such drunkards? Without doubt they must all go to hell, except they truly repent and turn to God. Drunkenness is so common amongst us, that even our young men, (and what is still more shocking) *young women* are not ashamed to get drunk. Our young men will get drunk as soon as they will eat when they are hungry.—It is generally esteemed among men more abominable for a woman to be drunk than a man; and yet there is nothing more common amongst us than female drunkards. Women ought to be more modest than men; the holy scriptures recommend modesty to women in particular;—But drunken women have no modesty at all. It is more intolerable for a woman to get drunk, if we consider further, that she is in great danger of falling into the hands of the sons of Belial, or wicked men and being shamefully treated by them.

And here I cannot but observe, we find in sacred writ, a wo denounced against men who put their bottles to their neighbours mouth to make them drunk, that they may see their nakedness: And no doubt there are such devilish men now in our days, as there were in the days of old.

And to conclude, Consider my poor kindred, you that are drunkards, into what a miserable condition you have brought yourselves. There is a dreadful wo thundering against you every day, and the Lord says, That drunkards shall not inherit the kingdom of heaven.

And now let me exhort you all to break off from your drunkenness, by a gospel repentance, and believe on the Lord Jesus and you shall be saved. Take warning by this doleful sight before us, and by all the dreadful judgments that have befallen poor drunkards. O let us all reform our lives, and live as becomes dying creatures, in time to come. Let us be persuaded that we are accountable creatures to God, and we must be called to an account in a few days. You that have been careless all your days, now awake to righteousness, and be concerned for your poor never-dying souls. Fight against all sins, and especially the sin that easily besets you, and behave in time to come as becomes rational creatures; and above all things receive and believe on the

Lord Jesus Christ, and you shall have eternal life; and when you come to die, your souls will be received into heaven, there to be with the Lord Jesus in eternal happiness, with all the saints in glory: Which God of his infinite mercy grant, through Jesus Christ our Lord.—AMEN.

1772

Briton Hammon fl. 1760

Briton Hammon's captivity narrative is widely recognized as the first African American prose text published in North America. Unfortunately, the historical record of Hammon's life is limited to the information contained within his narrative, from which Hammon explains he has "omitted a great many things." Thus we do not know for certain whether he was a servant or a slave, whether he wrote the narrative in its entirety, or what his life was like after his return to Massachusetts. Yet Hammon's narrative still raises intriguing questions about how a man of African descent who was in servitude gained access to the public sphere and how he made use of the conventions of one of the era's most popular genres, the captivity narrative.

With his master's permission, Hammon departed from Massachusetts in 1747 on a ship bound for Jamaica. After picking up its cargo, the ship foundered off the Florida coast and was attacked by sixty Native Americans. Hammon, the only survivor, was quickly taken into captivity. Although he soon escaped aboard a Spanish schooner, he was later imprisoned for more than four years in a dungeon in Spanish Cuba because he refused to serve on a Spanish ship. After escaping from his Spanish captors, Hammon worked in Cuba before signing on board a ship bound for London. In London, Hammon was happily reunited with his master, General Winslow, after almost thirteen years. Soon after returning to Boston with his master, he published the narrative of his "uncommon sufferings."

Although Hammon is believed to be the author of his narrative, some critics have suggested that the narrative's opening and closing (and perhaps even the narrative itself) might have been authored by a white editor or writer. Ironically, the very characteristic that has caused some to question his authorship—the narrative's rather formulaic opening and closing—was a characteristic shared by numerous other eighteenth-century texts presumably written by *white* men and women, whose authorship remains unquestioned. The questioning of Hammon's authorship is revealing, given that eighteenth-century notions about authorship and about the importance of originality differed from our own era's privileging of authorial status. Many early American literary genres relied on a strict adherence to convention rather than on originality to achieve their didactic aims. That the authorship of Hammon's narrative is unconfirmed is thus unremarkable.

Contemporary readers might find it surprising that Briton Hammon made little reference to his race in his work; indeed, only one phrase in his lengthy title identified him as "A Negro Man,—Servant to General Winslow." In fact, Hammon's class position was undoubtedly much more important than his race from the perspective of his readers, and it is his subordinate position that is emphasized within the text. As a young servant or slave returning to Boston in 1760 during the middle of the Seven Years' War, Hammon would have been welcomed into a city whose male population was significantly depleted. Like young Thomas Brown, whose narrative was also published in Boston in 1760, Hammon represented a whole class of servants whose otherwise marginal status was transformed within the wartime economy. Furthermore, it was during conflicts like the Seven Years' War that the popularity and political importance of captivity narratives increased.

Yet for figures like Hammon, the experience of captivity did not fit neatly into the conventions of his chosen genre. Hammon's initial escape from captivity among Native Americans did not restore him to his community but instead to a second captivity among the Spanish. And although Hammon, like Mary Rowlandson and John Williams before him, describes his captors as barbarians and savages, his description of his eventual return to Boston—his final redemption—is contradictory, for Hammon seems to have been redeemed into servitude rather than freedom. The nature of Hammon's redemption is further complicated by the fact that he may well have been more free—at least in terms of receiving wages for his labor—during the intervals surrounding his captivities among Native Americans and the Spanish than he was after returning to Boston with his "good Master." Hammon's narrative, one of only two eighteenth-century African American captivity narratives, thus adds a significant dimension to the study of an important early American literary genre.

Amy E. Winans
Susquehanna University

PRIMARY WORK

Narrative of the Uncommon Sufferings and Surprizing Deliverance of Briton Hammon, 1760.

Narrative of the Uncommon Sufferings and Surprizing Deliverance of Briton Hammon[1]

TO THE READER,

AS my Capacities and Condition of Life are very low, it cannot be expected that I should make those Remarks on the Sufferings I have met with, or the kind Providence of a good GOD for my Preservation, as one in a higher Station; but shall leave that to the Reader as he goes along, and so I shall only relate Matters of Fact as they occur to my Mind—

[1]The complete title of the Narrative was *Narrative of the Uncommon Sufferings and Surprizing Deliverance of* Briton Hammon, *A Negro Man,—Servant to General Winslow, of Marshfield, in New-England; Who returned to* Boston, *after having been absent almost Thirteen Years. Containing An Account of the many Hardships he underwent from the Time he left his Master's House, in the Year 1747, to the Time of his Return to* Boston.—*How he was Cast away in the Capes of* Florida;—*the horrid Cruelty and inhuman Barbarity of the* Indians *in murdering the whole Ship's Crew;—the Manner of his being carry'd by them into Captivity. Also, An Account of his being Confined Four Years and Seven Months in a close Dungeon,—And the remarkable Manner in which he met with his* good old Master *in* London; *who returned to* New-England, *a Passenger, in the same Ship.*

On Monday, 25th Day of *December,* 1747, with the leave of my Master, I went from *Marshfield,* with an Intention to go a Voyage to Sea, and the next Day, the 26th, got to *Plymouth,* where I immediately ship'd myself on board of a Sloop, Capt. *John Howland,* Master, bound to *Jamaica* and the *Bay*[2]—We sailed from *Plymouth* in a short Time, and after a pleasant Passage of about 30 Days, arrived at *Jamaica*; we was detain'd at *Jamaica* only 5 Days, from whence we sailed for the *Bay,* where we arrived safe in 10 Days. We loaded our Vessel with Logwood, and sailed from the *Bay* the 25th Day of May following, and the 15th Day of *June,* we were cast away on *Cape Florida* about 5 Leagues from the Shore; being now destitute of every Help,[3] we knew not what to do or what Course to take in this our sad Condition:—The Captain was advised, intreated, and beg'd on, by every Person on board, to heave over but only 20 Ton of the *Wood,* and we should get clear, which if he had done, might have sav'd his Vessel and Cargo, and not only so, but his own Life, as well as the Lives of the Mate and Nine Hands, as I shall presently relate.

After being upon this Reef two Days, the Captain order'd the Boat to be hoisted out, and then ask'd who were willing to tarry on board? The whole Crew was for going on Shore at this Time, but as the Boat would not carry 12 persons at once, and to prevent any Uneasiness, the Captain, a Passenger, and one Hand tarry'd on board, while the Mate, with Seven Hands besides myself, were order'd to go on Shore in the Boat, which as soon as we had reached, one half were to be Landed, and the other four to return to the Sloop, to fetch the Captain and the others on Shore. The Captain order'd us to take with us our Arms, Ammunition, Provisions and Necessaries for Cooking, as also a Sail to make a Tent of, to shelter us from the Weather; after having left the Sloop we stood towards the Shore, and being within Two Leagues of the same, we espy'd a Number of Canoes, which we at first took to be Rocks, but soon found our Mistake, for we perceiv'd they moved towards us; we presently saw an English Colour hoisted in one of the Canoes, at the Sight of which we were not a little rejoiced, but on our advancing yet nearer, we found them, to our very great Surprize, to be *Indians* of which there were Sixty; being now so near them we could not possibly make our Escape; they soon came up with and boarded us, took away all our Arms, Ammunition, and Provision. The whole Number of Canoes (being about Twenty,) then made for the Sloop, except Two which they left to guard us, who order'd us to follow on with them; the Eighteen which made for the Sloop, went so much faster than we that they got on board above Three Hours before we came along side, and had kill'd Captain *Howland,* the Passenger and the other hand; we came to the Larboard side of the Sloop, and they order'd us round to the Starboard, and as we were passing round the Bow,[4] we saw the whole Number of *Indians,* advancing forward and loading their Guns, upon which the Mate said, *"my Lads we are all dead Men,"* and before we had got round, they discharged their Small Arms upon us, and kill'd Three of our hands, viz. *Reuben Young* of *Cape-Cod,* Mate; *Joseph Little* and *Lemuel Doty* of *Plymouth,* upon which I immediately jump'd overboard, chusing rather to be drowned, than to be kill'd by those barbarous and inhuman Savages. In three or four Minutes

[2]John Howland was captain of the ship, not "master" to Hammon.

[3]Florida was held by Spain at this time.

[4]Evidently, they were on the left side (larboard) and were ordered to remove to the right side (starboard) of the ship, to which side they passed by moving around the ship by way of its front (bow).

after, I heard another Volley which dispatched the other five, viz. *John Nowland,* and *Nathaniel Rich,* both belonging to *Plymouth,* and *Elkanah Collymore,* and *James Webb,* Strangers, and *Moses Newmock,* Molatto. As soon as they had kill'd the whole of the People, one of the Canoes padled after me, and soon came up with me, hawled me into the Canoe, and beat me most terribly with a Cutlass, after that they ty'd me down, then this Canoe stood for the Sloop again and as soon as she came along side, the *Indians* on board the Sloop betook themselves to their Canoes, then set the Vessel on Fire, making a prodigious shouting and hallowing like so many Devils. As soon as the Vessel was burnt down to the Water's edge, the *Indians* stood for the Shore, together with our Boat, on board of which they put 5 hands. After we came to the Shore, they led me to their Hutts, where I expected nothing but immediate Death, and as they spoke broken English, were often telling me, while coming from the Sloop to the Shore, that they intended to roast me alive. But the Providence of God order'd it other ways, for He appeared for my Help, *in this Mount of Difficulty,* and they were better to me then my Fears, and soon unbound me, but set a Guard over me every Night. They kept me with them about five Weeks, during which Time they us'd me pretty well, and gave me boil'd Corn, which was what they often eat themselves. The Way I made my Escape from these Villains was this; A Spanish Schooner arriving there from *St. Augustine,* the Master of which, whose Name was *Romond,* asked the *Indians* to let me go on board his Vessel, which they granted, and the Captain[5] knowing me very well, weigh'd Anchor and carry'd me off to the *Havanna,*[6] and after being there four Days the *Indians* came after me, and insisted on having me again, as I was their Prisoner;—They made Application to the Governor, and demanded me again from him; in answer to which the Governor told them, that as they had put the whole Crew to Death, they should not have me again, and so paid them Ten Dollars for me, adding, that he would not have them kill any Person hereafter, but take as many of them as they could, of those that should be cast away, and bring them to him for which he would pay them Ten Dollars a-head. At the *Havanna* I lived with the Governor in the Castle about a Twelve-month, where I was walking thro' the Street, I met with a Press-Gang who immediately prest me, and put me into Gaol, and with a Number of others I was confin'd till next Morning,[7] when we were all brought out, and ask'd who would go on board the King's Ships, four of which having been lately built, were bound to *Old-Spain,* and on my refusing to serve on board, they put me in a close Dungeon, where I was confin'd *Four years and seven months,* during which time I often made application to the Governor, by Persons who came to see the Prisoners, but they never acquainted him with it, nor did he know all this Time what became of me, which was the means of my being confin'd there so long. But kind Providence so order'd it, that after I had been in this Place so long as the Time mention'd above the Captain of a Merchantman, belonging to *Boston,* having sprung a Leak was obliged to put into the *Havanna* to rest, and while he was at Din-

[5]Hammon's note reads: "The Way I came to know this Gentleman was, by his being taken last War by an *English* Privateer, and brought into *Jamaica,* while I was there."

[6]That is, Hammon boarded a Spanish ship from St. Augustine, Florida, which took him to Havanna, capital of the Spanish colony in present-day Cuba. Francisco Antonio Cagigal de la Vega (1695–1777) was governor of Cuba.

[7]Hammon was seized by an impressment crew, usually supported by the government, and held in jail (gaol) for possible service (pressment).

ner at Mrs. *Betty Howard's,* she told the Captain of my deplorable Condition, and said she would be glad, if he could by some means or other relieve me; The Captain told Mrs. *Howard* he would use his best Endeavours for my Relief and Enlargement.

Accordingly, after Dinner, [the Captain] came to the Prison, and ask'd the Keeper if he might see me; upon his Request I was brought out of the Dungeon, and after the Captain had Interrogated me, told me, he would intercede with the Governor for my Relief out of that miserable Place, which he did, and the next Day the Governor sent an order to release me; I lived with the Governor about a Year after I was delivered from the Dungeon, in which Time I endeavour'd three Times to make my Escape, the last of which proved effectual; the first Time I got on board of Captain *Marsh,* an *English* Twenty Gun Ship, with a Number of others, and lay on board conceal'd that Night; and the next Day the Ship being under sail, I thought myself safe, and so made my Appearance upon Deck, but as soon as we were discovered the Captain ordered the Boat out, and sent us all on Shore—I intreated the Captain to let me, in particular, tarry on board, begging, and crying to him, to commiserate my unhappy Condition, and added, that I had been confin'd almost five Years in a close Dungeon, but the Captain would not hearken to any Intreaties, for fear of having the Governor's Displeasure, and so I was obliged to go on Shore.

After being on Shore another Twelvemonth, I endeavour'd to make my Escape the second Time, by trying to get on board of a Sloop bound to *Jamaica,* and as I was going from the City to the Sloop, was unhappily taken by the Guard, and ordered back to the Castle, and there confined.—However, in a short Time I was set at Liberty, and order'd with a Number of others to carry the Bishop[8] from the Castle, thro' the Country, to confirm the old People, baptize Children, &c. for which he receives large Sums of Money.—I was employ'd in this Service about Seven Months, during which Time I lived very well, and then returned to the Castle again, where I had my Liberty to walk about the City, and do Work for my self;—The *Beaver,* an *English* Man of War then lay in the Harbour, and having been informed by some of the Ship's Crew that she was to sail in a few Days, I had nothing now to do, but to seek an Opportunity how I should make my Escape.

Accordingly one Sunday Night the Lieutenant of the Ship with a Number of the Barge Crew were in a Tavern, and Mrs. *Howard* who had before been a Friend to me, interceded with the Lieutenant to carry me on board: the Lieutenant said he would with all his Heart, and immediately I went on board in the Barge. The next Day the *Spaniards* came along side the *Beaver,* and demanded me again, with a Number of others who had made their Escape from them, and got on board the Ship, but just before I did; but the Captain, who was a true *Englishman,* refus'd them, and said he could not answer it, to deliver up any *Englishman* under *English* Colours.—In a few Days we set Sail for *Jamaica,* where we arrived safe, after a short and pleasant Passage.

After being at *Jamaica* a short Time we sail'd for *London,* as convoy to a Fleet of Merchantmen, who all arrived safe in the *Downs,* I was turned over to another Ship, the *Arcenceil,* and there remained about a Month. From this Ship I went on board the *Sandwich* of 90 Guns; on board the *Sandwich,* I tarry'd 6 Weeks, and then was

[8]The bishop at this time was Pedro Augustín Morell de Santa Cruz (1694–1768). Hammon's note reads: "He is carried (by Way of Respect) in a large Two-arm Chair; the Chair is lin'd with crimson Velvet, and supported by eight Persons."

order'd on board the *Hercules,* Capt. *John Porter,* a 74 Gun Ship, we sail'd on a Cruize, and met with a *French* 84 Gun Ship, and had a very smart Engagement, in which about 70 of our Hands were Kill'd and Wounded, the Captain lost his Leg in the Engagement, and I was Wounded in the Head by a small Shot.[9] We should have taken this Ship, if they had not cut away the most of our Rigging; however, in about three Hours after, a 64 Gun Ship, came up with and took her—I was discharged from the *Hercules* the 12th Day of *May* 1759 (having been on board of that Ship 3 Months) on account of my being disabled in the Arm, and render'd incapable of Service, after being honourably paid the Wages due to me. I was put into the *Greenwich* Hospital where I stay'd and soon recovered.—I then ship'd myself a Cook on board Captain *Martyn,* an arm'd Ship in the King's Service. I was on board this Ship almost Two Months, and after being paid my Wages, was discharg'd in the Month of *October.*—After my discharge from Captain *Martyn,* I was taken sick in *London* of a Fever, and was confin'd about 6 Weeks, where I expended all my Money, and left in very poor Circumstances; and unhappy for me I knew nothing of my *good Master's* being in *London* at this my very difficult Time. After I got well of my sickness, I ship'd myself on board of a large Ship bound to *Guinea,*[10] and being in a publick House one Evening, I overheard a Number of Persons talking about Rigging a Vessel bound to *New-England,* I ask'd them to what Part of *New-England* this Vessel was bound? They told me, to *Boston;* and having ask'd them who was Commander? they told me, Capt. *Watt;* in a few Minutes after this the Mate of the Ship came in, and I ask'd him if Captain Watt did not want a Cook, who told me he did, and that the Captain would be in, in a few Minutes; and in about half an Hour the Captain came in, and then I ship'd myself at once, after begging off from the Ship bound to *Guinea*; I work'd on board Captain *Watt's* Ship almost Three Months, before she sail'd, and one Day being at Work in the Hold, I overheard some Persons on board mention the Name of *Winslow,* at the Name of which I was very inquisitive, and having ask'd what *Winslow* they were talking about? They told me it was *General Winslow;* and that he was one of the Passengers, I ask'd them what *General Winslow*? For I never knew *my good Master,* by that Title before; but after enquiring more particularly I found it must be *Master,* and in a few Days Time the Truth was joyfully verify'd by a happy Sight of his Person, which so overcome me, that I could not speak to him for some Time—*My good Master* was exceeding glad to see me, telling me that I was like one arose from the Dead, for he thought I had been Dead a great many Years, having heard nothing of me for almost Thirteen Years.

I think I have not deviated from Truth, in any particular of this my Narrative, and tho' I have omitted a great many Things, yet what is wrote may suffice to convince the Reader, that I have been most grievously afflicted, and yet thro' the Divine Goodness, as miraculously preserved, and delivered out of many Dangers; of which I desire to retain a *grateful Remembrance,* as long as I live in the World.

And now, That in the Providence of that GOD, who delivered his Servant David out of the Paw of the Lion and out of the Paw of the Bear,[11] *I am freed from a* long

[9]Hammon's note about the "engagement" reads: "A particular Account of this Engagement, has been Publish'd in the *Boston* News-Papers."

[10]A ship bound for Guinea would have been a ship heading to Africa to acquire a load of slaves.

[11]See I Samuel 17:37.

and dreadful Captivity, among worse Savages than they; *And am return'd to my* own Native Land, to Shew how Great Things the Lord hath done for Me; *I would call upon all Men, and Say,* O Magnifie the Lord with Me, and let us Exalt his Name together![12]—O that Men would Praise the Lord for His Goodness, and for his Wonderful Works to the Children of Men!

1760

Prince Hall 1735?–1807

Prince Hall's organizational efforts took place at a propitious time in early African American political and social history. Following the upsurge of the black slave population in the mid-eighteenth century, the revolutionary and post-revolutionary periods saw an increase in the founding of black benevolent societies, churches, schools, and mutual-aid groups. Drawing upon a new sense of African identity, derived possibly from the presence of newly arrived countrymen, African American activists frequently denominated their institutions as "African." This racial self-consciousness was enhanced by the increasing formation of black households and kinship groups in New England, New York, and New Jersey, as slaves were freed.

If Prince Hall had not actually lived, he most certainly would have been invented—which is to say that the pioneering socialization he achieved for and among early black Americans would have been realized sooner or later by some colonial black American. Whether in seemingly passive enslavement or as modestly protesting free persons, blacks were clearly too vital, too fundamentally hardy, to have long been excluded from dignified social groupings, and, thereafter, from variously finding their own American way.

Hall organized some fourteen free black Bostonians in 1775 into a society that eventually became an official, degree-granting Masonic order, "African Lodge No. 459" (later No. 370) on May 6, 1787. As Master of this first lodge, Hall continued his work and brought together an association of black Masonic Grand Lodges that would proliferate into what is today a flourishing, worldwide fraternal society. (In 1977 there were more than 500,000 members of such lodges.) Hall is also remembered as one of the more prolific writers of early black America.

Born sometime between 1735 and 1738 at a place still unknown, Hall seems to have been a slave or indentured servant in the Boston household of leather-dresser William Hall from 1749 until 1770, when he was freed. Thereafter he made a decent living as a leather-dresser, caterer, and perhaps as a shop owner. From the year 1762, Hall was a member of the Reverend Andrew Crosswell's Congregational church on School Street, and "in full communication therewith, for a number of years," he may well have functioned as an unordained preacher to fellow Masons and other interested blacks on the premises of the School Street church, which was abandoned in 1764, when an epidemic of smallpox struck Boston.

From 1777 until four months before his death in December 1807, Prince Hall engaged in activities central to the development of a vital African American identity. He composed and published a group

[12]See Psalms 34:4.

of writings, including letters to London Masonic officials, the Countess of Huntingdon, Boston newspapers, and prominent blacks in Providence and Philadelphia, but most notably he published a series of petitions on behalf of his Masons and free blacks in general. He solicited the abolition of Massachusetts slavery (1777). He petitioned for the proffered but rejected military assistance of some 700 blacks for use by Governor James Bowdoin (who was trying to put down Shays's Rebellion in the western part of the state, 1786). In January of 1787, with 73 other blacks, Hall petitioned the General Court for financial or other assistance in support of plans for blacks to emigrate to Africa. In October of that year, he petitioned, unsuccessfully, for public education for children of taxpaying Boston blacks.

In his own home for most of 1789, Hall housed the Reverend John Marrant (1755–1791), then enroute back to London from a lengthy preaching tour of eastern Canada. In London in 1785, Marrant had become the first black American ordained minister. Hall also made Marrant a chaplain for his Lodge; for the Lodge Marrant preached at Fanueil Hall an inspirational sermon published later that year.

Hall himself is on record in the "Taxing Books" as having paid both real estate and poll taxes from 1780 onwards. He also petitioned, this time successfully, on behalf of three Boston blacks who were kidnapped into slavery but quickly released (1788). In 1792 he published a racially stimulating Charge to fellow Lodge members; in 1797 he published another such Charge. On May 6, 1806, Hall and a white man, John Vinal of Boston, once a member of Hall's School Street church, gave a deposition acknowledging joint receipt of three thousand dollars for the sale of the church property. Finally, on August 31, 1807, Hall signed another deposition, in effect a testimony of Vinal's character; both of these depositions remain in manuscript.

Prince Hall was much concerned with the organization and dignifying of his fellow Masons, to be sure, but he was just as concerned with the future of the enslaved black American: because black slavery was primarily a white American issue, he was necessarily concerned with the future of America and Americans.

William H. Robinson
Rhode Island College

Philip M. Richards
Colgate University

PRIMARY WORKS

A Charge, Delivered to the Brethren of the African Lodge on the 25th of June, 1792, At the Hall of Brother William Smith, in Charlestown. By the Right Worshipful Master Prince Hall. Printed at the Request of the Lodge. Printed and sold at the Bible and Heart, Cornhill, Boston, 1792; *A Charge Delivered to the African Lodge. June 24, 1797, at Menotomy. By the Right Worshipful Prince Hall. Published by the Desire of the Members of Said Lodge.* 1797.

A Charge, Delivered to the African Lodge, June 24, 1797, at Menotomy

By the Right Worshipful Prince Hall. Published by the Desire of the Members of Said Lodge. 1797.

Beloved Brethren of the African Lodge,

'Tis now five years since I deliver'd a Charge to you on some parts and points of Masonry. As one branch or superstructure on the foundation; when I endeavoured to shew you the duty of a Mason to a Mason, and charity or love to all mankind, as the mark and image of the great God, and the Father of the human race.[1]

I shall now attempt to shew you that it is our duty to sympathise with our fellow men under their troubles, the families of our brethren who are gone: we hope to the Grand Lodge above, here to return no more. But the cheerfulness that you have ever had to relieve them, and ease their burdens, under their forrows, will never be forgotten by them; and in this manner you will never be weary in doing good.

But my brethren, although we are to begin here, we must not end here; for only look around you and you will see and hear of numbers of our fellow men crying out with holy Job, Have pity on me, O my friends, for the hand of the Lord hath touched me. And this is not to be confined to parties or colours; not to towns or states; not to a kingdom, but to the kingdoms of the whole earth, over whom Christ the king is head and grand master.

Among these numerous sons and daughters of distress, I shall begin with our friends and brethren; and first, let us see them dragg'd from their native country by the iron hand of tyranny and oppression, from their dear friends and connections, with weeping eyes and aching hearts, to a strange land and strange people, whose tender mercies are cruel; and there to bear the iron yoke of slavery & cruelty till death as a friend shall relieve them. And must not the unhappy condition of these our fellow men draw forth our hearty prayer and wishes for their deliverance from these merchants and traders, whose characters you have in the xviii chap. of the Revelations 11, 12, & 13 verses,[2] and who knows but these same sort of traders may in a short time, in the like manner, bewail the loss of the African traffick, to their shame and confusion: and if I mistake not, it now begins to dawn in some of the West-India islands; which puts me in mind of a nation (that I have somewhere read of) called Ethiopeans, that cannot change their skin: But God can and will change their

[1]In 1792, Hall's Masons paid for the printing of *A Charge Delivered to the Brethren of the African Lodge on the 25th of June, 1792. At the Hall of Brother William Smith, In Charlestown. By the Right Worshipful Master Prince Hall. Printed at the Request of the Lodge. Printed and Sold at the Bible and Heart, Cornhill, Boston.* The printing of both the 1792 and the 1797 Charges was paid for by Hall's Masons, thereby documenting the earliest instance of cooperative black American publishing efforts. The most accurate version is in Dorothy's Porter's *Early Negro Writing, 1760–1837* (1971).

[2]"And the merchants of the earth shall weep and moan over her [great city of Babylon]; for no man buyeth their merchandise any more" (Revelation 18:11).

conditions, and their hearts too; and let Boston and the world know, that He hath no respect of persons; and that that bulwark of envy, pride, scorn and contempt, which is so visible to be seen in some and felt, shall fall, to rise no more.

When we hear of the bloody wars which are now in the world, and thousands of our fellow men slain; fathers and mothers bewailing the loss of their sons; wives for the loss of their husbands; towns and cities burnt and destroy'd; what must be the heart-felt sorrow and distress of these poor and unhappy people! Though we cannot help them, the distance being so great, yet we may sympathize with them in their troubles, and mingle a tear of sorrow with them, and do as we are exhorted to—weep with those that weep.

Thus my brethren we see what a chequered world we live in. Sometimes happy in having our wives and children like olive-branches about our tables; receiving the bounties of our great Benefactor. The next year, or month, or week we may be deprived of some of them, and we go mourning about the streets, so in societies; we are this day to celebrate this Feast of St. John's, and the next week we might be called upon to attend a funeral of some one here, as we have experienced since our last in this Lodge. So in the common affairs of life we sometimes enjoy health and prosperity; at another time sickness and adversity, crosses and disappointments.

So in states and kingdoms; sometimes in tranquility, then wars and tumults; rich today, and poor tomorrow; which shews that there is not an independent mortal on earth, but dependent one upon the other, from the king to the beggar.

The great law-giver, Moses, who instructed by his father-in-law, Jethro, an Ethiopean, how to regulate his courts of justice and what sort of men to choose for the different offices; hear now my words, said he, I will give you counsel, and God shall be with you; be thou for the people to Godward, that thou mayest bring the causes unto God, and thou shall teach them ordinances and laws, and shall shew the way wherein they must walk, and the work that they must do: moreover thou shall provide out of all the people, able men, such as fear God, men of truth, hating covetousness, and place such over them, to be rulers of thousands, of hundreds and of tens.

So Moses hearkened to the voice of his father-in-law, and did all that he said. Exodus xviii. 22–24.

This is the first and grandest lecture that Moses ever received from the mouth of man; for Jethro understood geometry as well as laws, *that* a Mason may plainly see: so a little captive servant maid by whose advice Nomen, the great general of Syria's army, was healed of his leprosy; and by a servant his proud spirit was brought down: 2 Kings v. 3–14.[3] The feelings of this little captive for this great man, her captor, was so great, that she forgot her state of captivity, and felt for the distress of her enemy. Would to God (said she to her mistress) my lord were with the prophets in Samaria, he should be healed of his leprosy: So after he went to the prophet, his proud host was so haughty that he not only disdain'd the prophet's direction, but derided the good old prophet; and had it not been for his servant he would have gone to his grave

[3]The Syrian general is Naaman; the captive maid is from Israel; the prophet in Samaria is Elisha.

with a double leprosy, the outward and the inward, in the heart, which is the worst of leprosies; a black heart is worse than a white leprosy.

How unlike was this great general's behaviour to that of as grand a character, and as well beloved by his prince as he was; I mean Obadiah, to a like prophet. See for this 1st Kings xviii. from 7 to the 16th.

And as Obadiah was in the way, behold Elijah met him, and he knew him, and fell on his face, and said, Art not thou, my Lord, Elijah, and he told him, Yea, go and tell thy Lord, behold Elijah is here: and so on to the 16th verse. Thus we see that great and good men have, and always will have, a respect for ministers and servants of God. Another instance of this is in Acts viii. 27 to 31, of the Ethiopian Eunuch, a man of great authority, to Philip, the apostle: here is mutual love and friendship between them. This minister of Jesus Christ did not think himself too good to receive the hand, and ride in a chariot with a black man in the face of day; neither did this great monarch (for so he was) think it beneath him to take a poor servant of the Lord by the hand, and invite him into his carriage, though but with a staff, one coat, and no money in his pocket. So our Grand Master, Solomon, was not asham'd to take the Queen of Sheba by the hand, and lead her into his court, at the hour of high twelve, and there converse with her on points of masonry (for if ever there was a female mason in the world she was one) and other curious matters; and gratified her, by shewing her all his riches and curious pieces of architecture in the temple, and in his house: After some time staying with her, he loaded her with much rich presents: he gave her the right hand of affection and parted in love.[4]

I hope that no one will dare openly (tho' in fact the behaviour of some implies as much) to say, as our Lord said on another occasion, Behold a greater than Solomon is here.[5] But yet let them consider that our Grand Master Solomon did not divide the living child, whatever he might do with the dead one, neither did he pretend to make a law to forbid the parties from having free intercourse with one another without the fear of censure, or be turned out of the synagogue.

Now my brethren, as we see and experience that all things here are frail and changeable and nothing here to be depended upon: Let us seek those things which are above, which are sure, and stedfast, and unchangeable, and at the same time let us pray to Almighty God, while we remain in the tabernacle, that he would give us the grace of patience and strength to bear up under all our troubles, which at this day God knows we have our share. Patience I say, for were we not possess'd of a great measure of it you could not bear up under the daily insults you meet with in the streets of Boston; much more on public days of recreation, how are you shamefully abus'd, and that at such a degree that you may truly be said to carry your lives in your hands, and the arrows of death are flying about your heads; helpless old women have their clothes torn off their backs, even to the exposing of their nakedness; and by whom are these disgraceful and abusive actions committed, not by the men born and bred in Boston, for they are better bred; but by a mob or horde of shameless, low-lived, envious, spiteful persons, some of them not long since, servants in gentlemen's kitchens, scouring knives, tending horses, and driving chaise. 'Twas said by a gentleman who saw that filthy behaviour in the common, that in all the places he had been

[4]See I Kings 10:1–13.

[5]See Matthew 12:42; also, Luke 11:31.

in, he never saw so cruel behaviour in all his life, and that a slave in the West-Indies, on Sunday or holidays enjoys himself and friends without any molestation. Not only this man, but many in town who hath seen their behaviour to you, and that without any provocation—twenty or thirty cowards fall upon one man—have wonder'd at the patience of the Blacks: 'tis not for want of courage in you, for they know that they dare not face you man for man, but in a mob, which we despise, and had rather suffer wrong than to do wrong, to the disturbance of the community and the disgrace of our reputation: for every good citizen doth honor to the laws of the State where he resides.

My brethren, let us not be cast down under these and many other abuses we at present labour under: for the darkest is before the break of day. My brethren, let us remember what a dark day it was with our African brethren six years ago,[6] in the French West-Indies. Nothing but the snap of the whip was heard from morning to evening; hanging, broken on the wheel, burning, and all manner of tortures inflicted on those unhappy people for nothing else but to gratify their masters pride, wantonness, and cruelty: but blessed be God, the scene is changed; they now confess that God hath no respect of persons, and therefore receive them as their friends, and treat them as brothers. Thus doth Ethiopia begin to stretch forth her hand, from a sink of slavery to freedom and equality.

Although you are deprived of the means of education,[7] yet you are not deprived of the means of meditation; by which I mean thinking, hearing and weighing matters, men, and things in your own mind, and making that judgment of them as you think reasonable to satisfy your minds and give an answer to those who may ask you a question. This nature hath furnished you with, without letter learning; and some have made great progress therein, some of those I have heard repeat psalms and hymns, and a great part of a sermon, only by hearing it read or preached and why not in other things in nature: how many of this class of our brethren that follow the seas can foretell a storm some days before it comes; whether it will be a heavy or light, a long or short one; foretell a hurricane, whether it will be destructive or moderate, without any other means than observation and consideration.

So in the observation of the heavenly bodies, this same class without a telescope or other apparatus have through a smoak'd glass observed the eclipse of the sun: One being ask'd what he saw through his smoaked glass, said, Saw, saw, de clipsey, or de clipseys.[8] And what do you think of it?—Stop, dere be two. Right, and what do they look like?—Look like, why if I tell you, they look like two ships sailing one bigger than tother; so they sail by one another, and make no noise. As simple as the answers are they have a meaning, and shew that God can out of the mouth of babes and Africans shew forth his glory; let us then love and adore him as the God who defends us and supports us and will support us under our pressures, let them be ever so heavy and pressing. Let us by the blessing of God, in whatsoever state we are, or may be in,

[6]In 1791, slave insurrections began against French rule in Saint Domingue which led eventually to the bloodily established Republic of Haiti in 1804.

[7]Although obliged to pay poll and real estate taxes, black Bostonians who were financially able were denied a city-wide, tax-supported school system until after the turn of the nineteenth century.

[8]This is the first recorded instance of black American written expression of black dialect.

to be content; for clouds and darkness are about him; but justice and truth is his habitation; who hath said. Vengeance is mine and I will repay it, therefore let us kiss the rod and be still, and see the works of the Lord.[9]

Another thing I would warn you against, is the slavish fear of man, which bringest a snare, saith Solomon.[10] This passion of fear, like pride and envy, hath slain its thousands.—What but this makes so many perjure themselves; for fear of offending them at home they are a little depending on for some trifles: A man that is under a panic of fear, is afraid to be alone; you cannot hear of a robbery or house broke open or set on fire, but he hath an accomplice with him, who must share the spoil with him; whereas if he was truly bold, and void of fear, he would keep the whole plunder to himself: so when either of them is detected and not the other, he may be call'd to oath to keep it secret, but through fear, (and that passion is so strong) he will not confess, till the fatal cord is put on his neck; then death will deliver him from the fear of man, and he will confess the truth when it will not be of any good to himself or the community: nor is this passion of fear only to be found in this class of men, but among the great.

What was the reason that our African kings and princes have plunged themselves and their peaceable kingdoms into bloody wars, to the destroying of towns and kingdoms, but the fear of the report of a great gun or the glittering of arms and swords, which struck these kings near the seaports with such a panic of fear, as not only to destroy the peace and happiness of their inland brethren, but plung'd millions of their fellow countrymen into slavery and cruel bondage.

So in other countries; see Felix trembling on his throne.[11] How many Emperors and kings have left their kingdoms and best friends at the sight of a handful of men in arms: how many have we seen that have left their estates and their friends and ran over to the stronger side as they thought; all through the fear of men, who is but a worm, and hath no more power to hurt his fellow worm, without the permission of God, than a real worm.

Thus we see, my brethren, what a miserable condition it is to be under the slavish fear of men; it is of such a destructive nature to mankind, that the scriptures every where from Genesis to the Revelations warns us against it; and even our blessed Saviour himself forbids us from this slavish fear of man, in his sermon on the mount; and the only way to avoid it is to be in the fear of God: let a man consider the greatness of his power, as the maker and upholder of all things here below, and that in Him we live, and move, and have our being, the giver of the mercies we enjoy here from day to day, and that our lives are in his hands, and that he made the heavens, the sun, moon and stars to move in their various orders; let us thus view the greatness of God, and then turn our eyes on mortal man, a worm, a shade, a wafer, and see whether he is an object of fear or not; on the contrary, you will think him in his best estate to be but vanity, feeble and a dependent mortal, and stands in need of your help, and cannot do without your assistance, in some way or other; and yet some of these poor mortals will try to make you believe they are Gods, but worship them not. My

[9]Romans 12:19.
[10]Proverbs 29:25.
[11]The governor of Caesarea who kept the apostle Paul in custody when a band of Jews conspired to kill him. See Acts 23:24 ff.

brethren, let us pay all due respect to all whom God hath put in places of honor over us: do justly and be faithful to them that hire you, and treat them with that respect they may deserve; but worship no man. Worship God, this much is your duty as christians and as masons.

We see then how becoming and necessary it is to have a fellow feeling for our distres'd brethren of the human race, in their troubles, both spiritual and temporal— How refreshing it is to a sick man, to see his sympathising friends around his bed, ready to administer all the relief in their power; although they can't relieve his bodily pain yet they may ease his mind by good instructions and cheer his heart by their company.

How doth it cheer up the heart of a man when his house is on fire, to see a number of friends coming to his relief; he is so transported that he almost forgets his loss and his danger, and fills him with love and gratitude; and their joys and sorrows are mutual.

So a man wreck'd at sea, how must it revive his drooping heart to see a ship bearing down for his relief.

How doth it rejoice the heart of a stranger in a strange land to see the people cheerful and pleasant and are ready to help him.

How did it, think you, cheer the heart of those our poor unhappy African brethren, to see a ship commissioned from God, and from a nation that without flattery faith, that all men are free and are brethren; I say to see them in an instant deliver such a number from their cruel bolts and galling chains, and to be fed like men and treated like brethren. Where is the man that has the least spark of humanity, that will not rejoice with them; and bless a righteous God who knows how and when to relieve the oppressed, as we see he did in the deliverance of the captives among the Algerines;[12] how sudden were they delivered by the sympathising members of the Congress of the United States, who now enjoy the free air of peace and liberty, to their great joy and surprize, to them and their friends. Here we see the hand of God in various ways bringing about his own glory for the good of mankind, by the mutual help of their fellow men; which ought to teach us in all our straits, be they what they may, to put our trust in Him, firmly believing that he is able and will deliver us and defend us against all our enemies; and that no weapon form'd against us shall prosper; only let us be steady and uniform in our walks, speech and behaviour; always doing to all men as we wish and desire they would do to us in the like cases and circumstances.

Live and act as Masons, that you may die as Masons; let those despisers see, altho' many of us cannot read, yet by our searches and researches into men and things, we have supplied that defect; and if they will let us we shall call ourselves a charter'd lodge of just and lawful Masons; be always ready to give an answer to those that ask you a question; give the right hand of affection and fellowship to whom it justly belongs; let their colour and complexion be what it will, let their nation be what it may, for they are your brethren, and it is your indispensable duty so to do; let them as Masons deny this, and we & the world know what to think of them be they ever so grand: for we know this was Solomon's creed, Solomon's creed did I say, it is the de-

[12]In 1796, Joel Barlow helped to free eighty-eight American sailors taken hostage by Algeria during the crisis of 1787 with Britain.

cree of the Almighty, and all Masons have learnt it: tis plain market language, and plain and true facts need no apologies.

I shall now conclude with an old poem which I found among some papers:[13]

Let blind admirers handsome faces praise,
And graceful features to great honor raise,
The glories of the red and white express,
I know no beauty but in holiness;
If God of beauty be the uncreate
Perfect idea, in this lower state,
The greatest beauties of an human mould
Who most resemble Him we justly hold;
Whom we resemble not in flesh and blood,
But being pure and holy, just and good:
May such a beauty fall but to my share,
For curious shape or face I'll never care.

1797

[13]John Rawlet (1642–1686), "True Beauty," in *Poetick Miscellanies of Mr. John Rawlet* (London, 1687).

Olaudah Equiano 1745–1797

More than twelve million Africans made the brutal Middle Passage from Africa to the Americas, but very few recorded this experience in writing. First published in 1789, *The Interesting Narrative of the Life of Olaudah Equiano, or Gustavus Vassa, the African. Written by Himself* is a work of paramount literary and historical significance as one of the first autobiographies by a former slave. Equiano's compelling depiction of an African childhood, Atlantic transit, enslavement, manumission, and life as a free black in Europe and the Americas was a commercial and literary success and a powerful political tool in the campaign to end the slave trade.

By his own account, Olaudah Equiano was born about 1745 in what is now eastern Nigeria. Kidnapped with his sister when he was ten years old, Equiano was shipped to Barbados and then was enslaved on a Virginia plantation. British naval officer Michael Henry Paschal purchased Equiano and renamed him Gustavus Vassa, after a sixteenth-century Swedish king and freedom fighter. Equiano traveled extensively with Paschal, learned to read and write from his fellow sailors, and participated in some of the key sea battles of the Seven Years' War (1756–1763) between the rival imperial powers Great Britain and France. Then he was sold to a Quaker merchant in whose service Equiano traveled through the West Indies, witnessing the horrific cruelty of Caribbean plantation slavery and managing to earn some money by importing and exporting island goods for sale. In July 1766, Equiano used these profits to purchase his freedom, and he moved to London.

Free blacks in the eighteenth-century occupied a position of tremendous social, political, and economic vulnerability. Street mobs and unscrupulous employers preyed upon them, as did kidnappers who sold their victims into slavery. Legal codes restricting travel, trade, work, recreation, and literacy were imposed on free and enslaved blacks alike. Equiano and his eighteenth-century counterparts participated in important military, commercial, and political endeavors around the Atlantic littoral, and they developed a "Black Atlantic" political culture based in the understanding that peoples of the African diaspora would have to defend their freedom vigilantly against the violent, predatory modern world.

As a free man in London, Equiano publicly advocated the welfare of his fellow Africans, African Americans, and Afro-Britons. He was spurred into activism by the infamous *Zong* tragedy (1781), when the captain of a disease-infested British slave ship ordered 133 living Africans cast overboard in order to claim insurance benefits providing compensation for slaves killed to prevent or punish rebellion but not for slaves lost to disease. Equiano subsequently joined efforts to resetttle impoverished Afro-Britons in Sierra Leone and the nascent movement to abolish the slave trade. Although England itself was never home to a large population of African slaves, British ships and businesses were deeply involved in the slave trade, transporting more than eighty thousand slaves annually in the late 1780s.

Equiano fully understood the power of writing to effect political change. During the 1780s, he published abolitionist letters and essays in London newspapers, and he carefully designed the *Interesting Narrative* to build the movement against the slave trade. He correctly anticipated that his graphic, first-person account of the horrible Middle Passage would raise consciousness even among readers who had no firsthand contact with the slave trade. He also developed an ingenious marketing strategy for the *Interesting Narrative* that included book tours and advance subscription sales. The names of hundreds of influential subscribers—including members of the royal family, the aristocracy, and the clergy—appeared in the opening pages of the book, as celebrity endorsements of Equiano's abolitionist message. Literary reviewers received his autobiography with praise, English feminist Mary Wollstonecraft wrote that Equiano's description of slavery was enough to "make the blood turn in its course." Dozens of editions of the *Interesting Narrative* were published in England, Ireland, the United States, and Canada, and translations appeared in Russia, Holland, and Germany.

When Parliament debated the legality of the slave trade in April 1792, Olaudah Equiano was in attendance. That same month, he married an Englishwoman named Susanna Cullen, with whom he had two daughters: Ann Mary, born in October 1793, and Joanna, born in April 1795. Olaudah Equiano died on March 31, 1797. Ten years later, in 1807, Great Britain outlawed participation in the international slave trade.

Equiano belonged to a transatlantic cohort of early black writers that included Phillis Wheatley, Jupiter Hammon, Ignatius Sancho, and James Albert Ukawsaw Gronniosaw, who understood that their writings would serve as evidence in public debates about race and slavery. Together, they built new traditions of African American and Afro-British literature, and they demonstrated their mutual respect by referencing one another in their writings. The trope of the talking book appears in several early black texts, including Equiano's *Interesting Narrative,* symbolizing the negotiation between traditional African oral literature and Europe-American print literacy. Equiano is also an important forerunner of nineteenth-century slave narrators such as Frederick Douglass and Harriet Jacobs, whom he anticipated in crafting his autobiography as a narrative of movement from slavery to freedom, from literacy to literary mastery, and from anonymity to public advocacy for black freedom. Like many slave narrators, he also paralleled his own emancipation with a narrative of Christian conversion.

Recently discovered church records document the 1759 baptism of Gustavus Vassa and give his birthplace as "Carolina"; an English Royal Navy muster list also indicates that South Carolina was Vassa's birthplace. Was Equiano born in Africa or in South Carolina? Are we to believe the *Interesting Narrative,* or these two documents, which suggest a competing account of Equiano's origins and upbringing? Scholars have not arrived at a consensus on this contentious issue. We do know that historical records often give incomplete, invented, or conflicting information about the lives of people of color in early America. Most slave births were not documented, and many slaves did not know their own birthdates. Such circumstances impelled famous slave narrators like Douglass to reconstruct their own early lives.

In this context of biographical uncertainty, it is important to remember that autobiography is always an act of self-invention. During the seventeenth and eighteenth centuries, tremendous changes in world politics and economies uprooted many traditional communities, thus making individual acts of self-creation—including self-creation through writing—newly possible and newly necessary. Benjamin Franklin used his *Autobiography* to construct a public persona as the prototypical American self-made man; Olaudah Equiano used his *Interesting Narrative* to construct a public persona as a representative survivor of the African slave trade, and he used this persona to campaign for an end to Great Britain's participation in the trade. In this way, the *Interesting Narrative* can be read as more than a story of a single individual: it is a collective autobiography for millions who survived the slave trade and a compelling view of the way that African men and women, torn forcibly from their homelands, created new identities and new lives for themselves as blacks of the diaspora.

Joanna Brooks
San Diego State University

PRIMARY WORK

The Interesting Narrative of the Life of Olaudah Equiano, or Gustavus Vassa, the African. Written by Himself, London, 1789.

from The Interesting Narrative of the Life of Olaudah Equiano, or Gustavus Vassa, the African. Written by Himself.

from Chapter 1

I believe it is difficult for those who publish their own memoirs to escape the imputation of vanity; nor is this the only disadvantage under which they labor: it is also their misfortune that what is uncommon is rarely, if ever, believed, and what is obvious we are apt to turn from with disgust, and to charge the writer with impertinence. People generally think those memoirs only worthy to be read or remembered which abound in great or striking events, those, in short, which in a high degree excite either admiration or pity; all others they consign to contempt and oblivion. It is therefore, I confess, not a little hazardous in a private and obscure individual, and a stranger too, thus to solicit the indulgent attention of the public, especially when I own I offer here the history of neither a saint, a hero, nor a tyrant. I believe there are few events in my life which have not happened to many; it is true the incidents of it are numerous, and, did I consider myself an European, I might say my sufferings were great; but when I compare my lot with that of most of my countrymen, I regard myself as a *particular favorite of heaven,* and acknowledge the mercies of Providence in every occurrence of my life. If, then, the following narrative does not appear sufficiently interesting to engage general attention, let my motive be some excuse for its publication. I am not so foolishly vain as to expect from it either immortality or literary reputation. If it affords any satisfaction to my numerous friends, at whose request it has been written, or in the smallest degree promotes the interests of humanity, the ends for which it was undertaken will be fully attained, and every wish of my heart gratified. Let it therefore be remembered, that, in wishing to avoid censure, I do not aspire to praise.

That part of Africa, known by the name of Guinea, to which the trade for slaves is carried on, extends along the coast above 3400 miles, from Senegal to Angola, and includes a variety of kingdoms. Of these the most considerable is the kingdom of Benin, both as to extent and wealth, the richness and cultivation of the soil, the power of its king, and the number and warlike disposition of the inhabitants. It is situated nearly under the line, and extends along the coast about 170 miles, but runs back into the interior part of Africa to a distance hitherto, I believe, unexplored by any traveller, and seems only terminated at length by the empire of Abyssinia, near 1500 miles from its beginning. This kingdom is divided into many provinces or districts, in one of the most remote and fertile of which, I was born, in the year 1745, situated in a charming fruitful vale, named Essaka.[1] The distance of this province from the capital of Benin and the sea coast must be very considerable, for I had never

[1]Equiano was born in the country that is now known as Nigeria. He claimed Benin because he was borrowing from books on Africa by Anthony Benezet, the Quaker anti-slavery writer [Ed.].

heard of white men or Europeans, nor of the sea; and our subjection to the king of Benin was little more than nominal, for every transaction of the government, as far as my slender observation extended, was conducted by the chief or elders of the place. The manners and government of a people who have little commerce with other countries are generally very simple, and the history of what passes in one family or village may serve as a specimen of the whole nation. My father was one of those elders or chiefs I have spoken of, and was styled Embrenche, a term, as I remember, importing the highest distinction, and signifying in our language a *mark* of grandeur. This mark is conferred on the person entitled to it, by cutting the skin across at the top of the forehead, and drawing it down to the eyebrows; and while it is in this situation applying a warm hand, and rubbing it until it shrinks up into a thick *weal* across the lower part of the forehead. Most of the judges and senators were thus marked; my father had long borne it; I had seen it conferred on one of my brothers, and I also was *destined* to receive it by my parents. Those Embrenche, or chief men, decided disputes and punished crimes, for which purpose they always assembled together. The proceedings were generally short, and in most cases the law of retaliation prevailed. I remember a man was brought before my father, and the other judges, for kidnapping a boy; and, although he was the son of a chief or senator, he was condemned to make recompense by a man or woman slave. Adultery, however, was sometimes punished with slavery or death, a punishment which I believe is inflicted on it throughout most of the nations of Africa,[2] so sacred among them is the honor of the marriage bed, and so jealous are they of the fidelity of their wives. Of this I recollect an instance—a woman was convicted before the judges of adultery, and delivered over, as the custom was, to her husband, to be punished. Accordingly he determined to put her to death; but it being found, just before her execution, that she had an infant at her breast, and no woman being prevailed on to perform the part of a nurse, she was spared on account of the child. The men, however, do not preserve the same constancy to their wives which they expect from them; for they indulge in a plurality, though seldom in more than two. Their mode of marriage is thus—both parties are usually betrothed when young by their parents (though I have known the males to betroth themselves). On this occasion a feast is prepared, and the bride and bridegroom stand up in the midst of all their friends, who are assembled for the purpose, while he declares she is henceforth to be looked upon as his wife, and that no other person is to pay any addresses to her. This is also immediately proclaimed in the vicinity, on which the bride retires from the assembly. Some time after, she is brought home to her husband, and then another feast is made, to which the relations of both parties are invited; her parents then deliver her to the bridegroom, accompanied with a number of blessings, and at the same time they tie round her waist a cotton string of the thickness of a goosequill, which none but married women are permitted to wear; she is now considered as completely his wife; and at this time the dowry is given to the new married pair, which generally consists of portions of land, slaves, and cattle, household goods, and implements of husbandry. These are offered by the friends of both parties; besides which the parents of the

[2]See Benezet's "Account of Guinea," throughout.

bridegroom present gifts to those of the bride, whose property she is looked upon before marriage; but after it she is esteemed the sole property of her husband. The ceremony being now ended, the festival begins, which is celebrated with bonfires and loud acclamations of joy, accompanied with music and dancing.

We are almost a nation of dancers, musicians, and poets. Thus every great event, such as a triumphant return from battle or other cause of public rejoicing, is celebrated in public dances, which are accompanied with songs and music suited to the occasion. The assembly is separated into four divisions, which dance either apart or in succession, and each with a character peculiar to itself. The first division contains the married men, who in their dances frequently exhibit feats of arms and the representation of a battle. To these succeed the married women, who dance in the second division. The young men occupy the third, and the maidens the fourth. Each represents some interesting scene of real life, such as a great achievement, domestic employment, a pathetic story, or some rural sport; and as the subject is generally founded on some recent event, it is therefore ever new. This gives our dances a spirit and variety which I have scarcely seen elsewhere.[3] We have many musical instruments, particularly drums of different kinds, a piece of music which resembles a guitar, and another much like a stickado.[4] These last are chiefly used by betrothed virgins, who play on them on all grand festivals.

As our manners are simple, our luxuries are few. The dress of both sexes is nearly the same. It generally consists of a long piece of calico, or muslin, wrapped loosely round the body, somewhat in the form of a highland plaid. This is usually dyed blue, which is our favorite color. It is extracted from a berry, and is brighter and richer than any I have seen in Europe. Besides this, our women of distinction wear golden ornaments, which they dispose with some profusion on their arms and legs. When our women are not employed with the men in tillage, their usual occupation is spinning and weaving cotton, which they afterwards dye, and make into garments. They also manufacture earthen vessels, of which we have many kinds. Among the rest, tobacco pipes, made after the same fashion, and used in the same manner, as those in Turkey.[5]

Our manner of living is entirely plain; for as yet the natives are unacquainted with those refinements in cookery which debauch the taste; bullocks, goats, and poultry supply the greatest part of their food. (These constitute likewise the principal wealth of the country, and the chief articles of its commerce.) The flesh is usually stewed in a pan; to make it savory we sometimes use pepper, and other spices, and we have salt made of wood ashes. Our vegetables are mostly plantains, eadas, yams, beans, and Indian corn. The head of the family usually eats alone; his wives and slaves have also their separate tables. Before we taste food we always wash our hands; indeed, our cleanliness on all occasions is extreme, but on this it is an indispensable ceremony. After washing, libation is made, by pouring out a small portion of the drink on the floor, and tossing a small quantity of the food in a certain place, for the spirits of departed relations, which the natives suppose to preside over their conduct

[3]When I was in Smyrna I have frequently seen the Greeks dance after this manner.

[4]Stickado: a xylophone-like instrument [Ed.].

[5]The bowl is earthen, curiously figured, to which a long reed is fixed as a tube. This tube is sometimes so long as to be borne by one, and frequently out of grandeur, two boys.

and guard them from evil. They are totally unacquainted with strong or spirituous liquors; and their principal beverage is palm wine. This is got from a tree of that name, by tapping it at the top and fastening a large gourd to it; and sometimes one tree will yield three or four gallons in a night. When just drawn it is of a most delicious sweetness; but in a few days it acquires a tartish and more spirituous flavor, though I never saw anyone intoxicated by it. The same tree also produces nuts and oil. Our principal luxury is in perfumes: one sort of these is an odoriferous wood of delicious fragrance, the other a kind of earth, a small portion of which thrown into the fire diffuses a most powerful odor.[6] We beat this wood into powder, and mix it with palm oil, with which both men and women perfume themselves.

In our buildings we study convenience rather than ornament. Each master of a family has a large square piece of ground, surrounded with a moat or fence, or enclosed with a wall made of red earth tempered, which, when dry, is as hard as brick. Within this, are his houses to accommodate his family and slaves, which, if numerous, frequently present the appearance of a village. In the middle, stands the principal building, appropriated to the sole use of the master and consisting of two apartments; in one of which he sits in the day with his family, the other is left apart for the reception of his friends. He has besides these a distinct apartment in which he sleeps, together with his male children. On each side are the apartments of his wives, who have also their separate day and night houses. The habitations of the slaves and their families are distributed throughout the rest of the enclosure. These houses never exceed one story in height; they are always built of wood, or stakes driven into the ground, crossed with wattles, and neatly plastered within and without. The roof is thatched with reeds. Our day houses are left open at the sides; but those in which we sleep are always covered, and plastered in the inside, with a composition mixed with cow-dung, to keep off the different insects, which annoy us during the night. The walls and floors also of these are generally covered with mats. Our beds consist of a platform, raised three or four feet from the ground, on which are laid skins, and different parts of a spongy tree, called plantain. Our covering is calico or muslin, the same as our dress. The usual seats are a few logs of wood, but we have benches, which are generally perfumed to accommodate strangers: these compose the greater part of our household furniture. Houses so constructed and furnished require but little skill to erect them. Every man is a sufficient architect for the purpose. The whole neighborhood afford their unanimous assistance in building them, and in return receive and expect no other recompense than a feast.

As we live in a country where nature is prodigal of her favors, our wants are few and easily supplied; of course we have few manufactures. They consist for the most part of calicoes, earthen ware, ornaments, and instruments of war and husbandry. But these make no part of our commerce, the principal articles of which, as I have observed, are provisions. In such a state, money is of little use; however, we have some small pieces of coin, if I may call them such. They are made something like an anchor, but I do not remember either their value or denomination. We have also

[6]When I was in Smyrna I saw the same kind of earth, and brought some of it with me to England; it resembles musk in strength, but is more delicious in scent, and is not unlike the smell of a rose.

markets, at which I have been frequently with my mother. These are sometimes visited by stout mahogany-colored men from the south-west of us: we call them *Oye-Eboe,* which term signifies red men living at a distance. They generally bring us fire-arms, gun-powder, hats, beads, and dried fish. The last we esteemed a great rarity, as our waters were only brooks and springs. These articles they barter with us for odoriferous woods and earth, and our salt of wood ashes. They always carry slaves through our land; but the strictest account is exacted of their manner of procuring them before they are suffered to pass. Sometimes, indeed, we sold slaves to them, but they were only prisoners of war, or such among us as had been convicted of kidnapping, or adultery, and some other crimes, which we esteemed heinous. This practice of kidnapping induces me to think, that, notwithstanding all our strictness, their principal business among us was to trepan[7] our people. I remember too, they carried great sacks along with them, which not long after, I had an opportunity of fatally seeing applied to that infamous purpose.

Our land is uncommonly rich and fruitful, and produces all kinds of vegetables in great abundance. We have plenty of Indian corn, and vast quantities of cotton and tobacco. Our pineapples grow without culture; they are about the size of the largest sugar-loaf, and finely flavored. We have also spices of different kinds, particularly pepper, and a variety of delicious fruits which I have never seen in Europe, together with gums of various kinds, and honey in abundance. All our industry is exerted to improve these blessings of nature. Agriculture is our chief employment; and everyone, even the children and women, are engaged in it. Thus we are all habituated to labor from our earliest years. Everyone contributes something to the common stock; and, as we are unacquainted with idleness, we have no beggars. The benefits of such a mode of living are obvious. The West India planters prefer the slaves of Benin or Eboe to those of any other part of Guinea, for their hardiness, intelligence, integrity, and zeal. Those benefits are felt by us in the general healthiness of the people, and in their vigor and activity; I might have added, too, in their comeliness. Deformity is indeed unknown amongst us, I mean that of shape. Numbers of the natives of Eboe now in London might be brought in support of this assertion: for, in regard to complexion, ideas of beauty are wholly relative. I remember while in Africa to have seen three Negro children who were tawny, and another quite white, who were universally regarded by myself, and the natives in general, as far as related to their complexions, as deformed. Our women, too, were, in my eye at least, uncommonly graceful, alert, and modest to a degree of bashfulness; nor do I remember to have heard of an instance of incontinence amongst them before marriage. They are also remarkably cheerful. Indeed, cheerfulness and affability are two of the leading characteristics of our nation.

Our tillage is exercised in a large plain or common, some hour's walk from our dwellings, and all the neighbors resort thither in a body. They use no beasts of husbandry; and their only instruments are hoes, axes, shovels, and beaks, or pointed iron, to dig with. Sometimes we are visited by locusts, which come in large clouds, so as to darken the air, and destroy our harvest. This, however, happens rarely, but when

[7]Trepan: to trick or deceive [Ed.].

it does, a famine is produced by it. I remember an instance or two wherein this happened. This common is often the theatre of war; and therefore when our people go out to till their land, they not only go in a body, but generally take their arms with them for fear of a surprise; and when they apprehend an invasion, they guard the avenues to their dwellings, by driving sticks into the ground, which are so sharp at one end as to pierce the foot, and are generally dipt in poison. From what I can recollect of these battles, they appear to have been irruptions of one little state or district on the other, to obtain prisoners or booty. Perhaps they were incited to this by those traders who brought the European goods I mentioned, amongst us. Such a mode of obtaining slaves in Africa is common; and I believe more are procured this way, and by kidnapping, than any other.[8] When a trader wants slaves, he applies to a chief for them, and tempts him with his wares. It is not extraordinary, if on this occasion he yields to the temptation with as little firmness, and accepts the price of his fellow creature's liberty, with as little reluctance as the enlightened merchant. Accordingly he falls on his neighbors, and a desperate battle ensues. If he prevails and takes prisoners, he gratifies his avarice by selling them; but, if his party be vanquished, and he falls into the hands of the enemy, he is put to death; for, as he has been known to foment their quarrels, it is thought dangerous to let him survive, and no ransom can save him, though all other prisoners may be redeemed. We have fire-arms, bows and arrows, broad two-edged swords and javelins; we have shields also which cover a man from head to foot. All are taught the use of these weapons; even our women are warriors, and march boldly out to fight along with the men. Our whole district is a kind of militia: on a certain signal given, such as the firing of a gun at night, they all rise in arms and rush upon their enemy. It is perhaps something remarkable, that when our people march to the field a red flag or banner is borne before them. I was once a witness to a battle in our common. We had been all at work in it one day as usual, when our people were suddenly attacked. I climbed a tree at some distance, from which I beheld the fight. There were many women as well as men on both sides; among others my mother was there, and armed with a broad sword. After fighting for a considerable time with great fury, and many had been killed, our people obtained the victory, and took their enemy's Chief a prisoner. He was carried off in great triumph, and, though he offered a large ransom for his life, he was put to death. A virgin of note among our enemies had been slain in the battle, and her arm was exposed in our marketplace, where our trophies were always exhibited. The spoils were divided according to the merit of the warriors. Those prisoners which were not sold or redeemed, we kept as slaves; but how different was their condition from that of the slaves in the West Indies! With us, they do no more work than other members of the community, even their master; their food, clothing, and lodging were nearly the same as theirs (except that they were not permitted to eat with those who were free-born); and there was scarce any other difference between them, than a superior degree of importance which the head of a family possesses in our state, and that authority which, as such, he exercises over every part of his household. Some of these slaves have even slaves under them as their own property, and for their own use.

[8]See Benezet's "Account of Africa," throughout.

As to religion, the natives believe that there is one Creator of all things, and that he lives in the sun, and is girted round with a belt; that he may never eat or drink, but, according to some, he smokes a pipe, which is our own favorite luxury. They believe he governs events, especially our deaths or captivity; but, as for the doctrine of eternity, I do not remember to have ever heard of it; some, however, believe in the transmigration of souls in a certain degree. Those spirits which were not transmigrated, such as their dear friends or relations, they believe always attend them, and guard them from the bad spirits or their foes. For this reason they always, before eating, as I have observed, put some small portion of the meat, and pour some of their drink, on the ground for them; and they often make oblations of the blood of beasts or fowls at their graves. I was very fond of my mother, and almost constantly with her. When she went to make these oblations at her mother's tomb, which was a kind of small solitary thatched house, I sometimes attended her. There she made her libations, and spent most of the night in cries and lamentations. I have been often extremely terrified on these occasions. The loneliness of the place, the darkness of the night, and the ceremony of libation, naturally awful and gloomy, were heightened by my mother's lamentations; and these concurring with the doleful cries of birds, by which these places were frequented, gave an inexpressible terror to the scene.

We compute the year, from the day on which the sun crosses the line, and on its setting that evening, there is a general shout throughout the land; at least, I can speak from my own knowledge, throughout our vicinity. The people at the same time make a great noise with rattles, not unlike the basket rattles used by children here, though much larger, and hold up their hands to heaven for a blessing. It is then the greatest offerings are made; and those children whom our wise men foretell will be fortunate are then presented to different people. I remember many used to come to see me, and I was carried about to others for that purpose. They have many offerings, particularly at full moons; generally two, at harvest, before the fruits are taken out of the ground; and when any young animals are killed, sometimes they offer up part of them as a sacrifice. These offerings, when made by one of the heads of a family, serve for the whole. I remember we often had them at my father's and my uncle's, and their families have been present. Some of our offerings are eaten with bitter herbs. We had a saying among us to anyone of a cross temper, "That if they were to be eaten, they should be eaten with bitter herbs."

We practised circumcision like the Jews, and made offerings and feasts on that occasion, in the same manner as they did. Like them also, our children were named from some event, some circumstance, or fancied foreboding, at the time of their birth. I was named *Olaudah,* which in our language signifies vicissitude, or fortunate; also, one favored, and having a loud voice and well spoken. I remember we never polluted the name of the object of our adoration; on the contrary, it was always mentioned with the greatest reverence; and we were totally unacquainted with swearing, and all those terms of abuse and reproach which find their way so readily and copiously into the language of more civilized people. The only expressions of that kind I remember were, "May you rot, or may you swell, or may a beast take you."

I have before remarked that the natives of this part of Africa are extremely cleanly. This necessary habit of decency was with us a part of religion, and therefore we had many purifications and washings; indeed almost as many, and used on the same occasions, if my recollection does not fail me, as the Jews. Those that touched the dead at any time were obliged to wash and purify themselves before they could enter a dwelling-house. Every woman, too, at certain times was forbidden to come into a dwelling-house, or touch any person, or anything we eat. I was so fond of my mother I could not keep from her, or avoid touching her at some of those periods, in consequence of which I was obliged to be kept out with her, in a little house made for that purpose, till offering was made, and then we were purified. . . .

Such is the imperfect sketch my memory has furnished me with, of the manners and customs of a people among whom I first drew my breath. And here I cannot forbear suggesting what has long struck me very forcibly, namely, the strong analogy which even by this sketch, imperfect as it is, appears to prevail in the manners and customs of my countrymen and those of the Jews, before they reached the land of promise, and particularly the patriarchs while they were yet in that pastoral state which is described in Genesis—an analogy, which alone would induce me to think that the one people had sprung from the other. Indeed, this is the opinion of Dr. Gill, who, in his commentary on Genesis, very ably deduces the pedigree of the Africans from Afer and Afra, the descendents of Abraham by Keturah his wife and concubine (for both these titles are applied to her). It is also conformable to the sentiments of Dr. John Clarke, formerly Dean of Sarum, in his truth of the Christian religion; both these authors concur in ascribing to us this original. The reasonings of those gentlemen are still further confirmed by the scripture chronology; and if any further corroboration were required, this resemblance in so many respects, is a strong evidence in support of the opinion. Like the Israelites in their primitive state, our government was conducted by our chiefs or judges, our wise men and elders; and the head of a family with us enjoyed a similar authority over his household, with that which is ascribed to Abraham and the other patriarchs. The law of retaliation obtained almost universally with us as with them: and even their religion appeared to have shed upon us a ray of its glory, though broken and spent in its passage, or eclipsed by the cloud with which time, tradition, and ignorance might have enveloped it; for we had our circumcision (a rule, I believe, peculiar to that people), we had also our sacrifices and burnt-offerings, our washings and purifications, and on the same occasions as they did.

As to the difference of color between the Eboan Africans and the modern Jews, I shall not presume to account for it. It is a subject which has engaged the pens of men of both genius and learning, and is far above my strength. The most able and Reverend Mr. T. Clarkson, however, in his much admired essay on the Slavery and Commerce of the Human Species, has ascertained the cause in a manner that at once solves every objection on that account, and, on my mind at least, has produced the fullest conviction. I shall therefore refer to that performance for the theory,[9] contenting myself with extracting a fact as related by Dr. Mitchel.[10] "The Spaniards, who have inhabited America, under the torrid zone, for any time, are become as dark colored as our native Indians of Virginia; of which *I myself have been a witness.*" There is also another instance[11] of a Portuguese settlement at Mitomba, a river in Sierra

[9]Pages 178 to 216.
[10]Philos. Trans. No. 476, Sec. 4, cited by Mr. Clarkson, p. 205.
[11]Same page.

Leone, where the inhabitants are bred from a mixture of the first Portuguese discoverers with the natives, and are now become in their complexion, and in the woolly quality of their hair, *perfect Negroes,* retaining however a smattering of the Portuguese language.

These instances, and a great many more which might be adduced, while they show how the complexions of the same persons vary in different climates, it is hoped may tend also to remove the prejudice that some conceive against the natives of Africa on account of their color. Surely the minds of the Spaniards did not change with their complexions! Are there not causes enough to which the apparent inferiority of an African may be ascribed, without limiting the goodness of God, and supposing he forebore to stamp understanding on certainly his own image, because "carved in ebony." Might it not naturally be ascribed to their situation? When they come among Europeans, they are ignorant of their language, religion, manners, and customs. Are any pains taken to teach them these? Are they treated as men? Does not slavery itself depress the mind, and extinguish all its fire and every noble sentiment? But, above all, what advantages do not a refined people possess, over those who are rude and uncultivated? Let the polished and haughty European recollect that his ancestors were once, like the Africans, uncivilized, and even barbarous. Did Nature make *them* inferior to their sons? and should *they too* have been made slaves? Every rational mind answers, No. Let such reflections as these melt the pride of their superiority into sympathy for the wants and miseries of their sable brethren, and compel them to acknowledge that understanding is not confined to feature or color. If, when they look round the world, they feel exultation, let it be tempered with benevolence to others, and gratitude to God, "who hath made of one blood all nations of men for to dwell on all the face of the earth";[12] "and whose wisdom is not our wisdom, neither are our ways his ways."

Chapter 2

I hope the reader will not think I have trespassed on his patience in introducing myself to him, with some account of the manners and customs of my country. They had been implanted in me with great care, and made an impression on my mind, which time could not erase, and which all the adversity and variety of fortune I have since experienced, served only to rivet and record: for, whether the love of one's country be real or imaginary, or a lesson of reason, or an instinct of nature, I still look back with pleasure on the first scenes of my life, though that pleasure has been for the most part mingled with sorrow.

I have already acquainted the reader with the time and place of my birth. My father, besides many slaves, had a numerous family, of which seven lived to grow up, including myself and sister, who was the only daughter. As I was the youngest of the sons, I became, of course, the greatest favorite with my mother, and was always with her; and she used to take particular pains to form my mind. I was trained up from my earliest years in the art of war: my daily exercise was shooting and throwing

[12]Acts 17:26.

javelins, and my mother adorned me with emblems, after the manner of our greatest warriors. In this way I grew up till I had turned the age of eleven, when an end was put to my happiness in the following manner: Generally, when the grown people in the neighborhood were gone far in the fields to labor, the children assembled together in some of the neighboring premises to play; and commonly some of us used to get up a tree to look out for any assailant, or kidnapper, that might come upon us—for they sometimes took those opportunities of our parents' absence, to attack and carry off as many as they could seize. One day as I was watching at the top of a tree in our yard, I saw one of those people come into the yard of our next neighbor but one, to kidnap, there being many stout young people in it. Immediately on this I gave the alarm of the rogue, and he was surrounded by the stoutest of them, who entangled him with cords, so that he could not escape, till some of the grown people came and secured him. But, alas! ere long it was my fate to be thus attacked, and to be carried off, when none of the grown people were nigh. One day, when all our people were gone out to their works as usual, and only I and my dear sister were left to mind the house, two men and a woman got over our walls, and in a moment seized us both, and, without giving us time to cry out, or make resistance, they stopped our mouths, and ran off with us into the nearest wood. Here they tied our hands, and continued to carry us as far as they could, till night came on, when we reached a small house, where the robbers halted for refreshment, and spent the night. We were then unbound, but were unable to take any food; and, being quite overpowered by fatigue and grief, our only relief was some sleep, which allayed our misfortune for a short time. The next morning we left the house, and continued travelling all the day. For a long time we had kept the woods, but at last we came into a road which I believed I knew. I had now some hopes of being delivered; for we had advanced but a little way before I discovered some people at a distance, on which I began to cry out for their assistance; but my cries had no other effect than to make them tie me faster and stop my mouth, and then they put me into a large sack. They also stopped my sister's mouth, and tied her hands; and in this manner we proceeded till we were out of sight of these people. When we went to rest the following night, they offered us some victuals, but we refused it and the only comfort we had was in being in one another's arms all that night, and bathing each other with our tears. But alas we were soon deprived of even the small comfort of weeping together. The next day proved a day of greater sorrow than I had yet experienced; for my sister and I were then separated, while we lay clasped in each other's arms. It was in vain that we had sought them not to part us; she was torn from me, and immediately carried away, while I was left in a state of distraction not to be described. I cried and grieved continually; and for several days did not eat anything but what they forced into my mouth. At length, after many days' travelling, during which I had often changed masters, I got into the hands of a chieftain, in a very pleasant country. This man had two wives and some children, and they all used me extremely well, and did all they could do to comfort me; particularly the first wife, who was something like my mother. Although I was a great many days' journey from my father's house, yet these people spoke exactly the same language with us. This first master of mine, as I may call him, was a smith, and my principal employment was working his bellows, which were the same kind as I had seen in my vicinity. They were in some respects not unlike the stoves here in gentlemen's kitchens, and were covered over with leather; and in the middle of that leather a stick was fixed, and a person stood up, and worked it in the same manner as is done to pump water out of a cask with a hand pump. I believe it was gold he worked, for it was of a lovely bright yellow color, and was worn by the women on their wrists and ankles. I was there I suppose about a month, and they at last used to trust me some little distance from the house. This liberty I used in embracing every opportunity to inquire the way to my own home; and I also sometimes, for the same purpose, went with the maidens, in the cool of the evenings, to bring pitchers of water from the springs for the use of the house. I had also remarked where the sun rose in the morning, and set in the evening, as I had travelled along; and I had observed that my father's house was towards the rising of the sun. I therefore determined to seize the first opportunity of making my escape, and to shape my course for that quarter; for I was quite oppressed and weighed down by grief after my mother and friends; and my love of liberty, ever great, was strengthened by the mortifying circumstance of not daring to eat with the free-born children, although I was mostly their companion. While I was projecting my escape one day, an unlucky event happened, which quite disconcerted my plan, and put an end to my hopes. I used to be sometimes employed in assisting an elderly slave to cook and take care of the poultry; and one morning, while I was feeding some chickens, I happened to toss a small pebble at one of them, which hit it on the middle, and directly killed it. The old slave, having soon after missed the chicken, inquired after it; and on my relating the accident (for I told her the truth, for my mother would never suffer me to tell a lie), she flew into a violent passion, and threatened that I should suffer for it; and, my master being out, she immediately went and told her mistress what I had done. This alarmed me very much, and I expected an instant flogging, which to me was uncommonly dreadful, for I had seldom been beaten at home. I therefore resolved to fly; and accordingly I ran into a thicket that was hard by, and hid myself in the bushes. Soon afterwards my mistress and the slave returned, and, not seeing me, they searched all the house, but not finding me, and I not making answer when they called to me, they thought I had run away, and the whole neighborhood was raised in the pursuit of me. In that part of the country, as in ours, the houses and villages were skirted with woods, or shrubberies, and the bushes were so thick that a man could readily conceal himself in them, so as to elude the strictest search. The neighbors continued the whole day looking for me, and several times many of them came within a few yards of the place where I lay hid. I expected every moment, when I heard a rustling among the trees, to be found out, and punished by my master; but they never discovered me, though they were often so near that I even heard their conjectures as they were looking about for me; and I now learned from them that any attempts to return home would be hopeless. Most of them supposed I had fled towards home; but the distance was so great, and the way so intricate, that they thought I could never reach it, and that I should be lost in the woods. When I heard this I was seized with a violent panic, and abandoned myself to despair. Night, too, began to approach, and aggravated all my fears. I had before entertained hopes of getting home, and had determined when it should be dark to make the attempt; but I was now convinced it was fruitless, and began to consider that, if possibly I could escape all other animals, I could not those of the human kind; and that, not knowing the way, I must perish in the woods. Thus was I like the hunted deer—

——Every leaf and every whisp'ring breath,
Convey'd a foe, and every foe a death.[13]

I heard frequent rustlings among the leaves, and being pretty sure they were snakes, I expected every instant to be stung by them. This increased my anguish, and the horror of my situation became now quite insupportable. I at length quitted the thicket, very faint and hungry, for I had not eaten or drank anything all the day, and crept to my master's kitchen, from whence I set out at first, which was an open shed, and laid myself down in the ashes with an anxious wish for death, to relieve me from all my pains. I was scarcely awake in the morning, when the old woman slave, who was the first up, came to light the fire, and saw me in the fireplace. She was very much surprised to see me, and could scarcely believe her own eyes. She now promised to intercede for me, and went for her master, who soon after came, and, having slightly reprimanded me, ordered me to be taken care of, and not ill treated.

Soon after this, my master's only daughter, and child by his first wife, sickened and died, which affected him so much that for sometime he was almost frantic, and really would have killed himself, had he not been watched and prevented. However, in a short time afterwards he recovered, and I was again sold. I was now carried to the left of the sun's rising, through many dreary wastes and dismal woods, amidst the hideous roarings of wild beasts. The people I was sold to used to carry me very often, when I was tired, either on their shoulders or on their backs. I saw many convenient well-built sheds along the road, at proper distances, to accommodate the merchants and travellers, who lay in those buildings along with their wives, who often accompany them; and they always go well armed.

From the time I left my own nation, I always found somebody that understood me till I came to the sea coast. The languages of different nations did not totally differ, nor were they so copious as those of the Europeans, particularly the English. They were therefore, easily learned; and, while I was journeying thus through Africa, I acquired two or three different tongues. In this manner I had been travelling for a considerable time, when, one evening, to my great surprise, whom should I see brought to the house where I was but my dear sister! As soon as she saw me, she gave a loud shriek, and ran into my arms—I was quite overpowered; neither of us could speak, but, for a considerable time, clung to each other in mutual embraces, unable to do anything but weep. Our meeting affected all who saw us; and, indeed, I must acknowledge, in honor of those sable destroyers of human rights, that I never met with any ill treatment, or saw any offered to their slaves, except tying them, when necessary, to keep them from running away. When these people knew we were brother and sister, they indulged us to be together; and the man, to whom I supposed we belonged, lay with us, he in the middle, while she and I held one another by the hands across his breast all night; and thus for a while we forgot our misfortunes, in the joy of being together; but even this small comfort was soon to have an end; for scarcely had the fatal morning appeared when she was again torn from me forever! I was now more miserable, if possible, than before. The small relief which her

[13]From John Denham's *Cooper's Hill* (1642) [Ed.].

presence gave me from pain, was gone, and the wretchedness of my situation was redoubled by my anxiety after her fate, and my apprehensions lest her sufferings should be greater than mine, when I could not be with her to alleviate them. Yes, thou dear partner of all my childish sports! thou sharer of my joys and sorrows! happy should I have ever esteemed myself to encounter every misery for you and to procure your freedom by the sacrifice of my own. Though you were early forced from my arms, your image has been always riveted in my heart, from which neither time nor fortune have been able to remove it; so that, while the thoughts of your sufferings have damped my prosperity, they have mingled with adversity and increased its bitterness. To that Heaven which protects the weak from the strong, I commit the care of your innocence and virtues, if they have not already received their full reward, and if your youth and delicacy have not long since fallen victims to the violence of the African trader, the pestilential stench of a Guinea ship, the seasoning in the European colonies or the lash and lust of a brutal and unrelenting overseer.

I did not long remain after my sister. I was again sold, and carried through a number of places, till after travelling a considerable time, I came to a town called Tinmah, in the most beautiful country I had yet seen in Africa. It was extremely rich, and there were many rivulets which flowed through it, and supplied a large pond in the centre of the town, where the people washed. Here I first saw and tasted cocoanuts, which I thought superior to any nuts I had ever tasted before; and the trees, which were loaded, were also interspersed among the houses, which had commodious shades adjoining, and were in the same manner as ours, the insides being neatly plastered and whitewashed. Here I also saw and tasted for the first time, sugar-cane. Their money consisted of little white shells, the size of the finger nail. I was sold here for one hundred and seventy-two of them, by a merchant who lived and brought me there. I had been about two or three days at his house, when a wealthy widow, a neighbor of his, came there one evening, and brought with her an only son, a young gentleman about my own age and size. Here they saw me; and, having taken a fancy to me, I was bought of the merchant, and went home with them. Her house and premises were situated close to one of those rivulets I have mentioned, and were the finest I ever saw in Africa: they were very extensive, and she had a number of slaves to attend her. The next day I was washed and perfumed, and when meal time came, I was led into the presence of my mistress, and ate and drank before her with her son. This filled me with astonishment; and I could scarce help expressing my surprise that the young gentleman should suffer me, who was bound, to eat with him who was free; and not only so, but that he would not at any time either eat or drink till I had taken first, because I was the eldest, which was agreeable to our custom. Indeed, every thing here, and all their treatment of me, made me forget that I was a slave. The language of these people resembled ours so nearly, that we understood each other perfectly. They had also the very same customs as we. There were likewise slaves daily to attend us, while my young master and I, with other boys, sported with our darts and bows and arrows, as I had been used to do at home. In this resemblance to my former happy state, I passed about two months; and I now began to think I was to be adopted into the family, and was beginning to be reconciled to my situation, and to forget by degrees my misfortunes, when all at once the delusion vanished; for, without the least previous knowledge, one morning early, while my dear master and companion was still asleep, I was awakened out of my reverie to fresh sorrow, and hurried away even amongst the uncircumcised.

Thus, at the very moment I dreamed of the greatest happiness, I found myself most miserable; and it seemed as if fortune wished to give me this taste of joy only to render the reverse more poignant. The change I now experienced was as painful as it was sudden and unexpected. It was a change indeed, from a state of bliss to a scene which is inexpressible by me, as it discovered to me an element I had never before beheld, and till then had no idea of, and wherein such instances of hardship and cruelty continually occurred, as I can never reflect on but with horror.

All the nations and people I had hitherto passed through, resembled our own in their manners, customs, and language; but I came at length to a country, the inhabitants of which differed from us in all those particulars. I was very much struck with this difference, especially when I came among a people who did not circumcise, and ate without washing their hands. They cooked also in iron pots, and had European cutlasses and cross bows, which were unknown to us, and fought with their fists among themselves. Their women were not so modest as ours, for they ate, and drank, and slept with their men. But above all, I was amazed to see no sacrifices or offerings among them. In some of those places the people ornamented themselves with scars, and likewise filed their teeth very sharp. They wanted sometimes to ornament me in the same manner, but I would not suffer them; hoping that I might some time be among a people who did not thus disfigure themselves, as I thought they did. At last I came to the banks of a large river which was covered with canoes, in which the people appeared to live with their household utensils and provisions of all kinds. I was beyond measure astonished at this, as I had never before seen any water larger than a pond or a rivulet; and my surprise was mingled with no small fear when I was put into one of these canoes, and we began to paddle and move along the river. We continued going on thus till night, and when we came to land, and made fires on the banks, each family by themselves; some dragged their canoes on shore, others stayed and cooked in theirs, and laid in them all night. Those on the land had mats, of which they made tents, some in the shape of little houses; in these we slept; and after the morning meal, we embarked again and proceeded as before. I was often very much astonished to see some of the women, as well as the men, jump into the water, dive to the bottom, come up again, and swim about. Thus I continued to travel, sometimes by land, sometimes by water, through different countries and various nations, till the end of six or seven months after I had been kidnapped, I arrived at the sea coast. It would be tedious and uninteresting to relate all the incidents which befell me during this journey, and which I have not yet forgotten; of the various hands I passed through, and the manners and customs of all the different people among whom I lived—I shall therefore only observe, that in all the places where I was, the soil was exceedingly rich; the pumpkins, eadas, plantains, yams, &c. &c., were in great abundance, and of incredible size. There were also vast quantities of different gums, though not used for any purpose, and everywhere a great deal of tobacco. The cotton even grew quite wild, and there was plenty of red-wood. I saw no mechanics whatever in all the way, except such as I have mentioned. The chief employment in all these countries was agriculture, and both the males and females, as with us, were brought up to it, and trained in the arts of war.

The first object which saluted my eyes when I arrived on the coast, was the sea, and a slave ship, which was then riding at anchor, and waiting for its cargo. These filled me with astonishment, which was soon converted into terror, when I was carried on board. I was immediately handled, and tossed up to see if I were sound, by some of the crew; and I was now persuaded that I had gotten into a world of bad spirits, and that they were going to kill me. Their complexions, too, differing so much from ours, their long hair, and the language they spoke (which was very different from any I had ever heard), united to confirm me in this belief. Indeed, such were the horrors of my views and fears at the moment, that, if ten thousand worlds had been my own, I would have freely parted with them all to have exchanged my condition with that of the meanest slave in my own country. When I looked round the ship too, and saw a large furnace of copper boiling, and a multitude of black people of every description chained together, every one of their countenances expressing dejection and sorrow, I no longer doubted of my fate; and, quite overpowered with horror and anguish, I fell motionless on the deck and fainted. When I recovered a little, I found some black people about me, who I believed were some of those who had brought me on board, and had been receiving their pay; they talked to me in order to cheer me, but all in vain. I asked them if we were not to be eaten by those white men with horrible looks, red faces, and long hair. They told me I was not, and one of the crew brought me a small portion of spirituous liquor in a wine glass; but, being afraid of him, I would not take it out of his hand. One of the blacks, therefore, took it from him and gave it to me, and I took a little down my palate, which, instead of reviving me, as they thought it would, threw me into the greatest consternation at the strange feeling it produced, having never tasted any such liquor before. Soon after this, the blacks who brought me on board went off, and left me abandoned to despair.

I now saw myself deprived of all chance of returning to my native country, or even the least glimpse of hope of gaining the shore, which I now considered as friendly; and I even wished for my former slavery in preference to my present situation, which was filled with horrors of every kind, still heightened by my ignorance of what I was to undergo. I was not long suffered to indulge my grief; I was soon put down under the decks, and there I received such a salutation in my nostrils as I had never experienced in my life: so that, with the loathsomeness of the stench, and crying together, I became so sick and low that I was not able to eat, nor had I the least desire to taste anything. I now wished for the last friend, death, to relieve me; but soon, to my grief, two of the white men offered me eatables; and, on my refusing to eat, one of them held me fast by the hands, and laid me across, I think, the windlass, and tied my feet, while the other flogged me severely. I had never experienced anything of this kind before, and, although not being used to the water, I naturally feared that element the first time I saw it, yet, nevertheless, could I have got over the nettings, I would have jumped over the side, but I could not; and besides, the crew used to watch us very closely who were not chained down to the decks, lest we should leap into the water; and I have seen some of these poor African prisoners most severely cut, for attempting to do so, and hourly whipped for not eating. This indeed was often the case with myself. In a little time after, amongst the poor chained men, I found some of my own nation, which in a small degree gave ease to my mind. I inquired of these what was to be done with us? They gave me to understand, we were to be carried to these white people's country to work for them. I then was a little revived, and thought, if it were no worse than working, my situation was not so desperate; but still I feared I should be put to death, the white people looked and acted, as I thought, in so savage a manner; for I had never seen among any people such instances of brutal cruelty; and this not only shown towards us blacks, but also to some of the whites themselves. One white man in particular I saw, when we were permitted to be on deck, flogged so unmercifully with a large rope near the foremast, that he died in consequence of it; and they tossed him over the side as they would have done a brute. This made me fear these people the more; and I expected nothing less than to be treated in the same manner. I could not help expressing my fears and apprehensions to some of my countrymen; I asked them if these people had no country, but lived in this hollow place (the ship)? They told me they did not, but came from a distant one. "Then," said I, "how comes it in all our country we never heard of them?" They told me because they lived so very far off. I then asked where were their women? had they any like themselves? I was told they had. "And why," said I, "do we not see them?" They answered, because they were left behind. I asked how the vessel could go? They told me they could not tell; but that there was cloth put upon the masts by the help of the ropes I saw, and then the vessel went on; and the white men had some spell or magic they put in the water when they liked, in order to stop the vessel. I was exceedingly amazed at this account, and really thought they were spirits. I therefore wished much to be from amongst them, for I expected they would sacrifice me; but my wishes were vain—for we were so quartered that it was impossible for any of us to make our escape.

While we stayed on the coast I was mostly on deck; and one day, to my great astonishment, I saw one of these vessels coming in with the sails up. As soon as the whites saw it, they gave a great shout, at which we were amazed; and the more so, as the vessel appeared larger by approaching nearer. At last, she came to an anchor in my sight, and when the anchor was let go, I and my countrymen who saw it, were lost in astonishment to observe the vessel stop—and were now convinced it was done by magic. Soon after this the other ship got her boats out, and they came on board of us, and the people of both ships seemed very glad to see each other. Several of the strangers also shook hands with us black people, and made motions with their hands, signifying I suppose, we were to go to their country, but we did not understand them.

At last when the ship we were in, had got in all her cargo, they made ready with many fearful noises, and we were all put under deck, so that we could not see how they managed the vessel. But this disappointment was the least of my sorrow. The stench of the hold while we were on the coast was so intolerably loathsome, that it was dangerous to remain there for any time, and some of us had been permitted to stay on the deck for the fresh air; but now that the whole ship's cargo were confined together, it became absolutely pestilential. The closeness of the place, and the heat of the climate, added to the number in the ship, which was so crowded that each had scarcely room to turn himself, almost suffocated us. This produced copious perspirations, so that the air soon became unfit for respiration, from a variety of loathsome smells, and brought on a sickness among the slaves, of which many died—thus falling victims to the improvident avarice, as I may call it, of their purchasers. This wretched situation was again aggravated by the galling of the chains, now became insupportable, and the filth of the necessary tubs, into which the children often fell, and were almost suffocated. The shrieks of the women, and the groans of the dying, rendered the whole a scene of horror almost inconceivable. Happily perhaps, for myself, I was soon reduced so low here that it was thought necessary to keep me almost always on deck; and from my extreme youth I was not put in fetters. In this situation I expected every hour to share the fate of my companions, some of whom were almost daily brought upon deck at the point of death, which I began to hope would soon put an end to my miseries. Often did I think many of the inhabitants of the deep much more happy than myself. I envied them the freedom they enjoyed, and as often wished I could change my condition for theirs. Every circumstance I met with, served only to render my state more painful, and heightened my apprehensions, and my opinion of the cruelty of the whites.

One day they had taken a number of fishes; and when they had killed and satisfied themselves with as many as they thought fit, to our astonishment who were on deck, rather than give any of them to us to eat, as we expected, they tossed the remaining fish into the sea again, although we begged and prayed for some as well as we could, but in vain; and some of my country men, being pressed by hunger, took an opportunity, when they thought no one saw them, of trying to get a little privately; but they were discovered, and the attempt procured them some very severe floggings. One day, when we had a smooth sea and moderate wind, two of my wearied countrymen who were chained together (I was near them at the time), preferring death to such a life of misery, somehow made through the nettings and jumped into the sea; immediately, another quite dejected fellow, who, on account of his illness, was suffered to be out of irons, also followed their example; and I believe many more would very soon have done the same, if they had not been prevented by the ship's crew, who were instantly alarmed. Those of us that were the most active, were in a moment put down under the deck; and there was such a noise and confusion amongst the people of the ship as I never heard before, to stop her, and get the boat out to go after the slaves. However, two of the wretches were drowned, but they got the other, and afterwards flogged him unmercifully, for thus attempting to prefer death to slavery. In this manner we continued to undergo more hardships than I can now relate, hardships which are inseparable from this accursed trade. Many a time we were near suffocation from the want of fresh air, which we were often without for whole days together. This, and the stench of the necessary tubs, carried off many.

During our passage, I first saw flying fishes, which surprised me very much; they used frequently to fly across the ship, and many of them fell on the deck. I also now first saw the use of the quadrant; I had often with astonishment seen the mariners make observations with it, and I could not think what it meant. They at last took notice of my surprise; and one of them, willing to increase it, as well as to gratify my curiosity, made me one day look through it. The clouds appeared to me to be land, which disappeared as they passed along. This heightened my wonder; and I was now more persuaded than ever, that I was in another world, and that every thing about me was magic. At last, we came in sight of the island of Barbadoes, at which the whites on board gave a great shout, and made many signs of joy to us. We did not know what to think of this; but as the vessel drew nearer, we plainly saw the harbor, and other ships of different kinds and sizes, and we soon anchored amongst them, off Bridgetown. Many merchants and planters now came on board, though it was in the evening. They put us in separate parcels, and examined us attentively. They also made us jump, and pointed to the land, signifying we were to go there. We thought by this, we should be eaten by these ugly men, as they appeared to us; and, when soon after we were all put down under the deck again, there was much dread and trembling among us, and nothing but bitter cries to be heard all the night from these apprehensions, insomuch, that at last the white people got some old slaves from the land to pacify us. They told us we were not to be eaten, but to work, and were soon to go on land, where we should see many of our country people. This report eased us much. And sure enough, soon after we were landed, there came to us Africans of all languages.

We were conducted immediately to the merchant's yard, where we were all pent up together, like so many sheep in a fold, without regard to sex or age. As every object was new to me, everything I saw filled me with surprise. What struck me first, was, that the houses were built with bricks and stories, and in every other respect different from those I had seen in Africa; but I was still more astonished on seeing people on horseback. I did not know what this could mean; and, indeed, I thought these people were full of nothing but magical arts. While I was in this astonishment, one of my fellow prisoners spoke to a countryman of his, about the horses, who said they were the same kind they had in their country. I understood them, though they were from a distant part of Africa; and I thought it odd I had not seen any horses there; but afterwards, when I came to converse with different Africans, I found they had many horses amongst them, and much larger than those I then saw.

We were not many days in the merchant's custody, before we were sold after their usual manner, which is this: On a signal given (as the beat of a drum), the buyers rush at once into the yard where the slaves are confined, and make choice of that parcel they like best. The noise and clamor with which this is attended and the eagerness visible in the countenances of the buyers, serve not a little to increase the apprehension of terrified Africans, who may well be supposed to consider them as the ministers of the destruction to which they think themselves devoted. In this manner, without scruple, are relations and friends separated, most of them never to see each other again. I remember, in the vessel in which I was brought over, in the men's apartment, there were several brothers, who, in the sale, were sold in different lots; and it was very moving on this occasion, to see and hear their cries at parting. O, ye nominal Christians! might not an African ask you—Learned you this from your God, who says unto you, Do unto all men as you would men should do unto you? Is it not enough that we are torn from our country and friends, to toil for your luxury and lust of gain? Must every tender feeling be likewise sacrificed to your avarice? Are the dearest friends and relations, now rendered more dear by their separation from their kindred, still to be parted from each other, and thus prevented from cheering the gloom of slavery, with the small comfort of being together, and mingling their sufferings and sorrows? Why are parents to lose their children, brothers their sisters, or husbands their wives? Surely, this is a new refinement in cruelty, which, while it has no advantage to atone for it, thus aggravates distress, and adds fresh horrors even to the wretchedness of slavery.

from Chapter 3

I now totally lost the small remains of comfort I had enjoyed in conversing with my countrymen; the women too, who used to wash and take care of me were all gone different ways, and I never saw one of them afterwards.

I stayed in this island for a few days, I believe it could not be above a fortnight, when I, and some few more slaves, that were not saleable amongst the rest, from very much fretting, were shipped off in a sloop for North America. On the passage we were better treated than when we were coming from Africa, and we had plenty of rice and fat pork. We were landed up a river a good way from the sea, about Virginia county, where we saw few or none of our native Africans, and not one soul who could talk to me. I was a few weeks weeding grass and gathering stones in a plantation; and at last all my companions were distributed different ways, and only myself was left. I was now exceedingly miserable, and thought myself worse off than any of the rest of my companions, for they could talk to each other, but I had no person to speak to that I could understand. In this state, I was constantly grieving and pining, and wishing for death rather than anything else. While I was in this plantation, the gentleman, to whom I suppose the estate belonged, being unwell, I was one day sent for to his dwelling-house to fan him; when I came into the room where he was I was very much affrighted at some things I saw, and the more so as I had seen a black woman slave as I came through the house, who was cooking the dinner, and the poor creature was cruelly loaded with various kinds of iron machines; she had one particularly on her head, which locked her mouth so fast that she could scarcely speak; and could not eat nor drink. I was much astonished and shocked at this contrivance, which I afterwards learned was called the iron muzzle. Soon after I had a fan put in my hand, to fan the gentleman while he slept; and so I did indeed with great fear. While he was fast asleep I indulged myself a great deal in looking about the room, which to me appeared very fine and curious. The first object that engaged my attention was a watch which hung on the chimney, and was going. I was quite surprised at the noise it made, and was afraid it would tell the gentleman anything I might do amiss; and when I immediately after observed a picture hanging in the room, which appeared constantly to look at me, I was still more affrighted, having never seen such things as these before. At one time I thought it was something relative to magic; and not seeing it move, I thought it might be some way the whites had to keep their great men when they died, and offer them libations as we used to do our friendly spirits. In this state of anxiety I remained till my master awoke, when I was dismissed out of the room, to my no small satisfaction and relief; for I thought that these people were all made up of wonders. In this place I was called Jacob; but on board the *African Snow,* I was called Michael. I had been some time in this miserable, forlorn, and much dejected state, without having anyone to talk to, which made my life a burden, when the kind and unknown hand of the Creator (who in very deed leads the blind in a way they know not) now began to appear, to my comfort; for one day the captain of a merchant ship, called the *Industrious Bee,* came on some business to my master's house. This gentleman, whose name was Michael Henry Pascal, was a lieutenant in the royal navy, but now commanded this trading ship, which was somewhere in the confines of the county many miles off. While he was at my master's house, it happened that he saw me, and liked me so well that he made a purchase of me. I think I have often heard him say he gave thirty or forty pounds sterling for me; but I do not remember which. However, he meant me for a present to some of his friends in England: and as I was sent accordingly from the house of my then master (one Mr. Campbell) to the place where the ship lay; I was conducted on horseback by an elderly black man (a mode of travelling which appeared very odd to me). When I arrived I was carried on board a fine large ship, loaded with tobacco, &c., and just ready to sail for England. I now thought my condition much mended; I had sails to lie on, and plenty of good victuals to eat; and everybody on board used me very kindly, quite contrary to what I had seen of any white people before; I therefore began to think that they were not all of the same disposition. A few days after I was on board we sailed for England. I was still at a loss to conjecture my destiny. By this time, however, I could smatter a little imperfect English; and I wanted to know as well as I could where we were going. Some of the people of the ship used to tell me they were going to carry me back to my own country, and this made me very happy. I was quite rejoiced at the idea of going back, and thought if I could get home what wonders I should have to tell. But I was reserved for another fate, and was soon undeceived when we came within sight of the English coast. While I was on board this ship, my captain and master named me *Gustavus Vassa.* I at that time began to understand him a little, and refused to be called so, and told him as well as I could that I would be called Jacob; but he said I should not, and still called me Gustavus: and when I refused to answer to my new name, which I at first did, it gained me many a cuff; so at length I submitted, and by which I have been known ever since. The ship had a very long passage, and on that account we had very short allowance of provisions. Towards the last, we had only one pound and a half of bread per week, and about the same quantity of meat, and one quart of water a day. We spoke with only one vessel the whole time we were at sea, and but once we caught a few fishes. In our extremities the captain and people told me in jest they would kill and eat me; but I thought them in earnest, and was depressed beyond measure, expecting every moment to be my last. While I was in this situation, one evening they caught, with a good deal of trouble, a large shark, and got it on board. This gladdened my poor heart exceedingly, as I thought it would serve the people to eat instead of their eating me; but very soon, to my astonishment, they cut off a small part of the tail, and tossed the rest over the side. This renewed my consternation; and I did not know what to think of these white people, though I very much feared they would kill and eat me. There was on board the ship a young lad who had never been at sea before, about four or five years older than myself: his name was Richard Baker. He was a native of America, had received an excellent education, and was of the most amiable temper. Soon after I went on board, he showed me a great deal of partiality and attention, and in return I grew extremely fond of him. We at length became inseparable; and, for the space of two years, he was of very great use to me, and was my constant companion and instructor. Although this dear youth had many slaves of his own, yet he and I have gone through many sufferings together on shipboard; and we have many nights lain in each other's bosoms when we were in great distress. Thus such a friendship was cemented between us as we cherished till his death, which, to my very great sorrow, happened in the year 1759, when he was up the Archipelago, on board his Majesty's ship the *Preston:* an event which I have never ceased to regret, as I lost at once a kind interpreter, an agreeable companion, and a faithful friend; who, at the age of fifteen, discovered a mind superior to prejudice; and who was not ashamed to notice, to associate with, and to be the friend and instructor of one who was ignorant, a stranger, of a different complexion, and a slave! My master had lodged in his mother's house in America; he respected him very much, and made him always eat with him in the cabin. He used often to tell him jocularly that he would kill and eat me. Sometimes he would say to me—the black people were not good to eat, and would ask me if we did not eat people in my country. I said, No; then he said he would kill Dick (as he always called him) first, and afterwards me. Though this hearing relieved my mind a little as to myself, I was alarmed for Dick, and whenever he was called I used to be very much afraid he was to be killed; and I would peep and watch to see if they were going to kill him; nor was I free from this consternation till we made the land. One night we lost a man overboard; and the cries and noise were so great and confused, in stopping the ship, that I, who did not know what was the matter, began, as usual, to be very much afraid, and to think they were going to make an offering with me, and perform some magic; which I still believed they dealt in. As the waves were very high, I thought the Ruler of the seas was angry, and I expected to be offered up to appease him. This filled my mind with agony, and I could not any more, that night, close my eyes again to rest. However, when daylight appeared, I was a little eased in my mind; but still, every time I was called, I used to think it was to be killed. Some time after this, we saw some very large fish, which I afterwards found were called grampusses. They looked to me exceedingly terrible, and made their appearance just at dusk, and were so near as to blow the water on the ship's deck. I believed them to be the rulers of the sea; and as the white people did not make any offerings at any time, I thought they were angry with them; and at last, what confirmed my belief was, the wind just then died away, and a calm ensued, and in consequence of it the ship stopped going. I supposed that the fish had performed this, and I hid myself in the fore part of the ship, through fear of being offered up to appease them, every minute peeping and quaking; but my good friend Dick came shortly towards me, and I took an opportunity to ask him, as well as I could, what these fish were. Not being able to talk much English, I could but just make him understand my question; and not at all, when I asked him if any offerings were to be made to them; however, he told me these fish would swallow anybody which sufficiently alarmed me. Here he was called away by the captain, who was leaning over the quarter-deck railing, and looking at the fish; and most of the people were busied in getting a barrel of pitch to light for them to play with. The captain now called me to him, having learned some of my apprehensions from Dick; and having diverted himself and others for some time with my fears, which appeared ludicrous enough in my crying and trembling, he dismissed me. The barrel of pitch was now lighted and put over the side into the water. By this time it was just dark, and the fish went after it; and to my great joy, I saw them no more.

However, all my alarms began to subside when we got sight of land; and at last the ship arrived at Falmouth, after a passage of thirteen weeks. Every heart on board seemed gladdened on our reaching the shore, and none more than mine. The captain immediately went on shore, and sent on board some fresh provisions, which we wanted very much. We made good use of them, and our famine was soon turned into feasting, almost without ending. It was about the beginning of the spring 1757, when I arrived in England and I was near twelve years of age at that time. I was very much struck with the buildings and the pavement of the streets in Falmouth; and, indeed, every object I saw, filled me with new surprise. One morning, when I got upon deck, I saw it covered all over with the snow that fell over night. As I had never seen anything of the kind before, I thought it was salt: so I immediately ran down to the mate, and desired him, as well as I could, to come and see how somebody in the night had thrown salt all over the deck. He, knowing what it was, desired me to bring some of it down to him. Accordingly I took up a handful of it, which I found very cold indeed; and when I brought it to him he desired me to taste it. I did so, and I was surprised beyond measure. I then asked him what it was; he told me it was snow, but I could not in anywise understand him. He asked me, if we had no such thing in my country; I told him, No. I then asked him the use of it, and who made it; he told me a great man in the heavens, called God. But here again I was to all intents and purposes at a loss to understand him; and the more so, when a little after I saw the air filled with it, in a heavy shower, which fell down on the same day. After this I went to church; and having never been at such a place before, I was again amazed at seeing and hearing the service. I asked all I could about it, and they gave me to understand it was worshipping God, who made us and all things. I was still at a great loss, and soon got into an endless field of inquiries, as well as I was able to speak and ask about things. However, my little friend Dick used to be my best interpreter; for I could make free with him, and he always instructed me with pleasure. And from what I could understand by him of this God, and in seeing these white people did not sell one another as we did, I was much pleased; and in this I thought they were much happier than we Africans. I was astonished at the wisdom of the white people in all things I saw; but was amazed at their not sacrificing, or making any offerings, and eating with unwashed hands, and touching the dead. I likewise could not help remarking the particular slenderness of their women, which I did not at first like; and I thought they were not so modest and shame-faced as the African women.

I had often seen my master and Dick employed in reading: and I had a great curiosity to talk to the books as I thought they did, and so to learn how all things had a beginning. For that purpose I have often taken up a book, and have talked to it, and then put my ears to it, when alone, in hopes it would answer me; and I have been very much concerned when I found it remained silent.

My master lodged at the house of a gentleman in Falmouth, who had a fine little daughter about six or seven years of age, and she grew prodigiously fond of me, insomuch that we used to eat together, and had servants to wait on us. I was so much caressed by this family that it often reminded me of the treatment I had received from my little noble African master. After I had been here a few days, I was sent on board of the ship; but the child cried so much after me that nothing could pacify her till I was sent for again. It is ludicrous enough, that I began to fear I should be betrothed to this young lady; and when my master asked me if I would stay there with her behind him, as he was going away with the ship, which had taken in the tobacco again, I cried immediately, and said I would not leave him. At last, by stealth, one night I was sent on board the ship again; and in a little time we sailed for Guernsey, where she was in part owned by a merchant, one Nicholas Doberry. As I was now amongst a people who had not their faces scarred, like some of the African nation where I had been, I was very glad I did not let them ornament me in that manner when I was with them. When we arrived at Guernsey, my master placed me to board and lodge with one of his mates, who had a wife and family there; and some months afterwards he went to England, and left me in care of this mate, together with my friend Dick. This mate had a little daughter, aged about five or six years, with whom I used to be much delighted. I had often observed that when her mother washed her face it looked very rosy, but when she washed mine it did not look so. I therefore tried oftentimes myself if I could not by washing make my face of the same color as my little play-mate, Mary, but it was all in vain; and I now began to be mortified at the difference in our complexions. This woman behaved to me with great kindness and attention, and taught me everything in the same manner as she did her own child, and, indeed, in every respect treated me as such. I remained here till the summer of the year 1757, when my master, being appointed first lieutenant of his Majesty's ship the *Roebuck,* sent for Dick and me, and his old mate. On this we all left Guernsey, and set out for England in a sloop, bound for London. As we were coming up towards the Nore, where the *Roebuck* lay, a man-of-war's boat came along side to press our people, on which each man ran to hide himself. I was very much frightened at this, though I did not know what it meant, or what to think or do. However I went and hid myself also under a hencoop. Immediately afterwards, the press-gang came on board with their swords drawn, and searched all about, pulled the people out by force, and put them into the boat. At last I was found out also; the man that found me held me up by the heels while they all made their sport of me, I roaring and crying out all the time most lustily; but at last the mate, who was my conductor, seeing this, came to my assistance, and did all he could to pacify me; but all to very little purpose, till I had seen the boat go off. Soon afterwards we came to the Nore, where the *Roebuck* lay; and, to our great joy, my master came on board to us, and brought us to the ship. When I went on board this large ship, I was amazed indeed to see the quantity of men and the guns. However, my surprise began to diminish as my knowledge increased; and I ceased to feel those apprehensions and alarms which had taken such strong possession of me when I first came among the Europeans, and for some time after. I began now to pass to an opposite extreme; I was so far from being afraid of anything new which I saw, that after I had been some time in this ship, I even began to long for an engagement. My griefs, too, which in young minds are not perpetual, were now wearing away; and I soon enjoyed myself pretty well, and felt tolerably easy in my present situation. There was a number of boys on board, which still made it more agreeable; for we were always together, and a great part of our time was spent in play. I remained in this ship a considerable time, during which we made several cruises, and visited a variety of places; among others we were twice in Holland, and brought over several persons of distinction from it, whose names I do not now remember. On the passage, one day, for the diversion of those gentlemen, all the boys were called on the quarter-deck, and were paired proportionably, and then made to fight; after which the gentlemen gave the combatants from five to nine shillings each. This was the first time I ever fought with a white boy; and I never knew what it was to have a bloody nose before. This made me fight most desperately, I suppose considerably more than an hour; and at last, both of us being weary, we were parted. I had a great deal of this kind of sport afterwards, in which the captain and the ship's company used very much to encourage me. . . .

from Chapter 7

Every day now brought me nearer my freedom, and I was impatient till we proceeded again to sea, that I might have an opportunity of getting a sum large enough to purchase it. I was not long ungratified; for, in the beginning of the year 1766, my master bought another sloop, named the *Nancy,* the largest I had ever seen. She was partly laden, and was to proceed to Philadelphia; our captain had his choice of three, and I was well pleased he chose this, which was the largest; for, from his having a large vessel, I had more room, and could carry a larger quantity of goods with me. Accordingly, when we had delivered our old vessel, the *Prudence,* and completed the lading of the *Nancy,* having made near three hundred per cent, by four barrels of pork I brought from Charleston, I laid in as large a cargo as I could, trusting to God's providence to prosper my undertaking. . . .

When we had unladen the vessel, and I had sold my venture, finding myself master of about forty-seven pounds—I consulted my true friend, the captain, how I should proceed in offering my master the money for my freedom. He told me to come on a certain morning, when he and my master would be at breakfast together. Accordingly, on that morning I went, and met the captain there, as he had appointed. When I went in I made my obeisance to my master, and with my money in my hand, and many fears in my heart, I prayed him to be as good as his offer to me, when he was pleased to promise me my freedom as soon as I could purchase it. This speech seemed to confound him, he began to recoil, and my heart that instant sunk within me. "What," said he, "give you your freedom? Why, where did you get the money? Have you got forty pounds sterling?" "Yes, sir," I answered. "How did you get it?" replied he. I told him, very honestly. The captain then said he knew I got the money honestly, and with much industry, and that I was particularly careful. On which my master replied, I got money much faster than he did; and said he would not have made me the promise he did if he had thought I should have got the money so soon. "Come, come," said my worthy captain, clapping my master on the back, "Come, Robert (which was his name), I think you must let him have his freedom; you have laid your money out very well; you have received a very good interest for it all this time, and here is now the principal at last. I know Gustavus has earned you more than a hundred a year, and he will save you money, as he will not leave you. Come, Robert, take the money." My master then said he would not be worse than his promise; and, taking the money, told me to go to the Secretary at the Register Office, and get my manumission drawn up. These words of my master were like a voice from heaven to me. In an instant all my trepidation was turned into unutterable bliss; and I most reverently bowed myself with gratitude, unable to express my feelings, but by the overflowing of my eyes, and a heart replete with thanks to God, while my true and worthy friend, the captain congratulated us both with a peculiar degree of heart-felt pleasure. As soon as the first transports of my joy were over, and that I had expressed my thanks to these my worthy friends, in the best manner I was able, I rose with a heart full of affection and reverence, and left the room, in order to obey my master's joyful mandate of going to the Register Office. As I was leaving the house I called to mind the words of the Psalmist, in the 126th Psalm, and like him, "I glorified God in my heart, in whom I trusted." These words had been impressed on my mind from the very day I was forced from Deptford to the present hour, and I now saw them, as I thought, fulfilled and verified. My imagination was all rapture as I flew to the Register Office; and, in this respect, like the apostle Peter[14] (whose deliverance from prison was so sudden and extraordinary that he

[14]Acts 12:9.

thought he was in a vision), I could scarcely believe I was awake. Heavens! who could do justice to my feelings at this moment! Not conquering heroes themselves, in the midst of a triumph—Not the tender mother who has just regained her long lost infant, and presses it to her heart—Not the weary hungry mariner, at the sight of the desired friendly port—Not the lover, when he once more embraces his beloved mistress, after she has been ravished from his arms! All within my breast was tumult, wildness, and delirium! My feet scarcely touched the ground, for they were winged with joy; and, like Elijah,[15] as he rose to Heaven, they "were with lightning sped as I went on." Everyone I met I told of my happiness, and blazed about the virtue of my amiable master and captain.

When I got to the office and acquainted the Register with my errand, he congratulated me on the occasion, and told me he would draw up my manumission for half price, which was a guinea. I thanked him for his kindness; and, having received it, and paid him, I hastened to my master to get him to sign it, that I might be fully released. Accordingly he signed the manumission that day; so that, before night, I, who had been a slave in the morning, trembling at the will of another, was become my own master, and completely free. I thought this was the happiest day I had ever experienced; and my joy was still heightened by the blessings and prayers of many of the sable race, particularly the aged, to whom my heart had ever been attached with reverence.

As the form of my manumission has something peculiar in it, and expresses the absolute power and dominion one man claims over his fellow, I shall beg leave to present it before my readers at full length.

Montserrat.

To all men unto whom these presents shall come: I, Robert King, of the parish of St. Anthony, in the said island, merchant, send greeting. Know ye, that I, the aforesaid Robert King, for and in consideration of the sum of seventy pounds current money of the said island, to me in hand paid, and to the intent that a Negro man slave, named Gustavus Vassa, shall and may become free, having manumitted, emancipated, enfranchised, and set free, and by these presents do manumit, emancipate, enfranchise, and set free, the aforesaid Negro man slave, named Gustavus Vassa, for ever; hereby giving, granting and releasing unto him, the said Gustavus Vassa, all right, title, dominion, sovereignty, and property, which, as lord and master over the aforesaid Gustavus Vassa, I had, or now have, or by any means whatsoever I may or can hereafter possibly have over him, the aforesaid Negro, for ever. In witness whereof, I, the above said Robert King, have unto these presents set my hand and seal, this tenth day of July, in the year of our Lord one thousand seven hundred and sixty-six.

ROBERT KING

Signed, sealed, and delivered in the presence of Terry Legay, Montserrat.
Registered the within manumission at full length, this eleventh day of July 1766, in liber. D.

TERRY LEGAY, Register

[15]In II Kings 2:1–18, Elijah ascends into heaven on a fiery chariot with horses of fire [Ed.].

In short, the fair as well as the black people immediately styled me by a new appellation, to me the most desirable in the world, which was freeman; and at the dances I gave, my Georgia superfine blue clothes made no indifferent appearance, as I thought. Some of the sable females, who formerly stood aloof, now began to relax and appear less coy; but my heart was still fixed on London, where I hoped to be ere long. So that my worthy captain and his owner, my late master, finding that the bent of my mind was towards London, said to me, "We hope you won't leave us, but that you will still be with the vessels." Here gratitude bowed me down; and none but the generous mind can judge of my feelings, struggling between inclination and duty. However, notwithstanding my wish to be in London, I obediently answered my benefactors, that I would go in the vessel, and not leave them; and from the day I was entered on board as an able-bodied sailor, at thirty-six shillings per month, besides what perquisites I could make. My intention was to make a voyage or two, entirely to please these my honored patrons; but I determined that the year following, if it pleased God, I would see old England once more, and surprise my old master, Captain Pascal, who was hourly in my mind; for I still loved him, notwithstanding his usage of me, and pleased myself with thinking what he would say, when he saw what the Lord had done for me in so short a time, instead of being, as he might perhaps suppose, under the cruel yoke of some planter. With these kind of reveries I used often to entertain myself, and shorten the time till my return; and now, being as in my original free African state, I embarked on board the *Nancy,* after having got all things ready for our voyage. In this state of serenity, we sailed for St. Eustatius; and having smooth seas and calm weather, we soon arrived there. After taking our cargo on board, we proceeded to Savannah, in Georgia, in August, 1766. While we were there, as usual, I used to go for the cargo up the rivers in boats; and on this business have been frequently beset by alligators, which were very numerous on that coast; and shot many of them when they have been near getting into our boats, which we have with great difficulty sometimes prevented, and have been very much frightened at them. I have seen a young one sold in Georgia alive for six pence. . . .

from Chapter 10

Our voyage to the north pole being ended, I returned to London with Doctor Irving, with whom I continued for some time, during which I began seriously to reflect on the dangers I had escaped, particularly those of my last voyage, which made a lasting impression on my mind, and, by the grace of God, proved afterwards a mercy to me; it caused me to reflect deeply on my eternal state, and to seek the Lord with full purpose of heart, ere it was too late. I rejoiced greatly; and heartily thanked the Lord for directing me to London, where I was determined to work out my own salvation, and, in so doing, procure a title to heaven; being the result of a mind blinded by ignorance and sin.

In process of time I left my master, Doctor Irving, the purifier of waters. I lodged in Coventry court, Haymarket, where I was continually oppressed and much concerned about the salvation of my soul, and was determined (in my own strength) to be a first-rate Christian. I used every means for this purpose; and, not being able to find any person amongst those with whom I was then acquainted that acquiesced with me in point of religion, or, in scripture language, that would show me any good, I was much dejected, and knew not where to seek relief; however, I first frequented the neighboring churches, St. James' and others, two or three times a day, for many weeks; still I came away dissatisfied: something was wanting that I could not obtain, and I really found more heart-felt relief in reading my Bible at home than in attending the church; and, being resolved to be saved, I pursued other methods. First I went among the Quakers, where the word of God was neither read or preached, so that I remained as much in the dark as ever. I then searched into the Roman Catholic principles, but was not in the least edified. I at length had recourse to the Jews, which availed me nothing, as the fear of eternity daily harassed my mind, and I knew not where to seek shelter from the wrath to come. However, this was my conclusion, at all events, to read the four evangelists, and whatever sect or party I found adhering thereto, such I would join. . . . Thus I continued to travel in much heaviness, and frequently murmured against the Almighty, particularly in his providential dealings; and, awful to think! I began to blaspheme, and wished often to be anything but a human being. In these severe conflicts the Lord answered me by awful "visions of the night, when deep sleep falleth upon men, in slumberings upon the bed" (Job 33:15). He was pleased, in much mercy, to give me to see, and in some measure understand, the great and awful scene of the judgment day, that "no unclean person, no unholy thing, can enter into the kingdom of God" (Eph. 5:5). I would then, if it had been possible, have changed my nature with the meanest worm on the earth; and was ready to say to the mountains and rocks "fall on me" (Rev. 6:16), but all in vain. I then, in the greatest agony, requested the divine Creator, that he would grant me a small space of time to repent of my follies and vile iniquities, which I felt were grievous. The Lord, in his manifold mercies, was pleased to grant my request, and, being yet in a state of time, the sense of God's mercies were so great on my mind when I awoke that my strength entirely failed me for many minutes, and I was exceedingly weak. This was the first spiritual mercy I ever was sensible of, and being on praying ground, as soon as I recovered a little strength, and got out of bed and dressed myself, I invoked heaven, from my inmost soul, and fervently begged that God would never again permit me to blaspheme his most holy name. The Lord, who is long-suffering and full of compassion to such poor rebels as we are, condescended to hear and answer. I felt that I was altogether unholy, and saw clearly what a bad use I had made of the faculties I was endowed with: they were given me to glorify God with; I thought, therefore, I had better want them here, and enter into life eternal, than abuse them and be cast into hell fire. I prayed to be directed, if there were any holier than those with whom I was acquainted, that the Lord would point them out to me. I appealed to the Searcher of hearts, whether I did not wish to love him more, and serve him better. Notwithstanding all this, the reader may easily discern, if a believer, that I was still in nature's darkness. At length I hated the house in which I lodged, because God's most holy name was blasphemed in it; then I saw the word of God verified, *viz.,* "Before they call, I will answer; and while they are yet speaking, I will hear."

I had a great desire to read the Bible the whole day at home; but not having a convenient place for retirement, I left the house in the day, rather than stay amongst the wicked ones; and that day, as I was walking, it pleased God to direct me to a house where there was an old sea-faring man, who experienced much of the love of

God shed abroad in his heart. He began to discourse with me; and, as I desired to love the Lord, his conversation rejoiced me greatly; and, indeed, I had never heard before the love of Christ to believers set forth in such a manner, and in so clear a point of view. Here I had more questions to put to the man than his time would permit him to answer; and in that memorable hour there came in a dissenting minister; he joined our discourse, and asked me some few questions; among others, where I heard the gospel preached? I knew not what he meant by hearing the gospel; I told him I had read the gospel; and he asked where I went to church, or whether I went at all or not? To which I replied, "I attended St. James's, St. Martin's, and St. Ann's Soho." "So," said he, "you are a churchman?" I answered, I was. He then invited me to a love-feast at his chapel that evening. I accepted the offer, and thanked him; and soon after he went away, I had some further discourse with the old Christian, added to some profitable reading, which made me exceedingly happy. When I left him he reminded me of coming to the feast; I assured him I would be there. Thus we parted, and I weighed over the heavenly conversation that passed between these two men, which cheered my then heavy and drooping spirit more than anything I had met with for many months. However, I thought the time long in going to my supposed banquet. I also wished much for the company of these friendly men; their company pleased me much; and I thought the gentleman very kind in asking me, a stranger, to a feast; but how singular did it appear to me, to have it in a chapel! When the wished-for hour came I went, and happily the old man was there, who kindly seated me, as he belonged to the place. I was much astonished to see the place filled with people, and no signs of eating and drinking. There were many ministers in the company. At last they began by giving out hymns, and between the singing, the ministers engaged in prayer; in short, I knew not what to make of this sight, having never seen anything of the kind in my life before now. Some of the guests began to speak their experience, agreeable to what I read in the Scriptures; much was said by every speaker of the providence of God, and his unspeakable mercies, to each of them. This I knew in a great measure and could most heartily join them. But when they spoke of a future state, they seemed to be altogether certain of their calling and election of God; and that no one could ever separate them from the love of Christ, or pluck them out of his hands. This filled me with utter consternation, intermingled with admiration. I was so amazed as not to know what to think of the company; my heart was attracted, and my affections were enlarged. I wished to be as happy as them, and was persuaded in my mind that they were different from the world "that lieth in wickedness" (I John 5:19). Their language and singing, &c., did well harmonize; I was entirely overcome, and wished to live and die thus. Lastly, some persons in the place produced some neat baskets full of buns, which they distributed about; and each person communicated with his neighbor, and sipped water out of different mugs, which they handed about to all who were present. This kind of Christian fellowship I had never seen, nor ever thought of seeing on earth; it fully reminded me of what I had read in the Holy Scriptures, of the primitive Christians, who loved each other and broke bread, in partaking of it, even from house to house. This entertainment (which lasted about four hours) ended in singing and prayer. It was the first soul feast I ever was present at. This last twenty-four hours produced me things, spiritual and temporal, sleeping and waking, judgment and mercy, that I could not but admire the goodness of God, in directing the blind, blasphemous sinner in the path that he knew not of, even among the just; and, instead of judgment, he has shewed mercy, and will hear and answer the prayers and supplications of every returning prodigal:

O! to grace how great a debtor
Daily I'm constrained to be![16]

After this I was resolved to win Heaven if possible; and if I perished I thought it should be at the feet of Jesus, in praying to him for salvation. After having been an eye-witness to some of the happiness which attended those who feared God, I knew not how, with any kind of propriety, to return to my lodgings, where the name of God was continually profaned, at which I felt the greatest horror; I paused in my mind for some time, not knowing what to do; whether to hire a bed elsewhere, or go home again. At last fearing an evil report might arise, I went home, with a farewell to card playing and vain jesting, &c. I saw that time was very short, eternity long, and very near; and I viewed those persons alone blessed who were found ready at midnight call, or when the judge of all, both quick and dead, cometh. . . . During this time I was out of employ, nor was I likely to get a situation for me, which obliged me to go once more to sea. I engaged as steward of a ship called the *Hope,* Captain Richard Strange, bound from London to Cadiz in Spain. In a short time after I was on board, I heard the name of God much blasphemed, and I feared greatly lest I should catch the horrible infection. I thought if I sinned again after having life and death set evidently before me, I should certainly go to hell. My mind was uncommonly chagrined, and I murmured much at God's providential dealings with me, and was discontented with the commandments, that I could not be saved by what I had done; I hated all things, and wished I had never been born; confusion seized me, and I wished to be annihilated. One day I was standing on the very edge of the stern of the ship, thinking to drown myself; but this scripture was instantly impressed on my mind—"That no murderer hath eternal life abiding in him" (I John 3:15). Then I paused and thought myself the unhappiest man living. Again I was convinced that the Lord was better to me than I deserved, and I was better off in the world than many. After this I began to fear death; I fretted, mourned, and prayed, till I became a burden to others, but more so to myself. At length I concluded to beg my bread on shore rather than go again to sea amongst a people who feared not God, and I entreated the captain three different times to discharge me; he would not, but each time gave me greater and greater encouragement to continue with him, and all on board shewed me very great civility: notwithstanding all this I was unwilling to embark again. At last some of my religious friends advised me, by saying it was my lawful calling, consequently it was my duty to obey, and that God was not confined to place, &c., &c. particularly Mr. G—— Smith, the governor of Tothil-fields, Bridewell, who pitied my case, and read the eleventh chapter of the Hebrews to me, with exhortations. He prayed for me, and I believed that he prevailed on my behalf, as my burden was then greatly removed, and I found a heartfelt resignation to the will of God. The good man gave me a pocket Bible and Alleine's *Alarm to the Unconverted.* We parted, and the next day I went on board again. We sailed for Spain, and I found favor with the captain. It was the fourth

[16] From a Methodist hymn by Robert Robinson (1735–1790) [Ed.].

of the month of September when we sailed from London; we had a delightful voyage to Cadiz, where we arrived the twenty-third of the same month. The place is strong, commands a fine prospect, and is very rich. The Spanish galleons frequent that port, and some arrived whilst we were there. I had many opportunities of reading the scriptures. I wrestled hard with God in fervent prayer, who had declared in his word that he would hear the groanings and deep sighs of the poor in spirit. I found this verified to my utter astonishment and comfort in the following manner.

On the morning of the 6th of October (I pray you to attend), all that day, I thought I should either see or hear something supernatural. I had a secret impulse on my mind of something that was to take place, which drove me continually for that time to a Throne of Grace. It pleased God to enable me to wrestle with him, as Jacob did: I prayed that if sudden death were to happen, and I perished, it might be at Christ's feet.

In the evening of the same day, as I was reading and meditating on the fourth chapter of Acts, twelfth verse, under the solemn apprehensions of eternity, and reflecting on my past actions, I began to think I had lived a moral life, and that I had a proper ground to believe I had an interest in the divine favor; but still meditating on the subject, not knowing whether salvation was to be had partly for our own good deeds or solely as the sovereign gift of God; in this deep consternation the Lord was pleased to break in upon my soul with his bright beams of heavenly light; and in an instant, as it were, removing the veil, and letting light into a dark place, I saw clearly with an eye of faith, the crucified Saviour bleeding on the cross on mount Calvary; the scriptures became an unsealed book; I saw myself a condemned criminal under the law, which came with its full force to my conscience, and when "the commandment came sin revived, and I died." I saw the Lord Jesus Christ in his humiliation, loaded and bearing my reproach, sin, and shame. I then clearly perceived that by the deeds of the law no flesh living could be justified. I was then convinced that by the first Adam sin came, and by the second Adam (the Lord Jesus Christ) all that are saved must be made alive. It was given me at that time to know what it was to be born again (John 3:5). I saw the eighth chapter to the Romans, and the doctrines of God's decrees, verified agreeable to his eternal, everlasting, and unchangeable purposes. The word of God was sweet to my taste, yea, sweeter than honey and the honeycomb. Christ was revealed to my soul as the chiefest among ten thousand. These heavenly moments were really as life to the dead, and what John calls an earnest of the Spirit.[17] This was indeed unspeakable, and I firmly believe undeniable by many. Now every leading providential circumstance that happened to me, from the day I was taken from my parents to that hour, was then in my view, as if it had but just then occurred. I was sensible of the invisible hand of God, which guided and protected me, when in truth I knew it not: still the Lord pursued me, although I slighted and disregarded it; this mercy melted me down. When I considered my poor wretched state I wept, seeing what a great debtor I was to sovereign free grace. Now the Ethiopian was willing to be saved by Jesus Christ, the sinner's only surety, and also to rely on none other person or thing for salvation. Self was obnoxious, and good works he had none, for it is God that worketh in us both to will and to do. Oh! the amazing things of that hour can

[17]John 16:13, 14, &c.

never be told—it was joy in the Holy Ghost! I felt an astonishing change; the burden of sin, the gaping jaws of hell, and the fears of death, that weighed me down before, now lost their horror; indeed I thought death would now be the best earthly friend I ever had. Such were my grief and joy as I believe are seldom experienced. I was bathed in tears, and said, What am I that God should thus look on me, the vilest of sinners? I felt a deep concern for my mother and friends, which occasioned me to pray with fresh ardor; and in the abyss of thought, I viewed the unconverted people of the world in a very awful state, being without God and without hope.

It pleased God to pour out on me the spirit of prayer and the grace of supplication, so that in loud acclamations I was enabled to praise and glorify his most holy name. When I got out of the cabin, and told some of the people what the Lord had done for me, alas! who could understand me or believe my report! None but to whom the arm of the Lord was revealed. I became a barbarian to them in talking of the love of Christ: his name was to me as ointment poured forth, indeed it was sweet to my soul, but to them a rock of offense. I thought my case singular, and every hour a day until I came to London, for I much longed to be with some to whom I could tell of the wonders of God's love towards me, and join in prayer to him whom my soul loved and thirsted after. I had uncommon commotions within, such as few can tell aught about. Now the Bible was my only companion and comfort; I prized it much, with many thanks to God that I could read it for myself, and was not left to be tossed about or led by man's devices and notions. The worth of a soul cannot be told. May the Lord give the reader an understanding in this. Whenever I looked in the Bible I saw things new, and many texts were immediately applied to me with great comfort, for I knew that to me was the word of salvation sent. Sure I was that the Spirit which indited the word opened my heart to receive the truth of it as it is in Jesus—that the same Spirit enabled me to act faith upon the promises that were precious to me, and enabled me to believe to the salvation of my soul. By free grace I was persuaded that I had a part in the first resurrection, and was enlightened with the "light of the living" (Job 33:30). I wished for a man of God with whom I might converse: my soul was like the chariots of Amminadib (Canticles 6:12). These, among others, were the precious promises that were so powerfully applied to me. "All things whatsoever ye shall ask in prayer, believing, ye shall receive" (Mat. 21:22). "Peace I leave with you, my peace I give unto you" (John 14:27). I saw the blessed Redeemer to be the fountain of life, and the well of salvation. I experienced him to be all in all; he had brought me by a way that I knew not, and he had made crooked paths straight. Then in his name I set up my Ebenezer,[18] saying, Hitherto he hath helped me: and could say to the sinners about me, Behold what a Saviour I have! Thus I was, by the teaching of that all-glorious Deity, the great One in Three, and Three in One, confirmed in the truths of the Bible, those oracles of everlasting truth, on which every soul living must stand or fall eternally, agreeable to Acts 4:12. "Neither is there salvation in any other, for there is none other name under heaven given among men whereby we must be saved, but only Christ Jesus." May God give the

[18]Biblical reference to a commemorative stone dedicated to God. 1 Samuel 7:12 [Ed.].

reader a right understanding in these facts! "To him that believeth, all things are possible, but to them that are unbelieving nothing is pure" (Titus 1:15).

During this period we remained at Cadiz until our ship got laden. We sailed about the fourth of November; and, having a good passage, we arrived in London the month following, to my comfort, with heartfelt gratitude to God for his rich and unspeakable mercies.

On my return I had but one text which puzzled me, or that the devil endeavored to buffet me with, *viz.,* Rom. 11:6, and, as I had heard of the Rev. Mr. Romaine, and his great knowledge in the scriptures, I wished much to hear him preach. One day I went to Blackfriars church, and, to my great satisfaction and surprise, he preached from that very text. He very clearly shewed the difference between human works and free election, which is according to God's sovereign will and pleasure. These glad tidings set me entirely at liberty, and I went out of the church rejoicing, seeing my spots were those of God's children. I went to Westminster Chapel, and saw some of my old friends, who were glad when they perceived the wonderful change that the Lord had wrought in me, particularly Mr. G——— S[mith], my worthy acquaintance, who was a man of a choice spirit and had great zeal for the Lord's service. I enjoyed his correspondence till he died, in the year 1784. I was again examined at that same chapel, and was received into church fellowship amongst them. I rejoiced in spirit, making melody in my heart to the God of all my mercies. Now my whole wish was to be dissolved, and to be with Christ—but, alas! I must wait mine appointed time.

1789

Judith Sargent Murray 1751–1820

Judith Sargent Murray's literary career flourished during the 1790s, a time when America was struggling to define itself as independent—politically and aesthetically—from Great Britain. Murray was engaged in this period of change, voicing her opinions on literary nationalism, the federalist system of government, the equality of women, and religious universalism. The seeds of these interests were planted early in Murray's life. She was born in Gloucester, Massachusetts, the eldest child of Captain Winthrop Sargent and Judith Saunders. A socially prominent family, the Sargents were distinguished by their political activity: Winthrop Sargent served in the provisional government during the Revolutionary War, and his son Winthrop was honored by Washington for his military activities. At an early age Judith Sargent exhibited so high a degree of intelligence that her parents encouraged her to study with her brother, who was preparing with a local Gloucester minister for entrance to Harvard. She thus gained an education far superior to that given most women: she studied the Latin and Greek languages and literatures and was introduced to the sciences, including mathematics and astronomy. The Sargent family became strong supporters of John Murray, who visited Gloucester in his mission to establish Universalism in America. By aligning themselves with this liberal branch of Protestantism, the Sargents elicited scorn from their religiously conservative neighbors.

At age eighteen, Judith Sargent married John Stevens, a prosperous sea captain and trader; the large Stevens house in Gloucester thereafter became a popular meeting-place in the town. Dating from this period are the author's earliest known writings, including several poems and an important essay in which she introduces her ideas on the equality of women, "Desultory Thoughts upon the Utility of encouraging a degree of Self-Complacency, especially in Female Bosoms" (1784). She signed her early work "Constantia," one of the many pseudonyms she would use throughout her career.

When her husband died in 1786, Stevens became a closer friend of John Murray, and they married in 1788. The couple shared both religious beliefs and intellectual interests. The Murrays' move to Boston in 1793 widened the author's literary involvement, and her career flourished. She wrote two plays for the newly reopened Federal Street Theatre, thereby aligning herself with such writers as Royall Tyler. With regular contributions to the *Massachusetts Magazine*—one of the most prestigious journals of the late eighteenth century—Murray established herself as a prominent essayist and poet. The three-volume edition of her *Gleaner* essays, published in 1798, attracted over 700 subscribers, among them President Adams and George Washington.

After 1800, Murray turned her attention to editing John Murray's biography and religious writings. Following the death of her husband in 1815, Murray moved to Natchez, Mississippi, to live with her only child, Julia, who had married a wealthy planter. Murray died in 1820.

An assessment of Murray's literary career must consider the fervor with which she addressed the most important issues of her day. The major outlets for these ideas were her two concurrent essay series—*The Repository* (largely religious in nature) and *The Gleaner*—which ran in the *Massachusetts Magazine* from 1792 to 1794. The imaginary author of the *Gleaner* essays, Mr. Vigillius, discussed such varied topics as the new Constitution, the dangers of political factionalism, and the progressive nature of history. Within *The Gleaner* series Murray included critical essays on drama at a time when many writers were concerned about the future of American literature. According to Murray's federalist agenda, the new American drama should reflect the virtues of the new republic: liberty, patriotism, and equality. By focusing on American virtues and scenes—as she did in her plays, *The Medium, or Virtue Triumphant* and *The Traveller Returned*—Murray upheld that national drama would be revitalized and could break away from the British tradition.

Murray also turned her attention toward a reconsideration of fiction with her brief novel, *The Story of Margaretta,* included within the framework of *The Gleaner.* Unlike most heroines of sentimental fiction, Margaretta is able to escape the cycle of seduction and destruction because of her superior education: she proves herself to be wise and virtuous and is rewarded with a loving husband. This link between education, virtuous filial conduct, and reward is an important aspect of Murray's philosophy. She argued that if women were given equal opportunity to develop their rational capacities, they would be able to exercise good judgment, thus escaping their supposedly female susceptibility to passion and sentimental emotionalism (both considered bad conduct). Murray predicts that advancements in education and thus in social place would allow young women to form "a new era in female history."

"On the Equality of the Sexes" (reportedly drafted in 1779; printed in the *Massachusetts Magazine* in April/May 1790, and signed "Constantia") is perhaps Murray's most influential essay. Here she radically questioned the system that held women subservient to men. She argued that the capacities of imagination and memory are verifiably equal in men and women, and the apparent inequalities in reason and judgment arise only from a difference in education. Murray argued that housework and needlework are mindless activities, ones that deny women any exercise of their intellectual faculties. If women were given the same education as men, Murray maintained, their reason and judgment would develop equally. It is interesting to note that Murray predicated the need for women's education not only on the equality of their rational capabilities but also on the equality of their souls. Feminist reform was linked, in Murray's theory, to the egalitarian promise of the new republic. If America were to achieve its destined level of greatness, it would have to develop and cherish the intellect and virtue of all citizens.

Amy M. Yerkes
Johns Hopkins University

PRIMARY WORKS

The Gleaner, Massachusetts Magazine, 1792–1794, later published as *The Gleaner; A Miscellaneous Production,* 3 vols., 1798; *The Repository, Massachusetts Magazine,* 1792–1794; *The Medium, or Virtue Triumphant,* 1795; *The Traveller Returned,* 1796; "Desultory Thoughts upon the Utility of encouraging A degree of Self-Complacency, especially in Female Bosoms," *Gentleman and Lady's Town and Country Magazine,* 1784; "On the Domestic Education of Children," *Massachusetts Magazine,* May 1790; "On the Equality of the Sexes," *Massachusetts Magazine,* March, April 1790.

Desultory Thoughts upon the Utility of encouraging a degree of Self-Complacency, especially in Female Bosoms[1]

Self estimation, kept within due bounds,
However oddly the assertion sounds,
May, of the fairest efforts be the root,
May yield the embow'ring shade—the mellow fruit;
May stimulate to most exalted deeds,
Direct the soul where blooming honor leads;
May give her there, to act a noble part,
To virtuous pleasures yield the willing heart.
Self-estimation will debasement shun,
And, in the path of wisdom, joy to run;
An unbecoming act in fears to do,
And still, its exaltation keeps in view.
"To rev'rence self," a Bard long since directed,
And, on each moral truth HE well reflected;

[1]Published in *Gentleman and Lady's Magazine,* October 22, 1784.

But, lost to conscious worth, to decent pride,
Compass nor helm there is, our course to guide:
Nor may we anchor cast, for rudely tost
In an unfathom'd sea, each motive's lost.
Wildly amid contending waves we're beat,
And rocks and quick sands, shoals and depths we meet;
'Till, dash'd in pieces, or, till found'ring, we
One common wreck of all our prospects see!
Nor, do we mourn, for we were lost to fame,
And never hap'd to reach a tow'ring name;
Ne'er taught to "rev'rence self," or to aspire;
Our bosoms never caught ambition's fire;
An indolence of virtue still prevail'd,
Nor the sweet gale of praise was e'er inhal'd;
Rous'd by a new stimulus, no kindling glow.
No soothing emulations gentle flow,
We judg'd that nature, not to us inclin'd,
In narrow bounds our progress had confin'd,
And, that our forms, to say the very best,
Only, not frightful, were by all confest.

I think, to teach young minds to aspire, ought to be the ground work of education: many a laudable achievement is lost, from a persuasion that our efforts are unequal to the arduous attainment. Ambition is a noble principle, which properly directed, may be productive of the most valuable consequences. It is amazing to what heights the mind by exertion may tow'r: I would, therefore, have my pupils believe, that every thing in the compass of mortality, was placed within their grasp, and that, the avidity of application, the intenseness of study, were only requisite to endow them with every external grace; and mental accomplishment. Thus I should impel them to progress on, if I could not lead them to the heights I would wish them to attain. It is too common with parents to expatiate in their hearing, upon all the foibles of their children, and to let their virtues pass, in appearance, unregarded: this they do, least they should, (were they to commend) swell their little hearts to pride, and implant in their tender minds, undue conceptions of their own importance. Those, for example, who have the care of a beautiful female, they assiduously guard every avenue, they arrest the stream of due admiration, and endeavour to divest her of all idea of the bounties of nature: what is the consequence? She grows up, and of course mixes with those who are self interested: strangers will be sincere; she encounters the tongue of the flatterer, he will exaggerate, she finds herself possessed of accomplishments which have been studiously concealed from her, she throws the reins upon the neck of fancy, and gives every encomiast full credit for his most extravagant eulogy. Her natural connections, her home is rendered disagreeable, and she hastes to the scenes, whence arise the sweet perfume of adulation, and when she can obtain the regard due to a merit, which she supposes altogether uncommon. Those who have made her acquainted with the dear secret, she considers as her best friends; and it is more than probable, that she will soon fall a sacrifice to some worthless character, whose interest may lead him to the most hyperbolical lengths in the round of flattery.

Now, I should be solicitous that my daughter should possess for me the fondest love, as well as that respect which gives birth to duty; in order to promote this wish of my soul, from my lips she should be accustomed to hear the most pleasing truths, and, as in the course of my instructions, I should doubtless find myself but too often impelled to wound the delicacy of youthful sensibility. I would therefore, be careful to avail myself of this exuberating balance: I would, from the early dawn of reason, address her as a rational being; hence, I apprehend, the most valuable consequences would result in some such language as this, she might from time to time be accosted. A pleasing form is undoubtedly advantageous. Nature, my dear, hath furnished you with an agreeable person, your glass, was I to be silent, would inform you that you are pretty, your appearance will sufficiently recommend you to a stranger, the flatterer will give a more than mortal finishing to every feature; but, it must be your part, my sweet girl, to render yourself worthy respect from higher motives: you must learn "to reverence yourself," that is, your intellectual existance; you must join my efforts, in endeavouring to adorn your mind, for, it is from the proper furnishing of that, you will become indeed a valuable person, you will, as I said, give birth to the most favorable impressions at first sight: but, how mortifying should this be all, if, upon a more extensive knowledge you should be discovered to possess no one mental charm, to be fit only at best, to be hung up as a pleasing picture among the paintings of some spacious hall. The FLATTERER, indeed, will still pursue you, but it will be from interested views, and he will smile at your undoing! Now, then, my best Love, is the time for you to lay in such a fund of useful knowledge as shall continue, and augment every kind sentiment in regard to you, as shall set you above the snares of the artful betrayer.

Thus, that sweet form, shall serve but as a polished casket, which will contain a most beautiful gem, highly finished, and calculated for advantage, as well as ornament. Was she, I say, habituated thus to reflect, she would be taught to aspire; she would learn to estimate every accomplishment, according to its proper value; and, when the voice of adulation should assail her ear, as she had early been initiated into its true meaning, and from youth been accustomed to the language of praise; her attention would not be captivated, the Siren's song would not borrow the aid of novelty, her young mind would not be enervated or intoxicated, by a delicious surprise, she would possess her soul in serenity, and by that means, rise superior to the deep laid schemes which, too commonly, encompass the steps of beauty.

Neither should those to whom nature had been parsimonious, be tortured by me with degrading comparisons; every advantage I would expatiate upon, and there are few who possess not some personal charms. I would teach them to gloss over their imperfections, inasmuch as, I do think, an agreeable form, a very necessary introduction to society, and of course it behoves us to render our appearance as pleasing as possible: I would, I must repeat, by all means guard them against a low estimation of self. I would leave no charm undiscovered or unmarked, for the penetrating eye of the pretended admirer, to make unto himself a merit by holding up to her view; thus, I would destroy the weapons of flattery, or render them useless, by leaving not the least room for their operation.

A young lady, growing up with the idea, that she possesses few, or no personal attractions, and that her mental abilities are of an inferior kind, imbibing at the same time, a most melancholly idea of a female, descending down the vale of life in an unprotected state; taught also to regard her character ridiculously contemptible, will, too probably, throw herself away upon the first who approaches her with tenders of love, however indifferent may be her chance of happiness, least if she omits the present day of grace, she may never be so happy as to meet a second offer, and must then inevitably be stigmatized with that dreaded title, an Old Maid, must rank with a class whom she has been accustomed to regard as burthens upon society, and objects whom she might with impunity turn into ridicule! Certainly love, friendship and esteem, ought to take place of marriage, but, the woman thus circumstanced, will seldom regard these previous requisites to felicity, if she can but insure the honors, which she, in idea, associates with a matrimonial connection—to prevent which great evil, I would early impress under proper regulations, a reverence of self; I would endeavour to rear to worth, and a consciousness thereof: I would be solicitous to inspire the glow of virtue, with that elevation of soul, that dignity, which is ever attendant upon self-approbation, arising from the genuine source of innate rectitude. I must be excused for thus insisting upon my hypothesis, as I am, from observation, persuaded, that many have suffered materially all their life long, from a depression of soul, early inculcated, in compliance to a false maxim, which hath supposed pride would thereby be eradicated. I know there is a contrary extreme, and I would, in almost all cases, prefer the happy medium. However, if these fugitive hints may induce some abler pen to improve thereon, the exemplification will give pleasure to the heart of CONSTANTIA.

October 22, 1784

On the Domestic Education of Children[1]

I hate severity to trembling youth,
Mildness should designate each useful truth;
My soul detests the rude unmanly part,
Which swells with bursting sighs the little heart.
What can an infant do to merit blows?
See, from his eyes a briny torrent flows.
Behold the pretty mourner! pale his cheek,
His tears are fruitless, and he dare not speak.
Lowly he bends beneath yon tyrant's rod;
Unfeeling pedagogue—who like some god
Fabled of old, of bloody savage mind,
To scourge, and not to mend the human race, design'd.

It would be well if every gentle method to form the young untutored mind, was essayed, previous to a harsher mode of procedure. Do blows ever produce a salutary effect upon a gentle or a generous disposition? It can hardly be presumed that they

[1]Published in *Massachusetts Magazine,* May 1790.

do; and if not upon the bosom, the feelings of which urbanity hath arranged, is it not more than probable that they tend to make an obstinate being still more perverse? Yet the reins of government I would not consign to children; the young idea I would direct; nor would I permit the dawn of life to pass uncultured by; nevertheless, to barbarous hands I would not yield the tender plant. Behind the pallid countenance of the little culprit, the tender sorrow, the imploring tear, the beseeching eye, the knee bent for forgiveness—and can the offences of a child be other than venial? But it is in vain—the inhuman preceptor continues obdurate—he retains his purpose, and the wretched sufferer receives those blows which only the malefactor can merit! Is there not some reason to suppose, that by a repetition of ignominious punishments, we shall eradicate from the young mind all sense of shame, thus throwing down a very essential barrier, and finally opening the floodgates of vice.

But what shall we substitute instead of those violent and coercive measures? I proceed to give an example. Martesia is blessed with a numerous offspring of both sexes—some of her young folks have discovered dispositions not a little refractory—caprice hath shown its head, and a number of little petulances early displayed themselves; yet, that weapon known by the name of a rod was never so much as heard of among them, nor do they know the meaning of a blow. How then doth Martesia manage, for it is certain that her salutary efforts have well nigh eradicated from her little circle every perverse humour. Her family is a well regulated Commonwealth, the moving spring of which is emulation, *a laudable kind of emulation, which never partakes of envy, save when virtue acknowledgeth the hue of vice.* She hath in her gift various posts of honour; these she distributes according to the merit of the pretender; they are conferred upon those who have made any improvement, and the whole company join to invest the distinguished candidate with his new dignity. Martesia makes it a rule never to appear ruffled before her children, and she is particularly careful to keep every irregular passion from their observation. That she is tenderly concerned for them, and takes a very deep interest in their happiness, is a truth which she daily inculcates. She wishes also to implant in their young minds the most elevated opinion of her understanding; and she conceives that they cannot be too early impressed with an idea of her possessing superiour abilities. The advantages which she will derive from this plan are obvious; her authority will be the more readily acknowledged, and her decisions will obtain the requisite weight. By reiterated petitions she is seldom persecuted, for as the little claimants are sensible of her attachment, and cannot call her judgment in question, they are not accustomed to repeat their requests. Yet, notwithstanding they are taught to believe Martesia ever under the government of reason, should a persevering spirit be found clamourously urgent, the pursuit, however, cannot be long continued, since but one answer will be given; which answer, though mild, is always peremptory and conclusive. To render prevalent in the minds of her children, sentiments of humanity and benevolence, is with Martesia an essential object. A *dignified* condescension to inferiority she also inculcates, and she early endeavours, by judicious advances, to bring them acquainted with that part of the economy of the Deity which hath made our obligations to each other reciprocal: Thus solicitous to enforce the idea of their dependence, even upon the meanest domestick, she exacts from her servants no extraordinary marks of humility toward them, for her view is to choke, if possible, the first buddings of unbecoming pride.

Doth she discover the smallest disposition to cruelty, or are her children deficient in divine sensibility, she is anxiously studious to exterminate the unhappy propensity, and to awaken, or to *create,* the finer feelings of the soul. To this end she hath ever at hand a number of well chosen tales, calculated to promote the interests of virtue, to excite commiseration, and suited to their tender years. Meantime she is sparing of reproaches, and would, if possible, avoid imparting to them a consciousness of the discovery which she hath made. Her rewards are always exactly and impartially proportioned—*the degree of merit she critically examines*—and as this is her invariable rule, a murmur in the little society can never arise, and they are constantly convinced of the propriety of her decisions. The highest honour by which they can be distinguished, is the investiture of a commission to convey to some worthy, but destitute family, a dinner, a garment, or a piece of money; and this office being always adjudged according to the magnitude of any particular action, it often happens that the most insensible are found in this department. Thus they are accustomed to acts of benevolence—they learn to feel, and become humane by habit.

The greatest felicity which our little family can experience, is in the presence of Martesia. They are free from every restraint—pursue, unmolested, their amusements—and of their innocent mirth she not seldom partakes. It is in the pleasure which they derive from her smiles, her approbation, and her society, that she sounds the basis of all her punishments.—When coercive measures are judged indispensable, if the fault is trivial, it remains a profound secret to all but Martesia and the little aggressor: But on the maternal countenance hands a cloud—cold and distant looks take place of benign complacency; nor doth returning tenderness manifest tokens of reconciliation, until full atonement is made for the errour. If the offence is of a more heinous die, it is immediately published throughout the house; from Martesia the culprit receiveth not the smallest attention; not a look, nor a word; while he or she is regarded by every one with studied indifference. Should the transgression be considered as capital, the criminal is forthwith excluded the parental presence—not even a domestick conceives him worthy of notice—and it is with difficulty that he can obtain the assistance of which he stands in need. At length his little heart is almost broke—he petitions for favour, he sueth for forgiveness. No mediator presents, for Martesia reserves to herself the merit of obliging. Well, the concessions of the pretty offender are sufficiently humble—it is judged that his sufferings are adequate to his fault—Martesia is appeased and the offense is cancelled. And it is to be observed, that when once the penitent is admitted into favour, his crime is entirely obliterated—it can no more be held up to view. Martesia, however, seldom hath occasion to exercise the last mentioned severity. Perverseness she hath at length well nigh subdued—and among her little flock a refractory spirit is now hardly known. To behold her in the midst of the sweetly smiling circle is truly charming.

When, for the completion of their education, she is obliged to part with her boys, with a firmness becoming her character she will submit; and should their preceptor pursue her plan, they will undoubtedly be rendered useful members of society; while her girls, continuing under such auspices, cannot be other than worthy and amiable women.

CONSTANTIA.

1790

On the Equality of the Sexes[1]

That minds are not alike, full well I know,
This truth each day's experience will show;
To heights surprising some great spirits soar,
With inborn strength mysterious depths explore;
Their eager gaze surveys the path of light,
Confest it stood to Newton's piercing sight.
  Deep science, like a bashful maid retires,
And but the *ardent* breast her worth inspires;
By perserverance the coy fair is won.
And Genius, led by Study, wears the crown.
  But some there are who wish not to improve,
Who never can the path of knowledge love,
Whose souls almost with the dull body one,
With anxious care each mental pleasure shun;
Weak is the level'd, enervated mind,
And but while here to vegetate design'd.
The torpid spirit mingling with its clod,
Can scarcely boast its origin from God;
Stupidly dull—they move progressing on—
They eat, and drink, and all their work is done.
While others, emulous of sweet applause,
Industrious seek for each event a cause,
Tracing the hidden springs whence knowledge flows,
Which nature all in beauteous order shows.
  Yet cannot I their sentiments imbibe,
Who this distinction to the sex ascribe,
As if a woman's form must needs enrol,
A weak, servile, an inferiour soul;
And that the guise of man must still proclaim,
Greatness of mind, and him, to be the same:
Yet as the hours revolve fair proofs arise,
Which the bright wreath of growing fame supplies;
And in past times some men have *sunk so low,*
That female records nothing *less* can show.
But imbecility is still confin'd,
And by the lordly sex to us consign'd;
They rob us of the power t' improve,
And then declare we only trifles love;
Yet haste the era, when the world shall know,

[1]Published in the *Massachusetts Magazine,* April and May 1790.

That such distinctions only dwell below;
The soul unfetter'd, to no sex confin'd,
Was for the abodes of cloudless day design'd.
  Mean time we emulate their manly fires,
Though erudition all their thoughts inspires,
Yet nature with *equality* imparts,
And *noble passions,* swell e'en *female hearts.*

Is it upon mature consideration we adopt the idea, that nature is thus partial in her distributions? Is it indeed a fact, that she hath yielded to one half of the human species so unquestionable a mental superiority? I know that to both sexes elevated understandings, and the reverse, are common. But, suffer me to ask, in what the minds of females are so notoriously deficient, or unequal. May not the intellectual powers be ranged under these four heads—imagination, reason, memory and judgment. The province of imagination hath long since been surrendered up to us, and we have been crowned undoubted sovereigns of the regions of fancy. Invention is perhaps the most arduous effort of the mind; this branch of imagination hath been particularly ceded to us, and we have been time out of mind invested with that creative faculty. Observe the variety of fashions (here I bar the contemptuous smile) which distinguish and adorn the female world; how continually are they changing, insomuch that they almost render the wise man's assertion problematical, and we are ready to say, *there is something new under the sun.* Now what a playfulness, what an exuberance of fancy, what strength of inventive imagination, doth this continual variation discover? Again, it hath been observed, that if the turpitude of the conduct of our sex, hath been ever so enormous, so extremely ready are we, that the very first thought presents us with an apology, so plausible, as to produce our actions even in an amiable light. Another instance of our creative powers, is our talent for slander; how ingenious are we at inventive scandal? what a formidable story can we in a moment fabricate merely from the force of a prolifick imagination? how many reputations, in the fertile brain of a female, have been utterly despoiled? how industrious are we at improving a hint? suspicion how easily do we convert into conviction, and conviction, embellished by the power of eloquence, stalks abroad to the surprise and confusion of unsuspecting innocence. Perhaps it will be asked if I furnish these facts as instances of excellency in our sex. Certainly not; but as proofs of a creative faculty, of a lively imagination. Assuredly great activity of mind is thereby discovered, and was this activity properly directed, what beneficial effects would follow. Is the needle and kitchen sufficient to employ the operations of a soul thus organized? I should conceive not. Nay, it is a truth that those very departments leave the intelligent principle vacant, and at liberty for speculation. Are we deficient in reason? we can only reason from what we know, and if an opportunity of acquiring knowledge hath been denied us, the inferiority of our sex cannot fairly be deduced from thence. Memory, I believe, will be allowed us in common, since every one's experience must testify, that a loquacious old woman is as frequently met with, as a communicative old man; their subjects are alike drawn from the fund of other times, and the transactions of their youth, or of maturer life, entertain, or perhaps fatigue you, in the evening of their lives. "But our judgment is not so strong—we do not distinguish so well."—Yet it may be questioned, from what doth this superiority, in this determining faculty of the soul, proceed. May we not trace its source in the difference of education, and continued advantages? Will it be said that the judgment of a male of two years old, is more sage than that of a female's of the same age? I believe the reverse is generally observed to be true. But from that period what partiality! how is the one exalted, and the other depressed, by the contrary modes of education which are adopted! the one is taught to aspire, and the other is early confined and limitted. As their years increase, the sister must be wholly domesticated, while the brother is led by the hand through all the flowery paths of science. Grant that their minds are by nature equal, yet who shall wonder at the *apparent* superiority, if indeed custom becomes *second nature;* nay if it taketh place of nature, and that it doth the experience of each day will evince. At length arrived at womanhood, the uncultivated fair one feels a void, which the employments allotted her are by no means capable of filling. What can she do? to books she may not apply; or if she doth, *to those only of the novel kind,* lest she merit the appellation of a *learned lady;* and what ideas have been affixed to this term, the observation of many can testify. Fashion, scandal, and sometimes what is still more reprehensible, are then called in to her relief; and who can say to what lengths the liberties she takes may proceed. Meantime she herself is most unhappy; she feels the want of a cultivated mind. Is she single, she in vain seeks to fill up time from sexual employments or amusements. Is she united to a person whose soul nature made equal to her own, education hath set him so far above her, that in those entertainments which are productive of such rational felicity, she is not qualified to accompany him. She experiences a mortifying consciousness of inferiority, which embitters every enjoyment. Doth the person to whom her adverse fate hath consigned her, posses a mind incapable of improvement, she is equally wretched, in being so closely connected with an individual whom she cannot but despise. Now, was she permitted the same instructors as her brother, (with an eye however to their particular departments) for the employment of a rational mind an ample field would be opened. In astronomy she might catch a glimpse of the immensity of the Deity, and thence she would form amazing conceptions of the august and supreme Intelligence. In geography she would admire Jehovah in the midst of his benevolence; thus adapting this globe to the various wants and amusements of its inhabitants. In natural philosophy she would adore the infinite majesty of heaven, clothed in condescension; and as she traversed the reptile world, she would hail the goodness of a creating God. A mind, thus filled, would have little room for the trifles with which our sex are, with too much justice, accused of amusing themselves, and they would thus be rendered fit companions for those, who should one day wear them as their crown. Fashions, in their variety, would then give place to conjectures, which might perhaps conduce to the improvement of the literary world; and there would be no leisure for slander or detraction. Reputation would not then be blasted, but serious speculations would occupy the lively imaginations of the sex. Unnecessary visits would be precluded, and that custom would only be indulged by way of relaxation, or to answer the demands of consanguinity and friendship. Females would become discreet, their judgments would be invigorated, and their partners for life being circumspectly chosen, an unhappy Hymen would then be as rare, as is now the reverse.

Will it be urged that those acquirements would supersede our domestick duties. I answer that every requisite in female economy is easily attained; and, with truth I can add, that when once attained, they require no further *mental attention.* Nay, while we are pursuing the needle, or the superintendency of the family, I repeat, that our minds are at full liberty for reflection; that imagination may exert itself in full vigor; and that if a just foundation is early laid, our ideas will then be worthy of rational beings. If we were industrious we might easily find time to arrange them upon paper, or should avocations press too hard for such an indulgence, the hours allotted for conversation would at least become more refined and rational. Should it still be vociferated, "Your domestick employments are sufficient"—I would calmly ask, is it reasonable, that a candidate for immortality, for the joys of heaven, an intelligent being, who is to spend an eternity in contemplating the works of Deity, should at present be so degraded, as to be allowed no other ideas, than those which are suggested by the mechanism of a pudding, or the sewing the seams of a garment? Pity that all such censurers of female improvement do not go one step further, and deny their future existence; to be consistent they surely ought.

Yes, ye lordly, ye haughty sex, our souls are by nature *equal* to yours; the same breath of God animates, enlivens, and invigorates us; and that we are not fallen lower than yourselves, let those witness who have greatly towered above the various discouragements by which they have been so heavily oppressed; and though I am unacquainted with the list of celebrated characters on either side, yet from the observations I have made in the contracted circle in which I have moved, I dare confidently believe, that from the commencement of time to the present day, there hath been as many females, as males, who, by the *mere force of natural powers,* have merited the crown of applause; who, *thus unassisted,* have seized the wreath of fame. I know there are who assert, that as the animal powers of the one sex are superiour, of course their mental faculties also must be stronger; thus attributing strength of mind to the transient organization of this earth born tenement. But if this reasoning is just, man must be content to yield the palm to many of the brute creation, since by not a few of his brethren of the field, he is far surpassed in bodily strength. Moreover, was this argument admitted, it would prove too much, for occular demonstration evinceth, that there are many robust masculine ladies, and effeminate gentlemen. Yet I fancy that Mr. Pope, though clogged with an enervated body, and distinguished by a diminutive stature, could nevertheless lay claim to greatness of soul; and perhaps there are many other instances which might be adduced to combat so unphilosophical an opinion. Do we not often see, that when the clay built tabernacle is well nigh dissolved, when it is just ready to mingle with the parent soil, the immortal inhabitant aspires to, and even attaineth heights the most sublime, and which were before wholly unexplored. Besides, were we to grant that animal strength proved any thing, taking into consideration the accustomed impartiality of nature, we should be induced to imagine, that she had invested the female mind with superiour strength as an equivalent for the bodily powers of man. But waving this however palpable advantage, for *equality only,* we wish to contend.

I am aware that there are many passages in the sacred oracles which seem to give the advantage to the other sex; but I consider all these as wholly metaphorical. Thus David was a man after God's own heart, yet see him enervated by his licentious passions! behold him following Uriah to the death, and shew me wherein could consist the immaculate Being's complacency. Listen to the curses which Job bestoweth upon the day of his nativity, and tell me where is his perfection, where his patience—*literally* it existed not. David and Job were types of him who was to come; and the superiority of man, as exhibited in scripture, being also emblematical, all arguments deduced from thence, of course fall to the ground. The exquisite delicacy of the female mind proclaimeth the exactness of its texture, while its nice sense of honour announceth its innate, its native grandeur. And indeed, in one respect, the preeminence seems to be tacitly allowed us, for after an education which limits and confines, and employments and recreations which naturally tend to enervate the body, and debilitate the mind; after we have from early youth been adorned with ribbons, and other gewgaws, dressed out like the ancient victims previous to a sacrifice, being taught by the care of our parents in collecting the most showy materials that the ornamenting our exteriour ought to be the principal object of our attention; after, I say, fifteen years thus spent, we are introduced into the world, amid the united adulation of every beholder. Praise is sweet to the soul; we are immediately intoxicated by large draughts of flattery, which being plentifully administered, is to the pride of our hearts the most acceptable incense. It is expected that with the other sex we should commence immediate war, and that we should triumph over the machinations of the most artful. We must be constantly upon our guard; prudence and discretion must be our characteristicks; and we must rise superiour to, and obtain a complete victory over those who have been long adding to the native strength of their minds, by an unremitted study of men and books, and who have, moreover, conceived from the loose characters which they have been portrayed in the extensive variety of their reading, a most contemptible opinion of the sex. Thus unequal, we are, notwithstanding, forced to the combat, and the infamy which is consequent upon the smallest deviation in our conduct, proclaims the high idea which was formed of our native strength; and thus, indirectly at least, is the preference acknowledged to be our due. And if we are allowed an equality of acquirement, let serious studies equally employ our minds, and we will bid our souls arise to equal strength. We will meet upon even ground, the despot man; we will rush with alacrity to the combat, and, crowned by success, we shall then answer the exalted expectations which are formed. Though sensibility, soft compassion, and gentle commiseration, are inmates in the female bosom, yet against every deep laid art, altogether fearless of the event, we will set them in array; for assuredly the wreath of victory will encircle the spotless brow. If we meet an equal, a sensible friend, we will reward him with the hand of amity, and through life we will be assiduous to promote his happiness; but from every deep laid scheme for our ruin, retiring into ourselves, amid the flowery paths of science, we will indulge in all the refined and sentimental pleasures of contemplation. And should it still be urged, that the studies thus inlisted upon would interfere with our more peculiar department, I must further reply, that *early hours,* and close application, will do wonders; and to her who is from the first dawn of reason taught to fill up time rationally, both the requisites will be easy. I grant that niggard fortune is too generally unfriendly to the mind; and that much of that valuable treasure, time, is necessarily expended upon the wants of the body; but it should be remembered, that in embarrassed circumstances our companions have as little leisure for literary improvement, as is afforded to us; for most certainly their provident care is at least as requisite as our exertions. Nay, we have even more leisure for sedentary pleasures, as our avocations are more retired, much less laborious, and, as hath been observed, by no means require that avidity of attention which is proper to the employments of the other sex. In high life, or, in other words, where the parties are in possession of affluence, the objection respecting time is wholly obviated, and of course falls to the ground; and it may also be repeated, that many of those hours which are at present swallowed up in fashion and scandal, might be redeemed, were we habituated to useful reflections. But in one respect, O ye arbiters of our fate! we confess that the superiority is indubitably yours; you are by nature formed for our protectors; we pretend not to vie with you in bodily strength; upon this point we will never contend for victory. Shield us then, we beseech you, from external evils, and in return we will transact *your* domestick affairs. Yes, *your,* for are you not equally interested in those matters with ourselves? Is not the elegancy of neatness as agreeable to your sight as to ours; is not the well favoured viand equally delightful to your taste; and doth not your sense of hearing suffer as much, from the discordant sounds prevalent in an ill regulated family, produced by the voices of children and many *et ceteras?*

CONSTANTIA.

By way of supplement to the foregoing pages, I subjoin the following extract from a letter, wrote to a friend in the December of 1780.

And now assist me, O thou genius of my sex, while I undertake the arduous task of endeavouring to combat that vulgar, that almost universal errour, which hath, it seems, enlisted even Mr. P—— under its banners. The superiority of your sex hath, I grant, been time out of mind esteemed a truth incontrovertible; in consequence of which persuasion, every plan of education hath been calculated to establish this favourite tenet. Not long since; weak and presuming as I was, I amused myself with selecting some arguments from nature, reason, and experience, against this so generally received idea. I confess that to sacred testimonies I had not recourse. I held them to be merely metaphorical, and thus regarding them, I could not persuade myself that there was any propriety in bringing them to decide in this *very important debate.* However, as you, sir, confine yourself entirely to the sacred oracles, I mean to bend the whole of my artillery against those supposed proofs, which you have from thence provided, and from which you have formed an intrenchment *apparently* so invulnerable. And first, to begin with our great progenitors; but here, suffer me to premise, that it is for mental strength I mean to contend, for with respect to animal powers, I yield them undisputed to that sex, which enjoys them in common with the lion, the tyger, and many other beasts of prey; therefore your observations respecting the *rib under the arm, at a distance from the head, &c. &c.* in no sort militate against my view. Well, but the woman was first in the transgression. Strange how blind *self love* renders you men; were you not wholly absorbed in a partial admiration of your own abilities, you would long since have acknowledged the force of what I am now going to urge. It is true some ignoramuses have absurdly enough informed us, that the beauteous fair of paradise, was seduced from her obedience, by a malignant demon, *in the guise of a baleful serpent;* but we, who are better informed, know that the fallen spirit presented himself to her view, *a shining angel still;* for thus, saith the criticks in the Hebrew tongue, ought the word to be rendered. Let us examine her motive—Hark! the seraph declares that she shall attain a perfection of knowledge; for is there aught which is not comprehended under one or other of the terms *good* and *evil.* It doth not appear that she was governed by any one sensual appetite;

but merely by a desire of adorning her mind; a laudable ambition fired her soul, and a thirst for knowledge impelled the predilection so fatal in its consequences. Adam could not plead the same deception; assuredly he was not deceived; nor ought we to admire his superiour strength, or wonder at his sagacity, when we so often confess that example is much more influential than precept. His gentle partner stood before him, a melancholy instance of the direful effects of disobedience; he saw her not possessed of that wisdom which she had fondly hoped to obtain, but he beheld the once blooming female, disrobed of that innocence, which had heretofore rendered her so lovely. To him then deception became impossible, as he had proof positive of the fallacy of the argument, which the deceiver had suggested. What then could be his inducement to burst the barriers, and to fly directly in the face of that command, which *immediately* from the mouth of deity *he* had received, since, I say, he could not plead that fascinating stimulous, the accumulation of knowledge, as indisputable conviction was so visibly portrayed before him. What mighty cause impelled him to sacrifice myriads of beings yet unborn, and by one impious act, which *he saw* would be productive of such fatal effects, entail undistinguished ruin upon a race of beings, which he was yet to produce. Blush, ye vaunters of fortitude; ye boasters of resolution; ye haughty lords of the creation; blush when ye remember, that he was influenced by no other motive than a bare pusillanimous attachment to a woman! by sentiments so exquisitely soft, that all his sons have, from that period, when they have designed to degrade them, described as highly feminine. Thus it should seem, that all the arts of the grand deceiver (since means adequate to the purpose are, I conceive, invariably pursued) were requisite to mislead our general mother, while the father of mankind forfeited his own, and relinquished the happines of posterity, merely in compliance with the blandishments of a female. The subsequent subjection the apostle Paul explains as a figure; after enlarging upon the subject, he adds, *"This is a great mystery; but I speak concerning Christ and the church."* Now we know with what consummate wisdom the unerring father of eternity hath formed his plans; all the types which he hath displayed, he hath permitted *materially* to fail, in the very virtue for which *they* were famed. The reason for this is obvious, we might otherwise mistake his economy, and render that honour to the creature, which is due only to the creator. I know that Adam was a figure of him who was to come. The grace contained in his figure, is the reason of my rejoicing, and while I am very far from prostrating before the shadow, I yield joyfully in all things the preeminence to the second federal head. Confiding faith is prefigured by Abraham, yet he exhibits a contrast to affiance, when he says of his fair companion, she is my sister. Gentleness was the characteristick of Moses, yet he hesitated not to reply to Jehovah himself, with unsaintlike tongue he murmured at the waters of strife, and with rash hands he break the tables, which were inscribed by the finger of divinity. David, dignified with the title of the man after God's own heart, and yet how stained was his life. Solomon was celebrated for wisdom, but folly is wrote in legible characters upon his almost every action. Lastly, let us turn our eyes to man in the aggregate. He is manifested as the figure of strength, but that we may not regard him as any thing more than a figure, his soul is formed in no sort superiour, but every way equal to the mind of her, who is the emblem of weakness, and whom he hails the gentle companion of his better days.

1790

Occasional Epilogue to *The Contrast;* a Comedy, Written by Royall Tyler, Esq.[1]

O Lud, O Lud, O Lud, what a farrago;
These poets do delight their parts to show.
Says I, pray give us something new and pithy,
Ideas fit for frolic, and for me.
An Epilogue, you know, should still be funny,
I like of all things this New England Johnny.[2]

Not but a verse, or two, may point the time,
And as I know you love to scribble rhyme;
Touching once more the panegyric string,
With countless bays, a fragrant sprig to fling,
Upon the close of this returning day,
You may contrive some pretty thing to say.

'Twas thus I chatter'd, reason'd, laugh'd, and talk'd,
As for the muse the destin'd path I chalk'd;
But—heaven bless us—had you seen the look,
The very blood my honest cheeks forsook,
So grave, so cool, unbending, and severe,
We love to fill with dignity our sphere.—

"Madam," and then a reprehending glance,
"If right I understand what you advance,
"You ask an Epilogue for Tyler's play!
"You ask a Garland for this golden day!
"You ask a jest, with humour, sense, and wit!
"On which the critics will in judgment sit.

"Madam, my Pegasus I never spur,
"If he resists an inch I cannot stir,
"But, buoyant on the feathery steed I'll float,
"And as he points—the ready line I'll note—
"Further I cannot promise—or design—
"For, madam—to command, was never mine."

[1]Published in the *Massachusetts Magazine,* March 1794. The editor's preface to the publication announced: "The Epilogue was composed at the request of a friend, and spoken at Gloucester, by Mrs. Solomon, upon the close of the President's *birth day*—1794." Tyler's play was first performed in New York City in 1787.

[2]The name Jonathan—or Johnny—was frequently used derisively to refer to country bumpkins in eighteenth-century America. Tyler uses this name, however, to accentuate the contrast between Jonathan—an uneducated but virtuous servant to the play's hero Colonel Manley—and Jessamy, the foolish servant of the play's foppish Billy Dimple.

She mounted, sure enough—and such a canter,
Upon my faith it is a downright ranter;
No features of an Epilogue appear,
But listen, beaus and belles, and you shall hear.

"Columbia, blest Columbia—thee I hail,
"Borne gently onward by the *peaceful* gale,
"Fleet are thy footsteps up the hill of fame,
"Vast are the honours of thy brightening name:

"The arts and sciences around thee press,
"While bards, recording bards, thy efforts bless;
"Thy Tyler's bosom, nerv'd by attic fire,
"Whom taste, and sense, and reason must admire;
"The Contrast who, in all its parts conceiv'd,
"Whatever virtuous firmness hath achiev'd;

"Who knew so well to paint the soldier's part
"Whose pen hath sketch'd the wily coxcomb's heart;
"Who could the soul of dauntless valour give,
"And bid a fluttering Billy Dimple live;[3]
"Smiling like Jessamy, and simple too,
"As ever yet an unform'd Yankee grew:
"Coarse as Vanrough—skill'd in the plodding page,
"No Smithfield bargainer could be more sage.

"With nicer touch portraying female worth,
"Or fashion's wild, and most eccentric growth.
"This universal genius, soaring still,
"Ascends with eclat the eventful hill.

"But fainter gems must all unmark'd remain,
"When this day's Hero sweeps along the plain.
"Bright gleam'd the hour, which usher'd in the morn,
"On seraphs wings it was revolving borne.
"Twas then, America; thy genius rose,
"Around thy world augmenting light she throws;
"And when she gave a Washington to thee,
"She gave thee empire, arms, and liberty.

[3]Billy Dimple is Colonel Manley's unsuccessful rival for the hand of the play's heroine, Maria. Just as Tyler accentuates the contrast between Jonathan and Jessamy (see note 2), he positions the foppish Dimple—who having visited England becomes a slavish and foolish imitator of that nation's manners—against Colonel Manley, who represents American virtues. Maria's father, van Rough, is a shrewd and practical businessman, another character type satirized in Tyler's play.

"Again thy weal no treacherous league shall stand,
"Discord in vain employs her murderous band;
"Thy patriot, warrior, statesman, yet remains,
"And all the weight of government sustains.
"Through dark arcanas his pervading ken,
"Unfolds the secrets of designing men;
"No foreign influence, with haughty stride,
"Shall sway thy councils, or thy chiefs divide;
"With native splendor, like the star of day,
"Thy Hero still pursues his radiant way;
"Nor shall he ever set in shades of night,
"Naught can diminish *heaven impressed* light,
"But when he fades from this our hemisphere,
"With added lustre, he shall then appear,
"Where stars, and suns, in floods of brightness rise,
"And where no opaque globe the veil supplies.
"Then shall ascend"—and then—and then—and then—

Oh, memory, confusion wraps my soul!
Of what remain'd I have forgot the whole!
I said, so many lines 'twas hard to con;
I did not get them till the day was done!

But, Candour, if that *you* my cause will plead,
I promise, on my faith, in very deed—
Whene'er our friends shall grace these walls again,
With studious care I will my part retain;
Meantime I bend, in meek obeisance low,
And for your patience all my thanks bestow.

CONSTANTIA.

1794

Ann Eliza Bleecker 1752–1783

Ann Eliza Bleecker never published anything in her lifetime. Instead, she enclosed her numerous poems and narratives in letters that she circulated among a small group of family and friends. With her fictionalized Indian captivity narrative, *The History of Maria Kittle,* she took this strategy one step further, presenting the story itself as a letter to her half-sister Susan Ten Eyck. She begins with the saluation "Dear Susan" and interrupts the plot intermittently to address Susan directly and comment on the action. In addition, Bleecker later included the narrative in another letter to her cousin, where she suggested that, like Susan, her young cousin might also benefit from the story. Indian captivity stories, such as those of Hannah Dustan and Mary Rowlandson, were tremendously popular in the late eighteenth century, and

Bleecker's fictionalized account invigorated the genre by giving it an explicitly didactic dimension that links it to the emerging genre of the didactic novel. Bleecker's mode of expression was influenced heavily by the eighteenth-century British cult of sensibility, and she wrote in the mannered, often hyperbolic, language of feeling popular in didactic fiction.

Bleecker was born in October 1752 in New York City to Margarette van Wyck and Brandt Schuyler, a prosperous merchant, and at a young age she acquired a local reputation for her precocious poetic talent. She often composed "extempore" in the midst of company and at the request of friends. Her poetry ranged from the sophisticated and witty to the satirical and sentimental, as illustrated by the samples below. At seventeen she married John J. Bleecker, and the couple settled on a bucolic estate in Tomhanick, a town eighteen miles north of Albany where John Bleecker had inherited land. Geographically isolated and far from the familiar urban context of her family and friends, Bleecker addressed all her work to friends to alleviate her loneliness. The move to Tomhanick represented the first in a series of losses that seemed to Bleecker to characterize her life. Her involvement in her grief suggests that she was self-consciously fashioning a poetic identity that drew heavily on the era's "sentimental" virtues.

The central event that provoked Bleecker's melancholia occurred early in the American Revolution, in the summer of 1777. Threatened by the approaching British troops of General John Burgoyne, who led an expedition from Canada against the colonies, the Bleecker family was forced to flee on foot to Albany with their two daughters, six-year-old Margaretta and the infant Abella. In the course of their journey, Abella died of dysentery. They continued on and were joined by Bleecker's mother in Red Hook, who also died on the journey. This death was followed by that of Bleecker's sister, Caty Swits, who had joined them for their return trip to Tomhanick. Every generation in Bleecker's supportive circle of women had been devastated. Four years later, in 1781, John Bleecker was kidnapped by a band of wandering British soldiers. Though he was soon returned to his family, the trauma of the event led Bleecker to miscarry. From that summer in 1777 until her death in 1783, Bleecker suffered from intense bouts of depression, and maternal loss figures prominently in much of her writing.

Maria Kittle contains many typical features of the Indian captivity narrative: it presents graphic scenes of violence, depicts Native Americans as treacherous savages who mercilessly slay infants and women, and recounts the hardships of Maria's journey as a captive. Yet in the last third of the narrative, *Maria Kittle* diverges from the genre by representing Maria's experiences in Canada after she has been redeemed. Indeed, the story of her captivity carries less emotional weight than this final section in which three colonial women tearfully recount their tales of maternal loss to a sympathetic group of British and French women. Significantly, these stories bear a number of similarities to Bleecker's experience of losing her own daughter as a result of the invasion of anti-insurrectionary British troops. In transposing her tale of maternal loss onto the Indian captivity narrative, Bleecker expresses the desire for a redemptive community of women who achieve a degree of agency through the acts of telling, hearing, and responding "appropriately" to stories. Yet this agency relies on the racist conventions of Indian captivity narratives that demonize Native Americans, and Bleecker deploys the powerful rhetorical strategies of sentimentalism in the construction of a national identity.

After her death in 1783, her daughter, Margaretta Faugères, also a poet (see her poetry in this anthology), published a significant portion of Bleecker's work, which included twenty-three letters, thirty-six poems, an unfinished short historical novel, *The History of Henry and Ann,* and *The History of Maria Kittle.* This material first appeared in *The New-York Magazine* in 1790 and 1791 and then in a collection entitled *The Posthumous Works of Ann Eliza Bleecker* in 1793. That *Maria Kittle* was republished separately in 1797 attests to its popularity.

Allison Giffen
New Mexico State University

PRIMARY WORK

The Posthumous Works of Ann Eliza Bleecker in Prose and Verse. To which is added, A Collection of Essays, Prose and Poetical, by Margaretta V. Faugères, ed. Margaretta Faugères, 1793.

Written in the Retreat from Burgoyne[1]

Was it for this, with thee a pleasing load,
I sadly wander'd through the hostile wood;
When I thought fortune's spite could do no more,
To see thee perish on a foreign shore?
Oh my lov'd babe! my treasures left behind
Ne'er sunk a cloud of grief upon my mind;
Rich in my children—on my arms I bore
My living treasures from the scalper's pow'r:

When I sat down to rest beneath some shade,
On the soft grass how innocent she play'd,
While her sweet sister, from the fragrant wild,
Collects the flow'rs to please my precious child;
Unconscious of her danger, laughing roves,
Nor dreads the painted savage in the groves.
Soon as the spires of Albany appear'd,
With fallacies my rising grief I cheer'd;
"Resign'd I bear," said I, "heaven's just reproof,
"Content to dwell beneath a stranger's roof;
"Content my babes should eat dependent bread,
"Or by the labor of my hands be fed:
"What though my houses, lands, and goods are gone,
"My babes remain—these I can call my own."

[1]John Burgoyne (1722–1792) led 6400 British soldiers from Canada into New York in 1777. Bleecker was forced to flee from her home in Tomhanick before Burgoyne's sudden invasion. Traveling on foot with her two small daughters, she headed south to Albany. Her husband John, away from home at the time of the invasion, joined them a day later. The youngest child, Abella, died of dysentery along the way. The family returned to Tomhanick after Burgoyne's defeat on October 17, 1777.

But soon my lov'd Abella hung her head,
From her soft cheek the bright carnation fled;
Her smooth transparent skin too plainly shew'd
How fierce through every vein the fever glow'd.
—In bitter anguish o'er her limbs I hung,
I wept and sigh'd, but sorrow chain'd my tongue;
At length her languid eyes clos'd from the day,
The idol of my soul was torn away;
Her spirit fled and left me ghastly clay!
Then—then my soul rejected all relief,
Comfort I wish'd not for, I lov'd my grief:
"Hear my Abella!" cried I, "hear me mourn,
"For one short moment, oh! my child return;
"Let my complaint detain thee from the skies,
"Though troops of angels urge thee on to rise."
All night I mourn'd—and when the rising day
Gilt her sad chest with his benignest ray,
My friends press round me with officious care,
Bid me suppress my sighs, nor drop a tear;
Of resignation talk'd—passions subdu'd,
Of souls serene and christian fortitude;
Bade me be calm, nor murmur at my loss,
But unrepining bear each heavy cross.
"Go!" cried I raging, "stoic bosoms go!
"Whose hearts vibrate not to the sound of woe;
"Go from the sweet society of men,
"Seek some unfeeling tiger's savage den,
"There calm—alone—of resignation preach,
"My Christ's examples better precepts teach."
Where the cold limbs of gentle Laz'rus[2] lay
I find him weeping o'er the humid clay;
His spirit groan'd, while the beholders said
(With gushing eyes) "see how he lov'd the dead!"
And when his thoughts on great Jerus'lem turn'd,
Oh! how pathetic o'er her fall he mourn'd!
And sad Gethsemene's nocturnal shade
The anguish of my weeping Lord survey'd:
Yes, 'tis my boast to harbor in my breast
The sensibilities by God exprest;
Nor shall the mollifying hand of time,
Which wipes off common sorrows, cancel mine.

October 29, 1777

[2]See John 11 for the account of Christ's raising Lazarus from the dead.

from The History of Maria Kittle[1]

In the afternoon Maria received her visitants in a neat little parlour. She was dressed in a plain suit of mourning, and wore a small muslin cap, from which her hair fell in artless curls on her fine neck: her face was pale, though not emaciated, and her eyes streamed a soft languor over her countenance, more bewitching than the sprightliest glances of vivacity. As they entered she arose, and advancing, modestly received their civilities, while Mrs. D—— handed them to chairs: but hearing a well-known voice, she hastily lifted up her eyes, and screamed out in an accent of surprise, "Good Heaven! may I credit my senses? My dear Mrs. Bratt, my kind neighbour, is it really you that I see?" Here she found herself clasped in her friend's arms, who, after a long subsiding sigh, broke into tears. The tumult of passion at length abating—"Could I have guessed, my Maria," said she, "that you was here, my visit should not have been deferred a moment after your arrival; but I have mourned with a sister in affliction, (permit me to present her to you,) and while our hearts were wrung with each other's distress, alas! we inquired after no foreign calamity." Being all seated, "I dare not," resumed Maria, "ask after your family; I am afraid you only have escaped to tell me of them."—"Not so, my sister," cried Mrs. Bratt; "but if you can bear the recollection of your misfortunes, do oblige me with the recital." The ladies joined their intreaty, and Mrs. Kittle complied in a graceful manner.

After some time spent in tears, and pleasing melancholy, tea was brought in; and towards sun-set Mrs. D—— invited the company to walk in the garden, which being very small, consisted only of a parterre,[2] at the farther end of which stood an arbour covered with a grape-vine. Here being seated, after some chat on indifferent subjects, Maria desired Mrs. Bratt, (if agreeable to the company) to acquaint her with the circumstances of her capture. They all bowed approbation; and after some hesitation Mrs. Bratt began:—

"My heart, ladies, shall ever retain a sense of the happiness I enjoyed in the society of Mrs. Kittle and several other amiable persons in the vicinage of *Schochticook,* where I resided. She in particular cheered my lonely hours of widowhood, and omitted nothing that she thought might conduce to my serenity. I had two sons; she recommended the education of them to my leisure hours. I accepted of her advice, and found a suspension of my sorrows in the execution of my duty. They soon improved beyond my capacity of teaching. Richard, my eldest, was passionately fond of books, which he studied with intense application. This naturally attached him to a sedentary life, and he became the constant instructive companion of my evening hours. My youngest son, Charles, was more volatile, yet not less agreeable; his person was charming, his wit sprightly, and his address elegant. They often importuned me, at the commencement of this war, to withdraw to *Albany;* but, as I apprehended no

[1] *The History of Maria Kittle* was first published in five installments in The *New-York Magazine* between September 1790 and January 1791. It was later collected in *The Posthumous Works of Ann Eliza Bleecker* (1793). This excerpt occurs toward the end of the narrative while Maria is in Montreal, where she has just been redeemed after having been kidnapped by Native Americans.

[2] An ornamental garden with paths between the flower beds.

danger, (the British troops being stationed above us, quite from *Saratoga* to the Lake) I ridiculed their fears.

"One evening as my sons were come in from reaping, and I was busied in preparing them a dish of tea, we were surprised by a discharge of musketry near us. We all three ran to the door, and beheld a party of Indians not twenty paces from us. Struck with astonishment, we had no power to move; and the savages again firing that instant, my Charles dropped down dead beside me. Good God! what were my emotions! But language would fail, should I attempt to describe them. My surviving son then turning to me, with a countenance expressive of the deepest horror, urged me to fly. "Let us be gone this instant," said he; "a moment determines our fate. O my mother! you are already lost." But despair had swallowed up my fears; I fell shrieking on the body of my child, and rending away my hair, endeavoured to recall him to life with unavailing laments. Richard, in the meanwhile, had quitted me, and the moment after I beheld him mounted on horseback, and stretching away to the city. The Indians fired a volley at him, but missed, and, I flatter myself that he arrived safe. And now, not all my prayers and tears could prevent the wretches from scalping my precious child. But when they rent me away from him, and dragged me from the house, my grief and rage burst forth like a hurricane. I execrated their whole race, and called for eternal vengeance to crush them to atoms. After a while I grew ashamed of my impetuosity: the tears began again to flow silently on my cheek; and, as I walked through the forest between two Indians, my soul grew suddenly sick and groaned in me; a darkness, more substantial than Egyptian night, fell upon it, and my existence became an insupportable burthen to me. I looked up to Heaven with a hopeless kind of awe, but I murmured no more at the dispensations of my God; and in this frame of sullen resignation I passed the rest of my journey, which being nearly similar to Mrs. Kittle's, I shall avoid the repetition of. And now permit me (said she, turning to the French ladies) to acknowledge your extreme goodness to me. I was a stranger, sick and naked, and you took me in. You indeed have proved the good Samaritan to me,[3] pouring oil and wine in my wounds."—"*Hush, hush!* (cried Madame De Roche,) you estimate our services at too high a rate. I see you are no connoisseur in minds; there is a great deal of honest hospitality in the world, though you have met with so little."

"I now reject, (interrupted Mrs. Bratt,) all prejudices of education. From my infancy have I been taught that the French were a cruel perfidious enemy, but I have found them quite the reverse."

Madame De R. willing to change the subject, accosted the other stranger,—"Dear Mrs. Willis, shall we not be interested likewise in your misfortunes?"—Ah! do, (added Mademoiselle V.) "my heart is now sweetly tuned to melancholy. I love to indulge these divine sensibilities, which your affecting histories are so capable of inspiring."—Maria then took hold of Mrs. Willis's hand, and pressed her to oblige them.—Mrs. Willis bowed. She dropt a few tears; but assuming a composed look, she began:—

"I am the daughter of a poor clergyman, who being confined to his chamber by sickness, for several years, amused himself by educating me. At his death, finding myself friendless, and without money, I accepted the hand of a young man who had

[3]See Luke 10:30–37.

taken a leased farm in Pennsylvania. He was very agreeable, and extravagantly fond of me. We lived happily for many years in a kind of frugal affluence. When the savages began to commit outrages on the frontier settlements, our neighbours, intimidated at their rapid approaches, erected a small fort, surrounded by a high palisade. Into this the more timorous drove their cattle at night; and one evening, as we were at supper, my husband (being ordered on guard) insisted that I should accompany him with the children (for I had two lovely girls, one turned of thirteen years, and another of six months.) My Sophia assented to the proposal with joy. "Mamma, (said she,) what a merry woman the Captain's wife is; she will divert us the whole evening, and she is very fond of your company: come, I will take our little Charlotte on my arm, and papa will carry the lantern." I acceded with a nod; and already the dear charmer had handed me my hat and gloves, when somebody thundered at the door. We were silent as death, and instantly after plainly could distinguish the voices of savages conferring together. Chilled as I was with fear, I flew to the cradle, and catching my infant, ran up into a loft. Sophia followed me all trembling, and panting for breath cast herself in my bosom. Hearing the Indians enter, I looked through a crevice in the floor, and saw them, with menacing looks, seat themselves round the table, and now and then address themselves to Mr. Willis, who, all pale and astonished, neither understood nor had power to answer them. I observed they took a great pleasure in terrifying him, by flourishing their knives, and gashing the table with their hatchets. Alas! this sight shot icicles to my soul; and, to increase my distress, my Sophia's little heart beat against my breast, with redoubled strokes, at every word they uttered.

Having finished their repast in a gluttinous manner, they laid a fire-brand in each corner of the chamber, and then departed, driving poor Mr. Willis before them. The smoke soon incommoded us; but we dreaded our barbarous enemy more than the fire. At length, however, the flames beginning to invade our retreat, trembling and apprehensive, we ventured down stairs; the whole house now glowed like a furnace; the flames rolled toward the stairs, which we hastily descended; but just as I sat my foot on the threshold of the door, a piece of timber, nearly consumed through, gave way, and fell on my left arm, which supported my infant, miserably fracturing the bone. I instantly caught up my fallen lamb, and hastened to overtake my Sophia. There was a large hollow tree contiguous to our house, with an aperture just large enough to admit so small a woman as I am. Here we had often laughingly proposed to hide our children, in case of a visit from the olive coloured natives. In this we now took shelter; and being seated some time, my soul seemed to awake as it were from a vision of horror: I lifted up my eyes, and beheld the cottage that lately circumscribed all my worldly wealth and delight, melting away before the devouring fire. I dropt a tear as our apostate first parents did when thrust out from *Eden*.

"The world lay all before them, where to chuse their place of rest, and Providence their guide."[4] Ah, Eve! thought I, hadst thou been like me, solitary, maimed, and unprotected, thy situation had been deplorable indeed. Then pressing my babe to my heart, "How quiet are thou, my angel, (said I;) sure—sure, Heaven has stilled thy little plaints in mercy to us."—"Ah! (sobbed Sophia,) now I am comforted again

[4]John Milton (1608–1674), *Paradise Lost*, bk. 12: 646–47.

that I hear my dear mamma's voice. I was afraid grief would have forever deprived me of that happiness." And here she kissed my babe and me with vehemence. When her transports were moderated, "How cold my sister is, (said she,) do wrap her up warmer, mamma; poor thing, she is not used to such uncomfortable lodging."

"The pain of my arm now called for all my fortitude and attention; but I forbore to mention this afflicting circumstance to my daughter.

"The cheerful swallow now began to usher in the dawn with melody; we timidly prepared to quit our hiding place; and turning round to the light, I cast an anxious eye of love on my innocent, wondering that she slept so long. But oh! horror and misery! I beheld her a pale, stiff corpse in my arms; (suffer me to weep, ladies, at the cruel recollection.) It seems the piece of wood that disabled me, had also crushed my Charlotte's tender skull, and no wonder my hapless babe was quiet. I could no longer sustain my sorrowful burden, but falling prostrate, almost insensible at the dreadful discovery, uttered nothing but groans. Sophia's little heart was too susceptible for so moving a scene. Distracted between her concern for me, and her grief for the loss of her dear sister, she cast herself beside me, and with the softest voice of sorrow, bewailed the fate of her beloved Charlotte—her sweet companion—her innocent, laughing play-fellow. At length we rose, and Sophia, clasping all that remained of my cherub in her arms, "Ah! (said she,) I did engage to carry you, my sister, but little did I expect in this distressing manner." "When we came in sight of the fort, though I endeavoured to spirit up my grieved child, yet I found my springs of action begin to move heavily, my heart fluttered, and I suddenly fainted away. Sophia, concluding I was dead, uttered so piercing a cry, that the centinel looking up, immediately called to those in the fort to assist us. When I recovered, I found myself in a bed encircled by my kind neighbours, who divided their expressions of love and condolement between me and my child. I remained in the fort after this; but, ladies, you may think, that bereft as I was of so kind a husband and endearing child, I soon found myself solitary and destitute. I wept incessantly; and hearing nothing from my dear Willis, I at length resolved to traverse the wilds of *Canada* in pursuit of him. When I communicated this to my friends, they all strongly opposed it; but finding me inflexible, they furnished me with some money and necessaries, and obtained a permission from the Governor to let me go under protection of a flag that was on the way. Hearing likewise that a cartel was drawn for an exchange of prisoners, I sat out, flushed with hope, and with indefatigable industry and painful solicitude, arrived at *Montreal,* worn to a skeleton (as you see ladies) with fatigue.

"I omitted not to inquire of every officer, the names of prisoners who had been brought in. At length I understood that Mr. Willis had perished in jail, on his first arrival, of a dysentery.—Here my expectations terminated in despair. I had no money to return with, and indeed but for my Sophia no inclination—the whole world seemed dark and cheerless to me as the fabled region of Cimmeria,[5] and I was nigh perishing for very want, when Mrs. Bratt, hearing of my distress, sought my acquaintance: she kindly participated my sorrows, and too—too generously shared her

[5]The Cimmerians were an ancient nomadic people, the earliest known inhabitants of what is now the Crimea. They were fabled by the ancients to live in perpetual darkness. Odysseus visits Cimmeria in Homer's *Odyssey,* Book XI.

purse and bed with me. This, ladies, is the story of a broken-hearted woman; nor should I have intruded it in any other but the house of mourning."

Here she concluded, while the ladies severally embracing her, expressed their acknowledgments for the painful task she had complied with to oblige their curiosity.—"Would to Heaven!" said Madame De R. that the brutal nations were extinct, for never—never can the united humanity of *France* and *Britain* compensate for the horrid cruelties of their savage allies."

They were soon after summoned to an elegant collation; and having spent the best part of the night together, the guests retired to their respective homes. . . .

Philip Freneau 1752–1832

Philip Morin Freneau, the most versatile and vitriolic of the patriot poets, was born in New York, the son of Pierre Fresneau, a tradesman, and Agnes Watson. His father's Huguenot (French Protestant) faith and his mother's Presbyterianism influenced Philip to enroll at the College at Nassau (Princeton), the bastion of New Light Christianity in America. Freneau joined the American Whig Society, the more libertarian of the college's two student clubs. There he taught himself to be a poet, mastering the techniques of satire in the paper wars against the other club, the Cliosophical Society, and the devices of polite literature in verse prepared for the commencement exercises. With fellow Whigs James Madison and Hugh Henry Brackenridge, he composed a farcical romance, *Father Bombo's Pilgrimmage to Mecca,* a work some scholars have been tempted to designate the first American novel. Of more lasting consequence were "The Power of Fancy," a personal testament to his devotion to imagination, and his commencement poem, a collaboration with Brackenridge, *A Poem on the Rising Glory of America,* which explored the myth of the westward course of empire and arts from the Old World to the New.

Freneau graduated in 1771 when the American market for literature was so undeveloped that no one could make a living from writing. Consequently, he conducted his career as a man of letters as an adjunct to other occupations—schoolmaster, captain of a merchant vessel, government bureaucrat, farmer, and newspaper editor. He advanced his literary reputation by substituting productivity and topicality for exquisiteness and finish in his work. Immersing himself in the print culture (the world of magazines, newspapers, and cheap books then coming into being)—Freneau turned his back on the older belletristic world of private clubs and salons. Every product of his adult pen found its way into print, and every issue of the day prompted him to write.

Freneau won an audience for his poetry in 1775 with a series of verse satires of British officials and Tories, of which "A Political Litany," has proved the most enduring. Having made himself anathema to the New York Tories, the poet embarked for the West Indies, where he lived for two years until joining the colonial forces as a blockade runner. In 1780, he was captured and incarcerated on a British prison vessel, an experience he memorialized bitterly in *The Prison Ship.* He attached himself to the *Freeman's Journal* in Philadelphia, and lambasted the British and the Tories with a fusillade of verse. The patriotic zeal and sardonic humor of these pieces won Freneau his reputation as "The Poet of the Revolution."

Despite his fame as a political poet, Freneau never restricted his literary concerns to affairs of state—not even when serving as the chief propagandist for Jeffersonian democracy as editor of the *National Gazette* (1790–1793). An encyclopedic curiosity led him to inquire into natural philosophy, speculative theology, history, aesthetics, and social manners. The quality of his work in these areas varies. As a poet of nature Freneau has earned lasting fame, his lyric on "The Wild Honey Suckle" being generally reckoned the inaugural poem in the romantic tradition furthered by William Cullen Bryant and the Transcendentalists. Freneau was less successful, though no less serious, as a theological poet. His susceptibility to ingenious theological speculation may be seen in the change of his beliefs from decade to decade. He espoused at various times deism, Swedenborgianism, and a neo-Epicurianism.

Freneau's importance as a poet is evident in his work in creating a language and a subject matter adjusted to the increasingly democratic ideology of newspapers and magazines. He was America's first public poet in the popular mold.

David S. Shields
University of Southern California

PRIMARY WORKS

A Poem, On the Rising Glory of America, 1772; *The Miscellaneous Works of Mr. Philip Freneau Containing his Essays, and Additional Poems,* 1788; Elihu Hubbard Smith, ed., *American Poems, Selected and Original* (vol. 1), 1793; *A Collection of Poems on American Affairs,* 1815; *The Poems of Philip Freneau, Poet of the American Revolution,* 3 vols., ed. Fred Lewis Pattee, 1902; *Poems of Freneau,* ed. Harry Hayden Clark, 1929; *The Last Poems of Philip Freneau,* ed. Lewis Leary, 1945; *The Newspaper Verse of Philip Freneau,* ed. Judith R. Hiltner, 1986.

The Power of Fancy[1]

Wakeful, vagrant, restless thing,
Ever wandering on the wing,
Who thy wondrous source can find,
Fancy, regent of the mind;
A spark from Jove's[2] resplendent throne,
But thy nature all unknown.
This spark of bright, celestial flame,
From Jove's seraphic altar came,
And hence alone in man we trace,
Resemblance to the immortal race.
Ah! what is all this mighty whole,

[1]Publication of Mark Akenside's *The Pleasures of Imagination* (1744) inspired many meditations on the power of fancy. Freneau composed his while an undergraduate at the College of New Jersey (Princeton).

[2]Chief god in the Roman pantheon.

These suns and stars that round us roll!
What are they all, where'er they shine,
But Fancies of the Power Divine!
What is this globe, these lands, and seas,
And heat, and cold, and flowers, and trees,
And life, and death, and beast, and man,
And time—that with the sun began—
But thoughts on reason's scale combin'd,
Ideas of the Almighty mind!
On the surface of the brain
Night after night she walks unseen,
Noble fabrics doth she raise
In the woods or on the seas,
On some high, steep, pointed rock,
Where the billows loudly knock
And the dreary tempests sweep
Clouds along the uncivil deep.
Lo! she walks upon the moon,
Listens to the chimy tune
Of the bright, harmonious spheres,[3]
And the song of angels hears;
Sees this earth a distant star,[4]
Pendant, floating in the air;
Leads me to some lonely dome,
Where Religion loves to come,
Where the bride of Jesus[5] dwells,
And the deep ton'd organ swells
In notes with lofty anthems join'd,
Notes that half distract the mind.
Now like lightning she descends
To the prison of the fiends,
Hears the rattling of their chains,
Feels their never ceasing pains—
But, O never may she tell
Half the frightfulness of hell.
Now she views Arcadian[6] rocks,
Where the shepherds guard their flocks,
And, while yet her wings she spreads,
Sees chrystal streams and coral beds,
Wanders to some desert deep,

[3]In ancient cosmology the heavens were envisioned as a layered stack of concentric, transparent spheres whose motion produced music.

[4]"Milton's *Paradise Lost,* B. II. v. 1052." [Freneau's note.]

[5]Revelation 21:2. The bride of Jesus is a metaphor for the New Jerusalem of Christian apocalyptic.

[6]The realm of rural contentment which poets identified with a mountainous region of ancient Greece.

Or some dark, enchanted steep,
By the full moonlight doth shew
Forests of a dusky blue,
Where, upon some mossy bed,
Innocence reclines her head.
Swift, she stretches o'er the seas
To the far off Hebrides,
Canvas on the lofty mast
Could not travel half so fast—
Swifter than the eagle's flight
Or instantaneous rays of light!
Lo! contemplative she stands
On Norwegia's[7] rocky lands—
Fickle Goddess, set me down
Where the rugged winters frown
Upon Orca's[8] howling steep,
Nodding o'er the northern deep,
Where the winds tumultuous roar,
Vext that Ossian[9] sings no more.
Fancy, to that land repair,
Sweetest Ossian slumbers there;
Waft me far to southern isles
Where the soften'd winter smiles,
To Bermuda's orange shades,
Or Demarara's[10] lovely glades;
Bear me o'er the sounding cape,
Painting death in every shape,
Where daring Anson[11] spread the sail
Shatter'd by the stormy gale—
Lo! she leads me wild and far,
Sense can never follow her—
Shape thy course o'er land and sea,
Help me to keep pace with thee,
Lead me to yon' chalky cliff,
Over rock and over reef,
Into Britain's fertile land,
Stretching far her proud command.
Look back and view, thro' many a year,
Cæsar, Julius Cæsar, there.[12]
Now to Tempe's[13] verdant wood,
Over the mid-ocean flood

[7]Norway's.

[8]The Orkney Islands off the Scottish coast.

[9]Gaelic hero of ancient lore popularized during the eighteenth century by a fantasy retelling of his tales by James Macpherson.

[10]Territory in British Guiana famed for sugar.

[11]Admiral George Anson circumnavigated the globe with a British fleet during the 1740s.

[12]Caesar came to Britain in 55 B.C.

[13]A vale in ancient Greece sacred to Apollo.

Lo! the islands of the sea—
Sappho,[14] Lesbos mourns for thee:
Greece, arouse thy humbled head,[15]
Where are all thy mighty dead,
Who states to endless ruin hurl'd
And carried vengeance through the world?—
Troy, thy vanish'd pomp resume,
Or, weeping at thy Hector's[16] tomb,
Yet those faded scenes renew,
Whose memory is to Homer due.
Fancy, lead me wandering still
Up to Ida's[17] cloud-topt hill;
Not a laurel there doth grow
But in vision thou shalt show,—
Every sprig on Virgil's[18] tomb
Shall in livelier colours bloom,
And every triumph Rome has seen
Flourish on the years between.
    Now she bears me far away
In the east to meet the day,
Leads me over Ganges'[19] streams,
Mother of the morning beams—
O'er the ocean hath she ran,
Places me on Tinian;[20]
Farther, farther in the east,
Till it almost meets the west,
Let us wandering both be lost
On Tahiti's sea-beat coast,
Bear me from that distant strand,
Over ocean, over land,
To California's golden shore—
Fancy, stop, and rove no more.
    Now, tho' late, returning home,
Lead me to Belinda's tomb;
Let me glide as well as you
Through the shroud and coffin too,
And behold, a moment, there,

[14]Sappho of the island of Lesbos was the greatest of Greek women poets; she wrote during the seventh century, B.C.

[15]At the time of Freneau's writing Greece was under Turkish rule; the country would win independence in 1829.

[16]Prince of Troy killed by Achilles in Homer's *Iliad.*

[17]The mountain from which Zeus witnessed the siege of Troy.

[18]The greatest Roman poet, author of the *Georgics, Eclogues,* and the *Aeneid;* lived from 70 to 19 B.C.

[19]The sacred river of the Hindu faith located in India.

[20]Pacific island.

All that once was good and fair—
Who doth here so soundly sleep?
Shall we break this prison deep?—
Thunders cannot wake the maid,
Lightnings cannot pierce the shade,
And tho' wintry tempests roar,
Tempests shall disturb no more.
    Yet must those eyes in darkness stay,
That once were rivals to the day?—
Like heaven's bright lamp beneath the main
They are but set to rise again.
    Fancy, thou the muses' pride,
In thy painted realms reside
Endless images of things,
Fluttering each on golden wings,
Ideal objects, such a store,
The universe could hold no more:
Fancy, to thy power I owe
Half my happiness below;
By thee Elysian[21] groves were made,
Thine were the notes that Orpheus play'd;
By thee was Pluto[22] charm'd so well
While rapture seiz'd the sons of hell—
Come, O come—perceiv'd by none,
You and I will walk alone.

1770, 1786

A Political Litany[1]

Libera Nos, Domine.—DELIVER US O LORD, not only from British Dependence, but also,

From a junto[2] that labour with absolute power,
Whose schemes disappointed have made them look sour,
From the lords of the council, who fight against freedom,
Who still follow on where delusion shall lead them.

[21]In the Greek underworld, the home of the virtuous dead.

[22]In Greek myth the poet Orpheus won release of his wife, Eurydice, from Pluto, overlord of Hades, by the power of his music.

[1]Published in New York, June 1775.

[2]A political circle.

From the group at St. James's,[3] who slight our petitions,
And fools that are waiting for further submissions—
From a nation whose manners are rough and severe,
From scoundrels and rascals,—do keep us all clear.

From pirates sent out by command of the king
To murder and plunder, but never to swing;
From *Wallace* and *Greaves,* and *Vipers* and *Roses,*[4]
Who, if heaven pleases, we'll give bloody noses.

From the valiant *Dunmore,*[5] with his crew of banditti,
Who plunder Virginians at *Williamsburg* city,
From hot-headed *Montague,*[6] mighty to swear,
The little fat man, with his pretty white hair.

From bishops in Britain, who butchers are grown,
From slaves, that would die for a smile from the throne,
From assemblies that vote against *Congress proceedings,*
(Who now see the fruit of their stupid misleadings.)

From *Tryon* the mighty,[7] who flies from our city,
And swelled with importance disdains the committee:[8]
(But since he is pleased to proclaim us his foes,
What the devil care we where the devil he goes.)

From the caitiff,[9] lord *North,*[10] who would bind us in chains,
From a royal king Log,[11] with his tooth-full of brains,
Who dreams, and is certain (when taking a nap)
He has conquered our lands, as they lay on his map.

From a kingdom that bullies, and hectors, and swears,
We send up to heaven our wishes and prayers
That we, disunited, may freemen be still,
And Britain go on—to be damned if she will.

1775

[3]The location of the royal court in London.

[4]Captains and ships in the British navy, then employed on the American coast. [Freneau's note.]

[5]Royal Governor of Virginia (1732–1809) whose troops (characterized by Freneau as bandits) seized the colony's gunpowder in April, 1775.

[6]British Admiral John Montagu (1719–1795).

[7]William Tryon (1725–1788), Royal Governor of New York, who fled the city at the outbreak of the Revolution.

[8]The Committee of Safety, the patriot circle directing the revolutionary effort in New York.

[9]Coward.

[10]Frederick North (1732–1792), Prime Minister of Great Britain during the revolutionary era.

[11]In Aesop's fable the frogs ask for a king. The king of the gods give them a log for a ruler. The allusion is applied to George III.

To Sir Toby[1]

A Sugar Planter in the interior parts of Jamaica, near the City of San Jago de la Vega, (Spanish Town) 1784

"The motions of his spirit are black as night,
And his affections dark as Erebus."
—SHAKESPEARE[2]

If there exists a hell—the case is clear—
Sir Toby's slaves enjoy that portion here:
Here are no blazing brimstone lakes—'tis true;
But kindled Rum too often burns as blue;
In which some fiend, whom nature must detest,
Steeps Toby's brand, and marks poor Cudjoe's breast.[3]
Here whips on whips excite perpetual fears,
And mingled howlings vibrate on my ears:
Here nature's plagues abound, to fret and tease,
Snakes, scorpions, despots, lizards, centipees—
No art, no care escapes the busy lash;
All have their dues—and all are paid in cash—
The eternal driver keeps a steady eye
On a black herd, who would his vengeance fly.
But chained, imprisoned, on a burning soil,
For the mean avarice of a tyrant, toil!
The lengthy cart-whip guards this monster's reign—
And cracks, like pistols, from the fields of cane.
Ye powers! who formed these wretched tribes, relate,
What had they done, to merit such a fate!
Why were they brought from Eboe's[4] sultry waste,
To see that plenty which they must not taste—
Food, which they cannot buy, and dare not steal;
Yams and potatoes—many a scanty meal!—
One, with a gibbet[5] wakes his Negro's fears,
One to the windmill nails him by the ears;
One keeps his slave in darkened dens, unfed,
One puts the wretch in pickle ere he's dead:
This, from a tree suspends him by the thumbs,

[1]Titled in some versions "The Island Field Negro." In its sentiments the poem resembles the anti-slavery verses of Bryan Edwards, Jamaica's foremost poet at the time of Freneau's visit in 1784.

[2]*The Merchant of Venice,* V, i, 79. Freneau quotes a corrupt text: "black as night" should be "dull as night."

[3]This passage has a reference to the West India custom (sanctioned by law) of branding a newly imported slave on the breast, with a red-hot iron, as evidence of the purchaser's property. [Freneau's note.]

[4]A small Negro kingdom near the river Senegal. [Freneau's note.]

[5]Gallows.

That, from his table grudges even the crumbs!
O'er yond' rough hills a tribe of females go,
Each with her gourd, her infant, and her hoe;
Scorched by a sun that has no mercy here,
Driven by a devil, whom men call overseer—
In chains, twelve wretches to their labors haste;
Twice twelve I saw, with iron collars graced!—
Are such the fruits that spring from vast domains?
Is wealth, thus got, Sir Toby, worth your pains!—
Who would your wealth on terms, like these, possess,
Where all we see is pregnant with distress—
Angola's[6] natives scourged by ruffian hands,
And toil's hard product shipp'd to foreign lands.
Talk not of blossoms, and your endless spring;
What joy, what smile, can scenes of misery bring?—
Though Nature, here, has every blessing spread,
Poor is the laborer—and how meanly fed!—
Here Stygian[7] paintings light and shade renew,
Pictures of hell, that Virgil's[8] pencil drew:
Here, surly Charons[9] make their annual trip,
And ghosts arrive in every Guinea ship,[10]
To find what beasts these western isles afford,
Plutonian[11] scourges, and despotic lords:—
Here, they, of stuff determined to be free,
Must climb the rude cliffs of the Liguanee;[12]
Beyond the clouds, in skulking haste repair,
And hardly safe from brother traitors[13] there.—

1792

The Wild Honey Suckle

Fair flower, that dost so comely grow,
Hid in this silent, dull retreat,
Untouched thy honied blossoms blow,
Unseen thy little branches greet:

[6]West African colony whence the Portuguese outshipped slaves.
[7]Black and hellish.
[8]Alluding to the Roman poet's description of Hades, *Aeneid,* VI.
[9]In classical myth the boatman who ferried souls over the river Styx to the netherworld.
[10]Slave ship.
[11]Hellish; Pluto was lord of the underworld.
[12]The mountains northward of Kingston. [Freneau's note.]
[13]Alluding to the *Independent* Negroes in the blue mountains, who for a stipulated reward, deliver up every fugitive that falls into their hands to the English Government. [Freneau's note.]

No roving foot shall crush thee here,
No busy hand provoke a tear.

By Nature's self in white arrayed,
She bade thee shun the vulgar eye,
And planted here the guardian shade,
And sent soft waters murmuring by;
Thus quietly thy summer goes,
Thy days declining to repose.

Smit with those charms, that must decay,
I grieve to see your future doom;
They died—nor were those flowers more gay,
The flowers that did in Eden bloom;
Unpitying frosts, and Autumn's power
Shall leave no vestige of this flower.

From morning suns and evening dews
At first thy little being came:
If nothing once, you nothing lose,
For when you die you are the same;
The space between, is but an hour,
The frail duration of a flower.

1786

from The Country Printer[1]

Part 2: The News

ALL is not *Truth* ('tis said) that travellers tell—
So much the better for this man of news:
For hence, the country round that know him well,
Will, if he prints some lies, his lies excuse.
Earthquakes, and battles, shipwrecks, myriads slain—
If false or truth—alike to him are gain.

But if this motley tribe say nothing new,
Then many a lazy, lounging look is cast
To watch the weary post-boy travelling through,

[1]*National Gazette,* December 22, 1791. Published in four installments from December 19, 1791, to January 5, 1792, "The Country Printer" treated (1) the printer's town, (2) the news, (3) "The Office," and (4) the printer's political role.

On horse's rump, his budget[2] buckled fast;
With letters safe in leathern prison pent
And, wet from press, full many a packet sent.

Not Argus[3] with his fifty pair of eyes
Look'd sharper for his prey than honest *Type*[4]
Explores each package of alluring size,
Prepar'd to seize them with a nimble gripe
Did not the post-boy watch his goods, and swear
That village *Type* shall only have his share.

Ask you what *matter* fills his various page?
A mere farrago 'tis of mingled things;
Whate'er is done on madam *Terra*'s Stage
He to the knowledge of his townsmen brings:
One while, he tells of Monarchs run away;
And now, of witches drown'd in Buzzard's bay.

Some miracles he makes, and some he steals;
Half nature's works are giants in his eyes:
Much, very much, in wonderment he deals,—
New-Hampshire apples grown to pompkin size,
Pompkins almost as large as country inns,
And ladies bearing each,—three lovely twins!

He, births and deaths with cold indifference views;
A paragraph from his is all they claim:
And here the rural 'squire, amongst the news
Sees the fair record of his father's fame;
All that was good, minutely brought to light,
All that was ill,—concealed from vulgar sight.

1791

On Observing a Large Red-streak Apple

In spite of ice, in spite of snow,
In spite of all the winds that blow,
In spite of hail and biting frost,
Suspended here I see you toss'd;

[2]Leather satchel.
[3]In Greek mythology, Argus had a hundred eyes and was thus deemed acutely vigilant. Upon Argus's death, Hera transferred his eyes to the tail of the peacock.
[4]The country printer's name.

You still retain your wonted hold
Though days are short and nights are cold.

Amidst this system of decay
How could you have one wish to stay?
If fate or fancy kept you there
They meant you for a *Solitaire.*[1]
Were it not better to descend,
Or in the cider mill to end
Than thus to shiver in the storm
And not a leaf to keep you warm—
A moment, then, had buried all,
Nor you have doomed so late a fall.

But should the stem to which you cling
Uphold you to another spring,
Another race would round you rise
And view the *stranger* with surprize,
And, peeping from the blossoms say
Away, old dotard, get away!

Alas! small pleasure can there be
To dwell, a hermit, on the tree—
Your old companions, all, are gone,
Have dropt, and perished, every one;
You only stay to face the blast,
A sad memento of the past.

Would fate or nature hear my prayer,
I would your bloom of youth repair
I would the wrongs of time restrain
And bring your blossom state again:
But fate and nature both say no;
And you, though late must perish too.

What can we say, what can we hope?
Ere from the branch I see you drop,
All I can do, all in my power
Will be to watch your parting hour:
When from the branch I see you fall,
A grave we dig a-south the wall.
There you shall sleep 'till from your core,
Of youngsters rises three or four;

[1]A gem whose ornamental effect depends on being set by itself.

These shall salute the coming spring
And Red streaks to perfection bring
When years have brought them to their prime
And they shall have their summers time:
This, this is all you can attain,
And thus, I bid you, live again!

1822

The Indian Burying Ground[1]

In spite of all the learned have said,
I still my old opinion keep;
The posture, that we give the dead,
Points out the soul's eternal sleep.

Not so the ancients of these lands—
The Indian, when from life released,
Again is seated with his friends,
And shares again the joyous feast.[2]

His imaged birds, and painted bowl,
And venison, for a journey dressed,
Bespeak the nature of the soul,
Activity, that knows no rest.

His bow, for action ready bent,
And arrows, with a head of stone,
Can only mean that life is spent,
And not the old ideas gone.

Thou, stranger, that shalt come this way,
No fraud upon the dead commit—
Observe the swelling turf, and say
They do not lie, but here they sit.

Here still a lofty rock remains,
On which the curious eye may trace

[1]Originally titled, "Lines occasioned by a visit to an old Indian burying ground" (1787). William Collins's "Pensive Ode, on the death of the poet Thomson," which contains a meditation on the grave of a druid, provided Freneau with a model for this popular poem.

[2]"The North American Indians bury their dead in a sitting posture; decorating the corpse with wampum, the images of birds, quadrupeds, &c: And (if that of a warrior) with bows, arrows, tomahawks, and other military weapons." [Freneau's note.]

(Now wasted, half, by wearing rains)
The fancies of a ruder race.

Here still an aged elm aspires,
Beneath whose far-projecting shade
(And which the shepherd still admires)
The children of the forest played!

There oft a restless Indian queen
(Pale Shebah,[3] with her braided hair)
And many a barbarous form is seen
To chide the man that lingers there.

By midnight moons, o'er moistening dews;
In habit for the chase arrayed,
The hunter still the deer pursues,
The hunter and the deer, a shade![4]

And long shall timorous fancy see
The painted chief, and pointed spear,
And Reason's self shall bow the knee
To shadows and delusions here.

1787

On the Causes of Political Degeneracy[1]

Oh! fatal day, when to this peaceful shore,
European despots sent this doctrine o'er,[2]
That man's vast race was born to lick the dust,
Feed on the winds, or toil thro' life accurst;
Poor and despis'd, that others might be great,
And swoln to Monarchs to devour the State.

Whence came these ills, or from what causes grew,
This vortex vast, that only spares the few;
Despotic sway, whose very plague combin'd,

[3]I Kings 10: the beautiful Queen of Sheba.

[4]A spirit. The Indian netherworld was popularly known as the "land of shades."

[1]Also titled "Reflections on the Gradual Progress of Nations from Democratical States to Despotic Empires."

[2]Absolute monarchy. The doctrine, associated with Louis XIV of France, in the New World was associated with the imperial programs of France in Canada and Spain in Latin America.

Distracts, degrades, and swallows up mankind?
Accuse not nature for the dreadful scene
That glooms her stage, or hides her sky serene;
She, equal she, in all her varying ways,
Her equal blessings through the world displays:
The Suns that now on northern climates glow,
Will soon retire, to melt Antarctic Snow;
The seas she robb'd, to make her clouds and rain,
Return in rivers to their breast again;
But man, wrong'd man, borne down, deceiv'd and vext,

Groans on thro' life, bewilder'd and perplext,
Few suns on him but suns of slavery shine,
Now starv'd in camps, now grovelling in the mine,
Chain'd fetter'd, tortur'd, sent from earth a slave,
To seek rewards in worlds beyond the grave.

If in her general system just to all,
We nature, our impartial parent call,
Why did she not on man's whole race bestow,
Those fine sensations spirits only know,
That, born with reason's uncorruptive mind,
Their proper bliss in common blessings find,
Which, shed o'er all, would all our race pervade,
In streams not niggard[3] by the tyrant made?

Leave this a secret in great Nature's breast;
Confess that all her works tend to the best,
Yet own that man's neglected reason here,
Breeds all the mischiefs that we feel or fear,
In all beside the skill to ride his race,
Man, wise and skillful, gives each part its place,
Each nice machine he plans, to reason true,
Adapting all things to the end in view;
But turn to this, the art himself to rule,
His sense is folly, and himself a fool.
Where the prime strength resides, there rests, 'tis plain,
The power mankind to govern and restrain—

Where lies this strength but in the social plan,
Design'd for all, the common good of man:
The power concentered by the general voice,
In honest men, an honest people's choice,
With constant change, to keep the patriot pure,

[3]Stingy.

And vain from views of power the heart secure;
There lies the secret, hid from Rome and Greece,
That holds the world in awe, and holds in peace.

See through this earth, in ages now retir'd,
Man foe to man, as policy requir'd:
At some proud tyrant's nod what millions rose,
To crush mankind, or make the world their foes.
View Asia ravaged, Europe drench'd in blood,

From feuds, whose cause no nation understood—
The cause, alas! of so much misery sown,
Known at the helm of state, and truly known.
Left to themselves, where'er mankind is found,
In peace they wish to walk life's little round,
In peace to sleep, in peace to till the soil,
Nor gain subsistence from a brother's toil,
All but the base, designing, cunning few,
Who seize on nations with a robber's view.
With crowns and sceptres awe the dazzled eye,
And priests, that hold the artillery of the sky;
These, these with armies, navies, potent grown,
Impoverish man, and bid the nations groan;
These, with pretended balance of free States,
Keep worlds at variance, breed eternal hates,
Make man the poor base slave of low design,
Degrade his nature and his tribes disjoin,
Shed hell's foul plagues o'er his exalted race,
And filch the hard earned mite, to make them base.

Shall views like these involve our happy land,
Where embrio monarchs thirst for wide command,[4]
Shall our young nation's strength and fair renown,
Be sacrified to prop a falling throne,
That ages past the world's great curse has stood,
To thrive on rapine, and to feed on blood—
Americans! will you controul such views!
Speak—for you must—you have no time to lose.

1798

[4]Freneau fears the federalist merchants in particular of setting up frontier fiefdoms.

Timothy Dwight 1752–1817

Timothy Dwight hailed from one of the most influential families in New England. His mother, Mary Edwards Dwight, was the third daughter of Jonathan Edwards; his father, Major Timothy Dwight, was a judge, military man, farmer, and merchant. His grandfather Jonathan Edwards had been especially instrumental in promoting Congregationalism during the Great Awakening (c. 1720–1740). His great-grandfather was Calvinist preacher Solomon Stoddard, and his great-great-grandfather was Puritan leader Thomas Hooker. Where Stoddard had been called the "Congregational Pope" of the Connecticut Valley for his immense power and influence, Timothy Dwight was nicknamed "Pope Dwight" for his autocratic ways at Yale College. From this dynamic lineage, Dwight inherited an intellectual enthusiasm befitting the eighteenth century: he was a poet, an essayist, a preacher, a politician, a teacher, a college president, and a travel writer.

Timothy Dwight was born at midcentury, on May 14, 1752, in Northampton, Massachusetts. Largely under his mother's tutelage, he was reading the Bible by age four and teaching catechism to local Indians by age seven. Although he had fulfilled the Yale entrance requirements by the age of eight, he had to wait until 1765 to enter college at the age of thirteen. After a momentary lapse into gambling, he allegedly studied fourteen hours a day, which, coupled with his pre-dawn reading habits to master Homer, resulted in progressively weakened eyesight. Dwight was awarded his B.A. in 1769 and his M.A. in 1772, delivering the commencement address entitled "A Dissertation on the History, Eloquence, and Poetry of the Bible." Despite an initial inclination to study law, he became a tutor at Yale from 1771 to 1777. He married Mary Woolsey in March 1777 and in June took up his first ministry, at Weathersfield. In October, he became chaplain at West Point. Two years later, in 1779, Dwight returned to Northampton upon his father's death. For the next five years, he supported his mother and twelve siblings, managed two farms, preached, and taught. In 1783, the Dwights moved to Greenfield, Connecticut, when he was granted a pastorate. During his twelve-year appointment, Dwight established a highly reputable coeducational academy, where female students could study the more classical forms of literature and thus presumably avoid the dangers of novel-reading. In 1795, Dwight succeeded Ezra Stiles as president of Yale College.

For twenty-two years, Timothy Dwight enthusiastically embraced his role as president of Yale and was credited with raising the college's profile and expanding its academic scope. He encouraged the study of medicine and chemistry and, in addition to his administrative duties, taught classes in rhetoric, theology, logic, and the belles-lettres. Dwight was apparently quite popular with the students and promoted a more congenial environment by abolishing a system of public punishments of undergraduates based upon fines and reinforced by physical abuse. He also ushered in several religious revivals associated with the Second Great Awakening (c. 1795–1835). In 1796, despite a youthful aversion to exercise that led him to experiment with eating only twelve mouthfuls per meal to maintain his weight rather then exercise, Dwight began making lengthy journeys through New York and New England. He traveled mostly by horseback during the fall when school was in recess, a break that allowed students to return home for the harvest. Eventually, he traveled over 18,000 miles, and his journals took up four volumes, approximately 2,000 pages. The *Travels* provide valuable social, botanical, and geographical data for early-American scholars. Dwight delivered numerous sermons, including one on dueling at Yale on September 9, 1804, two months after Aaron Burr killed Alexander Hamilton in a duel (Burr was Dwight's first cousin). In 1816, Dwight's health began to decline with the onset of cancer of the bladder, and on January 11, 1817, he died in New Haven, Connecticut.

Dwight came of age during the heady days of the Revolutionary War and the forming of the new American republic. During his college years, he became a member of a literary group at Yale known as the "Connecticut Wits" (or "Hartford Wits"). The primary group included Joel Barlow, David Humphreys, and John Trumbull, along with Noah Webster and Lemuel Hopkins. The group adopted the satirical form of Samuel Butler's *Hudibras* and Alexander Pope's *Dunciad* to espouse their conservative views and to criticize more liberal democratic figures such as Thomas Jefferson. They advocated a literature based upon American subjects. Fancying themselves as American bards in the Homeric tradition, their most famous work, *The Anarchiad: A Poem on the Restoration of Chaos and Substantial Night* (1786–1787), was a mock epic critical of states that were slow to ratify the Constitution. Vincent Freimarck compares the Wits to other student groups that, like the "Fugitives at Vanderbilt and the Beats at Columbia, [were] warmed by a sense of literary vocation and at odds with the curricular status quo." Despite their conservatism, Dwight and Trumbull advocated the radical notion of introducing "contemporary English literature as a subject of study" and encouraging their students to write poetry and essays. Their works were often didactic, disseminating the image of a virtuous America.

Dwight's published works were comprehensive in scope. *The Conquest of Canäan; a Poem, in Eleven Books* (1785), dedicated to George Washington, is based upon the narrative of Joshua. *The Triumph of Infidelity* (1788), dedicated to Voltaire, chronicles Satan's battles to undermine the virtues of the new republic. *Greenfield Hill* (1794), dedicated to John Adams, is a pastoral poem using Connecticut as the exemplar of the perfect society. *Travels in New England and New York* (4 vols., 1821–1822) is a collection of travel letters written from 1796 to 1815.

Dwight's *Greenfield Hill* is a seven-part 4,500-line poem modeled on the English poet John Denham's *Cooper's Hill* (1642). Its descriptions of beautiful scenery are overlaid with moral guidance and social commentary. The dedication to Vice President John Adams reads: "with Sentiments of the highest Respect for his Private Character, and for the important Services he has rendered to his Country." Dwight described the setting in his introduction: "In the parish of Greenfield, in the town of Fairfield, in Connecticut, there is a pleasant and beautiful eminence, called Greenfield Hill; at the distance of three miles from Long-Island Sound." The poet uses several narrators to convey Greenfield Hill as an American utopia. In Part II, excerpted here, he evokes Oliver Goldsmith's *The Deserted Village* by adopting the sentimental style and upholding the ideals of the simple country life; the narrator of this part is a poet-preacher. American virtue is contrasted with European corruption, and as Emory Elliott explains, the contrast exemplifies one of Dwight's favorite themes: "the decadence of Europe as opposed to the pristine and moral beauty of America." Greenfield Hill thus emerges as the superior social and moral locale. Part IV shifts our attention to war and the lessons of the Pequot War, whereupon past glory is tempered by the virtual annihilation of a noble race. Dwight's overall comparison between Europe and America favors his homeland as ultimately more virtuous, grounded as it was in an agrarian dream.

Susan Clair Imbarrato
Minnesota State University–Moorhead

PRIMARY WORK

Greenfield Hill, 1794, rpt. 1970.

from Greenfield Hill

Part II[1]
The Flourishing Village

Fair Verna! loveliest village of the west;[2]
Of every joy, and every charm, possess'd;
How pleas'd amid thy varied walks I rove,
Sweet, cheerful walks of innocence, and love,
And o'er thy smiling prospects cast my eyes,
And see the seats of peace, and pleasure, rise,
And hear the voice of Industry resound,
And mark the smile of Competence, around!
Hail, happy village! O'er the cheerful lawns,
With earliest beauty, spring delighted dawns;
The northward sun begins his vernal smile;
The spring-bird[3] carols o'er the cressy rill:
The shower, that patters in the ruffled stream,
The ploughboy's voice, that chides the lingering team,
The bee, industrious, with his busy song,
The woodman's axe, the distant groves among,

[1]Part II is written in heroic couplets and thematically linked to Goldsmith's *The Deserted Village.* Dwight's "Argument," preceding this section, identifies the sections of the poem: "View of the Village invested with the pleasing appearances of Spring—Recollection of the Winter—Pleasures of Winter—Of Nature and humble life—March—Original subject resumed—Freedom of the Villagers from manorial evils—Address to Competence, reciting its pleasures, charitable effects, virtues attendant upon it, and its utility to the public—Contrasted by European artificial society—Further effects of Competence on Society, particularly in improving the People at large—African appears—State of Negro Slavery in Connecticut—Effects of Slavery on the African, from his childhood through life—Slavery generally characterized—West-Indian Slavery—True cause of the calamities of the West-Indies—Church—Effects of the Sabbath—Academic School—School-matter—House of Sloth—Female Worthy—Inferior Schools—Female Visit—What is not, and what is, a social female visit—Pleasure of living in an improving state of society, contrasted by the dullness of stagnated society—Emigrations to the Western Country—Conclusion." The notes to the poem are Dwight's unless otherwise indicated.

[2]This part of the poem, though appropriated to the parish of Greenfield, may be considered as a general description of the towns and villages of New England. . . . Morose and gloomy persons, and perhaps some others, may think the description too highly colored. Persons of moderation and candor may possibly think otherwise. . . . The inhabitants of New England . . . [are] a singular example of virtue and happiness. . . . In this imperfect attempt, the writer wishes to exhibit the blessings, which flow from an equal division of property, and a general competence."

[3]A small bird, called in some parts of New England, by that name; which appears, very early in the spring, on the banks of brooks and small rivers, and sings a very sweet and sprightly note.

The wagon, rattling down the rugged steep,
The light wind, lulling every care to sleep,
All these, with mingled music, from below,
Deceive intruding sorrow, as I go.

How pleas'd, fond Recollection, with a smile,
Surveys the varied round of wintery toil!
How pleas'd, amid the flowers, that scent the plain,
Recalls the vanish'd frost, and sleeted rain;
The chilling damp, the ice-endangering street,
And treacherous earth that slump'd[4] beneath the feet.

Yet even stern winter's glooms could joy inspire:
Then social circles grac'd the nutwood[5] fire;
The axe resounded, at the sunny door;
The swain, industrious, trimm'd his flaxen store;
Or thresh'd, with vigorous flail, the bounding wheat,
His poultry round him pilfering for their meat;
Or slid his firewood on the creaking snow;
Or bore his produce to the main below;
Or o'er his rich returns exulting laugh'd;
Or pledg'd the healthful orchard's sparkling draught:
While, on his board, for friends and neighbors spread,
The turkey smok'd, his busy housewife fed;
And Hospitality look'd smiling round,
And Leisure told his tale, with gleeful sound.

Then too, the rough road hid beneath the sleigh,
The distant friend despis'd a length of way,
And join'd the warm embrace, and mingling smile,
And told of all his bliss, and all his toil;
And, many a month elaps'd, was pleas'd to view
How well the household far'd, the children grew;
While tales of sympathy deceiv'd the hour,
And Sleep, amus'd, resign'd his wonted power.

Yes! let the proud despise, the rich deride,
These humble joys, to Competence allied:
To me, they bloom, all fragrant to my heart,
Nor ask the pomp of wealth, nor gloss of art.
And as a bird, in prison long confin'd,
Springs from his open'd cage, and mounts the wind,

[4]From Dwight's notes: This word, said, in England, to be of North Country original, is customarily used in New England, to denote the sudden sinking of the foot in the earth, when partially thawn, as in the month of March. It is also used to denote the sudden sinking of the foot.

[5]Hickory.

Thro' fields of flowers, and fragrance, gaily flies,
Or reassumes his birth-right, in the skies:
Unprison'd thus from artificial joys,
Where pomp fatigues, and fussful fashion cloys,
The soul, reviving, loves to wander free
Thro' native scenes of sweet simplicity;
Thro' Peace' low vale, where Pleasure lingers long,
And every songster tunes his sweetest song,
And Zephyr hastes, to breathe his first perfume,
And Autumn stays, to drop his latest bloom:
'Till grown mature, and gathering strength to roam,
She lifts her lengthen'd wings, and seeks her home.

But now the wintery glooms are vanish'd all;
The lingering drift behind the shady wall;
The dark-brown spots, that patch'd the snowy field;
The surly frost, that every bud conceal'd;
The russet veil, the way with slime o'erspread,
And all the saddening scenes of March are fled.

Sweet-smiling village! loveliest of the hills!
How green thy groves! How pure thy glassy rills!
With what new joy, I walk thy verdant streets![6]
How often pause, to breathe thy gale of sweets;
To mark thy well-built walls! thy budding fields!
And every charm, that rural nature yields;
And every joy, to Competence allied,
And every good, that Virtue gains from Pride!

No griping landlord here alarms the door,
To halve, for rent, the poor man's little store.
No haughty owner drives the humble swain
To some far refuge from his dread domain;
Nor wastes, upon his robe of useless pride,
The wealth, which shivering thousands want beside;
Nor in one palace sinks a hundred cots;
Nor in one manor drowns a thousand lots;
Nor, on one table, spread for death and pain,
Devours what would a village well sustain.

O Competence, thou bless'd by Heaven's decree,[7]
How well exchang'd is empty pride for thee!

[6]In several parts of this country, the roads through villages are called streets.

[7]Men in middling circumstances appear greatly to excel the rich, in piety, charity, and public spirit; nor will a critical observer of human life hesitate to believe, that they enjoy more happiness.

Oft to thy cot my feet delighted turn,
To meet thy cheerful smile, at peep of morn;
To join thy toils, that bid the earth look gay;
To mark thy sports, that hail the eve of May;
To see thy ruddy children, at thy board,
And share thy temperate meal, and frugal hoard;
And every joy, by winning prattlers giv'n,
And every earnest of a future Heaven.

There the poor wanderer finds a table spread,
The fireside welcome, and the peaceful bed.
The needy neighbor, oft by wealth denied,
There finds the little aids of life supplied;
The horse, that bears to mill the hard-earn'd grain;
The day's work given, to reap the ripen'd plain;
The useful team, to house the precious food,
And all the offices of real good.

There too, divine Religion is a guest,
And all the Virtues join the daily feast.
Kind Hospitality attends the door,
To welcome in the stranger and the poor;
Sweet Chastity, still blushing as she goes;
And Patience smiling at her train of woes;
And meek-eyed Innocence, and Truth refin'd,
And Fortitude, of bold, but gentle mind.

Thou pay'st the tax, the rich man will not pay;
Thou feed'st the poor, the rich man drives away.
Thy sons, for freedom, hazard limbs, and life,
While pride applauds, but shuns the manly strife:
Thou prop'st religion's cause, the world around,
And show'st thy faith in works, and not in sound.

Say, child of passion! while, with idiot stare,
Thou seest proud grandeur wheel her sunny car;
While kings, and nobles, roll bespangled by,
And the tall palace lessens in the sky;
Say, while with pomp thy giddy brain runs round,
What joys, like these, in splendor can be found?
Ah, yonder turn thy wealth-enchanted eyes,
Where that poor, friendless wretch expiring lies!
Hear his sad partner shriek, beside his bed,
And call down curses on her landlord's head,
Who drove, from yon small cot, her household sweet,
To pine with want, and perish in the street.
See the pale tradesman toil, the livelong day,

To deck imperious lords, who never pay!
Who waste, at dice, their boundless breadth of soil,
But grudge the scanty meed of honest toil.
See hounds and horses riot on the store,
By Heaven created for the hapless poor!
See half a realm one tyrant scarce sustain,
While meager thousands round him glean the plain!
See, for his mistress' robe, a village sold,
Whose matrons shrink from nakedness and cold!
See too the Farmer prowl around the shed,[8]
To rob the starving household of their bread;
And seize, with cruel fangs, the helpless swain,
While wives, and daughters, plead, and weep, in vain;
Or yield to infamy themselves, to save
Their sire from prison, famine, and the grave.

There too foul luxury taints the putrid mind,
And slavery there imbrutes the reasoning kind:
There humble worth, in damps of deep despair,
Is bound by poverty's eternal bar:
No motives bright the ethereal aim impart,
Nor one fair ray of hope allures the heart.

But, O sweet Competence! how chang'd the scene,
Where thy soft footsteps lightly print the green!
Where Freedom walks erect, with manly port,
And all the blessings to his side resort,
In every hamlet, Learning builds her schools,
And beggars, children gain her arts, and rules;
And mild Simplicity o'er manners reigns,
And blameless morals Purity sustains.

From thee the rich enjoyments round me spring,
Where every farmer reigns a little king;
Where all to comfort, none to danger, rise;
Where pride finds few, but nature all supplies;
Where peace and sweet civility are seen,
And meek good-neighborhood endears the green.
Here every class (if classes those we call,
Where one extended class embraces all,
All mingling, as the rainbow's beauty blends,
Unknown where every hue begins or ends)
Each following, each, with uninvidious strife,
Wears every feature of improving life.

[8]Farmer of revenue: A superior kind of tax-gatherer, in some countries of Europe.

Each gains from other comeliness of dress,
And learns, with gentle mein to win and bless,
With welcome mild the stranger to receive,
And with plain, pleasing decency to live.
Refinement hence even humblest life improves;
Not the loose fair, that form and frippery loves;
But she, whose mansion is the gentle mind,
In thought, and action, virtuously refin'd.
Hence, wives and husbands act a lovelier part,
More just the conduct, and more kind the heart;
Hence brother, sister, parent, child, and friend,
The harmony of life more sweetly blend;
Hence labor brightens every rural scene;
Hence cheerful plenty lives along the green;
Still Prudence eyes her hoard, with watchful care,
And robes of thrift and neatness, all things wear.

from Part IV[9] The Destruction of the Pequods

. . . When pride and wrath awake the world to arms,[10]
How heaves thy snowy breast with fainting throe!
While lust and rapine trumpet death's alarms,
And men 'gainst men with fiery vengeance glow.
In Europe oft, that land of war, and woe,

[9]Part IV is written in Spenserian stanzas in imitation of James Beattie's "The Minstrel." [Ed.] Dwight notes in his "Argument preceding this section: "The Pequods inhabited the branches of the Thames, which empties itself into the Sound, at New London. This nation, from the first settlement of the English Colonists, regarded them with jealousy; and attempted to engage the neighboring tribes in a combination against them. Several of those tribes were, however, more jealous of the Pequods, than of the English, and rejected their solicitations. Not discouraged by these disappointments, they resolved to attempt the distraction of the English, with the strength of their own tribes only; and cruelly assassinated Captains Stone, Norton, and Oldham, as they were trading peaceably in their neighborhood. The English demanded the murderers; but were answered with disdain, and insult. Upon this, Captain Mason was dispatched into their country with a body of troops; and attacking one of their principal forts, destroyed it, together with a large number of their warriors. The rest of the nation fled. A large body of them came to a swamp, three miles westward of Fairfield. One of their number loitering behind the rest, was discovered by the English troops, then commanded by Captain Stoughton, of the Massachusetts; and was compelled to disclose their retreat. One hundred of them, it is said, surrendered. The rest, bravely resolving to live and die together, were attacked, and chiefly destroyed. On this piece of History, the following part of the Poem is founded. It is introduced by reflections on the changes, wrought in the world by time. Ancient Empires. Great Britain. America. Story related, with reflections on the savages. Conclusion."

[10]This section begins on line 217 of Part IV of *Greenfield Hill.* The narrator to this point has been a local mother who has told of Mason's defense against of Pequods. According to Kenneth Silverman, her narrative "prompts reflection on the nature of the Indians, on change, and on the inevitable collapse of empires." [Ed.]

As her sad steps the lingering mourner draws,
How slowly did thy feet entangled go,
Chain'd by vile tests, and prison'd round by laws;
While bigotry and rage in blood insteep'd thy cause!

* * *

When o'er th' Atlantic wild, by Angels borne,
Thy pilgrim barque explor'd it's western way,
With spring and beauty bloom'd the waste forlorn,
And night and chaos shrunk from new-born day.
Dumb was the savage howl; th' instinctive lay
Wav'd, with strange warblings, thro' the woodland's bound;
The village smil'd; the temple's golden ray
Shot high to heaven; fair culture clothed the ground;
Art blossom'd; cities sprang; and sails the ocean crown'd.

As on heaven's sacred hill, of hills the queen,
At thy command, contention foul shall cease,
Thy solar aspect, every storm serene,
And smooth the rugged wild of man to peace;
So here thy voice (fair earnest of the bliss!)
Transform'd the savage to the meekly child.
Hell saw, with pangs, her hideous realm decrease;
Wolves play'd with lambs; the tyger's heart grew mild;
And on his own bright work the GODHEAD, look'd and smil'd.

Hail Elliot! Mayhew[11] hail! by HEAVEN inform'd
With that pure love, which clasps the human kind;
To virtue's path even Indian feet you charm'd,
And lit, with wisdom's beam, the dusky mind:
From torture, blood, and treachery, refin'd,
The new-born convert lisp'd MESSIAH's name.
Mid Choirs complacent, in pure rapture join'd,
Your praise resounds, on yonder starry frame,
While souls, redeem'd from death, their earthly saviours claim.

Oh had the same bright spirit ever reign'd;[12]
Nor trader villains foul'd the Savage mind;
Nor Avarice pin'd for boundless breadth of land;
Nor, with slow death, the wretches been consign'd

[11]These excellent men have proved, beyond dispute, that the Indians may be civilized, and Christianized, by proper efforts. Their Apostolic piety ought to be remembered, with perpetual honor; and well deserves a public monument from the State, of which they were ornaments, as well as citizens." [Dwight's note.] John Eliot (1604–1690) was sympathetic toward the Indians in his attempts to shield them from more aggressive settlers. He established missionary towns and is referred to by the Puritans as "Apostle to the Indians." Thomas Mayhew (c. 1621–1657) ministered to the Wampanoag Indians. [Ed.]

[12]The greatest obstacle to Christianizing the Indians is now, as it usually has been, their riv-

To India's curse,[13] that poisons half mankind!
Then, O divine Religion! torture's blaze
Less frequent round thy tender heart had twin'd;
On the wild wigwam peace had cast it's rays,
And the tremendous whoop had chang'd to hymns of praise.

Fierce, dark, and jealous, is the exotic soul,
That, cell'd in secret, rules the savage breast.
There treacherous thoughts of gloomy vengeance roll,
And deadly deeds of malice unconfess'd;
The viper's poison rankling in it's nest.
Behind his tree, each Indian aims unseen:
No sweet oblivion soothes the hate impress'd:
Years fleet in vain: in vain realms intervene:
The victim's blood alone can quench the flames within.

Their knives the tawny tribes in slaughter steep,
When men, mistrustless, think them distant far;
And, when blank midnight shrouds the world in sleep,
The murderous yell announces first the war.
In vain sweet smiles compel the fiends to spare;
Th' unpitied victim screams, in tortures dire;
The life-blood stains the virgin's bosom bare;
Cherubic infants, limb by limb expire;
And silver'd Age sinks down in slowly-curling fire.

Yet savages are men. With glowing heat,
Fix'd as their hatred, friendship fills their mind;
By acts with justice, and with truth, replete,
Their iron breasts to softness are inclin'd.
But when could War of converts boast refin'd?
Or when Revenge to peace and sweetness move?
His heart, man yields alone to actions kind;
His faith, to creeds, whose soundness virtues prove,
Thawn in the April sun, and opening still to love.

Senate august! that sway'st Columbian climes,
Form'd of the wise, the noble, and humane,

eted persuasion, that the British Colonists, in all their correspondence with them, have aimed at their own benefit, not at the benefit of the Indians; at the acquisition of their lands, not at the salvation of their souls: a persuasion founded on too unequivocal and shameful proof. So long as those, who trade with them, are allowed to poison them by all the means of corruption, virtuous men can only regret their miserable condition. It is to be hoped, that the late act of Congress, regulating our correspondence with the Indians, together with several other humane and just measures of the same nature, measures which reflect the highest honor on that Body, will, in a good degree, remove these evils.

[13]Rum.

Cast back the glance through long-ascending times,
And think what nations fill'd the western plain.
Where are they now? What thoughts the bosom pain,
From mild Religion's eye how streams the tear,
To see so far outspread the waste of man,
And ask "How fell the myriads, HEAVEN plac'd here!"
Reflect, be just, and feel for Indian woes severe.[14]

But cease, foul Calumny! with sooty tongue,
No more the glory of our sires belie.
They felt, and they redress'd, each nation's wrong;
Even Pequod foes they view'd with generous eye,
And, pierc'd with injuries keen, that Virtue try,
The savage faith, and friendship, strove to gain:
And, had no base Canadian fiends been nigh,
Even now soft Peace had smil'd on every plain,
And tawny nations liv'd, and own'd MESSIAH'S reign.

Amid a circling marsh, expanded wide,
To a lone hill the Pequods wound their way;[15]
And none, but Heaven, the mansion had descried,
Close-tangled, wild, impervious to the day;
But one poor wanderer, loitering long astray.
Wilder'd in labyrinths of pathless wood,
In a tall tree embower'd, obscurely lay:
Strait summon'd down, the trembling suppliant show'd
Where lurk'd his vanish'd friends, within their drear abode.

To death, the murderers were anew requir'd,
A pardon proffer'd, and a peace assur'd;
And, though with vengeful heat their foes were fir'd,
Their lives, their freedom, and their lands, secur'd.
Some yielding heard. In fastness strong immur'd,

[14]The French settlers of Canada took unceasing and immense pains, to induce the Indians to quarrel with the English Colonists. To this conduct they were influenced not less by religious motives, than by those of policy, and by what has been called national enmity. [Dwight's note.] In the third edition of *The Heath Anthology of American Literature,* Carla Mulford suggests, "These lines probably refer to Little Turtle's War, which took place from 1786 to 1794, between the Shawnees, Miamis, and Ottawas of the Ohio Territory and the U.S. Government. President Washington eventually sent 'Mad Anthony' Wayne into battle with the Indians. In 1793 the Shawnees rejected newly offered U.S. peace terms; they eventually succumbed at the Battle of Fallen Timbers in August 1794. In August of 1795 the Treaty of (Fort) Greenville, securing white settlement on lands northwest of the Ohio River, established another so-called 'permanent' boundary for whites."

[15]The hill, to which the Pequods retired, has the appearance of being artificial.

The rest the terms refus'd, with brave disdain,
Near, and more near, the peaceful Herald lur'd;
Then bade a shower of arrows round him rain,
And wing'd him swift, from danger, to the distant plain.

Through the sole, narrow way, to vengeance led,
To final fight our generous heroes drew;
And Stoughton[16] now had pass'd the moor's black shade,
When hell's terrific region scream'd anew.
Undaunted, on their foes they fiercely flew;
As fierce, the dusky warriors crowd the fight;
Despair inspires; to combat's face they glue;
With groans, and shouts, they rage, unknowing slight,
And close their sullen eyes, in shades of endless night.

Indulge, my native land! indulge the tear,
That steals, impassion'd, o'er a nation's doom:
To me each twig, from Adam's stock, is dear,
And sorrows fall upon an Indian's tomb.
And, O ye Chiefs! in yonder starry home,
Accept the humble tribute of this rhyme.
Your gallant deeds, in Greece, or haughty Rome,[17]
By Maro[18] sung, or Homer's harp sublime,
Had charm'd the world's wide round, and triumph'd over time.

1794

Phillis Wheatley 1753–1784

Known best for her Christian verses reflecting orthodox piety, Phillis Wheatley (Peters) in fact wrote on a wide variety of topics. A kidnapped African slave child, aged about seven years old, she was sold from the South Market in Boston to well-to-do Susanna Wheatley. She was raised in a pious Christian household, and the precocious child evidently experienced special, much-indulged comfort and only token slavery. (Phillis Wheatley was manumitted by October 18, 1773.) Tutored by family members, she quickly learned English, Latin, and the Bible, and she began writing in 1765, four years after arriving in Boston harbor.

She wrote to Reverend Samson Occom, a converted Christian Mohican Indian minister, and she sent a poem to Reverend Joseph Sewall of Boston's Old South

[16]Israel Stoughton, the Massachusetts leader of 120 troops who pursued the fleeing Pequots into New York. [Ed.]

[17]The heroism, celebrated by Homer, Virgil, and other Greek and Latin Poets, principally consisted of feats of personal prowess, and the conduct of small parties. Such was the gallantry of the first American Colonists.

[18]Virgil, full name Publius Vergilius Maro (70–19 B.C.), a Roman poet best known for his epic, the *Aeneid.* [Ed.]

Church. Both this letter and poem are not extant, but a poem from this early period remains: in 1767, when she was about thirteen or fourteen years old, Phillis Wheatley published her first verses in a Newport, Rhode Island, newspaper. By 1772, she had composed enough poems to advertise twenty-eight of them in *The Boston Censor* for February 29, March 14, and April 11. She hoped to publish a volume of her poems that year in Boston.

The range of her topical concerns was already evident in these twenty-eight titles. Along with poems on morality and piety, the volume offered patriotic American pieces, an epithalamium, and a short, racially self-conscious poem, "Thoughts on Being Brought from Africa to America." Had enough subscribers for this volume come forward, it would have been printed. But advertisements brought no subscribers, for reasons in part racially motivated. Wheatley was encouraged by her doting and undaunted mistress to revise her manuscripts in preparation for a volume that Susanna Wheatley had arranged, with the prestigious cooperation of the Countess of Huntingdon, to have published in London in 1773, complete with an engraved likeness of the poet as a frontispiece. This was the first volume known to have been published by a black American, man or woman.

In the fall of 1779, she ran (six times) proposals for a projected third volume, of thirty-three poems and thirteen letters. The work was to be dedicated to Benjamin Franklin. But again, as in 1772 and 1773, these 1779 proposals were rejected by Bostonians. In the *Boston Magazine* for September, 1784, there would be printed a final solicitation for subscribers to this third volume, but there would be no such book in print by the time Phillis Wheatley died three months later on December 5. She was buried obscurely on December 8, along with the body of the last of three infant children.

Wheatley's poems ably and imaginatively suit the neoclassical poetic norms of her day, yet she was not accepted by whites of her generation. Indeed her life evidences the effects of racial injustice. Her first volume, the projected 1772 Boston publication, was advertised by printers, who although they knew better, claimed that they could not credit "ye performances to be by a Negro." But it was no secret that Wheatley was a black poet. In the half-dozen poems she published in America and London before and during the time she solicited Boston subscribers for her 1772 book, she was almost always identified as a black poet. While her second collection, published as *Poems,* went through at least four London printings for a run of about 1200 copies, in America the same volume fared poorly early on. Wheatley received a second lot of 300 copies of her *Poems* from London in May of 1774, but as late as 1778 she could write to a friend in New Haven and ask for return to her of copies of her "books that remain unsold," announcing with unfounded bravado that she "could easily dispose of them here for 12/Lm°" (that is, twelve pounds Legal money). Her book was never reprinted in America during her lifetime; the first American reprinting appeared in Philadelphia in 1786, two years after she had died.

But if her early rejection seems peculiarly American, so too were her gradual conscious tags, reminding readers that she was African. In more than thirty posthumously published letters and variants, and in several poems published after her 1773 volume, Phillis Wheatley would continue to register her racial awareness, but nowhere more bitingly than in her 1774 letter to Samson Occom.

Wheatley's sense of herself as an African and an American makes her in some ways a dual provincial in relationship to the eighteenth-century Anglo-Atlantic cosmopolitan center. The art of her poetry resides in her capacity to make her political, cultural, and poetic self-consciousness a literary subject in and of itself. In her acutely self-aware occasional poetry, she gives us one of the most searching portraits available of the American provincial consciousness.

Wheatley's London-published volume included not only Christian elegies, but also a highly original English translation from the Latin of Ovid, biblical paraphrases, and poems about nature, imagination, and memory. Like any good poet who sought patrons, Wheatley also included flattering salutes to an English captain and the Earl of Dartmouth, two happy pieces on the good fortunes of two ladies, and even a playful rebus to James Bowdoin. She included as well her poem on being brought from Africa to America, a metrical salute to a local black Boston artist, and several poems that spoke to the issues of racial self-acceptance leading to success here and hereafter. *Poems* was eventually reprinted more than two dozen times in America and Europe, and selections appear with regularity in American textbooks. An autographed copy of her book sells today for several thousands of dollars.

William H. Robinson
Rhode Island College

Philip M. Richards
Colgate University

PRIMARY WORKS

Poems, 1773; Anonymous, *Memoir and Poems of Phillis Wheatley, A Native African and a Slave,* 1834; Charles Deane, *Letters of Phillis Wheatley, the Negro Slave Poet of Boston,* 1864; Charles F. Heartman, *Phillis Wheatley (Phillis Peters). Poems and Letters. First Collected Edition,* 1915; Julian D. Mason, ed., *The Poems of Phillis Wheatley,* 1966.

To Mæcenas[1]

Mæcenas, you, beneath the myrtle shade,
Read o'er what poets sung, and shepherds play'd.
What felt those poets but you feel the same?
Does not your soul possess the sacred flame?
Their noble strains your equal genius shares
In softer language, and diviner airs.

While *Homer* paints lo! circumfus'd in air,
Celestial Gods in mortal forms appear;
Swift as they move hear each recess rebound,
Heav'n quakes, earth trembles, and the shores resound.
Great Sire of verse, before my mortal eyes,
The lightnings blaze across the vaulted skies,
And, as the thunder shakes the heav'nly plains,
A deep-felt horror thrills through all my veins.

[1]The Roman Gaius Cilnius Mæcenas was the special friend and patron of Horace and Virgil. This poem was not listed in the 1772 Proposals.

When gentler strains demand thy graceful song,
The length'ning line moves languishing along.
When great *Patroclus* courts *Achilles'* aid,
The grateful tribute of my tears is paid;
Prone on the shore he feels the pangs of love,
And stern *Pelides* tend'rest passions move.

Great *Maro's* strain in heav'nly numbers flows,
The *Nine* inspire, and all the bosom glows.
O could I rival thine and *Virgil's* page,
Or claim the *Muses* with the *Mantuan* Sage;
Soon the same beauties should my mind adorn,
And the same ardors in my soul should burn:
Then should my song in bolder notes arise,
And all my numbers pleasingly surprize;
But here I sit, and mourn a grov'ling mind,
That fain would mount, and ride upon the wind.

Not you, my friend, these plaintive strains become,
Not you, whose bosom is the *Muses* home;
When they from tow'ring *Helicon* retire,
They fan in you the bright immortal fire,
But I less happy, cannot raise the song,
The fault'ring music dies upon my tongue.

The happier *Terence*[2] all the choir inspir'd,
His soul replenish'd, and his bosom fir'd;
But say, ye *Muses,* why this partial grace,
To one alone of *Afric's* sable race;
From age to age transmitting thus his name
With the first glory in the rolls of fame?

Thy virtues, great *Mæcenas*! shall be sung
In praise of him, from whom those virtues sprung:
While blooming wreaths around thy temples spread,
I'll snatch a laurel from thine honour'd head,
While you indulgent smile upon the deed.

As long as *Thames* in streams majestic flows,
Or *Naiads* in their oozy beds repose,
While Phœbus reigns above the starry train,
While bright *Aurora* purples o'er the main,
So long, great Sir, the muse thy praise shall sing,

[2]He was an *African* by birth. [Wheatley's note.]

So long thy praise shall make *Parnassus* ring:
Then grant, *Mæcenas,* thy paternal rays,
Hear me propitious, and defend my lays.

Letter to the Right Hon'ble The Earl of Dartmouth per favour of Mr. Wooldridge[1]

Oct. 10, 1772

My Lord,

The Joyful occasion which has given me this Confidence in addressing your Lordship in the enclose'd, will, I hope, sufficiently apologize for this freedom from an African, who with the (now) happy America, exults with equal transport in the view of one of its greatest advocates Presiding, with the Special tenderness of a Fatherly heart, over the American department.

Nor can they, my Lord, be insensible of the Friendship so much exemplified in your endeavors in their behalf, during the late unhappy disturbances.[2] I sincerely wish your Lordship all Possible success, in your undertakings for the Interest of North America.

That the united Blessings of Heaven and Earth may attend you here, and the endless Felicity of the invisible state, in the presence of the Divine Benefactor may be your portion hereafter, is the hearty desire of, My Lord,

Your Lordship's most Ob[t]. &
devoted Hum[e]. Serv[t].
Phillis Wheatley
Boston, N.E. Oct 10, 1772

[1]William Legge (1753–1801), third Earl of Dartmouth, appointed Secretary for the North American colonies in August 1772, to the measured approval of some colonists who recognized Dartmouth's sympathetic ear for colonial grievances.

Thomas Wooldridge (d. 1794), a minor English functionary traveling throughout the colonies in the employ of Lord Dartmouth. Wooldridge visited and interviewed Phillis in Boston, promising that he would deliver the above poem and its cover letter, and he did so, the manuscripts of both being located among the Earl of Dartmouth's papers in the County Record Office, Stafford, England. Also located there is Wooldridge's letter in manuscript, dated "New York Nov. 24th 1772," which describes his interview with Phillis Wheatley.

[2]Wheatley refers to several riotous reactions to various British financial and legal impositions on the colonies.

To the Right Honourable William, Earl of Dartmouth, His Majesty's Principal Secretary of State for North-America, &c[1]

Hail, happy day, when, smiling like the morn,
Fair *Freedom* rose *New-England* to adorn:
The northern clime beneath her genial ray,
Dartmouth, congratulates thy blissful sway:
Elate with hope her race no longer mourns,
Each soul expands, each grateful bosom burns,
While in thine hand with pleasure we behold
The silken reins, and *Freedom's* charms unfold.
Long lost to realms beneath the northern skies
She shines supreme, while hated *faction* dies:
Soon as appear'd the *Goddess* long desir'd,
Sick at the view, she lanquish'd and expir'd;
Thus from the splendors of the morning light
The owl in sadness seeks the caves of night.

No more, *America,* in mournful strain
Of wrongs, and grievance unredress'd complain,
No longer shalt thou dread the iron chain,
Which wanton *Tyranny* with lawless hand
Had made, and with it meant t' enslave the land.

Should you, my lord, while you peruse my song,
Wonder from whence my love of *Freedom* sprung,
Whence flow these wishes for the common good,
By feeling hearts alone best understood,
I, young in life, by seeming cruel fate
Was snatch'd from *Afric's* fancy'd happy seat:
What pangs excruciating must molest,
What sorrows labour in my parent's breast?
Steel'd was that soul and by no misery mov'd
That from a father seiz'd his babe belov'd:
Such, such my case. And can I then but pray
Others may never feel tyrannic sway?

For favours past, great Sir, our thanks are due,
And thee we ask thy favours to renew,

[1]Dartmouth, sympathetic to Methodists in England, was a friend of the Countess of Huntingdon.

Since in thy pow'r, as in thy will before,
To sooth the griefs, which thou did'st once deplore.
May heav'nly grace the sacred sanction give
To all thy works, and thou for ever live
Not only on the wings of fleeting *Fame,*
Though praise immortal crowns the patriot's name,
But to conduct to heav'ns refulgent fane,
May fiery coursers sweep th' ethereal plain,
And bear thee upwards to that blest abode,
Where, like the prophet, thou shalt find thy God.

Letter to the Rt. Hon'ble the Countess of Huntingdon[1]

Oct. 25, 1770

Most noble Lady,

The occasion of my addressing your Ladiship will, I hope, apologize for this my boldness in doing it. it (sic) is to enclose a few lines on the decease of your worthy chaplain, the Rev'd Mr. Whitefield, in the loss of whom, I sincerely sympathize with your Ladiship: but your great loss which is his Greater gain, will, I hope, meet with infinite reparation, in the presence of God, the Divine Benefactor whose image you bear by filial imitation.

The Tongues of the learned are insufficient, much less the pen of an untutor'd African, to paint in lively characters, the excellencies of this Citizen of Zion! I beg an Interest in your Ladiship's Prayers, and am

With great humility
Your Ladiship's most Obedient
Humble Servant

Phillis Wheatley

Boston Oct. 25th 1770

[1]The Countess of Huntingdon, Selina Hastings (1702–1791), religious zealot, expended most of her considerable fortune for the support of her dissident form of English Methodism. It was the countess who acted as Wheatley's English patron when she allowed the poet to dedicate *Poems on Various Subjects, Religious and Moral* (London, 1773) to herself; and it was at the countess's insistence that Wheatley's portrait was painted and then engraved as a frontispiece for the collection of poems, the first known published volume by a black American. The text of this letter is from one of two manuscript versions, both housed among the Countess's papers in the Cheshunt Foundation at Cambridge University in England.

On the Death of the Rev. Mr. George Whitefield 1770[1]

Hail, happy saint, on thine immortal throne,
Possest of glory, life, and bliss unknown;
We hear no more the music of thy tongue,
Thy wonted auditories cease to throng.
Thy sermons in unequall'd accents flow'd,
And ev'ry bosom with devotion glow'd;
Thou didst in strains of eloquence refin'd
Inflame the heart, and captivate the mind.
Unhappy we the setting sun deplore,
So glorious once, but ah! it shines no more.

Behold the prophet in his tow'ring flight!
He leaves the earth for heav'n's unmeasur'd height,
And worlds unknown receive him from our sight.
There *Whitefield* wings with rapid course his way,
And sails to *Zion* through vast seas of day.
Thy pray'rs, great saint, and thine incessant cries
Have pierc'd the bosom of thy native skies.
Thou moon hast seen, and all the stars of light,
How he has wrestled with his God by night.
He pray'd that grace in ev'ry heart might dwell,
He long'd to see *America* excel;
He charg'd its youth that ev'ry grace divine
Should with full lustre in their conduct shine;
That Saviour, which his soul did first receive,
The greatest gift that ev'n a God can give,
He freely offer'd to the num'rous throng,
That on his lips with list'ning pleasure hung.

"Take him, ye wretched, for your only good,
"Take him[,] ye starving sinners, for your food;
"Ye thirsty, come to this life-giving stream,
"Ye preachers, take him for your joyful theme;
"Take him[,] my dear *Americans,*["] he said,

[1]From Phillis Wheatley, *Poems on Various Subjects, Religious and Moral,* (1773). Personal chaplain to Lady Huntingdon since 1749, the Reverend George Whitefield (1714–1770) was a fiery and enormously popular English evangelist who conducted frequent prayer visits to America. His favorite American undertaking was the establishment of Bethesda, an orphanage outside of Savannah, Georgia, which he built in 1764 with rationalized slave labor. The text, above, is a revision of the poem which first appeared as a 62-line broadside in Boston in October, 1770, and was widely reprinted in Boston, Newport, New York, Philadelphia, and London. Another revised version, in 64 lines, was published in London in 1771. The poem established Phillis Wheatley's international reputation.

"Be your complaints on his kind bosom laid:
"Take him, ye *Africans,* he longs for you,
"*Impartial Saviour* is his title due:
"Wash'd in the fountain of redeeming blood,
"You shall be son, and kings, and priests to God."

Great *Countess,*[2] we *Americans* revere
Thy name, and mingle in thy grief sincere;
New England deeply feels, the *Orphans* mourn,
Their more than father will no more return.

But, though arrested by the hand of death,
Whitefield no more exerts his lab'ring breath,
Yet let us view him in th'eternal skies,
Let ev'ry heart to this bright vision rise;
While the tomb safe retains its sacred trust,
Till life divine re-animates his dust.

1770

On the Death of Dr. Samuel Marshall 1771[1]

Through thickest glooms look back, immortal shade,
On that confusion which thy death has made;
Or from *Olympus'* height look down and see
A *Town* involv'd in grief bereft of thee.
Thy *Lucy* sees thee mingle with the dead,
And rends the graceful tresses from her head,
Wild in her woe, with grief unknown opprest[,]
Sigh follows sigh[,] deep heaving from her breast.

Too quickly fled, ah! whither art thou gone?
Ah! lost for ever to thy wife and son!

[2]The Countess of *Huntingdon,* to whom Mr. *Whitefield* was Chaplain. [Wheatley's note.]

[1]From Phillis Wheatley's *Poems* (1773), revised from the first appearance of the poem, also in 28 lines, in *The Boston Evening Post* (7 October, 1771), p. 3. Dr. Samuel Marshall (1735–1771) graduated from Harvard College in 1754, and prepared for a medical career in London hospitals, qualifying as an M.D. in 1761. He returned to Boston in 1765, married Lucy Tyler and purchased a newer home on Congress Street, not far from Phillis Wheatley's King Street (today's State Street) home. Marshall fathered one son who died on September 29, 1771. Widely respected, he was described in his obituary in *The Boston Evening Post* (30 September) as "highly esteemed . . . a very skillful Physician, Surgeon and Man Midwife . . . ; his death therefore is to be lamented as a public loss to the community. . . ." A relative of Wheatley's mistress, Marshall likely attended the poet in her chronic medical problems.

The hapless child, thine only hope and heir,
Clings round his mother's neck, and weeps his sorrows there.
The loss of thee on *Tyler's* soul returns,
And *Boston* for her dear physician mourns.

When sickness call'd for *Marshall's* healing hand,
With what compassion did his soul expand?
In him we found the father and the friend:
In life how lov'd! how honour'd in his end!

And must not then our *Aesculapius*[2] stay
To bring his ling'ring infant into day?
The babe unborn in the dark womb is tost,
And seems in anguish for its father lost.

Gone is *Apollo* from his house of earth,
But leaves the sweet memorials of his worth:
The common parent, whom we all deplore,
From yonder world unseen must come no more,
Yet 'midst our woes immortal hopes attend
The spouse, the sire, the universal friend.

1773

On Being Brought from Africa to America[1]

'Twas mercy brought me from my *Pagan* land,
Taught my benighted soul to understand
That there's a God, that there's a *Saviour* too:
Once I redemption neither sought nor knew.
Some view our sable race with scornful eye,
"Their colour is a diabolic die."
Remember, *Christians, Negros,* black as *Cain,*
May be refin'd, and join th'angelic train.

1773

[2]Aesculapius, the son of Phoebus Apollo and the princess Coronis, was regarded as "the father of medicine."

[1]This much-reprinted piece has been often cited as an instance of Phillis Wheatley's denigration of things black. Instead, it is a measuredly defiant refutation of the racist notions held by some white Christians, who argue that, by virtue of biblical dictate, black humanity has been forever removed from any hope of Christian membership. The poet defames Africa not because most of its peoples are black, but because she understood it to be a land of "pagans," i.e., non-Christians. The notion that pagan Africa was in critical need of Christianity was repeated by other literate, eighteenth-century blacks, and has persisted to this day. This printing is from Wheatley's 1773 volume of *Poems.*

A Farewell to America

To Mrs. S. W.[1]

Adieu, *New-England's* smiling meads,
Adieu, the flow'ry plain:
I leave thine op'ning charms, O spring,
And tempt the roaring main.

In vain for me the flow'rets rise,
And boast their gaudy pride,
While here beneath the Northern skies
I mourn for *health* deny'd.

Celestial maid of rosy hue,
O let me feel thy reign!
I languish till thy face I view
Thy vanish'd joys regain.

Susannah mourns, nor can I bear,
To see the crystal shower,
Or mark the tender falling tear
At sad departure's hour;

Not unregarding can I see
Her soul with grief opprest
But let no sigh, nor groans for me
Steal from her pensive breast.

In vain the feather'd warblers sing,
In vain the garden blooms,
And on the bosom of the spring
Breathes out her sweet perfumes

While for *Britannia's* distant shore
We sweep the liquid plain,
And with astonish'd eyes explore
The wide-extended main.

[1]Susanna Wheatley (1709–1774), Phillis Wheatley's mistress. Phillis Wheatley was traveling to England for her health, but also to promote her poetry. The poem hints, however, that another incentive may have been the recent decision by Lord Mansfield in the Somerset case of 1772, which held out asylum to all Africans forced to leave England. Wheatley returned and was freed by the Wheatleys.

Lo! *Health* appears! celestial dame!
Complacent and serene,
With *Hebe's*[2] mantle o'er her Frame,
With soul-delighting mien.

To mark the vale where *London* lies
With misty vapors crown'd
Which cloud *Aurora's*[3] thousand dyes,
And veil her charms around.

Why, *Phoebus,*[4] moves thy car so slow?
So slow thy rising ray?
Give us the famous town to view,
Thou glorious king of day!

For thee, *Britannia,* I resign
New-England's smiling fields;
To view again her charms divine,
What joy the prospect yields!

But thou! Temptation hence away,
With all thy fatal train
Nor once seduce my soul away,
By thine enchanting strain.

Thrice happy they, whose heav'nly shield
Secures their souls from harms
And fell *Temptation* on the field
Of all its pow'r disarms!

1773

To the University of Cambridge, in New England[1]

While an intrinsic ardor prompts to write,
The muses promise to assist my pen;
'Twas not long since I left my native shore
The land of errors, and *Egyptian* gloom:

[2]Goddess of youth, daughter of Hera and Zeus.
[3]Goddess of dawn.
[4]The sun personified, sometimes Apollo.
[1]The University of Cambridge, in New England, i.e., Harvard College in Cambridge, Massachusetts. The text is from Wheatley's *Poems* (1773).

Father of mercy, 'twas thy gracious hand
Brought me in safety from those dark abodes.

Students, to you 'tis giv'n to scan the heights
Above, to traverse the ethereal space,
And mark the systems of revolving worlds.
Still more, ye sons of science ye receive
The blissful news by messengers from heav'n,
How *Jesus'* blood for your redemption flows.
See him with hands out-strecht upon the cross;
Immense compassion in his bosom glows;
He hears revilers, nor resents their scorn:
What matchless mercy in the Son of God!
When the whole human race by sin has fall'n,
He deign'd to die that they might rise again,
And share with him in the sublimest skies,
Life without death, and glory without end.

Improve your privileges while they stay,
Ye pupils, and each hour redeem, that bears
Or good or bad report of you to heav'n.
Let sin, that baneful evil to the soul,
By you be shunn'd, nor once remit your guard;
Suppress the deadly serpent in its egg.
Ye blooming plants of human race divine,
An *Ethiop*[2] tells you 'tis your greatest foe;
Its transient sweetness turns to endless pain,
And in immense perdition sinks the soul.

1773

Philis's Reply to the Answer in our Last by the Gentleman in the Navy.[1]

For one bright moment, heavenly goddess! shine,
Inspire my song and form the lays divine.

[2]In several poems, both in her volume and in separately published pieces and variants, Wheatley variously registered her racial self-consciousness.

[1]This headnote was presumably written by Joseph Greenleaf, editor of *The Royal American Magazine,* in whose December 1774 issue Wheatley had published a poem, "To A Gentleman in the Navy"; in that same issue was also printed an anonymous poem, "The Answer," written by "the gentleman in the navy," a response to the poem. In the January 1775 issue of *The Royal American Magazine,* Wheatley published this poem.

Rochford,[2] attend. Beloved of Phoebus! hear,
A truer sentence never reach'd thine ear;
Struck with thy song, each vain conceit resign'd
A soft affection seiz'd my grateful mind,
While I each golden sentiment admire;
In thee, the muse's bright celestial fire.
The generous plaudit 'tis not mine to claim,
A muse untutor'd, an unknown to fame.

The heavenly sisters[3] pour thy notes along
And crown their bard with every grace of song.
My pen, least favour'd by the tuneful nine,
Can never rival, never equal thine;
Then fix the humble Afric muse's seat
At British Homer's[4] and Sir Isaac's[5] feet.
Those bards whose fame in deathless strains arise
Creation's boast, and fav'rites of the skies.
In fair description are thy powers display'd
In artless grottos, and the sylvan shade;
Charm'd with thy painting,[6] how my bosom burns!
And pleasing Gambia on my soul returns,[7]
With native grace in spring's luxuriant reign,
Smiles the gay mead, and Eden blooms again,
The various bower, the tuneful flowing stream,
The soft retreats, the lovers['] golden dream.
Her soil spontaneous, yields exhaustless stores;
For phoebus revels on her verdant shores.
Whose flowery births, a fragrant train appear,
And crown the youth throughout the smiling year.
There, as in Britain's favour'd isle, behold
The bending harvest ripen into gold!

[2]This name cannot be found among rosters of Royal Naval officers in Boston in 1774. Presumably, "Rochford" was a verse-writing Royal Naval officer who had served off the coast of Africa, and in 1774 was based in Boston, possibly billeted in the Wheatley household on King Street, where the poet may still have been living. She may be referring to William Henry Zuylestein, fourth Earl of Rochford (1723–1781), who, although not in Boston, had much to do with royal fleet actions abroad.

[3]The Greek muses.

[4]John Milton (1608–1674), poet, author of "Paradise Lost."

[5]Sir Isaac Newton (1642–1727), English natural philosopher and mathematician.

[6]In the anonymous poem, "The Answer," the writer was complimentary to Africa, which he calls ". . . the guilded shore, the happy land,/ Where spring and autumn gentle hand in hand."

[7]The poet may be remembering her African birthplace. Whether or not she is being autobiographical in her extended praises for things African (lines 21–34), she is the first black American poet to so rhapsodize about Africa.

Just are thy views of Afric's blissful plain,
On the warm limits of the land and main.
Pleas'd with the theme, see sportive fancy play,
In realms devoted to the God of day!
Europa's bard, who with great depth explor'd,
Of nature, and thro' boundless systems soar'd,
Thro' earth, thro' heaven, and hell's profound domain,
Where night eternal holds her awful reign.
But, lo! in him Britania's prophet dies,
And whence, ah! whence, shall other *Newtons* rise?
Muse, bid thy Rochford's matchless pen display
The charms of friendship in the sprightly lay:
Queen of his song, thro' all his numbers shine,
And plausive glories, goddess; shall be thine!
With partial grace thou mak'st his verse excel,
And *his* the glory to describe so well.
Cerulean bard![8] to thee these strains belong,
The Muse's darling and the prince of song.

December 5th, 1774

To His Excellency General Washington

SIR.

I Have taken the freedom to address your Excellency in the enclosed poem, and entreat your acceptance, though I am not insensible of its inaccuracies. Your being appointed by the Grand Continental Congress to be Generalissimo of the armies of North America, together with the fame of your virtues, excite sensations not easy to suppress. Your generosity, therefore, I presume, will pardon the attempt. Wishing your Excellency all possible success in the great cause you are so generously engaged in. I am,

Your Excellency's most obedient humble servant,
PHILLIS WHEATLEY.

Providence, Oct. 26, 1775.
His Excellency Gen. Washington.

Celestial choir! enthron'd in realms of light,
Columbia's[1] scenes of glorious toils I write.

[8]Rochford, whom Wheatley is poetically thanking for his complimentary poem, "The Answer." Uniforms of the Royal Naval officers were "cerulean," or sky-blue.

[1]America.

While freedom's cause her anxious breast alarms,
She flashes dreadful in refulgent arms.
See mother earth her offspring's fate bemoan,
And nations gaze at scenes before unknown!
See the bright beams of heaven's revolving light
Involved in sorrows and the veil of night!
The goddess comes, she moves divinely fair,
Olive and laurel binds her golden hair:
Wherever shines this native of the skies,
Unnumber'd charms and recent graces rise.
Muse! bow propitious while my pen relates
How pour her armies through a thousand gates,
As when Eolus[2] heaven's fair face deforms,
Enwrapp'd in tempest and a night of storms;
Astonish'd ocean feels the wild uproar,
The refluent surges beat the sounding shore;
Or thick as leaves in Autumn's golden reign,
Such, and so many, moves the warrior's train.
In bright array they seek the work of war,
Where high unfurl'd the ensign waves in air.
Shall I to Washington their praise recite?
Enough thou know'st them in the fields of fight.
Thee, first in peace and honours,—we demand
The grace and glory of thy martial band.
Fam'd for thy valour, for thy virtues more,
Hear every tongue thy guardian aid implore!
One century scarce perform'd its destined round,
When Gallic powers Columbia's fury found;[3]
And so may you, whoever dares disgrace
The land of freedom's heaven-defended race!
Fix'd are the eyes of nations on the scales,
For in their hopes Columbia's arm prevails.
Anon Britannia droops the pensive head,
While round increase the rising hills of dead.
Ah! cruel blindness to Columbia's state!
Lament thy thirst of boundless power too late.
Proceed, great chief, with virtue on thy side,
Thy ev'ry action let the goddess guide.
A crown, a mansion, and a throne that shine,
With gold unfading, WASHINGTON! be thine.

1776

[2]God of the winds.

[3]A reference to the French and Indian War (or the Seven Years War) 1756–1763, from which the colonists emerged triumphant over the French.

Liberty and Peace,

A Poem by Phillis Peters[1]

Lo! Freedom comes. Th'prescient Muse foretold,
All Eyes th'accomplish'd Prophecy behold:
Her Port describ'd, *"She moves divinely fair,*
"Olive and Laurel bind her golden Hair."
She, the bright Progeny of Heaven, descends,
And every grace her sovereign Step attends;
For now kind Heaven, indulgent to our Prayer,
In smiling *Peace* resolves the Din of *War.*
Fix'd in *Columbia* her illustrious Line,
And bids in thee her future Councils shine.
To every Realm her Portals open'd wide,
Receives from each the full commercial Tide.
Each Art and Science now with rising Charms,
Th' expanding Heart with Emulation warms.
E'en great *Britannia* sees with dread Surprize,
And from the dazzling Splendors turns her Eyes!
Britain, whose Navies swept th'*Atlantic* o'er,
And Thunder sent to every distant Shore:
E'en thou, in Manners cruel as thou art,
The Sword resign'd, resume the friendly Part!
For *Galia*'s Power espous'd *Columbia*'s Cause,
And new-born *Rome* shall give *Britannia* Law,
Nor unremember'd in the grateful Strain,
Shall princely *Louis'* friendly Deeds remain;
The generous Prince[2] th'impending Vengeance eye's,
Sees the fierce Wrong, and to the rescue flies.
Perish that Thirst of boundless Power, that drew
On *Albion*'s Head the Curse to Tyrants due.
But thou appeas'd submit to Heaven's decree,
That bids this Realm of Freedom rival thee!
Now sheathe the Sword that bade the Brave attone
With guiltless Blood for Madness not their own.
Sent from th'Enjoyment of their native Shore
Ill-fated—never to behold her more!
From every Kingdom on *Europa*'s Coast
Throng'd various Troops, their Glory, Strength and Boast.

[1]Wheatley married John Peters, a free, literate, and ambitious black shopkeeper of Boston in April of 1778, the two of them becoming parents to three children who all died in infancy.

[2]"The generous Prince": France joined the Americans as allies in June 1778.

With heart-felt pity fair *Hibernia* saw
Columbia menac'd by the Tyrant's Law:
On hostile Fields fraternal Arms engage,
And mutual Deaths, all dealt with mutual Rage;
The Muse's Ear hears mother Earth deplore
Her ample Surface smoak with kindred Gore:
The hostile Field destroys the social Ties,
And ever-lasting Slumber seals their Eyes.
Columbia mourns, the haughty Foes deride,
Her Treasures plunder'd, and her Towns destroy'd:
Witness how *Charlestown's* curling Smoaks arise,
In sable Columns to the clouded Skies!
The ample Dome, high-wrought with curious Toil,
In one sad Hour[3] the savage Troops despoil.
Descending *Peace* the Power of War confounds;
From every Tongue coelestial *Peace* resounds:
As from the East th'illustrious King of Day,
With rising Radiance drives the Shades away,
So Freedom comes array'd with Charms divine,
And in her Train Commerce and Plenty shine.
Britannia owns her Independent Reign,
Hibernia, Scotia, and the Realms of *Spain;*
And great *Germania*'s ample Coast admires
The generous Spirit that *Columbia* fires.
Auspicious Heaven shall fill with fav'ring Gales,
Where e'er *Columbia* spreads her swelling Sails:
To every Realm shall *Peace* her Charms display,
And Heavenly *Freedom* spreads her golden Ray.

1785

Lemuel Haynes 1753–1833

A significant black writer of the late eighteenth and early nineteenth centuries, Lemuel Haynes engaged in a sustained elaboration of the issues of freedom and autonomy so central to African American writing in his era. As a New Light minister—one of the few professions to which a black man of his social status might

[3]From three until four p.m. on June 17, 1776, the Battle of Bunker Hill, on the Charlestown peninsula, just across the bay from North Boston, was fought between outnumbered Americans and British troops, who finally achieved a costly victory, losing over 1000 of their own, while Americans suffered the losses of 450 men. Once ashore, the British troops vindictively burned down the town of Charlestown, then home for some 3000 persons, the flames burning all that afternoon and into that night, the rising smoke blackening the skies, or, as Wheatley puts it, "The ample Dome" was "high wrought with curious Toil."

aspire—Haynes fully extended the potential meanings of evangelical Protestantism for the blacks who so frequently absorbed it.

Paradoxically, Haynes's early life and intellectual experience is typical of that of his black contemporaries in the same way that his later life typifies the experiences of his white contemporaries of the conservative Calvinist ministry. Born July 18, 1753, in West Hartford, Connecticut, Haynes was raised by the evangelical family of David Rose in Middle Granville, Massachusetts. Although Haynes received cursory schooling, it appears that the bulk of his literary, theological, and spiritual instruction occurred within the Rose household. Here, Haynes was immersed in the Bible as well as in the writings of Isaac Watts, Edward Young, and George Whitefield. In an era when few blacks achieved the literacy demanded for serious literary activity, Haynes developed extensive and informed intellectual interests.

Haynes was one of several African Americans—including Jupiter Hammon and Phillis Wheatley—who generated the first significant body of African American writing that emerged from the confluence of revivalist awakening discourse and the Whig rhetoric of the Revolution. He joined the Continental Army in 1775 and fought during the Revolutionary War. Not surprisingly, the Revolution provided the young Lemuel Haynes with opportunities for some of his first literary initiatives. One of his first verses, which celebrates a battle, was partially entitled "A Poem on the inhuman Tragedy perpetuated on the 19th of April 1778 by a Number of the British Troops under the Command of Thomas Gage." Shortly afterward, Haynes wrote "Liberty Further Extended," a sustained attack on human bondage, which—borrowing from revolutionary political formulations and Calvinist theology—called for the immediate emancipation of blacks.

After the Revolution, Haynes declined the chance for schooling at Dartmouth College in order to study classical languages under Daniel Farrand and William Bradford while working on the Rose farm. He was licensed to preach, and with the approval of local ministers, he accepted a proposal of marriage from a white woman, Elizabeth Babbitt, who eventually had ten children with him. Haynes served as a preacher in the Granville church for five years before the church applied for his ordination by the conservative New Light Association of Ministers in Litchfield County, Connecticut. After ordination, he continued preaching in Torrington, Vermont, where he had supplied the pulpit since 1784. He preached there until he received a call from the West Parish of Rutland, Vermont, which provided him with his longest pulpit stay, from 1778 to 1818. He then preached in Manchester, Vermont, for four years, and finally in Granville, New York, for eleven years (until shortly before his death).

Haynes's adult life was atypical of many of his black contemporaries. At Rutland alone, he wrote 5,500 sermons, of which 400 were funeral sermons. In another sense, however, Haynes was very much a typical New Light evangelical Calvinist preacher. The social composition of the ministry changed in the late eighteenth century as a large number of lower- and middle-class men (many of them from rural families) entered the pastorate and got caught up in the revivalism of the period. Once in the profession, they faced difficult parish lives. The number of church separations increased sharply during this turbulent period as a result of theological and ecclesiastical divisions and geographical displacement from communal centers in eastern cities. Ministers often had short-lived pastorates and frequently found themselves preaching beyond the "frontiers" of New England. Haynes took over the pastorship of a separate congregation in the Torrington church, one that rejected the Half-Way Covenant. The church in West Rutland, Vermont, where he was a successful revivalist, was also a New Light congregation that rejected the Half-Way measures.

Haynes's commitment to the New Light principles, which led him to like-minded congregations and the frontier, decisively shaped his preaching. He takes not only New Light but also traditional New Divinity theological stances in his sermons on divine decrees, a voluntarist psychology locating sinfulness purely in the will and insisting upon natural ability and moral inability. Although Haynes's preaching was doctrinally grounded, it drew upon his own idiosyncratic system of New Light and New Divinity principles to create a powerful rhetoric that stressed the sinner's absolute voluntary resistance to godliness and correct doctrine as well as his or her obligation to transform immediately. This rhetoric formed the core of a revivalist message that stressed natural liberty, moral inability, and the obligation of immediate repentance, and his involvement in a federalism typical for New Light and New Divinity ministers in the early nineteenth century.

Within the context of Haynes's theological discourse, we see a full elaboration of the isolated elements of Calvinism found in earlier writers such as Wheatley, Hammon, and Equiano. Most important to this elaboration is that liberty is essential for a person's spiritual being to realize his or her moral and spiritual obligations. In other words, the moral obligations defined by Edwardsean theology implied moral right. Haynes's early commitment to Edwardsean theology, traditional Calvinism, and anti-slavery principles in his earliest writing, "Liberty Further Extended," was an important point of departure for an altogether typical New Light career. The much more famous discourse, "Universal Salvation," that provocatively links the doctrine of universalism with the devil's assault upon godliness is part of a sustained characterization of the sinful will, a characterization that shapes much of Haynes's preaching. His career suggests the nexus of thought that grounded the evangelical Protestant and libertarian principles of early black writers in the late eighteenth and the early nineteenth century.

Philip M. Richards
Colgate University

PRIMARY WORK

Black Preacher to White America: The Collected Writings of Lemuel Haynes, 1774–1833, ed. Richard Newman, 1990.

Liberty Further Extended: Or Free Thoughts on the Illegality of Slave-keeping[1]

We hold these truths to be self-Evident, that all men are created Equal, that they are Endowed By their Creator with Ceartain unalienable rights, that among these are Life, Liberty, and the pursuit of happyness.

Congress

The Preface. As *Tyrony* had its Origin from the infernal regions: so it is the Deuty, and honner of Every son of freedom to repel her first motions. But while we are Engaged in the important struggle, it cannot Be tho't impertinent for us to turn one Eye into our own Breast, for a little moment, and See, whether thro' some inadvertency, or a self-contracted Spirit, we Do not find the monster Lurking in our own Bosom; that now while we are inspir'd with so noble a Spirit and Becoming Zeal, we may Be Disposed to tear her from us. If the following would produce such an Effect the auther should rejoice.

It is Evident, by ocular demonstration, that man by his Depravety, hath procured many Courupt habits which are detrimental to society; And altho' there is a way pre[s]crib'd Whereby man may be re-instated into the favour of god, yet these courupt habits are Not Extirpated, nor can the subject of renovation Bost of perfection, 'till he Leaps into a state of immortal Existance. yet it hath pleas'd the majesty of Heaven to Exhibet his will to men, and Endow them With an intulect Which is susceptible of speculation; yet, as I observ'd before, man, in consequence of the fall is Liable to digressions. But to proceed,

Liberty, & freedom, is an innate principle, which is unmovebly placed in the human Species; and to see a man aspire after it, is not Enigmatical, seeing he acts no ways incompatible with his own Nature; consequently, he that would infring upon a mans Liberty may reasonably Expect to meet with oposision, seeing the Defendant cannot Comply to Non-resistance, unless he Counter-acts the very Laws of nature.

Liberty is a Jewel which was handed Down to man from the cabinet of heaven, and is Coaeval with his Existance. And as it proceed from the Supreme Legislature of the univers, so it is he which hath a sole right to take away; therefore, he that would take away a mans Liberty assumes a prerogative that Belongs to another, and acts out of his own domain.

One man may bost a superorety above another in point of Natural previledg; yet if he can produse no convincive arguments in vindication of this preheminence his hypothesis is to Be Suspected. To affirm, that an Englishman has a right to his Liberty, is a truth which has Been so clearly Evinced, Especially of Late, that to spend

[1]The full title of the text in manuscript reads: "Liberty Further Extended: Or Free thoughts on the illegality of Slave-keeping; Wherein those arguments that Are useed in its vindication Are plainly confuted. Together with an humble Address to such as are Concearned in the practise. By Lemuel Haynes."

This manuscript was first published in 1983, in *The William and Mary Quarterly.* We reproduce here the text as it was printed in *Black Preacher to White America,* ed. Richard Newman, 1990. Newman preserved all original spellings, structure, and punctuation.

time in illustrating this, would be But Superfluous tautology. But I query, whether Liberty is so contracted a principle as to be Confin'd to any nation under Heaven; nay, I think it not hyperbolical to affirm, that Even an african, has Equally as good a right to his Liberty in common with Englishmen.

I know that those that are concerned in the Slave-trade, Do pretend to Bring arguments in vindication of their practise; yet if we give them a candid Examination, we shall find them (Even those of the most cogent kind) to be Essencially Deficient. We live in a day wherein *Liberty* & *freedom* is the subject of many millions Concern; and the important Struggle hath alread caused great Effusion of Blood; men seem to manifest the most sanguine resolution not to Let their natural rights go without their Lives go with them; a resolution, one would think Every one that has the Least Love to his country, or futer posterity, would fully confide in, yet while we are so zelous to maintain, and foster our own invaded rights, it cannot be tho't impertinent for us Candidly to reflect on our own conduct, and I doubt not But that we shall find that subsisting in the midst of us, that may with propriety be stiled *Opression,* nay, much greater opression, than that which Englishmen seem so much to spurn at. I mean an oppression which they, themselves, impose upon others.

It is not my Business to Enquire into Every particular practise, that is practised in this Land, that may come under this Odeus Character; But, what I have in view, is humbly to offer som free thoughts, on the practise of *Slave-keeping.* Opression, is not spoken of, nor ranked in the sacred oracles, among the Least of those sins, that are the procureing Caus of those signal Judgments, which god is pleas'd to bring upon the Children of men. Therefore let us attend. I mean to white [write] with freedom, yet with the greatest Submission.

And the main proposition, which I intend for some Breif illustration is this, Namely, That an *African,* or, in other terms, *that a Negro may Justly Chalenge, and has an undeniable right to his* ["freed(om)" is blotted out] *Liberty: Consequently, the practise of Slave-keeping, which so much abounds in this Land is illicit.*

Every privilege that mankind Enjoy have their Origen from god; and whatever acts are passed in any Earthly Court, which are Derogatory to those Edicts that are passed in the Court of Heaven, the act is *void.* If I have a perticular previledg granted to me by god, and the act is not revoked nor the power that granted the benefit vacated, (as it is imposable but that god should Ever remain immutable) then he that would infringe upon my Benifit, assumes an unreasonable, and tyrannic power.

It hath pleased god to *make of one Blood all nations of men, for to dwell upon the face of the Earth.* Acts 17, 26. And as all are of one Species, so there are the same Laws, and aspiring principles placed in all nations; and the Effect that these Laws will produce, are Similar to Each other. Consequently we may suppose, that what is precious to one man, is precious to another, and what is irksom, or intolarable to one man, is so to another, consider'd in a Law of Nature. Therefore we may reasonably Conclude, that Liberty is Equally as pre[c]ious to a *Black man,* as it is to a *white one,* and Bondage Equally as intollarable to the one as it is to the other: Seeing it Effects the Laws of nature Equally as much in the one as it Does in the other. But, as I observed Before, those privileges that are granted to us By the Divine Being, no one has the Least right to take them from us without our consen[t]; and there is Not the Least precept, or practise, in the Sacred Scriptures, that constitutes a Black man a Slave, any more than a white one.

Shall a mans Couler Be the Decisive Criterion whereby to Judg of his natural right? or Becaus a man is not of the same couler with his Neighbour, shall he Be Deprived of those things that Distuingsheth [Distinguisheth] him from the Beasts of the field?

I would ask, whence is it that an Englishman is so far Distinguished from an African in point of Natural privilege? Did he recieve it in his origenal constitution? or By Some Subsequent grant? Or Does he Bost of some hygher Descent that gives him this pre-heminance? for my part I can find no such revelation. It is a Lamantable consequence of the fall, that mankind, have an insatiable thurst after Superorety one over another: So that however common or prevalent the practise may be, it Does not amount, Even to a Surcomstance, that the practise is warrentable.

God has been pleas'd to distiungs [distinguish] some men from others, as to natural abilitys, But not as to natural *right,* as they came out of his hands.

But sometimes men by their flagitious[2] practise forfeit their Liberty into the hands of men, By Becomeing unfit for society; But have the *affricans* Ever as a Nation, forfited their Liberty in this manner? What Ever individuals have done; yet, I Believe, no such Chaleng can be made upon them, as a Body. As there should be Some rule whereby to govern the conduct of men; so it is the Deuty, and intrest of a community, to form a system of *Law,* that is calculated to promote the commercial intrest of Each other: and so Long as it produses so Blessed an Effect, it should be maintained. But when, instead of contributing to the well Being of the community, it proves banefull to its subjects over whome it Extends, then it is hygh time to call it in question. Should any ask, where shall we find any system of Law whereby to regulate our moral Conduct? I think their is none so Explicit and indeffinite, as that which was given By the Blessed Saviour of the world. *As you would that men should do unto you, do you Even so to them.* One would think, that the mention of the precept, would strike conviction to the heart of these Slavetraders; unless an aviricious Disposision, governs the Laws of humanity.

If we strictly adhear to the rule, we shall not impose anything upon Others, But what we should Be willing should Be imposed upon us were we in their Condision.

I shall now go on to consider the manner in which the Slave-trade is carried on, By which it will plainly appear, that the practise is vile and atrocious, as well as the most inhuman. it is undoubtedly true that those that Emigrate slaves from *Africa* Do Endevour to rais mutanies among them in order to procure slaves. here I would make some Extracts from a pamphlet printed in Philadelphia, a few years ago: the varacity of which need not be scrupled, seeing it agrees with many other accounts.

N. *Brue,* Directory of the *French* factory at *Senegal,* who Lived twenty-seven years in that country says, "that the *Europeans* are far from desiring to act as peacemakers among the *Negros,* which would Be acting contrary to their intrest, since the greater the wars, the more slaves are procured." *William Boseman,* factor for the Duch at *Delmina,* where he resided sixteen years, relates, "that one of the former Comma[n]ders hired an army of the Negros, of *Jefferia,* and *Cabesteria,* for a Large Sum of money, to fight the Negros of *Commanry* [?], which occasioned a Battle, which was more Bloody than the wars of the Negros usually are: And that another Commander gave at one time five *hundred* pounds, and at another time Eight hundred pounds, to two other Negro nations, to induce them to take up arms against

[2]Criminal; extremely wicked.

their Country people." This is confirmed by *Barbot,* agent general of the french African company, who says, "The *Hollanders,* a people very zelous for their Commerce at the Coasts, were very studious to have the war carried on amongst the Blacks, to distract, as Long as possible, the trade of the other Europeans and to that Effect, were very ready to assist upon all occasions, the Blacks, their allies, that they mite Beat their Enemies, and so the Commerce fall into their hands." And one *William Smith,* who was sent By the *African* company, to visit their settlements in the year 1726, from the information he reciev'd from one, who had resided ten years, viz. "that the Discerning Natives accounted it their greatest unhappyness that they were Ever visited by the *Europeans*:—that we Christians introduced the traffick of Slaves, and that Before our comeing they Lived in peace; But, say they, it is observable, that Wherever Christianity comes, there comes with it a Sword, a gun, powder, and Ball." And thus it Brings ignominy upon our holy religion, and mak[e]s the Name of Christians sound Odious in the Ears of the heathen. O Christianity, how art thou Disgraced, how art thou reproached, By the vicious practises of those upon whome thou dost smile! Let us go on to consider the great hardships, and sufferings, those Slaves are put to, in order to be transported into these plantations. There are generally many hundred slaves put on board a vessel, and they are Shackkled together, two by two, wors than Crimanals going to the place of Execution; and they are Crouded together as close as posable, and almost naked; and their sufferings are so great, as I have Been Credibly informed, that it often Carries off one third of them on their passage; yea, many have put an End to their own Lives for very anguish; And as some have manifested a Disposision to rise in their Defence, they have Been put to the most Cruel torters, and Deaths as human art could inflict. And O! the Sorrows, the Greif the Distress, and anguish which attends them! and not onely them But their frinds also in their Own Country, when they must forever part with Each Other? What must be the plaintive noats that the tend[er] parents must assume for the Loss of their Exiled *Child*? Or the husband for his Departed wife? and how Do the Crys of their Departed friends Eccho from the watry Deep! Do not I really hear the fond mother Expressing her Sorrows, in accents that mite well peirce the most obdurate heart? "O! my Child, why why was thy Destiny hung on so precarious a theread! unhappy fate! O that I were a captive with thee or for thee! [About seventy-five words are crossed out and utterly illegible. The mother's words continue:] Cursed Be the Day wherein I Bare thee, and Let that inauspicious Night be remembered no more. Come, O King of terrors. Dissipate my greif, and send my woes into oblivion."

But I need Not stand painting the Dreery Sene. Let me rather appeal to tender parents, whether this is Exaggarating matters? Let me ask them what would be their Distress. Should one of their Dearest *Children* Be snach'd from them, in a Clendestine manner, and carried to *Africa,* or some othe forreign Land, to be under the most abject Slavery for Life, among a strang people? would it not imbitter all your Domestic Comforts? would he not Be Ever upon your mind? nay, Doth not nature Even recoil at the reflection?

And is not their many ready to say, (unless void of natural Effections) that it would not fail to Bring them Down with sorrow to the grave? And surely, this has Been the awfull fate of some of those *Negros* that have been Brought into these plantations; which is not to be wondered at, unless we suppose them to be without natural Effections: which is to rank them Below the very Beasts of the field.

O! what an Emens Deal of Affrican-Blood hath Been Shed by the inhuman Cruelty of Englishmen! that reside in a Christian Land! Both at home, and in their own Country? they being the fomenters of those wars, that is absolutely necessary, in order to carry on this cursed trade; and in their Emigration into these colonys? and By their merciless masters, in some parts at Least? O ye that have made yourselves Drunk with human Blood! altho' you may go with impunity here in this Life, yet God will hear the Crys of that innocent Blood, which crys from the Sea, and from the ground against you, Like the Blood of Abel, more pealfull [?] than thunder, *vengence! vengence!* What will you Do in that Day when God shall make inquisision for Blood? he will make you Drink the phials of his indignation which Like a potable Stream shall Be poured out without the Least mixture of mercy; Believe it, Sirs, their shall not a Drop of Blood, which you have Spilt unjustly, Be Lost in forgetfullness. But it Shall Bleed affresh, and testify against you, in the Day when God shall Deal with Sinners.

We know that under the Levitical Oeconomy,[3] *man-stealing* was to Be punished with Death; so [?] we Esteem those that Steal any of our Earthy Commadety gilty of a very heinous Crime:

What then must Be an adiquate punishment to Be inflicted on those that Seal [steal] men?

Men were made for more noble Ends than to be Drove to market, like Sheep and oxen. "Our being Christians, (says one) Does not give us the Least Liberty to trample on heathen, nor Does it give us the Least Superiority over them." And not only are they gilty of *man-stealing* that are the immediate actors in this trade, But those in these colonys that Buy them at their hands, ar far from Being guiltless: for when they saw the theif they consented with him. if men would forbear to Buy Slaves off the hands of the Slave-merchants, then the trade would of necessaty cease; if I buy a man, whether I am told he was stole, or not, yet I have no right to Enslave him, Because he is a human Being: and the immutable Laws of God, and indefeasible Laws of nature, pronounced him free.

Is it not exceeding strang that mankind should Become such mere vassals to their own carnal avarice as Even to imbrue their hands in inocent Blood? and to Bring such intollerable opressiones upon others, that were they themselves to feel them, perhaps they would Esteem Death preferable—pray consider the miserys of a Slave, Being under the absolute controul of another, subject to continual Embarisments, fatiuges, and corections at the will of a master; it is as much impossable for us to bring a man heartely to acquiesce in a passive obedience in this case, as it would be to stop a man's Breath, and yet have it caus no convulsion in nature. those negros amongst us that have Children, they, viz. their *Children* are brought up under a partial Disapilne: their white masters haveing but Little, or no Effection for them. So that we may suppose, that the abuses that they recieve from the hands of their masters are often very considerable; their parents Being placed in such a Situation as not being able to perform relative Deutys. Such are those restrictions they are kept under By their task-masters that they are render'd incapable of performing those morral Deutys Either to God or man that are infinitely binding on all the human race;

[3]The laws God gave to Moses in the Sinai desert that compose a ritual system administered by the tribe of Levi. On man-stealing, see Deuteronomy 24:7.

how often are they Seperated from Each other, here in this Land at many hundred miles Distance, Children from parents, and parents from Children, Husbands from wives, and wives from Husbands? those whom God hath Joined together, and pronounced one flesh, man assumes a prerogative to put asunder. What can be more abject than their condission? in short, if I may so speak 'tis a hell upon Earth; and all this for filthy Lucres sake:[4] Be astonished, O ye Heavens, at this! I believe it would Be much Better for these Colonys if their was never a Slave Brought into this Land; theirby our poor are put to great Extremitys, by reason of the plentifullness of Labour, which otherwise would fall into their hands.

I shall now go on to take under Consideration some of those *arguments* which those that are Concern'd in the Slave-trade Do use in vindication of their practise; which arguments, I shall Endevour to Shew, are Lame, and Defective.

The first argument that I shall take notice of is this viz. *that in all probability the Negros are of Canaans posterity, which ware Destined by the almighty to Slavery; theirfore the practise is warrantable.* To which I answer, Whethear the Negros are of Canaans posterity or not, perhaps is not known By any mortal under Heaven. But allowing they were actually of Canaans posterity, yet we have no reason to think that this Curs Lasted any Longer than the comeing of Christ: when that Sun of riteousness arose this wall of partition was Broken Down. Under the *Law,* their were many External Cerimonies that were tipecal of Spiritual things; or which Shadowed forth the purity, & perfection of the Gospel: as Corporeal *blemishes,* Spurious *Birth,* flagicious *practises,* debar'd them from the congregation of the Lord: theirby Shewing, the intrinsick purity of heart that a Conceal'd Gospel requir'd as the pre-requisite for heaven, and as *Ham* uncovered his fathers nakedness, that is, Did not Endevour to Conceal it, but gaz'd perhaps with a Lascivious Eye, which was repugnant to the Law which was afterwards given to the Children of Isarel [Israel]: So it was most [?] Necessary that god Should manifest his Signal Disapprobation of this hainous Sin, By makeing him and his posterity a publick Example to the world, that theirby they mite be set apart, and Seperated from the people of God as unclean. And we find it was a previlege Granted to God's people of old, that they mite Enslave the *heathen, and the Stranger that were in the Land*; theirby to Shew the Superior previleges God's people Enjoy'd above the rest of the world: So that we, Gentiles were then Subject to Slavery, Being then heathen; [illegible] So that if they will keep Close to the Letter they must own themselves yet Subject to the yoak; unless we Suppose them *free* By Being Brought into the same place, or haveing the same previleges with the Jews; then it follows, that we may inslave all Nations, be they White or Black, that are heathens, which they themselves will not allow. We find, under that Dispensation, God Declareing that he would *visit the iniquity of the fathers upon the Children, unto the third, and fourth generation, &c.* And we find it so in the case of *Ham,* as well as many others; their posterity Being Extrinsically unclean.

But now our glorious hygh preist hath visably appear'd in the flesh, and hath Establish'd a more glorious Oeconomy. he hath not only visably Broken Down that wall of partision that interposed Between the ofended majesty of Heaven and rebellious Sinners and removed those tedeous forms under the Law, which savoured so much

[4]The Apostles warned against the pursuit of material wealth. See 1 Timothy 3:3, 3:8; Peter 5:2.

of servitude, and which *could never make the comers thereunto perfect,* By rendering them obselete: But he has removed those many Embarisments, and Distinctions, that they were incident to, under so contracted a Dispensation. So that whatever *Bodily imperfections,* or whatever *Birth* we sustain, it Does not in the Least Debar us from Gospel previlege's. Or whatever hainous practise any may be gilty of, yet if they manifest a gospel [?] repentance, we have no right to Debar them from our Communion. and it is plain Beyond all Doubt, that at the comeing of Christ, this curse that was upon *Canaan,* was taken off; and I think there is not the Least force in this argument than there would Be to argue that an imperfect Contexture of *parts,* or Base *Birth,* Should Deprive any from Gospel previleges; or Bring up any of those antiquated Ceremonies from oblivion, and reduse them into practise.

But you will say that Slave-keeping was practised Even under the Gospel, for we find *paul,* and the other apostles Exhorting *Servants to be obedient to their masters.* to which I reply, that it mite be they were Speaking to Servants in *minority* in General; But Doubtless it was practised in the Days of the Apostles from what *St. paul* Says, *1. Corin. 7 21. art thou called, being a servant? care not for it; but if thou mayest Be made free, use it rather.* So that the Apostle seems to recommend freedom if attainable, q.d. "if it is thy unhappy Lot to be a slave, yet if thou art Spiritually free Let the former appear so minute a thing when compared with the Latter that it is comparitively unworthy of notice; yet Since freedom is so Exelent a Jewel, which none have a right to Extirpate, and if there is any hope of attaining it, use all Lawfull measures for that purpose." So that however Extant or preval[e]nt it mite Be in that or this age; yet it does not in the Least reverse the unchangeable Laws of God, or of nature; or make that Become Lawfull which is in itself unlawfull; neither is it Strange, if we consider the moral Depravity of mans nature, thro'out all ages of the world, that mankind should Deviate from the unering rules of Heaven. But again, another argument which some use to maintain their intollerable opression upon others is this, viz., *that those Negros that are Brought into these plantations are Generally prisoners, taken in their wars, and would otherwise fall a sacrifice to the resentment of their own people.* But this argument, I think, is plainly confuted By the forecited account which Mr. *Boasman* gives, as well as many others. Again, some say they *Came honestly By their Slaves, Becaus they Bought them of their parents,* (that is, those that Brought them from Africa) *and rewarded them well for them.* But without Doubt this is, for the most part fals; But allowing they Did actually Buy them of their parents, yet I query, whether parents have any right to sel their Children for Slaves: if parents have a right to Be free, then it follows that their Children have Equally as good a right to their freedom, Even *Hereditary.* So, (to use the words of a Learned writer) "one has no Body to Blame But himself, in case he shall find himself Deprived of a man whome he tho't By Buying for a price he had made his own; for he Dealt in a trade which was illicit, and was prohibited by the most obvious Dictates of Humanity. for these resons Every one of those unfortunate men who are pretended to be Slaves, has a right to Be Declared free, for he never Lost his Liberty; he could not Lose it; his prince had no power to Dispose of him. of cours the Sale was *ipso Jure* void."[5]

But I shall take notice of one argument more which these Slave-traders use, and it is this, viz. *that those Negros that are Emigrated into these colonies are brought out*

[5]By the operation of the Law itself (Latin).

of a Land of Darkness under the meridian Light of the Gospel; and so it is a great Blessing instead of a Curs. But I would ask, who is this that Darkneth counsel By words with out knoledg? Let us attend to the great appostle Speaking to us in *Rom. 3.8.* where he reproves some slanderers who told it as a maxim preached By the apostles that they said *Let us Do Evil that Good may come, whose Damnation* the inspired penman pronounces with an Emphasis *to Be Just.* And again *Chap.* 6 vers 1. where By way of interagation he asks, *Shall we continue in Sin that grace may abound?* The answer is obvious, *God forbid.* But that those Slavemerchants that trade upon the coasts of Africa do not aim at the Spiritual good of their Slaves, is Evident By their Behaviour towards them; if they had their Spiritual good at heart, we should Expect that those Slave-merchants that trade upon their coasts, would, insted of Causing quarrelings, and Blood-Shed among them, which is repugnant to Christianity, and below the Character of humanity, Be Sollicitous to Demean Exampleary among them, that By their wholesom conduct, those heathen mite be Enduced to Entertain hygh, and admiring tho'ts of our holy religion. Those Slaves in these Colonies are generally kept under the greatest ignorance, and Blindness, and they are scersly Ever told by their white masters whether there is a Supreme Being that governs the univers; or wheather there is any reward, or punishments Beyond the grave. Nay such are those restrictions that they are kept under that they Scersly know that they have a right to Be free, or if they Do they are not allowed to Speak in their defence; Such is their abject condission, that that *genius* that is peculiar to the human race, cannot have that Cultivation that the polite world is favour'd with, and therefore they are stiled the ignorant part of the world; whereas were they under the Same advantages to git knoledge with them, perhaps their progress in arts would not be inferior.

But should we give ourselves the trouble to Enquire into the grand motive that indulges men to concearn themselves in a trade So vile and abandon, we Shall find it to Be this, Namely, to Stimulate their Carnal avarice, and to maintain men in pride, Luxury, and idleness, and how much it hath Subserv'd to this vile purpose I Leave the Candid publick to Judge: I speak it with reverence yet I think all must give in that it hath such a tendency.

But altho god is of Long patience, yet it does not Last always, nay, he has *whet* his *glittering Sword, and his hand hath already taken hold on Judgement;*[6] for who knows how far that the unjust Oppression which hath abounded in this Land, may be the procuring cause of this very Judgement that now impends, which so much portends *Slavery*?

for this is God's way of working, Often he brings the Same Judgements, or Evils upon men, as they unriteously Bring upon others. As is plain from *Judges* 1 and on.

But Adoni-bezek fled, and they persued after him, and caut him, and cut off his thumbs, and his great toes.

And Adoni-besek said, threescore and ten kings haveing their thumbs and their great toes cut off gathered their meat under my table: as I have Done, So god hath requited me.

And as wicked *Ahab,* and *Jezebel* to gratify their covetousness caused *Naboth* to be put to Death, and as *Dogs* licked the Blood of *Naboth,* the word of the Lord was By the prophet *Elijah, thus Saith the Lord, in the place where Dogs Licked the Blood*

[6]Deuteronomy 32:4.

of Naboth, Shall Dogs Lick thy Blood Even thine. See 1 Kings 21. 19. And of Jezebel also Spake the Lord, Saying, The Dogs Shall Eat Jezebel By the walls of Jezreel. vers 23.

And we find the Judgement actually accomplished upon *Ahab* in the 22. Chap. & 38. vers.

And upon *Jezebel* in the 9 chap. 2 of *Kings.*

Again *Rev. 16.6. for they have Shed the Blood of Saints and prophets, and thou hast given them Blood to Drink; for they are worthy.* And *chap.* 18.6. *Reward her Even as She rewarded you.* I say this is often God's way of Dealing, by retaliating Back upon men the Same Evils that they unjustly Bring upon others. I Don't Say that we have reason to think that *Oppression* is the alone caus of this Judgement that God is pleas'd to Bring upon this Land, Nay, But we have the greatest reason to think that this is not one of the Least. And whatever some may think that I am instigated By a fals zeal; and all that I have Said upon the Subject is mere Novelty: yet I am not afraid to appeal to the consience of any rational and honnest man, as to the truth of what I have just hinted at; and if any will not confide in what I have humbly offer'd, I am persuaded it must be such Short-Sited persons whose Contracted Eyes never penitrate thro' the narrow confines of Self, and are mere Vassals to filthy Lucre.

But I Cannot persuade myself to make a period to this Small *Treatise,* without humbly addressing myself, more perticularly, unto all such as are Concearn'd in the practise of *Slave-keeping.*

Sirs, Should I persue the Dictates of nature, resulting from a sense of my own inability, I should be far from attempting to form this address: Nevertheless, I think that a mere Superficial reflection upon the merits of the Cause, may Serve as an ample apology, for this humble attempt. Therefore hopeing you will take it well at my hands, I persume, (tho' with the greatest Submission) to Crave your attention, while I offer you a few words.

Perhaps you will think the preceeding pages unworthy of Speculation: well, Let that be as it will; I would Sollicit you Seriously to reflect on your conduct, wheather you are not gilty of unjust Oppression. Can you wash your hands, and say, I am Clean from this Sin? Perhaps you will Dare to Say it Before men; But Dare you Say it Before the tremendous tribunal of that God Before Whome we must all, in a few precarious moments appear? then whatever fair glosses we may have put upon our Conduct, that god whose Eyes pervade the utmost Extent of human tho't, and Surveys with one intuitive view, the affairs of men; he will Examin into the matter himself, and will set Every thing upon its own Basis; and impartiallity Shall Be Seen flourishing throughout that Sollemn assembly. Alas! Shall men hazard their precious Souls for a little of the transetory things of time. O *Sirs!* Let that pity, and compassion, which is peculiar to mankind, Especially to Englishmen, no Longer Lie Dormant in your Breast: Let it run free thro' Disinterested Benevolence. then how would these iron yoaks Spontaneously fall from the gauled Necks of the oppress'd! And that Disparity, in point of Natural previlege, which is the Bane of Society, would Be Cast upon the utmost coasts of Oblivion. If this was the impulsive Exercise that animated all your actions, your Conscience's wold Be the onely Standard unto which I need appeal. think it nor uncharitable, nor Censorious to say, that whenever we Erect our Battery, so as it is Like to prove a Detriment to the intrest of any, we Loos their attention. or, if we Don't Entirely Loos that, yet if true Christian candour is wanting we cannot Be in a Sutiable frame for Speculation: So that the good Effect that these

Otherwise mite have, will prove abortive. If I could once persuade you to reflect upon the matter with a Single, and an impartial Eye, I am almost assured that no more need to be Said upon the Subject: But whether I shall Be so happy as to persuade you to Cherish such an Exercise I know not: yet I think it is very obvious from what I have humbly offer'd, that so far forth as you have Been Concerned in the *Slave-trade,* so far it is that you have assumed an oppressive, and tyrannic power. Therefore is it not hygh time to undo these heavy Burdens, and Let the Oppressed go free? And while you manifest such a noble and magnanimous Spirit, to maintain inviobly your own Natural rights, and militate so much against Despotism, as it hath respect unto yourselves, you do not assume the Same usurpations, and are no Less tyrannic. Pray let there be a congruity amidst you Conduct, Least you fall amongst that Class the inspir'd pen-man Speaks of. *Rom.* 2.21 and on. *thou therefore which teacheth another, teachest thou not thy Self? thou that preachest a man Should not Steal, Dost thou Steal? thou that sayest, a man Should not Commit adultery, Dost thou Commit adultery? thou that abhoreth idols, Dost thou Commit Sacrilege? thou that makest thy Bost of the Law, through Breaking the Law Dishonnerest thou God?* While you thus Sway your tyrant Scepter over others, you have nothing to Expect But to Share in the Bitter pill. 'Twas an Exelent note that I Lately read in a modern peice, and it was this. "O when shall America be consistantly Engaged in the Cause of Liberty!" If you have any Love to yourselves, or any Love to this Land, if you have any Love to your fellow-men, Break these intollerable yoaks, and Let their names Be remembered no more, Least they Be retorted on your own necks, and you Sink under them; for god will not hold you guiltless.

Sirs, the important Caus in which you are Engag'd in is of a[n] Exelent nature, 'tis ornamental to your Characters, and will, undoubtedly, immortalize your names thro' the Latest posterity. And it is pleasing to Behold that patriottick Zeal which fire's your Breast; But it is Strange that you Should want the Least Stimulation to further Expressions of so noble a Spirit. Some gentlemen have Determined to Contend in a Consistant manner: they have *Let the oppressed go free;* and I cannot think it is for the want of such a generous princaple in you, But thro' some inadvertancy that [end of extant manuscript].

1990

Universal Salvation[1]

Preface

There is no greater folly than for men to express anger and resentment because their religious sentiments are attacked. If their characters are impeached by their own creed, they only are to blame.

All that the antagonists can say, cannot make falsehood truth, nor truth, falsehood. The following discourse was delivered at Rutland, Vt., June, 1805, immediately after hearing Mr. Ballou, an Universal Preacher, zealously exhibit his sentiments. The author had been repeatedly solicited to hear and dispute with the above Preacher: and had been charged with dishonesty and cowardice for refusing. He felt that some kind of testimony, in opposition to what he calls error, ought to be made; and has been urged to let the same appear in print. But whether, on the whole, it is for the interest of truth, is left to the judgment of the candid.

A Sermon

Genesis 3, 4, And the serpent said unto the woman, ye shall not surely die.

The holy scriptures are a peculiar fund of instruction. They inform us of the origin of creation; of the primitive state of man; of his fall, or apostacy from God. It appears that he was placed in the garden of Eden, with full liberty to regale himself with all the delicious fruits that were to be found, except what grew on one tree—if he eat of that, that he should surely die, was the declaration of the Most High.

Happy were the human pair amidst this delightful Paradise, until a certain preacher, in his journey, came that way, and disturbed their peace and tranquility, by endeavoring to reverse the prohibition of the Almighty; as in our text, ye shall not surely die.

> She pluck'd, she ate,
> Earth felt the wound; nature from her seat,
> Sighing through all her works, gave signs of woe,
> That all was lost.
>
> MILTON[2]

We may attend,—To the character of the preacher; to the doctrines inculcated; to the hearer addressed; to the medium or instrument of the preaching.

I. As to the preacher, I shall observe, he has many names given him in the sacred writings; the most common is the devil. That it was he that disturbed the felicity of

[1]The original title of Hayne's most famous sermon is: "Universal Salvation: A Very Ancient Doctrine; With Some Account of the Life and Character of Its Author. A Sermon. Delivered at Rutland, West Parish, in the Year 1805." It is reprinted from *Black Preacher in White America,* ed. Richard Newman; the copy was taken directly from the manuscript held by the Schomberg Center for Research in Black Culture.

[2]John Milton, *Paradise Lost,* Book 9, lines 781–784.

our first parents, is evident from 2 Cor. 11:3, and many other passages of Scripture. He was once an angel of light and knew better than to preach such doctrine; he did violence to his own reason.—But to be a little more particular, let it be observed:

1. He is an old preacher. He lived above one thousand seven hundred years before Abraham; above two thousand four hundred and thirty years before Moses; four thousand and four years before Christ. It is now five thousand eight hundred and nine years since he commenced preaching. By this time he must have acquired great skill in the art.

2. He is a very cunning, artful preacher. When Elymas the sorcerer, came to turn away people from the faith, he is said to be full of all subtlety, and a child of the devil, not only because he was an enemy to all righteousness, but on account of his carnal cunning and craftiness.[3]

3. He is a very laborious, unweried preacher. He has been in the ministry almost six thousand years; and yet his zeal has not in the least abated. The apostle Peter compares him to a roaring lion, walking about seeking whom he may devour. When God inquired of this persevering preacher, Job 2:2, From whence camest thou? He answered the Lord, and said, From going to and fro in the earth, and from walking up and down in it. He is far from being circumscribed within the narrow limits of parish, state, or continental lines; but his haunt and travel is very large and extensive.

4. He is a heterogeneous preacher, if I may so express myself. He makes use of a Bible when he holds forth, as in his sermon to our Saviour; Matt. 4:6. He mixes truth with error, in order to make it go well, or to carry his point.

5. He is a very presumptuous preacher. Notwithstanding God had declared, in the most plain and positive terms, Thou shalt surely die, or In dying, thou shalt die, yet this audacious wretch had the impudence to confront omnipotence, and says ye shall not surely die!

6. He is a very successful preacher. He draws a great number after him. No preacher can command hearers like him. He was successful with our first parents, with the old world. Noah once preached to those spirits who are now in the prison of hell; and told them from God, that they should surely die;[4] but this preacher came along and declared the contrary, ye shall not surely die. The greater part it seems believed him and went to destruction. So it was with Sodom and Gomorrah. Lot preached to them; the substance of which was, up, get ye out of this place, for the Lord will destroy this city. Gen. 19:14. But this old declaimer told them, no danger, no danger, ye shall not surely die. To which they generally gave heed, and Lot seemed to them as one who mocked; they believed the universal preacher, and were consumed. Agreeably to the declaration of the apostle Jude, Sodom and Gomorrah and the cities about them, suffering the vengeance of eternal fire.

II. Let us attend to the doctrine inculcated by this preacher; ye shall not surely die. Bold assertion! without a single argument to support it. The death contained in the threatening was doubtless eternal death,—as nothing but this would express God's feelings towards sin, or render an infinite atonement necessary. To suppose it to be spiritual death, is to blend crime and punishment together; to suppose temporal

[3]See Acts 13:8.

[4]Noah and his family were the only ones saved when God decided to destroy the earth because of the wickedness he saw among people. See Genesis 6.

death to be the curse of the law, then believers are not delivered from it, according to Gal. 3:13. What Satan meant to preach, was that there is no hell, and that the wages of sin is not death, but eternal life.

III. We shall now take notice of the hearer addressed by the preacher. This we have in the text, And the serpent said unto the woman, etc. That Eve had not so much experience as Adam, is evident; and so was not equally able to withstand temptation. This doubtless was the reason why the devil chose her, with whom he might hope to be successful. Doubtless he took a time when she was separated from her husband.

That this preacher has had the greatest success in the dark and ignorant parts of the earth, is evident: his kingdom is a kingdom of darkness. He is a great enemy to light. St. Paul gives us some account of him in his day, 2 Tim. 3:6. For of this sort are they which creep into houses, and lead captive silly women, laden with sin led away with divers lusts. The same apostle observes, Rom. 16:17, 18. Now I beseech you, brethren, mark them which cause divisions and offences, contrary to the doctrine which ye have learned, and avoid them. For they that are such serve not the Lord Jesus Christ, but their own belly; and by good words and fair speeches deceive the simple.

IV. The instrument or medium made use of by the preacher will now be considered. This we have in the text: And the serpent said etc. But how came the devil to preach through the serpent?

1. To save his own character, and the better to carry his point. Had the devil come to our first parents personally and unmasked, they would have more easily seen the deception. The reality of a future punishment is at times so clearly impressed on the human mind, that even Satan is constrained to own that there is a hell; altho' at other times he denies it. He does not wish to have it known that he is a liar; therefore he conceals himself, that he may the better accomplish his designs, and save his own character.

2. The devil is an enemy to all good, to all happiness and excellence. He is opposed to the felicity of the brutes. He took delight in tormenting the swine. The serpent, before he set up preaching Universal Salvation, was a cunning, beautiful, and happy creature; but now his glory is departed; for the Lord said unto the serpent, because thou hast done this, thou art cursed above all cattle, and above every beast of the field, upon thy belly shalt thou go, and dust shalt thou eat all the days of thy life. There is therefore, a kind of duplicate cunning in the matter, Satan gets the preacher and hearers also.

> And is not this triumphant flattery,
> And more than simple conquest in the foe?
>
> YOUNG[5]

3. Another reason why Satan employs instruments in his service is, because his empire is large and he cannot be every where himself.

[5]From Edward Young (1683–1765), *Night Thoughts on Life, Death, and Immortality: In Nine Nights* (1742–1746), "Night Five," a defense of Christian orthodoxy against free-thinkers. The actual lines are: "And is not this triumphant treachery,/And more than simple conquest, in the fiend?"

4. He has a large number at his command, that love and approve of his work, delight in building up his kingdom, and stand ready to go at his call.

Inferences

1. The devil is not dead, but still lives; and is able to preach as well as ever, ye shall not surely die.

2. Universal Salvation is no new fangled scheme, but can boast of great antiquity.

3. See a reason why it ought to be rejected, because it is an ancient devilish doctrine.

4. See one reason why it is that Satan is such an enemy to the Bible, and to all who preach the gospel, because of that injunction, And he said unto them, go ye into all the world, and preach the gospel to every creature. He that believeth and is baptized shall be saved; but he that believeth not shall be damned.

5. See whence it was that Satan exerted himself so much to convince our first parents that there was no hell; because the denunciation of the Almighty was true, and he was afraid they would continue in the belief of it. Was there no truth in future punishment, or was it only a temporary evil, Satan would not be so busy, in trying to convince men that there is none. It is his nature and his element to lie. When he speaketh a lie, he speaketh of his own; for he is a liar, and the father of it.

6. We infer that ministers should not be proud of their preaching. If they preach the true gospel, they only, in substance, repeat Christ's sermons; if they preach ye shall not surely die, they only make use of the devil's old notes, that he delivered almost six thousand years ago.

7. It is probable that the doctrine of Universal Salvation will still prevail, since this preacher is yet alive, and not in the least superannuated; and every effort against him only enrages him more and more, and excites him to new inventions and exertions to build up his cause.

To close the subject: As the author of the foregoing discourse has confined himself wholly to the character of Satan, he trusts no one will feel himself personally injured by this short sermon: But should any imbibe a degree of friendship for this aged divine, and think that I have not treated this Universal Preacher with that respect and veneration which he justly deserves, let them be so kind as to point it out, and I will most cheerfully retract; for it has ever been a maxim with me, render unto all their dues.

1805

Joel Barlow 1754–1812

Joel Barlow aspired to write the great American epic and did so repeatedly, with his *Prospect of Peace* (1778), *The Vision of Columbus* (1787), and *The Columbiad* (1807). Yet he remains best remembered for his mock-heroic poem about his Connecticut childhood, *The Hasty Pudding* (1796). Barlow's accomplishments as poet, chaplain, newspaper editor, bookseller, real estate agent, publisher, and diplomat are impressive, but his simple celebration of American domesticity stands as his most endearing literary contribution.

Joel Barlow was born the eighth of nine children on a 170-acre farm in Redding, Connecticut, on March 24, 1754. His father, Samuel Barlow, was a wealthy farmer; his mother, Esther Hull, was a local Redding resident and Samuel's second wife. Joel Barlow left home when he was nineteen to attend college at Moor's Indian School at Hanover, New Hampshire, founded by Eleazar Wheelock, who characterized Barlow as a "middling scholar" possessed of "sober, regular, and good Behavior." In August 1774, he enrolled at Dartmouth College, but three months later his father died, and Barlow used his portion of the estate, about £100, to transfer to Yale in November. Shortly before he returned to Yale for his sophomore year, his mother died. In the summer of 1776, Barlow enlisted in the Continental Army to fight in the Battle of Long Island. On July 23, 1778, he graduated from Yale and, as class poet, read *The Prospect of Peace,* a patriotic tribute to the struggle for independence written in rhyming pairs of iambic pentameter known as heroic couplets. The style was significant, for as Timothy Steele reminds us, iambic pentameter was considered "the English measure most suitable for epic subjects," adopted accordingly by Milton for *Paradise Lost,* Dryden for his translation of Virgil, and Pope for his translation of Homer. Barlow clearly embraced the epic style of emulating the heroic couplets of Dryden and Pope in *The Prospect of Peace,* and in a later poem, *The Vision of Columbus* (1787), which opens with Columbus in prison at the end of his life and relays his vision for a New World founded, somewhat controversially, upon its indigenous inheritance. According to Cecelia Tichi, Barlow's major writings mythologize America as a "nation destined to begin a global epoch of transcendent peace and progress." For this ambitious plan, Barlow's use of the epic style and heroic couplet to narrate America's founding seems particularly appropriate.

Immediately after graduation, Barlow accepted a position as a schoolmaster, but changed his mind and, after borrowing money from his older brother Nathaniel, returned to Yale for a master's degree in theology. In 1779, he began boarding at the home of Michael Baldwin, blacksmith and father of his college friend Abraham Baldwin. Barlow became romantically involved with two women at this time, Ruth Baldwin, his landlord's daughter, and Elizabeth Whitman, a respected local poet. (Ten years later, Whitman died, a single woman, after giving birth to a stillborn child at the Bell Tavern in Danvers, Massachusetts. Her life was supposedly the model for Hannah Foster's 1797 sentimental novel, *The Coquette.*) Michael Baldwin was apparently unimpressed with Barlow's financial potential and sent his daughter off to the family home in Guilford, Connecticut. Barlow and Baldwin became secretly engaged, a risky decision because it was a misdemeanor in Connecticut for a woman to be betrothed without her father's consent. They married secretly in January 1781. Despite these complicated beginnings, the Barlows were happily married for thirty-one years.

During the 1780s, a group of Hartford

writers, all Yale graduates, began collaborating on verse and prose works addressing various local controversies. Initially called the "Wicked Wits," later the "Connecticut Wits," the group included Barlow, Timothy Dwight, John Trumbull, David Humphreys, Noah Webster, and Lemuel Hopkins. Their best-known composition is a mock-heroic epic, *The Anarchiad: A Poem on the Restoration of Chaos and Substantial Night* (1786–1787), directed against Daniel Shays and the general political unrest that followed the Revolutionary War. From 1780 to 1783, Barlow served as chaplain for the Third Massachusetts Brigade. In 1784, he founded the *American Mercury,* a weekly newspaper, with Elisha Babcock. The paper enjoyed a solid reputation but was financially troubled, causing Barlow to leave a year later and open a bookstore. In 1787, after eight years of composition, *The Vision of Columbus* was published in nine books with over 5,000 lines of heroic couplets. It was successfully received, and Barlow enjoyed immediate celebrity. He had been admitted to the bar in 1786, but law was not to be a lasting profession, for in 1788 he set sail for Europe as an agent for the Ohio-based Scioto Land Company. The trip was to have been a short one, but Barlow and his wife (who joined him in 1790) remained abroad until 1804.

Throughout the 1790s, the Barlows became patrons of the arts and actively involved in European culture and politics. From his associations with such prominent figures as Thomas Paine, Mary Wollstonecraft, and Thomas Jefferson, Barlow became more politically liberal and even assisted in publishing Paine's *The Age of Reason* (1794). The once-conservative Yale graduate began to embrace a more radicalized, anti-monarchical philosophy that forced a break from earlier colleagues, such as Dwight, who allegedly ordered Barlow's portrait removed from Yale. In 1792, Barlow became an honorary citizen of France. While he was campaigning for a seat in the French National Assembly, he was offered a dish of cornmeal mush. The gift of this American food prompted the nostalgic, mock-heroic, *The Hasty Pudding* (1793). His next project was *The Columbiad* (1807), a revised version of *The Vision of Columbus,* more consonant with Barlow's deistic beliefs and embrace of Jeffersonian republicanism.

Although Barlow supported the French Revolution, the Reign of Terror that followed caused him to leave France. In his position as U.S. consul to Algiers from 1795 to 1797, Barlow secured the release of over one hundred American seamen who had been taken hostage by pirates. He also negotiated treaties with Algiers, Tripoli, and Tunis. In 1811, President James Madison appointed Barlow minister plenipotentiary to France and sent him to negotiate a treaty with Napoleon. Barlow wrote his final poem, *Advice to a Raven in Russia,* in 1812 after witnessing the horrors of Napoleon's ill-fated Russian campaign. After Napoleon's defeat at Moscow, Barlow's delegation attempted to outrun pursuing Russian troops. Barlow traveled in a carriage for ten days, fifteen hours each day, in sub-zero temperatures. He died of pneumonia in Zarnowiec, Poland, near Cracow, on December 26, 1812. His body remains buried there.

Susan Clair Imbarrato
Minnesota State University–Moorhead

PRIMARY WORKS

Poems: *The Prospect of Peace,* 1778; *Poem, Spoken at the Public Commencement at Yale College,* 1781; *The Conspiracy of Kings,* 1792; *The Hasty Pudding,* 1793; *Advice to a Raven in Russia,* written 1812, published 1938. Multi-book "epic" poems: *The Vision of Columbus,* 1787; *The Columbiad,* 1807. Prose tracts: *Advice to the Privileged Orders in the Several States of Europe, Resulting from the Necessity and Propriety of a General Revolution in the Principle of Government,* 1792.

The Prospect of Peace[1]

The closing scenes of Tyrants' fruitless rage,
The opening prospects of a golden age,
The dread events that crown th' important year,
Wake the glad song, and claim th' attentive ear.
Long has Columbia rung with dire alarms,
While Freedom call'd her injur'd sons to arms;
While various fortune fir'd th' embattled field,
Conquest delay'd, and victory stood conceal'd;
While closing legions mark'd their dreadful way,
And Millions trembled for the dubious day.
In this grand conflict heaven's Eternal Sire,
At whose dread frown the sons of guilt expire,
Bade vengeance rise, with sacred fury driven,
On those who war with Innocence and Heaven.
Behold, where late the trembling squadrons fled,
Hosts bow'd in chains, and hapless numbers bled,
In different fields our numerous heroes rouse,
To crop the wreath from Britain's impious brows.
Age following age shall these events relate
'Till Time's old empire yield to destin'd Fate;
Historic truth our guardian chiefs proclaim,
Their worth, their actions, and their deathless fame;
Admiring crouds their life-touch'd forms behold
In breathing canvass, or in sculptur'd gold,
And hail the Leader of the favorite throng,
The rapt'rous theme of some heroic song.
And soon, emerging from the orient skies,
The blisful morn in glorious pomp shall rise,
Wafting fair Peace from Europe's fated coast;
Where wand'ring long, in mazy factions lost,
From realm to realm, by rage and discord driven,
She seem'd resolv'd to reascend her heaven.
This LEWIS view'd, and reach'd a friendly hand,[2]
Pointing her flight to this far-distant land;
Bade her extend her empire o'er the West,
And Europe's balance tremble on her crest!
Now, see the Goddess mounting on the day,[3]

[1]On July 23, 1778, Barlow, the class poet, delivered this poem at Yale's commencement. A local New Haven printer, Joseph Buckminster, immediately published it in pamphlet form. The text has been slightly modernized and taken from the first edition.

[2]France's King Louis XVI (1754–1793) provided naval and monetary aid to the American colonies during the Revolutionary War.

[3]Aurora or Eos is the goddess of dawn.

To these fair climes direct her circling way,
Willing to seek, once more, an earthly throne,
To cheer the globe, and emulate the sun.
With placid look she eyes the blissful shore,
Bids the loud-thundering cannon cease to roar;
Bids British navies from these ports be tost,
And hostile keels no more insult the coast;
Bids private feuds her sacred vengeance feel,
And bow submissive to the public weal;
Bids long, calm years adorn the happy clime,
And roll down blessings to remotest time.
Hail! heaven-born Peace, fair Nurse of Virtue hail!
Here, fix thy sceptre and exalt thy scale;
Hence, thro' the earth extend thy late domain,
'Till Heaven's own splendor shall absorb thy reign!
What scenes arise! what glories we behold!
See a broad realm its various charms unfold;
See crouds of patriots bless the happy land,
A godlike senate and a warlike band;
One friendly Genius fires the numerous whole,[4]
From glowing Georgia to the frozen pole.
Along these shores, amid these flowery vales,
The woodland shout the joyous ear assails;
Industrious crouds in different labors toil,
Those ply the arts, and these improve the soil.
Here the fond merchant counts his rising gain,
There strides the rustic o'er the furrow'd plain,
Here walks the statesman, pensive and serene,
And there the school boys gambol round the green.
See ripening harvests gild the smiling plains,
Kind Nature's bounty and the pride of swains;
Luxuriant vines their curling tendrils shoot,
And bow their heads to drop the clustering fruit;
In the gay fields, with rich profusion strow'd,
The orchard bends beneath its yellow load,
The lofty boughs their annual burden pour,
And juicy harvests swell th' autumnal store.
These are the blessings of impartial Heaven,
To each fond heart in just proportion given.
No grasping lord shall grind the neighbouring poor,
Starve numerous vassals to increase his store;
No cringing slave shall at his presence bend,
Shrink at his frown, and at his nod attend;
Afric's unhappy children, now no more

[4]The light of American Genius spread by poets will lead America to her destiny.

Shall feel the cruel chains they felt before,
But every State in this just mean agree,
To bless mankind, and set th' oppressed free.
Then, rapt in transport, each exulting slave
Shall taste that Boon which God and nature gave,
And, fir'd with virtue, join the common cause,
Protect our freedom and enjoy our laws.
At this calm period, see, in pleasing view,
Art vies with Art, and Nature smiles anew:
On the long, winding strand that meets the tide,
Unnumber'd cities lift their spiry pride;
Gay, flowery walks salute th' inraptur'd eyes,
Tall, beauteous domes in dazzling prospect rise;
There thronging navies stretch their wanton sails,
Tempt the broad main and catch the driving gales;
There commerce swells from each remotest shore,
And wafts in plenty to the smiling store.
To these throng'd seats the country wide resorts,
And rolls her treasures to the op'ning ports;
While, far remote, gay health and pleasure flow,
And calm retirement cheers the laboring brow.
No din of arms the peaceful patriot hears,
No parting sigh the tender matron fears,
No field of fame invites the youth to rove,
Nor virgins know a harsher sound than love.
Fair Science then her laurel'd beauty rears,
And soars with Genius to the radiant stars.
Her glimmering dawn from Gothic darkness rose,
And nations saw her shadowy veil disclose;
She cheer'd fair Europe with her rising smiles,
Beam'd a bright morning o'er the British isles,
Now soaring reaches her meridian height,
And blest Columbia hails the dazzling light!
Here, rapt in tho't, the philosophic soul
Shall look thro' Nature's parts and grasp the whole.
See Genius kindling at a FRANKLIN's fame,
See unborn sages catch th' electric flame,
Bid hovering clouds the threatening blast expire,
Curb the fierce stream and hold th' imprison'd fire!
See the pleas'd youth, with anxious study, rove,
In orbs excentric thro' the realms above,
No more perplex'd, while RITTENHOUSE appears
To grace the museum with the rolling spheres.[5]

[5]Lines 115–124 mark scientific advancements. Benjamin Franklin (1706–1790) and David Rittenhouse (1732–1796) were leading scientists and members of the American Philosophical Society. Franklin is credited with the discovery of electricity and Rittenhouse as an early observer of Venus's atmosphere.

See that young Genius, that inventive soul,
Whose laws the jarring elements control;
Who guides the vengeance of mechanic power,
To blast the watery world & guard the peaceful shore.
And where's the rising Sage, the unknown name,
That new advent'rer in the lists of fame,
To find the cause, in secret nature bound,
The unknown cause, and various charms of sound?
What subtil medium leads the devious way;
Why different tensions different sounds convey;
Why harsh, rough tones in grating discord roll,
Or mingling concert charms th' enraptur'd soul.
And tell the cause why sluggish vapors rise,
And wave, exalted, thro' the genial skies;
What strange contrivance nature forms to bear
The ponderous burden thro' the lighter air.
These last Displays the curious mind engage,
And fire the genius of the rising age;
While moral tho'ts the pleas'd attention claim,
Swell the warm soul, and wake the virtuous flame;
While Metaphysics soar a boundless height,
And launch with EDWARDS[6] to the realms of light.
See the blest Muses hail their roseate bowers,
Their mansions blooming with poetic flowers;
See listening Seraphs join the epic throng,
And unborn JOSHUAS[7] rise in future song.
Satire attends at Virtue's wakening call,
And Pride and Coquetry and Dulness fall.
Unnumber'd bards shall string the heavenly lyre,
To those blest strains which heavenly themes inspire;
Sing the rich Grace on mortal Man bestow'd,
The Virgin's Offspring and the *filial God*;
What love descends from heaven when JESUS dies!
What shouts attend him rising thro' the skies!
See Science now in lovelier charms appear,
Grac'd with new garlands from the blooming Fair.
See laurel'd nymphs in polish'd pages shine,
And Sapphic sweetness glow in every line.
No more the rougher Muse shall dare disgrace
The radiant charms that deck the blushing face;
But rising Beauties scorn the tinsel show,
The powder'd coxcomb and the flaunting beau;
While humble Merit, void of flattering wiles,

[6]Lines 141–146: In this new millenium, science and religion will harmoniously co-exist; Jonathan Edwards (1703–1758).

[7]Joshua was the biblical warrior who led Israel in the conquest of Canaan.

Claims the soft glance, and wakes th' enlivening smiles.
The opening lustre of an angel-mind,
Beauty's bright charms with sense superior join'd,
Bid Virtue shine, bid Truth and Goodness rise,
Melt from the voice, and sparkle from the eyes;
While the pleas'd Muse the gentle bosom warms,
The first in genius, as the first in charms.
Thus age and youth a smiling aspect wear,
Aw'd into virtue by the leading Fair;
While the bright offspring, rising to the stage,
Conveys the blessings to the future age.
  THESE are the views that Freedom's cause attend;
THESE shall endure 'till Time and Nature end.
With Science crown'd, shall Peace and Virtue shine,
And blest Religion beam a light divine.
Here the pure Church, descending from her God,
Shall fix on earth her long and last abode;
Zion arise, in radiant splendors dress'd,
By Saints admir'd, by Infidels confess'd;
Her opening courts, in dazzling glory, blaze,
Her walls salvation, and her portals praise.
  From each far corner of th' extended earth,
Her gathering sons shall claim their promis'd birth.
Thro' the drear wastes, beneath the setting day,
Where prowling natives haunt the wood for prey,
The swarthy Millions lift their wondring eyes,
And smile to see the Gospel morning rise:
Those who, thro' time, in savage darkness lay,
Wake to new light, and hail the glorious day!
In those dark regions, those uncultur'd wilds,
Fresh blooms the rose, the peaceful lilly smiles.
On the tall cliffs unnumber'd *Carmels* rise,[8]
And in each vale some beauteous *Sharon* lies.[9]
  From this fair Mount th' excinded stone shall roll,
Reach the far East and spread from pole to pole;
From one small Stock shall countless nations rise,
The world replenish and adorn the skies.
Earth's blood-stain'd empires, with their Guide the Sun,
From orient climes their gradual progress run;
And circling far, reach every western shore,
'Till earth-born empires rise and fall no more.
But see th' imperial GUIDE from heaven descend,

[8]Mt. Carmel, in northwestern Israel, is considered a holy place by many religions; for Christians it marks the scene of Elijah's confrontation with the false prophets of Baal.

[9]The Plain of Sharon, a coastal plain in Israel along the Mediterranean noted for its fertility and dense forests from antiquity to the eighteenth century.

Whose beams are Peace, whose kingdom knows no end;
From calm Vesperia, thro' th' etherial way,[10]
Back sweep the shades before th' effulgent day;
Thro' the broad East, the brightening splendor driven,
Reverses Nature and illumins heaven;
Astonish'd regions bless the gladdening sight,
And Suns and Systems own superior light.
As when th' asterial blaze o'er Bethl'em stood,
Which mark'd the birth-place of th' incarnate God;
When eastern priests the heavenly splendor view'd,
And numerous crouds the wonderous sign pursu'd:
So eastern kings shall view th' unclouded day
Rise in the West and streak its golden way:
That signal spoke a Savior's humble birth,
This speaks his long and glorious reign on earth!
THEN Love shall rule, and Innocence adore,
Discord shall cease, and Tyrants be no more;
'Till yon bright orb, and those celestial spheres,
In radiant circles, mark a thousand years;
'Till the grand *fiat* burst th' etherial frames,
Worlds crush on worlds, and Nature sink in flames!
The Church elect, from smouldering ruins, rise,
And sail triumphant thro' the yielding skies,
Hail'd by the Bridegroom! to the Father given,
The Joy of Angels, and the Queen of Heaven!

1778

[10]Vesperia, a variant of the Latin *vesper* and Greek *vesperus,* to denote Venus when it is the evening star.

The Hasty Pudding

A Poem, in Three Cantos[1]

Omne tulit punctum qui miscuit utile dulci.[2]
He makes a good breakfast who mixes pudding with molasses.

Canto I

Ye Alps audacious, thro' the Heavens that rise,
To cramp the day and hide me from the skies;
Ye Gallic flags, that o'er their heights unfurl'd,[3]
Bear death to kings, and freedom to the world,
I sing not you. A softer theme I chuse,
A virgin theme, unconscious of the Muse,
But fruitful, rich, well suited to inspire
The purest frenzy of poetic fire.
  Despise it not, ye Bards to terror steel'd,
Who hurl'd your thunders round the epic field;
Nor ye who strain your midnight throats to sing
Joys that the vineyard and the still-house[4] bring;
Or on some distant fair[5] your notes employ,
And speak of raptures that you ne'er enjoy.
I sing the sweets I know, the charms I feel,
My morning incense, and my evening meal,
The sweets of Hasty-Pudding. Come, dear bowl,
Glide o'er my palate, and inspire my soul.
The milk beside thee, smoking from the kine,[6]
Its substance mingled, married in with thine,
Shall cool and temper thy superior heat,
And save the pains of blowing while I eat.
  Oh! could the smooth, the emblematic song
Flow like thy genial juices o'er my tongue,
Could those mild morsels in my numbers[7] chime,
And, as they roll in substance, roll in rhyme,
No more thy aukward unpoetic name

[1]Written at an inn at Chambéry, Savoy, a region of France, in 1792 after Barlow had been served a dish of cornmeal mush, or hasty pudding as it was called in New England. It is a mock-heroic, a form of satire that adapts the classical epic, heroic style to a trivial subject. The poem was published in France in 1793; the text printed here is from the first American edition, 1796.

[2]Latin, from Horace (65–8 B.C.), *The Art of Poetry* (8? B.C.): "He who combines the useful and the pleasing wins the approval of all."

[3]French flags. Savoy, once part of Sardinia, was annexed by France in 1792.

[4]A distillery.

[5]Fair lady.

[6]Cattle.

[7]Meter, metrical verse.

Should shun the Muse, or prejudice thy fame;
But rising grateful to the accustom'd ear,
All Bards should catch it, and all realms revere!
Assist me first with pious toil to trace
Thro' wrecks of time thy lineage and thy race;
Declare what lovely squaw, in days of yore,
(Ere great Columbus sought thy native shore)
First gave thee to the world; her works of fame
Have liv'd indeed, but liv'd without a name.
Some tawny Ceres, goddess of her days,[8]
First learn'd with stones to crack the well-dry'd maize,
Thro' the rough sieve to shake the golden show'r,
In boiling water stir the yellow flour.
The yellow flour, bestrew'd and stir'd with haste,
Swells in the flood and thickens to a paste,
Then puffs and wallops,[9] rises to the brim,
Drinks the dry knobs that on the surface swim:
The knobs at last the busy ladle breaks,
And the whole mass its true consistence takes.
Could but her sacred name, unknown so long,
Rise like her labors, to the sons of song,
To her, to them, I'd consecrate my lays,
And blow her pudding with the breath of praise.
If 'twas Oella,[10] whom I sang before,
I here ascribe her one great virtue more.
Not thro' the rich Peruvian realms alone
The fame of Sol's sweet daughter should be known,
But o'er the world's wide climes should live secure,
Far as his rays extend, as long as they endure.
Dear Hasty-Pudding, what unpromis'd joy
Expands my heart, to meet thee in Savoy!
Doom'd o'er the world thro' devious paths to roam,
Each clime my country, and each house my home,
My soul is sooth'd, my cares have found an end,
I greet my long-lost, unforgotten friend.
For thee thro' Paris, that corrupted town,
How long in vain I wandered up and down,
Where shameless Bacchus,[11] with his drenching hoard
Cold from his cave usurps the morning board.
London is lost in smoke and steep'd in tea;
No Yankey there can lisp the name of thee:
The uncouth word, a libel on the town,

[8] Ceres, the Roman goddess of agriculture and grain.

[9] Boils and bubbles.

[10] Oella, a legendary Inca Indian, daughter of Sol, the sun, and inventor of spinning. Oella is also cited in Barlow's *Vision of Columbus* (1787).

[11] Bacchus or Dionysus is the Greek and Roman god of wine.

Would call a proclamation from the crown.[12]
For climes oblique, that fear the sun's full rays,
Chill'd in their fogs, exclude the generous maize;
A grain whose rich luxuriant growth requires
Short gentle showers, and bright etherial fires.
But here tho' distant from our native shore,
With mutual glee we meet and laugh once more,
The same! I know thee by that yellow face,
That strong complexion of true Indian race,
Which time can never change, nor soil impair,
Nor Alpine snows, nor Turkey's morbid air;
For endless years, thro' every mild domain,
Where grows the maize, there thou art sure to reign.
But man; more fickle, the bold licence claims,
In different realms to give thee different names.
Thee the soft nations round the warm Levant[13]
Palanta call, the French of course *Polante;*[14]
E'en in thy native regions, how I blush
To hear the Pennsylvanians call thee Mush!
On Hudson's banks, while men of Belgic spawn[15]
Insult and eat thee by the name *suppawn.*[16]
All spurious appellations, void of truth:
I've better known thee from my earliest youth,
Thy name is *Hasty-Pudding!* thus our sires
Were wont to greet thee fuming from their fires;
And while they argu'd in thy just defence
With logic clear, they thus explained the sense:—
"In *haste* the boiling cauldron o'er the blaze,
"Receives and cooks the ready-powder'd maize;
"In *haste* 'tis serv'd, and then in equal *haste,*
"With cooling milk, we make the sweet repast.
"No carving to be done, no knife to grate
"The tender ear, and wound the stony plate;
"But the smooth spoon, just fitted to the lip,
"And taught with art the yielding mass to dip,
"By frequent journies to the bowl well stor'd,
"Performs the hasty honors of the board."
Such is thy name, significant and clear,
A name, a sound to every Yankey dear,
But most to me, whose heart and palate chaste

[12]A certain king, at the time when this was written, was publishing proclamations to prevent American principles from being propagated in his country. [Barlow's note. The king is England's George III.]

[13]Eastern Mediterranean coast.

[14]Italian and French words for cooked cornmeal.

[15]Of Dutch ancestry.

[16]Algonkian Indian name for mush.

Preserve my pure hereditary taste.
There are who strive to stamp with disrepute
The luscious food, because it feeds the brute;
In tropes of high-strain'd wit, while gaudy prigs
Compare thy nursling man to pamper'd pigs;
With sovereign scorn I treat the vulgar jest,
Nor fear to share thy bounties with the beast.
What though the generous cow gives me to quaff
The milk nutritious; am I then a calf?
Or can the genius of the noisy swine,
Tho' nurs'd on pudding, thence lay claim to mine?
Sure the sweet song, I fashion to thy praise,
Runs more melodious than the notes they raise.
My song resounding in its grateful glee,
No merit claims; I praise myself in thee.
My father lov'd thee through his length of days:
For thee his fields were shaded o'er with maize;
From thee what health, what vigour he possest,
Ten sturdy freemen sprung from him attest;
Thy constellation rul'd my natal morn,
And all my bones were made of Indian corn.
Delicious grain! whatever form it take,
To roast or boil, to smother or to bake,
In every dish 'tis welcome still to me,
But most, my Hasty-Pudding, most in thee.
Let the green Succatash with thee contend,
Let beans and corn their sweetest juices blend,
Let butter drench them in its yellow tide,
And a long slice of bacon grace their side;
Not all the plate, how fam'd soe'er it be,
Can please my palate like a bowl of thee.
Some talk of Hoe-cake,[17] fair Virginia's pride,
Rich Johnny-cake[18] this mouth has often tri'd;
Both please me well, their virtues much the same;
Alike their fabric, as allied their fame,
Except in dear New-England, were the last
Receives a dash of pumpkin in the paste,
To give it sweetness and improve the taste.
But place them all before me, smoaking hot,
The big round dumplin rolling from the pot;
The pudding of the bag, whose quivering breast,
With suet lin'd leads on the Yankey feast;
The Charlotte[19] brown, within whose crusty sides

[17]Cornmeal, water, and salt batter baked on a hoe blade over an open fire.

[18]A lighter variation consisting of cornmeal, wheat flour, eggs, and milk.

[19]A fruit-filled dessert cake or custard.

A belly soft the pulpy apple hides;
The yellow bread, whose face like amber glows,
And all of Indian that the bake-pan knows—
You tempt me not—my fav'rite greets my eyes,
To that lov'd bowl my spoon by instinct flies.

Canto II

To mix the food by vicious rules of art,
To kill the stomach and to sink the heart,
To make mankind, to social virtue sour,
Cram o'er each dish, and be what they devour;
For this the kitchen Muse first framed her book,
Commanding sweats to stream from every cook;
Children no more their antic gambols tried,
And friends to physic[20] wonder'd why they died.
Not so the Yankey—his abundant feast,
With simples[21] furnished, and with plainness drest,
A numerous offspring gathers round the board,
And cheers alike the servant and the lord;
Whose well-bought hunger prompts the joyous taste,
And health attends them from the short repast.
While the full pail rewards the milk-maid's toil,
The mother sees the morning cauldron boil;
To stir the pudding next demands their care,
To spread the table and the bowls prepare;
To feed the children, as their portions cool,
And comb their heads, and send them off to school.
Yet may the simplest dish, some rules impart,
For nature scorns not all the aids of art.
E'en Hasty-Pudding, purest of all food,
May still be bad, indifferent, or good,
As sage experience the short process guides,
Or want of skill, or want of care presides.
Whoe'er would form it on the surest plan,
To rear the child and long sustain the man;
To shield the morals while it mends the size,
And all the powers of every food supplies,
Attend the lessons that the Muse shall bring,
Suspend your spoons, and listen while I sing.
But since, O man! thy life and health demand
Not food alone, but labour from thy hand,
First in the field, beneath the sun's strong rays,
Ask of thy mother earth the needful maize;
She loves the race that courts her yielding soil,

[20]Science or medicine.

[21]Herbs.

And gives her bounties to the sons of toil.
When now the ox, obedient to thy call,
Repays the loan that fill'd the winter stall,
Pursue his traces o'er the furrow'd plain,
And plant in measur'd hills the golden grain.
But when the tender germe begins to shoot,
And the green spire declares the sprouting root,
Then guard your nursling from each greedy foe,
Th' insidious worm, the all-devouring crow.
A little ashes, sprinkled round the spire,
Soon steep'd in rain, will bid the worm retire;
The feather'd robber with his hungry maw
Swift flies the field before your man of straw,
A frightful image, such as school boys bring
When met to burn the Pope, or hang the King.[22]
Thrice in the season, through each verdant row
Wield the strong plough-share and the faithful hoe;
The faithful hoe, a double task that takes,
To till the summer corn, and roast the winter cakes.[23]
Slow springs the blade, while check'd by chilling rains,
Ere yet the sun the seat of Cancer[24] gains;
But when his fiercest fires emblaze the land,
Then start the juices, then the roots expand;
Then, like a column of Corinthian[25] mould,
The stalk struts upward, and the leaves unfold;
The bushy branches all the ridges fill,
Entwine their arms, and kiss from hill to hill.
Here cease to vex them, all your cares are done;
Leave the last labours to the parent sun;
Beneath his genial smiles the well-drest field,
When autumn calls, a plenteous crop shall yield.
Now the strong foliage bears the standards high,
And shoots the tall top-gallants[26] to the sky;
The suckling ears their silky fringes bend,
And pregnant grown, their swelling coats distend;
The loaded stalk, while still the burthen grows,
O'erhangs the space that runs between the rows;
High as a hop-field waves the silent grove,

[22]In England, Guy Fawkes Day on November 5 marks the anniversary of the uncovering in 1605 of a Roman Catholic plot to blow up the king and Parliament. Effigies of the pope, Fawkes, and others are burned. Anti-Catholic sentiment gave way to anti-monarchical protest, and thus Barlow's allusion to King Louis XVI.

[23]Hoecakes.

[24]Zodiac sign that marks the summer solstice, June 21.

[25]Greek column embellished with leaves.

[26]A ship's upper masts and sails.

A safe retreat for little thefts of love,
When the pledg'd roasting-ears invite the maid,
To meet her swain beneath the new-form'd shade;
His generous hand unloads the cumbrous hill,
And the green spoils her ready basket fill;
Small compensation for the two-fold bliss,
The promis'd wedding and the present kiss.
Slight depredations these; but now the moon
Calls from his hollow tree the sly raccoon;
And while by night he bears the prize away,
The bolder squirrel labours through the day.
Both thieves alike, but provident of time,
A virtue, rare, that almost hides their crime.
Then let them steal the little stores they can,
And fill their gran'ries from the toils of man;
We've one advantage where they take no part,—
With all their wiles they ne'er have found the art
To boil the Hasty-Pudding; here we shine
Superior far to tenants of the pine;
This envied boon to man shall still belong,
Unshar'd by them in substance or in song.
At last the closing season browns the plain,
And ripe October gathers in the grain;
Deep loaded carts the spacious corn-house fill,
The sack distended marches to the mill;
The lab'ring mill beneath the burthen groans,
And show'rs the future pudding from the stones;[27]
Till the glad house-wife greets the powder'd gold,
And the new crop exterminates the old.

Canto III

The days grow short; but tho' the falling sun
To the glad swain proclaims his day's work done,
Night's pleasing shades his various task prolong,
And yield new subjects to my various song.
For now, the corn-house fill'd, the harvest home,
Th' invited neighbours to the *Husking*[28] come;
A frolic scene, where work, and mirth, and play,
Unite their charms, to chace the hours away.
Where the huge heap lies center'd in the hall,
The lamp suspended from the cheerful wall,
Brown corn-fed nymphs, and strong hard-handed beaux,

[27]Grindstones for milling corn.

[28]A party for husking corn.

Alternate rang'd, extend in circling rows,
Assume their seats, the solid mass attack;
The dry husks rustle, and the corn-cobs crack;
The song, the laugh, alternate notes resound,
And the sweet cider trips in silence round.
The laws of Husking ev'ry wight[29] can tell;
And sure no laws he ever keeps so well:
For each red ear a general kiss he gains,
With each smut[30] ear she smuts the luckless swains;
But when to some sweet maid a prize is cast,
Red as her lips, and taper as her waist,
She walks the round, and culls one favor'd beau,
Who leaps, the luscious tribute to bestow.
Various the sport, as are the wits and brains
Of well pleas'd lasses and contending swains:
Till the vast mound of corn is swept away,
And he that gets the last ear, wins the day.
Meanwhile the house-wife urges all her care,
The well-earn'd feast to hasten and prepare.
The sifted meal already waits her hand,
The milk is strain'd the bowls in order stand,
The fire flames high; and, as a pool (that takes
The headlong stream that o'er the mill-dam breaks)
Foams, roars and rages with incessant toils,
So the vext cauldron rages, roars and boils.
First with clean salt she seasons well the food,
Then strews the flour and thickens all the flood.
Long o'er the simmering fire she lets it stand:
To stir it well demands a stronger hand;
The husband takes his turn; and round and round
The ladle flies; at last the toil is crown'd;
When to the board the thronging huskers pour,
And take their seats as at the corn before.
I leave them to their feast. There still belong
More copious matters to my faithful song.
For rules there are, tho' ne'er unfolded yet,
Nice[31] rules and wise, how pudding should be ate.
Some with molasses line the luscious treat,
And mix, like Bards, the useful with the sweet.
A wholesome dish, and well-deserving praise,
A great resource in those bleak wintry days,
When the chill'd earth lies buried deep in snow,
And raging Boreas[32] drives the shivering cow.
Blest cow! thy praise shall still my notes employ,

[29]Individual.
[30]A fungus-blackened ear of corn.
[31]Precise and subtle rules.
[32]The north, and coldest, wind.

Great source of health, the only source of joy;
How oft thy teats these pious hands have prest!
How oft thy bounties prove my only feast!
How oft I've fed thee with my fav'rite grain!
And roar'd, like thee, to find thy children slain!
Ye swains who know her various worth to prize,
Ah! house her well from Winter's angry skies.
Potatoes, Pumpkins, should her sadness cheer,
Corn from your crib, and mashes[33] from your beer;
When Spring returns she'll well acquit the loan,
And nurse at once your infants and her own.
Milk then with pudding I should always chuse;
To this in future I confine my Muse,
Till she in haste some farther hints unfold,
Well for the young, nor useless to the old.
First in your bowl the milk abundant take,
Then drop with care along the silver lake
Your flakes of pudding; these at first will hide
Their little bulk beneath the swelling tide;
But when their growing mass no more can sink,
When the soft island looms above the brink,
Then check your hand: you've got the portion's due,
So taught our sires, and what they taught is true.
There is a choice in spoons. Tho' small appear
The nice distinction, yet to me 'tis clear,
The deep bowl'd Gallic spoon, contriv'd to scoop
In ample draughts the thin diluted soup,
Performs not well in those substantial things,
Whose mass adhesive to the metal clings;
Where the strong labial muscles must embrace,
The gentle curve, and sweep the hollow space.
With ease to enter and discharge the freight,
A bowl less concave but still more dilate,
Becomes the pudding best. The shape, the size,
A secret rests unknown to vulgar eyes.
Experienc'd feeders can alone impart
A rule so much above the lore of art.
These tuneful lips, that thousand spoons have tried,
With just precision could the point decide,
Tho' not in song; the muse but poorly shines
In cones, and cubes, and geometric lines.
Yet the true form, as near as she can tell,
Is that small section of a goose-egg-shell,

[33]A grain mixture from brewing beer.

Which in two equal portions shall divide
The distance from the centre to the side.
Fear not to slaver; 'tis no deadly sin,
Like the free Frenchman, from your joyous chin
Suspend the ready napkin; or, like me,
Poise with one hand your bowl upon your knee;
Just in the zenith your wise head project,
Your full spoon, rising in a line direct,
Bold as a bucket, heeds no drops that fall,
The wide mouth'd bowl will surely catch them all.

1793

Advice to a Raven in Russia[1]

December, 1812

Black fool, why winter here? These frozen skies,
Worn by your wings and deafened by your cries,
Should warn you hence, where milder suns invite,
And day alternates with his mother night.
You fear perhaps your food will fail you there,
Your human carnage, that delicious fare
That lured you hither, following still your friend
The great Napoleon to the world's bleak end.
You fear, because the southern climes poured forth
Their clustering nations to infest the north,
Bavarians, Austrians, those who drink the Po[2]
And those who skirt the Tuscan seas below,
With all Germania, Neustria, Belgia, Gaul,[3]
Doomed here to wade through slaughter to their fall,
You fear he left behind no wars, to feed
His feathered cannibals and nurse the breed.
Fear not, my screamer, call your greedy train,

[1]Barlow had been dispatched to Lithuania to conclude a treaty with the French. After the 23-day, 1,400-mile-journey through war-torn northern Europe, Barlow waited two-weeks for Napoleon, who allegedly passed by in the night fearing assassination by his own troops. The poem was written during this interval and bears witness to the carnage and destruction in the wake of Napoleon's frantic retreat across Poland. Barlow died of pneumonia as he and his nephew, Tom Barlow, attempted to stay ahead of the pursuing Russian army. The poem was first published by Leon Howard in *The Huntington Library Quarterly 2* (1938).

[2]A river in Italy flowing from the Alps to the Adriatic Sea.

[3]Germany, northern France, the Netherlands, France.

Sweep over Europe, hurry back to Spain,
You'll find his legions there; the valiant crew
Please best their master when they toil for you.
Abundant there they spread the country o'er.
And taint the breeze with every nation's gore,
Iberian, Lusian,[4] British widely strown,
But still more wide and copious flows their own.
Go where you will; Calabria,[5] Malta, Greece,
Egypt and Syria still his fame increase,
Domingo's[6] fattened isle and India's plains
Glow deep with purple drawn from Gallic veins.
No raven's wing can stretch the flight so far
As the torn bandrols[7] of Napoleon's war.
Choose then your climate, fix your best abode,
He'll make you deserts and he'll bring you blood.
How could you fear a dearth? have not mankind,
Though slain by millions, millions left behind?
Has not conscription still the power to wield
Her annual falchion[8] o'er the human field?
A faithful harvester! or if a man
Escape that gleaner, shall he scape the ban?
The triple ban, that like the hound of hell[9]
Gripes with three joles,[10] to hold his victim well.
Fear nothing then, hatch fast your ravenous brood,
Teach them to cry to Bonaparte for food;
They'll be like you, of all his suppliant train,
The only class that never cries in vain.
For see what mutual benefits you lend!
(The surest way to fix the mutual friend)
While on his slaughtered troops your tribes are fed,
You cleanse his camp and carry off his dead.
Imperial scavenger! but now you know
Your work is vain amid these hills of snow.
His tentless troops are marbled through with frost
And change to crystal when the breath is lost.
Mere trunks of ice, though limbed like human frames
And lately warmed with life's endearing flames,
They cannot taint the air, the world impest,[11]
Nor can you tear one fiber from their breast.
No! from their visual sockets, as they lie,

[4]Lusitania, present-day Portugal.
[5]In southern Italy.
[6]The West Indies.
[7]Flags carried in war.
[8]Sickle or sword.
[9]The third ban was the list for the youngest draftees into the French army; Greek mythology, the three-headed dog, Cerberus, guards the gates of Hades.
[10]Jaws.
[11]Infect.

With beak and claws you cannot pluck an eye.
The frozen orb, preserving still its form,
Defies your talons as it braves the storm,
But stands and stares to God, as if to know
In what cursed hands He leaves His world below.
  Fly then, or starve; though all the dreadful road
From Minsk[12] to Moscow with their bodies strowed
May count some myriads, yet they can't suffice
To feed you more beneath these dreary skies.
Go back, and winter in the wilds of Spain;
Feast there awhile, and in the next campaign
Rejoin your master; for you'll find him then,
With his new million of the race of men,
Clothed in his thunders, all his flags unfurled,
Raging and storming o'er the prostrate world.
  War after war his hungry soul requires,
State after state shall sink beneath his fires,
Yet other Spains in victim smoke shall rise
And other Moscows suffocate the skies,
Each land lie reeking with its people's slain
And not a stream run bloodless to the main.
Till men resume their souls, and dare to shed
Earth's total vengeance on the monster's head,
Hurl from his blood-built throne this king of woes,
Dash him to dust, and let the world repose.

1938

Royall Tyler 1757–1826

When Royall Tyler graduated from Harvard in July 1776, there was no formal commencement for the senior class. Graduation was overshadowed by the political turmoil resulting from the Declaration of Independence. Tyler went on to distinguish himself by becoming a lawyer, a judge, an essayist, an author, a professor, and the creator of *The Contrast* (1787), the first American play to be professionally produced and commercially successful.

Royall Tyler was born in Boston on July 18, 1757, the youngest of four children. His father was Royall Tyler, a wealthy merchant actively involved in politics, and his mother was Mary Steele, daughter of Captain John Steele. His birth name was William Clark Tyler, but upon his father's death in 1771, he legally changed it to Royall Tyler at the request of his mother. He attended the Boston Latin School, completing the seven years of study by the age of

[12]City located 400 miles southwest of Moscow. It is estimated that of the 600,000 troops engaged in Napoleon's retreat, only 24,000 returned.

fifteen, and entered Harvard on July 15, 1772. Tyler soon established a reputation as a good student with a quick wit who was apparently quite the practical joker. One tale has him sending a fishing line out of a dormitory window in order to catch a pig from the yard below, only to hook the wig of Samuel Langdon, the school's president. Tyler was also considered rather flamboyant if not profligate for squandering half of his inheritance while in college and during the years immediately after.

After graduation, Tyler began reading law, but in December his studies were interrupted when he joined the Continental Army, initially serving under Colonel John Hancock. In 1778, Tyler became a major and an aide to General John Sullivan. In late 1778, he returned to his legal studies, received his master's degree from Harvard in 1779, and was admitted to the Massachusetts bar on August 19, 1780. Two years later, he began his practice in Braintree, Massachusetts, eight miles outside of Boston, where he roomed with the family of Mary and Richard Cranch. Mary was the sister of Abigail Cranch Adams, and from these associations Tyler met Abigail ("Nabby") Adams, daughter of John and Abigail. With John Adams dispatched to Europe, Abigail Adams reported on the growing attachment between their seventeen-year-old-daughter and Tyler. In a December 23, 1782, letter to John, she describes Tyler as having "a sprightly fancy, a warm imagination and an agreeable person," but then adds, "he was rather negligent in pursueing (sic) his business . . . and dissipated two or 3 years of his Life and too much of his fortune for to reflect upon with pleasure; all of which he now laments but cannot recall." Although John Adams admits that he was impressed by Tyler's family and that he would prefer a lawyer for his daughter, he was not "looking for a Poet, nor a Professor of belle Letters." The attachment was broken off, and in 1786, young Abigail married Colonel William Stephens Smith. The match turned out to be an unfortunate one because Smith repeatedly failed in business ventures. As for Tyler, he was deeply depressed by the breakup and went into seclusion to live with his mother in Jamaica Plain. By the fall of 1786, however, he had resumed his law practice in Boston and begun boarding at the home of Joseph Pearse Palmer.

In 1787, Tyler played a role in suppressing Shays's Rebellion, a group of dissident farmers led by Daniel Shays fighting for land rights, and helped to negotiate a surrender. These events brought Tyler to Vermont, where he would live for thirty-five years. In 1790, Tyler briefly returned to Boston and renewed his acquaintance with Mary Palmer, daughter of Joseph and Elizabeth Palmer. In the winter of 1793, he proposed marriage to the eighteen-year-old Mary but immediately returned to Guilford, Vermont, to serve as the state's attorney for Windham County. They were married in 1794, a bond lasting thirty-two years, and had eleven children. In 1812, Mary Tyler published *Grandmother Tyler's Book,* a compendium of advice on child rearing, which went into a second edition in 1818.

In 1801, Tyler was elected to the Supreme Court of Vermont as an assistant judge at a salary of $900 a year; in 1807, he was elected chief justice at a salary of $1,000. As a circuit judge, Tyler spent ten months a year on the road. He was elected assistant judge six times and chief justice six times. In 1802, he became a trustee of the University of Vermont; in 1811, he was appointed professor of jurisprudence, a position he held until 1814. In 1812, Tyler ran unsuccessfully for the United States Senate. He lost in part because he had changed his political affiliation from Federalist to Republican and the Federalists were, at that moment, in power in Vermont. This defeat signaled a change in monetary fortune for the Tylers, but Mary's sewing and the generosity of family and neighbors sustained them. Royall Tyler continued writing into the final years of his life. He died on August 26, 1826, in Brattleboro, Vermont, after suffering from facial cancer for ten years.

In addition to legal tracts, Tyler wrote six plays, a musical drama, two long poems, a semifictional travel narrative, *The Yankey in London* (1809), numerous essays under the pseudonym "Spondee" with Joseph Dennie as "Colon," the novel *The Algerine Captive* (1797), and its unfinished revision, *The Bay Boy.* Tyler is best known for *The Contrast,* a comedy that addresses class issues with a series of contrasting characters: Jonathan, a rustic Yankee character; Colonel Henry Manly, a virtuous though bombastic Revolutionary War veteran; Billy Dimple, an English dandy; and Maria, a sentimental heroine romantically mismatched at her father's behest. Tyler wrote the play while in New York in March 1787; he had been sent there to solicit the state's support against the rebellious farmers aligned with Daniel Shays. Allegedly, Tyler saw a production of Richard Sheridan's *The School for Scandal* (1777) and was so inspired that he wrote *The Contrast* in less than a month. Tyler is credited with creating a memorable American type, the Yankee, whose backwoods dialect and humor became a model for other regional humorists, such as Augustus Baldwin Longstreet, Thomas Bangs Thorpe, and Mark Twain. *The Contrast* opened on April 16, 1787, at the John Street Theatre to successful reviews and was immediately reproduced on April 18, May 2, and May 12, an unprecedented four performances in one month. The play opened in Baltimore on August 12 and in Philadelphia on December 10, where Thomas Wignell, a popular actor, read it. *The Contrast* was published in Philadelphia in 1790, counting among its subscribers George Washington. Although the form was adapted from English drama, Tyler infused the play with a distinctively American theme, domestic simplicity over European pretense.

Susan Clair Imbarrato
Minnesota State University–Moorhead

PRIMARY WORKS

The Contrast, 1790; *The Algerine Captive,* 1797; *The Yankey in London,* 1809; *Four Plays by Royall Tyler,* ed. Arthur Wallace Peach and George Floyd Newbrough, 1941; *The Prose of Royall Tyler,* ed. Marius B. Peladeau, 1972; *The Verse of Royall Tyler,* ed. Marius B. Peladeau, 1968.

The Contrast, A Comedy in Five Acts

CHARACTERS

COL. MANLY	CHARLOTTE
DIMPLE	MARIA
VAN ROUGH	LETITIA
JESSAMY	JENNY
JONATHAN	

SERVANTS

SCENE. *New York*

Prologue

Written by a Young Gentleman of New York, and Spoken by Mr. Wignell[1]

EXULT, each patriot heart!—this night is shown
A piece, which we may fairly call our own;
Where the proud titles of "My Lord! Your Grace!"
To humble *Mr.* and plain *Sir* give place.
Our Author pictures not from foreign climes
The fashions or the follies of the times;
But has confin'd the subject of his work
To the gay scenes—the circles of New-York.
On native themes his Muse displays her pow'rs;
If ours the faults, the virtues too are ours.
Why should our thoughts to distant countries roam,
When each refinement may be found at home?
Who travels now to ape the rich or great
To deck an equipage and roll in state;
To court the graces, or to dance with ease,
Or by hypocrisy to strive to please?
Our free-born ancestors such arts despis'd;
Genuine sincerity alone they priz'd;
Their minds, with honest emulation fir'd;
To solid good—not ornament—aspir'd;
Or, if ambition rous'd a bolder flame,
Stern virtue throve, where indolence was shame.

But modern youths, with imitative sense,
Deem taste in dress the proof of excellence;
And spurn the meanness of your homespun arts,
Since homespun habits would obscure their parts;
Whilst all, which aims at splendour and parade,
Must come from Europe, *and be ready made.*
Strange! we should thus our native worth disclaim,
And check the progress of our rising fame.
Yet *one,* whilst imitation bears the sway,
Aspires to nobler heights, and points the way.
Be rous'd, my friends! his bold example view;
Let your own Bards be proud to copy *you!*
Should rigid critics reprobate our play,
At least the patriotic heart will say,
"Glorious our fall, since in a noble cause,
The bold *attempt alone* demands applause."
Still may the wisdom of the Comic Muse

[1]Thomas Wignell (c. 1753–1803) a popular comic actor who first played the role of Jonathan.

Exalt your merits, or your faults accuse.
But think not, 't is her aim be severe;—
We all are mortals, and as mortals err.
If candour pleases, we are truly blest;
Vice trembles, when compell'd to stand confess'd.
Let not light Censure on your faults offend,
Which aims not to expose them, but amend.
Thus does our Author to your candour trust;
Conscious, the *free* are generous, as just.

ACT I

SCENE. *an Apartment at* CHARLOTTE'S. CHARLOTTE *and* LETITIA *discovered*

LETITIA. And so, Charlotte, you really think the pocket-hoop[2] unbecoming.

CHARLOTTE. No, I don't say so. It may be very becoming to saunter round the house of a rainy day; to visit my grand-mamma, or to go to Quakers' meeting: but to swim in a minuet, with the eyes of fifty well-dressed beaux upon me, to trip it in the Mall, or walk on the battery,[3] give me the luxurious, jaunty, flowing, bellhoop. It would have delighted you to have seen me the last evening, my charming girl! I was dangling o'er the battery with Billy Dimple; a knot of young fellows were upon the platform; as I passed them I faltered with one of the most bewitching false steps you ever saw, and then recovered myself with such a pretty confusion, flirting my hoop to discover a jet black shoe and brilliant buckle. Gad! how my little heart thrilled to hear the confused raptures of—*"Demme,*[4] *Jack, what a delicate foot!" "Ha! General, what a well-turned——"*

LETITIA. Fie! fie! Charlotte [*stopping her mouth*], I protest you are quite a libertine.

CHARLOTTE. Why, my dear little prude, are we not all such libertines? Do you think, when I sat tortured two hours under the hands of my friseur,[5] and an hour more at my toilet, that I had any thoughts of my aunt Susan, or my cousin Betsey? though they are both allowed to be critical judges of dress.

LETITIA. Why, who should we dress to please, but those who are judges of its merit?

CHARLOTTE. Why, a creature who does not know *Buffon* from *Soufflé*[6]—Man!—my Letitia—Man! for whom we dress, walk, dance, talk, lisp, languish, and smile. Does not the grave Spectator[7] assure us that even our much bepraised diffidence, modesty, and blushes are all directed to make ourselves good wives and mothers as fast as we can? Why, I'll undertake with one flirt of this hoop to bring more beaux to my feet in one week than the grave Maria, and her sentimental circle, can do, by sighing sentiment till their hairs are grey.

LETITIA. Well, I won't argue with you; you always out-talk me; let us change the subject. I hear that Mr. Dimple and Maria are soon to be married.

[2]A type of hoop skirt.
[3]Battery Park, located at the southern end of Manhattan.
[4]"Damn me."
[5]Hairdresser.
[6]Georges de Buffon (1707–1788), a French naturalist. Tyler's pun on "Bouffant," or puffy and light, as in a hairdo, is then contrasted with "soufflé," a puffy, light egg dish.
[7]*The Spectator* was an eighteenth-century periodical known for its essays on morals and literature that were introduced by "Mr. Spectator."

CHARLOTTE. You hear true. I was consulted in the choice of the wedding clothes. She is to be married in a delicate white satin, and has a monstrous pretty brocaded lutestring[8] for the second day. It would have done you good to have seen with what an affected indifference the dear sentimentalist turned over a thousand pretty things, just as if her heart did not palpitate with her approaching happiness, and at last made her choice and arranged her dress with such apathy as if she did not know that plain white satin and a simple blond lace would show her clear skin and dark hair to the greatest advantage.

LETITIA. But they say her indifference to dress, and even to the gentleman himself, is not entirely affected.

CHARLOTTE. How?

LETITIA. It is whispered that if Maria gives her hand to Mr. Dimple, it will be without her heart.

CHARLOTTE. Though the giving the heart is one of the last of all laughable considerations in the marriage of a girl of spirit, yet I should like to hear what antiquated notions the dear little piece of old-fashioned prudery has got in her head.

LETITIA. Why, you know that old Mr. John-Richard-Robert-Jacob-Isaac-Abraham-Cornelius Van Dumpling, Billy Dimple's father (for he has thought fit to soften his name, as well as manners, during his English tour), was the most intimate friend of Maria's father. The old folks, about a year before Mr. Van Dumpling's death, proposed this match; the young folks were accordingly introduced, and told they must love one another. Billy was then a good-natured, decent-dressing young fellow, with a little dash of the coxcomb, such as our young fellows of fortune usually have. At this time, I really believe she thought she loved him; and had they then been married, I doubt not they might have jogged on, to the end of the chapter, a good kind of a sing-song lack-a-daysaical life, as other honest married folks do.

CHARLOTTE. Why did they not then marry?

LETITIA. Upon the death of his father, Billy went to England to see the world and rub off a little of the patroon rust. During his absence, Maria, like a good girl, to keep herself constant to her *nown true-love,* avoided company, and betook herself, for her amusement, to her books, and her dear Billy's letters. But, alas! how many ways has the mischievous demon of inconstancy of stealing into a woman's heart! Her love was destroyed by the very means she took to support it.

CHARLOTTE. How?—Oh! I have it—some likely young beau found the way to her study.

LETITIA. Be patient, Charlotte; your head so runs upon beaux. Why, she read *Sir Charles Grandison, Clarissa Harlowe,* Shenstone, and the *Sentimental Journey;*[9] and between whiles, as I said, Billy's letters. But, as her taste improved, her love declined. The contrast was so striking betwixt the good sense of her books and the flimsiness of her love-letters, that she discovered she had unthinkingly engaged her hand without her heart; and then the whole transaction, managed by the old folks, now appeared so unsentimental, and looked so like bargaining for a bale of

[8]Shiny, silk dress.

[9]*Sir Charles Grandison* (1753) and *Clarissa Harlowe* (1747), novels by Samuel Richardson (1689–1761); William Shenstone (1714–1763), a poet who wrote "Pastoral Ballad" (1755); *A Sentimental Journey,* a novel by Laurence Sterne (1713–1768).

goods, that she found she ought to have rejected, according to every rule of romance, even the man of her choice, if imposed upon her in that manner. Clary Harlowe would have scorned such a match.

CHARLOTTE. Well, how was it on Mr. Dimple's return? Did he meet a more favourable reception than his letters?

LETITIA. Much the same. She spoke of him with respect abroad, and with contempt in her closet. She watched his conduct and conversation, and found that he had by travelling acquired the wickedness of Lovelace[10] without his wit, and the politeness of Sir Charles Grandison without his generosity. The ruddy youth, who washed his face at the cistern every morning, and swore and looked eternal love and constancy, was now metamorphosed into a flippant, palid, polite beau, who devotes the morning to his toilet, reads a few pages of Chesterfield's letters,[11] and then minces out, to put the infamous principles in practice upon every woman he meets.

CHARLOTTE. But, if she is so apt at conjuring up these sentimental bugbears, why does she not discard him at once?

LETITIA. Why, she thinks her word too sacred to be trifled with. Besides, her father, who has a great respect for the memory of his deceased friend, is ever telling her how he shall renew his years in their union, and repeating the dying injunctions of old Van Dumpling.

CHARLOTTE. A mighty pretty story! And so you would make me believe that the sensible Maria would give up Dumpling manor, and the all-accomplished Dimple as a husband, for the absurd, ridiculous reason, forsooth, because she despises and abhors him. Just as if a lady could not be privileged to spend a man's fortune, ride in his carriage, be called after his name, and call him her *nown dear lovee* when she wants money, without loving and respecting the great he-creature. Oh! my dear girl, you are a monstrous prude.

LETITIA. I don't say what I would do; I only intimate how I suppose she wishes to act.

CHARLOTTE. No, no, no! A fig of sentiment. If she breaks, or wishes to break, with Mr. Dimple, depend upon it, she has some other man in her eye. A woman rarely discards one lover until she is sure of another. Letitia little thinks what a clue I have to Dimple's conduct. The generous man submits to render himself disgusting to Maria, in order that she may leave him at liberty to address me. I must change the subject. *[Aside, and rings a bell.*

Enter SERVANT.

Frank, order the horses to.——Talking of marriage, did you hear that Sally Bloomsbury is going to be married next week to Mr. Indigo, the rich Carolinian?

LETITIA. Sally Bloomsbury married!—why, she is not yet in her teens.

CHARLOTTE. I do not know how this is, but you may depend upon it, 'tis a done affair. I have it from the best authority. There is my aunt Wyerly's Hannah. You know Hannah; though a black, she is a wench that was never caught in a lie in her life. Now, Hannah has a brother who courts Sarah, Mrs. Catgut the milliner's girl,

[10]The villainous rake in *Clarissa Harlowe.*

[11]The earl of Chesterfield, Philip Stanhope (1694–1773), wrote a series of letters instructing his son on good manners. Published in 1774, they were judged hypocritical and superficial.

and she told Hannah's brother, and Hannah, who, as I said before, is a girl of undoubted veracity, told it directly to me, that Mrs. Catgut was making a new cap for Miss Bloomsbury, which, as it was very dressy, it is very probable is designed for a wedding cap. Now, as she is to be married, who can it be but to Mr. Indigo? Why, there is no other gentleman that visits at her papa's.

LETITIA. Say not a word more, Charlotte. Your intelligence is so direct and well grounded, it is almost a pity that it is not a piece of scandal.

CHARLOTTE. Oh! I am the pink of prudence. Though I cannot charge myself with ever having discredited a tea-party by my silence, yet I take care never to report anything of my acquaintance, especially if it is to their credit—*discredit,* I mean—until I have searched to the bottom of it. It is true, there is infinite pleasure in this charitable pursuit. Oh! how delicious to go and condole with the friends of some backsliding sister, or to retire with some old dowager or maiden aunt of the family, who love scandal so well that they cannot forbear gratifying their appetite at the expense of the reputation of their nearest relations! And then to return full fraught with a rich collection of circumstances, to retail to the next circle of our acquaintance under the strongest injunctions of secrecy—ha, ha, ha!—interlarding the melancholy tale with so many doleful shakes of the head, and more doleful "Ah! who would have thought it! so amiable, so prudent a young lady, as we all thought her, what a monstrous pity! well, I have nothing to charge myself with; I acted the part of a friend, I warned her of the principles of that rake, I told her what would be the consequence; I told her so, I told her so."—Ha, ha, ha!

LETITIA. Ha, ha, ha! Well, but, Charlotte, you don't tell me what you think of Miss Bloomsbury's match.

CHARLOTTE. Think! why I think it is probable she cried for a plaything, and they have given her a husband. Well, well, well, the puling chit[12] shall not be deprived of her plaything: 'tis only exchanging London dolls for American babies.—Apropos, of babies, have you heard what Mrs. Affable's high-flying notions of delicacy have come to?

LETITIA. Who, she that was Miss Lovely?

CHARLOTTE. The same; she married Bob Affable of Schenectady. Don't you remember?

Enter SERVANT.

SERVANT. Madam, the carriage is ready.

LETITIA. Shall we go to the stores first, or visiting?

CHARLOTTE. I should think it rather too early to visit, especially Mrs. Prim; you know she is so particular.

LETITIA. Well, but what of Mrs. Affable?

CHARLOTTE. Oh, I'll tell you as we go; come, come, let us hasten. I hear Mrs. Catgut has some of the prettiest caps arrived you ever saw. I shall die if I have not the first sight of them. [*Exeunt.*

[12]A childish, sniveling woman.

SCENE II

A Room in VAN ROUGH'S *House*

MARIA sitting disconsolate at a Table, with Books, & c.

SONG[13]

I

The sun sets in night, and the stars shun the day;
But glory remains when their lights fade away!
Begin, ye tormentors! your threats are in vain,
For the son of Alknomook shall never complain.

II

Remember the arrows he shot from his bow;
Remember your chiefs by his hatchet laid low:
Why so slow?—do you wait till I shrink from the pain?
No—the son of Alknomook will never complain.

III

Remember the wood where in ambush we lay,
And the scalps which we bore from your nation away:
Now the flame rises fast, you exult in my pain;
But the son of Alknomook can never complain.

IV

I go to the land where my father is gone;
His ghost shall rejoice in the fame of his son:
Death comes like a friend, he relieves me from pain;
And thy son, Oh Alknomook! has scorn'd to complain.

There is something in this song which ever calls forth my affections. The manly virtue of courage, that fortitude which steels the heart against the keenest misfortunes, which interweaves the laurel of glory amidst the instruments of torture and death, displays something so noble, so exalted, that in despite of the prejudices of education I cannot but admire it, even in a savage. The prepossession which our sex is supposed to entertain for the character of a soldier is, I know, a standing piece of raillery[14] among the wits. A cockade,[15] a lapell'd coat, and a feather, they will tell you, are irresistible by a female heart. Let it be so. Who is it that considers the helpless situation of our sex, that does not see that we each moment stand in need of a protector, and that a brave one too? Formed of the more delicate ma-

[13]Poet is unknown. The poem has been attributed to Royall Tyler and Philip Freneau, among others.

[14]Satire.

[15]A medallion worn on a hat as part of a military uniform.

terials of nature, endowed only with the softer passions, incapable, from our ignorance of the world, to guard against the wiles of mankind, our security for happiness often depends upon their generosity and courage. Alas! how little of the former do we find! How inconsistent! that man should be leagued to destroy that honour upon which solely rests his respect and esteem. Ten thousand temptations allure us, ten thousand passions betray us; yet the smallest deviation from the path of rectitude is followed by the contempt and insult of man, and the more remorseless pity of woman; years of penitence and tears cannot wash away the stain, nor a life of virtue obliterate its remembrance. Reputation is the life of woman; yet courage to protect it is masculine and disgusting; and the only safe asylum a woman of delicacy can find is in the arms of a man of honour. How naturally, then, should we love the brave and the generous; how gratefully should we bless the arm raised for our protection, when nerv'd by virtue and directed by honour! Heaven grant that the man with whom I may be connected—may be connected! Whither has my imagination transported me—whither does it now lead me? Am I not indissolubly engaged, by every obligation of honour which my own consent and my father's approbation can give, to a man who can never share my affections, and whom a few days hence it will be criminal for me to disapprove—to disapprove! would to heaven that were all—to despise. For, can the most frivolous manners, actuated by the most depraved heart, meet, or merit, anything but contempt from every woman of delicacy and sentiment?

[VAN ROUGH *without.* Mary!

Ha! my father's voice—Sir!—

Enter VAN ROUGH

VAN ROUGH. What, Mary, always singing doleful ditties, and moping over these plaguy books.

MARIA. I hope, Sir, that it is not criminal to improve my mind with books, or to divert my melancholy with singing, at my leisure hours.

VAN ROUGH. Why, I don't know that, child; I don't know that. They us'd to say, when I was a young man, that if a woman knew how to make a pudding, and to keep herself out of fire and water, she knew enough for a wife. Now, what good have these books done you? have they not made you melancholy? as you call it. Pray, what right has a girl of your age to be in the dumps? haven't you everything your heart can wish; an't you going to be married to a young man of great fortune; an't you going to have the quit-rent[16] of twenty miles square?

MARIA. One-hundredth part of the land, and a lease for life of the heart of a man I could love, would satisfy me.

VAN ROUGH. Pho, pho, pho! child; nonsense, downright nonsense, child. This comes of your reading your story-books; your Charles Grandisons, your Sentimental Journals, and your Robinson Crusoes,[17] and such other trumpery. No, no, no! child, it is money makes the mare go; keep your eye upon the main chance, Mary.

MARIA. Marriage, Sir, is, indeed, a very serious affair.

[16]A fixed fee.

[17]*Robinson Crusoe* (1719), a novel by Daniel Defoe (1660–1731).

VAN ROUGH. You are right, child; you are right. I am sure I found it so, to my cost.

MARIA. I mean, Sir, that as marriage is a portion for life, and so intimately involves our happiness, we cannot be too considerate in the choice of our companion.

VAN ROUGH. Right, child; very right. A young woman should be very sober when she is making her choice, but when she has once made it, as you have done, I don't see why she should not be as merry as a grig;[18] I am sure she has reason enough to be so. Solomon says that "there is a time to laugh, and a time to weep."[19] Now, a time for a young woman to laugh is when she has made sure of a good rich husband. Now, a time to cry, according to you, Mary, is when she is making choice of him; but I should think that a young woman's time to cry was when she despaired of *getting* one. Why, there was your mother, now: to be sure, when I popp'd the question to her she did look a little silly; but when she had once looked down on her apron-strings, as all modest young women us'd to do, and drawled out ye-s, she was as brisk and as merry as a bee.

MARIA. My honoured mother, Sir, had no motive to melancholy; she married the man of her choice.

VAN ROUGH. The man of her choice! And pray, Mary, an't you going to marry the man of your choice—what trumpery notion is this? It is these vile books [*throwing them away*]. I'd have you to know, Mary, if you won't make young Van Dumpling the man of *your* choice, you shall marry him as the man of *my* choice.

MARIA. You terrify me, Sir. Indeed, Sir, I am all submission. My will is yours.

VAN ROUGH. Why, that is the way your mother us'd to talk. "My will is yours, my dear Mr. Van Rough, my will is yours"; but she took special care to have her own way, though, for all that.

MARIA. Do not reflect upon my mother's memory, Sir——

VAN ROUGH. Why not, Mary, why not? She kept me from speaking my mind all her *life,* and do you think she shall henpeck me now she is *dead* too? Come, come; don't go to sniveling; be a good girl, and mind the main chance. I'll see you well settled in the world.

MARIA. I do not doubt your love, Sir, and it is my duty to obey you. I will endeavour to make my duty and inclination go hand in hand.

VAN ROUGH. Well, well, Mary; do you be a good girl, mind the main chance, and never mind inclination. Why, do you know that I have been down in the cellar this very morning to examine a pipe[20] of Madeira which I purchased the week you were born, and mean to tap on your wedding day?—That pipe cost me fifty pounds sterling. It was well worth sixty pounds; but I overreach'd Ben Bulkhead, the super-cargo. I'll tell you the whole story. You must know that——

Enter SERVANT

SERVANT. Sir, Mr. Transfer, the broker, is below. [*Exit.*

VAN ROUGH. Well, Mary, I must go. Remember, and be a good girl, and mind the main chance. [*Exit.*

MARIA [*alone*]. How deplorable is my situation! How distressing for a daughter to

[18]Cricket.

[19]From Ecclesiastes 3:4, "A time to weep, and a time to laugh."

[20]A wine cask.

find her heart militating with her filial duty! I know my father loves me tenderly; why then do I reluctantly obey him? Heaven knows! with what reluctance I should oppose the will of a parent, or set an example of filial disobedience; at a parent's command, I could wed awkwardness and deformity. Were the heart of my husband good, I would so magnify his good qualities with the eye of conjugal affection, that the defects of his person and manners should be lost in the emanation of his virtues. At a father's command, I could embrace poverty. Were the poor man my husband, I would learn resignation to my lot; I would enliven our frugal meal with good humour, and chase away misfortune from our cottage with a smile. At a father's command, I could almost submit to what every female heart knows to be the most mortifying, to marry a weak man, and blush at my husband's folly in every company I visited. But to marry a depraved wretch, whose only virtue is a polished exterior; who is actuated by the unmanly ambition of conquering the defenceless; whose heart, insensible to the emotions of patriotism, dilates at the plaudits of every unthinking girl; whose laurels are the sighs and tears of the miserable victims of his specious behaviour—can he, who has no regard for the peace and happiness of other families, ever have a due regard for the peace and happiness of his own? Would to heaven that my father were not so hasty in his temper? Surely, if I were to state my reasons for declining this match, he would not compel me to marry a man, whom, though my lips may solemnly promise to honour, I find my heart must ever despise. [*Exit.*

End of the First Act

ACT II. SCENE I

Enter CHARLOTTE *and* LETITIA

CHARLOTTE [*at entering*]. Betty, take those things out of the carriage and carry them to my chamber; see that you don't tumble them. My dear, I protest, I think it was the homeliest of the whole. I declare I was almost tempted to return and change it.

LETITIA. Why would you take it?

CHARLOTTE. Didn't Mrs. Catgut say it was the most fashionable?

LETITIA. But, my dear, it will never fit becomingly on you.

CHARLOTTE. I know that; but did not you hear Mrs. Catgut say it was fashionable?

LETITIA. Did you see that sweet airy cap with the white sprig?

CHARLOTTE. Yes, and I longed to take it; but, my dear, what could I do? Did not Mrs. Catgut say it was the most fashionable; and if I had not taken it, was not that awkward gawky, Sally Slender, ready to purchase it immediately?

LETITIA. Did you observe how she tumbled over the things at the next shop, and then went off without purchasing anything, nor even thanking the poor man for his trouble? But, of all the awkward creatures, did you see Miss Blouze endeavouring to thrust her unmerciful arm into those small kid gloves?

CHARLOTTE. Ha, ha, ha, ha!

LETITIA. Then did you take notice with what an affected warmth of friendship she and Miss Wasp met? when all their acquaintance know how much pleasure they take in abusing each other in every company.

CHARLOTTE. Lud![21] Letitia, is that so extraordinary? Why, my dear, I hope you are not going to turn sentimentalist. Scandal, you know, is but amusing ourselves with the faults, foibles, follies, and reputations of our friends; indeed, I don't know why we should have friends, if we are not at liberty to make use of them. But no person is so ignorant of the world as to suppose, because I amuse myself with a lady's faults, that I am obliged to quarrel with her person every time we meet; believe me, my dear, we should have very few acquaintance at that rate.

SERVANT *enters and delivers a letter to* CHARLOTTE, *and*—— [*Exit.*

CHARLOTTE. You'll excuse me, my dear.

[*Opens and reads to herself.*

LETITIA. Oh, quite excusable.

CHARLOTTE. As I hope to be married, my brother Henry is in the city.

LETITIA. What, your brother, Colonel Manly?

CHARLOTTE. Yes, my dear; the only brother I have in the world.

LETITIA. Was he never in this city?

CHARLOTTE. Never nearer than Harlem Heights,[22] where he lay with his regiment.

LETITIA. What sort of a being is this brother of yours? If he is as chatty, as pretty, as sprightly as you, half the belles in the city will be pulling caps for him.

CHARLOTTE. My brother is the very counterpart and reverse of me: I am gay, he is grave; I am airy, he is solid; I am ever selecting the most pleasing objects for my laughter, he has a tear for every pitiful one. And thus, whilst he is plucking the briars and thorns from the path of the unfortunate, I am strewing my own path with roses.

LETITIA. My sweet friend, not quite so poetical, and a little more particular.

CHARLOTTE. Hands off, Letitia. I feel the rage of simile upon me; I can't talk to you in any other way. My brother has a heart replete with the noblest sentiments, but then, it is like—it is like—Oh! you provoking girl, you have deranged all my ideas—it is like—Oh! I have it—his heart is like an old maiden lady's bandbox; it contains many costly things, arranged with the most scrupulous nicety, yet the misfortune is that they are too delicate, costly, and antiquated for common use.

LETITIA. By what I can pick out of your flowery description, your brother is no beau.

CHARLOTTE. No, indeed, he makes no pretension to the character. He'd ride, or rather fly, an hundred miles to relieve a distressed object, or to do a gallant act in the service of his country; but should you drop your fan or bouquet in his presence, it is ten to one that some beau at the farther end of the room would have the honour of presenting it to you before he had observed that it fell. I'll tell you one of his antiquated, anti-gallant notions. He said once in my presence, in a room full of company—would you believe it?—in a large circle of ladies, that the best evidence a gentleman could give a young lady of his respect and affection was to endeavour in a friendly manner to rectify her foibles. I protest I was crimson to the eyes, upon reflecting that I was known as his sister.

[21] A variant of "Lord!"

[22] A battle site in the American Revolution; now a neighborhood in New York City.

LETITIA. Insupportable creature! tell a lady of her faults! if he is so grave, I fear I have no chance of captivating him.

CHARLOTTE. His conversation is like a rich, old-fashioned brocade—it will stand alone; every sentence is a sentiment. Now you may judge what a time I had with him, in my twelve months' visit to my father. He read me such lectures, out of pure brotherly affection, against the extremes of fashion, dress, flirting, and coquetry, and all the other dear things which he knows I dote upon, that I protest his conversation made me as melancholy as if I had been at church; and heaven knows, though I never prayed to go there but on one occasion, yet I would have exchanged his conversation for a psalm and a sermon. Church is rather melancholy, to be sure; but then I can ogle the beaux, and be regaled with "here endeth the first lesson," but his brotherly *here,* you would think had no end. You captivate him! Why, my dear, he would as soon fall in love with a box of Italian flowers. There is Maria, now, if she were not engaged, she might do something. Oh! how I should like to see that pair of pensorosos[23] together, looking as grave as two sailors' wives of a stormy night, with a flow of sentiment meandering through their conversation like purling streams in modern poetry.

LETITIA. Oh! my dear fanciful—

CHARLOTTE. Hush! I hear some person coming through the entry.

Enter SERVANT

SERVANT. Madam, there's a gentleman below who calls himself Colonel Manly; do you choose to be at home?

CHARLOTTE. Show him in. [*Exit* SERVANT.] Now for a sober face.

Enter COLONEL MANLY

MANLY. My dear Charlotte, I am happy that I once more enfold you within the arms of fraternal affection. I know you are going to ask (amiable impatience!) how our parents do—the venerable pair transmit you their blessing by me. They totter on the verge of a well-spent life, and wish only to see their children settled in the world, to depart in peace.

CHARLOTTE. I am very happy to hear that they are well. [*Coolly.*] Brother, will you give me leave to introduce you to our uncle's ward, one of my most intimate friends?

MANLY. [*saluting* LETITIA]. I ought to regard your friends as my own.

CHARLOTTE. Come, Letitia, do give us a little dash of your vivacity; my brother is so sentimental and so grave, that I protest he'll give us the vapours.[24]

MANLY. Though sentiment and gravity, I know, are banished the polite world, yet I hoped they might find some countenance in the meeting of such near connections as brother and sister.

CHARLOTTE. Positively, brother, if you go one step further in this strain, you will set me crying, and that, you know, would spoil my eyes; and then I should never get the husband which our good papa and mamma have so kindly wished me—never be established in the world.

[23]Persons deeply engaged in thought.
[24]Melancholy, the blues.

MANLY. Forgive me, my sister—I am no enemy to mirth; I love your sprightliness; and I hope it will one day enliven the hours of some worthy man; but when I mention the respectable authors of my existence—the cherishers and protectors of my helpless infancy, whose hearts glow with such fondness and attachment that they would willingly lay down their lives for my welfare—you will excuse me if I am so unfashionable as to speak of them with some degree of respect and reverence.

CHARLOTTE. Well, well, brother; if you won't be gay, we'll not differ; I will be as grave as you wish. [*Affects gravity.*] And so, brother, you have come to the city to exchange some of your commutation notes[25] for a little pleasure?

MANLY. Indeed you are mistaken; my errand is not of amusement, but business; and as I neither drink nor game, my expenses will be so trivial, I shall have no occasion to sell my notes.

CHARLOTTE. Then you won't have occasion to do a very good thing. Why, here was the Vermont General—he came down some time since, sold all his musty notes at one stroke, and then laid the cash out in trinkets for his dear Fanny. I want a dozen pretty things myself; have you got the notes with you?

MANLY. I shall be ever willing to contribute, as far as it is in my power, to adorn or in any way to please my sister; yet I hope I shall never be obliged for this to sell my notes. I may be romantic, but I preserve them as a sacred deposit. Their full amount is justly due to me, but as embarrassments, the natural consequences of a long war, disable my country from supporting its credit, I shall wait with patience until it is rich enough to discharge them. If that is not in my day, they shall be transmitted as an honourable certificate to posterity, that I have humbly imitated our illustrious WASHINGTON, in having exposed my health and life in the service of my country, without reaping any other reward than the glory of conquering in so arduous a contest.

CHARLOTTE. Well said heroics. Why, my dear Henry, you have such a lofty way of saying things, that I protest I almost tremble at the thought of introducing you to the polite circles in the city. The belles would think you were a player run mad, with your head filled with old scraps of tragedy; and as to the beaux, they might admire, because they would not understand you. But, however, I must, I believe, introduce you to two or three ladies of my acquaintance.

LETITIA. And that will make him acquainted with thirty or forty beaux.

CHARLOTTE. Oh! brother, you don't know what a fund of happiness you have in store.

MANLY. I fear, sister, I have not refinement sufficient to enjoy it.

CHARLOTTE. Oh! you cannot fail being pleased.

LETITIA. Our ladies are so delicate and dressy.

CHARLOTTE. And our beaux so dressy and delicate.

LETITIA. Our ladies chat and flirt so agreeably.

CHARLOTTE. And our beaux simper and bow so gracefully.

LETITIA. With their hair so trim and neat.

CHARLOTTE. And their faces so soft and sleek.

[25]Promissory notes equal to five years' full pay given to officers after the Revolutionary War. Many officers cashed them in before they matured, suffering a large discount.

LETITIA. Their buckles so tonish[26] and bright.

CHARLOTTE. And their hands so slender and white.

LETITIA. I vow, Charlotte, we are quite poetical.

CHARLOTTE. And then, brother, the faces of the beaux are of such a lily-white hue! None of that horrid robustness of constitution, that vulgar cornfed glow of health, which can only serve to alarm an unmarried lady with apprehension, and prove a melancholy memento to a married one, that she can never hope for the happiness of being a widow. I will say this to the credit of our city beaux, that such is the delicacy of their complexion, dress, and address, that, even had I no reliance upon the honour of the dear Adonises,[27] I would trust myself in any possible situation with them, without the least apprehensions of rudeness.

MANLY. Sister Charlotte!

CHARLOTTE. Now, now, now, brother [*interrupting him*], now don't go to spoil my mirth with a dash of your gravity; I am so glad to see you, I am in tip-top spirits. Oh! that you could be with us at a little snug party. There is Billy Simper, Jack Chaffé, and Colonel Van Titter, Miss Promonade, and the two Miss Tambours, sometimes make a party, with some other ladies, in a side-box at the play. Everything is conducted with such decorum. First we bow round to the company in general, then to each one in particular, then we have so many inquiries after each other's health, and we are so happy to meet each other, and it is so many ages since we last had that pleasure, and if a married lady is in company, we have such a sweet dissertation upon her son Bobby's chin-cough;[28] then the curtain rises, then our sensibility is all awake, and then, by the mere force of apprehension, we torture some harmless expression into a double meaning, which the poor author never dreamt of, and then we have recourse to our fans, and then we blush, and then the gentlemen jog one another, peep under the fan, and make the prettiest remarks; and then we giggle and they simper, and they giggle and we simper, and then the curtain drops, and then for nuts and oranges, and then we bow, and it's pray, Ma'am, take it, and pray, Sir, keep it, and oh! not for the world, Sir; and then the curtain rises again, and then we blush and giggle and simper and bow all over again. Oh! the sentimental charms of a side-box conversation! [*All laugh.*

MANLY. Well, sister, I join heartily with you in the laugh; for, in my opinion, it is as justifiable to laugh at folly as it is reprehensible to ridicule misfortune.

CHARLOTTE. Well, but, brother, positively I can't introduce you in these clothes: why, your coat looks as if it were calculated for the vulgar purpose of keeping yourself comfortable.

MANLY. This coat was my regimental coat in the late war. The public tumults of our state[29] have induced me to buckle on the sword in support of that government which I once fought to establish. I can only say, sister, that there was a time when this coat was respectable, and some people even thought that those men who had endured so many winter campaigns in the service of their country, without bread, clothing, or pay, at least deserved that the poverty of their appearance should not be ridiculed.

[26]Fashionable.
[27]In Greek myth, Adonis was a beautiful young boy.
[28]Whooping cough.
[29]Reference to Shays's Rebellion in Massachusetts in 1786.

CHARLOTTE. We agree in opinion entirely, brother, though it would not have done for me to have said it: it is the coat makes the man respectable. In the time of the war, when we were almost frightened to death, why, your coat was respectable, that is, fashionable; now another kind of coat is fashionable, that is, respectable. And pray direct the tailor to make yours the height of the fashion.

MANLY. Though it is of little consequence to me of what shape my coat is, yet, as to the height of the fashion, there you will please to excuse me, sister. You know my sentiments on that subject. I have often lamented the advantage which the French have over us in that particular. In Paris, the fashions have their dawnings, their routine, and declensions, and depend as much upon the caprice of the day as in other countries; but there every lady assumes a right to deviate from the general *ton*[30] as far as will be of advantage to her own appearance. In America, the cry is, what is the fashion? and we follow it indiscriminately, because it is so.

CHARLOTTE. Therefore it is, that when large hoops are in fashion, we often see many a plump girl lost in the immensity of a hoop-petticoat, whose want of height and *en-bon-point*[31] would never have been remarked in any other dress. When the high head-dress is the mode, how then do we see a lofty cushion, with a profusion of gauze, feathers, and ribbon, supported by a face no bigger than an apple! whilst a broad full-faced lady, who really would have appeared tolerably handsome in a large head-dress, looks with her smart chapeau[32] as masculine as a soldier.

MANLY. But remember, my dear sister, and I wish all my fair country-women would recollect, that the only excuse a young lady can have for going extravagantly into a fashion is because it makes her look extravagantly handsome.—Ladies, I must wish you a good morning.

CHARLOTTE. But, brother, you are going to make home with us.

MANLY. Indeed I cannot. I have seen my uncle and explained that matter.

CHARLOTTE. Come and dine with us, then. We have a family dinner about half-past four o'clock.

MANLY. I am engaged to dine with the Spanish ambassador. I was introduced to him by an old brother officer; and instead of freezing me with a cold card of compliment to dine with him ten days hence, he, with the true old Castilian frankness, in a friendly manner, asked me to dine with him to-day—an honour I could not refuse. Sister, adieu—Madam, you most obedient—— [*Exit.*

CHARLOTTE. I will wait upon you to the door, brother; I have something particular to say to you.

[*Exit.*

LETITIA [*alone*]. What a pair!—She the pink of flirtation, he the essence of everything that is *outré*[33] and gloomy.—I think I have completely deceived Charlotte by my manner of speaking of Mr. Dimple; she's too much the friend of Maria to be confided in. He is certainly rendering himself disagreeable to Maria, in order to break with her and proffer his hand to me. This is what the delicate fellow hinted in our last conversation. [*Exit.*

[30]Fashion.
[31]Plumpness.
[32]Hat.
[33]Bizarre, odd.

SCENE II. The Mall

Enter JESSAMY

JESSAMY. Positively this Mall is a very pretty place. I hope the cits[34] won't ruin it by repairs. To be sure, it won't do to speak of in the same day with Ranelagh or Vauxhall;[35] however, it's a fine place for a young fellow to display his person to advantage. Indeed, nothing is lost here; the girls have taste, and I am very happy to find they have adopted the elegant London fashion of looking back, after a genteel fellow like me has passed them.—Ah! who comes here? This, by his awkwardness, must be the Yankee colonel's servant. I'll accost him.

Enter JONATHAN

Votre très-humble serviteur, Monsieur.[36] I understand Colonel Manly, the Yankee officer, has the honour of your services.

JONATHAN. Sir!——

JESSAMY. I say, Sir, I understand that Colonel Manly has the honour of having you for a servant.

JONATHAN. Servant! Sir, do you take me for a neger—I am Colonel Manly's waiter.

JESSAMY. A true Yankee distinction, egad, without a difference. Why, Sir, do you not perform all the offices of a servant? do you not even blacken his boots?

JONATHAN. Yes; I do grease them a bit sometimes; but I am a true blue son of liberty, for all that. Father said I should come as Colonel Manly's waiter, to see the world, and all that; but no man shall master me. My father has as good a farm as the colonel.

JESSAMY. Well, Sir, we will not quarrel about terms upon the eye of an acquaintance from which I promise myself so much satisfaction—therefore, sans ceremonie[37]——

JONATHAN. What?——

JESSAMY. I say I am extremely happy to see Colonel Manly's waiter.

JONATHAN. Well, and I vow, too, I am pretty considerably glad to see you; but what the dogs need of all this outlandish lingo? Who may you be, Sir, if I may be so bold?

JESSAMY. I have the honour to be Mr. Dimple's servant, or, if you please, waiter. We lodge under the same roof, and should be glad of the honour of your acquaintance.

JONATHAN. You a waiter! by the living jingo, you look so topping, I took you for one of the agents to Congress.

JESSAMY. The brute has discernment, notwithstanding his appearance.—Give me leave to say I wonder then at your familiarity.

JONATHAN. Why, as to the matter of that, Mr.——; pray, what's your name?

JESSAMY. Jessamy, at your service.

JONATHAN. Why, I swear we don't make any great matter of distinction in our state between quality and other folks.

[34]Derogatory term for "citizens."
[35]Public amusement parks around London.
[36]"Your most humble servant, Sir" (French).
[37]"without ceremony" (French).

JESSAMY. This is, indeed, a levelling principle.—I hope, Mr. Jonathan, you have not taken part with the insurgents.

JONATHAN. Why, since General Shays has sneaked off and given us the bag to hold, I don't care to give my opinion; but you'll promise not to tell—put your ear this way—you won't tell?—I vow I did think the sturgeons were right.

JESSAMY. I thought, Mr. Jonathan, you Massachusetts men always argued with a gun in your hand. Why didn't you join them?

JONATHAN. Why, the colonel is one of those folks called the Shin—Shin[38]—dang it all, I can't speak them lignum vitæ[39] words—you know who I mean—there is a company of them—they wear a china goose at their button-hole—a kind of gilt thing.—Now the colonel told father and brother—you must know there are, let me see—there is Elnathan, Silas, and Barnabas, Tabitha—no, no, she's a she—tarnation, now I have it—there's Elnathan, Silas, Barnabas, Jonathan, that's I—seven of us, six went into the wars, and I stayed at home to take care of mother. Colonel said that it was a burning shame for the true blue Bunker Hill sons of liberty, who had fought Governor Hutchinson, Lord North,[40] and the Devil, to have any hand in kicking up a cursed dust against a government which we had, every mother's son of us, a hand in making.

JESSAMY. Bravo!—Well, have you been abroad in the city since your arrival? What have you seen that is curious and entertaining?

JONATHAN. Oh! I have seen a power of fine sights. I went to see two marblestone men and a leaden horse that stands out in doors in all weathers; and when I came where they was, one had got no head, and t'other weren't there. They said as how the leaden man was a damn'd tory,[41] and that he took wit in his anger and rode off in the time of the troubles.

JESSAMY. But this was not the end of your excursion?

JONATHAN. Oh, no; I went to a place they call Holy Ground.[42] Now I counted this was a place where folks go to meeting; so I put my hymn-book in my pocket, and walked softly and grave as a minister; and when I came there, the dogs a bit of a meeting-house could I see. At last I spied a young gentlewoman standing by one of the seats which they have here at the doors. I took her to be the deacon's daughter, and she looked so kind, and so obliging, that I thought I would go and ask her the way to lecture, and—would you think it?—she called me dear, and sweeting, and honey, just as if we were married: by the living jingo, I had a month's mind to buss[43] her.

JESSAMY. Well, but how did it end?

JONATHAN. Why, as I was standing talking with her, a parcel of sailor men and boys got round me, the snarl-headed curs fell a-kicking and cursing of me at such a tarnal[44] rate, that I vow I was glad to take to my heels and split home, right off, tail on end, like a stream of chalk.

[38]The Society of Cincinnati founded in 1783 by officers who served in the Continental Army during the American Revolution.

[39]"Wood of life" (Latin).

[40]Thomas Hutchinson (1711–1780), royal governor of Massachusetts (1771–1774); Frederick North (1732–1792), prime minister of Britain (1770–1782).

[41]British supporter during the American Revolution.

[42]The land owned by Trinity Church and where the brothel district was located in New York City.

[43]Kiss.

[44]Damned

JESSAMY. Why, my dear friend, you are not acquainted with the city; that girl you saw was a—— [*Whispers.*

JONATHAN. Mercy on my soul! was that young woman a harlot!—Well! if this is New-York Holy Ground, what must the Holy-day Ground be!

JESSAMY. Well, you should not judge of the city too rashly. We have a number of elegant, fine girls that make a man's leisure hours pass very agreeably. I would esteem it an honour to announce you to some of them.—Gad! that announce is a select word; I wonder where I picked it up.

JONATHAN. I don't want to know them.

JESSAMY. Come, come, my dear friend, I see that I must assume the honour of being the director of your amusements. Nature has given us passions, and youth and opportunity stimulate to gratify them. It is no shame, my dear Blueskin,[45] for a man to amuse himself with a little gallantry.

JONATHAN. Girl huntry! I don't altogether understand. I never played at that game. I know how to play hunt the squirrel, but I can't play anything with the girls; I am as good as married.

JESSAMY. Vulgar, horrid brute! Married, and above a hundred miles from his wife, and thinks that an objection to his making love to every woman he meets! He never can have read, no, he never can have been in a room with a volume of the divine Chesterfield.—So you are married?

JONATHAN. No, I don't say so, I said I was as good as married, a kind of promise.

JESSAMY. As good as married!——

JONATHAN. Why, yes; there's Tabitha Wymen, the deacon's daughter, at home; she and I have been courting a great while, and folks say as how we are to be married; and so I broke a piece of money[46] with her when we parted, and she promised not to spark it with Solomon Dyer while I am gone. You wouldn't have me false to my true-love, would you?

JESSAMY. May be you have another reason for constancy; possibly the young lady has a fortune? Ha! Mr. Jonathan, the solid charms; the chains of love are never so binding as when the links are made of gold.

JONATHAN. Why, as to fortune, I must needs say her father is pretty dumb rich; he went representative for our town last year. He will give her—let me see—four times seven is—seven times four—nought and carry one—he will give her twenty acres of land—somewhat rocky though—a Bible, and a cow.

JESSAMY. Twenty acres of rock, a Bible, and a cow! Why, my dear Mr. Jonathan, we have servant-maids, or, as you would more elegantly express it, waitresses, in this city, who collect more in one year from their mistresses' cast clothes.

JONATHAN. You don't say so!——

JESSAMY. Yes, and I'll introduce you to one of them. There is a little lump of flesh and delicacy that lives at next door, waitress to Miss Maria; we often see her on the stoop.

JONATHAN. But are you sure she would be courted by me?

JESSAMY. Never doubt it; remember a faint heart never—blisters on my tongue—I was going to be guilty of a vile proverb; flat against the authority of Chesterfield.

[45]Slang for a supporter of the American Revolution, derived from the blue soldier's uniforms.

[46]Custom whereby a pledge is sealed when two parties break a coin and each person keeps a half.

I say there can be no doubt that the brilliancy of your merit will secure you a favourable reception.

JONATHAN. Well, but what must I say to her?

JESSAMY. Say to her! why, my dear friend, though I admire your profound knowledge on every other subject, yet, you will pardon my saying that your want of opportunity has made the female heart escape the poignancy of your penetration. Say to her! Why, when a man goes a-courting, and hopes for success, he must begin with doing, and not saying.

JONATHAN. Well, what must I do?

JESSAMY. Why, when you are introduced you must make five or six elegant bows.

JONATHAN. Six elegant bows! I understand that; six, you say? Well——

JESSAMY. Then you must press and kiss her hand; then press a kiss, and so on to her lips and cheeks; then talk as much as you can about hearts, darts, flames, nectar and ambrosia—the more incoherent the better.

JONATHAN. Well, but suppose she should be angry with I?

JESSAMY. Why, if she should pretend—please to observe, Mr. Jonathan—if she should pretend to be offended, you must——But I'll tell you how my master acted in such a case: He was seated by a young lady of eighteen upon a sofa, plucking with a wanton hand the blooming sweets of youth and beauty. When the lady thought it necessary to check his ardour, she called up a frown upon her lovely face, so irresistibly alluring, that it would have warmed the frozen bosom of age; remember, said she, putting her delicate arm upon his, remember your character and my honour. My master instantly dropped upon his knees, with eyes swimming with love, cheeks glowing with desire, and in the gentlest modulation of voice he said: My dear Caroline, in a few months our hands will be indissolubly united at the altar; our hearts I feel are already so; the favours you now grant as evidence of your affection are favours indeed; yet, when the ceremony is once past, what will now be received with rapture will then be attributed to duty.

JONATHAN. Well, and what was the consequence?

JESSAMY. The consequence!—Ah! forgive me, my dear friend, but you New England gentlemen have such a laudable curiosity of seeing the bottom of everything—why, to be honest, I confess I saw the blooming cherub of a consequence smiling in its angelic mother's arms, about ten months afterwards.

JONATHAN. Well, if I follow all your plans, make them six bows, and all that, shall I have such little cherubim consequences?

JESSAMY. Undoubtedly.—What are you musing upon?

JONATHAN. You say you'll certainly make me acquainted?—Why, I was thinking then how I should contrive to pass this broken piece of silver—won't it buy a sugar-dram?[47]

JESSAMY. What is that, the love-token from the deacon's daughter?—You come on bravely. But I must hasten to my master. Adieu, my dear friend.

JONATHAN. Stay, Mr. Jessamy—must I buss her when I am introduced to her?

JESSAMY. I told you, you must kiss her.

JONATHAN. Well, but must I buss her?

JESSAMY. Why kiss and buss, and buss and kiss, is all one.

[47] A drink of punch.

JONATHAN. Oh! my dear friend, though you have a profound knowledge of all, a pugnency[48] of tribulation, you don't know everything. [*Exit.*

JESSAMY [*alone*]. Well, certainly I improve; my master could not have insinuated himself with more address into the heart of a man he despised. Now will this blundering dog sicken Jenny with his nauseous pawings, until she flies into my arms for very ease. How sweet will the contrast be between the blundering Jonathan and the courtly and accomplished Jessamy!

End of the Second Act

ACT III. SCENE I

DIMPLE'S *Room*

DIMPLE *discovered at a Toilet*

DIMPLE [*reading*]: "Women have in general but one object, which is their beauty." Very true, my lord; positively very true. "Nature has hardly formed a woman ugly enough to be insensible to flattery upon her person." Extremely just, my lord; every day's delightful experience confirms this. "If her face is so shocking that she must, in some degree, be conscious of it, her figure and air, she thinks, make ample amends for it." The sallow Miss Wan is a proof of this. Upon my telling the distasteful wretch, the other day, that her countenance spoke the pensive language of sentiment, and that Lady Wortley Montagu[49] declared that if the ladies were arrayed in the garb of innocence, the face would be the last part which would be admired, as Monsieur Milton expresses it, she grinn'd horribly a ghastly smile.[50] "If her figure is deformed, she thinks her face counterbalances it."[51]

Enter JESSAMY *with letters*

Where got you these, Jessamy?

JESSAMY. Sir, the English packet is arrived.

DIMPLE [*opens and reads a letter enclosing notes*]:

"Sir,

"I have drawn bills on you in favour of Messers. Van Cash and Co. as per margin. I have taken up your note to Col. Piquet, and discharged your debts to my Lord Lurcher and Sir Harry Rook. I herewith enclose you copies of the bills, which I have no doubt will be immediately honoured. On failure, I shall empower some lawyer in your country to recover the amounts.

"I am, Sir,

"Your most humble servant,

"JOHN HAZARD."

[48]Perhaps "poignancy."

[49]English poet (1689–1762).

[50]From *Paradise Lost, Book 2,* by John Milton (1608–1674).

[51]Quoted from Chesterfield's letters.

Now, did not my lord expressly say that it was unbecoming a well-bred man to be in a passion, I confess I should be ruffled. [*Reads.*] "There is no accident so unfortunate, which a wise man may not turn to his advantage; nor any accident so fortunate, which a fool will not turn to his disadvantage." True, my lord; but how advantage can be derived from this I can't see. Chesterfield himself, who made, however, the worst practice of the most excellent precepts, was never in so embarrassing a situation. I love the person of Charlotte, and it is necessary I should command the fortune of Letitia. As to Maria!—I doubt not by my *sangfroid*[52] behaviour I shall compel her to decline the match; but the blame must not fall upon me. A prudent man, as my lord says, should take all the credit of a good action to himself, and throw the discredit of a bad one upon others. I must break with Maria, marry Letitia, and as for Charlotte—why, Charlotte must be a companion to my wife.—Here, Jessamy!

Enter JESSAMY
DIMPLE *folds and seals two letters*

DIMPLE. Here, Jessamy, take this letter to my love. [*Gives one.*

JESSAMY. To which of your honour's loves?—Oh! [*reading*] to Miss Letitia, your honour's rich love.

DIMPLE. And this [*delivers another*] to Miss Charlotte Manly. See that you deliver them privately.

JESSAMY. Yes, your honour. [*Going.*

DIMPLE. Jessamy, who are these strange lodgers that came to the house last night?

JESSAMY. Why, the master is a Yankee colonel; I have not seen much of him; but the man is the most unpolished animal your honour ever disgraced your eyes by looking upon. I have had one of the most *outré* conversations with him!—He really has a most prodigious effect upon my risibility.

DIMPLE. I ought, according to every rule of Chesterfield, to wait on him and insinuate myself into his good graces.——Jessamy, wait on the colonel with my compliments, and if he is disengaged I will do myself the honour of paying him my respects.—Some ignorant, unpolished boor——

JESSAMY *goes off and returns*

JESSAMY. Sir, the colonel is gone out, and Jonathan his servant says that he is gone to stretch his legs upon the Mall.—Stretch his legs! what an indelicacy of diction!

DIMPLE. Very well. Reach me my hat and sword. I'll accost him there, in my way to Letitia's, as by accident; pretend to be struck by his person and address, and endeavour to steal into his confidence. Jessamy, I have no business for you at present. [*Exit.*

JESSAMY. [*taking up the book*]. My master and I obtain our knowledge from the same source—though, gad! I think myself much the prettier fellow of the two. [*Surveying himself in the glass.*] That was a brilliant thought, to insinuate that I folded my master's letters for him; the folding is so neat, that it does honour to the operator. I once intended to have insinuated that I wrote his letters too; but that was before I saw them; it won't do now; no honour there, positively.—"Nothing looks more

[52]Composed, cool.

vulgar, [*reading affectedly*] ordinary, and illiberal than ugly, uneven, and ragged nails; the ends of which should be kept even and clean, not tipped with black, and cut in small segments of circles."[53]—Segments of circles! surely my lord did not consider that he wrote for the beaux. Segments of circles; what a crabbed term! Now I dare answer that my master, with all his learning, does not know that this means, according to the present mode, let the nails grow long, and then cut them off even at top. [*Laughing without.*] Ha! that's Jenny's titter. I protest I despair of ever teaching that girl to laugh; she has something so execrably natural in her laugh, that I declare it absolutely discomposes my nerves. How came she into our house! [*Calls.*] Jenny!

Enter JENNY

Prythee, Jenny, don't spoil your fine face with laughing.

JENNY. Why, mustn't I laugh, Mr. Jessamy?

JESSAMY. You may smile, but, as my lord says, nothing can authorise a laugh.

JENNY. Well, but I can't help laughing.—Have you see him, Mr. Jessamy? ha, ha, ha!

JESSAMY. Seen whom?

JENNY. Why, Jonathan, the New England colonel's servant. Do you know he was at the play last night, and the stupid creature don't know where he has been. He would not go to a play for the world; he thinks it was a show, as he calls it.

JESSAMY. As ignorant and unpolished as he is, do you know, Miss Jenny, that I propose to introduce him to the honour of your acquaintance?

JENNY. Introduce him to me! for what?

JESSAMY. Why, my lovely girl, that you may take him under your protection, as Madame Rambouillet did young Stanhope;[54] that you may, by your plastic hand, mould this uncouth cub into a gentleman. He is to make love to you.

JENNY. Make love to me!——

JESSAMY. Yes, Mistress Jenny, make love to you; and, I doubt not, when he shall become *domesticated* in your kitchen, that this boor, under your auspices, will soon become *un amiable petit Jonathan.*[55]

JENNY. I must say, Mr. Jessamy, if he copies after me, he will be vastly, monstrously polite.

JESSAMY. Stay here one moment, and I will call him.—Jonathan!—Mr. Jonathan!— [*Calls.*

JONATHAN (*within*]. Holla! there.—[*Enters.*] You promise to stand by me—six bows you say. [*Bows.*

JESSAMY. Mrs. Jenny, I have the honour of presenting Mr. Jonathan, Colonel Manly's waiter, to you. I am extremely happy that I have it in my power to make two worthy people acquainted with each other's merits.

JENNY. So, Mr. Jonathan, I hear you were at the play last night.

JONATHAN. At the play! why, did you think I went to the devil's drawing-room?

JENNY. The devil's drawing-room!

JONATHAN. Yes; why an't cards and dice the devil's device, and the play-house the

[53]Quoted from Chesterfield's letters.

[54]Catherine de Vivonne Rambouillet (1588–1665), a teacher of the arts of gentility and conversation whose life predates Philip Stanhope (1732–1768), Lord Chesterfield's son.

[55]"a courteous little Jonathan" (French).

shop where the devil hangs out the vanities of the world upon the tenterhooks of temptation? I believe you have not heard how they were acting the old boy one night, and the wicked one came among them sure enough, and went right off in a storm, and carried one quarter of the play-house with him. Oh! no, no, no! you won't catch me at a play-house, I warrant you.

JENNY. Well, Mr. Jonathan, though I don't scruple your veracity, I have some reasons for believing you were there: pray, where were you about six o'clock?

JONATHAN. Why, I went to see one Mr. Morrison, the *hocus pocus* man; they said as how he could eat a case knife.

JENNY. Well, and how did you find the place?

JONATHAN. As I was going about here and there, to and again, to find it, I saw a great crowd of folks going into a long entry that had lanterns over the door; so I asked a man whether that was not the place where they played *hocus pocus?* He was a civil, kind man, though he did speak like the Hessians;[56] he lifted up his eyes and said, "They play *hocus pocus* tricks enough there, Got knows, mine friend."

JENNY. Well—

JONATHAN. So I went right in, and they showed me away, clean up to the garret, just like meeting-house gallery. And so I saw a power of topping folks, all sitting round in little cabins,[57] "just like father's corn-cribs"; and then there was such a squeaking with the fiddles, and such a tarnal blaze with the lights, my head was near turned. At last the people that sat near me set up such a hissing—hiss—like so many mad cats; and then they went thump, thump, thump, just like our Peleg threshing wheat, and stamped away, just like the nation;[58] and called out for one Mr. Langolee—I suppose he helps act the tricks.

JENNY. Well, and what did you do all this time?

JONATHAN. Gor, I—I liked the fun, and so I thumped away, and hiss'd as lustily as the best of 'em. One sailor-looking man that sat by me, seeing me stamp, and knowing I was a cute fellow, because I could make a roaring noise, clapped me on the shoulder and said, "You are a d——d hearty cock, smite my timbers!" I told him so I was, but I thought he need not swear so, and make use of such naughty words.

JESSAMY. The savage!—Well, and did you see the man with his tricks?

JONATHAN. Why, I vow, as I was looking out for him, they lifted up a great green cloth and let us look right into the next neighbour's house. Have you a good many houses in New-York made so in that 'ere way?

JENNY. Not many; but did you see the family?

JONATHAN. Yes, swamp it; I see'd the family.

JENNY. Well, and how did you like them?

JONATHAN. Why, I vow they were pretty much like other families—there was a poor, good-natured, curse of a husband, and a sad rantipole[59] of a wife.

JENNY. But did you see no other folks.

JONATHAN. Yes. There was one youngster; they called him Mr. Joseph; he talked as

[56]German peasants from Hesse hired by the British as mercenary soldiers in the American Revolution.

[57]Theater boxes.

[58]Or, "damnation."

[59]Wild, unruly person.

sober and as pious as a minister; but, like some ministers that I know, he was a sly tike in his heart for all that. He was going to ask a young woman to spark it with him, and—the Lord have mercy on my soul!—she was another man's wife.

JESSAMY. The Wabash![60]

JENNY. And did you see any more folks?

JONATHAN. Why, they came on as thick as mustard. For my part, I thought the house was haunted. There was a soldier fellow, who talked about his row de dow, dow, and courted a young woman; but, of all the cute folk I saw, I liked one little fellow——

JENNY. Aye! who was he?

JONATHAN. Why, he had red hair, and a little round plump face like mine, only not altogether so handsome. His name was—Darby—that was his baptizing name; his other name I forgot. Oh! it was Wig—Wag—Wag-all Darby Wagall[61]—pray, do you know him?—I should like to take a sling with him, or a drap of cyder with a pepper-pod in it, to make it warm and confortable.

JENNY. I can't say I have that pleasure.

JONATHAN. I wish you did; he is a cute fellow. But there was one thing I didn't like in that Mr. Darby; and that was, he was afraid of some of them 'ere shooting irons, such as your troopers wear on training days. Now, I'm a true born Yankee American son of liberty, and I never was afraid of a gun yet in all my life.

JENNY. Well, Mr. Jonathan, you were certainly at the play-house.

JONATHAN. I at the play-house!—Why didn't I see the play then?

JENNY. Why, the people you saw were players.

JONATHAN. Mercy on my soul! did I see the wicked players?—Mayhap that 'ere Darby that I liked so was the old serpent himself, and had his cloven foot in his pocket. Why, I vow, now I come to think on't, the candles seemed to burn blue, and I am sure where I sat it smelt tarnally of brimstone.

JESSAMY. Well, Mr. Jonathan, from your account, which I confess is very accurate, you must have been at the play-house.

JONATHAN. Why, I vow, I began to smell a rat. When I came away, I went to the man for my money again; you want your money? says he; yes, says I; for what? says he; why, says I, no man shall jockey me out of my money; I paid my money to see sights, and the dogs a bit of a sight have I seen, unless you call listening to people's private business a sight. Why, says he, it is the School for Scandalization.[62]—The School for Scandalization!—Oh! ho! no wonder you New-York folks are so cute at it, when you go to school to learn it; and so I jogged off.

JESSAMY. My dear Jenny, my master's business drags me from you; would to heaven I knew no other servitude than to your charms.

JONATHAN. Well, but don't go; you won't leave me so——

JESSAMY. Excuse me.—Remember the cash.

[*Aside to him, and—Exit.*

[60]A cheat.

[61]A combination of Thomas Wignall, the actor, and Darby, a character that Wignall played in *The Poor Soldier* (1783).

[62]*The School for Scandal* (1777) by Richard Sheridan (1751–1816) was produced in New York shortly before *The Contrast* opened.

JENNY. Mr. Jonathan, won't you please to sit down? Mr. Jessamy tells me you wanted to have some conversation with me.

[*Having brought forward two chairs, they sit.*

JONATHAN. Ma'am!—
JENNY. Sir!——
JONATHAN. Ma'am!——
JENNY. Pray, how do you like the city, Sir?
JONATHAN. Ma'am!——
JENNY. I say, Sir, how do you like New-York?
JONATHAN. Ma'am!——
JENNY. The stupid creature! but I must pass some little time with him, if it is only to endeavour to learn whether it was his master that made such an abrupt entrance into our house and my young mistress's heart, this morning. [*Aside.*] As you don't seem to like to talk, Mr. Jonathan—do you sing?
JONATHAN. Gor, I—I am glad she asked that, for I forgot what Mr. Jessamy bid me say, and I dare as well be hanged as act what he bid me do, I'm so ashamed. [*Aside.*] Yes, Ma'am, I can sing—I can sing "Mear," "Old Hundred," and "Bangor."
JENNY. Oh! I don't mean psalm tunes. Have you no little song to please the ladies, such as "Roslin Castle," or the "Maid of the Mill?"
JONATHAN. Why, all my tunes are go to meeting tunes, save one, and I count you won't altogether like that 'ere.
JENNY. What is it called?
JONATHAN. I am sure you have heard folks talk about it; it is called "Yankee Doodle."
JENNY. Oh! it is the tune I am fond of; and if I know anything of my mistress, she would be glad to dance to it. Pray, sing!
JONATHAN [*sings*].

Father and I went up to camp,
Along with Captain Goodwin;
And there we saw the men and boys,
As thick as hasty-pudding.
Yankee doodle do, etc.

And there we saw a swamping gun,
Big as log of maple,
On a little deuced cart,
A load for father's cattle.
Yankee doodle do, etc.

And every time they fired it off
It took a horn of powder
It made a noise—like father's gun,
Only a nation louder.
Yankee doodle do, etc.

There was a man in our town,
His name was——

No, no, that won't do. Now, if I was with Tabitha Wymen and Jemima Cawley down at father Chase's, I shouldn't mind singing this all out before them—you would be affronted if I was to sing that, though that's a lucky thought; if you should be affronted, I have something dang'd cute, which Jessamy told me to say to you.

JENNY. Is that all! I assure you I like it of all things.

JONATHAN. No, no; I can sing more; some other time, when you and I are better acquainted, I'll sing the whole of it—no, no—that's a fib—I can't sing but a hundred and ninety verses; our Tabitha at home can sing it all.—— [*Sings.*

Marblehead's rocky place,
And Cape-Cod is sandy;
Charlestown is burnt down,
Boston is the dandy.
Yankee doddle, doodle do, etc.

I vow, my own town song has put me into such topping spirits that I believe I'll begin to do a little, as Jessamy says we must when we go a-courting—[*Runs and kisses her.*] Burning rivers! cooling flames! red-hot roses! pig-nuts! hasty-pudding and ambrosia!

JENNY. What means this freedom? you insulting wretch. [*Strikes him.*

JONATHAN. Are you affronted?

JENNY. Affronted! with what looks shall I express my anger?

JONATHAN. Looks! why as to the matter of looks, you look as cross as a witch.

JENNY. Have you no feeling for the delicacy of my sex?

JONATHAN. Feeling! Gor, I—I feel the delicacy of your sex pretty smartly [*rubbing his cheek*], though, I vow, I thought when you city ladies courted and married, and all that, you put feeling out of the question. But I want to know whether you are really affronted, or only pretend to be so? 'Cause, if you are certainly right down affronted, I am at the end of my tether; Jessamy didn't tell me what to say to you.

JENNY. Pretend to be affronted!

JONATHAN. Aye aye, if you only pretend, you shall hear how I'll go to work to make cherubim consequences. [*Runs up to her.*

JENNY. Begone, you brute!

JONATHAN. That looks like mad; but I won't lose my speech. My dearest Jenny—your name is Jenny, I think?—My dearest Jenny, though I have the highest esteem for the sweet favours you have just now granted me—Gor, that's a fib, though; but Jessamy says it is not wicked to tell lies to the women. [*Aside.*] I say, though I have the highest esteem for the favours you have just now granted me, yet you will consider that, as soon as the dissolvable knot is tied, they will no longer be favours, but only matters of duty and matters of course.

JENNY. Marry you! you audacious monster! get out of my sight, or, rather, let me fly from you. [*Exit hastily.*

JONATHAN. Gor! she's gone off in a swinging passion, before I had time to think of consequences. If this is the way with your city ladies, give me the twenty acres of rock, the Bible, the cow, and Tabitha, and a little peaceable bundling.[63]

SCENE II. The Mall

Enter MANLY

MANLY. It must be so, Montague! and it is not all the tribe of Mandevilles[64] that shall convince me that a nation, to become great, must first become dissipated. Luxury is surely the bane of a nation: Luxury! which enervates both soul and body, by opening a thousand new sources of enjoyment, opens, also, a thousand new sources of contention and want: Luxury! which renders a people weak at home, and accessible to bribery, corruption, and force from abroad. When the Grecian states knew no other tools than the axe and the saw, the Grecians were a great, a free and a happy people. The kings of Greece devoted their lives to the service of their country, and her senators knew no other superiority over their fellow-citizens than a glorious pre-eminence in danger and virtue. They exhibited to the world a noble spectacle—a number of independent states united by a similarity of language, sentiment, manners, common interest, and common consent in one grand mutual league of protection. And, thus united, long might they have continued the cherishers of arts and sciences, the protectors of the oppressed, the scourge of tyrants, and the safe asylum of liberty. But when foreign gold, and still more pernicious foreign luxury, had crept among them, they sapped the vitals of their virtue. The virtues of their ancestors were only found in their writings. Envy and suspicion, the vices of little minds, possessed them. The various states engendered jealousies of each other; and, more unfortunately, growing jealous of their great federal council, the Amphicytons,[65] they forgot that their common safety had existed, and would exist, in giving them an honourable extensive prerogative. The common good was lost in the pursuit of private interest; and that people who, by uniting, might have stood against the world in arms, by dividing, crumbled into ruin—their name is now only known in the page of the historian, and what they once were is all we have left to admire. Oh! that America! Oh! that my country, would, in this her day, learn the things which belong to her peace!

Enter DIMPLE

DIMPLE. You are Colonel Manly, I presume?

MANLY. At your service, Sir.

DIMPLE. My name is Dimple, Sir. I have the honour to be a lodger in the same house with you, and, hearing you were in the Mall, came hither to take the liberty of joining you.

[63]A courtship ritual where the couple shares the same bed fully dressed.

[64]Edward Montagu (1713–1776), author of *Reflections on the Rise and Fall of Ancient Republics* (1759). Bernard de Mandeville (1670–1733), author of *The Fable of the Bees* (1705). These authors wrote on the decline of civilizations and the follies of humankind.

[65]Religious assemblies of Greek states.

MANLY. You are very obliging, Sir.

DIMPLE. As I understand you are a stranger here, Sir, I have taken the liberty to introduce myself to your acquaintance, as possibly I may have it in my power to point out some things in this city worthy your notice.

MANLY. An attention to strangers is worthy a liberal mind, and must ever be gratefully received. But to a soldier, who has no fixed abode, such attentions are particularly pleasing.

DIMPLE. Sir, there is no character so respectable as that of a soldier. And, indeed, when we reflect how much we owe to those brave men who have suffered so much in the service of their country, and secured to us those inestimable blessings that we now enjoy, our liberty and independence, they demand every attention which gratitude can pay. For my own part, I never meet an officer, but I embrace him as my friend, nor a private in distress, but I insensibly extend my charity to him.—— I have hit the Bumkin off very tolerably. [*Aside.*

MANLY. Give me your hand, Sir! I do not proffer this hand to everybody; but you steal into my heart. I hope I am as insensible to flattery as most men; but I declare (it may be my weak side) that I never hear the name of soldier mentioned with respect, but I experience a thrill of pleasure which I never feel on any other occasion.

DIMPLE. Will you give me leave, my dear Colonel, to confer an obligation on myself, by showing you some civilities during your stay here, and giving a similar opportunity to some of my friends?

MANLY. Sir, I thank you; but I believe my stay in this city will be very short.

DIMPLE. I can introduce you to some men of excellent sense, in whose company you will esteem yourself happy; and, by way of amusement, to some fine girls, who will listen to your soft things with pleasure.

MANLY. Sir, I should be proud of the honour of being acquainted with those gentlemen—but, as for the ladies, I don't understand you.

DIMPLE. Why, Sir, I need not tell you, that when a young gentleman is alone with a young lady he must say some soft things to her fair cheek—indeed, the lady will expect it. To be sure, there is not much pleasure when a man of the world and a finished coquette meet, who perfectly know each other; but how delicious is it to excite the emotions of joy, hope, expectation, and delight in the bosom of a lovely girl who believes every tittle of what you say to be serious!

MANLY. Serious, Sir! In my opinion, the man who, under pretensions of marriage, can plant thorns in the bosom of an innocent, unsuspecting girl is more detestable than a common robber, in the same proportion as private violence is more despicable than open force, and money of less value than happiness.

DIMPLE. How he awes me by the superiority of his sentiments. [*Aside.*] As you say, Sir, a gentleman should be cautious how he mentions marriage.

MANLY. Cautious, Sir! No person more approves of an intercourse between the sexes than I do. Female conversation softens our manners, whilst our discourse, from the superiority of our literary advantages, improves their minds. But, in our young country, where there is no such thing as gallantry, when a gentleman speaks of love to a lady, whether he mentions marriage or not, she ought to conclude either that he meant to insult her or that his intentions are the most serious and honourable. How mean, how cruel, is it, by a thousand tender assiduities, to win the affections of an amiable girl, and, though you leave her virtue unspotted, to betray her into the appearance of so many tender partialities, that every man of delicacy would suppress his inclination towards her, by supposing her heart engaged! Can any man, for the trivial gratification of his leisure hours, affect the happiness of a whole life! His not having spoken of marriage may add to his perfidy, but can be no excuse for his conduct.

DIMPLE. Sir, I admire your sentiments—they are mine. The light observations that fell from me were only a principle of the tongue; they came not from the heart; my practice has ever disapproved these principles.

MANLY. I believe you, sir. I should with reluctance suppose that those pernicious sentiments could find admittance into the heart of a gentleman.

DIMPLE. I am now, Sir, going to visit a family, where, if you please, I will have the honour of introducing you. Mr. Manly's ward, Miss Letitia, is a young lady of immense fortune; and his niece, Miss Charlotte Manly, is a young lady of great sprightliness and beauty.

MANLY. That gentleman, Sir, is my uncle, and Miss Manly my sister.

DIMPLE. The devil she is! [*Aside.*] Miss Manly your sister, Sir? I rejoice to hear it, and feel a double pleasure in being known to you.—Plague on him! I wish he was at Boston again, with all my soul. [*Aside.*

MANLY. Come, Sir, will you go?

DIMPLE. I will follow you in a moment, Sir. [*Exit* MANLY.] Plague on it! this is unlucky. A fighting brother is a cursed appendage to a fine girl. Egad! I just stopped in time; had he not discovered himself, in two minutes more I should have told him how well I was with his sister. Indeed, I cannot see the satisfaction of an intrigue, if one can't have the pleasure of communicating it to our friends. [*Exit.*

End of the Third Act

ACT IV. SCENE I

CHARLOTTE'S *Apartment*

CHARLOTTE *leading in* MARIA

CHARLOTTE. This is so kind, my sweet friend, to come to see me at this moment. I declare, if I were going to be married in a few days, as you are, I should scarce have found time to visit my friends.

MARIA. Do you think, then, that there is an impropriety in it?—How should you dispose of your time?

CHARLOTTE. Why, I should be shut up in my chamber; and my head would so run upon—upon—upon the solemn ceremony that I was to pass through!—I declare, it would take me above two hours merely to learn that little monosyllable—*Yes.* Ah! my dear, your sentimental imagination does not conceive what that little tiny word implies.

MARIA. Spare me your raillery, my sweet friend; I should love your agreeable vivacity at any other time.

CHARLOTTE. Why, this is the very time to amuse you. You grieve me to see you look so unhappy.

MARIA. Have I not reason to look so?

CHARLOTTE. What new grief distresses you?

MARIA. Oh! how sweet it is, when the heart is borne down with misfortune, to recline and repose on the bosom of friendship! Heaven knows that, although it is improper for a young lady to praise a gentleman, yet I have ever concealed Mr. Dimple's foibles, and spoke of him as of one whose reputation I expected would be linked with mine; but his late conduct towards me has turned my coolness into contempt. He behaves as if he meant to insult and disgust me; whilst my father, in the last conversation on the subject of our marriage, spoke of it as a matter which lay near his heart, and in which he would not bear contradiction.

CHARLOTTE. This works well; oh! the generous Dimple. I'll endeavour to excite her to discharge him. [*Aside.*] But, my dear friend, your happiness depends on yourself. Why don't you discard him? Though the match has been of long standing, I would not be forced to make myself miserable: no parent in the world should oblige me to marry the man I did not like.

MARIA. Oh! my dear, you never lived with your parents, and do not know what influence a father's frowns have upon a daughter's heart. Besides, what have I to alledge against Mr. Dimple, to justify myself to the world? He carries himself so smoothly, that every one would impute the blame to me, and call me capricious.

CHARLOTTE. And call her capricious! Did ever such an objection start into the heart of woman? For my part, I wish I had fifty lovers to discard, for no other reason than because I did not fancy them. My dear Maria, you will forgive me; I know your candour and confidence in me; but I have at times, I confess, been led to suppose that some other gentleman was the cause of your aversion to Mr. Dimple.

MARIA. No, my sweet friend, you may be assured, that though I have seen many gentlemen I could prefer to Mr. Dimple, yet I never saw one that I thought I could give my hand to, until this morning.

CHARLOTTE. This morning!

MARIA. Yes; one of the strangest accidents in the world. The odious Dimple, after disgusting me with his conversation, had just left me, when a gentleman, who, it seems, boards in the same house with him, saw him coming out of our door, and, the houses looking very much alike, he came into our house instead of his lodgings; nor did he discover his mistake until he got into the parlour, where I was; he then bowed so gracefully, made such a genteel apology, and looked so manly and noble!——

CHARLOTTE. I see some folks, though it is so great an impropriety, can praise a gentleman, when he happens to be the man of their fancy. [*Aside.*

MARIA. I don't know how it was—I hope he did not think me indelicate—but I asked him, I believe, to sit down, or pointed to a chair. He sat down, and, instead of having recourse to observations upon the weather, or hackneyed criticisms upon the theatre, he entered readily into a conversation worthy a man of sense to speak, and a lady of delicacy and sentiment to hear. He was not strictly handsome, but he spoke the language of sentiment, and his eyes looked tenderness and honour.

CHARLOTTE. Oh! [eagerly] you sentimental, grave girls, when your hearts are once touched, beat us rattles a bar's length. And so you are quite in love with this he-angel?

MARIA. In love with him! How can you rattle so, Charlotte? am I not going to be miserable? [*Sighs.*] In love with a gentleman I never saw but one hour in my life, and don't know his name! No; I only wished that the man I shall marry may look, and talk, and act, just like him. Besides, my dear, he is a married man.

CHARLOTTE. Why, that was good-natured—he told you so, I suppose, in mere charity, to prevent you falling in love with him?

MARIA. He didn't tell me so; [*peevishly*] he looked as if he was married.

CHARLOTTE. How, my dear; did he look sheepish?

MARIA. I am sure he has a susceptible heart, and the ladies of his acquaintance must be very stupid not to——

CHARLOTTE. Hush! I hear some person coming.

Enter LETITIA

LETITIA. My dear Maria, I am happy to see you. Lud! what a pity it is that you have purchased your wedding clothes.

MARIA. I think so. [*Sighing.*

LETITIA. Why, my dear, there is the sweetest parcel of silks come over you ever saw! Nancy Brilliant has a full suit come; she sent over her measure, and it fits her to a hair; it is immensely dressy, and made for a court-hoop. I thought they said the large hoops were going out of fashion.

CHARLOTTE. Did you see the hat? Is it a fact that the deep laces round the border is still the fashion?

DIMPLE. [*within*]. Upon my honour, Sir.

MARIA. Ha! Dimple's voice! My dear, I must take leave of you. There are some things necessary to be done at our house. Can't I go through the other room?

Enter DIMPLE *and* MANLY

DIMPLE. Ladies, your most obedient.

CHARLOTTE. Miss Van Rough, shall I present my brother Henry to you? Colonel Manly, Maria—Miss Van Rough, brother.

MARIA. Her brother! [*Turns and sees* MANLY.] Oh! my heart! the very gentleman I have been praising.

MANLY. The same amiable girl I saw this morning!

CHARLOTTE. Why, you look as if you were acquainted.

MANLY. I unintentionally intruded into this lady's presence this morning, for which she was so good as to promise me her forgiveness.

CHARLOTTE. Oh! ho! is that the case! Have these two penserosos been together? Were they Henry's eyes that looked so tenderly? [*Aside.*] And so you promised to pardon him? and could you be so good-natured? have you really forgiven him? I beg you would do it for my sake [*whispering loud to* MARIA]. But, my dear, as you are in such haste, it would be cruel to detain you; I can show you the way through the other room.

MARIA. Spare me, my sprightly friend.

MANLY. The lady does not, I hope, intend to deprive us of the pleasure of her company so soon.

CHARLOTTE. She has only a mantua-maker[66] who waits for her at home. But, as I am to give my opinion of the dress, I think she cannot go yet. We were talking of the fashions when you came in, but I suppose the subject must be changed to something of more importance now. Mr. Dimple, will you favour us with an account of the public entertainments?

DIMPLE. Why, really, Miss Manly, you could not have asked me a question more *mal-apropos.*[67] For my part, I must confess that, to a man who has travelled, there is nothing that is worthy the name of amusement to be found in this city.

CHARLOTTE. Except visiting the ladies.

DIMPLE. Pardon me, Madam; that is the avocation of a man of taste. But for amusement, I positively know of nothing that can be called so, unless you dignify with that title the hopping once a fortnight to the sound of two or three squeaking fiddles, and the clattering of the old tavern windows, or sitting to see the miserable mummers, whom you call actors, murder comedy and make a farce of tragedy.

MANLY. Do you never attend the theatre, Sir?

DIMPLE. I was tortured there once.

CHARLOTTE. Pray, Mr. Dimple, was it a tragedy or a comedy?

DIMPLE. Faith, Madam, I cannot tell; for I sat with my back to the stage all the time, admiring a much better actress than any there—a lady who played the fine woman to perfection; though, by the laugh of the horrid creatures round me, I suppose it was comedy. Yet, on second thoughts, it might be some hero in a tragedy, dying so comically as to set the whole house in an uproar. Colonel, I presume you have been in Europe?

MANLY. Indeed, Sir, I was never ten leagues from the continent.

DIMPLE. Believe me, Colonel, you have an immense pleasure to come; and when you shall have seen the brilliant exhibitions of Europe, you will learn to despise the amusements of this country as much as I do.

MANLY. Therefore I do not wish to see them; for I can never esteem that knowledge valuable which tends to give me a distaste for my native country.

DIMPLE. Well, Colonel, though you have not travelled, you have read.

MANLY. I have, a little; and by it have discovered that there is a laudable partiality which ignorant, untravelled men entertain for everything that belongs to their native country. I call it laudable; it injures no one; adds to their own happiness; and, when extended, becomes the noble principle of patriotism. Travelled gentlemen rise superior, in their own opinion, to this; but if the contempt which they contract for their country is the most valuable acquisition of their travels, I am far from thinking that their time and money are well spent.

MARIA. What noble sentiments!

CHARLOTTE. Let my brother set out where he will in the fields of conversation, he is sure to end his tour in the temple of gravity.

MANLY. Forgive me, my sister. I love my country; it has its foibles undoubtedly—some foreigners will with pleasure remark them—but such remarks fall very ungracefully from the lips of her citizens.

[66]Dressmaker.

[67]"Inappropriate" (French).

DIMPLE. You are perfectly in the right, Colonel—America has her faults.

MANLY. Yes, Sir; and we, her children, should blush for them in private, and endeavour, as individuals, to reform them. But, if our country has its errors in common with other countries, I am proud to say America—I mean the United States—has displayed virtues and achievements which modern nations may admire, but of which they have seldom set us the example.

CHARLOTTE. But, brother, we must introduce you to some of our gay folks, and let you see the city, such as it is. Mr. Dimple is known to almost every family in town; he will doubtless take a pleasure in introducing you?

DIMPLE. I shall esteem every service I can render your brother an honour.

MANLY. I fear the business I am upon will take up all my time, and my family will be anxious to hear from me.

MARIA. His family! but what is it to me that he is married! [*Aside.*]. Pray, how did you leave your lady, Sir?

CHARLOTTE. My brother is not married [*observing her anxiety*]; it is only an odd way he has of expressing himself. Pray, brother, is this business, which you make your continual excuse, a secret?

MANLY. No, sister; I came hither to solicit the honourable Congress, that a number of my brave old soldiers may be put upon the pension-list, who were, at first, not judged to be so materially wounded as to need the public assistance. My sister says true [*to* MARIA]; I call my late soldiers my family. Those who were not in the field in the late glorious contest, and those who were, have their respective merits; but, I confess, my older brother-soldiers are dearer to me than the former description. Friendships made in adversity are lasting; our countrymen may forget us, but that is no reason why we should forget one another. But I must leave you; my time of engagement approaches.

CHARLOTTE. Well, but, brother, if you will go, will you please to conduct my fair friend home? You live in the same street——I was to have gone with her myself—[*Aside.*] A lucky thought.

MARIA. I am obliged to your sister, Sir, and was just intending to go. [*Going.*

MANLY. I shall attend her with pleasure.

Exit with MARIA, *followed by* DIMPLE *and* CHARLOTTE.

MARIA. Now, pray, don't betray me to your brother.

CHARLOTTE. [*Just as she sees him make a motion to take his leave.*] One word with you, brother, if you please. [*Follows them out.*

Manent[68] DIMPLE *and* LETITIA.

DIMPLE. You received the billet[69] I sent you, I presume?

LETITIA. Hush!—Yes.

DIMPLE. When shall I pay my respects to you?

LETITIA. At eight I shall be unengaged.

Reenter CHARLOTTE

[68]"There remain" (French). [69]A note.

DIMPLE. Did my lovely angel receive my billet? [*To* CHARLOTTE.]
CHARLOTTE. Yes.
DIMPLE. What hour shall I expect with impatience?
CHARLOTTE. At eight I shall be at home unengaged.
DIMPLE. Unfortunate! I have a horrid engagement of business at that hour. Can't you finish your visit earlier and let six be the happy hour?
CHARLOTTE. You know your influence over me. [*Exeunt severally.*

SCENE II

VAN ROUGH'S House

VAN ROUGH [*alone*]. It cannot possibly be true! The son of my old friend can't have acted so unadvisedly. Seventeen thousand pounds! in bills! Mr. Transfer must have been mistaken. He always appeared so prudent, and talked so well upon money matters, and even assured me that he intended to change his dress for a suit of clothes which would not cost so much, and look more substantial, as soon as he married. No, no, no! it can't be; it cannot be. But, however, I must look out sharp. I did not care what his principles or his actions were, so long as he minded the main chance. Seventeen thousand pounds! If he had lost it in trade, why the best men may have ill-luck; but to game it away, as Transfer says—why, at this rate, his whole estate may go in one night, and, what is ten times worse, mine into the bargain. No, no; Mary is right. Leave women to look out in these matters; for all they look as if they didn't know a journal from a ledger, when their interest is concerned they know what's what; they mind the main chance as well as the best of us. I wonder Mary did not tell me she knew of his spending his money so foolishly. Seventeen thousand pounds! Why, if my daughter was standing up to be married, I would forbid the banns,[70] if I found it was to a man who did not mind the main chance.—Hush! I hear somebody coming. 'Tis Mary's voice; a man with her too! I shouldn't be surprised if this should be the other string to her bow. Aye, aye, let them alone; women understand the main chance.—Though, i' faith, I'll listen a little. [*Retires into a closet.*

MANLY *leading in* MARIA

MANLY. I hope you will excuse my speaking upon so important a subject so abruptly; but, the moment I entered your room, you struck me as the lady whom I had long loved in imagination, and never hoped to see.
MARIA. Indeed, Sir, I have been led to hear more upon this subject than I ought.
MANLY. Do you, then, disapprove my suit, Madam, or the abruptness of my introducing it? If the latter, my peculiar situation, being obliged to leave the city in a few days, will, I hope, be my excuse; if the former, I will retire, for I am sure I would not give a moment's inquietude to her whom I could devote my life to please. I am not so indelicate as to seek your immediate approbation; permit me only to be near you, and by a thousand tender assiduities to endeavour to excite a grateful return.

[70]Wedding announcements.

MARIA. I have a father, whom I would die to make happy; he will disapprove——

MANLY. Do you think me so ungenerous as to seek a place in your esteem without his consent? You must—you ever ought to consider that man as unworthy of you seeks an interest in your heart contrary to a father's approbation. A young lady should reflect that the loss of a lover may be supplied, but nothing can compensate for the loss of a parent's affection. Yet, why do you suppose your father would disapprove? In our country, the affections are not sacrificed to riches or family aggrandizement; should you approve, my family is decent, and my rank honourable.

MARIA. You distress me, Sir.

MANLY. Then I will sincerely beg your excuse for obtruding so disagreeable a subject, and retire. [*Going.*

MARIA. Stay, Sir! your generosity and good opinion of me deserve a return; but why must I declare what, for these few hours, I have scarce suffered myself to think?—I am——

MANLY. What?

MARIA. Engaged, Sir; and, in a few days to be married to the gentleman you saw at your sister's.

MANLY. Engaged to be married! And I have been basely invading the rights of another? Why have you permitted this? Is this the return for the partiality I declared for you?

MARIA. You distress me, Sir. What would you have me say? you are too generous to wish the truth. Ought I to say that I dared not suffer myself to think of my engagement, and that I am going to give my hand without my heart? Would you have me confess a partiality for you? If so, your triumph is complete, and can be only more so when days of misery with the man I cannot love will make me think of him whom I could prefer.

MANLY [*after a pause*]. We are both unhappy; but it is your duty to obey your parent—mine to obey my honour. Let us, therefore, both follow the path of rectitude; and of this we may be assured, that if we are not happy, we shall, at least, deserve to be so. Adieu! I dare not trust myself longer with you. [*Exeunt severally.*

End of the Fourth Act

ACT V. SCENE I

DIMPLE'S *Lodgings*

JESSAMY *meeting* JONATHAN

JESSAMY. Well, Mr. Jonathan, what success with the fair?

JONATHAN. Why, such a tarnal cross tike you never saw! You would have counted she had lived upon crab-apples and vinegar for a fortnight. But what the rattle makes you look so tarnation glum?

JESSAMY. I was thinking, Mr. Jonathan, what could be the reason of her carrying herself so coolly to you.

JONATHAN. Coolly, do you call it? Why, I vow, she was fire-hot angry: may be it was because I buss'd her.

JESSAMY. No, no, Mr. Jonathan; there must be some other cause; I never yet knew a lady angry at being kissed.

JONATHAN. Well, if it is not the young woman's bashfulness, I vow I can't conceive why she shouldn't like me.

JESSAMY. May be it is because you have not the graces, Mr. Jonathan.

JONATHAN. Grace! Why, does the young woman expect I must be converted before I court her?

JESSAMY. I mean graces of person; for instance, my lord tells us that we must cut off our nails even at top, in small segments of circles—though you won't understand that; in the next place, you must regulate your laugh.

JONATHAN. Maple-log seize it! don't I laugh natural?

JESSAMY. That's the very fault, Mr. Jonathan. Besides, you absolutely misplace it. I w told by a friend of mine that you laughed outright at the play the other night, wh you ought only to have tittered.

JONATHAN. Gor! I—what does one go to see fun for if they can't laugh.

JESSAMY. You may laugh; but you must laugh by rule.

JONATHAN. Swamp it—laugh by rule! Well, I should like that tarnally.

JESSAMY. Why, you know, Mr. Jonathan, that to dance, a lady to play with her f a gentleman with his cane, and all other natural motions, are regulated by a master has composed an immensely pretty gamut, by which any lady or gent with a few years' close application, may learn to laugh as gracefully as if th born and bred to it.

JONATHAN. Mercy on my soul! A gamut for laughing—just like fa, la, sol?

JESSAMY. Yes. It comprises every possible display of jocularity, from an *af*o[71] smile to a *piano* titter, or full chorus *fortissimo* ha, ha, ha! My master er s his leisure hours in marking out the plays, like a cathedral chanting-book, he ignorant may know where to laugh; and that pit, box, and gallery may ke ne together, and not have a snigger in one part of the house, a broad grin i other, and a d——d grum[72] look in the third. How delightful to see the ence all smile together, then look on their books, then twist their mouths into greeable simper, than altogether shake the house with a general ha, ha, ha! as a full chorus of Handel's[73] at an Abbey commemoration.

JONATHAN. Ha, ha, ha! that's dang'd cute, I swear.

JESSAMY. The gentlemen, you see, will laugh the tenor; the ladie ll play the counter-tenor; the beaux will squeak the treble; and our jolly frien n the gallery a thorough base, ho, ho, ho!

JONATHAN. Well, can't you let me see that gamut?

JESSAMY. Oh! yes, Mr. Jonathan; here it is [*Takes out a book.*] Oh p, this is only a titter with its variations. Ah, here it is. [*Takes out another.*] Nov you must know, Mr. Jonathan, this is a piece written by Ben Jonson,[74] which I he set to my master's gamut. The places where you must smile, look grave, or ugh outright, are marked below the line. Now look over me. "There was a certa man"—now you must smile.

[71] "Affectionate," "soft," "loud" (Italian).

[72] Grim.

[73] George Frederick Handel (1685–1759), British composer. Refe to a performance at Westminster Abbeyn London.

[74] English dramatist (572–1637).

JONATHAN. Well, read it again; I warrant I'll mind my eye.

JESSAMY. "There was a certain man, who had a sad scolding wife"—now you must laugh.

JONATHAN. Tarnation! That's no laughing matter though.

JESSAMY. "And she lay sick a-dying"—now you must titter.

JONATHAN. What, snigger when the good woman's a-dying! Gor, I——

JESSAMY. Yes, the notes say you must—"and she asked her husband leave to make a will"—now you must begin to look grave; "and her husband said"——

JONATHAN. Ay, what did her husband say? Something dang'd cute, I reckon.

JESSAMY. "And her husband said, you have had your will all your life-time, and would you have it after you are dead, too?"

JONATHAN. Ho, ho, ho! There the old man was even with her; he was up to the notch—ha, ha, ha!

JESSAMY. But, Mr. Jonathan, you must not laugh so. Why you ought to have tittered *piano,* and you have laughed *fortissimo.* Look here; you see these marks, A, B, C, and so on; these are the references to the other part of the book. Let us turn to it, and you will see the directions how to manage the muscles. This [*turns over*] was note D you blundered at.—You must purse the mouth into a smile, then titter, discovering the lower part of the three front upper teeth.

ATHAN. How? read it again.

AMY. "There was a certain man"—very well!—"who had a sad scolding wife"—ıy don't you laugh?

THAN. Now, that scolding wife sticks in my gizzard so pluckily that I can't laugh the blood and nowns of me. Let me look grave here, and I'll laugh your belly where the old creature's a-dying.

JE . "And she asked her husband"—[*Bell rings.*] My master's bell! he's re- d, I fear.—Here, Mr. Jonathan, take this gamut; and I make no doubt but w few years' close application, you may be able to smile gracefully.

[*Exeunt severally.*

SCENE II

CHARLOTTE *Apartment*

Enter MANL

MANLY. What, one at home? How unfortunate to meet the only lady my heart was ever moved , to find her engaged to another, and confessing her partiality for me! Yet eng d to a man who, by her intimation, and his libertine conversation with me, I fea does not merit her. Aye! there's the sting; for, were I assured that Maria was hap , my heart is not so selfish but that it would dilate in knowing it, even though it ere with another. But to know she is unhappy!—I must drive these thoughts fr m me. Charlotte has some books; and this is what I believe she calls her little libr ry.

[*Enters a closet.*

Enter DIMPLE *leading* LETITIA

LETITIA. And will you pretend to say now, Mr. Dimple, that you propose to break with Maria? Are not the banns published? Are not the clothes purchased? Are not the friends invited? In short, is it not a done affair?

DIMPLE. Believe me, my dear Letitia, I would not marry her.

LETITIA. Why have you not broke with her before this, as you all along deluded me by saying you would?

DIMPLE. Because I was in hopes she would, ere this, have broke with me.

LETITIA. You could not expect it.

DIMPLE. Nay, but be calm a moment; 'twas from my regard to you that I did not di card her.

LETITIA. Regard to me!

DIMPLE. Yes; I have done everything in my power to break with her, but the foo girl is so fond of me that nothing can accomplish it. Besides, how can I offe my hand when my heart is indissolubly engaged to you?

LETITIA. There may be reason in this; but why so attentive to Miss Manly?

DIMPLE. Attentive to Miss Manly! For heaven's sake, if you have no better opir my constancy, pay not so ill a compliment to my taste.

LETITIA. Did I not see you whisper her to-day?

DIMPLE. Possibly I might—but something of so very trifling a nature that I ready forgot what it was.

LETITIA. I believe she has not forgot it.

DIMPLE. My dear creature, how can you for a moment suppose I should ha se-rious thoughts of that trifling, gay, flighty coquette, that disagreeable—

Enter CHARLOTTE

My dear Miss Manly, I rejoice to see you; there is a charm in your conv n that always marks your entrance into company as fortunate.

LETITIA. Where have you been, my dear?

CHARLOTTE. Why, I have been about to twenty shops, turning over pre ngs, and so have left twenty visits unpaid. I wish you would step into the carr nd whisk round, make my apology, and leave my cards where our friends ar t at home; that, you know, will serve as a visit. Come, do go.

LETITIA. So anxious to get me out! but I'll watch you. [*Aside.*] Oh! y ll go; I want a little exercise. Positively [DIMPLE *offering to accompany her*], Dimple, you shall not go; why, half my visits are cake and caudle visits; it wo o, you know, for you to go. [*Exit, but returns to the door in the back e and listens.*]

DIMPLE. This attachment of your brother to Maria is fortunate.

CHARLOTTE. How did you come to the knowledge of it?

DIMPLE. I read it in their eyes.

CHARLOTTE. And I had it from her mouth. It would have amus you to have seen her! She, that thought it so great an impropriety to praise entleman that she could not bring out one word in your favour, found a redun ncy to praise him.

DIMPLE. I have done everything in my power to assist his passio there: your delicacy, my dearest girl, would be shocked at half the instances of eglect and misbehaviour.

CHARLOTTE. I don't know how I should bear neglect; but M. Dimple must misbehave himself indeed, to forfeit my good opinion.

DIMPLE. Your good opinion, my angel, is the pride and pleasure of my heart; and if the most respectful tenderness for you, and an utter indifference for all your sex besides, can make me worthy of your esteem, I shall richly merit it.

CHARLOTTE. All my sex besides, Mr. Dimple!—you forgot your tête-à-tête[75] with Letitia.

DIMPLE. How can you, my lovely angel, cast a thought on that insipid, wry-mouthed, ugly creature!

CHARLOTTE. But her fortune may have charms.

DIMPLE. Not to a heart like mine. The man, who has been blessed with the good opinion of my Charlotte, must despise the allurements of fortune.

CHARLOTTE. I am satisfied.

DIMPLE. Let us think no more on the odious subject, but devote the present hour to happiness.

IARLOTTE. Can I be happy, when I see the man I prefer going to be married to another?

MPLE. Have I not already satisfied my charming angel, that I can never think of narrying the puling Maria? But, even if it were so, could that be any bar to our appiness? for, as the poet sings,

> "Love, free as air, at sight of human ties,
> Spreads his light wings, and in a moment flies."[76]

ne, then, my charming angel! why delay our bliss? The present moment is ours; ext is in the hand of fate. [*Kissing her.*

C TTE. Begone, Sir! By your delusions you had almost lulled my honour asleep.

DI Let me lull the demon to sleep again with kisses.

[*He struggles with her; she screams.*

En NLY

MANLY n, villain! and defend yourself.— [*Draws.*

VAN R *enters and beats down their swords*

VAN ROU s the devil in you? are you going to murder one another?

[*Holding* DIMPLE.

DIMPLE. H him, hold him—I can command my passion.

Enter JONA N

JONATHAN. W t the rattle ails you? Is the old one[77] in you? Let the colonel alone, can't you? I l chock-full of fight—do you want to kill the colonel?——

MANLY. Be still, nathan; the gentleman does not want to hurt me.

JONATHAN. Gor —I wish he did; I'd show him Yankee boys play, pretty quick.— Don't you see u have frightened the young woman into the *hystrikes?*

VAN ROUGH. Pray, ome of you explain this; what has been the occasion of all this racket?

[75] Private conversation.

[76] "Eloisa to Abelard" (717), by Alexander Pope (1688–1744).

[77] The devil.

MANLY. That gentleman can explain it to you; it will be a very diverting story for an intended father-in-law to hear.

VAN ROUGH. How was this matter, Mr. Van Dumpling?

DIMPLE. Sir—upon my honour—all I know is, that I was talking to this young lady, and this gentleman broke in on us in a very extraordinary manner.

VAN ROUGH. Why, all this is nothing to the purpose; can you explain it, Miss? [*To* CHARLOTTE.

Enter LETITIA *through the back scene*

LETITIA. I can explain it to that gentleman's confusion. Though long betrothed t your daughter [*to* VAN ROUGH], yet, allured by my fortune, it seems (with shar do I speak it) he has privately paid his addresses to me, I was drawn in to lister him by his assuring me that the match was made by his father without his cons and that he proposed to break with Maria, whether he married me or not. whatever were his intentions respecting your daughter, Sir, even to me he false; for he has repeated the same story, with some cruel reflections upon m son, to Miss Manly.

JONATHAN. What a tarnal curse!

LETITIA. Nor is this all, Miss Manly. When he was with me this very morning, h the same ungenerous reflections upon the weakness of your mind as he h cently done upon the defects of my person.

JONATHAN. What a tarnal curse and damn, too.

DIMPLE. Ha! since I have lost Letitia, I believe I had as good make it up wi ia. Mr. Van Rough, at present I cannot enter into particulars; but, I believe ex- plain everything to your satisfaction in private.

VAN ROUGH. There is another matter, Mr. Van Dumpling, which I woul you explain. Pray, Sir, have Messrs. Van Cash & Co. presented you th ls for acceptance?

DIMPLE. The deuce! Has he heard of those bills! Nay, then, all's up wit ia, too; but an affair of this sort can never prejudice me among the ladies; th ll rather long to know what the dear creature possesses to make him so agre [*Aside.*] Sir, you'll hear from me. [*to* MANLY.

MANLY. And you from me, Sir——

DIMPLE. Sir, you wear a sword——

MANLY. Yes, Sir. This sword was presented to me by that brave Galli ro, the Marquis De la Fayette.[78] I have drawn it in the service of my countr nd in private life, on the only occasion where a man is justified in drawing his rd, in defence of a lady's honour. I have fought too many battles in the service my country to dread the imputation of cowardice. Death from a man of honou would be a glory you do not merit; you shall live to bear the insult of man and th contempt of that sex whose general smiles afforded you all your happiness.

DIMPLE. You won't meet me, Sir? Then I'll post you for a cowar

[78]French general (1757–1834) who served in the Continental Army during the American Revolution.

MANLY. I'll venture that, Sir. The reputation of my life does not depend upon the breath of a Mr. Dimple. I would have you to know, however, Sir, that I have a cane to chastise the insolence of a scoundrel, and a sword and the good laws of my country to protect me from the attempts of an assassin——

DIMPLE. Mighty well! Very fine, indeed! Ladies and gentlemen, I take my leave; and you will please to observe in the case of my deportment the contrast between a gentleman who has read Chesterfield and received the polish of Europe and an unpolished, untravelled American. [*Exit*

Enter MARIA

MARIA. Is he indeed gone?——

LETITIA. I hope, never to return.

VAN ROUGH. I am glad I heard of those bills; though it's plaguy unlucky; I hoped to see Mary married before I did.

ANLY. Will you permit a gentleman, Sir, to offer himself as a suitor to your daughter? Though a stranger to you, he is not altogether so to her, or unknown in this city. You may find a son-in-law of more fortune, but you can never meet with one who is richer in love for her, or respect for you.

ROUGH. Why, Mary, you have not let this gentleman make love to you without y leave?

Y. I did not say, Sir——

. Say, Sir!——I—the gentleman, to be sure, met me accidentally.

UGH. Ha, ha, ha! Mark me, Mary; young folks think old folks to be fools; but olks know young folks to be fools. Why, I knew all about this affair. This was a cunning way I had to bring it about. Hark ye! I was in the closet when you e were at our house. [*Turns to the company.*] I heard that little baggage say s li ed her old father, and would die to make him happy! Oh! how I loved the ggage! And you talked very prudently, young man. I have inquired into yo racter, and find you to be a man of punctuality and mind the main chance. An as you love Mary and Mary loves you, you shall have my consent immediately e married. I'll settle my fortune on you, and go and live with you the remain f my life.

MANLY. S hope——

VAN ROUG ome, come, no fine speeches; mind the main chance, young man, and you and all always agree.

LETITIA. I si rely wish you joy [*advancing to* MARIA]; and hope your pardon for my conduct.

MARIA. I than ou for your congratulations, and hope we shall at once forget the wretch who s given us so much disquiet, and the trouble that he has occasioned.

CHARLOTTE. An I, my dear Maria—how shall I look up to you for forgiveness? I, who, in the p tice of the meanest arts, have violated the most sacred rights of friendship? I n er can forgive myself, or hope charity from the world; but, I confess, I have mu to hope from such a brother; and I am happy that I may soon say, such a sister.

MARIA. My dear, you distress me; you have all my love.

MANLY. And mine.

CHARLOTTE. If repentance can entitle me to forgiveness, I have already much merit;

for I despise the littleness of my past conduct. I now find that the heart of any worthy man cannot be gained by invidious attacks upon the rights and characters of others—by countenancing the addresses of a thousand—or that the finest assemblage of features, the greatest taste in dress, the genteelest address, or the most brilliant wit, cannot eventually secure a coquette from contempt and ridicule.

MANLY. And I have learned that probity, virtue, honour, though they should not have received the polish of Europe, will secure to an honest American the good graces of his fair countrywomen, and I hope, the applause of THE PUBLIC.

The End

Hannah Webster Foster 1758–1840

Along with Susanna Rowson's *Charlotte Temple* (1794) and William H. Brown's *The Power of Sympathy* (1789), Foster's *The Coquette; or, The History of Eliza Wharton* (1797) topped the American best-seller lists of the 1790s. Frequently reprinted in the nineteenth century, the novel has had several twentieth-century printings as well. The success of her work did not bring Foster wide recognition, however; the book appeared anonymously, as written by "A Lady of Massachusetts." Not until 1866—twenty-six years after her death—did Hannah Foster's name appear on the title page.

Born in Salisbury, Massachusetts, the eldest daughter of Hannah Wainwright and Grant Webster, a prosperous merchant, Hannah Webster began life in comfortable surroundings. Her mother died in 1762, and it is likely that Hannah Webster was then enrolled in an academy for young women, somewhat like the one she later described in *The Boarding School; or, Lessons of a Preceptress to Her Pupils* (1798). The wide range of historical and literary allusions included in her works reflects an excellent education. By 1771, the young woman was living in Boston, where she began writing political articles for local newspapers. Her publications attracted the attention of John Foster, a graduate of Dartmouth, whom she married on 1785. The couple lived in Brighton chusetts, where John Foster ser pastor until his retirement in 182 of

Before she reached her ten ear marriage, Foster bore six childr om- after the birth of her last child wing pleted *The Coquette,* and the , she year, *The Boarding School.* Th d de- returned to newspaper writ g writ- voted herself to encouraging , Foster ers. When John Foster died ir r daugh- moved to Montreal to be wi nd Eliza ters Harriet Vaughan Che hom were Lanesford Cushing, both also writers.

The Coquette follow e epistolary tradition first used by Sa Richardson in his novel *Pamela* (17 The story of Eliza Wharton's tempt n, seduction, distress, and doom is rev ed in letters between friends and confi nts. Eliza Wharton falls victim to the r e, Peter Sanford, referred to as "a secon Lovelace"—an allusion to the seducer Richardson's second novel, *Clarissa H lowe* (1747–1748). Like the heroines of cuntless novels, Eliza dies in childbirth. Y unlike those countless novels, *The Coquette* offers characters torn between love and their own worldly ambitions, between virtue and vice.

On another level, *The Coquette* serves as a prototype for the American quest-for-freedom novel, raising questions about the extent to which individuals can remain free in a society. Eliza is a coquette, but she is also an intelligent, spirited young woman unwilling to bury herself in a conventional marriage with a man (the Rev. Boyer) whom she finds agreeable but immensely dull. She would gladly enter an egalitarian marriage like that enjoyed by her friends the Richmans, but she finds herself without such an opportunity. For Eliza, "Marriage is the tomb of friendship. It appears o me a very selfish state" (Letter 12).

The letters in *The Coquette* treat sub-cts ranging from friendship and marriage economic security and social status. ey expose, according to Cathy N. idson, the fundamental injustices of a archal culture that places opportuni- or women within a limited domes- here. Given contemporary marriage d restrictive mores, the novel illus- he extent to which women and men nstrained by social expectation. In novel contrasts women's and ws of marriage.

r's novel is deeply embedded in the can experience. Her claim that *The C* *te* was "founded on fact" was not m a nod to the convention employed rly novelists to justify lurid or sensatio orks. She based her story on the exper e, nearly a decade earlier, of her husba distant cousin Elizabeth Whitman artford, Connecticut, the daughter of rents highly respected in clerical, political, and social circles. After rejecting two ministerial suitors, Whitman engaged in a clandestine affair that left her pregnant and abandoned. Her story became public knowledge when the *Salem Mercury* (July 29, 1788) reported that "a female stranger," secluded at the Bell Tavern in Danvers to await her husband's arrival, had given birth to a stillborn child and had subsequently died. Reporters and preachers cited Whitman's story as "a good moral lecture to young ladies." Foster's contemporaries had no difficulty identifying the real-life counterparts of the "coquette" and her ministerial associates, though the identity of her seducer remains subject to dispute.

Foster's second work, *The Boarding School,* does not fit easily into any literary category. The subtitle, however, suggests a didactic commentary on female education. The first portion of the work fulfills that expectation: a description of the finishing school run by Mrs. Maria Williams, it includes exhortations on social conduct, reading, and general preparations for survival. The second part, containing letters from the students to the preceptress and to each other, demonstrates the beneficial effects of Mrs. William's instruction. In Foster's day, *The Boarding School* may have seemed the predictable work of a minister's wife. Today, it illuminates the gender conflicts underlying Foster's classic, *The Coquette*.

Lucy M. Freibert
University of Louisville

PRIMARY W S

The Coquette; o e History of Eliza Wharton. A Novel Founded on Fact, 1797, rpt. 1986; *The Boarding School; Lessons of a Preceptress to Her Pupils,* 1798.

from The Coquette; or, the History of Eliza Wharton

[As the novel opens, Eliza has just escaped an unwanted marriage with an elderly clergyman, Mr. Haly, who died before her parents could get him to the altar. Delighted to be launched into "society" again, Eliza visits General and Mrs. Richman. Eliza soon receives the attentions of a minister named Boyer, but she cannot bring herself to marry him immediately. She flirts with Sanford against the advice of her friends.]

Letter I
To Miss Lucy Freeman

New-Haven.

An unusual sensation possesses my breast; a sensation, which I once thought could never pervade it on any occasion whatever. It is *pleasure;* pleasure, my dear Lucy, on leaving my paternal roof! Could you have believed that the darling child of an indulgent and dearly beloved mother would feel a gleam of joy at leaving her? but so it is. The melancholy, the gloom, the condolence, which surrounded me for a month after the death of Mr. Haly, had depressed my spirits, and palled every enjoyment of life. Mr. Haly was a man of worth; a man of real and substantial merit. He is therefore deeply, and justly regreted by *his* friends; he was chosen to be a future guardian, and companion for me, and was, therefore, beloved by *mine.* As their choice; as a good man, and a faithful friend, I esteemed him. But no one acquainted with the disparity of our tempers and dispositions, our views and designs, can suppose my heart much engaged in the alliance. Both nature and education had instilled into my mind an implicit obedience to the will and desires of my parents. To them, of course, I sacrificed my fancy in this affair; determined that my reason should concur with theirs; and on that to risk my future happiness. I was the more encouraged, as I saw, from our first acquaintance, his declining health; and expected, that the event would prove as it has. Think not, however, that I rejoice in his death. No; far be it from me; for though I believe that I never felt the passion of love for Mr. Haly; yet a habit of conversing with him, of hearing daily the most virtuous, tender, and affectionate sentiments from his lips, inspired emotions of the sincerest friendship, and esteem.

He is gone. His fate is unalterably, and I trust, happily fixed. He lived the life, and died the death of the righteous. O that my last end may be like his! This event will, I hope, make a suitable and abiding impression upon my mind; teach me the fading nature of all sublunary enjoyments, and the little dependence which is to be placed on earthly felicity. Whose situation was more agreeable; whose prospects more flattering, than Mr. Haly's? Social, domestic, and connubial joys were fondly anticipated, and friends, and fortune seemed ready to crown every wish! Yet animated by still brighter hopes, he cheerfully bid them all adieu. In conversation with me, but a few days before his exit; "There is" said he, "but one link in the chain of life, undissevered; that, my dear Eliza, is my attachment to you. But God is wise and good in all his ways; and in this, as in all other respects, I would cheerfully say, His will be done." . . .

The disposition of mind, which I now feel, I wish to cultivate. Calm, placid, and serene; thoughtful of my duty, and benevolent to all around me, I wish for no other connection than that of friendship,

This Letter is all egotism, I have even neglected to mention the respectable, and happy friends, with whom I reside; but will do it in my next. Write soon, and often; and believe me sincerely yours,

Eliza Wharton.

Letter II

To the Same

New-Haven.

Time, which effaces every occasional impression, I find gradually dispelling the pleasing pensiveness, which the melancholy event, the subject of my last, had diffused over my mind. Naturally cheerful, volatile, and unreflecting, the opposite disposition, I have found to contain sources of enjoyment, which I was before unconscious of possessing.

My friends, here, are the picture of conjugal felicity. The situation is delightful. The visiting parties perfectly agreeable. Every thing tends to facilitate the return of my accustomed vivacity. I have written to my mother, and received an answer. She praises my fortitude, and admires the philosophy which I have exerted, under, what she calls, my heavy bereavement. Poor woman! She little thinks that my heart was untouched; and when that is unaffected, other sentiments and passions make but a transient impression. I have been, for a month or two, excluded from the gay world; and, indeed, fancied myself soaring above it. It is now that I begin to descend, and find my natural propensity for mixing in the busy scenes and active pleasures of life returning. I have received your letter; your moral lecture rather; and be assured, my dear, your monitorial lessons and advice shall be attended to. I believe I shall never again resume those airs, which you term *coquettish,* but which I think deserve a softer appellation; as they proceed from an innocent heart, and are the effusions of a youthful, and cheerful mind. We are all envited to spend the day, to morrow, at Col. Farington's, who has an elegant seat in this neighbourhood. Both he and his Lady are strangers to me; but the friends, by whom I am introduced, will procure me a welcome reception. Adieu.

Eliza Wharton.

Letter III
To the Same

New-Haven.

Is it time for me to talk again of conquests? or must I only enjoy them in silence? I must write to you the impulses of my mind; or I must not write at all. You are not so morose, as to wish me to become a nun, would our country, and religion allow it. I ventured yesterday to throw aside the habiliments of mourning, and to array myself in those more adapted to my taste. We arrived at Col. Farington's about one o'clock. The Col. handed me out of the carriage, and introduced me to a large company assembled in the Hall. My name was pronounced with an *emphasis;* and I was received with the most flattering tokens of respect. When we were summoned to dinner, a young gentleman in a clerical dress offered me his hand, and led me to a table furnished with an elegant, and sumptuous repast, with more gallantry, and address than commonly fall to the share of students. He sat opposite me at table; and whenever I raised my eye, it caught his. The ease, and politeness of his manners, with his particular attention to me, raised my curiosity, and induced me to ask Mrs. Laiton who he was? She told me that his name was Boyer; that he was descended from a worthy family; had passed with honor and applause through the university where he was educated; had since studied divinity with success; and now had a call to settle as a minister in one of the first parishes in a neighbouring state.

The gates of a spacious garden were thrown open, at this instant; and I accepted with avidity an invitation to walk in it. Mirth, and hilarity prevailed, and the moments fled on downy wings; while we traced the beauties of art and nature, so liberally displayed, and so happily blended in this delightful retreat. An enthusiastic admirer of scenes like these, I had rambled some way from the company, when I was followed by Mrs. Laiton to offer her condolence on the supposed loss, which I had sustained, in the death of Mr. Haly. My heart rose against the woman, so ignorant of human nature, as to think such conversation acceptable at such a time. I made her little reply, and waved the subject, though I could not immediately dispel the gloom which it excited. . . .

We were soon joined by the gentlemen, who each selected his partner, and the walk was prolonged.

Mr. Boyer offered me his arm, which I gladly accepted; happy to be relieved from the impertinence of my female companion. We returned to tea, after which the ladies sung, and played by turns on the Piano Forte; while some of the gentlemen accompanied with the flute, the clarinet, and the violin, forming in the whole a very decent concert. An elegant supper, and half an hour's conversation after it, closed the evening; when we returned home, delighted with our entertainment and pleased with ourselves and each other. My imagination is so impressed with the festive scenes of the day, that Morpheus waves his ebon-wand in vain. The evening is fine beyond the power of description! all nature is serene and harmonious; in perfect unison with my present disposition of mind. I have been taking a retrospect of my past life; and a few juvenile follies excepted, which I trust the recording angel has blotted out with the tear of charity, find an approving conscience, and a heart at ease. Fortune, indeed, has not been very liberal of her gifts to me; but I presume on a large stock in the bank of friendship, which, united with health and innocence, give me some pleasing anticipations of future felicity.

Whatever my fate may be, I shall always continue your

Eliza Wharton.

Letter IV

To Mr. Selby

New-Haven.

You ask me, my friend, whether I am in pursuit of truth, or a lady? I answer, both. I hope and trust they are united; and really expect to find truth and the virtues and graces besides in a fair form. If you mean by the first part of your question, whether I am searching into the sublimer doctrines of religion? To these I would by no means be inattentive; but to be honest, my studies of that kind have been very much interrupted of late. The respectable circle of acquaintances with which I am honored here, has rendered my visits very frequent and numerous. In one of these I was introduced to Miss Eliza Wharton; a young lady whose elegant person, accomplished mind, and polished manners have been much celebrated. Her fame has often reached me; but, as the queen of Sheba said to Solomon, the half was not told me. You will think, that I talk in the style of a lover. I confess it, nor am I ashamed to rank myself among the professed admirers of this lovely fair one. I am in no danger, however, of becoming an enthusiastic devotee. No, I mean to act upon just and rational principles. Expecting soon to settle in an eligible situation, if such a companion as I am persuaded she will make me, may fall to my lot, I shall deem myself as happy as this state of imperfection will admit. She is now resident at Gen. Richman's. The general and his lady are her particular friends. They are warm in her praises. They tell me, however, that she is naturally of a gay disposition. No matter for that; it is an agreeable quality, where there is discretion sufficient for its regulation. A cheerful friend, much more a cheerful wife is peculiarly necessary to a person of a studious and sedentary life. They dispel the gloom of retirement, and exhilerate the spirits depressed by intense application. . . .

I have had several opportunities of conversing with her. She discovers an elevated mind, a ready apprehension, and an accurate knowledge of the various subjects which have been brought into view. I have not yet introduced the favorite subject of my heart. Indeed she seems studiously to avoid noticing any expression which leads towards it. But she must hear it soon. I am sure of the favor and interest of the friends with whom she resides. They have promised to speak previously in my behalf. I am to call as if accidentally this afternoon, just as they are to ride abroad. They are to refer me to Miss Wharton for entertainment, till their return. What a delightful opportunity for my purpose! I am counting the hours, nay, the very moments. Adieu. You shall soon hear again from your most obedient,

J. Boyer.

Letter V
To Miss Lucy Freeman

New-Haven.

These bewitching charms of mine have a tendency to keep my mind in a state of perturbation. I am so pestered with these admirers; not that I am so very handsome neither; but I don't know how it is, I am certainly very much the taste of the other sex. Followed, flattered, and caressed; I have cards and compliments in profusion. But I must try to be serious; for I have, alas! one serious lover. As I promised you to be particular in my writing, I suppose I must proceed methodically. Yesterday we had a party to dine. Mr. Boyer was of the number. His attention was immediately engrossed; and I soon perceived that every word, every action, and every look was studied to gain my approbation. As he sat next me at dinner, his assiduity and politeness were pleasing; and as we walked together afterwards, his conversation was improving. Mine was sentimental and sedate; perfectly adapted to the taste of my gallant. Nothing, however, was said particularly expressive of his apparent wishes. I studiously avoided every kind of discourse which might lead to this topic. I wish not for a declaration from any one, especially from one whom I could not repulse and do not intend to encourage at present. His conversation, so similar to what I had often heard from a similar character, brought a deceased friend to mind, and rendered me somewhat pensive. I retired directly after supper. Mr. Boyer had just taken leave.

Mrs. Richman came into my chamber as she was passing to her own. Excuse my intrusion, Eliza, said she; I thought I would just step in and ask you if you have passed a pleasant day?

Perfectly so, madam; and I have now retired to protract the enjoyment by recollection. What, my dear, is your opinion of our favorite Mr. Boyer? Declaring him your favorite, madam, is sufficient to render me partial to him. But to be frank, independent of that, I think him an agreeable man. Your heart, I presume, is now free? Yes, and I hope it will long remain so. Your friends, my dear, solicitous for your welfare, wish to see you suitably and agreeably connected. I hope my friends will never again interpose in my concerns of that nature. You, madam, who have ever known my heart, are sensible, that had the Almighty spared life, in a certain instance, I must have sacrificed my own happiness, or incurred their censure. I am young, gay, volatile. A melancholy event has lately extricated me from those shackles, which parental authority had imposed on my mind. Let me then enjoy that freedom which I so highly prize. Let me have opportunity, unbiassed by opinion, to gratify my natural disposition in a participation of those pleasures which youth and innocence afford. Of such pleasures, no one, my dear, would wish to deprive you. But beware, Eliza!—Though strowed[1] with flowers, when contemplated by your lively imagination, it is, after all, a slippery, thorny path. The round of fashionable dissipation is dangerous. A phantom is often pursued, which leaves its deluded votary the real form of wretchedness. She spoke with an emphasis, and taking up her candle, wished me a good night. I had not power to return the

[1]Strewn.

compliment. Something seemingly prophetic in her looks and expressions, cast a momentary gloom upon my mind! But I despise those contracted ideas which confine virtue to a cell. I have no notion of becoming a recluse. Mrs. Richman has ever been a beloved friend of mine; yet I always thought her rather prudish. Adieu,

Eliza Wharton.

Letter VI

To the Same

New-Haven.

I had scarcely seated myself at the breakfast table this morning, when a servant entered with a card of invitation from Major Sanford, requesting the happiness of my hand this evening, at a ball, given by Mr. Atkins, about three miles from this. I shewed the billet to Mrs. Richman, saying, I have not much acquaintance with this gentleman, madam; but I suppose his character sufficiently respectable to warrant an affirmative answer. He is a gay man, my dear, to say no more, and such are the companions we wish, when we join a party avowedly formed for pleasure. I then stepped into my apartment, wrote an answer, and dispatched the servant. When I returned to the parlour, something disapprobating appeared in the countenances of both my friends. I endeavored without seeming to observe, to dissipate it by chit chat; but they were better pleased with each other than with me; and soon rising, walked into the garden, and left me to amuse myself alone. My eyes followed them through the window. Happy pair, said I. Should it ever be my fate to wear the hymenial chain, may I be thus united! The purest and most ardent affection, the greatest consonance of taste and disposition, and the most congenial virtue and wishes distinguish this lovely couple. Health and wealth, with every attendant blessing preside over their favored dwelling, and shed their benign influence without alloy. The consciousness of exciting their displeasure gave me pain; but I consoled myself with the idea that it was ill founded.

They should consider, said I, that they have no satisfaction to look for beyond each other.

There every enjoyment is centered; but I am a poor solitary being, who need some amusement beyond what I can supply myself. The mind, after being confined at home for a while, sends the imagination abroad in quest of new treasures, and the body may as well accompany it, for ought I can see. . . .

Eliza Wharton.

Letter VIII

To Mr. Charles Deighton

New-Haven.

We had an elegant ball, last night, Charles; and what is still more to the taste of your old friend, I had an elegant partner; one exactly calculated to please my fancy; gay, volatile, apparently thoughtless of every thing but present enjoyment. It was Miss Eliza Wharton, a young lady, whose agreeable person, polished manners, and refined talents, have rendered her the toast of the country around for these two years; though for half that time she has had a clerical lover imposed on her by her friends; for I am told it was not agreeable to her inclination. By this same clerical lover of hers, she was for several months confined as a nurse. But his death has happily relieved her, and she now returns to the world with redoubled lustre. At present she is a visitor to Mrs. Richman, who is a relation. I first saw her on a party of pleasure at Mr. Frazier's where we walked, talked, sung, and danced together. I thought her cousin watched her with a jealous eye; for she is, you must know, a prude; and immaculate, more so than you or I must be the man who claims admission to her society. But I fancy this young lady is a coquette; and if so, I shall avenge my sex, by retaliating the mischiefs, she meditates against us. Not that I have any ill designs; but only to play off her own artillery, by using a little unmeaning gallantry. And let her beware of the consequences. A young clergyman came in at Gen. Richman's yesterday, while I was waiting for Eliza, who was much more cordially received by the general and his lady, than was your humble servant: but I lay that up.

When she entered the room, an air of mutual embarrassment was evident. The lady recovered her assurance much more easily than the gentleman. I am just going to ride, and shall make it in my way to call and inquire after the health of my dulcinea. Therefore, adieu for the present.

Peter Sanford.

Letter XI

To Mr. Charles Deighton

New-Haven.

Well, Charles, I have been manoeuvring to day, a little revengefully. That, you will say, is out of character. So baleful a passion does not easily find admission among those softer ones, which you well know I cherish. However, I am a mere Proteus, and can assume any shape that will best answer my purpose.

I called this forenoon, as I told you I intended, at Gen. Richman's. I waited some time in the parlor alone, before Eliza appeared; and when she did appear, the distant reserve of her manners and the pensiveness of her countenance convinced me that she had been vexed, and I doubted not but Peter Sanford was the occasion. Her wise cousin, I could have sworn, had been giving her a detail of the vices of her gallant; and warning her against the danger of associating with him in future. Notwithstanding, I took no notice of any alteration in her behavior; but entered with the utmost facetiousness into a conversation which I thought most to her taste. By degrees, she assumed her usual vivacity; cheerfulness and good humor again animated her countenance. I tarried as long as decency would admit. She having intimated that they were to dine at my friend Lawrence's, I caught at this information; and determined to follow them, and teaze the jealous Mrs. Richman, by playing off all the gallantry I was master of in her presence.

I went, and succeeded to the utmost of my wishes, as I read in the vexation, visible in the one; and the ease and attention displayed by the other. I believe too, that I have charmed the eye at least, of the amiable Eliza. Indeed, Charles, she is a fine girl. I think it would hurt my conscience to wound her mind or reputation. Were I disposed to marry, I am persuaded she would make an excellent wife; but that you know is no part of my plan, so long as I can keep out of the noose. Whenever I do submit to be shackled, it must be from a necessity of mending my fortune. This girl would be far from doing that. However, I am pleased with her acquaintance, and mean not to abuse her credulity and good nature, if I can help it.

Peter Sanford.

Letter XII

To Miss Lucy Freeman

New-Haven.

The heart of your friend is again besieged. Whether it will surrender to the assailants or not, I am unable at present to determine. Sometimes I think of becoming a predestinarian, and submitting implicitly to fate, without any exercise of free will; but, as mine seems to be a wayward one, I would counteract the operations of it, if possible.

Mrs. Richman told me this morning, that she hoped I should be as agreeably entertained this afternoon, as I had been the preceding; that she expected Mr. Boyer to dine, and take tea; and doubted not but he would be as attentive and sincere to me, if not as gay and polite as the gentleman who obtruded his civilities yesterday. I replied that I had no reason to doubt the sincerity of the one, or the other, having never put them to the test, nor did I imagine I ever should. Your friends, Eliza, said she, would be very happy to see you united to a man of Mr. Boyer's worth; and so agreeably settled, as he has a prospect of being. I hope, said I, that my friends are not so weary of my company, as to wish to dispose of me. I am too happy in my present connections to quit them for new ones. Marriage is the tomb of friendship. It appears to me a very selfish state. Why do people, in general, as soon as they are married, centre all their cares, their concerns, and pleasures in their own families? former acquaintances are neglected or forgotten. The tenderest ties between friends are weakened, or dissolved; and benevolence itself moves in a very limited sphere. It is the glory of the marriage state, she rejoined, to refine, by circumscribing our enjoyments. Here we can repose in safety.

"The friendships of the world are oft
Confed'racies in vice, or leagues in pleasure:
Our's has the purest virtue for its basis;
And such a friendship ends not but with life."

True, we cannot always pay that attention to former associates, which we may wish; but the little community which we superintend is quite as important an object; and certainly renders us more beneficial to the public. True benevolence, though it may change its objects, is not limited by time or place. Its effects are the same, and aided by a second self, are rendered more diffusive and salutary.

Some pleasantry passed, and we retired to dress. When summoned to dinner, I found Mr. Boyer below. If what is sometimes said be true, that love is diffident, reserved, and unassuming, this man must be tinctured with it. These symptoms were visible in his deportment when I entered the room. However, he soon recovered himself, and the conversation took a general turn. The festive board was crowned with sociability, and we found in reality, "The feast of reason, and the flow of soul." After we rose from table, a walk in the garden was proposed, an amusement we are all peculiarly fond of. Mr. Boyer offered me his arm. When at a sufficient distance from our company, he begged leave to congratulate himself on having an opportunity which he had ardently desired for some time, of declaring to me his attachment; and of soliciting an interest in my favor; or, if he might be allowed the term, affection. I replied, that, Sir, is indeed laying claim to an important interest. I believe you must substitute some more indifferent epithet for the present. Well then, said he, if it must be so, let it be esteem, or friendship. Indeed, Sir, said I, you are intitled to them both. Merit has always a share in that bank; and I know of none, who has a larger claim on that score, than Mr. Boyer. I suppose my manner was hardly serious enough for what he considered a weighty cause. He was a little disconcerted; but soon regaining his presence of mind, entreated me, with an air of earnestness, to encourage his suit, to admit his addresses, and, if possible, to reward his love. I told him, that this was rather a sudden affair to me; and that I could not answer him without consideration. Well then, said he, take what time you think proper, only relieve my suspense as soon as may be. Shall I visit you again to morrow? O, not so soon, said I. Next Monday, I believe will be early enough. I will endeavor to be at home. He thanked me even for that favor, recommended himself once more to my kindness; and we walked towards the company, returned with them to the house, and he soon took leave. I immediately retired to write this letter, which I shall close, without a single observation on the subject, until I know your opinion.

Eliza Wharton.

Letter XIII
To Miss Eliza Wharton

Hartford.

And so you wish to have my opinion before you know the result of your own. This is playing a little too much with my patience. But, however, I will gratify you this once, in hopes that my epistle may have a good effect. You will ask, perhaps, whether I would influence your judgment? I answer, no; provided you will exercise it yourself: but I am a little apprehensive that your fancy will mislead you. Methinks I can gather from your letters, a predilection for this Major Sanford. But he is a rake, my dear friend; and can a lady of your delicacy and refinement, think of forming a connection with a man of that character? I hope not. Nay, I am confident you do not. You mean only to exhibit a few more girlish airs, before you turn matron. But I am persuaded, if you wish to lead down the dance of life with regularity, you will not find a more excellent partner than Mr. Boyer. Whatever you can reasonably expect in a lover, husband, or friend, you may perceive to be united in this worthy man. His taste is undebauched, his manners not vitiated, his morals uncorrupted. His situation in life is, perhaps, as elevated as you have a right to claim. Forgive my plainness, Eliza. It is the task of friendship, sometimes to tell disagreeable truths. I know your ambition is to make a distinguished figure in the first class of polished society; to shine in the gay circle of fashionable amusements, and to bear off the palm amidst the votaries of pleasure. But these are fading honors, unsatisfactory enjoyments; incapable of gratifying those immortal principles of reason and religion, which have been implanted in your mind by nature; assiduously cultivated by the best of parents, and exerted, I trust, by yourself. Let me advise you then, in conducting this affair; an affair, big, perhaps, with your future fate, to lay aside those coquettish airs which you sometimes put on; and remember that you are not dealing with a fop, who will take advantage of every concession; but with a man of sense and honor, who will properly estimate your condescension, and frankness. Act then with that modest freedom, that dignified unreserve which bespeaks conscious rectitude and sincerity of heart.

I shall be extremely anxious to hear the process and progress of this business. Relieve my impatience, as soon as possible, and believe me yours, with undissembled affection.

Lucy Freeman.

Letter XVIII
To Mr. Charles Deighton

New-Haven.

Do you know, Charles, that I have commenced lover? I was always a general one; but now I am somewhat particular. I shall be the more interested, as I am likely to meet with difficulties; and it is the glory of a rake, as well as a Christian to combat obstacles. This same Eliza, of whom I have told you, has really made more impression on my heart, than I was aware of; or than the sex, take them as they rise, are wont to do. But she is besieged by a priest (a likely lad though.) I know not how it is, but they are commonly successful with the girls, even the gayest of them. This one, too, has the interest of all her friends, as I am told. I called yesterday, at General Richman's, and found this pair together, apparently too happy in each other's society for my wishes. I must own, that I felt a glow of jealousy, which I never experienced before; and vowed revenge for the pain it gave me, though but momentary. Yet Eliza's reception of me was visibly cordial; nay, I fancied my company as pleasing to her as that which she had before. I tarried not long, but left him to the enjoyment of that pleasure which I flatter myself will be short-lived. O, I have another plan in my head; a plan of necessity, which, you know, is the mother of invention. It is this: I am very much courted and caressed by the family of Mr. Lawrence, a man of large property in this neighborhood. He has only one child; a daughter, with whom I imagine the old folks intend to shackle me in the bonds of matrimony. The girl looks very well. She has no soul though, that I can discover. She is heiress, nevertheless, to a great fortune; and that is all the soul I wish for in a wife. In truth, Charles, I know of no other way to mend my circumstances. But lisp not a word of my embarrassments for your life. Show and equipage are my hobby-horse; and if any female wish to share them with me, and will furnish me with the means of supporting them, I have no objection. Could I conform to the sober rules of wedded life, and renounce those dear enjoyments of dissipation, in which I have so long indulged, I know not the lady in the world with whom I would sooner form a connection of this sort than with Eliza Wharton. But it will never do. If my fortune, or hers were better, I would risk a union; but as they are, no idea of the kind can be admitted. I shall endeavor, notwithstanding, to enjoy her company as long as possible. Though I cannot possess her wholly myself, I will not tamely see her the property of another.

I am now going to call at General Richman's, in hopes of an opportunity to profess my devotion to her. I know I am not a welcome visitor to the family; but I am independent of their censure or esteem, and mean to act accordingly.

Peter Sanford.

[After returning home, Eliza becomes engaged to Boyer yet continues to see Sanford. Boyer warns Eliza of the risk she is taking with her reputation. Finally, Boyer, discovering Eliza in intimate conversation with Sanford in her family's garden, breaks off the engagement. Eliza's efforts to retrieve Boyer's good will fail completely. Meanwhile, Sanford marries a wealthy woman but resumes his pursuit of Eliza. Eventually he seduces her. When she becomes pregnant, Eliza leaves home secretly with Sanford.]

Letter LXV

To Mr. Charles Deighton

Hartford.

Good news, Charles, good news! I have arrived to the utmost bounds of my wishes; the full possession of my adorable Eliza! I have heard a quotation from a certain book; but what book it was I have forgotten, if I ever knew. No matter for that; the quotation is, that "stolen waters are sweet, and bread eaten in secret is pleasant." If it has reference to the pleasures, which I have enjoyed with Eliza, I like it hugely, as Tristram Shandy's father said of Yorick's sermon; and I think it fully verified.

I had a long and tedious siege. Every method which love could suggest, or art invent, was adopted. I was sometimes ready to despair, under an idea that her resolution was unconquerable, her virtue impregnable. Indeed, I should have given over the pursuit long ago, but for the hopes of success I entertained from her parleying with me, and in reliance upon her own strength, endeavoring to combat, and counteract my designs. Whenever this has been the case, Charles, I have never yet been defeated in my plan. If a lady will consent to enter the lists against the antagonist of her honor, she may be sure of losing the prize. Besides, were her delicacy genuine, she would banish the man at once, who presumed to doubt, which he certainly does, who attempts to vanquish it!

But, far be it from me to criticise the pretensions of the sex. If I gain the rich reward of my dissimulation and gallantry, that you know is all I want.

To return then to the point. An unlucky, but not a miraculous accident, has taken place, which must soon expose our amour. What can be done? At the first discovery, absolute distraction seized the soul of Eliza, which has since terminated in a fixed melancholy. Her health too is much impaired. She thinks herself rapidly declining; and I tremble when I see her emaciated form!

My wife has been reduced very low, of late. She brought me a boy a few weeks past, a dead one though.

These circumstances give me neither pain nor pleasure. I am too much ingrossed by my divinity, to take an interest in any thing else. True, I have lately suffered myself to be somewhat engaged here and there by a few jovial lads, who assist me in dispelling the anxious thoughts, which my perplexed situation excites. I must, however, seek some means to relieve Eliza's distress. My finances are low; but the last fraction shall be expended in her service, if she need it.

Julia Granby is expected at Mrs. Wharton's every hour. I fear that her inquisitorial eye will soon detect our intrigue, and obstruct its continuation. Now there's a girl, Charles, I should never attempt to seduce; yet she is a most alluring object, I assure you. But the dignity of her manners forbid all assaults upon her virtue. Why, the very expression of her eye, blasts in the bud, every thought, derogatory to her honor; and tells you plainly, that the first insinuation of the kind, would be punished with eternal banishment and displeasure! Of her there is no danger! But I can write no more, except that I am, &c.

Peter Sanford.

Letter LXVIII

To Mrs. M. Wharton

Tuesday.

My Honored And Dear Mamma,

In what words, in what language shall I address you? What shall I say on a subject which deprives me of the power of expression? Would to God I had been totally deprived of that power before so fatal a subject required its exertion! Repentance comes too late, when it cannot prevent the evil lamented. For your kindness, your more than maternal affection towards me, from my infancy to the present moment, a long life of filial duty and unerring rectitude could hardly compensate. How greatly deficient in gratitude must I appear then, while I confess, that precept and example, counsel and advice, instruction and admonition, have been all lost upon me!

Your kind endeavors to promote my happiness have been repaid by the inexcusable folly of sacrificing it. The various emotions of shame, and remorse, penitence and regret, which torture and distract my guilty breast, exceed description. Yes, madam, your Eliza has fallen; fallen, indeed! She has become the victim of her own indiscretion, and of the intrigue and artifice of a designing libertine, who is the husband of another! She is polluted, and no more worthy of her parentage! She flies from you, not to conceal her guilt, that she humbly and penitently owns; but to avoid what she has never experienced, and feels herself unable to support, a mother's frown; to escape the heart-rending sight of a parent's grief, occasioned by the crimes of her guilty child!

I have become a reproach and disgrace to my friends. The consciousness of having forfeited their favor, and incurred their disapprobation and resentment, induces me to conceal from them the place of my retirement; but, lest your benevolence should render you anxious for my comfort in my present situation, I take the liberty to assure you that I am amply provided for.

I have no claim even upon your pity; but from my long experience of your tenderness, I presume to hope it will be extended to me. Oh, my mother, if you knew what the state of my mind is, and has been, for months past, you would surely compassionate my case! Could tears efface the stain, which I have brought upon my family, it would, long since have been washed away! But, alas, tears are vain; and vain is my bitter repentance! It cannot obliterate my crime, nor restore me to innocence and peace! In this life I have no ideas of happiness. These I have wholly resigned! The only hope which affords me any solace, is that of your forgiveness. If the deepest contrition can make an atonement; if the severest pains, both of body and mind, can restore me to your charity, you will not be inexorable! Oh, let my sufferings be deemed a sufficient punishment; and add not the insupportable weight of a parent's wrath! At present, I cannot see you. The effect of my crime is too obvious to be longer concealed, to elude the invidious eye of curiosity. This night, therefore, I leave your hospitable mansion! This night I become a wretched wanderer from thy paternal roof! Oh, that the grave were this night to be my lodging! Then should I lie down and be at rest! Trusting in the mercy of God, through the mediation of his son; I think I could meet my heavenly father with more composure and confidence, than my earthly parent!

Let not the faults and misfortunes of your daughter oppress your mind. Rather let the conviction of having faithfully discharged your duty to your lost child, support and console you in this trying scene.

Since I wrote the above, you have kindly granted me your forgiveness, though you knew not how great, how aggravated was my offence! You forgive me, you say: Oh, the harmonious, the transporting sound! It has revived my drooping spirits; and will enable me to encounter, with resolution, the trials before me!

Farewell, my dear mamma! pity and pray for your ruined child; and be assured, that affection and gratitude will be the last sentiments, which expire in the breast of your repenting daughter,

Eliza Wharton.

[Julia Granby, the friend who has been staying at the Whartons', reports Eliza's demise to Lucy Freeman, now Mrs. Sumner.]

Letter LXXI

To Mrs. Lucy Sumner

Hartford.

The drama is now closed! A tragical one indeed it has proved!

How sincerely, my dear Mrs. Sumner, must the friends of our departed Eliza, sympathize with each other; and with her afflicted, bereaved parent!

You have doubtless seen the account, in the public papers, which gave us the melancholy intelligence. But I will give you a detail of circumstances.

A few days after my last was written, we heard that Major Sanford's property was attached, and he a prisoner in his own house. He was the last man, to whom we wished to apply for information respecting the forlorn wanderer; yet we had no other resource. And after waiting a fortnight in the most cruel suspense, we wrote a billet, entreating him, if possible, to give some intelligence concerning her. He replied, that he was unhappily deprived of all means of knowing himself; but hoped soon to relieve his own, and our anxiety about her.

In this situation we continued, till a neighbor (purposely, we since concluded) sent us a Boston paper. Mrs. Wharton took it, and inconscious of its contents, observed that the perusal might divert her, a few moments. She read for some time; when it suddenly dropped upon the floor. She clasped her hands together, and raising her streaming eyes to heaven, exclaimed, It is the Lord; let him do what he will! Be still, O my soul, and know that he is God!

What madam, said I, can be the matter? She answered not; but with inexpressible anguish depicted in her countenance, pointed to the paper. I took it up, and soon found the fatal paragraph. I shall not attempt to paint our heart felt grief and lamentation upon this occasion; for we had no doubt of Eliza's being the person described, as a stranger, who died at Danvers, last July. Her delivery of a child; her dejected state of mind; the marks upon her linen; indeed, every circumstance in the advertisement convinced us beyond dispute that it could be no other. Mrs. Wharton retired immediately to her chamber, where she continued overwhelmed with sorrow that night and the following day. Such, in fact, has been her habitual frame ever since; though the endeavors of her friends, who have sought to console her, have rendered her somewhat more conversable. My testimony of Eliza's penitence, before her departure, is a source of comfort to this disconsolate parent. She fondly cherished the idea, that having expiated her offence by sincere repentance and amendment, her deluded child finally made a happy exchange of worlds. But the desperate resolution, which she formed, and executed of becoming a fugitive; of deserting her mother's house and protection, and of wandering and dying among strangers, is a most distressing reflection to her friends; especially to her mother, in whose breast so many painful ideas arise, that she finds it extremely difficult to compose herself to that resignation, which she evidently strives to exemplify.

Eliza's brother has been to visit her last retreat; and to learn the particulars of her melancholy exit. He relates, that she was well accommodated, and had every attention and assistance, which her situation required. The people where she resided appear to have a lively sense of her merit and misfortunes. They testify her modest deportment, her fortitude under the sufferings to which she was called, and the serenity and composure, with which she bid a last adieu to the world. Mr. Wharton has brought back several scraps of her writing, containing miscellaneous reflections on her situation, the death of her babe, and the absence of her friends. Some of these were written before, some after her confinement. These valuable testimonies of the affecting sense, and calm expectation she entertained of her approaching dissolution, are calculated to sooth and comfort the minds of mourning connections. They greatly alleviate the regret occasioned by her absence, at this awful period.

Her elopement can be equalled only by the infatuation which caused her ruin.

> "But let no one reproach her memory.
> Her life has paid the forfeit of her folly.
> Let that suffice."

I am told that Major Sanford is quite frantic. Sure I am that he has reason to be. If the mischiefs he has brought upon others return upon his own head, dreadful indeed must be his portion! His wife has left him, and returned to her parents. His estate, which has been long mortgaged, is taken from him; and poverty and disgrace await him! Heaven seldom leaves injured innocence unavenged! Wretch, that he is, he ought for ever to be banished from human society! I shall continue with Mrs. Wharton, till the lenient hand of time has assuaged her sorrows; and then make my promised visit to you. I will bring Eliza's posthumous papers with me, when I come to Boston, as I have not time to copy them now.

I foresee, my dear Mrs. Sumner, that this disastrous affair will suspend your enjoyments, as it has mine. But what are our feelings, compared with the pangs which rend a parent's heart? This parent, I here behold, inhumanly stripped of the best solace of her declining years, by the ensnaring machinations of a profligate debauchee! Not only the life, but what was still dearer, the reputation and virtue of the unfortunate Eliza, have fallen victims at the shrine of *libertinism!* Detested be the epithet! Let it henceforth bear its true signature, and candor itself shall call it *lust* and *brutality!*

Execrable is the man, however arrayed in magnificence, crowned with wealth, or decorated with the external graces and accomplishments of fashionable life, who shall presume to display them, at the expense of virtue and innocence! Sacred names! attended with real blessings; blessings too useful and important to be trifled away! My resentment at the base arts, which must have been employed to complete the seduction of Eliza, I cannot suppress. I wish them to be exposed, and stamped with universal ignominy! Nor do I doubt but you will join with me in execrating the measures by which *we* have been robbed of so valuable a friend; and *society,* of so ornamental a member. I am, &c.

Julia Granby.

Letter LXXII

To Mr. Charles Deighton

Hartford.

Confusion, horror and despair are the portion of your wretched, unhappy friend! Oh, Deighton, I am undone! Misery irremediable is my future lot! She is gone; yes, she is gone for ever! The darling of my soul, the centre of all my wishes and enjoyments is no more! Cruel fate has snatched her from me; and she is irretrievably lost! I rave, and then reflect: I reflect, and then rave! I have not patience to bear this calamity, nor power to remedy it! Where shall I fly from the upbraidings of my mind, which accuses me as the murderer of my Eliza? I would fly to death, and seek a refuge in the grave; but the forebodings of a retribution to come, I cannot away with! Oh, that I had seen her; that I had once more asked her forgiveness! But even that privilege, that consolation was denied me! The day on which I meant to visit her, most of my property was attached, and to secure the rest, I was obliged to shut my doors, and become a prisoner in my own house! High living, and old debts, incurred by extravagance, had reduced the fortune of my wife to very little, and I could not satisfy the clamorous demands of my creditors.

I would have given millions, had I possessed them, to have been at liberty to see, and to have had power to preserve Eliza from death! But in vain was my anxiety; it could not relieve; it could not liberate me! When I first heard the dreadful tidings of her exit, I believe I acted like a madman! Indeed, I am little else now!

I have compounded with my creditors, and resigned the whole of my property.

Thus, that splendor and equipage, to secure which, I have sacrificed a virtuous woman, is taken from me; that poverty, the dread of which prevented my forming an honorable connection with an amiable and accomplished girl, the only one I ever loved, has fallen, with redoubled vengeance, upon my guilty head; and I must become a vagabond in the earth!

I shall fly my country as soon as possible; I shall go from every object which reminds me of my departed Eliza! But never, never shall I eradicate from my bosom the idea of her excellence; or the painful remembrance of the injuries I have done her! Her shade will perpetually haunt me! The image of her, as she appeared when mounting the carriage which conveyed her for ever from my sight, she waved her hand in token of a last adieu, will always be present to my imagination! The solemn counsel she gave me before we parted, never more to meet, will not cease to resound in my ears!

While my being is prolonged, I must feel the disgraceful, and torturing effects of my guilt in seducing her! How madly have I deprived her of happiness, of reputation, of life! Her friends, could they know the pangs of contrition, and the horror of conscience which attend me, would be amply revenged!

It is said, she quitted the world with composure and peace. Well she might! She had not that insupportable weight of iniquity, which sinks me to despair! She found consolation in that religion, which I have ridiculed as priestcraft and hypocrisy! But whether it be true, or false, would to heaven I could now enjoy the comforts, which its votaries evidently feel!

My wife has left me. As we lived together without love, we parted without regret.

Now, Charles, I am to bid you a long, perhaps, a last farewell. Where I shall roam in future, I neither know nor care; I shall go where the name of Sanford is unknown; and his person and sorrows unnoticed.

In this happy clime I have nothing to induce my stay. I have not money to support me with my profligate companions; nor have I any relish, at present, for their society. By the virtuous part of the community, I am shunned as the pest and bane of social enjoyment. In short I am debarred from every kind of happiness. If I look back, I recoil with horror from the black catalogue of vices, which have stained my past life, and reduced me to indigence and contempt. If I look forward, I shudder at the prospects which my foreboding mind presents to view, both in this and a coming world! This is a deplorable, yet just picture of myself! How totally the reverse of what I once appeared!

Let it warn you, my friend, to shun the dangerous paths which I have trodden, that you may never be involved in the hopeless ignominy and wretchedness of.

Peter Sanford.

Letter LXXIII

To Miss Julia Granby

Boston.

A melancholy tale have you unfolded, my dear Julia; and tragic indeed is the concluding scene!

Is she then gone! gone in this most distressing manner! Have I lost my once loved friend; lost her in a way which I could never have conceived to be possible.

Our days of childhood were spent together in the same pursuits, in the same amusements. Our riper years encreased our mutual affection, and maturer judgment most firmly cemented our friendship. Can I then calmly resign her to so severe a fate! Can I bear the idea of her being lost to honor, to fame, and to life! No;

she shall still live in the heart of her faithful Lucy; whose experience of her numerous virtues and engaging qualities, has imprinted her image too deeply on the memory to be obliterated. However she may have erred, her sincere repentance is sufficient to restore her to charity.

Your letter gave me the first information of this awful event. I had taken a short excursion into the country, where I had not seen the papers; or if I had, paid little or no attention to them. By your directions I found the distressing narrative of her exit. The poignancy of my grief, and the unavailing lamentations which the intelligence excited, need no delineation. To scenes of this nature, you have been habituated in the mansion of sorrow, where you reside.

How sincerely I sympathize with the bereaved parent of the dear, deceased Eliza, I can feel, but have not power to express. Let it be her consolation, that her child is at rest. The resolution which carried this deluded wanderer thus far from her friends, and supported her through her various trials, is astonishing! Happy would it have been, had she exerted an equal degree of fortitude in repelling the first attacks upon her virtue! But she is no more; and heaven forbid that I should accuse or reproach her!

Yet, in what language shall I express my abhorrence of the monster, whose detestable arts have blasted one of the fairest flowers in creation? I leave him to God, and his own conscience! Already is he exposed in his true colors! Vengeance already begins to overtake him! His sordid mind must now suffer the deprivation of those sensual gratifications, beyond which he is incapable of enjoyment!

Upon your reflecting and steady mind, my dear Julia, I need not inculcate the lessons which may be drawn from this woe-fraught tale; but for the sake of my sex in general, I wish it engraved upon every heart, that virtue alone, independent of the trappings of wealth, the parade of equipage, and the adulation of gallantry, can secure lasting felicity. From the melancholy story of Eliza Wharton, let the American fair learn to reject with disdain every insinuation derogatory to their true dignity and honor. Let them despise, and for ever banish the man, who can glory in the seduction of innocence and the ruin of reputation. To associate, is to approve; to approve, is to be betrayed!

I am, &c.

Lucy Sumner.

Letter LXXIV

To Mrs. M. Wharton

Boston.

Dear Madam,

We have paid the last tribute of respect to your beloved daughter. The day after my arrival, Mrs. Sumner proposed that we should visit the sad spot which contains the remains of our once amiable friend. The grave of Eliza Wharton, said she, shall not be unbedewed by the tears of friendship.

Yesterday we went accordingly, and were much pleased with the apparent sincerity of the people, in their assurances that every thing in their power had been done to render her situation comfortable. The minutest circumstances were faithfully related; and from the state of her mind, in her last hours, I think much comfort may be derived to her afflicted friends.

We spent a mournful hour, in the place where she is interred, and then returned to the inn, while Mrs. Sumner gave orders for a decent stone to be erected over her grave, with the following inscription:

"THIS HUMBLE STONE,
IN MEMORY OF
ELIZA WHARTON,
IS INSCRIBED BY HER WEEPING FRIENDS,
TO WHOM SHE ENDEARED HERSELF BY UNCOMMON
TENDERNESS AND AFFECTION.
ENDOWED WITH SUPERIOR ACQUIREMENTS,
SHE WAS STILL MORE DISTINGUISHED BY
HUMILITY AND BENEVOLENCE.
LET CANDOR THROW A VEIL OVER HER FRAILTIES,
FOR GREAT WAS HER CHARITY TO OTHERS.
SHE SUSTAINED THE LAST
PAINFUL SCENE, FAR FROM EVERY FRIEND;
AND EXHIBITED AN EXAMPLE
OF CALM RESIGNATION.
HER DEPARTURE WAS ON THE 25TH DAY OF
JULY, A.D.——,
IN THE 37TH YEAR OF HER AGE,
AND THE TEARS OF STRANGERS WATERED HER
GRAVE."

I hope, madam, that you will derive satisfaction from these exertions of friendship, and that, united to the many other sources of consolation with which you are furnished, they may alleviate your grief; and while they leave the pleasing remembrance of her virtues, add the supporting persuasion, that your Eliza is happy.

I am, &c.

Julia Granby.

1797

Susanna Haswell Rowson 1762–1824

Susanna Haswell Rowson's *Charlotte Temple* (first published in London, in 1791, as *Charlotte, A Tale of Truth*) became the first American best-selling novel when it was republished in 1794 by Matthew Carey of Philadelphia. Susanna Haswell was born in Portsmouth, England, in 1762. Her mother, Susanna Musgrave Haswell, died from complications of childbirth, an event that surely influenced Rowson's fiction. Her father, Lieutenant William Haswell, left Susanna in the care of relatives and went to Massachusetts. Late in 1766, he brought his daughter, then almost five years old, through a perilous sea voyage to the colonies. Haswell had remarried, and soon young Susanna had two half-brothers.

The Haswells' loyalty to England made life in Massachusetts difficult for them during the Revolutionary War. They were first detained by an American guard and later conveyed by prisoner exchange to London. In England, Susanna Haswell worked as a governess and wrote poetry, short stories, and novels. In 1786, under the patronage of the Duchess of Devonshire, she published *Victoria,* a sentimental novel in the style popularized by Samuel Richardson. She continued to write prolifically in the following years, and her reputation and readership grew on both sides of the Atlantic Ocean.

In 1786, she married William Rowson, a hardware merchant. When the hardware business failed, the Rowsons decided to go on the stage. They toured in Britain and then signed with Thomas Wignell's theater company. In 1793, the company went to the United States, where Susanna Rowson not only acted but was also a playwright and lyricist. Her song "America, Commerce and Freedom," in celebration of her adopted country, was especially popular.

When the American edition of *Charlotte Temple* appeared in 1794, it quickly sold out, and Carey had it reprinted at least once and possibly twice in the same year. It has been estimated that the book went through over 200 editions and was read by as many as a half-million people. Its subtitle may in part account for its immense popularity in a growing nation with a puritanical past. Though novel-reading might have been regarded as a questionable activity, reading "a tale of truth" could be excused, especially if that tale had been written by an author who took every possible occasion to drive home a moral point, and in *Charlotte Temple* the moral is clear: Charlotte unwisely elopes to America with a man who falsely promises to marry her, is eventually forsaken by him, suffers both physical and mental anguish, and dies after bearing his child.

Rownson eventually gave up the stage and, in 1797, established a very successful school, Mrs. Rowson's Young Ladies' Academy, in Boston, where she earned renown as an educator, textbook author, and columnist for *Boston Weekly Magazine.* When she died, she was one of the most celebrated women in America. In 1828, a sequel to *Charlotte Temple,* a novel entitled *Charlotte's Daughter: or, The Three Orphans* (also called *Lucy Temple*) was published posthumously.

Though *Charlotte Temple* enjoyed enormous popularity throughout the nineteenth century, its literary merit was questioned. Some critics characterized Rowson's work as sentimental and melodramatic. Other critics defended the novel, citing its psychological power and insight, as well as its important portrayal of standards of morality prevalent in eighteenth-century America. Rowson's depiction of the Revolutionary War as the background of her romance has also been seen as significant in American literary history.

Literary scholars have also disagreed on the extent to which Rowson was a feminist. Certainly in her novels, and even more strikingly in some of her poetry, Rowson confirms the established view of women as weak and in need of protection—either from parents or a husband—although experiences from her own life belied this traditional assessment. Yet there is in her depiction of the subjected and precarious situation of women an incipient protest against it.

Critics who have not taken Rowson seriously as a literary figure emphasize her appeal to an audience of "housemaids and shopgirls"—in other words, to uneducated women employed in low-paying jobs—just the people who might be receptive to a protest, however mild and disguised, against the injustices women faced. Rowson's feminism does not consist of an open rejection of any established order or sentiment; instead, she vividly describes a world of endless woes faced by women: deceitful friends, false advisers, faithless lovers, disastrous pregnancies, and fatal childbirths. One can find in these melodramatic situations an incipient protest against the female condition and at the same time the source of Rowson's lasting power and appeal.

Laraine Fergenson
Bronx Community College
City University of New York

PRIMARY WORKS

Victoria, A Novel, (London, 1786); *The Inquisitor, or the Invisible Rambler* (London, 1788; first American edition, 1794); *Mentoria, or the Young Ladies' Friend* (London, 1791; first American edition, 1794); *Charlotte, a Tale of Truth* (London, 1791; first American edition, 1794; later published as *Charlotte Temple*; *Rebecca, or, The Fille de Chambre* (London, 1792; first American edition, 1794); *Trials of the Human Heart* (1795); *Reuben and Rachel, or Tales of Old Times* (1798); *Sarah; or, The Exemplary Wife* (1813); *Charlotte's Daughter; or, The Three Orphans* (1828; later published as *Lucy Temple*); Cathy N. Davidson, ed., *Charlotte Temple* (1987); Ann Douglas, ed., *Charlotte Temple and Lucy Temple* (1991).

from Charlotte Temple[1]

from Preface

For the perusal of the young and thoughtless of the fair sex, this Tale of Truth is designed; and I could wish my fair readers to consider it as not merely the effusion of Fancy, but as a reality. The circumstances on which I have founded this novel were related to me some little time since by an old lady who had personally known Charlotte, though she concealed the real names of the characters, and likewise the place where the unfortunate scenes were acted. . . . I have thrown over the whole a slight veil of fiction, and substituted names and places according to my own fancy. The principal characters in this little tale are now consigned to the silent tomb: it can therefore hurt the feelings of no one; and may, I flatter myself, be of service to some who are so unfortunate as to have neither friends to advise, or understanding to direct them, through the various and unexpected evils that attend a young and unprotected woman in her first entrance into life. . . .

[1]The following excerpts are taken from the first American edition (1794), but the title *Charlotte Temple,* by which the novel is better known, has been used here.

Sensible as I am that a novel writer, at a time when such a variety of works are ushered into the world under that name, stands but a poor chance for fame in the annals of literature, but conscious that I wrote with a mind anxious for the happiness of that sex whose morals and conduct have so powerful an influence on mankind in general; and convinced that I have not wrote a line that conveys a wrong idea to the head or a corrupt wish to the heart, I shall rest satisfied in the purity of my own intentions, and if I merit not applause, I feel that I dread not censure.

If the following tale should save one hapless fair one from the errors which ruined poor Charlotte, or rescue from impending misery the heart of one anxious parent, I shall feel a much higher gratification in reflecting on this trifling performance, than could possibly result from the applause which might attend the most elegant, finished piece of literature whose tendency might deprave the heart or mislead the understanding.

from Chapter I
A Boarding School

"Are you for a walk," said Montraville to his companion, as they arose from table; "are you for a walk? or shall we order the chaise and proceed to Portsmouth?" Belcour preferred the former; and they sauntered out to view the town, and to make remarks on the inhabitants, as they returned from church.

Montraville was a Lieutenant in the army: Belcour was his brother officer: they had been to take leave of their friends previous to their departure for America, and were now returning to Portsmouth, where the troops waited orders for embarkation. They had stopped at Chichester to dine; and knowing they had sufficient time to reach the place of destination before dark, and yet allow them a walk, had resolved, it being Sunday afternoon, to take a survey of the Chichester ladies as they returned from their devotions.

They had gratified their curiosity, and were preparing to return to the inn without honouring any of the belles with particular notice, when Madame Du Pont, at the head of her school, descended from the church. Such an assemblage of youth and innocence naturally attracted the young soldiers: they stopped; and, as the little cavalcade passed, almost involuntarily pulled off their hats. A tall, elegant girl looked at Montraville and blushed: he instantly recollected the features of Charlotte Temple, whom he had once seen and danced with at a ball at Portsmouth. At that time he thought on her only as a very lovely child, she being then only thirteen; but the improvement two years had made in her person, and the blush of recollection which suffused her cheeks as she passed, awakened in his bosom new and pleasing ideas. Vanity led him to think that pleasure at again beholding him might have occasioned the emotion he had witnessed, and the same vanity led him to wish to see her again.

"She is the sweetest girl in the world," said he, as he entered the inn. Belcour stared. "Did you not notice her?" continued Montraville: "she had on a blue bonnet, and with a pair of lovely eyes of the same colour, has contrived to make me feel devilish odd about the heart."

"Pho," said Belcour, "a musket ball from our friends, the Americans, may in less than two months make you feel worse."

"I never think of the future," replied Montraville; "but am determined to make the most of the present, and would willingly compound with any kind Familiar who would inform me who the girl is, and how I might be likely to obtain an interview."

But no kind Familiar at that time appearing, and the chaise[2] which they had ordered, driving up to the door, Montraville and his companion were obliged to take leave of Chichester and its fair inhabitant, and proceed on their journey.

But Charlotte had made too great an impression on his mind to be easily eradicated: having therefore spent three whole days in thinking on her and in endeavouring to form some plan for seeing her, he determined to set off for Chichester, and trust to chance either to favour or frustrate his designs. Arriving at the verge of the town, he dismounted, and sending the servant forward with the horses, proceeded toward the place, where, in the midst of an extensive pleasure ground, stood the mansion which contained the lovely Charlotte Temple. Montraville leaned on a broken gate, and looked earnestly at the house. The wall which surrounded it was high, and perhaps the Argus's[3] who guarded the Hesperian[4] fruit within, were more watchful than those famed of old.

"'Tis a romantic attempt," said he; "and should I even succeed in seeing and conversing with her, it can be productive of no good: I must of necessity leave England in a few days, and probably may never return; why then should I endeavour to engage the affections of this lovely girl, only to leave her a prey to a thousand inquietudes, of which at present she has no idea? I will return to Portsmouth and think no more about her."

The evening now was closed; a serene stillness reigned; and the chaste Queen of Night with her silver crescent faintly illuminated the hemisphere. The mind of Montraville was hushed into composure by the serenity of the surrounding objects. "I will think on her no more," said he, and turned with an intention to leave the place; but as he turned, he saw the gate which led to the pleasure grounds open, and two women come out, who walked arm-in-arm across the field.

"I will at least see who these are," said he. He overtook them, and giving them the compliments of the evening, begged leave to see them into the more frequented parts of the town: but how was he delighted, when, waiting for an answer, he discovered, under the concealment of a large bonnet, the face of Charlotte Temple.

He soon found means to ingratiate himself with her companion, who was a French teacher at the school, and, at parting, slipped a letter he had purposely written, into Charlotte's hand, and five guineas into that of Mademoiselle, who promised she would endeavour to bring her young charge into the field again the next evening.

[2]A light horse-drawn carriage.
[3]Misspelled plural of Argus, a mythological guardian, who had one hundred eyes.
[4]A reference to the mythological golden apples guarded by the Hesperides, the daughters of Atlas; here *Hesperian fruit* refers to the students at the school.

Chapter VI
An Intriguing Teacher

Madame Du Pont was a woman every way calculated to take the care of young ladies, had that care entirely devolved on herself; but it was impossible to attend the education of a numerous school without proper assistants; and those assistants were not always the kind of people whose conversation and morals were exactly such as parents of delicacy and refinement would wish a daughter to copy. Among the teachers at Madame Du Pont's school, was Mademoiselle La Rue, who added to a pleasing person and insinuating address, a liberal education and the manners of a gentlewoman. She was recommended to the school by a lady whose humanity overstepped the bounds of discretion: for though she knew Miss La Rue had eloped from a convent with a young officer, and, on coming to England, had lived with several different men in open defiance of all moral and religious duties; yet, finding her reduced to the most abject want, and believing the penitence which she professed to be sincere, she took her into her own family, and from thence recommended her to Madame Du Pont, as thinking the situation more suitable for a woman of her abilities. But Mademoiselle possessed too much of the spirit of intrigue to remain long without adventures. At church, where she constantly appeared, her person attracted the attention of a young man who was upon a visit at a gentleman's seat in the neighbourhood: she had met him several times clandestinely; and being invited to come out that evening, and eat some fruit and pastry in a summer-house belonging to the gentleman he was visiting, and requested to bring some of the ladies with her, Charlotte being her favourite, was fixed on to accompany her.

The mind of youth eagerly catches at promised pleasure: pure and innocent by nature, it thinks not of the dangers lurking beneath those pleasures, till too late to avoid them: when Mademoiselle asked Charlotte to go with her, she mentioned the gentleman as a relation, and spoke in such high terms of the elegance of his gardens, the sprightliness of his conversation, and the liberality with which he ever entertained his guests, that Charlotte thought only of the pleasure she should enjoy in the visit,—not on the imprudence of going without her governess's knowledge, or of the danger to which she exposed herself in visiting the house of a gay young man of fashion.

Madame Du Pont was gone out for the evening, and the rest of the ladies retired to rest, when Charlotte and the teacher stole out at the back gate, and in crossing the field, were accosted by Montraville, as mentioned in the first chapter.

Charlotte was disappointed in the pleasure she had promised herself from this visit. The levity of the gentlemen and the freedom of their conversation disgusted her. She was astonished at the liberties Mademoiselle permitted them to take; grew thoughtful and uneasy, and heartily wished herself at home again in her own chamber.

Perhaps one cause of that wish might be, an earnest desire to see the contents of the letter which had been put into her hand by Montraville.

Any reader who has the least knowledge of the world, will easily imagine the letter was made up of encomiums on her beauty, and vows of everlasting love and constancy; nor will he be surprised that a heart open to every gentle, generous sentiment, should feel itself warmed by gratitude for a man who professed to feel so much for her; nor is it improbable but her mind might revert to the agreeable person and martial appearance of Montraville.

In affairs of love, a young heart is never in more danger than when attempted by a handsome young soldier. A man of an indifferent appearance, will, when arrayed in a military habit, shew to advantage; but when beauty of person, elegance of manner, and an easy method of paying compliments, are united to the scarlet coat, smart cockade, and military sash, ah! well-a-day for the poor girl who gazes on him: she is in imminent danger; but if she listens to him with pleasure, 'tis all over with her, and from that moment she has neither eyes nor ears for any other object.

Now, my dear sober matron, (if a sober matron should deign to turn over these pages, before she trusts them to the eye of a darling daughter,) let me intreat you not to put on a grave face, and throw down the book in a passion and declare 'tis enough to turn the heads of half the girls in England; I do solemnly protest, my dear madam, I mean no more by what I have here advanced, than to ridicule those romantic girls, who foolishly imagine a red coat and silver epaulet constitute the fine gentleman; and should that fine gentleman make half a dozen fine speeches to them, they will imagine themselves so much in love as to fancy it a meritorious action to jump out of a two pair of stairs window, abandon their friends, and trust entirely to the honour of a man, who perhaps hardly knows the meaning of the word, and if he does, will be too much the modern man of refinement, to practice it in their favour.

Gracious heaven! when I think on the miseries that must rend the heart of a doating parent, when he sees the darling of his age at first seduced from his protection, and afterwards abandoned, by the very wretch whose promises of love decoyed her from the paternal roof—when he sees her poor and wretched, her bosom torn between remorse for her crime and love for her vile betrayer—when fancy paints to me the good old man stooping to raise the weeping penitent, while every tear from her eye is numbered by drops from his bleeding heart, my bosom glows with honest indignation, and I wish for power to extirpate those monsters of seduction from the earth.

Oh my dear girls—for to such only am I writing—listen not to the voice of love, unless sanctioned by paternal approbation: be assured, it is now past the days of romance: no woman can be run away with contrary to her own inclination: then kneel down each morning, and request kind heaven to keep you free from temptation, or, should it please to suffer you to be tried, pray for fortitude to resist the impulse of inclination when it runs counter to the precepts of religion and virtue.

from Chapter VII
Natural Sense of Propriety Inherent in the Female Bosom

"I cannot think we have done exactly right in going out this evening, Mademoiselle," said Charlotte, seating herself when she entered her apartment: "nay, I am sure it was not right; for I expected to be very happy, but was sadly disappointed."

"It was your own fault, then," replied Mademoiselle: "for I am sure my cousin omitted nothing that could serve to render the evening agreeable."

"True," said Charlotte: "but I thought the gentlemen were very free in their manner: I wonder you would suffer them to behave as they did."

"Prithee, don't be such a foolish little prude," said the artful woman, affecting anger: "I invited you to go in hopes it would divert you, and be an agreeable change of scene; however, if your delicacy was hurt by the behaviour of the gentlemen, you need not go again; so there let it rest."

"I do not intend to go again," said Charlotte, gravely taking off her bonnet, and beginning to prepare for bed: "I am sure, if Madame Du Pont knew we had been out to-night, she would be very angry; and it is ten to one but she hears of it by some means or other."

"Nay, Miss," said La Rue, "perhaps your mighty sense of propriety may lead you to tell her yourself: and in order to avoid the censure you would incur, should she hear of it by accident, throw the blame on me: but I confess I deserve it: it will be a very kind return for that partiality which led me to prefer you before any of the rest of the ladies; but perhaps it will give you pleasure," continued she, letting fall some hypocritical tears, "to see me deprived of bread, and for an action which by the most rigid could only be esteemed an inadvertency, lose my place and character, and be driven again into the world, where I have already suffered all the evils attendant on poverty."

This was touching Charlotte in the most vulnerable part: she rose from her seat, and taking Mademoiselle's hand—"You know, my dear La Rue," said she, "I love you too well, to do anything that would injure you in my governess's opinion: I am only sorry we went out this evening."

"I don't believe it, Charlotte," said she, assuming a little vivacity; "for if you had not gone out, you would not have seen the gentleman who met us crossing the field; and I rather think you were pleased with his conversation."

"I had seen him once before," replied Charlotte, "and thought him an agreeable man; and you know one is always pleased to see a person with whom one has passed several chearful hours. "But," said she pausing, and drawing the letter from her pocket, while a gentle suffusion of vermillion tinged her neck and face, "he gave me this letter; what shall I do with it?"

"Read it, to be sure," returned Mademoiselle.

"I am afraid I ought not," said Charlotte: "my mother has often told me, I should never read a letter given me by a young man, without first giving it to her."

"Lord bless you, my dear girl," cried the teacher smiling, "have you a mind to be in leading strings all your life time. Prithee open the letter, read it, and judge for yourself; if you show it your mother, the consequence will be, you will be taken from school, and a strict guard kept over you; so you will stand no chance of ever seeing the smart young officer again."

"I should not like to leave school yet," replied Charlotte, "till I have attained a greater proficiency in my Italian and music. But you can, if you please, Mademoiselle, take the letter back to Montraville, and tell him I wish him well, but cannot, with any propriety, enter into a clandestine correspondence with him." She laid the letter on the table, and began to undress herself.

"Well," said La Rue, "I vow you are an unaccountable girl: have you no curiosity to see the inside now? for my part I could no more let a letter addressed to me lie unopened so long, than I could work miracles: he writes a good hand," continued she, turning the letter, to look at the superscription.

" 'Tis well enough," said Charlotte, drawing it towards her.

"He is a genteel young fellow," said La Rue carelessly, folding up her apron at the same time; "but I think he is marked with the small pox."

"Oh you are greatly mistaken," said Charlotte eagerly; "he has a remarkable clear skin and fine complexion."

"His eyes, if I could judge by what I saw," said La Rue, "are grey and want expression."

"By no means," replied Charlotte; "they are the most expressive eyes I ever saw."

"Well, child, whether they are grey or black is of no consequence: you have determined not to read his letter; so it is likely you will never either see or hear from him again."

Charlotte took up the letter, and Mademoiselle continued—

"He is most probably going to America; and if ever you should hear any account of him, it may possibly be that he is killed; and though he loved you ever so fervently, though his last breath should be spent in a prayer for your happiness, it can be nothing to you: you can feel nothing for the fate of the man, whose letters you will not open, and whose sufferings you will not alleviate, by permitting him to think you would remember him when absent, and pray for his safety."

Charlotte still held the letter in her hand: her heart swelled at the conclusion of Mademoiselle's speech, and a tear dropped upon the wafer that closed it.

"The wafer is not dry yet," said she, "and sure there can be no great harm—" She hesitated. La Rue was silent. "I may read it, Mademoiselle, and return it afterwards."

"Certainly," replied Mademoiselle.

"At any rate I am determined not to answer it," continued Charlotte, as she opened the letter.

Here let me stop to make one remark, and trust me my very heart aches while I write it; but certain I am, that when once a woman has stifled the sense of shame in her own bosom, when once she has lost sight of the basis on which reputation, honour, every thing that should be dear to the female heart, rests, she grows hardened in guilt, and will spare no pains to bring down innocence and beauty to the shocking level with herself: and this proceeds from that diabolical spirit of envy, which repines at seeing another in the full possession of that respect and esteem which she can no longer hope to enjoy.

Mademoiselle eyed the unsuspecting Charlotte, as she perused the letter, with a malignant pleasure. She saw, that the contents had awakened new emotions in her youthful bosom: she encouraged her hopes, calmed her fears, and before they parted for the night, it was determined that she should meet Montraville the ensuing evening. . . .

Chapter IX
We Know Not What a Day May Bring Forth

Various were the sensations which agitated the mind of Charlotte, during the day preceding the evening in which she was to meet Montraville. Several times did she almost resolve to go to her governess, show her the letter, and be guided by her advice: but Charlotte had taken one step in the ways of imprudence; and when that is once done, there are always innumerable obstacles to prevent the erring person returning to the path of rectitude: yet these obstacles, however forcible they may appear in general, exist chiefly in imagination.

Charlotte feared the anger of her governess: she loved her mother, and the very idea of incurring her displeasure, gave her the greatest uneasiness: but there was a more forcible reason still remaining: should she show the letter to Madame Du Pont, she must confess the means by which it came into her possession; and what would be the consequence? Mademoiselle would be turned out of doors.

"I must not be ungrateful," said she. "La Rue is very kind to me; besides I can, when I see Montraville, inform him of the impropriety of our continuing to see or correspond with each other, and request him to come no more to Chichester."

However prudent Charlotte might be in these resolutions, she certainly did not take a proper method to confirm herself in them. Several times in the course of the day, she indulged herself in reading over the letter, and each time she read it, the contents sunk deeper in her heart. As evening drew near, she caught herself frequently consulting her watch. "I wish this foolish meeting was over," said she, by way of apology to her own heart, "I wish it was over; for when I have seen him, and convinced him my resolution is not to be shaken, I shall feel my mind much easier."

The appointed hour arrived. Charlotte and Mademoiselle eluded the eye of vigilance; and Montraville, who had waited their coming with impatience, received them with rapturous and unbounded acknowledgments for their condescension: he had wisely brought Belcour with him to entertain Mademoiselle, while he enjoyed an uninterrupted conversation with Charlotte.

Belcour was a man whose character might be comprised in a few words; and as he will make some figure in the ensuing pages, I shall here describe him. He possessed a genteel fortune, and had a liberal education; dissipated, thoughtless, and capricious, he paid little regard to the moral duties, and less to religious ones: eager in the pursuit of pleasure, he minded not the miseries he inflicted on others, so that his own wishes, however extravagant, were gratified. Self, darling self, was the idol he worshiped, and to that he would have sacrificed the interest and happiness of all mankind. Such was the friend of Montraville: will not the reader be ready to imagine that the man who could regard[5] such a character must be actuated by the same feelings, follow the same pursuits, and be equally unworthy with the person to whom he gave his confidence?

But Montraville was a different character: generous in his disposition, liberal in his opinions, and good-natured almost to a fault; yet eager and impetuous in the pursuit of a favorite object, he staid not to reflect on the consequence which might follow the attainment of his wishes; with a mind ever open to conviction, had he been so fortunate as to possess a friend who would have pointed out the cruelty of endeavouring to gain the heart of an innocent artless girl, when he knew it was utterly impossible for him to marry her, and when the gratification of his passion would be unavoidable infamy and misery to her, and a cause of never-ceasing remorse to himself: had these dreadful consequences been placed before him in a proper light, the humanity of his nature would have urged him to give up the pursuit: but Belcour was not this friend; he rather encouraged the growing passion of Montraville; and being

[5]have regard for, care for.

pleased with the vivacity of Mademoiselle, resolved to leave no argument untried, which he thought might prevail on her to be the companion of their intended voyage; and he made no doubt but her example, added to the rhetoric of Montraville, would persuade Charlotte to go with them.

Charlotte had, when she went out to meet Montraville, flattered herself that her resolution was not to be shaken, and that, conscious of the impropriety of her conduct in having a clandestine intercourse with a stranger, she would never repeat the indiscretion.

But alas! poor Charlotte, she knew not the deceitfulness of her own heart, or she would have avoided the trial of her stability.

Montraville was tender, eloquent, ardent, and yet respectful. "Shall I not see you once more," said he, "before I leave England? Will you not bless me by an assurance that when we are divided by a vast expanse of sea I shall not be forgotten?"

Charlotte sighed.

"Why that sigh, my dear Charlotte? Could I flatter myself that a fear for my safety, or a wish for my welfare occasioned it, how happy would it make me."

"I shall ever wish you well, Montraville," said she, "but we must meet no more."

"Oh, say not so, my lovely girl: reflect that when I leave my native land, perhaps a few short weeks may terminate my existence; the perils of the ocean—the dangers of war—."

"I can hear no more," said Charlotte, in a tremulous voice. "I must leave you."

"Say you will see me once again."

"I dare not," said she.

"Only for one half hour to-morrow evening: 'tis my last request. I shall never trouble you again, Charlotte."

"I know not what to say," cried Charlotte, struggling to draw her hands from him: "let me leave you now."

"And will you come to-morrow?" said Montraville.

"Perhaps I may," said she.

"Adieu then. I will live upon that hope till we meet again."

He kissed her hand. She sighed an adieu, and catching hold of Mademoiselle's arm, hastily entered the garden gate.

Chapter XI
Conflict of Love and Duty

Almost a week was now gone, and Charlotte continued every evening to meet Montraville, and in her heart every meeting was resolved to be the last; but alas! when Montraville at parting would earnestly entreat one more interview, that treacherous heart betrayed her; and, forgetful of its resolution, pleaded the cause of the enemy so powerfully, that Charlotte was unable to resist. Another and another meeting succeeded; and so well did Montraville improve each opportunity, that the heedless girl at length confessed no idea could be so painful to her as that of never seeing him again.

"Then we will never be parted," said he.

"Ah, Montraville," replied Charlotte, forcing a smile, "how can it be avoided? My parents would never consent to our union; and even could they be brought to approve of it, how should I bear to be separated from my kind, my beloved mother?"

"Then you love your parents more than you do me, Charlotte?"

"I hope I do," said she, blushing and looking down, "I hope my affection for them will ever keep me from infringing the laws of filial duty."

"Well, Charlotte," said Montraville gravely, and letting go her hand, "since that is the case, I find I have deceived myself with fallacious hopes. I had flattered my fond heart, that I was dearer to Charlotte than any thing in the world besides. I thought that you would for my sake have braved the danger of the ocean, that you would, by your affection and smiles, have softened the hardships of war, and, had it been my fate to fall, your tenderness would cheer the hour of death, and smooth my passage to another world. But farewell, Charlotte! I see you never loved me. I shall now welcome the friendly ball that deprives me of the sense of my misery."

"Oh stay, unkind Montraville," cried she, catching hold of his arm, as he pretended to leave her, "stay, and to calm your fears, I will here protest that was it not for the fear of giving pain to the best of parents, and returning their kindness with ingratitude, I would follow you through every danger, and, in studying to promote your happiness, insure my own. But I cannot break my mother's heart, Montraville; I must not bring the grey hairs of my doating grandfather with sorrow to the grave, or make my beloved father perhaps curse the hour that gave me birth." She covered her face with her hands, and burst into tears.

"All these distressing scenes, my dear Charlotte," cried Montraville, "are merely the chimeras of a disturbed fancy. Your parents might perhaps grieve at first; but when they heard from your own hand that you were with a man of honour, and that it was to insure your felicity by a union with him, to which you feared they would never have given their assent, that you left their protection, they will, be assured, forgive an error which love alone occasioned, and when we return from America, receive you with open arms and tears of joy."

Belcour and Mademoiselle heard this last speech, and conceiving it a proper time to throw in their advice and persuasions, approached Charlotte, and so well seconded the entreaties of Montraville, that finding Mademoiselle intended going with Belcour, and feeling her own treacherous heart too much inclined to accompany them, the hapless Charlotte, in an evil hour, consented that the next evening they should bring a chaise to the end of the town, and that she would leave her friends, and throw herself entirely on the protection of Montraville. "But should you," said she, looking earnestly at him, her eyes full of tears, "should you, forgetful of your promises, and repenting the engagements you here voluntarily enter into, forsake and leave me on a foreign shore—"

"Judge not so meanly of me," said he. "The moment we reach our place of destination, Hymen[6] shall sanctify our love; and when I shall forget your goodness, may heaven forget me!"

"Ah," said Charlotte, leaning on Mademoiselle's arm as they walked up the garden together, "I have forgot all that I ought to have remembered, in consenting to this intended elopement."

[6]The god of marriage.

"You are a strange girl," said Mademoiselle: "you never know your own mind two minutes at a time. Just now you declared Montraville's happiness was what you prized most in the world; and now I suppose you repent having insured that happiness by agreeing to accompany him abroad."

"Indeed I do repent," replied Charlotte, "from my soul: but while discretion points out the impropriety of my conduct, inclination urges me on to ruin."

"Ruin! fiddlesticks!" said Mademoiselle; "am I not going with you? and do I feel any of these qualms?"

"You do not renounce a tender father and mother," said Charlotte.

"But I hazard my dear reputation," replied Mademoiselle, bridling.

"True," replied Charlotte, "but you do not feet what I do." She then bade her good night: but sleep was a stranger to her eyes, and the tear of anguish watered her pillow.

from Chapter XII [How thou art fall'n!]

> [On the day that she plans to elope with Montraville, Charlotte receives a letter from her parents informing her that her grandfather will go to the school on the following day to take Charlotte home for a visit with her parents, who are planning a birthday celebration for her. This timely letter makes her reconsider her plan.]

. . . "Oh!" cried Charlotte . . . "let me reflect:—the irrevocable step is not yet taken: it is not too late to recede from the brink of a precipice, from which I can only behold the dark abyss of ruin, shame, and remorse!"

She arose from her seat, and flew to the apartment of La Rue. "Oh Mademoiselle!" said she, "I am snatched by a miracle from destruction! This letter has saved me: it has opened my eyes to the folly I was so near committing. I will not go, Mademoiselle; I will not wound the hearts of those dear parents who make my happiness the whole study of their lives."

"Well," said Mademoiselle, "do as you please, Miss; but pray understand that my resolution is taken, and it is not in your power to alter it. I shall meet the gentlemen at the appointed hour, and shall not be surprized at any outrage which Montraville may commit, when he finds himself disappointed. Indeed I should not be astonished, was he to come immediately here, and reproach you for your instability in the hearing of the whole school: and what will be the consequence? you will bear the odium of having formed the resolution of eloping, and every girl of spirit will laugh at your want of fortitude to put it in execution, while prudes and fools will load you with reproach and contempt. You will have lost the confidence of your parents, incurred their anger, and the scoffs of the world; and what fruit do you expect to reap from this piece of heroism, (for such no doubt you think it is?) you will have the pleasure to reflect, that you have deceived the man who adores you, and whom in your heart you prefer to all other men, and that you are separated from him for ever."

This eloquent harangue was given with such volubility, that Charlotte could not find an opportunity to interrupt her, or to offer a single word till the whole was finished, and then found her ideas so confused, that she knew not what to say.

At length she determined that she would go with Mademoiselle to the place of assignation, convince Montraville of the necessity of adhering to the resolution of remaining behind; assure him of her affection, and bid him adieu.

Charlotte formed this plan in her mind, and exulted in the certainty of its success. "How shall I rejoice," said she, "in this triumph of reason over inclination, and, when in the arms of my affectionate parents, lift up my soul in gratitude to heaven as I look back on the dangers I have escaped!"

The hour of assignation arrived: Mademoiselle put what money and valuables she possessed in her pocket, and advised Charlotte to do the same; but she refused; "my resolution is fixed," said she; "I will sacrifice love to duty."

Mademoiselle smiled internally; and they proceeded softly down the back stairs and out of the garden gate. Montraville and Belcour were ready to receive them.

"Now," said Montraville, taking Charlotte in his arms, "you are mine for ever."

"No," said she, withdrawing from his embrace, "I am come to take an everlasting farewell."

It would be useless to repeat the conversation that here ensued; suffice it to say, that Montraville used every argument that had formerly been successful, Charlotte's resolution began to waver, and he drew her almost imperceptibly towards the chaise.

"I cannot go," said she: "cease, dear Montraville, to persuade. I must not: religion, duty, forbid."

"Cruel Charlotte," said he, "if you disappoint my ardent hopes, by all that is sacred, this hand shall put a period to my existence. I cannot—will not live without you."

"Alas! my torn heart!" said Charlotte, "how shall I act?"

"Let me direct you," said Montraville, lifting her into the chaise.

"Oh! my dear forsaken parents!" cried Charlotte.

The chaise drove off. She shrieked, and fainted into the arms of her betrayer.

[In the following scene the news of Charlotte's elopement is conveyed by Mr. Temple to his wife.]

from Chapter XIV
Maternal Sorrow

. . . "Temple," said she, assuming a look of firmness and composure, "tell me the truth I beseech you. I cannot bear this dreadful suspense. What misfortune has befallen my child? Let me know the worst, and I will endeavour to bear it as I ought."

"Lucy," replied Mr. Temple, "imagine your daughter alive, and in no danger of death: what misfortune would you then dread?"

"There is one misfortune which is worse than death. But I know my child too well to suspect—"

"Be not too confident, Lucy."

"Oh heavens!" said she, "what horrid images do you start: is it possible she should forget—"

"She has forgot us all, my love; she has preferred the love of a stranger to the affectionate protection of her friends."

"Not eloped?" cried she eagerly.[7]

Mr. Temple was silent.

"You cannot contradict it," said she. "I see my fate in those tearful eyes. Oh Charlotte! Charlotte! how ill have you requited our tenderness! But, Father of Mercies," continued she, sinking on her knees, and raising her streaming eyes and clasped hands to heaven, "this once vouchsafe to hear a fond, a distracted mother's prayer. Oh let thy bounteous Providence watch over and protect the dear thoughtless girl, save her from the miseries which I fear will be her portion, and oh! of thine infinite mercy, make her not a mother, lest she should one day feel what I now suffer." . . .

1794

Charles Brockden Brown 1771–1810

Charles Brockden Brown was critically acclaimed in both America and Europe for his novels that adapted the Gothic style to the American landscape, substituting urban decay and untamed wilderness for castles and dungeons. In England, he was celebrated by the social reformer and novelist William Godwin and by the poets John Keats and Percy Bysshe Shelley. In the United States, where the admiration was largely posthumous, Brown was praised by Edgar Allan Poe, James Fenimore Cooper, Nathaniel Hawthorne, Margaret Fuller, Henry Wadsworth Longfellow, and John Greenleaf Whittier. Although recognition alluded him in his lifetime, as did monetary rewards, Brown did succeed in publishing six novels, as well as numerous political pamphlets and essays, and in founding two literary journals. Brown considered himself a "story-telling moralist," blending the didactic with the literary in consonance with an age still ambivalent about the benefits of reading fiction. Cathy N. Davidson acknowledges Brown's struggle with an audience predisposed against the novel and concludes, "Brown strove to educate the educated to the intellectual benefits of novel reading."

Charles Brockden Brown was born on January 17, 1771, in Philadelphia to Quaker parents, Elijah and Mary Armitt Brown. He grew up amid the excitement and turmoil of the colonies in revolt, even witnessing the arrest and temporary banishment to Virginia of his wealthy merchant father, whose Quaker pacifism led to accusations of being a British sympathizer. Brown entered the Friends Latin School in Philadelphia at the age of eleven and studied under the distinguished Robert Proud, graduating at the age of seventeen. Instead of attending college, Brown initially complied with his family's wishes and began working as a lawyer's apprentice to Alexander Wilcocks, but he became disenchanted with the profession by 1793. All the while, he continued to nurture his literary skills and in 1786 joined the Belles Letters Club of Philadelphia. In 1789, he

[7]Anxiously.

published a series of essays in *Columbian Magazine* under the title "The Rhapsodist," adopting the persona of a "hermit-explorer" who, as Emory Elliot explains, "spent months alone in the Ohio wilderness, meditating on human nature." Brown may have disappointed his family by not entering the family mercantile business, but his Quaker upbringing infused his writings with ethical and moral themes.

In 1796, Brown moved to New York and joined the Friendly Club, a group of intellectuals interested in the social reformist ideas of Mary Wollstonecraft and William Godwin. Club members included William Dunlap, a writer and artist who became Brown's first biographer, William Johnson, a friend, and Elihu Hubbard Smith, a poet, playwright, and medical student. In 1798, Brown shared bachelor quarters with Smith and Johnson in what must have been a stimulating environment, for in that year Brown published two novels: *Alcuin: A Dialogue* was a critique of marriage and its restrictions for women. *Wieland; Or, The Transformation. An American Tale* was based on a true story about a devoted father and brother who turns delusional and murderous. As the source of the delusion may be voices from God, *Wieland* also addresses what would become a recurrent theme in Brown's works: religious ambiguity. The year 1798 was also a time of tragedy. Johnson had welcomed into their home an Italian physician stricken with yellow fever. The man soon died, and Brown and Smith also fell ill. Brown survived, while Smith succumbed.

Brown drew upon his close encounter with disease in several of his works, notably *Ormond* (1799) and the first part of *Arthur Mervyn,* both published in 1799. In 1799, Brown also published his fourth novel, *Edgar Huntly,* which used sleepwalking as a framing device, a subject he explored in "Somnambulism," the "fragment" that appears in this anthology. Some critics have suggested that Brown employed this structure to explore themes of the subconscious and repressed impulses, another manifestation of the Gothic. During that prolific year, Brown turned his attentions to editing. In April 1799, he helped to found *The Monthly Magazine and American Review.* In addition to working as editor, he submitted many of his own writings. In December 1800, the magazine was renamed *The American Review and Literary Journal* and continued publication until 1802.

In 1801, Brown published two novels in the sentimental style, *Clara Howard* and *Jane Talbot.* Michael T. Gilmore observes that Brown's final novels appropriately addressed women's subjects in that "the romances constituted a last appeal to the already feminized reading public and capped his attempt to earn a living as a fiction writer." Despite these attempts, the works were not financially successful. At this point, Brown entered the family's trading business with his brothers. In 1803, he published two political pamphlets critical of Thomas Jefferson's policies regarding the purchase of the Louisiana Territory: *An Address to the Government of the United States, on the Cession of Louisiana to the French* and *Monroe's Embassy, or the Conduct of the Government, in Relation to Our Claims to the Navigation of the Mississippi.* Though Brown's motives in these pamphlets are not entirely clear, they were apparently quite popular and gave him the notoriety that had eluded him as a novelist. In 1803, Brown launched another periodical, *The Literary Magazine and American Register,* where he published "Somnambulism" in May 1805. This successful periodical ran until 1807, when it was reconfigured as the semi-annual *American Register, or General Repository of History, Politics, and Science,* which ran until 1810.

In 1804, Brown married Elizabeth Linn after a four-year courtship challenged by their families on religious grounds. Linn was the daughter of a Presbyterian minister. Brown's parents did not attend the

Presbyterian ceremony, and Brown was subsequently censored by his Quaker meeting in Philadelphia. Despite this family tension, the Browns enjoyed a brief but happy marriage that produced four children in five years. In 1804, Brown also translated and published with the original notes Volney's *A View of the Soil and Climate of the United States.* Geography had long been an interest for Brown. At the time of his death he was working on his own geographical study, "System of General Geography; Containing a Topological, Statistical, and Descriptive Survey of the Earth" (the manuscript has been lost). In 1809, he wrote another anti-Jeffersonian pamphlet, on the trade embargo, *An Address to the Congress of the United States on the Utility and Justice of Restrictions Upon Foreign Commerce.* This was his final publication. Brown died at the age of thirty-nine from tuberculosis in Philadelphia on February 22, 1810.

Susan Clair Imbarrato
Minnesota State University–Moorhead

PRIMARY WORKS

Wieland (1798); *Ormond* (1799); *Edgar Huntly* (1799); and *Arthur Mervyn* (1799–1800); *The Novels of Charles Brockden Brown,* 7 vols. (1827), 6 vols. (1887).

Somnambulism[1]

A fragment

[The following fragment will require no other preface or commentary than an extract from the Vienna Gazette of June 14, 1784. "At Great Clogau, in Silesia, the attention of physicians, and of the people, has been excited by the case of a young man, whose behaviour indicates perfect health in all respects but one. He has a habit of rising in his sleep, and performing a great many actions with as much order and exactness as when awake. This habit for a long time shewed itself in freaks and achievements merely innocent, or, at least, only troublesome and inconvenient, till about six weeks ago. At that period a shocking event took place about three leagues from the town, and in the neighbourhood where the youth's family resides. A young lady, travelling with her father by night, was shot dead upon the road, by some person unknown. The officers of justice took a good deal of pains to trace the author of the crime, and at length, by carefully comparing circumstances, a suspicion was fixed upon this youth. After an accurate scrutiny, by the tribunal of the circle, he has been declared author of the murder: but what renders the case truly extraordinary is, that there are good reasons for believing that the deed was perpetrated by the youth while asleep, and was entirely unknown to himself. The young woman was the object of his affection, and the journey in which she had engaged had given him the utmost anxiety for her safety."]

[1]Published in the *Literary Magazine and American Register* 3 (May 1805).

——Our guests were preparing to retire for the night, when somebody knocked loudly at the gate. The person was immediately admitted, and presented a letter to Mr. Davis. This letter was from a friend, in which he informed our guest of certain concerns of great importance, on which the letter-writer was extremely anxious to have a personal conference with his friend; but knowing that he intended to set out from——four days previous to his writing, he was hindered from setting out by the apprehension of missing him upon the way. Meanwhile, he had deemed it best to send a special messenger to quicken his motions, should he be able to find him.

The importance of this interview was such, that Mr. Davis declared his intention of setting out immediately. No solicitations could induce him to delay a moment. His daughter, convinced of the urgency of his motives, readily consented to brave the perils and discomforts of a nocturnal journey.

This event had not been anticipated by me. The shock that it produced in me was, to my own apprehension, a subject of surprise. I could not help perceiving that it was greater than the occasion would justify. The pleasures of this intercourse were, in a moment, to be ravished from me. I was to part from my new friend, and when we should again meet it was impossible to foresee. It was then that I recollected her expressions, that assured me that her choice was fixed upon another. If I saw her again, it would probably be as a wife. The claims of friendship, as well as those of love, would then be swallowed up by a superior and hateful obligation.

But, though betrothed, she was not wedded. That was yet to come; but why should it be considered as inevitable? Our dispositions and views must change with circumstances. Who was he that Constantia Davis had chosen? Was he born to outstrip all competitors in ardour and fidelity? We cannot fail of chusing that which appears to us most worthy of choice. He had hitherto been unrivalled; but was not this day destined to introduce to her one, to whose merits every competitor must yield? He that would resign this prize, without an arduous struggle, would, indeed, be of all wretches the most pusillanimous and feeble.

Why, said I, do I cavil at her present choice? I will maintain that it does honour to her discernment. She would not be that accomplished being which she seems, if she had acted otherwise. It would be sacrilege to question the rectitude of her conduct. The object of her choice was worthy. The engagement of her heart in his favour was unavoidable, because her experience had not hitherto produced one deserving to be placed in competition with him. As soon as his superior is found, his claims will be annihilated. Has not this propitious accident supplied the defects of her former observation? But soft! is she not betrothed? If she be, what have I to dread? The engagement is accompanied with certain conditions. Whether they be openly expressed or not, they necessarily limit it. Her vows are binding on condition that the present situation continues, and that another does not arise, previously to marriage, by whose claims those of the present lover will be justly superseded.

But how shall I contend with this unknown admirer? She is going whither it will not be possible for me to follow her. An interview of a few hours is not sufficient to accomplish the important purpose that I meditate; but even this is now at an end. I shall speedily be forgotten by her. I have done nothing that entitles me to a place in her remembrance. While my rival will be left at liberty to prosecute his suit, I shall be abandoned to solitude, and have no other employment than to ruminate on the bliss that has eluded my grasp. If scope were allowed to my exertions, I might hope that they would ultimately be crowned with success; but, as it is, I am manacled and powerless. The good would easily be reached, if my hands were at freedom: now that they are fettered, the attainment is impossible.

But is it true that such is my forlorn condition? What is it that irrecoverably binds me to this spot? There are seasons of respite from my present occupations, in which I commonly indulge myself in journeys. This lady's habitation is not at an immeasurable distance from mine. It may be easily comprised within the sphere of my excursions. Shall I want a motive or excuse for paying her a visit? Her father has claimed to be better acquainted with my uncle. The lady has intimated, that the sight of me, at any future period, will give her pleasure. This will furnish ample apology for visiting their house. But why should I delay my visit? Why not immediately attend them on their way? If not on their whole journey, at least for a part of it? A journey in darkness is not unaccompanied with peril. Whatever be the caution or knowledge of their guide, they cannot be supposed to surpass mine, who have trodden this part of the way so often, that my chamber floor is scarcely more familiar to me. Besides, there is danger, from which, I am persuaded, my attendance would be a sufficient, an indispensable safeguard.

I am unable to explain why I conceived this journey to be attended with uncommon danger. My mind was, at first, occupied with the remoter consequences of this untimely departure, but my thoughts gradually returned to the contemplation of its immediate effects. There were twenty miles to a ferry, by which the travellers designed to cross the river, and at which they expected to arrive at sun-rise the next morning. I have said that the intermediate way was plain and direct. Their guide professed to be thoroughly acquainted with it.—From what quarter, then, could danger be expected to arise? It was easy to enumerate and magnify possibilities; that a tree, or ridge, or stone unobserved might overturn the carriage; that their horse might fail, or be urged, by some accident, to flight, were far from being impossible. Still they were such as justified caution. My vigilance would, at least, contribute to their security. But I could not for a moment divest myself of the belief, that my aid was indispensable. As I pondered on this image my emotions arose to terror.

All men are, at times, influenced by inexplicable sentiments. Ideas haunt them in spite of all their efforts to discard them. Prepossessions are entertained, for which their reason is unable to discover any adequate cause. The strength of a belief, when it is destitute of any rational foundation, seems, of itself, to furnish a new ground for credulity. We first admit a powerful persuasion, and then, from reflecting on the insufficiency of the ground on which it is built, instead of being prompted to dismiss it, we become more forcibly attached to it.

I had received little of the education of design. I owed the formation of my character chiefly to accident. I shall not pretend to determine in what degree I was credulous or superstitious. A belief, for which I could not rationally account, I was sufficiently prone to consider as the work of some invisible agent; as an intimation from the great source of existence and knowledge. My imagination was vivid. My passions, when I allowed them sway, were incontroulable. My conduct, as my feelings, was characterised by precipitation and headlong energy.

On this occasion I was eloquent in my remonstrances. I could not suppress my opinion, that unseen danger lurked in their way. When called upon to state the reasons of my apprehensions, I could only enumerate possibilities of which they were already apprised, but which they regarded in their true light. I made bold enquiries into the importance of the motives that should induce them to expose themselves to the least hazard. They could not urge their horse beyond his real strength. They would be compelled to suspend their journey for some time the next day. A few hours were all that they could hope to save by their utmost expedition. Were a few hours of such infinite moment?

In these representations I was sensible that I had over-leaped the bounds of rigid decorum. It was not my place to weigh his motives and inducements. My age and situation, in this family, rendered silence and submission my peculiar province. I had hitherto confined myself within bounds of scrupulous propriety, but now I had suddenly lost sight of all regards but those which related to the safety of the travellers.

Mr. Davis regarded my vehemence with suspicion. He eyed me with more attention than I had hitherto received from him. The impression which this unexpected interference made upon him, I was, at the time, too much absorbed in other considerations to notice. It was afterwards plain that he suspected my zeal to originate in a passion for his daughter, which it was by no means proper for him to encourage. If this idea occurred to him, his humanity would not suffer it to generate indignation or resentment in his bosom. On the contrary, he treated my arguments with mildness, and assured me that I had over-rated the inconveniences and perils of the journey. Some regard was to be paid to his daughter's ease and health. He did not believe them to be materially endangered. They should make suitable provision of cloaks and caps against the inclemency of the air. Had not the occasion been extremely urgent, and of that urgency he alone could be the proper judge, he should certainly not consent to endure even these trivial inconveniences. "But you seem," continued he, "chiefly anxious for my daughter's sake. There is, without doubt, a large portion of gallantry in your fears. It is natural and venial in a young man to take infinite pains for the service of the ladies; but, my dear, what say you? I will refer this important question to your decision. Shall we go, or wait till the morning?"

"Go, by all means," replied she. "I confess the fears that have been expressed appear to be groundless. I am bound to our young friend for the concern he takes in our welfare, but certainly his imagination misleads him. I am not so much a girl as to be scared merely because it is dark."

I might have foreseen this decision; but what could I say? My fears and my repugnance were strong as ever.

The evil that was menaced was terrible. By remaining where they were till the next day they would escape it. Was no other method sufficient for their preservation? My attendance would effectually obviate the danger.

This scheme possessed irresistible attractions. I was thankful to the danger for suggesting it. In the fervour of my conceptions, I was willing to run to the world's end to show my devotion to the lady. I could sustain, with alacrity, the fatigue of many nights of travelling and watchfulness. I should unspeakably prefer them to warmth and ease, if I could thereby extort from this lady a single phrase of gratitude or approbation.

I proposed to them to bear them company, at least till the morning light. They would not listen to it. Half my purpose was indeed answered by the glistening eyes and affectionate looks of Miss Davis, but the remainder I was pertinaciously bent on likewise accomplishing. If Mr. Davis had not suspected my motives, he would probably have been less indisposed to compliance. As it was, however, his objections were insuperable. They earnestly insisted on my relinquishing my design. My uncle, also, not seeing any thing that justified extraordinary precautions, added his injunctions. I was conscious of my inability to show any sufficient grounds for my fears. As long as their representations rung in my ears, I allowed myself to be ashamed of my weakness, and conjured up a temporary persuasion that my attendance was, indeed, superfluous, and that I should show most wisdom in suffering them to depart alone.

But this persuasion was transient. They had no sooner placed themselves in their carriage, and exchanged the parting adieus, but my apprehensions returned upon me as forcibly as ever. No doubt part of my despondency flowed from the idea of separation, which, however auspicious it might prove to the lady, portended unspeakable discomforts to me. But this was not all. I was breathless with fear of some unknown and terrible disaster that awaited them. A hundred times I resolved to disregard their remonstrances, and hover near them till the morning. This might be done without exciting their displeasure. It was easy to keep aloof and be unseen by them. I should doubtless have pursued this method if my fears had assumed any definite and consistent form; if, in reality, I had been able distinctly to tell what it was that I feared. My guardianship would be of no use against the obvious sources of danger in the ruggedness and obscurity of the way. For that end I must have tendered them my services, which I knew would be refused, and, if pertinaciously obtruded on them, might justly excite displeasure. I was not insensible, too, of the obedience that was due to my uncle. My absence would be remarked. Some anger and much disquietude would have been the consequences with respect to him. And after all, what was this groundless and ridiculous persuasion that governed me? Had I profited nothing by experience of the effects of similar follies? Was I never to attend to the lessons of sobriety and truth? How ignominious to be thus the slave of a fortuitous and inexplicable impulse! To be the victim of terrors more chimerical than those which haunt the dreams of idiots and children! *They* can describe clearly, and attribute a real existence to the object of their terrors. Not so can I.

Influenced by these considerations, I shut the gate at which I had been standing, and turned towards the house. After a few steps I paused, turned, and listened to the distant sounds of the carriage. My courage was again on the point of yielding, and new efforts were requisite before I could resume my first resolutions.

I spent a drooping and melancholy evening. My imagination continually hovered over our departed guests. I recalled every circumstance of the road. I reflected by what means they were to pass that bridge, or extricate themselves from this slough. I imagined the possibility of their guide's forgetting the position of a certain oak that grew in the road. It was an ancient tree, whose boughs extended, on all sides, to an extraordinary distance. They seemed disposed by nature in that way in which they would produce the most ample circumference of shade. I could not recollect any other obstruction from which much was to be feared. This indeed was several miles distant, and its appearance was too remarkable not to have excited attention.

The family retired to sleep. My mind had been too powerfully excited to permit me to imitate their example. The incidents of the last two days passed over my fancy like a vision. The revolution was almost incredible which my mind had undergone, in consequence of these incidents. It was so abrupt and entire that my soul seemed to have passed into a new form. I pondered on every incident till the surrounding scenes disappeared, and I forgot my real situation. I mused upon the image of Miss Davis till my whole soul was dissolved in tenderness, and my eyes overflowed with tears. There insensibly arose a sort of persuasion that destiny had irreversably decreed that I should never see her more.

While engaged in this melancholy occupation, of which I cannot say how long it lasted, sleep overtook me as I sat. Scarcely a minute had elapsed during this period without conceiving the design, more or less strenuously, of sallying forth, with a view to overtake and guard the travellers; but this design was embarrassed with invincible objections, and was alternately formed and laid aside. At length, as I have said, I sunk into profound slumber, if that slumber can be termed profound, in which my fancy was incessantly employed in calling up the forms, into new combinations, which had constituted my waking reveries.—The images were fleeting and transient, but the events of the morrow recalled them to my remembrance with sufficient distinctness. The terrors which I had so deeply and unaccountably imbibed could not fail of retaining some portion of their influence, in spite of sleep.

In my dreams, the design which I could not bring myself to execute while awake I embraced without hesitation. I was summoned, me-thought, to defend this lady from the attacks of an assassin. My ideas were full of confusion and inaccuracy. All that I can recollect is, that my efforts had been unsuccessful to avert the stroke of the murderer. This, however, was not accomplished without drawing on his head a bloody retribution. I imagined myself engaged, for a long time, in pursuit of the guilty, and, at last, to have detected him in an artful disguise. I did not employ the usual preliminaries which honour prescribes, but, stimulated by rage, attacked him with a pistol and terminated his career by a mortal wound.

I should not have described these phantoms had there not been a remarkable coincidence between them and the real events of that night. In the morning, my uncle, whose custom it was to rise first in the family, found me quietly reposing in the chair in which I had fallen asleep. His summons roused and startled me. This posture was so unusual that I did not readily recover my recollection, and perceive in what circumstances I was placed.

I shook off the dreams of the night. Sleep had refreshed and invigorated my frame, as well as tranquillized my thoughts. I still mused on yesterday's adventures, but my reveries were more cheerful and benign. My fears and bodements were dispersed with the dark, and I went into the fields, not merely to perform the duties of the day, but to ruminate on plans for the future.

My golden visions, however, were soon converted into visions of despair. A messenger arrived before noon, intreating my presence, and that of my uncle, at the house of Dr. Inglefield, a gentleman who resided at the distance of three miles from our house. The messenger explained the intention of this request. It appeared that the terrors of the preceding evening had some mysterious connection with truth. By some deplorable accident, Miss Davis had been shot on the road, and was still lingering in dreadful agonies at the house of this physician. I was in a field near the road when the messenger approached the house. On observing me, he called me. His tale was meagre and imperfect, but the substance of it was easy to gather. I stood for a moment motionless and aghast. As soon as I recovered my thoughts I set off full speed, and made not a moment's pause till I reached the house of Inglefield.

The circumstances of this mournful event, as I was able to collect them at different times, from the witnesses, were these. After they had parted from us, they proceeded on their way for some time without molestation. The clouds disappearing, the star-light enabled them with less difficulty to discern their path. They met not a human being till they came within less than three miles of the oak which I have before described. Here Miss Davis looked forward with some curiosity and said to her father, "Do you not see some one in the road before us? I saw him this moment move across from the fence on the right hand and stand still in the middle of the road."

"I see nothing, I must confess," said the father: "but that is no subject of wonder; your young eyes will of course see farther than my old ones."

"I see him clearly at this moment," rejoined the lady. "If he remain a short time where he is, or seems to be, we shall be able to ascertain his properties. Our horse's head will determine whether his substance be impassive or not."

The carriage slowly advancing, and the form remaining in the same spot, Mr. Davis at length perceived it, but was not allowed a clearer examination, for the person, having, as it seemed, ascertained the nature of the cavalcade, shot across the road, and disappeared. The behaviour of this unknown person furnished the travellers with a topic of abundant speculation.

Few possessed a firmer mind than Miss Davis; but whether she was assailed, on this occasion, with a mysterious foreboding of her destiny; whether the eloquence of my fears had not, in spite of resolution, infected her; or, whether she imagined evils that my incautious temper might draw upon me, and which might originate in our late interview, certain it was that her spirits were visibly depressed. This accident made no sensible alteration in her. She was still disconsolate and incommunicative. All the efforts of her father were insufficient to inspire her with cheerfulness. He repeatedly questioned her as to the cause of this unwonted despondency. Her answer was, that her spirits were indeed depressed, but she believed that the circumstance was casual. She knew of nothing that could justify despondency. But such is humanity. Cheerfulness and dejection will take their turns in the best regulated bosoms, and come and go when they will, and not at the command of reason. This observation was succeeded by a pause. At length Mr. Davis said, "A thought has just occurred to me. The person whom we just now saw is young Althorpe."

Miss Davis was startled: "Why, my dear father, should you think so? It is too dark to judge, at this distance, by resemblance of figure. Ardent and rash as he appears to be, I should scarcely suspect him on this occasion. With all the fiery qualities of youth, unchastised by experience, untamed by adversity, he is capable no doubt of extravagant adventures, but what could induce him to act in this manner?"

"You know the fears that he expressed concerning the issue of this night's journey. We know not what foundation he might have had for these fears. He told us of no danger that ought to deter us, but it is hard to conceive that he should have been thus vehement without cause. We know not what motives might have induced him to conceal from us the sources of his terror. And since he could not obtain our consent to his attending us, he has taken these means, perhaps, of effecting his purpose. The darkness might easily conceal him, from our observation. He might have passed us without our noticing him, or he might have made a circuit in the woods we have just passed, and come out before us."

"That I own," replied the daughter, "is not improbable. If it be true, I shall be sorry for his own sake, but if there be any danger from which his attendance can secure us, I shall be well pleased for all our sakes. He will reflect with some satisfaction, perhaps, that he has done or intended us a service. It would be cruel to deny him a satisfaction so innocent."

"Pray, my dear, what think you of this young man? Does his ardour to serve us flow from a right source?"

"It flows, I have no doubt, from a double source. He has a kind heart, and delights to oblige others: but this is not all. He is likewise in love, and imagines that he cannot do too much for the object of his passion."

"Indeed!" exclaimed Mr. Davis, in some surprise. "You speak very positively. That is more than I suspected; but how came you to know it with so much certainty?"

"The information came to me in the directest manner. He told me so himself."

"So ho! why, the impertinent young rogue!"

"Nay, my dear father, his behaviour did not merit that epithet. He is rash and inconsiderate. That is the utmost amount of his guilt. A short absence will show him the true state of his feelings. It was unavoidable, in one of his character, to fall in love with the first woman whose appearance was in any degree specious. But attachments like these will be extinguished as easily as they are formed. I do not fear for him on this account."

"Have you reason to fear for him on any account?"

"Yes. The period of youth will soon pass away. Overweening and fickle, he will go on committing one mistake after another, incapable of repairing his errors, or of profiting by the daily lessons of experience. His genius will be merely an implement of mischief. His greater capacity will be evinced merely by the greater portion of unhappiness that, by means of it, will accrue to others or rebound upon himself."

"I see, my dear, that your spirits are low. Nothing else, surely, could suggest such melancholy presages. For my part, I question not, but he will one day be a fine fellow and a happy one. I like him exceedingly. I shall take pains to be acquainted with his future adventures, and do him all the good that I can."

"That intention," said his daughter, "is worthy of the goodness of your heart. He is no less an object of regard to me than to you. I trust I shall want neither the power nor inclination to contribute to his welfare. At present, however, his welfare will be best promoted by forgetting me. Hereafter, I shall solicit a renewal of intercourse."

"Speak lower," said the father. "If I mistake not, there is the same person again." He pointed to the field that skirted the road on the left hand. The young lady's better eyes enabled her to detect his mistake. It was the trunk of a cherry-tree that he had observed.

They proceeded in silence. Contrary to custom, the lady was buried in musing. Her father, whose temper and inclinations were moulded by those of his child, insensibly subsided into the same state.

The re-appearance of the same figure that had already excited their attention diverted them anew from their contemplations. "As I live," exclaimed Mr. Davis, "that thing, whatever it be, haunts us. I do not like it. This is strange conduct for young Althorpe to adopt. Instead of being our protector, the danger, against which he so pathetically warned us, may be, in some inscrutable way, connected with this personage. It is best to be upon your guard."

"Nay, my father," said the lady, "be not disturbed. What danger can be dreaded by two persons from one? This thing, I dare say, means us no harm. What is at present inexplicable might be obvious enough if we were better acquainted with this neighbourhood. It is not worth a thought. You see it is now gone." Mr. Davis looked again, but it was no longer discernible.

They were now approaching a wood. Mr. Davis called to the guide to stop. His daughter enquired the reason of this command. She found it arose from his uncertainty as to the propriety of proceeding.

"I know not how it is," said he, "but I begin to be affected with the fears of young Althorpe. I am half resolved not to enter this wood.—That light yonder informs that a house is near. It may not be unadvisable to stop. I cannot think of delaying our journey till morning; but, by stopping a few minutes, we may possibly collect some useful information. Perhaps it will be expedient and practicable to procure the attendance of another person. I am not well pleased with myself for declining our young friend's offer."

To this proposal Miss Davis objected the inconveniences that calling at a farmer's house, at this time of night, when all were retired to rest, would probably occasion. "Besides," continued she, "the light which you saw is gone: a sufficient proof that it was nothing but a meteor."

At this moment they heard a noise, at a small distance behind them, as of shutting a gate. They called. Speedily an answer was returned in a tone of mildness. The person approached the chaise, and enquired who they were, whence they came, whither they were going, and, lastly, what they wanted.

Mr. Davis explained to this inquisitive person, in a few words, the nature of their situation, mentioned the appearance on the road, and questioned him, in his turn, as to what inconveniences were to be feared from prosecuting his journey. Satisfactory answers were returned to these enquiries.

"As to what you seed in the road," continued he, "I reckon it was nothing but a sheep or a cow. I am not more scary than some folks, but I never goes out a' nights without I sees some *sich* thing as that, that I takes for a man or woman, and am scared a little oftentimes, but not much. I'm sure after to find that it's not nothing but a cow, or hog, or tree, or something. If it wasn't some sich thing you seed, I reckon it was *Nick Handyside*."

"Nick Handyside! who was he?"

"It was a fellow that went about the country a' nights. A shocking fool to be sure, that loved to plague and frighten people. Yes. Yes. It couldn't be nobody, he reckoned, but Nick. Nick was a droll thing. He wondered they'd never heard of Nick. He reckoned they were strangers in these here parts."

"Very true, my friend. But who is Nick? Is he a reptile to be shunned, or trampled on?"

"Why I don't know how as that. Nick is an odd soul to be sure; but he don't do nobody no harm, as ever I heard, except by scaring them. He is easily skeart though, for that matter, himself. He loves to frighten folks, but he's shocking apt to be frightened himself. I reckon you took Nick for a ghost. That's a shocking good story, I declare. Yet it's happened hundreds and hundreds of times, I guess, and more."

When this circumstance was mentioned, my uncle, as well as myself, was astonished at our own negligence. While enumerating, on the preceding evening, the obstacles and inconveniences which the travellers were likely to encounter, we entirely and unaccountably overlooked one circumstance, from which inquietude might reasonably have been expected. Near the spot where they now were, lived a Mr. Handyside, whose only son was an idiot. He also merited the name of monster, if a projecting breast, a mis-shapen head, features horrid and distorted, and a voice that resembled nothing that was ever before heard, could entitle him to that appellation. This being, besides the natural deformity of his frame, wore looks and practised gesticulations that were, in an inconceivable degree, uncouth and hideous. He was mischievous, but his freaks were subjects of little apprehension to those who were accustomed to them, though they were frequently occasions of alarm to strangers. He particularly delighted in imposing on the ignorance of strangers and the timidity of women. He was a perpetual rover. Entirely bereft of reason, his sole employment consisted in sleeping, and eating, and roaming. He would frequently escape at night, and a thousand anecdotes could have been detailed respecting the tricks which Nick Handyside had played upon way-farers.

Other considerations, however, had, in this instance, so much engrossed our minds, that Nick Handyside had never been once thought of or mentioned. This was the more remarkable, as there had very lately happened an adventure, in which this person had acted a principal part. He had wandered from home, and got bewildered in a desolate tract, known by the name of Norwood. It was a region, rude, sterile, and lonely, bestrewn with rocks, and embarrassed with bushes.

He had remained for some days in this wilderness. Unable to extricate himself, and, at length, tormented with hunger, he manifested his distress by the most doleful shrieks. These were uttered with most vehemence, and heard at greatest distance, by night. At first, those who heard them were panic-struck; but, at length, they furnished a clue by which those who were in search of him were guided to the spot. Notwithstanding the recentness and singularity of this adventure, and the probability that our guests would suffer molestation from this cause, so strangely forgetful had we been, that no caution on this head had been given. This caution, indeed, as the event testified, would have been superfluous, and yet I cannot enough wonder, that in hunting for some reason, by which I might justify my fears to them or to myself, I had totally overlooked this mischief-loving idiot. After listening to an ample description of Nick, being warned to proceed with particular caution in a part of the road that was near at hand, and being assured that they had nothing to dread from human-interference, they resumed their journey with new confidence.

Their attention was frequently excited by rustling leaves or stumbling footsteps; and the figure which they doubted not to belong to Nick Handyside, occasionally hovered in their sight. This appearance no longer inspired them with apprehension. They had been assured that a stern voice was sufficient to reprise him, when most importunate. This antic being treated all others as children. He took pleasure in the effects which the sight of his own deformity produced, and betokened his satisfaction by a laugh, which might have served as a model to the poet who has depicted the ghastly risibilities of Death. On this occasion, however, the monster behaved with unusual moderation. He never came near enough for his peculiarities to be distinguished by star-light. There was nothing fantastic in his motions, nor any thing surprising, but the celebrity of his transitions. They were unaccompanied by those howls, which reminded you at one time of a troop of hungry wolves, and had, at another, something in them inexpressibly wild and melancholy. This monster possessed a certain species of dexterity. His talents, differently applied, would have excited rational admiration. He was fleet as a deer. He was patient, to an incredible degree, of watchfulness, and cold, and hunger. He had improved the flexibility of his voice, till his cries, always loud and rueful, were capable of being diversified without end. Instances had been known, in which the stoutest heart was appalled by them; and some, particularly in the case of women, in which they had been productive of consequences truly deplorable.

When the travellers had arrived at that part of the wood where, as they had been informed, it was needful to be particularly cautious, Mr. Davis for their greater security, proposed to his daughter to alight. The exercise of walking, he thought, after so much time spent in a close carriage, would be salutary and pleasant. The young lady readily embraced the proposal. They forthwith alighted, and walked at a small distance before the chaise, which was not conducted by the servant. From this moment the spectre, which, till now, had been occasionally visible, entirely disappeared. This incident naturally led the conversation to this topic. So singular a specimen of the forms which human nature is found to assume could not fail of suggesting a variety of remarks.

They pictured to themselves many combinations of circumstances in which Handyside might be the agent, and in which the most momentous effects might flow from his agency, without its being possible for others to conjecture the true nature of the agent. The propensities of this being might contribute to realize, on an American road, many of those imaginary tokens and perils which abound in the wildest romance. He would be an admirable machine, in a plan whose purpose was to generate or foster, in a given subject, the frenzy of quixotism.—No theatre was better adapted than Norwood to such an exhibition. This part of the country had long been deserted by beasts of prey. Bears might still, perhaps, be found during a very rigorous season, but wolves which, when the country was a desert, were extremely numerous, had now, in consequence of increasing population, withdrawn to more savage haunts. Yet the voice of Handyside, varied with the force and skill of which he was known to be capable, would fill these shades with outcries as ferocious as those which are to be heard in Siamese or Abyssinian forests. The tale of his recent elopement had been told by the man with whom they had just parted, in a rustic but picturesque style.

"But why," said the lady, "did not our kind host inform us of this circumstance? He must surely have been well acquainted with the existence and habits of this Handyside. He must have perceived to how many groundless alarms our ignorance, in this respect, was likely to expose us. It is strange that he did not afford us the slightest intimation of it."

Mr. Davis was no less surprised at this omission. He was at a loss to conceive how this should be forgotten in the midst of those minute directions, in which every cause had been laboriously recollected from which he might incur danger or suffer obstruction.

This person, being no longer an object of terror, began to be regarded with a very lively curiosity. They even wished for his appearance and near approach, that they might carry away with them more definite conceptions of his figure. The lady declared she should be highly pleased by hearing his outcries, and consoled herself with the belief, that he would not allow them to pass the limits which he had prescribed to his wanderings, without greeting them with a strain or two. This wish had scarcely been uttered, when it was completely gratified.

The lady involuntarily started, and caught hold of her father's arm. Mr. Davis himself was disconcerted. A scream, dismally loud, and piercingly shrill, was uttered by one at less than twenty paces from them.

The monster had shown some skill in the choice of a spot suitable to his design. Neighbouring precipices, and a thick umbrage of oaks, on either side, contributed to prolong and to heighten his terrible notes. They were rendered more awful by the profound stillness that preceded and followed them. They were able speedily to quiet the trepidations which this hideous outcry, in spite of preparation and foresight, had produced, but they had not foreseen one of its unhappy consequences.

In a moment Mr. Davis was alarmed by the rapid sound of footsteps behind him. His presence of mind, on this occasion, probably saved himself and his daughter from instant destruction. He leaped out of the path, and, by a sudden exertion, at the same moment, threw the lady to some distance from the tract. The horse that drew the chaise rushed by them with the celerity of lightning. Affrighted at the sounds which had been uttered at a still less distance from the horse than from Mr. Davis, possibly with a malicious design to produce this very effect, he jerked the bridle from the hands that held it, and rushed forward with headlong speed. The man, before he could provide for his own safety, was beaten to the earth. He was considerably bruised by the fall, but presently recovered his feet, and went in pursuit of the horse.

This accident happened at about a hundred yards from the *oak,* against which so many cautions had been given. It was not possible, at any time, without considerable caution, to avoid it. It was not to be wondered at, therefore, that, in a few seconds, the carriage was shocked against the trunk, overturned, and dashed into a thousand fragments. The noise of the crash sufficiently informed them of this event. Had the horse been inclined to stop, a repetition, for the space of some minutes, of the same savage and terrible shrieks would have added tenfold to his consternation and to the speed of his flight. After this dismal strain had ended, Mr. Davis raised his daughter from the ground. She had suffered no material injury. As soon as they recovered from the confusion into which this accident had thrown them, they began to consult upon the measures proper to be taken upon this emergency. They were left alone. The servant had gone in pursuit of the flying horse. Whether he would be able to retake him was extremely dubious. Meanwhile they were surrounded by darkness. What was the distance of the next house could not be known. At that hour of the night they could not hope to be directed, by the far-seen taper, to any hospitable roof. The only alternative, therefore, was to remain where they were, uncertain of the fate of their companion, or to go forward with the utmost expedition.

They could not hesitate to embrace the latter. In a few minutes they arrived at the oak. The chaise appeared to have been dashed against a knotty projecture of the trunk, which was large enough for a person to be conveniently seated on it. Here they again paused.—Miss Davis desired to remain here a few minutes to recruit her exhausted strength. She proposed to her father to leave her here, and go forward in quest of the horse and the servant. He might return as speedily as he thought proper. She did not fear to be alone. The voice was still. Having accomplished his malicious purposes, the spectre had probably taken his final leave of them. At all events, if the report of the rustic was true, she had no personal injury to fear from him.

Through some deplorable infatuation, as he afterwards deemed it, Mr. Davis complied with her intreaties, and went in search of the missing. He had engaged in a most unpromising undertaking. The man and horse were by this time at a considerable distance. The former would, no doubt, shortly return. Whether his pursuit succeeded or miscarried, he would surely see the propriety of hastening his return with what tidings he could obtain, and to ascertain his master's situation. Add to this, the impropriety of leaving a woman, single and unarmed, to the machinations of this demoniac. He had scarcely parted with her when these reflections occurred to him. His resolution was changed. He turned back with the intention of immediately seeking her. At the same moment, he saw the flash and heard the discharge of a pistol. The light proceeded from the foot of the oak. His imagination was filled with horrible forebodings. He ran with all his speed to the spot. He called aloud upon the name of his daughter, but, alas! she was unable to answer him. He found her stretched at the foot of the tree, senseless, and weltering in her blood. He lifted her in his arms, and seated her against the trunk. He found himself stained with blood, flowing from a wound, which either the darkness of the night, or the confusion of his thoughts, hindered him from tracing. Overwhelmed with a catastrophe so dreadful and unexpected, he was divested of all presence of mind. The author of his calamity had vanished. No human being was at hand to succour him in his uttermost distress. He beat his head against the ground, tore away his venerable locks, and rent the air with his cries.

Fortunately there was a dwelling at no great distance from this scene. The discharge of a pistol produces a sound too loud not to be heard far and wide, in this lonely region. This house belonged to a physician. He was a man noted for his humanity and sympathy. He was roused, as well as most of his family, by a sound so uncommon. He rose instantly, and calling up his people, proceeded with lights to the road. The lamentations of Mr. Davis directed them to the place. To the physician the scene was inexplicable. Who was the author of this distress; by whom the pistol was discharged; whether through some untoward chance or with design, he was as yet uninformed, nor could he gain any information from the incoherent despair of Mr. Davis.

Every measure that humanity and professional skill could suggest were employed on this occasion. The dying lady was removed to the house. The ball had lodged in her brain, and to extract it was impossible. Why should I dwell on the remaining incidents of this tale? She languished till the next morning, and then expired.——

1805

Acknowledgments

Text

John Adams. From John A. Schutz and Douglas Adair, eds., *The Spur of Fame: Dialogues of John Adams and Benjamin Rush, 1805–1813* (1966), pp. 201–02. Reprinted with the permission of the Henry E. Huntington Library.

John Adams and Abigail Adams. From *The Adams Papers: Diary and Autobiography of John Adams* (4 vols.), ed. L. H. Butterfield et al. (Cambridge, MA: Belknap Press of Harvard University Press, 1963), vols. 3–4, reprinted by permission of the publisher, copyright © 1963, 1973 by the Massachusetts Historical Society.

From *The Adams Papers: Adams Family Correspondence* (8 vols.), ed. L. H. Butterfield et al. (Cambridge, MA: Belknap Press of Harvard University Press, 1963), vols. 1–3, reprinted by permission of the publisher, copyright © 1963, 1973 by the Massachusetts Historical Society.

Taiaiake Alfred. From Taiaiake Alfred, "Acknowledgements," *WASASE: Indigenous Pathways of Action and Freedom* (Peterborough, ON: Broadview, 2005), pp. 13–16. Copyright © 2005 by Taiaiake Alfred. Reprinted by permission of Broadview Press.

Arthur J. O. Anderson. "Two Songs," from *Grammatical Examples, Exercises, and Review*, for use with *Rules of the Aztec Language*, trans. Arthur J. O. Anderson (Salt Lake City: University of Utah, 1973). Permission granted by University of Utah Press.

William L. Andrews. From Elizabeth Ashbridge, *Some Account of the Fore Part of the Life of Elizabeth Ashbridge,* in William L. Andrews et al., eds., *Journeys in New Worlds: Early American Narratives* (1990), pp. 147–76. Copyright © 1990. Reprinted by permission of The University of Wisconsin Press.

Joel Barlow. Joel Barlow, "Advice to a Raven in Russia," *Huntington Library Quarterly* (1938). Reprinted with the permission of the Henry E. Huntington Library.

George S. Claghorn. "On Sarah Pierpont," from George S. Claghorn, ed., *Letters and Personal Writings by Jonathan Edwards*. Reprinted by permission of Yale University Press.

J. M. Cohen. From J. M. Cohen, ed. and trans., *The Four Voyages of Christopher Columbus* (Penguin Classics, 1969), copyright © J. M. Cohen, 1969. Reprinted by permission of Penguin Books, Ltd.

Jacob E. Cooke. Federalist Papers Nos. 6 and 10, from *The Federalist*, ed. Jacob E. Cooke (1961). Used by permission of the University Press of New England.

Benjamin Franklin. From *The Autobiography of Benjamin Franklin*, ed. Leonard W. Labaree. Reprinted by permission of Yale University Press.

Maynard J. Geiger. From Maynard J. Geiger, ed. and trans., *Palou's Life of Junípero Serra* (1955). Used with permission of the Academy of American Franciscan History.

Paul Gilroy. From Paul Gilroy, *The Black Atlantic: Modernity and Double Consciousness* (Cambridge, MA: Harvard University Press, 1993).

Lemuel Haynes. From Richard Newman, ed., *Black Preacher to White America: The Collected Writings of Lemuel Haynes, 1774–1833* (1990). Reprinted by permission of the Carlson Publishing Company.

C. L. R. James. Translation of "Letter to the Directory, 5 November 1797," from C. L. R. James, trans., *The Black Jacobins: Toussaint L'Ouverture and the San Domingo Revolution* (2nd ed.) (New York: Vintage Books, 1963), as it appeared in George F. Tyson, ed., *Great Lives Observed: Toussaint L'Ouverture* (New York: Simon & Schuster).

Thomas Jefferson. Letters of Thomas Jefferson to Peter Carr (August 10, 1787), to Charles Carroll (April 15, 1791), to Benjamin Hawkins (February 18, 1803), and to Nathaniel Burwell (March 14, 1818) and messages to Brother Handsom Lake (November 3, 1802) and The Wolf and People of the Mandan Nation (December 30, 1806) appear as published in *Jefferson: Writings* (New York: Library of America, 1984).

Allen Johnson. "Origin of the Sun Shower (Huron-Wendat)," in Allen Johnson, trans., *Huron-Wyandot Traditional Narratives in Translations and Native Texts.*

Basil Johnston. "Man's Dependence on Animals (Anishinaabe-Ojibway)," in Basil Johnston, *Ojibway Heritage,* reprinted by permission of the University of Nebraska Press. Copyright © 1976 by McClelland and Stewart.

Alan Kilpatrick. "Formula for Going to the Water," from Alan Kilpatrick, *The Night Has a Naked Soul: Witchcraft and Sorcery among the Western Cherokee* (Syracuse: Syracuse University Press, 1997), pp. 112–13. Reprinted by permission of Syracuse University Press.

Anna Gritts Kilpatrick and Jack Frederick Kilpatrick. "Formula to Attract a Woman," from Jack Frederick Kilpatrick and Anna Gritts Kilpatrick, eds., *Walk in Your Soul: Love Incantations of the Oklahoma Cherokees* (Dallas: Southern Methodist University Press, 1965), pp. 29–32. Reprinted by permission of Southern Methodist University Press.

Annette Kolodny. From Annette Kolodny, "Letting Go Our Grand Obsessions: Notes toward a New Literary History of the American Frontiers," *American Literature* 64.1 (March 1992): 1–18.

Tom Lowenstein. Eskimo Poems, from Tom Lowenstein, trans., *Eskimo Poems from Canada and Greenland.* Copyright © 1973 by Tom Lowenstein. Reprinted by permission of the translator.

James Mooney. "The Origin of Disease and Medicine (Cherokee)," from *Myths of the Cherokee,* collected by James Mooney (1900; Mineola, NY: Dover Publications, 1995), pp. 250–52.

Samuel Eliot Morison. From Samuel Eliot Morison, ed., *Of Plymouth Plantation 1620–1647,* copyright 1952 by Samuel Eliot Morison and renewed 1980 by Emily M. Beck. Used by permission of Alfred A. Knopf, a division of Random House, Inc.

Gary E. Moulton. From Meriwether Lewis and William Clark, *The Journals of the Lewis and Clark Expedition* (13 vols. and an abridged edition), ed. Gary E. Moulton (Lincoln: University of Nebraska Press, 1983–2001). © University of Nebraska Press.

Paula M. L. Moya and Ramón Saldívar. "Fictions of the Trans-American Imaginary," *Modern Fiction Studies* 49 (Spring 2003): 1–18.

Ely S. Parker. "Iroquois, or the Confederacy of the Five Nations," from *The Ely S. Parker Papers.* Reprinted by permission of the Buffalo and Erie County Historical Society.

Mary Louise Pratt. From Mary Louise Pratt, *Imperial Eyes: Travel Writing and Transculturation* (London: Routledge, 1992).

Donald E. Stanford. Poems from *The Poems of Edward Taylor,* ed. Donald E. Stanford (New Haven, CT: Yale University Press, 1960). Copyright © 1960, 1988 by Donald E. Stanford. Reprinted by permission.

Herbert J. Storing. "Anti-Federalist Paper," from *The Complete Anti-Federalist.* © 1981.

Brian Swann. "The Arrival of Whites (Lenape)" and "Song of the Drum (Lewis Mitchell, Passamaquoddy)" are reprinted from Brian Swann, ed., *Algonquian Spirit: Contemporary Translations of the Algonquian Literatures of North America,* by permission of the University of Nebraska Press. © 2005 by the Board of Regents of the University of Nebraska.

R. D. Theisz. "Iktomi and the Dancing Duck," from R. D. Theisz, ed., *Buckskin Tokens: Contemporary Oral Narratives of the Lakota.* Reprinted by permission.

M. Halsey Thomas. From *The Diary of Samuel Sewall: 1674–1729,* ed. M. Halsey Thomas. Copyright © 1973 by Farrar, Straus & Giroux, Inc. Reprinted by permission of Farrar, Straus and Giroux, LLC.

Richard Van Der Beets. From Richard Van Der Beets, ed., *Held Captive by Indians: Selected Narratives, 1642–1836.* Copyright © 1973 by The University of Tennessee Press. Reprinted by permission of The University of Tennessee Press.

Gaspar Pérez de Villagrà. Selections by Gaspar Pérez de Villagrà, from Miguel Encinias, Alfred Rodriguez, and Joseph P. Sanchez, ed. and trans.,

Historia de la Nueva Mexico, 1610, by Gaspar Perez de Villagra: A Critical and Annotated Spanish/English Edition (1992), pp. 3–6 (from Canto I), 260–66 (from Canto XXX). Used by permission.

James R. Walker. "Wohpe and the Gift of the Pipe," from James R. Walker, *Lakota Belief and Ritual*, ed. Raymond J. DeMallie and Elaine A. Jahner, reprinted by permission of the University of Nebraska Press. Copyright © 1980, 1991 by the University of Nebraska Press.

Mercy Otis Warren. From Mercy Warren, "A Thought on the Inestimable Blessing of Reason." Reprinted courtesy Massachusetts Historical Society.

Andrew Wiget. From Andrew Wiget, "Reading against the Grain: Origin Stories and American Literary History," *American Literary History* 3.2 (Summer 1991): 209–31.

Michael Wigglesworth. From Michael Wigglesworth, *The Poems of Michael Wigglesworth,* ed. Ronald A. Bosco (1989), pp. 11–12, 43–46, 57–58, 61–66.

Roger Williams. Roger Williams, "To the Town of Providence," from *The Correspondence of Roger Williams*, Vol. 2, *1654–1682*, ed. Glenn LaFantasie, reprinted by permission of the University Press of New England. Copyright © 1988 by the Rhode Island Historical Society.

From Roger Williams, *The Complete Writings of Roger Williams,* ed. Perry Miller (New York: Russell & Russell, 1963), reprinted with the permission of Scribner, an imprint of Simon & Schuster Adult Publishing Group.

From Roger Williams, preface, chapters 20–21, 29, and "Testimony of Roger Williams Relative to His First Coming into the Narragansett County," *A Key into the Language of America,* ed. with preface and notes by J. Hammond Trumbell and an introduction by Howard M. Chapin (New York: Russell & Russell, 1973), reprinted with the permission of Scribner, an imprint of Simon & Schuster Adult Publishing Group.

John Winthrop. From John Winthrop, "A Model of Christian Charity" and "Winthrop's Christian Experience," entries from *The Journal of John Winthrop*. Reprinted courtesy Massachusetts Historical Society.

John Woolman. From John Woolman, *The Journal and Major Essays of John Woolman*, ed. Phillips P. Moulton, copyright holder, published 1971 by Oxford University Press. Reprinted by permission.

Photos

Page 128: Theodor Galle, *America,* The Granger Collection.

Insert page 1, top: *Charta Cosmographia,* University of Georgia Hargrett Rare Book and Manuscript Library.

Insert page 1, bottom: Hopi pueblo, Denver Public Library, Western History Collection.

Insert page 2, Thomas Smith, *Self-Portrait,* Worcester Art Museum, Worcester, Massachusetts, museum purchase.

Insert page 3, top: Nicholaes Visscher, Early map of the Dutch colony of New Netherland, Library of Congress.

Insert page 3, bottom: Miguel Cabrera, *La Virgen de Guadalupe,* © Christie's Images Ltd.

Insert page 4: Benjamin Franklin, Diagram and explanation of a Franklin stove, Rare Book and Special Collections Division, Library of Congress.

Insert page 5, top: Advertisement for the sale of Africans, Library of Congress.

Insert page 5, bottom: Frontispiece and title page from Phillis Wheatley, *Poems on Various Subjects, Religious and Moral,* Pocumtuck Valley Memorial Association Library, Deerfield, Massachusetts.

Insert page 6, top: Thomas Jefferson, Draft of the Declaration of Independence, Library of Congress.

Insert page 6, bottom: Jane Pitford Braddick Peticolas, *Monticello,* Monticello / Thomas Jefferson Foundation, Inc.

Insert page 7: Abigail Adams Hobart, Sampler, Brown University Archives.

Insert page 8: *The New England Primer,* Special Collections, Monroe C. Gutman Library, Harvard Graduate School of Education.

Index of Authors, Titles, and First Lines of Poems